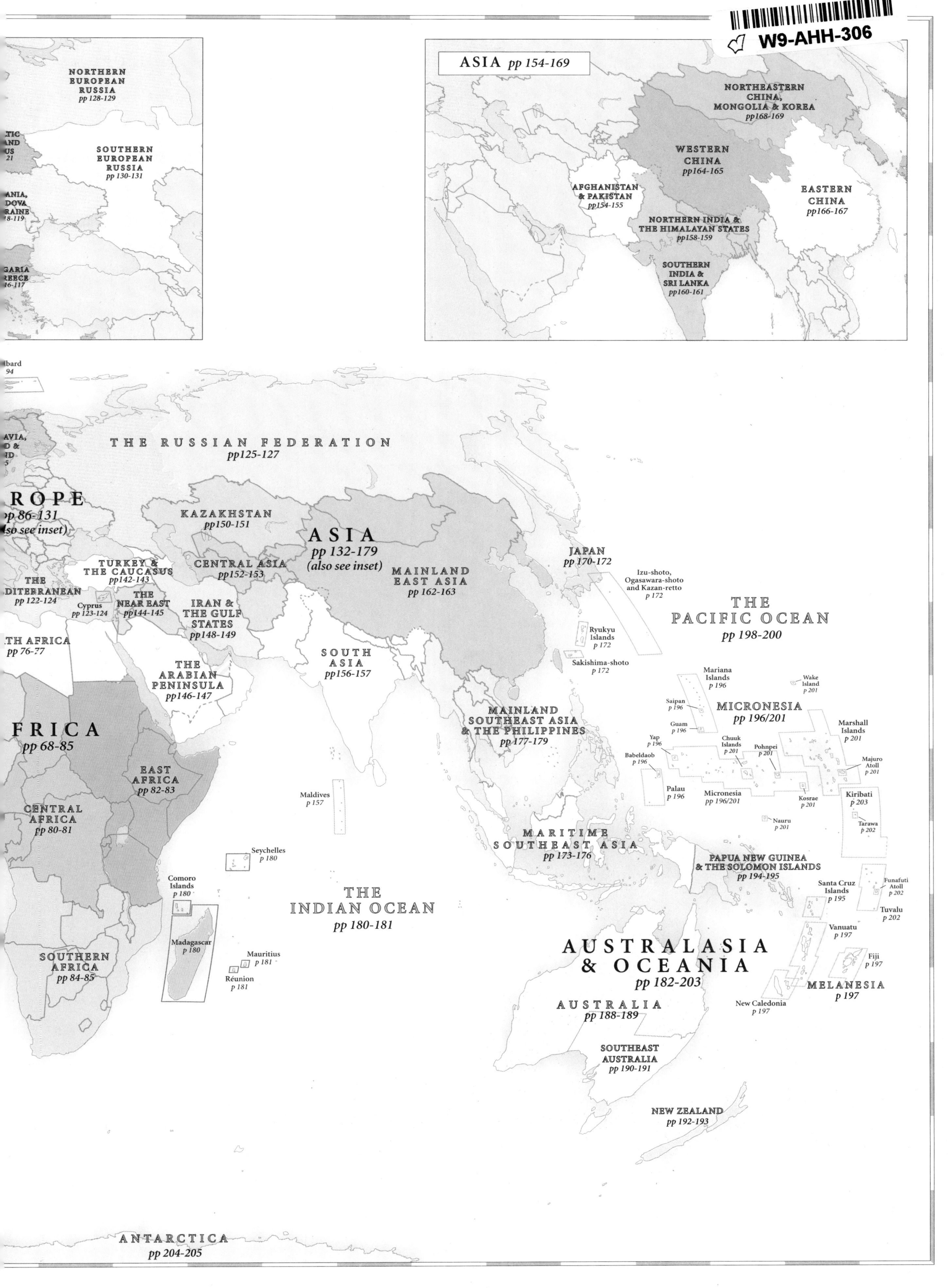

W9-AHH-306
NORTHERN EUROPEAN RUSSIA pp 128-129
SOUTHERN EUROPEAN RUSSIA pp 130-131
ASIA pp 154-169
NORTHEASTERN CHINA, MONGOLIA & KOREA pp168-169
WESTERN CHINA pp164-165
AFGHANISTAN & PAKISTAN pp154-155
EASTERN CHINA pp166-167
NORTHERN INDIA & THE HIMALAYAN STATES pp158-159
SOUTHERN INDIA & SRI LANKA pp160-161
THE RUSSIAN FEDERATION pp125-127
KAZAKHSTAN pp150-151
ASIA pp 132-179 (also see inset)
TURKEY & THE CAUCASUS pp142-143
CENTRAL ASIA pp152-153
MAINLAND EAST ASIA pp 162-163
JAPAN pp 170-172
Izu-shoto, Ogasawara-shoto and Kazan-retto p 172
Cyprus pp 123-124
THE NEAR EAST pp144-145
IRAN & THE GULF STATES pp148-149
Ryukyu Islands p 172
THE PACIFIC OCEAN pp 198-200
SOUTH ASIA pp156-157
Sakishima-shoto p 172
THE ARABIAN PENINSULA pp146-147
Mariana Islands p 196
Wake Island p 201
Saipan p 196
MICRONESIA pp 196/201
MAINLAND SOUTHEAST ASIA & THE PHILIPPINES pp 177-179
Guam p 196
Marshall Islands p 201
EAST AFRICA pp 82-83
Yap p 196
Chuuk Islands p 201
Pohnpei p 201
Babeldaob p 196
Majuro Atoll p 201
Maldives p 157
Palau p 196
Micronesia pp 196/201
Kosrae p 201
Kiribati p 203
CENTRAL AFRICA pp 80-81
Nauru p 201
Tarawa p 202
MARITIME SOUTHEAST ASIA pp 173-176
Seychelles p 180
PAPUA NEW GUINEA & THE SOLOMON ISLANDS pp 194-195
Comoro Islands p 180
THE INDIAN OCEAN pp 180-181
Santa Cruz Islands p 195
Funafuti Atoll p 202
Tuvalu p 202
Madagascar p 180
Vanuatu p 197
SOUTHERN AFRICA pp 84-85
Mauritius p 181
Réunion p 181
AUSTRALASIA & OCEANIA pp 182-203
Fiji p 197
MELANESIA p 197
New Caledonia p 197
AUSTRALIA pp 188-189
SOUTHEAST AUSTRALIA pp 190-191
NEW ZEALAND pp 192-193
ANTARCTICA pp 204-205

DK
WORLD
ATLAS

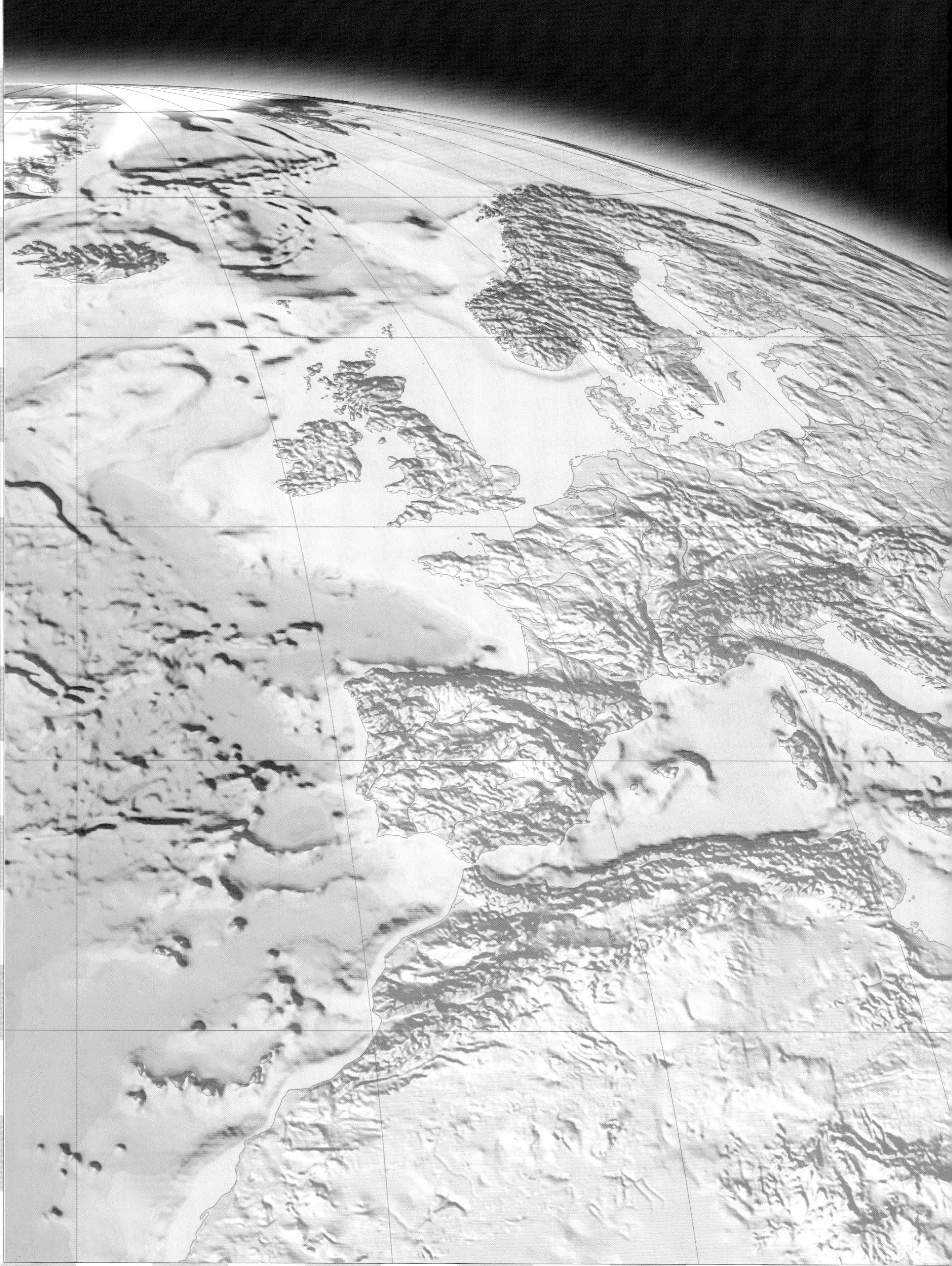

DK
WORLD
ATLAS

DK PUBLISHING, INC.

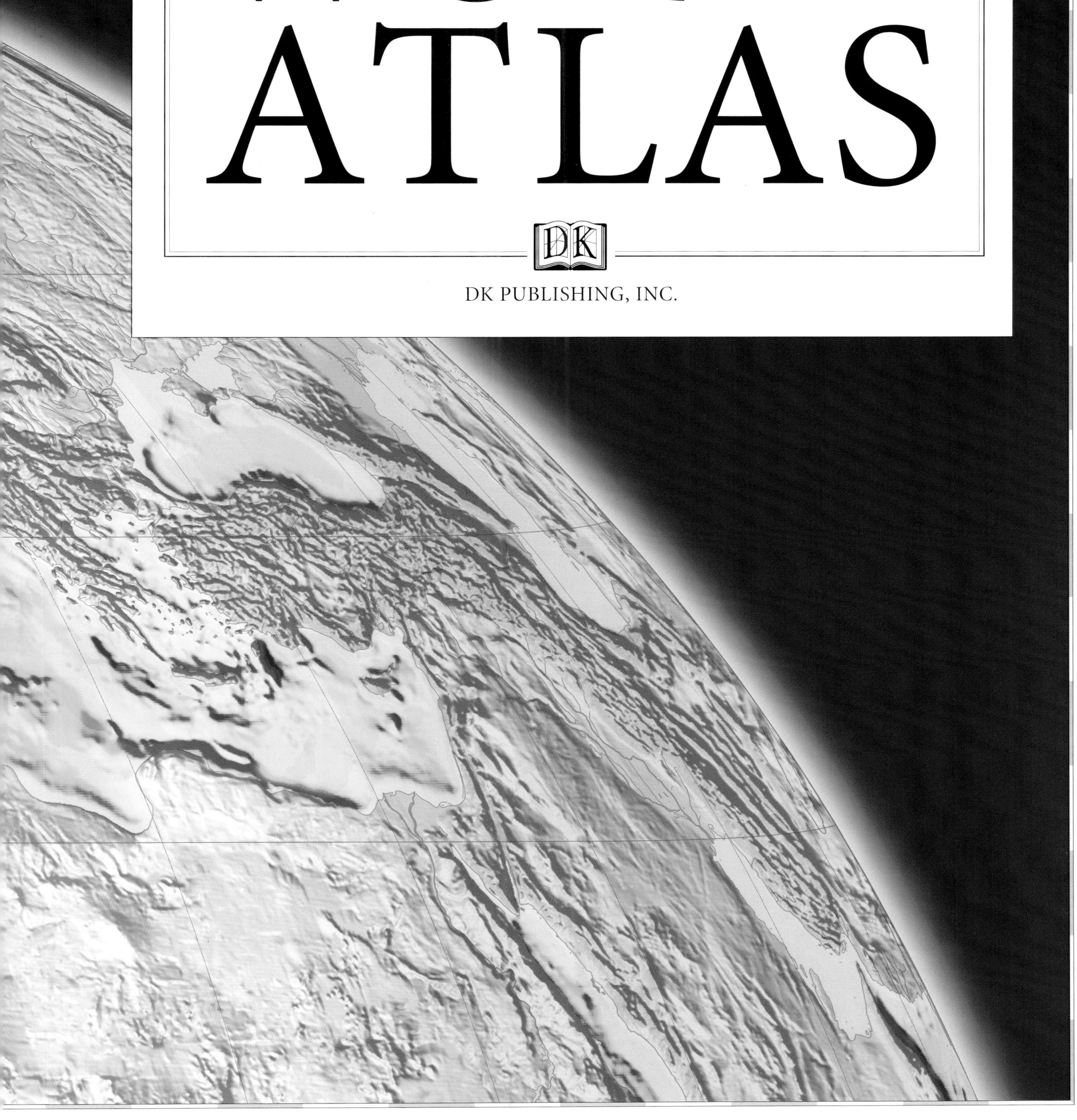

A DK PUBLISHING BOOK

GENERAL GEOGRAPHICAL CONSULTANTS

PHYSICAL GEOGRAPHY • Denys Brunsden, Emeritus Professor, Department of Geography, King's College, London, England

HUMAN GEOGRAPHY • Professor J. Malcolm Wagstaff, Department of Geography, University of Southampton, England

PLACE NAMES • Caroline Burgess, Permanent Committee on Geographical Names, London, England

BOUNDARIES • International Boundaries Research Unit, Mountjoy Research Centre, University of Durham, England

DIGITAL MAPPING CONSULTANTS

DK Cartopia developed by George Galfalvi and XMap Ltd., London, England

Professor Jan-Peter Muller, Department of Photogrammetry and Surveying, University College, London, England

Cover globes, planets, and information on the Solar System provided by Philip Eales and Kevin Tildsley, Planetary Visions Ltd., London, England

REGIONAL CONSULTANTS

NORTH AMERICA • Dr. David Green, Department of Geography, King's College, London • Jim Walsh, Head of Reference Services, Tisch Library, Tufts University, Medford, Massachussetts

SOUTH AMERICA • Dr. David Preston, School of Geography, University of Leeds, England

EUROPE • Dr. Edward M. Yates, formerly of the Department of Geography, King's College, London, England

AFRICA • Dr. Philip Amis, Development Administration Group, University of Birmingham, England • Dr. Ieuan Ll. Griffiths, Department of Geography, University of Sussex, England
Dr. Tony Binns, Department of Geography, University of Sussex, England

CENTRAL ASIA • Dr. David Turnock, Department of Geography, University of Leicester, England

SOUTH AND EAST ASIA • Dr. Jonathan Rigg, Department of Geography, University of Durham, England

AUSTRALASIA AND OCEANIA • Dr. Robert Allison, Department of Geography, University of Durham, England

ACKNOWLEDGMENTS

Digital terrain data created by Eros Data Center, Boulder, Colorado. Processed by GVS Images Inc., California, and Planetary Visions Ltd., London, England
CIRCA Research and Reference Information, Cambridge, England • Digitization by Robertson Research International, Swanley, England • Peter Clark

DORLING KINDERSLEY CARTOGRAPHY

EDITOR-IN-CHIEF
Andrew Heritage

MANAGING CARTOGRAPHER • David Roberts SENIOR CARTOGRAPHIC EDITOR • Roger Bullen

CARTOGRAPHERS
Pamela Alford • James Anderson • Sarah Baker-Ede • Caroline Bowie • Dale Buckton • Tony Chambers • Jan Clark • Bob Croser • Martin Darlison • Claire Ellam
Sally Gable • Jeremy Hepworth • Geraldine Horner • Chris Jackson • Christine Johnston • Julia Lunn • Michael Martin • James Mills-Hicks • Simon Mumford • John Plumer
John Scott • Ann Stephenson • Julie Turner • Jane Voss • Scott Wallace • Iorwerth Watkins • Bryony Webb • Alan Whitaker • Peter Winfield

DIGITAL MAPS CREATED IN DK CARTOPIA BY
Tom Coulson • Thomas Robertshaw
Philip Rowles • Rob Stokes

PLACE NAMES DATABASE TEAM
Natalie Clarkson • Ruth Duxbury • Caroline Falce • John Featherstone • Dan Gardiner
Ciárán Hynes • Margaret Hynes • Helen Rudkin • Margaret Stevenson • Annie Wilson

DATABASE MANAGER • Simon Lewis

MANAGING EDITOR
Lisa Thomas

EDITORS
Thomas Heath • Wim Jenkins • Jane Oliver
Constance Novis (US) • Siobhān Ryan • Elizabeth Wyse

EDITORIAL RESEARCH
Helen Dangerfield • Andrew Rebeiro-Hargrave

ADDITIONAL EDITORIAL ASSISTANCE
Debra Clapson • Robert Damon • Ailsa Heritage • Jayne Parsons • Chris Whitwell

MANAGING ART EDITOR
Philip Lord

DESIGNERS
Scott David • Carol Ann Davis • David Douglas
Rhonda Fisher • Karen Gregory • Nicola Liddiard • Paul Williams

ILLUSTRATIONS
Ciárán Hughes • Advanced Illustration, Congleton, England

PICTURE RESEARCH
Melissa Albany • James Clarke • Anna Lord • Christine Rista • Sarah Moule

EDITORIAL DIRECTION • Louise Cavanagh

ART DIRECTION • Chez Picthall

PRODUCTION
David Proffit • Hilary Stephens

First American Edition, 1997
Published in the United States by DK Publishing, Inc., 95 Madison Avenue, New York, New York 10016 • Visit us on the World Wide Web at http: // www.dk.com
2 4 6 8 10 9 7 5 3 1

Library of Congress Cataloging-in-Publication Data

DK Publishing, Inc.
DK world atlas
– Scales differ
p. cm.
Includes index/gazetteer
ISBN 0-7894-1974-2
1. Atlases. I. Title. II. Title: World atlas.
G1021 .D625 1997 <G&M> 97-12426
912--DC21 CIP
MAPS

Reproduction by Colourscan, Singapore, and The Printed Word, London. Printed and bound by in Italy by Mondadori.

INTRODUCTION

FOR MANY, THE OUTSTANDING LEGACY OF THE TWENTIETH CENTURY has been the way in which the Earth has shrunk. As we approach the end of this most dramatic of centuries, and the end of the second millennium, there is a greater need than ever for a clear vision of the world in which we live. The human population has increased fourfold since 1900. The last scraps of *terra incognita* – the polar regions and ocean depths – have been penetrated and mapped. New regions have been colonized, and previously hostile realms claimed for habitation. The advent of aviation technology and mass tourism has allowed many of us to travel farther, faster, and more frequently than ever before. In doing so we are given a bird's-eye view of the Earth's surface denied to our forebears.

AT THE SAME TIME, the amount of information about our world has grown enormously. Telecommunications can span the greatest distances in fractions of a second: our multimedia environment hurls uninterrupted streams of data at us, on the printed page, through the airwaves, and across our television and computer screens; events from all corners of the globe reach us instantaneously, and are witnessed as they unfold. Our sense of stability and certainty has been eroded; instead, we are aware that the world is in a constant state of flux and change. Natural disasters, man-made cataclysms, and conflicts between nations remind us daily of the enormity and fragility of our domain.

OUR CURRENT GLOBAL CULTURE has made the need greater than ever before for everyone to possess an atlas. The *DK World Atlas* has been conceived to meet this need. At its core, like all atlases, it seeks to define where places are, to describe their main characteristics, and to locate them in relation to other places. Every attempt has been made to make the information on the maps as clear and accessible as possible. In addition, each page of the atlas provides a wealth of further information, bringing the maps to life. Using photographs, diagrams, "at-a-glance" maps, introductory texts, and captions, the atlas builds up a detailed portait of those features – cultural, political, economic, and geomorphological – which make each region unique, and which are also the main agents of change.

A MAP PROVIDES ONLY A SNAPSHOT of the world at a given time. Drawing on the resources of a wide range of sciences and using the latest technology, the *DK World Atlas* is intended to equip the reader with the information needed to understand why the world today is the shape it is, and to recognize the processes of change that will determine its evolution in the next century.

PETER KINDERSLEY

CONTENTS

INTRODUCTION .... *v*

CONTENTS .... *vi–vii*

HOW TO USE THIS ATLAS .... *viii–ix*

THE WORLD TODAY

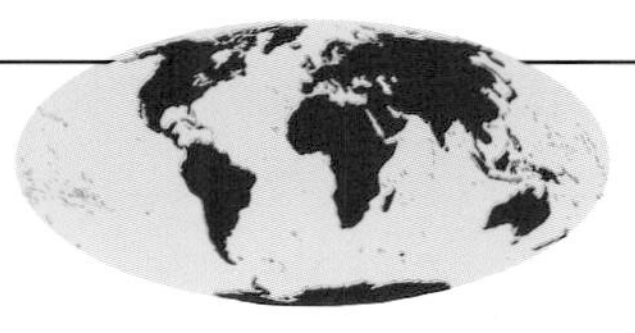

THE SOLAR SYSTEM .... *x–xi*

THE PHYSICAL WORLD .... *xii–xiii*

STRUCTURE OF THE EARTH .... *xiv–xv*

SHAPING THE LANDSCAPE .... *xvi–xvii*

THE WORLD'S OCEANS .... *xviii–xix*

THE GLOBAL CLIMATE .... *xx–xxi*

LIFE ON EARTH .... *xxii–xxiii*

POPULATION AND SETTLEMENT .... *xxiv–xxv*

THE ECONOMIC SYSTEM .... *xxvi–xxvii*

THE POLITICAL WORLD .... *xxviii–xxix*

STATES AND BOUNDARIES .... *xxx–xxxi*

INTERNATIONAL DISPUTES .... *xxxii*

ATLAS OF THE WORLD

NORTH AMERICA

NORTH AMERICA *1*

PHYSICAL NORTH AMERICA *2–3*

POLITICAL NORTH AMERICA *4–5*

NORTH AMERICAN RESOURCES *6–7*

CANADA: WESTERN PROVINCES *8–9*
Alberta, British Columbia, Manitoba, Saskatchewan, Yukon Territory

CANADA: EASTERN PROVINCES *10–11*
New Brunswick, Newfoundland & Labrador, Nova Scotia, Ontario, Prince Edward Island, Québec, St. Pierre & Miquelon

SOUTHEASTERN CANADA *12–13*
Southern Ontario, Southern Québec

CANADA *(gatefold)* *14–16*

UNITED STATES OF AMERICA *(gatefold)* . *17–19*

USA: NORTHEASTERN STATES *20–21*
Connecticut, Maine, Massachusetts, New Hampshire, New Jersey, New York, Pennsylvania, Rhode Island, Vermont

USA: MID-EASTERN STATES *22–23*
Delaware, District of Columbia, Kentucky, Maryland, North Carolina, South Carolina, Tennessee, Virginia, West Virginia

USA: SOUTHERN STATES *24–25*
Alabama, Florida, Georgia, Louisiana, Mississippi

USA: TEXAS *26–27*

USA: SOUTH MIDWESTERN STATES .. *28–29*
Arkansas, Kansas, Missouri, Oklahoma

USA: UPPER PLAINS STATES *30–31*
Iowa, Minnesota, Nebraska, North Dakota, South Dakota

USA: GREAT LAKES STATES *32–33*
Illinois, Indiana, Michigan, Ohio, Wisconsin

USA: NORTH MOUNTAIN STATES *34–35*
Idaho, Montana, Oregon, Washington, Wyoming

USA: CALIFORNIA & NEVADA *36–37*

USA: SOUTH MOUNTAIN STATES *38–39*
Arizona, Colorado, New Mexico, Utah

USA: HAWAII & ALASKA *40–41*

MEXICO *42–43*

CENTRAL AMERICA *44–45*
Belize, Costa Rica, El Salvador, Guatemala, Honduras, Nicaragua, Panama

THE CARIBBEAN *46–47*
Anguilla, Antigua & Barbuda, Aruba, Bahamas, Barbados, British Virgin Islands, Cayman Islands, Cuba, Dominica, Dominican Republic, Grenada, Guadeloupe, Haiti, Jamaica, Martinique, Montserrat, Navassa Island, Netherlands Antilles, Puerto Rico, St. Kitts & Nevis, St. Lucia, St. Vincent & the Grenadines, Trinidad & Tobago, Turks & Caicos Islands, US Virgin Islands

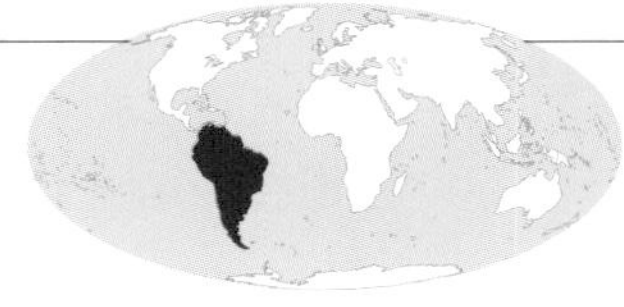

SOUTH AMERICA

SOUTH AMERICA *48–49*

PHYSICAL SOUTH AMERICA *50–51*

POLITICAL SOUTH AMERICA *52–53*

SOUTH AMERICAN RESOURCES *54–55*

NORTHERN SOUTH AMERICA *56–57*
Colombia, French Guiana, Guyana, Suriname, Venezuela

WESTERN SOUTH AMERICA *58–59*
Bolivia, Ecuador, Peru

BRAZIL *60–61*

EASTERN SOUTH AMERICA *62–63*
Uruguay, Northeast Argentina, Southeast Brazil

SOUTHERN SOUTH AMERICA *64–65*
Argentina, Chile, Paraguay

THE ATLANTIC OCEAN *66–67*

AFRICA

AFRICA *68–69*

PHYSICAL AFRICA *70–71*

POLITICAL AFRICA *72–73*

AFRICAN RESOURCES *74–75*

NORTH AFRICA *76–77*
Algeria, Egypt, Libya, Morocco, Tunisia, Western Sahara

WEST AFRICA *78–79*
Benin, Burkina, Cape Verde, Gambia, Ghana, Guinea, Guinea-Bissau, Ivory Coast, Liberia, Mali, Mauritania, Niger, Nigeria, Senegal, Sierra Leone, Togo

CENTRAL AFRICA *80–81*
Cameroon, Central African Republic, Chad, Congo, Congo (Democratic Republic of), Equatorial Guinea, Gabon, Sao Tome & Principe

EAST AFRICA *82–83*
Burundi, Djibouti, Eritrea, Ethiopia, Kenya, Rwanda, Somalia, Sudan, Tanzania, Uganda

SOUTHERN AFRICA *84–85*
Angola, Botswana, Lesotho, Malawi, Mozambique, Namibia, South Africa, Swaziland, Zambia, Zimbabwe

EUROPE

EUROPE ... 86–87

PHYSICAL EUROPE ... 88–89

POLITICAL EUROPE ... 90–91

EUROPEAN RESOURCES ... 92–93

SCANDINAVIA, FINLAND & ICELAND ... 94–95
Denmark, Finland, Iceland, Norway, Svalbard, Sweden

SOUTHERN SCANDINAVIA ... 96–97
Denmark, Southern Norway, Southern Sweden

THE BRITISH ISLES ... 98–99
United Kingdom, Republic of Ireland

THE LOW COUNTRIES ... 100–101
Belgium, Luxembourg, Netherlands

GERMANY ... 102–103

FRANCE ... 104–105
France, Monaco

THE IBERIAN PENINSULA ... 106–107
Andorra, Gibraltar, Portugal, Spain

THE ITALIAN PENINSULA ... 108–109
Italy, San Marino, Vatican City

THE ALPINE STATES ... 110–111
Austria, Liechtenstein, Slovenia, Switzerland

CENTRAL EUROPE ... 112–113
Czech Republic, Hungary, Poland, Slovakia

THE WESTERN BALKANS ... 114–115
Albania, Bosnia & Herzegovina, Croatia, Macedonia, Yugoslavia

BULGARIA & GREECE ... 116–117
(including European Turkey)

ROMANIA, MOLDOVA & UKRAINE ... 118–119

THE BALTIC STATES & BELARUS ... 120–121
Belarus, Estonia, Latvia, Lithuania, Kaliningrad

THE MEDITERRANEAN *(gatefold)* ... 122–124

THE RUSSIAN FEDERATION *(gatefold)* ... 125–127

NORTHERN EUROPEAN RUSSIA ... 128–129

SOUTHERN EUROPEAN RUSSIA ... 130–131

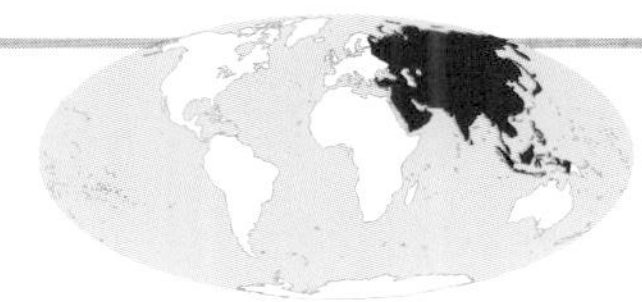

ASIA

ASIA ... 132–133

ASIAN RESOURCES ... 134–135

POLITICAL ASIA ... 136 / 141

PHYSICAL ASIA *(gatefold)* ... 137–140

TURKEY & THE CAUCASUS ... 142–143
Armenia, Azerbaijan, Georgia, Turkey

THE NEAR EAST ... 144–145
Iraq, Israel, Jordan, Lebanon, Syria

THE ARABIAN PENINSULA ... 146–147
Bahrain, Kuwait, Oman, Qatar, Saudi Arabia, United Arab Emirates, Yemen

IRAN & THE GULF STATES ... 148–149
Bahrain, Iran, Kuwait, Qatar, United Arab Emirates

KAZAKHSTAN ... 150–151

CENTRAL ASIA ... 152–153
Kyrgyzstan, Tajikistan, Turkmenistan, Uzbekistan

AFGHANISTAN & PAKISTAN ... 154–155

SOUTH ASIA ... 156–157
Bangladesh, Bhutan, India, Maldives, Nepal, Pakistan, Sri Lanka

NORTHERN INDIA & THE HIMALAYAN STATES ... 158–159
Bangladesh, Bhutan, Nepal, Northern India

SOUTHERN INDIA & SRI LANKA ... 160–161

MAINLAND EAST ASIA ... 162–163
China, Macao, Mongolia, North Korea, South Korea, Taiwan

WESTERN CHINA ... 164–165

EASTERN CHINA ... 166–167
Eastern China, Macao, Taiwan

NORTHEASTERN CHINA, MONGOLIA & KOREA ... 168–169
Mongolia, Northeastern China, North Korea, South Korea,

JAPAN *(gatefold)* ... 170–172

MARITIME SOUTHEAST ASIA *(gatefold)* ... 173–176
Brunei, Indonesia, Malaysia, Singapore

MAINLAND SOUTHEAST ASIA & THE PHILIPPINES *(gatefold)* ... 177–179
Cambodia, Laos, Myanmar, Paracel Islands, Philippines, Spratly Islands, Thailand, Vietnam

THE INDIAN OCEAN ... 180–181

AUSTRALASIA AND OCEANIA

AUSTRALASIA & OCEANIA ... 182–183

POLITICAL AUSTRALASIA & OCEANIA ... 184–185

AUSTRALASIAN & OCEANIAN RESOURCES ... 186–187

AUSTRALIA ... 188–189

SOUTHEAST AUSTRALIA ... 190–191
New South Wales, South Australia, Tasmania, Victoria

NEW ZEALAND ... 192–193

PAPUA NEW GUINEA & THE SOLOMON ISLANDS ... 194–195

MICRONESIA ... 196 / 201
Guam, Marshall Islands, Micronesia, Nauru, Northern Mariana Islands, Palau, Wake Island

MELANESIA ... 197
Fiji, New Caledonia, Vanuatu

THE PACIFIC OCEAN *(gatefold)* ... 198–200

POLYNESIA ... 202–203
Cook Islands, Easter Island, French Polynesia, Kiribati, Niue, Pitcairn Islands, Tokelau, Tuvalu, Wallis & Futuna

ANTARCTICA ... 204–205

THE ARCTIC ... 206–207

INDEX–GAZETTEER

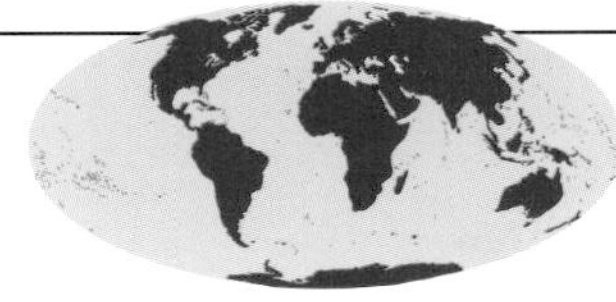

COUNTRIES OF THE WORLD
including World Timezones ... 208–214

GEOGRAPHICAL GLOSSARY ... 215–217

GEOGRAPHICAL NAMES ... 218

INDEX ... 219–338

ACKNOWLEDGMENTS ... 338

KEY TO REGIONAL MAPS

PHYSICAL FEATURES

elevation

- 6000m / 19,686ft
- 4000m / 13,124ft
- 3000m / 9843ft
- 2000m / 6562ft
- 1000m / 3281ft
- 500m / 1640ft
- 250m / 820ft
- 100m / 328ft
- sea level
- below sea level

- ▲ elevation above sea level (mountain height)
- ▲ volcano
- ⨯ pass
- ▼ elevation below sea level (depression depth)

- sand desert
- lava flow
- coastline
- reef
- atoll

sea depth

- sea level
- -250m / -820ft
- -500m / -1640ft
- -1000m / -3281ft
- -2000m / -6562ft
- -3000m / -9843ft

- ▲ seamount / guyot symbol
- ▼ undersea spot depth

DRAINAGE FEATURES

- main river
- secondary river
- tertiary river
- minor river
- main seasonal river
- secondary seasonal river
- canal
- waterfall
- rapids
- dam
- perennial lake
- seasonal lake
- perennial salt lake
- seasonal salt lake
- reservoir
- salt flat / salt pan
- marsh / salt marsh
- mangrove
- wadi
- spring / well / waterhole / oasis

ICE FEATURES

- ice cap / sheet
- ice shelf
- glacier
- summer pack ice limit
- winter pack ice limit

COMMUNICATIONS

- highway
- highway (under construction)
- major road
- minor road
- tunnel (road)
- main line
- minor line
- tunnel (railroad)
- ✈ international airport

BORDERS

- full international border
- undefined international border
- disputed de facto border
- disputed territorial claim border
- indication of country extent (Pacific only)
- indication of dependent territory extent (Pacific only)
- demarcation/ cease-fire line
- autonomous / federal region border
- 2nd order internal administrative border
- 3rd order internal administrative border

SETTLEMENTS

- built-up area

settlement population symbols

- more than 5 million
- 1 million to 5 million
- 500,000 to 1 million
- 100,000 to 500,000
- 50,000 to 100,000
- 10,000 to 50,000
- fewer than 10,000

- country/dependent territory capital city
- autonomous / federal region / 2nd order internal administrative center
- 3rd order internal administrative center

MISCELLANEOUS FEATURES

- ancient wall
- site of interest
- scientific station

GRATICULE FEATURES

- lines of latitude and longitude / Equator
- Tropics / Polar circles
- degrees of longitude / latitude

TYPOGRAPHIC KEY

PHYSICAL FEATURES

landscape features	*Namib Desert* *Massif Central* *ANDES*
headland	*Nordkapp*
elevation / volcano / pass	Mount Meru 4556 m
drainage features	*Lake Rudolf*
rivers / canals / spring / well / waterhole / oasis / waterfall / rapids / dam	*Mekong*
ice features	*Vatnajökull*
sea features	*Golfe de Lion* *Andaman Sea* *INDIAN OCEAN*
undersea features	*Barracuda Fracture Zone*

REGIONS

country	**ARMENIA**
dependent territory with parent state	NIUE (to NZ)
region outside feature area	ANGOLA
autonomous / federal region	MINAS GERAIS
2nd order internal administrative region	MINSKAYA VOBLASTS'
3rd order internal administrative region	Vaucluse
cultural region	New England

SETTLEMENTS

capital city	**BEIJING**
dependent territory capital city	FORT-DE-FRANCE
other settlements	Chicago Adana Tizi Ozou Yonezawa Farnham

MISCELLANEOUS

sites of interest / miscellaneous	Valley of the Kings
Tropics / Polar circles	*Antarctic Circle*

HOW TO USE THIS ATLAS

THE ATLAS IS ORGANIZED BY CONTINENT, moving eastward from the International Date Line. The opening section describes the world's structure, systems, and main features. It is followed by The Atlas of the World, a continent-by-continent guide to today's world, starting with a comprehensive insight into the physical, political, and economic structure of each continent, followed by integrated mapping and a description of each region or country.

THE WORLD

THE INTRODUCTORY SECTION of the Atlas deals with every aspect of the planet, from physical structure to human geography, providing an overall picture of the world we live in. Complex topics such as the landscape of the Earth, climate, oceans, population, and economic patterns are clearly explained with the aid of maps and diagrams drawn from the latest information.

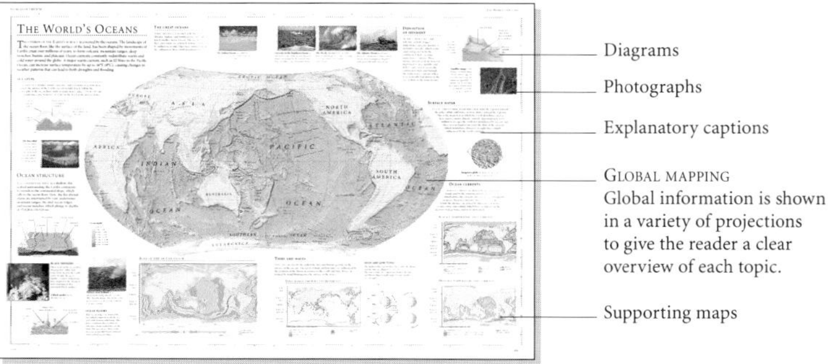
THE WORLD'S OCEANS
Diagrams
Photographs
Explanatory captions
GLOBAL MAPPING
Global information is shown in a variety of projections to give the reader a clear overview of each topic.
Supporting maps

THE POLITICAL CONTINENT

THE POLITICAL PORTRAIT of the continent is a vital reference point for every continental section, showing the position of countries relative to one another, and the relationship between human settlement and geographic location. The complex mosaic of languages spoken in each continent is mapped, along with the effect of communications networks on the pattern of settlement.

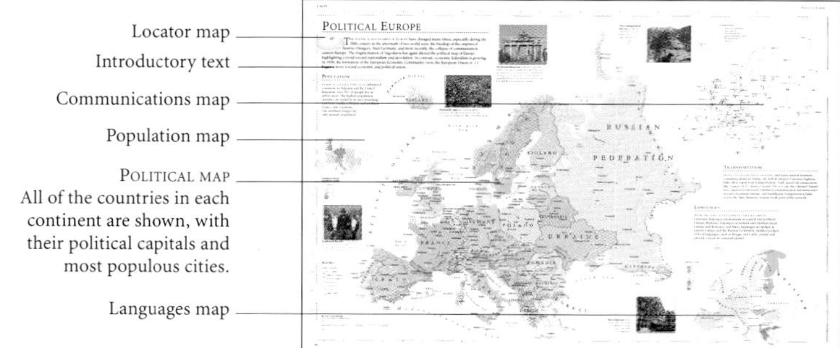
Locator map
Introductory text
Communications map
Population map
POLITICAL MAP
All of the countries in each continent are shown, with their political capitals and most populous cities.
Languages map
POLITICAL EUROPE

CONTINENTAL RESOURCES

THE EARTH'S RICH NATURAL RESOURCES, including oil, gas, minerals, and fertile land, have played a key role in the development of society. These pages show the location of minerals and agricultural resources on each continent, and how they have been instrumental in dictating industrial growth and the varieties of economic activity across the continent.

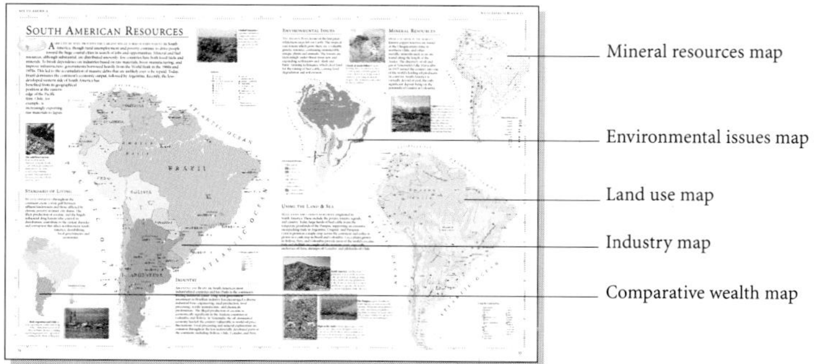
SOUTH AMERICAN RESOURCES
Mineral resources map
Environmental issues map
Land use map
Industry map
Comparative wealth map

THE PHYSICAL CONTINENT

THE ASTONISHING VARIETY of landforms, and the dramatic forces that created and continue to shape the landscape, are explained in the continental physical spread. Cross-sections, illustrations, and terrain maps highlight the different parts of the continent, showing how nature's forces have produced the landscapes we see today.

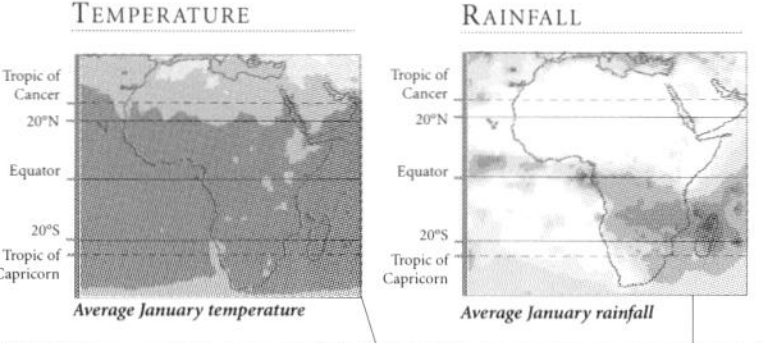

TEMPERATURE
RAINFALL
Tropic of Cancer
20°N
Equator
20°S
Tropic of Capricorn
Average January temperature
Average January rainfall

CLIMATE CHARTS
Rainfall and temperature charts clearly show the continental patterns of rainfall and temperature.

CLIMATE MAP
Climatic regions vary across each continent. The map displays the differing climatic regions, as well as daily hours of sunshine at selected weather stations.

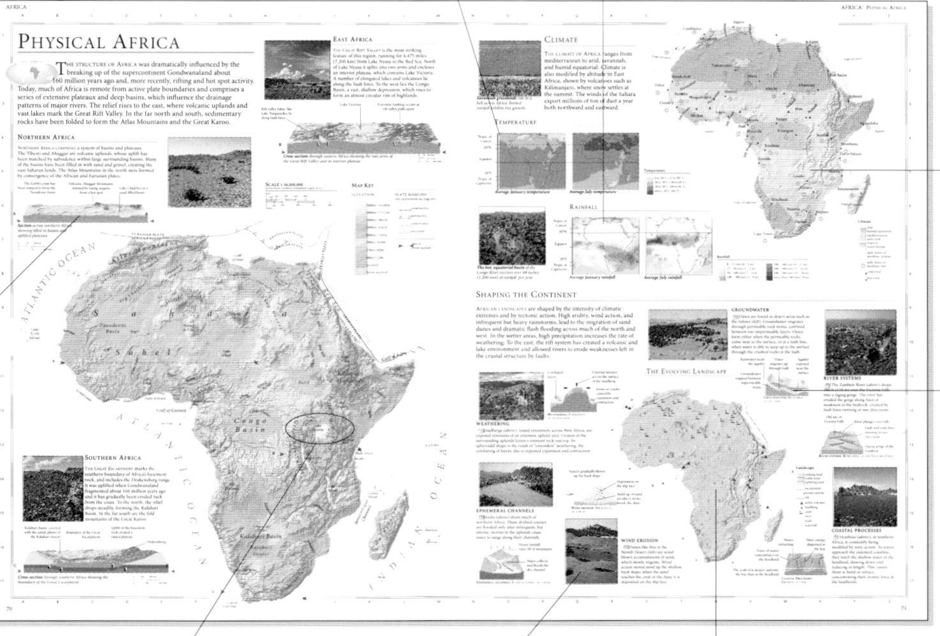

PHYSICAL AFRICA

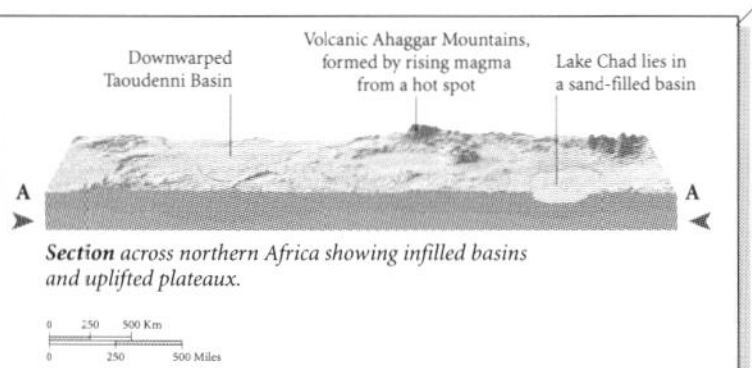

Downwarped Taoudenni Basin
Volcanic Ahaggar Mountains, formed by rising magma from a hot spot
Lake Chad lies in a sand-filled basin
A
A
Section across northern Africa showing infilled basins and uplifted plateaux.

CROSS-SECTIONS
Detailed cross-sections through selected parts of the continent show the underlying geomorphic structure.

Rainwater feeds the aquifer
Aquifer exposed near the surface
Groundwater trapped between impermeable strata
GROUNDWATER: FORMATION OF AN OASIS

LANDFORM DIAGRAMS
The complex formation of many typical landforms is summarized in these easy-to-understand illustrations.

MAIN PHYSICAL MAP
Detailed satellite data have been used to create an accurate and visually striking picture of the surface of the continent.

Albert
Lake Victoria
Great Rift Valley
Kilimanjaro 5895m
Lake Tanganyika
Pemba Island
Zanzibar

PHOTOGRAPHS
A wide range of beautiful photographs bring the world's regions to life.

LANDSCAPE EVOLUTION MAP
The physical shape of each continent is affected by a variety of forces that continually sculpt and modify the landscape. This map shows the major processes that affect different parts of the continent.

REGIONAL MAPPING

THE MAIN BODY of the Atlas is a unique regional map set, with detailed information on the terrain, the human geography of the region, and its infrastructure. Around the edge of the map, additional "at-a-glance" maps give an instant picture of regional industry, land use, and agriculture. The detailed terrain map (shown in perspective) focuses on the main physical features of the region, and is enhanced by annotated illustrations, and photographs of the physical structure.

REGIONAL LOCATOR
This small map shows the location of each country in relation to its continent.

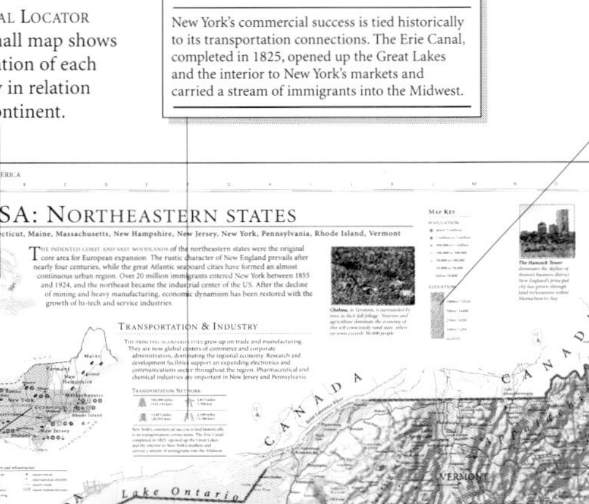

TRANSPORTATION NETWORK

340,090 miles (544,144 km)	4,813 miles 7,700 km
12,872 miles (20,592 km)	2,108 miles (3,389 km)

New York's commercial success is tied historically to its transportation connections. The Erie Canal, completed in 1825, opened up the Great Lakes and the interior to New York's markets and carried a stream of immigrants into the Midwest.

TRANSPORTATION NETWORK
The differing extent of the transportation network for each region is shown here, along with key facts about the transportation system.

KEY TO MAIN MAP
A key to the population symbols and land heights accompanies the main map.

WORLD LOCATOR
This locates the continent in which the region is found on a small world map.

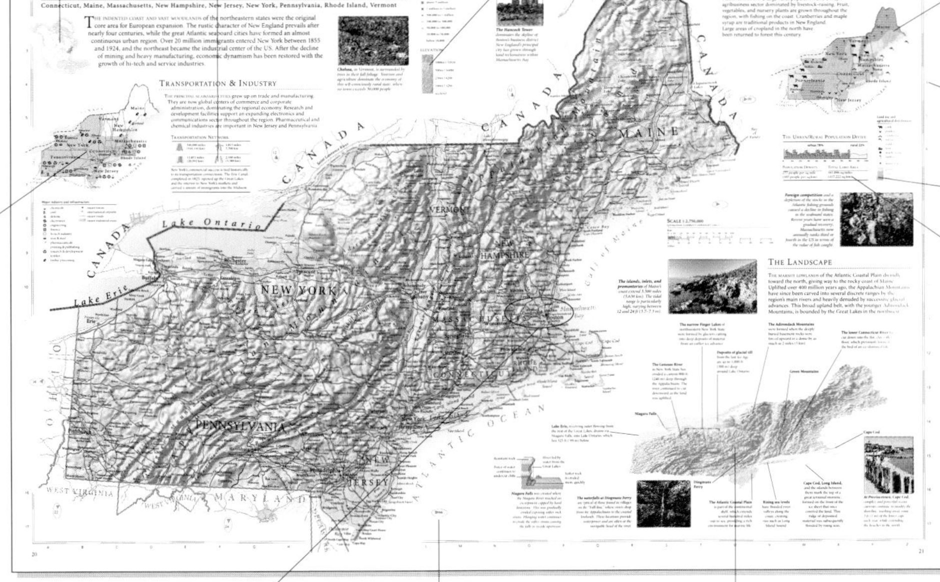

USA: NORTHEASTERN STATES

LAND USE MAP
This shows the different types of land use that characterize the region, as well as indicating the principal agricultural activities.

GRID REFERENCE
The framing grid provides a location reference for each place listed in the Index.

MAP KEYS
Each supporting map has its own key.

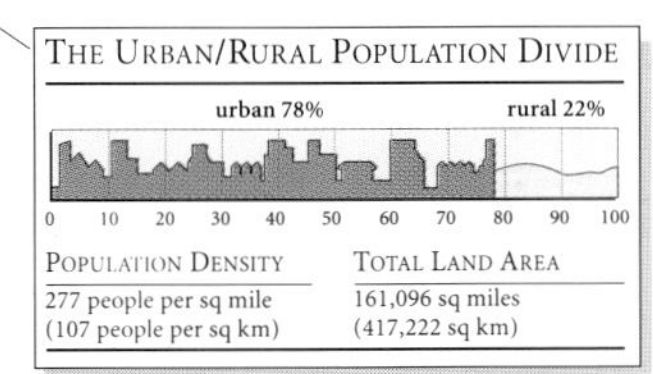

THE URBAN/RURAL POPULATION DIVIDE
urban 78%
rural 22%
0 10 20 30 40 50 60 70 80 90 100
POPULATION DENSITY
277 people per sq mile
(107 people per sq km)
TOTAL LAND AREA
161,096 sq miles
(417,222 sq km)

URBAN/RURAL POPULATION DIVIDE
The proportion of people in the region who live in urban and rural areas, as well as the overall population density and land area, are clearly shown in these simple graphics.

CANADA
Maine
Vermont
New Hampshire
New York
Massachusetts
Connecticut
Rhode Island
Pennsylvania
New Jersey
ATLANTIC OCEAN

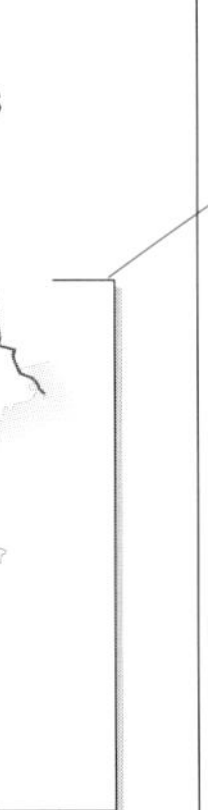

TRANSPORTATION AND INDUSTRY MAP
The main industrial areas are mapped, and the most important industrial and economic activities of the region are shown.

CONTINUATION SYMBOLS
These symbols indicate where adjacent maps can be found.

LANDSCAPE MAP
The computer-generated terrain model accurately portrays an oblique view of the landscape. Annotations highlight the most important geographic features of the region.

MASSACHUSETTS
Boston
Worcester
Springfield
Providence
Massachusetts Bay

MAIN REGIONAL MAP
A wealth of information is displayed on the main map, building up a rich portrait of the interaction between the physical landscape and the human and political geography of each region. The key to the regional maps can be found on page viii.

Jupiter

- **Diameter:** 88,846 miles (142,984 km)
- **Mass:** 1,900,000 million million million tons
- **Temperature:** -153°C (extremes not available)
- **Distance from Sun:** 483 million miles (778 million km)
- **Length of day:** 9.84 Earth hours
- **Length of year:** 11.86 Earth years
- **Surface gravity:** 1 kg = 2.53 kg

Mars

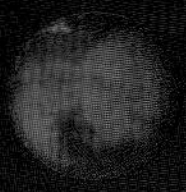

- **Diameter:** 4,217 miles (6,786 km)
- **Mass:** 642 million million million tons
- **Temperature:** -137 to 37°C
- **Distance from Sun:** 142 million miles (228 million km)
- **Length of day:** 24.623 Earth hours
- **Length of year:** 1.88 Earth years
- **Surface gravity:** 1 kg = 0.38 kg

Earth

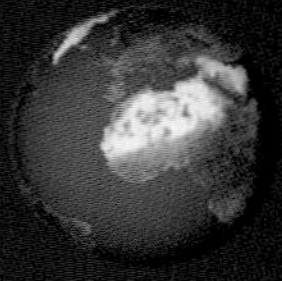

- **Diameter:** 7,926 miles (12,756 km)
- **Mass:** 5,976 million million million tons
- **Temperature:** -13 to 37°C
- **Distance from Sun:** 93 million miles (150 million km)
- **Length of day:** 23.92 hours
- **Length of year:** 365.25 days
- **Surface gravity:** 1 kg = 1 kg

Venus

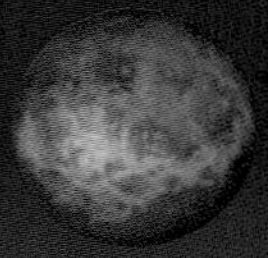

- **Diameter:** 7,520 miles (12,102 km)
- **Mass:** 4,870 million million million tons
- **Temperature:** 457°C (extremes not available)
- **Distance from Sun:** 67 million miles (108 million km)
- **Length of day:** 243.01 Earth days
- **Length of year:** 224.7 Earth days
- **Surface gravity:** 1 kg = 0.38 kg

Mercury

- **Diameter:** 3,031 miles (4,878 km)
- **Mass:** 330 million million million tons
- **Temperature:** -173 to 427°C
- **Distance from Sun:** 36 million miles (58 million km)
- **Length of day:** 58.65 Earth days
- **Length of year:** 87.97 Earth days
- **Surface gravity:** 1 kg = 0.38 kg

The Solar System

Nine major planets, their satellites, and countless minor planets (asteroids) orbit the Sun to form the Solar System. The Sun, our nearest star, creates energy from nuclear reactions deep within its interior, providing all the light and heat that make life on Earth possible. The Earth is unique in the solar system in that it supports life: its size, gravitational pull, and distance from the Sun have all created the optimum conditions for the evolution of life. The planetary images seen here are composites derived from actual spacecraft images (not shown to scale).

The Sun

- **Diameter:** 864,948 miles (1,392,000 km)
- **Mass:** 1990 million million million million tons

The Sun was formed when a swirling cloud of dust and gas contracted, pulling matter into its center. When the temperature at the center rose to 1,000,000°C, nuclear fusion – the fusing of hydrogen into helium, creating energy – occurred, releasing a constant stream of heat and light.

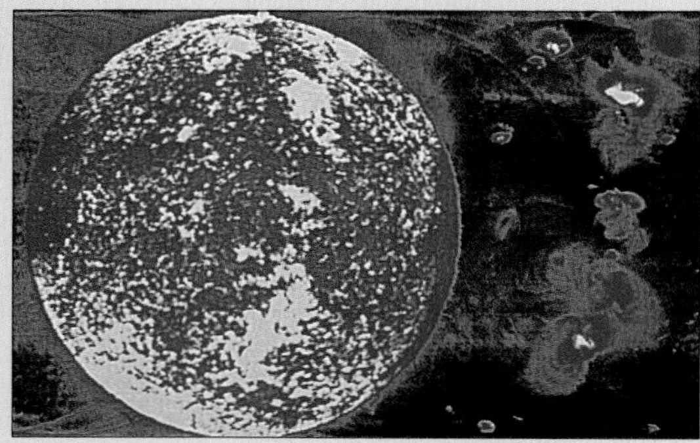

Solar flares are sudden bursts of energy from the Sun's surface. They can be 125,000 miles (200,000 km) long.

The formation of the Solar System

The cloud of dust and gas emitted by the Sun during its formation cooled to form the Solar System. The smaller planets nearest the Sun are formed of minerals and metals. The outer planets were formed at lower temperatures, and mainly consist of swirling clouds of gases.

The Milankovitch cycle

The amount of radiation from the Sun which reaches the Earth is affected by variations in the Earth's orbit and the tilt of the Earth's axis, as well as by "wobbles" in the axis. These variations cause three separate cycles, corresponding with the durations of recent ice ages.

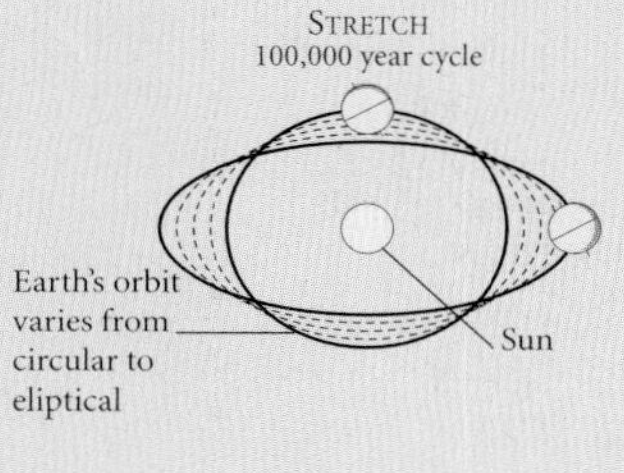
Stretch
100,000 year cycle
Earth's orbit varies from circular to eliptical
Sun

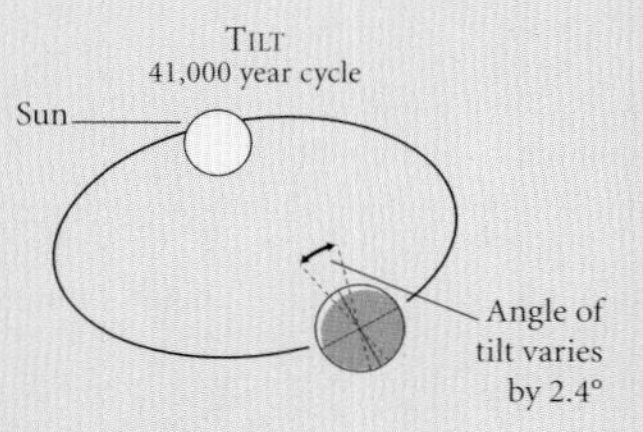
Tilt
41,000 year cycle
Sun
Angle of tilt varies by 2.4°

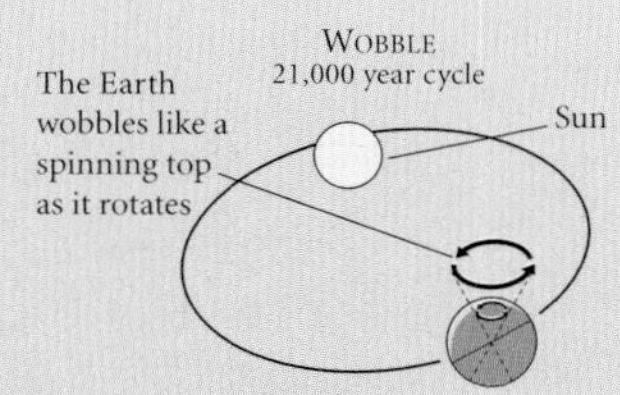
Wobble
21,000 year cycle
The Earth wobbles like a spinning top as it rotates
Sun

N O P Q R S T U V W X Y Z

Saturn

- **Diameter:** 74,974 miles (120,660 km)
- **Mass:** 570,000 million million million tons
- **Temperature:** -185°C (extremes not available)
- **Distance from Sun:** 887 million miles (1,427 million km)
- **Length of day:** 10.23 Earth hours
- **Length of year:** 29.46 Earth years
- **Surface gravity:** 1 kg = 1.07 kg

Uranus

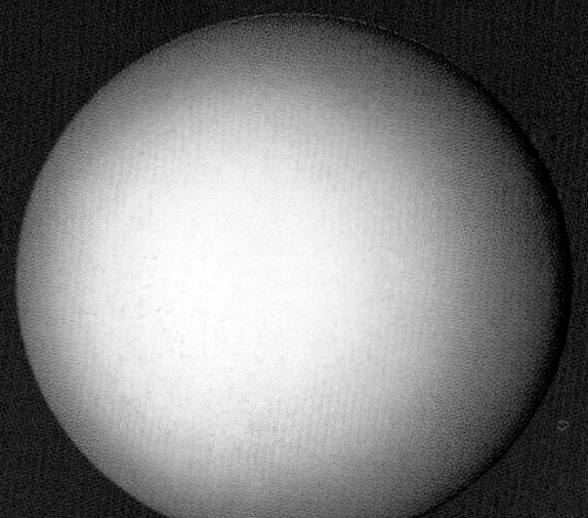

- **Diameter:** 31,763 miles (51,118 km)
- **Mass:** 86,800 million million million tons
- **Temperature:** -214°C (extremes not available)
- **Distance from Sun:** 1,783 million miles (2,870 million km)
- **Length of day:** 17.9 Earth hours
- **Length of year:** 84.01 Earth years
- **Surface gravity:** 1 kg = 0.92 kg

Space Debris

Millions of objects, remnants of planetary formation, circle the Sun in a zone lying between Mars and Jupiter, known as the asteroid belt. Fragments of asteroids break off to form meteoroids, which can reach the Earth's surface. Comets, composed of ice and dust, originated outside our solar system. Their elliptical orbit brings them close to the Sun and into the inner solar system.

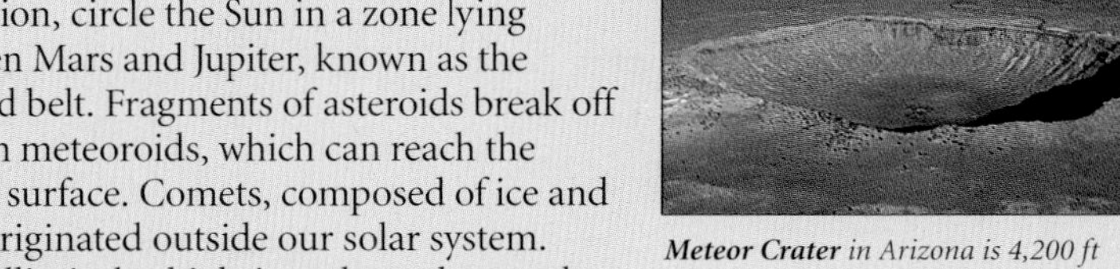

***Meteor Crater** in Arizona is 4,200 ft (1,300 m) wide and 660 ft (200 m) deep. It was formed over 10,000 years ago.*

Meteoroids

Meteoroids are fragments of asteroids that hurtle through space at great velocity. Although millions of meteoroids enter the Earth's atmosphere, the vast majority burn up on entry, and fall to the Earth as a meteor or shooting star. Large meteoroids traveling at speeds of 155,000 mph (250,000 kmh) can sometimes withstand the atmosphere and hit the Earth's surface with tremendous force, creating large craters on impact.

Possible and actual meteorite craters

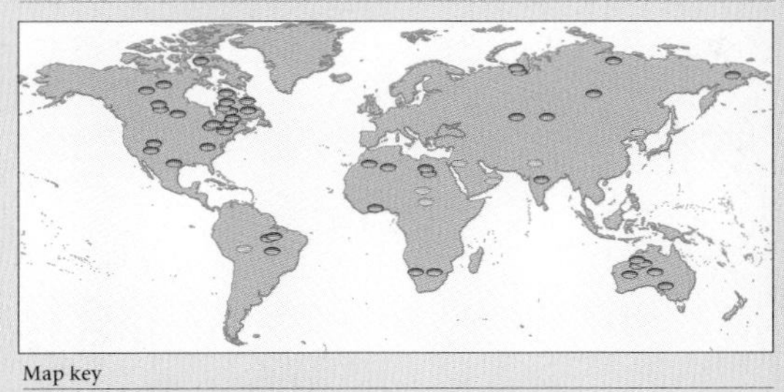

Map key
Possible impact craters
Meteorite impact craters

***The orbit of Halley's Comet** brings it past the Earth every 76 years. It last visited in 1986.*

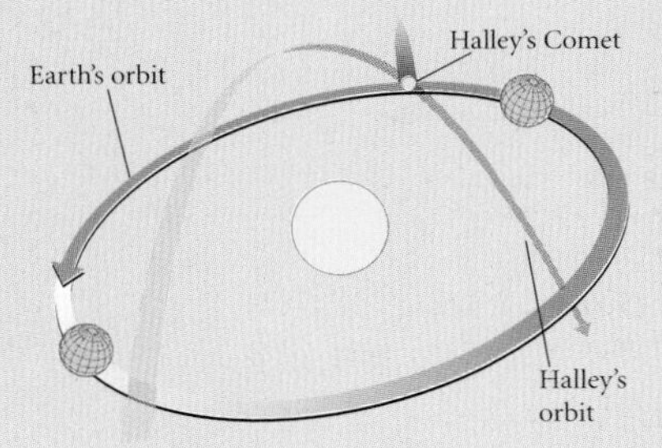
Earth's orbit
Halley's Comet
Halley's orbit

Orbit of Halley's Comet around the Sun

Neptune

- **Diameter:** 30,775 miles (49,528 km)
- **Mass:** 10,200 million million million tons
- **Temperature:** -225°C (extremes not available)
- **Distance from Sun:** 2,794 million miles (4,497 million km)
- **Length of day:** 19.2 Earth hours
- **Length of year:** 164.79 Earth years
- **Surface gravity:** 1 kg = 1.18 kg

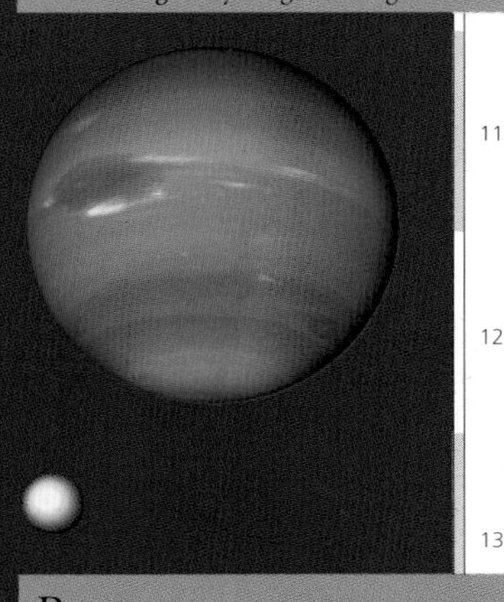

Pluto

- **Diameter:** 1,429 miles (2,300 km)
- **Mass:** 13 million million million tons
- **Temperature:** -236°C (extremes not available)
- **Distance from Sun:** 3,666 million miles (5,900 million km)
- **Length of day:** 6.39 Earth hours
- **Length of year:** 248.54 Earth years
- **Surface gravity:** 1 kg = 0.30 kg

The Earth's Atmosphere

During the early stages of the Earth's formation, ash, lava, carbon dioxide, and water vapor were discharged onto the surface of the planet by constant volcanic eruptions. The water formed the oceans, while carbon dioxide entered the atmosphere or was dissolved in the oceans. Clouds, formed of water droplets, reflected some of the Sun's radiation back into space. The Earth's temperature stabilized and early life forms began to emerge, converting carbon dioxide into life-giving oxygen.

__It is thought that the__ gases that make up the Earth's atmosphere originated deep within the interior, and were released many millions of years ago during intense volcanic activity, similar to this eruption at Mount St. Helens.

Order and relative distance from the Sun of planets

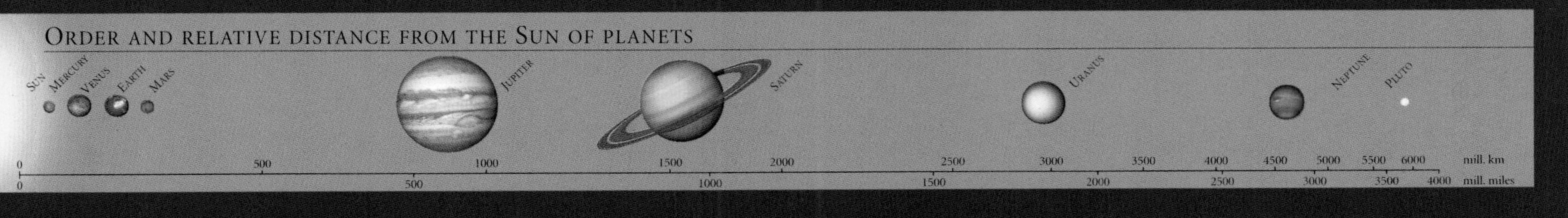
Sun
Mercury
Venus
Earth
Mars
Jupiter
Saturn
Uranus
Neptune
Pluto
0 500 1000 1500 2000 2500 3000 3500 4000 4500 5000 5500 6000 mill. km
0 500 1000 1500 2000 2500 3000 3500 4000 mill. miles

N O P Q R S T U V W X Y Z

The Physical World

The Earth's surface is constantly being transformed: it is uplifted, folded, and faulted by tectonic forces; weathered and eroded by wind, water, and ice. Sometimes change is dramatic, the spectacular results of earthquakes or floods. More often it is a slow process over millions of years. A physical map of the world represents a snapshot of the ever-evolving architecture of the Earth. This terrain map shows the whole surface of the Earth, both above and below the sea.

The World in Section

These cross-sections around the Earth, one in the northern hemisphere; one straddling the Equator, reveal the limited areas of land above sea level in comparison with the extent of the sea floor. The greater erosive effects of weathering by wind and water limit the upward elevation of land above sea level, while the deep oceans retain their dramatic mountain and trench profiles.

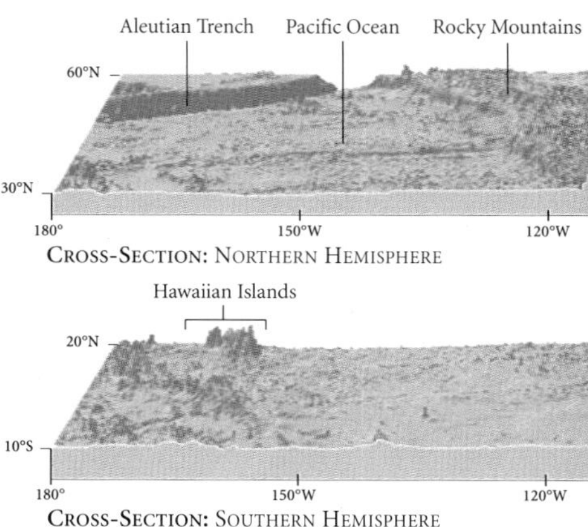
Aleutian Trench
Pacific Ocean
Rocky Mountains
60°N
30°N
180°
150°W
120°W
Hawaiian Islands
20°N
10°S

Cross-Section: Northern Hemisphere

Cross-Section: Southern Hemisphere

Map Key

Geographical regions

- ice
- tundra
- needleleaf forest
- broadleaf forest
- cultivated land
- hot desert
- cold desert
- tropical grassland
- tropical rain forest
- mountain
- submarine regions

Scale 1:66,000,000
(projection: Wagner VII)

Km 0 250 500 1,000 1,500 2,000
Miles 0 250 500 1,000 1,500 2,000

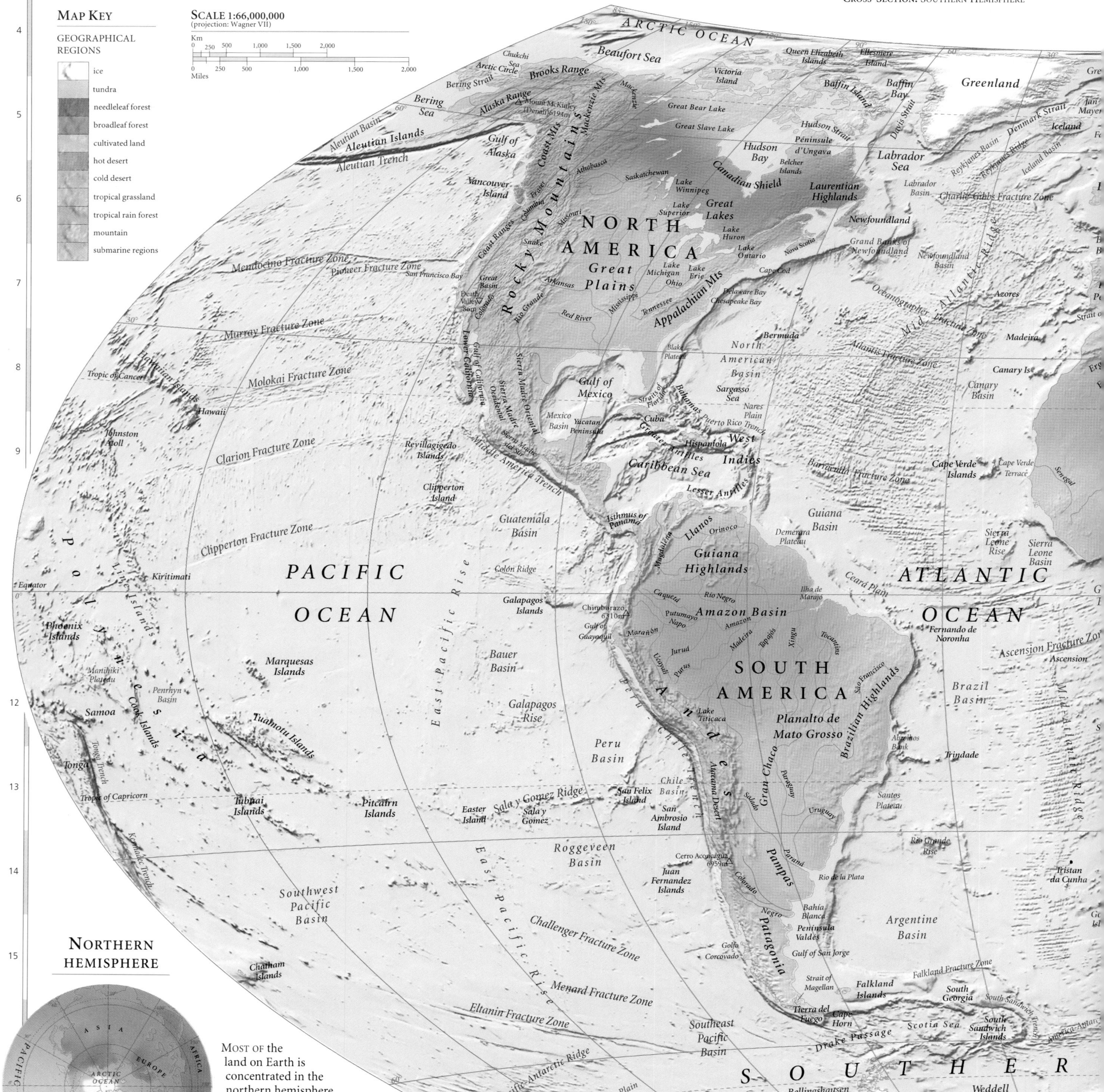

Northern Hemisphere

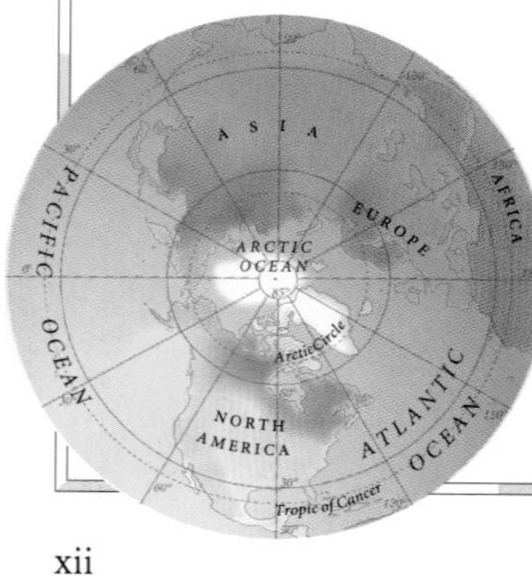

Most of the land on Earth is concentrated in the northern hemisphere, although Europe and North America are the only continents that lie wholly in the north.

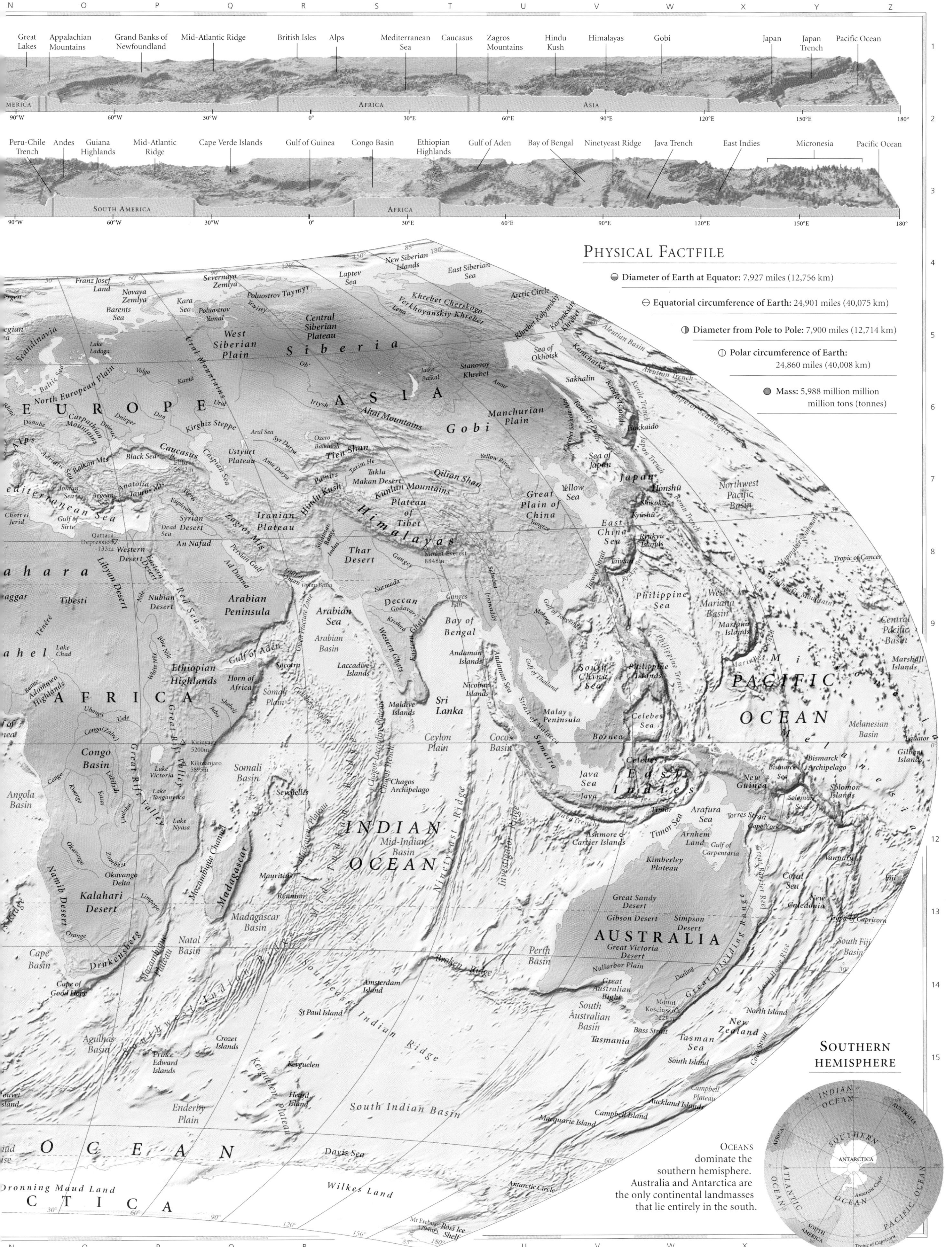

N O P Q R S T U V W X Y Z
Great Lakes
Appalachian Mountains
Grand Banks of Newfoundland
Mid-Atlantic Ridge
British Isles
Alps
Mediterranean Sea
Caucasus
Zagros Mountains
Hindu Kush
Himalayas
Gobi
Japan
Japan Trench
Pacific Ocean
Africa
Asia
90°W 60°W 30°W 0° 30°E 60°E 90°E 120°E 150°E 180°
Peru-Chile Trench
Andes
Guiana Highlands
Mid-Atlantic Ridge
Cape Verde Islands
Gulf of Guinea
Congo Basin
Ethiopian Highlands
Gulf of Aden
Bay of Bengal
Ninetyeast Ridge
Java Trench
East Indies
Micronesia
Pacific Ocean
South America
Africa
1 2 3 4 5 6 7 8 9 10 11 12 13 14 15
Franz Josef Land
Novaya Zemlya
Barents Sea
Severnaya Zemlya
Kara Sea
Poluostrov Taymyr
Laptev Sea
New Siberian Islands
East Siberian Sea
Arctic Circle
Khrebet Cherskogo
Verkhoyanskiy Khrebet
Central Siberian Plateau
West Siberian Plain
Siberia
Sea of Okhotsk
Kamchatka
Sakhalin
Aleutian Basin
Aleutian Trench
Emperor Seamounts
Kurile Trench
Kurile Islands
Stanovoy Khrebet
Lake Baikal
Scandinavia
Lake Ladoga
Baltic Sea
North European Plain
Volga
Kama
Ural Mountains
EUROPE
ASIA
Carpathian Mountains
Dnieper
Don
Danube
Alps
Kirghiz Steppe
Aral Sea
Syr Darya
Irtysh
Altai Mountains
Manchurian Plain
Gobi
Hokkaidō
Caucasus
Elbrus 5642m
Caspian Sea
Ustyurt Plateau
Amu Darya
Tien Shan
Black Sea
Balkan Mts
Adriatic Sea
Anatolia
Taurus Mts
Aegean Sea
Ionian Sea
Mediterranean Sea
Pamirs
Takla Makan Desert
Kunlun Mountains
Qilian Shan
Yellow River
Sea of Japan
Japan
Honshū
Shikoku
Kyushu
Japan Trench
Bonin Trench
Northwest Pacific Basin
Yellow Sea
Great Plain of China
Yangtze
East China Sea
Ryukyu Islands
Taiwan
Taiwan Strait
Chott el Jerid
Gulf of Sirte
Euphrates
Tigris
Syrian Desert
Dead Sea
Zagros Mts
Iranian Plateau
Hindu Kush
Plateau of Tibet
Himalayas
Qattara Depression -133m
Western Desert
An Nafud
Persian Gulf
Thar Desert
Ganges
Mount Everest 8848m
Sahara
Libyan Desert
Eastern Desert
Ad Dahna
Indus
Tropic of Cancer
Tibesti
Nile
Nubian Desert
Red Sea
Arabian Peninsula
Gulf of Oman
Narmada
Deccan
Ganges Fan
Irrawaddy
Mekong
Philippine Sea
West Mariana Basin
Mariana Islands
Central Pacific Basin
Marshall Islands
Arabian Sea
Arabian Basin
Western Ghats
Bay of Bengal
Andaman Islands
Gulf of Tonkin
Philippine Trench
Philippine Islands
Mariana Trench
Micronesia
Lake Chad
Sahel
Blue Nile
White Nile
Gulf of Aden
Socotra
Ethiopian Highlands
Horn of Africa
Laccadive Islands
Nicobar Islands
Andaman Sea
Gulf of Thailand
South China Sea
PACIFIC OCEAN
Adamawa Highlands
AFRICA
Ubangi
Uele
Juba
Shebeli
Somali Plain
Maldive Islands
Sri Lanka
Malay Peninsula
Strait of Malacca
Sumatra
Celebes Sea
Borneo
Melanesian Basin
Equator
Gilbert Islands
Congo (Zaire)
Congo Basin
Great Rift Valley
Kirinyaga 5200m
Kilimanjaro 5895m
Lake Victoria
Ceylon Plain
Cocos Basin
Java Sea
Java
Celebes
East Indies
New Guinea
Bismarck Sea
Bismarck Archipelago
Solomon Islands
Solomon Sea
Angola Basin
Kwango
Kasai
Lake Tanganyika
Somali Basin
Seychelles
Chagos Archipelago
Chagos Trench
Ninetyeast Ridge
Investigator Ridge
Timor
Arafura Sea
Torres Strait
Cape York
Lake Nyasa
INDIAN OCEAN
Mid-Indian Basin
Java Trench
Ashmore & Cartier Islands
Timor Sea
Arnhem Land
Gulf of Carpentaria
Vanuatu
Fiji
Okavango
Zambezi
Mozambique Channel
Madagascar
Mauritius
Réunion
Kimberley Plateau
Great Barrier Reef
Coral Sea
New Caledonia
Namib Desert
Okavango Delta
Kalahari Desert
Limpopo
Madagascar Basin
Great Sandy Desert
Gibson Desert
Simpson Desert
Great Dividing Range
Tropic of Capricorn
Orange
Natal Basin
Drakensberg
Mozambique Plateau
AUSTRALIA
Great Victoria Desert
South Fiji Basin
Cape Basin
Perth Basin
Broken Ridge
Nullarbor Plain
Darling
Lord Howe Rise
Cape of Good Hope
Amsterdam Island
Great Australian Bight
Mount Kosciuszko 2228m
North Island
St Paul Island
Southeast Indian Ridge
South Australian Basin
Bass Strait
New Zealand
Tasman Sea
Tasmania
South Island
Agulhas Basin
Southwest Indian Ridge
Crozet Islands
Prince Edward Islands
Kerguelen
Kerguelen Plateau
Heard Island
Campbell Plateau
Auckland Islands
Campbell Island
Macquarie Island
Enderby Plain
South Indian Basin
OCEAN
Davis Sea
Antarctic Circle
Dronning Maud Land
Wilkes Land
ANTARCTICA
Mt Erebus 3794m
Ross Ice Shelf
N O P Q R U V W X

Physical Factfile

- **Diameter of Earth at Equator:** 7,927 miles (12,756 km)
- **Equatorial circumference of Earth:** 24,901 miles (40,075 km)
- **Diameter from Pole to Pole:** 7,900 miles (12,714 km)
- **Polar circumference of Earth:** 24,860 miles (40,008 km)
- **Mass:** 5,988 million million million tons (tonnes)

Southern Hemisphere

Indian Ocean
Australia
Southern Ocean
Antarctica
Antarctic Circle
Atlantic Ocean
Pacific Ocean
South America
Africa
Tropic of Capricorn

Oceans dominate the southern hemisphere. Australia and Antarctica are the only continental landmasses that lie entirely in the south.

Structure of the Earth

EARTH TODAY IS JUST THE LATEST PHASE in a constant process of geological evolution that has occurred over the past 4.5 billion years. Earth's continents are neither fixed nor stable; over the course of Earth's history, propelled by currents rising from the intense heat at its center, the great plates on which they lie have moved, collided, joined together, and separated. These processes continue to mold and transform the surface of the Earth, causing earthquakes and volcanic eruptions and creating oceans, mountain ranges, deep ocean trenches, and island chains.

Inside the Earth

THE EARTH'S HOT INNER CORE is made up of solid iron, while the outer core is composed of liquid iron and nickel. The mantle nearest the core is viscous, while the rocky upper mantle is fairly rigid. The crust is the rocky outer shell of the Earth. Together, the upper mantle and the crust form the lithosphere.

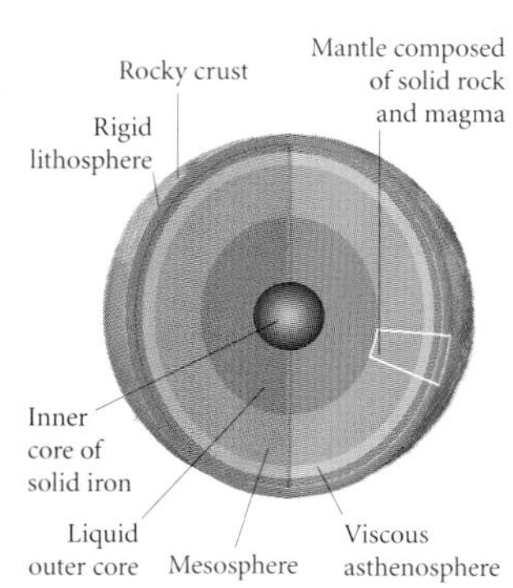

Rocky crust
Mantle composed of solid rock and magma
Rigid lithosphere
Inner core of solid iron
Liquid outer core
Mesosphere
Viscous asthenosphere

The Dynamic Earth

THE EARTH'S CRUST is made up of eight major (and several minor) rigid continental and oceanic tectonic plates, which fit closely together. The positions of the plates are not static. They are constantly moving relative to one another. The type of movement between plates affects how they alter the structure of the Earth. The oldest parts of the plates, known as shields, are the most stable parts of the Earth and little tectonic activity occurs here.

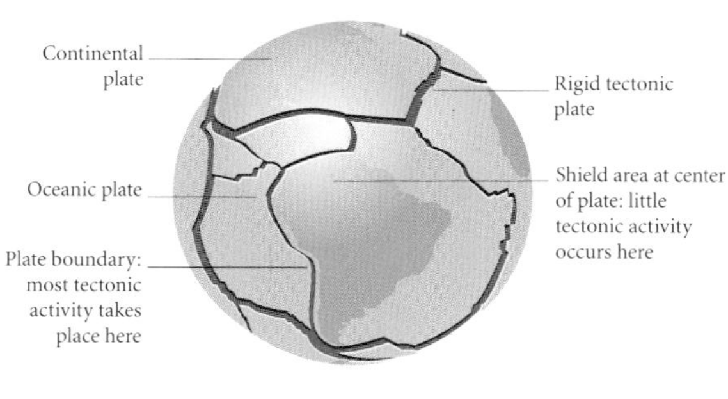

Continental plate
Oceanic plate
Plate boundary: most tectonic activity takes place here
Rigid tectonic plate
Shield area at center of plate: little tectonic activity occurs here

Convection currents

Inner core
Outer core
Subduction zone
Ocean crust
Movement of plate
Mid-ocean ridge
Lithosphere
Asthenosphere
Mesosphere
Continental crust

DEEP WITHIN THE EARTH, at its inner core, temperatures may exceed 8,100°F (4,000°C). This heat warms rocks in the mesosphere. These rise through the partially molten mantle, displacing cooler rocks just below the solid crust, which sink, and are warmed again by the heat of the mantle. This process is continuous, creating convection currents, which form the moving force beneath the Earth's crust.

Plate boundaries

THE BOUNDARIES BETWEEN THE PLATES are the areas where most tectonic activity takes place. Three types of movement occur at plate boundaries: the plates can either move toward each other, move apart, or slide past each other. The effect this has on the Earth's structure depends on whether the margin is between two continental plates, two oceanic plates, or an oceanic and continental plate.

The Mid-Atlantic Ridge rises above sea level in Iceland, producing geysers and volcanoes.

Mid-ocean ridges

Mid-ocean ridges are formed when two adjacent oceanic plates pull apart, forcing molten rocks onto the surface, which cool to form solid rock. Vast amounts of volcanic material are discharged at ocean ridges, and create the ocean floors. Submarine ocean ridges can reach heights of 10,000 ft (3,000 m).

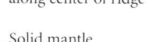

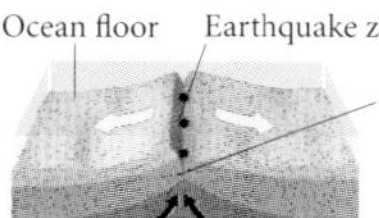

Ocean floor
Earthquake zone
Magma pushed upward along center of ridge
Solid mantle

FORMATION OF A MID-OCEAN RIDGE

Mount Pinatubo is an active volcano, lying on the Pacific "Ring of Fire."

Oceanic plates meeting

Oceanic crust is denser and thinner than continental crust; on average it is 3 miles (5 km) thick, while continental crust averages 18–24 miles (30–40 km). When oceanic plates of similar density meet, the crust is contorted as one plate overrides the other, forming deep sea trenches and volcanic island arcs above sea level.

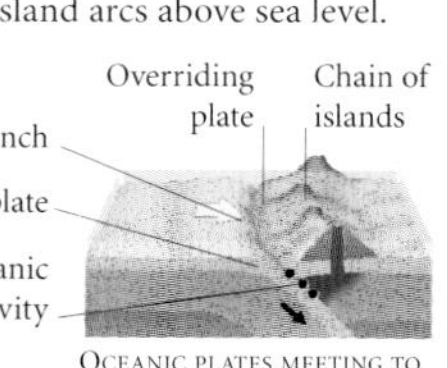

Ocean trench
Overriding plate
Chain of islands
Diving plate
Volcanic activity

OCEANIC PLATES MEETING TO FORM AN ISLAND ARC

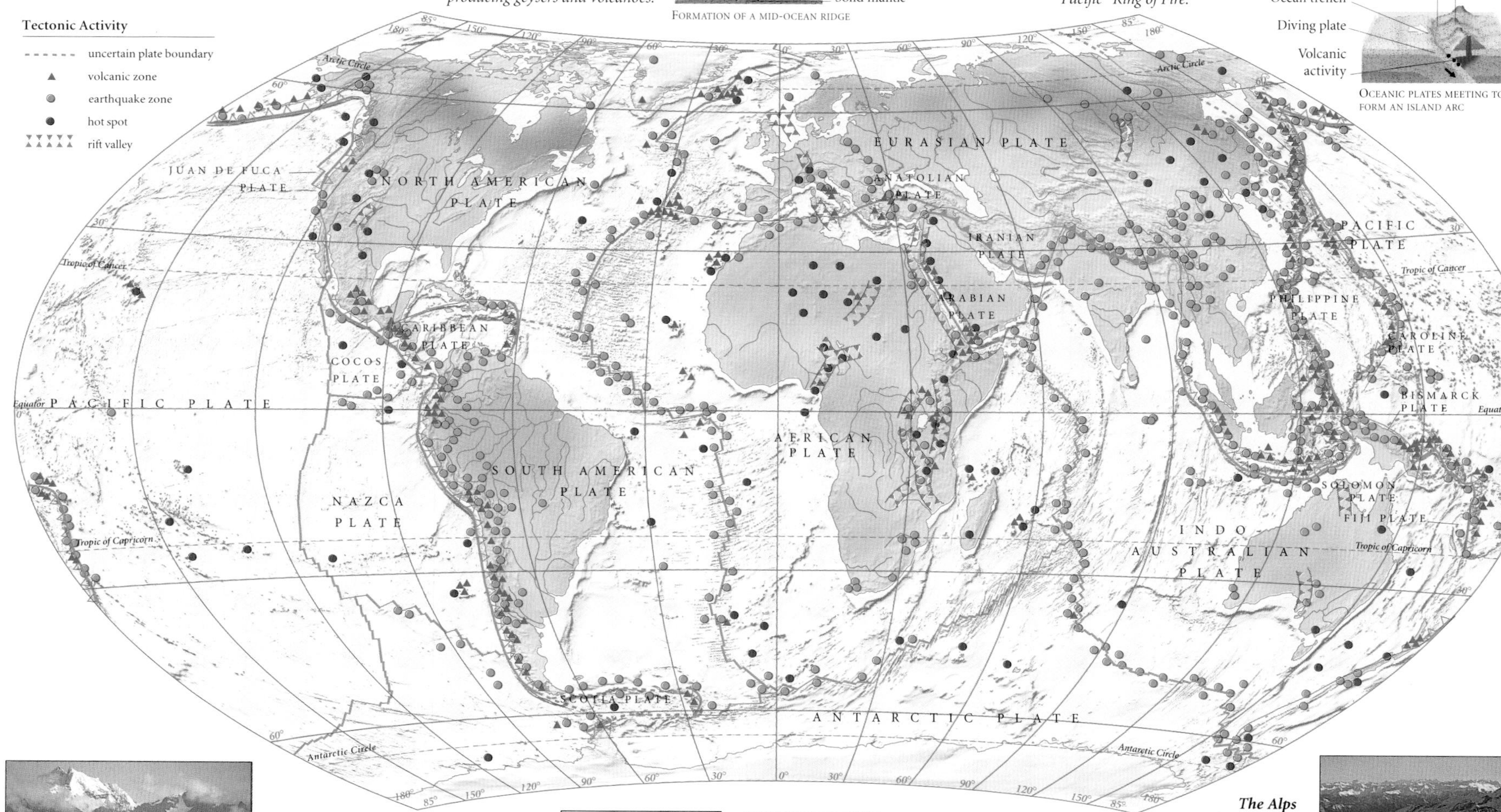

Tectonic Activity
uncertain plate boundary
volcanic zone
earthquake zone
hot spot
rift valley
JUAN DE FUCA PLATE
NORTH AMERICAN PLATE
EURASIAN PLATE
ANATOLIAN PLATE
IRANIAN PLATE
ARABIAN PLATE
CARIBBEAN PLATE
COCOS PLATE
PACIFIC PLATE
PHILIPPINE PLATE
CAROLINE PLATE
BISMARCK PLATE
AFRICAN PLATE
SOUTH AMERICAN PLATE
NAZCA PLATE
SOLOMON PLATE
FIJI PLATE
INDO AUSTRALIAN PLATE
SCOTIA PLATE
ANTARCTIC PLATE
Arctic Circle
Tropic of Cancer
Equator
Tropic of Capricorn
Antarctic Circle

Diving plates

When an oceanic and a continental plate meet, the denser oceanic plate is driven underneath the continental plate, which is crumpled by the collision into mountain ranges. As the oceanic plate plunges downward, it heats up, and molten rock (magma) is forced up to the surface.

The Andean mountain chain is the typical result of the impact of a diving plate.

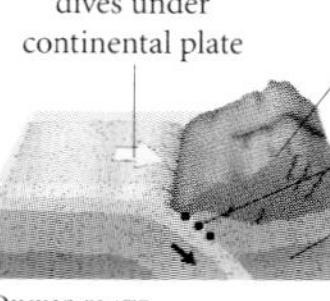

Oceanic plate dives under continental plate
Mountains thrust up by collision
Earthquake zone
Continental plate

DIVING PLATE

The deep fracture caused by the sliding plates of the San Andreas Fault can be clearly seen in parts of California.

Sliding plates

When two plates slide past each other, friction is caused along the fault line that divides them. The plates do not move smoothly and the uneven movement causes earthquakes.

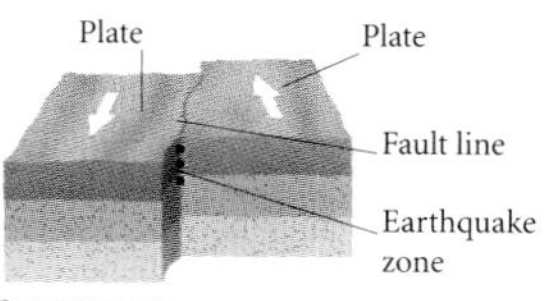

Plate
Plate
Fault line
Earthquake zone

SLIDING PLATES

The Alps were formed about 65 million years ago, when the African Plate collided with the Eurasian Plate.

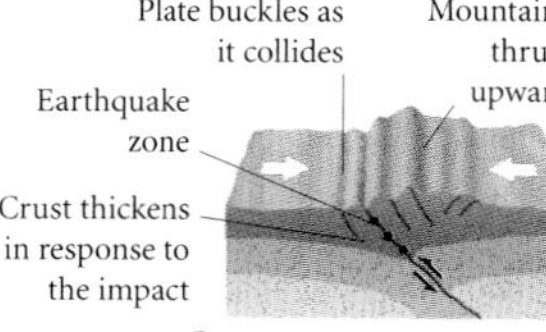

Plate buckles as it collides
Mountains thrust upward
Earthquake zone
Crust thickens in response to the impact

CONTINENTAL PLATES COLLIDING TO FORM A MOUNTAIN RANGE

Colliding plates

When two continental plates collide, great mountain chains are thrust upward as the crust buckles and folds under the force of the impact.

CONTINENTAL DRIFT

THE PLATES that make up the Earth's crust move only a few inches a year. Over the millions of years of Earth's history, however, its continents have moved many thousands of miles, creating new continents, oceans, and mountain chains.

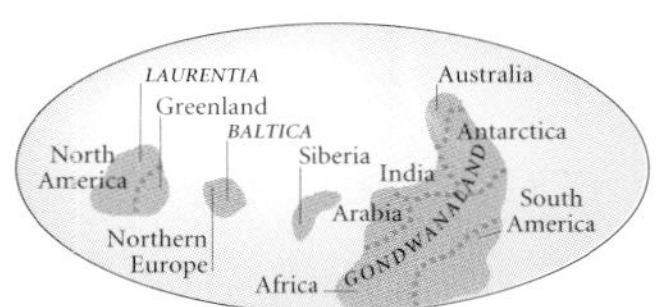
LAURENTIA
Greenland
BALTICA
Australia
North America
Siberia
Antarctica
India
Northern Europe
Arabia
South America
Africa
GONDWANALAND

1: CAMBRIAN PERIOD

570–510 million years ago. *Most continents are in tropical latitudes. The supercontinent of Gondwanaland reaches the South Pole.*

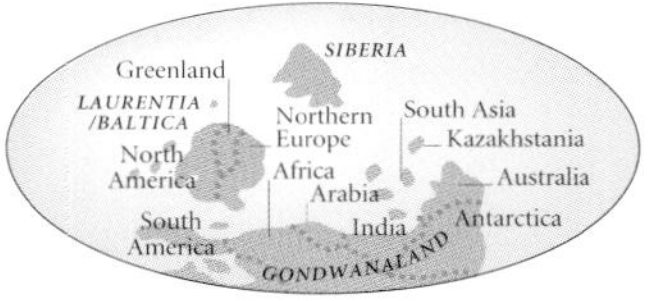
Greenland
SIBERIA
LAURENTIA /BALTICA
Northern Europe
South Asia
Kazakhstania
North America
Africa
Australia
Arabia
South America
India
Antarctica
GONDWANALAND

2: DEVONIAN PERIOD

408–362 million years ago. *The continents of Gondwanaland and Laurentia/Baltica are drifting northward.*

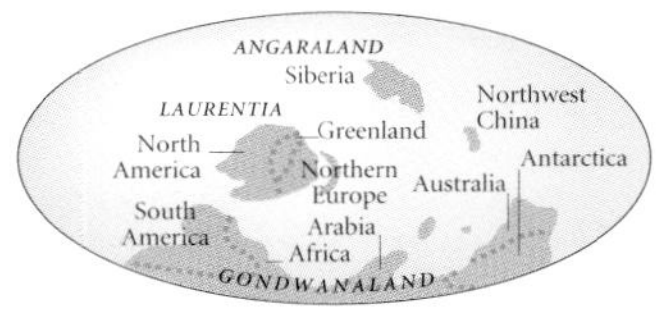
ANGARALAND
Siberia
LAURENTIA
Northwest China
North America
Greenland
Antarctica
Northern Europe
Australia
South America
Arabia
Africa
GONDWANALAND

3: CARBONIFEROUS PERIOD

362–290 million years ago. *Earth is dominated by three continents: Laurentia, Angaraland, and Gondwanaland.*

Greenland
Siberia
Manchuria
Northern Europe
China
Central Asia
Arabia
Southeast Asia
North America
Africa
India
South America
Australia
Antarctica
LAURASIA
PANGEA
GONDWANALAND

4: TRIASSIC PERIOD

245–208 million years ago. *All three major continents have joined to form the supercontinent of Pangea.*

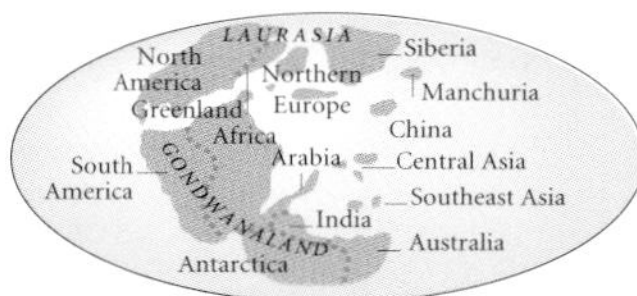
LAURASIA
North America
Siberia
Greenland
Northern Europe
Manchuria
China
Africa
South America
Arabia
Central Asia
Southeast Asia
India
Australia
Antarctica
GONDWANALAND

5: JURASSIC PERIOD

208–145 million years ago. *The supercontinent of Pangea begins to break up, causing an overall rise in sea levels.*

LAURASIA
Greenland
Siberia
Northern Europe
Manchuria
North America
Spain
China
Turkey
Central Asia
Africa
Arabia
Southeast Asia
South America
India
Australia
GONDWANALAND
Antarctica

6: CRETACEOUS PERIOD

145–65 million years ago. *Warm, shallow seas cover much of the land. Sea levels are about 80 ft (25 m) above present levels.*

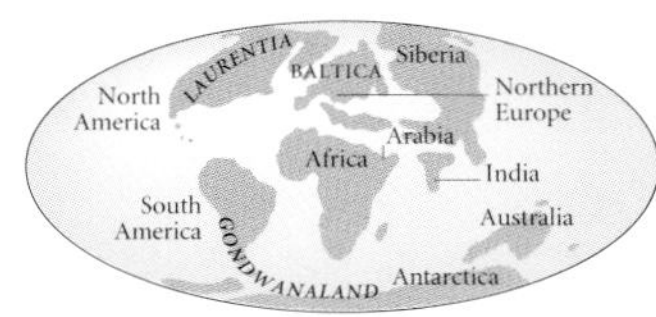
LAURENTIA
BALTICA
Siberia
North America
Northern Europe
Arabia
Africa
India
South America
Australia
GONDWANALAND
Antarctica

7: TERTIARY PERIOD

65–2 million years ago. *Although the world's geography is becoming more recognizable, major events, such as the creation of the Himalayan mountain chain, are still to occur during this period.*

CONTINENTAL SHIELDS

THE CENTERS OF THE EARTH'S CONTINENTS, known as shields, were established between 2,500 and 500 million years ago; some contain rocks more than two billion years old. They were formed by a series of turbulent events: plate movements, earthquakes, and volcanic eruptions. Since the Precambrian period, over 570 million years ago, the shields have experienced little tectonic activity. Today, these flat, low-lying slabs of solidified molten rock form the stable centers of the continents. They are bounded or covered by successive belts of younger sedimentary rock.

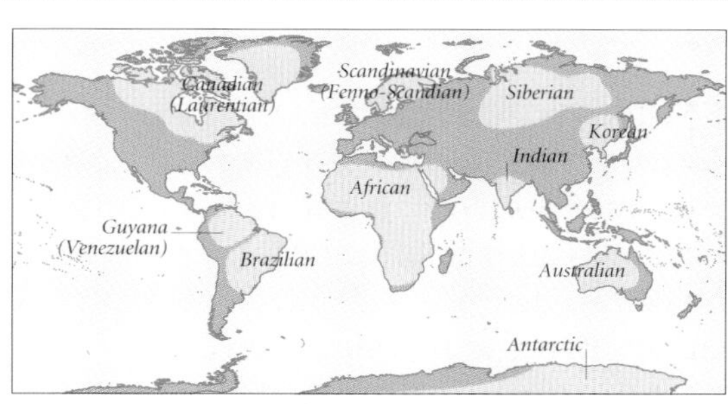
Canadian (Laurentian)
Scandinavian (Fenno-Scandian)
Siberian
Korean
Indian
African
Guyana (Venezuelan)
Brazilian
Australian
Antarctic

CREATION OF THE HIMALAYAS

BETWEEN 10 AND 20 MILLION YEARS AGO, the Indian subcontinent, part of the ancient continent of Gondwanaland, collided with the continent of Asia. The Indo-Australian Plate continued to move northward, displacing continental crust and uplifting the Himalayas, the world's highest mountain chain.

MOVEMENTS OF INDIA

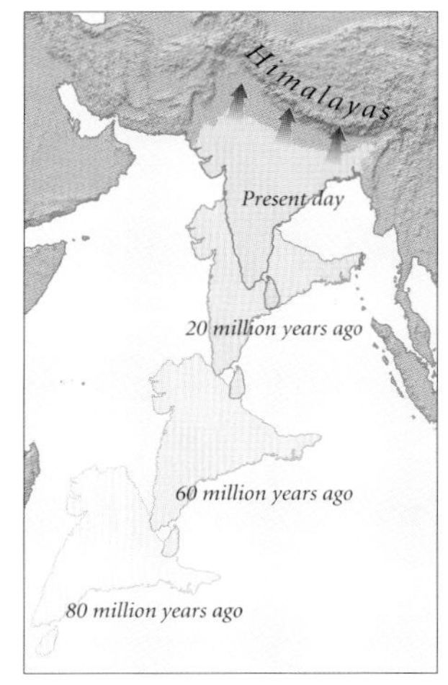
Himalayas
Present day
20 million years ago
60 million years ago
80 million years ago

Force of collision pushes up mountains

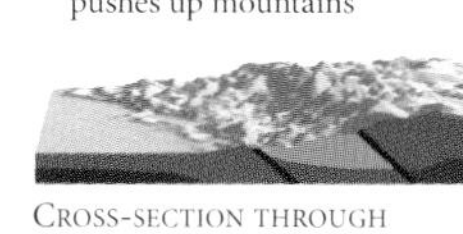

CROSS-SECTION THROUGH THE HIMALAYAS

The Himalayas *were uplifted when the Indian subcontinent collided with Asia.*

THE HAWAIIAN ISLAND CHAIN

A HOT SPOT lying deep beneath the Pacific Ocean pushes a plume of magma from the Earth's mantle up through the Pacific Plate to form volcanic islands. While the hot spot remains stationary, the plate on which the islands sit is moving slowly. A long chain of islands has been created as the plate passes over the hot spot.

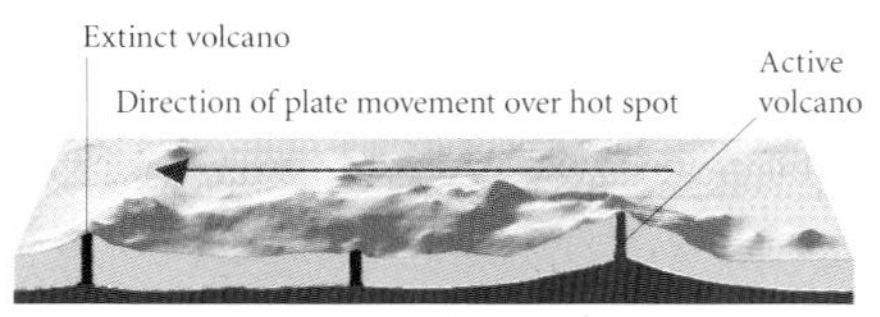
Extinct volcano
Active volcano
Direction of plate movement over hot spot

CROSS-SECTION THROUGH THE HAWAIIAN ISLANDS

EVOLUTION OF THE HAWAIIAN ISLANDS

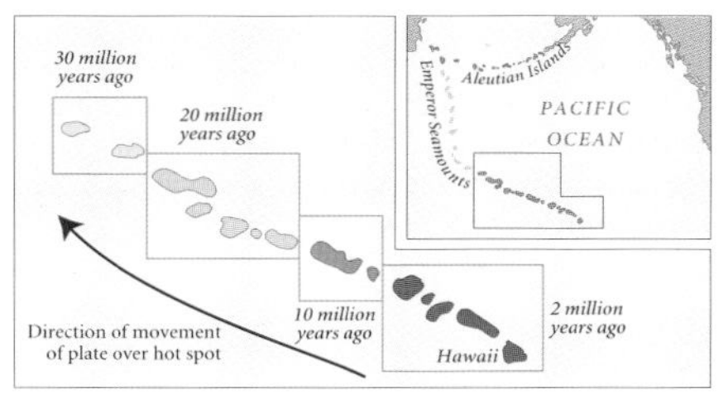
30 million years ago
20 million years ago
10 million years ago
2 million years ago
Hawaii
Direction of movement of plate over hot spot
Aleutian Islands
Emperor Seamounts
PACIFIC OCEAN

THE EARTH'S GEOLOGY

EARTH'S ROCKS ARE created in a continual cycle. Exposed rocks are weathered and eroded by wind, water, and chemicals and deposited as sediments. If they pass into the Earth's crust they will be transformed by high temperatures and pressures into metamorphic rocks or they will melt and solidify as igneous rocks.

GNEISS

Gneiss formations *in Norway's Jotunheimen Mountains.*

1 Gneiss is a metamorphic rock made at great depth during the formation of mountain chains, when intense heat and pressure transform sedimentary or igneous rocks.

***Basalt** columns at Giant's Causeway, Northern Ireland, UK.*

BASALT

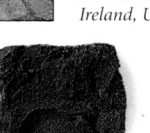

2 Basalt is an igneous rock, formed when small quantities of magma lying close to the Earth's surface cool rapidly.

LIMESTONE

3 Limestone is a sedimentary rock, formed mainly from the calcite skeletons of marine animals that have been compressed into rock.

Limestone hills, *Guilin, China.*

SANDSTONE

8 Sandstones are sedimentary rocks formed mainly in deserts, beaches, and deltas. Desert sandstones are formed of grains of quartz which have been well rounded by wind erosion.

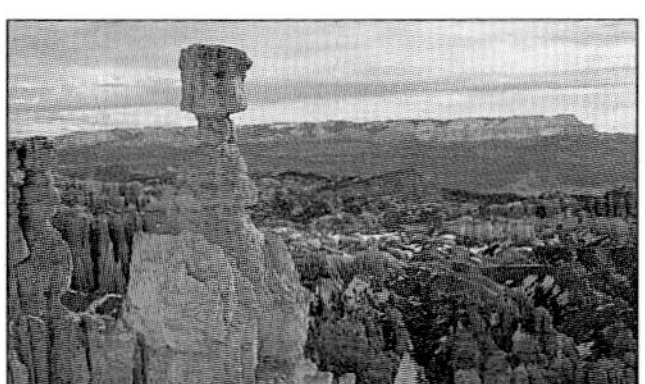

Rock stacks *of desert sandstone, at Bryce Canyon National Park, Utah.*

***Extrusive igneous rocks** are formed during volcanic eruptions, as here in Hawaii.*

ANDESITE

7 Andesite is an extrusive igneous rock formed from magma that has solidified on the Earth's crust after a volcanic eruption.

THE WORLD'S MAJOR GEOLOGICAL REGIONS

Geological Regions
- continental shield
- sedimentary cover
- coral formation
- igneous rock types

Mountain Ranges
- Alpine (new)
- Hercynian (old)
- Caledonian (ancient)

CORAL

4 Coral reefs are formed from the skeletons of millions of individual corals.

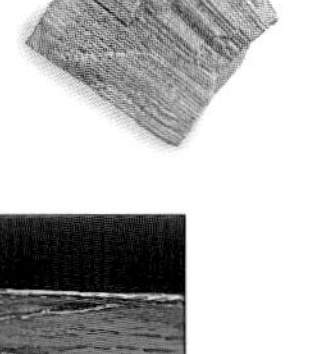

Great Barrier Reef, *Australia.*

SCHIST

6 Schist is a metamorphic rock formed during mountain-building, when temperature and pressure are comparatively high. Both mudstones and shales reform into schist under these conditions.

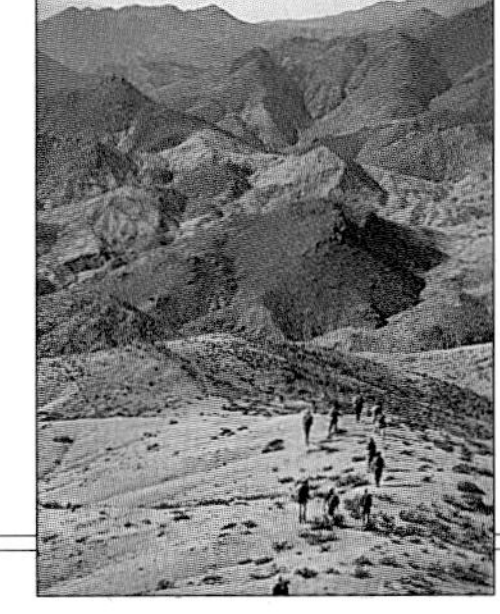

Schist formations *in the Atlas Mountains, northwestern Africa.*

GRANITE

5 Granite is an intrusive igneous rock formed from magma that has solidified deep within the Earth's crust. The magma cools slowly, producing a coarse-grained rock.

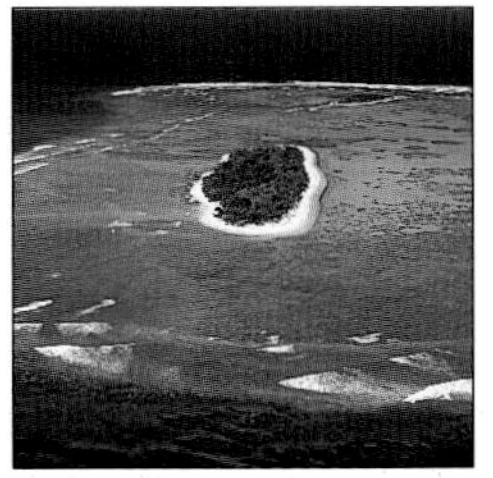

Namibia's *Namaqualand Plateau is formed of granite.*

Shaping the Landscape

The basic solid material of the Earth's surface is rock: valleys, deserts, soil, and sand are all evidence of the powerful agents of weathering, erosion, and deposition, which constantly shape and transform the Earth's landscapes. Water, either flowing continually in rivers or seas, or frozen and compacted into solid sheets of ice, has the most clearly visible impact on the Earth's surface. But wind can transport fragments of rock over huge distances and strip away protective layers of vegetation, exposing rock surfaces to the impact of extreme heat and cold.

Water

Less than 2% of the world's water is on the land, but it is the most powerful agent of landscape change. Water, as rainfall, groundwater, and rivers, can transform landscapes through both erosion and deposition. Eroded material carried by rivers forms the world's most fertile soils.

***Waterfalls** such as the Iguaçu Falls on the border between Argentina and southern Brazil erode the underlying rock, causing the falls to retreat.*

Coastal water

The world's coastlines are constantly changing; every day, tides deposit, sift, and sort sand and gravel on the shoreline. Over longer periods, powerful wave action erodes cliffs and headlands and carves out bays.

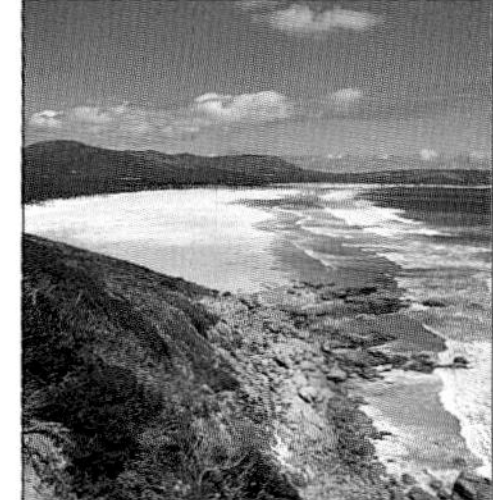

***A low, wide sandy beach** on South Africa's Cape Peninsula is continually reshaped by the action of the Atlantic waves.*

***The sheer chalk cliffs** at Seven Sisters in southern England are constantly under attack from waves.*

Groundwater

In regions where there are porous rocks like chalk, water is stored underground in large quantities; these reservoirs of water are called aquifers. Rain percolates through topsoil into the underlying bedrock, creating an underground store of water. The upper limit of the saturated zone is called the water table.

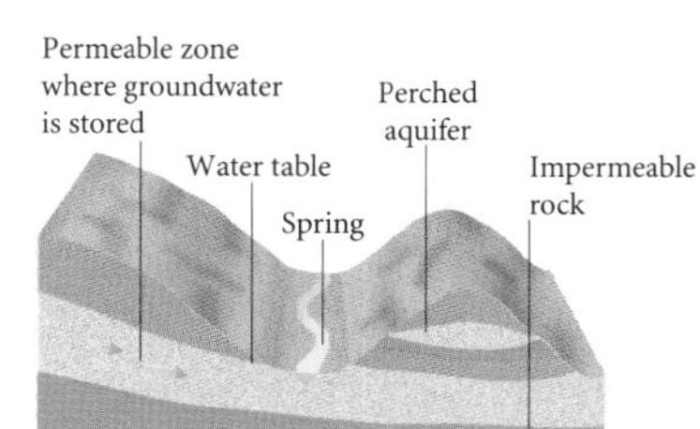

Permeable zone where groundwater is stored
Water table
Spring
Perched aquifer
Impermeable rock

Storage of groundwater in an aquifer

World river systems
drainage basin
World river systems:
Sediment deposited annually per drainage basin
tons per sq mile per year
9120
6080
1520
760
2400
1600
400
200 and less
tonnes per sq km per year
ARCTIC OCEAN
Yukon
Mackenzie
Nelson
St. Lawrence
Columbia
Colorado
Mississippi/Missouri
Rio Grande
ATLANTIC OCEAN
PACIFIC OCEAN
Orinoco
Amazon
São Francisco
Paraná
ATLANTIC OCEAN
Rhine
Danube
Volga
Ob'
Yenisey
Lena
Amur
Tigris/Euphrates
Indus
Ganges/Brahmaputra
Yellow River
Yangtze
Mekong
Niger
Nile
Congo
Zambezi
Orange
INDIAN OCEAN
PACIFIC OCEAN
Murray/Darling
Arctic Circle
Tropic of Cancer
Equator
Tropic of Capricorn
Antarctic Circle

Rivers

Rivers erode the land by grinding and dissolving rocks and stones. Most erosion occurs in the river's upper course as it flows through highland areas. Rock fragments move along the riverbed in fast-flowing water and are deposited in areas where the river slows down, such as flat plains, or where the river enters seas or lakes.

River valleys

Over long periods of time rivers erode uplands to form characteristic V-shaped valleys with smooth sides.

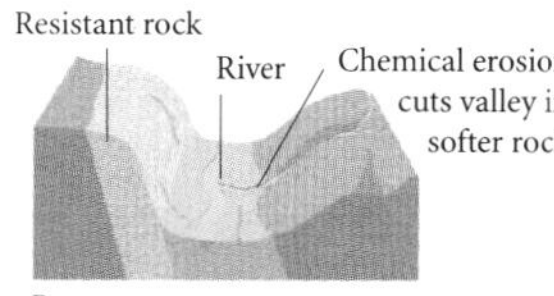

Resistant rock
River
Chemical erosion cuts valley in softer rock

River valley erosion

Deltas

When a river deposits its load of silt and sediment (alluvium) on entering the sea, it may form a delta. As this material accumulates, it chokes the mouth of the river, forcing it to create new channels to reach the sea.

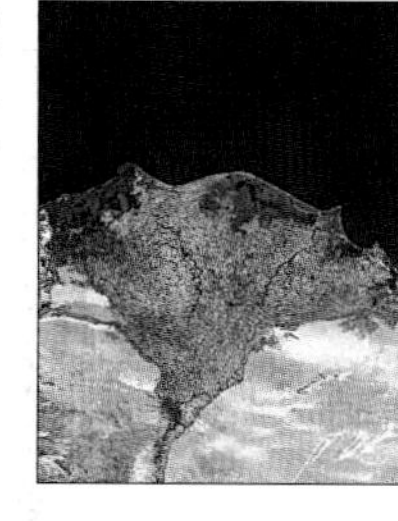

***The Nile** forms a broad delta as it flows into the Mediterranean.*

Drainage basins

The drainage basin is the area of land drained by a major trunk river and its smaller branch rivers or tributaries. Drainage basins are separated from one another by natural boundaries, known as watersheds.

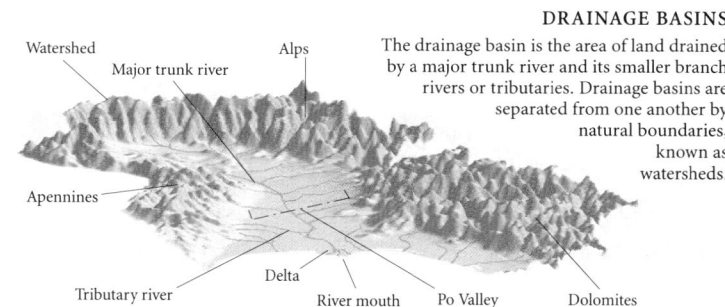

Watershed
Major trunk river
Alps
Apennines
Tributary river
Delta
River mouth
Po Valley
Dolomites

***The drainage basin** of the Po River, northern Italy.*

Meanders

In their lower courses, rivers flow slowly. As they flow across the lowlands, they form looping bends, called meanders *(left)*.

***The Mississippi River** forms meanders as it flows across the southern US.*

***The meanders** of Utah's San Juan River have become deeply incised.*

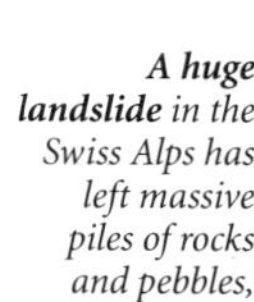

***Mud** is deposited by China's Yellow River in its lower course.*

Deposition

When rivers have deposited large quantities of fertile alluvium, they are forced to find new channels through the alluvium deposits, creating braided river systems.

Landslides

Heavy rain and associated flooding on slopes can loosen underlying rocks. These crumble, causing the top layers of rock and soil to slip.

***A huge landslide** in the Swiss Alps has left massive piles of rocks and pebbles, called scree.*

Gullies

In areas where soil is thin, rainwater is not effectively absorbed and can flow overland. The water runs downhill in channels, or gullies, and may lead to rapid erosion of soil.

***A deep gully** in the French Alps, caused by the scouring of upper layers of turf.*

Ice

During its long history, the Earth has experienced a number of glacial episodes when temperatures were considerably lower than today. During the last Ice Age, 18,000 years ago, ice covered an area three times larger than it does today. Over these periods, the ice has left a remarkable legacy of transformed landscapes.

Glaciers

Glaciers are formed by the compaction of snow into "rivers" of ice. As they move over the landscape, glaciers pick up and carry a load of rocks and boulders; erode the landscape which they pass over and are eventually deposited at the end of the glacier.

***A massive glacier** advancing down a valley in southern Argentina.*

Glacial valleys

Glaciers can erode much more powerfully than rivers. They form steep-sided, flat-bottomed valleys with a typical U-shaped profile. Valleys created by tributary glaciers, whose floors have not been eroded to the same depth as the main glacial valley floor, are called hanging valleys.

***The U-shaped profile** and piles of morainic debris are characteristic of a valley once filled by a glacier.*

***A series of hanging valleys** high up in the Chilean Andes.*

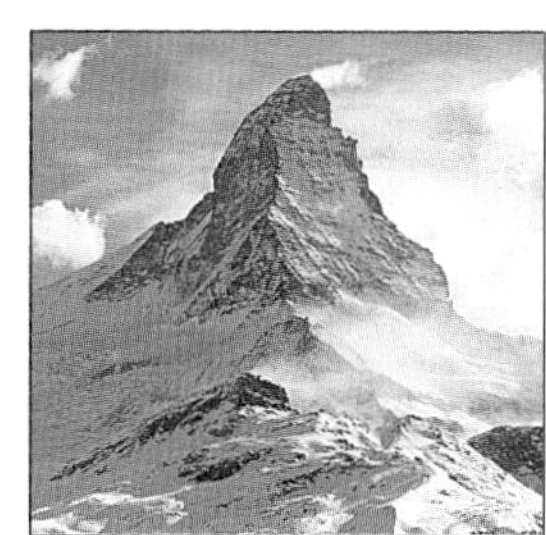

***The profile** of the Matterhorn has been formed by three cirques lying "back-to-back."*

Cirques

Cirques are basin-shaped hollows that mark the head of a glaciated valley. Where neighboring cirques meet, they are divided by sharp rock ridges, called arêtes. It is these arêtes which give the Matterhorn its characteristic profile.

Fjords

Fjords are ancient glacial valleys flooded by the sea following the end of a period of glaciation. Beneath the water, the valley floor can be 4,000 ft (1,300 m) deep.

***A fjord** fills a former glacial valley in southern New Zealand.*

Past and present world ice cover and glacial features

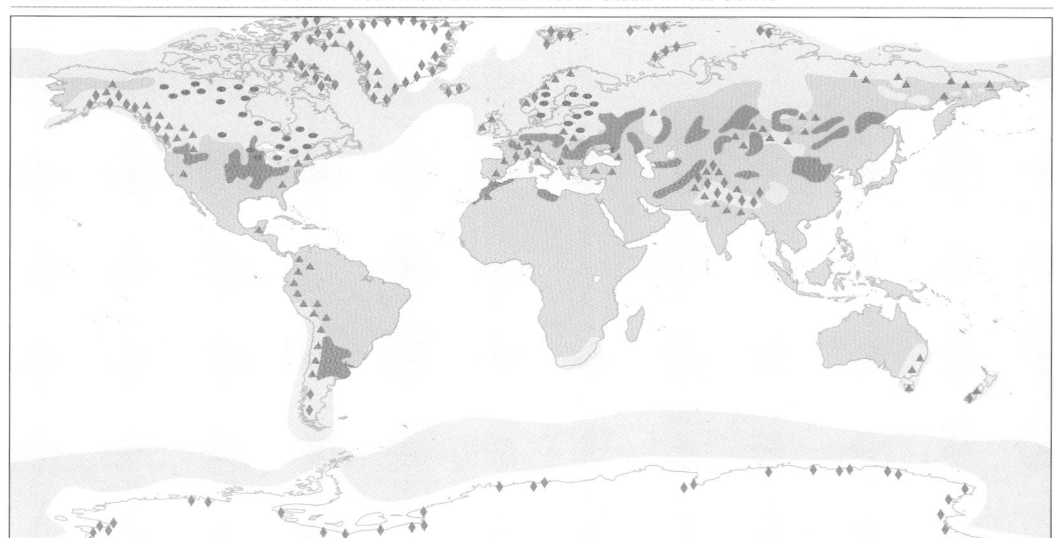

Past and present world ice cover and glacial features

- extent of last Ice Age
- loess deposits
- post-glacial feature
- glacial feature
- present day ice cover
- glacial field

Post-glacial features

When a glacial episode ends, the retreating ice leaves many features. These include depositional ridges, called moraines, which may be eroded into low hills, known as drumlins; sinuous ridges, called eskers; kames, which are rounded hummocks; depressions, known as kettle holes; and finely-ground loess deposits.

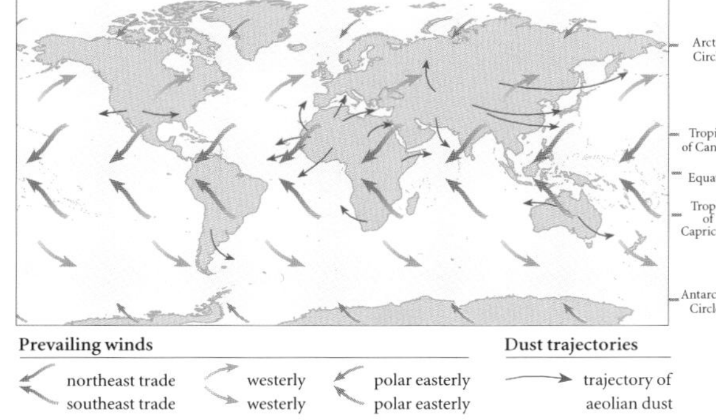
Kame terrace
Retreating glacier
Kettle hole
Drumlin
Esker
Terminal moraine
Braided river
Windblown loess
Glacial till
Bedrock

Post-glacial landscape features

Ice shattering

Water drips into fissures in rocks and freezes, expanding as it does so. The pressure weakens the rock, causing it to crack and eventually shatter into polygonal patterns.

***Irregular polygons** show through the sedge-grass tundra in the Yukon, Canada.*

Periglaciation

Periglacial areas occur near to the edge of ice sheets. A layer of frozen ground lying just beneath the surface of the land is known as permafrost. When the surface melts in the summer, the water is unable to drain into the frozen ground, and so "creeps" downhill, a process known as solifluction.

Wind

Strong winds can transport rock fragments great distances, especially where there is little vegetation to protect the rock. In desert areas, wind picks up loose, unprotected sand particles, carrying them over great distances. This powerfully abrasive debris is blasted at the surface by the wind, "weathering" the landscape into dramatic shapes.

Prevailing winds and dust trajectories

Arctic Circle
Tropic of Cancer
Equator
Tropic of Capricorn
Antarctic Circle

Prevailing winds: northeast trade, southeast trade; westerly, westerly; polar easterly, polar easterly

Dust trajectories: trajectory of aeolian dust

Deposition

The rocky, stony floors of the world's deserts are swept and scoured by strong winds. The smaller, finer particles of sand are shaped into surface ripples, dunes, or sand mountains, which rise to a height of 650 ft (200 m). Dunes usually form single lines, running perpendicular to the direction of the strongest wind. These long, straight ridges can extend for more than 100 miles (160 km).

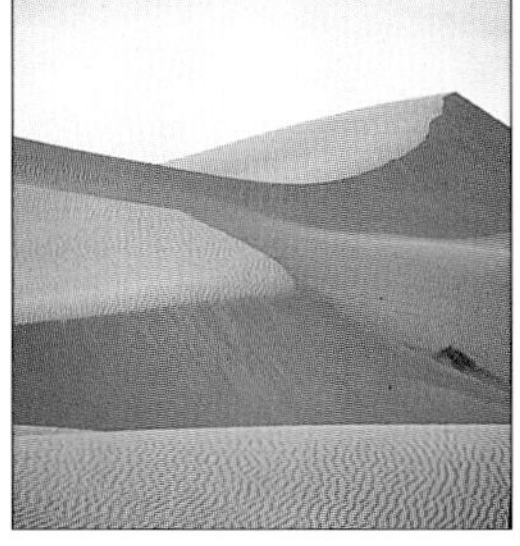

***Barchan dunes** in the Arabian Desert.*

***Complex dune system** in the Sahara.*

Dunes

Dunes are shaped by wind direction and sand supply. Where sand supply is limited, crescent-shaped barchan dunes are formed.

Types of Dune

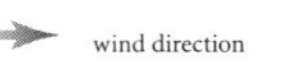

wind direction

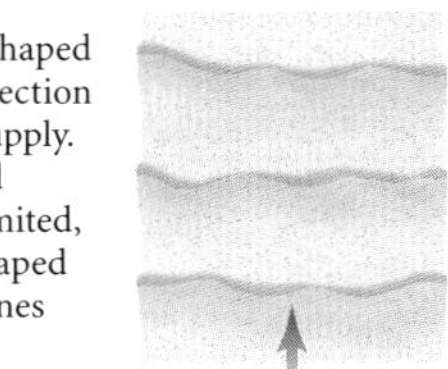

Transverse dune

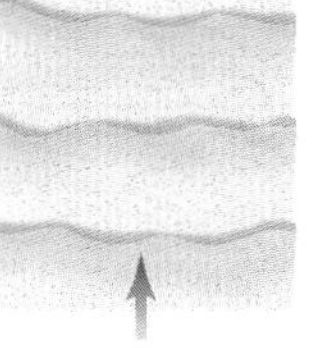

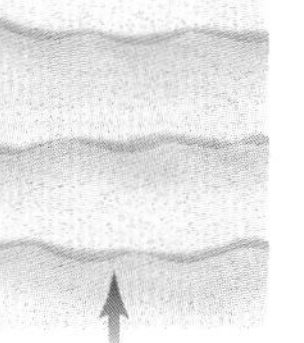

Barchan dune

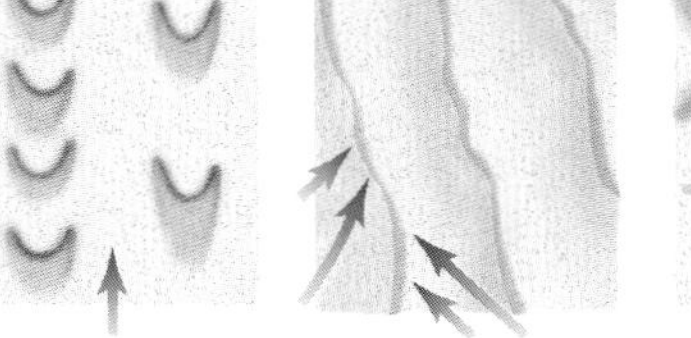

Linear dune

Star dune

Temperature

Hot and cold deserts

Main desert types: hot arid; semi-arid; cold polar

Most of the world's deserts are in the tropics. The cold deserts, which occur elsewhere, are arid because they are a long way from the rain-giving sea. Desert rocks are exposed because of lack of vegetation and are susceptible to changes in temperature. Extremes of heat and cold can cause both cracks and fissures to appear in the rock.

Heat

Fierce sun can heat the surface of rock, causing it to expand more rapidly than the cooler, underlying layers. This creates tensions that force the rock to crack or break up. In arid regions, the evaporation of water from rock surfaces dissolves certain minerals within the water, causing salt crystals to form in small openings in the rock. The hard crystals force the openings to widen into cracks and fissures.

***The cracked and parched** floor of Death Valley, California, one of the hottest deserts on Earth.*

Desert abrasion

Abrasion creates a wide range of desert landforms, from faceted pebbles and wind ripples in the sand, to large-scale features such as yardangs (low, streamlined ridges) and scoured desert pavements.

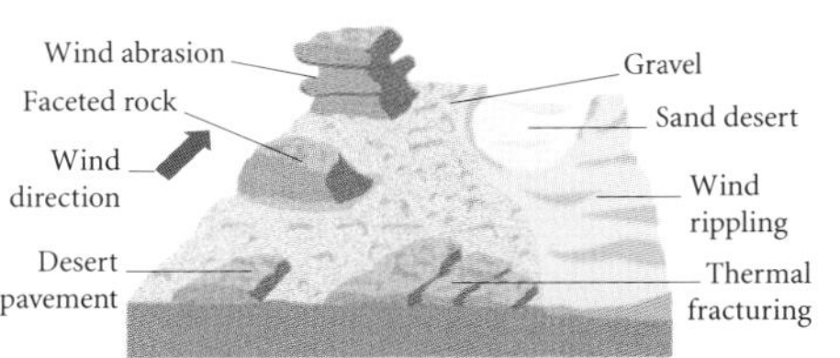
Wind abrasion
Gravel
Faceted rock
Sand desert
Wind direction
Wind rippling
Desert pavement
Thermal fracturing

Desert features formed by abrasion

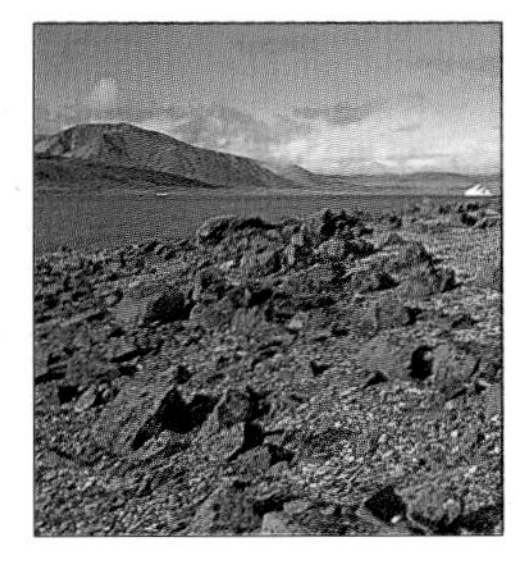

***This dry valley** at Ellesmere Island in the Canadian Arctic is an example of a cold desert. The cracked floor and scoured slopes are features also found in hot deserts.*

THE WORLD'S OCEANS

TWO-THIRDS OF THE EARTH'S SURFACE is covered by the oceans. The landscape of the ocean floor, like the surface of the land, has been shaped by movements of Earth's crust over millions of years, to form volcanic mountain ranges, deep trenches, basins, and plateaus. Ocean currents constantly redistribute warm and cold water around the globe. A major warm current, such as El Niño in the Pacific Ocean, can increase surface temperature by up to 46°F (8°C), causing changes in weather patterns that can lead to both droughts and flooding.

THE GREAT OCEANS

THERE ARE FIVE OCEANS on Earth: the Pacific, Atlantic, Indian, and Southern oceans, and the much smaller Arctic Ocean. The ocean basins as they exist today are relatively young – only about 80 million years old. One of the most recent plate collisions, between the Eurasian and African plates, created the present day arrangement of continents and oceans.

The Indian Ocean accounts for approximately 20% of the total area of the world's oceans.

SEA LEVEL

IF THE INFLUENCE of tides, winds, currents, and variations in gravity were ignored, the surface of the Earth's oceans would closely follow the topography of the ocean floor, with an underwater ridge 3,000 ft (915 m) high producing a rise of up to 3 ft (1 m) in the level of the surface water.

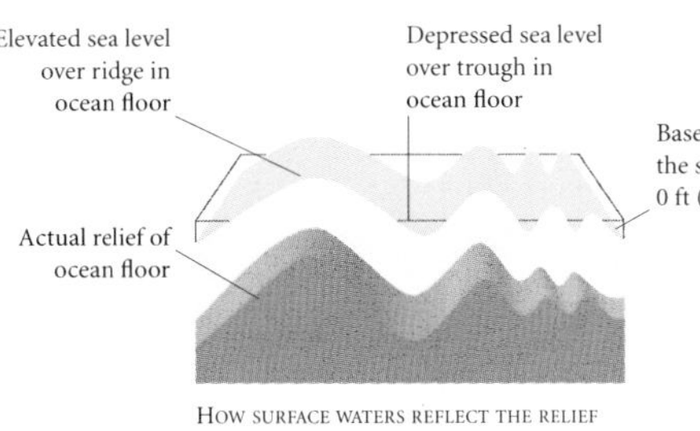
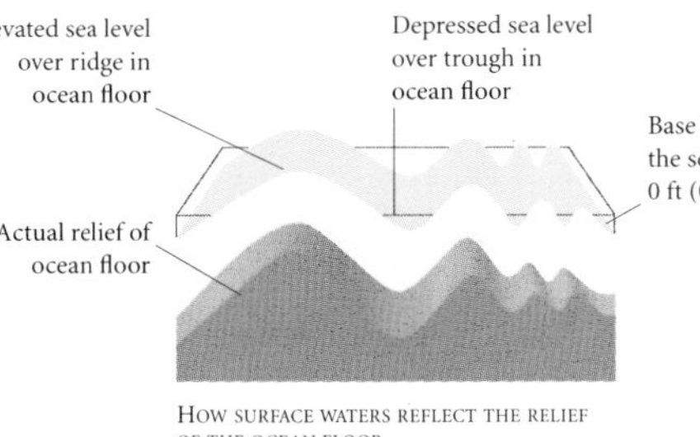
Elevated sea level over ridge in ocean floor
Depressed sea level over trough in ocean floor
Base level of the sea surface at 0 ft (0 m)
Actual relief of ocean floor

HOW SURFACE WATERS REFLECT THE RELIEF OF THE OCEAN FLOOR

***The low relief** of many small Pacific islands, such as these atolls at Huahine in French Polynesia, makes them vulnerable to changes in sea level.*

OCEAN STRUCTURE

THE CONTINENTAL SHELF is a shallow, flat seabed surrounding the Earth's continents. It extends to the continental slope, which falls to the ocean floor. Here, the flat abyssal plains are interrupted by vast, underwater mountain ranges, the mid-ocean ridges, and ocean trenches, which plunge to depths of 35,828 ft (10,920 m).

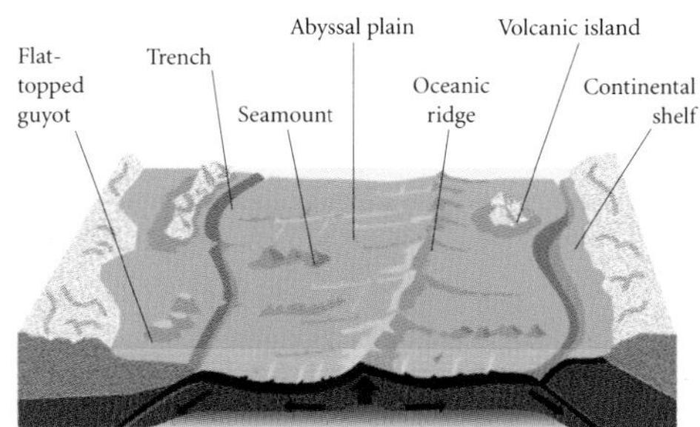
Flat-topped guyot
Trench
Seamount
Abyssal plain
Oceanic ridge
Volcanic island
Continental shelf

TYPICAL SEA-FLOOR FEATURES

ARCTIC
Arctic Circle
Barents Sea
Kara Sea
Laptev Sea
East Siberian Sea
North Sea
Baltic Sea
EUROPE
ASIA
Sea of Okhotsk
Black Sea
Caspian Sea
Adriatic Sea
Mediterranean Sea
Sea of Japan
Kurile Trench
Japan Trench
Northwest Pacific Basin
Yellow Sea
East China Sea
Persian Gulf
Tropic of Cancer
Red Sea
Arabian Sea
Bay of Bengal
Taiwan Strait
Mid-Pacific Mountains
Philippine Sea
Mariana Trench
AFRICA
Gulf of Thailand
South China Sea
Sunda Shelf
Strait of Malacca
Celebes Sea
Gulf of Guinea
Equator
Somali Basin
INDIAN
Carlsberg Ridge
Chagos-Laccadive Plateau
Mid-Indian Ridge
Mid-Indian Basin
Ninetyeast Ridge
Bismarck Sea
Melanesian Basin
Solomon Sea
Arafura Sea
Timor Sea
Angola Basin
Mozambique Channel
Mascarene Plateau
Coral Sea
Great Barrier Reef
Tropic of Capricorn
Walvis Ridge
Madagascar Basin
AUSTRALIA
Perth Basin
Cape Basin
Mozambique Plateau
Southwest Indian Ridge
OCEAN
South Australian Basin
Bass Strait
Tasman Sea
Southeast Indian Ridge
Agulhas Basin
Kerguelen Plateau
South Indian Basin
Enderby Plain
SOUTHERN
Antarctic Circle
ANTARCTICA
Ocean depth
Sea level
200m / 656ft
1000m / 3281ft
2000m / 6562ft
3000m / 9843ft
4000m / 13,124ft
5000m / 16,400ft
6000m / 19,686ft

BLACK SMOKERS

These vents in the ocean floor disgorge hot, sulfur-rich water from deep in the Earth's crust. Despite the great depths, a variety of lifeforms have adapted to the chemical-rich environment that surrounds black smokers.

***A black smoker** in the Atlantic Ocean.*

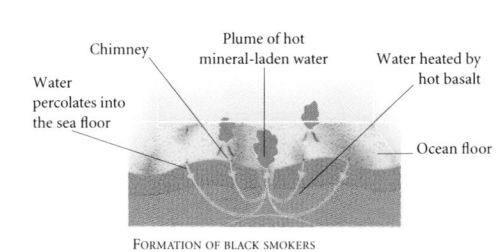

Chimney
Plume of hot mineral-laden water
Water heated by hot basalt
Water percolates into the sea floor
Ocean floor

FORMATION OF BLACK SMOKERS

***Surtsey, near Iceland,** is a volcanic island lying directly over the Mid-Atlantic Ridge. The many active geysers and volcanoes reflect intense volcanic activity.*

OCEAN FLOORS

Mid-ocean ridges are formed by lava which erupts beneath the sea and cools to form solid rock. This process mirrors the creation of volcanoes from cooled lava on the land. The ages of sea-floor rocks increase in parallel bands outward from central ocean ridges.

AGES OF THE OCEAN FLOOR

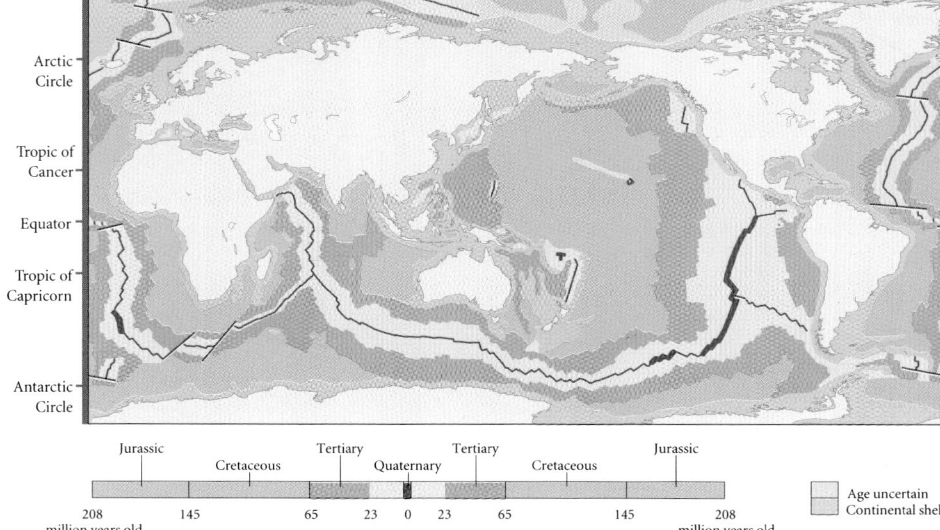
Arctic Circle
Tropic of Cancer
Equator
Tropic of Capricorn
Antarctic Circle
Jurassic
Cretaceous
Tertiary
Quaternary
Tertiary
Cretaceous
Jurassic
208 million years old
145
65
23
0
23
65
145
208 million years old
Age uncertain
Continental shelf

Currents in the Southern Ocean are driven by some of the world's fiercest winds, including the Roaring Forties, Furious Fifties, and Shrieking Sixties.

The Pacific Ocean is the world's largest and deepest ocean, covering over one-third of the surface of the Earth.

The Atlantic Ocean was formed when the landmasses of the eastern and western hemispheres began to drift apart 180 million years ago.

NORTH AMERICA

SOUTH AMERICA

ATLANTIC OCEAN

PACIFIC OCEAN

Beaufort Sea, Baffin Bay, Greenland Sea, Davis Strait, Arctic Circle, Hudson Strait, Hudson Bay, Labrador Sea, Gulf of Alaska, Mid-Atlantic Ridge, Newfoundland Basin, Mendocino Fracture Zone, Murray Fracture Zone, North American Basin, Gulf of Mexico, Sargasso Sea, Canary Basin, Tropic of Cancer, Molokai Fracture Zone, Yucatan Basin, Caribbean Sea, Barracuda Fracture Zone, Clarion Fracture Zone, Guatemala Basin, Clipperton Fracture Zone, Equator, Peru Basin, Brazil Basin, East Pacific Rise, Nazca Ridge, Chile Basin, Sala y Gomez Ridge, Tropic of Capricorn, Rio Grande Rise, Southwest Pacific Basin, Argentine Basin, Scotia Sea, Antarctic Ridge, Southeast Pacific Basin, Amundsen Sea, Bellingshausen Sea, Weddell Sea, Antarctic Circle

DEPOSITION OF SEDIMENT

STORMS, EARTHQUAKES, and volcanic activity trigger underwater currents, known as turbidity currents, which scour sand and gravel from the continental shelf, creating underwater canyons. These strong currents pick up material deposited at river mouths and deltas, and carry it across the continental shelf and through the underwater canyons, where it is eventually laid down on the ocean floor in the form of fans.

Sediment accumulates at head of underwater canyon

Continental shelf

Rocks and other debris, flow from shelf to ocean floor

Recently-deposited sediments overlay older rocks

Deep sea turbidity flow

HOW SEDIMENT IS DEPOSITED ON THE OCEAN FLOOR

***Satellite image** of the Yangtze (Chang Jiang) Delta, in which the land appears red. The river deposits immense quantities of silt into the East China Sea, much of which will eventually reach the deep ocean floor.*

SURFACE WATER

OCEAN CURRENTS move warm water away from the Equator toward the poles, while cold water, in turn, moves toward the Equator. This is the main way in which the Earth distributes surface heat and is a major climatic control. Approximately 4,000 million years ago, the Earth was dominated by oceans and there was no land to interrupt the flow of the currents, which would have flowed as straight lines, simply influenced by the Earth's rotation.

***Imaginary globe** showing the movement of water around a landless Earth.*

OCEAN CURRENTS

SURFACE CURRENTS are driven by the prevailing winds and by the spinning motion of the Earth, which drives the currents into circulating whirlpools, or gyres. Deep sea currents, over 330 ft (100 m) below the surface, are driven by differences in water temperature and salinity, which have an impact on the density of deep water and on its movement.

SURFACE TEMPERATURE AND CURRENTS

Arctic Circle
Tropic of Cancer
Equator
Tropic of Capricorn
Antarctic Circle

Surface temperature and currents
Ice-shelf (below 32°F / 0°C)
Sea-ice* (average) below 28°F / -2°C
Seawater 28–32°F / -2–0°C
* Seawater freezes at 28.4°F / -1.9°C
32–50°F / 0–10°C
50–68°F / 10–20°C
68–86°F / 20–30°C
warm current
cold current

TIDES AND WAVES

TIDES ARE CREATED by the pull of the Sun and Moon's gravity on the surface of the oceans. The levels of high and low tides are influenced by the position of the Moon in relation to the Earth and Sun. Waves are formed by wind blowing over the surface of the water.

TIDAL RANGE AND WAVE ENVIRONMENTS

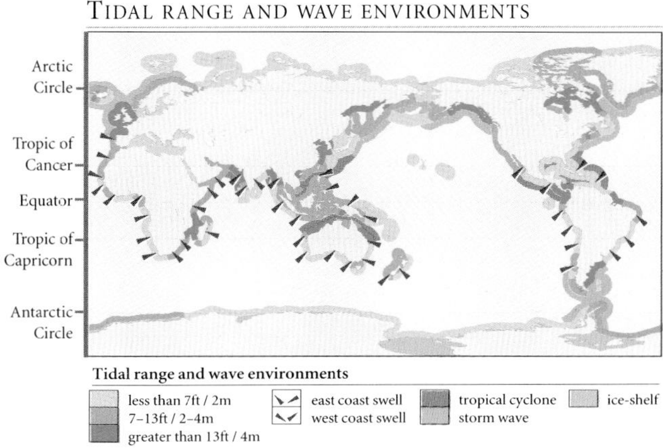
Arctic Circle
Tropic of Cancer
Equator
Tropic of Capricorn
Antarctic Circle
Tidal range and wave environments
less than 7ft / 2m
7–13ft / 2–4m
greater than 13ft / 4m
east coast swell
west coast swell
tropical cyclone storm wave
ice-shelf

HIGH AND LOW TIDES

The highest tides occur when the Earth, the Moon, and the Sun are aligned *(below left)*.
The lowest tides are experienced when the Sun and Moon align at right angles to one another *(below right)*.

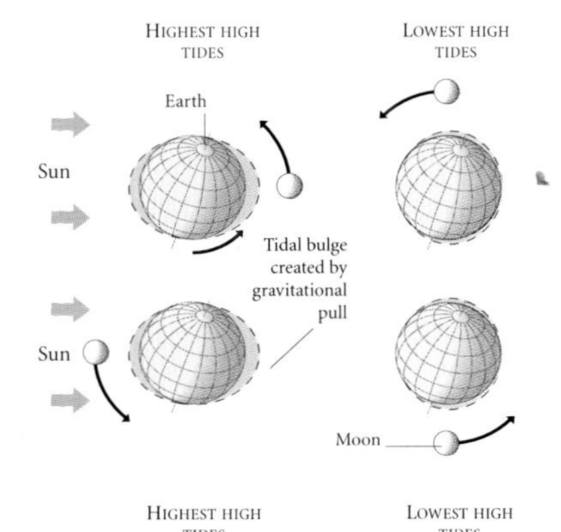
HIGHEST HIGH TIDES
LOWEST HIGH TIDES
Earth
Sun
Tidal bulge created by gravitational pull
Sun
Moon
HIGHEST HIGH TIDES
LOWEST HIGH TIDES

DEEP SEA TEMPERATURE AND CURRENTS

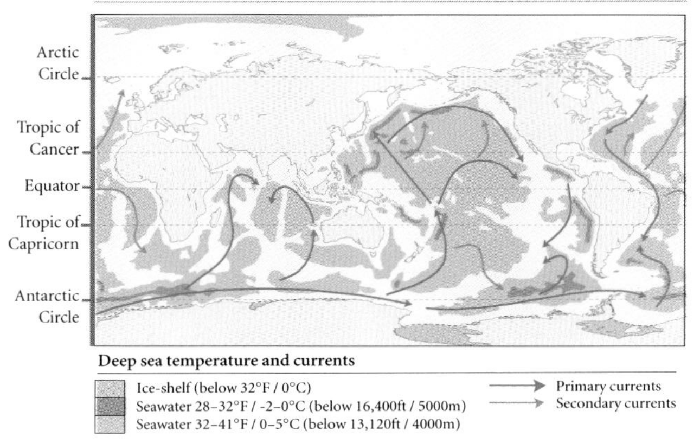
Arctic Circle
Tropic of Cancer
Equator
Tropic of Capricorn
Antarctic Circle
Deep sea temperature and currents
Ice-shelf (below 32°F / 0°C)
Seawater 28–32°F / -2–0°C (below 16,400ft / 5000m)
Seawater 32–41°F / 0–5°C (below 13,120ft / 4000m)
Primary currents
Secondary currents

The Global Climate

The Earth's climatic types consist of stable patterns of weather conditions averaged out over a long period of time. Different climates are categorized according to particular combinations of temperature and humidity. By contrast, weather consists of short-term fluctuations in wind, temperature, and humidity conditions. Different climates are determined by latitude, altitude, the prevailing wind, and the circulation of ocean currents. Longer-term changes in climate, such as global warming or the onset of ice ages, are punctuated by shorter-term events, which make up the day-to-day weather of a region, such as frontal depressions, hurricanes, and blizzards.

The Atmosphere, Wind & Weather

The Earth's atmosphere has been compared to a giant ocean of air that surrounds the planet. Its circulation patterns are similar to the currents in the oceans and are influenced by three factors; the Earth's orbit around the Sun; rotation around its axis, and variations in the amount of heat radiation received from the Sun. If both heat and moisture were not redistributed between the Equator and the poles, large areas of the Earth would be uninhabitable.

Heavy fogs, as here in southern England, form as moisture-laden air hovers over cold ground.

Temperature

The world can be divided into three major climatic zones, stretching like large belts across the latitudes: the tropics which are warm; the cold polar regions; and the temperate zones, which lie between them. Temperatures across the Earth range from above 30°C (86°F) in the deserts to as low as -55°C (-70°F) at the poles. Temperature is also influenced by altitude; because air becomes cooler and less dense the higher it gets, mountainous regions are typically colder than those areas which are at, or close to, sea level.

Average January temperatures

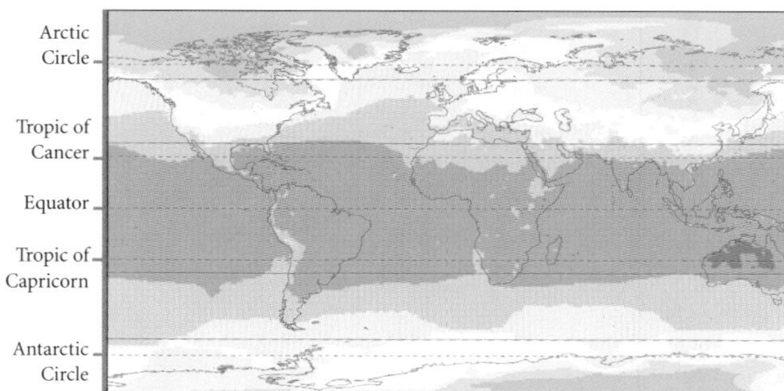

Arctic Circle
Tropic of Cancer
Equator
Tropic of Capricorn
Antarctic Circle

Average July temperatures

Arctic Circle
Tropic of Cancer
Equator
Tropic of Capricorn
Antarctic Circle

below -22°F (-30°C)
-22 to -4°F (-30 to -20°C)
-4 to 14°F (-20 to -10°C)
14 to 32°F (-10 to 0°C)
32 to 50°F (0 to 10°C)
50 to 68°F (10 to 20°C)
68 to 86°F (20 to 30°C)
above 86°F (30°C)

Global air circulation

Air does not simply flow from the equator to the poles, it circulates in giant cells, known as Hadley and Ferrel cells. As air warms it expands, becoming less dense and rising; this creates areas of low pressure. As the air rises it cools and condenses, causing heavy rainfall over the tropics and slight snowfall over the poles. This cool air then sinks, forming high pressure belts. At surface level in the tropics these sinking currents are deflected poleward as the westerlies and toward the equator as the trade winds. At the poles they become the polar easterlies.

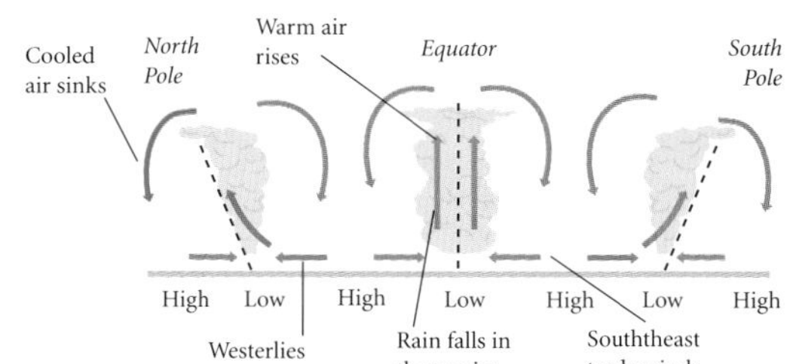

Cooled air sinks
North Pole
Warm air rises
Equator
South Pole
High
Low
High
Low
High
Low
High
Westerlies
Rain falls in the tropics
Southeast trade winds

The Antarctic pack ice expands its area by almost seven times during the winter as temperatures drop and surrounding seas freeze.

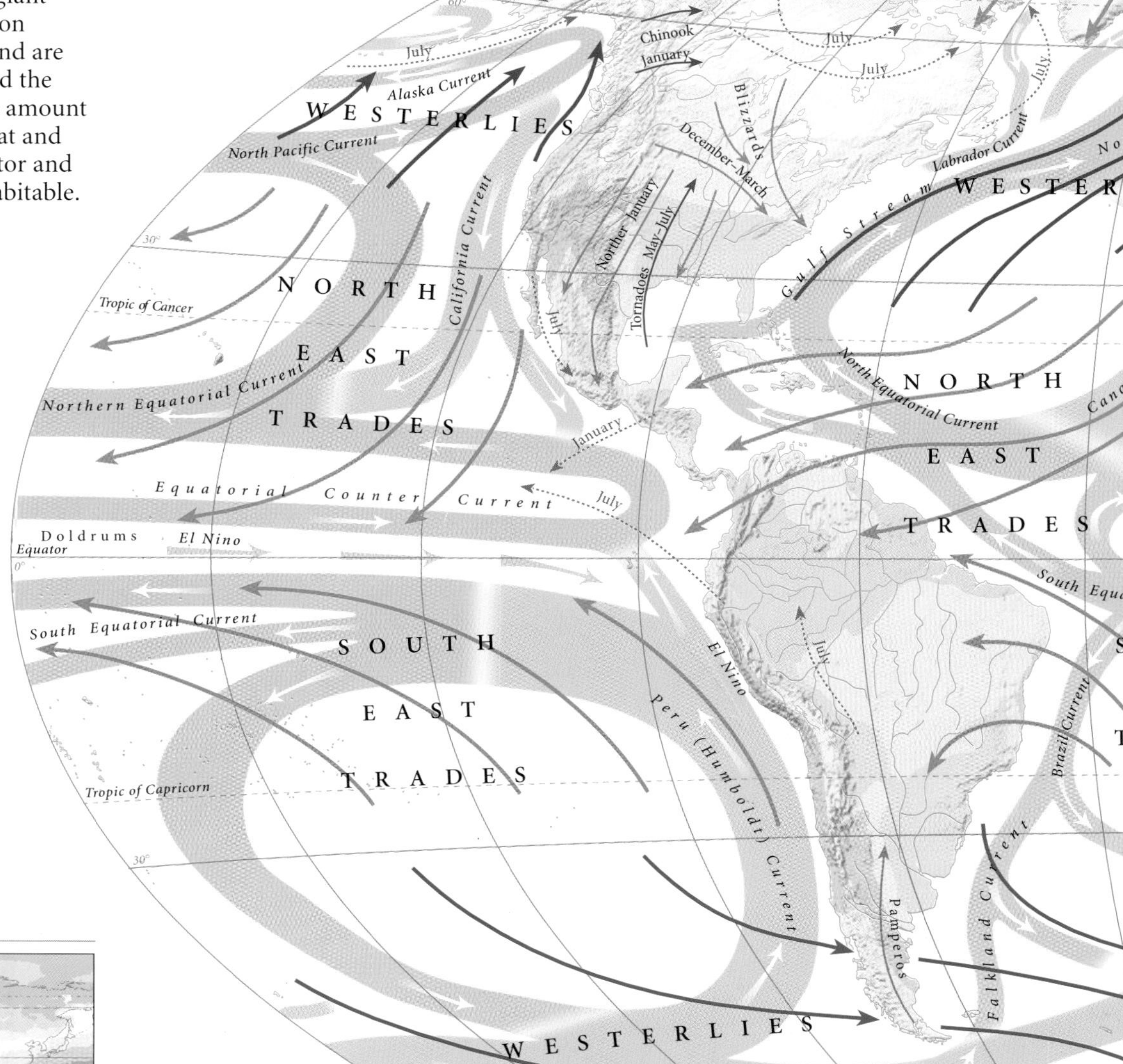

Arctic Circle
January
Chinook
January
July
July
July
POLAR
Alaska Current
WESTERLIES
North Pacific Current
Blizzards
December–March
Labrador Current
North Atlantic Drift
WESTERLIES
Gulf Stream
California Current
Northers January
Tornadoes May–July
July
Tropic of Cancer
NORTH EAST TRADES
Northern Equatorial Current
North Equatorial Current
NORTH EAST TRADES
Canary Current
January
Equatorial Counter Current
July
Doldrums
Equator
El Nino
Doldrums
South Equatorial Current
South Equatorial Current
SOUTH EAST TRADES
El Nino
July
Peru (Humboldt) Current
Brazil Current
SOUTH EAST TRADES
Tropic of Capricorn
Pamperos
Falkland Current
WESTERLIES
West Wind Drift
Antarctic Circle
POLAR

Climatic change

The Earth is currently in a warm phase between ice ages. Warmer temperatures result in higher sea levels as more of the polar ice caps melt. Most of the world's population lives near coasts, so any changes which might cause sea levels to rise could have a potentially disastrous impact.

This ice fair, painted by Pieter Brueghel the Younger in the 17th century, shows the Little Ice Age which peaked around 300 years ago.

The greenhouse effect

Gases such as carbon dioxide are known as "greenhouse gases" because they allow shortwave solar radiation to enter the Earth's atmosphere, but help to stop longwave radiation from escaping. This traps heat, raising the Earth's temperature. An excess of these gases, such as that which results from the burning of fossil fuels, helps to trap more heat and can lead to global warming.

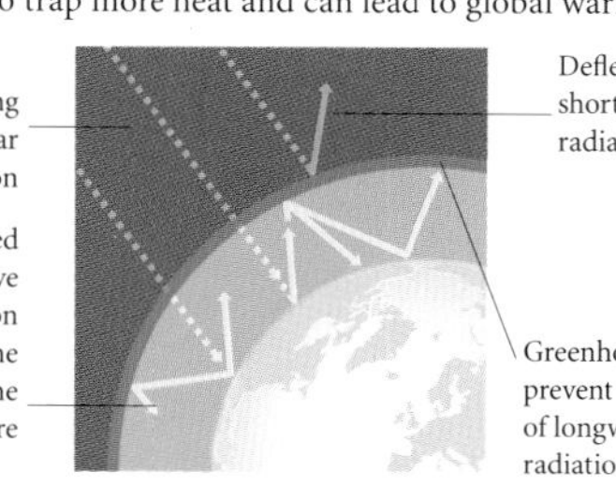

Incoming shortwave solar radiation
Deflected longwave radiation emitted by the Earth heats the atmosphere
Deflected shortwave solar radiation
Greenhouse gases prevent the escape of longwave radiation

The islands of the Caribbean, Mexico's Gulf coast, and the southeastern US are often hit by hurricanes formed far out in the Atlantic.

OCEANIC WATER CIRCULATION

IN GENERAL, OCEAN CURRENTS parallel the movement of winds across the Earth's surface. Incoming solar energy is greatest at the Equator and least at the poles. So, water in the oceans heats up most at the Equator and flows poleward, cooling as it moves north or south toward the Arctic or Antarctic. The flow is eventually reversed and cold water currents move back toward the equator. These ocean currents act as a vast system for moving heat from the Equator toward the poles and are a major influence on the distribution of the Earth's climates.

***In marginal climatic zones** years of drought can completely dry out the land and transform grassland to desert.*

TILT AND ROTATION

The tilt and rotation of the Earth during its annual orbit largely control the distribution of heat and moisture across its surface, which correspondingly controls its large-scale weather patterns. As the Earth annually rotates around the Sun, half its surface is receiving maximum radiation, creating summer and winter seasons. The angle of the Earth means that, on average, the tropics receive two and a half times as much heat from the Sun each day as the poles.

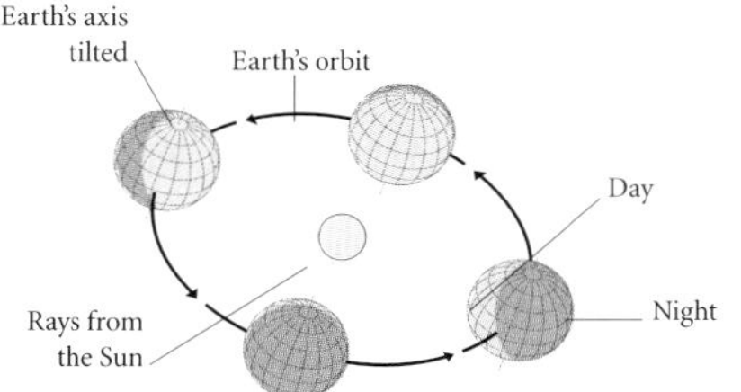
Earth's axis tilted
Earth's orbit
Day
Rays from the Sun
Night

MAP KEY

Climate zones: ice cap; tundra; subarctic; cool continental; warm humid; mediterranean; semiarid; arid; tropical; humid equatorial

Ocean currents: warm; cold

Prevailing winds: warm; cold

Local winds: warm; cold; seasonal*

* (seasonal winds which can either be warm or cold)

***The wide range** of environments found in the Andes is strongly related to their altitude, which modifies climatic influences. While the peaks are snowcapped, many protected interior valleys are semitropical.*

THE CORIOLIS EFFECT

The rotation of the Earth influences atmospheric circulation by deflecting winds and ocean currents. Winds blowing in the northern hemisphere are deflected to the right and those in the southern hemisphere are deflected to the left, creating large-scale patterns of wind circulation, such as the northeast and southeast trade winds and the westerlies. This effect is greatest at the poles and least at the Equator.

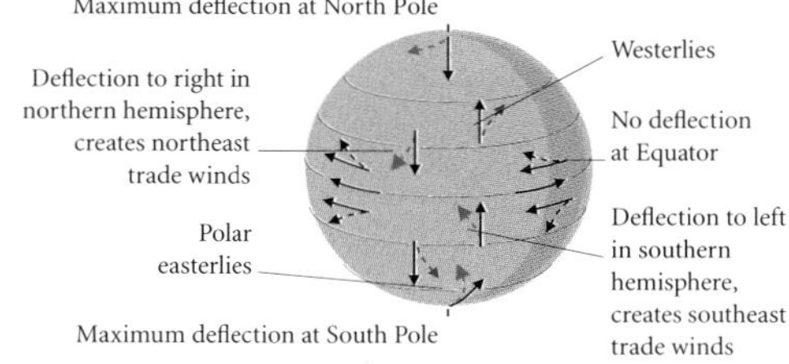
Maximum deflection at North Pole
Westerlies
Deflection to right in northern hemisphere, creates northeast trade winds
No deflection at Equator
Polar easterlies
Deflection to left in southern hemisphere, creates southeast trade winds
Maximum deflection at South Pole

PRECIPITATION

WHEN WARM AIR EXPANDS, it rises and cools, and the water vapor it carries condenses to form clouds. Heavy, regular rainfall is characteristic of the equatorial region, while the poles are cold and receive only slight snowfall. Tropical regions have marked dry and rainy seasons, while in the temperate regions rainfall is relatively unpredictable.

***Monsoon rains,** which affect southern Asia from May to September, are caused by sea winds blowing across the warm land.*

***Heavy tropical rainstorms** occur frequently in Papua New Guinea, often causing soil erosion and landslides in cultivated areas.*

AVERAGE JANUARY RAINFALL

Arctic Circle – Tropic of Cancer – Equator – Tropic of Capricorn – Antarctic Circle

AVERAGE JULY RAINFALL

Arctic Circle – Tropic of Cancer – Equator – Tropic of Capricorn – Antarctic Circle

0–1 in (0–25 mm); 1–2 in (25–50 mm); 2–4 in (50–100 mm); 4–8 in (100–200 mm); 8–12 in (200–300 mm); 12–16 in (300–400 mm); 16–20 in (400–500 mm); above 20 in (500 mm)

__The intensity of__ some blizzards in Canada and the northern US can give rise to snowdrifts higher than 10 ft (3 m).

***The Atacama Desert** in Chile is one of the driest places on Earth, with an average rainfall of less than 2 inches (50 mm) per year.*

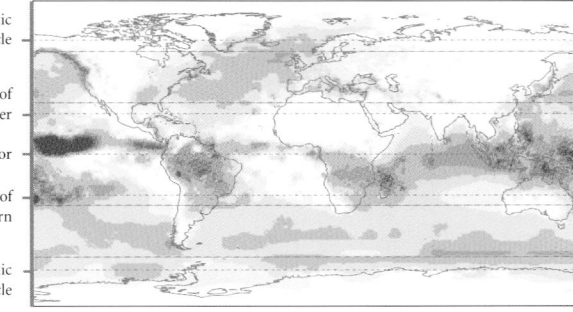

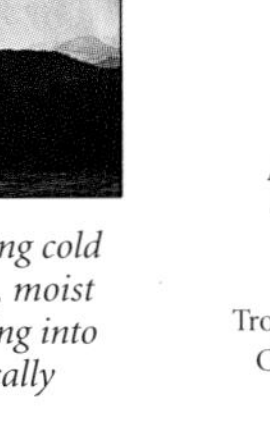

***Violent thunderstorms** occur along advancing cold fronts, when cold, dry air masses meet warm, moist air, which rises rapidly, its moisture condensing into thunderclouds. Rain and hail become electrically charged, causing lightning.*

THE RAINSHADOW EFFECT

When moist air is forced to rise by mountains, it cools and the water vapor falls as precipitation, either as rain or snow. Only the dry, cold air continues over the mountains, leaving inland areas with little or no rain. This is called the rainshadow effect and is one reason for the existence of the Mojave Desert in California, which lies east of the Sierra Nevada.

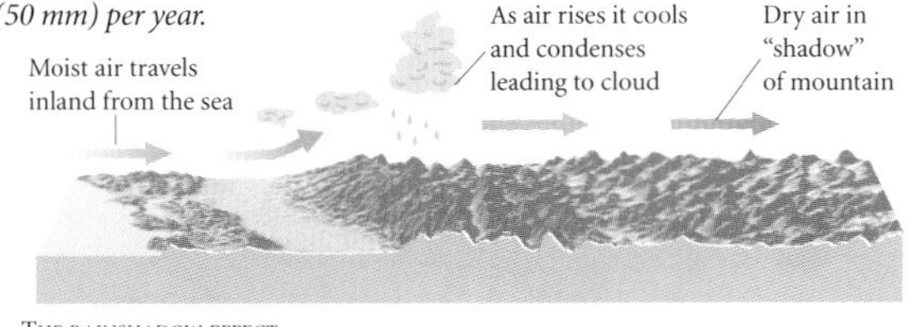
Moist air travels inland from the sea
As air rises it cools and condenses leading to cloud
Dry air in "shadow" of mountain

THE RAINSHADOW EFFECT

Life on Earth

A UNIQUE COMBINATION of an oxygen-rich atmosphere and plentiful water is the key to life on Earth. Apart from the polar ice caps, there are few areas that have not been colonized by animals or plants over the course of the Earth's history. Plants process sunlight to provide them with their energy, and ultimately all of the Earth's animals rely on plants for survival. Because of this reliance, plants are known as primary producers, and the availability of nutrients and the temperature of an area are defined as its primary productivity, which affects the quantity and type of animals that are able to live there. This index is affected by climatic factors – cold and aridity restrict the quantity of life, while warmth and regular rainfall allow a greater diversity of species.

Biogeographical Regions

THE EARTH CAN BE DIVIDED into a series of biogeographical regions, or biomes, ecological communities where certain species of plant and animal coexist within particular climatic conditions. Within these broad classifications, other factors, including soil richness, altitude, and human activities, such as urbanization, intensive agriculture, and deforestation, affect the local distribution of living species within each biome.

POLAR REGIONS

A layer of permanent ice at the Earth's poles covers both seas and land. Very little plant and animal life can exist in these harsh regions.

TUNDRA

A desolate region, tundra has long, dark freezing winters and short, cold summers. With virtually no soil and large areas of permanently frozen ground known as permafrost, the tundra is largely treeless, though it is briefly clothed by small flowering plants in the summer months.

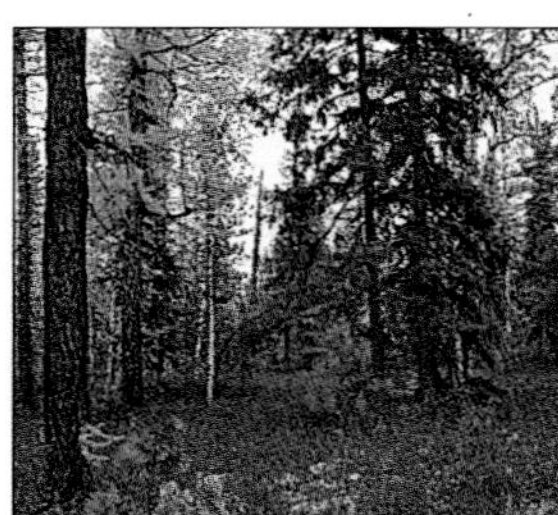

NEEDLELEAF FORESTS

With milder summers than the tundra and less wind, these areas are able to support large forests of coniferous trees.

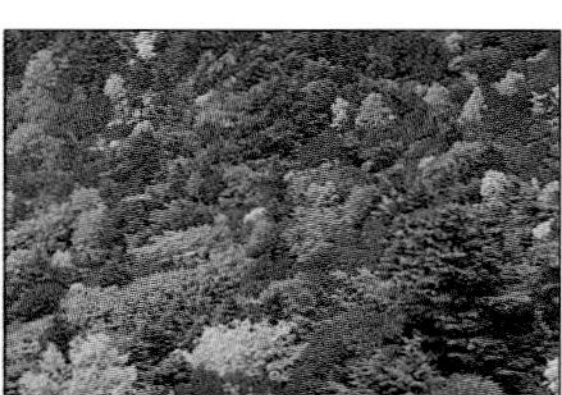

BROADLEAF FORESTS

Much of the northern hemisphere was once covered by deciduous forests, which occurred in areas with marked seasonal variations. Most deciduous forests have been cleared for human settlement.

TEMPERATE RAIN FORESTS

In warmer, wetter areas, such as southern China, temperate deciduous forests are replaced by evergreen forest.

DESERTS

Deserts are areas with negligible rainfall. Most hot deserts lie within the Tropics; cold deserts are dry because of their distance from the moisture-providing sea.

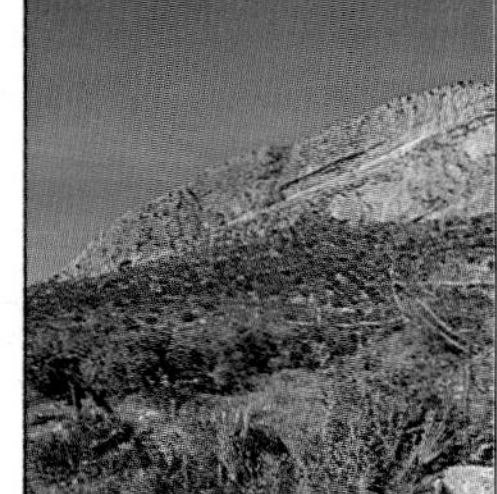

MEDITERRANEAN

Hot, dry summers and short winters typify these areas, which were once covered by evergreen shrubs and woodland, but have now been cleared by humans for agriculture.

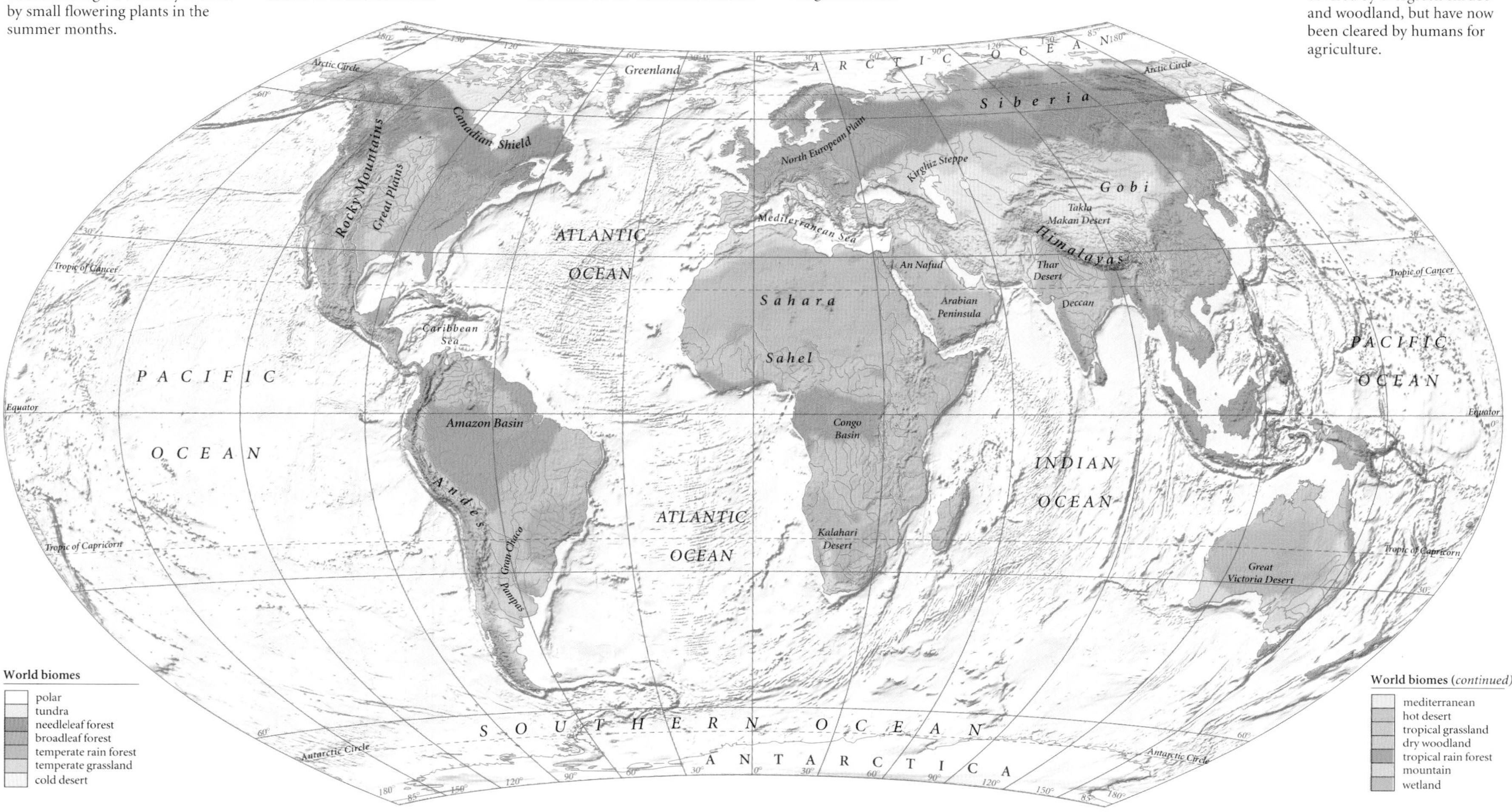

World biomes
- polar
- tundra
- needleleaf forest
- broadleaf forest
- temperate rain forest
- temperate grassland
- cold desert

World biomes (*continued*)
- mediterranean
- hot desert
- tropical grassland
- dry woodland
- tropical rain forest
- mountain
- wetland

TROPICAL AND TEMPERATE GRASSLANDS

The major grassland areas are found in the centers of the larger continental landmasses. In Africa's tropical savannah regions, seasonal rainfall alternates with drought. Temperate grasslands, also known as *steppes* and *prairies*, are found in the northern hemisphere and in South America, where they are known as the *pampas*.

DRY WOODLANDS

Trees and shrubs, adapted to dry conditions, grow widely spaced from one another, interspersed by savannah grasslands.

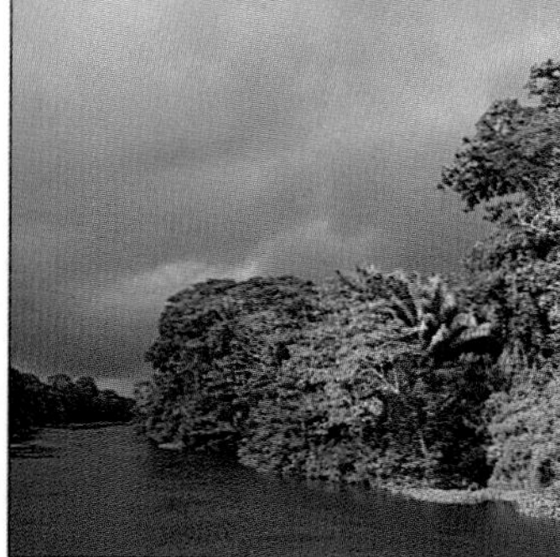

TROPICAL RAIN FORESTS

Characterized by year-round warmth and high rainfall, tropical rain forests contain the highest diversity of plant and animal species on Earth.

MOUNTAINS

Though the lower slopes of mountains may be thickly forested, only ground-hugging shrubs and other vegetation will grow above the tree line, which varies according to both altitude and latitude.

WETLANDS

Rarely lying above sea level, wetlands include marshes, swamps, and tidal flats. Some, with their moist, fertile soils, are rich feeding grounds for fish and breeding grounds for birds. Others have little soil structure and are too acidic to support much plant and animal life.

World Wealth Disparity

A global assessment of Gross Domestic Product (GDP) by nation reveals great disparities. The developed world, with only 25% of the world's population, has 80% of the world's manufacturing income. Civil war, conflict, and political instability further undermine the economic self-sufficiency of many of the world's poorest nations.

Cities such as Detroit *have been badly hit by the decline in heavy industry.*

Urban decay

Although the US still dominates the global economy, it faces deficits in both the federal budget and the balance of trade. Vast discrepancies in personal wealth, high levels of unemployment, and the dismantling of welfare provisions throughout the 1980s have led to severe deprivation in several of the inner cities of North America's industrial heartland.

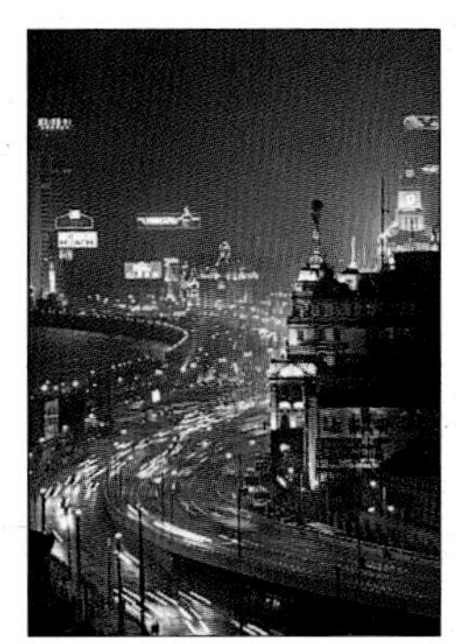

Booming cities

Since the 1980s the Chinese government has set up special industrial zones, such as Shanghai, where foreign investment is encouraged through tax incentives. Migrants from rural China pour into these regions in search of work, creating "boomtown" economies.

Foreign investment *has encouraged new infrastructure development in cities like Shanghai.*

Urban sprawl

Cities are expanding all over the developing world, attracting economic migrants in search of work and opportunities. In cities such as Rio de Janeiro, housing has not kept pace with the population explosion, and squalid shanty towns *(favelas)* rub shoulders with middle-class housing.

The favelas *of Rio de Janeiro sprawl over the hills surrounding the city.*

Comparative world wealth

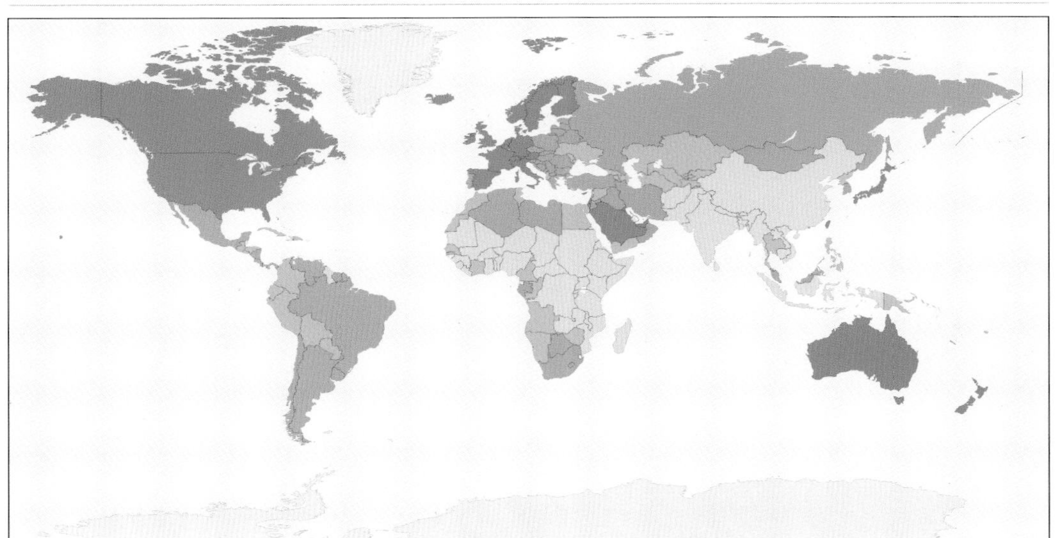

World economies
high income
upper-middle income
lower-middle income
low income
data unavailable

Economic "tigers"

The economic "tigers" of the Pacific Rim – Taiwan, Singapore, and South Korea – have grown faster than Europe and the US over the last decade. Their export- and service-led economies have benefited from stable government, low labor costs, and foreign investment.

Hong Kong*, with its fine natural harbor, is one of the most important ports in Asia.*

Agricultural economies

In parts of the developing world, people survive by subsistence farming – growing enough food only for themselves and their families. With no surplus product, they are unable to exchange goods for currency, the only means of escaping the poverty trap. In other countries, farmers have been encouraged to concentrate on growing a single crop for the export market. This reliance on cash crops leaves farmers vulnerable to crop failure and to changes in the market price of the crop.

The Ugandan uplands *are fertile, but poor infrastructure hampers the export of cash crops.*

A shopping arcade in Paris *displays a great profusion of luxury goods.*

The affluent West

The capital cities of many countries in the developed world are showcases for consumer goods, reflecting the increasing importance of the service sector, and particularly the retail sector, in the world economy. The idea of shopping as a leisure activity is unique to the western world. Luxury goods and services attract visitors, who in turn generate tourist revenue.

Tourism

In 1990, there were 425 million tourists worldwide. Tourism is now the world's biggest single industry, employing 127 million people, though frequently in low-paid unskilled jobs. While tourists are increasingly exploring newly-accessible and less-developed regions of the world, the benefits of the industry are not always felt at a local level. There are also worries about the environmental impact of tourism, as the world's last wildernesses increasingly become tourist attractions.

Botswana's Okavango Delta *is an area rich in wildlife. Tourists go on safaris in the region, but the impact of tourism is controlled.*

Money Flows

Foreign investment in the developing world during the 1970s led to a global financial crisis in the 1980s, when many countries were unable to meet their debt repayments. The International Monetary Fund (IMF) was forced to reschedule the debts and, in some cases, write them off completely. Within the developing world, austerity programs have been initiated to cope with the debt, leading in turn to high unemployment and galloping inflation. In many parts of Africa, stricken economies are now dependent on international aid.

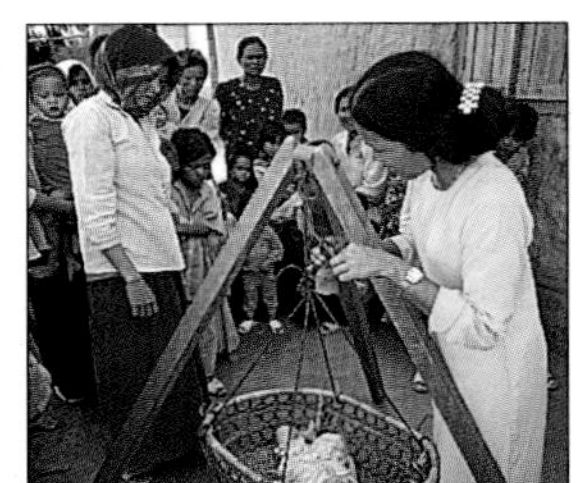

In rural Southeast Asia*, babies are given medical checks by UNICEF as part of a global aid program sponsored by the UN.*

Tourist arrivals

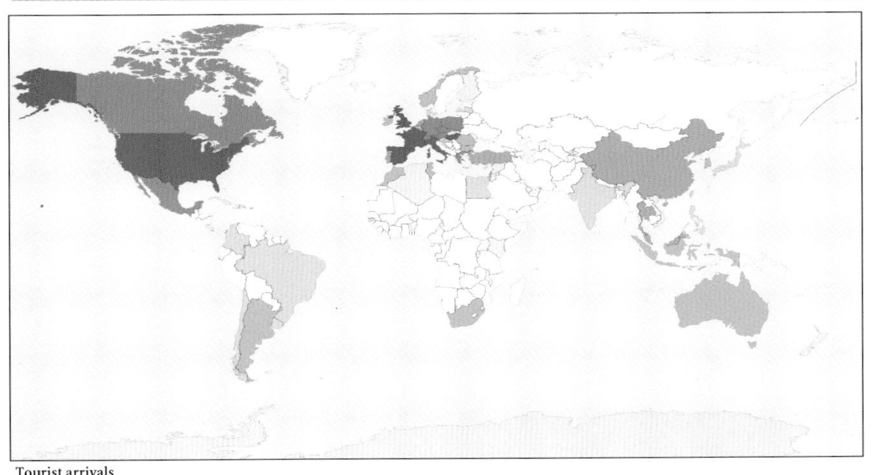

Tourist arrivals
over 20 million
10–20 million
5–10 million
2.5–5 million
1–2.5 million
700,000–999,000
under 700,000
data unavailable

International debt: donors and receivers

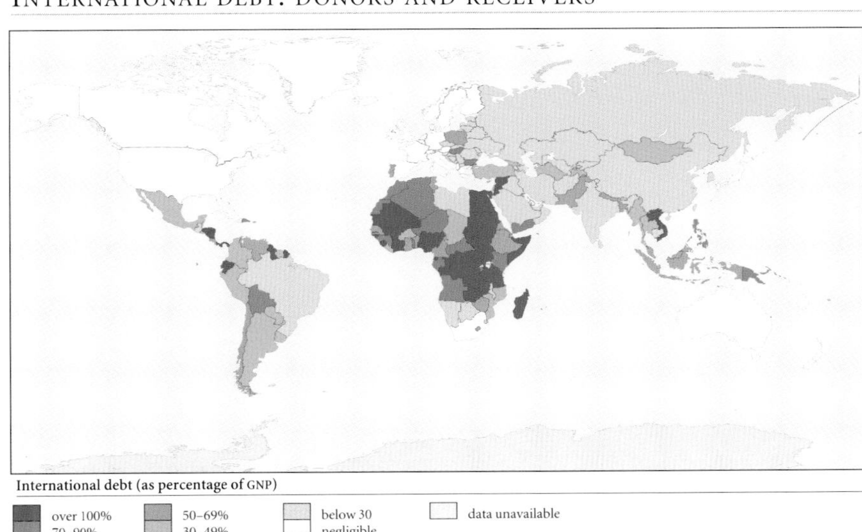

International debt (as percentage of GNP)
over 100%
70–90%
50–69%
30–49%
below 30
negligible
data unavailable

The Political World

There are 192 independent countries in the world today. With the exception of Antarctica, where territorial claims have been deferred by international treaty, every land area on the Earth's surface either belongs to, or is claimed by, one country or another. The largest country in the world is the Russian Federation; the smallest is Vatican City. Some 60 overseas dependent territories remain, administered variously by France, Australia, Denmark, New Zealand, Norway, Portugal, the UK, the US, and the Netherlands.

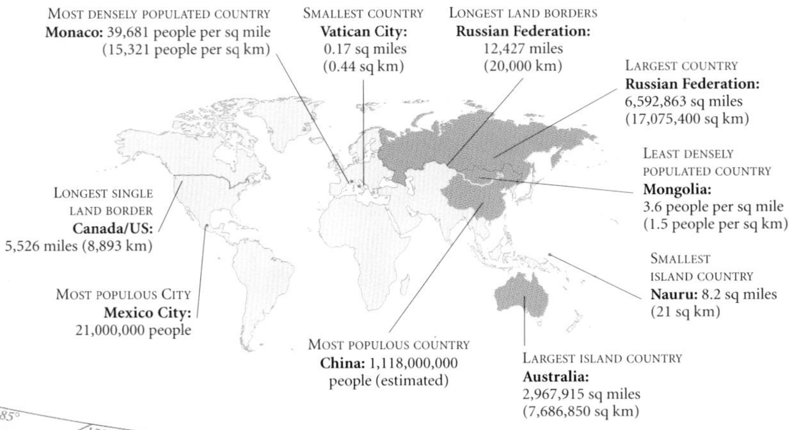

Most densely populated country
Monaco: 39,681 people per sq mile (15,321 people per sq km)

Smallest country
Vatican City: 0.17 sq miles (0.44 sq km)

Longest land borders
Russian Federation: 12,427 miles (20,000 km)

Largest country
Russian Federation: 6,592,863 sq miles (17,075,400 sq km)

Least densely populated country
Mongolia: 3.6 people per sq mile (1.5 people per sq km)

Longest single land border
Canada/US: 5,526 miles (8,893 km)

Smallest island country
Nauru: 8.2 sq miles (21 sq km)

Most populous City
Mexico City: 21,000,000 people

Most populous country
China: 1,118,000,000 people (estimated)

Largest island country
Australia: 2,967,915 sq miles (7,686,850 sq km)

International Borders

The map shows three main types of boundary between states. Full borders represent internationally agreed and recognized territorial boundaries. Undefined borders exist where no fixed boundary between states has been demarcated; the boundaries indicated in this way show approximate areas of sovereignty. A disputed border is indicated where a *de facto* territorial boundary exists, which is not agreed or is subject to arbitration.

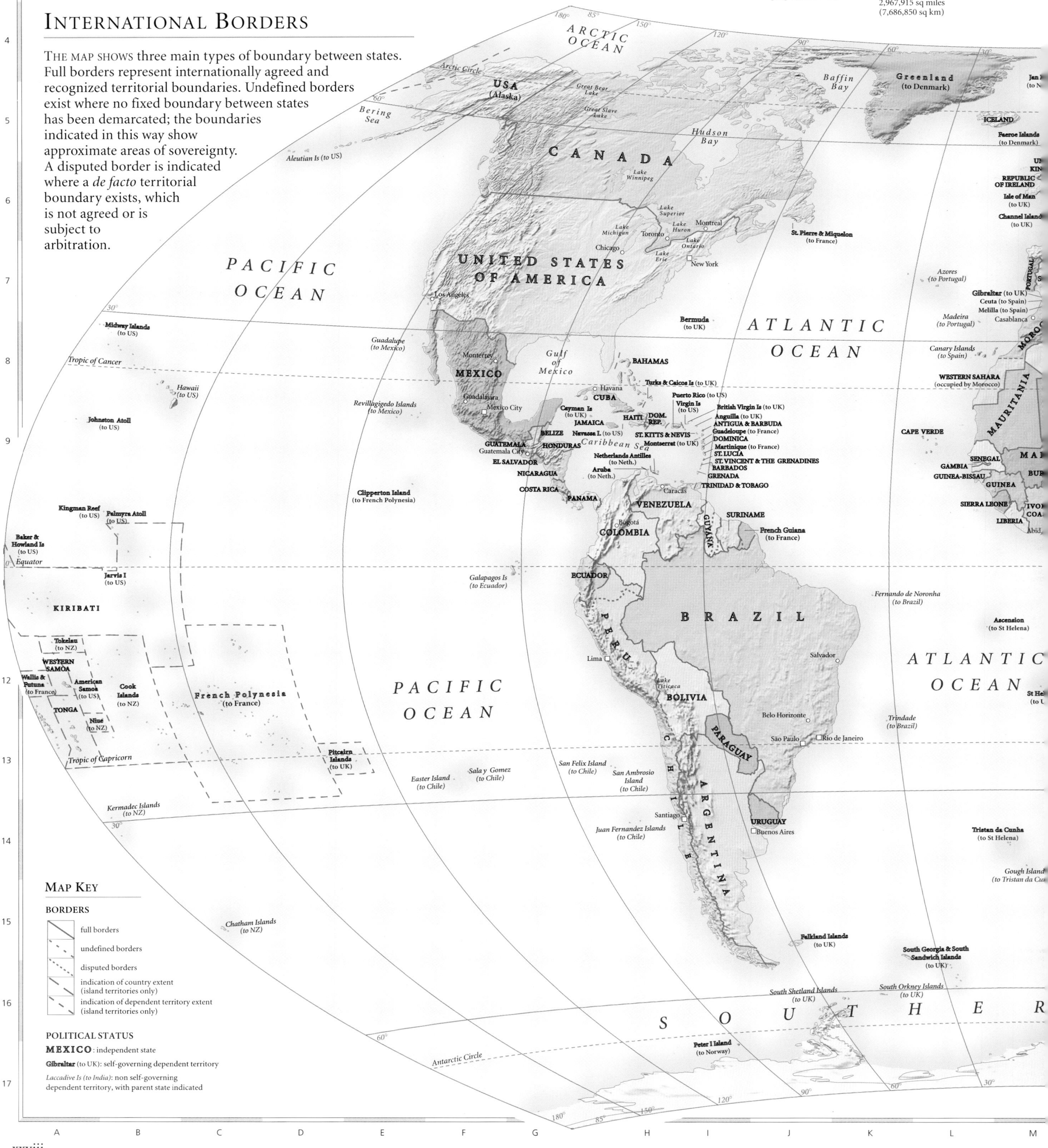

Map Key

Borders

- full borders
- undefined borders
- disputed borders
- indication of country extent (island territories only)
- indication of dependent territory extent (island territories only)

Political Status

MEXICO: independent state

Gibraltar (to UK): self-governing dependent territory

Laccadive Is (to India): non self-governing dependent territory, with parent state indicated

The World in 1914

The early years of the 20th century saw the mainly European colonial empires reaching their greatest extents by 1914. Two world wars inaugurated their disintegration, but even in 1950 there were only 82 independent countries. Since then, over 100 have gained their independence, culminating in the breakup of the former Soviet Union after 1990.

Percentage of Earth's Land Surface Controlled by Colonial Empires in 1914

- Independent: 29.8%
- Chinese: 6%
- Ottoman: 1.5%
- Russian: 15%
- Portuguese: 1%
- Spanish: 1%
- British: 21.5%
- Dutch: 1.4%
- Danish: 1.5%
- American: 7.6%
- Japanese: 0.4%
- German: 1.6%
- Italian: 1.8%
- Belgian: 1.6%
- French: 7.7%

Colonial Empires in 1914

Colonial Empires in 1914

- Belgian
- British
- Chinese
- Danish
- Dutch
- French
- German
- Italian
- Japanese
- Ottoman
- Portuguese
- Russian
- Spanish
- American
- Independent

SCALE 1:66,000,000
(projection: Wagner VII)

STATES AND BOUNDARIES

THERE ARE OVER 190 SOVEREIGN STATES in the world today; in 1950 there were only 82. Over the last half-century, national self-determination has been a driving force for many states with a history of colonialism and oppression. As more borders are added to the world map, the number of international border disputes increases. In many cases, where the impetus toward independence has been religious or ethnic, disputes with minority groups have also caused violent internal conflict. While many newly formed states have moved peacefully toward independence, successfully establishing government by multiparty democracy, dictatorship by military regime or individual despot is often the result of the internal power struggles that characterize the early stages in the lives of new nations.

THE CHANGING WORLD MAP

DECOLONIZATION

In 1950, large areas of the world remained under the control of a handful of European countries (*page xxviii*). The process of decolonization had begun in Asia, where, following the Second World War, much of southern and southeastern Asia sought and achieved self-determination. In the 1960s, a host of African states achieved independence, so that by 1965, most of the larger tracts of the European overseas empires had been substantially eroded. The final major stage in decolonization came with the breakup of the Soviet Union and the Eastern bloc after 1990. The process continues today, as the last toeholds of European colonialism, often tiny island nations, press increasingly for independence.

Icons of communism*, including statues of former leaders such as Lenin and Stalin, were destroyed when the Soviet bloc was dismantled in 1989, creating several new nations.*

NEW NATIONS 1945–1965

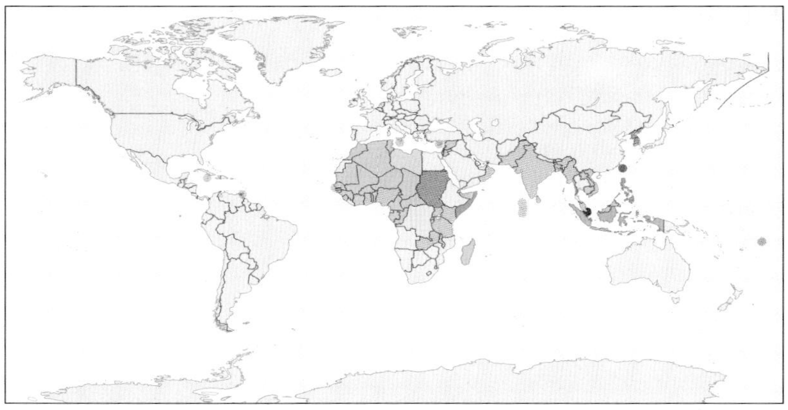

NEW NATIONS 1965–1996

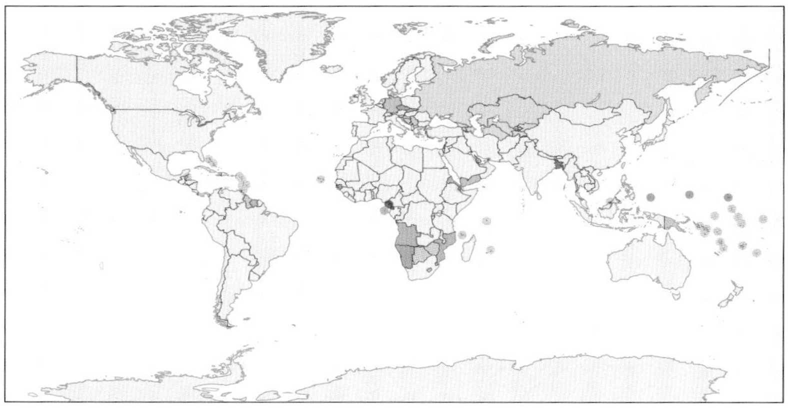

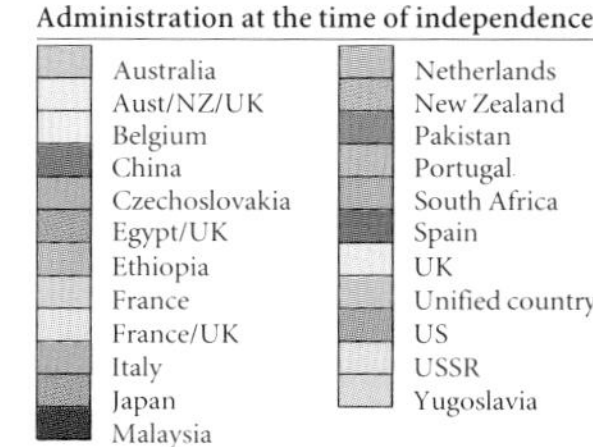

Administration at the time of independence

- Australia
- Aust/NZ/UK
- Belgium
- China
- Czechoslovakia
- Egypt/UK
- Ethiopia
- France
- France/UK
- Italy
- Japan
- Malaysia
- Netherlands
- New Zealand
- Pakistan
- Portugal
- South Africa
- Spain
- UK
- Unified country
- US
- USSR
- Yugoslavia

THE NATURE OF POLITICS

Democracy is a broad term: it can range from the ideal of multiparty elections and fair representation to, in countries such as Singapore and Indonesia, a thin disguise for single-party rule. In despotic regimes, on the other hand, a single, often personal authority has total power; institutions such as parliament and the military are mere instruments of the dictator.

The Stars and Stripes *is a potent symbol of the US's status as a federal democracy.*

Iran *is one of the world's true theocracies; Islam has an impact on every aspect of political life.*

North Korea *is an independent communist republic. Power is concentrated in the hands of Kim Jong Il.*

Saddam Hussein *overthrew his predecessor in 1979. Since then he has promoted an extreme personality cult, with autocratic control over 19.3 million Iraqis.*

South Africa *became a democracy in 1994, when elections ended 45 years of white rule.*

In Brunei *the Sultan has ruled by decree since 1962; power is closely tied to the royal family. The Sultan's brothers are responsible for finance and foreign affairs.*

Types of government

- Multiparty democracy for more than 10 yrs
- Multiparty/transitional democracy within last 10 yrs
- Single-party government
- Military regime
- Monarchy or theocracy
- State of unrest/civil war

Lines on the Map

The determination of international boundaries can be based on a variety of criteria. Many of the borders between older states follow physical boundaries; some mirror religious and ethnic differences; others are the legacy of complex histories of conflict and colonialism, while others have been imposed by international agreements or arbitration.

Post colonial borders

When the European colonial empires in Africa were dismantled during the second half of the 20th century, the outlines of the new African states mirrored colonial boundaries. These boundaries had been drawn up by colonial administrators, often based on inadequate geographical knowledge. Such arbitrary boundaries were imposed on people of different languages, racial groups, religions, and customs. This confused legacy often led to civil and international war.

WESTERN SAHARA
ALGERIA
MAURITANIA
MALI

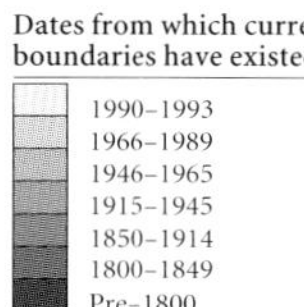
Dates from which current boundaries have existed
1990–1993
1966–1989
1946–1965
1915–1945
1850–1914
1800–1849
Pre-1800

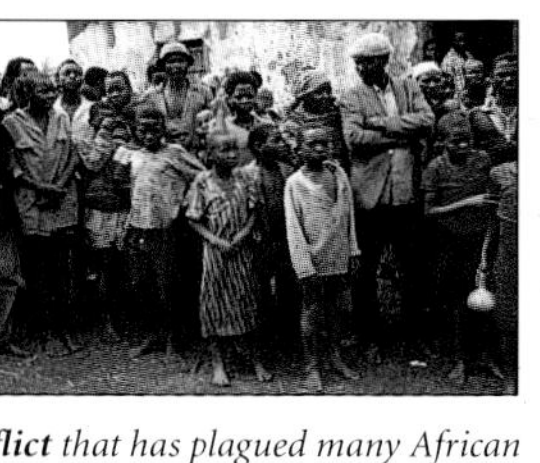
The conflict that has plagued many African countries since independence has caused millions of people to become refugees.

Enclaves

The shifting political map over the course of history has frequently led to anomalous situations. Parts of national territories may become isolated by territorial agreement, forming an enclave. The West German part of the city of Berlin, which until 1989 lay several hundred miles within East German territory, was a famous example.

Baltic Sea
ESTONIA
RUSSIAN FEDERATION
LATVIA
LITHUANIA
RUSS. FED. (Kaliningrad)
POLAND
BELARUS

Since the independence *of Lithuania and Belarus, the peoples of the Russian enclave of Kaliningrad have become physically isolated.*

Antarctica

When Antarctic exploration began a century ago, seven nations – Australia, Argentina, Britain, Chile, France, New Zealand, and Norway – laid claim to the new territory. In 1961 the Antarctic Treaty, signed by 39 nations, agreed to hold all territorial claims in abeyance.

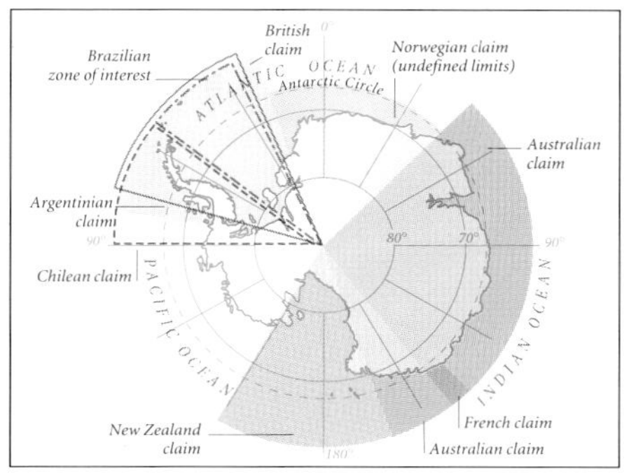
Brazilian zone of interest
British claim
Norwegian claim (undefined limits)
Antarctic Circle
Australian claim
Argentinian claim
Chilean claim
PACIFIC OCEAN
INDIAN OCEAN
New Zealand claim
French claim
Australian claim

World boundaries

Geometric borders

Straight lines and lines of longitude and latitude have occasionally been used to determine international boundaries. The world's longest international boundary, between Canada and the US, follows the 49th parallel for over one-third of its course. Many Canadian, American, and Australian internal administrative boundaries are similarly determined using a geometric solution.

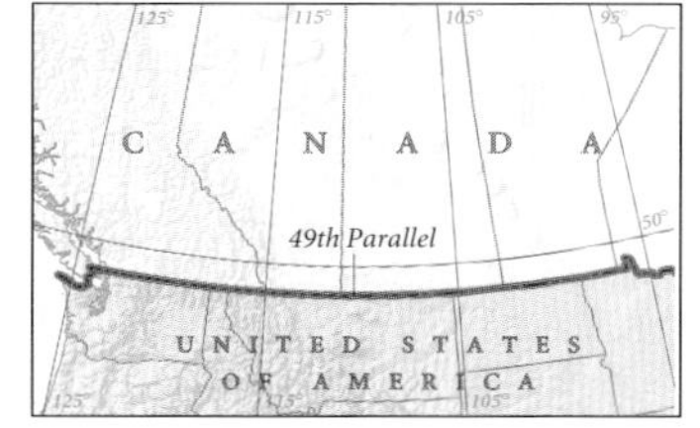
CANADA
49th Parallel
UNITED STATES OF AMERICA

The 49th parallel *forms the boundary between much of the US and Canada.*

Physical borders

Many of the world's countries are divided by physical borders: lakes, rivers, mountains. The demarcation of such boundaries can, however, lead to disputes. Control of waterways, water supplies and fisheries are frequent sources of international friction.

Lake borders

Countries that lie next to lakes usually place their borders in the middle of the lake. The Lake Nyasa border between Malawi and Tanzania, however, runs along Tanzania's shore.

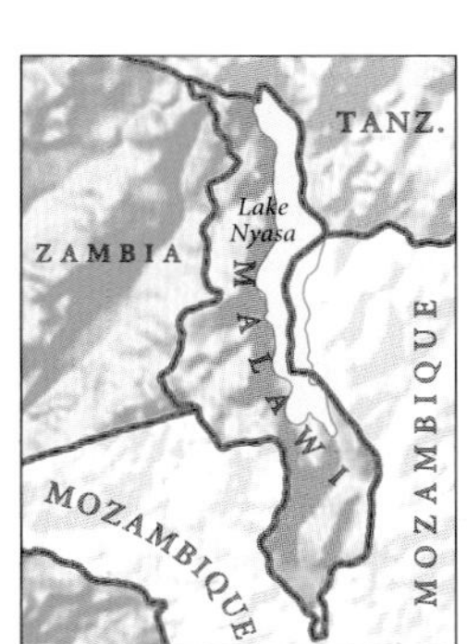
TANZ.
ZAMBIA
Lake Nyasa
MALAWI
MOZAMBIQUE
MOZAMBIQUE

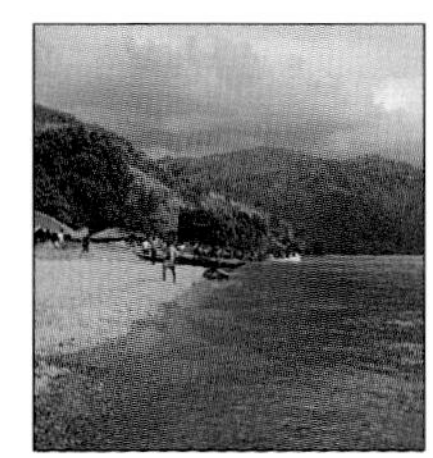
Complicated agreements *between colonial powers led to the awkward division of Lake Nyasa*

River borders

Rivers alone account for one-sixth of the world's borders. Many great rivers form boundaries between a number of countries. Changes in a river's course and interruptions of its natural flow can lead to disputes, particularly in areas where water is scarce. The center of the river's course is the nominal boundary line.

GERMANY
Danube
UKRAINE
SLOVAKIA
AUSTRIA
HUNGARY
ROMANIA
CROATIA
Danube
YUGOSLAVIA
BULGARIA

The Danube *forms all or part of the border between nine European nations.*

Mountain borders

Mountain ranges form natural barriers and are the basis for many major borders, particularly in Europe and Asia. The watershed is the conventional boundary demarcation line, but its accurate determination is often problematic.

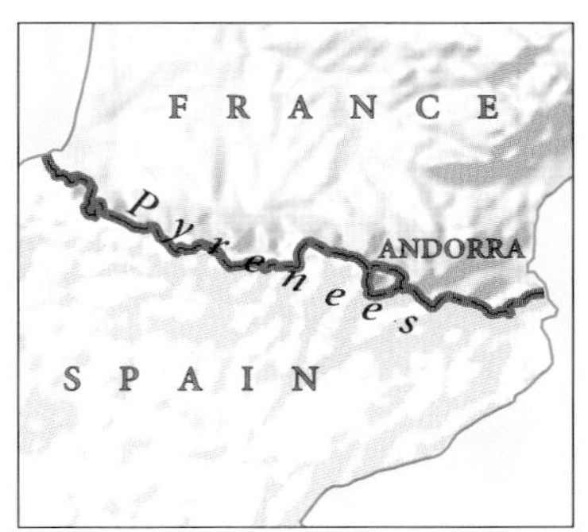
FRANCE
Pyrenees
ANDORRA
SPAIN

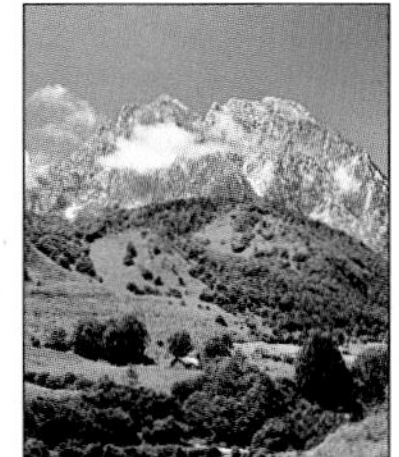
The Pyrenees *form a natural mountain border between France and Spain.*

Shifting boundaries – Poland

Borders between countries can change dramatically over time. The nations of eastern Europe have been particularly affected by changing boundaries. Poland is an example of a country whose boundaries have changed so significantly that it has literally moved around Europe. At the start of the 16th century, Poland was the largest nation in Europe. Between 1772 and 1795, it was absorbed into Prussia, Austria, and Russia, and it effectively ceased to exist. After the First World War, Poland became an independent country once more, but its borders changed again after the Second World War following invasions by both Soviet Russia and Nazi Germany.

Moscow
POLAND
Warsaw
Kiev
In 1634, *Poland was the largest nation in Europe, its eastern boundary reaching toward Moscow.*

Moscow
PRUSSIA
Warsaw
RUSSIA
AUSTRIA
Kiev
From 1772–1795, *Poland was gradually partitioned among Austria, Russia, and Prussia. Its eastern boundary receded by over 100 miles (160 km).*

Moscow
POLAND
Warsaw
Kiev
Following the First World War, *Poland was reinstated as an independent state, but it was less than half the size it had been in 1634.*

Moscow
POLAND
Warsaw
Kiev
After the Second World War, *the Baltic Sea border was extended westward, but much of the eastern territory was annexed by Russia.*

INTERNATIONAL DISPUTES

THERE ARE MORE THAN 60 DISPUTED BORDERS or territories in the world today. Although many of these disputes can be settled by peaceful negotiation, some areas have become a focus for international conflict. Ethnic tensions have been a major source of territorial disagreement throughout history, as has the ownership of and access to valuable natural resources. The turmoil of the post-colonial era in many parts of Africa is partly a result of the 19th-century "carve-up" of the continent, which created the potential for conflict by drawing often arbitrary lines through linguistic and cultural areas.

JAMMU AND KASHMIR

DISPUTES OVER JAMMU AND KASHMIR have caused three serious wars between India and Pakistan since 1947. Pakistan wishes to annex the largely Muslim territory, while India refuses to cede any territory or to hold a referendum, and also lays claim to the entire territory. Most international maps show the line of control agreed in 1972 as the de facto border. In addition, both Pakistan and India have territorial disputes with neighbouring China. The situation is further complicated by a Kashmiri independence movement, active since the late 1980s.

***Indian army troops** maintain their positions in the mountainous terrain of northern Kashmir.*

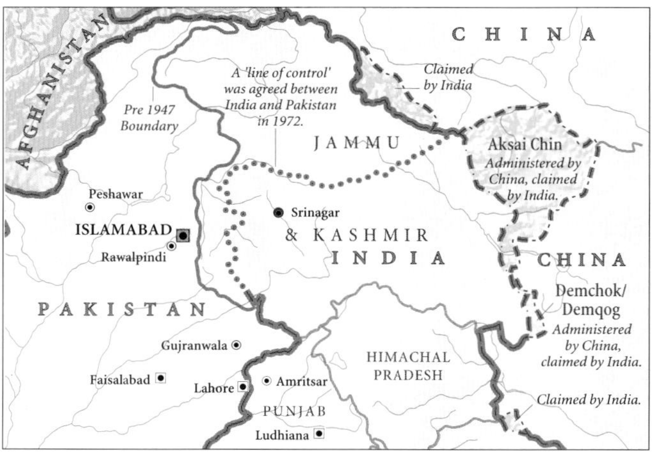
AFGHANISTAN
CHINA
A 'line of control' was agreed between India and Pakistan in 1972.
Claimed by India
Pre 1947 Boundary
JAMMU
Aksai Chin
Administered by China, claimed by India.
Peshawar
ISLAMABAD
Rawalpindi
Srinagar
& KASHMIR
INDIA
CHINA
PAKISTAN
Demchok/ Demqog
Administered by China, claimed by India.
Gujranwala
Faisalabad
Lahore
Amritsar
HIMACHAL PRADESH
PUNJAB
Ludhiana
Claimed by India.

NORTH AND SOUTH KOREA

SINCE 1953, the de facto border between North and South Korea has been a ceasefire line that straddles the 38th Parallel and is designated as a demilitarized zone. Both countries have heavy fortifications and troop concentrations behind this zone.

***Heavy fortifications** are in place on the border between North and South Korea.*

CYPRUS

CYPRUS WAS PARTITIONED in 1974, following an invasion by Turkish troops. The south is now the Greek Cypriot Republic of Cyprus, while the self-proclaimed Turkish Republic of Northern Cyprus is recognized only by Turkey.

***The so-called** green line divides Cyprus into Greek and Turkish sectors.*

TURKISH REPUBLIC OF NORTHERN CYPRUS
Karpasia
Mediterranean Sea
Kyrenia Mountains
NICOSIA
Troödos
UK Sovereign Base Area
Larnaka
CYPRUS
Lemesós (Limassol)
UK Sovereign Base Area
Mediterranean Sea

Disputed territories and borders

- Countries involved in active territorial or border disputes
- Disputed borders
- Undefined borders
- Disputed territories

THE FALKLAND ISLANDS

THE BRITISH DEPENDENT TERRITORY of the Falkland Islands was invaded by Argentina in 1982, sparking a full-scale war with the UK. In 1995, the UK and Argentina reached an agreement on the exploitation of oil reserves around the islands.

***British** warships exchange fire during the war with Argentina in 1982.*

ISRAEL

ISRAEL WAS CREATED IN 1947 following the UN Resolution (147) on Palestine. Until 1979 Israel had no borders, only ceasefire lines from a series of wars in 1948, 1967, and 1973. Treaties with Egypt in 1979 and Jordan in 1994 led to these borders being defined and agreed. Negotiations over disputed territories with Lebanon and Syria, and the issue of self-government with the Palestinians, continue.

- Israeli settlement
- Major settlement
- Palestinian settlement
- Area under Palestinian control

***Barbed-wire** fences surround a settlement in the Golan Heights.*

YUGOSLAVIA

FOLLOWING THE DISINTEGRATION in 1990 of the communist state of Yugoslavia, the breakaway states of Croatia and Bosnia-Herzegovina came into conflict with the parent state (consisting of Serbia and Montenegro). Warfare focused on ethnic and territorial ambitions in Bosnia. The tenuous Dayton Accord of 1995 sought to recognize the post-1990 borders, whilst providing for ethnic partition. It required international peace-keeping troops to maintain the terms of the peace.

- invaded by Serbia
- Muslim/Croat federation

***Most claimant states** have small military garrisons on the Spratly Islands.*

THE SPRATLY ISLANDS

THE SITE OF POTENTIAL OIL and natural gas reserves, the Spratly Islands in the South China Sea have been claimed by China, Vietnam, Taiwan, Malaysia, and the Philippines since the Japanese gave up a wartime claim in 1951.

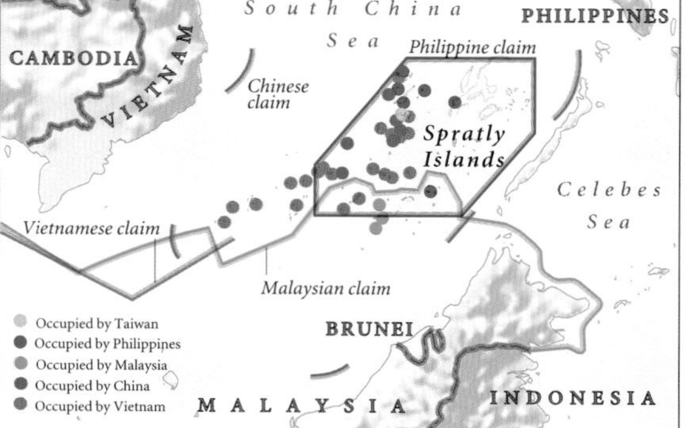
South China Sea
PHILIPPINES
CAMBODIA
VIETNAM
Philippine claim
Chinese claim
Spratly Islands
Celebes Sea
Vietnamese claim
Malaysian claim
BRUNEI
Occupied by Taiwan
Occupied by Philippines
Occupied by Malaysia
Occupied by China
Occupied by Vietnam
MALAYSIA
INDONESIA

ATLAS OF THE WORLD

THE MAPS IN THIS ATLAS ARE ARRANGED CONTINENT BY CONTINENT, STARTING FROM THE INTERNATIONAL DATE LINE AND MOVING EAST. THE MAPS PROVIDE A UNIQUE VIEW OF TODAY'S WORLD, COMBINING TRADITIONAL CARTOGRAPHIC TECHNIQUES WITH THE LATEST REMOTE-SENSED AND DIGITAL TECHNOLOGY.

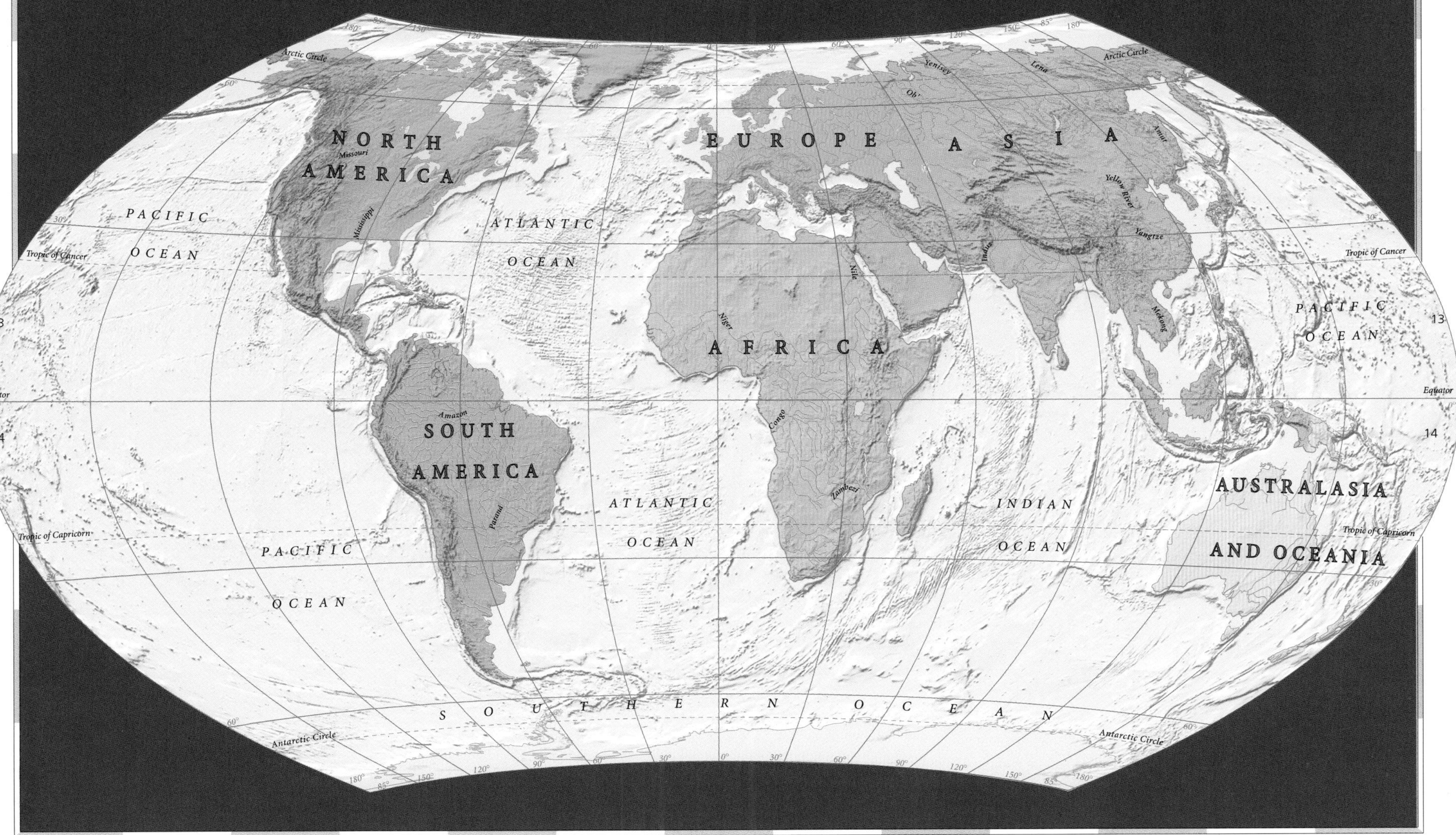

NORTH AMERICA
Missouri
Mississippi
EUROPE
ASIA
Yenisey
Lena
Ob'
Amur
Yellow River
Yangtze
Indus
Mekong
Nile
Niger
Congo
Zambezi
AFRICA
SOUTH AMERICA
Amazon
Paraná
AUSTRALASIA AND OCEANIA
PACIFIC OCEAN
ATLANTIC OCEAN
INDIAN OCEAN
SOUTHERN OCEAN
Arctic Circle
Tropic of Cancer
Equator
Tropic of Capricorn
Antarctic Circle
13
14

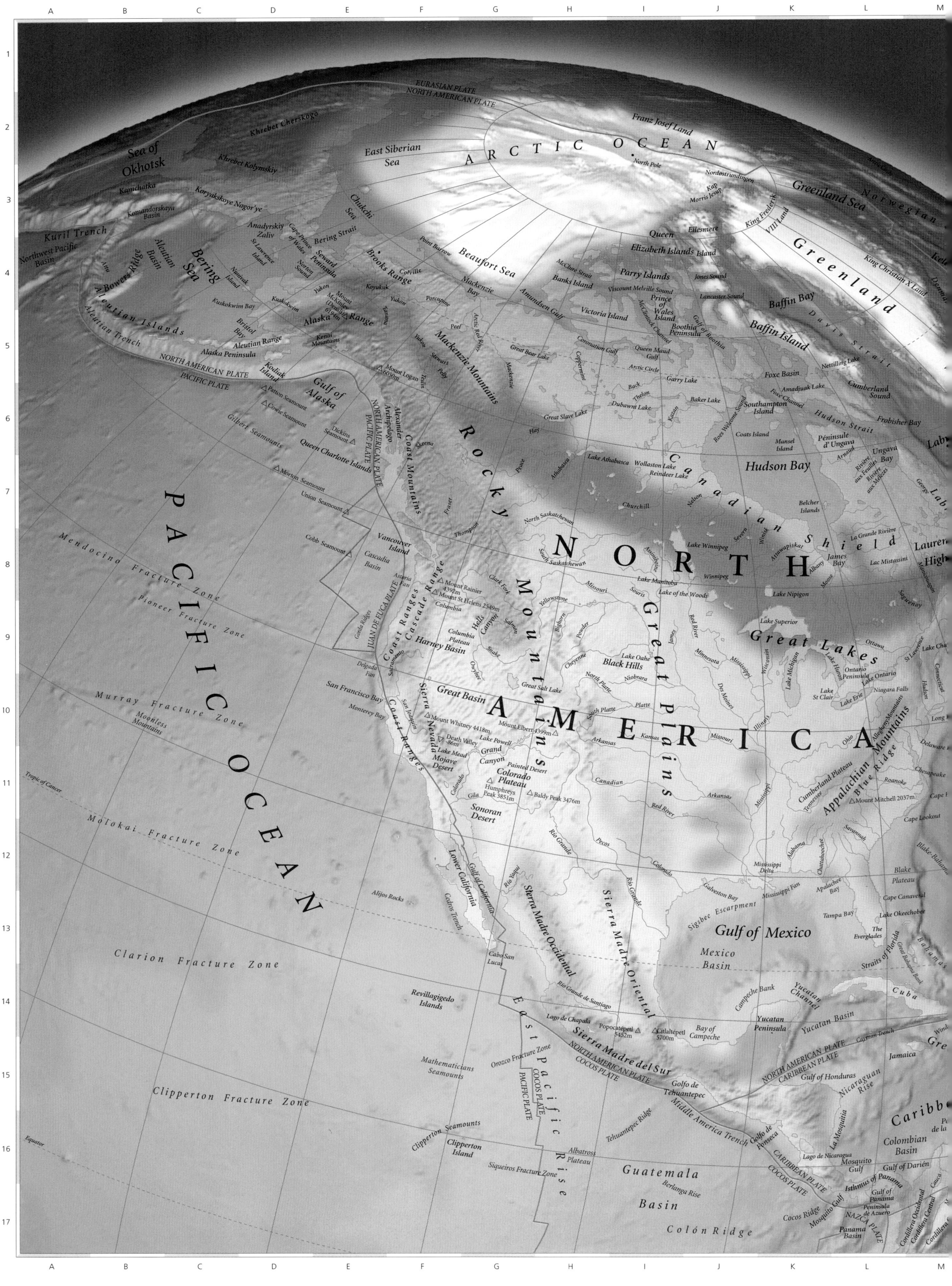

A B C D E F G H I J K L M

EURASIAN PLATE
NORTH AMERICAN PLATE
Franz Josef Land
Khrebet Cherskogo
Sea of Okhotsk
East Siberian Sea
ARCTIC OCEAN
North Pole
Khrebet Kolymskiy
Kamchatka
Koryakskoye Nagor'ye
Nordostrundingen
Greenland Sea
Norwegian
Kap Morris Jesup
Komandorskaya Basin
Chukchi Sea
Anadyrskiy Zaliv
Cape Prince of Wales
Bering Strait
Kuril Trench
Northwest Pacific Basin
Aleutian Basin
Bering Sea
St Lawrence Island
Seward Peninsula
Norton Sound
Point Barrow
Beaufort Sea
Queen Elizabeth Islands
Ellesmere Island
King Frederik VIII Land
Greenland
Brooks Range
Colville
Nunivak Island
Bowers Ridge
Yukon
Koyukuk
Mount McKinley (Denali) 6194m
Alaska Range
Tanana
Porcupine
Mackenzie Bay
Amundsen Gulf
McClure Strait
Banks Island
Parry Islands
Viscount Melville Sound
Prince of Wales Island
M'Clintock Channel
Jones Sound
Lancaster Sound
Baffin Bay
King Christian X Land
Aleutian Islands
Kuskokwim Bay
Kuskokwim
Bristol Bay
Aleutian Range
Kenai Mountains
Aleutian Trench
Alaska Peninsula
Peel
Arctic Red River
Victoria Island
Boothia Peninsula
Gulf of Boothia
Baffin Island
Davis Strait
Mackenzie Mountains
Coronation Gulf
Great Bear Lake
Coppermine
Queen Maud Gulf
Arctic Circle
NORTH AMERICAN PLATE
PACIFIC PLATE
Kodiak Island
Mount Logan 6050m
Stewart
Pelly
Teslin
Garry Lake
Foxe Basin
Nettilling Lake
Cumberland Sound
Amadjuak Lake
Foxe Channel
Back
Thelon
Dubawnt Lake
Baker Lake
Kazan
Southampton Island
Gulf of Alaska
Patton Seamount
Cowie Seamount
Alexander Archipelago
NORTH AMERICAN PLATE
PACIFIC PLATE
Gilbert Seamounts
Dickins Seamount
Coast Mountains
Skeena
Rocky
Great Slave Lake
Hay
Roes Welcome Sound
Hudson Strait
Frobisher Bay
Coats Island
Mansel Island
Péninsule d'Ungava
Queen Charlotte Islands
Peace
Athabasca
Lake Athabasca
Wollaston Lake
Reindeer Lake
Canadian Shield
Hudson Bay
Arnaud
Rivière aux Feuilles
Rivière aux Mélèzes
Ungava Bay
Morton Seamount
Fraser
Churchill
Nelson
Belcher Islands
Union Seamount
PACIFIC OCEAN
Thompson
North Saskatchewan
Severn
Winisk
Attawapiskat
La Grande Rivière
Mendocino Fracture Zone
Cobb Seamount
Vancouver Island
Cascadia Basin
NORTH
South Saskatchewan
Assiniboine
Lake Winnipeg
Albany
James Bay
Lac Mistassini
Laurentian Highlands
Winnipeg
Astoria Fan
Mount Rainier 4392m
Mount St Helens 2549m
Columbia
Clark Fork
Lake Manitoba
Missouri
Souris
Lake of the Woods
Moose
Lake Nipigon
Saguenay
Pioneer Fracture Zone
Gorda Ridges
JUAN DE FUCA PLATE
Coast Ranges
Cascade Range
Yellowstone
Bighorn
Powder
Rocky Mountains
Great Plains
James
Red River
Lake Superior
Great Lakes
Ottawa
Columbia Plateau
Hells Canyon
Salmon
Harney Basin
Snake
Owyhee
Cheyenne
Lake Oahe
Black Hills
Niobrara
Minnesota
Mississippi
Wisconsin
Lake Michigan
Lake Huron
Ontario Peninsula
Lake Ontario
St Lawrence
Lake Champlain
Connecticut
Hudson
Delgada Fan
Sacramento
San Francisco Bay
Monterey Bay
San Joaquin
Sierra Nevada
Great Basin
Great Salt Lake
North Platte
Platte
Des Moines
Lake St Clair
Lake Erie
Niagara Falls
Murray Fracture Zone
Moonless Mountains
AMERICA
South Platte
Mount Whitney 4418m
Mount Elbert 4399m
Death Valley -86m
Lake Powell
Lake Mead
Mojave Desert
Grand Canyon
Painted Desert
Colorado Plateau
Arkansas
Kansas
Missouri
Illinois
Ohio
Allegheny Mountains
Appalachian Mountains
Blue Ridge
Delaware Bay
Long Island
Chesapeake Bay
Cumberland Plateau
Tennessee
Roanoke
Mount Mitchell 2037m
Cape Hatteras
Tropic of Cancer
Colorado
Gila
Humphreys Peak 3851m
Baldy Peak 3476m
Canadian
Arkansas
Red River
Sonoran Desert
Cape Lookout
Molokai Fracture Zone
Rio Grande
Pecos
Colorado
Alabama
Chattahoochee
Savannah
Mississippi Delta
Blake-Bahama
Blake Plateau
Lower California
Gulf of California
Rio Yaqui
Sierra Madre Occidental
Sierra Madre Oriental
Rio Grande
Galveston Bay
Mississippi Fan
Apalachee Bay
Cape Canaveral
Alijos Rocks
Cedros Trench
Sigsbee Escarpment
Gulf of Mexico
Tampa Bay
Lake Okeechobee
The Everglades
Mexico Basin
Straits of Florida
Great Bahama Bank
Bahamas
Clarion Fracture Zone
Cabo San Lucas
Rio Grande de Santiago
Campeche Bank
Yucatan Channel
Cuba
Revillagigedo Islands
Lago de Chapala
Popocatépetl 5452m
Citlaltépetl 5700m
Bay of Campeche
Yucatan Peninsula
Yucatan Basin
Cayman Trench
Windward Passage
Sierra Madre del Sur
NORTH AMERICAN PLATE
COCOS PLATE
NORTH AMERICAN PLATE
CARIBBEAN PLATE
Jamaica
Mathematicians Seamounts
Orozco Fracture Zone
East Pacific Rise
PACIFIC PLATE
COCOS PLATE
Gulf of Honduras
Nicaraguan Rise
Clipperton Fracture Zone
Golfo de Tehuantepec
Tehuantepec Ridge
Middle America Trench
Golfo de Fonseca
La Mosquitia
Caribbean
Equator
Clipperton Seamounts
Clipperton Island
Albatross Plateau
Siqueiros Fracture Zone
Guatemala Basin
Lago de Nicaragua
CARIBBEAN PLATE
COCOS PLATE
Mosquito Gulf
Colombian Basin
Gulf of Darién
Isthmus of Panama
Gulf of Panama
Península de Azuero
Berlanga Rise
Cocos Ridge
Mosquito Gulf
NAZCA PLATE
Panama Basin
Colón Ridge
Cordillera Occidental
Cordillera Central

A B C D E F G H I J K L M

North America

North America is the world's third largest continent, with a total area of 9,358,340 sq miles (24,238,000 sq km) including Greenland and the Caribbean Islands. It lies wholly within the Northern Hemisphere.

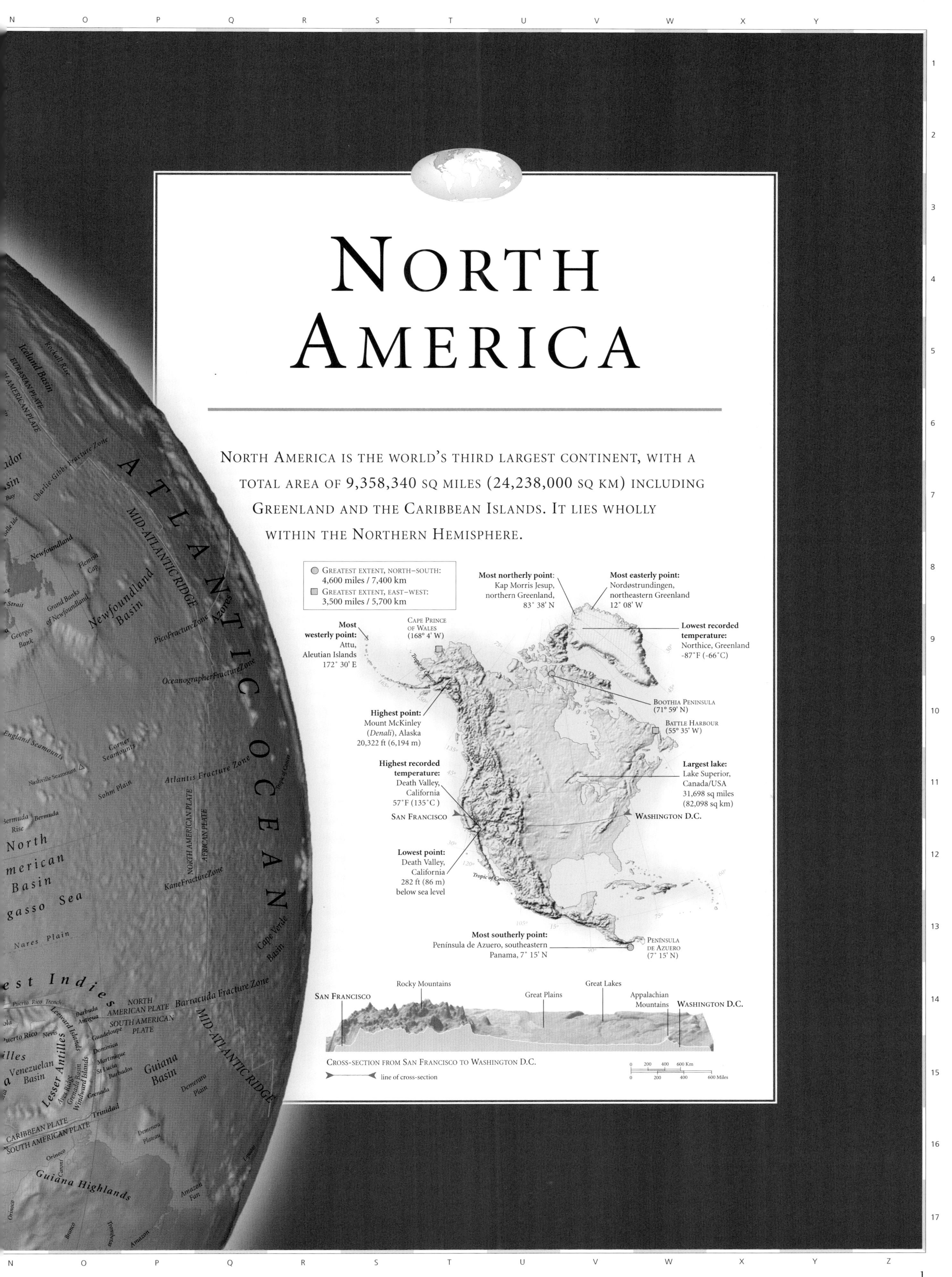

Greatest extent, north–south: 4,600 miles / 7,400 km
Greatest extent, east–west: 3,500 miles / 5,700 km
Most northerly point: Kap Morris Jesup, northern Greenland, 83° 38' N
Most easterly point: Nordøstrundingen, northeastern Greenland 12° 08' W
Most westerly point: Attu, Aleutian Islands 172° 30' E
Cape Prince of Wales (168° 4' W)
Lowest recorded temperature: Northice, Greenland -87°F (-66°C)
Boothia Peninsula (71° 59' N)
Battle Harbour (55° 35' W)
Highest point: Mount McKinley (Denali), Alaska 20,322 ft (6,194 m)
Highest recorded temperature: Death Valley, California 57°F (135°C)
Largest lake: Lake Superior, Canada/USA 31,698 sq miles (82,098 sq km)
San Francisco
Washington D.C.
Lowest point: Death Valley, California 282 ft (86 m) below sea level
Tropic of Cancer
Most southerly point: Península de Azuero, southeastern Panama, 7° 15' N
Península de Azuero (7° 15' N)
San Francisco
Rocky Mountains
Great Plains
Great Lakes
Appalachian Mountains
Washington D.C.
Cross-section from San Francisco to Washington D.C.
line of cross-section
0 200 400 600 Km
0 200 400 600 Miles
Atlantic Ocean
Mid-Atlantic Ridge
Newfoundland Basin
Newfoundland
Flemish Cap
Grand Banks of Newfoundland
Charlie-Gibbs Fracture Zone
Pico Fracture Zone
Oceanographer Fracture Zone
Azores
Iceland Basin
Rockall Rise
Corner Seamounts
Nashville Seamount
Sohm Plain
Atlantis Fracture Zone
North American Plate
African Plate
Kane Fracture Zone
North American Basin
Nares Plain
Cape Verde Basin
Barracuda Fracture Zone
North American Plate
South American Plate
Leeward Islands
Lesser Antilles
Venezuelan Basin
Guiana Basin
Demerara Plain
Trinidad
Caribbean Plate
South American Plate
Guiana Highlands
Amazon Fan
Amazon
Orinoco

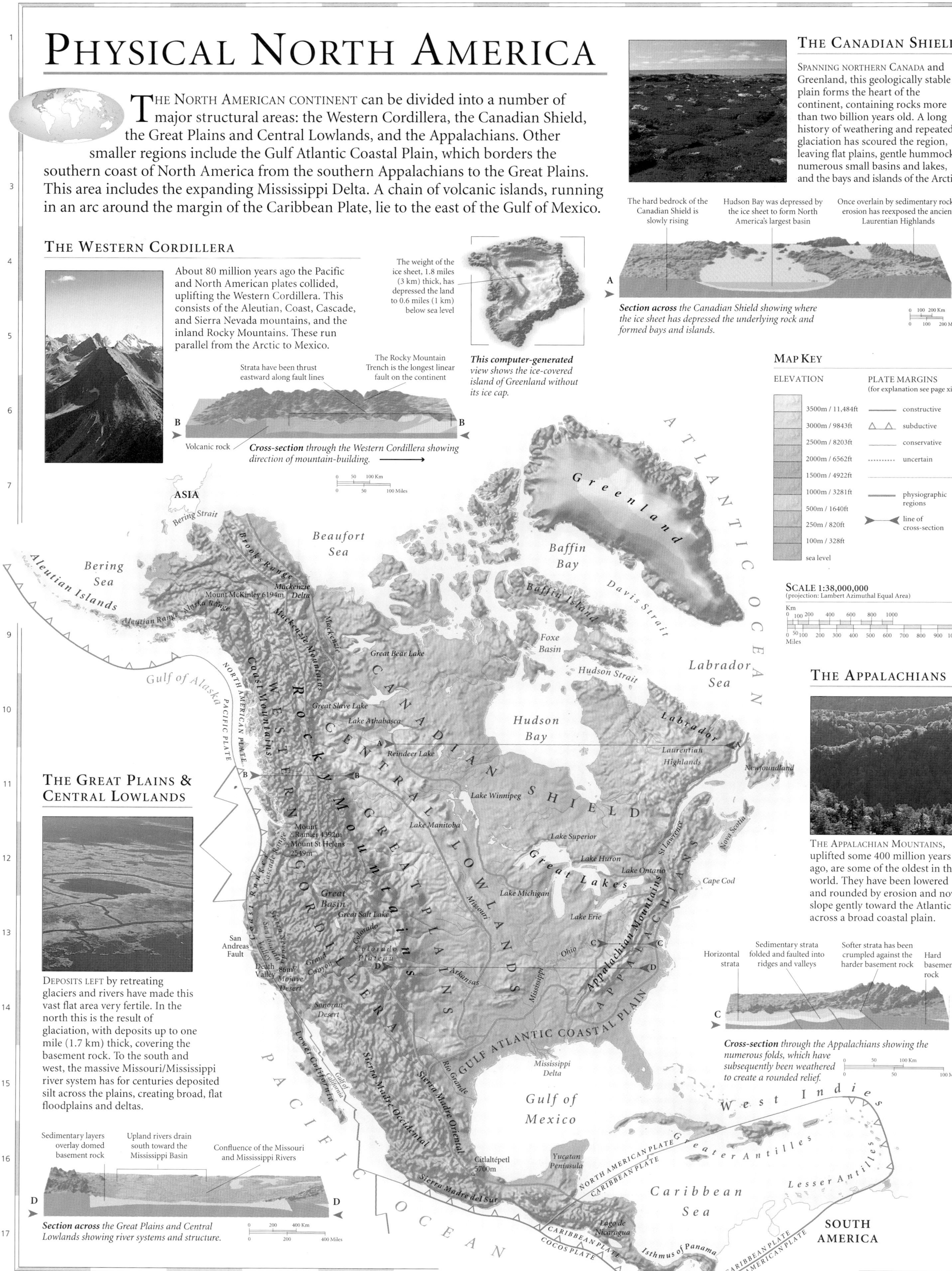

ASIA
Bering Strait
Beaufort Sea
Bering Sea
Aleutian Islands
Aleutian Range
Alaska Range
Mount McKinley 6194m
Brooks Range
Mackenzie Delta
Mackenzie Mountains
Mackenzie
Great Bear Lake
Great Slave Lake
Lake Athabasca
Reindeer Lake
Gulf of Alaska
NORTH AMERICAN PLATE
PACIFIC PLATE
Coast Mountains
WESTERN CORDILLERA
Rocky Mountains
CANADIAN SHIELD
CENTRAL LOWLANDS
GREAT PLAINS
Greenland
Baffin Bay
Baffin Island
Davis Strait
Foxe Basin
Hudson Strait
Hudson Bay
Labrador Sea
Labrador
Laurentian Highlands
Newfoundland
ATLANTIC OCEAN
Lake Winnipeg
Lake Manitoba
Lake Superior
Lake Huron
Lake Michigan
Lake Ontario
Lake Erie
Great Lakes
St Lawrence
Nova Scotia
Cape Cod
Mount Rainier 4392m
Mount St Helens 2549m
Cascade Range
Coast Ranges
Great Basin
Great Salt Lake
Sierra Nevada
San Joaquin Valley
San Andreas Fault
Death Valley -86m
Mojave Desert
Grand Canyon
Colorado
Colorado Plateau
Sonoran Desert
Missouri
Arkansas
Mississippi
Ohio
Appalachian Mountains
APPALACHIANS
GULF ATLANTIC COASTAL PLAIN
Mississippi Delta
Rio Grande
Lower California
Gulf of California
Sierra Madre Occidental
Sierra Madre Oriental
Sierra Madre del Sur
Citlaltépetl 5700m
Gulf of Mexico
Yucatan Peninsula
West Indies
Greater Antilles
Lesser Antilles
Caribbean Sea
Lago de Nicaragua
Isthmus of Panama
NORTH AMERICAN PLATE
CARIBBEAN PLATE
COCOS PLATE
SOUTH AMERICAN PLATE
SOUTH AMERICA
PACIFIC OCEAN
MAP KEY
ELEVATION
3500m / 11,484ft
3000m / 9843ft
2500m / 8203ft
2000m / 6562ft
1500m / 4922ft
1000m / 3281ft
500m / 1640ft
250m / 820ft
100m / 328ft
sea level
PLATE MARGINS
(for explanation see page xiv)
constructive
subductive
conservative
uncertain
physiographic regions
line of cross-section
SCALE 1:38,000,000
(projection: Lambert Azimuthal Equal Area)

Physical North America

The North American continent can be divided into a number of major structural areas: the Western Cordillera, the Canadian Shield, the Great Plains and Central Lowlands, and the Appalachians. Other smaller regions include the Gulf Atlantic Coastal Plain, which borders the southern coast of North America from the southern Appalachians to the Great Plains. This area includes the expanding Mississippi Delta. A chain of volcanic islands, running in an arc around the margin of the Caribbean Plate, lie to the east of the Gulf of Mexico.

The Western Cordillera

About 80 million years ago the Pacific and North American plates collided, uplifting the Western Cordillera. This consists of the Aleutian, Coast, Cascade, and Sierra Nevada mountains, and the inland Rocky Mountains. These run parallel from the Arctic to Mexico.

Strata have been thrust eastward along fault lines
The Rocky Mountain Trench is the longest linear fault on the continent
Volcanic rock

***Cross-section** through the Western Cordillera showing direction of mountain-building.*

The weight of the ice sheet, 1.8 miles (3 km) thick, has depressed the land to 0.6 miles (1 km) below sea level

***This computer-generated** view shows the ice-covered island of Greenland without its ice cap.*

The Canadian Shield

Spanning northern Canada and Greenland, this geologically stable plain forms the heart of the continent, containing rocks more than two billion years old. A long history of weathering and repeated glaciation has scoured the region, leaving flat plains, gentle hummocks, numerous small basins and lakes, and the bays and islands of the Arctic.

The hard bedrock of the Canadian Shield is slowly rising
Hudson Bay was depressed by the ice sheet to form North America's largest basin
Once overlain by sedimentary rocks, erosion has reexposed the ancient Laurentian Highlands

***Section across** the Canadian Shield showing where the ice sheet has depressed the underlying rock and formed bays and islands.*

The Great Plains & Central Lowlands

Deposits left by retreating glaciers and rivers have made this vast flat area very fertile. In the north this is the result of glaciation, with deposits up to one mile (1.7 km) thick, covering the basement rock. To the south and west, the massive Missouri/Mississippi river system has for centuries deposited silt across the plains, creating broad, flat floodplains and deltas.

Sedimentary layers overlay domed basement rock
Upland rivers drain south toward the Mississippi Basin
Confluence of the Missouri and Mississippi Rivers

***Section across** the Great Plains and Central Lowlands showing river systems and structure.*

The Appalachians

The Appalachian Mountains, uplifted some 400 million years ago, are some of the oldest in the world. They have been lowered and rounded by erosion and now slope gently toward the Atlantic across a broad coastal plain.

Horizontal strata
Sedimentary strata folded and faulted into ridges and valleys
Softer strata has been crumpled against the harder basement rock
Hard basement rock

***Cross-section** through the Appalachians showing the numerous folds, which have subsequently been weathered to create a rounded relief.*

CLIMATE

NORTH AMERICA'S climate includes extremes ranging from freezing Arctic conditions in Alaska and Greenland, to desert in the southwest, and tropical conditions in southeastern Florida, the Caribbean, and Central America. Central and southern regions can experience severe storms including tornadoes and hurricanes.

"Tornado alley" in the Mississippi Valley suffers frequent tornadoes.

Climate

- ice cap
- tundra
- subarctic
- cool continental
- warm humid
- semiarid
- arid
- humid equatorial
- tropical
- daily hours of sunshine, January
- daily hours of sunshine, July
- direction of hurricanes
- tornado zones

TEMPERATURE

Average January temperature

Average July temperature

Temperature

- below -22°F (-30°C)
- -22 to -4°F (-30 to -20°C)
- -4 to 14°F (-20 to -10°C)
- 14 to 32°F (-10 to 0°C)
- 32 to 50° F (0 to 10°C)
- 50°F (10 to 20°C)
- 68 to 86°F (20 to 30°C)
- above 86 °F (30°C)

Much of the southwest is semi-desert, receiving less than 12 inches (300 mm) of rainfall a year.

RAINFALL

Average January rainfall

Average July rainfall

Rainfall

- 0 – 1 in (0 – 25 mm)
- 1 – 2 in (25 – 50 mm)
- 2 – 4 in (50 – 100 mm)
- 4 – 8 in (100 – 200 mm)
- 8 – 12 in (200 – 300 mm)
- 12 – 16 in (300 – 400 mm)
- 16 – 20 in (400 – 500 mm)
- above 20 in (500 mm)

The lush, green mountains of the Lesser Antilles receive annual rainfall of up to 360 inches (9,000 mm).

SHAPING THE CONTINENT

GLACIAL PROCESSES affect much of northern Canada, Greenland, and the Western Cordillera. Along the western coast of North America, Central America, and the Caribbean, underlying plates moving together lead to earthquakes and volcanic eruptions. The vast river systems, fed by mountain streams, constantly erode and deposit material along their paths.

VOLCANIC ACTIVITY

1 Mount St. Helens volcano *(right)* in the Cascade Range erupted violently in May 1980, killing 57 people and leveling large areas of forest. The lateral blast filled a valley with debris for 15 miles (25 km).

Molten rock at volcano's core — Vertical eruption — Lateral explosion increases extent of damage — Landslide fills valley

VOLCANIC ACTIVITY: ERUPTION OF MOUNT ST. HELENS

PERIGLACIATION

2 The ground in the far north is nearly always frozen: the surface thaws only in summer. This freeze–thaw process produces features such as pingos *(left)*; formed by the freezing of groundwater. With each successive winter ice accumulates, producing a mound with a core of ice.

Ice core pushes up ground to form pingo — Unfrozen lake — Groundwater attracted to ice core

PERIGLACIATION: FORMATION OF A PINGO IN THE MACKENZIE DELTA

POST-GLACIAL LAKES

3 A chain of lakes from Great Bear Lake to the Great Lakes *(above)* was created as the ice retreated northward. Glaciers scoured hollows in the softer lowland rock. Glacial deposits at the lip of the hollows, and ridges of harder rock, trapped water to form lakes.

Retreating glacier — Ice-scoured hollow filled with glacial meltwater to form a lake — Harder rock creates a barrier between lakes — Softer lowland rock

POST-GLACIAL LAKES: FORMATION OF THE GREAT LAKES

THE EVOLVING LANDSCAPE

Landscape

- limestone region
- sinking land
- stable land
- uplifting land
- active volcano
- area of tectonic activity
- limit of permafrost
- maximum limit of glaciation
- ocean current

SEISMIC ACTIVITY

5 The San Andreas Fault *(above)* places much of the North America's West Coast under constant threat from earthquakes. It is caused by the Pacific Plate grinding at a faster rate past the North American Plate, though in the same direction.

Pacific Plate — San Andreas Fault — Fault is caused by faster movement of Pacific Plate — North American Plate

SEISMIC ACTIVITY: ACTION OF THE SAN ANDREAS FAULT

RIVER EROSION

6 The Grand Canyon *(above)* in the Colorado Plateau was created by the Colorado River, combined with the gradual uplift of the plateau, over the past 30 million years. The contours of the canyon formed as the softer rock layers eroded into gentle slopes, and the hard rock layers into cliffs. The depth varies from 3,855–6,560 ft (1,175–2,000 m).

Soft rock is easily eroded into gentle slopes — Hard rock resists erosion — Colorado River cuts down through rock

RIVER EROSION: FORMATION OF THE GRAND CANYON

WEATHERING

4 The Yucatan Peninsula is a vast, flat limestone plateau in southern Mexico. Weathering action from both rainwater and underground streams has enlarged fractures in the rock to form caves and hollows, called sinkholes *(above)*.

Porous limestone plateau — Rainwater erodes porous rock forming sinkholes — Sea level — Underground stream erodes rock further

WEATHERING: WATER EROSION ON THE YUCATAN PENINSULA

Political North America

Democracy is well established in some parts of the continent but is a recent phenomenon in others. The economically dominant nations of Canada and the US have a long democratic tradition but elsewhere, notably in the countries of Central America, political turmoil has been more common. In Nicaragua and Haiti, harsh dictatorships have only recently been superseded by democratically elected governments. North America's largest countries, Canada, Mexico, and the US have federal–state systems, sharing political power between national and state governments. The US has intervened militarily on several occasions in Central America and the Caribbean to protect its strategic interests.

Transportation

In the 19th century, railroads opened up the North American continent. Air transportation is now more common for long-distance passenger travel, although railroads are still extensively used for bulk freight transportation. Waterways like the Mississippi River are important for the transportation of bulk materials, and the Panama Canal is a vital link between the Pacific and Atlantic Oceans. In the 20th century, road transportation has increased dramatically, with the introduction of cheap, mass-produced cars and extensive highway construction.

This busy suburban interchange *in Los Angeles is part of the US Interstate freeway system. Construction of the 55,000 mile (88,500 km) freeway network began in the 1950s, and it now connects most major cities, and carries one-fifth of US road traffic.*

Transportation

- major roads and highways
- major railroads
- major canal
- international borders
- transportation intersections
- international airports
- major ports

The 40-mile (65-km) *long Panama Canal cuts through the Isthmus of Panama, a narrow strip of land connecting North and South America. Opened in 1914, the canal reduced the journey between the Atlantic and Pacific oceans by almost 8,000 nautical miles (14,800 km).*

Low-density housing developments *such as this one on the outskirts of Phoenix, Arizona, reflect the US's abundance of land and a dispersed population, dependent on the car for mobility.*

UNITED STATES OF AMERICA — HAWAII

SCALE 1:12,000,000
(projection: Lambert Conformal Conic)

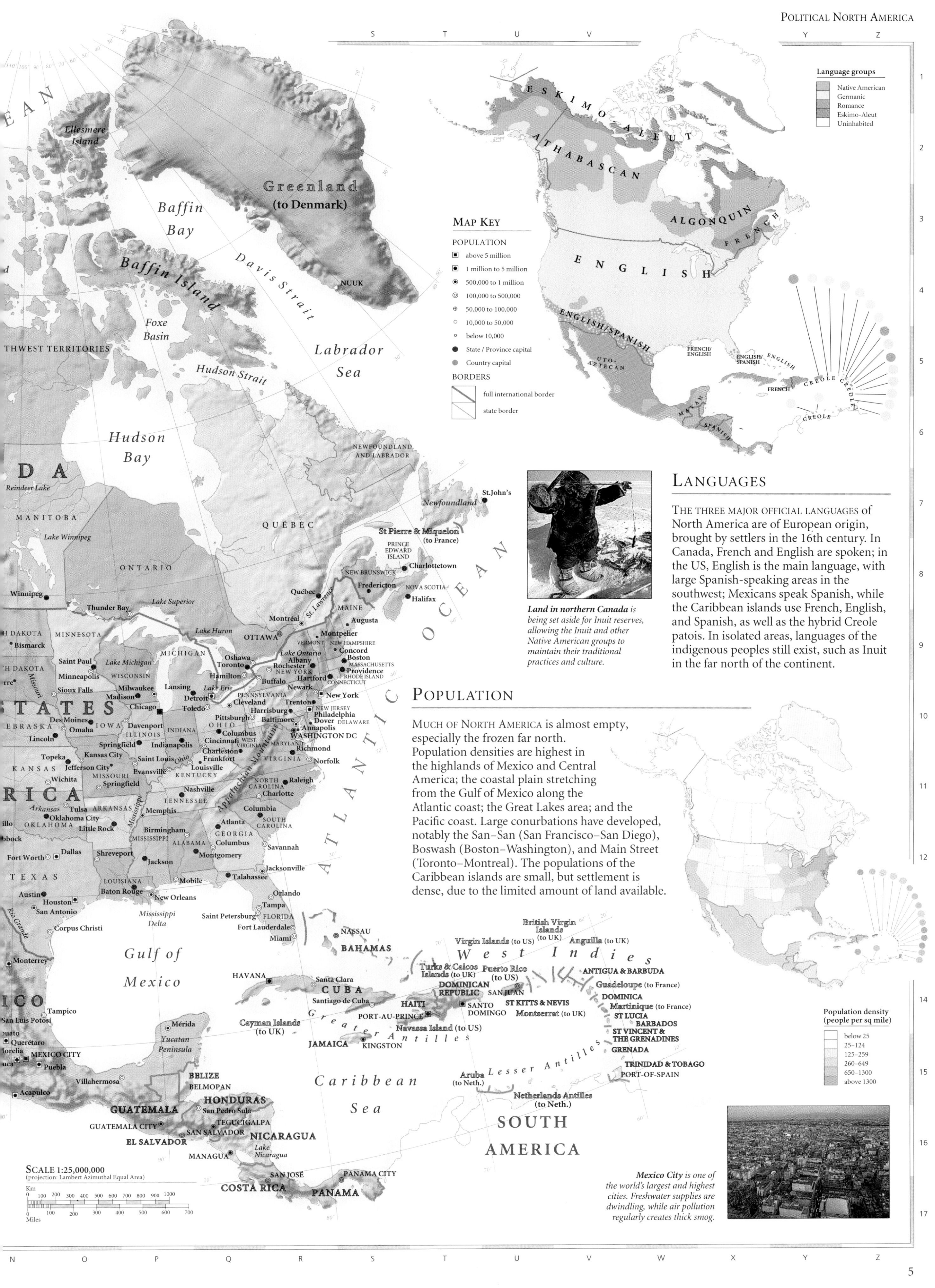

Ellesmere Island
Greenland (to Denmark)
Baffin Bay
Baffin Island
Davis Strait
NUUK
Foxe Basin
Labrador Sea
Hudson Strait
Hudson Bay
NEWFOUNDLAND AND LABRADOR
Newfoundland
St.John's
QUÉBEC
St Pierre & Miquelon (to France)
PRINCE EDWARD ISLAND
Charlottetown
NEW BRUNSWICK
Fredericton
NOVA SCOTIA
Halifax
MANITOBA
Lake Winnipeg
ONTARIO
Winnipeg
Thunder Bay
Lake Superior
Québec
Montréal
OTTAWA
MAINE
Augusta
Montpelier
VERMONT
NEW HAMPSHIRE
Concord
Boston
MASSACHUSETTS
Providence
RHODE ISLAND
Hartford
CONNECTICUT
New York
NEW JERSEY
Trenton
Philadelphia
Dover
DELAWARE
Annapolis
WASHINGTON DC
MARYLAND
Richmond
VIRGINIA
Norfolk
Raleigh
NORTH CAROLINA
Charlotte
Columbia
SOUTH CAROLINA
Atlanta
GEORGIA
Columbus
Savannah
Jacksonville
Talahassee
Orlando
Tampa
FLORIDA
Saint Petersburg
Fort Lauderdale
Miami
ATLANTIC OCEAN
Lake Huron
Lake Ontario
Lake Erie
Lake Michigan
MICHIGAN
Oshawa
Toronto
Hamilton
Rochester
Albany
NEW YORK
Buffalo
Newark
Lansing
Detroit
Toledo
Cleveland
PENNSYLVANIA
Harrisburg
Pittsburgh
Baltimore
OHIO
Columbus
Cincinnati
WEST VIRGINIA
Charleston
Frankfort
Louisville
KENTUCKY
Nashville
TENNESSEE
Appalachian Mountains
MINNESOTA
Saint Paul
Minneapolis
WISCONSIN
Milwaukee
Madison
Chicago
Sioux Falls
Des Moines
Omaha
IOWA
Davenport
ILLINOIS
INDIANA
Indianapolis
Springfield
Lincoln
Topeka
Kansas City
Jefferson City
Saint Louis
Evansville
MISSOURI
Springfield
Wichita
KANSAS
Tulsa
ARKANSAS
Oklahoma City
OKLAHOMA
Little Rock
Memphis
Mississippi
Birmingham
MISSISSIPPI
ALABAMA
Montgomery
Jackson
Shreveport
Dallas
Fort Worth
TEXAS
LOUISIANA
Baton Rouge
New Orleans
Mobile
Austin
Houston
San Antonio
Corpus Christi
Rio Grande
Mississippi Delta
Gulf of Mexico
Monterrey
Tampico
San Luis Potosí
Querétaro
MEXICO CITY
Puebla
Acapulco
Mérida
Yucatan Peninsula
Villahermosa
BELIZE
BELMOPAN
GUATEMALA
GUATEMALA CITY
HONDURAS
San Pedro Sula
TEGUCIGALPA
SAN SALVADOR
EL SALVADOR
NICARAGUA
MANAGUA
Lake Nicaragua
SAN JOSÉ
COSTA RICA
PANAMA CITY
PANAMA
SOUTH AMERICA
Caribbean Sea
HAVANA
Santa Clara
CUBA
Santiago de Cuba
Cayman Islands (to UK)
JAMAICA
KINGSTON
Greater Antilles
HAITI
PORT-AU-PRINCE
DOMINICAN REPUBLIC
SANTO DOMINGO
SAN JUAN
Puerto Rico (to US)
Turks & Caicos Islands (to UK)
Navassa Island (to US)
NASSAU
BAHAMAS
West Indies
Virgin Islands (to US)
British Virgin Islands (to UK)
Anguilla (to UK)
ANTIGUA & BARBUDA
Guadeloupe (to France)
DOMINICA
Martinique (to France)
ST KITTS & NEVIS
Montserrat (to UK)
ST LUCIA
BARBADOS
ST VINCENT & THE GRENADINES
GRENADA
TRINIDAD & TOBAGO
PORT-OF-SPAIN
Lesser Antilles
Aruba (to Neth.)
Netherlands Antilles (to Neth.)
SCALE 1:25,000,000
(projection: Lambert Azimuthal Equal Area)
MAP KEY
POPULATION
above 5 million
1 million to 5 million
500,000 to 1 million
100,000 to 500,000
50,000 to 100,000
10,000 to 50,000
below 10,000
State / Province capital
Country capital
BORDERS
full international border
state border
Language groups
Native American
Germanic
Romance
Eskimo-Aleut
Uninhabited
ESKIMO-ALEUT
ATHABASCAN
ALGONQUIN
FRENCH
ENGLISH
ENGLISH/SPANISH
UTO-AZTECAN
FRENCH/ENGLISH
ENGLISH/SPANISH
ENGLISH
FRENCH
CREOLE
MAYAN
SPANISH
Population density (people per sq mile)
below 25
25–124
125–259
260–649
650–1300
above 1300

LANGUAGES

THE THREE MAJOR OFFICIAL LANGUAGES of North America are of European origin, brought by settlers in the 16th century. In Canada, French and English are spoken; in the US, English is the main language, with large Spanish-speaking areas in the southwest; Mexicans speak Spanish, while the Caribbean islands use French, English, and Spanish, as well as the hybrid Creole patois. In isolated areas, languages of the indigenous peoples still exist, such as Inuit in the far north of the continent.

***Land in northern Canada** is being set aside for Inuit reserves, allowing the Inuit and other Native American groups to maintain their traditional practices and culture.*

POPULATION

MUCH OF NORTH AMERICA is almost empty, especially the frozen far north. Population densities are highest in the highlands of Mexico and Central America; the coastal plain stretching from the Gulf of Mexico along the Atlantic coast; the Great Lakes area; and the Pacific coast. Large conurbations have developed, notably the San–San (San Francisco–San Diego), Boswash (Boston–Washington), and Main Street (Toronto–Montreal). The populations of the Caribbean islands are small, but settlement is dense, due to the limited amount of land available.

***Mexico City** is one of the world's largest and highest cities. Freshwater supplies are dwindling, while air pollution regularly creates thick smog.*

NORTH AMERICAN RESOURCES

THE TWO NORTHERN COUNTRIES of Canada and the US are richly endowed with natural resources that have helped to fuel economic development. The US is the world's largest economy, although today it is facing stiff competition from the Far East. Mexico has relied on oil revenues but there are hopes that the North American Free Trade Agreement (NAFTA) will encourage trade growth with Canada and the US. The poorer countries of Central America and the Caribbean depend largely on cash crops and tourism.

STANDARD OF LIVING

THE US AND CANADA have one of the highest overall standards of living in the world. However, many people still live in poverty, especially in urban ghettos and some rural areas. Central America and the Caribbean are markedly poorer than their wealthier northern neighbors. Haiti is the poorest country in the western hemisphere.

Standard of Living (UN Human Development Index)

high

low

INDUSTRY

THE MODERN, INDUSTRIALIZED economies of the US and Canada contrast sharply with those of Mexico, Central America, and the Caribbean. Manufacturing is especially important in the US; vehicle production is concentrated around the Great Lakes, while electronic and hi-tech industries are increasingly found in the western and southern states. Mexico depends on oil exports and assembly work, taking advantage of cheap labor. Many Central American and Caribbean countries rely heavily on agricultural exports.

After its purchase from Russia in 1867, Alaska's frozen lands were largely ignored by the US. Oil reserves similar in magnitude to those in eastern Texas were discovered in Prudhoe Bay, Alaska, in 1968, but freezing temperatures and a fragile environment hamper oil extraction.

Fish such as cod, flounder, and plaice are caught in the Grand Banks off the Newfoundland coast, and processed in many North Atlantic coastal settlements.

South of San Francisco, "Silicon Valley" is both a national and international center for hi-tech industries, electronic industries, and research institutions.

CANADA
UNITED STATES OF AMERICA
MEXICO
Gulf of Mexico
ATLANTIC OCEAN
PACIFIC OCEAN
Caribbean Sea

***The twin towers** of the World Trade Center dominate the Manhattan skyline. New York is one of the world's leading trade and finance centers.*

***Multinational** companies rely on cheap labor and tax benefits to assemble vehicles in Mexican factories.*

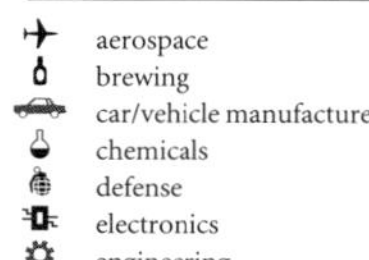

Industry

- aerospace
- brewing
- car/vehicle manufacture
- chemicals
- defense
- electronics
- engineering
- film industry
- finance
- food processing
- hi-tech industry
- iron & steel
- pharmaceuticals
- printing & publishing
- research & development
- shipbuilding
- sugar processing
- textiles
- timber processing
- tobacco processing
- coal
- oil
- gas
- industrial cities
- major industrial areas

GNP per capita (US$)

- 0–1999
- 2000–4999
- 5000–9999
- 10,000–19,999
- 20,000–24,999
- 25,000+

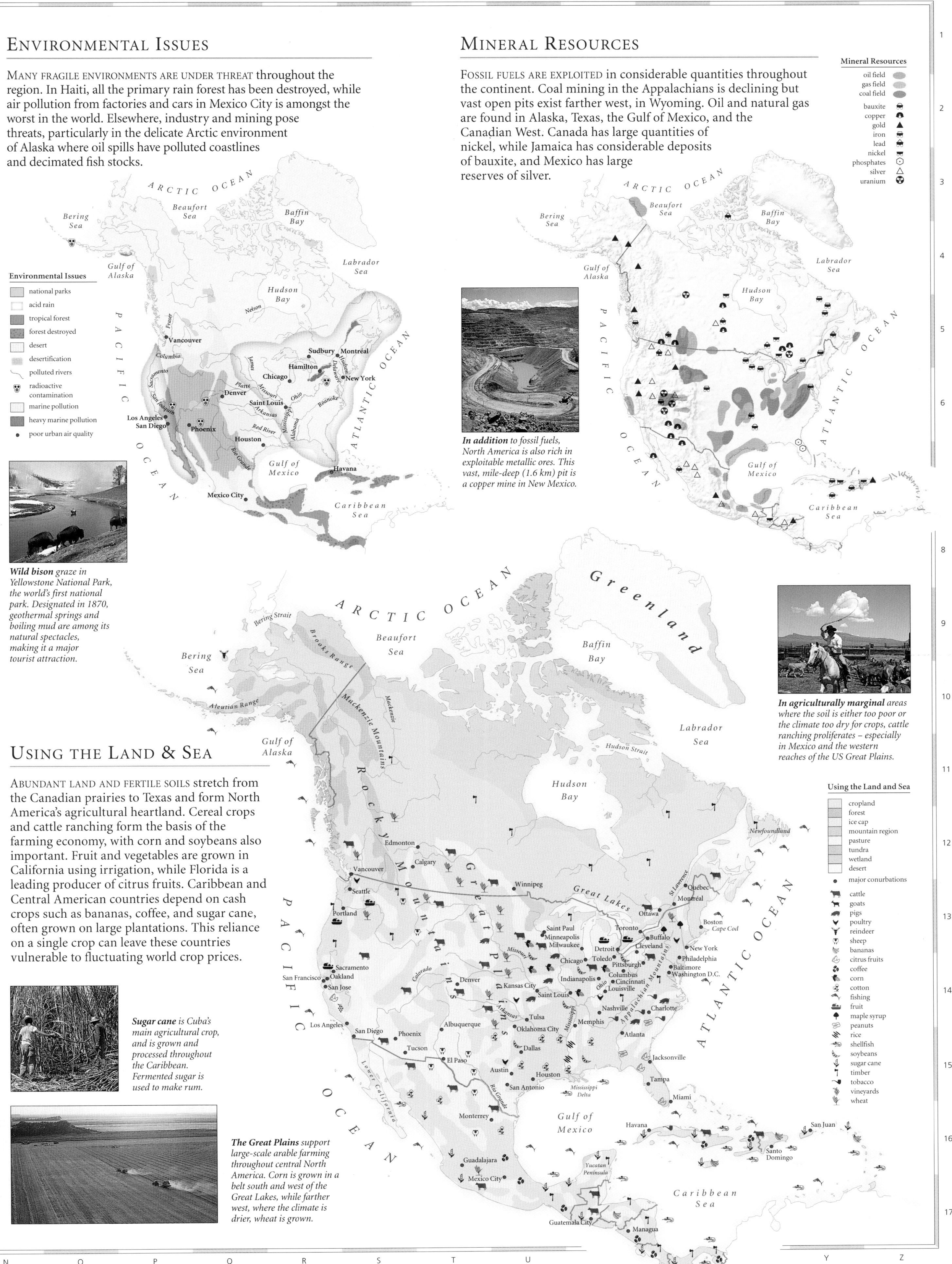

ENVIRONMENTAL ISSUES

MANY FRAGILE ENVIRONMENTS ARE UNDER THREAT throughout the region. In Haiti, all the primary rain forest has been destroyed, while air pollution from factories and cars in Mexico City is amongst the worst in the world. Elsewhere, industry and mining pose threats, particularly in the delicate Arctic environment of Alaska where oil spills have polluted coastlines and decimated fish stocks.

Environmental Issues
national parks
acid rain
tropical forest
forest destroyed
desert
desertification
polluted rivers
radioactive contamination
marine pollution
heavy marine pollution
poor urban air quality
ARCTIC OCEAN
Beaufort Sea
Bering Sea
Baffin Bay
Gulf of Alaska
Labrador Sea
Hudson Bay
PACIFIC OCEAN
ATLANTIC OCEAN
Gulf of Mexico
Caribbean Sea
Vancouver
Sudbury
Montréal
Hamilton
Chicago
New York
Denver
Saint Louis
Los Angeles
San Diego
Phoenix
Houston
Havana
Mexico City

***Wild bison** graze in Yellowstone National Park, the world's first national park. Designated in 1870, geothermal springs and boiling mud are among its natural spectacles, making it a major tourist attraction.*

MINERAL RESOURCES

FOSSIL FUELS ARE EXPLOITED in considerable quantities throughout the continent. Coal mining in the Appalachians is declining but vast open pits exist farther west, in Wyoming. Oil and natural gas are found in Alaska, Texas, the Gulf of Mexico, and the Canadian West. Canada has large quantities of nickel, while Jamaica has considerable deposits of bauxite, and Mexico has large reserves of silver.

Mineral Resources
oil field
gas field
coal field
bauxite
copper
gold
iron
lead
nickel
phosphates
silver
uranium
ARCTIC OCEAN
Beaufort Sea
Bering Sea
Baffin Bay
Gulf of Alaska
Labrador Sea
Hudson Bay
PACIFIC OCEAN
ATLANTIC OCEAN
Gulf of Mexico
Caribbean Sea

***In addition** to fossil fuels, North America is also rich in exploitable metallic ores. This vast, mile-deep (1.6 km) pit is a copper mine in New Mexico.*

USING THE LAND & SEA

ABUNDANT LAND AND FERTILE SOILS stretch from the Canadian prairies to Texas and form North America's agricultural heartland. Cereal crops and cattle ranching form the basis of the farming economy, with corn and soybeans also important. Fruit and vegetables are grown in California using irrigation, while Florida is a leading producer of citrus fruits. Caribbean and Central American countries depend on cash crops such as bananas, coffee, and sugar cane, often grown on large plantations. This reliance on a single crop can leave these countries vulnerable to fluctuating world crop prices.

Using the Land and Sea
cropland
forest
ice cap
mountain region
pasture
tundra
wetland
desert
major conurbations
cattle
goats
pigs
poultry
reindeer
sheep
bananas
citrus fruits
coffee
corn
cotton
fishing
fruit
maple syrup
peanuts
rice
shellfish
soybeans
sugar cane
timber
tobacco
vineyards
wheat
ARCTIC OCEAN
Greenland
Bering Strait
Brooks Range
Beaufort Sea
Baffin Bay
Bering Sea
Aleutian Range
Mackenzie Mountains
Mackenzie
Gulf of Alaska
Labrador Sea
Hudson Strait
Hudson Bay
Rocky Mountains
Great Plains
Great Lakes
Appalachian Mountains
PACIFIC OCEAN
ATLANTIC OCEAN
Gulf of Mexico
Caribbean Sea
Newfoundland
St Lawrence
Cape Cod
Lower California
Yucatan Peninsula
Mississippi Delta
Edmonton
Calgary
Vancouver
Seattle
Winnipeg
Portland
Québec
Montréal
Ottawa
Toronto
Boston
Saint Paul
Minneapolis
Milwaukee
Buffalo
Detroit
Cleveland
New York
Chicago
Toledo
Pittsburgh
Philadelphia
Baltimore
Washington D.C.
Sacramento
San Francisco
Oakland
San Jose
Denver
Kansas City
Indianapolis
Columbus
Cincinnati
Louisville
Saint Louis
Nashville
Charlotte
Los Angeles
San Diego
Phoenix
Albuquerque
Tulsa
Oklahoma City
Memphis
Atlanta
Tucson
El Paso
Dallas
Jacksonville
Austin
Houston
San Antonio
Tampa
Miami
Monterrey
Havana
San Juan
Santo Domingo
Guadalajara
Mexico City
Guatemala City
Managua

***In agriculturally marginal** areas where the soil is either too poor or the climate too dry for crops, cattle ranching proliferates – especially in Mexico and the western reaches of the US Great Plains.*

***Sugar cane** is Cuba's main agricultural crop, and is grown and processed throughout the Caribbean. Fermented sugar is used to make rum.*

***The Great Plains** support large-scale arable farming throughout central North America. Corn is grown in a belt south and west of the Great Lakes, while farther west, where the climate is drier, wheat is grown.*

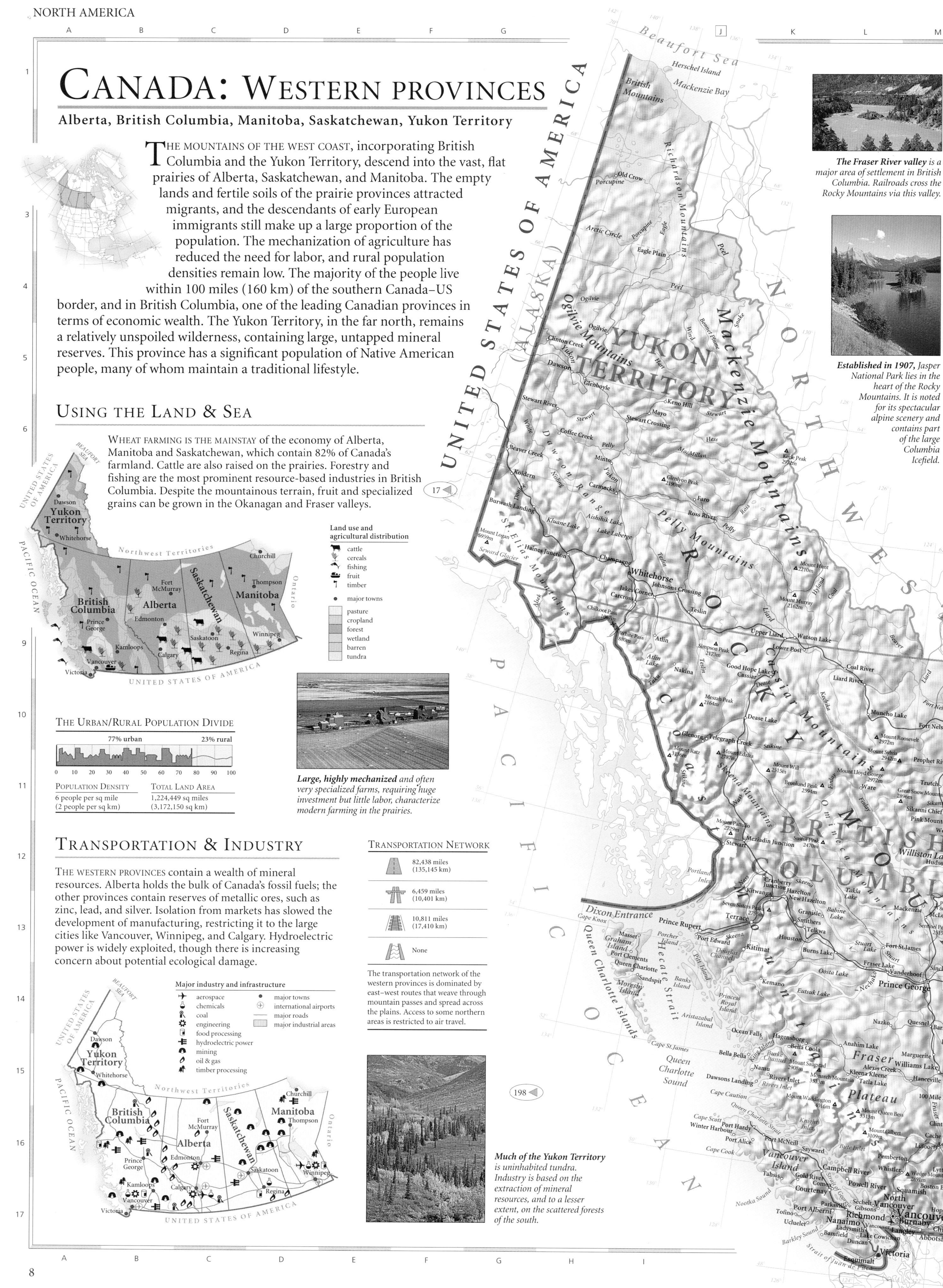

CANADA: WESTERN PROVINCES

Alberta, British Columbia, Manitoba, Saskatchewan, Yukon Territory

THE MOUNTAINS OF THE WEST COAST, incorporating British Columbia and the Yukon Territory, descend into the vast, flat prairies of Alberta, Saskatchewan, and Manitoba. The empty lands and fertile soils of the prairie provinces attracted migrants, and the descendants of early European immigrants still make up a large proportion of the population. The mechanization of agriculture has reduced the need for labor, and rural population densities remain low. The majority of the people live within 100 miles (160 km) of the southern Canada–US border, and in British Columbia, one of the leading Canadian provinces in terms of economic wealth. The Yukon Territory, in the far north, remains a relatively unspoiled wilderness, containing large, untapped mineral reserves. This province has a significant population of Native American people, many of whom maintain a traditional lifestyle.

USING THE LAND & SEA

WHEAT FARMING IS THE MAINSTAY of the economy of Alberta, Manitoba and Saskatchewan, which contain 82% of Canada's farmland. Cattle are also raised on the prairies. Forestry and fishing are the most prominent resource-based industries in British Columbia. Despite the mountainous terrain, fruit and specialized grains can be grown in the Okanagan and Fraser valleys.

Land use and agricultural distribution
cattle
cereals
fishing
fruit
timber
major towns
pasture
cropland
forest
wetland
barren
tundra

THE URBAN/RURAL POPULATION DIVIDE

77% urban
23% rural
0 10 20 30 40 50 60 70 80 90 100

POPULATION DENSITY	TOTAL LAND AREA
6 people per sq mile (2 people per sq km)	1,224,449 sq miles (3,172,150 sq km)

Large, highly mechanized and often very specialized farms, requiring huge investment but little labor, characterize modern farming in the prairies.

TRANSPORTATION & INDUSTRY

THE WESTERN PROVINCES contain a wealth of mineral resources. Alberta holds the bulk of Canada's fossil fuels; the other provinces contain reserves of metallic ores, such as zinc, lead, and silver. Isolation from markets has slowed the development of manufacturing, restricting it to the large cities like Vancouver, Winnipeg, and Calgary. Hydroelectric power is widely exploited, though there is increasing concern about potential ecological damage.

Major industry and infrastructure
aerospace
chemicals
coal
engineering
food processing
hydroelectric power
mining
oil & gas
timber processing
major towns
international airports
major roads
major industrial areas

TRANSPORTATION NETWORK

Roads	82,438 miles (135,145 km)
Highways	6,459 miles (10,401 km)
Railways	10,811 miles (17,410 km)
Waterways	None

The transportation network of the western provinces is dominated by east–west routes that weave through mountain passes and spread across the plains. Access to some northern areas is restricted to air travel.

Much of the Yukon Territory is uninhabited tundra. Industry is based on the extraction of mineral resources, and to a lesser extent, on the scattered forests of the south.

***The Fraser River valley** is a major area of settlement in British Columbia. Railroads cross the Rocky Mountains via this valley.*

***Established in 1907,** Jasper National Park lies in the heart of the Rocky Mountains. It is noted for its spectacular alpine scenery and contains part of the large Columbia Icefield.*

THE LANDSCAPE

THE MASSIVE ROCKY MOUNTAINS form a continental divide between rivers flowing eastward and westward. The interior plains lie east of the mountains, stretching from the Arctic Circle south into the US. Covered with glacial deposits from the last Ice Age, these are interspersed with hilly regions and long, steep escarpments.

MAP KEY

POPULATION

- 500,000 to 1 million
- 100,000 to 500,000
- 50,000 to 100,000
- 10,000 to 50,000
- below 10,000

ELEVATION

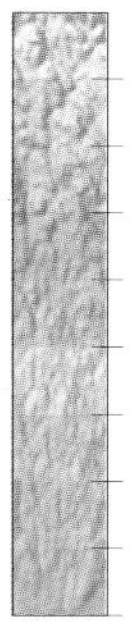

- 6000m / 19,686ft
- 4000m / 13,124ft
- 3000m / 9843ft
- 2000m / 6562ft
- 1000m / 3281ft
- 500m / 1640ft
- 250m / 820ft
- 100m / 328ft
- sea level

SCALE 1:7,500,000
(projection: Lambert Conformal Conic)

Km 0 25 50 100 150 200 250
Miles 0 25 50 100 150 200 250

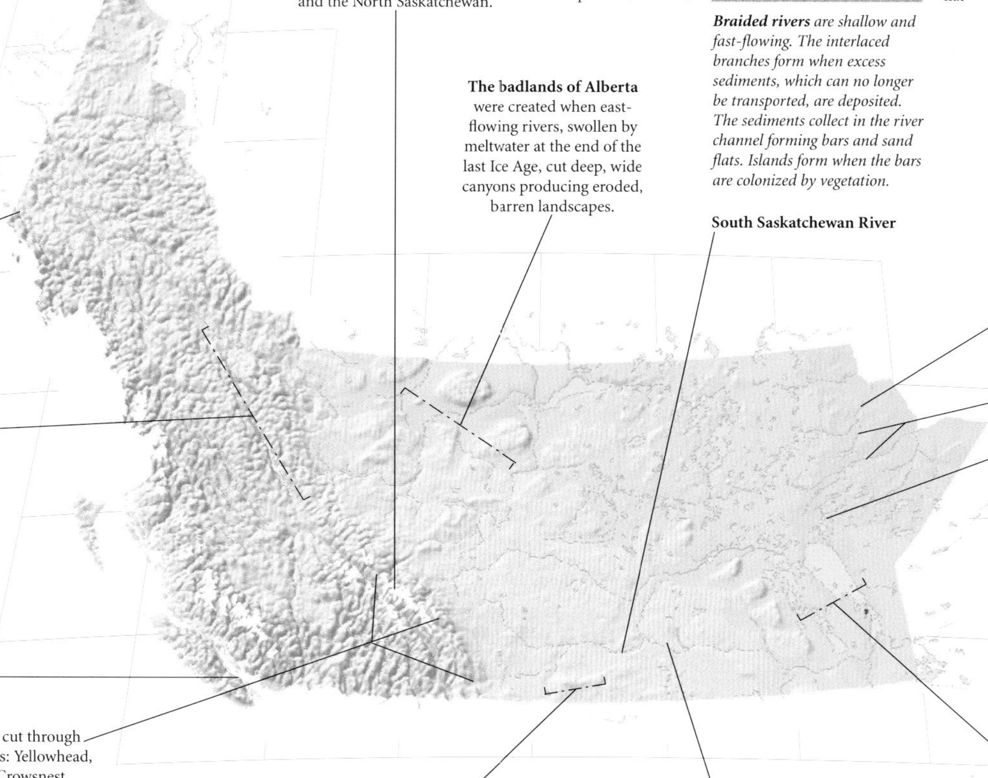

Mount Logan rises 19,551 ft (5,959 m). It is the highest peak in Canada.

The Rocky Mountain Trench is the longest linear fault in the world. It has formed a straight, flat-bottomed valley between 2 and 9 miles (4–15 km) wide, and up to 3,280 ft (1,000 m) deep.

Hundreds of islands dot the fjord-indented coast of British Columbia; the largest is Vancouver Island.

Three major passes cut through the Rocky Mountains: Yellowhead, Kicking Horse, and Crowsnest. They are all used as transportation routes through the mountains.

The Columbia Icefield in the Rocky Mountains is the source of two major rivers, the Athabasca and the North Saskatchewan.

The badlands of Alberta were created when east-flowing rivers, swollen by meltwater at the end of the last Ice Age, cut deep, wide canyons producing eroded, barren landscapes.

The Cypress Hills rise to 4,806 ft (1,465 m) above the surrounding plain. Having escaped the last glaciation, they contain unique plant and animal life. The silvery lupine, bunchberry, and lodgepole pine all grow in the cool, moist climate of the hills.

Vegetated island

River flow is diverted by deposited sediments

Bar

Sand flat

***Braided rivers** are shallow and fast-flowing. The interlaced branches form when excess sediments, which can no longer be transported, are deposited. The sediments collect in the river channel forming bars and sand flats. Islands form when the bars are colonized by vegetation.*

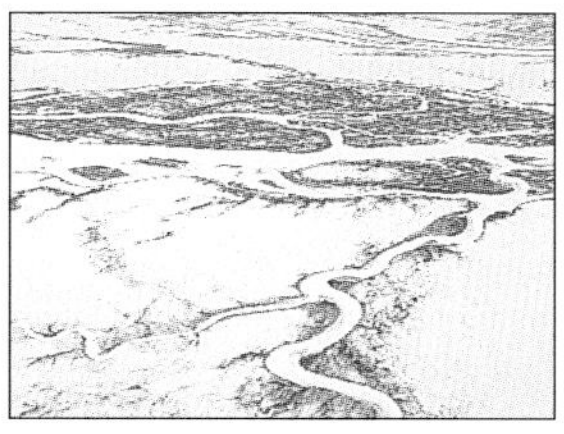

South Saskatchewan River

The Alberta and Saskatchewan plains bear strong testament to past glaciations. The Assiniboine, Saskatchewan, and Qu'Appelle Rivers occupy flat-bottomed, steep-sided valleys eroded during the last Ice Age by glacial meltwater.

***Across the tundra** of northern Manitoba, widespread permafrost inhibits water from permeating the soil. This causes rivers like the Churchill to flow in many channels, which can be frozen for up to six months during the winter.*

The Nelson and Churchill rivers drain northward across the Canadian Shield to Hudson Bay. The shield covers three-fifths of Saskatchewan.

Setting Lake

***Ancient granite outcrops**, part of the Canadian Shield, are scattered across the surface of Setting Lake, which was initially formed by meltwater from the last Ice Age.*

The lowlands of Manitoba are a basin that once held the vast post-glacial Lake Agassiz, remnants of which include Lake Winnipeg, Lake Winnipegosis, and Lake Manitoba.

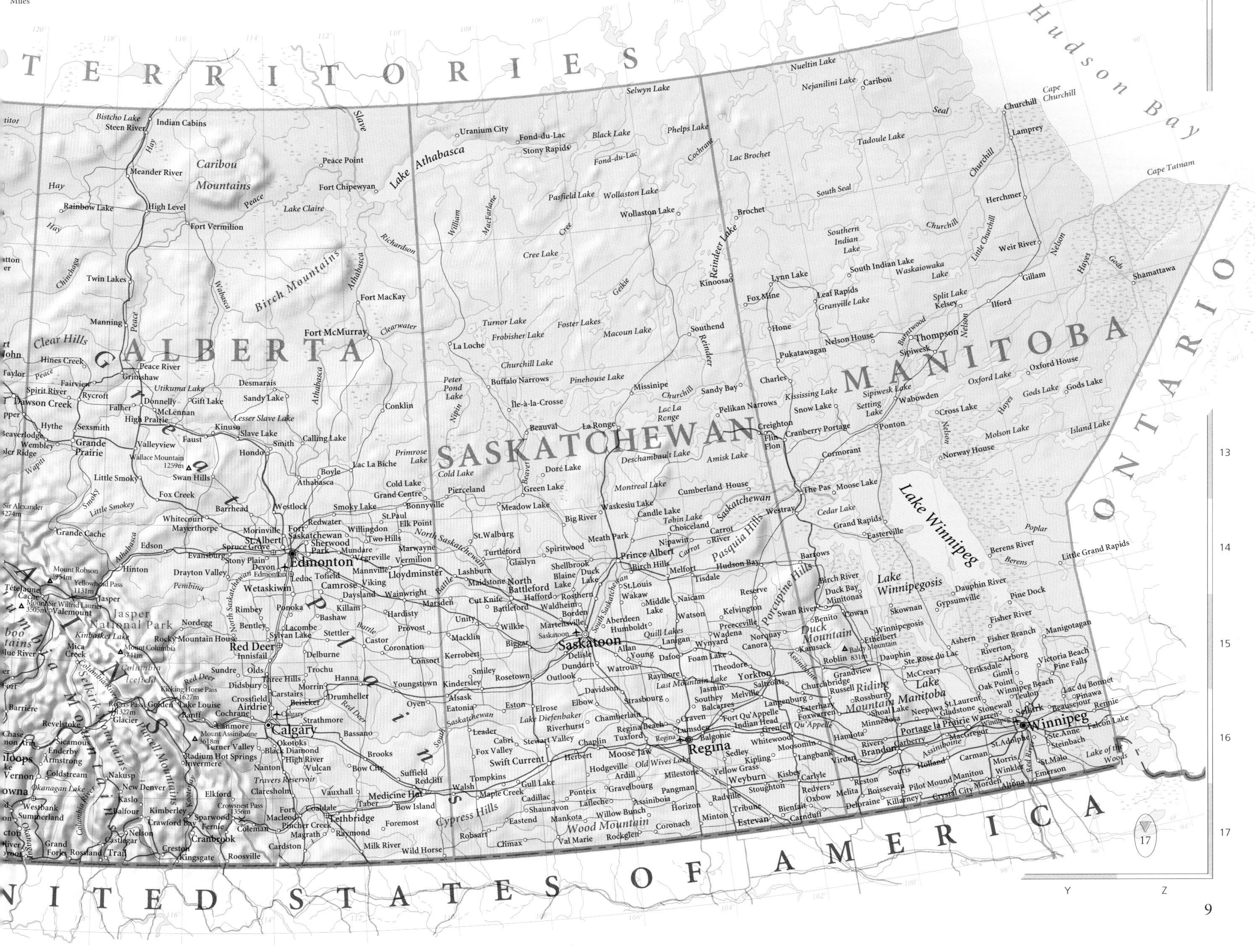

17

CANADA: EASTERN PROVINCES

New Brunswick, Newfoundland and Labrador, Nova Scotia, Ontario, Prince Edward Island, Québec, *St. Pierre & Miquelon* (to France)

COLONIZED BY BOTH THE ENGLISH AND THE FRENCH during the 16th century, Canada's eastern provinces are still marked by their dual influences. They contain the last fragment of once-sizeable French territories, the islands of St. Pierre and Miquelon. French remains Canada's second official language and Québec's first language. The population of the eastern provinces is highly concentrated in the south, especially along the border with the US. A recent decline in fishing in the Atlantic provinces has encouraged a steady flow of westerly migration to more properous regions. The north, around Hudson Bay, remains snow-covered for most of the year and the indigenous Inuit make up the bulk of its sparse population.

Rocher Percé is 290 ft (88 m) high. Lying off the southeastern coast of Québec, it is a sanctuary for seabirds.

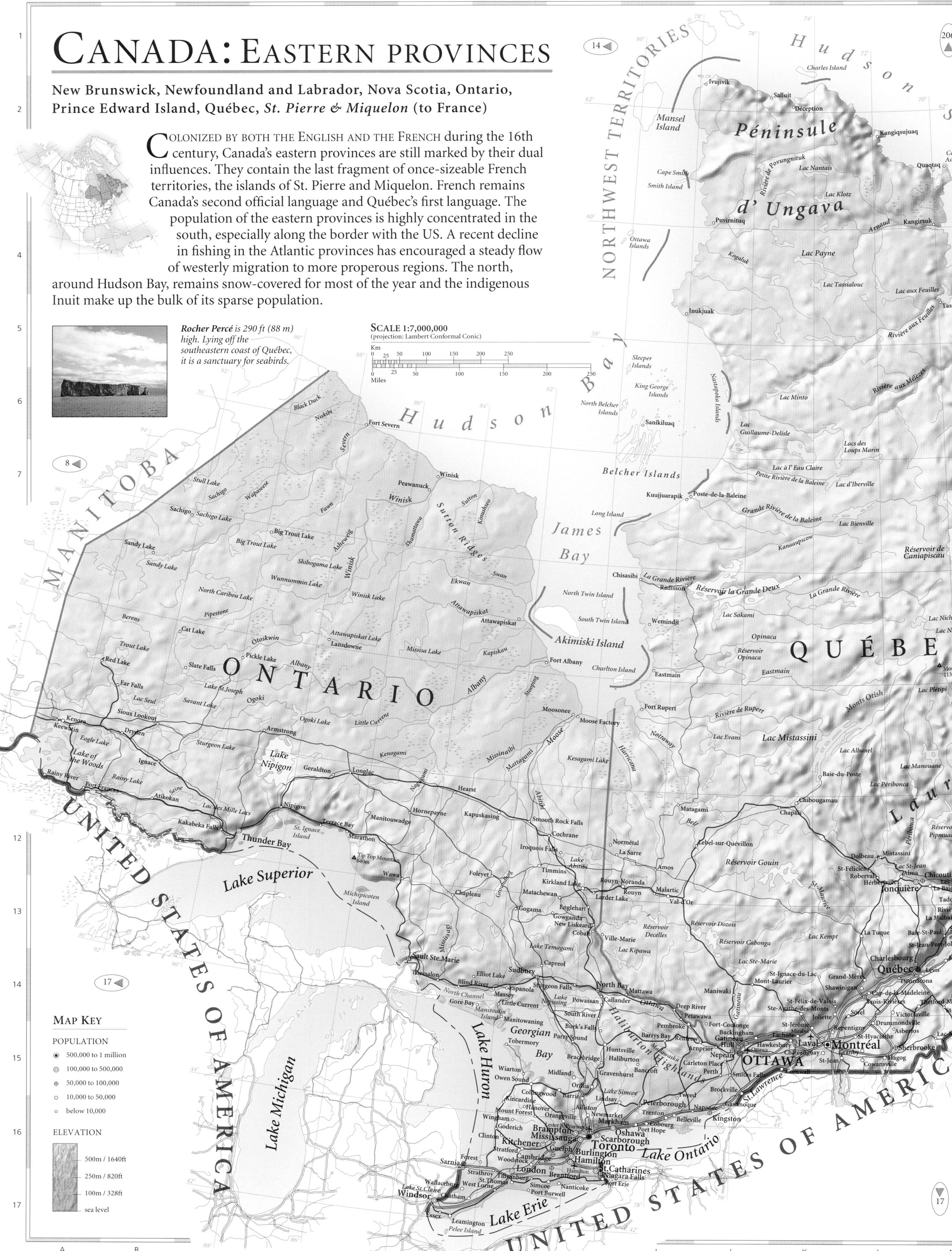

SCALE 1:7,000,000
(projection: Lambert Conformal Conic)
Km 0 25 50 100 150 200 250
Miles 0 25 50 100 150 200 250
MAP KEY
POPULATION
500,000 to 1 million
100,000 to 500,000
50,000 to 100,000
10,000 to 50,000
below 10,000
ELEVATION
500m / 1640ft
250m / 820ft
100m / 328ft
sea level
14
206
8
17
NORTHWEST TERRITORIES
MANITOBA
ONTARIO
QUÉBEC
UNITED STATES OF AMERICA
Hudson Bay
James Bay
Péninsule d' Ungava
Mansel Island
Belcher Islands
Akimiski Island
Lake Superior
Lake Michigan
Lake Huron
Lake Ontario
Lake Erie
Georgian Bay
Lake Nipigon
Lake of the Woods
Lac Mistassini
Réservoir Gouin
Sutton Ridges
Thunder Bay
Sault Ste.Marie
Sudbury
North Bay
Timmins
Moosonee
Kenora
Toronto
Hamilton
London
Windsor
Kitchener
Kingston
OTTAWA
Montréal
Québec
Laval
Chicoutimi
Ivujivik
Salluit
Puvirnituq
Inukjuak
Kuujjuarapik
Chisasibi
Fort Severn
Big Trout Lake
Attawapiskat
Fort Albany

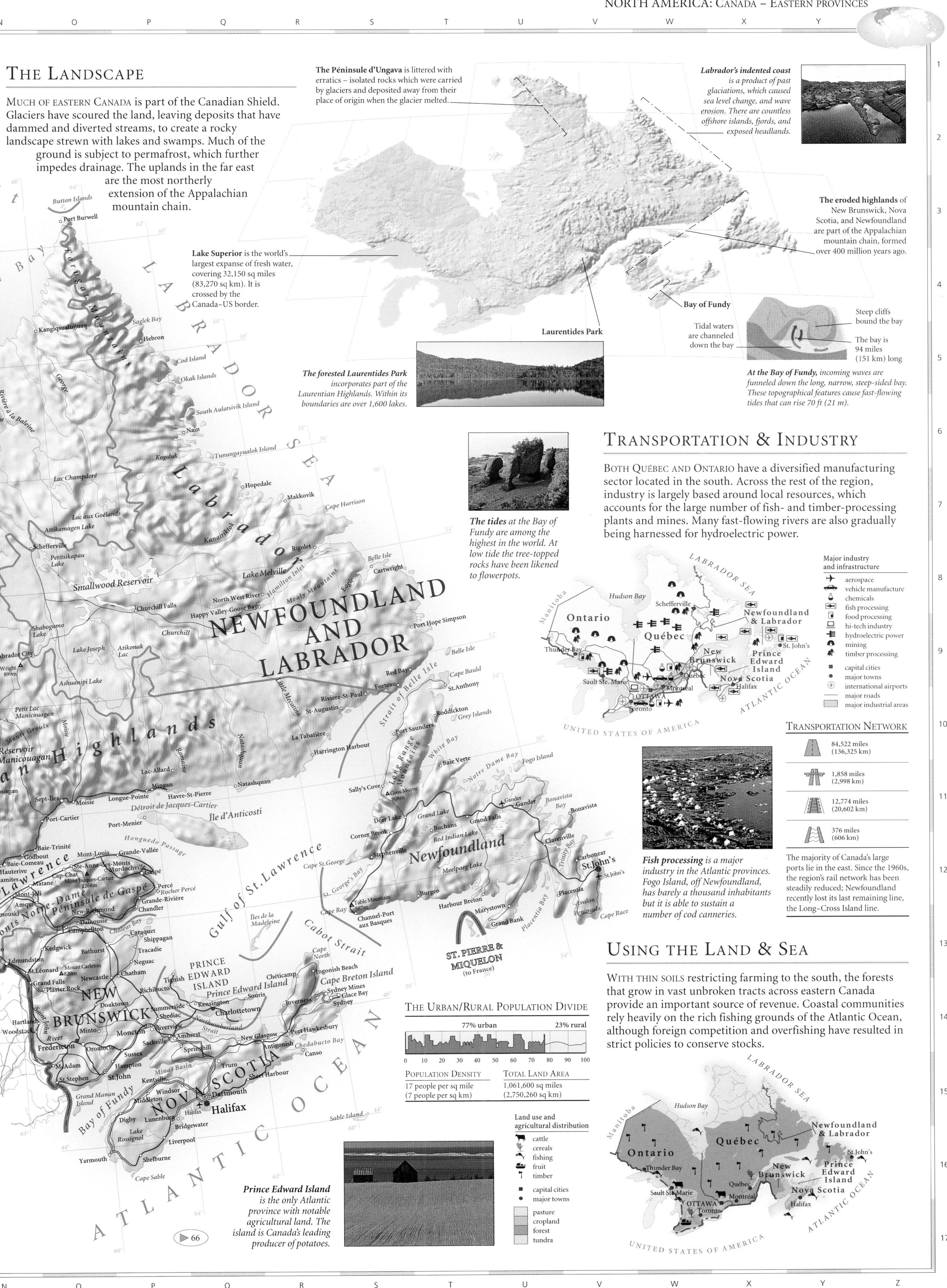
N O P Q R S T U V W X Y Z
LABRADOR SEA
Labrador
NEWFOUNDLAND AND LABRADOR
Newfoundland
Gulf of St. Lawrence
Cabot Strait
PRINCE EDWARD ISLAND
NEW BRUNSWICK
NOVA SCOTIA
ATLANTIC OCEAN
Halifax
St.John's
Charlottetown
Fredericton
ST. PIERRE & MIQUELON (to France)
Péninsule de Gaspé
Île d'Anticosti
Cape Breton Island
Bay of Fundy
Smallwood Reservoir
Lake Melville
Strait of Belle Isle

The Landscape

Much of eastern Canada is part of the Canadian Shield. Glaciers have scoured the land, leaving deposits that have dammed and diverted streams, to create a rocky landscape strewn with lakes and swamps. Much of the ground is subject to permafrost, which further impedes drainage. The uplands in the far east are the most northerly extension of the Appalachian mountain chain.

The Péninsule d'Ungava is littered with erratics – isolated rocks which were carried by glaciers and deposited away from their place of origin when the glacier melted.

Labrador's indented coast is a product of past glaciations, which caused sea level change, and wave erosion. There are countless offshore islands, fjords, and exposed headlands.

Lake Superior is the world's largest expanse of fresh water, covering 32,150 sq miles (83,270 sq km). It is crossed by the Canada–US border.

The eroded highlands of New Brunswick, Nova Scotia, and Newfoundland are part of the Appalachian mountain chain, formed over 400 million years ago.

Laurentides Park

Bay of Fundy

Tidal waters are channeled down the bay

Steep cliffs bound the bay

The bay is 94 miles (151 km) long

***The forested Laurentides Park** incorporates part of the Laurentian Highlands. Within its boundaries are over 1,600 lakes.*

***At the Bay of Fundy,** incoming waves are funneled down the long, narrow, steep-sided bay. These topographical features cause fast-flowing tides that can rise 70 ft (21 m).*

***The tides** at the Bay of Fundy are among the highest in the world. At low tide the tree-topped rocks have been likened to flowerpots.*

Transportation & Industry

Both Québec and Ontario have a diversified manufacturing sector located in the south. Across the rest of the region, industry is largely based around local resources, which accounts for the large number of fish- and timber-processing plants and mines. Many fast-flowing rivers are also gradually being harnessed for hydroelectric power.

Major industry and infrastructure: aerospace, vehicle manufacture, chemicals, fish processing, food processing, hi-tech industry, hydroelectric power, mining, timber processing, capital cities, major towns, international airports, major roads, major industrial areas

***Fish processing** is a major industry in the Atlantic provinces. Fogo Island, off Newfoundland, has barely a thousand inhabitants but it is able to sustain a number of cod canneries.*

Transportation Network

84,522 miles (136,325 km)

1,858 miles (2,998 km)

12,774 miles (20,602 km)

376 miles (606 km)

The majority of Canada's large ports lie in the east. Since the 1960s, the region's rail network has been steadily reduced; Newfoundland recently lost its last remaining line, the Long–Cross Island line.

Using the Land & Sea

With thin soils restricting farming to the south, the forests that grow in vast unbroken tracts across eastern Canada provide an important source of revenue. Coastal communities rely heavily on the rich fishing grounds of the Atlantic Ocean, although foreign competition and overfishing have resulted in strict policies to conserve stocks.

The Urban/Rural Population Divide

77% urban | 23% rural

Population Density	Total Land Area
17 people per sq mile (7 people per sq km)	1,061,600 sq miles (2,750,260 sq km)

Land use and agricultural distribution: cattle, cereals, fishing, fruit, timber, capital cities, major towns, pasture, cropland, forest, tundra

***Prince Edward Island** is the only Atlantic province with notable agricultural land. The island is Canada's leading producer of potatoes.*

▶ 66

SOUTHEASTERN CANADA

Southern Ontario, Southern Québec

THE SOUTHERN PARTS of Québec and Ontario form the economic heart of Canada. The two provinces are divided by their language and culture; in Québec, French is the main language, while English is spoken in Ontario. Separatist sentiment has led to a provincial referendum on the question of Québec having a sovereignty association with Canada. The region contains Canada's capital, Ottawa, and its two largest cities: Toronto, the center of commerce, and Montréal, the cultural and administrative heart of French Canada.

The port at Montréal *is situated on the St. Lawrence Seaway. A network of 16 locks allows oceangoing vessels access to routes once plied by fur-trappers and early settlers.*

TRANSPORTATION & INDUSTRY

THE CITIES OF SOUTHERN QUÉBEC AND ONTARIO, and their suburbs, form the heart of Canadian manufacturing industry. Toronto is Canada's leading financial center, and Ontario's motor and aerospace industries have developed around the city. A major center for nickel mining lies to the north of Toronto. Most of Québec's industry is located in Montréal, the oldest port in North America. Chemicals, paper manufacture, and the construction of transportation equipment are leading industrial activities.

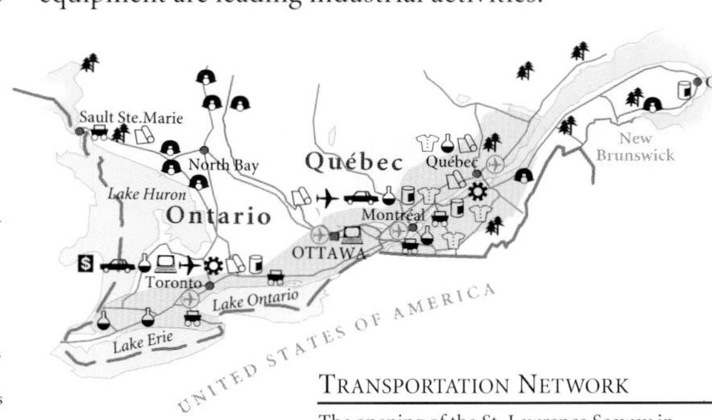
Sault Ste.Marie
North Bay
Québec
Lake Huron
Ontario
Montréal
Québec
OTTAWA
Toronto
Lake Ontario
Lake Erie
UNITED STATES OF AMERICA
Gaspé
New Brunswick

Niagara Falls *lies on the border between Canada and the US. It comprises a system of two falls: American Falls, in New York, is separated from Horseshoe Falls, in Ontario, by Goat Island. Horseshoe Falls, seen here, plunges 160 ft (48 m) and is 2,500 ft (762 m) wide.*

Major industry and infrastructure

- car manufacture
- chemicals
- engineering
- finance
- food processing
- hi-tech industry
- mining
- iron & steel
- textiles
- paper industry
- timber processing
- capital cities
- major towns
- international airports
- major roads
- major industrial areas

TRANSPORTATION NETWORK

The opening of the St. Lawrence Seaway in 1959 finally allowed oceangoing ships (up to 24,000 tons [tonnes]) access to the interior of Canada, creating a vital trading route.

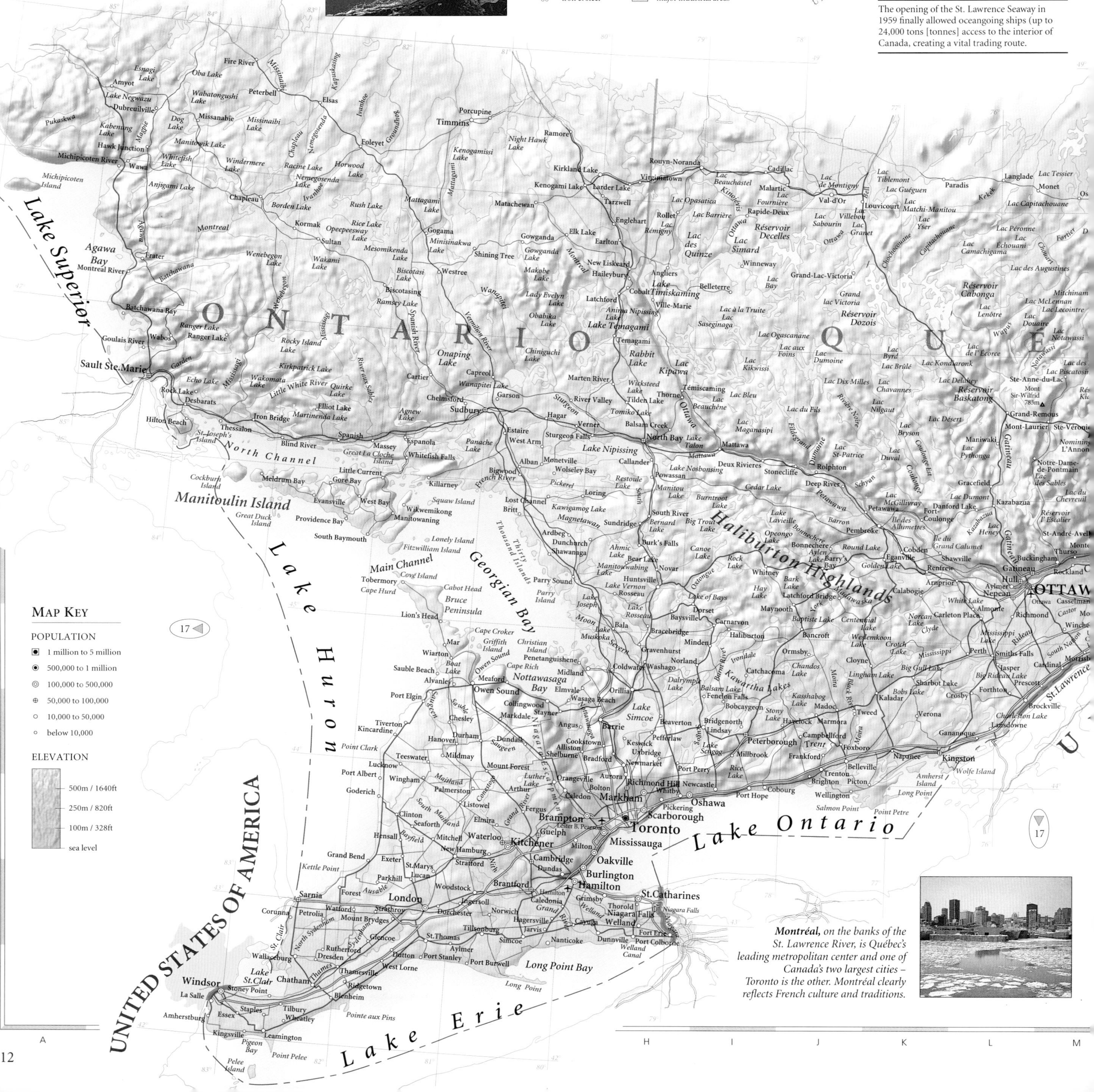

MAP KEY

POPULATION

- 1 million to 5 million
- 500,000 to 1 million
- 100,000 to 500,000
- 50,000 to 100,000
- 10,000 to 50,000
- below 10,000

ELEVATION

- 500m / 1640ft
- 250m / 820ft
- 100m / 328ft
- sea level

ONTARIO QUÉBEC

Lake Superior · Lake Huron · Georgian Bay · Lake Ontario · Lake Erie · UNITED STATES OF AMERICA

17

Montréal, *on the banks of the St. Lawrence River, is Québec's leading metropolitan center and one of Canada's two largest cities – Toronto is the other. Montréal clearly reflects French culture and traditions.*

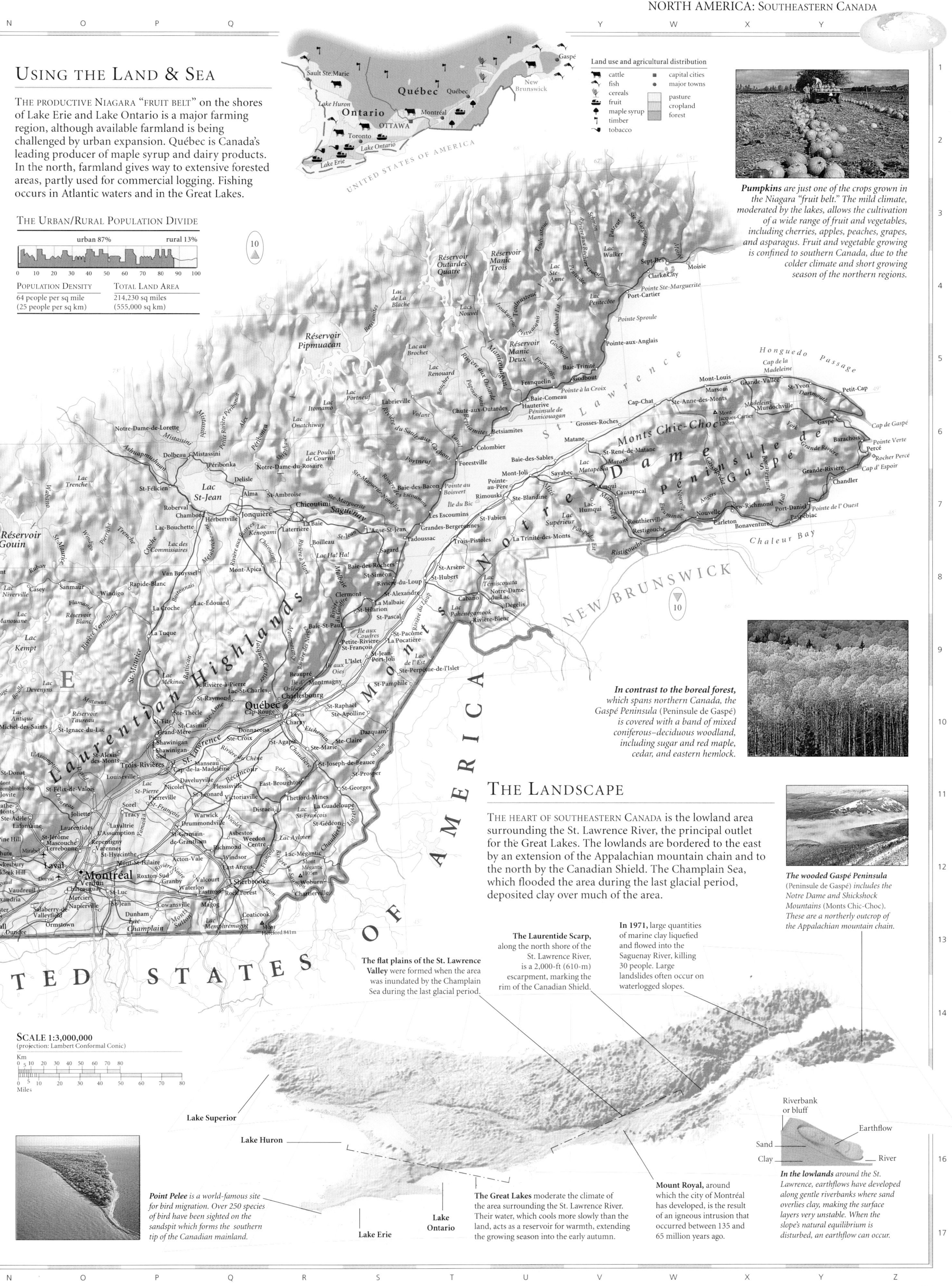
Land use and agricultural distribution
cattle
fish
cereals
fruit
maple syrup
timber
tobacco
capital cities
major towns
pasture
cropland
forest
Sault Ste.Marie
Québec
Ontario
Lake Huron
Montréal
OTTAWA
Toronto
Lake Ontario
Lake Erie
Gaspé
New Brunswick
UNITED STATES OF AMERICA
Réservoir Pipmuacan
Réservoir Manic Deux
Lac St-Jean
Chicoutimi
Saguenay
Québec
Trois-Rivières
Montréal
Laval
Sherbrooke
Laurentian Highlands
Notre Dame
Monts Chic-Choc
Péninsule de Gaspé
St Lawrence
Honguedo Passage
Chaleur Bay
NEW BRUNSWICK
UNITED STATES OF AMERICA
SCALE 1:3,000,000
(projection: Lambert Conformal Conic)
Km
Miles
Lake Superior
Lake Huron
Lake Erie
Lake Ontario
Riverbank or bluff
Earthflow
Sand
Clay
River

Using the Land & Sea

The productive Niagara "fruit belt" on the shores of Lake Erie and Lake Ontario is a major farming region, although available farmland is being challenged by urban expansion. Québec is Canada's leading producer of maple syrup and dairy products. In the north, farmland gives way to extensive forested areas, partly used for commercial logging. Fishing occurs in Atlantic waters and in the Great Lakes.

The Urban/Rural Population Divide

urban 87% rural 13%

Population Density 64 people per sq mile (25 people per sq km)

Total Land Area 214,230 sq miles (555,000 sq km)

***Pumpkins** are just one of the crops grown in the Niagara "fruit belt." The mild climate, moderated by the lakes, allows the cultivation of a wide range of fruit and vegetables, including cherries, apples, peaches, grapes, and asparagus. Fruit and vegetable growing is confined to southern Canada, due to the colder climate and short growing season of the northern regions.*

***In contrast to the boreal forest,** which spans northern Canada, the Gaspé Peninsula (Peninsule de Gaspé) is covered with a band of mixed coniferous–deciduous woodland, including sugar and red maple, cedar, and eastern hemlock.*

The Landscape

The heart of southeastern Canada is the lowland area surrounding the St. Lawrence River, the principal outlet for the Great Lakes. The lowlands are bordered to the east by an extension of the Appalachian mountain chain and to the north by the Canadian Shield. The Champlain Sea, which flooded the area during the last glacial period, deposited clay over much of the area.

***The wooded Gaspé Peninsula** (Peninsule de Gaspé) includes the Notre Dame and Shickshock Mountains (Monts Chic-Choc). These are a northerly outcrop of the Appalachian mountain chain.*

The flat plains of the St. Lawrence Valley were formed when the area was inundated by the Champlain Sea during the last glacial period.

The Laurentide Scarp, along the north shore of the St. Lawrence River, is a 2,000-ft (610-m) escarpment, marking the rim of the Canadian Shield.

In 1971, large quantities of marine clay liquefied and flowed into the Saguenay River, killing 30 people. Large landslides often occur on waterlogged slopes.

***Point Pelee** is a world-famous site for bird migration. Over 250 species of bird have been sighted on the sandspit which forms the southern tip of the Canadian mainland.*

The Great Lakes moderate the climate of the area surrounding the St. Lawrence River. Their water, which cools more slowly than the land, acts as a reservoir for warmth, extending the growing season into the early autumn.

Mount Royal, around which the city of Montréal has developed, is the result of an igneous intrusion that occurred between 135 and 65 million years ago.

***In the lowlands** around the St. Lawrence, earthflows have developed along gentle riverbanks where sand overlies clay, making the surface layers very unstable. When the slope's natural equilibrium is disturbed, an earthflow can occur.*

CANADA

CANADA IS THE SECOND LARGEST COUNTRY in the world, and with only about one-tenth of its land area inhabited, it is one of the most sparsely populated. Canada became a confederation in 1867, though Newfoundland did not join until 1949. As a founding member of the UN and of the Commonwealth, Canada has played an important role in international affairs. A constitutional crisis, focusing on the French-speaking Québécois, Inuit, and Native American land rights, has dominated politics in the 1990s. In 1999, part of the Northwest Territories, Nunavut, will become a self-governing Inuit homeland.

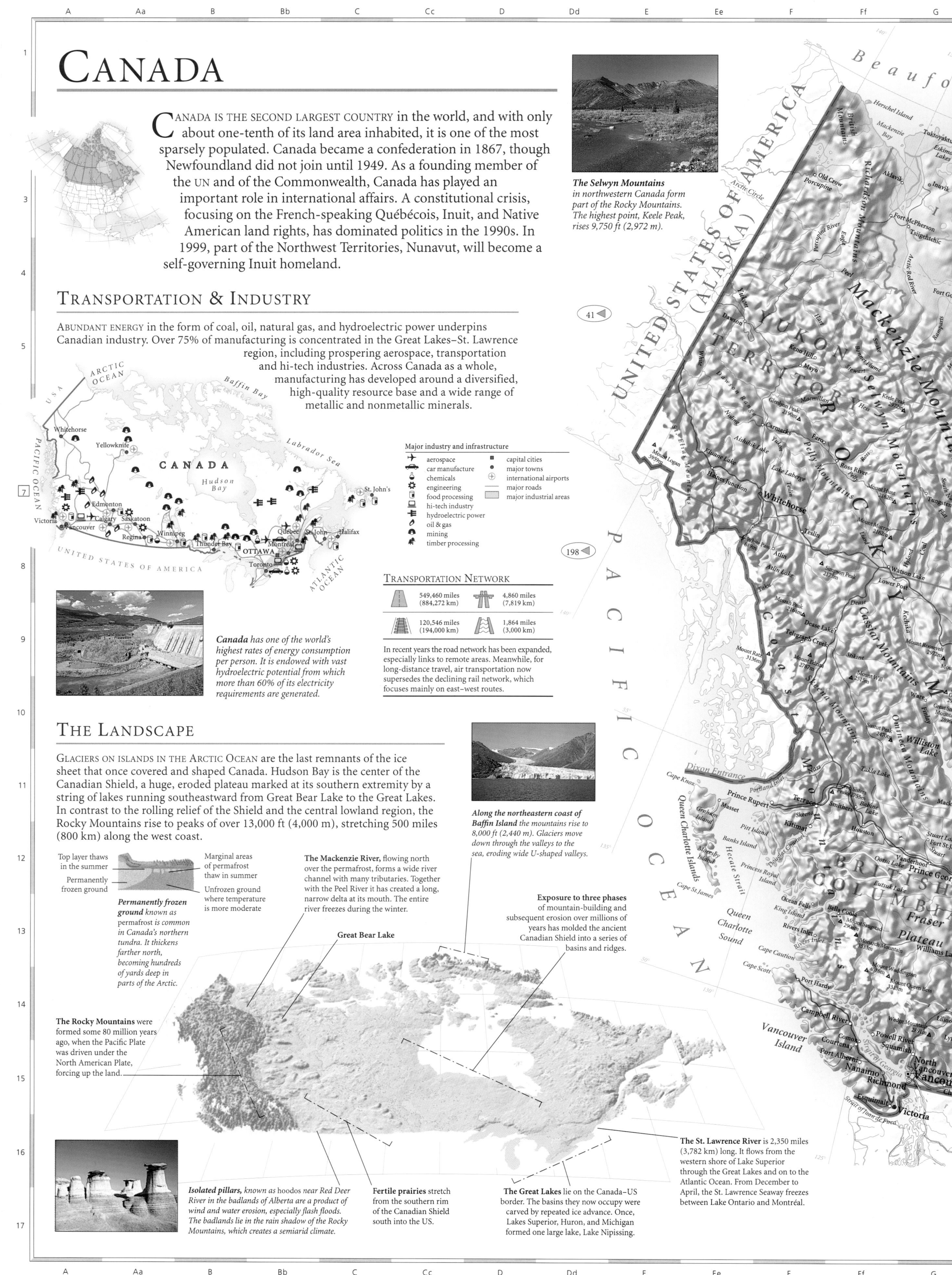

Beaufort
UNITED STATES OF AMERICA (ALASKA)
Arctic Circle
YUKON TERRITORY
Mackenzie Mountains
Selwyn Mountains
Richardson Mountains
British Mountains
Herschel Island
Mackenzie Bay
Tuktoyaktuk
Eskimo Lakes
Inuvik
Aklavik
Old Crow
Porcupine
Fort McPherson
Tsiigehtchic
Arctic Red River
Fort Good Hope
Dawson
Keno Hill
Mayo
Keele Peak 2972m
Glenlyon Peak 2190m
Carmacks
Faro
Ross River
Mount Logan 5959m
Kluane Lake
Haines Junction
Whitehorse
Lake Laberge
Teslin
Watson Lake
Lower Post
Atlin
Atlin Lake
White Pass
Dease Lake
Telegraph Creek
Cassiar Mountains
Omineca Mountains
Williston Lake
Skeena Mountains
Dixon Entrance
Cape Knox
Prince Rupert
Masset
Graham Island
Queen Charlotte Islands
Moresby Island
Hecate Strait
Banks Island
Pitt Island
Kitimat
Terrace
Smithers
Houston
Babine Lake
Takla Lake
Princess Royal Island
Cape St. James
Queen Charlotte Sound
Ocean Falls
King Island
Bella Coola
Rivers Inlet
Cape Caution
Cape Scott
Port Hardy
BRITISH COLUMBIA
Fraser Plateau
Williams Lake
Prince George
Vanderhoof
Fort St. James
Stuart Lake
Mount Waddington 4016m
Campbell River
Courtenay
Comox
Port Alberni
Nanaimo
Powell River
Squamish
North Vancouver
Vancouver
Richmond
Esquimalt
Victoria
Vancouver Island
Strait of Georgia
Strait of Juan de Fuca
PACIFIC OCEAN

The Selwyn Mountains in northwestern Canada form part of the Rocky Mountains. The highest point, Keele Peak, rises 9,750 ft (2,972 m).

41 ◀

198 ◀

TRANSPORTATION & INDUSTRY

ABUNDANT ENERGY in the form of coal, oil, natural gas, and hydroelectric power underpins Canadian industry. Over 75% of manufacturing is concentrated in the Great Lakes–St. Lawrence region, including prospering aerospace, transportation and hi-tech industries. Across Canada as a whole, manufacturing has developed around a diversified, high-quality resource base and a wide range of metallic and nonmetallic minerals.

ARCTIC OCEAN
Baffin Bay
Labrador Sea
CANADA
Hudson Bay
USA
PACIFIC OCEAN
UNITED STATES OF AMERICA
ATLANTIC OCEAN
Whitehorse
Yellowknife
Edmonton
Calgary
Saskatoon
Regina
Victoria
Vancouver
Winnipeg
Thunder Bay
OTTAWA
Toronto
Montreal
Quebec
St. John
Halifax
St. John's
Major industry and infrastructure
aerospace
car manufacture
chemicals
engineering
food processing
hi-tech industry
hydroelectric power
oil & gas
mining
timber processing
capital cities
major towns
international airports
major roads
major industrial areas

TRANSPORTATION NETWORK

549,460 miles (884,272 km)	4,860 miles (7,819 km)
120,546 miles (194,000 km)	1,864 miles (3,000 km)

In recent years the road network has been expanded, especially links to remote areas. Meanwhile, for long-distance travel, air transportation now supersedes the declining rail network, which focuses mainly on east–west routes.

***Canada** has one of the world's highest rates of energy consumption per person. It is endowed with vast hydroelectric potential from which more than 60% of its electricity requirements are generated.*

THE LANDSCAPE

GLACIERS ON ISLANDS IN THE ARCTIC OCEAN are the last remnants of the ice sheet that once covered and shaped Canada. Hudson Bay is the center of the Canadian Shield, a huge, eroded plateau marked at its southern extremity by a string of lakes running southeastward from Great Bear Lake to the Great Lakes. In contrast to the rolling relief of the Shield and the central lowland region, the Rocky Mountains rise to peaks of over 13,000 ft (4,000 m), stretching 500 miles (800 km) along the west coast.

*Along the northeastern coast of **Baffin Island** the mountains rise to 8,000 ft (2,440 m). Glaciers move down through the valleys to the sea, eroding wide U-shaped valleys.*

Top layer thaws in the summer
Permanently frozen ground
Marginal areas of permafrost thaw in summer
Unfrozen ground where temperature is more moderate

***Permanently frozen ground** known as permafrost is common in Canada's northern tundra. It thickens farther north, becoming hundreds of yards deep in parts of the Arctic.*

The Mackenzie River, flowing north over the permafrost, forms a wide river channel with many tributaries. Together with the Peel River it has created a long, narrow delta at its mouth. The entire river freezes during the winter.

Great Bear Lake

Exposure to three phases of mountain-building and subsequent erosion over millions of years has molded the ancient Canadian Shield into a series of basins and ridges.

The Rocky Mountains were formed some 80 million years ago, when the Pacific Plate was driven under the North American Plate, forcing up the land.

The St. Lawrence River is 2,350 miles (3,782 km) long. It flows from the western shore of Lake Superior through the Great Lakes and on to the Atlantic Ocean. From December to April, the St. Lawrence Seaway freezes between Lake Ontario and Montréal.

***Isolated pillars,** known as hoodoos near Red Deer River in the badlands of Alberta are a product of wind and water erosion, especially flash floods. The badlands lie in the rain shadow of the Rocky Mountains, which creates a semiarid climate.*

Fertile prairies stretch from the southern rim of the Canadian Shield south into the US.

The Great Lakes lie on the Canada–US border. The basins they now occupy were carved by repeated ice advance. Once, Lakes Superior, Huron, and Michigan formed one large lake, Lake Nipissing.

Using the Land & Sea

The majority of Canada's agricultural land is found in the prairies, which cover 140 million acres (57 million ha) and support wheat and grain-fed cattle. More specialized crops, such as fruit and vegetables, are grown in pockets of agricultural land in the east and west. Of Canada's many islands, only Prince Edward Island has notable farmland. Further north, boreal forests, exploited for timber, run in an almost unbroken arc, giving way to uncultivable tundra and ice sheets in the far north.

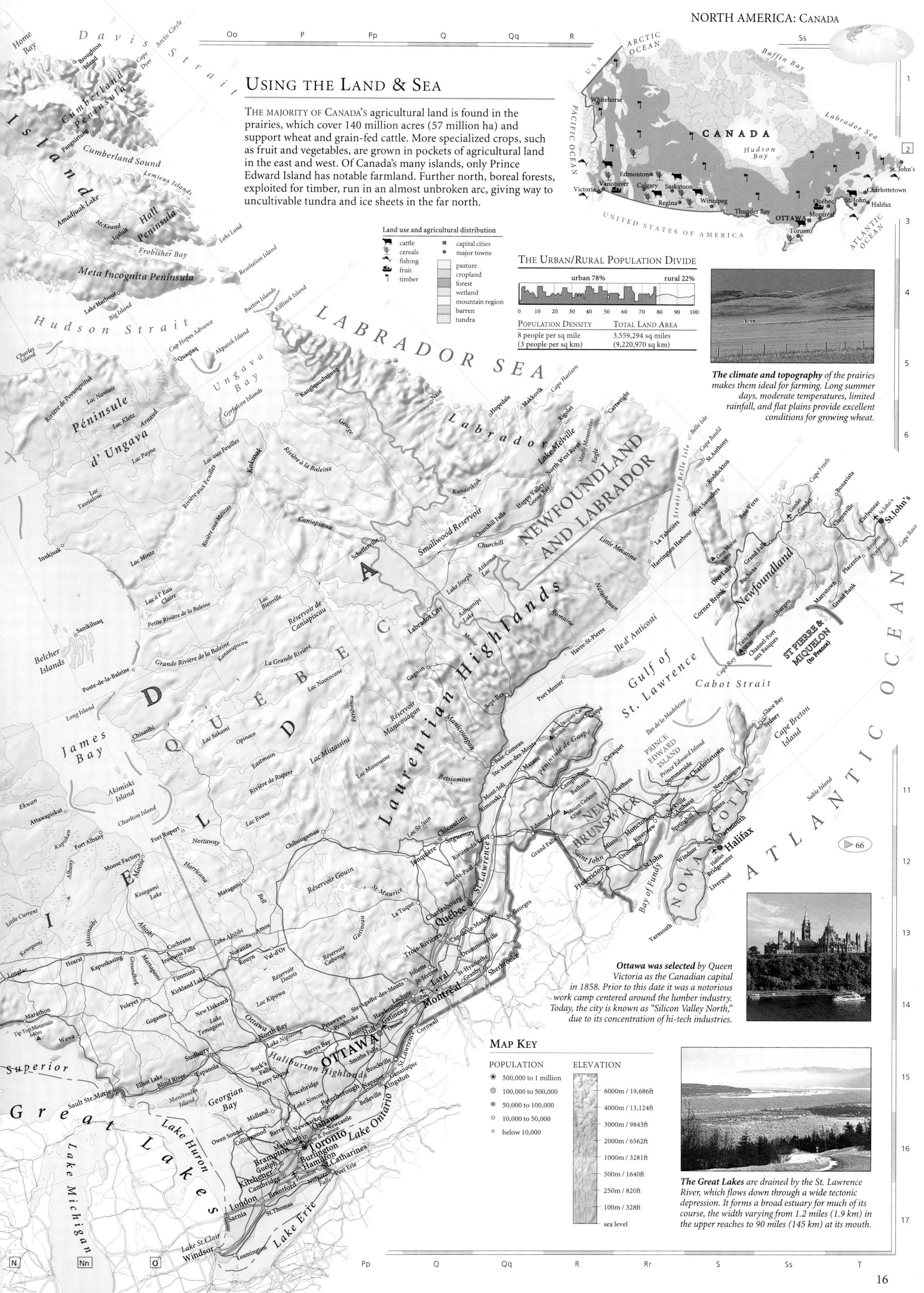
Land use and agricultural distribution
cattle
cereals
fishing
fruit
timber
capital cities
major towns
pasture
cropland
forest
wetland
mountain region
barren
tundra
ARCTIC OCEAN
PACIFIC OCEAN
CANADA
Hudson Bay
UNITED STATES OF AMERICA
ATLANTIC OCEAN
The Urban/Rural Population Divide
urban 78%
rural 22%
0 10 20 30 40 50 60 70 80 90 100
Population Density
8 people per sq mile
(3 people per sq km)
Total Land Area
3,559,294 sq miles
(9,220,970 sq km)
Map Key
POPULATION
500,000 to 1 million
100,000 to 500,000
50,000 to 100,000
10,000 to 50,000
below 10,000
ELEVATION
6000m / 19,686ft
4000m / 13,124ft
3000m / 9843ft
2000m / 6562ft
1000m / 3281ft
500m / 1640ft
250m / 820ft
100m / 328ft
sea level
LABRADOR SEA
QUEBEC
NEWFOUNDLAND AND LABRADOR
Laurentian Highlands
Gulf of St. Lawrence
ATLANTIC OCEAN
NEW BRUNSWICK
NOVA SCOTIA
PRINCE EDWARD ISLAND
ST PIERRE & MIQUELON (to France)
OTTAWA
Montréal
Québec
Toronto
Halifax
St.John's
Great Lakes
Lake Huron
Lake Michigan
Lake Ontario
Lake Erie
Superior
James Bay
Hudson Strait
Ungava Bay
Péninsule d'Ungava
Davis Strait
Baffin Island
Cabot Strait
66
Oo P Pp Q Qq R Rr S Ss T
N Nn O
1 2 3 4 5 6 11 12 13 14 15 16 17

The climate and topography *of the prairies makes them ideal for farming. Long summer days, moderate temperatures, limited rainfall, and flat plains provide excellent conditions for growing wheat.*

Ottawa was selected *by Queen Victoria as the Canadian capital in 1858. Prior to this date it was a notorious work camp centered around the lumber industry. Today, the city is known as "Silicon Valley North," due to its concentration of hi-tech industries.*

The Great Lakes *are drained by the St. Lawrence River, which flows down through a wide tectonic depression. It forms a broad estuary for much of its course, the width varying from 1.2 miles (1.9 km) in the upper reaches to 90 miles (145 km) at its mouth.*

THE UNITED STATES OF AMERICA

CONTERMINOUS US (FOR ALASKA AND HAWAII SEE PAGES 40-41)

THE US'S PROGRESSION FROM FRONTIER TERRITORY to economic and political superpower has taken less than 200 years. The 48 contiguous states, along with the outlying states of Alaska and Hawaii, are part of a federal union, held together by the guiding principles of the US Constitution, which embodies the ideals of democracy and liberty for all. Abundant fertile land and a rich resource base fueled and sustained US economic development. With the spread of agriculture and the growth of trade and industry came the need for a larger workforce, which was supplied by millions of immigrants, many seeking an escape from poverty and political or religious persecution. Immigration continues today, particularly from Central America and Asia.

***Mount Rainier** is a dormant volcano in the Cascade Range, Washington. This 14,090-ft (4,392-m) peak is flanked by the most extensive glacier outside Alaska.*

TRANSPORTATION & INDUSTRY

THE US HAS BEEN THE INDUSTRIAL POWERHOUSE of the world since the Second World War, pioneering mass production and the consumer lifestyle. Initially, heavy engineering and manufacturing in the northeast led the economy. Today, heavy industry has declined and the US economy is driven by service and financial industries, with the most important being defense, hi-tech, and electronics.

***Washington D.C.** was established as the nation's capital in 1790. It is home to the seat of national government, on Capitol Hill, as well as the President's official residence, the White House.*

Major industry and infrastructure

aerospace	research & development
car manufacture	textiles
chemicals	tourism
coal	capital cities
electronics	major towns
engineering	international airports
food processing	major roads
hi-tech industry	major industrial areas
oil & gas	

TRANSPORTATION NETWORK

3,955,393 miles (6,365,590 km)	52,419 miles (84,361 km)
148,308 miles (238,628 km)	25,482 miles (41,009 km)

Transportation in the US is dominated by the car which, with the extensive Interstate Highway system, allows great personal mobility. Today, internal air flights between major cities provide the most rapid cross-country travel.

THE LANDSCAPE

THE HIGH, RUGGED MOUNTAIN RANGES of the west are about 80 million years old, geologically young compared to the old, eroded, Appalachian mountain chain, which dates from when North America and Europe were joined together as part of the supercontinent Pangaea, 400 million years ago. In contrast, the Great Plains and Mississippi Basin have a low relief and fertile soils.

***Devils Tower, in Wyoming** is a 1,280-ft (390-m) intrusion of basalt rock, which cooled to form octagonal pillars. In 1906 it became the first US National Monument.*

Missouri River
Mississippi River
Ohio River
Mississippi Delta

***The massive drainage basin** of the Mississippi covers 1,250,000 sq miles (3,200,000 sq km). It includes all areas drained by the Mississippi and its chief tributaries, the Missouri and Ohio Rivers, and drains the entire region from the Appalachians to the Rockies.*

Mount Rainier

The Rocky Mountains form the backbone of the US, running from Alaska to New Mexico. They contain the country's highest mountains and many active volcanoes.

Hells Canyon, running through part of Idaho and Oregon, is North America's deepest gorge. It was formed by the down-cutting of the Snake River through the thick basalt rocks of the Columbia–Snake Plateau.

Death Valley, California, 282 ft (86 m) below sea level, is the lowest point in the western hemisphere, and one of the hottest places on Earth. Temperatures of 190° F (88° C) have been recorded here.

The Great Lakes

The Hudson-Mohawk Gap, lying at the point where the two rivers join, allows passage from the Atlantic Ocean to the continental interior.

Niagara Falls

Barrier beaches, bars, and spits are typical of the Atlantic coast. These sand formations around Cape Hatteras stretch along the coast for 200 miles (320 km).

The Great Smoky Mountains, part of the ancient Appalachian mountain chain, formed a natural barrier to early settlers attempting to penetrate the country's interior.

***Volcanically heated water** erupts every 40-80 minutes from Old Faithful geyser in Yellowstone National Park, Wyoming. The 170-ft (50-m) column of water and steam persists for 4 minutes.*

Monument Valley's striking sandstone spires and pillars *(buttes)* have been formed by the action of wind, water, heat, and cold.

The deep gullies of South Dakota's badlands are created by periodic torrential rainfall, which erodes the soft soils and rocks. Their form has been greatly affected by changes in land use.

Great Plains

Most of the US is drained by the great Mississippi River system. At its mouth, where levees are breached, floodwaters are carried to the swamps through a series of channels. This region is known as the bayou.

The US Gulf Coast is seriously affected by hurricane erosion, which reshapes its beaches and sandbanks.

The Everglades are a vast area of sawgrass swamp covering 4,000 sq miles (10,300 sq km) of southern Florida.

198

SCALE 1: 8,750,000
(projection: Lambert Azimuthal Equal Area)
Km
0 25 50 100 150 200 250 300
0 25 50 100 150 200 250
Miles
I Ii J Jj K Kk L Ll M
Gg H Hh I Ii J Jj K M
MAP KEY
POPULATION
above 5 million
1 million to 5 million
500,000 to 1 million
100,000 to 500,000
50,000 to 100,000
10,000 to 50,000
below 10,000
ELEVATION
4000m / 13,124ft
3000m / 9843ft
2000m / 6562ft
1000m / 3281ft
500m / 1640ft
250m / 820ft
100m / 328ft
sea level

***The Sonoran Desert** in southwestern Arizona stretches into Mexico and merges to the northwest with California's Mojave Desert. Much of the southwest is very arid, especially the "rain-starved" areas between the Coast Ranges and the Rocky Mountains.*

Viscount Melville Sound
Passage Point
Peel Point
Stefansson Island
206
Banks Island
Cape Kellett
Sachs Harbour
Prince of Wales Strait
Prince Albert Peninsula
Amundsen Gulf
Cape Bathurst
Cape Lambton
Cape Wollaston
Cape Parry
Holman
Franklin Bay
Cape Lyon
Paulatuk
Prince Albert Sound
Wollaston Peninsula
Dolphin & Union Strait
Hadley Bay
McClintock Channel
Zeta Lake
Victoria Island
Prince of Wales Island
Somerset Island
Peel Sound
Franklin Strait
Gateshead Island
Boothia Peninsula
Prince Regent Inlet
Gulf of Boothia
Larsen Sound
Brodeur Peninsula
Borden Peninsula
Admiralty Inlet
Baffin
Gifford
Rowley
Cape Henry Kater
Cape Englefield
Igloolik
Jens Munk Island
Rowley Island
Baird Peninsula
Hall Beach
Melville Peninsula
Prince Charles Island
Air Force Island
Nettilling Lake
Cape Chapman
Taloyoak
Kitikmeot
Cambridge Bay
King William Island
Gjoa Haven
Rae Strait
Jenny Lind Island
Pelly Bay
Simpson Peninsula
Committee Bay
Wales Island
Foxe Basin
Bowman Bay
Queen Maud Gulf
Adelaide Peninsula
Kent Peninsula
Bowes Point
Chantrey Inlet
Coronation Gulf
Cape Krusenstern
Bathurst Inlet
Ellice
Hayes
Repulse Bay
Vansittart Island
Cape Dorchester
Foxe Peninsula
Cape Dorset
Salisbury Island
Foxe Channel
Bluenose Lake
Rae
Coppermine
NORTHWEST TERRITORIES
Hood
Burnside
Coppermine
Takijuq Lake
Great Bear Lake
Echo Bay
Déline
Norman Wells
Hottah Lake
Back
Garry Lake
Wager Bay
Roes Welcome Sound
Southampton Island
Coral Harbour
Nottingham Island
Evans Strait
Ivujivik
Aberdeen Lake
Baker Lake
Quoich
Chesterfield Inlet
Cape Kendall
Cape Low
Fisher Strait
Coats Island
Mansel Island
Aylmer Lake
Thelon
Clinton-Colden Lake
Hanbury
Keewatin
Dubawnt Lake
Rankin Inlet
Yathkyed Lake
Whale Cove
Wrigley
Lac La Martre
Snare
Yellowknife
Fort Smith
Lac La Martre
Rae-Edzo
Willowlake
Reliance
Yellowknife
Fort Simpson
Lutselk'e
Snowdrift
Nonacho Lake
Kazan
Eskimo Point
Arviat
Ottawa Islands
Hudson Bay
Fort Providence
Great Slave Lake
Fort Resolution
Taltson
Dubawnt
Tha-Anne
Thlewiaza
Trout
Hay River
Pine Point
Thoa
Wholdaia Lake
Kasba Lake
Nueltin Lake
Petitot
Bistcho Lake
Steen River
Fort Smith
Slave
Selwyn Lake
Nejanilini Lake
Cape Churchill
Caribou Mountains
Uranium City
Phelps Lake
Seal
Churchill
Peace
Fort Chipewyan
Lake Athabasca
Black Lake
Lac Brochet
Tadoule Lake
High Level
Fort Vermilion
Lake Claire
William
MacFarlane
Pasfield Lake
Wollaston Lake
South Seal
Southern Indian Lake
Cape Tatnam
Fort Severn
Chinchaga
Clear Hills
Birch Mountains
Cree Lake
Cree
Geikie
Reindeer Lake
Nelson
Hayes
Gods
Severn
Winisk
Fort St. John
Manning
SASKATCHEWAN
Lynn Lake
Waskaiowaka Lake
Gillam
Grimshaw
Fairview
Peace River
Wabasca
Clearwater
Turnor Lake
Foster Lakes
Leaf Rapids
Granville Lake
Split Lake
Dawson Creek
Smoky
Athabasca
Fort McMurray
La Loche
Frobisher Lake
Macoun Lake
Thompson
Desmarais
Churchill Lake
Burntwood
ALBERTA
Utikuma Lake
Peter Pond Lake
Buffalo Narrows
Pinehouse Lake
Missinipe
Reindeer
Grande Prairie
Wapiti
High Prairie
Lesser Slave Lake
Churchill
Sipiwesk Lake
Oxford Lake
Gods Lake
Sachigo
Fawn
Valleyview
Slave Lake
Wallace Mountain 1259m
Swan Hills
Kississing Lake
Wabowden
Sachigo Lake
Big Trout Lake
Winisk Lake
Athabasca
Primrose Lake
La Ronge
Lac La Ronge
Flin Flon
Molson Lake
Beaver
Deschambault Lake
Creighton
Amisk Lake
Island Lake
Severn
Attawapiskat
Grande Cache
Whitecourt
Barrhead
Westlock
Cold Lake
Cold Lake
Grand Centre
MANITOBA
Montreal Lake
Meadow Lake
St. Paul
Morinville
Mount Robson 3954m
St. Albert
Fort Saskatchewan
Edmonton
Tobin Lake
Saskatchewan
The Pas
Cedar Lake
Grand Rapids
Lake Winnipeg
Poplar
Sandy Lake
Sandy Lake
North Caribou Lake
Attawapiskat Lake
Hinton
Edson
Spruce Grove
Stony Plain
Drayton Valley
Pembina
Devon
Leduc
Vegreville
Vermilion
North Saskatchewan
St. Walburg
Lloydminster
Prince Albert
Nipawin
Pasquia Hills
Hudson Bay
Lake Winnipegosis
Pipestone
ONTARIO
Camrose
Wetaskiwin
Wainwright
North Battleford
Melfort
Tisdale
Berens
Ogoki
Rocky Mountain House
Ponoka
Battleford
Porcupine Hills
Swan River
Trout Lake
Kinbasket Lake
Mount Columbia 3747m
North Saskatchewan
Sylvan Lake
Lacombe
Red Deer
Stettler
Battle
Unity
Martensville
Saskatoon
Saskatoon
Humboldt
Quill Lakes
Duck Mountain
Baldy Mountain 831m
Gypsumville
Lake St. Joseph
Armstrong
Lake Nipigon
Red Deer
Didsbury
Olds
Kicking Horse Pass
Golden
Banff
Airdrie
Drumheller
Biggar
Lanigan
Watrous
Wynyard
Canora
Kamsack
Lake Manitoba
Eriksdale
Red Lake
Ear Falls
Lac Seul
Sioux Lookout
Salmon Arm
Mount Assiniboine 3618m
Canmore
Calgary
Strathmore
Oyen
Rosetown
Kindersley
Outlook
Lake Diefenbaker
Last Mountain Lake
Yorkton
Melville
Dauphin
Riding Mountain
Gimli
Dryden
Nipigon
Okanagan Lake
Invermere
Okotoks
High River
South Saskatchewan
Fort Qu'Appelle
Indian Head
Esterhazy
Minnedosa
Neepawa
Portage la Prairie
Stonewall
Selkirk
Pinawa
Beausejour
Kenora
Eagle Lake
Lac des Milles Lacs
Kelowna
Claresholm
Travers Reservoir
Swift Current
Lumsden
Regina
Regina
Moose Jaw
Old Wives Lake
Moosomin
Qu'Appelle
Brandon
Assiniboine
Winnipeg
Winnipeg
Steinbach
Crowsnest Pass
Kimberley
Fort Macleod
Lethbridge
Redcliff
Medicine Hat
Taber
Coaldale
Maple Creek
Weyburn
Carlyle
Virden
Carman
Winkler
Morden
Altona
Red River
Rainy Lake
Atikokan
Thunder Bay
Nelson
Castlegar
Cranbrook
Pincher Creek
Raymond
Cardston
Milk River
Cypress Hills
Assiniboia
Val Marie
Wood Mountain
Rockglen
Estevan
Melita
Killarney
Lake of the Woods
Rainy River
Fort Frances
Lake
UNITED STATES OF AMERICA
SCALE 1:9,250,000
Projection: Lambert Azimuthal Equal Area)
50 100 150 200 250 300 350
25 50 100 150 200 250 300 350
17
H Hh I Ii J Jj K Kk L Ll M Mm

The clear waters of Niagara Falls *cascade 190 ft (58 m) into the gorge below. It is one of North America's most famous spectacles and a leading tourist attraction. The falls are slowly receding and the gorge may one day stretch from Lake Ontario to Lake Erie.*

USING THE LAND & SEA

OVER HALF OF THE US is used for agriculture, typified by the large cereal grain farms and cattle ranches of the Great Plains and Midwest prairie regions. Although wheat and corn are still primary crops, a diverse range of fruits and vegetables are grown in the fertile areas, particularly near the east and west coasts. Despite the abundance of cultivable land, inadequate soil management has resulted in a third of the topsoil being lost through wind and water erosion.

THE URBAN/RURAL POPULATION DIVIDE

urban 75% rural 25%

0 10 20 30 40 50 60 70 80 90 100

POPULATION DENSITY	TOTAL LAND AREA
72 people per sq mile (28 people per sq km)	3,538,307 sq miles (9,166,600 sq km)

Land use and agricultural distribution

cattle, pigs, poultry, citrus fruits, cotton, fishing, fruit, corn, peanuts, shellfish, soybeans, timber, tobacco, wheat, capital cities, major towns, pasture, cropland, forest, wetland, desert, mountain region

Fakahatchee Strand *is part of the extensive subtropical swamps in the Florida Everglades. The swamps support a wide variety of animal life, including many rare birds, fish, alligators, and crocodiles.*

Farming on the Great Plains *and in the Midwest is characterized by large-scale, mechanized wheat farms.*

USA: Northeastern States

Connecticut, Maine, Massachusetts, New Hampshire, New Jersey, New York, Pennsylvania, Rhode Island, Vermont

The indented coast and vast woodlands of the northeastern states were the original core area for European expansion. The rustic character of New England prevails after nearly four centuries, while the great Atlantic seaboard cities have formed an almost continuous urban region. Over 20 million immigrants entered New York between 1855 and 1924, and the northeast became the industrial center of the US. After the decline of mining and heavy manufacturing, economic dynamism has been restored with the growth of hi-tech and service industries.

Chelsea, in Vermont, is surrounded by trees in their fall foliage. Tourism and agriculture dominate the economy of this self-consciously rural state, where no town exceeds 30,000 people.

Map Key

Population

- above 5 million
- 1 million to 5 million
- 500,000 to 1 million
- 100,000 to 500,000
- 50,000 to 100,000
- 10,000 to 50,000
- below 10,000

Elevation

- 1000m / 3281ft
- 500m / 1640ft
- 250m / 820ft
- 100m / 328ft
- sea level

Transportation & Industry

The principal seaboard cities grew up on trade and manufacturing. They are now global centers of commerce and corporate administration, dominating the regional economy. Research and development facilities support an expanding electronics and communications sector throughout the region. Pharmaceutical and chemical industries are important in New Jersey and Pennsylvania.

Transportation Network

340,090 miles (544,144 km)	4,813 miles 7,700 km
12,872 miles (20,592 km)	2,108 miles (3,389 km)

New York's commercial success is tied historically to its transportation connections. The Erie Canal, completed in 1825, opened up the Great Lakes and the interior to New York's markets and carried a stream of immigrants into the Midwest.

CANADA
Maine
Vermont
Portland
New Hampshire
Syracuse
Albany
Rochester
Buffalo
New York
Massachusetts
Boston
Connecticut
Hartford
Providence
Rhode Island
Pennsylvania
Ohio
Pittsburgh
New York
Harrisburg
New Jersey
Philadelphia
ATLANTIC OCEAN
West Virginia
Maryland
Delaware

Major industry and infrastructure

- chemicals
- coal
- defense
- electronics
- engineering
- finance
- hi-tech industry
- iron & steel
- pharmaceuticals
- printing & publishing
- research & development
- textiles
- timber processing
- major towns
- international airports
- major roads
- major industrial area

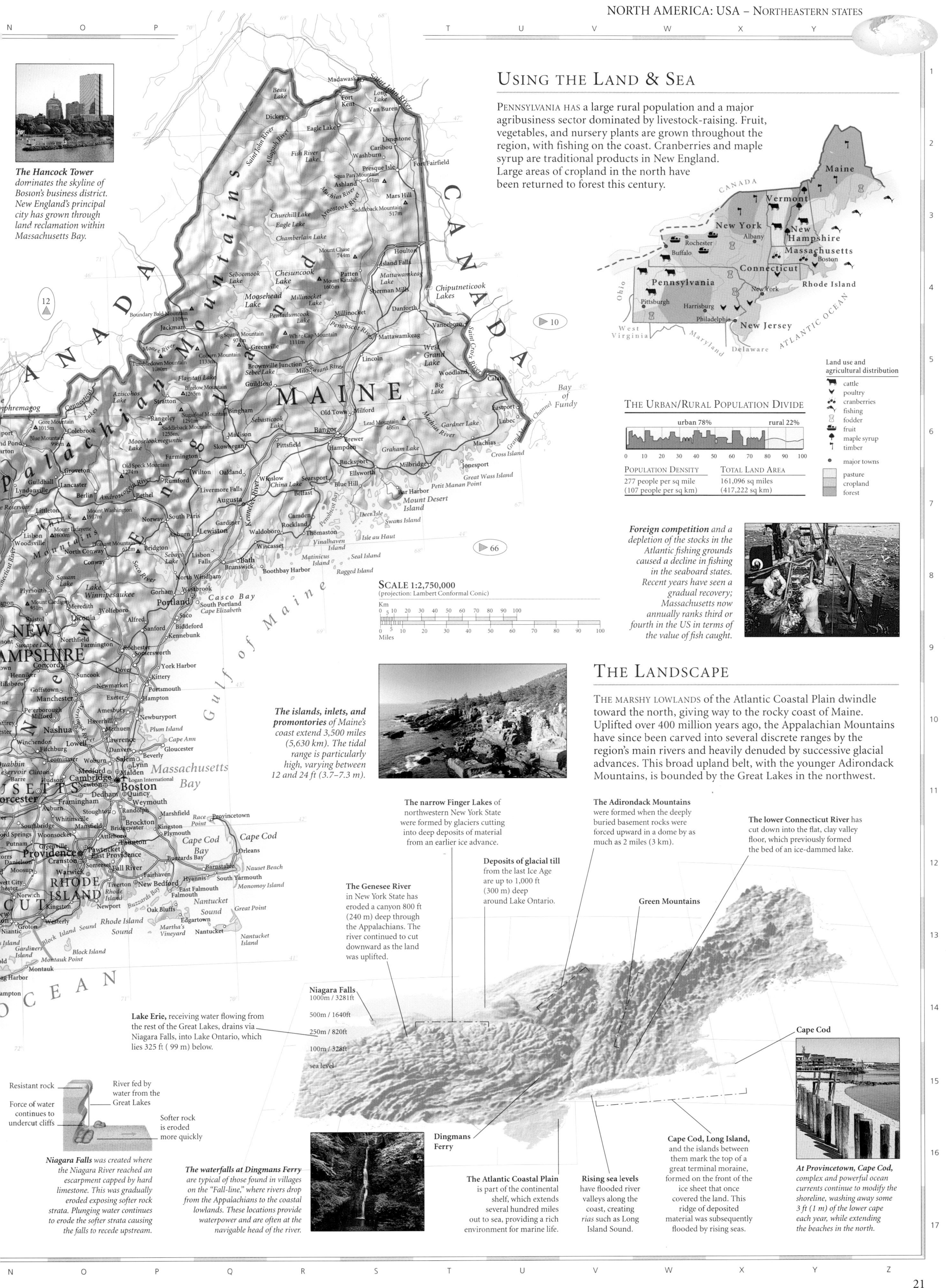
MAINE
CANADA
Gulf of Maine
Bay of Fundy
Massachusetts Bay
Cape Cod Bay
Casco Bay
Appalachian Mountains
New England
NEW HAMPSHIRE
RHODE ISLAND
ATLANTIC OCEAN
Boston
Providence
Portland
Bangor
Augusta
Niagara Falls
1000m / 3281ft
500m / 1640ft
250m / 820ft
100m / 328ft
sea level
Green Mountains
Cape Cod
Dingmans Ferry
Resistant rock
Force of water continues to undercut cliffs
River fed by water from the Great Lakes
Softer rock is eroded more quickly

The Hancock Tower dominates the skyline of Boston's business district. New England's principal city has grown through land reclamation within Massachusetts Bay.

Using the Land & Sea

Pennsylvania has a large rural population and a major agribusiness sector dominated by livestock-raising. Fruit, vegetables, and nursery plants are grown throughout the region, with fishing on the coast. Cranberries and maple syrup are traditional products in New England. Large areas of cropland in the north have been returned to forest this century.

Land use and agricultural distribution: cattle, poultry, cranberries, fishing, fodder, fruit, maple syrup, timber, major towns, pasture, cropland, forest

The Urban/Rural Population Divide

urban 78% — rural 22%

Population Density	Total Land Area
277 people per sq mile (107 people per sq km)	161,096 sq miles (417,222 sq km)

Foreign competition and a depletion of the stocks in the Atlantic fishing grounds caused a decline in fishing in the seaboard states. Recent years have seen a gradual recovery; Massachusetts now annually ranks third or fourth in the US in terms of the value of fish caught.

Scale 1:2,750,000 (projection: Lambert Conformal Conic)

The islands, inlets, and promontories of Maine's coast extend 3,500 miles (5,630 km). The tidal range is particularly high, varying between 12 and 24 ft (3.7–7.3 m).

The Landscape

The marshy lowlands of the Atlantic Coastal Plain dwindle toward the north, giving way to the rocky coast of Maine. Uplifted over 400 million years ago, the Appalachian Mountains have since been carved into several discrete ranges by the region's main rivers and heavily denuded by successive glacial advances. This broad upland belt, with the younger Adirondack Mountains, is bounded by the Great Lakes in the northwest.

The narrow Finger Lakes of northwestern New York State were formed by glaciers cutting into deep deposits of material from an earlier ice advance.

The Adirondack Mountains were formed when the deeply buried basement rocks were forced upward in a dome by as much as 2 miles (3 km).

The lower Connecticut River has cut down into the flat, clay valley floor, which previously formed the bed of an ice-dammed lake.

Deposits of glacial till from the last Ice Age are up to 1,000 ft (300 m) deep around Lake Ontario.

The Genesee River in New York State has eroded a canyon 800 ft (240 m) deep through the Appalachians. The river continued to cut downward as the land was uplifted.

Lake Erie, receiving water flowing from the rest of the Great Lakes, drains via Niagara Falls, into Lake Ontario, which lies 325 ft (99 m) below.

Niagara Falls was created where the Niagara River reached an escarpment capped by hard limestone. This was gradually eroded exposing softer rock strata. Plunging water continues to erode the softer strata causing the falls to recede upstream.

The waterfalls at Dingmans Ferry are typical of those found in villages on the "Fall-line," where rivers drop from the Appalachians to the coastal lowlands. These locations provide waterpower and are often at the navigable head of the river.

The Atlantic Coastal Plain is part of the continental shelf, which extends several hundred miles out to sea, providing a rich environment for marine life.

Rising sea levels have flooded river valleys along the coast, creating *rias* such as Long Island Sound.

Cape Cod, Long Island, and the islands between them mark the top of a great terminal moraine, formed on the front of the ice sheet that once covered the land. This ridge of deposited material was subsequently flooded by rising seas.

At Provincetown, Cape Cod, complex and powerful ocean currents continue to modify the shoreline, washing away some 3 ft (1 m) of the lower cape each year, while extending the beaches in the north.

USA: Mid-Eastern States

Delaware, District of Columbia, Kentucky, Maryland, North Carolina, South Carolina, Tennessee, Virginia, West Virginia

Key events in American history took place in this diverse region, which became the front line between the North and the South during the Civil War of the 1860s. Strong regional contrasts exist between the fertile coastal plains, the isolated upcountry of the Appalachian Mountains, and the cotton-growing areas of the Mississippi lowlands to the west. While coal mining, a traditional industry in the Appalachians, has declined in recent years leaving much rural poverty, service industries elsewhere have increased, especially in Washington D.C., the nation's capital.

Map Key

POPULATION
- 500,000 to 1 million
- 100,000 to 500,000
- 50,000 to 100,000
- 10,000 to 50,000
- below 10,000

ELEVATION
- 6000m / 19,686ft
- 4000m / 13,124ft
- 3000m / 9843ft
- 2000m / 6562ft
- 1000m / 3281ft
- 500m / 1640ft
- 250m / 820ft
- 100m / 328ft
- sea level

SCALE 1:3,000,000
(projection: Lambert Conformal Conic)

The Bluegrass region of Kentucky *centers on the town of Lexington. This exceptionally fertile rolling plain is well known for its thoroughbred horse-breeding ranches.*

Transportation & Industry

In the urbanized northeast, manufacturing remains important, alongside a burgeoning service sector. North Carolina is a major center for industrial research and development. Traditional industries include Tennessee whiskey and textiles in South Carolina. The decline of open-cast coal mining in the Appalachians has been hastened by environmental controls, although adventure tourism is a flourishing new industry.

Major industry and infrastructure
- adventure tourism
- car manufacture
- coal
- electronics
- engineering
- finance
- food processing
- hi-tech industry
- mining
- research & development
- textiles
- capital cities
- major towns
- international airports
- major roads
- major industrial areas

Transportation Network

452,218 miles (723,548 km)	5,737 miles (8,267 km)
18,336 miles (29,503 km)	4,404 miles (7,081 km)

Tennessee's rivers are part of an important inland bulk transportation network. Memphis connects with New Orleans in the south, and with cities as distant as Minneapolis, Sioux City, Chicago, and Pittsburgh, via the Mississippi and its tributaries.

The Landscape

The eastern tributaries of the Mississippi drain the interior lowlands. The Cumberland Plateau and the parallel ranges of the Appalachians have been successively uplifted and eroded over time, with the eastern side reduced to a series of foothills, known as the Piedmont. The broad coastal plain gradually falls away into salt marshes, lagoons, and offshore bars, broken by flooded estuaries along the shores of the Atlantic.

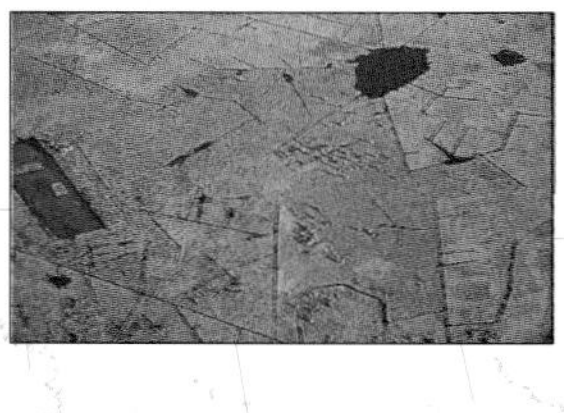

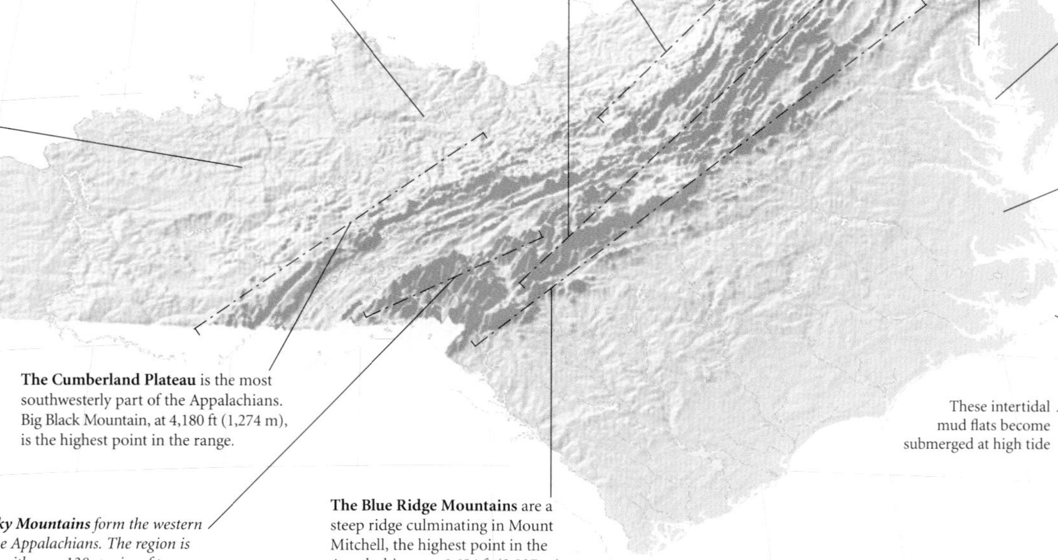

Natural Bridge in eastern Kentucky is an arch 78 ft (26 m) long and 65 ft (20 m) high. It has been shaped out of resistant sandstone by gradual weathering processes that removed the softer rock lying underneath.

The Allegheny Mountains form the northwestern edge of the Appalachian mountain chain. Continuous folding has formed rich seams of bituminous coal.

Appalachian Mountains

Farmland on the eastern shores of Chesapeake Bay is sustained by artificial drainage. The area also provides refuge for a variety of waterfowl.

The many inlets of Chesapeake Bay are the flooded tributaries of the main river valley, which have been inundated by rising sea levels.

Salt marshes such as Great Dismal Swamp develop where the coast is sheltered. Vast areas of such marshland have been reclaimed for farmland and settlement.

Cape Hatteras is the easternmost point of an offshore barrier island, a wave-deposited sandbar which has become permanent, establishing its own vegetation.

The Mammoth Cave is part of an extensive cave system in the limestone region of southwestern Kentucky. It stretches for over 300 miles (485 km) on five different levels and contains three rivers and three lakes.

The Mississippi River and its tributary the Ohio River form the western border of the region.

The Cumberland Plateau is the most southwesterly part of the Appalachians. Big Black Mountain, at 4,180 ft (1,274 m), is the highest point in the range.

Barrier islands

Tidal inlet

Barrier island

These intertidal mud flats become submerged at high tide

The Great Smoky Mountains form the western escarpment of the Appalachians. The region is heavily forested, with over 130 species of trees.

The Blue Ridge Mountains are a steep ridge culminating in Mount Mitchell, the highest point in the Appalachians, at 6,684 ft (2,037 m).

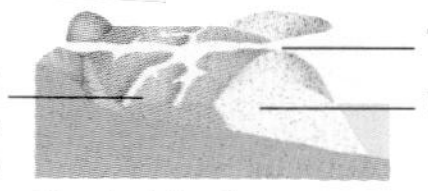

***Barrier islands** are common along the coasts of North and South Carolina. As sea levels rise, wave action builds up ridges of sand and pebbles parallel to the coast, separated by lagoons or intertidal mud flats, which are flooded at high tide.*

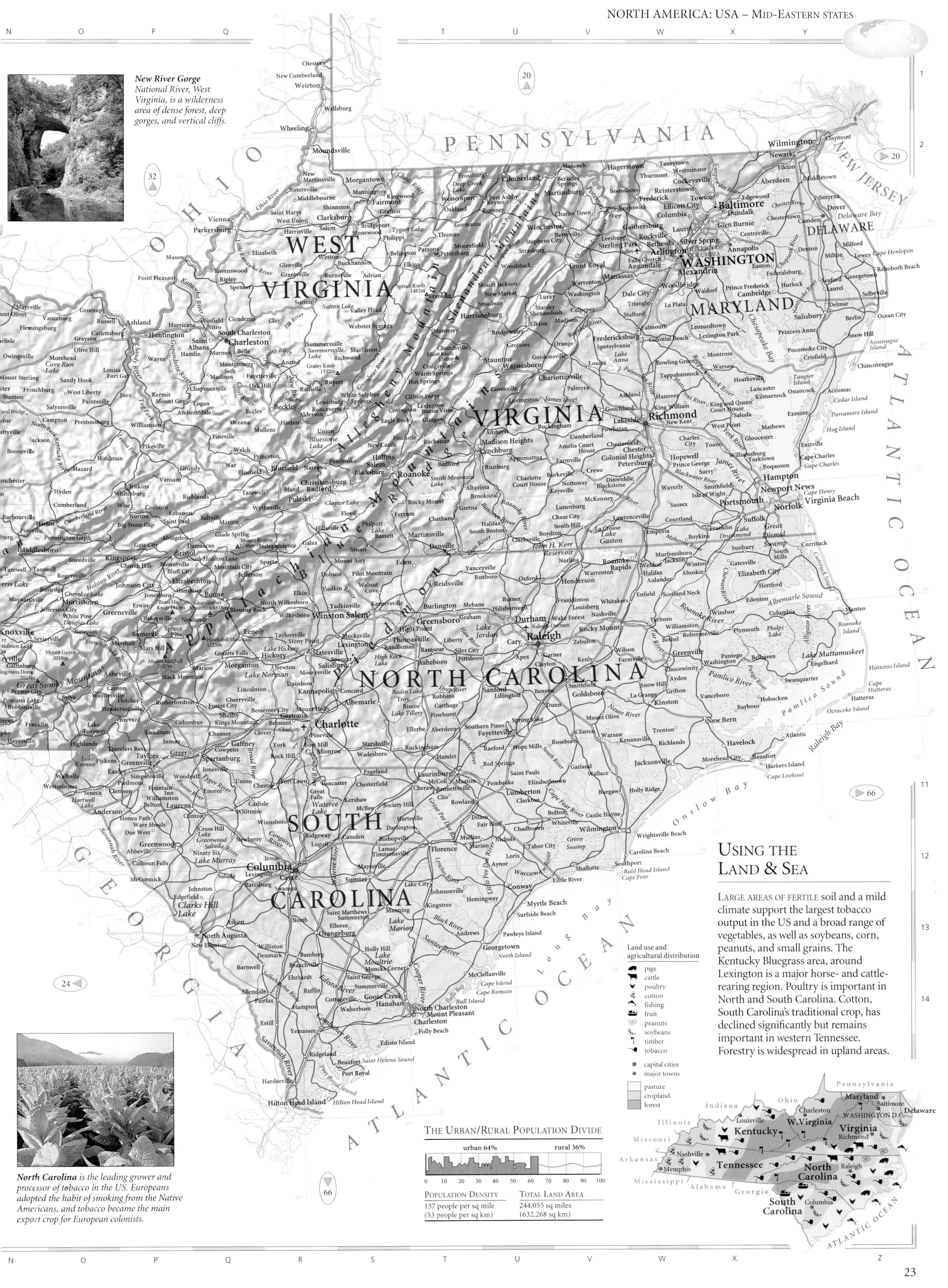
N O P Q R S T U V W X Y Z
PENNSYLVANIA
OHIO
WEST VIRGINIA
VIRGINIA
MARYLAND
DELAWARE
NEW JERSEY
NORTH CAROLINA
SOUTH CAROLINA
GEORGIA
ATLANTIC OCEAN
Appalachian Mountains
Allegheny Mountains
Blue Ridge
Shenandoah Mountains
Piedmont
Great Smoky Mountains
Chesapeake Bay
Delaware Bay
Albemarle Sound
Pamlico Sound
Onslow Bay
Long Bay
Raleigh Bay
WASHINGTON
Richmond
Raleigh
Columbia
Charleston
Baltimore
Norfolk
Virginia Beach
Charlotte
Greensboro
Durham
Winston Salem
Wilmington
Roanoke
Knoxville
Asheville
Myrtle Beach
Hilton Head Island
Cape Hatteras
Cape Lookout
Cape Fear
Land use and agricultural distribution
pigs
cattle
poultry
cotton
fishing
fruit
peanuts
soybeans
timber
tobacco
capital cities
major towns
pasture
cropland
forest
Pennsylvania
Ohio
Indiana
Illinois
Missouri
Arkansas
Mississippi
Alabama
Georgia
Kentucky
Tennessee
W.Virginia
Virginia
Maryland
Delaware
North Carolina
South Carolina
Louisville
Nashville
Memphis
Charleston
Baltimore
WASHINGTON D.C.
Richmond
Raleigh
Columbia

New River Gorge *National River, West Virginia, is a wilderness area of dense forest, deep gorges, and vertical cliffs.*

North Carolina *is the leading grower and processor of tobacco in the US. Europeans adopted the habit of smoking from the Native Americans, and tobacco became the main export crop for European colonists.*

Using the Land & Sea

Large areas of fertile soil and a mild climate support the largest tobacco output in the US and a broad range of vegetables, as well as soybeans, corn, peanuts, and small grains. The Kentucky Bluegrass area, around Lexington is a major horse- and cattle-rearing region. Poultry is important in North and South Carolina. Cotton, South Carolina's traditional crop, has declined significantly but remains important in western Tennessee. Forestry is widespread in upland areas.

The Urban/Rural Population Divide

urban 64% | rural 36%

0 10 20 30 40 50 60 70 80 90 100

Population Density
137 people per sq mile
(53 people per sq km)

Total Land Area
244,055 sq miles
(632,268 sq km)

USA: Southern states

Alabama, Florida, Georgia, Louisiana, Mississippi

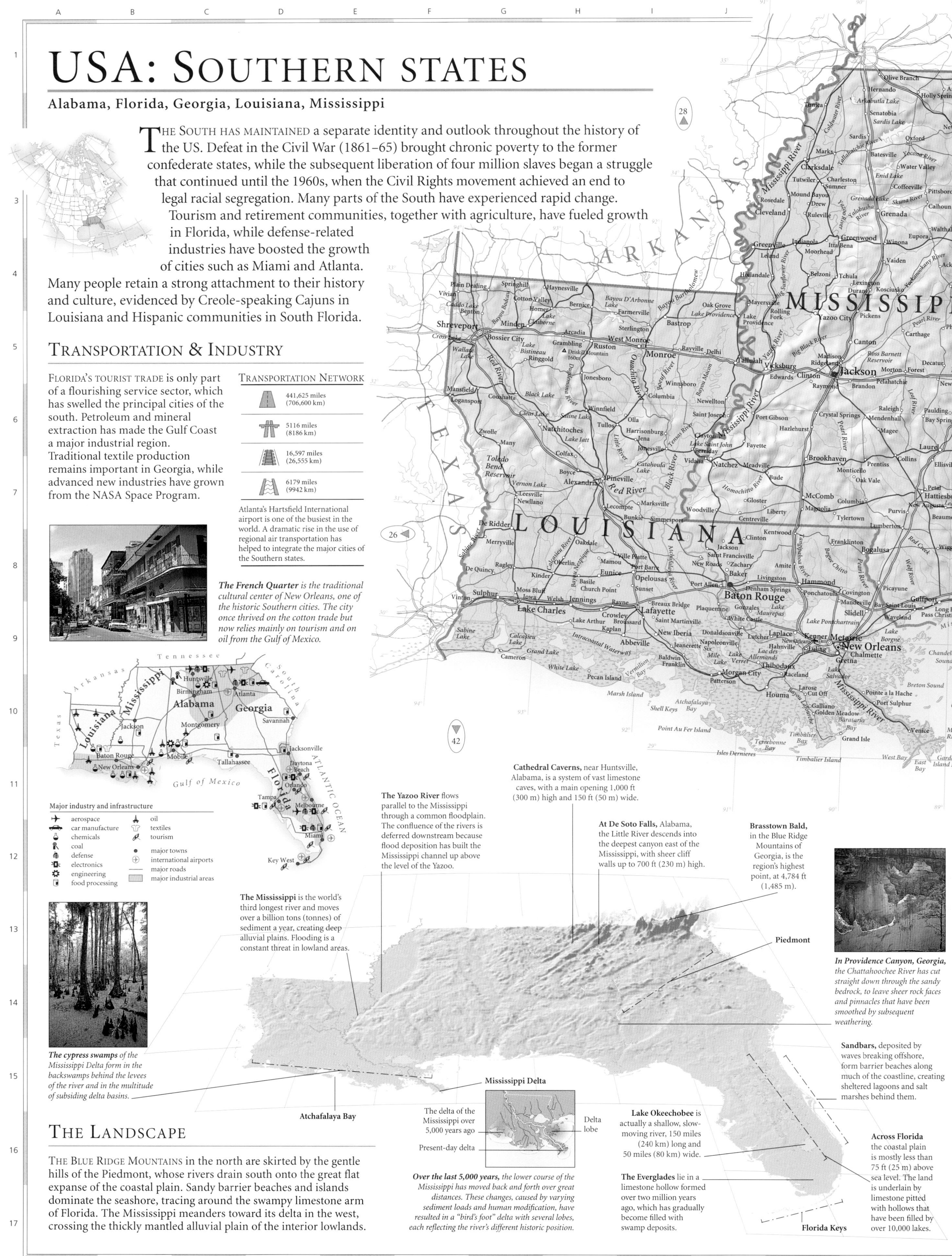

ARKANSAS
MISSISSIPPI
LOUISIANA
TEXAS
Shreveport
Monroe
Alexandria
Lake Charles
Lafayette
Baton Rouge
New Orleans
Jackson
Vicksburg
Natchez
Houma
Red River
Mississippi River

28

26

42

THE SOUTH HAS MAINTAINED a separate identity and outlook throughout the history of the US. Defeat in the Civil War (1861–65) brought chronic poverty to the former confederate states, while the subsequent liberation of four million slaves began a struggle that continued until the 1960s, when the Civil Rights movement achieved an end to legal racial segregation. Many parts of the South have experienced rapid change. Tourism and retirement communities, together with agriculture, have fueled growth in Florida, while defense-related industries have boosted the growth of cities such as Miami and Atlanta. Many people retain a strong attachment to their history and culture, evidenced by Creole-speaking Cajuns in Louisiana and Hispanic communities in South Florida.

Transportation & Industry

FLORIDA'S TOURIST TRADE is only part of a flourishing service sector, which has swelled the principal cities of the south. Petroleum and mineral extraction has made the Gulf Coast a major industrial region. Traditional textile production remains important in Georgia, while advanced new industries have grown from the NASA Space Program.

Transportation Network

441,625 miles (706,600 km)
5116 miles (8186 km)
16,597 miles (26,555 km)
6179 miles (9942 km)

Atlanta's Hartsfield International airport is one of the busiest in the world. A dramatic rise in the use of regional air transportation has helped to integrate the major cities of the Southern states.

The French Quarter is the traditional cultural center of New Orleans, one of the historic Southern cities. The city once thrived on the cotton trade but now relies mainly on tourism and on oil from the Gulf of Mexico.

Tennessee
Arkansas
South Carolina
Texas
Louisiana
Mississippi
Alabama
Georgia
Florida
Huntsville
Birmingham
Atlanta
Jackson
Montgomery
Savannah
Mobile
Baton Rouge
New Orleans
Tallahassee
Jacksonville
Daytona Beach
Orlando
Tampa
Melbourne
Miami
Key West
Gulf of Mexico
ATLANTIC OCEAN

Major industry and infrastructure

- aerospace
- car manufacture
- chemicals
- coal
- defense
- electronics
- engineering
- food processing
- oil
- textiles
- tourism
- major towns
- international airports
- major roads
- major industrial areas

The cypress swamps of the Mississippi Delta form in the backswamps behind the levees of the river and in the multitude of subsiding delta basins.

The Mississippi is the world's third longest river and moves over a billion tons (tonnes) of sediment a year, creating deep alluvial plains. Flooding is a constant threat in lowland areas.

The Yazoo River flows parallel to the Mississippi through a common floodplain. The confluence of the rivers is deferred downstream because flood deposition has built the Mississippi channel up above the level of the Yazoo.

Cathedral Caverns, near Huntsville, Alabama, is a system of vast limestone caves, with a main opening 1,000 ft (300 m) high and 150 ft (50 m) wide.

At De Soto Falls, Alabama, the Little River descends into the deepest canyon east of the Mississippi, with sheer cliff walls up to 700 ft (230 m) high.

Brasstown Bald, in the Blue Ridge Mountains of Georgia, is the region's highest point, at 4,784 ft (1,485 m).

Piedmont

In Providence Canyon, Georgia, the Chattahoochee River has cut straight down through the sandy bedrock, to leave sheer rock faces and pinnacles that have been smoothed by subsequent weathering.

Sandbars, deposited by waves breaking offshore, form barrier beaches along much of the coastline, creating sheltered lagoons and salt marshes behind them.

Atchafalaya Bay

Mississippi Delta

The delta of the Mississippi over 5,000 years ago

Present-day delta

Delta lobe

Over the last 5,000 years, the lower course of the Mississippi has moved back and forth over great distances. These changes, caused by varying sediment loads and human modification, have resulted in a "bird's foot" delta with several lobes, each reflecting the river's different historic position.

Lake Okeechobee is actually a shallow, slow-moving river, 150 miles (240 km) long and 50 miles (80 km) wide.

The Everglades lie in a limestone hollow formed over two million years ago, which has gradually become filled with swamp deposits.

Florida Keys

Across Florida the coastal plain is mostly less than 75 ft (25 m) above sea level. The land is underlain by limestone pitted with hollows that have been filled by over 10,000 lakes.

The Landscape

THE BLUE RIDGE MOUNTAINS in the north are skirted by the gentle hills of the Piedmont, whose rivers drain south onto the great flat expanse of the coastal plain. Sandy barrier beaches and islands dominate the seashore, tracing around the swampy limestone arm of Florida. The Mississippi meanders toward its delta in the west, crossing the thickly mantled alluvial plain of the interior lowlands.

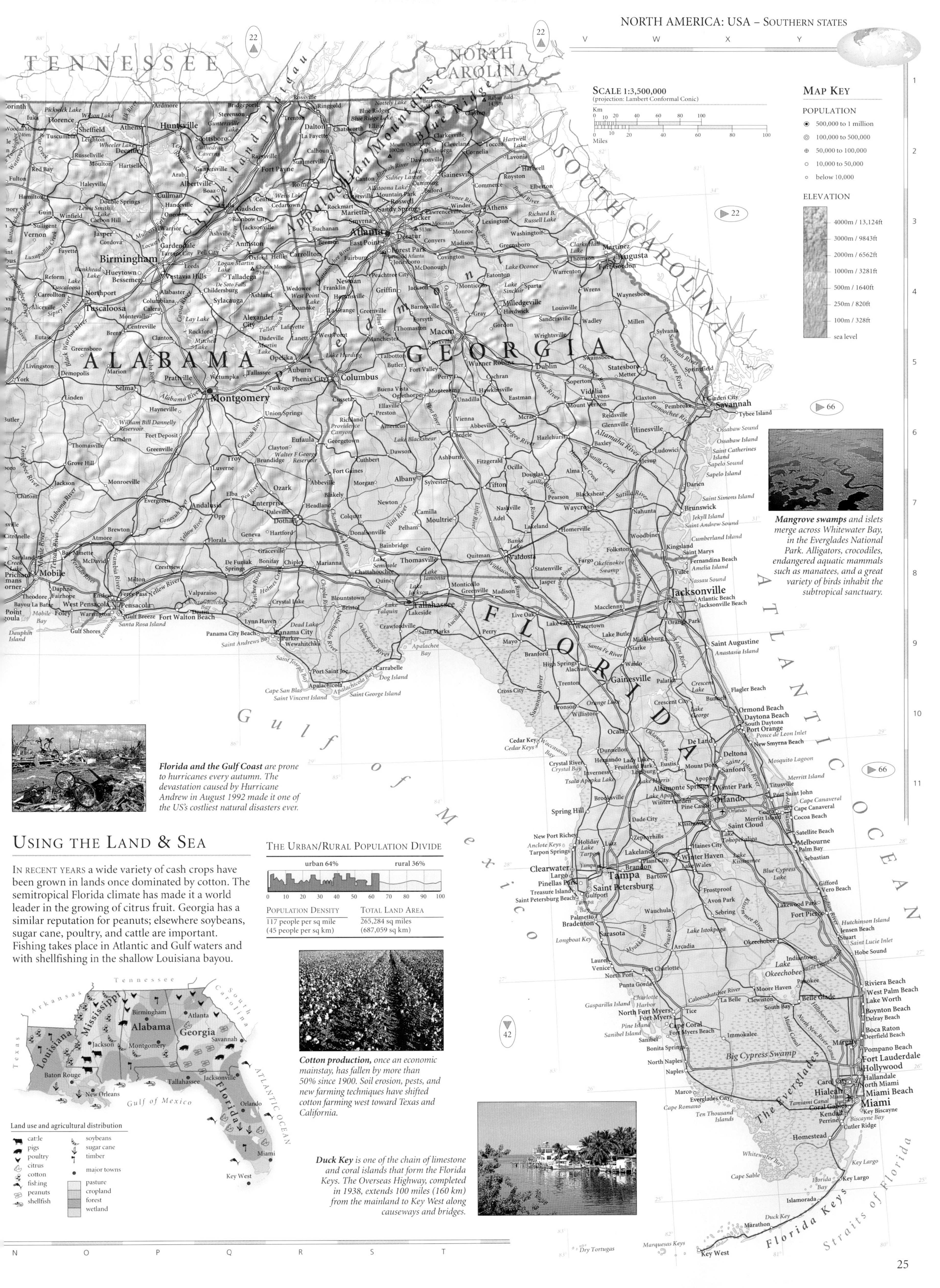

TENNESSEE
NORTH CAROLINA
SOUTH CAROLINA
ALABAMA
GEORGIA
FLORIDA
Gulf of Mexico
ATLANTIC OCEAN
Straits of Florida
Florida Keys
The Everglades
Big Cypress Swamp
Appalachian Mountains
Blue Ridge
Cumberland Plateau
Piedmont
Birmingham
Montgomery
Mobile
Atlanta
Columbus
Macon
Augusta
Savannah
Tallahassee
Jacksonville
Gainesville
Orlando
Tampa
Saint Petersburg
Miami
Fort Lauderdale
Key West
SCALE 1:3,500,000
(projection: Lambert Conformal Conic)
Km
Miles
MAP KEY
POPULATION
500,000 to 1 million
100,000 to 500,000
50,000 to 100,000
10,000 to 50,000
below 10,000
ELEVATION
4000m / 13,124ft
3000m / 9843ft
2000m / 6562ft
1000m / 3281ft
500m / 1640ft
250m / 820ft
100m / 328ft
sea level

Mangrove swamps *and islets merge across Whitewater Bay, in the Everglades National Park. Alligators, crocodiles, endangered aquatic mammals such as manatees, and a great variety of birds inhabit the subtropical sanctuary.*

Florida and the Gulf Coast *are prone to hurricanes every autumn. The devastation caused by Hurricane Andrew in August 1992 made it one of the US's costliest natural disasters ever.*

USING THE LAND & SEA

IN RECENT YEARS a wide variety of cash crops have been grown in lands once dominated by cotton. The semitropical Florida climate has made it a world leader in the growing of citrus fruit. Georgia has a similar reputation for peanuts; elsewhere soybeans, sugar cane, poultry, and cattle are important. Fishing takes place in Atlantic and Gulf waters and with shellfishing in the shallow Louisiana bayou.

THE URBAN/RURAL POPULATION DIVIDE

urban 64% | rural 36%

POPULATION DENSITY	TOTAL LAND AREA
117 people per sq mile (45 people per sq km)	265,284 sq miles (687,059 sq km)

Land use and agricultural distribution: cattle, pigs, poultry, citrus, cotton, fishing, peanuts, shellfish, soybeans, sugar cane, timber, major towns, pasture, cropland, forest, wetland

Cotton production, *once an economic mainstay, has fallen by more than 50% since 1900. Soil erosion, pests, and new farming techniques have shifted cotton farming west toward Texas and California.*

Duck Key *is one of the chain of limestone and coral islands that form the Florida Keys. The Overseas Highway, completed in 1938, extends 100 miles (160 km) from the mainland to Key West along causeways and bridges.*

A B C D E F G H I J K

USA: Texas

FIRST EXPLORED BY SPANIARDS moving north from Mexico in search of gold, Texas was controlled by Spain and then by Mexico, before becoming an independent republic in 1836 and joining the Union of States in 1845. During the 19th century, many migrants who came to Texas raised cattle on the abundant land; in the 20th century, they were joined by prospectors attracted by the promise of oil riches. Today, although natural resources, especially oil, still form the basis of its wealth, the diversified Texan economy includes thriving hi-tech and financial industries. The major urban centers, home to 80% of the population, lie in the south and east, and include Houston, the oil city, and Dallas–Fort Worth. Hispanic influences remain strong, especially in southern and western Texas.

Dallas was founded in 1841 *as a prairie trading post and its development was stimulated by the arrival of railroads. Cotton and then oil funded the town's early growth. Today, the modern, high-rise skyline of Dallas reflects the city's position as a leading center of banking, insurance, and the petroleum industry in the southwest.*

Using the Land

COTTON PRODUCTION AND LIVESTOCK-RAISING, particularly cattle, dominate farming, although crop failures and the demands of local markets have led to some diversification. Following the introduction of modern farming techniques, cotton production spread out of the east into the plains of western Texas. Cattle ranches are widespread, while sheep and goats are raised on the dry Edwards Plateau.

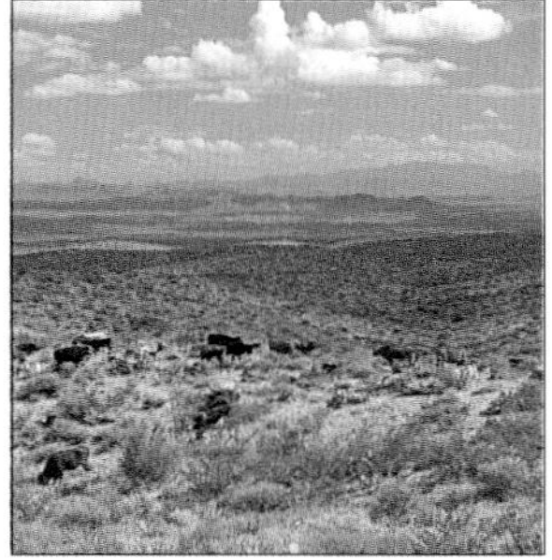

The huge cattle ranches of Texas *developed during the 19th century when land was plentiful and could be acquired cheaply. Today, more cattle and sheep are raised in Texas than in any other state.*

Land use and agricultural distribution

- cattle
- goats
- sheep
- cereals
- cotton
- major towns
- pasture
- cropland
- forest
- barren

The Urban/Rural Population Divide

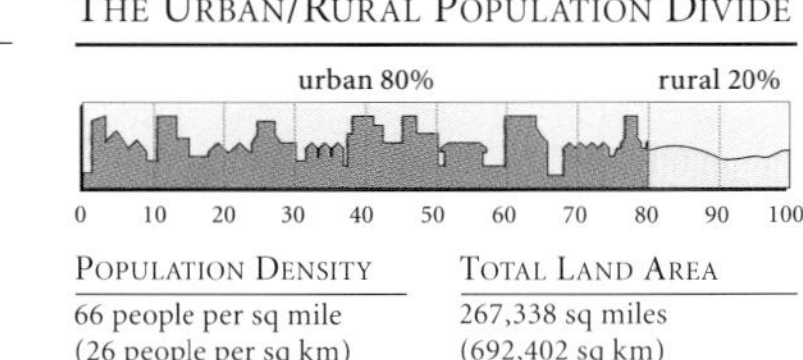
urban 80%
rural 20%
0 10 20 30 40 50 60 70 80 90 100

Population Density	Total Land Area
66 people per sq mile	267,338 sq miles
(26 people per sq km)	(692,402 sq km)

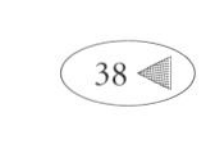
38

The Landscape

TEXAS IS MADE UP OF A SERIES of massive steps descending from the mountains and high plains of the west and northwest to the coastal lowlands in the southeast. Many of the state's borders are delineated by water. The Rio Grande flows from the Rocky Mountains to the Gulf of Mexico, marking the border with Mexico.

Cap Rock Escarpment *juts out of the plains, running 200 miles (320 km) from north to south. Its height varies from 300 ft (90 m) rising to sheer cliffs up to 1,000 ft (300 m).*

42

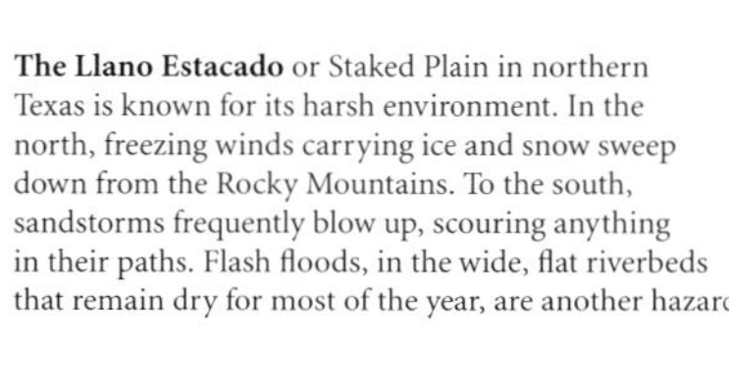

The Llano Estacado or Staked Plain in northern Texas is known for its harsh environment. In the north, freezing winds carrying ice and snow sweep down from the Rocky Mountains. To the south, sandstorms frequently blow up, scouring anything in their paths. Flash floods, in the wide, flat riverbeds that remain dry for most of the year, are another hazard.

The Guadalupe Mountains lie in the southern Rocky Mountains. They incorporate Guadalupe Peak, the highest in Texas, rising 8,749 ft (2,667 m).

The Red River flows for 1,300 miles (2,090 km), marking most of the northern border of Texas. A dam and reservoir along its course provide vital irrigation and hydroelectric power to the surrounding area.

The Rio Grande flows from the Rocky Mountains through semi-arid land, supporting sparse vegetation. The river actually shrinks along its course, losing more water through evaporation and seepage than it gains from its tributaries and rainfall.

Sabine River

Extensive forests of pine and cypress grow in the eastern corner of the coastal lowlands where the average rainfall is 45 inches (1,145 mm) a year. This is higher than the rest of the state and over twice the average in the west.

In the coastal lowlands of southeastern Texas the Earth's crust is warping, causing the land to subside and allowing the sea to invade. Around Galveston, the rate of downward tilting is 6 inches (15 cm) per year.

Big Bend National Park

Flowing through 1,500-ft (450-m) high gorges, *the shallow, muddy Rio Grande makes a 90° bend. This marks the southern border of Big Bend National Park, and gives it its name. The area is a mixture of forested mountains, deserts, and canyons.*

Edwards Plateau is a limestone outcrop. It is part of the Great Plains, bounded to the southeast by the Balcones Escarpment, which marks the southerly limit of the plains.

Padre Island

Laguna Madre in southern Texas has been almost completely cut off from the sea by Padre Island. This sandbank was created by wave action, carrying and depositing material along the coast, in a process known as longshore drift.

Oil deposits

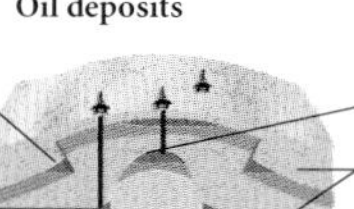
Oil trapped by fault
Oil deposits migrate through reservoir rocks such as shale
Oil accumulates beneath impermeable cap rock
Impermeable rock strata
Salt dome

Oil deposits *are found beneath much of Texas. They collect as oil migrates upward through porous layers of rock until it is trapped, either by a cap of rock above a salt dome or by a fault line that exposes impermeable rock through which the oil cannot rise.*

A B C D E F G H I J K L M

TRANSPORTATION & INDUSTRY

INDUSTRY IN THE 20TH CENTURY has largely concentrated on the processing of local raw materials, especially oil – deposits have been discovered underneath 65% of the state's area. The technological demands of the oil industry and defense-related institutions, particularly NASA, have stimulated the development of numerous electronics and hi-tech firms which, alongside many national corporate headquarters, are based in Dallas–Fort Worth and Houston.

Major industry and infrastructure

- chemicals
- defense
- engineering
- finance
- food processing
- gas
- hi-tech industry
- mining
- oil
- textiles
- major towns
- international airports
- major roads
- major industrial areas

TRANSPORTATION NETWORK

293,509 miles (496,614 km)	3,229 miles (5,166 km)
10,681 miles (17,089 km)	845 miles (1,359 km)

The sheer size of Texas promoted the development of an extensive road and rail network. The highway system, although well developed, is concentrated in the east.

The Texas hill country is the most southerly extension of the Great Plains. Although farming is the primary source of income, the beautiful hills, valleys, and lakes are a major tourist attraction.

Padre Island is a sandbank. It extends 113 miles (182 km) along the southern coast of Texas.

SCALE 1:3,250,000
(projection: Lambert Conformal Conic)

MAP KEY

POPULATION

- 1 million to 5 million
- 500,000 to 1 million
- 100,000 to 500,000
- 50,000 to 100,000
- 10,000 to 50,000
- below 10,000

ELEVATION

- 2000m / 6562ft
- 1000m / 3281ft
- 500m / 1640ft
- 250m / 820ft
- 100m / 328ft
- sea level

USA: South Midwestern States

Arkansas, Kansas, Missouri, Oklahoma

The expansion of the US focused on this region in the mid-19th century. Settlers spread from the confluence of the Missouri and Mississippi Rivers up onto the Great Plains. This treeless expanse, which early explorers had called the Great American Desert, was turned into one of the world's richest agricultural regions. But periodic droughts, coupled with overintensive farming, led to the "dustbowl" soil erosion crisis of the 1930s, the abandonment of many farms, and a mass exodus to the West Coast. The land has since recovered, although the mechanization of agriculture has led to a decline in the rural population. In recent years, suburban residential development has spread rapidly across the wooded Ozark Plateau in the east of the region.

Transportation & Industry

The processing of agricultural products, such as brewing and meatpacking, has traditionally been important in these states. In Kansas and Oklahoma, diversified manufacturing now supplements income from fossil fuels; Wichita has become a world center for aeronautical engineering, an industry that also employs many people in neighboring Missouri.

Major industry and infrastructure

- aerospace
- engineering
- finance
- food processing
- gas
- mining
- oil
- vehicle manufacture
- major towns
- international airports
- major roads
- major industrial areas

Agricultural produce from the plains is moved by barges along the Mississippi. The river now carries a far greater tonnage of freight than any other waterway system in the US.

Transportation Network

380,307 miles (608,491 km)	4,068 miles (6,508 km)
16,185 miles (25,896 km)	1,994 miles (3,208 km)

The Arkansas River and its tributaries allow access to over half of the US's navigable inland waterways. A system of locks and dams along the river provides Tulsa, in Oklahoma, with a navigable water route to the Gulf of Mexico.

Map Key

POPULATION

- 100,000 to 500,000
- 50,000 to 100,000
- 10,000 to 50,000
- below 10,000

ELEVATION

- 1000m / 3281ft
- 500m / 1640ft
- 250m / 820ft
- 100m / 328ft
- sea level

SCALE 1:3,000,000
(projection: Lambert Conformal Conic)

The Landscape

Most of the region consists of high, treeless plains, which gradually descend east from the Rocky Mountains. Drainage follows this slope, with rivers flowing toward the alluvial lowlands of the Mississippi in the southeast. Between the plains and the lowlands lie various ranges of wooded hills, including the deeply incised Ozark Plateau.

***The Mississippi,** North America's longest river, is joined by the Missouri, its main tributary, on a floodplain which spreads south to the Gulf of Mexico.*

Collapsed limestone caverns led to the formation of Big Basin in Kansas, a depression 100 ft (33 m) deep and 1 mile (1.6 km) wide.

Flint Hills is the region's easternmost major escarpment. Steep, grassy uplands are interspersed with rocky, wooded ravines and outcrops of limestone and chert.

The Ozark Plateau is a wooded, hilly region of rivers and narrow, winding lakes. The Lake of the Ozarks was created by the damming of the Osage River in 1930.

Missouri River

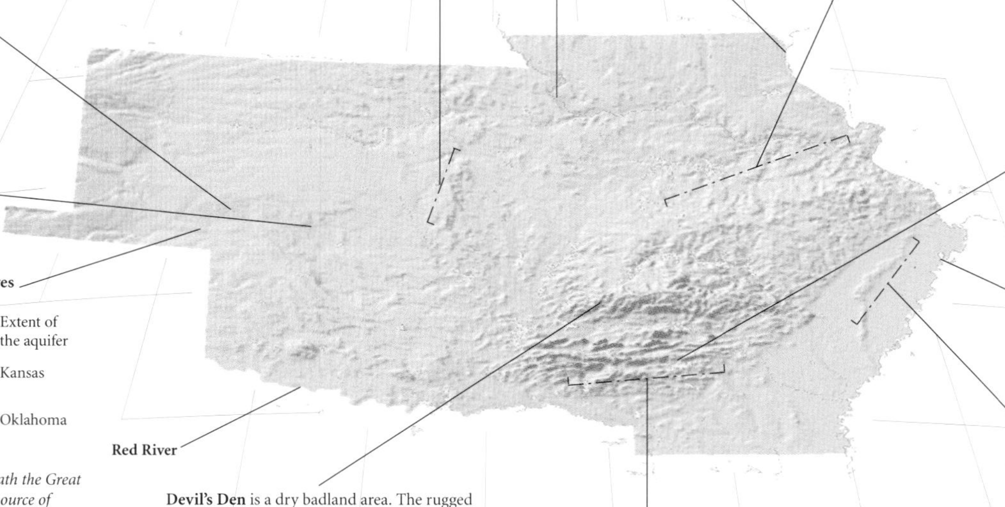

The Great Salt Plains of northern Oklahoma cover 45 sq miles (116 sq km). The arid, white flats were left by the gradual evaporation of an ancient salt lake.

***Lake Ouachita,** in Arkansas, is one of a number of irregularly-shaped lakes found among the ridges of the Ouachita Mountains.*

Underground water reserves

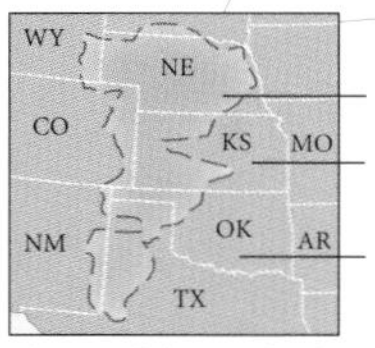

Extent of the aquifer

The Ogallala Aquifer, beneath the Great Plains, is the largest known source of underground water in the world. There is concern about the rapid depletion of this finite water supply by irrigation.

Mississippi River

Red River

Devil's Den is a dry badland area. The rugged landscape, strewn with large boulders, is the eroded remnant of a spur extending from the Arbuckle Mountains to the west.

Ouachita Mountains

Crowleys Ridge is a long, sandy ridge, rising from the Mississippi floodplain. It was formed over thousands of years, by the deposition of sand blown eastward from the Great Plains.

***The landscape of northeastern Kansas** is interlaced by rivers that have cut broad wooded valleys through the gentle hills. All the rivers in Kansas form part of the massive Missouri/Mississippi drainage basin.*

***Gateway Arch,** in Saint Louis, Missouri, is 634 ft (192 m) high. The huge steel arch symbolizes the city's historic role as the "Gateway to the West."*

USING THE LAND

THE PROBLEMS of a harsh continental climate, with severe winters and hot, dry summers, are partially offset by the rich soils of the plains. Kansas is a major cereal crop producer, ranking first in US production of wheat and sorghum. Rainfall increases toward the east, favoring the cultivation of soybeans, cotton, and rice, with corn concentrated in Missouri. Huge herds of cattle are raised in Oklahoma, Kansas, and Missouri.

***A combine harvester** works the land on the Great Plains. A hundred years ago this region, also known as the prairies – the French word for pasture – was covered with tall, wild grasses.*

THE URBAN/RURAL POPULATION DIVIDE

urban 65% | rural 35%

0 10 20 30 40 50 60 70 80 90 100

POPULATION DENSITY	TOTAL LAND AREA
48 people per sq mile (19 people per sq km)	274,900 sq miles (712,177 sq km)

Land use and agricultural distribution

- cattle
- poultry
- cereals
- corn
- cotton
- fodder
- rice
- soybeans
- major towns
- pasture
- cropland
- forest

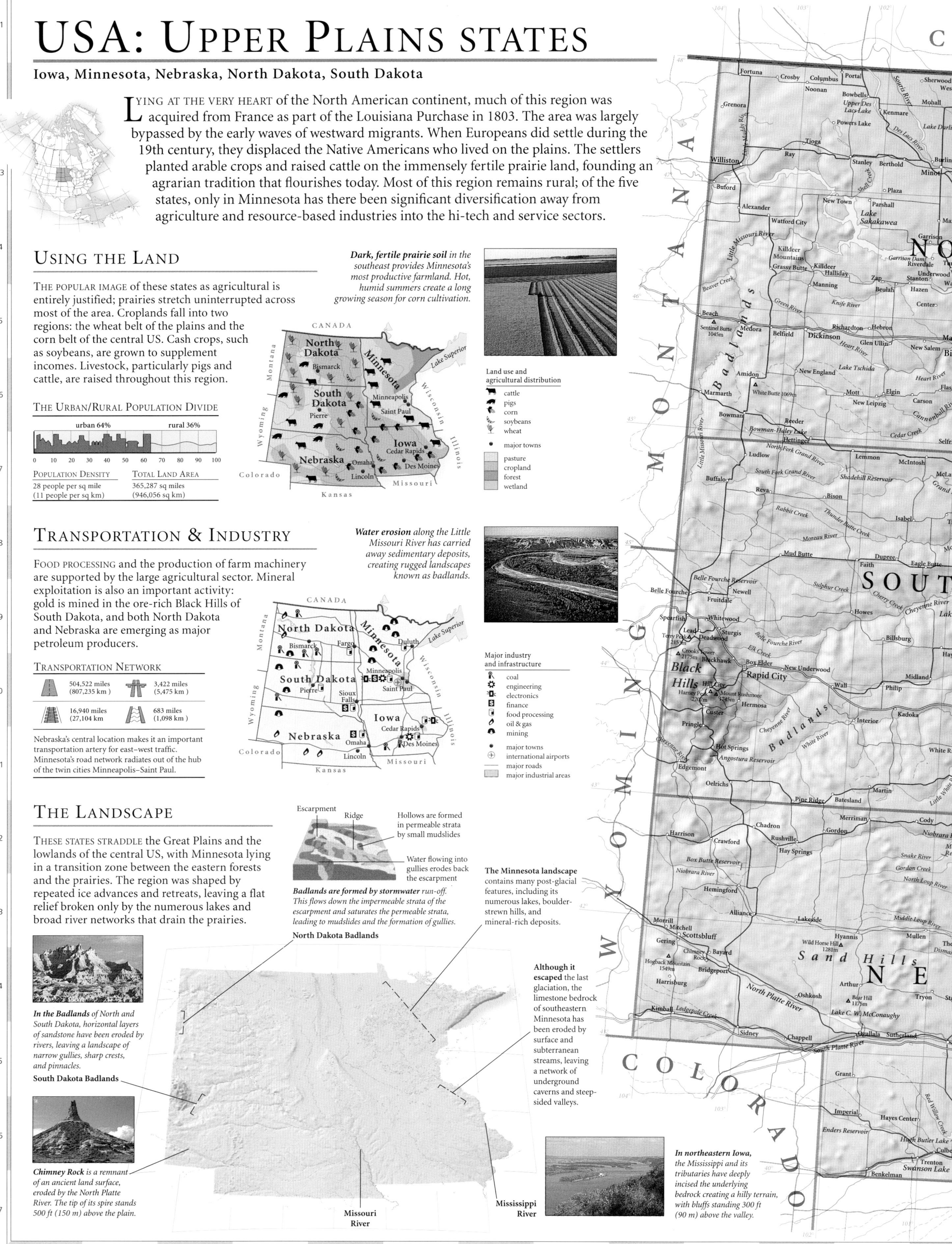

USA: Upper Plains states

Iowa, Minnesota, Nebraska, North Dakota, South Dakota

Lying at the very heart of the North American continent, much of this region was acquired from France as part of the Louisiana Purchase in 1803. The area was largely bypassed by the early waves of westward migrants. When Europeans did settle during the 19th century, they displaced the Native Americans who lived on the plains. The settlers planted arable crops and raised cattle on the immensely fertile prairie land, founding an agrarian tradition that flourishes today. Most of this region remains rural; of the five states, only in Minnesota has there been significant diversification away from agriculture and resource-based industries into the hi-tech and service sectors.

Using the Land

The popular image of these states as agricultural is entirely justified; prairies stretch uninterrupted across most of the area. Croplands fall into two regions: the wheat belt of the plains and the corn belt of the central US. Cash crops, such as soybeans, are grown to supplement incomes. Livestock, particularly pigs and cattle, are raised throughout this region.

The Urban/Rural Population Divide

urban 64%
rural 36%
0 10 20 30 40 50 60 70 80 90 100

Population Density	Total Land Area
28 people per sq mile (11 people per sq km)	365,287 sq miles (946,056 sq km)

Dark, fertile prairie soil in the southeast provides Minnesota's most productive farmland. Hot, humid summers create a long growing season for corn cultivation.

CANADA
North Dakota
Bismarck
Minnesota
Lake Superior
Montana
South Dakota
Pierre
Minneapolis
Saint Paul
Wisconsin
Wyoming
Iowa
Cedar Rapids
Des Moines
Illinois
Nebraska
Omaha
Lincoln
Colorado
Kansas
Missouri
Land use and agricultural distribution
cattle
pigs
corn
soybeans
wheat
major towns
pasture
cropland
forest
wetland

Transportation & Industry

Food processing and the production of farm machinery are supported by the large agricultural sector. Mineral exploitation is also an important activity: gold is mined in the ore-rich Black Hills of South Dakota, and both North Dakota and Nebraska are emerging as major petroleum producers.

Transportation Network

504,522 miles (807,235 km)	3,422 miles (5,475 km)
16,940 miles (27,104 km)	683 miles (1,098 km)

Nebraska's central location makes it an important transportation artery for east–west traffic. Minnesota's road network radiates out of the hub of the twin cities Minneapolis–Saint Paul.

Water erosion along the Little Missouri River has carried away sedimentary deposits, creating rugged landscapes known as badlands.

CANADA
North Dakota
Bismarck
Fargo
Minnesota
Duluth
Lake Superior
Montana
South Dakota
Pierre
Minneapolis
Saint Paul
Sioux Falls
Wisconsin
Wyoming
Iowa
Cedar Rapids
Des Moines
Illinois
Nebraska
Omaha
Lincoln
Colorado
Kansas
Missouri
Major industry and infrastructure
coal
engineering
electronics
finance
food processing
oil & gas
mining
major towns
international airports
major roads
major industrial areas

The Landscape

These states straddle the Great Plains and the lowlands of the central US, with Minnesota lying in a transition zone between the eastern forests and the prairies. The region was shaped by repeated ice advances and retreats, leaving a flat relief broken only by the numerous lakes and broad river networks that drain the prairies.

Escarpment
Ridge
Hollows are formed in permeable strata by small mudslides
Water flowing into gullies erodes back the escarpment

***Badlands are formed by stormwater** run-off. This flows down the impermeable strata of the escarpment and saturates the permeable strata, leading to mudslides and the formation of gullies.*

The Minnesota landscape contains many post-glacial features, including its numerous lakes, boulder-strewn hills, and mineral-rich deposits.

North Dakota Badlands

In the Badlands of North and South Dakota, horizontal layers of sandstone have been eroded by rivers, leaving a landscape of narrow gullies, sharp crests, and pinnacles.

South Dakota Badlands

Although it escaped the last glaciation, the limestone bedrock of southeastern Minnesota has been eroded by surface and subterranean streams, leaving a network of underground caverns and steep-sided valleys.

Chimney Rock is a remnant of an ancient land surface, eroded by the North Platte River. The tip of its spire stands 500 ft (150 m) above the plain.

Missouri River

Mississippi River

In northeastern Iowa, *the Mississippi and its tributaries have deeply incised the underlying bedrock creating a hilly terrain, with bluffs standing 300 ft (90 m) above the valley.*

MONTANA
WYOMING
COLORADO
NO
SOUT
NE
Williston
Minot
Lake Sakakawea
Dickinson
Badlands
Belle Fourche
Spearfish
Lead
Deadwood
Sturgis
Black Hills
Rapid City
Harney Peak 2207m
Mount Rushmore
Custer
Hot Springs
Pine Ridge
Chadron
Scottsbluff
Sand Hills
North Platte River
Ogallala
South Platte River

***Along the shores** of Lake Superior in Minnesota, the average number of frostfree days can be as few as 90, and frosts may occur in any month of the year.*

MINNESOTA

IOWA

MAP KEY

POPULATION

- ◎ 100,000 to 500,000
- ⊕ 50,000 to 100,000
- ○ 10,000 to 50,000
- ◦ below 10,000

ELEVATION

- 2000m / 6562ft
- 1000m / 3281ft
- 500m / 1640ft
- 250m / 820ft
- 100m / 328ft
- sea level

SCALE 1:3,250,000
(projection: Lambert Conformal Conic)

Km 0 10 20 40 60 80 100 120

Miles 0 10 20 40 60 80 100 120

USA: Great Lakes states

Illinois, Indiana, Michigan, Ohio, Wisconsin

The states bordering the Great Lakes developed rapidly in the second half of the 19th century as a result of improvements in communications: railroads to the west and waterways to the south and east. Fertile land and good links with growing eastern cities encouraged the development of agriculture and food processing. Migrants from Europe and other parts of the US flooded into the region and for much of this century the region's economy boomed. However, in recent years heavy industry has declined, earning the region the unwanted label, the "Rustbelt."

Transportation & Industry

The Great Lakes region is the center of the US car industry. Since the early part of this century, its prosperity has been closely linked to the fortunes of automobile manufacturing. Iron and steel production has expanded to meet demand from this industry. In the 1970s, nationwide recession, cheaper foreign competition in the automobile sector, pollution in and around the Great Lakes, and the collapse of the meatpacking industry, centered in Chicago, forced these states to diversify their industrial base. New industries have emerged, notably electronics, service, and financial industries.

Major industry and infrastructure

- car manufacture
- coal
- electronics
- engineering
- finance
- food processing
- iron & steel
- oil
- research & development
- textiles
- major towns
- international airports
- major roads
- major industrial areas

Transportation Network

540,682 miles (865,091 km)	6,550 miles (10,480 km)
24,928 miles (39,884 km)	2,330 miles (3,748 km)

Few areas of the US have a comparable system. Chicago is a principal transportation terminus with a dense network of roads, railroads, and Interstate freeways that radiates out from the city.

***Ever since Ransom Olds** and Henry Ford started mass-producing automobiles in Detroit early this century, the city's name has become synonymous with the American automotive industry.*

The Landscape

Much of this region shows the impact of glaciation, which lasted until about 10,000 years ago, and extended as far south as Illinois and Ohio. Although the relief of the region slopes toward the Great Lakes, because the ice sheets blocked northerly drainage, most of the rivers today flow southward, forming part of the massive Mississippi/Missouri drainage basin.

***The dunes near** Sleeping Bear Point rise 400 ft (120 m) from the banks of Lake Michigan. They are constantly resculpted by wind.*

Lake Michigan

Lake Erie is the shallowest of the five Great Lakes. Its average depth is about 62 ft (19 m). Storms sweeping across from Canada erode its shores and cause the silting of its harbors.

The many lakes and marshes of Wisconsin and Michigan are the result of the glacial erosion and deposition, which occurred during the last Ice Age.

Southwestern Wisconsin is known as a "driftless" area. Unlike most of the region, low hills protected it from erosion by the advancing ice sheet.

Most of the water used in northern Illinois is pumped from underground reservoirs. Due to increased demand, many areas now face a water shortage. Around Joliet, the water table has been lowered by more than 700 ft (210 m) over the 20th century.

The Appalachian Plateau stretches eastward from Ohio. It is dissected by streams flowing west into the Mississippi and Ohio Rivers.

Illinois plains

Mississippi River

Ohio River

The plains of Illinois are characteristic of drift landscapes, scoured and flattened by glacial erosion and covered with fertile glacial deposits.

Relic landforms from the last glaciation, such as shallow basins and ridges, cover all but the south of this region. Ridges, known as moraines, up to 300 ft (100 m) high, lie to the south of Lake Michigan.

Unlike the level prairie to the north, southern Indiana is relatively rugged. Limestone in the hills has been dissolved by water, producing features such as sinkholes and underground caves.

Glacial till

Present-day river or stream

Channels caused by outwash from melting glacier

Most recent till deposits

Older till sheet

Bedrock

***As a result of successive glacial depositions,** the total depth of till along the former southern margin of the Laurentide ice sheet can exceed 1,300 ft (400 m).*

30

28

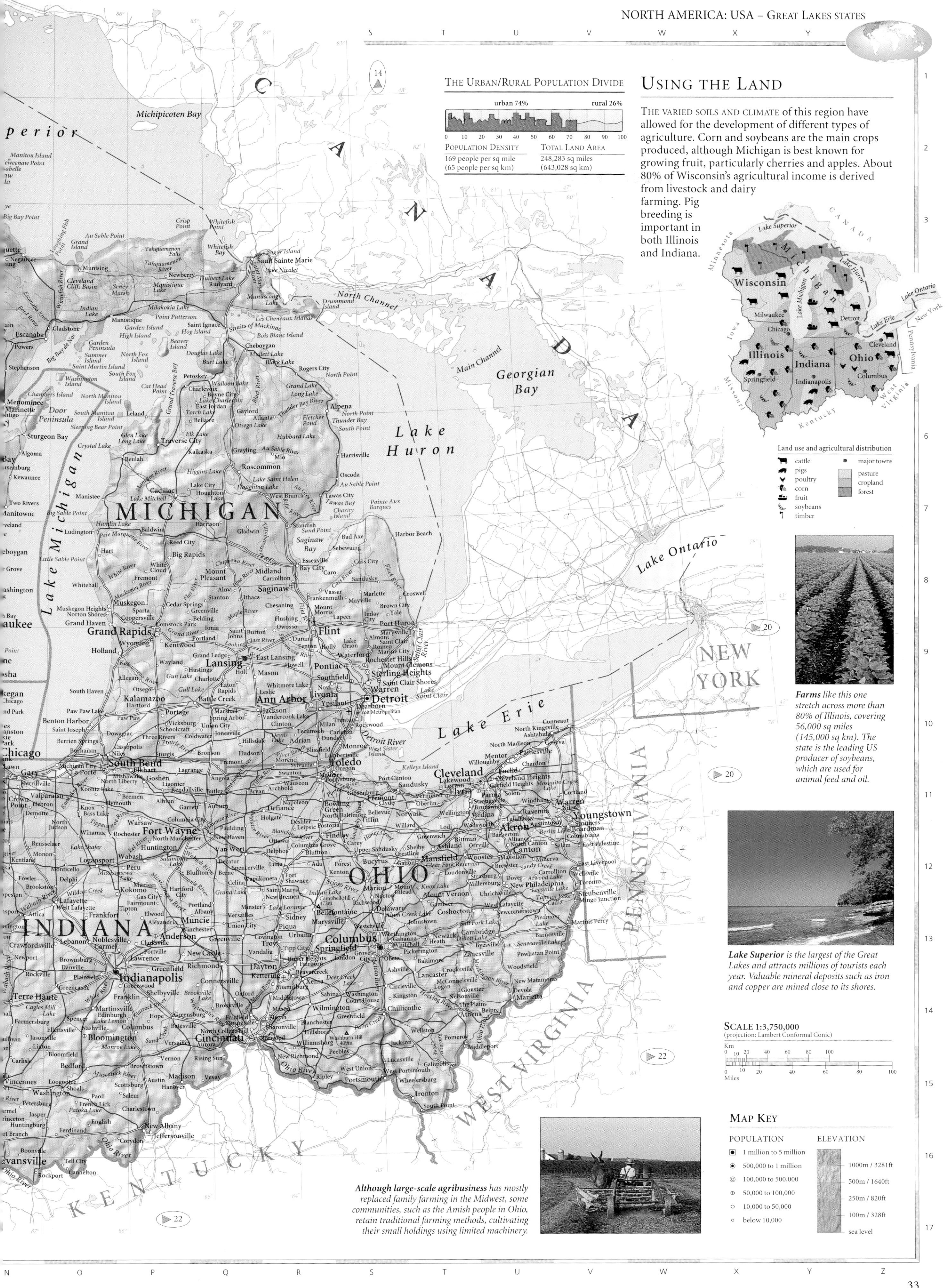

S T U V W X Y
CANADA
Michipicoten Bay
Lake Superior
Lake Michigan
Lake Huron
Georgian Bay
Main Channel
North Channel
Saginaw Bay
Lake Ontario
Lake Erie
MICHIGAN
OHIO
INDIANA
NEW YORK
PENNSYLVANIA
WEST VIRGINIA
KENTUCKY
Chicago
Detroit
Cleveland
Columbus
Indianapolis
Toledo
Fort Wayne
South Bend
Grand Rapids
Lansing
Flint
Saginaw
Ann Arbor
Akron
Youngstown
Dayton
Cincinnati
Canton
Evansville
Terre Haute
Sault Sainte Marie
Traverse City
Kalamazoo
Muncie
Anderson
Bloomington
Springfield
Mansfield
Port Huron
Warren
Sandusky
Ohio River
1 2 3 6 7 8 9 10 11 12 13 14 15 16 17
N O P Q R S T U V W X Y Z

The Urban/Rural Population Divide

urban 74% rural 26%

0 10 20 30 40 50 60 70 80 90 100

Population Density	Total Land Area
169 people per sq mile (65 people per sq km)	248,283 sq miles (643,028 sq km)

Using the Land

The varied soils and climate of this region have allowed for the development of different types of agriculture. Corn and soybeans are the main crops produced, although Michigan is best known for growing fruit, particularly cherries and apples. About 80% of Wisconsin's agricultural income is derived from livestock and dairy farming. Pig breeding is important in both Illinois and Indiana.

Lake Superior
Canada
Minnesota
Michigan
Wisconsin
Lake Michigan
Lake Huron
Lake Ontario
Lake Erie
New York
Pennsylvania
Iowa
Milwaukee
Chicago
Detroit
Cleveland
Illinois
Indiana
Ohio
Springfield
Indianapolis
Columbus
Missouri
Kentucky
West Virginia

Land use and agricultural distribution

cattle, pigs, poultry, corn, fruit, soybeans, timber, major towns, pasture, cropland, forest

***Farms** like this one stretch across more than 80% of Illinois, covering 56,000 sq miles (145,000 sq km). The state is the leading US producer of soybeans, which are used for animal feed and oil.*

***Lake Superior** is the largest of the Great Lakes and attracts millions of tourists each year. Valuable mineral deposits such as iron and copper are mined close to its shores.*

Scale 1:3,750,000
(projection: Lambert Conformal Conic)

Km 0 10 20 40 60 80 100
Miles 0 10 20 40 60 80 100

***Although large-scale agribusiness** has mostly replaced family farming in the Midwest, some communities, such as the Amish people in Ohio, retain traditional farming methods, cultivating their small holdings using limited machinery.*

Map Key

Population	Elevation
1 million to 5 million	1000m / 3281ft
500,000 to 1 million	500m / 1640ft
100,000 to 500,000	250m / 820ft
50,000 to 100,000	100m / 328ft
10,000 to 50,000	sea level
below 10,000	

USA: North Mountain states

Idaho, Montana, Oregon, Washington, Wyoming

The remoteness of the North Mountain states, coupled with their rugged landscape, ensured that this was one of the last areas settled by Europeans in the 19th century. Fur-trappers and gold-prospectors followed the Snake River westward as it wound its way through the Rocky Mountains. The states of the northwest have pioneered many conservationist policies, with the first US National Park opened in Yellowstone in 1872. More recently, the Cascades and Rocky Mountains have become havens for adventure tourism. The mountains still serve to isolate the western seaboard from the rest of the continent. This isolation has encouraged West Coast cities to expand their trade links with countries of the Pacific Rim.

The Snake River has cut down into the basalt of the Columbia Basin to form Hells Canyon, the deepest in the US, with cliffs up to 7,900 ft (2,408 m) high.

Map Key

Population	Elevation
500,000 to 1 million	4000m / 13,124ft
100,000 to 500,000	3000m / 9843ft
50,000 to 100,000	2000m / 6562ft
10,000 to 50,000	1000m / 3281ft
below 10,000	500m / 1640ft
	250m / 820ft
	100m / 328ft
	sea level

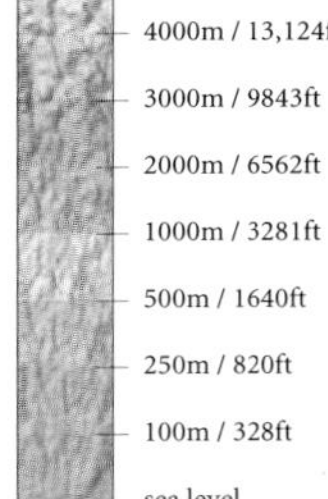

***Fine-textured volcanic soils** in the hilly Palouse region of eastern Washington are susceptible to erosion.*

Using the Land

Wheat farming in the east gives way to cattle ranching as rainfall decreases. Irrigated farming in the Snake River valley produces large yields of potatoes and other vegetables. Dairying and fruit-growing take place in the wet western lowlands between the mountain ranges.

The Urban/Rural Population Divide

urban 70% | rural 30%

0 10 20 30 40 50 60 70 80 90 100

Population Density	Total Land Area
20 people per sq mile (8 people per sq km)	493,782 sq miles (1,278,846 sq km)

Scale 1:3,750,000 (projection: Lambert Conformal Conic)

Km 0 10 20 40 60 80 100
Miles 0 10 20 40 60 80 100

Land use and agricultural distribution

- cattle
- poultry
- cereals
- fruit
- potatoes
- timber
- major towns
- pasture
- cropland
- forest

198

Transportation & Industry

Minerals and timber are extremely important in this region. Uranium, precious metals, copper, and coal are all mined, the latter in vast open-cast pits in Wyoming; oil and natural gas are extracted farther north. Manufacturing, notably related to the aerospace and electronics industries, is important in western cities.

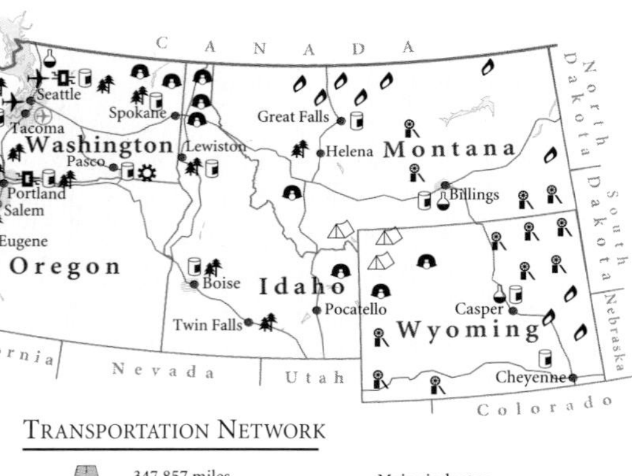

Transportation Network

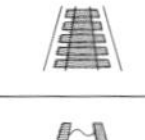

347,857 miles (556,571 km)
4,200 miles (6,720 km)
12,354 miles (19,766 km)
1,108 miles (1,782 km)

The Union Pacific Railroad has been in service across Wyoming since 1867. The route through the Rocky Mountains is now shared with the Interstate 80, a major east–west highway.

Major industry and infrastructure

- adventure tourism
- aerospace
- coal
- chemicals
- electronics
- food processing
- mining
- oil & gas
- timber processing
- major towns
- international airports
- major roads
- major industrial areas

***Seattle** lies in one of Puget Sound's many inlets. The city receives oil and other resources from Alaska, and benefits from expanding trade across the Pacific.*

***Crater Lake**, Oregon, is 6 miles (10 km) wide and 1,800 ft (600 m) deep. It marks the site of a volcanic cone, which collapsed after an eruption within the last 7,000 years.*

14 36 36

THE LANDSCAPE

THE ROCKY MOUNTAINS are flanked by lower parallel ranges, which spread onto the Great Plains in the east and surmount the broad lava plateau that extends westward. The Cascade Range divides the Columbia Basin from the coastlands, where the low areas around Puget Sound are broken by the steep, volcanic Olympic Mountains and the wooded hills of the Coast Ranges.

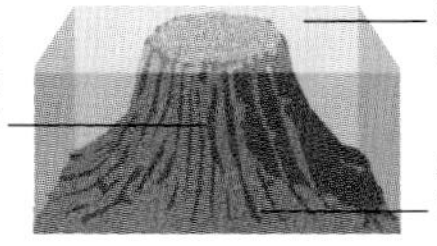

Molten rock cools, forming parallel columns

Surrounding strata eroded away

Molten rock wells up from the Earth's core

***Devil's Tower in Wyoming** is an igneous intrusion, formed below the Earth's surface. Molten rock intruded through cracks in the overlying strata and cooled. Over time, the softer rock layers have been eroded away, leaving only the tower standing.*

Glacial valleys on the seaward side of the Olympic Mountains receive about 142 inches (3,600 mm) of rain per year, supporting the only true rain forest of the northern hemisphere.

The Cascades are glacially scoured volcanic mountains, the highest of which is Mount Rainier, a dormant volcano 14,409 ft (4,392 m) high.

Coast Ranges

Mount St. Helens erupted in 1980, killing 57 people and devastating a huge area.

Puget Sound

Columbia Basin

Grand Coulee and the lesser *coulées* (ravines) were cut by cataclysmic floods, from the release of an ice-dammed lake, at the end of the last Ice Age.

The Continental Divide, or watershed, crosses the Lewis Range. From here, rivers flow west to Hudson Bay, south to the Gulf of Mexico and east to the Pacific Ocean.

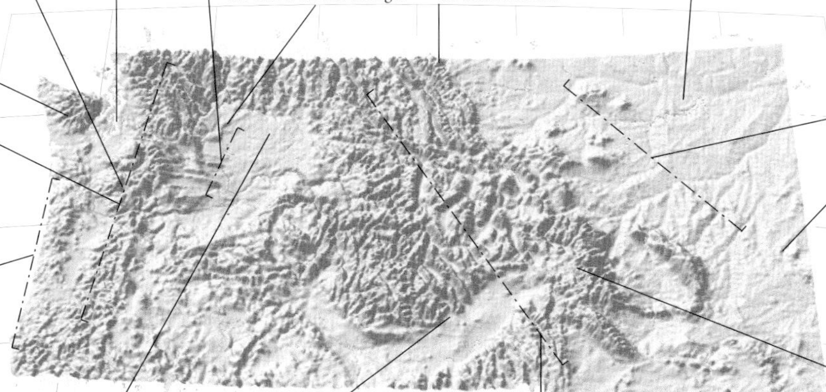

***Piney Buttes** are the remnants of an older, higher land surface gradually weathered and eroded into isolated outcrops with flat tops and steep sides.*

Great Plains

Devil's Tower

The plateaus of the Columbia and Snake Rivers represent one of the world's largest accumulations of lava. Over 5 million years ago, successive flows of molten basalt buried the existing land surface by up to 450 ft (150 m).

The contorted rock shapes at "Craters of the Moon" National Monument in Idaho were left 2,000 years ago by the sporadic upwelling of viscous lava from fissures in the basalt plateau.

Rocky Mountains

***Water from the hot springs** in Yellowstone National Park deposits minerals as it cools in rock pools. Long periods of deposition have created these rock terraces.*

USA: California & Nevada

The Gold Rush of 1849 attracted the first major wave of European settlers to the West Coast. The pleasant climate, beautiful scenery, and dynamic economy continue to attract immigrants – despite the ever-present danger of earthquakes – and California has become the US's most populous state. The overwhelmingly urban population is concentrated in the vast conurbations of Los Angeles, San Francisco, and San Diego; new immigrants include people from South Korea, the Philippines, Vietnam, and Mexico. Nevada's arid lands were initially exploited for minerals; in recent years, revenue from mining has been superseded by income from the tourist and gambling centers of Las Vegas and Reno.

Map Key

Population	Elevation
1 million to 5 million	4000m / 13,124ft
500,000 to 1 million	3000m / 9843ft
100,000 to 500,000	2000m / 6562ft
50,000 to 100,000	1000m / 3281ft
10,000 to 50,000	500m / 1640ft
below 10,000	250m / 820ft
	100m / 328ft
	sea level

Scale 1:3,000,000
(projection: Lambert Conformal Conic)

Km 0 5 10 20 30 40 50 60 70 80

Miles 0 5 10 20 30 40 50 60 70 80

Transportation & Industry

Nevada's rich mineral reserves ushered in a period of mining wealth that has now been replaced by revenue generated from gambling. California supports a broad set of activities including defense-related industries and research and development facilities. "Silicon Valley," near San Francisco, is a world-leading center for microelectronics, while tourism and the Los Angeles film industry also generate large incomes.

DUNES
OASIS
CASINO

Gambling was legalized in Nevada in 1931. Las Vegas has since become the center of this multimillion dollar industry.

Oregon
Idaho
Utah
Arizona
Nevada
California
Reno
Ely
Carson City
Sacramento
Oakland
San Francisco
San Jose
Bakersfield
Las Vegas
Los Angeles
San Diego
PACIFIC OCEAN
MEXICO
Major industry and infrastructure
aerospace
car manufacture
defense
film industry
finance
food processing
gambling
hi-tech industry
mining
pharmaceuticals
research & development
textiles
tourism
major towns
international airports
major roads
major industrial areas

Transportation Network

211,459 miles (338,334 km)
2,944 miles (4,710 km)
7,872 miles (12,595 km)
190 miles (306 km)

In California, the motor vehicle is a vital part of daily life, and an extensive freeway system runs throughout the state, which has a greater *per capita* car ownership than anywhere else in the world.

The Landscape

The broad Central Valley divides California's coastal mountains from the Sierra Nevada. The San Andreas Fault, running beneath much of the state, is the site of frequent earth tremors and sometimes more serious earthquakes. East of the Sierra Nevada, the landscape is characterized by the basin and range topography with stony deserts and many salt lakes.

Rising molten rock causes stretching of the Earth's crust
Extensive cracking (faulting) uplifted a series of ridges
As ridges are eroded they fill intervening valleys with sediments

Molten rock (magma) welling up to form a dome in the Earth's interior, causes the brittle surface rocks to stretch and crack. Some areas were uplifted to form mountains (ranges), while others sank to form flat valleys (basins).

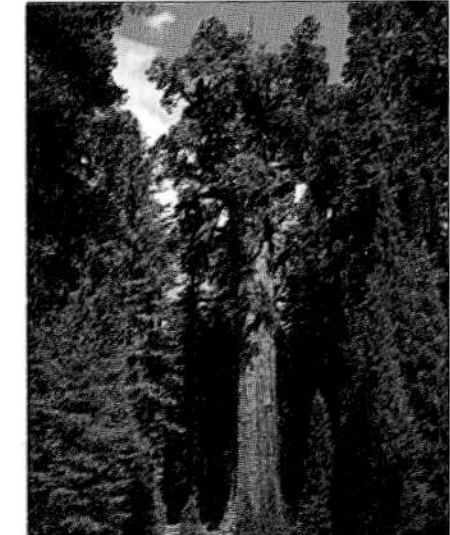

***The General Sherman** sequoia tree in Sequoia National Park is 3,000 years old. At 275 ft (84 m), it is one of the largest living things on Earth.*

Most of California's agriculture is confined to the fertile and extensively irrigated Central Valley, running between the Coast Ranges and the Sierra Nevada. It incorporates the San Joaquin and Sacramento valleys.

The dramatic granitic rock formations of Half Dome and El Capitan, and the verdant coniferous forests, attract millions of visitors annually to Yosemite National Park in the Sierra Nevada.

Sierra Nevada

The Great Basin dominates most of Nevada's topography, containing large open basins, punctuated by eroded features such as *buttes* and *mesas*. River flow tends to be seasonal, depending on spring showers and winter snowmelt.

Wheeler Peak is home to some of the world's oldest living trees, bristlecone pines, which live for up to 5,000 years.

When the Hoover Dam across the Colorado River was completed in 1936, it created Lake Mead, one of the largest artificial lakes in the world, extending for 115 miles (285 km) upstream.

The San Andreas Fault is a transverse fault which extends for 650 miles (1,050 km) through California. Major earthquakes occur when the land either side of the fault moves at different rates. San Francisco was devastated by an earthquake in 1906.

Death Valley

***Named by migrating settlers** in 1849, Death Valley is the driest, hottest place in North America, as well as being the lowest point on land in the western hemisphere, at 282 ft (86 m) below sea level.*

The sparsely populated Mojave Desert receives less than 8 inches (200 mm) of rainfall a year. It is used extensively for testing weapons and other military purposes.

The Salton Sea was created accidentally between 1905 and 1907 when an irrigation channel from the Colorado River broke its banks and formed this salty 300-sq-mile (777-sq-km) landlocked lake.

Amargosa Desert

***The Sierra Nevada** create a "rainshadow," preventing rain from reaching much of Nevada. Pacific air masses, passing over the mountains, are stripped of their moisture.*

Using the Land

California is the leading agricultural producer in the US, although low rainfall makes irrigation essential. The long growing season and abundant sunshine allow many crops to be grown in the fertile Central Valley, including grapes, citrus fruits, vegetables, and cotton. Almost 17 million acres (6.8 million ha) of California's forests are used commercially. Nevada's arid climate and poor soil are largely unsuitable for agriculture; 85% of its land is state-owned and large areas are used for underground of testing nuclear weapons.

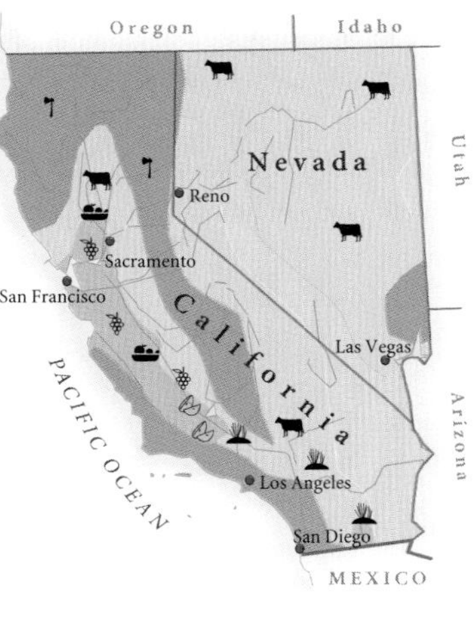

Land use and agricultural distribution
cattle
citrus fruits
fruit
irrigation
timber
vineyards
major towns
pasture
cropland
forest
desert
Oregon
Idaho
Utah
Arizona
Nevada
California
Reno
Sacramento
San Francisco
Las Vegas
Los Angeles
San Diego
PACIFIC OCEAN
MEXICO

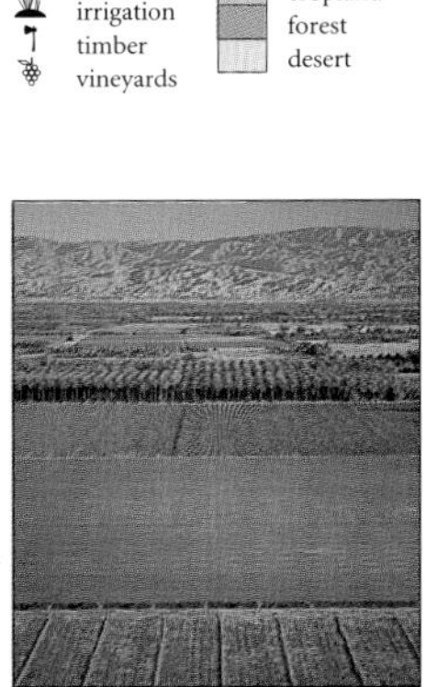

***Without considerable** irrigation, this fertile valley at Palm Springs would still be part of the Sonoran Desert. California's farmers account for about 80% of the state's total water usage.*

The Urban/Rural Population Divide

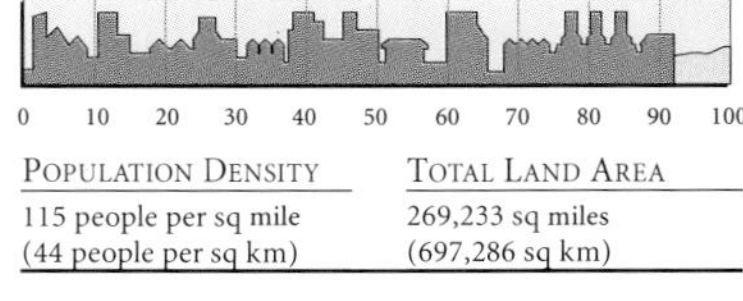

urban 92%
rural 8%
0 10 20 30 40 50 60 70 80 90 100

Population Density	Total Land Area
115 people per sq mile (44 people per sq km)	269,233 sq miles (697,286 sq km)

Smith River
Crescent City
Klamath Mountains
Siskiyou Mountains
Happy Camp
Klamath
Klamath River
Orick
Orleans
Salmon Mountains
Coast Ranges
Thompson 2741m
Mckinleyville
Arcata
Blue Lake
Eureka
Humboldt Bay
Trinity River
Weaverville
Ferndale
Fortuna
Rio Dell
Scotia
Hayfork
Cape Mendocino
Eel River
Weott
Garberville
Covelo
Snow Mountain 2151m
Laytonville
Fort Bragg
Willits
Mendocino
Ukiah
Upper Lake
Lakeport
Kelseyville
Point Arena
Boonville
Hopland
Gualala
Cloverdale
Healdsburg
Santa Rosa
Sebastopol
Bodega Head
Point Reyes
San Francisco
PACIFIC

198

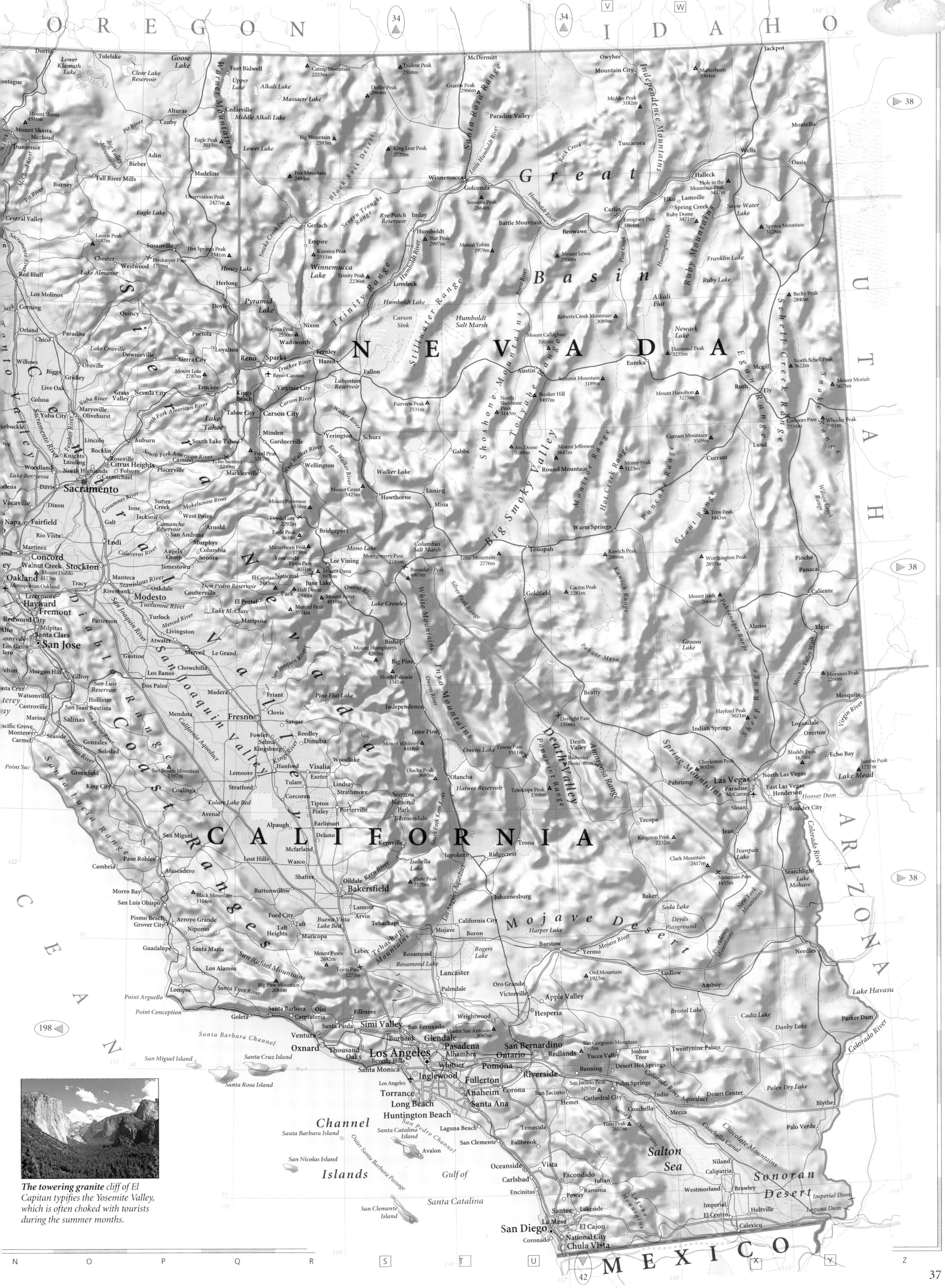

OREGON • IDAHO • NEVADA • CALIFORNIA • UTAH • ARIZONA • MEXICO

34 34 V W

Great Basin

Dorris, Tulelake, Lower Klamath Lake, Montague, Mount Shasta 4316m, Mccloud, Dunsmuir, Clear Lake Reservoir, Goose Lake, Upper Lake, Fort Bidwell, Alkali Lake, Cedarville, Alturas, Canby, Adin, Middle Alkali Lake, Eagle Peak 3015m, Catnip Mountain 2223m, Trident Peak 2558m, Duffer Peak 2864m, McDermitt, Owyhee, Mountain City, Jackpot, Matterhorn 3304m

Pit River, Burney, Fall River Mills, Bieber, Madeline, Observation Peak 2427m, Big Mountain 2593m, Fox Mountain 2494m, King Lear Peak 2720m, Paradise Valley, Winnemucca, Golconda, Tuscarora, Carlin, Elko, Lamoille, McAfee Peak 3182m, Wells, Oasis, Montello

Central Valley, Mount Shasta, Lassen Peak 3187m, Susanville, Honey Lake, Hot Springs Peak 2341m, Kumiva Peak 2511m, Sonoma Peak 2864m, Battle Mountain, Beowawe, Humboldt River, Mount Lewis 2990m, Spring Creek, Ruby Dome 3471m, Snow Water Lake, Spruce Mountain 3228m

Red Bluff, Los Molinos, Corning, Orland, Chico, Paradise, Chester, Westwood, Fredonyer Pass 1759m, Herlong, Doyle, Pyramid Lake, Nixon, Fernley, Fallon, Lahontan Reservoir, Star Peak 2997m, Mount Tobin 2979m, Humboldt Salt Marsh, Mount Callaghan 3105m, Roberts Creek Mountain 3089m, Newark Lake, Alkali Flat, Diamond Peak 3235m, Becky Peak 2840m, Franklin Lake, Ruby Lake, North Schell Peak 3622m

Willows, Biggs, Gridley, Live Oak, Colusa, Yuba City, Marysville, Olivehurst, Lincoln, Rocklin, Roseville, Citrus Heights, North Highlands, Carmichael, Grass Valley, Nevada City, Downieville, Sierra City, Mount Lola 2787m, Truckee, Kings Beach, Tahoe City, Lake Tahoe, Carson City, Virginia City, Yerington, Schurz, Gabbs, Round Mountain, Austin, Eureka, Summit Mountain 3189m, Bunker Hill 3497m, Mount Hamilton 3275m, Ruth, Ely, McGill, Mount Moriah 3679m, Wheeler Peak 3981m, Lund, Currant

Sacramento, Davis, Vacaville, Fairfield, Napa, Dixon, Rio Vista, Lodi, Galt, Ione, Jackson, Stockton, Concord, Walnut Creek, Mount Diablo 1173m, Oakland, Livermore, Hayward, Fremont, Redwood City, Milpitas, Santa Clara, San Jose, Morgan Hill, Gilroy, Los Banos, Dos Palos, Madera, Chowchilla, Merced, Le Grand, Fresno, Clovis, Sanger, Reedley, Dinuba, Bishop, Big Pine, North Palisade 4341m, Mount Humphreys 4263m, Mount Whitney 4418m, Lone Pine, Owens Lake, Towne Pass 1511m, Death Valley, Badwater, Beatty, Las Vegas, North Las Vegas, Henderson, Boulder City, Hoover Dam, Lake Mead, Mormon Peak 2260m, Mesquite, Logandale, Overton, Echo Bay, Jumbo Peak 1751m, Virgin River, Colorado River

San Jose, Watsonville, Castroville, Salinas, Hollister, San Juan Bautista, Pacific Grove, Monterey, Carmel, Seaside, Marina, Gonzales, Soledad, Greenfield, King City, Coalinga, Avenal, Hanford, Lemoore, Visalia, Exeter, Tulare, Corcoran, Tipton, Pixley, Porterville, Delano, McFarland, Wasco, Lost Hills, Shafter, Oildale, Bakersfield, Buttonwillow, Lamont, Arvin, Tehachapi, Mojave, California City, Boron, Barstow, Yermo, Ludlow, Amboy, Needles, Lake Havasu, Parker Dam

Point Sur, Cambria, Paso Robles, Atascadero, Morro Bay, San Luis Obispo, Pismo Beach, Grover City, Arroyo Grande, Nipomo, Guadalupe, Santa Maria, Los Alamos, Lompoc, Point Arguello, Point Conception, Goleta, Santa Barbara, Ojai, Carpinteria, Ventura, Oxnard, Fillmore, Simi Valley, San Fernando, Thousand Oaks, Burbank, Glendale, Pasadena, Los Angeles, Beverly Hills, Santa Monica, Inglewood, Torrance, Long Beach, Huntington Beach, Santa Ana, Anaheim, Fullerton, Whittier, Pomona, Ontario, San Bernardino, Redlands, Riverside, Corona, Hemet, San Jacinto, Banning, Palm Springs, Indio, Coachella, Mecca, Desert Center, Blythe, Palo Verde

Santa Barbara Channel, San Miguel Island, Santa Rosa Island, Santa Cruz Island, Anacapa Island, Santa Barbara Island, San Nicolas Island, San Clemente Island, Santa Catalina Island, Oceanside, Carlsbad, Encinitas, Escondido, Vista, Julian, Ramona, Poway, San Diego, El Cajon, La Mesa, Lakeside, Santee, National City, Chula Vista, Coronado, Imperial, El Centro, Calexico, Brawley, Westmorland, Calipatria, Niland, Salton Sea, Holtville, Sonoran Desert, Imperial Dam, Laguna Dam

MEXICO

198

***The towering granite** cliff of El Capitan typifies the Yosemite Valley, which is often choked with tourists during the summer months.*

38 38 38

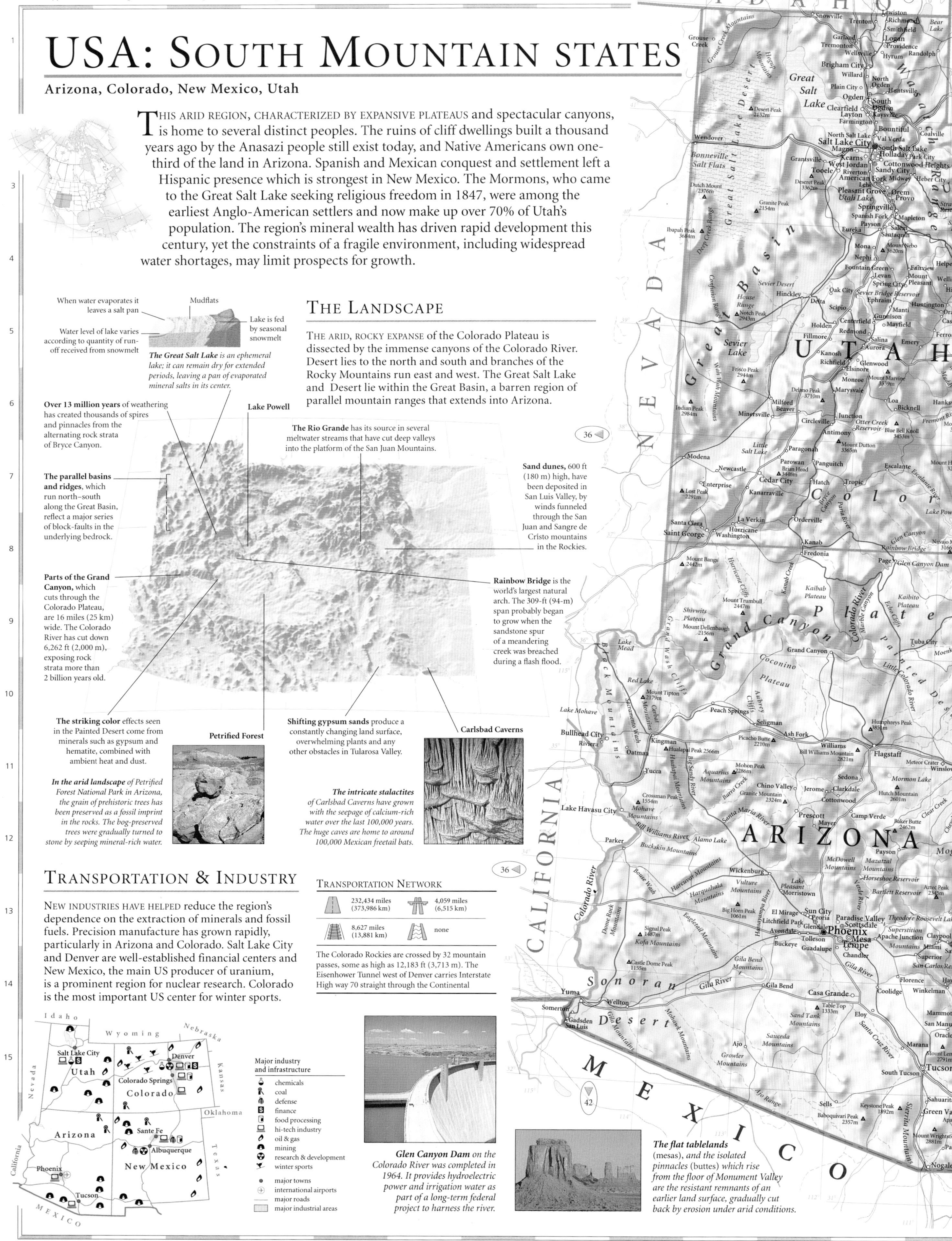

USA: South Mountain states

Arizona, Colorado, New Mexico, Utah

This arid region, characterized by expansive plateaus and spectacular canyons, is home to several distinct peoples. The ruins of cliff dwellings built a thousand years ago by the Anasazi people still exist today, and Native Americans own one-third of the land in Arizona. Spanish and Mexican conquest and settlement left a Hispanic presence which is strongest in New Mexico. The Mormons, who came to the Great Salt Lake seeking religious freedom in 1847, were among the earliest Anglo-American settlers and now make up over 70% of Utah's population. The region's mineral wealth has driven rapid development this century, yet the constraints of a fragile environment, including widespread water shortages, may limit prospects for growth.

The Landscape

The arid, rocky expanse of the Colorado Plateau is dissected by the immense canyons of the Colorado River. Desert lies to the north and south and branches of the Rocky Mountains run east and west. The Great Salt Lake and Desert lie within the Great Basin, a barren region of parallel mountain ranges that extends into Arizona.

When water evaporates it leaves a salt pan

Mudflats

Lake is fed by seasonal snowmelt

Water level of lake varies according to quantity of run-off received from snowmelt

The Great Salt Lake is an ephemeral lake; it can remain dry for extended periods, leaving a pan of evaporated mineral salts in its center.

Over 13 million years of weathering has created thousands of spires and pinnacles from the alternating rock strata of Bryce Canyon.

Lake Powell

The Rio Grande has its source in several meltwater streams that have cut deep valleys into the platform of the San Juan Mountains.

The parallel basins and ridges, which run north–south along the Great Basin, reflect a major series of block-faults in the underlying bedrock.

Sand dunes, 600 ft (180 m) high, have been deposited in San Luis Valley, by winds funneled through the San Juan and Sangre de Cristo mountains in the Rockies.

Parts of the Grand Canyon, which cuts through the Colorado Plateau, are 16 miles (25 km) wide. The Colorado River has cut down 6,262 ft (2,000 m), exposing rock strata more than 2 billion years old.

Rainbow Bridge is the world's largest natural arch. The 309-ft (94-m) span probably began to grow when the sandstone spur of a meandering creek was breached during a flash flood.

The striking color effects seen in the Painted Desert come from minerals such as gypsum and hematite, combined with ambient heat and dust.

Petrified Forest

In the arid landscape of Petrified Forest National Park in Arizona, the grain of prehistoric trees has been preserved as a fossil imprint in the rocks. The bog-preserved trees were gradually turned to stone by seeping mineral-rich water.

Shifting gypsum sands produce a constantly changing land surface, overwhelming plants and any other obstacles in Tularosa Valley.

Carlsbad Caverns

The intricate stalactites *of Carlsbad Caverns have grown with the seepage of calcium-rich water over the last 100,000 years. The huge caves are home to around 100,000 Mexican freetail bats.*

Transportation & Industry

New industries have helped reduce the region's dependence on the extraction of minerals and fossil fuels. Precision manufacture has grown rapidly, particularly in Arizona and Colorado. Salt Lake City and Denver are well-established financial centers and New Mexico, the main US producer of uranium, is a prominent region for nuclear research. Colorado is the most important US center for winter sports.

Transportation Network

(roads)	232,434 miles (373,986 km)	(highways)	4,059 miles (6,515 km)
(railways)	8,627 miles (13,881 km)	(waterways)	none

The Colorado Rockies are crossed by 32 mountain passes, some as high as 12,183 ft (3,713 m). The Eisenhower Tunnel west of Denver carries Interstate High way 70 straight through the Continental

Major industry and infrastructure: chemicals, coal, defense, finance, food processing, hi-tech industry, oil & gas, mining, research & development, winter sports, major towns, international airports, major roads, major industrial areas

Glen Canyon Dam *on the Colorado River was completed in 1964. It provides hydroelectric power and irrigation water as part of a long-term federal project to harness the river.*

The flat tablelands (mesas), and the isolated pinnacles (buttes) which rise from the floor of Monument Valley are the resistant remnants of an earlier land surface, gradually cut back by erosion under arid conditions.

34
36
36
42

***Bonneville Salt Flats** are in the Great Salt Lake. Sodium chloride (salt), magnesium, and other minerals are commercially extracted from these flats.*

SCALE 1:3,500,000
(projection: Lambert Conformal Conic)

Km 0 10 20 40 60 80 100

Miles 0 10 20 40 60 80 100

Map Key

POPULATION

- 500,000 to 1 million
- 100,000 to 500,000
- 50,000 to 100,000
- 10,000 to 50,000
- below 10,000

ELEVATION

- 4000m / 13124ft
- 3000m / 9843ft
- 2000m / 6562ft
- 1000m / 3281ft
- 500m / 1640ft
- 250m / 820ft
- 100m / 328ft
- sea level

WYOMING

NEBRASKA

KANSAS

OKLAHOMA

TEXAS

COLORADO

NEW MEXICO

ROCKY MOUNTAINS

MEXICO

***A glacially eroded valley** in Rocky Mountain National Park, Colorado. There are 1,500 peaks exceeding 10,000 ft (3,000 m) within the state, six times the number of major mountains found in the Swiss Alps.*

Using The Land

Livestock, particularly cattle ranching, is the main source of agricultural income. The region has a long growing season and areas of rich soil, but depends heavily on water for irrigation. Crops include corn and wheat in eastern areas and chili peppers, fruit, and cotton aided by additional irrigation.

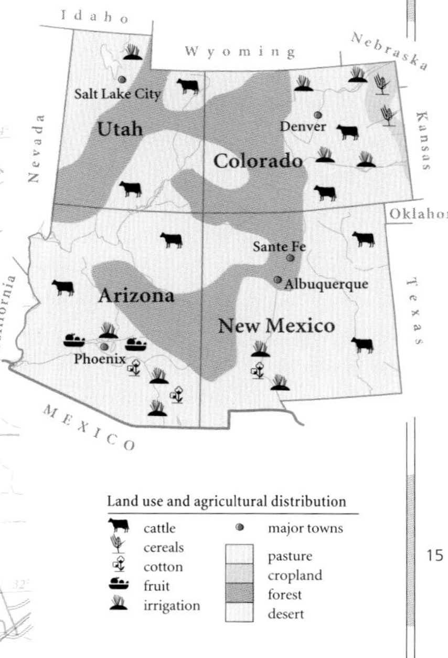

Idaho, Wyoming, Nebraska, Kansas, Oklahoma, Texas, Mexico, California, Nevada, Utah, Colorado, Arizona, New Mexico, Salt Lake City, Denver, Sante Fe, Albuquerque, Phoenix

Land use and agricultural distribution

- cattle
- cereals
- cotton
- fruit
- irrigation
- major towns
- pasture
- cropland
- forest
- desert

***Cattle ranching** was introduced to New Mexico via Texas in the last century, and has become the principal agricultural land use across this region.*

The Urban/Rural Population Divide

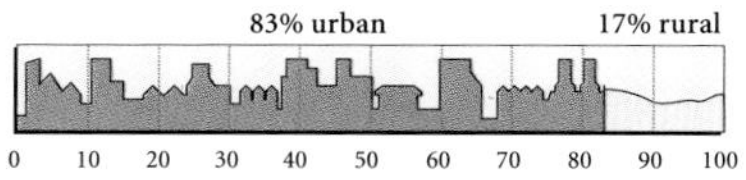

83% urban | 17% rural

0 10 20 30 40 50 60 70 80 90 100

Population Density	Total Land Area
9 people per sq mile (24 people per sq km)	424,738 sq miles (1,100,028 sq km)

USA: Hawaii

THE 122 ISLANDS of the Hawaiian archipelago, part of Polynesia, are the peaks of the world's largest volcanoes. They rise approximately 6 miles (9.7 km) from the floor of the Pacific Ocean. The largest, the island of Hawaii, remains highly active. Hawaii became the 50th state in 1959. A tradition of receiving immigrant workers is reflected in the islands' ethnic diversity, with peoples drawn from around the rim of the Pacific. Only 2% of the current population are native Polynesians.

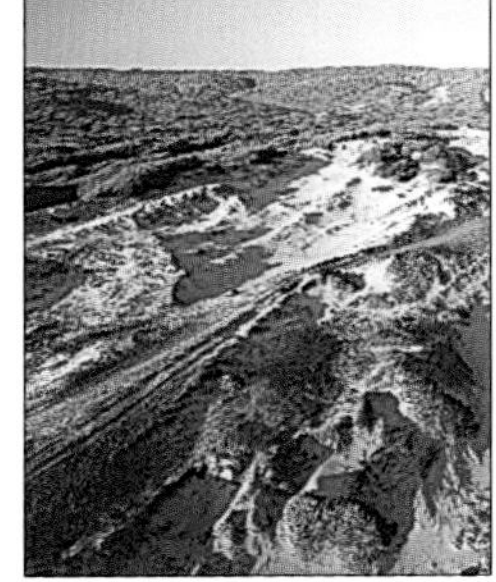

***The island of Molokai** is formed from volcanic rock. Mature sand dunes cover the rocks in coastal areas.*

Transportation & Industry

TOURISM DOMINATES the economy, with over half of the population employed in the service industry. The naval base at Pearl Harbor is also a major of employer. Industry is concentrated on the island of Oahu and relies mostly on imported materials, while agricultural produce is processed locally.

Transportation Network

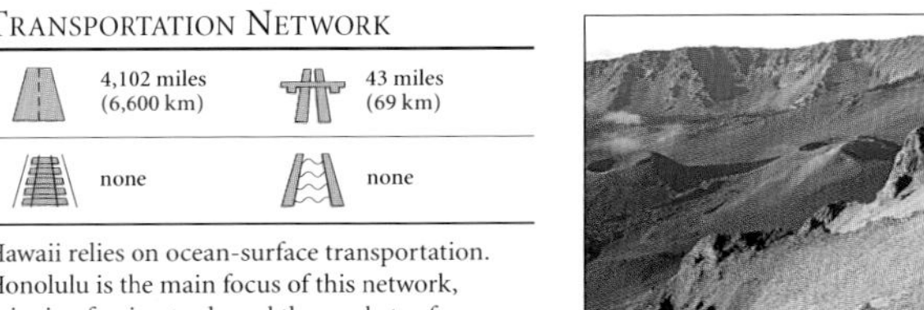

4,102 miles (6,600 km)	43 miles (69 km)
none	none

Hawaii relies on ocean-surface transportation. Honolulu is the main focus of this network, bringing foreign trade and the markets of mainland US to Hawaii's outer islands.

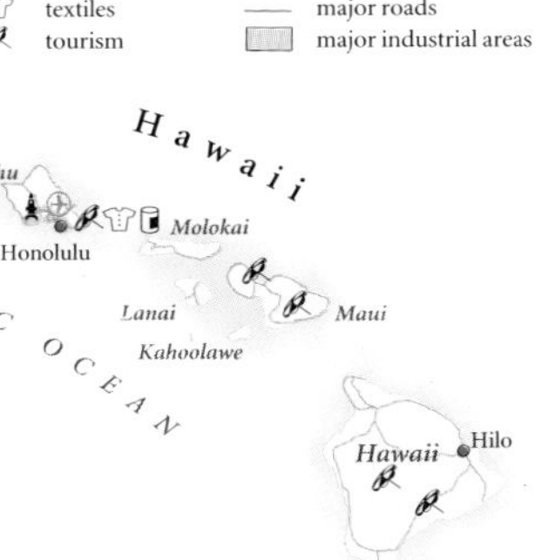

***Haleakala's extinct volcanic crater** is the world's largest. The giant caldera, containing many secondary cones, is 2,000 ft (600 m) deep and 20 miles (32 km) in circumference.*

Major industry and infrastructure
- food processing
- military base
- textiles
- tourism
- major towns
- international airports
- major roads
- major industrial areas

SCALE 1:3,500,000
(projection: Lambert Conformal Conic)

Map Key

POPULATION
- 100,000 to 500,000
- 50,000 to 100,000
- 10,000 to 50,000
- below 10,000

ELEVATION
- 4000m / 13,124ft
- 3000m / 9843ft
- 2000m / 6562ft
- 1000m / 3281ft
- 500m / 1640ft
- 250m / 820ft
- 100m / 328ft
- sea level

Using the Land & Sea

THE VOLCANIC SOILS are extremely fertile and the climate hot and humid on the lower slopes, supporting large commercial plantations growing sugar cane, bananas, pineapples, and other tropical fruit, as well as nursery plants and flowers. Some land is given to pasture, particularly for beef and dairy cattle.

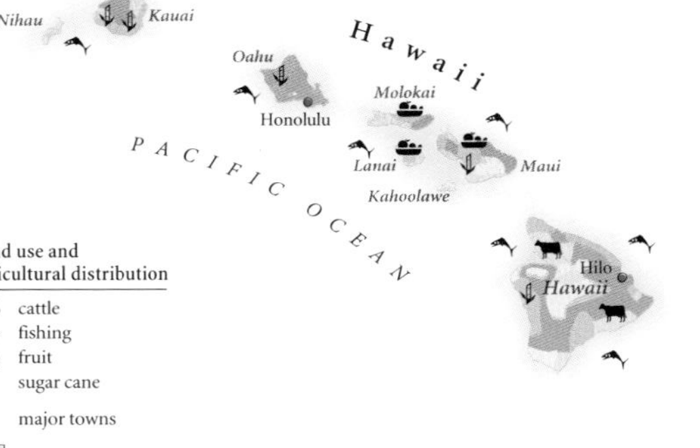

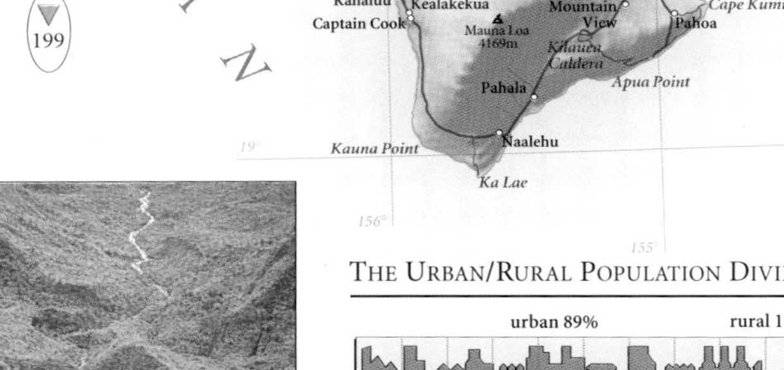

***The island of Kauai** is one of the wettest places in the world, receiving some 450 inches (11,500 mm) of rain a year.*

Land use and agricultural distribution

- cattle
- fishing
- fruit
- sugar cane
- major towns
- pasture
- cropland
- forest
- mountain region

The Urban/Rural Population Divide

urban 89% — rural 11%

Population Density	Total Land Area
180 people per sq mile (69 people per sq km)	592,704 sq miles (1,535,505 sq km)

Using the Land & Sea

THE ICE-FREE COASTLINE of Alaska provides access to salmon fisheries and more than 5.5 million acres (2.2 million ha) of forest. Most of Alaska is uncultivable, and around 90% of food is imported. Barley, hay, and hothouse products are grown around Anchorage, where dairy farming is also concentrated.

The Urban/Rural Population Divide

urban 68% — rural 32%

Population Density	Total Land Area
1 person per sq mile (0.3 people per sq km)	586,412 sq miles (1,518,800 sq km)

***A raft of timber** from the Tongass Forest is hauled by a tug, bound for the pulp mills of the Alaskan coast between Juneau and Ketchikan.*

Map Key

POPULATION
- 100,000 to 500,000
- 50,000 to 100,000
- 10,000 to 50,000
- below 10,000

ELEVATION
- 4000m / 13,124ft
- 3000m / 9843ft
- 2000m / 6562ft
- 1000m / 3281ft
- 500m / 1640ft
- 250m / 820ft
- 100m / 328ft
- sea level

SCALE 1:8,000,000
(projection: Lambert Conformal Conic)

125
199

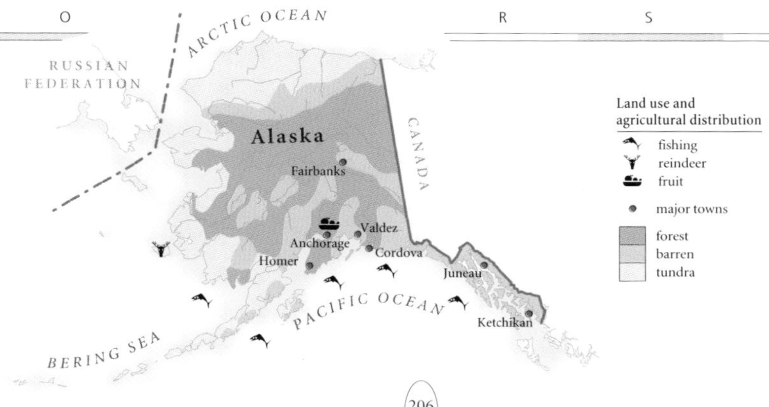

USA: ALASKA

JUST OVER HALF A MILLION people live in Alaska, a wilderness of ice, forest, mountains, and plains, purchased from Russia in 1867 and covering twice the area of Texas. The discovery of large oil reserves has brought prosperity to the US's "last frontier," while advancing the need to preserve natural habitats and the traditional livelihoods of indigenous peoples, such as the Aleuts and Inupiaq.

Land use and agricultural distribution

- fishing
- reindeer
- fruit
- major towns
- forest
- barren
- tundra

THE LANDSCAPE

THE MOUNTAINS OF THE PACIFIC COAST culminate in the heavily glaciated Alaska Range and extend west to the Alaska Peninsula and the great volcanic arc of the Aleutian Islands. The interior plains are drained by the Yukon River and bounded by the bare, jagged peaks of the Brooks Range to the north.

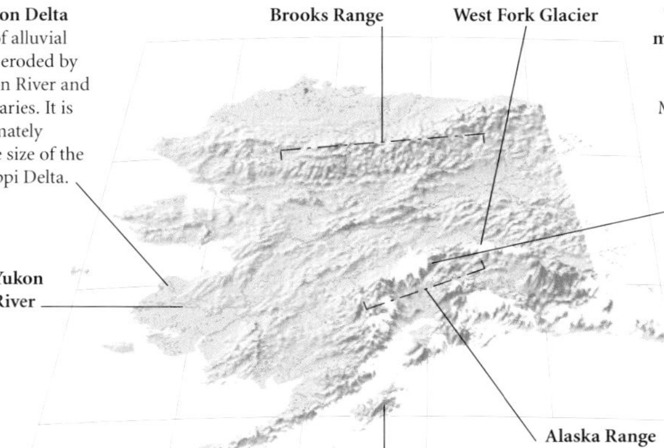

The Yukon Delta is a fan of alluvial material eroded by the Yukon River and its tributaries. It is approximately twice the size of the Mississippi Delta.

Brooks Range

West Fork Glacier

The ten highest mountains in the US are all in the Alaska Range; Mount McKinley *(Denali)*, at 20,321 ft (6,194 m), is the highest.

Yukon River

Alaska Range

The arc of the Aleutian Islands marks the boundary between the Eurasian and Pacific tectonic plates.

Fjords are found along the coast where valleys, deeply excavated by large glaciers, were inundated by rising seas.

***By August**, the Alaska Range is covered with autumnal tundra vegetation.*

West Fork Glacier

The surging ice mass shears along the glacier margin

Deep crevasses divide the front of the surging glacier into large ice blocks

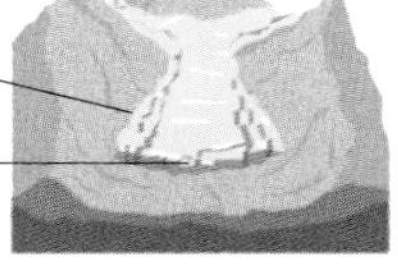

***Surging glaciers** make rapid and dramatic advances, normally after periods of snow accumulation. West Fork Glacier in the Susitna River Basin traveled 2.5 miles (4 km) in 1987.*

TRANSPORTATION & INDUSTRY

LARGE AREAS OF ALASKA are undeveloped, and much of the existing infrastructure is a legacy of Cold War military investment. Mineral ores, including gold, have been mined for over a century, but the oil business now dominates the economy. Processing industries such as paper-pulp mills supply Japan and other markets on the Pacific Rim.

TRANSPORTATION NETWORK

13,524 miles (21,760 km)	49 miles (78 km)
482 miles (772 km)	none

Nearly 80 million gallons of oil are pumped through the Trans-Alaska Pipeline every day. The oil takes six days to travel the 789 miles (1,262 km) from Prudhoe Bay to Valdez.

Major industry and infrastructure

- fish processing
- gold mining
- oil
- timber processing
- major towns
- international airports
- major roads

***The Trans-Alaska Pipeline** has carried crude oil from Prudhoe Bay since 1977. The oilfield is the largest in the US and is estimated to be equal to the biggest oilfields of the Persian Gulf.*

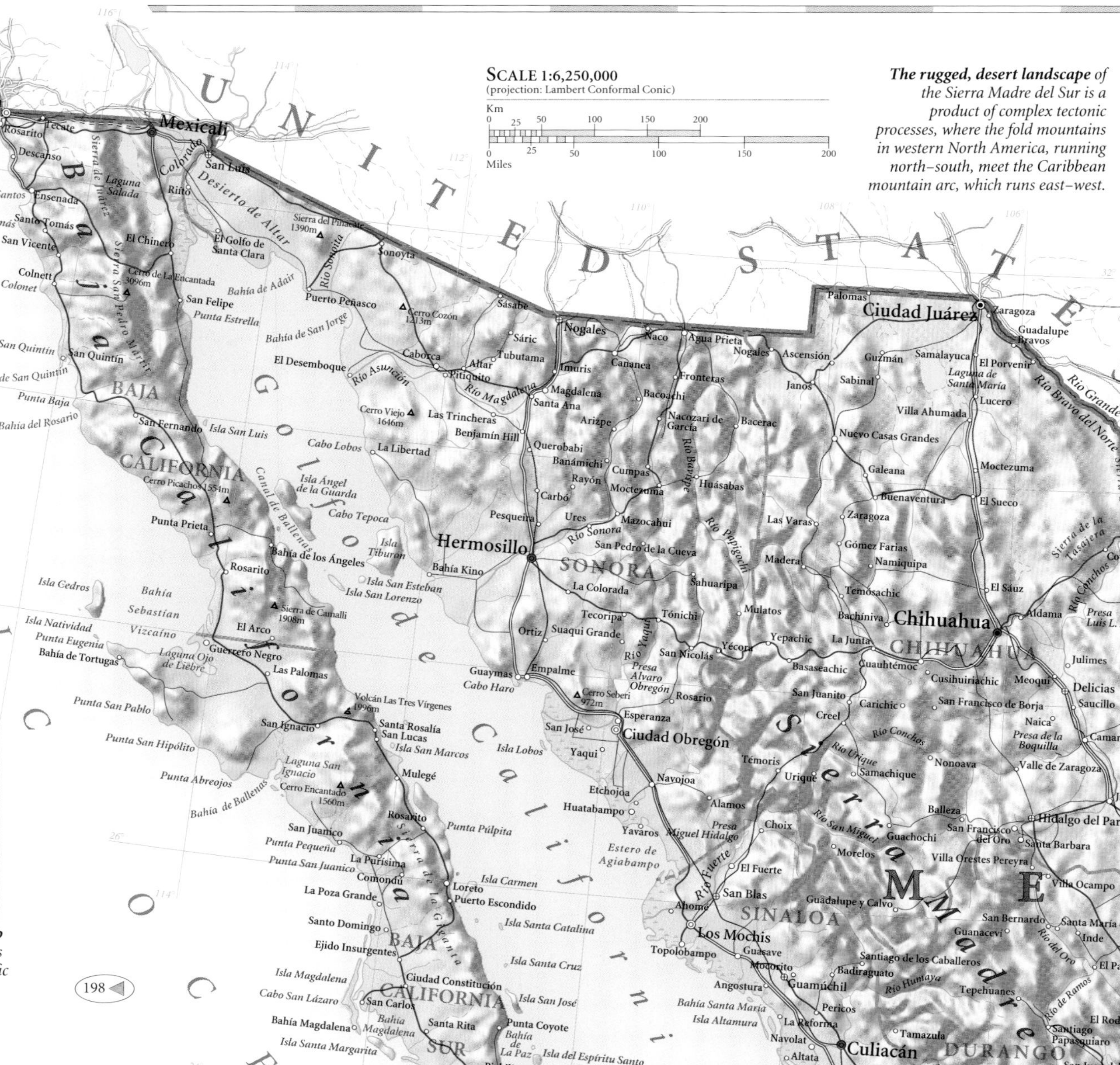

SCALE 1:6,250,000
(projection: Lambert Conformal Conic)

Km 0 25 50 100 150 200
Miles 0 25 50 100 150 200

The rugged, desert landscape *of the Sierra Madre del Sur is a product of complex tectonic processes, where the fold mountains in western North America, running north–south, meet the Caribbean mountain arc, which runs east–west.*

Wave action has cut steep cliffs *into the igneous rocks of Isla Cedros, off the Pacific coast of Baja California. The island is home to sea lions, reptiles, and deer.*

MEXICO

MEXICO POSSESSES rich mineral resources, limited agricultural land, and the world's largest and fastest growing Spanish-speaking population. Most Mexicans are *mestizo* – of Hispanic and Native American heritage – although Amerindian communities still exist in the south, 400 years after Spain destroyed the Aztec empire. Much of the arid north is sparsely inhabited, while Mexico City is becoming the world's most populous city. Conflict with the US has long overshadowed Mexico's development, but the North American Free Trade Agreement offers a more benign relationship, which may offset Mexico's hyperinflation, foreign debt, unequal wealth distribution, and political instability.

USING THE LAND & SEA

CORN OCCUPIES much of the cultivated area. Commercial plantations of coffee, sugar, vanilla, and cotton are found along the Gulf coastal plain and in irrigated parts of the arid north, which is otherwise used for extensive ranching. Fishing is important, particularly shellfish for export. A soaring population has created the need for grain imports since 1980.

THE URBAN/RURAL POPULATION DIVIDE

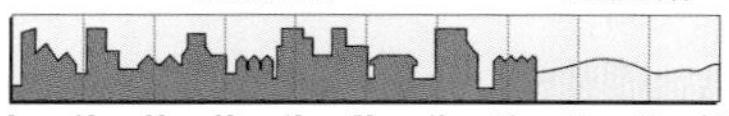

urban 74% rural 26%

0 10 20 30 40 50 60 70 80 90 100

POPULATION DENSITY	TOTAL LAND AREA
119 people per sq mile (46 people per sq km)	755,865 sq miles (1,958,200 sq km)

Land use and agricultural distribution

- cattle
- coffee
- corn
- cotton
- fishing
- shellfish
- sugar cane
- timber
- vanilla
- capital cities
- major towns
- pasture
- cropland
- forest
- desert

Coffee beans spread out to dry *in the sun. Coffee, grown mainly on the Gulf coastal plain, is Mexico's most valuable export crop.*

MEXICO: ADMINISTRATIVE REGIONS

① DISTRITO FEDERAL

MAP KEY

POPULATION

- above 5 million
- 1 million to 5 million
- 500,000 to 1 million
- 100,000 to 500,000
- 50,000 to 100,000
- 10,000 to 50,000
- below 10,000

ELEVATION

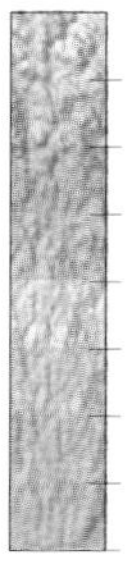

- 4000m / 13,124ft
- 3000m / 9843ft
- 2000m / 6562ft
- 1000m / 3281ft
- 500m / 1640ft
- 250m / 820ft
- 100m / 328ft
- sea level

THE LANDSCAPE

THE GREAT CENTRAL PLATEAU rises gently southward from the Rio Grande, isolated from the coastal plains by the Sierra Madre Oriental and Occidental. The two ranges converge from the east and west respectively, culminating in high volcanic peaks around Mexico City. Further ranges of the Sierra Madre rise to the south of the Balsas Basin, skirted by the low-lying Isthmus of Tehuantepec (*Istmo de Tehuantepec*) and Yucatan Peninsula.

Formation of the Gulf of California

Direction of plate movement

Baja California

Gulf of California

Transform fault

Spreading oceanic ridge

Edge of continental crust

The Gulf of California *(Golfo de California) began to open out about 4 million years ago as a result of rifting and plate displacement along transform faults.*

The long, narrow, extremely arid peninsula of Baja (lower) California is an elongated granite block, separated from the mainland by the flooded rift valley of the Gulf of California (*Golfo de California*).

Wave action has constructed sandbars that shelter lagoons along the shore of the Gulf coastal plain.

The dormant cone of Volcán Pico de Orizaba is, at 18,700 ft (5,700 m), the highest peak in Mexico. In North America, only Mount McKinley and Mount Logan are taller.

Tropical rain forest abounds *in the Yucatan Peninsula, a broad, low limestone shelf. Rivers are rare due to the porous nature of limestone, so the forest is fed mainly by streams and underground water.*

Sierra Madre Oriental

Rio Grande

The heavily forested Isthmus of Tehuantepec (*Istmo de Tehuantepec*) is a *graben*, a low-lying trough created by downward movement of the bedrock between two fault lines.

Sierra Madre Occidental

Río Balsas

Popocatépetl

Popocatépetl *is a dormant volcano, part of the Pacific "Ring of Fire." The crater is over half a mile (1 km) wide.*

The unstable, earthquake-prone, upland basin around Mexico City was once a region of shallow lakes. Flood control measures and domestic consumption over the last four centuries have caused the virtual disappearance of this surface water.

The highlands of Chiapas are a series of *horsts*, blocks of land thrust upward between two fault lines. Volcanic cones have developed where lava has flowed out from the faults.

TRANSPORTATION & INDUSTRY

OIL AND GAS ON THE GULF COAST are Mexico's main sources of export income. Metal mining has declined but the country remains a leading global producer of silver. Manufacturing is heavily concentrated around the metropolitan area of Mexico City, while the duty-free movement of goods in the US border region, under the *Maquiladora* (twin plant) scheme, has created new hi-tech and service growth centers.

Major industry and infrastructure

- brewing
- car manufacture
- chemicals
- electronics
- fish processing
- maquiladoras
- mining
- oil & gas
- textiles
- capital cities
- major towns
- international airports
- major roads
- major industrial areas

A stone figure *reclines by the Temple of Warriors, within the Mayan city of Chichén-Itzá. The Maya civilization flourished across the Yucatan Peninsula between 200 and 900* AD.

TRANSPORTATION NETWORK

151,951 miles (373,986 km)

1,935 miles (3,116 km)

12,684 miles (20,425 km)

1,801 miles (2,900 km)

Fast, modern highways or *autopistas* now link Mexico City with Toluca, Puebla, and other satellite cities, yet distant centers like Chihuahua are still served by narrow roads and an outdated railroad network.

17
60
44
44

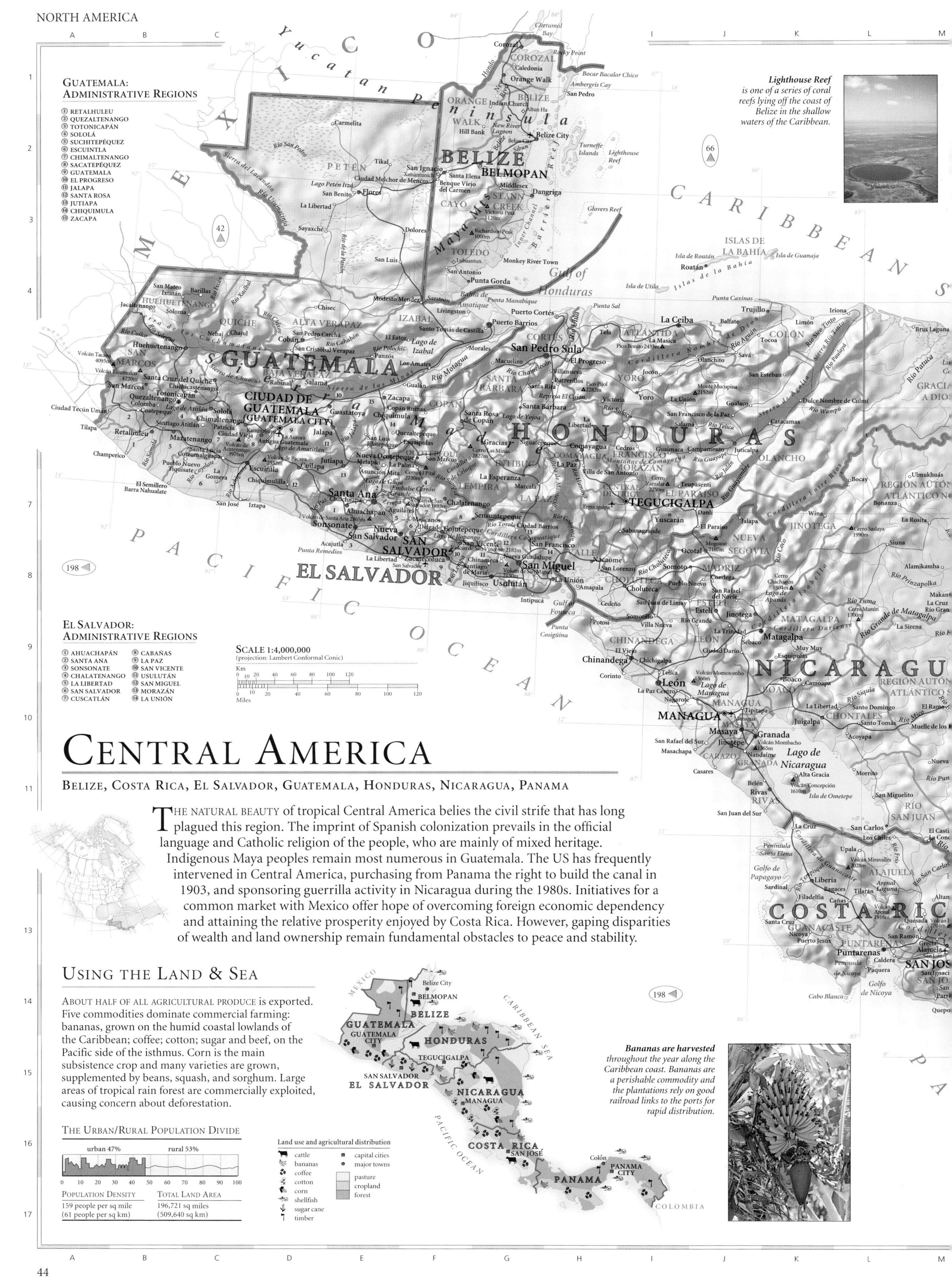
GUATEMALA: ADMINISTRATIVE REGIONS
① RETALHULEU
② QUEZALTENANGO
③ TOTONICAPÁN
④ SOLOLÁ
⑤ SUCHITEPÉQUEZ
⑥ ESCUINTLA
⑦ CHIMALTENANGO
⑧ SACATEPÉQUEZ
⑨ GUATEMALA
⑩ EL PROGRESO
⑪ JALAPA
⑫ SANTA ROSA
⑬ JUTIAPA
⑭ CHIQUIMULA
⑮ ZACAPA
EL SALVADOR: ADMINISTRATIVE REGIONS
① AHUACHAPÁN
② SANTA ANA
③ SONSONATE
④ CHALATENANGO
⑤ LA LIBERTAD
⑥ SAN SALVADOR
⑦ CUSCATLÁN
⑧ CABAÑAS
⑨ LA PAZ
⑩ SAN VICENTE
⑪ USULUTÁN
⑫ SAN MIGUEL
⑬ MORAZÁN
⑭ LA UNIÓN
SCALE 1:4,000,000
(projection: Lambert Conformal Conic)
Km
Miles
GUATEMALA
BELIZE
BELMOPAN
HONDURAS
TEGUCIGALPA
EL SALVADOR
SAN SALVADOR
NICARAGUA
MANAGUA
COSTA RICA
SAN JOSÉ
PANAMA
PANAMA CITY
COLOMBIA
CARIBBEAN SEA
PACIFIC OCEAN
Land use and agricultural distribution
cattle
bananas
coffee
cotton
corn
shellfish
sugar cane
timber
capital cities
major towns
pasture
cropland
forest

Lighthouse Reef is one of a series of coral reefs lying off the coast of Belize in the shallow waters of the Caribbean.

Central America

Belize, Costa Rica, El Salvador, Guatemala, Honduras, Nicaragua, Panama

The natural beauty of tropical Central America belies the civil strife that has long plagued this region. The imprint of Spanish colonization prevails in the official language and Catholic religion of the people, who are mainly of mixed heritage. Indigenous Maya peoples remain most numerous in Guatemala. The US has frequently intervened in Central America, purchasing from Panama the right to build the canal in 1903, and sponsoring guerrilla activity in Nicaragua during the 1980s. Initiatives for a common market with Mexico offer hope of overcoming foreign economic dependency and attaining the relative prosperity enjoyed by Costa Rica. However, gaping disparities of wealth and land ownership remain fundamental obstacles to peace and stability.

Using the Land & Sea

About half of all agricultural produce is exported. Five commodities dominate commercial farming: bananas, grown on the humid coastal lowlands of the Caribbean; coffee; cotton; sugar and beef, on the Pacific side of the isthmus. Corn is the main subsistence crop and many varieties are grown, supplemented by beans, squash, and sorghum. Large areas of tropical rain forest are commercially exploited, causing concern about deforestation.

The Urban/Rural Population Divide

urban 47% | rural 53%

Population Density	Total Land Area
159 people per sq mile (61 people per sq km)	196,721 sq miles (509,640 sq km)

Bananas are harvested throughout the year along the Caribbean coast. Bananas are a perishable commodity and the plantations rely on good railroad links to the ports for rapid distribution.

The Landscape

The Sierra Madre range spreads west from Mexico, between the narrow Pacific coastal plain and the limestone lowland of Petén. Parallel hill ranges sweep across Honduras and extend south, past the Caribbean Mosquito Coast, to Lakes Managua and Nicaragua. The Cordillera Central rises to the south, gradually descending to Lake Gatún *(Lago Gatún)*. A highly active volcanic belt runs along the Pacific seaboard from Mexico to Costa Rica.

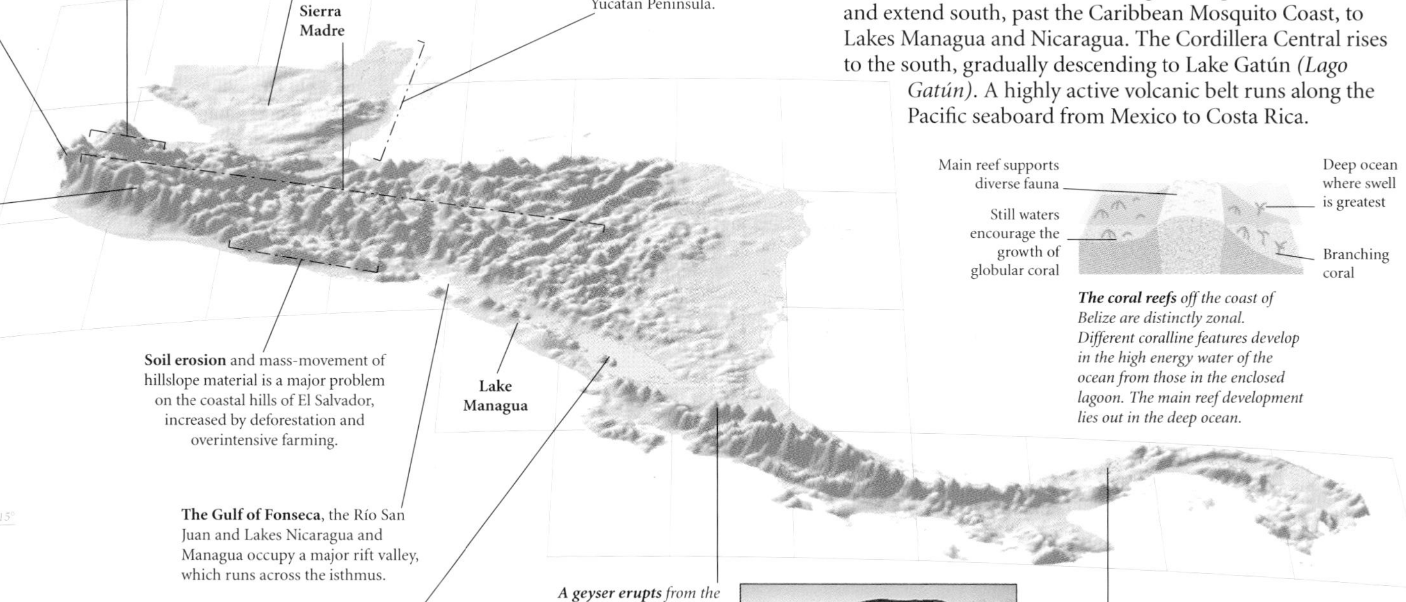

Over 40 active volcanoes line the Pacific coast north of Panama, including Volcán Tajumulco. At 13,846 ft (4,220 m), it is the highest point in Central America.

The high plateau of the Sierra de los Cuchumatanes is a *horst*, an upthrusted block of land. The limestone rock is deeply incised with canyons along the plateau edge.

Lake Petén Itzá is typical of the swampy depressions or *bajos* of the Petén region, formed by intense weathering of limestone in the hot and humid climate.

Low, white limestone cliffs, mangrove swamps, and coral reefs characterize the coast of Belize, which is part of the Yucatan Peninsula.

Sierra Madre

The 990-ft (300-m) deep crater *occupied by Lake Atitlán (Lago de Atitlán) was created after a volcanic explosion caused the original cone to collapse in on itself. Other volcanic cones lie on its shores.*

Soil erosion and mass-movement of hillslope material is a major problem on the coastal hills of El Salvador, increased by deforestation and overintensive farming.

Lake Managua

The Gulf of Fonseca, the Río San Juan and Lakes Nicaragua and Managua occupy a major rift valley, which runs across the isthmus.

Lake Nicaragua *(Lago de Nicaragua)* contains around 400 islands, some of which are active volcanoes. Unique freshwater species of shark and swordfish have evolved over the long period since the lake was cut off from the Pacific by a belt of volcanic cones.

A geyser erupts *from the central cone of Volcán Poás, an active volcano in the Cordillera Central of Costa Rica, which frequently produces spectacular lava flows.*

Main reef supports diverse fauna

Still waters encourage the growth of globular coral

Deep ocean where swell is greatest

Branching coral

The coral reefs *off the coast of Belize are distinctly zonal. Different coralline features develop in the high energy water of the ocean from those in the enclosed lagoon. The main reef development lies out in the deep ocean.*

Over half of the route of the Panama Canal runs through Lake Gatún *(Lago Gatún)*, the highest stretch of the journey. The freshwater lake also acts as a holding reservoir for the canal, providing water to operate the locks.

Transportation & Industry

Most manufacturing takes the form of cottage industries concentrated in the larger towns, and the production of food, tobacco, furniture, textiles, clothing, and footwear. The region's oil and metallic mineral potential is largely unexploited. The Panamanian economy is dominated by service industries, and the country has one of the world's largest free trade zones, in Colón.

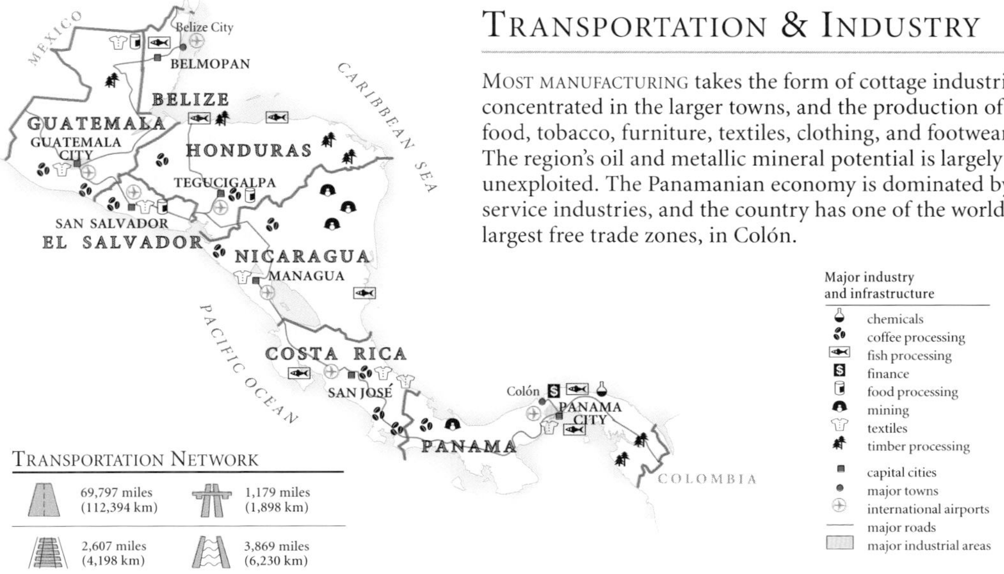

An ox-drawn plow *tills fields of tobacco in the Copán region of Honduras. Only about 25% of the land is cultivated in this sparsely-populated country.*

Major industry and infrastructure
- chemicals
- coffee processing
- fish processing
- finance
- food processing
- mining
- textiles
- timber processing
- capital cities
- major towns
- international airports
- major roads
- major industrial areas

Transportation Network

69,797 miles (112,394 km)	1,179 miles (1,898 km)
2,607 miles (4,198 km)	3,869 miles (6,230 km)

The completion of a major oil pipeline across Panama in 1982 has reduced crude oil shipments via the Panama Canal, further contributing to a long-term decline in canal traffic.

Map Key

POPULATION
- 500,000 to 1 million
- 100,000 to 500,000
- 50,000 to 100,000
- 10,000 to 50,000
- below 10,000

ELEVATION
- 4000m / 13,124ft
- 3000m / 9843ft
- 2000m / 6562ft
- 1000m / 3281ft
- 500m / 1640ft
- 250m / 820ft
- 100m / 328ft
- sea level

Panama's rain forests *are home to many mammals which originated in North America, including jaguars, tapirs, and deer, as well as sloths, anteaters, and armadillos, which migrated from South America long ago.*

166

128

56

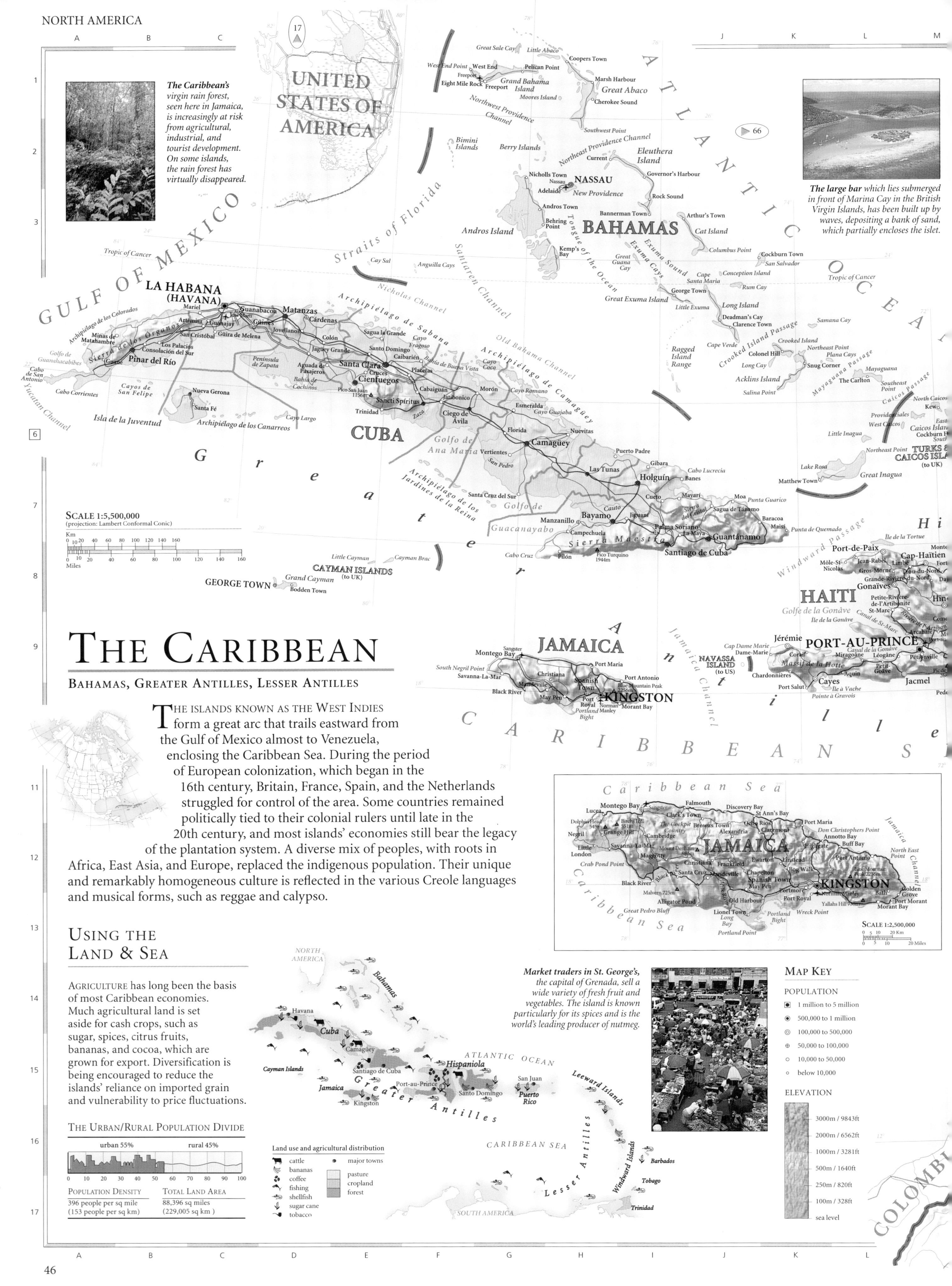
UNITED STATES OF AMERICA
GULF OF MEXICO
ATLANTIC OCEAN
BAHAMAS
NASSAU
New Providence
Andros Island
Great Abaco
Grand Bahama Island
Eleuthera Island
Cat Island
Great Exuma Island
Long Island
Acklins Island
Great Inagua
Matthew Town
TURKS & CAICOS ISLANDS (to UK)
Straits of Florida
Santaren Channel
Old Bahama Channel
Nicholas Channel
Tropic of Cancer
LA HABANA (HAVANA)
Matanzas
Pinar del Río
Santa Clara
Cienfuegos
Sancti Spíritus
Ciego de Ávila
Camagüey
Las Tunas
Holguín
Bayamo
Santiago de Cuba
Guantánamo
CUBA
Isla de la Juventud
Sierra Maestra
Pico Turquino 1944m
Golfo de Guacanayabo
Yucatan Channel
CAYMAN ISLANDS (to UK)
GEORGE TOWN
Grand Cayman
Little Cayman
Cayman Brac
Greater Antilles
JAMAICA
KINGSTON
Montego Bay
Jamaica Channel
NAVASSA ISLAND (to US)
HAITI
PORT-AU-PRINCE
Cap-Haïtien
Gonaïves
Jacmel
Windward Passage
CARIBBEAN SEA
SCALE 1:5,500,000
(projection: Lambert Conformal Conic)
Caribbean Sea
Falmouth
Ocho Rios
Port Antonio
Mandeville
Spanish Town
May Pen
Blue Mountain Peak 2256m
SCALE 1:2,500,000
NORTH AMERICA
Havana
Cuba
Camagüey
Santiago de Cuba
Cayman Islands
Jamaica
Kingston
Port-au-Prince
Hispaniola
Santo Domingo
San Juan
Puerto Rico
ATLANTIC OCEAN
Leeward Islands
Windward Islands
Lesser Antilles
Barbados
Tobago
Trinidad
SOUTH AMERICA
Land use and agricultural distribution
cattle
bananas
coffee
fishing
shellfish
sugar cane
tobacco
major towns
pasture
cropland
forest
MAP KEY
POPULATION
1 million to 5 million
500,000 to 1 million
100,000 to 500,000
50,000 to 100,000
10,000 to 50,000
below 10,000
ELEVATION
3000m / 9843ft
2000m / 6562ft
1000m / 3281ft
500m / 1640ft
250m / 820ft
100m / 328ft
sea level

The Caribbean's *virgin rain forest, seen here in Jamaica, is increasingly at risk from agricultural, industrial, and tourist development. On some islands, the rain forest has virtually disappeared.*

The large bar *which lies submerged in front of Marina Cay in the British Virgin Islands, has been built up by waves, depositing a bank of sand, which partially encloses the islet.*

The Caribbean

Bahamas, Greater Antilles, Lesser Antilles

The islands known as the West Indies form a great arc that trails eastward from the Gulf of Mexico almost to Venezuela, enclosing the Caribbean Sea. During the period of European colonization, which began in the 16th century, Britain, France, Spain, and the Netherlands struggled for control of the area. Some countries remained politically tied to their colonial rulers until late in the 20th century, and most islands' economies still bear the legacy of the plantation system. A diverse mix of peoples, with roots in Africa, East Asia, and Europe, replaced the indigenous population. Their unique and remarkably homogeneous culture is reflected in the various Creole languages and musical forms, such as reggae and calypso.

Using the Land & Sea

Agriculture has long been the basis of most Caribbean economies. Much agricultural land is set aside for cash crops, such as sugar, spices, citrus fruits, bananas, and cocoa, which are grown for export. Diversification is being encouraged to reduce the islands' reliance on imported grain and vulnerability to price fluctuations.

The Urban/Rural Population Divide

urban 55% | rural 45%

Population Density	Total Land Area
396 people per sq mile (153 people per sq km)	88,396 sq miles (229,005 sq km)

Market traders in St. George's, *the capital of Grenada, sell a wide variety of fresh fruit and vegetables. The island is known particularly for its spices and is the world's leading producer of nutmeg.*

Transportation & Industry

Caribbean industry remains, with few exceptions, agricultural and export-led, or service-based, supporting the flourishing tourist industry. However, several countries including Jamaica, Barbados, Trinidad and Tobago, and Puerto Rico have developed important mineral industries. Cuba is attempting to diversify its economy by importing capital goods to start up new manufacturing businesses.

Cruise ships, such as this one moored at Castries in St. Lucia, have become a popular mode for tourist travel around the Caribbean islands, stopping off at several islands for sightseeing and shopping.

Transportation Network

	60,831 miles (97,956 km)		357 miles (575 km)
	10,310 miles (16,602 km)		211 miles (340 km)

Air links are well developed between most of the Caribbean islands. The importance of the tourist trade has recently encouraged many countries to upgrade their paved roads.

Major industry and infrastructure

- fish processing
- finance
- mining
- oil refining
- sugar refining
- tourism
- major towns
- international airports
- major roads
- major industrial areas

This rock stack on the coast of St. Martin in the Leeward Islands has been created by wave action that undercuts the cliffs, forming an arch. Continued wave action weakened the arch, which eventually collapsed leaving a single tower of rock.

The Pitons, in St. Lucia, are two volcanic domes; the tallest is 2,620 ft (798 m) high. Their steep slopes are covered in thick forest.

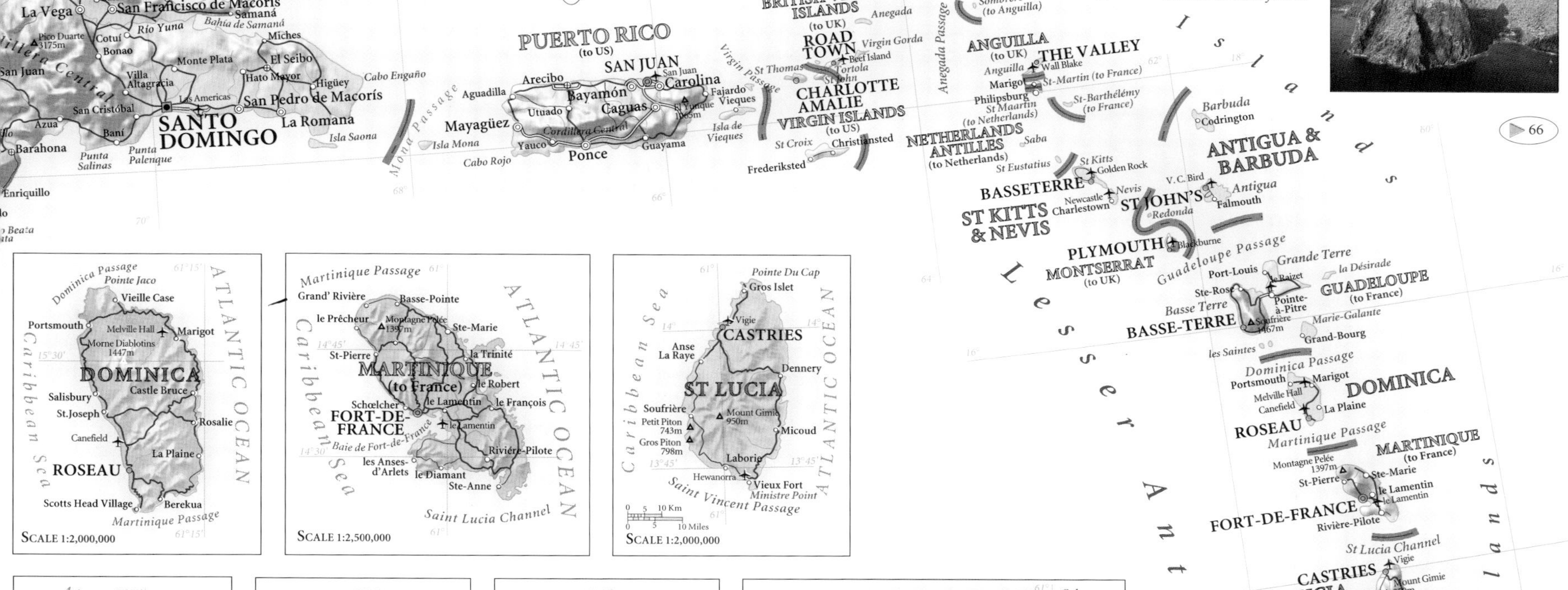

DOMINICAN REPUBLIC
SANTO DOMINGO
PUERTO RICO (to US)
SAN JUAN
BRITISH VIRGIN ISLANDS (to UK)
ROAD TOWN
CHARLOTTE AMALIE
VIRGIN ISLANDS (to US)
ANGUILLA (to UK)
THE VALLEY
NETHERLANDS ANTILLES (to Netherlands)
ANTIGUA & BARBUDA
ST JOHN'S
BASSETERRE
ST KITTS & NEVIS
PLYMOUTH
MONTSERRAT (to UK)
GUADELOUPE (to France)
BASSE-TERRE
DOMINICA
ROSEAU
MARTINIQUE (to France)
FORT-DE-FRANCE
ST LUCIA
CASTRIES
Leeward Islands
Lesser Antilles

South America

Reaching from the humid tropics down into the cold South Atlantic, South America has an area of 6,886,000 sq miles (17,835,000 sq km). There are 12 separate countries, with the largest, Brazil, covering almost half of the continent.

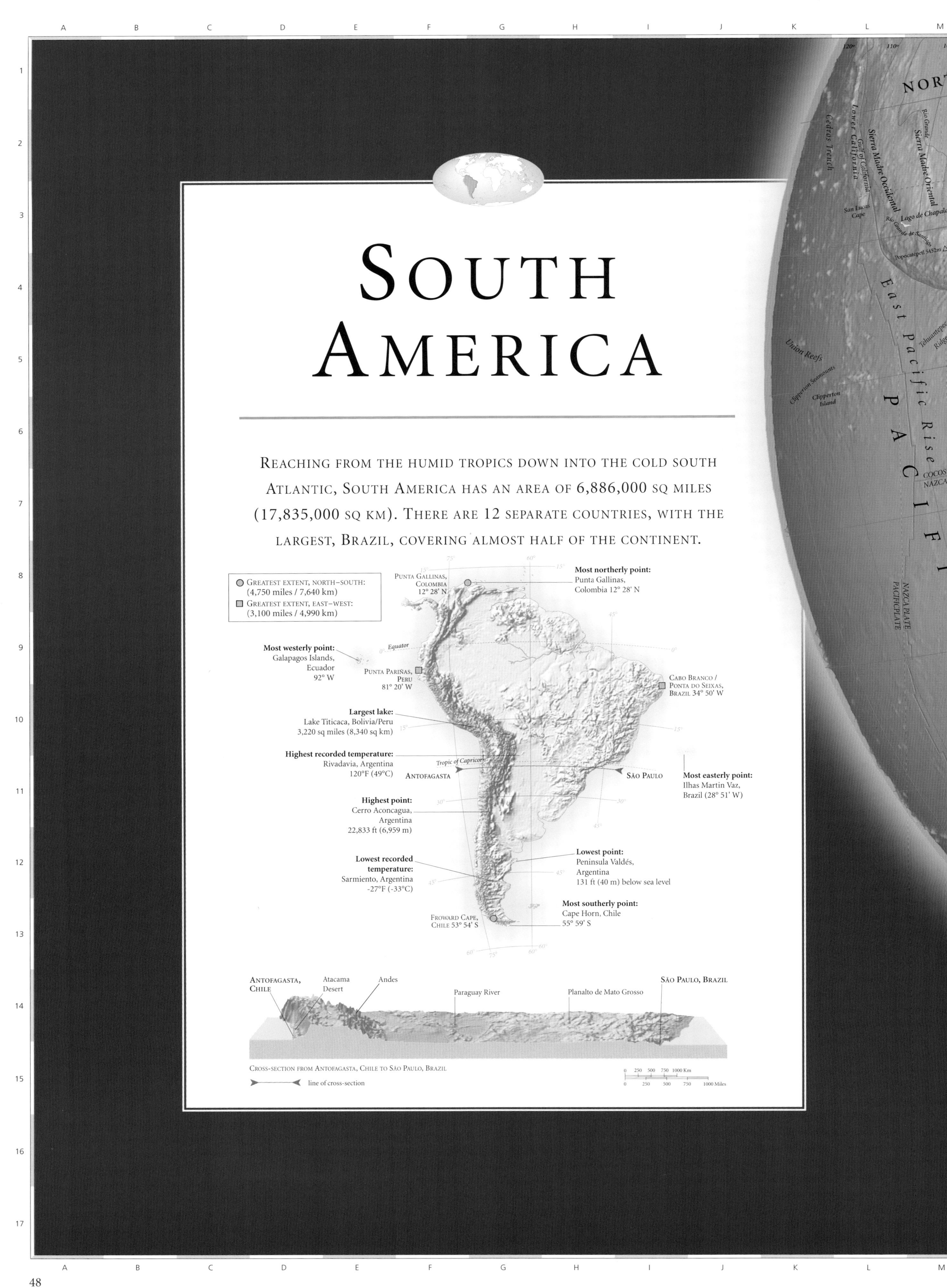

Greatest extent, north–south: (4,750 miles / 7,640 km)
Greatest extent, east–west: (3,100 miles / 4,990 km)
Punta Gallinas, Colombia 12° 28' N
Most northerly point: Punta Gallinas, Colombia 12° 28' N
Most westerly point: Galapagos Islands, Ecuador 92° W
Equator
Punta Pariñas, Peru 81° 20' W
Cabo Branco / Ponta do Seixas, Brazil 34° 50' W
Largest lake: Lake Titicaca, Bolivia/Peru 3,220 sq miles (8,340 sq km)
Highest recorded temperature: Rivadavia, Argentina 120°F (49°C)
Tropic of Capricorn
Antofagasta
São Paulo
Most easterly point: Ilhas Martin Vaz, Brazil (28° 51' W)
Highest point: Cerro Aconcagua, Argentina 22,833 ft (6,959 m)
Lowest point: Peninsula Valdés, Argentina 131 ft (40 m) below sea level
Lowest recorded temperature: Sarmiento, Argentina -27°F (-33°C)
Most southerly point: Cape Horn, Chile 55° 59' S
Froward Cape, Chile 53° 54' S
Antofagasta, Chile
Atacama Desert
Andes
Paraguay River
Planalto de Mato Grosso
São Paulo, Brazil
Cross-section from Antofagasta, Chile to São Paulo, Brazil
line of cross-section
0 250 500 750 1000 Km
0 250 500 750 1000 Miles
NORT
Cedros Trench
Lower California
Gulf of California
Sierra Madre Occidental
Sierra Madre Oriental
Río Grande
San Lucas Cape
Lago de Chapala
Río Grande de Santiago
Popocatépetl 5452m
East Pacific Rise
Tehuantepec Ridge
Union Reefs
Clipperton Seamounts
Clipperton Island
PACIFI
COCOS
NAZCA
NAZCA PLATE
PACIFIC PLATE

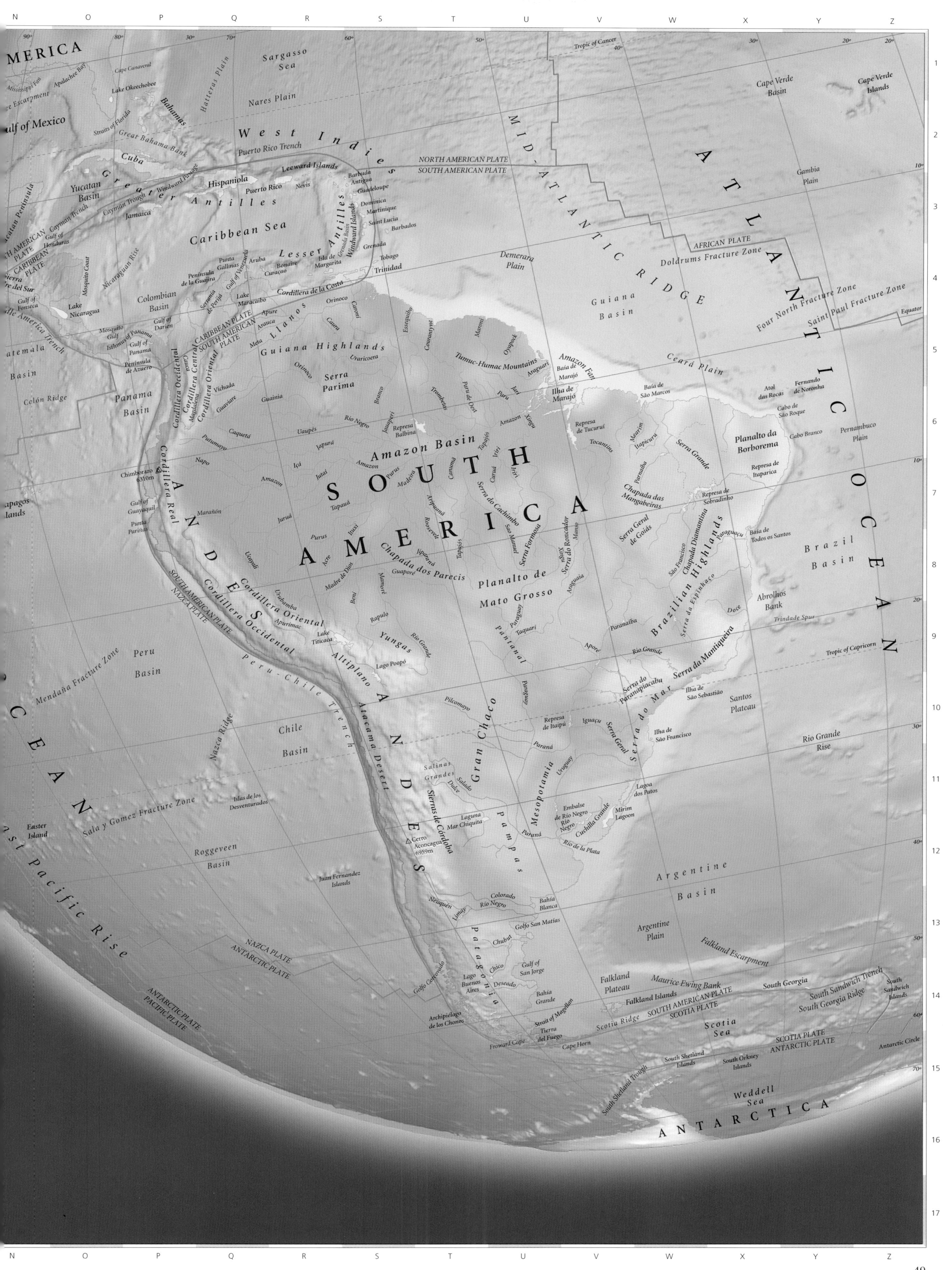

N O P Q R S T U V W X Y Z
1 2 3 4 5 6 7 8 9 10 11 12 13 14 15 16 17
MERICA
Sargasso Sea
Nares Plain
Cape Canaveral
Lake Okeechobee
Bahamas
Hatteras Plain
Apalachee Bay
Mississippi Fan
Escarpment
ulf of Mexico
Straits of Florida
Great Bahama Bank
West Indies
Puerto Rico Trench
Cuba
Yucatan Basin
Yucatan Peninsula
Greater Antilles
Cayman Trench
Cayman Trough
Windward Passage
Hispaniola
Puerto Rico
Leeward Islands
Nevis
Barbuda
Antigua
Guadeloupe
Dominica
Martinique
Saint Lucia
Barbados
Jamaica
Caribbean Sea
Lesser Antilles
Windward Islands
Grenada Basin
Grenada
Tobago
Trinidad
Aruba
Bonaire
Curaçao
Isla de Margarita
Punta Gallinas
Peninsula de la Guajira
Gulf of Venezuela
Serrania de Perija
Lake Maracaibo
Cordillera de la Costa
NORTH AMERICAN PLATE
CARIBBEAN PLATE
Gulf of Honduras
Mosquito Coast
Nicaraguan Rise
Colombian Basin
Gulf of Fonseca
Lake Nicaragua
Mosquito Gulf
Isthmus of Panama
Gulf of Panama
Gulf of Darién
Peninsula de Azuero
Middle America Trench
Guatemala Basin
Colón Ridge
Panama Basin
CARIBBEAN PLATE
SOUTH AMERICAN PLATE
Cordillera Occidental
Cordillera Central
Cordillera Oriental
Cauca
Magdalena
Apure
Arauca
Meta
Llanos
Orinoco
Caura
Caroni
Guiana Highlands
Uraricoera
Serra Parima
Vichada
Guaviare
Guainia
Essequibo
Courantyne
Maroni
Oyapock
Tumuc-Humac Mountains
Araguari
Demerara Plain
Guiana Basin
NORTH AMERICAN PLATE
SOUTH AMERICAN PLATE
MID-ATLANTIC RIDGE
Tropic of Cancer
AFRICAN PLATE
Doldrums Fracture Zone
Four North Fracture Zone
Saint Paul Fracture Zone
Equator
ATLANTIC OCEAN
Cape Verde Basin
Cape Verde Islands
Gambia Plain
Ceará Plain
Amazon Fan
Baía de Marajó
Ilha de Marajó
Jari
Paru
Paru de Oeste
Trombetas
Branco
Rio Negro
Jauaperi
Represa Balbina
Amazon
Xingu
Baía de São Marcos
Atol das Rocas
Fernando de Noronha
Cabo de São Roque
Cabo Branco
Pernambuco Plain
Planalto da Borborema
Represa de Itaparica
Represa de Tucuruí
Tocantins
Mearim
Itapicuru
Serra Grande
Parnaíba
Chapada das Mangabeiras
Represa de Sobradinho
Caquetá
Putumayo
Napo
Vaupés
Japurá
Amazon Basin
Tapajós
Curuá
Iriri
Içá
Jutaí
Purus
Madeira
Canumã
Chimborazo 6310m
Galapagos Islands
Gulf of Guayaquil
Punta Pariñas
Cordillera Real
Marañón
SOUTH AMERICA
Tapauá
Juruá
Ituxi
Aripuanã
Serra do Cachimbo
Roosevelt
Ji-paraná
Teles Pires
São Manuel
Serra Formosa
Xingu
Serra do Roncador
Manso
Serra Geral de Goiás
São Francisco
Chapada Diamantina
Brazilian Highlands
Paraguaçu
Baía de Todos os Santos
Brazil Basin
Ucayali
ANDES
Acre
Madre de Dios
Chapada dos Parecis
Guaporé
Mamoré
Beni
Planalto de Mato Grosso
Araguaia
Serra do Espinhaço
Doce
Abrolhos Bank
Trindade Spur
Urubamba
Cordillera Oriental
Cordillera Occidental
Apurimac
SOUTH AMERICAN PLATE
NAZCA PLATE
Lake Titicaca
Rapulo
Yungas
Rio Grande
Lago Poopó
Paraguay
Taquari
Pantanal
Paranaíba
Aporé
Rio Grande
Serra da Mantiqueira
Tropic of Capricorn
Peru Basin
Mendaña Fracture Zone
Peru-Chile Trench
Altiplano
Atacama Desert
Pilcomayo
Paraguay
Serra do Paranapiacaba
Serra do Mar
Ilha de São Sebastião
Santos Plateau
OCEAN
Nazca Ridge
Chile Basin
Gran Chaco
Represa de Itaipu
Iguaçu
Serra Geral
Paraná
Ilha de São Francisco
Rio Grande Rise
Salinas Grandes
Salado
Dulce
Sierras de Córdoba
Mesopotamia
Uruguay
Lagoa dos Patos
Islas de los Desventurados
Sala y Gomez Fracture Zone
Easter Island
Laguna Mar Chiquita
Cerro Aconcagua 6959m
Pampas
Embalse de Rio Negro
Rio Negro
Cuchilla Grande
Mirim Lagoon
Paraná
Río de la Plata
Roggeveen Basin
Juan Fernandez Islands
East Pacific Rise
Argentine Basin
Neuquén
Colorado
Rio Negro
Bahía Blanca
Limay
Golfo San Matías
Patagonia
Chubut
Argentine Plain
Falkland Escarpment
NAZCA PLATE
ANTARCTIC PLATE
ANTARCTIC PLATE
PACIFIC PLATE
Golfo Corcovado
Lago Buenos Aires
Chico
Deseado
Gulf of San Jorge
Bahía Grande
Falkland Plateau
Maurice Ewing Bank
Falkland Islands
South Georgia
South Sandwich Trench
South Sandwich Islands
South Georgia Ridge
Archipiélago de los Chonos
Strait of Magellan
Tierra del Fuego
Froward Cape
Cape Horn
Scotia Ridge
SOUTH AMERICAN PLATE
SCOTIA PLATE
Scotia Sea
SCOTIA PLATE
ANTARCTIC PLATE
Antarctic Circle
South Shetland Islands
South Orkney Islands
South Shetland Trough
Weddell Sea
ANTARCTICA

Physical South America

THREE MAJOR PHYSIOGRAPHICAL REGIONS characterize South America. The oldest, the ancient Brazilian Shield and the smaller Guyana and Patagonian shields, form the stable core of the continent. Stretching along the entire west coast are the younger Andean fold mountains with many summits rising to 20,000 ft (6,100 m). These two diverse regions are separated by a number of sedimentary basins carrying South America's large river systems to the sea. These include the massive Amazon Basin and the basin of the Gran Chaco.

The Amazon Basin and Guyana Shield

THE AMAZON RIVER occupies a large depression in the Earth's crust, formed by the uplift of the Andes. It is covered by thick volcanic deposits and layers of alluvium – these have been laid down by the Amazon's many tributaries. To the north is the smaller Guyana Shield.

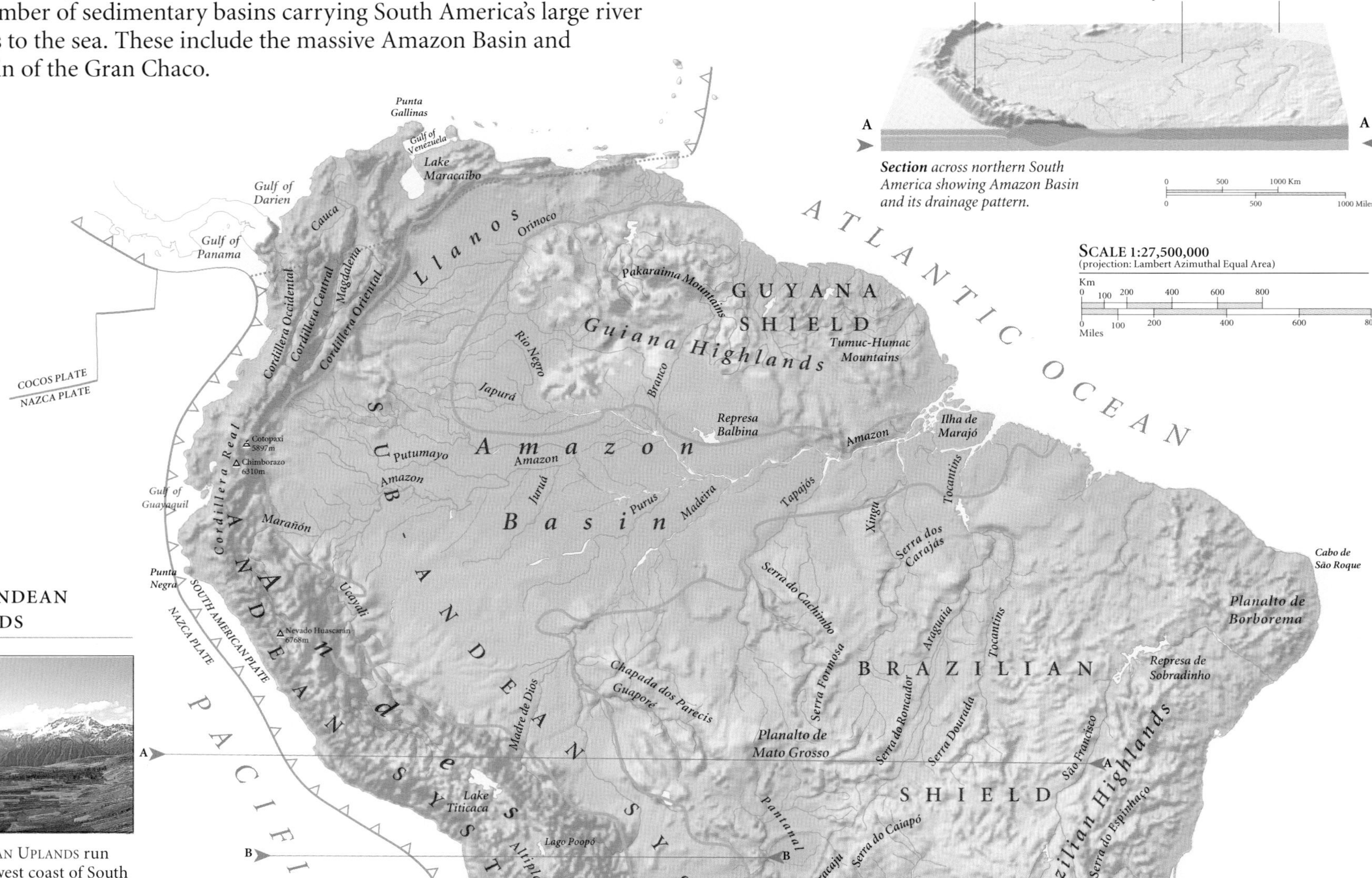

Headwaters of the Amazon rise in the Andes
Thick alluvium deposits
Mouths of the Amazon
A
A
Punta Gallinas
Gulf of Venezuela
Lake Maracaibo
Gulf of Darien
Gulf of Panama
Cauca
Magdalena
Cordillera Occidental
Cordillera Central
Cordillera Oriental
Llanos
Orinoco
Pakaraima Mountains
GUYANA SHIELD
Guiana Highlands
Tumuc-Humac Mountains
Rio Negro
Branco
Japurá
COCOS PLATE
NAZCA PLATE
ATLANTIC OCEAN
Cordillera Real
Cotopaxi 5897m
Chimborazo 6310m
Putumayo
Amazon
Amazon Basin
Represa Balbina
Ilha de Marajó
Gulf of Guayaquil
Marañón
Juruá
Purus
Madeira
Tapajós
Xingu
Tocantins
Serra dos Carajás
Cabo de São Roque
Punta Negra
SUB-ANDEAN SYSTEM
Ucayali
Nevado Huascarán 6768m
Serra do Cachimbo
Planalto de Borborema
SOUTH AMERICAN PLATE
NAZCA PLATE
Chapada dos Parecis
Guaporé
Madre de Dios
Serra Formosa
Araguaia
BRAZILIAN SHIELD
Represa de Sobradinho
Serra do Roncador
Serra Dourada
Tocantins
Planalto de Mato Grosso
São Francisco
Brazilian Highlands

Section across northern South America showing Amazon Basin and its drainage pattern.

SCALE 1:27,500,000 (projection: Lambert Azimuthal Equal Area)

The Andean Uplands

THE ANDEAN UPLANDS run along the west coast of South America. They are being uplifted as the Nazca Plate is subducted beneath the South American Plate. They contain some of the world's largest volcanoes, such as Cotopaxi, and Lake Titicaca, which occupies a dormant site. The far south has many large ice sheets and a fragmented coastline.

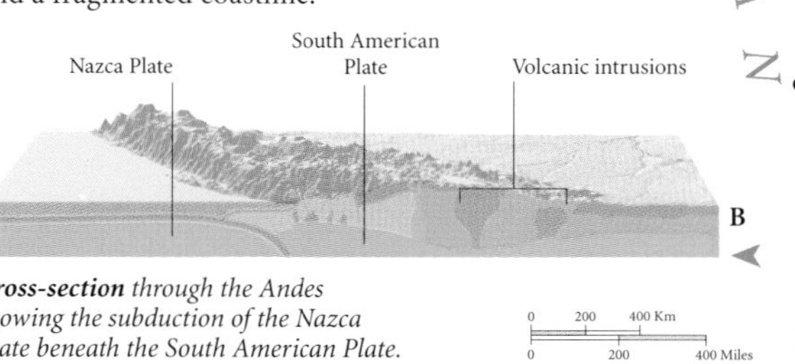

Nazca Plate
South American Plate
Volcanic intrusions
B
B

Cross-section through the Andes showing the subduction of the Nazca Plate beneath the South American Plate.

The Brazilian Shield and Gran Chaco

THE IMMENSE BRAZILIAN SHIELD underlies more than one-third of South America. It is pitted with numerous volcanic intrusions, and a large basaltic plateau exists between the Paraná River and the Atlantic Ocean. The flat Gran Chaco lies to the west of the Shield, covered by sedimentary deposits eroded from the Andes, and transported by South America's mighty rivers.

Young, folded Andes Mountains — Volcanic intrusions — Major rivers drain to the south through the Gran Chaco — Ancient resistant shield

Section across central South America showing the flat basin of the Gran Chaco and the ancient Brazilian Shield.

Map Key

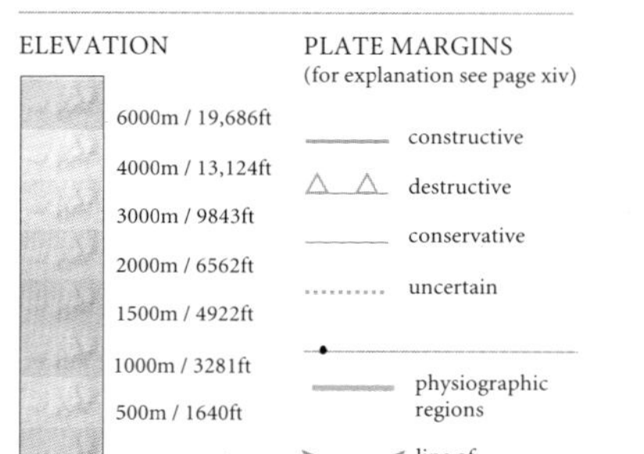

ELEVATION
6000m / 19,686ft
4000m / 13,124ft
3000m / 9843ft
2000m / 6562ft
1500m / 4922ft
1000m / 3281ft
500m / 1640ft
250m / 820ft
100m / 328ft
sea level
PLATE MARGINS
(for explanation see page xiv)
constructive
destructive
conservative
uncertain
physiographic regions
line of cross-section

Climate

The climate of South America is influenced by three principal factors: the seasonal shift of high pressure air masses over the tropics, cold ocean currents along the western coast, which affect temperature and precipitation, and the mountain barrier produced by by the Andes, which creates a rain shadow over much of the south.

***Mild winters** and cool summers typify the extensive Pampas grasslands of Argentina.*

***Chile's hyperarid** Atacama Desert is renowned as one of the driest places on Earth.*

Climate
- tundra
- cool continental
- warm humid
- semiarid
- arid
- humid equatorial
- tropical
- daily hours of sunshine, January
- daily hours of sunshine, July
- cold wind

Temperature

Average January temperature

Average July temperature

Temperature
- below -22°F (-30°C)
- -22 to -4°F (-30 to -20°C)
- -4 to 14° F (-20 to -10°C)
- 14 to 32°F (-10 to 0°C)
- 32 to 50°F (0 to 10°C)
- 50°F (10 to 20°C)
- 68 to 86°F (20 to 30°C)
- above 86°F (30°C)

Rainfall

Average January rainfall

Average July rainfall

Rainfall
- 0–1 in (0–25 mm)
- 1–2 in (25–50 mm)
- 2–4 in (50–100 mm)
- 4–8 in (100–200 mm)
- 8–12 in (200–300 mm)
- 12–16 in (300–400 mm)
- 16–20 in (400–500 mm)
- more than 20 in (500 mm)

***Tropical conditions** are found across more than half of South America. When both rainfall and temperatures are high, hot, humid rain forests prevail.*

Shaping the Continent

South America's active tectonic belt has been extensively folded over millions of years; landslides are still frequent in the mountains. The large river systems that erode the mountains flow across resistant shield areas, depositing sediment. Present-day glaciation affects the distinctive landscape of the far south.

Mass Movement

6 Debris slides are common in the highlands of South America *(left)*. They occur where soil on a slope is saturated with rainwater and therefore less stable. The actual slides are often triggered by earthquakes.

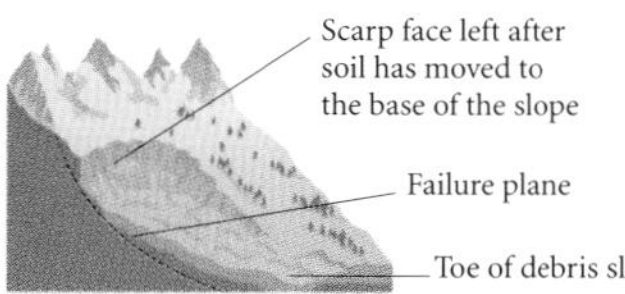
Scarp face left after soil has moved to the base of the slope
Failure plane
Toe of debris slide

Mass Movement: A section of a debris slide

Chemical Weathering

1 Table mountains *(left)* are the eroded remnants of an ancient upland. As water percolates along cracks in these high, flat-topped mountains it forms intricate cave systems. Chemical weathering also isolates large blocks which then collapse, accumulating as rockfalls at the foot of scarp slopes.

Smooth summit dissected by deep gorges
Rainfall
Runoff surges down caverns as waterfalls

Chemical Weathering: Erosion of the Guyana Shield

The Evolving Landscape

River Systems

2 Along the Amazon *(above)* there is a great variation in rates of erosion. As the headwaters of the Amazon flow down from the Andes, they erode and transport vast quantities of sediment, and are known as whitewaters. Across the shield areas erosion rates are very low. These rivers, carrying rotting vegetation, are called blackwaters.

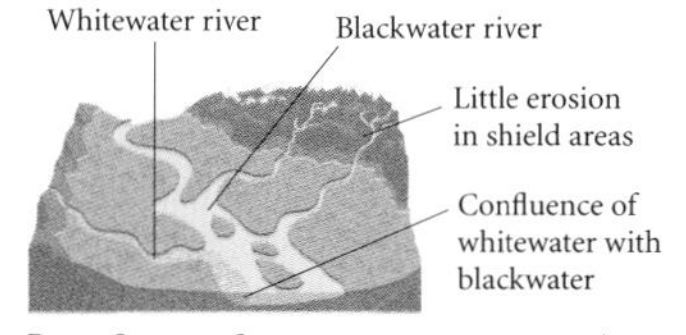
Whitewater river
Blackwater river
Little erosion in shield areas
Confluence of whitewater with blackwater

River Systems: Suspended sediments in the Amazon

Folding

5 Folding occurs beneath the surface under high temperatures and pressures. Rocks become sufficiently malleable to flow and not fracture as tectonic plates collide. In the Valley of the Moon in Chile *(above)*, anticlines (or upfolds) and synclines (or troughs) have been exploited by erosion.

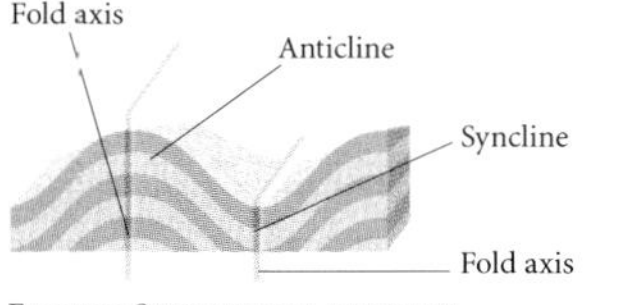
Fold axis
Anticline
Syncline
Fold axis

Folding: Synclines and anticlines

Deposition

4 Large alluvial fans are found extensively across South America *(above)*. Confined mountain rivers, carrying large quantities of eroded material, emerge from a mountain gorge onto the plains, where they deposit their load in huge fans.

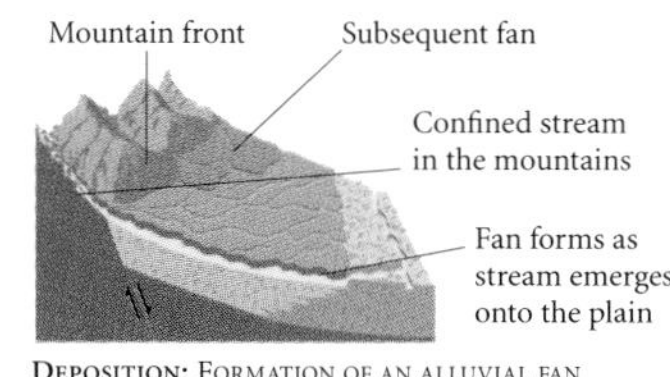
Mountain front
Subsequent fan
Confined stream in the mountains
Fan forms as stream emerges onto the plain

Deposition: Formation of an alluvial fan

Landscape
- uplifting land
- stable land
- sinking land
- glacier
- ocean current
- aluvial fan
- inselberg
- river

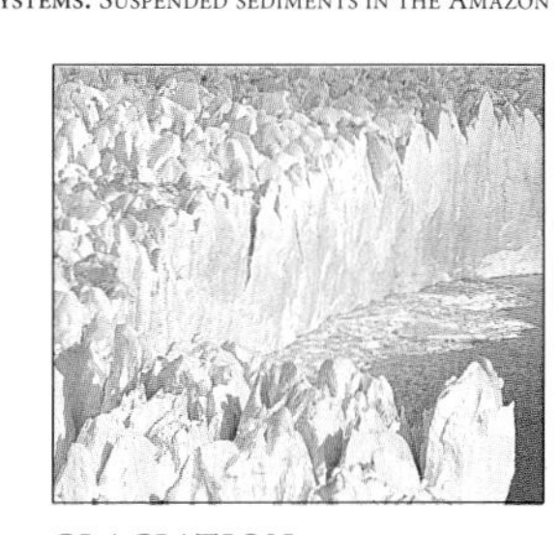
Unstable front in deep water, where ice is fracturing
Original extent of glacier
Icebergs
Stable front
Glacier was grounded against a shoal

Glaciation: Retreating glacier in Patagonia

Glaciation

3 As fjord glaciers in Patagonia *(above)* retreat, they become grounded on shoals. In deeper water the base of the glacier becomes unstable, and icebergs break off (calve) until the glacier snout grounds once more.

Political South America

Modern South America's political boundaries have their origins in the territorial endeavors of explorers during the 16th century, who claimed almost the entire continent for Portugal and Spain. The Portuguese land in the east later evolved into the federal state of Brazil, while the Spanish vice-royalties eventually emerged as separate independent nation-states in the early 19th century. South America's growing population has become increasingly urbanized, with the growth of coastal cities into large conurbations like Rio de Janeiro and Buenos Aires. In Brazil, Argentina, Chile, and Uruguay, a succession of military dictatorships has given way to fragile, but strengthening, democracies.

Europe retains a small *foothold in South America. Kourou in French Guiana is the site chosen by the European Space Agency to launch the Ariane rocket. As a result of its status as a French overseas department, French Guiana is actually part of the European Union.*

Scale 1:21,500,000
(projection: Lambert Azimuthal Equal Area)

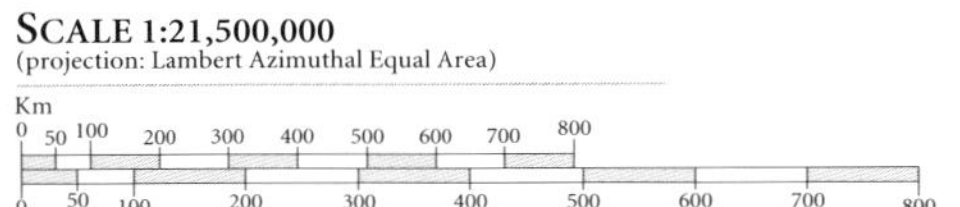
Km
0 50 100 200 300 400 500 600 700 800
0 50 100 200 300 400 500 600 700 800
Miles

Transportation

Most major road and rail routes are confined to the coastal regions by the imposing natural barriers of the Andes Mountains and the Amazon Basin. Few major cross-continental routes exist, although Buenos Aires serves as a transportation center for the main rail links to La Paz and Valparaíso, while the construction of the Trans-Amazon and Pan-American Highways have made direct road travel possible from Recife to Lima and from Puerto Montt up the coast into Central America. A new waterway project is planned to transform the Paraguay River into a major shipping route, although it involves considerable wetlands destruction.

South America's *most extensive rail network centers on the Argentinian capital, Buenos Aires. The construction of new rail lines outward from this important port allowed the colonization of the Pampas lands for agriculture.*

Transportation
- major roads and highways
- major railroads
- international borders
- transportation intersections
- international airports
- major ports

Languages

Prior to European exploration in the 16th century, a diverse range of indigenous languages were spoken across the continent. With the arrival of Iberian settlers, Spanish became the dominant language, with Portuguese spoken in Brazil, and Native American languages, such as Quechua and Guaraní, becoming concentrated in the continental interior. Today this pattern persists, although successive European colonization has led to Dutch being spoken in Suriname, English in Guyana, and French in French Guiana. In large urban areas, Japanese and Chinese are increasingly common.

Language groups
- American Indian
- Germanic
- Romance

Chile's main port, Valparaíso, *is a vital national shipping center, in addition to playing a key role in the growing trade with Pacific nations. The country's awkward, elongated shape means that sea transportation is frequently used for internal travel and communications in Chile.*

Indigenous South American lifestyles *have not been totally submerged by European cultures and languages. The continental interior, and particularly the Amazon Basin, is still home to many different native peoples.*

Lima's *magnificent cathedral reflects South America's colonial past with its unmistakably Spanish style. In July 1821, Peru became the last Spanish colony on the mainland to declare independence.*

In April 1960, *Brazil's government began the move from Rio de Janeiro to Brasília, a futuristic city built in the sparsely populated interior. Brasília is now the federal capital of Brazil.*

Rapid urbanization *has been a feature of most South American countries in the latter half of the 20th century. In many cases, this unchecked growth has led to the development of sprawling slums, lacking adequate water and sewage facilities.*

Perched high in the Andes *like many of the cities in western South America, La Paz, Bolivia is the world's highest capital city at over 11,500 ft (3,500 m).*

Map Key

POPULATION

- above 5 million
- 1 million to 5 million
- 500,000 to 1 million
- 100,000 to 500,000
- 50,000 to 100,000
- 10,000 to 50,000
- below 10,000
- Country capital
- State capital

BORDERS

- full international border
- disputed de facto border
- disputed territorial claim border
- state border

Population

Almost half of South America's population lives in Brazil but, due to the large uninhabited expanses of the Amazon Basin, its overall population density is much lower than in other countries. During the 20th century the most important population trend has been the movement from rural to urban areas, giving rise to great population concentrations in large cities like São Paulo, Rio de Janeiro, Caracas, Lima, Bogotá, and Buenos Aires.

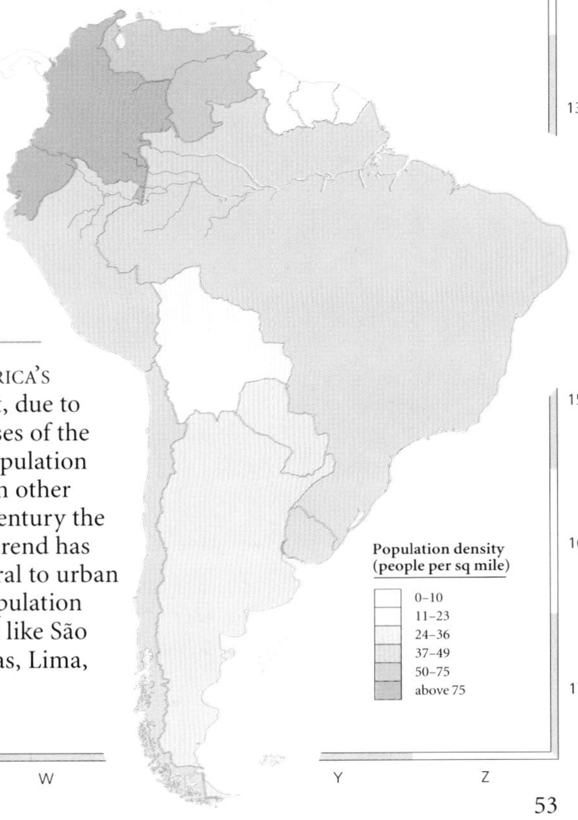

Population density (people per sq mile)

- 0–10
- 11–23
- 24–36
- 37–49
- 50–75
- above 75

South American Resources

Agriculture still provides the largest single form of employment in South America, though rural unemployment and poverty continue to drive people toward the huge coastal cities in search of jobs and opportunities. Mineral and fuel resources, although substantial, are distributed unevenly; few countries have both fossil fuels and minerals. To break dependence on industries based on raw materials, boost manufacturing, and improve infrastructure, governments borrowed heavily from the World Bank in the 1960s and 1970s. This led to the accumulation of massive debts that are unlikely to be repaid. Today, Brazil dominates the continent's economic output, followed by Argentina. Recently, the less-developed western side of South America has benefited from its geographical position at the eastern edge of the Pacific Rim. Chile, for example, is increasingly exporting raw materials to Japan.

Ciudad Guayana is a planned industrial complex in eastern Venezuela, built as an iron and steel center to exploit the nearby iron ore reserves.

Industry
aerospace
brewing
car/vehicle manufacture
chemicals
electronics
engineering
finance
fish processing
food processing
hi-tech industry
iron & steel
meat processing
metal refining
narcotics
pharmaceuticals
printing & publishing
shipbuilding
sugar processing
textiles
timber processing
tobacco processing
oil
gas
industrial cities
major industrial areas

***The cold Peru Current** flows north from the Antarctic along the Pacific coast of Peru, providing rich nutrients for one of the world's largest fishing grounds. Overexploitation has severely reduced Peru's anchovy catch.*

Standard of Living

Financial disparities throughout the continent create a wide gulf between affluent landowners and the chronically poor in inner-city slums. The illicit production of cocaine, and the hugely influential drug barons who control its distribution, contribute to the violent disorder and corruption that affect northwestern South America, destabilizing local governments and economies.

Standard of Living
(UN Human Development Index)
low
high

***Both Argentina and Chile** are now exploring the southernmost tip of the continent in search of oil. Here in Punta Arenas, a drilling rig is being prepared for exploratory drilling in the Strait of Magellen.*

GNP per capita (US$)
0–499
500–999
1,000–1,499
1,500–2,999
3,000–5,999
6,000+

Industry

Argentina and Brazil are South America's most industrialized countries and São Paulo is the continent's leading industrial center. Long-term government investment in Brazilian industry has encouraged a diverse industrial base; engineering, steel production, food processing, textile manufacture, and chemicals predominate. The illegal production of cocaine is economically significant in the Andean countries of Colombia and Bolivia. In Venezuela, the oil-dominated economy has left the country vulnerable to global price fluctuations. Food processing and mineral exploitation are common throughout the less industrially developed parts of the continent, including Bolivia, Chile, Ecuador, and Peru.

Environmental Issues

The Amazon Basin is one of the last great wilderness areas left on Earth. The tropical rain forests which grow there are a valuable genetic resource, containing innumerable unique plants and animals. The forests are increasingly under threat from new and expanding settlements and "slash and burn" farming techniques, which clear land for the raising of beef cattle, causing land degradation and soil erosion.

***Clouds of smoke billow** from the burning Amazon rain forest. Over 25,000 sq miles (60,000 sq km) of virgin rain forest are being cleared annually, destroying an ancient, irreplaceable, natural resource and biodiverse habitat.*

Environmental Issues

- national parks
- tropical forest
- forest destroyed
- desert
- desertification
- polluted rivers
- marine pollution
- heavy marine pollution
- poor urban air quality

Mineral Resources

Over a quarter of the world's known copper reserves are found at the Chuquicamata mine in northern Chile, and other metallic minerals such as tin are found along the length of the Andes. The discovery of oil and gas at Venezuela's Lake Maracaibo in 1917 turned the country into one of the world's leading oil producers. In contrast, South America is virtually devoid of coal, the only significant deposit being on the peninsula of Guajira in Colombia.

***Copper** is Chile's largest export, most of which is mined at Chuquicamata. Along the length of the Andes, metallic minerals like copper and tin are found in abundance, formed by the excessive pressures and heat involved in mountain-building.*

Mineral Resources

- oil field
- gas field
- coal field
- bauxite
- copper
- diamonds
- gold
- iron
- lead
- silver
- tin

Using the Land & Sea

Many foods now common worldwide originated in South America. These include the potato, tomato, squash, and cassava. Today, large herds of beef cattle roam the temperate grasslands of the Pampas, supporting an extensive meatpacking trade in Argentina, Uruguay, and Paraguay. Corn is grown as a staple crop across the continent and coffee is grown as a cash crop in Brazil and Colombia. Coca plants grown in Bolivia, Peru, and Colombia provide most of the world's cocaine. Fish and shellfish are caught off the western coast, especially anchovies off Peru, shrimps off Ecuador, and pilchards off Chile.

***South America**, and Brazil in particular, now leads the world in coffee production, mainly growing* Coffea arabica *in large plantations. Coffee beans are harvested, roasted, and brewed to produce the world's second most popular drink, after tea.*

***The Pampas** region of southeast South America is characterized by extensive, flat plains and populated by cattle and ranchers* (gauchos)*. Argentina is a major world producer of beef, much of which is exported to the US for use in hamburgers.*

***High in the Andes**, hardy alpacas graze on the barren land. Alpacas are thought to have been domesticated by the Incas, whose nobility wore robes made from their wool. Today, they are still reared and prized for their soft, warm fleeces.*

Using the Land and Sea

- barren land
- cropland
- desert
- forest
- mountain region
- pasture
- major conurbations
- cattle
- pigs
- sheep
- bananas
- corn
- citrus fruits
- cocoa
- cotton
- coffee
- fishing
- oil palms
- peanuts
- rubber
- shellfish
- soybeans
- sugar cane
- vineyards
- wheat

Northern South America

Colombia, Guyana, Suriname, Venezuela, ***French Guiana*** **(to France)**

Fringed by the Pacific and Atlantic oceans and the Caribbean Sea, South America's northern region has a rich range of natural resources, some exploited for centuries by colonial powers, including the Spanish, French, Dutch, and British, others still to be fully explored. The prospects for further economic development in Colombia, Guyana, and Suriname are blighted by drug-related violence and political instability. Venezuela, despite huge incomes from its oil reserves, remains less developed in other industrial sectors.

French Guiana is an overseas *département* of France, now seeking greater autonomy. Most of the major population centers, such as Bogotá, have grown up in the temperate conditions of the high Andes or, like Caracas, at strategic points along the Caribbean coast.

Flowers grown *in Colombia are exported all over the world, and include fine carnations and roses. Here, workers are cutting roses that have been grown in plastic greenhouses.*

Map Key

POPULATION

- 1 million to 5 million
- 500,000 to 1 million
- 100,000 to 500,000
- 50,000 to 100,000
- 10,000 to 50,000
- below 10,000

ELEVATION

- 4000m / 13,124ft
- 3000m / 9843ft
- 2000m / 6562ft
- 1000m / 3281ft
- 500m / 1640ft
- 250m / 820ft
- 100m / 328ft
- sea level

Large open squares, *like the Plaza Bolivia in Bogotá, are characteristic of many cities founded by the Spanish.*

Scattered farms *and villages have grown up on the gentle slopes of this Colombian river valley, utilizing the fertile soils for farming.*

Scale 1:6,500,000
(projection: Lambert Azimuthal Equal Area)

Km 0 25 50 100 150 200
Miles 0 25 50 100 150 200

The Orinoco River *flows from its source in the southern Guiana Highlands to form a broad delta on Venezuela's Atlantic coast. One of its distributary channels opens into a wide bay called the Serpent's Mouth.*

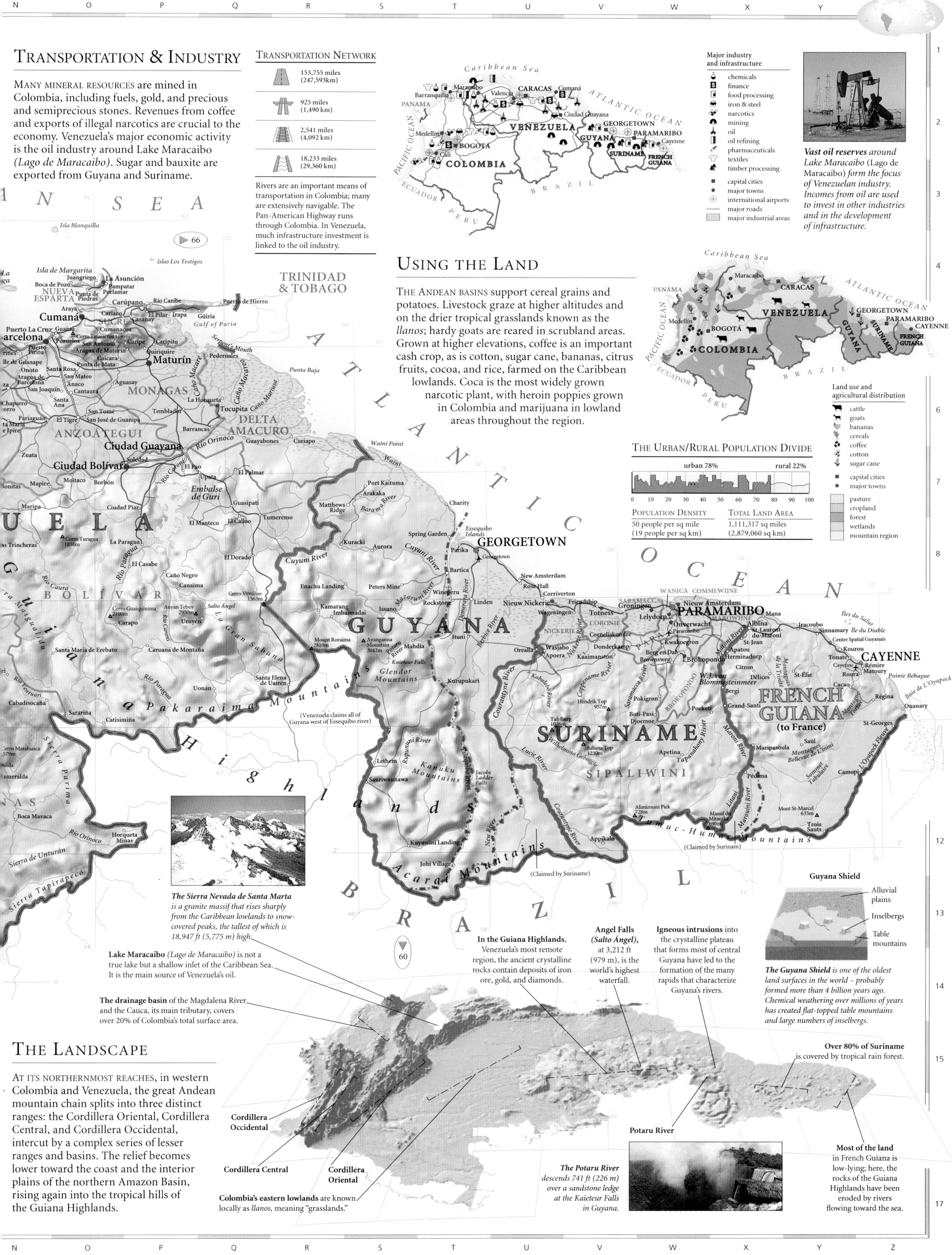
Transportation Network
153,755 miles (247,593km)
925 miles (1,490 km)
2,541 miles (4,092 km)
18,233 miles (29,360 km)
Major industry and infrastructure
chemicals
finance
food processing
iron & steel
narcotics
mining
oil
oil refining
pharmaceuticals
textiles
timber processing
capital cities
major towns
international airports
major roads
major industrial areas
Land use and agricultural distribution
cattle
goats
bananas
cereals
coffee
cotton
sugar cane
capital cities
major towns
pasture
cropland
forest
wetlands
mountain region
The Urban/Rural Population Divide
urban 78%
rural 22%
Population Density
50 people per sq mile (19 people per sq km)
Total Land Area
1,111,317 sq miles (2,879,060 sq km)
Guyana Shield
Alluvial plains
Inselbergs
Table mountains
Cordillera Occidental
Cordillera Central
Cordillera Oriental
Potaru River
GUYANA
SURINAME
FRENCH GUIANA (to France)
GEORGETOWN
PARAMARIBO
CAYENNE
ATLANTIC OCEAN

Transportation & Industry

Many mineral resources are mined in Colombia, including fuels, gold, and precious and semiprecious stones. Revenues from coffee and exports of illegal narcotics are crucial to the economy. Venezuela's major economic activity is the oil industry around Lake Maracaibo *(Lago de Maracaibo)*. Sugar and bauxite are exported from Guyana and Suriname.

Rivers are an important means of transportation in Colombia; many are extensively navigable. The Pan-American Highway runs through Colombia. In Venezuela, much infrastructure investment is linked to the oil industry.

***Vast oil reserves** around Lake Maracaibo (Lago de Maracaibo) form the focus of Venezuelan industry. Incomes from oil are used to invest in other industries and in the development of infrastructure.*

Using the Land

The Andean basins support cereal grains and potatoes. Livestock graze at higher altitudes and on the drier tropical grasslands known as the *llanos*; hardy goats are reared in scrubland areas. Grown at higher elevations, coffee is an important cash crop, as is cotton, sugar cane, bananas, citrus fruits, cocoa, and rice, farmed on the Caribbean lowlands. Coca is the most widely grown narcotic plant, with heroin poppies grown in Colombia and marijuana in lowland areas throughout the region.

▶ 66

▼ 60

***The Sierra Nevada de Santa Marta** is a granite massif that rises sharply from the Caribbean lowlands to snow-covered peaks, the tallest of which is 18,947 ft (5,775 m) high.*

Lake Maracaibo *(Lago de Maracaibo)* is not a true lake but a shallow inlet of the Caribbean Sea. It is the main source of Venezuela's oil.

The drainage basin of the Magdalena River and the Cauca, its main tributary, covers over 20% of Colombia's total surface area.

In the Guiana Highlands, Venezuela's most remote region, the ancient crystalline rocks contain deposits of iron ore, gold, and diamonds.

Angel Falls ***(Salto Ángel)***, at 3,212 ft (979 m), is the world's highest waterfall.

Igneous intrusions into the crystalline plateau that forms most of central Guyana have led to the formation of the many rapids that characterize Guyana's rivers.

***The Guyana Shield** is one of the oldest land surfaces in the world – probably formed more than 4 billion years ago. Chemical weathering over millions of years has created flat-topped table mountains and large numbers of inselbergs.*

Over 80% of Suriname is covered by tropical rain forest.

The Landscape

At its northernmost reaches, in western Colombia and Venezuela, the great Andean mountain chain splits into three distinct ranges: the Cordillera Oriental, Cordillera Central, and Cordillera Occidental, intercut by a complex series of lesser ranges and basins. The relief becomes lower toward the coast and the interior plains of the northern Amazon Basin, rising again into the tropical hills of the Guiana Highlands.

Colombia's eastern lowlands are known locally as *llanos*, meaning "grasslands."

***The Potaru River** descends 741 ft (226 m) over a sandstone ledge at the Kaieteur Falls in Guyana.*

Most of the land in French Guiana is low-lying; here, the rocks of the Guiana Highlands have been eroded by rivers flowing toward the sea.

Western South America

Bolivia, Ecuador, Peru

The three states of Western South America share a similar geography and recent history. Dominated by the Inca empire until Spanish conquest in the 16th century, they achieved independence from Spain in the early 19th century. The precipitous terrain of the Andes presents severe difficulties for overland transportation and continues to be a barrier to national unity and stability. Although Ecuador is now a relatively stable democracy, the military is highly influential in Peru and Bolivia, while the drug trade and associated corruption discourages external aid and economic progress. Wealth and power are still largely concentrated in the hands of a small elite of families who attained their position during the Spanish colonial period. Land rights and political recognition for indigenous peoples are becoming increasingly important issues, particularly in Ecuador.

The Landscape

Bolivia, Peru, and Ecuador each possess a high Andean mountain region and an eastern region consisting of tropical lowlands and the Andean slope leading down to them. Toward the south of the region, the mountains widen to form the high plateau of the Altiplano. Peru and Ecuador also have fertile lowland coastal plains. A wide variety of environments include *selva* (tropical rain forest), *montaña* (mountain forest), and grassland.

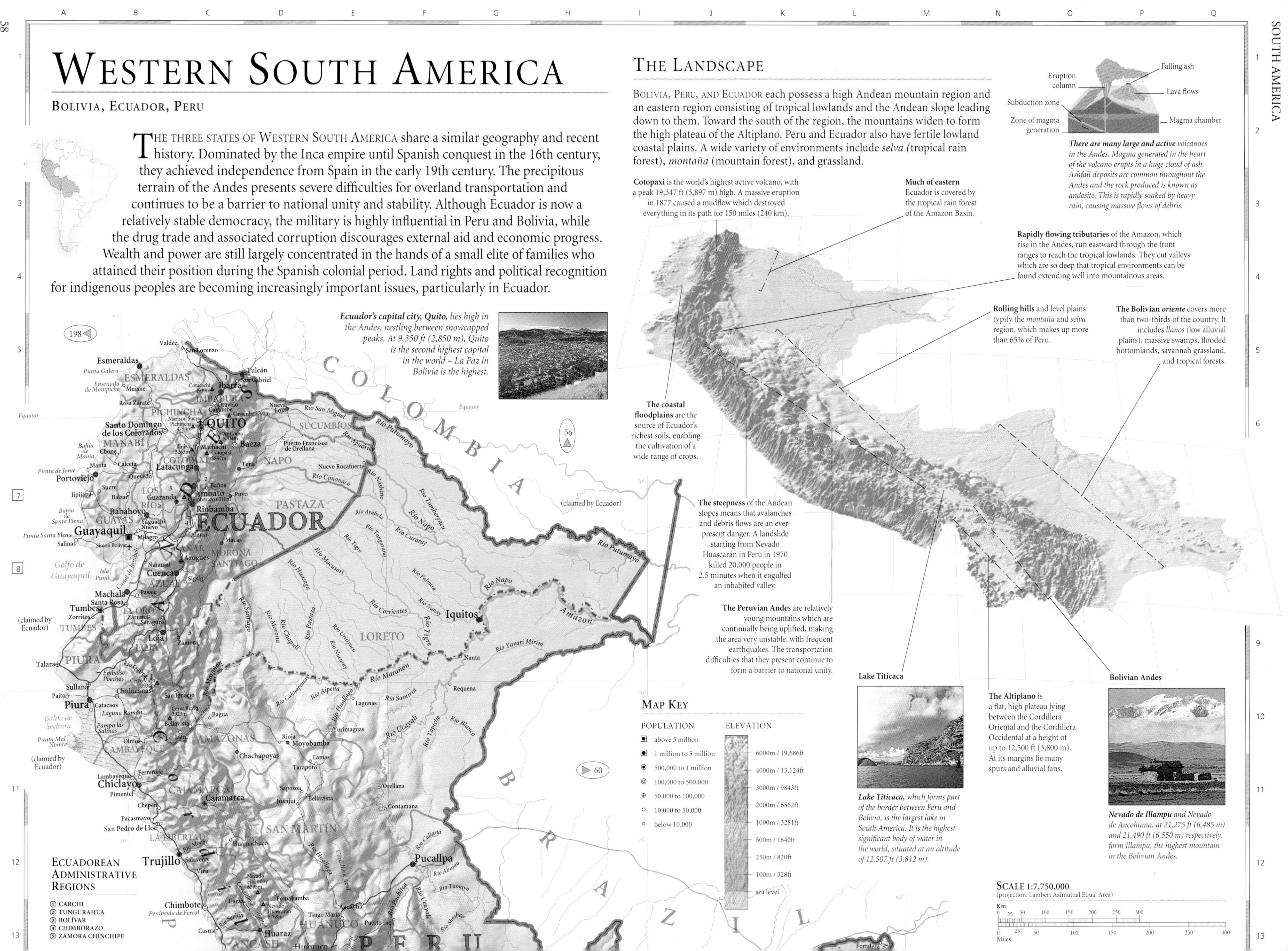

Eruption column
Falling ash
Lava flows
Subduction zone
Zone of magma generation
Magma chamber
Lake Titicaca
Bolivian Andes
MAP KEY
POPULATION
above 5 million
1 million to 5 million
500,000 to 1 million
100,000 to 500,000
50,000 to 100,000
10,000 to 50,000
below 10,000
ELEVATION
6000m / 19,686ft
4000m / 13,124ft
3000m / 9843ft
2000m / 6562ft
1000m / 3281ft
500m / 1640ft
250m / 820ft
100m / 328ft
sea level
SCALE 1:7,750,000
(projection: Lambert Azimuthal Equal Area)
ECUADOREAN ADMINISTRATIVE REGIONS
① CARCHI
② TUNGURAHUA
③ BOLÍVAR
④ CHIMBORAZO
⑤ ZAMORA CHINCHIPE
COLOMBIA
ECUADOR
PERU
BRAZIL
QUITO
Guayaquil
Iquitos
Pucallpa
Trujillo
Chiclayo
Piura
Chimbote
Cuenca
Ambato
Esmeraldas
Amazon
(claimed by Ecuador)
Equator

There are many large and active volcanoes in the Andes. Magma generated in the heart of the volcano erupts in a huge cloud of ash. Ashfall deposits are common throughout the Andes and the rock produced is known as andesite. This is rapidly soaked by heavy rain, causing massive flows of debris.

Cotopaxi is the world's highest active volcano, with a peak 19,347 ft (5,897 m) high. A massive eruption in 1877 caused a mudflow which destroyed everything in its path for 150 miles (240 km).

Much of eastern Ecuador is covered by the tropical rain forest of the Amazon Basin.

Rapidly flowing tributaries of the Amazon, which rise in the Andes, run eastward through the front ranges to reach the tropical lowlands. They cut valleys which are so deep that tropical environments can be found extending well into mountainous areas.

Rolling hills and level plains typify the *montaña* and *selva* region, which makes up more than 65% of Peru.

The Bolivian *oriente* covers more than two-thirds of the country. It includes *llanos* (low alluvial plains), massive swamps, flooded bottomlands, savannah grassland, and tropical forests.

The coastal floodplains are the source of Ecuador's richest soils, enabling the cultivation of a wide range of crops.

The steepness of the Andean slopes means that avalanches and debris flows are an ever-present danger. A landslide starting from Nevado Huascarán in Peru in 1970 killed 20,000 people in 2.5 minutes when it engulfed an inhabited valley.

The Peruvian Andes are relatively young mountains which are continually being uplifted, making the area very unstable, with frequent earthquakes. The transportation difficulties that they present continue to form a barrier to national unity.

The Altiplano is a flat, high plateau lying between the Cordillera Oriental and the Cordillera Occidental at a height of up to 12,500 ft (3,800 m). At its margins lie many spurs and alluvial fans.

Lake Titicaca, *which forms part of the border between Peru and Bolivia, is the largest lake in South America. It is the highest significant body of water in the world, situated at an altitude of 12,507 ft (3,812 m).*

Nevado de Illampu *and Nevado de Ancohuma, at 21,275 ft (6,485 m) and 21,490 ft (6,550 m) respectively, form Illampu, the highest mountain in the Bolivian Andes.*

Ecuador's capital city, Quito, *lies high in the Andes, nestling between snowcapped peaks. At 9,350 ft (2,850 m), Quito is the second highest capital in the world – La Paz in Bolivia is the highest.*

198 ◁ 56 △ ▷ 60

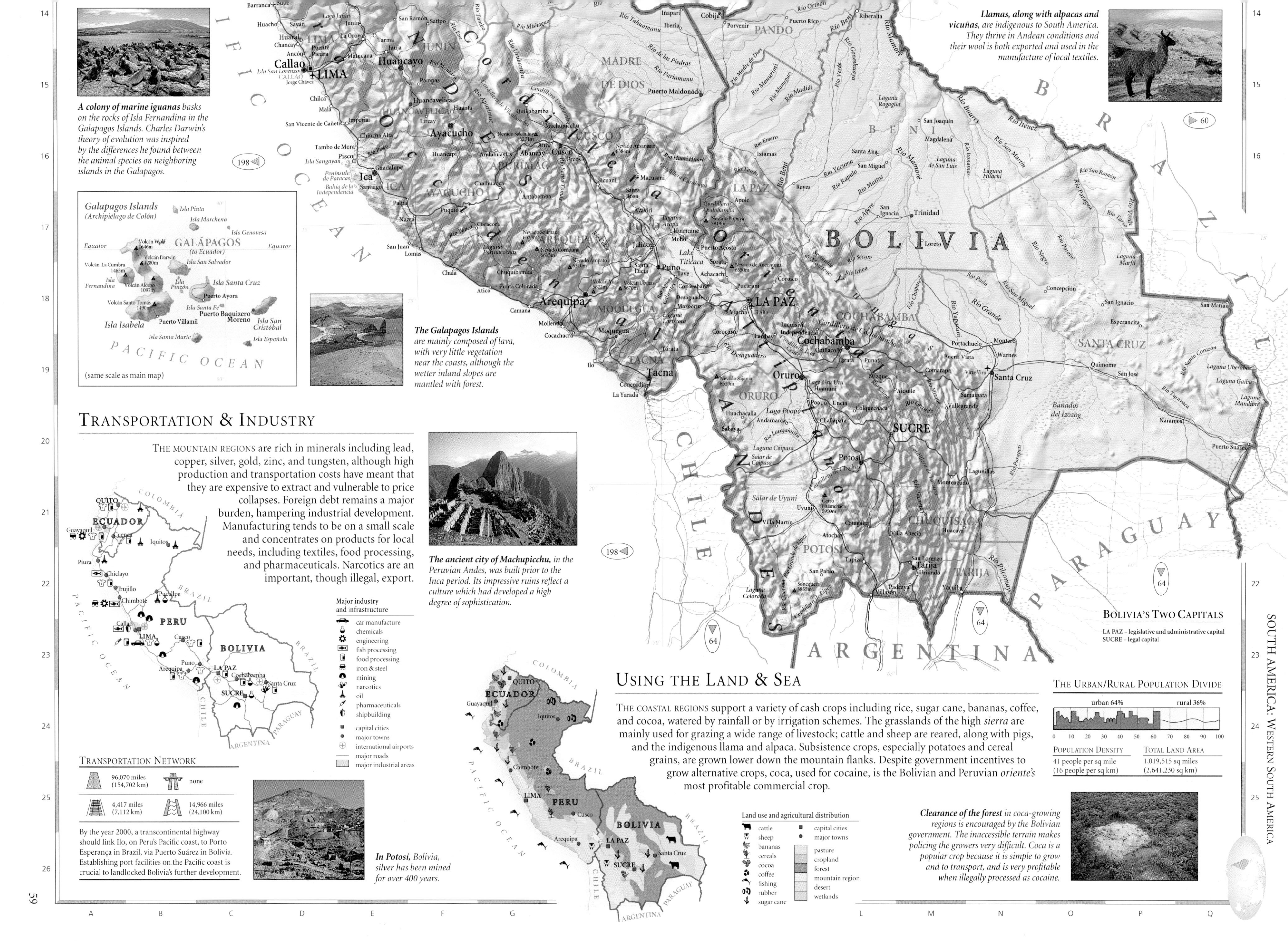

Bolivia's Two Capitals
La Paz – legislative and administrative capital
Sucre – legal capital
The Urban/Rural Population Divide
urban 64%
rural 36%
0 10 20 30 40 50 60 70 80 90 100
Population Density
41 people per sq mile
(16 people per sq km)
Total Land Area
1,019,515 sq miles
(2,641,230 sq km)
Major industry and infrastructure
car manufacture
chemicals
engineering
fish processing
food processing
iron & steel
mining
narcotics
oil
pharmaceuticals
shipbuilding
capital cities
major towns
international airports
major roads
major industrial areas
Transportation Network
96,070 miles (154,702 km)
none
4,417 miles (7,112 km)
14,966 miles (24,100 km)
Land use and agricultural distribution
cattle
sheep
bananas
cereals
cocoa
coffee
fishing
rubber
sugar cane
capital cities
major towns
pasture
cropland
forest
mountain region
desert
wetlands
Galapagos Islands (Archipiélago de Colón)
(same scale as main map)

A colony of marine iguanas *basks on the rocks of Isla Fernandina in the Galapagos Islands. Charles Darwin's theory of evolution was inspired by the differences he found between the animal species on neighboring islands in the Galapagos.*

The Galapagos Islands *are mainly composed of lava, with very little vegetation near the coasts, although the wetter inland slopes are mantled with forest.*

Llamas, along with alpacas and vicuñas, *are indigenous to South America. They thrive in Andean conditions and their wool is both exported and used in the manufacture of local textiles.*

The ancient city of Machupicchu, *in the Peruvian Andes, was built prior to the Inca period. Its impressive ruins reflect a culture which had developed a high degree of sophistication.*

Transportation & Industry

The mountain regions are rich in minerals including lead, copper, silver, gold, zinc, and tungsten, although high production and transportation costs have meant that they are expensive to extract and vulnerable to price collapses. Foreign debt remains a major burden, hampering industrial development. Manufacturing tends to be on a small scale and concentrates on products for local needs, including textiles, food processing, and pharmaceuticals. Narcotics are an important, though illegal, export.

By the year 2000, a transcontinental highway should link Ilo, on Peru's Pacific coast, to Porto Esperança in Brazil, via Puerto Suárez in Bolivia. Establishing port facilities on the Pacific coast is crucial to landlocked Bolivia's further development.

In Potosí, *Bolivia, silver has been mined for over 400 years.*

Using the Land & Sea

The coastal regions support a variety of cash crops including rice, sugar cane, bananas, coffee, and cocoa, watered by rainfall or by irrigation schemes. The grasslands of the high *sierra* are mainly used for grazing a wide range of livestock; cattle and sheep are reared, along with pigs, and the indigenous llama and alpaca. Subsistence crops, especially potatoes and cereal grains, are grown lower down the mountain flanks. Despite government incentives to grow alternative crops, coca, used for cocaine, is the Bolivian and Peruvian *oriente's* most profitable commercial crop.

Clearance of the forest *in coca-growing regions is encouraged by the Bolivian government. The inaccessible terrain makes policing the growers very difficult. Coca is a popular crop because it is simple to grow and to transport, and is very profitable when illegally processed as cocaine.*

Brazil

Brazil is the largest country in South America, with a population of nearly 160 million – greater than the combined total of the whole of the rest of the continent. The 26 states which make up the federal republic of Brazil are administered from the purpose-built capital, Brasília. Tropical rain forest, covering more than one-third of the country, contains rich natural resources, but great tracts are sacrificed on a daily basis to agriculture, industry, and urban expansion. Most of Brazil's multiethnic population now live in cities, some of which are vast areas of urban sprawl. São Paulo is one of the world's biggest conurbations, with more than 17 million inhabitants. Although prosperity is a reality for some, many people still live in great poverty, and mounting foreign debts continue to damage Brazil's prospects of economic advancement.

Using the Land

Brazil has immense natural resources, including minerals and hardwoods, many of which are found in the fragile rain forest. Brazil is the world's leading coffee grower and a major producer of livestock, sugar, and orange juice concentrate. Soybeans for animal feed, particularly for poultry, have become the country's most significant crop.

The Urban/Rural Population Divide

urban 77% · rural 23%

Population Density	Total Land Area
44 people per sq mile (17 people per sq km)	3,286,472 sq miles (8,511,970 sq km)

Land use and agricultural distribution
cattle
pigs
sheep
citrus fruits
coffee
cotton
soybeans
sugar cane
timber
capital cities
major towns
pasture
cropland
forest
BRAZIL
ATLANTIC OCEAN
Manaus
Belém
Fortaleza
Recife
Salvador
Carajás
BRASÍLIA
Belo Horizonte
Rio de Janeiro
São Paulo
Curitiba
Porto Alegre
COLOMBIA
VENEZUELA
GUYANA
SURINAME
FRENCH GUIANA
PERU
BOLIVIA
PARAGUAY
ARGENTINA
URUGUAY

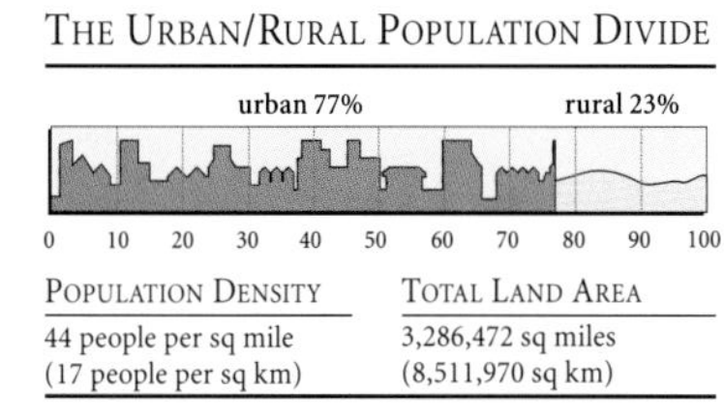

The fecundity of parts of Brazil's rain forest is the result of exceptionally high levels of rainfall and the quantities of silt deposited by the Amazon River system.

The Landscape

The Amazon Basin, containing the largest area of tropical rain forest on Earth, covers nearly half of Brazil. It is bordered by two shield areas: in the south by the Brazilian Highlands, and in the north by the Guiana Highlands. The east coast is dominated by a great escarpment which runs for 1,600 miles (2,565 km).

The Amazon Basin is the largest river basin in the world. The Amazon River and over a thousand tributaries drain an area of 2,375,000 sq miles (6,150,000 sq km) and carry one-fifth of the world's fresh water out to sea.

The ancient Brazilian Highlands have a varied topography. Their plateaus, hills, and deep valleys are bordered by highly-eroded mountains containing important mineral deposits. They are drained by three great river systems, the Amazon, the Paraguay–Paraná, and the São Francisco.

Guiana Highlands

The São Francisco Basin has a climate unique in Brazil. Known as the "drought polygon," it has almost no rain during the dry season, leading to regular disastrous droughts.

Brazil's highest mountain is the Pico da Neblina. It was discovered as recently as 1962. It is 9,888 ft (3,014 m) high.

The northeastern scrublands are known as the *caatinga*, a virtually impenetrable thorny woodland, sometimes intermixed with cacti where water is scarce.

The floodplains which border the Amazon River are made up of a variety of different features including shallow lakes and swamps, mangrove forests in the tidal delta area, and fertile levées on riverbanks and point bars.

Pantanal swamps

The Pantanal region in the south of Brazil is an extension of the Gran Chaco plain. The swamps and marshes of this area are renowned for their beauty and abundant and unique wildlife, including wildfowl and these caimans, a type of crocodile.

The famous Sugar Loaf Mountain (*Pão de Açúcar*) which overlooks Rio de Janeiro is a fine example of a volcanic plug – a domed core of solidified lava left after the slopes of the original volcano have eroded away.

The Iguaçu River surges over the spectacular Iguaçu Falls (Saltos do Iguaçu) toward the Paraná River. Falls like these are increasingly under pressure from large-scale hydroelectric projects such as that at Itaipú.

Hillslope gullying

Rainfall
Direction of growth
Water seeps through hillslope
Overland water flow
Gully

Large-scale gullies are common in Brazil, particularly on hillslopes from which vegetation has been removed. Gullies grow headward (up the slope), aided by a combination of erosion through water seepage and rainwater runoff.

Deep natural harbors such as Baia de Guanabara were created where the steep slopes of the Serra da Mantiqueira plunge directly into the ocean.

Map Key

Population	Elevation
above 5 million	3000m / 9843ft
1 million to 5 million	2000m / 6562ft
500,000 to 1 million	1000m / 3281ft
100,000 to 500,000	500m / 1640ft
50,000 to 100,000	250m / 820ft
10,000 to 50,000	100m / 328ft
below 10,000	sea level

56 · 56 · 56 · 56 · 56 · 66 · 56 · 58

VENEZUELA
GUYANA
SURINAME
FRENCH GUIANA (to France)
COLOMBIA
ATLANTIC OCEAN
Guiana Highlands
RORAIMA
AMAPÁ
Boa Vista
Macapá
Belém
Manaus
Santarém
São Luís
Parnaíba
Pakaraima Mountains
Tumuc-Humac Mountains
Acaraí Mountains
Serra Parima
Serra do Jatapu
Serra do Traíra
Mount Roraima 2810m
Pico da Neblina 3014m
Ilha de Marajó
Mouths of the Amazon
Planalto Maracanaquará
Rio Negro
Rio Branco
Rio Jari
Rio Trombetas
Rio Tocantins
Amazon
Equator

BRAZIL
PERU
BOLIVIA
PARAGUAY
ARGENTINA
URUGUAY
ATLANTIC OCEAN
ACRE
RONDÔNIA
MATO GROSSO
MATO GROSSO DO SUL
TOCANTINS
PIAUÍ
BAHIA
GOIÁS
DISTRITO FEDERAL
MINAS GERAIS
ESPÍRITO SANTO
RIO DE JANEIRO
SÃO PAULO
PARANÁ
SANTA CATARINA
RIO GRANDE DO SUL
PERNAMBUCO
PARAÍBA
RIO GRANDE DO NORTE
ALAGOAS
SERGIPE
Planalto Central
(Brazilian Highlands)
Planalto de Mato Grosso
Pantanal
Serra Geral
Serra do Mar
Chapada Diamantina
Chapada dos Parecis
Serra do Cachimbo
Serra dos Gradaús
Serra do Roncador
Espigão Mestre
Brasília
Rio de Janeiro
São Paulo
Belo Horizonte
Salvador
Recife
Porto Alegre
Curitiba
Florianópolis
Goiânia
Cuiabá
Campo Grande
Porto Velho
Rio Branco
Vitória
Aracaju
Maceió
Natal
João Pessoa
Tropic of Capricorn
Lagoa dos Patos
Mirim Lagoon
Lagoa Mangueira

SCALE 1:12,750,000
(projection: Lambert Azimuthal Equal Area)

Transportation & Industry

Brazilian industry is diverse and well developed, partly as a result of past government incentives, including the prohibition of imports. Industries which have benefited include car manufacture, petrochemicals, and microelectronics. Textiles, clothing, and footwear are among Brazil's most successful exports. The country's service and tourist industries are also expanding rapidly.

Transportation Network

- 1,032,008 miles (1,661,850 km)
- 2,105 miles (5,000 km)
- 13,738 miles (22,123 km)
- 31,069 miles (50,000 km)

An extensive new road network is being built to link Brazil's main centers. Investment is needed to update the antiquated railroad system. In São Paulo, the subway system is being extended to accommodate the expanding population.

Major industry and infrastructure

car manufacture	mining	capital cities
chemicals	oil	major towns
electronics	printing & publishing	international airports
finance	textiles	major roads
food processing	timber processing	major industrial areas
iron & steel	tourism	

Brazil's urban population *has grown by over 6% per year since the mid-1970s. At current population levels, this represents a rate of nearly 6 million people annually. In Rio de Janeiro prosperous neighborhoods exist alongside over 450 shantytowns or favelas, some of which house as many as 250,000 people.*

A gaucho *wearing traditional clothing herds beef cattle on the grasslands of the Rio Grande do Sul in southern Brazil.*

Picinguaba Beach *lies in Serra do Mar State Park in São Paulo state. São Paulo's beaches stretch for 240 miles (400 km) along the Atlantic coast.*

Eastern South America

Uruguay, Northeast Argentina, Southeast Brazil

The vast conurbations of Rio de Janeiro, São Paulo, and Buenos Aires form the core of South America's highly-urbanized eastern region. São Paulo state, with almost 34 million inhabitants, is among the world's 20 most powerful economies, and São Paulo is the fastest growing city on the continent. Rio de Janeiro and Buenos Aires, transformed in the last hundred years from port cities into great metropolitan areas each with more than 10 million inhabitants, typify the unstructured growth and wealth disparities of South America's great cities. In Uruguay, over half of the population lives in the capital, Montevideo, which faces Buenos Aires across the Plate River (*Río de la Plata*). Immigration from the countryside has created severe pressure on the urban infrastructure, particularly on available housing, leading to a profusion of crowded shanty settlements (*favelas* or *barrios*).

Using the Land

Most of Uruguay and the Pampas of northern Argentina are devoted to raising livestock, especially cattle and sheep, which are central to both countries' economies. Soybeans, first produced in Brazil's Rio Grande do Sul, are now more widely grown for large-scale export, as are cereal grains, sugar cane, and grapes. Subsistence crops, including potatoes, corn, and sugar beets, are grown on the remaining arable land.

Land use and agricultural distribution

- cattle
- sheep
- cereals
- coffee
- fruit
- soybeans
- sugar cane
- capital cities
- major towns
- pasture
- cropland
- forest
- wetlands
- barren land

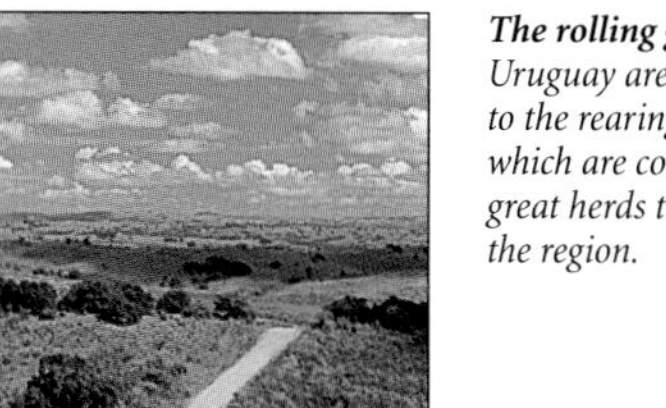

***The rolling grasslands** of Uruguay are ideally suited to the rearing of cattle, which are concentrated in great herds throughout the region.*

Scale 1:6,250,000
(projection: Lambert Azimuthal Equal Area)

***Soybeans** are harvested, pressed, and processed into soycake, which is used as animal feed. The cake is fed mainly to chickens on large-scale factory farms, and the growth in soy production has been an important factor in the expansion of the Brazilian poultry trade.*

Transportation & Industry

Southeast Brazil is home to much of the important motor and capital goods industry, largely based around São Paulo; iron and steel production is also concentrated in this region. Uruguay's economy continues to be based mainly on the export of livestock products, including meat and leather goods. Buenos Aires is Argentina's chief port, and the region has a varied and sophisticated economic base including service-based industries such as finance and publishing, as well as primary processing.

Major industry and infrastructure

- car manufacture
- chemicals
- engineering
- finance
- food processing
- iron & steel
- meat processing
- printing & publishing
- shipbuilding
- textiles
- timber processing
- capital cities
- major towns
- international airports
- major roads
- major industrial areas

Map Key

POPULATION	ELEVATION
above 5 million	2000m / 6562ft
1 million to 5 million	1000m / 3281ft
500,000 to 1 million	500m / 1640ft
100,000 to 500,000	250m / 820ft
50,000 to 100,000	100m / 328ft
10,000 to 50,000	sea level
below 10,000	

Transportation Network

Throughout the region, road networks need to be expanded to cope with urban development. Plans are underway to build a road tunnel under the Plate River (*Río de la Plata*) to link Montevideo and Buenos Aires.

***The Itaipú dam** on the Paraná River is one of the largest hydroelectric projects in the world, financed by both Brazil and Paraguay.*

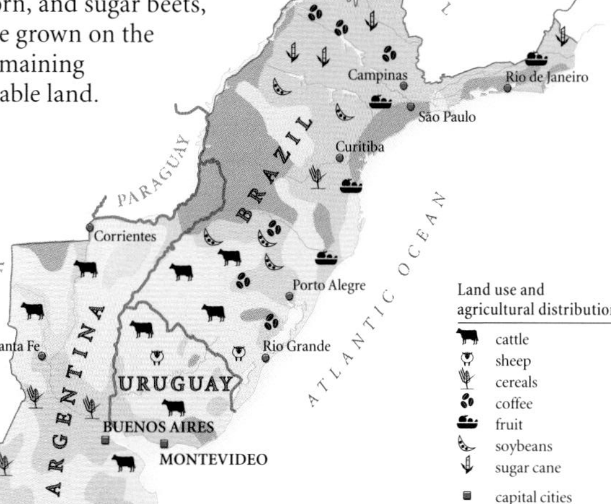

60

64

66

***Rio de Janeiro's** annual carnival, Mardi Gras, which ushers in the start of Lent, is an extravagant five-day parade through the city, characterized by fantastically decorated floats, exuberant dancing, and samba music.*

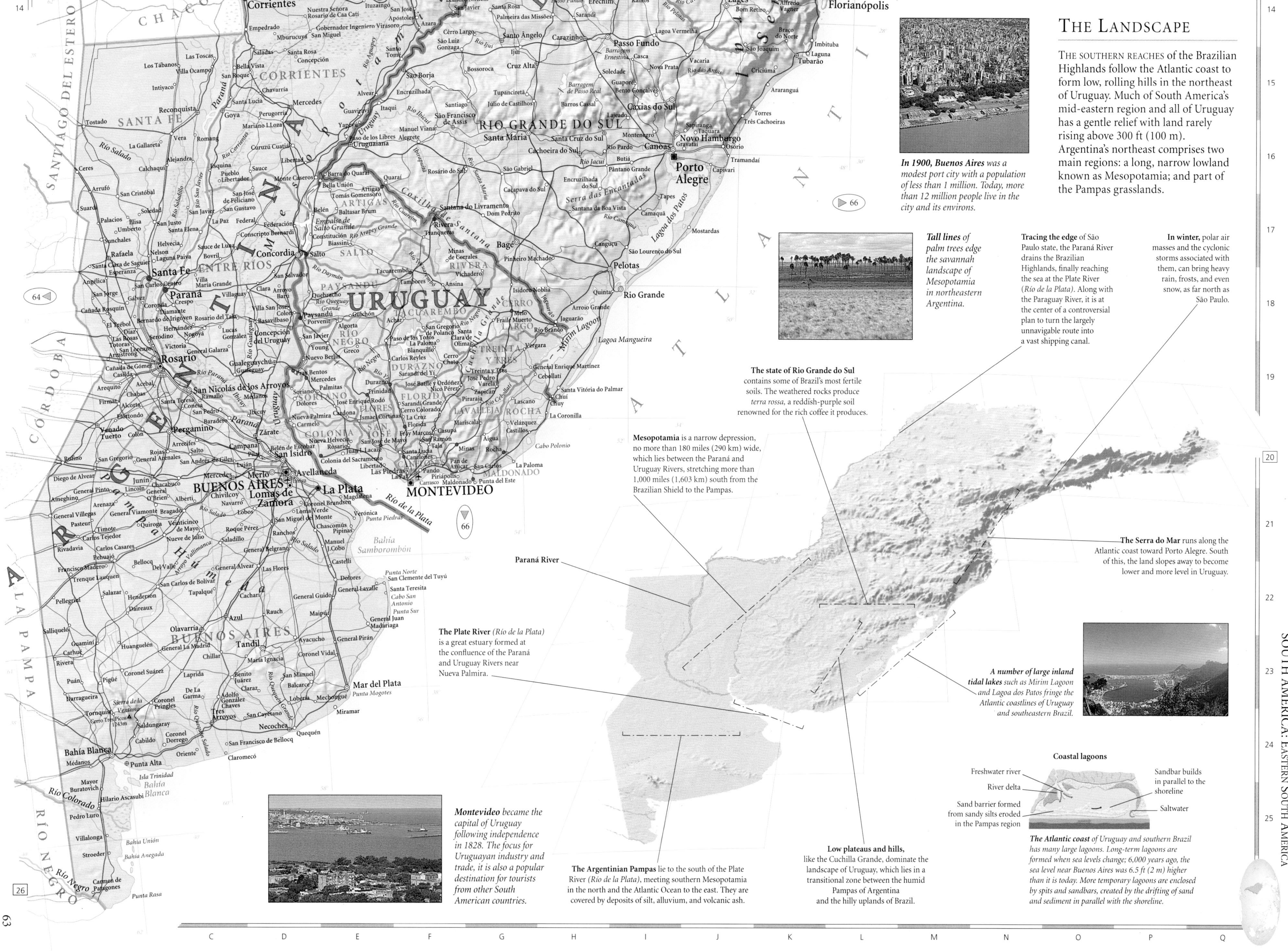

THE LANDSCAPE

THE SOUTHERN REACHES of the Brazilian Highlands follow the Atlantic coast to form low, rolling hills in the northeast of Uruguay. Much of South America's mid-eastern region and all of Uruguay has a gentle relief with land rarely rising above 300 ft (100 m). Argentina's northeast comprises two main regions: a long, narrow lowland known as Mesopotamia; and part of the Pampas grasslands.

***In 1900, Buenos Aires** was a modest port city with a population of less than 1 million. Today, more than 12 million people live in the city and its environs.*

***Tall lines** of palm trees edge the savannah landscape of Mesopotamia in northeastern Argentina.*

Tracing the edge of São Paulo state, the Paraná River drains the Brazilian Highlands, finally reaching the sea at the Plate River (*Río de la Plata*). Along with the Paraguay River, it is at the center of a controversial plan to turn the largely unnavigable route into a vast shipping canal.

In winter, polar air masses and the cyclonic storms associated with them, can bring heavy rain, frosts, and even snow, as far north as São Paulo.

The state of Rio Grande do Sul contains some of Brazil's most fertile soils. The weathered rocks produce *terra rossa*, a reddish-purple soil renowned for the rich coffee it produces.

Mesopotamia is a narrow depression, no more than 180 miles (290 km) wide, which lies between the Paraná and Uruguay Rivers, stretching more than 1,000 miles (1,603 km) south from the Brazilian Shield to the Pampas.

Paraná River

The Serra do Mar runs along the Atlantic coast toward Porto Alegre. South of this, the land slopes away to become lower and more level in Uruguay.

The Plate River (*Río de la Plata*) is a great estuary formed at the confluence of the Paraná and Uruguay Rivers near Nueva Palmira.

***A number of large inland tidal lakes** such as Mirim Lagoon and Lagoa dos Patos fringe the Atlantic coastlines of Uruguay and southeastern Brazil.*

Coastal lagoons

Freshwater river
River delta
Sand barrier formed from sandy silts eroded in the Pampas region
Sandbar builds in parallel to the shoreline
Saltwater

***The Atlantic coast** of Uruguay and southern Brazil has many large lagoons. Long-term lagoons are formed when sea levels change; 6,000 years ago, the sea level near Buenos Aires was 6.5 ft (2 m) higher than it is today. More temporary lagoons are enclosed by spits and sandbars, created by the drifting of sand and sediment in parallel with the shoreline.*

***Montevideo** became the capital of Uruguay following independence in 1828. The focus for Uruguayan industry and trade, it is also a popular destination for tourists from other South American countries.*

The Argentinian Pampas lie to the south of the Plate River (*Río de la Plata*), meeting southern Mesopotamia in the north and the Atlantic Ocean to the east. They are covered by deposits of silt, alluvium, and volcanic ash.

Low plateaus and hills, like the Cuchilla Grande, dominate the landscape of Uruguay, which lies in a transitional zone between the humid Pampas of Argentina and the hilly uplands of Brazil.

64 ◀ 66 ▶ 66 ▼

Southern South America

Argentina, Chile, Paraguay

South America's cone-shaped southern region is shared by Argentina and Chile, two overwhelmingly urbanized nations whose populations live mainly in or around the capital cities, Buenos Aires and Santiago. The people are largely *mestizo* or of European origin; in the early 20th century Argentina absorbed waves of new European immigrants, many from Italy and Germany. Paraguay is far less urbanized than its neighbors, with a homogeneous population of mixed Spanish and Guaraní origin, who retain their Indian roots through the Guaraní language. Though most Paraguayans live in the southeast, near Asunción, the indigenous Indians live in the sparsely populated Gran Chaco. The Gran Chaco is also home to some of Argentina's minority indigenous peoples, who otherwise live mainly in Andean regions. Chile's estimated 800,000 Mapauche Indians live almost exclusively in the south.

Transportation & Industry

Food processing and agricultural exports remain a fundamental part of Argentina's economy. The growth of manufacturing is regularly hampered by hyper-inflation and massive foreign debts. The world's most important copper producer and one of the top ten gold producers, Chile also has a thriving wine and grape industry. Most Paraguayan exports involve primary processing, although domestic goods are produced for home markets.

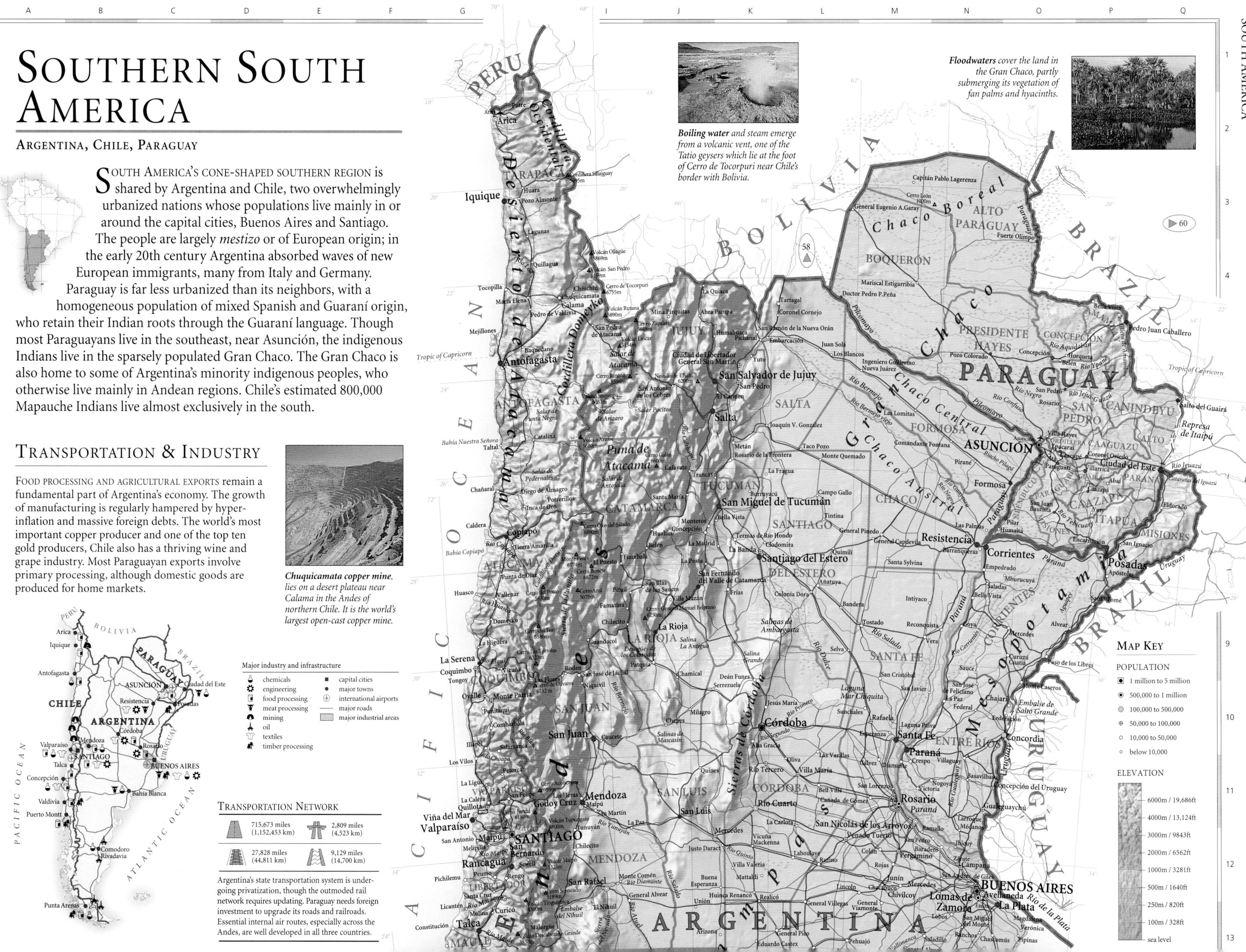

Major industry and infrastructure
chemicals
engineering
food processing
meat processing
mining
oil
textiles
timber processing
capital cities
major towns
international airports
major roads
major industrial areas
Transportation Network
715,673 miles (1,152,453 km)
2,809 miles (4,523 km)
27,828 miles (44,811 km)
9,129 miles (14,700 km)
Map Key
Population
1 million to 5 million
500,000 to 1 million
100,000 to 500,000
50,000 to 100,000
10,000 to 50,000
below 10,000
Elevation
6000m / 19,686ft
4000m / 13,124ft
3000m / 9843ft
2000m / 6562ft
1000m / 3281ft
500m / 1640ft
250m / 820ft
100m / 328ft
sea level
PARAGUAY
ASUNCIÓN
BRAZIL
BOLIVIA
PERU
URUGUAY
ARGENTINA
CHILE
BUENOS AIRES
SANTIAGO
PACIFIC OCEAN
ATLANTIC OCEAN

Argentina's state transportation system is undergoing privatization, though the outmoded rail network requires updating. Paraguay needs foreign investment to upgrade its roads and railroads. Essential internal air routes, especially across the Andes, are well developed in all three countries.

Chuquicamata copper mine, *lies on a desert plateau near Calama in the Andes of northern Chile. It is the world's largest open-cast copper mine.*

Boiling water *and steam emerge from a volcanic vent, one of the Tatio geysers which lie at the foot of Cerro de Tocorpuri near Chile's border with Bolivia.*

Floodwaters *cover the land in the Gran Chaco, partly submerging its vegetation of fan palms and hyacinths.*

▶ 60

THE LANDSCAPE

THE ANDES RUN FROM NORTH TO SOUTH, forming a precipitous natural border between Chile and Argentina. East of the Andes are the scrublands of the Gran Chaco and the plains of the Pampas, which extend northward toward Paraguay. In the far southwest, Chile's indented Pacific coastline has many features typical of areas which have been affected by glaciation.

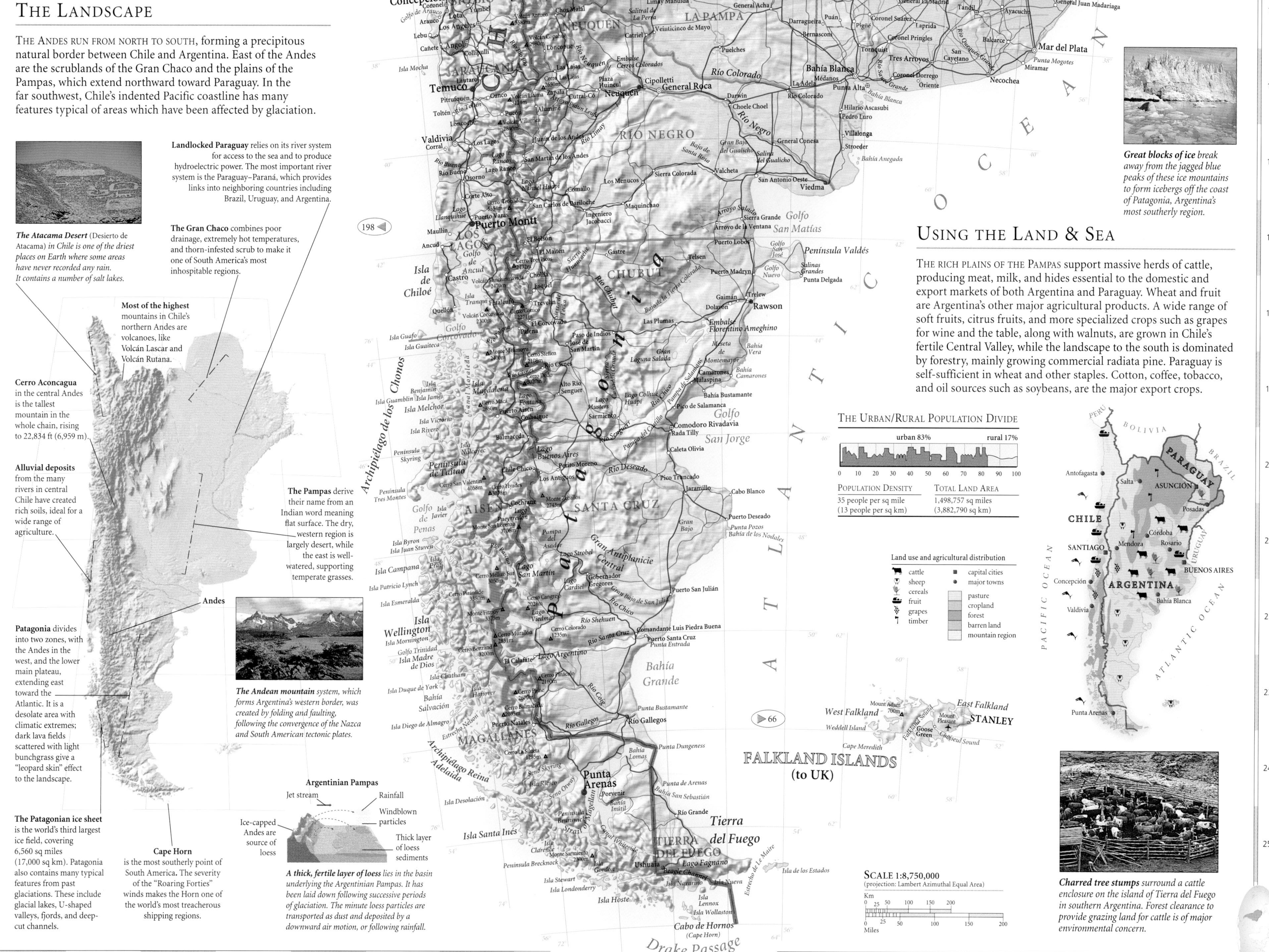
Andes
Argentinian Pampas
Jet stream
Rainfall
Windblown particles
Ice-capped Andes are source of loess
Thick layer of loess sediments
LA PAMPA
NEUQUÉN
RÍO NEGRO
CHUBUT
SANTA CRUZ
AISÉN
LOS LAGOS
MAGALLANES
TIERRA DEL FUEGO
Puerto Montt
Temuco
Valdivia
Punta Arenas
Bahía Blanca
Mar del Plata
Rawson
Viedma
Comodoro Rivadavia
Río Gallegos
Ushuaia
Isla de Chiloé
Archipiélago de los Chonos
Isla Wellington
Isla Santa Inés
Tierra del Fuego
Cabo de Hornos (Cape Horn)
Drake Passage
FALKLAND ISLANDS (to UK)
West Falkland
East Falkland
STANLEY
198
66
SCALE 1:8,750,000
(projection: Lambert Azimuthal Equal Area)
PERU
BOLIVIA
BRAZIL
PARAGUAY
ASUNCIÓN
CHILE
SANTIAGO
ARGENTINA
BUENOS AIRES
URUGUAY
PACIFIC OCEAN
ATLANTIC OCEAN
Antofagasta
Salta
Posadas
Córdoba
Mendoza
Rosario
Concepción
Valdivia
Bahía Blanca
Punta Arenas

The Atacama Desert *(Desierto de Atacama) in Chile is one of the driest places on Earth where some areas have never recorded any rain. It contains a number of salt lakes.*

Landlocked Paraguay relies on its river system for access to the sea and to produce hydroelectric power. The most important river system is the Paraguay–Paraná, which provides links into neighboring countries including Brazil, Uruguay, and Argentina.

The Gran Chaco combines poor drainage, extremely hot temperatures, and thorn-infested scrub to make it one of South America's most inhospitable regions.

Most of the highest mountains in Chile's northern Andes are volcanoes, like Volcán Lascar and Volcán Rutana.

Cerro Aconcagua in the central Andes is the tallest mountain in the whole chain, rising to 22,834 ft (6,959 m).

Alluvial deposits from the many rivers in central Chile have created rich soils, ideal for a wide range of agriculture.

The Pampas derive their name from an Indian word meaning flat surface. The dry, western region is largely desert, while the east is well-watered, supporting temperate grasses.

Patagonia divides into two zones, with the Andes in the west, and the lower main plateau, extending east toward the Atlantic. It is a desolate area with climatic extremes; dark lava fields scattered with light bunchgrass give a "leopard skin" effect to the landscape.

***The Andean mountain** system, which forms Argentina's western border, was created by folding and faulting, following the convergence of the Nazca and South American tectonic plates.*

The Patagonian ice sheet is the world's third largest ice field, covering 6,560 sq miles (17,000 sq km). Patagonia also contains many typical features from past glaciations. These include glacial lakes, U-shaped valleys, fjords, and deep-cut channels.

Cape Horn is the most southerly point of South America. The severity of the "Roaring Forties" winds makes the Horn one of the world's most treacherous shipping regions.

***A thick, fertile layer of loess** lies in the basin underlying the Argentinian Pampas. It has been laid down following successive periods of glaciation. The minute loess particles are transported as dust and deposited by a downward air motion, or following rainfall.*

***Great blocks of ice** break away from the jagged blue peaks of these ice mountains to form icebergs off the coast of Patagonia, Argentina's most southerly region.*

USING THE LAND & SEA

THE RICH PLAINS OF THE PAMPAS support massive herds of cattle, producing meat, milk, and hides essential to the domestic and export markets of both Argentina and Paraguay. Wheat and fruit are Argentina's other major agricultural products. A wide range of soft fruits, citrus fruits, and more specialized crops such as grapes for wine and the table, along with walnuts, are grown in Chile's fertile Central Valley, while the landscape to the south is dominated by forestry, mainly growing commercial radiata pine. Paraguay is self-sufficient in wheat and other staples. Cotton, coffee, tobacco, and oil sources such as soybeans, are the major export crops.

THE URBAN/RURAL POPULATION DIVIDE

urban 83% — rural 17%

POPULATION DENSITY	TOTAL LAND AREA
35 people per sq mile (13 people per sq km)	1,498,757 sq miles (3,882,790 sq km)

Land use and agricultural distribution: cattle, sheep, cereals, fruit, grapes, timber; capital cities, major towns; pasture, cropland, forest, barren land, mountain region

***Charred tree stumps** surround a cattle enclosure on the island of Tierra del Fuego in southern Argentina. Forest clearance to provide grazing land for cattle is of major environmental concern.*

The Atlantic Ocean

The Atlantic is the youngest of the world's oceans, formed about 180 million years ago when the landmasses of the eastern and western hemispheres separated. Its underwater topography is dominated by the Mid-Atlantic Ridge, a huge mountain system running north to south along the center of the ocean. Although most of the ridge's peaks lie below the sea, some emerge as volcanic islands, like Iceland and the Azores. The Atlantic contains a wealth of resources, including substantial oil and gas reserves and rich fishing grounds. Until the 1950s, the north Atlantic was the world's busiest shipping route; cheaper air transportation and alternate routes have shifted patterns of world trade.

Resources

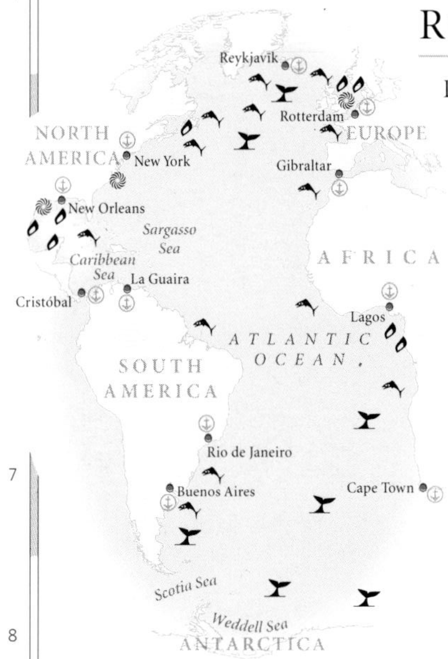

Development of the oil and gas reserves in the Atlantic began in the 1940s around the Gulf of Mexico. Since then other areas have been exploited, including the North Sea, the west coast of Africa and the area east of Newfoundland and Nova Scotia. There is also extensive mining of sand, gravel, and shell deposits by the US and UK. For centuries, the north Atlantic's fishing grounds have been more heavily utilized than other oceans, leading to a serious decline in many fish stocks.

Resources (including wildlife)

- fish
- whales
- aggregates
- oil & gas
- major towns
- major ports

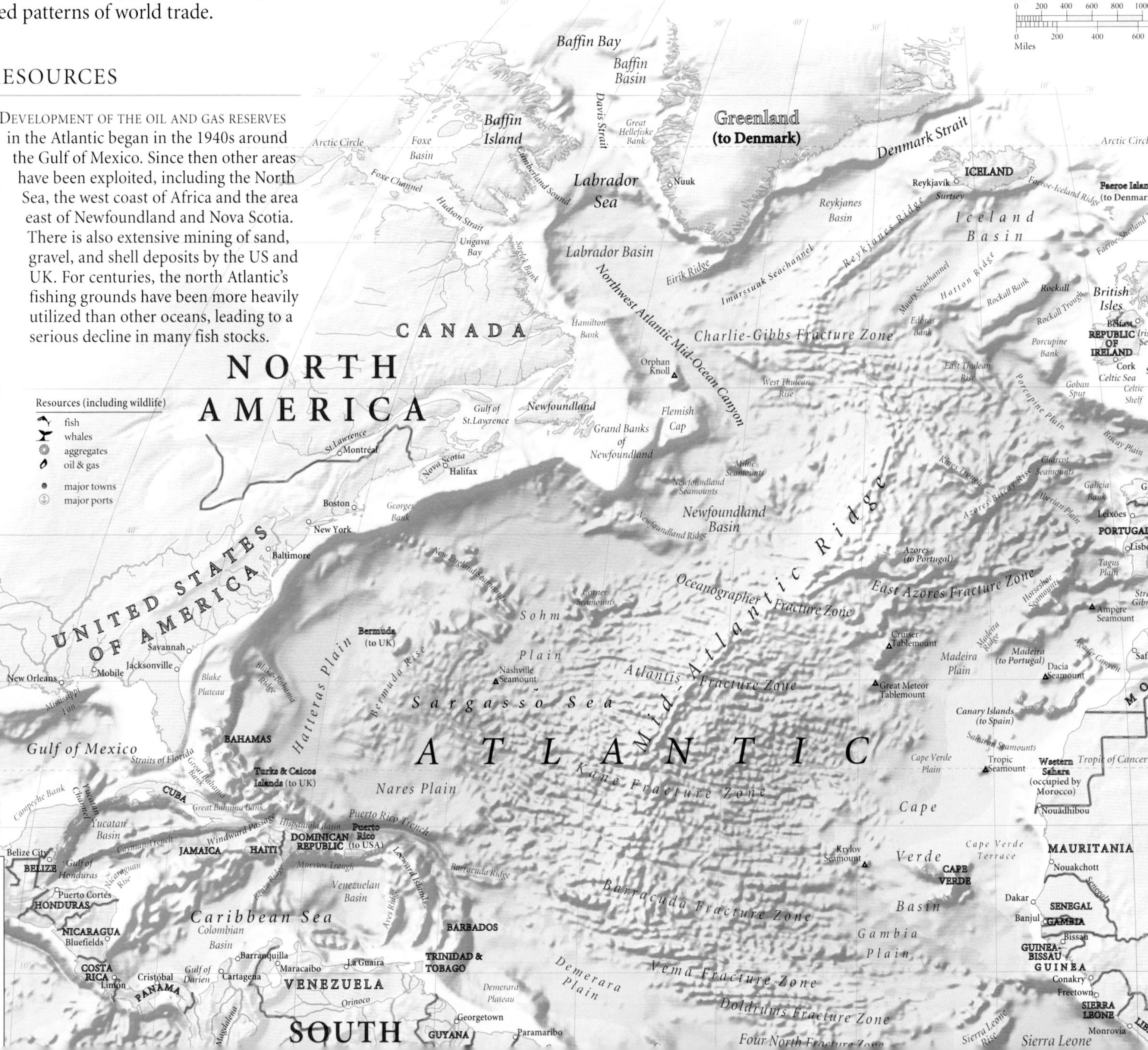

Surtsey near Iceland, *lies on the Mid-Atlantic Ridge. The island was formed in 1963 following a volcanic eruption caused by sea-floor spreading.*

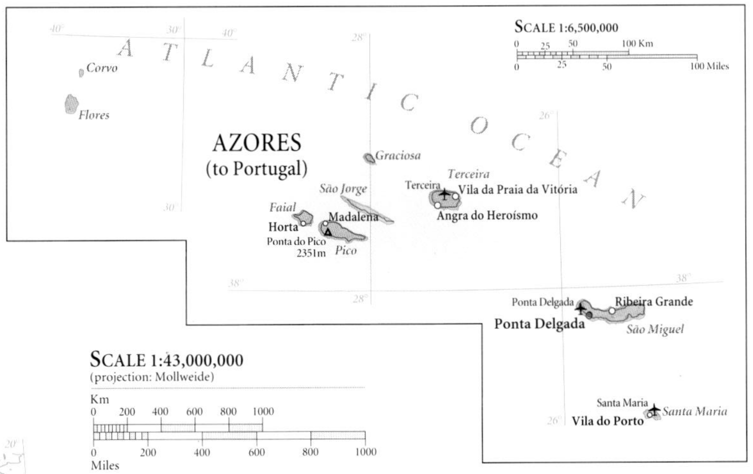

Fishing *in the seas around northwestern Europe dates back more than 1,500 years. The high nutrient content of the seas makes them ideal breeding grounds for many species of fish.*

On January 5, 1993, *the oil tanker Braer ran aground in the Shetland Islands, spilling 83,660 tons (85,000 tonnes) of light crude oil into the ocean, devastating the local marine ecosystem.*

SCALE 1:43,000,000 (projection: Mollweide)

AZORES (to Portugal) — SCALE 1:6,500,000

MADEIRA (to Portugal) — SCALE 1:2,500,000

ISLAS CANARIAS (CANARY ISLANDS) (to Spain) — SCALE 1:6,500,000

BERMUDA (to UK) — SCALE 1:500,000

NORTH AMERICA

CANADA

UNITED STATES OF AMERICA

EUROPE

AFRICA

ATLANTIC

SOUTH

THE LANDSCAPE

THE FLOOR OF THE ATLANTIC is spreading by about one inch (2.5 cm) a year. The South American and African plates are moving apart, drawing molten rock up from the Earth's core. The Mid-Atlantic Ridge lies along the boundary of the two plates, forming the world's longest mountain range and dividing the Atlantic floor into two parallel troughs. These troughs are subdivided into numerous smaller basins by transform faults. Most of the oceanic islands in the Atlantic are volcanic in origin and are part of the Mid-Atlantic Ridge or the Caribbean arc.

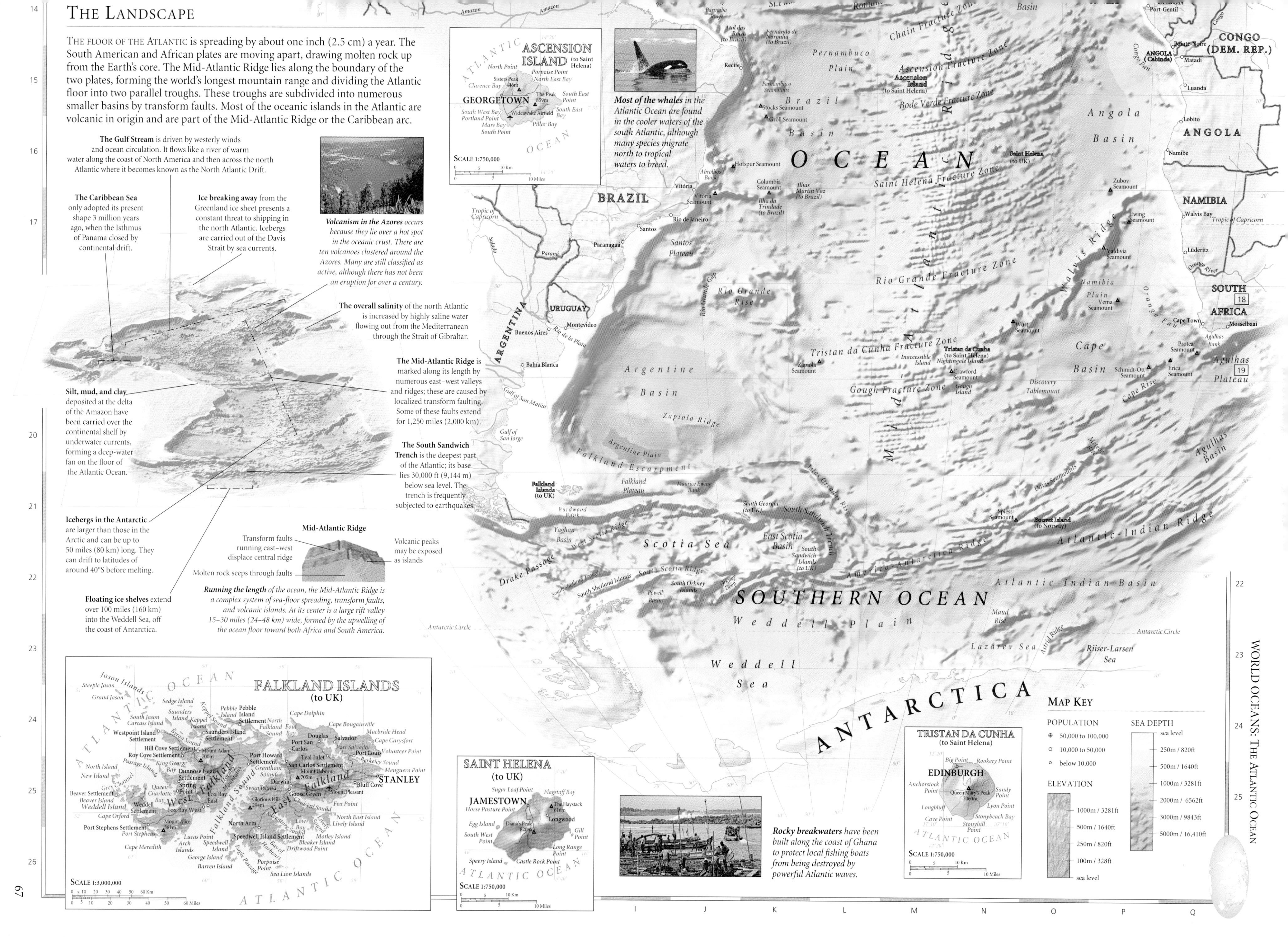

ASCENSION ISLAND (to Saint Helena)
GEORGETOWN
SAINT HELENA (to UK)
JAMESTOWN
TRISTAN DA CUNHA (to Saint Helena)
EDINBURGH
FALKLAND ISLANDS (to UK)
STANLEY
BRAZIL
URUGUAY
ARGENTINA
ANGOLA
NAMIBIA
SOUTH AFRICA
CONGO (DEM. REP.)
OCEAN
SOUTHERN OCEAN
ANTARCTICA
Mid-Atlantic Ridge
Transform faults running east–west displace central ridge
Volcanic peaks may be exposed as islands
Molten rock seeps through faults
MAP KEY
POPULATION
50,000 to 100,000
10,000 to 50,000
below 10,000
ELEVATION
1000m / 3281ft
500m / 1640ft
250m / 820ft
100m / 328ft
sea level
SEA DEPTH
sea level
250m / 820ft
500m / 1640ft
1000m / 3281ft
2000m / 6562ft
3000m / 9843ft
5000m / 16,410ft

The Gulf Stream is driven by westerly winds and ocean circulation. It flows like a river of warm water along the coast of North America and then across the north Atlantic where it becomes known as the North Atlantic Drift.

The Caribbean Sea only adopted its present shape 3 million years ago, when the Isthmus of Panama closed by continental drift.

Ice breaking away from the Greenland ice sheet presents a constant threat to shipping in the north Atlantic. Icebergs are carried out of the Davis Strait by sea currents.

***Volcanism in the Azores** occurs because they lie over a hot spot in the oceanic crust. There are ten volcanoes clustered around the Azores. Many are still classified as active, although there has not been an eruption for over a century.*

The overall salinity of the north Atlantic is increased by highly saline water flowing out from the Mediterranean through the Strait of Gibraltar.

The Mid-Atlantic Ridge is marked along its length by numerous east–west valleys and ridges; these are caused by localized transform faulting. Some of these faults extend for 1,250 miles (2,000 km).

Silt, mud, and clay deposited at the delta of the Amazon have been carried over the continental shelf by underwater currents, forming a deep-water fan on the floor of the Atlantic Ocean.

The South Sandwich Trench is the deepest part of the Atlantic; its base lies 30,000 ft (9,144 m) below sea level. The trench is frequently subjected to earthquakes.

Icebergs in the Antarctic are larger than those in the Arctic and can be up to 50 miles (80 km) long. They can drift to latitudes of around 40°S before melting.

Floating ice shelves extend over 100 miles (160 km) into the Weddell Sea, off the coast of Antarctica.

***Running the length** of the ocean, the Mid-Atlantic Ridge is a complex system of sea-floor spreading, transform faults, and volcanic islands. At its center is a large rift valley 15–30 miles (24–48 km) wide, formed by the upwelling of the ocean floor toward both Africa and South America.*

***Most of the whales** in the Atlantic Ocean are found in the cooler waters of the south Atlantic, although many species migrate north to tropical waters to breed.*

***Rocky breakwaters** have been built along the coast of Ghana to protect local fishing boats from being destroyed by powerful Atlantic waves.*

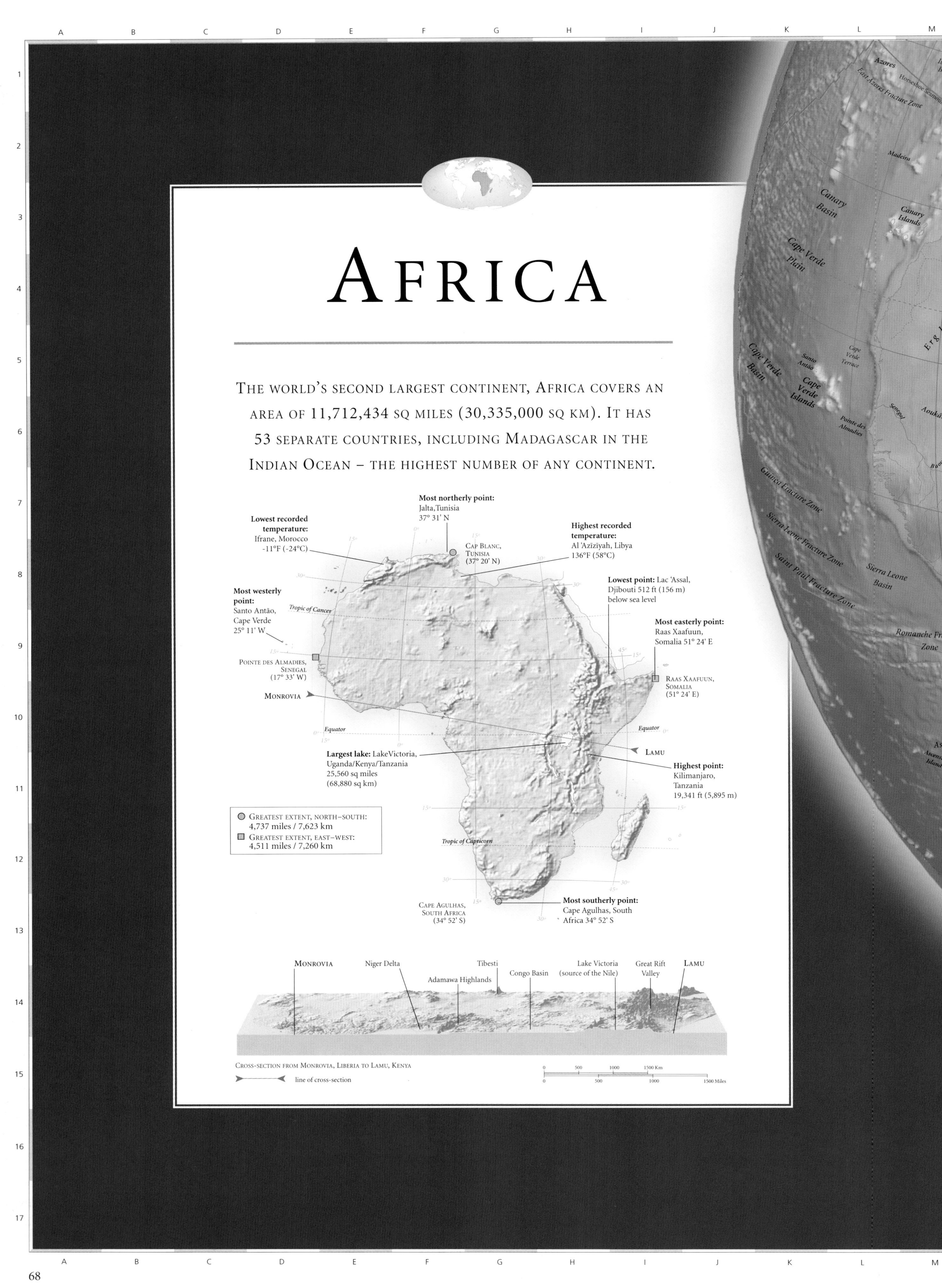
AFRICA
THE WORLD'S SECOND LARGEST CONTINENT, AFRICA COVERS AN AREA OF 11,712,434 SQ MILES (30,335,000 SQ KM). IT HAS 53 SEPARATE COUNTRIES, INCLUDING MADAGASCAR IN THE INDIAN OCEAN – THE HIGHEST NUMBER OF ANY CONTINENT.
Most northerly point: Jalta,Tunisia 37° 31' N
Lowest recorded temperature: Ifrane, Morocco -11°F (-24°C)
Highest recorded temperature: Al 'Azīzīyah, Libya 136°F (58°C)
Cap Blanc, Tunisia (37° 20' N)
Lowest point: Lac 'Assal, Djibouti 512 ft (156 m) below sea level
Most westerly point: Santo Antão, Cape Verde 25° 11' W
Tropic of Cancer
Most easterly point: Raas Xaafuun, Somalia 51° 24' E
Pointe des Almadies, Senegal (17° 33' W)
Raas Xaafuun, Somalia (51° 24' E)
Monrovia
Equator
Lamu
Largest lake: Lake Victoria, Uganda/Kenya/Tanzania 25,560 sq miles (68,880 sq km)
Highest point: Kilimanjaro, Tanzania 19,341 ft (5,895 m)
Greatest extent, north–south: 4,737 miles / 7,623 km
Greatest extent, east–west: 4,511 miles / 7,260 km
Tropic of Capricorn
Cape Agulhas, South Africa (34° 52' S)
Most southerly point: Cape Agulhas, South Africa 34° 52' S
Monrovia
Niger Delta
Tibesti
Adamawa Highlands
Congo Basin
Lake Victoria (source of the Nile)
Great Rift Valley
Lamu
Cross-section from Monrovia, Liberia to Lamu, Kenya
line of cross-section
0 500 1000 1500 Km
0 500 1000 1500 Miles
Azores
East Azores Fracture Zone
Madeira
Canary Basin
Canary Islands
Cape Verde Plain
Cape Verde Basin
Santo Antão
Cape Verde Islands
Cape Verde Terrace
Pointe des Almadies
Aoukâr
Guinea Fracture Zone
Sierra Leone Fracture Zone
Saint Paul Fracture Zone
Sierra Leone Basin

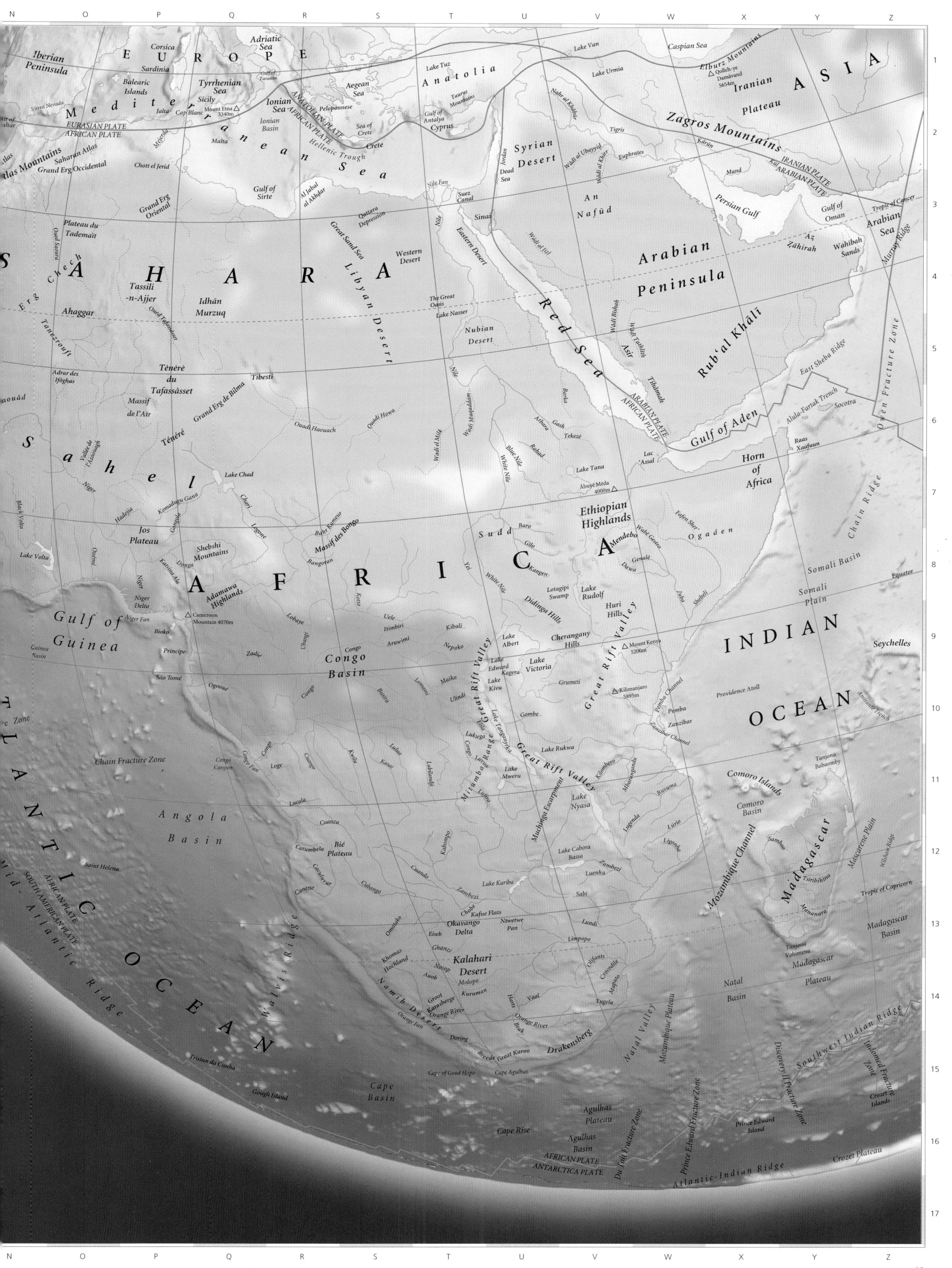

N O P Q R S T U V W X Y Z
1 2 3 4 5 6 7 8 9 10 11 12 13 14 15 16 17
EUROPE
ASIA
AFRICA
SAHARA
Sahel
Iberian Peninsula
Corsica
Sardinia
Balearic Islands
Adriatic Sea
Tyrrhenian Sea
Sicily
Mount Etna 3340m
Cap Blanc
Jalta
Malta
Gulf of Taranto
Ionian Sea
Ionian Basin
Aegean Sea
Peloponnese
Sea of Crete
Crete
Hellenic Trough
Mediterranean Sea
EURASIAN PLATE
AFRICAN PLATE
ANATOLIAN PLATE
Sierra Nevada
Atlas Mountains
Saharan Atlas
Grand Erg Occidental
Chott el Jerid
Grand Erg Oriental
Gulf of Sirte
Al Jabal al Akhdar
Qattara Depression
Great Sand Sea
Libyan Desert
Western Desert
Plateau du Tademaït
Oued Saoura
Erg Chech
Tassili -n-Ajjer
Idhān Murzuq
Ahaggar
Tanezrouft
Adrar des Ifôghas
Ténéré du Tafassâsset
Tibesti
Grand Erg de Bilma
Massif de l'Aïr
Ténéré
Ouadi Haouach
Ouadi Howa
Lake Chad
Komadugu Gana
Chari
Logone
Hadejia
Jos Plateau
Shebshi Mountains
Adamawa Highlands
Cameroon Mountain 4070m
Niger
Niger Delta
Niger Fan
Black Volta
Lake Volta
Oueme
Benue
Gulf of Guinea
Guinea Basin
Bioko
Príncipe
São Tomé
Bahr Aouk
Massif des Bongo
Bangoran
Lake Tuz
Anatolia
Taurus Mountains
Gulf of Antalya
Cyprus
Lake Van
Lake Urmia
Caspian Sea
Elburz Mountains
Qolleh-ye Damāvand 5654m
Iranian Plateau
Zagros Mountains
IRANIAN PLATE
ARABIAN PLATE
Tigris
Euphrates
Kārūn
Mand
Persian Gulf
Gulf of Oman
Tropic of Cancer
Arabian Sea
Murray Ridge
Nahr al Khābūr
Wādī al Ubayyid
Wadi al Khirr
Syrian Desert
Jordan
Dead Sea
Nile Fan
Suez Canal
Sinai
Nile
Eastern Desert
An Nafūd
Wādī al Ḥamḍ
Arabian Peninsula
Az Zāhirah
Wahībah Sands
Rubʻ al Khālī
Wādī Bīshah
Wādī Tathlīth
ʻAsīr
Tihāmah
Red Sea
The Great Oasis
Lake Nasser
Nubian Desert
Wadi al Milk
Wadi Muqaddam
Atbara
Gash
Tekezē
Barka
Rahad
Blue Nile
White Nile
Lake Tana
Abuyē Mēda 4000m
Lac ʻAssal
Gulf of Aden
ARABIAN PLATE
AFRICAN PLATE
Horn of Africa
Raas Xaafuun
Socotra
Alula-Fartak Trench
East Sheba Ridge
Owen Fracture Zone
Ethiopian Highlands
Mendebo
Wabē Gestro
Fafen Shet'
Ogaden
Genalē
Dawa
Juba
Shebeli
Sudd
Baro
Gilo
Kangen
Lotagipi Swamp
Didinga Hills
Lake Rudolf
Huri Hills
Yei
Kotto
Uele
Itimbiri
Aruwimi
Kibali
Nepoko
Lobaye
Ubangi
Zadie
Congo Basin
Congo
Ogooué
Maiko
Ulindi
Lomami
Busira
Lake Albert
Lake Edward
Kagera
Lake Kivu
Lake Victoria
Cherangany Hills
Mount Kenya 5200m
Great Rift Valley
Grumeti
Kilimanjaro 5895m
Gombe
Lake Tanganyika
Lake Rukwa
Lake Mweru
Luapula
Mitumba Range
Lukuga
Lualaba
Kilombero
Mbarangandu
Ruvuma
Lake Nyasa
Muchinga Escarpment
Lugenda
Lúrio
Ligonha
Pemba Channel
Pemba
Zanzibar
Zanzibar Channel
Providence Atoll
Seychelles
Amirante Trench
INDIAN OCEAN
Somali Basin
Somali Plain
Equator
Chain Ridge
Comoro Islands
Comoro Basin
Tanjona Bobaomby
Sambao
Madagascar
Mozambique Channel
Tsiribihina
Mangoro
Mananara
Tropic of Capricorn
Mascarene Plain
Wilshaw Ridge
Madagascar Basin
Tanjona Vohimena
Madagascar Plateau
Natal Basin
Chain Fracture Zone
Congo Canyon
Congo Fan
Loge
Cuango
Kwilu
Kasai
Lulua
Lubilanji
Lucala
Cuanza
Angola Basin
Bié Plateau
Catumbela
Cunene
Cuando
Cubango
Kabompo
Zambezi
Lake Kariba
Lake Cabora Bassa
Luenha
Sabi
Chobe
Kafue Flats
Okavango Delta
Ntwetwe Pan
Lundi
Limpopo
Olifants
Crocodile
Maputo
Tugela
Omatako
Eiseb
Ghanzi
Khomas Hochland
Nosop
Auob
Kalahari Desert
Molopo
Kuruman
Harts
Vaal
Orange River
Brak
Groot Karasberge
Orange Fan
Namib Desert
Doring
Breede
Great Karoo
Drakensberg
Cape of Good Hope
Cape Agulhas
Saint Helena
ATLANTIC OCEAN
Mid-Atlantic Ridge
SOUTH AMERICAN PLATE
AFRICAN PLATE
Walvis Ridge
Tristan da Cunha
Gough Island
Cape Basin
Cape Rise
Agulhas Plateau
Agulhas Basin
AFRICAN PLATE
ANTARCTICA PLATE
Du Toit Fracture Zone
Natal Valley
Mozambique Plateau
Prince Edward Fracture Zone
Discovery II Fracture Zone
Prince Edward Island
Southwest Indian Ridge
Indomed Fracture Zone
Crozet Islands
Crozet Plateau
Atlantic-Indian Ridge

Physical Africa

The structure of Africa was dramatically influenced by the breaking up of the supercontinent Gondwanaland about 160 million years ago and, more recently, rifting and hot spot activity. Today, much of Africa is remote from active plate boundaries and comprises a series of extensive plateaus and deep basins, which influence the drainage patterns of major rivers. The relief rises to the east, where volcanic uplands and vast lakes mark the Great Rift Valley. In the far north and south, sedimentary rocks have been folded to form the Atlas Mountains and the Great Karoo.

East Africa

The Great Rift Valley is the most striking feature of this region, running for 4,475 miles (7,200 km) from Lake Nyasa to the Red Sea. North of Lake Nyasa it splits into two arms and encloses an interior plateau, which contains Lake Victoria. A number of elongated lakes and volcanoes lie along the fault lines. To the west lies the Congo Basin, a vast, shallow depression, which rises to form an almost circular rim of highlands.

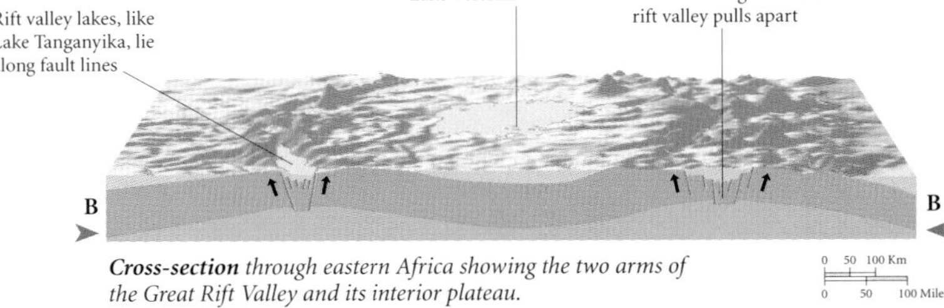
Rift valley lakes, like Lake Tanganyika, lie along fault lines
Lake Victoria
Extensive faulting occurs as rift valley pulls apart
B
B
0 50 100 Km
0 50 100 Miles

Cross-section through eastern Africa showing the two arms of the Great Rift Valley and its interior plateau.

Northern Africa

Northern Africa comprises a system of basins and plateaus. The Tibesti and Ahaggar are volcanic uplands, whose uplift has been matched by subsidence within large surrounding basins. Many of the basins have been filled in with sand and gravel, creating the vast Saharan lands. The Atlas Mountains in the north were formed by convergence of the African and Eurasian plates.

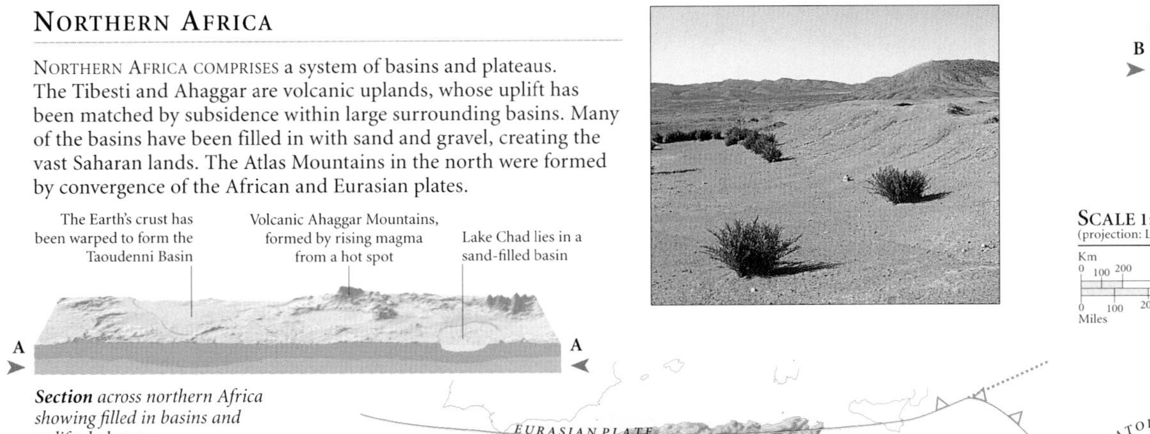
The Earth's crust has been warped to form the Taoudenni Basin
Volcanic Ahaggar Mountains, formed by rising magma from a hot spot
Lake Chad lies in a sand-filled basin
A
A
0 250 500 Km
0 250 500 Miles

***Section** across northern Africa showing filled in basins and uplifted plateaus.*

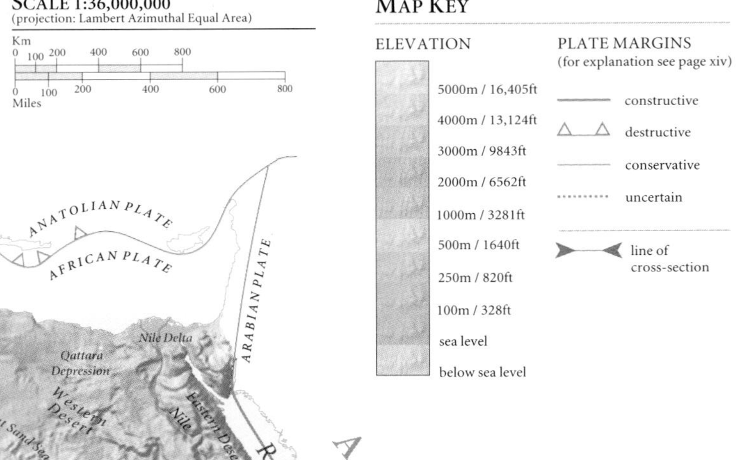
SCALE 1:36,000,000
(projection: Lambert Azimuthal Equal Area)
Km 0 100 200 400 600 800
Miles 0 100 200 400 600 800
MAP KEY
ELEVATION
5000m / 16,405ft
4000m / 13,124ft
3000m / 9843ft
2000m / 6562ft
1000m / 3281ft
500m / 1640ft
250m / 820ft
100m / 328ft
sea level
below sea level
PLATE MARGINS
(for explanation see page xiv)
constructive
destructive
conservative
uncertain
line of cross-section
ASIA
Red Sea
Nubian Desert
Lake Nasser
Nile
Eastern Desert
ARABIAN PLATE
AFRICAN PLATE
ANATOLIAN PLATE

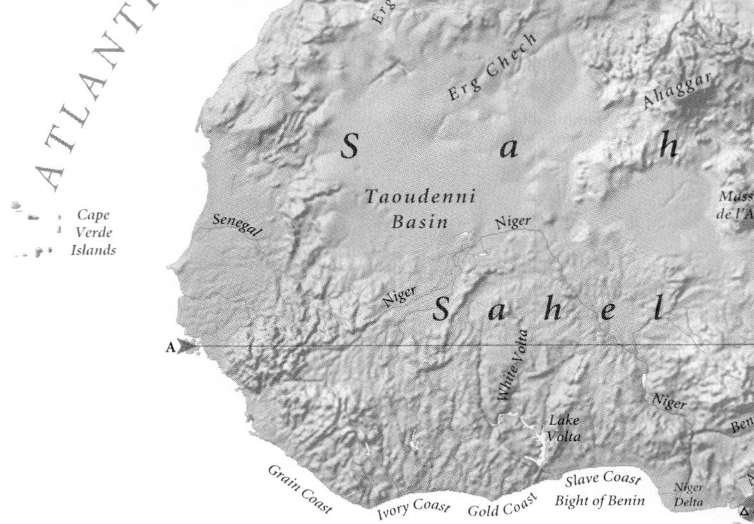
EURASIAN PLATE
AFRICAN PLATE
Atlas Mountains
ATLANTIC OCEAN
Grand Erg Occidental
Grand Erg Oriental
Erg Iguidi
Erg Chech
Ahaggar
Sahara
Taoudenni Basin
Massif de l'Aïr
Ténéré
Senegal
Niger
Sahel
Cape Verde Islands
White Volta
Lake Volta
Benue
Grain Coast
Ivory Coast
Gold Coast
Slave Coast
Bight of Benin
Niger Delta
Adamawa Highlands
Cameroon Mountain 4070m
Gulf of Guinea
São Tomé
Chott el Jerid
Gulf of Sirte
Qattara Depression
Western Desert
Great Sand Sea
Libyan Desert
Tibesti

Gulf of Aden
Horn of Africa
Lake Tana
Ethiopian Highlands
Blue Nile
White Nile
Sudd
Massif des Bongo
Ubangi
Congo (Zaire)
Congo Basin
Lake Albert
Lake Victoria
Lake Rudolf
Great Rift Valley
Kilimanjaro 5895m
Shebeli
Juba
Lake Tanganyika
Mitumba Range
Pemba Island
Zanzibar
Seychelles

Southern Africa

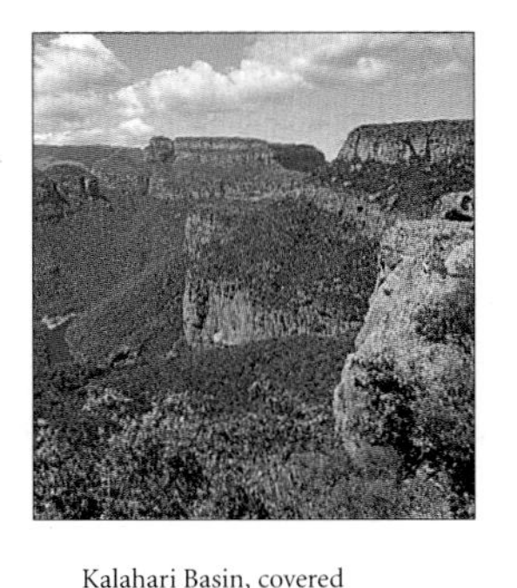

The Great Escarpment marks the southern boundary of Africa's basement rock, and includes the Drakensberg range. It was uplifted when Gondwanaland fragmented about 160 million years ago and it has gradually been eroded back from the coast. To the north, the relief drops steadily, forming the Kalahari Basin. In the far south are the fold mountains of the Great Karoo.

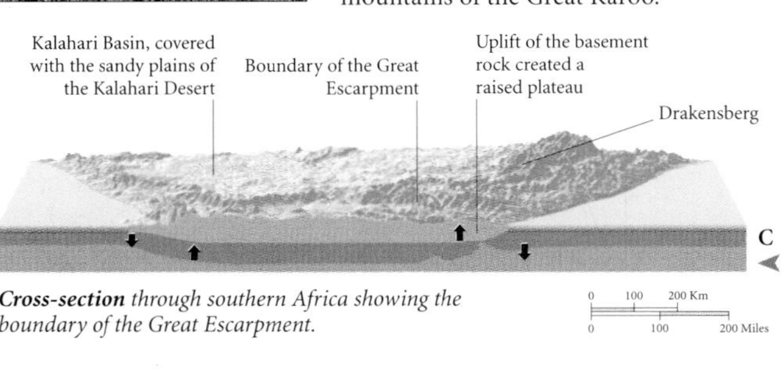
Kalahari Basin, covered with the sandy plains of the Kalahari Desert
Boundary of the Great Escarpment
Uplift of the basement rock created a raised plateau
Drakensberg
C
C
0 100 200 Km
0 100 200 Miles

***Cross-section** through southern Africa showing the boundary of the Great Escarpment.*

Bié Plateau
Lake Nyasa
Zambezi
Comoro Islands
Mozambique Channel
Madagascar
Mauritius
Réunion
INDIAN OCEAN
ATLANTIC OCEAN
Namib Desert
Okavango Delta
Kalahari Basin
Kalahari Desert
Limpopo
Orange River
Drakensberg
Great Karoo
Cape of Good Hope

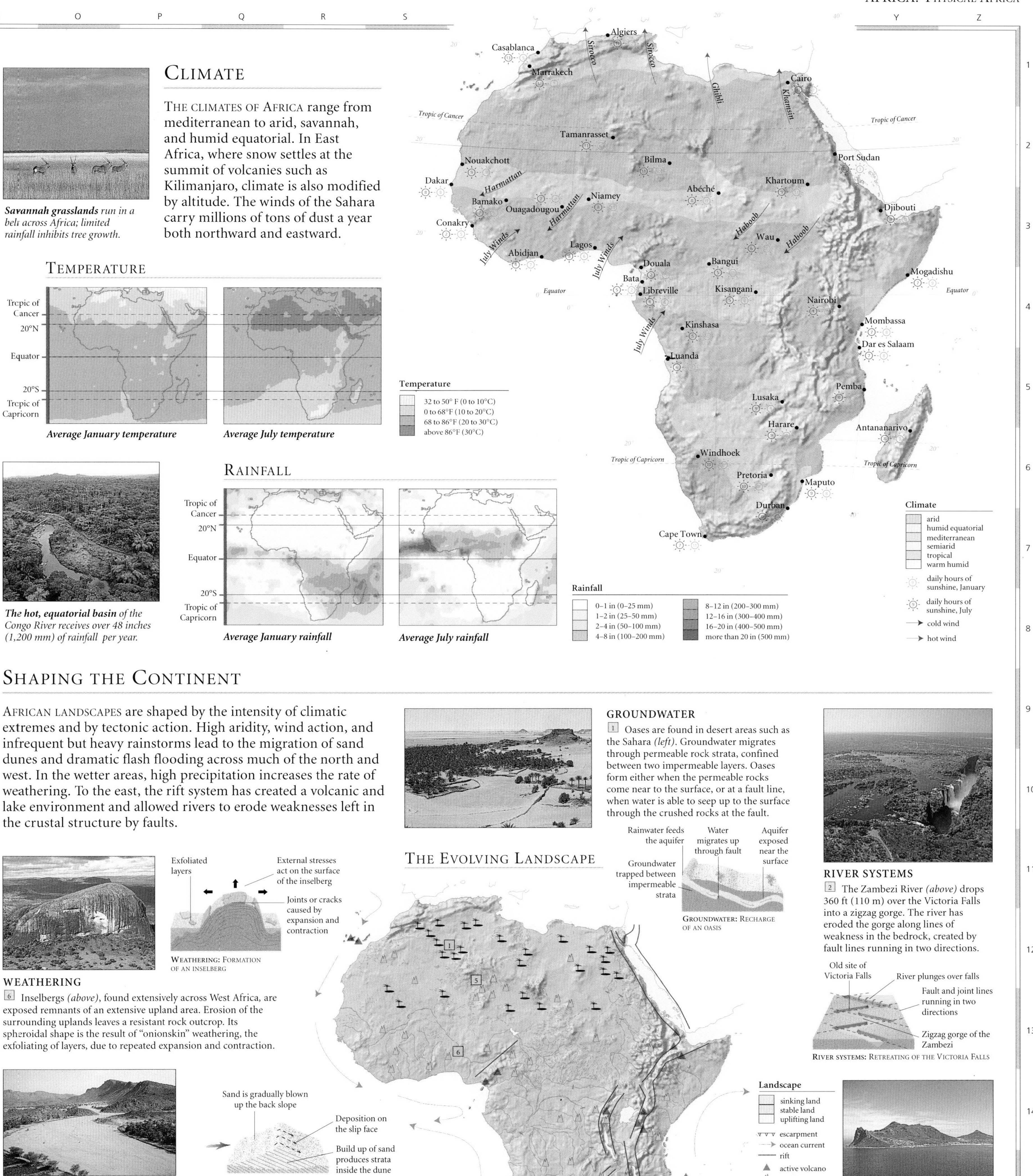

N O P Q R S Y Z
Casablanca
Algiers
Marrakech
Sirocco
Ghibli
Cairo
Khamsin
Tropic of Cancer
Tamanrasset
Nouakchott
Bilma
Port Sudan
Dakar
Harmattan
Abéché
Khartoum
Bamako
Niamey
Ouagadougou
Djibouti
Conakry
Haboob
Wau
July Winds
Abidjan
Lagos
Douala
Bangui
Bata
Libreville
Kisangani
Mogadishu
Equator
Nairobi
Kinshasa
Mombassa
Dar es Salaam
Luanda
Pemba
Lusaka
Harare
Antananarivo
Windhoek
Tropic of Capricorn
Pretoria
Maputo
Durban
Cape Town
Temperature
32 to 50° F (0 to 10°C)
0 to 68°F (10 to 20°C)
68 to 86°F (20 to 30°C)
above 86°F (30°C)
Rainfall
0–1 in (0–25 mm)
1–2 in (25–50 mm)
2–4 in (50–100 mm)
4–8 in (100–200 mm)
8–12 in (200–300 mm)
12–16 in (300–400 mm)
16–20 in (400–500 mm)
more than 20 in (500 mm)
Climate
arid
humid equatorial
mediterranean
semiarid
tropical
warm humid
daily hours of sunshine, January
daily hours of sunshine, July
cold wind
hot wind
Tropic of Cancer
20°N
Equator
20°S
Tropic of Capricorn
Landscape
sinking land
stable land
uplifting land
escarpment
ocean current
rift
active volcano
inselberg
oasis
river
wadi
waterfall

Climate

***Savannah grasslands** run in a belt across Africa; limited rainfall inhibits tree growth.*

THE CLIMATES OF AFRICA range from mediterranean to arid, savannah, and humid equatorial. In East Africa, where snow settles at the summit of volcanies such as Kilimanjaro, climate is also modified by altitude. The winds of the Sahara carry millions of tons of dust a year both northward and eastward.

Temperature

Average January temperature

Average July temperature

***The hot, equatorial basin** of the Congo River receives over 48 inches (1,200 mm) of rainfall per year.*

Rainfall

Average January rainfall

Average July rainfall

Shaping the Continent

AFRICAN LANDSCAPES are shaped by the intensity of climatic extremes and by tectonic action. High aridity, wind action, and infrequent but heavy rainstorms lead to the migration of sand dunes and dramatic flash flooding across much of the north and west. In the wetter areas, high precipitation increases the rate of weathering. To the east, the rift system has created a volcanic and lake environment and allowed rivers to erode weaknesses left in the crustal structure by faults.

The Evolving Landscape

Groundwater

1 Oases are found in desert areas such as the Sahara *(left)*. Groundwater migrates through permeable rock strata, confined between two impermeable layers. Oases form either when the permeable rocks come near to the surface, or at a fault line, when water is able to seep up to the surface through the crushed rocks at the fault.

Rainwater feeds the aquifer
Water migrates up through fault
Aquifer exposed near the surface
Groundwater trapped between impermeable strata

GROUNDWATER: RECHARGE OF AN OASIS

River Systems

2 The Zambezi River *(above)* drops 360 ft (110 m) over the Victoria Falls into a zigzag gorge. The river has eroded the gorge along lines of weakness in the bedrock, created by fault lines running in two directions.

Old site of Victoria Falls
River plunges over falls
Fault and joint lines running in two directions
Zigzag gorge of the Zambezi

RIVER SYSTEMS: RETREATING OF THE VICTORIA FALLS

Weathering

Exfoliated layers
External stresses act on the surface of the inselberg
Joints or cracks caused by expansion and contraction

WEATHERING: FORMATION OF AN INSELBERG

6 Inselbergs *(above)*, found extensively across West Africa, are exposed remnants of an extensive upland area. Erosion of the surrounding uplands leaves a resistant rock outcrop. Its spheroidal shape is the result of "onionskin" weathering, the exfoliating of layers, due to repeated expansion and contraction.

Ephemeral Channels

5 Wadis *(above)* drain much of northern Africa. These drybed courses are flooded only after infrequent, but intense, storms in the uplands cause water to surge along their channels.

Heavy rainfall runs off of mountains
Water collects and floods the dry channel

EPHEMERAL CHANNELS: FLASH FLOODING OF A WADI

Sand is gradually blown up the back slope
Deposition on the slip face
Build up of sand produces strata inside the dune

WIND EROSION: MIGRATION OF A DUNE

Wind Erosion

4 Dunes like this in the Namib Desert *(left)* are wind-blown accumulations of sand, which slowly migrate. Wind action moves sand up the shallow back slope; when the sand reaches the crest of the dune it is deposited on the slip face.

Waves refracting
Wave energy dispersed in the bay
Force of waves concentrates on the headland
The seabed is deeper opposite the bay than at the headland

COASTAL PROCESSES: EROSION OF A BAY

Coastal Processes

3 Houtbaai *(above)*, in southern Africa, is constantly being modified by wave action. As waves approach the indented coastline, they reach the shallow water of the headland, slowing down and reducing in length. This causes them to bend or refract, concentrating their erosive force at the headlands.

N O P Q R S T U V W X Y Z

Political Africa

THE CURRENT POLITICAL MAP OF MODERN AFRICA emerged after the Second World War. Over the next half-century, all of the countries formerly controlled by European powers gained independence from their colonial rulers – only Liberia and Ethiopia were never colonized. The postcolonial era has not been an easy period for many countries, but there have been moves toward multiparty democracy in much of West Africa, and in Zambia, Tanzania, and Kenya. In South Africa, democratic elections replaced the internationally-condemned apartheid system only in 1994. Other countries have still to find political stability; corruption in government and ethnic tensions are serious problems. National infrastructures, based on the colonial transportation systems built to exploit Africa's resources, are often inappropriate for independent economic development.

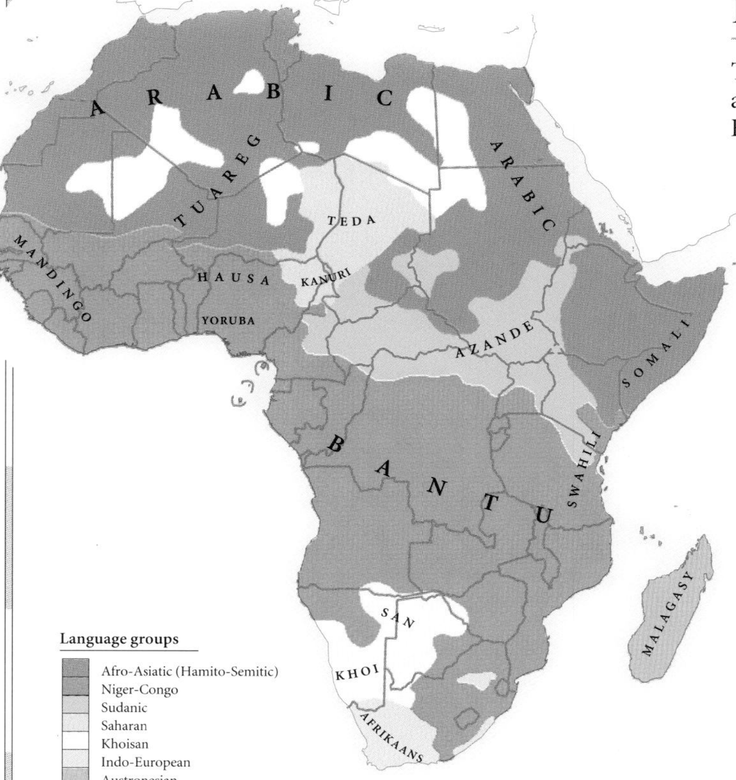
ARABIC
TUAREG
ARABIC
TEDA
MANDINGO
HAUSA
KANURI
YORUBA
AZANDE
SOMALI
BANTU
SWAHILI
MALAGASY
SAN
KHOI
AFRIKAANS
Language groups
Afro-Asiatic (Hamito-Semitic)
Niger-Congo
Sudanic
Saharan
Khoisan
Indo-European
Austronesian

Languages

THREE MAJOR WORLD LANGUAGES act as *lingua francas* across the African continent: Arabic in North Africa; English in southern and eastern Africa and Nigeria; and French in Central and West Africa and in Madagascar. A huge number of African languages are spoken as well – over 2,000 have been recorded, with more than 400 in Nigeria alone – reflecting the continuing importance of traditional cultures and values. In the north of the continent, the extensive use of Arabic reflects Middle Eastern influences while Bantu is widely spoken across much of southern Africa.

OFFICIAL AFRICAN LANGUAGES

Official languages
French
English
Arabic
Portuguese
Swahili
Ahmaric
Spanish
French/English
French/Arabic
English/Swahili

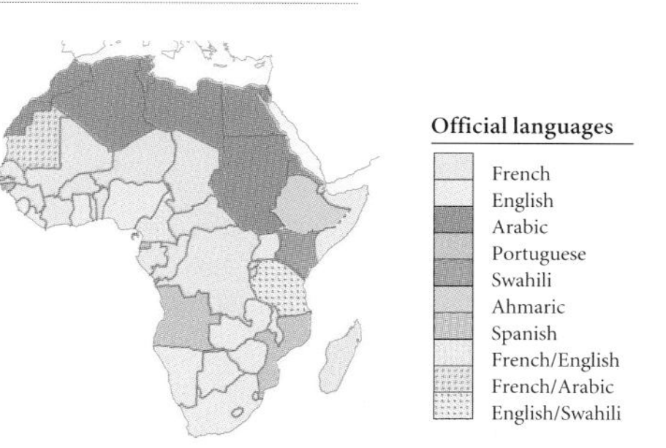

***Islamic influences** are evident throughout North Africa. The Great Mosque at Kairouan, Tunisia, is Africa's holiest Islamic place.*

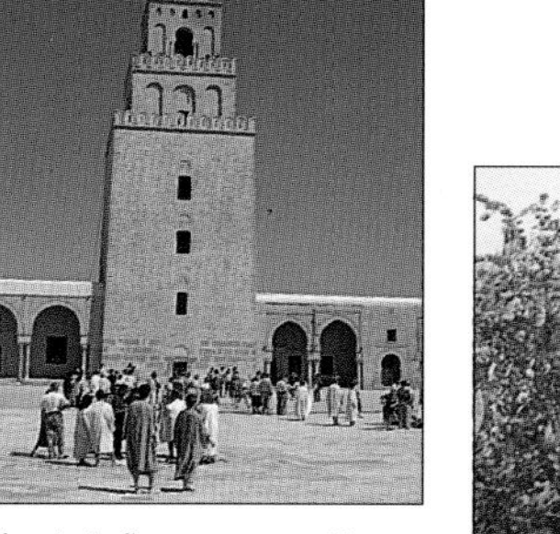

***In northeastern Nigeria,** people speak Kanuri – a dialect of the Saharan language group.*

Madeira (to Portugal)
Casab
Saf
Marrak
MOROCC
Agadir
Canary Islands (to Spain)
LAÂYOUNE
Western Sahara (Occupied by Morocco)
Tropic of Cancer
CAPE VERDE
PRAIA
MAURITANI
NOUAKCHOTT
Senegal
SENEGAL
DAKAR
Kaolack
GAMBIA
BANJUL
GUINEA-BISSAU
BISSAU
BAMAKO
GUINEA
CONAKRY
Koidu
FREETOWN
SIERRA LEONE
YAMOUSSOUK
MONROVIA
LIBERIA
PORTUG

Transportation

AFRICAN RAILROADS WERE BUILT to aid the exploitation of natural resources, and most offer passage only from the interior to the coastal cities, leaving large parts of the continent untouched – five landlocked countries have no railroads at all. The Congo (Zaire), Nile, and Niger River networks offer limited access to the continental interior, as a number of waterfalls and cataracts prevent navigation from the sea. Many roads were developed in the 1960s and 1970s, but economic difficulties make the maintenance and expansion of these networks difficult.

***South Africa** has the largest concentration of railroads in Africa. Over 20,000 miles (32,000 km) of routes have been built since 1870.*

***Traditional means of transportation,** such as the camel, are still widely used across the less accessible parts of Africa.*

***The Congo (Zaire) River,** though not suitable for river transportation along its entire length, forms a vital link for people and goods in its navigable inland reaches.*

Ceuta (to Spain)
Tanger
Rabat
Casablanca
Algiers
Oran
Skikda
Tunis
Tripoli
Agadir
Alexandria
Port Said
Suez
Cairo
Aswân
Wadi Halfa
Port Sudan
Tamanrasset
Nouâdhibou
Nouakchott
Dakar
Banjul
Bissau
Conakry
Freetown
Monrovia
Bamako
Ouagadougou
Niamey
Agadez
Kano
Maiduguri
Ndjamena
Nyala
Khartoum
Massawa
Assab
Djibouti
Addis Ababa
Abidjan
Accra
Cotonou
Lomé
Lagos
Warri
Douala
Malabo
Yaoundé
Bangui
Libreville
Port-Gentil
Kisangani
Kampala
Nairobi
Mogadishu
Bukavu
Mombasa
Pointe-Noire
Brazzaville
Kinshasa
Matadi
Kananga
Kalemie
Dodoma
Dar es Salaam
Luanda
Mbeya
Lobito
Lubumbashi
Namibe
Lusaka
Nampula
Livingstone
Harare
Tsumeb
Bulawayo
Beira
Antananarivo
Toamasina
Windhoek
Walvis Bay
Keetmanshoop
Pretoria
Johannesburg
Maputo
Durban
Cape Town
Port Elizabeth
Transportation
major roads and highways
major railroads
major canal
international borders
transportation intersections
international airports
major ports

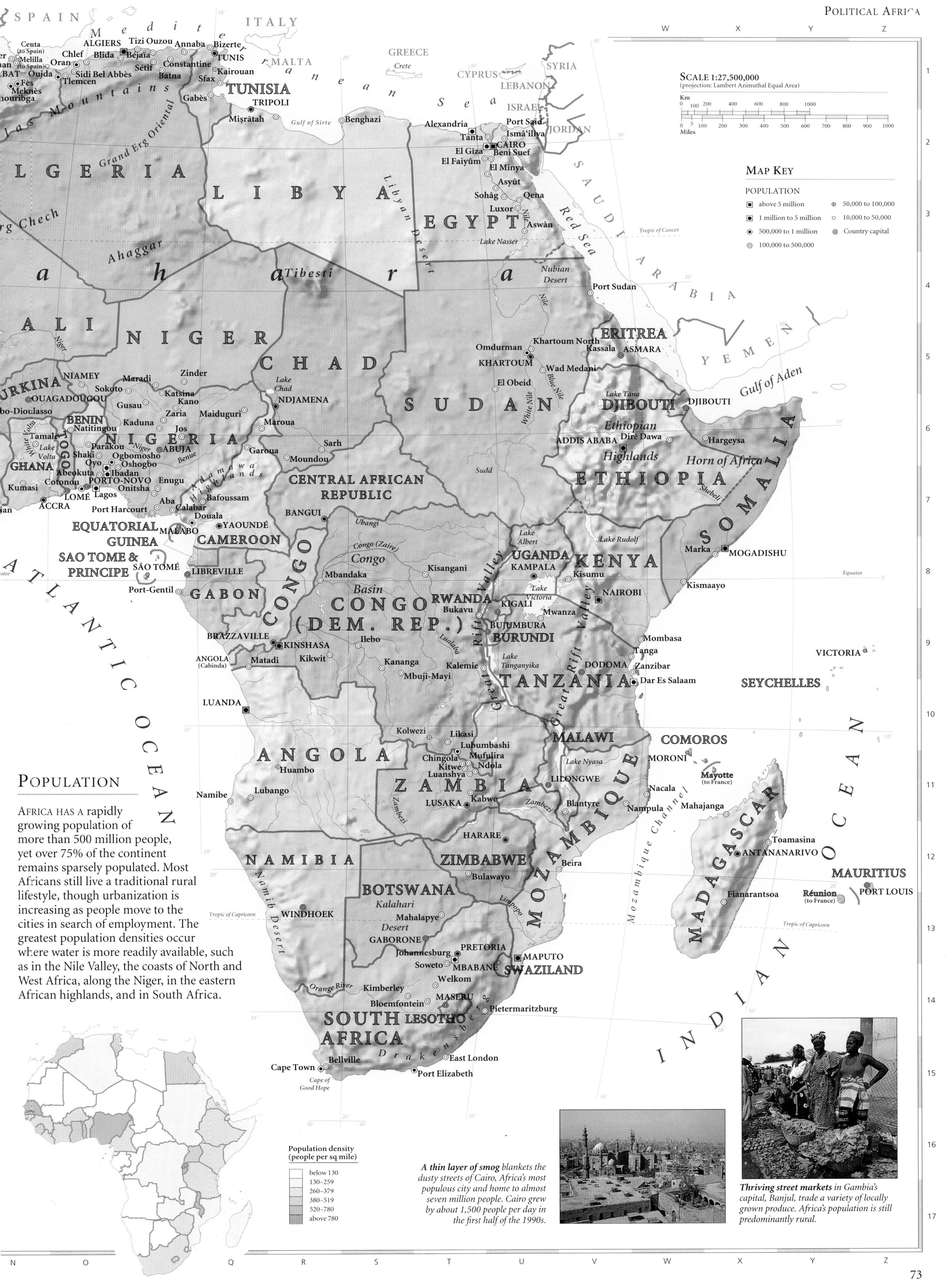
SCALE 1:27,500,000
(projection: Lambert Azimuthal Equal Area)
Km
Miles
MAP KEY
POPULATION
above 5 million
1 million to 5 million
500,000 to 1 million
100,000 to 500,000
50,000 to 100,000
10,000 to 50,000
Country capital
SPAIN
ITALY
GREECE
CYPRUS
SYRIA
LEBANON
ISRAEL
JORDAN
SAUDI ARABIA
YEMEN
Mediterranean Sea
MALTA
TUNISIA
TUNIS
Bizerte
Kairouan
Sfax
Gabès
TRIPOLI
Mişrātah
Gulf of Sirte
Benghazi
ALGERIA
ALGIERS
Tizi Ouzou
Annaba
Blida
Béjaïa
Constantine
Sétif
Batna
Chlef
Oran
Sidi Bel Abbès
Tlemcen
Oujda
Fès
Meknès
Ceuta (to Spain)
Melilla (to Spain)
Grand Erg Oriental
Atlas Mountains
Ahaggar
Sahara
Tibesti
LIBYA
Libyan Desert
EGYPT
Alexandria
Tanta
CAIRO
El Giza
Beni Suef
El Faiyûm
El Minya
Asyût
Sohâg
Qena
Luxor
Aswân
Port Said
Ismâ'iliya
Lake Nasser
Nile
Red Sea
Tropic of Cancer
Nubian Desert
Port Sudan
SUDAN
Omdurman
KHARTOUM
Khartoum North
Wad Medani
El Obeid
Kassala
Blue Nile
White Nile
Sudd
ERITREA
ASMARA
DJIBOUTI
Gulf of Aden
Lake Tana
Ethiopian Highlands
ADDIS ABABA
Dire Dawa
Hargeysa
Horn of Africa
ETHIOPIA
Shebeli
SOMALIA
MOGADISHU
Marka
Kismaayo
NIGER
NIAMEY
Zinder
Maradi
CHAD
Lake Chad
NDJAMENA
Sarh
Moundou
MALI
BURKINA
OUAGADOUGOU
Bobo-Dioulasso
BENIN
Natitingou
TOGO
GHANA
Tamale
Lake Volta
White Volta
Kumasi
ACCRA
LOMÉ
Cotonou
PORTO-NOVO
NIGERIA
Sokoto
Katsina
Kano
Gusau
Zaria
Kaduna
Maiduguri
Jos
ABUJA
Parakou
Shaki
Ogbomosho
Oyo
Oshogbo
Abeokuta
Ibadan
Lagos
Onitsha
Enugu
Aba
Port Harcourt
Calabar
Niger
Benue
Maroua
Garoua
Adamawa Highlands
Bafoussam
Douala
YAOUNDÉ
CAMEROON
EQUATORIAL GUINEA
MALABO
SAO TOME & PRINCIPE
SÃO TOMÉ
LIBREVILLE
Port-Gentil
GABON
CONGO
CENTRAL AFRICAN REPUBLIC
BANGUI
Ubangi
Congo (Zaire)
Congo Basin
Mbandaka
Kisangani
CONGO (DEM. REP.)
BRAZZAVILLE
KINSHASA
Ilebo
Kikwit
Matadi
ANGOLA (Cabinda)
Kananga
Mbuji-Mayi
Kalemie
Lualaba
UGANDA
KAMPALA
Lake Albert
Lake Rudolf
KENYA
Kisumu
NAIROBI
Lake Victoria
RWANDA
KIGALI
Bukavu
BURUNDI
BUJUMBURA
Mwanza
Great Rift Valley
Lake Tanganyika
TANZANIA
DODOMA
Mombasa
Tanga
Zanzibar
Dar Es Salaam
Equator
SEYCHELLES
VICTORIA
ATLANTIC OCEAN
LUANDA
ANGOLA
Huambo
Lubango
Namibe
Kolwezi
Likasi
Lubumbashi
Chingola
Mufulira
Kitwe
Ndola
Luanshya
ZAMBIA
LUSAKA
Kabwe
Zambezi
MALAWI
Lake Nyasa
LILONGWE
Blantyre
COMOROS
MORONI
Mayotte (to France)
Nacala
Nampula
MOZAMBIQUE
Mozambique Channel
Mahajanga
MADAGASCAR
Toamasina
ANTANANARIVO
Fianarantsoa
MAURITIUS
PORT LOUIS
Réunion (to France)
INDIAN OCEAN
Tropic of Capricorn
HARARE
ZIMBABWE
Bulawayo
Beira
Limpopo
NAMIBIA
Namib Desert
WINDHOEK
BOTSWANA
Kalahari Desert
Mahalapye
GABORONE
Johannesburg
PRETORIA
Soweto
MBABANE
MAPUTO
SWAZILAND
Welkom
Orange River
Kimberley
Bloemfontein
MASERU
LESOTHO
Pietermaritzburg
Drakensberg
SOUTH AFRICA
Cape Town
Bellville
East London
Port Elizabeth
Cape of Good Hope
Population density (people per sq mile)
below 130
130–259
260–379
380–519
520–780
above 780

POPULATION

AFRICA HAS A rapidly growing population of more than 500 million people, yet over 75% of the continent remains sparsely populated. Most Africans still live a traditional rural lifestyle, though urbanization is increasing as people move to the cities in search of employment. The greatest population densities occur where water is more readily available, such as in the Nile Valley, the coasts of North and West Africa, along the Niger, in the eastern African highlands, and in South Africa.

A thin layer of smog blankets the dusty streets of Cairo, Africa's most populous city and home to almost seven million people. Cairo grew by about 1,500 people per day in the first half of the 1990s.

Thriving street markets in Gambia's capital, Banjul, trade a variety of locally grown produce. Africa's population is still predominantly rural.

African Resources

The economies of most African countries are dominated by subsistence and cash crop agriculture, with limited industrialization. Manufacturing is largely confined to South Africa. Many countries depend on a single resource, such as copper or gold, or a cash crop, such as coffee, for export income, which can leave them vulnerable to fluctuations in world commodity prices. In order to diversify their economies and develop a wider industrial base, overseas investment is being actively sought by many African governments.

Industry

Many African industries concentrate on the extraction and processing of raw materials. These include the oil industry, food processing, mining, and textile production. South Africa accounts for more than half of the continent's industrial output, with much of the remainder coming from the countries along the northern coast. Over 60% of Africa's workforce is employed in agriculture.

The unspoiled natural splendor of wildlife reserves, like the Serengeti National Park in Tanzania, attract tourists from around the globe to Africa. The tourist industry in Kenya and Tanzania is particularly well developed, where it accounts for almost 10% of GNP.

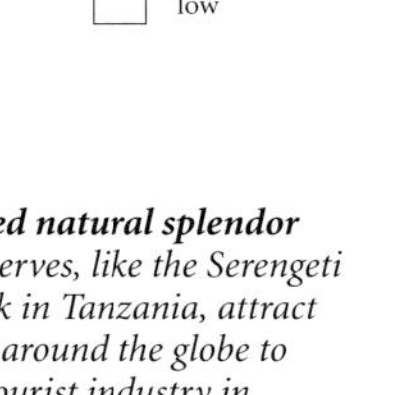

Standard of Living

Since the 1960s most countries in Africa have seen significant improvements in life expectancy, health care, and education. However, 18 of the 20 most deprived countries in the world are African, and the continent as a whole lies well behind the rest of the world in terms of many basic human needs.

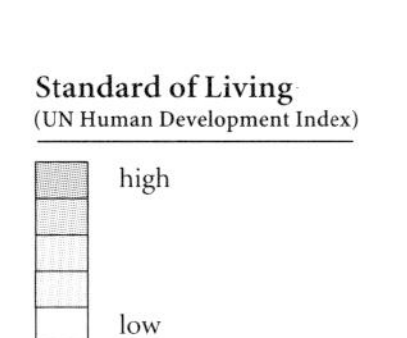
Standard of Living
(UN Human Development Index)
high
low

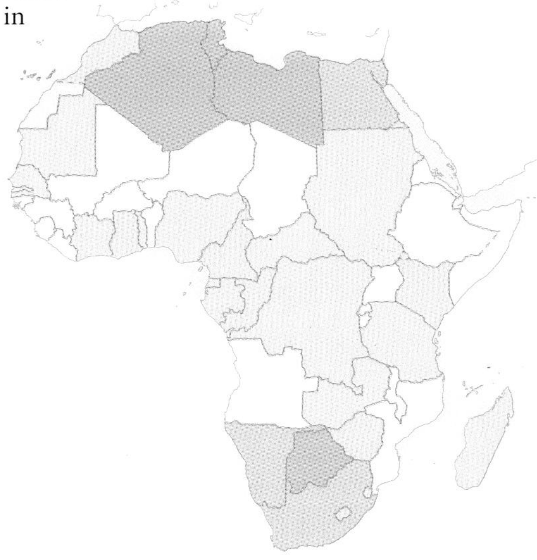

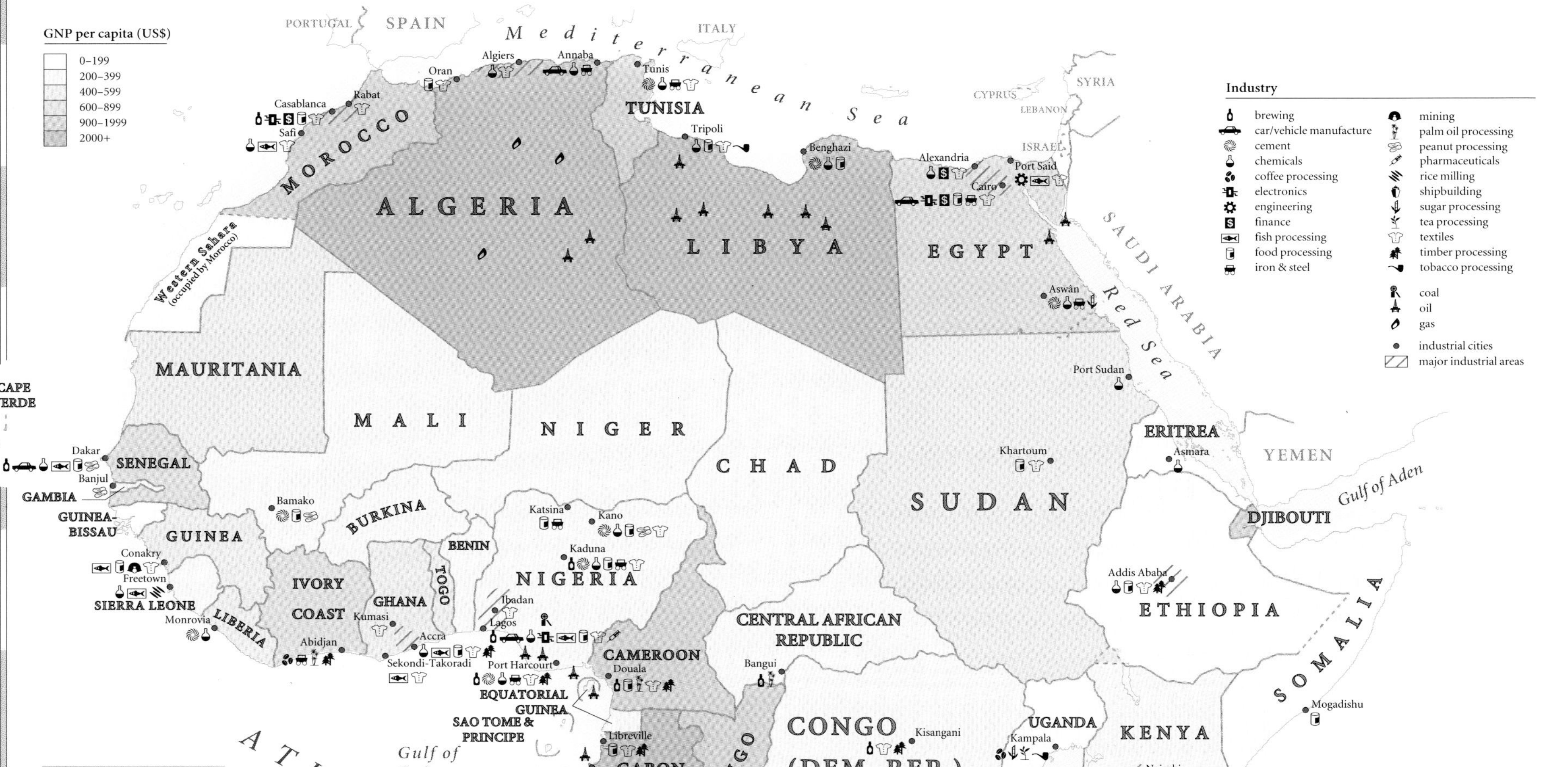

GNP per capita (US$)
0–199
200–399
400–599
600–899
900–1999
2000+

Industry
brewing
car/vehicle manufacture
cement
chemicals
coffee processing
electronics
engineering
finance
fish processing
food processing
iron & steel
mining
palm oil processing
peanut processing
pharmaceuticals
rice milling
shipbuilding
sugar processing
tea processing
textiles
timber processing
tobacco processing
coal
oil
gas
industrial cities
major industrial areas

PORTUGAL SPAIN ITALY Mediterranean Sea CYPRUS SYRIA LEBANON ISRAEL SAUDI ARABIA Red Sea YEMEN Gulf of Aden

Algiers Annaba Oran Tunis TUNISIA Tripoli Casablanca Rabat Safi MOROCCO ALGERIA LIBYA Benghazi Alexandria Port Said Cairo EGYPT Aswân Western Sahara (occupied by Morocco) MAURITANIA CAPE VERDE MALI NIGER CHAD SUDAN Port Sudan Khartoum ERITREA Asmara DJIBOUTI Dakar SENEGAL Banjul GAMBIA GUINEA-BISSAU GUINEA Bamako BURKINA Katsina Kano Kaduna BENIN NIGERIA Conakry Freetown SIERRA LEONE Monrovia LIBERIA IVORY COAST Abidjan Kumasi GHANA TOGO Accra Sekondi-Takoradi Ibadan Lagos Port Harcourt CAMEROON Douala CENTRAL AFRICAN REPUBLIC Bangui Addis Ababa ETHIOPIA SOMALIA Mogadishu EQUATORIAL GUINEA SAO TOME & PRINCIPE Gulf of Guinea Libreville GABON Port-Gentil CONGO CONGO (DEM. REP.) Kisangani UGANDA Kampala KENYA Nairobi RWANDA BURUNDI Bukavu Mombasa Brazzaville Pointe-Noire Kinshasa Kananga Dodoma Zanzibar Dar es Salaam TANZANIA SEYCHELLES Luanda ANGOLA Lobito Lubumbashi Ndola MALAWI COMOROS Mayotte (to France) ZAMBIA Lusaka Blantyre Harare ZIMBABWE Kwekwe Bulawayo Beira MOZAMBIQUE Mozambique Channel MADAGASCAR Antananarivo MAURITIUS Réunion (to France) NAMIBIA Windhoek Walvis Bay BOTSWANA Pretoria Johannesburg Maputo SWAZILAND Kimberley LESOTHO Durban SOUTH AFRICA East London Cape Town Port Elizabeth ATLANTIC OCEAN INDIAN OCEAN

The discovery of oil in the swampy Niger Delta during the 1960s made Nigeria one of Africa's richer nations. As world oil prices fell in the 1980s, the Nigerian economy faltered.

Exotic rugs and brightly colored textiles are sold in a street market along the banks of the Nile River in Luxor, Egypt.

The Rössing uranium mines in Namibia are the largest in the world. Africa and the US produce more than half of the world's uranium ore, used to fuel nuclear power plants. Elsewhere, South Africa and Niger also mine uranium on a large scale.

Environmental Issues

One of Africa's most serious environmental problems occurs in marginal areas such as the Sahel where scrub and forest clearance, often for cooking fuel, combined with overgrazing, is causing desertification. Game reserves in southern and eastern Africa have helped to preserve many endangered animals, although the needs of growing populations have led to conflict over land use, and poaching is a serious problem.

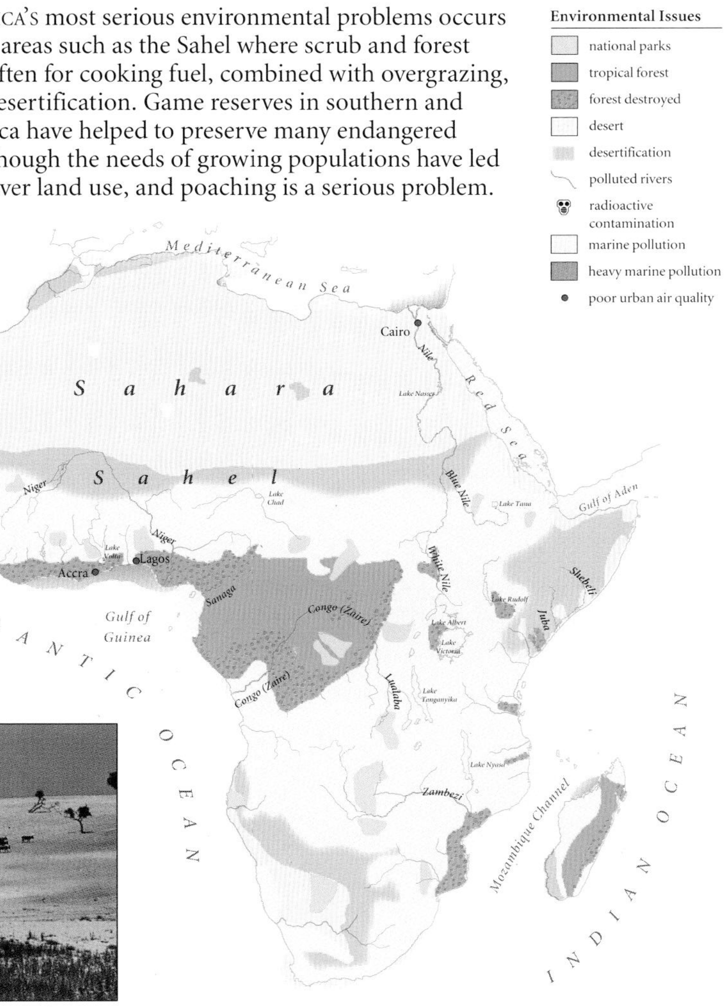

Environmental Issues

- national parks
- tropical forest
- forest destroyed
- desert
- desertification
- polluted rivers
- radioactive contamination
- marine pollution
- heavy marine pollution
- poor urban air quality

The Sahel's *delicate natural equilibrium is easily destroyed by the clearing of vegetation, drought, and overgrazing. This causes the Sahara to advance south, engulfing the savannah grasslands.*

Mineral Resources

Africa's ancient plateaus contain some of the world's most substantial reserves of precious stones and metals. Over 40% of the world's gold is mined in South Africa; Zambia has great copper deposits; and diamonds are mined in Botswana, Congo (Dem. Rep.), and South Africa. Oil has brought great economic benefits to Algeria, Libya, and Nigeria.

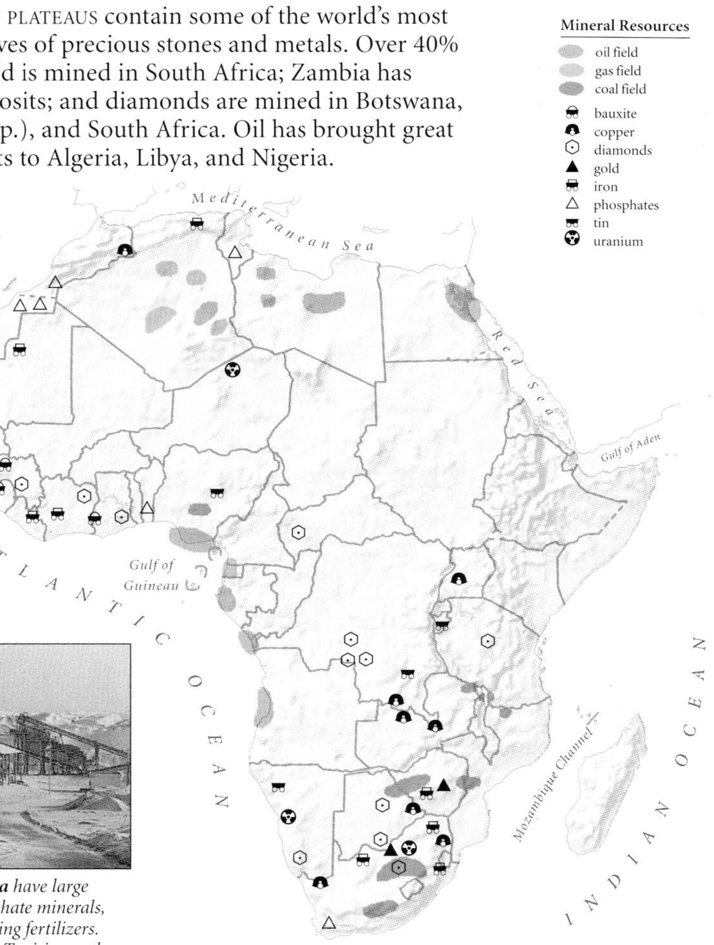

Mineral Resources

- oil field
- gas field
- coal field
- bauxite
- copper
- diamonds
- gold
- iron
- phosphates
- tin
- uranium

North and West Africa *have large deposits of white phosphate minerals, which are used in making fertilizers. Morocco, Senegal, and Tunisia are the continent's leading producers.*

Workers on a tea plantation *gather one of Africa's most important cash crops, providing a valuable source of income. Coffee, rubber, bananas, cotton, and cocoa are also widely grown as cash crops.*

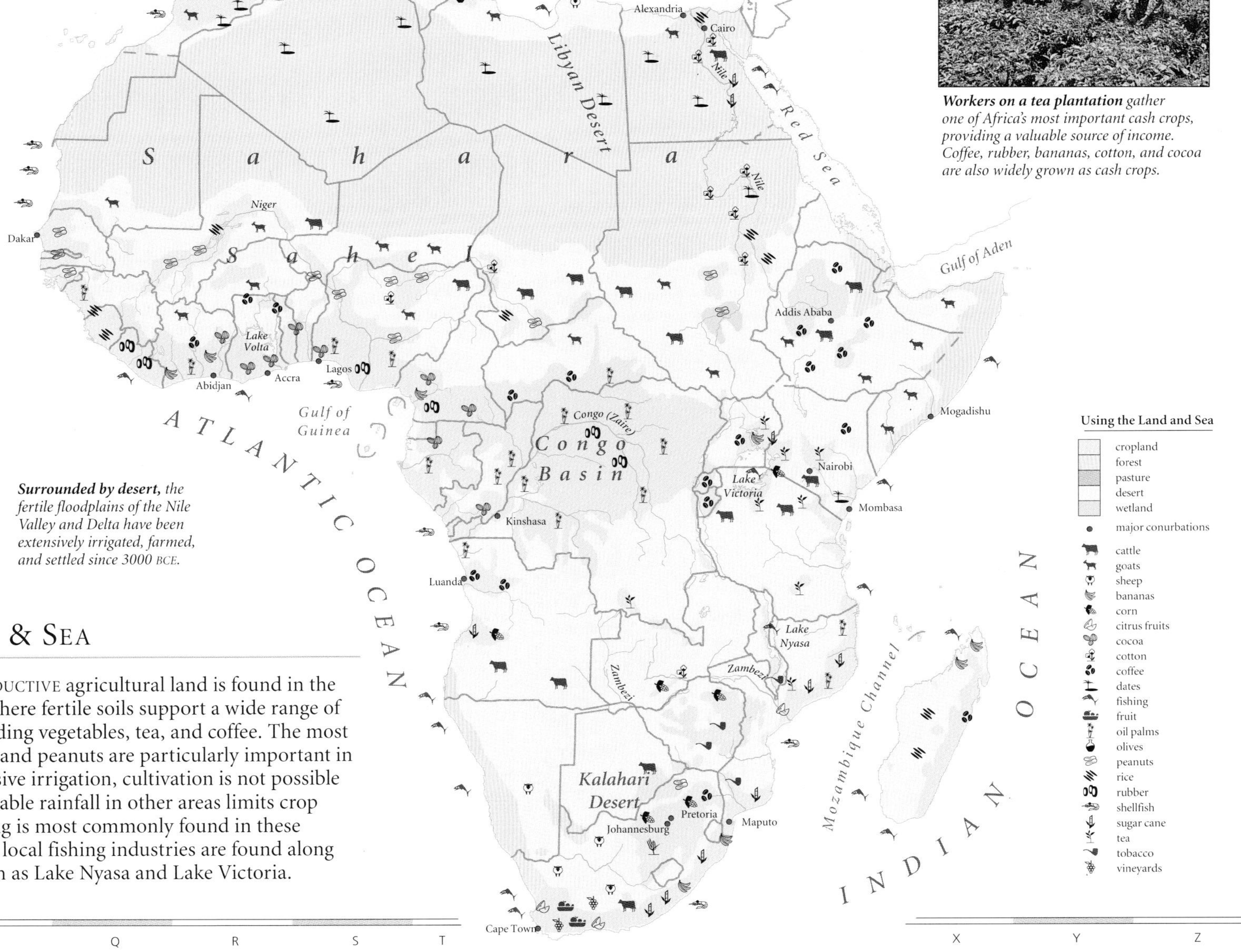

Surrounded by desert, *the fertile floodplains of the Nile Valley and Delta have been extensively irrigated, farmed, and settled since 3000 BCE.*

Using the Land & Sea

Some of Africa's most productive agricultural land is found in the eastern volcanic uplands, where fertile soils support a wide range of valuable export crops including vegetables, tea, and coffee. The most widely-grown crop is corn, and peanuts are particularly important in West Africa. Without intensive irrigation, cultivation is not possible in desert regions and unreliable rainfall in other areas limits crop production. Pastoral herding is most commonly found in these marginal lands. Substantial local fishing industries are found along coasts and in vast lakes such as Lake Nyasa and Lake Victoria.

Using the Land and Sea

- cropland
- forest
- pasture
- desert
- wetland
- major conurbations
- cattle
- goats
- sheep
- bananas
- corn
- citrus fruits
- cocoa
- cotton
- coffee
- dates
- fishing
- fruit
- oil palms
- olives
- peanuts
- rice
- rubber
- shellfish
- sugar cane
- tea
- tobacco
- vineyards

North Africa

Algeria, Egypt, Libya, Morocco, Tunisia, Western Sahara

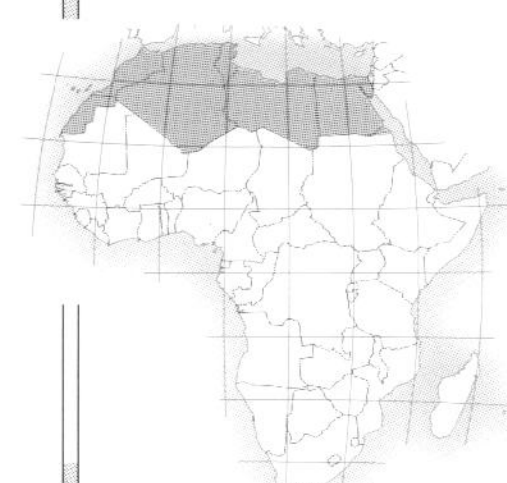

Fringed by the Mediterranean along the northern coast and by the arid Sahara in the south, North Africa reflects the influence of many invaders, both European and, most importantly, Arab, giving the region an almost universal Islamic flavor and a common Arabic language. The countries lying to the west of Egypt are often referred to as the Maghreb, an Arabic term for "west." Today, Morocco and Tunisia exploit their culture and landscape for tourism, while rich oil and gas deposits aid development in Libya and Algeria, despite political turmoil. Egypt, with its fertile, Nile-watered agricultural land and varied industrial base, is the most populous nation.

***These rock piles** in Algeria's Ahaggar Mountains are the result of weathering caused by extremes of temperature. Great cracks or joints appear in the rocks, which are then worn smooth by the wind.*

The Landscape

The Atlas Mountains, which run through much of Morocco, northern Algeria, and Tunisia, are part of the fold mountain system, which also runs through much of southern Europe. They recede to the south and east, becoming a steppe landscape before meeting the Sahara desert, which covers more than 90% of the region. The sediments of the Sahara overlie an ancient plateau of crystalline rock, some of which is more than four billion years old.

Map Key

Population

- above 5 million
- 1 million to 5 million
- 500,000 to 1 million
- 100,000 to 500,000
- 50,000 to 100,000
- 10,000 to 50,000
- below 10,000

Elevation

- 4000m / 13,124ft
- 3000m / 9843ft
- 2000m / 6562ft
- 1000m / 3281ft
- 500m / 1640ft
- 250m / 820ft
- 100m / 328ft
- sea level

Scale 1:11,000,000
(projection: Lambert Azimuthal Equal Area)

***The town of Tiznit**, Morocco, lies in an oasis in the desert. Crops and trees grow on the fertile land surrounding the town.*

***The Grand Erg Occidental** is one of Algeria's great Saharan sand seas. Wind force and direction determines the nature of landforms, such as the linear or seif dunes in the foreground.*

Using the Land & Sea

Sheltered valleys in the Atlas Mountains, the Nile Valley and Delta, and the Mediterranean coast are the main sources of good farmland. A wide variety of valuable crops, including cereals, rice, and cotton, and woods such as cedar and cork, are grown. Typical Mediterranean crops such as olives, figs, dates, and citrus fruits also thrive in these areas. The Nile Valley is particularly fertile, and most of Egypt's population lives close to the river. Elsewhere, irrigation is essential to improve crop yields on the desert margins.

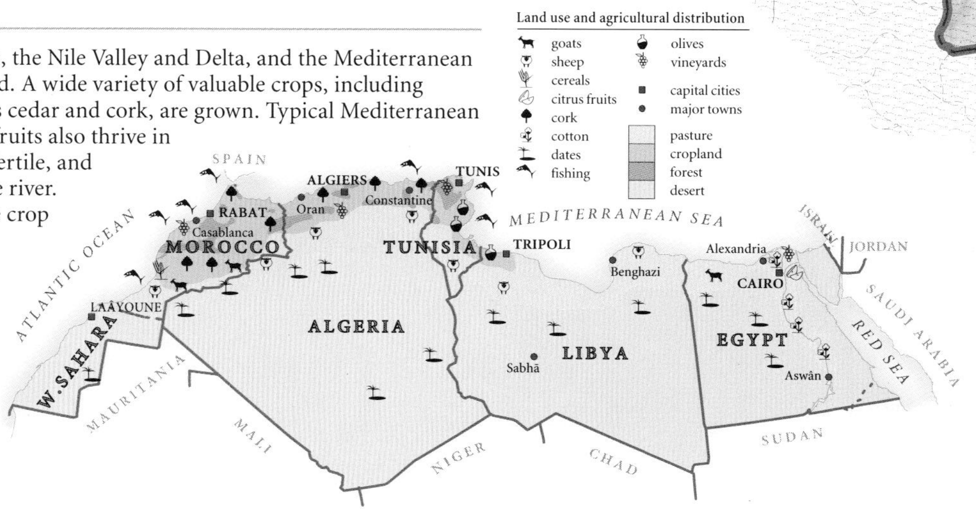

Land use and agricultural distribution

- goats
- sheep
- cereals
- citrus fruits
- cork
- cotton
- dates
- fishing
- olives
- vineyards
- capital cities
- major towns
- pasture
- cropland
- forest
- desert

The Urban/Rural Population Divide

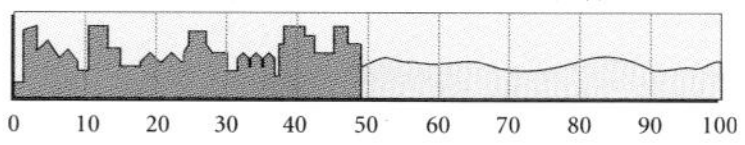

urban 49% — rural 51%

Population Density	Total Land Area
56 people per sq mile (22 people per sq km)	2,215,020 sq miles (5,738,394 sq km)

***Many North African nomads,** such as the Bedouin, maintain a traditional pastoral lifestyle on the desert fringes, moving their herds of sheep, goats, and camels from place to place and across country borders in order to find sufficient grazing land.*

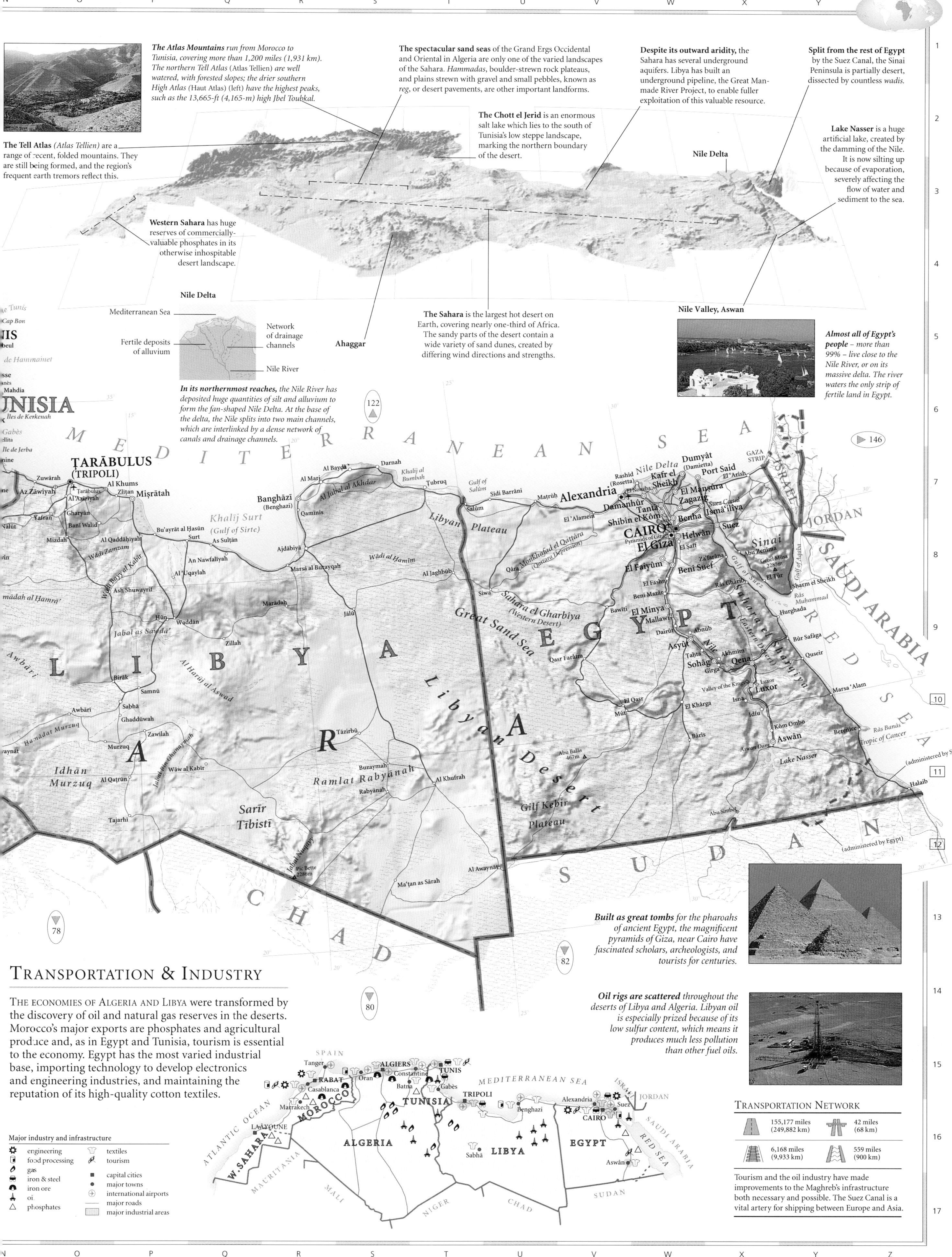

N O P Q R S T U V W X Y Z
1 2 3 4 5 6 7 8 9 10 11 12 13 14 15 16 17
The Tell Atlas (Atlas Tellien) are a range of recent, folded mountains. They are still being formed, and the region's frequent earth tremors reflect this.
Western Sahara has huge reserves of commercially-valuable phosphates in its otherwise inhospitable desert landscape.
The Chott el Jerid is an enormous salt lake which lies to the south of Tunisia's low steppe landscape, marking the northern boundary of the desert.
Nile Delta
Mediterranean Sea
Network of drainage channels
Fertile deposits of alluvium
Nile River
Ahaggar
The Sahara is the largest hot desert on Earth, covering nearly one-third of Africa. The sandy parts of the desert contain a wide variety of sand dunes, created by differing wind directions and strengths.
Nile Valley, Aswan
Lake Nasser is a huge artificial lake, created by the damming of the Nile. It is now silting up because of evaporation, severely affecting the flow of water and sediment to the sea.
122
146
78
82
80
MEDITERRANEAN SEA
TUNISIA
TARĀBULUS (TRIPOLI)
Zuwārah
Az Zāwiyah
Al Khums
Mişrātah
Gharyān
Banī Walīd
Mizdah
Yafran
Al Qaddāḩīyah
Wādī Zamzam
Khalīj Surt (Gulf of Sirte)
Surt
As Sulţān
Bu'ayrāt al Ḩasūn
An Nawfalīyah
Al 'Uqaylah
Banghāzī (Benghazi)
Qamīnis
Al Marj
Al Bayḑā
Darnah
Al Jabal al Akhḑar
Tubruq
Ajdābiyā
Marsá al Burayqah
Wādī al Ḩamīm
Al Jaghbūb
Jālū
Marādah
Ash Shuwayrif
Hūn
Waddān
Jabal as Sawdā'
Zillah
Al Haruj al Aswad
LIBYA
SAHARA
Birāk
Samnū
Sabhā
Ghaddūwah
Awbārī
Murzuq
Zawīlah
Ḩamādat Murzuq
Idhān Murzuq
Al Qaţrūn
Wāw al Kabīr
Tajarhī
Sarīr Tibistī
Tāzirbū
Buzaymah
Ramlat Rabyānah
Rabyānah
Al Khufrah
Al Awaynāt
Ma'ţan as Sārah
Pic Bette 2286m
Libyan Desert
Libyan Plateau
Gulf of Salûm
Salûm
Sidi Barrâni
Matrûh
Alexandria
El 'Alamein
Qattara Depression
Siwa
Sahara el Gharbîya (Western Desert)
Great Sand Sea
Bawiti
Qasr Farâfra
El Qasr
Mut
El Khârga
Bârîs
Gilf Kebir Plateau
Abu Balâs 467m
EGYPT
Nile Delta
Rashîd (Rosetta)
Dumyât (Damietta)
Port Said
Kafr el Sheikh
El Mansûra
Damanhûr
Tanta
Zagazig
Ismâ'ilîya
Suez Canal
Shibîn el Kôm
Benha
CAIRO
El Gîza
Pyramids of Giza
Helwân
Suez
El Faiyûm
Beni Suef
El Minya
Mallawi
Dairût
Asyût
Tahta
Sohâg
Girga
Akhmim
Qena
Valley of the Kings
Luxor
Isna
Idfu
Kôm Ombo
Aswân
Aswân Dam
Lake Nasser
Abu Simbel
Sinai
Gebel Mûsa 2285m
El Tûr
Gulf of Suez
Gulf of Aqaba
Sharm el Sheikh
Hurghada
Bûr Safâga
Quseir
Marsa 'Alam
Berenice
Râs Banâs
Tropic of Cancer
Halaib
(administered by Sudan)
(administered by Egypt)
Sahara el Sharqîya (Eastern Desert)
GAZA STRIP
ISRAEL
JORDAN
SAUDI ARABIA
RED SEA
SUDAN
CHAD

The Atlas Mountains *run from Morocco to Tunisia, covering more than 1,200 miles (1,931 km). The northern Tell Atlas* (Atlas Tellien) *are well watered, with forested slopes; the drier southern High Atlas* (Haut Atlas) *(left) have the highest peaks, such as the 13,665-ft (4,165-m) high Jbel Toubkal.*

The spectacular sand seas of the Grand Ergs Occidental and Oriental in Algeria are only one of the varied landscapes of the Sahara. *Hammadas*, boulder-strewn rock plateaus, and plains strewn with gravel and small pebbles, known as *reg*, or desert pavements, are other important landforms.

Despite its outward aridity, the Sahara has several underground aquifers. Libya has built an underground pipeline, the Great Man-made River Project, to enable fuller exploitation of this valuable resource.

Split from the rest of Egypt by the Suez Canal, the Sinai Peninsula is partially desert, dissected by countless *wadis*.

In its northernmost reaches, *the Nile River has deposited huge quantities of silt and alluvium to form the fan-shaped Nile Delta. At the base of the delta, the Nile splits into two main channels, which are interlinked by a dense network of canals and drainage channels.*

Almost all of Egypt's people *– more than 99% – live close to the Nile River, or on its massive delta. The river waters the only strip of fertile land in Egypt.*

Built as great tombs *for the pharoahs of ancient Egypt, the magnificent pyramids of Giza, near Cairo have fascinated scholars, archeologists, and tourists for centuries.*

Oil rigs are scattered *throughout the deserts of Libya and Algeria. Libyan oil is especially prized because of its low sulfur content, which means it produces much less pollution than other fuel oils.*

Transportation & Industry

The economies of Algeria and Libya were transformed by the discovery of oil and natural gas reserves in the deserts. Morocco's major exports are phosphates and agricultural produce and, as in Egypt and Tunisia, tourism is essential to the economy. Egypt has the most varied industrial base, importing technology to develop electronics and engineering industries, and maintaining the reputation of its high-quality cotton textiles.

Major industry and infrastructure

- engineering
- food processing
- gas
- iron & steel
- iron ore
- oil
- phosphates
- textiles
- tourism
- capital cities
- major towns
- international airports
- major roads
- major industrial areas

Transportation Network

155,177 miles (249,882 km)	42 miles (68 km)	6,168 miles (9,933 km)	559 miles (900 km)

Tourism and the oil industry have made improvements to the Maghreb's infrastructure both necessary and possible. The Suez Canal is a vital artery for shipping between Europe and Asia.

West Africa

Benin, Burkina, Cape Verde, Gambia, Ghana, Guinea, Guinea-Bissau, Ivory Coast, Liberia, Mali, Mauritania, Niger, Nigeria, Senegal, Sierra Leone, Togo

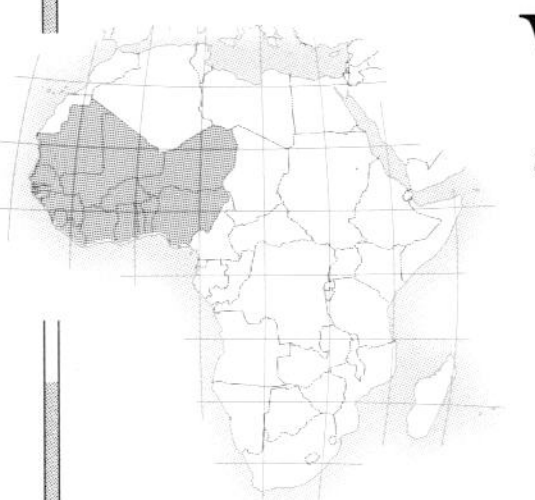

West Africa is an immensely diverse region, encompassing the desert landscapes and mainly Muslim populations of the southern Saharan countries, and the tropical rain forests of the more humid south, with a great variety of local languages and cultures. The rich natural resources and accessibility of the area were quickly exploited by Europeans; most of the Africans captured by slave traders came from this region, causing serious depopulation. The very different influences of West Africa's leading colonial powers, Britain and France, remain today, reflected in the languages and institutions of the countries they once governed.

The dry scrub of the Sahel is only suitable for grazing herd animals, like these cattle in Mali.

SCALE 1:9,000,000
(projection: Lambert Azimuth Equal Area)

Transportation & Industry

Abundant natural resources, including oil and metallic minerals, are found in much of West Africa, although investment is required for their further exploitation. Nigeria experienced an oil boom during the 1970s but subsequent growth has been sporadic. Most industry in other countries has a primary basis, including mining, logging, and food processing.

Transportation Network

231,966 miles (373,537 km)	433 miles (698 km)
6,658 miles (10,721 km)	9,526 miles (15,340 km)

The road and rail systems are most developed near the coasts. Some of the landlocked countries remain disadvantaged by the difficulty of access to ports, and their poor road networks.

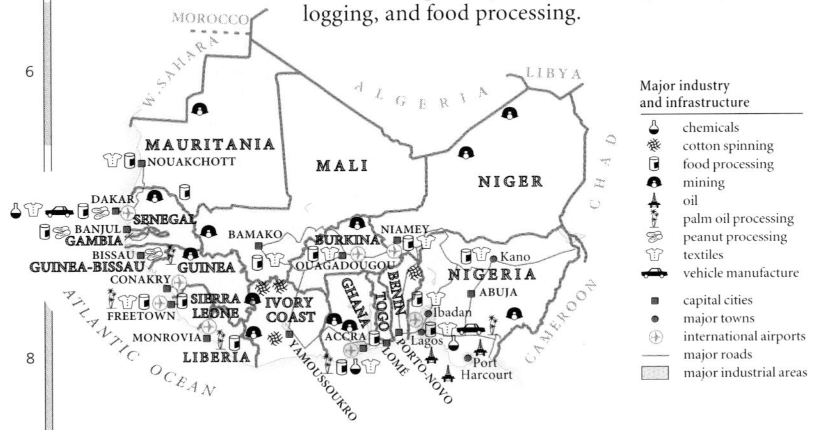

Major industry and infrastructure: chemicals; cotton spinning; food processing; mining; oil; palm oil processing; peanut processing; textiles; vehicle manufacture; capital cities; major towns; international airports; major roads; major industrial areas

Map Key

Population	Elevation
1 million to 5 million	2000m / 6562ft
500,000 to 1 million	1000m / 3281ft
100,000 to 500,000	500m / 1640ft
50,000 to 100,000	250m / 820ft
10,000 to 50,000	100m / 328ft
below 10,000	sea level

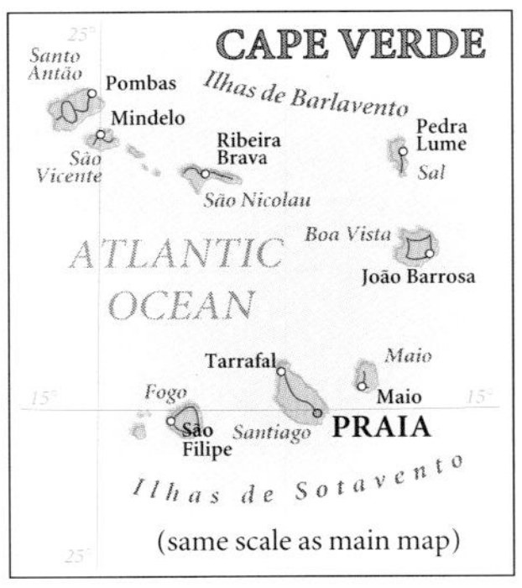

CAPE VERDE (same scale as main map)

The southern regions of West Africa still contain great swaths of tropical rain forest, including some of the world's most prized hardwood trees, such as mahogany and iroko.

Using the Land & Sea

The humid southern regions are most suitable for cultivation; in these areas, cash crops such as coffee, cotton, cocoa, and rubber are grown in large quantities. Peanuts are grown throughout West Africa. In the north, advancing desertification has made the Sahel increasingly uncultivable, and pastoral farming is more common. Huge herds of sheep, cattle, and goats are grazed on the savannah grasses. Fishing is important in coastal and delta areas.

The Gambia, mainland Africa's smallest country, produces great quantities of peanuts. Winnowing is used to separate the nuts from their stalks.

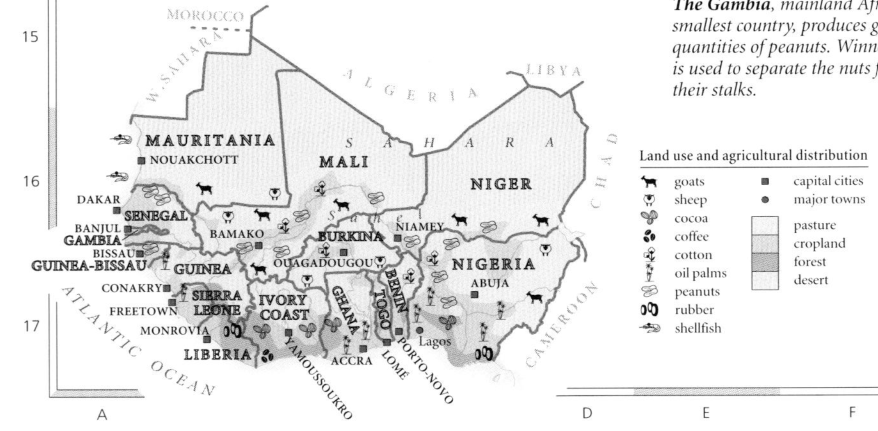

Land use and agricultural distribution: goats; sheep; cocoa; coffee; cotton; oil palms; peanuts; rubber; shellfish; capital cities; major towns; pasture; cropland; forest; desert

The Urban/Rural Population Divide

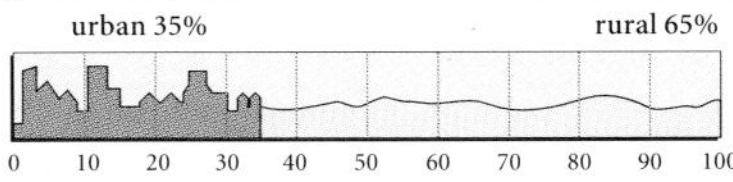

urban 35% — rural 65%

Population Density	Total Land Area
91 people per sq mile (35 people per sq km)	2,337,137 sq miles (6,054,760 sq km)

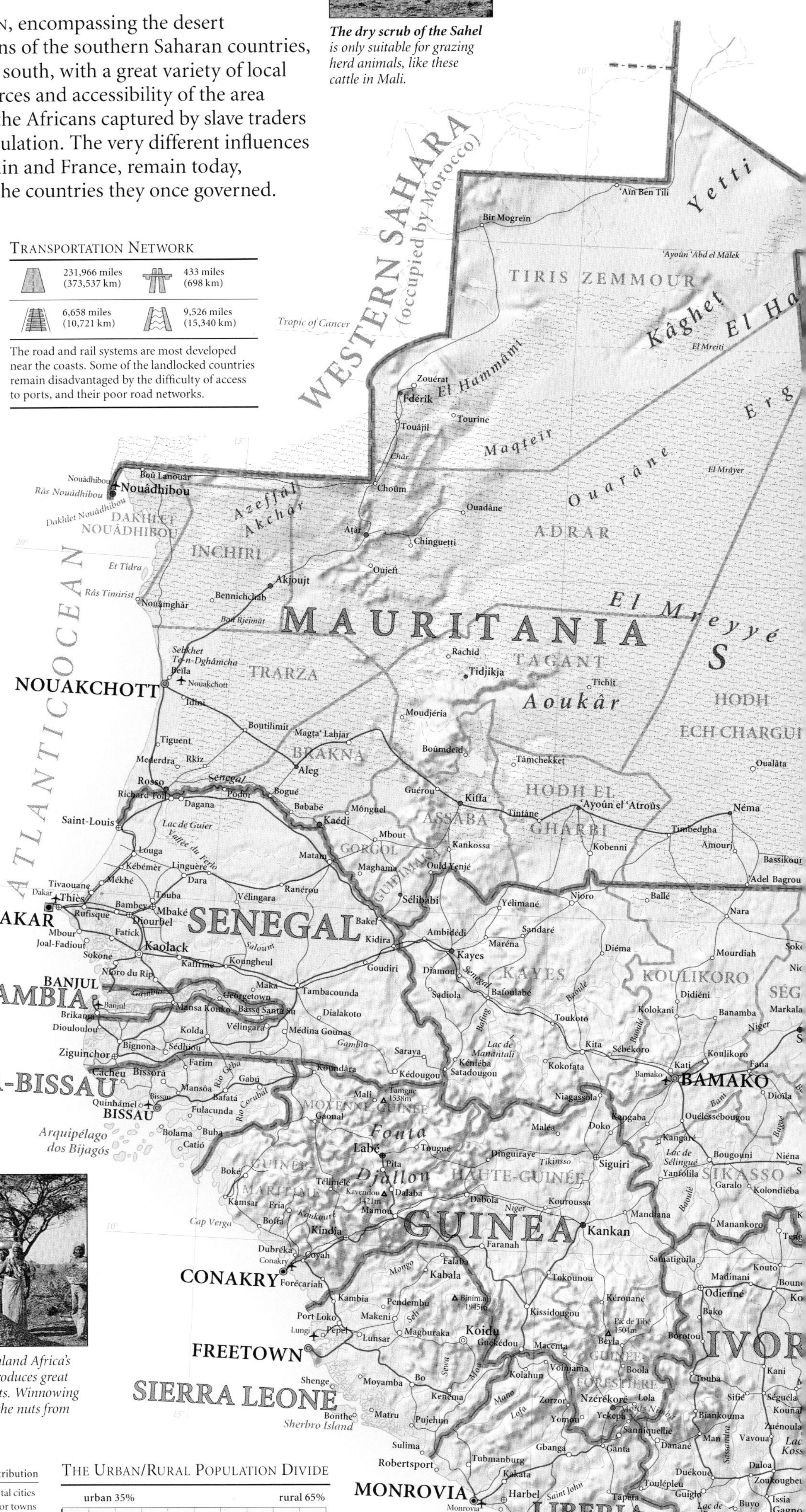

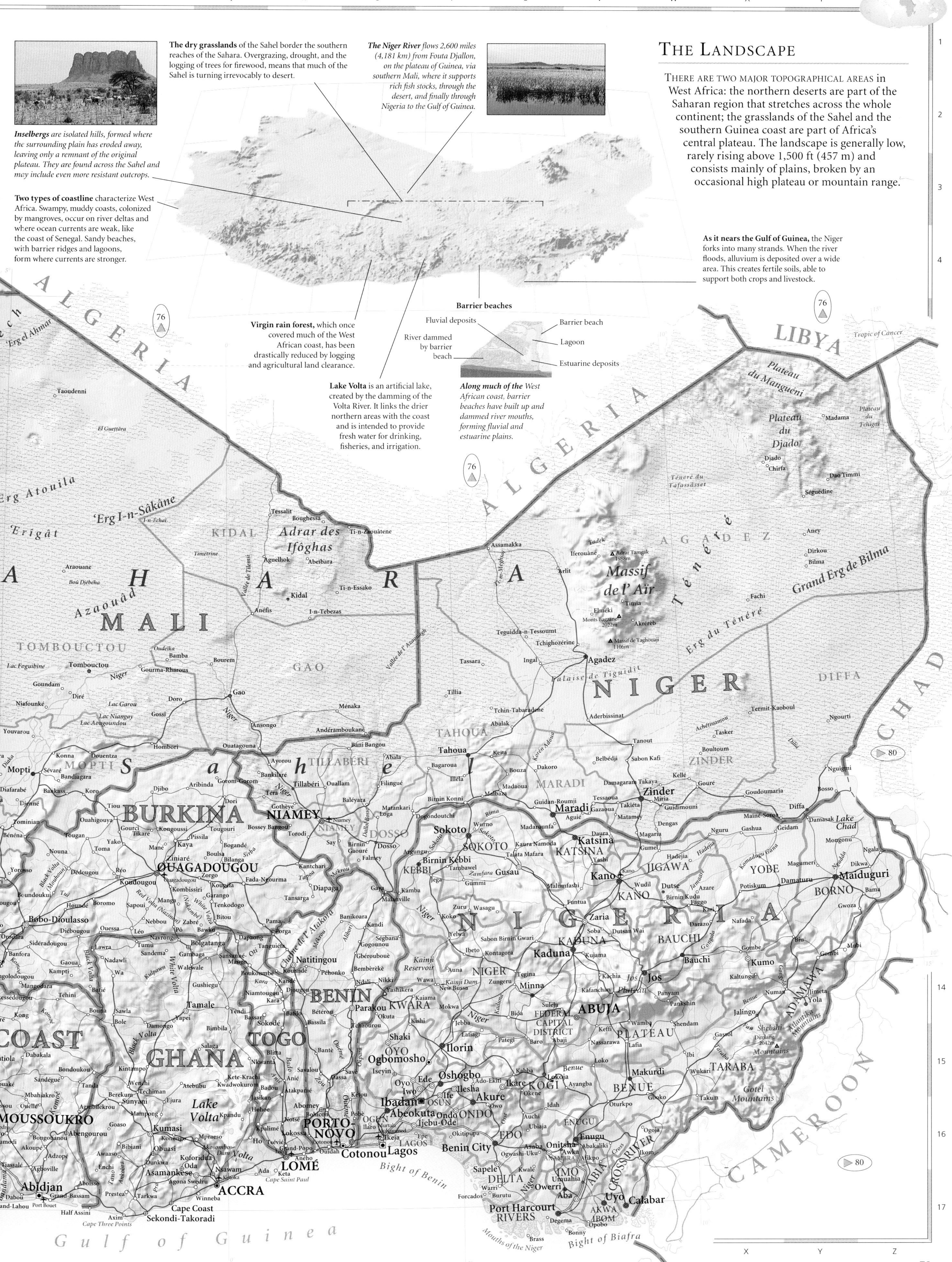
THE LANDSCAPE
THERE ARE TWO MAJOR TOPOGRAPHICAL AREAS in West Africa: the northern deserts are part of the Saharan region that stretches across the whole continent; the grasslands of the Sahel and the southern Guinea coast are part of Africa's central plateau. The landscape is generally low, rarely rising above 1,500 ft (457 m) and consists mainly of plains, broken by an occasional high plateau or mountain range.
Inselbergs are isolated hills, formed where the surrounding plain has eroded away, leaving only a remnant of the original plateau. They are found across the Sahel and may include even more resistant outcrops.
The dry grasslands of the Sahel border the southern reaches of the Sahara. Overgrazing, drought, and the logging of trees for firewood, means that much of the Sahel is turning irrevocably to desert.
The Niger River flows 2,600 miles (4,181 km) from Fouta Djallon, on the plateau of Guinea, via southern Mali, where it supports rich fish stocks, through the desert, and finally through Nigeria to the Gulf of Guinea.
Two types of coastline characterize West Africa. Swampy, muddy coasts, colonized by mangroves, occur on river deltas and where ocean currents are weak, like the coast of Senegal. Sandy beaches, with barrier ridges and lagoons, form where currents are stronger.
As it nears the Gulf of Guinea, the Niger forks into many strands. When the river floods, alluvium is deposited over a wide area. This creates fertile soils, able to support both crops and livestock.
Barrier beaches
Fluvial deposits
Barrier beach
Lagoon
River dammed by barrier beach
Estuarine deposits
Along much of the West African coast, barrier beaches have built up and dammed river mouths, forming fluvial and estuarine plains.
Virgin rain forest, which once covered much of the West African coast, has been drastically reduced by logging and agricultural land clearance.
Lake Volta is an artificial lake, created by the damming of the Volta River. It links the drier northern areas with the coast and is intended to provide fresh water for drinking, fisheries, and irrigation.
ALGERIA
LIBYA
MALI
NIGER
NIGERIA
BURKINA
GHANA
TOGO
BENIN
CHAD
CAMEROON
SAHARA
Sahel
NIAMEY
OUAGADOUGOU
ABUJA
ACCRA
LOMÉ
PORTO-NOVO
Massif de l'Aïr
Ténéré
Grand Erg de Bilma
Lake Volta
Lake Chad
Gulf of Guinea
Bight of Benin
Bight of Biafra
Tropic of Cancer
76
80

Central Africa

Cameroon, Central African Republic, Chad, Congo, Congo (Democratic Republic of), Equatorial Guinea, Gabon, Sao Tome & Principe

The great rain forest basin of the Congo (Zaire) River embraces most of remote Central Africa. The interior was largely unknown to Europeans until late in the 19th century, when its tribal kingdoms were split principally between France and Belgium, with Sao Tome and Principe the lone Portuguese territory, and Equatorial Guinea controlled by Spain. Open democracy and regional economic integration are important goals for these nations, several of which have only recently emerged from restrictive regimes, and investment is needed to improve transportation infrastructures. Many of the small, fast-growing, and increasingly urban population speak French, the regional *lingua franca,* along with several hundred Pygmy, Bantu, and Sudanic dialects.

The Landscape

Lake Chad lies in a desert basin bounded by the volcanic Tibesti Mountains in the north, plateaus in the east and, in the south, the broad watershed of the Congo Basin. The vast circular depression of the Congo is isolated from the coastal plain by the granite Massif du Chaillu. To the northwest, the volcanoes and fold mountains of the Cameroon Ridge *(Dorsale Camerounaise)* extend as islands into the Gulf of Guinea. The high fold mountains fringing the east of the Congo Basin fall steeply to the lakes of the Great Rift Valley.

A plug of resistant lava, *at the southwestern end of the Cameroon Ridge* (Dorsale Camerounaise), *is all that remains of an eroded volcano.*

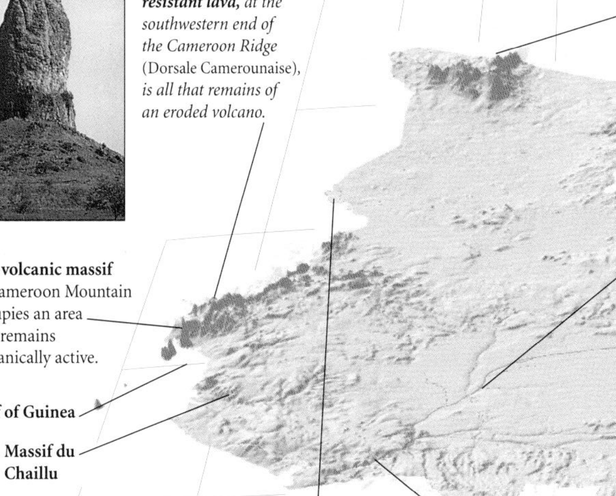

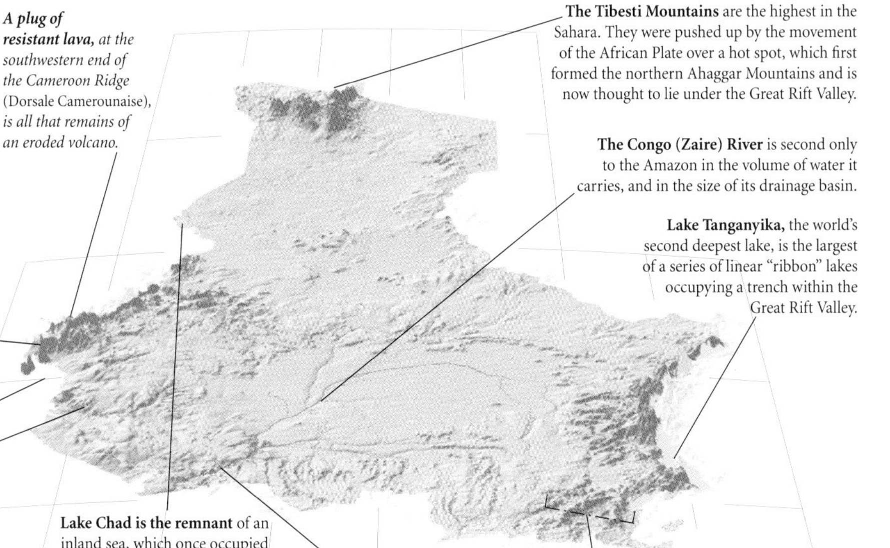

Gulf of Guinea
Massif du Chaillu

The volcanic massif of Cameroon Mountain occupies an area that remains volcanically active.

The Tibesti Mountains are the highest in the Sahara. They were pushed up by the movement of the African Plate over a hot spot, which first formed the northern Ahaggar Mountains and is now thought to lie under the Great Rift Valley.

The Congo (Zaire) River is second only to the Amazon in the volume of water it carries, and in the size of its drainage basin.

Lake Tanganyika, the world's second deepest lake, is the largest of a series of linear "ribbon" lakes occupying a trench within the Great Rift Valley.

Lake Chad is the remnant of an inland sea, which once occupied much of the surrounding basin. A series of droughts since the 1970s has reduced the area of this shallow freshwater lake to about 1,000 sq miles (2,599 sq km).

The lakelike expansion of the Congo (Zaire) River, in Stanley Pool, is the lowest point of the interior basin, though the river still descends more than 1,000 ft (300 m) to reach the sea.

Rich mineral deposits in "Copper Belt" of Congo (Dem. Rep.) were formed under intense heat and pressure, when the ancient African Shield was uplifted to form the region's mountains.

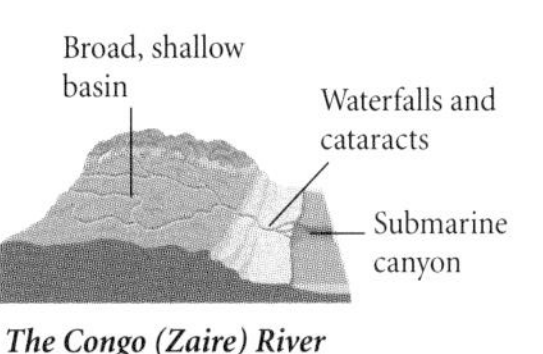

Broad, shallow basin
Waterfalls and cataracts
Submarine canyon

The Congo (Zaire) River *flows sluggishly through the rain forest of the interior basin. Toward the coast, the river drops steeply in a series of waterfalls and cataracts. At this point, the erosional power of the river becomes so great that it has formed a deep submarine canyon offshore.*

Virgin tropical rain forest *is found in the Ruwenzori range Congo (Dem. Rep.) and Ugandan border.*

The vast sandflats *surrounding Lake Chad were once covered by water. Changing climatic patterns caused the lake to shrink, and desert now covers much of its previous area.*

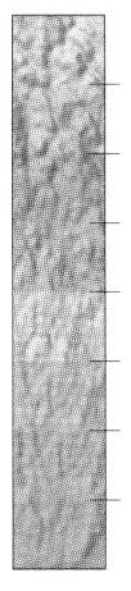

Transportation & Industry

Large reserves of valuable minerals are found in Central Africa: copper, cobalt, manganese, zinc, and tin are mined in Congo (Dem. Rep.) and Cameroon; diamonds in the Central African Republic; and manganese in Gabon. Cameroon, Gabon, Congo (Dem. Rep.), and Congo have oil deposits and oil has also been recently discovered in Chad. Other export industries are based on the processing of goods such as palm oil and rubber.

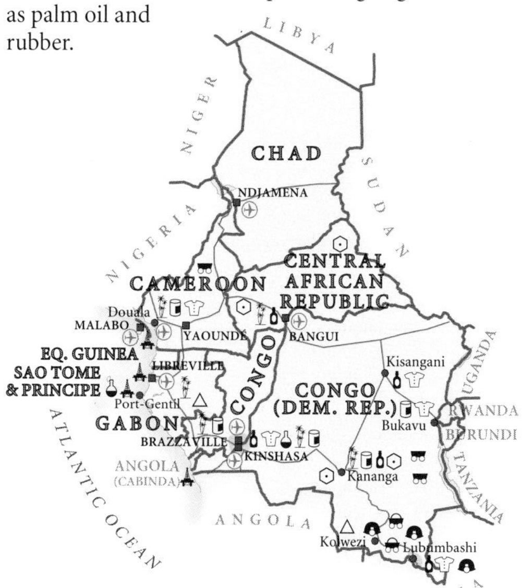

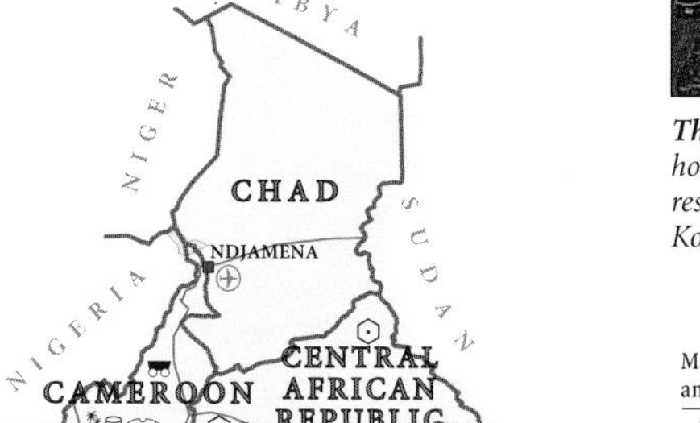

The ancient rocks *of Congo (Dem. Rep.) hold immense and varied mineral reserves. This open pit copper mine is at Kolwezi in the far south.*

Major industry and infrastructure: brewing, chemicals, cobalt, copper, diamonds, food processing, manganese, oil, palm oil processing, textiles, tin, capital cities, major towns, international airports, major roads, major industrial areas

Transportation Network

181,633 miles (292,485 km)	342 miles (550 km)
4,774 miles (7,688 km)	15,261 miles (24,475 km)

The Trans-Gabon railroad, which began operating in 1987, has opened up new sources of timber and manganese. Elsewhere, much investment is needed to update and improve road, rail, and water transportation.

Map Key

POPULATION
- 1 million to 5 million
- 500,000 to 1 million
- 100,000 to 500,000
- 50,000 to 100,000
- 10,000 to 50,000
- below 10,000

ELEVATION
- 4000m / 13,124ft
- 3000m / 9843ft
- 2000m / 6562ft
- 1000m / 3281ft
- 500m / 1640ft
- 250m / 820ft
- 100m / 328ft
- sea level

Scale 1:9,500,000 (projection: Lambert Azimuthal Equal Area)

76
78

CENTRAL AFRICAN REPUBLIC
CAMEROON
CONGO
GABON
CONGO (DEM. REP.)
EQUATORIAL GUINEA
SAO TOME & PRINCIPE
ANGOLA
ANGOLA (CABINDA)
ZAMBIA
TANZANIA
UGANDA
RWANDA
BURUNDI
ATLANTIC OCEAN
Gulf of Guinea
Bight of Biafra
Congo Basin
Lake Tanganyika
Lake Mweru
Lake Kivu
Lake Edward
Lake Albert
BANGUI
YAOUNDÉ
LIBREVILLE
MALABO
SÃO TOMÉ
BRAZZAVILLE
KINSHASA
Douala
Port-Gentil
Pointe-Noire
Mbandaka
Kisangani
Kananga
Mbuji-Mayi
Lubumbashi
Matadi
Bukavu
Goma
Kalemie
Bambari
Berbérati
Bandundu
82
66
84
Land use and agricultural distribution
cattle
cocoa
coffee
cotton
palms
peanuts
rubber
timber
capital cities
major towns
pasture
cropland
forest
desert
CHAD
NDJAMENA
CAMEROON
CENTRAL AFRICAN REPUBLIC
EQ. GUINEA
SAO TOME & PRINCIPE
GABON
CONGO
CONGO (DEM. REP.)
ANGOLA
ZAMBIA
LIBYA
NIGER
NIGERIA
SUDAN

The great Congo (Zaire) River forms part of the border between Congo and Congo (Dem. Rep.). The river flows quickly. A series of falls and rapids makes it only partly navigable.

Using the Land

Cash crops for export include cocoa, coffee, and rubber. Shifting cultivation is widely practiced, and plantains are the staple food of the equatorial region, grown with yam and taro. Cassava, guinea corn (sorghum), and millet are the main subsistence crops in savannah areas. Cattle farming is limited to areas free of tsetse fly, and fish from the interior rivers are an important protein source.

High-quality timber *is floated to Port-Gentil, Gabon, via the Ogooué River. Timber provides important export revenue for several countries, though there has been concern about the uncontrolled logging of rare tropical woods.*

The Urban/Rural Population Divide

urban 34% — rural 76%

0 10 20 30 40 50 60 70 80 90 100

Population Density	Total Land Area
33 people per sq mile (13 people per sq km)	2,023,939 sq miles (5,243,364 sq km)

East Africa

Burundi, Djibouti, Eritrea, Ethiopia, Kenya, Rwanda, Somalia, Sudan, Tanzania, Uganda

The countries of East Africa divide into two distinct cultural regions. Sudan and the "Horn" nations have been influenced by the Middle East. Ethiopia was the home of one of the earliest Christian civilizations, and Sudan reflects both Muslim and Christian influences. The southern countries share a closer cultural affinity with other sub-Saharan nations. Some of Africa's most densely populated countries lie in this region, and the needs of a growing number of people have put pressure on marginal lands and fragile environments. Although most East African economies remain strongly agricultural, Kenya has developed a varied industrial base.

The Landscape

East Africa's most significant landscape feature is the Great Rift Valley. This formed during the most recent phase of continental movement, when the rigid basement rocks cracked and buckled. Great blocks of land were raised and lowered, creating huge flat-bottomed valleys and steep escarpments, sometimes covered by volcanic extrusions in highland areas.

This dome at Gonder, *in Ethiopia, is a volcanic intrusion, formed when molten rock pushed up the surface of the Earth and then solidified, leaving an outcrop of igneous rock.*

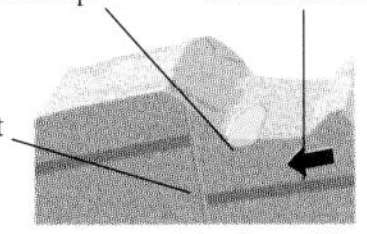

Ephemeral lake forms at far edge of slope

Central block slopes toward main fault

Boundary fault

The eastern arm *of the Great Rift Valley is gradually being pulled apart. The forces on one side are greater than the other, however, causing the land to slope. This affects regional drainage that migrates down the slope.*

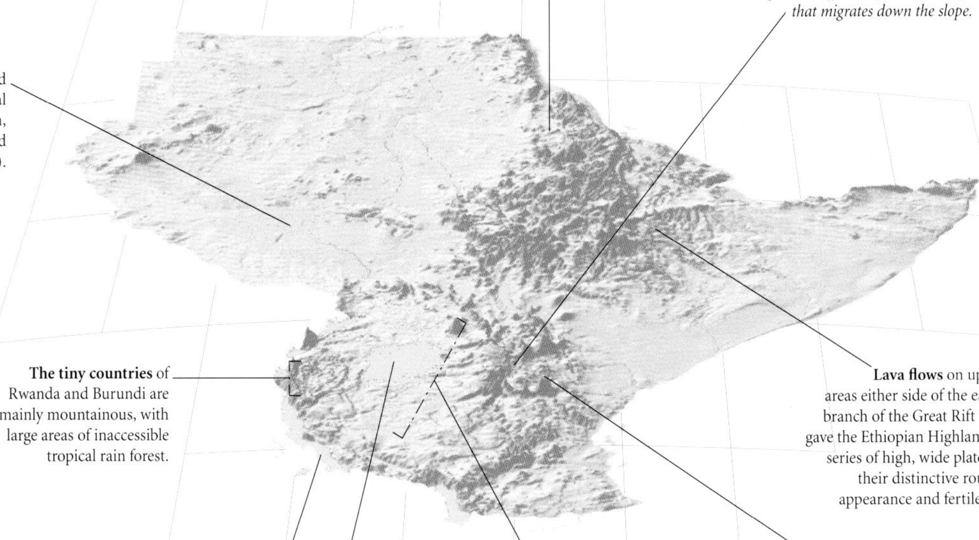

Much of northern Sudan is covered by desert. However, in the tropical wetlands of the southern Sudd region, annual rainfall can sometimes exceed 40 inches (1,000 mm).

The tiny countries of Rwanda and Burundi are mainly mountainous, with large areas of inaccessible tropical rain forest.

Lava flows on uplifted areas either side of the eastern branch of the Great Rift Valley gave the Ethiopian Highlands – a series of high, wide plateaus – their distinctive rounded appearance and fertile soils.

Kilimanjaro

Lake Tanganyika lies 8,202 ft (2,500 m) above sea level. It has a depth of nearly 16,400 ft (5,000 m). The lake traces the valley floor for some 400 miles (644 km) of the western arm of the Great Rift Valley.

Lake Victoria occupies a vast basin between the two arms of the Great Rift Valley. It is the world's second largest lake in terms of surface area, extending 26,828 sq miles (69,484 sq km). The lake contains numerous islands and coral reefs.

A vast plateau lies between the eastern and western rift valleys in Kenya, Uganda, and western Tanzania. It has been leveled by long periods of erosion to form a peneplain, but is dotted with inselbergs – outcrops of more resistant rocks.

An extinct volcano, *Kilimanjaro is Africa's highest mountain, rising 19,340 ft (5,895 m). It is one of the few places in Africa where snow settles, allowing glacier ice to form.*

The Kassala region *in eastern Sudan is watered by the Atbara River, an important tributary of the Nile. Most of the population is engaged in agriculture, growing cotton and cereals.*

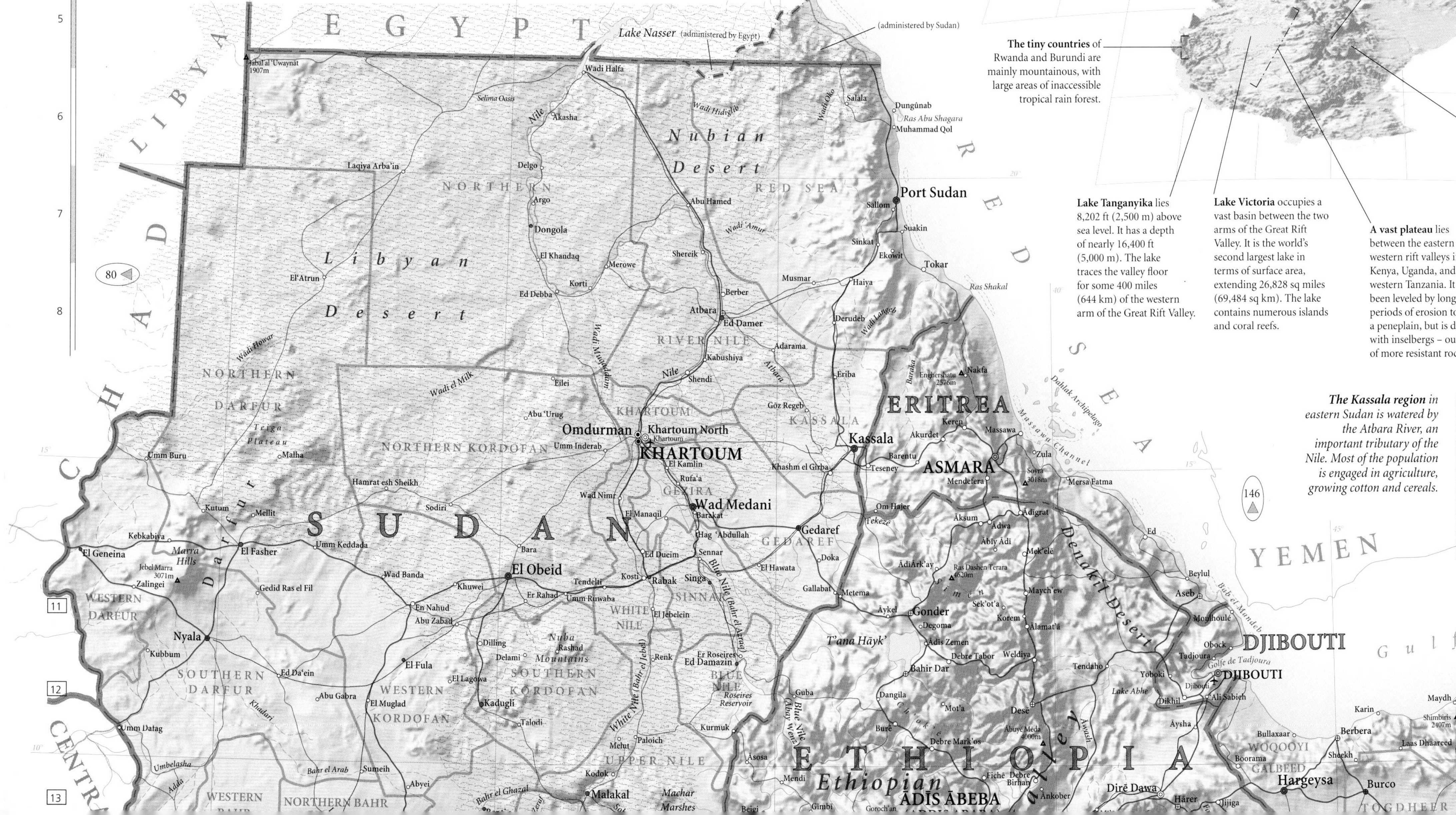

76
80
146

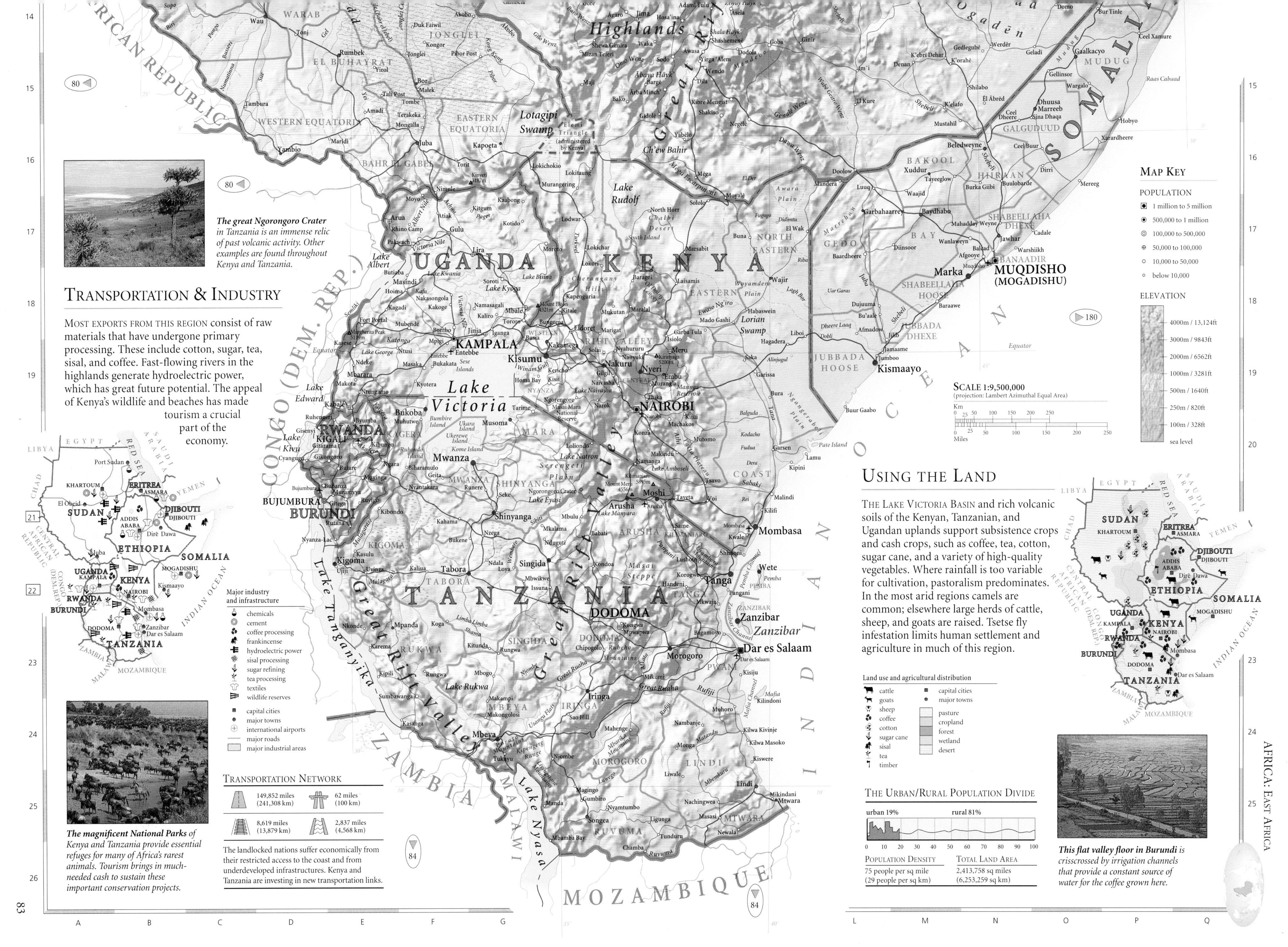
UGANDA
KENYA
TANZANIA
SOMALIA
RWANDA
BURUNDI
CONGO (DEM. REP.)
ZAMBIA
MALAWI
MOZAMBIQUE
KAMPALA
NAIROBI
DODOMA
MUQDISHO (MOGADISHU)
BUJUMBURA
KIGALI
Mombasa
Dar es Salaam
Zanzibar
Kismaayo
Lake Victoria
Lake Tanganyika
Lake Nyasa
Lake Rudolf
Great Rift Valley
INDIAN OCEAN
Map Key
POPULATION
1 million to 5 million
500,000 to 1 million
100,000 to 500,000
50,000 to 100,000
10,000 to 50,000
below 10,000
ELEVATION
4000m / 13,124ft
3000m / 9843ft
2000m / 6562ft
1000m / 3281ft
500m / 1640ft
250m / 820ft
100m / 328ft
sea level
SCALE 1:9,500,000
(projection: Lambert Azimuthal Equal Area)
Major industry and infrastructure
chemicals
cement
coffee processing
frankincense
hydroelectric power
sisal processing
sugar refining
tea processing
textiles
wildlife reserves
capital cities
major towns
international airports
major roads
major industrial areas
Land use and agricultural distribution
cattle
goats
sheep
coffee
cotton
sugar cane
sisal
tea
timber
capital cities
major towns
pasture
cropland
forest
wetland
desert

The great Ngorongoro Crater in Tanzania is an immense relic of past volcanic activity. Other examples are found throughout Kenya and Tanzania.

Transportation & Industry

Most exports from this region consist of raw materials that have undergone primary processing. These include cotton, sugar, tea, sisal, and coffee. Fast-flowing rivers in the highlands generate hydroelectric power, which has great future potential. The appeal of Kenya's wildlife and beaches has made tourism a crucial part of the economy.

Transportation Network

149,852 miles (241,308 km)	62 miles (100 km)	8,619 miles (13,879 km)	2,837 miles (4,568 km)

The landlocked nations suffer economically from their restricted access to the coast and from underdeveloped infrastructures. Kenya and Tanzania are investing in new transportation links.

The magnificent National Parks of Kenya and Tanzania provide essential refuges for many of Africa's rarest animals. Tourism brings in much-needed cash to sustain these important conservation projects.

Using the Land

The Lake Victoria Basin and rich volcanic soils of the Kenyan, Tanzanian, and Ugandan uplands support subsistence crops and cash crops, such as coffee, tea, cotton, sugar cane, and a variety of high-quality vegetables. Where rainfall is too variable for cultivation, pastoralism predominates. In the most arid regions camels are common; elsewhere large herds of cattle, sheep, and goats are raised. Tsetse fly infestation limits human settlement and agriculture in much of this region.

The Urban/Rural Population Divide

urban 19% — rural 81%

Population Density	Total Land Area
75 people per sq mile (29 people per sq km)	2,413,758 sq miles (6,253,259 sq km)

***This flat valley floor in Burundi** is crisscrossed by irrigation channels that provide a constant source of water for the coffee grown here.*

Southern Africa

Angola, Botswana, Lesotho, Malawi, Mozambique, Namibia, South Africa, Swaziland, Zambia, Zimbabwe

Africa's vast southern plateau has been a contested homeland for disparate peoples for many centuries. The European incursion began with the slave trade and quickened in the 19th century, when the discovery of enormous mineral wealth secured South Africa's regional economic dominance. The struggle against white minority rule led to strife in Namibia, Zimbabwe, and the former Portuguese territories of Angola and Mozambique. South Africa's notorious apartheid laws, which denied basic human rights to more than 75% of the people, led to the state being internationally ostracized until 1994, when the first fully democratic elections inaugurated a new era of racial justice.

Transportation & Industry

South Africa, the world's largest exporter of gold, has a varied economy that generates about 75% of the region's income and draws migrant labor from neighboring states. Angola exports petroleum; Botswana and Namibia rely on diamond mining; and Zambia is seeking to diversify its economy to compensate for declining copper reserves.

Almost all new mining ventures in Zimbabwe are now subject to government control. This mine at Bindura in northeastern Zimbabwe produces nickel, one of the country's top three minerals in terms of economic value.

CONGO (DEM. REP.)
TANZANIA
LUANDA
Lobito
ANGOLA
Ndola
ZAMBIA
LUSAKA
MALAWI
LILONGWE
Blantyre
HARARE
MOZAMBIQUE
ZIMBABWE
Bulawayo
Beira
NAMIBIA
WINDHOEK
Walvis Bay
BOTSWANA
GABORONE
PRETORIA
MAPUTO
Johannesburg
MBABANE
SWAZILAND
MASERU
LESOTHO
Durban
S.AFRICA
CAPE TOWN
Port Elizabeth
ATLANTIC OCEAN
INDIAN OCEAN

Major industry and infrastructure

car manufacture	gold	capital cities			
coal	oil	major towns			
copper	textiles	international airports			
diamonds	uranium	major roads			
food processing	wildlife reserves	major industrial areas			

Transportation Network

196,477 miles (316,388 km)	1,267 miles (2,040 km)
24,137 miles (38,868 km)	5,090 miles (8,196 km)

Southern Africa's Cape-gauge rail network is by far the largest on the continent. About two-thirds of the 20,000-mile (32,000-km) system lies within South Africa. Lines such as the Harare–Bulawayo route have become corridors for industrial growth.

The Landscape

Most of southern Africa rests on a concave plateau comprising the Kalahari basin and a mountainous fringe, skirted by a coastal plain that widens out in Mozambique. The plateau extends north, toward the Planalto de Bié in Angola, the Congo Basin, and the lake-filled troughs of the Great Rift Valley. The eastern region is drained by the Zambezi and Limpopo Rivers, and the Orange is the major western river.

Thousands of years of evaporating water have produced the Etosha Pan, one of the largest salt flats in the world. Lake and river sediments in the area indicate that the region was once less arid.

Finger Rock, near Khorixas, Namibia *is a remnant of a former land surface, which has been denuded by erosion over the last 5 million years. These occasional stacks of partially weathered rocks interrupt the plains of the dry southern interior.*

Following a series of droughts, *this baobab tree in Zimbabwe now stands alone in a field once filled by sugar cane. The thick trunk and small leaves of the baobab help it to conserve water, enabling it to survive even in drought conditions.*

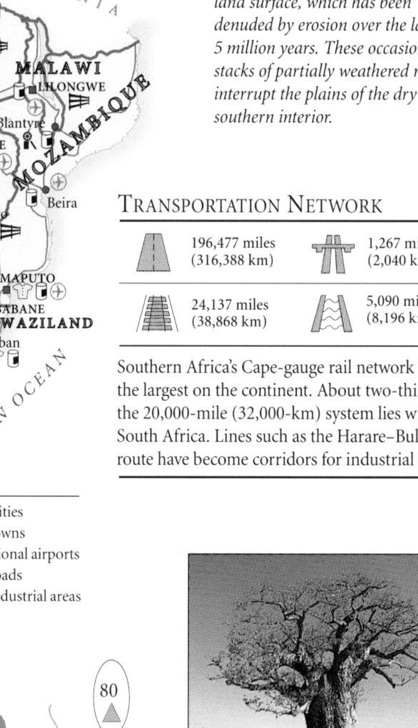

Planalto de Bié
Khorixas, Namibia
Namib Desert
Great Rift Valley
Bushveld intrusion
Limpopo River

The Okavango/Cubango River flows from the Planalto de Bié to the swamplands of the Okavango Delta, one of the world's largest inland deltas, where it divides into countless distributary channels, feeding out into the desert.

At Victoria Falls, the Zambezi River has cut a spectacular gorge by taking advantage of large joints in the basalt, which were first formed as the lava cooled and contracted.

The fast-flowing *Zambezi River cuts a deep, wide channel as it flows along the Zimbabwe/Zambia border.*

Lake Nyasa occupies one of the deep troughs of the Great Rift Valley, where the land has been displaced downward by as much as 3,000 ft (920 m).

Volcanic lava, over 250 million years old, caps the peaks of the Drakensberg range, which lie on the mountainous rim of southern Africa's interior plateau.

Broad, flat-topped mountains characterize the Great Karoo, which have been cut from level rock strata under extremely arid conditions.

The Kalahari Desert is the largest continuous sand surface in the world. Iron oxide gives a distinctive red color to the windblown sand, which, in eastern areas covers the bedrock to a depth of 200 ft (60 m).

The Orange River, one of the longest in Africa, rises in Lesotho and is the only major river in the south which flows westward, rather than to the east coast.

The mountains of the Little Karoo are composed of sedimentary rocks that have been substantially folded and faulted.

Bushveld intrusion

Gabbro and peridotite
Granite
Magnetite
Chromite
Platinum minerals

The Bushveld intrusion *lies on South Africa's high "veld." Molten magma intruded into the Earth's crust creating a saucer-shaped feature, more than 180 miles (300 km) across, containing regular layers of precious minerals, overlain by a dome of granite.*

South Africa's Three Capitals

PRETORIA – administrative capital
CAPE TOWN – legislative capital
BLOEMFONTEIN – judicial capital

Scale 1:9,500,000
(projection: Lambert Azimuthal Equal Area)

Km 0 25 50 100 150 200 250 300
Miles 0 25 50 100 150 200 250 300

Map Key

POPULATION

- 1 million to 5 million
- 500,000 to 1 million
- 100,000 to 500,000
- 50,000 to 100,000
- 10,000 to 50,000
- below 10,000

ELEVATION

- 3000m / 9843ft
- 2000m / 6562ft
- 1000m / 3281ft
- 500m / 1640ft
- 250m / 820ft
- 100m / 328ft
- sea level

80
82
12
13

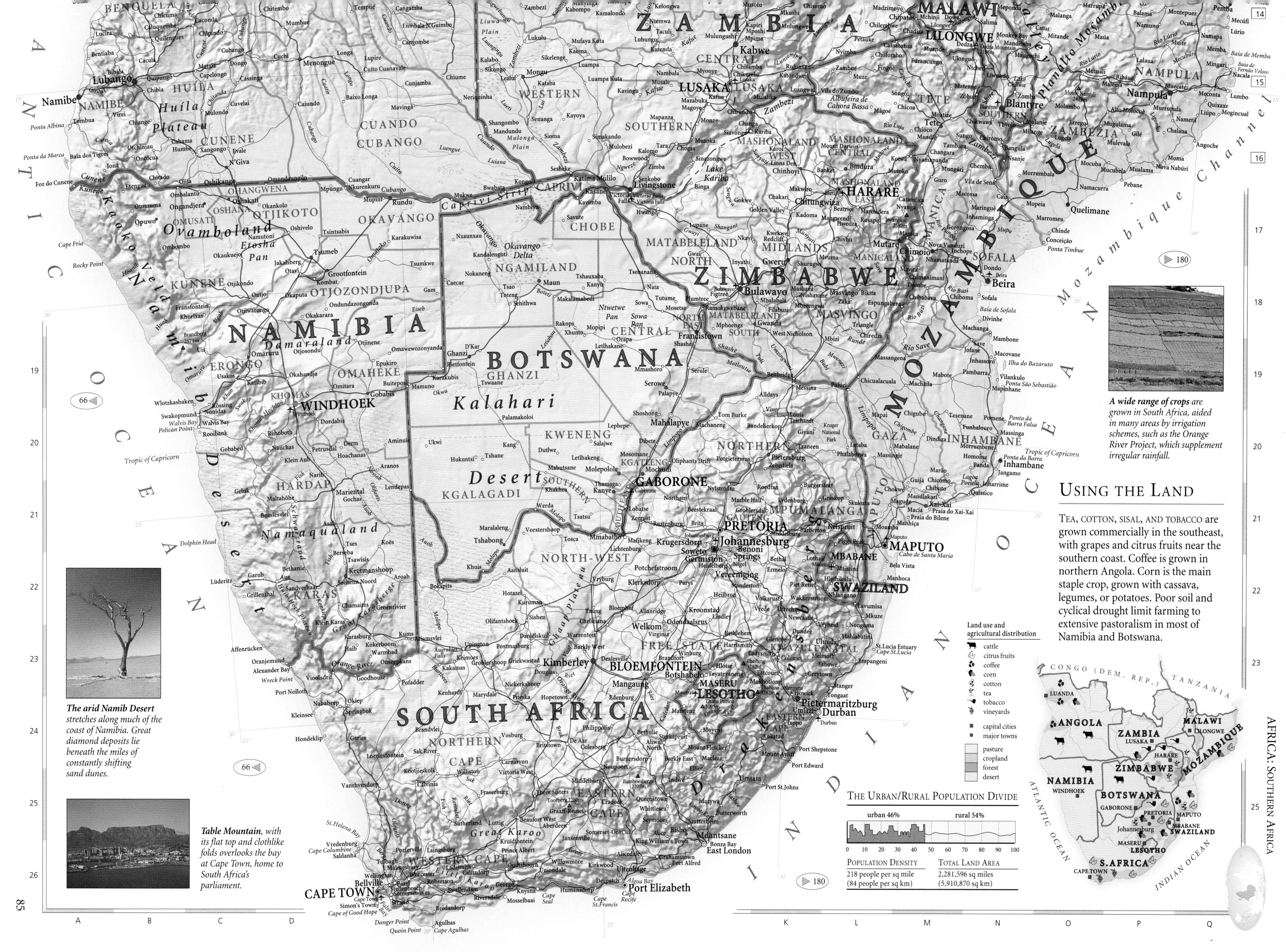
ZAMBIA
MALAWI
LILONGWE
LUSAKA
HARARE
ZIMBABWE
MOZAMBIQUE
NAMIBIA
WINDHOEK
BOTSWANA
GABORONE
SOUTH AFRICA
PRETORIA
Johannesburg
MAPUTO
MBABANE
SWAZILAND
MASERU
LESOTHO
BLOEMFONTEIN
CAPE TOWN
Durban
Port Elizabeth
East London
Kimberley
Bulawayo
Beira
Blantyre
Nampula
Quelimane
Inhambane
Kalahari
Desert
Namib Desert
Great Karoo
Mozambique Channel
ATLANTIC OCEAN
INDIAN OCEAN
Tropic of Capricorn
Land use and agricultural distribution
cattle
citrus fruits
coffee
corn
cotton
tea
tobacco
vineyards
capital cities
major towns
pasture
cropland
forest
desert
CONGO (DEM. REP.)
TANZANIA
ANGOLA
LUANDA
S. AFRICA

Using the Land

Tea, cotton, sisal, and tobacco are grown commercially in the southeast, with grapes and citrus fruits near the southern coast. Coffee is grown in northern Angola. Corn is the main staple crop, grown with cassava, legumes, or potatoes. Poor soil and cyclical drought limit farming to extensive pastoralism in most of Namibia and Botswana.

The Urban/Rural Population Divide

urban 46% — rural 54%

Population Density	Total Land Area
218 people per sq mile (84 people per sq km)	2,281,596 sq miles (5,910,870 sq km)

A wide range of crops are grown in South Africa, aided in many areas by irrigation schemes, such as the Orange River Project, which supplement irregular rainfall.

The arid Namib Desert stretches along much of the coast of Namibia. Great diamond deposits lie beneath the miles of constantly shifting sand dunes.

Table Mountain, with its flat top and clothlike folds overlooks the bay at Cape Town, home to South Africa's parliament.

A
B
C
D
E
F
G
H
I
J
K
L
M
1
2
3
4
5
6
7
8
9
10
11
12
13
14
15
16
17
ARCTIC OCEAN
North Pole
Ellesmere Island
Greenland
King Frederik VIII Land
King Christian X Land
Greenland Sea
NORTH AMERICAN PLATE
EURASIAN PLATE
Spitsbergen
Franz Josef Land
Ostrov Rudol'fa
Severnaya Zemlya
Laptev Sea
Poluostrov Taymyr
Kara Sea
Mys Zhelaniya
Novaya Zemlya
Barents Sea
Bjørnøya
Barents Trough
Poluostrov Yamal
Baydaratskaya Guba
Gulf of Ob
Yenisey
Kara Strait
North Cape
Nordkinn
Tromsøflaket
Fugløya Bank
Murmansk Rise
Ostrov Kolguyev
Poluostrov Kanin
Ob'
Pechora
West Siberian Plain
Ural Mountains
ASIA
Arctic Circle
Denmark Strait
Kolbeinsey Ridge
Iceland Plateau
Jan Mayen Ridge
Jan Mayen
Jan Mayen Fracture Zone
Norwegian Sea
Norwegian Basin
Voring Plateau
Vesterålen
Lofoten
Kebnekaise 2117m
Inarijärvi
Tornealven
Luleälven
Kemijoki
Kola Peninsula
Ozero Imandra
White Sea
Timanskiy Kryazh
Gora Narodnaya 1895m
Mezen'
Northern Dvina
Vychegda
Irtysh
Bjargtangar
Iceland
Vatnajökull
Reykjanes Ridge
Faeroe-Iceland Ridge
Traena Bank
Kölen
Scandinavia
Umeälven
Gulf of Bothnia
Oulujoki
Onega Bay
Ozero Vygozero
Lake Onega
Lake Ladoga
Onega
Vaga
Iceland Basin
Faeroe Islands
Bill Baileys Bank
Galdhøpiggen 2469m
Ljungan
Ljusnan
Glåma
Åland
Svir
Beloye Ozero
Sukhona
Yug
Kama
Tobol
Hatton Ridge
Faeroe-Shetland Trough
Shetland Islands
Viking Bank
Orkney Islands
Gulf of Finland
Lake Peipus
Msta
Lake Ilmen
Rybinsk Reservoir
Unzha
Gor'kiy Reservoir
Vyatka
Votkinsk Reservoir
Rockall Rise
Outer Hebrides
Ben Nevis 1343m
Grampian Mountains
Norwegian Trench
Vänern
Vättern
Gotland
Gulf of Riga
Lake Pskov
North European Plain
Kuybyshev Reservoir
Belaya
Sura
Oka
Moskva
Feni Ridge
Rockall Trough
North Channel
North Sea
Jutland Bank
Skagerrak
Kattegat
Great Fisher Bank
Jylland
Sjælland
Baltic Sea
Western Dvina
Neman
Tsna
Volga
Volga Upland
Samara
Ural
ATLANTIC OCEAN
British Isles
Ireland
Irish Sea
Pennines
Snowdon 1085m
Britain
Shannon
Trent
Severn
St. George's Channel
Dogger Bank
German Bight
Frisian Islands
Elbe
Oder
Warta
Vistula
Bug
Pripet Marshes
Byerezina
Dnieper
Khoper
Klyaz'ma
Don
Central Russian Upland
Desna
Seym
Porcupine Plain
Celtic Sea
Celtic Shelf
Bristol Channel
The Fens
Thames
Land's End
English Channel
Channel Islands
Strait of Dover
Ardennes
Rhine
Harz
EUROPE
Dnieper Lowlands
Kiev Reservoir
Kremenchuk Reservoir
Donets
Tsimlyansk Reservoir
Volga
Kirghiz
Yergeni
Seine
Marne
Meuse
Moselle
Vosges
Black Forest
Danube
Morava
Dniester
Podil's'ka Vysochina
Pivdennyy Buh
Don
Manych
Carpathian Mountains
Tisza
Siret
Prut
Black Sea Lowland
Sea of Azov
Kuban
Crimea
Kerch Strait
Lake Constance
Loire
Cher
Lake Geneva
Alps
Bakony
Lake Balaton
Great Hungarian Plain
Mureş
Transylvanian Alps
Charcot Seamounts
Azores-Biscay Rise
Bay of Biscay
Biscay Plain
Vienne
Massif Central
Dordogne
Garonne
Lot
Gévennes
Mont Blanc 4807m
Saône
Rhône
Lake Garda
Dolomites
Po
Drava
Sava
Tisza
Theta Gap
Galicia Bank
Miño
Cordillera Cantábrica
Pyrenees
Aneto 3404m
Aragón
Ebro
Gulf of Lion
Ligurian Sea
Arno
Apennines
Adriatic Sea
Dinaric Alps
Drina
Danube
Balkan Mountains
Black Sea
Iberian Peninsula
Iberian Plain
Douro
Duero
Sistema Central
Sistema Ibérico
Corno Grande 2912m
Tiber
Corsica
Strait of Bonifacio
Lake Scutari
Adriatic Basin
Rhodope Mountains
Maritsa
Tundzha
Vardar
Bosporus
Sea of Marmara
Lake Ohrid
Lake Prespa
Cabo da Roca
Tagus
Tagus Plain
Guadiana
Júcar
Sierra Morena
Gulf of Valencia
Balearic Islands
Balearic Plain
Sardinia
Tyrrhenian Sea
Tyrrhenian Basin
Gulf of Taranto
Strait of Otranto
Pindus Mountains
Aegean Sea
Anatolia
Lake Tuz
Gorringe Ridge
Cape Saint Vincent
Guadalquivir
Segura
Sistemas Beticos
Sierra Nevada
Mediterranean Sea
Strait of Messina
Strait of Sicily
Mount Etna 3340m
Ionian Sea
Peloponnese
Mirtoan Sea
Taurus Mountains
Gulf of Antalya
ARABIAN PLATE
AFRICAN PLATE
Horseshoe Seamounts
Ampère Seamount
Punta de Tarifa
Strait of Gibraltar
Alboran Sea
Oued Chiffa
Tell Atlas
EURASIAN PLATE
AFRICAN PLATE
Sicily
Malta
Ionian Basin
Sea of Crete
Karpathos Strait
Kasos Strait
Crete
Rhodes Basin
Cyprus
Cyprus Basin
Gávdos
Seine Plain
Seine Seamount
Rif
Sebou
Moulouya
Madeira
Mediterranean Ridge
Levantine Basin
Atlas Mountains
Middle Atlas
Oum er Rbia
High Atlas
Saharan Atlas
Agadir Canyon
Dacia Seamount
Chott el Jerid
Nile Fan
Gulf of Sidra
Canary Islands
Suez Canal
Nile
Gulf of Suez
Grand Erg Occidental
Grand Erg Oriental
Western Desert
Libyan Desert
AFRICA
'Erg Iguidi
Erg Chech
Sahara

EUROPE

EUROPE IS THE WORLD'S SECOND SMALLEST CONTINENT, COVERING 4,053,309 SQ MILES (10,498,000 SQ KM). IT COMPRISES 44 SEPARATE COUNTRIES, INCLUDING TURKEY AND THE RUSSIAN FEDERATION. THE GREATER PARTS OF THESE NATIONS, HOWEVER, LIE IN ASIA.

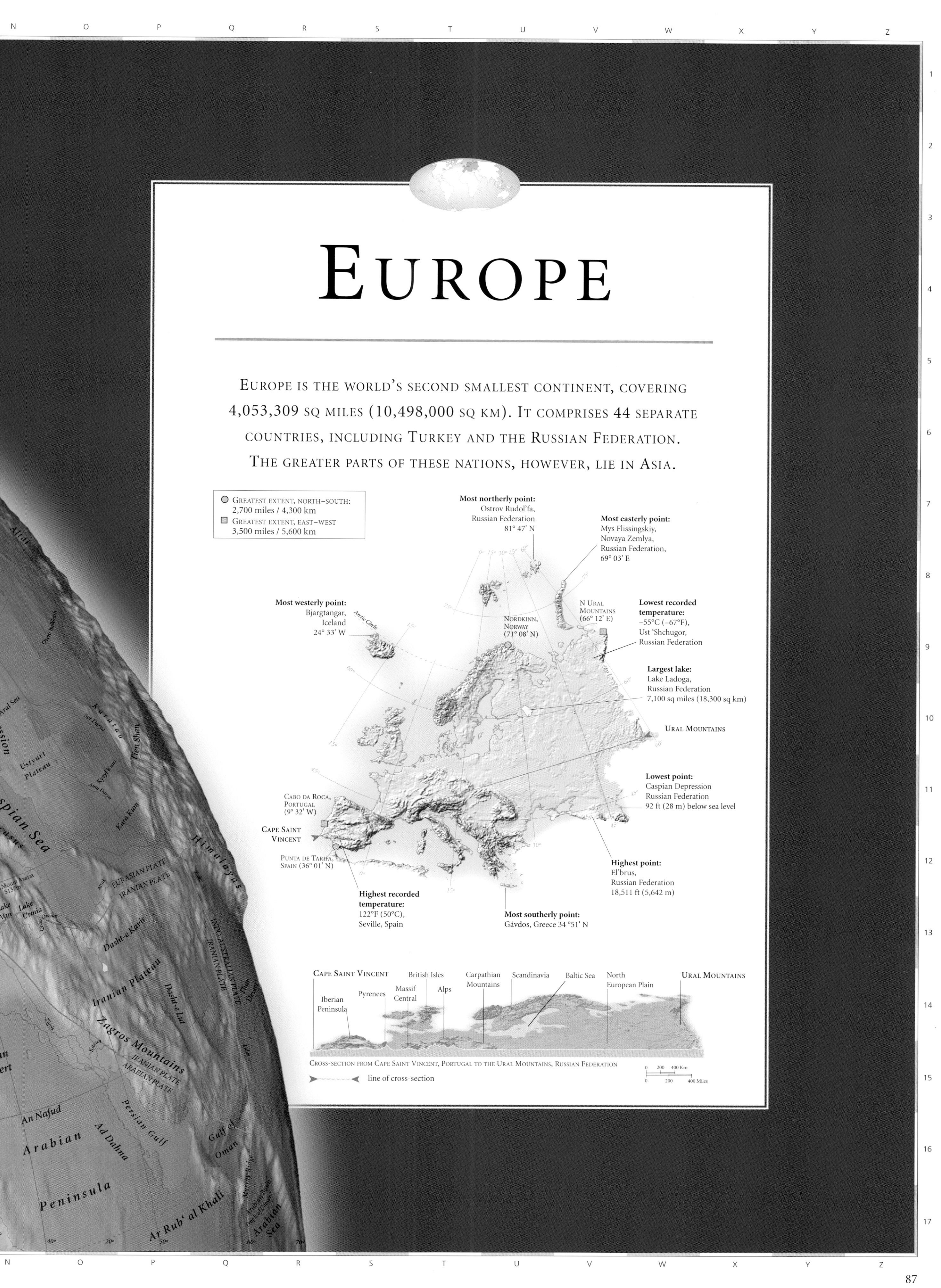

Greatest extent, north–south: 2,700 miles / 4,300 km
Greatest extent, east–west 3,500 miles / 5,600 km
Most northerly point: Ostrov Rudol'fa, Russian Federation 81° 47' N
Most easterly point: Mys Flissingskiy, Novaya Zemlya, Russian Federation, 69° 03' E
Most westerly point: Bjargtangar, Iceland 24° 33' W
Nordkinn, Norway (71° 08' N)
N Ural Mountains (66° 12' E)
Lowest recorded temperature: –55°C (–67°F), Ust 'Shchugor, Russian Federation
Largest lake: Lake Ladoga, Russian Federation 7,100 sq miles (18,300 sq km)
Ural Mountains
Lowest point: Caspian Depression Russian Federation 92 ft (28 m) below sea level
Cabo da Roca, Portugal (9° 32' W)
Cape Saint Vincent
Punta de Tarifa, Spain (36° 01' N)
Highest point: El'brus, Russian Federation 18,511 ft (5,642 m)
Highest recorded temperature: 122°F (50°C), Seville, Spain
Most southerly point: Gávdos, Greece 34 °51' N
Arctic Circle
Cape Saint Vincent
Iberian Peninsula
Pyrenees
Massif Central
British Isles
Alps
Carpathian Mountains
Scandinavia
Baltic Sea
North European Plain
Ural Mountains
Cross-section from Cape Saint Vincent, Portugal to the Ural Mountains, Russian Federation
line of cross-section
0 200 400 Km
0 200 400 Miles
Caspian Sea
Himalayas
Iranian Plateau
Zagros Mountains
Persian Gulf
Gulf of Oman
Arabian Sea
Arabian Peninsula
An Nafud
Ad Dahna
Ar Rub' al Khali
Dasht-e Kavir
Dasht-e Lut
Thar Desert
Kara Kum
Tien Shan
Ustyurt Plateau
Lake Urmia
Lake Van
Eurasian Plate
Iranian Plate
Arabian Plate
Indo-Australian Plate

Physical Europe

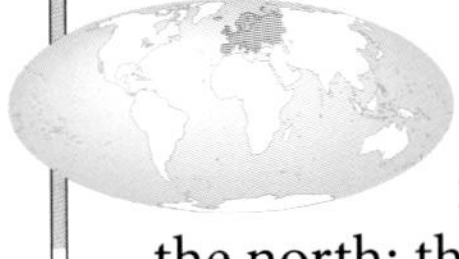

The physical diversity of Europe belies its relatively small size. To the northwest and south it is enclosed by mountains. The older, rounded Atlantic Highlands of Scandinavia and the British Isles lie to the north; the younger, rugged peaks of the Alpine Uplands are in the south. The North European Plain lies in between, stretching 2,485 miles (4,000 km) from The Fens in England to the Ural Mountains in Russia. South of the plain lies a series of gently folded sedimentary rocks separated by ancient plateaus, known as massifs.

The North European Plain

Rising less than 1,000 ft (300 m) above sea level, the North European Plain strongly reflects past glaciation. Ridges of both coarse moraine and finer, windblown deposits have accumulated over much of the region. The ice sheet also diverted a number of river channels from their original courses.

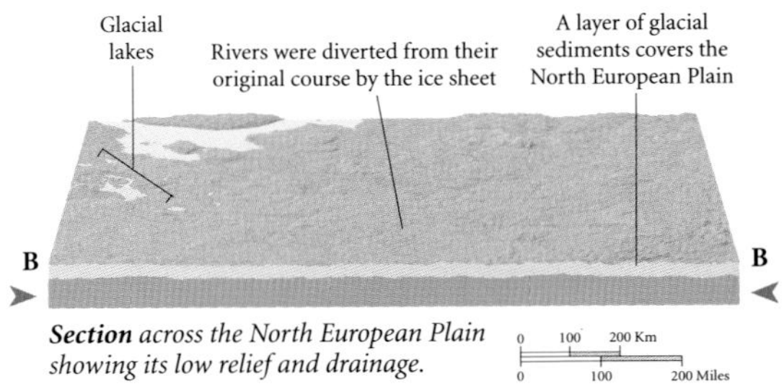

Glacial lakes

Rivers were diverted from their original course by the ice sheet

A layer of glacial sediments covers the North European Plain

B B

***Section** across the North European Plain showing its low relief and drainage.*

0 100 200 Km / 0 100 200 Miles

The Atlantic Highlands

The Atlantic Highlands were formed over 500 million years ago during the Caledonian mountain-building period, by compression against the Scandinavian Shield. The highlands were once part of a continuous mountain chain, now divided by the North Sea and a submerged rift valley.

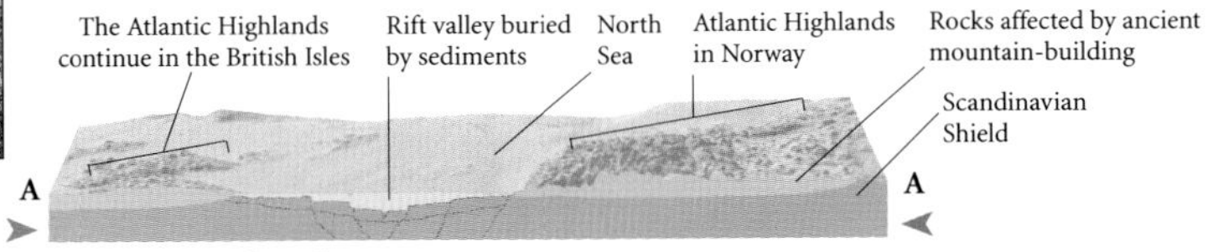

The Atlantic Highlands continue in the British Isles

Rift valley buried by sediments

North Sea

Atlantic Highlands in Norway

Rocks affected by ancient mountain-building

Scandinavian Shield

A A

***Cross-section** through northeastern Europe showing the continuous mountain chain and rift valley system.*

0 100 200 Km / 0 100 200 Miles

Scale 1:23,000,000
(projection: Lambert Azimuthal Equal Area)

Km 0 100 200 400 600
Miles 0 50 100 200 300 400 500 600

Map Key

ELEVATION

- 4000m / 13,124ft
- 3000m / 9843ft
- 2000m / 6562ft
- 1000m / 3281ft
- 500m / 1640ft
- 250m / 820ft
- 100m / 328ft
- sea level

PLATE MARGINS
(for explanation see page xiv)

- constructive
- destructive
- conservative
- uncertain
- physiographic regions
- line of cross-section

The Plateaus and Lowlands

The uplifted plateaus or massifs of southern central Europe are the result of long-term erosion, later followed by uplift. They are the source areas of many of the rivers that drain Europe's lowlands. In some of the higher reaches, fractures have enabled igneous rocks from deep in the Earth to reach the surface.

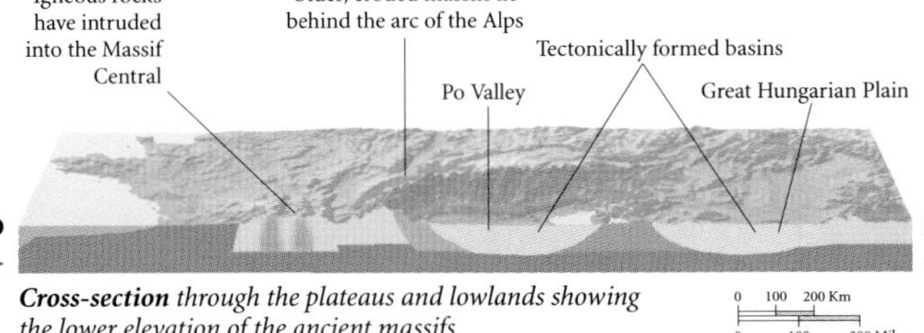
Igneous rocks have intruded into the Massif Central
Older, eroded massifs lie behind the arc of the Alps
Tectonically formed basins
Po Valley
Great Hungarian Plain
D
D

***Cross-section** through the plateaus and lowlands showing the lower elevation of the ancient massifs.*

0 100 200 Km / 0 100 200 Miles

The Alpine Uplands

The collision of the African and European continents, which began about 65 million years ago, folded and then uplifted a series of mountain ranges running across southern Europe and into Asia. Two major lines of folding can be traced: one includes the Pyrenees, the Alps, and the Carpathian Mountains; the other incorporates the Apennines and the Dinaric Alps.

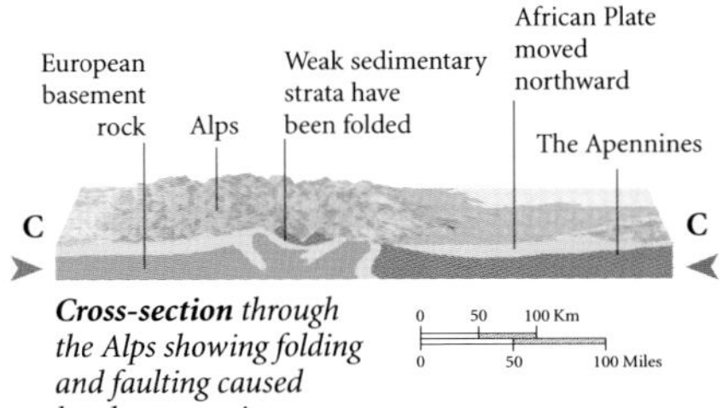
European basement rock
Alps
Weak sedimentary strata have been folded
African Plate moved northward
The Apennines
C
C

***Cross-section** through the Alps showing folding and faulting caused by plate tectonics.*

0 50 100 Km / 0 50 100 Miles

N O P Q R S T U V W X Z

Frost grips northern and eastern Europe during the long cold winters. Lakes and rivers frequently freeze.

CLIMATE

EUROPE EXPERIENCES few extremes in either rainfall or temperature, with the exception of the far north and south. Along the west coast, the warm currents of the North Atlantic Drift moderate temperatures. Although east–west air movement is relatively unimpeded by relief, the Alpine Uplands halt the progress of north–south air masses, protecting most of the Mediterranean from cold, north winds.

TEMPERATURE

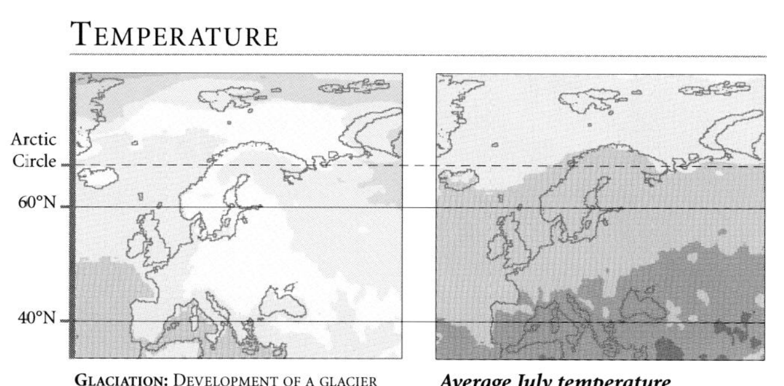

Arctic Circle
60°N
40°N

GLACIATION: DEVELOPMENT OF A GLACIER

Average July temperature

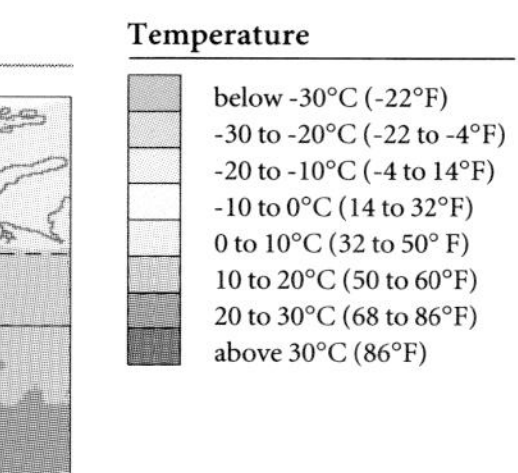

Temperature
below -30°C (-22°F)
-30 to -20°C (-22 to -4°F)
-20 to -10°C (-4 to 14°F)
-10 to 0°C (14 to 32°F)
0 to 10°C (32 to 50° F)
10 to 20°C (50 to 60°F)
20 to 30°C (68 to 86°F)
above 30°C (86°F)

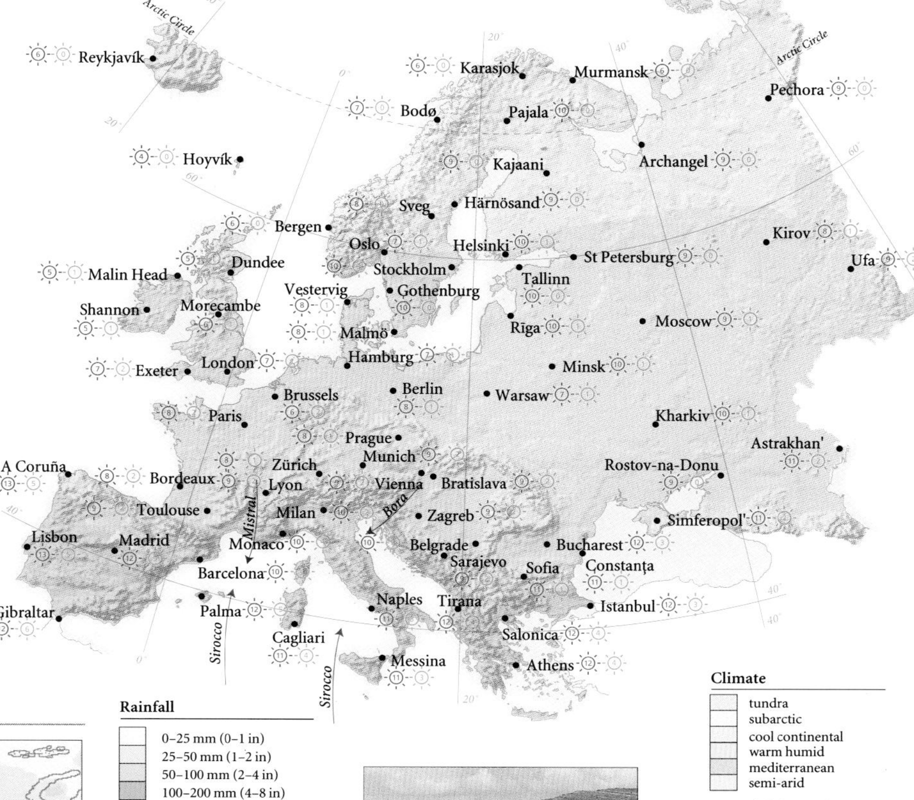

Arctic Circle
Reykjavík
Karasjok
Murmansk
Pechora
Bodø
Pajala
Hoyvík
Kajaani
Archangel
Sveg
Härnösand
Bergen
Oslo
Helsinki
Kirov
Ufa
Malin Head
Dundee
Stockholm
St Petersburg
Tallinn
Vestervig
Gothenburg
Shannon
Morecambe
Malmö
Riga
Moscow
Hamburg
Exeter
London
Minsk
Berlin
Brussels
Warsaw
Paris
Kharkiv
Prague
Astrakhan'
A Coruña
Munich
Zürich
Bordeaux
Vienna
Bratislava
Rostov-na-Donu
Lyon
Toulouse
Mistral
Milan
Zagreb
Bora
Simferopol'
Lisbon
Madrid
Monaco
Belgrade
Bucharest
Sarajevo
Sofia
Constanța
Barcelona
Naples
Tirana
Istanbul
Gibraltar
Palma
Salonica
Cagliari
Sirocco
Messina
Athens

Climate
tundra
subarctic
cool continental
warm humid
mediterranean
semi-arid
daily hours of sunshine, January
daily hours of sunshine, July
cold wind
hot wind

Mild temperatures and frequent rainfall contribute to the fertile farmland found over much of northwestern Europe.

RAINFALL

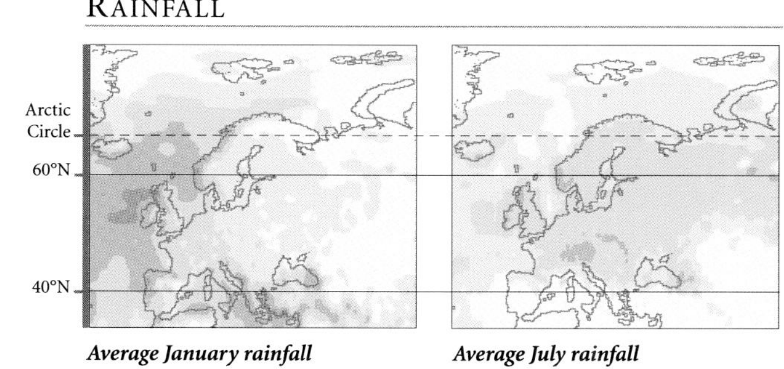

Arctic Circle
60°N
40°N

Average January rainfall

Average July rainfall

Rainfall
0–25 mm (0–1 in)
25–50 mm (1–2 in)
50–100 mm (2–4 in)
100–200 mm (4–8 in)
200–300 mm (8–12 in)
300–400 mm (12–16 in)
400–500 mm (16–20 in)
more than 500 mm (20 in)

Dusty Sirocco winds from Africa help to create the semiarid scrubland common across the Mediterranean coastlands of southern Europe.

SHAPING THE CONTINENT

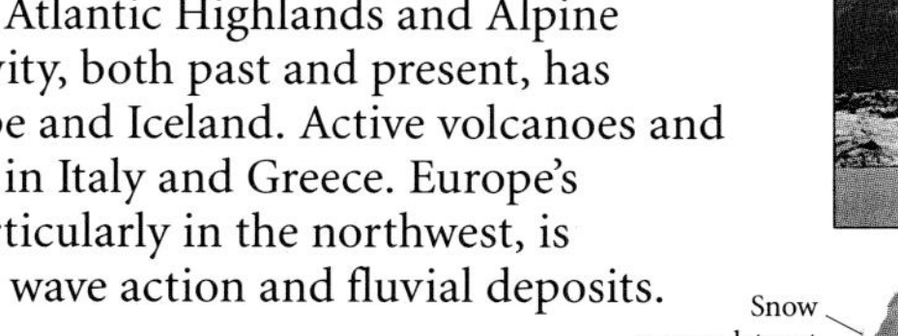

SUCCESSIVE ICE AGES have left many relic landforms across Europe. Present glaciers continue to carve peaks and valleys in the northern Atlantic Highlands and Alpine Uplands. Tectonic activity, both past and present, has shaped southern Europe and Iceland. Active volcanoes and earthquakes still occur in Italy and Greece. Europe's extensive coastline, particularly in the northwest, is constantly modified by wave action and fluvial deposits.

GLACIATION

1 Valley glaciers, such as this one *(left)* in Iceland, form in hollows at the top of valleys and flow downward, drawn by gravity. Their growth is dynamic; new snowfall constantly accumulates at the head of the glacier, while the snout melts, depositing material eroded and carried by the glacier.

Snow accumulates at the head of glacier
Glacier movement erodes valley
Glacier snout melts, depositing eroded debris

GLACIATION: DEVELOPMENT OF A GLACIER

RIVER SYSTEMS

2 Rivers are continuously transporting eroded material toward the sea. Slow-moving, low-gradient rivers, like this one in western Russia *(above)*, deposit their alluvium load, filling in valleys and creating a floodplain. Subsequent climatic and tectonic fluctuations may erode the floodplain to form terraces.

Terrace created by erosion
Floodplain
Deposited alluvium
River channel

RIVER SYSTEMS: FORMATION OF A FLOODPLAIN AND TERRACES

COASTAL PROCESSES

5 Spits are narrow bands of sand or shingle, formed by longshore drift, a process where waves carry material along the beach. They usually form where the coastline changes direction, and their growth is then halted by an opposing river current, as at Spurn Head, in the British Isles *(left)*. Coastal features such as these are constantly being created and destroyed.

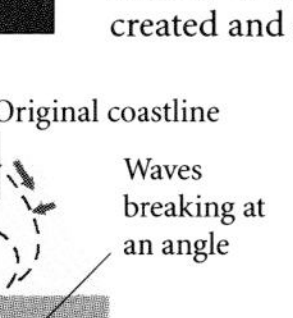
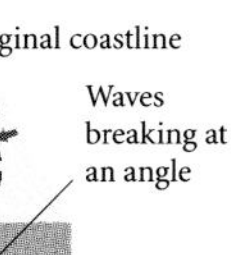
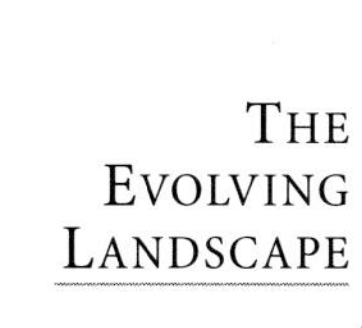

Sand and shingle spit
Original coastline
Waves breaking at an angle
Opposing river current

COASTAL PROCESSES: FORMATION OF A SPIT

THE EVOLVING LANDSCAPE

1
2
3
4
5
Landscape
uplifting land
stable land
sinking land
limestone region
glacier
active volcano
ocean current
area of tectonic activity
maximum limit of glaciation

WEATHERING

3 As surface water filters through permeable limestone, the rock dissolves to form underground caves, like Postojna in the Karst region of Slovenia *(above)*. Stalactites grow downward as lime-enriched water seeps from roof fractures; stalagmites grow upward where drips splash down.

Stalagmites created by drips
Underground cavern
River flowing underground dissolves rocks and creates caves
Stalactites formed by seeping water

WEATHERING: FORMATION OF A CAVE

EROSION AND WEATHERING

4 Much of Europe was once subjected to folding and faulting, exposing hard and soft rock layers. Subsequent erosion and weathering has worn away the softer strata, leaving up-ended layers of hard rock, as in the French Pyrenees *(above)*.

Exposed up-ended rocks
Soft rock
Outline of original folded strata
Hard rock
Hard rock
Hard rock

EROSION AND WEATHERING: MODIFICATION OF A FOLD

N O P Q R S T U V W X Y Z

POLITICAL EUROPE

THE POLITICAL BOUNDARIES OF EUROPE have changed many times, especially during the 20th century in the aftermath of two world wars, the breakup of the empires of Austria–Hungary, Nazi Germany, and more recently, the collapse of communism in eastern Europe. The fragmentation of the former Yugoslavia has again altered the political map of Europe, highlighting a trend toward nationalism and devolution. In contrast, economic federalism is growing. In 1958, the formation of the European Economic Community (now the European Union or EU) began a move toward economic and political union.

***The Brandenburg Gate** in Berlin is a potent symbol of German reunification. In 1961 a wall was built in the road beneath it to stop the flow of refugees to the West. The road was opened again in 1989 when the wall was destroyed and East and West Germany were reunited.*

POPULATION

EUROPE IS A DENSELY POPULATED, urbanized continent; in Belgium and the United Kingdom, over 90% of people live in urban areas. The highest population densities are found in an area stretching east from southern Britain and northern France, into Germany. The northern fringes are only sparsely populated.

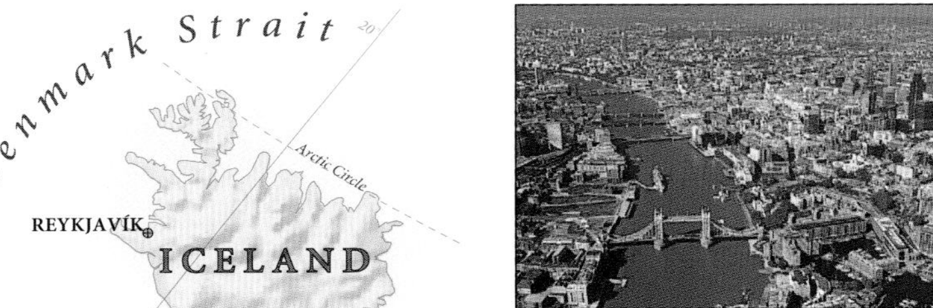

***Demand for space** in densely populated European cities like London has led to the development of high-rise offices and urban sprawl.*

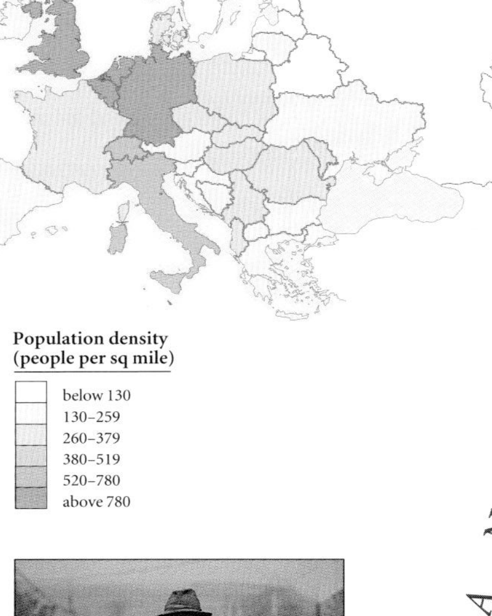

Population density (people per sq mile)

- below 130
- 130–259
- 260–379
- 380–519
- 520–780
- above 780

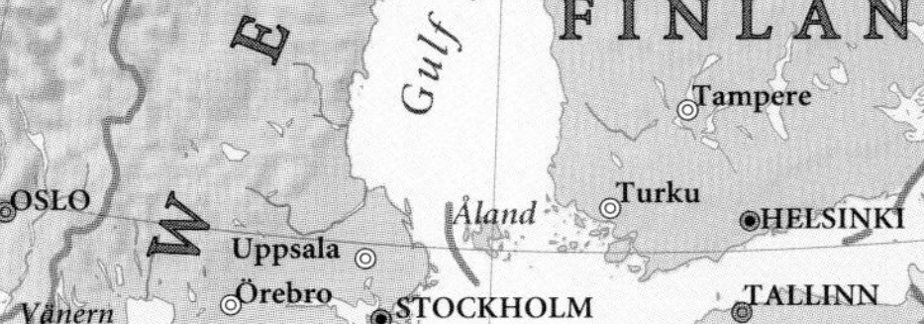

***Traditional lifestyles** still persist in many remote and rural parts of Europe, especially in the south, east, and in the far north.*

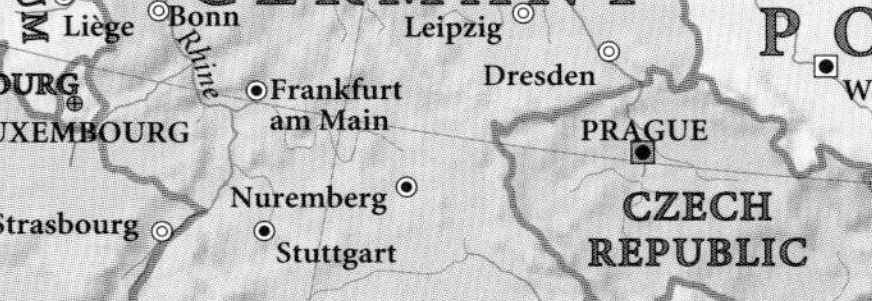

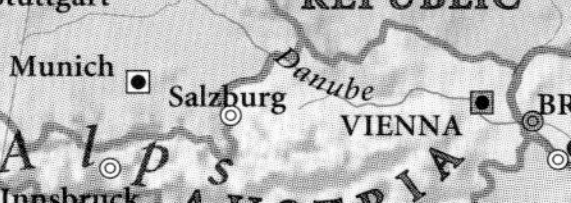

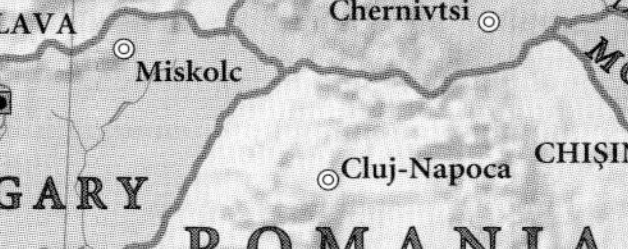

MAP KEY

POPULATION

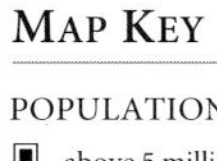

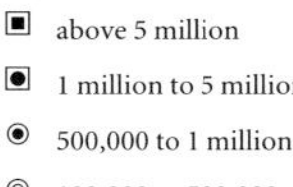

- above 5 million
- 1 million to 5 million
- 500,000 to 1 million
- 100,000 to 500,000
- 50,000 to 100,000
- 10,000 to 50,000
- Country capital

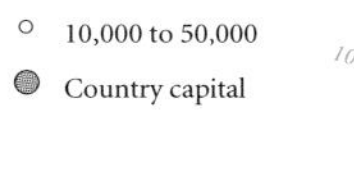

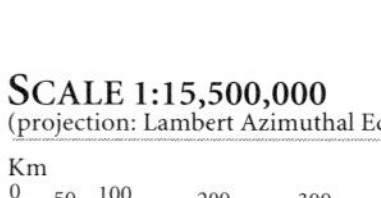

SCALE 1:15,500,000
(projection: Lambert Azimuthal Equal Area)

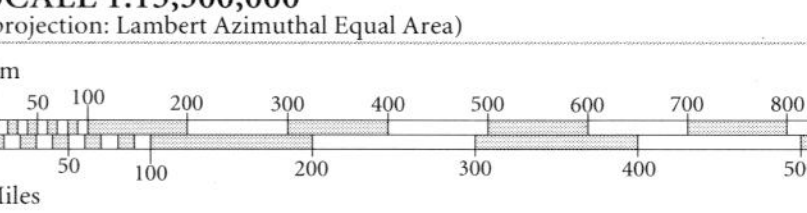

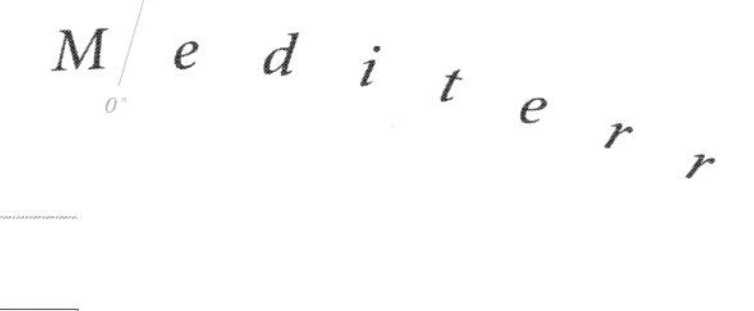

Overcoming natural barriers, *the Brenner Autobahn, one of the main routes across the Alps, links Innsbruck, Austria, with Verona, Italy.*

Transportation

- major roads and highways
- major railroads
- international borders
- transportation intersections
- major international airports
- major ports

TRANSPORTATION

DESPITE ITS FRAGMENTED GEOGRAPHY and many natural frontiers, communications in Europe are well developed. Extensive highway links allow rapid road transportation. High-speed rail connections like France's TGV (*Train à Grande Vitesse*), and the Channel Tunnel have improved rail travel. Outdated communication infrastructures in parts of eastern Europe, and insufficient transportation links across the Alps, however, remain weak parts of the network.

LANGUAGES

THERE ARE THREE MAIN EUROPEAN language groups: Germanic languages predominate in central and northern Europe; Romance languages in western and Mediterranean Europe and Romania; and Slavic languages are spoken in eastern Europe and the Russian Federation. Isolated pockets of local languages, such as Basque and Gaelic, persist and frequently provide a focus for national identity.

Language groups

- Turkic
- Albanian
- Finnic/Ugric
- Germanic
- Slavic
- Romance
- Basque
- Baltic
- Celtic
- Greek

The architecture *of the Grand Place lies at the heart of Brussels – home city to one of the EU headquarters.*

European Resources

EUROPE'S LARGE TRACTS OF FERTILE, accessible land, combined with its generally temperate climate, have allowed a greater percentage of land to be used for agricultural purposes than on any other continent. Extensive coal and iron ore deposits were used to create steel and manufacturing industries during the 19th and 20th centuries. Today, although natural resources have been largely exploited, and heavy industry is of declining importance, the growth of hi-tech and service industries has enabled Europe to maintain its wealth.

Industry

EUROPE'S WEALTH WAS GENERATED by the rise of industry and colonial exploitation during the 19th century. The mining of abundant natural resources made Europe the industrial center of the world. Adaptation has been essential in the changing world economy, and a move to service-based industries has been widespread except in eastern Europe, where heavy industry still dominates.

***Countries like** Hungary are still struggling to modernize inefficient factories left over from extensive, centrally-planned industrialization during the communist era.*

***Frankfurt am Main** is an example of a modern service-based city. The skyline is dominated by headquarters from the worlds of banking and commerce.*

***Other power sources** are becoming more attractive as fossil fuels run out; 16% of Europe's electricity is now provided by hydroelectric power.*

Standard of Living

LIVING STANDARDS IN WESTERN EUROPE are among the highest in the world, although there is a growing sector of homeless, jobless people. Eastern Europeans have lower overall standards of living – a legacy of stagnated economies.

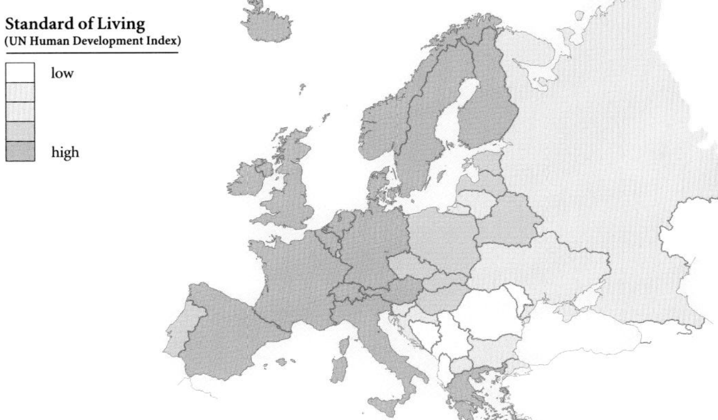
Standard of Living
(UN Human Development Index)
low
high

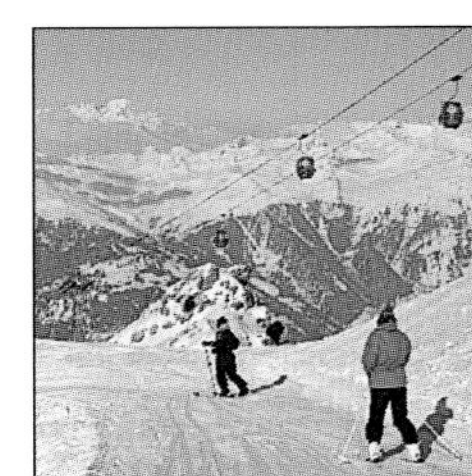

***Skiing brings millions** of tourists to the slopes every year. This means that even unproductive, marginal land generates income in the French, Swiss, Italian, and Austrian Alps.*

Novaya Zemlya

Ostrov Kolguyev

Barents Sea

Norwegian Sea

ATLANTIC OCEAN

North Sea

Baltic Sea

Gulf of Bothnia

Bay of Biscay

Mediterranean Sea

Tyrrhenian Sea

Adriatic Sea

Ionian Sea

Aegean Sea

Black Sea

Caspian Sea

ICELAND, Reykjavík, Faeroe Islands (to Denmark), NORWAY, Trondheim, Bergen, Oslo, SWEDEN, Stockholm, Gothenburg, Malmö, FINLAND, Turku, Helsinki, RUSSIAN FEDERATION, Murmansk, Archangel, St Petersburg, Cherepovets, Yaroslavl, Ivanovo, Nizhniy Novgorod, Kazan', Perm', Ufa, Moscow, Ryazan', Tula, Tol'yatti, Samara, Saratov, Voronezh, Kursk, Volgograd, Rostov-na-Donu, ESTONIA, Tallinn, LATVIA, Riga, LITHUANIA, Vilnius, RUSS. FED. (Kaliningrad), BELARUS, Minsk, UKRAINE, Kiev, Kharkiv, Dnipropetrovs'k, Donets'k, Kryvyy Rih, Odesa, MOLDOVA, POLAND, Gdańsk, Poznań, Łódź, Warsaw, Katowice, Kraków, REPUBLIC OF IRELAND, Dublin, UNITED KINGDOM, Glasgow, Belfast, Newcastle upon Tyne, Isle of Man (to UK), Liverpool, Manchester, Birmingham, Cardiff, London, Channel Islands (to UK), DENMARK, Copenhagen, NETH., Amsterdam, Rotterdam, BELG., Antwerp, Brussels, Liège, LUX., GERMANY, Hamburg, Berlin, Essen, Cologne, Leipzig, Dresden, Frankfurt am Main, Stuttgart, Munich, CZECH REP., Prague, SLOVAKIA, Bratislava, AUSTRIA, Linz, Vienna, HUNGARY, Budapest, FRANCE, Lille, Rouen, Paris, Metz, Strasbourg, Nantes, Bordeaux, Lyon, Toulouse, Marseille, SWITZ., Zürich, LIECH., MONACO, ANDORRA, SPAIN, A Coruña, Bilbao, Madrid, Barcelona, Seville, PORTUGAL, Porto, Lisbon, Gibraltar (to UK), Ceuta (to Spain), Melilla (to Spain), MOROCCO, Balearic Islands, Corsica, Sardinia, Sicily, MALTA, ITALY, Turin, Milan, Venice, Genoa, Bologna, SAN MARINO, VATICAN CITY, Rome, Naples, Taranto, Palermo, SLVN., Zagreb, CROATIA, BOSNIA & HERZ., YUGOSLAVIA, Belgrade, ALBANIA, MACED., GREECE, Salonica, Piraeus, Athens, Crete, ROMANIA, Ploiești, Bucharest, Constanța, BULGARIA, Sofia, Varna, TURKEY, Istanbul, GEORGIA, KAZAKHSTAN

GNP per capita (US$)
below 1,999
2,000–4,999
5,000–9,999
10,000–19,999
20,000–24,999
above 25,000

Industry
aerospace
brewing
car/vehicle manufacture
chemicals
defense
electronics
engineering
finance
food processing
hi-tech industry
iron & steel
pharmaceuticals
printing & publishing
shipbuilding
textiles
timber processing
wine
coal
oil
gas
industrial cities
major industrial areas

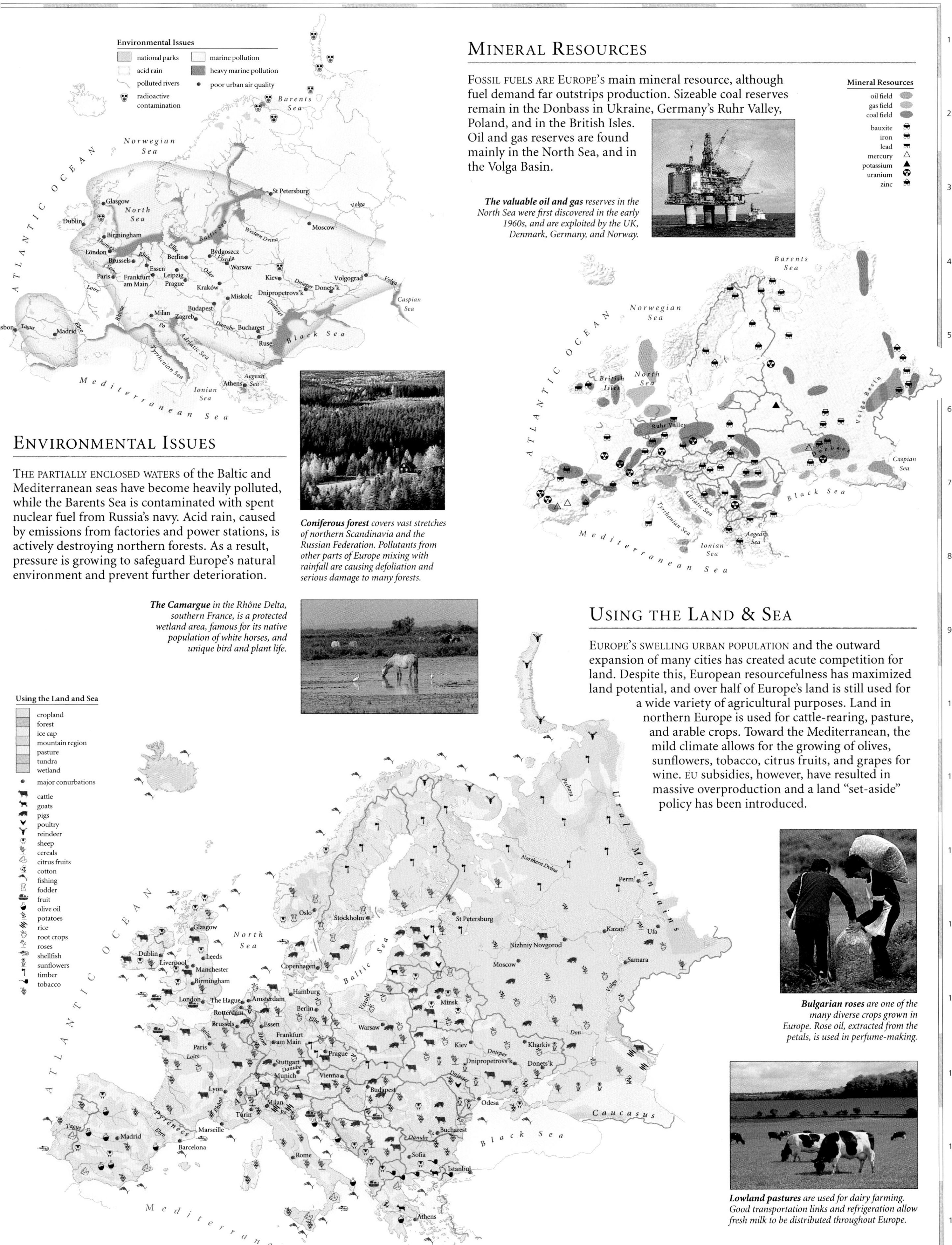

Environmental Issues
national parks
marine pollution
acid rain
heavy marine pollution
polluted rivers
poor urban air quality
radioactive contamination
Mineral Resources
oil field
gas field
coal field
bauxite
iron
lead
mercury
potassium
uranium
zinc
Using the Land and Sea
cropland
forest
ice cap
mountain region
pasture
tundra
wetland
major conurbations
cattle
goats
pigs
poultry
reindeer
sheep
cereals
citrus fruits
cotton
fishing
fodder
fruit
olive oil
potatoes
rice
root crops
roses
shellfish
sunflowers
timber
tobacco

Mineral Resources

Fossil fuels are Europe's main mineral resource, although fuel demand far outstrips production. Sizeable coal reserves remain in the Donbass in Ukraine, Germany's Ruhr Valley, Poland, and in the British Isles. Oil and gas reserves are found mainly in the North Sea, and in the Volga Basin.

***The valuable oil and gas** reserves in the North Sea were first discovered in the early 1960s, and are exploited by the UK, Denmark, Germany, and Norway.*

Environmental Issues

The partially enclosed waters of the Baltic and Mediterranean seas have become heavily polluted, while the Barents Sea is contaminated with spent nuclear fuel from Russia's navy. Acid rain, caused by emissions from factories and power stations, is actively destroying northern forests. As a result, pressure is growing to safeguard Europe's natural environment and prevent further deterioration.

***Coniferous forest** covers vast stretches of northern Scandinavia and the Russian Federation. Pollutants from other parts of Europe mixing with rainfall are causing defoliation and serious damage to many forests.*

***The Camargue** in the Rhône Delta, southern France, is a protected wetland area, famous for its native population of white horses, and unique bird and plant life.*

Using the Land & Sea

Europe's swelling urban population and the outward expansion of many cities has created acute competition for land. Despite this, European resourcefulness has maximized land potential, and over half of Europe's land is still used for a wide variety of agricultural purposes. Land in northern Europe is used for cattle-rearing, pasture, and arable crops. Toward the Mediterranean, the mild climate allows for the growing of olives, sunflowers, tobacco, citrus fruits, and grapes for wine. EU subsidies, however, have resulted in massive overproduction and a land "set-aside" policy has been introduced.

***Bulgarian roses** are one of the many diverse crops grown in Europe. Rose oil, extracted from the petals, is used in perfume-making.*

***Lowland pastures** are used for dairy farming. Good transportation links and refrigeration allow fresh milk to be distributed throughout Europe.*

Scandinavia, Finland & Iceland

Denmark, Norway, Sweden, Finland, Iceland

Jutting into the Arctic Circle, this northern swath of Europe has some of the continent's harshest environments, but benefits from great reserves of oil, gas, and natural evergreen forests. While most early settlers came from the south, migrants to Finland came from the east, bringing a distinct language and culture. Since the late 19th century, the Scandinavian states have developed strong egalitarian traditions. Today, their social welfare systems are among the most extensive in the world, and standards of living are high. The Lapps, or Saami, maintain their traditional lifestyle in the northern regions of Norway, Sweden, and Finland.

The Landscape

Glaciers up to 10,000 ft (3,000 m) deep covered most of Scandinavia and Finland during the last Ice Age. The effects of glaciation mark the entire landscape, from the mountains to the lowlands, across the tundra landscape of Lapland and the lake districts of Sweden and Finland.

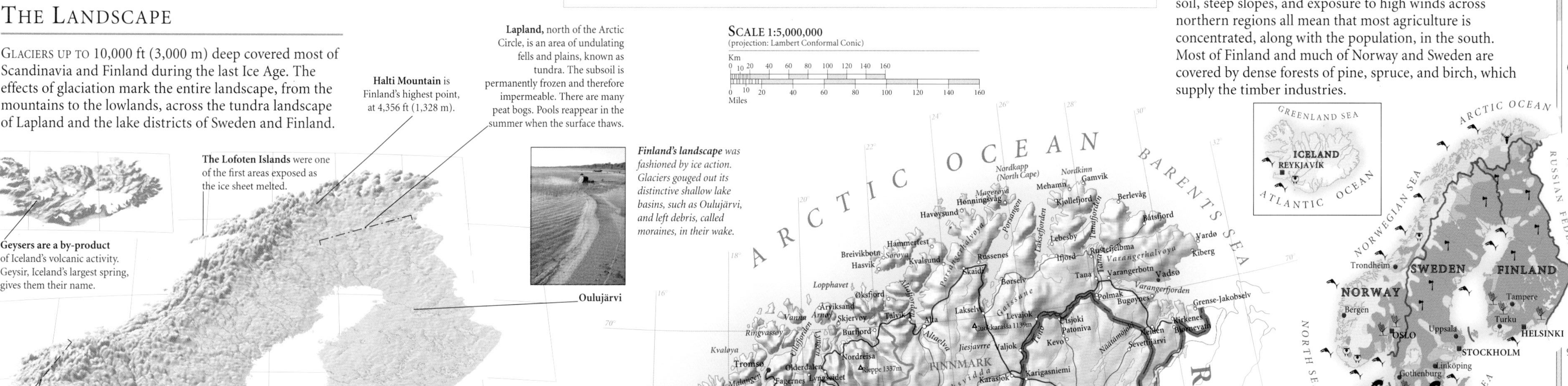

Halti Mountain is Finland's highest point, at 4,356 ft (1,328 m).

Lapland, north of the Arctic Circle, is an area of undulating fells and plains, known as tundra. The subsoil is permanently frozen and therefore impermeable. There are many peat bogs. Pools reappear in the summer when the surface thaws.

The Lofoten Islands were one of the first areas exposed as the ice sheet melted.

Geysers are a by-product of Iceland's volcanic activity. Geysir, Iceland's largest spring, gives them their name.

Oulujärvi

Finland's landscape was *fashioned by ice action. Glaciers gouged out its distinctive shallow lake basins, such as Oulujärvi, and left debris, called moraines, in their wake.*

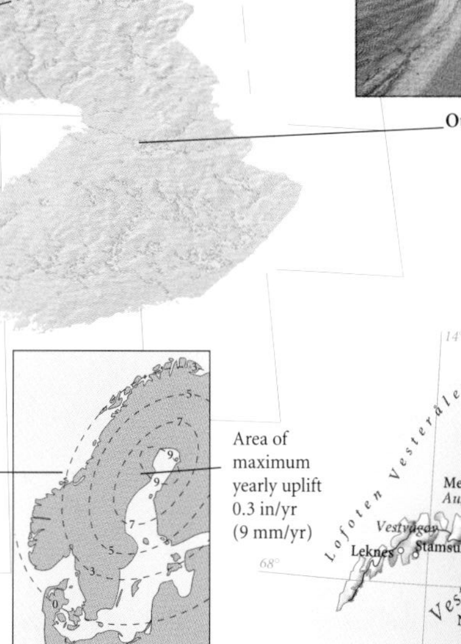
Slower rates of uplift 0.1 in/yr (3 mm/yr)
Area of maximum yearly uplift 0.3 in/yr (9 mm/yr)

***Scandinavia** is still recovering from the last Ice Age, when ice depressed the land by 2,000 ft (600 m). This gradual uplift is known as isostatic rebound.*

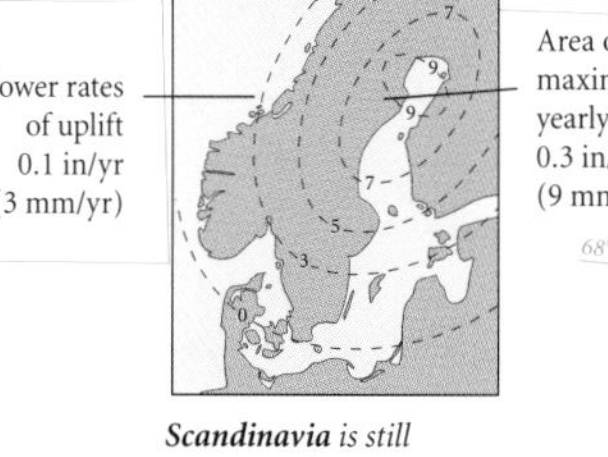

Sjælland coast

***On the coast of Sjælland,** these cliffs have been eroded by the sea, exposing layers of chalk and limestone.*

Fjords

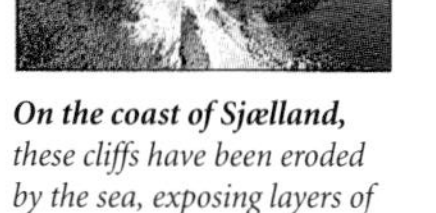

***The fjords** on the western coast of Norway were once gentle river valleys. Their deep floors and steep sides were carved out by glaciers during the last Ice Age, and they were later flooded by the sea.*

Scale 1:5,000,000
(projection: Lambert Conformal Conic)

(same scale as main map)

Scale 1:8,000,000
(projection: Lambert Conformal Conic)

▶125

Using the Land & Sea

The cold climate, short growing season, poorly developed soil, steep slopes, and exposure to high winds across northern regions all mean that most agriculture is concentrated, along with the population, in the south. Most of Finland and much of Norway and Sweden are covered by dense forests of pine, spruce, and birch, which supply the timber industries.

Land use and agricultural distribution
fishing, pigs, reindeer, sheep, cereals, timber
capital cities, major towns
pasture, cropland, forest, mountain region, tundra

The Urban/Rural Population Divide

urban 84% — rural 16%

Population Density
269 people per sq mile (104 people per sq km)

Total Land Area
329,380 sq miles (853,090 sq km)

Along with traditional reindeer *herding, many Lapp herders now also earn their living by fishing and farming, or working in cities. Tourism provides some with an extra source of income.*

Sweden is one *of the world's largest producers of wood and wood-based products. The traditional transportation of logs, by floating them down rivers, has now been largely replaced by the use of trucks.*

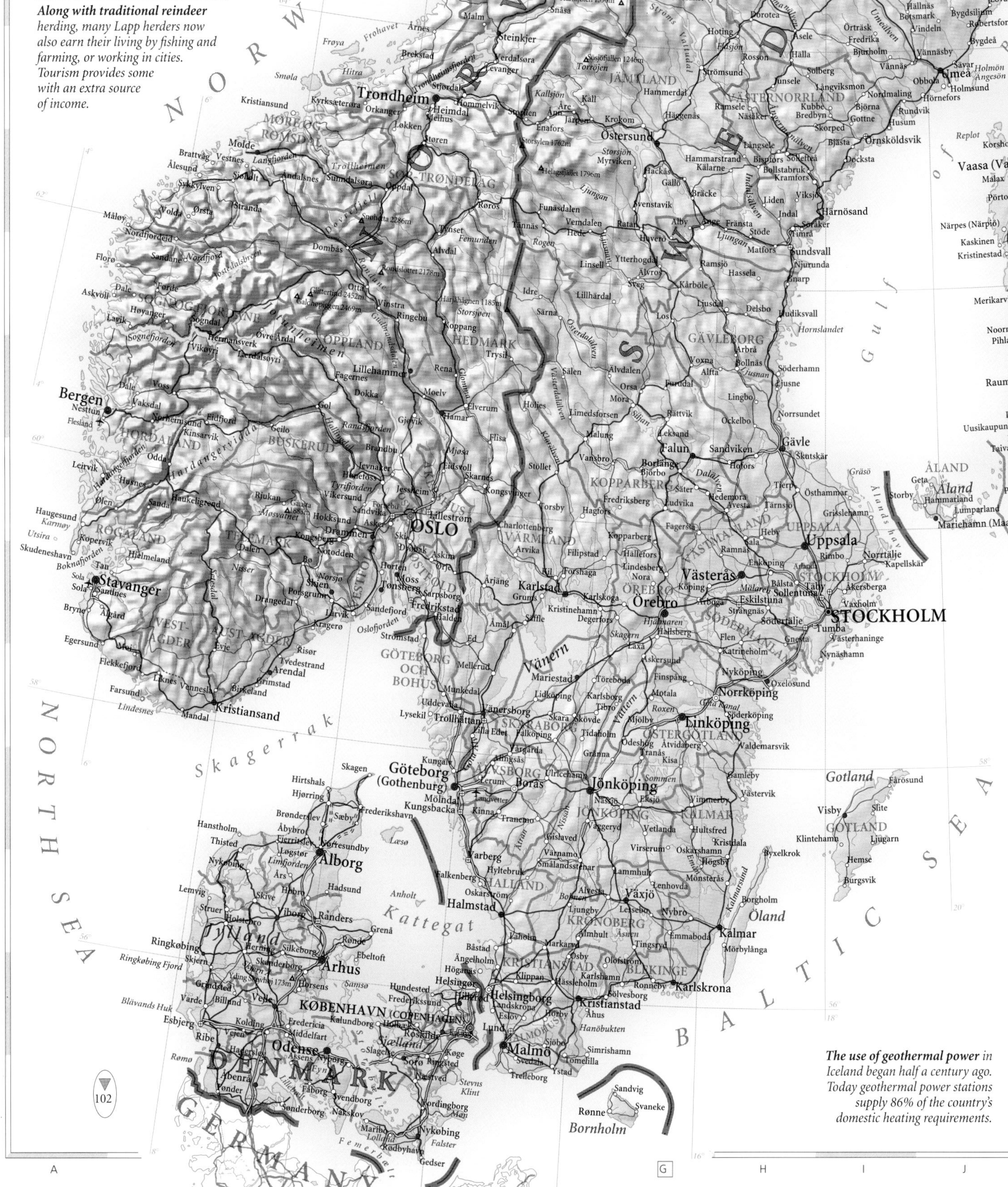

Map Key

POPULATION

- 500,000 to 1 million
- 100,000 to 500,000
- 50,000 to 100,000
- 10,000 to 50,000
- below 10,000

ELEVATION

- 2000m / 6562ft
- 1000m / 3281ft
- 500m / 1640ft
- 250m / 820ft
- 100m / 328ft
- sea level

Transportation & Industry

Norway derives its premier industry, the production of oil and gas, from the North Sea, while Denmark exploits its own oil and gas reserves. Hydroelectric power is a major industry, particularly in Sweden and Iceland. Timber processing remains significant in Finland and Sweden, but metal and engineering industries are increasingly important. In Iceland, fish products are the main source of export earnings.

Transportation Network

238,725 miles (384,192 km)

1,255 miles (2,020 km)

14,903 miles (23,984 km)

15,715 miles (25,292 km)

Roads now reach most areas, but the railroads are less developed. Much of the north is not served by rail and must rely on air and sea transportation for long distance travel and for transporting freight.

Major industry and infrastructure

- car manufacture
- engineering
- fish processing
- geothermal power
- hydroelectric power
- nuclear power
- oil & gas
- timber processing
- capital cities
- major towns
- international airports
- major roads
- major industrial areas

The use of geothermal power *in Iceland began half a century ago. Today geothermal power stations supply 86% of the country's domestic heating requirements.*

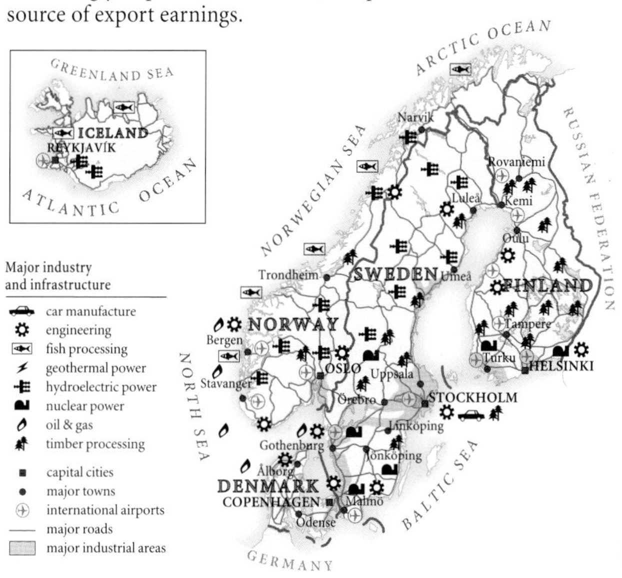

102

Southern Scandinavia

Denmark, Southern Norway, Southern Sweden

Scandinavia's economic and political hub is the more habitable and accessible southern region. Many of the area's major cities are on the southern coasts, including Oslo and Stockholm, the capitals of Norway and Sweden. In Denmark, most of the population and the capital, Copenhagen, are located on its many islands. A cultural unity links the three Scandinavian countries. Their main languages, Danish, Swedish, and Norwegian, are mutually intelligible, and they all retain their monarchies, though the parliaments have legislative control.

Using the Land

Agriculture in southern Scandinavia is highly mechanized, even though farms are small. Denmark is the most intensively farmed country and its western pastureland is used mainly for pig farming. Cereal crops, including wheat, barley, and oats, predominate in eastern Denmark and in the far south of Sweden. Southern Norway and Sweden have large tracts of forest, which are exploited for logging.

The Urban/Rural Population Divide

urban 87% · rural 13%

Population Density	Total Land Area
152 people per sq mile (61 people per sq km)	173,487 sq miles (456,564 sq km)

Land use and agricultural distribution: cattle, pigs, sheep, cereals, fodder, root crops, timber; capital cities, major towns; pasture, cropland, forest, mountain region

The Landscape

Southern Scandinavia, with the exception of Norway, has a flatter terrain than the rest of the region. Denmark and southern Sweden are both extensions of the North European Plain. In this area, because of glacial deposition rather than erosion, the soils are deeper and more fertile.

In the past, glaciers such as this one in Olden, Norway, were much larger. Today, many are retreating to yield the spectacular glacial scenery.

Distinctive low ridges, called eskers, are found across southern Sweden. They are formed from sand and gravel deposits left by retreating glaciers.

Limestone pillars *eroded by the sea dot the coast of Gotland and surrounding islands.*

The peak of Glittertind in the Jotunheimen mountains is 8,044 ft (2,452 m) high.

Acid rain, caused by industrial pollution carried north from elsewhere in Europe, harms plant and animal life in Scandinavian forests and lakes. The region's surface rocks lack lime to neutralize the acid, making the problem more serious.

Olden

Sognefjorden

The lakes of southern Sweden are all that remains of a time when the land was completely flooded. The land rose as the ice that covered the area melted, leaving lakes in shallow, ice-scoured depressions. Sweden has over 90,000 lakes.

Vänern, in Sweden, is the largest lake in Scandinavia. It covers an area of 2,080 sq miles (5,390 sq km).

Denmark's flat and fertile soils are formed on glacial deposits between 100–160 ft (30–50 m) deep.

Erosion by glaciers deepened existing river valleys

Sea level

When the ice retreated, the valley was flooded by the sea

Old valley floor

Sognefjorden *is the deepest of Norway's many fjords. It drops to 4,291 ft (1,308 m) below sea level.*

In Norway, *winters are longer and colder inland than in coastal areas, where the warm current of the North Atlantic Drift moderates the climate.*

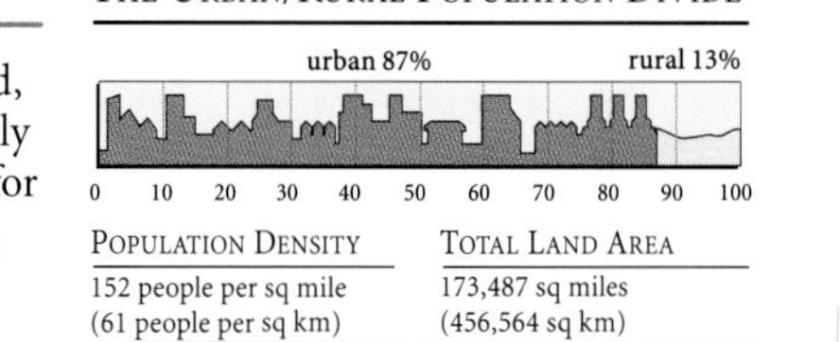

Scale 1:2,900,000

(projection: Lambert Conformal Conic)

Map Key

Population: 500,000 to 1 million; 100,000 to 500,000; 50,000 to 100,000; 10,000 to 50,000; below 10,000

Elevation: 2000m / 6562ft; 1000m / 3281ft; 500m / 1640ft; 250m / 820ft; 100m / 328ft; sea level

98 ◀ ▶ 94 ▶ 94

FINLAND
SWEDEN
DENMARK
GERMANY
NORTH SEA
BALTIC SEA
Skagerrak
Kattegat
Ålands Hav
Hanöbukten
Jammerbugten
Vänern
Vättern
Mälaren
Götaland
Småland
Jylland
Sjælland
Fyn
Gotland
Öland
Bornholm
STOCKHOLM
OSLO
KØBENHAVN (COPENHAGEN)
Göteborg (Gothenburg)
Malmö
Uppsala
Västerås
Örebro
Norrköping
Linköping
Jönköping
Karlstad
Halmstad
Helsingborg
Kristianstad
Karlskrona
Kalmar
Växjö
Visby
Stavanger
Kristiansand
Ålborg
Århus
Odense
Esbjerg
HORDALAND
ROGALAND
TELEMARK
BUSKERUD
AKERSHUS
ØSTFOLD
VESTFOLD
VEST-AGDER
AUST-AGDER
VÄRMLAND
UPPSALA
VÄSTMANLAND
ÖREBRO
SÖDERMANLAND
STOCKHOLM
ÖSTERGÖTLAND
SKARABORG
ÄLVSBORG
GÖTEBORG OCH BOHUS
HALLAND
JÖNKÖPING
KRONOBERG
KALMAR
BLEKINGE
KRISTIANSTAD
MALMÖHUS
GOTLAND
NORDJYLLAND
VIBORG
ÅRHUS
RINGKØBING
VEJLE
RIBE
SØNDERJYLLAND
FYN
VESTSJÆLLAND
STORSTRØM
FREDERIKSBORG
ROSKILDE
BORNHOLM
FAEROE ISLANDS (to Denmark)
TÓRSHAVN
ATLANTIC OCEAN
(same scale as main map)
98
102
112
A B C D E F G H I J K L M N O P Q
14 15 16 17 18 19 20 21 22 23 24 25 26

Shipbuilding in Gothenburg has declined in recent years while manufacturers in other sectors have come to the fore. One of these is the car firm, Volvo, a major employer in Gothenburg.

Transportation & Industry

In Denmark and Norway, food processing is a major industry. Swedish iron and steel production supports car manufacturers, such as Saab and Volvo. Nearly half of Norway's income comes from North Sea oil and gas reserves. Denmark's successful hi-tech, high-profit electronics and light engineering industries largely use imported raw materials.

NORWEGIAN SEA
NORTH SEA
BALTIC SEA
GERMANY
NORWAY
SWEDEN
DENMARK
Trondheim
Bergen
Stavanger
Kristiansand
Drammen
OSLO
Örebro
Västerås
Uppsala
STOCKHOLM
Linköping
Jönköping
Borås
Gothenburg
Ålborg
Randers
Århus
Odense
COPENHAGEN
Helsingborg
Malmö
Major industry and infrastructure
car manufacture
electronics
engineering
furniture industry
iron & steel
shipbuilding
food processing
capital cities
major towns
international airports
major roads
major industrial areas

Transportation Network

133,712 miles (215,666 km)

1,160 miles (1,872 km)

8,180 miles (13,195 km)

3,668 miles (5,197 km)

In this region, major additions to the transportation network are the new bridge and tunnel projects currently being planned to connect Denmark's main islands and forge links with Sweden and Germany.

More than half of the *land in Denmark is used for agriculture. Grains, particularly wheat and barley, are the main cultivated crops.*

Sand deposited by glaciers *at the end of the last Ice Age has been fashioned by wind and waves into dunes, creating heathlands along the northwestern coast of Jylland.*

The British Isles

United Kingdom, Republic of Ireland

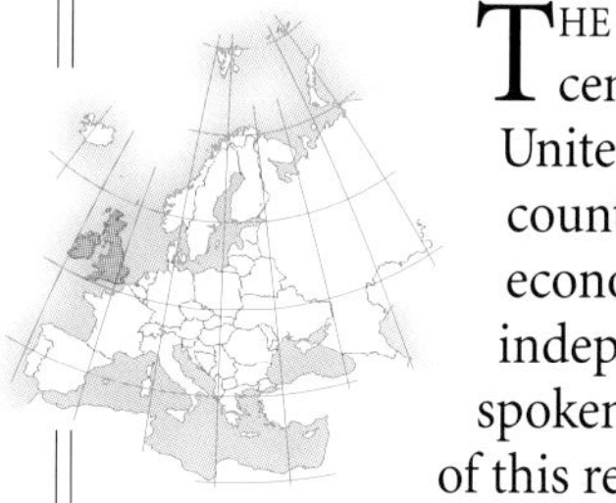

The British Isles have played a central role in European and world history for centuries. England, Wales, Scotland, and Northern Ireland together form the United Kingdom (UK), while the southern portion of Ireland is an independent country, self-governing since 1921. England has often been the politically and economically dominant partner in the UK. The other partners, however, maintain independent cultures and distinct national identities, and Celtic languages are still spoken by some people. Southeastern England is the most densely populated part of this region, with more than nine million people living in and around London.

The valley of Glen Coe in the Scottish Highlands is a U-shaped valley, typical of the north and west of the British Isles, where glaciers shaped much of the landscape.

Transportation & Industry

The British Isles' industrial base was founded primarily on coal, iron, and textiles, situated largely in the north. Today, the most productive sectors include hi-tech industries clustered mainly in southeastern England, chemicals, finance, and the service sector, particularly tourism.

Major industry and infrastructure

- car manufacture
- chemicals
- engineering
- hi-tech industry
- iron & steel
- tourism
- capital cities
- major towns
- international airports
- major roads
- major industrial areas

Transportation Network

278,898 miles (448,844 km)	1,927 miles (3,101 km)
11,514 miles (18,530 km)	2,255 miles (3,629 km)

The UK's congested roads have become a major focus of environmental concern in recent years. No longer an island, the UK was finally linked to continental Europe by the Channel Tunnel in 1994.

Clew Bay, in western Ireland, is characteristic of the heavily indented west coast, where deep wide-mouthed bays separate the mountains of Mayo, Donegal, and Kerry as they thrust out into the Atlantic Ocean.

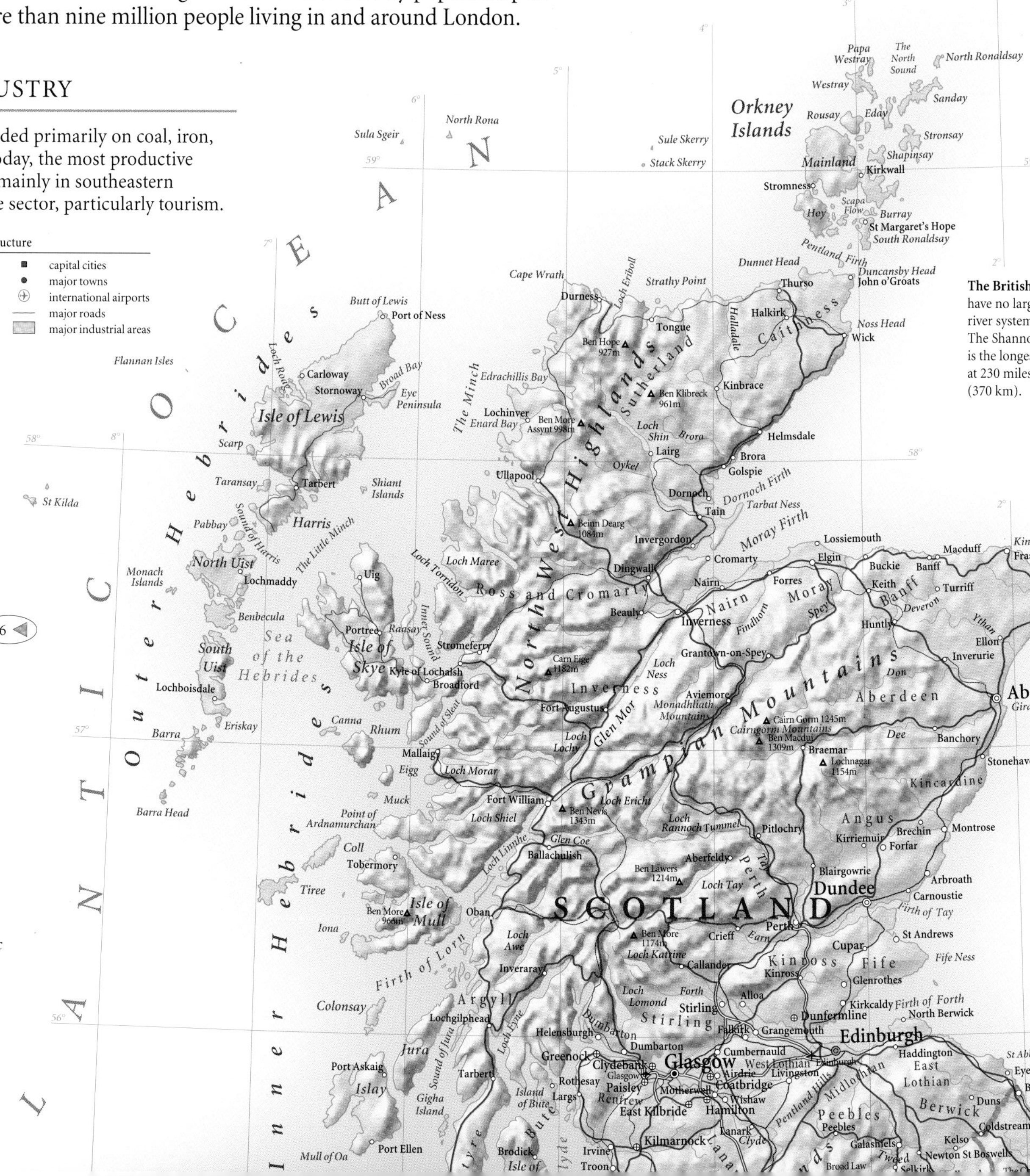

66

94

The Landscape

Rugged uplands dominate the landscape of Scotland, Wales, and northern England. All of the peaks in the British Isles over 4,000 ft (1,219 m) lie in highland Scotland. Lowland England rises into several ranges of rolling hills, including the older Mendips, and the Cotswolds and the Chilterns, which were formed at the same time as the Alps in southern Europe.

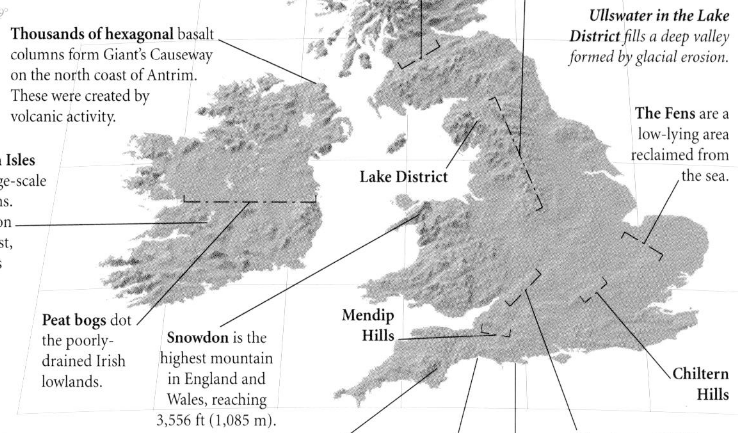

The lowlands of Scotland, drained by the Tay, Forth, and Clyde Rivers, are centered on a rift valley. The region contains valuable coal reserves.

The Pennines, sometimes called "the backbone of England," are formed of limestones and grits.

Ben Nevis, at 4,409 ft (1,343 m), is the highest peak in the UK.

Over 600 islands, mostly uninhabited, lie west and north of the Scottish mainland.

Ullswater in the Lake District fills a deep valley formed by glacial erosion.

Thousands of hexagonal basalt columns form Giant's Causeway on the north coast of Antrim. These were created by volcanic activity.

The Fens are a low-lying area reclaimed from the sea.

Lake District

The British Isles have no large-scale river systems. The Shannon is the longest, at 230 miles (370 km).

Peat bogs dot the poorly-drained Irish lowlands.

Snowdon is the highest mountain in England and Wales, reaching 3,556 ft (1,085 m).

Mendip Hills

Chiltern Hills

The Cotswold Hills are characterized by a series of limestone ridges overlooking clay vales.

Dartmoor, *studded with tors, is an exposed part of a vast granite dome, formed when molten rock intruded into the Earth's crust.*

Durdle Door

Black Ven, Lyme Regis

Water, Mudslide, Sea, Cracks, Sandstone, Clay, Limestone

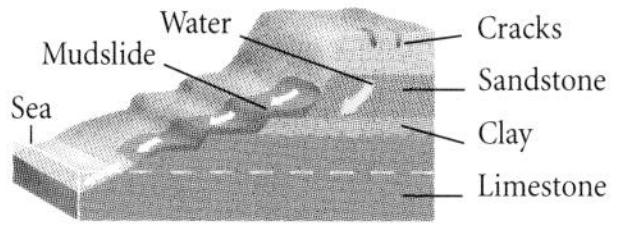

Much of the south coast *is subject to landslides. Following rain, porous sandstones feed water into the underlying, less permeable clays, which then crumble and slide into the sea.*

Coastal erosion *around the British Isles forms striking features, such as this limestone arch, known as Durdle Door, in Dorset.*

Map Key

POPULATION

- above 5 million
- 1 million to 5 million
- 500,000 to 1 million
- 100,000 to 500,000
- 50,000 to 100,000
- 10,000 to 50,000
- below 10,000

ELEVATION

- 1000m / 3281ft
- 500m / 1640ft
- 250m / 820ft
- 100m / 328ft
- sea level

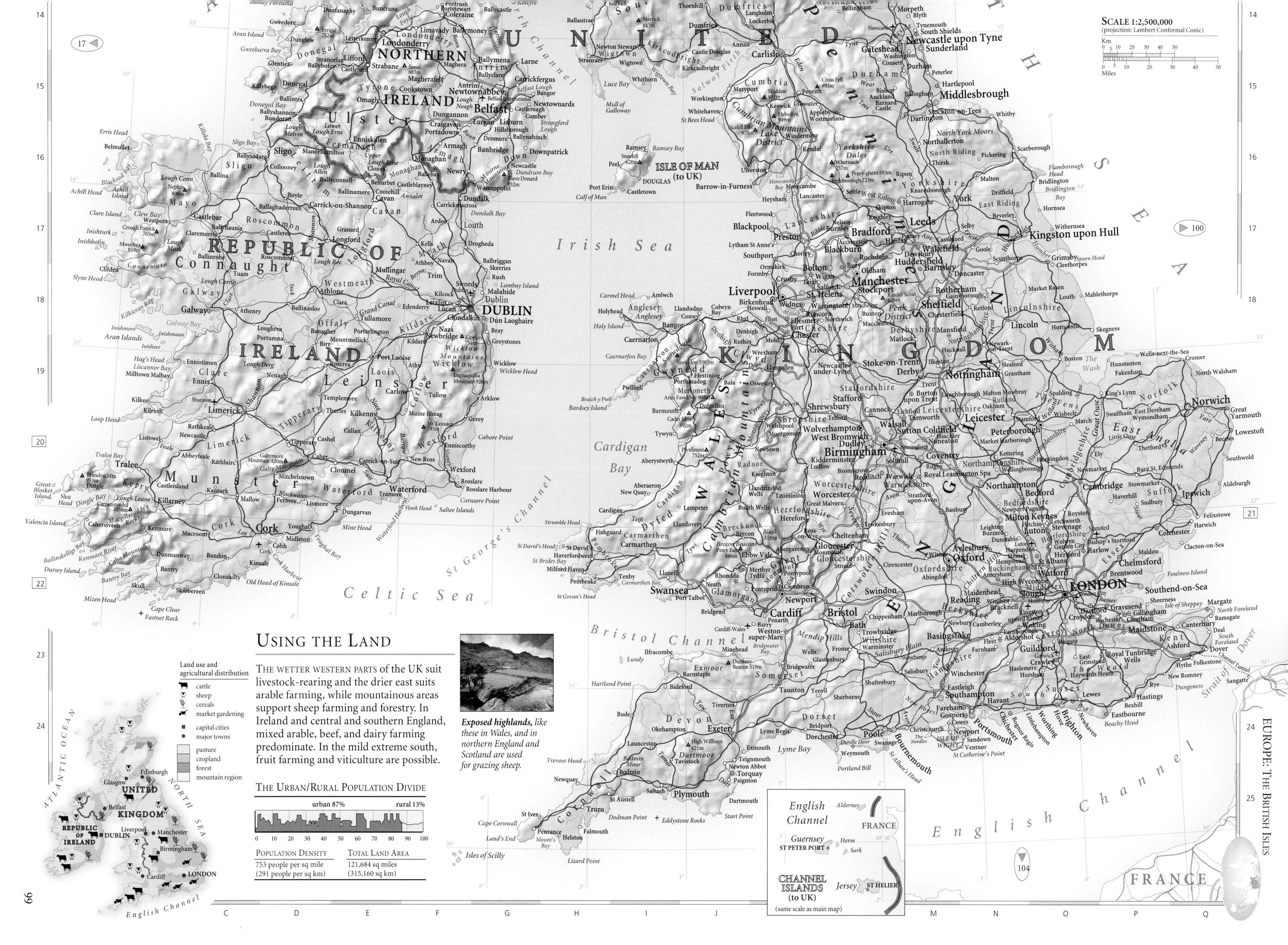
SCALE 1:2,500,000
(projection: Lambert Conformal Conic)
UNITED KINGDOM
REPUBLIC OF IRELAND
NORTHERN IRELAND
WALES
ISLE OF MAN (to UK)
Irish Sea
Celtic Sea
St George's Channel
Bristol Channel
English Channel
North Channel
NORTH SEA
Cardigan Bay
FRANCE
LONDON
DUBLIN
Birmingham
Manchester
Liverpool
Leeds
Bradford
Sheffield
Newcastle upon Tyne
Kingston upon Hull
Belfast
Cork
Cardiff
Bristol
Southampton
Portsmouth
Plymouth
Norwich
CHANNEL ISLANDS (to UK)
(same scale as main map)
Guernsey
ST PETER PORT
Jersey
ST HELIER
Alderney
Herm
Sark
Isles of Scilly

Using the Land

THE WETTER WESTERN PARTS of the UK suit livestock-rearing and the drier east suits arable farming, while mountainous areas support sheep farming and forestry. In Ireland and central and southern England, mixed arable, beef, and dairy farming predominate. In the mild extreme south, fruit farming and viticulture are possible.

***Exposed highlands,** like these in Wales, and in northern England and Scotland are used for grazing sheep.*

The Urban/Rural Population Divide

urban 87% · rural 13%

Population Density	Total Land Area
753 people per sq mile	121,684 sq miles
(291 people per sq km)	(315,160 sq km)

Land use and agricultural distribution: cattle, sheep, cereals, market gardening, capital cities, major towns, pasture, cropland, forest, mountain region

The Low Countries

Belgium, Luxembourg, Netherlands

One of northwestern Europe's strategic crossroads, the Low Countries are united by a common history. They have often been used as a battleground in European wars. For over a thousand years they were ruled by foreign powers. Even after they achieved independence, the three countries maintained close links, later forming the world's first totally free labor and goods market, the Benelux Economic Union, which became the core of the European Community (now the European Union or EU). These states have remained at the forefront of wider European cooperation; Brussels, The Hague, and Luxembourg host the major institutions of the EU.

The Landscape

The main geographical regions of the Netherlands are the northern glacial heathlands, the low-lying lands of the Rhine and Maas/Meuse, the reclaimed polders, and the dune coast and islands. Belgium includes part of the Ardennes, together with the coalfields on its northern flanks, and the fertile Flanders Plain.

Heathlands are found along the coast of the Netherlands. Much of the coast was breached by the sea in the 5th century, creating its distinctive inlets and islands.

Schoorl

Dune system

Sea

Polder

Drainage ditch

***Extensive sand dune** systems along the coast have prevented flooding of the land. Behind the dunes, marshy land is drained to form polders, usable land suitable for agriculture.*

Sand dunes

***One-third of the Netherlands** lies below sea level and flooding is a constant threat. Dams have been built across the mouths of many rivers to contain floodwaters.*

Since the Middle Ages the people of the Netherlands have used ditches and drainage dykes to reclaim land from the sea. These reclaimed areas are known as polders.

The parallel valleys of the Maas/Meuse and Rhine Rivers were created when the Rhine was deflected from its previous course by the ice sheet which formed during the last Ice Age.

Silts and sands eroded by the Rhine throughout its course are deposited to form a delta on the west coast of the Netherlands.

The loess soils of the Flanders Plain in western Belguim provide excellent conditions for arable farming.

Ardennes

***Uplifted and folded** 220 million years ago, the Ardennes have since been reduced to relatively level plateaus, then sharply incised by rivers such as the Maas/Meuse.*

Hautes Fagnes is the highest part of Belgium. The bogs and streams in this upland region are the result of high rainfall and low temperatures.

Transportation & Industry

In the western Netherlands, a massive, sprawling industrialized zone encompasses many new hi-tech and service industries. Belgium's central region has emerged as the country's light manufacturing and services center. Luxembourg city is home to more than 160 banks and the European headquarters of many international companies.

Transportation Network

155,154 miles (249,697 km)

1,065 miles (1,714 km)

4,280 miles (6,888 km)

4,369 miles (7,031 km)

The Low Countries hold a key position on the North Sea, containing Europe's two largest ports, Rotterdam and Antwerp, which are connected to a comprehensive system of inland waterways.

Major industry and infrastructure

- aerospace
- finance
- engineering
- hi-tech industry
- pharmaceuticals
- textiles
- capital cities
- major towns
- international airports
- major roads
- major industrial areas

▶ 102

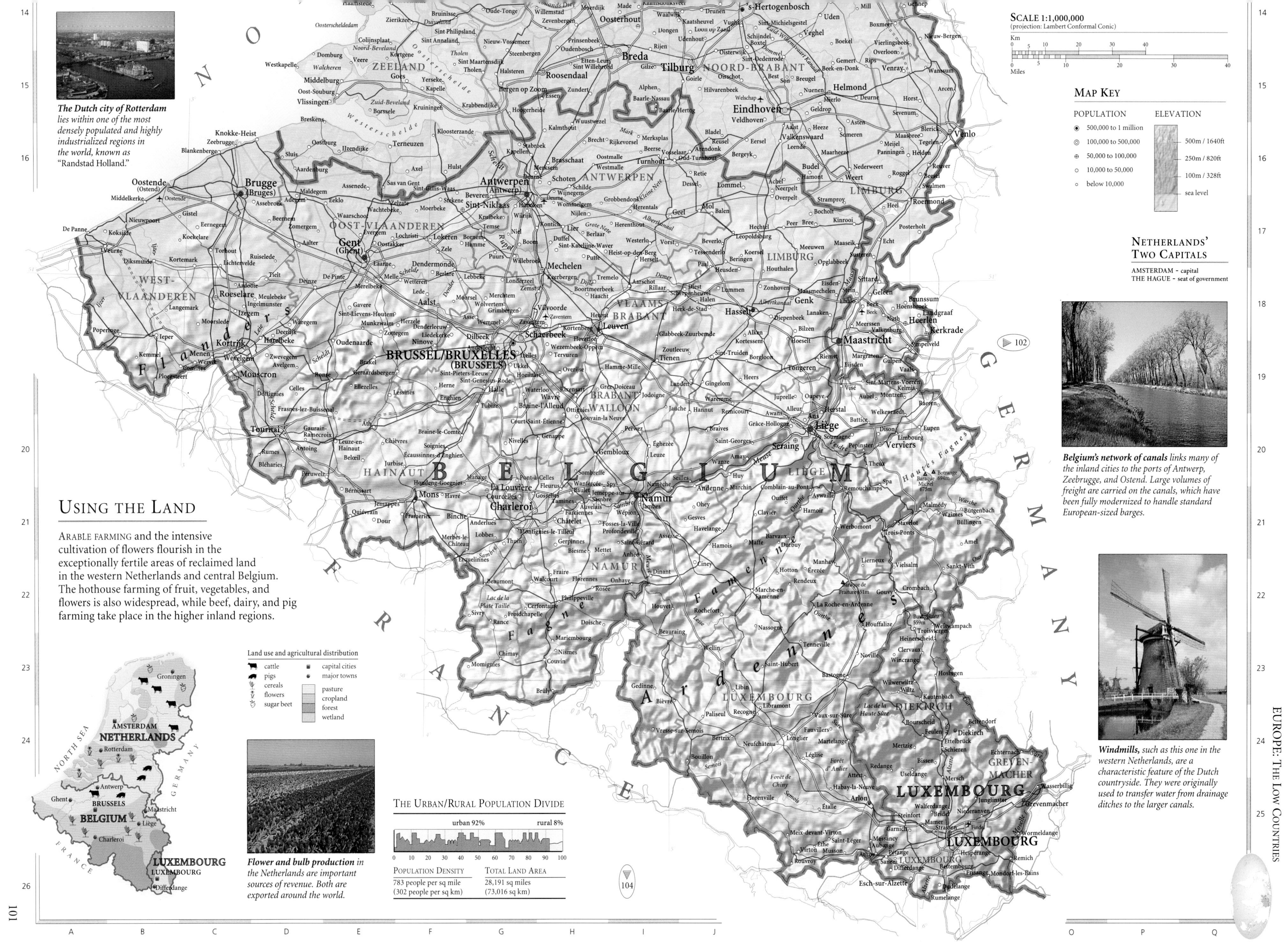
NORTH SEA
GERMANY
FRANCE
BELGIUM
LUXEMBOURG
ZEELAND
NOORD-BRABANT
LIMBURG
ANTWERPEN
OOST-VLAANDEREN
WEST-VLAANDEREN
VLAAMS BRABANT
BRABANT WALLON
HAINAUT
NAMUR
LIÈGE
LUXEMBOURG
DIEKIRCH
GREVENMACHER
Flanders
Fagne
Famenne
Ardennes
Hautes Fagnes
BRUSSEL/BRUXELLES (BRUSSELS)
Antwerpen (Antwerp)
Gent (Ghent)
Brugge (Bruges)
Oostende (Ostend)
Liège
Charleroi
Namur
Mons
Leuven
Mechelen
Maastricht
Eindhoven
Breda
Tilburg
's-Hertogenbosch
Venlo
Luxembourg
Esch-sur-Alzette
102
104
Scale 1:1,000,000
(projection: Lambert Conformal Conic)
Km
Miles
Map Key
Population
500,000 to 1 million
100,000 to 500,000
50,000 to 100,000
10,000 to 50,000
below 10,000
Elevation
500m / 1640ft
250m / 820ft
100m / 328ft
sea level
Land use and agricultural distribution
cattle
pigs
cereals
flowers
sugar beet
capital cities
major towns
pasture
cropland
forest
wetland
AMSTERDAM
NETHERLANDS
Groningen
Rotterdam
Antwerp
Ghent
BRUSSELS
Maastricht
Liège
Charleroi
LUXEMBOURG
Differdange
The Urban/Rural Population Divide
urban 92%
rural 8%
0 10 20 30 40 50 60 70 80 90 100

The Dutch city of Rotterdam *lies within one of the most densely populated and highly industrialized regions in the world, known as "Randstad Holland."*

Netherlands' Two Capitals

AMSTERDAM - capital
THE HAGUE - seat of government

Belgium's network of canals *links many of the inland cities to the ports of Antwerp, Zeebrugge, and Ostend. Large volumes of freight are carried on the canals, which have been fully modernized to handle standard European-sized barges.*

Windmills, *such as this one in the western Netherlands, are a characteristic feature of the Dutch countryside. They were originally used to transfer water from drainage ditches to the larger canals.*

Using the Land

Arable farming and the intensive cultivation of flowers flourish in the exceptionally fertile areas of reclaimed land in the western Netherlands and central Belgium. The hothouse farming of fruit, vegetables, and flowers is also widespread, while beef, dairy, and pig farming take place in the higher inland regions.

Flower and bulb production *in the Netherlands are important sources of revenue. Both are exported around the world.*

Population Density	Total Land Area
783 people per sq mile (302 people per sq km)	28,191 sq miles (73,016 sq km)

Germany

Despite the devastation of its industry and infrastructure during the Second World War and its separation from East Germany during the Cold War, West Germany made a rapid recovery in the following generation to become Europe's most formidable economic power. When the Berlin Wall was dismantled in 1989, Germany was politically united for the first time in 40 years. Complete social and economic unity remain a longer-term goal, as East German industry and society adapt to a free market. Germany has been a key player in the creation of the European Union (EU) and in moves toward adopting a single European currency.

Using the Land

Germany has a large, efficient agricultural sector, producing more than three-quarters of its own food. The major crops grown are cereals and sugar beet on the more fertile soils, and root crops, rye, oats, and fodder on the poorer soils of the northern plains and central uplands. Southern Germany is also a principal producer of high-quality wines. Vineyards cover the slopes surrounding the Rhine and its tributaries.

Land use and agricultural distribution: cattle, pigs, cereals, sugar beet, vineyards, capital cities, major towns, pasture, cropland, forest

The Urban/Rural Population Divide

urban 86% / rural 14%

Population Density	Total Land Area
593 people per sq mile (229 people per sq km)	13,804 sq miles (356,910 sq km)

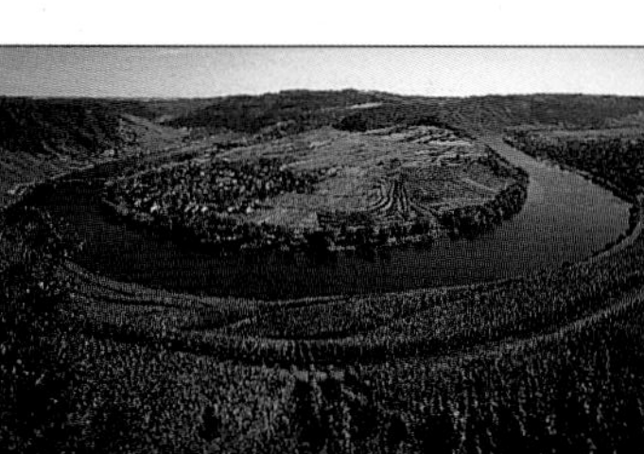

The Moselle River flows through the Rhine State Uplands (Rheinisches Schiefergebirge). *During a period of uplift, preexisting river meanders were deeply incised, to form its present dramatic contours.*

The Landscape

The plains of northern Germany, the volcanic plateaus and mountains of the central uplands, and the Bavarian Alps are the three principal geographic regions in Germany. North to south the land rises steadily from barely 300 ft (90 m) in the plains to 6,500 ft (2,000 m) in the Bavarian Alps, which are a small but distinct region in the far south.

***The heathlands** of northern Germany are covered by glacial deposits of sandy outwash soil, which makes them largely infertile. They only support sheep and solitary trees.*

Müritz Lake covers 45 sq miles (117 sq km), but is only 108 ft (33 m) deep. It lies in a shallow valley formed by meltwater flowing out from a retreating ice sheet. These valleys are known as *Urstromtäler*.

Lüneburg Heath (*Lüneburger Heide*)

Much of the landscape of northern Germany has been shaped by glaciation. During the last Ice Age, the ice sheet advanced as far the northern slopes of the central uplands.

Fault lines · Rhine · Downfaulted block

***Part of the floor** of the Rhine Rift Valley was let down between two parallel faults in the Earth's crust.*

Rhine Rift Valley

The Harz Mountains were formed 300 million years ago. They are block-faulted mountains, formed when a section of the Earth's crust was thrust up between two faults.

Elbe River

***The Elbe** flows in wide meanders across the North German Plain to the North Sea. At its mouth it is 10 miles (16 km) wide.*

The Rhine is Germany's principal waterway and one of Europe's longest rivers, flowing 820 miles (1,320 km).

Zugspitze, the highest peak in Germany at 9,719 ft (2,962 m), was formed during the Alpine mountain-building period, 30 million years ago.

The Danube rises in the Black Forest (*Schwarzwald*) and flows east, across a wide valley, on its course to the Black Sea.

Scale 1:2,250,000 (projection: Lambert Conformal Conic)

95 · 98 · 100 · 112

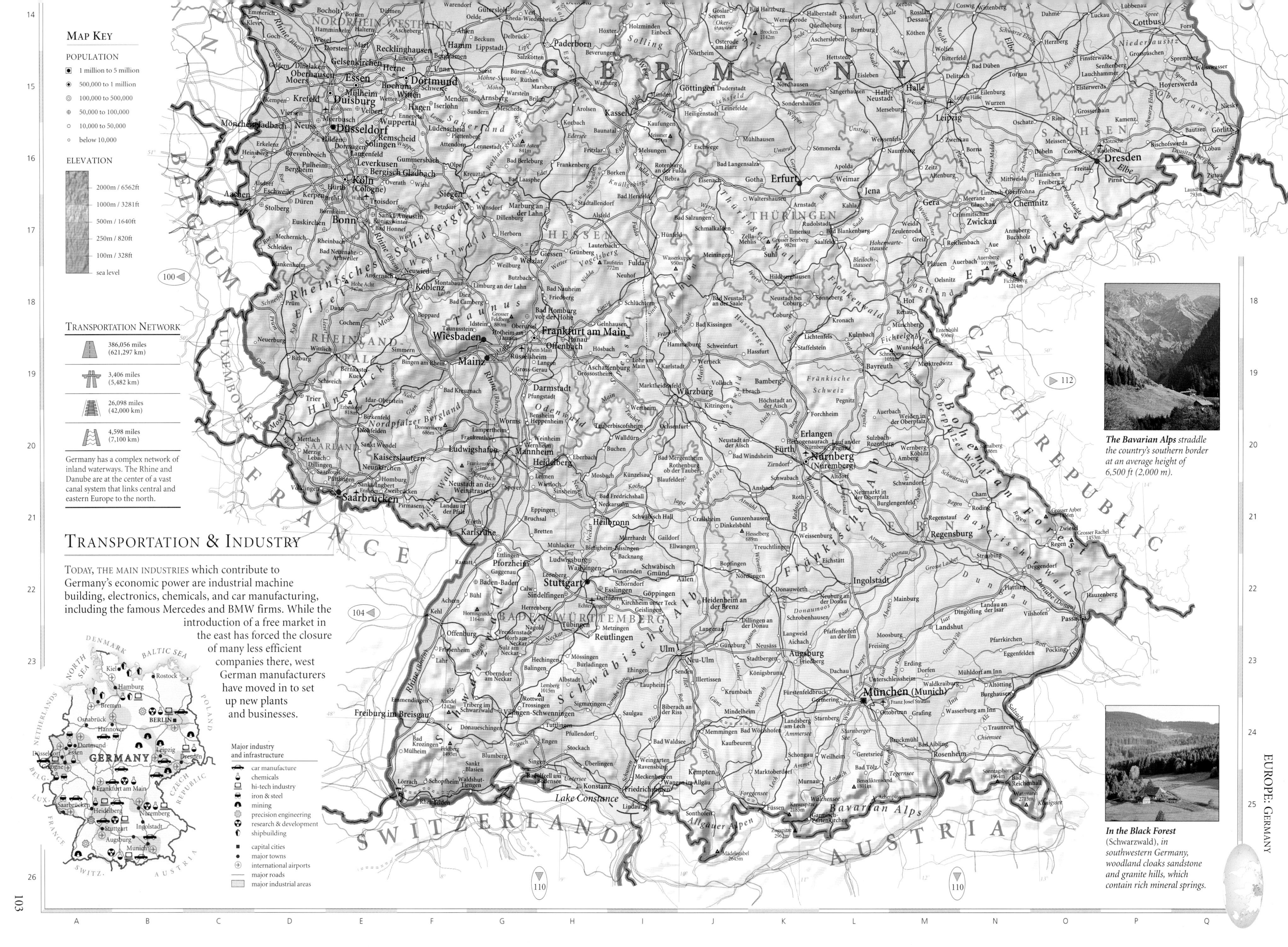

MAP KEY
POPULATION
1 million to 5 million
500,000 to 1 million
100,000 to 500,000
50,000 to 100,000
10,000 to 50,000
below 10,000
ELEVATION
2000m / 6562ft
1000m / 3281ft
500m / 1640ft
250m / 820ft
100m / 328ft
sea level
TRANSPORTATION NETWORK
386,056 miles (621,297 km)
3,406 miles (5,482 km)
26,098 miles (42,000 km)
4,598 miles (7,100 km)
Germany has a complex network of inland waterways. The Rhine and Danube are at the center of a vast canal system that links central and eastern Europe to the north.
GERMANY
BELGIUM
LUXEMBOURG
FRANCE
SWITZERLAND
AUSTRIA
CZECH REPUBLIC
Major industry and infrastructure
car manufacture
chemicals
hi-tech industry
iron & steel
mining
precision engineering
research & development
shipbuilding
capital cities
major towns
international airports
major roads
major industrial areas

TRANSPORTATION & INDUSTRY

TODAY, THE MAIN INDUSTRIES which contribute to Germany's economic power are industrial machine building, electronics, chemicals, and car manufacturing, including the famous Mercedes and BMW firms. While the introduction of a free market in the east has forced the closure of many less efficient companies there, west German manufacturers have moved in to set up new plants and businesses.

The Bavarian Alps *straddle the country's southern border at an average height of 6,500 ft (2,000 m).*

In the Black Forest (Schwarzwald), *in southwestern Germany, woodland cloaks sandstone and granite hills, which contain rich mineral springs.*

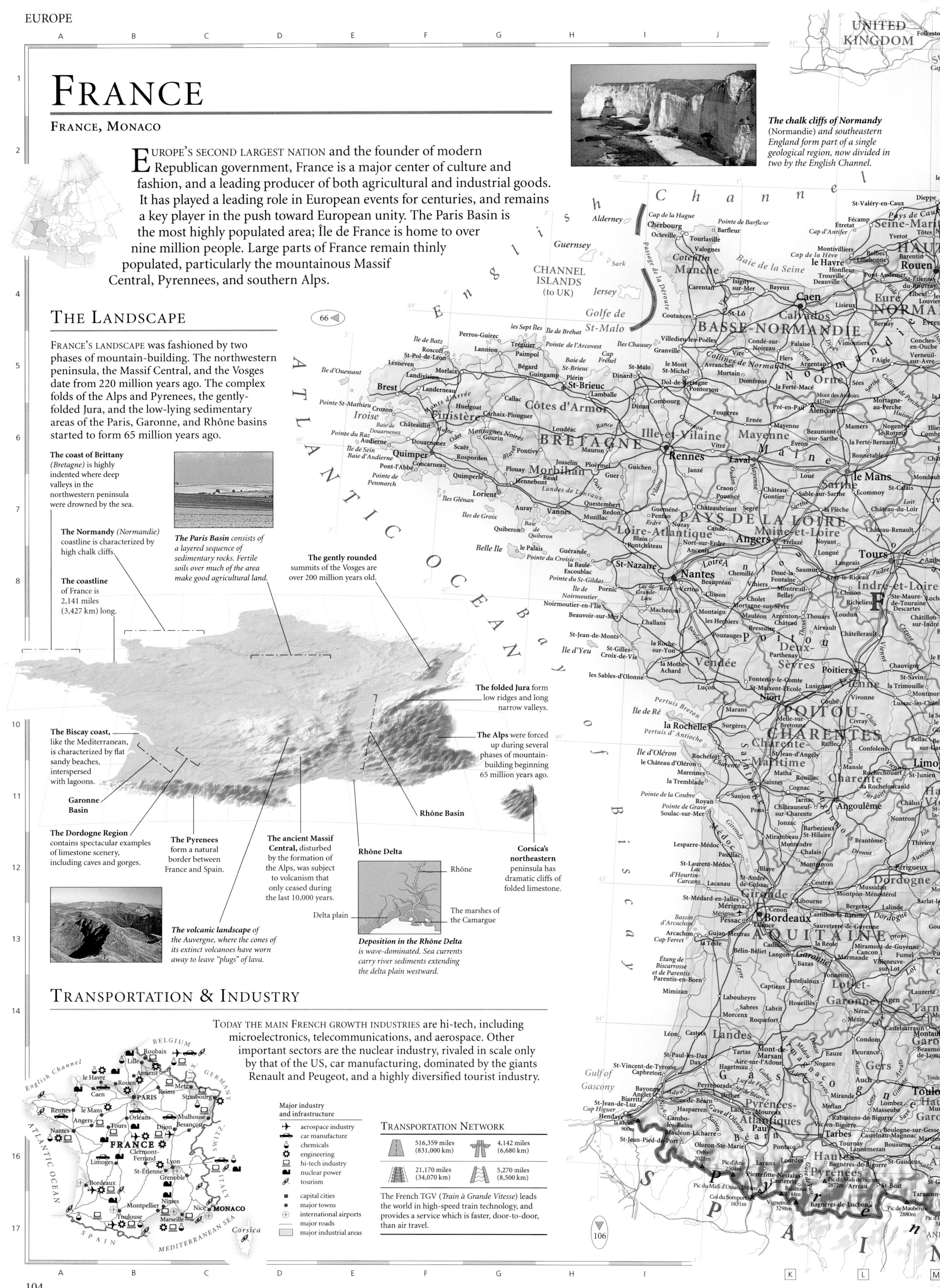

FRANCE

FRANCE, MONACO

EUROPE'S SECOND LARGEST NATION and the founder of modern Republican government, France is a major center of culture and fashion, and a leading producer of both agricultural and industrial goods. It has played a leading role in European events for centuries, and remains a key player in the push toward European unity. The Paris Basin is the most highly populated area; Île de France is home to over nine million people. Large parts of France remain thinly populated, particularly the mountainous Massif Central, Pyrenees, and southern Alps.

The chalk cliffs of Normandy *(Normandie) and southeastern England form part of a single geological region, now divided in two by the English Channel.*

THE LANDSCAPE

FRANCE'S LANDSCAPE was fashioned by two phases of mountain-building. The northwestern peninsula, the Massif Central, and the Vosges date from 220 million years ago. The complex folds of the Alps and Pyrenees, the gently-folded Jura, and the low-lying sedimentary areas of the Paris, Garonne, and Rhône basins started to form 65 million years ago.

The coast of Brittany *(Bretagne)* is highly indented where deep valleys in the northwestern peninsula were drowned by the sea.

The Normandy *(Normandie)* coastline is characterized by high chalk cliffs.

The coastline of France is 2,141 miles (3,427 km) long.

The Paris Basin *consists of a layered sequence of sedimentary rocks. Fertile soils over much of the area make good agricultural land.*

The gently rounded summits of the Vosges are over 200 million years old.

The folded Jura form low ridges and long narrow valleys.

The Alps were forced up during several phases of mountain-building beginning 65 million years ago.

The Biscay coast, like the Mediterranean, is characterized by flat sandy beaches, interspersed with lagoons.

Garonne Basin

The Dordogne Region contains spectacular examples of limestone scenery, including caves and gorges.

The Pyrenees form a natural border between France and Spain.

The ancient Massif Central, disturbed by the formation of the Alps, was subject to volcanism that only ceased during the last 10,000 years.

Rhône Delta

Rhône Basin

Corsica's northeastern peninsula has dramatic cliffs of folded limestone.

Rhône
Delta plain
The marshes of the Camargue

Deposition in the Rhône Delta *is wave-dominated. Sea currents carry river sediments extending the delta plain westward.*

The volcanic landscape *of the Auvergne, where the cones of its extinct volcanoes have worn away to leave "plugs" of lava.*

TRANSPORTATION & INDUSTRY

TODAY THE MAIN FRENCH GROWTH INDUSTRIES are hi-tech, including microelectronics, telecommunications, and aerospace. Other important sectors are the nuclear industry, rivaled in scale only by that of the US, car manufacturing, dominated by the giants Renault and Peugeot, and a highly diversified tourist industry.

BELGIUM
GERMANY
SWITZ.
ITALY
English Channel
ATLANTIC OCEAN
MEDITERRANEAN SEA
SPAIN
Corsica
MONACO
FRANCE
PARIS
Lille
Roubaix
Amiens
le Havre
Rouen
Caen
Reims
Metz
Strasbourg
Rennes
le Mans
Orléans
Mulhouse
Angers
Nantes
Tours
Dijon
Besançon
Clermont-Ferrand
Limoges
Lyon
St-Étienne
Grenoble
Bordeaux
Nîmes
Montpellier
Nice
Marseille
Toulouse
Major industry and infrastructure
aerospace industry
car manufacture
chemicals
engineering
hi-tech industry
nuclear power
tourism
capital cities
major towns
international airports
major roads
major industrial areas

TRANSPORTATION NETWORK

516,359 miles (831,000 km)	4,142 miles (6,680 km)
21,170 miles (34,070 km)	5,270 miles (8,500 km)

The French TGV (*Train à Grande Vitesse*) leads the world in high-speed train technology, and provides a service which is faster, door-to-door, than air travel.

UNITED KINGDOM
English Channel
CHANNEL ISLANDS (to UK)
Alderney
Guernsey
Sark
Jersey
Golfe de St-Malo
ATLANTIC OCEAN
Bay of Biscay
Gulf of Gascony
BASSE-NORMANDIE
BRETAGNE
PAYS DE LA LOIRE
POITOU-CHARENTES
AQUITAINE
Normandie
Finistère
Côtes d'Armor
Morbihan
Ille-et-Vilaine
Mayenne
Sarthe
Manche
Calvados
Orne
Loire-Atlantique
Maine-et-Loire
Vendée
Deux-Sèvres
Vienne
Charente-Maritime
Charente
Gironde
Dordogne
Landes
Lot-et-Garonne
Pyrénées-Atlantiques
Hautes-Pyrénées
Gers
Brest
Quimper
Lorient
Vannes
St-Brieuc
St-Malo
Rennes
Caen
Cherbourg
le Havre
Rouen
Laval
le Mans
Angers
Nantes
St-Nazaire
Tours
Poitiers
Niort
la Rochelle
Angoulême
Limoges
Périgueux
Bordeaux
Agen
Mont-de-Marsan
Bayonne
Biarritz
Pau
Tarbes
Toulouse
SPAIN
ANDORRA

66

106

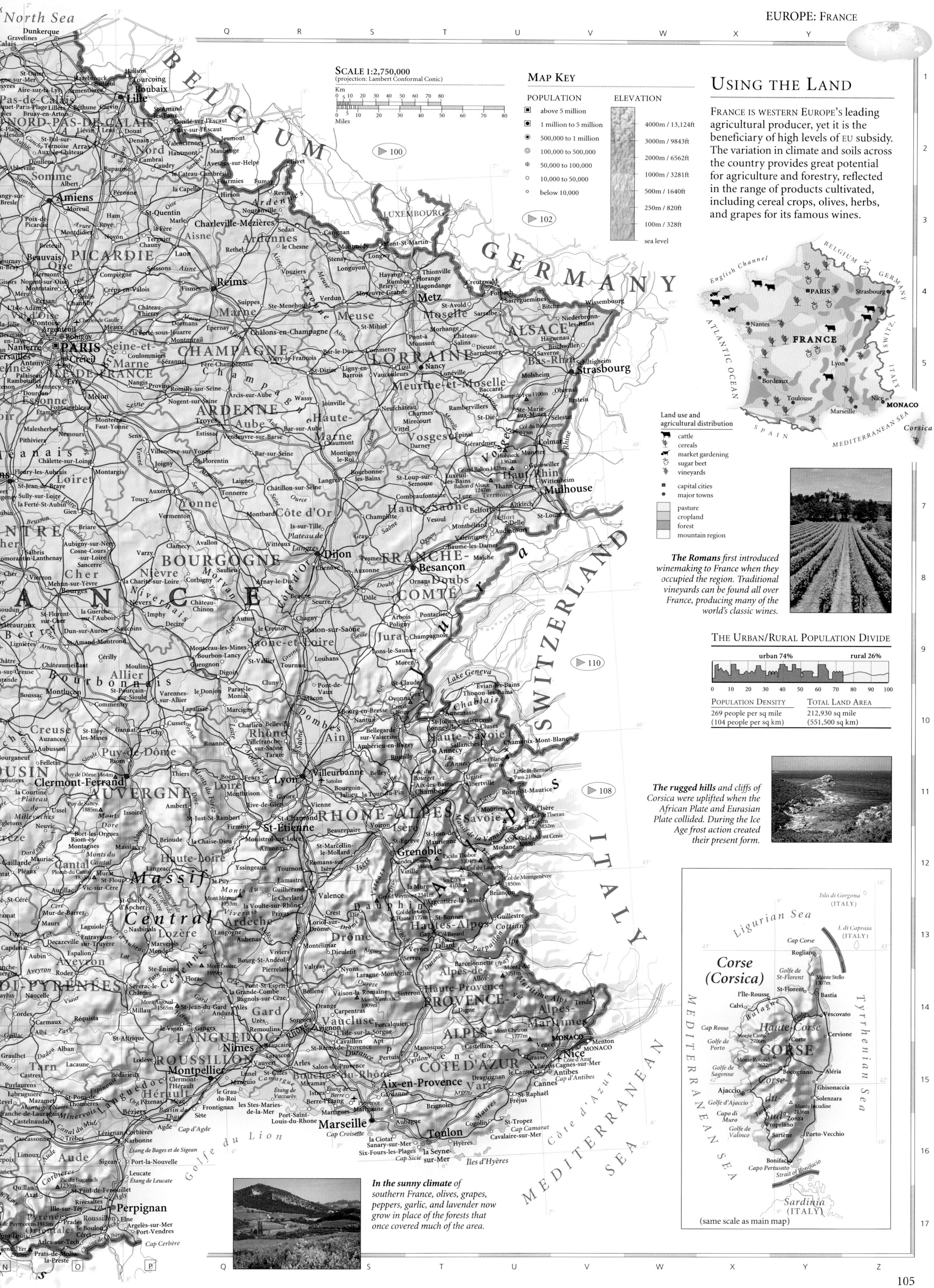
SCALE 1:2,750,000
(projection: Lambert Conformal Conic)
Km
Miles
MAP KEY
POPULATION
above 5 million
1 million to 5 million
500,000 to 1 million
100,000 to 500,000
50,000 to 100,000
10,000 to 50,000
below 10,000
ELEVATION
4000m / 13,124ft
3000m / 9843ft
2000m / 6562ft
1000m / 3281ft
500m / 1640ft
250m / 820ft
100m / 328ft
sea level
100
102
110
108
North Sea
BELGIUM
LUXEMBOURG
GERMANY
SWITZERLAND
ITALY
MONACO
MEDITERRANEAN SEA
Golfe du Lion
Côte d'Azur
Land use and agricultural distribution
cattle
cereals
market gardening
sugar beet
vineyards
capital cities
major towns
pasture
cropland
forest
mountain region
English Channel
ATLANTIC OCEAN
SPAIN
FRANCE
PARIS
Corse (Corsica)
Ligurian Sea
Tyrrhenian Sea
Sardinia (ITALY)
(same scale as main map)
THE URBAN/RURAL POPULATION DIVIDE
urban 74%
rural 26%
POPULATION DENSITY
269 people per sq mile
(104 people per sq km)
TOTAL LAND AREA
212,930 sq mile
(551,500 sq km)

Using the Land

France is western Europe's leading agricultural producer, yet it is the beneficiary of high levels of EU subsidy. The variation in climate and soils across the country provides great potential for agriculture and forestry, reflected in the range of products cultivated, including cereal crops, olives, herbs, and grapes for its famous wines.

The Romans first introduced winemaking to France when they occupied the region. Traditional vineyards can be found all over France, producing many of the world's classic wines.

The rugged hills and cliffs of Corsica were uplifted when the African Plate and Eurasian Plate collided. During the Ice Age frost action created their present form.

In the sunny climate of southern France, olives, grapes, peppers, garlic, and lavender now grow in place of the forests that once covered much of the area.

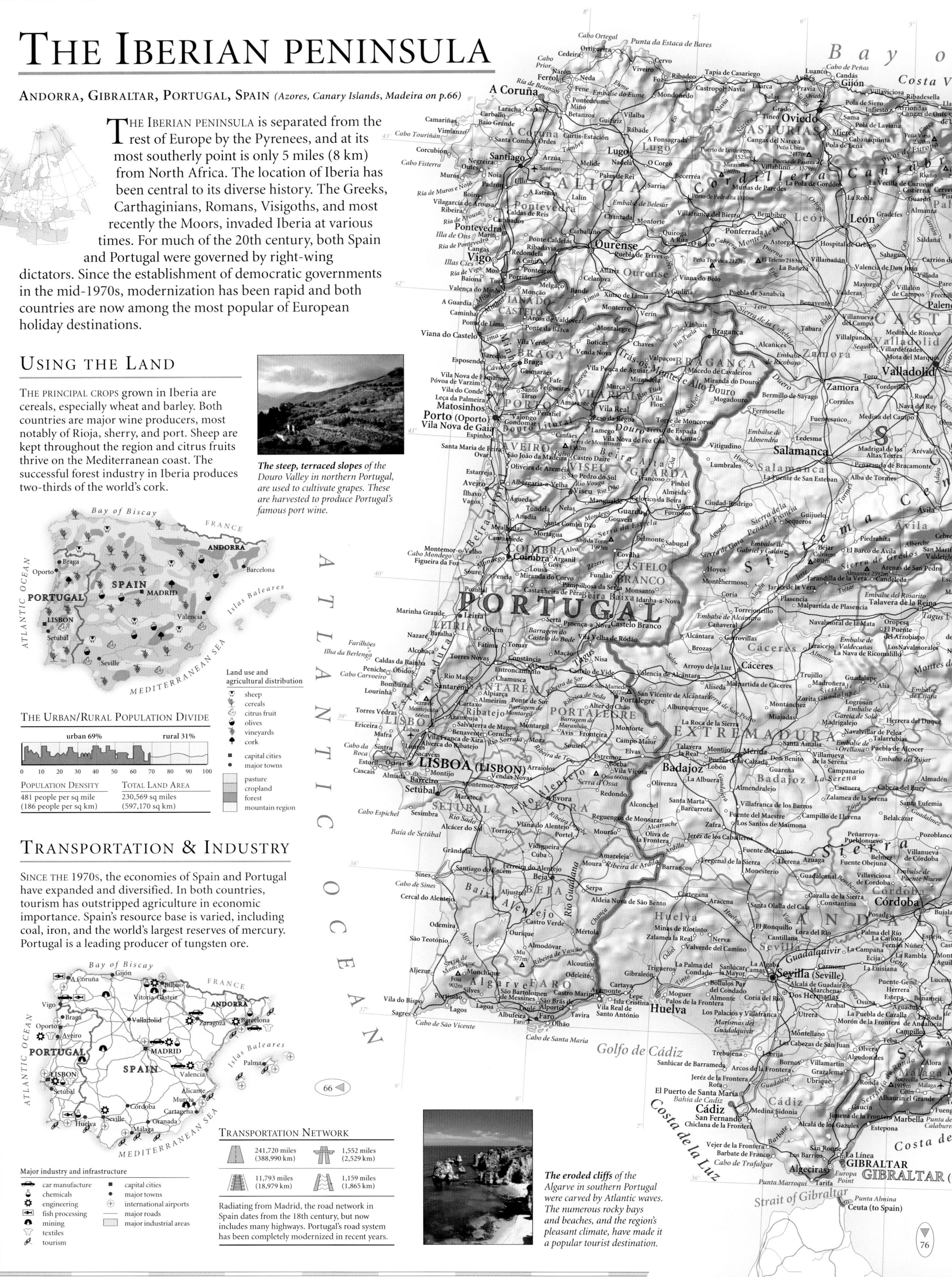
Bay of Biscay
Costa Verde
ATLANTIC OCEAN
Golfo de Cádiz
Costa de la Luz
Costa del Sol
Strait of Gibraltar
PORTUGAL
LISBOA (LISBON)
Porto (Oporto)
GIBRALTAR
MOROCCO
Ceuta (to Spain)
Cordillera Cantábrica
Sistema Central
A Coruña
Santiago
Vigo
Ourense
Lugo
Oviedo
Gijón
León
Valladolid
Salamanca
Zamora
Bragança
Braga
Coimbra
Setúbal
Faro
Huelva
Sevilla (Seville)
Cádiz
Córdoba
Badajoz
Cáceres
Mérida
Algeciras
Cabo de São Vicente
66
76

The Iberian peninsula

Andorra, Gibraltar, Portugal, Spain *(Azores, Canary Islands, Madeira on p.66)*

The Iberian peninsula is separated from the rest of Europe by the Pyrenees, and at its most southerly point is only 5 miles (8 km) from North Africa. The location of Iberia has been central to its diverse history. The Greeks, Carthaginians, Romans, Visigoths, and most recently the Moors, invaded Iberia at various times. For much of the 20th century, both Spain and Portugal were governed by right-wing dictators. Since the establishment of democratic governments in the mid-1970s, modernization has been rapid and both countries are now among the most popular of European holiday destinations.

Using the Land

The principal crops grown in Iberia are cereals, especially wheat and barley. Both countries are major wine producers, most notably of Rioja, sherry, and port. Sheep are kept throughout the region and citrus fruits thrive on the Mediterranean coast. The successful forest industry in Iberia produces two-thirds of the world's cork.

***The steep, terraced slopes** of the Douro Valley in northern Portugal, are used to cultivate grapes. These are harvested to produce Portugal's famous port wine.*

Bay of Biscay · FRANCE · ANDORRA · ATLANTIC OCEAN · Oporto · Braga · PORTUGAL · SPAIN · MADRID · Barcelona · Islas Baleares · LISBON · Setúbal · Valencia · Seville · MEDITERRANEAN SEA

Land use and agricultural distribution
- sheep
- cereals
- citrus fruit
- olives
- vineyards
- cork
- capital cities
- major towns
- pasture
- cropland
- forest
- mountain region

The Urban/Rural Population Divide

urban 69% · rural 31%

0 10 20 30 40 50 60 70 80 90 100

Population Density	Total Land Area
481 people per sq mile (186 people per sq km)	230,569 sq miles (597,170 sq km)

Transportation & Industry

Since the 1970s, the economies of Spain and Portugal have expanded and diversified. In both countries, tourism has outstripped agriculture in economic importance. Spain's resource base is varied, including coal, iron, and the world's largest reserves of mercury. Portugal is a leading producer of tungsten ore.

Bay of Biscay · Gijón · A Coruña · Bilbao · Vitoria-Gasteiz · FRANCE · ANDORRA · Vigo · Braga · Oporto · Aveiro · Valladolid · Zaragoza · Barcelona · PORTUGAL · MADRID · Islas Baleares · Palma · LISBON · SPAIN · Valencia · Setúbal · Alicante · Murcia · Córdoba · Cartagena · Seville · Granada · Huelva · Málaga · ATLANTIC OCEAN · MEDITERRANEAN SEA

Major industry and infrastructure
- car manufacture
- chemicals
- engineering
- fish processing
- mining
- textiles
- tourism
- capital cities
- major towns
- international airports
- major roads
- major industrial areas

Transportation Network

241,720 miles (388,990 km)	1,552 miles (2,529 km)
11,793 miles (18,979 km)	1,159 miles (1,865 km)

Radiating from Madrid, the road network in Spain dates from the 18th century, but now includes many highways. Portugal's road system has been completely modernized in recent years.

***The eroded cliffs** of the Algarve in southern Portugal were carved by Atlantic waves. The numerous rocky bays and beaches, and the region's pleasant climate, have made it a popular tourist destination.*

MAP KEY
POPULATION
1 million to 5 million
500,000 to 1 million
100,000 to 500,000
50,000 to 100,000
10,000 to 50,000
below 10,000
ELEVATION
3000m / 9843ft
2000m / 6562ft
1000m / 3281ft
500m / 1640ft
250m / 820ft
100m / 328ft
sea level
SCALE 1:2,750,000
(projection: Lambert Conformal Conic)
FRANCE
Pyrenees
ANDORRA
MEDITERRANEAN SEA
Golfo de Valencia
Islas Baleares (Balearic Islands)
Costa Brava
Costa Blanca
Costa del Sol
Mallorca (Majorca)
Menorca (Minorca)
Eivissa (Ibiza)
Formentera
Barcelona
Valencia
Zaragoza
Madrid
Cordillera Cantábrica
Douro/Duero River
Tagus River
Sierra Morena
Mountain front
Weathered material
Pediment

The climate in northwestern Spain is milder in both summer and winter than in the rest of the country, creating a verdant environment more commonly associated with northwestern Europe.

THE LANDSCAPE

A VAST PLATEAU, the Meseta dominates the center of the peninsula, enclosed by the Cordillera Cantábrica to the north and the Sierra Morena to the south. It is drained by three major rivers, the Douro/Duero, the Tagus, and the Guadalquivir. The peninsula experiences great variations in climate and rainfall, both regionally and locally.

The Pyrenees form Iberia's northeastern boundary, running for some 270 miles (440 km) and dividing it from the rest of Europe.

The Ebro River has formed the peninsula's largest delta. Recently, sediment flows have been seriously disturbed by nearby reservoirs.

On the northeastern coast, sea level changes are evident from wave-cut beaches which rise up to 200 ft (60 m) above the present sea level.

The Meseta averages 1,970 ft (600 m) in height and is now largely dry and treeless.

The Balearic Islands *(Islas Baleares)* are characterized by jagged limestones and plains.

***Pediments** are characteristic of semiarid lands across Iberia. A pediment is a flat, low-lying, eroded platform, cut into the bedrock. Weathered material is transported by streams and deposited in broad fan shapes on the pediment.*

The Guadalquivir River brings vital irrigation water to the plains, and like many of Iberia's rivers, it is prone to flooding.

The Sierra Nevada in southern Spain contain Iberia's highest peak, Mulhacén, which rises 11,418 ft (3,481 m).

***In the Sierra de los Filabres** deforestation and overgrazing, which cause soil erosion, have created semidesert badlands.*

The Italian peninsula

Italy, San Marino, Vatican City

The Italian peninsula is a land of great contrasts. Until unification in 1860, Italy was a collection of independent city states, whose competitiveness during the Renaissance resulted in the architectural and artistic magnificence of cities such as Rome, Florence, and Venice. The majority of Italy's population and economic activity is concentrated in the north, centered on the sophisticated industrial city of Milan. Southern Italy, called the *Mezzogiorno*, has a harsh and difficult terrain, and remains far less developed than the north. Attempts to attract industry and investment in the south are frequently deterred by the entrenched network of organized crime and corruption.

The Landscape

The mainly mountainous and hilly Italian peninsula took its present form following a collision between the African and Eurasian tectonic plates. The Alps in the northwest rise to a high point of 15,772 ft (4,807 m) at Mont Blanc *(Monte Bianco)* on the French border, while the Apennines *(Appennino)* form a rugged backbone that runs the entire length of the country.

***The island of Sardinia** is an ancient land mass, an uplifted section of very old igneous rocks. Its rugged mountainous regions provide pasture for sheep and goats, while its valleys support some agriculture.*

Costa Smeralda

Mont Blanc *(Monte Bianco)*

***The Dolomites** (Alpi Dolomitiche) are formed of thick limestones, overlying weaker marine strata. They have distinctive serrated peaks and many massive landslides occur.*

The Po Valley once formed part of the Adriatic Sea. Sediments of gravel, sand, and clay washed down from the Alps gradually filled it to form a broad, cultivable plain.

The distinctive square shape of the Gulf of Taranto *(Golfo di Taranto)* was defined by numerous block faults. Earthquakes are common in this region.

The Apennines *(Appennino)* are the source of most of Italy's rivers. They run 823 miles (1,324 km) down the length of the peninsula.

Sardinia is the second largest island in the Mediterranean Sea. The highest point is Punta La Marmora at 6,017 ft (1,834 m).

The Pontine Marshes *(Agro Pontino)* are bounded by low sandhills that prevent natural drainage.

Vesuvius *(Vesuvio)*

Sicily is the largest island in the Mediterranean at 9,926 sq miles (25,708 sq km).

The southeastern tip of Sicily lies 95 miles (152 km) from the northern African mainland and is part of the same geological region.

The Strait of Messina *(Stretto di Messina)* is between 2 and 12 miles (3–19 km) wide. It is a rich fishing ground.

Vesuvius *(Vesuvio)*

Monte Somma
Old crater
Present-day crater has developed within the old crater of Monte Somma
Old crater

***There have been four volcanoes** on the site of Vesuvius since volcanic activity began here more than 10,000 years ago.*

Using the Land

Italy produces 95% of its own food. The best farming land is in the Po Valley in northern Italy, where soft wheat and rice are grown. Irrigation is essential to agriculture in much of the south. Italy is a major producer and exporter of citrus fruits, olives, tomatoes, and wine.

The Urban/Rural Population Divide

urban 69%
rural 31%
0 10 20 30 40 50 60 70 80 90 100

Population Density	Total Land Area
497 people per sq mile (196 people per sq km)	116,320 sq miles (301,270 sq km)

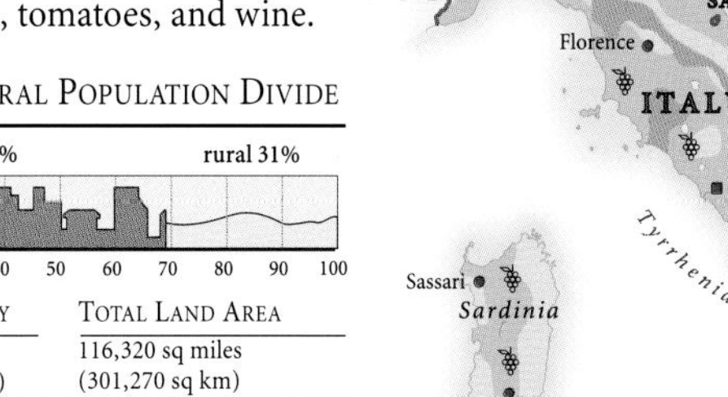
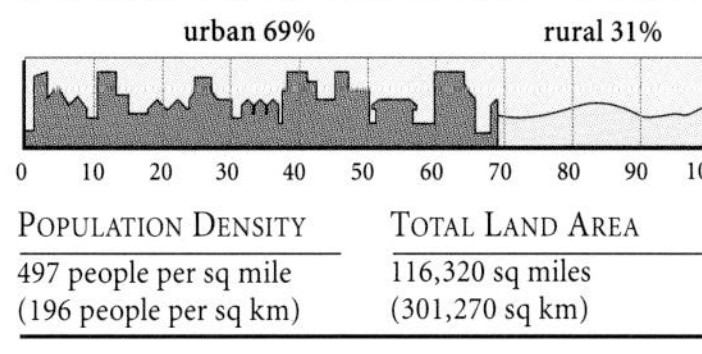
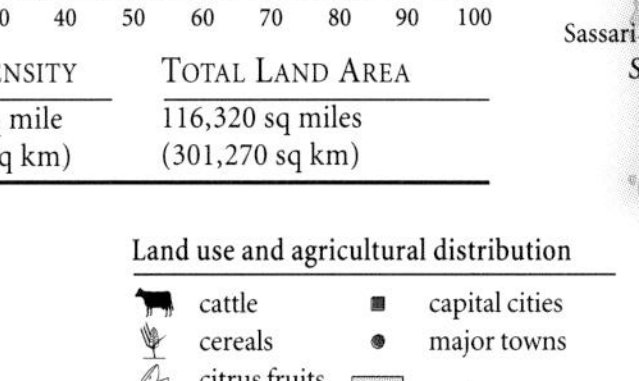
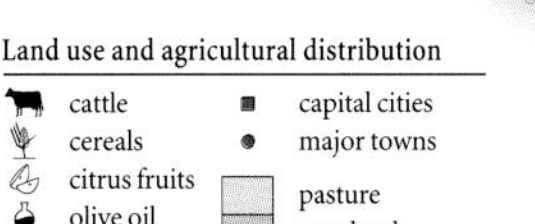
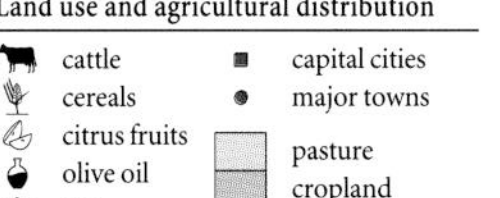

SWITZERLAND
AUSTRIA
SLOVENIA
CROATIA
FRANCE
Milan
Turin
Genoa
Bologna
SAN MARINO
Florence
ITALY
ROME
Naples
Bari
Adriatic Sea
Tyrrhenian Sea
Ionian Sea
Sardinia
Sassari
Cagliari
Palermo
Sicily
Catania
MEDITERRANEAN SEA

Land use and agricultural distribution

- cattle
- cereals
- citrus fruits
- olive oil
- rice
- vineyards
- capital cities
- major towns
- pasture
- cropland
- forest
- mountain region

SWITZERLAND
AUSTRIA
SLOVENIA
CROATIA
FRANCE
MONACO
Lepontine Alps
Alpi Dolomitiche
TRENTINO-ALTO ADIGE
LOMBARDIA
VALLE D'AOSTA
PIEMONTE
LIGURIA
EMILIA-ROMAGNA
VENETO
FRIULI-VENEZIA GIULIA
TOSCANA
MARCHE
SAN MARINO
Po Valley
Gulf of Venice
Golfo di Genova
Ligurian Sea
Milano (Milan)
Torino (Turin)
Genova (Genoa)
Venezia (Venice)
Bologna
Firenze (Florence)
Verona
Trento
Bolzano
Trieste
Ancona
Perugia
Rimini
Parma
Modena
Padova (Padua)
Brescia
Bergamo
Monte Bianco 4807m
Monte Cervino 4478m
Gran Paradiso 4061m

Scale 1:2,500,000
(projection: Lambert Conformal Conic)

110
110
110
114
122
104

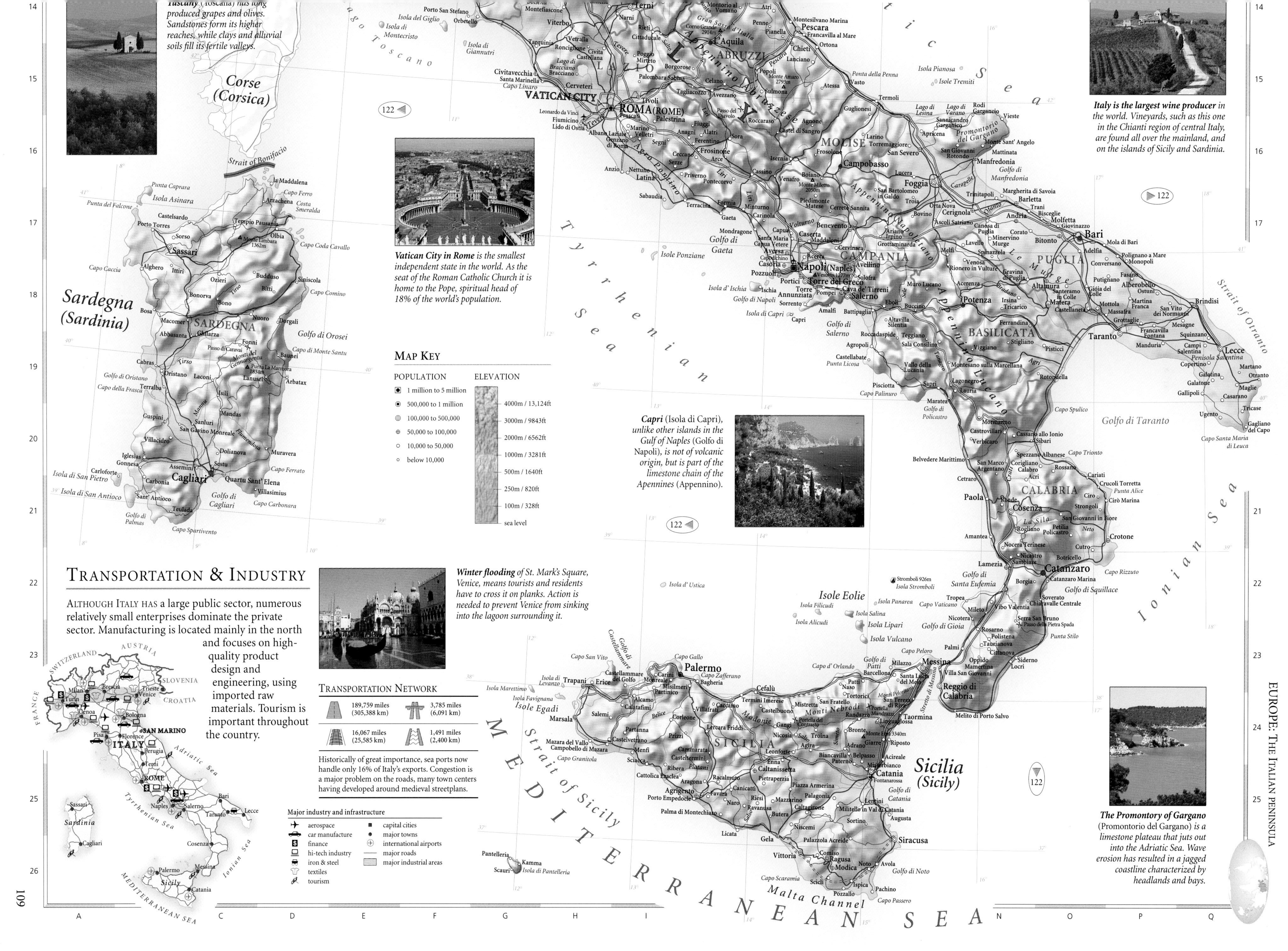
Corse (Corsica)
Strait of Bonifacio
Sardegna (Sardinia)
SARDEGNA
Sassari
Cagliari
Golfo di Orosei
Golfo di Cagliari
Isola di San Pietro
Isola di San Antioco
Tyrrhenian Sea
Mar Ligure
LAZIO
ABRUZZI
MOLISE
CAMPANIA
PUGLIA
BASILICATA
CALABRIA
SICILIA
VATICAN CITY
ROMA (ROME)
Napoli (Naples)
Bari
Taranto
Brindisi
Lecce
Foggia
Pescara
Campobasso
Potenza
Salerno
Catanzaro
Reggio di Calabria
Palermo
Messina
Catania
Siracusa
Sicilia (Sicily)
Isole Eolie
Isole Egadi
Golfo di Taranto
Strait of Otranto
Ionian Sea
Strait of Sicily
Malta Channel
MEDITERRANEAN SEA
Appennino Abruzzese
Appennino Napoletano
Appennino Lucano
Promontorio del Gargano
Isola d' Ustica
Pantelleria
122
A C D E F G H I N O P Q
14 15 16 17 18 19 20 21 22 23 24 25 26

Tuscany (Toscana) has long produced grapes and olives. Sandstones form its higher reaches, while clays and alluvial soils fill its fertile valleys.

Italy is the largest wine producer in the world. Vineyards, such as this one in the Chianti region of central Italy, are found all over the mainland, and on the islands of Sicily and Sardinia.

Vatican City in Rome is the smallest independent state in the world. As the seat of the Roman Catholic Church it is home to the Pope, spiritual head of 18% of the world's population.

Capri (Isola di Capri), unlike other islands in the Gulf of Naples (Golfo di Napoli), is not of volcanic origin, but is part of the limestone chain of the Apennines (Appennino).

The Promontory of Gargano (Promontorio del Gargano) is a limestone plateau that juts out into the Adriatic Sea. Wave erosion has resulted in a jagged coastline characterized by headlands and bays.

Map Key

POPULATION	ELEVATION
1 million to 5 million	4000m / 13,124ft
500,000 to 1 million	3000m / 9843ft
100,000 to 500,000	2000m / 6562ft
50,000 to 100,000	1000m / 3281ft
10,000 to 50,000	500m / 1640ft
below 10,000	250m / 820ft
	100m / 328ft
	sea level

Transportation & Industry

Although Italy has a large public sector, numerous relatively small enterprises dominate the private sector. Manufacturing is located mainly in the north and focuses on high-quality product design and engineering, using imported raw materials. Tourism is important throughout the country.

Winter flooding of St. Mark's Square, Venice, means tourists and residents have to cross it on planks. Action is needed to prevent Venice from sinking into the lagoon surrounding it.

Transportation Network

189,759 miles (305,388 km)	3,785 miles (6,091 km)
16,067 miles (25,585 km)	1,491 miles (2,400 km)

Historically of great importance, sea ports now handle only 16% of Italy's exports. Congestion is a major problem on the roads, many town centers having developed around medieval streetplans.

Major industry and infrastructure

- aerospace
- car manufacture
- finance
- hi-tech industry
- iron & steel
- textiles
- tourism
- capital cities
- major towns
- international airports
- major roads
- major industrial areas

THE ALPINE STATES

AUSTRIA, LIECHTENSTEIN, SLOVENIA, SWITZERLAND

THE ALPINE COUNTRIES of Austria, Switzerland, Liechtenstein, and Slovenia form a narrow strip across western Europe's geographical core, lying on the main north–south trading routes across the Alps. Switzerland, politically neutral since 1815, is an important international meeting place and houses one of the headquarters of the United Nations, although not a member itself. Once at the heart of the great Habsburg Empire, Austria has been a fully independent nation since 1955, and maintains a deserved reputation as an international center of culture. Slovenia declared independence from the former Yugoslavia in 1991 and despite initial economic hardship, is now starting to achieve the prosperity enjoyed by its Alpine neighbors.

USING THE LAND

THE ALPINE REGION'S mountainous terrain discourages cultivation over much of the land area. The primary agricultural activity is raising dairy and beef cattle on the pastureland of the lower mountain slopes. Austria is self-supporting in grains, and crops such as wheat, barley, and grapes are grown in the eastern Austrian lowlands. Woodlands are more prevalent in the eastern Alps; both Austria and Slovenia have large tracts of forest.

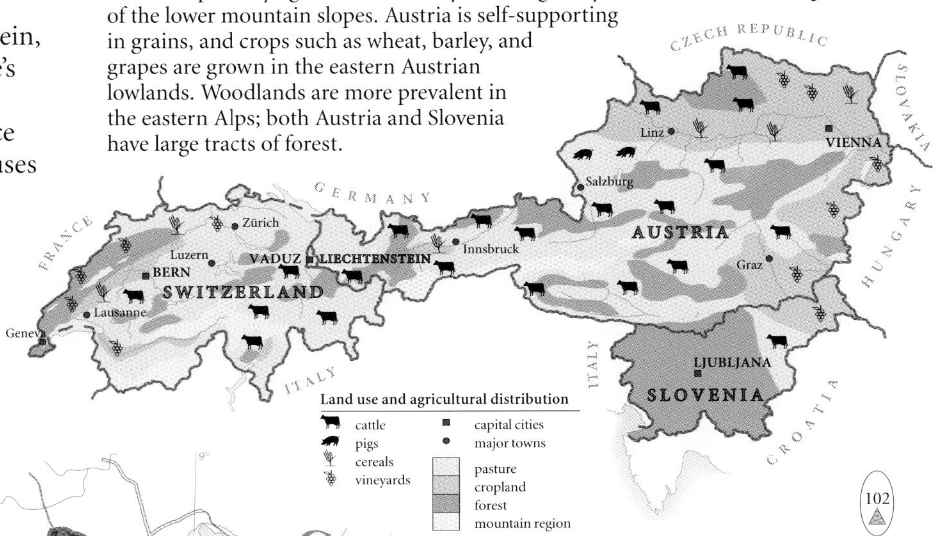

Land use and agricultural distribution

cattle
pigs
cereals
vineyards
capital cities
major towns
pasture
cropland
forest
mountain region

The Matterhorn, on the Swiss–Italian border, is one of the highest mountains in the Alps, at 14,692 ft (4,478 m). The term "horn" refers to its distinctive peak, formed by three glaciers eroding hollows, known as cirques, in each of its sides.

102

104

108

104

THE LANDSCAPE

THE ALPS OCCUPY THREE-FIFTHS OF SWITZERLAND, most of southern Austria, and the northwest of Slovenia. They were formed by the collision of the African and Eurasian tectonic plates, which began 65 million years ago. Their complex geology is reflected in the differing heights and rock types of the various ranges. The Rhine flows along Liechtenstein's border with Switzerland, creating a broad floodplain in the north and west of Liechtenstein. In the far northeast and east are a number of lowland regions, including the Vienna Basin, Burgenland, and the plain of the Danube. Slovenia's major rivers flow across the lower eastern regions; in the west, the rivers flow underground through the limestone Karst region.

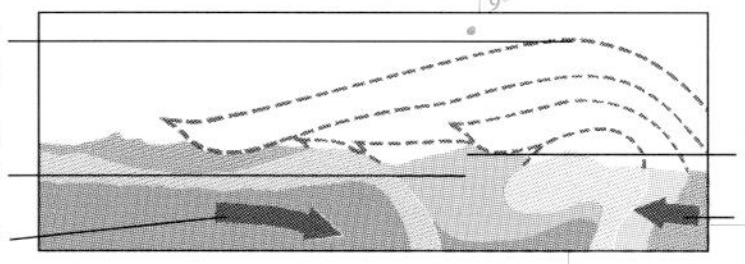

Original height after uplift and folding
Folded strata are overturned, creating a *nappe*
Eurasian Plate
Present-day height of Alps
African Plate

***The convergence of the African and Eurasian plates** compressed and folded huge masses of rock strata. As the plates continued to move together, the folded strata were overturned, creating complex nappes. Much of the rock strata has since been eroded, resulting in the current topography of the Alps.*

***Constricted as it cuts** through ridges in the Alps, the Danube meanders across the lowlands, where uplift combined with river erosion has deepened meanders.*

The Vienna Basin lies mainly below 390 ft (120 m). It gradually subsided and filled with sediment as the Alps were uplifted.

Neusiedler See straddles the border of Austria and Hungary; the area around it provides some of the best wine-growing land in Austria.

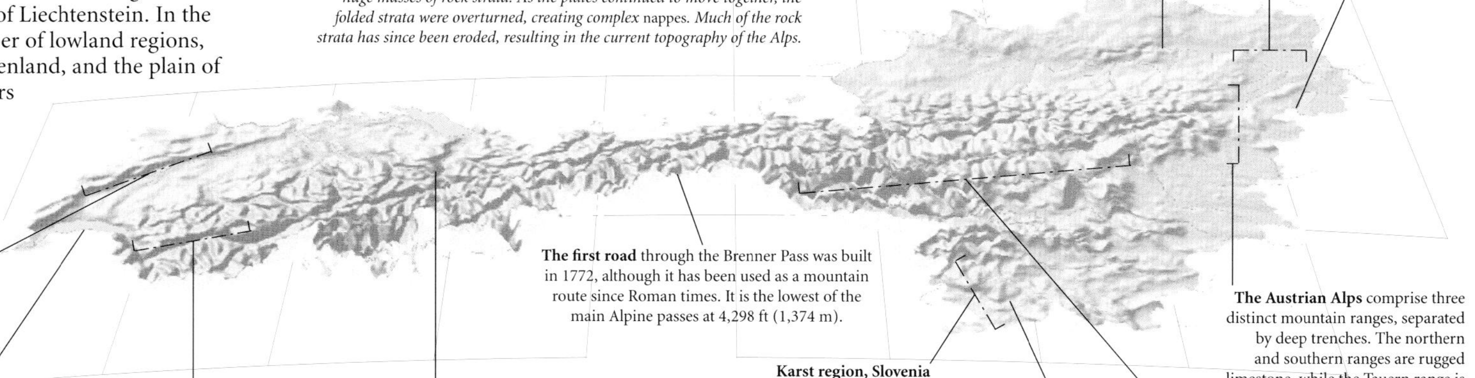

The mountains of the Jura form a natural border between Switzerland and France. Their marine limestones date from more than 200 million years ago. When the Alps were formed, the Jura were folded into a series of parallel ridges and troughs.

The first road through the Brenner Pass was built in 1772, although it has been used as a mountain route since Roman times. It is the lowest of the main Alpine passes at 4,298 ft (1,374 m).

The Austrian Alps comprise three distinct mountain ranges, separated by deep trenches. The northern and southern ranges are rugged limestone, while the Tauern range is made of crystalline rocks.

Tectonic activity has resulted in dramatic changes in land height over very short distances. Lake Geneva, lying at 1,221 ft (372 m) is only 43 miles (70 km) away from the 15,772-ft (4,807-m) peak of Mont Blanc, on the France–Italy border.

The Bernese Alps (*Berner Alpen*) contain the Aletsch, which at 15 miles (24 km)is the longest Alpine glacier.

The Rhine, like other major Alpine rivers, follows a broad, flat trough between the mountains. Along part of its course, the Rhine forms the boundary between Switzerland and Liechtenstein.

Karst region, Slovenia

***The deep, blue lakes** of the Karst region of Slovenia are part of a drainage network that runs largely underground through this limestone area.*

The limestone cave system at Postojna extends for more than 10 miles (16 km) and includes caverns reaching 125 ft (40 m) in height and width.

The Tauern range in the central Austrian Alps contains the highest mountain in Austria, the towering Grossglockner, rising 12,461 ft (3,798 m).

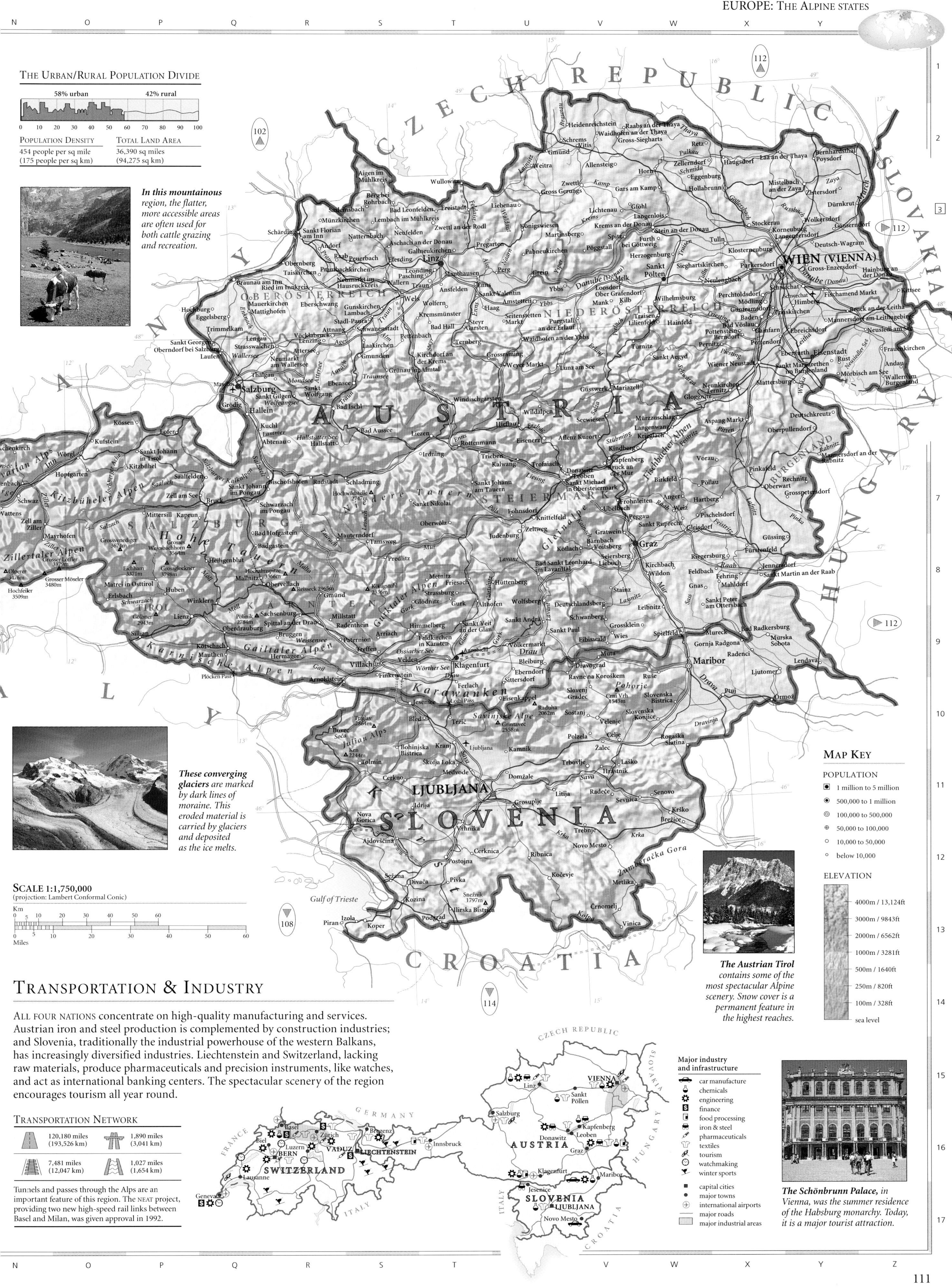
N O P Q R S T U V W X Y
THE URBAN/RURAL POPULATION DIVIDE
58% urban
42% rural
0 10 20 30 40 50 60 70 80 90 100
POPULATION DENSITY
454 people per sq mile
(175 people per sq km)
TOTAL LAND AREA
36,390 sq miles
(94,275 sq km)
CZECH REPUBLIC
SLOVAKIA
HUNGARY
AUSTRIA
SLOVENIA
CROATIA
ITALY
GERMANY
WIEN (VIENNA)
LJUBLJANA
Salzburg
Linz
Graz
Innsbruck
Klagenfurt
Maribor
Gulf of Trieste
SCALE 1:1,750,000
(projection: Lambert Conformal Conic)
MAP KEY
POPULATION
1 million to 5 million
500,000 to 1 million
100,000 to 500,000
50,000 to 100,000
10,000 to 50,000
below 10,000
ELEVATION
4000m / 13,124ft
3000m / 9843ft
2000m / 6562ft
1000m / 3281ft
500m / 1640ft
250m / 820ft
100m / 328ft
sea level
TRANSPORTATION NETWORK
120,180 miles (193,526 km)
1,890 miles (3,041 km)
7,481 miles (12,047 km)
1,027 miles (1,654 km)
Major industry and infrastructure
car manufacture
chemicals
engineering
finance
food processing
iron & steel
pharmaceuticals
textiles
tourism
watchmaking
winter sports
capital cities
major towns
international airports
major roads
major industrial areas
SWITZERLAND
LIECHTENSTEIN
VADUZ
BERN
111

In this mountainous region, the flatter, more accessible areas are often used for both cattle grazing and recreation.

These converging glaciers are marked by dark lines of moraine. This eroded material is carried by glaciers and deposited as the ice melts.

The Austrian Tirol contains some of the most spectacular Alpine scenery. Snow cover is a permanent feature in the highest reaches.

TRANSPORTATION & INDUSTRY

ALL FOUR NATIONS concentrate on high-quality manufacturing and services. Austrian iron and steel production is complemented by construction industries; and Slovenia, traditionally the industrial powerhouse of the western Balkans, has increasingly diversified industries. Liechtenstein and Switzerland, lacking raw materials, produce pharmaceuticals and precision instruments, like watches, and act as international banking centers. The spectacular scenery of the region encourages tourism all year round.

Tunnels and passes through the Alps are an important feature of this region. The NEAT project, providing two new high-speed rail links between Basel and Milan, was given approval in 1992.

The Schönbrunn Palace, in Vienna, was the summer residence of the Habsburg monarchy. Today, it is a major tourist attraction.

Central Europe

Czech Republic, Hungary, Poland, Slovakia

When Slovakia and the Czech Republic became separate countries in 1993, they joined Hungary and Poland in a new role as independent nation states, following centuries of shifting boundaries and imperial strife. This turbulent history bequeathed the region a rich cultural heritage, shared through the works of its many great writers and composers, and celebrated in the vibrant historic capitals of Prague, Budapest, and Warsaw. Having shaken off Soviet domination in 1989, these states are facing the challenge of winning commercial investment to modernize outmoded industry, while bearing the severe environmental impact from forty years of large-scale industrialization.

The Landscape

The forested Carpathian Mountains, uplifted with the Alps, lie southeast of the older Bohemian massif, which contains the Sudeten and Krušné Hory *(Erzgebirge)* ranges. They divide the fertile plains of the Danube to the south and the Vistula *(Wisła)*, which flows north across vast expanses of glacial deposits into the Baltic Sea.

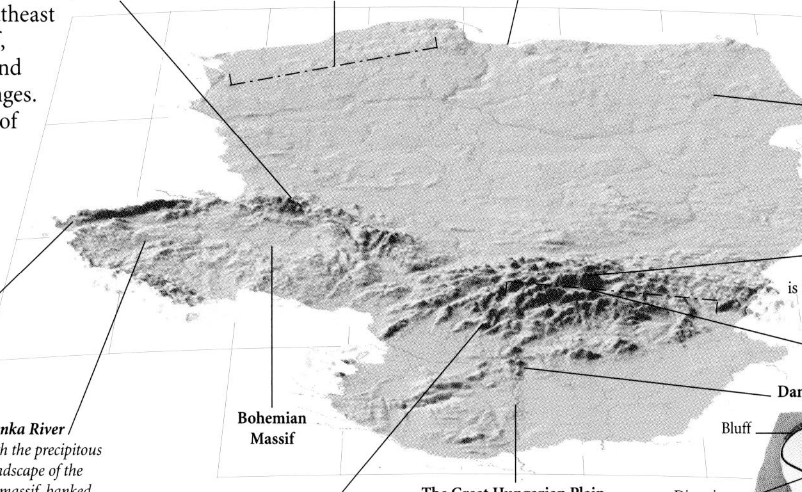

Hot mineral springs occur where geothermally heated water wells up through faults and fractures in the rocks of the Sudeten Mountains.

Pomerania is a sandy coastal region of glacially formed lakes stretching west from the Vistula *(Wisła)*.

Longshore currents moving east along the Baltic coast have built a 40-mile (65-km) spit composed of material from the Vistula *(Wisła)* River.

The Biebrza River *has left meanders and oxbow lakes as it flows across low-lying ground.*

Gerlachovský Štít, in the Tatra Mountains, is Slovakia's highest mountain, at 8,711ft (2,655 m).

Carpathian Mountains

Danube River

Krušné Hory *(Erzgebirge)*

The Berounka River *cuts through the precipitous wooded landscape of the Bohemian massif, banked by a broad floodplain.*

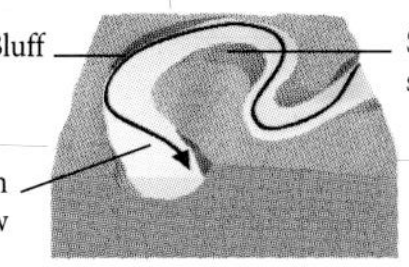

Bohemian Massif

The Slovak Ore Mountains *(Slovenské Rudohorie)* are noted for their mineral resources, including high-grade iron ore.

The Great Hungarian Plain formed by the floodplain of the Danube is a mixture of steppe and cultivated land, covering nearly half of Hungary's total area.

Bluff — Slip-off slope — Direction of flow

Meanders *form as rivers flow across plains at a low gradient. A steep cliff, or bluff, forms on the outside curve, and a gentler slip-off slope on the inside bend.*

Transportation & Industry

Heavy industry has dominated postwar life in Central Europe. Poland has large coal reserves, having inherited the Silesian coalfield from Germany after the Second World War, allowing the export of large quantities of coal, along with other minerals. Hungary specializes in consumer goods and services, while Slovakia's industrial base is still relatively small. The Czech Republic's traditional glassworks and breweries bring some stability to its precarious Soviet-built manufacturing sector.

Major industry and infrastructure

- car manufacture
- chemicals
- engineering
- food processing
- mining
- shipbuilding
- tourism
- capital cities
- major towns
- international airports
- major roads
- major industrial areas

Transportation Network

338,659 miles (546,224 km)		722 miles (1,165 km)	
28,970 miles (46,727 km)		3,822 miles (6,165 km)	

The huge growth of tourism and business has prompted major investment in the transportation infrastructure, with new roadbuilding planned within and between the main cities of the region.

Budapest, *the capital of Hungary, straddles the Danube. It comprises the historic towns of Buda, on the west bank, and Pest, which contains the Parliament Building, seen here on the far bank.*

▶ 120
▶ 120

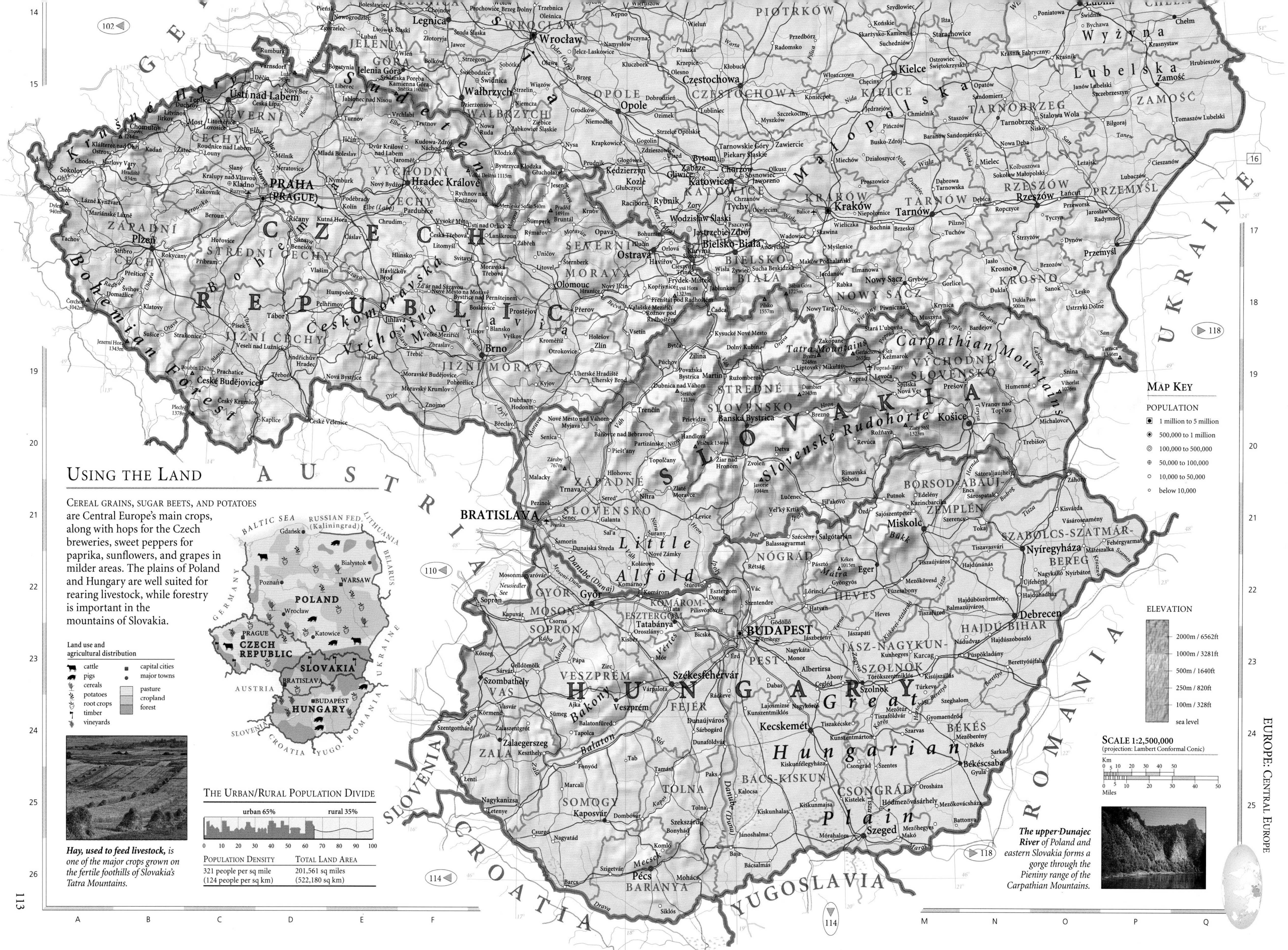
CZECH REPUBLIC
SLOVAKIA
HUNGARY
POLAND
GERMANY
AUSTRIA
SLOVENIA
CROATIA
YUGOSLAVIA
ROMANIA
UKRAINE
PRAHA (PRAGUE)
BRATISLAVA
BUDAPEST
Map Key
POPULATION
1 million to 5 million
500,000 to 1 million
100,000 to 500,000
50,000 to 100,000
10,000 to 50,000
below 10,000
ELEVATION
2000m / 6562ft
1000m / 3281ft
500m / 1640ft
250m / 820ft
100m / 328ft
sea level
SCALE 1:2,500,000
(projection: Lambert Conformal Conic)

Using the Land

Cereal grains, sugar beets, and potatoes are Central Europe's main crops, along with hops for the Czech breweries, sweet peppers for paprika, sunflowers, and grapes in milder areas. The plains of Poland and Hungary are well suited for rearing livestock, while forestry is important in the mountains of Slovakia.

Land use and agricultural distribution: cattle, pigs, cereals, potatoes, root crops, timber, vineyards; capital cities, major towns; pasture, cropland, forest

***Hay, used to feed livestock,** is one of the major crops grown on the fertile foothills of Slovakia's Tatra Mountains.*

The Urban/Rural Population Divide

urban 65% — rural 35%

Population Density	Total Land Area
321 people per sq mile (124 people per sq km)	201,561 sq miles (522,180 sq km)

***The upper Dunajec River** of Poland and eastern Slovakia forms a gorge through the Pieniny range of the Carpathian Mountains.*

The Western Balkans

Albania, Bosnia & Herzegovina, Croatia, Macedonia, Yugoslavia

For 46 years the federation of Yugoslavia held together the most diverse ethnic region in Europe, along the picturesque mountain hinterland of the Dalmatian coast. Economic collapse resulted in internal tensions. The Serbian government regained central control over the previously autonomous regions of Kosovo and Vojvodina. In June 1991 Croatia and Slovenia (page 110) declared independence and Yugoslavia fragmented into five new nations. Bosnia and Herzegovina was devastated as Serbs and Croats struggled to establish ethnically exclusive territories, while the Bosnian government sought to preserve the country's multiethnic character. Albania is slowly emerging from the long isolation imposed by the communist Hoxha regime.

***Hot, dry summers** and mild winters offer excellent conditions for viticulture in Montenegro. The precipitous Dinaric Alps have kept this region relatively isolated for centuries.*

SCALE 1:2,500,000
(projection: Lambert Conformal Conic)

The Landscape

The Tisza, Sava, and Drava Rivers drain the broad northern lowland, meeting the Danube after it crosses the Hungarian border. In the west, the Dinaric Alps divide the Adriatic Sea from the interior. Mainland valleys and elongated islands run parallel to the steep Dalmatian *(Dalmacija)* coastline, following alternating bands of resistant limestone.

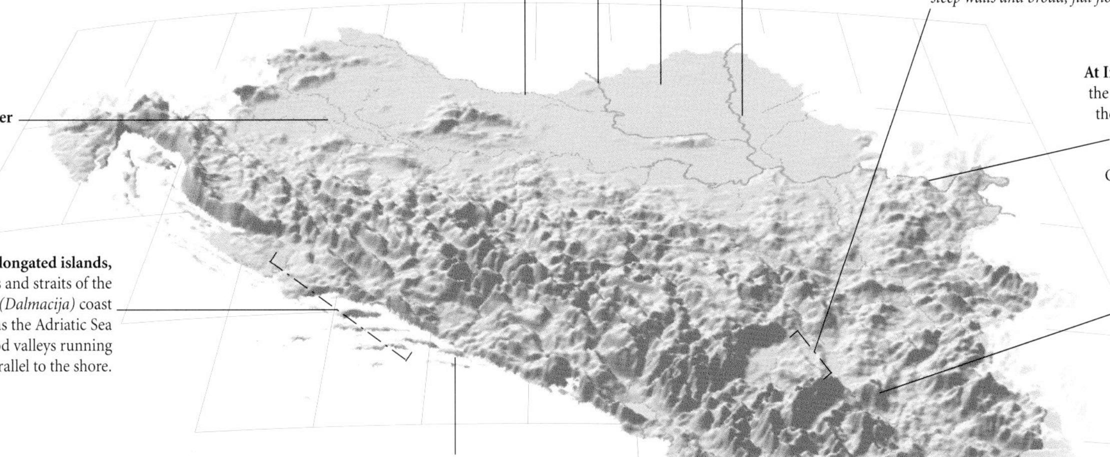

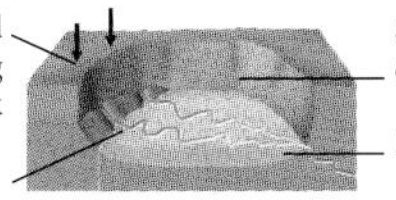

At least 70% of all fresh water in the Western Balkans drains into the Black Sea, mostly via the Danube *(Dunav)*.

The river floodplains of the Pannonian Basin are flanked by terraces of gravel and wind-blown glacial deposits, known as loess.

Drava River

Tisza River

Sava River

***Poljes* in the Kosovo region**

Underground drainage along joints in the rock

Spring at foot of cliff

Sheer limestone walls enclose all sides

Flat polje floor

***Rain and underground water** dissolve limestone along massive vertical joints (cracks). This creates poljes: depressions several miles across with steep walls and broad, flat floors.*

At Iron Gate *(Đerdap)*, on the border with Romania, the Danube narrows and cuts through foothills of the Balkan and Carpathian mountains, forming the deepest gorge in Europe.

The elongated islands, promontories and straits of the Dalmatian *(Dalmacija)* coast were formed as the Adriatic Sea rose to flood valleys running parallel to the shore.

A major earthquake at Skopje, Macedonia, in 1963 killed 1,000 people. The whole region lies on an active crustal plate margin.

Dalmatian *(Dalmacija)* coast

***Limestone cliffs** along the Dalmatian* (Dalmacija) *shoreline are heavily eroded, as saltwater dissolves the rock along existing horizontal cracks, or joints. This tends to form a platform of rock at the foot of the cliff.*

A series of river valleys breaking through the Dinaric Alps from the lowlands of western Albania give access to the interior.

Lake Ohrid

***Lake Ohrid** borders Albania and Macedonia. Ohrid is the deepest lake in the Western Balkans, reaching depths of 938 ft (286 m).*

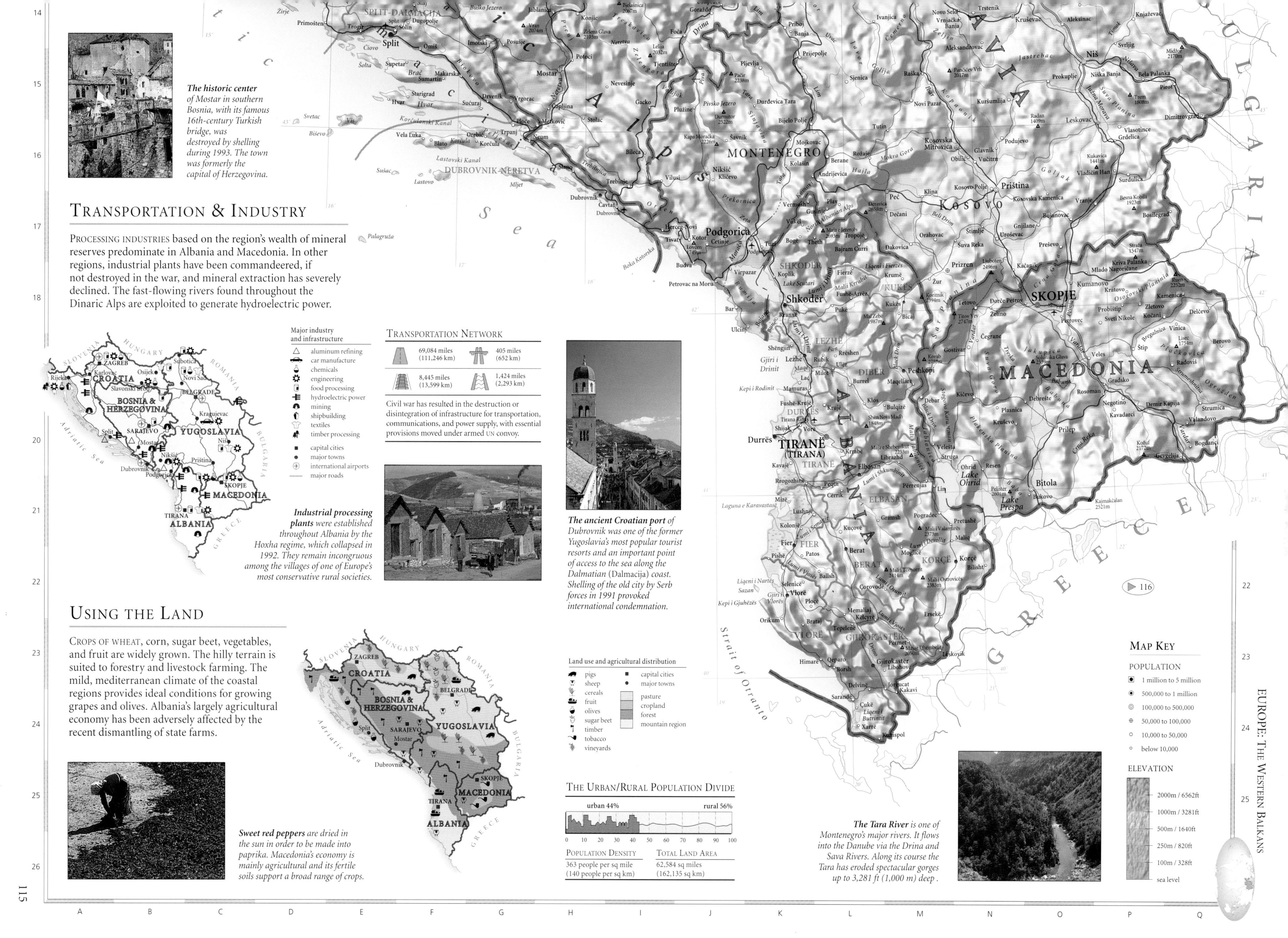
BULGARIA
YUGOSLAVIA
MONTENEGRO
KOSOVO
MACEDONIA
ALBANIA
GREECE
Dinaric Alps
Adriatic Sea
Strait of Otranto
SKOPJE
TIRANË (TIRANA)
Podgorica
Priština
Shkodër
Durrës
Bitola
Lake Ohrid
Lake Prespa
DUBROVNIK-NERETVA
SPLIT-DALMACIJA
▶ 116

MAP KEY
POPULATION
1 million to 5 million
500,000 to 1 million
100,000 to 500,000
50,000 to 100,000
10,000 to 50,000
below 10,000
ELEVATION
2000m / 6562ft
1000m / 3281ft
500m / 1640ft
250m / 820ft
100m / 328ft
sea level

The historic center of Mostar in southern Bosnia, with its famous 16th-century Turkish bridge, was destroyed by shelling during 1993. The town was formerly the capital of Herzegovina.

Transportation & Industry

Processing industries based on the region's wealth of mineral reserves predominate in Albania and Macedonia. In other regions, industrial plants have been commandeered, if not destroyed in the war, and mineral extraction has severely declined. The fast-flowing rivers found throughout the Dinaric Alps are exploited to generate hydroelectric power.

Major industry and infrastructure
aluminum refining
car manufacture
chemicals
engineering
food processing
hydroelectric power
mining
shipbuilding
textiles
timber processing
capital cities
major towns
international airports
major roads

Transportation Network

69,084 miles (111,246 km)	405 miles (652 km)
8,445 miles (13,599 km)	1,424 miles (2,293 km)

Civil war has resulted in the destruction or disintegration of infrastructure for transportation, communications, and power supply, with essential provisions moved under armed UN convoy.

Industrial processing plants *were established throughout Albania by the Hoxha regime, which collapsed in 1992. They remain incongruous among the villages of one of Europe's most conservative rural societies.*

The ancient Croatian port *of Dubrovnik was one of the former Yugoslavia's most popular tourist resorts and an important point of access to the sea along the Dalmatian (Dalmacija) coast. Shelling of the old city by Serb forces in 1991 provoked international condemnation.*

Using the Land

Crops of wheat, corn, sugar beet, vegetables, and fruit are widely grown. The hilly terrain is suited to forestry and livestock farming. The mild, mediterranean climate of the coastal regions provides ideal conditions for growing grapes and olives. Albania's largely agricultural economy has been adversely affected by the recent dismantling of state farms.

Land use and agricultural distribution
pigs
sheep
cereals
fruit
olives
sugar beet
timber
tobacco
vineyards
capital cities
major towns
pasture
cropland
forest
mountain region

The Urban/Rural Population Divide

urban 44% | rural 56%

Population Density	Total Land Area
363 people per sq mile (140 people per sq km)	62,584 sq miles (162,135 sq km)

Sweet red peppers *are dried in the sun in order to be made into paprika. Macedonia's economy is mainly agricultural and its fertile soils support a broad range of crops.*

The Tara River *is one of Montenegro's major rivers. It flows into the Danube via the Drina and Sava Rivers. Along its course the Tara has eroded spectacular gorges up to 3,281 ft (1,000 m) deep.*

Bulgaria & Greece

Including **European Turkey**

Greece is renowned as the original hearth of Western civilization. Its rugged terrain and numerous islands have profoundly affected its development, creating a strong agricultural and maritime tradition. In the past 50 years, this formerly rural society has rapidly urbanized, with more than half of the population now living in the capital, Athens, and in the northern city of Salonica. Bulgaria, dominated for centuries by the Ottoman Turks, became part of the eastern bloc after the Second World War, only slowly emerging from Soviet influence in 1989. Moves toward democracy have led to some political instability and Bulgaria has been slow to align its economy with the rest of Europe.

Transportation & Industry

Soviet investment introduced heavy industry into Bulgaria and the processing of agricultural produce, such as tobacco, is important throughout the country. Both countries have substantial shipyards and Greece has one of the world's largest merchant fleets. Many small craft workshops, producing textiles and processed foods, are clustered around Greek cities. The service and construction sectors have profited from the successful tourist industry.

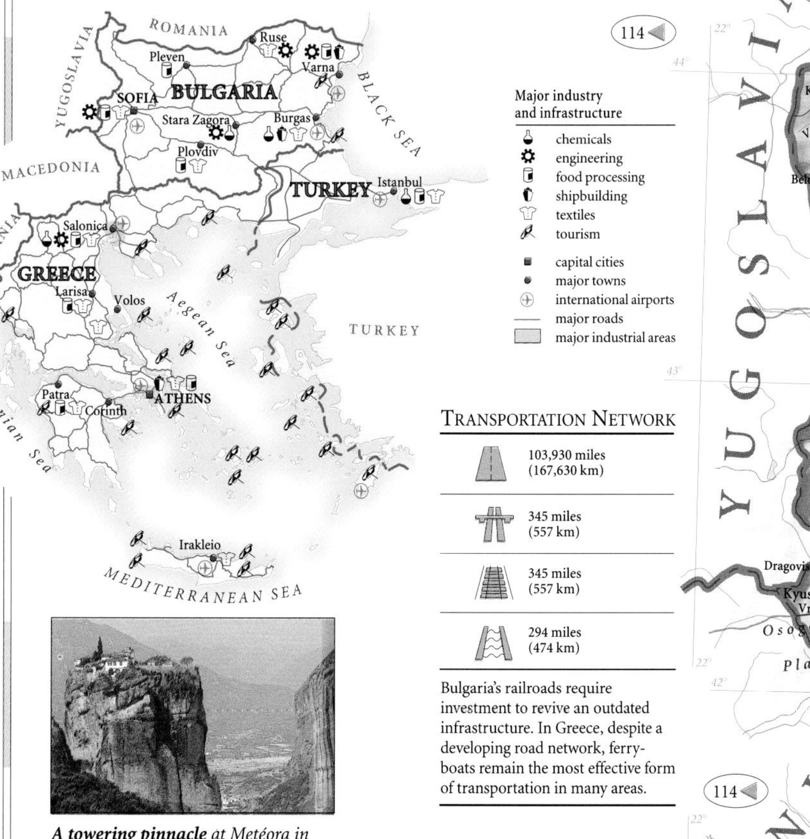
ROMANIA
YUGOSLAVIA
BULGARIA
SOFIA
Pleven
Ruse
Varna
Stara Zagora
Burgas
Plovdiv
BLACK SEA
TURKEY
Istanbul
MACEDONIA
ALBANIA
Salonica
GREECE
Larisa
Volos
Aegean Sea
ATHENS
Patra
Corinth
Ionian Sea
Irakleio
MEDITERRANEAN SEA
Major industry and infrastructure
chemicals
engineering
food processing
shipbuilding
textiles
tourism
capital cities
major towns
international airports
major roads
major industrial areas

Transportation Network

103,930 miles (167,630 km)

345 miles (557 km)

345 miles (557 km)

294 miles (474 km)

Bulgaria's railroads require investment to revive an outdated infrastructure. In Greece, despite a developing road network, ferry-boats remain the most effective form of transportation in many areas.

***A towering pinnacle** at Metéora in central Greece is home to the monastery of Roussanou. The 24 rock towers that dominate the plain of Thessaly (Thessalía) are remnants of an old plateau. Long-term weathering along fissures in the rock has worn away the rest of the plateau.*

The Landscape

Bulgaria's Balkan Mountains divide the Danubian Plain *(Dunavska Ravnina)* and Maritsa Basin, meeting the Black Sea in the east along sandy beaches. The steep Rhodope Mountains form a natural barrier with Greece, while the younger Pindus form a rugged central spine. This descends into the Aegean Sea to give a vast archipelago of more than 2,000 islands, the largest of which is Crete.

The Danube, Europe's second longest river, forms most of Bulgaria's northern border. The Danubian Plain *(Dunavska Ravnina)*, extending from the southern bank, is extremely fertile.

Balkan Mountains

Maritsa Basin

Rhodope Mountains

Pindus Mountains

Corinth Canal *(Doíryga Korinthou)*

Kýthira

Crete

Kárpathos

Rhodes

***The Arda River** cuts through the Rhodope Mountains in rugged, rocky gorges.*

Mount Olympus is the mythical home of the Greek Gods and, at 9,570 ft (2,917 m), the highest mountain in Greece.

The islands of Crete, Kýthira, Kárpathos, and Rhodes are part of an arc that bends southeastward from the Peloponnese, forming the southern boundary of the Aegean.

Limestone rocks exposed by erosion of metamorphic rocks

Mount Olympus

Younger limestones created in shallow seas

Ancient metamorphic rock, formed miles below the surface

***Mount Olympus** is a composite of rocks formed by two major tectonic events. First the older metamorphic rocks were thrust over the limestones, then two million years ago regional warping and subsequent erosion reexposed the limestone.*

The Peloponnese consist of several mountainous peninsulas, linked to the mainland by the Isthmus of Corinth. The Corinth Canal *(Doíryga Korinthou)*, built in 1893, cuts through the isthmus, linking the Aegean and Ionian Seas.

***Layers of black volcanic ash** still cover the island of Thíra. This volcano last erupted 3,500 years ago, but still shows signs of volcanic activity.*

Scale 1:2,500,000
(projection: Lambert Conformal Conic)

114

118

114

GREECE
TURKEY
ALBANIA
Aegean Sea
Ionian Sea
MEDITERRANEAN SEA
Pindos (Pindus Mountains)
Ionioi Nísoi (Ionian Islands)
Vóreioi Sporádes
Évvoia (Euboea)
Kykládes (Cyclades)
Dodekánisos (Dodecanese)
Kríti (Crete)
Kritikó Pélagos (Sea of Crete)
Karpáthio Pélagos
Mirtóo Pelagos
VÓREION AIGAÍON
NÓTION AIGAÍON
PELOPONNISOS
ATTIKÍ
STEREÁ ELLÁS
DYTIKÍ ELLÁS
IPEIROS
THESSALÍA
DYTIKÍ MAKEDONÍA
KENTRIKÍ MAKEDONÍA
ÁGION ÓROS
ATHÍNA (ATHENS)
Peiraías (Piraeus)
Thessaloníki (Salonica)
Pátra
Lárisa
Irákleio
Ródos (Rhodes)
Lésvos (Lesbos)
Chíos
Sámos
114
142
122
MAP KEY
POPULATION
above 5 million
1 million to 5 million
500,000 to 1 million
100,000 to 500,000
50,000 to 100,000
10,000 to 50,000
below 10,000
ELEVATION
3000m / 9843ft
2000m / 6562ft
1000m / 3281ft
500m / 1640ft
250m / 820ft
100m / 328ft
sea level
Land use and agricultural distribution
cattle
fishing
goats
sheep
cereals
citrus fruits
cotton
olives
roses
tobacco
vineyards
capital cities
major towns
pasture
cropland
forest
mountain region
ROMANIA
BULGARIA
SOFIA
Pleven
Shumen
Varna
Stara Zagora
Burgas
Plovdiv
Edirne
Kirklareli
Istanbul
Tekirdağ
BLACK SEA
YUGOSLAVIA
MACEDONIA
ALBANIA
Salonica
Larisa
Volos
Patra
Corinth
ATHENS
Irakleio
Aegean Sea
Ionian Sea
MEDITERRANEAN SEA
THE URBAN/RURAL POPULATION DIVIDE
urban 65%
rural 35%
0 10 20 30 40 50 60 70 80 90 100
POPULATION DENSITY
245 people per sq mile
(95 people per sq km)
TOTAL LAND AREA
102,353 sq miles
(265,164 sq km)

USING THE LAND & SEA

THE FERTILE PLAINS of Bulgaria support cattle, fruit, vegetable cultivation, tobacco, and cereals; while also providing traditional industries with grapes for wine, roses for perfume, and sunflowers for oil. More than half of Greece is barren upland. Citrus fruit, olives, and tobacco are widely exported, yet much of rural life is still characterized by subsistence farming and goat herding.

***The dry scrubland** seen here at Vasilikí in Crete, is characteristic of much of southern Greece, and is caused by centuries of forest clearance and soil degradation. Landslides are also common.*

***These terraces,** built on the hillside at Náxos, an island of the Cyclades group, help to guard against soil erosion.*

Romania, Moldova & Ukraine

The industrial, social, and cultural makeup of Romania and the former Soviet states of Moldova and Ukraine still bears the imprint of their communist past. As part of the USSR, Ukraine was a leading agricultural, industrial, and energy producer. These industries, like those in Moldova and Romania, are now being reoriented more firmly toward Western markets. As a result of shifting borders, and Soviet policy actively encouraging Russian immigration into other Soviet states like Ukraine and Moldova, all three countries contain large numbers of foreign nationals. Moldovans and Romanians are still close in terms of language and culture, although Moldova is striving to remain an independent nation.

112

Using the Land

The fertile black soils of Ukraine, often called "the breadbasket of Europe," have enabled the cultivation of a variety of cereals and vegetables, which are widely exported. Romania and Moldova also grow cereals, sunflowers, and vegetables, and are noted particularly for the quality of their wines.

The fertile lands and tolerant climate of Moldova are ideally suited to growing grapes for wine.

112

Land use and agricultural distribution
- cattle
- pigs
- poultry
- sheep
- cereals
- cotton
- sugar beet
- sunflowers
- vineyards
- capital cities
- major towns
- pasture
- cropland
- forest
- wetland

The Urban/Rural Population Divide

urban 62% | rural 38%

0 10 20 30 40 50 60 70 80 90 100

Population Density	Total Land Area
238 people per sq mile (92 people per sq km)	334,947 sq miles (867,740 sq km)

***Glacial lakes** are found throughout the Transylvanian Alps (Carpaţii Meridionali), although the mountains no longer have any permanent snow cover.*

Transportation & Industry

Heavy industry using local raw materials characterizes much of this region. The industrial heartland of Ukraine, specializing in metal and machine-building industries, is based around its vast mineral reserves in the Donbass region. In Moldova, food processing draws on produce from its agricultural sector. Romanian industry relies both on local raw materials and imported iron, steel, and oil.

114

Major industry and infrastructure
- car manufacture
- chemicals
- coal
- engineering
- food processing
- mining
- oil & gas
- textiles
- tourism
- capital cities
- major towns
- international airports
- major roads
- major industrial areas

Transportation Network

223,834 miles (361,024 km)	70 miles (113 km)
21,989 miles (35,466 km)	3,796 miles (6,124 km)

Increased industrialization has necessitated the upgrading of road and rail networks in all three countries. Modernization has tended to focus only on major cities and industrial areas.

116

***During the 1960s and 1970s**, many industries, like this carbon factory, developed using the mineral resources on the flanks of the Transylvanian Alps (Carpaţii Meridionali).*

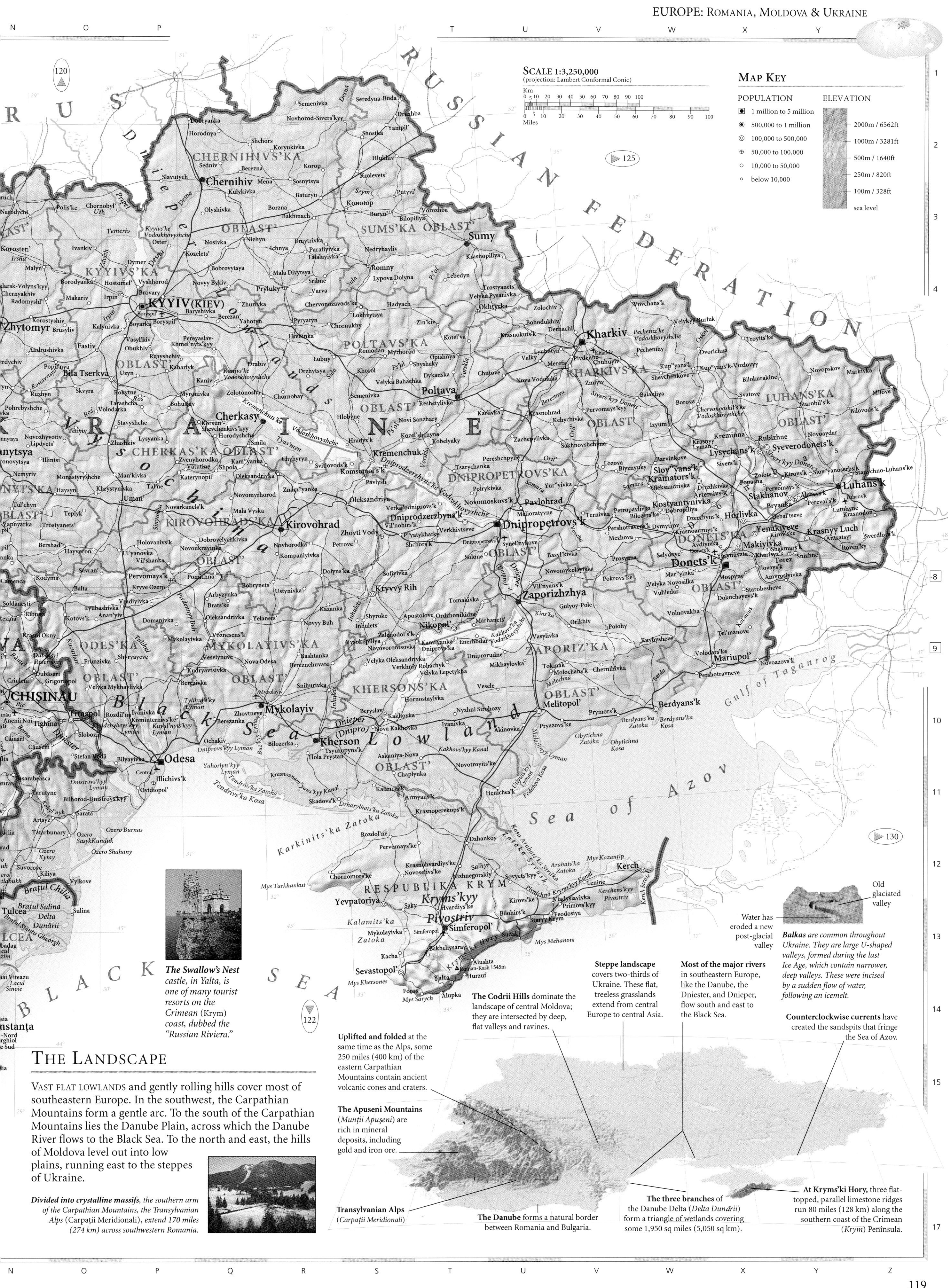
SCALE 1:3,250,000
(projection: Lambert Conformal Conic)
Km
Miles
MAP KEY
POPULATION
1 million to 5 million
500,000 to 1 million
100,000 to 500,000
50,000 to 100,000
10,000 to 50,000
below 10,000
ELEVATION
2000m / 6562ft
1000m / 3281ft
500m / 1640ft
250m / 820ft
100m / 328ft
sea level
RUSSIAN FEDERATION
UKRAINE
CHERNIHIVS'KA OBLAST'
SUMS'KA OBLAST'
KYYIVS'KA OBLAST'
POLTAVS'KA OBLAST'
KHARKIVS'KA OBLAST'
LUHANS'KA OBLAST'
CHERKAS'KA OBLAST'
DNIPROPETROVS'KA OBLAST'
KIROVOHRADS'KA OBLAST'
DONETS'KA OBLAST'
ODES'KA OBLAST'
MYKOLAYIVS'KA OBLAST'
KHERSONS'KA OBLAST'
ZAPORIZ'KA OBLAST'
RESPUBLIKA KRYM
KYYIV (KIEV)
Chernihiv
Sumy
Kharkiv
Poltava
Cherkasy
Kremenchuk
Kirovohrad
Dnipropetrovs'k
Donets'k
Luhans'k
Zaporizhzhya
Kryvyy Rih
Mykolayiv
Kherson
Odesa
Melitopol'
Mariupol'
Berdyans'k
CHISINAU
Simferopol'
Sevastopol'
Yalta
Kerch
Dnieper Lowland
Black Sea Lowland
Sea of Azov
Gulf of Taganrog
BLACK SEA
Krymskyy Pivostriv
Karkinits'ka Zatoka
Old glaciated valley
Water has eroded a new post-glacial valley
Balkas are common throughout Ukraine. They are large U-shaped valleys, formed during the last Ice Age, which contain narrower, deep valleys. These were incised by a sudden flow of water, following an icemelt.
Steppe landscape covers two-thirds of Ukraine. These flat, treeless grasslands extend from central Europe to central Asia.
Most of the major rivers in southeastern Europe, like the Danube, the Dniester, and Dnieper, flow south and east to the Black Sea.
The Codrii Hills dominate the landscape of central Moldova; they are intersected by deep, flat valleys and ravines.
Counterclockwise currents have created the sandspits that fringe the Sea of Azov.
Uplifted and folded at the same time as the Alps, some 250 miles (400 km) of the eastern Carpathian Mountains contain ancient volcanic cones and craters.
The Apuseni Mountains (*Munții Apuseni*) are rich in mineral deposits, including gold and iron ore.
Transylvanian Alps (*Carpații Meridionali*)
The Danube forms a natural border between Romania and Bulgaria.
The three branches of the Danube Delta (*Delta Dunării*) form a triangle of wetlands covering some 1,950 sq miles (5,050 sq km).
At Kryms'ki Hory, three flat-topped, parallel limestone ridges run 80 miles (128 km) along the southern coast of the Crimean (*Krym*) Peninsula.

The Swallow's Nest castle, in Yalta, is one of many tourist resorts on the Crimean (Krym) *coast, dubbed the "Russian Riviera."*

THE LANDSCAPE

VAST FLAT LOWLANDS and gently rolling hills cover most of southeastern Europe. In the southwest, the Carpathian Mountains form a gentle arc. To the south of the Carpathian Mountains lies the Danube Plain, across which the Danube River flows to the Black Sea. To the north and east, the hills of Moldova level out into low plains, running east to the steppes of Ukraine.

***Divided into crystalline massifs,** the southern arm of the Carpathian Mountains, the Transylvanian Alps* (Carpații Meridionali), *extend 170 miles (274 km) across southwestern Romania.*

The Baltic States & Belarus

Belarus, Estonia, Latvia, Lithuania, Kaliningrad

Occupying Europe's main corridor to Russia, the four distinct cultures of Estonia, Latvia, Lithuania, and Belarus share a history of struggle for nationhood against the interests of more powerful neighbors. As the first republics to declare their independence from the Soviet Union in 1990–91, the Baltic states of Estonia, Latvia, and Lithuania have sought an economic role in the EU, while reaffirming their European cultural roots through the church and a strong musical tradition. Meanwhile, Belarus has shown economic and political allegiance to Russia by joining the Commonwealth of Independent States.

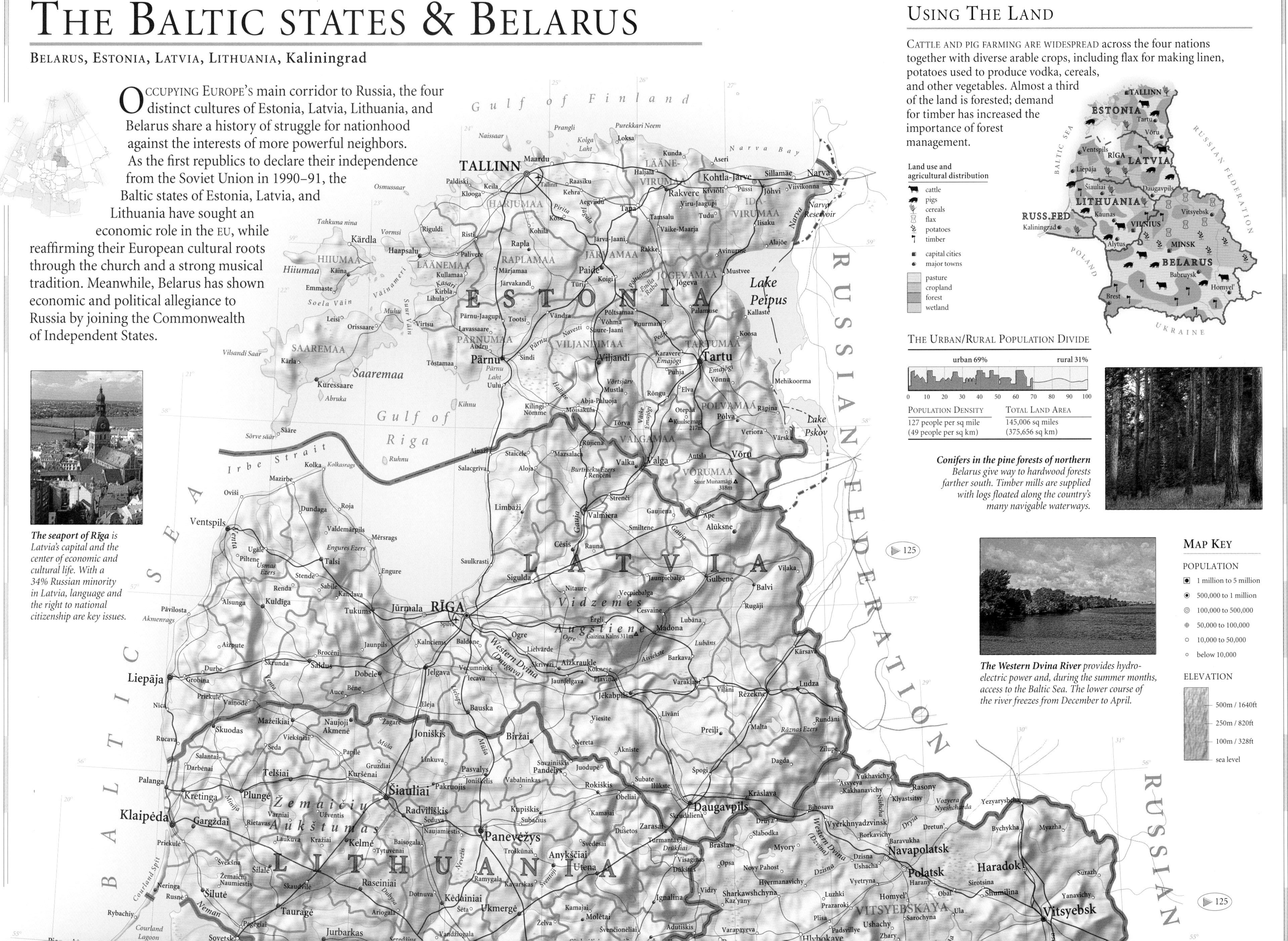
Gulf of Finland
TALLINN
ESTONIA
Gulf of Riga
Irbe Strait
BALTIC SEA
LATVIA
RĪGA
LITHUANIA
RUSSIAN FEDERATION
Lake Peipus
Lake Pskov
Western Dvina (Daugava)
Vidzemes
Saaremaa
Hiiumaa
Ventspils
Liepāja
Klaipėda
Šiauliai
Panevėžys
Daugavpils
Tartu
Pärnu
Narva
Navapolatsk
Polatsk
Vitsyebsk
Haradok
125

The seaport of Rīga is Latvia's capital and the center of economic and cultural life. With a 34% Russian minority in Latvia, language and the right to national citizenship are key issues.

Using The Land

Cattle and pig farming are widespread across the four nations together with diverse arable crops, including flax for making linen, potatoes used to produce vodka, cereals, and other vegetables. Almost a third of the land is forested; demand for timber has increased the importance of forest management.

Land use and agricultural distribution
cattle
pigs
cereals
flax
potatoes
timber
capital cities
major towns
pasture
cropland
forest
wetland
TALLINN
ESTONIA
RIGA
LATVIA
LITHUANIA
VILNIUS
MINSK
BELARUS
RUSS.FED
Kaliningrad
RUSSIAN FEDERATION
POLAND
UKRAINE
BALTIC SEA

The Urban/Rural Population Divide

urban 69%
rural 31%
0 10 20 30 40 50 60 70 80 90 100

Population Density	Total Land Area
127 people per sq mile (49 people per sq km)	145,006 sq miles (375,656 sq km)

Conifers in the pine forests of northern Belarus give way to hardwood forests farther south. Timber mills are supplied with logs floated along the country's many navigable waterways.

The Western Dvina River provides hydro-electric power and, during the summer months, access to the Baltic Sea. The lower course of the river freezes from December to April.

Map Key

POPULATION
1 million to 5 million
500,000 to 1 million
100,000 to 500,000
50,000 to 100,000
10,000 to 50,000
below 10,000
ELEVATION
500m / 1640ft
250m / 820ft
100m / 328ft
sea level

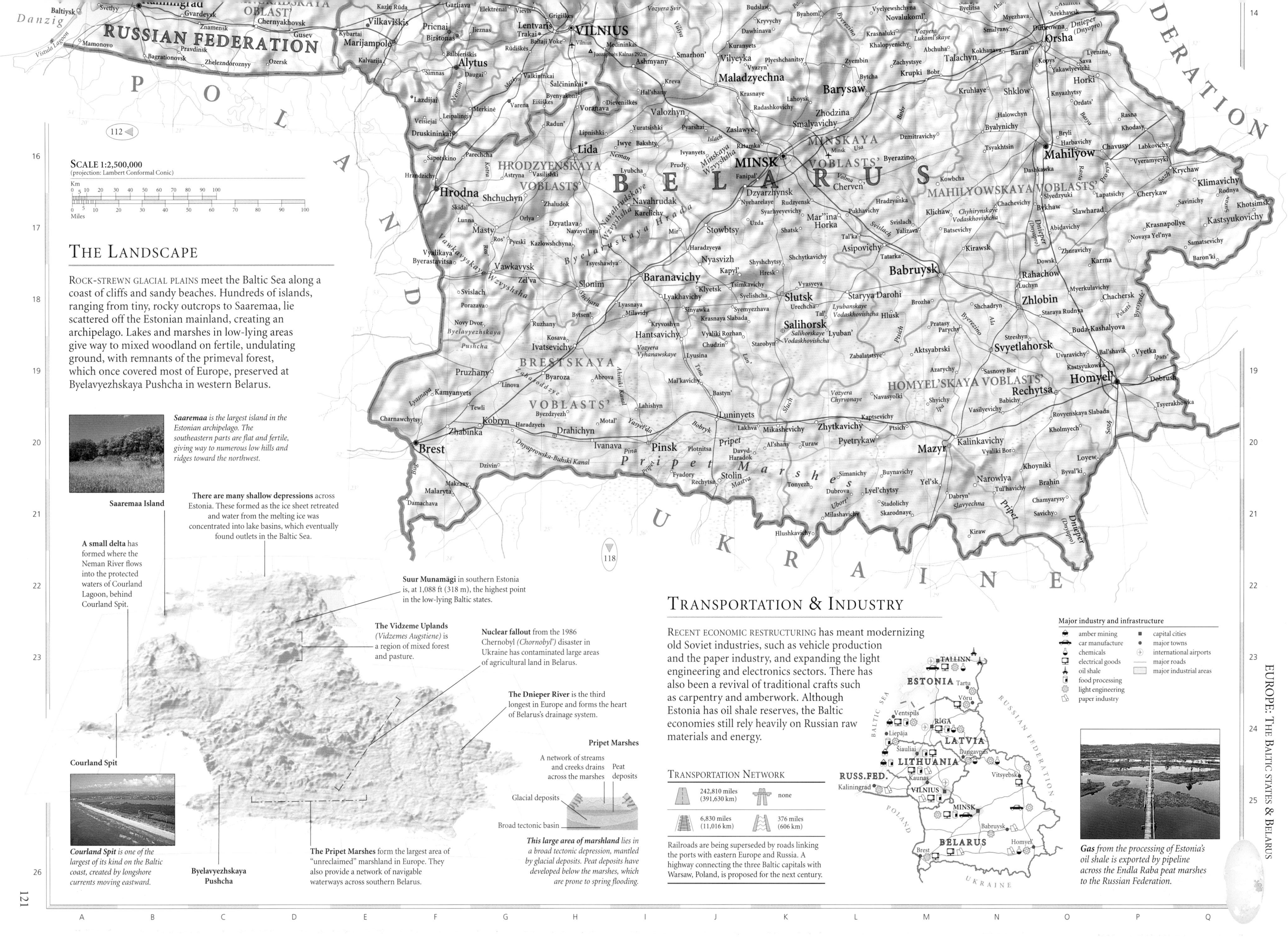
RUSSIAN FEDERATION
POLAND
BELARUS
UKRAINE
FEDERATION
HRODZYENSKAYA VOBLASTS'
MINSKAYA VOBLASTS'
MAHILYOWSKAYA VOBLASTS'
BRESTSKAYA VOBLASTS'
HOMYEL'SKAYA VOBLASTS'
VILNIUS
MINSK
Hrodna
Brest
Pinsk
Mahilyow
Homyel'
Babruysk
Baranavichy
Barysaw
Orsha
Pripet Marshes
112
118
SCALE 1:2,500,000
(projection: Lambert Conformal Conic)
Major industry and infrastructure
amber mining
car manufacture
chemicals
electrical goods
oil shale
food processing
light engineering
paper industry
capital cities
major towns
international airports
major roads
major industrial areas

The Landscape

Rock-strewn glacial plains meet the Baltic Sea along a coast of cliffs and sandy beaches. Hundreds of islands, ranging from tiny, rocky outcrops to Saaremaa, lie scattered off the Estonian mainland, creating an archipelago. Lakes and marshes in low-lying areas give way to mixed woodland on fertile, undulating ground, with remnants of the primeval forest, which once covered most of Europe, preserved at Byelavyezhskaya Pushcha in western Belarus.

Saaremaa is the largest island in the Estonian archipelago. The southeastern parts are flat and fertile, giving way to numerous low hills and ridges toward the northwest.

Saaremaa Island

There are many shallow depressions across Estonia. These formed as the ice sheet retreated and water from the melting ice was concentrated into lake basins, which eventually found outlets in the Baltic Sea.

A small delta has formed where the Neman River flows into the protected waters of Courland Lagoon, behind Courland Spit.

Suur Munamägi in southern Estonia is, at 1,088 ft (318 m), the highest point in the low-lying Baltic states.

The Vidzeme Uplands *(Vidzemes Augstiene)* is a region of mixed forest and pasture.

Nuclear fallout from the 1986 Chernobyl *(Chornobyl')* disaster in Ukraine has contaminated large areas of agricultural land in Belarus.

The Dnieper River is the third longest in Europe and forms the heart of Belarus's drainage system.

Pripet Marshes

A network of streams and creeks drains across the marshes

Peat deposits

Glacial deposits

Broad tectonic basin

***This large area of marshland** lies in a broad tectonic depression, mantled by glacial deposits. Peat deposits have developed below the marshes, which are prone to spring flooding.*

Courland Spit

***Courland Spit** is one of the largest of its kind on the Baltic coast, created by longshore currents moving eastward.*

Byelavyezhskaya Pushcha

The Pripet Marshes form the largest area of "unreclaimed" marshland in Europe. They also provide a network of navigable waterways across southern Belarus.

Transportation & Industry

Recent economic restructuring has meant modernizing old Soviet industries, such as vehicle production and the paper industry, and expanding the light engineering and electronics sectors. There has also been a revival of traditional crafts such as carpentry and amberwork. Although Estonia has oil shale reserves, the Baltic economies still rely heavily on Russian raw materials and energy.

Transportation Network

242,810 miles (391,630 km)	none
6,830 miles (11,016 km)	376 miles (606 km)

Railroads are being superseded by roads linking the ports with eastern Europe and Russia. A highway connecting the three Baltic capitals with Warsaw, Poland, is proposed for the next century.

***Gas** from the processing of Estonia's oil shale is exported by pipeline across the Endla Raba peat marshes to the Russian Federation.*

The Mediterranean

The Mediterranean Sea stretches over 2,500 miles (4,000 km) east to west, separating Europe from Africa. At its westernmost point it is connected to the Atlantic Ocean through the Strait of Gibraltar. In the east, the Suez Canal, opened in 1869, gives passage to the Indian Ocean. In the northeast, linked by the Sea of Marmara, lies the Black Sea. The Mediterranean is bordered by 28 states and territories, and more than 100 million people live on its shores and islands. Throughout history, the Mediterranean has been a focal area for many great empires and civilizations, reflected in the variety of cultures found on its shores. Since the 1960s, development along the southern coast of Europe has expanded rapidly to accommodate increasing numbers of tourists and to enable the exploitation of oil and gas reserves. This has resulted in rising levels of pollution, threatening the future of the sea.

Using the Land & Sea

A quarter of the fish species found in the Mediterranean are economically important. Sardines are the main catch in northern and western regions and aquaculture, including oyster farming, is becoming increasingly important in the eastern Mediterranean. Olives, citrus fruit, cork trees, and grapes thrive in the Mediterranean climate, enjoying hot, dry summers and mild, wet winters. Italy and Spain are world leaders in commercial olive production.

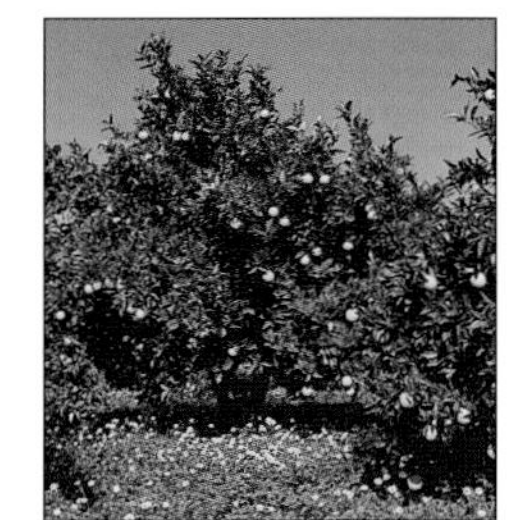

The growing of citrus fruits, such as lemons, limes, oranges, and grapefruit, is common along the coasts surrounding the Mediterranean.

Land use and agricultural distribution

- goats
- sheep
- cereals
- citrus fruits
- cork
- fishing
- olive oil
- sunflowers
- tobacco
- vineyards
- major towns
- pasture
- cropland
- forest
- mountain region
- wetland
- desert

The Landscape

The Mediterranean Sea is almost totally landlocked, joined to the Atlantic Ocean through the Strait of Gibraltar, which is only 8 miles (13 km) wide. Lying on an active plate margin, sea floor movements have formed a variety of basins, troughs, and ridges. A submarine ridge running from Tunisia to the island of Sicily divides the Mediterranean into two distinct basins. The western basin is characterized by broad, smooth abyssal (ocean) plains. In contrast, the eastern basin is dominated by a large ridge system, running east to west.

The narrow Strait of Gibraltar inhibits water exchange between the Mediterranean Sea and the Atlantic Ocean, producing a high degree of salinity and a low tidal range within the Mediterranean. The lack of tides has encouraged the build-up of pollutants in many semienclosed bays.

Main surface current

Dense currents sink below surface

Denser, more saline currents flow back to Atlantic

***Because the Mediterranean** is almost enclosed by land, its circulation is quite different from the oceans. There is one major current which flows in from the Atlantic and moves east. Currents flowing back to the Atlantic are denser and flow below the main current.*

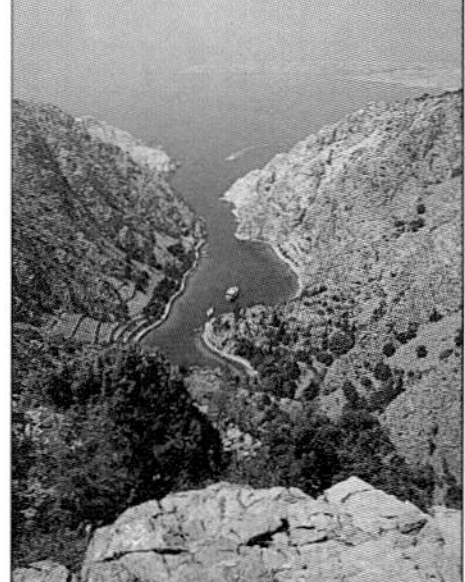

***The Dalmatian** (Dalmacija) **coast** has many long, elongated islands parallel to the mainland. These were created when rising sea levels drowned valleys running parallel with the coast.*

Transportation & Industry

The opening of the Suez Canal in 1869 made the Mediterranean a key shipping route to Asia. Oil and gas reserves, although comparatively small on a world scale, are being explored and exploited off the coasts of Libya, Greece, Italy, Spain, and Tunisia. The Mediterranean's greatest natural resources are its miles of beaches and warm sea. Over half the world's income from tourism is generated in the Mediterranean.

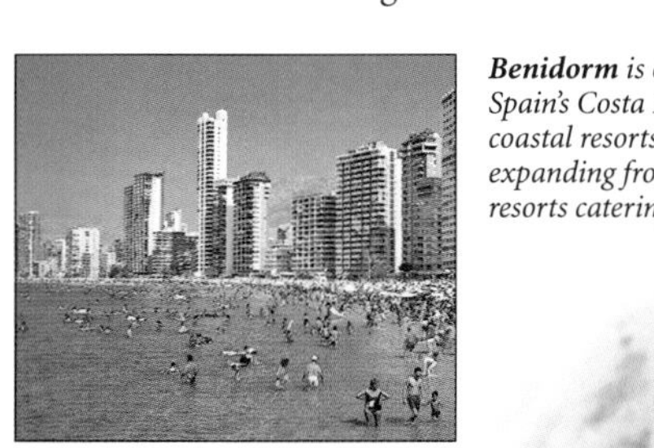

***Benidorm** is one of the most popular resorts on Spain's Costa Blanca. Many of the Mediterranean's coastal resorts have grown up since the 1950s, expanding from small fishing villages to large resorts catering almost exclusively to tourists.*

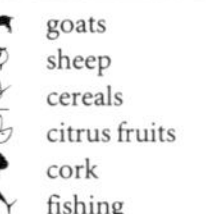

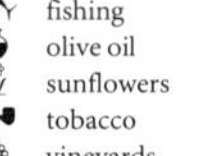

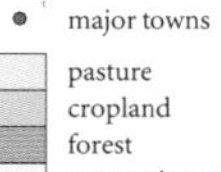

66

66

76

The Ionian Basin is the deepest in the Mediterranean, reaching depths of 16,800 ft (5,121 m).

Industrial pollution flowing from the Dnie[ster] and Danube Rivers has destroyed a la[rge] proportion of the fish population that use[d to] inhabit the upper layers of the Black S[ea].

The eastern basin of the Mediterranean contains many features which indicate the force of a colliding plate margin, including volcanoes, earthquake zones, ridges, and seamounts.

***The Atlas Mountains** are a range of fold mountains that lie in Morocco and Algeria. They run parallel to the Mediterranean, forming a topographical and climatic divide between the Mediterranean coast and the western Sahara.*

The edge of the Eurasian Plate is edged by a continental shelf. In the Mediterranean Sea this is widest at the Ebro Fan, where it extends 60 miles (96 km).

Beneath the Strait of Sicily lies a submarine ridge which rises to 1,200 ft (360 m) below sea level. It divides the eastern and western basins of the Mediterranean.

An arc of active submarine, island, and mainland volcanoes, including Etna and Vesuvius, lie in and around southern Italy. The area is also susceptible to earthquakes and landslides.

The shallow basin of the Aegean contains numerous small islands, many of volcanic origin.

Nutrient-flows into the east[ern] Mediterranean and sediment-fl[ows] to the Nile Delta have been seve[rely] decreased by the building of [the] Aswan Dam across the Nile in Eg[ypt], causing the delta to shri[nk].

Zemlya Frantsa-Iosifa
ARCTIC OCEAN
KARSKOYE MORE
MORE LAPTEVYKH
Novosibirskiye Ostrova
Ostrov Komsomolets
Ostrov Oktyabr'skoy Revolyutsii
Ostrov Bol'shevik
Poluostrov Taymyr
Gora Byrranga
Severo-Sibirskaya Nizmennost'
Poluostrov Yamal
TAYMYRSKIY (DOLGANO-NENETSKIY) AVTONOMNYY OKRUG
YAMALO-NENETSKIY AVTONOMNYY OKRUG
Plato Putorana
Zapadno-Sibirskaya Ravnina
Srednesibirskoye Ploskogor'ye
EVENKIYSKIY AVTONOMNYY OKRUG
RESPUBLIKA SAKHA (YAKUTIYA)
Verkhoyanskiy Khrebet
SIBIR' (SIBERIA)
RUSSIAN FEDERATION
TOMSKAYA OBLAST'
NOVOSIBIRSKAYA OBLAST'
KRASNOYARSKIY KRAY
IRKUTSKAYA OBLAST'
CHITINSKAYA OBLAST'
AMURSKAYA OBLAST'
RESPUBLIKA BURYATIYA
RESPUBLIKA TYVA
RESPUBLIKA ALTAY
ALTAYSKIY KRAY
Altai Mountains
Eastern Sayans
Zapadnyy Sayan
Yablonovyy Khrebet
Ozero Baykal
Noril'sk
Yakutsk
Tomsk
Novosibirsk
Kemerovo
Novokuznetsk
Barnaul
Krasnoyarsk
Abakan
Kyzyl
Irkutsk
Angarsk
Bratsk
Ulan-Ude
Chita
Blagoveshchensk
MONGOLIA
CHINA
Amur
Lena
Yenisey
Ob'

A fishing trawler lies at anchor in the icy waters of Karaginskiy Zaliv, at the northern end of the Kamchatka Peninsula (Poluostrov Kamchatka) in eastern Siberia. The Russian Federation's fishing fleet is the largest in the world and operates worldwide.

The shores of Lake Baikal (Ozero Baykal) are a mixture of forest and the grassy steppe seen here. The lake freezes to a depth of 33 ft (10 m) in winter.

SCALE 1:13,800,000
(projection: Lambert Conformal Conic)

206

168

EUROPE
ATLANTIC OCEAN
BLACK SEA
MEDITERRANEAN SEA
AFRICA
ASIA
Madrid
Barcelona
Valencia
Malaga
Oran
Algiers
Marseille
Nice
Livorno
Venice
Rome
Naples
Palermo
Tunis
Sfax
Tripoli
Benghazi
Alexandria
Cairo
Port Said
Suez
Tel Aviv-Yafo
Beirut
Antalya
Izmir
Athens
Istanbul
Ankara
Burgas
Constanța
Sevastopol'
Novorossiysk
Trabzon
Sofia
Dubrovnik
Major industry and infrastructure
fishing port
oil & gas
tourism
major towns
international airports
major roads
major industrial areas
CYPRUS
Kornuçam Burnu (Akrotiri Kormakiti)
Güzelyurt Körfezi (Kólpos Mórfou)
Kólpos Chrysochoú
Akrotiri Arnaoúti
Pólis
Lefke (Léfka)
Kámpos
Pedoulas
Páno Panagia
Pégeia
Páfos
Koúklia
Kólpos Episkopí
Sovereign Base Area (to UK)
Akrotiri
Kk
L
Ll
M
Mm
H
Hh
I
Ii
J
Jj
K
110
104
114
76
Bay of Biscay
FRANCE
SWITZERLAND
AUSTRIA
SLOVENIA
CROATIA
BOSNIA & HERZEGOVINA
YUGOSLAVIA
ALBANIA
ANDORRA
MONACO
SAN MARINO
ITALIA
MADRID
Bordeaux
Lyon
Villeurbanne
St-Étienne
Grenoble
Toulouse
Montpellier
Nîmes
Aix-en-Provence
Marseille
Toulon
Nice
Cannes
Perpignan
Massif Central
Pyrénées
Golfe du Lion
Côte d'Azur
Ligurian Sea
Golfo di Genova
Torino (Turin)
Milano (Milan)
Genova (Genoa)
Novara
Monza
Bergamo
Brescia
Verona
Padova
Venezia (Venice)
Chioggia
Trento
Bolzano
Udine
Trieste
LJUBLJANA
ZAGREB
Maribor
Rijeka
Pula
Gulf of Venice
Alessandria
Piacenza
Parma
Reggio nell' Emilia
Modena
Ferrara
Bologna
Forlì
Ravenna
Rimini
La Spezia
Prato
Firenze (Florence)
Pisa
Livorno
Perugia
Ancona
Terni
Pescara
Civitavecchia
ROMA (ROME)
Napoli (Naples)
Torre del Greco
Salerno
Foggia
Bari
Brindisi
Taranto
Lecce
Otranto
Cosenza
Catanzaro
Crotone
Reggio di Calabria
Messina
Palermo
Catania
Siracusa
Agrigento
Sicilia (Sicily)
Adriatic Sea
Adriatic Basin
Tyrrhenian Sea
Tyrrhenian Basin
Ionian Sea
Ionian Basin
Golfo di Taranto
Strait of Messina
Strait of Sicily
Corse (Corsica) (to France)
Ajaccio
Sardegna (Sardinia) (to Italy)
Sassari
Cagliari
Strait of Bonifacio
Isola d'Elba
Mallorca (Majorca)
Menorca (Minorca)
Palma
Eivissa (Ibiza)
Formentera
Islas Baleares (Balearic Islands)
Algerian Basin
MEDITERRANEAN
Donostia-San Sebastián
Bilbao
Vitoria-Gasteiz
Pamplona
Logroño
Zaragoza
Lleida
Barcelona
Sabadell
Mataró
Tarragona
Costa Brava
Castelló de la Plana
Valencia
Golfo de Valencia
Albacete
Alicante
Elche
Benidorm
Murcia
Cartagena
Costa Blanca
ALGER (ALGIERS)
Oran
Mostaganem
Chlef
Blida
Tizi Ouzou
Béjaïa
Skikda
Annaba
Constantine
Sétif
Batna
Tlemcen
Sidi Bel Abbès
Atlas Tellien
ALGERIA
Haut Plateaux
Atlas Saharien
Massif de l'Aurès
Chott El Hodna
TUNISIA
Bizerte
TUNIS
Golfe de Hammamet
Sousse
Sfax
Golfe de Gabès
Gabès
Île de Jerba
Médenine
Îles de Kerkenah
VALLETTA
MALTA
Isole Pelagie (to Italy)
Pantelleria (to Italy)
ṬARĀBULUS (TRIPOLI)
Zuwārah
Al 'Azīzīyah
Gharyān
Al Khums
Miṣrātah
Khalīj Surt (Gulf of Sirte)
Surt
As Sulṭān
An Nawfalīyah
Ajdābiyā
Banghāzī (Benghazi)
LIBYA
Sabkhat Ghuzayyil
Ionioi Nisoi (Ionian Islands)
Kérkyra (Corfu)
Kefallinía
Lefkada
Sarajevo
Banja Luka
Tuzla
Zenica
Mostar
Split
Zadar
Dubrovnik
Podgorica
TIRANË (TIRANA)
Durrës
MALTA
Gozo
Victoria
Nadur
Għajnsielem
Comino (Kemmuna)
Mellieħa
Malta
San Pawl il-Baħar
Mosta
St Julian's
Sliema
VALLETTA
Rabat
Paola
Birżebbuġa
Marsaxlokk Bay
Il-Kullana
Mediterranean Sea
SCALE 1:900,000
(projection: Lambert Conformal Conic)

Monte Carlo *is just one of the luxurious resorts scattered along the Riviera, which stretches along the coast from Cannes in France to La Spezia in Italy. The region's mild winters and hot summers have attracted wealthy tourists since the early 19th century.*

IN 1974 ... while G... Cyprus ... zone cur... north of... Republic... recogniz...

The city of Venice *is built on an archipelago of islands and mudflats in the middle of a lagoon at the head of the Adriatic Sea. The city's numerous canals follow water routes between the original 118 islands.*

Oxygen in the Black Sea is dissolved only in its upper layers; at depths below 230–300 ft (70–100 m) the sea is "dead" and can support no life other than specially adapted bacteria.

Cyprus is the third largest *Mediterranean island after Sardinia and Sicily. The island is mountainous and contains two main ranges, the Troodos and the Kyrenia Mountains.*

Both the Dead Sea in Jordan and the Gulf of Aqaba are extensions of the Great Rift Valley, which runs through eastern Africa.

The Suez Canal, opened in 1869, extends 100 miles (160 km) from Port Said to the Gulf of Suez.

Commercial fisheries *are found throughout the Mediterranean. Operations have traditionally been small-scale. As elsewhere, high demand has caused a decline in fish stocks.*

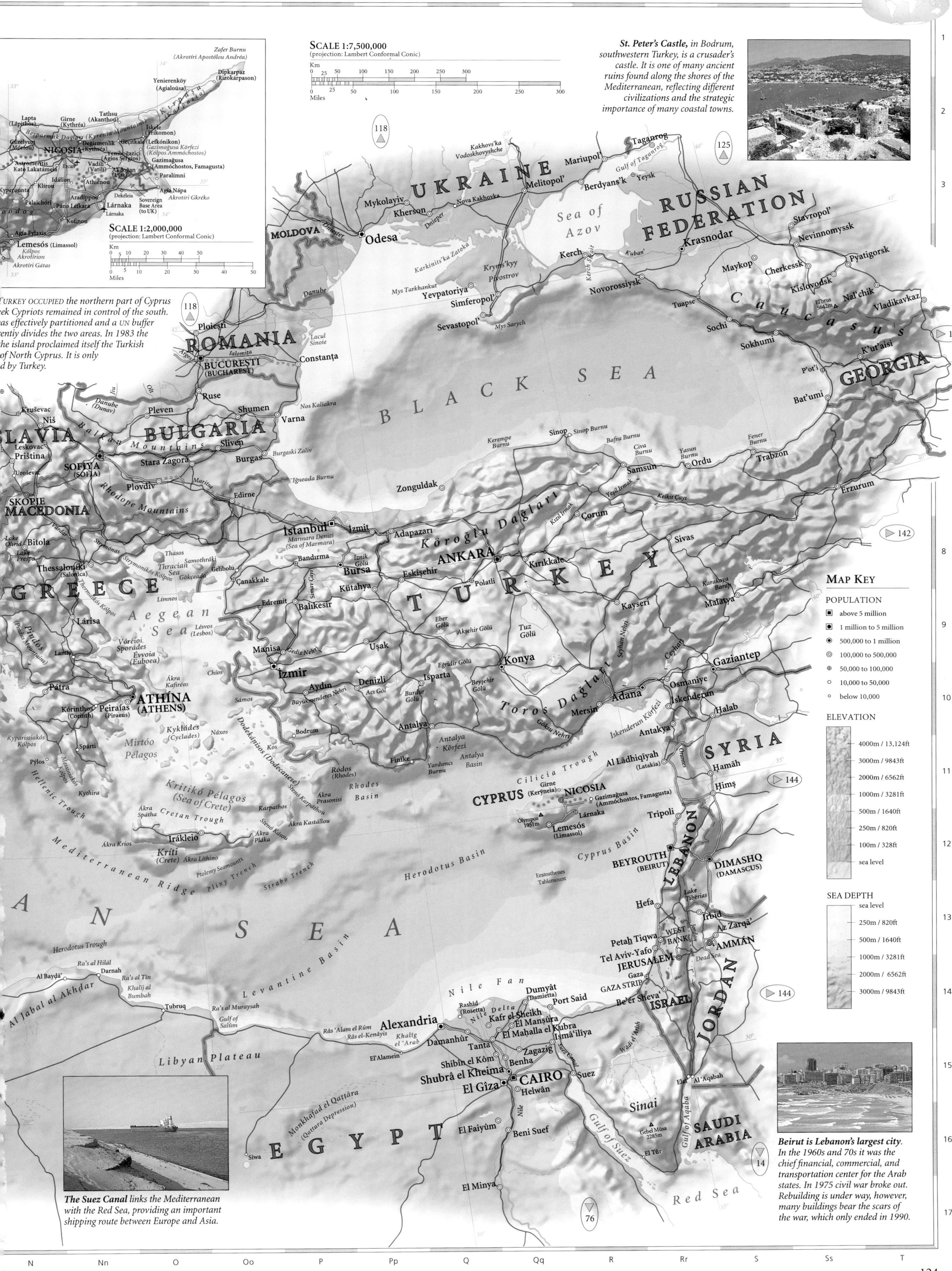

N Nn O Oo P Pp Q Qq R Rr S Ss T
1 2 3 8 9 10 11 12 13 14 15 16 17
SCALE 1:7,500,000
(projection: Lambert Conformal Conic)
Km 0 25 50 100 150 200 250 300
Miles 0 25 50 100 150 200 250 300
SCALE 1:2,000,000
(projection: Lambert Conformal Conic)
Km 0 5 10 20 30 40 50
Miles 0 5 10 20 30 40 50
Zafer Burnu (Akrotíri Apostólou Andréa)
Dipkarpaz (Rizokárpason)
Yenierenköy (Agialoúsa)
Lapta (Lápithos)
Girne (Kythréa)
Tatlısu (Akanthoú)
Güzelyurt (Mórfou)
NICOSIA
Değirmenlik (Kythréa)
Geçitkale (Lefkónikon)
İskele (Trikomon)
Gazimağusa Körfezi (Kólpos Ammóchostos)
Gazimağusa (Ammóchostos, Famagusta)
Paralímni
Agia Nápa
Akrotíri Gkréko
Idálion
Athíenou
Lárnaka
Kofinou
Sovereign Base Area (to UK)
Lemesós (Limassol)
Kólpos Akrotíriou
Akrotíri Gátas
118
125
142
144
14
76
UKRAINE
MOLDOVA
RUSSIAN FEDERATION
ROMANIA
BUCUREŞTI (BUCHAREST)
BULGARIA
SOFIYA (SOFIA)
MACEDONIA
SKOPJE
GREECE
ATHÍNA (ATHENS)
TURKEY
ANKARA
İstanbul
İzmir
GEORGIA
SYRIA
LEBANON
BEYROUTH (BEIRUT)
DIMASHQ (DAMASCUS)
CYPRUS
NICOSIA
ISRAEL
JERUSALEM
JORDAN
AMMAN
EGYPT
CAIRO
Alexandria
SAUDI ARABIA
BLACK SEA
Sea of Azov
Aegean Sea
MEDITERRANEAN SEA
Red Sea
Odesa
Mykolayiv
Kherson
Sevastopol'
Simferopol'
Yevpatoriya
Melitopol'
Mariupol'
Berdyans'k
Taganrog
Krasnodar
Novorossiysk
Sochi
Sokhumi
Stavropol'
Nevinnomyssk
Pyatigorsk
Vladikavkaz
Nal'chik
Bat'umi
K'ut'aisi
Constanţa
Varna
Burgas
Ruse
Pleven
Shumen
Sliven
Stara Zagora
Plovdiv
Edirne
Thessaloníki (Salonica)
Lárisa
Pátra
Irákleio
Kríti (Crete)
Ródos (Rhodes)
Bursa
Eskişehir
Kütahya
Balıkesir
Manisa
Aydın
Denizli
Isparta
Antalya
Konya
Kayseri
Sivas
Samsun
Trabzon
Erzurum
Malatya
Gaziantep
Adana
Mersin
İskenderun
Antakya
Halab
Hamāh
Ḩimş
Tripoli
Al Lādhiqīyah (Latakia)
Hefa
Tel Aviv-Yafo
Gaza
GAZA STRIP
WEST BANK
Port Said
Suez
El Gîza
Sinai
Gulf of Suez
Gulf of Aqaba
MAP KEY
POPULATION
above 5 million
1 million to 5 million
500,000 to 1 million
100,000 to 500,000
50,000 to 100,000
10,000 to 50,000
below 10,000
ELEVATION
4000m / 13,124ft
3000m / 9843ft
2000m / 6562ft
1000m / 3281ft
500m / 1640ft
250m / 820ft
100m / 328ft
sea level
SEA DEPTH
sea level
250m / 820ft
500m / 1640ft
1000m / 3281ft
2000m / 6562ft
3000m / 9843ft

St. Peter's Castle, in Bodrum, southwestern Turkey, is a crusader's castle. It is one of many ancient ruins found along the shores of the Mediterranean, reflecting different civilizations and the strategic importance of many coastal towns.

TURKEY OCCUPIED the northern part of Cyprus ...ek Cypriots remained in control of the south. ...as effectively partitioned and a UN buffer ...ently divides the two areas. In 1983 the ...he island proclaimed itself the Turkish ...of North Cyprus. It is only ...d by Turkey.

The Suez Canal links the Mediterranean with the Red Sea, providing an important shipping route between Europe and Asia.

Beirut is Lebanon's largest city. In the 1960s and 70s it was the chief financial, commercial, and transportation center for the Arab states. In 1975 civil war broke out. Rebuilding is under way, however, many buildings bear the scars of the war, which only ended in 1990.

THE RUSSIAN FEDERATION

MAP KEY
POPULATION
above 5 million
1 million to 5 million
500,000 to 1 million
100,000 to 500,000
50,000 to 100,000
10,000 to 50,000
below 10,000
ELEVATION
4000m / 13,124ft
3000m / 9843ft
2000m / 6562ft
1000m / 3281ft
500m / 1640ft
250m / 820ft
100m / 328ft
sea level
BARENTS SEA
NORWAY
FINLAND
ESTONIA
LATVIA
LITHUANIA
BELARUS
UKRAINE
KAZAKHSTAN
BLACK SEA
Caspian Sea
Sea of Azov
Beloye More
Murmansk
Arkhangel'sk (Archangel)
Sankt-Peterburg
Novgorod
Pskov
Smolensk
Bryansk
Kaluga
Tula
Orel
Kursk
Belgorod
Voronezh
Lipetsk
Tambov
Ryazan'
Vladimir
Ivanovo
Yaroslavl'
Kostroma
Vologda
Cherepovets
Petrozavodsk
Syktyvkar
Ukhta
Vorkuta
Kirov
Nizhniy Novgorod
Cheboksary
Yoshkar-Ola
Kazan'
Izhevsk
Perm'
Ul'yanovsk
Saransk
Penza
Saratov
Samara
Tol'yatti
Ufa
Yekaterinburg
Chelyabinsk
Kurgan
Tyumen'
Omsk
Orenburg
Orsk
Volgograd
Astrakhan'
Elista
Rostov-na-Donu
Krasnodar
Maykop
Stavropol'
Cherkessk
Nal'chik
Vladikavkaz
Groznyy
Makhachkala
Kaliningrad
MOSKVA (MOSCOW)
Ural'skiye Gory
RUSSIA
94
120
118
142
150
USING THE LAND
Land use and agricultural distribution
cattle
cereals
root crops
timber
capital cities
major towns
pasture
cropland
forest
desert
mountain region
barren
RUSSIAN FEDERATION
Siberia
ARCTIC OCEAN
Barents Sea
Bering Sea
Sea of Okhotsk
Sea of Japan
Black Sea
Caspian Sea
KAZAKHSTAN
MONGOLIA
CHINA
Murmansk
St. Petersburg
Archangel
MOSCOW
Nizhniy Novgorod
Volgograd
Novosibirsk
Irkutsk
Yakutsk
Magadan
Yuzhno-Sakhalinsk
Vladivostok
THE URBAN/RURAL POPULATION DIVIDE
urban 74%
rural 26%
0
10
20
30
40
50
60
70
80
90
100

Summer beds of moss and lichen scatter a 90% surface cover of ice across the islands of Franz Josef Land (Zemlya Frantsa-Iosifa), the northernmost land in the eastern hemisphere.

THE COLD WAR ERA OF GLOBAL RELATIONS was concluded in 1991 with the formal dissolution of the Soviet Union. The Russian Federation declared its separate sovereignty from the foundering communist empire following independence declarations from a number of former Soviet republics. As the leading member of the Commonwealth of Independent States, the Russian Federation has a central role in the development of post-Soviet Eurasia. Crossing 11 time zones, the Russian Federation is almost twice the size of the US, and with more than 150 ethnic minorities and 21 autonomous republics, regionalist dissent within its own territory remains a danger.

USING THE LAND

THE MAIN AGRICULTURAL REGIONS follow the belt of rich, black *chernozem* soils between Ukraine and Novosibirsk, producing cereals, fodder, and a broad range of crops for industrial use. Small pockets of pastureland are also found in this region. Large areas of terrain are uncultivable, and the constraints of a severe climate force the Federation to be partly dependent on imported grain. The wilds of Siberia are given over to hunting and reindeer herding, and contain the world's largest timber reserves.

THE RUSSIAN FEDERATION: ADMINISTRATIVE REGIONS

1. PSKOVSKAYA OBLAST'
2. YAROSLAVSKAYA OBLAST'
3. IVANOVSKAYA OBLAST'
4. SMOLENSKAYA OBLAST'
5. MOSKOVSKAYA OBLAST
6. VLADIMIRSKAYA OBLAST'
7. RESPUBLIKA MARIY EL
8. CHUVASHSKAYA RESPUBLIKA
9. KALUZHSKAYA OBLAST'
10. TUL'SKAYA OBLAST'
11. RYAZANSKAYA OBLAST'
12. RESPUBLIKA MORDOVIYA
13. UL'YANOVSKAYA OBLAST'
14. SAMARSKAYA OBLAST'
15. BRYANSKAYA OBLAST'
16. ORLOVSKAYA OBLAST'
17. LIPETSKAYA OBLAST'
18. TAMBOVSKAYA OBLAST'
19. KURSKAYA OBLAST'
20. BELGORODSKAYA OBLAST'
21. VORONEZHSKAYA OBLAST'
22. KRASNODARSKIY KRAY
23. RESPUBLIKA ADYGEYA
24. KARACHAYEVO-CHERKESSKAYA RESPUBLIKA
25. KABARDINO-BALKARSKAYA RESPUBLIKA
26. RESPUBLIKA SEVERNAYA OSETIYA
27. INGUSHSKAYA RESPUBLIKA
28. CHECHENSKAYA RESPUBLIKA
29. YEVREYSKAYA AVTONOMNAYA OBLAST'

POPULATION DENSITY

23 people per sq mile
(9 people per sq km)

TOTAL LAND AREA

65,592,800 sq miles
(17,075,400 sq km)

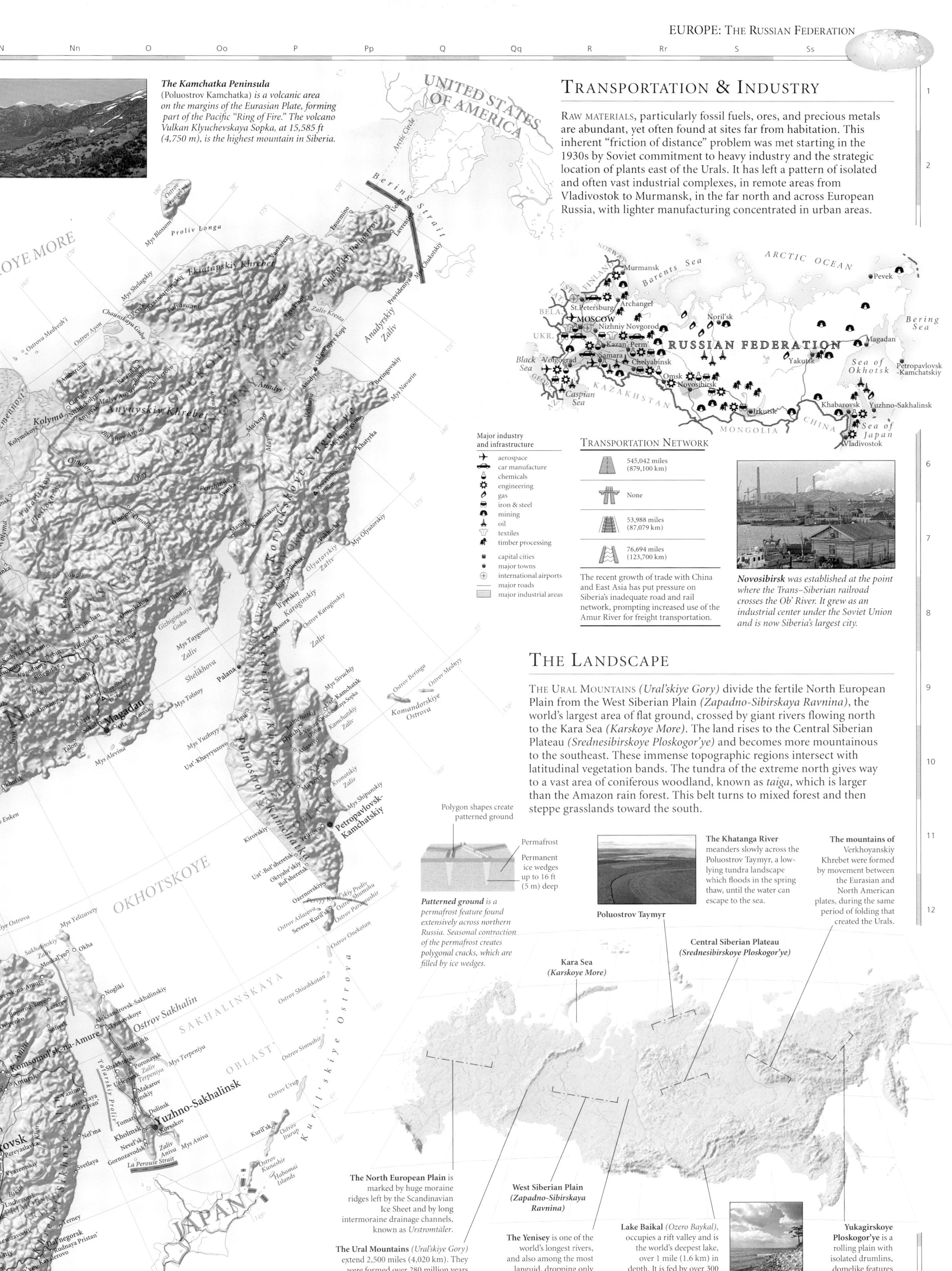

The Kamchatka Peninsula (Poluostrov Kamchatka) *is a volcanic area on the margins of the Eurasian Plate, forming part of the Pacific "Ring of Fire." The volcano Vulkan Klyuchevskaya Sopka, at 15,585 ft (4,750 m), is the highest mountain in Siberia.*

Transportation & Industry

RAW MATERIALS, particularly fossil fuels, ores, and precious metals are abundant, yet often found at sites far from habitation. This inherent "friction of distance" problem was met starting in the 1930s by Soviet commitment to heavy industry and the strategic location of plants east of the Urals. It has left a pattern of isolated and often vast industrial complexes, in remote areas from Vladivostok to Murmansk, in the far north and across European Russia, with lighter manufacturing concentrated in urban areas.

Major industry and infrastructure
aerospace
car manufacture
chemicals
engineering
gas
iron & steel
mining
oil
textiles
timber processing
capital cities
major towns
international airports
major roads
major industrial areas
RUSSIAN FEDERATION
ARCTIC OCEAN
Barents Sea
Bering Sea
Sea of Okhotsk
Sea of Japan
Black Sea
Caspian Sea
KAZAKHSTAN
MONGOLIA
CHINA
Murmansk
St.Petersburg
Archangel
MOSCOW
Nizhniy Novgorod
Kazan
Perm'
Samara
Volgograd
Chelyabinsk
Omsk
Novosibirsk
Irkutsk
Noril'sk
Yakutsk
Magadan
Pevek
Petropavlovsk-Kamchatskiy
Khabarovsk
Yuzhno-Sakhalinsk
Vladivostok

Transportation Network

545,042 miles (879,100 km)	
None	
53,988 miles (87,079 km)	
76,694 miles (123,700 km)	

The recent growth of trade with China and East Asia has put pressure on Siberia's inadequate road and rail network, prompting increased use of the Amur River for freight transportation.

Novosibirsk *was established at the point where the Trans-Siberian railroad crosses the Ob' River. It grew as an industrial center under the Soviet Union and is now Siberia's largest city.*

The Landscape

THE URAL MOUNTAINS *(Ural'skiye Gory)* divide the fertile North European Plain from the West Siberian Plain *(Zapadno-Sibirskaya Ravnina)*, the world's largest area of flat ground, crossed by giant rivers flowing north to the Kara Sea *(Karskoye More)*. The land rises to the Central Siberian Plateau *(Srednesibirskoye Ploskogor'ye)* and becomes more mountainous to the southeast. These immense topographic regions intersect with latitudinal vegetation bands. The tundra of the extreme north gives way to a vast area of coniferous woodland, known as *taiga*, which is larger than the Amazon rain forest. This belt turns to mixed forest and then steppe grasslands toward the south.

Polygon shapes create patterned ground
Permafrost
Permanent ice wedges up to 16 ft (5 m) deep

Patterned ground *is a permafrost feature found extensively across northern Russia. Seasonal contraction of the permafrost creates polygonal cracks, which are filled by ice wedges.*

The Khatanga River meanders slowly across the Poluostrov Taymyr, a low-lying tundra landscape which floods in the spring thaw, until the water can escape to the sea.

The mountains of Verkhoyanskiy Khrebet were formed by movement between the Eurasian and North American plates, during the same period of folding that created the Urals.

Poluostrov Taymyr
Central Siberian Plateau (Srednesibirskoye Ploskogor'ye)
Kara Sea (Karskoye More)
West Siberian Plain (Zapadno-Sibirskaya Ravnina)

The North European Plain is marked by huge moraine ridges left by the Scandinavian Ice Sheet and by long intermoraine drainage channels, known as *Urstromtäler*.

The Ural Mountains *(Ural'skiye Gory)* extend 2,500 miles (4,020 km). They were formed over 280 million years ago, folded as the East European and Siberian plates moved closer together.

The Yenisey is one of the world's longest rivers, and also among the most languid, dropping only 500 ft (152 m) over 1,200 miles (2,000 km).

Lake Baikal *(Ozero Baykal)*, occupies a rift valley and is the world's deepest lake, over 1 mile (1.6 km) in depth. It is fed by over 300 rivers and drained by just one, the Angara.

Yukagirskoye Ploskogor'ye is a rolling plain with isolated drumlins, domelike features resulting from glacial deposition.

UNITED STATES OF AMERICA
Bering Strait
Arctic Circle
OKHOTSKOYE
Ostrov Sakhalin
Yuzhno-Sakhalinsk
Magadan
Petropavlovsk-Kamchatskiy
Poluostrov Kamchatka
Sredinnyy Khrebet
Komandorskiye Ostrova
Kuril'skiye Ostrova
La Perouse Strait
JAPAN
Vladivostok
Nakhodka
Khabarovsk
Komsomol'sk-na-Amure
Anadyr'
Proliv Longa
Ostrov Vrangelya
Chukotskiy Poluostrov
Koryakskoye Nagor'ye
Kolyma
Palana

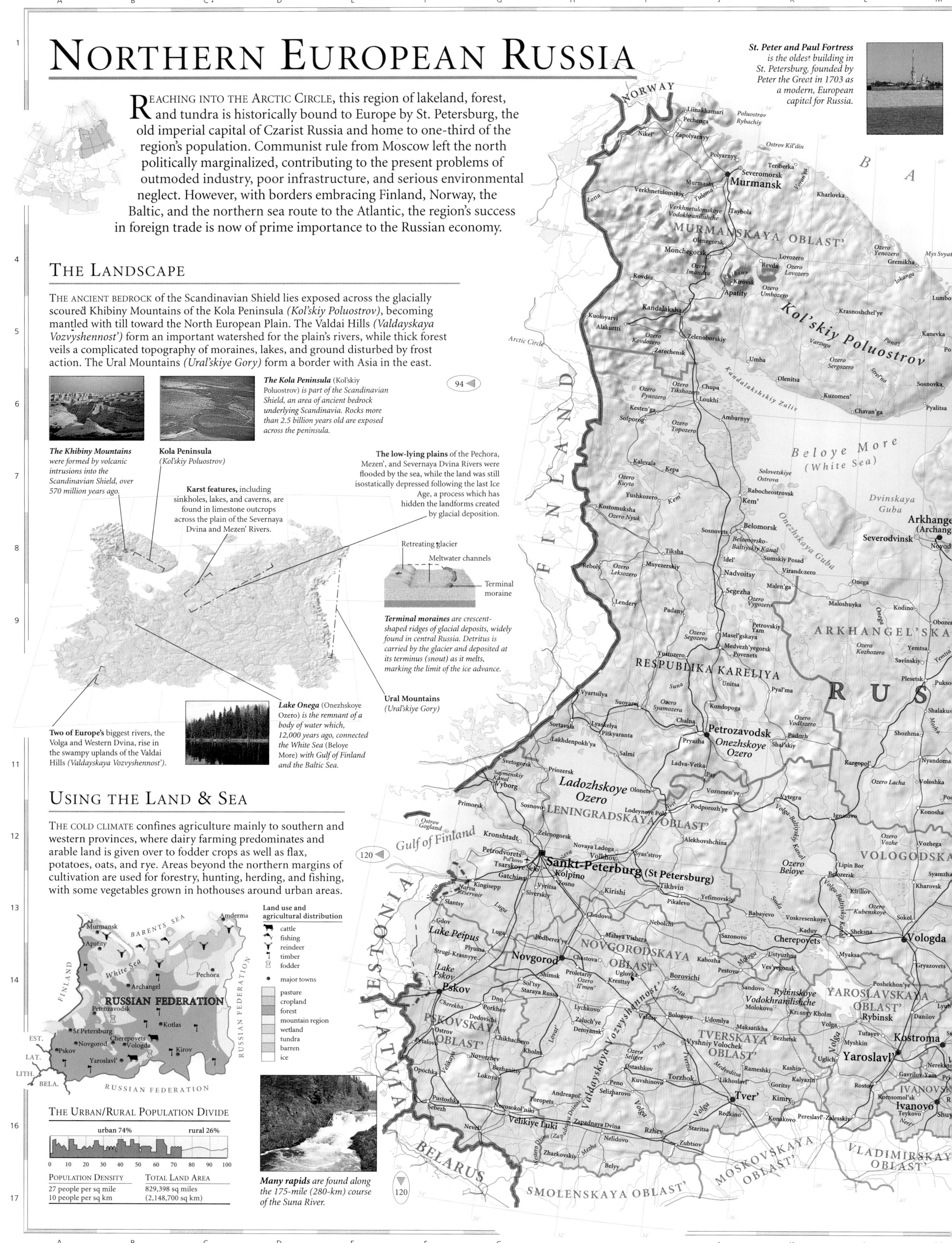

Northern European Russia

Reaching into the Arctic Circle, this region of lakeland, forest, and tundra is historically bound to Europe by St. Petersburg, the old imperial capital of Czarist Russia and home to one-third of the region's population. Communist rule from Moscow left the north politically marginalized, contributing to the present problems of outmoded industry, poor infrastructure, and serious environmental neglect. However, with borders embracing Finland, Norway, the Baltic, and the northern sea route to the Atlantic, the region's success in foreign trade is now of prime importance to the Russian economy.

St. Peter and Paul Fortress *is the oldest building in St. Petersburg, founded by Peter the Great in 1703 as a modern, European capital for Russia.*

The Landscape

The ancient bedrock of the Scandinavian Shield lies exposed across the glacially scoured Khibiny Mountains of the Kola Peninsula *(Kol'skiy Poluostrov)*, becoming mantled with till toward the North European Plain. The Valdai Hills *(Valdayskaya Vozvyshennost')* form an important watershed for the plain's rivers, while thick forest veils a complicated topography of moraines, lakes, and ground disturbed by frost action. The Ural Mountains *(Ural'skiye Gory)* form a border with Asia in the east.

The Khibiny Mountains *were formed by volcanic intrusions into the Scandinavian Shield, over 570 million years ago.*

Kola Peninsula *(Kol'skiy Poluostrov)*

The Kola Peninsula (Kol'skiy Poluostrov) *is part of the Scandinavian Shield, an area of ancient bedrock underlying Scandinavia. Rocks more than 2.5 billion years old are exposed across the peninsula.*

Karst features, including sinkholes, lakes, and caverns, are found in limestone outcrops across the plain of the Severnaya Dvina and Mezen' Rivers.

The low-lying plains of the Pechora, Mezen', and Severnaya Dvina Rivers were flooded by the sea, while the land was still isostatically depressed following the last Ice Age, a process which has hidden the landforms created by glacial deposition.

Retreating glacier
Meltwater channels
Terminal moraine

Terminal moraines *are crescent-shaped ridges of glacial deposits, widely found in central Russia. Detritus is carried by the glacier and deposited at its terminus (snout) as it melts, marking the limit of the ice advance.*

Ural Mountains *(Ural'skiye Gory)*

Lake Onega (Onezhskoye Ozero) *is the remnant of a body of water which, 12,000 years ago, connected the White Sea* (Beloye More) *with Gulf of Finland and the Baltic Sea.*

Two of Europe's biggest rivers, the Volga and Western Dvina, rise in the swampy uplands of the Valdai Hills *(Valdayskaya Vozvyshennost')*.

Using the Land & Sea

The cold climate confines agriculture mainly to southern and western provinces, where dairy farming predominates and arable land is given over to fodder crops as well as flax, potatoes, oats, and rye. Areas beyond the northern margins of cultivation are used for forestry, hunting, herding, and fishing, with some vegetables grown in hothouses around urban areas.

Land use and agricultural distribution
cattle
fishing
reindeer
timber
fodder
major towns
pasture
cropland
forest
mountain region
wetland
tundra
barren
ice
RUSSIAN FEDERATION
BARENTS SEA
White Sea
FINLAND
EST.
LAT.
LITH.
BELA.
Murmansk
Apatity
Amderma
Pechora
Archangel
Petrozavodsk
St Petersburg
Cherepovets
Novgorod
Vologda
Kotlas
Pskov
Yaroslavl'
Kirov

The Urban/Rural Population Divide

urban 74%
rural 26%
0 10 20 30 40 50 60 70 80 90 100

Population Density	Total Land Area
27 people per sq mile	829,398 sq miles
10 people per sq km	(2,148,700 sq km)

Many rapids *are found along the 175-mile (280-km) course of the Suna River.*

NORWAY
FINLAND
ESTONIA
LATVIA
BELARUS
Murmanskaya Oblast'
Kol'skiy Poluostrov
Beloye More (White Sea)
Respublika Kareliya
Arkhangel'skaya
Ladozhskoye Ozero
Onezhskoye Ozero
Leningradskaya Oblast'
Gulf of Finland
Sankt-Peterburg (St Petersburg)
Novgorodskaya Oblast'
Pskovskaya Oblast'
Tverskaya Oblast'
Vologodskaya
Yaroslavskaya Oblast'
Smolenskaya Oblast'
Moskovskaya Oblast'
Vladimirskaya Oblast'
Valdayskaya Vozvyshennost'
Murmansk
Petrozavodsk
Arkhangel'sk
Novgorod
Pskov
Vologda
Tver'
Yaroslavl'
Kostroma
Ivanovo

94
120
120

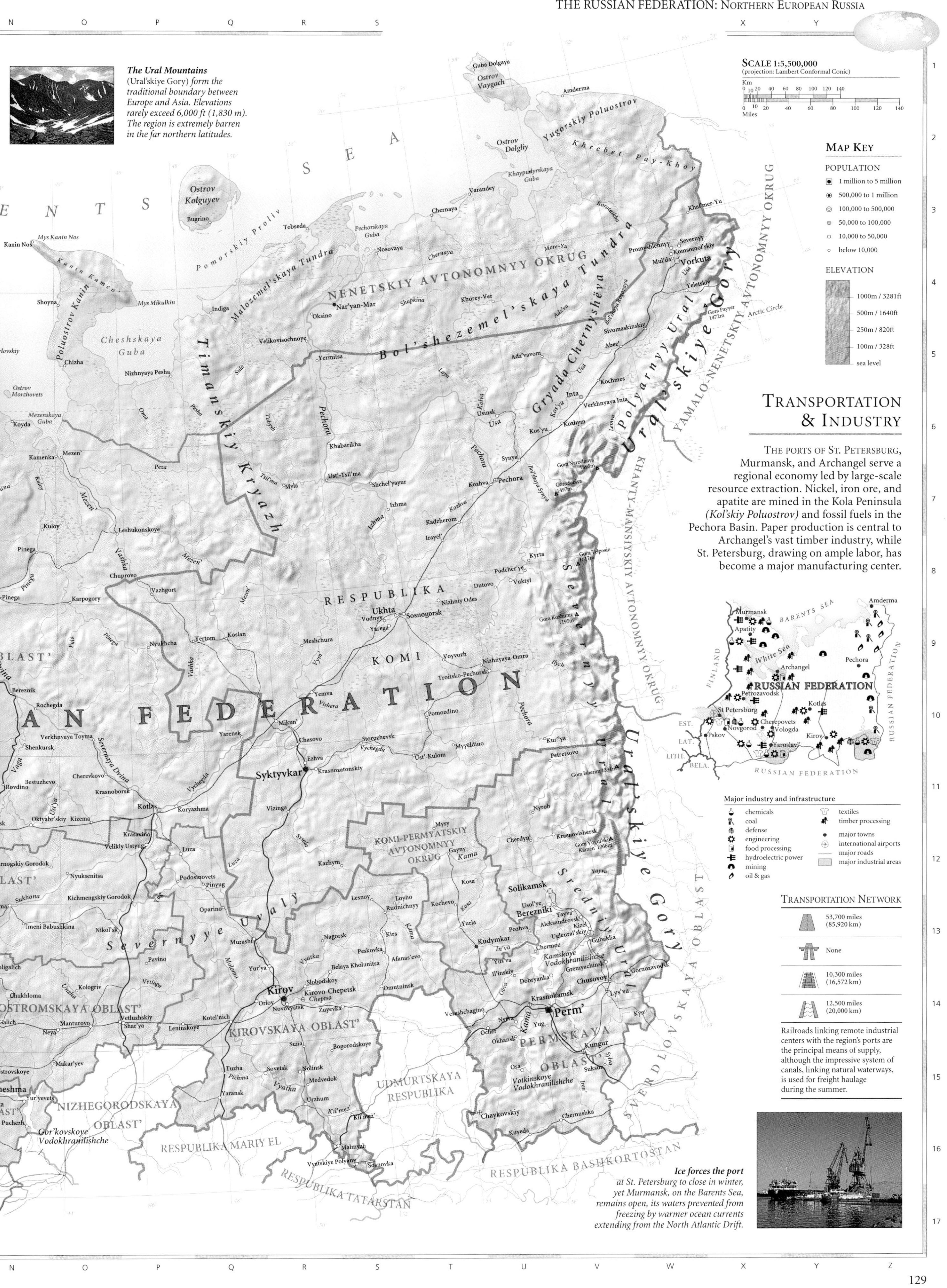

N O P Q R S X Y
SCALE 1:5,500,000
(projection: Lambert Conformal Conic)
Km 0 10 20 40 60 80 100 120 140
Miles 0 10 20 40 60 80 100 120 140
MAP KEY
POPULATION
1 million to 5 million
500,000 to 1 million
100,000 to 500,000
50,000 to 100,000
10,000 to 50,000
below 10,000
ELEVATION
1000m / 3281ft
500m / 1640ft
250m / 820ft
100m / 328ft
sea level
Major industry and infrastructure
chemicals
coal
defense
engineering
food processing
hydroelectric power
mining
oil & gas
textiles
timber processing
major towns
international airports
major roads
major industrial areas
TRANSPORTATION NETWORK
53,700 miles (85,920 km)
None
10,300 miles (16,572 km)
12,500 miles (20,000 km)
Murmansk
Apatity
BARENTS SEA
White Sea
Archangel
Pechora
Amderma
RUSSIAN FEDERATION
Petrozavodsk
St Petersburg
Cherepovets
Vologda
Novgorod
Pskov
Kotlas
Kirov
Yaroslavl'
FINLAND
EST.
LAT.
LITH.
BELA.
Ostrov Vaygach
Guba Dolgaya
Amderma
Yugorskiy Poluostrov
Khrebet Pay-Khoy
Ostrov Dolgiy
Khaypudyrskaya Guba
Varandey
Ostrov Kolguyev
Bugrino
Pomorskiy Proliv
Mys Kanin Nos
Kanin Nos
Kanin Kamen'
Mys Mikulkin
Poluostrov Kanin
Cheshskaya Guba
Ostrov Morzhovets
Mezenskaya Guba
Malozemel'skaya Tundra
Bol'shezemel'skaya Tundra
NENETSKIY AVTONOMNYY OKRUG
Nar'yan-Mar
Vorkuta
Inta
Usinsk
Pechora
Polyarnyy Ural
Ural'skiye Gory
Gryada Chernysheva
Timanskiy Kryazh
YAMALO-NENETSKIY AVTONOMNYY OKRUG
KHANTY-MANSIYSKIY AVTONOMNYY OKRUG
Arctic Circle
Gora Payyer 1472m
Gora Narodnaya 1895m
Gora Sabyla 1497m
Gora Telposiz 1617m
Gora Kozhimiz 1195m
Severnyy Ural
RESPUBLIKA KOMI
Ukhta
Sosnogorsk
Syktyvkar
RUSSIAN FEDERATION
Kotlas
Velikiy Ustyug
Severnyye Uvaly
KOMI-PERMYATSKIY AVTONOMNYY OKRUG
Solikamsk
Berezniki
Kudymkar
Perm'
PERMSKAYA OBLAST'
Sredniy Ural
Kamskoye Vodokhranilishche
Votkinskoye Vodokhranilishche
SVERDLOVSKAYA OBLAST'
Kirov
KIROVSKAYA OBLAST'
KOSTROMSKAYA OBLAST'
NIZHEGORODSKAYA OBLAST'
Gor'kovskoye Vodokhranilishche
RESPUBLIKA MARIY EL
UDMURTSKAYA RESPUBLIKA
RESPUBLIKA TATARSTAN
RESPUBLIKA BASHKORTOSTAN
Chaykovskiy
N O P Q R S T U V W X Y Z
1 2 3 4 5 6 7 8 9 10 11 12 13 14 15 16 17

The Ural Mountains *(Ural'skiye Gory) form the traditional boundary between Europe and Asia. Elevations rarely exceed 6,000 ft (1,830 m). The region is extremely barren in the far northern latitudes.*

TRANSPORTATION & INDUSTRY

THE PORTS OF ST. PETERSBURG, Murmansk, and Archangel serve a regional economy led by large-scale resource extraction. Nickel, iron ore, and apatite are mined in the Kola Peninsula *(Kol'skiy Poluostrov)* and fossil fuels in the Pechora Basin. Paper production is central to Archangel's vast timber industry, while St. Petersburg, drawing on ample labor, has become a major manufacturing center.

Railroads linking remote industrial centers with the region's ports are the principal means of supply, although the impressive system of canals, linking natural waterways, is used for freight haulage during the summer.

Ice forces the port *at St. Petersburg to close in winter, yet Murmansk, on the Barents Sea, remains open, its waters prevented from freezing by warmer ocean currents extending from the North Atlantic Drift.*

BALTIC SEA
LITHUANIA
POLAND
BELARUS
UKRAINE
KALININGRADSKAYA OBLAST'
Kaliningrad
Smolensk
MOSKVA (MOSCOW)
Kaluga
Tula
Bryansk
Orël
Kursk
Belgorod
Voronezh
Lipetsk
Ryazan'
Vladimir
Rostov-na-Donu
Taganrog
Krasnodar
Maykop
Novorossiysk
Sochi
Sea of Azov
BLACK SEA
120
112
118

SOUTHERN EUROPEAN RUSSIA

THIS REGION, DIVIDED FROM ASIA by desert, seas, and mountains, has exerted a powerful influence both east and west since the 13th century. More than 70 years of communist rule produced a highly urbanized, industrial society dominated by Moscow, which was the capital of the Soviet Union until 1991. Almost two-thirds of the Russian Federation's population live in this core area, with a relatively high *per capita* share of its wealth. However, the rapid growth of a market economy has caused great social upheaval, with rising crime and political instability.

***Kaliningrad** has been a Russian enclave since 1945. The port is an important center for the Russian Federation's Baltic fishing fleet.*

***St. Basil's Cathedral**, completed in 1561, stands in Moscow's Red Square next to the Kremlin, which was the original fortified stronghold of the city.*

THE LANDSCAPE

ANCIENT FOLDS in the deep sedimentary strata of the North European Plain have created a sequence of high and low regions. The Central Russian Upland *(Srednerusskaya Vozvyshennost')* in the west is deeply incised by rivers draining into the lowland of the Oka and Don rivers. In the east, the Volga, Europe's longest river, divides the Volga Uplands *(Privolzhskaya Vozvyshennost')* from the foothills of the Ural Mountains *(Ural'skiye Gory)*, flowing south to the Caspian Sea. The Caucasus Mountains and the Black Sea form a natural border to the southwest.

***A plantation of Scots pine** helps consolidate the loose sandy soils of the Meshchera Lowland* (Meshcherskaya Nizina), *which lies on the bed of an old glacial lake.*

The Smolensk-Moscow Upland *(Smolensko-Moskovskaya Vozvyshennost')* is a series of terminal moraine ridges marking the southern extent of the last glaciation.

Glacial till covers the bedrock to the north of the North European Plain, giving a gentle surface relief.

The lowland of the Oka and Don Rivers lies over a broad trough, between the upfolds of the Volga Uplands *(Privolzhskaya Vozvyshennost')* to the east, and the Central Russian Upland *(Srednerusskaya Vozvyshennost')* to the west.

The southern Ural Mountains *(Ural'skiye Gory)* consist of several parallel ranges of ancient fold mountains running from north to south.

Ice and water have formed escarpments and columns in the resistant chalk strata south of the Central Russian Upland *(Srednerusskaya Vozvyshennost')*.

The floodplain of the Volga forms a long oasis of verdant vegetation, contrasting with the aridity of the surrounding Caspian hinterland.

The marshlands of the Volga Delta are visited by over 260 species of bird each year, migrating between South Africa and Arctic Siberia.

The Caspian Depression is a large downfold (or syncline) which became flooded, forming the Caspian Sea. The shoreline is 98 ft (30 m) below sea level.

Drifting sand occupies large areas of the south, creating dunes up to 50 ft (15 m) high.

***The Caucasus Mountains** run from the Black Sea to the Caspian Sea and include El'brus which, at 18,511 ft (5,642 m), is the highest point in all of Europe.*

Salt dome

Salt dome is forced up and through the rock strata

Sedimentary strata

Salts are forced upward by denser overlying strata

***Salt domes**, rounded hills up to 500 ft (150 m) high, are produced as less dense rock salts are displaced under the extreme pressure of denser, overlying strata and forced up toward the surface creating domes. They are widespread in the Caspian Depression.*

SCALE 1:5,500,000
(projection: Lambert Conformal Conic)
Km
Miles
MAP KEY
POPULATION
above 5 million
1 million to 5 million
500,000 to 1 million
100,000 to 500,000
50,000 to 100,000
10,000 to 50,000
below 10,000
ELEVATION
4000m / 13,124ft
3000m / 9843ft
2000m / 6562ft
1000m / 3281ft
500m / 1640ft
250m / 820ft
100m / 328ft
sea level
KIROVSKAYA OBLAST'
PERMSKAYA OBLAST'
SVERDLOVSKAYA OBLAST'
CHELYABINSKAYA OBLAST'
KOSTROMSKAYA OBLAST'
NIZHEGORODSKAYA OBLAST'
UDMURTSKAYA RESPUBLIKA
RESPUBLIKA MARIY EL
CHUVASHSKAYA RESPUBLIKA
RESPUBLIKA TATARSTAN
RESPUBLIKA BASHKORTOSTAN
RESPUBLIKA MORDOVIYA
UL'YANOVSKAYA OBLAST'
PENZENSKAYA OBLAST'
SAMARSKAYA OBLAST'
ORENBURGSKAYA OBLAST'
SARATOVSKAYA OBLAST'
VOLGOGRADSKAYA OBLAST'
ASTRAKHANSKAYA OBLAST'
RESPUBLIKA KALMYKIYA
STAVROPOL'SKIY KRAY
CHECHENSKAYA RESPUBLIKA
RESPUBLIKA DAGESTAN
KAZAKHSTAN
GEORGIA
AZERBAIJAN
RUSSIAN FEDERATION
Caspian Sea
Caspian Depression
Ural'skiye Gory
Nizhniy Novgorod
Kazan'
Samara
Tol'yatti
Ul'yanovsk
Saratov
Volgograd
Astrakhan'
Orenburg
Ufa
Izhevsk
Cheboksary
Penza
Saransk
Elista
Makhachkala
Groznyy
Vladikavkaz
Nal'chik
Naberezhnyye Chelny
Sterlitamak
Orsk
Kuybyshevskoye Vodokhranilishche
Volgogradskoye Vodokhranilishche
Saratovskoye Vodokhranilishche
Tsimlyanskoye Vodokhranilishche
Nizhnekamskoye Vodokhranilishche
Volga
Kama
Ural

USING THE LAND

IN THE COLD, HUMID NORTH and in the southern Urals *(Ural'skiye Gory)*, small grains, potatoes, and flax are commonly rotated with legumes, which support livestock farming. The rich *chernozem* (black earth) areas support diverse crops such as sugar beet, hemp, sunflowers, millet, and vegetables. Farther south, aridity restricts husbandry to extensive grazing, with intensive fruit and rice cultivation along the oasis of the Volga.

THE URBAN/RURAL POPULATION DIVIDE

urban 65% | rural 35%

0 10 20 30 40 50 60 70 80 90 100

POPULATION DENSITY	TOTAL LAND AREA
129 people per sq mile (50 people per sq km)	705,916 sq miles (1,828,800 sq km)

Land use and agricultural distribution
sheep
flax
potatoes
rice
sunflowers
sugar beet
timber
capital cities
major towns
pasture
cropland
forest
wetland
mountain region
tundra
RUSSIAN FEDERATION
MOSCOW
Nizhniy Novgorod
Ufa
Samara
Voronezh
Orsk
Rostov-na-Donu
Astrakhan'
Groznyy
BELARUS
UKRAINE
KAZAKHSTAN
Sea of Azov
BLACK SEA
GEORGIA
AZERB.
Caspian Sea

TRANSPORTATION & INDUSTRY

MANUFACTURING is largely based around Moscow and the Volga region, which became a major industrial area during the Second World War. Both Moscow and Nizhniy Novgorod are centers of skilled labor for light manufacturing and engineering. Most of Russia's main chemical plants are located along the Volga, and one of the world's largest car factories was recently opened in Tol'yatti. Processing and machine construction plants use oil, gas, and hydroelectric power from the Volga Basin and metallic minerals from the Urals *(Ural'skiye Gory)* and Kursk.

Industrial plants are massed along the Volga. Environmental stress from decades of unbridled industrial development has prompted widespread concern about pollution levels.

TRANSPORTATION NETWORK

250,000 miles (402,000 km)	None
28,000 miles (44,800 km)	16,300 miles (26,080 km)

Seventy private and national flag airlines have been created from the reorganization of the state airline Aeroflot, which maintained the world's largest fleet of aircraft during the Soviet era.

Major industry and infrastructure
aerospace
car manufacture
chemicals
defense
electronics
engineering
gas
mining
oil
textiles
capital cities
major towns
international airports
major roads
major industrial areas
RUSSIAN FEDERATION
MOSCOW
Nizhniy Novgorod
Kazan'
Ufa
Tula
Ryazan'
Ul'yanovsk
Bryansk
Penza
Tol'yatti
Samara
Kursk
Voronezh
Saratov
Belgorod
Orsk
Volgograd
Rostov-na-Donu
Astrakhan'
Stavropol'
Groznyy
BELARUS
UKRAINE
KAZAKHSTAN
Sea of Azov
BLACK SEA
GEORGIA
AZERB.
Caspian Sea

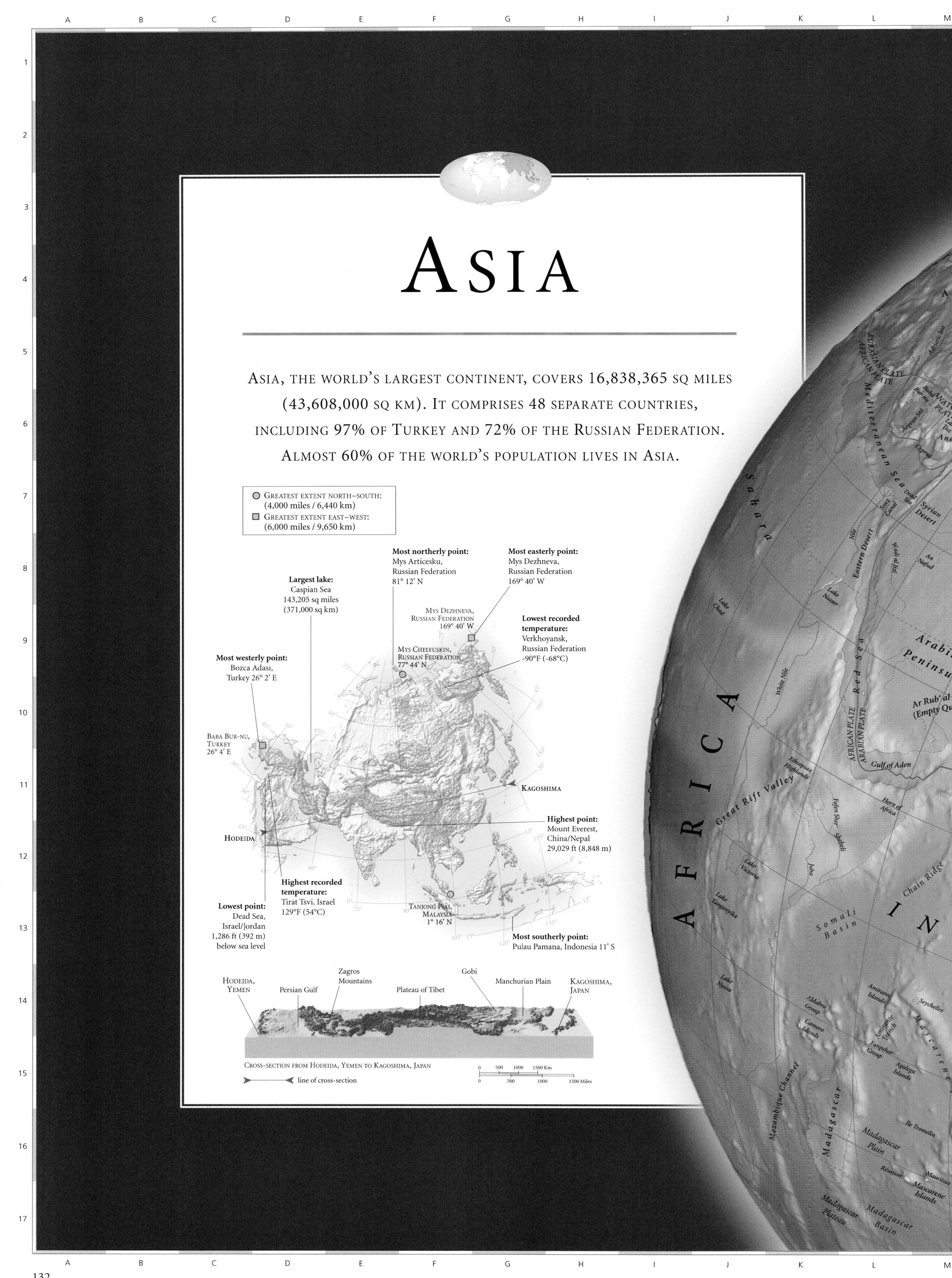

ASIA
ASIA, THE WORLD'S LARGEST CONTINENT, COVERS 16,838,365 SQ MILES (43,608,000 SQ KM). IT COMPRISES 48 SEPARATE COUNTRIES, INCLUDING 97% OF TURKEY AND 72% OF THE RUSSIAN FEDERATION. ALMOST 60% OF THE WORLD'S POPULATION LIVES IN ASIA.
GREATEST EXTENT NORTH–SOUTH: (4,000 miles / 6,440 km)
GREATEST EXTENT EAST–WEST: (6,000 miles / 9,650 km)
Most northerly point: Mys Articesku, Russian Federation 81° 12' N
Most easterly point: Mys Dezhneva, Russian Federation 169° 40' W
Largest lake: Caspian Sea 143,205 sq miles (371,000 sq km)
MYS DEZHNEVA, RUSSIAN FEDERATION 169° 40' W
Lowest recorded temperature: Verkhoyansk, Russian Federation -90°F (-68°C)
MYS CHELYUSKIN, RUSSIAN FEDERATION 77° 44' N
Most westerly point: Bozca Adası, Turkey 26° 2' E
BABA BUR-NU, TURKEY 26° 4' E
KAGOSHIMA
Highest point: Mount Everest, China/Nepal 29,029 ft (8,848 m)
HODEIDA
Highest recorded temperature: Tirat Tsvi, Israel 129°F (54°C)
Lowest point: Dead Sea, Israel/Jordan 1,286 ft (392 m) below sea level
TANJONG PIAI, MALAYSIA 1° 16' N
Most southerly point: Pulau Pamana, Indonesia 11' S
HODEIDA, YEMEN
Persian Gulf
Zagros Mountains
Plateau of Tibet
Gobi
Manchurian Plain
KAGOSHIMA, JAPAN
CROSS-SECTION FROM HODEIDA, YEMEN TO KAGOSHIMA, JAPAN
line of cross-section
0 500 1000 1500 Km
0 500 1000 1500 Miles
AFRICA
Sahara
Mediterranean Sea
EURASIAN PLATE
AFRICAN PLATE
ANATOLIAN PLATE
Aegean Sea
Cyprus
Dead Sea
Suez Canal
Syrian Desert
Nile
Eastern Desert
An Nafud
Lake Nasser
Lake Chad
Red Sea
Arabian Peninsula
White Nile
AFRICAN PLATE
ARABIAN PLATE
Ar Rub' al Khali (Empty Quarter)
Ethiopian Highlands
Gulf of Aden
Great Rift Valley
Horn of Africa
Shebeli
Lake Victoria
Juba
Chain Ridge
Lake Tanganyika
Somali Basin
Lake Nyasa
Amirante Islands
Seychelles
Aldabra Group
Comoro Islands
Amirante Trench
Farquhar Group
Agalega Islands
Mozambique Channel
Madagascar
Madagascar Plain
Île Tromelin
Réunion
Mauritius
Mascarene Islands
Madagascar Plateau
Madagascar Basin

N O P Q R S T U V W X Y Z

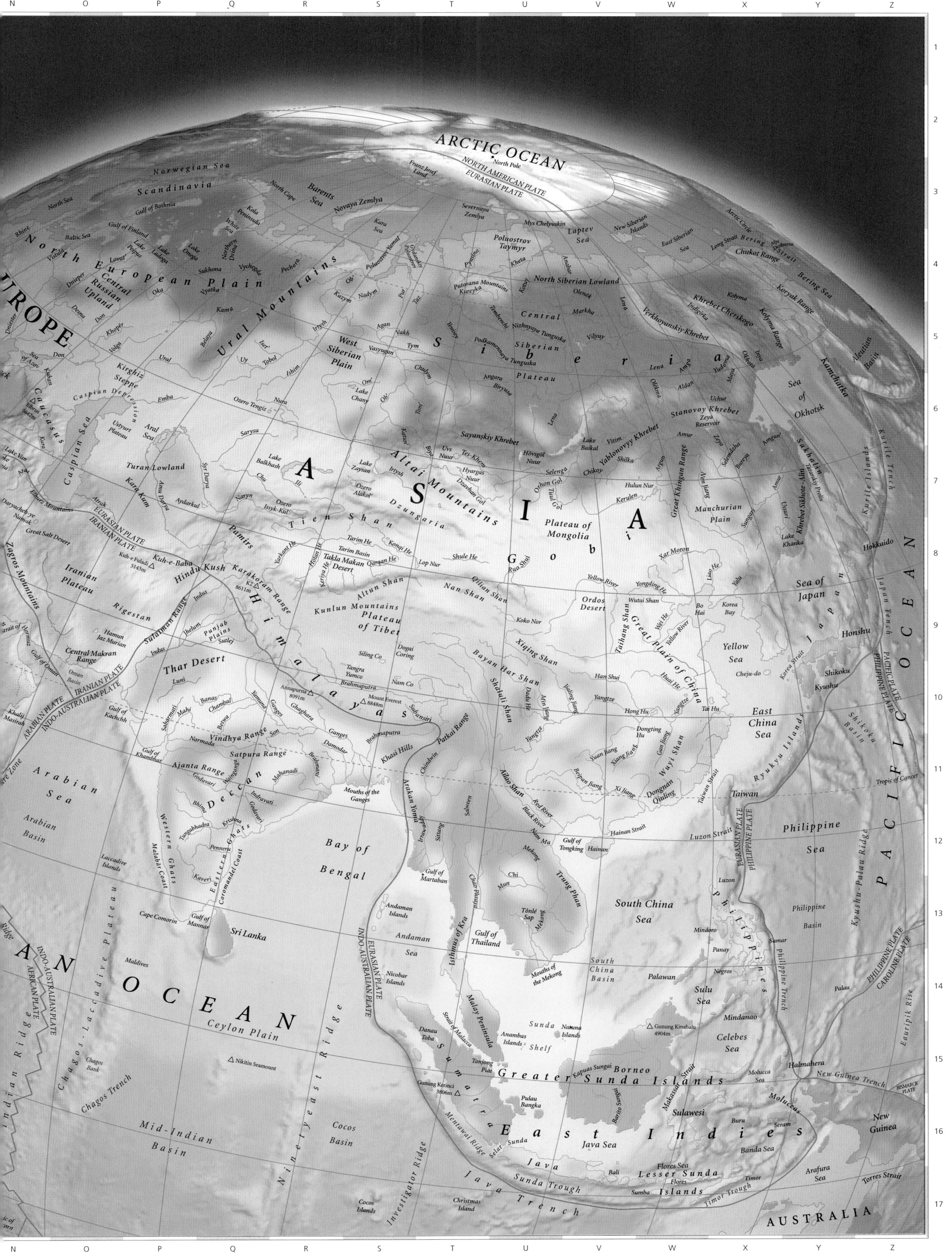
ARCTIC OCEAN
A S I A
EUROPE
PACIFIC OCEAN
INDIAN OCEAN
AUSTRALIA

1 2 3 4 5 6 7 8 9 10 11 12 13 14 15 16 17

N O P Q R S T U V W X Y Z

Asian Resources

ALTHOUGH AGRICULTURE REMAINS THE ECONOMIC MAINSTAY of most Asian countries, the number of people employed in agriculture has steadily declined, as new industries have been developed during the past 30 years. China, Indonesia, Malaysia, Thailand, and Turkey have all experienced far-reaching structural changes in their economies, while the breakup of the former Soviet Union has created a new economic challenge in the Central Asian republics. The countries of the Persian Gulf illustrate the rapid transformation from rural nomadism to modern, urban society, which oil wealth has brought to parts of the continent. Asia's most economically dynamic countries, Japan, Singapore, South Korea, and Taiwan, fringe the Pacific Ocean and are known as the Pacific Rim. In contrast, other Southeast Asian countries like Laos and Cambodia remain both economically and industrially underdeveloped.

Standard of Living

DESPITE JAPAN'S HIGH STANDARDS OF LIVING, and southwestern Asia's oil-derived wealth, immense disparities exist throughout the continent. Afghanistan remains one of the world's most underdeveloped nations, as do the mountain states of Nepal and Bhutan. Rapid population growth is exacerbating poverty and overcrowding in many parts of India and Bangladesh.

Standard of Living
(UN Human Development Index)

low
high

Industry

JAPANESE INDUSTRY LEADS THE CONTINENT in both productivity and efficiency; electronics, hi-tech industries, car manufacture, and shipbuilding are important. In recent years, the so-called economic "tigers" of the Pacific Rim such as Taiwan and South Korea are now challenging Japan's economic dominance. Heavy industries such as engineering, chemicals, and steel typify the industrial complexes along the corridor created by the Trans–Siberian Railway, the Fergana Valley in Central Asia, and also much of the huge industrial plain of east China. The discovery of oil in the Persian Gulf has brought immense wealth to countries that previously relied on subsistence agriculture on marginal desertland.

Industry

- aerospace
- brewing
- car/vehicle manufacture
- cement
- chemicals
- electronics
- engineering
- finance
- fish processing
- food processing
- hi-tech industry
- iron & steel
- pharmaceuticals
- printing & publishing
- shipbuilding
- sugar processing
- tea processing
- textiles
- timber processing
- tobacco processing
- coal
- oil
- gas
- industrial cities
- major industrial areas

GNP per capita (US$)

- 0–499
- 500–999
- 1,000–4,999
- 5,000–9,999
- 10,000–19,999
- 2,0000+

On a small island *on the southern tip of the Malay Peninsula lies Singapore, one of the Pacific Rim's most vibrant economic centers. Multinational banking and finance form the core of the city's wealth.*

Iron and steel, *engineering, and shipbuilding typify the industries of eastern China's industrial cities, especially the nation's leading manufacturing center, Shanghai.*

Traditional industries *are still crucial to many rural economies across Asia. Here, on the Vietnamese coast, salt has been extracted from seawater by evaporation and is being loaded into a truck to take to market.*

ENVIRONMENTAL ISSUES

THE TRANSFORMATION OF UZBEKISTAN by the former Soviet Union into the world's second largest producer of cotton led to the diversion of several major rivers for irrigation. Starved of this water, the Aral Sea diminished in volume by over 50% in 30 years, irreversibly altering the ecology of the area. Heavy industries in eastern China have polluted coastal waters, rivers, and urban air, while in Myanmar, Malaysia, and Indonesia, ancient hardwood rain forests are being cut down faster than they can regenerate.

Environmental Issues

- tropical forest
- forest destroyed
- desert
- desertification
- acid rain
- polluted rivers
- marine pollution
- heavy marine pollution
- radioactive contamination
- poor urban air quality

***The long-term environmental impact** of the Gulf War (1991) is still uncertain. As Iraqi troops left Kuwait, equipment was abandoned to rust and thousands of oil wells were set on fire, pouring crude oil into the Persian Gulf.*

***Although Siberia remains** a quintessentially frozen, inhospitable wasteland, vast untapped mineral reserves – especially the oil and gas of the West Siberian Plain – have lured industrial development to the area since the 1950s and 1960s.*

MINERAL RESOURCES

AT LEAST 60% OF THE WORLD'S known oil and gas deposits are found in Asia; notably the vast oil fields of the Persian Gulf, and the less-exploited oil and gas fields of the Ob' Basin in western Siberia. Immense coal reserves in Siberia and China have been utilized to support large steel industries. Southeast Asia has some of the world's largest deposits of tin, found in a belt running down the Malay Peninsula to Indonesia.

Mineral Resources

- oil field
- gas field
- coal field
- chromite
- copper
- gold
- iron
- lead
- nickel
- platinum
- tin
- wolfram

USING THE LAND & SEA

VAST AREAS OF ASIA REMAIN UNCULTIVATED as a result of unsuitable climatic and soil conditions. In favorable areas such as river deltas, farming is intensive. Rice is the staple crop of most Asian countries, grown in paddy fields on waterlogged alluvial plains and terraced hillsides, and often irrigated for higher yields. Across the black-earth region of the Eurasian steppe in southern Siberia and Kazakhstan, wheat farming is the dominant activity. Cash crops, like tea in Sri Lanka and dates in the Arabian Peninsula, are grown for export, and provide valuable income. The sovereignty of the rich fishing grounds in the South China Sea is disputed by China, Malaysia, Taiwan, the Philippines, and Vietnam, because of potential oil reserves.

***Date palms** have been cultivated in oases throughout the Arabian Peninsula since antiquity. In addition to the fruit, palms are used for timber, fuel, rope, and for making vinegar, syrup, and a liquor known as arrack.*

***Rice terraces blanket the landscape** across the small Indonesian island of Bali. The large amounts of water needed to grow rice have resulted in Balinese farmers organizing water-control cooperatives.*

Using the Land and Sea

- cropland
- desert
- forest
- mountain region
- pasture
- tundra
- wetland
- major conurbations
- cattle
- pigs
- goats
- sheep
- coconuts
- corn
- cotton
- dates
- fishing
- fruit
- jute
- oil palms
- peanuts
- rice
- rubber
- shellfish
- soy beans
- sugar beet
- sugar cane
- tea
- timber
- wheat

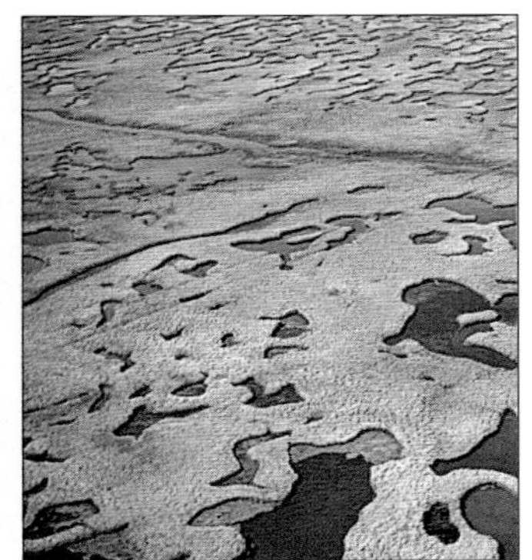

Siberian Plateau and Plain

The West Siberian Plain is one of the largest in the world, and contains a vast system of marshes. The whole area is covered by glacial deposits, underlain by the Angara Shield, a remnant of the ancient continent of Laurasia. The flat relief of the region and thick surface deposits result in poor drainage; this, combined with the freezing and thawing of the extensive permafrost layer, leads to the formation of the vast swamps that cover the area. Many of the north-flowing rivers are also frozen for up to half of the year.

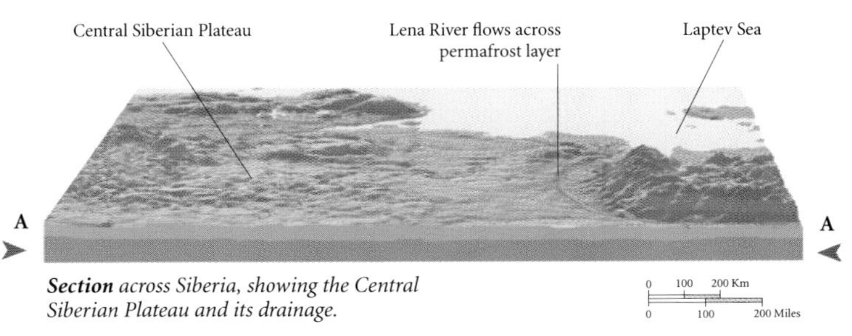
Central Siberian Plateau
Lena River flows across permafrost layer
Laptev Sea
A
A
0 100 200 Km
0 100 200 Miles

***Section** across Siberia, showing the Central Siberian Plateau and its drainage.*

The Arabian Shield and Iranian Plateau

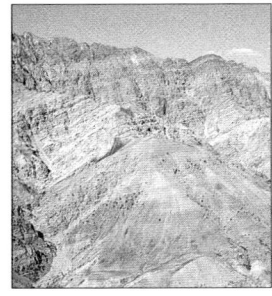

Approximately five million years ago, rifting of the continental crust split the Arabian Plate from the African Plate and flooded the Red Sea. As this rift spread, the Arabian Plate collided with the Eurasian Plate, transforming part of the Tethys seabed into the Zagros Mountains, which run northwest–southeast across western Iran.

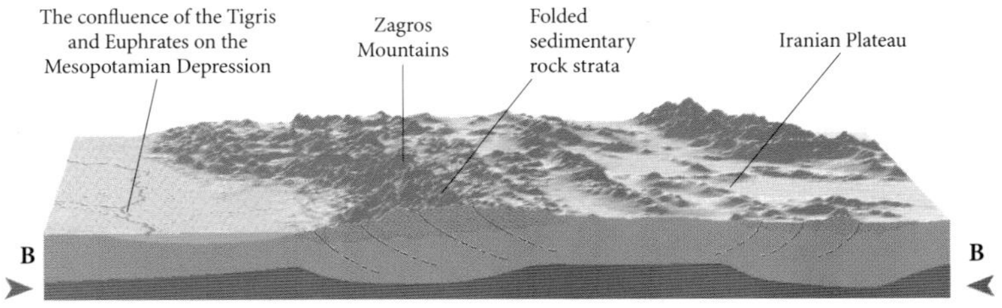

The confluence of the Tigris and Euphrates on the Mesopotamian Depression
Zagros Mountains
Folded sedimentary rock strata
Iranian Plateau
B
B
0 50 100 Km
0 50 100 Miles

***Cross-section** through southwestern Asia, showing the Mesopotamian Depression, the folded Zagros Mountains, and the Iranian Plateau.*

The Turan Basin and Kazakh Uplands

The Turan Basin and Kazakh Uplands are a complex mixture of mountain foothills, an arid limestone plateau, and deserts including the Kyzl Kum and Kara Kum. In the center of the Turan Lowland – an area of inland drainage – is the desiccated Aral Sea, reduced to a fraction of its former size because of the diversion of its flow into irrigation channels. The only rivers with sufficient water to cross this arid region are the Syr Dayra and Amu Dayra.

The Indian Shield and Himalayan System

The large shield area beneath the Indian subcontinent is between 2.5 and 3.5 billion years old. As the floor of the southern Indian Ocean spread, it pushed the Indian Shield north. It was eventually driven beneath the Plateau of Tibet. This process closed up the ancient Tethys Sea and uplifted the world's highest mountain chain, the Himalayas. Much of the uplifted rock strata was from the seabed of the Tethys Sea, partly accounting for the weakness of the rocks and the high levels of erosion found in the Himalayas.

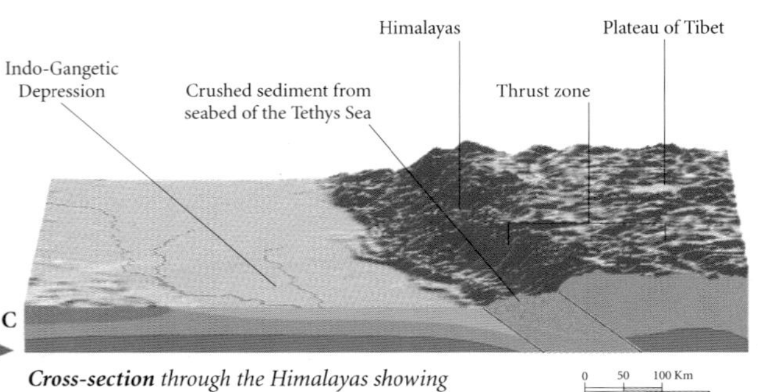
Himalayas
Plateau of Tibet
Indo-Gangetic Depression
Crushed sediment from seabed of the Tethys Sea
Thrust zone
C
C
0 50 100 Km
0 50 100 Miles

***Cross-section** through the Himalayas showing thrust faulting of the rock strata.*

Central Asian Plateaus and Basins

The Plateau of Tibet lies north of the Himalayas and covers 965,250 sq miles (2,500,000 sq km); its average elevation is 16,500 ft (5,000 m). The region is noted for its extreme aridity. In the south, the Himalayan mountain belt blocks moisture-bearing winds. The pressure from the Indo-Australian Plate against the plateau is causing both uplift and, when combined with the downward force caused by the weight of the plateau, extension east and west of the more malleable underlying crust. The brittle upper rock layers are extensively faulted.

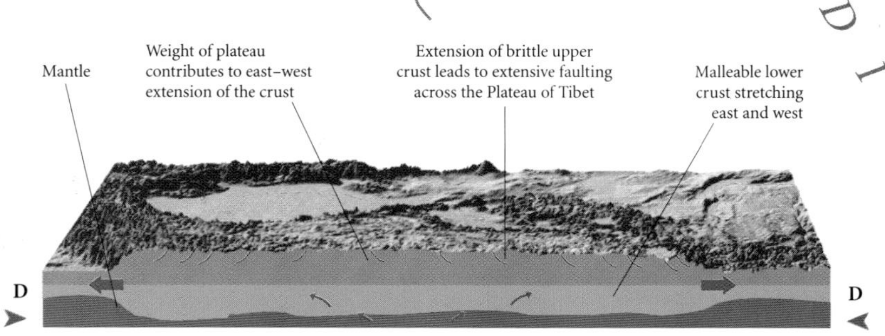

Mantle
Weight of plateau contributes to east–west extension of the crust
Extension of brittle upper crust leads to extensive faulting across the Plateau of Tibet
Malleable lower crust stretching east and west
D
D
0 200 400 Km
0 200 400 Miles

***Cross-section** across the Plateau of Tibet, showing uplift and crustal extension caused by the collision of the Indo-Australian and Eurasian plates.*

Physical Asia

The structure of Asia can be divided into two distinct regions. The landscape of northern Asia consists of old mountain chains, shields, plateaus, and basins, like the Ural Mountains in the west and the Central Siberian Plateau in the east. To the south of this region are a series of plateaus and basins, including the vast Plateau of Tibet and the Tarim Basin. In contrast, the landscapes of southern Asia are much younger, formed by tectonic activity beginning about 65 million years ago, leading to an almost continuous mountain chain running from Europe, across much of Asia, and culminating in the mighty Himalayan mountain belt, formed when the Indo-Australian Plate collided with the Eurasian Plate. These mountains are still being uplifted. North of the mountains lies a belt of deserts, including the Gobi and the Takla Makan. In the far south, tectonic activity has formed narrow island arcs, extending over 4,000 miles (7,000 km). To the west lies the Arabian Shield, once part of the African Plate. As it was rifted apart from Africa, the Arabian Plate collided with the Eurasian Plate, uplifting the Zagros Mountains.

Shaping the Landscape

In the north, melting of extensive permafrost leads to typical periglacial features such as thermokarst. In the arid areas, wind action transports sand, creating extensive dune systems. An active tectonic margin in the south causes continued uplift and volcanic and seismic activity, but also high rates of weathering and erosion. Across the continent, huge rivers erode and transport vast quantities of sediment, depositing it on the plains or forming large deltas.

Periglaciation

1 Permafrost is widespread across northern Siberia. When ground ice, which makes up a large proportion of the soil layer, melts, it contracts and extensive ground subsidence occurs. Over time, this process leads to depressions in the landscape and the gradual movement of soil down slopes. Eventually the accumulation of water in the depressions leads to thermokarstic lakes *(left)*.

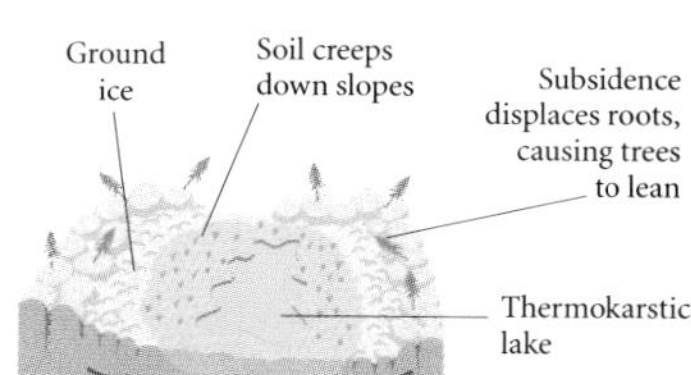

Ground ice
Soil creeps down slopes
Subsidence displaces roots, causing trees to lean
Thermokarstic lake

Periglaciation: formation of thermokarst

The Evolving Landscape

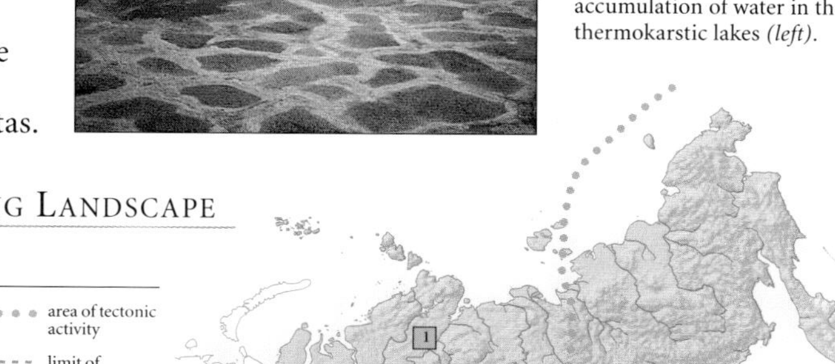

Landscape
limestone region
sinking land
stable land
uplifting land
active volcano
area of tectonic activity
limit of permafrost
ocean current

Tectonic Activity

7 The Dead Sea *(above)* lies in a pull-apart basin. The sliding of the African Plate against the Arabian Plate, at unequal rates, led to the sinking of blocks of crust. This depression has been filled by the waters of the Dead Sea and Lake Tiberias *(Sea of Galilee)*. The plates continue to move, causing intermittent earthquakes.

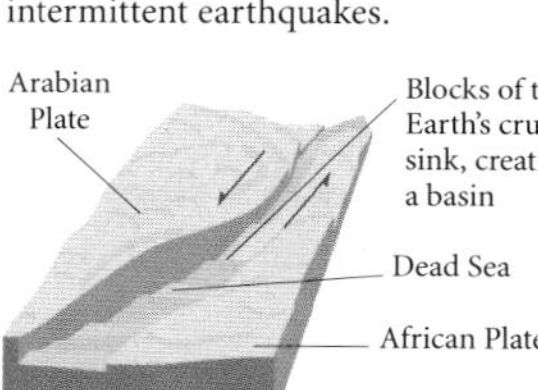

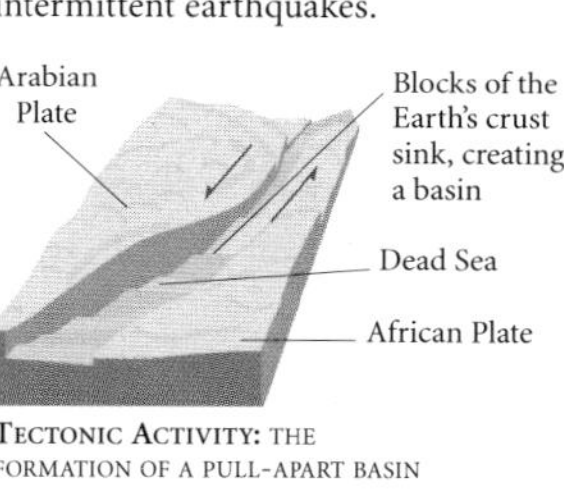

Arabian Plate
Blocks of the Earth's crust sink, creating a basin
Dead Sea
African Plate

Tectonic Activity: the formation of a pull-apart basin

River Systems

2 Vast river systems flow across Asia, many originating in the Himalayas and the Plateau of Tibet. Seasonal melting of snow and monsoon rains swell the river flow, leading to flooding and erosion. The Yellow River *(above)* gets its color from the high level of eroded material from the loess plateau.

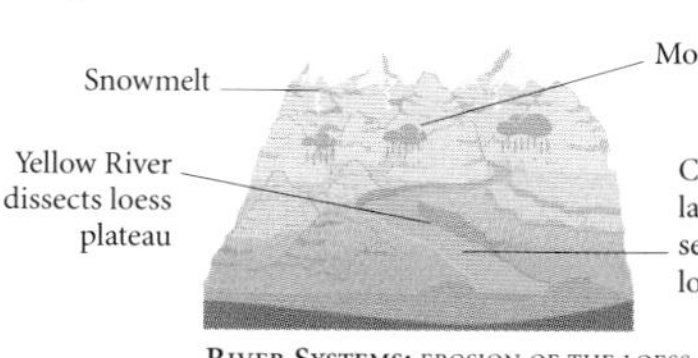

Snowmelt
Monsoon rains
Yellow River dissects loess plateau
Carries large sediment load

River Systems: erosion of the loess plateau by the Yellow River

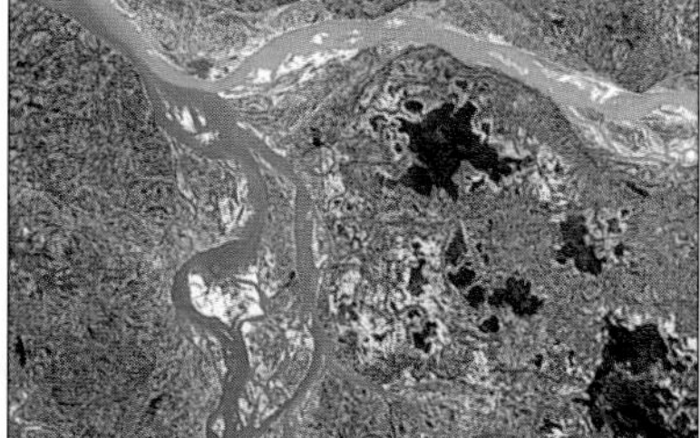

Sedimentation

6 The Ganges/Brahmaputra is a tide-dominated delta *(above)*. The two rivers transport huge quantities of mountain sediment, which is deposited on the delta plain. This debris is then redistributed by tidal currents, to form extensions to the bars, beach ridges, and deltaic deposits.

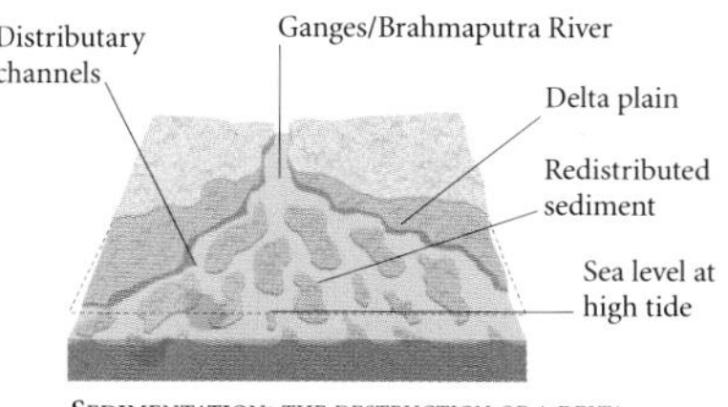

Distributary channels
Ganges/Brahmaputra River
Delta plain
Redistributed sediment
Sea level at high tide

Sedimentation: the destruction of a delta

Coastal Erosion

5 The erosion of cliffs along the coast of Indonesia *(above)* and Thailand occurs when waves and currents undermine the base leading to the collapse of material. The surf then gradually erodes this material away, exposing the cliff to further undercutting. This process eventually creates shore platforms.

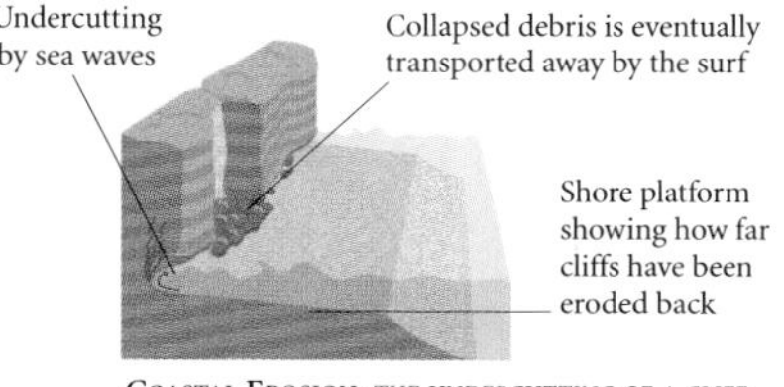

Undercutting by sea waves
Collapsed debris is eventually transported away by the surf
Shore platform showing how far cliffs have been eroded back

Coastal Erosion: the undercutting of a cliff

Volcanic Activity

4 Volcanic eruptions occur frequently across Southeast Asia's island arcs *(above)*. Low-level eruptions occur when groundwater, superheated by underlying magma, becomes pressurized, forcing hot fluid and rocks up through cracks in the volcanic cone. This is known as a phreatic eruption.

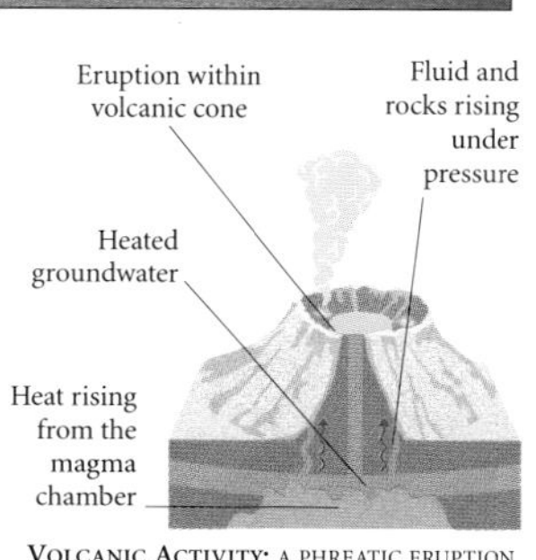

Eruption within volcanic cone
Fluid and rocks rising under pressure
Heated groundwater
Heat rising from the magma chamber

Volcanic Activity: a phreatic eruption

Chemical Weathering

3 Tower karsts are widespread across southern China *(above)* and Vietnam. It is thought that the karstic towers were formed under a soil cover, where small depressions in the limestone bedrock began to be weathered by soil water acids, eventually creating larger hollows. This process continued over millions of years, deepening the hollows and leaving steep-sided limestone hills.

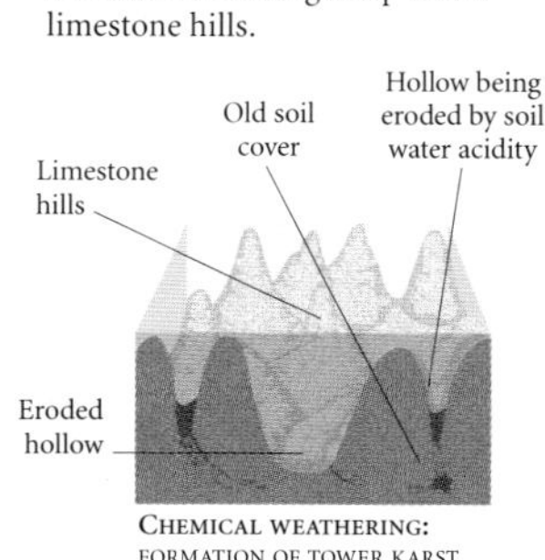

Limestone hills
Old soil cover
Hollow being eroded by soil water acidity
Eroded hollow

Chemical weathering: formation of tower karst

Political Asia

Asia is the world's largest continent, encompassing many different and discrete realms, from the desert Arab lands of the southwest to the subtropical archipelago of Indonesia; from the vast barren wastes of Siberia to the fertile river valleys of China and South Asia, seats of some of the world's most ancient civilizations. The collapse of the Soviet Union has fragmented the north of the continent into the Siberian portion of the Russian Federation and the new republics of Central Asia. Strong religious traditions heavily influence the politics of South and Southwest Asia. Hindu and Muslim rivalries threaten to upset the political equilibrium in South Asia, where India – in terms of population – remains the world's largest democracy. Communist China is the last great world empire. A population giant, it is still relatively closed to the western world, while on its doorstep, the economically progressive and dynamic Pacific Rim countries, led by Japan, continue to assert their worldwide economic force.

Population density
(people per sq mile)

- below 25
- 26–124
- 125–259
- 260–649
- 650–10,400
- above 10,400

Population

Some of the world's most populous and least populous regions are in Asia. The plains of eastern China, the Ganges River in India, Japan, and the Indonesian island of Java, all have very high population densities. In contrast, parts of Siberia and the Plateau of Tibet are virtually uninhabited. China has the world's greatest population – 20% of the globe's total – while India, with the second largest, is likely to overtake China within 20 years.

Calcutta's 12 million *inhabitants bustle through a maze of crowded, narrow streets. The population density in India's largest city reaches almost 85,000 per sq mile (33,000 per sq km).*

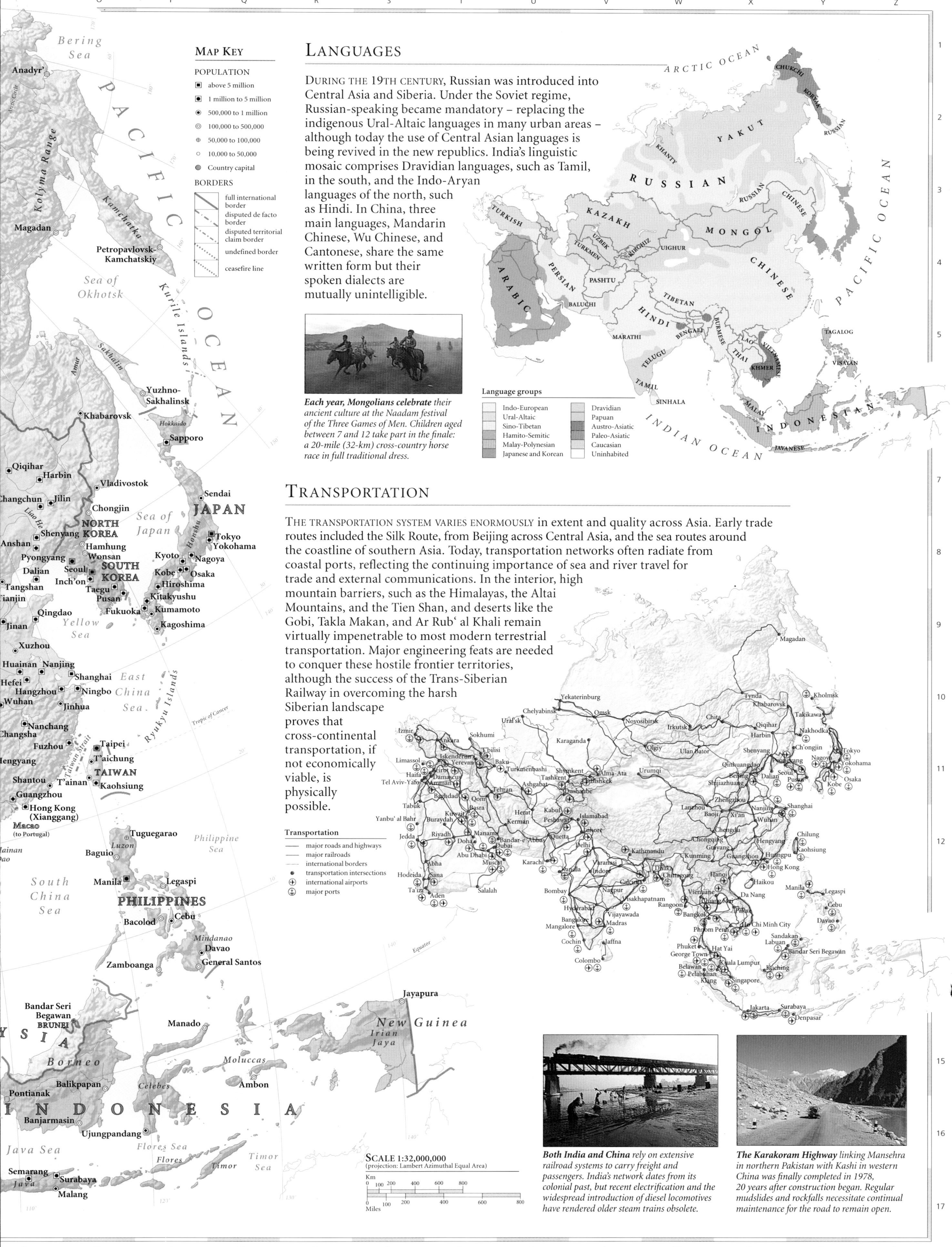
O P Q R S T U V W X Y Z
1 2 3 4 5 7 8 9 10 11 12 15 16 17
MAP KEY
POPULATION
above 5 million
1 million to 5 million
500,000 to 1 million
100,000 to 500,000
50,000 to 100,000
10,000 to 50,000
Country capital
BORDERS
full international border
disputed de facto border
disputed territorial claim border
undefined border
ceasefire line
Bering Sea
PACIFIC OCEAN
Anadyr'
Kolyma Range
Magadan
Kamchatka
Petropavlovsk-Kamchatskiy
Sea of Okhotsk
Kurile Islands
Sakhalin
Amur
Yuzhno-Sakhalinsk
Khabarovsk
Hokkaido
Sapporo
Qiqihar
Harbin
Vladivostok
Changchun
Jilin
Chongjin
Sea of Japan
Sendai
JAPAN
Honshu
Tokyo
Yokohama
Shenyang
NORTH KOREA
Hamhung
Wonsan
Anshan
Pyongyang
SOUTH KOREA
Seoul
Inch'on
Dalian
Taegu
Pusan
Kyoto
Nagoya
Kobe
Osaka
Hiroshima
Kitakyushu
Fukuoka
Kumamoto
Kagoshima
Tangshan
Tianjin
Qingdao
Jinan
Yellow Sea
Xuzhou
Huainan
Nanjing
Hefei
Shanghai
East China Sea
Hangzhou
Ningbo
Wuhan
Jinhua
Ryukyu Islands
Tropic of Cancer
Nanchang
Changsha
Fuzhou
Taipei
T'aichung
TAIWAN
Taiwan Strait
Hengyang
Shantou
T'ainan
Kaohsiung
Guangzhou
Hong Kong (Xianggang)
Macao (to Portugal)
Tuguegarao
Luzon
Philippine Sea
Baguio
South China Sea
Manila
Legaspi
PHILIPPINES
Bacolod
Cebu
Mindanao
Davao
Zamboanga
General Santos
Equator
Jayapura
Bandar Seri Begawan
BRUNEI
Manado
New Guinea
Irian Jaya
Borneo
Moluccas
Balikpapan
Celebes
Ambon
Pontianak
INDONESIA
Banjarmasin
Ujungpandang
Java Sea
Flores Sea
Flores
Timor
Timor Sea
Semarang
Java
Surabaya
Malang
ARCTIC OCEAN
CHUKCHI
KORYAK
RUSSIAN
YAKUT
KHANTY
RUSSIAN
KAZAKH
TURKISH
UZBEK
TURKMEN
KIRGHIZ
UIGHUR
MONGOL
CHINESE
ARABIC
PERSIAN
PASHTU
BALUCHI
TIBETAN
HINDI
MARATHI
BENGALI
BURMESE
LAO
THAI
VIETNAMESE
KHMER
TELUGU
TAMIL
SINHALA
MALAY
INDONESIAN
JAVANESE
TAGALOG
VISAYAN
INDIAN OCEAN
Language groups
Indo-European
Ural-Altaic
Sino-Tibetan
Hamito-Semitic
Malay-Polynesian
Japanese and Korean
Dravidian
Papuan
Austro-Asiatic
Paleo-Asiatic
Caucasian
Uninhabited
Transportation
major roads and highways
major railroads
international borders
transportation intersections
international airports
major ports
SCALE 1:32,000,000
(projection: Lambert Azimuthal Equal Area)
Km 0 100 200 400 600 800
Miles 0 100 200 400 600 800

Languages

During the 19th century, Russian was introduced into Central Asia and Siberia. Under the Soviet regime, Russian-speaking became mandatory – replacing the indigenous Ural-Altaic languages in many urban areas – although today the use of Central Asian languages is being revived in the new republics. India's linguistic mosaic comprises Dravidian languages, such as Tamil, in the south, and the Indo-Aryan languages of the north, such as Hindi. In China, three main languages, Mandarin Chinese, Wu Chinese, and Cantonese, share the same written form but their spoken dialects are mutually unintelligible.

***Each year, Mongolians celebrate** their ancient culture at the Naadam festival of the Three Games of Men. Children aged between 7 and 12 take part in the finale: a 20-mile (32-km) cross-country horse race in full traditional dress.*

Transportation

The transportation system varies enormously in extent and quality across Asia. Early trade routes included the Silk Route, from Beijing across Central Asia, and the sea routes around the coastline of southern Asia. Today, transportation networks often radiate from coastal ports, reflecting the continuing importance of sea and river travel for trade and external communications. In the interior, high mountain barriers, such as the Himalayas, the Altai Mountains, and the Tien Shan, and deserts like the Gobi, Takla Makan, and Ar Rub' al Khali remain virtually impenetrable to most modern terrestrial transportation. Major engineering feats are needed to conquer these hostile frontier territories, although the success of the Trans-Siberian Railway in overcoming the harsh Siberian landscape proves that cross-continental transportation, if not economically viable, is physically possible.

***Both India and China** rely on extensive railroad systems to carry freight and passengers. India's network dates from its colonial past, but recent electrification and the widespread introduction of diesel locomotives have rendered older steam trains obsolete.*

***The Karakoram Highway** linking Mansehra in northern Pakistan with Kashi in western China was finally completed in 1978, 20 years after construction began. Regular mudslides and rockfalls necessitate continual maintenance for the road to remain open.*

Climate

The climate of Asia exhibits marked differences from region to region, with freezing polar conditions in the north, hot and cold deserts in central regions, and subtropical conditions throughout the south. Much of this variation can be attributed to enormous mountain barriers and internal depressions found across the continent. Monsoon winds, which reverse semiannually, cause alternate wet and dry seasons across southern Asia. These air masses moving north from the ocean are stripped of their moisture over the Himalayas, causing arid conditions across the Plateau of Tibet. Both the south and east are susceptible to tropical cyclones or typhoons.

Treeless, frozen plains, *with permanently frozen soil layers characterize much of Siberia. Even during the summer, only the top 2–3 ft (1 m) of soil thaws.*

Tundralike marshes *are found alongside vast sand dunes in the Takla Makan Desert in China. In the spring, windstorms of hurricane force can send dust as high as 13,000 ft (4,000 m) into the air.*

The Gobi Desert *experiences major extremes in climate, with winter temperatures sometimes falling below -40°F (-40°C) and summer temperatures exceeding 113°F (45°C).*

Anadyr' · Mys Chelyuskin · Salekhard · Yakutsk · Okhotsk · Petropavlovsk-Kamchatskiy · Stony Tunguska · Yekaterinburg · Omsk · Novosibirsk · Khabarovsk · Sapporo · Irkutsk · Harbin · Vladivostok · Karaganda · Ankara · Fort-Shevchenko · T'bilisi · Tokyo · Urumqi · Beijing · Seoul · Osaka · Jerusalem · Tashkent · Ashgabat · Taiyuan · Nagasaki · Baghdad · Tehran · Lanzhou · Shanghai · Kabul · Wuhan · Kuwait · Lahore · Chengdu · Taipei · Bandar-e 'Abbas · New Delhi · Kathmandu · Kunming · Hong Kong (Xianggang) · Muscat · Karachi · Dhaka · Hanoi · Calcutta · Bombay · Chiang Mai · Vientiane · Rangoon · Bangkok · Madras · Port Blair · Phnom Penh · Ho Chi Minh City · Colombo · Bandar Seri Begawan · Manokwari · Phuket · Ambon · Singapore · Padang · Jakarta · Kupang

Arctic Circle · Tropic of Cancer · Equator · Buran · Typhoon · Cyclone

Climate

- tundra
- subarctic
- cool continental
- warm humid
- mediterranean
- semiarid
- arid
- humid equatorial
- tropical
- daily hours of sunshine, January
- daily hours of sunshine, July
- cyclone
- typhoon
- cold/dry monsoon
- warm/wet monsoon
- cold wind

Temperature

Arctic Circle · 60°N · 40°N · Tropic of Cancer · 20°N · Equator · 20°S · Tropic of Capricorn · 40°S

Average January temperature · *Average July temperature*

Temperature

- below -22°F (-30°C)
- -22 to -4°F (-30 to -20°C)
- -4 to 14°F (-20 to -10°C)
- 14 to 32°F (-10 to 0°C)
- 32 to 50° F (0 to 10°C)
- 50°F (10 to 20°C)
- 68 to 86°F (20 to 30°C)
- 86 °F (above 30°C)

Tropical cyclones *occur principally during late summer and early autumn. The intense winds and heavy rainfall can devastate entire villages.*

Throughout India, *the southwest monsoon, which brings heavy rainfall from May to September, accounts for 80% of annual precipitation.*

Rainfall

Arctic Circle · 60°N · 40°N · Tropic of Cancer · 20°N · Equator · 20°S · Tropic of Capricorn · 40°S

Average January rainfall · *Average July rainfall*

Rainfall

- 0–1 in (0–25 mm)
- 1–2 in (25–50 mm)
- 2–4 in (50–100 mm)
- 4–8 in (100–200 mm)
- 8–12 in (200–300 mm)
- 12–16 in (300–400 mm)
- 16–20 in (400–500 mm)
- 20 in (more than 500 mm)

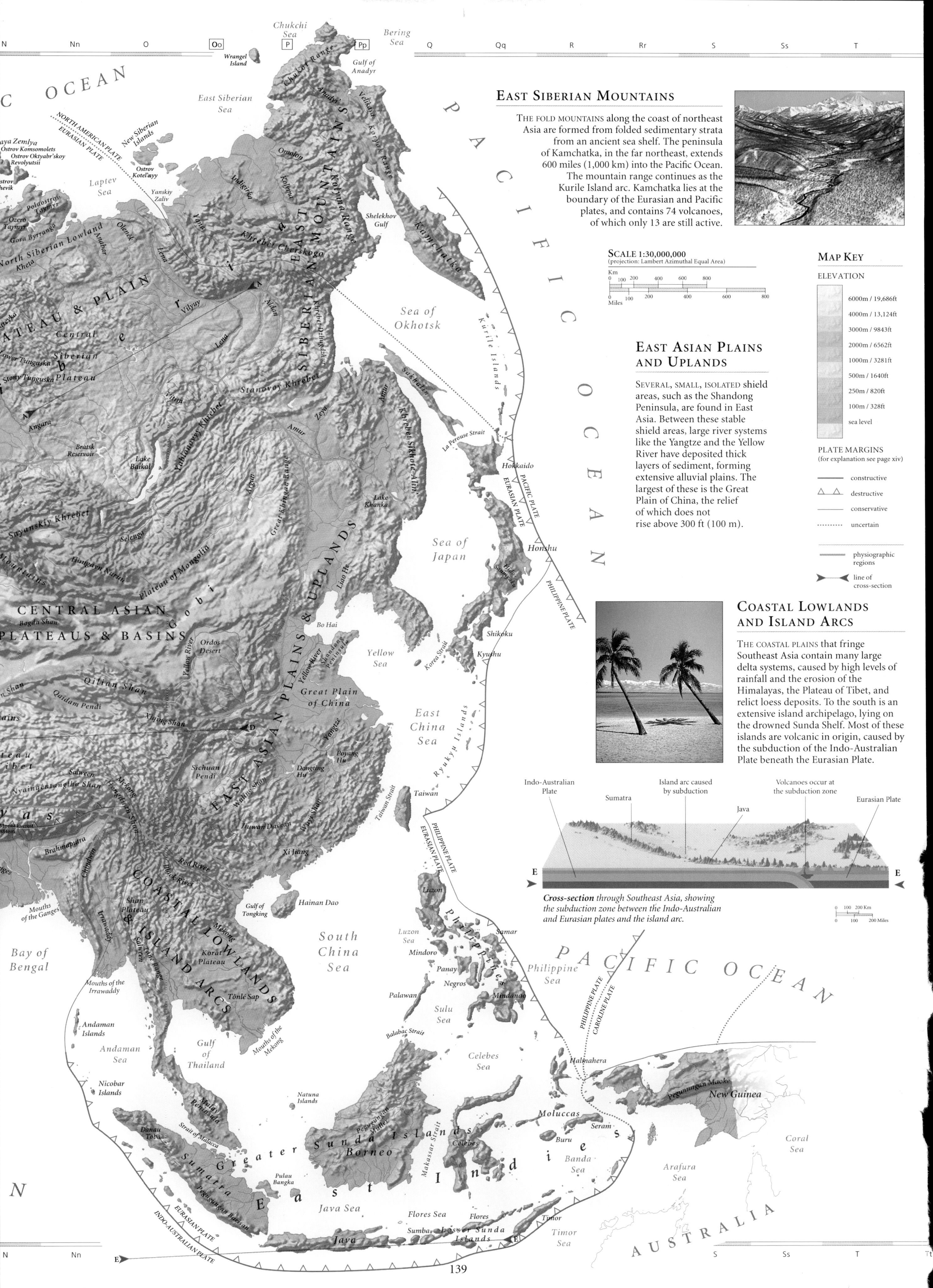

Chukchi Sea
Bering Sea
Wrangel Island
Gulf of Anadyr
East Siberian Sea
New Siberian Islands
NORTH AMERICAN PLATE
EURASIAN PLATE
Ostrov Komsomolets
Ostrov Oktyabr'skoy Revolyutsii
Ostrov Kotel'nyy
Laptev Sea
Yanskiy Zaliv
Chukot Range
Anadyr'
Velikaya
Koryak Range
Omolon
Kolyma
Kolyma Range
Indigirka
Yana
Khrebet Cherskogo
Shelekhov Gulf
Kamchatka
Olenek
Anabar
Lena
North Siberian Lowland
Gora Byrranga
Ozero Taymyr
Vilyuy
Aldan
EAST SIBERIAN MOUNTAINS
Central Siberian Plateau
Lower Tunguska
Stony Tunguska
Sea of Okhotsk
Kurile Islands
Stanovoy Khrebet
Sakhalin
Amur
Zeya
Vitim
Angara
Bratsk Reservoir
Lake Baikal
Yablonovyy Khrebet
La Perouse Strait
Hokkaido
PACIFIC PLATE
EURASIAN PLATE
Khrebet Sikhote-Alin'
Lake Khanka
Argun
Great Khingan Range
Sayanskiy Khrebet
Selenga
Hangayn Nuruu
Plateau of Mongolia
Sea of Japan
Honshu
PHILIPPINE PLATE
Liao He
Gobi
CENTRAL ASIAN PLATEAUS & BASINS
Bogda Shan
Ordos Desert
Yellow River
Bo Hai
Shandong Peninsula
Yellow Sea
Korea Strait
Shikoku
Kyushu
Qilian Shan
Qaidam Pendi
Great Plain of China
Xiqing Shan
EAST ASIAN PLAINS & UPLANDS
East China Sea
Ryukyu Islands
Yangtze
Poyang Hu
Dongting Hu
Sichuan Pendi
Salween
Mekong
Nyainqentanglha Shan
Mount Everest
Brahmaputra
Taiwan
Taiwan Strait
Xi Jiang
Red River
Black River
Chindwin
Irrawaddy
Shan Plateau
Mouths of the Ganges
Gulf of Tongking
Hainan Dao
Bay of Bengal
COASTAL LOWLANDS & ISLAND ARCS
Korat Plateau
Tônlé Sap
Mouths of the Irrawaddy
Mouths of the Mekong
South China Sea
Luzon
Luzon Sea
Philippines
Samar
Mindoro
Panay
Negros
Palawan
Mindanao
Philippine Sea
PACIFIC OCEAN
CAROLINE PLATE
Sulu Sea
Balabac Strait
Andaman Islands
Andaman Sea
Gulf of Thailand
Nicobar Islands
Celebes Sea
Halmahera
Natuna Islands
Malay Peninsula
Strait of Malacca
Danau Toba
Sumatra
Borneo
Celebes
Makassar Strait
Moluccas
Seram
Buru
Banda Sea
New Guinea
Pegunungan Maoke
Coral Sea
Arafura Sea
Greater Sunda Islands
East Indies
Pulau Bangka
Java Sea
Java
Flores Sea
Flores
Sumba
Lesser Sunda Islands
Timor
Timor Sea
AUSTRALIA
INDO-AUSTRALIAN PLATE
EURASIAN PLATE
N Nn O Oo P Pp Q Qq R Rr S Ss T
SCALE 1:30,000,000
(projection: Lambert Azimuthal Equal Area)
Km 0 100 200 400 600 800
Miles 0 100 200 400 600 800
MAP KEY
ELEVATION
6000m / 19,686ft
4000m / 13,124ft
3000m / 9843ft
2000m / 6562ft
1000m / 3281ft
500m / 1640ft
250m / 820ft
100m / 328ft
sea level
PLATE MARGINS
(for explanation see page xiv)
constructive
destructive
conservative
uncertain
physiographic regions
line of cross-section
Indo-Australian Plate
Sumatra
Island arc caused by subduction
Java
Volcanoes occur at the subduction zone
Eurasian Plate
E
E
0 100 200 Km
0 100 200 Miles

East Siberian Mountains

The fold mountains along the coast of northeast Asia are formed from folded sedimentary strata from an ancient sea shelf. The peninsula of Kamchatka, in the far northeast, extends 600 miles (1,000 km) into the Pacific Ocean. The mountain range continues as the Kurile Island arc. Kamchatka lies at the boundary of the Eurasian and Pacific plates, and contains 74 volcanoes, of which only 13 are still active.

East Asian Plains and Uplands

Several, small, isolated shield areas, such as the Shandong Peninsula, are found in East Asia. Between these stable shield areas, large river systems like the Yangtze and the Yellow River have deposited thick layers of sediment, forming extensive alluvial plains. The largest of these is the Great Plain of China, the relief of which does not rise above 300 ft (100 m).

Coastal Lowlands and Island Arcs

The coastal plains that fringe Southeast Asia contain many large delta systems, caused by high levels of rainfall and the erosion of the Himalayas, the Plateau of Tibet, and relict loess deposits. To the south is an extensive island archipelago, lying on the drowned Sunda Shelf. Most of these islands are volcanic in origin, caused by the subduction of the Indo-Australian Plate beneath the Eurasian Plate.

***Cross-section** through Southeast Asia, showing the subduction zone between the Indo-Australian and Eurasian plates and the island arc.*

Turkey & the Caucasus

Armenia, Azerbaijan, Georgia, Turkey

This region occupies the fragmented junction between Europe, Asia, and the Russian Federation. Sunni Islam provides a common identity for the secular state of Turkey, which the revered leader Kemal Atatürk established out of the remnants of the Ottoman Empire after the First World War. Turkey has a broad resource base and expanding trade links with Europe, but the east is relatively undeveloped and strife between the state and a large Kurdish minority has yet to be resolved. Georgia is similarly challenged by ethnic separatism, while the Christian state of Armenia and the mainly Muslim and oil-rich Azerbaijan are locked in conflict over the territory of Nagornyy Karabakh.

Transportation & Industry

Turkey leads the region's well diversified economy. Petrochemicals, textiles, engineering, and food processing are the main industries. Azerbaijan is able to export oil, while the other states rely heavily on hydro-electric power and imported fuel. Georgia produces precision machinery. War and earthquake damage have devastated Armenia's infrastructure.

Azerbaijan has substantial oil reserves, located in and around the Caspian Sea. They were some of the earliest oil fields in the world to be exploited.

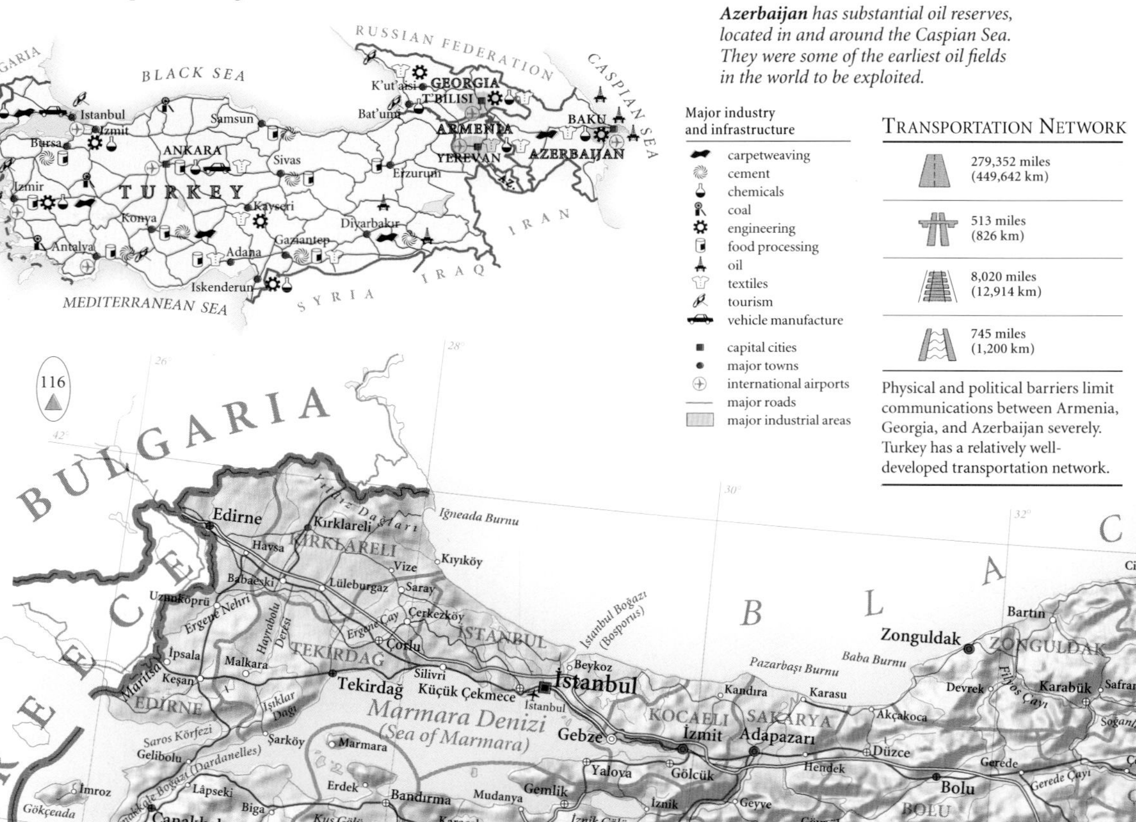

RUSSIAN FEDERATION
BLACK SEA
CASPIAN SEA
BULGARIA
GREECE
Istanbul
İzmit
Bursa
İzmir
Samsun
ANKARA
Sivas
TURKEY
Konya
Kayseri
Antalya
Adana
Gaziantep
Diyarbakır
Erzurum
İskenderun
K'ut'aisi
GEORGIA
T'BILISI
Bat'umi
ARMENIA
YEREVAN
BAKU
AZERBAIJAN
IRAN
IRAQ
SYRIA
MEDITERRANEAN SEA

Major industry and infrastructure
- carpetweaving
- cement
- chemicals
- coal
- engineering
- food processing
- oil
- textiles
- tourism
- vehicle manufacture
- capital cities
- major towns
- international airports
- major roads
- major industrial areas

Transportation Network

- 279,352 miles (449,642 km)
- 513 miles (826 km)
- 8,020 miles (12,914 km)
- 745 miles (1,200 km)

Physical and political barriers limit communications between Armenia, Georgia, and Azerbaijan severely. Turkey has a relatively well-developed transportation network.

Using the Land & Sea

Turkey is largely self-sufficient in food. The irrigated Black Sea coastlands have the world's highest yields of hazelnuts. Tobacco, cotton, golden raisins, tea, and figs are the region's main cash crops and a great range of fruit and vegetables are grown. Wine grapes are among the labor-intensive crops that allow full use of limited agricultural land in the Caucasus. Sturgeon fishing is particularly important in Azerbaijan.

RUSSIAN FEDERATION
BLACK SEA
CASPIAN SEA
BULGARIA
GREECE
Istanbul
Samsun
ANKARA
İzmir
Konya
TURKEY
Antalya
Adana
Diyarbakır
GEORGIA
T'BILISI
ARMENIA
YEREVAN
BAKU
AZERBAIJAN
IRAN
IRAQ
SYRIA
MEDITERRANEAN SEA

Land use and agricultural distribution
- cattle
- goats
- cotton
- fishing
- fruit
- hazelnuts
- olives
- sugar beet
- tobacco
- vineyards
- capital cities
- major towns
- pasture
- cropland
- forest

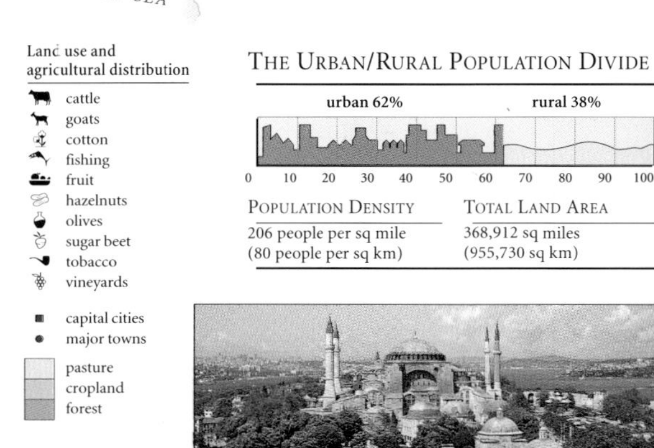

The Urban/Rural Population Divide

urban 62% | rural 38%

0 10 20 30 40 50 60 70 80 90 100

Population Density	Total Land Area
206 people per sq mile (80 people per sq km)	368,912 sq miles (955,730 sq km)

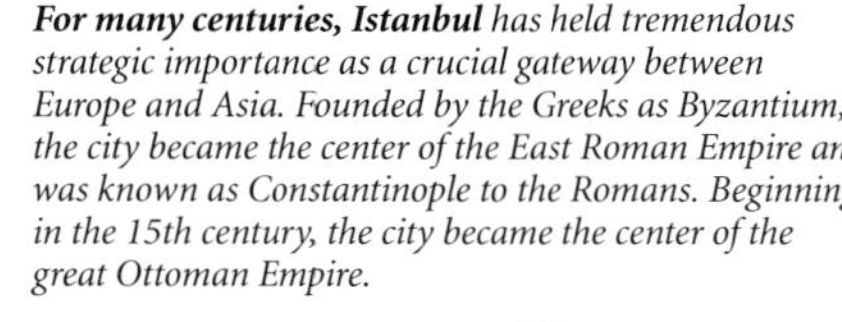

For many centuries, Istanbul has held tremendous strategic importance as a crucial gateway between Europe and Asia. Founded by the Greeks as Byzantium, the city became the center of the East Roman Empire and was known as Constantinople to the Romans. Beginning in the 15th century, the city became the center of the great Ottoman Empire.

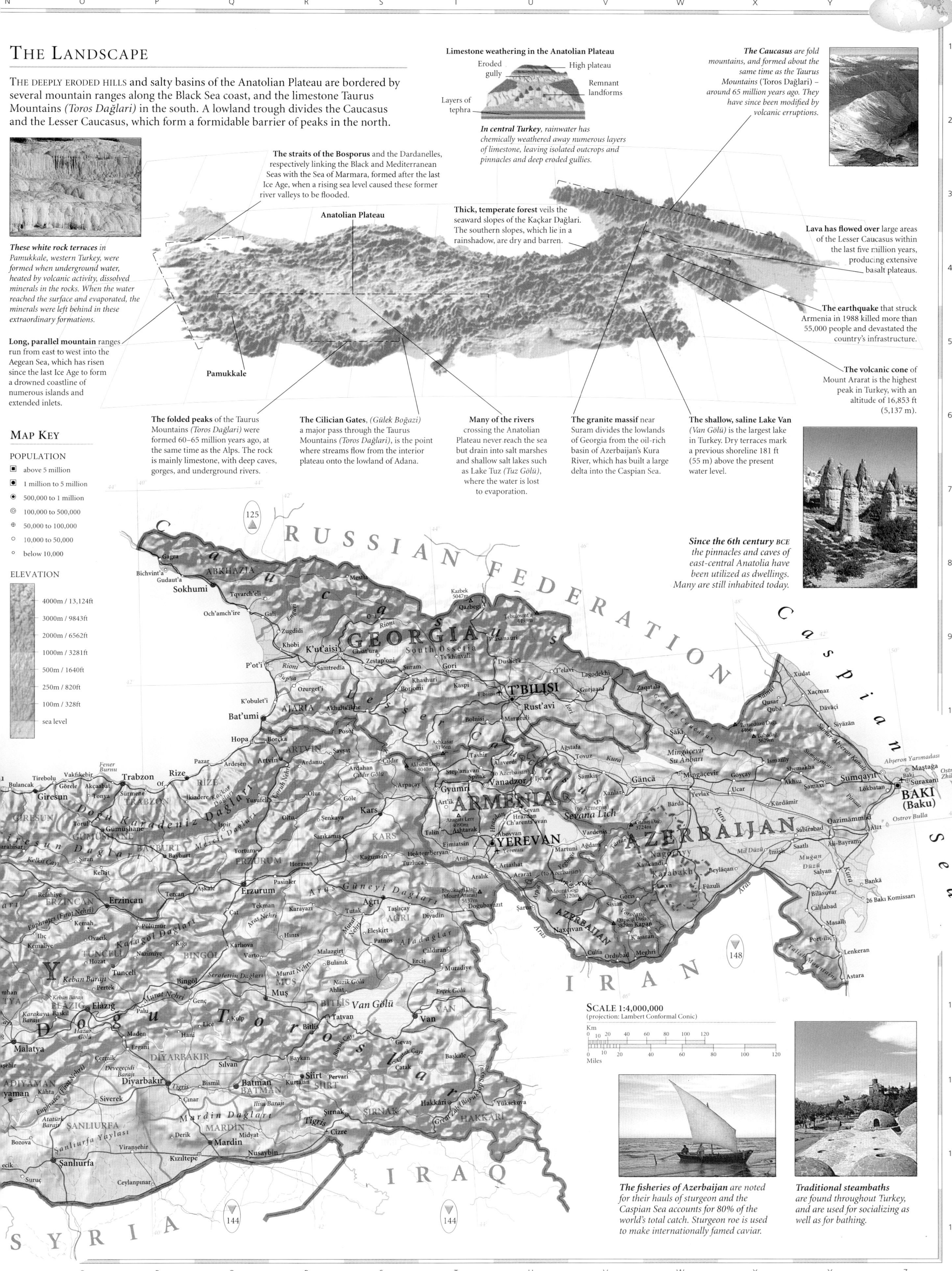
N O P Q R S T U V W X Y
Eroded gully
High plateau
Remnant landforms
Layers of tephra
Anatolian Plateau
Pamukkale
MAP KEY
POPULATION
above 5 million
1 million to 5 million
500,000 to 1 million
100,000 to 500,000
50,000 to 100,000
10,000 to 50,000
below 10,000
ELEVATION
4000m / 13,124ft
3000m / 9843ft
2000m / 6562ft
1000m / 3281ft
500m / 1640ft
250m / 820ft
100m / 328ft
sea level
RUSSIAN FEDERATION
GEORGIA
ARMENIA
AZERBAIJAN
IRAN
IRAQ
SYRIA
Caspian Sea
T'BILISI
YEREVAN
BAKI (Baku)
125
148
144
144
SCALE 1:4,000,000
(projection: Lambert Conformal Conic)
Km
Miles
O P Q R S T U V W X Y Z

The Landscape

THE DEEPLY ERODED HILLS and salty basins of the Anatolian Plateau are bordered by several mountain ranges along the Black Sea coast, and the limestone Taurus Mountains *(Toros Dağlari)* in the south. A lowland trough divides the Caucasus and the Lesser Caucasus, which form a formidable barrier of peaks in the north.

These white rock terraces *in Pamukkale, western Turkey, were formed when underground water, heated by volcanic activity, dissolved minerals in the rocks. When the water reached the surface and evaporated, the minerals were left behind in these extraordinary formations.*

Long, parallel mountain ranges run from east to west into the Aegean Sea, which has risen since the last Ice Age to form a drowned coastline of numerous islands and extended inlets.

The straits of the Bosporus and the Dardanelles, respectively linking the Black and Mediterranean Seas with the Sea of Marmara, formed after the last Ice Age, when a rising sea level caused these former river valleys to be flooded.

Limestone weathering in the Anatolian Plateau

In central Turkey, *rainwater has chemically weathered away numerous layers of limestone, leaving isolated outcrops and pinnacles and deep eroded gullies.*

The Caucasus *are fold mountains, and formed about the same time as the Taurus Mountains (Toros Dağlari) – around 65 million years ago. They have since been modified by volcanic eruptions.*

Thick, temperate forest veils the seaward slopes of the Kaçkar Dağlari. The southern slopes, which lie in a rainshadow, are dry and barren.

Lava has flowed over large areas of the Lesser Caucasus within the last five million years, producing extensive basalt plateaus.

The earthquake that struck Armenia in 1988 killed more than 55,000 people and devastated the country's infrastructure.

The volcanic cone of Mount Ararat is the highest peak in Turkey, with an altitude of 16,853 ft (5,137 m).

The folded peaks of the Taurus Mountains *(Toros Dağlari)* were formed 60–65 million years ago, at the same time as the Alps. The rock is mainly limestone, with deep caves, gorges, and underground rivers.

The Cilician Gates, *(Gülek Boğazi)* a major pass through the Taurus Mountains *(Toros Dağlari)*, is the point where streams flow from the interior plateau onto the lowland of Adana.

Many of the rivers crossing the Anatolian Plateau never reach the sea but drain into salt marshes and shallow salt lakes such as Lake Tuz *(Tuz Gölü)*, where the water is lost to evaporation.

The granite massif near Suram divides the lowlands of Georgia from the oil-rich basin of Azerbaijan's Kura River, which has built a large delta into the Caspian Sea.

The shallow, saline Lake Van *(Van Gölü)* is the largest lake in Turkey. Dry terraces mark a previous shoreline 181 ft (55 m) above the present water level.

Since the 6th century BCE *the pinnacles and caves of east-central Anatolia have been utilized as dwellings. Many are still inhabited today.*

The fisheries of Azerbaijan *are noted for their hauls of sturgeon and the Caspian Sea accounts for 80% of the world's total catch. Sturgeon roe is used to make internationally famed caviar.*

Traditional steambaths *are found throughout Turkey, and are used for socializing as well as for bathing.*

THE NEAR EAST

IRAQ, ISRAEL, JORDAN, LEBANON, SYRIA

SOME OF THE WORLD'S OLDEST CIVILIZATIONS developed in this region – the Fertile Crescent – which is venerated by Jews, Muslims, and Christians, but torn by competing religious, ethnic, and national claims to the land. Turkish Ottoman rule ended with the First World War and the region was divided into areas administered by Britain and France. The UN endorsed calls for a Jewish homeland in what was then Palestine and in 1948 the state of Israel was declared. Hostility toward the Jewish state led to a series of wars but since 1977, and especially since 1993, a peace process between Israel and her neighbors has been evolving. Since independence, Syria has played a leading role in Middle Eastern politics. The once-prosperous state of Lebanon is emerging from a ruinous factional war, while Iraq's great oil wealth has funded military campaigns against Iran and Kuwait and the stifling of internal dissent, leading to international ostracization.

USING THE LAND & SEA

WATER SCARCITY limits cropland to the north and to areas watered principally by the Tigris, Euphrates, and Jordan Rivers. In Israel, new irrigation techniques are allowing cultivation in the arid Negev. Wheat is the chief grain and large areas of scrub support herds of livestock. Commercial produce includes dates, tobacco, citrus fruits, olives, grapes, and cotton, which is Syria's main export crop. Fishing is still important in the Mediterranean.

THE URBAN/RURAL POPULATION DIVIDE

urban 63% | rural 37%

0 10 20 30 40 50 60 70 80 90 100

POPULATION DENSITY	TOTAL LAND AREA
145 people per sq mile (56 people per sq km)	325,460 sq miles (843,160 sq km)

Land use and agricultural distribution

- sheep
- cereals
- citrus fruits
- cotton
- dates
- fishing
- rice
- tobacco
- capital cities
- major towns
- pasture
- cropland
- wetland
- desert

TRANSPORTATION & INDUSTRY

THE PETROCHEMICAL INDUSTRY is well established, and central to the economies of Syria and Iraq, which was the world's second largest oil exporter before the war with Iran which began in 1980. Lebanon has traditionally been a center for commerce, while Israel has a well-diversified economy with an expanding tourist industry, despite few natural resources.

TRANSPORTATION NETWORK

- 62,624 miles (100,844 km)
- 1,000 miles (1,600 km)
- 3,897 miles (6,275 km)
- 498 miles (802 km)

Jordan's seaport of Al 'Aqabah is connected to Damascus in Syria by road and rail. This route to the Red Sea provides for large exports of phosphate and trade with states in the Persian Gulf.

Major industry and infrastructure

- car manufacture
- cement
- chemicals
- electronics
- finance
- food processing
- iron & steel
- oil
- oil refining
- textiles
- capital cities
- major towns
- international airports
- major roads
- major industrial areas

***The Dome of the Rock** in Jerusalem is a magnificent mosque, revered by Muslims. Close by is the Western Wall, the city's most sacred Jewish landmark and the Church of the Holy Sepulchre, a famous Christian place of worship.*

***The city of Petra**, carved from spectacular rose-colored limestone, lies deep within a canyon in southern Jordan. Revenues from the spice trade funded the construction of the city which was built by the Nabatean people in about 400 BCE.*

***Water and wind erosion** over thousands of years have created the Canyon of the Oasis at En 'Avedat in the Negev Desert (HaNegev). Extreme diurnal temperature fluctuations, coupled with wind erosion have caused layers of rock to crack and peel away.*

THE LANDSCAPE

THE AL JAZIRAH PLATEAU divides the Euphrates and Tigris Rivers, which cross the Mesopotamian plain to reach their confluence in the southeast. The rocky Syrian Desert extends west to the northern extremity of the Great Rift Valley, which runs from the mountains of Lebanon to the Gulf of Aqaba. The Jordan River flows south along this trough into the Dead Sea, divided from the Mediterranean coastal plain by a steep-sided plateau.

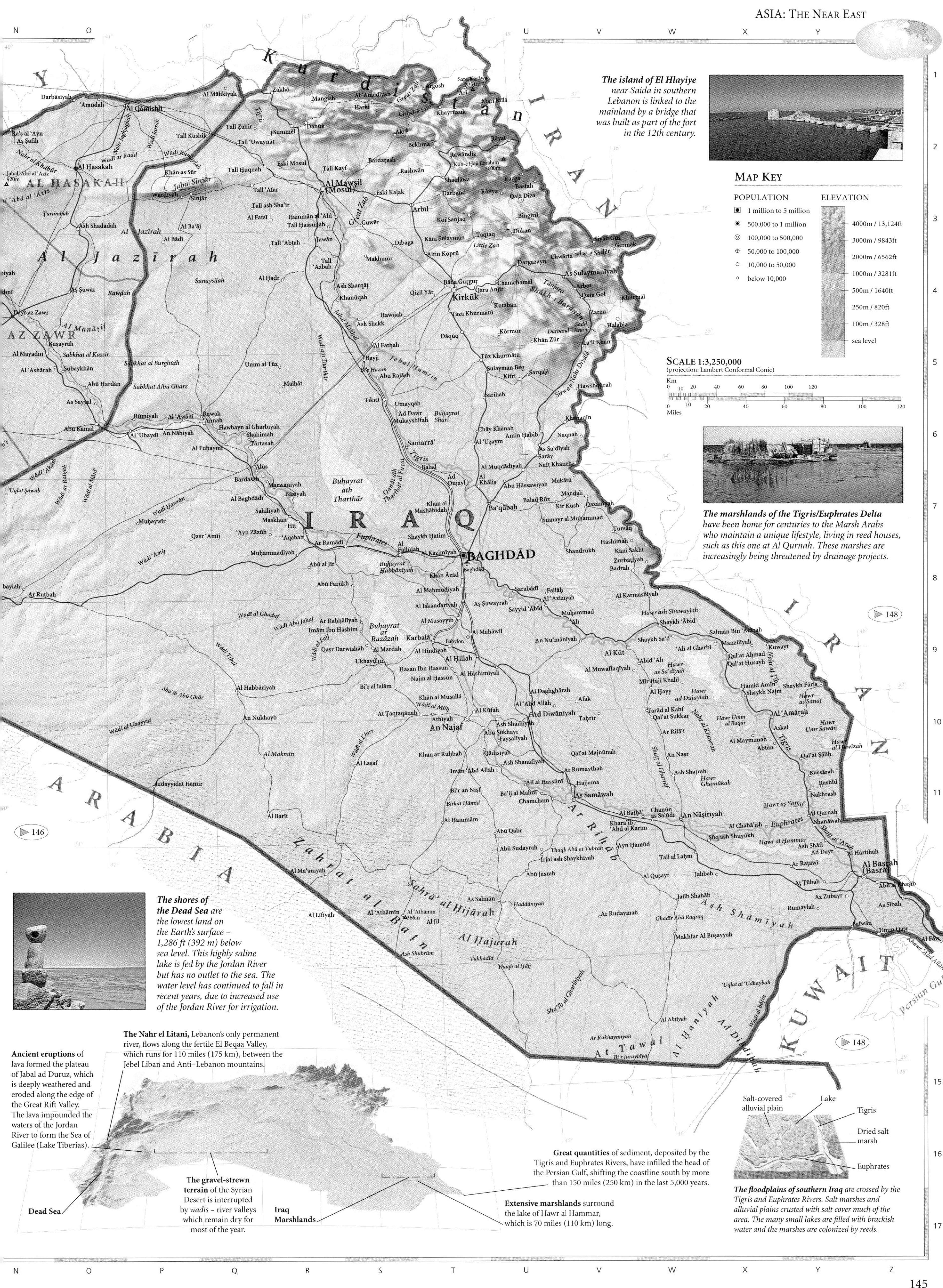
IRAQ
IRAN
ARABIA
KUWAIT
Kurdistan
Al Jazīrah
BAGHDĀD
Persian Gulf
MAP KEY
POPULATION
1 million to 5 million
500,000 to 1 million
100,000 to 500,000
50,000 to 100,000
10,000 to 50,000
below 10,000
ELEVATION
4000m / 13,124ft
3000m / 9843ft
2000m / 6562ft
1000m / 3281ft
500m / 1640ft
250m / 820ft
100m / 328ft
sea level
SCALE 1:3,250,000
(projection: Lambert Conformal Conic)
Km
Miles
146
148
148
Salt-covered alluvial plain
Lake
Tigris
Dried salt marsh
Euphrates
Dead Sea
Iraq Marshlands

The island of El Hlayiye near Saida in southern Lebanon is linked to the mainland by a bridge that was built as part of the fort in the 12th century.

***The marshlands of the Tigris/Euphrates Delta** have been home for centuries to the Marsh Arabs who maintain a unique lifestyle, living in reed houses, such as this one at Al Qurnah. These marshes are increasingly being threatened by drainage projects.*

***The shores of the Dead Sea** are the lowest land on the Earth's surface – 1,286 ft (392 m) below sea level. This highly saline lake is fed by the Jordan River but has no outlet to the sea. The water level has continued to fall in recent years, due to increased use of the Jordan River for irrigation.*

Ancient eruptions of lava formed the plateau of Jabal ad Duruz, which is deeply weathered and eroded along the edge of the Great Rift Valley. The lava impounded the waters of the Jordan River to form the Sea of Galilee (Lake Tiberias).

The Nahr el Litani, Lebanon's only permanent river, flows along the fertile El Beqaa Valley, which runs for 110 miles (175 km), between the Jebel Liban and Anti-Lebanon mountains.

The gravel-strewn terrain of the Syrian Desert is interrupted by *wadis* – river valleys which remain dry for most of the year.

Great quantities of sediment, deposited by the Tigris and Euphrates Rivers, have infilled the head of the Persian Gulf, shifting the coastline south by more than 150 miles (250 km) in the last 5,000 years.

Extensive marshlands surround the lake of Hawr al Hammar, which is 70 miles (110 km) long.

***The floodplains of southern Iraq** are crossed by the Tigris and Euphrates Rivers. Salt marshes and alluvial plains crusted with salt cover much of the area. The many small lakes are filled with brackish water and the marshes are colonized by reeds.*

THE ARABIAN PENINSULA

BAHRAIN, KUWAIT, OMAN, QATAR, SAUDI ARABIA, UNITED ARAB EMIRATES (UAE), YEMEN

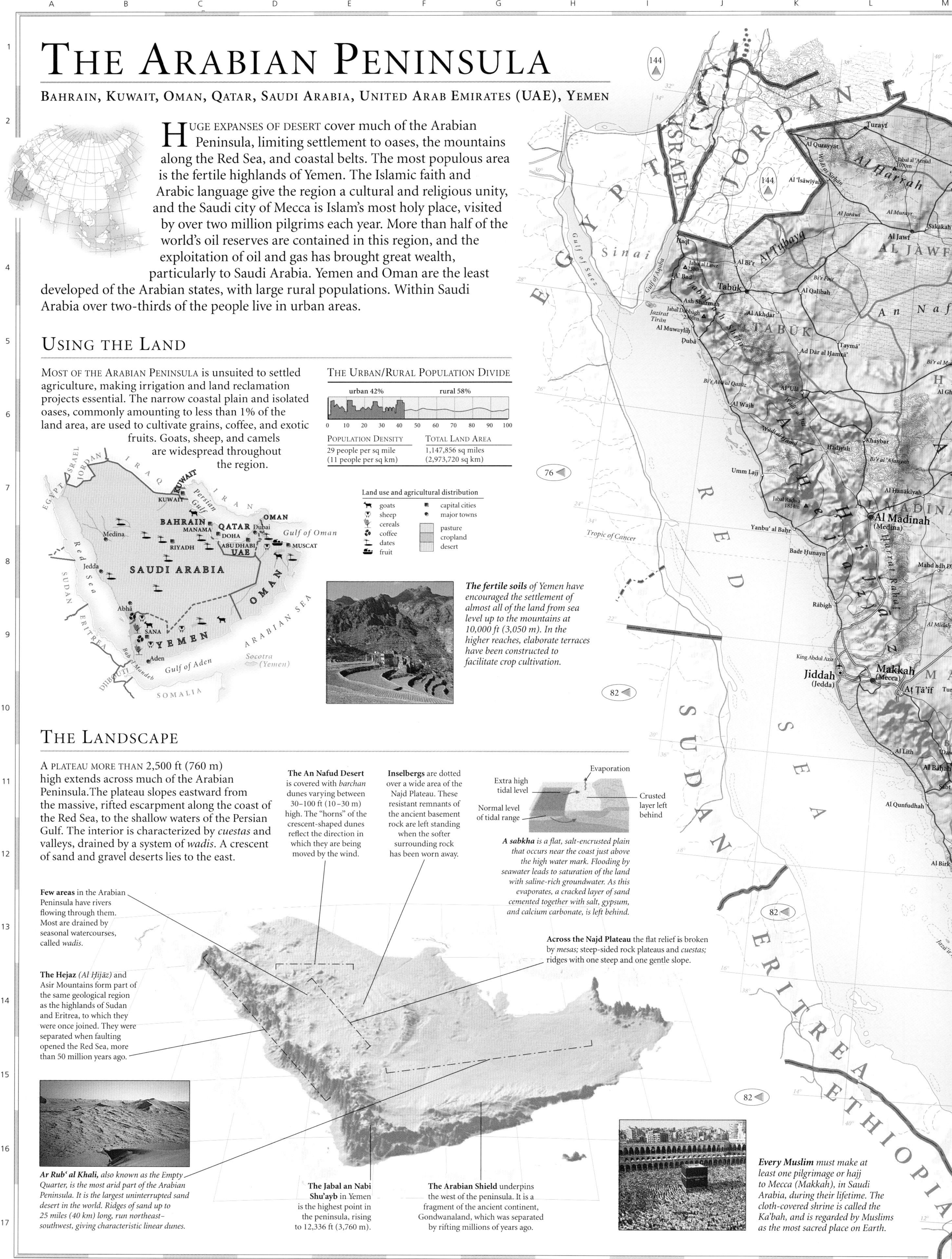

144
EGYPT
ISRAEL
JORDAN
Sinai
Gulf of Suez
Gulf of Aqaba
Tropic of Cancer
RED SEA
SUDAN
ERITREA
ETHIOPIA
TABŪK
AL HIJAZ
AL JAWF
Al Harrah
Turayf
Al Qurayyat
Al 'Isāwiyah
Al Jawf
Sakākah
Tabūk
Haql
Ash Sharmah
Al Muwaylih
Dubā
Taymā'
Al 'Ulā
Al Wajh
Umm Lajj
Yanbu' al Bahr
Khaybar
Al Hanākiyah
Al Madīnah (Medina)
Badr Hunayn
Rābigh
King Abdul Aziz
Jiddah (Jedda)
Makkah (Mecca)
At Tā'if
Al Līth
Al Bāhah
Al Qunfudhah
76
82

Huge expanses of desert cover much of the Arabian Peninsula, limiting settlement to oases, the mountains along the Red Sea, and coastal belts. The most populous area is the fertile highlands of Yemen. The Islamic faith and Arabic language give the region a cultural and religious unity, and the Saudi city of Mecca is Islam's most holy place, visited by over two million pilgrims each year. More than half of the world's oil reserves are contained in this region, and the exploitation of oil and gas has brought great wealth, particularly to Saudi Arabia. Yemen and Oman are the least developed of the Arabian states, with large rural populations. Within Saudi Arabia over two-thirds of the people live in urban areas.

Using the Land

Most of the Arabian Peninsula is unsuited to settled agriculture, making irrigation and land reclamation projects essential. The narrow coastal plain and isolated oases, commonly amounting to less than 1% of the land area, are used to cultivate grains, coffee, and exotic fruits. Goats, sheep, and camels are widespread throughout the region.

The Urban/Rural Population Divide

urban 42% | rural 58%

Population Density	Total Land Area
29 people per sq mile (11 people per sq km)	1,147,856 sq miles (2,973,720 sq km)

Land use and agricultural distribution: goats, sheep, cereals, coffee, dates, fruit, capital cities, major towns, pasture, cropland, desert

The fertile soils of Yemen have encouraged the settlement of almost all of the land from sea level up to the mountains at 10,000 ft (3,050 m). In the higher reaches, elaborate terraces have been constructed to facilitate crop cultivation.

The Landscape

A plateau more than 2,500 ft (760 m) high extends across much of the Arabian Peninsula. The plateau slopes eastward from the massive, rifted escarpment along the coast of the Red Sea, to the shallow waters of the Persian Gulf. The interior is characterized by *cuestas* and valleys, drained by a system of *wadis*. A crescent of sand and gravel deserts lies to the east.

The An Nafud Desert is covered with *barchan* dunes varying between 30–100 ft (10–30 m) high. The "horns" of the crescent-shaped dunes reflect the direction in which they are being moved by the wind.

Inselbergs are dotted over a wide area of the Najd Plateau. These resistant remnants of the ancient basement rock are left standing when the softer surrounding rock has been worn away.

Evaporation · Extra high tidal level · Normal level of tidal range · Crusted layer left behind

***A sabkha** is a flat, salt-encrusted plain that occurs near the coast just above the high water mark. Flooding by seawater leads to saturation of the land with saline-rich groundwater. As this evaporates, a cracked layer of sand cemented together with salt, gypsum, and calcium carbonate, is left behind.*

Few areas in the Arabian Peninsula have rivers flowing through them. Most are drained by seasonal watercourses, called *wadis*.

The Hejaz *(Al Ḩijāz)* and Asir Mountains form part of the same geological region as the highlands of Sudan and Eritrea, to which they were once joined. They were separated when faulting opened the Red Sea, more than 50 million years ago.

Across the Najd Plateau the flat relief is broken by *mesas*; steep-sided rock plateaus and *cuestas*; ridges with one steep and one gentle slope.

***Ar Rub' al Khali**, also known as the Empty Quarter, is the most arid part of the Arabian Peninsula. It is the largest uninterrupted sand desert in the world. Ridges of sand up to 25 miles (40 km) long, run northeast–southwest, giving characteristic linear dunes.*

The Jabal an Nabi Shu'ayb in Yemen is the highest point in the peninsula, rising to 12,336 ft (3,760 m).

The Arabian Shield underpins the west of the peninsula. It is a fragment of the ancient continent, Gondwanaland, which was separated by rifting millions of years ago.

***Every Muslim** must make at least one pilgrimage or hajj to Mecca (Makkah), in Saudi Arabia, during their lifetime. The cloth-covered shrine is called the Ka'bah, and is regarded by Muslims as the most sacred place on Earth.*

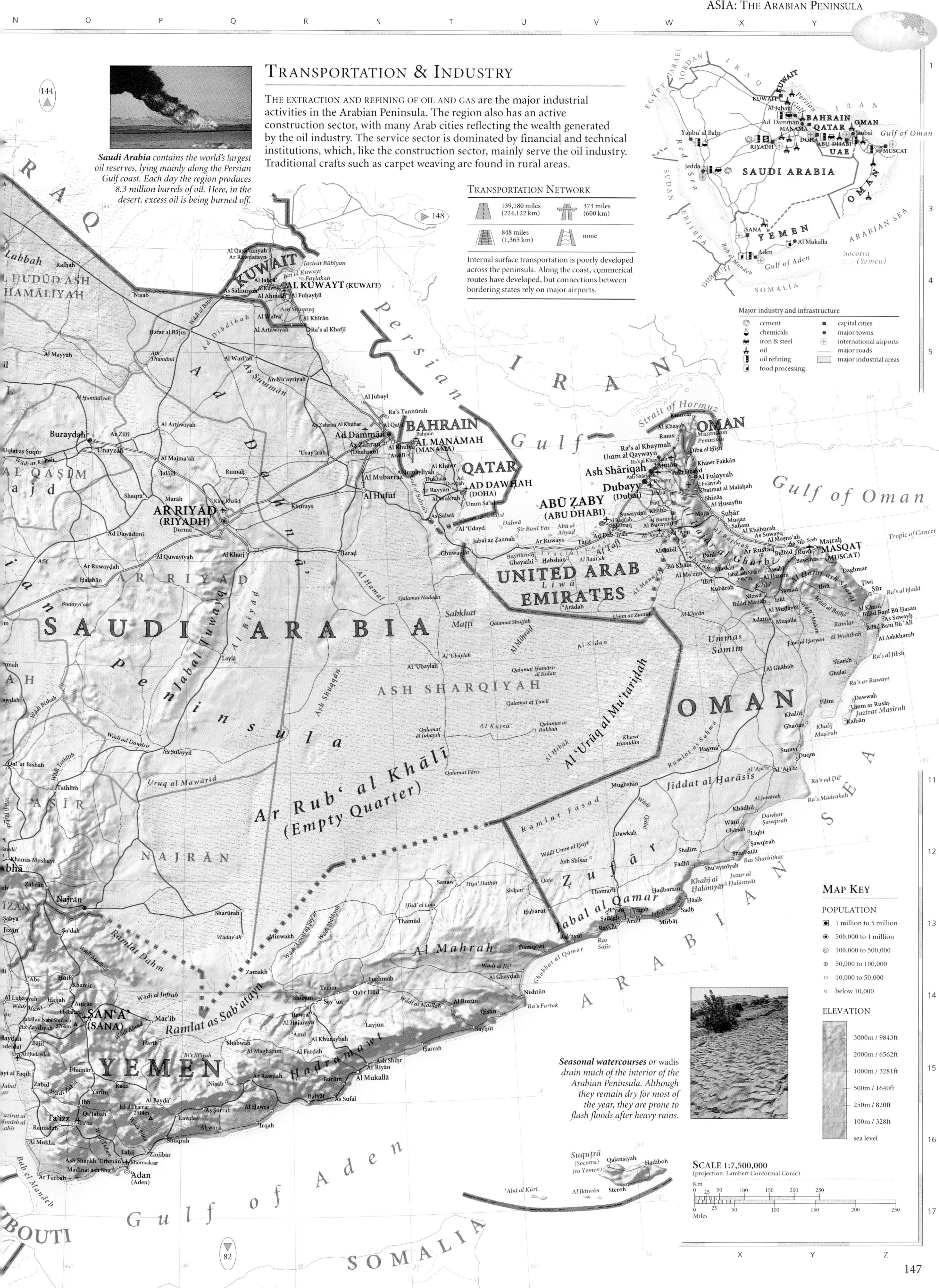
N O P Q R S T U V W X Y
Z
1
3
4
5
11
12
13
14
15
16
17
144
148
82
IRAQ
KUWAIT
AL KUWAYT (KUWAIT)
Persian Gulf
IRAN
BAHRAIN
AL MANĀMAH (MANAMA)
QATAR
AD DAWḤAH (DOHA)
ABŪ ẒABY (ABU DHABI)
Dubayy (Dubai)
Ash Shāriqah
UNITED ARAB EMIRATES
Strait of Hormuz
Gulf of Oman
MASQAT (MUSCAT)
OMAN
SAUDI ARABIA
AR RIYĀḌ (RIYADH)
Ad Dammām
Al Hufūf
Ad Dahnā'
Arabian Peninsula
Ar Rub' al Khālī (Empty Quarter)
ASH SHARQĪYAH
NAJRĀN
YEMEN
SAN'A' (SANA)
'Adan (Aden)
Al Mukallā
Ḥaḍramawt
Al Mahrah
Ẓufār
Jabal al Qamar
Ramlat as Sab'atayn
ARABIAN SEA
Gulf of Aden
SOMALIA
DJIBOUTI
Bab el Mandeb
Suquṭrā (Socotra) (to Yemen)
Tropic of Cancer
Major industry and infrastructure
cement
chemicals
iron & steel
oil
oil refining
food processing
capital cities
major towns
international airports
major roads
major industrial areas
SCALE 1:7,500,000
(projection: Lambert Conformal Conic)
Km
Miles
X Y Z

TRANSPORTATION & INDUSTRY

THE EXTRACTION AND REFINING OF OIL AND GAS are the major industrial activities in the Arabian Peninsula. The region also has an active construction sector, with many Arab cities reflecting the wealth generated by the oil industry. The service sector is dominated by financial and technical institutions, which, like the construction sector, mainly serve the oil industry. Traditional crafts such as carpet weaving are found in rural areas.

***Saudi Arabia** contains the world's largest oil reserves, lying mainly along the Persian Gulf coast. Each day the region produces 8.3 million barrels of oil. Here, in the desert, excess oil is being burned off.*

TRANSPORTATION NETWORK

road	139,180 miles (224,122 km)	railway	373 miles (600 km)
rail	848 miles (1,365 km)	waterway	none

Internal surface transportation is poorly developed across the peninsula. Along the coast, commerical routes have developed, but connections between bordering states rely on major airports.

***Seasonal watercourses** or wadis drain much of the interior of the Arabian Peninsula. Although they remain dry for most of the year, they are prone to flash floods after heavy rains.*

MAP KEY

POPULATION

- 1 million to 5 million
- 500,000 to 1 million
- 100,000 to 500,000
- 50,000 to 100,000
- 10,000 to 50,000
- below 10,000

ELEVATION

- 3000m / 9843ft
- 2000m / 6562ft
- 1000m / 3281ft
- 500m / 1640ft
- 250m / 820ft
- 100m / 328ft
- sea level

Iran & the Gulf States

Bahrain, Iran, Kuwait, Qatar, United Arab Emirates (UAE)

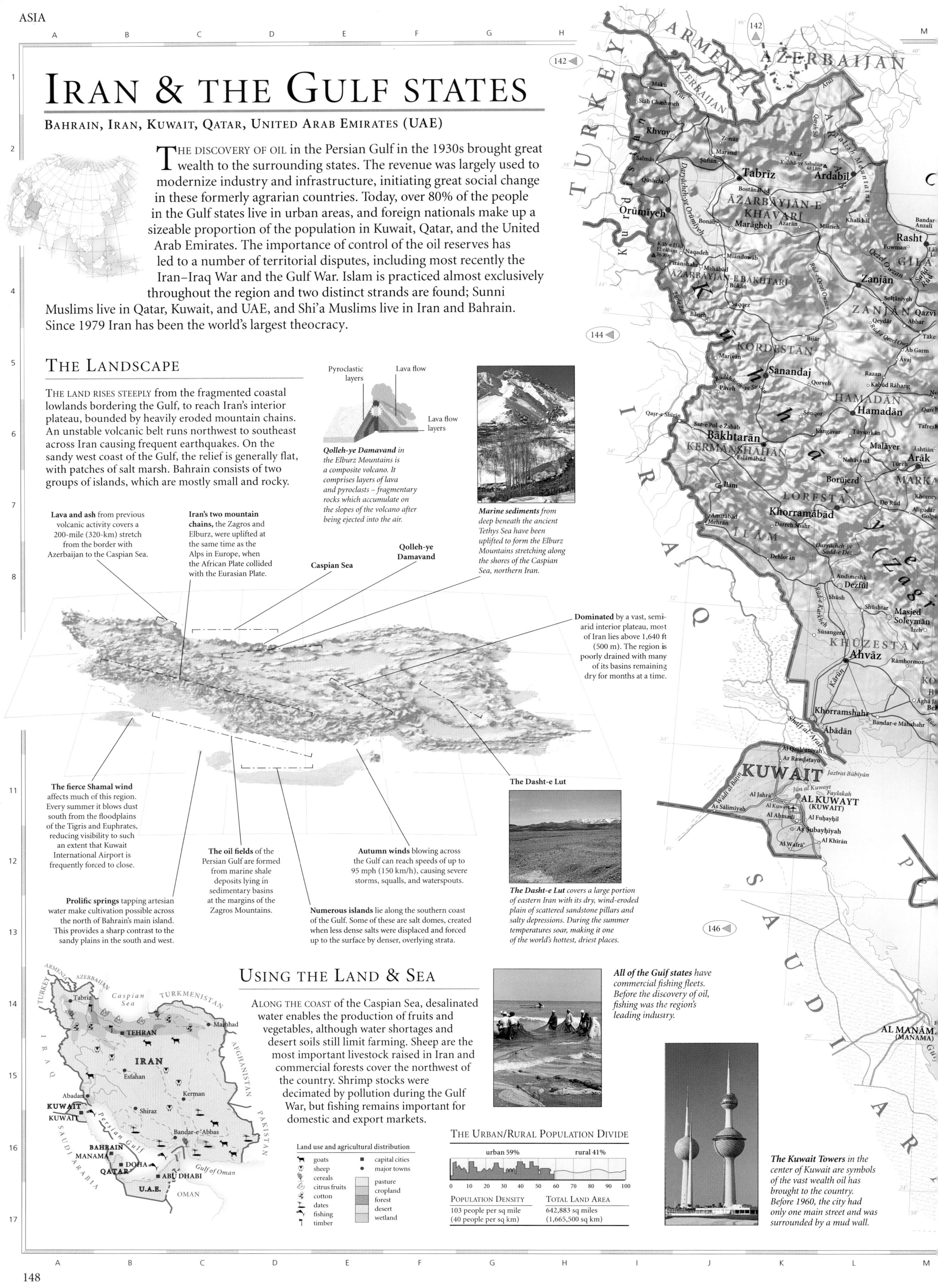

The discovery of oil in the Persian Gulf in the 1930s brought great wealth to the surrounding states. The revenue was largely used to modernize industry and infrastructure, initiating great social change in these formerly agrarian countries. Today, over 80% of the people in the Gulf states live in urban areas, and foreign nationals make up a sizeable proportion of the population in Kuwait, Qatar, and the United Arab Emirates. The importance of control of the oil reserves has led to a number of territorial disputes, including most recently the Iran–Iraq War and the Gulf War. Islam is practiced almost exclusively throughout the region and two distinct strands are found; Sunni Muslims live in Qatar, Kuwait, and UAE, and Shi'a Muslims live in Iran and Bahrain. Since 1979 Iran has been the world's largest theocracy.

The Landscape

The land rises steeply from the fragmented coastal lowlands bordering the Gulf, to reach Iran's interior plateau, bounded by heavily eroded mountain chains. An unstable volcanic belt runs northwest to southeast across Iran causing frequent earthquakes. On the sandy west coast of the Gulf, the relief is generally flat, with patches of salt marsh. Bahrain consists of two groups of islands, which are mostly small and rocky.

Pyroclastic layers
Lava flow
Lava flow layers

Qolleh-ye Damavand in the Elburz Mountains is a composite volcano. It comprises layers of lava and pyroclasts – fragmentary rocks which accumulate on the slopes of the volcano after being ejected into the air.

***Marine sediments** from deep beneath the ancient Tethys Sea have been uplifted to form the Elburz Mountains stretching along the shores of the Caspian Sea, northern Iran.*

Lava and ash from previous volcanic activity covers a 200-mile (320-km) stretch from the border with Azerbaijan to the Caspian Sea.

Iran's two mountain chains, the Zagros and Elburz, were uplifted at the same time as the Alps in Europe, when the African Plate collided with the Eurasian Plate.

Caspian Sea

Qolleh-ye Damavand

Dominated by a vast, semi-arid interior plateau, most of Iran lies above 1,640 ft (500 m). The region is poorly drained with many of its basins remaining dry for months at a time.

The fierce Shamal wind affects much of this region. Every summer it blows dust south from the floodplains of the Tigris and Euphrates, reducing visibility to such an extent that Kuwait International Airport is frequently forced to close.

Prolific springs tapping artesian water make cultivation possible across the north of Bahrain's main island. This provides a sharp contrast to the sandy plains in the south and west.

The oil fields of the Persian Gulf are formed from marine shale deposits lying in sedimentary basins at the margins of the Zagros Mountains.

Numerous islands lie along the southern coast of the Gulf. Some of these are salt domes, created when less dense salts were displaced and forced up to the surface by denser, overlying strata.

Autumn winds blowing across the Gulf can reach speeds of up to 95 mph (150 km/h), causing severe storms, squalls, and waterspouts.

The Dasht-e Lut

***The Dasht-e Lut** covers a large portion of eastern Iran with its dry, wind-eroded plain of scattered sandstone pillars and salty depressions. During the summer temperatures soar, making it one of the world's hottest, driest places.*

Using the Land & Sea

Along the coast of the Caspian Sea, desalinated water enables the production of fruits and vegetables, although water shortages and desert soils still limit farming. Sheep are the most important livestock raised in Iran and commercial forests cover the northwest of the country. Shrimp stocks were decimated by pollution during the Gulf War, but fishing remains important for domestic and export markets.

Tabriz
Caspian Sea
TURKMENISTAN
Mashhad
TEHRAN
IRAN
Esfahan
Kerman
Shiraz
Abadan
KUWAIT
Bandar-e 'Abbas
BAHRAIN
MANAMA
DOHA
QATAR
ABU DHABI
U.A.E.
OMAN
Gulf of Oman
Persian Gulf
AFGHANISTAN
PAKISTAN
SAUDI ARABIA
IRAQ
TURKEY
ARMENIA
AZERBAIJAN
Land use and agricultural distribution
goats
sheep
cereals
citrus fruits
cotton
dates
fishing
timber
capital cities
major towns
pasture
cropland
forest
desert
wetland

All of the Gulf states have commercial fishing fleets. Before the discovery of oil, fishing was the region's leading industry.

The Urban/Rural Population Divide

urban 59%
rural 41%
0 10 20 30 40 50 60 70 80 90 100

Population Density	Total Land Area
103 people per sq mile (40 people per sq km)	642,883 sq miles (1,665,500 sq km)

***The Kuwait Towers** in the center of Kuwait are symbols of the vast wealth oil has brought to the country. Before 1960, the city had only one main street and was surrounded by a mud wall.*

142 144 146

Many volcanoes lie in Iran's 1,200-mile (1,930-km) volcanic belt, including the country's highest peak, the now-extinct Qolleh-ye Damavand at 18,600 ft (5,671 m).

152

Extensive oil and gas exploitation in the Gulf region has allowed the economic transformation of the Gulf states. Kuwait and the United Arab Emirates today have the highest per capita incomes in the world.

Transportation & Industry

Both onshore and offshore oil reserves are exploited throughout the region. Kuwait not only extracts but also refines 80% of its oil. Bahrain has diversified its economy to become the main commercial and financial center in the Gulf. Iran produces a wide range of products: textile mills are widespread and carpet weaving is an important export industry.

N O P Q R S T U V W X Y
TURKMENISTAN
Caspian Sea
IRAN
AFGHANISTAN
PAKISTAN
OMAN
QATAR
BAHRAIN
UNITED ARAB EMIRATES
Gulf of Oman
Strait of Hormuz
Makran Coast
Trucial Coast
Dasht-e Kavīr
Dasht-e Lūt
Iranian Plateau
KHORĀSĀN
SEMNĀN
ESFAHĀN
YAZD
KERMĀN
FĀRS
HORMOZGĀN
SĪSTĀN VA BALUCHESTĀN
MĀZANDARĀN
TEHRĀN
TEHRAN
Qom
Kāshān
Esfahān
Yazd
Kermān
Shīrāz
Bandar-e Būshehr
Bandar-e 'Abbās
Zāhedān
Mashhad
Neyshābūr
Sabzevār
Gorgān
Sārī
Bābol
Āmol
Semnān
Bam
Mīnāb
Qeshm
Ra's al Khaymah
Umm al Qaywayn
'Ajman
Ash Shāriqah
Dubayy (Dubai)
Al Fujayrah
Khawr Fakkān
Dibā al Ḩişn
AD DAWḨAH (DOHA)
Al Khawr
Al Wakrah
Umm Sa'īd
ABŪ ẒABY (ABU DHABI)
Al 'Ayn
Al Buraymī
Liwā
Caspian Sea
TURKMENISTAN
IRAN
TEHRAN
Tabriz
Rasht
Gorgan
Mashhad
Qom
Bakhtaran
Esfahan
Birjand
Ahvaz
Abadan
KUWAIT
Shiraz
Kerman
Zahedan
Bandar-e Bushehr
Bandar-e 'Abbas
BAHRAIN
MANAMA
DOHA
QATAR
ABU DHABI
Dubai
U.A.E.
OMAN
SAUDI ARABIA
IRAQ
AFGHANISTAN
PAKISTAN
Gulf of Oman
Persian Gulf
Major industry and infrastructure
carpet manufacture
chemicals
finance
food processing
oil
oil refining
textiles
capital city
major towns
international airports
major roads
major industrial areas
TRANSPORTATION NETWORK
92,308 miles (148,644 km)
478 miles (770 km)
3,010 miles (4,847 km)
81 miles (130 km)
MAP KEY
POPULATION
above 5 million
1 million to 5 million
500,000 to 1 million
100,000 to 500,000
50,000 to 100,000
10,000 to 50,000
below 10,000
ELEVATION
4000m / 13,124ft
3000m / 9843ft
2000m / 6562ft
1000m / 3281ft
500m / 1640ft
250m / 820ft
100m / 328ft
sea level
SCALE 1:5,500,000
(projection: Lambert Conformal Conic)
Km
Miles
154

Major towns and neighboring countries are linked by adequate road networks, although rural areas are less well served. Bahrain is linked to the mainland by a 15-mile (25-km) causeway.

KAZAKHSTAN

ABUNDANT NATURAL RESOURCES lie in the immense steppe grasslands, deserts, and central plateau of the former Soviet republic of Kazakhstan. An intensive program of industrial and agricultural development to exploit these resources during the Soviet era resulted in catastrophic industrial pollution, including fallout from nuclear testing and the shrinkage of the Aral Sea. Since independence, the government has encouraged foreign investment and liberalized the economy to promote growth. The adoption of Kazakh as the national language is intended to encourage a new sense of national identity in a state where living conditions for the majority remain harsh, both in cramped urban centers and impoverished rural areas.

TRANSPORTATION & INDUSTRY

THE SINGLE MOST IMPORTANT INDUSTRY in Kazakhstan is mining, based around extensive oil deposits near the Caspian Sea, the world's largest chromium mine, and vast reserves of iron ore. Recent foreign investment has helped to develop industries including food processing and steel manufacture, and to expand the exploitation of mineral resources. The Russian space program is still based in Baykonur, near Zhezkazgan, in central Kazakhstan.

Major industry and infrastructure

- chemicals
- engineering
- fish processing
- food processing
- iron & steel
- metallurgy
- mining
- oil
- capital cities
- major towns
- international airports
- major roads
- major industrial areas

TRANSPORTATION NETWORK

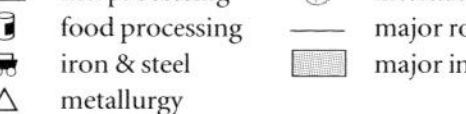

- 103,623 miles (166,864 km)
- none
- 8,786 miles (14,148 km)
- none

Industrial areas in the north and east are well-connected to Russia. Air and rail links with Germany and China have been established through foreign investment. Better access to Baltic ports is being sought.

Foreign investment is being actively sought by the Kazakh government in order to fully exploit the potential of the country's rich mineral reserves, found in such places as this open-cast coal mine, in Kazakhstan.

USING THE LAND & SEA

THE REARING OF LARGE HERDS of sheep and goats on the steppe grasslands forms the core of Kazakh agriculture. Arable cultivation and cotton-growing in pasture and desert areas was encouraged during the Soviet era, but relative yields are low. The heavy use of fertilizers and the diversion of natural water sources for irrigation has degraded much of the land.

THE URBAN/RURAL POPULATION DIVIDE

urban 58% — rural 42%

POPULATION DENSITY	TOTAL LAND AREA
16 people per sq mile (6 people per sq km)	1,048,878 sq miles (2,717,300 sq km)

Land use and agricultural distribution

- cattle
- goats
- sheep
- cotton
- fishing
- wheat
- capital cities
- major towns
- pasture
- cropland
- forest
- mountain region
- desert

The nomadic peoples who moved their herds around the steppe grasslands are now largely settled, although echoes of their traditional lifestyle, in particular their superb riding skills, remain.

125

152

MAP KEY

POPULATION

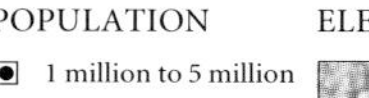

- 1 million to 5 million
- 500,000 to 1 million
- 100,000 to 500,000
- 50,000 to 100,000
- 10,000 to 50,000
- below 10,000

ELEVATION

- 4000m / 13,124ft
- 3000m / 9843ft
- 2000m / 6562ft
- 1000m / 3281ft
- 500m / 1640ft
- 250m / 820ft
- 100m / 328ft
- sea level

SCALE 1:6,250,000 (projection: Lambert Conformal Conic)

The Landscape

STRETCHING MORE THAN 1,250 MILES (2,000 km) from the Caspian Sea in the west to China in the east, more than 40% of Kazakhstan is covered by steppe grasslands, which give way to barren desert in the south. The land rises eastward toward the mineral-rich central plateau, to form the Altai Mountains.

1960
1996
2010
The Caspian Sea is the largest body of inland water in the world.
The desert of Peski Bol'shiye Barsuki is mainly sandy, displaying a number of classic dune formations. Groundwater supports a small amount of vegetation.
A large number of salt lakes fill depressions in the rolling uplands of central Kazakhstan.
The Altai Mountains lie on Kazakhstan's eastern borders with China and the Russian Federation. Cold and largely barren, they are the source of many of the rivers which flow across the steppe.
Altai Mountains
Tien Shan
Aral Sea
Khrebet Kanchingiz
Its waters taken for industry and irrigation, the Syr Darya, one of Kazakhstan's major rivers, now barely reaches the Aral Sea, which it used to fill. Like many Kazakh rivers it has been heavily polluted with chemicals and its flow has been restricted by up to 60%.
The waters of Lake Balkhash (*Ozero Balkhash*), unlike those of the Aral Sea, are still able to support a fishing industry.
The central Kazakh Uplands (*Kazakhskiy Melkosopochnik*) contain much of the country's mineral riches. The landscape is largely flat with occasional rocky outcrops and hillocks.
Immense stretches of steppe grasslands characterize much of the Kazakh landscape. These lowland areas have been used for arable cultivation in recent years, although problems with irrigation have meant that much of the land is being allowed to revert to its natural vegetation and pastoral usage.
N O P Q R S T U V W X Y
R S T U V W X Y Z
1 2 4 5 6 7 8 13 14 15 16 17
125
162
152
FEDERATION
KAZAKHSTAN
KYRGYZSTAN
CHINA
Petropavlovsk
SEVERNYY KAZAKHSTAN
KOKSHETAU
Kokshetau
Kulunda Steppe
Pavlodar
PAVLODAR
AKMOLA
Akmola
Kazakhskiy Melkosopochnik
TURGAY
Arkalyk
Temirtau
Karaganda
KARAGANDA
Semipalatinsk
Ust'-Kamenogorsk
SEMIPALATINSK
VOSTOCHNYY KAZAKHSTAN
Altai Mountains
Ozero Zaysan
Khrebet Tarbagatay
Zhezkazgan
ZHEZKAZGAN
Ozero Balkhash
Balkhash
TALDYKORGAN
Taldykorgan
Betpak-Dala
ZHAMBYL
ALMATY
Peski Saryesik-Atyrau
Peski Taukum
Peski Moyynkum
Kzyl-Orda
YUZHNYY KAZAKHSTAN
Khrebet Karatau
Zhambyl
Shymkent
Kyzyl Kum
ALMATY (ALMA-ATA)
Kirghiz Range
Tien Shan
Khan Tengri Pk 6398m

Since 1960, the Aral Sea has shrunk by 40%, become extremely saline, and lost all but five of its once-abundant fish species. Factors in this ecological disaster include the excessive use of fertilizers, defoliants, and the diversion of its main source rivers for the irrigation of desert lands.

Rows of pine trees edge this valley near Alma-Ata, the capital of Kazakhstan. The snow-covered slopes in the background are used for skiing.

Central Asia

Kyrgyzstan, Tajikistan, Turkmenistan, Uzbekistan

The four republics that declared independence in 1991 were created in the early years of the former Soviet Union, promoting ethnic divisions in a region whose common focus, since the 8th century, has been Islam. Traditional rural, nomadic ways of life have survived the Soviet era, while the benefits of modern industry and grand irrigation schemes have resulted in severe pollution in the delicate, arid steppe environment, particularly in Uzbekistan. Many ethnic minority groups are scattered among the four republics, with isolated communities in the mountains of Kyrgyzstan. The current Islamic revival has brought hope of greater regional unity, in spite of religious factionalism which, in 1992, plunged Tajikistan into civil war.

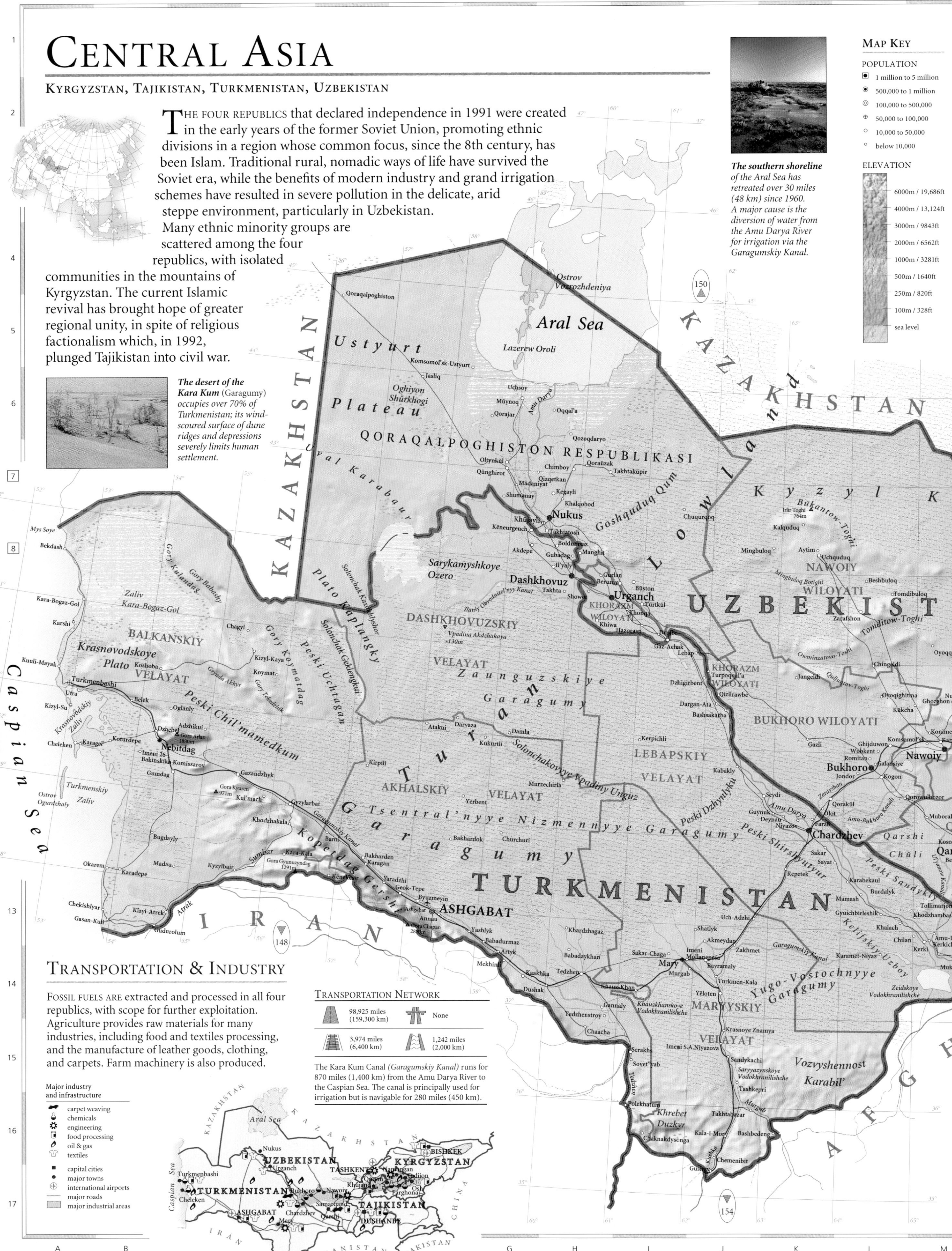

Map Key
POPULATION
1 million to 5 million
500,000 to 1 million
100,000 to 500,000
50,000 to 100,000
10,000 to 50,000
below 10,000
ELEVATION
6000m / 19,686ft
4000m / 13,124ft
3000m / 9843ft
2000m / 6562ft
1000m / 3281ft
500m / 1640ft
250m / 820ft
100m / 328ft
sea level
KAZAKHSTAN
UZBEKISTAN
TURKMENISTAN
IRAN
Aral Sea
Caspian Sea
Ustyurt Plateau
QORAQALPOGHISTON RESPUBLIKASI
Sarykamyshkoye Ozero
Nukus
Dashkhovuz
Urganch
ASHGABAT
Nebitdag
Turkmenbashi
Bukhoro
Chardzhev
Mary
Nawoiy
BALKANSKIY VELAYAT
DASHKHOVUZSKIY VELAYAT
AKHALSKIY VELAYAT
LEBAPSKIY VELAYAT
MARYYSKIY VELAYAT
BUKHORO WILOYATI
NAWOIY WILOYATI
KHORAZM WILOYATI
Tsentral'nyye Garagumy
Zaunguzskiye Garagumy
Kyzyl Kum
Turan Lowland
Garagumskiy Kanal
Amu Darya
Kopetdag
Krasnovodskoye Plato
Zaliv Kara-Bogaz-Gol
Vozvyshennost Karabil'
150
148
154
TRANSPORTATION NETWORK
98,925 miles (159,300 km)
None
3,974 miles (6,400 km)
1,242 miles (2,000 km)
Major industry and infrastructure
carpet weaving
chemicals
engineering
food processing
oil & gas
textiles
capital cities
major towns
international airports
major roads
major industrial areas

The southern shoreline *of the Aral Sea has retreated over 30 miles (48 km) since 1960. A major cause is the diversion of water from the Amu Darya River for irrigation via the Garagumskiy Kanal.*

The desert of the Kara Kum (Garagumy) *occupies over 70% of Turkmenistan; its wind-scoured surface of dune ridges and depressions severely limits human settlement.*

Transportation & Industry

Fossil fuels are extracted and processed in all four republics, with scope for further exploitation. Agriculture provides raw materials for many industries, including food and textiles processing, and the manufacture of leather goods, clothing, and carpets. Farm machinery is also produced.

The Kara Kum Canal *(Garagumskiy Kanal)* runs for 870 miles (1,400 km) from the Amu Darya River to the Caspian Sea. The canal is principally used for irrigation but is navigable for 280 miles (450 km).

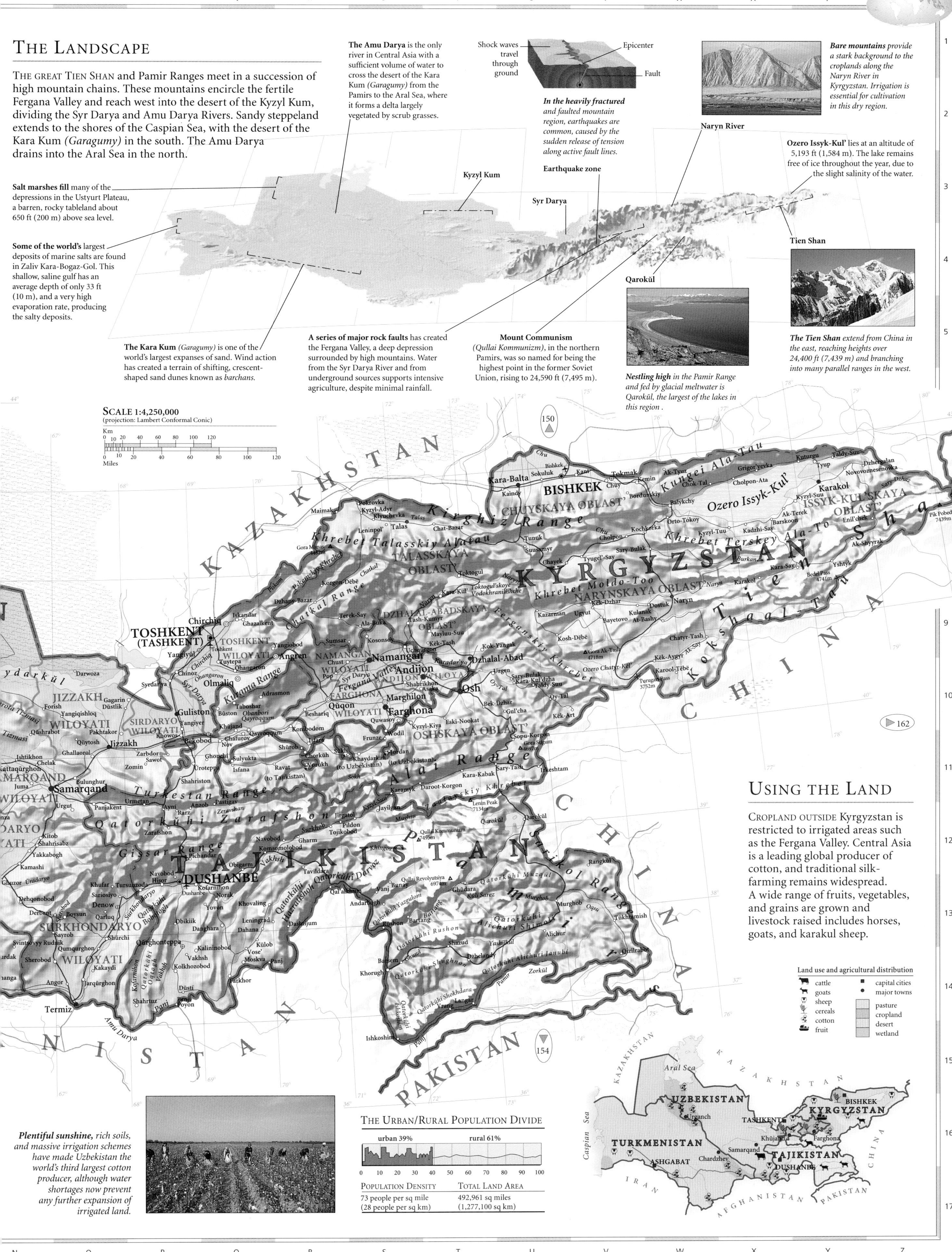

N O P Q R S T U V W X Y
Shock waves travel through ground
Epicenter
Fault
Kyzyl Kum
Syr Darya
Earthquake zone
Naryn River
Tien Shan
Qarokŭl
SCALE 1:4,250,000
(projection: Lambert Conformal Conic)
KAZAKHSTAN
KYRGYZSTAN
TAJIKISTAN
CHINA
PAKISTAN
BISHKEK
TOSHKENT (TASHKENT)
DUSHANBE
Ozero Issyk-Kul'
Kirghiz Range
Fergana Valley
Alai Range
Samarqand
Namangan
Andijon
Osh
Farghona
Termiz
Land use and agricultural distribution
cattle
goats
sheep
cereals
cotton
fruit
capital cities
major towns
pasture
cropland
desert
wetland
UZBEKISTAN
TURKMENISTAN
KYRGYZSTAN
TAJIKISTAN
ASHGABAT
IRAN
AFGHANISTAN
Aral Sea
Caspian Sea

THE LANDSCAPE

THE GREAT TIEN SHAN and Pamir Ranges meet in a succession of high mountain chains. These mountains encircle the fertile Fergana Valley and reach west into the desert of the Kyzyl Kum, dividing the Syr Darya and Amu Darya Rivers. Sandy steppeland extends to the shores of the Caspian Sea, with the desert of the Kara Kum *(Garagumy)* in the south. The Amu Darya drains into the Aral Sea in the north.

The Amu Darya is the only river in Central Asia with a sufficient volume of water to cross the desert of the Kara Kum *(Garagumy)* from the Pamirs to the Aral Sea, where it forms a delta largely vegetated by scrub grasses.

In the heavily fractured *and faulted mountain region, earthquakes are common, caused by the sudden release of tension along active fault lines.*

Bare mountains *provide a stark background to the croplands along the Naryn River in Kyrgyzstan. Irrigation is essential for cultivation in this dry region.*

Ozero Issyk-Kul' lies at an altitude of 5,193 ft (1,584 m). The lake remains free of ice throughout the year, due to the slight salinity of the water.

Salt marshes fill many of the depressions in the Ustyurt Plateau, a barren, rocky tableland about 650 ft (200 m) above sea level.

Some of the world's largest deposits of marine salts are found in Zaliv Kara-Bogaz-Gol. This shallow, saline gulf has an average depth of only 33 ft (10 m), and a very high evaporation rate, producing the salty deposits.

The Kara Kum *(Garagumy)* is one of the world's largest expanses of sand. Wind action has created a terrain of shifting, crescent-shaped sand dunes known as *barchans.*

A series of major rock faults has created the Fergana Valley, a deep depression surrounded by high mountains. Water from the Syr Darya River and from underground sources supports intensive agriculture, despite minimal rainfall.

Mount Communism *(Qullai Kommunizm)*, in the northern Pamirs, was so named for being the highest point in the former Soviet Union, rising to 24,590 ft (7,495 m).

Nestling high *in the Pamir Range and fed by glacial meltwater is Qarokŭl, the largest of the lakes in this region .*

The Tien Shan *extend from China in the east, reaching heights over 24,400 ft (7,439 m) and branching into many parallel ranges in the west.*

USING THE LAND

CROPLAND OUTSIDE Kyrgyzstan is restricted to irrigated areas such as the Fergana Valley. Central Asia is a leading global producer of cotton, and traditional silk-farming remains widespread. A wide range of fruits, vegetables, and grains are grown and livestock raised includes horses, goats, and karakul sheep.

Plentiful sunshine, *rich soils, and massive irrigation schemes have made Uzbekistan the world's third largest cotton producer, although water shortages now prevent any further expansion of irrigated land.*

THE URBAN/RURAL POPULATION DIVIDE

urban 39% — rural 61%

POPULATION DENSITY	TOTAL LAND AREA
73 people per sq mile (28 people per sq km)	492,961 sq miles (1,277,100 sq km)

AFGHANISTAN & PAKISTAN

PAKISTAN WAS CREATED by the partition of British India in 1947, becoming the western arm of a new Islamic state for Indian Muslims. The eastern sector, in Bengal, seceded to become the separate country of Bangladesh in 1971. Over half of Pakistan's 122 million people live in the Punjab, at the fertile head of the great Indus Basin. The river sustains a national economy based on irrigated agriculture, including cotton for the vital textiles industry. Afghanistan, a mountainous, landlocked country with an ancient and independent culture, has been wracked by war since 1979, when calls for help from a beleaguered government led to a Soviet invasion. Despite the Soviet withdrawal, factional strife continues and five million Afghan refugees remain over the border in Pakistan.

***The town of Bamian** lies high in the Hindu Kush, 250 miles (420 km) west of the Afghan capital, Kabul. It contains two huge statues of Buddha and a number of sanctuaries and cells carved in the rock. In 1222, the ancient city was destroyed by Chinghiz Khan.*

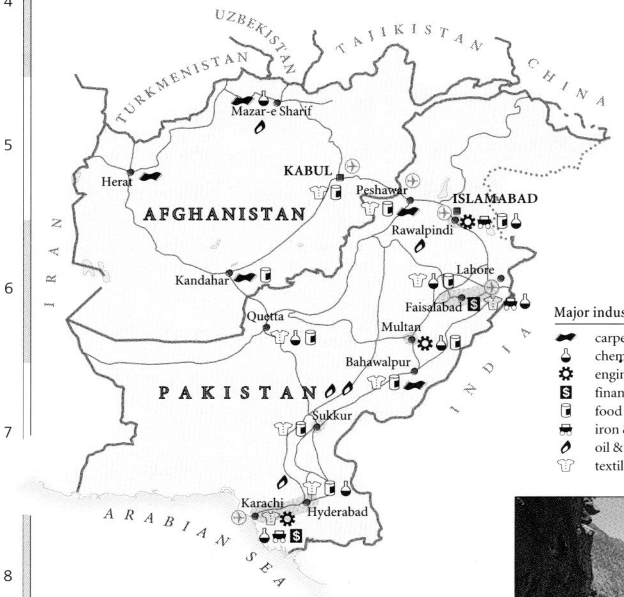

TRANSPORTATION & INDUSTRY

PAKISTAN IS HIGHLY dependent on the cotton textiles industry, although diversified manufacture is expanding around cities such as Karachi and Lahore. Afghanistan's limited industry is based mainly on the processing of agricultural raw materials and includes traditional crafts such as carpet weaving.

UZBEKISTAN
TAJIKISTAN
TURKMENISTAN
CHINA
IRAN
INDIA
ARABIAN SEA
AFGHANISTAN
PAKISTAN
Mazar-e Sharif
KABUL
Herat
Kandahar
Peshawar
ISLAMABAD
Rawalpindi
Lahore
Quetta
Faisalabad
Multan
Bahawalpur
Sukkur
Karachi
Hyderabad

Major industry and infrastructure

carpet weaving	capital cities
chemicals	major towns
engineering	international airports
finance	major roads
food processing	major industrial areas
iron & steel	
oil & gas	
textiles	

TRANSPORTATION NETWORK

82,740 miles (133,237 km)
None
7,855 miles (12,649 km)
745 miles (1,200 km)

The Karakoram Highway was completed after 20 years of construction in 1978. It breaches the Himalayan mountain barrier and provides a commercial motor route linking lowland Pakistan and China.

***The Karakoram Highway** is one of the highest major roads in the world. It took over 24,000 workers almost 20 years to complete.*

THE LANDSCAPE

AFGHANISTAN'S TOPOGRAPHY is dominated by the mountains of the Hindu Kush, which spread south and west into numerous mountain spurs. The dry plateau of southwestern Afghanistan extends into Pakistan and the hills which overlook the great Indus Basin. In northern Pakistan the Hindu Kush, Himalayan and Karakoram ranges meet to form one of the world's highest mountain regions.

***The Hunza River** rises in the northern Karakoram Range, running for 120 miles (193 km) before joining the Gilgit River.*

***The arid Hindu Kush** makes much of Afghanistan uninhabitable, with over 50% of the land lying above 6,500 ft (2,000 m).*

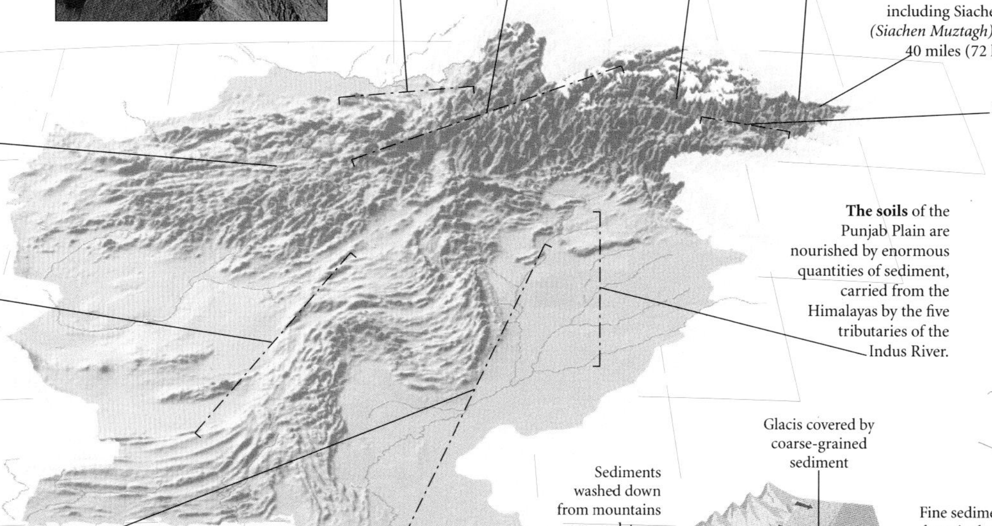

Hunza River
Hindu Kush
Himalayas

The plains and foothills which extend from the northern slopes of the Hindu Kush are part of the great grassy steppe of Central Asia.

K2 (Mount Godwin Austen), in the Karakoram Range, is the second highest mountain in the world, at an altitude of 28,251 ft (8,611 m).

Some of the largest glaciers outside the polar regions are found in the Karakoram Range, including Siachen Glacier (Siachen Muztagh), which is 40 miles (72 km) long.

Frequent earthquakes mean that mountain-building processes are continuing in this region, as the Indo-Australian Plate drifts northward, colliding with the Eurasian Plate.

Mountain chains running southwest from the Hindu Kush into Pakistan form a barrier to the humid winds that blow from the Indian Ocean, creating arid conditions across southern Afghanistan.

The soils of the Punjab Plain are nourished by enormous quantities of sediment, carried from the Himalayas by the five tributaries of the Indus River.

The Indus Basin is part of the Indus–Ganges lowland, a vast depression which has been filled with layers of sediment over the last 50 million years. These deposits are estimated to be over 16,400 ft (5,000 m) deep.

The Indus Delta is prone to heavy flooding and high levels of salinity. It remains a largely uncultivated wilderness area.

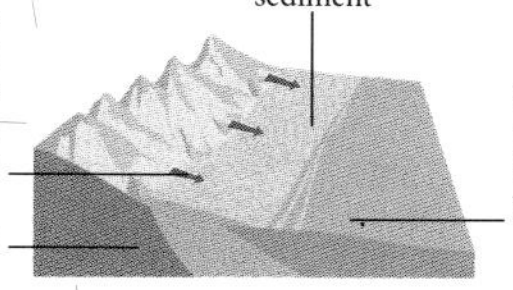

Glacis covered by coarse-grained sediment
Sediments washed down from mountains accumulate on glacis slopes
Bedrock
Fine sediments deposited on salt flats are removed by wind erosion.

***Glacis** are gentle, debris-covered slopes which lead into saltflats or deserts. They typically occur at the base of mountains in arid regions such as Afghanistan.*

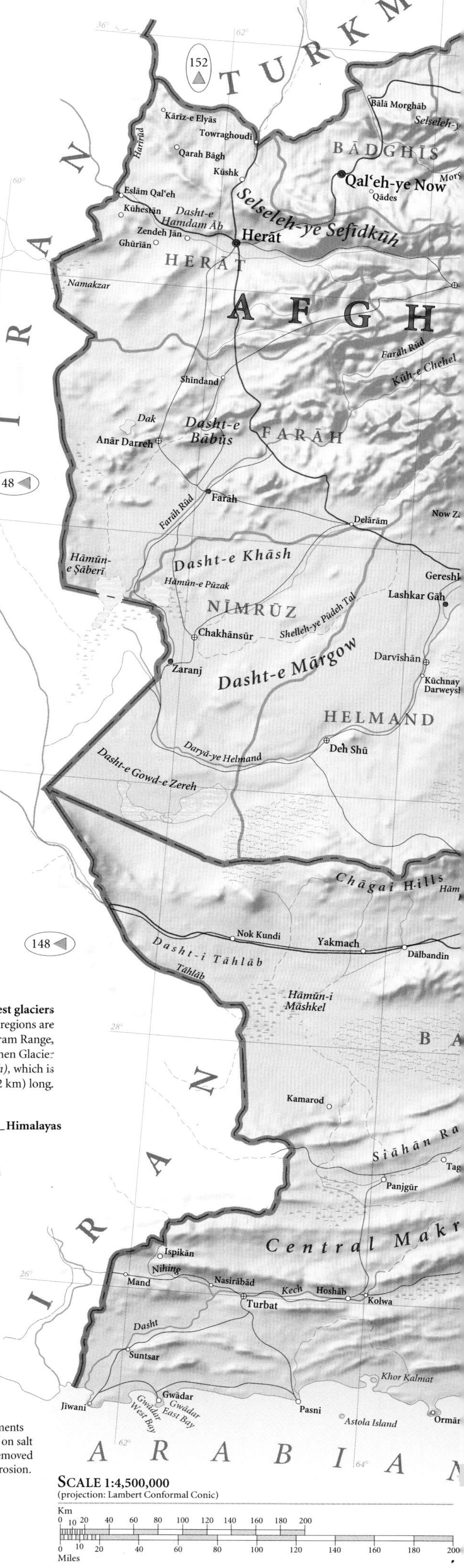

TURKMEN
IRAN
AFGH
ARABIAN
152
148
148
Kāriz-e Elyās
Towraghoudi
Qarah Bāgh
Kūshk
Bālā Morghāb
BĀDGHĪS
Qal'eh-ye Now
Eslām Qal'eh
Kūhestān
Dasht-e Hamdam Āb
Zendeh Jān
Ghūriān
Selseleh-ye Sefīdkūh
Herāt
HERĀT
Namakzar
Shīndand
Dak
Anār Darreh
Dasht-e Bābūs
FARĀH
Farāh
Farāh Rūd
Delārām
Hāmūn-e Şāberī
Dasht-e Khāsh
Hāmūn-e Pūzak
NĪMRŪZ
Chakhānsūr
Zaranj
Dasht-e Mārgow
Lashkar Gāh
Darvīshān
HELMAND
Deh Shū
Daryā-ye Helmand
Dasht-e Gowd-e Zereh
Chāgai Hills
Nok Kundi
Yakmach
Dālbandin
Dasht-i Tāhlāb
Hāmūn-i Māshkel
Kamarod
Siāhān Range
Panjgūr
Central Makran
Ispikān
Nihing
Mand
Nasirābād
Kech
Hoshāb
Turbat
Kolwa
Dasht
Suntsar
Jiwani
Gwādar
Gwādar West Bay
Gwādar East Bay
Pasni
Khor Kalmat
Astola Island
Ormāra

SCALE 1:4,500,000
(projection: Lambert Conformal Conic)

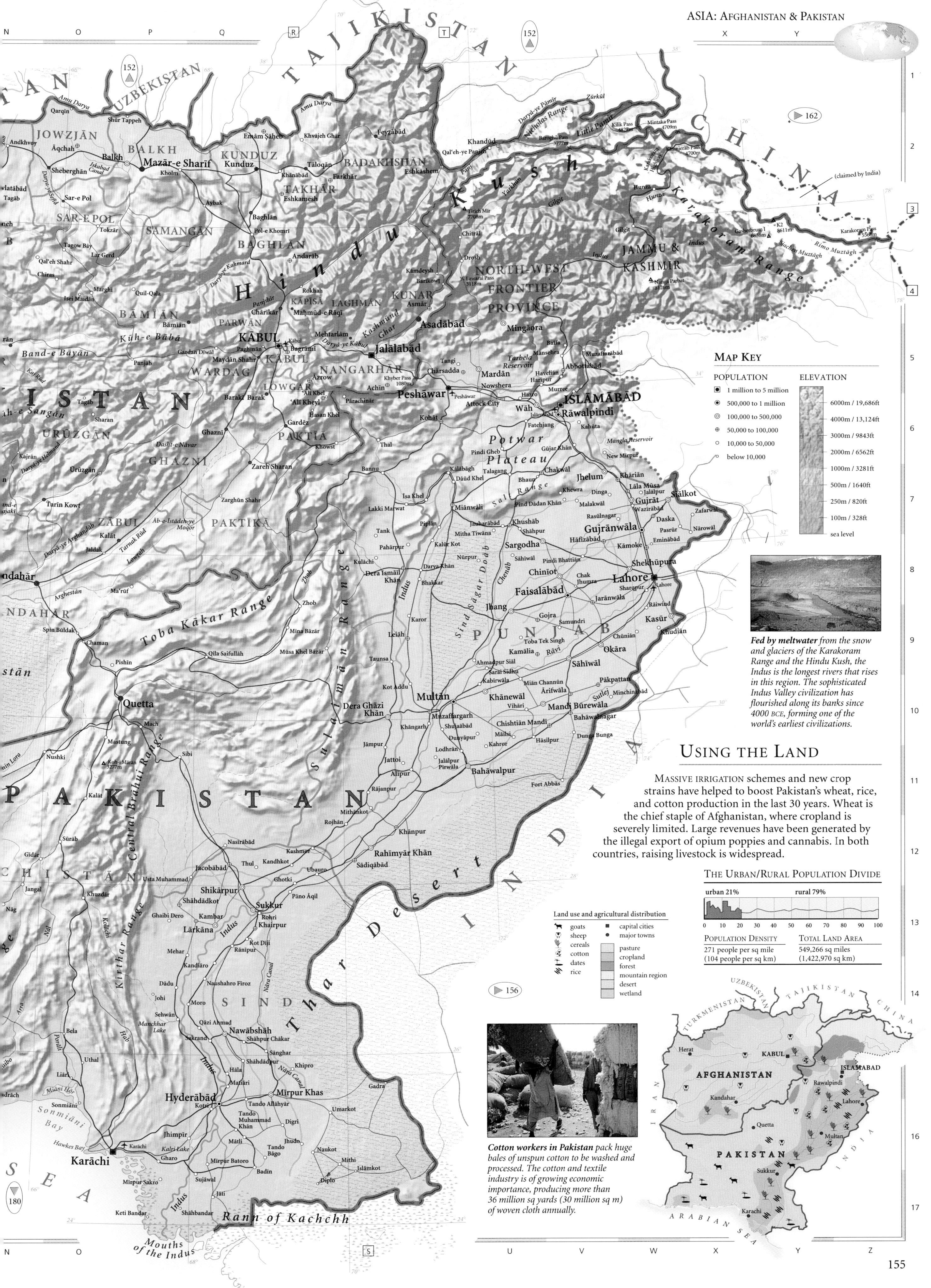
MAP KEY
POPULATION
1 million to 5 million
500,000 to 1 million
100,000 to 500,000
50,000 to 100,000
10,000 to 50,000
below 10,000
ELEVATION
6000m / 19,686ft
4000m / 13,124ft
3000m / 9843ft
2000m / 6562ft
1000m / 3281ft
500m / 1640ft
250m / 820ft
100m / 328ft
sea level
Land use and agricultural distribution
goats
sheep
cereals
cotton
dates
rice
capital cities
major towns
pasture
cropland
forest
mountain region
desert
wetland

Fed by meltwater from the snow and glaciers of the Karakoram Range and the Hindu Kush, the Indus is the longest rivers that rises in this region. The sophisticated Indus Valley civilization has flourished along its banks since 4000 BCE, forming one of the world's earliest civilizations.

Using the Land

Massive irrigation schemes and new crop strains have helped to boost Pakistan's wheat, rice, and cotton production in the last 30 years. Wheat is the chief staple of Afghanistan, where cropland is severely limited. Large revenues have been generated by the illegal export of opium poppies and cannabis. In both countries, raising livestock is widespread.

The Urban/Rural Population Divide

urban 21% | rural 79%

Population Density

271 people per sq mile (104 people per sq km)

Total Land Area

549,266 sq miles (1,422,970 sq km)

Cotton workers in Pakistan pack huge bales of unspun cotton to be washed and processed. The cotton and textile industry is of growing economic importance, producing more than 36 million sq yards (30 million sq m) of woven cloth annually.

SOUTH ASIA

BANGLADESH, BHUTAN, INDIA, MALDIVES, NEPAL, PAKISTAN, SRI LANKA

MORE THAN ONE-FIFTH of the world's population lives in the South Asian subcontinent. Great cultural diversity has come from a long succession of foreign invaders, including Hindu Aryans, Islamic Moguls, and the British, whose empire incorporated the princely states of the Maharajas and extended to the borders of Nepal and Bhutan in the Himalayas. Half a century after independence, India is the world's largest democracy, and at the current rate of growth, may overtake China as the world's most populous country within the next century. There are points of tension in the region over claims for independence by the Sikhs in the Indian Punjab and the Tamil separatists in Sri Lanka, and the long-standing dispute with Pakistan over Jammu and Kashmir in the north.

THE LANDSCAPE

SOUTHERN ASIA is effectively isolated from the rest of Asia by desert along the western flank of Pakistan, and a continuous wall of mountains, dominated by the Himalayas, to the north and east. The great basins of the Indus and Ganges separate this mountain fringe from the rolling plateau of the Indian peninsula, which is bordered by a line of coastal hills, the Eastern and Western Ghats.

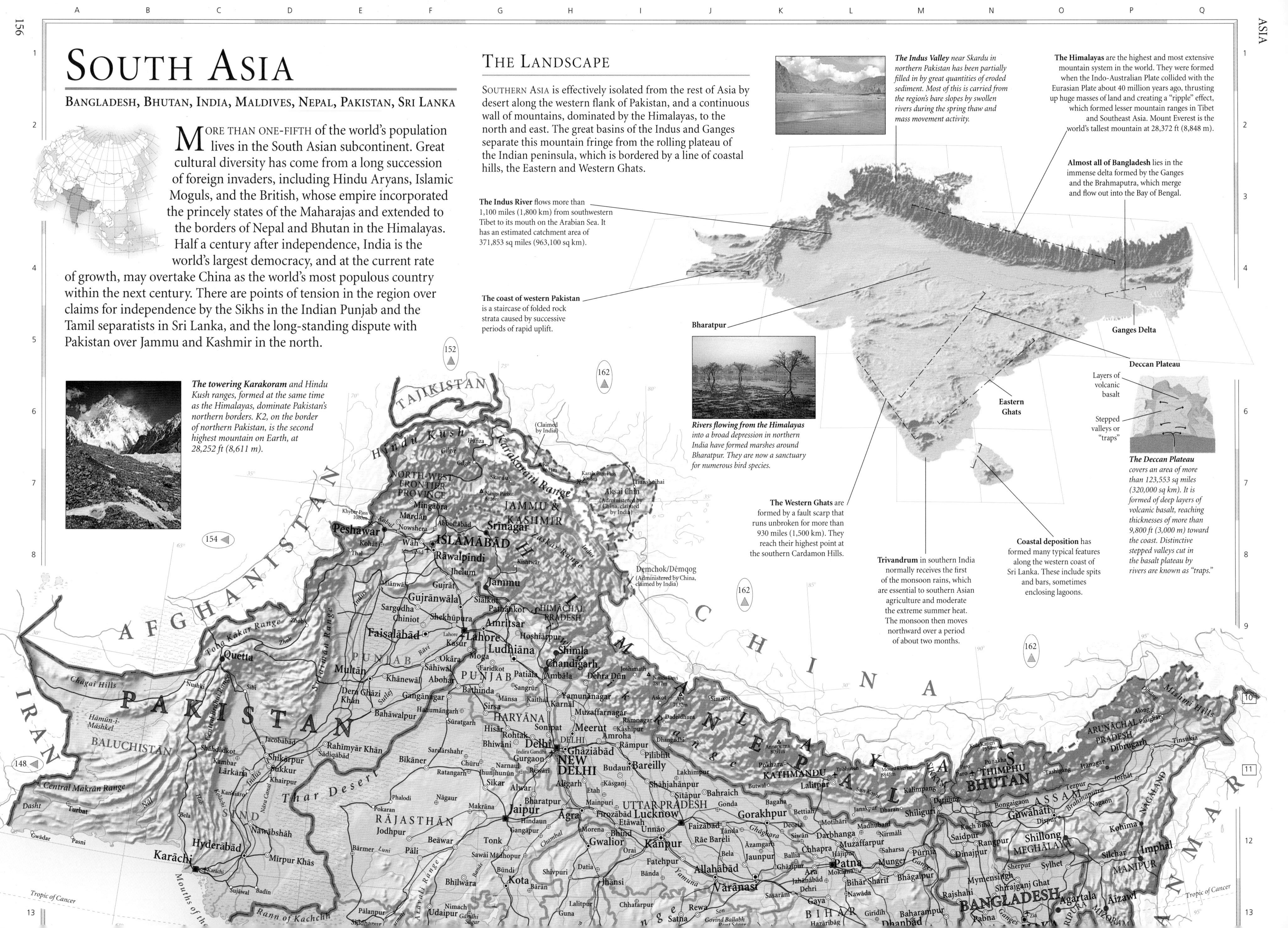
Ganges Delta
Deccan Plateau
Layers of volcanic basalt
Stepped valleys or "traps"
Eastern Ghats
Bharatpur
AFGHANISTAN
PAKISTAN
CHINA
NEPAL
BHUTAN
BANGLADESH
TAJIKISTAN
IRAN

The Indus River flows more than 1,100 miles (1,800 km) from southwestern Tibet to its mouth on the Arabian Sea. It has an estimated catchment area of 371,853 sq miles (963,100 sq km).

The coast of western Pakistan is a staircase of folded rock strata caused by successive periods of rapid uplift.

The Indus Valley *near Skardu in northern Pakistan has been partially filled in by great quantities of eroded sediment. Most of this is carried from the region's bare slopes by swollen rivers during the spring thaw and mass movement activity.*

The Himalayas are the highest and most extensive mountain system in the world. They were formed when the Indo-Australian Plate collided with the Eurasian Plate about 40 million years ago, thrusting up huge masses of land and creating a "ripple" effect, which formed lesser mountain ranges in Tibet and Southeast Asia. Mount Everest is the world's tallest mountain at 28,372 ft (8,848 m).

Almost all of Bangladesh lies in the immense delta formed by the Ganges and the Brahmaputra, which merge and flow out into the Bay of Bengal.

Rivers flowing from the Himalayas *into a broad depression in northern India have formed marshes around Bharatpur. They are now a sanctuary for numerous bird species.*

The Deccan Plateau *covers an area of more than 123,553 sq miles (320,000 sq km). It is formed of deep layers of volcanic basalt, reaching thicknesses of more than 9,800 ft (3,000 m) toward the coast. Distinctive stepped valleys cut in the basalt plateau by rivers are known as "traps."*

The towering Karakoram *and Hindu Kush ranges, formed at the same time as the Himalayas, dominate Pakistan's northern borders. K2, on the border of northern Pakistan, is the second highest mountain on Earth, at 28,252 ft (8,611 m).*

The Western Ghats are formed by a fault scarp that runs unbroken for more than 930 miles (1,500 km). They reach their highest point at the southern Cardamon Hills.

Trivandrum in southern India normally receives the first of the monsoon rains, which are essential to southern Asian agriculture and moderate the extreme summer heat. The monsoon then moves northward over a period of about two months.

Coastal deposition has formed many typical features along the western coast of Sri Lanka. These include spits and bars, sometimes enclosing lagoons.

152 154 162 162 162 148

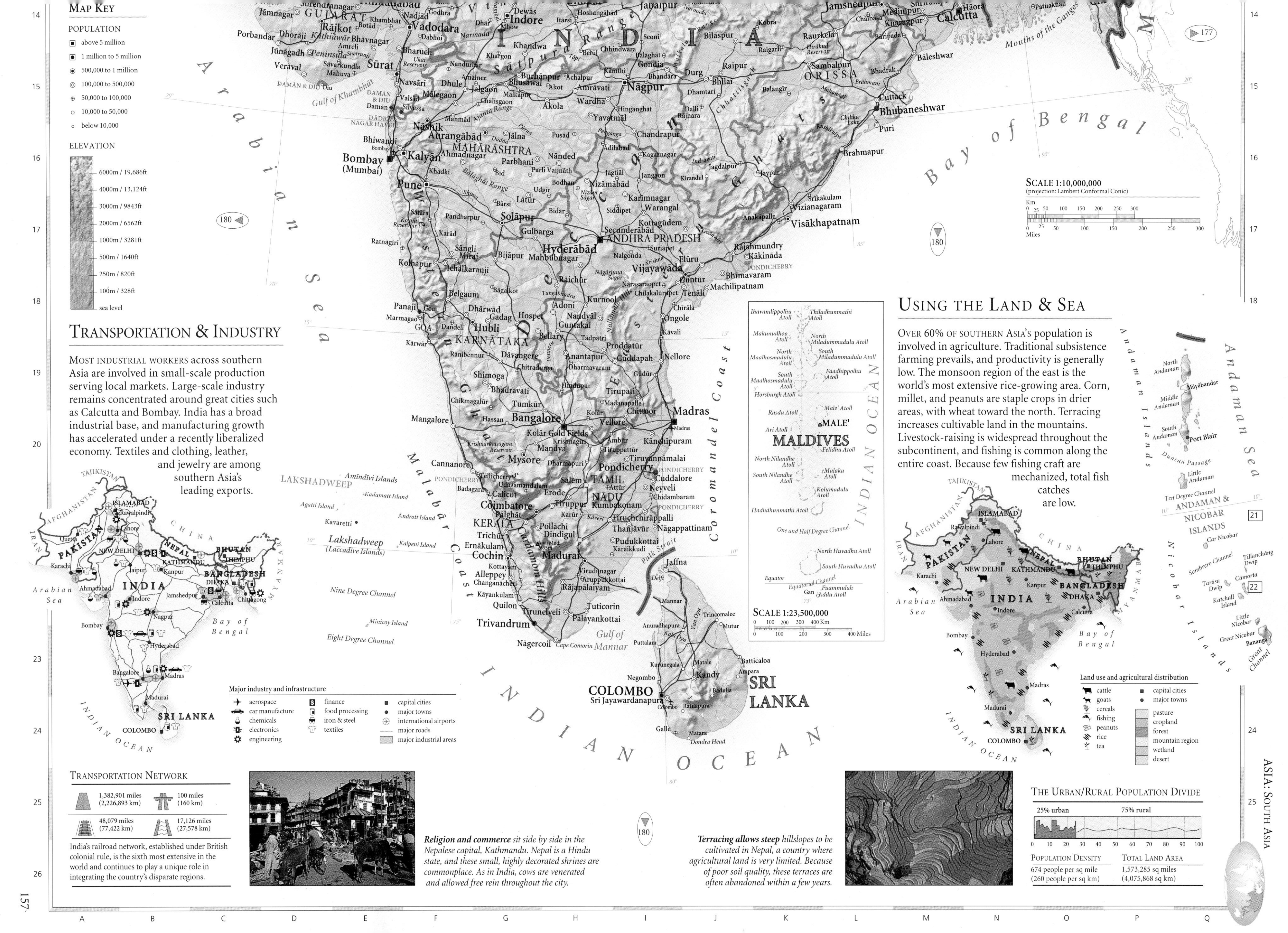
MAP KEY
POPULATION
above 5 million
1 million to 5 million
500,000 to 1 million
100,000 to 500,000
50,000 to 100,000
10,000 to 50,000
below 10,000
ELEVATION
6000m / 19,686ft
4000m / 13,124ft
3000m / 9843ft
2000m / 6562ft
1000m / 3281ft
500m / 1640ft
250m / 820ft
100m / 328ft
sea level
SCALE 1:10,000,000
(projection: Lambert Conformal Conic)
SCALE 1:23,500,000
INDIA
Arabian Sea
Bay of Bengal
INDIAN OCEAN
SRI LANKA
MALDIVES
Andaman Sea
Andaman Islands
Nicobar Islands
ANDAMAN & NICOBAR ISLANDS
Major industry and infrastructure
aerospace
car manufacture
chemicals
electronics
engineering
finance
food processing
iron & steel
textiles
capital cities
major towns
international airports
major roads
major industrial areas
Land use and agricultural distribution
cattle
goats
cereals
fishing
peanuts
rice
tea
capital cities
major towns
pasture
cropland
forest
mountain region
wetland
desert
1,382,901 miles (2,226,893 km)
100 miles (160 km)
48,079 miles (77,422 km)
17,126 miles (27,578 km)
25% urban
75% rural

Transportation & Industry

Most industrial workers across southern Asia are involved in small-scale production serving local markets. Large-scale industry remains concentrated around great cities such as Calcutta and Bombay. India has a broad industrial base, and manufacturing growth has accelerated under a recently liberalized economy. Textiles and clothing, leather, and jewelry are among southern Asia's leading exports.

Transportation Network

India's railroad network, established under British colonial rule, is the sixth most extensive in the world and continues to play a unique role in integrating the country's disparate regions.

***Religion and commerce** sit side by side in the Nepalese capital, Kathmandu. Nepal is a Hindu state, and these small, highly decorated shrines are commonplace. As in India, cows are venerated and allowed free rein throughout the city.*

Using the Land & Sea

Over 60% of southern Asia's population is involved in agriculture. Traditional subsistence farming prevails, and productivity is generally low. The monsoon region of the east is the world's most extensive rice-growing area. Corn, millet, and peanuts are staple crops in drier areas, with wheat toward the north. Terracing increases cultivable land in the mountains. Livestock-raising is widespread throughout the subcontinent, and fishing is common along the entire coast. Because few fishing craft are mechanized, total fish catches are low.

***Terracing allows steep** hillslopes to be cultivated in Nepal, a country where agricultural land is very limited. Because of poor soil quality, these terraces are often abandoned within a few years.*

The Urban/Rural Population Divide

Population Density
674 people per sq mile
(260 people per sq km)

Total Land Area
1,573,285 sq miles
(4,075,868 sq km)

Northern India & the Himalayan States

Bangladesh, Bhutan, Nepal, Arunachal Pradesh, Assam, Bihar, Chandigarh, Delhi, Haryana, Himachal Pradesh, Jammu & Kashmir, Manipur, Meghalaya, Mizoram, Nagaland, Punjab, Rajasthan, Sikkim, Tripura, Uttar Pradesh, West Bengal

The Ganges and Brahmaputra river basins and the massive mountain barrier of the Himalayas define this region's landscape and have served to reinforce potent cultural and religious differences among its people. Hinduism pervades most aspects of national life and is a growing political force within India, a secular country that also encompasses the center of Sikhism in Amritsar and the world's largest Muslim minority. Nepal is a crowded mountain state that faces severe ecological problems due to deforestation, while the tiny Himalayan Buddhist kingdom of Bhutan is emerging from long-term isolation to welcome selected visitors. The Muslim state of Bangladesh, formerly East Pakistan, is one of the world's most densely populated countries and one of the poorest, with more than 120 million people living largely on the massive Ganges/Brahmaputra Delta. Many Bangladeshis live under threat of repeated, catastrophic floods.

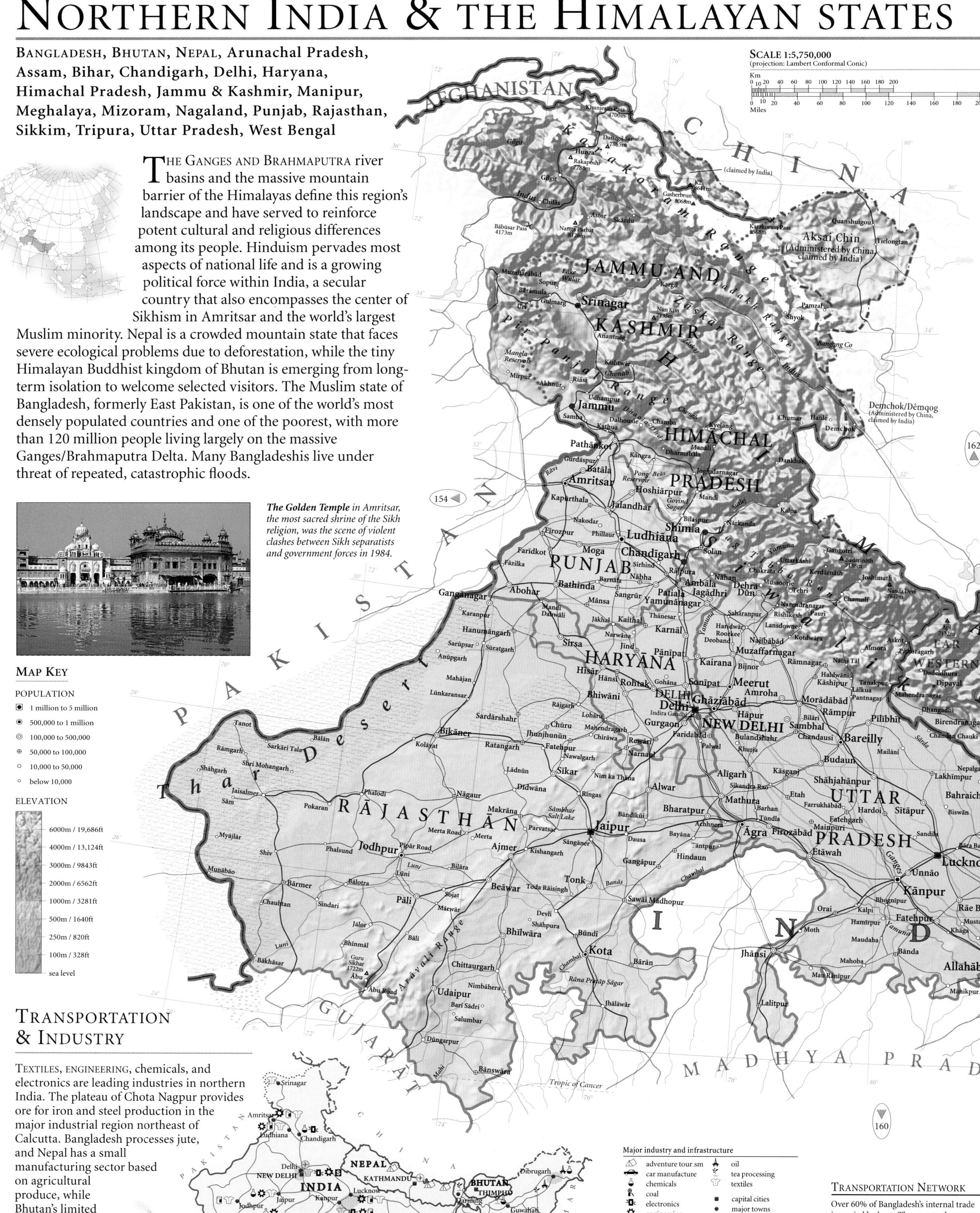

SCALE 1:5,750,000
(projection: Lambert Conformal Conic)
Km
Miles
AFGHANISTAN
CHINA
PAKISTAN
Thar Desert
GUJARAT
MADHYA PRADESH
JAMMU AND KASHMIR
HIMACHAL PRADESH
PUNJAB
HARYANA
RĀJASTHĀN
UTTAR PRADESH
INDIA
Aksai Chin (Administered by China, claimed by India)
Demchok/Dêmqog (Administered by China, claimed by India)
(claimed by India)
Karakoram Range
Ladakh Range
Zaskar Range
Pir Panjal Range
Dhaula Dhar
Siwalik Range
Aravalli Range
Srinagar
Jammu
Amritsar
Ludhiāna
Chandīgarh
Shimla
Delhi
NEW DELHI
Ghāziābād
Meerut
Jaipur
Jodhpur
Ajmer
Āgra
Kānpur
Lucknow
Bareilly
Kota
Udaipur
Bīkaner
Tropic of Cancer
154
160
162

The Golden Temple in Amritsar, the most sacred shrine of the Sikh religion, was the scene of violent clashes between Sikh separatists and government forces in 1984.

Map Key

POPULATION
- 1 million to 5 million
- 500,000 to 1 million
- 100,000 to 500,000
- 50,000 to 100,000
- 10,000 to 50,000
- below 10,000

ELEVATION
- 6000m / 19,686ft
- 4000m / 13,124ft
- 3000m / 9843ft
- 2000m / 6562ft
- 1000m / 3281ft
- 500m / 1640ft
- 250m / 820ft
- 100m / 328ft
- sea level

Transportation & Industry

Textiles, engineering, chemicals, and electronics are leading industries in northern India. The plateau of Chota Nagpur provides ore for iron and steel production in the major industrial region northeast of Calcutta. Bangladesh processes jute, and Nepal has a small manufacturing sector based on agricultural produce, while Bhutan's limited industry is concentrated in the southern lowland area.

Major industry and infrastructure
- adventure tour.sm
- car manufacture
- chemicals
- coal
- electronics
- engineering
- finance
- food processing
- iron & steel
- jute processing
- oil
- tea processing
- textiles
- capital cities
- major towns
- international airports
- major roads
- major industrial areas

Transportation Network

Over 60% of Bangladesh's internal trade is carried by boat. The country has a very disjointed land transportation network, with no bridges over the Brahmaputra and few road crossings on the Ganges River.

THE LANDSCAPE

MOST OF THE REGION is drained by the Ganges River, which meets the Brahmaputra in Bangladesh to form an immense delta before flowing into the Bay of Bengal. The Himalayas extend eastward over 1,500 miles (2,400 km) from the parallel ranges running through Jammu and Kashmir. The Thar Desert occupies the southwest.

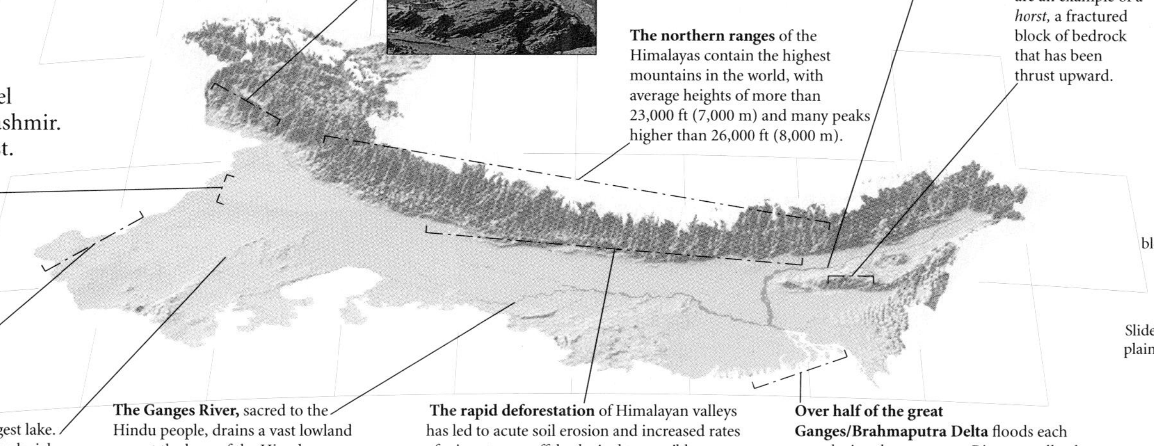

The Indian Punjab lies mainly to the west of the Ganges watershed, and its rivers flow into the Indus. Control of this water resource has been a cause of great friction with neighboring Pakistan.

The border between India and Pakistan runs through the Thar Desert, an area of sandy *seif* dunes 50–100 ft (15–30 m) in height. Fossils found in the desert indicate that the dunes, stabilized by vegetation, have been in their current position for about 3,000 years.

Sambhar Salt Lake in Rajasthan is India's largest lake. Unlike most of the Himalayan lakes, which are glacial in origin – formed in ice-scoured basins or as the result of depositional damming – it is an ephemeral salt lake filled periodically by flash flooding.

The Pir Panjal Range *in southwestern Kashmir rises to elevations of 12,500 ft (3,810 m). Despite the freezing conditions, settlements and extensive pastures are found above the tree line.*

The Ganges River, sacred to the Hindu people, drains a vast lowland area at the base of the Himalayas. The northern plains are covered by sandy deposits, broken by mud banks formed when the river floods.

The rapid deforestation of Himalayan valleys has led to acute soil erosion and increased rates of rainwater runoff, both cited as possible causes of the worsening floods downstream in the Ganges/Brahmaputra Delta. Natural runoff rates are high, however, and may be the real cause.

In the last 40 million years, the course of the Brahmaputra has been diverted hundreds of miles to the east by the rising landmass of the Himalayas.

The northern ranges of the Himalayas contain the highest mountains in the world, with average heights of more than 23,000 ft (7,000 m) and many peaks higher than 26,000 ft (8,000 m).

Over half of the great Ganges/Brahmaputra Delta floods each year during the monsoon. Rivers, swollen by meltwater from the Himalayas and by excess rainwater, break their banks and fertilize the land with nutrient-rich sediment.

The Khasi Hills are an example of a *horst*, a fractured block of bedrock that has been thrust upward.

The summit of Machhapuchhre *rises to 22,942 ft (6,993 m). It is also known as the "Fish's Tail" because of its distinctive peak.*

Debris slides in the middle Himalayas

Soil blocks

Debris fans at base of slope

Slide plain

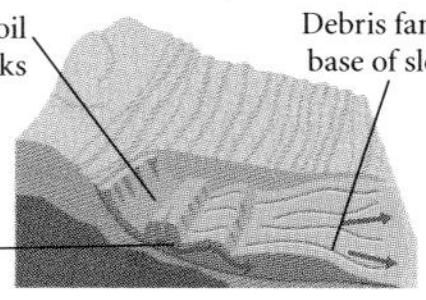

Soil loss *in the middle Himalayas has largely been attributed to debris slides, where large blocks of soil are mobilized by saturation along a slide plane. Once mobile, the soil slides down the slope, gaining speed and thinning to form a fan at the base of the slope.*

USING THE LAND

GRAIN PRODUCTION dominates land use. Rice is grown most widely in the east. Irrigation and new crop strains have dramatically increased yields in the Punjab, a major wheat-producing area. River floodplains are intensively farmed and livestock herding is widespread, particularly in Bhutan. Regional crops include jute in Bangladesh, tea in Assam, cardamom in Sikkim, and saffron in Kashmir.

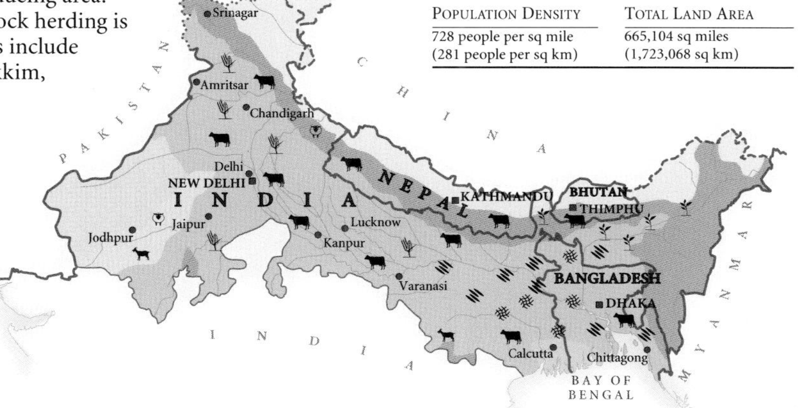

THE URBAN/RURAL POPULATION DIVIDE

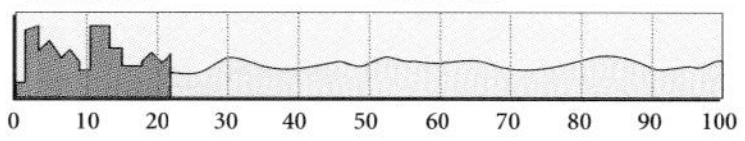

urban 22% rural 78%

0 10 20 30 40 50 60 70 80 90 100

POPULATION DENSITY	TOTAL LAND AREA
728 people per sq mile (281 people per sq km)	665,104 sq miles (1,723,068 sq km)

Land use and agricultural distribution

cattle, goats, sheep, cereals, jute, rice, tea, capital cities, major towns, pasture, cropland, forest, mountain region, wetland, desert

An adverse climate, *steep slopes, and poor soils limit crop cultivation in Bhutan, which is a largely agrarian economy. Rice, corn, and wheat are the main staples, although orchards are being established since the soil and climate suit this type of farming.*

Flooded streets *in Dhaka, Bangladesh, are a testament to the region's vulnerability to flooding. In 1988 alone, 75% of the country was flooded, leaving thousands of people dead and over 25 million homeless.*

162 177 180

Southern India & Sri Lanka

Sri Lanka, Andhra Pradesh, Dadra & Nagar Haveli, Daman & Diu, Goa, Gujarat, Karnataka, Kerala, Lakshadweep, Madhya Pradesh, Maharashtra, Orissa, Pondicherry, Tamil Nadu

The unique and highly independent southern states of India reflect the diverse and decentralized nature of that country, which has fourteen official languages. The southern half of the peninsula was beyond the reach of early invaders from the north and retained the distinct and ancient culture of Dravidian peoples such as the Tamils, whose language is spoken in preference to Hindi throughout southern India. The interior plateau of southern India is less densely populated than the coastal lowlands, where the European colonial imprint is strongest. Urban and industrial growth is accelerating, but southern India's vast population remains predominantly rural. The island of Sri Lanka has two distinct cultural groups; the mainly Buddhist Sinhalese majority, and the Tamil minority whose struggle for a homeland in the northeast has led to prolonged civil war.

Using the Land & Sea

Rice is the main staple in the east, in Sri Lanka, and along the humid Malabar Coast. Peanuts are grown on the Deccan Plateau, with wheat, corn, and chickpeas, toward the north. Sri Lanka is a leading exporter of tea, coconuts, and rubber. Cotton plantations supply local mills around Nagpur and Bombay. Fishing supports many communities in Kerala and the Laccadive Islands.

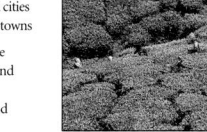

Land use and agricultural distribution

cattle	capital cities
goats	major towns
cereals	pasture
cotton	cropland
fishing	forest
peanuts	wetland
rice	
rubber	
tea	

Commercial plantations, growing tea (seen here), cardamom, coffee, coconuts, and rubber, occupy about half the agricultural land in Kerala, necessitating food imports for local consumption.

The Urban/Rural Population Divide

urban 29% — rural 71%

Population Density	Total Land Area
650 people per sq mile (251 people per sq km)	698,295 sq miles (1,809,054 sq km)

The Landscape

The undulating Deccan Plateau underlies most of southern India. It slopes gently down toward the east and is largely enclosed by the Ghats coastal hill ranges. The Western Ghats run continuously along the Arabian Sea coast, while the Eastern Ghats are interrupted by rivers which follow the slope of the plateau and flow across broad lowlands into the Bay of Bengal. The plateaus and basins of Sri Lanka's central highlands are surrounded by a broad plain.

Along the northern boundary of the Deccan Plateau, old basement rocks are interspersed with younger sedimentary strata. This creates spectacular scarplands that are cut by numerous waterfalls, along the softer sedimentary strata.

The Rann of Kachchh tidal marshes encircle the low-lying Kachchh Peninsula. For several months during the rainy season the water level of the marshes rises and Kachchh becomes an island.

The Konkan coast, which runs between Daman and Goa, is characterized by rocky headlands and bays with crescent shaped beaches. Flooded river valleys known as *rias* extend inland.

The interior uplands of southern India are broadly known as the Deccan Plateau. River erosion of the plateau's volcanic rock has created distinctive stepped valleys called *traps*.

Deep layers of river sediment have created a broad lowland plain along the eastern coast, with rivers such as the Krishna forming extensive deltas.

***The Western Ghats** run north–south marking the western boundary of the Deccan Plateau. Their height rises to the south where their summits reach altitudes of 8,000 ft (2,500 m).*

The island of Sri Lanka is essentially an extension of the Deccan Plateau. It lies on the Indian continental shelf and is composed of the same hard, crystalline rocks.

Adam's Bridge

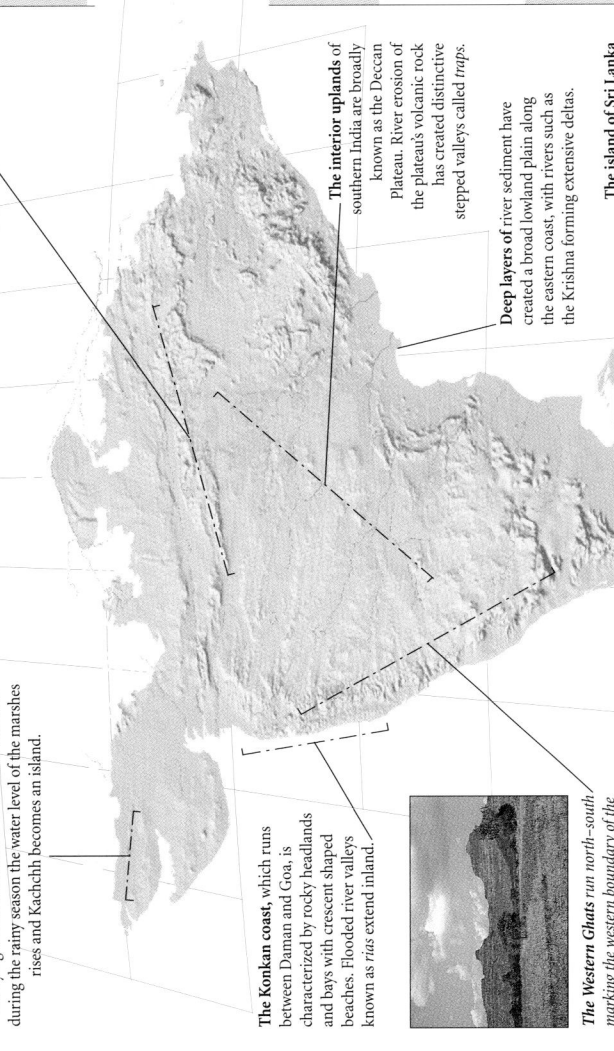

Relict of ancient tombolo
Adam's Bridge
Ocean currents cause sediment build up
Sri Lanka

***Adam's Bridge (Rama's Bridge)** is a chain of sandy shoals lying about 4 ft (1.2 m) under the sea between India and Sri Lanka. They once formed the world's longest tombolo, or land bridge, before the sea level began to rise several thousand years ago.*

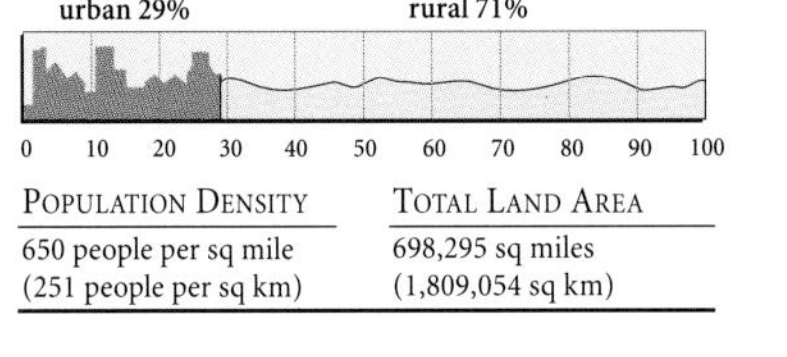
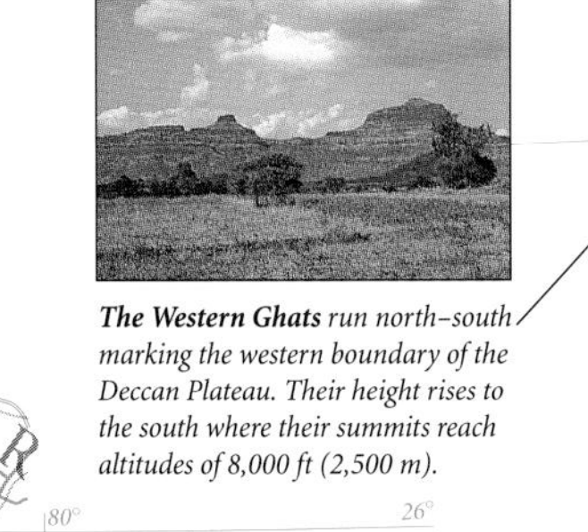
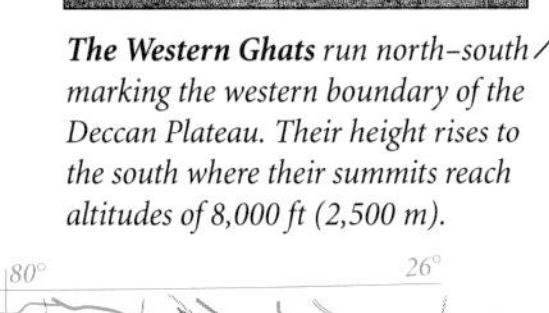
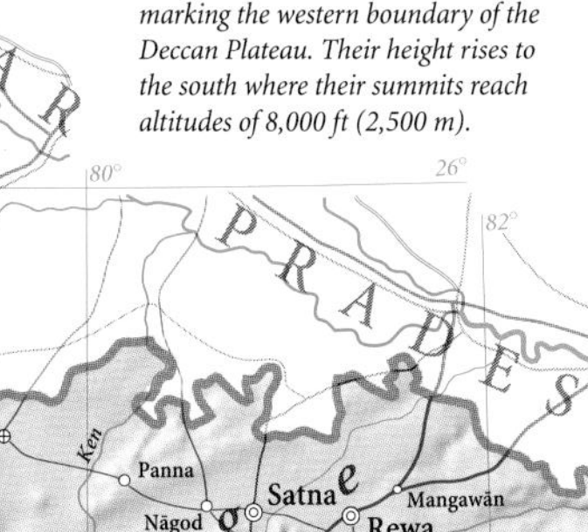

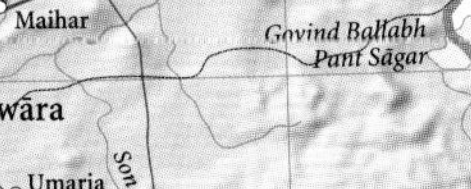

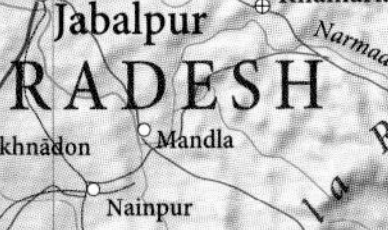
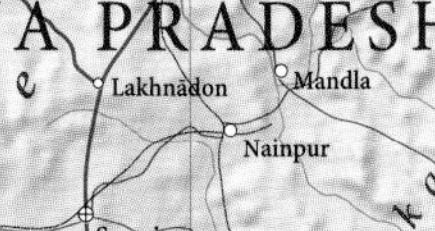

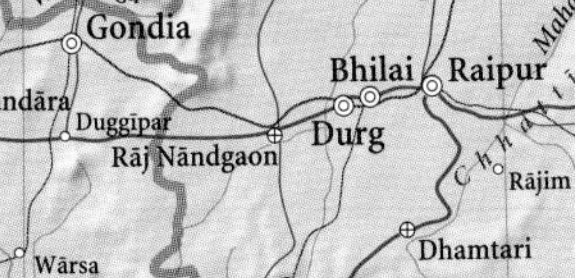

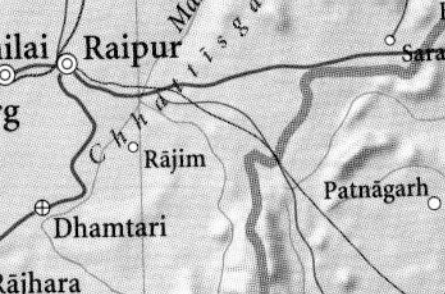
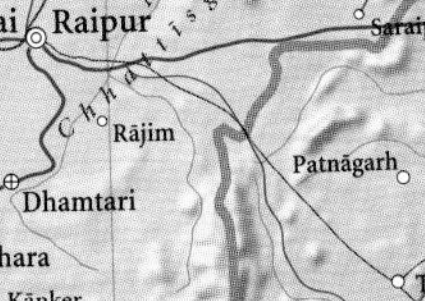
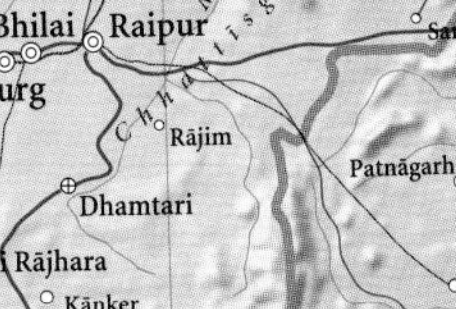
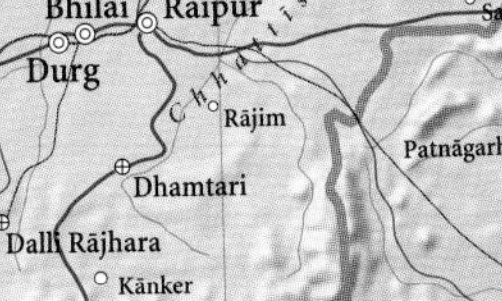

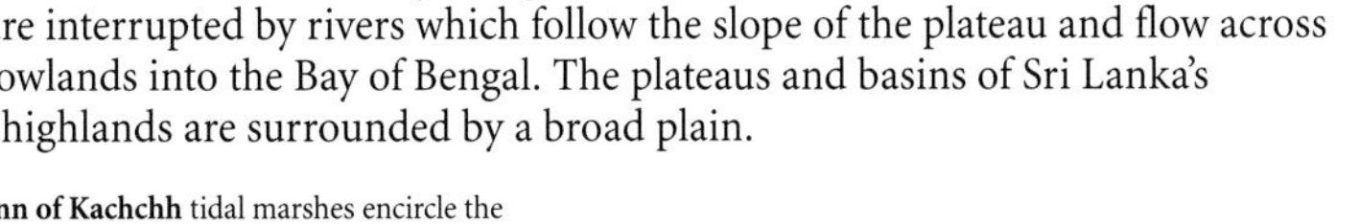

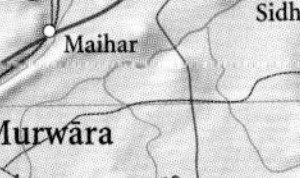
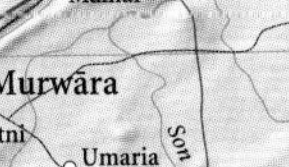

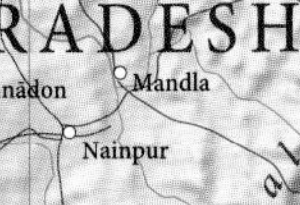
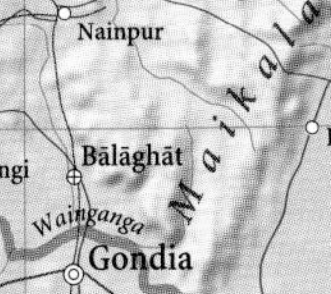

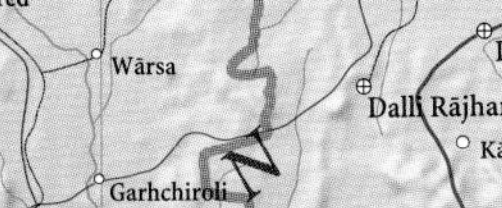
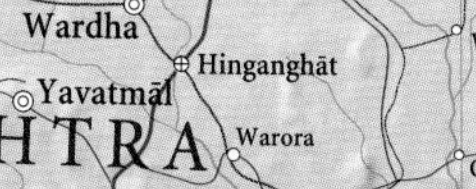
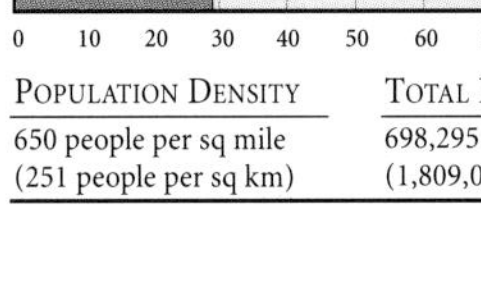
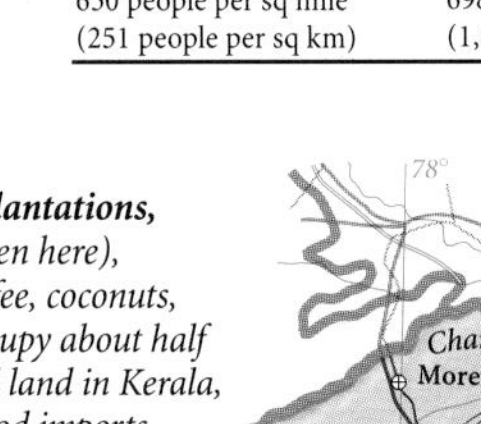
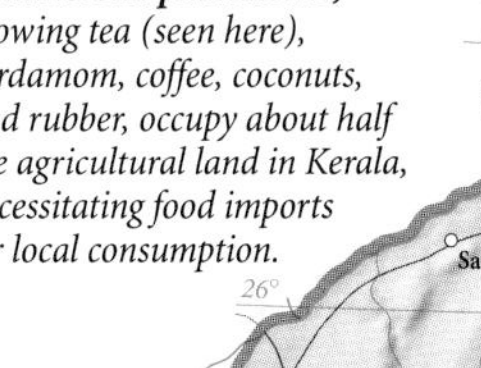

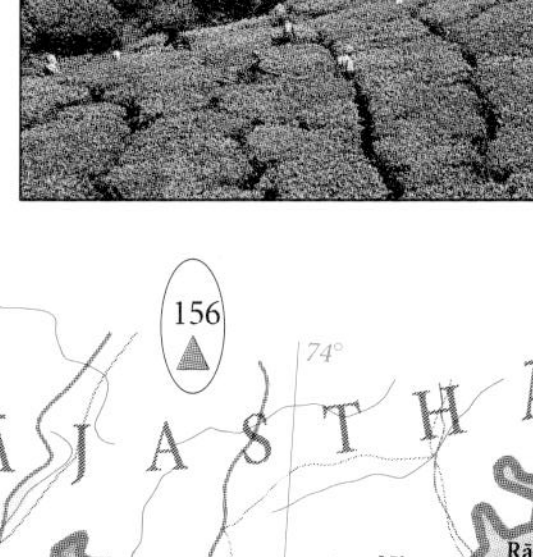
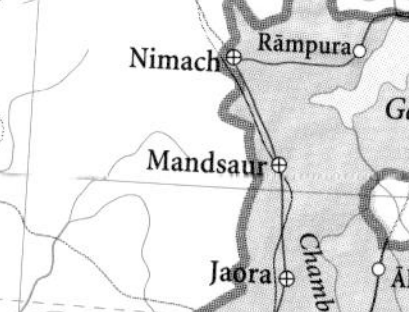
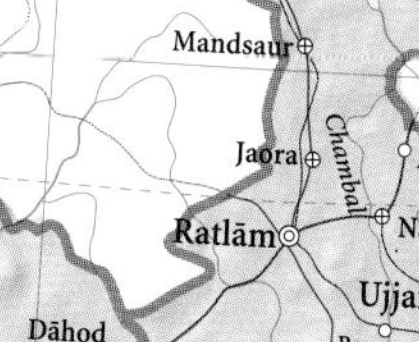
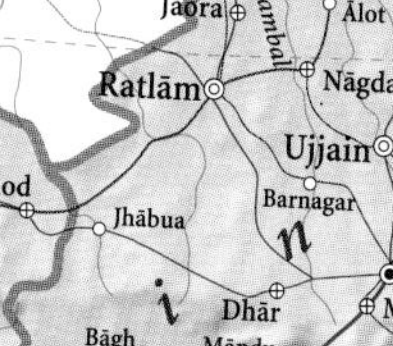

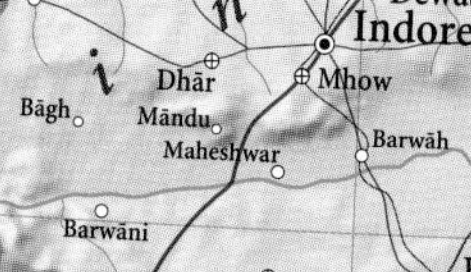

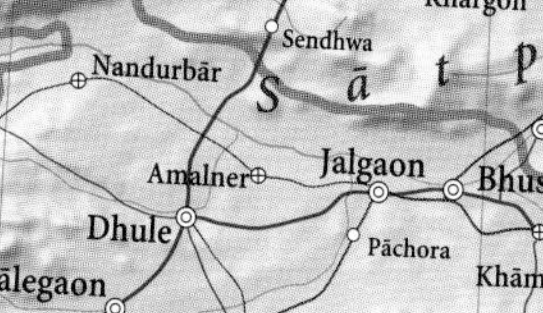
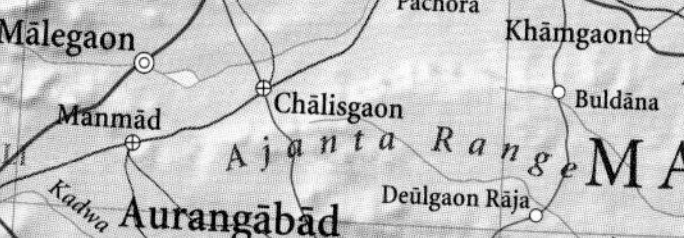

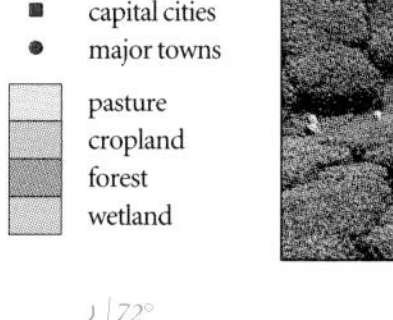
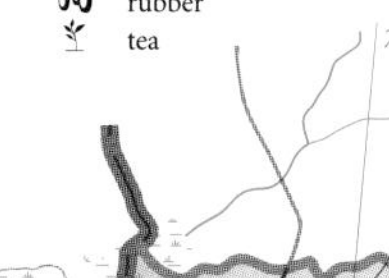

PAKISTAN
RĀJASTHĀN
UTTAR PRADESH
GUJARĀT
MADHYA PRADESH
MAHĀRĀSHTRA
ORISSA
BIHĀR
WEST BENGAL
Ahmadābād
Vadodara
Sūrat
Indore
Bhopāl
Jabalpur
Nāgpur
Gwalior
Cuttack
Bhubaneshwar
Gulf of Khambhat
Gulf of Kachchh
Rann of Kachchh
Tropic of Cancer

154
156
180

Map Key

POPULATION

- above 5 million
- 1 million to 5 million
- 500,000 to 1 million
- 100,000 to 500,000
- 50,000 to 100,000
- 10,000 to 50,000
- below 10,000

ELEVATION

- 2000m / 6562ft
- 1000m / 3281ft
- 500m / 1640ft
- 250m / 820ft
- 100m / 328ft
- sea level

Sea pencils *thrive on the coral reefs around the coast of the Laccadive Islands and Sri Lanka. The reefs support an amazing diversity of marine life, but are increasingly under threat from growing coastal populations.*

Local fisheries around Sri Lanka *afford great potential for exploitation. Development, however, has been hampered by technological constraints. Most fishermen live on the coastal fringes and operate on a small scale.*

SCALE 1:6,250,000
(projection: Lambert Conformal Conic)

The great triumphal arch *of Charminar, built in 1591, epitomizes the fine Islamic architecture, which the Moghuls brought from the north to Hyderabad, the capital of Andhra Pradesh.*

Transportation & Industry

SOUTH INDIA HAS a broad industrial base, with three leading regions around Bombay, Bangalore, and Ahmadabad. Cotton mills and chemical plants make use of cheap hydroelectric power generated in the Western Ghats. Light engineering and textiles are well established to the south and west of Madras. Sri Lanka's industry is based mainly on the processing of agricultural products.

Major industry and infrastructure

- aerospace
- car manufacture
- chemicals
- electronics
- engineering
- food processing
- iron & steel
- pharmaceuticals
- printing & publishing
- shipbuilding
- tea processing
- textiles
- tobacco processing
- capital cities
- major towns
- international airports
- major roads
- major industrial areas

Transportation Network

India's hard-surfaced road network has grown almost tenfold since independence, yet many villages are still only accessible on foot, even in densely-populated rural areas.

Bombay *is one of the largest and most densely populated cities in the world. It is the center of India's textile trade and has important finance and commerce sectors.*

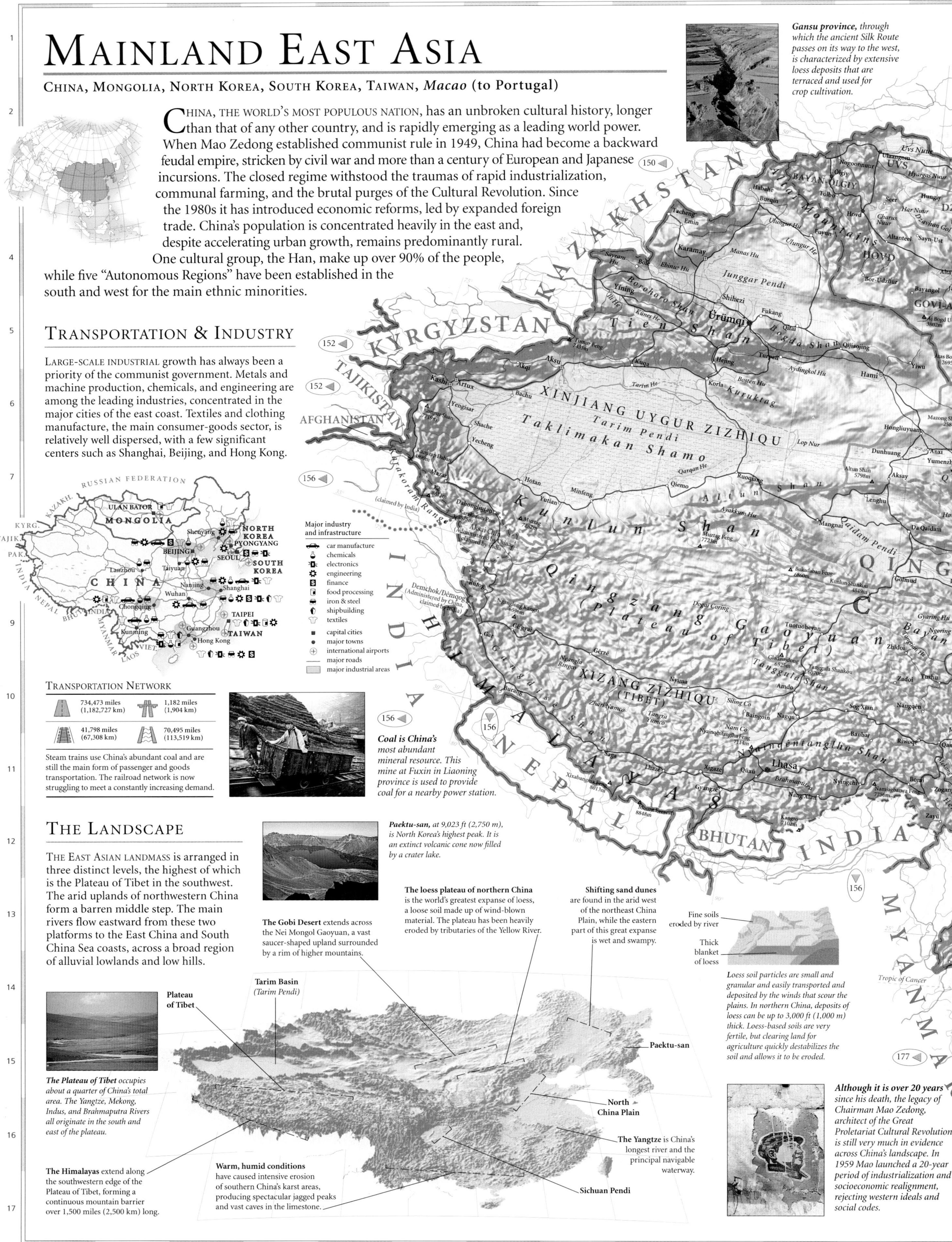

Mainland East Asia

China, Mongolia, North Korea, South Korea, Taiwan, *Macao* (to Portugal)

China, the world's most populous nation, has an unbroken cultural history, longer than that of any other country, and is rapidly emerging as a leading world power. When Mao Zedong established communist rule in 1949, China had become a backward feudal empire, stricken by civil war and more than a century of European and Japanese incursions. The closed regime withstood the traumas of rapid industrialization, communal farming, and the brutal purges of the Cultural Revolution. Since the 1980s it has introduced economic reforms, led by expanded foreign trade. China's population is concentrated heavily in the east and, despite accelerating urban growth, remains predominantly rural. One cultural group, the Han, make up over 90% of the people, while five "Autonomous Regions" have been established in the south and west for the main ethnic minorities.

Gansu province, *through which the ancient Silk Route passes on its way to the west, is characterized by extensive loess deposits that are terraced and used for crop cultivation.*

Transportation & Industry

Large-scale industrial growth has always been a priority of the communist government. Metals and machine production, chemicals, and engineering are among the leading industries, concentrated in the major cities of the east coast. Textiles and clothing manufacture, the main consumer-goods sector, is relatively well dispersed, with a few significant centers such as Shanghai, Beijing, and Hong Kong.

RUSSIAN FEDERATION
KAZAKH.
KYRG.
TAJIK.
PAK.
INDIA
NEPAL
BHUTAN
MYANMAR
LAOS
VIET.
ULAN BATOR
MONGOLIA
NORTH KOREA
PYONGYANG
SOUTH KOREA
SEOUL
BEIJING
Shenyang
Taiyuan
Lanzhou
CHINA
Nanjing
Shanghai
Wuhan
Chongqing
TAIPEI
TAIWAN
Guangzhou
Hong Kong
Kunming
Major industry and infrastructure
car manufacture
chemicals
electronics
engineering
finance
food processing
iron & steel
shipbuilding
textiles
capital cities
major towns
international airports
major roads
major industrial areas

Transportation Network

734,473 miles (1,182,727 km)		1,182 miles (1,904 km)	
41,798 miles (67,308 km)		70,495 miles (113,519 km)	

Steam trains use China's abundant coal and are still the main form of passenger and goods transportation. The railroad network is now struggling to meet a constantly increasing demand.

***Coal is China's** most abundant mineral resource. This mine at Fuxin in Liaoning province is used to provide coal for a nearby power station.*

The Landscape

The East Asian landmass is arranged in three distinct levels, the highest of which is the Plateau of Tibet in the southwest. The arid uplands of northwestern China form a barren middle step. The main rivers flow eastward from these two platforms to the East China and South China Sea coasts, across a broad region of alluvial lowlands and low hills.

***Paektu-san,** at 9,023 ft (2,750 m), is North Korea's highest peak. It is an extinct volcanic cone now filled by a crater lake.*

The Gobi Desert extends across the Nei Mongol Gaoyuan, a vast saucer-shaped upland surrounded by a rim of higher mountains.

The loess plateau of northern China is the world's greatest expanse of loess, a loose soil made up of wind-blown material. The plateau has been heavily eroded by tributaries of the Yellow River.

Shifting sand dunes are found in the arid west of the northeast China Plain, while the eastern part of this great expanse is wet and swampy.

Fine soils eroded by river
Thick blanket of loess

Loess soil particles are small and granular and easily transported and deposited by the winds that scour the plains. In northern China, deposits of loess can be up to 3,000 ft (1,000 m) thick. Loess-based soils are very fertile, but clearing land for agriculture quickly destabilizes the soil and allows it to be eroded.

Plateau of Tibet
Tarim Basin (Tarim Pendi)
Paektu-san
North China Plain
Sichuan Pendi

***The Plateau of Tibet** occupies about a quarter of China's total area. The Yangtze, Mekong, Indus, and Brahmaputra Rivers all originate in the south and east of the plateau.*

The Himalayas extend along the southwestern edge of the Plateau of Tibet, forming a continuous mountain barrier over 1,500 miles (2,500 km) long.

Warm, humid conditions have caused intensive erosion of southern China's karst areas, producing spectacular jagged peaks and vast caves in the limestone.

The Yangtze is China's longest river and the principal navigable waterway.

***Although it is over 20 years** since his death, the legacy of Chairman Mao Zedong, architect of the Great Proletarian Cultural Revolution, is still very much in evidence across China's landscape. In 1959 Mao launched a 20-year period of industrialization and socioeconomic realignment, rejecting western ideals and social codes.*

KAZAKHSTAN
KYRGYZSTAN
TAJIKISTAN
AFGHANISTAN
INDIA
NEPAL
BHUTAN
MYANMAR
XINJIANG UYGUR ZIZHIQU
Tarim Pendi
Taklimakan Shamo
Junggar Pendi
Tien Shan
Ürümqi
Kashi
Aksu
Hami
Kunlun Shan
Altun Shan
Qingzang Gaoyuan (Plateau of Tibet)
XIZANG ZIZHIQU (TIBET)
Lhasa
HIMALAYAS
Karakoram Range
Nyainqentanglha Shan
Mount Everest 8848m

150
152
152
156
156
156
156
177

SCALE 1:12,500,000
(projection: Lambert Conformal Conic)
Km 0 25 50 100 150 200 250 300 350 400 450 500
Miles 0 25 50 100 150 200 250 300 350 400 450 500
MAP KEY
POPULATION
above 5 million
1 million to 5 million
500,000 to 1 million
100,000 to 500,000
50,000 to 100,000
10,000 to 50,000
below 10,000
ELEVATION
6000m / 19,686ft
4000m / 13,124ft
3000m / 9843ft
2000m / 6562ft
1000m / 3281ft
500m / 1640ft
250m / 820ft
100m / 328ft
sea level
RUSSIAN FEDERATION
MONGOLIA
CHINA
NORTH KOREA
SOUTH KOREA
JAPAN
TAIWAN
VIETNAM
LAOS
SEA OF JAPAN
Yellow Sea
EAST CHINA SEA
SOUTH CHINA SEA
Gulf of Tongking
Gobi
ULAANBAATAR (ULAN BATOR)
BEIJING (PEKING)
P'YŎNGYANG
SŎUL (SEOUL)
T'AIPEI
Shanghai
Hong Kong (Xianggang)
MACAO (to Portugal)
Tropic of Cancer
Land use and agricultural distribution
pigs
sheep
corn
cotton
fishing
fruit
rice
sugar cane
soybeans
capital cities
major towns
pasture
cropland
forest
mountain region

The Great Wall of China remains one of the world's largest-ever construction projects, and is so vast that it is visible from space. Finally completed in CE *214, it runs for over 4,000 miles (6,400 km) from the Yellow Sea, stretching into Central Asia.*

USING THE LAND & SEA

AROUND 90% OF China is unsuitable for cultivation, being either climactically or topographically adverse, or lacking sufficiently fertile soils. Most of the west is used for nomadic herding, while farmland is concentrated in the eastern monsoon region, with rice grown in the tropical and subtropical south. Cereals and soybeans predominate as rainfall and temperatures decline farther north.

THE URBAN/RURAL POPULATION DIVIDE

urban 30% | rural 70%

0 10 20 30 40 50 60 70 80 90 100

POPULATION DENSITY	TOTAL LAND AREA
297 people per sq mile (115 people per sq km)	4,288,672 sq miles (11,110,550 sq km)

Beijing *(formerly Peking) is China's capital city and, with Shanghai, one of its leading industrial and cultural centers. The morning and evening rush hours are dominated by bicycles, which constitute the bulk of traffic.*

Western China

Gansu, Ningxia, Qinghai, Tibet, Xinjiang

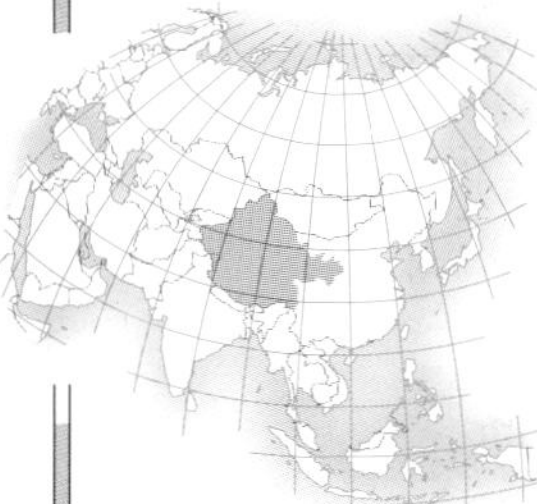

The plateaus and basins of China's dry, desolate western domain are sparsely populated and largely undeveloped, although they have rich mineral reserves; they also form a critical buffer zone for China, in a geographically important and culturally sensitive part of the Asian continent. Across most of the west, the Han Chinese are outnumbered by a range of cultural groups, including the Uygur, the largest group of the various seminomadic Muslim peoples from Central Asia. The remote, inhospitable Plateau of Tibet is the world's coldest and highest plateau. It has been occupied by the Chinese since 1958. Tibet is one of western China's five "Autonomous Regions," but its reclusive Buddhist culture has been systematically undermined by the Chinese government.

Map Key

POPULATION

- 1 million to 5 million
- 500,000 to 1 million
- 100,000 to 500,000
- 50,000 to 100,000
- 10,000 to 50,000
- below 10,000

ELEVATION

- 6000m / 19,686ft
- 4000m / 13,124ft
- 3000m / 9843ft
- 2000m / 6562ft
- 1000m / 3281ft
- 500m / 1640ft
- 250m / 820ft
- 100m / 328ft
- sea level

SCALE 1:7,000,000
(projection: Lambert Conformal Conic)

Km 0 25 50 100 150 200 250 300
Miles 0 25 50 100 150 200 250 300

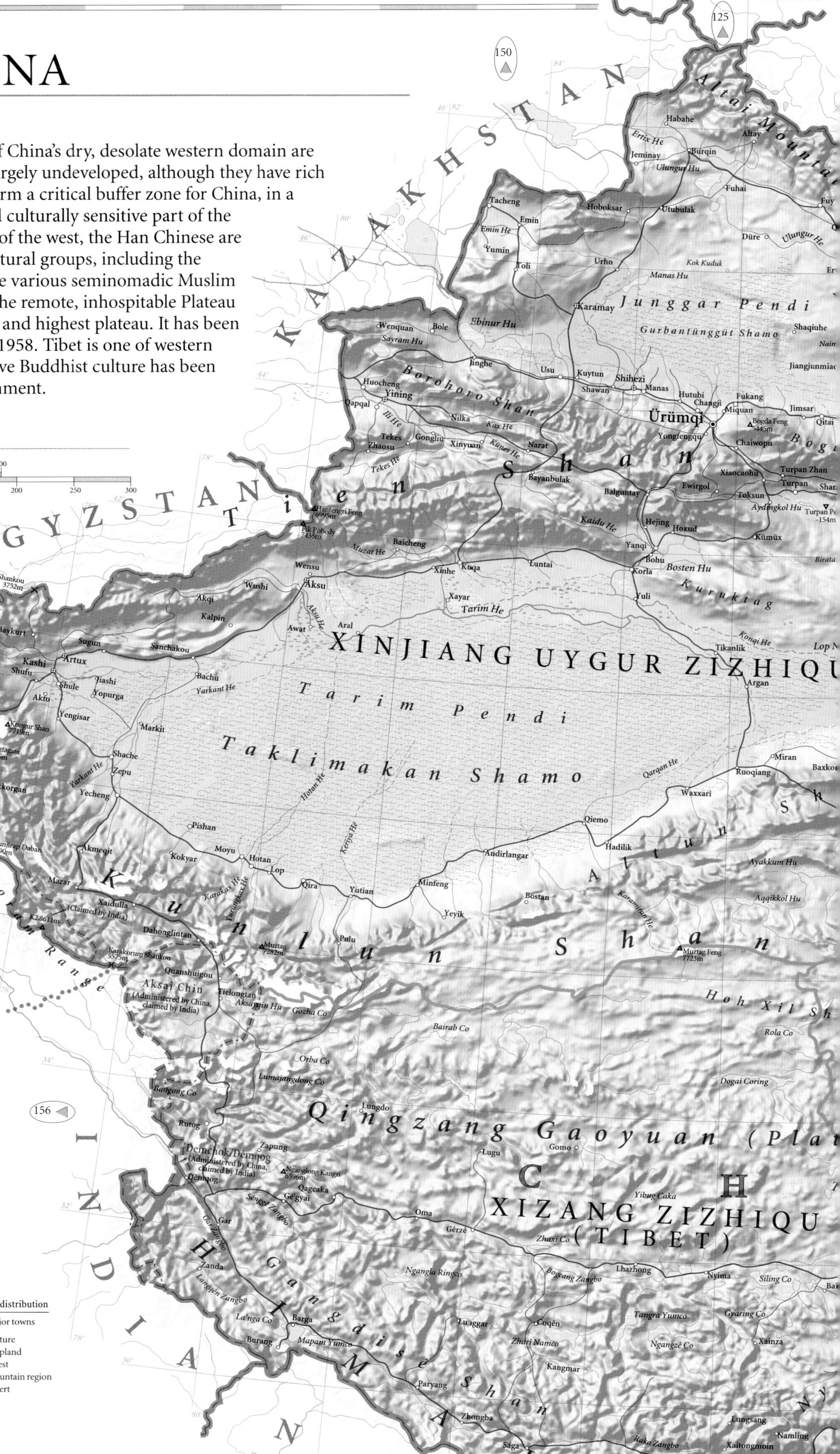

The Lhasa He *is one of the many rivers that drains the vast Plateau of Tibet. From its source in the Nyainqêntanglha Shan range and fed by the spring meltwater, it eventually joins the upper Brahmaputra 40 miles (65 km) southeast of Lhasa.*

Using the Land

Agriculture is constrained by the cold, dry climate and lack of fertile soils in the region, although irrigation and greenhouse farming are increasing agricultural potential. Large quantities of fruits, like melons and grapes, are grown at the oases of Hami and Turpan in Xinjiang, and new irrigation schemes have greatly increased cotton and wheat production in the Tarim Basin *(Tarim Pendi)*. Most of the great area of Tibet and Qinghai is devoted to pastoralism. Sheep are the principal livestock.

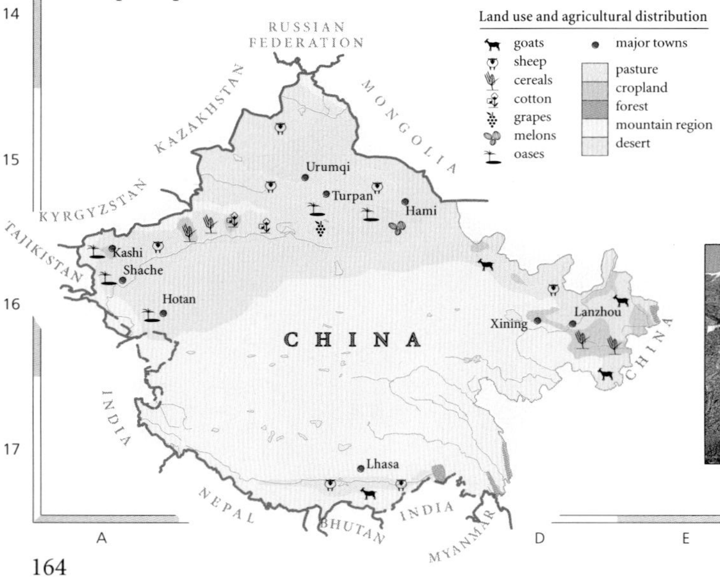

Land use and agricultural distribution

- goats
- sheep
- cereals
- cotton
- grapes
- melons
- oases
- major towns
- pasture
- cropland
- forest
- mountain region
- desert

The Potola Palace, *in Tibet's capital, Lhasa, was the former residence of the Dalai Lama, Tibetan Buddhism's spiritual leader. Tibet remains only sparsely populated; forming more than 20% of China's landmass, it supports less than 1% of its population.*

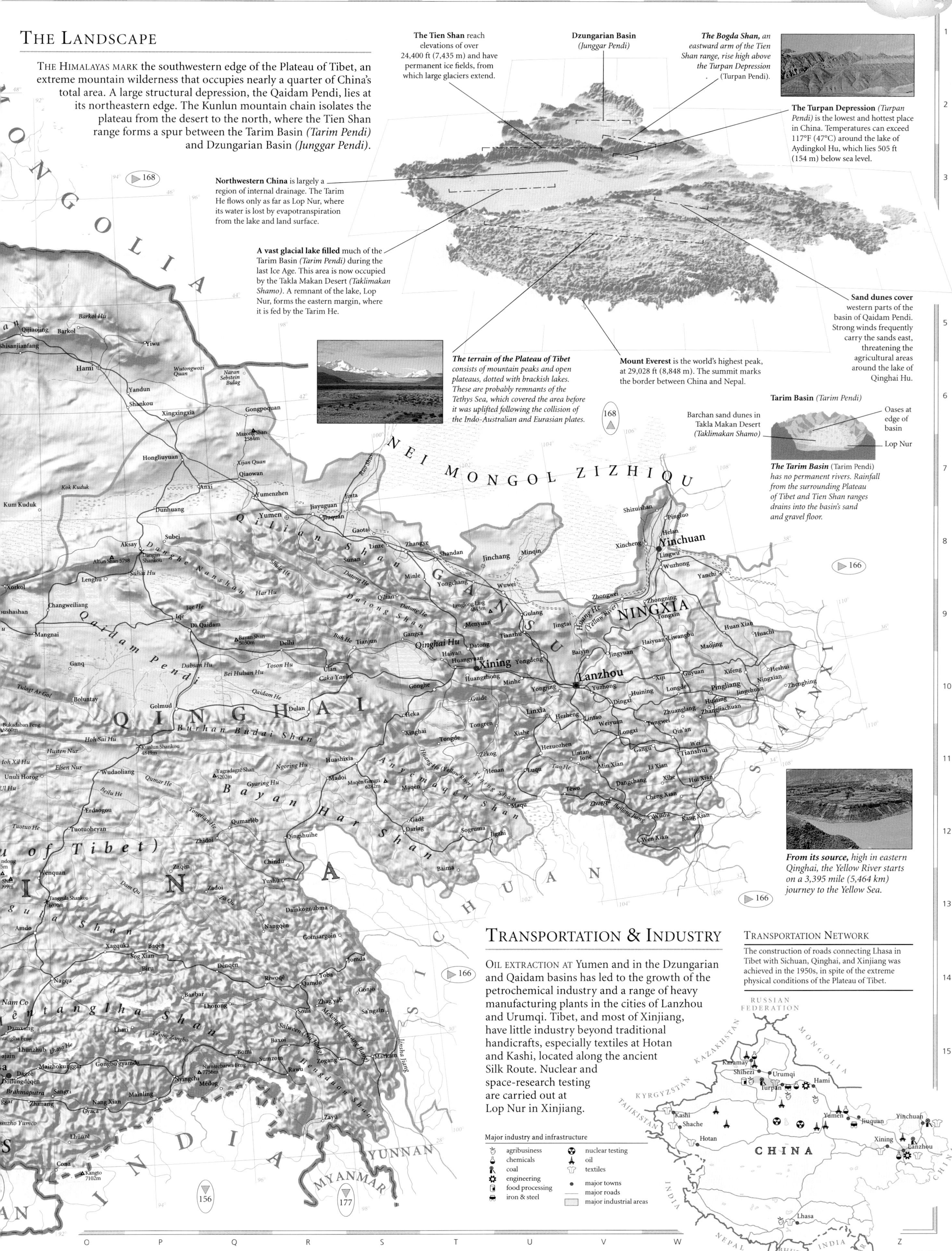

N O P Q R S T U V W X Y

THE LANDSCAPE

THE HIMALAYAS MARK the southwestern edge of the Plateau of Tibet, an extreme mountain wilderness that occupies nearly a quarter of China's total area. A large structural depression, the Qaidam Pendi, lies at its northeastern edge. The Kunlun mountain chain isolates the plateau from the desert to the north, where the Tien Shan range forms a spur between the Tarim Basin *(Tarim Pendi)* and Dzungarian Basin *(Junggar Pendi)*.

The Tien Shan reach elevations of over 24,400 ft (7,435 m) and have permanent ice fields, from which large glaciers extend.

Dzungarian Basin *(Junggar Pendi)*

The Bogda Shan, *an eastward arm of the Tien Shan range, rise high above the Turpan Depression (Turpan Pendi).*

The Turpan Depression *(Turpan Pendi)* is the lowest and hottest place in China. Temperatures can exceed 117°F (47°C) around the lake of Aydingkol Hu, which lies 505 ft (154 m) below sea level.

Northwestern China is largely a region of internal drainage. The Tarim He flows only as far as Lop Nur, where its water is lost by evapotranspiration from the lake and land surface.

A vast glacial lake filled much of the Tarim Basin *(Tarim Pendi)* during the last Ice Age. This area is now occupied by the Takla Makan Desert *(Taklimakan Shamo)*. A remnant of the lake, Lop Nur, forms the eastern margin, where it is fed by the Tarim He.

Sand dunes cover western parts of the basin of Qaidam Pendi. Strong winds frequently carry the sands east, threatening the agricultural areas around the lake of Qinghai Hu.

The terrain of the Plateau of Tibet *consists of mountain peaks and open plateaus, dotted with brackish lakes. These are probably remnants of the Tethys Sea, which covered the area before it was uplifted following the collision of the Indo-Australian and Eurasian plates.*

Mount Everest is the world's highest peak, at 29,028 ft (8,848 m). The summit marks the border between China and Nepal.

Tarim Basin *(Tarim Pendi)*
Barchan sand dunes in Takla Makan Desert *(Taklimakan Shamo)*
Oases at edge of basin
Lop Nur

The Tarim Basin *(Tarim Pendi) has no permanent rivers. Rainfall from the surrounding Plateau of Tibet and Tien Shan ranges drains into the basin's sand and gravel floor.*

168
166
MONGOLIA
NEI MONGOL ZIZHIQU
GANSU
NINGXIA
QINGHAI
Qaidam Pendi
SICHUAN
INDIA
MYANMAR
YUNNAN
Hami
Yumen
Dunhuang
Jiayuguan
Zhangye
Jinchang
Wuwei
Yinchuan
Shizuishan
Xining
Lanzhou
Qinghai Hu
Golmud
Delhi
Madoi
Yushu
Tianshui
Pingliang
Guyuan
Linxia
Qilian Shan
Bayan Har Shan
A'nyêmaqên Shan
Burhan Budai Shan
Hengduan Shan
Nyingchi
Nagqu
Nam Co

From its source, *high in eastern Qinghai, the Yellow River starts on a 3,395 mile (5,464 km) journey to the Yellow Sea.*

TRANSPORTATION & INDUSTRY

OIL EXTRACTION AT Yumen and in the Dzungarian and Qaidam basins has led to the growth of the petrochemical industry and a range of heavy manufacturing plants in the cities of Lanzhou and Urumqi. Tibet, and most of Xinjiang, have little industry beyond traditional handicrafts, especially textiles at Hotan and Kashi, located along the ancient Silk Route. Nuclear and space-research testing are carried out at Lop Nur in Xinjiang.

TRANSPORTATION NETWORK

The construction of roads connecting Lhasa in Tibet with Sichuan, Qinghai, and Xinjiang was achieved in the 1950s, in spite of the extreme physical conditions of the Plateau of Tibet.

Major industry and infrastructure
agribusiness
chemicals
coal
engineering
food processing
iron & steel
nuclear testing
oil
textiles
major towns
major roads
major industrial areas

RUSSIAN FEDERATION
KAZAKHSTAN
MONGOLIA
KYRGYZSTAN
TAJIKISTAN
CHINA
INDIA
NEPAL
BHUTAN
Karamay
Shihezi
Urumqi
Turpan
Hami
Kashi
Shache
Hotan
Yumen
Jiuquan
Yinchuan
Xining
Lanzhou
Lhasa

156
177
O P Q R S T U V W X Y Z

EASTERN CHINA

TAIWAN, Anhui, Beijing, Fujian, Guangdong, Guangxi, Guizhou, Hainan, Hebei, Henan, Hubei, Hunan, Jiangsu, Jiangxi, Shaanxi, Shandong, Shanghai, Shanxi, Sichuan, Tianjin, Yunnan, Zhejiang, *Macao* (to Portugal)

THE EAST IS CHINA'S HEARTLAND. Since 1949, massive industrial development has transformed much of the densely populated rural landscape, in a region still prone to flooding and drought. Over 20 cities have populations of more than a million, including the giant metropolis of Shanghai and the capital Beijing, which has been China's cultural and political center since the 13th century. The ethnically diverse southwest and the oil-rich interior provinces of Sichuan and Shaanxi have largely missed out on the remarkable economic growth occurring in designated free-trade areas along the coasts of the South and East China Seas. The republic of Taiwan was established in 1949 by Chinese nationalists ousted from the mainland by the victorious communist forces. Taiwan now has one of the strongest economies in the world, but its sovereignty is not recognized by China. Hong Kong provides a major international trade link for China, the and 99-year "lease" period of British control ended in 1997.

In Shaanxi province, north of the Qin Ling range, is an agriculturally fertile region covered with fine, wind-blown deposits and known as the loess plateau. The loose sediments are vulnerable to water erosion.

USING THE LAND & SEA

THIS IS A REGION of intensive cultivation. Wheat, millet, sorghum, and cotton are the main crops of the Yellow River basin. South of Sichuan, rice becomes the principal crop, grown with wheat, corn, and cotton along the Yangtze River. Tea is produced in the hills and sugar cane along the coast of the southeast, where flat land is limited. Pigs and poultry are raised in great numbers.

Land use and agricultural distribution

- cattle
- pigs
- cereals
- corn
- cotton
- fishing
- peanuts
- rice
- sugar cane
- tea
- capital cities
- major towns
- pasture
- cropland
- forest
- mountain region
- wetland
- tundra

On the hills above the North China Plain, slopes are terraced to utilize the rich loess soils of the Taihang Shan Range.

Since the transferral of Hong Kong from the UK to China, only the Portuguese territory of Macao, with its colonial architecture, bars, and casinos, remains as a vestige of Europe's territorial exploits in the Far East. Macao reverts to Chinese rule in 1999.

MAP KEY

POPULATION

- above 5 million
- 1 million to 5 million
- 500,000 to 1 million
- 100,000 to 500,000
- 50,000 to 100,000
- 10,000 to 50,000
- below 10,000

ELEVATION

- 6000m / 19,686ft
- 4000m / 13,124ft
- 3000m / 9843ft
- 2000m / 6562ft
- 1000m / 3281ft
- 500m / 1640ft
- 250m / 820ft
- 100m / 328ft
- sea level

SCALE 1:7,750,000
(projection: Lambert Conformal Conic)

Km 0 25 50 100 150 200 250 300
Miles 0 25 50 100 150 200 250 300

THE LANDSCAPE

THE SICHUAN PENDI (Red Basin) lies at the foot of the Plateau of Tibet between the Qin Ling range in the north and the limestone uplands of Yunnan and Guizhou to the south. Hills extend from Yunnan to the rocky southeastern coast, dividing the Yangtze and Xi Jiang basins. The North China Plain is composed of sediment carried by the Yellow River from the loess plateau in the northwest.

The Yellow River carries more sediment than any other river on Earth – approximately 1.6 billion tons (tonnes) per year. Floods caused by the breaching of the river's high banks have claimed many millions of human lives through history.

Intensive weathering of a great mass of limestone has left spectacular sheer-sided limestone pinnacles around Guilin in Guangxi. They rise abruptly from flat valley floors composed of deposited sediment. Limestone landforms are widespread in the southeast.

Loess plateau

North China Plain

Qin Ling

Yangtze River

The vast Sichuan Pendi is one of China's leading rice-producing areas. The humid climate and accelerated weathering have produced a rich soil, while its climate is moderated by the encircling mountains.

Xi Jiang

Yun Gui Gaoyuan

The terraced rice paddies of southeastern China illustrate the significance of over 7,000 years of cultivation in shaping the landscape.

The eroded rocky features of the Yun Gui Gaoyuan are testament to the Earth's forces that have folded and eroded this limestone region to produce dramatic, incised river valleys, gorges, and karst features.

Wu Jiang Gorge

***The Wu Jiang Gorge** is the result of tectonic uplift on the Yun Gui Gaoyuan Plateau, which has caused the rapid downcutting of rivers across the region, creating deep, steep-sided valleys.*

Course of the Yellow River

Pre 4BC

4BC–AD1

1234–1891

***Over the past 2,000** years, the downstream course of the Yellow River has altered dramatically, veering unpredictably to the north and south across the North China Plain, and flooding vast expanses of land.*

TRANSPORTATION & INDUSTRY

MODERN INDUSTRY IS CONCENTRATED in the coastal provinces, with dramatic new growth in Guangdong, based on foreign investment. Chemicals, iron and steel production, engineering, and textiles are leading activities around Beijing and Shanghai, the two largest industrial centers. In the interior provinces, large fossil-fuel reserves support heavy industry around major cities such as Wuhan and Chengdu. Taiwan's broadly based manufacturing economy specializes in hi-tech goods. Hong Kong is a major financial center and international entrepôt.

Major industry and infrastructure

- car manufacture
- chemicals
- electronics
- engineering
- finance
- food processing
- iron & steel
- pharmaceuticals
- shipbuilding
- textiles
- capital cities
- major towns
- international airports
- major roads
- major industrial areas

***The former British colony** of Hong Kong was ceded to China in 1997, marking the beginning of a new chapter in the history of this small territory. A vibrant mixture of eastern and western cultures, the booming textile industry, and subsequent electronics and financial industries have driven immense growth and brought economic prosperity since the 1950s.*

***Taiwan** is one of the Pacific Rim's economic "tigers," specializing in hi-tech and electronics industries.*

TRANSPORTATION NETWORK

China's Grand Canal *(Da Yunhe)*, built in the 13th century, is the world's longest artificial waterway, running 1,100 miles (1,770 km) from Beijing to Hangzhou. Despite restoration work, not all of the canal is currently navigable.

Northeastern China, Mongolia & Korea

Mongolia, North Korea, South Korea, Heilongjiang, Inner Mongolia, Jilin, Liaoning

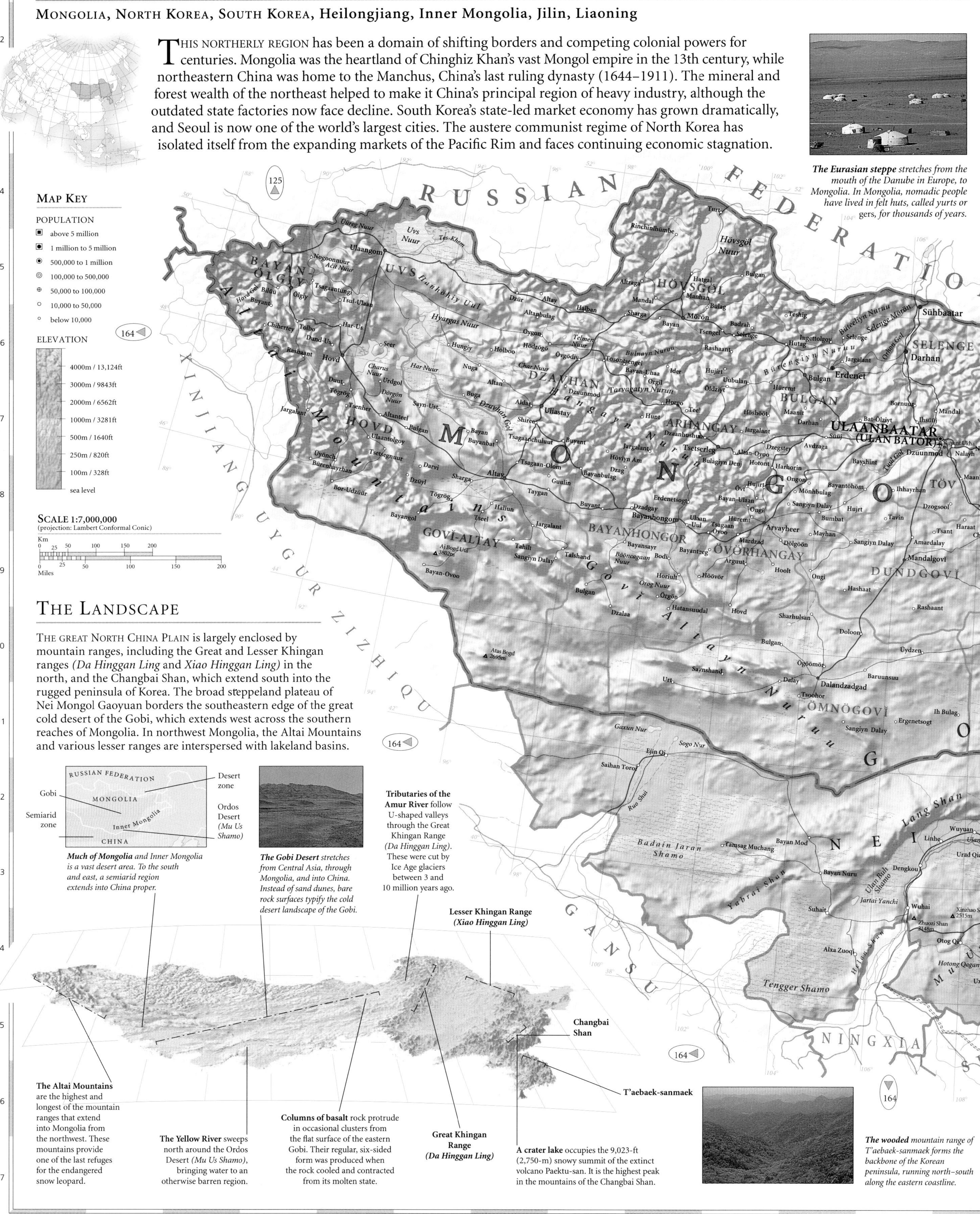

This northerly region has been a domain of shifting borders and competing colonial powers for centuries. Mongolia was the heartland of Chinghiz Khan's vast Mongol empire in the 13th century, while northeastern China was home to the Manchus, China's last ruling dynasty (1644–1911). The mineral and forest wealth of the northeast helped to make it China's principal region of heavy industry, although the outdated state factories now face decline. South Korea's state-led market economy has grown dramatically, and Seoul is now one of the world's largest cities. The austere communist regime of North Korea has isolated itself from the expanding markets of the Pacific Rim and faces continuing economic stagnation.

The Eurasian steppe stretches from the mouth of the Danube in Europe, to Mongolia. In Mongolia, nomadic people have lived in felt huts, called yurts or gers, for thousands of years.

Map Key
POPULATION
above 5 million
1 million to 5 million
500,000 to 1 million
100,000 to 500,000
50,000 to 100,000
10,000 to 50,000
below 10,000
ELEVATION
4000m / 13,124ft
3000m / 9843ft
2000m / 6562ft
1000m / 3281ft
500m / 1640ft
250m / 820ft
100m / 328ft
sea level
SCALE 1:7,000,000
(projection: Lambert Conformal Conic)
RUSSIAN FEDERATION
MONGOLIA
XINJIANG UYGUR ZIZHIQU
GANSU
NINGXIA
ULAANBAATAR (ULAN BATOR)
Altai Mountains
Gobi Altayn Nuruu
Badain Jaran Shamo
Tengger Shamo

The Landscape

The great North China Plain is largely enclosed by mountain ranges, including the Great and Lesser Khingan ranges *(Da Hinggan Ling* and *Xiao Hinggan Ling)* in the north, and the Changbai Shan, which extend south into the rugged peninsula of Korea. The broad steppeland plateau of Nei Mongol Gaoyuan borders the southeastern edge of the great cold desert of the Gobi, which extends west across the southern reaches of Mongolia. In northwest Mongolia, the Altai Mountains and various lesser ranges are interspersed with lakeland basins.

RUSSIAN FEDERATION
MONGOLIA
Inner Mongolia
CHINA
Gobi
Semiarid zone
Desert zone
Ordos Desert (Mu Us Shamo)

Much of Mongolia and Inner Mongolia is a vast desert area. To the south and east, a semiarid region extends into China proper.

The Gobi Desert stretches from Central Asia, through Mongolia, and into China. Instead of sand dunes, bare rock surfaces typify the cold desert landscape of the Gobi.

Tributaries of the Amur River follow U-shaped valleys through the Great Khingan Range *(Da Hinggan Ling)*. These were cut by Ice Age glaciers between 3 and 10 million years ago.

Lesser Khingan Range *(Xiao Hinggan Ling)*

Changbai Shan

T'aebaek-sanmaek

The Altai Mountains are the highest and longest of the mountain ranges that extend into Mongolia from the northwest. These mountains provide one of the last refuges for the endangered snow leopard.

The Yellow River sweeps north around the Ordos Desert *(Mu Us Shamo)*, bringing water to an otherwise barren region.

Columns of basalt rock protrude in occasional clusters from the flat surface of the eastern Gobi. Their regular, six-sided form was produced when the rock cooled and contracted from its molten state.

Great Khingan Range *(Da Hinggan Ling)*

A crater lake occupies the 9,023-ft (2,750-m) snowy summit of the extinct volcano Paektu-san. It is the highest peak in the mountains of the Changbai Shan.

The wooded mountain range of T'aebaek-sanmaek forms the backbone of the Korean peninsula, running north–south along the eastern coastline.

TRANSPORTATION & INDUSTRY

NORTH KOREA'S CENTRALLY PLANNED ECONOMY is strongly oriented toward heavy industry, while South Korea has a broad manufacturing base that includes textiles, steel, electronics, and one of the world's largest shipbuilding industries. Mongolia and Inner Mongolia's great mineral resource potential is largely undeveloped. The heavy industrial region around Shenyang produces iron, steel, chemicals, and cement on a massive scale.

TRANSPORTATION NETWORK

Liaoning has China's most comprehensive railroad network, the legacy of the Japanese occupation of Manchuria, earlier this century. The railroads are used primarily for freight transportation.

***Ulan Bator**, the Mongolian capital, bears many of the hallmarks of Soviet-style central planning. This is the result of economic and industrial assistance from the Soviet Union following Mongolian independence in 1921.*

Major industry and infrastructure

- car manufacture
- chemicals
- coal
- electronics
- engineering
- finance
- food processing
- iron & steel
- pharmaceuticals
- shipbuilding
- textiles
- capital cities
- major towns
- international airports
- major roads
- major industrial areas

***While North Korea** has remained politically and economically isolated from the rest of the world, South Korea has enjoyed immense economic growth. It has benefited considerably from US economic aid in the aftermath of the Korean War of 1950–1953.*

USING THE LAND & SEA

MONGOLIA AND INNER MONGOLIA rely heavily on livestock farming, with only about 1% of the land area cultivated. Northeastern China produces wheat, corn, soybeans, and sugar beet. The cool climate limits the range of crops, and large upland areas of the northeast remain forested. Rice is the staple food of North and South Korea. The latter has become a leading ocean-fishing nation.

Land use and agricultural distribution

- goats
- pigs
- sheep
- corn
- fishing
- rice
- soybeans
- sugar beet
- wheat
- capital cities
- major towns
- pasture
- cropland
- forest
- mountain region
- desert

JAPAN

IN THE YEARS SINCE THE END of the Second World War, Japan has become the most dynamic industrial nation in the world. The country is composed of a string of over 4,000 islands. They lie in the northwest Pacific in a great northeast–southwest arc. Four major islands – Hokkaido, Honshu, Shikoku, and Kyushu – are home to the great majority of Japan's population of 124 million people, although the mountainous terrain of the central region means that most cities are situated on the coast. A densely populated industrial belt stretches along much of Honshu's southern coast, and includes Japan's crowded capital, Tokyo. Alongside its spectacular economic growth and the increasing westernization of its cities, Japan still maintains a highly individual culture, reflected in its traditional food, formal behavioral codes, unique Shinto religion, and reverence for the emperor, who is officially regarded as a god.

USING THE LAND & SEA

ALTHOUGH ONLY ABOUT 11% OF JAPAN is suitable for cultivation, substantial government support, a favorable climate, and intensive farming methods enable the country to be virtually self-sufficient in rice production. Northern Hokkaido, the largest and most productive farming region, has an open terrain and climate similar to that of the American Midwest, and produces more than half of Japan's cereal grain requirements. Farmers are being encouraged to diversify by growing fruits, vegetables, and wheat, as well as raising livestock.

Sea of Japan
Sapporo
Hachinohe
Toyama
Fukushima
Nagasaki
Fukuoka
Hiroshima
Tsuruga
Kobe
JAPAN
Osaka
Nagoya
Kagoshima
TOKYO
Hitachi
Yokohama
PACIFIC OCEAN

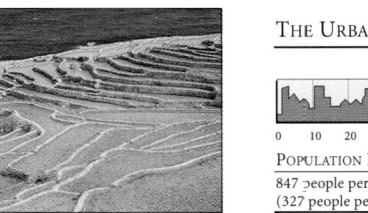

Land use and agricultural distribution
- cattle
- pigs
- fishing
- cereals
- citrus fruits
- fruit
- herbs
- rice
- root crops
- tobacco
- capital cities
- major towns
- pasture
- cropland
- forest

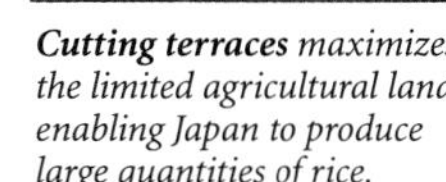

Cutting terraces maximizes the limited agricultural land, enabling Japan to produce large quantities of rice.

THE URBAN/RURAL POPULATION DIVIDE

urban 77% | rural 23%

0 10 20 30 40 50 60 70 80 90 100

POPULATION DENSITY	TOTAL LAND AREA
847 people per sq mile (327 people per sq km)	145,869 sq miles (377,800 sq km)

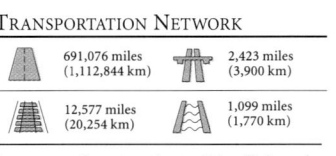

TRANSPORTATION & INDUSTRY

JAPAN IS THE WORLD'S second largest market economy, outranked only by the US. Technological development, particularly of computers, electronic goods, cars, and motorcycles, is second to none. Japanese industry invests in its workforce and in long-term research and development to maintain the high standard of its products and a reputation for innovation. Japanese businesses are now global, both in their manufacturing bases and in the distribution of goods.

Wakkanai
Sapporo
Kushiro
Sea of Japan
Hachinohe
Kitakyushu
Tokuyama
Nagasaki
Fukuoka
Hiroshima
Kumamoto
Matsuyama
Kagoshima
Kobe
Tsuruga
Toyama
Kyoto
Osaka
Nagoya
JAPAN
Sendai
Fukushima
Hitachi
Yaizu
TOKYO
Chiba
Yokohama
PACIFIC OCEAN

Major industry and infrastructure
- brewing
- car manufacture
- chemicals
- hi-tech industry
- engineering
- finance
- iron & steel
- research & development
- shipbuilding
- textiles
- winter sports
- capital cities
- major towns
- international airports
- major roads
- major industrial areas

***The Kobe earthquake** in January 1995 highlighted Japan's vulnerability to earthquakes, despite technological advances. It shattered much of the infrastructure of this important port. More than 5,000 people died as buildings and overhead highways collapsed and fires broke out.*

TRANSPORTATION NETWORK

691,076 miles (1,112,844 km)	2,423 miles (3,900 km)
12,577 miles (20,254 km)	1,099 miles (1,770 km)

Japanese road construction traditionally lagged behind that of its extensive and technologically advanced railroad network. The road network's relative lack of development has led to severe urban congestion, although expressways have now been built in some cities.

***Known in the west** as the "bullet train," the Shinkansen is the second-fastest train in the world. It speeds past the snow-capped peak of Mount Fuji between the cities of Tokyo and Osaka.*

***A number of new volcanoes** have emerged in Japan this century, existing alongside older cones. This volcano, on the island of Kyushu in Aso-Kuju National Park, is now dormant and covered with grass.*

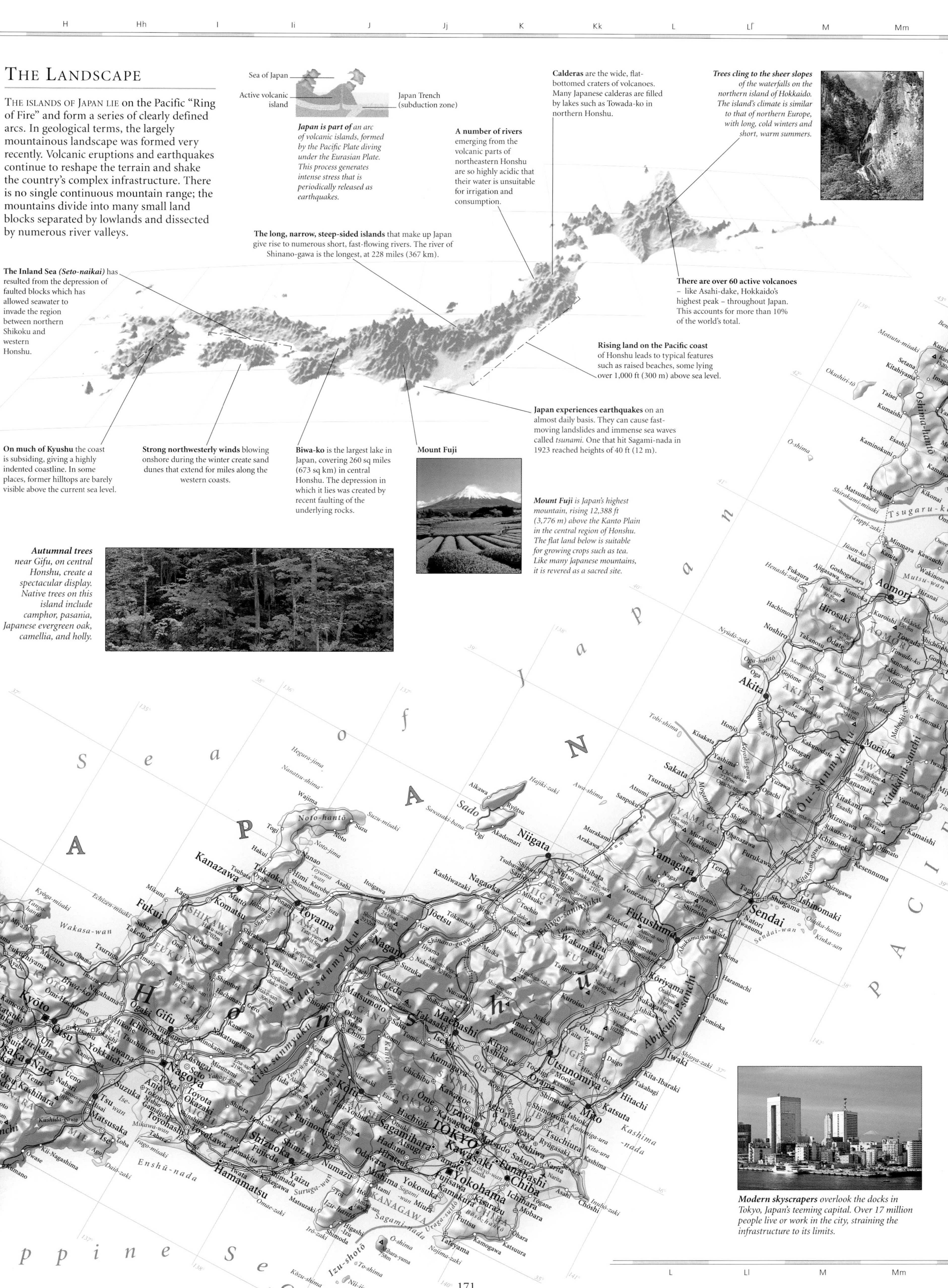

THE LANDSCAPE

THE ISLANDS OF JAPAN LIE on the Pacific "Ring of Fire" and form a series of clearly defined arcs. In geological terms, the largely mountainous landscape was formed very recently. Volcanic eruptions and earthquakes continue to reshape the terrain and shake the country's complex infrastructure. There is no single continuous mountain range; the mountains divide into many small land blocks separated by lowlands and dissected by numerous river valleys.

Sea of Japan
Active volcanic island
Japan Trench (subduction zone)

***Japan is part of** an arc of volcanic islands, formed by the Pacific Plate diving under the Eurasian Plate. This process generates intense stress that is periodically released as earthquakes.*

A number of rivers emerging from the volcanic parts of northeastern Honshu are so highly acidic that their water is unsuitable for irrigation and consumption.

Calderas are the wide, flat-bottomed craters of volcanoes. Many Japanese calderas are filled by lakes such as Towada-ko in northern Honshu.

***Trees cling to the sheer slopes** of the waterfalls on the northern island of Hokkaido. The island's climate is similar to that of northern Europe, with long, cold winters and short, warm summers.*

The long, narrow, steep-sided islands that make up Japan give rise to numerous short, fast-flowing rivers. The river of Shinano-gawa is the longest, at 228 miles (367 km).

The Inland Sea *(Seto-naikai)* has resulted from the depression of faulted blocks which has allowed seawater to invade the region between northern Shikoku and western Honshu.

There are over 60 active volcanoes – like Asahi-dake, Hokkaido's highest peak – throughout Japan. This accounts for more than 10% of the world's total.

Rising land on the Pacific coast of Honshu leads to typical features such as raised beaches, some lying over 1,000 ft (300 m) above sea level.

Japan experiences earthquakes on an almost daily basis. They can cause fast-moving landslides and immense sea waves called *tsunami.* One that hit Sagami-nada in 1923 reached heights of 40 ft (12 m).

On much of Kyushu the coast is subsiding, giving a highly indented coastline. In some places, former hilltops are barely visible above the current sea level.

Strong northwesterly winds blowing onshore during the winter create sand dunes that extend for miles along the western coasts.

Biwa-ko is the largest lake in Japan, covering 260 sq miles (673 sq km) in central Honshu. The depression in which it lies was created by recent faulting of the underlying rocks.

Mount Fuji

***Mount Fuji** is Japan's highest mountain, rising 12,388 ft (3,776 m) above the Kanto Plain in the central region of Honshu. The flat land below is suitable for growing crops such as tea. Like many Japanese mountains, it is revered as a sacred site.*

***Autumnal trees** near Gifu, on central Honshu, create a spectacular display. Native trees on this island include camphor, pasania, Japanese evergreen oak, camellia, and holly.*

Sea of Japan
Pacific
Honshu
Japan
Philippine Sea
Tokyo
Yokohama
Nagoya
Kyoto
Sendai
Niigata
Sado
Noto-hanto

***Modern skyscrapers** overlook the docks in Tokyo, Japan's teeming capital. Over 17 million people live or work in the city, straining the infrastructure to its limits.*

Gg H Hh I Ii J Jj K Kk L Ll M Mm
MALAYSIA
SOUTH CHINA SEA
THAILAND
Kota Bharu
Kuala Terengganu
Kuantan
KUALA LUMPUR
Seremban
Melaka
Johor Bahru
SINGAPORE
Ipoh
Natuna Sea
Kepulauan Anambas
Kepulauan Natuna
Pulau Natuna Besar
Kepulauan Riau
Kepulauan Lingga
Pekanbaru
Jambi
Palembang
Bengkulu
Bandarlampung
Pulau Bangka
Pulau Belitung
Selat Karimata
Pontianak
Kuching
KALIMANTAN BARAT
KALIMANTAN TENGAH
Java Sea
JAKARTA
Bandung
Semarang
Yogyakarta
Surabaya
Malang
Pulau Madura
Pulau Bawean
Pulau Enggano
SUMATERA BARAT
SUMATERA SELATAN
LAMPUNG
BENGKULU
JAWA BARAT
JAWA TENGAH
JAWA TIMUR
YOGYAKARTA
180
180

Malaysia exports a greater tonnage of tropical timber than any other country in the world. Much of it comes from Sarawak in Borneo. Although in principle logging is allowed only on a sustainable basis, environmentalists fear that the rain forest in Sarawak will have disappeared by the early 21st century.

This tiny island near Kota Kinabalu, in Sabah, eastern Malaysia, is a part of a designated national park. Thickly forested, it is surrounded by broad, sandy beaches and shallow inland seas.

Throughout Southeast Asia, where agricultural land is at a premium, terraces are cut into the slopes to maximize the area available for cultivation. These terraces on the Indonesian island of Bali are used to support rice paddies.

MAP KEY

POPULATION
- above 5 million
- 1 million to 5 million
- 500,000 to 1 million
- 100,000 to 500,000
- 50,000 to 100,000
- 10,000 to 50,000
- below 10,000

ELEVATION
- 4000m / 13,124ft
- 3000m / 9843ft
- 2000m / 6562ft
- 1000m / 3281ft
- 500m / 1640ft
- 250m / 820ft
- 100m / 328ft
- sea level

SCALE 1:6,250,000
(projection: Mercator)

Km 0 25 50 100 150
Miles 0 25 50 100 150

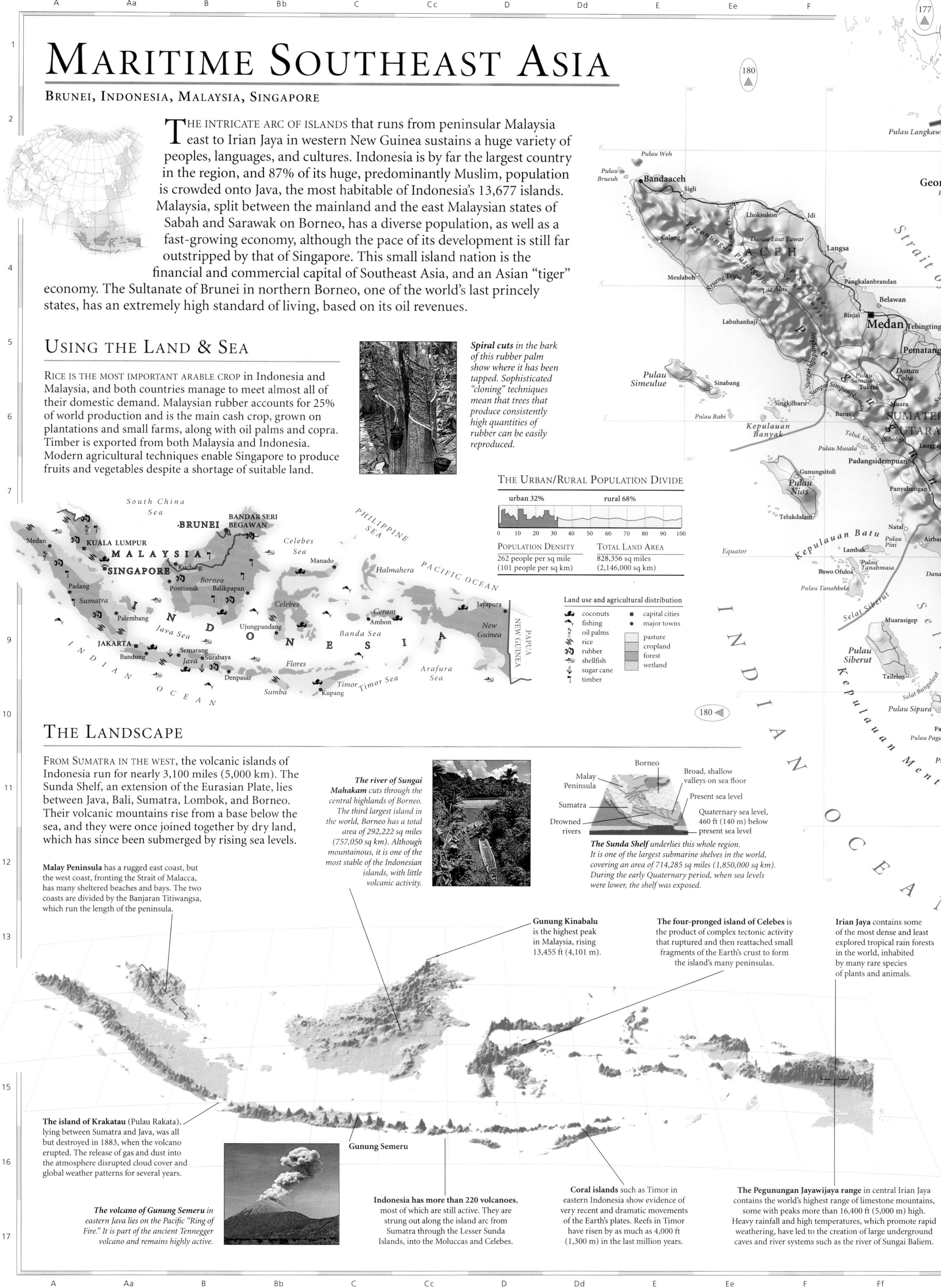

Pulau Weh
Pulau Brueuh
Bandaaceh
Sigli
Lhoksukon
Idi
Calang
Danau Laut Tawar
ACEH
Langsa
Meulaboh
Lac Alas
Pangkalanbrandan
Belawan
Binjai
Medan
Tebingtinggi
Labuhanhaji
Pematangsiantar
Pulau Simeulue
Sinabang
Pulau Samosir
Tukuk
Danau Toba
Singkilbaru
Muara
Pulau Rabi
Kepulauan Banyak
Baras
SUMATERA UTARA
Teluk Sibolga
Sibolga
Pulau Musala
Padangsidempuan
Gunungsitoli
Pulau Nias
Panyabungan
Telukdalam
Natal
Equator
Kepulauan Batu
Lambak
Pulau Pini
Airbangis
Pulau Tanahmasa
Bawo Ofuloa
Pulau Tanahbela
Selat Siberut
Muarasigep
Pulau Siberut
Taileleo
Selat Bungalaut
Pulau Sipura
Kepulauan Mentawai
Pasapa
Pulau Pagai Utara
Pulau Langkawi
George Town
Strait of Malacca
INDIAN OCEAN

Maritime Southeast Asia

Brunei, Indonesia, Malaysia, Singapore

The intricate arc of islands that runs from peninsular Malaysia east to Irian Jaya in western New Guinea sustains a huge variety of peoples, languages, and cultures. Indonesia is by far the largest country in the region, and 87% of its huge, predominantly Muslim, population is crowded onto Java, the most habitable of Indonesia's 13,677 islands. Malaysia, split between the mainland and the east Malaysian states of Sabah and Sarawak on Borneo, has a diverse population, as well as a fast-growing economy, although the pace of its development is still far outstripped by that of Singapore. This small island nation is the financial and commercial capital of Southeast Asia, and an Asian "tiger" economy. The Sultanate of Brunei in northern Borneo, one of the world's last princely states, has an extremely high standard of living, based on its oil revenues.

Using the Land & Sea

Rice is the most important arable crop in Indonesia and Malaysia, and both countries manage to meet almost all of their domestic demand. Malaysian rubber accounts for 25% of world production and is the main cash crop, grown on plantations and small farms, along with oil palms and copra. Timber is exported from both Malaysia and Indonesia. Modern agricultural techniques enable Singapore to produce fruits and vegetables despite a shortage of suitable land.

***Spiral cuts** in the bark of this rubber palm show where it has been tapped. Sophisticated "cloning" techniques mean that trees that produce consistently high quantities of rubber can be easily reproduced.*

The Urban/Rural Population Divide

urban 32% — rural 68%

0 10 20 30 40 50 60 70 80 90 100

Population Density	Total Land Area
262 people per sq mile (101 people per sq km)	828,356 sq miles (2,146,000 sq km)

South China Sea
BRUNEI
BANDAR SERI BEGAWAN
Medan
KUALA LUMPUR
MALAYSIA
SINGAPORE
Kuching
Borneo
Pontianak
Balikpapan
Padang
Sumatra
Palembang
INDONESIA
Java Sea
JAKARTA
Bandung
Semarang
Java
Surabaya
Denpasar
INDIAN OCEAN
Celebes Sea
Manado
PHILIPPINE SEA
Halmahera
PACIFIC OCEAN
Celebes
Ujungpandang
Ceram
Ambon
Banda Sea
Jayapura
New Guinea
PAPUA NEW GUINEA
Flores
Sumba
Timor
Kupang
Timor Sea
Arafura Sea
Land use and agricultural distribution
coconuts
fishing
oil palms
rice
rubber
shellfish
sugar cane
timber
capital cities
major towns
pasture
cropland
forest
wetland

The Landscape

From Sumatra in the west, the volcanic islands of Indonesia run for nearly 3,100 miles (5,000 km). The Sunda Shelf, an extension of the Eurasian Plate, lies between Java, Bali, Sumatra, Lombok, and Borneo. Their volcanic mountains rise from a base below the sea, and they were once joined together by dry land, which has since been submerged by rising sea levels.

***The river of Sungai Mahakam** cuts through the central highlands of Borneo. The third largest island in the world, Borneo has a total area of 292,222 sq miles (757,050 sq km). Although mountainous, it is one of the most stable of the Indonesian islands, with little volcanic activity.*

Borneo
Malay Peninsula
Broad, shallow valleys on sea floor
Present sea level
Sumatra
Quaternary sea level, 460 ft (140 m) below present sea level
Drowned rivers

***The Sunda Shelf** underlies this whole region. It is one of the largest submarine shelves in the world, covering an area of 714,285 sq miles (1,850,000 sq km). During the early Quaternary period, when sea levels were lower, the shelf was exposed.*

Malay Peninsula has a rugged east coast, but the west coast, fronting the Strait of Malacca, has many sheltered beaches and bays. The two coasts are divided by the Banjaran Titiwangsa, which run the length of the peninsula.

Gunung Kinabalu is the highest peak in Malaysia, rising 13,455 ft (4,101 m).

The four-pronged island of Celebes is the product of complex tectonic activity that ruptured and then reattached small fragments of the Earth's crust to form the island's many peninsulas.

Irian Jaya contains some of the most dense and least explored tropical rain forests in the world, inhabited by many rare species of plants and animals.

The island of Krakatau (Pulau Rakata), lying between Sumatra and Java, was all but destroyed in 1883, when the volcano erupted. The release of gas and dust into the atmosphere disrupted cloud cover and global weather patterns for several years.

Gunung Semeru

***The volcano of Gunung Semeru** in eastern Java lies on the Pacific "Ring of Fire." It is part of the ancient Tennegger volcano and remains highly active.*

Indonesia has more than 220 volcanoes, most of which are still active. They are strung out along the island arc from Sumatra through the Lesser Sunda Islands, into the Moluccas and Celebes.

Coral islands such as Timor in eastern Indonesia show evidence of very recent and dramatic movements of the Earth's plates. Reefs in Timor have risen by as much as 4,000 ft (1,300 m) in the last million years.

The Pegunungan Jayawijaya range in central Irian Jaya contains the world's highest range of limestone mountains, some with peaks more than 16,400 ft (5,000 m) high. Heavy rainfall and high temperatures, which promote rapid weathering, have led to the creation of large underground caves and river systems such as the river of Sungai Baliem.

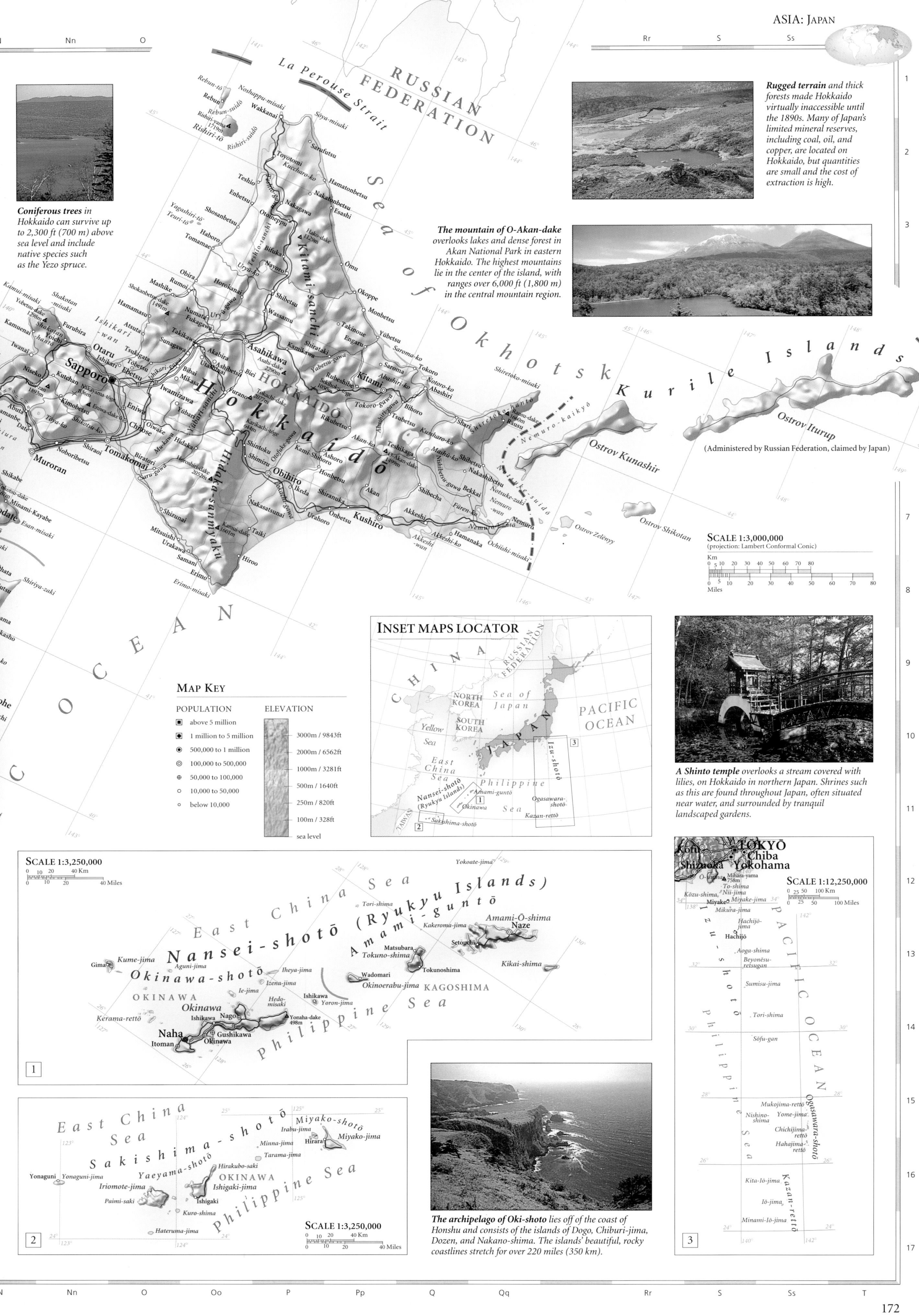
RUSSIAN FEDERATION
La Perouse Strait
Sea of Okhotsk
Kurile Islands
Ostrov Iturup
(Administered by Russian Federation, claimed by Japan)
Ostrov Kunashir
Ostrov Shikotan
Ostrov Zelenyy
Nemuro-kaikyō
Hokkaidō
HOKKAIDŌ
Kitami-sanchi
Hidaka-sanmyaku
Ishikari-wan
Sapporo
Asahikawa
Obihiro
Kushiro
Kitami
Abashiri
Muroran
Tomakomai
Otaru
Wakkanai
Rebun-tō
Rishiri-tō
Sōya-misaki
Shiretoko-misaki
Erimo-misaki
Nemuro
OCEAN
SCALE 1:3,000,000
(projection: Lambert Conformal Conic)
Km
Miles
INSET MAPS LOCATOR
CHINA
NORTH KOREA
SOUTH KOREA
JAPAN
Sea of Japan
Yellow Sea
East China Sea
PACIFIC OCEAN
Philippine Sea
TAIWAN
MAP KEY
POPULATION
above 5 million
1 million to 5 million
500,000 to 1 million
100,000 to 500,000
50,000 to 100,000
10,000 to 50,000
below 10,000
ELEVATION
3000m / 9843ft
2000m / 6562ft
1000m / 3281ft
500m / 1640ft
250m / 820ft
100m / 328ft
sea level
SCALE 1:3,250,000
East China Sea
Nansei-shotō (Ryukyu Islands)
Amami-guntō
Amami-Ō-shima
Naze
Tokuno-shima
Okinoerabu-jima
KAGOSHIMA
Okinawa-shotō
OKINAWA
Okinawa
Naha
Nago
Kume-jima
Kerama-rettō
Philippine Sea
Sakishima-shotō
Miyako-shotō
Miyako-jima
Yaeyama-shotō
Iriomote-jima
Ishigaki-jima
Ishigaki
Yonaguni-jima
Hateruma-jima
TOKYŌ
Chiba
Yokohama
SCALE 1:12,250,000
Izu-shotō
PACIFIC OCEAN
Philippine Sea
Hachijō-jima
Miyake-jima
Ogasawara-shotō
Kazan-rettō
Iō-jima
Chichijima-rettō
Hahajima-rettō
Mukojima-rettō

***Coniferous trees** in Hokkaido can survive up to 2,300 ft (700 m) above sea level and include native species such as the Yezo spruce.*

***Rugged terrain** and thick forests made Hokkaido virtually inaccessible until the 1890s. Many of Japan's limited mineral reserves, including coal, oil, and copper, are located on Hokkaido, but quantities are small and the cost of extraction is high.*

***The mountain of O-Akan-dake** overlooks lakes and dense forest in Akan National Park in eastern Hokkaido. The highest mountains lie in the center of the island, with ranges over 6,000 ft (1,800 m) in the central mountain region.*

***A Shinto temple** overlooks a stream covered with lilies, on Hokkaido in northern Japan. Shrines such as this are found throughout Japan, often situated near water, and surrounded by tranquil landscaped gardens.*

***The archipelago of Oki-shoto** lies off of the coast of Honshu and consists of the islands of Dogo, Chiburi-jima, Dozen, and Nakano-shima. The islands' beautiful, rocky coastlines stretch for over 220 miles (350 km).*

Mainland Southeast Asia & the Philippines

Cambodia, Laos, Myanmar, Philippines, Thailand, Vietnam

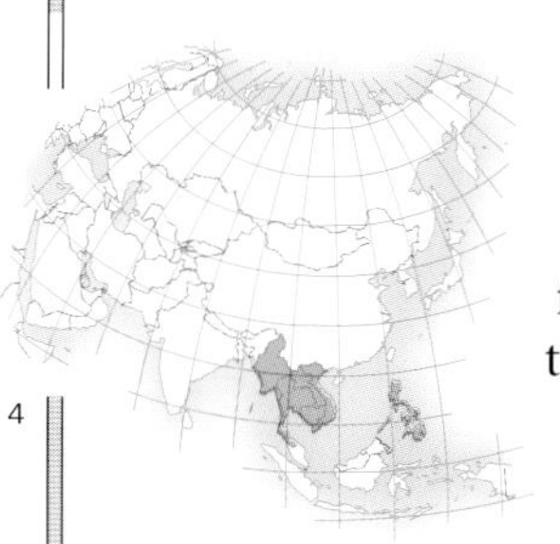

Thickly forested mountains intercut by the broad valleys of five great rivers characterize the landscape of Southeast Asia's mainland countries. Agriculture remains the main activity for much of the population, which is concentrated in the river floodplains and deltas. Linked ethnic and cultural roots give the region a distinct identity. Most people on the mainland are Theravada Buddhists, and the Philippines is the only predominantly Christian country in Southeast Asia. Foreign intervention began in the 16th century with the opening of the spice trade; Cambodia, Laos, and Vietnam were French colonies until the end of the Second World War; Myanmar was under British control; and the Philippines was controlled by Spain and the US in the 20th century. Only Thailand was never colonized. Today, Thailand and the Philippines are poised to play a leading role in the economic development of the Pacific Rim, and Laos and Vietnam have begun to mend the devastation of the Vietnam War, and to develop their economies. With continuing political instability and a shattered infrastructure, Cambodia faces an uncertain future, while Myanmar is seeking investment and the ending of its 30-year isolation from the world community.

The Irrawaddy River is Myanmar's vital central artery, watering the rice paddies and providing a rich source of fish, as well as an important transportation link, particularly for local traffic.

Commercial logging, still widespread in Myanmar, has now been stopped in Thailand because of overexploitation of the tropical rain forest.

The Landscape

A series of mountain ranges runs north–south through the mainland, formed as the result of the collision between the Eurasian Plate and the Indian subcontinent, which created the Himalayas. They are interspersed by the valleys of a number of great rivers. On their passage to the sea, these rivers have deposited sediment, forming huge, fertile floodplains and deltas. The Philippines' 7,000 islands are mountainous and volcanic, with narrow coastal plains.

Lake Taal on the Philippine island of Luzon lies within the crater of an immense volcano that has erupted twice in the 20th century, first in 1911 and again in 1965, causing the deaths of more than 3,200 people.

The Irrawaddy River runs virtually north–south, draining the plains of northern Myanmar. The Irrawaddy Delta is the country's main rice-growing area.

Hkakabo Razi is the highest point in mainland Southeast Asia. It rises 19,300 ft (5,885 m) at the border between China and Myanmar.

Mountains dominate the Laotian landscape, with more than 90% of the land lying more than 600 ft (180 m) above sea level. The mountains of the Chaîne Annamitique form the country's eastern border.

The Red River Delta in northern Vietnam is fringed to the north by steep-sided, round-topped limestone hills, typical of karst scenery.

Mindanao has five mountain ranges, many of which have large numbers of active volcanoes. Lying just west of the Philippine Trench, which forms the boundary between the colliding Philippine and Eurasian plates, the entire island chain is subject to earthquakes and volcanic activity.

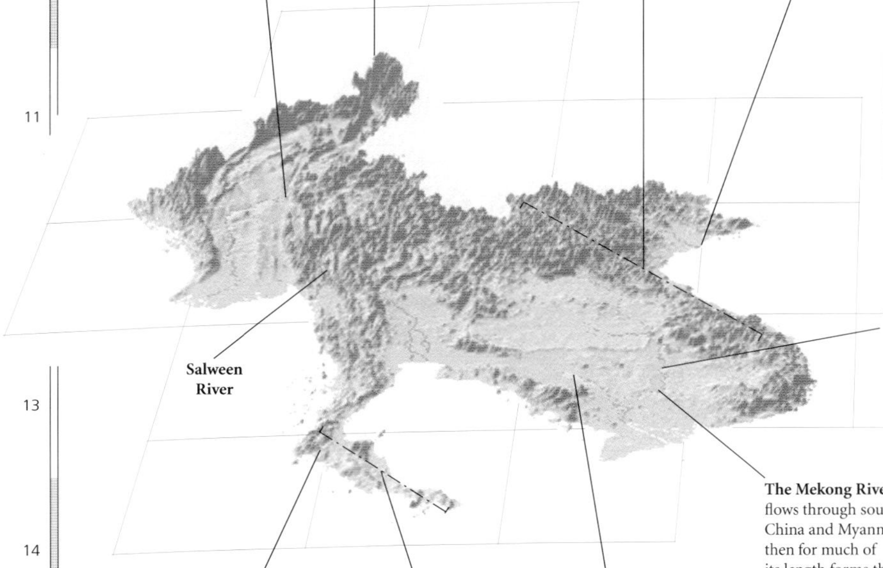

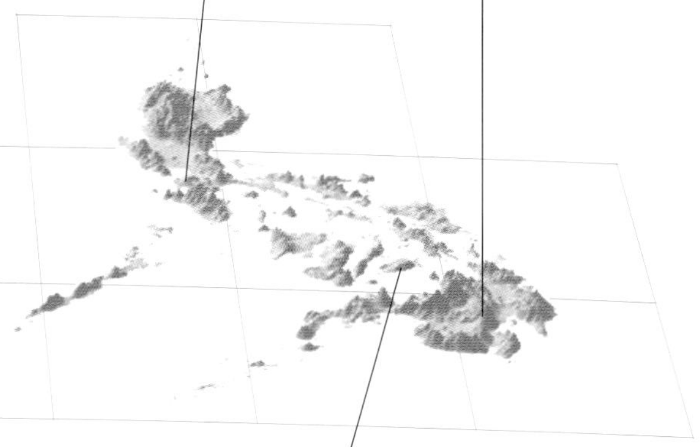

The fast-flowing waters of the Mekong River cascade over this waterfall in Champasak province in Laos. The force of the water erodes rocks at the base of the fall.

Salween River

The Mekong River flows through southern China and Myanmar, then for much of its length forms the border between Laos and Thailand, flowing through Cambodia before terminating in a vast delta on the southern Vietnamese coast.

Malay Peninsula

Tonle Sap, a freshwater lake, drains into the Mekong Delta via the Mekong River. It is the largest lake in Southeast Asia.

Thailand

Bohol

The coast of the Isthmus of Kra, in southeast Thailand, has many small, precipitous islands like these, formed by chemical erosion on limestone, which is weathered along vertical cracks. The humidity of the climate in Southeast Asia increases the rate of weathering.

The coastline of the Isthmus of Kra

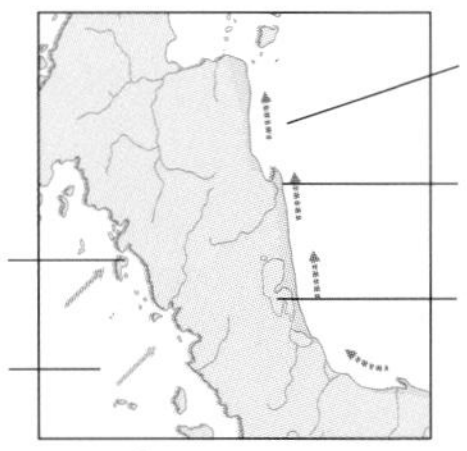

Longshore drift
Spit
Lagoon
Eroded coastline
Wave attack

The east and west coasts of the Isthmus of Kra differ greatly. The tectonically uplifting west coast is exposed to the harsh southwesterly monsoon and is heavily eroded. On the east coast, longshore currents produce depositional features such as spits and lagoons.

Bohol in the southern Philippines is famous for its so-called "chocolate hills." There are more than 1,000 of these regular mounds on the island. The hills are limestone in origin, the smoothed remains of an earlier cycle of erosion. Their brown appearance in the dry season gives the hills their name.

TRANSPORTATION & INDUSTRY

SINGAPORE HAS A THRIVING ECONOMY based on international trade and finance. Annual trade through the port is among the highest of any port in the world. Indonesia still depends on natural resources, particularly wood, petroleum, and gas, although the economy is rapidly diversifying, with manufactured exports including garments, consumer electronics, and footwear. A high-profile aircraft industry has developed in Bandung. Malaysia has a fast-growing and varied manufacturing sector, although oil, gas, and timber remain important resource-based industries.

Major industry and infrastructure

- aerospace
- copra processing
- chemicals
- electronics
- engineering
- finance
- food processing
- iron & steel
- oil
- shipbuilding
- timber processing
- textiles

- capital cities
- major towns
- international airports
- major roads
- major industrial areas

Ranks of gleaming skyscrapers, new highways, and infrastructure construction reflect the investment that is pouring into Southeast Asian cities like the Malaysian capital, Kuala Lumpur. Traditional housing and markets still exist between the new developments. Many of the city's inhabitants subsist at a level far removed from the prosperity implied by its outward modernity.

TRANSPORTATION NETWORK

160,350 miles (258,213 km)
188 miles (302 km)
5,482 miles (8,828 km)
15,523 miles (32,903km)

Singapore's subway system, completed in 1991, is among the most efficient in the world. Malaysia has several fast, modern highways and most roads are paved. Indonesia's many islands make improvement of the shipping infrastructure a priority.

Although Indonesia is now a mainly Muslim country, relicts of other civilizations are found throughout its many islands. These scattered columns are the ruins of a Hindu settlement that flourished on Java more than a thousand years ago.

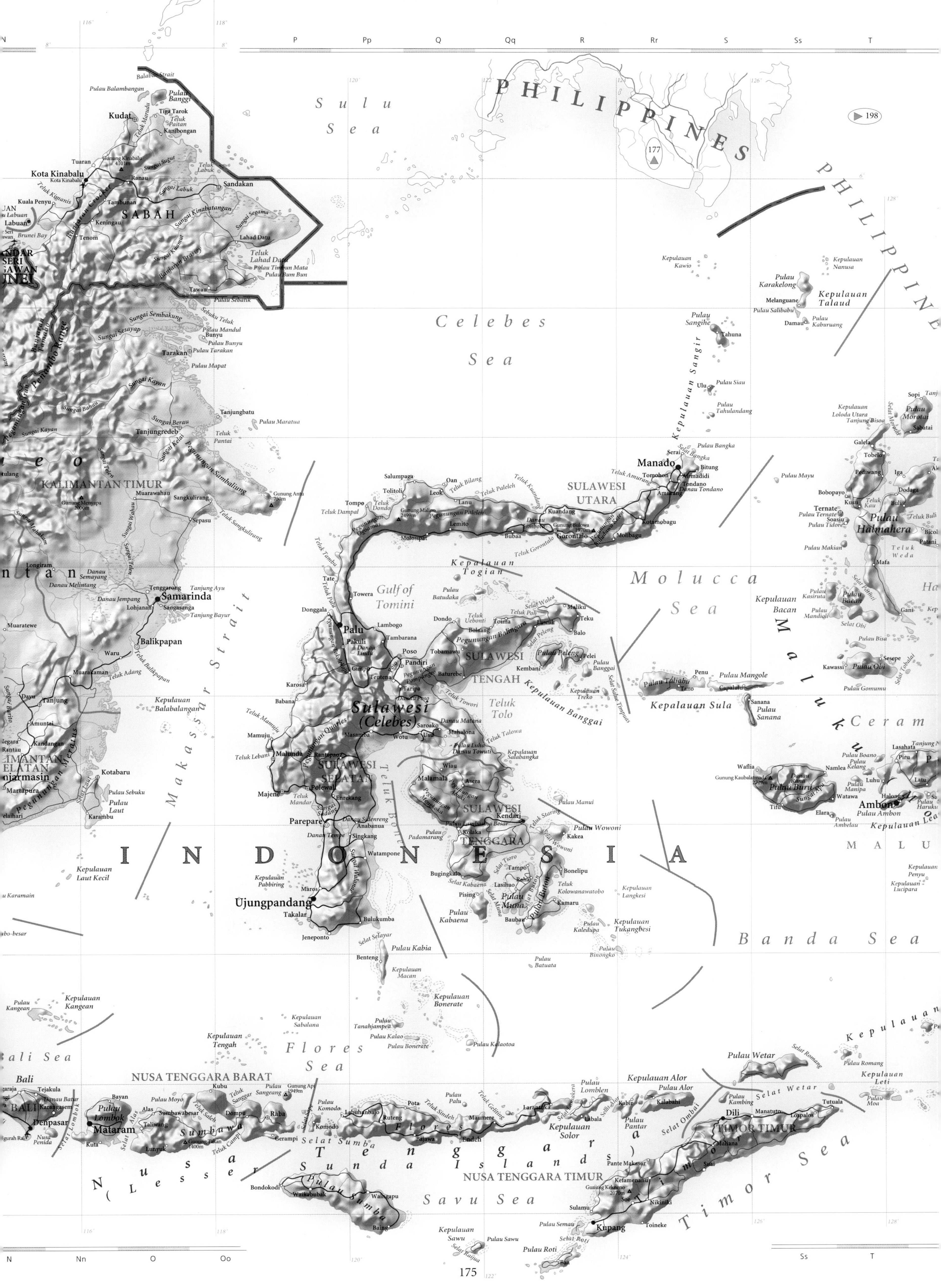

N
P
Pp
Q
Qq
R
Rr
S
Ss
T
116°
118°
120°
122°
124°
126°
128°
198
177
Sulu Sea
PHILIPPINES
PHILIPPINE
Balabac Strait
Pulau Balambangan
Pulau Banggi
Kudat
Tiga Tarok
Teluk Paitan
Kanibongan
Tuaran
Gunung Kinabalu 4101m
Kota Kinabalu
Ranau
Sandakan
Teluk Labuk
Sungai Labuk
Kuala Penyu
Teluk Kimanis
Tambunan
SABAH
Sungai Kinabatangan
Sungai Segama
Labuan
Keningau
Brunei Bay
Tenom
Lahad Datu
Teluk Lahad Datu
Pulau Timbun Mata
Pulau Bum Bun
Tawau
Pulau Sebatik
Sebuku Teluk
Sungai Sembakung
Sungai Sesayap
Pulau Mandul
Bunyu
Pulau Bunyu
Tarakan
Pulau Tarakan
Pulau Mapat
Sungai Kayan
Sungai Bahau
Tanjungbatu
Pulau Maratua
Sungai Berau
Tanjungredeb
Teluk Pantai
Pegunungan Sambaliung
KALIMANTAN TIMUR
Gunung Menyapa 2000m
Muarawahau
Sangkulirang
Gunung Antu 750m
Sepasu
Teluk Sangkulirang
Sungai Wahau
Longiram
Danau Semayang
Danau Melintang
Danau Jempang
Tenggarong
Tanjung Ayu
Samarinda
Lohjanan
Sangasanga
Tanjung Bayur
Muaratewe
Balikpapan
Waru
Teluk Balikpapan
Muarakaman
Teluk Adang
Dayu
Tanjung
Amuntai
Kandangan
Kotabaru
Pulau Sebuku
Pulau Laut
Karambu
Martapura
Pegunungan Meratus
Kepulauan Balabalangan
Makassar Strait
Celebes Sea
Kepulauan Kawio
Kepulauan Nanusa
Pulau Karakelong
Melanguane
Pulau Salibabu
Kepulauan Talaud
Damau
Pulau Kaburuang
Pulau Sangihe
Tahuna
Kepulauan Sangir
Ulu
Pulau Siau
Pulau Tahulandang
Pulau Bangka
Selat Bangka
Serai
Manado
Bitung
Airmadidi
Tomohon
Tondano
Danau Tondano
Amurang
Teluk Amurang
Kotamobagu
SULAWESI UTARA
Kuandang
Gorontalo
Molibagu
Danau Limboto
Bubaa
Teluk Gorontalo
Salumpaga
Tolitoli
Oan
Teluk Bilang
Teluk Paleleh
Leok
Lanu
Pegunungan Paleleh
Lemito
Tompo
Teluk Dondo
Teluk Dampal
Gunung Malino 2499m
Molosipat
Teluk Tambu
Kepalauan Togian
Tate
Towera
Gulf of Tomini
Pulau Batudaka
Donggala
Palu
Lambogo
Tambarana
Pakuli
Danau Lindu
Poso
Pandiri
Gimpu
Tentena
Danau Poso
Karosa
Babana
Sulawesi (Celebes)
Teluk Mamuju
Mamuju
Pegunungan Quarles
Masamba
Wotu
Saroako
Danau Matana
Mahalona
Usu
Teluk Lebani
Malunda
SULAWESI SELATAN
Rantepao
Polewali
Enrekang
Majene
Teluk Mandar
Parepare
Danau Sidenreng
Anabanua
Danau Tempe
Singkang
Watampone
Teluk Bone
Kepulauan Pabbiring
Maros
Ujungpandang
Takalar
Bulukumba
Jeneponto
Selat Selayar
Benteng
Pulau Kabia
Kepulauan Macan
Kepulauan Bonerate
Dondo
Teluk Uebonti
Bolaang
Toima
Teluk Poh
Luwuk
Maliku
Teku
Balo
Selat Walea
Pegunungan Balingara
Tobamawu
SULAWESI TENGAH
Baturebe
Pulau Peleng
Selat Peleng
Kembani
Pelei
Pulau Banggai
Kepulauan Treko
Kepulauan Banggai
Selat Salue Timpaus
Teluk Towori
Teluk Tolo
Teluk Talowa
Pulau Luhu
Danau Towuti
Kepulauan Salabangka
Wiau
Malamala
Asera
SULAWESI TENGGARA
Kendari
Teluk Staring
Pulau Manui
Pulau Wowoni
Kakea
Pulau Padamarang
Kolaka
Bonelipu
Selat Tioro
Tampo
Raha
Lasihao
Bugingkalo
Selat Kabaena
Pising
Pulau Kabaena
Selat Muna
Pulau Muna
Pulau Buton
Teluk Kolowanawatobo
Kamaru
Baubau
Kepulauan Langkesi
Pulau Kaledupa
Kepulauan Tukangbesi
Pulau Binongko
Pulau Batuata
Molucca Sea
Kepulauan Bacan
Pulau Taliabu
Tano
Penu
Pulau Mangole
Capalulu
Kepalauan Sula
Sanana
Pulau Sanana
Maluku
Ceram
Sopi
Pulau Morotai
Sabatai
Kepulauan Loloda Utara
Tanjung Bisoa
Galela
Tobelo
Pulau Mayu
Pediwang
Iga
Dodaga
Bobopayo
Kusu
Teluk Kau
Buli
Ternate
Pulau Ternate
Soasiu
Pulau Tidore
Pulau Halmahera
Teluk Buli
Bicoli
Patani
Pulau Makian
Teluk Weda
Mafa
Pulau Kasiruta
Pulau Bacan
Pulau Mandioli
Gani
Selat Obi
Pulau Bisa
Kawassi
Pulau Obi
Sesepe
Selat Tobalai
Pulau Gomumu
Waflia
Gunung Kaubalatmada 2729m
Danau Rana
Pulau Buru
Namlea
Pulau Kelang
Pulau Manipa
Luhu
Watawa
Tifu
Elara
Pulau Ambelau
Ambon
Pulau Ambon
Pulau Haruku
Lasahata
Piru
Latu
Halong
Kepulauan Lease
MALUKU
Kepulauan Penyu
Kepulauan Lucipara
Banda Sea
INDONESIA
Kepulauan Laut Kecil
Pulau Kangean
Kepulauan Kangean
Bali Sea
Kepulauan Sabalana
Kepulauan Tengah
Pulau Tanahjampea
Pulau Kalao
Pulau Bonerate
Pulau Kalaotoa
Flores Sea
NUSA TENGGARA BARAT
Bali
Tejakula
Danau Batur
Karangasem
BALI
Denpasar
Nusa Penida
Selat Lombok
Pulau Lombok
Mataram
Kuta
Bayan
Pulau Moyo
Alas
Selat Alas
Sumbawabesar
Taliwang
Lunyuk
Sumbawa
Gunung Tambora
Kubu
Teluk Saleh
Dompu
Teluk Sanggar
Pulau Sangeang
Gunung Api 1949m
Raba
Selat Sape
Pulau Komodo
Komodo
Gerampi
Labuhanbajo
Ruteng
Pota
Bajawa
Flores
Pulau Palu
Teluk Sindeh
Maumere
Teluk Geliting
Endeh
Larantuka
Pulau Lomblen
Lebala
Kepulauan Solor
Kepulauan Alor
Pulau Alor
Kalabahi
Kabir
Pulau Pantar
Selat Ombai
Pulau Wetar
Selat Romang
Pulau Romang
Kepulauan Leti
Pulau Moa
Pulau Kambing
Selat Wetar
Dili
Manatuto
Lospalos
Tutuala
TIMOR TIMUR
Mahana
Suai
Timor
Pante Makasar
Kefamenanu
NUSA TENGGARA TIMUR
Gunung Kekneno 2070m
Soe
Nikiniki
Sulamu
Kupang
Toineke
Pulau Semau
Selat Roti
Pulau Roti
Kepulauan Sawu
Pulau Sawu
Selat Raijua
Savu Sea
Timor Sea
Nusa Tenggara (Lesser Sunda Islands)
Bondokodi
Waikabubak
Pulau Sumba
Waingapu
Baing
Selat Sumba
Nn
O
Oo

Land use and agricultural distribution
cattle
pigs
bananas
coconuts
fishing
oil palms
rice
rubber
sugar cane
timber
capital cities
major towns
pasture
cropland
forest
mountain region
The Urban/Rural Population Divide
urban 22%
rural 78%
0 10 20 30 40 50 60 70 80 90 100
Population Density
253 people per sq mile
(98 people per sq km)
Total Land Area
733,828 sq miles
(1,901,110 sq km)
MYANMAR
THAILAND
LAOS
CAMBODIA
VIETNAM
PHILIPPINES
MALAYSIA
BRUNEI
Gulf of Thailand
South China Sea
PARACEL ISLANDS (disputed)
KRUNG THEP (BANGKOK)
PHNUM PENH (PHNOM PENH)
VIANGCHAN (VIENTIANE)
HANOI
Hô Chi Minh
Gulf of Tongking
Gulf of Thailand

Using the Land & Sea

The fertile floodplains of rivers such as the Mekong and Salween, and the humid climate, enable the production of rice throughout the region. Cambodia, Myanmar, and Laos still have substantial forests, producing hardwoods such as teak and rosewood. Cash crops include tropical fruits such as coconuts, bananas, and pineapples, rubber, oil palm, sugar cane, and the jute substitute, kenaf. Pigs and cattle are the main livestock raised. Large quantities of marine and freshwater fish are caught throughout the region.

The Paracel Islands and the Spratly Islands *are two strategically sensitive island groups, disputed by several surrounding countries. The Paracels are claimed by China, Taiwan, and Vietnam, though only China has actually occupied them. The Spratlys are claimed by China, Taiwan, Vietnam, Malaysia, and the Philippines and are particularly important because they lie on oil and gas deposits.*

The walled city of Hue, *in central Vietnam, was built in the 19th century in the style of a Chinese city. It is the site of a number of religious monuments, including the Thien-Mu Pagoda.*

TRANSPORTATION & INDUSTRY

INDUSTRIAL MANUFACTURING has become increasingly important in Thailand, Vietnam, and the Philippines in recent years. The assembling of component-based electrical and electronic goods is becoming more common throughout this region, with foreign companies benefiting from low labor costs and the upgrading of technology. The economies of Myanmar and Cambodia are still based on agricultural produce and the processing of raw materials. Tin is the region's most important metal, and nickel, copper, and chromite are also mined, although the quantities produced are not significant on a global scale. Thailand's successful tourist industry is the country's highest earner of foreign exchange.

TRANSPORTATION NETWORK

130,235 miles (209,718 km)	None
7,087 miles (11,413 km)	20,433 miles (32,903 km)

Transportation development has concentrated on the building of road networks. Water and sea transportation remain important, although air links have improved, particularly in Thailand and the Philippines.

Major industry and infrastructure

- chemicals
- electronics
- engineering
- finance
- food processing
- iron & steel
- oil & gas
- mining
- shipbuilding
- textiles
- timber processing
- capital cities
- major towns
- international airports
- major roads
- major industrial areas

***Opium poppies** are destroyed under army supervision in Thailand. This action is part of a government-sponsored initiative to reduce the trade in drugs such as heroin, which is derived from these plants. Drug trafficking is a major problem throughout the region; the area is known as the "Golden Triangle," and Laos is the third-largest producer of opium poppies in the world.*

***The terracing of land** to restrict soil erosion and create flat surfaces for agriculture is a common practice throughout Southeast Asia, particularly where land is scarce. These terraces are on Luzon in the Philippines.*

***…w and timber dwellings** …been built close to the …of the beach on this …nd near Palawan, … of the most westerly …nds in the Philippines.*

SCALE 1:7,750,000
(projection: Lambert Conformal Conic)

Km 0 25 50 100 150 200
Miles 0 25 50 100 150 200

MAP KEY

POPULATION

- above 5 million
- 1 million to 5 million
- 500,000 to 1 million
- 100,000 to 500,000
- 50,000 to 100,000
- 10,000 to 50,000
- below 10,000

ELEVATION

- 4000m / 13,124ft
- 3000m / 9843ft
- 2000m / 6562ft
- 1000m / 3281ft
- 500m / 1640ft
- 250m / 820ft
- 100m / 328ft
- sea level

198

The Indian Ocean

Despite being the smallest of the three major oceans, the evolution of the Indian Ocean was the most complex. The ocean basin was formed during the breakup of the supercontinent Gondwanaland, when the Indian subcontinent moved northeast, Africa moved west, and Australia separated from Antarctica. Like the Pacific Ocean, the warm waters of the Indian Ocean are punctuated by coral atolls and islands. About one-fifth of the world's population – over a billion people – live on its shores. Those people living along the northern coasts are constantly threatened by flooding and typhoons caused by the monsoon winds.

The Landscape

The Indian Ocean began forming about 150 million years ago, but in its present form it is relatively young, only about 36 million years old. Along the three subterranean mountain chains of its mid-ocean ridge the sea floor is still spreading. The Indian Ocean has fewer trenches than other oceans and only a narrow continental shelf around most of its surrounding land.

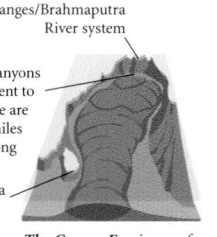

Sediments come from Ganges/Brahmaputra River system

Submarine canyons transport sediment to fan – some of these are more than 1,500 miles (2,500 km) long

Sri Lanka

The mid-oceanic ridge runs from the Arabian Sea. It diverges east of Madagascar. One arm runs southwest to join the Mid-Atlantic Ridge, the other branches southeast, joining the Pacific-Antarctic Ridge, southeast of Tasmania.

The Ninetyeast Ridge takes its name from the line of longitude it follows. It is the world's longest and straightest undersea ridge.

Indus River

Two of the world's largest rivers flow into the Indian Ocean; the Indus and the Ganges/Brahmaputra. Both have deposited enormous fans of sediment.

The Ganges Fan *is one of the world's largest submarine accumulations of sediment, extending far beyond Sri Lanka. It is fed by the Ganges/Brahmaputra River system, whose sediment is carried through a network of underwater canyons at the edge of the continental shelf.*

A large proportion *of the coast of Thailand, on the Isthmus of Kra, is stabilized by mangrove thickets. They act as an important breeding ground for wildlife.*

The Java Trench is the world's longest. Running 1,600 miles (2,570 km) from the southwest of Java, it is only 50 miles (80 km) wide.

The relief of Madagascar rises from a low-lying coastal strip in the east, to the central plateau. The plateau is also a major watershed separating Madagascar's three main river basins.

The central group *of the Seychelles are mountainous, granite islands. They have a narrow coastal belt and lush, tropical vegetation cloaks the highlands.*

The Kerguelen Islands in the Southern Ocean were created by a hot spot in the Earth's crust. The islands were formed in succession as the Antarctic Plate moved slowly over the hot spot.

The circulation in the northern Indian Ocean is controlled by the monsoon winds. Biannually these winds reverse their pattern, causing a reversal in the surface currents and alternating high and low pressure conditions over Asia and Australia.

Resources

Many of the small islands in the Indian Ocean rely exclusively on tuna-fishing and tourism to maintain their economies. Most fisheries are artisanal, although large-scale tuna-fishing does take place in the Seychelles, Mauritius, and the western Indian Ocean. Nonliving resources include oil in the Persian Gulf, pearls in the Red Sea, and tin from deposits off the shores of Burma, Thailand, and Indonesia.

Resources (including wildlife): fish; penguins; shellfish; whales; oil & gas; tin deposits; tourism; major towns; major ports

The recent use of large *dragnets for tuna-fishing has not only threatened the livelihoods of many small-scale fisheries, but also caused widespread environmental concern about the potential impact on other marine species.*

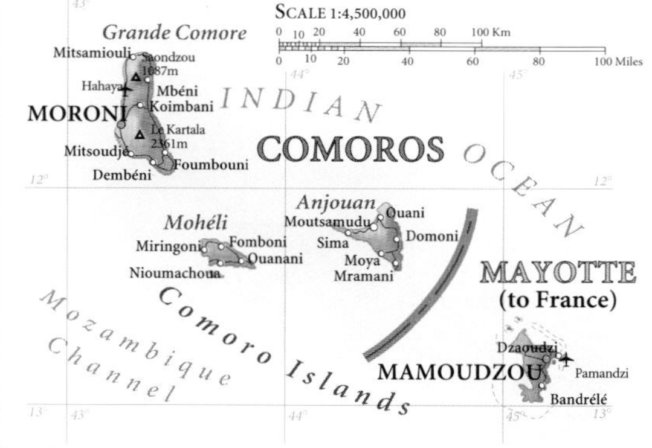
Scale 1:4,500,000
Grande Comore
Mitsamiouli
Hahaya
Mbéni
Koimbani
MORONI
Kartala
2361m
Mitsoudjé
Foumbouni
Dembéni
INDIAN OCEAN
COMOROS
Mohéli
Miringoni
Fomboni
Nioumachoua
Ouanani
Anjouan
Mutsamudu
Ouani
Domoni
Sima
Moya
Mramani
MAYOTTE
(to France)
Mozambique Channel
Comoro Islands
MAMOUDZOU
Dzaoudzi
Pamandzi
Bandrélé

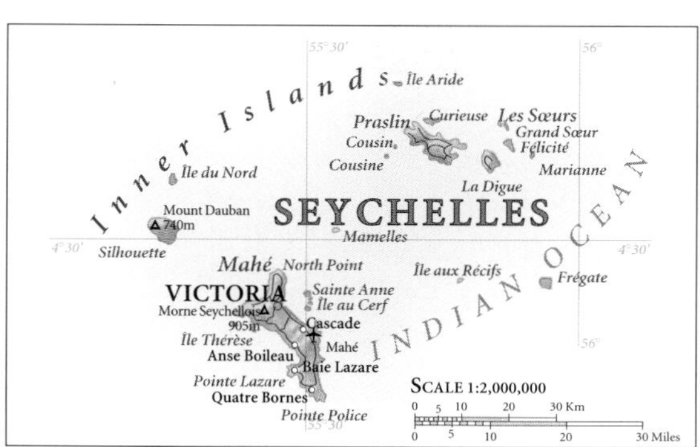
Inner Islands
Ile Aride
Praslin
Curieuse
Les Sœurs
Grand Sœur
Félicité
Cousin
Cousine
Marianne
La Digue
Ile du Nord
Mount Dauban
740m
SEYCHELLES
Mamelles
Silhouette
Mahé
North Point
Ile aux Récifs
VICTORIA
Morne Seychellois
905m
Sainte Anne
Ile au Cerf
Frégate
Ile Thérèse
Cascade
Anse Boileau
Baie Lazare
Pointe Lazare
Quatre Bornes
Pointe Police
INDIAN OCEAN
Scale 1:2,000,000

Coral reefs *support an enormous diversity of animal and plant life. Many species of tiny tropical fish, like these squirrel fish, live and feed around the profusion of reefs and atolls in the Indian Ocean.*

N O P Q R S T U V W X Y
SCALE 1:42,000,000
(projection: Mollweide)
Km
0 200 400 600 800 1000
0 200 400 600 800 1000
Miles
IRAN
Bandar-e 'Abbās
UAE
QATAR
Doha
Abu Dhabi
Dubai
Gwādar
PAKISTAN
Karāchi
Mīnā' Qābūs
OMAN
Salalah
ASIA
Indus
Brahmaputra
Ganges
BANGLADESH
Dhaka
Chittagong
Calcutta
Bhāvnagar
Narmada
INDIA
Bombay
Godavari
Krishna
Visākhapatnam
Ganges Fan
Bay of Bengal
Madras
Mangalore
Cochin
Tuticorin
Trincomalee
Sri Lanka
Colombo
SRI LANKA
Laccadive Islands (to India)
MYANMAR
Irrawaddy
Salween
Rangoon
Mekong
CHINA
LAOS
Gulf of Tongking
VIETNAM
THAILAND
CAMBODIA
Gulf of Thailand
Andaman Islands (to India)
Andaman Sea
Andaman Basin
Nicobar Islands (to India)
Bedawan
Strait of Malacca
MALAYSIA
Klang
Singapore
Sumatra
Kepulauan Mentawai
East China Sea
Ryukyu Islands
TAIWAN
Tropic of Cancer
South China Sea
Philippine Sea
PHILIPPINES
Sulu Sea
Celebes Sea
Borneo
INDONESIA
Makassar Strait
Celebes
Molucca Sea
Ceram Sea
Banda Sea
Java Sea
Java
Bali
Lombok Basin
Sumbawa
Timor
Savu
Pulau Sumba
Java Ridge
Java Trench
New Guinea
Equator
Arafura Sea
Timor Trough
Timor Sea
Joseph Bonaparte Gulf
Sahul Shelf
Darwin
Gulf of Carpentaria
Wyndham
Ashmore & Cartier Islands (to Australia)
Christmas Island (to Australia)
Roo Rise
North Australian Basin
Rowley Shoals
Broome
Gascoyne Plain
Exmouth Plateau
Port Hedland
Wallaby Plateau
Cuvier Basin
Cuvier Plateau
Shark Bay
Tropic of Capricorn
AUSTRALIA
Geraldton
Perth Basin
Fremantle
Bunbury
Albany
Naturaliste Plateau
Great Australian Bight
Port Augusta
Darling
Murray
Spencer Gulf
Adelaide
Kangaroo Island
Melbourne
King Island
Bass Strait
South Australian Basin
Tasmania
South Australian Plain
Tasman Plateau
Murray Ridge
Indus Fan
Arabian Sea
Arabian Basin
Owen Fracture Zone
Sheba Ridge
Alula-Fartak Trench
Socotra (to Yemen)
Error Tablemount
Carlsberg Ridge
Chain Ridge
Andrew Tablemount
Coco-de-Mer Seamounts
Mahé
Seychelles Bank
Amirante Islands
SEYCHELLES
Amirante Trench
Mascarene Plateau
Saya de Malha Bank
Agalega Islands (to Mauritius)
Mascarene Basin
Nazareth Bank
Cargados Carajos Bank
MAURITIUS
Mascarene Islands
Réunion (to France)
Mascarene Plain
Madagascar Basin
Rodrigues (to Mauritius)
Egeria Fracture Zone
Argo Fracture Zone
Vema Fracture Zone
Mid-Indian Ridge
Chagos-Laccadive Plateau
MALDIVES
Chagos Trench
Chagos Archipelago
Diego Garcia
British Indian Ocean Territory (to UK)
Ceylon Plain
Mid-Indian Basin
Ninetyeast Ridge
Cocos Basin
Cocos Islands (to Australia)
Osborn Plateau
Investigator Ridge
Wharton Basin
INDIAN OCEAN
East Indiaman Ridge
Batavia Seamount
Gulden Draak Seamount
Hartog Ridge
Broken Ridge
Diamantina Fracture Zone
Naturaliste Fracture Zone
Southwest Indian Ridge
Crozet Basin
Amsterdam Fracture Zone
Amsterdam Island
St. Paul Island
Crozet Plateau
Crozet Islands
French Southern & Antarctic Territories (to France)
Kerguelen
Kerguelen Plateau
Heard & McDonald Islands (to Australia)
Lena Tablemount
Southeast Indian Ridge
SOUTHERN OCEAN
South Indian Basin
Banzare Seamounts
Plain
ANTARCTICA
Prydz Bay
Antarctic Circle
RÉUNION (to France)
SCALE 1:2,000,000
0 5 10 20 30 Km
0 5 10 20 30 Miles
ST-DENIS
Ste-Marie
Le Port
Gillot
Ste-Suzanne
St-André
St-Paul
St-Gilles-les-Bains
Salazie
St-Benoit
Pointe des Aigrettes
Piton des Neiges 3070m
Cilaos
Trois-Bassins
St-Leu
La Plaine-des-Palmistes
Ste-Rose
Pointe au Sel
Piton de la Fournaise 2632m
Le Tampon
St-Louis
St-Pierre
Point de la Rivière St-Etienne
St-Joseph
St-Philippe
Pointe de la Table
INDIAN OCEAN
INSET MAP KEY
POPULATION
500,000 to 1 million
100,000 to 500,000
50,000 to 100,000
10,000 to 50,000
below 10,000
ELEVATION
3000m / 9843ft
2000m / 6562ft
1000m / 3281ft
500m / 1640ft
250m / 820ft
100m / 328ft
sea level
OCEAN MAP KEY
SEA DEPTH
sea level
250m / 820ft
500m / 1640ft
1000m / 3281ft
2000m / 6562ft
3000m / 9843ft
MAURITIUS
Round Island
Flat Island
Gunner's Quoin
Canonniers Point
Île D'Ambre
Triolet
Pamplemousses
Goodlands
PORT LOUIS
Rivière du Rempart
Beau Bassin
Rose Hill
Centre de Flacq
Bel Air
Quatre Bornes
Mont du Rempart
Vacoas
Tamarin
Curepipe
Piton de la Petite Rivière Noire 828m
Rose Belle
Mahebourg
Sir Seewoosagur Ramgoolam
Pointe Sud Ouest
Chemin Grenier
Souillac
SCALE 1:2,000,000
0 5 10 20 30 Km
0 5 10 20 30 Miles
N O P Q R S T U V W X Y Z

***The steeper eastern side** of Madagascar is drained by numerous short, fast-flowing rivers. In contrast, larger, more languid rivers flow across the west. Both erode huge quantities of Madagascar's red soil.*

***There are over 1,300** small coral islands in the Maldives, but only about 200 are inhabited. Based around an ancient submerged volcanic mountain range, all the islands are low-lying and none rise more than 6 ft (1.8 m) above sea level.*

***The island of Mauritius** is volcanic in origin. Its central plateau is bounded by mountains which may once have formed the rim of a volcanic crater.*

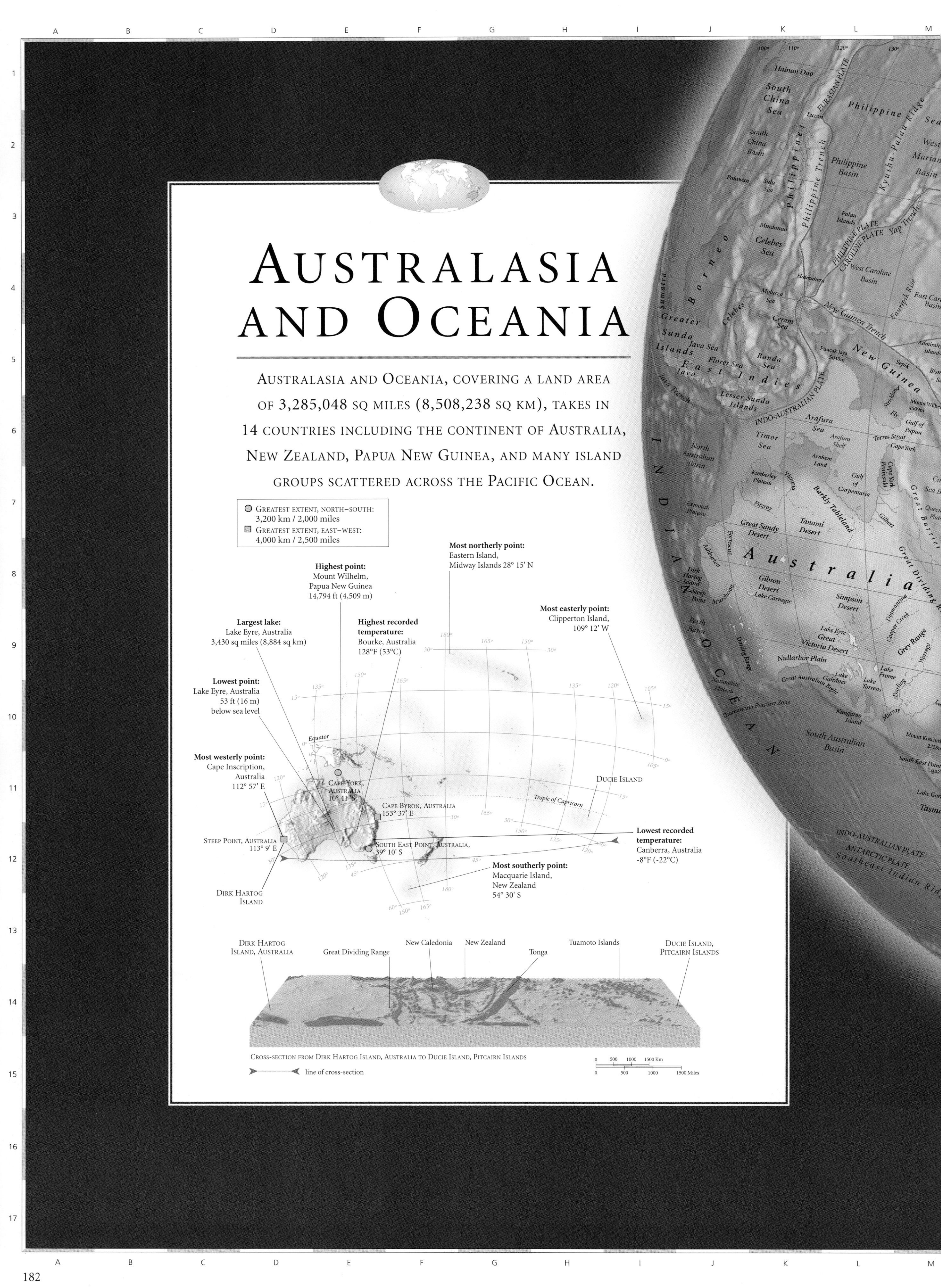

AUSTRALASIA AND OCEANIA
AUSTRALASIA AND OCEANIA, COVERING A LAND AREA OF 3,285,048 SQ MILES (8,508,238 SQ KM), TAKES IN 14 COUNTRIES INCLUDING THE CONTINENT OF AUSTRALIA, NEW ZEALAND, PAPUA NEW GUINEA, AND MANY ISLAND GROUPS SCATTERED ACROSS THE PACIFIC OCEAN.
GREATEST EXTENT, NORTH–SOUTH: 3,200 km / 2,000 miles
GREATEST EXTENT, EAST–WEST: 4,000 km / 2,500 miles
Most northerly point: Eastern Island, Midway Islands 28° 15' N
Highest point: Mount Wilhelm, Papua New Guinea 14,794 ft (4,509 m)
Most easterly point: Clipperton Island, 109° 12' W
Largest lake: Lake Eyre, Australia 3,430 sq miles (8,884 sq km)
Highest recorded temperature: Bourke, Australia 128°F (53°C)
Lowest point: Lake Eyre, Australia 53 ft (16 m) below sea level
Most westerly point: Cape Inscription, Australia 112° 57' E
Equator
CAPE YORK, AUSTRALIA 10° 41' S
DUCIE ISLAND
Tropic of Capricorn
CAPE BYRON, AUSTRALIA 153° 37' E
STEEP POINT, AUSTRALIA 113° 9' E
SOUTH EAST POINT, AUSTRALIA, 39° 10' S
Lowest recorded temperature: Canberra, Australia -8°F (-22°C)
Most southerly point: Macquarie Island, New Zealand 54° 30' S
DIRK HARTOG ISLAND
DIRK HARTOG ISLAND, AUSTRALIA
Great Dividing Range
New Caledonia
New Zealand
Tonga
Tuamoto Islands
DUCIE ISLAND, PITCAIRN ISLANDS
CROSS-SECTION FROM DIRK HARTOG ISLAND, AUSTRALIA TO DUCIE ISLAND, PITCAIRN ISLANDS
line of cross-section
0 500 1000 1500 Km
0 500 1000 1500 Miles
Hainan Dao
South China Sea
Philippine Sea
Philippines
Philippine Trench
Philippine Basin
West Mariana Basin
Celebes Sea
Borneo
Greater Sunda Islands
Java Sea
Flores Sea
Banda Sea
East Indies
New Guinea
Arafura Sea
Timor Sea
INDIAN OCEAN
Great Sandy Desert
Tanami Desert
Australia
Gibson Desert
Simpson Desert
Great Victoria Desert
Nullarbor Plain
Great Australian Bight
South Australian Basin
Gulf of Carpentaria
Great Barrier Reef
Great Dividing Range
INDO-AUSTRALIAN PLATE
ANTARCTIC PLATE
Southeast Indian Ridge

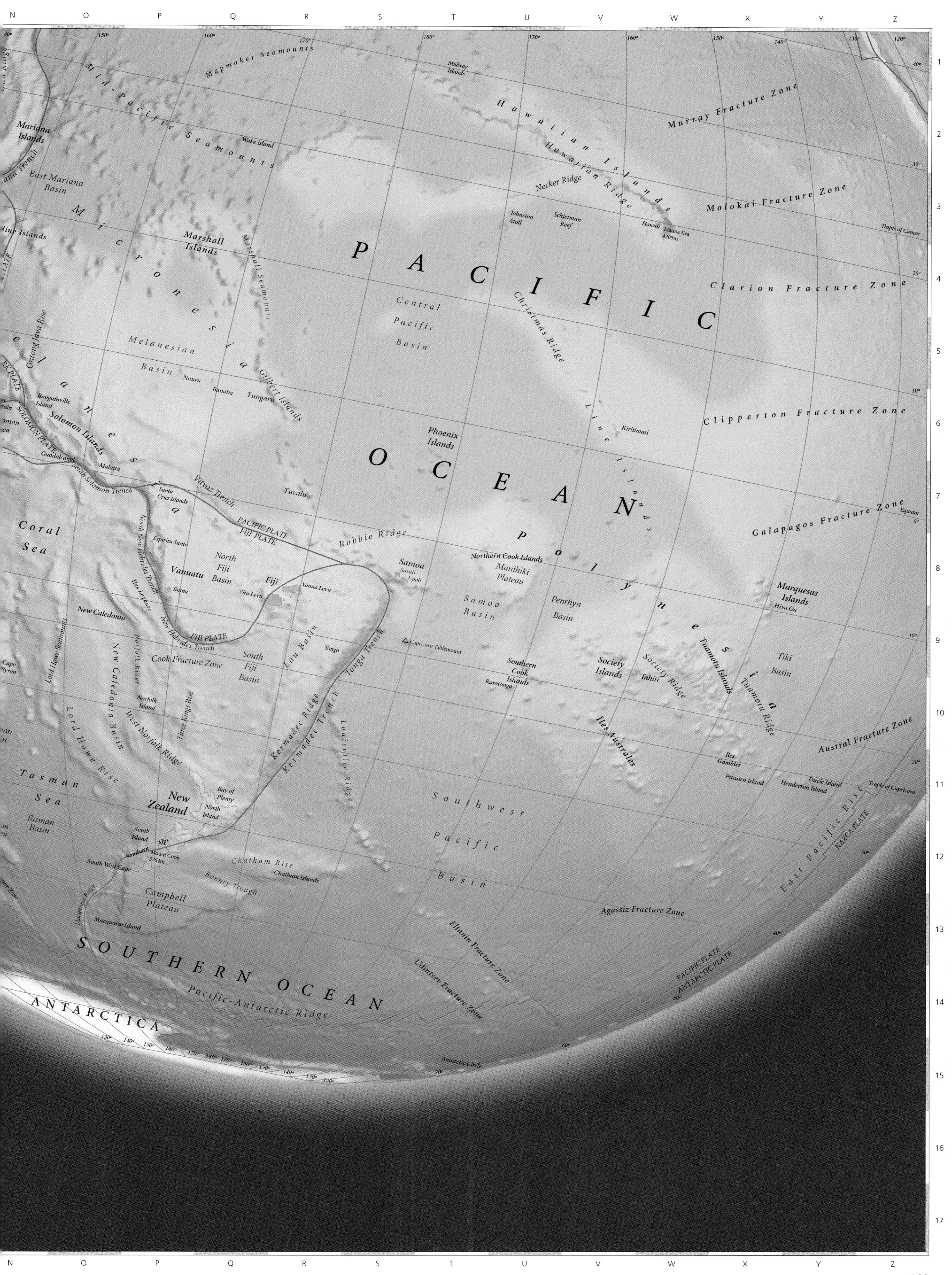
PACIFIC OCEAN
Mapmaker Seamounts
Mid-Pacific Seamounts
Midway Islands
Hawaiian Islands
Hawaiian Ridge
Murray Fracture Zone
Mariana Islands
Wake Island
East Mariana Basin
Necker Ridge
Molokai Fracture Zone
Micronesia
Johnston Atoll
Schjetman Reef
Hawaii
Mauna Kea 4205m
Tropic of Cancer
Marshall Islands
Marshall Seamounts
Clarion Fracture Zone
Central Pacific Basin
Christmas Ridge
Ontong Java Rise
Melanesian Basin
Melanesia
Nauru
Banaba
Tungaru
Gilbert Islands
Bougainville Island
Solomon Islands
Clipperton Fracture Zone
Line Islands
Kiritimati
Phoenix Islands
SOLOMON PLATE
Guadalcanal
Malaita
South Solomon Trench
Santa Cruz Islands
Vityaz Trench
Tuvalu
Galapagos Fracture Zone
Equator
Coral Sea
PACIFIC PLATE
FIJI PLATE
Robbie Ridge
Polynesia
Espiritu Santo
North New Hebrides Trench
North Fiji Basin
Vanuatu
Samoa
Savaii
Upoli
Northern Cook Islands
Manihiki Plateau
Marquesas Islands
Hiva Oa
Fiji
Vanua Levu
Viti Levu
Tanna
Iles Loyauté
New Caledonia
Samoa Basin
Penrhyn Basin
New Hebrides Trench
FIJI PLATE
Lau Basin
Tonga
Tonga Trench
Capricorn Tablemount
Lord Howe Seamounts
Norfolk Ridge
New Caledonia Basin
Cook Fracture Zone
South Fiji Basin
Southern Cook Islands
Rarotonga
Society Islands
Tahiti
Society Ridge
Tuamotu Islands
Tuamotu Ridge
Tiki Basin
Cape Byron
Norfolk Island
West Norfolk Ridge
Three Kings Rise
Kermadec Ridge
Kermadec Trench
Louisville Ridge
Iles Australes
Lord Howe Rise
Austral Fracture Zone
Iles Gambier
Pitcairn Island
Henderson Island
Ducie Island
Tropic of Capricorn
Tasman Sea
New Zealand
Bay of Plenty
North Island
Tasman Basin
South Island
Southwest Pacific Basin
Southern Alps
Mount Cook 3764m
South West Cape
Chatham Rise
Chatham Islands
Bounty Trough
East Pacific Rise
NAZCA PLATE
Campbell Plateau
Macquarie Ridge
Macquarie Island
Agassiz Fracture Zone
Eltanin Fracture Zone
SOUTHERN OCEAN
Udintsev Fracture Zone
PACIFIC PLATE
ANTARCTIC PLATE
Pacific-Antarctic Ridge
ANTARCTICA
Antarctic Circle

Political Australasia and Oceania

Vast expanses of ocean separate this geographically fragmented realm, characterized more by each country's isolation than by any political unity. Australia's and New Zealand's traditional ties with the UK, as members of the British Commonwealth, are now in question as Australasian and Oceanian nations increasingly look to forge new relationships with neighboring Asian countries like Japan. External influences have featured strongly in the politics of the islands of the Pacific; the various territories of Micronesia were largely under American control until the late 1980s. France, New Zealand, the US, and the UK still have territories under colonial rule in Polynesia. The testing of nuclear weapons by Western superpowers was widespread during the Cold War period, but has now been discontinued.

Western Australia's mineral wealth has transformed its state capital, Perth, into one of Australia's major cities. Perth is one of the world's most isolated cities. It is more than 2,500 miles (4,000 km) from the population centers of the eastern seaboard.

Population

Density of settlement in the region is generally low. Australia is one of the least densely populated countries on Earth with over 80% of its population living within 25 miles (40 km) of the coast – mostly in the southeast of the country. New Zealand, and the island groups of Melanesia, Micronesia, and Polynesia, are much more densely populated, although many of the smaller islands remain uninhabited.

Population density (people per sq mile)
- below 10
- 10–62
- 63–130
- 131–259
- 260–519
- 520–780
- above 780

The myriad of small coral islands *that are scattered across the Pacific Ocean are often uninhabited. They offer little shelter from the weather, often no fresh water, and only limited food supplies.*

The planes *of the Australian Royal Flying Doctor Service are able to cover large expanses of barren land quickly, bringing medical treatment to the most inaccessible and faraway places.*

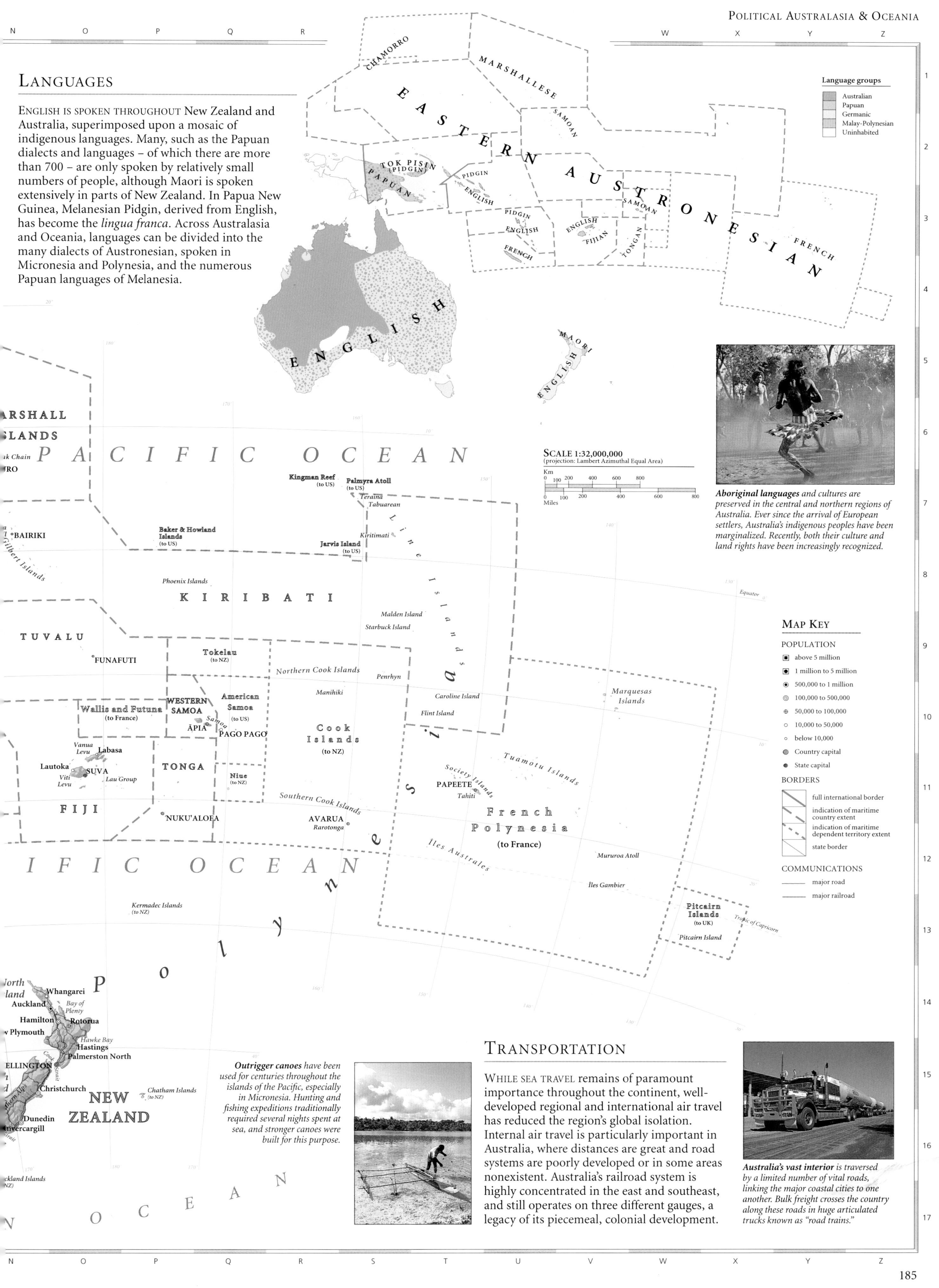

Language groups
Australian
Papuan
Germanic
Malay-Polynesian
Uninhabited
EASTERN AUSTRONESIAN
CHAMORRO
MARSHALLESE
SAMOAN
TOK PISIN (PIDGIN)
PAPUAN
PIDGIN
ENGLISH
FRENCH
FIJIAN
TONGAN
MAORI
ENGLISH
SCALE 1:32,000,000
(projection: Lambert Azimuthal Equal Area)
Km
Miles
PACIFIC OCEAN
Kingman Reef (to US)
Palmyra Atoll (to US)
Teraina
Tabuarean
Kiritimati
Line Islands
Baker & Howland Islands (to US)
Jarvis Island (to US)
BAIRIKI
Phoenix Islands
KIRIBATI
Malden Island
Starbuck Island
TUVALU
FUNAFUTI
Tokelau (to NZ)
Northern Cook Islands
Penrhyn
Manihiki
Caroline Island
Flint Island
Marquesas Islands
WESTERN SAMOA
APIA
American Samoa (to US)
PAGO PAGO
Wallis and Futuna (to France)
Cook Islands (to NZ)
Vanua Levu
Labasa
Lautoka
SUVA
Viti Levu
Lau Group
FIJI
TONGA
Niue (to NZ)
NUKU'ALOFA
Southern Cook Islands
AVARUA
Rarotonga
Society Islands
PAPEETE
Tahiti
Tuamotu Islands
French Polynesia (to France)
Iles Australes
Mururoa Atoll
Iles Gambier
Pitcairn Islands (to UK)
Pitcairn Island
Tropic of Capricorn
Equator
Kermadec Islands (to NZ)
Polynesia
Whangarei
Auckland
Bay of Plenty
Hamilton
Rotorua
Hawke Bay
Hastings
Palmerston North
Christchurch
Dunedin
Chatham Islands (to NZ)
NEW ZEALAND
MAP KEY
POPULATION
above 5 million
1 million to 5 million
500,000 to 1 million
100,000 to 500,000
50,000 to 100,000
10,000 to 50,000
below 10,000
Country capital
State capital
BORDERS
full international border
indication of maritime country extent
indication of maritime dependent territory extent
state border
COMMUNICATIONS
major road
major railroad

Languages

English is spoken throughout New Zealand and Australia, superimposed upon a mosaic of indigenous languages. Many, such as the Papuan dialects and languages – of which there are more than 700 – are only spoken by relatively small numbers of people, although Maori is spoken extensively in parts of New Zealand. In Papua New Guinea, Melanesian Pidgin, derived from English, has become the *lingua franca*. Across Australasia and Oceania, languages can be divided into the many dialects of Austronesian, spoken in Micronesia and Polynesia, and the numerous Papuan languages of Melanesia.

Aboriginal languages *and cultures are preserved in the central and northern regions of Australia. Ever since the arrival of European settlers, Australia's indigenous peoples have been marginalized. Recently, both their culture and land rights have been increasingly recognized.*

Outrigger canoes *have been used for centuries throughout the islands of the Pacific, especially in Micronesia. Hunting and fishing expeditions traditionally required several nights spent at sea, and stronger canoes were built for this purpose.*

Transportation

While sea travel remains of paramount importance throughout the continent, well-developed regional and international air travel has reduced the region's global isolation. Internal air travel is particularly important in Australia, where distances are great and road systems are poorly developed or in some areas nonexistent. Australia's railroad system is highly concentrated in the east and southeast, and still operates on three different gauges, a legacy of its piecemeal, colonial development.

Australia's vast interior *is traversed by a limited number of vital roads, linking the major coastal cities to one another. Bulk freight crosses the country along these roads in huge articulated trucks known as "road trains."*

Australasian and Oceanian Resources

Natural resources are of major economic importance throughout Australasia and Oceania. Australia in particular is a top world exporter of raw materials such as coal, iron ore, and bauxite, while New Zealand's agricultural economy is dominated by sheep-raising. Trade with western Europe has declined significantly in the last 20 years, and the Pacific Rim countries of Southeastern Asia are now the main trading partners, as well as a source of new settlers to the region. Australasia and Oceania's greatest resources are its climate and environment; tourism increasingly provides a vital source of income for the whole continent.

__The largely unpolluted__ waters of the Pacific Ocean support rich and varied marine life, much of which is farmed commercially. Here, oysters are gathered for market off the coast of New Zealand's South Island.

__Huge flocks of sheep__ are a common sight in New Zealand, where they outnumber people by 20 to 1. New Zealand is one of the world's largest exporters of wool and frozen lamb.

Standard of Living

In marked contrast to its neighbor, Australia, with one of the world's highest life expectancies and standards of living, Papua New Guinea is one of the world's least developed countries. In addition, high population growth and urbanization rates throughout the islands of the Pacific contribute to overcrowding. In Australia and New Zealand, the Aboriginal and Maori people have been isolated, although recently their land ownership rights have begun to be recognized in an effort to ease their social and economic isolation, and to improve living standards.

Standard of Living
(UN Human Development Index)
low
high
figures unavailable

Environmental Issues

The prospect of rising sea levels poses a threat to many low-lying islands in the Pacific. The testing of nuclear weapons, once common throughout the region, was finally discontinued in 1996. Australia's ecological balance has been irreversibly altered by the introduction of alien species. Although it has the world's largest underground water reserve, the Great Artesian Basin, the availability of fresh water in Australia remains critical. Periodic droughts combined with overgrazing lead to desertification and increase the risk of devastating bush fires.

Environmental Issues
- national parks
- tropical forest
- forest destroyed
- desert
- desertification
- polluted rivers
- radioactive contamination
- marine pollution
- heavy marine pollution
- poor urban air quality

__In 1946 Bikini Atoll,__ in the Marshall Islands, was chosen as the site for Operation Crossroads – investigating the effects of atomic bombs upon naval vessels. Further nuclear tests continued until 1958. The long-term environmental effects are unknown.

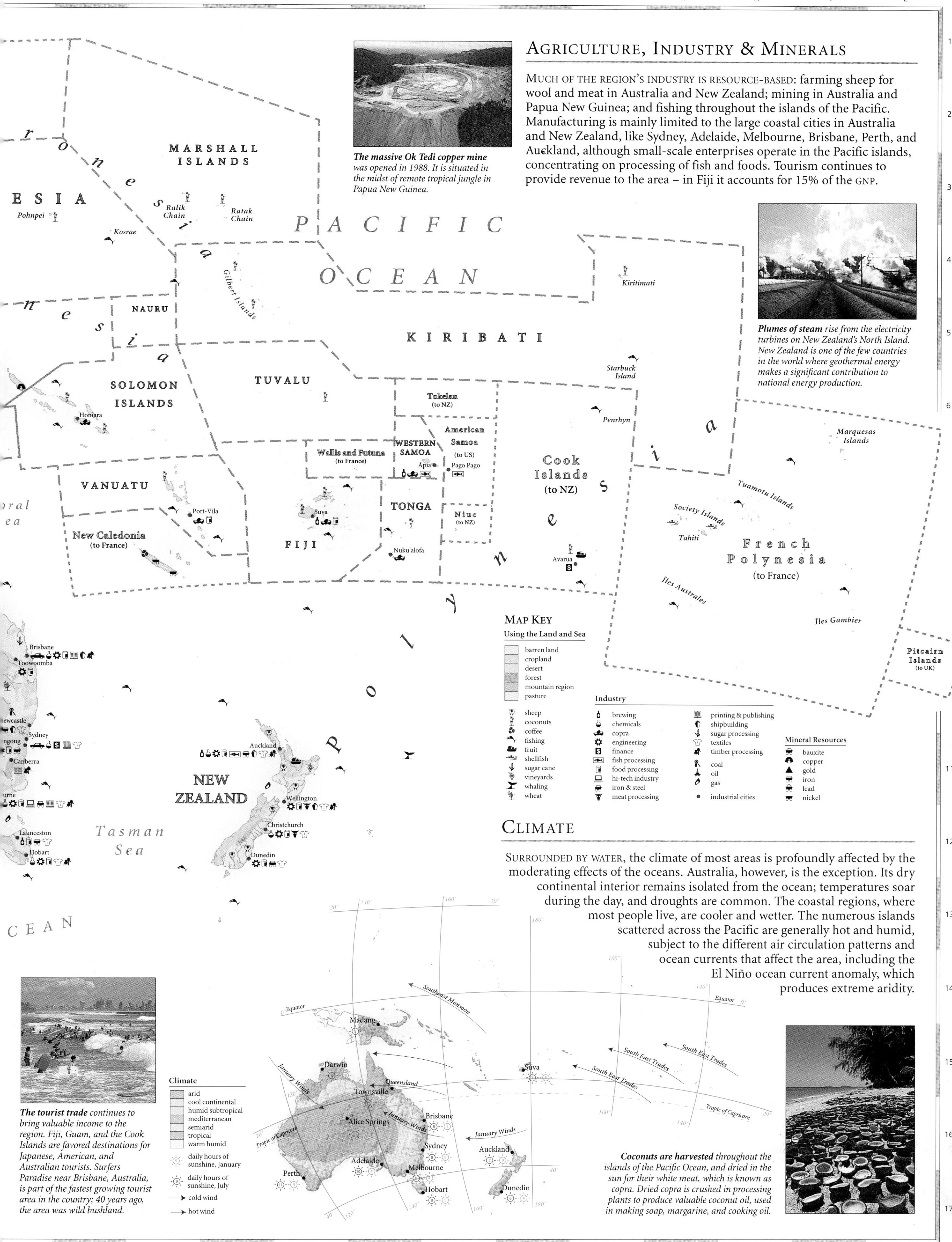

MARSHALL ISLANDS
Ralik Chain
Ratak Chain
Pohnpei
Kosrae
PACIFIC OCEAN
Gilbert Islands
NAURU
KIRIBATI
Kiritimati
Starbuck Island
SOLOMON ISLANDS
Honiara
TUVALU
Tokelau (to NZ)
American Samoa (to US)
Pago Pago
WESTERN SAMOA
Apia
Wallis and Futuna (to France)
Cook Islands (to NZ)
Penrhyn
Avarua
Marquesas Islands
Tuamotu Islands
Society Islands
Tahiti
French Polynesia (to France)
Iles Australes
Iles Gambier
Pitcairn Islands (to UK)
VANUATU
Port-Vila
New Caledonia (to France)
FIJI
Suva
TONGA
Nuku'alofa
Niue (to NZ)
Polynesia
Brisbane
Toowoomba
Newcastle
Sydney
Canberra
Launceston
Hobart
Tasman Sea
NEW ZEALAND
Auckland
Wellington
Christchurch
Dunedin
MAP KEY
Using the Land and Sea
barren land
cropland
desert
forest
mountain region
pasture
sheep
coconuts
coffee
fishing
fruit
shellfish
sugar cane
vineyards
whaling
wheat
Industry
brewing
chemicals
copra
engineering
finance
fish processing
food processing
hi-tech industry
iron & steel
meat processing
printing & publishing
shipbuilding
sugar processing
textiles
timber processing
coal
oil
gas
industrial cities
Mineral Resources
bauxite
copper
gold
iron
lead
nickel
Climate
arid
cool continental
humid subtropical
mediterranean
semiarid
tropical
warm humid
daily hours of sunshine, January
daily hours of sunshine, July
cold wind
hot wind
Equator
Southeast Monsoon
South East Trades
January Winds
Tropic of Capricorn
Madang
Darwin
Queensland
Townsville
Alice Springs
Brisbane
Sydney
Adelaide
Melbourne
Perth
Hobart
Auckland
Dunedin
Suva

AGRICULTURE, INDUSTRY & MINERALS

MUCH OF THE REGION'S INDUSTRY IS RESOURCE-BASED: farming sheep for wool and meat in Australia and New Zealand; mining in Australia and Papua New Guinea; and fishing throughout the islands of the Pacific. Manufacturing is mainly limited to the large coastal cities in Australia and New Zealand, like Sydney, Adelaide, Melbourne, Brisbane, Perth, and Auckland, although small-scale enterprises operate in the Pacific islands, concentrating on processing of fish and foods. Tourism continues to provide revenue to the area – in Fiji it accounts for 15% of the GNP.

The massive Ok Tedi copper mine *was opened in 1988. It is situated in the midst of remote tropical jungle in Papua New Guinea.*

Plumes of steam *rise from the electricity turbines on New Zealand's North Island. New Zealand is one of the few countries in the world where geothermal energy makes a significant contribution to national energy production.*

CLIMATE

SURROUNDED BY WATER, the climate of most areas is profoundly affected by the moderating effects of the oceans. Australia, however, is the exception. Its dry continental interior remains isolated from the ocean; temperatures soar during the day, and droughts are common. The coastal regions, where most people live, are cooler and wetter. The numerous islands scattered across the Pacific are generally hot and humid, subject to the different air circulation patterns and ocean currents that affect the area, including the El Niño ocean current anomaly, which produces extreme aridity.

The tourist trade *continues to bring valuable income to the region. Fiji, Guam, and the Cook Islands are favored destinations for Japanese, American, and Australian tourists. Surfers Paradise near Brisbane, Australia, is part of the fastest growing tourist area in the country; 40 years ago, the area was wild bushland.*

Coconuts are harvested *throughout the islands of the Pacific Ocean, and dried in the sun for their white meat, which is known as copra. Dried copra is crushed in processing plants to produce valuable coconut oil, used in making soap, margarine, and cooking oil.*

AUSTRALIA

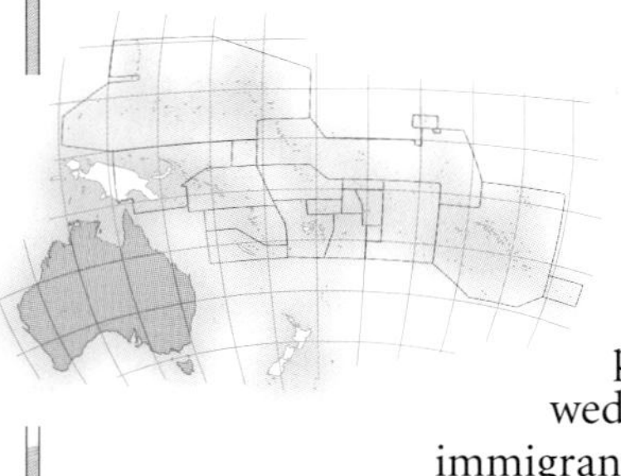

AUSTRALIA IS THE WORLD'S smallest continent, a stable landmass lying between the Indian and Pacific oceans. Previously home to its aboriginal peoples only, since the end of the 18th century immigration has transformed the face of the country. Initially settlers came mainly from western Europe, particularly the UK, and for years Australia remained wedded to its British colonial past. More recent immigrants have come from eastern Europe, and from Asian countries such as Japan, South Korea, and Indonesia. Australia is now forging strong trading links with these "Pacific Rim" countries and its economic future seems to lie with Asia and the Americas, rather than Europe, its traditional partner.

Uluru (***Ayers Rock***), *the world's largest freestanding rock, is a massive outcrop of red sandstone in Australia's desert center. Wind and sandstorms have ground the rock into the smooth curves seen here. Uluru is revered as a sacred site by many aboriginal peoples.*

SCALE 1:10,500,000
(projection: Lambert Conformal Conic)

Km 0 25 50 100 150 200 250 300 350
Miles 0 25 50 100 150 200 250 300 350

MAP KEY

POPULATION	ELEVATION
1 million to 5 million	2000m / 6562ft
500,000 to 1 million	1000m / 3281ft
100,000 to 500,000	500m / 1640ft
50,000 to 100,000	250m / 820ft
10,000 to 50,000	100m / 328ft
below 10,000	sea level

160

USING THE LAND

OVER 165 MILLION SHEEP are dispersed in vast herds around the country, contributing to a major export industry. Cattle-ranching is important, particularly in the west. Wheat, and grapes for Australia's wine industry, are grown mainly in the south. Much of the country is desert, unsuitable for agriculture unless irrigation is used.

THE URBAN/RURAL POPULATION DIVIDE

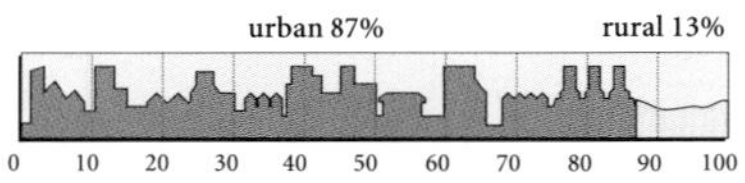

urban 87% — rural 13%

0 10 20 30 40 50 60 70 80 90 100

POPULATION DENSITY	TOTAL LAND AREA
5 people per sq mile (2 people per sq km)	2,967,893 sq miles (7,686,850 sq km)

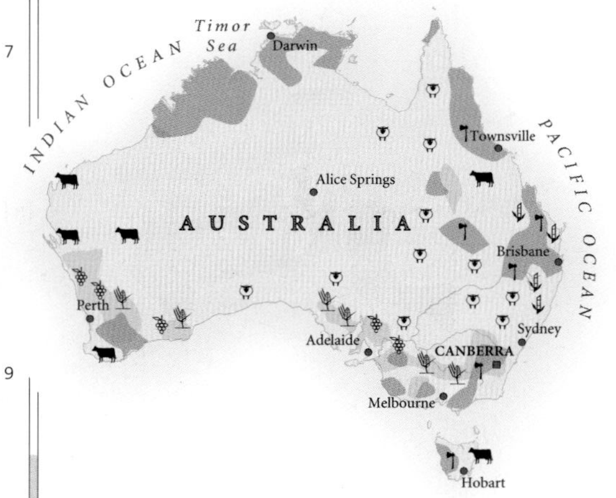

Land use and agricultural distribution

cattle, sheep, cereals, sugar cane, timber, vineyards, capital cities, major towns, pasture, cropland, forest, desert, mountain region

Lines of ripening vines stretch for miles in Barossa Valley, a major wine-growing region near Adelaide.

THE LANDSCAPE

AUSTRALIA CONSISTS OF MANY ERODED PLATEAUS, lying firmly in the middle of the Indo-Australian Plate. It is the world's flattest continent, and the driest, after Antarctica. The coasts tend to be more hilly and fertile, especially in the east. The mountains of the Great Dividing Range form a natural barrier between the eastern coastal areas and the flat, dry plains and desert regions of the Australian "outback."

The Great Barrier Reef *is the world's largest area of coral islands and reefs. It runs for about 1,240 miles (2,000 km) along the Queensland coast.*

The Pinnacles *are a series of rugged sandstone pillars. Their strange shapes have been formed by water and wind erosion.*

The ancient Kimberley Plateau is the source of some of Australia's richest mineral deposits, including diamonds.

Arnhem Land

Uluru (Ayers Rock)

The tropical rain forest of the Cape York Peninsula contains more than 600 different varieties of tree.

Great Artesian Basin

The Great Dividing Range forms a watershed between east- and west-flowing rivers. Erosion has created deep valleys, gorges, and waterfalls where rivers tumble over escarpments on their way to the sea.

More than half of Australia rests on a uniform shield over 600 million years old. It is one of the Earth's original geological plates.

Murray/Darling River

Australian Alps

The Nullarbor Plain is a low-lying limestone plateau which is so flat that the Trans-Australian Railway runs through it in a straight line for more than 300 miles (483 km).

The Simpson Desert has a number of large salt pans, created by the evaporation of past rivers and now sourced by seasonal rains. Some are crusted with gypsum, but most are covered by common salt crystals.

The Lake Eyre Basin, lying 51 ft (16 m) below sea level, is one of the largest inland drainage systems in the world, covering an area of more than 500,000 sq miles (1,300,000 sq km).

Tasmania has the same geological structure as the Australian Alps. During the last period of glaciation, 18,000 years ago, sea levels were some 300 ft (100 m) lower and it was joined to the mainland.

Great Artesian Basin

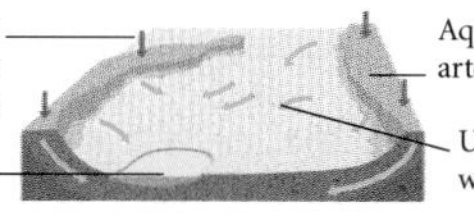

Rainwater replenishes aquifer — Aquifers from which artesian water is obtained — Lake Eyre — Underground water movements

The Great Artesian Basin *underlies nearly 20% of the total area of Australia, providing a valuable store of underground water, essential to Australian agriculture. The ephemeral rivers which drain the northern part of the basin have highly braided courses and, in consequence, the area is known as "channel country."*

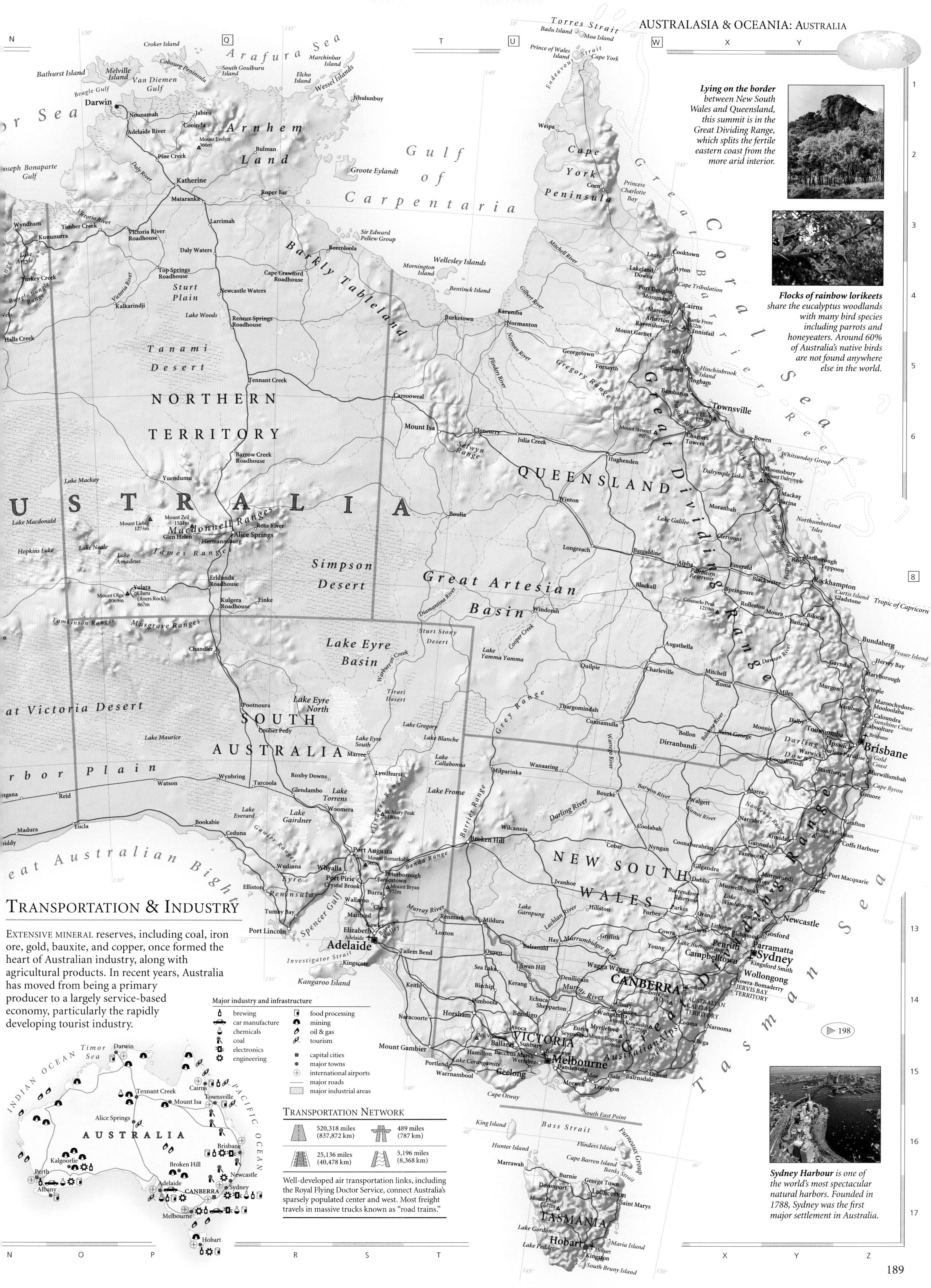
Arafura Sea
Timor Sea
Gulf of Carpentaria
Coral Sea
Tasman Sea
Great Australian Bight
Torres Strait
Bass Strait
Arnhem Land
Cape York Peninsula
NORTHERN TERRITORY
QUEENSLAND
SOUTH AUSTRALIA
NEW SOUTH WALES
VICTORIA
TASMANIA
AUSTRALIAN CAPITAL TERRITORY
JERVIS BAY TERRITORY
CANBERRA
AUSTRALIA
Great Barrier Reef
Great Dividing Range
Great Artesian Basin
Simpson Desert
Tanami Desert
Sturt Plain
Barkly Tableland
Lake Eyre Basin
Lake Eyre North
Lake Eyre South
Nullarbor Plain
Great Victoria Desert
Sturt Stony Desert
Tirari Desert
Macdonnell Ranges
Musgrave Ranges
Flinders Ranges
Australian Alps
Darwin
Alice Springs
Brisbane
Sydney
Melbourne
Adelaide
Hobart
Townsville
Cairns
Newcastle
Wollongong
Mount Isa
Tennant Creek
Katherine
Tropic of Capricorn
Melville Island
Bathurst Island
Groote Eylandt
Wellesley Islands
Whitsunday Group
Fraser Island
Kangaroo Island
King Island
Flinders Island
Furneaux Group
Cape York
Yorke Peninsula
Eyre Peninsula
Spencer Gulf
Uluru (Ayers Rock) 867m
Mount Kosciuszko 2228m
Lake Frome
Lake Torrens
Lake Gairdner
Lake Amadeus
Lake Mackay
▶ 198

Lying on the border between New South Wales and Queensland, this summit is in the Great Dividing Range, which splits the fertile eastern coast from the more arid interior.

Flocks of rainbow lorikeets share the eucalyptus woodlands with many bird species including parrots and honeyeaters. Around 60% of Australia's native birds are not found anywhere else in the world.

Sydney Harbour is one of the world's most spectacular natural harbors. Founded in 1788, Sydney was the first major settlement in Australia.

Transportation & Industry

Extensive mineral reserves, including coal, iron ore, gold, bauxite, and copper, once formed the heart of Australian industry, along with agricultural products. In recent years, Australia has moved from being a primary producer to a largely service-based economy, particularly the rapidly developing tourist industry.

Major industry and infrastructure
- brewing
- car manufacture
- chemicals
- coal
- electronics
- engineering
- food processing
- mining
- oil & gas
- tourism
- capital cities
- major towns
- international airports
- major roads
- major industrial areas

Transportation Network

520,318 miles (837,872 km)	489 miles (787 km)
25,136 miles (40,478 km)	5,196 miles (8,368 km)

Well-developed air transportation links, including the Royal Flying Doctor Service, connect Australia's sparsely populated center and west. Most freight travels in massive trucks known as "road trains."

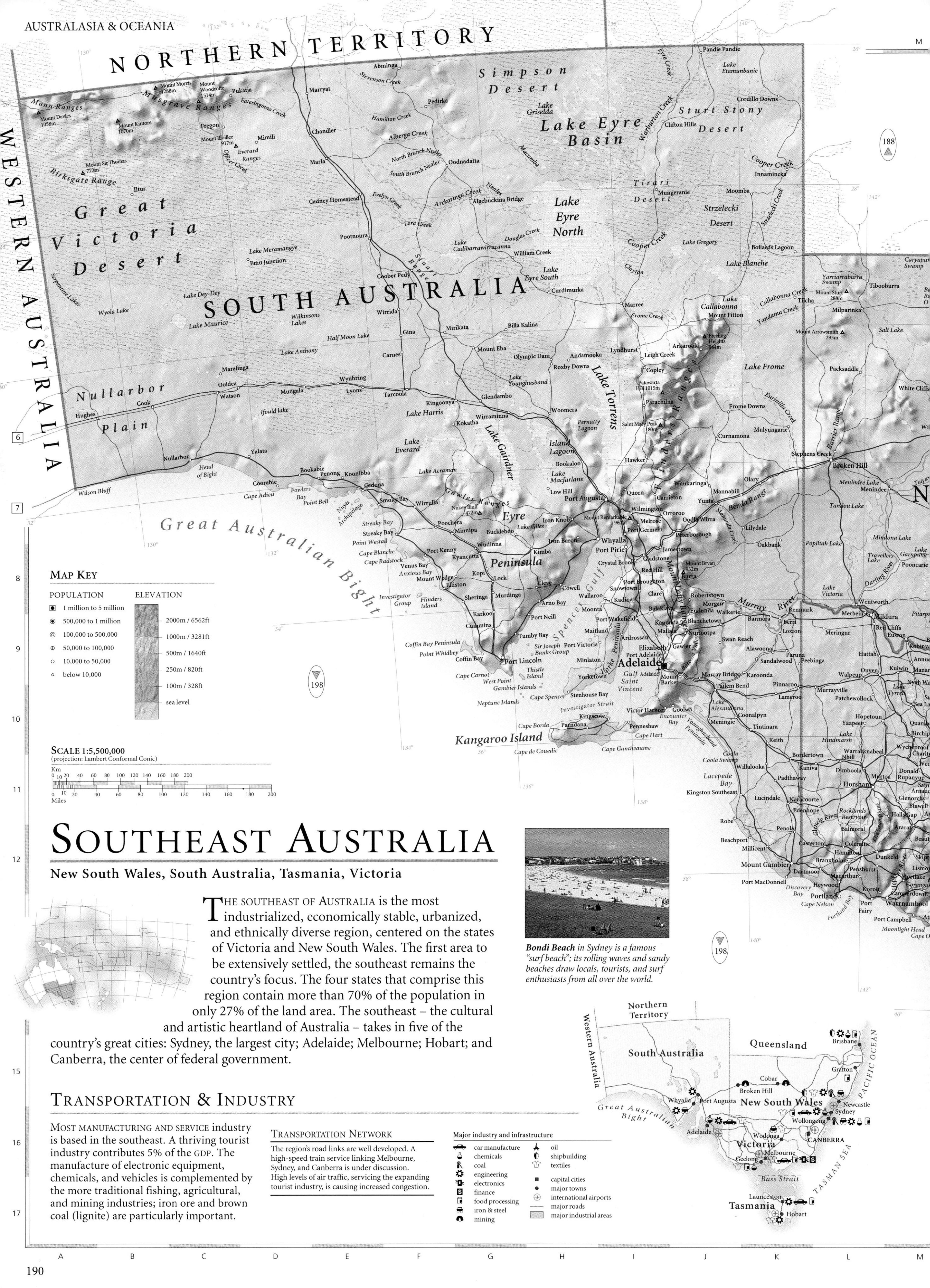
NORTHERN TERRITORY
WESTERN AUSTRALIA
SOUTH AUSTRALIA
Simpson Desert
Lake Eyre Basin
Sturt Stony Desert
Great Victoria Desert
Lake Eyre North
Lake Eyre South
Tirari Desert
Strzelecki Desert
Nullarbor Plain
Great Australian Bight
Eyre Peninsula
Lake Torrens
Lake Gairdner
Flinders Ranges
Spencer Gulf
Gulf Saint Vincent
Kangaroo Island
Adelaide
Port Augusta
Whyalla
Port Pirie
Port Lincoln
Broken Hill
Mount Gambier
Murray River
Lake Frome
Coober Pedy
Musgrave Ranges
Stuart Ranges
Gawler Ranges
Investigator Strait
Mildura
MAP KEY
POPULATION
1 million to 5 million
500,000 to 1 million
100,000 to 500,000
50,000 to 100,000
10,000 to 50,000
below 10,000
ELEVATION
2000m / 6562ft
1000m / 3281ft
500m / 1640ft
250m / 820ft
100m / 328ft
sea level
SCALE 1:5,500,000
(projection: Lambert Conformal Conic)
Km
Miles
Northern Territory
Western Australia
South Australia
Queensland
New South Wales
Victoria
Tasmania
Great Australian Bight
Bass Strait
TASMAN SEA
PACIFIC OCEAN
Brisbane
Grafton
Cobar
Broken Hill
Whyalla
Port Augusta
Newcastle
Sydney
Wollongong
Adelaide
Wodonga
CANBERRA
Melbourne
Geelong
Launceston
Hobart

SOUTHEAST AUSTRALIA

New South Wales, South Australia, Tasmania, Victoria

THE SOUTHEAST OF AUSTRALIA is the most industrialized, economically stable, urbanized, and ethnically diverse region, centered on the states of Victoria and New South Wales. The first area to be extensively settled, the southeast remains the country's focus. The four states that comprise this region contain more than 70% of the population in only 27% of the land area. The southeast – the cultural and artistic heartland of Australia – takes in five of the country's great cities: Sydney, the largest city; Adelaide; Melbourne; Hobart; and Canberra, the center of federal government.

Bondi Beach *in Sydney is a famous "surf beach"; its rolling waves and sandy beaches draw locals, tourists, and surf enthusiasts from all over the world.*

TRANSPORTATION & INDUSTRY

MOST MANUFACTURING AND SERVICE industry is based in the southeast. A thriving tourist industry contributes 5% of the GDP. The manufacture of electronic equipment, chemicals, and vehicles is complemented by the more traditional fishing, agricultural, and mining industries; iron ore and brown coal (lignite) are particularly important.

TRANSPORTATION NETWORK

The region's road links are well developed. A high-speed train service linking Melbourne, Sydney, and Canberra is under discussion. High levels of air traffic, servicing the expanding tourist industry, is causing increased congestion.

Major industry and infrastructure

- car manufacture
- chemicals
- coal
- engineering
- electronics
- finance
- food processing
- iron & steel
- mining
- oil
- shipbuilding
- textiles
- capital cities
- major towns
- international airports
- major roads
- major industrial areas

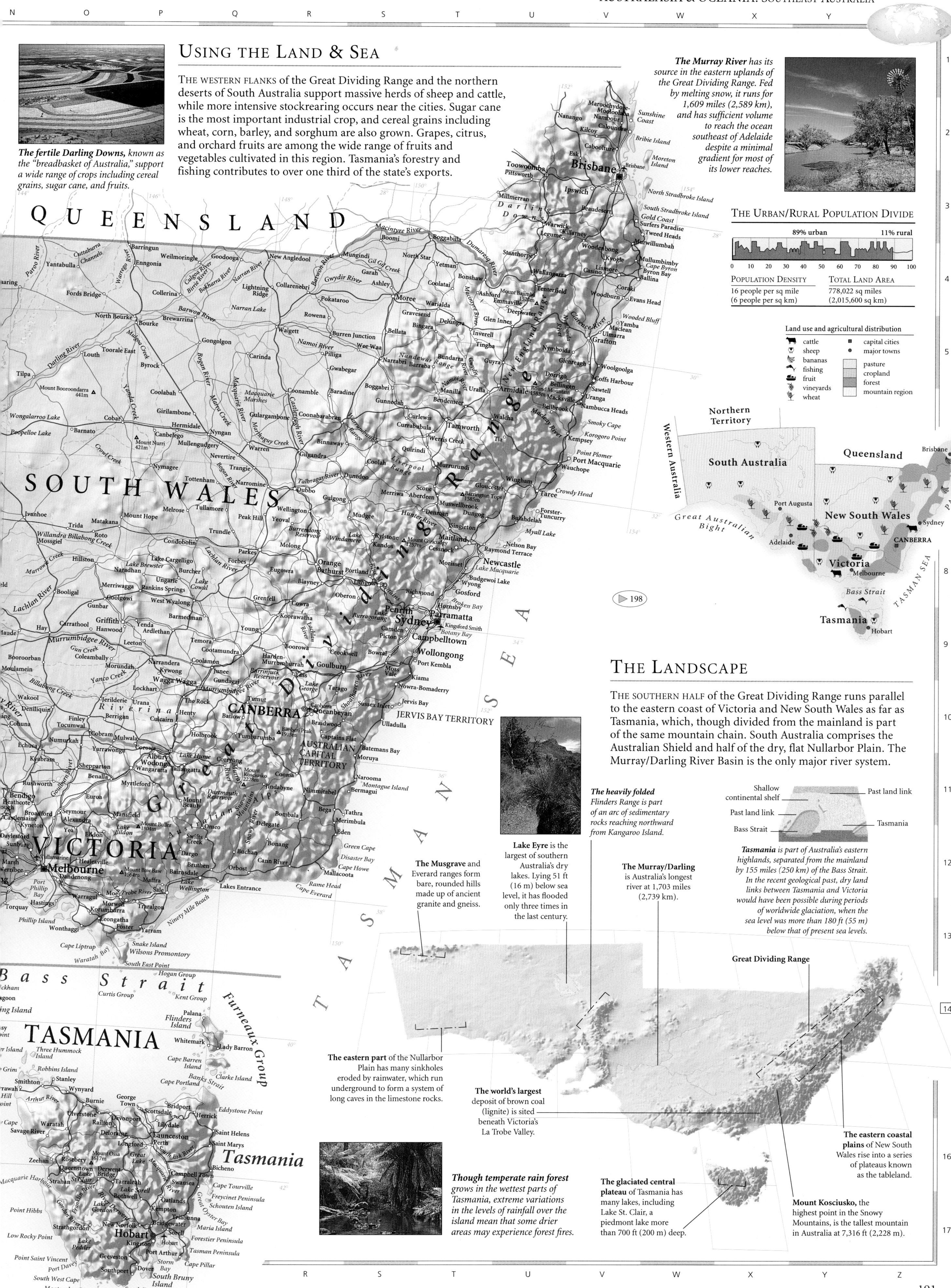
QUEENSLAND
NEW SOUTH WALES
VICTORIA
TASMANIA
TASMAN SEA
Bass Strait
Great Dividing Range
Brisbane
Sydney
CANBERRA
Melbourne
Hobart
Newcastle
Wollongong
AUSTRALIAN CAPITAL TERRITORY
JERVIS BAY TERRITORY
198
THE URBAN/RURAL POPULATION DIVIDE
89% urban
11% rural
0 10 20 30 40 50 60 70 80 90 100
POPULATION DENSITY
16 people per sq mile
(6 people per sq km)
TOTAL LAND AREA
778,022 sq miles
(2,015,600 sq km)
Land use and agricultural distribution
cattle
sheep
bananas
fishing
fruit
vineyards
wheat
capital cities
major towns
pasture
cropland
forest
mountain region
Northern Territory
Western Australia
South Australia
Queensland
New South Wales
Victoria
Tasmania
Great Australian Bight
PACIFIC OCEAN
Port Augusta
Adelaide
Shallow continental shelf
Past land link
Bass Strait
Tasmania
Great Dividing Range

USING THE LAND & SEA

THE WESTERN FLANKS of the Great Dividing Range and the northern deserts of South Australia support massive herds of sheep and cattle, while more intensive stockrearing occurs near the cities. Sugar cane is the most important industrial crop, and cereal grains including wheat, corn, barley, and sorghum are also grown. Grapes, citrus, and orchard fruits are among the wide range of fruits and vegetables cultivated in this region. Tasmania's forestry and fishing contributes to over one third of the state's exports.

The fertile Darling Downs, *known as the "breadbasket of Australia," support a wide range of crops including cereal grains, sugar cane, and fruits.*

The Murray River *has its source in the eastern uplands of the Great Dividing Range. Fed by melting snow, it runs for 1,609 miles (2,589 km), and has sufficient volume to reach the ocean southeast of Adelaide despite a minimal gradient for most of its lower reaches.*

THE LANDSCAPE

THE SOUTHERN HALF of the Great Dividing Range runs parallel to the eastern coast of Victoria and New South Wales as far as Tasmania, which, though divided from the mainland is part of the same mountain chain. South Australia comprises the Australian Shield and half of the dry, flat Nullarbor Plain. The Murray/Darling River Basin is the only major river system.

The heavily folded *Flinders Range is part of an arc of sedimentary rocks reaching northward from Kangaroo Island.*

Tasmania *is part of Australia's eastern highlands, separated from the mainland by 155 miles (250 km) of the Bass Strait. In the recent geological past, dry land links between Tasmania and Victoria would have been possible during periods of worldwide glaciation, when the sea level was more than 180 ft (55 m) below that of present sea levels.*

Lake Eyre is the largest of southern Australia's dry lakes. Lying 51 ft (16 m) below sea level, it has flooded only three times in the last century.

The Musgrave and Everard ranges form bare, rounded hills made up of ancient granite and gneiss.

The Murray/Darling is Australia's longest river at 1,703 miles (2,739 km).

The eastern part of the Nullarbor Plain has many sinkholes eroded by rainwater, which run underground to form a system of long caves in the limestone rocks.

The world's largest deposit of brown coal (lignite) is sited beneath Victoria's La Trobe Valley.

The eastern coastal plains of New South Wales rise into a series of plateaus known as the tableland.

Though temperate rain forest *grows in the wettest parts of Tasmania, extreme variations in the levels of rainfall over the island mean that some drier areas may experience forest fires.*

The glaciated central plateau of Tasmania has many lakes, including Lake St. Clair, a piedmont lake more than 700 ft (200 m) deep.

Mount Kosciusko, the highest point in the Snowy Mountains, is the tallest mountain in Australia at 7,316 ft (2,228 m).

New Zealand

Lying 1,500 miles east-southeast of Australia, New Zealand was originally settled by the Maori people of Polynesia. It was visited by Europeans for the first time only as recently as the 1770s. The islands' rugged topography means that most settlement has concentrated in coastal areas. People of European origin make up more than 85% of the 3.5 million population, following immigration which began in the 1920s. Many recent settlers have come from Asia, including India and China, and a number of the Pacific islands. The Maori now make up a minority of less than half a million. Their ancient claims to at least half of national territory, however, are gaining increasing legal credence.

The Landscape

New Zealand comprises two large islands and many scattered smaller islands. On South Island, the Alpine Fault marks the boundary between the Pacific and Indo-Australian plates. Tectonic activity has strongly influenced the formation of the Southern Alps, snowcapped mountains with several peaks over 9,800 ft (3,000 m). North Island has a lower and less extensive mountain region, containing forested hills, a central volcanic plateau, and downlands.

Mountain-building in the Southern Alps
South Island
North Island
Southern Alps
Alpine Fault
Indo-Australian Plate
Pacific Plate
Northland
Rotorua
Probable location of Alpine Fault
SCALE 1:2,750,000
(projection: Lambert Conformal Conic)
Km
Miles
PACIFIC OCEAN
TASMAN SEA
NEW ZEALAND
North Island
NORTHLAND
AUCKLAND
WAIKATO
BAY OF PLENTY
GISBORNE
HAWKE'S BAY
TARANAKI
MANAWATU-WANGANUI
Ninety Mile Beach
Auckland
Hamilton
Rotorua
Tauranga
New Plymouth
Napier
Hastings
Gisborne
Palmerston North
Wanganui
Whangarei
Lake Taupo
Bay of Plenty
Hawke Bay
Coromandel Peninsula
Hauraki Gulf
Great Barrier Island
North Taranaki Bight
South Taranaki Bight
198

The Southern Alps have been formed by "slip" faulting. The Indo-Australian and Pacific plates run in opposite directions along the Alpine Fault. Although they slide past each other, they are also being thrust over one another, causing the continental crust of the Pacific Plate to be uplifted to form the Alps.

The Northland region is characterized by many coastal inlets. These are lined by mangrove swamps, signaling the change to a subtropical climate in the far north of the island.

The Rotorua and Taupo valleys have some of the largest and most spectacular thermal springs in New Zealand. These occur when superheated groundwater rises to the surface through joints in the rocks.

Mount Taranaki, rising 8,261 ft (2,518 m), is an isolated, dormant volcano.

The boundary between the Indo-Australian Plate and the Pacific Plate runs through the center of North Island, leading to many typical volcanic features. The plateau which rises from the slopes of Lake Taupo contains a string of active volcanoes.

Lake Taupo is New Zealand's largest inland lake. It occupies the crater of an extinct volcano.

The Southern Alps run for more than 300 miles, (483 km) forming the backbone of South Island. They were uplifted following the collision of the Pacific and Indo-Australian plates.

Fiordland in the far southwest, contains a large number of flooded glacial valleys.

The Tasman Glacier, the largest glacier in New Zealand, flows for 18 miles (29 km), down the slopes of New Zealand's highest mountain, Mount Cook.

The coastal Canterbury Plains are the result of glacial outwash. They are the only major flat area in New Zealand.

The Southern Alps contain more than 360 glaciers, including the Murchison, Mueller, and Godley glaciers on the eastern slopes and the Fox and Franz Josef glaciers to the west.

High levels of rainfall and a steep topography make New Zealand's rivers run swiftly. In the southern reaches of both islands, rivers such as the Mokoreta form broad, braided streams.

Clouds of steam rise from White Island, an active, offshore volcano lying in the Bay of Plenty, off the northern coast of North Island.

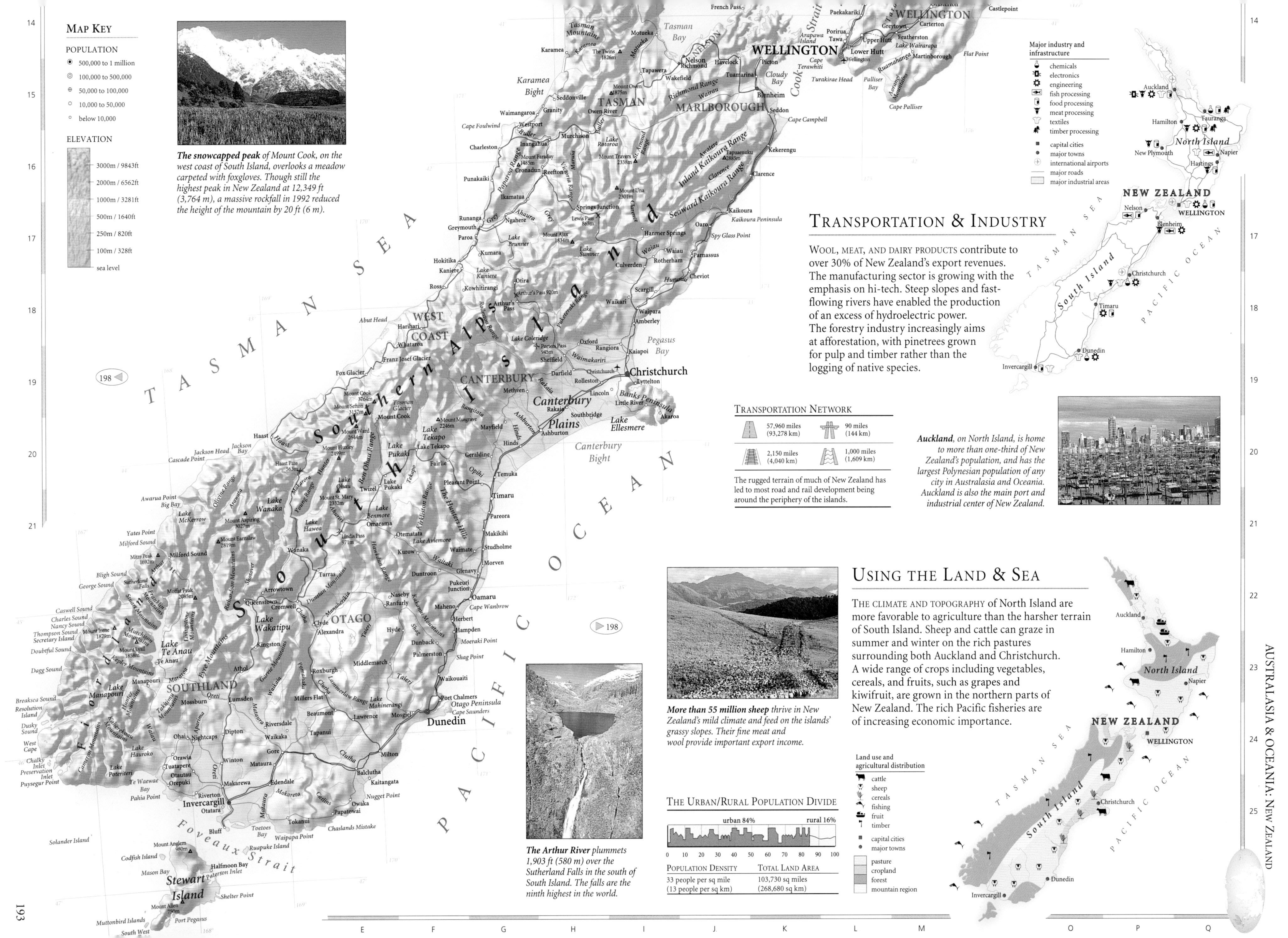
MAP KEY
POPULATION
500,000 to 1 million
100,000 to 500,000
50,000 to 100,000
10,000 to 50,000
below 10,000
ELEVATION
3000m / 9843ft
2000m / 6562ft
1000m / 3281ft
500m / 1640ft
250m / 820ft
100m / 328ft
sea level
TASMAN SEA
PACIFIC OCEAN
Southern Alps
South Island
Stewart Island
Foveaux Strait
Cook Strait
WELLINGTON
Christchurch
Dunedin
Invercargill
Canterbury Plains
CANTERBURY
WEST COAST
TASMAN
MARLBOROUGH
NELSON
OTAGO
SOUTHLAND
Fiordland
198
Major industry and infrastructure
chemicals
electronics
engineering
fish processing
food processing
meat processing
textiles
timber processing
capital cities
major towns
international airports
major roads
major industrial areas
NEW ZEALAND
North Island
Auckland
Hamilton
Tauranga
New Plymouth
Napier
Hastings
Nelson
Blenheim
Timaru
Land use and agricultural distribution
cattle
sheep
cereals
fishing
fruit
timber
capital cities
major towns
pasture
cropland
forest
mountain region

The snowcapped peak of Mount Cook, on the west coast of South Island, overlooks a meadow carpeted with foxgloves. Though still the highest peak in New Zealand at 12,349 ft (3,764 m), a massive rockfall in 1992 reduced the height of the mountain by 20 ft (6 m).

Transportation & Industry

WOOL, MEAT, AND DAIRY PRODUCTS contribute to over 30% of New Zealand's export revenues. The manufacturing sector is growing with the emphasis on hi-tech. Steep slopes and fast-flowing rivers have enabled the production of an excess of hydroelectric power. The forestry industry increasingly aims at afforestation, with pinetrees grown for pulp and timber rather than the logging of native species.

Transportation Network

57,960 miles (93,278 km)	90 miles (144 km)
2,150 miles (4,040 km)	1,000 miles (1,609 km)

The rugged terrain of much of New Zealand has led to most road and rail development being around the periphery of the islands.

Auckland, on North Island, is home to more than one-third of New Zealand's population, and has the largest Polynesian population of any city in Australasia and Oceania. Auckland is also the main port and industrial center of New Zealand.

Using the Land & Sea

THE CLIMATE AND TOPOGRAPHY of North Island are more favorable to agriculture than the harsher terrain of South Island. Sheep and cattle can graze in summer and winter on the rich pastures surrounding both Auckland and Christchurch. A wide range of crops including vegetables, cereals, and fruits, such as grapes and kiwifruit, are grown in the northern parts of New Zealand. The rich Pacific fisheries are of increasing economic importance.

More than 55 million sheep thrive in New Zealand's mild climate and feed on the islands' grassy slopes. Their fine meat and wool provide important export income.

The Urban/Rural Population Divide

urban 84% — rural 16%

Population Density	Total Land Area
33 people per sq mile (13 people per sq km)	103,730 sq miles (268,680 sq km)

The Arthur River plummets 1,903 ft (580 m) over the Sutherland Falls in the south of South Island. The falls are the ninth highest in the world.

Papua New Guinea & The Solomon Islands

Cut off by inaccessible, largely mountainous terrain, the peoples of Papua New Guinea have maintained a remarkable diversity of language and culture. There are over 750 separate languages, and yet more distinct tribes. Much of the country remains isolated, with many of the indigenous inhabitants of the interior living as hunter-gatherers. To the east of Papua New Guinea, the Solomons form an archipelago of several hundred islands, scattered over an area of 252,897 sq miles (655,000 sq km). The Solomon Islanders, a mainly Melanesian people, live on the six largest islands.

Transportation & Industry

Papua New Guinea has substantial mineral resources including the world's largest copper reserves at Panguna on Bougainville Island; gold, and potential oil and natural gas. Political instability on Bougainville and an undeveloped infrastructure deters the investment necessary for exploitation of these reserves. The Solomon Islanders rely mainly on copra and timber with some production of palm oil and cocoa. Traditional crafts are made for the tourist market and for export.

Transportation Network

Roads	416 miles (670 km)
Motorways	None
Railways	None
Waterways	6,794 miles (10,940 km)

Much of Papua New Guinea and the Solomons is inaccessible by road. A network of airstrips serves even remote villages on the islands. The Solomons' airport has been extended to take jumbo jets to improve connections for tourism.

PACIFIC OCEAN
Manus I.
Bismarck Archipelago
Kavieng
Wewak
Bismarck Sea
Rabaul
PAPUA NEW GUINEA
Bougainville Island
INDONESIA
Mount Hagen
Madang
Ok Tedi
Lae
New Britain
Panguna
Kieta
New Guinea
Solomon Sea
SOLOMON ISLANDS
Auki
PORT MORESBY
HONIARA
CORAL SEA
Louisiade Archipelago

Major industry and infrastructure
- beverages
- coffee processing
- copra processing
- food processing
- mining
- textiles
- timber processing
- capital cities
- major towns
- international airports
- major roads

The slopes of this extinct volcano near Talasea on the island of New Britain have been almost entirely colonized by rain forest vegetation.

Using the Land & Sea

Most agriculture in Papua New Guinea is at a subsistence level, with more than two-thirds of the land used for rough grazing, particularly for pigs. The tropical rain forest is a rich timber resource. The Solomon Islanders rely heavily on coconuts for export revenue and fishing, mainly for tuna, is a staple industry.

Land use and agricultural distribution
- bananas
- cocoa
- coconuts
- fishing
- oil palms
- rubber
- timber
- capital cities
- major towns
- cropland
- forest
- wetland

***Over 70% of Papua New Guinea** is covered by dense, tropical rain forest, sustained by high levels of rainfall. Uncontrolled logging in the formerly inaccessible rain forest has led to species loss and soil erosion on steep slopes.*

The Urban/Rural Population Divide

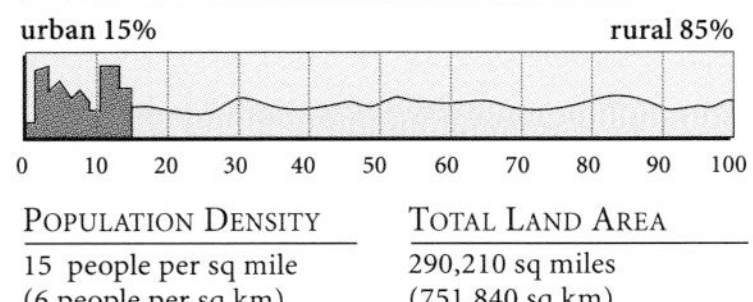

urban 15%
rural 85%
0 10 20 30 40 50 60 70 80 90 100

Population Density	Total Land Area
15 people per sq mile (6 people per sq km)	290,210 sq miles (751,840 sq km)

Map Key

Population	Elevation
100,000 to 500,000	4000m / 13,124ft
50,000 to 100,000	3000m / 9843ft
10,000 to 50,000	2000m / 6562ft
below 10,000	1000m / 3281ft
	500m / 1640ft
	250m / 820ft
	100m / 328ft
	sea level

173

***Huli tribesmen** from Southern Highlands Province in Papua New Guinea parade in ceremonial dress, their powdered wigs decorated with exotic plumage and their faces and bodies painted with colored pigments.*

SCALE 1:5,500,000
(projection: Mercator)

Km 0 10 20 40 60 80 100 120 140 160 180 200
Miles 0 10 20 40 60 80 100 120 140 160 180 200

THE LANDSCAPE

THE PLATE MARGIN between the Pacific and Indo-Australian plates runs through the mainland of Papua New Guinea, which is dominated by steep and forested mountain ranges. The 600 or so outer islands are mainly high, volcanic islands, fringed by coral reefs. The Solomons comprise six large volcanic islands which form two parallel chains, and several hundred small islands and atolls.

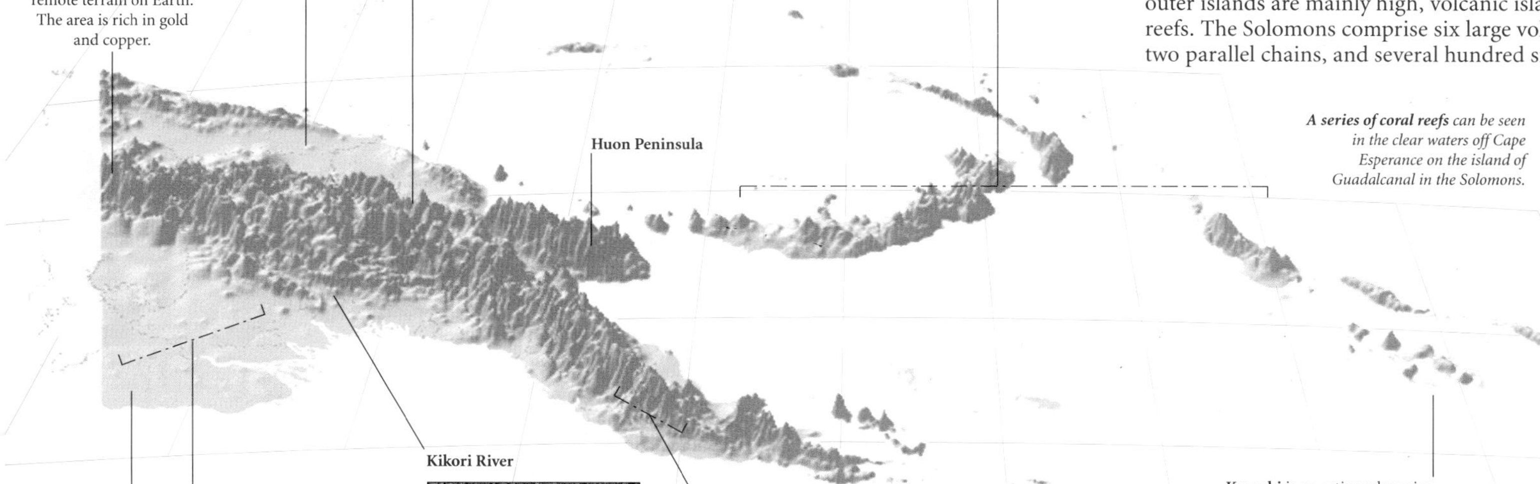

The Sepik River drains the lowlands north of the Central Range, flowing eastward into the Bismarck Sea.

The Bismarck Range is precipitous, rugged, and covered in dense vegetation, rising to 14,793 ft (4,509 m) at Mount Wilhelm in central Papua New Guinea.

Most of Papua New Guinea's outlying islands, including New Britain, Bougainville Island, and New Ireland, are precipitous and of volcanic origin.

The Star Mountains include some of the most remote terrain on Earth. The area is rich in gold and copper.

Huon Peninsula

A series of coral reefs can be seen in the clear waters off Cape Esperance on the island of Guadalcanal in the Solomons.

Cape Esperance

Kikori River

Southern Papua New Guinea is part of the Indo-Australian Plate. New Guinea only became separated physically from Australia about 8,000 years ago, following the flooding of the Torres Strait.

The lowland plains in the south and north of the main island are swampy, and contain fertile alluvial soil. This contrasts with the mountainous islands in the rest of Papua New Guinea where soils are generally thin and nutrients are retained in the existing vegetation.

Papua New Guinea's rivers, *though fairly short, carry extremely high sediment loads, largely due to soil erosion. This is caused by a combination of very steep slopes and heavy rainfall, and is made worse by forest clearance, particularly "slash and burn" techniques and road or mine operations.*

Kavachi is an active submarine volcano near New Georgia, which erupts every few years.

The Owen Stanley Range contains several of Papua New Guinea's highest peaks, the greatest of which is Mount Victoria at 13,200 ft (4,035 m).

The Louisiade Archipelago contains 10 volcanic islands and numerous coral islets. Tagula Island is the largest of the islands, containing the archipelago's highest peak at 2,645 ft (806 m).

Huon Peninsula

Caves and undercut cliffs mark former shoreline

Stream cuts down through recently exposed land

Former level of beach

Current beach

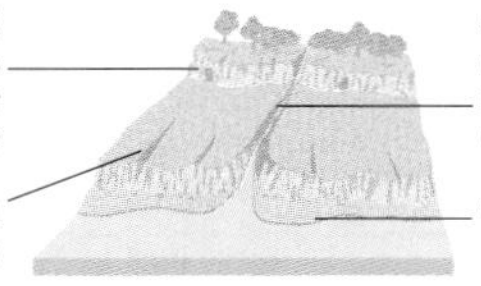

Uplift of the land *in tectonically active regions can lead to former coastlines being lifted beyond the reach of the sea. New cliffs and caves are formed at a lower level, and rivers cut down through the lower land to reach sea level once more.*

(same scale as main map)

Lying close to the banks *of the Sepik River in northern Papua New Guinea, this building is known as the Spirit House. It is constructed from leaves and twigs, ornately woven and trimmed into geometric patterns. The house is decorated with a mask and topped by a carved statue.*

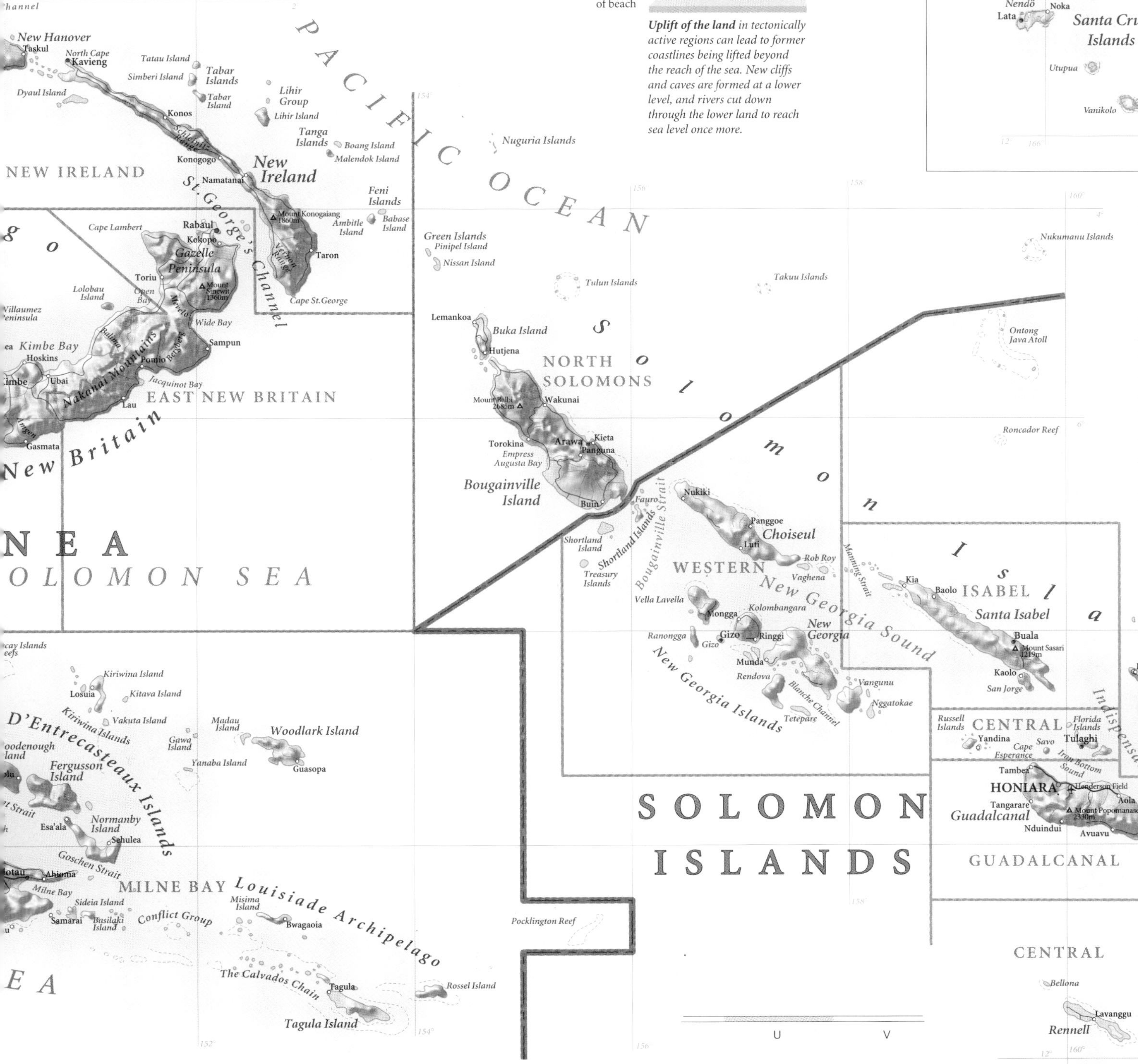

THE PACIFIC OCEAN

THE PACIFIC IS THE WORLD'S LARGEST AND DEEPEST OCEAN. It is nearly twice the area of the Atlantic and contains almost three times as much water. The ocean is dotted with islands and surrounded by some of the world's most populous states; over half the world's population lives on its shores. The Pacific is bordered by active plate margins known as the "Ring of Fire," causing earthquakes and tsunamis, and creating volcanic islands and subterranean mountain chains. The largest underwater mountains break the surface as island arcs. The fisheries of the Pacific are some of the most productive in the world and provide a vital resource for many of the Pacific islands. Since the Second World War there has been a shift in trading patterns, with a considerable growth in trade between the US and the countries of the Pacific Rim.

INSET MAP KEY

POPULATION
∘ below 10,000

ELEVATION
1000m / 3281ft
500m / 1640ft
250m / 820ft
100m / 328ft
sea level

OCEAN MAP KEY

SEA DEPTH
sea level
250m / 820ft
500m / 1640ft
1000m / 3281ft
2000m / 6562ft
3000m / 9843ft
5000m / 16,410ft

SCALE 1:50,000,000
(projection: Mollweide)

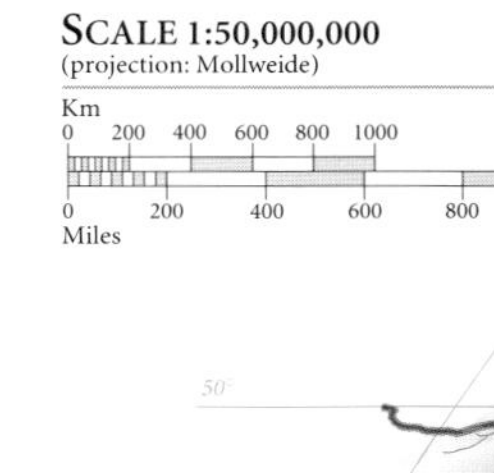

AMERICAN SAMOA AND WESTERN SAMOA

AMERICAN SAMOA AND WESTERN SAMOA are part of the island archipelago of Polynesia. The two most populous islands are Tutuila in American Samoa and Upolu in Western Samoa. Although the economies of both of these states remain predominantly resource-based, both are expanding their light manufacturing sectors, and the US administration is the primary employer in American Samoa. Fishing is particularly important: 25% of all tuna consumed in the US is processed and canned in Pago Pago.

Japan is one of the major trading nations within the Pacific, importing iron and steel from Australia, and grain from the US. The major exports from the Pacific Rim are electronics, precision equipment, and motor cars.

WESTERN SAMOA · AMERICAN SAMOA (to US) · PACIFIC OCEAN · SCALE 1:3,000,000

Many of the buildings in Western Samoa reflect the country's colonial past. Once a colony of New Zealand, Western Samoa is now an independent state; American Samoa remains an unincorporated territory of the US.

THE RING OF FIRE

THE ACTIVE PLATE MARGINS surrounding the Pacific have created numerous land and island volcanoes along its border. The actual basin of the Pacific is made up of a number of separate tectonic plates which move away from each other, colliding with other plates. When they collide, the thinner oceanic plates are forced beneath the thicker continental plates, forming deep ocean trenches and high ridges. These collision zones, known as subduction zones, are characterized by intense seismic and volcanic activity.

RESOURCES

MANY OF THE SMALL ISLANDS in the Pacific rely heavily on marine resources to provide valuable export incomes. These fisheries tend to be small-scale and are forced to compete with the large commercial fleets from Japan and the Russian Federation. Although many metallic mineral deposits have been discovered in the Pacific, few are exploited. The major areas of oil and gas extraction are off the coast of Vietnam, along the Kamchatka Peninsula, and off the coast of Alaska. The numerous reefs which fringe the islands of the Pacific are harvested for corals.

Farms such as this black pearl oyster farm in Tahiti are widespread throughout the Pacific. The culturing or farming of marine organisms, such as mollusks and crustaceans, has been practiced for hundreds of years.

Resources
fish
shellfish
whales
oil & gas
major towns
major ports

Ring of Fire
plate boundaries
major volcanoes

Mayon Volcano in the Philippines is one of many active volcanoes on the Pacific "Ring of Fire." It is noted for its perfect conical shape; the base of the cone is 80 miles (130 km) in circumference.

The Hawaiian volcanoes lie in the center of a plate, not on a plate margin, and are known as intraplate volcanoes. They are associated with hot spots, where a plume of hot molten rock rises to the surface as the plate moves over it.

MELANESIA

FIJI, VANUATU, *New Caledonia* (to France)

THREE MAIN ISLAND groups make up the area of southern Melanesia in the southwestern Pacific: the independent countries of Fiji and Vanuatu and the French overseas territory of New Caledonia. The major Melanesian island group, the Solomon Islands, lies to the east of Papua New Guinea (pages 194–95). Most of the larger islands are volcanic in origin; the smaller ones are mainly coral atolls and are largely uninhabited. The economy in all three island groups is increasingly driven by tourism, not necessarily to the benefit of other economic activities.

VANUATU

A STRING OF MOUNTAINOUS VOLCANIC ISLANDS covering more than 800 sq miles (1,300 sq km) of the south Pacific, Vanuatu achieved independence from France and the UK in 1980. The majority of the population relies on subsistence fishing and agriculture. Once-important copra and cocoa exports are declining as a result of cost-effective substitutes from elsewhere, and alternatives are being explored. There is further resource potential in the forests and fishing grounds, and beef and arable farming are of growing importance. Tourism, accounting for 40% of the GDP, is the fastest-growing sector of the economy, and further expansion is planned.

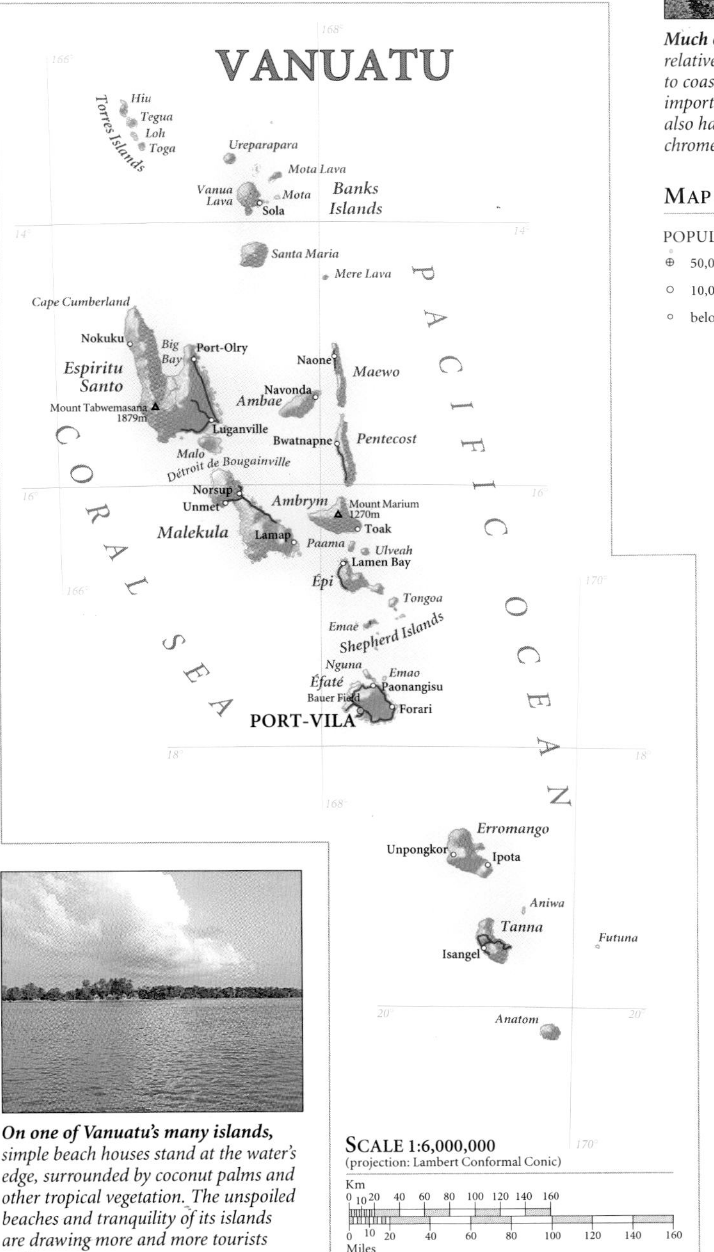
VANUATU
Torres Islands
Hiu
Tegua
Loh
Toga
Ureparapara
Mota Lava
Vanua Lava
Mota
Sola
Banks Islands
Santa Maria
Mere Lava
Cape Cumberland
Nokuku
Big Bay
Port-Olry
Espiritu Santo
Mount Tabwemasana 1879m
Naone
Maewo
Navonda
Ambae
Luganville
Bwatnapne
Pentecost
Malo
Détroit de Bougainville
Norsup
Unmet
Ambrym
Mount Marium 1270m
Toak
Malekula
Lamap
Paama
Ulveah
Lamen Bay
Epi
Tongoa
Emae
Shepherd Islands
Nguna
Emao
Éfaté
Bauer Field
Paonangisu
Forari
PORT-VILA
CORAL SEA
PACIFIC OCEAN
Erromango
Unpongkor
Ipota
Aniwa
Tanna
Isangel
Futuna
Anatom
SCALE 1:6,000,000
(projection: Lambert Conformal Conic)

On one of Vanuatu's many islands, simple beach houses stand at the water's edge, surrounded by coconut palms and other tropical vegetation. The unspoiled beaches and tranquility of its islands are drawing more and more tourists to Vanuatu.

SCALE 1:6,000,000
(projection: Lambert Conformal Conic)

CORAL SEA

NEW CALEDONIA (to France)

Much of New Caledonia is volcanic, with relatively high interior plateaus descending to coastal plains. Nickel is the most important mineral resource, but the hills also harbor metallic deposits including chrome, cobalt, iron, gold, silver, and copper.

MAP KEY

POPULATION
- 50,000 to 100,000
- 10,000 to 50,000
- below 10,000

ELEVATION
- 1000m / 3281ft
- 500m / 1640ft
- 250m / 820ft
- 100m / 328ft
- sea level

NEW CALEDONIA (France)

NEW CALEDONIA, a French overseas territory known as Kanaky by its indigenous peoples, comprises a large main island 260 miles (418 km) long and many smaller islands and atolls. Socioeconomic inequality, unemployment, and the issue of independence have caused tension between the Kanaks and the French-speaking expatriate population. This has resulted in a long history of political violence, although a referendum on independence is promised for 1998. New Caledonia produces 25% of the world's nickel, and improved incomes from tourism and agriculture have benefited the economy.

FIJI

FIJI IS A VOLCANIC ARCHIPELAGO in the southwestern Pacific consisting of two large islands and 880 smaller islets, and covering a total area of 7,054 sq miles (18,270 sq km). The majority of the population lives on the two largest islands. The people are split fairly evenly between Indo-Fijians, who arrived when Fiji was still a British colony, and the indigenous Fijians who have, since 1987, controlled the government. Sugar and copra are the most important crops in a diversified agricultural base and forestry is becoming increasingly important. A relatively varied economy has potential for mineral and hydroelectric exploitation, while Fiji's climate and location on the main Pacific air routes are an impetus to tourism.

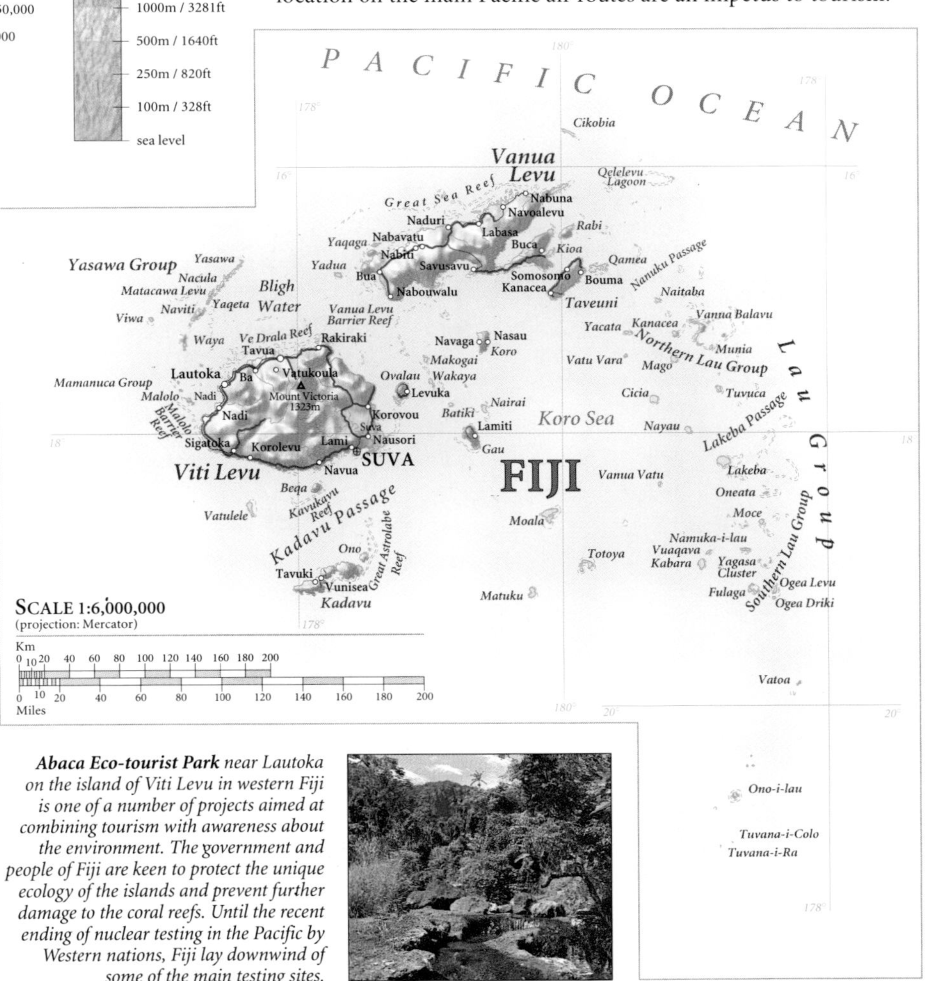
PACIFIC OCEAN
FIJI
Cikobia
Vanua Levu
Great Sea Reef
Nabuna
Navoalevu
Labasa
Rabi
Buca
Kioa
Yasawa Group
Yasawa
Nacula
Matacawa Levu
Naviti
Viwa
Yaqeta
Bligh Water
Vanua Levu Barrier Reef
Savusavu
Nabouwalu
Somosomo
Bouma
Kanacea
Taveuni
Waya
Rakiraki
Lautoka
Ba
Vatukoula
Mount Victoria 1323m
Nadi
Sigatoka
Korolevu
Viti Levu
Nausori
SUVA
Navua
Levuka
Koro Sea
Lakeba
Moala
Totoya
Matuku
Kadavu
Kadavu Passage
Vunisea
Lau Group
Southern Lau Group
Northern Lau Group
Vatoa
Ono-i-lau
Tuvana-i-Colo
Tuvana-i-Ra
SCALE 1:6,000,000
(projection: Mercator)

Abaca Eco-tourist Park *near Lautoka on the island of Viti Levu in western Fiji is one of a number of projects aimed at combining tourism with awareness about the environment. The government and people of Fiji are keen to protect the unique ecology of the islands and prevent further damage to the coral reefs. Until the recent ending of nuclear testing in the Pacific by Western nations, Fiji lay downwind of some of the main testing sites.*

MICRONESIA

MARSHALL ISLANDS, MICRONESIA, NAURU, PALAU,
Guam, Northern Mariana Islands, Wake Island

THE MICRONESIAN ISLANDS lie in the western reaches of the Pacific Ocean and are all part of the same volcanic zone. The Federated States of Micronesia is the largest group, with more than 600 atolls and forested volcanic islands in an area of more than 1,120 sq miles (2,900 sq km). Micronesia is a mixture of former colonies, overseas territories, and dependencies. Most of the region still relies on aid and subsidies to sustain economies limited by resources, isolation, and an emigrating population drawn to New Zealand and Australia by the attractions of a western lifestyle.

PALAU

PALAU IS AN ARCHIPELAGO OF OVER 200 ISLANDS, only eight of which are inhabited. It was the last remaining UN Trust Territory in the Pacific, controlled by the US until 1994, when it became independent. The economy operates on a subsistence level, with coconuts and cassava as the principal crops. Fishing licenses and tourism provide foreign currency.

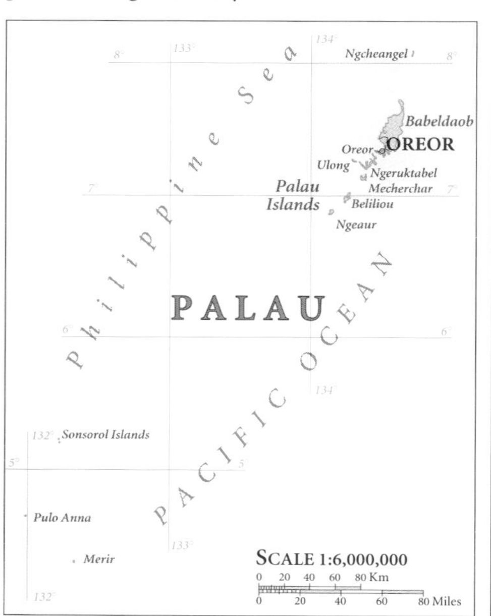
Philippine Sea
Ngcheangel
Babeldaob
OREOR
Oreor
Ulong
Ngeruktabel
Mecherchar
Palau Islands
Beliliou
Ngeaur
PALAU
PACIFIC OCEAN
Sonsorol Islands
Pulo Anna
Merir
SCALE 1:6,000,000
0 20 40 60 80 Km
0 20 40 60 80 Miles

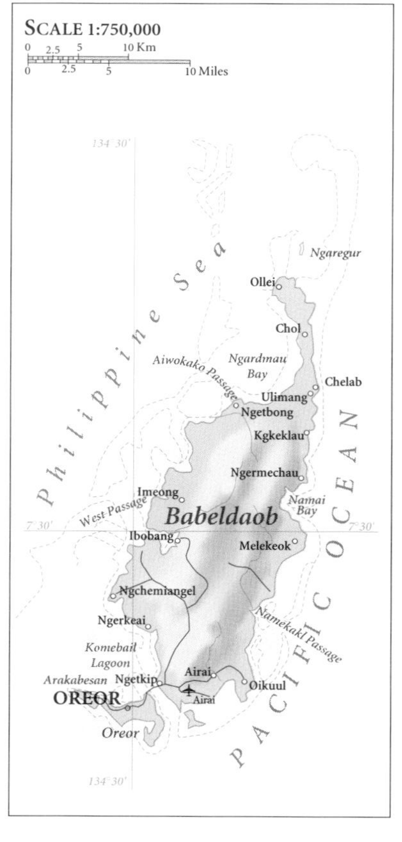
SCALE 1:750,000
0 2.5 5 10 Km
0 2.5 5 10 Miles
Philippine Sea
Ngaregur
Ollei
Chol
Aiwokako Passage
Ngardmau Bay
Chelab
Ulimang
Ngetbong
Ngkeklau
Ngermechau
Imeong
West Passage
Namai Bay
Babeldaob
Ibobang
Melekeok
Ngchemiangel
Ngerkeai
Namekakl Passage
Komebail Lagoon
Arakabesan
Ngetkip
Airai
Oikuul
OREOR
Oreor
PACIFIC OCEAN

NORTHERN MARIANA ISLANDS (to US)

A US COMMONWEALTH TERRITORY, the Northern Marianas comprise the whole of the Mariana archipelago except for Guam. The islands retain their close links with the US and continue to receive American aid. Tourism, though bringing in much-needed revenue, has speeded the decline of the traditional subsistence economy. Most of the population lives on Saipan.

Philippine Sea
Puntan Sabaneta
Punta Lagua Lichan
Bird Island
San Roque
Managaha
Puetton Tanapag
Tanapag
Kalabera
Capitol Hill
Garapan
Mount Tapochau 465m
Saipan
Oleai
San Vicente
Susupe
Chalan Kanoa
Magicienne Bay
Kagman Point
San Antonio
Saipan International
Saipan Channel
Puntan I Naftan
PACIFIC OCEAN
SCALE 1:500,000
0 2 4 8 Km
0 2 4 8 Miles

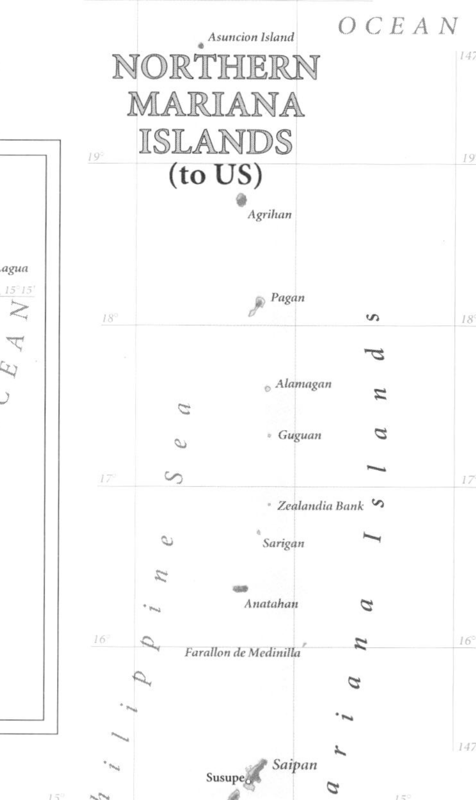
Farallon de Pajaros
Supply Reef
Maug Islands
PACIFIC OCEAN
Asuncion Island
NORTHERN MARIANA ISLANDS (to US)
Agrihan
Pagan
Alamagan
Guguan
Zealandia Bank
Sarigan
Anatahan
Farallon de Medinilla
Philippine Sea
Mariana Islands
Saipan
Susupe
San Jose
Tinian
Aguijan
Rota
GUAM (to US)
AGANA
Dededo
PACIFIC OCEAN
SCALE 1:5,000,000
0 20 40 80 Km
0 20 40 80 Miles

The Palau Islands have numerous hidden lakes and lagoons. These sustain their own ecosystems, which have developed in isolation. This has produced adaptations in the animals and plants that are often unique to each lake.

GUAM (to US)

LYING AT THE SOUTHERN END of the Mariana Islands, Guam is an important US military base and tourist destination. Social and political life is dominated by the indigenous Chamorro, who make up just under half of the population, although the increasing prevalence of western culture threatens Guam's traditional social stability.

The tranquility *of these coastal lagoons, at Inarajan in southern Guam, belies the fact that the island lies in a region where typhoons are common.*

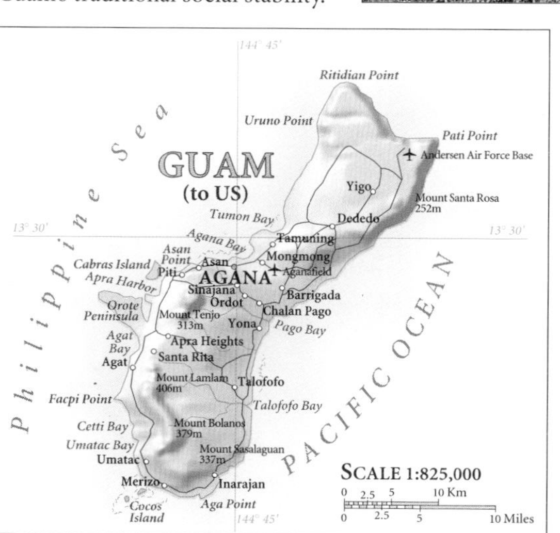
Ritidian Point
Uruno Point
Pati Point
Andersen Air Force Base
GUAM (to US)
Philippine Sea
Yigo
Mount Santa Rosa 252m
Tumon Bay
Dededo
Agana Bay
Tamuning
Asan Point
Mongmong
Cabras Island
Piti
Asan
AGANA
Apra Harbor
Sinajana
Barrigada
Orote Peninsula
Mount Tenjo 313m
Ordot
Chalan Pago
Yona
Pago Bay
Agat Bay
Apra Heights
Agat
Santa Rita
Mount Lamlam 406m
Talofofo
Facpi Point
Talofofo Bay
Cetti Bay
Mount Bolanos 379m
Umatac Bay
Umatac
Mount Sasalaguan 337m
Merizo
Inarajan
Cocos Island
Aga Point
PACIFIC OCEAN
SCALE 1:825,000
0 2.5 5 10 Km
0 2.5 5 10 Miles

MICRONESIA

A MIXTURE OF HIGH VOLCANIC ISLANDS and low-lying coral atolls, the Federated States of Micronesia include all of the Caroline Islands except Palau. Pohnpei, Kosrae, Chuuk, and Yap are the four main island cluster states, each of which has its own language, with English remaining the official language. Nearly half of the population is concentrated on Pohnpei, the largest island. Independent since 1979, the islands continue to receive considerable aid from the US that supplements an economy based primarily on fishing and copra processing.

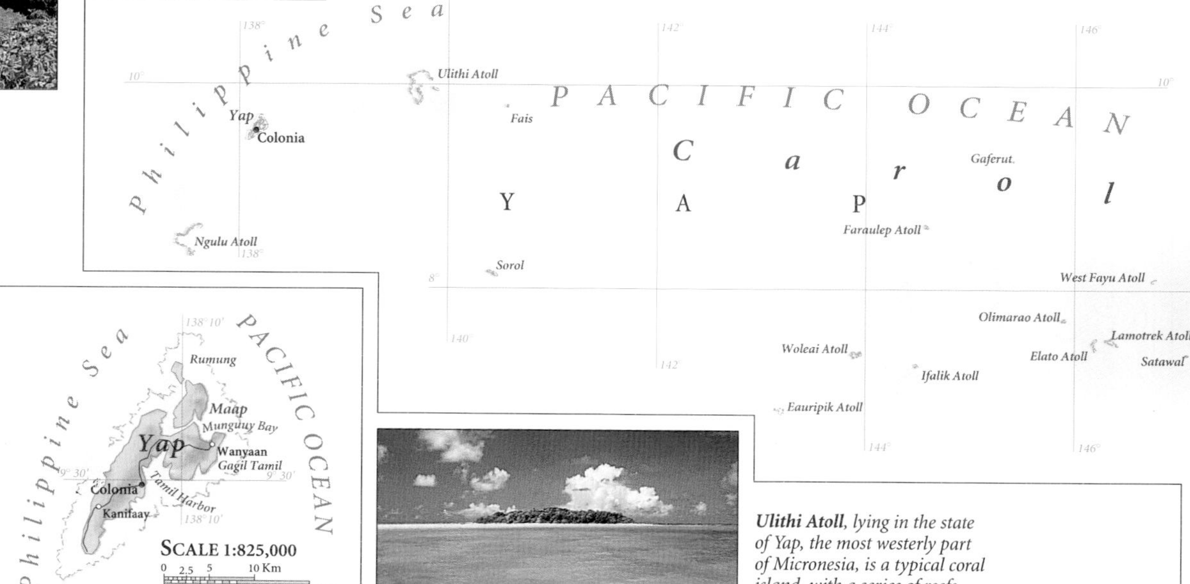
Philippine Sea
Ulithi Atoll
Fais
PACIFIC OCEAN
Yap
Colonia
Caroli
YAP
Gaferut
Faraulep Atoll
Ngulu Atoll
Sorol
West Fayu Atoll
Olimarao Atoll
Lamotrek Atoll
Woleai Atoll
Elato Atoll
Satawal
Ifalik Atoll
Eauripik Atoll
PACIFIC OCEAN
Rumung
Maap
Munguuy Bay
Yap
Wanyaan
Gagil Tamil
Tamil Harbor
Colonia
Kanifaay
SCALE 1:825,000
0 2.5 5 10 Km
0 2.5 5 10 Miles

Ulithi Atoll*, lying in the state of Yap, the most westerly part of Micronesia, is a typical coral island, with a series of reefs enclosing a large lagoon.*

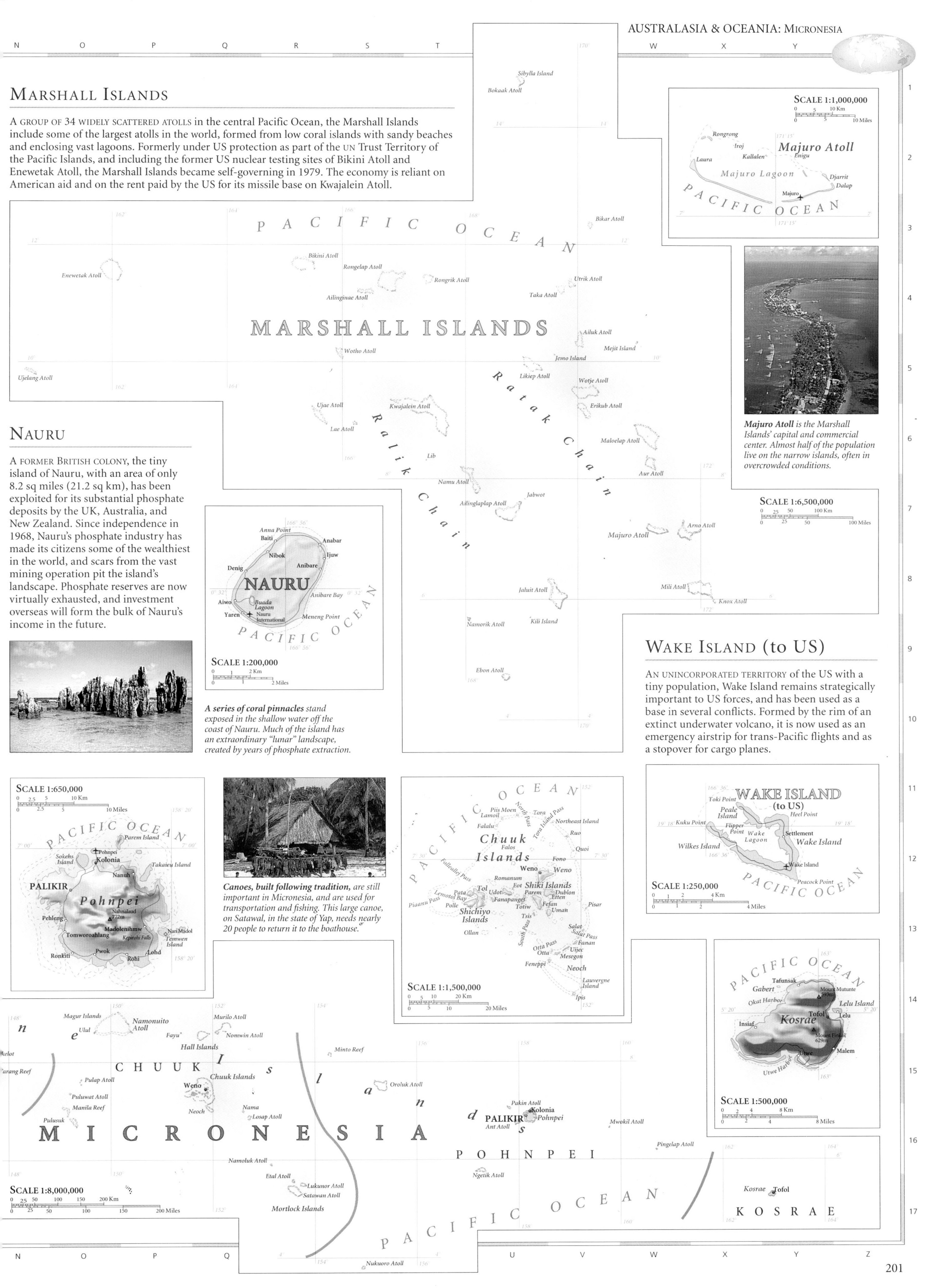

PACIFIC OCEAN
MARSHALL ISLANDS
Sibylla Island
Bokaak Atoll
Bikar Atoll
Bikini Atoll
Rongelap Atoll
Rongrik Atoll
Enewetak Atoll
Utrik Atoll
Ailinginae Atoll
Taka Atoll
Ailuk Atoll
Mejit Island
Wotho Atoll
Jemo Island
Ujelang Atoll
Likiep Atoll
Wotje Atoll
Ujae Atoll
Kwajalein Atoll
Erikub Atoll
Lae Atoll
Ratak Chain
Ralik Chain
Maloelap Atoll
Lib
Aur Atoll
Namu Atoll
Jabwot
Ailinglaplap Atoll
Arno Atoll
Majuro Atoll
Mili Atoll
Knox Atoll
Jaluit Atoll
Kili Island
Namorik Atoll
Ebon Atoll
SCALE 1:6,500,000
SCALE 1:1,000,000
Majuro Atoll
Rongrong
Iroj
Kallalen
Enigu
Laura
Majuro Lagoon
Djarrit
Dalap
Majuro
PACIFIC OCEAN
NAURU
Anna Point
Baiti
Anabar
Nibok
Ijuw
Denig
Anibare
Anibare Bay
Aiwo
Buada Lagoon
Yaren
Nauru International
Meneng Point
PACIFIC OCEAN
SCALE 1:200,000
WAKE ISLAND (to US)
Toki Point
Peale Island
Heel Point
Kuku Point
Flipper Point
Wake Lagoon
Settlement
Wilkes Island
Wake Island
Peacock Point
PACIFIC OCEAN
SCALE 1:250,000
SCALE 1:650,000
PACIFIC OCEAN
Parem Island
Pohnpei
Kolonia
Sokehs Island
Takaieu Island
Nanuh
PALIKIR
Pohnpei
Nahnalaud 772m
Pehleng
Madolenihmw
Tomworoahlang
Kepirohi Falls
Nan Madol
Temwen Island
Ronkiti
Pwok
Rohi
Lohd
OCEAN
PACIFIC
Chuuk Islands
Piis Moen
Lamoil
Tora
Northeast Island
Falalu
Ruo
Quoi
Falos
Fono
Weno
Romanum
Eot
Shiki Islands
Udot
Parem
Dublon
Tol
Fanapanges
Etten
Pata
Totiw
Fefan
Uman
Polle
Shichiyo Islands
Tsis
Pisar
Ollan
Salat
Fanan
Otta
Uijec
Mesegon
Feneppi
Neoch
Lauvergne Island
Ipis
SCALE 1:1,500,000
PACIFIC OCEAN
Tafunsak
Gabert
Mount Mutunte
Okat Harbor
Lelu Island
Tofol
Lelu
Kosrae
Insiaf
Mount Finkol 629m
Utwe
Malem
Utwe Harbor
SCALE 1:500,000
Micronesia
Magur Islands
Namonuito Atoll
Murilo Atoll
Ulul
Fayu
Nomwin Atoll
Hall Islands
Minto Reef
CHUUK
Chuuk Islands
Pulap Atoll
Weno
Oroluk Atoll
Puluwat Atoll
Manila Reef
Neoch
Nama
Losap Atoll
Pakin Atoll
Kolonia
PALIKIR
Pohnpei
Ant Atoll
Mwokil Atoll
Pulusuk
MICRONESIA
Namoluk Atoll
POHNPEI
Pingelap Atoll
Etal Atoll
Lukunor Atoll
Satawan Atoll
Ngetik Atoll
Mortlock Islands
Kosrae
Tofol
KOSRAE
PACIFIC OCEAN
Nukuoro Atoll
SCALE 1:8,000,000

MARSHALL ISLANDS

A GROUP OF 34 WIDELY SCATTERED ATOLLS in the central Pacific Ocean, the Marshall Islands include some of the largest atolls in the world, formed from low coral islands with sandy beaches and enclosing vast lagoons. Formerly under US protection as part of the UN Trust Territory of the Pacific Islands, and including the former US nuclear testing sites of Bikini Atoll and Enewetak Atoll, the Marshall Islands became self-governing in 1979. The economy is reliant on American aid and on the rent paid by the US for its missile base on Kwajalein Atoll.

Majuro Atoll is the Marshall Islands' capital and commercial center. Almost half of the population live on the narrow islands, often in overcrowded conditions.

NAURU

A FORMER BRITISH COLONY, the tiny island of Nauru, with an area of only 8.2 sq miles (21.2 sq km), has been exploited for its substantial phosphate deposits by the UK, Australia, and New Zealand. Since independence in 1968, Nauru's phosphate industry has made its citizens some of the wealthiest in the world, and scars from the vast mining operation pit the island's landscape. Phosphate reserves are now virtually exhausted, and investment overseas will form the bulk of Nauru's income in the future.

***A series of coral pinnacles** stand exposed in the shallow water off the coast of Nauru. Much of the island has an extraordinary "lunar" landscape, created by years of phosphate extraction.*

WAKE ISLAND (to US)

AN UNINCORPORATED TERRITORY of the US with a tiny population, Wake Island remains strategically important to US forces, and has been used as a base in several conflicts. Formed by the rim of an extinct underwater volcano, it is now used as an emergency airstrip for trans-Pacific flights and as a stopover for cargo planes.

***Canoes, built following tradition,** are still important in Micronesia, and are used for transportation and fishing. This large canoe, on Satawal, in the state of Yap, needs nearly 20 people to return it to the boathouse.*

The Landscape

Although it is still the largest ocean, the basin of the Pacific has been gradually decreasing in size due to the movement of the Indo-Australian Plate. Its oldest parts are about 135 million years old. The eastern border of the Pacific is characterized by a continuous mountain chain running the length of the North and South American continents. The eastern basin has a low, uninterrupted relief, at depths averaging 15,000 ft (4,570 m). In contrast, the western Pacific is scattered with island arcs and bounded by a series of deep ocean trenches. An almost continuous chain of volcanoes surrounds the ocean and an active mid-ocean ridge runs northeast–southwest.

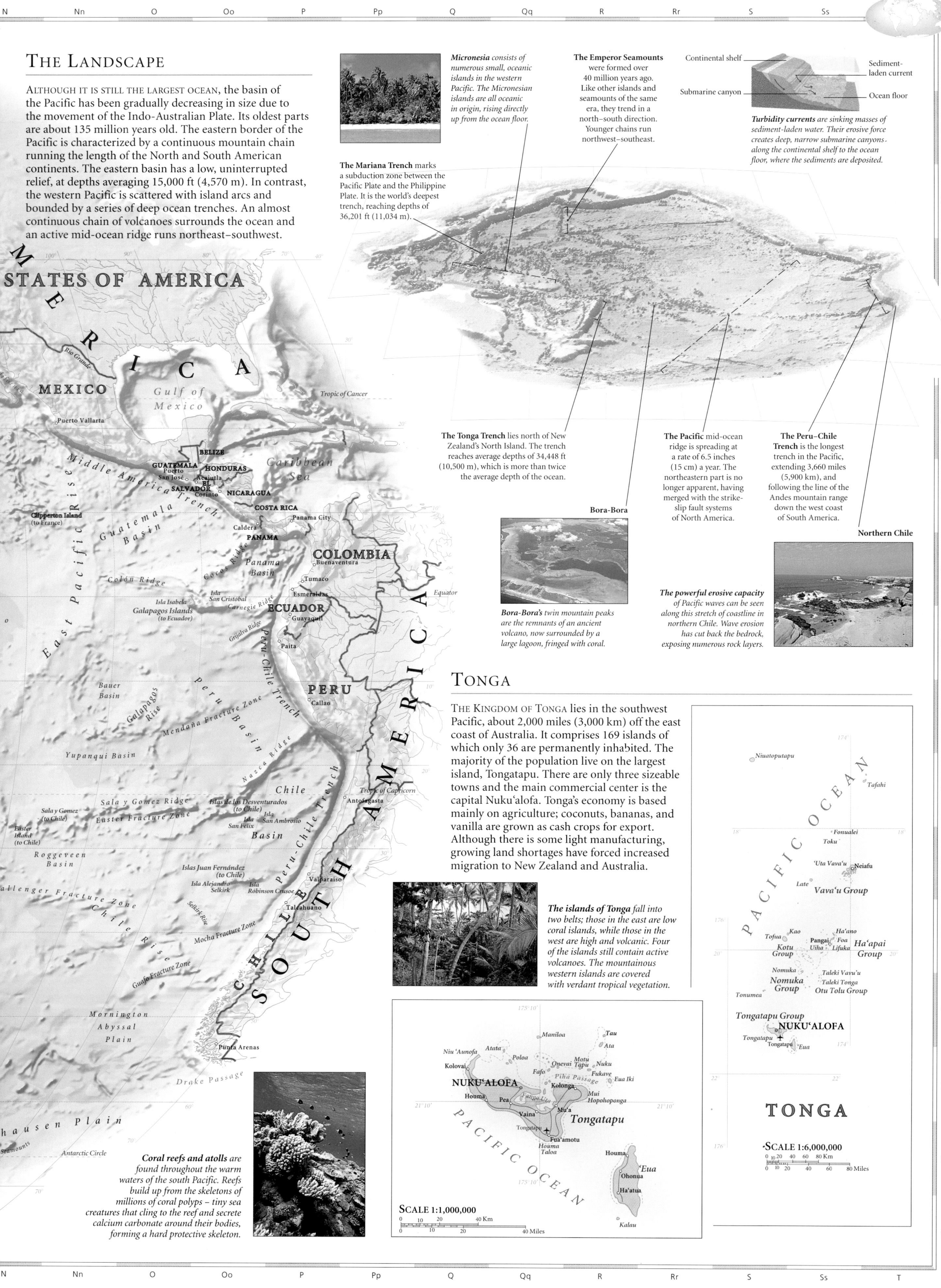

N Nn O Oo P Pp Q Qq R Rr S Ss T
1 2 3 4 6 7 8 9 10 11 12 13 14 15 16 17
Continental shelf
Submarine canyon
Sediment-laden current
Ocean floor
STATES OF AMERICA
AMERICA
MEXICO
Gulf of Mexico
Rio Grande
Tropic of Cancer
Puerto Vallarta
BELIZE
GUATEMALA
HONDURAS
Puerto San José
Acajutla
EL SALVADOR
Corinto
NICARAGUA
Caribbean Sea
Middle America Trench
Clipperton Island (to France)
COSTA RICA
Caldera
Panama City
PANAMA
Guatemala Basin
Panama Basin
Cocos Ridge
COLOMBIA
Buenaventura
Tumaco
Esmeraldas
Equator
Colón Ridge
Isla Isabela
Isla San Cristóbal
Galapagos Islands (to Ecuador)
Carnegie Ridge
ECUADOR
Guayaquil
Grijalva Ridge
Paita
East Pacific Rise
Peru-Chile Trench
Bauer Basin
Galapagos Rise
Peru Basin
PERU
Callao
Mendaña Fracture Zone
Yupanqui Basin
Nazca Ridge
Chile Basin
Sala y Gomez (to Chile)
Sala y Gomez Ridge
Easter Fracture Zone
Easter Island (to Chile)
Islas de los Desventurados (to Chile)
Isla San Félix
Isla San Ambrosio
Tropic of Capricorn
Antofagasta
Roggeveen Basin
Islas Juan Fernández (to Chile)
Isla Alejandro Selkirk
Isla Robinson Crusoe
Valparaíso
Challenger Fracture Zone
Chile Rise
Talcahuano
Selkirk Rise
Mocha Fracture Zone
Guafo Fracture Zone
CHILE
SOUTH AMERICA
Mornington Abyssal Plain
Punta Arenas
Drake Passage
Antarctic Circle
Seamounts
Niuatoputapu
Tafahi
PACIFIC OCEAN
Fonualei
Toku
'Uta Vava'u
Neiafu
Late
Vava'u Group
Kao
Tofua
Kotu Group
Ha'ano
Pangai
Foa
Uiha
Lifuka
Ha'apai Group
Nomuka
Nomuka Group
Tonumea
Taleki Vavu'u
Taleki Tonga
Otu Tolu Group
Tongatapu Group
NUKU'ALOFA
Tongatapu
'Eua
TONGA
SCALE 1:6,000,000
0 10 20 40 60 80 Km
0 10 20 40 60 80 Miles
Tau
Ata
Maniloa
Atata
Niu 'Aunofa
Poloa
Kolovai
Onevai
Motu Tapu
Nuku
Fafa
Fukave
Piha Passage
Eua Iki
NUKU'ALOFA
Kolonga
Houma
Pea
Mui Hopohoponga
Vaina
Mu'a
Tongatapu
Fua'amotu
Houma Taloa
Houma
Ohonua
Ha'atua
Kalau
PACIFIC OCEAN
SCALE 1:1,000,000
0 10 20 40 Km
0 10 20 40 Miles

Micronesia *consists of numerous small, oceanic islands in the western Pacific. The Micronesian islands are all oceanic in origin, rising directly up from the ocean floor.*

The Emperor Seamounts were formed over 40 million years ago. Like other islands and seamounts of the same era, they trend in a north–south direction. Younger chains run northwest–southeast.

Turbidity currents *are sinking masses of sediment-laden water. Their erosive force creates deep, narrow submarine canyons along the continental shelf to the ocean floor, where the sediments are deposited.*

The Mariana Trench marks a subduction zone between the Pacific Plate and the Philippine Plate. It is the world's deepest trench, reaching depths of 36,201 ft (11,034 m).

The Tonga Trench lies north of New Zealand's North Island. The trench reaches average depths of 34,448 ft (10,500 m), which is more than twice the average depth of the ocean.

The Pacific mid-ocean ridge is spreading at a rate of 6.5 inches (15 cm) a year. The northeastern part is no longer apparent, having merged with the strike-slip fault systems of North America.

The Peru–Chile Trench is the longest trench in the Pacific, extending 3,660 miles (5,900 km), and following the line of the Andes mountain range down the west coast of South America.

Bora-Bora

Bora-Bora's *twin mountain peaks are the remnants of an ancient volcano, now surrounded by a large lagoon, fringed with coral.*

Northern Chile

The powerful erosive capacity *of Pacific waves can be seen along this stretch of coastline in northern Chile. Wave erosion has cut back the bedrock, exposing numerous rock layers.*

Tonga

The Kingdom of Tonga lies in the southwest Pacific, about 2,000 miles (3,000 km) off the east coast of Australia. It comprises 169 islands of which only 36 are permanently inhabited. The majority of the population live on the largest island, Tongatapu. There are only three sizeable towns and the main commercial center is the capital Nuku'alofa. Tonga's economy is based mainly on agriculture; coconuts, bananas, and vanilla are grown as cash crops for export. Although there is some light manufacturing, growing land shortages have forced increased migration to New Zealand and Australia.

The islands of Tonga *fall into two belts; those in the east are low coral islands, while those in the west are high and volcanic. Four of the islands still contain active volcanoes. The mountainous western islands are covered with verdant tropical vegetation.*

Coral reefs and atolls *are found throughout the warm waters of the south Pacific. Reefs build up from the skeletons of millions of coral polyps – tiny sea creatures that cling to the reef and secrete calcium carbonate around their bodies, forming a hard protective skeleton.*

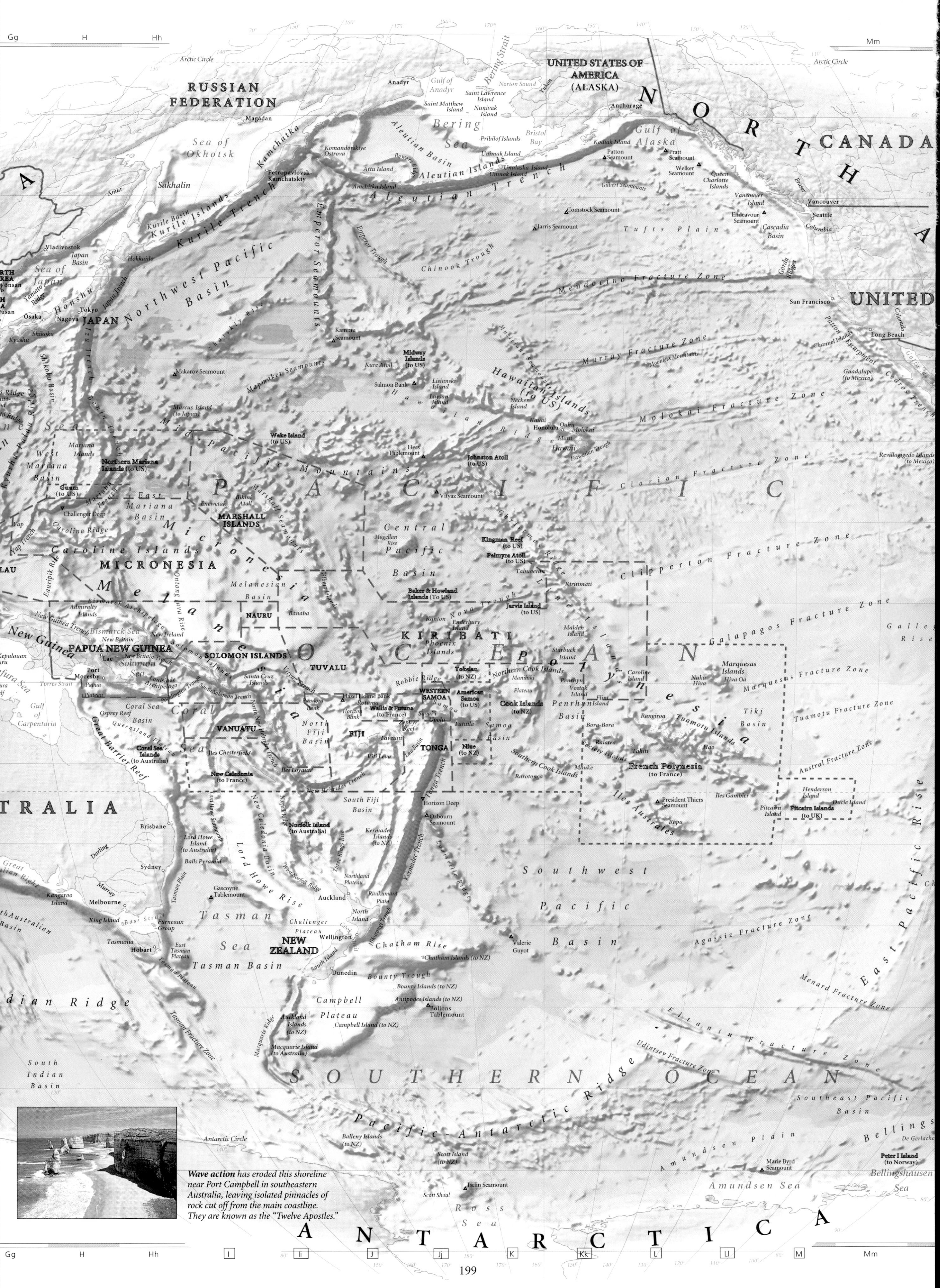

Gg
H
Hh
Mm
Arctic Circle
RUSSIAN FEDERATION
UNITED STATES OF AMERICA (ALASKA)
NORTH A
CANADA
Anadyr
Gulf of Anadyr
Bering Strait
Norton Sound
Yukon
Saint Lawrence Island
Saint Matthew Island
Nunivak Island
Anchorage
Magadan
Bering Sea
Pribilof Islands
Bristol Bay
Gulf of Alaska
Kodiak Island
Pratt Seamount
Patton Seamount
Welker Seamount
Queen Charlotte Islands
Sea of Okhotsk
Kamchatka
Komandorskiye Ostrova
Aleutian Basin
Bowers Ridge
Attu Island
Aleutian Islands
Unimak Island
Unalaska Island
Umnak Island
Aleutian Trench
Gilbert Seamounts
Petropavlovsk-Kamchatskiy
Amchitka Island
Sakhalin
Amur
Kurile Basin
Kurile Islands
Kurile Trench
Emperor Seamounts
Emperor Trough
Vancouver Island
Vancouver
Fraser
Seattle
Columbia
Endeavour Seamount
Cascadia Basin
Comstock Seamount
Harris Seamount
Tufts Plain
Chinook Trough
Vladivostok
Japan Basin
Sea of Japan
Hokkaido
Northwest Pacific Basin
Mendocino Fracture Zone
Gorda Ridge
San Francisco
UNITED
Honshu
Japan Trench
Tokyo
Osaka
Nagoya
JAPAN
Shikoku
Kyushu
Yamato Ridge
Shatsky Rise
Kammu Seamount
Midway Islands (to US)
Kure Atoll
Musicians Seamounts
Murray Fracture Zone
Moonless Mountains
Patton Escarpment
Channel Islands
Long Beach
Colorado
Izu Trench
Shikoku Basin
Makarov Seamount
Mapmaker Seamounts
Salmon Bank
Lisianski Island
Laysan Island
Hawaiian Islands (to US)
Hawaiian Ridge
Necker Island
Guadalupe (to Mexico)
Cedros Trench
Molokai Fracture Zone
Bonin Trench
Marcus Island (to Japan)
Kauai
Oahu
Honolulu
Molokai
Maui
Hawaii
Hawaiian Trough
Kyushu-Palau Ridge
West Mariana Basin
Mariana Islands
Northern Mariana Islands (to US)
Mid-Pacific Mountains
Wake Island (to US)
Hess Tablemount
Johnston Atoll (to US)
Revillagigedo Islands (to Mexico)
Clarion Fracture Zone
Guam (to US)
Mariana Trench
Challenger Deep
East Mariana Basin
Enewetak
Bikini Atoll
Vityaz Seamount
PACIFIC
Yap
Yap Trench
Caroline Ridge
Marshall Seamounts
MARSHALL ISLANDS
Central Pacific Basin
Magellan Rise
Christmas Ridge
Kingman Reef (to US)
Palmyra Atoll (to US)
Tabuaeran
Kiritimati
Clipperton Fracture Zone
Caroline Islands
MICRONESIA
Micronesia
Eauripik Rise
Ontong Java Rise
Melanesian Basin
Gilbert Islands
Baker & Howland Islands (To US)
Jarvis Island (to US)
Line Islands
Nova Trough
Galapagos Fracture Zone
Galapagos Rise
Melanesia
Admiralty Islands
Bismarck Archipelago
NAURU
Banaba
Kanton
Enderbury Island
KIRIBATI
Phoenix Islands
Malden Island
New Guinea Trench
Bismarck Sea
New Ireland
New Britain
New Guinea
PAPUA NEW GUINEA
Lae
New Britain Trench
SOLOMON ISLANDS
Solomon Sea
Solomon Islands
OCEAN
Starbuck Island
Polynesia
Marquesas Islands
Nuku Hiva
Hiva Oa
Kepulauan Aru
Port Moresby
Papua
Torres Strait
Louisiade Archipelago
Santa Cruz Islands
South Solomon Trench
Vitiaz Trench
TUVALU
Robbie Ridge
Tokelau (to NZ)
Northern Cook Islands
Manihiki Plateau
Penrhyn
Vostok Island
Caroline Island
Marquesas Fracture Zone
Gulf of Carpentaria
Coral Sea Basin
Coral Sea
Queensland Plateau
Osprey Reef
Hazel Holme Bank
Rotuma
Pandora Bank
Horizon Bank
Wallis & Futuna (to France)
WESTERN SAMOA
Savai'i
Upolu
American Samoa (to US)
Tutuila
Samoa Basin
Cook Islands (to NZ)
Penrhyn Basin
Flint Island
Tiki Basin
Tuamotu Fracture Zone
Great Barrier Reef
VANUATU
North Fiji Basin
FIJI
Zephyr Reef
Taveuni
Vanua Levu
Viti Levu
Lau Ridge
TONGA
Niue (to NZ)
Bora-Bora
Raiatea
Society Islands
Tahiti
Rangiroa
Tuamotu Islands
Hao
French Polynesia (to France)
Coral Sea Islands (to Australia)
Iles Chesterfield
New Hebrides Trench
Iles Loyauté
New Caledonia (to France)
Tonga Trench
Southern Cook Islands
Rarotonga
Mauke
Iles Gambier
Austral Fracture Zone
Henderson Island
Ducie Island
Pitcairn Island
Pitcairn Islands (to UK)
AUSTRALIA
Lord Howe Seamounts
New Caledonia Basin
Norfolk Ridge
South Fiji Basin
Horizon Deep
Ozbourn Seamount
Iles Australes
President Thiers Seamount
Rapa
Brisbane
Norfolk Island (to Australia)
Kermadec Islands (to NZ)
Three Kings Ridge
Lord Howe Island (to Australia)
Balls Pyramid
Darling
Lord Howe Rise
West Norfolk Ridge
Kermadec Trench
Louisville Ridge
Southwest Pacific Basin
Sydney
Tasman Plain
Northland Plateau
Great Australian Bight
Murray
Kangaroo Island
Melbourne
Gascoyne Tablemount
Auckland
Raukumara Plain
South Australian Basin
King Island
Bass Strait
Furneaux Group
Tasman Sea
Challenger Plateau
North Island
Hikurangi Trench
Cook Strait
Valerie Guyot
Agassiz Fracture Zone
Tasmania
Hobart
East Tasman Plateau
Wellington
NEW ZEALAND
Chatham Rise
Chatham Islands (to NZ)
Tasman Basin
South Island
Dunedin
Bounty Trough
Bounty Islands (to NZ)
East Pacific Rise
Menard Fracture Zone
Indian Ridge
Tasman Plateau
Campbell Plateau
Antipodes Islands (to NZ)
Bollons Tablemount
Eltanin Fracture Zone
Auckland Islands (to NZ)
Campbell Island (to NZ)
Macquarie Ridge
Tasman Fracture Zone
Macquarie Island (to Australia)
Udintsev Fracture Zone
South Indian Basin
SOUTHERN OCEAN
Southeast Pacific Basin
Pacific-Antarctic Ridge
Bellingshausen Plain
De Gerlache
Antarctic Circle
Balleny Islands (to NZ)
Scott Island (to NZ)
Amundsen Plain
Peter I Island (to Norway)
Marie Byrd Seamount
Bellingshausen Sea
Iselin Seamount
Scott Shoal
Amundsen Sea
Ross Sea
ANTARCTICA
Gg
H
Hh
I
Ii
J
Jj
K
Kk
L
Ll
M
Mm

Wave action *has eroded this shoreline near Port Campbell in southeastern Australia, leaving isolated pinnacles of rock cut off from the main coastline. They are known as the "Twelve Apostles."*

POLYNESIA

KIRIBATI, TUVALU, *Cook Islands, Easter Island, French Polynesia, Niue, Pitcairn Islands, Tokelau, Wallis & Futuna*

THE NUMEROUS ISLAND GROUPS OF POLYNESIA lie to the east of Australia, scattered over a vast area in the south Pacific. The islands are a mixture of low-lying coral atolls, some of which enclose lagoons, and the tips of great underwater volcanoes. The populations on the islands are small, and most people are of Polynesian origin, as are the Maori of New Zealand. Local economies remain simple, relying mainly on subsistence crops, mineral deposits, many of which are now exhausted, fishing, and tourism.

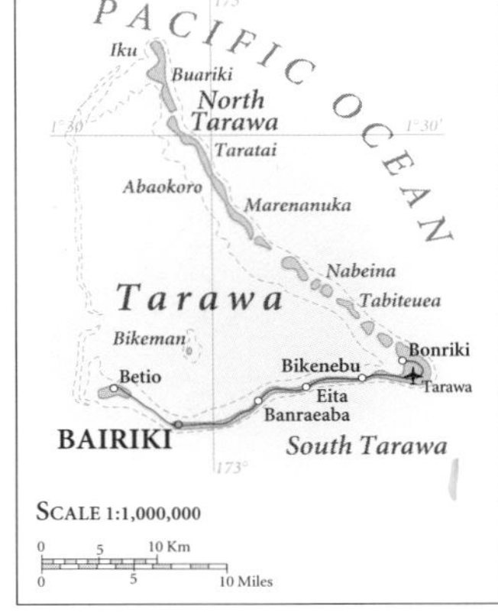
PACIFIC OCEAN
Iku
Buariki
North Tarawa
Taratai
Abaokoro
Marenanuka
Nabeina
Tabiteuea
Tarawa
Bikeman
Betio
Bikenebu
Bonriki
Tarawa
Eita
Banraeaba
BAIRIKI
South Tarawa
SCALE 1:1,000,000

With the exception of Banaba, all the islands in Kiribati's three groups are low-lying coral atolls. This aerial view shows the sparsely vegetated islands, intercut by many small lagoons.

KIRIBATI

A FORMER BRITISH COLONY, Kiribati became independent in 1979. Banaba's phosphate deposits ran out in 1980, following decades of exploitation by the British. Economic development remains slow and most agriculture is at a subsistence level, although coconuts provide export income, and underwater agriculture is being developed.

TUVALU

TUVALU IS A CHAIN of nine coral atolls, 360 miles (579 km) long with a land area of just over 9 sq miles (23 sq km). It is one of the world's smallest and most isolated states. As the Ellice Islands, Tuvalu was linked to the Gilbert Islands (now part of Kiribati) as a British colony until independence in 1978. Politically and socially conservative, Tuvaluans live by fishing and subsistence farming.

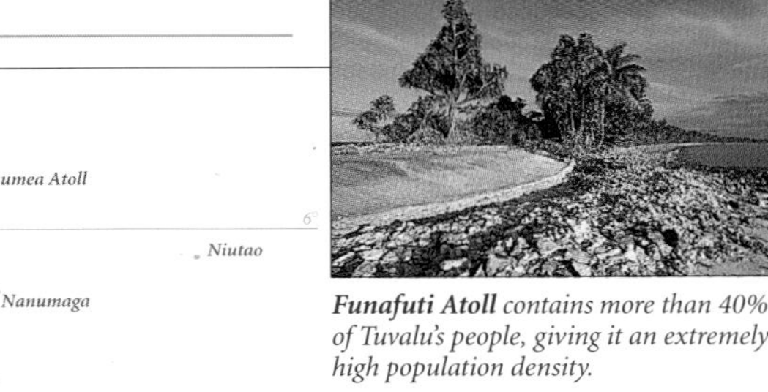

Funafuti Atoll *contains more than 40% of Tuvalu's people, giving it an extremely high population density.*

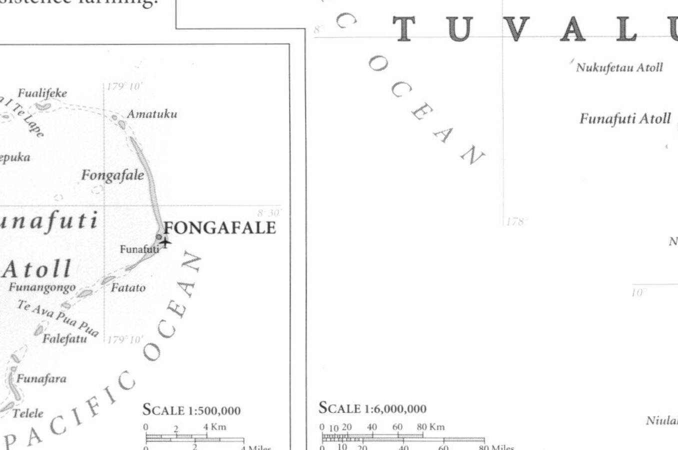
Nanumea Atoll
Niutao
Nanumaga
PACIFIC OCEAN
Nui Atoll
Vaitupu
TUVALU
Nukufetau Atoll
Funafuti Atoll
FONGAFALE
Nukulaelae Atoll
Niulakita
SCALE 1:6,000,000
Te Ava I Te Lape
Fualifeke
Amatuku
Tepuka
Fongafale
Fualopa
Funafuti Atoll
FONGAFALE
Fuafatu
Funafuti
Te Ava Fuagea
Vasafua
Funangongo
Fatato
Fuagea
Te Ava Pua Pua
Falefatu
Tefala
Funafara
Teafuafou
Telele
PACIFIC OCEAN
SCALE 1:500,000

TOKELAU (to New Zealand)

A LOW-LYING CORAL ATOLL, Tokelau is a dependent territory of New Zealand with few natural resources. Although a 1990 cyclone destroyed crops and infrastructure, a tuna cannery and the sale of fishing licenses have raised revenue. A catamaran link between the islands has increased their potential for tourism. Tokelau's small size and economic weakness make independence from New Zealand unlikely.

Fishermen cast their nets *to catch small fish in the shallow waters off Atafu Atoll, the most westerly island in Tokelau.*

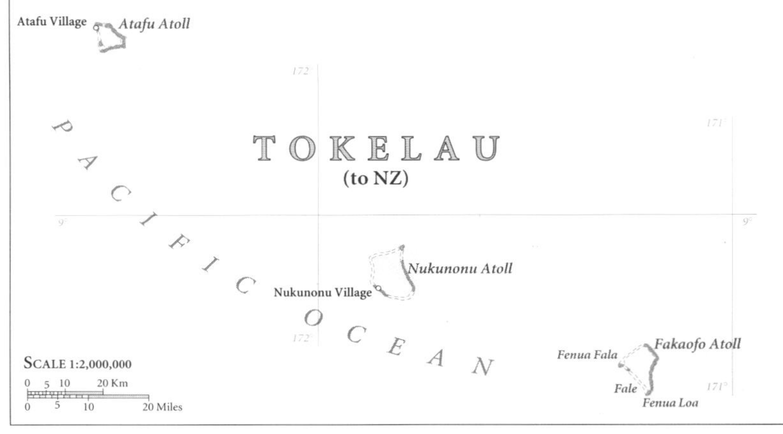
Atafu Village
Atafu Atoll
TOKELAU
(to NZ)
PACIFIC OCEAN
Nukunonu Atoll
Nukunonu Village
Fenua Fala
Fakaofo Atoll
Fale
Fenua Loa
SCALE 1:2,000,000

WALLIS & FUTUNA (to France)

IN CONTRAST TO OTHER FRENCH overseas territories in the south Pacific, the inhabitants of Wallis and Futuna have shown little desire for greater autonomy. A subsistence economy produces a variety of tropical crops, while foreign currency remittances come from expatriates and from the sale of licenses to Japanese and Korean fishing fleets.

PACIFIC OCEAN
Pointe Fatua
Pointe Matapu
Île Futuna
Toloke
Mont Puke 524m
Leava
Mala'e
Kolia
Pointe Vele
Alofitai
Pointe Matalesina
Mont Kolofau 417m
Pointe Sauma
Île Alofi
SCALE 1:1,000,000

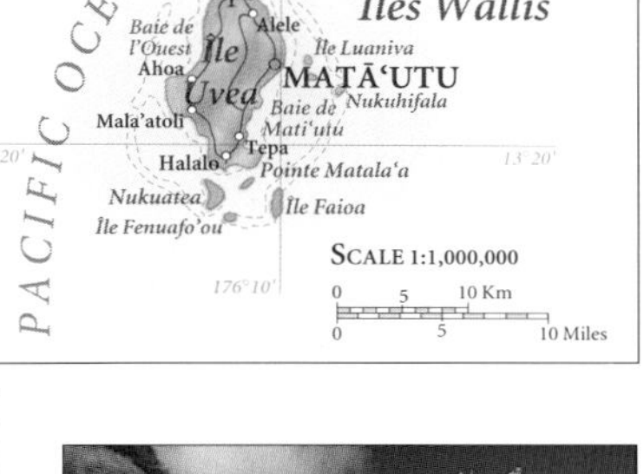
PACIFIC OCEAN
Nukuloa
Nukutapu
Hihifo
Vaitupu
Îles Wallis
Baie de l'Ouest
Île Uvea
Ahoa
Alele
Île Luaniva
MATĀ'UTU
Baie de Mati'utu
Nukuhifala
Mala'atoli
Halalo
Tepa
Pointe Matala'a
Nukuatea
Île Fenuafo'ou
Île Faioa
SCALE 1:1,000,000

NIUE (to New Zealand)

NIUE, the world's largest coral island, is self-governing but exists in free association with New Zealand. Tropical fruits are grown for local consumption; tourism and the sale of postage stamps provide foreign currency. The lack of local job prospects has led more than 10,000 Niueans to emigrate to New Zealand, which has now invested heavily in Niue's economy in the hope of reversing this trend.

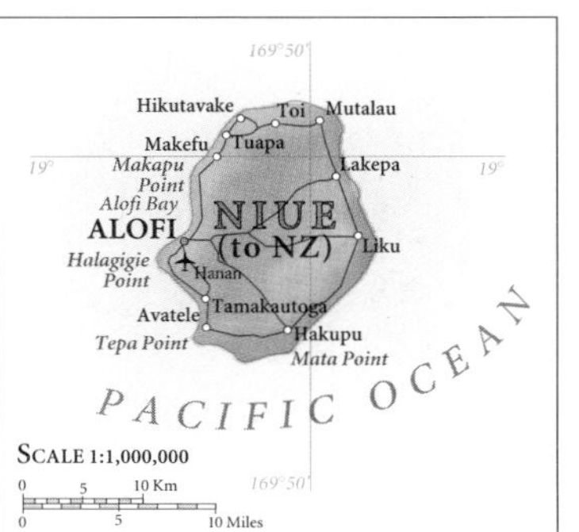
Hikutavake
Toi
Mutalau
Makefu
Tuapa
Makapu Point
Lakepa
Alofi Bay
ALOFI
NIUE (to NZ)
Liku
Halagigie Point
Hanan
Tamakautoga
Avatele
Hakupu
Tepa Point
Mata Point
PACIFIC OCEAN
SCALE 1:1,000,000

Waves have cut back *the original coastline, exposing a sandy beach, near Mutalau in the northeast corner of Niue.*

Palm trees *fringe the white sands of a beach on Aitutaki in the Southern Cook Islands, where tourism is of increasing economic importance.*

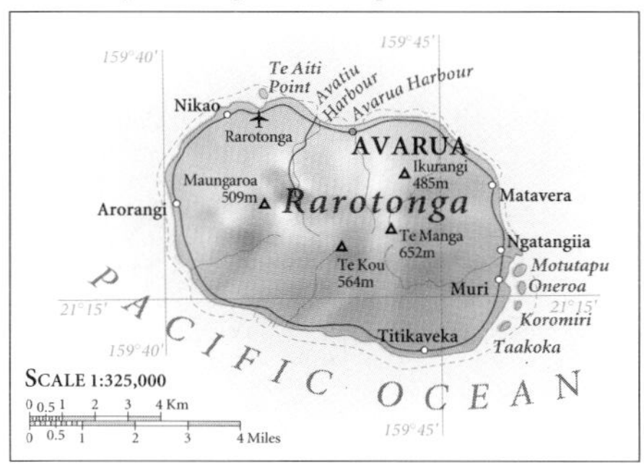
Te Aiti Point
Avatiu Harbour
Avarua Harbour
Nikao
Rarotonga
AVARUA
Ikurangi 485m
Maungaroa 509m
Rarotonga
Matavera
Arorangi
Te Manga 652m
Te Kou 564m
Ngatangiia
Motutapu
Oneroa
Muri
Koromiri
Titikaveka
Taakoka
PACIFIC OCEAN
SCALE 1:325,000

COOK ISLANDS (to New Zealand)

A MIXTURE OF CORAL ATOLLS and volcanic peaks, the Cook Islands achieved self-government in 1965 but exist in free association with New Zealand. A diverse economy includes pearl and giant-clam farming and an ostrich farm, as well as tourism and banking. A 1991 friendship treaty with France provides for French surveillance of territorial waters.

Penrhyn
Rakahanga
Pukapuka
Nassau
Manihiki
Northern Cook Islands
Suwarrow
COOK ISLANDS
(to NZ)
PACIFIC OCEAN
Palmerston
Southern Cook Islands
Aitutaki
Manuae
Takutea
Mitiaro
Atiu
Mauke
Rarotonga
AVARUA
Mangaia
SCALE 1:20,000,000

N O P Q R S T U V W X Y

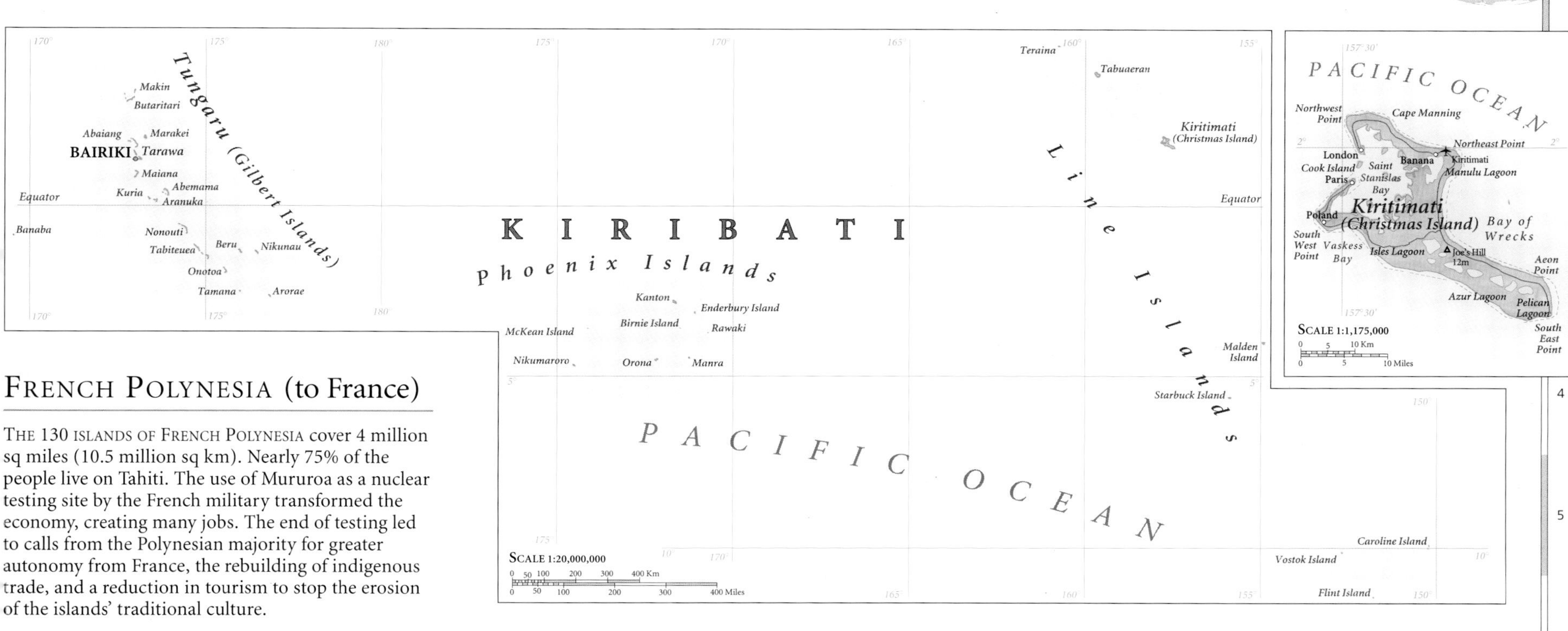
Makin
Butaritari
Abaiang
Marakei
BAIRIKI
Tarawa
Maiana
Abemama
Kuria
Aranuka
Equator
Banaba
Nonouti
Tabiteuea
Beru
Nikunau
Onotoa
Tamana
Arorae
Tungaru (Gilbert Islands)
KIRIBATI
Phoenix Islands
Kanton
Enderbury Island
Birnie Island
Rawaki
McKean Island
Nikumaroro
Orona
Manra
Teraina
Tabuaeran
Kiritimati (Christmas Island)
Line Islands
Malden Island
Starbuck Island
PACIFIC OCEAN
SCALE 1:20,000,000
Caroline Island
Vostok Island
Flint Island
PACIFIC OCEAN
Northwest Point
Cape Manning
Northeast Point
London
Cook Island
Banana
Kiritimati
Saint Stanislas Bay
Paris
Manulu Lagoon
Poland
Kiritimati (Christmas Island)
Bay of Wrecks
South West Point
Vaskess Bay
Isles Lagoon
Joe's Hill 12m
Aeon Point
Azur Lagoon
Pelican Lagoon
SCALE 1:1,175,000
South East Point

FRENCH POLYNESIA (to France)

THE 130 ISLANDS OF FRENCH POLYNESIA cover 4 million sq miles (10.5 million sq km). Nearly 75% of the people live on Tahiti. The use of Mururoa as a nuclear testing site by the French military transformed the economy, creating many jobs. The end of testing led to calls from the Polynesian majority for greater autonomy from France, the rebuilding of indigenous trade, and a reduction in tourism to stop the erosion of the islands' traditional culture.

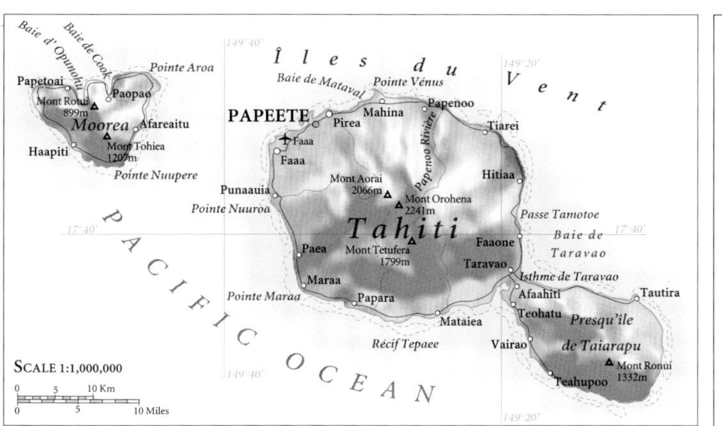
Baie d'Opunohu
Baie de Cook
Pointe Aroa
Papetoai
Paopao
Mont Rotui 899m
Moorea
Afareaitu
Haapiti
Mont Tohiea 1207m
Pointe Nuupere
Îles du Vent
Baie de Matavai
Pointe Vénus
Papenoo
PAPEETE
Pirae
Mahina
Tiarei
Faaa
Hitiaa
Punaauia
Pointe Nuuroa
Mont Aorai 2066m
Mont Orohena 2241m
Tahiti
Passe Tamotoe
Baie de Taravao
Paea
Mont Tetufera 1799m
Faaone
Taravao
Isthme de Taravao
Maraa
Papara
Afaahiti
Tautira
Pointe Maraa
Mataiea
Teohatu
Presqu'île de Taiarapu
Récif Tepaee
Vairao
Mont Ronui 1332m
Teahupoo
PACIFIC OCEAN
SCALE 1:1,000,000

Hatutu
Eiao
Îles Marquises
Nuku Hiva
Taiohae
Ua Huka
Ua Pu
Atuona
Hiva Oa
Tahuata
Motane
Fatu Hiva
Omoa

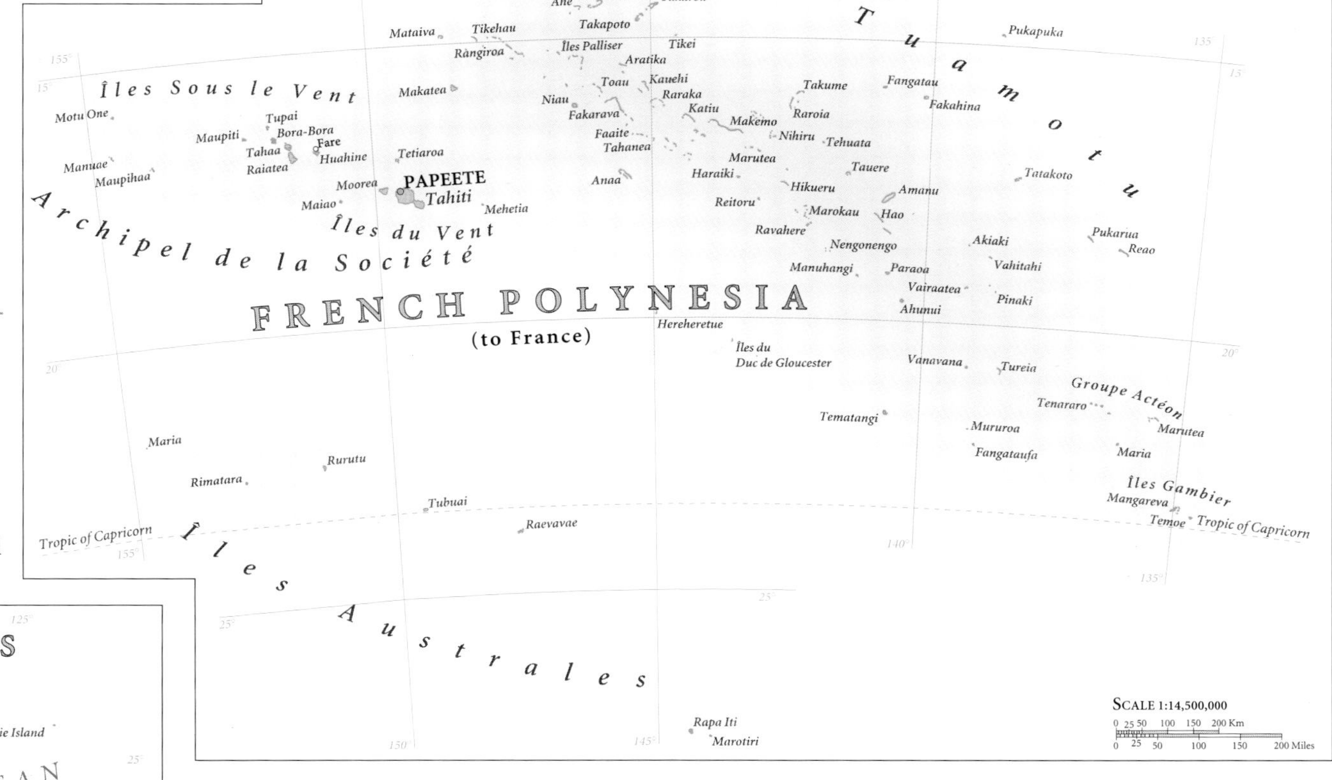
PACIFIC OCEAN
Îles Tuamotu
Îles du Roi George
Îles du Désappointement
Ahe
Manihi
Takaroa
Tepoto
Napuka
Takapoto
Mataiva
Tikehau
Rangiroa
Îles Palliser
Tikei
Pukapuka
Aratika
Îles Sous le Vent
Makatea
Toau
Kauehi
Raraka
Takume
Fangatau
Niau
Fakarava
Katiu
Raroia
Fakahina
Motu One
Tupai
Bora-Bora
Maupiti
Faaite
Makemo
Tahanea
Nihiru
Tehuata
Tahaa
Fare
Raiatea
Huahine
Tetiaroa
Manuae
Maupihaa
Marutea
Tauere
Tatakoto
Moorea
PAPEETE
Tahiti
Anaa
Haraiki
Hikueru
Amanu
Maiao
Mehetia
Reitoru
Marokau
Hao
Îles du Vent
Ravahere
Akiaki
Pukarua
Reao
Archipel de la Société
Nengonengo
Vahitahi
Manuhangi
Paraoa
Vairaatea
Pinaki
Ahunui
FRENCH POLYNESIA
(to France)
Hereheretue
Îles du Duc de Gloucester
Vanavana
Tureia
Groupe Actéon
Tenararo
Tematangi
Marutea
Mururoa
Fangataufa
Maria
Maria
Rurutu
Rimatara
Îles Gambier
Mangareva
Temoe
Tubuai
Tropic of Capricorn
Raevavae
Îles Australes
Rapa Iti
Marotiri
SCALE 1:14,500,000

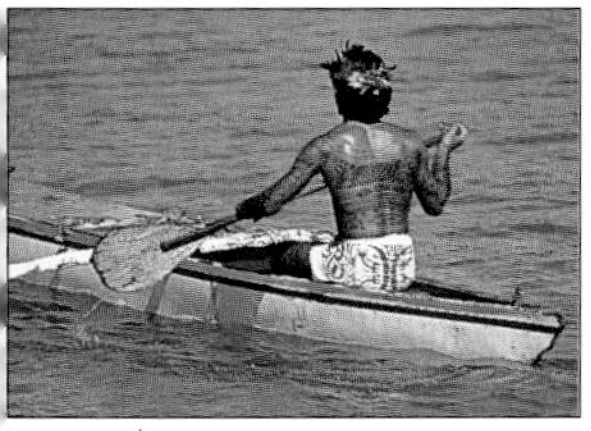
The traditional Tahitian welcome for visitors, who are greeted by parties of canoes, has become a major tourist attraction.

PITCAIRN ISLANDS (to UK)

BRITAIN'S MOST ISOLATED DEPENDENCY, Pitcairn Island was first populated by mutineers from the HMS *Bounty* in 1790. Emigration is further depleting the already limited gene pool of the island's inhabitants, with associated social and health problems. Barter, fishing, and subsistence farming form the basis of the economy, although postage stamp sales provide foreign currency earnings, and offshore mineral exploitation may boost the economy in future.

Oeno Island
PITCAIRN ISLANDS
(to UK)
Henderson Island
Ducie Island
Pitcairn Island
PACIFIC OCEAN
SCALE 1:10,000,000

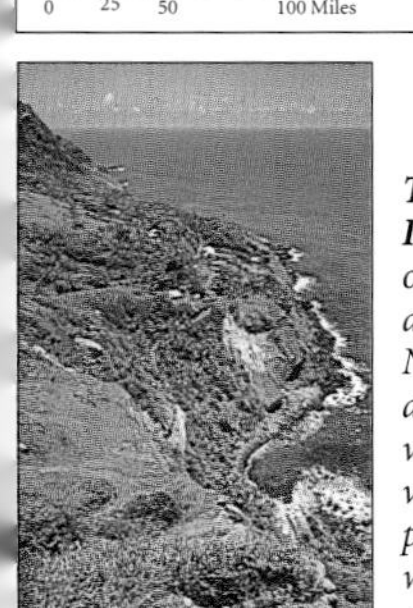
The Pitcairn Islanders rely on regular airdrops from New Zealand and periodic visits by supply vessels to provide them with basic commodities.

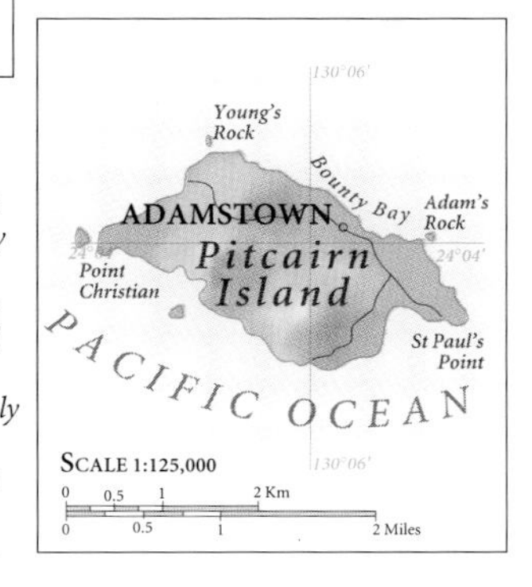
Young's Rock
Bounty Bay
Adam's Rock
ADAMSTOWN
Pitcairn Island
Point Christian
St Paul's Point
PACIFIC OCEAN
SCALE 1:125,000

EASTER ISLAND (to Chile)

ONE OF THE MOST EASTERLY ISLANDS in Polynesia, Easter Island *(Isla de Pascua)* – also known as Rapa Nui – is part of Chile. The mainly Polynesian inhabitants support themselves by farming, which is mainly of a subsistence nature, and includes cattle rearing and growing crops such as sugar cane, bananas, corn, gourds, and potatoes. In recent years, tourism has become the most important source of income, and the island sustains a small commercial airport.

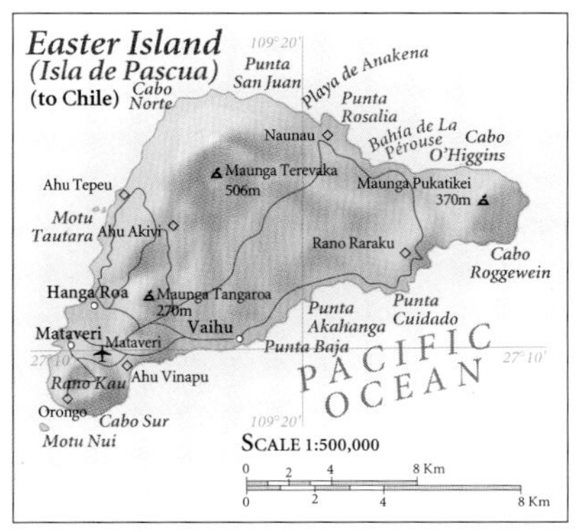
Easter Island
(Isla de Pascua)
(to Chile)
Cabo Norte
Punta San Juan
Playa de Anakena
Punta Rosalia
Naunau
Bahia de La Pérouse
Cabo O'Higgins
Maunga Terevaka 506m
Maunga Pukatikei 370m
Ahu Tepeu
Motu Tautara
Ahu Akivi
Rano Raraku
Cabo Roggewein
Hanga Roa
Maunga Tangaroa 270m
Punta Cuidado
Mataveri
Vaihu
Punta Akahanga
Punta Baja
Rano Kau
Ahu Vinapu
PACIFIC OCEAN
Orongo
Cabo Sur
Motu Nui
SCALE 1:500,000

***The Naunau**, a series of huge stone statues, overlook Playa de Anakena, on Easter Island. Carved out of a soft volcanic rock, they were erected between 400 and 900 years ago.*

ANTARCTICA

THE ICE-COVERED CONTINENT of Antarctica, which is the Earth's most southerly region, has drawn explorers and entrepreneurs seeking challenge and riches in its wintry lands for over 200 years. The extreme climate has deterred any large-scale settlement of the continent, and though commercial hunters built outposts in the past, habitation is now limited to scientific bases. The Antarctic Treaty, which came into force in 1961, provides for international governance and scientific cooperation instead of potential territorial conflict.

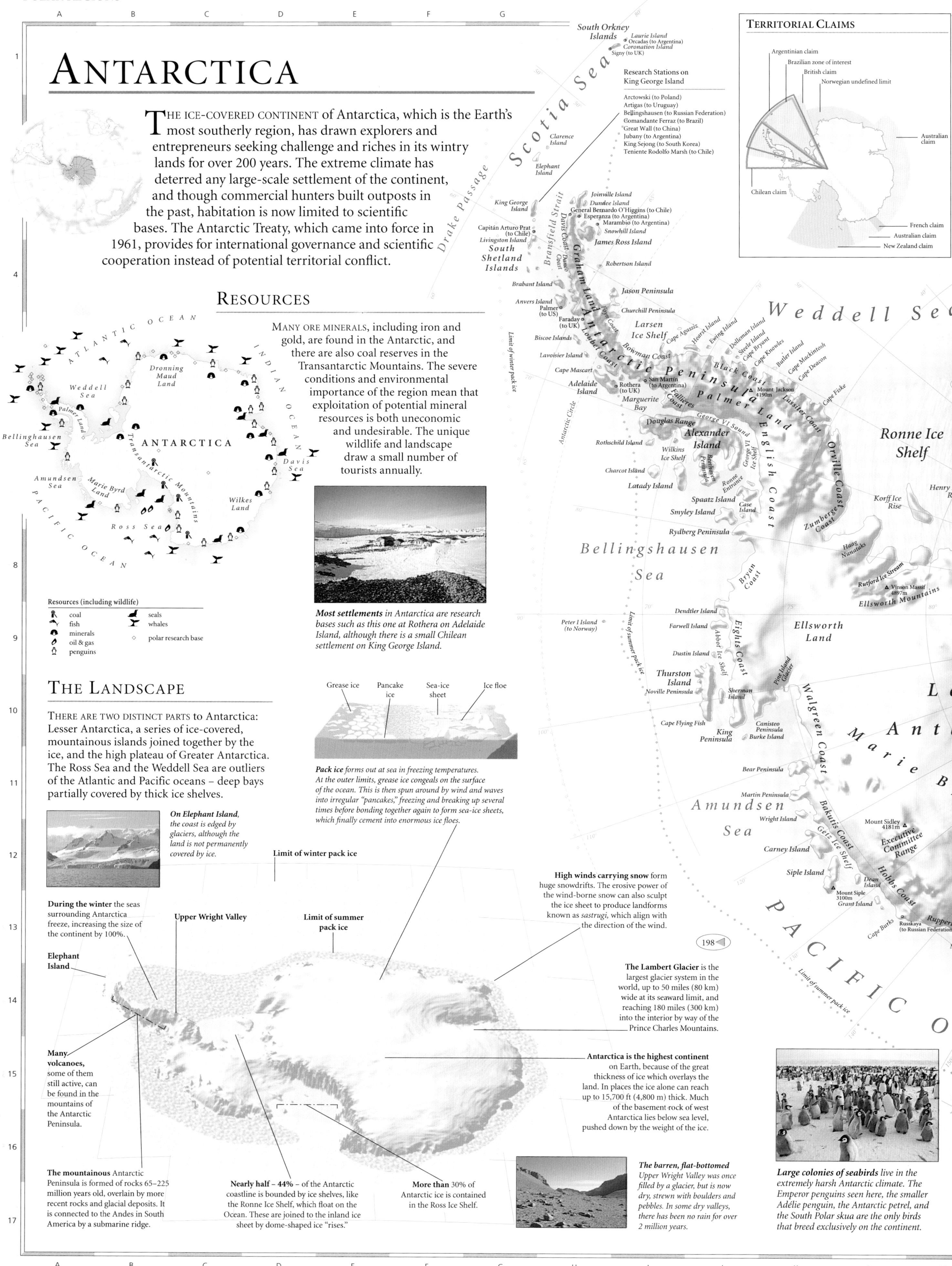

TERRITORIAL CLAIMS
Argentinian claim
Brazilian zone of interest
British claim
Norwegian undefined limit
Australian claim
Chilean claim
French claim
Australian claim
New Zealand claim
South Orkney Islands
Laurie Island
Orcadas (to Argentina)
Coronation Island
Signy (to UK)
Research Stations on King George Island
Arctowski (to Poland)
Artigas (to Uruguay)
Bellingshausen (to Russian Federation)
Comandante Ferraz (to Brazil)
Great Wall (to China)
Jubany (to Argentina)
King Sejong (to South Korea)
Teniente Rodolfo Marsh (to Chile)
Scotia Sea
Drake Passage
Weddell Sea
Bellingshausen Sea
Amundsen Sea
PACIFIC OCEAN
Ronne Ice Shelf
Ellsworth Land
Antarctic Peninsula
Palmer Land
Graham Land
Alexander Island
Thurston Island
Ellsworth Mountains
Vinson Massif 4897m
Mount Jackson 4190m
Mount Sidley 4181m
Mount Siple 3100m
Peter I Island (to Norway)
Russkaya (to Russian Federation)
Limit of winter pack ice
Limit of summer pack ice
Resources (including wildlife)
coal
fish
minerals
oil & gas
penguins
seals
whales
polar research base
ATLANTIC OCEAN
INDIAN OCEAN
PACIFIC OCEAN
ANTARCTICA
Dronning Maud Land
Weddell Sea
Palmer Land
Bellingshausen Sea
Amundsen Sea
Marie Byrd Land
Transantarctic Mountains
Ross Sea
Wilkes Land
Davis Sea
Grease ice
Pancake ice
Sea-ice sheet
Ice floe
Limit of winter pack ice
Upper Wright Valley
Limit of summer pack ice
Elephant Island

RESOURCES

MANY ORE MINERALS, including iron and gold, are found in the Antarctic, and there are also coal reserves in the Transantarctic Mountains. The severe conditions and environmental importance of the region mean that exploitation of potential mineral resources is both uneconomic and undesirable. The unique wildlife and landscape draw a small number of tourists annually.

***Most settlements** in Antarctica are research bases such as this one at Rothera on Adelaide Island, although there is a small Chilean settlement on King George Island.*

THE LANDSCAPE

THERE ARE TWO DISTINCT PARTS to Antarctica: Lesser Antarctica, a series of ice-covered, mountainous islands joined together by the ice, and the high plateau of Greater Antarctica. The Ross Sea and the Weddell Sea are outliers of the Atlantic and Pacific oceans – deep bays partially covered by thick ice shelves.

***On Elephant Island,** the coast is edged by glaciers, although the land is not permanently covered by ice.*

***Pack ice** forms out at sea in freezing temperatures. At the outer limits, grease ice congeals on the surface of the ocean. This is then spun around by wind and waves into irregular "pancakes," freezing and breaking up several times before bonding together again to form sea-ice sheets, which finally cement into enormous ice floes.*

During the winter the seas surrounding Antarctica freeze, increasing the size of the continent by 100%.

Many volcanoes, some of them still active, can be found in the mountains of the Antarctic Peninsula.

The mountainous Antarctic Peninsula is formed of rocks 65–225 million years old, overlain by more recent rocks and glacial deposits. It is connected to the Andes in South America by a submarine ridge.

Nearly half – 44% – of the Antarctic coastline is bounded by ice shelves, like the Ronne Ice Shelf, which float on the Ocean. These are joined to the inland ice sheet by dome-shaped ice "rises."

More than 30% of Antarctic ice is contained in the Ross Ice Shelf.

High winds carrying snow form huge snowdrifts. The erosive power of the wind-borne snow can also sculpt the ice sheet to produce landforms known as *sastrugi*, which align with the direction of the wind.

The Lambert Glacier is the largest glacier system in the world, up to 50 miles (80 km) wide at its seaward limit, and reaching 180 miles (300 km) into the interior by way of the Prince Charles Mountains.

Antarctica is the highest continent on Earth, because of the great thickness of ice which overlays the land. In places the ice alone can reach up to 15,700 ft (4,800 m) thick. Much of the basement rock of west Antarctica lies below sea level, pushed down by the weight of the ice.

***The barren, flat-bottomed** Upper Wright Valley was once filled by a glacier, but is now dry, strewn with boulders and pebbles. In some dry valleys, there has been no rain for over 2 million years.*

***Large colonies of seabirds** live in the extremely harsh Antarctic climate. The Emperor penguins seen here, the smaller Adélie penguin, the Antarctic petrel, and the South Polar skua are the only birds that breed exclusively on the continent.*

198

66
ATLANTIC OCEAN
INDIAN OCEAN
ANTARCTICA
Greater Antarctica
Dronning Maud Land
Fimbutheimen
Princess Astrid Kyst
Prinsesse Ragnhild Kyst
Prins Harald Kyst
Kronprins Olav Kyst
Kronprinsesse Märtha Kyst
Borg Massif
Maudheimvidda
Riiser-Larsen Ice Shelf
Cape Norvegia
Georg von Neumayer (to Germany)
Sanae (to South Africa)
Fimbul Ice Shelf
Maitri (to India)
Novolazarevskaya (to Russian Federation)
Mühlig-Hofmann Mountains
Wohlthat Mountains
Asuka (to Japan)
Sør Rondane Mountains
Thorshavnheiane
Belgica Mountains
Mount Victor 2588m
Limit of summer pack ice
Antarctic Circle
Riiser-Larsen Peninsula
Lützow Holmbukta
Syowa (to Japan)
Molodezhnaya (to Russian Federation)
Thyer Glacier
Casey Bay
Amundsen Bay
Nye Mountains
Napier Mountains
Cape Batterbee
Mount Elkins 2300m
Enderby Land
Dismal Mountains
Edward VIII Gulf
Law Promontory
Kemp Land
Hansen Mountains
Mawson Coast
Mawson (to Australia)
Gustav Bull Mountains
Mac. Robertson Land
Mount Menzies 3355m
Prince Charles Mountains
Lars Christensen Coast
Cape Darnley
Lambert Glacier
Amery Ice Shelf
Gillock Island
Mackenzie Bay
Ingrid Christensen Coast
Zhongshan (to China)
Prydz Bay
Davis (to Australia)
Princess Elizabeth Land
West Ice Shelf
King Leopold and Queen Astrid Land
Mikhaylov Island
Philippi Glacier
Wilhelm II Land
Wilhelm II Coast
Davis Sea
Mirny (to Russian Federation)
Queen Mary Coast
Masson Island
Northcliffe Glacier
Denman Glacier
Shackleton Ice Shelf
Scott Glacier
Mill Island
Bowman Island
Knox Coast
Vincennes Bay
Wilkes Land
Casey (to Australia)
Budd Coast
Cape Poinsett
Cape Waldron
Sabrina Coast
Dalton Iceberg Tongue
Banzare Coast
Cape Goodenough
Porpoise Bay
Terre Adélie
Wilkes Coast
Cape Keltie
Dibble Iceberg Tongue
Adélie Coast
Dumont d'Urville (to France)
Cape Garry
Mertz Glacier
Ninnis Glacier
George V Coast
Cape Freshfield
George V Land
Cape Hudson
Leningradskaya
Cape Cheetham
Oates Land
Rennick Glacier
Mount Minto 4163m
Cape Adare
Borchgrevink Coast
Coulman Island
Dumont d'Urville Sea
Balleny Islands
Scott Island
Lyddan Island
Brunt Ice Shelf
Stancomb-Wills Glacier
Halley (to UK)
Caird Coast
Luitpold Coast
Coats Land
Belgrano II (to Argentina)
Theron Mountains
Slessor Glacier
Filchner Ice Shelf
Recovery Glacier
Support Force Glacier
Pensacola Mountains
Foundation Ice Stream
South Pole
Amundsen-Scott (to US)
Transantarctic Mountains
Vostok (to Russian Federation)
South Geomagnetic Pole
Whitmore Mountains
Seelig
Horlick Mountains
Watson Escarpment
Queen Maud Mountains
Amundsen Coast
Gould Coast
Beardmore Glacier
Dufek Coast
Mount Kirkpatrick 4528m
Mount Markham 4351m
Nimrod Glacier
Shackleton Coast
Byrd Glacier
Mount McClintock 3492m
Hillary Coast
Victoria Land
Siple Coast
Rockefeller Plateau
Shirase Coast
Ross Ice Shelf
Roosevelt Island
Saunders Coast
Sulzberger Bay
Edward VII Peninsula
Mount Lister 4026m
Scott Base (to NZ)
McMurdo Base (to US)
Ross Island
Mount Erebus 3794m
Scott Coast
Drygalski Ice Tongue
Ross Sea
180
MAP KEY
ELEVATION
ice cap
ice shelf
exposed land
SCALE 1:14,750,000
(projection: Lambert Azimuthal Equal Area)
Km
0 25 50 100 150 200 250 300 350 400 450 500
0 25 50 100 150 200 250 300 350 400 450 500
Miles
V W X Y
N O P Q R S T U V W X Y Z
1 2 3 4 5 6 7 8 13 14 15 16 17

The sun sets over the Antarctic Peninsula for more than six months during the winter. However, there are more hours of sunshine during the brief Antarctic summer than most equatorial countries receive in a whole year.

Immense, flat-topped icebergs are formed when blocks of ice break away from the main ice sheet. Though the exposed area is enormous, the volume of ice concealed beneath the water may be many times greater.

The Arctic

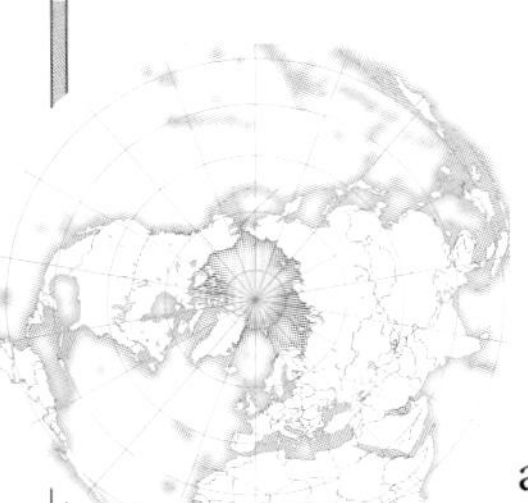

THREE CONTINENTS, ASIA, NORTH AMERICA, AND EUROPE, reach into the Arctic Circle at their northernmost limits, almost entirely encircling the Arctic Ocean. Despite the region's extraordinarily harsh climate, it has been inhabited for thousands of years by peoples such as the European Lapps, the Russian Nenet, and the North American Inuit, who draw a living from fishing, herding, and hunting. More recently, particularly in the Russian Arctic, opportunities to exploit oil and other mineral reserves have encouraged immigration. Pollution of the Arctic's unique ecology and damage to the traditional lifestyles of many native peoples have been the unfortunate results of this activity, and international cooperation is needed to safeguard the future of the region.

Map Key

POPULATION
- above 5 million
- 1 million to 5 million
- 500,000 to 1 million
- 100,000 to 500,000
- 50,000 to 100,000
- 10,000 to 50,000
- below 10,000

SEA DEPTH
- sea level
- 250m / 820ft
- 500m / 1640ft
- 1000m / 3281ft
- 2000m / 6562ft
- 3000m / 9843ft

SCALE 1:21,000,000
(projection: Lambert Azimuthal Equal Area)

Windblown snow etches deep patterns in the ice sheet. Known as sastrugi, the patterns align with the direction of the wind.

Resources

LARGE QUANTITIES of coal, oil, and natural gas are to be found in the basins of the Arctic Ocean and in northern Canada, Alaska, and the Russian Federation. The cost and difficulty of extraction and, more recently, awareness of damage to the environment have limited exploitation to coastal regions. The unfrozen waters have stocks of fish, including cod, flounder, and haddock. Quotas have now been put in place to restrict the number of fish caught annually. Reindeer are herded in large numbers by many of the native Arctic peoples. Most grain and vegetables are imported from elsewhere.

Bering Sea
ASIA
NORTH AMERICA
ARCTIC OCEAN
Inuvik
Tiksi
Noril'sk
Qaanaaq
Murmansk
Reykjavík
ATLANTIC OCEAN
EUROPE

Icebreakers are ships with specially strengthened hulls designed to break a path through the ice. They are used to keep important routes open during the winter, when falling temperatures cause much of the Arctic Ocean to freeze over.

Resources
- coal
- fish
- mining
- oil & gas
- radioactive contamination
- major towns
- major ports

The Landscape

THE ARCTIC OCEAN comprises two large ocean basins divided by three submarine ridges, the greatest of which, the Lomonosov Ridge, is a huge underwater mountain range that has an average height of more than 10,000 ft (3,000 m). The lands that encircle the Arctic Ocean are underlain by great shield areas of ancient rocks, which were heavily glaciated during the last Ice Age.

Icebergs are constantly broken up and reshaped by wind and the oceans. This flat-topped iceberg has been undercut, leaving a craggy ice cliff.

A complex and ancient mountain system, extending from the Queen Elizabeth Islands to eastern Greenland, was formed more than 245 million years ago.

The Arctic Ocean is the world's smallest ocean, with a total area of 5,440,000 sq miles (15,100,000 sq km).

At a latitude of more than 75° N, the Arctic Ocean is almost permanently covered with pack ice, though high winds and the movement of the seas can cause the ice to crack and break up.

In the more southerly reaches of the Arctic, like Siberia, much of the land is covered by permafrost. In the summer, higher temperatures warm the frozen ground, causing a number of typical phenomena. These include solifluction, the fast downhill movement of topsoil layers; freeze/thaw activity, which patterns the ground into regular polygonal shapes; and the formation of large domes with a frozen ice core, known as pingos.

The Canadian Shield underlies almost all of the Canadian Arctic. A very stable plateau of ancient rock, it is now covered by glacial lakes and sediment, that supports tundra vegetation.

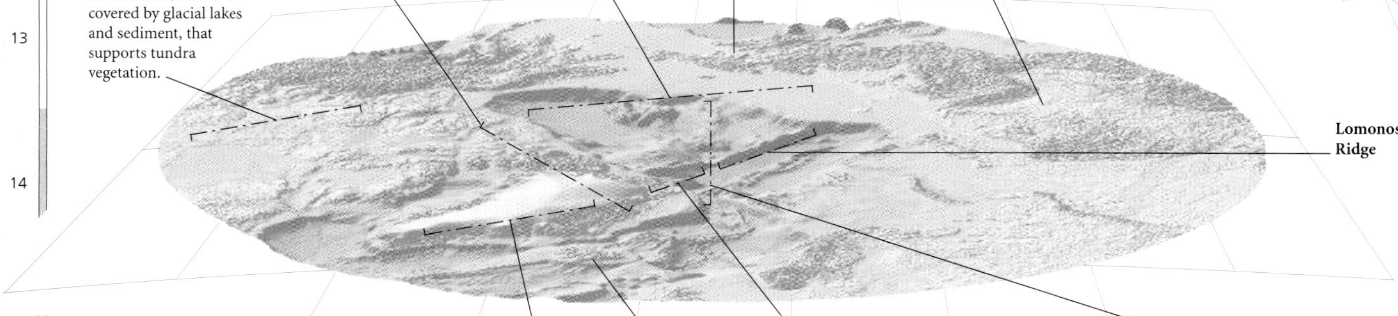

Lomonosov Ridge

Lomonosov Ridge

Arctic ice shelf

Much of Greenland *is covered by a massive ice sheet more than 650,000 sq miles (1,683,400 sq km) in extent. The weight of the ice has depressed the central land area to form a basin lying more than 1,000 ft (300 m) below sea level. Only at the edges of the island is bare rock visible.*

Iceland has five major glaciers, sustained by heavy snowfall. Parts of the ice cap cover active volcanoes, such as Bárdharbunga, which periodically erupt causing the melted ice to form a great lake at the glacier margins.

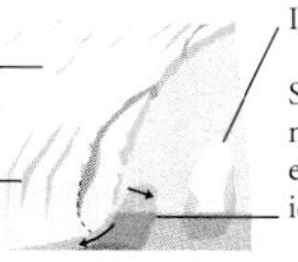

Ice sheet
Iceberg
Crevasses occur at the edge of the ice sheet
Seawater melts the edge of the ice sheet

At the boundary *of the Arctic ice shelves, seawater flows under the ice, causing melting and forming crevasses on the surface. This eventually weakens blocks of ice, which break away as icebergs. This process is known as calving.*

CANADA
NORTH AMERICA
Great Bear Lake
Great Slave Lake
Coppermine
Bathurst Inlet
Cambridge Bay
Churchill
Nelson
Southampton Island
Hudson Bay
Coats Island
Repulse Bay
Melville Peninsula
Mansel Island
Ivujivik
Foxe Basin
Prince Charles Island
Foxe Peninsula
Inukjuak
Hudson Strait
Baffin Isla
Lake Harbour
Cumberland Sound
Ungava Bay
Cape Chidley
Davis Str
Labrador Sea
Nain
Maniitsoq
NUUK
Paamiut
Ivittuut
Labrador Basin
Qaqortoq
Nanortalik
Eirik Ridge
ATLAN

198 ◀
14 ◀
14 ◀
▼ 66

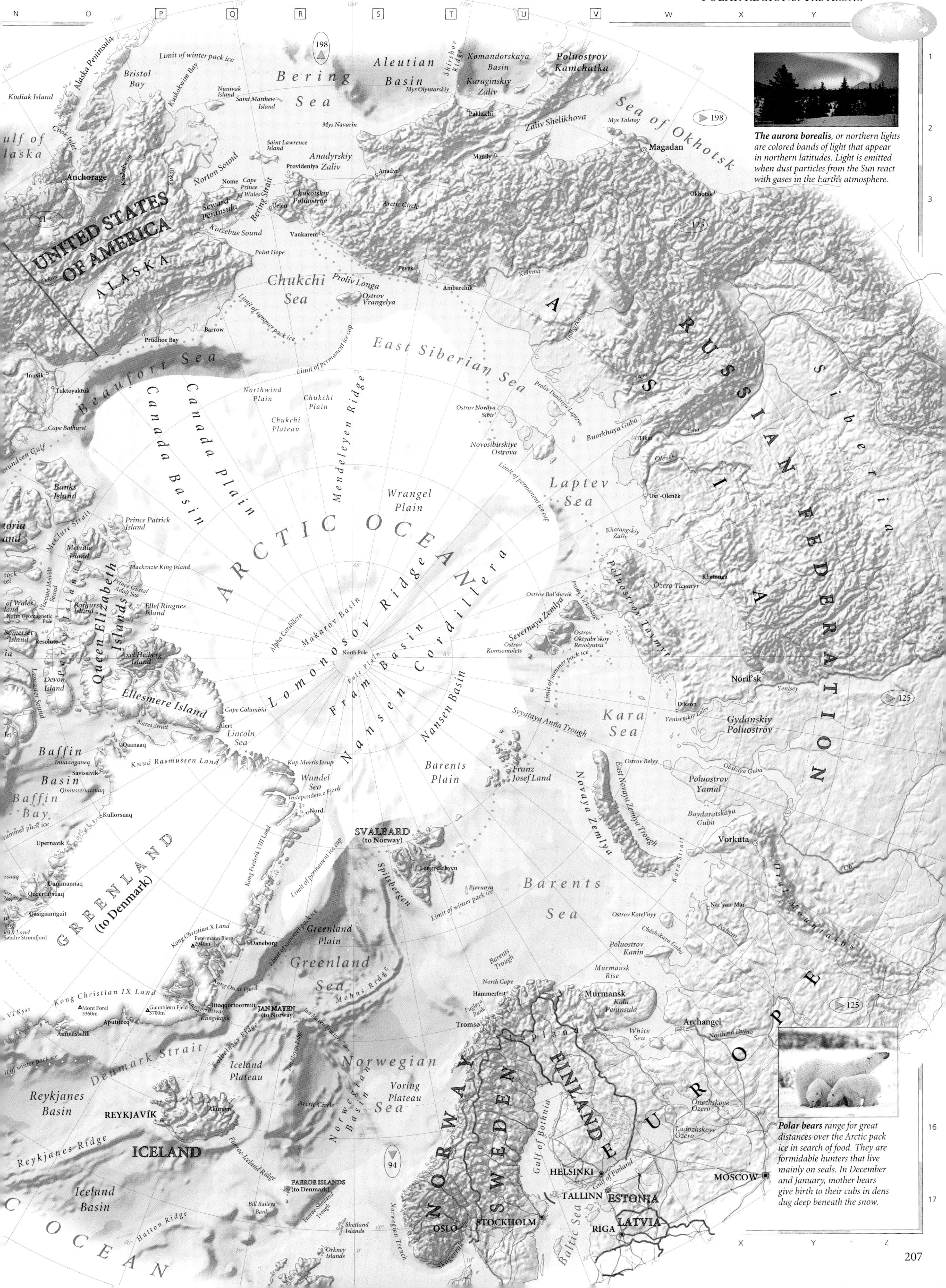

The aurora borealis, *or northern lights are colored bands of light that appear in northern latitudes. Light is emitted when dust particles from the Sun react with gases in the Earth's atmosphere.*

Polar bears *range for great distances over the Arctic pack ice in search of food. They are formidable hunters that live mainly on seals. In December and January, mother bears give birth to their cubs in dens dug deep beneath the snow.*

THE TIME ZONES

–2 –1 0 +1 +2 +3 +4 +5 +6 +7 +8 +9 +10 +11 +12 –12 –11 –10 –9 –8 –7 –6 –5 –4 –3 –2
ARCTIC OCEAN
Severnaya Zemlya
Franz Josef Land
SVALBARD (to Norway)
New Siberian Islands
Queen Elizabeth Islands
GREENLAND (to Denmark)
JAN MAYEN (to Norway)
Novaya Zemlya
International Dateline
Baffin Island
Arctic Circle
ICELAND
FAEROE ISLANDS (to Denmark)
NORWAY
SWEDEN
FINLAND
RUSSIAN FEDERATION
European Russia
Asian Russia
Alaska (to US)
REPUBLIC OF IRELAND
UNITED KINGDOM
DENMARK
CHANNEL ISLANDS (to UK)
KAZAKHSTAN
MONGOLIA
Kurile Islands (to Rus. Fed.)
CANADA
Newfoundland
ST. PIERRE & MIQUELON (to France)
Azores (to Portugal)
GIBRALTAR (to UK)
Madeira (to Portugal)
Canary Islands (to Spain)
WESTERN SAHARA
SPAIN
PORT.
ANDORRA
ITALY
TURKEY
GREECE
UZBEK.
TURKMEN.
KYRG.
TAJ.
IRAN
AFGH.
CHINA
N. KOREA
S. KOREA
JAPAN
PACIFIC OCEAN
UNITED STATES OF AMERICA
ATLANTIC OCEAN
BERMUDA (to UK)
TUNISIA
MALTA
CYPRUS
SYRIA
ISRAEL
JORDAN
IRAQ
KUWAIT
BAHRAIN
QATAR
SAUDI ARABIA
PAKISTAN
NEPAL
BHUTAN
BANGLADESH
INDIA
MACAO (to Portugal)
TAIWAN
MIDWAY ISLANDS (to US)
ALGERIA
LIBYA
EGYPT
MOROCCO
MAURITANIA
MALI
NIGER
CHAD
SUDAN
ERITREA
YEMEN
OMAN
DJIBOUTI
ETHIOPIA
SOMALIA
LAOS
MYAN.
THAI.
VIETNAM
CAMB.
Paracel Islands (disputed)
NORTHERN MARIANA ISLANDS (to US)
GUAM (to US)
WAKE ISLAND (to US)
MARSHALL ISLANDS
Hawaii (to US)
JOHNSTON ATOLL (to US)
MEXICO
CAPE VERDE
SENEGAL
GAMBIA
GUINEA-BISSAU
GUINEA
SIERRA LEONE
LIBERIA
IVORY COAST
GHANA
TOGO
BENIN
NIGERIA
CAMEROON
C.A.R.
UGANDA
KENYA
Laccadive Islands (to India)
Andaman Islands (to India)
SRI LANKA
MALDIVES
SINGAPORE
MALAYSIA
BRUNEI
PHILIPPINES
Spratly Islands (disputed)
MICRONESIA
PALAU
NAURU
KIRIBATI
WALLIS & FUTUNA (to France)
KINGMAN REEF (to US)
PALMYRA ATOLL (to US)
BAKER & HOWLAND ISLANDS (to US)
JARVIS ISLAND (to US)
Clipperton Island (to France)
GUATEMALA
EL SALVADOR
NICARAGUA
COSTA RICA
PANAMA
COLOMBIA
VENEZUELA
GUYANA
SURINAME
FRENCH GUIANA (to France)
Equator
ASCENSION ISLAND (to St Helena)
SAO TOME & PRINCIPE
GABON
CONGO
RWANDA
BURUNDI
ZAIRE
TANZANIA
ST HELENA (to UK)
ANGOLA
ZAMBIA
MALAWI
MOZAMBIQUE
ZIMB.
NAMIBIA
BOTS.
SOUTH AFRICA
SWAZILAND
LESOTHO
COMOROS
MAYOTTE (to France)
SEYCHELLES
MAURITIUS
REUNION (to France)
BRITISH INDIAN OCEAN TERRITORY (to UK)
CHRISTMAS ISLAND (to Australia)
COCOS (KEELING) ISLANDS (to Australia)
ASHMORE & CARTIER ISLANDS (to Australia)
INDONESIA
PAPUA NEW GUINEA
SOLOMON ISLANDS
TUVALU
TOKELAU (to NZ)
VANUATU
FIJI
NEW CALEDONIA (to France)
W. SAMOA
AMERICAN SAMOA (to US)
COOK ISLANDS (to NZ)
NIUE (to NZ)
TONGA
FRENCH POLYNESIA (to France)
Iles Marquises
Galápagos Islands (to Ecuador)
ECUADOR
PERU
BRAZIL
BOLIVIA
PARAGUAY
Tropic of Capricorn
CHILE
ARGENTINA
URUGUAY
ATLANTIC OCEAN
INDIAN OCEAN
AUSTRALIA
CORAL SEA ISLANDS (to Australia)
NORFOLK ISLAND (to Australia)
Kermadec Island (to NZ)
PITCAIRN ISLANDS (to UK)
Easter Island (to Chile)
San Felix Island (to Chile)
San Ambrosia Island (to Chile)
Juan Fernandez Island (to Chile)
TRISTAN DA CUNHA (to St Helena)
Gough Island (to Tristan da Cunha)
Greenwich Meridian
Prince Edward Islands (to South Africa)
FRENCH SOUTHERN & ANTARCTIC TERRITORIES (to France)
HEARD & MCDONALD ISLANDS (to Australia)
Tasmania
NEW ZEALAND
Chatham Island (to NZ)
Bounty Island (to NZ)
Campbell Island (to NZ)
Macquarie Island (to Australia)
PACIFIC OCEAN
FALKLAND ISLANDS (to UK)
11:00 12:00 13:00 14:00 15:00 16:00 17:00 18:00 19:00 20:00 21:00 22:00 23:00 24:00 01:00 02:00 03:00 04:00 05:00 06:00 07:00 08:00 09:00 10:00
ANTARCTICA (except for Graham Land, Antarctica is not subject to any time zone)
ANTARCTICA Graham Land
Antarctic Circle

The numbers at the top of the map indicate the number of hours each time zone is ahead or behind Greenwich Mean Time (GMT). The clocks and 24-hour times given at the bottom of the map show the time in each time zone when it is 12:00 hours noon GMT.

COUNTRIES OF THE WORLD

THERE ARE CURRENTLY 192 independent countries in the world – more than at any previous time – and 59 dependencies. Antarctica is the only land area on Earth that is not officially part of, and does not belong to, any single country.

In 1950, the world comprised 82 countries. In the decades following, many more states came into being as they achieved independence from their former colonial rulers. Most recently, the breakup of the former Soviet Union in 1991, and the former Yugoslavia in 1992, swelled the ranks of independent states.

COUNTRY FACTFILE KEY

Formation Date of independence / date current borders were established
Population Total population / population density – based on total *land* area / percentage of urban-based population
Languages An asterisk (*) denotes the official language(s)
Calorie consumption Average number of calories consumed daily per person

AFGHANISTAN
Central Asia

Official name Islamic State of Afghanistan
Formation 1919 / 1919
Capital Kabul
Population 20.1 million / 80 people per sq mile (31 people per sq km) / 20%
Total area 251,770 sq miles (652,090 sq km)
Languages Persian*, Pashtu*, Dari, Uzbek, Turkmen
Religions Sunni Muslim 84%, Shi'a Muslim 15%, other 1%
Ethnic mix Pashtun 38%, Tajik 25%, Hazara 19%, Uzbek 6%, other 12%
Government Mujahideen coalition
Currency Afghani = 100 puls
Literacy rate 29%
Calorie consumption 1,523 kilocalories

ALBANIA
Southeastern Europe

Official name Republic of Albania
Formation 1912 / 1913
Capital Tirana
Population 3.4 million / 321 people per sq mile (124 people per sq km) / 36%
Total area 11,100 sq miles (28,750 sq km)
Languages Albanian*, Greek, Macedonian
Religions Muslim 70%, Greek Orthodox 20%, Roman Catholic 10%
Ethnic mix Albanian 96%, Greek 2%, other (including Macedonian) 2%
Government Multiparty republic
Currency Lek = 100 qindars
Literacy rate 72%
Calorie consumption 2,605 kilocalories

ALGERIA
Northern Africa

Official name Democratic and Popular Republic of Algeria
Formation 1962 / 1962
Capital Algiers
Population 27.9 million / 31 people per sq mile (12 people per sq km) / 53%
Total area 919,590 sq miles (2,381,740 sq km)
Languages Arabic*, Berber, French
Religions Muslim 99%, Christian & Jewish 1%
Ethnic mix Arab and Berber 99%, European 1%
Government Military regime
Currency Dinar = 100 centimes
Literacy rate 57%
Calorie consumption 2,897 kilocalories

ANDORRA
Southwestern Europe

Official name Principality of Andorra
Formation 1278 / 1278
Capital Andorra la Vella
Population 64,000 / 357 people per sq mile (138 people per sq km) / 94%
Total area 181 sq miles (468 sq km)
Languages Catalan*, Spanish, French, Portuguese
Religions Roman Catholic 86%, other 14%
Ethnic mix Catalan 61%, Spanish Castilian 30%, other 9%
Government Parliamentary democracy
Currency French franc, Spanish peseta
Literacy rate 100%
Calorie consumption 3,708 kilocalories

ANGOLA
Southern Africa

Official name Republic of Angola
Formation 1975 / 1975
Capital Luanda
Population 11.1 million / 23 people per sq mile (9 people per sq km) / 30%
Total area 481,551 sq miles (1,246,700 sq km)
Languages Portuguese*, Umbundu, Kimbundu, Kongo
Religions Roman Catholic / Protestant 64%, traditional beliefs 34%, other 2%
Ethnic mix Ovimbundu 37%, Kimbundu 25%, Bakongo 13%, other 25%
Government Multiparty republic
Currency Kwanza = 100 lwei
Literacy rate 42%
Calorie consumption 1,839 kilocalories

ANTIGUA & BARBUDA
West Indies

Official name Antigua and Barbuda
Formation 1981 / 1981
Capital St. John's
Population 65,000 / 384 people per sq mile (148 people per sq km) / 36%
Total area 170 sq miles (440 sq km)
Languages English*, English Creole
Religions Protestant 87%, Roman Catholic 10%, other 3%
Ethnic mix Black 98%, other 2%
Government Parliamentary democracy
Currency E. Caribbean $ = 100 cents
Literacy rate 96%
Calorie consumption 2,458 kilocalories

ARGENTINA
South America

Official name Republic of Argentina
Formation 1816 / 1925
Capital Buenos Aires
Population 34.6 million / 34 people per sq mile (13 people per sq km) / 87%
Total area 1,068,296 sq miles (2,766,890 sq km)
Languages Spanish*, Italian, English, German, French, Amerindian languages
Religions Roman Catholic 90%, Jewish 2%, other 8%
Ethnic mix White 85%, other (including *mestizo* and Amerindian) 15%
Government Multiparty republic
Currency Peso = 100 centavos
Literacy rate 95%
Calorie consumption 2,880 kilocalories

ARMENIA
Southwestern Asia

Official name Republic of Armenia
Formation 1991 / 1991
Capital Yerevan
Population 3.6 million / 314 people per sq mile (121 people per sq km) / 68%
Total area 11,505 sq miles (29,000 sq km)
Languages Armenian*, Azerbaijani, Russian, Kurdish
Religions Armenian Apostolic 90%, other Christian and Muslim 10%
Ethnic mix Armenian 93%, Azerbaijani 3%, Russian, Kurdish 4%
Government Multiparty republic
Currency Dram = 100 louma
Literacy rate 99%
Calorie consumption NOT AVAILABLE

AUSTRALIA
Australasia & Oceania

Official name Commonwealth of Australia
Formation 1901 / 1901
Capital Canberra
Population 17.8 million / 5 people per sq mile (2 people per sq km) / 85%
Total area 2,967,893 sq miles (7,686,850 sq km)
Languages English*, Greek, Italian, Malay, Vietnamese, Aboriginal
Religions Protestant 60%, Roman Catholic 26%, other 14%
Ethnic mix Caucasian 95%, Asian 4%, Aboriginal and other 1%
Government Parliamentary democracy
Currency Australian $ = 100 cents
Literacy rate 99%
Calorie consumption 3,179 kilocalories

AUSTRIA
Central Europe

Official name Republic of Austria
Formation 1918 / 1945
Capital Vienna
Population 8 million / 251 people per sq mile (97 people per sq km) / 55%
Total area 32,375 sq miles (83,850 sq km)
Languages German*, Croatian, Slovene, Hungarian (Magyar)
Religions Roman Catholic 85%, Protestant 6%, other 9%
Ethnic mix German 99%, other (including Hungarian, Slovene, Croat) 1%
Government Multiparty republic
Currency Schilling = 100 groschen
Literacy rate 99%
Calorie consumption 3,497 kilocalories

AZERBAIJAN
Southwestern Asia

Official name Azerbaijani Republic
Formation 1991 / 1991
Capital Baku
Population 7.6 million / 228 people per sq mile (88 people per sq km) / 55%
Total area 33,436 sq miles (86,600 sq km)
Languages Azerbaijani*, Russian, Armenian
Religions Muslim 83%, Armenian Apostolic, Russian Orthodox 17%
Ethnic mix Azerbaijani 83%, Russian 6%, Armenian 6%, other 5%
Government Multiparty republic
Currency Manat = 100 gopik
Literacy rate 97%
Calorie consumption NOT AVAILABLE

BAHAMAS
West Indies

Official name Commonwealth of the Bahamas
Formation 1973 / 1973
Capital Nassau
Population 300,000 / 78 people per sq mile (30 people per sq km)/ 85%
Total area 5,359 sq miles (13,880 sq km)
Languages English*, English Creole
Religions Protestant 76%, Roman Catholic 19%, other 5%
Ethnic mix Black 85%, White 15%
Government Parliamentary democracy
Currency Bahamian $ = 100 cents
Literacy rate 98%
Calorie consumption 2,624 kilocalories

Bahrain
Southwestern Asia

Official name State of Bahrain
Formation 1971 / 1971
Capital Manama
Population 600,000 / 2,286 people per sq mile (882 people per sq km) / 89%
Total area 263 sq miles (680 sq km)
Languages Arabic*, English, Urdu
Religions Muslim (Shi'a majority) 85%, Christian 7%, other 8%
Ethnic mix Arab 73%, South Asian 14%, Persian 8%, other 5%
Government Absolute monarchy (emirate)
Currency Dinar = 1,000 fils
Literacy rate 84%
Calorie consumption NOT AVAILABLE

Bangladesh
Southern Asia

Official name People's Republic of Bangladesh
Formation 1971 / 1971
Capital Dhaka
Population 120.4 million / 2,330 people per sq mile (899 people per sq km) / 17%
Total area 55,598 sq miles (143,998 sq km)
Languages Bengali*, Urdu, Chakma, Marma, Garo, Khasi
Religions Muslim 83%, Hindu 16%, other 1%
Ethnic mix Bengali 98%, other 2%
Government Multiparty republic
Currency Taka = 100 paisa
Literacy rate 35%
Calorie consumption 2,019 kilocalories

Barbados
West Indies

Official name Barbados
Formation 1966 / 1966
Capital Bridgetown
Population 300,000 / 1,809 people per sq mile (698 people per sq km) / 46%
Total area 166 sq miles (430 sq km)
Languages English*, English Creole
Religions Protestant 94%, Roman Catholic 5%, other 1%
Ethnic mix Black 80%, mixed 15%, White 4%, other 1%
Government Parliamentary democracy
Currency Barbados $ = 100 cents
Literacy rate 99%
Calorie consumption 3,207 kilocalories

Belarus
Eastern Europe

Official name Republic of Belarus
Formation 1991 / 1991
Capital Minsk
Population 10.1 million / 127 people per sq mile (49 people per sq km) / 68%
Total area 80,154 sq miles (207,600 sq km)
Languages Belarus*, Russian
Religions Russian Orthodox 60%, Roman Catholic 8%, other 32%
Ethnic mix Belarus 78%, Russian 13%, Polish 4%, other 5%
Government Multiparty republic
Currency Rouble = 100 kopeks
Literacy rate 98%
Calorie consumption NOT AVAILABLE

Belgium
Northwestern Europe

Official name Kingdom of Belgium
Formation 1830 / 1830
Capital Brussels
Population 10.1 million / 798 people per sq mile (308 people per sq km) / 97%
Total area 12,780 sq miles (33,100 sq km)
Languages French*, Dutch*, German, Flemish
Religions Roman Catholic 75%, other 25%
Ethnic mix Flemish 58%, Walloon 32%, other European 6%, other 4%
Government Constitutional monarchy
Currency Franc = 100 centimes
Literacy rate 99%
Calorie consumption: 3,681 kilocalories

Belize
Central America

Official name Belize
Formation 1981 / 1981
Capital Belmopan
Population 200,000 /23 people per sq mile (9 people per sq km) / 47%
Total area 8,865 sq miles (22,960 sq km)
Languages English*, English Creole, Spanish
Religions Christian 87%, other 13%
Ethnic mix *mestizo* 44%, Creole 30%, Indian 11%, Garifuna 8%, other 7%
Government Parliamentary democracy
Currency Belizean $ =100 cents
Literacy rate 95%
Calorie consumption 2,662 kilocalories

Benin
Western Africa

Official name Republic of Benin
Formation 1960 / 1960
Capital Porto-Novo
Population 5.4 million / 127 people per sq mile (49 people per sq km) / 30%
Total area 43,480 sq miles (112,620 sq km)
Languages French*, Fon, Adja, Yoruba
Religions Traditional beliefs 70%, Muslim 15%, Christian 15%
Ethnic mix Fon 39%, Yoruba 12%, Adja 10%, other 39%
Government Multiparty republic
Currency CFA franc = 100 centimes
Literacy rate 23%
Calorie consumption 2,532 kilocalories

Bhutan
Southeastern Asia

Official name Kingdom of Bhutan
Formation 1949 / 1865
Capital Thimphu
Population 1.6 million / 88 people per sq mile (34 people per sq km) / 6%
Total area 18,147 sq miles (47,000 sq km)
Languages Dzongkha*, Nepali, Assamese
Religions Mahayana Buddhist 70%, Hindu 24%, Muslim 5%, other 1%
Ethnic mix Bhutia 61%, Gurung 15%, Assamese 13%, other 11%
Government Constitutional monarchy
Currency Ngultrum = 100 chetrum
Literacy rate 38%
Calorie consumption 2,553 kilocalories

Bolivia
South America

Official name Republic of Bolivia
Formation 1825 / 1938
Capitals La Paz / Sucre
Population 7.4 million / 18 people per sq mile (7 people per sq km) / 58%
Total area 424,162 sq miles (1,098,580 sq km)
Languages Spanish*, Quechua*, Aymará*
Religions Roman Catholic 95%, other 5%
Ethnic mix Indian 55%, *mestizo* 27%, White 10%, other 8%
Government Multiparty republic
Currency Boliviano = 100 centavos
Literacy rate 83%
Calorie consumption 2,094 kilocalories

Bosnia & Herzegovina
Southeastern Europe

Official name Republic of Bosnia and Herzegovina
Formation 1992 / 1992
Capital Sarajevo
Population 3.5 million / 176 people per sq mile (68 people per sq km) / 36%
Total area 19,741 sq miles (51,130 sq km)
Languages Serbian*, Croatian*
Religions Muslim 40%, Orthodox Catholic 31%, other 29%
Ethnic mix Bosnian 44%, Serb 31%, Croat 17%, other 8%
Government Multiparty republic
Currency Dinar = 100 para
Literacy rate 93%
Calorie consumption NOT AVAILABLE

Botswana
Southern Africa

Official name Republic of Botswana
Formation 1966 / 1966
Capital Gaborone
Population 1.5 million / 8 people per sq mile (3 people per sq km) / 25%
Total area 224,600 sq miles (581,730 sq km)
Languages English*, Tswana, Shona, San
Religions Traditional beliefs 50%, Christian 50%
Ethnic mix Tswana 75%, Shona 12%, San 3%, other 10%
Government Multiparty republic
Currency Pula = 100 thebe
Literacy rate 67%
Calorie consumption 2,266 kilocalories

Brazil
South America

Official name Federative Republic of Brazil
Formation 1822 / 1929
Capital Brasília
Population 161.8 million / 49 people per sq mile (19 people per sq km) / 76%
Total area 3,286,472 sq miles (8,511,970 sq km)
Languages Portuguese*, German, Italian
Religions Roman Catholic 90%, other 10%
Ethnic mix White (Portuguese, Italian, German, Japanese) 55%, mixed 38%, Black 6%, other 1%
Government Multiparty republic
Currency Real = 100 centavos
Literacy rate 80%
Calorie consumption 2,824 kilocalories

Brunei
Southeastern Asia

Official name Sultanate of Brunei
Formation 1984 / 1984
Capital Bandar Seri Begawan
Population 300,000 / 148 people per sq mile (57 people per sq km) / 58%
Total area 2,228 sq miles (5,770 sq km)
Languages Malay*, English, Chinese
Religions Muslim 63%, Buddhist 14%, Christian 10%, other 13%
Ethnic mix Malay 69%, Chinese 18%, other 13%
Government Absolute monarchy
Currency Brunei $ = 100 cents
Literacy rate 89%
Calorie consumption 2,745 kilocalories

Bulgaria
Southeastern Europe

Official name Republic of Bulgaria
Formation 1908 / 1923
Capital Sofia
Population 8.8 million / 207 people per sq mile (80 people per sq km) / 69%
Total area 42,822 sq miles (110,910 sq km)
Languages Bulgarian*, Turkish, Macedonian, Romany, Armenian
Religions Christian 85%, Muslim 13%, Jewish 1%, other 1%
Ethnic mix Bulgarian 85%, Turkish 9%, Macedonian 3%, Gypsy 3%
Government Multiparty republic
Currency Lev = 100 stoninki
Literacy rate 98%
Calorie consumption 2,831 kilocalories

Burkina
Western Africa

Official name Burkina Faso
Formation 1960 / 1960
Capital Ouagadougou
Population 10.3 million / 98 people per sq mile (38 people per sq km) / 22%
Total area 105,870 sq miles (274,200 sq km)
Languages French*, Mossi, Fulani
Religions Traditional beliefs 65%, Muslim 25%, Christian 10%
Ethnic mix Mossi 45%, Mande 10%, Fulani 10%, other 35%
Government Multiparty republic
Currency CFA franc = 100 centimes
Literacy rate 18%
Calorie consumption 2,387 kilocalories

Burundi
Central Africa

Official name Republic of Burundi
Formation 1962 / 1962
Capital Bujumbura
Population 6.4 million / 648 people per sq mile (250 people per sq km) / 7%
Total area 10,750 sq miles (27,830 sq km)
Languages Kirundi*, French*, Swahili
Religions Christian 68%, traditional beliefs 32%
Ethnic mix Hutu 85%, Tutsi 13%, Twa pygmy 1%, other 1%
Government Multiparty republic
Currency Franc = 100 centimes
Literacy rate 50%
Calorie consumption 1,941 kilocalories

Cambodia
Southeastern Asia

Official name Kingdom of Cambodia
Formation 1953 / 1953
Capital Phnom Penh
Population 10.3 million / 150 people per sq mile (58 people per sq km) / 19%
Total area 69,000 sq miles (181,040 sq km)
Languages Khmer*, French, Chinese, Vietnamese
Religions Buddhist 88%, Muslim 2%, other 10%
Ethnic mix Khmer 94%, Chinese 4%, other 2%
Government Constitutional monarchy
Currency Riel = 100 sen
Literacy rate 35%
Calorie consumption 2,021 kilocalories

Cameroon
Central Africa

Official name Republic of Cameroon
Formation 1960 / 1960
Capital Yaoundé
Population 12.5 million / 73 people per sq mile (28 people per sq km) / 42%
Total area 183,570 miles (475,440 sq km)
Languages English*, French*, Fang, Bulu, Yaundé, Duala
Religions Traditional beliefs 51%, Christian 33%, Muslim 16%
Ethnic mix Bamileke and Manum 20%, Fang 19%, other 61%
Government Multiparty republic
Currency CFA franc = 100 centimes
Literacy rate 54%
Calorie consumption 1,981 kilocalories

Canada
North America

Official name Canada
Formation 1867 / 1949
Capital Ottawa
Population 29.5 million / 8 people per sq mile (3 people per sq km) / 77%
Total area 3,851,788 sq miles (9,976,140 sq km)
Languages English*, French*, Chinese, Italian, German, Portuguese, Inuit
Religions Roman Catholic 46%, Protestant 30%, other 24%
Ethnic mix British origin 40%, French origin 27%, other 33%
Government Parliamentary democracy
Currency Canadian $ = 100 cents
Literacy rate 96%
Calorie consumption 3,094 kilocalories

Cape Verde
Atlantic Ocean

Official Name Republic of Cape Verde
Formation 1975 / 1975
Capital Praia
Population 400,000 / 257 people per sq mile (99 people per sq km) / 49%
Total area 1,556 sq miles (4,030 sq km)
Languages Portuguese*, Creole
Religions Roman Catholic 98%, Protestant 2%
Ethnic mix Creole (*mestizo*) 71%, Black 28%, White 1%
Government Multiparty republic
Currency Escudo = 100 centavos
Literacy rate 63%
Calorie consumption 2,805 kilocalories

Central African Republic
Central Africa

Official name Central African Republic
Formation 1960 / 1960
Capital Bangui
Population 3.3 million / 13 people per sq mile (5 people per sq km) / 38%
Total area 240,530 sq miles (622,980 sq km)
Languages French*, Sango, Banda, Gbaya
Religions Christian 50%, traditional beliefs 27%, Muslim 15%, other 8%
Ethnic mix Baya 34%, Banda 27%, Mandjia 21%, other 18%
Government Multiparty republic
Currency CFA franc = 100 centimes
Literacy rate 38%
Calorie consumption 1,690 kilocalories

Chad
Central Africa

Official name Republic of Chad
Formation 1960 / 1960
Capital N'Djamena
Population 6.4 million / 19 people per sq mile (5 people per sq km) / 21%
Total area 495,752 sq miles (1,284,000 sq km)
Languages French*, Sara, Maba
Religions Muslim 44%, Christian 33%, traditional beliefs 23%
Ethnic mix Bagirmi, Sara, and Kreish 31%, Sudanic Arab 26%, Teda 7%, other 36%
Government Transitional
Currency CFA franc = 100 centimes
Literacy rate 45%
Calorie consumption 1,989 kilocalories

Chile
South America

Official name Republic of Chile
Formation 1818 / 1929
Capital Santiago
Population 14.3 million / 49 people per sq mile (19 people per sq km) / 84%
Total area 292,258 sq miles (756,950 sq km)
Languages Spanish*, Indian languages
Religions Roman Catholic 89%, Protestant 11%
Ethnic mix White and *mestizo* 92%, Indian 6%, other 2%
Government Multiparty republic
Currency Peso = 100 centavos
Literacy rate 94%
Calorie consumption 2,582 kilocalories

China
Eastern Asia

Official name People's Republic of China
Formation 1949 / 1950
Capital Beijing
Population 1.2 billion / 340 people per sq mile (131 people per sq km) / 28%
Total area 3,628,166 sq miles (9,396,960 sq km)
Languages Mandarin*, Wu, Cantonese, Hsiang, Min, Hakka, Kan
Religions Confucianist 20%, Buddhist 6%, Taoist 2%, other 72%
Ethnic mix Han 93%, Zhaung 1%, other 6%
Government Single-party republic
Currency Yuan = 10 jiao = 100 fen
Literacy rate 78%
Calorie consumption 2,727 kilocalories

Colombia
South America

Official name Republic of Colombia
Formation 1819 / 1922
Capital Bogotá
Population 35.1 million / 88 people per sq mile (34 people per sq km) / 71%
Total area 439,733 sq miles (1,138,910 sq km)
Languages Spanish*, Amerindian languages, English Creole
Religions Roman Catholic 95%, other 5%
Ethnic mix *mestizo* 58%, White 20%, mixed 14%, other 8%
Government Multiparty republic
Currency Peso = 100 centavos
Literacy rate 87%
Calorie consumption 2,677 kilocalories

Comoros
Indian Ocean

Official name Federal Islamic Republic of the Comoros
Formation 1975 / 1975
Capital Moroni
Population 600,000 / 814 people per sq mile (314 people per sq km) / 29%
Total area 861 sq miles (2,230 sq km)
Languages Arabic*, French*, Comoran
Religions Muslim 86%, Roman Catholic 14%
Ethnic mix Comorian 96%, other 4%
Government Islamic republic
Currency Franc = 100 centimes
Literacy rate 48%
Calorie consumption 1,897 kilocalories

Congo
Central Africa

Official name Republic of the Congo
Formation 1960 / 1960
Capital Brazzaville
Population 2.6 million / 21 people per sq km (8 people per sq km) / 56%
Total area 132,040 sq miles (342,000 sq km)
Languages French*, Kongo, Teke, Lingala
Religions Roman Catholic 50%, traditional beliefs 48%, other 2%
Ethnic mix Bakongo 48%, Teke 17%, Mboshi 17%, other 18%
Government Multiparty republic
Currency CFA franc = 100 centimes
Literacy rate 57%
Calorie consumption 2,296 kilocalories

Congo (Democratic Republic of) *see* **Zaire**

Costa Rica
Central America

Official name Republic of Costa Rica
Formation 1821 / 1838
Capital San José
Population 3.4 million / 174 people per sq mile (67 people per sq km) / 48%
Total area 19,730 miles (51,100 sq km)
Languages Spanish*, English Creole, Bribri, Cabecar
Religions Roman Catholic 95%, other 5%
Ethnic mix White / *mestizo* 96%, Black 2%, Amerindian 2%
Government Multiparty republic
Currency Colón = 100 centimos
Literacy rate 93%
Calorie consumption 2,883 kilocalories

Croatia
Southeastern Europe

Official name Republic of Croatia
Formation 1991 / 1991
Capital Zagreb
Population 4.5 million / 207 people per sq mile (80 people per sq km) / 51%
Total area 21,830 sq miles (56,540 sq km)
Languages Croatian*, Serbian, Hungarian (Magyar), Slovenian
Religions Roman Catholic 77%, Eastern Orthodox 11%, Protestant 1%, Muslim 1%, other 10%
Ethnic mix Croat 80%, Serb 12%, Hungarian, Slovenian, other 8%
Government Multiparty republic
Currency Kuna = 100 lipa
Literacy rate 97%
Calorie consumption NOT AVAILABLE

Cuba
West Indies

Official name Republic of Cuba
Formation 1902 / 1898
Capital Havana
Population 10.8 million / 251 people per sq mile (97 people per sq km) / 75%
Total area 42,803 sq miles (110,860 sq km)
Languages Spanish*, English, French
Religions Roman Catholic 85%, other 15%
Ethnic mix White 66%, Afro-European 22%, other 12%
Government Socialist republic
Currency Peso = 100 centavos
Literacy rate 94%
Calorie consumption 2,833 kilocalories

Cyprus
Southeastern Europe

Official name Republic of Cyprus
Formation 1960 / 1983
Capital Nicosia
Population 700,000 / 197 people per sq mile (76 people per sq km) / 53%
Total area 3,572 sq miles (9,251 sq km)
Languages Greek*, Turkish, English
Religions Greek Orthodox 77%, Muslim 18%, other 5%
Ethnic mix Greek 77%, Turkish 18%, other (mainly British) 5%
Government Multiparty republic
Currency Cypriot £ / Turkish lira
Literacy rate 94%
Calorie consumption 3,779 kilocalories

Czech Republic
Central Europe

Official name Czech Republic
Formation 1993 / 1993
Capital Prague
Population 10.3 million / 339 people per sq mile (131 people per sq km) / 65%
Total area 30,260 sq miles (78,370 sq km)
Languages Czech*, Slovak, Romany, Hungarian (Magyar)
Religions Roman Catholic 44%, Protestant 6%, other Christian 12%, other 38%
Ethnic mix Czech 85%, Moravian 13%, other 2%
Government Multiparty republic
Currency Koruna = 100 halura
Literacy rate 99%
Calorie consumption 3,156 kilocalories

Denmark
Northern Europe

Official name Kingdom of Denmark
Formation AD 960 / 1953
Capital Copenhagen
Population 5.2 million / 319 people per sq mile (123 people per sq km) / 85%
Total area 16,629 sq miles (43,069 sq km)
Languages Danish*, Faeroese, Inuit
Religions Evangelical Lutheran 91% other Christian 9%
Ethnic mix Danish 96%, Faeroese & Inuit 1%, other 3%
Government Constitutional monarchy
Currency Krone = 100 øre
Literacy rate 100%
Calorie consumption 3,664 kilocalories

Djibouti
East Africa

Official name Republic of Djibouti
Formation 1977 / 1977
Capital Djibouti
Population 600,000 / 67 people per sq mile (26 people per sq km) / 81%
Total area 8,958 sq miles (23,200 sq km)
Languages Arabic*, French*, Somali, Afar
Religions Christian 87%, other 13%
Ethnic mix Issa 35%, Afar 20%, Gadaboursis and Isaaks 28%, other 17%
Government Single-party republic
Currency Franc = 100 centimes
Literacy rate 43%
Calorie consumption 2,338 kilocalories

Dominica
West Indies

Official name Commonwealth of Dominica
Formation 1978 / 1978
Capital Roseau
Population 71,000 / 246 people per sq mile (95 people per sq km)/ 57%
Total area 290 sq miles (750 sq km)
Languages English*, French Creole, Carib, Cocoy
Religions Roman Catholic 77%, Protestant 15%, other 8%
Ethnic mix Black 98%, Amerindian 2%
Government Multiparty republic
Currency E. Caribbean $ = 100 cents
Literacy rate 97%
Calorie consumption 2,778 kilocalories

Dominican Republic
West Indies

Official name Dominican Republic
Formation 1865 / 1865
Capital Santo Domingo
Population 7.8 million / 417 people per sq mile (161 people per sq km) / 62%
Total area 18,815 sq miles (48,730 sq km)
Languages Spanish*, French Creole
Religions Roman Catholic 95%, other 5%
Ethnic mix Afro-European 73%, White 16%, Black 11%
Government Multiparty republic
Currency Peso = 100 centavos
Literacy rate 83%
Calorie consumption 2,286 kilocalories

Ecuador
South America

Official name Republic of Ecuador
Formation 1830 / 1942
Capital Quito
Population 11.5 million / 109 people per sq mile (42 people per sq km) / 56%
Total area 109,483 sq miles (283,560 sq km)
Languages Spanish*, Quechua, other Amerindian languages
Religions Roman Catholic 95%, other 5%
Ethnic mix *mestizo* 55%, Amerindian 25%, Black 10%, White 10%
Government Multiparty republic
Currency Sucre = 100 centavos
Literacy rate 87%
Calorie consumption 2,583 kilocalories

Egypt
Northern Africa

Official name Arab Republic of Egypt
Formation 1936 / 1982
Capital Cairo
Population 62.9 million / 163 people per sq mile (63 people per sq km) / 44%
Total area 386,660 sq miles (1,001,450 sq km)
Languages Arabic*, French, English, Berber, Greek, Armenian
Religions Muslim 94%, other 6%
Ethnic mix Eastern Hamitic 90%, other (including Greek, Armenian) 10%
Government Multiparty republic
Currency Pound = 100 piastres
Literacy rate 48%
Calorie consumption 3,335 kilocalories

El Salvador
Central America

Official name Republic of El Salvador
Formation 1856 / 1838
Capital San Salvador
Population 5.8 million / 726 people per sq mile (280 people per sq km) / 44%
Total area 8,124 sq miles (21,040 sq km)
Languages Spanish*, Nahua
Religions Roman Catholic 75%, other 25%
Ethnic mix *mestizo* 89%, Amerindian 10%, White 1%
Government Multiparty republic
Currency Colón = 100 centavos
Literacy rate 73%
Calorie consumption 2,663 kilocalories

Equatorial Guinea
Central Africa

Official name Republic of Equatorial Guinea
Formation 1968 / 1968
Capital Malabo
Population 400,000 / 36 people per sq mile (14 people per sq km) / 39%
Total area 10,830 sq miles (28,050 sq km)
Languages Spanish*, Fang, Bubi
Religions Christian 89%, other 11%
Ethnic mix Fang 72%, Bubi 14%, Duala 3%, other 11%
Government Multiparty republic
Currency CFA franc = 100 centimes
Literacy rate 50%
Calorie consumption NOT AVAILABLE

Eritrea
Eastern Africa

Official name State of Eritrea
Formation 1993 / 1993
Capital Asmara
Population 3.5 million / 96 people per sq mile (37 people per sq km) / 22%
Total area 36,170 sq miles (93,680 sq km)
Languages Tigrinya*, Arabic*, Tigre
Religions Coptic Christian 45%, Muslim 45%, other 10%
Ethnic mix Nine main ethnic groups
Government Provisional military government
Currency Ethiopian birr = 100 cents
Literacy rate 20%
Calorie consumption 1,610 kilocalories

Estonia
Northeastern Europe

Official name Republic of Estonia
Formation 1991 / 1991
Capital Tallinn
Population 1.6 million / 86 people per sq mile (37 people per sq km) / 72%
Total area 17,423 sq miles (45,125 sq km)
Languages Estonian*, Russian
Religions Evangelical Lutheran 98%, Eastern Orthodox, Baptist 2%
Ethnic mix Estonian 62%, Russian 30%, Ukrainian 3%, other 5%
Government Multiparty republic
Currency Kroon = 100 cents
Literacy rate 99%
Calorie consumption NOT AVAILABLE

Ethiopia
Eastern Africa

Official name Federal Democratic Republic of Ethiopia
Formation 1903 / 1993
Capital Addis Ababa
Population 55.1 million / 130 people per sq mile (50 people per sq km) / 13%
Total area 435,605 sq miles (1,128,221 sq km)
Languages Amharic*, English, Arabic
Religions Muslim 43%, Christian 37%, traditional beliefs, other 20%,
Ethnic mix Oromo 40%, Amhara and Tigrean 32%, other 28%
Government Multiparty republic
Currency Birr = 100 cents
Literacy rate 24%
Calorie consumption 1,610 kilocalories

Fiji
Australasia & Oceania

Official name Sovereign Democratic Republic of Fiji
Formation 1970 / 1970
Capital Suva
Population 800,000 / 114 people per sq mile (44 people per sq km) / 40%
Total area 7,054 sq miles (18,270 sq km)
Languages English*, Fijian, Hindu, Urdu
Religions Christian 52%, Hindu 8%, Muslim 38%, other 2%
Ethnic mix Native Fijian 49%, Indo-Fijian 46%, other 5%
Government Multiparty republic
Currency Fiji $ = 100 cents
Literacy rate 87%
Calorie consumption 3,089 kilocalories

Finland
Northern Europe

Official name Republic of Finland
Formation 1917 / 1917-1920
Capital Helsinki
Population 5.1 million / 44 people per sq mile (17 people per sq km) / 62%
Total area 130,552 sq miles (338,130 sq km)
Languages Finnish*, Swedish*, Lappish
Religions Evangelical Lutheran 89%, Greek Orthodox 1%, other 10%
Ethnic mix Finnish 93%, Swedish 6%, other (including Sami) 1%
Government Multiparty republic
Currency Markka = 100 pennia
Literacy rate 99%
Calorie consumption 3,018 kilocalories

France
Western Europe

Official name French Republic
Formation 1685 / 1919–1920
Capital Paris
Population 58 million / 272 people per sq mile (105 people per sq km) / 73%
Total area 212,930 sq miles (551,500 sq km)
Languages French*, Provençal, Breton, Catalan, Basque
Religions Roman Catholic 90%, Protestant 2%, Jewish 1%, other 7%
Ethnic mix French 92%, North African 3%, other 5%
Government Multiparty republic
Currency Franc = 100 centimes
Literacy rate 99%
Calorie consumption 3,633 kilocalories

Gabon
Central Africa

Official name Gabonese Republic
Formation 1960 / 1960
Capital Libreville
Population 1.3 million / 13 people per sq mile (5 people per sq km) / 48%
Total area 103,347 sq miles (267,670 sq km)
Languages French*, Fang, Punu, Sira, Nzebi, Mpongwe
Religions Roman Catholic, other Christian 96%, Muslim 2%, other 2%
Ethnic mix Fang 36%, Mpongwe 15%, Mbete 14%, other 35%
Government Multiparty republic
Currency CFA franc = 100 centimes
Literacy rate 61%
Calorie consumption 2,500 kilocalories

Gambia
Western Africa

Official name Republic of the Gambia
Formation 1965 / 1965
Capital Banjul
Population 1.1 million / 286 people per sq mile (110 people per sq km) / 24%
Total area 4,363 sq miles (11,300 sq km)
Languages English*, Mandinka, Fulani, Wolof, Diola, Soninke
Religions Muslim 85%, Christian 9%, traditional beliefs 6%
Ethnic mix Mandinka 41%, Fulani 14%, Wolof 13%, other 32%
Government Military regime
Currency Dalasi = 100 butut
Literacy rate 64%
Calorie consumption 2,360 kilocalories

Georgia
Southwestern Asia

Official name Republic of Georgia
Formation 1991 / 1991
Capital Tbilisi
Population 5.5 million / 206 people per sq mile (79 people per sq km) / 57%
Total area 26,911 sq miles (69,700 sq km)
Languages Georgian*, Russian
Religions Georgian Orthodox 70%, Russian Orthodox 10%, other 20%
Ethnic mix Georgian 69%, Armenian 9%, Russian 6%, other 16%
Government Republic
Currency Coupons
Literacy rate 99%
Calorie consumption NOT AVAILABLE

Germany
Northern Europe

Official name Federal Republic of Germany
Formation 1871 / 1990
Capital Berlin
Population 81.6 million / 604 people per sq mile (33 people per sq km) / 86%
Total area 137,800 sq miles (356,910 sq km)
Languages German*, Sorbian, Turkish
Religions Protestant 45%, Roman Catholic 37%, other 18%
Ethnic mix German 92%, other 8%
Government Multiparty republic
Currency Deutsche Mark = 100 pfennigs
Literacy rate 99%
Calorie consumption 3,344 kilocalories

Ghana
Western Africa

Official name Republic of Ghana
Formation 1957 / 1957
Capital Accra
Population 17.5 million / 197 people per sq mile (76 people per sq km) / 35%
Total area 92,100 sq miles (238,540 sq km)
Languages English*, Akan, Mossi, Ewe
Religions Traditional beliefs 38%, Muslim 30%, Christian 24%, other 8%
Ethnic mix Akan 52%, Mossi 15%, Ewe 12%, Ga 8%, other 13%
Government Multiparty republic
Currency Cedi = 100 pesewas
Literacy rate 61%
Calorie consumption 2,199 kilocalories

Greece
Southeastern Europe

Official name Hellenic Republic
Formation 1830 / 1945–1947
Capital Athens
Population 10.5 million / 207 people per sq mile (80 people per sq km) / 64%
Total area 50,961 sq miles (131,990 sq km)
Languages Greek*, Turkish, Albanian, Macedonian
Religions Greek Orthodox 98%, Muslim 1%, other 1%
Ethnic mix Greek 98%, other 2%
Government Multiparty republic
Currency Drachma = 100 lepta
Literacy rate 95%
Calorie consumption 3,815 kilocalories

Grenada
West Indies

Official name Grenada
Formation 1974 / 1974
Capital St. George's
Population 92,000 / 705 people per sq mile (271 people per sq km) / 17%
Total area 131 sq miles (340 sq km)
Languages English*, English Creole
Religions Roman Catholic 68%, Protestant 32%
Ethnic mix Black 84%, Afro-European 13%, South Asian 3%
Government Parliamentary democracy
Currency E. Caribbean $ = 100 cents
Literacy rate 98%
Calorie consumption 2,402 kilocalories

Guatemala
Central America

Official name Republic of Guatemala
Formation 1838 / 1838
Capital Guatemala City
Population 10.6 million / 255 people per sq mile (98 people per sq km) / 40%
Total area 42,043 sq miles (108,890 sq km)
Languages Spanish*, Quiché, Mam, Kekchí
Religions Christian 99%, other 1%
Ethnic mix Amerindian 55%, *ladino* (European-Amerindian, White) 45%
Government Multiparty republic
Currency Quetzal = 100 centavos
Literacy rate 54%
Calorie consumption 2,255 kilocalories

Guinea
Western Africa

Official name Republic of Guinea
Formation 1958 / 1958
Capital Conakry
Population 6.7 million / 70 people per sq mile (27 people per sq km) / 28%
Total area 94,926 sq miles (245,860 sq km)
Languages French*, Fulani, Malinke, Soussou, Kissi
Religions Muslim 85%, Christian 8%, traditional beliefs 7%
Ethnic mix Fulani 40%, Malinke 25%, Susu 12%, other 23%
Government Multiparty republic
Currency Franc = 100 centimes
Literacy rate 33%
Calorie consumption 2,389 kilocalories

Guinea-Bissau
Western Africa

Official name Republic of Guinea-Bissau
Formation 1974 / 1974
Capital Bissau
Population 1.1 million / 102 people per sq mile (39 people per sq km) / 21%
Total area 13,940 sq miles (36,120 sq km)
Languages Portuguese*, Balante, Fulani, Malinke
Religions Traditional beliefs 54%, Muslim 38%, Christian 8%
Ethnic mix Balante 27%, Fulani 22%, Malinke 12%, other 39%
Government Multiparty republic
Currency Peso = 100 centavos
Literacy rate 36%
Calorie consumption 2,556 kilocalories

Guyana
South America

Official name Cooperative Republic of Guyana
Formation 1966 / 1966
Capital Georgetown
Population 800,000 / 10 people per sq mile (4 people per sq km) / 35%
Total area 83,000 sq miles (214,970 sq km)
Languages English*, English Creole, Hindi, Tamil, English
Religions Christian 57%, Hindu 33%, Muslim 9%, other 1%
Ethnic mix South Asian 51%, Black and mixed 43%, other 6%
Government Multiparty republic
Currency Guyana $ =100 cents
Literacy rate 98%
Calorie consumption 2,384 kilocalories

Haiti
West Indies

Official name Republic of Haiti
Formation 1804 / 1804
Capital Port-au-Prince
Population 7.2 million / 679 people per sq mile (261 people per sq km) / 30%
Total area 10,714 sq miles (27,750 sq km)
Languages French*, French Creole*,
Religions Roman Catholic 80%, Protestant 16%, Voodoo 4%
Ethnic mix Black 95%, Afro-European 5%
Government Multiparty republic
Currency Gourde = 100 centimes
Literacy rate 35%
Calorie consumption 1,706 kilocalories

Honduras
Central America

Official name Republic of Honduras
Formation 1838 / 1838
Capital Tegucigalpa
Population 5.7 million / 133 people per sq mile (51 people per sq km) / 42%
Total area 43,278 sq miles (112,090 sq km)
Languages Spanish*, English Creole, Garifuna, Amerindian languages
Religions Roman Catholic 97%, other 3%
Ethnic mix *mestizo* 90%, Amerindian 7%, Garifuna (Black Carib) 2%, White 1%
Government Multiparty republic
Currency Lempira = 100 centavos
Literacy rate 71%
Calorie consumption 2,305 kilocalories

Hungary
Central Europe

Official name Republic of Hungary
Formation 1918 / 1945
Capital Budapest
Population 10.1 million / 282 people per sq mile (109 people per sq km) / 63%
Total area 35,919 sq miles (93,030 sq km)
Languages Hungarian (Magyar)*, German, Slovak
Religions Roman Catholic 68%, Protestant 25%, other 7%
Ethnic mix Hungarian (Magyar) 90%, German 2%, other 8%
Government Multiparty republic
Currency Forint = 100 filler
Literacy rate 99%
Calorie consumption 3,503 kilocalories

ICELAND
Northwestern Europe

Official name Republic of Iceland
Formation 1944 / 1944
Capital Reykjavík
Population 300,000 / 8 people per sq mile (3 people per sq km) / 91%
Total area 39,770 sq miles (103,000 sq km)
Languages Icelandic*, English
Religions Evangelical Lutheran 96%, other Christian 3%, other 1%
Ethnic mix Icelandic (Norwegian-Celtic descent) 98%, other 2%
Government Constitutional republic
Currency Krona = 100 aurar
Literacy rate 100%
Calorie consumption 3,058 kilocalories

INDIA
Southern Asia

Official name Republic of India
Formation 1947 / 1961
Capital New Delhi
Population 935.7 million / 816 people per sq mile (315 people per sq km) / 26%
Total area 1,269,338 sq miles (3,287,590 sq km)
Languages Hindi*, English*, Urdu, Bengali, Marathi, Telugu, Tamil, Bihari
Religions Hindu 83%, Muslim 11%, Christian 2%, Sikh 2%, other 2%
Ethnic mix Indo-Aryan 72%, Dravidian 25%, Mongoloid and other 3%
Government Multiparty republic
Currency Rupee = 100 paisa
Literacy rate 52%
Calorie consumption 2,395 kilocalories

INDONESIA
Southeastern Asia

Official name Republic of Indonesia
Formation 1949 / 1963
Capital Jakarta
Population 197.6 million / 282 people per sq mile (109 people per sq km) / 33%
Total area 735,555 sq miles (1,904,570 sq km)
Languages Bahasa Indonesia*, 250 (est.) languages or dialects
Religions Muslim 87%, Christian 10%, Hindu 2%, Buddhist 1%
Ethnic mix Javanese 45%, Sundanese 14%, Madurese 8%, other 33%
Government Multiparty republic
Currency Rupiah = 100 sen
Literacy rate 82%
Calorie consumption 2,752 kilocalories

IRAN
Southwestern Asia

Official name Islamic Republic of Iran
Formation 1906 / 1906
Capital Tehran
Population 67.3 million / 106 people per sq mile (41 people per sq km) / 57%
Total area 636,293 sq miles (1,648,000 sq km)
Languages Farsi (Persian)*, Azerbaijani, Giaki, Mazanderani, Kurdish, Baluchi, Arabic, Turkmen
Religions Shi'a Muslim 95%, Sunni Muslim 4%, other 1%
Ethnic mix Persian 52%, Azerbaijani 24%, Kurdish 9%, other 15%
Government Islamic Republic
Currency Rial = 100 dinars
Literacy rate 72%
Calorie consumption 2,860 kilocalories

IRAQ
Southwestern Asia

Official name Republic of Iraq
Formation 1932 / 1981
Capital Baghdad
Population 20.4 million / 122 people per sq mile (47 people per sq km) / 73%
Total area 169,235 sq miles (438,320 sq km)
Languages Arabic*, Kurdish, Turkish, Farsi (Persian)
Religions Shi'a Muslim 63%, Sunni Muslim 34%, other 3%
Ethnic mix Arab 79%, Kurdish 16%, Persian 3%, Turkish 2%
Government Single-party republic
Currency Dinar = 1,000 fils
Literacy rate 60%
Calorie consumption 2,121 kilocalories

IRELAND
Northwestern Europe

Official name Republic of Ireland
Formation 1921 / 1922
Capital Dublin
Population 3.6 million / 135 people per sq mile (52 people per sq km) / 57%
Total area 27,155 sq miles (70,280 sq km)
Languages English*, Irish Gaelic*
Religions Roman Catholic 93%, Protestant 5%, other 2%
Ethnic mix Irish 95%, other 5%
Government Multiparty republic
Currency Irish pound = 100 pence
Literacy rate 99%
Calorie consumption 3,847 kilocalories

ISRAEL
Southwestern Asia

Official name State of Israel
Formation 1948 / 1982
Capital Jerusalem
Population 5.6 million / 713 people per sq mile (275 people per sq km) / 91%
Total area 7,992 sq miles (20,700 sq km)
Languages Hebrew*, Arabic, Yiddish
Religions Jewish 83%, Muslim 13%, Christian 2%, other 2%
Ethnic mix Jewish 83%, Arab 17%
Government Multiparty republic
Currency New shekel = 100 agorat
Literacy rate 95%
Calorie consumption 3,050 kilocalories

ITALY
Southern Europe

Official name Italian Republic
Formation 1871 / 1954
Capital Rome
Population 57.2 million / 505 people per sq mile (195 people per sq km) / 67%
Total area 116,320 sq miles (301,270 sq km)
Languages Italian*, German, French, Rhaeto-Romanic, Sardinian
Religions Roman Catholic 99%, other 1%
Ethnic mix Italian 98%, other 2%
Government Multiparty republic
Currency Lira = 100 centesimi
Literacy rate 97%
Calorie consumption 3,561 kilocalories

IVORY COAST
Western Africa

Official name Republic of the Ivory Coast
Formation 1960 / 1960
Capital Yamoussoukro
Population 14.5 million / 117 people per sq mile (45 people per sq km) / 42%
Total area 124,503 sq miles (322,463 sq km)
Languages French*, Akran, Kru, Voltaic
Religions Traditional beliefs 63%, Muslim 25%, Christian 12%
Ethnic mix Baoule 23%, Bété 18%, Kru 17%, Malinke 15%, other 27%
Government Multiparty republic
Currency CFA franc = 100 centimes
Literacy rate 54%
Calorie consumption 2,491 kilocalories

JAMAICA
West Indies

Official name Jamaica
Formation 1962 / 1962
Capital Kingston
Population 2.4 million / 577 people per sq mile (222 people per sq km) / 52%
Total area 4,243 sq miles (10,990 sq km)
Languages English*, English Creole
Religions Christian 60%, other 40%
Ethnic mix Black 75%, mixed 15%, South Asian 5%, other 5%
Government Parliamentary democracy
Currency Jamaican $ = 100 cents
Literacy rate 98%
Calorie consumption 2,607 kilocalories

JAPAN
Eastern Asia

Official name Japan
Formation 1868 / 1945
Capital Tokyo
Population 125.1 million / 834 people per sq mile (322 people per sq km) / 77%
Total area 145,869 sq miles (377,800 sq km)
Languages Japanese*, Korean, Chinese
Religions Shinto and Buddhist 76%, Buddhist 16%, other 8%
Ethnic mix Japanese 99.4%, other 0.6%
Government Constitutional monarchy
Currency Yen = 100 sen
Literacy rate 99%
Calorie consumption 2,903 kilocalories

JORDAN
Southwestern Asia

Official name Hashemite Kingdom of Jordan
Formation 1946 / 1976
Capital Amman
Population 5.4 million / 159 people per sq mile (61 people per sq km) / 70%
Total area 34,440 sq miles (89,210 sq km)
Languages Arabic*
Religions Muslim 95%, Christian 5%
Ethnic mix Arab 98%, (Palestinian 49%), Armenian 1%, Circassian 1%
Government Constitutional monarchy
Currency Dinar = 1,000 fils
Literacy rate 83% Urban
Calorie consumption 3,022 kilocalories

KAZAKHSTAN
Central Asia

Official Name Republic of Kazakhstan
Formation 1991 / 1991
Capital Alma-Ata
Population 17.1 million / 16 people per sq mile (6 people per sq km) / 58%
Total area 1,049,150 sq miles (2,717,300 sq km)
Languages Kazakh*, Russian, German
Religions Muslim 47%, other 53% (mostly Russian Orthodox and Lutheran)
Ethnic mix Kazakh 40%, Russian 38%, Ukrainian 6%, other 16%
Government Multiparty republic
Currency Tenge = 100 tein
Literacy rate 97%
Calorie consumption NOT AVAILABLE

KENYA
Eastern Africa

Official name Republic of Kenya
Formation 1963 / 1963
Capital Nairobi
Population 28.3 million / 130 people per sq mile (108 people per sq km) / 25%
Total area 224,081 sq miles (580,370 sq km)
Languages Swahili*, English, Kikuyu, Luo, Kamba
Religions Christian 66%, traditional beliefs 26%, other 8%
Ethnic mix Kikuyu 21%, Luhya 14%, Kamba 11%, other 54%
Government Multiparty republic
Currency Shilling = 100 cents
Literacy rate 69%
Calorie consumption 2,075 kilocalories

KIRIBATI
Australasia & Oceania

Official Name Republic of Kiribati
Formation 1979 / 1979
Capital Bairiki
Population 77,000 / 281 people per sq mile (108 people per sq km) / 36%
Total area 274 sq miles (710 sq km)
Languages English*, Kiribati
Religions Roman Catholic 53%, Protestant 40%, other Christian 4%, other 3%
Ethnic mix I-Kiribati 98%, other 2%
Government Multiparty republic
Currency Australian $ = 100 cents
Literacy rate 98%
Calorie consumption 2,651 kilocalories

KUWAIT
Southwestern Asia

Official name State of Kuwait
Formation 1961 / 1981
Capital Kuwait
Population 1.5 million / 218 people per sq mile (84 people per sq km) / 95%
Total area 6,880 sq miles (17,820 sq km)
Languages Arabic*, English
Religions Muslim 92%, Christian 6%, other 2%
Ethnic mix Arab 85%, South Asian 9%, Persian 4%, other 2%
Government Constitutional monarchy
Currency Dinar = 1,000 fils
Literacy rate 73%
Calorie consumption 2,523 kilocalories

KYRGYZSTAN
Central Asia

Official name Kyrgyz Republic
Formation 1991 / 1991
Capital Bishkek
Population 4.7 million / 62 people per sq mile (24 people per sq km) / 39%
Total area 76,640 sq miles (198,500 sq km)
Languages Kyrgyz*, Russian*, Uzbek
Religions Muslim 65%, other (mostly Russian Orthodox) 35%
Ethnic mix Kyrgyz 52%, Russian 21%, Uzbek 13%, other (mostly Kazakh and Tajik) 14%
Government Multiparty republic
Currency Som = 100 teen
Literacy rate 97%
Calorie consumption NOT AVAILABLE

LAOS
Southeastern Asia

Official name Lao People's Democratic Republic
Formation 1953 / 1953
Capital Vientiane
Population 4.9 million / 54 people per sq mile (21 people per sq km) / 20%
Total area 91, 428 sq miles (236,800 sq km)
Languages Lao*, Miao, Yao
Religions Buddhist 85%, Christian 2%, other 13%
Ethnic mix Lao Loum 56%, Lao Theung 34%, Lao Soung 10%
Government Single-party republic
Currency Kip = 100 cents
Literacy rate 57%
Calorie consumption 2,259 kilocalories

LATVIA
Northeastern Europe

Official name Republic of Latvia
Formation 1991 / 1991
Capital Riga
Population 2.6 million / 104 people per sq mile (40 people per sq km) / 72%
Total area 24,938 sq miles (64,589 sq km)
Languages Latvian*, Russian
Religions Evangelical Lutheran 85%, other Christian 15%
Ethnic mix Latvian 52%, Russian 34%, Belarus 5%, other 9%
Government Multiparty republic
Currency Lats = 100 santimi
Literacy rate 99%
Calorie consumption NOT AVAILABLE

LEBANON
Southwestern Asia

Official name Republic of Lebanon
Formation 1944 / 1944
Capital Beirut
Population 3 million / 762 people per sq mile (293 people per sq km) / 86%
Total area 4,015 sq miles (10,400 sq km)
Languages Arabic*, French, Armenian,
Religions Muslim (mainly Shi'a) 57%, Christian (mainly Maronite) 43%
Ethnic mix Arab 93% (Lebanese 83%, Palestinian 10%), other 7%
Government Multiparty republic
Currency Pound = 100 piastres
Literacy rate 91%
Calorie consumption 3,317 kilocalories

LESOTHO
Southern Africa

Official name Kingdom of Lesotho
Formation 1966 / 1966
Capital Maseru
Population 2.1 million / 10 people per sq mile (27 people per sq km) / 21%
Total area 11,718 sq miles (30,350 sq km)
Languages English*, Sesotho*, Zulu
Religions Christian 93%, other 7%
Ethnic mix Basotho 99%, other 1%
Government Constitutional monarchy
Currency Loti = 100 lisente
Literacy rate 69%
Calorie consumption 2,201 kilocalories

LIBERIA
Western Africa

Official name Republic of Liberia
Formation 1847 / 1889–1907
Capital Monrovia
Population 3 million / 80 people per sq mile (27 people per sq km) / 44%
Total area 43,000 sq miles (111,370 sq km)
Languages English*, Kpelle, Bassa, Vai, Kru, Grebo, Kissi, Gola
Religions Traditional beliefs 70%, Muslim 20%, Christian 10%
Ethnic mix Kpelle 20%, Bassa 14%, Americo-Liberians 5%, other 61%
Government Transitional
Currency Liberian $ = 100 cents
Literacy rate 39%
Calorie consumption 1,640 kilocalories

LIBYA
Northern Africa

Official name Socialist People's Libyan Arab Jamahiriya
Formation 1951 / 1951
Capital Tripoli
Population 5.4 million / 8 people per sq mile (3 people per sq km) / 84%
Total area 679,358 sq miles (1,759,540 sq km)
Languages Arabic*, Tuareg
Religions Muslim 97%, other 3%
Ethnic mix Arab and Berber 97%, other 3%
Government Socialist *jamahiriya* (state of the masses)
Currency Dinar = 1,000 dirhams
Literacy rate 64%
Calorie consumption 3,308 kilocalories

LIECHTENSTEIN
Southeastern Europe

Official name Principality of Liechtenstein
Formation 1719 / 1719
Capital Vaduz
Population 30,630 / 495 people per sq mile (191 people per sq km) / 87%
Total area 62 sq miles (160 sq km)
Languages German*, Alemannish, Italian
Religions Roman Catholic 87%, Protestant 8%, other 5%
Ethnic mix Liechtensteiner 63%, Swiss 15%, German 9%, other 13%
Government Constitutional monarchy
Currency Swiss franc = 100 centimes
Literacy rate 100%
Calorie consumption NOT AVAILABLE

LITHUANIA
Northeastern Europe

Official name Republic of Lithuania
Formation 1991 / 1991
Capital Vilnius
Population 3.7 million / 148 people per sq mile (57 people per sq km) / 70%
Total area 25,174 sq miles (65,200 sq km)
Languages Lithuanian*, Russian
Religions Roman Catholic 87%, Russian Orthodox 10%, other 3%
Ethnic mix Lithuanian 80%, Russian 9%, Polish 8%, other 3%
Government Multiparty republic
Currency Litas = 100 centas
Literacy rate 98%
Calorie consumption NOT AVAILABLE

LUXEMBOURG
Northwestern Europe

Official name Grand Duchy of Luxembourg
Formation 1890 / 1890
Capital Luxembourg
Population 400,000 / 403 people per sq mile (155 people per sq km) / 88%
Total area 998 sq miles (2,586 sq km)
Languages Letzeburgish*, French, Portuguese, Italian
Religions Roman Catholic 97%, other 3%
Ethnic mix Luxemburger 72%, Portuguese 9%, Italian 5%, other 14%
Government Constitutional monarchy
Currency Franc = 100 centimes
Literacy rate 99% Urban
Calorie consumption 3,681 kilocalories

MACEDONIA
Southeastern Europe

Official name Former Yugoslav Republic of Macedonia
Formation 1991 / 1991
Capital Skopje
Population 2.2 million / 223 people per sq mile (86 people per sq km) / 59%
Total area 9,929 sq miles (25,715 sq km)
Languages Macedonian, Serbian, Croatian (no official language)
Religions Christian 80%, Muslim 20%
Ethnic mix Macedonian 67%, Albanian 20%, Turkish 4%, other 9%
Government Multiparty republic
Currency Denar = 100 deni
Literacy rate 89%
Calorie consumption NOT AVAILABLE

MADAGASCAR
Indian Ocean

Official name Democratic Republic of Madagascar
Formation 1960 / 1960
Capital Antananarivo
Population 14.8 million / 65 people per sq mile (25 people per sq km) / 25%
Total area 226,660 sq miles (587,040 sq km)
Languages Malagasy*, French*
Religions Traditional beliefs 52%, Christian 41%, Muslim 7%
Ethnic mix Merina 26%, Betsimisaraka 15%, Betsileo 12%, other 47%
Government Multiparty republic
Currency Franc = 100 centimes
Literacy rate 81%
Calorie consumption 2,135 kilocalories

MALAWI
Southern Africa

Official name Republic of Malawi
Formation 1964 / 1964
Capital Lilongwe
Population 11.1 million / 307 people per sq mile (118 people per sq km) / 12%
Total area 45,745 sq miles (118,480 sq km)
Languages English*, Chewa, Lomwe, Yao
Religions Christian 66%, traditional beliefs 18%, other 16%
Ethnic mix Maravi 55%, Lomwe 17%, Yao 13%, other 15%
Government Multiparty republic
Currency Kwacha = 100 tambala
Literacy rate 49%
Calorie consumption 1,825 kilocalories

MALAYSIA
Southeastern Asia

Official name Malaysia
Formation 1957 / 1965
Capital Kuala Lumpur
Population 20.1 million / 158 people per sq mile (61 people per sq km) / 51%
Total area 127,317 sq miles (329,750 sq km)
Languages Malay*, Chinese, Tamil
Religions Muslim 53%, Buddhist and Confucianist 30%, other 17%
Ethnic mix Malay and Aboriginal 60%, Chinese 30%, Indian 8%, other 2%
Government Federal constitutional monarchy
Currency Ringgit = 100 cents
Literacy rate 78%
Calorie consumption 2,888 kilocalories

MALDIVES
Indian Ocean

Official name Republic of Maldives
Formation 1965 / 1965
Capital Male
Population 300,000 / 2,591 people per sq mile (1,000 people per sq km) / 26%
Total area 116 sq miles (300 sq km)
Languages Divehi (Maldivian)*, Sinhala, Tamil
Religions Sunni Muslim 100%
Ethnic mix Maldivian 99%, other 1%
Government Republic
Currency Rufiyaa = 100 laari
Literacy rate 91%
Calorie consumption 2,580 kilocalories

MALI
Western Africa

Official name Republic of Mali
Formation 1960 / 1960
Capital Bamako
Population 10.8 million / 24 people per sq mile (9 people per sq km) / 25%
Total area 478,837 sq miles (1,240,190 sq km)
Languages French*, Bambara, Fulani, Senufo, Soninké
Religions Muslim 80%, traditional beliefs 18%, Christian 2%
Ethnic mix Bambara 31%, Fulani 13%, Senufo 12%, other 44%
Government Multiparty republic
Currency CFA franc = 100 centimes
Literacy rate 32%
Calorie consumption 2,278 kilocalories

MALTA
Southern Europe

Official name Republic of Malta
Formation 1964 / 1964
Capital Valletta
Population 400,000 / 3,239 people per sq mile (1,250 people per sq km) / 88%
Total area 124 sq miles (320 sq km)
Languages Maltese*, English*
Religions Roman Catholic 98%, other (mostly Anglican) 2%
Ethnic mix Maltese (mixed Arab, Sicilian, Norman, Spanish, Italian, English) 98%, other 2%
Government Multiparty republic
Currency Lira = 100 cents
Literacy rate 86%
Calorie consumption 3,486 kilocalories

MARSHALL ISLANDS
Australasia & Oceania

Official name Republic of the Marshall Islands
Formation 1986 / 1986
Capital Majuro
Population 52,000 / 744 people per sq mile (287 people per sq km) / 28%
Total area 70 sq miles (181 sq km)
Languages English*, Marshallese*
Religions Protestant 80%, Roman Catholic 15%, other 5%
Ethnic mix Marshallese 90%, other Pacific Islanders 10%
Government Republic
Currency US $ = 100 cents
Literacy rate 91%
Calorie consumption NOT AVAILABLE

MAURITANIA
Western Africa

Official name Islamic Republic of Mauritania
Formation 1960 / 1960
Capital Nouakchott
Population 2.3 million / 5 people per sq mile (2 people per sq km) / 50%
Total area 395,953 sq miles (1,025,520 sq km)
Languages French*, Hassaniyah Arabic, Wolof
Religions Muslim 100%
Ethnic mix Maure 80%, Wolof 7%, Tukulor 5%, other 8%
Government Multiparty republic
Currency Ouguiya = 5 khoums
Literacy rate 34%
Calorie consumption 2,685 kilocalories

MAURITIUS
Indian Ocean

Official name Republic of Mauritius
Formation 1968 / 1968
Capital Port Louis
Population 1.1 million / 1,542 people per sq mile (595 people per sq km) / 41%
Total area 718 sq miles (1,860 sq km)
Languages English*, French Creole, Hindi, Urdu, Tamil, Chinese
Religions Hindu 52%, Roman Catholic, 26%, Muslim 17%, other 5%
Ethnic mix Creole 55%, South Asian 40%, Chinese 3%, other 2%
Government Multiparty republic
Currency Rupee = 100 cents
Literacy rate 79%
Calorie consumption 2,690 kilocalories

MEXICO
North America

Official name United Mexican States
Formation 1836 / 1867
Capital Mexico City
Population 93.7 million / 127 people per sq mile (49 people per sq km) / 74%
Total area 756,061 sq miles (1,958,200 sq km)
Languages Spanish*, Mayan dialects
Religions Roman Catholic 89%, Protestant 6%, other 5%
Ethnic mix *mestizo* 55%, Amerindian 30%, White 6%, other 9%
Government Multiparty republic
Currency Peso = 100 centavos
Literacy rate 89%
Calorie consumption 3,146 kilocalories

MICRONESIA
Australasia & Oceania

Official name Federated States of Micronesia
Formation 1986 / 1986
Capital Palikir
Population 107,000 / 394 people per sq mile (152 people per sq km) / 36%
Total area 1,120 sq miles (2,900 sq km)
Languages English*, Trukese, Pohnpeian, Mortlockese, Kosrean
Religions Roman Catholic 50%, Protestant 48%, other 2%
Ethnic mix Micronesian 99%, other 1%
Government Republic
Currency US $ = 100 cents
Literacy rate 90%
Calorie consumption NOT AVAILABLE

MOLDOVA
Southeastern Europe

Official name Republic of Moldova
Formation 1991 / 1991
Capital Chişinău
Population 4.4 million / 339 people per sq mile (131 people per sq km) / 49%
Total area 13,000 sq miles (33, 700 sq km)
Languages Moldovan*, Russian, Romanian
Religions Romanian Orthodox 98%, Jewish 1%, other 1%
Ethnic mix Moldovan (Romanian) 65%, Ukrainian 14%, Russian 13%, other 8%
Government Multiparty republic
Currency Leu = 100 bani
Literacy rate 96%
Calorie consumption NOT AVAILABLE

MONACO
Southern Europe

Official name Principality of Monaco
Formation 1861 / 1861
Capital Monaco
Population 31,000 / 41,332 people per sq mile (15,897 people per sq km) / 100%
Total area 0.75 sq miles (1.95 sq km)
Languages French*, Italian, Monégasque, English
Religions Roman Catholic 95%, other 5%
Ethnic mix French 47%, Monégasque 17%, Italian 16%, other 20%
Government Constitutional monarchy
Currency French franc = 100 centimes
Literacy rate 99%
Calorie consumption NOT AVAILABLE

MONGOLIA
Eastern Asia

Official name Mongolia
Formation 1924 / 1911
Capital Ulan Bator
Population 2.4 million / 5 people per sq mile (2 people per sq km) / 59%
Total area 604,247 sq miles (1,565,000 sq km)
Languages Khalkha Mongol*, Turkic, Russian, Chinese
Religions Predominantly Tibetan Buddhist, with a Muslim minority
Ethnic mix Khalkha Mongol 90%, Kazakh 4%, Chinese 2%, other 4%
Government Multiparty republic
Currency Tughrik = 100 möngös
Literacy rate 81%
Calorie consumption 1,899 kilocalories

MOROCCO
Northern Africa

Official name Kingdom of Morocco
Formation 1956 / 1956
Capital Rabat
Population 27 million / 155 people per sq mile (60 people per sq km) / 47%
Total area 269,757 sq miles (698,670 sq km)
Religions Muslim 99%, other 1%
Ethnic mix Arab and Berber 99%, European 1%
Government Constitutional monarchy
Currency Dirham = 100 centimes
Literacy rate 44%
Calorie consumption 2,984 kilocalories

MOZAMBIQUE
Southern Africa

Official name Republic of Mozambique
Formation 1975 / 1975
Capital Maputo
Population 16 million / 135 people per sq mile (20 people per sq km) / 30%
Total area 309,493 sq miles (801,590 sq km)
Languages Portuguese*, Makua, Tsonga, Sena, Lomwe
Religions Traditional beliefs 60%, Christian 30%, Muslim 10%
Ethnic mix Makua-Lomwe 47%, Tsonga 23%, Malawi 12%, other 18%
Government Multiparty republic
Currency Metical = 100 centavos
Literacy rate 40%
Calorie consumption 1,680 kilocalories

MYANMAR
Southeastern Asia

Official name Union of Myanmar
Formation 1948 / 1948
Capital Rangoon
Population 46.5 million / 184 people per sq mile (71 people per sq km) / 25%
Total area 261,200 sq miles (676,550 sq km)
Languages Burmese*, Karen, Mon
Religions Buddhist 89%, Muslim 4%, other 7%
Ethnic mix Burman 68%, Shan 9%, Karen 6%, Rakhine 4%, other 13%
Government Military regime
Currency Kyat = 100 pyas
Literacy rate 81%
Calorie consumption 2,598 kilocalories

NAMIBIA
Southern Africa

Official name Republic of Namibia
Formation 1990 / 1994
Capital Windhoek
Population 1.5 million / 5 people per sq mile (2 people per sq km) / 34%
Total area 318,260 sq miles (824,290 sq km)
Languages English*, Afrikaans, Ovambo, Kavango, Bergdama
Religions Christian 90%, other 10%
Ethnic mix Ovambo 50%, Kavango 9%, Herero 7%, Damara 7%, other 27%
Government Multiparty republic
Currency Rand = 100 cents
Literacy rate 40%
Calorie consumption 2,134 kilocalories

NAURU
Australasia & Oceania

Official name Republic of Nauru
Formation 1968 / 1968
Capital No official capital
Population 10,000 / 1,233 people per sq mile (476 people per sq km) / 100%
Total area 8.2 sq miles (21.2 sq km)
Languages Nauruan*, English, Kiribati, Chinese, Tuvaluan
Religions Christian 95%, other 5%
Ethnic mix Nauruan 58%, other Pacific Islanders 26%, Chinese 8%, European 8%
Government Parliamentary democracy
Currency Australian $ = 100 cents
Literacy rate 99%
Calorie consumption NOT AVAILABLE

NEPAL
Southern Asia

Official name Kingdom of Nepal
Formation 1769 / 1769
Capital Kathmandu
Population 21.4 million / 404 people per sq mile (156 people per sq km) / 12%
Total area 54,363 sq miles (140,800 sq km)
Languages Nepali*, Maithilli, Bhojpuri
Religions Hindu 90%, Buddhist 5%, Muslim 3%, other 2%
Ethnic mix Nepalese 58%, Bihari 19%, Tamang 6%, other 17%
Government Constitutional monarchy
Currency Rupee = 100 paisa
Literacy rate 26%
Calorie consumption 1,957 kilocalories

NETHERLANDS
Northwestern Europe

Official name Kingdom of the Netherlands
Formation 1815 / 1890
Capitals Amsterdam, The Hague
Population 15.5 million / 1,188 people per sq mile (457 people per sq km) / 89%
Total area 14,410 sq miles (37,330 sq km)
Languages Dutch*, Frisian
Religions Roman Catholic 36%, Protestant 27%, other 37%
Ethnic mix Dutch 96%, other 4%
Government Constitutional monarchy
Currency Guilder = 100 cents
Literacy rate 99%
Calorie consumption 3,222 kilocalories

NEW ZEALAND
Australasia & Oceania

Official name New Zealand
Formation 1947 / 1947
Capital Wellington
Population 3.6 million / 34 people per sq mile (13 people per sq km) / 86%
Total area 103,730 sq miles (268,680 sq km)
Languages English, Maori
Religions Protestant 62%, Roman Catholic 18%, other 20%
Ethnic mix European 88%, Maori 9%, other 3%
Government Constitutional monarchy
Currency NZ $ = 100 cents
Literacy rate 99%
Calorie consumption 3,669 kilocalories

NICARAGUA
Central America

Official name Republic of Nicaragua
Formation 1838 / 1838
Capital Managua
Population 4.4 million / 96 people per sq mile (37 people per sq km) / 62%
Total area 50,193 sq miles (130,000 sq km)
Languages Spanish*, English Creole, Miskito
Religions Roman Catholic 95%, other 5%
Ethnic mix *mestizo* 69%, White 17%, Black 9%, Amerindian 5%
Government Multiparty republic
Currency Córdoba = 100 pence
Literacy rate 65%
Calorie consumption 2,293 kilocalories

NIGER
Western Africa

Official name Republic of Niger
Formation 1960 / 1960
Capital Niamey
Population 9.2 million / 18 people per sq mile (7 people per sq km) / 16%
Total area 489,188 sq miles (1,267,000 sq km)
Languages French*, Hausa, Djerma, Fulani, Tuareg, Teda
Religions Muslim 85%, traditional beliefs 14%, Christian 1%
Ethnic mix Hausa 56%, Djerma 22%, Fulani 9%, other 13%
Government Multiparty republic
Currency CFA franc = 100 centimes
Literacy rate 28%
Calorie consumption 2,257 kilocalories

NIGERIA
Western Africa

Official name Federal Republic of Nigeria
Formation 1960 / 1960
Capital Abuja
Population 111.7 million / 319 people per sq mile (123 people per sq km) / 37%
Total area 356,668 sq miles (923,770 sq km)
Languages English*, Hausa, Yoruba, Ibo
Religions Muslim 50%, Christian 40%, traditional beliefs 10%
Ethnic mix Hausa 21%, Yoruba 20%, Ibo 17%, Fulani 9%, other 33%
Government Military regime
Currency Naira = 100 kobo
Literacy rate 53%
Calorie consumption 2,124 kilocalories

NORTH KOREA
Eastern Asia

Official name Democratic People's Republic of Korea
Formation 1948 / 1948
Capital Pyongyang
Population 23.9 million / 515 people per sq mile (198 people per sq km) / 60%
Total area 46,540 sq miles (120,540 sq km)
Languages Korean*, Chinese
Religions Traditional beliefs 16%, Ch'ondogyo 14%, Buddhist 2%, nonreligious 68%
Ethnic mix Korean 99%, other 1%
Government Single-party republic
Currency Won = 100 chon
Literacy rate 99%
Calorie consumption 2,833 kilocalories

NORWAY
Northern Europe

Official name Kingdom of Norway
Formation 1905 / 1930
Capital Oslo
Population 4.3 million / 36 people per sq mile (14 people per sq km) / 73%
Total area 125,060 sq miles (323,900 sq km)
Languages Norwegian* (Bokmal and *Nynorsk*), Lappish, Finnish
Religions Evangelical Lutheran 88%, other Christian 12%
Ethnic mix Norwegian 95%, Lapp 1%, other 4%
Government Constitutional monarchy
Currency Krone = 100 øre
Literacy rate 99%
Calorie consumption 3,244 kilocalories

OMAN
Southwestern Asia

Official name Sultanate of Oman
Formation 1650 / 1951
Capital Muscat
Population 2.2 million / 26 people per sq mile (10 people per sq km) / 12%
Total area 82,030 sq miles (212,460 sq km)
Languages Arab*, Baluchi
Religions Ibadi Muslim 75%, other Muslim 11%, Hindu 14%
Ethnic mix Arab 75%, Baluchi 15%, Other 15%
Government Monarchy with Consultative Council
Currency Rial = 1,000 baizas
Literacy rate 44%
Calorie consumption 3,013 kilocalories

PAKISTAN
Southern Asia

Official name Islamic Republic of Pakistan
Formation 1947 / 1972
Capital Islamabad
Population 140.5 million / 472 people per sq mile (182 people per sq km) / 33%
Total area 307,374 sq miles (796,100 sq km)
Main languages Urdu*, Punjabi, Sindhi, Pashtu, Baluchi
Religions Sunni Muslim 77%, Shi'a Muslim 20%, Hindu 2%, Christian 1%
Ethnic mix Punjabi 56%, Sindhi 13%, Pashtun 8%, other 23%
Government Multiparty republic
Currency Rupee = 100 paisa
Literacy rate 38% Urban
Calorie consumption 2,315 kilocalories

PALAU
Australasia & Oceania

Official name Palau
Formation 1994 / 1994
Capital Oreor
Population 16,200 /83 people per sq mile (32 people per sq km) / 52%
Total area 192 sq miles (497 sq km)
Languages Palauan, English, Sonsorolese-Tobian (no official language)
Religions Christian 70%, traditional beliefs 30%
Ethnic mix Palauan 99%, 1% Other
Government Multiparty republic
Currency US $ = 100 cents
Literacy rate 92%
Calorie consumption NOT AVAILABLE

PANAMA
Central America

Official name Republic of Panama
Formation 1903 / 1914
Capital Panama City
Population 2.6 million / 88 people per sq mile (34 people per sq km) / 52%
Total area 29,761 sq miles (77,080 sq km)
Languages Spanish*, English Creole, Amerindian languages
Religions Roman Catholic 93%, other 7%
Ethnic mix *mestizo* 70%, Black 14%, White 10%, Amerindian 6%
Government Multiparty republic
Currency Balboa = 100 centesimos
Literacy rate 91%
Calorie consumption 2,242 kilocalories

PAPUA NEW GUINEA
Australasia & Oceania

Official name Independent State of Papua New Guinea
Formation 1975 / 1975
Capital Port Moresby
Population 4.3 million / 23 people per sq mile (9 people per sq km) / 15%
Total area 178,700 sq miles (462, 840 sq km)
Languages Pidgin English*, Motu*, 750 (est.) native languages
Religions Christian 66%, other 34%
Ethnic mix Papuan 85%, other 15%
Government Parliamentary democracy
Currency Kina = 100 toea
Literacy rate 72%
Calorie consumption 2,613 kilocalories

PARAGUAY
South America

Official name Paraguay
Formation 1811 / 1938
Capital Asunción
Population 5 million / 34 people per sq mile (13 people per sq km) / 51%
Total area 157,046 sq miles (406,750 sq km)
Languages Spanish*, Guaraní
Religions Roman Catholic 90%, other 10%
Ethnic mix *mestizo* 95%, White 3%, Amerindian 2%
Government Multiparty republic
Literacy rate 92%
Calorie consumption 2,670 kilocalories

Peru
South America

Official name Republic of Peru
Formation 1824 / 1942
Capital Lima
Population 23.8 million / 49 people per sq mile (19 people per sq km) / 71%
Total area 496,223 sq miles (1,285,220 sq km)
Languages Spanish*, Quechua, Aymará
Religions Roman Catholic 95%, other 5%
Ethnic mix Amerindian 45%, *mestizo* 37%, White 15%, other 3%
Government Multiparty republic
Currency New sol = 100 centimos
Literacy rate 89%
Calorie consumption 1,882 kilocalories

Philippines
Southwestern Asia

Official name Republic of the Philippines
Formation 1946 / 1946
Capital Manila
Population 67.6 million / 588 people per sq mile (227 people per sq km) / 51%
Total area 115,831 sq miles (300,000 sq km)
Languages Pilipino*, English, Cebuano, Hiligaynon, Samaran, Bikol
Religions Roman Catholic 83%, Protestant 9%, Muslim 5%, other 3%
Ethnic mix Filipino 96%, Chinese 2%, other 2%
Government Multiparty republic
Currency Peso = 100 centavos
Literacy rate 95%
Calorie consumption 2,257 kilocalories

Poland
Northern Europe

Official name Republic of Poland
Formation 1918 / 1945
Capital Warsaw
Population 38.4 million / 327 people per sq mile (126 people per sq km) / 63%
Total area 120,720 sq miles (312,680 sq km)
Languages Polish*, German
Religions Roman Catholic 95%, other Christian 5%
Ethnic mix Polish 98%, other 2%
Government Multiparty republic
Currency Zloty = 100 groszy
Literacy rate 99%
Calorie consumption 3,301 kilocalories

Portugal
Southwestern Europe

Official name Republic of Portugal
Formation 1140 / 1640
Capital Lisbon
Population 9.8 million / 277 people per sq mile (107 people per sq km) / 34%
Total area 35,670 sq miles (92,390 sq km)
Languages Portuguese*
Religions Roman Catholic 97%, Protestant 1%, other 2%
Ethnic mix Portuguese 98%, African 1%, other 1%
Government Multiparty republic
Currency Escudo = 100 centavos
Literacy rate 86%
Calorie consumption 3,634 kilocalories

Qatar
Southwestern Asia

Official name State of Qatar
Formation 1971 / 1971
Capital Doha
Population 600,000 / 143 people per sq mile (55 people per sq km) / 90%
Total area 4,247 sq miles (11,000 sq km)
Languages Arabic*, Farsi (Persian), Urdu, Hindi, English
Religions Sunni Muslim 86%, Hindu 10%, Christian 4%
Ethnic mix Arab 40%, South Asian 35%, Persian 12%, other 13%
Government Absolute monarchy
Currency Riyal = 100 dirhams
Literacy rate 79%
Calorie consumption NOT AVAILABLE

Romania
Southeastern Europe

Official name Romania
Formation 1947 / 1947
Capital Bucharest
Population 22.8 million /257 people per sq mile (99 people per sq km) / 54%
Total area 91,700 sq miles (237,500 sq km)
Languages Romanian*, Hungarian,
Religions Romanian Orthodox 70%, Roman Catholic 6%, Protestant 6%, other 18%
Ethnic mix Romanian 89%, Hungarian 8%, other (including Gypsy) 3%
Government Multiparty republic
Currency Leu = 100 bani
Literacy rate 97%
Calorie consumption 3,051 kilocalories

Russian Federation
Europe / Asia

Official name Russian Federation
Formation 1991 / 1991
Capital Moscow
Population 147 million /23 people per sq mile (9 people per sq km) / 75%
Total area 6,592,800 sq miles (17,075,400 sq km)
Languages Russian*, Tatar, Ukrainian
Religions Russian Orthodox 80%, other (including Jewish, Muslim) 20%
Ethnic mix Russian 80%, Tatar 4%, Ukrainian 3%, other 13%
Currency Rouble = 100 kopeks
Literacy rate 98%
Calorie consumption NOT AVAILABLE

Rwanda
Central Africa

Official name Rwandese Republic
Formation 1962 / 1962
Capital Kigali
Population 8 million / 788 people per sq mile (304 people per sq km) / 6%
Total area 10,170 sq miles (26,340 sq km)
Languages Kinyarwanda*, French*, Kiswahili, English
Religions Christian 74%, traditional beliefs 25%, other 1%
Ethnic mix Hutu 90%, Tutsi 9%, Twa pygmy 1%
Government Multiparty republic
Currency Franc = 100 centimes
Literacy rate 61%
Calorie consumption 1,821 kilocalories

Saint Kitts & Nevis
West Indies

Official name Federation of Saint Christopher and Nevis
Formation 1983 / 1983
Capital Basseterre
Population 44,000 / 295 people per sq mile (114 people per sq km) / 41%
Total area 139 sq miles (360 sq km)
Languages English*, English Creole
Religions Protestant 85%, Roman Catholic 10%, other Christian 5%
Ethnic mix Black 95%, mixed 5%
Government Parliamentary democracy
Currency E. Caribbean $ = 100 cents
Literacy rate 97%
Calorie consumption 2,419 kilocalories

Saint Lucia
West Indies

Official name Saint Lucia
Formation 1979 / 1979
Capital Castries
Population 145,000 / 617 people per sq mile (238 people per sq km) / 47%
Total area 239 sq miles (620 sq km)
Languages English*, French Creole, Hindi, Urdu
Religions Roman Catholic 90%, other 10%
Ethnic mix Black 90%, Afro-European 6%, South Asian 4%
Government Parliamentary democracy
Currency E. Caribbean $ = 100 cents
Literacy rate 93%
Calorie consumption 2,588 kilocalories

Saint Vincent & the Grenadines
West Indies

Official name Saint Vincent and the Grenadines
Formation 1979 / 1979
Capital Kingstown
Population 111,000 / 845 people per sq mile (326 people per sq km) / 43%
Total area 131 sq miles (340 sq km)
Languages English*, English Creole
Religions Protestant 62% Roman Catholic 19%, other 19%
Ethnic mix Black 82%, mixed 14%, White 3%, South Asian 1%
Government Parliamentary democracy
Currency E. Caribbean $ = 100 cents
Literacy rate 84%
Calorie consumption 2,347 kilocalories

San Marino
Southern Europe

Official name Republic of San Marino
Formation CE 301 / 1862
Capital San Marino
Population 24,000 / 1,018 people per sq mile (393 people per sq km) / 90%
Total area 24 sq miles (61 sq km)
Languages Italian*
Religions Roman Catholic 96%, other 4%
Ethnic mix Sammarinese 95%, other 5%
Government Multiparty republic
Currency Italian lira = 100 centesimi
Literacy rate 96%
Calorie consumption 3,561 kilocalories

Sao Tome & Principe
Western Africa

Official name Democratic Republic of Sao Tome and Principe
Formation 1975 / 1975
Capital São Tomé
Population 125,000 / 337 people per sq mile (130 people per sq km) / 44%
Total area 372 sq miles (964 sq km)
Languages Portuguese, Portuguese Creole
Religions Roman Catholic 90%, other Christian 10%
Ethnic mix Black 90%, Portuguese and Creole 10%
Government Multiparty republic
Currency Dobra = 100 centimos
Literacy rate 57%
Calorie consumption 2,129 kilocalories

Saudi Arabia
Southwestern Asia

Official name Kingdom of Saudi Arabia
Formation 1932 / 1981
Capital Riyadh
Population 17.9 million / 21 people per sq mile (8 people per sq km) / 78%
Total area 829,995 sq miles (2,149,690 sq km)
Languages Arabic*
Religions Sunni Muslim 85%, Shi'a Muslim 14%, Christian 1%
Ethnic mix Arab 90%, Yemeni 8%, other Arab 1%, other 1%
Government Absolute monarchy
Currency Riyal = 100 malalah
Literacy rate 63%
Calorie consumption 2,735 kilocalories

Senegal
Western Africa

Official name Republic of Senegal
Formation 1960 / 1960
Capital Dakar
Population 8.3 million /111 people per sq mile (43 people per sq km) / 41%
Total area 75,950 sq miles (196,720 sq km)
Languages French*, Wolof, Fulani, Serer
Religions Muslim 92%, traditional beliefs 6%, Christian 2%
Ethnic mix Wolof 46%, Fulani 25%, Serer 16%, other 13%
Government Multiparty republic
Currency CFA franc = 100 centimes
Literacy rate 33%
Calorie consumption 2,262 kilocalories

Seychelles
Indian Ocean

Official name Republic of Seychelles
Formation 1976 / 1976
Capital Victoria
Population 73,000 / 700 people per sq mile (270 people per sq km) / 52%
Total area 108 sq miles (280 sq km)
Languages Creole*, French, English
Religions Roman Catholic 90%, other 10%
Ethnic mix Seychellois (mixed African, South Asian and European) 95%, Chinese and South Asian 5%
Government Multiparty republic
Currency Rupee = 100 cents
Literacy rate 58%
Calorie consumption 2,287 kilocalories

Sierra Leone
Western Africa

Official name Republic of Sierra Leone
Formation 1961 / 1961
Capital Freetown
Population 4.5 million / 163 people per sq mile (63 people per sq km) / 34%
Total area 27,699 sq miles (71,740 sq km)
Languages English*, Krio (Creole), Mende, Temne
Religions Traditional beliefs 52%, Muslim 40%, Christian 8%
Ethnic mix Mende 34%, Temne 31%, Limba 9%, Kono 5%, other 21%
Government Military regime
Currency Leone = 100 cents
Literacy rate 31%
Calorie consumption 1,694 kilocalorie

Singapore
Southeastern Asia

Official name Republic of Singapore
Formation 1965 / 1965
Capital Singapore
Population 2.8 million / 11,894 people per sq mile (4,590 people per sq km) / 100%
Total area 239 sq miles (620 sq km)
Languages Malay*, Chinese, Tamil, English
Religions Buddhist 30%, Christian 20%, Muslim 17%, other 33%
Ethnic mix Chinese 76%, Malay 15%, South Asian 7%, other 2%
Government Multiparty democracy
Currency Singapore $ = 100 cents
Literacy rate 91%
Calorie consumption 3,128 kilocalories

Slovakia
Central Europe

Official name Slovak Republic
Formation 1993 / 1993
Capital Bratislava
Population 5.4 million / 285 people per sq mile (110 people per sq km) / 57%
Total area 19,100 sq miles (49,500 sq km)
Languages Slovak*, Hungarian (Magyar), Romany, Czech
Religions Roman Catholic 80%, Protestant 12%, other 8%
Ethnic mix Slovak 85%, Hungarian 9%, Czech 1%, other 5%
Government Multiparty republic
Currency Koruna = 100 halierov
Literacy rate 99%
Calorie consumption 3,156 kilocalories

Slovenia
Central Europe

Official name Republic of Slovenia
Formation 1991 / 1991
Capital Ljubljana
Population 1.9 million / 244 people per sq mile (94 people per sq km) / 62%
Total area 7,820 sq miles (20,250 sq km)
Languages Slovene*, Serbian, Croatian
Religions Roman Catholic 96%, Muslim 1%, other 3%
Ethnic mix Slovene 92%, Croat 3%, Serb 1%, other 4%
Government Multiparty republic
Currency Tolar = 100 stotins
Literacy rate 99%
Calorie consumption NOT AVAILABLE

Solomon Islands
Australasia & Oceania

Official name Solomon Islands
Formation 1978 / 1978
Capital Honiara
Population 400,000 / 36 people per sq mile (14 people per sq km) / 16%
Total area 111,583 sq miles (289,000 sq km)
Languages English*, 87 (established) native languages
Religions Christian 91%, other 9%
Ethnic mix Melanesian 94%, other 6%
Government Parliamentary democracy
Currency Solomon Is $ = 100 cents
Literacy rate 24%
Calorie consumption 2,173 kilocalories

Somalia
Eastern Africa

Official name Somali Democratic Republic
Formation 1960 / 1960
Capital Mogadishu
Population 9.3 million / 39 people per sq mile (15 people per sq km) / 25%
Total area 246,200 sq miles (637,660 sq km)
Languages Somali*, Arabic, English
Religions Sunni Muslim 99%, other (including Christian) 1%
Ethnic mix Somali 98%, Bantu, Arab and other 2%
Government Transitional
Currency Shilling = 100 cents
Literacy rate 24%
Calorie consumption 1,499 kilocalories

South Africa
Southern Africa

Official name Republic of South Africa
Formation 1910 / 1934
Capitals Pretoria, Cape Town, Bloemfontein
Population 41.5 million / 88 people per sq mile (34 people per sq km) / 50%
Total area 471,443 sq miles (1,221,040 sq km)
Languages Afrikaans*, English, 11 African languages
Religions Protestant 55%, Roman Catholic 9%, Hindu 1%, Muslim 1%, other 34%
Ethnic mix Black 75%, White 14%, mixed 9%, South Asian 2%
Government Multiparty republic
Currency Rand = 100 cents
Literacy rate 82%
Calorie consumption 2,695 kilocalories

South Korea
Eastern Asia

Official name Republic of Korea
Formation 1948 / 1948
Capital Seoul
Population 45 million / 1,182 people per sq mile (456 people per sq km) / 77%
Total area 38,232 sq miles (99,020 sq km)
Languages Korean*, Chinese
Religions Mahayana Buddhist 47%, Protestant 38%, Roman Catholic 11%, Confucianist 3%, other 1%
Ethnic mix Korean 99.9% other 0.1%
Government Multiparty republic
Currency Won = 100 chon
Literacy rate 97%
Calorie consumption 3,285 kilocalories

Spain
Southeastern Europe

Official name Kingdom of Spain
Formation 1492 / 1713
Capital Madrid
Population 39.6 million / 205 people per sq mile (79 people per sq km) / 76%
Total area 194,900 sq miles (504,780 sq km)
Languages Castilian Spanish*, Catalan*, Galician*, Basque*
Religions Roman Catholic 99%, other 1%
Ethnic mix Castilian Spanish 72%, Catalan 16%, Galician 7%, other 5%
Government Constitutional monarchy
Currency Peseta = 100 céntimos
Literacy rate 95%
Calorie consumption 3,708 kilocalories

Sri Lanka
Southern Asia

Official name Democratic Socialist Republic of Sri Lanka
Formation 1948 / 1948
Capital Colombo
Population 18.4 million / 736 people per sq mile (284 people per sq km) / 22%
Total area 25,332 sq miles (65,610 sq km)
Languages Sinhala*, Tamil, English
Religions Buddhist 70%, Hindu 15%, Christian 8%, Muslim 7%
Ethnic mix Sinhalese 74%, Tamil 18%, other 8%
Government Multiparty republic
Currency Rupee = 100 cents
Literacy rate 90%
Calorie consumption 2,273 kilocalories

Sudan
Eastern Africa

Official name Republic of Sudan
Formation 1956 / 1956
Capital Khartoum
Population 28.1 million / 31 people per sq mile (12 people per sq km) / 23%
Total area 967,493 sq miles (2,505,815 sq km)
Languages Arabic*, Dinka, Nuer, Nubian, Beja, Zande, Bari, Fur
Religions Muslim 70%, traditional beliefs 20%, Christian 5%, other 5%
Ethnic mix Arab 51%, Dinka 13%, Nuba 9%, Beja 7%, other 20%
Government Military regime
Currency Pound = 100 piastres
Literacy rate 46%
Calorie consumption 2,202 kilocalories

Suriname
South America

Official name Republic of Suriname
Formation 1975 / 1975
Capital Paramaribo
Population 400,000 / 5 people per sq mile (2 people per sq km) / 49%
Total area 63,039 sq miles (163,270 sq km)
Languages Dutch*, Pidgin English (Taki-Taki), Hindi, Javanese, Carib
Religions Christian 48%, Hindu 27%, Muslim 20%, other 5%
Ethnic mix South Asian 37%, Creole 31%, Javanese 15%, other 17%
Government Multiparty republic
Currency Guilder = 100 cents
Literacy rate 93%
Calorie consumption 2,547 kilocalories

Swaziland
Southern Africa

Official name Kingdom of Swaziland
Formation 1968 / 1968
Capital Mbabane
Population 900,000 / 135 people per sq mile (52 people per sq km) / 29%
Total area 6,703 sq miles (17,360 sq km)
Languages Siswati*, English*, Zulu
Religions Christian 60%, traditional beliefs 40%
Ethnic mix Swazi 95%, other 5%
Government Executive monarchy
Currency Lilangeni = 100 cents
Literacy rate 77%
Calorie consumption 2,706 kilocalories

Sweden
Northern Europe

Official name Kingdom of Sweden
Formation 1809 / 1905
Capital Stockholm
Population 8.8 million / 50 people per sq mile (20 people per sq km) / 83%
Total area 173,730 sq miles (449,960 sq km)
Languages Swedish*, Finnish, Lappish,
Religions Evangelical Lutheran 94%, Roman Catholic 2%, other 4%
Ethnic mix Swedish 87%, Finnish and Lapp 1%, other European 12%
Government Constitutional monarchy
Currency Krona = 100 öre
Literacy rate 99%
Calorie consumption 2,972 kilocalories

Switzerland
Central Europe

Official name Swiss Confederation
Formation 1815 / 1815
Capital Bern
Population 7.2 million / 469 people per sq mile (181 people per sq km) / 60%
Total area 15,940 sq miles (41,290 sq km)
Languages German*, French*, Italian*, Romansch*
Religions Roman Catholic 48%, Protestant 44%, other 8%
Ethnic mix German 65%, French 18%, Italian 10%, other 7%
Government Federal republic
Currency Franc = 100 centimes
Literacy rate 99%
Calorie consumption 3,379 kilocalories

Syria
Southwestern Asia

Official name Syrian Arab Republic
Formation 1946 / 1946
Capital Damascus
Population 14.7 million / 207 people per sq mile (80 people per sq km) / 51%
Total area 71,500 sq miles (185,180 sq km)
Languages Arabic*, French, Kurdish, Armenian, Circassian, Turkmen
Religions Sunni Muslim 74%, other Muslim 16%, Christian 10%
Ethnic mix Arab 90%, other 10%
Government Single-party republic
Currency Pound = 100 piastres
Literacy rate 71%
Calorie consumption 3,175 kilocalories

Taiwan
Eastern Asia

Official name Republic of China
Formation 1949 / 1949
Capital Taipei
Population 20.9 million / 1,682 people per sq mile (649 people per sq km) / 69%
Total area 13,969 sq miles (36,179 sq km)
Languages Mandarin*, Amoy Chinese, Hakka Chinese
Religions Buddhist, Confucianist, Taoist 93%, other 7%
Ethnic mix Taiwanese 84%, mainland Chinese 14%, other 2%
Government Multiparty republic
Currency New Taiwan $ = 100 cents
Literacy rate 94%
Calorie consumption NOT AVAILABLE

Tajikistan
Central Asia

Official name Republic of Tajikistan
Formation 1991 / 1991
Capital Dushanbe
Population 6.1 million / 111 people per sq mile (43 people per sq km) / 32%
Total area 55,251 sq miles (143,100 sq km)
Main languages Tajik*, Uzbek, Russian
Religions Sunni Muslim 85%, Shi'a Muslim 5%, other 10%
Ethnic mix Tajik 62%, Uzbek 24%, Russian 4%, Tatar 2%, other 8%
Government Single-party republic
Currency Tajik rouble = 100 kopeks
Literacy rate 98%
Calorie consumption NOT AVAILABLE

Tanzania
Eastern Africa

Official name United Republic of Tanzania
Formation 1964 / 1964
Capital Dodoma
Population 29.7 million / 88 people per sq mile (34 people per sq km) / 22%
Total area 364,900 sq miles (945,090 sq km)
Languages English*, Swahili, Sukuma, Chagga, Nyamwezi, Hehe, Makonde
Religions Traditional beliefs 42%, Muslim 31%, Christian 27%
Ethnic mix 120 ethnic Bantu groups 99%, other 1%
Government Single-party republic
Currency Shilling = 100 cents
Literacy rate 68%
Calorie consumption 2,018 kilocalories

Thailand
Southeastern Asia

Official name Kingdom of Thailand
Formation 1882 / 1887
Capital Bangkok
Population 58.8 million / 298 people per sq mile (115 people per sq km) / 19%
Total area 198,116 sq miles (513,120 sq km)
Languages Thai*, Chinese, Malay, Khmer, Mon, Karen
Religions Buddhist 95%, other 5%
Ethnic mix Thai 75%, Chinese 14%, Malay 4%, other 7%
Government Constitutional monarchy
Currency Baht = 100 stangs
Literacy rate 94%
Calorie consumption 2,432 kilocalories

Togo
Western Africa

Official name Togolese Republic
Formation 1960 / 1960
Capital Lomé
Population 4.1 million / 195 people per sq mile (75 people per sq km) / 30%
Total area 21,927 sq miles (56,790 sq km)
Languages French*, Ewe, Kabye, Gurma
Religions Traditional beliefs 70%, Christian 20%, Muslim 10%
Ethnic mix Ewe 43%, Kabye 26%, Gurma 16%, other 15%
Government Multiparty republic
Currency CFA franc = 100 centimes
Literacy rate 52%
Calorie consumption 2,242 kilocalories

Tonga
Australasia & Oceania

Official name Kingdom of Tonga
Formation 1970 / 1970
Capital Nuku'alofa
Population 98,000 / 352 people per sq mile (136 people per sq km) / 21%
Total area 290 sq miles (750 sq km)
Languages Tongan*, English
Religions Protestant 82%, Roman Catholic 18%
Ethnic mix Tongan 98%, other 2%
Government Constitutional monarchy
Currency Pa'anga = 100 seniti
Literacy rate 99%
Calorie consumption 2,946 kilocalories

Trinidad & Tobago
West Indies

Official name Republic of Trinidad and Tobago
Formation 1962 / 1962
Capital Port-of-Spain
Population 1.3 million / 656 people per sq mile (253 people per sq km) / 70%
Total area 1,981 sq miles (5,130 sq km)
Languages English*, English Creole, Hindi, French, Spanish
Religions Christian 58%, Hindu 30%, Muslim 8%, other 4%
Ethnic mix Black 43%, South Asian 40%, mixed 14%, other 3%
Government Multiparty republic
Currency Trinidad & Tobago $ = 100 cents
Literacy rate 98%
Calorie consumption 2,585 kilocalories

Tunisia
Northern Africa

Official name Republic of Tunisia
Formation 1956 / 1956
Capital Tunis
Population 8.9 million / 148 people per sq mile (57 people per sq km) / 56%
Total area 63,170 sq miles (163,610 sq km)
Languages Arabic*, French
Religions Muslim 98%, Christian 1%, other 1%
Ethnic mix Arab and Berber 98%, European 1%, other 1%
Government Multiparty republic
Currency Dinar = 1,000 millimes
Literacy rate 67%
Calorie consumption 3,330 kilocalories

Turkey
Asia / Europe

Official name Republic of Turkey
Formation 1923 / 1939
Capital Ankara
Population 61.9 million / 207 people per sq mile (80 people per sq km) / 64%
Total area 300,950 sq miles (779,450 sq km)
Languages Turkish*, Kurdish, Arabic, Circassian, Armenian
Religions Muslim 99%, other 1%
Ethnic mix Turkish 80%, Kurdish 17%, other 3%
Government Multiparty republic
Currency Turkish lira = 100 krural
Literacy rate 82%
Calorie consumption 3,429 kilocalories

Turkmenistan
Central Asia

Official name Turkmenistan
Formation 1991 / 1991
Capital Ashgabat
Population 4.1 million / 21 people per sq mile (8 people per sq km) / 45%
Total area 188,455 sq miles (488,100 sq km)
Languages Turkmen*, Uzbek, Russian
Religions Muslim 85%, Eastern Orthodox 10%, other 5%
Ethnic mix Turkmen 72%, Russian 9%, Uzbek 9%, other 10%
Government Single-party republic
Currency Manat = 100 tenge
Literacy rate 98%
Calorie consumption NOT AVAILABLE

Tuvalu
Australasia & Oceania

Official name Tuvalu
Formation 1978 / 1978
Capital Fongafale
Population 9,000 / 997 people per sq mile (346 people per sq km) / 31%
Total area 10 sq miles (26 sq km)
Languages Tuvaluan*, Kiribati, English
Religions Protestant 97%, other 3%
Ethnic mix Tuvaluan 95% other 5%
Government Constitutional monarchy
Currency Australian $ = 100 cents
Literacy rate 95%
Calorie consumption NOT AVAILABLE

Uganda
Eastern Africa

Official name Republic of Uganda
Formation 1962 / 1962
Capital Kampala
Population 21.3 million / 277 people per sq mile (107 people per sq km) / 12%
Total area 91,073 sq miles (235,880 sq km)
Languages English*, Luganda, Nkole, Chiga, Lango, Acholi, Teso
Religions Christian 66%, traditional beliefs 18%, Muslim 16%
Ethnic mix Buganda 18%, Banyoro 14%, Teso 9%, other 59%
Government Multiparty republic
Currency Shilling = 100 cents
Literacy rate 62%
Calorie consumption 2,159 kilocalories

Ukraine
Eastern Europe

Official name Ukraine
Formation 1991 / 1991
Capital Kiev
Population 51.4 million / 220 people per sq mile (85 people per sq km) / 69%
Total area 223,090 sq miles (603,700 sq km)
Languages Ukrainian*, Russian, Tatar
Religions Mostly Ukrainian Orthodox, with Roman Catholic, Protestant and Jewish minorities
Ethnic mix Ukrainian 73%, Russian 22%, other (including Tatar) 5%
Government Multiparty republic
Currency Karbovanets (coupons)
Literacy rate 98%
Calorie consumption NOT AVAILABLE

United Arab Emirates
Southwestern Asia

Official name United Arab Emirates
Formation 1971 / 1971
Capital Abu Dhabi
Population 1.9 million / 9 people per sq mile (23 people per sq km) / 82%
Total area 32,278 sq miles (83,600 sq km)
Languages Arabic*, Farsi (Persian), Urdu, Hindi, English
Religions Sunni Muslim 77%, Shi'a Muslim 19%, other 4%
Ethnic mix South Asian 50%, Emirian 19%, other Arab 23%, other 8%
Government Federation of monarchs
Currency Dirham = 100 fils
Literacy rate 79%
Calorie consumption 3,384 kilocalories

United Kingdom
Northwestern Europe

Official name United Kingdom of Great Britain and Northern Ireland
Formation 1801 / 1922
Capital London
Population 58.3 million / 625 people per sq mile (241 people per sq km) / 89%
Total area 94,550 sq miles (244,880 sq km)
Languages English*, Welsh, Scottish, Gaelic
Religions Protestant 52%, Roman Catholic 9%, Muslim 3%, other 36%
Ethnic mix English 81%, Scottish 10%, Welsh 2%, other 7%
Government Constitutional monarchy
Currency Pound sterling = 100 pence
Literacy rate 99%
Calorie consumption 3,317 kilocalories

United States
North America

Official name United States of America
Formation 1787 / 1959
Capital Washington D.C.
Population 263.3 million / 75 people per sq mile (29 people per sq km) / 76%
Total area 3,681,760 sq miles (9,372,610 sq km)
Languages English*, Spanish, Italian, German, French, Polish, Chinese, Greek
Religions Protestant 56%, Roman Catholic 28%, Jewish 2%, other 14%
Ethnic mix White (including Hispanic) 83%, Black 13%, other 4%
Government Multiparty republic
Currency US $ = 100 cents
Literacy rate 99%
Calorie consumption 3,732 kilocalories

Uruguay
South America

Official name Oriental Republic of Uruguay
Formation 1828 / 1909
Capital Montevideo
Population 3.2 million / 122 people per sq mile (18 people per sq km) / 90%
Total area 67,494 sq miles (174,810 sq km)
Languages Spanish*
Religions Roman Catholic 66%, Protestant 2%, Jewish 2%, other 30%
Ethnic mix European 88%, *mestizo* 8% Black 4%
Government Multiparty republic
Currency Peso = 100 centimes
Literacy rate 97%
Calorie consumption 2,750 kilocalories

Uzbekistan
Central Asia

Official name Republic of Uzbekistan
Formation 1991 / 1991
Capital Tashkent
Population 22.8 million / 132 people per sq mile (51 people per sq km) / 41%
Total area 439,733 sq miles (1,138,910 sq km)
Languages Uzbek*, Russian
Religions Muslim 88%, other (mostly Eastern Orthodox) 12%
Ethnic mix Uzbek 71%, Russian 8%, Tajik 5%, Kazakh 4%, other 12%
Government Single-party republic
Currency Sum = 100 teen
Literacy rate 97%
Calorie consumption NOT AVAILABLE

Vanuatu
Australasia & Oceania

Official name Republic of Vanuatu
Formation 1980 / 1980
Capital Port-Vila
Population 200,000 / 41 people per sq mile (16 people per sq km) / 19%
Total area 4,706 sq miles (12,190 sq km)
Languages Bislama*, English, French
Religions Protestant 77%, Roman Catholic 15%, traditional beliefs 8%
Ethnic mix Ni-Vanuatu 98%, other 2%
Government Multiparty republic
Currency Vatu = 100 centimes
Literacy rate 70%
Calorie consumption 2,739 kilocalories

Vatican City
Southern Europe

Official name Vatican City State
Formation 1929 / 1929
Capital Not applicable
Population 1,000 / 5,890 people per sq mile (2,273 people per sq km) /100%
Total area 0.17 sq miles (0.44 sq km)
Languages Italian*, Latin*
Religions Roman Catholic 100%
Ethnic mix Italian 90%, Swiss 10% (including the Swiss Guard, responsible for papal security)
Government Papal Commission
Currency Italian lira = 100 centesimi
Literacy rate 100%
Calorie consumption 3,561 kilocalories

Venezuela
South America

Official name Republic of Venezuela
Formation 1830 / 1929
Capital Caracas
Population 21.8 million / 65 people per sq mile (25 people per sq km) / 91%
Total area 352,143 sq miles (912,050 sq km)
Languages Spanish*, Amerindian languages
Religions Roman Catholic 96%, Protestant 2%, other 2%
Ethnic mix *mestizo* 67%, White 21%, Black 10%, Amerindian 2%
Government Multiparty republic
Currency Bolívar = 100 centimos
Literacy rate 91%
Calorie consumption 2,618 kilocalories

Vietnam
Southeastern Asia

Official name Socialist Republic of Vietnam
Formation 1976 / 1976
Capital Hanoi
Population 74.5 million / 593 people per sq mile (229 people per sq km) / 20%
Total area 127,243 sq miles (329,560 sq km)
Languages Vietnamese*, Chinese, Thai, Khmer, Muong
Religions Buddhist 55%, Roman Catholic 7%, Muslim 1%, other 37%
Ethnic mix Vietnamese 88%, Chinese 4%, Thai 2%, other 6%
Government Single-party republic
Currency Dong = 10 hao = 100 xu
Literacy rate 94%
Calorie consumption 2,250 kilocalories

Western Samoa
Australasia & Oceania

Official name Independent State of Western Samoa
Formation 1962 / 1962
Capital Apia
Population 169,000 / 155 people per sq mile (60 people per sq km) / 21%
Total area 1,027 sq miles (2,840 sq km)
Languages Samoan*, English*
Religions Protestant 74%, Roman Catholic 26%
Ethnic mix Samoan 93%, other 7%
Government Parliamentary state
Currency Tala = 100 sene
Literacy rate 92%
Calorie consumption 2,828 kilocalories

Yemen
Southwestern Asia

Official name Republic of Yemen
Formation 1990 / 1990
Capital Sana
Population 14.5 million / 70 people per sq mile (27 people per sq km) / 31%
Total area 203,849 sq miles (527,970 sq km)
Languages Arabic*, Hindi, Tamil, Urdu
Religions Sunni Muslim 55%, Shi'a Muslim 42%, other 3%
Ethnic mix Arab 95%, Afro-Arab 3%, South Asian, African, European 2%
Government Multiparty republic
Currency Rial (North), Dinar (South) – both are legal currency
Literacy rate 41%
Calorie consumption 2,203 kilocalories

Yugoslavia (Serbia & Montenegro) *Europe*

Official name Federal Republic of Yugoslavia
Formation 1992 / 1992
Capital Belgrade
Population 10.8 million / 1,088 people per sq mile (420 people per sq km) / 50%
Total area 9,929 sq miles (25,715 sq km)
Languages Serbian*, Croatian, Albanian
Religions Roman Catholic, Eastern Orthodox 65%, Muslim 19%, other 16%
Ethnic mix Serb 63%, Albanian 14%, Montenegrin 6%, other 17%
Government Multiparty republic
Currency Dinar = 100 para
Literacy rate 93%
Calorie consumption NOT AVAILABLE

Zaire *now called* Congo (Democratic Republic of)
Central Africa

Official name Republic of Zaire
Formation 1960 / 1960
Capital Kinshasa
Population 43.9 million / 49 people per sq mile (19 people per sq km) / 29%
Total area 905,563 sq miles (2,345,410 sq km)
Languages French*, Kiswahili, Tshiluba, Lingala
Religions Christian 70%, traditional beliefs 20%, Muslim 10%
Ethnic mix Bantu 23%, Hamitic 23%, other 54%
Government Transitional
Currency New zaire = 100 makuta
Literacy rate 77%
Calorie consumption 2,060 kilocalories

Zambia
Southern Africa

Official name Republic of Zambia
Formation 1964 / 1964
Capital Lusaka
Population 9.5 million / 34 people per sq mile (13 people per sq km) / 42%
Total area 285,992 sq miles (740,720 sq km)
Languages English*, Bemba*, Nyanja*, Tonga, Kaonde, Lunda
Religions Christian 63%, Traditional beliefs 35%, other 2%
Ethnic mix Bemba 36%, Maravi 18%, Tonga 15%, other 31%
Government Multiparty republic
Currency Kwacha = 100 ngwee
Literacy rate 78%
Calorie consumption 1,931 kilocalories

Zimbabwe
Southern Africa

Official name Republic of Zimbabwe
Formation 1980 / 1980
Capital Harare
Population 11.3 million / 75 people per sq mile (29 people per sq km) / 30%
Total area 150,800 sq miles (390,580 sq km)
Languages English*, Shona, Ndebele
Religions Syncretic (Christian and traditional beliefs) 50%, Christian 26%, traditional beliefs 24%
Ethnic mix Shona 71%, Ndebele 16%, other 11%, White, Asian 2%
Government Multiparty republic
Currency Zimbabwe $ = 100 cents
Literacy rate 85%
Calorie consumption 1,985 kilocalories

GLOSSARY

THIS GLOSSARY lists most geographical, technical, and foreign language terms that appear in the text, followed by a brief definition of the term. Any acronyms used in the text are also listed. Terms in italics are for cross-reference and indicate that the word is defined separately in the glossary.

A

Aboriginal The original (*indigenous*) inhabitants of a country or continent. Particularly used in reference to Australia.

Abyssal plain A broad *plain* found in the depths of the ocean, more than 10,000 ft (3,000 m) below sea level.

Acid rain Rain, sleet, snow, or mist that has absorbed waste gases from fossil-fueled power stations and vehicle exhaust fumes, becoming more acid. It causes severe environmental damage.

Adaptation The gradual evolution of plants and animals to enhance their abilites to survive and reproduce in their *environment*.

Afforestation The planting of new forest in areas that were once forested but have been cleared.

Agribusiness A term applied to activities such as growing crops, rearing animals, or manufacturing of farm machinery, that eventually leads to the supply of agricultural produce at market.

Air mass A huge, homogeneous mass of air, within which horizontal patterns of temperature and *humidity* are consistent. Air masses are separated by *fronts*.

Alliance An agreement between two or more nations, to work together to achieve common purposes.

Alluvial fan A large fan-shaped deposit of fine sediments deposited by a river as it emerges from a narrow, mountain valley onto a broad, open *plain*.

Alluvium Material deposited by rivers. Today usually applied only to finer particles of silt and clay.

Alpine Mountain *environment* between the *tree line* and the level of permanent snow cover.

Alpine mountains Ranges of mountains formed from 30 million to 65 million years ago by *folding*, in west and central Europe.

Amerindian A term applied to people *indigenous* to Mexico, Central and South America.

Animal husbandry The business of rearing animals.

Antarctic circle The parallel that lies at a *latitude* of 66° 32' S.

Anticline A geological *fold* that forms an arch shape, curving upward in the rock *strata*.

Anticyclone An area of relatively high atmospheric pressure.

Aquaculture Collective term for the farming of produce derived from the sea, including fish-farming and the cultivation of shellfish and plants such as seaweed.

Aquifer A body of rock that can absorb water. Also applied to any rock strata that have sufficient porosity to yield *groundwater* through wells or springs.

Arable Land that has been plowed and is in use for cultivation, or is suitable for growing crops.

Archipelago A group or chain of islands.

Arctic Circle The parallel that lies at a *latitude* of 66° 32' N.

Arête A thin, jagged mountain ridge that divides two adjacent *cirques*, found in regions where *glaciation* has occurred.

Arid Dry. An area of low rainfall, where the rate of *evaporation* may be greater than that of *precipitation*. Often defined as those areas that receive less than one inch (25 mm) of rain a year. Only drought-resistant plants can survive in these areas.

Artesian well A naturally occurring source of underground water, stored in an *aquifer*.

Artisanal Small-scale, manual operation, such as fishing, using little or no machinery.

ASEAN Association of Southeast Asian Nations. Established in 1967 to promote economic, social, and cultural cooperation. Its members include Brunei, Indonesia, Malaysia, Philippines, Singapore, and Thailand.

Aseismic A region where *earthquake* activity has ceased.

Asteroid A minor planet circling the Sun, mainly between the orbits of Mars and Jupiter.

Asthenosphere A zone of hot, partially melted rock, which underlies the *lithosphere*, within the Earth's *crust*.

Atmosphere The envelope of odorless, colorless, and tasteless gases surrounding the Earth, consisting of *oxygen* (23%), *nitrogen* (75%), argon (1%), and *carbon dioxide* (0.03%), as well as tiny proportions of other gases.

Atmospheric pressure The pressure created by the action of gravity on the gases surrounding the Earth.

Atoll A ring-shaped island or *coral reef* often enclosing a *lagoon* of seawater.

Avalanche The rapid movement of a mass of snow and ice down a steep slope. Similar movements of other materials are described as rock avalanches or *landslides* and sand avalanches.

B

Badlands A landscape that has been heavily eroded and dissected by rainwater, and supports little or no vegetation.

Back slope The gentler windward slope of a sand *dune* or gentler slope of a *cuesta*.

Bajos An *alluvial fan* deposited by a river at the base of mountains and hills that encircle *desert* areas.

Bar, coastal An offshore strip of sand or shingle, either above or below the water. Usually parallel to the shore but sometimes crescent-shaped or at an oblique angle.

Barchan A crescent-shaped sand *dune*, formed where wind direction is very consistent. The horns of the crescent point downwind, and where there is enough sand, the barchan is mobile.

Barrio A Spanish term for the shantytowns – settlements of shacks – that are clustered around many South and Central American cities (*see also Favela*).

Basalt Dark, fine-grained *igneous rock* that is formed near the Earth's surface from rapidly cooling *lava*.

Base level The level below which flowing water cannot erode the land.

Basement rock A mass of ancient rock, often of *Precambrian age*, covered by a layer of more recent *sedimentary rocks*. Commonly associated with *shield* areas.

Beach Shore of a sea or lake where waves break and there is an accumulation of loose sand, mud, gravel, or pebbles.

Bedrock Solid, consolidated, and relatively unweathered rock, found on the surface of the land or just below a layer of soil or *weathered* rock.

Biodiversity The quantity of animal or plant species in a given area.

Biomass The total mass of organic matter – plants and animals – in a given area. It is usually measured in kilograms per square meter. Plant biomass is proportionally greater than that of animals, except in cities.

Biosphere The zone just above and below the Earth's surface where all plants and animals live.

Blizzard A severe windstorm with snow and sleet. Visibility is often severely restricted.

Bluff The steep bank of a *meander*, formed by the erosive action of a river.

Boreal forest Tracts of mainly coniferous forest found in northern *latitudes*.

Breccia A type of rock composed of sharp fragments, cemented by a fine-grained material such as clay.

Butte An isolated, flat-topped hill with steep or vertical sides, buttes are the eroded remnants of a former land surface.

C

Caatinga Portuguese (Brazilian) term for thorny woodland growing in areas of pale granitic soils.

CACM Central American Common Market. Established in 1960 to further economic ties between its members, which are Costa Rica, El Salvador, Guatemala, Honduras, and Nicaragua.

Calcite Hexagonal crystals of calcium carbonate.

Caldera A huge volcanic vent, often containing a number of smaller vents, and sometimes a crater lake.

Carbon cycle The transfer of carbon to and from the *atmosphere*. This occurs on land through *photosynthesis*. In the sea, *carbon dioxide* is absorbed, some returning to the air and some taken up into the bodies of sea creatures.

Carbon dioxide A colorless, odorless gas (CO_2) that makes up 0.03% of the *atmosphere*.

Carbonation The process in which rocks are broken down by carbonic acid. Carbon dioxide in the air dissolves in rainwater, forming carbonic acid. *Limestone* terrain can be eaten away rapidly.

Cash crop A single crop grown specifically for export sale, instead of local use. Typical examples include coffee, tea, and citrus fruits.

Cassava A type of grain meal, used to produce tapioca. A staple crop in many parts of Africa.

Castle kopje Hill or rock outcrop, especially in southern Africa, where steep sides, and a summit composed of blocks, give a castlelike appearance.

Cataracts A series of stepped waterfalls created as a river flows over a band of hard, resistant rock.

Causeway A raised route through marshland or a body of water.

CEEAC Economic Community of Central African States. Established in 1983 to promote regional cooperation and if possible, establish a common market between 11 Central African nations.

Chemical weathering The chemical reactions leading to the decomposition of rocks. Types of chemical weathering include *carbonation*, *hydrolysis*, and *oxidation*.

Chernozem A fertile soil, also known as "black earth" consisting of a layer of dark topsoil rich in decaying vegetation, overlying a lighter chalky layer.

Cirque Found in mountain regions, an armchair-shaped basin with a steep back, or rear, wall and a raised rock lip, often containing a lake (or *tarn*). The cirque floor has been eroded by a *glacier*, while the back wall is eroded both by a *glacier* and by *weathering*.

Climate The average weather conditions in a given area over a period of years, sometimes defined as 30 years or more.

Cold War A period of hostile relations between the US and the former Soviet Union and their allies after World War II.

Composite volcano Also known as a strato-volcano, the volcanic cone is composed of alternating deposits of *lava* and *pyroclastic* material.

Compound A substance made up of *elements* chemically combined in a consistent way.

Condensation The process in which a gas changes into a liquid. For example, water vapor in the *atmosphere* condenses around tiny airborne particles to form droplets of water.

Confluence The point at which two rivers meet.

Conglomerate Rock composed of large, water worn, or rounded pebbles, held together by a natural cement.

Coniferous forest A forest type containing trees that are generally, but not necessarily, *evergreen* and have slender, needlelike leaves. Coniferous trees reproduce by means of seeds contained in a cone.

Continental drift The theory that the continents of today are fragments of one or more prehistoric *supercontinents* that have moved across the Earth's surface, creating ocean basins. The theory has been superseded by a more sophisticated theory, known as *plate tectonics*.

Continental shelf An area of the continental *crust*, below sea level, that slopes gently. It is separated from the deep ocean by a much more steeply inclined *continental slope*.

Continental slope A steep slope running from the edge of the *continental shelf* to the ocean floor.

Conurbation A vast metropolitan area created by the expansion of towns and cities into a virtually continuous urban area.

Cool continental A rainy *climate* with warm summers [warmest month below 76°F (22°C)] and often severe winters [coldest month below 32°F (0°C)].

Copra The dried white kernel of a coconut, from which coconut oil is extracted.

Coral reef An underwater barrier created by colonies of the coral polyp. Polyps secrete a protective skeleton of calcium carbonate, and reefs develop as live polyps build on the skeletons of dead generations.

Core The center of the Earth, consisting of a dense mass of iron and nickel. It is thought that the outer core is molten or liquid, and that the hot inner core is solid due to extremely high pressures.

Coriolis effect A deflecting force caused by the rotation of the Earth. In the northern hemisphere a body, such as an *air mass* or ocean current, is deflected to the right, and in the southern hemisphere to the left. This prevents winds from blowing straight from areas of high to low pressure.

Coulée A term for a ravine or gully created by river *erosion*.

Craton A large block of the Earth's *crust* that has remained stable for a long period of *geological time*. It is made up of ancient *shield* rocks.

Cretaceous A period of *geological time* beginning about 145 million years ago and lasting until about 65 million years ago.

Crevasse A deep crack in a *glacier*.

Crust The hard, thin, outer shell of the Earth. The crust floats on the *mantle*, which is softer and more dense. Under the oceans (oceanic crust) the crust is 3.7–6.8 miles (6–11 km) thick. Continental crust averages 18–24 miles (30–40 km).

Crystalline rock Rocks formed when molten *magma* crystallizes (*igneous rocks*) or when heat or pressure cause recrystallization (*metamorphic rocks*). Crystalline rocks are distinct from *sedimentary rocks*.

Cuesta A hill that rises into a steep slope on one side but has a gentler gradient on its other slope.

Cyclone An area of low *atmospheric pressure*, occurring where the air is warm and relatively low in density, causing low level winds to spiral. *Hurricanes* and *typhoons* are tropical cyclones.

D

De facto
1 Government or other activity that takes place, or exists in reality if not by right.
2 A border that exists in practice, but is not officially recognized by all of the countries it adjoins.

Deciduous forest A forest of trees that shed their leaves annually at a particular time or season. In *temperate* climates the fall of leaves occurs in the autumn. Some *coniferous* trees, such as the larch, are deciduous. Deciduous vegetation contrasts with *evergreen*, which keeps its leaves for more than a year.

Defoliant Chemical spray used to remove foliage (leaves) from trees.

Deforestation The act of cutting down and clearing large areas of forest for human activities, such as agriculture or urban development.

Delta Low-lying, fan-shaped area at the mouth of a river, formed by the *deposition* of successive layers of *sediment*. Slowing as it enters the sea, a river deposits sediment and may, as a result, split into numerous smaller channels, known as *distributaries*.

Denudation The combined effect of *weathering*, *erosion*, and *mass movement*, which, over long periods of time, exposes underlying rocks.

Deposition The laying down of material that has accumulated:
(*1*) after being *eroded* and then transported by physical forces such as wind, ice, or water;
(*2*) as organic remains, such as coal and coral;
(*3*) as the result of *evaporation* and chemical *precipitation*.

Depression
1 In climatic terms, a large low pressure system.
2 A complex *fold*, producing a large valley that incorporates both a *syncline* and an *anticline*.

Desert An *arid* region of low rainfall with little vegetation or animal life, except that which has adapted to the dry conditions. The term is now applied not only to hot tropical and subtropical regions, but to arid areas of the continental interiors and to the ice deserts of the *Arctic* and *Antarctic*.

Desertification The gradual extension of *desert* conditions in *arid* or *semiarid* regions, as a result of climatic change or human activity, such as overgrazing and *deforestation*.

Despot A ruler with absolute power. Despots are often associated with oppressive regimes.

Detritus Piles of rock deposited by an erosive agent such as a river or *glacier*.

Distributary Common at *deltas*, a minor branch of a river that does not rejoin the main stream.

Diurnal Something that occurs on a daily basis. Diurnal temperature refers to the variation in temperature over the course of a full day and night.

Divide A term describing the area of high ground separating two *drainage basins*.

Donga A steep-sided *gully*, resulting from *erosion* by a river or by floods.

Dormant A term used to describe a *volcano* that is not currently erupting. Dormant *volcanoes* are different from extinct *volcanoes* since they are still considered likely to erupt in the future.

Drainage basin The area drained by a single river system. Its boundary is marked by a *watershed* or *divide*.

Drought A long period of continuously low rainfall.

Drumlin A long, streamlined hillock composed of material deposited by a *glacier*. They often occur in groups known as swarms.

Dune A mound or ridge of sand, shaped, and often moved, by the wind. They are found in hot *deserts* and on low-lying coasts where onshore winds blow across sandy beaches.

Dyke A wall constructed in low-lying areas to contain floodwaters or protect the land from high tides.

E

Earthflow The rapid movement of soil and other loose surface material down a slope, when saturated with water. It is similar to a *mudflow* but does not flow as fast due to a lower percentage of water.

Earthquake Sudden movements of the Earth's *crust*, causing the ground to shake. Frequently occurring at *tectonic plate* margins, the shock, or series of shocks, spreads out from an *epicenter*.

EC The European Community (*see* EU).

Ecosystem A system of living organisms – plants and animals – interacting with their *environment*.

ECOWAS Economic Community of West African States. Established in 1975, it incorporates 16 West African states and aims to promote closer regional and economic cooperation.

Element
1 A constituent of the *climate* – *precipitation*, *humidity*, temperature, *atmospheric pressure*, or wind.
2 A substance that cannot be separated into simpler substances by chemical means.

El Niño A climatic phenomenon, the El Niño effect occurs about 14 times every century and leads to major shifts in global air circulation. It is associated with unusually warm currents off the coasts of Peru, Ecuador, and Chile. The anomaly can last for up to two years.

Environment The conditions created by the surroundings (both natural and artificial) within which an organism lives. In human geography the word includes the surrounding economic, cultural, and social conditions.

Eon (aeon) Traditionally a long, but not indefinite, period of *geological time*.

Ephemeral A nonpermanent feature, the term is often used in connection with seasonal rivers or lakes in dry areas.

Epicenter The point on the Earth's surface directly above the underground origin – or focus – of an *earthquake*.

Equator The line of *latitude* that lies equidistant between the North and South Poles.

Erg An extensive area of sand *dunes*, particularly in the Sahara Desert.

Erosion The processes that wear away the surface of the land. *Glaciers*, wind, rivers, waves, and currents all carry debris that causes erosion. Some definitions also include *mass movement* due to gravity as an agent of erosion.

Escarpment A steep slope at the margin of a level, upland surface. In a landscape created by *folding*, escarpments (or scarps) frequently lie behind a more gentle backward slope.

Esker A narrow, winding ridge of sand and gravel deposited by streams of water flowing beneath or at the edge of a *glacier*.

Erratic A rock transported by a *glacier* and deposited some distance from its place of origin.

Eustacy A worldwide fall or rise in ocean levels.

EU The European Union. Established in 1965, it was formerly known as the EEC (European Economic Community) and then the EC (European Community). Its members are Austria, Belgium, Denmark, Finland, France, Germany, Greece, Ireland, Italy, Luxembourg, Netherlands, Portugal, Spain, Sweden, and the UK. It seeks to establish an integrated European common market and eventual federation.

Evaporation The process in which a liquid or solid is turned into a gas or vapor. It also refers to the diffusion of water vapor into the *atmosphere* from exposed water surfaces such as lakes and seas.

Evapotranspiration The loss of moisture from the Earth's surface through a combination of *evaporation*, and *transpiration* from the leaves of plants.

Evergreen Plants with long-lasting leaves that are not shed annually or seasonally.

Exfoliation A type of *weathering* in which scalelike flakes of rock are peeled or broken off by the development of salt crystals in water within the rocks. *Groundwater*, which contains dissolved salts, seeps to the surface and evaporates, precipitating a film of salt crystals. These crystals expand and cause fine cracks. As the cracks grow, flakes of rock break off.

Extrusive rock *Igneous* rock formed when molten material, *magma*, pours forth at the Earth's surface and cools rapidly. It usually has a glassy texture.

F

Factionalism The actions of one or more minority political group acting against the interests of the majority government.

Fault A fracture or crack in rock, where strains (*tectonic* movement) have caused blocks to move, vertically or laterally, relative to each other.

Fauna Collective name for the animals of a particular period of time, or region.

Favela Brazilian term for the shantytowns of temporary huts that lie around the edge of many South and Central American cities.

Ferrel cell A component in the global pattern of air circulation, which rises in the colder *latitudes* (60° N and S) and descends in warmer *latitudes* (30° N and S). The Ferrel cell forms part of the world's three-cell air circulation pattern, with the *Hadley* and Polar cells.

Fissure A deep crack in a rock or a *glacier*.

Fjord A deep, narrow inlet, created when the sea inundates the *U-shaped valley* created by a *glacier*.

Flash flood A sudden, short-lived rise in the water level of a river or stream, or surge of water down a dry river channel, or *wadi*, caused by heavy rainfall.

Flax A plant used to make linen.

Floodplain The broad, flat part of a river valley, adjacent to the river itself, formed by *sediment* deposited during flooding.

Flora The collective name for the plants of a particular period of time or region.

Flow The movement of a river within its banks, particularly in terms of the speed and volume of water.

Fold A bend in the rock *strata* of the Earth's *crust*, resulting from compression.

Fossil The remains, or traces, of a dead organism preserved in the Earth's *crust*.

Fossil dune A *dune* formed in a once-*arid* region that is now wetter. *Dunes* normally move with the wind, but in these cases vegetation makes them stable.

Fossil fuel Fuel – coal, natural gas, or oil – composed of the fossilized remains of plants and animals.

Front The boundary between two *air masses* that contrast sharply in temperature and *humidity*.

Frontal depression An area of low pressure caused by rising warm air. They are generally 600–1,200 miles (1,000–2,000 km) in diameter. Within *depressions* there are both warm and cold fronts.

Frost shattering A form of *weathering* where water freezes in cracks, causing expansion. As temperatures fluctuate and the ice melts and refreezes, it eventually causes the rocks to shatter and fragments of rock to break off.

G

Gaucho South American term for a stock herder or cowboy who works on the grassy *plains* of Paraguay, Uruguay, and Argentina.

Geological timescale The chronology of the Earth's history as revealed in its rocks. Geological time is divided into a number of periods: eon, era, period, epoch, age, and chron (the shortest). These units are not of uniform length.

Geosyncline A concave fold (*syncline*) or large depression in the Earth's *crust*, extending hundreds of miles. This basin contains a deep layer of sediment, especially at its center, from the land masses around it.

Geothermal energy Heat derived from hot rocks within the Earth's *crust* and resulting in hot springs, steam, or hot rocks at the surface. The energy is generated by rock movements, and from the breakdown of radioactive elements occurring under intense pressure.

GDP Gross Domestic Product. The total value of goods and services produced by a country excluding income from foreign countries.

Geyser A jet of steam and hot water that intermittently erupts from vents in the ground in areas that are, or were, *volcanic*. Some geysers occasionally reach heights of 196 ft (60 m).

Ghetto An area of a city or region occupied by an overwhelming majority of people from one racial or religious group, who may be subject to persecution or containment.

Glaciation The growth of *glaciers* and *ice sheets*, and their impact on the landscape.

Glacier A body of ice moving downslope under the influence of gravity and consisting of compacted and frozen snow. A glacier is distinct from an *ice sheet*, which is wider and less confined by features of the landscape.

Glacio-eustacy A worldwide change in the level of the oceans, caused when the formation of *ice sheets* takes up water or when their melting returns water to the ocean. The formation of *ice sheets* in the *Pleistocene* epoch, for example, caused sea level to drop by about 320 ft (100 m).

Glaciofluvial To do with glacial *meltwater*, the landforms it creates, and its processes; *erosion*, transportation, and *deposition*. Glaciofluvial effects are more powerful and rapid when they occur within or beneath the *glacier*, rather than beyond its edge.

Glacis A gentle slope or *pediment*.

Global warming An increase in the average temperature of the Earth. At present the *greenhouse effect* is thought to contribute to this.

GNP Gross National Product. The total value of goods and services produced by a country.

Gondwanaland The *supercontinent* thought to have existed over 200 million years ago in the southern hemisphere. Gondwanaland is believed to have comprised today's Africa, Madagascar, Australia, parts of South America, *Antarctica*, and the Indian subcontinent.

Graben A block of rock let down between two parallel *faults*. Where the graben occurs within a valley, the structure is known as a *rift valley*.

Grease ice Slicks of ice that form in *Antarctic* seas, when ice crystals are bonded together by wind and wave action.

Greenhouse effect A change in the temperature of the *atmosphere*. Short-wave solar radiation travels through the *atmosphere* unimpeded to the Earth's surface, while outgoing, long-wave terrestrial radiation is absorbed by materials that reradiate it back to the Earth. Radiation trapped in this way, by water vapor, carbon dioxide, and other "greenhouse gases," keeps the Earth warm. As more *carbon dioxide* is released into the atmosphere by the burning of *fossil fuels*, the greenhouse effect may cause a global increase in temperature.

Groundwater Water that has seeped into the pores, cavities, and cracks of rocks or into soil and water held in an *aquifer*.

Gully A deep, narrow channel eroded in the landscape by *ephemeral* streams.

Guyot A small, flat-topped submarine mountain, formed as a result of subsidence that occurs during *sea-floor spreading*.

Gypsum A soft mineral *compound* (hydrated calcium sulfate), used as the basis of many forms of plaster, including plaster of Paris.

H

Hadley cell A large-scale component in the global pattern of air circulation. Warm air rises over the *Equator* and blows at high altitude toward the poles, sinking in subtropical regions (30° N and 30° S) and creating high pressure. The air then flows at the surface toward the *Equator* in the form of trade winds. There is one cell in each hemisphere. The Hadley cell is named after G. Hadley, who published his theory in 1735.

Hamada An Arabic word for a plateau of bare rock in a *desert*.

Hanging valley A tributary valley that ends suddenly, high above the bed of the main valley. The effect is found where the main valley has been more deeply eroded by a *glacier*, than has the tributary valley. A stream in a hanging valley will descend to the floor of the main valley as a waterfall or *cataract*.

Headward The action of a river eroding back upstream, as opposed to the normal process of downstream *erosion*. Headward *erosion* is often associated with *gullying*.

Hoodos Pinnacles of rock that have been worn away by *weathering* in *semiarid* regions.

Horst A block of the Earth's *crust* that has been left protruding from the Earth's surface by the sinking of adjoining blocks along fault lines.

Hot spot A region of the Earth's *crust* where high thermal activity occurs, often leading to volcanic eruptions. Hot spots often occur far from plate boundaries, but their movement is associated with *plate tectonics*.

Humid equatorial Rainy *climate* with no winter, where the coolest month is generally above 64°F (18°C).

Humidity The relative amount of moisture held in the Earth's *atmosphere*.

Hurricane
1 A tropical *cyclone* occurring in the Caribbean and western North Atlantic.
2 A wind of more than 65 knots (47 mph).

Hydroelectric power Energy produced by harnessing the rapid movement of water down steep mountain slopes to drive turbines that generate electricity.

Hydrolysis The chemical breakdown of rocks in reaction with water, forming new compounds.

I

Ice Age A period in the Earth's history when surface temperatures in the temperate *latitudes* were much lower and *ice sheets* expanded considerably. There have been *ice ages* from *Precambrian* times onward. The most recent began two million years ago and ended 10,000 years ago.

Ice cap A permanent dome of ice in highland areas. The term ice cap is often seen as distinct from *ice sheet*, which denotes a much wider covering of ice. The term is also used to describe the very extensive *polar* and Greenland ice caps.

Ice floe A large, flat mass of ice floating free on the ocean surface. It is usually formed after the breakup of winter ice by heavy storms.

Ice sheet A continuous, very thick layer of ice and snow. The term is usually used to denote ice masses that are continental in extent.

Ice shelf A floating mass of ice attached to the edge of a coast. The seaward edge is usually a sheer cliff up to 100 ft (30 m) high.

Ice wedge Massive blocks of ice up to 6.5 ft (2 m) wide at the top and extending 32 ft (10 m) deep. They are found in cracks in *polygonally-patterned* ground in *periglacial* regions.

Iceberg A large mass of ice in a lake or a sea that has broken off from a floating *ice sheet* (an *ice shelf*) or from a *glacier*.

Igneous rock Rock formed when molten material, *magma*, from the hot, lower layers of the Earth's *crust* cools, solidifies, and crystallizes, either within the Earth's *crust* (*intrusive*) or on the surface (*extrusive*).

IMF International Monetary Fund. Established in 1944 as a UN agency, it contains 175 members from around the world and is concerned with world monetary stability and economic development.

Incised meander A *meander* where the river, following its original course, cuts deeply into *bedrock*. This may occur when a mature, meandering river begins to erode its bed much more vigorously after the surrounding land has been uplifted.

Indigenous People, plants, or animals that are native to a particular region.

Infrastructure The communications and services – roads, railroads, and telecommunications – necessary for the functioning of a country or region.

Inselberg An isolated, steep-sided hill, rising from a low *plain* in *semiarid* and *savannah* landscapes. Inselbergs are usually composed of a rock, such as granite, which resists *erosion*.

Interglacial A period of global *climate*, between two *ice ages*, when temperatures rise and *ice sheets* and *glaciers* retreat.

Intraplate volcano A *volcano* that lies in the center of one of the Earth's *tectonic plates*, instead of, as is more common, at its edge. They are thought to have been formed by a *hot spot*.

Intrusion (intrusive igneous rock) Rock formed when molten material, *magma*, penetrates existing rocks below the Earth's surface before cooling and solidifying. These rocks cool more slowly than extrusive rock and therefore tend to have coarser grains.

Irrigation The artificial supply of agricultural water to dry areas, often involving the creation of canals and the diversion of natural watercourses.

Island arc A curved chain of islands. Typically, such an arc fringes an ocean trench, formed at the margin between two *tectonic plates*. As one plate overrides another, *earthquakes* and volcanic activity are common. The islands themselves are often volcanic cones.

Isostasy The state of equilibrium that the Earth's *crust* maintains as its lighter and heavier parts float on the denser underlying mantle.

Isthmus A narrow strip of land connecting two larger landmasses or islands.

J

Jet stream A narrow belt of westerly winds in the *troposphere*, at altitudes above 39,000 ft (12,000 m). Jet streams tend to blow more strongly in winter and include: the subtropical jet stream; the *polar* front jet stream in mid-*latitudes*; the *Arctic* jet stream; and the *polar*-night jet stream.

Joint A crack in a rock, formed where blocks of rock have not shifted relative to each other, as is the case with a *fault*. Joints are created by *folding*; by shrinkage in *igneous rock* as it cools or *sedimentary rock* as it dries out; and by the release of pressure in a rock mass when overlying materials are removed by *erosion*.

Jute A plant fiber used to make coarse ropes, sacks, and matting.

K

Kame A mound of stratified sand and gravel with steep sides, deposited in a *crevasse* by *meltwater* running over a *glacier*. When the ice retreats, this forms an undulating terrain of hummocks.

Karst A barren *limestone* landscape created by carbonic acid in streams and rainwater, in areas where *limestone* is close to the surface. Typical features include caverns, towerlike hills, *sinkholes*, and flat limestone pavements.

Kettle hole A round hollow formed in a glacial deposit by a detached block of glacial ice, which later melted. They can fill with water to form kettle-lakes.

L

Lagoon A shallow stretch of coastal saltwater behind a partial barrier such as a sandbank or *coral reef*. Lagoon is also used to describe the water encircled by an *atoll*.

LAIA Latin American Integration Association. Established in 1980, its members are Argentina, Bolivia, Brazil, Chile, Colombia, Ecuador, Mexico, Paraguay, Peru, Uruguay, and Venezuela. It aims to promote economic cooperation between member states.

Landslide The sudden downslope movement of a mass of rock or earth on a slope, caused either by heavy rain, the impact of waves, an *earthquake*, or human activity.

Laterite A hard red deposit left by *chemical weathering* in tropical conditions, and consisting mainly of oxides of iron and aluminum.

Latitude The angular distance from the *Equator* to a given point on the Earth's surface. Imaginary lines of *latitude* running parallel to the Equator encircle the Earth, and are measured in degrees north or south of the Equator. The Equator is 0°, the poles 90° South and North respectively. Also called parallels.

Laurasia In the theory of *continental drift*, the northern part of the great *supercontinent* of *Pangaea*. Laurasia is said to consist of North America, Greenland, and all of Eurasia north of the Indian subcontinent.

Lava The molten rock, *magma*, that erupts onto the Earth's surface through a *volcano*, or through a *fault* or crack in the Earth's *crust*. Lava refers to the rock both in its molten, and in its later solidified, form.

Leaching The process in which water dissolves minerals and moves them down through layers of soil or rock.

Levée A raised bank alongside the channel of a river. Levées are either manufactured or formed naturally in times of flood when the river overflows its channel, slows, and deposits much of its *sediment* load.

Lichen An organism that is the symbiotic product of an algae and a fungus. Lichens form in tight crusts on stones and trees, and are resistant to extreme cold. They are often found in tundra regions.

Lignite Low-grade coal, also known as brown coal. Found in large deposits in eastern Europe.

Limestone A porous *sedimentary* rock formed from carbonate materials.

Lingua franca The language adopted as the common language between speakers whose native languages are different. This is common in former colonial nations.

Lithosphere The rigid upper layer of the Earth, consisting of the *crust* and the upper part of the *mantle*.

Llanos Vast grassland *plains* of northern South America.

Loess Fine-grained, yellow deposits of unstratified silts and sands. Loess is believed to be wind-carried *sediment* created in the last *Ice Age*. Some deposits may have been redistributed by rivers later. Loess-derived soils are of a high quality, fertile, and easy to work.

Longitude A division of the Earth that pinpoints how far east or west a given place is from the Prime Meridian (0°) which runs through the Royal Observatory at Greenwich, England (UK). Imaginary lines of longitude are drawn around the world from pole to pole. The world is divided into 360 degrees.

Longshore drift The movement of sand and silt along the coast, carried by waves hitting the beach at an angle.

M

Magma Underground, molten rock that is very hot and highly charged with gas. It is generated at great pressure, at depths 10 miles (16 km) or more below the Earth's surface. It can issue as *lava* at the Earth's surface or, more often, solidify below the surface as *intrusive igneous rock*.

Mantle The layer of the Earth between the *crust* and the *core*. It is about 1,800 miles (2,900 km) thick. The uppermost layer of the mantle is the soft, 125-mile (200-km) thick *asthenosphere* on which the more rigid *lithosphere* floats.

Maquiladoras Factories on the Mexican side of the Mexico/US border, that are allowed to import raw materials and components duty-free and use low-cost labor to assemble the goods, finally exporting them for sale in the US.

Market gardening The intensive growing of fruits and vegetables close to large local markets.

Mass movement Downslope movement of weathered materials such as rock, often helped by rainfall or glacial *meltwater*. Mass movement may be a gradual process or rapid, as in a *landslide* or rockfall.

Massif A single very large mountain or an area of mountains with uniform characteristics and clearly defined boundaries.

Meander A looplike bend in a river. It is usually found in the lower, mature reaches of a river but can form wherever the valley is wide and the slope is gentle.

Mediterranean climate A temperate *climate* of hot, dry summers and warm, damp winters. This is typical of the western fringes of the world's continents in the warm temperate regions between *latitudes* of 30° and 40° (north and south).

Meltwater Water resulting from the melting of a *glacier* or *ice sheet*.

Mesa A broad, flat-topped hill, characteristic of *arid* regions.

Mesosphere A layer of the Earth's *atmosphere*, between the *stratosphere* and the *thermosphere*. Extending from about 25–50 miles (40–80 km) above the surface of the Earth.

Mestizo A person of mixed *Amerindian* and European origin.

Metallurgy The refining and working of metals.

Metamorphic rocks Rocks that have been altered from their original form, in terms of texture, composition, and structure by intense heat, pressure, or by the introduction of new chemical substances, or a combination of more than one of these.

Meteor A body of rock, metal, or other material that travels through space at great speeds. Meteors are visible as they enter the Earth's *atmosphere* as shooting stars and fireballs.

Meteorite The remains of a *meteor* that has fallen to Earth.

Meteoroid A *meteor* that is still traveling in space, outside the Earth's *atmosphere*.

Mezzogiorno A term applied to the southern portion of Italy.

Milankovitch hypothesis A theory suggesting that there are a series of cycles that slightly alter the Earth's position when rotating around the Sun. The cycles identified all affect the amount of *radiation* that the Earth receives at different *latitudes*. The theory is seen as a key factor in the cause of *ice ages*.

Millet A grain crop, forming part of the staple diet in much of Africa.

Mistral A strong, dry, cold, northerly or northwesterly wind that blows from the Massif Central of France to the Mediterranean Sea. It is common in winter and its cold blasts can cause crop damage in the Rhône Delta, in France.

Mohorovičić discontinuity (Moho) The structural divide at the margin between the Earth's *crust* and the *mantle*. On average it is 20 miles (35 km) below the continents and 6 miles (10 km) below the oceans. The different densities of the *crust* and the mantle cause *earthquake* waves to accelerate at this point.

Monarchy A form of government in which the head of state is a single hereditary monarch. The monarch may be a mere figurehead, or may retain significant authority.

Monsoon A wind that changes direction biannually. The change is caused by the reversal of pressure over landmasses and the adjacent oceans. Because the inflowing moist winds bring rain, the term monsoon is also used to refer to the rain itself. The term is derived from and most commonly refers to the seasonal winds of southern and eastern Asia.

Montaña Mountain areas along the west coast of South America.

Moraine Debris, transported and deposited by a *glacier* or *ice sheet* in unstratified, mixed piles of rock, boulders, pebbles, and clay.

Mountain-building The formation of *fold* mountains by tectonic activity. Also known as orogeny, mountain-building often occurs on the margin where two *tectonic plates* collide. The periods when most mountain-building occurred are known as orogenic phases and lasted many millions of years.

Mudflow An *avalanche* of mud that occurs when a mass of soil is drenched by rain or melting snow. It is a type of *mass movement* and is faster than an *earthflow* because it is lubricated by water.

N

Nappe A mass of rocks that has been overfolded by repeated thrust *faulting*.

NAFTA The North American Free Trade Association. Established in 1994 between Canada, Mexico, and the US to set up a free-trade zone.

NASA The North American Space Agency. It is a government body and was established in 1958 to develop manned and unmanned space programs.

NATO The North Atlantic Trade Organization. Established in 1949 to promote mutual defense and cooperation between its members, which are Belgium, Canada, Denmark, France, Germany, Greece, Iceland, Italy, Luxembourg, the Netherlands, Norway, Portugal, Spain, Turkey, UK, and US.

Nitrogen The odorless, colorless gas that makes up 78% of the atmosphere. Within the soil, it is a vital nutrient for plants.

Nomads (nomadic) Wandering communities that move around in search of suitable pasture for their herds of animals.

Nuclear fusion A technique used to create a new nucleus by the merging of two lighter ones, resulting in the release of large quantities of energy.

O

Oasis A fertile area in the middle of a *desert*, usually watered by an underground *aquifer*.

Oceanic ridge A mid-ocean ridge formed, according to the theory of *plate tectonics*, when plates drift apart and hot *magma* pours through to form new oceanic *crust*.

Oligarchy The government of a state by a small, exclusive group of people, such as an elite class or a family group.

Onionskin weathering The *weathering* away or *exfoliation* of a rock or outcrop by the peeling off of surface layers.

Oriente A flatter region lying to the east of the Andes in South America.

Outwash plain *Glaciofluvial* material (typically clay, sand, and gravel) carried beyond an *ice sheet* by *meltwater* streams, forming a broad, flat deposit.

Oxbow lake A crescent-shaped lake formed on a river *floodplain* when a river erodes the outside bend of a *meander*, making the neck of the *meander* narrower until the river cuts across the neck. The meander is cut off and is dammed off with sediment, creating an oxbow lake. Also known as a cut-off lake or horseshoe lake.

Oxidation A form of *chemical weathering* where *oxygen* dissolved in water reacts with minerals in rocks – particularly iron – to form oxides. Oxidation causes brown or yellow staining on rocks and eventually leads to the breakdown of the rock.

Oxygen A colorless, odorless gas that is one of the main constituents of the Earth's *atmosphere* and is essential to life on Earth.

Ozone layer A layer of enriched *oxygen* (O_3) within the stratosphere, mostly between 18–50 miles (30–80 km) above the Earth's surface. It is vital to the existence of life on Earth because it absorbs harmful shortwave ultraviolet radiation, while allowing beneficial longer wave ultraviolet radiation to penetrate to the Earth's surface.

P

Pacific Rim The name given to the economically dynamic countries bordering the Pacific Ocean.

Pack ice Ice masses more than 10 ft (3 m) thick that form on the sea surface and are not attached to a landmass.

Pancake ice Thin disks of ice, up to 8 ft (2.4 m) wide, that form when slicks of *grease ice* are tossed together by winds and stormy seas.

Pangaea In the theory of *continental drift*, Pangaea is the original great land mass that began to split about 190 million years ago. The southern portion is called *Gondwanaland* and the northern is called *Laurasia*. They were separated by the Tethys Sea.

Pastoralism Grazing of livestock–usually sheep, goats, or cattle. Pastoralists in many drier areas have traditionally been *nomadic*.

Parallel *see Latitude.*

Peat Ancient, partially decomposed vegetation found in wet, boggy conditions where there is little *oxygen*. It is the first stage in the development of coal and is often dried for use as fuel. It is also used to improve soil quality.

Pediment A gently sloping ramp of *bedrock* below a steeper slope, often found at mountain edges in *desert* areas, but also in other climatic zones. Pediments may include depositional elements such as *alluvial fans*.

Peninsula A thin strip of land surrounded on three of its sides by water. Large examples include Florida and Korea.

Per capita Latin term meaning "for each person."

Periglacial Regions on the edges of *ice sheets* or *glaciers* or, more commonly, cold regions experiencing intense frost action, *permafrost*, or both. Periglacial climates bring long, freezing winters and short, mild summers.

Permafrost Permanently frozen ground, typical of *Arctic* regions. Although a layer of soil above the permafrost melts in summer, the melted water does not drain through the permafrost.

Permeable rocks Rocks through which water can seep, because they are either porous or cracked.

Pharmaceuticals The manufacture of medicinal drugs.

Phreatic eruption A volcanic eruption that occurs when *lava* combines with *groundwater*, superheating the water and causing a sudden emission of steam at the surface.

Physical weathering (mechanical weathering) The breakdown of rocks by physical, as opposed to chemical, processes. Examples include: changes in pressure or temperature; the effect of windblown sand; the pressure of expanding salt crystals in cracks within rock; and the expansion and contraction of water within rock as it freezes and thaws.

Pingo A dome of earth with a core of ice, found in *tundra* regions. Pingos are formed either when *groundwater* freezes and expands, pushing up the land surface, or when trapped, freezing water in a lake expands and pushes up lake *sediments* to form the pingo dome.

Placer A belt of mineral-bearing rock *strata* lying at or close to the Earth's surface, from which minerals can be extracted easily.

Plain A flat, level region of land, often relatively low-lying.

Plateau A highland tract of flat land.

Plate *see Tectonic plates.*

Plate tectonics The study of *tectonic plates* that helps to explain *continental drift*, mountain formation, and volcanic activity. The movement of tectonic plates may be explained by the currents of rock rising and falling from within the Earth's *mantle* as it heats up and then cools. The boundaries of the plates are known as plate margins and most mountains, *earthquakes*, and *volcanoes* occur at these margins. Constructive margins are moving apart; destructive margins are crunching together; and conservative margins are sliding past one another.

Pleistocene A period of *geological time* spanning from about 5.2 million years ago to 1.6 million years ago.

Plutonic rock *Igneous* rocks found deep below the surface. They are coarse-grained because they cooled and solidified slowly.

Polar The zones within the *Arctic* and *Antarctic* circles.

Polje A long, broad *depression* found in *karst* (*limestone*) regions.

Polygonal patterning The ground patterning that is typically found in areas where the soil is subject to severe frost action, often in *periglacial* regions.

Porosity A measure of how much water can be held within a rock or a soil. Porosity is measured as the percentage of holes or pores in a material, compared to its total volume. For example, the porosity of slate is less than 1%, while that of gravel is 25–35%.

Prairies Originally a French word for grassy *plains* with few or no trees.

Precambrian The earliest period of *geological time* dating from over 570 million years ago.

Precipitation The fall of moisture from the *atmosphere* onto the surface of the Earth, whether as dew, hail, rain, sleet, or snow.

Pyramidal peak A steep, isolated mountain summit, formed when the back walls of three or more *cirques* are cut back and move toward each other. The cliffs around such a horned peak, or horn, are divided by sharp *arêtes*. The Matterhorn in the Swiss Alps is an example.

Pyroclasts Fragments of rock ejected during volcanic eruptions.

Q

Quaternary The current period of *geological time*, which started about 1.6 million years ago.

R

Radiation The emission of energy in the form of particles or waves. Radiation from the sun includes heat, light, ultraviolet rays, gamma rays, and X-rays. Only some of the solar energy radiated into space reaches the Earth.

Rain forest Dense forests in tropical zones with high rainfall, temperature, and *humidity*. Strictly, the term applies to the equatorial rain forest in tropical lowlands with constant rainfall and no seasonal change. The Congo and Amazon basins are examples. The term is applied more loosely to lush forest in other climates. Within rain forests organic life is dense and varied: at least 40% of all plant and animal species are found here and there may be as many as 100 tree species per 2.5 acres (1 ha).

Rainshadow An area that experiences low rainfall because of its position on the leeward side of a mountain range.

Reg A large area of stony *desert*, where tightly packed gravel lies on top of clayey sand. A reg is formed where the wind blows away the finer sand.

Remote-sensing Method of obtaining information about the *environment* using unmanned equipment, such as a satellite, that relays the information to a point where it is collected and used.

Resistance The capacity of a rock to resist *denudation*, by processes such as *weathering* and *erosion*.

Ria A flooded *V-shaped river valley* or estuary, flooded by a rise in sea level (*eustacy*) or sinking land. It is shorter than a *fjord* and gets deeper as it meets the sea.

Rift valley A long, narrow depression in the Earth's *crust*, formed by the sinking of rocks between two *faults*.

River channel The trough that contains a river and is molded by the flow of water within it.

Roche moutonée A rock found in a glaciated valley. The side facing the flow of the *glacier* has been smoothed and rounded, while the other side has been left more rugged because the *glacier*, as it flowed over the rock, has plucked out frozen fragments and carried them away.

Runoff Water draining from a land surface by flowing across it.

S

Sabkha The floor of an isolated *depression* that occurs in an *arid environment*. It is usually covered by salt deposits and devoid of vegetation.

SADC Southern African Development Community. Established in 1992 to promote economic integration between its member states, which are Angola, Botswana, Lesotho, Malawi, Mauritius, Mozambique, Namibia, South Africa, Swaziland, Tanzania, Zambia, and Zimbabwe.

Salt plug A rounded hill produced by the upward doming of rock *strata* caused by the movement of salt or other evaporite deposits under intense pressure.

Sastrugi Ice ridges formed by wind action. They lie parallel to the direction of the wind.

Savannah Open grassland found between the zone of *deserts*, and that of tropical *rain forests* in the tropics and subtropics. Scattered trees and shrubs are found in some kinds of savannah. A savannah *climate* usually has wet and dry seasons.

Scarp *see Escarpment.*

Scree Piles of rock fragments beneath a cliff or rock face, caused by mechanical *weathering*, especially *frost shattering*, where the expansion and contraction of freezing and thawing water within the rock gradually breaks it up.

Sea-floor spreading The process where *tectonic plates* move apart, allowing hot *magma* to erupt and solidify. This forms a new sea floor and, ultimately, widens the ocean.

Seamount An isolated, submarine mountain or hill, probably of volcanic origin.

Season A period of time linked to regular changes in the weather, especially the intensity of solar *radiation*.

Sediment Grains of rock transported and deposited by rivers, sea, ice, or wind.

Sedimentary rocks Rocks formed from the debris of preexisting rocks or of organic material. They are found in many *environments* – on the ocean floor, on beaches, in rivers, and in *deserts*. Organically-formed sedimentary rocks include coal and chalk. Other sedimentary rocks, such as flint, are formed by chemical processes. Most of these rocks contain *fossils*, which can be used to date them.

Seif A sand *dune* that lies parallel to the direction of the prevailing wind. Seifs form steep-sided ridges, sometimes extending for miles.

Seismic activity Movement within the Earth, such as an *earthquake* or *tremor*.

Selva A region of wet forest found in the Amazon Basin.

Semiarid, semidesert The *climate* and landscape that lies between *savannah* and *desert* or between *savannah* and a *mediterranean* climate. In semiarid conditions there is a little more moisture than in a true *desert*. More patches of drought-resistant vegetation can survive here.

Shale (marine shale) A compacted *sedimentary rock*, with fine-grained particles. Marine shale is formed on the seabed. Fuel such as oil may be extracted from it.

Sheetwash Water that runs downhill in thin sheets without forming channels. It can cause *sheet erosion*.

Sheet erosion The washing away of soil by a thin film or sheet of water, known as *sheetwash*.

Shield A vast stable block of the Earth's *crust* that has experienced little or no *mountain-building*.

Sierra The Spanish word for mountains.

Sinkhole A circular *depression* in a *limestone* region. They are formed by the collapse of an underground cave system or the *chemical weathering* of the *limestone*.

Sisal A plant fiber used to make matting.

Slash and burn A farming technique involving the cutting down and burning of scrub forest, to create agricultural land. After a number of seasons this land is abandoned and the process is repeated. This practice is common in Africa and South America.

Slip face The steep leeward side of a sand *dune* or slope. Opposite side to a *back slope*.

Soil A thin layer of rock particles mixed with the remains of dead plants and animals. This occurs naturally on the surface of the Earth and provides a medium for plants to grow in.

Soil creep The very gradual downslope movement of rock debris and soil, under the influence of gravity. This is a type of *mass movement*.

Soil erosion The wearing away of soil more quickly than it is replaced by natural processes. Soil can be carried away by wind as well as by water. Human activities, such as overgrazing and the clearing of land for farming, accelerate the process in many areas.

Solar energy Energy derived from the Sun. Solar energy is converted into other forms of energy. For example, the wind and waves, as well as the creation of plant material in photosynthesis, depend on solar energy.

Solifluction A kind of *soil creep*, where water in the surface layer has saturated the soil and rock debris, which slips slowly downhill. It often happens when frozen top-layer deposits thaw, leaving behind the frozen layers below.

Sorghum A type of grass found in South America, similar to sugar cane. When refined it is used to make molasses.

Spit A thin linear deposit of sand or shingle extending from the seashore. Spits are formed as angled waves shift sand along the beach, eventually extending a ridge of sand beyond a change in the angle of the coast. Spits are common where the coastline bends, especially at estuaries.

Squash A type of edible gourd.

Stack A tall, isolated pillar of rock near a coastline, created as wave action erodes away the adjacent rock.

Stalactite A tapering cylinder of mineral deposit, hanging from the roof of a cave in a *karst* area. It is formed by calcium carbonate dissolved in water that drips through the roof of a *limestone* cavern.

Stalagmite A cone of calcium carbonate, similar to a *stalactite*, rising from the floor of a *limestone* cavern and formed when drops of water fall from the roof of a *limestone* cave. If the water has dripped from a *stalactite* above the stalagmite, the two may join to form a continuous pillar.

Staple crop The main crop upon which a country is economically and or physically reliant. For example, the major crop grown for large-scale local consumption in southern Asia is rice.

Steppe Large areas of dry grassland in the northern hemisphere – particularly found in southeastern Europe and central Asia.

Strata The plural of stratum, a distinct, virtually horizontal layer of deposited material, lying parallel to other layers.

Stratosphere A layer of the *atmosphere*, above the *troposphere*, extending from about 7–30 miles (11–50 km) above the Earth's surface. In the lower part of the stratosphere, the temperature is relatively stable and there is little moisture.

Strike-slip fault Occurs where plates move sideways past each other and blocks of rocks move horizontally in relation to each other, not up or down as is the case with normal *faults*.

Subduction zone A region where two *tectonic plates* collide, forcing one beneath the other. Typically, a dense oceanic plate dips below a lighter continental plate, melting in the heat of the *asthenosphere*. This is why the zone is also called a destructive margin (*see Plate tectonics*). These zones are characterized by *earthquakes*, *volcanoes*, *mountain-building*, and the development of *oceanic trenches* and *island arcs*.

Submarine canyon A steep-sided valley that extends along the *continental shelf* to the ocean floor. Often formed by *turbidity currents*.

Submarine fan Deposits of silt and *alluvium*, carried by large rivers forming great fan-shaped deposits on the ocean floor.

Subsistence agriculture An agricultural practice in which enough food is produced to support the farmer and his or her dependents, but not providing any surplus to generate an income.

Subtropical A term loosely applied to *climates* that are nearly tropical or tropical for a part of the year – areas north or south of the *tropics* but outside the *temperate zone*.

Supercontinent A large continent that breaks up to form smaller continents or that forms when smaller continents merge. In the theory of *continental drift*, the supercontinents are *Pangaea*, *Gondwanaland*, and *Laurasia*.

Sustainable development An approach to development, particularly applied to economies around the world that exploit natural resources without destroying them or damaging the *environment*.

Syncline A basin-shaped downfold in rock *strata*, created when the *strata* are compressed, for example, where *tectonic plates* collide.

T

Tableland A highland area with a flat or gently undulating surface.

Taiga The belt of *coniferous* forest found in the north of Asia and North America. The conifers are adapted to survive low temperatures and long periods of snowfall.

Tarn A Scottish term for a small mountain lake, usually found at the head of a *glacier*.

Tectonic plates Plates, or tectonic plates, are the rigid slabs that form the Earth's outer shell, the *lithosphere*. Eight big plates and several smaller ones have been identified.

Temperate A moderate *climate* without extremes of temperature, typical of the mid-*latitudes* between the *tropics* and the *polar* circles.

Theocracy A state governed by religious laws. Today, the world's largest theocracy is Iran.

Thermokarst Subsidence created by the thawing of ground ice in *periglacial* areas, creating depressions.

Thermosphere A layer of the Earth's *atmosphere* that lies above the *mesosphere*, about 60–300 miles (100–500 km) above the Earth

Terraces Steps cut into steep slopes to create flat surfaces for cultivating crops. They also help to reduce soil *erosion* on unconsolidated slopes. They are most common in heavily populated parts of Southeast Asia.

Till Unstratified glacial deposits or drift left by a *glacier* or *ice sheet*. Till includes mixtures of clay, sand, gravel, and boulders.

Topography The typical shape and features of a given area such as land height and terrain.

Tombolo A large sand *spit* that attaches part of the mainland to an island.

Tornado A violent, spiraling windstorm with a center of very low pressure. Wind speeds reach 200 mph (320 km/h) and there is often thunder and heavy rain.

Transform fault In *plate tectonics*, a *fault* of continental scale, such as the San Andreas Fault, where two plates slide past each other, staying close together. The jerky, uneven movement creates *earthquakes* but does not destroy or add to the Earth's *crust*

Transpiration The loss of water vapor through the pores (or stomata) of plants. The process helps return moisture to the *atmosphere*.

Trap An area of fine-grained *igneous rock* that has been extruded and cooled on the Earth's surface in stages, forming a series of steps or terraces.

Tree line The line beyond which trees cannot grow, dependent on *latitude* and altitude, as well as local factors such as soil.

Tremor A slight *earthquake*.

Trench (oceanic trench) A long, deep trough in the ocean floor, formed, according to the theory of *plate tectonics*, when two plates collide and one dives under the other, creating a *subduction zone*.

Tropics The zone between the *Tropic of Cancer* and the *Tropic of Capricorn* where the *climate* is hot. The term can also be applied to denote areas even further north or south of the *Equator*, where the climate is similar to that of the true tropics.

Tropic of Cancer A line of *latitude* or an imaginary circle around the Earth, lying at 23° 28' N.

Tropic of Capricorn A line of *latitude* or an imaginary circle around the Earth, lying at 23° 28' S.

Troposphere The lowest layer of the Earth's *atmosphere*. From the surface, it reaches a height of between 4–10 miles (7–16 km). It is the most turbulent zone of the atmosphere and accounts for the generation of most of the world's weather. The layer above it is called the *stratosphere*.

Tsunami A huge wave created by shock waves from an *earthquake* under the sea. Reaching speeds of up to 600 mph (960 km/h), the wave may increase to heights of 50 ft (15 m) on entering coastal waters. It can cause great damage.

Tundra The treeless *plains* of the *Arctic Circle*, found south of the *polar* region of permanent ice and snow, and north of the belt of *coniferous* forests known as *taiga*. In this region of long, very cold winters, vegetation is usually limited to mosses, *lichens*, sedges, and rushes, although flowers and dwarf shrubs blossom in the brief summer.

Turbidity current An oceanic feature. A turbidity current is a mass of *sediment*-laden water that has substantial erosive power. Turbidity currents are thought to contribute to the formation of *submarine canyons*.

Typhoon A kind of *hurricane* (or tropical cyclone) bringing violent winds and heavy rain, a typhoon can do great damage. They occur in the South China Sea, especially around the Philippines.

U

U-shaped valley A river valley that has been deepened and widened by a *glacier*. They are characteristically flat-bottomed and steep-sided and generally much deeper than river valleys.

UN United Nations. Established in 1945, it contains 184 nations and aims to maintain international peace and security, and to promote cooperation over economic, social, cultural, and humanitarian problems.

UNICEF United Nations Children's Fund. A UN organization set up to promote family- and child-related programs.

Urstromtäler A German word used to describe *meltwater* channels that flowed along the front edge of the advancing *ice sheet* during the last *Ice Age*, 18,000–20,000 years ago.

V

V-shaped valley A typical valley eroded by a river in its upper course.

Virgin rain forest Tropical *rain forest* in its original state, untouched by human activity, such as logging, clearance for agriculture, settlement, or roadbuilding.

Viticulture The cultivation of grapes for wine.

Volcano An opening or vent in the Earth's *crust* where molten rock, *magma*, erupts. Volcanoes tend to be conical but may also occur as a crack in the Earth's surface or a hole blasted through a mountain. The *magma* is accompanied by other materials such as gas, steam, and fragments of rock, known as *pyroclasts*. Volcanoes tend to occur on destructive or constructive *tectonic plate* margins.

W–Z

Wadi The dry bed left by a torrent of water. Wadis are also classified as an *ephemeral* stream, found in *arid* and *semiarid* regions that are subject to sudden and often severe flash flooding.

Warm humid climate A rainy climate with warm summers and mild winters.

Water cycle The continuous circulation of water between the Earth's surface and the *atmosphere*. The processes include *evaporation* and *transpiration* of moisture into the atmosphere, and its return as *precipitation*, some of which flows into lakes and oceans.

Water table The upper level of *groundwater* saturation in permeable rock *strata*.

Watershed The dividing line between one *drainage basin* – an area where all streams flow into a single river system – and another. Watershed also means the whole drainage basin of a single river system, referred to as its catchment area.

Waterspout A rotating column of water in the form of cloud, mist, and spray that form on open water. Often has the appearance of a small *tornado*.

Weathering The decay and breakup of rocks at or near the Earth's surface, caused by water, wind, heat, ice, organic material, or the *atmosphere*. *Physical weathering* includes the effects of frost and temperature changes. Biological weathering includes the effects of plant roots, burrowing animals, and the acids produced by animals, especially as they decay after death. *Carbonation* and *hydrolysis* are among many kinds of *chemical weathering*.

Geographical Names

The following glossary lists all geographical terms occurring on the maps and in main-entry names in the Index-Gazetteer. These terms may precede, follow, or be run together with the proper element of the name; where they precede it the term is reversed for indexing purposes, for example, Poluostrov Yamal is indexed as Yamal, Puluostrov.

Key
Geographical term *Language*, Term

A

Å *Danish, Norwegian*, River
Āb *Persian*, River
Adrar *Berber*, Mountains
Agía, Ágios *Greek*, Saint
Air *Indonesian*, River
Ákra *Greek*, Cape, point
Alpen *German*, Alps
Alt- *German*, Old
Altiplanicie *Spanish*, Plateau
Älve(en) *Swedish*, River
-ån *Swedish*, River
Anse *French*, Bay
'Aqabat *Arabic*, Pass
Archipiélago *Spanish*, Archipelago
Arcipelago *Italian*, Archipelago
Arquipélago *Portuguese*, Archipelago
Arrecife(s) *Spanish*, Reef(s)
Aru *Tamil*, River
Augstiene *Latvian*, Upland
Aukštuma *Lithuanian*, Upland
Aust- *Norwegian*, Eastern
Avtonomnyy Okrug *Russian*, Autonomous district
Āw *Kurdish*, River
'Ayn *Arabic*, Spring, well
'Ayoûn *Arabic*, Wells

B

Baelt *Danish*, Strait
Bahía *Spanish*, Bay
Baḥr *Arabic*, River
Baía *Portuguese*, Bay
Baie *French*, Bay
Bañado *Spanish*, Marshland
Bandao *Chinese*, Peninsula
Banjaran *Malay*, Mountain range
Barajı *Turkish*, Dam
Barragem *Portuguese*, Reservoir
Bassin *French*, Basin
Batang *Malay*, Stream
Beinn, Ben *Gaelic*, Mountain
-berg *Afrikaans, Norwegian*, Mountain
Besar *Indonesian, Malay*, Big
Birkat, Birket *Arabic*, Lake, well, cistern
Boğazi *Turkish*, Lake
Boka *Serbo-Croatian*, Bay
Bol'sh-aya, -iye, -oy, -oye *Russian*, Big
Botigh(i) *Uzbek*, Depression basin
-bre(en) *Norwegian*, Glacier
Bredning *Danish*, Bay
Bucht *German*, Bay
Bugt(en) *Danish*, Bay
Buḥayrat *Arabic*, Lake, reservoir
Buḥeiret *Arabic*, Lake
Bukit *Malay*, Mountain
-bukta *Norwegian*, Bay
bukten *Swedish*, Bay
Bulag *Mongolian*, Spring
Bulak *Uighur*, Spring
Burnu *Turkish*, Cape, point
Buuraha *Somali*, Mountains

C

Cabo *Portuguese*, Cape
Caka *Tibetan*, Salt lake
Canal *Spanish*, Channel
Cap *French*, Cape
Capo *Italian*, Cape, headland
Cascada *Portuguese*, Waterfall
Cayo(s) *Spanish*, Islet(s), rock(s)
Cerro *Spanish*, Mountain
Chaîne *French*, Mountain range
Chapada *Portuguese*, Hills, upland
Chau *Cantonese*, Island
Chāy *Turkish*, River
Chhâk *Cambodian*, Bay
Chhu *Tibetan*, River
-chŏsuji *Korean*, Reservoir
Chott *Arabic*, Depression, salt lake
Chŭli *Uzbek*, Grassland, steppe
Ch'ün-tao *Chinese*, Island group
Chuŏr Phnum *Cambodian*, Mountains
Ciudad *Spanish*, City, town
Co *Tibetan*, Lake
Colline(s) *French*, Hill(s)
Cordillera *Spanish*, Mountain range
Costa *Spanish*, Coast
Côte *French*, Coast
Coxilha *Portuguese*, Mountains
Cuchilla *Spanish*, Mountains

D

Daban *Mongolian, Uighur*, Pass
Daği *Azerbaijani, Turkish*, Mountain
Dağlari *Azerbaijani, Turkish*, Mountains
-dake *Japanese*, Peak
-dal(en) *Norwegian*, Valley
Danau *Indonesian*, Lake
Dao *Chinese*, Island
Đao *Vietnamese*, Island
Daryā *Persian*, River
Daryācheh *Persian*, Lake
Dasht *Persian*, Desert, plain
Dawḥat *Arabic*, Bay
Denizi *Turkish*, Sea
Dere *Turkish*, Stream
Desierto *Spanish*, Desert
Dili *Azerbaijani*, Spit
-do *Korean*, Island
Dooxo *Somali*, Valley
Düzü *Azerbaijani*, Steppe
-dwīp *Bengali*, Island

E

-eilanden *Dutch*, Islands
Embalse *Spanish*, Reservoir
Ensenada *Spanish*, Bay
Erg *Arabic*, Dunes
Estany *Catalan*, Lake
Estero *Spanish*, Inlet
Estrecho *Spanish*, Strait
Étang *French*, Lagoon, lake
-ey *Icelandic*, Island
Ezero *Bulgarian, Macedonian*, Lake
Ezers *Latvian*, Lake

F

Feng *Chinese*, Peak
Fjord *Danish*, Fjord
-fjord(en) *Danish, Norwegian, Swedish*, fjord
-fjørdhur *Faeroese*, Fjord
Fleuve *French*, River
Fliegu *Maltese*, Channel
-fljór *Icelandic*, River
-flói *Icelandic*, Bay
Forêt *French*, Forest

G

-gan *Japanese*, Rock
-gang *Korean*, River
Ganga *Hindi, Nepali, Sinhala*, River
Gaoyuan *Chinese*, Plateau
Garagumy *Turkmen*, Sands
-gawa *Japanese*, River
Gebel *Arabic*, Mountain
-gebirge *German*, Mountain range
Ghadīr *Arabic*, Well
Ghubbat *Arabic*, Bay
Gjiri *Albanian*, Bay
Gol *Mongolian*, River
Golfe *French*, Gulf
Golfo *Italian, Spanish*, Gulf
Göl(ü) *Turkish*, Lake
Golyam, -a *Bulgarian*, Big
Gora *Russian, Serbo-Croatian*, Mountain
Góra *Polish*, Mountain
Gory *Russian*, Mountain
Gryada *Russian*, Ridge
Guba *Russian*, Bay
-gundo *Korean*, Island group
Gunung *Malay*, Mountain

H

Ḥadd *Arabic*, Spit
-haehyŏp *Korean*, Strait
Haff *German*, Lagoon
Hai *Chinese*, Bay, lake, sea
Haixia *Chinese*, Strait
Hamada *Arabic*, Plateau
Ḥammādat *Arabic*, Plateau
Hāmūn *Persian*, Lake
-hantō *Japanese*, Peninsula
Har, Haré *Hebrew*, Mountain
Ḥarrat *Arabic*, Lava-field
Hav(et) *Danish, Swedish*, Sea
Hawr *Arabic*, Lake
Hāyk' *Amharic*, Lake
He *Chinese*, River
-hegység *Hungarian*, Mountain range
Heide *German*, Heath, moorland
Helodrano *Malagasy*, Bay
Higashi- *Japanese*, East(ern)
Ḥiṣā' *Arabic*, Well
Hka *Burmese*, River
-ho *Korean*, Lake
Hô *Korean*, Reservoir
Ḥolot *Hebrew*, Dunes
Hora *Belarus, Czech*, Mountain
Hrada *Belarus*, Mountain, ridge
Hsi *Chinese*, River
Hu *Chinese*, Lake
Huk *Danish*, Point

I

Île(s) *French*, Island(s)
Ilha(s) *Portuguese*, Island(s)
Ilhéu(s) *Portuguese*, Islet(s)
Imeni *Russian*, In the name of
Inish- *Gaelic*, Island
Insel(n) *German*, Island(s)
Irmağı, Irmak *Turkish*, River
Isla(s) *Spanish*, Island(s)
Isola (Isole) *Italian*, Island(s)

J

Jabal *Arabic*, Mountain
Jāl *Arabic*, Ridge
-järv *Estonian*, Lake
-järvi *Finnish*, Lake
Jazā'ir *Arabic*, Islands
Jazīrat *Arabic*, Island
Jazīreh *Persian*, Island
Jebel *Arabic*, Mountain
Jezero *Serbo-Croatian*, Lake
Jezioro *Polish*, Lake
Jiang *Chinese*, River
-jima *Japanese*, Island
Jižní *Czech*, Southern
-jōgi *Estonian*, River
-joki *Finnish*, River
-jökull *Icelandic*, Glacier
Jūn *Arabic*, Bay
Juzur *Arabic*, Islands

K

Kaikyō *Japanese*, Strait
-kaise *Lappish*, Mountain
Kali *Nepali*, River
Kalnas *Lithuanian*, Mountain
Kalns *Latvian*, Mountain
Kang *Chinese*, Harbor
Kangri *Tibetan*, Mountain(s)
Kaôh *Cambodian*, Island
Kapp *Norwegian*, Cape
Káto *Greek*, Lower
Kavīr *Persian*, Desert
K'edi *Georgian*, Mountain range
Kediet *Arabic*, Mountain
Kepi *Albanian*, Cape, point
Kepulauan *Indonesian, Malay*, Island group
Khalīg, Khalīj *Arabic*, Gulf
Khawr *Arabic*, Inlet
Khola *Nepali*, River
Khrebet *Russian*, Mountain range
Ko *Thai*, Island
-ko *Japanese*, Inlet, lake
Kólpos *Greek*, Bay
-kopf *German*, Peak
Körfäzi *Azerbaijani*, Bay
Körfezi *Turkish*, Bay
Kõrgustik *Estonian*, Upland
Kosa *Russian, Ukrainian*, Spit
Koshi *Nepali*, River
Kou *Chinese*, Rivermouth
Kowtal *Persian*, Pass
Kray *Russian*, Region, territory
Kryazh *Russian*, Ridge
Kuduk *Uighur*, Well
Kūh(hā) *Persian*, Mountain(s)
-kul' *Russian*, Lake
Kŭl(i) *Tajik, Uzbek*, Lake
-kundo *Korean*, Island group
-kysten *Norwegian*, Coast
Kyun *Burmese*, Island

L

Laaq *Somali*, Watercourse
Lac *French*, Lake
Lacul *Romanian*, Lake
Lagh *Somali*, Stream
Lago *Italian, Portuguese, Spanish*, Lake
Lagoa *Portuguese*, Lagoon
Laguna *Italian, Spanish*, Lagoon, lake
Laht *Estonian*, Bay
Laut *Indonesian*, Bay
Lembalemba *Malagasy*, Plateau
Lerr *Armenian*, Mountain
Lerrnashght'a *Armenian*, Mountain range
Les *Czech*, Forest
Lich *Armenian*, Lake
Liehtao *Chinese*, Island group
Liqeni *Albanian*, Lake
Límni *Greek*, Lake
Ling *Chinese*, Mountain range
Llano *Spanish*, Plain, prairie
Lumi *Albanian*, River
Lyman *Ukrainian*, Estuary

M

Madīnat *Arabic*, City, town
Mae Nam *Thai*, River
-mägi *Estonian*, Hill
Maja *Albanian*, Mountain
Mal *Albanian*, Mountains
Mal-aya, -oye, -yy, *Russian*, Small
-man *Korean*, Bay
Mar *Spanish*, Lake
Marios *Lithuanian*, Lake
Massif *French*, Mountains
Meer *German*, Lake
-meer *Dutch*, Lake
Melkosopochnik *Russian*, Plain
-meri *Estonian*, Sea
Mifraz *Hebrew*, Bay
Minami- *Japanese*, South(ern)
-misaki *Japanese*, Cape, point
Monkhafad *Arabic*, Depression
Montagne(s) *French*, Mountain(s)
Montañas *Spanish*, Mountains
Mont(s) *French*, Mountain(s)
Monte *Italian, Portuguese*, Mountain
More *Russian*, Sea
Mörön *Mongolian*, River
Mys *Russian*, Cape, point

N

-nada *Japanese*, Open stretch of water
Nagor'ye *Russian*, Upland
Naḥal *Hebrew*, River
Nahr *Arabic*, River
Nam *Laotian*, River
Namakzār *Persian*, Salt desert
Né-a, -on, -os *Greek*, New
Nedre- *Norwegian*, Lower
-neem *Estonian*, Cape, point
Nehri *Turkish*, River
-nes *Norwegian*, Cape, point
Nevado *Spanish*, Mountain (snow-capped)
Nieder- *German*, Lower
Nishi- *Japanese*, West(ern)
-nísi *Greek*, Island
Nisoi *Greek*, Islands
Nizhn-eye, -iy, -iye, -yaya *Russian*, Lower
Nizmennost' *Russian*, Lowland, plain
Nord *Danish, French, German*, North
Norte *Portuguese, Spanish*, North
Nos *Bulgarian*, Point, spit
Nosy *Malagasy*, Island
Nov-a, -i, *Bulgarian, Serbo-Croatian*, New
Nov-aya, -o, -oye, -yy, -yye *Russian*, New
Now-a, -e, -y *Polish*, New
Nur *Mongolian*, Lake
Nuruu *Mongolian*, Mountains
Nuur *Mongolian*, Lake
Nyzovyna *Ukrainian*, Lowland, plain

O

-ø *Danish*, Island
Ober- *German*, Upper
Oblast' *Russian*, Province
Órmos *Greek*, Bay
Orol(i) *Uzbek*, Island
Øster- *Norwegian*, Eastern
Ostrov(a) *Russian*, Island(s)
Otok *Serbo-Croatian*, Island
Oued *Arabic*, Watercourse
-oy *Faeroese*, Island
-øy(a) *Norwegian*, Island
Oya *Sinhala*, River
Ozero *Russian, Ukrainian*, Lake

P

Passo *Italian*, Pass
Pegunungan *Indonesian, Malay*, Mountain range
Pélagos *Greek*, Sea
Pendi *Chinese*, Basin
Penisola *Italian*, Peninsula
Pertuis *French*, Strait
Peski *Russian*, Sands
Phanom *Thai*, Mountain
Phou *Laotian*, Mountain
Pi *Chinese*, Point
Pic *Catalan, French*, Peak
Pico *Portuguese, Spanish*, Peak
-piggen *Danish*, Peak
Pik *Russian*, Peak
Pivostriv *Ukrainian*, Peninsula
Planalto *Portuguese*, Plateau
Planina, Planini *Bulgarian, Macedonian, Serbo-Croatian*, Mountain range
Plato *Russian*, Plateau
Ploskogor'ye *Russian*, Upland
Poluostrov *Russian*, Peninsula
Ponta *Portuguese*, Point
Porthmós *Greek*, Strait
Pótamos *Greek*, River
Presa *Spanish*, Dam
Prokhod *Bulgarian*, Pass
Proliv *Russian*, Strait
Pulau *Indonesian, Malay*, Island
Pulu *Malay*, Island
Punta *Spanish*, Point
Pushcha *Belarus*, Forest
Puszcza *Polish*, Forest

Q

Qā' *Arabic*, Depression
Qalamat *Arabic*, Well
Qatorkŭh(i) *Tajik*, Mountain
Qiuling *Chinese*, Hills
Qolleh *Persian*, Mountain
Qu *Tibetan*, Stream
Quan *Chinese*, Well
Qulla(i) *Tajik*, Peak
Qundao *Chinese*, Island group

R

Raas *Somali*, Cape
-rags *Latvian*, Cape
Ramlat *Arabic*, Sands
Ra's *Arabic*, Cape, headland, point
Ravnina *Bulgarian, Russian*, Plain
Récif *French*, Reef
Recife *Portuguese*, Reef
Reka *Bulgarian*, River
Represa (Rep.) *Portuguese, Spanish*, Reservoir
Reshteh *Persian*, Mountain range
Respublika *Russian*, Republic, first-order administrative division
Respublika(si) *Uzbek*, Republic, first-order administrative division
-retsugan *Japanese*, Chain of rocks
-rettō *Japanese*, Island chain
Riacho *Spanish*, Stream
Riban' *Malagasy*, Mountains
Rio *Portuguese*, River
Río *Spanish*, River
Riu *Catalan*, River
Rivier *Dutch*, River
Rivière *French*, River
Rowd *Pashtu*, River
Rt *Serbo-Croatian*, Point
Rūd *Persian*, River
Rūdkhāneh *Persian*, River
Rudohorie *Slovak*, Mountains
Ruisseau *French*, Stream

S

-saar *Estonian*, Island
-saari *Finnish*, Island
Sabkhat *Arabic*, Salt marsh
Sāgar(a) *Hindi*, Lake, reservoir
Ṣaḥrā' *Arabic*, Desert
Saint, Sainte *French*, Saint
Salar *Spanish*, Salt pan
Salto *Portuguese, Spanish*, Waterfall
Samudra *Sinhala*, Reservoir
-san *Japanese, Korean*, Mountain
-sanchi *Japanese*, Mountains
-sandur *Icelandic*, Beach
Sankt *German, Swedish*, Saint
-sanmaek *Korean*, Mountain range
-sanmyaku *Japanese*, Mountain range
San, Santa, Santo *Italian, Portuguese, Spanish*, Saint
São *Portuguese*, Saint
Sarīr *Arabic*, Desert
Sebkha, Sebkhet *Arabic*, Depression, salt marsh
Sedlo *Czech*, Pass
See *German*, Lake
Selat *Indonesian*, Strait
Selatan *Indonesian*, Southern
-selkä *Finnish*, Lake, ridge
Selseleh *Persian*, Mountain range
Serra *Portuguese*, Mountain
Serranía *Spanish*, Mountain
-seto *Japanese*, Channel, strait
Sever-naya, -noye, -nyy, -o *Russian*, Northern
Sha'ib *Arabic*, Watercourse
Shākh *Kurdish*, Mountain
Shamo *Chinese*, Desert
Shan *Chinese*, Mountain(s)
Shankou *Chinese*, Pass
Shanmo *Chinese*, Mountain range
Shaṭṭ *Arabic*, Distributary
Shet' *Amharic*, River
Shi *Chinese*, Municipality
-shima *Japanese*, Island
Shiqqat *Arabic*, Depression
-shotō *Japanese*, Group of islands
Shuiku *Chinese*, Reservoir
Shŭrkhog(i) *Uzbek*, Salt marsh
Sierra *Spanish*, Mountains
Sint *Dutch*, Saint
-sjø(en) *Norwegian*, Lake
-sjön *Swedish*, Lake
Solonchak *Russian*, Salt lake
Solonchakovyye Vpadiny *Russian*, Salt basin, wetlands
Sơn *Vietnamese*, Mountain
Sông *Vietnamese*, River
Sør- *Norwegian*, Southern
-spitze *German*, Peak
Star-á, -é *Czech*, Old
Star-aya, -oye, -yy, -yye *Russian*, Old
Stenó *Greek*, Strait
Step' *Russian*, Steppe
Štít *Slovak*, Peak
Stœng *Cambodian*, River
Stolovaya Strana *Russian*, Plateau
Stredné *Slovak*, Middle
Střední *Czech*, Middle
Stretto *Italian*, Strait
Su Anbari *Azerbaijani*, Reservoir
-suidō *Japanese*, Channel, strait
Sund *Swedish*, Sound, strait
Sungai *Indonesian, Malay*, River
Suu *Turkish*, River

T

Tal *Mongolian*, Plain
Tandavan' *Malagasy*, Mountain range
Tangorombohitr' *Malagasy*, Mountain massif
Tanjung *Indonesian, Malay*, Cape, point
Tao *Chinese*, Island
Ṭaraq *Arabic*, Hills
Tassili *Berber*, Mountain, plateau
Tau *Russian*, Mountain(s)
Taungdan *Burmese*, Mountain range
Techníti Límni *Greek*, Reservoir
Tekojärvi *Finnish*, Reservoir
Teluk *Indonesian, Malay*, Bay
Tengah *Indonesian*, Middle
Terara *Amharic*, Mountain
Timur *Indonesian*, Eastern
-tind(an) *Norwegian*, Peak
Tizma(si) *Uzbek*, Mountain range, ridge
-tō *Japanese*, Island
Tog *Somali*, Valley
-tōge *Japanese*, Pass
Togh(i) *Uzbek*, Mountain
Tônlé *Cambodian*, Lake
Top *Dutch*, Peak
-tunturi *Finnish*, Mountain
Ṭurāq *Arabic*, Hills
Tur'at *Arabic*, Channel

U

Udde(n) *Swedish*, Cape, point
'Uqlat *Arabic*, Well
Utara *Indonesian*, Northern
Uul *Mongolian*, Mountains

V

Väin *Estonian*, Strait
Vallée *French*, Valley
-vatn *Icelandic*, Lake
-vatnet *Norwegian*, Lake
Velayat *Turkmen*, Province
-vesi *Finnish*, Lake
Vestre- *Norwegian*, Western
-vidda *Norwegian*, Plateau
-vík *Icelandic*, Bay
-viken *Swedish*, Bay, inlet
Vinh *Vietnamese*, Bay
Víztárloló *Hungarian*, Reservoir
Vodaskhovishcha *Belarus*, Reservoir
Vodokhranilishche (Vdkhr.) *Russian*, Reservoir
Vodoskhovyshche (Vdskh.) *Ukrainian*, Reservoir
Volcán *Spanish*, Volcano
Vostochn-o, yy *Russian*, Eastern
Vozvyshennost' *Russian*, Upland, plateau
Vozyera *Belarus*, Lake
Vpadina *Russian*, Depression
Vrchovina *Czech*, Mountains
Vrha *Macedonian*, Peak
Vychodné *Slovak*, Eastern
Vysochyna *Ukrainian*, Upland
Vysočina *Czech*, Upland

W

Waadi *Somali*, Watercourse
Wādī *Arabic* Watercourse
Wāḥat, Wâhat *Arabic*, Oasis
Wald *German*, Forest
Wan *Chinese*, Bay
Way *Indonesian*, River
Webi *Somali*, River
Wenz *Amharic*, River
Wiloyat(i) *Uzbek*, Province
Wyżyna *Polish*, Upland
Wzgórza *Polish*, Upland
Wzvyshsha *Belarus*, Upland

X

Xé *Laotian*, River
Xi *Chinese*, Stream

Y

-yama *Japanese*, Mountain
Yanchi *Chinese*, Salt lake
Yang *Chinese*, Bay
Yanhu *Chinese*, Salt lake
Yarımadası *Azerbaijani, Turkish*, Peninsula
Yaylası *Turkish*, Plateau
Yazovir *Bulgarian*, Reservoir
Yoma *Burmese*, Mountains
Ytre- *Norwegian*, Outer
Yü *Chinese*, Island
Yunhe *Chinese*, Canal
Yuzhn-o, -yy *Russian*, Southern

Z

-zaki *Japanese*, Cape, point
Zaliv *Bulgarian, Russian*, Bay
-zan *Japanese*, Mountain
Zangbo *Tibetan*, River
Zapadn-aya, -o, -yy *Russian*, Western
Západné *Slovak*, Western
Západní *Czech*, Western
Zatoka *Polish, Ukrainian*, Bay
-zee *Dutch*, Sea
Zemlya *Russian*, Earth, land
Zizhiqu *Chinese*, Autonomous region

Index

Glossary of Abbreviations

This glossary provides a comprehensive guide to the abbreviations used in this Atlas and in the Index-Gazetteer.

A
abbrev. abbreviated
Afr. Afrikaans
Alb. Albanian
Amh. Amharic
anc. ancient
approx. approximately
Ar. Arabic
Arm. Armenian
ASEAN Association of South East Asian Nations
ASSR Autonomous Soviet Socialist Republic
Aust. Australian
Az. Azerbaijani
Azerb. Azerbaijan

B
Basq. Basque
BCE Before the Common Era
Bel. Belarus
Ben. Bengali
Ber. Berber
B-H Bosnia-Herzegovina
bn billion (one thousand million)
BP British Petroleum
Bret. Breton
Brit. British
Bul. Bulgarian
Bur. Burmese

C
C central
C. Cape
°C degrees (Centigrade)
CACM Central America Common Market
Cam. Cambodian
Cant. Cantonese
CAR Central African Republic
Cast. Castilian
Cat. Catalan
CE Common Era
CEEAC Central America Common Market
Chin. Chinese
CIS Commonwealth of Independent States
cm centimeter(s)
Cro. Croat
Cz. Czech
Czech Rep. Czech Republic

D
Dan. Danish
Dom. Rep. Dominican Republic
Dut. Dutch

E
E east
EC see EU
EEC see EU
ECOWAS Economic Community of West African States
ECU European Currency Unit
EMS European Monetary System
Eng. English
est estimated
Est. Estonian
EU European Union (previously European Community [EC], European Economic Community [EEC])

F
°F degrees Fahrenheit
Faer. Faeroese
Fij. Fijian
Fin. Finnish
Fr. French
Fris. Frisian
ft foot/feet
FYROM Former Yugoslav Republic of Macedonia

G
g gram(s)
Gael. Gaelic
Gal. Galician
GDP Gross Domestic Product (the total value of goods and services produced by a country excluding income from foreign countries)
Geor. Georgian
Ger. German
Gk Greek
GNP Gross National Product (the total value of goods and services produced by a country)

H
Heb. Hebrew
HEP hydroelectric power
Hind. Hindi
hist. historical
Hung. Hungarian

I
I. Island
Icel. Icelandic
in inch(es)
In. Inuit (Eskimo)
Ind. Indonesian
Intl International
Ir. Irish
Is Islands
It. Italian

J
Jap. Japanese

K
Kaz. Kazakh
kg kilogram(s)
Kir. Kirghiz
km kilometer(s)
km² square kilometer (singular)
Kor. Korean
Kurd. Kurdish

L
L. Lake
LAIA Latin American Integration Association
Lao. Laotian
Lapp. Lappish
Lat. Latin
Latv. Latvian
Liech. Liechtenstein
Lith. Lithuanian
Lux. Luxembourg

M
m million/meter(s)
Mac. Macedonian
Maced. Macedonia
Mal. Malay
Malg. Malagasy
Malt. Maltese
mi. mile(s)
Mong. Mongolian
Mt. Mountain
Mts Mountains

N
N north
NAFTA North American Free Trade Agreement
Nep. Nepali
Neth. Netherlands
Nic. Nicaraguan
Nor. Norwegian
NZ New Zealand

P
Pash. Pashtu
PNG Papua New Guinea
Pol. Polish
Poly. Polynesian
Port. Portuguese
prev. previously

R
Rep. Republic
Res. Reservoir
Rmsch. Romansch
Rom. Romanian
Rus. Russian
Russ. Fed. Russian Federation

S
S south
SADC Southern Africa Development Community
SCr. Serbo-Croatian
Sinh. Sinhala
Slvk. Slovak
Slvn. Slovene
Som. Somali
Sp. Spanish
St., St Saint
Strs. Straits
Swa. Swahili
Swe. Swedish
Switz. Switzerland

T
Taj. Tajik
Th. Thai
Thai. Thailand
Tib. Tibetan
Turk. Turkish
Turkm. Turkmenistan

U
UAE United Arab Emirates
Uigh. Uighur
UK United Kingdom
Ukr. Ukrainian
UN United Nations
Urd. Urdu
US/USA United States of America
USSR Union of Soviet Socialist Republic
Uzb. Uzbek

V
var. variant
Vdkhr. Vodokhranilishche (Russian for reservoir)
Vdskh. Vodoskhovyshche (Ukrainian for reservoir)
Vtn. Vietnamese

W
W west
Wel. Welsh

Y
Yugo. Yugoslavia

This index lists all the placenames and features shown on the regional and continental maps in this Atlas. Placenames are referenced to the largest scale map on which they appear. The policy followed throughout the Atlas is to use the local spelling or local name at regional level; commonly-used English language names may occasionally be added (in parentheses) where this is an aid to identification e.g. Firenze (Florence). English names, where they exist, have been used for all international features e.g. oceans and country names; they are also used on the continental maps and in the introductory World Today section; these are then fully cross-referenced to the local names found on the regional maps. The index also contains commonly-found alternative names and variant spellings, which are also fully cross-referenced.

All main entry names are those of settlements unless otherwise indicated by the use of italicized definitions or representative symbols, which are keyed at the foot of each page.

1

25 de Mayo *see* Veinticinco de Mayo
143 *Y13* **26 Bakı Komissarı** *Rus.* Imeni 26 Bakinskikh Komissarov. SE Azerbaijan
26 Baku Komissarlary Adyndaky *see* Imeni 26 Bakinskikh Komissarov
8 *M16* **100 Mile House** *var.* Hundred Mile House. British Columbia, SW Canada

A

Aa *see* Gauja
Aabenraa *see* Åbenrå
Aabybro *see* Åbybro
103 *C16* **Aachen** *Dut.* Aken, *Fr.* Aix-la-Chapelle; *anc.* Aquae Grani, Aquisgranum. Nordrhein-Westfalen, W Germany
Aaiún *see* Laâyoune
Aakirkeby *see* Åkirkeby
Aalborg *see* Ålborg
Aalborg Bugt *see* Ålborg Bugt
103 *J21* **Aalen** Baden-Württemberg, S Germany
Aalestrup *see* Ålestrup
100 *I11* **Aalsmeer** Noord-Holland, C Netherlands
101 *F18* **Aalst** *Fr.* Alost. Oost-Vlaanderen, C Belgium
101 *K18* **Aalst** Noord-Brabant, S Netherlands
100 *O12* **Aalten** Gelderland, E Netherlands
101 *D17* **Aalter** Oost-Vlaanderen, NW Belgium
Aanaar *see* Inari
Aanaarjävri *see* Inarijärvi
95 *M17* **Äänekoski** Keski-Suomi, C Finland
144 *H7* **Aanjar** *var.* 'Anjar. C Lebanon
85 *G21* **Aansluit** Northern Cape, N South Africa
Aar *see* Aare
110 *F7* **Aarau** Aargau, N Switzerland
110 *D8* **Aarberg** Bern, W Switzerland
101 *D16* **Aardenburg** Zeeland, SW Netherlands
110 *D8* **Aare** *var.* Aar. ≈ W Switzerland
110 *F7* **Aargau** *Fr.* Argovie. ◈ *canton* N Switzerland
Aarhus *see* Århus
Aarlen *see* Arlon
Aars *see* Års
101 *I17* **Aarschot** Vlaams Brabant, C Belgium
Aassi, Nahr el *see* Orontes
Aat *see* Ath
166 *G7* **Aba** *prev.* Ngawa. Sichuan, C China
79 *V17* **Aba** Abia, S Nigeria
81 *P16* **Aba** Haut-Zaïre, NE Zaire
146 *J6* **Abā al Qazāz, Bi'r** *well* NW Saudi Arabia
Abā as Su'ūd *see* Najrān
61 *G14* **Abacaxis, Rio** ≈ NW Brazil
Abaco Island *see* Great Abaco/Little Abaco
Abaco Island *see* Great Abaco, N Bahamas
148 *K10* **Ābādān** Khūzestān, SW Iran
149 *O10* **Ābādeh** Fārs, C Iran
76 *H8* **Abadla** W Algeria
61 *M20* **Abaeté** Minas Gerais, SE Brazil
169 *Q10* **Abag Qi** *var.* Xin Hot. Nei Mongol Zizhiqu, N China
64 *P7* **Abaí** Caazapá, S Paraguay
203 *O2* **Abaiang** *var.* Apia; *prev.* Charlotte Island. *atoll* Tungaru, W Kiribati
Abaj *see* Abay
79 *U15* **Abaji** Federal Capital District, C Nigeria
39 *O7* **Abajo Peak** ▲ Utah, W USA
79 *V16* **Abakaliki** Enugu, S Nigeria
126 *Hh15* **Abakan** Respublika Khakasiya, S Russian Federation
126 *Hh15* **Abakan** ≈ S Russian Federation
79 *S11* **Abala** Tillabéri, SW Niger
79 *U11* **Abalak** Tahoua, C Niger
121 *N14* **Abalyanka** *Rus.* Obolyanka. ≈ N Belarus
126 *Ii14* **Aban** Krasnoyarskiy Kray, S Russian Federation
149 *P9* **Āb Anbār-e Kān Sorkh** Yazd, C Iran
59 *G16* **Abancay** Apurímac, SE Peru
202 *H2* **Abaokoro** *atoll* Tungaru, W Kiribati
Abariringa *see* Kanton
149 *P10* **Abarkū** Yazd, C Iran
172 *Qq5* **Abashiri** *var.* Abasiri. Hokkaidō, NE Japan
172 *Q6* **Abashiri-gawa** ≈ Hokkaidō, NE Japan
172 *Q5* **Abashiri-ko** ◎ Hokkaidō, NE Japan
Abasiri *see* Abashiri
43 *P10* **Abasolo** Tamaulipas, C Mexico
194 *L16* **Abau** Central, S PNG
151 *R10* **Abay** *var.* Abaj. Karaganda, C Kazakhstan
83 *I15* **Ābaya Hāyk'** *Eng.* Lake Margherita, *It.* Abbaia. ◎ SW Ethiopia
Ābay Wenz *see* Blue Nile
126 *Hh15* **Abaza** Respublika Khakasiya, S Russian Federation
Abbaia *see* Ābaya Hāyk'
149 *Q13* **Āb Bārīk** Fārs, S Iran
109 *C18* **Abbasanta** Sardegna, Italy, C Mediterranean Sea
Abbatis Villa *see* Abbeville
32 *M3* **Abbaye, Point** *headland* Michigan, N USA
Abbazia *see* Opatija
Abbé, Lake *see* Abhe, Lake
105 *N2* **Abbeville** *anc.* Abbatis Villa. Somme, N France
25 *R7* **Abbeville** Alabama, S USA
25 *U6* **Abbeville** Georgia, SE USA
24 *I9* **Abbeville** Louisiana, S USA
23 *P12* **Abbeville** South Carolina, SE USA
99 *B20* **Abbeyfeale** *Ir.* Mainistir na Féile. SW Ireland
108 *D8* **Abbiategrasso** Lombardia, NW Italy
95 *I14* **Abborrträsk** Norrbotten, N Sweden
204 *J9* **Abbot Ice Shelf** *ice shelf* Antarctica
8 *M17* **Abbotsford** British Columbia, SW Canada
32 *K6* **Abbotsford** Wisconsin, N USA
155 *U5* **Abbottābād** North-West Frontier Province, NW Pakistan
121 *M14* **Abchuha** *Rus.* Obchuga. Minskaya Voblasts', NW Belarus
100 *I10* **Abcoude** Utrecht, C Netherlands
145 *N2* **'Abd al 'Azīz, Jabal** ▲▲ NE Syria
147 *U17* **'Abd al Kūrī** *island* SE Yemen
145 *Z13* **'Abd Allāh, Khawr** *bay* Iraq/Kuwait
131 *U6* **Abdulino** Orenburgskaya Oblast', W Russian Federation
80 *J10* **Abéché** *var.* Abécher, Abeshr. Ouaddaï, SE Chad
Abécher *see* Abéché
149 *S8* **Āb-e Garm va Sard** Khorāsān, E Iran
79 *R8* **Abeïbara** Kidal, NE Mali
107 *P5* **Abejar** Castilla-León, N Spain
56 *E9* **Abejorral** Antioquia, W Colombia
Abela *see* Ávila
Abellinum *see* Avellino
94 *Q2* **Abeløya** *island* Kong Karls Land, E Svalbard
82 *I13* **Ābeltī** C Ethiopia
203 *O2* **Abemama** *var.* Apamama; *prev.* Roger Simpson Island. *atoll* Tungaru, W Kiribati
176 *Yy14* **Abemaree** *var.* Abemarre. Irian Jaya, E Indonesia
79 *O16* **Abengourou** E Ivory Coast
97 *G24* **Åbenrå** *var.* Aabenraa, *Ger.* Apenrade. Sønderjylland, SW Denmark
103 *L22* **Abens** ≈ SE Germany
79 *S16* **Abeokuta** Ogun, SW Nigeria
99 *I20* **Aberaeron** SW Wales, UK
Aberbrothock *see* Arbroath
Abercorn *see* Mbala
31 *R6* **Abercrombie** North Dakota, N USA
191 *T7* **Aberdeen** New South Wales, SE Australia
9 *T15* **Aberdeen** Saskatchewan, S Canada
85 *H25* **Aberdeen** Eastern Cape, S South Africa
98 *L9* **Aberdeen** *anc.* Devana. NE Scotland, UK
23 *X2* **Aberdeen** Maryland, NE USA
25 *N3* **Aberdeen** Mississippi, S USA
23 *T10* **Aberdeen** North Carolina, SE USA
31 *P8* **Aberdeen** South Dakota, N USA
34 *F8* **Aberdeen** Washington, NW USA
98 *K9* **Aberdeen** *cultural region* NE Scotland, UK
15 *K6* **Aberdeen Lake** ◎ Northwest Territories, NE Canada
98 *J10* **Aberfeldy** C Scotland, UK
99 *K21* **Abergavenny** *anc.* Gobannium. SE Wales, UK
Abergwaun *see* Fishguard
Abermarre *see* Abemaree
27 *N5* **Abernathy** Texas, SW USA
Abersee *see* Wolfgangsee
Abertawe *see* Swansea
Aberteifi *see* Cardigan
34 *I15* **Abert, Lake** ◎ Oregon, NW USA
99 *I20* **Aberystwyth** W Wales, UK
Abeshr *see* Abéché
108 *F10* **Abetone** Toscana, C Italy
129 *V5* **Abez'** Respublika Komi, NW Russian Federation
148 *M5* **Āb Garm** Zanjān, NW Iran
147 *N12* **Abhā** 'Asīr, SW Saudi Arabia
148 *M5* **Abhar** Zanjān, NW Iran
Abhé Bad/Ābhē Bid Hāyk' *see* Abhe, Lake
82 *K12* **Abhe, Lake** *var.* Lake Abbé, *Amh.* Ābhē Bid Hāyk', *Som.* Abhé Bad. ◎ Djibouti/Ethiopia
79 *V17* **Abia** ◈ *state* SE Nigeria
145 *V9* **'Abīd 'Alī** E Iraq
121 *O17* **Abidavichy** *Rus.* Obidovichi. Mahilyowskaya Voblasts', E Belarus
117 *L15* **Abide** Çanakkale, NW Turkey
79 *N17* **Abidjan** S Ivory Coast
Āb-i-Istāda *see* Īstādeh-ye Moqor, Āb-e-
29 *N4* **Abilene** Kansas, C USA
27 *Q7* **Abilene** Texas, SW USA
Abindonia *see* Abingdon
99 *M21* **Abingdon** *anc.* Abindonia. S England, UK
32 *K12* **Abingdon** Illinois, N USA
23 *P8* **Abingdon** Virginia, NE USA
Abingdon *see* Pinta, Isla
20 *J15* **Abington** Pennsylvania, NE USA
130 *K14* **Abinsk** Krasnodarskiy Kray, SW Russian Federation
39 *R9* **Abiquiu Reservoir** ⊠ New Mexico, SW USA
94 *I10* **Abisko** Norrbotten, N Sweden
10 *G12* **Abitibi** ≈ Ontario, S Canada
10 *H12* **Abitibi, Lake** ◎ Ontario, S Canada
82 *J10* **Ābīy Ādī** N Ethiopia
120 *H6* **Abja-Paluoja** Viljandimaa, S Estonia
143 *Q8* **Abkhazia** ◈ *autonomous republic* NW Georgia
190 *F1* **Abminga** South Australia
77 *W9* **Abnûb** C Egypt
Åbo *see* Turku
Åbo-Björneborg *see* Turku-Pori
158 *G9* **Abohar** Punjab, N India
79 *O17* **Aboisso** SE Ivory Coast
80 *H5* **Abo, Massif d'** ▲▲ NW Chad
79 *R16* **Abomey** S Benin
81 *F16* **Abong Mbang** Est, SE Cameroon
113 *L23* **Abony** Pest, C Hungary
80 *J11* **Abou-Déïa** Salamat, SE Chad
Aboudouhour *see* Abū aḍ Ḍuhūr
Abou Kémal *see* Abū Kamāl
Abou Simbel *see* Abu Simbel
143 *T12* **Abovyan** C Armenia
179 *P8* **Abra** ≈ Luzon, N Philippines
147 *P15* **Abrād, Wādī** *seasonal river* W Yemen
Abraham Bay *see* The Carlton
106 *G10* **Abrantes** *var.* Abrántes. Santarém, C Portugal
64 *J4* **Abra Pampa** Jujuy, N Argentina
Abrashlare *see* Brezovo
56 *G7* **Abrego** Norte de Santander, N Colombia
Abrene *see* Pytalovo
42 *C7* **Abreojos, Punta** *headland* W Mexico
67 *J16* **Abrolhos Bank** *undersea feature* W Atlantic Ocean
121 *H19* **Abrova** *Rus.* Obrovo. Brestskaya Voblasts', SW Belarus
118 *G11* **Abrud** *Ger.* Gross-Schlatten, *Hung.* Abrudbánya. Alba, SW Romania
Abrudbánya *see* Abrud
120 *E6* **Abruka** *island* SW Estonia
109 *J15* **Abruzzese, Appennino** ▲▲ C Italy
109 *J14* **Abruzzi** ◈ *region* C Italy
147 *N14* **'Abs** *var.* Sūq 'Abs. W Yemen
35 *T12* **Absaroka Range** ▲▲ Montana/Wyoming, NW USA
143 *Z11* **Abşeron Yarımadası** *Rus.* Apsheronskiy Poluostrov. *peninsula* E Azerbaijan
149 *N6* **Āb Shīrīn** Eşfahān, C Iran
145 *X10* **Abtān** SE Iraq
111 *R6* **Abtenau** Salzburg, NW Austria
170 *Dd12* **Abu** Yamaguchi, Honshū, SW Japan
158 *E14* **Ābu** Rājasthān, N India
144 *I4* **Abū aḍ Ḍuhūr** *Fr.* Aboudouhour. Idlib, NW Syria
149 *P17* **Abū al Abyaḍ** *island* C UAE
144 *K10* **Abū al Ḥuşayn, Khabrat** ◎ N Jordan
145 *R8* **Abū al Jīr** C Iraq
145 *Y12* **Abū al Khaşīb** *var.* Abul Khasib. SE Iraq
145 *U12* **Abū at Tubrah, Thaqb** *well* S Iraq
77 *V11* **Abu Balâs** ▲ SW Egypt
Abu Dhabi *see* Abū Ẓaby
145 *R8* **Abū Farūkh** C Iraq
82 *C12* **Abu Gabra** Southern Darfur, W Sudan
145 *P10* **Abū Ghār, Sha'īb** *dry watercourse* S Iraq
82 *G7* **Abu Hamed** River Nile, N Sudan
145 *O5* **Abū Ḥardān** *var.* Hajîne. Dayr az Zawr, E Syria
145 *T7* **Abū Ḥāssawīyah** E Iraq
144 *K10* **Abū Ḥifnah, Wādī** *dry watercourse* N Jordan
79 *V15* **Abuja** ● (Nigeria) Federal Capital District, C Nigeria
145 *R9* **Abū Jahaf, Wādī** *dry watercourse* C Iraq
58 *F12* **Abujao, Río** ≈ E Peru
145 *U12* **Abū Jasrah** S Iraq
145 *O6* **Abū Kamāl** *Fr.* Abou Kémal. Dayr az Zawr, E Syria
175 *Q11* **Abuki, Pegunungan** ▲▲ Sulawesi, C Indonesia
171 *Ll14* **Abukuma-gawa** ≈ Honshū, C Japan
171 *Ll15* **Abukuma-sanchi** ▲▲ Honshū, C Japan
Abula *see* Ávila
Abul Khasib *see* Abū al Khaşīb
81 *K16* **Abumombazi** *var.* Abumonbazi. Equateur, N Zaire
Abumonbazi *see* Abumombazi
61 *D15* **Abunã** Rondônia, W Brazil
58 *K13* **Abunã, Rio** *var.* Río Abuná. ≈ Bolivia/Brazil
144 *G10* **Abū Nuşayr** *var.* Abu Nuseir. 'Ammān, W Jordan
Abu Nuseir *see* Abū Nuşayr
145 *T12* **Abū Qabr** S Iraq
144 *K5* **Abū Raḩbah, Jabal** ▲▲ C Syria
145 *S5* **Abū Rajāsh** N Iraq
145 *W13* **Abū Raqrāq, Ghadīr** *well* S Iraq
158 *E14* **Ābu Road** Rājasthān, N India
82 *I6* **Abu Shagara, Ras** *headland* NE Sudan
77 *W12* **Abu Simbel** *var.* Abou Simbel, Abū Sunbul. *ancient monument* S Egypt
145 *U12* **Abū Sudayrah** S Iraq
145 *T10* **Abū Şukhayr** S Iraq
Abū Sunbul *see* Abu Simbel
172 *Nn6* **Abuta** Hokkaidō, NE Japan
193 *E18* **Abut Head** *headland* South Island, NZ
82 *E9* **Abu 'Urug** Northern Kordofan, C Sudan
82 *K12* **Ābuyē Mēda** ▲ C Ethiopia
179 *R13* **Abuyog** Leyte, C Philippines
82 *D11* **Abu Zabad** Western Kordofan, C Sudan
Abū Ẓabī *see* Abū Ẓaby
149 *P16* **Abū Ẓaby** *var.* Abū Ẓabī, *Eng.* Abu Dhabi. ● (UAE) Abū Ẓaby, C UAE
77 *X8* **Abu Zenîma** E Egypt
97 *N17* **Åby** Östergötland, S Sweden
Abyaḍ, Al Baḩr al *see* White Nile
97 *G20* **Åbybro** *var.* Aabybro. Nordjylland, N Denmark
82 *D13* **Abyei** Western Kordofan, S Sudan
Abyla *see* Ávila
Abymes *see* les Abymes
Abyssinia *see* Ethiopia
Açâba *see* Assaba
56 *F11* **Acacias** Meta, C Colombia
60 *L13* **Açailandia** Maranhão, E Brazil
Acaill *see* Achill Island
44 *E8* **Acajutla** Sonsonate, W El Salvador
81 *D17* **Acalayong** SW Equatorial Guinea

◆ Country
● Country Capital
◇ Dependent Territory
○ Dependent Territory Capital
◈ Administrative Region
✈ International Airport
▲ Mountain
▲▲ Mountain Range
Volcano
≈ River
◎ Lake
⊠ Reservoir

43 N13 **Acámbaro** Guanajuato, C Mexico
56 C6 **Acandí** Chocó, NW Colombia
106 H4 **A Cañiza** *var.* La Cañiza. Galicia, NW Spain
42 J11 **Acaponeta** Nayarit, C Mexico
42 J11 **Acaponeta, Río de** ≈ C Mexico
43 O16 **Acapulco** *var.* Acapulco de Juárez. Guerrero, S Mexico
Acapulco de Juárez *see* Acapulco
57 T13 **Acarai Mountains** *Sp.* Serra Acaraí. ⛰ Brazil/Guyana
Acaraí, Serra *see* Acarai Mountains
60 O13 **Acaraú** Ceará, NE Brazil
56 J6 **Acarigua** Portuguesa, N Venezuela
44 C6 **Acatenango, Volcán de** 🌋 S Guatemala
43 Q15 **Acatlán** *var.* Acatlán de Osorio. Puebla, S Mexico
Acatlán de Osorio *see* Acatlán
43 S15 **Acayucan** *var.* Acayucán. Veracruz-Llave, E Mexico
Accho *see* 'Akko
23 Y5 **Accomac** Virginia, NE USA
79 Q17 **Accra** ● (Ghana) SE Ghana
99 L17 **Accrington** NW England, UK
63 B19 **Acebal** Santa Fe, C Argentina
173 Ee4 **Aceh** *off.* Daerah Istimewa Aceh, *var.* Acheen, Achin, Atchin, Atjeh. ◈ *autonomous district* NW Indonesia
109 M18 **Acerenza** Basilicata, S Italy
109 K17 **Acerra** *anc.* Acerrae. Campania, S Italy
Acerrae *see* Acerra
Ach'asar Lerr *see* Achkasar
59 J17 **Achacachi** La Paz, W Bolivia
56 K7 **Achaguas** Apure, C Venezuela
160 H12 **Achalpur** *prev.* Elichpur, Ellichpur. Mahārāshtra, C India
63 F18 **Achar** Tacuarembó, C Uruguay
117 H19 **Acharnés** *var.* Aharnes; *prev.* Akharnaí. Attikí, C Greece
Acheen *see* Aceh
101 K16 **Achel** Limburg, NE Belgium
117 D16 **Achelóos** *var.* Akhelóös, Aspropótamos; *anc.* Achelous. ≈ W Greece
Achelous *see* Achelóos
169 W8 **Acheng** Heilongjiang, NE China
111 N6 **Achenkirch** Tirol, W Austria
103 L24 **Achenpass** *pass* Austria/Germany
111 N7 **Achensee** ◎ W Austria
103 F22 **Achern** Baden-Württemberg, SW Germany
117 C16 **Acherón** ≈ W Greece
79 W11 **Achétinamou** ≈ S Niger
158 J12 **Achhnera** Uttar Pradesh, N India
44 C7 **Achiguate, Río** ≈ S Guatemala
99 A16 **Achill Head** *Ir.* Ceann Acla. *headland* W Ireland
99 A16 **Achill Island** *Ir.* Acaill. *island* W Ireland
102 H11 **Achim** Niedersachsen, NW Germany
155 S5 **Achīn** Nangarhār, E Afghanistan
Achin *see* Aceh
126 Hh14 **Achinsk** Krasnoyarskiy Kray, S Russian Federation
168 E5 **Achit Nuur** ◎ NW Mongolia
143 T11 **Achkasar** *Arm.* Ach'asar Lerr. ▲ Armenia/Georgia
130 K13 **Achuyevo** Krasnodarskiy Kray, SW Russian Federation
83 F16 **Achwa** *var.* Aswa. ≈ N Uganda
142 E15 **Acıgöl** *salt lake* SW Turkey
109 L24 **Acireale** Sicilia, Italy, C Mediterranean Sea
Aciris *see* Agri
27 N7 **Ackerly** Texas, SW USA
24 M4 **Ackerman** Mississippi, S USA
31 W13 **Ackley** Iowa, C USA
46 J5 **Acklins Island** *island* SE Bahamas
Acla, Ceann *see* Achill Head
64 H11 **Aconcagua, Cerro** ▲ W Argentina
Açores/Açores, Arquipélago dos/Açores, Ilhas dos *see* Azores
106 H2 **A Coruña** *Cast.* La Coruña, *Eng.* Corunna; *anc.* Caronium. Galicia, NW Spain
44 L10 **Acoyapa** Chontales, S Nicaragua
108 H13 **Acquapendente** Lazio, C Italy
108 J13 **Acquasanta Terme** Marche, C Italy
108 I13 **Acquasparta** Lazio, C Italy
108 C9 **Acqui Terme e Bagni** Piemonte, NW Italy
Acrae *see* Palazzola Acreide
190 F7 **Acraman, Lake** *salt lake* South Australia
61 A15 **Acre** *off.* Estado do Acre. ◈ *state* W Brazil
Acre *see* 'Akko
61 C16 **Acre, Rio** ≈ W Brazil
109 N20 **Acri** Calabria, SW Italy
Acte *see* Ágion Óros
203 Y12 **Actéon, Groupe** *island group* Îles Tuamotu, SE French Polynesia
13 P12 **Acton-Vale** Québec, SE Canada
43 P13 **Actopan** *var.* Actopán. Hidalgo, C Mexico
61 P14 **Açu** *var.* Assu. Rio Grande do Norte, E Brazil
Acunum Acusio *see* Montélimar
79 Q17 **Ada** SE Ghana
31 R5 **Ada** Minnesota, N USA
33 R12 **Ada** Ohio, N USA
29 O12 **Ada** Oklahoma, C USA
114 L8 **Ada** Serbia, N Yugoslavia
Ada Bazar *see* Adapazarı
42 D3 **Adair, Bahía de** *bay* NW Mexico
106 M7 **Adaja** ≈ N Spain
40 H17 **Adak Island** *island* Aleutian Islands, Alaska, USA
Adalia *see* Antalya
Adalia, Gulf of *see* Antalya Körfezi
147 X9 **Adam** N Oman
Adama *see* Nazrēt
62 I8 **Adamantina** São Paulo, S Brazil
81 E14 **Adamaoua** *Eng.* Adamawa. ◈ *province* N Cameroon
70 F11 **Adamaoua, Massif d'** *Eng.* Adamawa Highlands. *plateau* NW Cameroon
79 Y14 **Adamawa** ◈ *state* E Nigeria
Adamawa *see* Adamaoua
Adamawa Highlands *see* Adamaoua, Massif d'
108 F6 **Adamello** ▲ N Italy
83 J14 **Ādamī Tulu** C Ethiopia
65 M23 **Adam, Mount** ▲ West Falkland, Falkland Islands
31 R16 **Adams** Nebraska, C USA
20 H8 **Adams** New York, NE USA
31 Q3 **Adams** North Dakota, N USA
161 I23 **Adam's Bridge** *chain of shoals* NW Sri Lanka
34 H10 **Adams, Mount** ▲ Washington, NW USA
Adam's Peak *see* Sri Pada
203 R16 **Adam's Rock** *island* Pitcairn Island, Pitcairn Islands
203 P16 **Adamstown** ○ (Pitcairn Islands) Pitcairn Island, Pitcairn Islands
22 G10 **Adamsville** Tennessee, S USA
27 S9 **Adamsville** Texas, SW USA
147 O17 **'Adan** *Eng.* Aden. SW Yemen
142 K16 **Adana** *var.* Seyhan. Adana, S Turkey
142 K16 **Adana** *var.* Seyhan. ◈ *province* S Turkey
Adâncata *see* Horlivka
175 Nn10 **Adang, Teluk** *bay* Borneo, C Indonesia
142 F11 **Adapazarı** *prev.* Ada Bazar. Sakarya, NW Turkey
82 H8 **Adarama** River Nile, NE Sudan
205 Q16 **Adare, Cape** *headland* Antarctica
108 E6 **Adda** *anc.* Addua. ≈ N Italy
82 A13 **Adda** ≈ W Sudan
149 Q17 **Aḍ Ḍab'īyah** Abū Ẓaby, C UAE
149 O18 **Aḍ Ḍafrah** *desert* S UAE
147 Q6 **Ad Dahnā'** *desert* E Saudi Arabia
76 A11 **Ad Dakhla** *var.* Dakhla. SW Western Sahara
Ad Dalanj *see* Dilling
Ad Damar *see* Ed Damer
Ad Damazīn *see* Ed Damazin
Ad Dāmir *see* Ed Damer
181 N2 **Ad Dammām** *desert* NE Saudi Arabia
147 R6 **Ad Dammān** *var.* Dammām. Ash Sharqīyah, NE Saudi Arabia
Ad Dāmūr *see* Damoûr
146 K5 **Ad Dār al Ḥamrā'** Tabūk, NW Saudi Arabia
146 M13 **Ad Darb** Jīzān, SW Saudi Arabia
147 O8 **Ad Dawādimī** Ar Riyāḍ, C Saudi Arabia
149 N16 **Ad Dawḥah** *Eng.* Doha. ● (Qatar) C Qatar
149 N16 **Ad Dawḥah** *Eng.* Doha. ✕ C Qatar
145 S6 **Ad Dawr** N Iraq
145 Y12 **Ad Dayr** *var.* Dayr, Shahbān. E Iraq
Addi Arkay *see* Ādī Ārk'ay
145 X15 **Ad Dibdibah** *physical region* Iraq/Kuwait
Aḍ Ḍiffah *see* Libyan Plateau
Addis Ababa *see* Ādīs Ābeba
Addison *see* Webster Springs
145 U10 **Ad Dīwānīyah** *var.* Diwaniyah. C Iraq
Addua *see* Adda
157 K22 **Addu Atoll** *atoll* S Maldives
Ad Dujail *see* Ad Dujayl
145 T7 **Ad Dujayl** *var.* Ad Dujail. N Iraq
Ad Duwaym/Ad Duwēm *see* Ed Dueim
101 D16 **Adegem** Oost-Vlaanderen, NW Belgium
25 U7 **Adel** Georgia, SE USA
31 U14 **Adel** Iowa, C USA
190 I9 **Adelaide** South Australia
46 H2 **Adelaide** New Providence, N Bahamas
190 I9 **Adelaide** ✕ South Australia
204 H6 **Adelaide Island** *island* Antarctica
15 K4 **Adelaide Peninsula** *peninsula* Northwest Territories, N Canada
189 P2 **Adelaide River** Northern Territory, N Australia
78 M10 **'Adel Bagrou** Hodh ech Chargui, SE Mauritania
194 I11 **Adelbert Range** ⛰ N PNG
188 K3 **Adele Island** *island* Western Australia
109 O17 **Adelfia** Puglia, SE Italy
205 V16 **Adélie Coast** *physical region* Antarctica
205 V14 **Adélie, Terre** *physical region* Antarctica
Adelnau *see* Odolanów
Adelsberg *see* Postojna
Aden *see* 'Adan
147 Q17 **Aden, Gulf of** *gulf* SW Arabian Sea
79 V10 **Aderbissinat** Agadez, C Niger
Adhaim *see* Al 'Uẓaym
149 R16 **Adh Dhayd** *var.* Al Dhaid. Ash Shāriqah, NE UAE
146 M4 **'Adhfā'** *spring/well* NW Saudi Arabia
144 I13 **'Ādhriyāt, Jabāl al** ⛰ S Jordan
194 L12 **Adi** ≈ New Britain, C PNG
82 I10 **Ādī Ārk'ay** *var.* Addi Arkay. N Ethiopia
190 C7 **Adieu, Cape** *headland* South Australia
108 H8 **Adige** *Ger.* Etsch. ≈ N Italy
82 J10 **Ādīgrat** N Ethiopia
160 I13 **Ādilabād** *var.* Ādilābād. Andhra Pradesh, C India
37 P2 **Adin** California, W USA
176 Vv12 **Adi, Pulau** *island* E Indonesia
20 K8 **Adirondack Mountains** ⛰ New York, NE USA
82 J13 **Ādīs Ābeba** *Eng.* Addis Ababa. ● (Ethiopia) C Ethiopia
82 J13 **Ādīs Ābeba** ✕ C Ethiopia
82 I11 **Ādīs Zemen** NW Ethiopia
Adi Ugri *see* Mendefera
143 N15 **Adıyaman** Adıyaman, SE Turkey
143 N15 **Adıyaman** ◈ *province* S Turkey
118 L11 **Adjud** Vrancea, E Romania
47 T6 **Adjuntas** C Puerto Rico
Adjuntas, Presa de las *see* Vicente Guerrero, Presa
Ādkup *see* Erikub Atoll
130 L15 **Adler** Krasnodarskiy Kray, SW Russian Federation
Adler *see* Orlice
110 G7 **Adliswil** Zürich, NW Switzerland
15 L1 **Admiralty Inlet** *fjord* Baffin Island, Northwest Territories, NE Canada
34 G7 **Admiralty Inlet** *inlet* Washington, NW USA
41 X13 **Admiralty Island** *island* Alexander Archipelago, Alaska, USA
194 K8 **Admiralty Islands** *island group* N PNG
142 B14 **Adnan Menderes** ✕ (İzmir) İzmir, W Turkey
39 V6 **Adobe Creek Reservoir** ⊡ Colorado, C USA
79 T16 **Ado-Ekiti** Ondo, SW Nigeria
Adola *see* Kibre Mengist
63 C23 **Adolfo González Chaues** Buenos Aires, E Argentina
161 H17 **Ādoni** Andhra Pradesh, C India
104 K15 **Adour** *anc.* Aturus. ≈ SW France
Adowa *see* Ādwa
107 O15 **Adra** Andalucía, S Spain
109 L24 **Adrano** Sicilia, Italy, C Mediterranean Sea
76 I9 **Adrar** C Algeria
78 K7 **Adrar** ◈ *region* C Mauritania
76 L11 **Adrar** ⛰ SE Algeria
76 A12 **Adrar Souttouf** ⛰ SW Western Sahara
Adrasman *see* Adrasmon
153 Q10 **Adrasmon** *Rus.* Adrasman. NW Tajikistan
80 K10 **Adré** Ouaddaï, E Chad
108 H9 **Adria** *anc.* Atria, Hadria, Hatria. Veneto, NE Italy
33 R10 **Adrian** Michigan, N USA
31 S11 **Adrian** Minnesota, N USA
29 R5 **Adrian** Missouri, C USA
26 M2 **Adrian** Texas, SW USA
23 S4 **Adrian** West Virginia, NE USA
Adrianople/Adrianopolis *see* Edirne
123 Mm8 **Adriatic Basin** *undersea feature* Adriatic Sea, N Mediterranean Sea
Adriatico, Mare *see* Adriatic Sea
108 L13 **Adriatic Sea** *Alb.* Deti Adriatik, *It.* Mare Adriatico, *SCr.* Jadransko More, *Slvn.* Jadransko Morje. *sea* N Mediterranean Sea
Adriatik, Deti *see* Adriatic Sea
Adua *see* Ādwa
Aduana del Sásabe *see* Sásabe
81 O17 **Adusa** Haut-Zaïre, NE Zaire
120 J13 **Adutiškis** Švenčionys, E Lithuania
29 Y7 **Advance** Missouri, C USA
67 D25 **Adventure Sound** *bay* East Falkland, Falkland Islands
82 J10 **Ādwa** *var.* Adowa, *It.* Adua. N Ethiopia
126 M8 **Adycha** ≈ NE Russian Federation
130 L14 **Adygeya, Respublika** ◈ *autonomous republic* SW Russian Federation
152 C11 **Adzhikui** *Turkm.* Ajyguyy. Balkanskiy Velayat, W Turkmenistan
79 N17 **Adzopé** SE Ivory Coast
129 U4 **Adz'va** ≈ NW Russian Federation
129 U5 **Adz'vavom** Respublika Komi, NW Russian Federation
Ædua *see* Autun
117 K19 **Aegean Islands** *island group* Greece/Turkey
Aegean North *see* Vóreion Aigaíon
117 I17 **Aegean Sea** *Gk.* Aigaíon Pélagos, Aigaío Pélagos, *Turk.* Ege Denizi. *sea* NE Mediterranean Sea
Aegean South *see* Nótion Aigaíon
120 H3 **Aegviidu** *Ger.* Charlottenhof. Harjumaa, NW Estonia
Aegyptus *see* Egypt
Aelana *see* Al 'Aqabah
Aelok *see* Ailuk Atoll
Aelōninae *see* Ailinginae Atoll
Aeļōnļapļap *see* Ailinglaplap Atoll
Æmilia *see* Emilia-Romagna
Æmilianum *see* Millau
Aemona *see* Ljubljana
Aenaria *see* Ischia
Aeolian Islands *see* Eolie, Isole
203 Z3 **Aeon Point** *headland* Kiritimati, NE Kiribati
97 G24 **Ærø** *Ger.* Arrö. *island* C Denmark
97 H24 **Ærøskøbing** Fyn, C Denmark
Æsernia *see* Isernia
106 G3 **A Estrada** Galicia, NW Spain
117 C18 **Aetós** Itháki, Iónioi Nísoi, Greece, C Mediterranean Sea
203 Q8 **Afaahiti** Tahiti, W French Polynesia
145 U10 **'Afak** C Iraq
Afanasjevo *see* Afanas'yevo
129 T14 **Afanas'yevo** *var.* Afanasjevo. Kirovskaya Oblast', NW Russian Federation
Afándou *see* Afántou
117 O23 **Afántou** *var.* Afándou. Ródos, Dodekánisos, Greece, Aegean Sea
Afar Depression *see* Danakil Desert
203 O7 **Afareaitu** Moorea, W French Polynesia
146 L7 **'Afariyah, Bi'r al** *well* NW Saudi Arabia
Afars et des Issas, Territoire Français des *see* Djibouti
85 D22 **Affenrücken** Karas, SW Namibia
Afghānestān, Dowlat-e Eslāmī-ye *see* Afghanistan
154 M6 **Afghanistan** *off.* Islamic State of Afghanistan, *Per.* Dowlat-e Eslāmī-ye Afghānestān; *prev.* Republic of Afghanistan. ◆ *islamic state* C Asia
Afgoi *see* Afgooye
83 N17 **Afgooye** *It.* Afgoi. Shabeellaha Hoose, S Somalia
147 N8 **'Afīf** Ar Riyāḍ, C Saudi Arabia
79 V17 **Afikpo** Abia, S Nigeria
Afiun Karahissar *see* Afyon
96 H7 **Åfjord** Sør-Trøndelag, C Norway
111 V6 **Aflenz Kurort** Steiermark, E Austria
76 J6 **Aflou** N Algeria
83 L18 **Afmadow** Jubbada Hoose, S Somalia
41 Q14 **Afognak Island** *island* Alaska, USA
106 J2 **A Fonsagrada** Galicia, NW Spain
194 L15 **Afore** Northern, S PNG
61 O15 **Afrânio** Pernambuco, E Brazil
68-69 **Africa** *continent*
70 L11 **Africa, Horn of** *physical region* Ethiopia/Somalia
180 K11 **Africana Seamount** *undersea feature* SW Indian Ocean
88 A14 **African Plate** *tectonic feature*
144 I2 **'Afrīn** Ḥalab, N Syria
142 M15 **Afşin** Kahramanmaraş, C Turkey
100 J7 **Afsluitdijk** *dam* N Netherlands
31 U15 **Afton** Iowa, C USA
31 W9 **Afton** Minnesota, N USA
29 R8 **Afton** Oklahoma, C USA
142 F14 **Afyon** *prev.* Afyonkarahisar. Afyon, W Turkey
142 F14 **Afyon** *var.* Afiun Karahissar, Afyonkarahisar. ◈ *province* W Turkey
Afyonkarahisar *see* Afyon
Agadès *see* Agadez
79 V10 **Agadez** *prev.* Agadès. Agadez, C Niger
79 W8 **Agadez** ◈ *department* N Niger
76 E8 **Agadir** SW Morocco
66 M9 **Agadir Canyon** *undersea feature* SE Atlantic Ocean
151 R12 **Agadyr'** Zhezkazgan, C Kazakhstan
181 O7 **Agalega Islands** *island group* N Mauritius
44 K6 **Agalta, Sierra de** ⛰ E Honduras
126 Gg10 **Agan** ≈ C Russian Federation
196 B16 **Agana** *var.* Agaña. ○ (Guam) NW Guam
196 B15 **Agana Bay** *bay* NW Guam
196 C16 **Agana Field** ✕ (Agana) C Guam
171 Kk13 **Agano-gawa** ≈ Honshū, C Japan
196 B17 **Aga Point** *headland* S Guam
160 G9 **Agar** Madhya Pradesh, C India
83 I14 **Āgaro** W Ethiopia
159 V15 **Agartala** Tripura, NE India
204 I5 **Agassiz, Cape** *headland* Antarctica
183 V13 **Agassiz Fracture Zone** *tectonic feature* S Pacific Ocean
196 B16 **Agat** W Guam
196 B16 **Agat Bay** *bay* W Guam
151 P13 **Agat, Gory** *hill* C Kazakhstan
Agatha *see* Agde
117 M20 **Agathónisi** *island* Dodekánisos, Greece, Aegean Sea
176 Y13 **Agats** Irian Jaya, E Indonesia
161 C21 **Agatti Island** *island* Lakshadweep, India, N Indian Ocean
40 D16 **Agattu Island** *island* Aleutian Islands, Alaska, USA
40 D16 **Agattu Strait** *strait* Aleutian Islands, Alaska, USA
12 B8 **Agawa** ≈ Ontario, S Canada
12 B8 **Agawa Bay** *lake bay* Ontario, S Canada
79 N17 **Agboville** SE Ivory Coast
143 V12 **Ağdam** *Rus.* Agdam. SW Azerbaijan
105 P16 **Agde** *anc.* Agatha. Hérault, S France
105 P16 **Agde, Cap d'** *headland* S France
Agedabia *see* Ajdābiyā
104 L14 **Agen** *anc.* Aginnum. Lot-et-Garonne, SW France
Agendicum *see* Sens
171 K16 **Ageo** Saitama, Honshū, S Japan
111 R5 **Ager** ≈ N Austria
Agere Hiywet *see* Hāgere Hiywet
110 G8 **Ägerisee** ◎ W Switzerland
148 M10 **Āghā Jārī** Khūzestān, SW Iran
41 P15 **Aghiyuk Island** *island* Alaska, USA
76 B12 **Aghouinit** SE Western Sahara
Aghri Dagh *see* Büyükağrı Dağı
76 B10 **Aghzoumal, Sebkhet** *var.* Sebjet Agsumal. *salt lake* E Western Sahara
117 F15 **Agiá** *var.* Ayiá. Thessalía, C Greece
42 G7 **Agiabampo, Estero de** *estuary* NW Mexico
124 Nn4 **Agía Fýlaxis** *var.* Ayia Phyla. S Cyprus
Agialoúsa *see* Yenierenköy
117 M21 **Agía Marína** Léros, Dodekánisos, Greece, Aegean Sea
124 Oo3 **Agía Nápa** *var.* Ayia Napa. E Cyprus
117 L16 **Agía Paraskeví** Lésvos, E Greece
117 J15 **Agías Eirínis, Ákra** *headland* Límnos, E Greece
117 L17 **Agiasós** *var.* Ayiásos, Ayiássos. Lésvos, E Greece
Aginnum *see* Agen
126 K16 **Aginskiy Buryatskiy Avtonomnyy Okrug** ◈ *autonomous district* S Russian Federation
126 Kk16 **Aginskoye** Aginskiy Buryatskiy Avtonomnyy Okrug, S Russian Federation
117 I14 **Ágion Óros** *Eng.* Mount Athos. ◈ *monastic republic* NE Greece
117 H14 **Ágion Óros** *var.* Akte, Aktí; *anc.* Acte. *peninsula* NE Greece
116 D13 **Ágios Achílleios** *religious building* Dytikí Makedonía, N Greece
117 J16 **Ágios Efstrátios** *var.* Áyios Evstrátios, Hagios Evstrátios. *island* E Greece
117 H20 **Ágios Geórgios** *island* Kykládes, Greece, Aegean Sea
117 Q23 **Ágios Geórgios** *island* SE Greece
117 E21 **Ágios Ilías** ▲ S Greece
117 K25 **Ágios Ioannis, Ákra** *headland* Kríti, Greece, E Mediterranean Sea
117 L20 **Ágios Kírykos** *var.* Áyios Kírikos. Ikaría, Dodekánisos, Greece, Aegean Sea
117 D16 **Ágios Nikolaos** Thessalía, C Greece
117 K25 **Ágios Nikólaos** *var.* Áyios Nikólaos. Kríti, Greece, E Mediterranean Sea
Ágios Sérgios *see* Yeniboğaziçi
117 H14 **Agíou Órous, Kólpos** *gulf* N Greece
109 K24 **Agira** *anc.* Agyrium. Sicilia, Italy, C Mediterranean Sea
117 G20 **Agkístri** *island* S Greece
116 G12 **Ágkistro** *var.* Angistro. ▲ NE Greece
105 O17 **Agly** ≈ S France
Agnetheln *see* Agnita
12 E10 **Agnew Lake** ◎ Ontario, S Canada
79 O16 **Agnibilékrou** E Ivory Coast
118 I11 **Agnita** *Ger.* Agnetheln, *Hung.* Szentágota. Sibiu, SW Romania
109 K15 **Agnone** Molise, C Italy
171 Hh17 **Ago** Mie, Honshū, SW Japan
108 C8 **Agogna** ≈ N Italy
79 P17 **Agona Swedru** *var.* Swedru. SE Ghana
Agordat *see* Akurdet
Agosta *see* Augusta
105 N15 **Agout** ≈ S France
158 J12 **Āgra** Uttar Pradesh, N India
Agra and Oudh, United Provinces of *see* Uttar Pradesh
Agram *see* Zagreb
107 U5 **Agramunt** Cataluña, NE Spain
107 Q5 **Agreda** Castilla-León, N Spain
143 S13 **Ağrı** *var.* Karaköse; *prev.* Karakılısse. Ağrı, NE Turkey
143 S13 **Ağrı** ◈ *province* NE Turkey
109 N19 **Agri** *anc.* Aciris. ≈ S Italy
Agri Dagi *see* Büyükağrı Dağı
109 J24 **Agrigento** *Gk.* Akragas; *prev.* Girgenti. Sicilia, Italy, C Mediterranean Sea
196 K4 **Agrihan** *island* N Northern Mariana Islands
117 D18 **Agrínio** *prev.* Agrinion. Dytikí Ellás, W Greece
Agrinion *see* Agrínio
117 G17 **Agriovótano** Évvoia, C Greece
109 L18 **Agropoli** Campania, S Italy
131 T3 **Agryz** Udmurtskaya Respublika, NW Russian Federation
143 U11 **Ağstafa** *Rus.* Akstafa. NW Azerbaijan
Agsumal, Sebjet *see* Aghzoumal, Sebkhet
42 J11 **Agua Brava, Laguna** *lagoon* W Mexico
56 F7 **Aguachica** Cesar, N Colombia
61 J20 **Água Clara** Mato Grosso do Sul, SW Brazil
46 D5 **Aguada de Pasajeros** Cienfuegos, C Cuba
56 J5 **Aguada Grande** Lara, N Venezuela
47 S5 **Aguadilla** W Puerto Rico
45 S16 **Aguadulce** Coclé, S Panama
106 L14 **Aguadulce** Andalucía, S Spain
43 O8 **Agualeguas** Nuevo León, NE Mexico
42 L9 **Aguanaval, Río** ≈ C Mexico
44 J5 **Aguán, Río** ≈ N Honduras
27 R16 **Agua Nueva** Texas, SW USA
62 J8 **Aguapeí, Rio** ≈ S Brazil
63 E14 **Aguapey, Río** ≈ NE Argentina
42 G3 **Agua Prieta** Sonora, NW Mexico
106 G5 **A Guardia** *var.* Laguardia, La Guardia. Galicia, NW Spain
58 E6 **Aguarico, Río** ≈ Ecuador/Peru
57 O6 **Aguasay** Monagas, NE Venezuela
42 M12 **Aguascalientes** Aguascalientes, C Mexico
42 L12 **Aguascalientes** ◈ *state* C Mexico
59 I18 **Aguas Calientes, Río** ≈ S Peru
107 R7 **Aguasvivas** ≈ NE Spain
62 J7 **Água Vermelha, Represa de** ⊡ S Brazil
58 E12 **Aguaytía** Ucayali, C Peru
106 I5 **A Gudiña** *var.* La Gudiña. Galicia, NW Spain
106 G7 **Águeda** Aveiro, N Portugal
106 J8 **Águeda** ≈ Portugal/Spain
79 Q8 **Aguelhok** Kidal, NE Mali
79 V12 **Aguié** Maradi, S Niger
196 K8 **Aguijan** *island* S Northern Mariana Islands
106 M14 **Aguilar** *var.* Aguilar de la Frontera. Andalucía, S Spain
106 M3 **Aguilar de Campóo** Castilla-León, N Spain
Aguilar de la Frontera *see* Aguilar
44 F7 **Aguilares** San Salvador, C El Salvador
107 Q14 **Aguilas** Murcia, SE Spain
42 L15 **Aguililla** Michoacán de Ocampo, SW Mexico
85 F26 **Agulhas** *var.* L'Agulhas. Western Cape, SW South Africa
180 J11 **Agulhas Bank** *undersea feature* SW Indian Ocean
180 K11 **Agulhas Basin** *undersea feature* SW Indian Ocean
85 F26 **Agulhas, Cape** *Afr.* Kaap Agulhas. *headland* SW South Africa
Agulhas, Kaap *see* Agulhas, Cape
62 O9 **Agulhas Negras, Pico das** ▲ SE Brazil
180 K11 **Agulhas Plateau** *undersea feature* SW Indian Ocean
172 Oo14 **Aguni-jima** *island* Nansei-shotō, SW Japan
Agurain *see* Salvatierra
179 Rr15 **Agusan** ≈ Mindanao, S Philippines
56 G5 **Agustín Codazzi** *var.* Codazzi. Cesar, N Colombia
Agyrium *see* Agira
76 L12 **Ahaggar** *high plateau region* SE Algeria
Ahal Welayaty *see* Akhalskiy Velayat
148 K2 **Ahar** Āżarbāyjān-e Khāvarī, NW Iran
Aharnes *see* Acharnés
144 J3 **Aḥaş, Jabal** ▲ NW Syria
144 J3 **Aḥaş, Jebal** ⛰ W Syria
193 G16 **Ahaura** ≈ South Island, NZ
102 E13 **Ahaus** Nordrhein-Westfalen, NW Germany
203 U9 **Ahe** *atoll* Îles Tuamotu, C French Polynesia
192 N10 **Ahimanawa Range** ⛰ North Island, NZ
121 I19 **Ahinski Kanal** *Rus.* Oginskiy Kanal. *canal* SW Belarus
195 N16 **Ahioma** SE PNG
192 I2 **Ahipara** Northland, North Island, NZ
192 I2 **Ahipara Bay** *bay* SE Tasman Sea
41 N13 **Ahklun Mountains** ⛰ Alaska, USA
143 R14 **Ahlat** Bitlis, E Turkey
103 F14 **Ahlen** Nordrhein-Westfalen, W Germany
160 D10 **Ahmadābād** *var.* Ahmedabad. Gujarāt, W India
149 R10 **Ahmadābād** Kermān, C Iran
Ahmadi *see* Al Aḥmadī
Ahmad Khel *see* Ḥasan Khēl
161 F14 **Ahmadnagar** *var.* Ahmednagar. Mahārāshtra, W India
155 T9 **Ahmadpur Siāl** Punjab, E Pakistan
79 N5 **Aḥmar, 'Erg el** *desert* N Mali
82 K13 **Ahmar Mountains** ⛰ C Ethiopia
Ahmedabad *see* Ahmadābād
Ahmednagar *see* Ahmadnagar
116 N12 **Ahmetbey** Kırklareli, NW Turkey
12 H12 **Ahmic Lake** ◎ Ontario, S Canada
202 G12 **Ahoa** Île Uvea, E Wallis and Futuna
42 G8 **Ahomé** Sinaloa, C Mexico
23 X8 **Ahoskie** North Carolina, SE USA
103 D17 **Ahr** ≈ W Germany
149 N12 **Ahram** *var.* Ahrom. Būshehr, S Iran
102 J9 **Ahrensburg** Schleswig-Holstein, N Germany
Ahrom *see* Ahram
95 L17 **Ähtäri** Vaasa, W Finland
42 K12 **Ahuacatlán** Nayarit, C Mexico
44 E7 **Ahuachapán** Ahuachapán, W El Salvador
44 A9 **Ahuachapán** ◈ *department* W El Salvador
203 V16 **Ahu Akivi** *var.* Siete Moai. *ancient monument* Easter Island, Chile, E Pacific Ocean
203 W11 **Ahunui** *atoll* Îles Tuamotu, C French Polynesia
193 E20 **Ahuriri** ≈ South Island, NZ
97 L22 **Åhus** Kristianstad, S Sweden
Ahu Tahira *see* Ahu Vinapu
203 V16 **Ahu Tepeu** *ancient monument* Easter Island, Chile, E Pacific Ocean
203 V17 **Ahu Vinapu** *var.* Ahu Tahira. *ancient monument* Easter Island, Chile, E Pacific Ocean
148 L9 **Ahvāz** *var.* Ahwāz; *prev.* Nāsiri. Khūzestān, SW Iran
Ahvenanmaa *see* Åland
147 Q16 **Aḥwar** SW Yemen
Ahwāz *see* Ahvāz
Aibak *see* Āybak
103 K22 **Aichach** Bayern, SE Germany
171 I16 **Aichi** *off.* Aichi-ken, *var.* Aiti. ◈ *prefecture* Honshū, SW Japan
Aïdin *see* Aydın
176 Ww12 **Aiduna** Irian Jaya, E Indonesia
Aidussina *see* Ajdovščina
194 F13 **Aiema** ≈ W PNG
Aifir, Clochán an *see* Giant's Causeway
Aigaíon Pélagos/Aigaío Pélagos *see* Aegean Sea
111 S3 **Aigen im Mülkreis** Oberösterreich, N Austria
117 G20 **Aígina** *var.* Aíyina, Egina. Aígina, C Greece
117 G20 **Aígina** *island* S Greece
117 E18 **Aígio** *var.* Egio; *prev.* Aíyion. Dytikí Ellás, S Greece
110 C10 **Aigle** Vaud, SW Switzerland
105 P14 **Aigoual, Mont** ▲ S France
181 O16 **Aigrettes, Pointe des** *headland* W Réunion
63 G19 **Aiguá** *var.* Aigua. Maldonado, S Uruguay
105 S13 **Aigues** ≈ SE France
105 N10 **Aigurande** Indre, C France
Ai-hun *see* Heihe
171 K11 **Aikawa** Niigata, Sado, C Japan
23 Q13 **Aiken** South Carolina, SE USA
27 N4 **Aiken** Texas, SW USA
166 F13 **Ailao Shan** ⛰ SW China
45 W14 **Ailigandí** San Blas, NE Panama
201 R4 **Ailinginae Atoll** *var.* Aelōninae. *atoll* Ralik Chain, SW Marshall Islands
201 T7 **Ailinglaplap Atoll** *var.* Aelōnlaplap. *atoll* Ralik Chain, S Marshall Islands
Aillionn, Loch *see* Allen, Lough
98 H13 **Ailsa Craig** *island* SW Scotland, UK
201 V5 **Ailuk Atoll** *var.* Aelok. *atoll* Ratak Chain, NE Marshall Islands
126 Mm12 **Aim** Khabarovskiy Kray, E Russian Federation
105 R11 **Ain** ◈ *department* E France
105 S10 **Ain** ≈ E France
Aïn Aïssa *see* Ayn 'Īsá
120 G7 **Ainaži** *Est.* Heinaste, *Ger.* Hainasch. Limbaži, N Latvia
76 L6 **Aïn Beida** NE Algeria
78 K4 **'Aïn Ben Tili** Tiris Zemmour, N Mauritania
76 J5 **Aïn Defla** *var.* Aïn Eddefla. N Algeria
Aïn Eddefla *see* Aïn Defla
76 L5 **Ain El Bey** ✕ (Constantine) NE Algeria
Ain Īsa *see* Ayn 'Īsá
117 C19 **Aínos** ▲ Kefallinía, Iónioi Nísoi, Greece, C Mediterranean Sea
107 T4 **Ainsa** Aragón, NE Spain
76 I7 **Aïn Sefra** NW Algeria
31 N13 **Ainsworth** Nebraska, C USA
Aintab *see* Gaziantep
76 H5 **Aïn Témouchent** N Algeria
194 H11 **Aiome** Madang, N PNG
Aïoun el Atrous/Aïoun el Atroûss *see* 'Ayoûn el 'Atroûs
56 E11 **Aipe** Huila, C Colombia
58 D9 **Aipena, Río** ≈ N Peru
59 L19 **Aiquile** Cochabamba, C Bolivia
Aïr *see* Aïr, Massif de l'
196 E10 **Airai** Babeldaob, C Palau
196 E10 **Airai** ✕ (Oreor) Babeldaob, N Palau
173 Ff8 **Airbangis** Sumatera, NW Indonesia
9 Q16 **Airdrie** Alberta, SW Canada
98 I12 **Airdrie** S Scotland, UK
Air du Azbine *see* Aïr, Massif de l'
99 M17 **Aire** ≈ N England, UK
104 K15 **Aire-sur-l'Adour** Landes, SW France
105 O1 **Aire-sur-la-Lys** Pas-de-Calais, N France
16 N2 **Air Force Island** *island* Baffin Island, Northwest Territories, NE Canada
174 L11 **Airhitam, Teluk** *bay* Borneo, C Indonesia
175 Rr7 **Airmadidi** Sulawesi, N Indonesia
79 V8 **Aïr, Massif de l'** *var.* Aïr, Air du Azbine, Asben. ⛰ NC Niger
110 G10 **Airolo** Ticino, S Switzerland
104 K9 **Airvault** Deux-Sèvres, W France
103 K19 **Aisch** ≈ S Germany
65 G20 **Aisén** *off.* Región Aisén del General Carlos Ibañez del Campo, *var.* Aysen. ◈ *region* S Chile
8 H7 **Aishihik Lake** ◎ Yukon Territory, W Canada
105 P3 **Aisne** ◈ *department* N France
105 R4 **Aisne** ≈ NE France
111 T4 **Aist** ≈ N Austria
116 K13 **Aisými** Anatolikí Makedonía kai Thráki, NE Greece
107 S11 **Aitana** ▲ E Spain
194 F9 **Aitape** *var.* Eitape. Sandaun, NW PNG
Aiti *see* Aichi
31 V6 **Aitkin** Minnesota, N USA
117 D18 **Aitolikó** *var.* Etoliko; *prev.* Aitolikón. Dytikí Ellás, C Greece
Aitolikón *see* Aitolikó
202 L15 **Aitutaki** *island* S Cook Islands
118 H11 **Aiud** *Ger.* Strassburg, *Hung.* Nagyenyed; *prev.* Engeten. Alba, SW Romania
120 I9 **Aiviekste** ≈ C Latvia
201 Q8 **Aiwo** SW Nauru
196 E8 **Aiwokako Passage** *passage* Babeldaob, N Palau
Aix *see* Aix-en-Provence
105 S15 **Aix-en-Provence** *var.* Aix; *anc.* Aquae Sextiae. Bouches-du-Rhône, SE France
Aix-la-Chapelle *see* Aachen
105 T11 **Aix-les-Bains** Savoie, E France
194 E11 **Aiyang, Mount** ▲ NW PNG
Aíyina *see* Aígina
Aíyion *see* Aígio
159 W15 **Āīzawl** Mizoram, NE India
120 H9 **Aizkraukle** Aizkraukle, S Latvia
120 C9 **Aizpute** Liepāja, W Latvia
171 L14 **Aizu-Wakamatsu** *var.* Aizuwakamatu. Fukushima, Honshū, C Japan
Aizuwakamatu *see* Aizu-Wakamatsu
104 E2 **Ajaccio** Corse, France, C Mediterranean Sea
104 E2 **Ajaccio, Golfe d'** *gulf* Corse, France, C Mediterranean Sea
43 Q15 **Ajalpán** Puebla, S Mexico
160 F13 **Ajanta Range** ⛰ C India
143 R10 **Ajaria** ◈ *autonomous republic* SW Georgia
Ajastan *see* Armenia
95 G14 **Ajaureforsen** Västerbotten, N Sweden
193 H17 **Ajax, Mount** ▲ South Island, NZ

◆ Country ● Country Capital ◇ Dependent Territory ○ Dependent Territory Capital ◈ Administrative Region ✕ International Airport ▲ Mountain ⛰ Mountain Range 🌋 Volcano ≈ River ◎ Lake ⊡ Reservoir

168 F9 **Aj Bogd Uul** ▲ SW Mongolia
77 R8 **Ajdābiyā** var. Agedabia, Ajdābiyah. NE Libya
Ajdābiyah see Ajdābiyā
111 S12 **Ajdovščina** Ger. Haidenschaft, It. Aidussina. W Slovenia
171 Mm8 **Ajigasawa** Aomori, Honshū, C Japan
Ajjinena see El Geneina
113 H23 **Ajka** Veszprém, W Hungary
144 G9 **'Ajlūn** Irbid, N Jordan
144 H9 **'Ajlūn, Jabal** ▲▲ W Jordan
149 R15 **'Ajmān** var. Ajman, 'Ujmān. 'Ajmān, NE UAE
158 G12 **Ajmer** var. Ajmere. Rājasthān, N India
38 J15 **Ajo** Arizona, SW USA
107 N2 **Ajo, Cabo de** headland N Spain
38 J16 **Ajo Range** ▲▲ Arizona, SW USA
Ajyguyy see Adzhikui
Akaba see Al 'Aqabah
172 P5 **Akabira** Hokkaidō, NE Japan
171 K12 **Akadomari** Niigata, Sado, C Japan
83 E20 **Akagera** var. Kagera. ≈ Rwanda/Tanzania see also Kagera
203 W16 **Akahanga, Punta** headland Easter Island, Chile, E Pacific Ocean
171 Ii16 **Akaishi-dake** ▲ Honshū, S Japan
171 J16 **Akaishi-sanmyaku** ▲▲ Honshū, S Japan
82 J13 **Āk'ak'i** C Ethiopia
161 G15 **Akalkot** Mahārāshtra, W India
Akamagaseki see Shimonoseki
172 Q7 **Akan** Hokkaidō, NE Japan
172 Q6 **Akan-ko** ◎ Hokkaidō, NE Japan
Akanthoú see Tatlısu
193 I19 **Akaroa** Canterbury, South Island, NZ
82 E6 **Akasha** Northern, N Sudan
170 G14 **Akashi** var. Akasi. Hyōgo, Honshū, SW Japan
145 N7 **'Akāsh, Wādī** var. Wādī 'Ukash. dry watercourse W Iraq
Akasi see Akashi
94 K11 **Äkäsjokisuu** Lappi, N Finland
143 S11 **Akbaba Dağı** ▲ Armenia/Turkey
142 B15 **Akbük Limanı** bay W Turkey
131 V8 **Akbulak** Orenburgskaya Oblast', W Russian Federation
143 O11 **Akçaabat** Trabzon, NE Turkey
143 N15 **Akçadağ** Malatya, C Turkey
142 G11 **Akçakoca** Bolu, NW Turkey
Akchakaya, Vpadina see Akdzhakaya, Vpadina
78 H7 **Akchâr** desert W Mauritania
151 S12 **Akchatau** Kaz. Aqshataū. Zhezkazgan, C Kazakhstan
142 L13 **Akdağlar** ▲▲ C Turkey
142 E17 **Ak Dağları** ▲▲ SW Turkey
142 K13 **Akdağmadeni** Yozgat, C Turkey
Akdar, Jebel see Akhḍar al Jabal
152 G8 **Akdepe** prev. Ak-Tepe, Leninsk, Turkm. Lenin. Dashkhovuzskiy Velayat, N Turkmenistan
Ak-Dere see Byala
124 O3 **Akdoğan** Gk. Lýsi. C Cyprus
126 Hh16 **Ak-Dovurak** Respublika Tyva, S Russian Federation
152 F9 **Akdzhakaya, Vpadina** var. Vpadina Akchakaya. depression N Turkmenistan
175 Tt7 **Akelamo** Pulau Halmahera, E Indonesia
Aken see Aachen
Akermanceaster see Bath
97 P15 **Åkersberga** Stockholm, C Sweden
97 H15 **Akershus** ◈ county S Norway
81 L16 **Aketi** Haut-Zaïre, N Zaire
Akgyr Erezi see Gryada Akkyr
152 E12 **Akhalskiy Velayat** Turkm. Ahal Welayaty. ◈ province C Turkmenistan
143 S10 **Akhalts'ikhe** SW Georgia
Akhangaran see Ohangaron
Akharnaí see Acharnés
77 R7 **Akhḍar, Al Jabal al** hill range NE Libya
Akhelóös see Achelóos
41 Q15 **Akhiok** Kodiak Island, Alaska, USA
142 C13 **Akhisar** Manisa, W Turkey
77 X10 **Akhmīm** anc. Panopolis. C Egypt
158 H6 **Akhnūr** Jammu and Kashmir, NW India
131 P11 **Akhtuba** ≈ SW Russian Federation
131 P11 **Akhtubinsk** Astrakhanskaya Oblast', SW Russian Federation
Akhtyrka see Okhtyrka
170 F15 **Aki** Kōchi, Shikoku, SW Japan
41 N12 **Akiachak** Alaska, USA
41 N12 **Akiak** Alaska, USA
203 X11 **Akiaki** atoll Îles Tuamotu, E French Polynesia
10 H9 **Akimiski Island** island Northwest Territories, C Canada
142 K17 **Akıncı Burnu** headland S Turkey
Akıncılar see Selçuk
119 U10 **Akinovka** Zaporiz'ka Oblast', S Ukraine
97 M24 **Åkirkeby** var. Aakirkeby. Bornholm, E Denmark
171 M10 **Akita** Akita, Honshū, C Japan
171 M10 **Akita** off. Akita-ken. ◈ prefecture Honshū, C Japan
78 H8 **Akjoujt** prev. Fort-Repoux. Inchiri, W Mauritania
94 H11 **Akkajaure** ◎ N Sweden
Akkala see Oqqal'a
161 L25 **Akkaraipattu** Eastern Province, E Sri Lanka
94 H11 **Akkavare** ▲ N Sweden
151 P13 **Akkense** Zhezkazgan, C Kazakhstan
Akkerman see Bilhorod-Dnistrovs'kyy
131 W8 **Akkermanovka** Orenburgskaya Oblast', W Russian Federation
172 Qq7 **Akkeshi** Hokkaidō, NE Japan
172 Qq7 **Akkeshi-ko** ◎ Hokkaidō, NE Japan
172 Qq8 **Akkeshi-wan** bay NW Pacific Ocean
144 F8 **'Akko** Eng. Acre, Fr. Saint-Jean-d'Acre; Bibl. Accho, Ptolemaïs. Northern, N Israel
151 T14 **Akkol'** Kaz. Aqkōl. Almaty, SE Kazakhstan
151 Q16 **Akkol'** Kaz. Aqkōl. Zhambyl, S Kazakhstan
150 M11 **Akkol', Ozero** prev. Ozero Zhaman-Akkol'. ◎ C Kazakhstan
100 L6 **Akkrum** Friesland, N Netherlands
150 F12 **Akkystau** Kaz. Aqqystaū. Atyrau, SW Kazakhstan
14 Ff3 **Aklavik** Northwest Territories, NW Canada
120 B9 **Akmenrags** headland W Latvia
164 E9 **Akmeqit** Xinjiang Uygur Zizhiqu, NW China
152 J14 **Akmeydan** Maryyskiy Velayat, C Turkmenistan
151 Q9 **Akmola** Kaz. Aqmola; prev. Akmolinsk, Tselinograd. Akmola, N Kazakhstan
151 P9 **Akmola** off. Akmolinskaya Oblast', Kaz. Aqmola Oblysy; prev. Tselinogradskaya Oblast. ◈ province C Kazakhstan
Akmolinsk/Akmolinskaya Oblast' see Akmola
Aknavásár see Târgu Ocna
120 I11 **Aknīste** Jēkabpils, S Latvia
170 G14 **Akō** Hyōgo, Honshū, SW Japan
83 G14 **Akobo** Jonglei, SE Sudan
83 G14 **Akobo** var. Ākobowenz. ≈ Ethiopia/Sudan
Ākobowenz see Akobo
160 H12 **Akola** Mahārāshtra, C India
Akordat see Akurdet
79 Q16 **Akosombo Dam** dam SE Ghana
160 H12 **Akot** Mahārāshtra, C India
79 N16 **Akoupé** SE Ivory Coast
10 M3 **Akpatok Island** island Northwest Territories, E Canada
164 G7 **Akqi** Xinjiang Uygur Zizhiqu, NW China
144 I2 **Akrād, Jabal al** ▲▲ N Syria
Akragas see Agrigento
94 H3 **Akranes** Vesturland, W Iceland
145 S2 **Ākrē** Ar. 'Aqrah. N Iraq
97 C16 **Åkrehamn** Rogaland, S Norway
79 V9 **Akréréb** Agadez, C Niger
117 D22 **Akrítas, Ákra** headland S Greece
39 V3 **Akron** Colorado, C USA
31 R12 **Akron** Iowa, C USA
33 U12 **Akron** Ohio, N USA
Akrotiri see Akrotírion
Akrotiri Bay see Akrotírion, Kólpos
124 N4 **Akrotírion** var. Akrotiri. UK air base S Cyprus
124 Nn4 **Akrotírion, Kólpos** var. Akrotiri Bay. bay S Cyprus
123 Mm4 **Akrotiri Sovereign Base Area** UK military installation S Cyprus
164 F11 **Aksai Chin** Chin. Aksayqin. disputed region China/India
Aksaj see Aksay
142 I15 **Aksaray** Aksaray, C Turkey
142 I15 **Aksaray** ◈ province C Turkey
165 P8 **Aksay** var. Aksay Kazakzu Zizhixian. Gansu, N China
150 G8 **Aksay** var. Aksaj, Kaz. Aqsay. Zapadnyy Kazakhstan, NW Kazakhstan
131 O11 **Aksay** Volgogradskaya Oblast', SW Russian Federation
153 W10 **Aksay** var. Toxkan He. ≈ China/Kyrgyzstan
Aksay Kazakzu Zizhixian see Aksay
Aksayqin see Aksai Chin
164 G11 **Aksayqin Hu** ◎ NW China
142 G14 **Akşehir** Konya, W Turkey
142 G14 **Akşehir Gölü** ◎ C Turkey
142 G16 **Akseki** Antalya, SW Turkey
126 L15 **Aksenovo-Zilovskoye** Chitinskaya Oblast', S Russian Federation
126 Kk16 **Aksha** Chitinskaya Oblast', S Russian Federation
151 V11 **Akshatau, Khrebet** ▲▲ E Kazakhstan
153 Y8 **Ak-Shyyrak** Issyk-Kul'skaya Oblast', E Kyrgyzstan
Akstafa see Ağstafa
164 H7 **Aksu** Xinjiang Uygur Zizhiqu, NW China
151 R8 **Aksu** Kaz. Aqsū. Akmola, N Kazakhstan
151 T8 **Aksu** var. Jermak, Kaz. Ermak; prev. Yermak. Pavlodar, NE Kazakhstan
151 W13 **Aksu** Kaz. Aqsū. Taldykorgan, SE Kazakhstan
151 V13 **Aksu** Kaz. Aqsū. ≈ SE Kazakhstan
151 X11 **Aksuat** Kaz. Aqsūat. Semipalatinsk, E Kazakhstan
151 Y11 **Aksuat** Kaz. Aqsūat. Vostochnyy Kazakhstan, SE Kazakhstan
131 S4 **Aksubayevo** Respublika Tatarstan, W Russian Federation
164 H7 **Aksu He** Rus. Sary-Dzhaz. ≈ China/Kyrgyzstan see also Sary-Dzhaz
82 J10 **Āksum** N Ethiopia
151 O12 **Aktas** Kaz. Aqtas. Zhezkazgan, C Kazakhstan
Aktash see Oqtosh
153 Y9 **Ak-Tash, Gora** ▲ C Kyrgyzstan
151 R10 **Aktau** Kaz. Aqtaū. Karaganda, C Kazakhstan
150 E11 **Aktau** Kaz. Aqtaū; prev. Shevchenko. Mangistau, W Kazakhstan
Aktau, Khrebet see Oqtogh, SW Tajikistan
Aktau, Khrebet see Oqtow Tizmasi, C Uzbekistan
Akte see Ágion Óros
Ak-Tepe see Akdepe
153 X7 **Ak-Terek** Issyk-Kul'skaya Oblast', E Kyrgyzstan
Aktí see Ágion Óros
164 E8 **Akto** Xinjiang Uygur Zizhiqu, W China
151 V12 **Aktogay** Kaz. Aqtoghay. Semipalatinsk, E Kazakhstan
151 T12 **Aktogay** Kaz. Aqtoghay. Zhezkazgan, C Kazakhstan
121 M18 **Aktsyabrski** Rus. Oktyabr'skiy; prev. Karpilovka. Homyel'skaya Voblasts', SE Belarus
150 I10 **Aktyubinsk** Kaz. Aqtōbe. Aktyubinsk, NW Kazakhstan
150 H11 **Aktyubinsk** off. Aktyubinskaya Oblast', Kaz. Aqtōbe Oblysy. ◈ province W Kazakhstan
153 W7 **Ak-Tyuz** var. Aktyuz. Chuyskaya Oblast', N Kyrgyzstan
81 J17 **Akula** Equateur, NW Zaire
170 Bb15 **Akune** Kagoshima, Kyūshū, SW Japan
40 L16 **Akun Island** island Aleutian Islands, Alaska, USA
82 J9 **Akurdet** var. Agordat, Akordat. C Eritrea
79 T16 **Akure** Ondo, SW Nigeria
94 J2 **Akureyri** Nordhurland Eystra, N Iceland
40 L17 **Akutan** Akutan Island, Alaska, USA
40 K17 **Akutan Island** island Aleutian Islands, Alaska, USA
79 V17 **Akwa Ibom** ◈ state SE Nigeria
Akyab see Sittwe
131 W7 **Ak"yar** Respublika Bashkortostan, W Russian Federation
151 Y11 **Akzhar** Kaz. Aqzhar. Vostochnyy Kazakhstan, E Kazakhstan
96 F13 **Ål** Buskerud, S Norway
121 N18 **Ala** Rus. Ola. ≈ SE Belarus
22 H11 **Alabama** off. State of Alabama; also known as Camellia State, Heart of Dixie, The Cotton State, Yellowhammer State. ◈ state S USA
25 P6 **Alabama River** ≈ Alabama, S USA
25 P4 **Alabaster** Alabama, S USA
145 U10 **Al 'Abd Allāh** var. Al Abdullah. S Iraq
Al Abdullah see Al 'Abd Allāh
145 W14 **Al Abṭīyah** well S Iraq
153 S9 **Ala-Buka** Dzhalal-Abadskaya Oblast', W Kyrgyzstan
194 K15 **Alabule** ≈ C PNG
142 J12 **Alaca** Çorum, N Turkey
142 K10 **Alaçam** Samsun, N Turkey
Alacant see Alicante
25 V9 **Alachua** Florida, SE USA
143 S13 **Aladağlar** ▲▲ W Turkey
142 K15 **Ala Dağları** ▲▲ C Turkey
131 O16 **Alagir** Respublika Severnaya Osetiya, SW Russian Federation
108 B6 **Alagna Valsesia** Valle d'Aosta, NW Italy
105 P12 **Alagnon** ≈ C France
61 P16 **Alagoas** off. Estado de Alagoas. ◈ state E Brazil
61 P17 **Alagoinhas** Bahia, E Brazil
107 R5 **Alagón** Aragón, NE Spain
106 J9 **Alagón** ≈ W Spain
95 K16 **Alahärmä** Vaasa, W Finland
al Ahdar see Al Akhḍar
148 K12 **Al Aḥmadī** var. Ahmadi. E Kuwait
Al Ain see Al 'Ayn
107 Z8 **Alaior** prev. Alayor. Menorca, Spain, W Mediterranean Sea
153 T11 **Alai Range** Rus. Alayskiy Khrebet. ▲▲ Kyrgyzstan/Tajikistan
Alais see Alès
147 X11 **Al 'Ajā'iz** E Oman
147 X11 **Al 'Ajā'iz** oasis SE Oman
95 L16 **Alajärvi** Vaasa, W Finland
120 K4 **Alajõe** Ida-Virumaa, NE Estonia
44 M13 **Alajuela** Alajuela, C Costa Rica
44 L12 **Alajuela** off. Provincia de Alajuela. ◈ province N Costa Rica
45 T14 **Alajuela, Lago** ◎ C Panama
40 M11 **Alakanuk** Alaska, USA
146 K5 **Al Akhḍar** var. al Ahdar. Tabūk, NW Saudi Arabia
Alakol' see Alakol', Ozero
151 X13 **Alakol', Ozero** Kaz. Alaköl. ◎ SE Kazakhstan
128 I5 **Alakurtti** Murmanskaya Oblast', NW Russian Federation
40 F10 **Alalakeiki Channel** channel Hawaii, USA, C Pacific Ocean
Al 'Alamayn see El 'Alamein
145 R1 **Al 'Amādīyah** N Iraq
196 K5 **Alamagan** island C Northern Mariana Islands
145 X10 **Al 'Amārah** var. Amara. E Iraq
82 J11 **Ālamat'ā** N Ethiopia
39 R11 **Alameda** New Mexico, SW USA
124 Pp15 **'Alam el Rûm, Râs** headland N Egypt
Alamícamba see Alamikamba
44 M8 **Alamikamba** var. Alamícamba. Región Autónoma Atlántico Norte, NE Nicaragua
26 K11 **Alamito Creek** ≈ Texas, SW USA
42 M8 **Alamitos, Sierra de los** ▲ NE Mexico
37 X9 **Alamo** Nevada, W USA
22 F9 **Alamo** Tennessee, S USA
43 Q12 **Álamo** Veracruz-Llave, C Mexico
39 S14 **Alamogordo** New Mexico, SW USA
38 J12 **Alamo Lake** ▣ Arizona, SW USA
42 H7 **Alamos** Sonora, NW Mexico
39 S7 **Alamosa** Colorado, C USA
95 J20 **Åland** var. Aland Islands, Fin. Ahvenanmaa. ◈ province SW Finland
95 J19 **Åland** Fin. Ahvenanmaa. island SW Finland
90 K9 **Åland** var. Aland Islands, Fin. Ahvenanmaa. island group SW Finland
Aland Islands see Åland
Aland Sea see Ålands Hav
97 Q14 **Ålands Hav** var. Aland Sea. strait Baltic Sea/Gulf of Bothnia
45 P16 **Alanje** Chiriquí, SW Panama
27 O2 **Alanreed** Texas, SW USA
142 G17 **Alanya** Antalya, S Turkey
25 U7 **Alapaha River** ≈ Florida/Georgia, SE USA
125 Ee11 **Alapayevsk** Sverdlovskaya Oblast', C Russian Federation
Alappuzha see Alleppey
144 F14 **Al 'Aqabah** var. Akaba, Aqaba, 'Aqaba; anc. Aelana, Elath. Ma'ān, SW Jordan
Al 'Arabīyah as Su'ūdīyah see Saudi Arabia
al Araïch see Larache
107 O10 **Alarcón** Castilla-La Mancha, C Spain
107 Q9 **Alarcón, Embalse de** ▣ C Spain
144 J2 **Al 'Arīmah** Fr. Arime. Ḥalab, N Syria
Al 'Arīsh see El 'Arîsh
147 R5 **Al Arṭāwīyah** SE Kuwait
147 P6 **Al Arṭāwīyah** Ar Riyāḍ, N Saudi Arabia
175 O16 **Alas** Sumbawa, S Indonesia
Alasca, Golfo de see Alaska, Gulf of
142 D14 **Alaşehir** Manisa, W Turkey
145 N5 **Al 'Ashārah** var. Ashara. Dayr az Zawr, E Syria
Al Ashkhara see Al Ashkharah
147 Z9 **Al Ashkharah** var. Al Ashkhara. NE Oman
41 P8 **Alaska** off. State of Alaska; also known as Land of the Midnight Sun, The Last Frontier, Seward's Folly; prev. Russian America. ◈ state NW USA
41 T13 **Alaska, Gulf of** var. Golfo de Alasca. gulf Canada/USA
41 O15 **Alaska Peninsula** peninsula Alaska, USA
41 Q11 **Alaska Range** ▲▲ Alaska, USA
173 Ee4 **Alas, Lae** ≈ Sumatera, NW Indonesia
Al-Asnam see Chlef
175 O16 **Alas, Selat** strait Nusa Tenggara, C Indonesia
108 B10 **Alassio** Liguria, NW Italy
Alat see Olot
143 Y12 **Älät** Rus. Alyat; prev. Alyaty-Pristan'. SE Azerbaijan
145 S13 **Al 'Athāmīn** S Iraq
41 P7 **Alatna River** ≈ Alaska, USA
109 J15 **Alatri** Lazio, C Italy
Alattio see Alta
131 P5 **Alatyr'** Chuvashskaya Respublika, W Russian Federation
58 C7 **Alausí** Chimborazo, C Ecuador
107 O3 **Álava** Basq. Araba. ◈ province País Vasco, N Spain
143 T11 **Alaverdi** N Armenia
Alavo see Alavus
95 N14 **Ala-Vuokki** Oulu, E Finland
95 K17 **Alavus** Swe. Alavo. Vaasa, W Finland
Al 'Awābī see Awābī
145 P6 **Al 'Awānī** W Iraq
77 U12 **Al Awaynāt** SE Libya
Al Awaynāt see Al 'Uwaynāt
190 K9 **Alawoona** South Australia
Alaykel'/Alay-Kuu see Këk-Art
149 R17 **Al 'Ayn** var. Al Ain. Abū Ẓaby, E UAE
149 R17 **Al 'Ayn** var. Al Ain. ✕ Abū Ẓaby, E UAE
144 G12 **Al 'Aynā** Al Karak, W Jordan
Alayor see Alaior
Alayskiy Khrebet see Alai Range
127 N7 **Alazeya** ≈ NE Russian Federation
145 U8 **Al 'Azīzīyah** var. Aziziya. E Iraq
123 L14 **Al 'Azīzīyah** NW Libya
144 I10 **Al Azraq al Janūbī** Az Zarqā', N Jordan
108 B9 **Alba** anc. Alba Pompeia. Piemonte, NW Italy
27 V6 **Alba** Texas, SW USA
118 G11 **Alba** ◈ county W Romania
145 P3 **Al Ba'āj** N Iraq
144 J2 **Al Bāb** Ḥalab, N Syria
118 G10 **Albac** Hung. Fehérvölgy; prev. Álbák. Alba, SW Romania
107 Q11 **Albacete** Castilla-La Mancha, C Spain
107 P11 **Albacete** ◈ province Castilla-La Mancha, C Spain
146 I4 **Al Bad'** Tabūk, NW Saudi Arabia
106 L7 **Alba de Tormes** Castilla-León, N Spain
145 P3 **Al Bādī** N Iraq
147 V8 **Al Badī'ah** ✕ (Abū Ẓaby) Abū Ẓaby, C UAE
149 P17 **Al Badī'ah** var. Al Bedei'ah. spring/well C UAE
145 Q7 **Al Baghdādī** var. Khān al Baghdādī. SW Iraq
Al Bāha see Al Bāḥah
146 M11 **Al Bāḥah** var. Al Bāha. Al Bāḥah, SW Saudi Arabia
146 M11 **Al Bāḥah** off. Minṭaqat al Bāḥah. ◈ province W Saudi Arabia
Al Baḥrayn see Bahrain
107 S11 **Albaida** País Valenciano, E Spain
118 H11 **Alba Iulia** Ger. Weissenburg, Hung. Gyulafehérvár; prev. Bălgrad, Karlsburg, Károly-Fehérvár. Alba, W Romania
Álbák see Albac
144 G10 **Al Balqā'** off. Muḥāfaẓat al Balqā', var. Balqā'. ◈ governorate NW Jordan
12 F11 **Alban** Ontario, S Canada
105 O15 **Alban** Tarn, S France
10 K11 **Albanel, Lac** ◎ Québec, SE Canada
115 L20 **Albania** off. Republic of Albania, Alb. Republika e Shqipërisë, Shqipëria; prev. People's Socialist Republic of Albania. ◆ republic SE Europe
Albania see Aubagne
109 H15 **Albano Laziale** Lazio, C Italy
188 J14 **Albany** Western Australia
25 S7 **Albany** Georgia, SE USA
33 P13 **Albany** Indiana, N USA
22 L8 **Albany** Kentucky, S USA
31 U7 **Albany** Minnesota, N USA
29 R2 **Albany** Missouri, C USA
20 L10 **Albany** state capital New York, NE USA
34 G12 **Albany** Oregon, NW USA
27 Q6 **Albany** Texas, SW USA
10 F10 **Albany** ≈ Ontario, S Canada
Alba Pompeia see Alba
Alba Regia see Székesfehérvár
144 J6 **Al Bāridah** var. Bāridah. Ḥimṣ, C Syria
145 Q11 **Al Barīt** S Iraq
107 R8 **Albarracín** Aragón, NE Spain
145 Y12 **Al Baṣrah** Eng. Basra; hist. Busra, Bussora. SE Iraq
145 V11 **Al Baṭḥā'** SE Iraq
147 X8 **Al Bāṭinah** var. Batinah. coastal region N Oman
1 H16 **Albatross Plateau** undersea feature E Pacific Ocean
Al Batrūn see Batroûn
124 Nn14 **Al Bayḍā'** var. Beida. NE Libya
147 P16 **Al Bayḍā'** var. Al Beida. SW Yemen
Al Bedei'ah see Al Badī'ah
Al Beida see Al Bayḍā'
23 S10 **Albemarle** var. Albermarle. North Carolina, SE USA
Albemarle Island see Isabela, Isla
23 N8 **Albemarle Sound** inlet W Atlantic Ocean
108 B10 **Albenga** Liguria, NW Italy
106 L8 **Alberche** ≈ C Spain
105 O17 **Albères, Chaîne des** var. les Albères, Montes Albères. ▲▲ France/Spain
Albères, Montes see Albères, Chaîne des
190 F2 **Alberga Creek** seasonal river South Australia
106 G7 **Albergaria-a-Velha** Aveiro, N Portugal
107 S10 **Alberic** País Valenciano, E Spain
Albermarle see Albemarle
109 P18 **Alberobello** Puglia, SE Italy
110 J7 **Alberschwende** Vorarlberg, W Austria
105 O3 **Albert** Somme, N France
9 O12 **Alberta** ◈ province SW Canada
194 K14 **Albert Edward, Mount** ▲ S PNG
Albert Edward Nyanza see Edward, Lake
63 C20 **Alberti** Buenos Aires, E Argentina
113 K23 **Albertirsa** Pest, C Hungary
101 I16 **Albertkanaal** canal N Belgium
81 P17 **Albert, Lake** var. Albert Nyanza, Lac Mobutu Sese Seko. ◎ Uganda/Zaire
31 V11 **Albert Lea** Minnesota, N USA
83 F16 **Albert Nile** ≈ NW Uganda
Albert Nyanza see Albert, Lake
105 T11 **Albertville** Savoie, E France
25 Q2 **Albertville** Alabama, S USA
Albertville see Kalemie
105 N15 **Albi** anc. Albiga. Tarn, S France
31 W15 **Albia** Iowa, C USA
Albiga see Albi
57 X9 **Albina** Marowijne, NE Suriname
85 A15 **Albina, Ponta** headland SW Angola
32 M16 **Albion** Illinois, N USA
33 P11 **Albion** Indiana, N USA
31 P14 **Albion** Nebraska, C USA
20 E9 **Albion** New York, NE USA
20 B12 **Albion** Pennsylvania, NE USA
Al Biqā' see El Beqaa
146 J4 **Al Bi'r** var. Bi'r Ibn Hirmās. Tabūk, NW Saudi Arabia
146 M12 **Al Birk** Makkah, SW Saudi Arabia
147 Q9 **Al Biyāḍ** desert C Saudi Arabia
100 H13 **Alblasserdam** Zuid-Holland, SW Netherlands
107 T8 **Albocácer** var. Albocasser. País Valenciano, E Spain
Albocasser see Albocácer
97 H19 **Albæk** Nordjylland, N Denmark
Albona see Labin
107 O17 **Alborán, Isla de** island S Spain
Alborán, Mar de see Alboran Sea
107 N17 **Alboran Sea** Sp. Mar de Alborán. sea SW Mediterranean Sea
97 G20 **Ålborg** var. Aalborg, Ålborg-Nørresundby; anc. Alburgum. Nordjylland, N Denmark
97 H21 **Ålborg Bugt** var. Aalborg Bugt. bay N Denmark
Ålborg-Nørresundby see Ålborg
149 O5 **Alborz, Reshteh-ye Kūhhā-ye** Eng. Elburz Mountains. ▲▲ N Iran
107 Q14 **Albox** Andalucía, S Spain
103 H23 **Albstadt** Baden-Württemberg, SW Germany
106 G14 **Albufeira** Beja, S Portugal
145 P5 **Albū Gharz, Sabkhat** ◎ W Iraq
107 O15 **Albuñol** Andalucía, S Spain
39 Q11 **Albuquerque** New Mexico, SW USA
147 W8 **Al Buraymī** var. Buraimi. N Oman
149 R17 **Al Buraymī** var. Buraimi. spring/well Oman/UAE
Al Burayqah see Marsá al Burayqah
Alburgum see Ålborg
106 I10 **Alburquerque** Extremadura, W Spain
189 V14 **Albury** New South Wales, SE Australia
191 P11 **Albury-Wodonga** New South Wales/Victoria, SE Australia
147 T14 **Al Buzūn** SE Yemen
95 G17 **Alby** Västernorrland, C Sweden
Albyn, Glen see Mor, Glen
106 G12 **Alcácer do Sal** Setúbal, W Portugal
Alcalá de Chisvert see Alcalà de Chivert
107 T8 **Alcalà de Chivert** var. Alcalá de Chisvert. País Valenciano, E Spain
106 K14 **Alcalá de Guadaira** Andalucía, S Spain
107 O8 **Alcalá de Henares** Ar. Alkal'a; anc. Complutum. Madrid, C Spain
106 K16 **Alcalá de los Gazules** Andalucía, S Spain
107 N14 **Alcalá La Real** Andalucía, S Spain
109 I23 **Alcamo** Sicilia, Italy, C Mediterranean Sea
107 T4 **Alcanadre** ≈ NE Spain
107 U6 **Alcanar** Cataluña, NE Spain
106 J5 **Alcañices** Castilla-León, N Spain
107 T7 **Alcañiz** Aragón, NE Spain
106 I9 **Alcántara** Extremadura, W Spain
106 J9 **Alcántara, Embalse de** ▣ W Spain
107 R13 **Alcantarilla** Murcia, SE Spain
107 P11 **Alcaraz** Castilla-La Mancha, C Spain
107 P12 **Alcaraz, Sierra de** ▲ C Spain
106 I12 **Alcarrache** ≈ SW Spain
107 T6 **Alcarràs** Cataluña, NE Spain
107 N14 **Alcaudete** Andalucía, S Spain
Alcázar see Ksar-el-Kebir
107 O10 **Alcázar de San Juan** anc. Alce. Castilla-La Mancha, C Spain
Alcazarquivir see Ksar-el-Kebir
Alce see Alcázar de San Juan
59 B17 **Alcebo, Volcán** ✺ Galapagos Islands, Ecuador, E Pacific Ocean
145 X12 **Al Chabā'ish** var. Al Kaba'ish. SE Iraq
119 Y7 **Alchevs'k** prev. Kommunarsk, Voroshilovsk. Luhans'ka Oblast', E Ukraine
Alcira see Alzira
23 N9 **Alcoa** Tennessee, S USA
106 F9 **Alcobaça** Leiria, C Portugal
107 N8 **Alcobendas** Madrid, C Spain
Alcoi see Alcoy
107 P7 **Alcolea del Pinar** Castilla-La Mancha, C Spain
106 I11 **Alconchel** Extremadura, W Spain
107 S9 **Alcora** País Valenciano, E Spain
107 N8 **Alcorcón** Madrid, C Spain
107 S7 **Alcorisa** Aragón, NE Spain
63 B19 **Alcorta** Santa Fe, C Argentina
106 H14 **Alcoutim** Faro, S Portugal
35 W15 **Alcova** Wyoming, C USA
107 S11 **Alcoy** var. Alcoi. País Valenciano, E Spain
107 Y9 **Alcúdia, Badia d'** bay Mallorca, Spain, W Mediterranean Sea
180 M7 **Aldabra Group** island group SW Seychelles
145 U10 **Al Daghghārah** C Iraq
42 J5 **Aldama** Chihuahua, N Mexico
43 P11 **Aldama** Tamaulipas, C Mexico
126 Ll12 **Aldan** Respublika Sakha (Yakutiya), NE Russian Federation
126 Mm12 **Aldan** ≈ NE Russian Federation
168 G7 **Aldar** Dzavhan, W Mongolia
al Dar al Baida see Rabat
99 Q20 **Aldeburgh** E England, UK
107 P5 **Aldehuela de Calatañazor** Castilla-León, N Spain
Aldeia Nova see Aldeia Nova de São Bento
106 H13 **Aldeia Nova de São Bento** var. Aldeia Nova. Beja, S Portugal
31 V11 **Alden** Minnesota, N USA
192 N6 **Aldermen Islands, The** island group N NZ
99 L25 **Alderney** island Channel Islands
99 N22 **Aldershot** S England, UK
23 R6 **Alderson** West Virginia, NE USA
Al Dhaid see Adh Dhayd
32 J11 **Aledo** Illinois, N USA
78 H9 **Aleg** Brakna, SW Mauritania
66 Q10 **Alegranza** island Islas Canarias, Spain, NE Atlantic Ocean
39 P12 **Alegres Mountain** ▲ New Mexico, SW USA
63 F15 **Alegrete** Rio Grande do Sul, S Brazil
63 C16 **Alejandra** Santa Fe, C Argentina
200 Oo12 **Alejandro Selkirk, Isla** island Islas Juan Fernández, Chile, E Pacific Ocean
128 I12 **Alekhovshchina** Leningradskaya Oblast', NW Russian Federation
41 O13 **Aleknagik** Alaska, USA
Aleksandriya see Oleksandriya
Aleksandropol' see Gyumri
130 L3 **Aleksandrov** Vladimirskaya Oblast', W Russian Federation
115 N14 **Aleksandrovac** Serbia, C Yugoslavia
131 R9 **Aleksandrov Gay** Saratovskaya Oblast', W Russian Federation
131 U6 **Aleksandrovka** Orenburgskaya Oblast', W Russian Federation
Aleksandrovka see Oleksandrivka
116 J8 **Aleksandrovo** Loveshka Oblast, N Bulgaria
129 V13 **Aleksandrovsk** Permskaya Oblast', NW Russian Federation
Aleksandrovsk see Zaporizhzhya
131 N14 **Aleksandrovskoye** Stavropol'skiy Kray, SW Russian Federation
127 O14 **Aleksandrovsk-Sakhalinskiy** Ostrov Sakhalin, Sakhalinskaya Oblast', SE Russian Federation
112 J10 **Aleksandrów Kujawski** Włocławek, C Poland
112 K12 **Aleksandrów Łódzki** Łódź, C Poland
Alekseevka see Alekseyevka
151 Q8 **Alekseyevka** Kaz. Alekseevka. Akmola, C Kazakhstan
151 P7 **Alekseyevka** Kaz. Alekseevka. Kokshetau, N Kazakhstan
151 Z10 **Alekseyevka** Kaz. Alekseevka. Vostochnyy Kazakhstan, E Kazakhstan
131 S7 **Alekseyevka** Samarskaya Oblast', W Russian Federation
126 Jj13 **Alekseyevsk** Irkutskaya Oblast', C Russian Federation
131 R4 **Alekseyevskoye** Respublika Tatarstan, W Russian Federation
130 K5 **Aleksin** Tul'skaya Oblast', W Russian Federation
115 O14 **Aleksinac** Serbia, SE Yugoslavia
202 G11 **Alele** Île Uvea, E Wallis and Futuna
97 N20 **Älem** Kalmar, S Sweden
104 L6 **Alençon** Orne, N France
60 I12 **Alenquer** Pará, NE Brazil
40 G10 **Alenuihaha Channel** channel Hawaii, USA, C Pacific Ocean
Alep/Aleppo see Ḥalab
104 F2 **Aléria** Corse, France, C Mediterranean Sea
207 Q11 **Alert** Ellesmere Island, Northwest Territories, N Canada
105 Q14 **Alès** prev. Alais. Gard, S France
118 G9 **Aleşd** Hung. Élesd. Bihor, SW Romania
108 C9 **Alessandria** Fr. Alexandrie. Piemonte, N Italy
97 G21 **Ålestrup** var. Aalestrup. Viborg, NW Denmark
96 D9 **Ålesund** Møre og Romsdal, S Norway
110 E10 **Aletschhorn** ▲ SW Switzerland
207 S1 **Aleutian Basin** undersea feature Bering Sea
40 H17 **Aleutian Islands** island group Alaska, USA
41 P14 **Aleutian Range** ▲▲ Alaska, USA
1 B5 **Aleutian Trench** undersea feature S Bering Sea
127 O10 **Alevina, Mys** headland E Russian Federation
13 Q6 **Alex** ≈ Québec, SE Canada
30 J3 **Alexander** North Dakota, N USA
41 W14 **Alexander Archipelago** island group Alaska, USA
Alexanderbaai see Alexander Bay
85 D23 **Alexander Bay** Afr. Alexanderbaai. Northern Cape, W South Africa
25 Q5 **Alexander City** Alabama, S USA
204 J6 **Alexander Island** island Antarctica
Alexander Range see Kirghiz Range
191 O12 **Alexandra** Victoria, SE Australia
193 D22 **Alexandra** Otago, South Island, NZ
117 F14 **Alexándreia** var. Alexándria. Kentrikí Makedonía, N Greece
Alexandretta see İskenderun
Alexandretta, Gulf of see İskenderun Körfezi
13 N13 **Alexandria** Ontario, SE Canada
124 Q15 **Alexandria** Ar. Al Iskandarīyah. N Egypt
46 J12 **Alexandria** C Jamaica
118 J15 **Alexandria** Teleorman, S Romania
33 P13 **Alexandria** Indiana, N USA
22 M4 **Alexandria** Kentucky, S USA
24 H7 **Alexandria** Louisiana, S USA
31 T7 **Alexandria** Minnesota, N USA
31 Q11 **Alexandria** South Dakota, N USA
23 W4 **Alexandria** Virginia, NE USA
Alexándria see Alexándreia
20 I7 **Alexandria Bay** New York, NE USA
Alexandrie see Alessandria
190 J10 **Alexandrina, Lake** ◎ South Australia
116 K13 **Alexandroúpoli** var. Alexandroúpolis, Turk. Dedeagaç, Dedeagach. Anatolikí Makedonía kai Thráki, NE Greece
Alexandroúpolis see Alexandroúpoli
8 L15 **Alexis Creek** British Columbia, SW Canada
126 Gg15 **Aleysk** Altayskiy Kray, S Russian Federation
145 S8 **Al Fallūjah** var. Falluja. C Iraq
107 R8 **Alfambra** ≈ E Spain
Al Faqa see Faq'
147 R15 **Al Farḍah** C Yemen
107 Q4 **Alfaro** La Rioja, N Spain
107 U5 **Alfarràs** Cataluña, NE Spain
Al Fāshir see El Fasher
Al Fashn see El Fashn
116 M7 **Alfatar** Razgradska Oblast, NE Bulgaria
145 S5 **Al Fatḥah** C Iraq
145 Q3 **Al Fatsī** N Iraq
145 Z13 **Al Fāw** var. Fao. SE Iraq
Al Fayyūm see El Faiyûm
117 D20 **Alfeiós** prev. Alfiós, anc. Alpheius, Alpheus. ≈ S Greece
102 I13 **Alfeld** Niedersachsen, C Germany
Alfiós see Alfeiós

◆ Country ● Country Capital ◇ Dependent Territory ○ Dependent Territory Capital ◈ Administrative Region ✕ International Airport ▲ Mountain ▲▲ Mountain Range ✺ Volcano ≈ River ◎ Lake ▣ Reservoir

Alföld *see* Great Hungarian Plain
96 *C11* **Ålfotbreen** *glacier* S Norway
21 *P9* **Alfred** Maine, NE USA
20 *F11* **Alfred** New York, NE USA
63 *K14* **Alfredo Vagner** Santa Catarina, S Brazil
96 *M12* **Alfta** Gävleborg, C Sweden
146 *K12* **Al Fuḩayḩīl** *var.* Fahaheel. SE Kuwait
145 *Q6* **Al Fuḩaymī** C Iraq
149 *S16* **Al Fujayrah** *Eng.* Fujairah. Al Fujayrah, NE UAE
149 *S16* **Al Fujayrah** *Eng.* Fujairah. ✈ Al Fujayrah, NE UAE
Al Furāt *see* Euphrates
150 *I10* **Alga** *Kaz.* Algha. Aktyubinsk, NW Kazakhstan
150 *G9* **Algabas** Zapadnyy Kazakhstan, NW Kazakhstan
97 *C17* **Ålgård** Rogaland, S Norway
106 *G14* **Algarve** *cultural region* S Portugal
190 *G3* **Algebuckina Bridge** South Australia
106 *K16* **Algeciras** Andalucía, SW Spain
107 *S10* **Algemesí** País Valenciano, E Spain
Al-Genain *see* El Geneina
123 *I11* **Alger** *var.* Algiers, El Djazaïr, Al Jazair. ● (Algeria) N Algeria
76 *H9* **Algeria** *off.* Democratic and Popular Republic of Algeria. ◆ *republic* N Africa
123 *J9* **Algerian Basin** *var.* Balearic Plain *undersea feature* W Mediterranean Sea
Algha *see* Alga
144 *I4* **Al Ghāb** ◎ NW Syria
147 *X10* **Al Ghābah** *var.* Ghaba. C Oman
147 *U14* **Al Ghayḍah** E Yemen
146 *M6* **Al Ghazālah** Ḩā'il, NW Saudi Arabia
109 *B17* **Alghero** Sardegna, Italy, C Mediterranean Sea
97 *M20* **Älghult** Kronoberg, S Sweden
Al Ghurdaqah *see* Hurghada
Algiers *see* Alger
107 *S10* **Alginet** País Valenciano, E Spain
85 *I26* **Algoa Bay** *bay* S South Africa
106 *L15* **Algodonales** Andalucía, S Spain
107 *N9* **Algodor** 〰 C Spain
Al Golea *see* El Goléa
33 *N6* **Algoma** Wisconsin, N USA
31 *U12* **Algona** Iowa, C USA
22 *L8* **Algood** Tennessee, S USA
107 *O2* **Algorta** País Vasco, N Spain
63 *E18* **Algorta** Río Negro, W Uruguay
Al Haba *see* Haba
145 *Q10* **Al Habbārīyah** S Iraq
Al Hadhar *see* Al Ḩaḑr
145 *Q4* **Al Ḩaḑr** *var.* Al Hadhar; *anc.* Hatra. NW Iraq
145 *T13* **Al Ḩajarah** *desert* S Iraq
147 *W8* **Al Ḩajār al Gharbī** ▲▲ N Oman
147 *Y8* **Al Ḩajar ash Sharqī** ▲▲ NE Oman
147 *R15* **Al Hajarayn** C Yemen
144 *L10* **Al Ḩamād** *desert* Jordan/Saudi Arabia
Al Hamad *see* Syrian Desert
77 *N9* **Al Ḩamādah al Ḩamrā'** *var.* Al Ḩamrā'. *desert* NW Libya
107 *N15* **Alhama de Granada** Andalucía, S Spain
107 *R13* **Alhama de Murcia** Murcia, SE Spain
37 *T15* **Alhambra** California, W USA
145 *T12* **Al Ḩammām** S Iraq
147 *X8* **Al Ḩamrā'** NE Oman
Al Ḩamrā' *see* Al Ḩamādah al Ḩamrā'
147 *O6* **Al Ḩamūdīyah** *spring/well* N Saudi Arabia
146 *M7* **Al Ḩanākīyah** Al Madīnah, W Saudi Arabia
145 *W14* **Al Ḩanīyah** *escarpment* Iraq/Saudi Arabia
145 *Y12* **Al Hārithah** SE Iraq
146 *L3* **Al Ḩarrah** *desert* NW Saudi Arabia
77 *Q10* **Al Harūj al Aswad** *desert* C Libya
Al Hasaifin *see* Al Ḩusayfīn
145 *N2* **Al Ḩasakah** *var.* Al Hasijah, El Haseke, *Fr.* Hassetché. Al Ḩasakah, NE Syria
145 *O2* **Al Ḩasakah** *off.* Muḩāfaz̧at al Ḩasakah, *var.* Al Hasakah, Āl Hasakah, Hasakah, Hassakeh. ◈ *governorate* NE Syria
145 *T9* **Al Hāshimīyah** C Iraq
144 *G13* **Al Hāshimīyah** Ma'ān, S Jordan
Al Hasijah *see* Al Ḩasakah
106 *M15* **Alhaurín el Grande** Andalucía, S Spain
147 *Q16* **Al Ḩawrā** S Yemen
145 *V10* **Al Ḩayy** *var.* Kut al Hai, Kūt al Ḩayy. E Iraq
147 *U11* **Al Ḩibāk** *desert* E Saudi Arabia
144 *H8* **Al Hījānah** *var.* Hejanah, Hijanah. Dimashq, W Syria
146 *K7* **Al Ḩijāz** *Eng.* Hejaz. *physical region* NW Saudi Arabia
Al Hilbeh *see* 'Ulayyānīyah, Bi'r al
145 *T9* **Al Ḩillah** *var.* Hilla. C Iraq
145 *T9* **Al Hindīyah** *var.* Hindiya. C Iraq
144 *G12* **Al Ḩisā** Aţ Ţafīlah, W Jordan
76 *G5* **Al-Hoceïma** *var.* al Hoceima, Al-Hoceima, Alhucemas; *prev.* Villa Sanjurjo. N Morocco
Alhucemas *see* Al-Hoceïma
107 *N17* **Alhucemas, Peñon de** *island group* S Spain
147 *N15* **Al Ḩudaydah** *Eng.* Hodeida. W Yemen
147 *N15* **Al Ḩudaydah** *Eng.* Hodeida. ✈ W Yemen
146 *M4* **Al Ḩudūd ash Shamālīyah** *var.* Minţaqat al Ḩudūd ash Shamālīyah, *Eng.* Northern Border Region. ◈ *province* N Saudi Arabia
147 *S7* **Al Hufūf** *var.* Hofuf. Ash Sharqīyah, NE Saudi Arabia
al-Hurma *see* Al Khurmah
147 *X7* **Al Ḩusayfīn** *var.* Al Hasaifin. N Oman
144 *G9* **Al Ḩuşn** *var.* Husn. Irbid, N Jordan
145 *U9* **'Alī** E Iraq
106 *L10* **Alia** Extremadura, W Spain
149 *P9* **'Alīābād** Yazd, C Iran
'Alīābad *see* Qā'emshahr
107 *S7* **Aliaga** Aragón, NE Spain
142 *B13* **Aliağa** İzmir, W Turkey
Aliákmon *see* Aliákmonas
117 *F14* **Aliákmonas** *prev.* Aliákmon, *anc.* Haliacmon. 〰 N Greece
145 *W9* **'Alī al Gharbī** E Iraq
145 *U11* **'Alī al Ḩassūnī** S Iraq
117 *G18* **Alíartos** Stereá Ellás, C Greece
143 *Y12* **Äli-Bayramlı** *Rus.* Ali-Bayramly. SE Azerbaijan
Ali-Bayramly *see* Äli-Bayramlı
116 *P12* **Alibey Barajı** ⊠ NW Turkey
79 *S13* **Alibori** 〰 N Benin
114 *M10* **Alibunar** Serbia, NE Yugoslavia
107 *S12* **Alicante** *Cat.* Alacant; *Lat.* Lucentum. País Valenciano, SE Spain
107 *S12* **Alicante** ◈ *province* País Valenciano, SE Spain
107 *S12* **Alicante** ✈ Murcia, E Spain
85 *I25* **Alice** Eastern Cape, S South Africa
27 *S14* **Alice** Texas, SW USA
85 *I25* **Alicedale** Eastern Cape, S South Africa
67 *B25* **Alice, Mount** *hill* West Falkland, Falkland Islands
109 *P20* **Alice, Punta** *headland* S Italy
189 *Q7* **Alice Springs** Northern Territory, C Australia
25 *N4* **Aliceville** Alabama, S USA
153 *U13* **Alichur** SE Tajikistan
153 *U14* **Alichuri Janubí, Qatorkŭhi** *Rus.* Yuzhno-Alichurskiy Khrebet. ▲▲ SE Tajikistan
153 *U13* **Alichuri Shimolí, Qatorkŭhi** *Rus.* Severo-Alichurskiy Khrebet. ▲▲ SE Tajikistan
109 *K22* **Alicudi, Isola** *island* Isole Eolie, S Italy
158 *J11* **Alīgarh** Uttar Pradesh, N India
148 *M7* **Alīgūdarz** Lorestān, W Iran
1 *F12* **Alijos, Islas** *island group* California, SW USA
155 *R6* **'Alī Kbel** *Pash.* 'Alī Khēl. Paktīkā, E Afghanistan
Ali Khel *see* 'Alī Kheyl, Paktīā, Afghanistan
'Alī Khēl *see* 'Alī Kbel, Paktīkā, Afghanistan
155 *R6* **'Alī Kheyl** *var.* Ali Khel, Jajı. Paktīā, SE Afghanistan
147 *V17* **Al Ikhwān** *island group* SE Yemen
Aliki *see* Alykí
81 *H19* **Alima** 〰 C Congo
Al Imārāt al 'Arabīyah al Muttaḩidah *see* United Arab Emirates
194 *M12* **Alimbit** 〰 New Britain, C PNG
117 *N23* **Alimía** *island* Dodekánisos, Greece, Aegean Sea
57 *V12* **Alimimuni Piek** ▲ S Suriname
81 *K15* **Alindao** Basse-Kotto, S Central African Republic
97 *J18* **Alingsås** Älvsborg, S Sweden
83 *K18* **Alinjugul** *spring/well* E Kenya
155 *S11* **Alīpur** Punjab, E Pakistan
159 *T12* **Alīpur Duār** West Bengal, NE India
20 *B14* **Aliquippa** Pennsylvania, NE USA
82 *L12* **'Ali Sabieh** *var.* 'Alī Sabīḩ. S Djibouti
'Alī Sabīḩ *see* 'Ali Sabieh
146 *K3* **Al 'Īsāwīyah** Al Jawf, NW Saudi Arabia
106 *J10* **Aliseda** Extremadura, W Spain
145 *T8* **Al Iskandarīyah** C Iraq
Al Iskandarīyah *see* Alexandria
127 *Oo5* **Aliskerovo** Chukotskiy Avtonomnyy Okrug, NE Russian Federation
116 *H13* **Alistráti** Kentrikí Makedonía, NE Greece
41 *P15* **Alitak Bay** *bay* Kodiak Island, Alaska, USA
Al Ittiḩād *see* Madīnat ash Sha'b
117 *H18* **Alivéri** *var.* Alivérion. Évvoia, C Greece
Alivérion *see* Alivéri
Aliwal-Noord *see* Aliwal North
85 *I24* **Aliwal North** *Afr.* Aliwal-Noord. Eastern Cape, SE South Africa
124 *Nn15* **Al Jabal al Akhḑar** ▲▲ NE Libya
144 *H13* **Al Jafr** Ma'ān, S Jordan
77 *T8* **Al Jaghbūb** NE Libya
148 *K11* **Al Jahrā'** *var.* Al Jahrah, Jahra. C Kuwait
Al Jahrah *see* Al Jahrā'
Al Jamāhīrīyah al 'Arabīyah al Lībīyah ash Sha'bīyah al Ishtirāk *see* Libya
146 *K3* **Al Jarāwī** *spring/well* NW Saudi Arabia
147 *X11* **Al Jawārah** *oasis* SE Oman
146 *L3* **Al Jawf** *var.* Jauf. Al Jawf, NW Saudi Arabia
146 *L4* **Al Jawf** *off.* Minţaqat al Jawf. ◈ *province* N Saudi Arabia
Al Jawlān *see* Golan Heights
Al Jazair *see* Alger
145 *N4* **Al Jazīrah** *physical region* Iraq/Syria
106 *F14* **Aljezur** Faro, S Portugal
145 *S13* **Al Jil** S Iraq
144 *G11* **Al Jīzah** *var.* Jiza. 'Ammān, N Jordan
Al Jīzah *see* El Gîza
Al Jubail *see* Al Jubayl
147 *S6* **Al Jubayl** *var.* Al Jubail. Ash Sharqīyah, NE Saudi Arabia
147 *T10* **Āl Juḩaysh, Qalamat** *well* SE Saudi Arabia
149 *N15* **Al Jumaylīyah** N Qatar
Al Junaynah *see* El Geneina
106 *G13* **Aljustrel** Beja, S Portugal
Al Kaba'ish *see* Al Chabā'ish
Al-Kadhimain *see* Al Kāz̧imīyah
Al Kāf *see* El Kef
Alkal'a *see* Alcalá de Henares
37 *W4* **Alkali Flat** *salt flat* Nevada, W USA
37 *Q1* **Alkali Lake** ◎ Nevada, W USA
147 *Z9* **Al Kāmil** NE Oman
144 *G11* **Al Karak** *var.* El Kerak, Karak, Kerak; *anc.* Kir Moab, Kir of Moab. Al Karak, W Jordan
144 *G12* **Al Karak** *off.* Muḩāfaz̧at al Karak. ◈ *governorate* W Jordan
145 *W8* **Al Karmashīyah** E Iraq
Al-Kashaniya *see* Al Qash'ānīyah
Al-Kasr al-Kebir *see* Ksar-el-Kebir
145 *T8* **Al Kāz̧imīyah** *var.* Al-Kadhimain, Kadhimain. C Iraq
101 *J18* **Alken** Limburg, NE Belgium
147 *X8* **Al Khābūrah** *var.* Khabura. N Oman
Al Khalīl *see* Hebron
145 *T7* **Al Khāliş** C Iraq
Al Khaluf *see* Khalūf
Al Khārijah *see* El Khârga
147 *Q8* **Al Kharj** Ar Riyāḑ, C Saudi Arabia
147 *W6* **Al Khaşab** *var.* Khasab. N Oman
Al Khaur *see* Al Khawr
149 *N15* **Al Khawr** *var.* Al Khaur, Al Khor. N Qatar
148 *K12* **Al Khīrān** *var.* Al Khiran. SE Kuwait
147 *W9* **Al Khīrān** *spring/well* NW Oman
Al Khiyām *see* El Khiyam
Al-Khobar *see* Al Khubar
Al Khor *see* Al Khawr
147 *S6* **Al Khubar** *var.* Al-Khobar. Ash Sharqīyah, NE Saudi Arabia
77 *T11* **Al Khufrah** SE Libya
123 *L14* **Al Khums** *var.* Homs, Khoms, Khums. NW Libya
147 *R15* **Al Khuraybah** C Yemen
146 *M9* **Al Khurmah** *var.* al-Hurma. Makkah, W Saudi Arabia
147 *V9* **Al Kidan** *desert* NE Saudi Arabia
100 *H9* **Alkmaar** Noord-Holland, NW Netherlands
145 *T10* **Al Kūfah** *var.* Kufa. S Iraq
147 *T10* **Al Kursū'** *desert* E Saudi Arabia
145 *V9* **Al Kūt** *var.* Kūt al 'Amārah, Kut al Imara. E Iraq
Al-Kuwait *see* Al Kuwayt
Al Kuwayr *see* Guwēr
148 *K11* **Al Kuwayt** *var.* Al-Kuwait, *Eng.* Kuwait, Kuwait City; *prev.* Qurein. ● (Kuwait) E Kuwait
148 *K11* **Al Kuwayt** ✈ C Kuwait
117 *G19* **Alkyonidón, Kólpos** *gulf* C Greece
147 *N4* **Al Labbah** *physical region* N Saudi Arabia
144 *G4* **Al Lādhiqīyah** *Eng.* Latakia, *Fr.* Lattaquié; *anc.* Laodicea, Laodicea ad Mare. Al Lādhiqīyah, W Syria
144 *H4* **Al Lādhiqīyah** *off.* Muḩāfaz̧at al Ļādhiqīyah, *var.* Al Lathqiyah, Latakia, Lattakia. ◈ *governorate* W Syria
21 *R2* **Allagash River** 〰 Maine, NE USA
158 *M13* **Allahābād** Uttar Pradesh, N India
149 *S3* **Allāh Dāgh, Reshteh-ye** ▲▲ NE Iran
41 *Q8* **Allakaket** Alaska, USA
126 *Mm11* **Allakh-Yun'** 〰 NE Russian Federation
9 *T15* **Allan** Saskatchewan, S Canada
177 *Ff6* **Allanmyo** Magwe, C Myanmar
85 *I22* **Allanridge** Free State, C South Africa
106 *H4* **Allariz** Galicia, NW Spain
145 *R11* **Al Laşaf** *var.* Al Lussuf. S Iraq
Al Lathqiyah *see* Al Lādhiqīyah
25 *S2* **Allatoona Lake** ⊠ Georgia, SE USA
85 *J19* **Alldays** Northern, NE South Africa
Alle *see* Łyna
33 *P10* **Allegan** Michigan, N USA
19 *Qq8* **Allegheny Mountains** ▲▲ NE USA
20 *E12* **Allegheny Plateau** ▲▲ New York/Pennsylvania, NE USA
20 *D11* **Allegheny Reservoir** ⊠ New York/Pennsylvania, NE USA
20 *E12* **Allegheny River** 〰 New York/Pennsylvania, NE USA
24 *K9* **Allemands, Lac des** ◎ Louisiana, S USA
27 *U6* **Allen** Texas, SW USA
23 *R14* **Allendale** South Carolina, SE USA
43 *N6* **Allende** Coahuila de Zaragoza, NE Mexico
43 *O9* **Allende** Nuevo León, NE Mexico
99 *D16* **Allen, Lough** *Ir.* Loch Aillionn. ◎ NW Ireland
193 *B26* **Allen, Mount** ▲ Stewart Island, Southland, SW NZ
111 *V2* **Allensteig** Niederösterreich, N Austria
Allenstein *see* Olsztyn
20 *I14* **Allentown** Pennsylvania, NE USA
161 *G23* **Alleppey** *var.* Alappuzha; *prev.* Alleppi. Kerala, SW India
Alleppi *see* Alleppey
102 *J12* **Aller** 〰 NW Germany
31 *V16* **Allerton** Iowa, C USA
101 *K19* **Alleur** Liège, E Belgium
103 *J25* **Allgäuer Alpen** ▲▲ Austria/Germany
30 *J13* **Alliance** Nebraska, C USA
33 *U12* **Alliance** Ohio, N USA
105 *O10* **Allier** ◈ *department* N France
145 *R13* **Al Līfīyah** S Iraq
46 *J13* **Alligator Pond** C Jamaica
23 *Y9* **Alligator River** 〰 North Carolina, SE USA
31 *W12* **Allison** Iowa, C USA
12 *G14* **Alliston** Ontario, S Canada
146 *L11* **Al Līth** Makkah, SW Saudi Arabia
Al Liwā' *see* Līwā
98 *J12* **Alloa** C Scotland, UK
105 *U14* **Allos** Alpes-de-Haute-Provence, SE France
110 *D6* **Allschwil** Basel-Land, NW Switzerland
Al Lubnān *see* Lebanon
147 *N14* **Al Luḩayyah** W Yemen
12 *K12* **Allumettes, Île des** *island* Québec, SE Canada
Al Lussuf *see* Al Laşaf
111 *S5* **Alm** 〰 N Austria
13 *Q7* **Alma** Québec, SE Canada
29 *S10* **Alma** Arkansas, C USA
25 *V7* **Alma** Georgia, SE USA
29 *P4* **Alma** Kansas, C USA
33 *Q8* **Alma** Michigan, N USA
31 *O17* **Alma** Nebraska, C USA
32 *I7* **Alma** Wisconsin, N USA
145 *R12* **Al Ma'ānīyah** S Iraq
Alma-Ata/Alma-Atinskaya Oblast' *see* Almaty
Almacellas *see* Almacelles
107 *T5* **Almacelles** *var.* Almacellas. Cataluña, NE Spain
106 *F11* **Almada** Setúbal, W Portugal
106 *L11* **Almadén** Castilla-La Mancha, C Spain
68 *L6* **Almadies, Pointe des** *headland* W Senegal
146 *L7* **Al Madīnah** *Eng.* Medina. Al Madīnah, W Saudi Arabia
146 *L7* **Al Madīnah** *off.* Minţaqat al Madīnah. ◈ *province* W Saudi Arabia
144 *H9* **Al Mafraq** *var.* Mafraq. Al Mafraq, N Jordan
144 *J10* **Al Mafraq** *off.* Muḩāfaz̧at al Mafraq. ◈ *governorate* NW Jordan
147 *R15* **Al Maghārīm** C Yemen
107 *N11* **Almagro** Castilla-La Mancha, C Spain
Al Maḩallah al Kubrá *see* El Maḩalla el Kubra
145 *T9* **Al Maḩāwīl** *var.* Khān al Maḩāwīl. C Iraq
Al Mahdīyah *see* Mahdia
145 *T8* **Al Maḩmūdīyah** *var.* Mahmudiya. C Iraq
147 *T14* **Al Mahrah** ▲▲ E Yemen
147 *P7* **Al Majma'ah** Ar Riyāḑ, C Saudi Arabia
145 *Q11* **Al Makmīn** *well* S Iraq
145 *Q1* **Al Mālikīyah** *var.* Malkiye. Al Ḩasakah, N Syria
Almalyk *see* Olmaliq
Al Mamlakah al Urdunīyah al Hāshimīyah *see* Jordan
Al Mamlakah *see* Morocco
149 *Q18* **Al Manādir** *var.* Al Manadir. *desert* Oman/UAE
148 *L15* **Al Manāmah** *Eng.* Manama. ● (Bahrain) N Bahrain
145 *O5* **Al Manāşif** ▲▲ E Syria
37 *O4* **Almanor, Lake** ⊠ California, W USA
107 *R11* **Almansa** Castilla-La Mancha, C Spain
Al Manşūrah *see* El Manşûra
106 *L3* **Almanza** Castilla-León, N Spain
106 *L8* **Almanzor** ▲ W Spain
107 *P14* **Almanzora** 〰 SE Spain
145 *S9* **Al Mardah** C Iraq
Al-Mariyya *see* Almería
77 *R7* **Al Marj** *var.* Barka, *It.* Barce. NE Libya
144 *L2* **Al Mashrafah** Ar Raqqah, N Syria
147 *X8* **Al Maşna'ah** *var.* Al Muşana'a. NE Oman
107 *T9* **Almassora** País Valenciano, E Spain
Almatinskaya Oblast' *see* Almaty
151 *U15* **Almaty** *var.* Alma-Ata. ● (Kazakhstan) Almaty, SE Kazakhstan
151 *S14* **Almaty** *off.* Almatinskaya Oblast', *Kaz.* Almaty Oblysy; *prev.* Alma-Atinskaya Oblast'. ◈ *province* SE Kazakhstan
151 *U15* **Almaty** ✈ Almaty, SE Kazakhstan
Almaty Oblysy *see* Almaty
al-Mawailih *see* Al Muwayliḩ
145 *R3* **Al Mawşil** *Eng.* Mosul. N Iraq
145 *N5* **Al Mayādīn** *var.* Mayadin, *Fr.* Meyadine. Dayr az Zawr, E Syria
145 *X10* **Al Maymūnah** *var.* Maimuna. SE Iraq
147 *N5* **Al Mayyāh** Ḩā'il, N Saudi Arabia
Al Ma'zam *see* Al Ma'zim
107 *P6* **Almazán** Castilla-León, N Spain
147 *W8* **Al Ma'zim** *var.* Al Ma'zam. NW Oman
126 *Kk11* **Almaznyy** Respublika Sakha (Yakutiya), NE Russian Federation
Al Mazra' *see* Al Mazra'ah
144 *G11* **Al Mazra'ah** *var.* Al Mazra', Mazra'a. Al Karak, W Jordan
103 *G15* **Alme** 〰 W Germany
106 *I7* **Almeida** Guarda, N Portugal
106 *G10* **Almeirim** Santarém, C Portugal
100 *O10* **Almelo** Overijssel, E Netherlands
107 *S9* **Almenara** País Valenciano, E Spain
107 *P12* **Almenaras** ▲ S Spain
107 *P5* **Almenar de Soria** Castilla-León, N Spain
106 *J6* **Almendra, Embalse de** ⊠ Castilla-León, NW Spain
106 *J11* **Almendralejo** Extremadura, W Spain
100 *J10* **Almere** *var.* Almere-stad. Flevoland, C Netherlands
100 *J10* **Almere-Buiten** Flevoland, C Netherlands
100 *J10* **Almere-Haven** Flevoland, C Netherlands
Almere-stad *see* Almere
107 *P15* **Almería** *Ar.* Al-Mariyya; *anc.* Unci, *Lat.* Portus Magnus. Andalucía, S Spain
107 *P14* **Almería** ◈ *province* Andalucía, S Spain
107 *P15* **Almería, Golfo de** *gulf* S Spain
131 *S5* **Al'met'yevsk** Respublika Tatarstan, W Russian Federation
97 *L21* **Älmhult** Kronoberg, S Sweden
147 *U9* **Al Miḩrāḑ** *desert* NE Saudi Arabia
Al Mīnā' *see* El Mina
106 *L17* **Almina, Punta** *headland* Ceuta, Spain, N Africa
Al Minyā *see* El Minya
Al Miqdādīyah *see* Al Muqdādīyah
45 *P14* **Almirante** Bocas del Toro, NW Panama
Almirós *see* Almyrós
146 *M9* **Al Mislaḩ** *spring/well* W Saudi Arabia
Almissa *see* Omiš
106 *G13* **Almodôvar** *var.* Almodóvar. Beja, S Portugal
106 *M11* **Almodóvar del Campo** Castilla-La Mancha, C Spain
107 *Q9* **Almodóvar del Pinar** Castilla-La Mancha, C Spain
33 *S9* **Almont** Michigan, N USA
12 *L13* **Almonte** Ontario, SE Canada
106 *J14* **Almonte** Andalucía, S Spain
106 *K9* **Almonte** 〰 W Spain
158 *K9* **Almora** Uttar Pradesh, N India
106 *M8* **Almorox** Castilla-La Mancha, C Spain
147 *S7* **Al Mubarraz** Ash Sharqīyah, E Saudi Arabia
Al Muḑaibī *see* Al Muḑaybī
144 *G15* **Al Mudawwarah** Ma'ān, SW Jordan
147 *Y9* **Al Muḑaybī** *var.* Al Muḑaibī. NE Oman
Almudébar *see* Almudévar
107 *S5* **Almudévar** *var.* Almudébar. Aragón, NE Spain
147 *S15* **Al Mukallā** *var.* Mukalla. SE Yemen
147 *N16* **Al Mukhā** *Eng.* Mocha. SW Yemen
107 *N15* **Almuñécar** Andalucía, S Spain
145 *U7* **Al Muqdādīyah** *var.* Al Miqdādīyah. C Iraq
146 *L3* **Al Murayr** *spring/well* NW Saudi Arabia
142 *M12* **Almus** Tokat, N Turkey
Al Muşana'a *see* Al Maşna'ah
145 *T9* **Al Musayyib** *var.* Musaiyib. C Iraq
145 *V9* **Al Muwaffaqīyah** S Iraq
144 *H10* **Al Muwaqqar** *var.* El Muwaqqar. 'Ammān, W Jordan
146 *J5* **Al Muwayliḩ** *var.* al-Mawailih. Tabūk, NW Saudi Arabia
117 *F17* **Almyrós** *var.* Almirós. Thessalía, C Greece
117 *I24* **Almyroú, Órmos** *bay* Krití, Greece, E Mediterranean Sea
Al Nūwfalīyah *see* An Nawfalīyah
98 *L13* **Alnwick** N England, UK
Al Obayyid *see* El Obeid
Al Odaid *see* Al 'Udayd
202 *B16* **Alofi** ○ (Niue) W Niue
202 *A16* **Alofi Bay** *bay* W Niue, C Pacific Ocean
202 *E13* **Alofi, Île** *island* S Wallis and Futuna
202 *E13* **Alofitai** Île Alofi, W Wallis and Futuna
Aloha State *see* Hawaii
120 *G7* **Aloja** Limbaži, N Latvia
159 *X10* **Along** Arunāchel Pradesh, NE India
117 *H16* **Alónnisos** *island* Vóreioi Sporádes, Greece, Aegean Sea
106 *M15* **Álora** Andalucía, S Spain
175 *Rr15* **Alor, Kepulauan** *island group* E Indonesia
175 *Rr16* **Alor, Pulau** *prev.* Ombai. *island* Kepulauan Alor, E Indonesia
175 *R16* **Alor, Selat** *strait* Flores Sea/Savu Sea
173 *G2* **Alor Setar** *var.* Alor Star, Alur Setar. Kedah, Peninsular Malaysia
Alost *see* Aalst
160 *F9* **Ālot** Madhya Pradesh, C India
195 *N16* **Alotau** Milne Bay, SE PNG
176 *Yy15* **Alotip** Irian Jaya, E Indonesia
Al Oued *see* El Oued
37 *R12* **Alpaugh** California, W USA
Alpen *see* Alps
33 *R6* **Alpena** Michigan, N USA
Alpes *see* Alps
105 *S14* **Alpes-de-Haute-Provence** ◈ *department* SE France
105 *U14* **Alpes-Maritimes** ◈ *department* SE France
189 *W8* **Alpha** Queensland, E Australia
207 *R9* **Alpha Cordillera** *var.* Alpha Ridge. *undersea feature* Arctic Ocean
Alpha Ridge *see* Alpha Cordillera
Alpheius *see* Alfeiós
101 *I15* **Alphen** Noord-Brabant, S Netherlands
100 *H11* **Alphen aan den Rijn** *var.* Alphen. Zuid-Holland, C Netherlands
Alpheus *see* Alfeiós
Alpi *see* Alps
106 *G10* **Alpiarça** Santarém, C Portugal
26 *K10* **Alpine** Texas, SW USA
110 *F8* **Alpnach** Unterwalden, W Switzerland
110 *D11* **Alps** *Fr.* Alpes, *Ger.* Alpen, *It.* Alpi. ▲▲ C Europe
147 *W8* **Al Qābil** *var.* Qabil. N Oman
Al Qaḑārif *see* Gedaref
77 *P8* **Al Qaddāḩīyah** N Libya
Al Qadmouss *see* Al Qadmūs
Al Qāhirah *see* Cairo
146 *K4* **Al Qalībah** Tabūk, NW Saudi Arabia
145 *O1* **Al Qāmishlī** *var.* Kamishli, Qamishly. Al Ḩasakah, NE Syria
144 *I6* **Al Qaryatayn** *var.* Qaryatayn, *Fr.* Qariateïne. Ḩimş, C Syria
148 *K11* **Al Qash'ānīyah** *var.* Al-Kashaniya. NE Kuwait
147 *N7* **Al Qaşīm** *off.* Minţaqat Qaşīm, Qassim. ◈ *province* C Saudi Arabia
144 *J5* **Al Qaşr** Ḩimş, C Syria
Al Qaşr *see* El Qaşr
Al Qaşrayn *see* Kasserine
147 *S6* **Al Qaţīf** Ash Sharqīyah, NE Saudi Arabia
144 *G11* **Al Qaţrānah** *var.* El Qatrani, Qatrana. Al Karak, W Jordan
77 *P11* **Al Qaţrūn** SW Libya
Al Qayrawān *see* Kairouan
Al-Qsar al-Kbir *see* Ksar-el-Kebir
Al Qubayyāt *see* Qoubaïyât
Al Qudayr *see* Al Qadr
Al Quds/Al Quds ash Sharīf *see* Jerusalem
144 *G8* **Al Qunayţirah** *var.* El Kuneitra, El Quneitra, Kuneitra, Qunaytra. Al Qunayţirah, SW Syria
144 *G8* **Al Qunayţirah** *off.* Muḩāfaz̧at al Qunayţirah, *var.* El Q'unayţirah, Qunaytirah, *Fr.* Kuneitra. ◈ *governorate* SW Syria
146 *M11* **Al Qunfudhah** Makkah, SW Saudi Arabia
146 *K2* **Al Qurayyāt** Al Jawf, NW Saudi Arabia
145 *Y11* **Al Qurnah** *var.* Kurna. SE Iraq
145 *V12* **Al Quşayr** S Iraq
144 *I6* **Al Quşayr** *var.* El Quseir, Quşayr, *Fr.* Kousseir. Ḩimş, W Syria
Al Quşayr *see* Quseir
144 *H7* **Al Quţayfah** *var.* Quţayfah, Qutayfe, Quteife, *Fr.* Kouteifé. Dimashq, W Syria
147 *P8* **Al Quwayīyah** Ar Riyāḑ, C Saudi Arabia
Al Quwayr *see* Guwēr
144 *F14* **Al Quwayrah** *var.* El Quweira. Ma'ān, SW Jordan
Al Rayyan *see* Ar Rayyān
Al Rbeil *see* Ar Rubayl
Al Ruweis *see* Ar Ruways
97 *G24* **Als** *Ger.* Alsen. *island* SW Denmark
105 *U5* **Alsace** *Ger.* Elsass; *anc.* Alsatia. ◈ *region* NE France
9 *R16* **Alsask** Saskatchewan, S Canada
107 *P3* **Alsasua** Navarra, N Spain
Alsatia *see* Alsace
103 *C16* **Alsdorf** Nordrhein-Westfalen, W Germany
8 *G8* **Alsek** 〰 Canada/USA
Alsen *see* Als
103 *F19* **Alsenz** 〰 W Germany
103 *H17* **Alsfeld** Hessen, C Germany
121 *K20* **Al'shany** *Rus.* Ol'shany. Brestskaya Voblasts', SW Belarus
Alsókubin *see* Dolný Kubín
120 *C9* **Alsunga** Kuldīga, W Latvia
Alt *see* Olt
94 *K9* **Alta** *Fin.* Alattio. Finnmark, N Norway
31 *T12* **Alta** Iowa, C USA
110 *I7* **Altach** Vorarlberg, W Austria
94 *K9* **Altaelva** 〰 N Norway
94 *J8* **Altafjorden** *fjord* NE Norwegian Sea
64 *K10* **Alta Gracia** Córdoba, C Argentina
44 *K11* **Alta Gracia** Rivas, SW Nicaragua
56 *H4* **Altagracia** Zulia, NW Venezuela
56 *M5* **Altagracia de Orituco** Guárico, N Venezuela
Altai *see* Altai Mountains
133 *T7* **Altai Mountains** *var.* Altai, *Chin.* Altay Shan, *Rus.* Altay. ▲▲ Asia/Europe
25 *V6* **Altamaha River** 〰 Georgia, SE USA
60 *J13* **Altamira** Pará, NE Brazil
56 *D12* **Altamira** Huila, S Colombia
44 *M13* **Altamira** Alajuela, N Costa Rica
43 *Q11* **Altamira** Tamaulipas, C Mexico
32 *L15* **Altamont** Illinois, N USA
29 *Q7* **Altamont** Kansas, C USA
34 *H16* **Altamont** Oregon, NW USA
22 *K10* **Altamont** Tennessee, S USA
25 *X11* **Altamonte Springs** Florida, SE USA
109 *O17* **Altamura** *anc.* Lupatia. Puglia, SE Italy
42 *H9* **Altamura, Isla** *island* C Mexico
168 *G7* **Altan** Dzavhan, W Mongolia
168 *G6* **Altanbulag** Dzavhan, N Mongolia
Altan Emel *see* Xin Barag Youqi
168 *J8* **Altan-Ovoo** Arhangay, C Mongolia
168 *E7* **Altanteel** Hovd, W Mongolia
42 *F3* **Altar** Sonora, NW Mexico
42 *D2* **Altar, Desierto de** *var.* Sonoran Desert. *desert* Mexico/USA *see also* Sonoran Desert
107 *Q8* **Alta, Sierra** ▲ N Spain
42 *H9* **Altata** Sinaloa, C Mexico
44 *D4* **Alta Verapaz** *off.* Departamento de Alta Verapaz. ◈ *department* C Guatemala
109 *L18* **Altavilla Silentia** Campania, S Italy
23 *T7* **Altavista** Virginia, NE USA
164 *L2* **Altay** Xinjiang Uygur Zizhiqu, NW China
168 *G5* **Altay** Dzavhan, N Mongolia
168 *G8* **Altay** Govĭ-Altay, W Mongolia
Altay *see* Altai Mountains
126 *H16* **Altay, Respublika** *var.* Gornyy Altay; *prev.* Gorno-Altayskaya Respublika. ◈ *autonomous republic* S Russian Federation
Altay Shan *see* Altai Mountains
125 *G15* **Altayskiy Kray** ◈ *territory* S Russian Federation
Altbetsche *see* Bečej
103 *L20* **Altdorf** Bayern, SE Germany
110 *G8* **Altdorf** *var.* Altorf. Uri, C Switzerland
107 *T11* **Altea** País Valenciano, E Spain
102 *L10* **Alte Elde** 〰 N Germany
103 *M16* **Altenburg** Thüringen, E Germany
Altenburg *see* Bucureşti, Romania
Altenburg *see* Baia de Criş, Romania
102 *P12* **Alte Oder** 〰 NE Germany
106 *H10* **Alter do Chão** Portalegre, C Portugal
94 *I10* **Altevatnet** ◎ N Norway
29 *V12* **Altheimer** Arkansas, C USA
111 *T9* **Althofen** Kärnten, S Austria
116 *H7* **Altimir** Oblast Montana, NW Bulgaria
142 *K11* **Altınkaya Barajı** ⊠ N Turkey
145 *S3* **Altin Köprü** *var.* Altun Kupri. N Iraq
142 *E13* **Altıntaş** Kütahya, W Turkey
59 *K18* **Altiplano** *physical region* W South America
Altkanischa *see* Kanjiža
105 *U7* **Altkirch** Haut-Rhin, NE France
Altlublau *see* Stará L'ubovňa
102 *L12* **Altmark** *cultural region* N Germany
Altmoldowa *see* Moldova Veche
27 *W8* **Alto** Texas, SW USA
106 *H11* **Alto Alentejo** *physical region* S Portugal
61 *I19* **Alto Araguaia** Mato Grosso, C Brazil
60 *L12* **Alto Bonito** Pará, NE Brazil
85 *O15* **Alto Molócuè** Zambézia, NE Mozambique
32 *K15* **Alton** Illinois, N USA
29 *W8* **Alton** Missouri, C USA
9 *X17* **Altona** Manitoba, S Canada
20 *E14* **Altoona** Pennsylvania, NE USA
32 *J6* **Altoona** Wisconsin, N USA
64 *N3* **Alto Paraguay** *off.* Departamento del Alto Paraguay. ◈ *department* N Paraguay
61 *L17* **Alto Paraíso de Goiás** Goiás, S Brazil
64 *P6* **Alto Paraná** *off.* Departamento del Alto Paraná. ◈ *department* E Paraguay
Alto Paraná *see* Paraná
61 *L15* **Alto Parnaíba** Maranhão, E Brazil
58 *H13* **Alto Purús, Río** 〰 E Peru
Altorf *see* Altdorf
65 *H19* **Alto Río Senguer** *var.* Alto Río Senguerr. Chubut, S Argentina
43 *Q13* **Altotonga** Veracruz-Llave, E Mexico
103 *N23* **Altötting** Bayern, SE Germany
Altpasua *see* Stara Pazova
168 *I5* **Altraga** Hövsgöl, N Mongolia
Alt-Schwanenburg *see* Gulbene
Altsohl *see* Zvolen
110 *I7* **Altstätten** Sankt Gallen, NE Switzerland
44 *G1* **Altun Ha** *ruins* Belize, N Belize
Altun Kupri *see* Altin Köprü
164 *D8* **Altun Shan** ▲ C China
164 *L9* **Altun Shan** *var.* Altyn Tagh. ▲▲ NW China
37 *P2* **Alturas** California, W USA
28 *K12* **Altus** Oklahoma, C USA
28 *K11* **Altus Lake** ⊠ Oklahoma, C USA
Altvater *see* Praděd
Altyn Tagh *see* Altun Shan
Alu *see* Shortland Island
al-'Ubaila *see* Al 'Ubaylah
145 *O6* **Al 'Ubaydī** W Iraq
147 *T9* **Al 'Ubaylah** *var.* al-'Ubaila. Ash Sharqīyah, E Saudi Arabia
147 *T9* **Al 'Ubaylah** *spring/well* E Saudi Arabia
Al Ubayyiḑ *see* El Obeid
147 *T7* **Al 'Udayd** *var.* Al Odaid. Abū Z̧aby, W UAE
120 *J8* **Alūksne** *Ger.* Marienburg. Alūksne, NE Latvia
146 *K6* **Al 'Ulā** Al Madīnah, NW Saudi Arabia
181 *N4* **Alula-Fartak Trench** *var.* Illaue Fartak Trench. *undersea feature* W Indian Ocean
144 *I11* **Al 'Umarī** 'Ammān, E Jordan
33 *S13* **Alum Creek Lake** ⊠ Ohio, N USA
65 *H15* **Aluminé** Neuquén, C Argentina
97 *O14* **Alunda** Uppsala, C Sweden
119 *T14* **Alupka** Respublika Krym, S Ukraine
77 *P8* **Al 'Uqaylah** N Libya
Al Uqşur *see* Luxor
Al Urdunn *see* Jordan
173 *G6* **Alur Panal** *bay* Sumatera, W Indonesia
147 *V10* **Al 'Urūq al Mu'tariḑah** *salt lake* SE Saudi Arabia
145 *Q7* **Ālūs** C Iraq
119 *T13* **Alushta** Respublika Krym, S Ukraine
77 *N11* **Al 'Uwaynāt** *var.* Al Awaynāt. SW Libya
145 *T6* **Al 'Uz̧aym** *var.* Adhaim. E Iraq
28 *L8* **Alva** Oklahoma, C USA
106 *H8* **Alva** 〰 N Portugal
97 *J18* **Älvängen** Älvsborg, S Sweden
12 *F14* **Alvanley** Ontario, S Canada
43 *S14* **Alvarado** Veracruz-Llave, E Mexico
27 *T7* **Alvarado** Texas, SW USA
60 *D13* **Alvarães** Amazonas, NW Brazil
42 *G6* **Alvaro Obregón, Presa** ⊠ W Mexico

◆ Country
● Country Capital
◇ Dependent Territory
○ Dependent Territory Capital
◈ Administrative Region
✈ International Airport
▲ Mountain
▲▲ Mountain Range
Volcano
〰 River
◎ Lake
⊠ Reservoir

96 H10 **Alvdal** Hedmark, S Norway
96 K12 **Älvdalen** Kopparberg, C Sweden
63 E15 **Alvear** Corrientes, NE Argentina
106 F10 **Alverca do Ribatejo** Lisboa, C Portugal
97 L20 **Alvesta** Kronoberg, S Sweden
96 D13 **Ålvik** Hordaland, S Norway
27 W12 **Alvin** Texas, SW USA
96 O13 **Älvkarleby** Uppsala, C Sweden
27 S5 **Alvord** Texas, SW USA
95 G18 **Älvros** Jämtland, C Sweden
97 J19 **Älvsborg** ⬖ county S Sweden
94 J13 **Älvsbyn** Norrbotten, N Sweden
148 K12 **Al Wafrā'** SE Kuwait
146 J6 **Al Wajh** Tabūk, NW Saudi Arabia
149 N16 **Al Wakrah** var. Wakra. C Qatar
144 M8 **al Walaj, Sha'īb** dry watercourse W Iraq
158 I11 **Alwar** Rājasthān, N India
147 Q5 **Al Wari'ah** Ash Sharqīyah, N Saudi Arabia
161 G22 **Alwaye** Kerala, SW India
168 K14 **Alxa Zuoqi** var. Ehen Hudag. Nei Mongol Zizhiqu, N China
Al Yaman see Yemen
144 G9 **Al Yarmūk** Irbid, N Jordan
Alyat/Alyaty-Pristan' see Ālät
117 I14 **Alykí** var. Aliki. Thásos, N Greece
121 F14 **Alytus** Pol. Olita. Alytus, S Lithuania
103 N23 **Alz** ≈ SE Germany
35 Y11 **Alzada** Montana, NW USA
126 Ii14 **Alzamay** Irkutskaya Oblast', S Russian Federation
101 M25 **Alzette** ≈ S Luxembourg
107 S10 **Alzira** var. Alcira ; anc. Saetabicula, Suero. País Valenciano, E Spain
Al Zubair see Az Zubayr
189 O8 **Amadeus, Lake** seasonal lake Northern Territory, C Australia
83 E15 **Amadi** Western Equatoria, SW Sudan
16 Nn3 **Amadjuak Lake** ◎ Baffin Island, Northwest Territories, N Canada
97 J23 **Amager** island E Denmark
170 Cc13 **Amagi** Fukuoka, Kyūshū, SW Japan
171 J17 **Amagi-san** ▲ Honshū, S Japan
175 Tt11 **Amahai** var. Masohi. Pulau Seram, E Indonesia
40 M16 **Amak Island** island Alaska, USA
170 Bb14 **Amakusa-nada** gulf Kyūshū, SW Japan
97 J16 **Åmål** Älvsborg, S Sweden
56 E8 **Amalfi** Antioquia, N Colombia
109 L18 **Amalfi** Campania, S Italy
117 D19 **Amaliáda** var. Amaliás. Dytikí Ellás, S Greece
Amaliás see Amaliáda
160 F12 **Amalner** Mahārāshtra, C India
176 X12 **Amamapare** Irian Jaya, E Indonesia
61 H21 **Amambaí, Serra de** var. Cordillera de Amambay, Serra de Amambay. ▲▲ Brazil/Paraguay see also Amambay, Cordillera de
64 P4 **Amambay** off. Departamento del Amambay. ⬖ department E Paraguay
64 P5 **Amambay, Cordillera de** var. Serra de Amambaí, Serra de Amambay. ▲▲ Brazil/Paraguay see also Amambaí, Serra de
Amambay, Serra de see Amambaí, Serra de/Amambay, Cordillera de
172 Q13 **Amami-guntō** island group SW Japan
172 Qq13 **Amami-Ō-shima** island S Japan
194 E10 **Amanab** Sandaun, NW PNG
108 J13 **Amandola** Marche, C Italy
109 N21 **Amantea** Calabria, SW Italy
203 W10 **Amanu** island Îles Tuamotu, C French Polynesia
60 J10 **Amapá** Amapá, NE Brazil
60 J11 **Amapá** off. Estado de Amapá; prev. Território de Amapá. ⬖ state NE Brazil
44 H8 **Amapala** Valle, S Honduras
Amara see Al 'Amārah
106 H6 **Amarante** Porto, N Portugal
177 G5 **Amarapura** Mandalay, C Myanmar
168 L9 **Amardalay** Dundgovĭ, C Mongolia
106 I12 **Amareleja** Beja, S Portugal
37 V11 **Amargosa Range** ▲▲ California, W USA
27 N2 **Amarillo** Texas, SW USA
Amarinthos see Amárynthos
109 K15 **Amaro, Monte** ▲ C Italy
117 H18 **Amárynthos** var. Amarinthos. Évvoia, C Greece
Amasia see Amasya
142 K12 **Amasya** anc. Amasia. Amasya, N Turkey
142 K11 **Amasya** ⬖ province N Turkey
44 F4 **Amatique, Bahía de** bay Gulf of Honduras, W Caribbean Sea
44 D6 **Amatitlán, Lago de** ◎ S Guatemala
109 J14 **Amatrice** Lazio, C Italy
202 C8 **Amatuku** atoll C Tuvalu
101 J20 **Amay** Liège, E Belgium
50 F7 **Amazon** Sp. Amazonas. ≈ Brazil/Peru
61 C14 **Amazonas** off. Estado do Amazonas. ⬖ state N Brazil
56 G15 **Amazonas** off. Comisaria del Amazonas. ⬖ province SE Colombia
58 C10 **Amazonas** off. Departamento de Amazonas. ⬖ department N Peru
56 M12 **Amazonas** off. Territorio Amazonas. ⬖ federal territory S Venezuela
Amazonas see Amazon
50 F7 **Amazon Basin** basin N South America
49 V5 **Amazon Fan** undersea feature W Atlantic Ocean
60 K11 **Amazon, Mouths of the** delta NE Brazil
197 C12 **Ambae** var. Aoba, Omba. island C Vanuatu
158 I9 **Ambāla** Haryāna, NW India
161 J26 **Ambalangoda** Southern Province, SW Sri Lanka
161 K26 **Ambalantota** Southern Province, S Sri Lanka
180 I6 **Ambalavao** Fianarantsoa, C Madagascar
56 E10 **Ambalema** Tolima, C Colombia
81 E17 **Ambam** Sud, S Cameroon
180 J2 **Ambanja** Antsirañana, N Madagascar
127 O5 **Ambarchik** Respublika Sakha (Yakutiya), NE Russian Federation
64 K9 **Ambargasta, Salinas de** salt lake C Argentina
128 J6 **Ambarnyy** Respublika Kareliya, NW Russian Federation
58 C7 **Ambato** Tungurahua, C Ecuador
180 I5 **Ambatolampy** Antananarivo, C Madagascar
180 H4 **Ambatomainty** Mahajanga, W Madagascar
180 J4 **Ambatondrazaka** Toamasina, C Madagascar
175 Ss12 **Ambelau, Pulau** see Ambelau, Pulau
103 L20 **Amberg** var. Amberg in der Oberpfalz. Bayern, SE Germany
Amberg in der Oberpfalz see Amberg
44 H1 **Ambergris Cay** island NE Belize
105 S11 **Ambérieu-en-Bugey** Ain, E France
193 I18 **Amberley** Canterbury, South Island, NZ
105 P11 **Ambert** Puy-de-Dôme, C France
Ambianum see Amiens
78 J11 **Ambidédi** Kayes, SW Mali
160 M10 **Ambikāpur** Madhya Pradesh, C India
180 J2 **Ambilobe** Antsirañana, N Madagascar
195 Q10 **Ambitle Island** island Feni Islands, NE PNG
41 O7 **Ambler** Alaska, USA
Amblève see Amel
Ambo see Hägere Hiywet
180 I8 **Amboasary** Toliara, S Madagascar
180 J4 **Ambodifotatra** var. Ambodifototra. Toamasina, E Madagascar
Amboenten see Ambunten
180 I5 **Ambohidratrimo** Antananarivo, C Madagascar
180 I6 **Ambohimahasoa** Fianarantsoa, SE Madagascar
180 K3 **Ambohitralanana** Antsirañana, NE Madagascar
176 X10 **Amboi, Kepulauan** island group E Indonesia
Amboina see Ambon
104 M8 **Amboise** Indre-et-Loire, C France
175 T11 **Ambon** prev. Amboina, Amboyna. Pulau Ambon, E Indonesia
175 T12 **Ambon, Pulau** island E Indonesia
83 I20 **Amboseli, Lake** ◎ Kenya/Tanzania
180 I6 **Ambositra** Fianarantsoa, SE Madagascar
180 I8 **Ambovombe** Toliara, S Madagascar
37 W14 **Amboy** California, W USA
32 L11 **Amboy** Illinois, N USA
Amboyna see Ambon
Ambracia see Árta
20 B14 **Ambridge** Pennsylvania, NE USA
Ambrim see Ambrym
84 A11 **Ambriz** Bengo, NW Angola
Ambrizete see N'Zeto
197 C13 **Ambrym** var. Ambrim. island C Vanuatu
174 Mm14 **Ambunten** prev. Amboenten. Pulau Madura, E Indonesia
194 G10 **Ambunti** East Sepik, NW PNG
161 I20 **Āmbūr** Tamil Nādu, SE India
40 E17 **Amchitka Island** island Aleutian Islands, Alaska, USA
40 F17 **Amchitka Pass** strait Aleutian Islands, Alaska, USA
147 R15 **'Amd** C Yemen
80 J10 **Am Dam** Ouaddaï, E Chad
176 Uu15 **Amdassa** Pulau Yamdena, E Indonesia
129 U1 **Amderma** Nenetskiy Avtonomnyy Okrug, NW Russian Federation
165 N14 **Amdo** Xizang Zizhiqu, W China
42 K13 **Ameca** Jalisco, SW Mexico
43 P14 **Amecameca** var. Amecameca de Juárez. México, C Mexico
Amecameca de Juárez see Amecameca
63 A20 **Ameghino** Buenos Aires, E Argentina
101 M21 **Amel** Fr. Amblève. Liège, E Belgium
100 K4 **Ameland** Fris. It Amelân. island Waddeneilanden, N Netherlands
Amelân, It see Ameland
109 H14 **Amelia** Umbria, C Italy
23 V6 **Amelia Court House** Virginia, NE USA
25 W8 **Amelia Island** island Florida, SE USA
20 L12 **Amenia** New York, NE USA
America see United States of America
67 M21 **America-Antarctica Ridge** undersea feature S Atlantic Ocean
America in Miniature see Maryland
62 L9 **Americana** São Paulo, S Brazil
35 Q15 **American Falls** Idaho, NW USA
35 Q15 **American Falls Reservoir** ▣ Idaho, NW USA
38 L3 **American Fork** Utah, W USA
198 D8 **American Samoa** ◇ US unincorporated territory W Polynesia
25 S6 **Americus** Georgia, SE USA
100 K12 **Amerongen** Utrecht, C Netherlands
100 K11 **Amersfoort** Utrecht, C Netherlands
99 N21 **Amersham** SE England, UK
32 I5 **Amery** Wisconsin, N USA
205 W6 **Amery Ice Shelf** ice shelf Antarctica
31 V13 **Ames** Iowa, C USA
21 P10 **Amesbury** Massachusetts, NE USA
Amestratus see Mistretta
117 F18 **Amfíkleia** var. Amfíklia. Stereá Ellás, C Greece
Amfíklia see Amfíkleia
117 D17 **Amfilochía** var. Amfilokhía. Dytikí Ellás, C Greece
Amfilokhía see Amfilochía
116 H13 **Amfípoli** anc. Amphipolis. site of ancient city Kentrikí Makedonía, NE Greece
117 F18 **Ámfissa** Stereá Ellás, C Greece
126 M11 **Amga** Respublika Sakha (Yakutiya), NE Russian Federation
126 M11 **Amga** ≈ NE Russian Federation
Amgalang see Xin Barag Zuoqi
195 N12 **Amgen** ≈ New Britain, C PNG
127 P4 **Amguema** ≈ NE Russian Federation
127 Nn14 **Amgun'** ≈ SE Russian Federation
11 P15 **Amherst** Nova Scotia, SE Canada
20 M11 **Amherst** Massachusetts, NE USA
20 D10 **Amherst** New York, NE USA
26 M4 **Amherst** Texas, SW USA
23 U6 **Amherst** Virginia, NE USA
Amherst see Kyaikkami
12 C18 **Amherstburg** Ontario, S Canada
23 Q6 **Amherstdale** West Virginia, NE USA
12 K15 **Amherst Island** island Ontario, SE Canada
Amida see Diyarbakır
30 J6 **Amidon** North Dakota, N USA
105 O3 **Amiens** anc. Ambianum, Samarobriva. Somme, N France
145 P8 **'Āmij, Wādī** var. Wadi 'Amīq. dry watercourse W Iraq
142 L17 **Amik Ovası** ◎ S Turkey
Amilḩayt, Wādī see Umm al Ḩayt, Wādī
Amíndaion/Amindeo see Amýntaio
161 C21 **Amīndīvi Islands** island group Lakshadweep, India, N Indian Ocean
145 U6 **Amīn Ḩabīb** E Iraq
85 E20 **Aminuis** Omaheke, E Namibia
'Amīq, Wadi see 'Āmij, Wādī
148 J7 **Amīrābād** Īlām, NW Iran
Amirante Bank see Amirante Ridge
181 N6 **Amirante Basin** undersea feature W Indian Ocean
181 N6 **Amirante Islands** var. Amirantes Group. island group C Seychelles
181 N7 **Amirante Ridge** var. Amirante Bank. undersea feature W Indian Ocean
Amirantes Group see Amirante Islands
181 N7 **Amirante Trench** undersea feature W Indian Ocean
176 Z12 **Amisibil** Irian Jaya, E Indonesia
9 U13 **Amisk Lake** ◎ Saskatchewan, C Canada
Amistad, Presa de la see Amistad Reservoir
27 O12 **Amistad Reservoir** var. Presa de la Amistad. ▣ Mexico/USA
Amisus see Samsun
24 K8 **Amite** var. Amite City. Louisiana, S USA
Amite City see Amite
29 T12 **Amity** Arkansas, C USA
160 H11 **Amla** prev. Amulla. Madhya Pradesh, C India
40 I17 **Amlia Island** island Aleutian Islands, Alaska, USA
99 I18 **Amlwch** NW Wales, UK
Ammaia see Portalegre
144 H10 **'Ammān** var. Amman; anc. Philadelphia, Bibl. Rabbah Ammon, Rabbath Ammon. ● (Jordan) 'Ammān, NW Jordan
144 H10 **'Ammān** off. Muḩāfaz̧at 'Ammān. ⬖ governorate NW Jordan
95 N14 **Ämmänsaari** Oulu, E Finland
94 H13 **Ammarnäs** Västerbotten, N Sweden
207 O15 **Ammassalik** var. Angmagssalik. S Greenland
103 K24 **Ammer** ≈ SE Germany
103 K24 **Ammersee** ◎ SE Germany
100 J13 **Ammerzoden** Gelderland, C Netherlands
Ammóchostos see Gazimağusa
Ammóchostos, Kólpos see Gazimağusa Körfezi
Amnok-kang see Yalu
Amoea see Portalegre
Amoentai see Amuntai
Amoerang see Amurang
149 O4 **Āmol** var. Amul. Māzandarān, N Iran
117 K21 **Amorgós** Amorgós, Kykládes, Greece, Aegean Sea
117 K22 **Amorgós** island Kykládes, Greece, Aegean Sea
25 N3 **Amory** Mississippi, S USA
10 I13 **Amos** Québec, SE Canada
97 G15 **Åmot** Buskerud, S Norway
97 E15 **Åmot** Telemark, S Norway
97 J15 **Åmotfors** Värmland, C Sweden
78 L10 **Amourj** Hodh ech Chargui, SE Mauritania
Amoy see Xiamen
180 H7 **Ampanihy** Toliara, SW Madagascar
161 L25 **Ampara** var. Amparai. Eastern Province, E Sri Lanka
180 J4 **Amparafaravola** Toamasina, E Madagascar
Amparai see Ampara
62 M9 **Amparo** São Paulo, S Brazil
180 J5 **Ampasimanolotra** Toamasina, E Madagascar
59 H17 **Ampato, Nevado** ▲ S Peru
103 L23 **Amper** ≈ SE Germany
66 M9 **Ampère Seamount** undersea feature E Atlantic Ocean
Amphipolis see Amfípoli
178 M10 **Amphitrite Group** island group N Paracel Islands
176 U15 **Amplawas** var. Emplawas. Pulau Babar, E Indonesia
107 U7 **Amposta** Cataluña, NE Spain
13 V7 **Amqui** Québec, SE Canada
147 O14 **'Amrān** W Yemen
Amraoti see Amrāvati
160 H12 **Amrāvati** prev. Amraoti. Mahārāshtra, C India
160 C11 **Amreli** Gujarāt, W India
110 H6 **Amriswil** Thurgau, NE Switzerland
144 H5 **'Amrīt** ruins Ţarţūs, W Syria
158 H7 **Amritsar** Punjab, N India
158 J10 **Amroha** Uttar Pradesh, N India
102 G7 **Amrum** island NW Germany
95 I15 **Åmsele** Västerbotten, N Sweden
100 I10 **Amstelveen** Noord-Holland, C Netherlands
100 I10 **Amsterdam** ● (Netherlands) Noord-Holland, C Netherlands
20 K10 **Amsterdam** New York, NE USA
181 Q11 **Amsterdam Fracture Zone** tectonic feature S Indian Ocean
181 R11 **Amsterdam Island** island NE French Southern and Antarctic Territories
111 U4 **Amstetten** Niederösterreich, N Austria
80 J11 **Am Timan** Salamat, SE Chad
152 L12 **Amu-Bukhoro Kanali** var. Aral-Bukhorskiy Kanal. canal C Uzbekistan
145 O1 **'Āmūdah** var. Amude. Al Ḩasakah, N Syria
152 M14 **Amu-Dar'ya** Lebapskiy Velayat, NE Turkmenistan
153 O15 **Amu Darya** Rus. Amudar'ya, Taj. Dar"yoi Amu, Turkm. Amyderya, Uzb. Amudaryo; anc. Oxus. ≈ C Asia
Amudar'ya/Amudaryo/Amu, Dar"yoi see Amu Darya
Amude see 'Āmūdah
146 L3 **'Amūd, Jabal al** ▲ NW Saudi Arabia
40 J17 **Amukta Island** island Aleutian Islands, Alaska, USA
40 I17 **Amukta Pass** strait Aleutian Islands, Alaska, USA
Amul see Āmol
Amulla see Amla
Amundsen Basin see Fram Basin
205 X3 **Amundsen Bay** bay Antarctica
205 P10 **Amundsen Coast** physical region Antarctica
15 H2 **Amundsen Gulf** gulf Northwest Territories, N Canada
199 Ll16 **Amundsen Plain** undersea feature S Pacific Ocean
205 Q9 **Amundsen-Scott** US research station Antarctica
204 J11 **Amundsen Sea** sea S Pacific Ocean
96 M12 **Amungen** ◎ C Sweden
175 N10 **Amuntai** prev. Amoentai. Borneo, C Indonesia
133 W6 **Amur** Chin. Heilong Jiang. ≈ China/Russian Federation
175 Rr7 **Amurang** prev. Amoerang. Sulawesi, C Indonesia
175 Rr7 **Amurang, Teluk** bay Sulawesi, C Indonesia
107 O3 **Amurrio** País Vasco, N Spain
127 Nn15 **Amursk** Khabarovskiy Kray, SE Russian Federation
126 M14 **Amurskaya Oblast'** ⬖ province SE Russian Federation
82 G7 **'Amur, Wadi** ≈ NE Sudan
117 C17 **Amvrakikós Kólpos** gulf W Greece
Amvrosiyevka see Amvrosiyivka
119 X8 **Amvrosiyivka** Rus. Amvrosiyevka. Donets'ka Oblast', SE Ukraine
Amyderya see Amu Darya
116 E13 **Amýntaio** var. Amindeo; prev. Amíndaion. Dytikí Makedonía, N Greece
12 B6 **Amyot** Ontario, S Canada
203 U10 **Anaa** atoll Îles Tuamotu, C French Polynesia
Anabanoea see Anabanua
175 Pp12 **Anabanua** prev. Anabanoea. Sulawesi, C Indonesia
201 R8 **Anabar** NE Nauru
126 K7 **Anabar** ≈ NE Russian Federation
An Abhainn Mhór see Blackwater
57 O6 **Anaco** Anzoátegui, NE Venezuela
35 Q10 **Anaconda** Montana, NW USA
34 H7 **Anacortes** Washington, NW USA
28 M11 **Anadarko** Oklahoma, C USA
116 N12 **Ana Dere** ≈ NW Turkey
106 G8 **Anadia** Aveiro, N Portugal
Anadolu Dağları see Doğu Karadeniz Dağları
127 Pp5 **Anadyr'** Chukotskiy Avtonomnyy Okrug, NE Russian Federation
127 P5 **Anadyr'** ≈ NE Russian Federation
Anadyr, Gulf of see Anadyrskiy Zaliv
133 X4 **Anadyrskiy Khrebet** var. Chukot Range. ▲▲ NE Russian Federation
127 Q4 **Anadyrskiy Zaliv** Eng. Gulf of Anadyr. gulf NE Russian Federation
117 K22 **Anáfi** anc. Anaphe. island Kykládes, Greece, Aegean Sea
109 J15 **Anagni** Lazio, C Italy
'Ānah see 'Annah
37 T15 **Anaheim** California, W USA
8 L15 **Anahim Lake** British Columbia, SW Canada
40 B8 **Anahola** Kauai, Hawaii, USA, C Pacific Ocean
27 X11 **Anahuac** Texas, SW USA
43 O7 **Anáhuac** Nuevo León, NE Mexico
161 G22 **Anai Mudi** ▲ S India
Anaiza see 'Unayzah
161 M15 **Anakāpalle** Andhra Pradesh, E India
203 W15 **Anakena, Playa de** beach Easter Island, Chile, E Pacific Ocean
41 Q7 **Anaktuvuk Pass** Alaska, USA
41 Q6 **Anaktuvuk River** ≈ Alaska, USA
180 J3 **Analalava** Mahajanga, NW Madagascar
46 F6 **Ana Maria, Golfo de** gulf C Cuba
Anambas Islands see Anambas, Kepulauan
174 Ii5 **Anambas, Kepulauan** var. Anambas Islands island group W Indonesia
79 U17 **Anambra** ⬖ state SE Nigeria
31 N4 **Anamoose** North Dakota, N USA
31 Y13 **Anamosa** Iowa, C USA
142 H17 **Anamur** İçel, S Turkey
142 H17 **Anamur Burnu** headland S Turkey
170 Ff16 **Anan** Tokushima, Shikoku, SW Japan
160 O12 **Ānandadur** Orissa, E India
161 H18 **Anantapur** Andhra Pradesh, S India
158 H5 **Anantnāg** var. Islamabad. Jammu and Kashmir, NW India
Ananyev see Anan'yiv
119 O9 **Anan'yiv** Rus. Ananyev. Odes'ka Oblast', SW Ukraine
130 J14 **Anapa** Krasnodarskiy Kray, SW Russian Federation
Anaphe see Anáfi
61 K18 **Anápolis** Goiás, C Brazil
149 R10 **Anār** Kermān, C Iran
Anár see Inari
149 P7 **Anārak** Eşfahān, C Iran
Anar Dara see Anār Darreh
154 J7 **Anār Darreh** var. Anar Dara. Farāh, W Afghanistan
Anárjohka see Inarijoki
25 X9 **Anastasia Island** island Florida, SE USA
196 K7 **Anatahan** island C Northern Mariana Islands
132 M6 **Anatolia** plateau C Turkey
88 F14 **Anatolian Plate** tectonic feature Asia/Europe
116 H13 **Anatolikí Makedonía kai Thráki** Eng. Macedonia East and Thrace. ⬖ region NE Greece
197 D17 **Anatom** var. Aneityum; prev. Kéamu. island S Vanuatu
64 L8 **Añatuya** Santiago del Estero, N Argentina
An Baile Meánach see Ballymena
An Bhearú see Barrow
An Bhóinn see Boyne
An Blascaod Mór see Great Blasket Island
An Cabhán see Cavan
An Caisleán Nua see Newcastle
An Caisleán Riabhach see Castlereagh, Northern Ireland, UK
An Caisleán Riabhach see Castlerea, Ireland
58 C13 **Ancash** off. Departamento de Ancash. ⬖ department W Peru
An Cathair see Caher
104 J8 **Ancenis** Loire-Atlantique, NW France
An Chanáil Ríoga see Royal Canal
An Cheacha see Caha Mountains
41 R11 **Anchorage** Alaska, USA
41 R12 **Anchorage** ✈ Alaska, USA
41 Q13 **Anchor Point** Alaska, USA
An Chorr Chríochach see Cookstown
67 M24 **Anchorstack Point** headland W Tristan da Cunha
An Clár see Clare
An Clochán see Clifden
An Clochán Liath see Dunglow
25 U12 **Anclote Keys** island group Florida, SE USA
An Cóbh see Cobh
59 J17 **Ancohuma, Nevado de** ▲ W Bolivia
An Comar see Comber
59 D14 **Ancón** Lima, W Peru
108 J12 **Ancona** Marche, C Italy
Ancuabe see Ancuabi
84 Q13 **Ancuabi** var. Ancuabe. Cabo Delgado, NE Mozambique
65 F17 **Ancud** prev. San Carlos de Ancud. Los Lagos, S Chile
65 G17 **Ancud, Golfo de** gulf S Chile
Ancyra see Ankara
169 V8 **Anda** Heilongjiang, NE China
59 G16 **Andahuaylas** Apurímac, S Peru
An Daingean see Dingle
159 R15 **Andāl** West Bengal, NE India
96 E9 **Åndalsnes** Møre og Romsdal, S Norway
106 K13 **Andalucía** Eng. Andalusia. ⬖ autonomous community S Spain
25 P7 **Andalusia** Alabama, S USA
Andalusia see Andalucía
157 Q21 **Andaman and Nicobar Islands** var. Andamans and Nicobars. ⬖ union territory India, NE Indian Ocean
181 T4 **Andaman Basin** undersea feature NE Indian Ocean
157 P19 **Andaman Islands** island group India, NE Indian Ocean
181 T4 **Andaman Sea** sea NE Indian Ocean
59 K19 **Andamarca** Oruro, C Bolivia
176 V10 **Andamata** Irian Jaya, E Indonesia
190 H5 **Andamooka** South Australia
147 Y9 **'Andām, Wādī** seasonal river NE Oman
180 J3 **Andapa** Antsirañana, NE Madagascar
155 R4 **Andarāb** var. Banow. Baghlān, NE Afghanistan
Andarbag see Andarbogh
153 S13 **Andarbogh** Rus. Andarbag, Anderbak. S Tajikistan
111 Z5 **Andau** Burgenland, E Austria
Andaung Pech see Bâ Kêv
110 I10 **Andeer** Graubünden, S Switzerland
94 H9 **Andenes** Nordland, C Norway
101 J20 **Andenne** Namur, SE Belgium
79 S11 **Andéramboukane** Gao, E Mali
Anderbak see Andarbogh
101 G18 **Anderlecht** Brussels, C Belgium
101 G21 **Anderlues** Hainaut, S Belgium
110 G9 **Andermatt** Uri, C Switzerland
103 E17 **Andernach** anc. Antunnacum. Rheinland-Pfalz, SW Germany
196 D15 **Andersen Air Force Base** air base NE Guam
41 R9 **Anderson** Alaska, USA
37 N4 **Anderson** California, W USA
33 P13 **Anderson** Indiana, N USA
29 R8 **Anderson** Missouri, C USA
23 P11 **Anderson** South Carolina, SE USA
27 V10 **Anderson** Texas, SW USA
15 Gg3 **Anderson** ≈ Northwest Territories, NW Canada
97 K20 **Anderstorp** Jönköping, S Sweden
56 D9 **Andes** Antioquia, W Colombia
49 P7 **Andes** ▲▲ W South America
31 P12 **Andes, Lake** ◎ South Dakota, N USA
94 H9 **Andfjorden** fjord E Norwegian Sea
161 H16 **Andhra Pradesh** ⬖ state E India
100 J8 **Andijk** Noord-Holland, NW Netherlands
153 S10 **Andijon** Rus. Andizhan. Andijon Wiloyati, E Uzbekistan
153 S10 **Andijon Wiloyati** Rus. Andizhanskaya Oblast'. ⬖ province E Uzbekistan
Andikíthira see Antikýthira
180 J4 **Andilamena** Toamasina, C Madagascar
148 L8 **Andīmeshk** var. Andimishk; prev. Salehābād. Khūzestān, SW Iran
Andimishk see Andīmeshk
Andipáros see Antíparos
Andipaxi see Antípaxoi
Andípsara see Antípsara
142 L16 **Andırın** Kahramanmaraş, S Turkey
164 J8 **Andirlangar** Xinjiang Uygur Zizhiqu, NW China
Andírrion see Antírrio
Ándissa see Ántissa
Andizhan see Andijon
Andizhanskaya Oblast' see Andijon Wiloyati
155 N2 **Andkhvoy** Fāryāb, N Afghanistan
107 Q2 **Andoain** País Vasco, N Spain
176 W9 **Andoi** Irian Jaya, E Indonesia
169 Y15 **Andong** Jap. Antō. E South Korea
111 R4 **Andorf** Oberösterreich, N Austria
107 S7 **Andorra** Aragón, NE Spain
107 V4 **Andorra** off. Principality of Andorra, Cat. Valls d'Andorra, Fr. Vallée d'Andorre. ◆ monarchy SW Europe
Andorra see Andorra la Vella
107 V4 **Andorra la Vella** var. Andorra, Fr. Andorre la Vielle, Sp. Andorra la Vieja. ● (Andorra) C Andorra
Andorra la Vieja see Andorra la Vella
Andorra, Valls d'/Andorre, Vallée d' see Andorra
Andorre la Vielle see Andorra la Vella
99 M22 **Andover** S England, UK
29 N6 **Andover** Kansas, C USA
94 G10 **Andøya** island C Norway
62 I8 **Andradina** São Paulo, S Brazil
Andraitx see Andratx
41 N10 **Andreafsky River** ≈ Alaska, USA
40 H17 **Andreanof Islands** island group Aleutian Islands, Alaska, USA
128 H16 **Andreapol'** Tverskaya Oblast', W Russian Federation
Andreas, Cape see Zafer Burnu
Andreevka see Andreyevka
23 N10 **Andrews** North Carolina, SE USA
23 T13 **Andrews** South Carolina, SE USA
26 M7 **Andrews** Texas, SW USA
181 N5 **Andrew Tablemount** var. Gora Andryu. undersea feature W Indian Ocean
151 W13 **Andreyevka** Kaz. Andreevka. Taldykorgan, SW Kazakhstan
109 N17 **Andria** Puglia, SE Italy
115 K16 **Andrijevica** Montenegro, SW Yugoslavia
117 E20 **Andrítsaina** Pelopónnisos, S Greece
An Droichead Nua see Newbridge
Androna see Khirbat al Andarīn
Andropov see Rybinsk
117 J19 **Ándros** Ándros, Kykládes, Greece, Aegean Sea
117 J20 **Ándros** island Kykládes, Greece, Aegean Sea
21 O7 **Androscoggin River** ≈ Maine/New Hampshire, NE USA
46 F3 **Andros Island** island NW Bahamas
131 R7 **Androsovka** Samarskaya Oblast', W Russian Federation
46 G3 **Andros Town** Andros Island, NW Bahamas
161 D21 **Āndrott Island** island Lakshadweep, India, N Indian Ocean
119 N5 **Andrushivka** Zhytomyrs'ka Oblast', N Ukraine
113 K17 **Andrychów** Bielsko-Biała, S Poland
Andryu, Gora see Andrew Tablemount
94 I10 **Andselv** Troms, N Norway
81 O17 **Andudu** Haut-Zaïre, NE Zaire
107 N13 **Andújar** anc. Illiturgis. Andalucía, SW Spain
84 C12 **Andulo** Bié, W Angola
105 Q14 **Anduze** Gard, S France
An Earagail see Errigal
97 L19 **Aneby** Jönköping, S Sweden
Anécho see Aného
79 Q9 **Anéfis** Kidal, NE Mali
47 U8 **Anegada** island NE British Virgin Islands
63 B25 **Anegada, Bahía** bay E Argentina
47 U9 **Anegada Passage** passage Anguilla/British Virgin Islands
79 R17 **Aného** var. Anécho; prev. Petit-Popo. S Togo
Aneityum see Anatom
119 N10 **Anenii Noi** Rus. Novyye Aneny. C Moldova
194 L12 **Anepmete** New Britain, E PNG
107 U4 **Aneto** ▲ NE Spain
Änew see Annau
Änewetak see Enewetak Atoll
79 Y8 **Aney** Agadez, NE Niger
An Fheoir see Nore
126 Ii13 **Angara** ≈ C Russian Federation
126 J15 **Angarsk** Irkutskaya Oblast', S Russian Federation
95 G17 **Ånge** Västernorrland, C Sweden
Angel see Úhlava
42 D4 **Ángel de la Guarda, Isla** island NW Mexico
179 P10 **Angeles** off. Angeles City. Luzon, N Philippines
Angeles City see Angeles
Angel Falls see Ángel, Salto
97 J22 **Ängelholm** Kristianstad, S Sweden
63 A17 **Angélica** Santa Fe, C Argentina
27 W8 **Angelina River** ≈ Texas, SW USA
57 Q9 **Ángel, Salto** Eng. Angel Falls. waterfall E Venezuela
97 M15 **Ängelsberg** Västmanland, C Sweden
37 P8 **Angels Camp** California, W USA
111 W7 **Anger** Steiermark, SE Austria
Angerapp see Ozersk
Angerburg see Węgorzewo
95 H15 **Ångermanälven** ≈ N Sweden
102 P11 **Angermünde** Brandenburg, NE Germany
104 K7 **Angers** anc. Juliomagus. Maine-et-Loire, NW France
13 W7 **Angers** ≈ Québec, SE Canada
95 J16 **Ängesön** island N Sweden
Angistro see Ágkistro
116 H13 **Angítis** ≈ NE Greece
178 J14 **Ângk Tasaôm** prev. Angtassom. Takêv, S Cambodia
193 C25 **Anglem, Mount** ▲ Stewart Island, Southland, SW NZ
99 I18 **Anglesey** cultural region NW Wales, UK
99 I18 **Anglesey** island NW Wales, UK
104 I15 **Anglet** Pyrénées-Atlantiques, SW France
27 W12 **Angleton** Texas, SW USA
Anglia see England
12 H9 **Angliers** Québec, SE Canada
Anglo-Egyptian Sudan see Sudan
Angmagssalik see Ammassalik
178 Ii8 **Ang Nam Ngum** ◎ C Laos
81 N16 **Ango** Haut-Zaïre, N Zaire
85 Q15 **Angoche** Nampula, E Mozambique
65 G14 **Angol** Araucanía, C Chile
33 Q11 **Angola** Indiana, N USA
84 A9 **Angola** off. Republic of Angola; prev. People's Republic of Angola, Portuguese West Africa. ◆ republic SW Africa
67 P15 **Angola Basin** undersea feature E Atlantic Ocean
41 X13 **Angoon** Admiralty Island, Alaska, USA
153 O14 **Angor** Surkhondaryo Wiloyati, S Uzbekistan
Angora see Ankara
194 H10 **Angoram** East Sepik, NW PNG
42 H8 **Angostura** Sinaloa, C Mexico
Angostura see Ciudad Bolívar
43 U17 **Angostura, Presa de la** ▣ SE Mexico
30 J11 **Angostura Reservoir** ▣ South Dakota, N USA
104 L11 **Angoulême** anc. Iculisma. Charente, W France
104 K11 **Angoumois** cultural region W France
66 O2 **Angra do Heroísmo** Terceira, Azores, Portugal, NE Atlantic Ocean

◆ Country
● Country Capital
◇ Dependent Territory
○ Dependent Territory Capital
⬖ Administrative Region
✈ International Airport
▲ Mountain
▲▲ Mountain Range
⛰ Volcano
≈ River
◎ Lake
▣ Reservoir

62 O10 **Angra dos Reis** Rio de Janeiro, SE Brazil
Angra Pequena *see* Lüderitz
153 Q10 **Angren** Toshkent Wiloyati, E Uzbekistan
Angtassom *see* Ângk Tasaôm
178 Hh11 **Ang Thong** *var.* Angthong. Ang Thong, C Thailand
81 M16 **Angu** Haut-Zaïre, N Zaire
107 S5 **Angües** Aragón, NE Spain
47 U9 **Anguilla** ◇ *UK dependent territory* E West Indies
47 V9 **Anguilla** *island* E West Indies
46 F4 **Anguilla Cays** *islets* SW Bahamas
Angul *see* Anugul
167 N1 **Anguli Nur** ◎ E China
81 O18 **Angumu** Haut-Zaïre, E Zaire
12 G14 **Angus** Ontario, S Canada
98 J10 **Angus** *cultural region* E Scotland, UK
61 K19 **Anhangüera** Goiás, S Brazil
101 I21 **Anhée** Namur, S Belgium
97 I21 **Anholt** *island* C Denmark
166 M11 **Anhua** *prev.* Dongping. Hunan, S China
167 P8 **Anhui** *var.* Anhui Sheng, Anhwei, Wan. ◈ *province* E China
Anhui Sheng/Anhwei *see* Anhui
41 O11 **Aniak** Alaska, USA
41 O12 **Aniak River** ≈ Alaska, USA
An Iarmhí *see* Westmeath
201 R8 **Anibare** E Nauru
201 R8 **Anibare Bay** *bay* E Nauru, W Pacific Ocean
Anicium *see* le Puy
117 K22 **Ánidro** *island* Kykládes, Greece, Aegean Sea
79 R15 **Anié** C Togo
79 Q15 **Anié** ≈ C Togo
104 J16 **Anie, Pic d'** ▲ SW France
131 Y7 **Anikhovka** Orenburgskaya Oblast', W Russian Federation
12 G9 **Anima Nipissing Lake** ◎ Ontario, S Canada
39 O16 **Animas** New Mexico, SW USA
39 P16 **Animas Peak** ▲ New Mexico, SW USA
39 P16 **Animas Valley** *valley* New Mexico, SW USA
118 F13 **Anina** *Ger.* Steierdorf, *Hung.* Stájerlakanina; *prev.* Ştaierdorf-Anina, Steierdorf-Anina, Steyerlak-Anina. Caraş-Severin, SW Romania
31 U14 **Anita** Iowa, C USA
127 Oo16 **Aniva, Mys** *headland* Ostrov Sakhalin, SE Russian Federation
127 Oo16 **Aniva, Zaliv** *bay* SE Russian Federation
197 E16 **Aniwa** *island* S Vanuatu
95 M19 **Anjalankoski** Kymi, S Finland
'Anjar *see* Aanjar
Anjiangying *see* Luanping
12 B8 **Anjigami Lake** ◎ Ontario, S Canada
171 Hh16 **Anjō** *var.* Anzyô. Aichi, Honshū, SW Japan
104 J8 **Anjou** *cultural region* NW France
180 I13 **Anjouan** *var.* Nzwani, Johanna Island. *island* SE Comoros
180 J4 **Anjozorobe** Antananarivo, C Madagascar
169 W13 **Anju** W North Korea
100 M5 **Anjum** *Fris.* Eanjum. Friesland, N Netherlands
180 G6 **Ankaboa, Tanjona** *headland* W Madagascar
166 L7 **Ankang** *prev.* Xing'an. Shaanxi, C China
142 I12 **Ankara** *prev.* Angora, *anc.* Ancyra. ● (Turkey) Ankara, C Turkey
142 H12 **Ankara** ◈ *province* C Turkey
97 N19 **Ankarsrum** Kalmar, S Sweden
180 H6 **Ankazoabo** Toliara, SW Madagascar
180 I4 **Ankazobe** Antananarivo, C Madagascar
31 V14 **Ankeny** Iowa, C USA
178 Kk11 **An Khê** Gia Lai, C Vietnam
102 O9 **Anklam** Mecklenburg-Vorpommern, NE Germany
82 K13 **Ānkober** C Ethiopia
79 O17 **Ankobra** ≈ S Ghana
81 N22 **Ankoro** Shaba, SE Zaire
101 L24 **Anlier, Forêt d'** *forest* SE Belgium
166 I13 **Anlong** Guizhou, S China
An Longfort *see* Longford
178 Ii11 **Ânlong Vêng** Siĕmréab, NW Cambodia
An Lorgain *see* Lurgan
167 N8 **Anlu** Hubei, C China
An Mhí *see* Meath
An Mhuir Cheilteach *see* Celtic Sea
An Muileann gCearr *see* Mullingar
95 F16 **Ånn** Jämtland, C Sweden
130 M8 **Anna** Voronezhskaya Oblast', W Russian Federation
32 L17 **Anna** Illinois, N USA
27 U5 **Anna** Texas, SW USA
76 L5 **Annaba** *prev.* Bône. NE Algeria
An Nabatīyah at Taḥtā *see* Nabatîyé
103 N17 **Annaberg-Buchholz** Sachsen, E Germany
111 T9 **Annabichl** ✕ (Klagenfurt) Kärnten, S Austria
146 M5 **An Nafūd** *desert* NW Saudi Arabia
145 P6 **'Annah** *var.* 'Ānah. NW Iraq
145 P6 **An Nāḩiyah** W Iraq
145 T10 **An Najaf** *var.* Najaf. S Iraq
23 V5 **Anna, Lake** ⊠ Virginia, NE USA
99 F16 **Annalee** ≈ N Ireland
178 Jj9 **Annamitique, Chaîne** ▲▲ C Laos
99 J14 **Annan** S Scotland, UK
31 U8 **Annandale** Minnesota, N USA
23 W4 **Annandale** Virginia, NE USA
201 Q7 **Anna Point** *headland* N Nauru
23 X3 **Annapolis** *state capital* Maryland, NE USA
196 A10 **Anna, Pulo** *island* S Palau
159 O10 **Annapurna** ▲ C Nepal
An Nāqūrah *see* En Nâqoûra
33 R10 **Ann Arbor** Michigan, N USA
An Nás *see* Naas
145 W12 **An Nāşirīyah** *var.* Nasiriya. SE Iraq
145 W11 **An Naşr** E Iraq
152 F13 **Annau** *Turkm.* Änew. Akhalskiy Velayat, C Turkmenistan
123 Mm16 **An Nawfalīyah** *var.* Al Nūwfalīyah. N Libya
21 P10 **Ann, Cape** *headland* Massachusetts, NE USA
188 I10 **Annean, Lake** ◎ Western Australia
Anneciacum *see* Annecy
105 T11 **Annecy** *anc.* Anneciacum. Haute-Savoie, E France
105 T11 **Annecy, Lac d'** ◎ E France
105 T10 **Annemasse** Haute-Savoie, E France
41 Z14 **Annette Island** *island* Alexander Archipelago, Alaska, USA
An Nhon *see* Binh Đinh
An Nīl al Abyaḑ *see* White Nile
An Nīl al Azraq *see* Blue Nile
25 Q3 **Anniston** Alabama, S USA
81 A19 **Annobón** *island* W Equatorial Guinea
105 R12 **Annonay** Ardèche, E France
46 K12 **Annotto Bay** C Jamaica
147 R5 **An Nu'ayrīyah** *var.* Narıya. Ash Sharqīyah, NE Saudi Arabia
190 M9 **Annuello** Victoria, SE Australia
145 Q10 **An Nukhayb** S Iraq
145 U9 **An Nu'mānīyah** E Iraq
Áno Arkhánai *see* Epáno Archánes
117 J25 **Anógeia** *var.* Anogia, Anóyia. Kríti, Greece, E Mediterranean Sea
Anogia *see* Anógeia
31 V8 **Anoka** Minnesota, N USA
An Ómaigh *see* Omagh
180 I1 **Anorontany, Tanjona** *headland* N Madagascar
180 J5 **Anosibe An'Ala** Toamasina, E Madagascar
Anóyia *see* Anógeia
An Pointe *see* Warrenpoint
167 P9 **Anqing** Anhui, E China
167 Q5 **Anqiu** Shandong, E China
An Ráth *see* Ráthluirc
An Ribhéar *see* Kenmare River
An Ros *see* Rush
101 K19 **Ans** Liège, E Belgium
Anşāb *see* Nişāb
176 Ww10 **Ansas** Irian Jaya, E Indonesia
103 J20 **Ansbach** Bayern, SE Germany
An Sciobairín *see* Skibbereen
An Scoil *see* Skull
An Seancheann *see* Old Head of Kinsale
47 Y5 **Anse-Bertrand** Grande Terre, N Guadeloupe
180 H17 **Anse Boileau** Mahé, NE Seychelles
47 S11 **Anse La Raye** NW Saint Lucia
56 D9 **Anserma** Caldas, W Colombia
111 T4 **Ansfelden** Oberösterreich, N Austria
169 U12 **Anshan** Liaoning, NE China
166 J12 **Anshun** Guizhou, S China
63 F17 **Ansina** Tacuarembó, C Uruguay
31 O15 **Ansley** Nebraska, C USA
27 P6 **Anson** Texas, SW USA
79 Q10 **Ansongo** Gao, E Mali
An Srath Bán *see* Strabane
23 R5 **Ansted** West Virginia, NE USA
176 Yy10 **Ansudu** Irian Jaya, E Indonesia
59 G15 **Anta** Cusco, S Peru
59 G16 **Antabamba** Apurímac, C Peru
Antafalva *see* Kovačica
142 L17 **Antakya** *anc.* Antioch, Antiochia. Hatay, S Turkey
180 K3 **Antalaha** Antsirañana, NE Madagascar
142 F17 **Antalya** *prev.* Adalia, *anc.* Attaleia, *Bibl.* Attalia. Antalya, SW Turkey
142 F17 **Antalya** ◈ *province* SW Turkey
142 F16 **Antalya** ✕ Antalya, SW Turkey
124 Qq11 **Antalya Basin** *undersea feature* E Mediterranean Sea
Antalya, Gulf of *see* Antalya Körfezi
142 F16 **Antalya Körfezi** *var.* Gulf of Adalia, *Eng.* Gulf of Antalya. *gulf* SW Turkey
180 J5 **Antanambao Manampotsy** Toamasina, E Madagascar
180 I5 **Antananarivo** *prev.* Tananarive. ● (Madagascar) Antananarivo, C Madagascar
180 I4 **Antananarivo** ◈ *province* C Madagascar
180 J5 **Antananarivo** ✕ Antananarivo, C Madagascar
An tAonach *see* Nenagh
204-205 **Antarctica** *continent*
204 I5 **Antarctic Peninsula** *peninsula* Antarctica
63 J15 **Antas, Rio das** ≈ S Brazil
201 U16 **Ant Atoll** *atoll* Caroline Islands, E Micronesia
An Teampall Mór *see* Templemore
Antep *see* Gaziantep
106 M15 **Antequera** *anc.* Anticaria, Antiquaria. Andalucía, S Spain
Antequera *see* Oaxaca
39 S5 **Antero Reservoir** ⊠ Colorado, C USA
28 M7 **Anthony** Kansas, C USA
39 R16 **Anthony** New Mexico, SW USA
190 D5 **Anthony, Lake** *salt lake* South Australia
76 E8 **Anti-Atlas** ▲▲ SW Morocco
105 U15 **Antibes** *anc.* Antipolis. Alpes-Maritimes, SE France
105 U15 **Antibes, Cap d'** *headland* SE France
Anticaria *see* Antequera
11 Q11 **Anticosti, Île d'** *Eng.* Anticosti Island. *island* Québec, E Canada
Anticosti Island *see* Anticosti, Île d'
104 K3 **Antifer, Cap d'** *headland* N France
32 L6 **Antigo** Wisconsin, N USA
11 Q15 **Antigonish** Nova Scotia, SE Canada
66 P11 **Antigua** Fuerteventura, Islas Canarias, NE Atlantic Ocean
47 X10 **Antigua** *island* S Antigua and Barbuda, Leeward Islands
Antigua *see* Antigua Guatemala
47 W9 **Antigua and Barbuda** ◆ *commonwealth republic* E West Indies
44 C6 **Antigua Guatemala** *var.* Antigua. Sacatepéquez, SW Guatemala
43 P11 **Antiguo Morelos** *var.* Antiguo-Morelos. Tamaulipas, C Mexico
117 F19 **Antíkyras, Kólpos** *gulf* C Greece
117 G24 **Antikýthira** *var.* Andikíthira. *island* S Greece
144 I7 **Anti-Lebanon** *var.* Jebel esh Sharqi, *Ar.* Al Jabal ash Sharqī, *Fr.* Anti-Liban. ▲▲ Lebanon/Syria
Anti-Liban *see* Anti-Lebanon
117 I22 **Antímilos** *island* Kykládes, Greece, Aegean Sea
38 L6 **Antimony** Utah, W USA
An tInbhear Mór *see* Arklow
32 M10 **Antioch** Illinois, N USA
Antioch *see* Antakya
104 I10 **Antioche, Pertuis d'** *inlet* W France
Antiochia *see* Antakya
56 D8 **Antioquia** Antioquia, C Colombia
56 E8 **Antioquia** *off.* Departamento de Antioquia. ◈ *province* C Colombia
117 J21 **Antíparos** *var.* Andipáros. *island* Kykládes, Greece, Aegean Sea
117 B17 **Antípaxoi** *var.* Andipaxi. *island* Iónioi Nísoi, Greece, C Mediterranean Sea
126 H7 **Antipayuta** Yamalo-Nenetskiy Avtonomnyy Okrug, N Russian Federation
199 J14 **Antipodes Islands** *island group* S NZ
Antipolis *see* Antibes
117 J18 **Antípsara** *var.* Andípsara. *island* E Greece
Antiquaria *see* Antequera
13 N10 **Antique, Lac** ◎ Québec, SE Canada
117 E18 **Antírrio** *var.* Andírrion. Dytikí Ellás, C Greece
117 K16 **Ántissa** *var.* Ándissa. Lésvos, E Greece
An tIúr *see* Newry
Antivari *see* Bar
58 C6 **Antizana** ▲ N Ecuador
29 Q13 **Antlers** Oklahoma, C USA
95 J14 **Antnäs** Norrbotten, N Sweden
Antō *see* Andong
64 G5 **Antofagasta** Antofagasta, N Chile
64 G6 **Antofagasta** *off.* Región de Antofagasta. ◈ *region* N Chile
64 I7 **Antofalla, Salar de** *salt lake* NW Argentina
101 D20 **Antoing** Hainaut, SW Belgium
26 M5 **Anton** Texas, SW USA
45 S16 **Antón** Coclé, C Panama
39 T11 **Anton Chico** New Mexico, SW USA
62 K12 **Antonina** Paraná, S Brazil
105 O5 **Antony** Hauts-de-Seine, N France
Antratsit *see* Antratsyt
119 Y8 **Antratsyt** *Rus.* Antratsit. Luhans'ka Oblast', E Ukraine
99 G15 **Antrim** *Ir.* Aontroim. NE Northern Ireland, UK
99 G14 **Antrim** *Ir.* Aontroim. *cultural region* NE Northern Ireland, UK
99 G14 **Antrim Mountains** ▲▲ NE Northern Ireland, UK
180 H5 **Antsalova** Mahajanga, W Madagascar
Antserana *see* Antsirañana
An tSionainn *see* Shannon
180 J2 **Antsirañana** *var.* Antserana; *prev.* Antsirane, Diégo-Suarez. Antsirañana, N Madagascar
180 J2 **Antsirañana** ◈ *province* N Madagascar
Antsirane *see* Antsirañana
An tSiúir *see* Suir
120 I7 **Antsla** *Ger.* Anzen. Võrumaa, SE Estonia
An tSláine *see* Slaney
180 J3 **Antsohihy** Mahajanga, NW Madagascar
65 G14 **Antuco, Volcán** ▲ C Chile
175 P7 **Antu, Gunung** ▲ Borneo, N Indonesia
An Tullach *see* Tullow
An-tung *see* Dandong
Antunnacum *see* Andernach
Antwerp *see* Antwerpen
101 G16 **Antwerpen** *Eng.* Antwerp, *Fr.* Anvers. Antwerpen, N Belgium
101 H16 **Antwerpen** *Eng.* Antwerp. ◈ *province* N Belgium
An Uaimh *see* Navan
160 N12 **Anugul** *var.* Angul. Orissa, E India
158 F9 **Anūpgarh** Rājasthān, NW India
160 K10 **Anūppur** Madhya Pradesh, C India
161 K24 **Anuradhapura** North Central Province, C Sri Lanka
Anvers *see* Antwerpen
204 G4 **Anvers Island** *island* Antarctica
41 N11 **Anvik** Alaska, USA
41 N10 **Anvik River** ≈ Alaska, USA
40 F17 **Anvil Peak** ▲ Semisopochnoi Island, Alaska, USA
165 P7 **Anxi** Gansu, N China
190 F8 **Anxious Bay** *bay* South Australia
167 O5 **Anyang** Henan, C China
165 S11 **A'nyêmaqên Shan** ▲▲ C China
120 H12 **Anykščiai** Anykščiai, E Lithuania
167 P13 **Anyuan** Jiangxi, S China
127 O6 **Anyuysk** Chukotskiy Avtonomnyy Okrug, NE Russian Federation
127 Oo5 **Anyuyskiy Khrebet** ▲▲ NE Russian Federation
56 D8 **Anza** Antioquia, C Colombia
Anzen *see* Antsla
126 H13 **Anzhero-Sudzhensk** Kemerovskaya Oblast', S Russian Federation
109 I16 **Anzio** Lazio, C Italy
57 O6 **Anzoátegui** *off.* Estado Anzoátegui. ◈ *state* NE Venezuela
153 P12 **Anzob** W Tajikistan
Anzyô *see* Anjō
Aoba *see* Ambae
172 Ss13 **Aoga-shima** *island* Izu-shotō, SE Japan
169 T12 **Aohan Qi** Nei Mongol Zizhiqu, N China
107 R3 **Aoiz** Navarra, N Spain
195 X16 **Aola** *var.* Tenaghau. Guadalcanal, C Solomon Islands
178 Gg15 **Ao Luk Nua** Krabi, SW Thailand
Aomen *see* Macao
172 N8 **Aomori** Aomori, Honshū, C Japan
171 Mm9 **Aomori** *off.* Aomori-ken. ◈ *prefecture* Honshū, C Japan
Aontroim *see* Antrim
117 C15 **Aóos** *var.* Vijosa, Vijosë, *Alb.* Lumi i Vjosës,. ≈ Albania/Greece *see also* Vjosës, Lumi i
203 Q7 **Aorai, Mont** ⛰ Tahiti, W French Polynesia
Aoraki *see* Cook, Mount
178 Ii13 **Aôral, Phnum** *prev.* Phnom Aural. ▲ W Cambodia
Aorangi *see* Cook, Mount
193 L15 **Aorangi Mountains** ▲▲ North Island, NZ
192 H13 **Aorere** ≈ South Island, NZ
108 A7 **Aosta** *anc.* Augusta Praetoria. Valle d'Aosta, NW Italy
79 O11 **Aougoundou, Lac** ◎ S Mali
78 K9 **Aoukâr** *var.* Aouker. *plateau* C Mauritania
80 J13 **Aouk, Bahr** ≈ Central African Republic/Chad
Aouker *see* Aoukâr
76 B11 **Aousard** SE Western Sahara
170 G12 **Aoya** Tottori, Honshū, SW Japan
80 H5 **Aozou** Borkou-Ennedi-Tibesti, N Chad
28 M11 **Apache** Oklahoma, C USA
38 L14 **Apache Junction** Arizona, SW USA
26 J9 **Apache Mountains** ▲▲ Texas, SW USA
38 M16 **Apache Peak** ▲ Arizona, SW USA
118 H10 **Apahida** Cluj, NW Romania
25 T9 **Apalachee Bay** *bay* Florida, SE USA
25 T3 **Apalachee River** ≈ Georgia, SE USA
25 S10 **Apalachicola** Florida, SE USA
25 S10 **Apalachicola Bay** *bay* Florida, SE USA
25 R9 **Apalachicola River** ≈ Florida, SE USA
Apam *see* Apan
Apamama *see* Abemama
43 P14 **Apan** *var.* Apam. Hidalgo, C Mexico
44 J8 **Apanás, Lago de** ◎ NW Nicaragua
56 H14 **Apaporis, Río** ≈ Brazil/Colombia
193 C23 **Aparima** ≈ South Island, NZ
179 P7 **Aparri** Luzon, N Philippines
114 J9 **Apatin** Serbia, NW Yugoslavia
128 J4 **Apatity** Murmanskaya Oblast', NW Russian Federation
57 X9 **Apatou** NW French Guiana
42 M14 **Apatzingán** *var.* Apatzingán de la Constitución. Michoacán de Ocampo, SW Mexico
176 Y9 **Apauwar** Irian Jaya, E Indonesia
Apaxtla *see* Apaxtla de Castrejón
43 O15 **Apaxtla de Castrejón** *var.* Apaxtla. Guerrero, S Mexico
120 J7 **Ape** Alūksne, NE Latvia
100 L11 **Apeldoorn** Gelderland, E Netherlands
Apennines *see* Appennino
Apenrade *see* Åbenrå
59 L17 **Apere, Río** ≈ C Bolivia
57 W11 **Apetina** Sipaliwini, SE Suriname
23 U9 **Apex** North Carolina, SE USA
81 M16 **Api** Haut-Zaïre, N Zaire
158 M9 **Api** ▲ NW Nepal
Apia *see* Abaiang
198 Bb8 **Āpia** ● (Western Samoa) Upolu, SE Western Samoa
62 K11 **Apiaí** São Paulo, S Brazil
175 P16 **Api, Gunung** ▲ Pulau Sangeang, S Indonesia
195 Y16 **Apio** Maramasike Island, N Solomon Islands
43 O15 **Apipilulco** Guerrero, S Mexico
43 P14 **Apizaco** Tlaxcala, S Mexico
57 U9 **Apoera** Sipaliwini, NW Suriname
117 O23 **Apolakkiá** Ródos, Dodekánisos, Greece, Aegean Sea
103 L16 **Apolda** Thüringen, C Germany
198 B8 **Apolima Strait** *strait* C Pacific Ocean
190 M13 **Apollo Bay** Victoria, SE Australia
Apollonia *see* Sozopol
59 J16 **Apolo** La Paz, W Bolivia
59 J16 **Apolobamba, Cordillera** ▲▲ Bolivia/Peru
179 Rr16 **Apo, Mount** ⛰ Mindanao, S Philippines
25 W11 **Apopka** Florida, SE USA
25 W11 **Apopka, Lake** ◎ Florida, SE USA
61 J19 **Aporé, Rio** ≈ SW Brazil
32 K2 **Apostle Islands** *island group* Wisconsin, N USA
Apostolas Andreas, Cape *see* Zafer Burnu
63 F14 **Apóstoles** Misiones, NE Argentina
Apostólou Andréa, Akrotíri *see* Zafer Burnu
119 S9 **Apostolove** *Rus.* Apostolovo. Dnipropetrovs'ka Oblast', E Ukraine
Apostolovo *see* Apostolove
19 Qq9 **Appalachian Mountains** ▲▲ E USA
97 K14 **Äppelbo** Kopparberg, C Sweden
100 N7 **Appelscha** *Fris.* Appelskea. Friesland, N Netherlands
Appelskea *see* Appelscha
108 G11 **Appennino** *Eng.* Apennines. ▲▲ Italy/San Marino
109 L17 **Appennino Napoletano** ▲▲ C Italy
110 I7 **Appenzell** Appenzell, NW Switzerland
110 H7 **Appenzell** ◈ *canton* NE Switzerland
57 V12 **Appikalo** Sipaliwini, S Suriname
100 O5 **Appingedam** Groningen, NE Netherlands
27 X8 **Appleby** Texas, SW USA
99 L15 **Appleby-in-Westmorland** NW England, UK
32 K10 **Apple River** ≈ Illinois, N USA
32 I5 **Apple River** ≈ Wisconsin, N USA
27 W9 **Apple Springs** Texas, SW USA
31 S8 **Appleton** Minnesota, N USA
32 M7 **Appleton** Wisconsin, N USA
29 S5 **Appleton City** Missouri, C USA
37 U14 **Apple Valley** California, W USA
31 V9 **Apple Valley** Minnesota, N USA
23 U6 **Appomattox** Virginia, NE USA
196 B16 **Apra Harbour** *harbor* W Guam
196 B16 **Apra Heights** W Guam
108 F6 **Aprica, Passo dell'** *pass* N Italy
109 M15 **Apricena** *anc.* Hadria Picena. Puglia, SE Italy
130 L14 **Apsheronsk** Krasnodarskiy Kray, SW Russian Federation
Apsheronskiy Poluostrov *see* Abşeron Yarımadası
105 S15 **Apt** *anc.* Apta Julia. Vaucluse, SE France
Apta Julia *see* Apt
40 H12 **Apua Point** *headland* Hawaii, USA, C Pacific Ocean
62 I10 **Apucarana** Paraná, S Brazil
Apulia *see* Puglia
56 K8 **Apure** *off.* Estado Apure. ◈ *state* C Venezuela
56 J7 **Apure, Río** ≈ W Venezuela
59 F16 **Apurímac** *off.* Departamento de Apurímac. ◈ *department* C Peru
59 F15 **Apurímac, Río** ≈ S Peru
118 G10 **Apuseni, Munţii** ▲▲ W Romania
207 P15 **Aputiteeq** *var.* Aputitêq. C Greenland
Aputitêq *see* Aputiteeq
Aqaba/'Aqaba *see* Al 'Aqabah
144 F15 **Aqaba, Gulf of** *var.* Gulf of Elat, *Ar.* Khalīj al 'Aqabah; *anc.* Sinus Aelaniticus. *gulf* NE Red Sea
145 R7 **'Aqabah** C Iraq
'Aqabah, Khalīj al *see* Aqaba, Gulf of
155 O2 **Āqchah** *var.* Āqcheh. Jowzjān, N Afghanistan
Āqcheh *see* Āqchah
Aqköl *see* Akkol'
Aqmola/Aqmola Oblysy *see* Akmola
164 L10 **Aqqikkol Hu** ◎ NW China
Aqqystaū *see* Akkystau
'Aqrah *see* Ākrē
Aqsay *see* Aksay
Aqshataū *see* Akchatau
Aqsū *see* Aksu
Aqsūat *see* Aksuat
Aqtas *see* Aktas
Aqtaū *see* Aktau
Aqtöbe/Aqtöbe Oblysy *see* Aktyubinsk
Aqtoghay *see* Aktogay
Aquae Augustae *see* Dax
Aquae Calidae *see* Bath
Aquae Flaviae *see* Chaves
Aquae Grani *see* Aachen
Aquae Panoniae *see* Baden
Aquae Sextiae *see* Aix-en-Provence
Aquae Solis *see* Bath
Aquae Tarbelicae *see* Dax
38 J11 **Aquarius Mountains** ▲▲ Arizona, SW USA
64 O5 **Aquidabán, Río** ≈ E Paraguay
61 H20 **Aquidauana** Mato Grosso do Sul, S Brazil
42 L15 **Aquila** Michoacán de Ocampo, S Mexico
Aquila/Aquila degli Abruzzi *see* L'Aquila
27 T8 **Aquilla** Texas, SW USA
46 L9 **Aquin** S Haiti
Aquisgranum *see* Aachen
104 J13 **Aquitaine** ◈ *region* SW France
Aqzhar *see* Akzhar
159 P13 **Āra** *prev.* Arrah. Bihār, N India
107 S4 **Ara** ≈ NE Spain
25 P2 **Arab** Alabama, S USA
Araba *see* Álava
144 G12 **'Arabah, Wādī al** *Heb.* Ha'Arava. *dry watercourse* Israel/Jordan
119 U12 **Arabats'ka Strilka, Kosa** *spit* S Ukraine
119 U12 **Arabats'ka Zatoka** *gulf* S Ukraine
'Arab, Baḩr al *see* Arab, Bahr el
82 C12 **Arab, Bahr el** *var.* Baḩr al 'Arab. ≈ S Sudan
58 E7 **Arabela, Río** ≈ N Peru
181 O4 **Arabian Basin** *undersea feature* N Arabian Sea
Arabian Desert *see* Sahara el Sharqîya
147 N9 **Arabian Peninsula** *peninsula* SW Asia
87 P15 **Arabian Plate** *tectonic feature* Africa/Asia/Europe
147 W14 **Arabian Sea** *sea* NW Indian Ocean
Arabicus, Sinus *see* Red Sea
'Arabī, Khalīj al *see* Persian Gulf
Arabistan *see* Khūzestān
'Arabīyah as Su'ūdīyah, Al Mamlakah al *see* Saudi Arabia
'Arabīyah Jumhūrīyah, Mişr al *see* Egypt
144 I9 **'Arab, Jabal al** ▲▲ S Syria
124 Pp14 **'Arab, Khalîg el** *Eng.* Arabs Gulf. *gulf* N Egypt
Arab Republic of Egypt *see* Egypt
Arabs Gulf *see* 'Arab, Khalîg el
145 Y12 **'Arab, Shaţţ al** *Eng.* Shatt al Arab, *Per.* Arvand Rūd. ≈ Iran/Iraq
142 I11 **Araç** Kastamonu, N Turkey
61 P16 **Aracaju** *state capital* Sergipe, E Brazil
56 F5 **Aracataca** Magdalena, N Colombia
60 P13 **Aracati** Ceará, E Brazil
62 J8 **Araçatuba** São Paulo, S Brazil
106 J13 **Aracena** Andalucía, S Spain
117 F20 **Arachnaío** ▲▲ S Greece
117 D16 **Árachthos** *var.* Arta; *prev.* Árakhthos, *anc.* Arachthus. ≈ W Greece
Arachthus *see* Árachthos
61 N19 **Araçuai** Minas Gerais, SE Brazil
142 I11 **Araç Çayı** ≈ N Turkey
144 F11 **'Arad** Southern, S Israel
118 F11 **Arad** Arad, W Romania
118 F11 **Arad** ◈ *county* W Romania
80 J9 **Arada** Biltine, NE Chad
149 P18 **'Arādah** Abū Z̧aby, S UAE
Aradhippou *see* Aradíppou
124 O3 **Aradíppou** *var.* Aradhippou. SE Cyprus
182 K6 **Arafura Sea** *Ind.* Laut Arafuru. *sea* W Pacific Ocean
182 L6 **Arafura Shelf** *undersea feature* C Arafura Sea
Arafuru, Laut *see* Arafura Sea
61 J18 **Aragarças** Goiás, C Brazil
Aragats, Gora *see* Aragats Lerr
143 T12 **Aragats Lerr** *Rus.* Gora Aragats. ▲ W Armenia
34 E14 **Arago, Cape** *headland* Oregon, NW USA
107 R6 **Aragón** ◈ *autonomous community* E Spain
107 Q4 **Aragón** ≈ NE Spain
109 I24 **Aragona** Sicilia, Italy, C Mediterranean Sea
107 Q7 **Aragoncillo** ▲ C Spain
56 L5 **Aragua** *off.* Estado Aragua. ◈ *state* N Venezuela
57 N6 **Aragua de Barcelona** Anzoátegui, NE Venezuela
57 O5 **Aragua de Maturín** Monagas, NE Venezuela
61 K15 **Araguaia, Río** *var.* Araguaya. ≈ C Brazil
61 K19 **Araguari** Minas Gerais, SE Brazil
60 J11 **Araguari, Rio** ≈ SW Brazil
Araguaya *see* Araguaia, Río
106 K14 **Arahal** Andalucía, S Spain
171 Jj13 **Arai** Niigata, Honshū, C Japan
Árainn *see* Inishmore
Árainn Mhór *see* Aran Island
Ara Jovis *see* Aranjuez
76 J11 **Arak** C Algeria
176 Yy15 **Arak** Irian Jaya, E Indonesia
148 M7 **Arāk** *prev.* Sultānābād. Markazī, W Iran
196 D10 **Arakabesan** *island* Palau Islands, N Palau
57 S7 **Arakaka** NW Guyana
177 Ff6 **Arakan State** *var.* Rakhine State. ◈ *state* W Myanmar
177 Ff5 **Arakan Yoma** ▲▲ W Myanmar
171 Kk12 **Arakawa** Niigata, Honshū, C Japan
Árakhthos *see* Árachthos
Araks/Arak's *see* Aras
164 H7 **Aral** Xinjiang Uygur Zizhiqu, NW China
Aral *see* Aral'sk, Kazakhstan
Aral *see* Vose', Tajikistan
Aral-Bukhorskiy Kanal *see* Amu-Bukhoro Kanali
143 T12 **Aralık** Kars, E Turkey
152 H5 **Aral Sea** *Kaz.* Aral Tengizi, *Rus.* Aral'skoye More, *Uzb.* Orol Dengizi. *inland sea* Kazakhstan/Uzbekistan
150 L13 **Aral'sk** *Kaz.* Aral. Kzyl-Orda, SW Kazakhstan
Aral'skoye More/Aral Tengizi *see* Aral Sea
43 O10 **Aramberri** Nuevo León, NE Mexico
194 F14 **Aramia** ≈ SW PNG
149 N6 **Ārān** *var.* Golārā. Eşfahān, C Iran
107 N5 **Aranda de Duero** Castilla-León, N Spain
114 M12 **Aranđelovac** *prev.* Arandjelovac. Serbia, C Yugoslavia
Arandjelovac *see* Aranđelovac
99 J19 **Aran Fawddwy** ▲ NW Wales, UK
99 C14 **Aran Island** *Ir.* Árainn Mhór. *island* NW Ireland
99 A18 **Aran Islands** *island group* W Ireland
107 N9 **Aranjuez** *anc.* Ara Jovis. Madrid, C Spain
85 E20 **Aranos** Hardap, SE Namibia
27 U14 **Aransas Bay** *inlet* Texas, SW USA
27 T14 **Aransas Pass** Texas, SW USA
203 O3 **Aranuka** *prev.* Nanouki. *atoll* Tungaru, W Kiribati
178 I11 **Aranyaprathet** Prachin Buri, S Thailand
Aranyosasztal *see* Zlatý Stôl
Aranyosgyéres *see* Câmpia Turzii
Aranyosmarót *see* Zlaté Moravce
170 Cc14 **Arao** Kumamoto, Kyūshū, SW Japan
79 O8 **Araouane** Tombouctou, N Mali
28 L10 **Arapaho** Oklahoma, C USA
31 N16 **Arapahoe** Nebraska, C USA
59 I16 **Arapa, Laguna** ◎ SE Peru
193 K14 **Arapawa Island** *island* C NZ
63 E17 **Arapey Grande, Río** ≈ N Uruguay
61 P16 **Arapiraca** Alagoas, E Brazil
146 M3 **'Ar'ar** Al Ḩudūd ash Shamālīyah, NW Saudi Arabia
56 G15 **Araracuara** Caquetá, S Colombia
63 K15 **Araranguá** Santa Catarina, S Brazil
62 L8 **Araraquara** São Paulo, S Brazil
61 I14 **Araras** Ceará, E Brazil
60 O13 **Araras** Pará, N Brazil
62 L9 **Araras** São Paulo, S Brazil
62 H11 **Araras, Serra das** ▲▲ S Brazil
143 U12 **Ararat** S Armenia
190 M12 **Ararat** Victoria, SE Australia
Ararat, Mount *see* Büyükağrı Dağı
146 M3 **'Ar'ar, Wādī** *dry watercourse* Iraq/Saudi Arabia
133 N7 **Aras** *Arm.* Arak's, *Az.* Araz Nehri, *Per.* Rūd-e Aras, *Rus.* Araks; *prev.* Araxes. ≈ SW Asia
107 R9 **Aras de Alpuente** País Valenciano, E Spain
143 S13 **Aras Güneyi Dağları** ▲▲ NE Turkey
Aras, Rūd-e *see* Aras
203 U9 **Aratika** *atoll* Îles Tuamotu, C French Polynesia
Aratürük *see* Yiwu
56 I8 **Arauca** Arauca, NE Colombia
56 I8 **Arauca** *off.* Intendencia de Arauca. ◈ *province* NE Colombia
65 G15 **Araucanía** *off.* Región de la Araucanía. ◈ *region* C Chile
56 L7 **Arauca, Río** ≈ Colombia/Venezuela
65 F14 **Arauco** Bío Bío, C Chile
65 F14 **Arauco, Golfo de** *gulf* S Chile
56 H8 **Arauquita** Arauca, C Colombia
Arausio *see* Orange
158 F13 **Arāvali Range** ▲▲ N India
195 S12 **Arawa** Bougainville Island, NE PNG
193 C20 **Arawata** ≈ South Island, NZ
194 L12 **Arawe Islands** *island group* E PNG
61 L20 **Araxá** Minas Gerais, SE Brazil
Araxes *see* Aras
57 O5 **Araya** Sucre, N Venezuela
Araz Nehri *see* Aras
107 R4 **Arba** ≈ N Spain
83 I15 **Ārba Minch'** SW Ethiopia
145 U4 **Arbat** NE Iraq
109 D19 **Arbatax** Sardegna, Italy, C Mediterranean Sea
Arbe *see* Rab
Arbela *see* Arbīl
145 S3 **Arbīl** *var.* Erbil, Irbīl, *Kurd.* Hawlēr; *anc.* Arbela. N Iraq
97 M16 **Arboga** Västmanland, C Sweden
97 M16 **Arbogaån** ≈ C Sweden
105 S9 **Arbois** Jura, E France
56 D6 **Arboletes** Antioquia, NW Colombia
9 X15 **Arborg** Manitoba, S Canada
96 N12 **Arbrå** Gävleborg, C Sweden
98 K10 **Arbroath** *anc.* Aberbrothock. E Scotland, UK
37 N6 **Arbuckle** California, W USA
29 N12 **Arbuckle Mountains** ▲▲ Oklahoma, C USA
Arbuzinka *see* Arbyzynka
119 Q8 **Arbyzynka** *Rus.* Arbuzinka. Mykolayivs'ka Oblast', S Ukraine
105 U12 **Arc** ≈ E France
104 J13 **Arcachon** Gironde, SW France
104 J13 **Arcachon, Bassin d'** *inlet* SW France
20 E10 **Arcade** New York, NE USA
25 W14 **Arcadia** Florida, SE USA
24 H5 **Arcadia** Louisiana, S USA
32 J7 **Arcadia** Wisconsin, N USA
Arcae Remorum *see* Châlons-en-Champagne
46 L9 **Arcahaie** C Haiti
36 K3 **Arcata** California, W USA
37 U6 **Arc Dome** ▲ Nevada, W USA
109 J16 **Arce** Lazio, C Italy
43 O15 **Arcelia** Guerrero, S Mexico
101 M15 **Arcen** Limburg, SE Netherlands
Archangel *see* Arkhangel'sk
Archangel Bay *see* Chëshskaya Guba
117 O23 **Archángelos** *var.* Arhangelos, Arkhángelos. Ródos, Dodekánisos, Greece, Aegean Sea
116 F7 **Archar** ≈ NW Bulgaria
33 R11 **Archbold** Ohio, N USA
107 R12 **Archena** Murcia, SE Spain
27 R5 **Archer City** Texas, SW USA
106 M14 **Archidona** Andalucía, S Spain
67 B25 **Arch Islands** *island group* SW Falkland Islands
108 G13 **Arcidosso** Toscana, C Italy
105 Q5 **Arcis-sur-Aube** Aube, N France
190 F3 **Arckaringa Creek** *seasonal river* South Australia
108 G7 **Arco** Trentino-Alto Adige, N Italy
35 Q14 **Arco** Idaho, NW USA
32 M14 **Arcola** Illinois, N USA
107 P6 **Arcos de Jalón** Castilla-León, N Spain

◆ Country
● Country Capital
◇ Dependent Territory
○ Dependent Territory Capital
◈ Administrative Region
✕ International Airport
▲ Mountain
▲▲ Mountain Range
⛰ Volcano
≈ River
◎ Lake
⊠ Reservoir

106 *K15* **Arcos de la Frontera** Andalucía, S Spain
106 *G5* **Arcos de Valdevez** Viana do Castelo, N Portugal
61 *P15* **Arcoverde** Pernambuco, E Brazil
104 *H5* **Arcovest, Pointe de l'** *headland* NW France
Arctic-Mid Oceanic Ridge *see* Nansen Cordillera
207 *R8* **Arctic Ocean** *ocean*
14 *G4* **Arctic Red River** ≈ Northwest Territories/Yukon Territory, NW Canada
Arctic Red River *see* Tsiigehtchic
41 *S6* **Arctic Village** Alaska, USA
204 *H1* **Arctowski** *Polish research station* South Shetland Islands, Antarctica
116 *I12* **Arda** *var.* Ardhas, *Gk.* Ardas. ≈ Bulgaria/Greece *see also* Ardas
148 *L2* **Ardabīl** *var.* Ardebil. Ardabīl, NW Iran
148 *L2* **Ardabīl** *off.* Ostān-e Ardabīl. ◈ *province* NW Iran
143 *R11* **Ardahan** Kars, NE Turkey
149 *P8* **Ardakān** Yazd, C Iran
96 *E12* **Årdalstangen** Sogn og Fjordane, S Norway
143 *R11* **Ardanuç** Artvin, NE Turkey
116 *L12* **Ardas** *var.* Ardhas, *Bul.* Arda. ≈ Bulgaria/Greece *see also* Arda
144 *I13* **Arḍ aş Şawwān** *var.* Ardh es Suwwān. *plain* S Jordan
131 *P5* **Ardatov** Respublika Mordoviya, W Russian Federation
12 *G12* **Ardbeg** Ontario, S Canada
Ardeal *see* Transylvania
Ardebil *see* Ardabīl
105 *Q13* **Ardèche** ≈ C France
105 *Q13* **Ardèche** ◈ *department* E France
99 *F17* **Ardee** *Ir.* Baile Átha Fhirdhia. NE Ireland
105 *Q3* **Ardennes** ◈ *department* NE France
101 *J23* **Ardennes** *physical region* Belgium/France
143 *Q11* **Ardeşen** Rize, NE Turkey
149 *O7* **Ardestān** *var.* Ardistan. Eşfahān, C Iran
110 *J9* **Ardez** Graubünden, SE Switzerland
Ardhas *see* Arda/Ardas
Ardh es Suwwān *see* Arḍ aş Şawwān
106 *I12* **Ardila, Ribeira de** *Sp.* Ardilla. ≈ Portugal/Spain *see also* Ardilla
9 *T17* **Ardill** Saskatchewan, S Canada
106 *I12* **Ardilla** *Port.* Ribeira de Ardila. ≈ Portugal/Spain *see also* Ardila, Ribeira de
42 *M11* **Ardilla, Cerro la** ▲ C Mexico
116 *J12* **Ardino** Khaskovska Oblast, S Bulgaria
Ardistan *see* Ardestān
191 *P9* **Ardlethan** New South Wales, SE Australia
Ard Mhacha *see* Armagh
25 *P1* **Ardmore** Alabama, S USA
29 *N13* **Ardmore** Oklahoma, C USA
22 *J10* **Ardmore** Tennessee, S USA
98 *G10* **Ardnamurchan, Point of** *headland* N Scotland, UK
101 *C17* **Ardooie** West-Vlaanderen, W Belgium
190 *I9* **Ardrossan** South Australia
118 *H9* **Ardusat** *Hung.* Erdőszáda. Maramureş, N Romania
95 *F16* **Åre** Jämtland, C Sweden
81 *P16* **Arebi** Haut-Zaïre, NE Zaire
47 *T5* **Arecibo** C Puerto Rico
176 *W10* **Aredo** Irian Jaya, E Indonesia
61 *P14* **Areia Branca** Rio Grande do Norte, E Brazil
121 *O14* **Arekhawsk** *Rus.* Orekhovsk. Vitsyebskaya Voblasts', N Belarus
Arel *see* Arlon
Arelas/Arelate *see* Arles
Arenal, Embalse de *see* Arenal Laguna
44 *L12* **Arenal Laguna** *var.* Embalse de Arenal. ◎ NW Costa Rica
44 *L13* **Arenal, Volcán** ⛰ NW Costa Rica
36 *K6* **Arena, Point** *headland* California, W USA
61 *H17* **Arenápolis** Mato Grosso, W Brazil
42 *G10* **Arena, Punta** *headland* W Mexico
106 *L8* **Arenas de San Pedro** Castilla-León, N Spain
65 *I24* **Arenas, Punta de** *headland* S Argentina
63 *B20* **Arenaza** Buenos Aires, E Argentina
97 *F17* **Arendal** Aust-Agder, S Norway
101 *J16* **Arendonk** Antwerpen, N Belgium
45 *T15* **Arenosa** Panamá, N Panama
Arensburg *see* Kuressaare
107 *W5* **Arenys de Mar** Cataluña, NE Spain
108 *C9* **Arenzano** Liguria, NW Italy
117 *F22* **Areópoli** *prev.* Areópolis. Pelopónnisos, S Greece
Areópolis *see* Areópoli
59 *H18* **Arequipa** Arequipa, SE Peru
59 *G17* **Arequipa** *off.* Departamento de Arequipa. ◈ *department* SW Peru
63 *B19* **Arequito** Santa Fe, C Argentina
106 *M7* **Arévalo** Castilla-León, N Spain
108 *H12* **Arezzo** *anc.* Arretium. Toscana, C Italy
107 *Q4* **Arga** ≈ N Spain
Argaeus *see* Erciyes Dağı
117 *G17* **Argalastí** Thessalía, C Greece
107 *O10* **Argamasilla de Alba** Castilla-La Mancha, C Spain
164 *L8* **Argan** Xinjiang Uygur Zizhiqu, NW China
107 *O8* **Arganda** Madrid, C Spain
106 *H8* **Arganil** Coimbra, N Portugal
179 *Qq14* **Argao** Cebu, C Philippines
159 *V15* **Argartala** Tripura, NE India
126 *K9* **Arga-Sala** ≈ NE Russian Federation
105 *P17* **Argelès-sur-Mer** Pyrénées-Orientales, S France
105 *T15* **Argens** ≈ SE France
108 *H9* **Argenta** Emilia-Romagna, N Italy
104 *K5* **Argentan** Orne, N France
105 *N12* **Argentat** Corrèze, C France
108 *A9* **Argentera** Piemonte, NE Italy
105 *N5* **Argenteuil** Val-d'Oise, N France
64 *K13* **Argentina** *off.* Republic of Argentina. ◆ *republic* S South America
Argentina Basin *see* Argentine Basin
Argentine Abyssal Plain *see* Argentine Plain
67 *I19* **Argentine Basin** *var.* Argentina Basin. *undersea feature* SW Atlantic Ocean
67 *I20* **Argentine Plain** *var.* Argentine Abyssal Plain. *undersea feature* SW Atlantic Ocean
Argentine Rise *see* Falkland Plateau
65 *H22* **Argentino, Lago** ◎ S Argentina
104 *K8* **Argenton-Château** Deux-Sèvres, W France
104 *M9* **Argenton-sur-Creuse** Indre, C France
Argentoratum *see* Strasbourg
118 *I12* **Argeş** ◈ *county* S Romania
118 *K14* **Argeş** ≈ S Romania
155 *O8* **Arghandāb, Daryā-ye** ≈ SE Afghanistan
Arghastān *see* Arghestān
155 *O8* **Arghestān** *Pash.* Arghastān. ≈ SE Afghanistan
Argirocastro *see* Gjirokastër
82 *E7* **Argo** Northern, N Sudan
181 *P7* **Argo Fracture Zone** *tectonic feature* C Indian Ocean
117 *F20* **Argolikós Kólpos** *gulf* S Greece
105 *R4* **Argonne** *physical region* NE France
174 *Mm15* **Argopuro, Gunung** ▲ Jawa, S Indonesia
117 *F20* **Árgos** Pelopónnisos, S Greece
145 *S1* **Argōsh** N Iraq
117 *D14* **Árgos Orestikó** Dytikí Makedonía, N Greece
117 *B19* **Argostóli** *var.* Argostólion. Kefallinía, Iónioi Nísoi, Greece, C Mediterranean Sea
Argostólion *see* Argostóli
Argovie *see* Aargau
37 *O14* **Arguello, Point** *headland* California, W USA
131 *P16* **Argun** Chechenskaya Respublika, SW Russian Federation
163 *T2* **Argun** *Chin.* Ergun He, *Rus.* Argun'. ≈ China/Russian Federation
79 *T12* **Argungu** Kebbi, NW Nigeria
168 *J9* **Arguut** Övörhangay, C Mongolia
189 *N3* **Argyle, Lake** *salt lake* Western Australia
98 *G12* **Argyll** *cultural region* W Scotland, UK
Argyrokastron *see* Gjirokastër
168 *I7* **Arhangay** ◈ *province* C Mongolia
Arhangelos *see* Archángelos
97 *P14* **Arholma** Stockholm, C Sweden
97 *G22* **Århus** *var.* Aarhus. Århus, C Denmark
97 *G22* **Århus** ◈ *county* C Denmark
145 *T1* **Ārī** E Iraq
194 *M12* **Aria** ≈ New Britain, E PNG
Aria *see* Herāt
170 *C13* **Ariake-kai** *bay* NE East China Sea
85 *F22* **Ariamsvlei** Karas, SE Namibia
109 *L17* **Ariano Irpino** Campania, S Italy
56 *F11* **Ariari, Río** ≈ C Colombia
157 *K19* **Ari Atoll** *atoll* C Maldives
79 *P11* **Aribinda** N Burkina
64 *G2* **Arica** *hist.* San Marcos de Arica. Tarapacá, N Chile
56 *H16* **Arica** Amazonas, S Colombia
64 *G2* **Arica** ✕ Tarapacá, N Chile
170 *G16* **Arida** Wakayama, Honshū, SW Japan
116 *E13* **Aridaía** *var.* Aridea, Aridhaía. Dytikí Makedonía, N Greece
Aridea *see* Aridaía
180 *I15* **Aride, Île** *island* Inner Islands, NE Seychelles
Aridhaía *see* Aridaía
105 *N17* **Ariège** ◈ *department* S France
104 *M16* **Ariège** *var.* la Riege. ≈ Andorra/France
118 *H11* **Arieş** ≈ W Romania
155 *U10* **Ārifwāla** Punjab, E Pakistan
Ariguaní *see* El Difícil
144 *G11* **Arīhā** Al Karak, W Jordan
144 *I3* **Arīḩā** *var.* Arīhā. Idlib, W Syria
Arīḩā *see* Jericho
39 *W4* **Arikaree River** ≈ Colorado/Nebraska, C USA
170 *Bb12* **Arikawa** Nagasaki, Nakadōri-jima, SW Japan
114 *L13* **Arilje** Serbia, W Yugoslavia
47 *U14* **Arima** Trinidad, Trinidad and Tobago
Arime *see* Al ʻArīmah
Ariminum *see* Rimini
61 *H16* **Arinos, Rio** ≈ W Brazil
42 *M14* **Ario de Rosales** *var.* Ario de Rosáles. Michoacán de Ocampo, SW Mexico
120 *F12* **Ariogala** Raseiniai, C Lithuania
49 *T7* **Aripuanā** ≈ W Brazil
61 *E15* **Ariquemes** Rondônia, W Brazil
124 *Rr15* **ʻArîsh, Wâdi el** ≈ NE Egypt
56 *K6* **Arismendi** Barinas, C Venezuela
8 *J14* **Aristazabal Island** *island* SW Canada
62 *F13* **Aristóbulo del Valle** Misiones, NE Argentina
180 *I5* **Arivonimamo** ✕ (Antananarivo) Antananarivo, C Madagascar
Arixang *see* Wenquan
107 *Q6* **Ariza** Aragón, NE Spain
64 *I6* **Arizaro, Salar de** *salt lake* NW Argentina
64 *K13* **Arizona** San Luis, C Argentina
38 *J12* **Arizona** *off.* State of Arizona; also known as Copper State, Grand Canyon State. ◈ *state* SW USA
42 *G4* **Arizpe** Sonora, NW Mexico
97 *J16* **Årjäng** Värmland, C Sweden
149 *P8* **Arjenān** Yazd, C Iran
94 *I13* **Arjeplog** Norrbotten, N Sweden
56 *E5* **Arjona** Bolívar, N Colombia
107 *N13* **Arjona** Andalucía, S Spain
127 *N11* **Arka** Khabarovskiy Kray, E Russian Federation
24 *L2* **Arkabutla Lake** ▣ Mississippi, S USA
131 *O7* **Arkadak** Saratovskaya Oblast', W Russian Federation
29 *T13* **Arkadelphia** Arkansas, C USA
117 *J25* **Arkalochóri** *prev.* Arkalohori, Arkalokhórion. Kríti, Greece, E Mediterranean Sea
Arkalohori/Arkalokhórion *see* Arkalochóri
151 *O10* **Arkalyk** *Kaz.* Arqalyq. Turgay, C Kazakhstan
29 *U10* **Arkansas** *off.* State of Arkansas; also known as The Land of Opportunity. ◈ *state* S USA
29 *W14* **Arkansas City** Arkansas, C USA
29 *O7* **Arkansas City** Kansas, C USA
18 *Kk10* **Arkansas River** ≈ C USA
190 *J5* **Arkaroola** South Australia
Arkhángelos *see* Archángelos
128 *L8* **Arkhangel'sk** *Eng.* Archangel. Arkhangel'skaya Oblast', NW Russian Federation
128 *L9* **Arkhangel'skaya Oblast'** ◈ *province* NW Russian Federation
131 *O14* **Arkhangel'skoye** Stavropol'skiy Kray, SW Russian Federation
127 *N16* **Arkhara** Amurskaya Oblast', S Russian Federation
99 *G19* **Arklow** *Ir.* An tInbhear Mór. SE Ireland
117 *M20* **Arkoí** *island* Dodekánisos, Greece, Aegean Sea
29 *R11* **Arkoma** Oklahoma, C USA
102 *O7* **Arkona, Kap** *headland* NE Germany
97 *N17* **Arkösund** Östergötland, S Sweden
126 *H4* **Arkticheskogo Instituta, Ostrova** *island* N Russian Federation
97 *O15* **Arlanda** ✕ (Stockholm) Stockholm, C Sweden
152 *C11* **Arlan, Gora** ▲ W Turkmenistan
107 *O5* **Arlanza** ≈ N Spain
107 *N5* **Arlanzón** ≈ N Spain
105 *R15* **Arles** *var.* Arles-sur-Rhône; *anc.* Arelas, Arelate. Bouches-du-Rhône, SE France
Arles-sur-Rhône *see* Arles
105 *O17* **Arles-sur-Tech** Pyrénées-Orientales, S France
31 *U9* **Arlington** Minnesota, N USA
31 *R15* **Arlington** Nebraska, C USA
34 *J11* **Arlington** Oregon, NW USA
31 *R10* **Arlington** South Dakota, N USA
22 *E10* **Arlington** Tennessee, S USA
27 *T6* **Arlington** Texas, SW USA
23 *W4* **Arlington** Virginia, NE USA
34 *H7* **Arlington** Washington, NW USA
32 *M10* **Arlington Heights** Illinois, N USA
79 *U8* **Arlit** Agadez, C Niger
101 *L24* **Arlon** *Dut.* Aarlen, *Ger.* Arel; *Lat.* Orolaunum. Luxembourg, SE Belgium
29 *R7* **Arma** Kansas, C USA
99 *F16* **Armagh** *Ir.* Ard Mhacha. S Northern Ireland, UK
99 *F16* **Armagh** *cultural region* S Northern Ireland, UK
104 *K15* **Armagnac** *cultural region* S France
105 *Q7* **Armançon** ≈ C France
62 *K10* **Armando Laydner, Represa** ▣ S Brazil
117 *M24* **Armathía** *island* SE Greece
130 *M14* **Armavir** Krasnodarskiy Kray, SW Russian Federation
56 *E10* **Armenia** Quindío, W Colombia
143 *T12* **Armenia** *off.* Republic of Armenia, *var.* Ajastan, *Arm.* Hayastani Hanrapetut'yun; *prev.* Armenian Soviet Socialist Republic. ◆ *republic* SW Asia
Armenierstadt *see* Gherla
105 *O1* **Armentières** Nord, N France
42 *K14* **Armería** Colima, SW Mexico
191 *T5* **Armidale** New South Wales, SE Australia
31 *P11* **Armour** South Dakota, N USA
63 *B18* **Armstrong** Santa Fe, C Argentina
9 *N16* **Armstrong** British Columbia, SW Canada
10 *D11* **Armstrong** Ontario, S Canada
31 *U11* **Armstrong** Iowa, C USA
27 *S16* **Armstrong** Texas, SW USA
119 *S11* **Armyans'k** *Rus.* Armyansk. Respublika Krym, S Ukraine
117 *H14* **Arnaía** *var.* Arnea. Kentrikí Makedonía, N Greece
123 *Mm3* **Arnaoúti, Akrotíri** *var.* Arnaoútis, Cape Arnaouti. *headland* W Cyprus
Arnaouti, Cape/Arnaoútis *see* Arnaoúti, Akrotíri
10 *L4* **Arnaud** ≈ Québec, E Canada
105 *Q8* **Arnay-le-Duc** Côte d'Or, C France
Arnea *see* Arnaía
107 *Q4* **Arnedo** La Rioja, N Spain
97 *I14* **Årnes** Akershus, S Norway
95 *E15* **Årnes** Sør-Trøndelag, S Norway
28 *K9* **Arnett** Oklahoma, C USA
100 *L12* **Arnhem** Gelderland, SE Netherlands
189 *Q2* **Arnhem Land** *physical region* Northern Territory, N Australia
108 *F11* **Arno** ≈ C Italy
Arṇo *see* Arno Atoll
201 *W7* **Arno Atoll** *var.* Arṇo. *atoll* Ratak Chain, NE Marshall Islands
190 *H8* **Arno Bay** South Australia
37 *Q8* **Arnold** California, W USA
29 *X5* **Arnold** Missouri, C USA
31 *N15* **Arnold** Nebraska, C USA
111 *R10* **Arnoldstein** *Slvn.* Pod Klošter. Kärnten, S Austria
105 *N9* **Arnon** ≈ C France
47 *P14* **Arnos Vale** ✕ (Kingstown) Saint Vincent, SE Saint Vincent and the Grenadines
94 *I8* **Arnøy** *island* N Norway
12 *L12* **Arnprior** Ontario, SE Canada
103 *G15* **Arnsberg** Nordrhein-Westfalen, W Germany
103 *K16* **Arnstadt** Thüringen, C Germany
Arnswalde *see* Choszczno
56 *K5* **Aroa** Yaracuy, N Venezuela
85 *E21* **Aroab** Karas, SE Namibia
117 *E19* **Ároania** ▲▲ S Greece
203 *O6* **Aroa, Pointe** *headland* Moorea, W French Polynesia
Aroe Islands *see* Aru, Kepulauan
103 *H15* **Arolsen** Niedersachsen, C Germany
108 *C7* **Arona** Piemonte, NE Italy
21 *R3* **Aroostook River** ≈ Canada/USA
Arop Island *see* Long Island
40 *M12* **Aropuk Lake** ◎ Alaska, USA
203 *P4* **Arorae** *atoll* Tungaru, W Kiribati
202 *G16* **Arorangi** Rarotonga, S Cook Islands
110 *I9* **Arosa** Graubünden, S Switzerland
106 *F4* **Arousa, Ría de** *estuary* E Atlantic Ocean
176 *Uu16* **Aro Usu, Tanjung** *headland* Pulau Selaru, SE Indonesia
192 *P8* **Arowhana** ▲ North Island, NZ
143 *V12* **Arp'a** *Az.* Arpaçay. ≈ Armenia/Azerbaijan
143 *S11* **Arpaçay** Kars, NE Turkey
Arpaçay *see* Arp'a
Arqalyq *see* Arkalyk
155 *N14* **Arra** ≈ SW Pakistan
Arrabona *see* Győr
Arrah *see* Āra
Ar Rahad *see* Er Rahad
145 *R9* **Ar Raḩḩālīyah** C Iraq
62 *Q10* **Arraial do Cabo** Rio de Janeiro, SE Brazil
106 *H11* **Arraiolos** Évora, S Portugal
145 *R8* **Ar Ramādī** *var.* Ramadi, Rumadiya. SW Iraq
144 *J6* **Ar Rāmī** Ḩimş, C Syria
Ar Rams *see* Rams
144 *H9* **Ar Ramthā** *var.* Ramtha. Irbid, N Jordan
98 *H13* **Arran, Isle of** *island* SW Scotland, UK
144 *L3* **Ar Raqqah** *var.* Rakka; *anc.* Nicephorium. Ar Raqqah, N Syria
144 *L3* **Ar Raqqah** *off.* Muḩāfaẓat al Raqqah, *var.* Raqqah, *Fr.* Rakka. ◈ *governorate* N Syria
105 *O2* **Arras** *anc.* Nemetocenna. Pas-de-Calais, N France
Ar Raşāfah *see* Ar Ruşāfah
Arrasate *see* Mondragón
144 *G12* **Ar Rashādīyah** Aţ Ţafīlah, W Jordan
144 *I5* **Ar Rastān** *var.* Rastâne. Ḩimş, W Syria
145 *X12* **Ar Raţāwī** E Iraq
104 *L15* **Arrats** ≈ S France
147 *N10* **Ar Rawḑah** Makkah, S Saudi Arabia
147 *Q15* **Ar Rawḑah** S Yemen
148 *K11* **Ar Rawḑatayn** *var.* Raudhatain. N Kuwait
149 *N16* **Ar Rayyān** *var.* Al Rayyan. C Qatar
104 *L17* **Arreau** Hautes-Pyrénées, S France
66 *Q11* **Arrecife** *var.* Arrecife de Lanzarote, Puerto Arrecife. Lanzarote, Islas Canarias, NE Atlantic Ocean
Arrecife de Lanzarote *see* Arrecife
45 *P6* **Arrecife Edinburgh** *reef* NE Nicaragua
63 *C19* **Arrecifes** Buenos Aires, E Argentina
45 *O5* **Arrecifes de la Media Luna** *reef* E Honduras
104 *F6* **Arrée, Monts d'** ▲▲ NW France
Ar Refā'ī *see* Ar Rifā'ī
Arretium *see* Arezzo
Arriaca *see* Guadalajara
111 *S9* **Arriach** Kärnten, S Austria
43 *T16* **Arriaga** Chiapas, SE Mexico
43 *N12* **Arriaga** San Luis Potosí, C Mexico
145 *W10* **Ar Rifā'ī** *var.* Ar Refā'ī. SE Iraq
145 *V12* **Ar Riḩāb** *salt flat* S Iraq
106 *L2* **Arriondas** Asturias, N Spain
147 *R7* **Ar Riyāḑ** *Eng.* Riyadh. ● (Saudi Arabia) Ar Riyāḑ, C Saudi Arabia
147 *O8* **Ar Riyāḑ** *off.* Minţaqat ar Riyāḑ. ◈ *province* C Saudi Arabia
147 *S15* **Ar Riyān** S Yemen
Arrö *see* Ærø
63 *H18* **Arroio Grande** Rio Grande do Sul, S Brazil
104 *K15* **Arros** ≈ S France
105 *Q9* **Arroux** ≈ C France
27 *R5* **Arrowhead, Lake** ▣ Texas, SW USA
190 *L5* **Arrowsmith, Mount** *hill* New South Wales, SE Australia
193 *D21* **Arrowtown** Otago, South Island, NZ
63 *D17* **Arroyo Barú** Entre Ríos, E Argentina
106 *J10* **Arroyo de la Luz** Extremadura, W Spain
65 *J16* **Arroyo de la Ventana** Río Negro, SE Argentina
37 *P13* **Arroyo Grande** California, W USA
Ar Ru'ays *see* Ar Ruways
147 *R11* **Ar Rubʻ al Khālī** *Eng.* Empty Quarter, Great Sandy Desert. *desert* SW Asia
145 *V13* **Ar Ruḑaymah** S Iraq
63 *A16* **Arrufó** Santa Fe, C Argentina
144 *I7* **Ar Ruḩaybah** *var.* Ruhaybeh, *Fr.* Rouhaïbé. Dimashq, W Syria
145 *V15* **Ar Rukhaymīyah** *well* S Iraq
145 *U11* **Ar Rumaythah** *var.* Rumaitha. S Iraq
147 *X8* **Ar Rustāq** *var.* Rostak, Rustaq. N Oman
145 *N8* **Ar Ruţbah** *var.* Rutba. SW Iraq
146 *M3* **Ar Rūthīyah** *spring/well* NW Saudi Arabia
ar-Ruwaida *see* Ar Ruwayḑah
147 *O8* **Ar Ruwayḑah** *var.* ar-Ruwaida. Jīzān, C Saudi Arabia
149 *N15* **Ar Ruways** *var.* Al Ruweis, Ar Ru'ays, Ruwais. N Qatar
149 *O17* **Ar Ruways** *var.* Ar Ru'ays, Ruwaisv. Abū Ẓaby, W UAE
97 *G21* **Års** *var.* Aars. Nordjylland, N Denmark
Arsanias *see* Murat Nehri
127 *Nn18* **Arsen'yev** Primorskiy Kray, SE Russian Federation
161 *G19* **Arsikere** Karnātaka, W India
131 *R3* **Arsk** Respublika Tatarstan, W Russian Federation
96 *N10* **Årskogen** Gävleborg, C Sweden
124 *N3* **Ársos** C Cyprus
96 *N13* **Årsunda** Gävleborg, C Sweden
Arta *see* Árachthos
117 *C17* **Árta** *anc.* Ambracia. Ípeiros, W Greece
143 *T12* **Artashat** S Armenia
42 *M15* **Arteaga** Michoacán de Ocampo, SW Mexico
127 *Nn18* **Artem** Primorskiy Kray, SE Russian Federation
46 *C4* **Artemisa** La Habana, W Cuba
119 *W7* **Artemivs'k** Donets'ka Oblast', E Ukraine
126 *I14* **Artemovsk** Krasnoyarskiy Kray, S Russian Federation
126 *Kk13* **Artemovskiy** Irkutskaya Oblast', C Russian Federation
125 *Ee13* **Artemovskiy** Sverdlovskaya Oblast', C Russian Federation
107 *U5* **Artesa de Segre** Cataluña, NE Spain
39 *U14* **Artesia** New Mexico, SW USA
27 *Q14* **Artesia Wells** Texas, SW USA
110 *G8* **Arth** Schwyz, C Switzerland
12 *F15* **Arthur** Ontario, S Canada
32 *M14* **Arthur** Illinois, N USA
30 *L14* **Arthur** Nebraska, C USA
31 *Q5* **Arthur** North Dakota, N USA
193 *B21* **Arthur** ≈ South Island, NZ
20 *B13* **Arthur, Lake** ▣ Pennsylvania, NE USA
191 *N15* **Arthur River** ≈ Tasmania, SE Australia
193 *G18* **Arthur's Pass** Canterbury, South Island, NZ
193 *G17* **Arthur's Pass** *pass* South Island, NZ
46 *I3* **Arthur's Town** Cat Island, C Bahamas
46 *M9* **Artibonite, Rivière de l'** ≈ C Haiti
63 *E16* **Artigas** *prev.* San Eugenio, San Eugenio del Cuareim. Artigas, N Uruguay
63 *E16* **Artigas** ◈ *department* N Uruguay
204 *H1* **Artigas** *Uruguayan research station* Antarctica
143 *T11* **Art'ik** W Armenia
197 *G4* **Art, Île** *island* Îles Belep, W New Caledonia
105 *O2* **Artois** *cultural region* N France
142 *L12* **Artova** Tokat, N Turkey
107 *Y9* **Artrutx, Cap d'** *var.* Cabo Dartuch. *headland* Menorca, Spain, W Mediterranean Sea
Artsiz *see* Artsyz
119 *N11* **Artsyz** *Rus.* Artsiz. Odes'ka Oblast', SW Ukraine
164 *E7* **Artux** Xinjiang Uygur Zizhiqu, NW China
143 *R11* **Artvin** Artvin, NE Turkey
143 *R11* **Artvin** ◈ *province* NE Turkey
152 *G14* **Artyk** Akhalskiy Velayat, C Turkmenistan
81 *Q16* **Aru** Haut-Zaïre, NE Zaire
106 *I4* **A Rúa** *var.* La Rúa. Galicia, NW Spain
83 *E17* **Arua** NW Uganda
Aruângua *see* Luangwa
47 *O15* **Aruba** *var.* Oruba. ◇ *Dutch autonomous region* S West Indies
49 *Q4* **Aruba** *island* Aruba, Lesser Antilles
Aru Islands *see* Aru, Kepulauan
176 *Ww14* **Aru, Kepulauan** *Eng.* Aru Islands; *prev.* Aroe Islands. *island group* E Indonesia
159 *W10* **Arunāchal Pradesh** *prev.* North East Frontier Agency, North East Frontier Agency of Assam. ◈ *state* NE India
169 *U7* **Arun Qi** Nei Mongol Zizhiqu, N China
161 *H23* **Aruppukkottai** Tamil Nādu, SE India
176 *Ww9* **Aruri, Selat** *strait* Irian Jaya, E Indonesia
83 *I20* **Arusha** Arusha, N Tanzania
83 *I21* **Arusha** ◈ *region* E Tanzania
83 *I20* **Arusha** ✕ Arusha, N Tanzania
56 *C9* **Arusí, Punta** *headland* NW Colombia
174 *Ll10* **Arut, Sungai** ≈ Borneo, C Indonesia
161 *J23* **Aruvi Aru** ≈ NW Sri Lanka
81 *M17* **Aruwimi** *var.* Ituri (upper course). ≈ NE Zaire
Árva *see* Orava
39 *T4* **Arvada** Colorado, C USA
Arvand Rūd *see* ʻArab, Shaţţ al
168 *J8* **Arvayheer** Övörhangay, C Mongolia
15 *L8* **Arviat** *prev.* Eskimo Point. Northwest Territories, C Canada
95 *I14* **Arvidsjaur** Norrbotten, N Sweden
97 *J15* **Arvika** Värmland, C Sweden
94 *J8* **Årviksand** Troms, N Norway
37 *S13* **Arvin** California, W USA
151 *P7* **Arykbalyk** *Kaz.* Aryqbalyq. Kokshetau, N Kazakhstan
Aryqbalyq *see* Arykbalyk
151 *P17* **Arys'** *Kaz.* Arys. Yuzhnyy Kazakhstan, S Kazakhstan
Arys *see* Orzysz
Arys Köli *see* Arys, Ozero
151 *O14* **Arys, Ozero** *Kaz.* Arys Köli. ◎ C Kazakhstan
109 *D16* **Arzachena** Sardegna, Italy, C Mediterranean Sea
131 *O4* **Arzamas** Nizhegorodskaya Oblast', W Russian Federation
147 *V13* **Arzāt** S Oman
106 *H3* **Arzúa** Galicia, NW Spain
113 *A16* **Aš** *Ger.* Asch. Západní Čechy, W Czech Republic
97 *H15* **Ås** Akershus, S Norway
97 *H20* **Aså** Nordjylland, N Denmark
85 *E21* **Asab** Karas, S Namibia
79 *U16* **Asaba** Delta, S Nigeria
155 *S4* **Asadābād** *var.* Asadābād; *prev.* Chaghasarāy. Kunar, E Afghanistan
144 *K3* **Asad, Buḩayrat al** ◎ N Syria
65 *H20* **Asador, Pampa del** *plain* S Argentina
171 *Kk17* **Asahi** Chiba, Honshū, S Japan
171 *J13* **Asahi** Toyama, Honshū, SW Japan
172 *Pp5* **Asahi-dake** ▲ Hokkaidō, N Japan
170 *Ff13* **Asahi-gawa** ≈ Honshū, SW Japan
172 *P5* **Asahikawa** Hokkaidō, N Japan
153 *S10* **Asaka** *Rus.* Assake; *prev.* Leninsk. Andijon Wiloyati, E Uzbekistan
79 *P17* **Asamankese** SE Ghana
171 *Jj15* **Asama-yama** ▲ Honshū, S Japan
196 *B15* **Asan** W Guam
196 *B15* **Asan Point** *headland* W Guam
159 *R15* **Āsānsol** West Bengal, NE India
176 *V9* **Asbakin** Irian Jaya, E Indonesia
Asben *see* Aïr, Massif de l'
125 *Ee11* **Asbest** Sverdlovskaya Oblast', C Russian Federation
13 *Q12* **Asbestos** Québec, SE Canada
31 *Y13* **Asbury** Iowa, C USA
20 *K15* **Asbury Park** New Jersey, NE USA
43 *Z12* **Ascención, Bahiá de la** *bay* NW Caribbean Sea
42 *I3* **Ascensión** Chihuahua, N Mexico
67 *M14* **Ascension Fracture Zone** *tectonic feature* C Atlantic Ocean
67 *G14* **Ascension Island** ◇ *dependency of St.Helena* C Atlantic Ocean
67 *N16* **Ascension Island** *island* C Atlantic Ocean
Asch *see* Aš
111 *S3* **Aschach an der Donau** Oberösterreich, N Austria
103 *H18* **Aschaffenburg** Bayern, SW Germany
103 *F14* **Ascheberg** Nordrhein-Westfalen, W Germany
103 *L14* **Aschersleben** Sachsen-Anhalt, C Germany
108 *G12* **Asciano** Toscana, C Italy
108 *J13* **Ascoli Piceno** *anc.* Asculum Picenum. Marche, C Italy
109 *M17* **Ascoli Satriano** *anc.* Asculub, Ausculum Apulum. Puglia, SE Italy
110 *G11* **Ascona** Ticino, S Switzerland
Asculub *see* Ascoli Satriano
Asculum Picenum *see* Ascoli Piceno
82 *L11* **Aseb** *var.* Assab, *Amh.* Āseb. SE Eritrea
97 *M20* **Åseda** Kronoberg, S Sweden
131 *T6* **Asekeyevo** Orenburgskaya Oblast', W Russian Federation
194 *J13* **Aseki** Morobe, C PNG
83 *J14* **Āsela** *var.* Asella, Aselle, Asselle. C Ethiopia
95 *H15* **Åsele** Västerbotten, N Sweden
Asella/Aselle *see* Āsela
96 *K12* **Åsen** Kopparberg, C Sweden
116 *J11* **Asenovgrad** *prev.* Stanimaka. Plovdivska Oblast, S Bulgaria
175 *Q11* **Asera** Sulawesi, C Indonesia
97 *E17* **Åseral** Vest-Agder, S Norway
120 *J3* **Aseri** *var.* Asserien, *Ger.* Asserin. Ida-Virumaa, NE Estonia
42 *J10* **Aserradero** Durango, W Mexico
97 *H16* **Åsgårdstrand** Vestfold, S Norway
125 *E11* **Asha** Chelyabinskaya Oblast', C Russian Federation
Ashara *see* Al ʻAshārah
25 *T6* **Ashburn** Georgia, SE USA
193 *G19* **Ashburton** Canterbury, South Island, NZ
193 *G19* **Ashburton** ≈ South Island, NZ
188 *H8* **Ashburton River** ≈ Western Australia
151 *V10* **Ashchysu** ≈ E Kazakhstan
8 *M16* **Ashcroft** British Columbia, SW Canada
144 *E10* **Ashdod** *anc.* Azotos, *Lat.* Azotus. Central, W Israel
29 *S14* **Ashdown** Arkansas, C USA
23 *T9* **Asheboro** North Carolina, SE USA
9 *X15* **Ashern** Manitoba, S Canada
23 *P10* **Asheville** North Carolina, SE USA
10 *E8* **Asheweig** ≈ Ontario, C Canada
29 *V9* **Ash Flat** Arkansas, C USA
191 *T4* **Ashford** New South Wales, SE Australia
99 *P22* **Ashford** SE England, UK
38 *K11* **Ash Fork** Arizona, SW USA
152 *F13* **Ashgabat** *prev.* Ashkhabad, Poltoratsk. ● (Turkmenistan) Akhalskiy Velayat, C Turkmenistan
152 *F13* **Ashgabat** ✕ Akhalskiy Velayat, C Turkmenistan
29 *T7* **Ash Grove** Missouri, C USA
171 *K15* **Ashikaga** *var.* Asikaga. Tochigi, Honshū, S Japan
171 *Mm10* **Ashiro** Iwate, Honshū, C Japan
170 *E16* **Ashizuri-misaki** *headland* Shikoku, SW Japan
Ashkelon *see* Ashqelon
Ashkhabad *see* Ashgabat
25 *Q4* **Ashland** Alabama, S USA
28 *K7* **Ashland** Kansas, C USA
23 *P5* **Ashland** Kentucky, S USA
21 *S2* **Ashland** Maine, NE USA
24 *M1* **Ashland** Mississippi, S USA
29 *U4* **Ashland** Missouri, C USA
31 *S15* **Ashland** Nebraska, C USA
33 *T12* **Ashland** Ohio, N USA
34 *G15* **Ashland** Oregon, NW USA
23 *W6* **Ashland** Virginia, NE USA
32 *K3* **Ashland** Wisconsin, N USA
22 *I8* **Ashland City** Tennessee, S USA
191 *S4* **Ashley** New South Wales, SE Australia
31 *O7* **Ashley** North Dakota, N USA
181 *W7* **Ashmore and Cartier Islands** ◇ *Australian external territory* E Indian Ocean
121 *I14* **Ashmyany** *Rus.* Oshmyany. Hrodzyenskaya Voblasts', W Belarus
20 *K12* **Ashokan Reservoir** ▣ New York, NE USA
172 *Pp6* **Ashoro** Hokkaidō, NE Japan
144 *E10* **Ashqelon** *var.* Ashkelon. Southern, C Israel
Ashraf *see* Behshahr
145 *O3* **Ash Shadādah** *var.* Ash Shaddādah, Jisr ash Shadadi, Shaddādī, Shedadi, Tell Shedadi. Al Ḩasakah, NE Syria
Ash Shaddādah *see* Ash Shadādah
145 *Y12* **Ash Shāfī** E Iraq
145 *R4* **Ash Shakk** *var.* Shaykh. C Iraq
Ash Sham/Ash Shām *see* Dimashq
145 *T10* **Ash Shāmīyah** *var.* Shamiya. C Iraq
145 *Y13* **Ash Shāmīyah** *var.* Al Bādiyah al Janūbīyah. *desert* S Iraq
145 *T11* **Ash Shanāfīyah** *var.* Ash Shināfīyah. S Iraq
144 *G13* **Ash Sharāh** *var.* Esh Sharā. ▲▲ W Jordan
149 *R16* **Ash Shāriqah** *Eng.* Sharjah. Ash Shāriqah, NE UAE
149 *R16* **Ash Shāriqah** *var.* Sharjah. ✕ Ash Shāriqah, NE UAE
146 *I4* **Ash Sharmah** *var.* Šarma. Tabūk, NW Saudi Arabia
145 *R4* **Ash Sharqāţ** NW Iraq
147 *S10* **Ash Sharqīyah** *off.* Al Minţaqah ash Sharqīyah, *Eng.* Eastern Region. ◈ *province* E Saudi Arabia
145 *W11* **Ash Shaţrah** *var.* Shatra. SE Iraq
144 *G13* **Ash Shawbak** Ma'ān, W Jordan
144 *L5* **Ash Shaykh Ibrāhīm** Ḩimş, C Syria
147 *O17* **Ash Shaykh ʻUthmān** SW Yemen
147 *S15* **Ash Shiḩr** SE Yemen
Ash Shināfīyah *see* Ash Shanāfīyah
147 *V12* **Ash Shişar** *var.* Shisur. SW Oman
145 *S13* **Ash Shubrūm** *well* S Iraq
147 *R4* **Ash Shuqayq** *var.* As Shageeg. *desert* S Kuwait
147 *R10* **Ash Shuqqān** *desert* E Saudi Arabia
77 *O9* **Ash Shuwayrif** *var.* Ash Shwayrif. N Libya
Ash Shwayrif *see* Ash Shuwayrif
33 *U10* **Ashtabula** Ohio, N USA
31 *Q5* **Ashtabula, Lake** ▣ North Dakota, N USA
143 *T12* **Ashtarak** W Armenia
148 *M6* **Āshtīān** *var.* Āshtiyān. Markazī, W Iran
Āshtiyān *see* Āshtīān
35 *R13* **Ashton** Idaho, NW USA
11 *O10* **Ashuanipi Lake** ◎ Newfoundland and Labrador, E Canada
13 *P6* **Ashuapmushuan** ≈ Québec, SE Canada
25 *Q3* **Ashville** Alabama, S USA
33 *S14* **Ashville** Ohio, N USA
32 *K3* **Ashwabay, Mount** *hill* Wisconsin, N USA
176 *Uu7* **Asia, Kepulauan** *island group* E Indonesia
160 *N13* **Āsika** Orissa, E India
Asikaga *see* Ashikaga
95 *M18* **Asikkala** *var.* Vääksy. Häme, SW Finland
76 *G5* **Asilah** N Morocco
ʻAşī, Nahr al *see* Orontes
109 *B16* **Asinara, Isola** *island* W Italy
126 *H13* **Asino** Tomskaya Oblast', C Russian Federation
121 *O14* **Asintorf** *Rus.* Osintorf. Vitsyebskaya Voblasts', N Belarus
121 *L17* **Asipovichy** *Rus.* Osipovichi. Mahilyowskaya Voblasts', C Belarus
147 *N12* **ʻAsīr** *off.* Minţaqat ʻAsīr. ◈ *province* SW Saudi Arabia

◆ Country
● Country Capital
◇ Dependent Territory
○ Dependent Territory Capital
◈ Administrative Region
✕ International Airport
▲ Mountain
▲▲ Mountain Range
⛰ Volcano
≈ River
◎ Lake
▣ Reservoir

146 M11 **'Asīr** *Eng.* Asīr. ▲ SW Saudi Arabia
145 X10 **Askal** E Iraq
143 P13 **Aşkale** Erzurum, NE Turkey
119 T11 **Askaniya-Nova** Khersons'ka Oblast', S Ukraine
97 H15 **Asker** Akershus, S Norway
97 L17 **Askersund** Örebro, C Sweden
Askī Kalak *see* Eski Kaļak
97 I15 **Askim** Østfold, S Norway
131 V3 **Askino** Respublika Bashkortostan, W Russian Federation
117 D14 **Áskio** ▲ N Greece
158 L9 **Askot** Uttar Pradesh, N India
96 C12 **Askvoll** Sogn og Fjordane, S Norway
142 A13 **Aslan Burnu** *headland* W Turkey
142 L16 **Aslantaş Barajı** ▣ S Turkey
155 S4 **Asmār** *var.* Bar Kunar. Kunar, E Afghanistan
82 I9 **Asmara** *Amh.* Āsmera. ● (Eritrea) C Eritrea
Āsmera *see* Asmara
97 L21 **Åsnen** ◎ S Sweden
117 F19 **Asopós** ≈ S Greece
176 X10 **Asori** Irian Jaya, E Indonesia
82 G12 **Āsosa** W Ethiopia
34 M10 **Asotin** Washington, NW USA
Aspadana *see* Eşfahān
Aspang *see* Aspang Markt
111 X6 **Aspang Markt** *var.* Aspang. Niederösterreich, E Austria
107 S12 **Aspe** País Valenciano, E Spain
39 R5 **Aspen** Colorado, C USA
27 P6 **Aspermont** Texas, SW USA
Asphaltites, Lacus *see* Dead Sea
Aspinwall *see* Colón
193 C20 **Aspiring, Mount** ▲ South Island, NZ
117 B16 **Asprókavos, Ákra** *headland* Kérkyra, Iónioi Nísoi, Greece, C Mediterranean Sea
Aspropótamos *see* Achelóos
Assab *see* Aseb
78 J10 **Assaba** *var.* Açâba. ◈ *region* S Mauritania
144 L4 **As Sabkhah** *var.* Sabkha. Ar Raqqah, NE Syria
145 U6 **As Sa'dīyah** E Iraq
Assad, Lake *see* Asad, Buḩayrat al
144 I8 **Aş Şafā** ▲ S Syria
144 I10 **Aş Şafāwī** Al Mafraq, N Jordan
Aş Şaff *see* El Şaff
145 N2 **Aş Şafīḩ** Al Ḩasakah, N Syria
Aş Şaḩrā' al Gharbīyah *see* Sahara el Gharbîya
Aş Şaḩrā' ash Sharqīyah *see* Sahara el Sharqîya
Assake *see* Asaka
As Salamīyah *see* Salamīyah
147 Q4 **As Salimi** *var.* Salemy. SW Kuwait
148 J11 **As Sālimīyah** W Kuwait
69 W7 **'Assal, Lac** ◎ C Djibouti
As Sallūm *see* Salûm
145 T13 **As Salmān** S Iraq
144 G10 **As Salţ** *var.* Salt. Al Balqā', NW Jordan
148 M16 **As Salwā** *var.* Salwa, Salwah. S Qatar
159 V12 **Assam** ◈ *state* NE India
Assamaka *see* Assamakka
79 T8 **Assamakka** *var.* Assamaka. Agadez, NW Niger
145 U11 **As Samāwah** *var.* Samawa. S Iraq
As Saqia al Hamra *see* Saguia al Hamra
144 J4 **Aş Şā'rān** Ḩamāh, C Syria
144 G9 **Aş Şarīḩ** Irbid, N Jordan
23 Z5 **Assateague Island** *island* Maryland, NE USA
145 O6 **As Sayyāl** *var.* Sayyāl. Dayr az Zawr, E Syria
101 G18 **Asse** Vlaams Brabant, C Belgium
101 D16 **Assebroek** West-Vlaanderen, NW Belgium
Asselle *see* Āsela
109 C20 **Assemini** Sardegna, Italy, C Mediterranean Sea
100 N7 **Assen** Drenthe, NE Netherlands
101 E16 **Assenede** Oost-Vlaanderen, NW Belgium
97 G24 **Assens** Fyn, C Denmark
Asserien/Asserin *see* Aseri
101 I21 **Assesse** Namur, SE Belgium
As Shageeg *see* Ash Shuqayq
147 Y8 **As Sīb** *var.* Seeb. NE Oman
145 Z13 **As Sībah** *var.* Sibah. SE Iraq
9 T17 **Assiniboia** Saskatchewan, S Canada
9 V15 **Assiniboine** ≈ Manitoba, S Canada
9 P16 **Assiniboine, Mount** ▲ Alberta/British Columbia, SW Canada
Assiout *see* Asyût
62 J9 **Assis** São Paulo, S Brazil
108 I13 **Assisi** Umbria, C Italy
Assiut *see* Asyût
Assling *see* Jesenice
Assouan *see* Aswân
Assu *see* Açu
Assuan *see* Aswân
148 K12 **Aş Şubayḩīyah** *var.* Subiyah. S Kuwait
147 R16 **As Sufāl** S Yemen
144 L5 **As Sukhnah** *var.* Sukhne, *Fr.* Soukhné. Ḩimş, C Syria
145 U4 **As Sulaymānīyah** *var.* Sulaimaniya, *Kurd.* Slēmānī. NE Iraq
147 P11 **As Sulayyil** Ar Riyāḑ, S Saudi Arabia
123 M16 **As Sulţān** N Libya
147 Q5 **Aş Şummān** *desert* N Saudi Arabia
147 Q16 **Aş Şurrah** SW Yemen
145 N4 **Aş Şuwār** *var.* Şuwār. Dayr az Zawr, E Syria
144 H9 **As Suwaydā'** *var.* El Suweida, Es Suweida, Suweida, *Fr.* Soueida. As Suwaydā', SW Syria
144 H9 **As Suwaydā'** *off.* Muḩāfaẓat as Suwaydā', *var.* As Suwaydā, Suwaydá, Suweida, *Fr.* Soueida. ◈ *governorate* S Syria
147 Z9 **As Suwayḩ** NE Oman
147 X8 **As Suwayq** *var.* Suwaik. N Oman
145 T8 **Aş Şuwayrah** *var.* Suwaira. E Iraq
As Suways *see* Suez
Asta Colonia *see* Asti
Astacus *see* İzmit
117 M23 **Astakída** *island* SE Greece
148 M3 **Āstāneh** Gīlān, NW Iran
Asta Pompeia *see* Asti
143 Y14 **Astara** S Azerbaijan
Astarabad *see* Gorgān
101 L15 **Asten** Noord-Brabant, SE Netherlands
Asterābād *see* Gorgān
108 C8 **Asti** *anc.* Asta Colonia, Asta Pompeia, Hasta Colonia, Hasta Pompeia. Piemonte, NW Italy
Astigi *see* Ecija
Astipálaia *see* Astypálaia
154 L16 **Astola Island** *island* SW Pakistan
158 H4 **Astor** Jammu and Kashmir, NW India
106 K4 **Astorga** *anc.* Asturica Augusta. Castilla-León, N Spain
34 F10 **Astoria** Oregon, NW USA
1 F8 **Astoria Fan** *undersea feature* E Pacific Ocean
97 J22 **Åstorp** Kristianstad, S Sweden
Astrabad *see* Gorgān
131 Q13 **Astrakhan'** Astrakhanskaya Oblast', SW Russian Federation
Astrakhan-Bazar *see* Cälilabad
131 Q11 **Astrakhanskaya Oblast'** ◈ *province* SW Russian Federation
95 J15 **Åsträsk** Västerbotten, N Sweden
Astrida *see* Butare
67 O22 **Astrid Ridge** *undersea feature* S Atlantic Ocean
194 J11 **Astrolabe Bay** *inlet* N PNG
197 I4 **Astrolabe, Récifs de l'** *reef* C New Caledonia
124 Nn3 **Astromerítis** N Cyprus
117 F20 **Ástros** Pelopónnisos, S Greece
121 G16 **Astryna** *Rus.* Ostryna. Hrodzyenskaya Voblasts', W Belarus
106 J2 **Asturias** ◈ *autonomous community* NW Spain
Asturias *see* Oviedo
Asturica Augusta *see* Astorga
117 L22 **Astypálaia** *var.* Astipálaia, *It.* Stampalia. *island* Kykládes, Greece, Aegean Sea
198 Aa8 **Āsuisui, Cape** *headland* Savai'i, W Western Samoa
205 S2 **Asuka** *Japanese research station* Antarctica
64 O6 **Asunción** ● (Paraguay) Central, S Paraguay
64 O6 **Asunción** × Central, S Paraguay
196 K3 **Asuncion Island** *island* N Northern Mariana Islands
44 E6 **Asunción Mita** Jutiapa, SE Guatemala
Asunción Nochixtlán *see* Nochixtlán
42 E3 **Asunción, Río** ≈ NW Mexico
97 M18 **Åsunden** ◎ S Sweden
120 K11 **Asvyeya** *Rus.* Osveya. Vitsyebskaya Voblasts', N Belarus
Aswa *see* Achwa
77 X11 **Aswân** *var.* Assouan, Assuan; *anc.* Syene. SE Egypt
77 X11 **Aswân High Dam** *dam* SE Egypt
77 W9 **Asyût** *var.* Assiout, Assiut, Siut; *anc.* Lycopolis. C Egypt
200 R15 **Ata** *island* Tongatapu Group, SW Tonga
64 G8 **Atacama** *off.* Región de Atacama. ◈ *region* C Chile
Atacama Desert *see* Atacama, Desierto de
64 H4 **Atacama, Desierto de** *Eng.* Atacama Desert. *desert* N Chile
64 I6 **Atacama, Puna de** ▲ NW Argentina
64 I5 **Atacama, Salar de** *salt lake* N Chile
56 E11 **Ataco** Tolima, C Colombia
202 H8 **Atafu Atoll** *island* NW Tokelau
202 H8 **Atafu Village** Atafu Atoll, NW Tokelau
76 K12 **Atakor** ▲ SE Algeria
79 R14 **Atakora, Chaîne de l'** *var.* Atakora Mountains. ▲ N Benin
Atakora Mountains *see* Atakora, Chaîne de l'
79 R16 **Atakpamé** C Togo
152 F11 **Atakui** Akhalskiy Velayat, C Turkmenistan
60 B13 **Atalaia do Norte** Amazonas, N Brazil
171 J17 **Atami** Shizuoka, Honshū, S Japan
78 I7 **Aţâr** Adrar, W Mauritania
168 G10 **Atas Bogd** ▲ SW Mongolia
37 P12 **Atascadero** California, W USA
27 S13 **Atascosa River** ≈ Texas, SW USA
151 R11 **Atasu** Zhezkazgan, C Kazakhstan
151 R12 **Atasu** ≈ C Kazakhstan
200 Qq15 **Atata** *island* Tongatapu Group, S Tonga
142 H10 **Atatürk** × (İstanbul) İstanbul, NW Turkey
143 N16 **Atatürk Barajı** ▣ S Turkey
Atax *see* Aude
82 G8 **Atbara** *var.* 'Aţbārah. River Nile, NE Sudan
82 H8 **Atbara** *var.* Nahr 'Aţbarah. ≈ Eritrea/Sudan
'Aţbārah/'Aţbarah, Nahr *see* Atbara
151 P9 **Atbasar** Akmola, N Kazakhstan
At-Bashi *see* At-Bashy
153 W9 **At-Bashy** *var.* At-Bashi. Narynskaya Oblast', C Kyrgyzstan
24 I10 **Atchafalaya Bay** *bay* Louisiana, S USA
24 I8 **Atchafalaya River** ≈ Louisiana, S USA
Atchin *see* Aceh
29 Q3 **Atchison** Kansas, C USA
79 P16 **Atebubu** C Ghana
107 Q6 **Ateca** Aragón, NE Spain
42 K11 **Atengo, Río** ≈ C Mexico
Aternum *see* Pescara
109 K15 **Atessa** Abruzzi, C Italy
Ateste *see* Este
101 E19 **Ath** *var.* Aat. Hainaut, SW Belgium
9 Q13 **Athabasca** Alberta, SW Canada
9 Q12 **Athabasca** *var.* Athabaska. ≈ Alberta, SW Canada
9 R10 **Athabasca, Lake** ◎ Alberta/Saskatchewan, SW Canada
Athabaska *see* Athabasca
117 C16 **Athamánon** ▲ C Greece
99 F17 **Athboy** *Ir.* Baile Átha Buí. E Ireland
Athenae *see* Athína
99 C18 **Athenry** *Ir.* Baile Átha an Rí. W Ireland
25 P2 **Athens** Alabama, S USA
25 T3 **Athens** Georgia, SE USA
33 T14 **Athens** Ohio, N USA
22 M10 **Athens** Tennessee, S USA
27 V7 **Athens** Texas, SW USA
Athens *see* Athína
117 B18 **Athéras, Ákra** *headland* Kefallinía, Iónioi Nísoi, Greece, C Mediterranean Sea
189 W4 **Atherton** Queensland, NE Australia
83 I19 **Athi** ≈ S Kenya
124 O3 **Athiénou** SE Cyprus
117 H19 **Athína** *Eng.* Athens; *prev.* Athínai, *anc.* Athenae. ● (Greece) Attikí, C Greece
Athínai *see* Athína
145 S10 **Athīyah** C Iraq
99 D18 **Athlone** *Ir.* Baile Átha Luain. C Ireland
161 F16 **Athni** Karnātaka, W India
193 C23 **Athol** Southland, South Island, NZ
21 N11 **Athol** Massachusetts, NE USA
117 I15 **Áthos** ▲ NE Greece
Athos, Mount *see* Ágion Óros
Ath Thawrah *see* Madīnat ath Thawrah
147 P5 **Ath Thumāmī** *spring/well* N Saudi Arabia
101 L25 **Athus** Luxembourg, SE Belgium
99 E19 **Athy** *Ir.* Baile Átha Í. C Ireland
80 I10 **Ati** Batha, C Chad
83 F16 **Atiak** NW Uganda
59 G17 **Atico** Arequipa, SW Peru
107 O6 **Atienza** Castilla-La Mancha, C Spain
41 Q6 **Atigun Pass** *pass* Alaska, USA
10 B12 **Atikokan** Ontario, S Canada
11 O9 **Atikonak Lac** ◎ Newfoundland and Labrador, E Canada
44 C6 **Atitlán, Lago de** ◎ W Guatemala
202 L16 **Atiu** *island* S Cook Islands
Atjeh *see* Aceh
127 O9 **Atka** Magadanskaya Oblast', E Russian Federation
40 H17 **Atka** Atka Island, Alaska, USA
40 H17 **Atka Island** *island* Aleutian Islands, Alaska, USA
131 O7 **Atkarsk** Saratovskaya Oblast', W Russian Federation
29 U11 **Atkins** Arkansas, C USA
31 O13 **Atkinson** Nebraska, C USA
176 U10 **Atkri** Irian Jaya, E Indonesia
43 O13 **Atlacomulco** *var.* Atlacomulco de Fabela. México, C Mexico
Atlacomulco de Fabela *see* Atlacomulco
25 S3 **Atlanta** *state capital* Georgia, SE USA
33 R6 **Atlanta** Michigan, N USA
27 X6 **Atlanta** Texas, SW USA
31 T15 **Atlantic** Iowa, C USA
23 Y10 **Atlantic** North Carolina, SE USA
25 W8 **Atlantic Beach** Florida, SE USA
20 J17 **Atlantic City** New Jersey, NE USA
180 L14 **Atlantic-Indian Basin** *undersea feature* SW Indian Ocean
180 K13 **Atlantic-Indian Ridge** *undersea feature* SW Indian Ocean
56 E4 **Atlántico** *off.* Departamento del Atlántico. ◈ *province* NW Colombia
66-67 **Atlantic Ocean** *ocean*
44 K7 **Atlántico Norte, Región Autónoma** *prev.* Zelaya Norte. ◈ *autonomous region* NE Nicaragua
44 L10 **Atlántico Sur, Región Autónoma** *prev.* Zelaya Sur. ◈ *autonomous region* SE Nicaragua
44 I5 **Atlántida** ◈ *department* N Honduras
79 Y15 **Atlantika Mountains** ▲ E Nigeria
66 J10 **Atlantis Fracture Zone** *tectonic feature* NW Atlantic Ocean
76 H7 **Atlas Mountains** ▲ NW Africa
127 Pp13 **Atlasova, Ostrov** *island* SE Russian Federation
127 Pp10 **Atlasovo** Kamchatskaya Oblast', E Russian Federation
123 H13 **Atlas Saharien** *var.* Saharan Atlas. ▲ Algeria/Morocco
Atlas, Tell *see* Atlas Tellien
123 Gg10 **Atlas Tellien** *Eng.* Tell Atlas. ▲ N Algeria
8 I9 **Atlin** British Columbia, W Canada
8 I9 **Atlin Lake** ◎ British Columbia, W Canada
43 P14 **Atlixco** Puebla, S Mexico
96 B11 **Atløyna** *island* S Norway
161 I17 **Ātmakūr** Andhra Pradesh, C India
25 O8 **Atmore** Alabama, S USA
103 J20 **Atmühl** ≈ S Germany
96 H11 **Atna** ≈ S Norway
170 E12 **Atō** Yamaguchi, Honshū, SW Japan
59 L21 **Atocha** Potosí, S Bolivia
29 P12 **Atoka** Oklahoma, C USA
29 O12 **Atoka Lake** *var.* Atoka Reservoir. ▣ Oklahoma, C USA
Atoka Reservoir *see* Atoka Lake
35 Q14 **Atomic City** Idaho, NW USA
42 L10 **Atotonilco** Zacatecas, C Mexico
42 M13 **Atotonilco el Alto** *var.* Atotonilco. Jalisco, SW Mexico
79 N7 **Atouila, 'Erg** *desert* N Mali
43 N16 **Atoyac** *var.* Atoyac de Alvarez. Guerrero, S Mexico
Atoyac de Alvarez *see* Atoyac
43 P15 **Atoyac, Río** ≈ S Mexico
41 O5 **Atqasuk** Alaska, USA
152 C13 **Atrak** *Per.* Rūd-e Atrak, *Rus.* Atrek, *Turkm.* Etrek. ≈ Iran/Turkmenistan
Atrak, Rūd-e *see* Atrak
97 J20 **Ätran** ≈ S Sweden
56 C7 **Atrato, Río** ≈ NW Colombia
Atrek *see* Atrak
109 K14 **Atri** Abruzzi, C Italy
Atria *see* Adria
171 Jj16 **Atsugi** *var.* Atugi. Kanagawa, Honshū, S Japan
171 L12 **Atsumi** Yamagata, Honshū, C Japan
172 Oo4 **Atsuta** Hokkaidō, NE Japan
176 Y13 **Atsy** Irian Jaya, E Indonesia
149 Q17 **Aţ Ţaff** *desert* C UAE
144 G12 **Aţ Ţafīlah** *var.* Et Tafila, Tafila. Aţ Ţafīlah, W Jordan
144 G12 **Aţ Ţafīlah** *off.* Muḩāfaẓat aţ Ţafīlah. ◈ *governorate* W Jordan
146 L10 **Aţ Ţā'if** Makkah, W Saudi Arabia
Attaleia/Attalia *see* Antalya
25 Q3 **Attalla** Alabama, S USA
144 L2 **At Tall al Abyaḑ** *var.* Tall al Abyaḑ, Tell Abyad, *Fr.* Tell Abiad. Ar Raqqah, N Syria
144 L7 **Aţ Ţanf** Ḩimş, S Syria
Attapu *see* Samakhixai
145 S10 **At Ţaqţaqānah** C Iraq
117 O23 **Attávytos** ▲ Ródos, Dodekánisos, Greece, Aegean Sea
145 V15 **At Tawal** *desert* Iraq/Saudi Arabia
10 G9 **Attawapiskat** Ontario, C Canada
10 F9 **Attawapiskat** ≈ Ontario, S Canada
10 D9 **Attawapiskat Lake** ◎ Ontario, C Canada
At Taybé *see* Ţayyibah
103 F16 **Attendorn** Nordrhein-Westfalen, W Germany
111 R5 **Attersee** Salzburg, NW Austria
111 R5 **Attersee** ◎ N Austria
101 L24 **Attert** Luxembourg, SE Belgium
144 M4 **At Tibnī** *var.* Tibnī. Dayr az Zawr, NE Syria
33 N13 **Attica** Indiana, N USA
20 E10 **Attica** New York, NE USA
Attica *see* Attikí
11 N7 **Attikamagen Lake** ◎ Newfoundland and Labrador, E Canada
117 H20 **Attikí** *Eng.* Attica. ◈ *region* C Greece
21 O12 **Attleboro** Massachusetts, NE USA
111 R5 **Attnang** Oberösterreich, N Austria
155 U6 **Attock City** Punjab, E Pakistan
Attopeu *see* Samakhixai
27 X8 **Attoyac River** ≈ Texas, SW USA
40 D16 **Attu** Attu Island, Alaska, USA
145 Y12 **Aţ Ţūbah** E Iraq
146 K4 **Aţ Ţubayq** *plain* Jordan/Saudi Arabia
40 C16 **Attu Island** *island* Aleutian Islands, Alaska, USA
Aţ Ţūr *see* El Ţûr
161 I21 **Āttūr** Tamil Nādu, SE India
147 N17 **At Turbah** SW Yemen
64 I12 **Atuel, Río** ≈ C Argentina
Atugi *see* Atsugi
203 X7 **Atuona** Hiva Oa, NE French Polynesia
Aturus *see* Adour
97 M18 **Åtvidaberg** Östergötland, S Sweden
37 P9 **Atwater** California, W USA
31 T8 **Atwater** Minnesota, N USA
28 I2 **Atwood** Kansas, C USA
33 U12 **Atwood Lake** ▣ Ohio, N USA
131 P5 **Atyashevo** Respublika Mordoviya, W Russian Federation
150 F12 **Atyrau** *prev.* Gur'yev. Atyrau, W Kazakhstan
150 E11 **Atyrau** *off.* Atyrauskaya Oblast', var. *Kaz.* Atyraū Oblysy; *prev.* Gur'yevskaya Oblast'. ◈ *province* W Kazakhstan
Atyraū Oblysy/Atyrauskaya Oblast' *see* Atyrau
110 J7 **Au** Vorarlberg, NW Austria
194 G8 **Aua Island** *island* NW PNG
105 S16 **Aubagne** *anc.* Albania. Bouches-du-Rhône, SE France
101 L25 **Aubange** Luxembourg, SE Belgium
105 Q6 **Aube** ◈ *department* N France
105 R6 **Aube** ≈ N France
101 L19 **Aubel** Liège, E Belgium
105 Q13 **Aubenas** Ardèche, E France
105 O8 **Aubigny-sur-Nère** Cher, C France
105 O13 **Aubin** Aveyron, S France
105 O13 **Aubrac, Monts d'** ▲ S France
38 J10 **Aubrey Cliffs** *cliff* Arizona, SW USA
25 R5 **Auburn** Alabama, S USA
37 P6 **Auburn** California, W USA
32 K14 **Auburn** Illinois, N USA
33 Q11 **Auburn** Indiana, N USA
22 J7 **Auburn** Kentucky, S USA
21 P8 **Auburn** Maine, NE USA
21 N11 **Auburn** Massachusetts, NE USA
31 S16 **Auburn** Nebraska, C USA
20 H10 **Auburn** New York, NE USA
34 H8 **Auburn** Washington, NW USA
105 N11 **Aubusson** Creuse, C France
120 E10 **Auce** *Ger.* Autz. Dobele, SW Latvia
104 L15 **Auch** *Lat.* Augusta Auscorum, Elimberrum. Gers, S France
79 U16 **Auchi** Edo, S Nigeria
25 T9 **Aucilla River** ≈ Florida/Georgia, SE USA
192 L6 **Auckland** Auckland, North Island, NZ
192 K5 **Auckland** *off.* Auckland Region. ◈ *region* North Island, NZ
192 L6 **Auckland** × Auckland, North Island, NZ
199 Ii15 **Auckland Islands** *island group* S NZ
105 O16 **Aude** ◈ *department* S France
105 N16 **Aude** *anc.* Atax. ≈ S France
Audenarde *see* Oudenaarde
Audern *see* Audru
104 E6 **Audierne** Finistère, NW France
104 E6 **Audierne, Baie d'** *bay* NW France
105 U7 **Audincourt** Doubs, E France
120 G5 **Audru** *Ger.* Audern. Pärnumaa, SW Estonia
31 T14 **Audubon** Iowa, C USA
103 N17 **Aue** Sachsen, E Germany
102 H12 **Aue** ≈ NW Germany
102 L9 **Auerbach** Bayern, SE Germany
103 M17 **Auerbach** Sachsen, E Germany
110 I10 **Auererrhein** ≈ SW Switzerland
103 N17 **Auersberg** ▲ E Germany
189 W9 **Augathella** Queensland, E Australia
33 Q12 **Auglaize River** ≈ Ohio, N USA
85 F22 **Augrabies Falls** *waterfall* W South Africa
33 R7 **Au Gres River** ≈ Michigan, N USA
Augsbourg *see* Augsburg
103 K22 **Augsburg** *Fr.* Augsbourg; *anc.* Augusta Vindelicorum. Bayern, S Germany
188 I14 **Augusta** Western Australia
109 L25 **Augusta** *It.* Agosta. Sicilia, Italy, C Mediterranean Sea
29 O6 **Augusta** Arkansas, C USA
25 V3 **Augusta** Georgia, SE USA
29 W11 **Augusta** Kansas, C USA
21 Q7 **Augusta** *state capital* Maine, NE USA
35 Q8 **Augusta** Montana, NW USA
Augusta *see* London
Augusta Auscorum *see* Auch
Augusta Emerita *see* Mérida
Augusta Praetoria *see* Aosta
Augusta Suessionum *see* Soissons
Augusta Trajana *see* Stara Zagora
Augusta Treverorum *see* Trier
Augusta Vangionum *see* Worms
Augusta Vindelicorum *see* Augsburg
97 G24 **Augustenborg** *Ger.* Augustenburg. Sønderjylland, SW Denmark
Augustenburg *see* Augustenborg
41 Q13 **Augustine Island** *island* Alaska, USA
12 L9 **Augustines, Lac des** ◎ Québec, SE Canada
Augustobona Tricassium *see* Troyes
Augustodunum *see* Autun
Augustodurum *see* Bayeux
Augustoritum Lemovicensium *see* Limoges
112 O8 **Augustów** *Rus.* Avgustov. Suwałki, NE Poland
Augustow Canal *see* Augustowski, Kanał
112 O8 **Augustowski, Kanał** *Eng.* Augustow Canal, *Rus.* Avgustovskiy Kanal. *canal* NE Poland
188 I9 **Augustus, Mount** ▲ Western Australia
195 X15 **Auki** Malaita, N Solomon Islands
23 W8 **Aulander** North Carolina, SE USA
188 L7 **Auld, Lake** *salt lake* Western Australia
Aulie Ata/Auliye-Ata *see* Zhambyl
108 E10 **Aulla** Toscana, C Italy
104 F6 **Aulne** ≈ NW France
Aulong *see* Ulong
39 T3 **Ault** Colorado, C USA
105 N3 **Aumale** Seine-Maritime, N France
Auminzatau, Gory *see* Owminzatovo-Toshi
79 T14 **Auna** Niger, W Nigeria
97 H21 **Auning** Århus, C Denmark
198 Cc9 **Aunu'u Island** *island* W American Samoa
85 E20 **Auob** *var.* Oup. ≈ Namibia/South Africa
95 K19 **Aura** Turku-Pori, SW Finland
111 R5 **Aurach** ≈ N Austria
Aural, Phnom *see* Aôral, Phnum
159 O14 **Aurangābād** Bihār, N India
160 F13 **Aurangābād** Mahārāshtra, C India
201 V7 **Aur Atoll** *atoll* E Marshall Islands
104 G7 **Auray** Morbihan, NW France
96 G13 **Aurdal** Oppland, S Norway
96 F8 **Aure** Møre og Romsdal, S Norway
31 T12 **Aurelia** Iowa, C USA
Aurelia Aquensis *see* Baden-Baden
Aurelianum *see* Orléans
123 J12 **Aurès, Massif de l'** ▲ NE Algeria
102 F10 **Aurich** Niedersachsen, NW Germany
105 O13 **Aurillac** Cantal, C France
Aurine, Alpi *see* Zillertaler Alpen
Aurium *see* Ourense
12 H15 **Aurora** Ontario, S Canada
57 S8 **Aurora** NW Guyana
39 T4 **Aurora** Colorado, C USA
32 M11 **Aurora** Illinois, N USA
33 Q15 **Aurora** Indiana, N USA
31 W4 **Aurora** Minnesota, N USA
29 S8 **Aurora** Missouri, C USA
31 P16 **Aurora** Nebraska, C USA
38 J5 **Aurora** Utah, W USA
Aurora *see* San Francisco, Philippines
Aurora *see* Maewo, Vanuatu
96 F10 **Aursjøen** ◎ S Norway
96 I9 **Aursunden** ◎ S Norway
85 D21 **Aus** Karas, SW Namibia
Ausa *see* Vic
12 E16 **Ausable** ≈ Ontario, S Canada
33 O3 **Au Sable Point** *headland* Michigan, N USA
33 S7 **Au Sable Point** *headland* Michigan, N USA
33 R6 **Au Sable River** ≈ Michigan, N USA
59 H16 **Ausangate, Nevado** ▲ C Peru
Auschwitz *see* Oświęcim
Ausculum Apulum *see* Ascoli Satriano
107 Q4 **Ausejo** La Rioja, N Spain
Aussig *see* Ústí nad Labem
97 F17 **Aust-Agder** ◈ *county* S Norway
94 P2 **Austfonna** *glacier* NE Svalbard
33 P15 **Austin** Indiana, N USA
31 W11 **Austin** Minnesota, N USA
37 U5 **Austin** Nevada, W USA
27 S10 **Austin** *state capital* Texas, S USA
188 J10 **Austin, Lake** *salt lake* Western Australia
33 V11 **Austintown** Ohio, N USA
27 V9 **Austonio** Texas, SW USA
Australes, Archipel des *see* Australes, Îles
Australes et Antarctiques Françaises, Terres *see* French Southern and Antarctic Territories
203 T14 **Australes, Îles** *var.* Archipel des Australes, Îles Tubuai, Tubuai Islands, *Eng.* Austral Islands. *island group* SW French Polynesia
183 Y11 **Austral Fracture Zone** *tectonic feature* S Pacific Ocean
189 O7 **Australia** *off.* Commonwealth of Australia. ◆ *commonwealth republic*
182 M8 **Australia** *continent*
191 Q12 **Australian Alps** ▲ SE Australia
191 R11 **Australian Capital Territory** *prev.* Federal Capital Territory. ◈ *territory* SE Australia
Australie, Bassin Nord de l' *see* North Australian Basin
Austral Islands *see* Australes, Îles
Austrava *see* Ostrov
111 T6 **Austria** *off.* Republic of Austria, *Ger.* Österreich. ◆ *republic* C Europe
94 K3 **Austurland** ◈ *region* SE Iceland
94 G10 **Austvågøy** *island* C Norway
60 G13 **Autazes** Amazonas, N Brazil
104 M16 **Auterive** Haute-Garonne, S France
Autesiodorum *see* Auxerre
105 N2 **Authie** ≈ N France
Autissiodorum *see* Auxerre
42 K14 **Autlán** *var.* Autlán de Navarro. Jalisco, SW Mexico
Autlán de Navarro *see* Autlán
Autricum *see* Chartres
105 Q9 **Autun** *anc.* Ædua, Augustodunum. Saône-et-Loire, C France
Autz *see* Auce
101 H20 **Auvelais** Namur, S Belgium
105 P11 **Auvergne** ◈ *region* C France
104 M12 **Auvézère** ≈ W France
105 P7 **Auxerre** *anc.* Autesiodorum, Autissiodorum. Yonne, C France
105 N2 **Auxi-le-Château** Pas-de-Calais, N France
105 S8 **Auxonne** Côte d'Or, C France
57 P9 **Auyan Tebuy** ▲ SE Venezuela
105 O10 **Auzances** Creuse, C France
29 U8 **Ava** Missouri, C USA
148 M5 **Āvaj** Zanjān, W Iran
97 C15 **Avaldsnes** Rogaland, S Norway
105 Q8 **Avallon** Yonne, C France
104 K6 **Avaloirs, Mont des** ▲ NW France
37 S16 **Avalon** Santa Catalina Island, California, W USA
20 J17 **Avalon** New Jersey, NE USA
11 V13 **Avalon Peninsula** *peninsula* Newfoundland, Newfoundland and Labrador, E Canada
62 K10 **Avaré** São Paulo, S Brazil
Avaricum *see* Bourges
202 H16 **Avarua** ○ (Cook Islands) Rarotonga, S Cook Islands
202 H16 **Avarua Harbour** *harbor* Rarotonga, S Cook Islands
Avasfelsőfalu *see* Negreşti-Oaş
40 L17 **Avatanak Island** *island* Aleutian Islands, Alaska, USA
202 B16 **Avatele** S Niue
202 H16 **Avatiu** Rarotonga, S Cook Islands
202 H15 **Avatiu Harbour** *harbor* Rarotonga, S Cook Islands
Avdeyevka *see* Avdiyivka
116 J13 **Ávdira** Anatolikí Makedonía kai Thráki, NE Greece
119 X8 **Avdiyivka** *Rus.* Avdeyevka. Donets'ka Oblast', SE Ukraine
168 K7 **Avdzaga** C Monogolia
106 G6 **Ave** ≈ N Portugal
106 G7 **Aveiro** *anc.* Talabriga. Aveiro, W Portugal
106 G7 **Aveiro** ◈ *district* N Portugal
Avela *see* Ávila
101 D18 **Avelgem** West-Vlaanderen, W Belgium
63 D20 **Avellaneda** Buenos Aires, E Argentina
109 L17 **Avellino** *anc.* Abellinum. Campania, S Italy
37 Q12 **Avenal** California, W USA
Avenio *see* Avignon
96 E8 **Averoya** *island* S Norway
109 K17 **Aversa** Campania, S Italy
35 N9 **Avery** Idaho, NW USA
27 W5 **Avery** Texas, SW USA
Aves, Islas de *see* Las Aves, Islas
Avesnes *see* Avesnes-sur-Helpe
105 Q2 **Avesnes-sur-Helpe** *var.* Avesnes. Nord, N France
66 G12 **Aves Ridge** *undersea feature* SE Caribbean Sea
97 M14 **Avesta** Kopparberg, C Sweden
105 O14 **Aveyron** ◈ *department* S France
105 N14 **Aveyron** ≈ S France
109 J15 **Avezzano** Abruzzi, C Italy
117 D16 **Avgó** ▲ C Greece
Avgustov *see* Augustów
Avgustovskiy Kanal *see* Augustowski, Kanał
98 J9 **Aviemore** N Scotland, UK
193 F21 **Aviemore, Lake** ◎ South Island, NZ
105 R15 **Avignon** *anc.* Avenio. Vaucluse, SE France
106 M7 **Ávila** *var.* Avila; *anc.* Abela, Abula, Abyla, Avela. Castilla-León, C Spain
106 L8 **Ávila** ◈ *province* Castilla-León, C Spain
106 K2 **Avilés** Asturias, NW Spain
120 J4 **Avinurme** *Ger.* Awwinorm. Ida-Virumaa, NE Estonia
106 H10 **Avis** Portalegre, C Portugal
97 F22 **Avlum** Ringkøbing, C Denmark
190 M11 **Avoca** Victoria, SE Australia
31 T14 **Avoca** Iowa, C USA
190 M11 **Avoca River** ≈ Victoria, SE Australia
109 L25 **Avola** Sicilia, Italy, C Mediterranean Sea
20 F10 **Avon** New York, NE USA
31 P12 **Avon** South Dakota, N USA
99 M23 **Avon** ≈ S England, UK
99 L20 **Avon** ≈ C England, UK
38 K13 **Avondale** Arizona, SW USA
25 X13 **Avon Park** Florida, SE USA
104 J5 **Avranches** Manche, N France
105 O3 **Avre** ≈ N France
195 X16 **Avuavu** *var.* Kolotambu. Guadalcanal, C Solomon Islands
Avveel *see* Ivalo, Finland
Avveel *see* Ivalojoki, Finland
Avvil *see* Ivalo
79 O17 **Awaaso** *var.* Awaso. SW Ghana
147 X8 **Awābī** *var.* Al 'Awābī. NE Oman
170 G15 **Awaji-shima** *island* SW Japan
192 L9 **Awakino** Waikato, North Island, NZ
148 M15 **'Awālī** C Bahrain
101 K19 **Awans** Liège, E Belgium
192 I2 **Awanui** Northland, North Island, NZ
154 M14 **Awārān** Baluchistān, SW Pakistan
83 K16 **Awara Plain** *plain* NE Kenya
82 M13 **Āwarē** E Ethiopia
144 M6 **'Awāriḑ, Wādī** *dry watercourse* E Syria
193 B20 **Awarua Point** *headland* South Island, NZ
83 J14 **Āwasa** S Ethiopia
82 K13 **Āwash** C Ethiopia
82 K12 **Āwash** *var.* Hawash. ≈ C Ethiopia
171 Kk11 **Awa-shima** *island* C Japan
Awaso *see* Awaaso
164 H7 **Awat** Xinjiang Uygur Zizhiqu, NW China
193 J15 **Awatere** ≈ South Island, NZ
77 O10 **Awbārī** SW Libya
77 N9 **Awbāri, Idhān** *var.* Edeyen d'Oubari. *desert* Algeria/Libya
82 C13 **Aweil** Northern Bahr el Ghazal, SW Sudan
98 H11 **Awe, Loch** ◎ W Scotland, UK
79 U16 **Awka** Anambra, SW Nigeria
41 O6 **Awuna River** ≈ Alaska, USA
Awwinorm *see* Avinurme
Ax *see* Dax
Axarfjördhur *see* Öxarfjördhur
105 N17 **Axat** Aude, S France
101 F16 **Axel** Zeeland, SW Netherlands
207 P9 **Axel Heiberg Island** *var.* Axel Heiburg. *island* Northwest Territories, N Canada
Axel Heiburg *see* Axel Heiberg Island
79 O17 **Axim** S Ghana
116 F13 **Axiós** *var.* Vardar. ≈ Greece/FYR Macedonia *see also* Vardar
105 N17 **Ax-les-Thermes** Ariège, S France
171 Gg14 **Ayabe** Kyōto, Honshū, SW Japan
122 F13 **Ayachi, Jbel** ▲ C Morocco
63 D22 **Ayacucho** Buenos Aires, E Argentina
59 F15 **Ayacucho** Ayacucho, S Peru
59 E16 **Ayacucho** *off.* Departamento de Ayacucho. ◈ *department* SW Peru
151 W11 **Ayaguz** *Kaz.* Ayaköz; *prev.* Sergiopol. Semipalatinsk, E Kazakhstan
151 V12 **Ayaguz** *Kaz.* Ayaköz. ≈ E Kazakhstan
Ayakagytma *see* Oyoqighitma

◆ Country
● Country Capital
◇ Dependent Territory
○ Dependent Territory Capital
◈ Administrative Region
× International Airport
▲ Mountain
▲ Mountain Range
Volcano
≈ River
◎ Lake
▣ Reservoir

Ayakkuduk *see* Oyoqquduq
164 *L10* **Ayakkum Hu** ◎ NW China
Ayaköz *see* Ayaguz
106 *H14* **Ayamonte** Andalucía, S Spain
127 *N12* **Ayan** Khabarovskiy Kray, E Russian Federation
142 *J10* **Ayancık** Sinop, N Turkey
57 *S9* **Ayanganna Mountain** ▲ C Guyana
79 *U16* **Ayangba** Kogi, C Nigeria
127 *P6* **Ayanka** Koryakskiy Avtonomnyy Okrug, E Russian Federation
56 *E7* **Ayapel** Córdoba, NW Colombia
142 *H12* **Ayaş** Ankara, N Turkey
59 *I16* **Ayaviri** Puno, S Peru
155 *P3* **Āybak** *var.* Aibak, Haibak; *prev.* Samangān. Samangān, NE Afghanistan
153 *N10* **Aydarkŭl** *Rus.* Ozero Aydarkul'. ◎ C Uzbekistan
Aydarkul', Ozero *see* Aydarkŭl
23 *W10* **Ayden** North Carolina, SE USA
142 *C15* **Aydın** *var.* Aïdin; *anc.* Tralles. Aydın, SW Turkey
142 *C15* **Aydın** *var.* Aïdin. ◆ *province* SW Turkey
142 *I17* **Aydıncık** İçel, S Turkey
142 *C15* **Aydın Dağları** ▲ W Turkey
164 *L6* **Aydingkol Hu** ◎ NW China
131 *X7* **Aydyrlinskiy** Orenburgskaya Oblast', W Russian Federation
107 *S4* **Ayerbe** Aragón, NE Spain
Ayers Rock *see* Uluru
Ayeyarwady *see* Irrawaddy
Ayiá *see* Agiá
Ayia Napa *see* Agía Nápa
Ayia Phyla *see* Agía Fýlaxis
Ayiásos/Ayiássos *see* Agiasós
Áyios Evstrátios *see* Ágios Efstrátios
Áyios Kírikos *see* Ágios Kírykos
Áyios Nikólaos *see* Ágios Nikólaos
Ayios Seryios *see* Yeniboğaziçi
82 *I11* **Āykel** NW Ethiopia
126 *K10* **Aykhal** Respublika Sakha (Yakutiya), NE Russian Federation
12 *J12* **Aylen Lake** ◎ Ontario, SE Canada
99 *N21* **Aylesbury** SE England, UK
107 *O6* **Ayllón** Castilla-León, N Spain
12 *F17* **Aylmer** Ontario, S Canada
12 *L12* **Aylmer** Québec, SE Canada
13 *R12* **Aylmer, Lac** ◎ Québec, SE Canada
15 *J6* **Aylmer Lake** ◎ Northwest Territories, NW Canada
151 *V14* **Aynabulak** Taldykorgan, SE Kazakhstan
144 *K2* **'Ayn al 'Arab** Ḩalab, N Syria
Aynayn *see* 'Aynīn
145 *V12* **'Ayn Ḩamūd** S Iraq
153 *P12* **Ayní** *prev.* Rus. Varzimanor Ayni. W Tajikistan
146 *M10* **'Aynīn** *var.* Aynayn. *spring/well* SW Saudi Arabia
23 *U12* **Aynor** South Carolina, SE USA
145 *Q7* **'Ayn Zāzūh** C Iraq
159 *N12* **Ayodhya** Uttar Pradesh, N India
127 *O5* **Ayon, Ostrov** *island* NE Russian Federation
107 *R11* **Ayora** País Valenciano, E Spain
79 *Q11* **Ayorou** Tillabéri, W Niger
81 *E16* **Ayos** Centre, S Cameroon
78 *L5* **'Ayoûn 'Abd el Mâlek** *well* N Mauritania
78 *K10* **'Ayoûn el 'Atroûs** *var.* Aïoun el Atrous, Aïoun el Atroûss. Hodh el Gharbi, SE Mauritania
98 *I13* **Ayr** W Scotland, UK
98 *I13* **Ayr** ↝ W Scotland, UK
98 *I13* **Ayrshire** *cultural region* SW Scotland, UK
Aysen *see* Aisén
82 *L12* **Āysha** E Ethiopia
152 *K8* **Aytim** Nawoiy Wiloyati, N Uzbekistan
189 *W4* **Ayton** Queensland, NE Australia
116 *M9* **Aytos** Burgaska Oblast, E Bulgaria
176 *Uu7* **Ayu, Kepulauan** *island group* E Indonesia
A Yun Pa *see* Cheo Reo
175 *O8* **Ayu, Tanjung** *headland* Borneo, N Indonesia
42 *K13* **Ayutla** Jalisco, C Mexico
43 *P16* **Ayutlá** *var.* Ayutla de los Libres. Guerrero, S Mexico
Ayutla de los Libres *see* Ayutlá
178 *H11* **Ayutthaya** *var.* Phra Nakhon Si Ayutthaya. Phra Nakhon Si Ayutthaya, C Thailand
142 *B13* **Ayvalık** Balıkesir, W Turkey
101 *L20* **Aywaille** Liège, E Belgium
147 *R13* **'Aywat aş Şay'ar, Wādī** *seasonal river* N Yemen
Azaffal *see* Azeffâl
107 *T9* **Azahar, Costa del** *coastal region* E Spain
107 *S6* **Azaila** Aragón, NE Spain
106 *F10* **Azambuja** Lisboa, C Portugal
159 *N13* **Āzamgarh** Uttar Pradesh, N India
79 *O9* **Azaouâd** *desert* C Mali
79 *S10* **Azaouagh, Vallée de l'** *var.* Azaouak. ↝ W Niger
Azaouak *see* Azaouagh, Vallée de l'
63 *F14* **Azara** Misiones, NE Argentina
148 *K3* **Āzarān** Āzarbāyjān-e Khāvarī, N Iran
Azärbaycan/Azärbaycan Respublikası *see* Azerbaijan
148 *I4* **Āzarbāyjān-e Bākhtarī** *off.* Ostān-e Āzarbāyjān-e Bākhtarī, *var.* Āzarbāyjān-e Gharbī, *Eng.* West Azerbaijan. ◆ *province* NW Iran
Āzarbāyjān-e Gharbī *see* Āzarbāyjān-e Bākhtarī
148 *J3* **Āzarbāyjān-e Khāvarī** *off.* Ostān-e Āzarbāyjān-e Khāvarī, *var.* Āzarbāyjān-e Sharqī, *Eng.* East Azerbaijan. ◆ *province* NW Iran
Āzarbāyjān-e Sharqī *see* Āzarbāyjān-e Khāvarī
79 *W13* **Azare** Bauchi, N Nigeria
121 *M19* **Azarychy** *Rus.* Ozarichi. Homyel'skaya Voblasts', SE Belarus
104 *L8* **Azay-le-Rideau** Indre-et-Loire, C France
144 *I2* **A'zāz** Ḩalab, NW Syria
78 *H7* **Azeffâl** *var.* Azaffal. *desert* Mauritania/Western Sahara
143 *V12* **Azerbaijan** *off.* Azerbaijani Republic, *Az.* Azärbaycan, Azärbaycan Respublikası; *prev.* Azerbaijan SSR. ◆ *republic* SE Asia
151 *T7* **Azhbulat, Ozero** ◎ NE Kazakhstan
76 *F7* **Azilal** C Morocco
Azimabad *see* Patna
21 *O6* **Aziscohos Lake** ⊠ Maine, NE USA
Azizbekov *see* Vayk'
Azizie *see* Telish
Aziziya *see* Al 'Azīzīyah
131 *T4* **Aznakayevo** Respublika Tatarstan, W Russian Federation
58 *C8* **Azogues** Cañar, S Ecuador
66 *N2* **Azores** *var.* Açores, Ilhas dos Açores, *Port.* Arquipélago dos Açores. *island group* Portugal, NE Atlantic Ocean
66 *L8* **Azores-Biscay Rise** *undersea feature* E Atlantic Ocean
Azotos/Azotus *see* Ashdod
80 *K11* **Azoum, Bahr** *seasonal river* SE Chad
130 *L12* **Azov** Rostovskaya Oblast', SW Russian Federation
130 *J13* **Azov, Sea of** *Rus.* Azovskoye More, *Ukr.* Azovs'ke More. *sea* NE Black Sea
Azovs'ke More/Azovskoye More *see* Azov, Sea of
Azraq, Bahr el *see* Blue Nile
144 *I10* **Azraq, Wāḩat al** *oasis* N Jordan
Āzro *see* Āzrow
76 *G6* **Azrou** C Morocco
155 *R5* **Āzrow** *var.* Āzro. Lowgar, E Afghanistan
39 *P8* **Aztec** New Mexico, SW USA
38 *M13* **Aztec Peak** ▲ Arizona, SW USA
47 *N9* **Azua** *var.* Azua de Compostela. S Dominican Republic
Azua de Compostela *see* Azua
106 *K12* **Azuaga** Extremadura, W Spain
58 *B8* **Azuay** ◆ *province* W Ecuador
170 *Bb11* **Azuchi-Ō-shima** *island* SW Japan
107 *O11* **Azuer** ↝ C Spain
45 *S17* **Azuero, Península de** *peninsula* S Panama
64 *I6* **Azufre, Volcán** *var.* Volcán Lastarria. ▲ N Chile
118 *J12* **Azuga** Prahova, SE Romania
63 *C22* **Azul** Buenos Aires, E Argentina
64 *I8* **Azul, Cerro** ▲ NW Argentina
58 *E12* **Azul, Cordillera** ▲ C Peru
171 *Ll14* **Azuma-san** ▲ Honshū, C Japan
105 *V15* **Azur, Côte d'** *coastal region* SE France
203 *Z3* **Azur Lagoon** ◎ Kiritimati, E Kiribati
'Azza *see* Gaza
Az Zāb al Kabīr *see* Great Zab
144 *H7* **Az Zabdānī** *var.* Zabadani. Dimashq, W Syria
147 *W8* **Az̧ Z̧āhirah** *desert* NW Oman
147 *S6* **Az̧ Z̧ahrān** *Eng.* Dhahran. Ash Sharqīyah, NE Saudi Arabia
147 *R6* **Az̧ Z̧ahrān al Khubar** *var.* Dhahran Al Khobar. ✕ Ash Sharqīyah, NE Saudi Arabia
Az Zaqāzīq *see* Zagazig
144 *H10* **Az Zarqā'** *var.* Zarqa. Az Zarqā', NW Jordan
144 *I11* **Az Zarqā'** *off.* Muḩāfaz̧at az Zarqā', *var.* Zarqa. ◆ *governorate* N Jordan
77 *O7* **Az Zāwiyah** *var.* Zawia. NW Libya
147 *N15* **Az Zaydīyah** W Yemen
76 *I11* **Azzel Matti, Sebkha** *var.* Sebkra Azz el Matti. *salt flat* C Algeria
147 *P6* **Az Zilfī** Ar Riyāḑ, N Saudi Arabia
145 *Y13* **Az Zubayr** *var.* Al Zubair. SE Iraq
Az Zuqur *see* Jabal Zuuqar, Jazirat

B

197 *H14* **Ba** *prev.* Mba. Viti Levu, W Fiji
Ba *see* Đa Răng
175 *R18* **Baa** Pulau Rote, C Indonesia
197 *G5* **Baaba, Île** *island* Îles Belep, W New Caledonia
144 *H7* **Baalbek** *var.* Ba'labakk; *anc.* Heliopolis. E Lebanon
110 *G8* **Baar** Zug, N Switzerland
83 *L17* **Baardheere** *var.* Bardere, *It.* Bardera. Gedo, SW Somalia
82 *Q12* **Baargaal** Bari, NE Somalia
101 *I15* **Baarle-Hertog** Antwerpen, N Belgium
101 *I15* **Baarle-Nassau** Antwerpen, N Belgium
100 *J11* **Baarn** Utrecht, C Netherlands
116 *D13* **Baba** *var.* Buševa, *Gk.* Varnoús. ▲ FYR Macedonia/Greece
78 *H10* **Bababé** Brakna, W Mauritania
142 *G10* **Baba Burnu** *headland* NW Turkey
119 *N13* **Babadag** Tulcea, SE Romania
143 *X10* **Babadağ Dağı** ▲ NE Azerbaijan
Babadayhan *see* Babadaýhan
152 *H14* **Babadaýhan** *Turkm.* Babadayhan; *prev.* Kirovsk. Akhalskiy Velayat, C Turkmenistan
152 *G14* **Babadurmaz** Akhalskiy Velayat, C Turkmenistan
116 *M12* **Babaeski** Kırklareli, NW Turkey
145 *T4* **Bāba Gurgur** N Iraq
58 *B7* **Babahoyo** *prev.* Bodegas. Los Ríos, C Ecuador
155 *P5* **Bābā, Kūh-e** ▲ C Afghanistan
175 *P10* **Babana** Sulawesi, C Indonesia
176 *U16* **Babar, Kepulauan** *island group* E Indonesia
176 *U15* **Babar, Pulau** *island* Kepulauan Babar, E Indonesia
158 *G4* **Bābāsar Pass** *pass* India/Pakistan
195 *Q10* **Babase Island** *island* Feni Islands, NE PNG
152 *C9* **Babashy** ▲ W Turkmenistan
174 *Ll15* **Babat** Jawa, S Indonesia
174 *I10* **Babat** Sumatera, W Indonesia
Babatag, Khrebet *see* Bobotogh, Qatorkŭhi
83 *H21* **Babati** Arusha, NE Tanzania
128 *J13* **Babayevo** Vologodskaya Oblast', NW Russian Federation
131 *Q15* **Babayurt** Respublika Dagestan, SW Russian Federation
35 *P6* **Babb** Montana, NW USA
31 *X4* **Babbitt** Minnesota, N USA
196 *E9* **Babeldaob** *var.* Babeldaop, Babelthuap. *island* N Palau
Babeldaop *see* Babeldaob
147 *N17* **Bab el Mandeb** *strait* Gulf of Aden/Red Sea
Babelthuap *see* Babeldaob
113 *K17* **Babia Góra** *var.* Babia Hora. ▲ Czech Republic/Poland
Babia Hora *see* Babia Góra
Babian Jiang *see* Black River
Babichi *see* Babichy
121 *N19* **Babichy** *Rus.* Babichi. Homyel'skaya Voblasts', SE Belarus
114 *I10* **Babina Greda** Vukovar-Srijem, E Croatia
8 *K13* **Babine Lake** ◎ British Columbia, SW Canada
176 *Vv10* **Babo** Irian Jaya, E Indonesia
149 *O4* **Bābol** *var.* Babul, Balfrush, Barfrush; *prev.* Barfurush. Māzandarān, N Iran
149 *O4* **Bābolsar** *var.* Babulsar; *prev.* Meshed-i-Sar. Māzandarān, N Iran
38 *L16* **Baboquivari Peak** ▲ Arizona, SW USA
81 *G15* **Baboua** Nana-Mambéré, W Central African Republic
121 *M17* **Babruysk** *Rus.* Bobruysk. Mahilyowskaya Voblasts', E Belarus
Babu *see* Hexian
Babul *see* Bābol
Babulsar *see* Bābolsar
115 *O19* **Babuna** ↝ C FYR Macedonia
115 *O19* **Babuna** ▲ C FYR Macedonia
154 *K7* **Bābūs, Dasht-e** *Pash.* Bebas, Dasht-i. ▲ W Afghanistan
126 *Jj16* **Babushkin** Respublika Buryatiya, S Russian Federation
179 *P7* **Babuyan Channel** *channel* N Philippines
179 *Pp7* **Babuyan Island** *island* N Philippines
145 *T9* **Babylon** *site of ancient city* C Iraq
114 *J9* **Bač** *Ger.* Batsch. Serbia, NW Yugoslavia
60 *M13* **Bacabal** Maranhão, E Brazil
43 *Y14* **Bacalar** Quintana Roo, SE Mexico
43 *Y14* **Bacalar Chico, Boca** *strait* SE Mexico
175 *Ss8* **Bacan, Kepulauan** *island group* E Indonesia
175 *T8* **Bacan, Pulau** *prev.* Batjan. *island* Maluku, E Indonesia
118 *L10* **Bacău** *Hung.* Bákó. Bacău, NE Romania
118 *K11* **Bacău** ◆ *county* E Romania
Bắc Bô, Vịnh *see* Tongking, Gulf of
178 *Jj5* **Bắc Can** Bắc Thai, N Vietnam
105 *T5* **Baccarat** Meurthe-et-Moselle, NE France
191 *N12* **Bacchus Marsh** Victoria, SE Australia
42 *H4* **Bacerac** Sonora, NW Mexico
118 *L10* **Băceşti** Vaslui, E Romania
178 *Jj6* **Bắc Giang** Ha Bắc, N Vietnam
56 *I5* **Bachaquero** Zulia, NW Venezuela
Bacher *see* Pohorje
120 *M13* **Bacheykava** *Rus.* Bocheykovo. Vitsyebskaya Voblasts', N Belarus
42 *I5* **Bachíniva** Chihuahua, N Mexico
164 *G8* **Bachu** Xinjiang Uygur Zizhiqu, NW China
15 *J6* **Back** ↝ Northwest Territories, N Canada
114 *K10* **Bačka Palanka** *prev.* Palanka. Serbia, NW Yugoslavia
114 *K8* **Bačka Topola** *Hung.* Topolya; *prev. Hung.* Bácstopolya. Serbia, N Yugoslavia
97 *J17* **Bäckefors** Älvsborg, S Sweden
Bäckermühle Schulzenmühle *see* Żywiec
97 *L16* **Bäckhammar** Värmland, C Sweden
114 *K9* **Bački Petrovac** *Hung.* Petrőcz; *prev.* Petrovac, Petrovácz. Serbia, NW Yugoslavia
103 *I21* **Backnang** Baden-Württemberg, SW Germany
178 *J15* **Bac Liêu** *var.* Vinh Loi. Minh Hai, S Vietnam
178 *Jj6* **Bắc Ninh** Ha Bắc, N Vietnam
42 *G4* **Bacoachi** Sonora, NW Mexico
179 *Q13* **Bacolod** *off.* Bacolod City. Negros, C Philippines
179 *P12* **Baco, Mount** ▲ Mindoro, N Philippines
113 *K25* **Bácsalmás** Bács-Kiskun, S Hungary
Bácsjózseffalva *see* Žednik
113 *J24* **Bács-Kiskun** *off.* Bács-Kiskun Megye. ◆ *county* S Hungary
Bácsszenttamás *see* Srbobran
Bácstopolya *see* Bačka Topola
Bactra *see* Balkh
161 *F21* **Badagara** Kerala, SW India
103 *M24* **Bad Aibling** Bayern, SE Germany
168 *I13* **Badain Jaran Shamo** *desert* N China
106 *I11* **Badajoz** *anc.* Pax Augusta. Extremadura, W Spain
106 *J11* **Badajoz** ◆ *province* Extremadura, W Spain
155 *S2* **Badakhshān** ◆ *province* NE Afghanistan
107 *W6* **Badalona** *anc.* Baetulo. Cataluña, E Spain
160 *O11* **Bādāmapāhārh** Orissa, E India
158 *K8* **Badarīnāth** ▲ N India
174 *Jj8* **Badas, Kepulauan** *island group* W Indonesia
111 *S6* **Bad Aussee** Salzburg, E Austria
33 *S8* **Bad Axe** Michigan, N USA
103 *G16* **Bad Berleburg** Nordrhein-Westfalen, W Germany
103 *L17* **Bad Blankenburg** Thüringen, C Germany
Bad Borseck *see* Borsec
103 *G18* **Bad Camberg** Hessen, W Germany
102 *L8* **Bad Doberan** Mecklenburg-Vorpommern, N Germany
103 *N14* **Bad Düben** Sachsen, E Germany
111 *X4* **Baden** *var.* Baden bei Wien; *anc.* Aquae Panoniae, Thermae Pannonicae. Niederösterreich, NE Austria
110 *F9* **Baden** Aargau, N Switzerland
103 *G21* **Baden-Baden** *anc.* Aurelia Aquensis. Baden-Württemberg, SW Germany
Baden bei Wien *see* Baden
103 *G22* **Baden-Württemberg** *Fr.* Bade-Wurtemberg. ◆ *state* SW Germany
114 *A10* **Baderna** Istra, NW Croatia
Bade-Wurtemberg *see* Baden-Württemberg
103 *H20* **Bad Fredrichshall** Baden-Württemberg, S Germany
102 *P11* **Bad Freienwalde** Brandenburg, NE Germany
111 *Q8* **Badgastein** *var.* Gastein. Salzburg, NW Austria
Badger State *see* Wisconsin
154 *L4* **Bādghīs** ◆ *province* NW Afghanistan
111 *T5* **Bad Hall** Oberösterreich, N Austria
103 *J14* **Bad Harzburg** Niedersachsen, C Germany
103 *I16* **Bad Hersfeld** Hessen, C Germany
100 *I10* **Badhoevedorp** Noord-Holland, C Netherlands
111 *Q8* **Bad Hofgastein** Salzburg, NW Austria
Bad Homburg *see* Bad Homburg vor der Höhe
103 *G18* **Bad Homburg vor der Höhe** *var.* Bad Homburg. Hessen, W Germany
103 *E17* **Bad Honnef** Nordrhein-Westfalen, W Germany
155 *Q17* **Badin** Sind, SE Pakistan
23 *S10* **Badin Lake** ◎ North Carolina, SE USA
42 *I8* **Badiraguato** Sinaloa, C Mexico
111 *R6* **Bad Ischl** Oberösterreich, N Austria
Badjawa *see* Bajawa
103 *J18* **Bad Kissingen** Bayern, SE Germany
Bad Königswart *see* Lázně Kynžvart
103 *F19* **Bad Kreuznach** Rheinland-Pfalz, SW Germany
103 *F24* **Bad Krozingen** Baden-Württemberg, SW Germany
103 *G16* **Bad Laasphe** Nordrhein-Westfalen, W Germany
30 *J6* **Badlands** *physical region* North Dakota, N USA
103 *K16* **Bad Langensalza** Thüringen, C Germany
111 *T3* **Bad Leonfelden** Oberösterreich, N Austria
103 *I20* **Bad Mergentheim** Baden-Württemberg, SW Germany
103 *H17* **Bad Nauheim** Hessen, W Germany
103 *E17* **Bad Neuenahr-Ahrweiler** Rheinland-Pfalz, W Germany
Bad Neustadt *see* Bad Neustadt an der Saale
103 *J18* **Bad Neustadt an der Saale** *var.* Bad Neustadt. Berlin, C Germany
Badnur *see* Betūl
176 *Yy15* **Bado** Irian Jaya, E Indonesia
102 *H13* **Bad Oeynhausen** Nordrhein-Westfalen, NW Germany
102 *J9* **Bad Oldesloe** Schleswig-Holstein, N Germany
79 *Q16* **Badou** C Togo
Bad Polzin *see* Połczyn-Zdrój
102 *H13* **Bad Pyrmont** Niedersachsen, C Germany
111 *X9* **Bad Radkersburg** Steiermark, SE Austria
145 *V8* **Badrah** E Iraq
168 *J6* **Badrah** Hövsgöl, N Mongolia
103 *N24* **Bad Reichenhall** Bayern, SE Germany
146 *K8* **Badr Ḩunayn** Al Madīnah, W Saudi Arabia
30 *M10* **Bad River** ↝ South Dakota, N USA
32 *K4* **Bad River** ↝ Wisconsin, N USA
102 *H13* **Bad Salzuflen** Nordrhein-Westfalen, NW Germany
103 *J16* **Bad Salzungen** Thüringen, C Germany
111 *V8* **Bad Sankt Leonhard im Lavanttal** Kärnten, S Austria
102 *K9* **Bad Schwartau** Schleswig-Holstein, N Germany
103 *L24* **Bad Tölz** Bayern, SE Germany
189 *U1* **Badu Island** *island* Queensland, NE Australia
161 *K25* **Badulla** Uva Province, C Sri Lanka
111 *X5* **Bad Vöslau** Niederösterreich, NE Austria
103 *I24* **Bad Waldsee** Baden-Württemberg, S Germany
37 *U11* **Badwater Basin** *depression* California, W USA
103 *J20* **Bad Windsheim** Bayern, C Germany
103 *J23* **Bad Wörishofen** Bayern, S Germany
102 *G10* **Bad Zwischenahn** Niedersachsen, NW Germany
106 *M13* **Baena** Andalucía, S Spain
Baeterrae/Baeterrae Septimanorum *see* Béziers
Baetic Cordillera/Baetic Mountains *see* Béticos, Sistemas
Baetulo *see* Badalona
59 *K18* **Baeza** Napo, NE Ecuador
107 *N13* **Baeza** Andalucía, S Spain
81 *D15* **Bafang** Ouest, W Cameroon
78 *H12* **Bafatá** C Guinea-Bissau
155 *U5* **Baffa** North-West Frontier Province, NW Pakistan
15 *Ll1* **Baffin** ◆ *district* Northwest Territories, NE Canada
207 *O11* **Baffin Basin** *undersea feature* N Labrador Sea
207 *N12* **Baffin Bay** *bay* Canada/Greenland
27 *T15* **Baffin Bay** *inlet* Texas, SW USA
206 *M12* **Baffin Island** *island* Northwest Territories, NE Canada
81 *E15* **Bafia** Centre, C Cameroon
79 *R14* **Bafilo** NE Togo
78 *J12* **Bafing** *headstream* W Africa
78 *J12* **Bafoulabé** Kayes, W Mali
81 *D15* **Bafoussam** Ouest, W Cameroon
149 *R9* **Bāfq** Yazd, C Iran
142 *L10* **Bafra** Samsun, N Turkey
142 *L10* **Bafra Burnu** *headland* N Turkey
149 *S12* **Bāft** Kermān, S Iran
81 *N18* **Bafwabalinga** Haut-Zaïre, NE Zaire
81 *N18* **Bafwaboli** Haut-Zaïre, NE Zaire
81 *N17* **Bafwasende** Haut-Zaïre, NE Zaire
194 *J11* **Bagabag Island** *island* N PNG
44 *K13* **Bagaces** Guanacaste, NW Costa Rica
159 *O12* **Bagaha** Bihār, N India
161 *F16* **Bāgalkot** Karnātaka, W India
83 *J22* **Bagamoyo** Pwani, E Tanzania
174 *Gg4* **Bagan Datuk** *var.* Bagan Datok. Perak, Peninsular Malaysia
179 *Rr15* **Baganga** Mindanao, S Philippines
174 *Gg6* **Bagansiapiapi** *var.* Pasirpangarayan. Sumatera, W Indonesia
Bagaria *see* Bagheria
79 *T11* **Bagaroua** Tahoua, W Niger
81 *I20* **Bagata** Bandundu, W Zaire
Bagdad *see* Baghdād
126 *Kk15* **Bagdarin** Respublika Buryatiya, S Russian Federation
63 *G17* **Bagé** Rio Grande do Sul, S Brazil
Bagenalstown *see* Muine Bheag
105 *P16* **Bages et de Sigean, Étang de** ◎ S France
35 *W17* **Baggs** Wyoming, C USA
160 *F11* **Bāgh** Madhya Pradesh, C India
145 *T8* **Baghdād** *var.* Bagdad, *Eng.* Baghdad. ● (Iraq) C Iraq
145 *T8* **Baghdād** ✕ C Iraq
159 *T16* **Bagherhat** Khulna, S Bangladesh
109 *J23* **Bagheria** *var.* Bagaria. Sicilia, Italy, C Mediterranean Sea
149 *S10* **Bāghīn** Kermān, C Iran
155 *Q3* **Baghlān** Baghlān, NE Afghanistan
155 *Q3* **Baghlān** *var.* Bāghlān. ◆ *province* NE Afghanistan
154 *M7* **Bāghrān** Helmand, S Afghanistan
31 *T4* **Bagley** Minnesota, N USA
108 *H10* **Bagnacavallo** Emilia-Romagna, C Italy
104 *K16* **Bagnères-de-Bigorre** Hautes-Pyrénées, S France
104 *L17* **Bagnères-de-Luchon** Hautes-Pyrénées, S France
108 *F11* **Bagni di Lucca** Toscana, C Italy
108 *H11* **Bagno di Romagna** Emilia-Romagna, C Italy
105 *R14* **Bagnols-sur-Cèze** Gard, S France
168 *M14* **Bag Nur** ◎ N China
179 *Q13* **Bago** *off.* Bago City. Negros, C Philippines
Bago *see* Pegu
78 *M13* **Bagoé** ↝ Ivory Coast/Mali
Bagrāmē *see* Bagrāmī
155 *R5* **Bagrāmī** *var.* Bagrāmē. Kābul, E Afghanistan
121 *B14* **Bagrationovsk** *Ger.* Preussisch Eylau. Kaliningradskaya Oblast', W Russian Federation
Bagrax *see* Bohu
Bagrax Hu *see* Bosten Hu
58 *C10* **Bagua** Amazonas, NE Peru
179 *P9* **Baguio** *off.* Baguio City. Luzon, N Philippines
79 *V9* **Bagzane, Monts** ▲ N Niger
Bāḩah, Minţaqat al *see* Al Bāḩah
Bahama Islands *see* Bahamas
46 *H3* **Bahamas** *off.* Commonwealth of the Bahamas. ◆ *commonwealth republic* N West Indies
1 *L13* **Bahamas** *var.* Bahama Islands. *island group* N West Indies
159 *S15* **Baharampur** *prev.* Berhampore. West Bengal, NE India
175 *Nn6* **Bahau, Sungai** ↝ Borneo, N Indonesia
155 *U10* **Bahāwalnagar** Punjab, E Pakistan
155 *T11* **Bahāwalpur** Punjab, E Pakistan
142 *L16* **Bahçe** Adana, S Turkey
166 *J8* **Ba He** ↝ C China
Bäherden *see* Bakharden
61 *N16* **Bahia** *off.* Estado da Bahia. ◆ *state* E Brazil
63 *B24* **Bahía Blanca** Buenos Aires, E Argentina
42 *L15* **Bahía Bufadero** Michoacán de Ocampo, SW Mexico
65 *J19* **Bahía Bustamante** Chubut, SE Argentina
42 *D5* **Bahía de los Ángeles** Baja California, NW Mexico
42 *C6* **Bahía de Tortugas** Baja California Sur, W Mexico
44 *J4* **Bahía, Islas de la** *Eng.* Bay Islands. *island group* N Honduras
42 *E5* **Bahía Kino** Sonora, NW Mexico
42 *E9* **Bahía Magdalena** *var.* Puerto Magdalena. Baja California Sur, W Mexico
56 *C8* **Bahía Solano** *var.* Ciudad Mutis, Solano. Chocó, W Colombia
82 *I11* **Bahir Dar** *var.* Bahr Dar, Bahrdar Giyorgis. NW Ethiopia
147 *X8* **Bahlā'** *var.* Bahlah, Bahlat. NW Oman
Bāhla *see* Bālān
Bahlah/Bahlat *see* Bahlā'
158 *M11* **Bahraich** Uttar Pradesh, N India
149 *M14* **Bahrain** *off.* State of Bahrain, Dawlat al Bahrayn, *Ar.* Al Baḩrayn; *prev.* Bahrein, *anc.* Tylos or Tyros. ◆ *monarchy* SW Asia
148 *M14* **Bahrain** ✕ C Bahrain
148 *M15* **Bahrain, Gulf of** *gulf* Persian Gulf, NW Arabian Sea
144 *I7* **Baḩrat Mallāḩah** ◎ W Syria
Bahrayn, Dawlat al *see* Bahrain
Bahr Dar/Bahrdar Giyorgis *see* Bahir Dar
Bahrein *see* Bahrain
83 *E16* **Bahr el Gabel** ◆ *state* S Sudan
82 *E13* **Bahr ez Zaref** ↝ C Sudan
69 *R8* **Bahr Kameur** ↝ N Central African Republic
Bahr Tabariya, Sea of *see* Tiberias, Lake
149 *W15* **Bāhū Kalāt** Sīstān va Balūchestān, SE Iran
120 *N13* **Bahushewsk** *Rus.* Bogushëvsk. Vitsyebskaya Voblasts', NE Belarus
Bai *see* Tagow Bāy
118 *G13* **Baia de Aramă** Mehedinţi, SW Romania
118 *G11* **Baia de Criş** *Ger.* Altenburg, *Hung.* Körösbánya. Hunedoara, SW Romania
85 *A16* **Baia dos Tigres** Namibe, SW Angola
84 *A13* **Baia Farta** Benguela, W Angola
118 *H9* **Baia Mare** *Ger.* Frauenbach, *Hung.* Nagybánya; *prev.* Neustadt. Maramureş, NW Romania
118 *H8* **Baia Sprie** *Ger.* Mittelstadt, *Hung.* Felsőbánya. Maramureş, NW Romania
80 *G13* **Baïbokoum** Logone-Oriental, SW Chad
166 *F12* **Baicao Ling** ▲ SW China
169 *U9* **Baicheng** *var.* Pai-ch'eng; *prev.* T'aon-an. Jilin, NE China
164 *I6* **Baicheng** *var.* Bay. Xinjiang Uygur Zizhiqu, NW China
118 *J13* **Băicoi** Prahova, SE Romania
Baidoa *see* Baydhabo
13 *U6* **Baie-Comeau** Québec, SE Canada
13 *T7* **Baie-des-Bacon** Québec, SE Canada
13 *S8* **Baie-des-Rochers** Québec, SE Canada
13 *U6* **Baie-des-Sables** Québec, SE Canada
10 *K11* **Baie-du-Poste** Québec, SE Canada
180 *H17* **Baie Lazare** Mahé, NE Seychelles
47 *Y5* **Baie-Mahault** Basse Terre, C Guadeloupe
13 *R9* **Baie-St-Paul** Québec, SE Canada
13 *V5* **Baie-Trinité** Québec, SE Canada
11 *T11* **Baie Verte** Newfoundland, Newfoundland and Labrador, SE Canada
Baiguan *see* Shangyu
145 *U11* **Bā'ij al Mahdī** S Iraq
Baiji *see* Bayjī
Baikal, Lake *see* Baykal, Ozero
Bailădila *see* Kirandul
Baile an Chaistil *see* Ballycastle
Baile an Róba *see* Ballinrobe
Baile an tSratha *see* Ballintra
Baile Átha an Rí *see* Athenry
Baile Átha Buí *see* Athboy
Baile Átha Cliath *see* Dublin
Baile Átha Fhirdhia *see* Ardee
Baile Átha Í *see* Athy
Baile Átha Luain *see* Athlone
Baile Átha Troim *see* Trim
Baile Brigín *see* Balbriggan
Baile Easa Dara *see* Ballysadare
118 *I13* **Băile Govora** Vâlcea, SW Romania
118 *F13* **Băile Herculane** *Ger.* Herkulesbad, *Hung.* Herkulesfürdő. Caraş-Severin, SW Romania
Baile Locha Riach *see* Loughrea
Baile Mhistéala *see* Mitchelstown
Baile Monaidh *see* Ballymoney
107 *N12* **Bailén** Andalucía, S Spain
Baile na hInse *see* Ballynahinch
Baile na Lorgan *see* Castleblayney
Baile na Mainistreach *see* Newtownabbey
Baile Nua na hArda *see* Newtownards
118 *I12* **Băile Olăneşti** Vâlcea, SW Romania
118 *H14* **Băileşti** Dolj, SW Romania
Bailingmiao *see* Darhan Muminggan Lianheqi
60 *K11* **Bailique, Ilha** *island* NE Brazil
105 *O1* **Bailleul** Nord, N France
80 *H12* **Ba Illi** Chari-Baguirmi, SW Chad
165 *V12* **Bailong Jiang** ↝ C China
84 *C13* **Bailundo** *Port.* Vila Teixeira da Silva. Huambo, C Angola
165 *T13* **Baima** *var.* Sêraitang. Qinghai, C China
176 *W14* **Baimun** Pulau Workai, E Indonesia
194 *H14* **Baimuru** Gulf, S PNG
164 *M16* **Bainang** Xizang Zizhiqu, W China
25 *S8* **Bainbridge** Georgia, SE USA
175 *Pp17* **Baing** Pulau Sumba, SE Indonesia
164 *M14* **Baingoin** Xizang Zizhiqu, W China
106 *G2* **Baio Grande** Galicia, NW Spain
106 *G4* **Baiona** Galicia, NW Spain
169 *V7* **Baiquan** Heilongjiang, NE China
Bā'ir *see* Bāyir
164 *I11* **Bairab Co** ◎ W China
27 *Q7* **Baird** Texas, SW USA
41 *N7* **Baird Mountains** ▲ Alaska, USA
15 *Mm2* **Baird Peninsula** *peninsula* Baffin Island, Northwest Territories, NE Canada
Baireuth *see* Bayreuth
202 *H3* **Bairiki** ● (Kiribati) Tarawa, NW Kiribati
169 *S11* **Bairin Youqi** *var.* Daban. Nei Mongol Zizhiqu, N China
169 *S10* **Bairin Zuoqi** *var.* Lindong. Nei Mongol Zizhiqu, N China
151 *P17* **Bairkum** *Kaz.* Bayyrqum. Yuzhnyy Kazakhstan, S Kazakhstan
191 *P12* **Bairnsdale** Victoria, SE Australia
179 *Q14* **Bais** Negros, S Philippines
104 *L15* **Baïse** *var.* Baise. ↝ S France
169 *W11* **Baishan** *prev.* Hunjiang. Jilin, NE China
120 *F12* **Baisogala** Radviliškis, C Lithuania
201 *Q7* **Baiti** N Nauru
106 *G13* **Baixo Alentejo** *physical region* S Portugal
66 *P5* **Baixo, Ilhéu de** *island* Madeira, Portugal, NE Atlantic Ocean
85 *E15* **Baixo Longa** Cuando Cubango, SE Angola
165 *V10* **Baiyin** Gansu, C China
166 *E8* **Baiyü** Sichuan, C China
167 *N14* **Baiyun** ✕ (Guangzhou) Guangdong, S China
166 *K4* **Baiyu Shan** ▲ C China
113 *J25* **Baja** Bács-Kiskun, S Hungary
42 *C4* **Baja California** ◆ *state* NW Mexico
42 *C4* **Baja California** *Eng.* Lower California. *peninsula* NW Mexico
42 *E9* **Baja California Sur** ◆ *state* W Mexico
Bājah *see* Béja
Bajan *see* Bayan
203 *V16* **Baja, Punta** *headland* Easter Island, Chile, E Pacific Ocean
42 *B4* **Baja, Punta** *headland* NW Mexico
57 *R5* **Baja, Punta** *headland* NE Venezuela
44 *D5* **Baja Verapaz** *off.* Departamento de Baja Verapaz. ◆ *department* C Guatemala
175 *Q16* **Bajawa** *prev.* Badjawa. Flores, S Indonesia
159 *S16* **Baj Baj** *prev.* Budge-Budge. West Bengal, E India
147 *N15* **Bājil** W Yemen
191 *U4* **Bajimba, Mount** ▲ New South Wales, SE Australia
114 *K13* **Bajina Bašta** Serbia, W Yugoslavia
159 *U14* **Bajitpur** Dhaka, E Bangladesh
114 *K8* **Bajmok** Serbia, NW Yugoslavia
Bajo Boquete *see* Boquete
115 *L17* **Bajram Curri** Kukës, N Albania
81 *J14* **Bakala** Ouaka, C Central African Republic
131 *T4* **Bakaly** Respublika Bashkortostan, W Russian Federation
Bakan *see* Shimonoseki
151 *U14* **Bakanas** *Kaz.* Baqanas. Almaty, SE Kazakhstan
151 *V12* **Bakanas** *Kaz.* Baqanas. ↝ E Kazakhstan
151 *U14* **Bakbakty** *Kaz.* Baqbaqty. Almaty, SE Kazakhstan
126 *Gg13* **Bakchar** Tomskaya Oblast', C Russian Federation
78 *I11* **Bakel** E Senegal
37 *W13* **Baker** California, W USA
24 *J8* **Baker** Louisiana, S USA
35 *Y9* **Baker** Montana, NW USA
34 *L12* **Baker** Oregon, NW USA
199 *Jj8* **Baker and Howland Islands** ◆ *US unincorporated territory* W Polynesia
38 *I12* **Baker Butte** ▲ Arizona, SW USA
41 *X15* **Baker Island** *island* Alexander Archipelago, Alaska, USA
15 *Kk6* **Baker Lake** Northwest Territories, N Canada
15 *Kk6* **Baker Lake** ◎ Northwest Territories, N Canada

◆ Country ● Country Capital ◇ Dependent Territory ○ Dependent Territory Capital ◆ Administrative Region ✕ International Airport ▲ Mountain ▲ Mountain Range ▲ Volcano ↝ River ◎ Lake ⊠ Reservoir

37 R13 **Bakersfield** California, W USA
26 M9 **Bakersfield** Texas, SW USA
23 P9 **Bakersville** North Carolina, SE USA
Bakhābī *see* Bū Khābī
152 E12 **Bakharden** *Turkm.* Bäherden; *prev.* Bakherden. Akhalskiy Velayat, C Turkmenistan
152 F12 **Bakhardok** *Turkm.* Bokurdak. Akhalskiy Velayat, C Turkmenistan
149 U5 **Bākharz, Kuhhā-ye** ▲ NE Iran
158 D13 **Bākhāsar** Rājasthān, NW India
Bakhchisaray *see* Bakhchysaray
119 T13 **Bakhchysaray** *Rus.* Bakhchisaray. Respublika Krym, S Ukraine
Bakherden *see* Bakharden
119 R3 **Bakhmach** Chernihivs'ka Oblast', N Ukraine
126 Hh11 **Bakhta** Krasnoyarskiy Kray, C Russian Federation
148 K6 **Bākhtarān** *prev.* Kermānshāh, Qahremānshahr. Kermānshāhān, W Iran
Bākhtarān *see* Kermānshāhān
149 Q11 **Bakhtegān, Daryācheh-ye** ◎ C Iran
151 X12 **Bakhty** Semipalatinsk, E Kazakhstan
143 Z11 **Bakı** *Eng.* Baku. ● (Azerbaijan) E Azerbaijan
143 Z11 **Bakı** ✕ E Azerbaijan
142 C13 **Bakır Çayı** ≈ W Turkey
94 L1 **Bakkafjördhur** Austurland, NE Iceland
94 L1 **Bakkaflói** *sea area* W Norwegian Sea
83 I15 **Bako** SW Ethiopia
78 L15 **Bako** NW Ivory Coast
Bákó *see* Bacău
113 H23 **Bakony** *Eng.* Bakony Mountains, *Ger.* Bakonywald. ▲ W Hungary
Bakony Mountains/ Bakonywald *see* Bakony
83 M16 **Bakool** *off.* Gobolka Bakool. ◆ *region* W Somalia
81 L15 **Bakouma** Mbomou, SE Central African Republic
131 N15 **Baksan** Kabardino-Balkarskaya Respublika, SW Russian Federation
121 I16 **Bakshty** Hrodzyenskaya Voblasts', W Belarus
Baku *see* Bakı
204 K12 **Bakutis Coast** *physical region* Antarctica
Bakwanga *see* Mbuji-Mayi
151 O15 **Bakyrly** Yuzhnyy Kazakhstan, S Kazakhstan
12 H13 **Bala** Ontario, S Canada
99 J19 **Bala** NW Wales, UK
142 I13 **Balâ** Ankara, C Turkey
179 O16 **Balabac Island** *island* W Philippines
Balabac, Selat *see* Balabac Strait
175 O1 **Balabac Strait** *var.* Selat Balabac. *strait* Malaysia/Philippines
Ba'labakk *see* Baalbek
175 O10 **Balabalangan, Kepulauan** *island group* N Indonesia
197 H4 **Balabio, Île** *island* Province Nord, W New Caledonia
118 I14 **Balaci** Teleorman, S Romania
145 S7 **Balad** N Iraq
145 U7 **Balad Rūz** E Iraq
126 J15 **Balagansk** Irkutskaya Oblast', S Russian Federation
160 J11 **Bālāghāt** Madhya Pradesh, C India
161 F14 **Bālāghāt Range** ▲ W India
104 E1 **Balagne** *physical region* Corse, France, C Mediterranean Sea
107 U5 **Balaguer** Cataluña, NE Spain
107 S3 **Balaïtous** *var.* Pic de Balaitous, Pic de Balaïtous. ▲ France/Spain
Balaitous, Pic de *see* Balaïtous
131 O3 **Balakhna** Nizhegorodskaya Oblast', W Russian Federation
126 I14 **Balakhta** Krasnoyarskiy Kray, S Russian Federation
190 I9 **Balaklava** South Australia
Balakleya *see* Balakliya
119 V6 **Balakliya** *Rus.* Balakleya. Kharkivs'ka Oblast', E Ukraine
131 Q7 **Balakovo** Saratovskaya Oblast', W Russian Federation
85 P14 **Balama** Cabo Delgado, N Mozambique
175 Nn1 **Balambangan, Pulau** *island* East Malaysia
154 L3 **Bālā Morghāb** Laghmān, NW Afghanistan
158 E11 **Bālān** *prev.* Bāhla. Rājasthān, NW India
118 J10 **Bălan** *Hung.* Balánbánya. Harghita, C Romania
Balánbánya *see* Bălan
179 P10 **Balanga** Luzon, N Philippines
160 M12 **Balāngīr** *prev.* Bolangir. Orissa, E India
131 N8 **Balashov** Saratovskaya Oblast', W Russian Federation
Balasore *see* Bāleshwar
113 K21 **Balassagyarmat** Nógrád, N Hungary
31 S10 **Balaton** Minnesota, N USA
113 H24 **Balaton** *var.* Lake Balaton, *Ger.* Plattensee. ◎ W Hungary
113 I23 **Balatonfüred** *var.* Füred. Veszprém, W Hungary
Balaton, Lake *see* Balaton
118 I11 **Bălăuşeri** *Ger.* Bladenmarkt, *Hung.* Balavásár. Mureş, C Romania
Balavásár *see* Bălăuşeri
107 Q11 **Balazote** Castilla-La Mancha, C Spain
Balázsfalva *see* Blaj
121 F14 **Balbieriškis** Prienai, S Lithuania
195 S12 **Balbi, Mount** ▲ Bougainville Island, NE PNG
60 F11 **Balbina, Represa** ▣ NW Brazil
45 T15 **Balboa** Panamá, C Panama
99 G17 **Balbriggan** *Ir.* Baile Brigín. E Ireland
Balbunar *see* Kubrat
83 N17 **Balcad** Shabeellaha Dhexe, C Somalia
63 D23 **Balcarce** Buenos Aires, E Argentina
9 U16 **Balcarres** Saskatchewan, S Canada
116 O8 **Balchik** Varnenska Oblast, NE Bulgaria
193 E24 **Balclutha** Otago, South Island, NZ
27 Q12 **Balcones Escarpment** *escarpment* Texas, SW USA
20 F14 **Bald Eagle Creek** ≈ Pennsylvania, NE USA
Baldenburg *see* Biały Bór
23 V12 **Bald Head Island** *island* North Carolina, SE USA
29 W10 **Bald Knob** Arkansas, C USA
32 K17 **Bald Knob** *hill* Illinois, N USA
Baldohn *see* Baldone
120 G9 **Baldone** *Ger.* Baldohn. Rīga, W Latvia
24 I9 **Baldwin** Louisiana, S USA
33 P7 **Baldwin** Michigan, N USA
29 Q4 **Baldwin City** Kansas, C USA
41 N8 **Baldwin Peninsula** *headland* Alaska, USA
20 H9 **Baldwinsville** New York, NE USA
25 N2 **Baldwyn** Mississippi, S USA
9 W15 **Baldy Mountain** ▲ Manitoba, S Canada
35 T7 **Baldy Mountain** ▲ Montana, NW USA
39 O13 **Baldy Peak** ▲ Arizona, SW USA
Bâle *see* Basel
107 X9 **Baleares** ◆ *autonomous community* E Spain
107 X11 **Baleares, Islas** *Eng.* Balearic Islands. *island group* Spain, W Mediterranean Sea
Baleares Major *see* Mallorca
Balearic Islands *see* Baleares, Islas
Balearic Plain *see* Algerian Basin
Balearis Minor *see* Menorca
174 M6 **Baleh, Batang** ≈ East Malaysia
10 J8 **Baleine, Grande Rivière de la** ≈ Québec, E Canada
10 K7 **Baleine, Petite Rivière de la** ≈ Québec, SE Canada
11 N6 **Baleine, Rivière à la** ≈ Québec, E Canada
101 J16 **Balen** Antwerpen, N Belgium
179 P9 **Baler** Luzon, N Philippines
160 P11 **Bāleshwar** *prev.* Balasore. Orissa, E India
126 L16 **Baley** Chitinskaya Oblast', S Russian Federation
79 S12 **Baléyara** Tillabéri, W Niger
131 T1 **Balezino** Udmurtskaya Respublika, NW Russian Federation
44 J4 **Balfate** Colón, N Honduras
9 O17 **Balfour** British Columbia, SW Canada
31 N3 **Balfour** North Dakota, N USA
Balfrush *see* Bābol
126 I16 **Balgazyn** Respublika Tyva, S Russian Federation
9 U16 **Balgonie** Saskatchewan, S Canada
Bălgrad *see* Alba Iulia
83 J19 **Balguda** *spring/well* S Kenya
164 K6 **Balguntay** Xinjiang Uygur Zizhiqu, NW China
147 R16 **Balḩāf** S Yemen
158 F13 **Bāli** Rājasthān, N India
175 N15 **Bali** ◆ *province* S Indonesia
175 N16 **Bali** *island* C Indonesia
113 K16 **Balice** ✕ (Kraków) Kraków, S Poland
176 Yy13 **Baliem, Sungai** ≈ Irian Jaya, E Indonesia
142 C12 **Balıkesir** Balıkesir, W Turkey
142 C12 **Balıkesir** ◆ *province* NW Turkey
144 L3 **Balīkh, Nahr** ≈ N Syria
175 O9 **Balikpapan** Borneo, C Indonesia
175 O9 **Balikpapan, Teluk** *bay* Borneo, C Indonesia
Bali, Laut *see* Bali Sea
195 O11 **Balima** ≈ New Britain, C PNG
179 P17 **Balimbing** Tawitawi, SW Philippines
194 G14 **Balimo** Western, SW PNG
Bálinc *see* Balinţ
175 Qq9 **Balingara, Pegunungan** ▲ Sulawesi, N Indonesia
103 H23 **Balingen** Baden-Württemberg, SW Germany
118 F11 **Balinţ** *Hung.* Bálinc. Timiş, W Romania
179 Pp6 **Balintang Channel** *channel* N Philippines
144 K3 **Bālis** Ḩalab, N Syria
175 N15 **Bali Sea** *Ind.* Laut Bali. *sea* C Indonesia
175 N16 **Bali, Selat** *strait* C Indonesia
100 K7 **Balk** Friesland, N Netherlands
124 O7 **Balkan Mountains** *Bul./SCr.* Stara Planina. ▲ Bulgaria/Yugoslavia
152 B9 **Balkanskiy Velayat** *Turkm.* Balkan Welaýaty. ◆ *province* W Turkmenistan
Balkan Welayaty *see* Balkanskiy Velayat
151 P8 **Balkashino** Akmola, N Kazakhstan
155 O2 **Balkh** *anc.* Bactra. Balkh, N Afghanistan
155 P2 **Balkh** ◆ *province* N Afghanistan
151 T13 **Balkhash** *Kaz.* Balqash. Zhezkazgan, SE Kazakhstan
Balkhash, Lake *see* Balkhash, Ozero
151 T13 **Balkhash, Ozero** *Eng.* Lake Balkhash, *Kaz.* Balqash. ◎ SE Kazakhstan
Balla Balla *see* Mbalabala
98 H10 **Ballachulish** N Scotland, UK
188 M12 **Balladonia** Western Australia
99 C16 **Ballaghaderreen** *Ir.* Bealach an Doirín. C Ireland
94 H10 **Ballangen** Nordland, NW Norway
99 H14 **Ballantrae** W Scotland, UK
191 N12 **Ballarat** Victoria, SE Australia
188 K11 **Ballard, Lake** *salt lake* Western Australia
Ballari *see* Bellary
78 L11 **Ballé** Koulikoro, W Mali
42 D7 **Ballenas, Bahía de** *bay* W Mexico
42 D5 **Ballenas, Canal de** *channel* NW Mexico
205 R17 **Balleny Islands** *island group* Antarctica
42 J7 **Balleza** *var.* San Pablo Balleza. Chihuahua, N Mexico
116 M13 **Ballı** Tekirdağ, NW Turkey
159 O13 **Ballia** Uttar Pradesh, N India
191 V4 **Ballina** New South Wales, SE Australia
99 C16 **Ballina** *Ir.* Béal an Átha. W Ireland
99 D16 **Ballinamore** *Ir.* Béal an Átha Móir. NW Ireland
99 D18 **Ballinasloe** *Ir.* Béal Átha na Sluaighe. W Ireland
27 P8 **Ballinger** Texas, SW USA
99 C17 **Ballinrobe** *Ir.* Baile an Róba. W Ireland
99 A21 **Ballinskelligs Bay** *Ir.* Bá na Scealg. *inlet* SW Ireland
99 D15 **Ballintra** *Ir.* Baile an tSratha. NW Ireland
105 T7 **Ballon d'Alsace** ▲ NE France
Ballon de Guebwiller *see* Grand Ballon
115 K21 **Ballsh** *var.* Ballshi. Fier, SW Albania
Ballshi *see* Ballsh
100 K4 **Ballum** Friesland, N Netherlands
99 F16 **Ballybay** *Ir.* Béal Átha Beithe. N Ireland
99 E14 **Ballybofey** *Ir.* Bealach Féich. NW Ireland
99 G14 **Ballycastle** *Ir.* Baile an Chaistil. N Northern Ireland, UK
99 G15 **Ballyclare** *Ir.* Bealach Cláir. E Northern Ireland, UK
99 E16 **Ballyconnell** *Ir.* Béal Átha Conaill. N Ireland
99 C17 **Ballyhaunis** *Ir.* Beál Átha hAmhnais. W Ireland
99 G14 **Ballymena** *Ir.* An Baile Meánach. NE Northern Ireland, UK
99 F14 **Ballymoney** *Ir.* Baile Monaidh. NE Northern Ireland, UK
99 G15 **Ballynahinch** *Ir.* Baile na hInse. SE Northern Ireland, UK
99 D16 **Ballysadare** *Ir.* Baile Easa Dara. NW Ireland
99 D15 **Ballyshannon** *Ir.* Béal Átha Seanaidh. NW Ireland
65 H19 **Balmaceda** Aisén, S Chile
65 G23 **Balmaceda, Cerro** ▲ S Chile
113 N22 **Balmazújváros** Hajdú-Bihar, E Hungary
110 E10 **Balmhorn** ▲ SW Switzerland
190 L12 **Balmoral** Victoria, SE Australia
26 K9 **Balmorhea** Texas, SW USA
Balneario Claromecó *see* Claromecó
175 R9 **Balo** Sulawesi, N Indonesia
Balochistān *see* Baluchistān
84 B13 **Balombo** *Port.* Norton de Matos, Vila Norton de Matos. Benguela, W Angola
84 B13 **Balombo** ≈ W Angola
189 X10 **Balonne River** ≈ Queensland, E Australia
158 E13 **Bālotra** Rājasthān, N India
Balqā'/Balqā', Muḩāfaẓat al *see* Al Balqā'
Balqash *see* Balkhash/ Balkhash, Ozero
158 M12 **Balrāmpur** Uttar Pradesh, N India
190 M9 **Balranald** New South Wales, SE Australia
118 H14 **Balş** Olt, S Romania
12 H11 **Balsam Creek** Ontario, S Canada
32 I5 **Balsam Lake** Wisconsin, N USA
12 I14 **Balsam Lake** ◎ Ontario, SE Canada
61 M14 **Balsas** Maranhão, E Brazil
42 M15 **Balsas, Río** *var.* Río Mexcala. ≈ S Mexico
45 W16 **Balsas, Río** ≈ SE Panama
121 O18 **Bal'shavik** *Rus.* Bol'shevik. Homyel'skaya Voblasts', SE Belarus
97 O15 **Bålsta** Uppsala, C Sweden
110 E7 **Balsthal** Solothurn, NW Switzerland
119 O8 **Balta** Odes'ka Oblast', SW Ukraine
121 H14 **Baltaji Voke** Vilnius, SE Lithuania
107 N5 **Baltanás** Castilla-León, N Spain
63 E16 **Baltasar Brum** Artigas, N Uruguay
118 M9 **Bălţi** *Rus.* Bel'tsy. N Moldova
Baltic Port *see* Paldiski
120 B10 **Baltic Sea** *Ger.* Ostee, *Rus.* Baltiyskoye More. *sea* N Europe
23 X3 **Baltimore** Maryland, NE USA
33 T13 **Baltimore** Ohio, N USA
Baltischport/Baltiski *see* Paldiski
Baltiskoye More *see* Baltic Sea
121 A14 **Baltiysk** *Ger.* Pillau. Kaliningradskaya Oblast', W Russian Federation
Baltkrievija *see* Belarus
194 K9 **Baluan Island** *island* N PNG
Balūchestān va Sīstān *see* Sīstān va Balūchestān
154 M12 **Baluchistān** *var.* Balochistān, Beluchistan. ◆ *province* SW Pakistan
179 Q12 **Balud** Masbate, N Philippines
174 Mm6 **Balui, Batang** ≈ East Malaysia
159 S13 **Bālurghat** West Bengal, NE India
120 J8 **Balvi** Balvi, NE Latvia
194 H12 **Balyer River** Western Highlands, C PNG
153 W7 **Balykchy** *Kir.* Ysyk-Köl; *prev.* Issyk-Kul', Rybach'ye. Issyk-Kul'skaya Oblast', NE Kyrgyzstan
58 B7 **Balzar** Guayas, W Ecuador
110 I8 **Balzers** S Liechtenstein
149 T12 **Bam** Kermān, SE Iran
79 Y13 **Bama** Borno, NE Nigeria
78 L12 **Bamako** ● (Mali) Capital District, SW Mali
79 P10 **Bamba** Gao, C Mali
44 M8 **Bambana, Río** ≈ NE Nicaragua
81 J15 **Bambari** Ouaka, C Central African Republic
189 W5 **Bambaroo** Queensland, NE Australia
103 K19 **Bamberg** Bayern, SE Germany
23 R14 **Bamberg** South Carolina, SE USA
81 M16 **Bambesa** Haut-Zaïre, N Zaire
78 G11 **Bambey** W Senegal
81 H16 **Bambio** Sangha-Mbaéré, SW Central African Republic
85 I24 **Bamboesberge** ▲ S South Africa
81 D14 **Bamenda** Nord-Ouest, W Cameroon
8 K17 **Bamfield** Vancouver Island, British Columbia, SW Canada
152 E12 **Bami** *Turkm.* Bamy. Akhalskiy Velayat, C Turkmenistan
155 P4 **Bāmīān** *var.* Bāmiān. Bāmīān, NE Afghanistan
155 O4 **Bāmīān** ◆ *province* C Afghanistan
81 J14 **Bamingui** Bamingui-Bangoran, C Central African Republic
80 J13 **Bamingui** ≈ N Central African Republic
80 J13 **Bamingui-Bangoran** ◆ *prefecture* N Central African Republic
149 V13 **Bampūr** Sīstān va Balūchestān, SE Iran
194 G14 **Bamu** ≈ SW PNG
Bamy *see* Bami
Bān *see* Bánovce nad Bebravou
83 N17 **Banaadir** *off.* Gobolka Banaadir. ◆ *region* S Somalia
203 N3 **Banaba** *var.* Ocean Island. *island* Tungaru, W Kiribati
61 O14 **Banabuiú, Açude** ▣ NE Brazil
59 O19 **Bañados del Izozog** *salt lake* SE Bolivia
99 D18 **Banagher** *Ir.* Beannchar. C Ireland
81 M17 **Banalia** Haut-Zaïre, N Zaire
78 L12 **Banamba** Koulikoro, W Mali
42 G4 **Banámichi** Sonora, NW Mexico
189 Y9 **Banana** Queensland, E Australia
203 Z2 **Banana** *prev.* Main Camp. Kiritimati, E Kiribati
61 K16 **Bananal, Ilha do** *island* C Brazil
25 Y12 **Banana River** *lagoon* Florida, SE USA
157 Q22 **Bananga** Andaman and Nicobar Islands, India, NE Indian Ocean
Banaras *see* Vārānasi
116 N13 **Banarlı** Tekirdağ, NW Turkey
158 H12 **Banās** ≈ N India
77 Z11 **Banâs, Râs** *headland* E Egypt
114 N10 **Banatski Karlovac** Serbia, NE Yugoslavia
147 P16 **Banā, Wādī** *dry watercourse* SW Yemen
142 E14 **Banaz** Uşak, W Turkey
142 E14 **Banaz Çayı** ≈ W Turkey
165 P14 **Banbar** Xizang Zizhiqu, W China
99 G15 **Banbridge** *Ir.* Droichead na Banna. SE Northern Ireland, UK
Ban Bua Yai *see* Bua Yai
99 M21 **Banbury** S England, UK
178 H7 **Ban Chiang Dao** Chiang Mai, NW Thailand
98 K9 **Banchory** NE Scotland, UK
12 J13 **Bancroft** Ontario, SE Canada
35 R15 **Bancroft** Idaho, NW USA
31 U11 **Bancroft** Iowa, C USA
160 I9 **Bānda** Madhya Pradesh, C India
158 L13 **Bānda** Uttar Pradesh, N India
173 E3 **Bandaaceh** *var.* Banda Atjeh; *prev.* Koetaradja, Kutaradja, Kutaraja. Sumatera, W Indonesia
Banda Atjeh *see* Bandaaceh
176 U12 **Banda, Kepulauan** *island group* E Indonesia
Banda, Laut *see* Banda Sea
79 N17 **Bandama** *var.* Bandama Fleuve. ≈ S Ivory Coast
79 N15 **Bandama Blanc** ≈ C Ivory Coast
Bandama Fleuve *see* Bandama
Bandar 'Abbās *see* Bandar-e 'Abbās
159 W16 **Bandarban** Chittagong, SE Bangladesh
82 Q13 **Bandarbeyla** *var.* Bender Beila, Bender Beyla. Bari, NE Somalia
149 R14 **Bandar-e 'Abbās** *var.* Bandar 'Abbās; *prev.* Gombroon. Hormozgān, S Iran
148 M3 **Bandar-e Anzalī** Gīlān, NW Iran
149 N12 **Bandar-e Būshehr** *var.* Būshehr, *Eng.* Bushire. Būshehr, S Iran
148 M11 **Bandar-e Gonāveh** *var.* Ganāveh; *prev.* Gonāveh. Būshehr, SW Iran
149 R14 **Bandar-e Khamīr** Hormozgān, S Iran
149 Q14 **Bandar-e Langeh** *var.* Bandar-e Lengeh, Lingeh. Hormozgān, S Iran
Bandar-e Lengeh *see* Bandar-e Langeh
148 L10 **Bandar-e Māhshahr** *var.* Māh-Shahr; *prev.* Bandar-e Ma'shūr. Khūzestān, SW Iran
Bandar-e Ma'shūr *see* Bandar-e Māhshahr
149 O14 **Bandar-e Nakhīlū** Hormozgān, S Iran
Bandar-e Shāh *see* Bandar-e Torkaman
149 P4 **Bandar-e Torkaman** *var.* Bandar-e Torkeman, Bandar-e Torkman; *prev.* Bandar-e Shāh. Māzandarān, N Iran
Bandar-e Torkeman/Bandar-e Torkman *see* Bandar-e Torkaman
Bandar Kassim *see* Boosaaso
174 Ii13 **Bandarlampung** *prev.* Tanjungkarang, Teloekbetoeng, Telukbetung. Sumatera, W Indonesia
Bandar Maharani *see* Muar
Bandar Masulipatnam *see* Machilipatnam
Bandar Penggaram *see* Batu Pahat
175 N3 **Bandar Seri Begawan** *prev.* Brunei Town. ● (Brunei) N Brunei
174 Mm3 **Bandar Seri Begawan** ✕ N Brunei
175 Ss13 **Banda Sea** *var.* Laut Banda. *sea* E Indonesia
106 H5 **Bande** Galicia, NW Spain
61 G15 **Bandeirantes** Mato Grosso, W Brazil
61 N20 **Bandeira, Pico da** ▲ SE Brazil
85 K19 **Bandelierkop** Northern, NE South Africa
64 L8 **Bandera** Santiago del Estero, N Argentina
27 Q11 **Bandera** Texas, SW USA
42 J13 **Banderas, Bahía de** *bay* W Mexico
79 O11 **Bandiagara** Mopti, C Mali
158 I12 **Bāndīkūi** Rājasthān, N India
142 C11 **Bandırma** *var.* Penderma. Balıkesir, NW Turkey
Bandjarmasin *see* Banjarmasin
Bandoeng *see* Bandung
99 C21 **Bandon** *Ir.* Droicheadna Bandan. SW Ireland
34 E14 **Bandon** Oregon, NW USA
178 J8 **Ban Dong Bang** Nong Khai, E Thailand
178 I6 **Ban Donkon** Oudômxai, N Laos
180 J14 **Bandrélé** SE Mayotte
81 H20 **Bandundu** *prev.* Banningville. Bandundu, W Zaire
81 I21 **Bandundu** *off.* Région de Bandundu. ◆ *region* W Zaire
174 Jj14 **Bandung** *prev.* Bandoeng. Jawa, C Indonesia
118 L15 **Băneasa** Constanţa, SW Romania
148 J4 **Bāneh** Kordestān, N Iran
46 I7 **Banes** Holguín, E Cuba
9 P16 **Banff** Alberta, SW Canada
98 K8 **Banff** NE Scotland, UK
98 K8 **Banff** *cultural region* NE Scotland, UK
Bánffyhunyad *see* Huedin
79 N14 **Banfora** SW Burkina
161 H19 **Bangalore** Karnātaka, S India
159 S16 **Bangaon** West Bengal, NE India
179 P9 **Bangar** Luzon, N Philippines
81 L15 **Bangassou** Mbomou, SE Central African Republic
194 K12 **Bangeta, Mount** ▲ C PNG
175 Qq10 **Banggai, Kepulauan** *island group* C Indonesia
175 R9 **Banggai, Pulau** *island* Kepulauan Banggai, N Indonesia
176 X11 **Banggelapa** Irian Jaya, E Indonesia
Banggi *see* Banggi, Pulau
175 O1 **Banggi, Pulau** *var.* Banggi. *island* East Malaysia
124 N15 **Banghāzī** *Eng.* Bengazi, Benghazi, *It.* Bengasi. NE Libya
Bang Hieng *see* Xé Banghiang
174 K8 **Bangkai, Tanjung** *var.* Bankai. *headland* Borneo, N Indonesia
174 M14 **Bangkalan** Pulau Madura, C Indonesia
175 S6 **Bangka, Pulau** *island* N Indonesia
174 J10 **Bangka, Pulau** *island* W Indonesia
174 Ii10 **Bangka, Selat** *strait* Sumatera, W Indonesia
175 Rr6 **Bangka, Selat** *var.* Selat Likupang. *strait* Sulawesi, N Indonesia
174 Gg8 **Bangkinang** Sumatera, W Indonesia
174 H10 **Bangko** Sumatera, W Indonesia
Bangkok *see* Krung Thep
Bangkok, Bight of *see* Krung Thep, Ao
159 T14 **Bangladesh** *off.* People's Republic of Bangladesh; *prev.* East Pakistan. ◆ *republic* S Asia
178 Kk13 **Ba Ngoi** Khanh Hoa, S Vietnam
158 K5 **Bangong Co** *var.* Pangong Tso. ◎ China/India *see also* Pangong Tso
99 G15 **Bangor** *Ir.* Beannchar. E Northern Ireland, UK
99 I18 **Bangor** NW Wales, UK
21 R6 **Bangor** Maine, NE USA
20 I14 **Bangor** Pennsylvania, NE USA
69 R8 **Bangoran** ≈ S Central African Republic
Bang Phra *see* Trat
Bang Pla Soi *see* Chon Buri
27 Q8 **Bangs** Texas, SW USA
178 H13 **Bang Saphan** *var.* Bang Saphan Yai. Prachuap Khiri Khan, SW Thailand
Bang Saphan Yai *see* Bang Saphan
38 I8 **Bangs, Mount** ▲ Arizona, SW USA
95 E15 **Bangsund** Nord-Trøndelag, C Norway
179 P8 **Bangued** Luzon, N Philippines
81 I15 **Bangui** ● (Central African Republic) Ombella-Mpoko, SW Central African Republic
81 I15 **Bangui** ✕ Ombella-Mpoko, SW Central African Republic
85 N16 **Bangula** Southern, S Malawi
Bangwaketse *see* Southern
84 K12 **Bangweulu, Lake** *var.* Lake Bengweulu. ◎ N Zambia
Banhā *see* Benha
Ban Hat Yai *see* Hat Yai
178 I8 **Ban Hin Heup** Viangchan, C Laos
Ban Houayxay/Ban Houei Sai *see* Houayxay
178 H12 **Ban Hua Hin** *var.* Hua Hin. Prachuap Khiri Khan, SW Thailand
81 L14 **Bani** Haute-Kotto, E Central African Republic
79 N12 **Bani** ≈ S Mali
47 O9 **Baní** S Dominican Republic
Banias *see* Bāniyās
79 S11 **Bani Bangou** Tillabéri, SW Niger
78 M12 **Banifing** *var.* Ngorolaka. ≈ Burkina/Mali
79 R13 **Banikoara** N Benin
Banī Mazār *see* Beni Mazâr
116 K8 **Baniski Lom** ≈ N Bulgaria
23 U7 **Banister River** ≈ Virginia, NE USA
Banī Suwayf *see* Beni Suef
77 O8 **Banī Walīd** NW Libya
144 H5 **Bāniyās** *var.* Banias, Baniyas, Paneas. Ţarţūs, W Syria
115 K14 **Banja** Serbia, W Yugoslavia
Banjak, Kepulauan *see* Banyak, Kepulauan
114 J12 **Banja Koviljača** Serbia, W Yugoslavia
114 G11 **Banja Luka** NW Bosnia and Herzegovina
175 N11 **Banjarmasin** *prev.* Bandjarmasin. Borneo, C Indonesia
Banjoewangi *see* Banyuwangi
78 F11 **Banjul** *prev.* Bathurst. ● (Gambia) W Gambia
78 F11 **Banjul** ✕ W Gambia
Banjuwangi *see* Banyuwangi
Bank *see* Bankä
143 Y13 **Bankä** *Rus.* Bank. SE Azerbaijan
178 Jj11 **Ban Kadian** *var.* Ban Kadiene. Champasak, S Laos
Ban Kadiene *see* Ban Kadian
Bankai *see* Bangkai, Tanjung
178 Gg15 **Ban Kam Phuam** Phangnga, SW Thailand
Ban Kantang *see* Kantang
79 O11 **Bankass** Mopti, S Mali
97 L19 **Bankeryd** Jönköping, S Sweden
85 K16 **Banket** Mashonaland West, N Zimbabwe
178 Jj11 **Ban Khamphô** Attapu, S Laos
25 O4 **Bankhead Lake** ▣ Alabama, S USA
79 Q11 **Bankilaré** Tillabéri, SW Niger
Banks, Îles *see* Banks Islands
8 I14 **Banks Island** *island* British Columbia, SW Canada
15 Hh1 **Banks Island** *island* Banks Island, Northwest Territories, NW Canada
197 C10 **Banks Islands** *Fr.* Îles Banks. *island group* N Vanuatu
25 U8 **Banks Lake** ◎ Georgia, SE USA
34 K8 **Banks Lake** ▣ Washington, NW USA
193 I19 **Banks Peninsula** *peninsula* South Island, NZ
191 Q15 **Banks Strait** *strait* SW Tasman Sea
Ban Kui Nua *see* Kui Buri
159 R16 **Bānkura** West Bengal, NE India
178 J8 **Ban Lakxao** *var.* Lak Sao. Bolikhamxai, C Laos
178 H17 **Ban Lam Phai** Songkhla, SW Thailand
Ban Mae Sot *see* Mae Sot
Ban Mae Suai *see* Mae Suai
Ban Mak Khaeng *see* Udon Thani
177 G3 **Banmauk** Sagaing, N Myanmar
Banmo *see* Bhamo
178 Jj10 **Ban Mun-Houamuang** S Laos
99 F14 **Bann** *var.* Lower Bann, Upper Bann. ≈ N Northern Ireland, UK
178 Jj10 **Ban Nadou** Salavan, S Laos
178 J10 **Ban Nakala** Savannakhét, S Laos
178 I8 **Ban Nakha** Viangchan, C Laos
178 Jj9 **Ban Nakham** Khammouan, S Laos
178 I8 **Ban Namoun** Xaignabouli, N Laos
178 Hh17 **Ban Nang Sata** Yala, SW Thailand
178 Gg15 **Ban Na San** Surat Thani, SW Thailand
178 I7 **Ban Nasi** Xiangkhoang, N Laos
46 I3 **Bannerman Town** Eleuthera Island, C Bahamas
37 V15 **Banning** California, W USA
Banningville *see* Bandundu
178 Jj11 **Ban Nongsim** Champasak, S Laos
155 S7 **Bannu** *prev.* Edwardesabad. North-West Frontier Province, NW Pakistan
Bañolas *see* Banyoles
58 C7 **Baños** Tungurahua, C Ecuador
Bánovce *see* Bánovce nad Bebravou
113 I19 **Bánovce nad Bebravou** *var.* Bánovce, *Hung.* Bán. Západné Slovensko, W Slovakia
114 I12 **Banovići** E Bosnia and Herzegovina
Banow *see* Andarāb
Ban Pak Phanang *see* Pak Phanang
178 Hh7 **Ban Pan Nua** Lampang, NW Thailand
178 I10 **Ban Phai** Khon Kaen, E Thailand
178 Jj9 **Ban Phou A Douk** Khammouan, C Laos
178 I8 **Ban Phu** Uthai Thani, W Thailand
178 H11 **Ban Pong** Ratchaburi, W Thailand
202 I3 **Banraeaba** Tarawa, W Kiribati
178 Gg11 **Ban Sai Yok** Kanchanaburi, W Thailand
Ban Sattahip/Ban Sattahipp *see* Sattahip
Ban Sichon *see* Sichon
Ban Si Racha *see* Siracha
113 J19 **Banská Bystrica** *Ger.* Neusohl, *Hung.* Besztercebánya. Stredné Slovensko, C Slovakia
178 J8 **Ban Sôppheung** Bolikhamxai, C Laos
Ban Sop Prap *see* Sop Prap
158 G15 **Bānswāra** Rājasthān, N India
178 Gg15 **Ban Ta Khun** Surat Thani, SW Thailand
Ban Takua Pa *see* Takua Pa
178 Jj9 **Ban Talak** Khammouan, C Laos
79 R15 **Bantè** W Benin
178 Ii8 **Ban Thabôk** Bolikhamxai, C Laos
178 Jj10 **Ban Tôp** Savannakhét, S Laos
99 B21 **Bantry** *Ir.* Beanntraí. SW Ireland
99 A21 **Bantry Bay** *Ir.* Bá Bheanntraí. *bay* SW Ireland
174 L15 **Bantul** *prev.* Bantoel. Jawa, C Indonesia
161 F19 **Bantvāl** *var.* Bantwāl. Karnātaka, E India
Bantwāl *see* Bantvāl
116 N9 **Banya** Burgaska Oblast, E Bulgaria
173 Ee6 **Banyak, Kepulauan** *prev.* Kepulauan Banjak. *island group* NW Indonesia
107 U8 **Banya, La** *headland* E Spain
81 E14 **Banyo** Adamaoua, NW Cameroon
107 X4 **Banyoles** *var.* Bañolas. Cataluña, NE Spain
178 H16 **Ban Yong Sata** Trang, SW Thailand
174 Mm16 **Banyuwangi** *var.* Banjuwangi; *prev.* Banjoewangi. Jawa, S Indonesia
205 X14 **Banzare Coast** *physical region* Antarctica
181 Q14 **Banzare Seamounts** *undersea feature* S Indian Ocean
Banzart *see* Bizerte
Baochang *see* Taibus Qi
167 O3 **Baoding** *var.* Pao-ting; *prev.* Tsingyuan. Hebei, E China
Baoebaoe *see* Baubau
Baoi, Oileán *see* Dursey Island
166 J6 **Baoji** *var.* Pao-chi, Paoki. Shaanxi, C China
195 V14 **Baolo** Santa Isabel, N Solomon Islands
178 K13 **Bao Lôc** Lâm Đông, S Vietnam
169 Z7 **Baoqing** Heilongjiang, NE China
Baoqing *see* Shaoyang
81 H15 **Baoro** Nana-Mambéré, W Central African Republic
166 E12 **Baoshan** *var.* Pao-shan. Yunnan, SW China
169 N13 **Baotou** *var.* Pao-t'ou, Paotow. Nei Mongol Zizhiqu, N China
78 L14 **Baoulé** ≈ S Mali
78 K12 **Baoulé** ≈ W Mali
105 O2 **Bapaume** Pas-de-Calais, N France
12 J13 **Baptiste Lake** ◎ Ontario, SE Canada
Baqanas *see* Bakanas
Baqbaqty *see* Bakbakty
165 P14 **Baqên** *var.* Dartang. Xizang Zizhiqu, W China
144 F14 **Bāqir, Jabal** ▲ S Jordan
145 T7 **Ba'qūbah** *var.* Qubba. C Iraq
64 H5 **Baquedano** Antofagasta, N Chile
118 M6 **Bar** Vinnyts'ka Oblast', C Ukraine
115 J18 **Bar** *It.* Antivari. Montenegro, SW Yugoslavia
82 E10 **Bara** Northern Kordofan, C Sudan
83 M18 **Baraawe** *It.* Brava. Shabeellaha Hoose, S Somalia
158 M12 **Bāra Banki** Uttar Pradesh, N India
125 G13 **Barabinsk** Novosibirskaya Oblast', C Russian Federation
32 L8 **Baraboo** Wisconsin, N USA
32 K8 **Baraboo Range** *hill range* Wisconsin, N USA
Baracaldo *see* San Vicente de Barakaldo
13 Y6 **Barachois** Québec, SE Canada
46 J7 **Baracoa** Guantánamo, E Cuba
63 C19 **Baradero** Buenos Aires, E Argentina
191 R6 **Baradine** New South Wales, SE Australia
Baraf Daja Islands *see* Damar, Kepulauan
160 M12 **Baragarh** Orissa, E India
83 I17 **Baragoi** Rift Valley, W Kenya
47 N9 **Barahona** SW Dominican Republic
159 W13 **Barail Range** ▲ NE India
82 I9 **Baraka** *var.* Barka, *Ar.* Khawr Barakah. *seasonal river* Eritrea/Sudan
82 G10 **Barakat** Gezira, C Sudan
Barakī *see* Barakī Barak
155 Q6 **Barakī Barak** *var.* Barakī, Baraki Rajan. Lowgar, E Afghanistan

◆ Country ● Country Capital ◇ Dependent Territory ○ Dependent Territory Capital ◆ Administrative Region ✕ International Airport ▲ Mountain ▲ Mountain Range Volcano ≈ River ◎ Lake ▣ Reservoir

Barakī Rajan see Barakī Barak
160 N11 Bārākot Orissa, E India
Baram see Baram, Batang
57 S7 Barama River ~ N Guyana
161 E14 Bārāmati Mahārāshtra, W India
174 Mm4 Baram, Batang var. Baram, Barram. ~ East Malaysia
158 H5 Bāramūla Jammu and Kashmir, NW India
121 N14 Baran' Vitsyebskaya Voblasts', NE Belarus
158 I14 Bārān Rājasthān, N India
145 U4 Barānān, Shākh-i ▲▲ E Iraq
121 I17 Baranavichy Pol. Baranowicze, Rus. Baranovichi. Brestskaya Voblasts', SW Belarus
127 Oo5 Baranikha Chukotskiy Avtonomnyy Okrug, NE Russian Federation
118 M4 Baranivka Zhytomyrs'ka Oblast', N Ukraine
41 W14 Baranof Island island Alexander Archipelago, Alaska, USA
Baranovichi/Baranowicze see Baranavichy
113 N15 Baranów Sandomierski Tarnobrzeg, SE Poland
113 I26 Baranya off. Baranya Megye. ◈ county S Hungary
159 R13 Barāri Bihār, NE India
24 L10 Barataria Bay bay Louisiana, S USA
Barat Daya, Kepulauan see Damar, Kepulauan
120 L12 Baravukha Rus. Borovukha. Vitsyebskaya Voblasts', N Belarus
56 E11 Baraya Huila, C Colombia
61 M21 Barbacena Minas Gerais, SE Brazil
56 B13 Barbacoas Nariño, SW Colombia
56 L6 Barbacoas Aragua, N Venezuela
47 Z13 Barbados ◆ commonwealth republic SE West Indies
49 S3 Barbados island Barbados
107 U11 Barbaria, Cap de var. Cabo de Berberia. headland Formentera, E Spain
116 N13 Barbaros Tekirdağ, NW Turkey
76 A11 Barbas, Cap headland S Western Sahara
107 T5 Barbastro Aragón, NE Spain
106 K16 Barbate ~ SW Spain
106 K16 Barbate de Franco Andalucía, S Spain
85 K21 Barberton Mpumalanga, NE South Africa
33 U12 Barberton Ohio, N USA
104 K12 Barbezieux-St-Hilaire Charente, W France
56 G9 Barbosa Santander, C Colombia
23 N7 Barbourville Kentucky, S USA
47 W9 Barbuda island N Antigua and Barbuda
189 W8 Barcaldine Queensland, E Australia
Barcarozsnyó see Râşnov
106 I11 Barcarrota Extremadura, W Spain
Barcău see Berettyó
Barce see Al Marj
109 L23 Barcellona var. Barcellona Pozzo di Gotto. Sicilia, Italy, C Mediterranean Sea
Barcellona Pozzo di Gotto see Barcellona
107 W6 Barcelona anc. Barcino, Barcinona. Cataluña, E Spain
57 N5 Barcelona Anzoátegui, NE Venezuela
107 S5 Barcelona ◈ province Cataluña, NE Spain
107 W6 Barcelona ✕ Cataluña, E Spain
105 U14 Barcelonnette Alpes-de-Haute-Provence, SE France
60 E12 Barcelos Amazonas, N Brazil
106 G5 Barcelos Braga, N Portugal
112 I10 Barcin Ger. Bartschin. Bydgoszcz, C Poland
Barcino/Barcinona see Barcelona
Barcoo see Cooper Creek
113 H26 Barcs Somogy, SW Hungary
143 W11 Bärdä Rus. Barda. C Azerbaijan
80 H5 Bardaï Borkou-Ennedi-Tibesti, N Chad
145 R2 Bardaṛash N Iraq
145 Q7 Bardasah SW Iraq
159 S16 Barddhamān West Bengal, NE India
113 N18 Bardejov Ger. Bartfeld, Hung. Bártfa. Východné Slovensko, NE Slovakia
107 R4 Bárdenas Reales physical region N Spain
Bardera/Bardere see Baardheere
Bardesīr see Bardsīr
94 K3 Bardharbunga ▲ C Iceland
Bardhë, Drini i see Beli Drim
108 E9 Bardi Emilia-Romagna, C Italy
108 A8 Bardonecchia Piemonte, W Italy
99 H19 Bardsey Island island NW Wales, UK
149 S11 Bardsīr var. Bardesīr, Mashīz. Kermān, C Iran
22 L6 Bardstown Kentucky, S USA
Barduli see Barletta
22 G7 Bardwell Kentucky, S USA
158 K11 Bareilly var. Bareli. Uttar Pradesh, N India
Bareli see Bareilly
100 H13 Barendrecht Zuid-Holland, SW Netherlands
104 M3 Barentin Seine-Maritime, N France
94 N3 Barentsburg Spitsbergen, W Svalbard
Barentsevo More/Barents Havet see Barents Sea
94 O3 Barentsøya island E Svalbard
207 T11 Barents Plain undersea feature N Barents Sea
129 P3 Barents Sea Nor. Barents Havet, Rus. Barentsevo More. sea Arctic Ocean
207 U14 Barents Trough undersea feature SW Barents Sea
82 I9 Barentu W Eritrea
104 J3 Barfleur Manche, N France
104 J3 Barfleur, Pointe de headland N France
Barfrush/Barfurush see Bābol
164 H14 Barga Xizang Zizhiqu, W China
107 N9 Bargas Castilla-La Mancha, C Spain
83 I15 Bargē SW Ethiopia
108 A9 Barge Piemonte, NE Italy
159 U16 Barguna Khulna, S Bangladesh
Bärguşad see Vorotan
126 K15 Barguzin Respublika Buryatiya, S Russian Federation
159 O13 Barhaj Uttar Pradesh, N India
191 N10 Barham New South Wales, SE Australia
158 J12 Barhan Uttar Pradesh, N India
21 S7 Bar Harbor Mount Desert Island, Maine, NE USA
159 R14 Barharwa Bihār, NE India
159 P15 Barhi Bihār, N India
109 O17 Bari var. Bari delle Puglie; anc. Barium. Puglia, SE Italy
82 P12 Bari off. Gobolka Bari. ◈ region NE Somalia
178 K14 Ba Ria Ba Ria-Vung Tau, S Vietnam
Bāridah see Al Bāridah
Bari delle Puglie see Bari
Barikot see Barīkowṭ
155 T4 Barīkowṭ var. Barikot. Kunar, NE Afghanistan
44 C4 Barillas var. Santa Cruz Barillas. Huehuetenango, NW Guatemala
56 J6 Barinas Barinas, W Venezuela
56 I7 Barinas off. Estado Barinas; prev. Zamora. ◈ state C Venezuela
56 I6 Barinitas Barinas, NW Venezuela
160 P11 Bāripada Orissa, E India
62 K9 Bariri São Paulo, S Brazil
77 W11 Bârîs S Egypt
158 G14 Bari Sādri Rājasthān, N India
159 U16 Barisal Khulna, S Bangladesh
173 G7 Barisan, Pegunungan ▲▲ Sumatera, W Indonesia
175 N10 Barito, Sungai ~ Borneo, C Indonesia
Barium see Bari
Barka see Baraka
Barka see Al Marj
166 H8 Barkam Sichuan, C China
120 J9 Barkava Madona, C Latvia
8 M15 Barkerville British Columbia, SW Canada
12 J12 Bark Lake ◎ Ontario, SE Canada
22 H7 Barkley, Lake ▣ Kentucky/Tennessee, S USA
8 K17 Barkley Sound inlet British Columbia, W Canada
85 J24 Barkly East Afr. Barkly-Oos. Eastern Cape, SE South Africa
Barkly-Oos see Barkly East
189 S4 Barkly Tableland plateau Northern Territory/Queensland, N Australia
Barkly-Wes see Barkly West
85 H22 Barkly West Afr. Barkly-Wes. Northern Cape, N South Africa
165 O5 Barkol var. Barkol Kazak Zizhixian. Xinjiang Uygur Zizhiqu, NW China
165 O5 Barkol Hu ◎ NW China
Barkol Kazak Zizhixian see Barkol
32 J3 Bark Point headland Wisconsin, N USA
27 P11 Barksdale Texas, SW USA
Bar Kunar see Asmār
118 L11 Bârlad prev. Bîrlad. Vaslui, E Romania
118 M11 Bârlad prev. Bîrlad. ~ E Romania
78 D9 Barlavento, Ilhas de var. Windward Islands. island group N Cape Verde
105 R5 Bar-le-Duc var. Bar-sur-Ornain. Meuse, NE France
188 K11 Barlee, Lake ◎ Western Australia
188 H8 Barlee Range ▲▲ Western Australia
109 N16 Barletta anc. Barduli. Puglia, SE Italy
112 E10 Barlinek Ger. Berlinchen. Gorzów, W Poland
29 S11 Barling Arkansas, C USA
176 Vv10 Barma Irian Jaya, E Indonesia
191 Q9 Barmedman New South Wales, SE Australia
Barmen-Elberfeld see Wuppertal
158 D12 Bārmer Rājasthān, NW India
190 K9 Barmera South Australia
99 I19 Barmouth NW Wales, UK
160 F10 Barnagar Madhya Pradesh, C India
158 H9 Barnāla Punjab, NW India
99 L15 Barnard Castle N England, UK
191 O6 Barnato New South Wales, SE Australia
126 H14 Barnaul Altayskiy Kray, C Russian Federation
111 V8 Bärnbach Steiermark, SE Austria
20 K16 Barnegat New Jersey, NE USA
25 S4 Barnesville Georgia, SE USA
31 R6 Barnesville Minnesota, N USA
33 U13 Barnesville Ohio, N USA
100 K11 Barneveld var. Barnveld. Gelderland, C Netherlands
27 O9 Barnhart Texas, SW USA
29 P8 Barnsdall Oklahoma, C USA
99 M17 Barnsley N England, UK
21 Q12 Barnstable Massachusetts, NE USA
99 I23 Barnstaple SW England, UK
Barnveld see Barneveld
23 Q14 Barnwell South Carolina, SE USA
69 U8 Baro var. Baro Wenz. ~ Ethiopia/Sudan
79 U15 Baro Niger, C Nigeria
Baro see Baro Wenz
Baroda see Vadodara
155 U2 Baroghil Pass var. Kowtal-e Barowghīl. pass Afghanistan/Pakistan
121 Q17 Baron'ki Rus. Boron'ki. Mahilyowskaya Voblasts', E Belarus
190 J9 Barossa Valley valley South Australia
Baroui see Salisbury
83 H14 Baro Wenz var. Baro, Nahr Barū. ~ Ethiopia/Sudan
159 U12 Barpeta Assam, NE India
33 S7 Barques, Pointe Aux headland Michigan, N USA
56 I5 Barquisimeto Lara, NW Venezuela
61 N16 Barra Bahia, E Brazil
98 E9 Barra island NW Scotland, UK
191 T5 Barraba New South Wales, SE Australia
62 L9 Barra Bonita São Paulo, S Brazil
66 J12 Barracuda Fracture Zone var. Fifteen Twenty Fracture Zone. tectonic feature SW Atlantic Ocean
66 G11 Barracuda Ridge undersea feature N Atlantic Ocean
45 N12 Barra del Colorado Limón, NE Costa Rica
45 N9 Barra de Río Grande Región Autónoma Atlántico Sur, E Nicaragua
84 A11 Barra do Cuanza Luanda, NW Angola
62 O9 Barra do Piraí Rio de Janeiro, SE Brazil
63 D16 Barra do Quaraí Rio Grande do Sul, SE Brazil
61 G14 Barra do São Manuel Pará, N Brazil
85 N19 Barra Falsa, Ponta da headland S Mozambique
98 E10 Barra Head headland NW Scotland, UK
Barram see Baram, Batang
62 O9 Barra Mansa Rio de Janeiro, SE Brazil
59 D14 Barranca Lima, W Peru
56 F8 Barrancabermeja Santander, N Colombia
56 H4 Barrancas La Guajira, N Colombia
56 J6 Barrancas Barinas, NW Venezuela
57 Q6 Barrancas Monagas, NE Venezuela
56 F6 Barranco de Loba Bolívar, N Colombia
106 I12 Barrancos Beja, S Portugal
64 N7 Barranqueras Chaco, N Argentina
56 E4 Barranquilla Atlántico, N Colombia
85 N20 Barra, Ponta da headland S Mozambique
107 P11 Barrax Castilla-La Mancha, C Spain
21 N11 Barre Massachusetts, NE USA
20 M7 Barre Vermont, NE USA
61 M17 Barreiras Bahia, E Brazil
106 F11 Barreiro Setúbal, W Portugal
67 C26 Barren Island island S Falkland Islands
22 K7 Barren River Lake ▣ Kentucky, S USA
62 L7 Barretos São Paulo, S Brazil
9 P14 Barrhead Alberta, SW Canada
12 G14 Barrie Ontario, S Canada
9 N16 Barrière British Columbia, SW Canada
12 H8 Barrière, Lac ◎ Québec, SE Canada
190 L6 Barrier Range hill range New South Wales, SE Australia
44 G3 Barrier Reef reef E Belize
196 C16 Barrigada C Guam
Barrington Island see Santa Fe, Isla
191 T7 Barrington Tops ▲ New South Wales, SE Australia
191 O4 Barringun New South Wales, SE Australia
61 K18 Barro Alto Goiás, S Brazil
61 N14 Barro Duro Piauí, NE Brazil
32 I5 Barron Wisconsin, N USA
12 J12 Barron ~ Ontario, SE Canada
63 H15 Barros Cassal Rio Grande do Sul, S Brazil
47 P14 Barrouallie Saint Vincent, W Saint Vincent and the Grenadines
41 O4 Barrow Alaska, USA
99 E20 Barrow Ir. An Bhearú. ~ SE Ireland
189 Q6 Barrow Creek Roadhouse Northern Territory, N Australia
99 J16 Barrow-in-Furness NW England, UK
188 G7 Barrow Island island Western Australia
41 O4 Barrow, Point headland Alaska, USA
9 V14 Barrows Manitoba, S Canada
99 J22 Barry S Wales, UK
12 J12 Barry's Bay Ontario, SE Canada
150 K14 Barsakel'mes, Ostrov island SW Kazakhstan
Baršć Łužyca see Forst
153 S14 Barsem S Tajikistan
151 V11 Barshatas Semipalatinsk, E Kazakhstan
161 F14 Bārsi Mahārāshtra, W India
102 I13 Barsinghausen Niedersachsen, C Germany
153 X8 Barskoon Issyk-Kul'skaya Oblast', E Kyrgyzstan
102 F10 Barssel Niedersachsen, NW Germany
37 U14 Barstow California, W USA
26 L8 Barstow Texas, SW USA
105 R6 Bar-sur-Aube Aube, NE France
Bar-sur-Ornain see Bar-le-Duc
105 Q6 Bar-sur-Seine Aube, N France
153 S13 Bartang S Tajikistan
153 T13 Bartang ~ SE Tajikistan
Bartenstein see Bartoszyce
Bártfa/Bartfeld see Bardejov
102 N7 Barth Mecklenburg-Vorpommern, NE Germany
29 W13 Bartholomew, Bayou ~ Arkansas/Louisiana, S USA
57 T8 Bartica N Guyana
142 H10 Bartın Zonguldak, N Turkey
189 W4 Bartle Frere ▲ Queensland, E Australia
29 P8 Bartlesville Oklahoma, C USA
31 P14 Bartlett Nebraska, C USA
22 E10 Bartlett Tennessee, S USA
27 T9 Bartlett Texas, SW USA
38 L13 Bartlett Reservoir ▣ Arizona, SW USA
21 N6 Barton Vermont, NE USA
112 L7 Bartoszyce Ger. Bartenstein. Olsztyn, N Poland
25 W12 Bartow Florida, SE USA
Bartschin see Barcin
176 V10 Baru Irian Jaya, E Indonesia
173 G6 Barumun, Sungai ~ Sumatera, W Indonesia
Barū, Nahr see Baro Wenz
174 M16 Barung, Nusa island S Indonesia
173 Fj6 Barus Sumatera, NW Indonesia
168 L10 Baruunsuu Ömnögovĭ, S Mongolia
169 P8 Baruun-Urt Sühbaatar, E Mongolia
45 P15 Barú, Volcán var. Volcán de Chiriquí. ⛰ W Panama
101 K21 Barvaux Luxembourg, SE Belgium
44 M13 Barva, Volcán ⛰ NW Costa Rica
119 W6 Barvinkove Kharkivs'ka Oblast', E Ukraine
160 G11 Barwāh Madhya Pradesh, C India
Bärwalde Neumark see Mieszkowice
160 F11 Barwāni Madhya Pradesh, C India
191 P5 Barwon River ~ New South Wales, SE Australia
121 L15 Barysaw Rus. Borisov. Minskaya Voblasts', NE Belarus
131 Q6 Barysh Ul'yanovskaya Oblast', W Russian Federation
119 Q4 Baryshivka Kyyivs'ka Oblast', N Ukraine
81 J17 Basankusu Equateur, NW Zaire
119 N11 Basarabeasca Rus. Bessarabka. SE Moldova
118 M14 Basarabi Constanța, SW Romania
42 H6 Basaseachic Chihuahua, NW Mexico
107 O2 Basauri País Vasco, N Spain
63 D18 Basavilbaso Entre Ríos, E Argentina
110 E6 Basel Eng. Basle, Fr. Bâle. Basel-Stadt, NW Switzerland
110 E7 Basel Eng. Basle, Fr. Bâle. ◈ canton NW Switzerland
149 T14 Bashākerd, Kūhhā-ye ▲▲ SE Iran
9 Q15 Bashaw Alberta, SW Canada
152 K16 Bashbedeng Maryyskiy Velayat, S Turkmenistan
85 J24 Bashee ~ S South Africa
167 T15 Bashi Channel Chin. Pa-shih Hai-hsia. channel Philippines/Taiwan
Bashkiria see Bashkortostan, Respublika
125 Dd12 Bashkortostan, Respublika prev. Bashkiria. ◈ autonomous republic W Russian Federation
131 N6 Bashmakovo Penzenskaya Oblast', W Russian Federation
152 J10 Bashsakarba Lebapskiy Velayat, NE Turkmenistan
119 R9 Bashtanka Mykolayivs'ka Oblast', S Ukraine
195 O17 Basilaki Island island SE PNG
24 H8 Basile Louisiana, S USA
109 M18 Basilicata ◈ region S Italy
35 V13 Basin Wyoming, C USA
99 N22 Basingstoke S England, UK
149 U8 Bāsīrān Khorāsān, E Iran
114 B10 Baška It. Bescanuova. Primorje-Gorski Kotar, NW Croatia
143 T15 Başkale Van, SE Turkey
12 L10 Baskatong, Réservoir ▣ Québec, SE Canada
143 O14 Baskil Elâzığ, E Turkey
Basle see Basel
160 H9 Bāsoda Madhya Pradesh, C India
81 L17 Basoko Haut-Zaïre, N Zaire
Basque Country, The see País Vasco
Basra see Al Başrah
105 U5 Bas-Rhin ◈ department NE France
Bassam see Grand-Bassam
9 Q16 Bassano Alberta, SW Canada
108 H7 Bassano del Grappa Veneto, NE Italy
79 Q15 Bassar var. Bassari. NW Togo
Bassari see Bassar
180 L9 Bassas da India island group W Madagascar
110 D7 Bassecourt Jura, W Switzerland
177 Ff8 Bassein var. Pathein. Irrawaddy, SW Myanmar
81 J15 Basse-Kotto ◈ prefecture S Central African Republic
107 V5 Bassella Cataluña, NE Spain
104 J5 Basse-Normandie Eng. Lower Normandy. ◈ region N France
47 Q11 Basse-Pointe N Martinique
78 H12 Basse Santa Su E Gambia
Basse-Saxe see Niedersachsen
47 X6 Basse-Terre ○ (Guadeloupe) Basse Terre, SW Guadeloupe
47 X6 Basse Terre island W Guadeloupe
47 V10 Basseterre ● (Saint Kitts and Nevis) Saint Kitts, Saint Kitts and Nevis
31 O13 Bassett Nebraska, C USA
23 S7 Bassett Virginia, NE USA
39 N15 Bassett Peak ▲ Arizona, SW USA
78 M10 Bassikounou Hodh ech Chargui, SE Mauritania
79 R15 Bassila W Benin
Bass, Îlots de see Marotiri
33 O11 Bass Lake Indiana, N USA
191 O14 Bass Strait strait SE Australia
102 H11 Bassum Niedersachsen, NW Germany
31 X3 Basswood Lake ◎ Canada/USA
97 J21 Båstad Kristianstad, S Sweden
145 U2 Baṣṭah E Iraq
159 N12 Basti Uttar Pradesh, N India
104 F1 Bastia Corse, France, C Mediterranean Sea
101 L23 Bastogne Luxembourg, SE Belgium
24 I5 Bastrop Louisiana, S USA
27 T11 Bastrop Texas, SW USA
95 J15 Bastuträsk Västerbotten, N Sweden
121 J19 Bastyn' Rus. Bostyn'. Brestskaya Voblasts', SW Belarus
Basuo see Dongfang
Basutoland see Lesotho
121 O15 Basya ~ E Belarus
119 V8 Basyl'kivka Dnipropetrovs'ka Oblast', E Ukraine
81 F21 Bas-Zaïre off. Région du Bas-Zaïre. ◈ region SW Zaire
81 D17 Bata NW Equatorial Guinea
81 D17 Bata ✕ S Equatorial Guinea
Batae Coritanorum see Leicester
126 M8 Batagay Respublika Sakha (Yakutiya), NE Russian Federation
126 Ll8 Batagay-Alyta Respublika Sakha (Yakutiya), NE Russian Federation
114 L10 Batajnica Serbia, N Yugoslavia
142 H15 Batakık Gölü ◎ S Turkey
116 H11 Batak, Yazovir ▣ SW Bulgaria
158 H7 Batāla Punjab, N India
106 F9 Batalha Leiria, C Portugal
81 N17 Batama Haut-Zaïre, NE Zaire
126 Ll10 Batamay Respublika Sakha (Yakutiya), NE Russian Federation
174 I7 Batam, Pulau island Kepulauan Riau, W Indonesia
166 F9 Batang Sichuan, C China
174 Kk14 Batang Jawa, C Indonesia
81 I14 Batangafo Ouham, NW Central African Republic
179 P11 Batangas off. Batangas City. Luzon, N Philippines
Bătania see Battonya
179 Pp6 Batan Islands island group N Philippines
62 L8 Batatais São Paulo, S Brazil
20 E10 Batavia New York, NE USA
Batavia see Jakarta
181 T9 Batavia Seamount undersea feature E Indian Ocean
130 L12 Bataysk Rostovskaya Oblast', SW Russian Federation
12 B9 Batchawana ~ Ontario, S Canada
12 B9 Batchawana Bay Ontario, S Canada
178 Ii12 Bătdâmbâng prev. Battambang. Bătdâmbâng, NW Cambodia
81 G20 Batéké, Plateaux plateau S Congo
191 S11 Batemans Bay New South Wales, SE Australia
23 Q13 Batesburg South Carolina, SE USA
30 K12 Batesland South Dakota, N USA
29 V10 Batesville Arkansas, C USA
33 Q14 Batesville Indiana, N USA
24 L2 Batesville Mississippi, S USA
27 Q13 Batesville Texas, SW USA
46 L13 Bath E Jamaica
99 L22 Bath hist. Akermanceaster, anc. Aquae Calidae, Aquae Solis. SW England, UK
21 Q8 Bath Maine, NE USA
20 F11 Bath New York, NE USA
Bath see Berkeley Springs
80 I10 Batha off. Préfecture du Batha. ◈ prefecture C Chad
80 I10 Batha seasonal river C Chad
147 Y8 Baṭḥā', Wādī al dry watercourse NE Oman
158 H9 Bathinda Punjab, NW India
100 M11 Bathmen Overijssel, E Netherlands
47 Z14 Bathsheba E Barbados
191 R8 Bathurst New South Wales, SE Australia
11 O13 Bathurst New Brunswick, SE Canada
Bathurst see Banjul
15 Gg2 Bathurst, Cape headland Northwest Territories, NW Canada
206 L8 Bathurst Inlet Northwest Territories, N Canada
15 J4 Bathurst Inlet inlet Northwest Territories, N Canada
189 N1 Bathurst Island island Northern Territory, N Australia
207 O9 Bathurst Island island Parry Islands, Northwest Territories, N Canada
79 O14 Batié SW Burkina
197 J14 Batiki prev. Mbatiki. island C Fiji
Batinah see Al Bāṭinah
147 Y9 Bāṭin, Wādī al dry watercourse SW Asia
13 P9 Batiscan ~ Québec, SE Canada
142 F16 Batı Toroslar ▲▲ SW Turkey
Batjan see Bacan, Pulau
Batlle y Ordóñez see José Batlle y Ordóñez
191 Q10 Batlow New South Wales, SE Australia
143 Q15 Batman var. İluh. Batman, SE Turkey
143 Q15 Batman ◈ province SE Turkey
76 L6 Batna NE Algeria
Batoe see Batu, Kepulauan
168 K7 Bat-Öldziyt Töv, C Mongolia
24 J8 Baton Rouge state capital Louisiana, S USA
81 G15 Batouri Est, E Cameroon
144 G14 Batrā', Jibāl al ▲▲ S Jordan
144 G6 Batroûn var. Al Batrūn. N Lebanon
Batsch see Bač
Batsevichi see Batsevichy
121 M17 Batsevichy Rus. Batsevichi. Mahilyowskaya Voblasts', E Belarus
94 M7 Båtsfjord Finnmark, N Norway
Battambang see Bătdâmbâng
205 X3 Batterbee, Cape headland Antarctica
161 L24 Batticaloa Eastern Province, E Sri Lanka
101 L19 Battice Liège, E Belgium
109 L18 Battipaglia Campania, S Italy
9 R15 Battle ~ Alberta/Saskatchewan, SW Canada
Battle Born State see Nevada
33 Q10 Battle Creek Michigan, N USA
29 T7 Battlefield Missouri, C USA
9 S15 Battleford Saskatchewan, S Canada
31 S6 Battle Lake Minnesota, N USA
37 U3 Battle Mountain Nevada, W USA
113 M25 Battonya Rom. Bătania. Békés, SE Hungary
175 Qq14 Batuata, Pulau island C Indonesia
175 Q8 Batudaka, Pulau island N Indonesia
173 F8 Batu, Kepulauan prev. Batoe. island group W Indonesia
143 Q10 Bat'umi W Georgia
174 H6 Batu Pahat prev. Bandar Penggaram. Johor, Peninsular Malaysia
175 Q10 Baturebe Sulawesi, N Indonesia
126 H13 Baturino Tomskaya Oblast', C Russian Federation
119 R3 Baturyn Chernihivs'ka Oblast', N Ukraine
144 F10 Bat Yam Tel Aviv, C Israel
131 Q4 Batyrevo Chuvashskaya Respublika, W Russian Federation
Batys Qazaqstan Oblysy see Zapadnyy Kazakhstan
104 F5 Batz, Île de island NW France
174 L7 Bau Sarawak, East Malaysia
179 P9 Bauang Luzon, N Philippines
175 Qq13 Baubau var. Baoebaoe. Pulau Buton, C Indonesia
79 W14 Bauchi Bauchi, NE Nigeria
79 W14 Bauchi ◈ state C Nigeria
104 H7 Baud Morbihan, NW France
31 T2 Baudette Minnesota, N USA
200 Nn10 Bauer Basin undersea feature E Pacific Ocean
197 C14 Bauer Field var. Port Vila. ✕ (Port-Vila) Éfaté, C Vanuatu
11 T9 Bauld, Cape headland Newfoundland, Newfoundland and Labrador, E Canada
105 T8 Baume-les-Dames Doubs, E France
195 X15 Baunani Malaita, N Solomon Islands
103 I15 Baunatal Hessen, C Germany
109 D18 Baunei Sardegna, Italy, C Mediterranean Sea
59 M15 Baures, Río ~ N Bolivia
62 K9 Bauru São Paulo, S Brazil
Baushar see Bawshar
120 G10 Bauska Ger. Bauske. Bauska, S Latvia
Bauske see Bauska
103 Q15 Bautzen Lus. Budyšin. Sachsen, E Germany
Bauzanum see Bolzano
Bavaria see Bayern
111 N7 Bavarian Alps Ger. Bayrische Alpen. ▲▲ Austria/Germany
Bavière see Bayern
42 H4 Bavispe, Río ~ NW Mexico
131 T5 Bavly Respublika Tatarstan, W Russian Federation
174 Kk10 Bawal, Pulau island N Indonesia
174 Mm10 Bawan Borneo, C Indonesia
191 O12 Baw Baw, Mount ▲ Victoria, SE Australia
176 W11 Bawe Irian Jaya, E Indonesia
174 M15 Bawean, Pulau island S Indonesia
174 L15 Bawen Jawa, S Indonesia
77 V9 Bawīṭi N Egypt
79 Q13 Bawku N Ghana
178 Gg7 Bawlakè Kayah State, C Myanmar
173 Ff8 Bawo Ofuloa Pulau Tanahmasa, W Indonesia
147 Y8 Bawshar var. Baushar. NE Oman
Ba Xian see Bazhou
164 M8 Baxkorgan Xinjiang Uygur Zizhiqu, W China
25 V6 Baxley Georgia, SE USA
165 R15 Baxoi Xizang Zizhiqu, W China
31 W14 Baxter Iowa, C USA
31 U6 Baxter Minnesota, N USA
29 R8 Baxter Springs Kansas, C USA
83 M17 Bay off. Gobolka Bay. ◈ region SW Somalia
Bay see Baicheng
46 H7 Bayamo Granma, E Cuba
47 U5 Bayamón E Puerto Rico
169 W8 Bayan Heilongjiang, NE China
175 Nn16 Bayan prev. Bajan. Pulau Lombok, C Indonesia
168 I6 Bayan Arhangay, C Mongolia
169 P7 Bayan Dornod, E Mongolia
169 N9 Bayan Dornogovĭ, SE Mongolia
168 F7 Bayan Govĭ-Altay, W Mongolia
169 O8 Bayan Hentiy, C Mongolia
158 I12 Bayāna Rājasthān, N India
155 N5 Bāyān, Band-e ▲▲ C Afghanistan
168 H8 Bayanbulag Bayanhongor, C Mongolia
169 N7 Bayanbulag Hentiy, C Mongolia
164 J5 Bayanbulak Xinjiang Uygur Zizhiqu, W China
126 Jj15 Bayanday Ust'-Ordynskiy Buryatskiy Avtonomnyy Okrug, S Russian Federation
Bayan Gol see Dengkou
168 F8 Bayangol Govĭ-Altay, SW Mongolia
165 R12 Bayan Har Shan var. Bayan Khar. ▲▲ C China
168 I8 Bayanhongor Bayanhongor, C Mongolia
168 H9 Bayanhongor ◈ province C Mongolia
Bayan Khar see Bayan Har Shan
173 G3 Bayan Lepas ✕ (George Town) Pinang, Peninsular Malaysia
168 K13 Bayan Mod Nei Mongol Zizhiqu, N China
168 K13 Bayan Nuru Nei Mongol Zizhiqu, N China
169 N12 Bayan Obo Nei Mongol Zizhiqu, N China
45 V15 Bayano, Lago ◎ E Panama
168 C5 Bayan-Ölgiy ◈ province NW Mongolia
168 F9 Bayan-Ovoo Govĭ-Altay, SW Mongolia
168 H9 Bayansayr Bayanhongor, C Mongolia
165 Q9 Bayan Shan ▲ C China
168 J9 Bayanteeg Övörhangay, C Mongolia
168 L8 Bayantöhöm Töv, C Mongolia
168 H6 Bayan-Uhaa Dzavhan, C Mongolia
168 J8 Bayan-Ulaan Övörhangay, C Mongolia
Bayan Ul Hot see Xi Ujimqin Qi
30 J14 Bayard Nebraska, C USA
39 P15 Bayard New Mexico, SW USA
105 T13 Bayard, Col pass SE France
169 O8 Bayasgalant Sühbaatar, E Mongolia
142 J12 Bayat Çorum, N Turkey
179 Q14 Bayawan Negros, C Philippines
149 R10 Bayāẓ Kermān, C Iran
179 R13 Baybay Leyte, C Philippines
23 X10 Bayboro North Carolina, SE USA
143 P12 Bayburt Bayburt, NE Turkey
143 P12 Bayburt ◈ province NE Turkey
33 R8 Bay City Michigan, N USA
27 V12 Bay City Texas, SW USA
125 G7 Baydaratskaya Guba var. Baydarata Bay. bay N Russian Federation
83 M16 Baydhabo var. Baydhowa, Isha Baydhabo, It. Baidoa. Bay, SW Somalia
Baydhowa see Baydhabo
103 N21 Bayerischer Wald ▲▲ SE Germany
103 K21 Bayern Eng. Bavaria, Fr. Bavière. ◈ state SE Germany
153 V9 Bayetovo Narynskaya Oblast', C Kyrgyzstan
104 K4 Bayeux anc. Augustodurum. Calvados, N France
12 E15 Bayfield ~ Ontario, S Canada
151 O15 Baygakum Kaz. Bäygequm. Kzyl-Orda, S Kazakhstan
Bäygequm see Baygakum
142 C14 Bayındır İzmir, SW Turkey
144 H12 Bāyir var. Bā'ir. Ma'ān, S Jordan
Bay Islands see Bahía, Islas de la
145 R5 Bayjī var. Baiji. N Iraq
151 Q16 Baykadam Kaz. Bayqadam. Zhambyl, S Kazakhstan
126 K15 Baykal, Ozero Eng. Lake Baikal. ◎ S Russian Federation
126 J16 Baykal'sk Irkutskaya Oblast', S Russian Federation
143 R15 Baykan Siirt, SE Turkey
126 Ii12 Baykit Evenkiyskiy Avtonomnyy Okrug, C Russian Federation
151 N12 Baykonur Zhezkazgan, C Kazakhstan
164 E7 Baykurt Xinjiang Uygur Zizhiqu, W China
12 I9 Bay, Lac ◎ Québec, SE Canada
179 Pp11 Bay, Laguna de ◎ Luzon, N Philippines
131 W6 Baymak Respublika Bashkortostan, W Russian Federation
25 O8 Bay Minette Alabama, S USA
149 O17 Baynūnah desert W UAE
192 O8 Bay of Plenty off. Bay of Plenty Region. ◈ region North Island, NZ
203 Z3 Bay of Wrecks bay Kiritimati, E Kiribati
179 P9 Bayombong Luzon, N Philippines
104 I15 Bayonne anc. Lapurdum. Pyrénées-Atlantiques, SW France
24 H4 Bayou D'Arbonne Lake ▣ Louisiana, S USA
25 N9 Bayou La Batre Alabama, S USA
Bayou State see Mississippi
Bayqadam see Baykadam
Bayram-Ali see Bayramaly
152 J14 Bayramaly prev. Bayram-Ali. Maryyskiy Velayat, S Turkmenistan
103 L19 Bayreuth var. Baireuth. Bayern, SE Germany
Bayrische Alpen see Bavarian Alps
Bayrūt see Beyrouth
24 L9 Bay Saint Louis Mississippi, S USA
Baysān see Bet She'an
168 L8 Bayshint Töv, C Mongolia

◆ Country ● Country Capital ◇ Dependent Territory ○ Dependent Territory Capital ◈ Administrative Region ✕ International Airport ▲ Mountain ▲▲ Mountain Range ⛰ Volcano ~ River ◎ Lake ▣ Reservoir

12 H13 **Bays, Lake of** ◎ Ontario, S Canada
24 M6 **Bay Springs** Mississippi, S USA
Bay State see Massachusetts
Baysun see Boysun
12 H13 **Baysville** Ontario, S Canada
147 N15 **Bayt al Faqīh** W Yemen
164 M4 **Baytik Shan** ▲▲ China/Mongolia
Bayt Laḥm see Bethlehem
27 W11 **Baytown** Texas, SW USA
175 O9 **Bayur, Tanjung** headland Borneo, N Indonesia
123 Ll16 **Bayy al Kabīr, Wādī** dry watercourse NW Libya
Bayyrqum see Bairkum
107 P14 **Baza** Andalucía, S Spain
143 X10 **Bazardüzü Dağı** Rus. Gora Bazardyuzyu. ▲ N Azerbaijan
Bazardyuzyu, Gora see Bazardüzü Dağı
Bazargic see Dobrich
85 N18 **Bazaruto, Ilha do** island SE Mozambique
104 K14 **Bazas** Gironde, SW France
107 O14 **Baza, Sierra de** ▲▲ S Spain
166 J8 **Bazhong** Sichuan, C China
167 P3 **Bazhou** prev. Baxian, Ba Xian. Hebei, E China
12 M9 **Bazin** ≈ Québec, SE Canada
Bazin see Pezinok
145 Q7 **Bāzīyah** C Iraq
144 H6 **Bcharré** var. Bcharreh, Bsharri, Bsherri. NE Lebanon
Bcharreh see Bcharré
30 J5 **Beach** North Dakota, N USA
190 K12 **Beachport** South Australia
99 O23 **Beachy Head** headland SE England, UK
20 K13 **Beacon** New York, NE USA
65 J25 **Beagle Channel** channel Argentina/Chile
189 O1 **Beagle Gulf** gulf Northern Territory, N Australia
Bealach an Doirín see Ballaghaderreen
Bealach Cláir see Ballyclare
Bealach Féich see Ballybofey
180 J3 **Bealanana** Mahajanga, NE Madagascar
Béal an Átha see Ballina
Béal an Átha Móir see Ballinamore
Béal an Mhuirhead see Belmullet
Béal Átha Beithe see Ballybay
Béal Átha Conaill see Ballyconnell
Béal Átha hAmhnais see Ballyhaunis
Béal Átha na Sluaighe see Ballinasloe
Béal Átha Seanaidh see Ballyshannon
Bealdovuopmi see Peltovuoma
Béal Feirste see Belfast
Béal Tairbirt see Belturbet
Beanna Boirche see Mourne Mountains
Beannchar see Banagher, Ireland
Beannchar see Bangor, Northern Ireland, UK
Beanntraí see Bantry
25 N2 **Bear Creek** ≈ Alabama/Mississippi, S USA
32 J13 **Bear Creek** ≈ Illinois, N USA
29 U13 **Bearden** Arkansas, C USA
205 Q10 **Beardmore Glacier** glacier Antarctica
32 K13 **Beardstown** Illinois, N USA
30 L14 **Bear Hill** ▲ Nebraska, C USA
Bear Island see Bjørnøya
12 H12 **Bear Lake** Ontario, S Canada
38 M1 **Bear Lake** ◎ Idaho/Utah, NW USA
41 U11 **Bear, Mount** ▲ Alaska, USA
104 J16 **Béarn** cultural region SW France
204 J11 **Bear Peninsula** peninsula Antarctica
158 I7 **Beās** ≈ India/Pakistan
107 P3 **Beasain** País Vasco, N Spain
107 O12 **Beas de Segura** Andalucía, S Spain
47 N10 **Beata, Cabo** headland SW Dominican Republic
47 N10 **Beata, Isla** island SW Dominican Republic
66 F11 **Beata Ridge** undersea feature N Caribbean Sea
31 R17 **Beatrice** Nebraska, C USA
85 L16 **Beatrice** Mashonaland East, NE Zimbabwe
9 N11 **Beatton** ≈ British Columbia, W Canada
9 N11 **Beatton River** British Columbia, W Canada
37 V10 **Beatty** Nevada, W USA
23 N6 **Beattyville** Kentucky, S USA
181 X16 **Beau Bassin** W Mauritius
105 R15 **Beaucaire** Gard, S France
12 I8 **Beauchastel, Lac** ◎ Québec, SE Canada
12 I10 **Beauchêne, Lac** ◎ Québec, SE Canada
191 V3 **Beaudesert** Queensland, E Australia
190 M12 **Beaufort** Victoria, SE Australia
23 X11 **Beaufort** North Carolina, SE USA
23 R15 **Beaufort** South Carolina, SE USA
40 M11 **Beaufort Sea** sea Arctic Ocean
Beaufort-Wes see Beaufort West
85 G25 **Beaufort West** Afr. Beaufort-Wes. Western Cape, SW South Africa
105 N7 **Beaugency** Loiret, C France
21 R1 **Beau Lake** ⊠ Maine, NE USA
98 I8 **Beauly** N Scotland, UK
101 G21 **Beaumont** Hainaut, S Belgium
193 E23 **Beaumont** Otago, South Island, NZ
24 M7 **Beaumont** Mississippi, S USA
27 X10 **Beaumont** Texas, SW USA
104 M15 **Beaumont-de-Lomagne** Tarn-et-Garonne, S France
104 L6 **Beaumont-sur-Sarthe** Sarthe, NW France
105 R8 **Beaune** Côte d'Or, C France
13 R9 **Beaupré** Québec, SE Canada
104 J8 **Beaupréau** Maine-et-Loire, NW France
101 I22 **Beauraing** Namur, SE Belgium
105 R12 **Beaurepaire** Isère, E France
9 Y16 **Beausejour** Manitoba, S Canada
105 N4 **Beauvais** anc. Bellovacum, Caesaromagus. Oise, N France
9 S13 **Beauval** Saskatchewan, C Canada
104 I9 **Beauvoir-sur-Mer** Vendée, NW France
41 R8 **Beaver** Alaska, USA
28 J8 **Beaver** Oklahoma, C USA
20 B14 **Beaver** Pennsylvania, NE USA
38 K6 **Beaver** Utah, W USA
8 L9 **Beaver** ≈ British Columbia/Yukon Territory, W Canada
9 S13 **Beaver** ≈ Saskatchewan, C Canada
31 N17 **Beaver City** Nebraska, C USA
8 G6 **Beaver Creek** Yukon Territory, W Canada
33 R14 **Beavercreek** Ohio, N USA
41 S8 **Beaver Creek** ≈ Alaska, USA
28 H3 **Beaver Creek** ≈ Kansas/Nebraska, C USA
30 J5 **Beaver Creek** ≈ Montana/North Dakota, N USA
31 Q14 **Beaver Creek** ≈ Nebraska, C USA
27 Q4 **Beaver Creek** ≈ Texas, SW USA
32 M8 **Beaver Dam** Wisconsin, N USA
32 M8 **Beaver Dam Lake** ◎ Wisconsin, N USA
20 B14 **Beaver Falls** Pennsylvania, NE USA
35 P12 **Beaverhead Mountains** ▲▲ Idaho/Montana, NW USA
35 Q12 **Beaverhead River** ≈ Montana, NW USA
67 A25 **Beaver Island** island W Falkland Islands
33 P5 **Beaver Island** island Michigan, N USA
29 S9 **Beaver Lake** ⊠ Arkansas, C USA
9 N13 **Beaverlodge** Alberta, W Canada
20 I8 **Beaver River** ≈ New York, NE USA
28 J8 **Beaver River** ≈ Oklahoma, C USA
20 B13 **Beaver River** ≈ Pennsylvania, NE USA
67 A25 **Beaver Settlement** Beaver Island, W Falkland Islands
Beaver State see Oregon
12 H14 **Beaverton** Ontario, S Canada
34 G11 **Beaverton** Oregon, NW USA
158 G12 **Beāwar** Rājasthān, N India
Bebas, Dasht-i see Bābūs, Dasht-e
62 L8 **Bebedouro** São Paulo, S Brazil
103 I16 **Bebra** Hessen, C Germany
43 W12 **Becal** Campeche, SE Mexico
13 Q11 **Bécancour** ≈ Québec, SE Canada
99 Q19 **Beccles** E England, UK
114 L9 **Bečej** Ger. Altbetsche, Hung. Óbecse, Rácz-Becse; prev. Magyar-Becse, Stari Bečej. Serbia, N Yugoslavia
106 I3 **Becerreá** Galicia, NW Spain
76 H7 **Béchar** prev. Colomb-Béchar. W Algeria
41 O14 **Becharof Lake** ◎ Alaska, USA
118 H15 **Bechet** var. Bechetu. Dolj, SW Romania
Bechetu see Bechet
23 R6 **Beckley** West Virginia, NE USA
103 G14 **Beckum** Nordrhein-Westfalen, W Germany
27 X7 **Beckville** Texas, SW USA
37 X4 **Becky Peak** ▲ Nevada, W USA
118 I9 **Beclean** Hung. Bethlen; prev. Betlen. Bistriţa-Năsăud, N Romania
Bécs see Wien
113 H18 **Bečva** Ger. Betschau, Pol. Beczwa. ≈ E Czech Republic
Beczwa see Bečva
105 P15 **Bédarieux** Hérault, S France
122 Dd12 **Beddouza, Cap** headland W Morocco
82 I13 **Bedelē** W Ethiopia
153 Y8 **Bedel Pass** Rus. Pereval Bedel. pass China/Kyrgyzstan
Bedel, Pereval see Bedel Pass
97 H22 **Beder** Århus, C Denmark
99 N20 **Bedford** E England, UK
33 O15 **Bedford** Indiana, N USA
31 U16 **Bedford** Iowa, C USA
22 L4 **Bedford** Kentucky, S USA
20 D15 **Bedford** Pennsylvania, NE USA
23 T6 **Bedford** Virginia, NE USA
99 N20 **Bedfordshire** cultural region E England, UK
131 N5 **Bednodem'yanovsk** Penzenskaya Oblast', W Russian Federation
100 N5 **Bedum** Groningen, NE Netherlands
29 V11 **Beebe** Arkansas, C USA
47 T9 **Beef Island** ✕ (Road Town) Tortola, E British Virgin Islands
Beehive State see Utah
101 L18 **Beek** Limburg, SE Netherlands
101 L18 **Beek** ✕ (Maastricht) Limburg, SE Netherlands
101 K14 **Beek-en-Donk** Noord-Brabant, S Netherlands
144 F13 **Be'er Menuḥa** Southern, S Israel
101 D16 **Beernem** West-Vlaanderen, NW Belgium
101 I16 **Beerse** Antwerpen, N Belgium
Beersheba see Be'ér Sheva'
144 E11 **Be'ér Sheva'** var. Beersheba, Ar. Bir es Saba. Southern, S Israel
100 J13 **Beesd** Gelderland, C Netherlands
101 M16 **Beesel** Limburg, SE Netherlands
85 J21 **Beestekraal** North-West, N South Africa
204 J7 **Beethoven Peninsula** peninsula Alexander Island, Antarctica
Beetstersweach see Beetsterzwaag
100 M6 **Beetsterzwaag** Fris. Beetstersweach. Friesland, N Netherlands
27 S13 **Beeville** Texas, SW USA
81 J18 **Befale** Equateur, NW Zaire
Befandriana see Befandriana Avaratra
180 J3 **Befandriana Avaratra** var. Befandriana, Befandriana Nord. Mahajanga, NW Madagascar
Befandriana Nord see Befandriana Avaratra
81 K18 **Befori** Equateur, N Zaire
180 I7 **Befotaka** Fianarantsoa, S Madagascar
191 R11 **Bega** New South Wales, SE Australia
104 G5 **Bégard** Côtes d'Armor, NW France
114 M9 **Begejski Kanal** canal NE Yugoslavia
151 V9 **Begen'** Semipalatinsk, E Kazakhstan
96 G13 **Begna** ≈ S Norway
Begoml' see Byahoml'
Begovat see Bekobod
159 Q13 **Begusarai** Bihār, NE India
149 R9 **Behābād** Yazd, C Iran
Behagle see Laï
57 Z10 **Béhague, Pointe** headland E French Guiana
Behar see Bihār
148 M10 **Behbahān** var. Behbehān. Khūzestān, SW Iran
Behbehān see Behbahān
46 G3 **Behring Point** Andros Island, W Bahamas
149 P4 **Behshahr** prev. Ashraf. Māzandarān, N Iran
169 V6 **Bei'an** Heilongjiang, NE China
Beibunar see Sredishte
Beibu Wan see Tongking, Gulf of
Beida see Al Bayḍā'
82 H13 **Beigi** W Ethiopia
166 L16 **Beihai** Guangxi Zhuangzu Zizhiqu, S China
165 Q10 **Bei Hulsan Hu** ◎ C China
167 N13 **Bei Jiang** ≈ S China
167 O2 **Beijing** var. Pei-ching, Eng. Peking; prev. Pei-p'ing. country/municipality capital (China) Beijing Shi, E China
167 P2 **Beijing** ✕ Beijing Shi, E China
Beijing see Beijing Shi
167 O2 **Beijing Shi** var. Beijing, Jing, Pei-ching, Eng. Peking; prev. Pei-p'ing. ◐ municipality E China
78 G8 **Beïla** Trarza, W Mauritania
100 N7 **Beilen** Drenthe, NE Netherlands
166 L15 **Beiliu** Guangxi Zhuangzu Zizhiqu, S China
165 O12 **Beilu He** ≈ W China
Beilul see Beylul
98 H8 **Beinn Dearg** ▲ N Scotland, UK
Beinn MacDuibh see Ben Macdui
166 I12 **Beipan Jiang** ≈ S China
169 T12 **Beipiao** Liaoning, NE China
85 N17 **Beira** Sofala, C Mozambique
85 N17 **Beira** ✕ Sofala, C Mozambique
106 I7 **Beira Alta** former province N Portugal
106 H9 **Beira Baixa** former province C Portugal
106 G8 **Beira Litoral** former province N Portugal
Beirut see Beyrouth
Beisān see Bet She'an
9 Q16 **Beiseker** Alberta, SW Canada
85 K19 **Beitbridge** Matabeleland South, S Zimbabwe
118 G10 **Beiuş** Hung. Belényes. Bihor, NW Romania
169 U12 **Beizhen** Liaoning, NE China
106 H12 **Beja** anc. Pax Julia. Beja, SE Portugal
106 G13 **Beja** ◐ district S Portugal
76 M5 **Béja** var. Bājah. N Tunisia
123 Ii11 **Bejaïa** var. Bejaïa, Fr. Bougie; anc. Saldae. NE Algeria
106 K8 **Béjar** Castilla-León, N Spain
Bejraburi see Phetchaburi
Bekaa Valley see El Beqaa
Bekabad see Bekobod
Békás see Bicaz
174 J14 **Bekasi** Jawa, C Indonesia
Bek-Budi see Qarshi
152 A8 **Bekdash** Balkanskiy Velayat, NW Turkmenistan
153 T10 **Bek-Dzhar** Oshskaya Oblast', SW Kyrgyzstan
113 N24 **Békés** Rom. Bichiş. Békés, SE Hungary
113 M24 **Békés** off. Békés Megye. ◐ county SE Hungary
113 M24 **Békéscsaba** Rom. Bichiş-Ciaba. Békés, SE Hungary
145 S2 **Bēkhma** E Iraq
180 H7 **Bekily** Toliara, S Madagascar
172 Qq7 **Bekkai** Hokkaidō, NE Japan
153 Q11 **Bekobod** Rus. Bekabad; prev. Begovat. Toshkent Wiloyati, E Uzbekistan
131 O7 **Bekovo** Penzenskaya Oblast', W Russian Federation
Bél see Beliu
158 M13 **Bela** Uttar Pradesh, N India
155 N15 **Bela** Baluchistān, SW Pakistan
81 F15 **Bélabo** Est, C Cameroon
114 N10 **Bela Crkva** Ger. Weisskirchen, Hung. Fehértemplom. Serbia, W Yugoslavia
181 Y16 **Bel Air** var. Rivière Sèche. E Mauritius
106 L12 **Belalcázar** Andalucía, S Spain
115 P15 **Bela Palanka** Serbia, SE Yugoslavia
121 H16 **Belarus** off. Republic of Belarus, var. Belorussia, Latv. Baltkrievija; prev. Belorussian SSR, Rus. Belorusskaya SSR. ◆ republic E Europe
Belau see Palau
61 H21 **Bela Vista** Mato Grosso do Sul, SW Brazil
85 L21 **Bela Vista** Maputo, S Mozambique
173 Ff4 **Belawan** Sumatera, W Indonesia
Běla Woda see Weisswasser
131 U4 **Belaya** ≈ W Russian Federation
127 N7 **Belaya Gora** Respublika Sakha (Yakutiya), NE Russian Federation
130 M11 **Belaya Kalitva** Rostovskaya Oblast', SW Russian Federation
129 R14 **Belaya Kholunitsa** Kirovskaya Oblast', NW Russian Federation
Belaya Tserkov' see Bila Tserkva
79 V11 **Belbédji** Zinder, S Niger
112 K13 **Bełchatów** var. Belchatow. Piotrków, C Poland
Belcher, Îles see Belcher Islands
10 H7 **Belcher Islands** Fr. Îles Belcher. island group Northwest Territories, SE Canada
107 S6 **Belchite** Aragón, NE Spain
31 O2 **Belcourt** North Dakota, N USA
33 P9 **Belding** Michigan, N USA
131 U5 **Belebey** Respublika Bashkortostan, W Russian Federation
83 N16 **Beledweyne** var. Belet Huen, It. Belet Uen. Hiiraan, C Somalia
152 B10 **Belek** Balkanskiy Velayat, W Turkmenistan
60 L12 **Belém** var. Pará. state capital Pará, N Brazil
67 I14 **Belém Ridge** undersea feature C Atlantic Ocean
39 R12 **Belen** New Mexico, SW USA
64 I7 **Belén** Catamarca, NW Argentina
56 G9 **Belén** Boyacá, C Colombia
44 J11 **Belén** Rivas, SW Nicaragua
64 O5 **Belén** Concepción, C Paraguay
63 D16 **Belén** Salto, N Uruguay
63 D20 **Belén de Escobar** Buenos Aires, E Argentina
116 J7 **Belene** Loveshka Oblast, N Bulgaria
116 J7 **Belene, Ostrov** island N Bulgaria
45 R15 **Belén, Río** ≈ C Panama
Belényes see Beiuş
197 G4 **Belep, Îles** island group W New Caledonia
106 H3 **Belesar, Embalse de** ⊠ NW Spain
Belet Huen/Belet Uen see Beledweyne
130 J5 **Belëv** Tul'skaya Oblast', W Russian Federation
99 G15 **Belfast** Ir. Béal Feirste. ◐ E Northern Ireland, UK
21 R7 **Belfast** Maine, NE USA
99 G15 **Belfast International** ✕ E Northern Ireland, UK
99 G15 **Belfast Lough** Ir. Loch Lao inlet E Northern Ireland, UK
30 K5 **Belfield** North Dakota, N USA
105 U7 **Belfort** Territoire-de-Belfort, E France
Belgard see Białogard
161 E17 **Belgaum** Karnātaka, W India
Belgian Congo see Zaire
205 T3 **Belgica Mountains** ▲▲ Antarctica
België/Belgique see Belgium
101 F20 **Belgium** off. Kingdom of Belgium, Dut. België, Fr. Belgique. ◆ monarchy NW Europe
130 J8 **Belgorod** Belgorodskaya Oblast', W Russian Federation
Belgorod-Dnestrovskiy see Bilhorod-Dnistrovs'kyy
130 J8 **Belgorodskaya Oblast'** ◐ province W Russian Federation
Belgrad see Beograd
31 T8 **Belgrade** Minnesota, N USA
35 S11 **Belgrade** Montana, NW USA
Belgrade see Beograd
205 N5 **Belgrano II** Argentinian research station Antarctica
23 X9 **Belhaven** North Carolina, SE USA
109 I23 **Belice** anc. Hypsas. ≈ Sicilia, Italy, C Mediterranean Sea
Belice see Belize/Belize City
115 M16 **Beli Drim** Alb. Drini i Bardhë. ≈ Albania/Yugoslavia
Beligrad see Berat
196 C8 **Beliliou** prev. Peleliu. island S Palau
116 L8 **Beli Lom, Yazovir** ⊠ NE Bulgaria
114 I8 **Beli Manastir** Hung. Pélmonostor; prev. Monostor. Osijek-Baranja, NE Croatia
104 J13 **Bélin-Béliet** Gironde, SW France
81 F17 **Bélinga** Ogooué-Ivindo, NE Gabon
23 S4 **Belington** West Virginia, NE USA
131 O6 **Belinskiy** Penzenskaya Oblast', W Russian Federation
174 I19 **Belinyu** Pulau Bangka, W Indonesia
174 Jj11 **Belitung, Pulau** island W Indonesia
118 F10 **Beliu** Hung. Bél. Arad, W Romania
116 I9 **Beli Vit** ≈ NW Bulgaria
44 G2 **Belize** Sp. Belice; prev. British Honduras, Colony of Belize. ◆ commonwealth republic Central America
44 F2 **Belize** Sp. Belice. ◐ district NE Belize
44 G2 **Belize** ≈ Belize/Guatemala
Belize see Belize City
44 G2 **Belize City** var. Belize, Sp. Belice. Belize, NE Belize
44 G2 **Belize City** ✕ Belize, NE Belize
Beljak see Villach
41 N16 **Belkofski** Alaska, USA
126 L4 **Bel'kovskiy, Ostrov** island Novosibirskiye Ostrova, NE Russian Federation
12 J8 **Bell** ≈ Québec, SE Canada
8 J15 **Bella Bella** British Columbia, SW Canada
104 M10 **Bellac** Haute-Vienne, C France
8 K15 **Bella Coola** British Columbia, SW Canada
108 D6 **Bellagio** Lombardia, N Italy
33 P6 **Bellaire** Michigan, N USA
108 D6 **Bellano** Lombardia, N Italy
161 G17 **Bellary** var. Ballari. Karnātaka, S India
191 S5 **Bellata** New South Wales, SE Australia
63 D16 **Bella Unión** Artigas, N Uruguay
63 C14 **Bella Vista** Corrientes, NE Argentina
64 J7 **Bella Vista** Tucumán, N Argentina
64 P4 **Bella Vista** Amambay, C Paraguay
58 B10 **Bellavista** Cajamarca, N Peru
58 D11 **Bellavista** San Martín, N Peru
191 U6 **Bellbrook** New South Wales, SE Australia
29 V5 **Belle** Missouri, C USA
23 Q5 **Belle** West Virginia, NE USA
33 R13 **Bellefontaine** Ohio, N USA
20 F14 **Bellefonte** Pennsylvania, NE USA
30 J9 **Belle Fourche** South Dakota, N USA
30 J9 **Belle Fourche Reservoir** ⊠ South Dakota, N USA
30 K9 **Belle Fourche River** ≈ South Dakota/Wyoming, N USA
105 S10 **Bellegarde-sur-Valserine** Ain, E France
25 Y14 **Belle Glade** Florida, SE USA
104 G8 **Belle Île** island NW France
11 T9 **Belle Isle** island Belle Isle, Newfoundland and Labrador, E Canada
11 S10 **Belle Isle, Strait of** strait Newfoundland and Labrador, E Canada
Bellenz see Bellinzona
31 W14 **Belle Plaine** Iowa, C USA
31 V9 **Belle Plaine** Minnesota, N USA
12 I9 **Belleterre** Québec, SE Canada
12 J15 **Belleville** Ontario, SE Canada
105 R10 **Belleville** Rhône, E France
32 K15 **Belleville** Illinois, N USA
29 N3 **Belleville** Kansas, C USA
31 Z13 **Bellevue** Iowa, C USA
31 S15 **Bellevue** Nebraska, C USA
33 S11 **Bellevue** Ohio, N USA
27 S5 **Bellevue** Texas, SW USA
34 H8 **Bellevue** Washington, NW USA
57 Y11 **Bellevue de l'Inini, Montagnes** ▲▲ S French Guiana
105 S11 **Belley** Ain, E France
Bellin see Kangirsuk
191 V6 **Bellingen** New South Wales, SE Australia
99 L14 **Bellingham** N England, UK
34 H6 **Bellingham** Washington, NW USA
Belling Hausen Mulde see Southeast Pacific Basin
204 H2 **Bellingshausen** Russian research station South Shetland Islands, Antarctica
Bellingshausen see Motu One
Bellingshausen Abyssal Plain see Bellingshausen Plain
200 N16 **Bellingshausen Plain** var. Bellingshausen Abyssal Plain. undersea feature SE Pacific Ocean
204 I8 **Bellingshausen Sea** sea Antarctica
100 P6 **Bellingwolde** Groningen, NE Netherlands
110 H11 **Bellinzona** Ger. Bellenz. Ticino, S Switzerland
27 T8 **Bellmead** Texas, SW USA
56 E8 **Bello** Antioquia, W Colombia
63 B21 **Bellocq** Buenos Aires, E Argentina
Bello Horizonte see Belo Horizonte
195 W17 **Bellona** var. Mungiki. island S Solomon Islands
Bellovacum see Beauvais
190 D7 **Bell, Point** headland South Australia
22 F9 **Bells** Tennessee, S USA
27 U5 **Bells** Texas, SW USA
94 N3 **Bellsund** inlet SW Svalbard
108 H6 **Belluno** Veneto, NE Italy
64 L11 **Bell Ville** Córdoba, C Argentina
85 E26 **Bellville** Western Cape, SW South Africa
27 U11 **Bellville** Texas, SW USA
106 L12 **Belmez** Andalucía, S Spain
31 V12 **Belmond** Iowa, C USA
20 E11 **Belmont** New York, NE USA
23 R10 **Belmont** North Carolina, SE USA
61 O18 **Belmonte** Bahia, E Brazil
106 I8 **Belmonte** Castelo Branco, C Portugal
107 P10 **Belmonte** Castilla-La Mancha, C Spain
44 G2 **Belmopan** ● (Belize) Cayo, C Belize
99 B16 **Belmullet** Ir. Béal an Mhuirhead. W Ireland
126 Mm15 **Belogorsk** Amurskaya Oblast', SE Russian Federation
Belogorsk see Bilohirs'k
116 F7 **Belogradchik** Oblast Montana, NW Bulgaria
180 H8 **Beloha** Toliara, S Madagascar
61 M20 **Belo Horizonte** prev. Bello Horizonte. state capital Minas Gerais, SE Brazil
28 M3 **Beloit** Kansas, C USA
32 L9 **Beloit** Wisconsin, N USA
Belokorovichi see Bilokorovychi
126 H15 **Belokurikha** Altayskiy Kray, S Russian Federation
128 J8 **Belomorsk** Respublika Kareliya, NW Russian Federation
128 J8 **Belomorsko-Baltiyskiy Kanal** Eng. White Sea-Baltic Canal, White Sea Canal. canal NW Russian Federation
159 V15 **Belonia** Tripura, NE India
Belopol'ye see Bilopillya
107 O4 **Belorado** Castilla-León, N Spain
130 L14 **Belorechensk** Krasnodarskiy Kray, SW Russian Federation
131 W5 **Beloretsk** Respublika Bashkortostan, W Russian Federation
Belorussia see Belarus
Belorussian SSR see Belarus
Belorusskaya Gryada see Byelaruskaya Hrada
Belorusskaya SSR see Belarus
Beloshchel'ye see Nar'yan-Mar
116 N8 **Beloslav** Varnenska Oblast, NE Bulgaria
Belostok see Białystok
180 H5 **Belo Tsiribihina** var. Belo-sur-Tsiribihina. Toliara, W Madagascar
Belovár see Bjelovar
Belovezhskaya Pushcha see Białowieska, Puszcza/Byelavyezhskaya Pushcha
116 H10 **Belovo** Plovdivska Oblast, W Bulgaria
126 H14 **Belovo** Kemerovskaya Oblast', S Russian Federation
Belovodsk see Bilovods'k
125 Ff9 **Beloyarskiy** Khanty-Mansiyskiy Avtonomnyy Okrug, N Russian Federation
128 K7 **Beloye More** Eng. White Sea. sea NW Russian Federation
128 K13 **Beloye, Ozero** ◎ NW Russian Federation
116 J10 **Belozem** Plovdivska Oblast, C Bulgaria
128 K13 **Belozërsk** Vologodskaya Oblast', NW Russian Federation
101 E20 **Belœil** Hainaut, SW Belgium
110 D8 **Belp** Bern, W Switzerland
110 D8 **Belp** ✕ (Bern) Bern, C Switzerland
109 L24 **Belpasso** Sicilia, Italy, C Mediterranean Sea
33 U14 **Belpre** Ohio, N USA
100 M8 **Belterwijde** ◎ N Netherlands
29 R4 **Belton** Missouri, C USA
23 P11 **Belton** South Carolina, SE USA
27 T9 **Belton** Texas, SW USA
27 S9 **Belton Lake** ⊠ Texas, SW USA
Bel'tsy see Bălţi
99 E16 **Belturbet** Ir. Béal Tairbirt. N Ireland
Beluchistan see Baluchistān
151 Z9 **Belukha, Gora** ▲ Kazakhstan/Russian Federation
109 M20 **Belvedere Marittimo** Calabria, SW Italy
32 L10 **Belvidere** Illinois, N USA
20 J14 **Belvidere** New Jersey, NE USA
Bely see Belyy
131 V8 **Belyayevka** Orenburgskaya Oblast', W Russian Federation
Belynichi see Byalynichy
128 H17 **Belyy** var. Bely, Beyj. Tverskaya Oblast', W Russian Federation
130 I6 **Belyye Berega** Bryanskaya Oblast', W Russian Federation
126 H5 **Belyy, Ostrov** island N Russian Federation
126 H12 **Belyy Yar** Tomskaya Oblast', C Russian Federation
102 N13 **Belzig** Brandenburg, NE Germany
24 K4 **Belzoni** Mississippi, S USA
180 H4 **Bemaraha** var. Plateau du Bemaraha. ▲▲ W Madagascar
84 B10 **Bembe** Uíge, NW Angola
79 S14 **Bembèrèkè** var. Bimbéréké. N Benin
106 K12 **Bembézar** ≈ SW Spain
106 J3 **Bembibre** Castilla-León, N Spain
31 T4 **Bemidji** Minnesota, N USA
100 L12 **Bemmel** Gelderland, SE Netherlands
176 U11 **Bemu** Pulau Seram, E Indonesia
Benāb see Bonāb
107 T5 **Benabarre** var. Benavarn. Aragón, NE Spain
Benaco see Garda, Lago di
81 L20 **Bena-Dibele** Kasai Oriental, C Zaire
107 R9 **Benageber, Embalse de** ⊠ E Spain
191 O11 **Benalla** Victoria, SE Australia
106 M14 **Benamejí** Andalucía, S Spain
Benares see Vārānasi
Benavarn see Benabarre
106 F10 **Benavente** Santarém, C Portugal
106 K5 **Benavente** Castilla-León, N Spain
27 S15 **Benavides** Texas, SW USA
98 F8 **Benbecula** island NW Scotland, UK
Bencovazzo see Benkovac
34 H13 **Bend** Oregon, NW USA
190 K7 **Benda Range** ▲▲ South Australia
191 T6 **Bendemeer** New South Wales, SE Australia
Bender see Tighina
Bender Beila/Bender Beyla see Bandarbeyla
Bender Cassim/Bender Qaasim see Boosaaso
Bendery see Tighina
191 N11 **Bendigo** Victoria, SE Australia
120 E10 **Bēne** Dobele, SW Latvia
100 K13 **Beneden-Leeuwen** Gelderland, C Netherlands
103 L24 **Benediktenwand** ▲ S Germany
Benemérita de San Cristóbal see San Cristóbal
79 N12 **Bénéna** Ségou, S Mali
180 I7 **Benenitra** Toliara, S Madagascar
Beneschau see Benešov
Beneški Zaliv see Venice, Gulf of
113 D17 **Benešov** Ger. Beneschau. Střední Čechy, W Czech Republic
126 Ll3 **Benetta, Ostrov** island Novosibirskiye Ostrova, NE Russian Federation
109 L17 **Benevento** anc. Beneventum, Malventum. Campania, S Italy
Beneventum see Benevento
181 S3 **Bengal, Bay of** bay N Indian Ocean
81 M17 **Bengamisa** Haut-Zaïre, N Zaire
Bengasi see Banghāzī
174 Ll15 **Bengawan, Sungai** ≈ Jawa, S Indonesia
Bengazi see Banghāzī
167 P7 **Bengbu** var. Peng-pu. Anhui, E China
34 L9 **Benge** Washington, NW USA
Benghazi see Banghāzī
174 H7 **Bengkalis** Pulau Bengkalis, W Indonesia
174 H6 **Bengkalis, Pulau** island W Indonesia
174 Kk7 **Bengkayang** Borneo, C Indonesia
Bengkoelen/Bengkoeloe see Bengkulu
174 H12 **Bengkulu** prev. Bengkoeloe, Benkoelen, Benkulen. Sumatera, W Indonesia
174 H11 **Bengkulu** off. Propinsi Bengkulu; prev. Bengkoelen, Benkoelen, Benkulen. ◐ province W Indonesia
84 A11 **Bengo** ◐ province W Angola
97 J16 **Bengtsfors** Älvsborg, S Sweden
84 B13 **Benguela** var. Benguella. Benguela, W Angola
85 A14 **Benguela** ◐ province W Angola
Benguella see Benguela
Bengweulu, Lake see Bangweulu, Lake
124 Qq15 **Benha** var. Banhā. N Egypt
198 G6 **Benham Seamount** undersea feature W Philippine Sea
98 H6 **Ben Hope** ▲ N Scotland, UK
81 P18 **Beni** Nord Kivu, NE Zaire
59 L15 **Beni** var. El Beni. ◐ department N Bolivia
76 H8 **Beni Abbès** W Algeria
107 T8 **Benicarló** País Valenciano, E Spain
107 T9 **Benicasim** País Valenciano, E Spain
107 T12 **Benidorm** País Valenciano, SE Spain
77 W9 **Beni Mazâr** var. Banī Mazār. C Egypt
122 F12 **Beni-Mellal** C Morocco
79 R14 **Benin** off. Republic of Benin; prev. Dahomey. ◆ republic W Africa
79 S17 **Benin, Bight of** gulf W Africa
79 U16 **Benin City** Edo, SW Nigeria
59 K16 **Beni, Río** ≈ N Bolivia
123 Gg11 **Beni Saf** var. Beni-Saf. NW Algeria
107 T11 **Benissa** País Valenciano, E Spain
124 Qq17 **Beni Suef** var. Banī Suwayf. N Egypt
9 V15 **Benito** Manitoba, S Canada
Benito see Uolo, Río
63 C23 **Benito Juárez** Buenos Aires, E Argentina
43 P14 **Benito Juaréz Internacional** ✕ (México) México, S Mexico
27 P5 **Benjamin** Texas, SW USA
60 B13 **Benjamin Constant** Amazonas, N Brazil
42 F4 **Benjamin Hill** Sonora, NW Mexico
65 F19 **Benjamín, Isla** island Archipiélago de los Chonos, S Chile
172 N5 **Benkei-misaki** headland Hokkaidō, NE Japan
30 L17 **Benkelman** Nebraska, C USA
98 I7 **Ben Klibreck** ▲ N Scotland, UK
Benkoelen see Bengkulu
114 D13 **Benkovac** It. Bencovazzo. Zadar-Knin, S Croatia
Benkulen see Bengkulu
98 I11 **Ben Lawers** ▲ C Scotland, UK
98 J9 **Ben Macdui** var. Beinn MacDuibh. ▲ C Scotland, UK
98 G11 **Ben More** ▲ W Scotland, UK
98 I11 **Ben More** ▲ C Scotland, UK
98 H7 **Ben More Assynt** ▲ N Scotland, UK
193 E20 **Benmore, Lake** ◎ South Island, NZ
100 L12 **Bennekom** Gelderland, SE Netherlands
23 T11 **Bennettsville** South Carolina, SE USA
98 H10 **Ben Nevis** ▲ N Scotland, UK
192 M9 **Benneydale** Waikato, North Island, NZ
Bennichab see Bennichchâb
78 H8 **Bennichchâb** var. Bennichab. Inchiri, W Mauritania
20 L10 **Bennington** Vermont, NE USA
193 E20 **Ben Ohau Range** ▲▲ South Island, NZ
85 J21 **Benoni** Gauteng, NE South Africa
180 J2 **Be, Nosy** var. Nossi-Bé. island NW Madagascar
Bénoué see Benue
44 F2 **Benque Viejo del Carmen** Cayo, W Belize
103 G19 **Bensheim** Hessen, W Germany
39 N16 **Benson** Arizona, SW USA
31 S8 **Benson** Minnesota, N USA
23 U10 **Benson** North Carolina, SE USA
175 Pp14 **Benteng** Pulau Selayar, C Indonesia
85 A14 **Bentiaba** Namibe, SW Angola
189 T4 **Bentinck Island** island Wellesley Islands, Queensland, N Australia

◆ Country ● Country Capital ◇ Dependent Territory ○ Dependent Territory Capital ◐ Administrative Region ✕ International Airport ▲ Mountain ▲▲ Mountain Range Volcano ≈ River ◎ Lake ⊠ Reservoir

82 E13 **Bentiu** Wahda, S Sudan
144 G8 **Bent Jbaïl** *var.* Bint Jubayl. S Lebanon
9 Q15 **Bentley** Alberta, SW Canada
63 I15 **Bento Gonçalves** Rio Grande do Sul, S Brazil
29 Y7 **Benton** Arkansas, C USA
32 L16 **Benton** Illinois, N USA
22 H7 **Benton** Kentucky, S USA
24 G5 **Benton** Louisiana, S USA
29 U12 **Benton** Missouri, C USA
22 M10 **Benton** Tennessee, S USA
33 O10 **Benton Harbor** Michigan, N USA
29 S9 **Bentonville** Arkansas, C USA
79 V16 **Benue** ◆ *state* SE Nigeria
80 F13 **Benue** *Fr.* Bénoué. ⁓ Cameroon/Nigeria
174 Hh6 **Benut** Johor, Peninsular Malaysia
169 V12 **Benxi** *prev.* Pen-ch'i, Penhsihu, Penki. Liaoning, NE China
Benyakoni *see* Byenyakoni
114 K10 **Beočin** Serbia, N Yugoslavia
Beodericsworth *see* Bury St Edmunds
114 M11 **Beograd** *Eng.* Belgrade, *Ger.* Belgrad; *anc.* Singidunum. ● (Yugoslavia) Serbia, N Yugoslavia
114 L11 **Beograd** *Eng.* Belgrade. ✕ Serbia, N Yugoslavia
78 M16 **Béoumi** C Ivory Coast
37 V3 **Beowawe** Nevada, W USA
176 Ww8 **Bepondi, Pulau** *see* Bepondi, Pulau
170 D13 **Beppu** Ōita, Kyūshū, SW Japan
170 Dd14 **Beppu-wan** *bay* SW Japan
197 H15 **Beqa** *prev.* Mbengga. *island* W Fiji
Beqa Barrier Reef *see* Kavukavu Reef
47 Y14 **Bequia** *island* C Saint Vincent and the Grenadines
115 L16 **Berane** *prev.* Ivangrad. Montenegro, SW Yugoslavia
115 L21 **Berat** *var.* Berati, *SCr.* Beligrad. Berat, C Albania
115 L21 **Berat** ◆ *district* C Albania
Berătău *see* Berettyó
Berati *see* Berat
Beraun *see* Berounka, Czech Republic
Beraun *see* Beroun, Czech Republic
175 O6 **Berau, Sungai** ⁓ Borneo, N Indonesia
176 V10 **Berau, Teluk** *var.* MacCluer Gulf. *bay* Irian Jaya, E Indonesia
82 G8 **Berber** River Nile, NE Sudan
82 N12 **Berbera** Woqooyi Galbeed, NW Somalia
81 H16 **Berbérati** Mambéré-Kadéï, SW Central African Republic
Berberia, Cabo de *see* Barbaria, Cap de
57 T9 **Berbice River** ⁓ NE Guyana
Berchid *see* Berrechid
105 N2 **Berck-Plage** Pas-de-Calais, N France
27 T13 **Berclair** Texas, SW USA
119 W10 **Berda** ⁓ SE Ukraine
Berdichev *see* Berdychiv
126 Ll11 **Berdigestyakh** Respublika Sakha (Yakutiya), NE Russian Federation
126 H14 **Berdsk** Novosibirskaya Oblast', C Russian Federation
119 W10 **Berdyans'k** *Rus.* Berdyansk; *prev.* Osipenko. Zaporiz'ka Oblast', SE Ukraine
119 W10 **Berdyans'ka Kosa** *spit* SE Ukraine
119 V10 **Berdyans'ka Zatoka** *gulf* S Ukraine
119 N5 **Berdychiv** *Rus.* Berdichev. Zhytomyrs'ka Oblast', N Ukraine
22 M6 **Berea** Kentucky, S USA
Beregovo/Beregszász *see* Berehove
118 G8 **Berehove** *Cz.* Berehovo, *Hung.* Beregszász, *Rus.* Beregovo. Zakarpats'ka Oblast', W Ukraine
Berehovo *see* Berehove
194 J15 **Bereina** Central, S PNG
47 O12 **Berekua** S Dominica
79 O16 **Berekum** W Ghana
77 Y11 **Berenice** *var.* Minâ Baranîs. SE Egypt
15 L14 **Berens** ⁓ Manitoba/Ontario, C Canada
9 X14 **Berens River** Manitoba, C Canada
31 R12 **Beresford** South Dakota, N USA
118 J4 **Berestechko** Volyns'ka Oblast', NW Ukraine
118 M11 **Bereşti** Galaţi, E Romania
119 U6 **Berestova** ⁓ E Ukraine
Beretău *see* Berettyó
113 N23 **Berettyó** *Rom.* Barcău; *prev.* Berătău, Beretău. ⁓ Hungary/Romania
113 N23 **Berettyóújfalu** Hajdú-Bihar, E Hungary
Bereza/Bereza Kartuska *see* Byaroza
119 Q4 **Berezan'** Kyyivs'ka Oblast', N Ukraine
119 Q10 **Berezanka** Mykolayivs'ka Oblast', S Ukraine
118 J6 **Berezhany** *Pol.* Brzeżany. Ternopil's'ka Oblast', W Ukraine
Berezina *see* Byerezino
Berezino *see* Byerazino
119 P10 **Berezivka** *Rus.* Berezovka. Odes'ka Oblast', SW Ukraine
119 Q2 **Berezna** Chernihivs'ka Oblast', NE Ukraine
118 L3 **Berezne** Rivnens'ka Oblast', NW Ukraine
119 R9 **Bereznehuvate** Mykolayivs'ka Oblast', S Ukraine
129 N10 **Bereznik** Arkhangel'skaya Oblast', NW Russian Federation
129 U13 **Berezniki** Permskaya Oblast', NW Russian Federation
Berezovka *see* Berezivka
125 Ff9 **Berezovo** Khanty-Mansiyskiy Avtonomnyy Okrug, N Russian Federation
131 O9 **Berezovskaya** Volgogradskaya Oblast', SW Russian Federation
126 H14 **Berezovskiy** Kemerovskaya Oblast', S Russian Federation
127 N14 **Berezovyy** Khabarovskiy Kray, E Russian Federation
85 E25 **Berg** ⁓ W South Africa
Berg *see* Berg bei Rohrbach
107 V4 **Berga** Cataluña, NE Spain
97 N20 **Berga** Kalmar, S Sweden
142 B13 **Bergama** İzmir, W Turkey
108 E7 **Bergamo** *anc.* Bergomum. Lombardia, N Italy
107 P3 **Bergara** País Vasco, N Spain
111 S3 **Berg bei Rohrbach** *var.* Berg. Oberösterreich, N Austria
195 O11 **Bergberg** ⁓ New Britain, C Papau New Guinea
102 I11 **Bergen** Mecklenburg-Vorpommern, NE Germany
103 O16 **Bergen** Niedersachsen, NW Germany
100 H8 **Bergen** Noord-Holland, NW Netherlands
96 C13 **Bergen** Hordaland, S Norway
Bergen *see* Mons
57 W9 **Berg en Dal** Brokopondo, C Suriname
101 G15 **Bergen op Zoom** Noord-Brabant, S Netherlands
104 L13 **Bergerac** Dordogne, SW France
101 J16 **Bergeyk** Noord-Brabant, S Netherlands
103 D16 **Bergheim** Nordrhein-Westfalen, W Germany
57 X10 **Bergi** Sipaliwini, E Suriname
103 E16 **Bergisch Gladbach** Nordrhein-Westfalen, W Germany
103 F14 **Bergkamen** Nordrhein-Westfalen, W Germany
97 N21 **Bergkvara** Kalmar, S Sweden
Bergomum *see* Bergamo
100 K13 **Bergse Maas** ⁓ S Netherlands
97 P15 **Bergshamra** Stockholm, C Sweden
96 N10 **Bergsjö** Gävleborg, C Sweden
95 J14 **Bergsviken** Norrbotten, N Sweden
100 L6 **Bergum** *Fris.* Burgum. Friesland, N Netherlands
100 M6 **Bergumer Meer** ◎ N Netherlands
96 N12 **Bergviken** ◎ C Sweden
174 I9 **Berhala, Selat** *strait* Sumatera, W Indonesia
Berhampore *see* Baharampur
127 Q9 **Beringa, Ostrov** *island* E Russian Federation
101 J17 **Beringen** Limburg, NE Belgium
41 T12 **Bering Glacier** *glacier* Alaska, USA
Beringov Proliv *see* Bering Strait
127 Q5 **Beringovskiy** Chukotskiy Avtonomnyy Okrug, NE Russian Federation
199 K2 **Bering Sea** *sea* N Pacific Ocean
40 L9 **Bering Strait** *Rus.* Beringov Proliv. *strait* Bering Sea/ Chukchi Sea
Berislav *see* Beryslav
107 O15 **Berja** Andalucía, S Spain
96 H9 **Berkåk** Sør-Trøndelag, S Norway
101 M16 **Berkel** ⁓ Germany/Netherlands
37 N8 **Berkeley** California, W USA
67 E24 **Berkeley Sound** *sound* NE Falkland Islands
23 V2 **Berkeley Springs** *var.* Bath. West Virginia, NE USA
205 N6 **Berkner Island** *island* Antarctica
116 G8 **Berkovitsa** Oblast Montana, NW Bulgaria
99 M22 **Berkshire** *cultural region* S England, UK
101 H17 **Berlaar** Antwerpen, N Belgium
Berlanga *see* Berlanga de Duero
107 P6 **Berlanga de Duero** *var.* Berlanga. Castilla-León, N Spain
1 I16 **Berlanga Rise** *undersea feature* E Pacific Ocean
101 F17 **Berlare** Oost-Vlaanderen, NW Belgium
106 E9 **Berlenga, Ilha da** *island* C Portugal
94 M7 **Berlevåg** Finnmark, N Norway
102 O12 **Berlin** ● (Germany) Berlin, NE Germany
23 Z4 **Berlin** Maryland, NE USA
21 O7 **Berlin** New Hampshire, NE USA
20 D16 **Berlin** Pennsylvania, NE USA
32 L7 **Berlin** Wisconsin, N USA
102 O12 **Berlin** ◆ *state* NE Germany
Berlinchen *see* Barlinek
33 U12 **Berlin Lake** ⊞ Ohio, N USA
191 R11 **Bermagui** New South Wales, SE Australia
42 L8 **Bermejillo** Durango, C Mexico
64 M6 **Bermejo (viejo), Río** ⁓ N Argentina
64 L5 **Bermejo, Río** ⁓ N Argentina
64 I10 **Bermejo, Río** ⁓ W Argentina
107 P2 **Bermeo** País Vasco, N Spain
106 K6 **Bermillo de Sayago** Castilla-León, N Spain
108 E6 **Bermina, Pizzo** *Rmsch.* Piz Bernina. ▲ Italy/Switzerland *see also* Bernina, Piz
66 A12 **Bermuda** *var.* Bermuda Islands, Bermudas; *prev.* Somers Islands. ◇ *UK crown colony* NW Atlantic Ocean
1 N11 **Bermuda** *var.* Great Bermuda, Long Island, Main Island. *island* Bermuda
Bermuda Islands *see* Bermuda
Bermuda-New England Seamount Arc *see* New England Seamounts
1 N11 **Bermuda Rise** *undersea feature* C Sargasso Sea
Bermudas *see* Bermuda
110 D8 **Bern** *Fr.* Berne. ● (Switzerland) Bern, W Switzerland
110 D9 **Bern** *Fr.* Berne. ◆ *canton* W Switzerland
39 R11 **Bernalillo** New Mexico, SW USA
12 H12 **Bernard Lake** ◎ Ontario, S Canada
63 B18 **Bernardo de Irigoyen** Santa Fe, NE Argentina
20 J14 **Bernardsville** New Jersey, NE USA
65 K14 **Bernasconi** La Pampa, C Argentina
102 O12 **Bernau** Brandenburg, NE Germany
104 L4 **Bernay** Eure, N France
103 L14 **Bernburg** Sachsen-Anhalt, C Germany
111 X5 **Berndorf** Niederösterreich, NE Austria
33 Q12 **Berne** Indiana, N USA
Berne *see* Bern
110 D10 **Berner Alpen** *var.* Berner Oberland, *Eng.* Bernese Oberland. ▲ SW Switzerland
Berner Oberland/Bernese Oberland *see* Berner Alpen
111 Y2 **Bernhardsthal** Niederösterreich, N Austria
24 H4 **Bernice** Louisiana, S USA
29 Y8 **Bernie** Missouri, C USA
188 G9 **Bernier Island** *island* Western Australia
Bernina Pass *see* Bernina, Passo del
110 J10 **Bernina, Passo del** *Eng.* Bernina Pass. *pass* SE Switzerland
110 J10 **Bernina, Piz** *It.* Pizzo Bermina. ▲ Italy/Switzerland *see also* Bermina, Pizzo
101 E20 **Bernissart** Hainaut, SW Belgium
103 E18 **Bernkastel-Kues** Rheinland-Pfalz, W Germany
Beroea *see* Ḥalab
180 H6 **Beroroha** Toliara, SW Madagascar
Béroubouay *see* Gbéroubouè
113 C17 **Beroun** *Ger.* Beraun. Střední Čechy, W Czech Republic
113 C16 **Berounka** *Ger.* Beraun. ⁓ W Czech Republic
115 Q18 **Berovo** E FYR Macedonia
76 F6 **Berrechid** *var.* Berchid. W Morocco
105 R15 **Berre, Étang de** ◎ SE France
105 S15 **Berre-l'Étang** Bouches-du-Rhône, SE France
190 K9 **Berri** South Australia
33 O10 **Berrien Springs** Michigan, N USA
191 O10 **Berrigan** New South Wales, SE Australia
105 N9 **Berry** *cultural region* C France
37 N7 **Berryessa, Lake** ◎ California, W USA
46 G2 **Berry Islands** *island group* N Bahamas
29 T9 **Berryville** Arkansas, C USA
23 V3 **Berryville** Virginia, NE USA
85 D21 **Berseba** Karas, S Namibia
119 O8 **Bershad'** Vinnyts'ka Oblast', C Ukraine
30 L3 **Berthold** North Dakota, N USA
39 T3 **Berthoud** Colorado, C USA
39 S4 **Berthoud Pass** *pass* Colorado, C USA
81 F15 **Bertoua** Est, E Cameroon
27 S10 **Bertram** Texas, SW USA
65 G22 **Bertrand, Cerro** ▲ S Argentina
101 J23 **Bertrix** Luxembourg, SE Belgium
203 P3 **Beru** *var.* Peru. *atoll* Tungaru, W Kiribati
Beruni *see* Beruniy
152 I9 **Beruniy** *var.* Biruni, *Rus.* Beruni. Qoraqalpoghiston Respublikasi, W Uzbekistan
60 F13 **Beruri** Amazonas, NW Brazil
20 H14 **Berwick** Pennsylvania, NE USA
98 K12 **Berwick** *cultural region* SE Scotland, UK
98 L12 **Berwick-upon-Tweed** N England, UK
119 S10 **Beryslav** *Rus.* Berislav. Khersons'ka Oblast', S Ukraine
Berytus *see* Beyrouth
180 H4 **Besalampy** Mahajanga, W Madagascar
105 T8 **Besançon** *anc.* Besontium, Vesontio. Doubs, E France
105 P10 **Besbre** ⁓ C France
Bescanuova *see* Baška
Besdan *see* Bezdan
Besed' *see* Byesyedz'
153 R10 **Beshariq** *Rus.* Besharyk; *prev.* Kirovo. Farghona Wiloyati, E Uzbekistan
Besharyk *see* Beshariq
152 L9 **Beshbuloq** *Rus.* Beshulak. Nawoiy Wiloyati, N Uzbekistan
Beshenkovichi *see* Byeshankovichy
152 M13 **Beshkent** Qashqadaryo Wiloyati, S Uzbekistan
Beshulak *see* Beshbuloq
176 Uu8 **Besir** Irian Jaya, E Indonesia
114 L10 **Beška** Serbia, N Yugoslavia
Beskra *see* Biskra
131 O16 **Beslan** Respublika Severnaya Osetiya, SW Russian Federation
115 P16 **Besna Kobila** ▲ SE Yugoslavia
143 N16 **Besni** Adıyaman, S Turkey
Besontium *see* Besançon
124 Nn2 **Beşparmak Dağları** *Eng.* Kyrenia Mountains. ▲ N Cyprus
Bessarabka *see* Basarabeasca
94 O2 **Bessels, Kapp** *headland* C Svalbard
25 P4 **Bessemer** Alabama, S USA
32 K3 **Bessemer** Michigan, N USA
23 Q10 **Bessemer City** North Carolina, SE USA
104 M10 **Bessines-sur-Gartempe** Haute-Vienne, C France
101 K15 **Best** Noord-Brabant, S Netherlands
27 N9 **Best** Texas, SW USA
129 O11 **Bestuzhevo** Arkhangel'skaya Oblast', NW Russian Federation
126 M11 **Bestyakh** Respublika Sakha (Yakutiya), NE Russian Federation
Beszterce *see* Bistriţa
Besztercebánya *see* Banská Bystrica
180 I5 **Betafo** Antananarivo, C Madagascar
106 H2 **Betanzos** Galicia, NW Spain
106 G2 **Betanzos, Ría de** *estuary* NW Spain
81 G15 **Bétaré Oya** Est, E Cameroon
107 S9 **Bétera** País Valenciano, E Spain
79 R15 **Bétérou** C Benin
85 K21 **Bethal** Mpumalanga, NE South Africa
32 K15 **Bethalto** Illinois, N USA
85 D21 **Bethanie** *var.* Bethanien, Bethany. Karas, S Namibia
Bethanien *see* Bethanie
29 N10 **Bethany** Missouri, C USA
29 S2 **Bethany** Oklahoma, C USA
Bethany *see* Bethanie
41 N12 **Bethel** Alaska, USA
21 P7 **Bethel** Maine, NE USA
23 W9 **Bethel** North Carolina, SE USA
20 B15 **Bethel Park** Pennsylvania, NE USA
23 W3 **Bethesda** Maryland, NE USA
85 J22 **Bethlehem** Free State, C South Africa
20 I14 **Bethlehem** Pennsylvania, NE USA
144 F10 **Bethlehem** *Ar.* Bayt Laḥm, *Heb.* Bet Leḥem. C West Bank
Bethlen *see* Beclean
85 J24 **Bethulie** Free State, C South Africa
105 O1 **Béthune** Pas-de-Calais, N France
104 M3 **Béthune** ⁓ N France
106 M14 **Béticos, Sistemas** *var.* Sistema Penibético, *Eng.* Baetic Cordillera, Baetic Mountains. ▲ S Spain
56 I6 **Betijoque** Trujillo, NW Venezuela
61 M20 **Betim** Minas Gerais, SE Brazil
202 H3 **Betio** Tarawa, W Kiribati
180 H7 **Betioky** Toliara, S Madagascar
Bet Leḥem *see* Bethlehem
Betlen *see* Beclean
178 H17 **Betong** Yala, SW Thailand
81 I16 **Bétou** La Likouala, N Congo
151 P14 **Betpak-Dala** *Kaz.* Betpaqdala. *plateau* S Kazakhstan
Betpaqdala *see* Betpak-Dala
180 H7 **Betroka** Toliara, S Madagascar
Betschau *see* Bečva
144 G9 **Bet She'an** *Ar.* Baysān, Beisān; *anc.* Scythopolis. Northern, N Israel
13 T6 **Betsiamites** Québec, SE Canada
13 T6 **Betsiamites** ⁓ Québec, SE Canada
180 J4 **Betsiboka** ⁓ N Madagascar
101 M25 **Bettembourg** Luxembourg, S Luxembourg
101 M23 **Bettendorf** Diekirch, NE Luxembourg
31 Z14 **Bettendorf** Iowa, C USA
77 R13 **Bette, Pic** *var.* Bikkū Bīttī, *It.* Picco Bette. ▲ S Libya
Bette, Picco *see* Bette, Pic
159 P12 **Bettiah** Bihār, N India
41 Q7 **Bettles** Alaska, USA
97 N17 **Bettna** Södermanland, C Sweden
160 H11 **Betūl** *prev.* Badnur. Madhya Pradesh, C India
160 H9 **Betwa** ⁓ C India
103 F16 **Betzdorf** Rheinland-Pfalz, W Germany
84 C9 **Béu** Uíge, NW Angola
33 P6 **Beulah** Michigan, N USA
30 L5 **Beulah** North Dakota, N USA
100 M8 **Beulakerwijde** ◎ N Netherlands
100 L13 **Beuningen** Gelderland, SE Netherlands
Beuthen *see* Bytom
105 N7 **Beuvron** ⁓ C France
101 F16 **Beveren** Oost-Vlaanderen, N Belgium
23 T9 **B.Everett Jordan Reservoir** *var.* Jordan Lake. ⊞ North Carolina, SE USA
99 N17 **Beverley** E England, UK
Beverley *see* Beverly
101 J17 **Beverlo** Limburg, NE Belgium
21 P11 **Beverly** Massachusetts, NE USA
34 J9 **Beverly** *var.* Beverley. Washington, NW USA
37 S15 **Beverly Hills** California, W USA
103 I14 **Beverungen** Nordrhein-Westfalen, C Germany
100 H9 **Beverwijk** Noord-Holland, W Netherlands
110 C10 **Bex** Vaud, W Switzerland
99 P23 **Bexhill** *var.* Bexhill-on-Sea. SE England, UK
Bexhill-on-Sea *see* Bexhill
142 E17 **Bey Dağları** ▲ SW Turkey
Beyj *see* Belyy
142 E10 **Beykoz** İstanbul, NW Turkey
78 K15 **Beyla** Guinée-Forestière, SE Guinea
143 X12 **Beyläqan** *prev.* Zhdanov. SW Azerbaijan
82 L10 **Beylul** *var.* Beilul. SE Eritrea
150 H14 **Beyneu** *Kaz.* Beyneū. Mangistau, SW Kazakhstan
Beyneū *see* Beyneu
172 Ss14 **Beyonēsu-retsugan** *Eng.* Bayonnaise Rocks. *island group* SE Japan
142 G12 **Beypazarı** Ankara, NW Turkey
161 F21 **Beypore** Kerala, SW India
144 G7 **Beyrouth** *var.* Bayrūt, *Eng.* Beirut; *anc.* Berytus. ● (Lebanon) W Lebanon
144 G7 **Beyrouth** ✕ W Lebanon
142 G15 **Beyşehir** Konya, SW Turkey
142 G15 **Beyşehir Gölü** ◎ C Turkey
110 J7 **Bezau** Vorarlberg, NW Austria
114 J8 **Bezdan** *Ger.* Besdan, *Hung.* Bezdán. Serbia, NW Yugoslavia
Bezdezh *see* Byezdzyezh
128 G15 **Bezhanitsy** Pskovskaya Oblast', W Russian Federation
128 K15 **Bezhetsk** Tverskaya Oblast', W Russian Federation
105 P16 **Béziers** *anc.* Baeterrae, Baeterrae Septimanorum, Julia Beterrae. Hérault, S France
Bezmein *see* Byuzmeyin
Bezwada *see* Vijayawāda
160 P12 **Bhadrak** *var.* Bhadrakh. Orissa, E India
Bhadrakh *see* Bhadrak
161 F19 **Bhadra Reservoir** ⊞ SW India
161 F18 **Bhadrāvati** Karnātaka, SW India
159 R14 **Bhāgalpur** Bihār, NE India
Bhairab *see* Bhairab Bazar
159 U14 **Bhairab Bazar** *var.* Bhairab. Dhaka, C Bangladesh
159 O11 **Bhairahawa** Western, S Nepal
155 S8 **Bhakkar** Punjab, E Pakistan
159 P11 **Bhaktapur** Central, C Nepal
178 Gg3 **Bhamo** *var.* Banmo. Kachin State, N Myanmar
Bhāmragad *see* Bhāmragarh
160 K13 **Bhāmragarh** *var.* Bhāmragad. Mahārāshtra, C India
160 J12 **Bhandāra** Mahārāshtra, C India
Bhārat *see* India
158 J12 **Bharatpur** *prev.* Bhurtpore. Rājasthān, N India
160 D11 **Bharūch** Gujarāt, W India
161 E18 **Bhatkal** Karnātaka, W India
159 O13 **Bhatni** *var.* Bhatni Junction. Uttar Pradesh, N India
Bhatni Junction *see* Bhatni
159 S16 **Bhātpāra** West Bengal, NE India
155 U7 **Bhaun** Punjab, E Pakistan
Bhaunagar *see* Bhāvnagar
160 M13 **Bhavānīpātna** Orissa, E India
161 H21 **Bhavānīsāgar Reservoir** ⊞ S India
160 D11 **Bhāvnagar** *prev.* Bhaunagar. Gujarāt, W India
Bheanntraí, Bá *see* Bantry Bay
Bheara, Béal an *see* Gweebarra Bay
160 K12 **Bhilai** Madhya Pradesh, C India
158 G13 **Bhīlwāra** Rājasthān, N India
161 E14 **Bhīma** ⁓ S India
161 K16 **Bhīmavaram** Andhra Pradesh, E India
160 I7 **Bhind** Madhya Pradesh, C India
158 E13 **Bhīnmāl** Rājasthān, N India
Bhir *see* Bīd
160 D13 **Bhiwandi** Mahārāshtra, W India
158 H10 **Bhiwāni** Haryāna, N India
158 L13 **Bhognīpur** Uttar Pradesh, N India
159 U16 **Bhola** Khulna, S Bangladesh
160 H10 **Bhopāl** Madhya Pradesh, C India
161 J14 **Bhopālpatnam** Madhya Pradesh, C India
161 E14 **Bhor** Mahārāshtra, W India
160 O12 **Bhubaneshwar** *prev.* Bhubaneswar, Bhuvaneshwar. Orissa, E India
Bhubaneswar *see* Bhubaneshwar
160 B9 **Bhuj** Gujarāt, W India
Bhuket *see* Phuket
Bhurtpore *see* Bharatpur
Bhusaval *see* Bhusāwal
160 G12 **Bhusāwal** *prev.* Bhusaval. Mahārāshtra, C India
159 T12 **Bhutan** *off.* Kingdom of Bhutan, *var.* Druk-yul. ◆ *monarchy* S Asia
Bhuvaneshwar *see* Bhubaneshwar
149 T15 **Bīābān, Kūh-e** ▲ S Iran
79 V18 **Biafra, Bight of** *var.* Bight of Bonny. *bay* W Africa
176 X9 **Biak** Irian Jaya, E Indonesia
176 Ww9 **Biak, Pulau** *island* E Indonesia
112 P12 **Biała Podlaska** Biała Podlaska, E Poland
112 O12 **Biała Podlaska** *off.* Województwo Bialskopodlaskie. ◆ *province* E Poland
112 F7 **Białogard** *Ger.* Belgard. Koszalin, NW Poland
Białostockie, Województwo *see* Białystok
112 P10 **Białowieska, Puszcza** *Bel.* Byelavyezhskaya Pushcha, *Rus.* Belovezhskaya Pushcha. *physical region* Belarus/Poland *see also* Byelavyezhskaya Pushcha
Bialskopodlaskie, Województwo *see* Biała Podlaska
112 G8 **Biały Bór** *Ger.* Baldenburg. Koszalin, NW Poland
112 P9 **Białystok** *Rus.* Belostok, Bielostok. Białystok, E Poland
112 O10 **Białystok** *off.* Województwo Białostockie, *Rus.* Belostok, Bielostok. ◆ *province* E Poland
109 L24 **Biancavilla** *prev.* Inessa. Sicilia, Italy, C Mediterranean Sea
Bianco, Monte *see* Blanc, Mont
78 L15 **Biankouma** W Ivory Coast
178 Ii7 **Bia, Phou** *var.* Pou Bia. ▲ C Laos
Bia, Pou *see* Bia, Phou
149 R5 **Biārjmand** Semnān, N Iran
104 I15 **Biarritz** Pyrénées-Atlantiques, SW France
110 H10 **Biasca** Ticino, S Switzerland
63 E17 **Biassini** Salto, N Uruguay
172 Oo5 **Bibai** Hokkaidō, NE Japan
85 B15 **Bibala** *Port.* Vila Arriaga. Namibe, SW Angola
106 I4 **Bibéi** ⁓ NW Spain
Biberach *see* Biberach an der Riss
103 I23 **Biberach an der Riss** *var.* Biberach, *Ger.* Biberach an der Riß. Baden-Württemberg, S Germany
110 E7 **Biberist** Solothurn, NW Switzerland
79 O16 **Bibiani** SW Ghana
114 C13 **Bibinje** Zadar-Knin, W Croatia
Biblical Gebal *see* Jbail
118 I5 **Bibrka** *Pol.* Bóbrka, *Rus.* Bobrka. L'vivs'ka Oblast', NW Ukraine
119 N10 **Bic** ⁓ S Moldova
115 M18 **Bicaj** Kukës, NE Albania
118 K10 **Bicaz** *Hung.* Békás. Neamţ, NE Romania
191 Q16 **Bicheno** Tasmania, SE Australia
Bichiş *see* Békés
Bichiş-Ciaba *see* Békéscsaba
Bichitra *see* Phichit
143 P8 **Bichvint'a** *Rus.* Pitsunda. NW Georgia
13 T7 **Bic, Île du** *island* Québec, SE Canada
34 J10 **Bickleton** Washington, NW USA
38 L6 **Bicknell** Utah, W USA
175 Tt7 **Bicoli** Pulau Halmahera, E Indonesia
113 J22 **Bicske** Fejér, C Hungary
161 F14 **Bīd** *prev.* Bhir. Mahārāshtra, W India
79 U15 **Bida** Niger, C Nigeria
161 H15 **Bīdar** Karnātaka, C India
147 Y8 **Bidbid** NE Oman
21 P9 **Biddeford** Maine, NE USA
100 L9 **Biddinghuizen** Flevoland, C Netherlands
35 X11 **Biddle** Montana, NW USA
99 J23 **Bideford** SW England, UK
84 D13 **Bié** ◆ *province* C Angola
37 O2 **Bieber** California, W USA
112 O9 **Biebrza** ⁓ NE Poland
172 P5 **Biei** Hokkaidō, NE Japan
110 D8 **Biel** *Fr.* Bienne. Bern, W Switzerland
102 G13 **Bielefeld** Nordrhein-Westfalen, NW Germany
110 D8 **Bieler See** *Fr.* Lac de Bienne. ◎ W Switzerland
Bielitz/Bielitz-Biala *see* Bielsko-Biała
108 C7 **Biella** Piemonte, N Italy
Bielostok *see* Białystok
Bielskie, Województwo/Bielsko *see* Bielsko-Biała
113 J17 **Bielsko-Biała** *Ger.* Bielitz, Bielitz-Biala. Bielsko-Biała, S Poland
113 J17 **Bielsko-Biała** *off.* Województwo Bielskie, *var.* Bielsko. ◆ *province* S Poland
112 P10 **Bielsk Podlaski** Białystok, E Poland
Bien Bien *see* Điện Biên
Biên Đông *see* South China Sea
9 V17 **Bienfait** Saskatchewan, S Canada
178 Jj14 **Biên Hoa** Đông Nai, S Vietnam
Bienne *see* Biel
Bienne, Lac de *see* Bieler See
10 K8 **Bienville, Lac** ◎ Québec, C Canada
84 D13 **Bié, Planalto do** *var.* Bié Plateau. *plateau* C Angola
Bié Plateau *see* Bié, Planalto do
110 B9 **Bière** Vaud, W Switzerland
100 O4 **Bierum** Groningen, NE Netherlands
100 I13 **Biesbos** *var.* Biesbosch. *wetland* S Netherlands
Biesbosch *see* Biesbos
101 H21 **Biesme** Namur, S Belgium
103 H21 **Bietigheim-Bissingen** Baden-Württemberg, SW Germany
101 J23 **Bièvre** Namur, SE Belgium
81 D18 **Bifoun** Moyen-Ogooué, NW Gabon
172 Pp3 **Bifuka** Hokkaidō, NE Japan
142 C11 **Biga** Çanakkale, NW Turkey
142 C13 **Bigadiç** Balıkesir, W Turkey
28 J7 **Big Basin** *basin* Kansas, C USA
193 B20 **Big Bay** *bay* South Island, NZ
197 B12 **Big Bay** *bay* C Vanuatu
33 O5 **Big Bay de Noc** ◎ Michigan, N USA
33 N3 **Big Bay Point** *headland* Michigan, N USA
35 R10 **Big Belt Mountains** ▲ Montana, NW USA
31 N10 **Big Bend Dam** *dam* South Dakota, N USA
26 K12 **Big Bend National Park** *national park* Texas, S USA
24 K5 **Big Black River** ⁓ Mississippi, S USA
29 O3 **Big Blue River** ⁓ Kansas/Nebraska, C USA
26 M10 **Big Canyon** ⁓ Texas, SW USA
35 N12 **Big Creek** Idaho, NW USA
25 N8 **Big Creek Lake** ⊞ Alabama, S USA
25 X15 **Big Cypress Swamp** *wetland* Florida, SE USA
41 S9 **Big Delta** Alaska, USA
32 K6 **Big Eau Pleine Reservoir** ⊞ Wisconsin, N USA
21 P5 **Bigelow Mountain** ▲ Maine, NE USA
31 U3 **Big Falls** Minnesota, N USA
35 P8 **Bigfork** Montana, NW USA
31 U3 **Big Fork River** ⁓ Minnesota, N USA
9 S15 **Biggar** Saskatchewan, S Canada
188 L3 **Bigge Island** *island* Western Australia
37 O5 **Biggs** California, W USA
34 I11 **Biggs** Oregon, NW USA
12 K13 **Big Gull Lake** ◎ Ontario, SE Canada
39 P16 **Big Hachet Peak** ▲ New Mexico, SW USA
35 P11 **Big Hole River** ⁓ Montana, NW USA
35 V13 **Bighorn Basin** *basin* Wyoming, C USA
35 U11 **Bighorn Lake** ◎ Montana/Wyoming, N USA
35 W13 **Bighorn Mountains** ▲ Wyoming, C USA
38 J13 **Big Horn Peak** ▲ Arizona, SW USA
35 V11 **Bighorn River** ⁓ Montana/ Wyoming, NW USA
16 O5 **Big Island** *island* Northwest Territories, NE Canada
41 O16 **Big Koniuji Island** *island* Shumagin Islands, Alaska, USA
27 N9 **Big Lake** Texas, SW USA
21 T5 **Big Lake** ◎ Maine, NE USA
32 I3 **Big Manitou Falls** *waterfall* Wisconsin, N USA
37 R2 **Big Mountain** ▲ Nevada, W USA
110 G10 **Bignasco** Ticino, S Switzerland
31 R16 **Big Nemaha River** ⁓ Nebraska, C USA
78 G12 **Bignona** SW Senegal
Bigorra *see* Tarbes
Bigosovo *see* Bihosava
37 S10 **Big Pine** California, W USA
37 Q14 **Big Pine Mountain** ▲ California, W USA
29 V6 **Big Piney Creek** ⁓ Missouri, C USA
67 M24 **Big Point** *headland* N Tristan da Cunha
33 P8 **Big Rapids** Michigan, N USA
32 K6 **Big Rib River** ⁓ Wisconsin, N USA
12 L14 **Big Rideau Lake** ◎ Ontario, SE Canada
9 T14 **Big River** Saskatchewan, C Canada
29 X5 **Big River** ⁓ Missouri, C USA
33 N7 **Big Sable Point** *headland* Michigan, N USA
35 S7 **Big Sandy** Montana, NW USA
27 W6 **Big Sandy** Texas, SW USA
39 V5 **Big Sandy Creek** ⁓ Colorado, C USA
31 Q16 **Big Sandy Creek** ⁓ Nebraska, C USA
31 V5 **Big Sandy Lake** ◎ Minnesota, N USA
38 J11 **Big Sandy River** ⁓ Arizona, SW USA
23 P5 **Big Sandy River** ⁓ S USA
25 V6 **Big Satilla Creek** ⁓ Georgia, SE USA
31 R12 **Big Sioux River** ⁓ Iowa/South Dakota, N USA
37 U7 **Big Smoky Valley** *valley* Nevada, W USA
27 N7 **Big Spring** Texas, SW USA
21 Q5 **Big Squaw Mountain** ▲ Maine, NE USA
23 O7 **Big Stone Gap** Virginia, NE USA
31 Q8 **Big Stone Lake** ◎ Minnesota/ South Dakota, N USA
24 K4 **Big Sunflower River** ⁓ Mississippi, S USA
35 T11 **Big Timber** Montana, NW USA
10 D8 **Big Trout Lake** Ontario, C Canada
12 I12 **Big Trout Lake** ◎ Ontario, SE Canada
37 Q2 **Big Valley Mountains** ▲ California, W USA
27 Q13 **Big Wells** Texas, SW USA
12 F11 **Bigwood** Ontario, S Canada
114 D11 **Bihać** NW Bosnia and Herzegovina
159 P14 **Bihār** *prev.* Behar. ◆ *state* N India
Bihār *see* Bihār Sharīf
83 F20 **Biharamulo** Kagera, NW Tanzania
159 R13 **Bihārīganj** Bihār, NE India
159 P14 **Bihār Sharīf** *var.* Bihār. Bihār, N India
118 F10 **Bihor** ◆ *county* NW Romania
172 Q6 **Bihoro** Hokkaidō, NE Japan
120 K11 **Bihosava** *Rus.* Bigosovo. Vitsyebskaya Voblasts', NW Belarus
Bijagos Archipelago *see* Bijagós, Arquipélago dos
78 G13 **Bijagós, Arquipélago dos** *var.* Bijagos Archipelago. *island group* W Guinea-Bissau
161 F16 **Bijāpur** Karnātaka, C India
148 K5 **Bījār** Kordestān, W Iran
114 J11 **Bijeljina** NE Bosnia and Herzegovina
115 K15 **Bijelo Polje** Montenegro, SW Yugoslavia
166 E11 **Bijiang** *prev.* Zhiziluo. Yunnan, SW China
166 I11 **Bijie** Guizhou, S China
158 J10 **Bijnor** Uttar Pradesh, N India
158 F11 **Bīkāner** Rājasthān, NW India
201 V3 **Bikar Atoll** *var.* Pikaar. *atoll* Ratak Chain, N Marshall Islands
202 H3 **Bikeman** *atoll* Tungaru, W Kiribati
202 I3 **Bikenebu** Tarawa, W Kiribati
127 Nn16 **Bikin** Khabarovskiy Kray, SE Russian Federation
127 Nn16 **Bikin** ⁓ SE Russian Federation
201 R3 **Bikini Atoll** *var.* Pikinni. *atoll* Ralik Chain, NW Marshall Islands
85 L17 **Bikita** Masvingo, E Zimbabwe
Bikkū Bīttī *see* Bette, Pic
81 I19 **Bikoro** Equateur, W Zaire
147 Z9 **Bilād Banī Bū 'Alī** NE Oman
147 Z9 **Bilād Banī Bū Ḥasan** NE Oman
147 X9 **Bilād Manaḥ** *var.* Manaḥ. NE Oman
79 Q12 **Bilanga** C Burkina

◆ Country ● Country Capital ◇ Dependent Territory ○ Dependent Territory Capital ◆ Administrative Region ✕ International Airport ▲ Mountain ▲ Mountain Range Volcano ⁓ River ◎ Lake ⊞ Reservoir

175 Q7 **Bilang, Teluk** *bay* Sulawesi, N Indonesia
158 F12 **Bilāra** Rājasthān, N India
158 K10 **Bilāri** Uttar Pradesh, N India
144 J5 **Bil'ās, Jabal al** ▲▲ C Syria
158 I8 **Bilāspur** Himāchal Pradesh, N India
160 L11 **Bilāspur** Madhya Pradesh, C India
173 G6 **Bila, Sungai** ≈ Sumatera, W Indonesia
143 Y13 **Biläsuvar** ***Rus.*** Bilyasuvar; ***prev.*** Pushkino. SE Azerbaijan
119 O5 **Bila Tserkva** ***Rus.*** Belaya Tserkov'. Kyyivs'ka Oblast', N Ukraine
178 H11 **Bilauktaung Range** ***var.*** Thanintari Taungdan. ▲▲ Myanmar/Thailand
107 O2 **Bilbao** ***Basq.*** Bilbo. País Vasco, N Spain
Bilbo *see* Bilbao
94 H2 **Bíldudalur** Vestfirdhir, NW Iceland
115 I16 **Bileća** S Bosnia and Herzegovina
142 E12 **Bilecik** Bilecik, NW Turkey
142 F12 **Bilecik** ⬖ *province* NW Turkey
118 E11 **Biled** ***Ger.*** Billed, ***Hung.*** Billéd. Timiș, W Romania
113 O15 **Biłgoraj** Zamość, SE Poland
119 P11 **Bilhorod-Dnistrovs'kyy** ***Rus.*** Belgorod-Dnestrovskiy, ***Rom.*** Cetatea Albă; ***prev.*** Akkerman, ***anc.*** Tyras. Odes'ka Oblast', SW Ukraine
81 M16 **Bili** Haut-Zaïre, N Zaire
127 Oo5 **Bilibino** Chukotskiy Avtonomnyy Okrug, NE Russian Federation
178 Gg8 **Bilin** Mon State, S Myanmar
179 Qq12 **Biliran Island** *island* C Philippines
115 N21 **Bilisht** ***var.*** Bilishti. Korçë, SE Albania
Bilishti *see* Bilisht
191 N10 **Billabong Creek** ***var.*** Moulamein Creek. *seasonal river* New South Wales, SE Australia
190 G4 **Billa Kalina** South Australia
207 Q17 **Bill Baileys Bank** *undersea feature* N Atlantic Ocean
Billed/Billéd *see* Biled
159 N14 **Billi** Uttar Pradesh, N India
99 M15 **Billingham** N England, UK
35 U11 **Billings** Montana, NW USA
97 J16 **Billingsfors** Älvsborg, S Sweden
Bill of Cape Clear, The *see* Clear, Cape
30 L9 **Billsburg** South Dakota, N USA
97 F23 **Billund** Ribe, W Denmark
38 L11 **Bill Williams Mountain** ▲ Arizona, SW USA
38 I12 **Bill Williams River** ≈ Arizona, SW USA
79 Y8 **Bilma** Agadez, NE Niger
79 Y8 **Bilma, Grand Erg de** *desert* NE Niger
189 Y9 **Biloela** Queensland, E Australia
114 G8 **Bilo Gora** ▲▲ N Croatia
119 U13 **Bilohirs'k** ***Rus.*** Belogorsk; ***prev.*** Karasubazar. Respublika Krym, S Ukraine
118 M3 **Bilokorovychi** ***Rus.*** Belokorovichi. Zhytomyrs'ka Oblast', N Ukraine
119 X5 **Bilokurakine** Luhans'ka Oblast', E Ukraine
119 T3 **Bilopillya** ***Rus.*** Belopol'ye. Sums'ka Oblast', NE Ukraine
119 Y6 **Bilovods'k** ***Rus.*** Belovodsk. Luhans'ka Oblast', E Ukraine
24 M9 **Biloxi** Mississippi, S USA
119 R10 **Bilozerka** Khersons'ka Oblast', S Ukraine
119 W7 **Bilozers'ke** Donets'ka Oblast', E Ukraine
100 J11 **Bilthoven** Utrecht, C Netherlands
80 K9 **Biltine** Biltine, E Chad
80 J9 **Biltine** ***off.*** Préfecture de Biltine. ⬖ *prefecture* E Chad
168 D5 **Bilüü** Bayan-Ölgiy, W Mongolia
Bilwi *see* Puerto Cabezas
Bilyasuvar *see* Biläsuvar
119 O11 **Bilyayivka** Odes'ka Oblast', SW Ukraine
101 K18 **Bilzen** Limburg, NE Belgium
Bimbéréké *see* Bembèrèkè
191 R10 **Bimberi Peak** ▲ New South Wales, SE Australia
79 Q15 **Bimbila** E Ghana
81 I15 **Bimbo** Ombella-Mpoko, SW Central African Republic
46 F2 **Bimini Islands** *island group* W Bahamas
160 I9 **Bīna** Madhya Pradesh, C India
149 T4 **Bīnālūd, Kūh-e** ▲▲ NE Iran
101 F20 **Binche** Hainaut, S Belgium
Bindloe Island *see* Marchena, Isla
85 L16 **Bindura** Mashonaland Central, NE Zimbabwe
107 T5 **Binefar** Aragón, NE Spain
85 J16 **Binga** Matabeleland North, W Zimbabwe
191 T5 **Bingara** New South Wales, SE Australia
103 F18 **Bingen am Rhein** Rheinland-Pfalz, SW Germany
28 M11 **Binger** Oklahoma, C USA
Bingerau *see* Węgrów
Bin Ghalfān, Jazā'ir *see* Ḩalāniyāt, Juzur al
21 Q6 **Bingham** Maine, NE USA
20 H11 **Binghamton** New York, NE USA
Bin Ghanīmah, Jabal *see* Bin Ghunaymah, Jabal
77 P11 **Bin Ghunaymah, Jabal** ***var.*** Jabal Bin Ghanīmah. ▲▲ C Libya
145 U3 **Bingird** NE Iraq
143 P14 **Bingöl** Bingöl, E Turkey
143 P14 **Bingöl** ⬖ *province* E Turkey
167 R6 **Binhai** ***var.*** Binhai Xian, Dongkan. Jiangsu, E China
Binhai Xian *see* Binhai
178 Kk12 **Binh Đinh** ***var.*** An Nhon. Binh Đinh, C Vietnam
178 Kk10 **Binh Sơn** ***var.*** Châu Ô. Quang Ngai, C Vietnam
Binimani *see* Bintimani
173 Ff5 **Binjai** Sumatera, W Indonesia
191 R6 **Binnaway** New South Wales, SE Australia
110 E6 **Binningen** Basel-Land, NW Switzerland
175 R13 **Binongko, Pulau** *island* Kepulauan Tukangbesi, C Indonesia
174 Gg3 **Bintang, Banjaran** ▲▲ Peninsular Malaysia
174 I7 **Bintan, Pulau** *island* Kepulauan Riau, W Indonesia
78 J14 **Bintimani** ***var.*** Binimani. ▲ NE Sierra Leone
Bint Jubayl *see* Bent Jbaïl
174 M5 **Bintulu** Sarawak, East Malaysia
176 Vv10 **Bintuni** ***prev.*** Steenkool. Irian Jaya, E Indonesia
176 Vv10 **Bintuni, Teluk** *bay* Irian Jaya, E Indonesia
169 W8 **Bin Xian** Heilongjiang, NE China
166 K14 **Binyang** Guangxi Zhuangzu Zizhiqu, S China
167 Q4 **Binzhou** Shandong, E China
65 G14 **Bío Bío** ***off.*** Región del Bío Bío. ⬖ *region* C Chile
65 G14 **Bío Bío, Río** ≈ C Chile
81 C16 **Bioco, Isla de** ***var.*** Bioko, ***Eng.*** Fernando Po, ***Sp.*** Fernando Póo; ***prev.*** Macías Nguema Biyogo. *island* NW Equatorial Guinea
114 D13 **Biograd na Moru** ***It.*** Zaravecchia. Zadar-Knin, S Croatia
Bioko *see* Bioco, Isla de
115 F14 **Biokovo** ▲▲ S Croatia
Biorra *see* Birr
Bipontium *see* Zweibrücken
149 W13 **Bīrag, Kūh-e** ▲▲ SE Iran
77 O10 **Birāk** ***var.*** Brak. C Libya
145 S10 **Bi'r al Islām** C Iraq
160 N11 **Biramitrapur** Orissa, E India
145 T11 **Bi'r an Nişf** S Iraq
80 L12 **Birao** Vakaga, NE Central African Republic
164 M6 **Biratar Bulak** *well* NW China
159 R12 **Biratnagar** Eastern, SE Nepal
172 Oo6 **Biratori** Hokkaidō, NE Japan
41 S8 **Birch Creek** Alaska, USA
40 M11 **Birch Creek** ≈ Alaska, USA
9 T14 **Birch Hills** Saskatchewan, S Canada
190 M10 **Birchip** Victoria, SE Australia
31 X4 **Birch Lake** ◎ Minnesota, N USA
9 Q11 **Birch Mountains** ▲▲ Alberta, W Canada
9 V15 **Birch River** Manitoba, S Canada
46 H12 **Birchs Hill** *hill* W Jamaica
41 R11 **Birchwood** Alaska, USA
196 I5 **Bird Island** *island* S Northern Mariana Islands
143 N16 **Birecik** Şanlıurfa, S Turkey
158 M10 **Birendranagar** ***var.*** Surkhet. Mid Western, W Nepal
Bir es Saba *see* Be'ér Sheva'
76 A12 **Bir-Gandouz** SW Western Sahara
159 P12 **Birganj** Central, C Nepal
83 B14 **Biri** ≈ W Sudan
Bi'r Ibn Hirmās *see* Al Bi'r
176 Yy10 **Biri, Sungai** ≈ Irian Jaya, E Indonesia
149 U8 **Bīrjand** Khorāsān, E Iran
145 T11 **Birkat Ḩāmid** *well* S Iraq
97 F18 **Birkeland** Aust-Agder, S Norway
103 E19 **Birkenfeld** Rheinland-Pfalz, SW Germany
99 K18 **Birkenhead** NW England, UK
111 W7 **Birkfeld** Steiermark, SE Austria
190 A2 **Birksgate Range** ▲▲ South Australia
Bîrlad *see* Bârlad
99 K20 **Birmingham** C England, UK
25 P4 **Birmingham** Alabama, S USA
99 M20 **Birmingham** ✕ C England, UK
Bir Moghrein *see* Bîr Mogreïn
78 J4 **Bîr Mogreïn** ***var.*** Bir Moghrein; ***prev.*** Fort-Trinquet. Tiris Zemmour, N Mauritania
203 S4 **Birnie Island** *atoll* Phoenix Islands, C Kiribati
Birni-Ngaouré *see* Birnin Gaouré
79 S12 **Birnin Gaouré** ***var.*** Birni-Ngaouré. Dosso, SW Niger
79 S12 **Birnin Kebbi** Kebbi, NW Nigeria
Birni-Nkonni *see* Birnin Konni
79 T12 **Birnin Konni** ***var.*** Birni-Nkonni. Tahoua, SW Niger
79 W13 **Birnin Kudu** Jigawa, N Nigeria
127 N16 **Birobidzhan** Yevreyskaya Avtonomnaya Oblast', SE Russian Federation
99 D18 **Birr** ***var.*** Parsonstown, ***Ir.*** Biorra. C Ireland
191 P4 **Birrie River** ≈ New South Wales/Queensland, SE Australia
110 D7 **Birse** ≈ NW Switzerland
Birsen *see* Biržai
110 E6 **Birsfelden** Basel-Land, NW Switzerland
131 U4 **Birsk** Respublika Bashkortostan, W Russian Federation
121 F14 **Birštonas** Prienai, C Lithuania
165 P14 **Biru** Xinjiang Uygur Zizhiqu, W China
Biruni *see* Beruniy
126 Ii14 **Biryusa** ≈ C Russian Federation
126 Ii14 **Biryusinsk** Irkutskaya Oblast', C Russian Federation
120 G10 **Biržai** ***Ger.*** Birsen. Biržai, NE Lithuania
123 Jj17 **Birżebbuġa** SE Malta
Bisanthe *see* Tekirdağ
175 T9 **Bisa, Pulau** *island* Maluku, E Indonesia
39 N17 **Bisbee** Arizona, SW USA
31 O2 **Bisbee** North Dakota, N USA
Biscaia, Baía de *see* Biscay, Bay of
104 I13 **Biscarrosse et de Parentis, Étang de** ◎ SW France
106 M1 **Biscay, Bay of** ***Sp.*** Golfo de Vizcaya, ***Port.*** Baía de Biscaia. *bay* France/Spain
25 Z16 **Biscayne Bay** *bay* Florida, SE USA
66 M7 **Biscay Plain** *undersea feature* SE Bay of Biscay
109 N17 **Bisceglie** Puglia, SE Italy
Bischoflack *see* Škofja Loka
Bischofsburg *see* Biskupiec
111 Q7 **Bischofshofen** Salzburg, NW Austria
103 P15 **Bischofswerda** Sachsen, E Germany
105 V5 **Bischwiller** Bas-Rhin, NE France
23 T10 **Biscoe** North Carolina, SE USA
204 G5 **Biscoe Islands** *island group* Antarctica
12 E9 **Biscotasi Lake** ◎ Ontario, S Canada
12 E9 **Biscotasing** Ontario, S Canada
56 J6 **Biscucuy** Portuguesa, NW Venezuela
116 K11 **Biser** Khaskovska Oblast, SE Bulgaria
115 D15 **Biševo** ***It.*** Busi. *island* SW Croatia
147 N12 **Bīshah, Wādī** *dry watercourse* C Saudi Arabia
153 U7 **Bishkek** ***var.*** Pishpek; ***prev.*** Frunze. ● (Kyrgyzstan) Chuyskaya Oblast', N Kyrgyzstan
153 U7 **Bishkek** ✕ Chuyskaya Oblast', N Kyrgyzstan
159 R16 **Bishnupur** West Bengal, NE India
85 J25 **Bisho** Eastern Cape, S South Africa
37 S9 **Bishop** California, W USA
27 S15 **Bishop** Texas, SW USA
99 L15 **Bishop Auckland** N England, UK
Bishop's Lynn *see* King's Lynn
99 O21 **Bishop's Stortford** E England, UK
23 S12 **Bishopville** South Carolina, SE USA
144 M5 **Bishrī, Jabal** ▲▲ E Syria
169 U4 **Bishui** Heilongjiang, NE China
83 G17 **Bisina, Lake** ***prev.*** Lake Salisbury. ◎ E Uganda
Biskara *see* Biskra
76 L6 **Biskra** ***var.*** Beskra, Biskara. NE Algeria
112 M8 **Biskupiec** ***Ger.*** Bischofsburg. Olsztyn, N Poland
179 Rr15 **Bislig** Mindanao, S Philippines
29 X6 **Bismarck** Missouri, C USA
30 M5 **Bismarck** *state capital* North Dakota, N USA
194 K9 **Bismarck Archipelago** *island group* NE PNG
133 Z16 **Bismarck Plate** *tectonic feature* W Pacific Ocean
194 I12 **Bismarck Range** ▲▲ N PNG
194 J10 **Bismarck Sea** *sea* W Pacific Ocean
143 P15 **Bismil** Dıyarbakır, SE Turkey
45 N6 **Bismuna, Laguna** *lagoon* NE Nicaragua
Bisnulok *see* Phitsanulok
175 T6 **Bisoa, Tanjung** *headland* Pulau Halmahera, N Indonesia
30 K7 **Bison** South Dakota, N USA
95 H17 **Bispfors** Jämtland, C Sweden
78 G13 **Bissau** ● (Guinea-Bissau) W Guinea-Bissau
78 G13 **Bissau** ✕ W Guinea-Bissau
101 M24 **Bissen** Luxembourg, C Luxembourg
78 G12 **Bissorã** W Guinea-Bissau
9 O10 **Bistcho Lake** ◎ Alberta, W Canada
24 G5 **Bistineau, Lake** ⊠ Louisiana, S USA
Bistrica *see* Ilirska Bistrica
118 I9 **Bistrița** ***Ger.*** Bistritz, ***Hung.*** Beszterce; ***prev.*** Nösen. Bistrița-Năsăud, N Romania
118 K10 **Bistrița** ***Ger.*** Bistritz. ≈ NE Romania
118 I9 **Bistrița-Năsăud** ⬖ *county* N Romania
Bistritz *see* Bistrița
Bistritz ober Pernstein *see* Bystřice nad Pernštejnem
158 L11 **Biswān** Uttar Pradesh, N India
112 M7 **Bisztynek** Olsztyn, N Poland
81 E17 **Bitam** Woleu-Ntem, N Gabon
103 D18 **Bitburg** Rheinland-Pfalz, SW Germany
105 U4 **Bitche** Moselle, NE France
80 I11 **Bitkine** Guéra, C Chad
143 R15 **Bitlis** Bitlis, SE Turkey
143 R14 **Bitlis** ⬖ *province* E Turkey
Bitoeng *see* Bitung
115 N20 **Bitola** ***Turk.*** Monastir; ***prev.*** Bitolj. S FYR Macedonia
Bitolj *see* Bitola
109 O17 **Bitonto** ***anc.*** Butuntum. Puglia, SE Italy
79 Q13 **Bitou** ***var.*** Bittou. SE Burkina
161 C20 **Bitra Island** *island* Lakshadweep, India, N Indian Ocean
103 M14 **Bitterfeld** Sachsen-Anhalt, E Germany
34 O9 **Bitterroot Range** ▲▲ Idaho/Montana, NW USA
35 P10 **Bitterroot River** ≈ Montana, NW USA
109 D18 **Bitti** Sardegna, Italy, C Mediterranean Sea
Bittou *see* Bitou
175 S7 **Bitung** ***prev.*** Bitoeng. Sulawesi, C Indonesia
62 I12 **Bituruna** Paraná, S Brazil
79 Y13 **Biu** Borno, E Nigeria
Biumba *see* Byumba
171 H14 **Biwa-ko** ◎ Honshū, SW Japan
176 Y13 **Biwarlaut** Irian Jaya, E Indonesia
29 P10 **Bixby** Oklahoma, C USA
126 H15 **Biya** ≈ S Russian Federation
Biy-Khem *see* Bol'shoy Yenisey
126 H15 **Biysk** Altayskiy Kray, S Russian Federation
170 Ff14 **Bizen** Okayama, Honshū, SW Japan
Bizerta *see* Bizerte
123 K11 **Bizerte** ***Ar.*** Banzart, ***Eng.*** Bizerta. N Tunisia
Bizkaia *see* Vizcaya
94 G2 **Bjargtangar** *headland* W Iceland
Bjärnå *see* Perniö
97 K22 **Bjärnum** Kristianstad, S Sweden
95 I16 **Bjästa** Västernorrland, C Sweden
115 I14 **Bjelašnica** ▲ SE Bosnia and Herzegovina
114 C10 **Bjelolasica** ▲ NW Croatia
114 F8 **Bjelovar** ***Hung.*** Belovár. Bjelovar-Bilogora, N Croatia
114 F8 **Bjelovar-Bilogora** ***off.*** Bjelovarsko-Bilogorska Županija. ⬖ *province* NE Croatia
Bjelovarsko-Bilogorska Županija *see* Bjelovar-Bilogora
94 H10 **Bjerkvik** Nordland, C Norway
97 G21 **Bjerringbro** Viborg, NW Denmark
Bjeshkët e Namuna *see* North Albanian Alps
97 L14 **Björbo** Kopparberg, C Sweden
97 I15 **Bjørkelangen** Akershus, S Norway
97 O14 **Björklinge** Uppsala, C Sweden
95 I14 **Björksele** Västerbotten, N Sweden
95 I16 **Björna** Västernorrland, C Sweden
97 C14 **Bjørnafjorden** *fjord* S Norway
97 L16 **Björneborg** Värmland, C Sweden
Björneborg *see* Pori
97 E14 **Bjornesfjorden** ◎ S Norway
94 M9 **Bjørnevatn** Finnmark, N Norway
207 T13 **Bjørnøya** ***Eng.*** Bear Island. *island* N Norway
95 I15 **Bjurholm** Västerbotten, N Sweden
97 J22 **Bjuv** Malmöhus, S Sweden
78 M12 **Bla** Ségou, W Mali
189 W8 **Blackall** Queensland, E Australia
31 V2 **Black Bay** *lake bay* Minnesota, N USA
29 N9 **Black Bear Creek** ≈ Oklahoma, C USA
99 K17 **Blackburn** NW England, UK
47 W10 **Blackburne** ✕ (Plymouth) E Montserrat
41 T11 **Blackburn, Mount** ▲ Alaska, USA
37 N5 **Black Butte Lake** ⊠ California, W USA
204 J5 **Black Coast** *physical region* Antarctica
9 Q16 **Black Diamond** Alberta, SW Canada
20 K11 **Black Dome** ▲ New York, NE USA
115 L18 **Black Drin** ***Alb.*** Lumi i Drinit të Zi, ***SCr.*** Crni Drim. ≈ Albania/FYR Macedonia
10 D6 **Black Duck** ≈ Ontario, C Canada
31 U4 **Blackduck** Minnesota, N USA
35 R14 **Blackfoot** Idaho, NW USA
35 P9 **Blackfoot River** ≈ Montana, NW USA
Black Forest *see* Schwarzwald
30 J10 **Blackhawk** South Dakota, N USA
30 I10 **Black Hills** ▲▲ South Dakota/Wyoming, N USA
9 T10 **Black Lake** ◎ Saskatchewan, C Canada
33 Q5 **Black Lake** ◎ Michigan, N USA
20 I7 **Black Lake** ◎ New York, NE USA
24 G6 **Black Lake** ⊠ Louisiana, S USA
28 F7 **Black Mesa** ▲ Oklahoma, C USA
23 P10 **Black Mountain** North Carolina, SE USA
37 P13 **Black Mountain** ▲ California, W USA
39 Q2 **Black Mountain** ▲ Colorado, C USA
98 K1 **Black Mountains** ▲▲ SE Wales, UK
38 H10 **Black Mountains** ▲▲ Arizona, SW USA
35 Q16 **Black Pine Peak** ▲ Idaho, NW USA
99 K17 **Blackpool** NW England, UK
39 Q14 **Black Range** ▲▲ New Mexico, SW USA
46 I12 **Black River** W Jamaica
12 J14 **Black River** ≈ Ontario, SE Canada
133 U12 **Black River** ***Chin.*** Babian Jiang, Lixian Jiang, ***Fr.*** Rivière Noire, ***Vtn.*** Sông Đa. ≈ China/Vietnam
46 I12 **Black River** ≈ W Jamaica
41 T7 **Black River** ≈ Alaska, USA
39 N13 **Black River** ≈ Arizona, SW USA
29 X7 **Black River** ≈ Arkansas/Missouri, C USA
24 I7 **Black River** ≈ Louisiana, S USA
33 S8 **Black River** ≈ Michigan, N USA
33 Q5 **Black River** ≈ Michigan, N USA
20 I8 **Black River** ≈ New York, NE USA
23 T13 **Black River** ≈ South Carolina, SE USA
32 J7 **Black River** ≈ Wisconsin, N USA
32 J7 **Black River Falls** Wisconsin, N USA
37 R3 **Black Rock Desert** *desert* Nevada, W USA
Black Sand Desert *see* Garagumy
23 S7 **Blacksburg** Virginia, NE USA
142 H10 **Black Sea** ***var.*** Euxine Sea, ***Bul.*** Cherno More, ***Rom.*** Marea Neagră, ***Rus.*** Chernoye More, ***Turk.*** Karadeniz, ***Ukr.*** Chorne More. *sea* Asia/Europe
119 Q10 **Black Sea Lowland** ***Ukr.*** Prychornomors'ka Nyzovyna. *depression* SE Europe
35 S17 **Blacks Fork** ≈ Wyoming, C USA
25 V7 **Blackshear** Georgia, SE USA
25 S6 **Blackshear, Lake** ⊠ Georgia, SE USA
99 A16 **Blacksod Bay** ***Ir.*** Cuan an Fhóid Duibh. *inlet* W Ireland
23 V7 **Blackstone** Virginia, NE USA
79 O14 **Black Volta** ***var.*** Borongo, Mouhoun, Moun Hou, ***Fr.*** Volta Noire. ≈ W Africa
25 O5 **Black Warrior River** ≈ Alabama, S USA
189 X8 **Blackwater** Queensland, E Australia
99 D20 **Blackwater** ***Ir.*** An Abhainn Mhór. ≈ S Ireland
29 T4 **Blackwater River** ≈ Missouri, C USA
23 W7 **Blackwater River** ≈ Virginia, NE USA
Blackwater State *see* Nebraska
29 N8 **Blackwell** Oklahoma, C USA
27 P7 **Blackwell** Texas, SW USA
101 J15 **Bladel** Noord-Brabant, S Netherlands
Bladenmarkt *see* Bălăușeri
116 G11 **Blagoevgrad** ***prev.*** Gorna Dzhumaya. Sofiyska Oblast, W Bulgaria
126 Gg14 **Blagoveshchenka** Altayskiy Kray, S Russian Federation
126 M16 **Blagoveshchensk** Amurskaya Oblast', SE Russian Federation
131 V4 **Blagoveshchensk** Respublika Bashkortostan, W Russian Federation
104 I7 **Blain** Loire-Atlantique, NW France
31 V8 **Blaine** Minnesota, N USA
34 H6 **Blaine** Washington, NW USA
9 T15 **Blaine Lake** Saskatchewan, S Canada
31 S14 **Blair** Nebraska, C USA
98 J10 **Blairgowrie** C Scotland, UK
20 C15 **Blairsville** Pennsylvania, NE USA
118 H11 **Blaj** ***Ger.*** Blasendorf, ***Hung.*** Balázsfalva. Alba, SW Romania
66 F9 **Blake-Bahama Ridge** *undersea feature* W Atlantic Ocean
25 S7 **Blakely** Georgia, SE USA
66 E10 **Blake Plateau** ***var.*** Blake Terrace. *undersea feature* W Atlantic Ocean
32 M1 **Blake Point** *headland* Michigan, N USA
Blake Terrace *see* Blake Plateau
63 B24 **Blanca, Bahía** *bay* E Argentina
58 C12 **Blanca, Cordillera** ▲▲ W Peru
107 T12 **Blanca, Costa** *physical region* SE Spain
39 S7 **Blanca Peak** ▲ Colorado, C USA
26 I9 **Blanca, Sierra** ▲ Texas, SW USA
123 K11 **Blanc, Cap** *headland* N Tunisia
Blanc, Cap *see* Nouâdhibou, Râs
33 R12 **Blanchard River** ≈ Ohio, N USA
190 E8 **Blanche, Cape** *headland* South Australia
195 U15 **Blanche Channel** *channel* NW Solomon Islands
190 J4 **Blanche, Lake** ◎ South Australia
33 R14 **Blanchester** Ohio, N USA
190 J9 **Blanchetown** South Australia
47 U13 **Blanchisseuse** Trinidad, Trinidad and Tobago
105 T11 **Blanc, Mont** ***It.*** Monte Bianco. ▲ France/Italy
27 R11 **Blanco** Texas, SW USA
44 K14 **Blanco, Cabo** *headland* NW Costa Rica
34 D14 **Blanco, Cape** *headland* Oregon, NW USA
64 H10 **Blanco, Río** ≈ W Argentina
58 F10 **Blanco, Río** ≈ NE Peru
13 O9 **Blanc, Réservoir** ⊠ Québec, SE Canada
23 R7 **Bland** Virginia, NE USA
94 I2 **Blanda** ≈ N Iceland
39 O7 **Blanding** Utah, W USA
107 X5 **Blanes** Cataluña, NE Spain
105 N3 **Blangy-sur-Bresle** Seine-Maritime, N France
113 C18 **Blanice** ***Ger.*** Blanitz. ≈ SE Czech Republic
Blanitz *see* Blanice
101 C16 **Blankenberge** West-Vlaanderen, NW Belgium
103 D17 **Blankenheim** Nordrhein-Westfalen, W Germany
27 R8 **Blanket** Texas, SW USA
57 O3 **Blanquilla, Isla** ***var.*** La Blanquilla. *island* N Venezuela
Blanquilla, La *see* Blanquilla, Isla
63 F18 **Blanquillo** Durazno, C Uruguay
113 G18 **Blansko** ***Ger.*** Blanz. Jižní Morava, SE Czech Republic
85 N15 **Blantyre** ***var.*** Blantyre-Limbe. Southern, S Malawi
85 N15 **Blantyre** ✕ Southern, S Malawi
Blantyre-Limbe *see* Blantyre
Blanz *see* Blansko
100 J10 **Blaricum** Noord-Holland, C Netherlands
Blasendorf *see* Blaj
Blatnitsa *see* Durankulak
115 F15 **Blato** ***It.*** Blatta. Dubrovnik-Neretva, S Croatia
Blatta *see* Blato
110 E10 **Blatten** Valais, SW Switzerland
103 J20 **Blaufelden** Baden-Württemberg, SW Germany
97 E23 **Blåvands Huk** *headland* W Denmark
104 G6 **Blavet** ≈ NW France
104 J12 **Blaye** Gironde, SW France
191 R8 **Blayney** New South Wales, SE Australia
67 D25 **Bleaker Island** *island* SE Falkland Islands
111 T10 **Bled** ***Ger.*** Veldes. NW Slovenia
101 D20 **Bléharies** Hainaut, SW Belgium
111 U9 **Bleiburg** ***Slvn.*** Pliberk. Kärnten, S Austria
103 L17 **Bleiloch-Stausee** ⊠ C Germany
100 H12 **Bleiswijk** Zuid-Holland, W Netherlands
97 L22 **Blekinge** ⬖ *county* S Sweden
12 D17 **Blenheim** Ontario, S Canada
193 K15 **Blenheim** Marlborough, South Island, NZ
101 M15 **Blerick** Limburg, SE Netherlands
Blesae *see* Blois
27 V13 **Blessing** Texas, SW USA
12 I10 **Bleu, Lac** ◎ Québec, SE Canada
Blibba *see* Blitta
123 I11 **Blida** ***var.*** El Boulaida, El Boulaïda. N Algeria
97 P15 **Blidö** Stockholm, C Sweden
97 K18 **Blidsberg** Älvsborg, S Sweden
193 A21 **Bligh Sound** *sound* South Island, NZ
197 H13 **Bligh Water** *strait* NW Fiji
12 D11 **Blind River** Ontario, S Canada
33 R11 **Blissfield** Michigan, N USA
174 Ll16 **Blitar** Jawa, C Indonesia
79 R15 **Blitta** ***prev.*** Blibba. C Togo
21 O13 **Block Island** *island* Rhode Island, NE USA
21 O13 **Block Island Sound** *sound* Rhode Island, NE USA
100 H10 **Bloemendaal** Noord-Holland, W Netherlands
85 H23 **Bloemfontein** ***var.*** Mangaung. ● (South Africa-judicial capital) Free State, C South Africa
85 I22 **Bloemhof** North-West, NW South Africa
104 M7 **Blois** ***anc.*** Blesae. Loir-et-Cher, C France
100 L8 **Blokzijl** Overijssel, N Netherlands
97 N20 **Blomstermåla** Kalmar, S Sweden
94 I2 **Blönduós** Nordhurland Vestra, N Iceland
112 L11 **Błonie** Warszawa, C Poland
99 C14 **Bloody Foreland** ***Ir.*** Cnoc Fola. *headland* NW Ireland
33 N15 **Bloomfield** Indiana, N USA
31 X16 **Bloomfield** Iowa, C USA
29 Y8 **Bloomfield** Missouri, C USA
39 P9 **Bloomfield** New Mexico, SW USA
27 U7 **Blooming Grove** Texas, SW USA
31 W10 **Blooming Prairie** Minnesota, N USA
32 L13 **Bloomington** Illinois, N USA
33 O15 **Bloomington** Indiana, N USA
31 V9 **Bloomington** Minnesota, N USA
27 U13 **Bloomington** Texas, SW USA
20 H14 **Bloomsburg** Pennsylvania, NE USA
189 X7 **Bloomsbury** Queensland, NE Australia
174 Ll14 **Blora** Jawa, C Indonesia
20 G12 **Blossburg** Pennsylvania, NE USA
27 V5 **Blossom** Texas, SW USA
127 Oo3 **Blossom, Mys** *headland* Wrangel Island, NE Russian Federation
25 R8 **Blountstown** Florida, SE USA
23 P8 **Blountville** Tennessee, S USA
23 Q9 **Blowing Rock** North Carolina, SE USA
110 J8 **Bludenz** Vorarlberg, W Austria
38 L6 **Blue Bell Knoll** ▲ Utah, W USA
25 Y12 **Blue Cypress Lake** ◎ Florida, SE USA
31 U11 **Blue Earth** Minnesota, N USA
23 Q7 **Bluefield** Virginia, NE USA
23 R7 **Bluefield** West Virginia, NE USA
45 N10 **Bluefields** Región Autónoma Atlántico Sur, SE Nicaragua
45 N10 **Bluefields, Bahía de** *bay* W Caribbean Sea
31 Z14 **Blue Grass** Iowa, C USA
Bluegrass State *see* Kentucky
Blue Hen State *see* Delaware
21 S7 **Blue Hill** Maine, NE USA
31 P16 **Blue Hill** Nebraska, C USA
32 J5 **Blue Hills** *hill range* Wisconsin, N USA
36 L3 **Blue Lake** California, W USA
Blue Law State *see* Connecticut
39 Q6 **Blue Mesa Reservoir** ⊠ Colorado, C USA
29 S12 **Blue Mountain** ▲ Arkansas, C USA
21 O6 **Blue Mountain** ▲ New Hampshire, NE USA
20 K8 **Blue Mountain** ▲ New York, NE USA
20 H15 **Blue Mountain** *ridge* Pennsylvania, NE USA
46 H10 **Blue Mountain Peak** ▲ E Jamaica
191 S8 **Blue Mountains** ▲▲ New South Wales, SE Australia
34 L11 **Blue Mountains** ▲▲ Oregon/Washington, NW USA
82 G12 **Blue Nile** ⬖ *state* E Sudan
82 H12 **Blue Nile** ***var.*** Abai, Bahr el Azraq, ***Amh.*** Ābay Wenz, ***Ar.*** An Nīl al Azraq. ≈ Ethiopia/Sudan
15 Hh4 **Bluenose Lake** ◎ Northwest Territories, NW Canada
29 O3 **Blue Rapids** Kansas, C USA
25 S1 **Blue Ridge** Georgia, SE USA
19 Q10 **Blue Ridge** ***var.*** Blue Ridge Mountains. ▲▲ North Carolina/Virginia, E USA
25 S1 **Blue Ridge Lake** ⊠ Georgia, SE USA
Blue Ridge Mountains *see* Blue Ridge
9 N15 **Blue River** British Columbia, SW Canada
29 O12 **Blue River** ≈ Oklahoma, C USA
29 R4 **Blue Springs** Missouri, C USA
23 R6 **Bluestone Lake** ⊠ West Virginia, NE USA
193 C25 **Bluff** Southland, South Island, NZ
39 O8 **Bluff** Utah, W USA
23 P8 **Bluff City** Tennessee, S USA
67 E24 **Bluff Cove** East Falkland, Falkland Islands
27 S7 **Bluff Dale** Texas, SW USA
191 N15 **Bluff Hill Point** *headland* Tasmania, SE Australia
33 Q12 **Bluffton** Indiana, N USA
33 R12 **Bluffton** Ohio, N USA
27 T7 **Blum** Texas, SW USA
103 G24 **Blumberg** Baden-Württemberg, SW Germany
62 K13 **Blumenau** Santa Catarina, S Brazil
31 N9 **Blunt** South Dakota, N USA
34 H15 **Bly** Oregon, NW USA
41 R13 **Blying Sound** *sound* Alaska, USA
99 M14 **Blyth** N England, UK
37 Y16 **Blythe** California, W USA
29 Y9 **Blytheville** Arkansas, C USA
119 V7 **Blyznyuky** Kharkivs'ka Oblast', E Ukraine
78 I15 **Bo** S Sierra Leone
97 G16 **Bø** Telemark, S Norway
179 Pp11 **Boac** Marinduque, N Philippines
44 K10 **Boaco** Boaco, S Nicaragua
44 J10 **Boaco** ⬖ *department* C Nicaragua
81 I15 **Boali** Ombella-Mpoko, SW Central African Republic
Boalsert *see* Bolsward
194 K13 **Boana** Morobe, C PNG
195 Q10 **Boang Island** *island* Tanga Islands, NE PNG
33 V12 **Boardman** Ohio, N USA
34 J11 **Boardman** Oregon, NW USA
12 F13 **Boat Lake** ◎ Ontario, S Canada
60 F10 **Boa Vista** *state capital* Roraima, NW Brazil
78 D9 **Boa Vista** *island* Ilhas de Barlavento, E Cape Verde
25 Q2 **Boaz** Alabama, S USA
166 L15 **Bobai** Guangxi Zhuangzu Zizhiqu, S China
180 J1 **Bobaomby, Tanjona** ***Fr.*** Cap d'Ambre. *headland* N Madagascar
161 M14 **Bobbili** Andhra Pradesh, E India
108 D9 **Bobbio** Emilia-Romagna, C Italy
12 I14 **Bobcaygeon** Ontario, SE Canada
Bober *see* Bóbr
105 O5 **Bobigny** Seine-St-Denis, N France
79 N13 **Bobo-Dioulasso** SW Burkina
112 G8 **Bobolice** ***Ger.*** Bublitz. Koszalin, NW Poland
175 T7 **Bobopayo** Pulau Halmahera, E Indonesia
153 P13 **Bobotogh, Qatorkŭhi** ***Rus.*** Khrebet Babatag. ▲▲ Tajikistan/Uzbekistan
116 G10 **Bobovdol** Sofiyska Oblast, W Bulgaria
121 M15 **Bobr** Minskaya Voblasts', NW Belarus
121 M15 **Bobr** ≈ C Belarus
113 E14 **Bóbr** ***Eng.*** Bobrawa, ***Ger.*** Bober. ≈ SW Poland
Bobrawa *see* Bóbr
Bobrik *see* Bobryk
Bobrinets *see* Bobrynets'
Bobrka/Bóbrka *see* Bibrka
130 L8 **Bobrov** Voronezhskaya Oblast', W Russian Federation
119 Q4 **Bobrovytsya** Chernihivs'ka Oblast', N Ukraine
Bobruysk *see* Babruysk
121 J19 **Bobryk** ***Rus.*** Bobrik. ≈ SW Belarus
119 Q8 **Bobrynets'** ***Rus.*** Bobrinets. Kirovohrads'ka Oblast', C Ukraine
12 K14 **Bobs Lake** ◎ Ontario, SE Canada
56 I6 **Bobures** Zulia, NW Venezuela
44 H1 **Boca Bacalar Chico** *headland* N Belize
114 G11 **Bočac** NW Bosnia and Herzegovina
43 R14 **Boca del Río** Veracruz-Llave, S Mexico
57 O4 **Boca de Pozo** Nueva Esparta, NE Venezuela
61 C15 **Boca do Acre** Amazonas, N Brazil
57 N12 **Boca Mavaca** Amazonas, S Venezuela
81 G14 **Bocaranga** Ouham-Pendé, W Central African Republic
25 Z15 **Boca Raton** Florida, SE USA
45 P14 **Bocas del Toro** Bocas del Toro, NW Panama
45 P15 **Bocas del Toro** ***off.*** Provincia de Bocas del Toro. ⬖ *province* NW Panama
45 P15 **Bocas del Toro, Archipiélago de** *island group* NW Panama
44 L7 **Bocay** Jinotega, N Nicaragua
107 N6 **Boceguillas** Castilla-León, N Spain
Bocheykovo *see* Bacheykava
113 L17 **Bochnia** Tarnów, SE Poland
101 K16 **Bocholt** Limburg, NE Belgium
103 D14 **Bocholt** Nordrhein-Westfalen, W Germany

◆ Country
● Country Capital
◇ Dependent Territory
○ Dependent Territory Capital
⬖ Administrative Region
✕ International Airport
▲ Mountain
▲▲ Mountain Range
Ѫ Volcano
≈ River
◎ Lake
⊠ Reservoir

103 E15 **Bochum** Nordrhein-Westfalen, W Germany
104 F2 **Bocognano** Corse, France, C Mediterranean Sea
56 I6 **Boconó** Trujillo, NW Venezuela
118 F12 **Bocşa** *Ger.* Bokschen, *Hung.* Boksánbánya. Caraş-Severin, SW Romania
81 H15 **Boda** Lobaye, SW Central African Republic
96 L12 **Boda** Kopparberg, C Sweden
97 O20 **Böda** Kalmar, S Sweden
97 L19 **Bodafors** Jönköping, S Sweden
126 Kk13 **Bodaybo** Irkutskaya Oblast', E Russian Federation
24 G5 **Bodcau, Bayou** *var.* Bodcau Creek. ~ Louisiana, S USA
Bodcau Creek *see* Bodcau, Bayou
46 D8 **Bodden Town** *var.* Boddentown. Grand Cayman, SW Cayman Islands
103 K14 **Bode** ~ C Germany
36 L7 **Bodega Head** *headland* California, W USA
Bodegas *see* Babahoyo
100 H11 **Bodegraven** Zuid-Holland, C Netherlands
80 H8 **Bodélé** *depression* W Chad
94 J13 **Boden** Norrbotten, N Sweden
Bodensee *see* Constance, Lake, C Europe
67 M15 **Bode Verde Fracture Zone** *tectonic feature* E Atlantic Ocean
161 H14 **Bodhan** Andhra Pradesh, C India
168 I9 **Bodĭ** Bayanhongor, C Mongolia
161 H22 **Bodinäyakkanür** Tamil Nādu, SE India
110 H10 **Bodio** Ticino, S Switzerland
99 I24 **Bodmin** SW England, UK
99 I24 **Bodmin Moor** *moorland* SW England, UK
94 G12 **Bodø** Nordland, C Norway
61 H20 **Bodoquena, Serra da** ▲▲ SW Brazil
142 B16 **Bodrum** Muğla, SW Turkey
Bodzafordulő *see* Întorsura Buzăului
101 L14 **Boekel** Noord-Brabant, SE Netherlands
Boeloekoemba *see* Bulukumba
105 Q11 **Boën** Loire, E France
81 K18 **Boende** Equateur, C Zaire
27 R11 **Boerne** Texas, SW USA
Boeroe *see* Buru, Pulau
Boetoeng *see* Buton, Pulau
24 I5 **Boeuf River** ~ Arkansas/ Louisiana, S USA
78 H14 **Boffa** Guinée-Maritime, W Guinea
Bó Finne, Inis *see* Inishbofin
Boga *see* Bogë
177 Ff9 **Bogale** Irrawaddy, SW Myanmar
24 L8 **Bogalusa** Louisiana, S USA
79 Q12 **Bogandé** C Burkina
81 I15 **Bogangolo** Ombella-Mpoko, C Central African Republic
191 Q7 **Bogan River** ~ New South Wales, SE Australia
27 W5 **Bogata** Texas, SW USA
113 D14 **Bogatynia** *Ger.* Reichenau. Jelenia Góra, SW Poland
142 K13 **Boğazlıyan** Yozgat, C Turkey
81 J17 **Bogbonga** Equateur, NW Zaire
164 J14 **Bogcang Zangbo** ~ W China
164 L5 **Bogda Feng** ▲ NW China
116 I9 **Bogdan** ▲ C Bulgaria
115 Q20 **Bogdanci** SE FYR Macedonia
164 M5 **Bogda Shan** *var.* Po-ko-to Shan. ▲▲ NW China
115 K17 **Bogë** *var.* Boga. Shkodër, N Albania
Bogendorf *see* Łuków
97 G23 **Bogense** Fyn, C Denmark
191 T3 **Boggabilla** New South Wales, SE Australia
191 S6 **Boggabri** New South Wales, SE Australia
194 I10 **Bogia** Madang, N PNG
99 N23 **Bognor Regis** SE England, UK
179 Qq13 **Bogo** Cebu, C Philippines
Bogodukhov *see* Bohodukhiv
189 V15 **Bogong, Mount** ▲ Victoria, SE Australia
174 J14 **Bogor** *Dut.* Buitenzorg. Jawa, C Indonesia
130 L5 **Bogoroditsk** Tul'skaya Oblast', W Russian Federation
131 O3 **Bogorodsk** Nizhegorodskaya Oblast', W Russian Federation
Bogorodskoje *see* Bogorodskoye
127 Nn14 **Bogorodskoye** Khabarovskiy Kray, SE Russian Federation
129 R15 **Bogorodskoye** *var.* Bogorodskoje. Kirovskaya Oblast', NW Russian Federation
56 F10 **Bogotá** *prev.* Santa Fe, Santa Fe de Bogotá. ● (Colombia) Cundinamarca, C Colombia
159 T14 **Bogra** Rajshahi, N Bangladesh
Bogschan *see* Boldu
126 Ii13 **Boguchany** Krasnoyarskiy Kray, C Russian Federation
130 M9 **Boguchar** Voronezhskaya Oblast', W Russian Federation
78 H10 **Bogué** Brakna, SW Mauritania
24 K8 **Bogue Chitto** ~ Louisiana/Mississippi, S USA
Bogushëvsk *see* Bahushewsk
Boguslav *see* Bohuslav
46 K12 **Bog Walk** C Jamaica
167 Q3 **Bo Hai** *var.* Gulf of Chihli. *gulf* NE China
167 R3 **Bohai Haixia** *strait* NE China
167 Q3 **Bohai Wan** *bay* NE China
113 C17 **Bohemia** *Cz.* Čechy, *Ger.* Böhmen. *cultural and historical region* W Czech Republic
113 B18 **Bohemian Forest** *Cz.* Ceský Les, Šumava, *Ger.* Böhmerwald. ▲▲ C Europe
Bohemian-Moravian Highlands *see* Českomoravská Vrchovina
79 R16 **Bohicon** S Benin
111 S11 **Bohinjska Bistrica** *Ger.* Wocheiner Feistritz. NW Slovenia
Bohkká *see* Pokka
Böhmen *see* Bohemia
Böhmerwald *see* Bohemian Forest
Böhmisch-Krumau *see* Český Krumlov
Böhmisch-Leipa *see* Česká Lípa
Böhmisch-Mährische Höhe *see* Českomoravská Vrchovina
Böhmisch-Trübau *see* Česká Třebová
119 U5 **Bohodukhiv** *Rus.* Bogodukhov. Kharkivs'ka Oblast', E Ukraine
179 Qq14 **Bohol** *island* C Philippines
179 Qq15 **Bohol Sea** *var.* Mindanao Sea. *sea* S Philippines
118 I7 **Bohorodchany** Ivano-Frankivs'ka Oblast', W Ukraine
168 M9 **Bohöt** Dundgovĭ, C Mongolia
164 K6 **Bohu** *var.* Bagrax. Xinjiang Uygur Zizhiqu, NW China
113 I17 **Bohumín** *Ger.* Oderberg; *prev.* Neuoderberg, Nový Bohumín. Severní Morava, E Czech Republic
119 P6 **Bohuslav** *Rus.* Boguslav. Kyyivs'ka Oblast', N Ukraine
60 F11 **Boiaçu** Roraima, N Brazil
109 K16 **Boiano** Molise, C Italy
13 R8 **Boilleau** Québec, SE Canada
61 O17 **Boipeba, Ilha de** *island* SE Brazil
106 G3 **Boiro** Galicia, NW Spain
33 Q5 **Bois Blanc Island** *island* Michigan, N USA
31 R7 **Bois de Sioux River** ~ Minnesota, N USA
35 N14 **Boise** *var.* Boise City. *state capital* Idaho, NW USA
28 G8 **Boise City** Oklahoma, C USA
35 N14 **Boise River, Middle Fork** ~ Idaho, NW USA
Bois, Lac des *see* Woods, Lake of the
Bois-le-Duc *see* 's-Hertogenbosch
9 W17 **Boissevain** Manitoba, S Canada
13 T7 **Boisvert, Pointe au** *headland* Québec, SE Canada
102 K10 **Boizenburg** Mecklenburg-Vorpommern, N Germany
Bojador *see* Boujdour
115 K18 **Bojana** *Alb.* Bunë. ~ Albania/ Yugoslavia *see also* Bunë
149 S3 **Bojnūrd** *var.* Bujnurd. Khorāsān, N Iran
174 Ll15 **Bojonegoro** *prev.* Bodjonegoro. Jawa, C Indonesia
201 T1 **Bokaak Atoll** *var.* Bokak, Taongi. *atoll* Ratak Chain, NE Marshall Islands
Bokak *see* Bokaak Atoll
159 Q15 **Bokāro** Bihār, N India
81 I18 **Bokatola** Equateur, NW Zaire
78 H13 **Boké** Guinée-Maritime, W Guinea
Bokhara *see* Bukhoro
191 Q4 **Bokhara River** ~ New South Wales/Queensland, SE Australia
Bo Kheo *see* Bâ Kêv
97 C16 **Boknafjorden** *fjord* S Norway
80 H11 **Bokoro** Chari-Baguirmi, W Chad
81 K19 **Bokota** Equateur, NW Zaire
178 Gg13 **Bokpyin** Tenasserim, S Myanmar
Boksánbánya/ Bokschen *see* Bocşa
85 F21 **Bokspits** Kgalagadi, SW Botswana
81 K18 **Bokungu** Equateur, C Zaire
Bokurdak *see* Bakhardok
80 G10 **Bol** Lac, W Chad
175 Qq9 **Bolaang** Sulawesi, N Indonesia
78 G13 **Bolama** SW Guinea-Bissau
Bolangir *see* Balāngīr
Bolanos *see* Bolaños, Mount, Guam
Bolaños *see* Bolaños de Calatrava, Spain
107 N11 **Bolaños de Calatrava** *var.* Bolaños. Castilla-La Mancha, C Spain
196 B17 **Bolanos, Mount** *var.* Bolaños. ▲ S Guam
42 L12 **Bolaños, Río** ~ C Mexico
117 M14 **Bolayır** Çanakkale, NW Turkey
104 L3 **Bolbec** Seine-Maritime, N France
118 L13 **Boldu** *var.* Bogschan. Buzău, SE Romania
152 H8 **Boldumsaz** *prev.* Kalinin, Kalininsk, Porsy. Dashkhovuzskiy Velayat, N Turkmenistan
164 I4 **Bole** *var.* Bortala. Xinjiang Uygur Zizhiqu, NW China
79 O15 **Bole** NW Ghana
81 J19 **Boleko** Equateur, W Zaire
113 E14 **Bolesławiec** *Ger.* Bunzlau. Jelenia Góra, SW Poland
131 R4 **Bolgar** *prev.* Kuybyshev. Respublika Tatarstan, W Russian Federation
79 P14 **Bolgatanga** N Ghana
Bolgrad *see* Bolhrad
119 N12 **Bolhrad** *Rus.* Bolgrad. Odes'ka Oblast', SW Ukraine
169 Y8 **Boli** Heilongjiang, NE China
81 I19 **Bolia** Bandundu, W Zaire
95 J14 **Boliden** Västerbotten, N Sweden
176 Uu11 **Bolifar** Pulau Seram, E Indonesia
179 Oo9 **Bolinao** Luzon, N Philippines
29 T6 **Bolivar** Missouri, C USA
22 F10 **Bolivar** Tennessee, S USA
56 C12 **Bolívar** Cauca, SW Colombia
56 F7 **Bolívar** *off.* Departmento de Bolívar. ◆ *province* N Colombia
58 A13 **Bolívar** ◆ *province* C Ecuador
57 N9 **Bolívar** *off.* Estado Bolívar. ◆ *state* SE Venezuela
27 X12 **Bolivar Peninsula** *headland* Texas, SW USA
56 I6 **Bolívar, Pico** ▲ W Venezuela
59 K17 **Bolivia** *off.* Republic of Bolivia. ◆ *republic* W South America
114 O13 **Boljevac** Serbia, E Yugoslavia
Bolkenhain *see* Bolków
130 J5 **Bolkhov** Orlovskaya Oblast', W Russian Federation
113 F14 **Bolków** *Ger.* Bolkenhain. Jelenia Góra, SW Poland
190 K3 **Bollards Lagoon** South Australia
105 R14 **Bollene** Vaucluse, SE France
96 N12 **Bollnäs** Gävleborg, C Sweden
189 W10 **Bollon** Queensland, C Australia
199 Jj14 **Bollons Tablemount** *undersea feature* S Pacific Ocean
95 H17 **Bollstabruk** Västernorrland, C Sweden
Bollulos de Par del Condado *see* Bollullos Par del Condado
106 J14 **Bollullos Par del Condado** *var.* Bolluilos de Par del Condado. Andalucía, S Spain
97 K21 **Bolmen** ◎ S Sweden
143 T10 **Bolnisi** S Georgia
81 H19 **Bolobo** Bandundu, W Zaire
127 N14 **Bolodek** Khabarovskiy Kray, SE Russian Federation
108 G10 **Bologna** Emilia-Romagna, N Italy
128 I15 **Bologoye** Tverskaya Oblast', W Russian Federation
81 J18 **Bolomba** Equateur, NW Zaire
43 X13 **Bolonchén de Rejón** *var.* Bolonchén de Rejón. Campeche, SE Mexico
126 H14 **Bolotnoye** Novosibirskaya Oblast', C Russian Federation
116 J13 **Boloústra, Ákra** *headland* NE Greece
178 Jj10 **Bolovens, Plateau des** *plateau* S Laos
108 H13 **Bolsena** Lazio, C Italy
109 G14 **Bolsena, Lago di** ◎ C Italy
130 B3 **Bol'shakovo** *Ger.* Kreuzingen; *prev.* Gross-Skaisgirren. Kaliningradskaya Oblast', W Russian Federation
126 J6 **Bol'shaya Balakhnya** ~ N Russian Federation
Bol'shaya Berëstovitsa *see* Vyalikaya Byerastavitsa
131 S7 **Bol'shaya Chernigovka** Samarskaya Oblast', W Russian Federation
131 S7 **Bol'shaya Glushitsa** Samarskaya Oblast', W Russian Federation
150 H9 **Bol'shaya Khobda** *Kaz.* Ülkenqobda. ~ Kazakhstan/ Russian Federation
126 Jj8 **Bol'shaya Kuonamka** ~ NE Russian Federation
130 M12 **Bol'shaya Martynovka** Rostovskaya Oblast', SW Russian Federation
126 I13 **Bol'shaya Murta** Krasnoyarskiy Kray, C Russian Federation
129 V4 **Bol'shaya Rogovaya** ~ NW Russian Federation
129 U7 **Bol'shaya Synya** ~ NW Russian Federation
151 V9 **Bol'shaya Vladimirovka** Semipalatinsk, E Kazakhstan
125 G13 **Bol'sherech'ye** Omskaya Oblast', C Russian Federation
127 Pp12 **Bol'sheretsk** Kamchatskaya Oblast', E Russian Federation
131 W3 **Bol'sheust'ikinskoye** Respublika Bashkortostan, W Russian Federation
Bol'shevik *see* Bal'shavik
126 Ii3 **Bol'shevik, Ostrov** *island* Severnaya Zemlya, N Russian Federation
129 U4 **Bol'shezemel'skaya Tundra** *physical region* NW Russian Federation
150 J13 **Bol'shiye Barsuki, Peski** *desert* SW Kazakhstan
125 Ff12 **Bol'shiye Uki** Omskaya Oblast', C Russian Federation
127 O6 **Bol'shoy Anyuy** ~ NE Russian Federation
126 K6 **Bol'shoy Begichev, Ostrov** *island* NE Russian Federation
131 O4 **Bol'shoye Murashkino** Nizhegorodskaya Oblast', W Russian Federation
131 W4 **Bol'shoy Iremel'** ▲ W Russian Federation
131 R7 **Bol'shoy Irgiz** ~ W Russian Federation
126 M5 **Bol'shoy Lyakhovskiy, Ostrov** *island* NE Russian Federation
126 Ll13 **Bol'shoy Nimnyr** Respublika Sakha (Yakutiya), NE Russian Federation
Bol'shoy Rozhan *see* Vyaliki Rozhan
150 E10 **Bol'shoy Uzen'** *Kaz.* Ülkenözen. ~ Kazakhstan/Russian Federation
126 Ii15 **Bol'shoy Yenisey** *var.* Biy-Khem. ~ S Russian Federation
42 K6 **Bolson de Mapimi** ▲▲ NW Mexico
100 K6 **Bolsward** *Fris.* Boalsert. Friesland, N Netherlands
107 T4 **Boltaña** Aragón, NE Spain
12 G15 **Bolton** Ontario, S Canada
99 K17 **Bolton** *prev.* Bolton-le-Moors. NW England, UK
23 V12 **Bolton** North Carolina, SE USA
Bolton-le-Moors *see* Bolton
142 G11 **Bolu** Bolu, NW Turkey
142 G11 **Bolu** ◆ *province* NW Turkey
195 N15 **Bolubolu** Goodenough Island, S PNG
94 H1 **Bolungarvík** Vestfirdhir, NW Iceland
165 O10 **Boluntay** Qinghai, W China
142 F14 **Bolvadin** Afyon, W Turkey
116 M10 **Bolyarovo** *prev.* Pashkeni. Burgaska Oblast, SE Bulgaria
108 G6 **Bolzano** *Ger.* Bozen; *anc.* Bauzanum. Trentino-Alto Adige, N Italy
81 F22 **Boma** Bas-Zaïre, W Zaire
191 R12 **Bombala** New South Wales, SE Australia
106 F10 **Bombarral** Leiria, C Portugal
160 D13 **Bombay** *Guj.* Mumbai. Mahārāshtra, W India
160 D13 **Bombay** × Mahārāshtra, W India
176 Vv11 **Bomberai** ~ Irian Jaya, E Indonesia
176 Vv11 **Bomberai, Jazirah** *peninsula* Irian Jaya, E Indonesia
176 Vv11 **Bomberai, Semenanjung** *headland* Irian Jaya, E Indonesia
83 F18 **Bombo** S Uganda
81 I17 **Bomboma** Equateur, NW Zaire
61 I14 **Bom Futuro** Pará, N Brazil
165 Q15 **Bomi** *var.* Bowo, Zhamo. Xizang Zizhiqu, W China
81 N17 **Bomili** Haut-Zaïre, NE Zaire
61 N17 **Bom Jesus da Lapa** Bahia, E Brazil
62 Q8 **Bom Jesus do Itabapoana** Rio de Janeiro, SE Brazil
97 C15 **Bømlafjorden** *fjord* S Norway
97 B15 **Bømlo** *island* S Norway
126 M14 **Bomnak** Amurskaya Oblast', SE Russian Federation
81 I17 **Bomongo** Equateur, NW Zaire
63 K14 **Bom Retiro** Santa Catarina, S Brazil
81 L15 **Bomu** *var.* Mbomou, Mbomu, M'Bomu. ~ Central African Republic/Zaire
148 J3 **Bonāb** *var.* Benāb, Bunab. Āžarbāyjān-e Khāvarī, N Iran
47 Q16 **Bonaire** *island* E Netherlands Antilles
41 U11 **Bona, Mount** ▲ Alaska, USA
194 M16 **Bonando** ~ SE Papau New Guinea
191 Q12 **Bonang** Victoria, SE Australia
44 L7 **Bonanza** Región Autónoma Atlántico Norte, NE Nicaragua
39 O4 **Bonanza** Utah, W USA
47 O9 **Bonao** C Dominican Republic
188 L3 **Bonaparte Archipelago** *island group* Western Australia
34 K6 **Bonaparte, Mount** ▲ Washington, NW USA
41 N11 **Bonasila Dome** ▲ Alaska, USA
47 T15 **Bonasse** Trinidad, Trinidad and Tobago
13 X7 **Bonaventure** Québec, SE Canada
13 X7 **Bonaventure** ~ Québec, SE Canada
11 V11 **Bonavista** Newfoundland, Newfoundland and Labrador, SE Canada
11 U11 **Bonavista Bay** *inlet* NW Atlantic Ocean
123 Kk11 **Bon, Cap** *headland* N Tunisia
81 E19 **Bonda** Ogooué-Lolo, C Gabon
131 N6 **Bondari** Tambovskaya Oblast', W Russian Federation
108 G9 **Bondeno** Emilia-Romagna, C Italy
32 L4 **Bond Falls Flowage** ◎ Michigan, N USA
81 L16 **Bondo** Haut-Zaïre, N Zaire
175 P17 **Bondokodi** Pulau Sumba, S Indonesia
79 O15 **Bondoukou** E Ivory Coast
Bondoukui/Bondoukuy *see* Boundoukui
174 Mm15 **Bondowoso** Jawa, C Indonesia
35 S14 **Bondurant** Wyoming, C USA
Bone *see* Watampone, Indonesia
Bône *see* Annaba, Algeria
32 I5 **Bone Lake** ◎ Wisconsin, N USA
175 R12 **Bonelipu** Pulau Buton, C Indonesia
175 Q14 **Bonerate, Kepulauan** *var.* Macan. *island group* C Indonesia
175 Pp15 **Bonerate, Pulau** *island* Kepulauan Bonerate, C Indonesia
31 O12 **Bonesteel** South Dakota, N USA
64 I8 **Bonete, Cerro** ▲ N Argentina
175 Pp11 **Bone, Teluk** *bay* Sulawesi, C Indonesia
110 D6 **Bonfol** Jura, NW Switzerland
159 U12 **Bongaigaon** Assam, NE India
81 K17 **Bongandanga** Equateur, NW Zaire
80 L13 **Bongo, Massif des** *var.* Chaîne des Mongos. ▲▲ NE Central African Republic
80 G12 **Bongor** Mayo-Kébbi, SW Chad
79 N16 **Bongouanou** E Ivory Coast
178 Kk11 **Bông Sơn** *var.* Hoai Nhơn. Bình Định, C Vietnam
27 U5 **Bonham** Texas, SW USA
Bonhard *see* Bonyhád
105 U6 **Bonhomme, Col du** *pass* NE France
104 F3 **Bonifacio** Corse, France, C Mediterranean Sea
Bonifacio, Bocche de/Bonifacio, Bouches de *see* Bonifacio, Strait of
104 F3 **Bonifacio, Strait of** *Fr.* Bouches de Bonifacio, *It.* Bocche de Bonifacio. *strait* C Mediterranean Sea
25 Q8 **Bonifay** Florida, SE USA
Bonin Islands *see* Ogasawara-shotō
199 H6 **Bonin Trench** *undersea feature* NW Pacific Ocean
25 W15 **Bonita Springs** Florida, SE USA
44 I5 **Bonito, Pico** ▲ N Honduras
103 E17 **Bonn** Nordrhein-Westfalen, W Germany
94 H11 **Bonnåsjøen** Nordland, C Norway
12 J12 **Bonnechere** Ontario, SE Canada
12 J12 **Bonnechere** ~ Ontario, SE Canada
35 N7 **Bonners Ferry** Idaho, NW USA
29 R4 **Bonner Springs** Kansas, C USA
104 L6 **Bonnétable** Sarthe, NW France
29 X6 **Bonne Terre** Missouri, C USA
8 J5 **Bonnet Plume** ~ Yukon Territory, NW Canada
104 M6 **Bonneval** Eure-et-Loir, C France
105 T10 **Bonneville** Haute-Savoie, E France
38 J3 **Bonneville Salt Flats** *salt flat* Utah, W USA
79 U18 **Bonny** Rivers, S Nigeria
Bonny, Bight of *see* Biafra, Bight of
39 W4 **Bonny Reservoir** ⊟ Colorado, C USA
9 R14 **Bonnyville** Alberta, SW Canada
109 C18 **Bono** Sardegna, Italy, C Mediterranean Sea
176 Xx10 **Bonoi** Irian Jaya, E Indonesia
Bononia *see* Vidin, Bulgaria
Bononia *see* Boulogne-sur-Mer, France
109 B18 **Bonorva** Sardegna, Italy, C Mediterranean Sea
32 M15 **Bonpas Creek** ~ Illinois, N USA
202 I3 **Bonriki** Tarawa, W Kiribati
191 T4 **Bonshaw** New South Wales, SE Australia
78 I16 **Bonthe** SW Sierra Leone
179 P8 **Bontoc** Luzon, N Philippines
194 M16 **Bonua** ~ S PNG
27 Y9 **Bon Wier** Texas, SW USA
113 J25 **Bonyhád** *Ger.* Bonhard. Tolna, S Hungary
Bonzabaai *see* Bonza Bay
85 J25 **Bonza Bay** *Afr.* Bonzabaai. Eastern Cape, S South Africa
190 D7 **Bookabie** South Australia
190 H6 **Bookaloo** South Australia
39 P5 **Book Cliffs** *cliff* Colorado/Utah, W USA
175 T9 **Boo, Kepulauan** *island group* E Indonesia
27 P1 **Booker** Texas, SW USA
78 K15 **Boola** Guinée-Forestière, SE Guinea
191 O8 **Booligal** New South Wales, SE Australia
101 G17 **Boom** Antwerpen, N Belgium
45 N6 **Boom** *var.* Boon. Región Autónoma Atlántico Norte, NE Nicaragua
191 S3 **Boomi** New South Wales, SE Australia
Boon *see* Boom
31 V13 **Boone** Iowa, C USA
23 Q8 **Boone** North Carolina, SE USA
29 S11 **Booneville** Arkansas, C USA
23 N6 **Booneville** Kentucky, S USA
25 N2 **Booneville** Mississippi, S USA
23 V3 **Boonsboro** Maryland, NE USA
168 H9 **Böön Tsagaan Nuur** ◎ S Mongolia
36 L6 **Boonville** California, W USA
33 N16 **Boonville** Indiana, N USA
29 U4 **Boonville** Missouri, C USA
20 I9 **Boonville** New York, NE USA
82 M12 **Boorama** Woqooyi Galbeed, NW Somalia
191 O6 **Booroondarra, Mount** *hill* New South Wales, SE Australia
191 N9 **Booroorban** New South Wales, SE Australia
191 R9 **Boorowa** New South Wales, SE Australia
101 H17 **Boortmeerbeek** Vlaams Brabant, C Belgium
82 P11 **Boosaaso** *var.* Bandar Kassim, Bender Qaasim, Bosaso, *It.* Bender Cassim. Bari, N Somalia
21 Q8 **Boothbay Harbor** Maine, NE USA
Boothia Felix *see* Boothia Peninsula
15 Kk2 **Boothia, Gulf of** *gulf* Northwest Territories, NE Canada
15 K2 **Boothia Peninsula** *prev.* Boothia Felix. *peninsula* Northwest Territories, NE Canada
81 E18 **Booué** Ogooué-Ivindo, NE Gabon
103 J21 **Bopfingen** Baden-Württemberg, S Germany
103 F18 **Boppard** Rheinland-Pfalz, W Germany
64 M4 **Boquerón** *off.* Departamento de Boquerón. ◆ *department* W Paraguay
45 P15 **Boquete** *var.* Bajo Boquete. Chiriquí, W Panama
42 J6 **Boquilla, Presa de la** ⊟ N Mexico
42 L5 **Boquillas** *var.* Boquillas del Carmen. Coahuila de Zaragoza, NE Mexico
Boquillas del Carmen *see* Boquillas
126 I11 **Bor** Krasnoyarskiy Kray, C Russian Federation
83 F15 **Bor** Jonglei, S Sudan
97 L20 **Bor** Jönköping, S Sweden
142 J15 **Bor** Niğde, S Turkey
114 P12 **Bor** Serbia, E Yugoslavia
203 S10 **Bora-Bora** *island* Îles Sous le Vent, W French Polynesia
178 Ii10 **Borabu** Maha Sarakham, E Thailand
35 P13 **Borah Peak** ▲ Idaho, NW USA
Boralday *see* Burunday
97 J19 **Borås** Älvsborg, S Sweden
149 N11 **Borāzjān** *var.* Borazjān. Būshehr, S Iran
Borazjān *see* Borāzjān
60 G13 **Borba** Amazonas, N Brazil
106 H11 **Borba** Évora, S Portugal
Borbetomagus *see* Worms
57 O7 **Borbón** Bolívar, E Venezuela
61 Q15 **Borborema, Planalto da** *plateau* NE Brazil
118 M14 **Borcea, Braţul** ~ S Romania
Borchalo *see* Marneuli
205 R15 **Borchgrevink Coast** *physical region* Antarctica
143 Q11 **Borçka** Artvin, NE Turkey
100 N11 **Borculo** Gelderland, E Netherlands
190 G10 **Borda, Cape** *headland* South Australia
104 K13 **Bordeaux** *anc.* Burdigala. Gironde, SW France
9 T15 **Borden** Saskatchewan, S Canada
12 D8 **Borden Lake** ◎ Ontario, S Canada
15 L1 **Borden Peninsula** *peninsula* Baffin Island, Northwest Territories, NE Canada
190 K11 **Bordertown** South Australia
94 H2 **Bordheyri** Vestfirdhir, NW Iceland
108 B11 **Bordighera** Liguria, NW Italy
76 K5 **Bordj-Bou-Arreridj** *var.* Bordj Bou Arreridj, Bordj Bou Arréridj. N Algeria
123 I10 **Bordj El Bahri, Cap de** *headland* N Algeria
76 L10 **Bordj Omar Driss** E Algeria
149 N13 **Bord Khūn** Hormozgān, S Iran
153 V7 **Bordunskiy** Chuyskaya Oblast', N Kyrgyzstan
97 M17 **Borensberg** Östergötland, S Sweden
Borgå *see* Porvoo
94 L2 **Borgarfjördhur** Austurland, NE Iceland
94 H3 **Borgarnes** Vesturland, W Iceland
95 G14 **Børgefjellet** ▲ C Norway
100 O7 **Borger** Drenthe, NE Netherlands
27 N2 **Borger** Texas, SW USA
97 N20 **Borgholm** Kalmar, S Sweden
109 N22 **Borgia** Calabria, SW Italy
101 J18 **Borgloon** Limburg, NE Belgium
205 P2 **Borg Massif** ▲▲ Antarctica
24 L9 **Borgne, Lake** ◎ Louisiana, S USA
108 C7 **Borgomanero** Piemonte, NE Italy
108 G10 **Borgo Panigale** × (Bologna) Emilia-Romagna, N Italy
109 J15 **Borgorose** Lazio, C Italy
108 A9 **Borgo San Dalmazzo** Piemonte, N Italy
108 G11 **Borgo San Lorenzo** Toscana, C Italy
108 C7 **Borgosesia** Piemonte, NE Italy
108 E9 **Borgo Val di Taro** Emilia-Romagna, C Italy
108 G6 **Borgo Valsugana** Trentino-Alto Adige, N Italy
169 O11 **Borhoyn Tal** Dornogovĭ, SE Mongolia
178 Ii8 **Borikhan** *var.* Borikhane. Bolikhamxai, C Laos
Borikhane *see* Borikhan
Borislav *see* Boryslav
131 N8 **Borisoglebsk** Voronezhskaya Oblast', W Russian Federation
Borisov *see* Barysaw
Borisovgrad *see* Pŭrvomay
Borispol' *see* Boryspil'
180 I3 **Boriziny** Mahajanga, NW Madagascar
107 Q5 **Borja** Aragón, NE Spain
Borjas Blancas *see* Les Borges Blanques
143 S10 **Borjomi** *Rus.* Borzhomi. C Georgia
120 L12 **Borkavichy** *Rus.* Borkovichi. Vitsyebskaya Voblasts', N Belarus
103 H16 **Borken** Hessen, C Germany
103 E14 **Borken** Nordrhein-Westfalen, W Germany
94 H10 **Borkenes** Troms, N Norway
80 H7 **Borkou-Ennedi-Tibesti** *off.* Préfecture du Borkou-Ennedi-Tibesti. ◆ *prefecture* N Chad
Borkovichi *see* Borkavichy
102 E9 **Borkum** *island* NW Germany
83 K17 **Bor, Lagh** *var.* Lak Bor. *dry watercourse* NE Kenya
Bor, Lak *see* Bor, Lagh
97 M14 **Borlänge** Kopparberg, C Sweden
108 C9 **Bormida** ~ NW Italy
108 F6 **Bormio** Lombardia, N Italy
103 M16 **Borna** Sachsen, E Germany
100 O10 **Borne** Overijssel, E Netherlands
101 F17 **Bornem** Antwerpen, N Belgium
174 M6 **Borneo** *island* Brunei/Indonesia/Malaysia
103 E16 **Bornheim** Nordrhein-Westfalen, W Germany
97 L24 **Bornholm** ◆ *county* E Denmark
97 L24 **Bornholm** *island* E Denmark
79 Y13 **Borno** ◆ *state* NE Nigeria
106 K15 **Bornos** Andalucía, S Spain
168 L7 **Bornuur** Töv, C Mongolia
126 I14 **Borodino** Krasnoyarskiy Kray, S Russian Federation
119 O4 **Borodyanka** Kyyivs'ka Oblast', N Ukraine
126 M10 **Borogontsy** Respublika Sakha (Yakutiya), NE Russian Federation
164 I5 **Borohoro Shan** ▲▲ NW China
79 O13 **Boromo** SW Burkina
37 T13 **Boron** California, W USA
179 R12 **Borongan** Samar, C Philippines
Borongo *see* Black Volta
Boron'ki *see* Baron'ki
Borosjenő *see* Ineu
Borossebes *see* Sebiş
78 L15 **Borotou** NW Ivory Coast
119 W6 **Borova** Kharkivs'ka Oblast', E Ukraine
116 H8 **Borovan** Oblast Montana, NW Bulgaria
128 I14 **Borovichi** Novgorodskaya Oblast', W Russian Federation
Borovlje *see* Ferlach
114 J9 **Borovo** Vukovar-Srijem, NE Croatia
151 Q7 **Borovoye** *Kaz.* Būrabay. Kokshetau, N Kazakhstan
130 K4 **Borovsk** Kaluzhskaya Oblast', W Russian Federation
125 F12 **Borovskiy** Tyumenskaya Oblast', C Russian Federation
151 N7 **Borovskoy** Kustanay, N Kazakhstan
Borovukha *see* Baravukha
97 L23 **Borrby** Kristianstad, S Sweden
189 R3 **Borroloola** Northern Territory, N Australia
118 F9 **Bors** Bihor, NW Romania
118 I9 **Borşa** *Hung.* Borsa. Maramureş, N Romania
118 J10 **Borsec** *Ger.* Bad Borseck, *Hung.* Borszék. Harghita, C Romania
94 K8 **Børselv** Finnmark, N Norway
115 L23 **Borsh** *var.* Borshi. Vlorë, S Albania
Borshchev *see* Borshchiv
118 K7 **Borshchiv** *Pol.* Borszczów, *Rus.* Borshchev. Ternopil's'ka Oblast', W Ukraine
Borshi *see* Borsh
113 L20 **Borsod-Abaúj-Zemplén** *off.* Borsod-Abaúj-Zemplén Megye. ◆ *county* NE Hungary
101 E15 **Borssele** Zeeland, SW Netherlands
Borszczów *see* Borshchiv
Borszék *see* Borsec
Bortala *see* Bole
105 O12 **Bort-les-Orgues** Corrèze, C France
Bor u České Lípy *see* Nový Bor
168 E8 **Bor-Udzüür** Hovd, W Mongolia
149 N9 **Borūjen** Chahār Maḩall va Bakhtiārī, C Iran
148 L7 **Borūjerd** *var.* Burujird. Lorestān, W Iran
118 H6 **Boryslav** *Pol.* Borysław, *Rus.* Borislav. L'vivs'ka Oblast', NW Ukraine
Borysław *see* Boryslav
119 P4 **Boryspil'** *Rus.* Borispol'. Kyyivs'ka Oblast', N Ukraine
119 P4 **Boryspil'** *Rus.* Borispol'. × (Kyyiv) Kyyivs'ka Oblast', N Ukraine
Borzhomi *see* Borjomi
119 R3 **Borzna** Chernihivs'ka Oblast', NE Ukraine
126 L16 **Borzya** Chitinskaya Oblast', S Russian Federation
109 B18 **Bosa** Sardegna, Italy, C Mediterranean Sea
114 F10 **Bosanska Dubica** NW Bosnia and Herzegovina
114 G10 **Bosanska Gradiška** N Bosnia and Herzegovina
114 F10 **Bosanska Kostajnica** NW Bosnia and Herzegovina
114 E11 **Bosanska Krupa** NW Bosnia and Herzegovina
114 H10 **Bosanski Brod** N Bosnia and Herzegovina
114 E10 **Bosanski Novi** NW Bosnia and Herzegovina
114 E11 **Bosanski Petrovac** NW Bosnia and Herzegovina
114 I10 **Bosanski Šamac** N Bosnia and Herzegovina
114 E12 **Bosansko Grahovo** W Bosnia and Herzegovina
Bosaso *see* Boosaaso
194 G13 **Bosavi, Mount** ⛰ W PNG
166 J14 **Bose** Guangxi Zhuangzu Zizhiqu, S China
167 Q5 **Boshan** Shandong, E China
115 P16 **Bosilegrad** *prev.* Bosiljgrad. Serbia, SE Yugoslavia
Bosiljgrad *see* Bosilegrad
Bösing *see* Pezinok
100 H12 **Boskoop** Zuid-Holland, C Netherlands
113 G18 **Boskovice** *Ger.* Boskowitz. Jižní Morava, SE Czech Republic
Boskowitz *see* Boskovice
114 I10 **Bosna** ~ N Bosnia and Herzegovina
176 X9 **Bosnabraidi** Irian Jaya, E Indonesia
114 H12 **Bosnia and Herzegovina** *off.* Republic of Bosnia and Herzegovina. ◆ *republic* SE Europe
81 J16 **Bosobolo** Equateur, NW Zaire
171 K17 **Bōsō-hantō** *peninsula* Honshū, S Japan
Bosora *see* Buşrá ash Shām
Bosphorus/Bosporus *see* İstanbul Boğazı
Bosporus Cimmerius *see* Kerch Strait
Bosporus Thracius *see* İstanbul Boğazı
Bosra *see* Buşrá ash Shām
81 H14 **Bossangoa** Ouham, C Central African Republic
Bossé Bangou *see* Bossey Bangou
81 I15 **Bossembélé** Ombella-Mpoko, C Central African Republic
81 H15 **Bossentélé** Ouham-Pendé, W Central African Republic
79 R12 **Bossey Bangou** *var.* Bossé Bangou. Tillabéri, SW Niger
24 G5 **Bossier City** Louisiana, S USA
85 D20 **Bossiesvlei** Hardap, S Namibia
79 Y11 **Bosso** Diffa, SE Niger
63 F15 **Bossoroca** Rio Grande do Sul, S Brazil
164 J10 **Bostan** Xinjiang Uygur Zizhiqu, W China
148 K3 **Bostānābād** Āžarbāyjān-e Khāvarī, N Iran
164 K6 **Bosten Hu** *var.* Bagrax Hu. ◎ NW China
99 O18 **Boston** *prev.* St.Botolph's Town. E England, UK
21 O11 **Boston** *state capital* Massachusetts, NE USA
8 M17 **Boston Bar** British Columbia, SW Canada
29 T10 **Boston Mountains** ▲▲ Arkansas, C USA

◆ Country
● Country Capital
◇ Dependent Territory
○ Dependent Territory Capital
◆ Administrative Region
× International Airport
▲ Mountain
▲▲ Mountain Range
⛰ Volcano
~ River
◎ Lake
⊟ Reservoir

- 13 *P8* **Bostonnais** ≈ Québec, SE Canada
- **Bostyn'** *see* Bastyn'
- 114 *J10* **Bosut** ≈ E Croatia
- 160 *C11* **Botād** Gujarāt, W India
- 191 *T9* **Botany Bay** *inlet* New South Wales, SE Australia
- 85 *G18* **Boteti** *var.* Botletle. ≈ N Botswana
- 116 *J9* **Botev** ▲ C Bulgaria
- 116 *H9* **Botevgrad** ***prev.*** Orkhaniye. Sofiyska Oblast, W Bulgaria
- 95 *J16* **Bothnia, Gulf of *Fin.*** Pohjanlahti, ***Swe.*** Bottniska Viken. *gulf* N Baltic Sea
- 191 *P17* **Bothwell** Tasmania, SE Australia
- 106 *H5* **Boticas** Vila Real, N Portugal
- 57 *W10* **Boti-Pasi** Sipaliwini, C Suriname
- **Botletle** *see* Boteti
- 131 *P16* **Botlikh** Chechenskaya Respublika, SW Russian Federation
- 119 *N10* **Botna** ≈ E Moldova
- 118 *I9* **Botoşani *Hung.*** Botosány. Botoşani, NE Romania
- 118 *K8* **Botoşani** ◈ *county* NE Romania
- **Botosány** *see* Botoşani
- 167 *P4* **Botou *prev.*** Bozhen. Hebei, E China
- 101 *M20* **Botrange** ▲ E Belgium
- 109 *O21* **Botricello** Calabria, SW Italy
- 85 *I23* **Botshabelo** Free State, C South Africa
- 95 *J15* **Botsmark** Västerbotten, N Sweden
- 85 *G19* **Botswana *off.*** Republic of Botswana. ◆ *republic* S Africa
- 31 *N2* **Bottineau** North Dakota, N USA
- **Bottniska Viken** *see* Bothnia, Gulf of
- 62 *L9* **Botucatu** São Paulo, S Brazil
- 78 *M16* **Bouaflé** C Ivory Coast
- 79 *N16* **Bouaké** *var.* Bwake. C Ivory Coast
- 81 *G14* **Bouar** Nana-Mambéré, W Central African Republic
- 76 *H7* **Bouarfa** NE Morocco
- 113 *B19* **Boubín** ▲ SW Czech Republic
- 81 *I14* **Bouca** Ouham, W Central African Republic
- 13 *T5* **Boucher** ≈ Québec, SE Canada
- 105 *R15* **Bouches-du-Rhône** ◈ *department* SE France
- 76 *C9* **Bou Craa** *var.* Bu Craa. NW Western Sahara
- 79 *O9* **Boû Djébéha** *oasis* C Mali
- 110 *C8* **Boudry** Neuchâtel, W Switzerland
- 188 *L2* **Bougainville, Cape** *headland* Western Australia
- 67 *E24* **Bougainville, Cape** *headland* East Falkland, Falkland Islands
- 197 *B12* **Bougainville, Détroit de *Eng.*** Bougainville Strait. *strait* C Vanuatu
- 195 *S13* **Bougainville Island** *island* NE PNG
- 195 *T13* **Bougainville Strait** *strait* N Solomon Islands
- **Bougainville Strait** *see* Bougainville, Détroit de
- 176 *U8* **Bouganville, Selat** *strait* Irian Jaya, E Indonesia
- 123 *J11* **Bougaroun, Cap** *headland* NE Algeria
- 79 *R8* **Boughessa** Kidal, NE Mali
- **Bougie** *see* Béjaïa
- 78 *L13* **Bougouni** Sikasso, SW Mali
- 101 *J24* **Bouillon** Luxembourg, SE Belgium
- 76 *K5* **Bouira** *var.* Bouïra. N Algeria
- 76 *D8* **Bou-Izakarn** SW Morocco
- 76 *B9* **Boujdour** *var.* Bojador. W Western Sahara
- 76 *G5* **Boukhalef** ✕ (Tanger) N Morocco
- **Boukombé** *see* Boukoumbé
- 79 *R14* **Boukoumbé** *var.* Boukombé. C Benin
- 78 *G6* **Boû Lanouâr** Dakhlet Nouâdhibou, W Mauritania
- 39 *T4* **Boulder** Colorado, C USA
- 35 *R10* **Boulder** Montana, NW USA
- 37 *X12* **Boulder City** Nevada, W USA
- 189 *T7* **Boulia** Queensland, C Australia
- 13 *N10* **Boullé** ≈ Québec, SE Canada
- 104 *J9* **Boulogne** ≈ NW France
- **Boulogne** *see* Boulogne-sur-Mer
- 104 *L16* **Boulogne-sur-Gesse** Haute-Garonne, S France
- 105 *N1* **Boulogne-sur-Mer** *var.* Boulogne; ***anc.*** Bononia, Gesoriacum, Gessoriacum. Pas-de-Calais, N France
- 197 *I7* **Bouloupari** Province Sud, S New Caledonia
- 79 *Q12* **Boulsa** C Burkina
- 79 *W11* **Boultoum** Zinder, C Niger
- 197 *K13* **Bouma** Taveuni, N Fiji
- 81 *G16* **Boumba** ≈ SE Cameroon
- 78 *J9* **Boûmdeïd** *var.* Boumdeït. Assaba, S Mauritania
- **Boumdeït** *see* Boûmdeïd
- 117 *C17* **Boumistós** ▲ W Greece
- 79 *O15* **Bouna** NE Ivory Coast
- 21 *P4* **Boundary Bald Mountain** ▲ Maine, NE USA
- 37 *S8* **Boundary Peak** ▲ Nevada, W USA
- 78 *M14* **Boundiali** N Ivory Coast
- 81 *G19* **Boundji** Cuvette, C Congo
- 79 *O13* **Boundoukui** *var.* Bondoukui, Bondoukuy. W Burkina
- 38 *L2* **Bountiful** Utah, W USA
- **Bounty Basin** *see* Bounty Trough
- 203 *Q16* **Bounty Bay** *bay* Pitcairn Island, C Pacific Ocean
- 199 *Jj14* **Bounty Islands** *island group* S NZ
- 183 *Q13* **Bounty Trough** ***var.*** Bounty Basin. *undersea feature* S Pacific Ocean
- 197 *I6* **Bourail** Province Sud, C New Caledonia
- 29 *V5* **Bourbeuse River** ≈ Missouri, C USA
- 105 *Q9* **Bourbon-Lancy** Saône-et-Loire, C France
- 33 *N11* **Bourbonnais** Illinois, N USA
- 105 *O10* **Bourbonnais** *cultural region* C France
- 105 *S7* **Bourbonne-les-Bains** Haute-Marne, N France
- **Bourbon Vendée** *see* la Roche-sur-Yon
- 76 *M8* **Bourdj Messaouda** E Algeria
- 79 *Q10* **Bourem** Gao, C Mali
- **Bourg** *see* Bourg-en-Bresse
- 105 *N11* **Bourganeuf** Creuse, C France
- **Bourgas** *see* Burgas
- **Bourge-en-Bresse** *see* Bourg-en-Bresse
- 105 *S10* **Bourg-en-Bresse** *var.* Bourg, Bourge-en-Bresse. Ain, E France
- 105 *O8* **Bourges** ***anc.*** Avaricum. Cher, C France
- 105 *T11* **Bourget, Lac du** ◎ E France
- 105 *P8* **Bourgogne *Eng.*** Burgundy. ◈ *region* E France
- 105 *S11* **Bourgoin-Jallieu** Isère, E France
- 105 *R14* **Bourg-St-Andéol** Ardèche, E France
- 105 *U11* **Bourg-St-Maurice** Savoie, E France
- 110 *C11* **Bourg St.Pierre** Valais, SW Switzerland
- 78 *H8* **Boû Rjeimât** *well* W Mauritania
- 191 *P5* **Bourke** New South Wales, SE Australia
- 99 *M24* **Bournemouth** S England, UK
- 101 *M23* **Bourscheid** Diekirch, NE Luxembourg
- 76 *K6* **Bou Saâda** *var.* Bou Saada. N Algeria
- 38 *I13* **Bouse Wash** ≈ Arizona, SW USA
- 105 *N10* **Boussac** Creuse, C France
- 104 *M16* **Boussens** Haute-Garonne, S France
- 80 *H12* **Bousso *prev.*** Fort-Bretonnet. Chari-Baguirmi, S Chad
- 78 *H9* **Boutilimit** Trarza, SW Mauritania
- 67 *D21* **Bouvet Island** ◇ *Norwegian dependency* S Atlantic Ocean
- 79 *U11* **Bouza** Tahoua, SW Niger
- 111 *R10* **Bovec *Ger.*** Flitsch, ***It.*** Plezzo. NW Slovenia
- 100 *J8* **Bovenkarspel** Noord-Holland, NW Netherlands
- 31 *V5* **Bovey** Minnesota, N USA
- 34 *M9* **Bovill** Idaho, NW USA
- 26 *L4* **Bovina** Texas, SW USA
- 109 *M17* **Bovino** Puglia, SE Italy
- 63 *C17* **Bovril** Entre Ríos, E Argentina
- 30 *L2* **Bowbells** North Dakota, N USA
- 9 *Q16* **Bow City** Alberta, SW Canada
- 31 *O8* **Bowdle** South Dakota, N USA
- 189 *X6* **Bowen** Queensland, NE Australia
- 198 *B4* **Bowers Ridge** *undersea feature* S Bering Sea
- 15 *Jj4* **Bowes Point** *headland* Northwest Territories, N Canada
- 27 *S5* **Bowie** Texas, SW USA
- 9 *R17* **Bow Island** Alberta, SW Canada
- **Bowkān** *see* Būkān
- 22 *J7* **Bowling Green** Kentucky, S USA
- 29 *V3* **Bowling Green** Missouri, C USA
- 33 *R11* **Bowling Green** Ohio, N USA
- 23 *W5* **Bowling Green** Virginia, NE USA
- 30 *J6* **Bowman** North Dakota, N USA
- 16 *N3* **Bowman Bay** *bay* NW Atlantic Ocean
- 204 *I5* **Bowman Coast** *physical region* Antarctica
- 30 *J7* **Bowman-Haley Lake** ⊠ North Dakota, N USA
- 205 *Z11* **Bowman Island** *island* Antarctica
- **Bowo** *see* Bomi
- 191 *S9* **Bowral** New South Wales, SE Australia
- 194 *K14* **Bowutu Mountains** ▲▲ C PNG
- 85 *I16* **Bowwood** Southern, S Zambia
- 30 *I12* **Box Butte Reservoir** ⊠ Nebraska, C USA
- 30 *J10* **Box Elder** South Dakota, N USA
- 97 *M18* **Boxholm** Östergötland, S Sweden
- **Bo Xian/Boxian** *see* Bozhou
- 167 *Q4* **Boxing** Shandong, E China
- 101 *L14* **Boxmeer** Noord-Brabant, SE Netherlands
- 101 *J14* **Boxtel** Noord-Brabant, S Netherlands
- 142 *J10* **Boyabat** Sinop, N Turkey
- 56 *F9* **Boyacá *off.*** Departamento de Boyacá. ◈ *province* C Colombia
- 119 *O4* **Boyarka** Kyyivs'ka Oblast', N Ukraine
- 24 *H7* **Boyce** Louisiana, S USA
- 35 *U11* **Boyd** Montana, NW USA
- 27 *S6* **Boyd** Texas, SW USA
- 23 *V8* **Boydton** Virginia, NE USA
- **Boyer Ahmadī va Kohkīlūyeh** *see* Kohkīlūyeh va Būyer Aḩmadī
- 31 *T13* **Boyer River** ≈ Iowa, C USA
- 23 *W8* **Boykins** Virginia, NE USA
- 9 *Q13* **Boyle** Alberta, SW Canada
- 99 *D16* **Boyle *Ir.*** Mainistirna Búille. C Ireland
- 99 *F17* **Boyne *Ir.*** An Bhóinn. ≈ E Ireland
- 33 *Q5* **Boyne City** Michigan, N USA
- 25 *Z14* **Boynton Beach** Florida, SE USA
- 153 *O13* **Boysun *Rus.*** Baysun. Surkhondaryo Wiloyati, S Uzbekistan
- **Bozau** *see* Întorsura Buzăului
- 142 *C14* **Boz Dağları** ▲▲ W Turkey
- 35 *S11* **Bozeman** Montana, NW USA
- **Bozen** *see* Bolzano
- 81 *J16* **Bozene** Equateur, NW Zaire
- 167 *P7* **Bozhou** ***var.*** Boxian, Bo Xian. Anhui, E China
- 142 *H16* **Bozkır** Konya, S Turkey
- 142 *K13* **Bozok Yaylası** *plateau* C Turkey
- 81 *H14* **Bozoum** Ouham-Pendé, W Central African Republic
- 143 *N16* **Bozova** Sanlıurfa, S Turkey
- **Bozrah** *see* Buşrá ash Shām
- 142 *E12* **Bozüyük** Bilecik, NW Turkey
- 108 *B9* **Bra** Piemonte, NW Italy
- 204 *G4* **Brabant Island** *island* Antarctica
- 115 *F15* **Brač** *var.* Brach, ***It.*** Brazza; ***anc.*** Brattia. *island* S Croatia
- **Bracara Augusta** *see* Braga
- 109 *H15* **Bracciano** Lazio, C Italy
- 109 *H14* **Bracciano, Lago di** ◎ C Italy
- 12 *H13* **Bracebridge** Ontario, S Canada
- **Brach** *see* Brač
- 95 *G17* **Bräcke** Jämtland, C Sweden
- 27 *P12* **Brackettville** Texas, SW USA
- 99 *N22* **Bracknell** S England, UK
- 63 *K14* **Braço do Norte** Santa Catarina, S Brazil
- 118 *G11* **Brad *Hung.*** Brád. Hunedoara, SW Romania
- 109 *N18* **Bradano** ≈ S Italy
- 25 *V13* **Bradenton** Florida, SE USA
- 12 *H14* **Bradford** Ontario, S Canada
- 99 *L17* **Bradford** N England, UK
- 29 *W10* **Bradford** Arkansas, C USA
- 20 *D12* **Bradford** Pennsylvania, NE USA
- 29 *T15* **Bradley** Arkansas, C USA
- 27 *P7* **Bradshaw** Texas, SW USA
- 27 *Q9* **Brady** Texas, SW USA
- 27 *Q9* **Brady Creek** ≈ Texas, SW USA
- 98 *J10* **Braemar** NE Scotland, UK
- 118 *K8* **Brăeşti** Botoşani, NW Romania
- 106 *G5* **Braga *anc.*** Bracara Augusta. Braga, NW Portugal
- 106 *G5* **Braga** ◈ *district* N Portugal
- 118 *J15* **Bragadiru** Teleorman, S Romania
- 63 *C20* **Bragado** Buenos Aires, E Argentina
- 106 *J5* **Bragança *Eng.*** Braganza; ***anc.*** Julio Briga. Bragança, NE Portugal
- 106 *I5* **Bragança** ◈ *district* N Portugal
- 62 *N9* **Bragança Paulista** São Paulo, S Brazil
- **Braganza** *see* Bragança
- **Bragin** *see* Brahin
- 31 *V7* **Braham** Minnesota, N USA
- **Brahe** *see* Brda
- **Brahestad** *see* Raahe
- 121 *O20* **Brahin *Rus.*** Bragin. Homyel'skaya Voblasts', SE Belarus
- 159 *U15* **Brahmanbaria** Chittagong, E Bangladesh
- 160 *O12* **Brāhmani** ≈ E India
- 160 *N13* **Brahmapur** Orissa, E India
- 133 *S10* **Brahmaputra** *var.* Padma, Tsangpo, ***Ben.*** Jamuna, ***Chin.*** Yarlung Zangbo Jiang, ***Ind.*** Bramaputra, Dihang, Siang. ≈ S Asia
- 99 *H19* **Braich y Pwll** *headland* NW Wales, UK
- 191 *R10* **Braidwood** New South Wales, SE Australia
- 32 *M11* **Braidwood** Illinois, N USA
- 118 *M13* **Brăila** Brăila, E Romania
- 118 *L13* **Brăila** ◈ *county* SE Romania
- 101 *G19* **Braine-l'Alleud** Walloon Brabant, C Belgium
- 101 *F19* **Braine-le-Comte** Hainaut, SW Belgium
- 31 *U6* **Brainerd** Minnesota, N USA
- 101 *J19* **Braives** Liège, E Belgium
- 85 *H23* **Brak** ≈ C South Africa
- **Brak** *see* Birāk
- 101 *E18* **Brakel** Oost-Vlaanderen, SW Belgium
- 100 *J13* **Brakel** Gelderland, C Netherlands
- 78 *H9* **Brakna** ◈ *region* S Mauritania
- 97 *J17* **Brålanda** Älvsborg, S Sweden
- **Bramaputra** *see* Brahmaputra
- 97 *F23* **Bramming** Ribe, W Denmark
- 12 *G15* **Brampton** Ontario, S Canada
- 102 *F12* **Bramsche** Niedersachsen, NW Germany
- 118 *J12* **Bran *Ger.*** Törzburg, ***Hung.*** Törcsvár. Braşov, S Romania
- 31 *W8* **Branch** Minnesota, N USA
- 23 *R14* **Branchville** South Carolina, SE USA
- 49 *Y6* **Branco, Cabo** *headland* E Brazil
- 60 *F11* **Branco, Rio** ≈ N Brazil
- 110 *J8* **Brand** Vorarlberg, W Austria
- 85 *B18* **Brandberg** ▲ NW Namibia
- 97 *H14* **Brandbu** Oppland, S Norway
- 97 *F22* **Brande** Ringkøbing, W Denmark
- **Brandebourg** *see* Brandenburg
- 102 *M12* **Brandenburg** *var.* Brandenburg an der Havel. Brandenburg, NE Germany
- 22 *K5* **Brandenburg** Kentucky, S USA
- 102 *N12* **Brandenburg *off.*** Freie und Hansestadt Hamburg, ***Fr.*** Brandebourg. ◈ *state* NE Germany
- **Brandenburg an der Havel** *see* Brandenburg
- 85 *I23* **Brandfort** Free State, C South Africa
- 9 *W16* **Brandon** Manitoba, S Canada
- 25 *V12* **Brandon** Florida, SE USA
- 24 *L6* **Brandon** Mississippi, S USA
- 99 *A20* **Brandon Mountain *Ir.*** Cnoc Bréanainn. ▲ SW Ireland
- **Brandsen** *see* Coronel Brandsen
- 97 *I14* **Brandval** Hedmark, S Norway
- 85 *F24* **Brandvlei** Northern Cape, W South Africa
- 25 *U9* **Branford** Florida, SE USA
- 112 *K7* **Braniewo *Ger.*** Braunsberg. Elbląg, N Poland
- 204 *H3* **Bransfield Strait** *strait* Antarctica
- 39 *U8* **Branson** Colorado, C USA
- 29 *T8* **Branson** Missouri, C USA
- 12 *G16* **Brantford** Ontario, S Canada
- 104 *L12* **Brantôme** Dordogne, SW France
- 190 *L12* **Branxholme** Victoria, SE Australia
- **Brasil** *see* Brazil
- 61 *C16* **Brasiléia** Acre, W Brazil
- 61 *K18* **Brasília** ● (Brazil) Distrito Federal, C Brazil
- **Braslav** *see* Braslaw
- 120 *J12* **Braslaw *Pol.*** Brasław, ***Rus.*** Braslav. Vitsyebskaya Voblasts', N Belarus
- 118 *J12* **Braşov *Ger.*** Kronstadt, ***Hung.*** Brassó; ***prev.*** Oraşul Stalin. Braşov, C Romania
- 118 *I12* **Braşov** ◈ *county* C Romania
- 176 *W7* **Bras, Pulau** *island* Kepulauan Mapia, E Indonesia
- 79 *U18* **Brass** Rivers, S Nigeria
- 101 *H16* **Brasschaat** *var.* Brasschaet. Antwerpen, N Belgium
- **Brasschaet** *see* Brasschaat
- 175 *O4* **Brassey, Banjaran** *var.* Brassey Range. ▲▲ East Malaysia
- **Brassey Range** *see* Brassey, Banjaran
- **Brassó** *see* Braşov
- 25 *T1* **Brasstown Bald** ▲ Georgia, SE USA
- 115 *K22* **Brataj** Vlorë, SW Albania
- 116 *J10* **Bratan** *var.* Morozov. ▲ C Bulgaria
- 113 *F21* **Bratislava *Ger.*** Pressburg, ***Hung.*** Pozsony. ● (Slovakia) Západné Slovensko, SW Slovakia
- 116 *H10* **Bratiya** ▲ C Bulgaria
- 126 *J14* **Bratsk** Irkutskaya Oblast', C Russian Federation
- 119 *Q8* **Brats'ke** Mykolayivs'ka Oblast', S Ukraine
- 126 *J14* **Bratskoye Vodokhranilishche *Eng.*** Bratsk Reservoir. ⊠ S Russian Federation
- **Bratsk Reservoir** *see* Bratskoye Vodokhranilishche
- **Brattia** *see* Brač
- 96 *D9* **Brattvåg** Møre og Romsdal, S Norway
- 114 *K12* **Bratunac** E Bosnia and Herzegovina
- 116 *J10* **Bratya Daskalovi *prev.*** Grozdovo. Khaskovska Oblast, C Bulgaria
- 111 *U2* **Braunau** ≈ N Austria
- **Braunau** *see* Braunau am Inn
- 111 *Q4* **Braunau am Inn** *var.* Braunau. Oberösterreich, N Austria
- **Braunsberg** *see* Braniewo
- 102 *J13* **Braunschweig *Eng./Fr.*** Brunswick. Niedersachsen, N Germany
- **Brava** *see* Baraawe
- 107 *Y6* **Brava, Costa** *coastal region* NE Spain
- 45 *V16* **Brava, Punta** *headland* E Panama
- 97 *N17* **Bråviken** *inlet* S Sweden
- 58 *B10* **Bravo, Cerro** ▲ N Peru
- **Bravo del Norte, Río/Bravo, Río** *see* Grande, Rio
- 37 *X17* **Brawley** California, W USA
- 99 *G18* **Bray *Ir.*** Bré. E Ireland
- 61 *G16* **Brazil *off.*** Federative Republic of Brazil, ***Port.*** Repùblica Federativa do Brasil, ***Sp.*** Brasil; ***prev.*** United States of Brazil. ◆ *federal republic* South America
- 67 *K15* **Brazil Basin** *var.* Brazilian Basin, Brazil'skaya Kotlovina. *undersea feature* W Atlantic Ocean
- **Brazilian Basin** *see* Brazil Basin
- **Brazilian Highlands** *see* Central, Planalto
- **Brazil'skaya Kotlovina** *see* Brazil Basin
- 27 *U10* **Brazos River** ≈ Texas, SW USA
- 176 *Yy13* **Brazza** ≈ Irian Jaya, E Indonesia
- **Brazza** *see* Brač
- 81 *G21* **Brazzaville** ● (Congo) Capital District, S Congo
- 81 *G21* **Brazzaville** ✕ Le Pool, S Congo
- 114 *J11* **Brčko** NE Bosnia and Herzegovina
- 112 *H8* **Brda *Ger.*** Brahe. ≈ N Poland
- **Bré** *see* Bray
- 193 *A23* **Breaksea Sound** *sound* South Island, NZ
- 192 *L4* **Bream Bay** *bay* North Island, NZ
- 192 *L4* **Bream Head** *headland* North Island, NZ
- **Bréanainn, Cnoc** *see* Brandon Mountain
- 47 *S6* **Brea, Punta** *headland* W Puerto Rico
- 24 *I9* **Breaux Bridge** Louisiana, S USA
- 118 *J13* **Breaza** Prahova, SE Romania
- 174 *K14* **Brebes** Jawa, C Indonesia
- 98 *K10* **Brechin** E Scotland, UK
- 101 *H15* **Brecht** Antwerpen, N Belgium
- 39 *S4* **Breckenridge** Colorado, C USA
- 31 *R6* **Breckenridge** Minnesota, N USA
- 27 *R6* **Breckenridge** Texas, SW USA
- 99 *J21* **Brecknock** *cultural region* SE Wales, UK
- 65 *G25* **Brecknock, Península** *headland* S Chile
- 113 *G19* **Břeclav *Ger.*** Lundenburg. Jižní Morava, SE Czech Republic
- 99 *J21* **Brecon** E Wales, UK
- 99 *J21* **Brecon Beacons** ▲▲ S Wales, UK
- 101 *I14* **Breda** Noord-Brabant, S Netherlands
- 97 *K20* **Bredaryd** Jönköping, S Sweden
- 85 *F26* **Bredasdorp** Western Cape, SW South Africa
- 95 *H16* **Bredbyn** Västernorrland, N Sweden
- 125 *E13* **Bredy** Chelyabinskaya Oblast', C Russian Federation
- 101 *K17* **Bree** Limburg, NE Belgium
- 69 *T15* **Breede** ≈ S South Africa
- 100 *I7* **Breezand** Noord-Holland, NW Netherlands
- 115 *P18* **Bregalnica** ≈ E FYR Macedonia
- 110 *I6* **Bregenz *anc.*** Brigantium. Vorarlberg, W Austria
- 110 *J7* **Bregenzer Wald** ▲▲ W Austria
- 116 *F6* **Bregovo** Oblast Montana, NW Bulgaria
- 104 *H5* **Bréhat, Île de** *island* NW France
- 94 *H2* **Breidhafjördhur** *bay* W Iceland
- 94 *L3* **Breidhdalsvík** Austurland, E Iceland
- 110 *H9* **Breil *Ger.*** Brigels. Graubünden, S Switzerland
- 94 *J8* **Breivikbotn** Finnmark, N Norway
- 96 *I9* **Brekken** Sør-Trøndelag, S Norway
- 96 *G7* **Brekstad** Sør-Trøndelag, S Norway
- 96 *B10* **Bremangerlandet** *island* S Norway
- **Brême** *see* Bremen
- 102 *H11* **Bremen *Fr.*** Brême. Bremen, NW Germany
- 25 *R3* **Bremen** Georgia, SE USA
- 33 *O11* **Bremen** Indiana, N USA
- 102 *H10* **Bremen *off.*** Freie Hansestadt Bremen, ***Fr.*** Brême. ◈ *state* N Germany
- 102 *G9* **Bremerhaven** Bremen, NW Germany
- **Bremersdorp** *see* Manzini
- 34 *G8* **Bremerton** Washington, NW USA
- 102 *H10* **Bremervörde** Niedersachsen, NW Germany
- 27 *U9* **Bremond** Texas, SW USA
- 27 *U10* **Brenham** Texas, SW USA
- 110 *M8* **Brenner** Tirol, W Austria
- **Brenner, Col du/Brennero, Passo del** *see* Brenner Pass
- 110 *M8* **Brenner Pass** *var.* Brenner Sattel, ***Fr.*** Col du Brenner, ***Ger.*** Brennerpass, ***It.*** Passo del Brennero. *pass* Austria/Italy
- **Brenner Sattel** *see* Brenner Pass
- 110 *G10* **Brenno** ≈ SW Switzerland
- 108 *F7* **Breno** Lombardia, N Italy
- 25 *O5* **Brent** Alabama, S USA
- 108 *H7* **Brenta** ≈ NE Italy
- 99 *P21* **Brentwood** E England, UK
- 20 *L14* **Brentwood** Long Island, New York, NE USA
- 108 *F7* **Brescia** ***anc.*** Brixia. Lombardia, N Italy
- 101 *D15* **Breskens** Zeeland, SW Netherlands
- **Breslau** *see* Wrocław
- 108 *H5* **Bressanone *Ger.*** Brixen. Trentino-Alto Adige, N Italy
- 98 *M2* **Bressay** *island* NE Scotland, UK
- 104 *K9* **Bressuire** Deux-Sèvres, W France
- 121 *F20* **Brest *Pol.*** Brześć nad Bugiem, ***Rus.*** Brest-Litovsk; ***prev.*** Brześć Litewski. Brestskaya Voblasts', SW Belarus
- 104 *F5* **Brest** Finistère, NW France
- **Brest-Litovsk** *see* Brest
- 114 *A10* **Brestova** Istra, NW Croatia
- **Brestskaya Oblast'** *see* Brestskaya Voblasts'
- 121 *G19* **Brestskaya Voblasts' *prev.*** Rus. Brestskaya Oblast'. ◈ *province* SW Belarus
- 104 *G6* **Bretagne *Eng.*** Brittany; ***Lat.*** Britannia Minor. ◈ *region* NW France
- 118 *G12* **Bretea-Română *Hung.*** Oláhbrettye; ***prev.*** Bretea-Romînă. Hunedoara, W Romania
- **Bretea-Romînă** *see* Bretea-Română
- 105 *O3* **Breteuil** Oise, N France
- 104 *I10* **Breton, Pertuis** *inlet* W France
- 24 *L10* **Breton Sound** *sound* Louisiana, S USA
- 192 *K2* **Brett, Cape** *headland* North Island, NZ
- 103 *G21* **Bretten** Baden-Württemberg, SW Germany
- 101 *K15* **Breugel** Noord-Brabant, S Netherlands
- 108 *B6* **Breuil *It.*** Cervinia. Valle d'Aosta, NW Italy
- 100 *I11* **Breukelen** Utrecht, C Netherlands
- 23 *P10* **Brevard** North Carolina, SE USA
- 40 *L9* **Brevig Mission** Alaska, USA
- 97 *G16* **Brevik** Telemark, S Norway
- 191 *P5* **Brewarrina** New South Wales, SE Australia
- 21 *R6* **Brewer** Maine, NE USA
- 31 *T11* **Brewster** Minnesota, N USA
- 31 *N14* **Brewster** Nebraska, C USA
- 33 *U12* **Brewster** Ohio, N USA
- 191 *O8* **Brewster, Lake** ◎ New South Wales, SE Australia
- 25 *P7* **Brewton** Alabama, S USA
- **Brezhnev** *see* Naberezhnyye Chelny
- 111 *W12* **Brežice *Ger.*** Rann. E Slovenia
- 116 *G9* **Breznik** Sofiyska Oblast, W Bulgaria
- 113 *K19* **Brezno *Ger.*** Bries, Briesen, ***Hung.*** Breznóbánya; ***prev.*** Brezno nad Hronom. Stredné Slovensko, C Slovakia
- **Breznóbánya/Brezno nad Hronom** *see* Brezno
- 118 *I12* **Brezoi** Vâlcea, SW Romania
- 116 *J10* **Brezovo *prev.*** Abrashlare. Plovdivska Oblast, C Bulgaria
- 81 *K14* **Bria** Haute-Kotto, C Central African Republic
- 105 *U13* **Briançon** ***anc.*** Brigantio. Hautes-Alpes, SE France
- 38 *K7* **Brian Head** ▲ Utah, W USA
- 105 *O7* **Briare** Loiret, C France
- 191 *V2* **Bribie Island** *island* Queensland, E Australia
- 45 *O14* **Bribrí** Limón, E Costa Rica
- 118 *L8* **Briceni** *var.* Brinceni, ***Rus.*** Brichany. N Moldova
- **Bricgstow** *see* Bristol
- **Brichany** *see* Briceni
- 101 *M24* **Bridel** Luxembourg, C Luxembourg
- 99 *J22* **Bridgend** S Wales, UK
- 12 *I14* **Bridgenorth** Ontario, SE Canada
- 25 *Q1* **Bridgeport** Alabama, S USA
- 37 *R8* **Bridgeport** California, W USA
- 20 *L13* **Bridgeport** Connecticut, NE USA
- 33 *N15* **Bridgeport** Illinois, N USA
- 30 *J14* **Bridgeport** Nebraska, C USA
- 27 *S6* **Bridgeport** Texas, SW USA
- 23 *S3* **Bridgeport** West Virginia, NE USA
- 27 *S5* **Bridgeport, Lake** ⊠ Texas, SW USA
- 35 *U11* **Bridger** Montana, NW USA
- 20 *I17* **Bridgeton** New Jersey, NE USA
- 188 *J14* **Bridgetown** Western Australia
- 47 *Y14* **Bridgetown** ● (Barbados) SW Barbados
- 191 *P17* **Bridgewater** Tasmania, SE Australia
- 11 *P16* **Bridgewater** Nova Scotia, SE Canada
- 21 *P12* **Bridgewater** Massachusetts, NE USA
- 31 *Q11* **Bridgewater** South Dakota, N USA
- 23 *U5* **Bridgewater** Virginia, NE USA
- 21 *P8* **Bridgton** Maine, NE USA
- 99 *K23* **Bridgwater** SW England, UK
- 99 *K22* **Bridgwater Bay** *bay* SW England, UK
- 99 *O16* **Bridlington** E England, UK
- 99 *O16* **Bridlington Bay** *bay* E England, UK
- 191 *P15* **Bridport** Tasmania, SE Australia
- 99 *K24* **Bridport** S England, UK
- 105 *O5* **Brie** *cultural region* N France
- **Brieg** *see* Brzeg
- **Briel** *see* Brielle
- 100 *G12* **Brielle** *var.* Briel, Bril, ***Eng.*** The Brill. Zuid-Holland, SW Netherlands
- 110 *E9* **Brienz** Bern, C Switzerland
- 110 *E9* **Brienzer See** ◎ SW Switzerland
- **Bries/Briesen** *see* Brezno
- **Brietzig** *see* Brzesko
- 105 *S4* **Briey** Meurthe-et-Moselle, NE France
- 110 *E10* **Brig *Fr.*** Brigue, ***It.*** Briga. Valais, SW Switzerland
- **Briga** *see* Brig
- 103 *G24* **Brigach** ≈ S Germany
- 20 *K17* **Brigantine** New Jersey, NE USA
- **Brigantio** *see* Briançon
- **Brigantium** *see* Bregenz
- **Brigels** *see* Breil
- 27 *S9* **Briggs** Texas, SW USA
- 38 *L1* **Brigham City** Utah, W USA
- 12 *J15* **Brighton** Ontario, SE Canada
- 99 *O23* **Brighton** SE England, UK
- 39 *T4* **Brighton** Colorado, C USA
- 32 *K15* **Brighton** Illinois, N USA
- 105 *T16* **Brignoles** Var, W France
- **Brigue** *see* Brig
- 107 *O7* **Brihuega** Castilla-La Mancha, C Spain
- 114 *A10* **Brijuni *It.*** Brioni. *island group* NW Croatia
- 78 *G12* **Brikama** W Gambia
- **Bril** *see* Brielle
- **Brill, The** *see* Brielle
- 103 *G15* **Brilon** Nordrhein-Westfalen, W Germany
- **Brinceni** *see* Briceni
- 109 *Q18* **Brindisi *anc.*** Brundisium, Brundusium. Puglia, SE Italy
- 29 *W11* **Brinkley** Arkansas, C USA
- **Brioni** *see* Brijuni
- 105 *P12* **Brioude *anc.*** Brivas. Haute-Loire, C France
- **Briovera** *see* St-Lô
- 191 *U2* **Brisbane** Queensland, E Australia
- 191 *V2* **Brisbane** ✕ Queensland, E Australia
- 27 *P2* **Briscoe** Texas, SW USA
- 108 *H10* **Brisighella** Emilia-Romagna, C Italy
- 110 *G11* **Brissago** Ticino, S Switzerland
- 99 *K22* **Bristol *anc.*** Bricgstow. SW England, UK
- 20 *M12* **Bristol** Connecticut, NE USA
- 25 *R9* **Bristol** Florida, SE USA
- 21 *N9* **Bristol** New Hampshire, NE USA
- 31 *Q8* **Bristol** South Dakota, N USA
- 23 *P8* **Bristol** Tennessee, S USA
- 20 *M8* **Bristol** Vermont, NE USA
- 41 *N14* **Bristol Bay** *bay* Alaska, USA
- 99 *I22* **Bristol Channel** *inlet* England/Wales, UK
- 37 *W14* **Bristol Lake** ◎ California, W USA
- 29 *P10* **Bristow** Oklahoma, C USA
- 88 *C10* **Britain** *var.* Great Britain. *island* UK
- **Britannia Minor** *see* Bretagne
- 8 *L12* **British Columbia *Fr.*** Colombie-Britannique. ◈ *province* SW Canada
- **British Guiana** *see* Guyana
- **British Honduras** *see* Belize
- 181 *Q7* **British Indian Ocean Territory** ◇ *UK dependent territory* C Indian Ocean
- 88 *B9* **British Isles** *island group* NW Europe
- 8 *I1* **British Mountains** ▲▲ Yukon Territory, NW Canada
- **British North Borneo** *see* Sabah
- **British Solomon Islands Protectorate** *see* Solomon Islands
- 47 *S8* **British Virgin Islands** ***var.*** Virgin Islands. ◇ *UK dependent territory* E West Indies
- 85 *J21* **Brits** North-West, N South Africa
- 85 *H24* **Britstown** Northern Cape, W South Africa
- 12 *F12* **Britt** Ontario, S Canada
- 31 *V12* **Britt** Iowa, C USA
- **Brittany** *see* Bretagne
- 31 *Q7* **Britton** South Dakota, N USA
- **Briva Curretia** *see* Brive-la-Gaillarde
- **Briva Isarae** *see* Pontoise
- **Brivas** *see* Brioude
- **Brive** *see* Brive-la-Gaillarde
- 104 *M12* **Brive-la-Gaillarde *prev.*** Brive, ***anc.*** Briva Curretia. Corrèze, C France
- 107 *O4* **Briviesca** Castilla-León, N Spain
- **Brixen** *see* Bressanone
- **Brixia** *see* Brescia
- 151 *S15* **Brlik *prev.*** Novotroickoje, Novotroitskoye. Zhambyl, SE Kazakhstan
- 113 *G18* **Brno *Ger.*** Brünn. Jižní Morava, SE Czech Republic
- 98 *G7* **Broad Bay** *bay* NW Scotland, UK
- 27 *X8* **Broaddus** Texas, SW USA
- 191 *O12* **Broadford** Victoria, SE Australia
- 98 *G9* **Broadford** N Scotland, UK
- 98 *J13* **Broad Law** ▲ S Scotland, UK
- 25 *U3* **Broad River** ≈ Georgia, SE USA
- 23 *N8* **Broad River** ≈ North Carolina/South Carolina, SE USA
- 189 *Y8* **Broadsound Range** ▲▲ Queensland, E Australia
- 35 *X11* **Broadus** Montana, NW USA
- 23 *U4* **Broadway** Virginia, NE USA
- 120 *E9* **Brocēni** Saldus, SW Latvia
- 9 *U11* **Brochet** Manitoba, C Canada
- 9 *U10* **Brochet, Lac** ◎ Manitoba, C Canada
- 13 *S5* **Brochet, Lac au** ◎ Québec, SE Canada
- 103 *K14* **Brocken** ▲ C Germany
- 21 *O12* **Brockton** Massachusetts, NE USA
- 12 *L14* **Brockville** Ontario, SE Canada
- 20 *D13* **Brockway** Pennsylvania, NE USA
- **Brod/Bród** *see* Slavonski Brod
- 15 *Kk1* **Brodeur Peninsula** *peninsula* Baffin Island, Northwest Territories, NE Canada
- 98 *H13* **Brodick** W Scotland, UK
- **Brod na Savi** *see* Slavonski Brod
- 112 *K9* **Brodnica *Ger.*** Buddenbrock. Toruń, N Poland
- 114 *G10* **Brod-Posavina *off.*** Brodsko-Posavska Županija. ◈ *province* NE Croatia
- 118 *J5* **Brody** L'vivs'ka Oblast', NW Ukraine
- 97 *G22* **Brædstrup** Vejle, C Denmark
- 100 *I10* **Broek-in-Waterland** Noord-Holland, C Netherlands
- 34 *L13* **Brogan** Oregon, NW USA
- 112 *N10* **Brok** Ostrołęka, E Poland
- 29 *P9* **Broken Arrow** Oklahoma, C USA
- 191 *T9* **Broken Bay** *bay* New South Wales, SE Australia
- 31 *N15* **Broken Bow** Nebraska, C USA
- 29 *R13* **Broken Bow** Oklahoma, C USA
- 29 *R12* **Broken Bow Lake** ⊠ Oklahoma, C USA
- 190 *L6* **Broken Hill** New South Wales, SE Australia
- 181 *S10* **Broken Ridge** *undersea feature* S Indian Ocean
- 194 *H10* **Broken Water Bay** *bay* W Bismarck Sea
- 57 *W10* **Brokopondo** Brokopondo, NE Suriname
- 57 *W10* **Brokopondo** ◈ *district* C Suriname
- **Bromberg** *see* Bydgoszcz
- 97 *L22* **Bromölla** Kristianstad, S Sweden
- 99 *L20* **Bromsgrove** W England, UK
- 97 *G20* **Brønderslev** Nordjylland, N Denmark
- 108 *D8* **Broni** Lombardia, N Italy
- 8 *K11* **Bronlund Peak** ▲ British Columbia, W Canada
- 95 *F14* **Brønnøysund** Nordland, C Norway
- 25 *V10* **Bronson** Florida, SE USA
- 33 *Q11* **Bronson** Michigan, N USA
- 27 *X8* **Bronson** Texas, SW USA
- 109 *L24* **Bronte** Sicilia, Italy, C Mediterranean Sea
- 27 *P8* **Bronte** Texas, SW USA
- 27 *Y9* **Brookeland** Texas, SW USA
- 179 *O15* **Brooke's Point** Palawan, W Philippines
- 29 *T3* **Brookfield** Missouri, C USA
- 24 *K7* **Brookhaven** Mississippi, S USA
- 34 *E16* **Brookings** Oregon, NW USA
- 31 *R10* **Brookings** South Dakota, N USA
- 31 *W14* **Brooklyn** Iowa, C USA
- 31 *U8* **Brooklyn Park** Minnesota, N USA
- 23 *U7* **Brookneal** Virginia, NE USA
- 9 *R16* **Brooks** Alberta, SW Canada
- 27 *V11* **Brookshire** Texas, SW USA
- 40 *L8* **Brooks Mountain** ▲ Alaska, USA
- 40 *M11* **Brooks Range** ▲▲ Alaska, USA
- 33 *O12* **Brookston** Indiana, N USA
- 25 *V11* **Brooksville** Florida, SE USA
- 25 *N4* **Brooksville** Mississippi, S USA
- 188 *J13* **Brookton** Western Australia
- 33 *Q14* **Brookville** Indiana, N USA
- 20 *D13* **Brookville** Pennsylvania, NE USA

◆ Country
● Country Capital
◇ Dependent Territory
○ Dependent Territory Capital
◈ Administrative Region
✕ International Airport
▲ Mountain
▲▲ Mountain Range
Volcano
≈ River
◎ Lake
⊠ Reservoir

33 Q14 **Brookville Lake** ⊠ Indiana, N USA
188 K5 **Broome** Western Australia
39 S4 **Broomfield** Colorado, C USA
Broos *see* Orăştie
98 J7 **Brora** N Scotland, UK
98 I7 **Brora** ≈ N Scotland, UK
97 F23 **Brørup** Ribe, W Denmark
97 L23 **Brösarp** Kristianstad, S Sweden
118 J9 **Broşteni** Suceava, NE Romania
104 M6 **Brou** Eure-et-Loir, C France
Broucsella *see* Brussel/Bruxelles
Broughton Bay *see* Tongjosŏn-man
16 O1 **Broughton Island** Northwest Territories, NE Canada
144 G7 **Broummâna** C Lebanon
24 I9 **Broussard** Louisiana, S USA
100 E13 **Brouwersdam** *dam* SW Netherlands
100 E13 **Brouwershaven** Zeeland, SW Netherlands
119 P4 **Brovary** Kyyivs'ka Oblast', N Ukraine
97 G20 **Brovst** Nordjylland, N Denmark
33 S8 **Brown City** Michigan, N USA
26 M6 **Brownfield** Texas, SW USA
35 Q7 **Browning** Montana, NW USA
35 R6 **Brown, Mount** ▲ Montana, NW USA
194 K15 **Brown River** ≈ S PNG
1 M9 **Browns Bank** *undersea feature* NW Atlantic Ocean
33 O14 **Brownsburg** Indiana, N USA
20 J16 **Browns Mills** New Jersey, NE USA
46 J12 **Browns Town** C Jamaica
33 P15 **Brownstown** Indiana, N USA
31 R8 **Browns Valley** Minnesota, N USA
22 K7 **Brownsville** Kentucky, S USA
22 F9 **Brownsville** Tennessee, S USA
27 T17 **Brownsville** Texas, SW USA
57 W10 **Brownsweg** Brokopondo, C Suriname
31 U9 **Brownton** Minnesota, N USA
21 R5 **Brownville Junction** Maine, NE USA
27 R8 **Brownwood** Texas, SW USA
27 R8 **Brownwood Lake** ⊠ Texas, SW USA
106 I9 **Brozas** Extremadura, W Spain
121 M18 **Brozha** Mahilyowskaya Voblasts', E Belarus
105 O2 **Bruay-en-Artois** Pas-de-Calais, N France
105 P2 **Bruay-sur-l'Escaut** Nord, N France
12 F13 **Bruce Peninsula** *peninsula* Ontario, S Canada
22 H9 **Bruceton** Tennessee, S USA
27 T9 **Bruceville** Texas, SW USA
103 G21 **Bruchsal** Baden-Württemberg, SW Germany
111 Q7 **Bruck** Salzburg, NW Austria
Bruck *see* Bruck an der Mur
111 Y4 **Bruck an der Leitha** Niederösterreich, NE Austria
111 V7 **Bruck an der Mur** *var.* Bruck. Steiermark, C Austria
103 M24 **Bruckmühl** Bayern, SE Germany
173 Dd3 **Brueuh, Pulau** *island* NW Indonesia
Bruges *see* Brugge
110 F6 **Brugg** Aargau, NW Switzerland
101 C16 **Brugge** *Fr.* Bruges. West-Vlaanderen, NW Belgium
111 R9 **Bruggen** Kärnten, S Austria
103 E16 **Brühl** Nordrhein-Westfalen, W Germany
101 F14 **Bruinisse** Zeeland, SW Netherlands
174 L5 **Bruit, Pulau** *island* East Malaysia
12 K10 **Brûlé, Lac** ◎ Québec, SE Canada
32 M4 **Brule River** ≈ Michigan/Wisconsin, N USA
101 H23 **Brûly** Namur, S Belgium
61 N17 **Brumado** Bahia, E Brazil
100 M11 **Brummen** Gelderland, E Netherlands
96 H13 **Brumunddal** Hedmark, S Norway
25 Q6 **Brundidge** Alabama, S USA
Brundisium/Brundusium *see* Brindisi
35 N15 **Bruneau River** ≈ Idaho, NW USA
Bruneck *see* Brunico
174 Mm4 **Brunei** *off.* Sultanate of Brunei, *Mal.* Negara Brunei Darussalam. ◆ *monarchy* SE Asia
175 N3 **Brunei Bay** *var.* Teluk Brunei. *bay* N Brunei
Brunei, Teluk *see* Brunei Bay
Brunei Town *see* Bandar Seri Begawan
108 H5 **Brunico** *Ger.* Bruneck. Trentino-Alto Adige, N Italy
Brünn *see* Brno
193 G17 **Brunner, Lake** ◎ South Island, NZ
101 M18 **Brunssum** Limburg, SE Netherlands
25 W7 **Brunswick** Georgia, SE USA
21 Q8 **Brunswick** Maine, NE USA
23 V3 **Brunswick** Maryland, NE USA
29 T3 **Brunswick** Missouri, C USA
33 T11 **Brunswick** Ohio, N USA
Brunswick *see* Braunschweig
65 H24 **Brunswick, Península** *headland* S Chile
113 H17 **Bruntál** *Ger.* Freudenthal. Severní Morava, E Czech Republic
205 N3 **Brunt Ice Shelf** *ice shelf* Antarctica
Brusa *see* Bursa
39 U3 **Brush** Colorado, C USA
44 M5 **Brus Laguna** Gracias a Dios, E Honduras
62 K13 **Brusque** Santa Catarina, S Brazil
Brussa *see* Bursa
101 E18 **Brussel** *var.* Brussels, *Fr.* Bruxelles, *Ger.* Brüssel; *anc.* Broucsella. ● (Belgium) Brussels, C Belgium *see also* Bruxelles
Brüssel/Brussels *see* Brussel/Bruxelles
119 O5 **Brusyliv** Zhytomyrs'ka Oblast', N Ukraine
191 Q12 **Bruthen** Victoria, SE Australia
Bruttium *see* Calabria
Brüx *see* Most
101 E18 **Bruxelles** *var.* Brussels, *Dut.* Brussel, *Ger.* Brüssel; *anc.* Broucsella. ● (Belgium) Brussels, C Belgium *see also* Brussel
56 J7 **Bruzual** Apure, W Venezuela
33 Q11 **Bryan** Ohio, N USA
27 U10 **Bryan** Texas, SW USA
204 J4 **Bryan Coast** *physical region* Antarctica
126 I13 **Bryanka** Krasnoyarskiy Kray, C Russian Federation
119 Y7 **Bryanka** Luhans'ka Oblast', E Ukraine
190 J8 **Bryan, Mount** ▲ South Australia
130 I6 **Bryansk** Bryanskaya Oblast', W Russian Federation
130 H6 **Bryanskaya Oblast'** ◈ *province* W Russian Federation
204 J5 **Bryant, Cape** *headland* Antarctica
29 U8 **Bryant Creek** ≈ Missouri, C USA
38 K8 **Bryce Canyon** *canyon* Utah, W USA
121 O15 **Bryli** *Rus.* Bryli. Mahilyowskaya Voblasts', E Belarus
97 C17 **Bryne** Rogaland, S Norway
27 R6 **Bryson** Texas, SW USA
23 N10 **Bryson City** North Carolina, SE USA
12 K11 **Bryson, Lac** ◎ Québec, SE Canada
130 K13 **Bryukhovetskaya** Krasnodarskiy Kray, SW Russian Federation
113 H15 **Brzeg** *Ger.* Brieg; *anc.* Civitas Altae Ripae. Opole, SW Poland
113 G14 **Brzeg Dolny** *Ger.* Dyhernfurth. Wrocław, SW Poland
Brześć Litewski/Brześć nad Bugiem *see* Brest
113 L17 **Brzesko** *Ger.* Brietzig. Tarnów, SE Poland
Brzeżany *see* Berezhany
112 K12 **Brzeziny** Skierniewice, C Poland
Brzostowica Wielka *see* Vyalikaya Byerastavitsa
113 O17 **Brzozów** Krosno, SE Poland
Bsharrī/Bsherri *see* Bcharré
197 I13 **Bua** Vanua Levu, N Fiji
97 J20 **Bua** Halland, S Sweden
84 M13 **Bua** ≈ C Malawi
Bua *see* Čiovo
83 L18 **Bu'aale** *It.* Buale. Jubbada Dhexe, SW Somalia
201 Q8 **Buada Lagoon** *lagoon* Nauru, C Pacific Ocean
195 W14 **Buala** Santa Isabel, E Solomon Islands
Buale *see* Bu'aale
202 H1 **Buariki** *atoll* Tungaru, W Kiribati
178 I10 **Bua Yai** *var.* Ban Bua Yai. Nakhon Ratchasima, E Thailand
77 P8 **Bu'ayrāt al Ḩasūn** *var.* Buwayrāt al Hasūn. C Libya
78 H13 **Buba** S Guinea-Bissau
175 Qq7 **Bubaa** Sulawesi, N Indonesia
83 D20 **Bubanza** NW Burundi
85 K18 **Bubi** *prev.* Bubye. ≈ S Zimbabwe
148 L11 **Būbīyan, Jazīrat** *island* E Kuwait
Bublitz *see* Bobolice
Bubye *see* Bubi
197 J13 **Buca** *prev.* Mbutha. Vanua Levu, N Fiji
142 F16 **Bucak** Burdur, SW Turkey
56 G8 **Bucaramanga** Santander, N Colombia
109 M18 **Buccino** Campania, S Italy
118 K9 **Bucecea** Botoşani, NE Romania
118 J6 **Buchach** *Pol.* Buczacz. Ternopil's'ka Oblast', W Ukraine
191 Q12 **Buchan** Victoria, SE Australia
78 J17 **Buchanan** *prev.* Grand Bassa. SW Liberia
25 R3 **Buchanan** Georgia, SE USA
33 O11 **Buchanan** Michigan, N USA
23 T6 **Buchanan** Virginia, NE USA
27 R10 **Buchanan Dam** Texas, SW USA
27 R10 **Buchanan, Lake** ⊠ Texas, SW USA
98 L8 **Buchan Ness** *headland* NE Scotland, UK
11 T12 **Buchans** Newfoundland, Newfoundland and Labrador, SE Canada
Bucharest *see* Bucureşti
103 H20 **Buchen** Baden-Württemberg, SW Germany
102 I10 **Buchholz in der Nordheide** Niedersachsen, NW Germany
110 I8 **Buchs** Aargau, N Switzerland
110 F7 **Buchs** Sankt Gallen, NE Switzerland
102 H13 **Bückeburg** Niedersachsen, NW Germany
38 K14 **Buckeye** Arizona, SW USA
Buckeye State *see* Ohio
23 S4 **Buckhannon** West Virginia, NE USA
27 T9 **Buckholts** Texas, SW USA
98 K8 **Buckie** NE Scotland, UK
12 M12 **Buckingham** Québec, SE Canada
23 U6 **Buckingham** Virginia, NE USA
99 N21 **Buckinghamshire** *cultural region* SE England, UK
41 N8 **Buckland** Alaska, USA
190 G7 **Buckleboo** South Australia
28 K7 **Bucklin** Kansas, C USA
29 T3 **Bucklin** Missouri, C USA
38 I12 **Buckskin Mountains** ▲▲ Arizona, SW USA
21 R7 **Bucksport** Maine, NE USA
84 A9 **Buco Zau** Cabinda, NW Angola
Bu Craa *see* Bou Craa
118 K14 **Bucureşti** *Eng.* Bucharest, *Ger.* Bukarest; *prev.* Altenburg, *anc.* Cetatea Damboviţei. ● (Romania) Bucureşti, S Romania
33 S12 **Bucyrus** Ohio, N USA
Buczacz *see* Buchach
96 E9 **Bud** Møre og Romsdal, S Norway
27 S11 **Buda** Texas, SW USA
121 O18 **Buda-Kashalyova** *Rus.* Buda-Koshelëvo. Homyel'skaya Voblasts', SE Belarus
Buda-Koshelëvo *see* Buda-Kashalyova
177 G4 **Budalin** Sagaing, C Myanmar
113 J22 **Budapest** *off.* Budapest Főváros, *SCr.* Budimpešta. ● (Hungary) Pest, N Hungary
158 K11 **Budaun** Uttar Pradesh, N India
147 O9 **Budayyi'ah** *oasis* C Saudi Arabia
205 Y12 **Budd Coast** *physical region* Antarctica
Buddenbrock *see* Brodnica
109 C17 **Budduso** Sardegna, Italy, C Mediterranean Sea
99 I23 **Bude** SW England, UK
24 J7 **Bude** Mississippi, S USA
101 K16 **Budel** Noord-Brabant, SE Netherlands
102 I8 **Büdelsdorf** Schleswig-Holstein, N Germany
131 O14 **Budënnovsk** Stavropol'skiy Kray, SW Russian Federation
118 K14 **Budeşti** Călăraşi, SE Romania
Budgewoi *see* Budgewoi Lake
191 T8 **Budgewoi Lake** *var.* Budgewoi. New South Wales, SE Australia
94 I2 **Búdhardalur** Vesturland, W Iceland
Budimpešta *see* Budapest
81 J16 **Budjala** Equateur, NW Zaire
108 G10 **Budrio** Emilia-Romagna, C Italy
Budslav *see* Budslaw
121 K14 **Budslaw** *Rus.* Budslav. Minskaya Voblasts', N Belarus
Budua *see* Budva
174 Ll5 **Budu, Tanjung** *headland* East Malaysia
115 J17 **Budva** *It.* Budua. Montenegro, SW Yugoslavia
Budweis *see* České Budějovice
Budyšin *see* Bautzen
81 D16 **Buea** Sud-Ouest, SW Cameroon
105 S13 **Buëch** ≈ SE France
20 J17 **Buena** New Jersey, NE USA
64 K12 **Buena Esperanza** San Luis, C Argentina
56 C11 **Buenaventura** Valle del Cauca, W Colombia
42 I4 **Buenaventura** Chihuahua, N Mexico
59 M18 **Buena Vista** Santa Cruz, C Bolivia
42 G10 **Buenavista** Baja California Sur, W Mexico
39 S5 **Buena Vista** Colorado, C USA
25 S5 **Buena Vista** Georgia, SE USA
23 T6 **Buena Vista** Virginia, NE USA
46 F5 **Buena Vista, Bahia de** *bay* N Cuba
37 R13 **Buena Vista Lake Bed** ◎ California, W USA
107 P8 **Buendía, Embalse de** ⊠ C Spain
65 F16 **Bueno, Río** ≈ S Chile
64 N12 **Buenos Aires** *hist.* Santa Maria del Buen Aire. ● (Argentina) Buenos Aires, E Argentina
45 O15 **Buenos Aires** Puntarenas, SE Costa Rica
63 C20 **Buenos Aires** *off.* Provincia de Buenos Aires. ◈ *province* E Argentina
65 H19 **Buenos Aires, Lago** *var.* Lago General Carrera. ◎ Argentina/Chile
56 C13 **Buesaco** Nariño, SW Colombia
31 U8 **Buffalo** Minnesota, N USA
28 K8 **Buffalo** Missouri, C USA
20 D10 **Buffalo** New York, NE USA
29 T6 **Buffalo** Oklahoma, C USA
30 J7 **Buffalo** South Dakota, N USA
27 V8 **Buffalo** Texas, SW USA
35 W12 **Buffalo** Wyoming, C USA
31 U11 **Buffalo Center** Iowa, C USA
26 M3 **Buffalo Lake** ⊠ Texas, SW USA
32 K7 **Buffalo Lake** ⊠ Wisconsin, N USA
9 S12 **Buffalo Narrows** Saskatchewan, C Canada
29 U9 **Buffalo River** ≈ Arkansas, C USA
31 R5 **Buffalo River** ≈ Minnesota, N USA
22 I10 **Buffalo River** ≈ Tennessee, S USA
32 J6 **Buffalo River** ≈ Wisconsin, N USA
46 L12 **Buff Bay** E Jamaica
25 T3 **Buford** Georgia, SE USA
30 J3 **Buford** North Dakota, N USA
35 Y17 **Buford** Wyoming, C USA
118 J14 **Buftea** Bucureşti, S Romania
86 I9 **Bug** *Bel.* Zakhodni Buh, *Eng.* Western Bug, *Rus.* Zapadnyy Bug, *Ukr.* Zakhidnyy Buh. ≈ E Europe
56 D11 **Buga** Valle del Cauca, W Colombia
168 F7 **Buga** Dzavhan, W Mongolia
105 O17 **Bugarach, Pic du** ▲ S France
152 B12 **Bugdayly** Balkanskiy Velayat, W Turkmenistan
Buggs Island Lake *see* John H.Kerr Reservoir
Bughotu *see* Santa Isabel
175 Q12 **Bugingkalo** Sulawesi, C Indonesia
Bugingkaro *see* Bungingkolu, Tanjung
66 P6 **Bugio** *island* Madeira, Portugal, NE Atlantic Ocean
94 M8 **Bugøynes** Finnmark, N Norway
129 Q3 **Bugrino** Nenetskiy Avtonomnyy Okrug, NW Russian Federation
131 T5 **Bugul'ma** Respublika Tatarstan, W Russian Federation
Bügür *see* Luntai
131 T6 **Buguruslan** Orenburgskaya Oblast', W Russian Federation
165 R9 **Buh He** ≈ C China
35 O15 **Buhl** Idaho, NW USA
103 F22 **Bühl** Baden-Württemberg, SW Germany
118 K10 **Buhuşi** Bacău, E Romania
Buie d'Istria *see* Buje
99 J20 **Builth Wells** E Wales, UK
195 S13 **Buin** Bougainville Island, NE PNG
110 J9 **Buin, Piz** ▲ Austria/Switzerland
131 Q4 **Buinsk** Chuvashskaya Respublika, W Russian Federation
131 Q4 **Buinsk** Respublika Tatarstan, W Russian Federation
169 R8 **Buir Nur** *Mong.* Buyr Nuur. ◎ China/Mongolia *see also* Buyr Nuur
100 M5 **Buitenpost** *Fris.* Bûtenpost. Friesland, N Netherlands
Buitenzorg *see* Bogor
85 F19 **Buitepos** Omaheke, E Namibia
107 N7 **Buitrago del Lozoya** Madrid, C Spain
Buj *see* Buy
106 M13 **Bujalance** Andalucía, S Spain
115 O17 **Bujanovac** Serbia, SE Yugoslavia
107 S6 **Bujaraloz** Aragón, NE Spain
114 A9 **Buje** *It.* Buie d'Istria. Istra, NW Croatia
Bujnurd *see* Bojnūrd
83 D21 **Bujumbura** *prev.* Usumbura. ● (Burundi) W Burundi
83 D20 **Bujumbura** ✕ W Burundi
126 L15 **Bukachacha** Chitinskaya Oblast', S Russian Federation
165 N11 **Bukadaban Feng** ▲ C China
195 R11 **Buka Island** *island* NE PNG
83 F18 **Bukakata** S Uganda
81 N24 **Bukama** Shaba, SE Zaire
148 J4 **Būkān** *var.* Bowkān. Āẕarbāyjān-e Bākhtarī, NW Iran
Bukantau, Gory *see* Bŭkantow-Toghi
152 K8 **Bŭkantow-Toghi** *Rus.* Gory Bukantau. ▲▲ N Uzbekistan
Bukarest *see* Bucureşti
81 O19 **Bukavu** *prev.* Costermansville. Sud Kivu, E Zaire
83 F21 **Bukene** Tabora, NW Tanzania
147 W8 **Bū Khābī** *var.* Bakhābī. NW Oman
Bukhara *see* Bukhoro
Bukharskaya Oblast' *see* Bukhoro Wiloyati
152 L11 **Bukhoro** *var.* Bokhara, *Rus.* Bukhara. Bukhoro Wiloyati, C Uzbekistan
152 J11 **Bukhoro Wiloyati** *Rus.* Bukharskaya Oblast'. ◈ *province* C Uzbekistan
174 I12 **Bukitkemuning** Sumatera, W Indonesia
173 G8 **Bukittinggi** *prev.* Fort de Kock. Sumatera, W Indonesia
113 L21 **Bükk** ▲▲ NE Hungary
83 F19 **Bukoba** Kagera, NW Tanzania
115 N20 **Bukovo** S FYR Macedonia
110 G6 **Bülach** Zürich, NW Switzerland
Būlaevo *see* Bulayevo
168 I6 **Bulag** Hövsgöl, N Mongolia
168 M7 **Bulag** Töv, C Mongolia
168 I8 **Bulagiyn Denj** Arhangay, C Mongolia
191 U7 **Bulahdelah** New South Wales, SE Australia
176 Yy15 **Bulaka, Sungai** ≈ Irian Jaya, E Indonesia
179 Qq12 **Bulan** Luzon, N Philippines
143 N11 **Bulancak** Giresun, N Turkey
158 J10 **Bulandshahr** Uttar Pradesh, N India
143 R14 **Bulanık** Muş, E Turkey
131 V7 **Bulanovo** Orenburgskaya Oblast', W Russian Federation
85 J17 **Bulawayo** *var.* Buluwayo. Matabeleland North, SW Zimbabwe
85 J17 **Bulawayo** ✕ Matabeleland North, SW Zimbabwe
151 Q6 **Bulayevo** *Kaz.* Būlaevo. Severnyy Kazakhstan, N Kazakhstan
142 D15 **Buldan** Denizli, SW Turkey
160 G12 **Buldāna** Mahārāshtra, C India
40 E16 **Buldir Island** *island* Aleutian Islands, Alaska, USA
Buldur *see* Burdur
168 H9 **Bulgan** Bayanhongor, C Mongolia
168 K6 **Bulgan** Bulgan, N Mongolia
168 F7 **Bulgan** Hovd, W Mongolia
168 J5 **Bulgan** Hövsgöl, N Mongolia
168 J10 **Bulgan** Ömnogövĭ, S Mongolia
168 J7 **Bulgan** ◈ *province* N Mongolia
116 H10 **Bulgaria** *off.* Republic of Bulgaria, *Bul.* Bŭlgariya; *prev.* People's Republic of Bulgaria. ◆ *republic* SE Europe
Bŭlgariya *see* Bulgaria
116 L9 **Bŭlgarka** ▲ E Bulgaria
175 T7 **Buli** Pulau Halmahera, E Indonesia
175 Tt7 **Buli, Teluk** *bay* Pulau Halmahera, E Indonesia
166 J13 **Buliu He** ≈ S China
Bullange *see* Büllingen
106 M11 **Bullaque** ≈ C Spain
107 Q13 **Bullas** Murcia, SE Spain
82 M12 **Bullaxaar** Woqooyi Galbeed, NW Somalia
110 C9 **Bulle** Fribourg, SW Switzerland
193 G15 **Buller** ≈ South Island, NZ
191 P12 **Buller, Mount** ▲ Victoria, SE Australia
38 H11 **Bullhead City** Arizona, SW USA
101 N21 **Büllingen** *Fr.* Bullange. Liège, E Belgium
Bullion State *see* Missouri
23 T14 **Bull Island** *island* South Carolina, SE USA
190 M4 **Bulloo River Overflow** *wetland* New South Wales, SE Australia
192 M12 **Bulls** Manawatu-Wanganui, North Island, NZ
23 T14 **Bulls Bay** *bay* South Carolina, SE USA
29 U9 **Bull Shoals Lake** ⊠ Arkansas/Missouri, C USA
189 Q2 **Bulman** Northern Territory, N Australia
168 I6 **Bulnayn Nuruu** ▲▲ N Mongolia
194 J13 **Bulolo** Morobe, C PNG
175 Qq7 **Bulowa, Gunung** ▲ Sulawesi, N Indonesia
Bulqiza *see* Bulqizë
115 L19 **Bulqizë** *var.* Bulqiza. Dibër, C Albania
Bulsar *see* Valsād
175 R7 **Buludawa Keten, Pegunungan** ▲▲ Sulawesi, N Indonesia
175 Pp13 **Bulukumba** *prev.* Boeloekoemba. Sulawesi, C Indonesia
153 O11 **Bulunghur** *Rus.* Bulungur; *prev.* Krasnogvardeysk. Samarqand Wiloyati, C Uzbekistan
81 I21 **Bulungu** Bandundu, SW Zaire
Bulungur *see* Bulunghur
Buluwayo *see* Bulawayo
81 K17 **Bumba** Equateur, N Zaire
124 O15 **Bumbah, Khalīj al** *gulf* N Libya
168 K8 **Bumbat** Övörhangay, C Mongolia
83 F19 **Bumbire Island** *island* N Tanzania
175 Oo4 **Bum Bun, Pulau** *island* East Malaysia
83 J17 **Buna** North Eastern, NE Kenya
27 Y10 **Buna** Texas, SW USA
Bunab *see* Bonāb
Bunai *see* M'bunai
153 S13 **Bunay** S Tajikistan
188 I13 **Bunbury** Western Australia
99 E14 **Buncrana** *Ir.* Bun Cranncha. NW Ireland
Bun Cranncha *see* Buncrana
189 Z9 **Bundaberg** Queensland, E Australia
191 T5 **Bundarra** New South Wales, SE Australia
102 G13 **Bünde** Nordrhein-Westfalen, NW Germany
158 H13 **Būndi** Rājasthān, N India
194 I12 **Bundi** Madang, N PNG
Bun Dobhráin *see* Bundoran
99 D15 **Bundoran** *Ir.* Bun Dobhráin. NW Ireland
115 K18 **Bunë** *SCr.* Bojana. ≈ Albania/Yugoslavia *see also* Bojana
179 R16 **Bunga** ≈ Mindanao, S Philippines
173 Ff10 **Bungalaut, Selat** *strait* W Indonesia
178 Ii8 **Bung Kan** Nong Khai, E Thailand
189 N4 **Bungle Bungle Range** ▲▲ Western Australia
84 C10 **Bungo** Uíge, NW Angola
83 G18 **Bungoma** Western, W Kenya
170 Dd15 **Bungo-suidō** *strait* SW Japan
170 Dd13 **Bungo-Takada** Ōita, Kyūshū, SW Japan
102 K8 **Bungsberg** *hill* N Germany
Bungur *see* Bunyu
81 P17 **Bunia** Haut-Zaïre, NE Zaire
37 U6 **Bunker Hill** ▲ Nevada, W USA
24 I7 **Bunkie** Louisiana, S USA
25 X10 **Bunnell** Florida, SE USA
107 S10 **Buñol** País Valenciano, E Spain
100 K11 **Bunschoten** Utrecht, C Netherlands
142 K14 **Bünyan** Kayseri, C Turkey
175 Oo5 **Bunyu** *var.* Bungur. Borneo, N Indonesia
175 Oo5 **Bunyu, Pulau** *island* N Indonesia
Bunzlau *see* Bolesławiec
Buoddobohki *see* Patoniva
126 Ll6 **Buorkhaya Guba** *bay* N Russian Federation
176 Z15 **Bupul** Irian Jaya, E Indonesia
83 K19 **Bura** Coast, SE Kenya
82 P12 **Buraan** Sanaag, N Somalia
Būrabay *see* Borovoye
Buraida *see* Buraydah
Buraimi *see* Al Buraymī
151 Y11 **Buran** Vostochnyy Kazakhstan, E Kazakhstan
164 G15 **Burang** Xizang Zizhiqu, W China
Burao *see* Burco
144 H8 **Burāq** Dar'ā, S Syria
147 O6 **Buraydah** *var.* Buraida. Al Qaşīm, N Saudi Arabia
37 S15 **Burbank** California, W USA
33 N11 **Burbank** Illinois, N USA
191 Q8 **Burcher** New South Wales, SE Australia
82 N13 **Burco** *var.* Burao, Bur'o. Togdheer, NW Somalia
152 L13 **Burdalyk** Lebapskiy Velayat, E Turkmenistan
189 W6 **Burdekin River** ≈ Queensland, NE Australia
29 O7 **Burden** Kansas, C USA
Burdigala *see* Bordeaux
142 E15 **Burdur** *var.* Buldur. Burdur, SW Turkey
142 E15 **Burdur** *var.* Buldur. ◈ *province* SW Turkey
142 E15 **Burdur Gölü** *salt lake* SW Turkey
67 H21 **Burdwood Bank** *undersea feature* SW Atlantic Ocean
82 I12 **Burē** NW Ethiopia
82 H13 **Burē** W Ethiopia
95 J15 **Bureå** Västerbotten, N Sweden
103 G14 **Büren** Nordrhein-Westfalen, W Germany
168 K6 **Bürengiyn Nuruu** ▲▲ N Mongolia
168 E8 **Bürenhayrhan** Hovd, W Mongolia
Būrewāla *see* Mandi Būrewāla
127 N17 **Bureya** ≈ SE Russian Federation
94 J9 **Burfjord** Troms, N Norway
102 L13 **Burg** *var.* Burg an der Ihle, Burg bei Magdeburg. Sachsen-Anhalt, C Germany
Burg an der Ihle *see* Burg
116 N10 **Burgas** *var.* Bourgas. Burgaska Oblast, E Bulgaria
116 N9 **Burgas** ✕ Burgaska Oblast, E Bulgaria
Burgas *see* Burgaska Oblast
116 L9 **Burgaska Oblast** *var.* Burgas. ◈ *province* E Bulgaria
116 N10 **Burgaski Zaliv** *gulf* E Bulgaria
116 M10 **Burgasko Ezero** *lagoon* E Bulgaria
23 V11 **Burgaw** North Carolina, SE USA
Burg bei Magdeburg *see* Burg
110 E8 **Burgdorf** Bern, NW Switzerland
111 Y7 **Burgenland** *off.* Land Burgenland. ◈ *state* SE Austria
11 S13 **Burgeo** Newfoundland, Newfoundland and Labrador, SE Canada
85 I24 **Burgersdorp** Eastern Cape, SE South Africa
85 K20 **Burgersfort** Mpumalanga, NE South Africa
103 N23 **Burghausen** Bayern, SE Germany
145 O5 **Burghūth, Sabkhat al** ◎ E Syria
103 M20 **Burglengenfeld** Bayern, SE Germany
43 P9 **Burgos** Tamaulipas, C Mexico
107 N4 **Burgos** Castilla-León, N Spain
107 N4 **Burgos** ◈ *province* Castilla-León, N Spain
Burgstadlberg *see* Hradiště
97 P20 **Burgsvik** Gotland, SE Sweden
Burgum *see* Bergum
Burgundy *see* Bourgogne
165 Q11 **Burhan Budai Shan** ▲▲ C China
142 B12 **Burhaniye** Balıkesir, W Turkey
160 G12 **Burhānpur** Madhya Pradesh, C India
179 Q11 **Burias Island** *island* C Philippines
131 W7 **Buribay** Respublika Bashkortostan, W Russian Federation
45 O17 **Burica, Punta** *headland* Costa Rica/Panama
178 Ii10 **Buriram** *var.* Buri Ram, Puriramya. Buri Ram, E Thailand
107 S10 **Burjassot** País Valenciano, E Spain
83 N16 **Burka Giibi** Hiiraan, C Somalia
153 X8 **Burkan** ≈ E Kyrgyzstan
27 R4 **Burkburnett** Texas, SW USA
31 O12 **Burke** South Dakota, N USA
8 K15 **Burke Channel** *channel* British Columbia, W Canada
204 J10 **Burke Island** *island* Antarctica
22 L7 **Burkesville** Kentucky, S USA
189 T4 **Burketown** Queensland, NE Australia
27 Q8 **Burkett** Texas, SW USA
27 Y9 **Burkeville** Texas, SW USA
23 V7 **Burkeville** Virginia, NE USA
79 O12 **Burkina** *off.* Burkina Faso; *prev.* Upper Volta. ◆ *republic* W Africa
Burkina Faso *see* Burkina
204 L13 **Burks, Cape** *headland* Antarctica
12 H12 **Burk's Falls** Ontario, S Canada
103 H23 **Burladingen** Baden-Württemberg, S Germany
27 T7 **Burleson** Texas, SW USA
35 P15 **Burley** Idaho, NW USA
150 G8 **Burlin** Zapadnyy Kazakhstan, NW Kazakhstan
12 G16 **Burlington** Ontario, S Canada
39 W4 **Burlington** Colorado, C USA
31 Y15 **Burlington** Iowa, C USA
29 P5 **Burlington** Kansas, C USA
23 T9 **Burlington** North Carolina, SE USA
30 M3 **Burlington** North Dakota, N USA
20 L7 **Burlington** Vermont, NE USA
32 M9 **Burlington** Wisconsin, N USA
29 Q1 **Burlington Junction** Missouri, C USA
Burma *see* Myanmar
8 L17 **Burnaby** British Columbia, SW Canada
119 O12 **Burnas, Ozero** ◎ SW Ukraine
27 S10 **Burnet** Texas, SW USA
37 O3 **Burney** California, W USA
191 O16 **Burnie** Tasmania, SE Australia
99 L17 **Burnley** NW England, UK
151 Q16 **Burnoye** Zhambyl, S Kazakhstan
159 R15 **Burnpur** West Bengal, NE India
34 K14 **Burns** Oregon, NW USA
28 K11 **Burns Flat** Oklahoma, C USA
22 M7 **Burnside** Kentucky, S USA
15 Ii5 **Burnside** ≈ Northwest Territories, NW Canada
34 L15 **Burns Junction** Oregon, NW USA
8 L13 **Burns Lake** British Columbia, SW Canada
31 V9 **Burnsville** Minnesota, N USA
23 P9 **Burnsville** North Carolina, SE USA
23 R4 **Burnsville** West Virginia, NE USA
12 I13 **Burnt River** ≈ Ontario, SE Canada
12 I11 **Burntroot Lake** ◎ Ontario, SE Canada
9 W12 **Burntwood** ≈ Manitoba, C Canada
Bur'o *see* Burco
164 L2 **Burqin** Xinjiang Uygur Zizhiqu, NW China
190 J8 **Burra** South Australia
191 S9 **Burragorang, Lake** ⊠ New South Wales, SE Australia
98 K5 **Burray** *island* NE Scotland, UK
115 L19 **Burrel** *var.* Burreli. Dibër, C Albania
Burreli *see* Burrel
191 R8 **Burrendong Reservoir** ⊠ New South Wales, SE Australia
191 R5 **Burren Junction** New South Wales, SE Australia
107 T9 **Burriana** País Valenciano, E Spain
191 R10 **Burrinjuck Reservoir** ⊠ New South Wales, SE Australia
38 J12 **Burro Creek** ≈ Arizona, SW USA
42 M5 **Burro, Serranías del** ▲▲ NW Mexico
64 K7 **Burruyacú** Tucumán, N Argentina
142 E12 **Bursa** *var.* Brussa; *prev.* Brusa, *anc.* Prusa. Bursa, NW Turkey
142 D12 **Bursa** *var.* Brusa, Brussa. ◈ *province* NW Turkey
77 Y9 **Bûr Safâga** *var.* Būr Safājah. E Egypt
Būr Safājah *see* Bûr Safâga
Būr Sa'īd *see* Port Said
83 O14 **Bur Tinle** Mudug, C Somalia
33 Q5 **Burt Lake** ◎ Michigan, N USA
Burtnieks *see* Burtnieku Ezers
120 H7 **Burtnieku Ezers** *var.* Burtnieks. ◎ N Latvia
33 Q9 **Burton** Michigan, N USA
Burton on Trent *see* Burton upon Trent
99 M19 **Burton upon Trent** *var.* Burton on Trent, Burton-upon-Trent. C England, UK
95 J15 **Burträsk** Västerbotten, N Sweden
151 S14 **Burubaytal** *prev.* Burylbaytal. Zhambyl, SE Kazakhstan
Burujird *see* Borūjerd
Burultokay *see* Fuhai
147 R15 **Burūm** SE Yemen
151 U16 **Burunday** *Kaz.* Boralday. Almaty, SE Kazakhstan
83 D21 **Burundi** *off.* Republic of Burundi; *prev.* Kingdom of Burundi, Urundi. ◆ *republic* C Africa
175 S11 **Buru, Pulau** *prev.* Boeroe. *island* E Indonesia
79 T17 **Burutu** Delta, S Nigeria
8 G7 **Burwash Landing** Yukon Territory, W Canada
31 O14 **Burwell** Nebraska, C USA
99 L17 **Bury** NW England, UK
126 K15 **Buryatiya, Respublika** *prev.* Buryatskaya ASSR. ◈ *autonomous republic* S Russian Federation
Buryatskaya ASSR *see* Buryatiya, Respublika
Burylbaytal *see* Burubaytal
119 S3 **Buryn'** Sums'ka Oblast', NE Ukraine
99 P20 **Bury St Edmunds** *hist.* Beodericsworth. E England, UK
116 G8 **Bŭrziya** ≈ NW Bulgaria
108 D9 **Busalla** Liguria, NW Italy
179 R17 **Busa, Mount** ▲ Mindanao, S Philippines
Busan *see* Pusan
145 N5 **Buşayrah** Dayr az Zawr, E Syria
Buševa *see* Baba
149 N12 **Būshehr** *off.* Ostān-e Būshehr. ◈ *province* SW Iran
Būshehr/Bushire *see* Bandar-e Būshehr
27 N2 **Bushland** Texas, SW USA
32 J12 **Bushnell** Illinois, N USA
Busi *see* Biševo
83 G18 **Busia** SE Uganda
Busiasch *see* Buziaş
81 K16 **Businga** Equateur, NW Zaire
81 J18 **Busira** ≈ NW Zaire
118 I5 **Bus'k** *Rus.* Busk. L'vivs'ka Oblast', W Ukraine
97 E14 **Buskerud** ◈ *county* S Norway
115 F14 **Buško Jezero** ⊠ SW Bosnia and Herzegovina
113 M15 **Busko-Zdrój** Kielce, SE Poland
Busra *see* Al Başrah, Iraq
Buşrá *see* Buşrá ash Shām, Syria
144 H9 **Buşrá ash Shām** *var.* Bosora, Bosra, Bozrah, Buşrá. Dar'ā, S Syria
188 I13 **Busselton** Western Australia
83 C14 **Busseri** ≈ W Sudan
108 E9 **Busseto** Emilia-Romagna, C Italy
108 A8 **Bussoleno** Piemonte, NE Italy
Bussora *see* Al Başrah
100 J10 **Bussum** Noord-Holland, C Netherlands
43 N7 **Bustamante** Nuevo León, NE Mexico
65 I23 **Bustamante, Punta** *headland* S Argentina
Bustan *see* Bŭston
118 J12 **Buşteni** Prahova, SE Romania
108 D7 **Busto Arsizio** Lombardia, N Italy
153 Q10 **Bŭston** *Rus.* Buston. NW Tajikistan
152 I9 **Bŭston** *Rus.* Bustan. Qoraqalpoghiston Respublikasi, W Uzbekistan
179 P12 **Busuanga Island** *island* Calamian Group, W Philippines
102 H8 **Büsum** Schleswig-Holstein, N Germany
81 M16 **Buta** Haut-Zaïre, N Zaire
83 E20 **Butare** *prev.* Astrida. S Rwanda
203 O2 **Butaritari** *atoll* Tungaru, W Kiribati
Butawal *see* Butwal

◆ Country
● Country Capital
◇ Dependent Territory
○ Dependent Territory Capital
◈ Administrative Region
✕ International Airport
▲ Mountain
▲▲ Mountain Range
Volcano
≈ River
◎ Lake
⊠ Reservoir

98 *H13* **Bute** *cultural region* SW Scotland, UK
168 *K6* **Büteeliyn Nuruu** ▲ N Mongolia
8 *L16* **Bute Inlet** *fjord* British Columbia, W Canada
98 *H12* **Bute, Island of** *island* SW Scotland, UK
81 *P18* **Butembo** Nord Kivu, NE Zaire
Bütenpost *see* Buitenpost
109 *K25* **Butera** Sicilia, Italy, C Mediterranean Sea
101 *M20* **Bütgenbach** Liège, E Belgium
Butha Qi *see* Zalantun
177 *F5* **Buthidaung** Arakan State, W Myanmar
63 *I16* **Butiá** Rio Grande do Sul, S Brazil
83 *F17* **Butiaba** NW Uganda
25 *N6* **Butler** Alabama, S USA
25 *S5* **Butler** Georgia, SE USA
33 *Q11* **Butler** Indiana, N USA
29 *R5* **Butler** Missouri, C USA
20 *B14* **Butler** Pennsylvania, NE USA
204 *K5* **Butler Island** *island* Antarctica
23 *U8* **Butner** North Carolina, SE USA
175 *Qq13* **Buton, Pulau** *var.* Pulau Butung; *prev.* Boetoeng. *island* C Indonesia
175 *Qq13* **Buton, Selat** *strait* C Indonesia
Bütow *see* Bytów
115 *L23* **Butrintit, Liqeni i** ◎ S Albania
25 *N3* **Buttahatchee River** ⇝ Alabama/Mississippi, S USA
35 *Q10* **Butte** Montana, NW USA
31 *O12* **Butte** Nebraska, C USA
173 *G3* **Butterworth** Pinang, Peninsular Malaysia
85 *J25* **Butterworth** *var.* Gcuwa. Eastern Cape, SE South Africa
11 *O3* **Button Islands** *island group* Northwest Territories, NE Canada
37 *R13* **Buttonwillow** California, W USA
179 *R14* **Butuan** *off.* Butuan City. Mindanao, S Philippines
Butung, Pulau *see* Buton, Pulau
Butuntum *see* Bitonto
130 *M8* **Buturlinovka** Voronezhskaya Oblast', W Russian Federation
159 *O11* **Butwal** *var.* Butawal. Western, C Nepal
103 *G17* **Butzbach** Hessen, W Germany
102 *L9* **Bützow** Mecklenburg-Vorpommern, N Germany
82 *N13* **Buuhoodle** Togdheer, N Somalia
83 *N16* **Buulobarde** *var.* Buulo Berde. Hiiraan, C Somalia Africa
Buulo Berde *see* Buulobarde
82 *P12* **Buuraha Cal Miskaat** ▲ NE Somalia
83 *L19* **Buur Gaabo** Jubbada Hoose, S Somalia
101 *M22* **Buurgplaatz** ▲ N Luxembourg
Buwayrāt al Hasūn *see* Bu'ayrāt al Ḩasūn
102 *I10* **Buxtehude** Niedersachsen, NW Germany
99 *L18* **Buxton** C England, UK
128 *M14* **Buy** *var.* Buj. Kostromskaya Oblast', NW Russian Federation
168 *G7* **Buyanbat** Govĭ-Altay, W Mongolia
168 *H8* **Buyant** Bayanhongor, C Mongolia
168 *D6* **Buyant** Bayan-Ölgiy, W Mongolia
168 *H7* **Buyant** Dzavhan, C Mongolia
169 *N9* **Buyant** Hentiy, C Mongolia
169 *N10* **Buyant-Uhaa** Dornogovĭ, SE Mongolia
168 *M7* **Buyant Ukha** ✕ (Ulaanbaatar) Töv, N Mongolia
131 *Q16* **Buynaksk** Respublika Dagestan, SW Russian Federation
121 *L20* **Buynavichy** *Rus.* Buynovichi. Homyel'skaya Voblasts', SE Belarus
Buynovichi *see* Buynavichy
78 *L16* **Buyo** SW Ivory Coast
78 *L16* **Buyo, Lac de** ▣ W Ivory Coast
169 *R7* **Buyr Nuur** *var.* Buir Nur. ◎ China/Mongolia *see also* Buir Nur
143 *T13* **Büyükağrı Dağı** *var.* Aghri Dagh, Agri Dagi, Koh I Noh, Masis, *Eng.* Great Ararat, Mount Ararat. ▲ E Turkey
143 *R15* **Büyük Çayı** ⇝ NE Turkey
116 *O13* **Büyük Çekmece** İstanbul, NW Turkey
116 *N12* **Büyükkarıştıran** Kırklareli, NW Turkey
117 *L14* **Büyükkemikli Burnu** *headland* NW Turkey
142 *E15* **Büyükmenderes Nehri** ⇝ SW Turkey
Büyükzap Suyu *see* Great Zab
104 *M9* **Buzançais** Indre, C France
118 *K13* **Buzău** Buzău, SE Romania
118 *K13* **Buzău** ◆ *county* SE Romania
118 *L12* **Buzău** ⇝ E Romania
77 *S11* **Buzaymah** *var.* Bzīmah. SE Libya
170 *D13* **Buzen** Fukuoka, Kyūshū, SW Japan
118 *F12* **Buziaş** *Ger.* Busiasch, *Hung.* Buziásfürdő; *prev.* Buziás. Timiş, W Romania
Buziásfürdő *see* Buziaş
85 *M18* **Búzi, Rio** ⇝ C Mozambique
119 *Q10* **Buz'kyy Lyman** *bay* S Ukraine
Büzmeyin *see* Byuzmeyin
151 *O8* **Buzuluk** Turgay, C Kazakhstan
131 *T6* **Buzuluk** Orenburgskaya Oblast', W Russian Federation
131 *N8* **Buzuluk** ⇝ SW Russian Federation
21 *P12* **Buzzards Bay** Massachusetts, NE USA
21 *P13* **Buzzards Bay** *bay* Massachusetts, NE USA
85 *G16* **Bwabata** Caprivi, NE Namibia
195 *P17* **Bwagaoia** Misima Island, SE PNG
Bwake *see* Bouaké
197 *C12* **Bwatnapne** Pentecost, C Vanuatu
121 *K14* **Byahoml'** *Rus.* Begoml'. Vitsyebskaya Voblasts', N Belarus
116 *J8* **Byala** Razgradska Oblast, N Bulgaria
116 *N9* **Byala** *prev.* Ak-Dere. Varnenska Oblast, NE Bulgaria
Byala Reka *see* Erydropótamos
116 *H8* **Byala Slatina** Oblast Montana, NW Bulgaria
121 *N15* **Byalynichy** *Rus.* Belynichi. Mahilyowskaya Voblasts', E Belarus
121 *G19* **Byaroza** *Pol.* Bereza Kartuska, *Rus.* Berëza. Brestskaya Voblasts', SW Belarus
Bybles *see* Jbail
113 *O14* **Bychawa** Lublin, SE Poland
Bychikha *see* Bychykha
120 *N11* **Bychykha** *Rus.* Bychikha. Vitsyebskaya Voblasts', NE Belarus
113 *I14* **Byczyna** *Ger.* Pitschen. Opole, SW Poland
Bydgoskie, Województwo *see* Bydgoszcz
112 *I10* **Bydgoszcz** *Ger.* Bromberg. Bydgoszcz, W Poland
112 *H9* **Bydgoszcz** *off.* Województwo Bydgoskie, *Ger.* Bromberg. ◆ *province* W Poland
121 *I17* **Byelaruskaya Hrada** *Rus.* Belorusskaya Gryada. *ridge* N Belarus
121 *G18* **Byelavyezhskaya Pushcha** *Pol.* Puszcza Białowieska, *Rus.* Belovezhskaya Pushcha. *forest* Belarus/Poland *see also* Białowieska, Puszcza
121 *H15* **Byenyakoni** *Rus.* Benyakoni. Hrodzyenskaya Voblasts', W Belarus
121 *M16* **Byerazino** *Rus.* Berezino. Minskaya Voblasts', C Belarus
120 *L13* **Byerazino** *Rus.* Berezino. Vitsyebskaya Voblasts', N Belarus
121 *L14* **Byerezino** *Rus.* Berezina. ⇝ C Belarus
120 *M13* **Byeshankovichy** *Rus.* Beshenkovichi. Vitsyebskaya Voblasts', N Belarus
33 *U13* **Byesville** Ohio, N USA
121 *P18* **Byesyedz'** *Rus.* Besed'. ⇝ SE Belarus
121 *H19* **Byezdzyezh** *Rus.* Bezdezh. Brestskaya Voblasts', SW Belarus
95 *J15* **Bygdeå** Västerbotten, N Sweden
96 *F12* **Bygdin** ◎ S Norway
95 *J15* **Bygdsiljum** Västerbotten, N Sweden
97 *E17* **Bygland** Aust-Agder, S Norway
97 *E17* **Byglandsfjord** Aust-Agder, S Norway
121 *N16* **Bykhaw** *Rus.* Bykhov. Mahilyowskaya Voblasts', E Belarus
Bykhov *see* Bykhaw
131 *P9* **Bykovo** Volgogradskaya Oblast', SW Russian Federation
126 *L6* **Bykovskiy** Respublika Sakha (Yakutiya), NE Russian Federation
205 *R12* **Byrd Glacier** *glacier* Antarctica
12 *K10* **Byrd, Lac** ◎ Québec, SE Canada
191 *P5* **Byrock** New South Wales, SE Australia
32 *L10* **Byron** Illinois, N USA
191 *V4* **Byron Bay** New South Wales, SE Australia
191 *V4* **Byron, Cape** *headland* New South Wales, E Australia
65 *F21* **Byron, Isla** *island* S Chile
Byron Island *see* Nikunau
67 *B24* **Byron Sound** *sound* NW Falkland Islands
126 *J5* **Byrranga, Gora** ▲ N Russian Federation
95 *J14* **Byske** Västerbotten, N Sweden
113 *K18* **Bystrá** ▲ N Slovakia
113 *F18* **Bystřice nad Pernštejnem** *Ger.* Bistritz ober Pernstein. Jižní Morava, SE Czech Republic
Bystrovka *see* Kemin
113 *G16* **Bystrzyca Kłodzka** *Ger.* Habelschwerdt. Wałbrzych, SW Poland
113 *I18* **Bytča** Stredné Slovensko, NW Slovakia
121 *L15* **Bytcha** *Rus.* Bytcha. Minskaya Voblasts', NE Belarus
Byteń/Byten' *see* Bytsyen'
113 *J16* **Bytom** *Ger.* Beuthen. Katowice, S Poland
112 *H7* **Bytów** *Ger.* Bütow. Słupsk, NW Poland
121 *H18* **Bytsyen'** *Pol.* Byteń, *Rus.* Byten'. Brestskaya Voblasts', SW Belarus
83 *E19* **Byumba** *var.* Biumba. N Rwanda
152 *F13* **Byuzmeyin** *Turkm.* Büzmeyin; *prev.* Bezmein. Akhalskiy Velayat, C Turkmenistan
121 *O20* **Byval'ki** Homyel'skaya Voblasts', SE Belarus
97 *O20* **Byxelkrok** Kalmar, S Sweden
Byzantium *see* İstanbul
Bzīmah *see* Buzaymah

C

64 *O6* **Caacupé** Cordillera, S Paraguay
64 *P6* **Caaguazú** *off.* Departamento de Caaguazú. ◆ *department* C Paraguay
84 *C13* **Caála** *var.* Kaala, Robert Williams, *Port.* Vila Robert Williams. Huambo, C Angola
64 *P7* **Caazapá** Caazapá, S Paraguay
64 *P7* **Caazapá** *off.* Departamento de Caazapá. ◆ *department* SE Paraguay
83 *P15* **Cabaad, Raas** *headland* C Somalia
179 *R14* **Cabadbaran** Mindanao, S Philippines
57 *N10* **Cabadisocaña** Amazonas, S Venezuela
46 *F5* **Cabaiguán** Sancti Spíritus, C Cuba
Caballeria, Cabo *see* Cavalleria, Cap de
39 *Q14* **Caballo Reservoir** ▣ New Mexico, SW USA
42 *L6* **Caballos Mesteños, Llano de los** *plain* N Mexico
106 *L2* **Cabañaquinta** Asturias, N Spain
44 *B9* **Cabañas** ◆ *department* E El Salvador
179 *P10* **Cabanatuan** *off.* Cabanatuan City. Luzon, N Philippines
13 *T8* **Cabano** Québec, SE Canada
106 *L11* **Cabeza del Buey** Extremadura, W Spain
47 *V5* **Cabezas de San Juan** *headland* E Puerto Rico
107 *N2* **Cabezón de la Sal** Cantabria, N Spain
Cabhán *see* Cavan
63 *B23* **Cabildo** Buenos Aires, E Argentina
Cabillonum *see* Chalon-sur-Saône
56 *H5* **Cabimas** Zulia, NW Venezuela
84 *A9* **Cabinda** *var.* Kabinda. Cabinda, NW Angola
84 *A9* **Cabinda** *var.* Kabinda. ◆ *province* NW Angola
35 *N7* **Cabinet Mountains** ▲ Idaho/Montana, NW USA
84 *B11* **Cabiri** Bengo, NW Angola
65 *J20* **Cabo Blanco** Santa Cruz, SE Argentina
84 *P13* **Cabo Delgado** *off.* Província de Capo Delgado. ◆ *province* NE Mozambique
12 *L9* **Cabonga, Réservoir** ▣ Québec, SE Canada
29 *V7* **Cabool** Missouri, C USA
191 *V2* **Caboolture** Queensland, E Australia
Cabora Bassa, Lake *see* Cahora Bassa, Albufeira de
42 *F3* **Caborca** Sonora, NW Mexico
Cabo San Lucas *see* San Lucas
29 *V11* **Cabot** Arkansas, C USA
12 *F12* **Cabot Head** *headland* Ontario, S Canada
16 *Ss10* **Cabot Strait** *strait* E Canada
Cabo Verde, Ilhas do *see* Cape Verde
106 *M14* **Cabra** Andalucía, S Spain
109 *B19* **Cabras** Sardegna, Italy, C Mediterranean Sea
196 *A15* **Cabras Island** *island* W Guam
47 *O8* **Cabrera** N Dominican Republic
107 *X10* **Cabrera** *anc.* Capraria. *island* Islas Baleares, Spain, W Mediterranean Sea
106 *J4* **Cabrera** ⇝ NW Spain
107 *Q15* **Cabrera, Sierra** ▲ S Spain
9 *S16* **Cabri** Saskatchewan, S Canada
107 *R10* **Cabriel** ⇝ E Spain
56 *M7* **Cabruta** Guárico, C Venezuela
179 *Oo8* **Cabugao** Luzon, N Philippines
56 *G10* **Cabuyaro** Meta, C Colombia
62 *I13* **Caçador** Santa Catarina, S Brazil
44 *G8* **Cacaguatique, Cordillera** *var.* Cordillera. ▲ NE El Salvador
114 *L13* **Čačak** Serbia, C Yugoslavia
57 *Y10* **Cacao** NE French Guiana
63 *H16* **Caçapava do Sul** Rio Grande do Sul, S Brazil
23 *U3* **Cacapon River** ⇝ West Virginia, NE USA
109 *J23* **Caccamo** Sicilia, Italy, C Mediterranean Sea
109 *A17* **Caccia, Capo** *headland* Sardegna, Italy, C Mediterranean Sea
61 *G18* **Cáceres** Mato Grosso, W Brazil
106 *J10* **Cáceres** *Ar.* Qazris. Extremadura, W Spain
106 *J9* **Cáceres** ◆ *province* Extremadura, W Spain
Cachacrou *see* Scotts Head Village
63 *C21* **Cacharí** Buenos Aires, E Argentina
28 *L12* **Cache** Oklahoma, C USA
8 *M16* **Cache Creek** British Columbia, SW Canada
37 *N6* **Cache Creek** ⇝ California, W USA
39 *S3* **Cache La Poudre River** ⇝ Colorado, C USA
Cacheo *see* Cacheu
29 *W11* **Cache River** ⇝ Arkansas, C USA
32 *L17* **Cache River** ⇝ Illinois, N USA
78 *G12* **Cacheu** *var.* Cacheo. W Guinea-Bissau
61 *I15* **Cachimbo** Pará, NE Brazil
61 *H15* **Cachimbo, Serra do** ▲ C Brazil
84 *D13* **Cachingues** Bié, C Angola
56 *G7* **Cáchira** Norte de Santander, N Colombia
63 *H16* **Cachoeira do Sul** Rio Grande do Sul, S Brazil
61 *O20* **Cachoeiro de Itapemirim** Espírito Santo, SE Brazil
84 *E12* **Cacolo** Lunda Sul, NE Angola
85 *C14* **Caconda** Huíla, C Angola
84 *A9* **Cacongo** Cabinda, NW Angola
37 *U9* **Cactus Peak** ▲ Nevada, W USA
84 *A11* **Cacuaco** Luanda, NW Angola
85 *B14* **Cacula** Huíla, SW Angola
69 *R12* **Caculuvar** ⇝ SW Angola
61 *O19* **Caçumba, Ilha** *island* SE Brazil
57 *N11* **Cacuri** Amazonas, S Venezuela
83 *N17* **Cadale** Shabeellaha Dhexe, E Somalia
107 *X4* **Cadaqués** Cataluña, NE Spain
113 *J18* **Čadca** *Hung.* Csaca. Stredné Slovensko, N Slovakia
29 *P13* **Caddo** Oklahoma, C USA
27 *R6* **Caddo** Texas, SW USA
27 *X6* **Caddo Lake** ▣ Louisiana/ Texas, SW USA
29 *S12* **Caddo Mountains** ▲ Arkansas, C USA
43 *O8* **Cadereyta** Nuevo León, NE Mexico
99 *J19* **Cader Idris** ▲ NW Wales, United Kingdom
190 *F3* **Cadibarrawirracanna, Lake** *salt lake* South Australia
12 *I7* **Cadillac** Québec, SE Canada
9 *T17* **Cadillac** Saskatchewan, S Canada
104 *K13* **Cadillac** Gironde, SW France
33 *P7* **Cadillac** Michigan, N USA
107 *V4* **Cadí, Torre de** ▲ NE Spain
179 *Q13* **Cadiz** *off.* Cadiz City. Negros, C Philippines
22 *H7* **Cadiz** Kentucky, S USA
33 *U13* **Cadiz** Ohio, N USA
106 *J15* **Cádiz** *anc.* Gades, Gadier, Gadir, Gadire. Andalucía, SW Spain
106 *K15* **Cádiz** ◆ *province* Andalucía, SW Spain
106 *I15* **Cadiz, Bahía de** *bay* SW Spain
Cadiz City *see* Cadiz
106 *H15* **Cadiz, Golfo de** *Eng.* Gulf of Cadiz. *gulf* Portugal/Spain
Cadiz, Gulf of *see* Cádiz, Golfo de
37 *X14* **Cadiz Lake** ◎ California, W USA
190 *E2* **Cadney Homestead** South Australia
Cadurcum *see* Cahors
85 *F17* **Caecae** Ngamiland, NW Botswana
104 *K4* **Caen** Calvados, N France
Caene/Caenepolis *see* Qena
Caerdydd *see* Cardiff
Caer Glou *see* Gloucester
Caer Gybi *see* Holyhead
Caerleon *see* Chester
Caer Luel *see* Carlisle
99 *I18* **Caernarfon** *var.* Caernarvon, Carnarvon. NW Wales, UK
99 *H18* **Caernarfon Bay** *bay* NW Wales, UK
99 *I19* **Caernarvon** *cultural region* NW Wales, UK
Caernarvon *see* Caernarfon
Caesaraugusta *see* Zaragoza
Caesarea Mazaca *see* Kayseri
Caesarobriga *see* Talavera de la Reina
Caesarodunum *see* Tours
Caesaromagus *see* Beauvais
Caesena *see* Cesena
61 *N17* **Caetité** Bahia, E Brazil
64 *J6* **Cafayate** Salta, N Argentina
179 *Pp9* **Cagayan** ⇝ Luzon, N Philippines
179 *R15* **Cagayan de Oro** *off.* Cagayan de Oro City. Mindanao, S Philippines
179 *Oo17* **Cagayan de Tawi Tawi** *island* S Philippines
179 *Pp14* **Cagayan Islands** *island group* C Philippines
33 *O14* **Cagles Mill Lake** ▣ Indiana, N USA
108 *I12* **Cagli** Marche, C Italy
109 *C20* **Cagliari** *anc.* Caralis. Sardegna, Italy, C Mediterranean Sea
109 *C20* **Cagliari, Golfo di** *gulf* Sardegna, Italy, C Mediterranean Sea
105 *U15* **Cagnes-sur-Mer** Alpes-Maritimes, SE France
56 *L5* **Cagua** Aragua, N Venezuela
179 *Pp8* **Cagua, Mount** ▲ Luzon, N Philippines
56 *F13* **Caguán, Río** ⇝ SW Colombia
47 *U6* **Caguas** E Puerto Rico
25 *P5* **Cahaba River** ⇝ Alabama, S USA
44 *E5* **Cahabón, Río** ⇝ C Guatemala
85 *B15* **Cahama** Cunene, SW Angola
99 *B21* **Caha Mountains** *Ir.* An Cheacha. ▲ SW Ireland
99 *D20* **Caher** *Ir.* An Cathair. S Ireland
99 *A21* **Cahersiveen** *Ir.* Cathair Saidhbhín. SW Ireland
32 *K15* **Cahokia** Illinois, N USA
85 *L15* **Cahora Bassa, Albufeira de** *var.* Lake Cabora Bassa. ▣ NW Mozambique
99 *G20* **Cahore Point** *Ir.* Rinn Chathóir. *headland* SE Ireland
104 *M14* **Cahors** *anc.* Cadurcum. Lot, S France
58 *D9* **Cahuapanas, Río** ⇝ N Peru
118 *M12* **Cahul** *Rus.* Kagul. S Moldova
Cahul, Lacul *see* Kahul, Ozero
85 *N16* **Caia** Sofala, C Mozambique
61 *J19* **Caiapó, Serra do** ▲ C Brazil
46 *F5* **Caibarién** Villa Clara, C Cuba
57 *O5* **Caicara** Monagas, NE Venezuela
61 *P14* **Caicó** Rio Grande do Norte, E Brazil
46 *M6* **Caicos Islands** *island group* W Turks and Caicos Islands
46 *L5* **Caicos Passage** *strait* Bahamas/Turks and Caicos Islands
167 *O9* **Caidian** *prev.* Hanyang. Hubei, C China
Caiffa *see* Ḩefa
188 *M12* **Caiguna** Western Australia
Caillí, Ceann *see* Hag's Head
42 *J11* **Caimanero, Laguna del** *var.* Laguna del Camaronero. *lagoon* E Pacific Ocean
119 *N10* **Căinari** *Rus.* Kaynary. C Moldova
59 *L19* **Caine, Río** ⇝ C Bolivia
Caiphas *see* Ḩefa
205 *N4* **Caird Coast** *physical region* Antarctica
98 *J9* **Cairn Gorm** ▲ C Scotland, UK
98 *J9* **Cairngorm Mountains** ▲ C Scotland, UK
41 *P12* **Cairn Mountain** ▲ Alaska, USA
189 *W4* **Cairns** Queensland, NE Australia
124 *Qq16* **Cairo** *Ar.* Al Qāhirah, *var.* El Qâhira. ● (Egypt) N Egypt
25 *T8* **Cairo** Georgia, SE USA
32 *L17* **Cairo** Illinois, N USA
77 *V8* **Cairo** ✕ C Egypt
Caiseal *see* Cashel
Caisleán an Bharraigh *see* Castlebar
Caisleán na Finne *see* Castlefinn
98 *J6* **Caithness** *cultural region* N Scotland, UK
85 *D15* **Caiundo** Cuando Cubango, S Angola
58 *C11* **Cajamarca** *prev.* Caxamarca. Cajamarca, NW Peru
58 *B11* **Cajamarca** *off.* Departamento de Cajamarca. ◆ *department* N Peru
105 *N14* **Cajarc** Lot, S France
179 *Q12* **Cajidiocan** Sibuyan Island, C Philippines
44 *G6* **Cajón, Represa El** ▣ NW Honduras
60 *N12* **Caju, Ilha do** *island* NE Brazil
Cakaubalavu Reef *see* Kavukavu Reef
165 *R10* **Caka Yanhu** ◎ C China
114 *E7* **Čakovec** *Ger.* Csakathurn, *Hung.* Csáktornya; *prev. Ger.* Tschakathurn. Medimurje, N Croatia
79 *V17* **Calabar** Cross River, S Nigeria
12 *K13* **Calabogie** Ontario, SE Canada
56 *L6* **Calabozo** Guárico, C Venezuela
109 *N20* **Calabria** *anc.* Bruttium. ◆ *region* SW Italy
106 *M16* **Calaburra, Punta de** *headland* S Spain
118 *G14* **Calafat** Dolj, SW Romania
Calafate *see* El Calafate
107 *Q4* **Calahorra** La Rioja, N Spain
105 *N1* **Calais** Pas-de-Calais, N France
21 *T5* **Calais** Maine, NE USA
Calais, Pas de *see* Dover, Strait of
Calalen *see* Kallalen
64 *H4* **Calama** Antofagasta, N Chile
Calamianes *see* Calamian Group
179 *P13* **Calamian Group** *var.* Calamianes. *island group* W Philippines
107 *R7* **Calamocha** Aragón, NE Spain
31 *N14* **Calamus River** ⇝ Nebraska, C USA
118 *G12* **Călan** *Ger.* Kalan, *Hung.* Pusztakalán. Hunedoara, SW Romania
107 *S7* **Calanda** Aragón, NE Spain
173 *E4* **Calang** Sumatera, W Indonesia
179 *P11* **Calapan** Mindoro, N Philippines
Călăras *see* Călăraşi
118 *M9* **Călăraşi** *var.* Călăras, *Rus.* Kalarash. C Moldova
118 *L14* **Călăraşi** Călăraşi, SE Romania
118 *K14* **Călăraşi** ◆ *county* SE Romania
56 *E10* **Calarca** Quindío, W Colombia
107 *Q12* **Calasparra** Murcia, SE Spain
109 *I23* **Calatafimi** Sicilia, Italy, C Mediterranean Sea
107 *Q6* **Calatayud** Aragón, NE Spain
179 *Pp11* **Calauag** Luzon, N Philippines
37 *P8* **Calaveras River** ⇝ California, W USA
179 *Oo11* **Calavite, Cape** *headland* Mindoro, N Philippines
179 *Qq12* **Calbayog** *off.* Calbayog City. Samar, C Philippines
179 *R12* **Calbiga** Samar, C Philippines
24 *G9* **Calcasieu Lake** ◎ Louisiana, S USA
24 *H8* **Calcasieu River** ⇝ Louisiana, S USA
58 *B6* **Calceta** Manabí, W Ecuador
63 *B16* **Calchaquí** Santa Fe, C Argentina
64 *J6* **Calchaquí, Río** ⇝ NW Argentina
60 *J10* **Calçoene** Amapá, NE Brazil
159 *S16* **Calcutta** West Bengal, NE India
159 *S16* **Calcutta** ✕ West Bengal, N India
56 *E9* **Caldas** *off.* Departamento de Caldas. ◆ *province* W Colombia
106 *F10* **Caldas da Rainha** Leiria, W Portugal
106 *G3* **Caldas de Reis** *var.* Caldas de Reyes. Galicia, NW Spain
Caldas de Reyes *see* Caldas de Reis
60 *F13* **Caldeirão** Amazonas, NW Brazil
64 *G7* **Caldera** Atacama, N Chile
44 *L14* **Caldera** Puntarenas, W Costa Rica
107 *N10* **Calderina** ▲ C Spain
143 *T13* **Çaldıran** Van, E Turkey
34 *M14* **Caldwell** Idaho, NW USA
29 *N8* **Caldwell** Kansas, C USA
12 *G15* **Caledon** Ontario, S Canada
85 *I23* **Caledon** *var.* Mohokare. ⇝ Lesotho/South Africa
44 *G1* **Caledonia** Corozal, N Belize
12 *G16* **Caledonia** Ontario, S Canada
31 *X11* **Caledonia** Minnesota, N USA
107 *X5* **Calella** *var.* Calella de la Costa. Cataluña, NE Spain
Calella de la Costa *see* Calella
25 *P4* **Calera** Alabama, S USA
65 *I19* **Caleta Olivia** Santa Cruz, SE Argentina
37 *X17* **Calexico** California, W USA
99 *H16* **Calf of Man** *island* SW Isle of Man
9 *Q16* **Calgary** Alberta, SW Canada
9 *Q16* **Calgary** ✕ Alberta, SW Canada
39 *U5* **Calhan** Colorado, C USA
66 *O5* **Calheta** Madeira, Portugal, NE Atlantic Ocean
25 *R2* **Calhoun** Georgia, SE USA
22 *I6* **Calhoun** Kentucky, S USA
24 *M3* **Calhoun City** Mississippi, S USA
23 *P12* **Calhoun Falls** South Carolina, SE USA
56 *D11* **Cali** Valle del Cauca, W Colombia
29 *V9* **Calico Rock** Arkansas, C USA
161 *F21* **Calicut** *var.* Kozhikode. Kerala, SW India
37 *Y9* **Caliente** Nevada, W USA
29 *U5* **California** Missouri, C USA
20 *B15* **California** Pennsylvania, NE USA
37 *Q12* **California** *off.* State of California; also known as El Dorado, The Golden State. ◆ *state* W USA
37 *P11* **California Aqueduct** *aqueduct* California, W USA
37 *T13* **California City** California, W USA
42 *F6* **California, Golfo de** *Eng.* Gulf of California; *prev.* Sea of Cortez. *gulf* W Mexico
California, Gulf of *see* California, Golfo de
143 *Y13* **Cälilabad** *Rus.* Dzhalilabad; *prev.* Astrakhan-Bazar. S Azerbaijan
118 *I12* **Călimăneşti** Vâlcea, SW Romania
118 *J9* **Călimani, Munţii** ▲ N Romania
Calinisc *see* Cupcina
37 *X17* **Calipatria** California, W USA
Calisia *see* Kalisz
36 *M7* **Calistoga** California, W USA
85 *G25* **Calitzdorp** Western Cape, SW South Africa
43 *W12* **Calkiní** Campeche, E Mexico
190 *K4* **Callabonna Creek** *var.* Tilcha Creek. *seasonal river* New South Wales/South Australia
190 *J4* **Callabonna, Lake** ◎ South Australia
104 *G5* **Callac** Côtes d'Armor, NW France
37 *U5* **Callaghan, Mount** ▲ Nevada, W USA
Callain *see* Callan
99 *E19* **Callan** *Ir.* Callain. S Ireland
12 *H11* **Callander** Ontario, S Canada
98 *I11* **Callander** C Scotland, UK
100 *H7* **Callantsoog** Noord-Holland, NW Netherlands
59 *D14* **Callao** Callao, W Peru
59 *D15* **Callao** *off.* Departamento del Callao. ◆ *constitutional province* W Peru
58 *F11* **Callaria, Río** ⇝ E Peru
Callatis *see* Mangalia
9 *Q13* **Calling Lake** Alberta, W Canada
Callosa de Ensarriá *see* Callosa d'En Sarrià
107 *T11* **Callosa d'En Sarrià** *var.* Callosa de Ensarriá. País Valenciano, E Spain
107 *S12* **Callosa de Segura** País Valenciano, E Spain
31 *X11* **Calmar** Iowa, C USA
Calmar *see* Kalmar
45 *R16* **Calobre** Veraguas, C Panama
179 *P10* **Caloocan** *municipality* Luzon, N Philippines
25 *X14* **Caloosahatchee River** ⇝ Florida, SE USA
191 *V2* **Caloundra** Queensland, E Australia
107 *T11* **Calpe** País Valenciano, E Spain
43 *P14* **Calpulalpan** Tlaxcala, S Mexico
109 *K25* **Caltagirone** Sicilia, Italy, C Mediterranean Sea
109 *J24* **Caltanissetta** Sicilia, Italy, C Mediterranean Sea
84 *E11* **Caluango** Lunda Norte, NE Angola
84 *C12* **Calucinga** Bié, W Angola
84 *B12* **Calulo** Cuanza Sul, NW Angola
85 *B14* **Caluquembe** Huíla, W Angola
82 *Q11* **Caluula** Bari, NE Somalia
104 *K4* **Calvados** ◆ *department* N France
195 *P17* **Calvados Chain, The** *island group* SE PNG
27 *U9* **Calvert** Texas, SW USA
22 *H7* **Calvert City** Kentucky, S USA
104 *E1* **Calvi** Corse, France, C Mediterranean Sea
42 *L12* **Calvillo** Aguascalientes, C Mexico
85 *F24* **Calvinia** Northern Cape, W South Africa
106 *K8* **Calvitero** ▲ W Spain
103 *G22* **Calw** Baden-Württemberg, SW Germany
Calydon *see* Kalydón
107 *N11* **Calzada de Calatrava** Castilla-La Mancha, C Spain
Cama *see* Kama
84 *C11* **Camabatela** Cuanza Norte, NW Angola
66 *Q5* **Camacha** Porto Santo, Madeira, Portugal, NE Atlantic Ocean
12 *L8* **Camachigama, Lac** ◎ Québec, SE Canada
42 *M9* **Camacho** Zacatecas, C Mexico
84 *D13* **Camacupa** *var.* General Machado, *Port.* Vila General Machado. Bié, C Angola
56 *L7* **Camaguán** Guárico, C Venezuela
46 *G6* **Camagüey** *prev.* Puerto Príncipe. Camagüey, C Cuba
46 *G5* **Camagüey, Archipiélago de** *island group* C Cuba
42 *D5* **Camalli, Sierra de** ▲ NW Mexico
59 *G18* **Camana** *var.* Camaná. Arequipa, SW Peru
31 *Z14* **Camanche** Iowa, C USA
37 *P8* **Camanche Reservoir** ▣ California, W USA
63 *I16* **Camaquã** Rio Grande do Sul, S Brazil
63 *H16* **Camaquã, Rio** ⇝ S Brazil
66 *P6* **Câmara de Lobos** Madeira, Portugal, NE Atlantic Ocean
105 *U16* **Camarat, Cap** *headland* SE France
43 *O8* **Camargo** Tamaulipas, C Mexico
105 *R15* **Camargue** *physical region* SE France
106 *F2* **Camariñas** Galicia, NW Spain
Camaronero, Laguna del *see* Caimanero, Laguna del
65 *J18* **Camarones** Chaco, S Argentina
65 *J18* **Camarones, Bahía** *bay* S Argentina
106 *J14* **Camas** Andalucía, S Spain
178 *J15* **Ca Mau** *prev.* Quan Long. Minh Hai, S Vietnam
84 *E11* **Camaxilo** Lunda Norte, NE Angola
106 *G3* **Cambados** Galicia, NW Spain
Cambay, Gulf of *see* Khambhāt, Gulf of
Camberia *see* Chambéry
99 *N22* **Camberley** SE England, UK
178 *Ii12* **Cambodia** *off.* Kingdom of Cambodia, *var.* Democratic Kampuchea, Roat Kampuchea, *Cam.* Kampuchea; *prev.* People's Democratic Republic of Kampuchea. ◆ *republic* SE Asia
104 *I16* **Cambo-les-Bains** Pyrénées-Atlantiques, SW France
105 *P2* **Cambrai** *Flem.* Kambryk; *prev.* Cambray, *anc.* Cameracum. Nord, N France
Cambray *see* Cambrai
106 *H2* **Cambre** Galicia, NW Spain
37 *O12* **Cambria** California, W USA
99 *J20* **Cambrian Mountains** ▲ C Wales, UK
12 *G16* **Cambridge** Ontario, S Canada
46 *I12* **Cambridge** W Jamaica
192 *M8* **Cambridge** Waikato, North Island, NZ
99 *O20* **Cambridge** *Lat.* Cantabrigia. E England, UK
34 *M12* **Cambridge** Idaho, NW USA
32 *K11* **Cambridge** Illinois, N USA
23 *Y4* **Cambridge** Maryland, NE USA
21 *O11* **Cambridge** Massachusetts, NE USA
31 *V7* **Cambridge** Minnesota, N USA
31 *N16* **Cambridge** Nebraska, C USA
33 *U13* **Cambridge** Ohio, NE USA
15 *J3* **Cambridge Bay** *district capital* Victoria Island, Northwest Territories, NW Canada
99 *O20* **Cambridgeshire** *cultural region* E England, UK
107 *U6* **Cambrils de Mar** Cataluña, NE Spain
Cambundi-Catembo *see* Nova Gaia
143 *N11* **Çam Burnu** *headland* N Turkey
191 *S9* **Camden** New South Wales, SE Australia
25 *O6* **Camden** Alabama, S USA
29 *U14* **Camden** Arkansas, C USA
23 *Y3* **Camden** Delaware, NE USA
21 *R7* **Camden** Maine, NE USA
20 *I16* **Camden** New Jersey, NE USA
20 *I9* **Camden** New York, NE USA
23 *R12* **Camden** South Carolina, SE USA
22 *H8* **Camden** Tennessee, S USA
27 *X9* **Camden** Texas, SW USA
41 *S5* **Camden Bay** *bay* S Beaufort Sea
29 *U6* **Camdenton** Missouri, C USA
Camellia State *see* Alabama
20 *M7* **Camels Hump** ▲ Vermont, NE USA
119 *N8* **Camenca** *Rus.* Kamenka. N Moldova
Cameracum *see* Cambrai
24 *G9* **Cameron** Louisiana, S USA
27 *T9* **Cameron** Texas, SW USA
32 *J5* **Cameron** Wisconsin, N USA
8 *M12* **Cameron** ⇝ British Columbia, W Canada
193 *A24* **Cameron Mountains** ▲ South Island, NZ
81 *D15* **Cameroon** *off.* Republic of Cameroon, *Fr.* Cameroun. ◆ *republic* W Africa
81 *D15* **Cameroon Mountain** ▲ SW Cameroon
Cameroon Ridge *see* Camerounaise, Dorsale
Cameroun *see* Cameroon
81 *E14* **Camerounaise, Dorsale** *Eng.* Cameroon Ridge. *ridge* NW Cameroon
179 *R14* **Camiguin Island** *island* S Philippines
179 *P10* **Camiling** Luzon, N Philippines
25 *T7* **Camilla** Georgia, SE USA
106 *G5* **Caminha** Viana do Castelo, N Portugal
37 *P7* **Camino** California, W USA
142 *B15* **Çamiçi Gölü** ◎ SW Turkey
109 *J24* **Cammarata** Sicilia, Italy, C Mediterranean Sea
44 *K10* **Camoapa** Boaco, S Nicaragua
60 *O13* **Camocim** Ceará, E Brazil
108 *D10* **Camogli** Liguria, NW Italy
189 *S5* **Camooweal** Queensland, C Australia
57 *Y11* **Camopi** E French Guiana
157 *Q22* **Camorta** *island* Nicobar Islands, India, NE Indian Ocean
179 *R13* **Camotes Sea** *sea* C Philippines
44 *I6* **Campamento** Olancho, C Honduras
63 *D19* **Campana** Buenos Aires, E Argentina
65 *F21* **Campana, Isla** *island* S Chile
106 *K11* **Campanario** Extremadura, W Spain
109 *L17* **Campania** *Eng.* Champagne. ◆ *region* S Italy
29 *Y8* **Campbell** Missouri, C USA
193 *K15* **Campbell, Cape** *headland* South Island, NZ
12 *J14* **Campbellford** Ontario, SE Canada
33 *R13* **Campbell Hill** *hill* Ohio, N USA
199 *J14* **Campbell Island** *island* S NZ
183 *P13* **Campbell Plateau** *undersea feature* SW Pacific Ocean
8 *K17* **Campbell River** Vancouver Island, British Columbia, SW Canada
22 *L6* **Campbellsville** Kentucky, S USA

11 O13 **Campbellton** New Brunswick, SE Canada
191 P16 **Campbell Town** Tasmania, SE Australia
191 S9 **Campbelltown** New South Wales, SE Australia
98 G13 **Campbeltown** W Scotland, UK
43 W13 **Campeche** Campeche, SE Mexico
43 W14 **Campeche** ◆ state SE Mexico
43 T14 **Campeche, Bahía de** *Eng.* Bay of Campeche. bay E Mexico
Campeche, Banco de see Campeche Bank
66 C11 **Campeche Bank** *Sp.* Banco de Campeche, Sonda de Campeche. undersea feature S Gulf of Mexico
Campeche, Bay of see Campeche, Bahía de
Campeche, Sonda de see Campeche Bank
46 H7 **Campechuela** Granma, E Cuba
190 M13 **Camperdown** Victoria, SE Australia
178 K6 **Cẩm Pha** Quang Ninh, N Vietnam
118 H10 **Câmpia Turzii** *Ger.* Jerischmarkt, *Hung.* Aranyosgyéres; *prev.* Cîmpia Turzii, Ghiriş, Gyéres. Cluj, NW Romania
106 K12 **Campillo de Llerena** Extremadura, W Spain
106 L15 **Campillos** Andalucía, S Spain
118 J13 **Câmpina** *prev.* Cîmpina. Prahova, SE Romania
61 Q15 **Campina Grande** Paraíba, E Brazil
62 L9 **Campinas** São Paulo, S Brazil
40 L10 **Camp Kulowiye** Saint Lawrence Island, Alaska, USA
81 D17 **Campo** *var.* Kampo. Sud, SW Cameroon
Campo see Ntem
61 N15 **Campo Alegre de Lourdes** Bahia, E Brazil
109 L16 **Campobasso** Molise, C Italy
109 H24 **Campobello di Mazara** Sicilia, Italy, C Mediterranean Sea
Campo Criptana see Campo de Criptana
107 O10 **Campo de Criptana** *var.* Campo Criptana. Castilla-La Mancha, C Spain
61 I16 **Campo de Diauarum** *var.* Pôsto Diuarum. Mato Grosso, W Brazil
56 E5 **Campo de la Cruz** Atlántico, N Colombia
107 P11 **Campo de Montiel** physical region C Spain
Campo dos Goitacazes see Campos
62 H12 **Campo Erê** Santa Catarina, S Brazil
64 L7 **Campo Gallo** Santiago del Estero, N Argentina
61 I20 **Campo Grande** state capital Mato Grosso do Sul, SW Brazil
62 K12 **Campo Largo** Paraná, S Brazil
60 N13 **Campo Maior** Piauí, E Brazil
106 I10 **Campo Maior** Portalegre, C Portugal
62 H10 **Campo Mourão** Paraná, S Brazil
62 Q9 **Campos** *var.* Campo dos Goitacazes. Rio de Janeiro, SE Brazil
61 L17 **Campos Belos** Goiás, S Brazil
62 N9 **Campos do Jordão** São Paulo, S Brazil
62 I13 **Campos Novos** Santa Catarina, S Brazil
61 O14 **Campos Sales** Ceará, E Brazil
27 Q9 **Camp San Saba** Texas, SW USA
23 N6 **Campton** Kentucky, S USA
118 I13 **Câmpulung** *prev.* Câmpulung-Muşcel, Cîmpulung. Argeş, S Romania
118 J9 **Câmpulung Moldovenesc** *var.* Cîmpulung Moldovenesc, *Ger.* Kimpolung, *Hung.* Hosszúmezjő. Suceava, NE Romania
Câmpulung-Muşcel see Câmpulung
Campus Stellae see Santiago
38 L12 **Camp Verde** Arizona, SW USA
27 P11 **Camp Wood** Texas, SW USA
178 Kk13 **Cam Ranh** Khanh Hoa, S Vietnam
9 Q15 **Camrose** Alberta, SW Canada
Camulodunum see Colchester
142 B12 **Çan** Çanakkale, NW Turkey
20 L12 **Canaan** Connecticut, NE USA
15 Kk13 **Canada** ◆ commonwealth republic N North America
207 P6 **Canada Basin** undersea feature Arctic Ocean
63 B18 **Cañada de Gómez** Santa Fe, C Argentina
207 P6 **Canada Plain** undersea feature Arctic Ocean
63 A18 **Cañada Rosquín** Santa Fe, C Argentina
27 P1 **Canadian** Texas, SW USA
18 Kk11 **Canadian River** ≈ SW USA
15 K12 **Canadian Shield** physical region Canada
65 I18 **Cañadón Grande, Sierra** ▲▲ S Argentina
57 P9 **Canaima** Bolívar, SE Venezuela
142 B11 **Çanakkale** *var.* Dardanelli; *prev.* Chanak, Kale Sultanie. Çanakkale, W Turkey
142 B12 **Çanakkale** ◆ province NW Turkey
142 B11 **Çanakkale Boğazı** *Eng.* Dardanelles. strait NW Turkey
197 I6 **Canala** Province Nord, C New Caledonia
61 A15 **Canamari** Amazonas, W Brazil
20 G10 **Canandaigua** New York, NE USA
20 F10 **Canandaigua Lake** ◎ New York, NE USA
42 G3 **Cananea** Sonora, NW Mexico
58 B8 **Cañar** ◆ province C Ecuador
66 N10 **Canarias, Islas** *Eng.* Canary Islands. ◆ autonomous community Spain, NE Atlantic Ocean
Canaries Basin see Canary Basin
46 C6 **Canarreos, Archipiélago de los** island group W Cuba
68 K3 **Canary Basin** *var.* Canaries Basin, Monaco Basin. undersea feature E Atlantic Ocean
Canary Islands see Canarias, Islas
44 L13 **Cañas** Guanacaste, NW Costa Rica
20 I10 **Canastota** New York, NE USA
Canati see Felanitx
42 K9 **Canatlán** Durango, C Mexico
106 J9 **Cañaveral** Extremadura, W Spain
25 Y11 **Canaveral, Cape** headland Florida, SE USA
61 O18 **Canavieiras** Bahia, E Brazil
45 R16 **Cañazas** Veraguas, W Panama
108 H6 **Canazei** Trentino-Alto Adige, N Italy
191 P6 **Canbelego** New South Wales, SE Australia
191 R10 **Canberra** ● (Australia) Australian Capital Territory, SE Australia
191 R10 **Canberra** ✕ Australian Capital Territory, SE Australia
37 P2 **Canby** California, W USA
31 S9 **Canby** Minnesota, N USA
105 N2 **Canche** ≈ N France
104 L13 **Cancon** Lot-et-Garonne, SW France
43 Z11 **Cancún** Quintana Roo, SE Mexico
106 K2 **Candás** Asturias, N Spain
104 J7 **Cande** Maine-et-Loire, NW France
43 W14 **Candelaria** Campeche, SE Mexico
26 J11 **Candelaria** Texas, SW USA
43 W15 **Candelaria, Río** ≈ Guatemala/Mexico
106 L8 **Candeleda** Castilla-León, N Spain
Candia see Irákleio
43 P8 **Cándido Aguilar** Tamaulipas, C Mexico
41 N8 **Candle** Alaska, USA
9 T14 **Candle Lake** Saskatchewan, C Canada
20 L13 **Candlewood, Lake** ▣ Connecticut, NE USA
31 O3 **Cando** North Dakota, N USA
179 P8 **Candon** Luzon, N Philippines
Canea see Chaniá
47 O12 **Canefield** ✕ (Roseau) SW Dominica
63 F20 **Canelones** *prev.* Guadalupe. Canelones, S Uruguay
63 E20 **Canelones** ◆ department S Uruguay
Canendiyú see Canindeyú
65 F14 **Cañete** Bío Bío, C Chile
107 Q9 **Cañete** Castilla-La Mancha, C Spain
Cañete see San Vicente de Cañete
29 P8 **Caney** Kansas, C USA
29 P8 **Caney River** ≈ Kansas/Oklahoma, C USA
107 S3 **Canfranc-Estación** Aragón, NE Spain
85 E14 **Cangamba** *Port.* Vila de Aljustrel. Moxico, E Angola
84 C12 **Cangandala** Malanje, NW Angola
106 G4 **Cangas** Galicia, NW Spain
106 J2 **Cangas del Narcea** Asturias, N Spain
106 L2 **Cangas de Onís** Asturias, N Spain
167 S11 **Cangnan** *prev.* Lingxi. Zhejiang, SE China
84 C10 **Cangola** Uíge, NW Angola
85 E14 **Cangombe** Moxico, E Angola
65 H21 **Cangrejo, Cerro** ▲ S Argentina
63 H17 **Canguçu** Rio Grande do Sul, S Brazil
167 P3 **Cangzhou** Hebei, E China
10 M7 **Caniapiscau** ≈ Québec, E Canada
10 M8 **Caniapiscau, Réservoir de** ▣ Québec, C Canada
109 J24 **Canicattì** Sicilia, Italy, C Mediterranean Sea
142 L11 **Canik Dağları** ▲▲ N Turkey
107 P14 **Caniles** Andalucía, S Spain
61 B16 **Canindé** Acre, W Brazil
64 P6 **Canindeyú** *var.* Canendiyú, Canindiyú. ◆ department E Paraguay
Canindiyú see Canindeyú
204 J10 **Canisteo Peninsula** peninsula Antarctica
20 F11 **Canisteo River** ≈ New York, NE USA
42 M10 **Cañitas** *var.* Cañitas de Felipe Pescador. Zacatecas, C Mexico
Cañitas de Felipe Pescador see Cañitas
107 P15 **Canjáyar** Andalucía, S Spain
142 I12 **Çankırı** *var.* Chankiri; *anc.* Gangra, Germanicopolis. Çankın, N Turkey
142 I11 **Çankırı** *var.* Chankiri. ◆ province N Turkey
179 Qq13 **Canlaon Volcano** 🌋 Negros, C Philippines
9 P16 **Canmore** Alberta, SW Canada
98 F9 **Canna** island NW Scotland, UK
161 F20 **Cannanore** *var.* Kananur, Kannur. Kerala, SW India
33 O17 **Cannelton** Indiana, N USA
105 U15 **Cannes** Alpes-Maritimes, SE France
41 R5 **Canning River** ≈ Alaska, USA
108 C6 **Cannobio** Piemonte, NE Italy
99 L19 **Cannock** C England, UK
30 M6 **Cannonball River** ≈ North Dakota, N USA
31 W9 **Cannon Falls** Minnesota, N USA
20 I11 **Cannonsville Reservoir** ▣ New York, NE USA
191 R12 **Cann River** Victoria, SE Australia
63 I16 **Canoas** Rio Grande do Sul, S Brazil
63 I14 **Canoas, Rio** ≈ S Brazil
12 I12 **Canoe Lake** ◎ Ontario, SE Canada
62 J12 **Canoinhas** Santa Catarina, S Brazil
39 T6 **Canon City** Colorado, C USA
57 P8 **Caño Negro** Bolívar, SE Venezuela
181 X15 **Canonniers Point** headland N Mauritius
25 W6 **Canoochee River** ≈ Georgia, SE USA
9 V15 **Canora** Saskatchewan, S Canada
47 Y14 **Canouan** island S Saint Vincent and the Grenadines
11 R15 **Canso** Nova Scotia, SE Canada
106 M3 **Cantabria** ◆ autonomous community N Spain
106 K3 **Cantábrica, Cordillera** ▲▲ N Spain
Cantabrigia see Cambridge
105 O12 **Cantal** ◆ department C France
107 N6 **Cantalejo** Castilla-León, N Spain
105 O12 **Cantal, Monts du** ▲▲ C France
106 G8 **Cantanhede** Coimbra, C Portugal
Cantaño see Cataño
57 O6 **Cantaura** Anzoátegui, NE Venezuela
118 M11 **Cantemir** *Rus.* Kantemir. S Moldova
99 Q22 **Canterbury** *hist.* Cantwaraburh, *anc.* Durovernum, *Lat.* Cantuaria. SE England, UK
193 F19 **Canterbury** *off.* Canterbury Region. ◆ region South Island, NZ
193 H20 **Canterbury Bight** bight South Island, NZ
193 H19 **Canterbury Plains** plain South Island, NZ
178 Jj15 **Cần Thơ** Cần Thơ, S Vietnam
106 K13 **Cantillana** Andalucía, S Spain
61 N15 **Canto do Buriti** Piauí, NE Brazil
25 S2 **Canton** Georgia, SE USA
32 K12 **Canton** Illinois, N USA
24 L5 **Canton** Mississippi, S USA
29 V2 **Canton** Missouri, C USA
20 J7 **Canton** New York, NE USA
23 O10 **Canton** North Carolina, SE USA
33 U12 **Canton** Ohio, N USA
28 L9 **Canton** Oklahoma, C USA
20 G12 **Canton** Pennsylvania, NE USA
31 R11 **Canton** South Dakota, N USA
27 V7 **Canton** Texas, SW USA
Canton see Guangzhou
Canton Island see Kanton
28 L9 **Canton Lake** ▣ Oklahoma, C USA
108 D7 **Cantù** Lombardia, N Italy
Cantuaria/Cantwaraburh see Canterbury
41 R10 **Cantwell** Alaska, USA
61 O16 **Canudos** Bahia, E Brazil
49 T7 **Canumã, Rio** ≈ N Brazil
Canusium see Puglia, Canosa di
26 G7 **Canutillo** Texas, SW USA
27 N3 **Canyon** Texas, SW USA
35 S12 **Canyon** Wyoming, C USA
34 K13 **Canyon City** Oregon, NW USA
35 R10 **Canyon Ferry Lake** ◎ Montana, NW USA
27 S11 **Canyon Lake** ▣ Texas, SW USA
178 Jj5 **Cao Bằng** *var.* Caobang. Cao Bằng, N Vietnam
166 J12 **Caodu He** ≈ S China
178 J14 **Cao Lanh** Đông Thap, S Vietnam
84 C11 **Caombo** Malanje, NW Angola
Caorach, Cuan na g see Sheep Haven
Caozhou see Heze
175 S10 **Capalulu** Pulau Mangole, E Indonesia
56 K8 **Capanaparo, Río** ≈ Colombia/Venezuela
60 L12 **Capanema** Pará, NE Brazil
62 L10 **Capão Bonito** São Paulo, S Brazil
62 I13 **Capão Doce, Morro do** ▲ S Brazil
56 I4 **Capatárida** Falcón, N Venezuela
104 I15 **Capbreton** Landes, SW France
Cap-Breton, Île du see Cape Breton Island
13 W6 **Cap-Chat** Québec, SE Canada
13 P11 **Cap-de-la-Madeleine** Québec, SE Canada
105 N13 **Capdenac** Aveyron, S France
191 Q15 **Cape Barren Island** island Furneaux Group, Tasmania, SE Australia
67 O18 **Cape Basin** undersea feature S Atlantic Ocean
11 R14 **Cape Breton Island** *Fr.* Île du Cap-Breton. island Nova Scotia, SE Canada
25 Y11 **Cape Canaveral** Florida, SE USA
23 Y6 **Cape Charles** Virginia, NE USA
79 P17 **Cape Coast** *prev.* Cape Coast Castle. S Ghana
Cape Coast Castle see Cape Coast
21 Q12 **Cape Cod Bay** bay Massachusetts, NE USA
25 W15 **Cape Coral** Florida, SE USA
189 R4 **Cape Crawford Roadhouse** Northern Territory, N Australia
16 N4 **Cape Dorset** Baffin Island, Northwest Territories, NE Canada
23 N8 **Cape Fear River** ≈ North Carolina, SE USA
29 Y7 **Cape Girardeau** Missouri, C USA
23 T14 **Cape Island** island South Carolina, SE USA
194 E11 **Capella** ▲ NW PNG
100 H12 **Capelle aan den IJssel** Zuid-Holland, SW Netherlands
85 C15 **Capelongo** Huíla, C Angola
20 J17 **Cape May** New Jersey, NE USA
20 J17 **Cape May Court House** New Jersey, NE USA
Cape Palmas see Harper
15 H2 **Cape Parry** Northwest Territories, N Canada
67 P19 **Cape Rise** undersea feature SW Indian Ocean
Cape Saint Jacques see Vung Tau
Capesterre see Capesterre-Belle-Eau
47 Y6 **Capesterre-Belle-Eau** *var.* Capesterre. Basse Terre, S Guadeloupe
85 D26 **Cape Town** *var.* Ekapa, *Afr.* Kaapstad, Kapstad. ● (South Africa-legislative capital) Western Cape, SW South Africa
85 E26 **Cape Town** ✕ Western Cape, SW South Africa
78 D9 **Cape Verde** *off.* Republic of Cape Verde, *Port.* Cabo Verde, Ilhas do Cabo Verde. ◆ republic E Atlantic Ocean
66 L11 **Cape Verde Basin** undersea feature E Atlantic Ocean
68 K5 **Cape Verde Islands** island group E Atlantic Ocean
66 L10 **Cape Verde Plain** undersea feature E Atlantic Ocean
Cape Verde Plateau/Cape Verde Rise see Cape Verde Terrace
66 L11 **Cape Verde Terrace** *var.* Cape Verde Plateau, Cape Verde Rise. undersea feature E Atlantic Ocean
189 V2 **Cape York Peninsula** peninsula Queensland, N Australia
46 M8 **Cap-Haïtien** *var.* Le Cap. N Haiti
45 T15 **Capira** Panamá, C Panama
12 K8 **Capitachouane** ≈ Québec, SE Canada
12 L8 **Capitachouane, Lac** ◎ Québec, SE Canada
39 T13 **Capitan** New Mexico, SW USA
204 G3 **Capitán Arturo Prat** Chilean research station South Shetland Islands, Antarctica
39 S13 **Capitan Mountains** ▲▲ New Mexico, SW USA
64 M3 **Capitán Pablo Lagerenza** *var.* Mayor Pablo Lagerenza. Chaco, N Paraguay
39 T13 **Capitan Peak** ▲ New Mexico, SW USA
196 H5 **Capitol Hill** Saipan, S Northern Mariana Islands
62 I9 **Capivara, Represa** ▣ S Brazil
63 J16 **Capivari** Rio Grande do Sul, S Brazil
115 H15 **Čapljina** S Bosnia and Herzegovina
85 M15 **Capoche** *var.* Kapoche. ≈ Mozambique/Zambia
Capo Delgado, Província de see Cabo Delgado
109 K17 **Capodichino** ✕ (Napoli) Campania, S Italy
Capodistria see Koper
108 E12 **Capraia, Isola di** island Archipelago Toscano, C Italy
109 B16 **Caprara, Punta** *var.* Punta dello Scorno. headland Isola Asinara, W Italy
Capraria see Cabrera
12 F10 **Capreol** Ontario, S Canada
109 K18 **Capri** Campania, S Italy
183 S9 **Capricorn Tablemount** undersea feature W Pacific Ocean
109 J18 **Capri, Isola di** island S Italy
85 G16 **Caprivi** ◆ district NE Namibia
Caprivi Concession see Caprivi Strip
85 F16 **Caprivi Strip** *Ger.* Caprivizipfel; *prev.* Caprivi Concession. cultural region NE Namibia
Caprivizipfel see Caprivi Strip
27 O5 **Cap Rock Escarpment** cliffs Texas, SW USA
13 R10 **Cap-Rouge** Québec, SE Canada
Cap Saint-Jacques see Vung Tau
40 F12 **Captain Cook** Hawaii, USA, C Pacific Ocean
191 R10 **Captains Flat** New South Wales, SE Australia
104 K14 **Captieux** Gironde, SW France
109 K17 **Capua** Campania, S Italy
56 F14 **Caquetá** *off.* Departamento del Caquetá. ◆ province S Colombia
56 E13 **Caquetá, Río** *var.* Rio Japurá, Yapurá. ≈ Brazil/Colombia see also Japurá, Rio
CAR see Central African Republic
Cara see Kara
59 I16 **Carabaya, Cordillera** ▲▲ E Peru
56 K5 **Carabobo** *off.* Estado Carabobo. ◆ state N Venezuela
118 I14 **Caracal** Olt, S Romania
60 F10 **Caracaraí** Rondônia, W Brazil
56 L5 **Caracas** ● (Venezuela) Distrito Federal, N Venezuela
56 I5 **Carache** Trujillo, N Venezuela
62 N10 **Caraguatatuba** São Paulo, S Brazil
50 I7 **Carajás, Serra dos** ▲▲ N Brazil
Caralis see Cagliari
56 E9 **Caramanta** Antioquia, W Colombia
179 Q11 **Caramoan** Catanduanes Island, N Philippines
Caramurat see Mihail Kogălniceanu
118 F12 **Caransebeş** *Ger.* Karansebesch, *Hung.* Karánsebes. Caraş-Severin, SW Romania
Carapella see Carapelle
109 M16 **Carapelle** *var.* Carapella. ≈ SE Italy
57 O9 **Carapo** Bolívar, SE Venezuela
11 P13 **Caraquet** New Brunswick, SE Canada
Caras see Caraz
118 F12 **Caraşova** *Hung.* Krassóvár. Caraş-Severin, SW Romania
118 F12 **Caraş-Severin** ◆ county SW Romania
44 M5 **Caratasca, Laguna de** lagoon NE Honduras
60 C13 **Carauari** Amazonas, NW Brazil
Caravaca see Caravaca de la Cruz
107 Q12 **Caravaca de la Cruz** *var.* Caravaca. Murcia, SE Spain
108 E7 **Caravaggio** Lombardia, N Italy
109 C18 **Caravai, Passo di** pass Sardegna, Italy, C Mediterranean Sea
61 O19 **Caravelas** Bahia, E Brazil
58 C12 **Caraz** *var.* Caras. Ancash, W Peru
63 H14 **Carazinho** Rio Grande do Sul, S Brazil
44 J11 **Carazo** ◆ department SW Nicaragua
106 H4 **Carballiño** Galicia, NW Spain
106 G2 **Carballo** Galicia, NW Spain
9 W16 **Carberry** Manitoba, S Canada
42 F4 **Carbó** Sonora, NW Mexico
109 C20 **Carbonara, Capo** headland Sardegna, Italy, C Mediterranean Sea
39 Q5 **Carbondale** Colorado, C USA
32 L17 **Carbondale** Illinois, N USA
29 Q4 **Carbondale** Kansas, C USA
20 I13 **Carbondale** Pennsylvania, NE USA
11 V12 **Carbonear** Newfoundland, Newfoundland and Labrador, SE Canada
107 Q9 **Carboneras de Guadazaón** *var.* Carboneras de Guadazón. Castilla-La Mancha, C Spain
Carboneras de Guadazón see Carboneras de Guadazaón
25 O3 **Carbon Hill** Alabama, S USA
109 B20 **Carbonia** *var.* Carbonia Centro. Sardegna, Italy, C Mediterranean Sea
Carbonia Centro see Carbonia
107 S10 **Carcaixent** País Valenciano, E Spain
Carcaso see Carcassonne
67 B24 **Carcass Island** island NW Falkland Islands
105 O16 **Carcassonne** *anc.* Carcaso. Aude, S France
107 R12 **Carche** ▲ S Spain
58 A13 **Carchi** ◆ province N Ecuador
8 I8 **Carcross** Yukon Territory, W Canada
Cardamomes, Chaîne des see Krâvanh, Chuŏr Phnum
161 G22 **Cardamom Hills** ▲▲ SW India
Cardamom Mountains see Krâvanh, Chuŏr Phnum
106 M12 **Cardeña** Andalucía, S Spain
46 D4 **Cárdenas** Matanzas, W Cuba
43 O11 **Cárdenas** San Luis Potosí, C Mexico
43 U15 **Cárdenas** Tabasco, SE Mexico
65 H21 **Cardiel, Lago** ◎ S Argentina
99 K22 **Cardiff** *Wel.* Caerdydd. ● S Wales, UK
99 J22 **Cardiff-Wales** ✕ S Wales, UK
99 I21 **Cardigan** *Wel.* Aberteifi. SW Wales, UK
99 I20 **Cardigan** cultural region W Wales, UK
99 I20 **Cardigan Bay** bay W Wales, UK
21 N8 **Cardigan, Mount** ▲ New Hampshire, NE USA
12 M13 **Cardinal** Ontario, SE Canada
107 V5 **Cardona** Cataluña, NE Spain
63 E19 **Cardona** Soriano, SW Uruguay
107 V4 **Cardoner** ≈ NE Spain
9 Q17 **Cardston** Alberta, SW Canada
189 W5 **Cardwell** Queensland, NE Australia
118 G8 **Carei** *Ger.* Gross-Karol, Karol, *Hung.* Nagykároly; *prev.* Careii-Mari. Satu Mare, NW Romania
Careii-Mari see Carei
60 F13 **Careiro** Amazonas, NW Brazil
104 J4 **Carentan** Manche, N France
106 M2 **Cares** ≈ N Spain
35 P14 **Carey** Idaho, NW USA
33 S12 **Carey** Ohio, N USA
27 P4 **Carey** Texas, SW USA
188 L11 **Carey, Lake** ◎ Western Australia
181 O8 **Cargados Carajos Bank** undersea feature C Indian Ocean
104 G6 **Carhaix-Plouguer** Finistère, NW France
63 A22 **Carhué** Buenos Aires, E Argentina
57 O5 **Cariaco** Sucre, NE Venezuela
109 O20 **Cariati** Calabria, SW Italy
2 H17 **Caribbean Plate** tectonic feature
46 I11 **Caribbean Sea** sea W Atlantic Ocean
9 N15 **Cariboo Mountains** ▲▲ British Columbia, SW Canada
9 W9 **Caribou** Manitoba, C Canada
21 S2 **Caribou** Maine, NE USA
9 P10 **Caribou Mountains** ▲▲ Alberta, SW Canada
Caribrod see Dimitrovgrad
42 I6 **Carichic** Chihuahua, N Mexico
179 Qq13 **Carigara** Leyte, C Philippines
105 R3 **Carignan** Ardennes, N France
191 Q5 **Carinda** New South Wales, SE Australia
107 R6 **Cariñena** Aragón, NE Spain
109 I23 **Carini** Sicilia, Italy, C Mediterranean Sea
109 K17 **Carinola** Campania, S Italy
Carinthi see Kärnten
57 O5 **Caripe** Monagas, NE Venezuela
57 P5 **Caripito** Monagas, NE Venezuela
13 W7 **Carleton** Québec, SE Canada
33 S10 **Carleton** Michigan, N USA
11 O14 **Carleton, Mount** ▲ New Brunswick, SE Canada
12 L13 **Carleton Place** Ontario, SE Canada
37 V3 **Carlin** Nevada, W USA
32 K14 **Carlinville** Illinois, N USA
99 K14 **Carlisle** *anc.* Caer Luel, Luguvallium, Luguvallum. NW England, UK
29 V11 **Carlisle** Arkansas, C USA
33 N15 **Carlisle** Indiana, N USA
31 V14 **Carlisle** Iowa, C USA
23 N5 **Carlisle** Kentucky, S USA
20 F15 **Carlisle** Pennsylvania, NE USA
23 Q11 **Carlisle** South Carolina, SE USA
40 J17 **Carlisle Island** island Aleutian Islands, Alaska, USA
29 R7 **Carl Junction** Missouri, C USA
109 A20 **Carloforte** Sardegna, Italy, C Mediterranean Sea
Carlopago see Karlobag
63 B21 **Carlos Casares** Buenos Aires, E Argentina
63 E18 **Carlos Reyles** Durazno, C Uruguay
63 A21 **Carlos Tejedor** Buenos Aires, E Argentina
99 F19 **Carlow** *Ir.* Ceatharlach. SE Ireland
99 F19 **Carlow** *Ir.* Cheatharlach. cultural region SE Ireland
98 F7 **Carloway** NW Scotland, UK
Carlsbad see Karlovy Vary
37 U17 **Carlsbad** California, W USA
39 U15 **Carlsbad** New Mexico, SW USA
133 N13 **Carlsberg Ridge** undersea feature S Arabian Sea
Carlsruhe see Karlsruhe
31 W6 **Carlton** Minnesota, N USA
9 V17 **Carlyle** Saskatchewan, S Canada
32 L15 **Carlyle** Illinois, N USA
32 L15 **Carlyle Lake** ▣ Illinois, N USA
8 H7 **Carmacks** Yukon Territory, W Canada
108 B9 **Carmagnola** Piemonte, NW Italy
9 X16 **Carman** Manitoba, S Canada
Carmana/Carmania see Kermān
99 I21 **Carmarthen** SW Wales, UK
99 I21 **Carmarthen** cultural region SW Wales, UK
99 I22 **Carmarthen Bay** inlet SW Wales, UK
105 N14 **Carmaux** Tarn, S France
37 N11 **Carmel** California, W USA
33 O13 **Carmel** Indiana, N USA
20 L13 **Carmel** New York, NE USA
99 H18 **Carmel Head** headland NW Wales, UK
44 E2 **Carmelita** Petén, N Guatemala
63 D19 **Carmelo** Colonia, SW Uruguay
43 V14 **Carmen** *var.* Ciudad del Carmen. Campeche, SE Mexico
63 A25 **Carmen de Patagones** Buenos Aires, E Argentina
42 F8 **Carmen, Isla** island W Mexico
42 M5 **Carmen, Sierra del** ▲▲ NW Mexico
32 M16 **Carmi** Illinois, N USA
37 O7 **Carmichael** California, W USA
Carmiel see Karmi'él
27 U11 **Carmine** Texas, SW USA
106 K14 **Carmona** Andalucía, S Spain
Carmona see Uíge
Carnaro see Kvarner
12 I13 **Carnarvon** Ontario, SE Canada
85 G24 **Carnarvon** Northern Cape, W South Africa
Carnarvon see Caernarfon
188 K9 **Carnarvon Range** ▲▲ Western Australia
188 G9 **Carnarvon** Western Australia
Carn Domhnach see Carndonagh
98 E13 **Carndonagh** *Ir.* Carn Domhnach. NW Ireland
9 V17 **Carnduff** Saskatchewan, S Canada
28 L11 **Carnegie** Oklahoma, C USA
188 L9 **Carnegie, Lake** salt lake Western Australia
200 Oo8 **Carnegie Ridge** undersea feature E Pacific Ocean
98 H9 **Carn Eige** ▲ N Scotland, UK
190 F5 **Carnes** South Australia
204 J12 **Carney Island** island Antarctica
20 H16 **Carneys Point** New Jersey, NE USA
Carniche, Alpi see Karnische Alpen
157 Q21 **Car Nicobar** island Nicobar Islands, India, NE Indian Ocean
81 H15 **Carnot** Mambéré-Kadéï, W Central African Republic
190 F10 **Carnot, Cape** headland South Australia
98 K11 **Carnoustie** E Scotland, UK
99 F20 **Carnsore Point** *Ir.* Ceann an Chairn. headland SE Ireland
15 Gg4 **Carnwath** ≈ Northwest Territories, NW Canada
33 R8 **Caro** Michigan, N USA
25 Z15 **Carol City** Florida, SE USA
61 L14 **Carolina** Maranhão, E Brazil
47 U5 **Carolina** E Puerto Rico
23 V12 **Carolina Beach** North Carolina, SE USA
203 Y5 **Caroline Island** *prev.* Thornton Island. atoll Line Islands, E Kiribati
201 N15 **Caroline Islands** island group C Micronesia
133 Z14 **Caroline Plate** tectonic feature
199 H7 **Caroline Ridge** undersea feature E Philippine Sea
Carolopois see Châlons-en-Champagne
47 V14 **Caroni Arena Dam** ▣ Trinidad, Trinidad and Tobago
Caronie, Monti see Nebrodi, Monti
57 P7 **Caroní, Río** ≈ E Venezuela
47 U14 **Caroni River** ≈ Trinidad, Trinidad and Tobago
Caronium see A Coruña
56 J5 **Carora** Lara, N Venezuela
88 F12 **Carpathian Mountains** *var.* Carpathians, *Cz./Pol.* Karpaty, *Ger.* Karpaten,. ▲▲ E Europe
Carpathians see Carpathian Mountains
Carpathos/Carpathus see Kárpathos
118 H12 **Carpaţii Meridionali** *var.* Alpi Transilvaniei, Carpaţii Sudici, *Eng.* South Carpathians, Transylvanian Alps, *Ger.* Südkarpaten, Transsylvanische Alpen, *Hung.* Déli-Kárpátok, Erdélyi-Havasok. ▲▲ C Romania
Carpaţii Sudici see Carpaţii Meridionali
182 L7 **Carpentaria, Gulf of** gulf N Australia
Carpentoracte see Carpentras
105 R14 **Carpentras** *anc.* Carpentoracte. Vaucluse, SE France
108 F9 **Carpi** Emilia-Romagna, N Italy
118 E11 **Cărpiniş** *Hung.* Gyertyámos. Timiş, W Romania
37 R14 **Carpinteria** California, W USA
25 S9 **Carrabelle** Florida, SE USA
Carraig Aonair see Fastnet Rock
Carraig Fhearghais see Carrickfergus
Carraig Mhachaire Rois see Carrickmacross
Carraig na Siúire see Carrick-on-Suir
Carrantual see Carrauntoohil
108 E10 **Carrara** Toscana, C Italy
63 F20 **Carrasco** ✕ (Montevideo) Canelones, S Uruguay
107 P9 **Carrascosa del Campo** Castilla-La Mancha, C Spain
56 H4 **Carrasquero** Zulia, NW Venezuela
191 O9 **Carrathool** New South Wales, SE Australia
Carrauntohil see Carrauntoohil
99 B21 **Carrauntoohil** *Ir.* Carrantual, Carrauntohil, Corrán Tuathail. ▲ SW Ireland
47 Y15 **Carriacou** island N Grenada
99 G15 **Carrickfergus** *Ir.* Carraig Fhearghais. NE Northern Ireland, UK
99 F16 **Carrickmacross** *Ir.* Carraig Mhachaire Rois. N Ireland
99 D16 **Carrick-on-Shannon** *Ir.* Cora Droma Rúisc. NW Ireland
99 E20 **Carrick-on-Suir** *Ir.* Carraig na Siúire. S Ireland
190 I7 **Carrieton** South Australia
42 L7 **Carrillo** Chihuahua, N Mexico
31 O4 **Carrington** North Dakota, N USA
106 M4 **Carrión** ≈ N Spain
106 M4 **Carrión de los Condes** Castilla-León, N Spain
27 P13 **Carrizo Springs** Texas, SW USA
39 S13 **Carrizozo** New Mexico, SW USA
31 T13 **Carroll** Iowa, C USA
25 N4 **Carrollton** Alabama, S USA
25 R3 **Carrollton** Georgia, SE USA
32 K14 **Carrollton** Illinois, N USA
22 L4 **Carrollton** Kentucky, S USA
33 R8 **Carrollton** Michigan, N USA
29 T3 **Carrollton** Missouri, C USA
33 U12 **Carrollton** Ohio, N USA
27 T6 **Carrollton** Texas, SW USA
9 U14 **Carrot** ≈ Saskatchewan, S Canada
9 U14 **Carrot River** Saskatchewan, C Canada
20 J7 **Carry Falls Reservoir** ▣ New York, NE USA
142 L11 **Çarşamba** Samsun, N Turkey
30 L6 **Carson** North Dakota, N USA
37 Q6 **Carson City** state capital Nevada, W USA
37 R6 **Carson River** ≈ Nevada, W USA
37 S5 **Carson Sink** salt flat Nevada, W USA
9 Q16 **Carstairs** Alberta, SW Canada
Carstensz, Puntjak see Jaya, Puncak
56 E5 **Cartagena** *var.* Cartagena de los Indes. Bolívar, NW Colombia
107 R13 **Cartagena** *anc.* Carthago Nova. Murcia, SE Spain
Cartagena de los Indes see Cartagena
56 D10 **Cartago** Valle del Cauca, W Colombia
45 N14 **Cartago** Cartago, C Costa Rica
44 M14 **Cartago** *off.* Provincia de Cartago. ◆ province C Costa Rica
27 O11 **Carta Valley** Texas, SW USA
106 F10 **Cartaxo** Santarém, C Portugal
106 I14 **Cartaya** Andalucía, S Spain
Carteret Islands see Tulun Islands
31 S15 **Carter Lake** Iowa, C USA
25 S3 **Cartersville** Georgia, SE USA
193 M14 **Carterton** Wellington, North Island, NZ
32 J13 **Carthage** Illinois, N USA
24 L5 **Carthage** Mississippi, S USA
29 R7 **Carthage** Missouri, C USA
20 I8 **Carthage** New York, NE USA
23 T10 **Carthage** North Carolina, SE USA
22 K8 **Carthage** Tennessee, S USA
27 X7 **Carthage** Texas, SW USA
76 M5 **Carthage** ✕ (Tunis) N Tunisia
Carthago Nova see Cartagena
12 E10 **Cartier** Ontario, S Canada
56 E13 **Cartogena de Chaira** Caquetá, S Colombia

11 S8 **Cartwright** Newfoundland and Labrador, E Canada
57 P9 **Caruana de Montaña** Bolívar, SE Venezuela
61 Q15 **Caruaru** Pernambuco, E Brazil
57 P5 **Carúpano** Sucre, NE Venezuela
Carusbur *see* Cherbourg
60 M12 **Carutapera** Maranhão, E Brazil
29 Y9 **Caruthersville** Missouri, C USA
105 O1 **Carvin** Pas-de-Calais, N France
60 E12 **Carvoeiro** Amazonas, NW Brazil
106 E10 **Carvoeiro, Cabo** *headland* C Portugal
23 U9 **Cary** North Carolina, SE USA
190 M3 **Caryapundy Swamp** *wetland* New South Wales/Queensland, SE Australia
67 E24 **Carysfort, Cape** *headland* East Falkland, Falkland Islands
76 F6 **Casablanca** *Ar.* Dar-el-Beida. NW Morocco
62 M8 **Casa Branca** São Paulo, S Brazil
38 L14 **Casa Grande** Arizona, SW USA
108 C8 **Casale Monferrato** Piemonte, NW Italy
108 E8 **Casalpusterlengo** Lombardia, N Italy
56 H10 **Casanare** *off.* Intendencia de Casanare. ◆ *province* C Colombia
57 P5 **Casanay** Sucre, NE Venezuela
26 K11 **Casa Piedra** Texas, SW USA
109 Q19 **Casarano** Puglia, SE Italy
44 J11 **Casares** Carazo, W Nicaragua
107 R10 **Casas Ibáñez** Castilla-La Mancha, C Spain
63 I14 **Casca** Rio Grande do Sul, S Brazil
180 I17 **Cascade** Mahé, NE Seychelles
35 N13 **Cascade** Idaho, NW USA
31 Y13 **Cascade** Iowa, C USA
35 R9 **Cascade** Montana, NW USA
193 B20 **Cascade Point** *headland* South Island, NZ
34 G13 **Cascade Range** ▲▲ Oregon/Washington, NW USA
35 N12 **Cascade Reservoir** ▣ Idaho, NW USA
1 E8 **Cascadia Basin** *undersea feature* NE Pacific Ocean
106 E11 **Cascais** Lisboa, C Portugal
13 W7 **Cascapédia** ≈ Québec, SE Canada
61 I22 **Cascavel** Ceará, E Brazil
62 G11 **Cascavel** Paraná, S Brazil
108 I13 **Cascia** Umbria, C Italy
108 F11 **Casciana** Toscana, C Italy
21 Q8 **Casco Bay** *bay* Maine, NE USA
204 J7 **Case Island** *island* Antarctica
108 B8 **Caselle** ✕ (Torino) Piemonte, NW Italy
109 K17 **Caserta** Campania, S Italy
13 N8 **Casey** Québec, SE Canada
32 M14 **Casey** Illinois, N USA
205 Y12 **Casey** *Australian research station* Antarctica
205 W3 **Casey Bay** *bay* Antarctica
82 Q11 **Caseyr, Raas** *headland* NE Somalia
99 D20 **Cashel** *Ir.* Caiseal. S Ireland
56 G6 **Casigua** Zulia, W Venezuela
63 B19 **Casilda** Santa Fe, C Argentina
Casim *see* General Toshevo
191 V4 **Casino** New South Wales, SE Australia
Casinum *see* Cassino
113 E17 **Čáslav** *Ger.* Tschaslau. Střední Čechy, C Czech Republic
58 C13 **Casma** Ancash, C Peru
178 J7 **Ca, Sông** ≈ N Vietnam
109 K17 **Casoria** Campania, S Italy
107 T6 **Caspe** Aragón, NE Spain
35 X15 **Casper** Wyoming, C USA
86 M10 **Caspian Depression** *Kaz.* Kaspiy Mangy Oypaty, *Rus.* Prikaspiyskaya Nizmennost'. *depression* Kazakhstan/Russian Federation
139 Kk8 **Caspian Sea** *Az.* Xäzär Dänizi, *Kaz.* Kaspiy Tengizi, *Per.* Baḥr-e Khazar, Daryā-ye Khazar, *Rus.* Kaspiyskoye More. *inland sea* Asia/Europe
85 L14 **Cassacatiza** Tete, NW Mozambique
Cassai *see* Kasai
84 F13 **Cassamba** Moxico, E Angola
109 N20 **Cassano allo Ionio** Calabria, SE Italy
33 S8 **Cass City** Michigan, N USA
Cassel *see* Kassel
12 M13 **Casselman** Ontario, SE Canada
31 R5 **Casselton** North Dakota, N USA
61 M16 **Cássia** *var.* Santa Rita de Cassia. Bahia, E Brazil
8 J9 **Cassiar** British Columbia, W Canada
8 K10 **Cassiar Mountains** ▲▲ British Columbia, W Canada
85 C15 **Cassinga** Huíla, SW Angola
109 J16 **Cassino** *prev.* San Germano; *anc.* Casinum. Lazio, C Italy
31 T4 **Cass Lake** Minnesota, N USA
31 T4 **Cass Lake** ◎ Minnesota, N USA
33 P10 **Cassopolis** Michigan, N USA
33 S8 **Cass River** ≈ Michigan, N USA
29 S8 **Cassville** Missouri, C USA
Castamoni *see* Kastamonu
60 L12 **Castanhal** Pará, NE Brazil
106 G8 **Castanheira de Pêra** Leiria, C Portugal
43 N7 **Castaños** Coahuila de Zaragoza, NE Mexico
110 I10 **Castasegna** Graubünden, SE Switzerland
108 D8 **Casteggio** Lombardia, N Italy
109 K23 **Castelbuono** Sicilia, Italy, C Mediterranean Sea
109 K15 **Castel di Sangro** Abruzzi, C Italy
108 H7 **Castelfranco Veneto** Veneto, NE Italy
104 K14 **Casteljaloux** Lot-et-Garonne, SW France
109 L18 **Castellabate** *var.* Santa Maria di Castellabate. Campania, S Italy
109 I23 **Castellammare del Golfo** Sicilia, Italy, C Mediterranean Sea
109 H22 **Castellammare, Golfo di** *gulf* Sicilia, Italy, C Mediterranean Sea
105 U15 **Castellane** Alpes-de-Haute-Provence, SE France
109 O18 **Castellaneta** Puglia, SE Italy
108 E9 **Castel l'Arquato** Emilia-Romagna, C Italy
63 E21 **Castelli** Buenos Aires, E Argentina
107 T9 **Castelló de la Plana** *var.* Castellón. País Valenciano, E Spain
107 S8 **Castellón** ◆ *province* País Valenciano, E Spain
Castellón *see* Castelló de la Plana
107 S7 **Castellote** Aragón, NE Spain
105 N16 **Castelnaudary** Aude, S France
104 L16 **Castelnau-Magnoac** Hautes-Pyrénées, S France
108 F10 **Castelnovo ne' Monti** Emilia-Romagna, C Italy
Castelnuovo *see* Herceg-Novi
106 H9 **Castelo Branco** Castelo Branco, C Portugal
106 H8 **Castelo Branco** ◆ *district* C Portugal
106 I10 **Castelo de Vide** Portalegre, C Portugal
106 G9 **Castelo do Bode, Barragem do** ▣ C Portugal
108 G10 **Castel San Pietro** Emilia-Romagna, C Italy
109 B17 **Castelsardo** Sardegna, Italy, C Mediterranean Sea
104 M14 **Castelsarrasin** Tarn-et-Garonne, S France
109 I24 **Casteltermini** Sicilia, Italy, C Mediterranean Sea
109 H24 **Castelvetrano** Sicilia, Italy, C Mediterranean Sea
190 L12 **Casterton** Victoria, SE Australia
104 J15 **Castets** Landes, SW France
108 H12 **Castiglione del Lago** Umbria, C Italy
108 F13 **Castiglione della Pescaia** Toscana, C Italy
108 F8 **Castiglione delle Stiviere** Lombardia, N Italy
106 M9 **Castilla-La Mancha** ◆ *autonomous community* NE Spain
106 L5 **Castilla-León** *var.* Castillia y Leon. ◆ *autonomous community* NW Spain
107 N10 **Castilla Nueva** *cultural region* C Spain
107 N6 **Castilla Vieja** *cultural region* N Spain
Castillia y Leon *see* Castilla-León
Castillo de Locubim *see* Castillo de Locubín
107 N14 **Castillo de Locubín** *var.* Castillo de Locubim. Andalucía, S Spain
104 K13 **Castillon-la-Bataille** Gironde, SW France
65 I19 **Castillo, Pampa del** *plain* S Argentina
63 G19 **Castillos** Rocha, SE Uruguay
99 B16 **Castlebar** *Ir.* Caisleán an Bharraigh. W Ireland
99 F16 **Castleblayney** *Ir.* Baile na Lorgan. N Ireland
47 O11 **Castle Bruce** E Dominica
38 M5 **Castle Dale** Utah, W USA
38 I14 **Castle Dome Peak** ▲ Arizona, SW USA
99 J14 **Castle Douglas** S Scotland, UK
99 E14 **Castlefinn** *Ir.* Caisleán na Finne. NW Ireland
99 M17 **Castleford** N England, UK
9 O17 **Castlegar** British Columbia, SW Canada
66 B12 **Castle Harbour** *inlet* Bermuda, NW Atlantic Ocean
23 V12 **Castle Hayne** North Carolina, SE USA
99 B20 **Castleisland** *Ir.* Oileán Ciarral. SW Ireland
191 N12 **Castlemaine** Victoria, SE Australia
39 R5 **Castle Peak** ▲ Colorado, C USA
35 O13 **Castle Peak** ▲ Idaho, NW USA
192 N13 **Castlepoint** Wellington, North Island, NZ
99 D17 **Castlerea** *Ir.* An Caisleán Riabhach. W Ireland
99 G15 **Castlereagh** *Ir.* An Caisleán Riabhach. N Northern Ireland, UK
191 R6 **Castlereagh River** ≈ New South Wales, SE Australia
39 T5 **Castle Rock** Colorado, C USA
32 K7 **Castle Rock Lake** ▣ Wisconsin, N USA
67 G25 **Castle Rock Point** *headland* S Saint Helena
99 I16 **Castletown** SE Isle of Man
31 R9 **Castlewood** South Dakota, N USA
9 R15 **Castor** Alberta, SW Canada
12 M13 **Castor** ≈ Ontario, SE Canada
29 X7 **Castor River** ≈ Missouri, C USA
Castra Albiensium *see* Castres
Castra Regina *see* Regensburg
105 N15 **Castres** *anc.* Castra Albiensium. Tarn, S France
100 H9 **Castricum** Noord-Holland, W Netherlands
47 S11 **Castries** ● (Saint Lucia) N Saint Lucia
62 J11 **Castro** Paraná, S Brazil
65 F17 **Castro** Los Lagos, W Chile
106 H7 **Castro Daire** Viseu, N Portugal
106 M13 **Castro del Río** Andalucía, S Spain
Castrogiovanni *see* Enna
106 H14 **Castro Marim** Faro, S Portugal
106 J2 **Castropol** Asturias, N Spain
107 O2 **Castro-Urdiales** *var.* Castro Urdiales. Cantabria, N Spain
106 G13 **Castro Verde** Beja, S Portugal
109 N19 **Castrovillari** Calabria, SW Italy
37 N10 **Castroville** California, W USA
27 R12 **Castroville** Texas, SW USA
106 K11 **Castuera** Extremadura, W Spain
63 F19 **Casupá** Florida, S Uruguay
193 A22 **Caswell Sound** *sound* South Island, NZ
143 Q13 **Çat** Erzurum, NE Turkey
44 K6 **Catacamas** Olancho, C Honduras
58 A10 **Catacaos** Piura, NW Peru
24 I7 **Catahoula Lake** ◎ Louisiana, S USA
143 S15 **Çatak** Van, SE Turkey
143 S15 **Çatak Çayi** ≈ SE Turkey
116 O12 **Çatalca** İstanbul, NW Turkey
116 O12 **Çatalca Yarımadası** *physical region* NW Turkey
64 H6 **Catalina** Antofagasta, N Chile
Catalonia *see* Cataluña
107 U5 **Cataluña** *Cat.* Catalunya; *Eng.* Catalonia. ◆ *autonomous community* N Spain
Catalunya *see* Cataluña
64 I7 **Catamarca** *off.* Provincia de Catamarca. ◆ *province* NW Argentina
Catamarca *see* San Fernando del Valle de Catamarca
179 Pp11 **Catanauan** Luzon, N Philippines
85 M16 **Catandica** Manica, C Mozambique
179 Qq11 **Catanduanes Island** *island* N Philippines
62 K8 **Catanduva** São Paulo, S Brazil
109 L24 **Catania** Sicilia, Italy, C Mediterranean Sea
109 M24 **Catania, Golfo di** *gulf* Sicilia, Italy, C Mediterranean Sea
47 U5 **Cataño** *var.* Cantaño. E Puerto Rico
109 O21 **Catanzaro** Calabria, SW Italy
109 O22 **Catanzaro Marina** *var.* Marina di Catanzaro. Calabria, S Italy
27 Q14 **Catarina** Texas, SW USA
179 Qq12 **Catarman** Samar, C Philippines
107 S10 **Catarroja** País Valenciano, E Spain
23 R11 **Catawba River** ≈ North Carolina/South Carolina, SE USA
179 R12 **Catbalogan** Samar, C Philippines
12 I14 **Catchacoma** Ontario, SE Canada
43 S15 **Catemaco** Veracruz-Llave, SE Mexico
Cathair na Mart *see* Westport
Cathair Saidhbhín *see* Cahersiveen
33 P5 **Cat Head Point** *headland* Michigan, N USA
25 Q2 **Cathedral Caverns** *cave* Alabama, S USA
37 V16 **Cathedral City** California, W USA
26 K10 **Cathedral Mountain** ▲ Texas, SW USA
34 G10 **Cathlamet** Washington, NW USA
78 G13 **Catió** S Guinea-Bissau
57 O10 **Catisimiña** Bolívar, SE Venezuela
46 J3 **Cat Island** *island* C Bahamas
10 B9 **Cat Lake** Ontario, S Canada
23 P5 **Catlettsburg** Kentucky, S USA
193 D24 **Catlins** ≈ South Island, NZ
37 R1 **Catnip Mountain** ▲ Nevada, W USA
43 Z11 **Catoche, Cabo** *headland* SE Mexico
29 P9 **Catoosa** Oklahoma, C USA
43 N10 **Catorce** San Luis Potosí, C Mexico
65 I14 **Catriel** Río Negro, C Argentina
64 K13 **Catriló** La Pampa, C Argentina
60 F11 **Catrimani** Roraima, N Brazil
60 E10 **Catrimani, Rio** ≈ N Brazil
20 K11 **Catskill** New York, NE USA
20 K11 **Catskill Creek** ≈ New York, NE USA
20 J11 **Catskill Mountains** ▲▲ New York, NE USA
20 D11 **Cattaraugus Creek** ≈ New York, NE USA
Cattaro *see* Kotor
Cattaro, Bocche di *see* Kotorska, Boka
109 I24 **Cattolica Eraclea** Sicilia, Italy, C Mediterranean Sea
85 B14 **Catumbela** ≈ W Angola
85 N14 **Catur** Niassa, N Mozambique
84 C10 **Cauale** ≈ NE Angola
179 Pp9 **Cauayan** Luzon, N Philippines
56 C12 **Cauca** *off.* Departamento del Cauca. ◆ *province* SW Colombia
49 P5 **Cauca** ≈ SE Venezuela
60 P13 **Caucaia** Ceará, E Brazil
56 E7 **Cauca, Río** ≈ N Colombia
56 E7 **Caucasia** Antioquia, NW Colombia
143 Q8 **Caucasus** *Rus.* Kavkaz. ▲▲ Georgia/Russian Federation
64 I10 **Caucete** San Juan, W Argentina
107 R11 **Caudete** Castilla-La Mancha, C Spain
105 P2 **Caudry** Nord, N France
84 D11 **Caungula** Lunda Norte, NE Angola
64 G13 **Cauquenes** Maule, C Chile
57 N8 **Caura, Río** ≈ C Venezuela
13 V7 **Causapscal** Québec, SE Canada
119 N10 **Căuşeni** *Rus.* Kaushany. E Moldova
104 M14 **Caussade** Tarn-et-Garonne, S France
104 K17 **Cauterets** Hautes-Pyrénées, S France
8 J15 **Caution, Cape** *headland* British Columbia, SW Canada
46 H7 **Cauto** ≈ E Cuba
Cauvery *see* Kāveri
104 L3 **Caux, Pays de** *physical region* N France
109 L18 **Cava de' Tirreni** Campania, S Italy
106 G6 **Cávado** ≈ N Portugal
Cavaia *see* Kavajë
105 R15 **Cavaillon** Vaucluse, SE France
105 U16 **Cavalaire-sur-Mer** Var, SE France
108 G6 **Cavalese** *Ger.* Gablös. Trentino-Alto Adige, N Italy
31 Q2 **Cavalier** North Dakota, N USA
78 L17 **Cavalla** *var.* Cavally, Cavally Fleuve. ≈ Ivory Coast/Liberia
107 Y8 **Cavalleria, Cap de** *var.* Cabo Caballeria. *headland* Menorca, Spain, W Mediterranean Sea
192 K2 **Cavalli Islands** *island group* N NZ
Cavally/Cavally Fleuve *see* Cavalla
99 E16 **Cavan** *Ir.* Cabhán. N Ireland
99 E16 **Cavan** *Ir.* An Cabhán. *cultural region* N Ireland
108 H8 **Cavarzare** Veneto, NE Italy
29 W9 **Cave City** Arkansas, C USA
22 K7 **Cave City** Kentucky, S USA
67 M25 **Cave Point** *headland* S Tristan da Cunha
23 N5 **Cave Run Lake** ▣ Kentucky, S USA
60 K11 **Caviana de Fora, Ilha** *var.* Ilha Caviana. *island* N Brazil
Caviana, Ilha *see* Caviana de Fora, Ilha
115 I16 **Cavtat** *It.* Ragusavecchia. Dubrovnik-Neretva, SE Croatia
Cawnpore *see* Kānpur
Caxamarca *see* Cajamarca
60 N13 **Caxias** Amazonas, W Brazil
60 A13 **Caxias** Maranhão, E Brazil
63 I15 **Caxias do Sul** Rio Grande do Sul, S Brazil
44 J4 **Caxinas, Punta** *headland* N Honduras
84 B11 **Caxito** Bengo, NW Angola
142 F14 **Çay** Afyon, W Turkey
42 L15 **Cayacal, Punta** *var.* Punta Mongrove. *headland* S Mexico
58 C6 **Cayambe** Pichincha, N Ecuador
58 C6 **Cayambe** ▲ N Ecuador
23 R12 **Cayce** South Carolina, SE USA
57 Y10 **Cayenne** ○ (French Guiana) NE French Guiana
57 Y10 **Cayenne** ✕ NE French Guiana
46 K10 **Cayes** *var.* Les Cayes. SW Haiti
47 U6 **Cayey** C Puerto Rico
47 U6 **Cayey, Sierra de** ▲ E Puerto Rico
105 N14 **Caylus** Tarn-et-Garonne, S France
46 E8 **Cayman Brac** *island* E Cayman Islands
46 D8 **Cayman Islands** ◇ *UK dependent territory* W West Indies
66 D11 **Cayman Trench** *undersea feature* NW Caribbean Sea
49 O3 **Cayman Trough** *undersea feature* NW Caribbean Sea
82 O13 **Caynabo** Togdheer, N Somalia
44 F3 **Cayo** ◆ *district* SW Belize
Cayo *see* San Ignacio
45 N9 **Cayos Guerrero** *reef* E Nicaragua
45 O9 **Cayos King** *reef* E Nicaragua
46 E4 **Cay Sal** *islet* SW Bahamas
12 G16 **Cayuga** Ontario, S Canada
27 V8 **Cayuga** Texas, SW USA
20 G10 **Cayuga Lake** ◎ New York, NE USA
106 K13 **Cazalla de la Sierra** Andalucía, S Spain
118 L14 **Căzănești** Ialomița, SE Romania
104 M16 **Cazères** Haute-Garonne, S France
114 E10 **Cazin** NW Bosnia and Herzegovina
84 G13 **Cazombo** Moxico, E Angola
107 O13 **Cazorla** Andalucía, S Spain
Cazza *see* Sušac
106 L4 **Cea** ≈ NW Spain
Ceadâr-Lunga *see* Ciadîr-Lunga
Ceanannas *see* Kells
Ceann Toirc *see* Kanturk
60 O13 **Ceará** *off.* Estado do Ceará. ◆ *state* C Brazil
Ceará *see* Fortaleza
Ceara Abyssal Plain *see* Ceará Plain
61 Q14 **Ceará Mirim** Rio Grande do Norte, E Brazil
66 J13 **Ceará Plain** *var.* Ceara Abyssal Plain. *undersea feature* W Atlantic Ocean
66 I13 **Ceará Ridge** *undersea feature* C Atlantic Ocean
Ceatharlach *see* Carlow
45 Q17 **Cébaco, Isla** *island* SW Panama
42 K7 **Ceballos** Durango, C Mexico
63 G19 **Cebollatí** Rocha, E Uruguay
63 G19 **Cebollatí, Río** ≈ E Uruguay
107 P5 **Cebollera** ▲ N Spain
106 M8 **Cebreros** Castilla-León, N Spain
179 Qq14 **Cebu** *off.* Cebu City. Cebu, C Philippines
179 Qq13 **Cebu** *island* C Philippines
109 J16 **Ceccano** Lazio, C Italy
Čechy *see* Bohemia
108 F12 **Cecina** Toscana, C Italy
28 K4 **Cedar Bluff Reservoir** ▣ Kansas, C USA
32 M8 **Cedarburg** Wisconsin, N USA
38 J7 **Cedar City** Utah, W USA
27 T11 **Cedar Creek** Texas, SW USA
30 L7 **Cedar Creek** ≈ North Dakota, N USA
27 U7 **Cedar Creek Reservoir** ▣ Texas, SW USA
31 W13 **Cedar Falls** Iowa, C USA
33 N8 **Cedar Grove** Wisconsin, N USA
23 Y6 **Cedar Island** *island* Virginia, NE USA
25 U11 **Cedar Key** Cedar Keys, Florida, SE USA
25 U11 **Cedar Keys** *island group* Florida, SE USA
9 V14 **Cedar Lake** ◎ Manitoba, C Canada
12 I11 **Cedar Lake** ◎ Ontario, SE Canada
26 M6 **Cedar Lake** ◎ Texas, SW USA
31 X13 **Cedar Rapids** Iowa, C USA
31 X14 **Cedar River** ≈ Iowa/Minnesota, C USA
31 O14 **Cedar River** ≈ Nebraska, C USA
33 P8 **Cedar Springs** Michigan, N USA
25 R3 **Cedartown** Georgia, SE USA
29 O7 **Cedar Vale** Kansas, C USA
37 Q2 **Cedarville** California, W USA
106 H1 **Cedeira** Galicia, NW Spain
44 H8 **Cedeño** Choluteca, S Honduras
43 N10 **Cedral** San Luis Potosí, C Mexico
44 I6 **Cedros** Francisco Morazán, C Honduras
42 M9 **Cedros** Zacatecas, C Mexico
42 B5 **Cedros, Isla** *island* W Mexico
199 Mm6 **Cedros Trench** *undersea feature* E Pacific Ocean
190 E7 **Ceduna** South Australia
112 D10 **Cedynia** *Ger.* Zehden. Szczecin, W Poland
82 P12 **Ceelaayo** Sanaag, N Somalia
83 O16 **Ceel Buur** *It.* El Bur; Galguduud, C Somalia
83 N15 **Ceel Dheere** *var.* Ceel Dher, *It.* El Dere. Galguduud, C Somalia
Ceel Dher *see* Ceel Dheere
83 P14 **Ceel Xamure** Mudug, E Somalia
82 O12 **Ceerigaabo** *var.* Erigabo, Erigavo. Sanaag, N Somalia
109 J23 **Cefalù** *anc.* Cephaloedium. Sicilia, Italy, C Mediterranean Sea
107 N6 **Cega** ≈ N Spain
113 K23 **Cegléd** *prev.* Czegléd. Pest, C Hungary
115 N18 **Čegrane** W FYR Macedonia
107 Q13 **Cehegín** Murcia, SE Spain
142 K12 **Çekerek** Yozgat, N Turkey
109 J15 **Celano** Abruzzi, C Italy
106 H4 **Celanova** Galicia, NW Spain
44 F6 **Celaque, Cordillera de** ▲▲ W Honduras
43 N13 **Celaya** Guanajuato, C Mexico
Celebes *see* Sulawesi
198 Ff8 **Celebes Basin** *undersea feature* SE South China Sea
175 Qq4 **Celebes Sea** *Ind.* Laut Sulawesi. *sea* Indonesia/Philippines
43 W12 **Celestún** Yucatán, E Mexico
33 Q12 **Celina** Ohio, N USA
22 L8 **Celina** Tennessee, S USA
27 U5 **Celina** Texas, SW USA
114 G11 **Čelinac Donji** N Bosnia and Herzegovina
111 V10 **Celje** *Ger.* Cilli. C Slovenia
113 G23 **Celldömölk** Vas, W Hungary
102 J12 **Celle** *var.* Zelle. Niedersachsen, N Germany
101 D19 **Celles** Hainaut, SW Belgium
106 I7 **Celorico da Beira** Guarda, N Portugal
Celovec *see* Klagenfurt
66 M7 **Celtic Sea** *Ir.* An Mhuir Cheilteach. *sea* SW British Isles
66 N7 **Celtic Shelf** *undersea feature* E Atlantic Ocean
116 L13 **Çeltik Gölü** ◎ NW Turkey
115 M14 **Čemerno** ▲ C Yugoslavia
175 Oo16 **Cempi, Teluk** *bay* Nusa Tenggara, S Indonesia
107 Q12 **Cenajo, Embalse del** ▣ S Spain
107 P4 **Cenicero** La Rioja, N Spain
108 E9 **Ceno** ≈ NW Italy
104 K13 **Cenon** Gironde, SW France
12 K13 **Centennial Lake** ◎ Ontario, SE Canada
Centennial State *see* Colorado
39 S7 **Center** Colorado, C USA
31 Q13 **Center** Nebraska, C USA
30 M5 **Center** North Dakota, N USA
27 X8 **Center** Texas, SW USA
31 W8 **Center City** Minnesota, N USA
38 L5 **Centerfield** Utah, W USA
22 K9 **Center Hill Lake** ▣ Tennessee, S USA
31 X13 **Center Point** Iowa, C USA
27 R11 **Center Point** Texas, SW USA
31 W16 **Centerville** Iowa, C USA
29 W7 **Centerville** Missouri, C USA
31 R12 **Centerville** South Dakota, N USA
22 I9 **Centerville** Tennessee, S USA
27 V9 **Centerville** Texas, SW USA
42 M5 **Centinela, Picacho del** ▲ NE Mexico
108 G9 **Cento** Emilia-Romagna, N Italy
Centrafricaine, République *see* Central African Republic
41 S8 **Central** Alaska, USA
39 P15 **Central** New Mexico, SW USA
85 H18 **Central** ◆ *district* E Botswana
144 E10 **Central** ◆ *district* C Israel
83 I19 **Central** ◆ *province* C Kenya
84 M13 **Central** ◆ *region* C Malawi
159 P12 **Central** ◆ *zone* C Nepal
194 J15 **Central** ◆ *province* S PNG
65 I21 **Central** ◆ *department* C Paraguay
195 W15 **Central** *off.* Central Province. ◆ *province* S Solomon Islands
85 J14 **Central** ◆ *province* C Zambia
119 P11 **Central** ✕ (Odesa) Odes'ka Oblast', SW Ukraine
Central *see* Centre
81 H14 **Central African Republic** *var.* République Centrafricaine, *abbrev.* CAR; *prev.* Ubangi-Shari, Oubangui-Chari, Territoire de l'Oubangui-Chari. ◆ *republic* C Africa
198 G6 **Central Basin Trough** *undersea feature* W Pacific Ocean
Central Borneo *see* Kalimantan Tengah
155 P12 **Central Brāhui Range** ▲▲ W Pakistan
Central Celebes *see* Sulawesi Tengah
31 Y13 **Central City** Iowa, C USA
22 I6 **Central City** Kentucky, S USA
31 P15 **Central City** Nebraska, C USA
50 D6 **Central, Cordillera** ▲▲ W Bolivia
56 D11 **Central, Cordillera** ▲▲ W Colombia
44 M13 **Central, Cordillera** ▲▲ C Costa Rica
47 N9 **Central, Cordillera** ▲▲ C Dominican Republic
45 R16 **Central, Cordillera** ▲▲ C Panama
179 P8 **Central, Cordillera** ▲▲ Luzon, N Philippines
47 S6 **Central, Cordillera** ▲▲ Puerto Rico
44 H7 **Central District** *var.* Tegucigalpa. ◆ *district* C Honduras
32 L15 **Centralia** Illinois, N USA
29 U4 **Centralia** Missouri, C USA
34 G9 **Centralia** Washington, NW USA
Central Indian Ridge *see* Mid-Indian Ridge
Central Java *see* Jawa Tengah
Central Kalimantan *see* Kalimantan Tengah
154 L14 **Central Makrān Range** ▲▲ W Pakistan
199 J8 **Central Pacific Basin** *undersea feature* C Pacific Ocean
61 M19 **Central, Planalto** *var.* Brazilian Highlands. ▲ E Brazil
34 F15 **Central Point** Oregon, NW USA
161 K25 **Central Province** ◆ *province* C Sri Lanka
Central Provinces and Berar *see* Madhya Pradesh
194 G11 **Central Range** ▲▲ NW PNG
Central Russian Upland *see* Srednerusskaya Vozvyshennost'
Central Siberian Plateau/Central Siberian Uplands *see* Srednesibirskoye Ploskogor'ye
106 K8 **Central, Sistema** ▲▲ C Spain
Central Sulawesi *see* Sulawesi Tengah
37 N3 **Central Valley** California, W USA
37 P8 **Central Valley** *valley* California, W USA
25 Q3 **Centre** Alabama, S USA
81 E15 **Centre** *Eng.* Central. ◆ *province* C Cameroon
104 M8 **Centre** ◆ *region* N France
181 Y16 **Centre de Flacq** E Mauritius
57 Y9 **Centre Spatial Guyanais** *space station* N French Guiana
25 O5 **Centreville** Alabama, S USA
23 X3 **Centreville** Maryland, NE USA
24 J7 **Centreville** Mississippi, S USA
Centum Cellae *see* Civitavecchia
166 M14 **Cenxi** Guangxi Zhuangzu Zizhiqu, S China
Ceos *see* Kéa
Cephaloedium *see* Cefalù
114 I9 **Čepin** *Hung.* Csepén. Osijek-Baranja, E Croatia
174 Ll15 **Cepu** *prev.* Tjepoe, Tjepu. Jawa, C Indonesia
Ceram *see* Seram, Pulau
175 T10 **Ceram Sea** *Ind.* Laut Seram. *sea* E Indonesia
198 G9 **Ceram Trough** *undersea feature* W Pacific Ocean
Cerasus *see* Giresun
38 I10 **Cerbat Mountains** ▲▲ Arizona, SW USA
105 P17 **Cerbère, Cap** *headland* S France
106 F13 **Cercal do Alentejo** Setúbal, S Portugal
113 A18 **Čerchov** *Ger.* Czerkow. ▲ W Czech Republic
105 O13 **Cère** ≈ C France
63 A16 **Ceres** Santa Fe, C Argentina
61 K18 **Ceres** Goiás, C Brazil
Ceresio *see* Lugano, Lago di
105 O17 **Céret** Pyrénées-Orientales, S France
56 E6 **Cereté** Córdoba, NW Colombia
180 I17 **Cerf, Île au** *island* Inner Islands, NE Seychelles
101 G22 **Cerfontaine** Namur, S Belgium
Cergy-Pontoise *see* Pontoise
109 N16 **Cerignola** Puglia, SE Italy
Cerigo *see* Kýthira
105 O9 **Cérilly** Allier, C France
142 I11 **Çerkeş** Çankırı, N Turkey
142 D10 **Çerkezköy** Tekirdağ, NW Turkey
111 T12 **Cerknica** *Ger.* Zirknitz. SW Slovenia
111 S11 **Cerkno** W Slovenia
118 F10 **Cermei** *Hung.* Csermő. Arad, W Romania
143 O15 **Çermik** Dıyarbakır, SE Turkey
114 I10 **Cerna** Vukovar-Srijem, E Croatia
Cernăuţi *see* Chernivtsi
118 M14 **Cernavodă** Constanța, SW Romania
105 U7 **Cernay** Haut-Rhin, NE France
Černice *see* Schwarzach
43 O8 **Cerralvo** Nuevo León, NE Mexico
42 G9 **Cerralvo, Isla** *island* W Mexico
109 L16 **Cerreto Sannita** Campania, S Italy
115 L20 **Cërrik** *var.* Cerriku. Elbasan, C Albania
Cerriku *see* Cërrik
43 O11 **Cerritos** San Luis Potosí, C Mexico
62 K11 **Cerro Azul** Paraná, S Brazil
63 F18 **Cerro Chato** Treinta y Tres, E Uruguay
63 F19 **Cerro Colorado** Florida, S Uruguay
58 E13 **Cerro de Pasco** Pasco, C Peru
63 G18 **Cerro Largo** ◆ *department* NE Uruguay
63 G14 **Cêrro Largo** Rio Grande do Sul, S Brazil
44 E7 **Cerrón Grande, Embalse** ▣ N El Salvador
65 I14 **Cerros Colorados, Embalse** ◎ W Argentina
107 V5 **Cervera** Cataluña, NE Spain
106 M3 **Cervera del Pisuerga** Castilla-León, N Spain
107 Q5 **Cervera del Río Alhama** La Rioja, N Spain
109 H15 **Cerveteri** Lazio, C Italy
108 H10 **Cervia** Emilia-Romagna, N Italy
108 J7 **Cervignano del Friuli** Friuli-Venezia Giulia, NE Italy
109 L17 **Cervinara** Campania, S Italy
Cervinia *see* Breuil
108 B6 **Cervino, Monte** *var.* Matterhorn. ▲ Italy/Switzerland *see also* Matterhorn
104 F2 **Cervione** Corse, France, C Mediterranean Sea
106 I1 **Cervo** Galicia, NW Spain
56 F5 **Cesar** *off.* Departamento del Cesar. ◆ *province* N Colombia
108 H10 **Cesena** *anc.* Caesena. Emilia-Romagna, N Italy
108 I10 **Cesenatico** Emilia-Romagna, N Italy
120 H8 **Cēsis** *Ger.* Wenden. Cēsis, C Latvia
113 D15 **Česká Lípa** *Ger.* Böhmisch-Leipa. Severní Čechy, N Czech Republic
Česká Republika *see* Czech Republic
113 F17 **Česká Třebová** *Ger.* Böhmisch-Trübau. Východní Čechy, E Czech Republic
113 D19 **České Budějovice** *Ger.* Budweis. Jižní Čechy, SW Czech Republic
113 D19 **České Velenice** Jižní Čechy, S Czech Republic
113 E18 **Českomoravská Vrchovina** *var.* Českomoravská Vysočina, *Eng.* Bohemian-Moravian Highlands, *Ger.* Böhmisch-Mährische Höhe. ▲▲ S Czech Republic
Českomoravská Vysočina *see* Českomoravská Vrchovina
113 C19 **Český Krumlov** *var.* Böhmisch-Krumau, *Ger.* Krummau. Jižní Čechy, SW Czech Republic
Český Les *see* Bohemian Forest
114 F8 **Česma** ≈ N Croatia
142 A14 **Çeşme** İzmir, W Turkey
Cess *see* Cestos
191 T8 **Cessnock** New South Wales, SE Australia
78 K17 **Cestos** *var.* Cess. ≈ S Liberia
120 I9 **Cesvaine** Madona, E Latvia
118 G14 **Cetate** Dolj, SW Romania
Cetatea Albă *see* Bilhorod-Dnistrovs'kyy
115 J17 **Cetinje** *It.* Cettigne. Montenegro, SW Yugoslavia
109 N20 **Cetraro** Calabria, S Italy
Cette *see* Sète
196 A17 **Cetti Bay** *bay* SW Guam
Cettigne *see* Cetinje
106 L17 **Ceuta** *var.* Sebta. Ceuta, Spain, N Africa
90 C16 **Ceuta** *enclave* Spain, N Africa
108 B9 **Ceva** Piemonte, NE Italy
105 P14 **Cévennes** ▲▲ S France
110 G10 **Cevio** Ticino, S Switzerland
142 K16 **Ceyhan** Adana, S Turkey
142 K17 **Ceyhan Nehri** ≈ S Turkey
143 P17 **Ceylanpınar** Şanlıurfa, SE Turkey
Ceylon *see* Sri Lanka
181 R6 **Ceylon Plain** *undersea feature* N Indian Ocean
Ceyre to the Caribs *see* Marie-Galante
105 Q14 **Cèze** ≈ S France
152 H15 **Chaacha** *Turkm.* Chäche. Akhalskiy Velayat, S Turkmenistan
131 P6 **Chaadayevka** Penzenskaya Oblast', W Russian Federation
178 H12 **Cha-Am** Phetchaburi, SW Thailand
149 W15 **Chābahār** *var.* Chāh Bahār, Chahbar. Sīstān va Balūchestān, SE Iran
63 B19 **Chabas** Santa Fe, C Argentina
105 T10 **Chablais** *physical region* E France
63 B20 **Chacabuco** Buenos Aires, E Argentina
44 K8 **Chachagón, Cerro** ▲ N Nicaragua
58 C10 **Chachapoyas** Amazonas, NW Peru
Chäche *see* Chaacha
121 O18 **Chachersk** *Rus.* Chechersk. Homyel'skaya Voblasts', SE Belarus
121 N16 **Chachevichy** *Rus.* Chechevichi. Mahilyowskaya Voblasts', E Belarus
63 B14 **Chaco** *off.* Provincia de Chaco. ◆ *province* NE Argentina
Chaco *see* Gran Chaco
64 M6 **Chaco Austral** *physical region* N Argentina
64 M3 **Chaco Boreal** *physical region* N Paraguay
64 M6 **Chaco Central** *physical region* N Argentina
41 Y15 **Chacon, Cape** *headland* Prince of Wales Island, Alaska, USA
80 H9 **Chad** *off.* Republic of Chad, *Fr.* Tchad. ◆ *republic* C Africa
126 Hh16 **Chadan** Respublika Tyva, S Russian Federation

● Country
◆ Country Capital
◇ Dependent Territory
○ Dependent Territory Capital
◆ Administrative Region
✕ International Airport
▲ Mountain
▲▲ Mountain Range
Volcano
≈ River
◎ Lake
▣ Reservoir

23 U12 **Chadbourn** North Carolina, SE USA
85 L14 **Chadiza** Eastern, E Zambia
69 Q7 **Chad, Lake** Fr. Lac Tchad. ◎ C Africa
126 J13 **Chadobets** ~ C Russian Federation
30 J12 **Chadron** Nebraska, C USA
Chadyr-Lunga see Ciadîr-Lunga
169 W14 **Chaeryŏng** SW North Korea
107 P17 **Chafarinas, Islas** island group S Spain
29 Y7 **Chaffee** Missouri, C USA
154 L12 **Chāgai Hills** var. Chāh Gay. ▲ Afghanistan/Pakistan
126 M12 **Chagda** Respublika Sakha (Yakutiya), NE Russian Federation
Chaghasarāy see Asadābād
155 N5 **Chaghcharān** var. Chakhcharan, Cheghcheran, Qala Āhangarān. Ghowr, C Afghanistan
105 R9 **Chagny** Saône-et-Loire, C France
181 Q7 **Chagos Archipelago** var. Oil Islands. island group British Indian Ocean Territory
133 O15 **Chagos Bank** undersea feature C Indian Ocean
133 O14 **Chagos-Laccadive Plateau** undersea feature N Indian Ocean
181 Q7 **Chagos Trench** undersea feature N Indian Ocean
45 T14 **Chagres, Río** ~ C Panama
47 U14 **Chaguanas** Trinidad, Trinidad and Tobago
56 M6 **Chaguaramas** Guárico, N Venezuela
152 C9 **Chagyl** Balkanskiy Velayat, NW Turkmenistan
Chahārmahāl and Bakhtiyāri see Chahār Maḩall va Bakhtīārī
148 M9 **Chahār Maḩall va Bakhtīārī** off. Ostān-e Chahār Maḩall va Bakhtīārī, var. Chahārmahāl and Bakhtiyāri. ◈ province SW Iran
Chāh Bahār/Chahbar see Chābahār
149 V13 **Chāh Derāz** Sīstān va Balūchestān, SE Iran
Chāh Gay see Chāgai Hills
178 Hh10 **Chai Badan** Lop Buri, C Thailand
159 Q16 **Chāībāsa** Bihār, N India
81 E19 **Chaillu, Massif du** ▲ C Gabon
178 Hh10 **Chai Nat** var. Chainat, Jainat, Jayanath. Chai Nat, C Thailand
67 M14 **Chain Fracture Zone** tectonic feature E Atlantic Ocean
181 N5 **Chain Ridge** undersea feature W Indian Ocean
Chairn, Ceann an see Carnsore Point
164 L5 **Chaiwopu** Xinjiang Uygur Zizhiqu, W China
178 I10 **Chaiyaphum** var. Jayabum. Chaiyaphum, C Thailand
64 N10 **Chajarí** Entre Ríos, E Argentina
44 C5 **Chajul** Quiché, W Guatemala
85 K16 **Chakari** Mashonaland West, N Zimbabwe
154 J9 **Chakhānsūr** Nīmrūz, SW Afghanistan
Chakhānsūr see Nīmrūz
Chakhcharan see Chaghcharān
155 V8 **Chak Jhumra** var. Jhumra. Punjab, E Pakistan
152 I16 **Chaknakdysonga** Akhalskiy Velayat, S Turkmenistan
159 P16 **Chakradharpur** Bihār, N India
158 J8 **Chakrāta** Uttar Pradesh, N India
155 U7 **Chakwāl** Punjab, NE Pakistan
59 F17 **Chala** Arequipa, SW Peru
104 K12 **Chalais** Charente, W France
110 D10 **Chalais** Valais, SW Switzerland
117 J20 **Chalándri** var. Halandri; prev. Khalándrion. prehistoric site Sýros, Kykládes, Greece, Aegean Sea
196 H6 **Chalan Kanoa** Saipan, S Northern Mariana Islands
196 C16 **Chalan Pago** C Guam
Chalap Dalam/Chalap Dalan see Chehel Abdālān, Kūh-e
44 F7 **Chalatenango** Chalatenango, N El Salvador
44 A9 **Chalatenango** ◈ department NW El Salvador
85 P15 **Chalaua** Nampula, NE Mozambique
83 I16 **Chalbi Desert** desert N Kenya
44 D7 **Chalchuapa** Santa Ana, W El Salvador
Chalcidice see Chalkidikí
Chalcis see Chalkída
105 N6 **Châlette-sur-Loing** Loiret, C France
13 X8 **Chaleur Bay** Fr. Baie des Chaleurs. bay New Brunswick/Québec, E Canada
Chaleurs, Baie des see Chaleur Bay
59 G16 **Chalhuanca** Apurímac, S Peru
160 F12 **Chālisgaon** Mahārāshtra, C India
117 N23 **Chálki** island Dodekánisos, Greece, Aegean Sea
117 F16 **Chalkiádes** Thessalía, C Greece
117 H18 **Chalkída** var. Halkida; prev. Khalkís, anc. Chalcis. Evvoia, E Greece
117 G14 **Chalkidikí** var. Khalkidhikí; anc. Chalcidice. peninsula NE Greece
193 A24 **Chalky Inlet** inlet South Island, NZ
41 S7 **Chalkyitsik** Alaska, USA
104 I9 **Challans** Vendée, NW France
59 K19 **Challapata** Oruro, SW Bolivia
199 H7 **Challenger Deep** undersea feature W Pacific Ocean
200 Nn12 **Challenger Fracture Zone** tectonic feature SE Pacific Ocean
199 Ii13 **Challenger Plateau** undersea feature E Tasman Sea
35 P13 **Challis** Idaho, NW USA
24 L9 **Chalmette** Louisiana, S USA
128 J11 **Chalna** Respublika Kareliya, NW Russian Federation
105 Q5 **Châlons-en-Champagne** prev. Châlons-sur-Marne, hist. Arcae Remorum, anc. Carolopois. Marne, NE France
Châlons-sur-Marne see Châlons-en-Champagne
105 R9 **Chalon-sur-Saône** anc. Cabillonum. Saône-et-Loire, C France
Chaltel, Cerro see Fitzroy, Monte
149 N4 **Chālūs** Māzandarān, N Iran
104 M11 **Châlus** Haute-Vienne, C France
103 N20 **Cham** Bayern, SE Germany
110 F7 **Cham** Zug, N Switzerland
39 R8 **Chama** New Mexico, SW USA
Cha Mai see Thung Song
85 E22 **Chamaites** Karas, S Namibia
155 O9 **Chaman** Baluchistān, SW Pakistan
39 R9 **Chama, Rio** ~ New Mexico, SW USA
158 I6 **Chamba** Himāchal Pradesh, N India
83 I25 **Chamba** Ruvuma, S Tanzania
156 H12 **Chambal** ~ C India
9 U16 **Chamberlain** Saskatchewan, S Canada
31 O11 **Chamberlain** South Dakota, N USA
21 R3 **Chamberlain Lake** ◎ Maine, NE USA
41 S5 **Chamberlin, Mount** ▲ Alaska, USA
39 O11 **Chambers** Arizona, SW USA
20 F16 **Chambersburg** Pennsylvania, NE USA
33 N5 **Chambers Island** island Wisconsin, N USA
105 T11 **Chambéry** anc. Camberia. Savoie, E France
84 L12 **Chambeshi** Northern, NE Zambia
84 L12 **Chambeshi** ~ NE Zambia
76 M6 **Chambi, Jebel** var. Jabal ash Sha'nabi. ▲ W Tunisia
13 Q7 **Chambord** Québec, SE Canada
194 G10 **Chambri Lake** ◎ W PNG
145 U11 **Chamcham** S Iraq
145 T4 **Chamchamāl** N Iraq
42 J14 **Chamela** Jalisco, SW Mexico
44 G5 **Chamelecón, Río** ~ NW Honduras
64 J9 **Chamical** La Rioja, C Argentina
117 L23 **Chamilí** island Kykládes, Greece, Aegean Sea
178 Ii13 **Châmnar** Kaôh Kông, SW Cambodia
158 K9 **Chamoli** Uttar Pradesh, N India
105 U11 **Chamonix-Mont-Blanc** Haute-Savoie, E France
160 L11 **Chāmpa** Madhya Pradesh, C India
8 H8 **Champagne** Yukon Territory, W Canada
105 Q5 **Champagne** cultural region N France
Champagne see Campania
105 Q5 **Champagne-Ardenne** ◈ region N France
105 S9 **Champagnole** Jura, E France
32 M13 **Champaign** Illinois, N USA
178 Jj11 **Champasak** Champasak, S Laos
105 U6 **Champ de Feu** ▲ NE France
11 O7 **Champdoré, Lac** ◎ Québec, NE Canada
44 B6 **Champerico** Retalhuleu, SW Guatemala
110 C11 **Champéry** Valais, SW Switzerland
20 L6 **Champlain** New York, NE USA
20 L9 **Champlain Canal** canal New York, NE USA
13 P13 **Champlain, Lac** ◎ Québec, SE Canada
20 L7 **Champlain, Lake** ◎ Canada/USA
105 S7 **Champlitte** Haute-Saône, E France
43 W13 **Champotón** Campeche, SE Mexico
106 G10 **Chamusca** Santarém, C Portugal
121 O20 **Chamyarysy** Rus. Chemerisy. Homyel'skaya Voblasts', SE Belorussia
131 P5 **Chamzinka** Respublika Mordoviya, W Russian Federation
Chanáil Mhór, An see Grand Canal
Chanak see Çanakkale
64 G7 **Chañaral** Atacama, N Chile
106 H13 **Chança** var. Chanza. ~ Portugal/Spain
59 D14 **Chancay** Lima, W Peru
Chan-chiang/Chanchiang see Zhanjiang
41 R7 **Chandalar** Alaska, USA
41 R6 **Chandalar River** ~ Alaska, USA
158 L10 **Chandan Chauki** Uttar Pradesh, N India
159 S16 **Chandannagar** prev. Chandernagore. West Bengal, E India
158 K10 **Chandausi** Uttar Pradesh, N India
24 M10 **Chandeleur Islands** island group Louisiana, S USA
24 M9 **Chandeleur Sound** sound N Gulf of Mexico
158 I8 **Chandīgarh** Punjab, N India
159 Q16 **Chāndil** Bihār, NE India
190 D2 **Chandler** South Australia
13 Y7 **Chandler** Québec, SE Canada
38 L14 **Chandler** Arizona, SW USA
29 O10 **Chandler** Oklahoma, C USA
27 V7 **Chandler** Texas, SW USA
41 Q6 **Chandler River** ~ Alaska, USA
58 H13 **Chandles, Río** ~ E Peru
169 N9 **Chandmanĭ** Dornogovĭ, SE Mongolia
12 J13 **Chandos Lake** ◎ Ontario, SE Canada
159 U15 **Chandpur** Chittagong, C Bangladesh
160 I13 **Chandrapur** Mahārāshtra, C India
85 J15 **Changa** Southern, S Zambia
Changan see Xi'an, Shaanxi, China
Chang'an see Rong'an, Guangxi Zhuangzu Zizhiqu, China
161 G23 **Changanācheri** Kerala, SW India
85 M19 **Changane** ~ S Mozambique
85 M16 **Changara** Tete, NW Mozambique
169 X11 **Changbai** var. Changbai Chaoxianzu Zizhixian. Jilin, NE China
Changbai Chaoxianzu Zizhixian see Changbai
169 X11 **Changbai Shan** ▲▲ NE China
169 V10 **Changchun** var. Ch'angch'un, Ch'ang-ch'un; prev. Hsinking. Jilin, NE China
166 M10 **Changde** Hunan, S China
167 S13 **Changhua** Jap. Shōka. C Taiwan
174 I7 **Changi** ✕ (Singapore) E Singapore
164 L5 **Changji** Xinjiang Uygur Zizhiqu, NW China
163 O13 **Chang Jiang** var. Yangtze Kiang, Eng. Yangtze. ~ C China
166 L17 **Changjiang** prev. Shiliu. Hainan, S China
167 S8 **Changjiang Kou** delta E China
178 I13 **Chang, Ko** island S Thailand
167 Q2 **Changli** Hebei, E China
169 V10 **Changling** Jilin, NE China
167 N11 **Changsha** var. Ch'angsha, Ch'ang-sha. Hunan, S China
167 Q10 **Changshan** Zhejiang, SE China
169 V14 **Changshan Qundao** island group NE China
167 S8 **Changshu** var. Ch'ang-shu. Jiangsu, E China
169 V11 **Changtu** Liaoning, NE China
45 P14 **Changuinola** Bocas del Toro, NW Panama
165 N9 **Changweiliang** Qinghai, W China
166 K6 **Changwu** Shaanxi, C China
169 U13 **Changxing Dao** island N China
166 M9 **Changyang** Hubei, C China
169 W14 **Changyŏn** SW North Korea
167 N5 **Changzhi** Shanxi, C China
167 R8 **Changzhou** Jiangsu, E China
117 H24 **Chaniá** var. Hania, Khaniá, Eng. Canea; anc. Cydonia. Kríti, Greece, E Mediterranean Sea
64 J5 **Chañi, Nevado de** ▲ NW Argentina
117 H24 **Chanión, Kólpos** gulf Kríti, Greece, E Mediterranean Sea
Chankiri see Çankırı
32 M11 **Channahon** Illinois, N USA
161 H20 **Channapatna** Karnātaka, E India
99 K26 **Channel Islands** Fr. Îles Normandes. island group S English Channel
37 R16 **Channel Islands** island group California, W USA
11 S13 **Channel-Port aux Basques** Newfoundland, Newfoundland and Labrador, SE Canada
Channel, The see English Channel
99 Q23 **Channel Tunnel** tunnel France/UK
26 M2 **Channing** Texas, SW USA
Chantabun/Chantaburi see Chanthaburi
106 H3 **Chantada** Galicia, NW Spain
178 I12 **Chanthaburi** var. Chantabun, Chantaburi. Chantaburi, S Thailand
105 O4 **Chantilly** Oise, N France
15 Kk4 **Chantrey Inlet** inlet Northwest Territories, N Canada
145 V12 **Chanūn as Sa'ūdī** S Iraq
29 Q6 **Chanute** Kansas, C USA
125 G13 **Chany, Ozero** ◎ C Russian Federation
Chanza see Chança
Ch'ao-an/Chaochow see Chaozhou
167 P8 **Chao Hu** ◎ E China
178 Hh11 **Chao Phraya, Mae Nam** ~ C Thailand
169 T8 **Chaor He** ~ NE China
Chaouèn see Chefchaouen
167 P14 **Chaoyang** Guangdong, S China
169 T12 **Chaoyang** Liaoning, NE China
Chaoyang see Huinan, Jilin, China
Chaoyang see Jiayin, Heilongjiang, China
167 Q14 **Chaozhou** var. Chaoan, Chao'an, Ch'ao-an; prev. Chaochow. Guangdong, SE China
60 N13 **Chapadinha** Maranhão, E Brazil
10 K12 **Chapais** Québec, SE Canada
42 L13 **Chapala** Jalisco, SW Mexico
42 L13 **Chapala, Lago de** ◎ C Mexico
152 F13 **Chapan, Gora** ▲ C Turkmenistan
59 M18 **Chapare, Río** ~ C Bolivia
56 E11 **Chaparral** Tolima, C Colombia
150 F9 **Chapayevo** Zapadnyy Kazakhstan, NW Kazakhstan
126 Kk12 **Chapayevo** Respublika Sakha (Yakutiya), NE Russian Federation
131 R6 **Chapayevsk** Samarskaya Oblast', W Russian Federation
62 H13 **Chapecó** Santa Catarina, S Brazil
62 I13 **Chapecó, Rio** ~ S Brazil
22 J9 **Chapel Hill** Tennessee, S USA
46 J12 **Chapelton** C Jamaica
12 C8 **Chapleau** Ontario, SE Canada
12 D7 **Chapleau** ~ Ontario, S Canada
9 T16 **Chaplin** Saskatchewan, S Canada
130 M6 **Chaplygin** Lipetskaya Oblast', W Russian Federation
119 S11 **Chaplynka** Khersons'ka Oblast', S Ukraine
15 L3 **Chapman, Cape** headland Northwest Territories, NE Canada
27 T15 **Chapman Ranch** Texas, SW USA
Chapman's see Okwa
23 P5 **Chapmanville** West Virginia, NE USA
30 K15 **Chappell** Nebraska, C USA
Chapra see Chhapra
58 D9 **Chapuli, Río** ~ N Peru
78 I6 **Châr** well N Mauritania
126 Kk13 **Chara** Chitinskaya Oblast', S Russian Federation
126 Kk13 **Chara** ~ C Russian Federation
56 G8 **Charala** Santander, C Colombia
43 N10 **Charcas** San Luis Potosí, C Mexico
27 T13 **Charco** Texas, SW USA
204 H7 **Charcot Island** island Antarctica
66 M8 **Charcot Seamounts** undersea feature E Atlantic Ocean
151 P17 **Chardara** Yuzhnyy Kazakhstan, S Kazakhstan
151 P17 **Chardarinskoye Vodokhranilishche** ⊠ S Kazakhstan
33 U11 **Chardon** Ohio, N USA
46 K9 **Chardonnières** SW Haiti
152 K12 **Chardzhev** prev. Chardzhou, Chardzhui, Leninsk-Turkmenski, Turkm. Chärjew. Lebapskiy Velayat, E Turkmenistan
Chardzhevskaya Oblast' see Lebapskiy Velayat
Chardzhou/Chardzhui see Chardzhev
104 L11 **Charente** ◈ department W France
104 J11 **Charente** ~ W France
104 J10 **Charente-Maritime** ◈ department W France
143 U12 **Ch'arents'avan** C Armenia
80 I12 **Chari** var. Shari. ~ Central African Republic/Chad
80 G11 **Chari-Baguirmi** off. Préfecture du Chari-Baguirmi. ◈ prefecture SW Chad
155 Q4 **Chārīkār** Parwān, NE Afghanistan
31 V15 **Chariton** Iowa, C USA
29 U3 **Chariton River** ~ Missouri, C USA
57 T7 **Charity** NW Guyana
33 R7 **Charity Island** island Michigan, N USA
Chärjew see Chardzhev
Chärjew Oblasty see Lebapskiy Velayat
Charkhlik/Charkhliq see Ruoqiang
101 G20 **Charleroi** Hainaut, S Belgium
9 V12 **Charles** Manitoba, C Canada
13 R10 **Charlesbourg** Québec, SE Canada
23 Y7 **Charles, Cape** headland Virginia, NE USA
31 W12 **Charles City** Iowa, C USA
23 W6 **Charles City** Virginia, NE USA
105 O5 **Charles de Gaulle** ✕ (Paris) Seine-et-Marne, N France
10 K1 **Charles Island** island Northwest Territories, NE Canada
Charles Island see Santa María, Isla
18 Mm5 **Charles-Lindbergh** ✕ (Minneapolis/Saint Paul) Minnesota, N USA
32 K9 **Charles Mound** hill Illinois, N USA
193 A22 **Charles Sound** sound South Island, NZ
193 G15 **Charleston** West Coast, South Island, NZ
29 Z7 **Charleston** Arkansas, C USA
32 M14 **Charleston** Illinois, N USA
24 L3 **Charleston** Mississippi, S USA
29 S11 **Charleston** Missouri, C USA
23 T15 **Charleston** South Carolina, SE USA
23 Q5 **Charleston** state capital West Virginia, NE USA
12 L14 **Charleston Lake** ◎ Ontario, SE Canada
37 W11 **Charleston Peak** ▲ Nevada, W USA
47 W10 **Charlestown** Nevis, Saint Kitts and Nevis
33 P16 **Charlestown** Indiana, N USA
20 M9 **Charlestown** New Hampshire, NE USA
23 V3 **Charles Town** West Virginia, NE USA
189 W9 **Charleville** Queensland, E Australia
105 R3 **Charleville-Mézières** Ardennes, N France
33 P5 **Charlevoix** Michigan, N USA
33 Q6 **Charlevoix, Lake** ◎ Michigan, N USA
41 T9 **Charley River** ~ Alaska, USA
66 J6 **Charlie-Gibbs Fracture Zone** tectonic feature N Atlantic Ocean
105 Q10 **Charlieu** Loire, E France
33 Q9 **Charlotte** Michigan, N USA
23 R10 **Charlotte** North Carolina, SE USA
22 I8 **Charlotte** Tennessee, S USA
27 R13 **Charlotte** Texas, SW USA
23 R10 **Charlotte** ✕ North Carolina, SE USA
47 T9 **Charlotte Amalie** prev. Saint Thomas. ○ (Virgin Islands (US)) Saint Thomas, N Virgin Islands (US)
23 U7 **Charlotte Court House** Virginia, NE USA
25 W14 **Charlotte Harbor** inlet Florida, SE USA
Charlotte Island see Abaiang
97 J15 **Charlottenberg** Värmland, C Sweden
Charlottenhof see Aegviidu
23 U5 **Charlottesville** Virginia, NE USA
Charlotte Town see Roseau, Dominica
Charlotte Town see Gouyave, Grenada
11 Q14 **Charlottetown** Prince Edward Island, Prince Edward Island, SE Canada
47 Z16 **Charlotteville** Tobago, Trinidad and Tobago
190 M11 **Charlton** Victoria, SE Australia
10 H10 **Charlton Island** island Northwest Territories, C Canada
105 T6 **Charmes** Vosges, NE France
121 F19 **Charnawchytsy** Rus. Chernavchitsy. Brestskaya Voblasts', SW Belorussia
13 R10 **Charny** Québec, SE Canada
155 T5 **Chārsadda** North-West Frontier Province, NW Pakistan
152 M14 **Charshanga** prev. Charshangy, Turkm. Charshangngy. Lebapskiy Velayat, E Turkmenistan
Charshangngy/Charshangy see Charshanga
151 W10 **Charsk** Semipalatinsk, E Kazakhstan
189 W6 **Charters Towers** Queensland, NE Australia
13 R12 **Chartierville** Québec, SE Canada
104 M6 **Chartres** anc. Autricum, Civitas Carnutum. Eure-et-Loir, C France
151 W15 **Charyn** Kaz. Sharyn. Almaty, SE Kazakhstan
63 D21 **Chascomús** Buenos Aires, E Argentina
9 N16 **Chase** British Columbia, SW Canada
23 U7 **Chase City** Virginia, NE USA
21 S4 **Chase, Mount** ▲ Maine, NE USA
120 M13 **Chashniki** Rus. Chashniki. Vitsyebskaya Voblasts', N Belorussia
117 D15 **Chásia** ▲▲ C Greece
31 V9 **Chaska** Minnesota, N USA
193 D25 **Chaslands Mistake** headland South Island, NZ
129 R11 **Chasovo** Respublika Komi, NW Russian Federation
Chasovo see Vazhgort
128 H14 **Chastova** Novgorodskaya Oblast', NW Russian Federation
149 R3 **Chāt** Māzandarān, N Iran
Chatak see Chhatak
41 R9 **Chatanika** Alaska, USA
41 R9 **Chatanika River** ~ Alaska, USA
153 T8 **Chat-Bazar** Talasskaya Oblast', NW Kyrgyzstan
47 Y14 **Chateaubelair** Saint Vincent, W Saint Vincent and the Grenadines
104 J7 **Châteaubriant** Loire-Atlantique, NW France
105 Q8 **Château-Chinon** Nièvre, C France
110 C10 **Château d'Oex** Vaud, W Switzerland
104 L7 **Château-du-Loir** Sarthe, NW France
104 M6 **Châteaudun** Eure-et-Loir, C France
104 K7 **Château-Gontier** Mayenne, NW France
13 O13 **Châteauguay** Québec, SE Canada
104 F6 **Châteaulin** Finistère, NW France
105 N9 **Châteaumeillant** Cher, C France
104 K11 **Châteauneuf-sur-Charente** Charente, W France
104 M7 **Château-Renault** Indre-et-Loire, C France
105 N9 **Châteauroux** prev. Indreville. Indre, C France
105 T5 **Château-Salins** Moselle, NE France
105 P4 **Château-Thierry** Aisne, N France
101 H21 **Châtelet** Hainaut, S Belgium
Châtelherault see Châtellerault
104 L9 **Châtellerault** var. Châtelherault. Vienne, W France
31 X10 **Chatfield** Minnesota, N USA
11 O14 **Chatham** New Brunswick, SE Canada
12 D17 **Chatham** Ontario, S Canada
99 P22 **Chatham** SE England, UK
32 K14 **Chatham** Illinois, N USA
23 T7 **Chatham** Virginia, NE USA
65 F22 **Chatham, Isla** island S Chile
183 R12 **Chatham Island** island Chatham Islands, NZ
Chatham Island see San Cristóbal, Isla
Chatham Island Rise see Chatham Rise
199 Jj14 **Chatham Islands** island group NZ, SW Pacific Ocean
183 Q12 **Chatham Rise** var. Chatham Island Rise. undersea feature S Pacific Ocean
41 X13 **Chatham Strait** strait Alaska, USA
Chathóir, Rinn see Cahore Point
104 M9 **Châtillon-sur-Indre** Indre, C France
105 Q7 **Châtillon-sur-Seine** Côte d'Or, C France
153 S8 **Chatkal** Uzb. Chotqol. ~ Kyrgyzstan/Uzbekistan
153 R9 **Chatkal Range** Rus. Chatkal'skiy Khrebet. ▲▲ Kyrgyzstan/Uzbekistan
Chatkal'skiy Khrebet see Chatkal Range
25 N7 **Chatom** Alabama, S USA
Chatrapur see Chhatrapur
149 S10 **Chatrūd** Kermān, C Iran
25 S2 **Chatsworth** Georgia, SE USA
Chāttagām see Chittagong
25 S8 **Chattahoochee** Florida, SE USA
25 R8 **Chattahoochee River** ~ SE USA
22 L10 **Chattanooga** Tennessee, S USA
153 V10 **Chatyr-Kël', Ozero** ◎ C Kyrgyzstan
153 W9 **Chatyr-Tash** Narynskaya Oblast', C Kyrgyzstan
13 R12 **Chaudière** ~ Québec, SE Canada
178 J14 **Châu Đốc** var. Chauphu, Chau Phu. An Giang, S Vietnam
158 D13 **Chauhtan** prev. Chohtan. Rājasthān, NW India
177 Ff5 **Chauk** Magwe, W Myanmar
105 R6 **Chaumont** prev. Chaumont-en-Bassigny. Haute-Marne, N France
Chaumont-en-Bassigny see Chaumont
127 O4 **Chaunskaya Guba** bay NE Russian Federation
105 P3 **Chauny** Aisne, N France
Châu Ô see Binh Sơn
Chau Phu see Châu Đốc
104 I5 **Chausey, Îles** island group N France
Chausy see Chavusy
20 C11 **Chautauqua Lake** ◎ New York, NE USA
104 L9 **Chauvigny** Vienne, W France
128 L6 **Chavan'ga** Murmanskaya Oblast', NW Russian Federation
12 K10 **Chavannes, Lac** ◎ Québec, SE Canada
Chavantes, Represa de see Xavantes, Represa de
63 D15 **Chavarría** Corrientes, NE Argentina
Chavash Respubliki see Chuvashskaya Respublika
106 I5 **Chaves** anc. Aquae Flaviae. Vila Real, N Portugal
Chávez, Isla see Santa Cruz, Isla
84 G13 **Chavuma** North Western, NW Zambia
121 O16 **Chavusy** Rus. Chausy. Mahilyowskaya Voblasts', E Belorussia
151 Q16 **Chayan** Yuzhnyy Kazakhstan, S Kazakhstan
153 U8 **Chayek** Narynskaya Oblast', C Kyrgyzstan
145 T6 **Chāy Khānah** E Iraq
129 T16 **Chaykovskiy** Permskaya Oblast', NW Russian Federation
178 K12 **Chbar** Môndól Kiri, E Cambodia
25 Q4 **Cheaha Mountain** ▲ Alabama, S USA
Cheatharlach see Carlow
23 S2 **Cheat River** ~ NE USA
113 A16 **Cheb** Ger. Eger. Západní Čechy, W Czech Republic
131 Q3 **Cheboksary** Chuvashskaya Respublika, W Russian Federation
33 Q5 **Cheboygan** Michigan, N USA
Chechaouèn see Chefchaouen
Chechenia see Chechenskaya Respublika
131 O15 **Chechenskaya Respublika** Eng. Chechenia, Chechnia, Rus. Chechnya. ◈ autonomous republic SW Russian Federation
69 N4 **Chech, Erg** desert Algeria/Mali
Chechersk see Chachersk
Chechevichi see Chachevichy
Che-chiang see Zhejiang
Chechnia/Chechnya see Chechenskaya Respublika
169 Y15 **Chech'ŏn** Jap. Teisen. N South Korea
113 L15 **Chęciny** Kielce, S Poland
29 Q10 **Checotah** Oklahoma, C USA
11 R15 **Chedabucto Bay** inlet Nova Scotia, E Canada
177 F7 **Cheduba Island** island W Myanmar
39 T5 **Cheesman Lake** ⊠ Colorado, C USA
205 S16 **Cheetham, Cape** headland Antarctica
76 G5 **Chefchaouen** var. Chaouèn, Chechaouèn, Sp. Xauen. N Morocco
Chefoo see Yantai
40 M12 **Chefornak** Alaska, USA
126 Mm15 **Chegdomyn** Khabarovskiy Kray, SE Russian Federation
78 M4 **Chegga** Tiris Zemmour, NE Mauritania
Cheghcheran see Chaghcharān
34 G9 **Chehalis** Washington, NW USA
34 G9 **Chehalis River** ~ Washington, NW USA
154 M6 **Chehel Abdālān, Kūh-e** var. Chalap Dalam, Pash. Chalap Dalan. ▲▲ C Afghanistan
117 D14 **Cheimadítis, Límni** ◎ N Greece
105 U15 **Cheiron, Mont** ▲ SE France
169 X17 **Cheju** Jap. Saishū. S South Korea
169 Y17 **Cheju** ✕ S South Korea
169 Y17 **Cheju-do** Jap. Saishū; prev. Quelpart. island S South Korea
169 X17 **Cheju-haehyŏp** strait S South Korea
Chekiang see Zhejiang
Chekichler see Chekishlyar
152 B13 **Chekishlyar** Turkm. Chekichler. Balkanskiy Velayat, W Turkmenistan
196 F8 **Chelab** Babeldaob, N Palau
153 N11 **Chelak** Rus. Chelek. Samarqand Wiloyati, C Uzbekistan
34 J7 **Chelan, Lake** ⊠ Washington, NW USA
Chelek see Chelak
152 A11 **Cheleken** Balkanskiy Velayat, W Turkmenistan
Chélif/Chéliff see Chelif, Oued
76 J5 **Chelif, Oued** var. Chélif, Chéliff, Chellif, Shellif. ~ N Algeria
150 K12 **Chelkar** Aktyubinsk, W Kazakhstan
Chelkar, Ozero see Shalkar, Ozero
Chellif see Chelif, Oued
113 P14 **Chełm** Rus. Kholm. Chełm, SE Poland
113 P14 **Chełm** off. Województwo Chełmskie, Rus. Kholm. ◈ province SE Poland
112 I9 **Chełmno** Ger. Culm, Kulm. Toruń, N Poland
12 F10 **Chelmsford** Ontario, S Canada
99 P21 **Chelmsford** E England, UK
Chełmskie, Województwo see Chełm
112 J9 **Chełmża** Ger. Culmsee, Kulmsee. Toruń, N Poland
29 Q8 **Chelsea** Oklahoma, C USA
20 M8 **Chelsea** Vermont, NE USA
99 L21 **Cheltenham** C England, UK
107 R9 **Chelva** País Valenciano, E Spain
125 Ee12 **Chelyabinsk** Chelyabinskaya Oblast', C Russian Federation
125 E12 **Chelyabinskaya Oblast'** ◈ province C Russian Federation
126 Jj4 **Chelyuskin, Mys** headland N Russian Federation
126 H15 **Chemal** Altayskiy Kray, S Russian Federation
43 Y12 **Chemax** Yucatán, SE Mexico
85 N16 **Chemba** Sofala, C Mozambique
84 J13 **Chembe** Luapula, NE Zambia
152 J17 **Chemenibit** Maryyskiy Velayat, S Turkmenistan
Chemerisy see Chamyarysy
118 K7 **Chemerivtsi** Khmel'nyts'ka Oblast', W Ukraine
104 J8 **Chemillé** Maine-et-Loire, NW France
181 X17 **Chemin Grenier** S Mauritius
103 N16 **Chemnitz** prev. Karl-Marx-Stadt. Sachsen, E Germany
Chemulpo see Inch'ŏn
34 H14 **Chemult** Oregon, NW USA
20 G12 **Chemung River** ~ New York/Pennsylvania, NE USA
155 U8 **Chenāb** ~ India/Pakistan
41 S9 **Chena Hot Springs** Alaska, USA
20 I11 **Chenango River** ~ New York, NE USA
174 Gg3 **Chenderoh, Tasik** ◎ Peninsular Malaysia
13 Q11 **Chêne, Rivière du** ~ Québec, SE Canada
34 L8 **Cheney** Washington, NW USA
28 M6 **Cheney Reservoir** ⊠ Kansas, C USA
Chengchiatun see Liaoyuan
Ch'eng-chou/Chengchow see Zhengzhou
167 P1 **Chengde** var. Jehol. Hebei, E China
166 I9 **Chengdu** var. Chengtu, Ch'eng-tu. Sichuan, C China
167 Q14 **Chenghai** Guangdong, S China
Chenghsien see Zhengzhou
166 L17 **Chengmai** Hainan, S China
Chengtu/Ch'eng-tu see Chengdu
165 W12 **Cheng Xian** Gansu, C China
Chenkiang see Zhenjiang
Chennai see Madras
105 R8 **Chenôve** Côte d'Or, C France
Chenstokhov see Częstochowa
166 L11 **Chenxi** Hunan, S China
Chen Xian/Chenxian/Chen Xiang see Chenzhou
167 N12 **Chenzhou** var. Chenxian, Chen Xian, Chen Xiang. Hunan, S China
178 Kk12 **Cheo Reo** var. A Yun Pa. Gia Lai, S Vietnam
116 I11 **Chepelare** Plovdivska Oblast, S Bulgaria
116 I11 **Chepelarska Reka** ~ S Bulgaria
58 B11 **Chepén** La Libertad, C Peru
64 J10 **Chepes** La Rioja, C Argentina
45 U14 **Chepo** Panamá, C Panama
Chepping Wycombe see High Wycombe
129 R14 **Cheptsa** ~ NW Russian Federation
32 K3 **Chequamegon Point** headland Wisconsin, N USA
105 O8 **Cher** ◈ department C France
104 M8 **Cher** ~ C France
Cherangani Hills see Cherangany Hills
83 H17 **Cherangany Hills** var. Cherangani Hills. ▲▲ W Kenya
23 S11 **Cheraw** South Carolina, SE USA
104 I3 **Cherbourg** anc. Carusbur. Manche, N France
131 R5 **Cherdakly** Ul'yanovskaya Oblast', W Russian Federation
129 U12 **Cherdyn'** Permskaya Oblast', NW Russian Federation
128 J14 **Cherekha** ~ W Russian Federation
126 J15 **Cheremkhovo** Irkutskaya Oblast', S Russian Federation
126 Hh15 **Cheremushki** Respublika Khakasiya, S Russian Federation
Cheren see Keren
128 K14 **Cherepovets** Vologodskaya Oblast', NW Russian Federation
129 O11 **Cherevkovo** Arkhangel'skaya Oblast', NW Russian Federation
76 I6 **Chergui, Chott ech** salt lake NW Algeria
Cherikov see Cherykaw
119 P6 **Cherkas'ka Oblast'** var. Cherkasy, Rus. Cherkasskaya Oblast'. ◈ province C Ukraine
Cherkasskaya Oblast' see Cherkas'ka Oblast'
Cherkassy see Cherkasy
119 Q6 **Cherkasy** Rus. Cherkassy. Cherkas'ka Oblast', C Ukraine

◆ Country
● Country Capital
◇ Dependent Territory
○ Dependent Territory Capital
◈ Administrative Region
✕ International Airport
▲ Mountain
▲▲ Mountain Range
Volcano
~ River
◎ Lake
⊠ Reservoir

Cherkasy *see* Cherkas'ka Oblast'
130 M15 **Cherkessk** Karachayevo-Cherkesskaya Respublika, SW Russian Federation
125 G13 **Cherlak** Omskaya Oblast', C Russian Federation
125 Fj14 **Cherlakskiy** Omskaya Oblast', C Russian Federation
129 U13 **Chermoz** Permskaya Oblast', NW Russian Federation
Chernavchitsy *see* Charnawchytsy
129 T3 **Chernaya** Nenetskiy Avtonomnyy Okrug, NW Russian Federation
129 T4 **Chernaya** ∿ NW Russian Federation
Chernigov *see* Chernihiv
Chernigovskaya Oblast' *see* Chernihivs'ka Oblast'
119 Q2 **Chernihiv** *Rus.* Chernigov. Chernihivs'ka Oblast', NE Ukraine
Chernihiv *see* Chernihivs'ka Oblast'
119 V9 **Chernihivka** Zaporiz'ka Oblast', SE Ukraine
119 P2 **Chernihivs'ka Oblast'** *var.* Chernihiv, *Rus.* Chernigovskaya Oblast'. ◈ *province* NE Ukraine
116 I9 **Cherni Osŭm** ∿ N Bulgaria
118 J8 **Chernivets'ka Oblast'** *var.* Chernivtsi, *Rus.* Chernovitskaya Oblast'. ◈ *province* W Ukraine
116 I9 **Cherni Vit** ∿ NW Bulgaria
116 G10 **Cherni Vrŭkh** ▲ W Bulgaria
118 K8 **Chernivtsi** *Ger.* Czernowitz, *Rom.* Cernăuţi, *Rus.* Chernovtsy. Chernivets'ka Oblast', W Ukraine
118 M7 **Chernivtsi** Vinnyts'ka Oblast', C Ukraine
Chernivtsi *see* Chernivets'ka Oblast'
Chernobyl' *see* Chornobyl'
126 Hh15 **Chernogorsk** Respublika Khakasiya, S Russian Federation
Cherno More *see* Black Sea
Chernomorskoye *see* Chornomors'ke
151 T7 **Chernoretskoye** Pavlodar, NE Kazakhstan
Chernovitskaya Oblast' *see* Chernivets'ka Oblast'
Chernovtsy *see* Chernivtsi
151 U8 **Chernoye** Pavlodar, NE Kazakhstan
Chernoye More *see* Black Sea
129 U16 **Chernushka** Permskaya Oblast', NW Russian Federation
119 N4 **Chernyakhiv** *Rus.* Chernyakhov. Zhytomyrs'ka Oblast', N Ukraine
Chernyakhov *see* Chernyakhiv
121 C14 **Chernyakhovsk** *Ger.* Insterburg. Kaliningradskaya Oblast', W Russian Federation
130 K8 **Chernyanka** Belgorodskaya Oblast', W Russian Federation
129 V5 **Chernyshëva, Gryada** ▲ NW Russian Federation
150 J14 **Chernyshëva, Zaliv** *gulf* SW Kazakhstan
126 L15 **Chernyshevsk** Chitinskaya Oblast', S Russian Federation
126 K11 **Chernyshevskiy** Respublika Sakha (Yakutiya), NE Russian Federation
131 P13 **Chërnyye Zemli** *plain* SW Russian Federation
Chërnyy Irtysh *see* Ertix He
131 V7 **Chernyy Otrog** Orenburgskaya Oblast', W Russian Federation
31 T12 **Cherokee** Iowa, C USA
28 M8 **Cherokee** Oklahoma, C USA
27 R9 **Cherokee** Texas, SW USA
23 O8 **Cherokee Lake** ⊡ Tennessee, S USA
Cherokees, Lake O' The *see* Grand Lake O' The Cherokees
46 H1 **Cherokee Sound** Great Abaco, N Bahamas
159 V13 **Cherrapunji** Meghālaya, NE India
30 L9 **Cherry Creek** ∿ South Dakota, N USA
20 J16 **Cherry Hill** New Jersey, NE USA
29 Q7 **Cherryvale** Kansas, C USA
23 Q10 **Cherryville** North Carolina, SE USA
Cherski Range *see* Cherskogo, Khrebet
127 O5 **Cherskiy** Respublika Sakha (Yakutiya), NE Russian Federation
126 Mm8 **Cherskogo, Khrebet** *var.* Cherski Range. ▲ NE Russian Federation
Cherso *see* Cres
130 L10 **Chertkovo** Rostovskaya Oblast', SW Russian Federation
Cherven' *see* Chervyen'
116 H8 **Cherven Bryag** Loveshka Oblast, NW Bulgaria
118 M4 **Chervonoarmiys'k** Zhytomyrs'ka Oblast', N Ukraine
Chervonograd *see* Chervonohrad
118 I4 **Chervonohrad** *Rus.* Chervonograd. L'vivs'ka Oblast', NW Ukraine
119 W6 **Chervonooskil's'ke Vodoskhovyshche** *Rus.* Krasnoosol'skoye Vodokhranilishche. ⊡ NE Ukraine
Chervonoye, Ozero *see* Chyrvonaye, Vozyera
119 S4 **Chervonozavods'ke** Poltavs'ka Oblast', C Ukraine
121 L16 **Chervyen'** *Rus.* Cherven'. Minskaya Voblasts', C Belorussia
121 P16 **Cherykaw** *Rus.* Cherikov. Mahilyowskaya Voblasts', E Belorussia
33 R9 **Chesaning** Michigan, N USA
23 X5 **Chesapeake Bay** *inlet* NE USA
Cheshevlya *see* Tsyeshawlya
99 K18 **Cheshire** *cultural region* C England, UK
129 P5 **Chëshskaya Guba** *var.* Archangel Bay, Chesha Bay, Dvina Bay. *bay* NW Russian Federation
12 F14 **Chesley** Ontario, S Canada
23 Q10 **Chesnee** South Carolina, SE USA
99 K18 **Chester** *Wel.* Caerleon; *hist.* Legaceaster, *Lat.* Deva, Devana Castra. C England, UK
37 O4 **Chester** California, W USA
32 K16 **Chester** Illinois, N USA
35 S7 **Chester** Montana, NW USA
20 I16 **Chester** Pennsylvania, NE USA
23 R1 **Chester** South Carolina, SE USA
27 X9 **Chester** Texas, SW USA
23 W6 **Chester** Virginia, NE USA
23 R11 **Chester** West Virginia, NE USA
99 M18 **Chesterfield** C England, UK
23 S11 **Chesterfield** South Carolina, SE USA
23 W6 **Chesterfield** Virginia, NE USA
199 I10 **Chesterfield, Îles** *island group* NW New Caledonia
15 Ll6 **Chesterfield Inlet** Northwest Territories, NW Canada
15 L6 **Chesterfield Inlet** *inlet* Northwest Territories, N Canada
23 Y3 **Chester River** ∿ Delaware/Maryland, NE USA
23 X3 **Chestertown** Maryland, NE USA
21 R4 **Chesuncook Lake** ◎ Maine, NE USA
32 J5 **Chetek** Wisconsin, N USA
11 R14 **Chéticamp** Nova Scotia, SE Canada
29 Q8 **Chetopa** Kansas, C USA
43 Y14 **Chetumal** *var.* Payo Obispo. Quintana Roo, SE Mexico
Chetumal, Bahia/Chetumal, Bahía de *see* Chetumal Bay
44 G1 **Chetumal Bay** *var.* Bahia Chetumal, Bahía de Chetumal. *bay* Belize/Mexico
8 M13 **Chetwynd** British Columbia, W Canada
40 M11 **Chevak** Alaska, USA
38 M12 **Chevelon Creek** ∿ Arizona, SW USA
193 J17 **Cheviot** Canterbury, South Island, NZ
98 L13 **Cheviot Hills** *hill range* England/Scotland, UK
98 L13 **Cheviot, The** ▲ NE England, UK
12 M11 **Chevreuil, Lac du** ◎ Québec, SE Canada
83 I16 **Ch'ew Bahir** *var.* Lake Stefanie. ◎ Ethiopia/Kenya
34 L7 **Chewelah** Washington, NW USA
28 K10 **Cheyenne** Oklahoma, C USA
35 Z17 **Cheyenne** *state capital* Wyoming, C USA
28 L5 **Cheyenne Bottoms** ◎ Kansas, C USA
18 Kk6 **Cheyenne River** ∿ South Dakota/Wyoming, N USA
39 W5 **Cheyenne Wells** Colorado, C USA
110 C9 **Cheyres** Vaud, W Switzerland
Chezdi-Oşorheiu *see* Târgu Secuiesc
159 P13 **Chhapra** *prev.* Chapra. Bihār, N India
159 V13 **Chhatak** *var.* Chatak. Chittagong, NE Bangladesh
160 J9 **Chhatarpur** Madhya Pradesh, C India
160 N13 **Chhatrapur** *prev.* Chatrapur. Orissa, E India
160 L12 **Chhattīsgarh** *plain* C India
160 I11 **Chhindwāra** Madhya Pradesh, C India
Chhlong *see* Phumĭ Chhlong
Chhuk *see* Phumĭ Chhuk
159 T12 **Chhukha** SW Bhutan
167 S14 **Chiai** *var.* Chia-i, Chiayi, Kiayi, Jiayi, *Jap.* Kagi. C Taiwan
Chia-mu-ssu *see* Jiamusi
85 B15 **Chiange** *Port.* Vila de Almoster. Huíla, SW Angola
Chiang-hsi *see* Jiangxi
167 S12 **Chiang Kai-shek** ✕ (T'aipei) N Taiwan
178 I8 **Chiang Khan** Loei, E Thailand
178 H7 **Chiang Mai** *var.* Chiangmai, Chiengmai, Kiangmai. Chiang Mai, NW Thailand
178 H7 **Chiang Mai** ✕ Chiang Mai, NW Thailand
178 Hh6 **Chiang Rai** *var.* Chianpai, Chienrai, Muang Chiang Rai. Chiang Rai, NW Thailand
Chiang-su *see* Jiangsu
Chianning/Chian-ning *see* Nanjing
Chianpai *see* Chiang Rai
108 G12 **Chianti** *cultural region* C Italy
Chiapa *see* Chiapa de Corzo
43 U16 **Chiapa de Corzo** *var.* Chiapa. Chiapas, SE Mexico
43 V16 **Chiapas** ◈ *state* SE Mexico
108 J12 **Chiaravalle** Marche, C Italy
109 N22 **Chiaravalle Centrale** Calabria, SW Italy
108 E7 **Chiari** Lombardia, N Italy
110 H12 **Chiasso** Ticino, S Switzerland
143 S9 **Chiat'ura** C Georgia
43 P15 **Chiautla** *var.* Chiautla de Tapia. Puebla, S Mexico
Chiautla de Tapia *see* Chiautla
108 D10 **Chiavari** Liguria, NW Italy
108 E6 **Chiavenna** Lombardia, N Italy
Chiayi *see* Chiai
Chiazza *see* Piazza Armerina
172 Ss12 **Chiba** *var.* Tiba. Chiba, Honshū, S Japan
171 K17 **Chiba** *off.* Chiba-ken, *var.* Tiba. ◈ *prefecture* Honshū, S Japan
85 M18 **Chibabava** Sofala, C Mozambique
85 B15 **Chibia** *Port.* João de Almeida, Vila João de Almeida. Huíla, SW Angola
85 M18 **Chiboma** Sofala, C Mozambique
84 J12 **Chibondo** Luapula, N Zambia
84 K11 **Chibote** Luapula, NE Zambia
10 K12 **Chibougamau** Québec, SE Canada
170 Ff11 **Chiburi-jima** *island* Oki-shotō, SW Japan
85 M20 **Chibuto** Gaza, S Mozambique
33 N11 **Chicago** Illinois, N USA
33 N11 **Chicago Heights** Illinois, N USA
13 W6 **Chic-Chocs, Monts** *Eng.* Shickshock Mountains. ▲ Québec, SE Canada
41 W13 **Chichagof Island** *island* Alexander Archipelago, Alaska, USA
59 K20 **Chichas, Cordillera de** ▲ SW Bolivia
43 X12 **Chichén-Itzá, Ruinas** *ruins* Yucatán, SE Mexico
99 N23 **Chichester** SE England, UK
171 Jj16 **Chichibu** *var.* Titibu. Saitama, Honshū, S Japan
44 C5 **Chichicastenango** Quiché, W Guatemala
44 I9 **Chichigalpa** Chinandega, NW Nicaragua
Ch'i-ch'i-ha-erh *see* Qiqihar
172 T16 **Chichijima-rettō** *Eng.* Beechy Group. *island group* SE Japan
56 K4 **Chichiriviche** Falcón, N Venezuela
41 R11 **Chickaloon** Alaska, USA
22 L10 **Chickamauga Lake** ⊡ Tennessee, S USA
25 N7 **Chickasawhay River** ∿ Mississippi, S USA
28 M11 **Chickasha** Oklahoma, C USA
41 T9 **Chicken** Alaska, USA
106 J16 **Chiclana de la Frontera** Andalucía, S Spain
58 B11 **Chiclayo** Lambayeque, NW Peru
37 N5 **Chico** California, W USA
85 L15 **Chicoa** Tete, NW Mozambique
85 M20 **Chicomo** Gaza, S Mozambique
20 M11 **Chicopee** Massachusetts, NE USA
65 I19 **Chico, Río** ∿ SE Argentina
65 I20 **Chico, Río** ∿ S Argentina
29 W14 **Chicot, Lake** ◎ Arkansas, C USA
13 R7 **Chicoutimi** Québec, SE Canada
13 Q8 **Chicoutimi** ∿ Québec, SE Canada
85 L19 **Chicualacuala** Gaza, SW Mozambique
85 B14 **Chicuma** Benguela, C Angola
161 J21 **Chidambaram** Tamil Nādu, SE India
206 K13 **Chidley, Cape** *headland* Newfoundland and Labrador, E Canada
103 N24 **Chiemsee** ◎ SE Germany
Chiengmai *see* Chiang Mai
Chienrai *see* Chiang Rai
108 B8 **Chieri** Piemonte, NW Italy
108 F8 **Chiese** ∿ N Italy
109 K14 **Chieti** *var.* Teate. Abruzzi, C Italy
101 E19 **Chièvres** Hainaut, SW Belgium
169 S12 **Chifeng** *var.* Ulanhad. Nei Mongol Zizhiqu, N China
84 F13 **Chifumage** ∿ E Angola
84 M13 **Chifunda** Eastern, NE Zambia
151 S14 **Chiganak** *var.* Čiganak. Zhambyl, SE Kazakhstan
41 P15 **Chiginagak, Mount** ▲ Alaska, USA
Chigirin *see* Chyhyryn
43 P13 **Chignahuapan** Puebla, S Mexico
41 O15 **Chignik** Alaska, USA
85 M19 **Chigombe** ∿ S Mozambique
56 D7 **Chigorodó** Antioquia, NW Colombia
85 M19 **Chigubo** Gaza, S Mozambique
168 D6 **Chihertey** Bayan-Ölgiy, W Mongolia
Chih-fu *see* Yantai
Chihli *see* Hebei
Chihli, Gulf of *see* Bo Hai
42 J6 **Chihuahua** Chihuahua, NW Mexico
42 I6 **Chihuahua** ◈ *state* N Mexico
151 O15 **Chiili** Kzyl-Orda, S Kazakhstan
28 M7 **Chikaskia River** ∿ Kansas/Oklahoma, C USA
161 H19 **Chik Ballāpur** Karnātaka, W India
128 G15 **Chikhachevo** Pskovskaya Oblast', W Russian Federation
161 F19 **Chikmagalūr** Karnātaka, W India
133 V7 **Chikoy** ∿ C Russian Federation
85 J15 **Chikumbi** Lusaka, C Zambia
84 M13 **Chikwa** Eastern, NE Zambia
Chikwana *see* Chikwawa
85 N15 **Chikwawa** *var.* Chikwana. Southern, S Malawi
161 J16 **Chilakalūrupet** Andhra Pradesh, E India
152 L14 **Chilan** Lebapskiy Velayat, E Turkmenistan
Chilapa *see* Chilapa de Alvarez
43 P16 **Chilapa de Alvarez** *var.* Chilapa. Guerrero, S Mexico
161 J25 **Chilaw** North Western Province, W Sri Lanka
59 D15 **Chilca** Lima, W Peru
25 Q4 **Childersburg** Alabama, S USA
27 P4 **Childress** Texas, SW USA
65 G14 **Chile** *off.* Republic of Chile. ◆ *republic* SW South America
49 R10 **Chile Basin** *undersea feature* E Pacific Ocean
65 H20 **Chile Chico** Aisén, W Chile
64 I9 **Chilecito** La Rioja, NW Argentina
64 H12 **Chilecito** Mendoza, W Argentina
85 L14 **Chilembwe** Eastern, E Zambia
200 O13 **Chile Rise** *undersea feature* SE Pacific Ocean
119 N13 **Chilia Braţul** ∿ SE Romania
Chilia-Nouă *see* Kiliya
151 V15 **Chilik** Almaty, SE Kazakhstan
151 V15 **Chilik** ∿ SE Kazakhstan
160 O13 **Chilika Lake** *var.* Chilka Lake. ◎ E India
84 J13 **Chililabombwe** Copperbelt, C Zambia
Chi-lin *see* Jilin
Chilka Lake *see* Chilika Lake
8 H9 **Chilkoot Pass** *pass* British Columbia, W Canada
Chill Ala, Cuan *see* Killala Bay
64 G13 **Chillán** Bío Bío, C Chile
63 C22 **Chillar** Buenos Aires, E Argentina
Chill Chiaráin, Cuan *see* Kilkieran Bay
32 K12 **Chillicothe** Illinois, N USA
29 S3 **Chillicothe** Missouri, C USA
33 S14 **Chillicothe** Ohio, N USA
27 Q4 **Chillicothe** Texas, SW USA
8 M17 **Chilliwack** British Columbia, SW Canada
Chill Mhantáin, Ceann *see* Wicklow Head
Chill Mhantáin, Sléibhte *see* Wicklow Mountains
110 C10 **Chillon** Vaud, W Switzerland
152 C11 **Chil'mamedkum, Peski** *Turkm.* Chilmämetgum. *desert* W Turkmenistan
Chilmämetgum *see* Chil'mamedkum, Peski
65 F17 **Chiloé, Isla de** *var.* Isla Grande de Chiloé. *island* W Chile
34 H15 **Chiloquin** Oregon, NW USA
43 O16 **Chilpancingo** *var.* Chilpancingo de los Bravos. Guerrero, S Mexico
Chilpancingo de los Bravos *see* Chilpancingo
99 N21 **Chiltern Hills** *hill range* S England, UK
32 M7 **Chilton** Wisconsin, N USA
84 F11 **Chiluage** Lunda Sul, NE Angola
84 N12 **Chilumba** *prev.* Deep Bay. Northern, N Malawi
167 T12 **Chilung** *var.* Keelung, *Jap.* Kirun, Kirun'; *prev. Sp.* Santissima Trinidad. N Taiwan
85 N15 **Chilwa, Lake** *var.* Lago Chirua, Lake Shirwa. ◎ SE Malawi
178 J10 **Chi, Mae Nam** ∿ E Thailand
44 C6 **Chimaltenango** Chimaltenango, C Guatemala
44 A2 **Chimaltenango** *off.* Departamento de Chimaltenango. ◈ *department* S Guatemala
45 V15 **Chimán** Panamá, E Panama
85 M17 **Chimanimani** *prev.* Mandidzudzure, Melsetter. Manicaland, E Zimbabwe
101 G22 **Chimay** Hainaut, S Belgium
39 S10 **Chimayo** New Mexico, SW USA
Chimbay *see* Chimboy
58 A13 **Chimborazo** ◈ *province* C Ecuador
58 C7 **Chimborazo** ▲ C Ecuador
58 C12 **Chimbote** Ancash, W Peru
152 H7 **Chimboy** *Rus.* Chimbay. Qoraqalpoghiston Respublikasi, NW Uzbekistan
194 H12 **Chimbu** ◈ *province* C PNG
56 F6 **Chimichagua** Cesar, N Colombia
Chimishliya *see* Cimişlia
Chimkent *see* Shymkent
Chimkentskaya Oblast' *see* Yuzhnyy Kazakhstan
30 I14 **Chimney Rock** *rock* Nebraska, C USA
85 M17 **Chimoio** Manica, C Mozambique
84 K11 **Chimpembe** Northern, NE Zambia
43 O8 **China** Nuevo León, NE Mexico
162 M9 **China** *off.* People's Republic of China, *Chin.* Chung-hua Jen-min Kung-ho-kuo, Zhonghua Renmin Gongheguo; *prev.* Chinese Empire. ◆ *republic* E Asia
21 Q7 **China Lake** ◎ Maine, NE USA
44 F8 **Chinameca** San Miguel, E El Salvador
Chi-nan/Chinan *see* Jinan
44 H9 **Chinandega** Chinandega, NW Nicaragua
44 H9 **Chinandega** ◈ *department* NW Nicaragua
China, People's Republic of *see* China
China, Republic of *see* Taiwan
26 J11 **Chinati Mountains** ▲ Texas, SW USA
Chinaz *see* Chinoz
59 E15 **Chincha Alta** Ica, SW Peru
9 N11 **Chinchaga** ∿ Alberta, SW Canada
Chin-chiang *see* Quanzhou
Chinchilla *see* Chinchilla de Monte Aragón
107 Q11 **Chinchilla de Monte Aragón** *var.* Chinchilla. Castilla-La Mancha, C Spain
56 D10 **Chinchiná** Caldas, W Colombia
107 O8 **Chinchón** Madrid, C Spain
43 Z14 **Chinchorro, Banco** *island* SE Mexico
Chin-chou/Chinchow *see* Jinzhou
23 Z5 **Chincoteague** Assateague Island, Virginia, NE USA
85 O17 **Chinde** Zambézia, NE Mozambique
169 X17 **Chin-do** *Jap.* Chin-tō. *island* SW South Korea
165 R13 **Chindu** Qinghai, C China
177 G2 **Chindwin** ∿ N Myanmar
Chinese Empire *see* China
152 L10 **Chingeldi** *Rus.* Chingildi. Nawoiy Wiloyati, N Uzbekistan
Ch'ing Hai *see* Qinghai Hu
Chinghai *see* Qinghai
Chingildi *see* Chingeldi
150 H9 **Chingirlau** *Kaz.* Shyngghyrlaū. Zapadnyy Kazakhstan, W Kazakhstan
84 J13 **Chingola** Copperbelt, C Zambia
Ching-Tao/Ch'ing-tao *see* Qingdao
84 C13 **Chinguar** Huambo, C Angola
78 I7 **Chinguețți** *var.* Chinguetti. Adrar, C Mauritania
169 Z16 **Chinhae** *Jap.* Chinkai. S South Korea
177 Ff4 **Chin Hills** ▲ W Myanmar
85 K16 **Chinhoyi** *prev.* Sinoia. Mashonaland West, N Zimbabwe
Chinhsien *see* Jinzhou
41 Q14 **Chiniak, Cape** *headland* Kodiak Island, Alaska, USA
12 G10 **Chiniguchi Lake** ◎ Ontario, S Canada
155 U8 **Chiniot** Punjab, NE Pakistan
169 Y16 **Chinju** *Jap.* Shinshū. S South Korea
Chinkai *see* Chinhae
80 M13 **Chinko** ∿ E Central African Republic
39 O9 **Chinle** Arizona, SW USA
167 R13 **Chinmen Tao** *var.* Jinmen Dao, Quemoy. *island* W Taiwan
Chinnchâr *see* Shinshār
Chinnereth *see* Tiberias, Lake
171 J15 **Chino** *var.* Tino. Nagano, Honshū, S Japan
104 L8 **Chinon** Indre-et-Loire, C France
35 T7 **Chinook** Montana, NW USA
Chinook State *see* Washington
199 Jj3 **Chinook Trough** *undersea feature* N Pacific Ocean
38 K11 **Chino Valley** Arizona, SW USA
153 P10 **Chinoz** *Rus.* Chinaz. Toshkent Wiloyati, E Uzbekistan
84 L12 **Chinsali** Northern, NE Zambia
177 F4 **Chin State** ◈ *state* W Myanmar
Chinsura *see* Chunchura
Chin-tō *see* Chin-do
56 E6 **Chinú** Córdoba, NW Colombia
101 K24 **Chiny, Forêt de** *forest* SE Belgium
85 M15 **Chioco** Tete, NW Mozambique
108 H8 **Chioggia** *anc.* Fossa Claudia. Veneto, NE Italy
116 H12 **Chionótrypa** ▲ NE Greece
117 L18 **Chíos** *var.* Hios, Khíos, *It.* Scio, *Turk.* Sakiz-Adasi. Chíos, E Greece
117 K18 **Chíos** *var.* Khíos. *island* E Greece
85 M14 **Chipata** *prev.* Fort Jameson. Eastern, E Zambia
85 C14 **Chipindo** Huíla, C Angola
25 R8 **Chipley** Florida, SE USA
161 D15 **Chiplūn** Mahārāshtra, W India
83 H22 **Chipogolo** Dodoma, C Tanzania
25 R8 **Chipola River** ∿ Florida, SE USA
99 L22 **Chippenham** S England, UK
32 J6 **Chippewa Falls** Wisconsin, N USA
32 J4 **Chippewa, Lake** ⊡ Wisconsin, N USA
33 Q8 **Chippewa River** ∿ Michigan, N USA
32 I6 **Chippewa River** ∿ Wisconsin, N USA
Chipping Wycombe *see* High Wycombe
116 G8 **Chiprovtsi** Oblast Montana, NW Bulgaria
21 T4 **Chiputneticook Lakes** *lakes* Canada/USA
58 D13 **Chiquián** Ancash, W Peru
43 Y11 **Chiquilá** Quintana Roo, SE Mexico
44 E6 **Chiquimula** Chiquimula, SE Guatemala
44 A3 **Chiquimula** *off.* Departamento de Chiquimula. ◈ *department* SE Guatemala
44 D7 **Chiquimulilla** Santa Rosa, S Guatemala
56 F9 **Chiquinquirá** Boyacá, C Colombia
161 J17 **Chīrāla** Andhra Pradesh, E India
155 N4 **Chīras** Ghowr, N Afghanistan
158 H11 **Chirāwa** Rājasthān, N India
Chirchik *see* Chirchiq
153 Q9 **Chirchiq** *Rus.* Chirchik. Toshkent Wiloyati, E Uzbekistan
153 P10 **Chirchiq** ∿ E Uzbekistan
Chire *see* Shire
85 L18 **Chiredzi** Masvingo, SE Zimbabwe
27 X8 **Chireno** Texas, SW USA
79 X7 **Chirfa** Agadez, NE Niger
39 O16 **Chiricahua Mountains** ▲ Arizona, SW USA
39 O16 **Chiricahua Peak** ▲ Arizona, SW USA
56 F6 **Chiriguaná** Cesar, N Colombia
41 P15 **Chirikof Island** *island* Alaska, USA
45 P16 **Chiriquí** *off.* Provincia de Chiriquí. ◈ *province* SW Panama
45 P17 **Chiriquí, Golfo de** *Eng.* Chiriqui Gulf. *gulf* SW Panama
45 P15 **Chiriquí Grande** Bocas del Toro, W Panama
Chiriqui Gulf *see* Chiriquí, Golfo de
45 P15 **Chiriquí, Laguna de** *lagoon* NW Panama
45 O16 **Chiriquí Viejo, Río** ∿ W Panama
Chiriquí, Volcán de *see* Barú, Volcán
85 N15 **Chiromo** Southern, S Malawi
116 J10 **Chirpan** Khaskovska Oblast, C Bulgaria
45 N14 **Chirripó Atlántico, Río** ∿ E Costa Rica
Chirripó, Cerro *see* Chirripó Grande, Cerro
45 N14 **Chirripó Grande, Cerro** *var.* Cerro Chirripó. ▲ SE Costa Rica
45 N13 **Chirripó, Río** *var.* Río Chirripó del Pacífico. ∿ NE Costa Rica
Chirua, Lago *see* Chilwa, Lake
85 J15 **Chirundu** Southern, S Zambia
31 W8 **Chisago City** Minnesota, N USA
85 J14 **Chisamba** Central, C Zambia
41 T10 **Chisana** Alaska, USA
84 I13 **Chisasa** North Western, NW Zambia
10 I9 **Chisasibi** Québec, C Canada
44 D4 **Chisec** Alta Verapaz, C Guatemala
131 U5 **Chishmy** Respublika Bashkortostan, W Russian Federation
31 V4 **Chisholm** Minnesota, N USA
155 U10 **Chishtiān Mandi** Punjab, E Pakistan
166 I11 **Chishui He** ∿ C China
Chisimaio/Chisimayu *see* Kismaayo
119 N10 **Chişinău** *Rus.* Kishinev. ● (Moldova) C Moldova
119 N10 **Chişinău** ✕ S Moldova
Chişinău-Criş *see* Chişineu-Criş
118 F10 **Chişineu-Criş** *Hung.* Kişjenő; *prev.* Chişinău-Criş. Arad, W Romania
85 K14 **Chisomo** Central, C Zambia
108 A8 **Chisone** ∿ NW Italy
26 K12 **Chisos Mountains** ▲ Texas, SW USA
41 T10 **Chistochina** Alaska, USA
131 R4 **Chistopol'** Respublika Tatarstan, W Russian Federation
151 O8 **Chistopol'ye** Kokshetau, N Kazakhstan
126 Kk16 **Chita** Chitinskaya Oblast', S Russian Federation
85 B16 **Chitado** Cunene, SW Angola
Chitaldroog/Chitaldrug *see* Chitradurga
85 C15 **Chitanda** ∿ S Angola
Chitangwiza *see* Chitungwiza
84 F10 **Chitato** Lunda Norte, NE Angola
85 C14 **Chitembo** Bié, C Angola
41 T11 **Chitina** Alaska, USA
41 T11 **Chitina River** ∿ Alaska, USA
126 Kk14 **Chitinskaya Oblast'** ◈ *province* S Russian Federation
84 M11 **Chitipa** Northern, NW Malawi
172 Oo6 **Chitose** *var.* Titose. Hokkaidō, NE Japan
161 G18 **Chitradurga** *prev.* Chitaldroog, Chitaldrug. Karnātaka, W India
155 T3 **Chitrāl** North-West Frontier Province, NW Pakistan
45 S16 **Chitré** Herrera, S Panama
159 V16 **Chittagong** *Ben.* Chāttagām. Chittagong, SE Bangladesh
159 U16 **Chittagong** ◈ *division* E Bangladesh
159 Q15 **Chittaranjan** West Bengal, NE India
158 G14 **Chittaurgarh** Rājasthān, N India
161 I19 **Chittoor** Andhra Pradesh, E India
161 G21 **Chittūr** Kerala, SW India
85 K16 **Chitungwiza** *prev.* Chitangwiza. Mashonaland East, NE Zimbabwe
64 H4 **Chiúchíu** Antofagasta, N Chile
84 F12 **Chiumbe** *var.* Tshiumbe. ∿ Angola/Zaire
85 F15 **Chiume** Moxico, E Angola
84 K13 **Chiundaponde** Northern, NE Zambia
108 H13 **Chiusi** Toscana, C Italy
56 J5 **Chivacoa** Yaracuy, N Venezuela
108 B8 **Chivasso** Piemonte, NW Italy
85 L17 **Chivhu** *prev.* Enkeldoorn. Midlands, C Zimbabwe
63 C20 **Chivilcoy** Buenos Aires, E Argentina
84 N12 **Chiweta** Northern, N Malawi
44 D4 **Chixoy, Río** *var.* Río Negro, Río Salinas. ∿ Guatemala/Mexico
84 H13 **Chizela** North Western, NW Zambia
129 O5 **Chizha** Nenetskiy Avtonomnyy Okrug, NW Russian Federation
170 G13 **Chizu** Tottori, Honshū, SW Japan
Chkalov *see* Orenburg
76 J5 **Chlef** *var.* Ech Cheliff, Ech Chleff; *prev.* Al-Asnam, El Asnam, Orléansville. NW Algeria
117 G18 **Chlómo** ▲ C Greece
113 M15 **Chmielnik** Kielce, S Poland
178 J11 **Chŏâm Khsant** Preăh Vihéar, N Cambodia
64 G10 **Choapa, Río** *var.* Choapo. ∿ C Chile
Choapas *see* Las Choapas
Choarta *see* Chwārtā
85 H17 **Chobe** ◈ *district* NE Botswana
69 T13 **Chobe** ∿ N Botswana
12 K8 **Chochocouane** ∿ Québec, SE Canada
112 E13 **Chocianów** *Ger.* Kotzenan. Legnica, SW Poland
56 C9 **Chocó** *off.* Departamento del Chocó. ◈ *province* W Colombia
37 X16 **Chocolate Mountains** ▲ California, W USA
23 W9 **Chocowinity** North Carolina, SE USA
29 N10 **Choctaw** Oklahoma, C USA
25 Q8 **Choctawhatchee Bay** *bay* Florida, SE USA
25 Q8 **Choctawhatchee River** ∿ Florida, SE USA
Chodau *see* Chodov
169 V14 **Chŏ-do** *island* SW North Korea
Chodorów *see* Khodoriv
113 A16 **Chodov** *Ger.* Chodau. Západní Čechy, W Czech Republic
112 G10 **Chodzież** Piła, NW Poland
65 J15 **Choele Choel** Río Negro, C Argentina
85 L14 **Chofombo** Tete, NW Mozambique
Chohtan *see* Chauhtan
9 U14 **Choiceland** Saskatchewan, C Canada
195 U13 **Choiseul** *var.* Lauru. *island* NW Solomon Islands
65 M23 **Choiseul Sound** *sound* East Falkland, Falkland Islands
42 H7 **Choix** Sinaloa, C Mexico
112 D10 **Chojna** Szczecin, W Poland
112 H8 **Chojnice** *Ger.* Konitz. Bydgoszcz, NW Poland
113 F14 **Chojnów** *Ger.* Hainau, Haynau. Legnica, W Poland
171 Ll11 **Chōkai-san** ▲ Honshū, C Japan
178 I11 **Chok Chai** Nakhon Ratchasima, C Thailand
82 I12 **Ch'ok'ē** *var.* Choke Mountains. ▲ NW Ethiopia
27 R13 **Choke Canyon Lake** ⊡ Texas, SW USA
Choke Mountains *see* Ch'ok'ē
151 T15 **Chokpar** *Kaz.* Shoqpar. Zhambyl, S Kazakhstan
153 W7 **Chok-Tal** *var.* Choktal. Issyk-Kul'skaya Oblast', E Kyrgyzstan
Chókué *see* Chokwé
126 Mm6 **Chokurdakh** Respublika Sakha (Yakutiya), NE Russian Federation
85 L20 **Chokwé** *var.* Chókué. Gaza, S Mozambique
196 F8 **Chol** Babeldaob, N Palau
166 E8 **Chola Shan** ▲ C China
104 J8 **Cholet** Maine-et-Loire, NW France
65 H17 **Cholila** Chubut, W Argentina
Cholo *see* Thyolo
153 V8 **Cholpon** Narynskaya Oblast', C Kyrgyzstan
153 X7 **Cholpon-Ata** Issyk-Kul'skaya Oblast', E Kyrgyzstan
43 P14 **Cholula** Puebla, S Mexico
44 I8 **Choluteca** Choluteca, S Honduras
44 H8 **Choluteca** ◈ *department* S Honduras
44 G6 **Choluteca, Río** ∿ SW Honduras
85 I15 **Choma** Southern, S Zambia
159 T11 **Chomo Lhari** ▲ NW Bhutan
178 H7 **Chom Thong** Chiang Mai, NW Thailand
113 B15 **Chomutov** *Ger.* Komotau. Severní Čechy, NW Czech Republic
126 K12 **Chona** ∿ C Russian Federation
169 X15 **Ch'ŏnan** *Jap.* Tenan. W South Korea
178 Hh12 **Chon Buri** *prev.* Bang Pla Soi. Chon Buri, S Thailand
58 B6 **Chone** Manabí, W Ecuador
169 W13 **Ch'ŏngch'ŏn-gang** ∿ W North Korea
169 Y11 **Ch'ŏngjin** NE North Korea
169 W13 **Chŏngju** W North Korea
167 S8 **Chongming Dao** *island* E China
166 J10 **Chongqing** *var.* Ch'ung-ching, Ch'ung-ch'ing, Chungking, Pahsien, Tchongking, Yuzhou. Sichuan, C China
Chŏngup *see* Chŏnju
167 O10 **Chongyang** Hubei, C China
169 Y16 **Chŏnju** *prev.* Chŏngup, *Jap.* Seiyu. SW South Korea
169 Y15 **Chŏnju** *Jap.* Zenshū. SW South Korea
Chonnacht *see* Connaught
169 Q9 **Chonogol** Sühbaatar, E Mongolia
65 F19 **Chonos, Archipiélago de los** *island group* S Chile
44 K10 **Chontales** ◈ *department* S Nicaragua
178 Jj14 **Chơn Thanh** Sông Be, S Vietnam
164 K17 **Cho Oyu** *var.* Qowowuyag. ▲ China/Nepal *see also* Qowowuyag
118 G7 **Chop** *Cz.* Čop, *Hung.* Csap. Zakarpats'ka Oblast', W Ukraine
23 Y3 **Choptank River** ∿ Maryland, NE USA
Chorcai, Cuan *see* Cork Harbour
45 P15 **Chorcha, Cerro** ▲ W Panama
Chorku *see* Chorkŭh
153 R11 **Chorkŭh** *Rus.* Chorku. N Tajikistan
99 K17 **Chorley** NW England, UK
Chorne More *see* Black Sea
119 R5 **Chornobay** Cherkas'ka Oblast', C Ukraine
119 O3 **Chornobyl'** *Rus.* Chernobyl'. Kyyivs'ka Oblast', N Ukraine
119 R12 **Chornomors'ke** *Rus.* Chernomorskoye. Respublika Krym, S Ukraine
119 R4 **Chornukhy** Poltavs'ka Oblast', C Ukraine
Chorokh/Chorokhi *see* Çoruh Nehri
112 O9 **Choroszcz** Białystok, NE Poland
118 K6 **Chortkiv** *Rus.* Chortkov. Ternopil's'ka Oblast', W Ukraine
Chortkov *see* Chortkiv
Chorum *see* Çorum
112 M9 **Chorzele** Ostrołęka, NE Poland
113 J16 **Chorzów** *Ger.* Königshütte; *prev.* Królewska Huta. Katowice, S Poland
169 W12 **Ch'osan** N North Korea
Chōsen-kaikyō *see* Korea Strait
171 Kk17 **Chōshi** *var.* Tyôsi. Chiba, Honshū, S Japan
65 H14 **Chos Malal** Neuquén, W Argentina
Chosŏn-minjujuŭi-inmin-kanghwaguk *see* North Korea
112 E9 **Choszczno** *Ger.* Arnswalde. Gorzów, W Poland
159 O15 **Chota Nāgpur** *plateau* N India
35 R8 **Choteau** Montana, NW USA
Chotqol *see* Chatkal
12 M8 **Chouart** ∿ Québec, SE Canada
78 I7 **Choûm** Adrar, C Mauritania
29 Q9 **Chouteau** Oklahoma, C USA
23 X8 **Chowan River** ∿ North Carolina, SE USA

◆ Country ● Country Capital ◇ Dependent Territory ○ Dependent Territory Capital ◈ Administrative Region ✕ International Airport ▲ Mountain ▲ Mountain Range ▲ Volcano ∿ River ◎ Lake ⊡ Reservoir

37 Q10 **Chowchilla** California, W USA
169 P7 **Choybalsan** Dornod, E Mongolia
168 M9 **Choyr** Dornogovĭ, C Mongolia
193 I19 **Christchurch** Canterbury, South Island, NZ
99 M24 **Christchurch** S England, UK
193 I18 **Christchurch** × Canterbury, South Island, NZ
46 J12 **Christiana** C Jamaica
85 H22 **Christiana** Free State, C South Africa
117 J23 **Christiáni** *island* Kykládes, Greece, Aegean Sea
Christiania *see* Oslo
12 G13 **Christian Island** *island* Ontario, S Canada
203 P16 **Christian, Point** *headland* Pitcairn Island, Pitcairn Islands
40 M11 **Christian River** ~ Alaska, USA
Christiansand *see* Kristiansand
23 S7 **Christiansburg** Virginia, NE USA
97 G23 **Christiansfeld** Sønderjylland, SW Denmark
Christianshåb *see* Qasigiannguit
41 X14 **Christian Sound** *inlet* Alaska, USA
47 T9 **Christiansted** Saint Croix, S Virgin Islands (US)
Christiansund *see* Kristiansund
27 R13 **Christine** Texas, SW USA
181 U7 **Christmas Island** ◇ *Australian external territory* E Indian Ocean
133 T17 **Christmas Island** *island* E Indian Ocean
Christmas Island *see* Kiritimati
199 K8 **Christmas Ridge** *undersea feature* C Pacific Ocean
32 L16 **Christopher** Illinois, N USA
27 P9 **Christoval** Texas, SW USA
113 F17 **Chrudim** Východní Čechy, C Czech Republic
117 K25 **Chrýsi** *island* SE Greece
123 Mm3 **Chrysochoú, Kólpos** *var.* Khrysokhou Bay. *bay* E Mediterranean Sea
116 I13 **Chrysoúpoli** *var.* Hrisoupoli; *prev.* Khrisoúpolis. Anatolikí Makedonía kai Thráki, NE Greece
113 K16 **Chrzanów** *var.* Chrzanow, *Ger.* Zaumgarten. Katowice, S Poland
133 Q7 **Chu** *Kaz.* Shū. ~ Kazakhstan/Kyrgyzstan
44 C5 **Chuacús, Sierra de** ▲ W Guatemala
159 S15 **Chuadanga** Khulna, W Bangladesh
Chuan *see* Sichuan
Ch'uan-chou *see* Quanzhou
41 O11 **Chuathbaluk** Alaska, USA
194 I12 **Chuave** Chimbu, W PNG
Chubek *see* Moskva
65 I17 **Chubut** *off.* Provincia de Chubut. ◆ *province* S Argentina
65 I17 **Chubut, Río** ~ SE Argentina
45 V15 **Chucanti, Cerro** ▲ E Panama
Ch'u-chiang *see* Shaoguan
45 W15 **Chucunaque, Río** ~ E Panama
Chudin *see* Chudzin
118 M5 **Chudniv** Zhytomyrs'ka Oblast', N Ukraine
128 H13 **Chudovo** Novgorodskaya Oblast', W Russian Federation
Chudskoye Ozero *see* Peipus, Lake
121 J18 **Chudzin** *Rus.* Chudin. Brestskaya Voblasts', SW Belorussia
41 Q13 **Chugach Islands** *island group* Alaska, USA
41 S11 **Chugach Mountains** ▲ Alaska, USA
170 Ee12 **Chūgoku-sanchi** ▲ Honshū, SW Japan
Chuguyev *see* Chuhuyiv
119 V5 **Chuhuyiv** *var.* Chuguyev. Kharkivs'ka Oblast', E Ukraine
63 H19 **Chuí** Rio Grande do Sul, S Brazil
Chuí *see* Chuy
151 S15 **Chu-Iliyskiye Gory** *Kaz.* Shū-Ile Taūlary. ▲ S Kazakhstan
Chukai *see* Cukai
Chukchi Avtonomnyy Okrug *see* Chukotskiy Avtonomnyy Okrug
Chukchi Peninsula *see* Chukotskiy Poluostrov
207 R6 **Chukchi Plain** *undersea feature* Arctic Ocean
207 R6 **Chukchi Plateau** *undersea feature* Arctic Ocean
207 R4 **Chukchi Sea** *Rus.* Chukotskoye More. *sea* Arctic Ocean
129 N14 **Chukhloma** Kostromskaya Oblast', NW Russian Federation
Chukotka *see* Chukotskiy Avtonomnyy Okrug
Chukot Range *see* Anadyrskiy Khrebet
127 Oo5 **Chukotskiy Avtonomnyy Okrug** *var.* Chukchi Avtonomnyy Okrug, Chukotka. ◆ *autonomous district* NE Russian Federation
127 Q4 **Chukotskiy, Mys** *headland* NE Russian Federation
127 Pp4 **Chukotskiy Poluostrov** *Eng.* Chukchi Peninsula. *peninsula* NE Russian Federation
Chukotskoye More *see* Chukchi Sea
Chukurkak *see* Chuqurqoq
151 P15 **Chulakkurgan** Yuzhnyy Kazakhstan, S Kazakhstan
37 U17 **Chula Vista** California, W USA
126 Ll13 **Chul'man** Respublika Sakha (Yakutiya), NE Russian Federation
58 B9 **Chulucanas** Piura, NW Peru
126 Gg14 **Chulym** Novosibirskaya Oblast', C Russian Federation
126 H13 **Chulym** ~ C Russian Federation
158 K6 **Chumar** Jammu and Kashmir, N India
116 K9 **Chumerna** ▲ C Bulgaria
127 N13 **Chumikan** Khabarovskiy Kray, E Russian Federation
178 I9 **Chum Phae** Khon Kaen, C Thailand
178 Gg14 **Chumphon** *var.* Jumporn. Chumphon, SW Thailand
178 Hh10 **Chumsaeng** *var.* Chum Saeng. Nakhon Sawan, C Thailand
126 H14 **Chumysh** ~ S Russian Federation
126 Ii13 **Chuna** ~ C Russian Federation
167 R9 **Chun'an** *var.* Pailing. Zhejiang, SE China
167 S13 **Chunan** N Taiwan
169 Y14 **Ch'unch'ŏn** *Jap.* Shunsen. N South Korea
159 S16 **Chunchura** *prev.* Chinsura. West Bengal, NE India
151 W15 **Chundzha** Almaty, SE Kazakhstan
Ch'ung-ch'ing/Ch'ung-ching *see* Chongqing
Chung-hua Jen-min Kung-ho-kuo *see* China
169 Y15 **Ch'ungju** *Jap.* Chūshū. C South Korea
Chungking *see* Chongqing
167 T14 **Chungyang Shanmo** *Chin.* Taiwan Shan. ▲ C Taiwan
155 V9 **Chūniān** Punjab, E Pakistan
126 Ii14 **Chunskiy** Irkutskaya Oblast', S Russian Federation
126 J11 **Chunya** ~ C Russian Federation
128 J6 **Chupa** Respublika Kareliya, NW Russian Federation
129 P8 **Chuprovo** Respublika Komi, NW Russian Federation
59 G17 **Chuquibamba** Arequipa, SW Peru
64 H4 **Chuquicamata** Antofagasta, N Chile
59 L21 **Chuquisaca** ◆ *department* S Bolivia
Chuquisaca *see* Sucre
152 I8 **Chuqurqoq** *Rus.* Chukurkak. Qoraqalpoghiston Respublikasi, NW Uzbekistan
131 T2 **Chur** Udmurtskaya Respublika, NW Russian Federation
110 I9 **Chur** *Fr.* Coire, *It.* Coira, *Rmsch.* Cuera, Quera; *anc.* Curia Rhaetorum. Graubünden, E Switzerland
126 M11 **Churapcha** Respublika Sakha (Yakutiya), NE Russian Federation
9 V16 **Churchbridge** Saskatchewan, S Canada
23 O8 **Church Hill** Tennessee, S USA
9 X9 **Churchill** Manitoba, C Canada
9 X10 **Churchill** ~ Manitoba/Saskatchewan, C Canada
11 P9 **Churchill** ~ Newfoundland and Labrador, E Canada
9 Y9 **Churchill, Cape** *headland* Manitoba, C Canada
11 P9 **Churchill Falls** Newfoundland and Labrador, E Canada
9 S12 **Churchill Lake** ◎ Saskatchewan, C Canada
21 Q3 **Churchill Lake** ⊠ Maine, NE USA
204 I5 **Churchill Peninsula** *peninsula* Antarctica
24 H8 **Church Point** Louisiana, S USA
31 O3 **Churchs Ferry** North Dakota, N USA
152 G12 **Churchuri** Akhalskiy Velayat, C Turkmenistan
23 T5 **Churchville** Virginia, NE USA
158 G10 **Chūru** Rājasthān, NW India
56 J4 **Churuguara** Falcón, N Venezuela
150 J12 **Chushkakul, Gory** ▲ SW Kazakhstan
Chūshū *see* Ch'ungju
39 O9 **Chuska Mountains** ▲ Arizona/New Mexico, SW USA
Chu, Sông *see* Sam, Nam
125 Ee11 **Chusovaya** ~ W Russian Federation
129 V14 **Chusovoy** Permskaya Oblast', NW Russian Federation
153 R10 **Chust** Namangan Wiloyati, E Uzbekistan
Chust *see* Khust
13 U6 **Chute-aux-Outardes** Québec, SE Canada
119 U5 **Chutove** Poltavs'ka Oblast', C Ukraine
201 O15 **Chuuk** *var.* Truk. ◆ *state* C Micronesia
201 P15 **Chuuk Islands** *var.* Hogoley Islands; *prev.* Truk Islands. *island group* Caroline Islands, C Micronesia
Chuvashia *see* Chuvashskaya Respublika
131 P4 **Chuvashskaya Respublika** *var.* Chavash Respubliki, *Eng.* Chuvashia. ◆ *autonomous republic* W Russian Federation
Chuwārtah *see* Chwārtā
Chu Xian/Chuxian *see* Chuzhou
166 G13 **Chuxiong** Yunnan, SW China
153 V7 **Chuy** Chuyskaya Oblast', N Kyrgyzstan
63 H19 **Chuy** *var.* Chuí. Rocha, E Uruguay
126 K12 **Chuya** Respublika Sakha (Yakutiya), NE Russian Federation
Chüy Oblasty *see* Chuyskaya Oblast'
153 U8 **Chuyskaya Oblast'** *Kir.* Chüy Oblasty. ◆ *province* N Kyrgyzstan
167 Q7 **Chuzhou** *var.* Chuxian, Chu Xian. Anhui, E China
145 U3 **Chwārtā** *var.* Choarta, Chuwārtah. NE Iraq
121 N16 **Chyhirynskaye Vodaskhovishcha** ⊠ E Belorussia
119 R6 **Chyhyryn** *Rus.* Chigirin. Cherkas'ka Oblast', N Ukraine
Chyrvonaya Slabada *see* Krasnaya Slabada
121 L19 **Chyrvonaye, Vozyera** *Rus.* Ozero Chervonoye. ◎ SE Belorussia
178 K12 **Ch, Srê** Gia Lai, C Vietnam
119 N11 **Ciadîr-Lunga** *var.* Ceadâr-Lunga, *Rus.* Chadyr-Lunga. S Moldova
174 K15 **Ciamis** *prev.* Tjiamis. Jawa, C Indonesia
174 J14 **Cianjur** *prev.* Tjiandjoer. Jawa, C Indonesia
62 H10 **Cianorte** Paraná, S Brazil
Ciarraí *see* Kerry
114 N13 **Ćićevac** Serbia, E Yugoslavia
197 K14 **Cicia** *prev.* Thithia. *island* Lau Group, E Fiji
107 P4 **Cidacos** ~ N Spain
142 I10 **Cide** Kastamonu, N Turkey
112 L10 **Ciechanów** *prev.* Zichenau. Ciechanów, C Poland
112 L10 **Ciechanów** *off.* Województwo Ciechanowskie. ◆ *province* C Poland
112 O10 **Ciechanowiec** *Ger.* Rudelstadt. Łomża, E Poland
Ciechanowskie, Województwo *see* Ciechanów
112 J10 **Ciechocinek** Włocławek, C Poland
46 F6 **Ciego de Ávila** Ciego de Ávila, C Cuba
56 F4 **Ciénaga** Magdalena, N Colombia
56 E6 **Ciénaga de Oro** Córdoba, NW Colombia
46 E5 **Cienfuegos** Cienfuegos, C Cuba
106 F4 **Cíes, Illas** *island group* NW Spain
113 P16 **Cieszanów** Przemyśl, SE Poland
113 J17 **Cieszyn** *Cz.* Těšín, *Ger.* Teschen. Bielsko-Biała, S Poland
107 R12 **Cieza** Murcia, SE Spain
142 F13 **Çifteler** Eskişehir, W Turkey
107 P7 **Cifuentes** Castilla-La Mancha, C Spain
Çiganak *see* Chiganak
107 P9 **Cigüela** ~ C Spain
142 H14 **Cihanbeyli** Konya, C Turkey
142 H14 **Cihanbeyli Yaylası** *plateau* C Turkey
106 L10 **Cíjara, Embalse de** ⊠ C Spain
174 K15 **Cikalong** Jawa, S Indonesia
174 Ii14 **Cikawung** Jawa, S Indonesia
197 K12 **Cikobia** *prev.* Thikombia. *island* N Fiji
174 K15 **Cilacap** *prev.* Tjilatjap. Jawa, C Indonesia
181 O16 **Cilaos** C Réunion
143 S11 **Çıldır** Kars, NE Turkey
143 S11 **Çıldır Gölü** ◎ NE Turkey
174 K14 **Ciledug** *prev.* Tjiledoeg. Jawa, SW Indonesia
166 M10 **Cili** Hunan, S China
124 R12 **Cilicia Trough** *undersea feature* E Mediterranean Sea
Cill Airne *see* Killarney
Cill Chainnigh *see* Kilkenny
Cill Chaoi *see* Kilkee
Cill Choca *see* Kilcock
Cill Dara *see* Kildare
107 N3 **Cilleruelo de Bezana** Castilla-León, N Spain
Cilli *see* Celje
Cill Mhantáin *see* Wicklow
Cill Rois *see* Kilrush
28 J6 **Cimarron** Kansas, C USA
39 T9 **Cimarron** New Mexico, SW USA
28 M9 **Cimarron River** ~ Kansas/Oklahoma, C USA
119 N11 **Cimişlia** *Rus.* Chimishliya. S Moldova
Cimpia Turzii *see* Câmpia Turzii
Cimpina *see* Câmpina
Cimpulung *see* Câmpulung
Cimpulung Moldovenesc *see* Câmpulung Moldovenesc
143 P15 **Çınar** Dıyarbakır, SE Turkey
56 J8 **Cinaruco, Río** ~ Colombia/Venezuela
Cina Selatan, Laut *see* South China Sea
107 T5 **Cinca** ~ NE Spain
114 G13 **Cincar** ▲ SW Bosnia and Herzegovina
33 Q15 **Cincinnati** Ohio, N USA
22 M4 **Cincinnati** × Kentucky, S USA
Cinco de Outubro *see* Xá-Muteba
142 C15 **Çine** Aydın, SW Turkey
101 J21 **Ciney** Namur, SE Belgium
106 H6 **Cinfães** Viseu, N Portugal
108 J12 **Cingoli** Marche, C Italy
43 U16 **Cintalapa** *var.* Cintalapa de Figueroa. Chiapas, SE Mexico
Cintalapa de Figueroa *see* Cintalapa
104 E1 **Cinto, Monte** ▲ Corse, France, C Mediterranean Sea
Cintra *see* Sintra
107 Q5 **Cintruénigo** Navarra, N Spain
Cionn tSáile *see* Kinsale
118 K13 **Ciorani** Prahova, SE Romania
115 E14 **Čiovo** *It.* Bua. *island* S Croatia
174 J14 **Cipanas** Jawa, S Indonesia
Cipiúr *see* Kippure
65 I15 **Cipolletti** Río Negro, C Argentina
123 L8 **Circeo, Capo** *headland* C Italy
41 S8 **Circle** *var.* Circle City. Alaska, USA
35 X8 **Circle** Montana, NW USA
Circle City *see* Circle
33 S14 **Circleville** Ohio, N USA
38 K6 **Circleville** Utah, W USA
174 K14 **Cirebon** *prev.* Tjirebon. Jawa, S Indonesia
99 L21 **Cirencester** *anc.* Corinium, Corinium Dobunorum. C England, UK
Cirkvenica *see* Crikvenica
109 O20 **Cirò** Calabria, SW Italy
109 O20 **Cirò Marina** Calabria, S Italy
104 K14 **Ciron** ~ SW France
Cirquenizza *see* Crikvenica
27 R7 **Cisco** Texas, SW USA
118 I12 **Cisnădie** *Ger.* Heltau, *Hung.* Nagydisznód. Sibiu, SW Romania
65 G18 **Cisnes, Río** ~ S Chile
27 T11 **Cistern** Texas, SW USA
106 L3 **Cistierna** Castilla-León, N Spain
174 Ii14 **Citeureup** Jawa, S Indonesia
Citharista *see* la Ciotat
Citlaltépetl *see* Orizaba, Volcán Pico de
57 X10 **Citron** NW French Guiana
25 N7 **Citronelle** Alabama, S USA
37 O7 **Citrus Heights** California, W USA
108 H7 **Cittadella** Veneto, NE Italy
108 H13 **Città della Pieve** Umbria, C Italy
108 H12 **Città di Castello** Umbria, C Italy
109 I14 **Cittaducale** Lazio, C Italy
109 N22 **Cittanova** Calabria, SW Italy
Cittavecchia *see* Starigrad
118 G10 **Ciucea** *Hung.* Csucsa. Cluj, NW Romania
118 M13 **Ciucurova** Tulcea, SE Romania
43 N5 **Ciudad Acuña** *var.* Villa Acuña. Coahuila de Zaragoza, NE Mexico
43 N15 **Ciudad Altamirano** Guerrero, S Mexico
44 G7 **Ciudad Barrios** San Miguel, NE El Salvador
56 I7 **Ciudad Bolívar** Barinas, NW Venezuela
57 N7 **Ciudad Bolívar** *prev.* Angostura. Bolívar, E Venezuela
42 K6 **Ciudad Camargo** Chihuahua, N Mexico
42 E8 **Ciudad Constitución** Baja California Sur, W Mexico
Ciudad Cortés *see* Cortés
43 V17 **Ciudad Cuauhtémoc** Chiapas, SE Mexico
44 J9 **Ciudad Darío** *var.* Dario. Matagalpa, W Nicaragua
Ciudad de Dolores Hidalgo *see* Dolores Hidalgo
44 C6 **Ciudad de Guatemala** *Eng.* Guatemala City; *prev.* Santiago de los Caballeros. ● (Guatemala) Guatemala, C Guatemala
Ciudad del Carmen *see* Carmen
64 Q6 **Ciudad del Este** *prev.* Cuidad Presidente Stroessner, Presidente Stroessner, Puerto Presidente Stroessner. Alto Paraná, SE Paraguay
64 K5 **Ciudad de Libertador General San Martín** *var.* Libertador General San Martín. Jujuy, C Argentina
Ciudad Delicias *see* Delicias
43 O11 **Ciudad del Maíz** San Luis Potosí, C Mexico
Ciudad de México *see* México
56 J7 **Ciudad de Nutrias** Barinas, NW Venezuela
Ciudad de Panamá *see* Panamá
57 P7 **Ciudad Guayana** *prev.* San Tomé de Guayana, Santo Tomé de Guayana. Bolívar, NE Venezuela
42 K14 **Ciudad Guzmán** Jalisco, SW Mexico
43 V17 **Ciudad Hidalgo** Chiapas, SE Mexico
43 N14 **Ciudad Hidalgo** Michoacán de Ocampo, SW Mexico
42 J3 **Ciudad Juárez** Chihuahua, N Mexico
42 L8 **Ciudad Lerdo** Durango, C Mexico
43 Q11 **Ciudad Madero** *var.* Villa Cecilia. Tamaulipas, C Mexico
43 P11 **Ciudad Mante** Tamaulipas, C Mexico
44 F2 **Ciudad Melchor de Mencos** *var.* Melchor de Mencos. Petén, NE Guatemala
43 P8 **Ciudad Miguel Alemán** Tamaulipas, C Mexico
Ciudad Mutis *see* Bahía Solano
42 G6 **Ciudad Obregón** Sonora, NW Mexico
56 I5 **Ciudad Ojeda** Zulia, NW Venezuela
57 P7 **Ciudad Piar** Bolívar, E Venezuela
Ciudad Porfirio Díaz *see* Piedras Negras
Ciudad Quesada *see* Quesada
107 N11 **Ciudad Real** Castilla-La Mancha, C Spain
107 N11 **Ciudad Real** ◆ *province* Castilla-La Mancha, C Spain
106 J7 **Ciudad-Rodrigo** Castilla-León, N Spain
44 A6 **Ciudad Tecún Umán** San Marcos, SW Guatemala
Ciudad Trujillo *see* Santo Domingo
43 P12 **Ciudad Valles** San Luis Potosí, C Mexico
43 O10 **Ciudad Victoria** Tamaulipas, C Mexico
44 C6 **Ciudad Vieja** Suchitepéquez, S Guatemala
118 L8 **Ciuhuru** *var.* Reuţel. ~ N Moldova
Ciutadella *see* Ciutadella de Menorca
107 Z8 **Ciutadella de Menorca** *var.* Ciutadella. Menorca, Spain, W Mediterranean Sea
142 L11 **Civa Burnu** *headland* N Turkey
108 J7 **Cividale del Friuli** Friuli-Venezia Giulia, NE Italy
109 H14 **Civita Castellana** Lazio, C Italy
108 J12 **Civitanova Marche** Marche, C Italy
Civitas Altae Ripae *see* Brzeg
Civitas Carnutum *see* Chartres
Civitas Eburovicum *see* Évreux
Civitas Nemetum *see* Speyer
109 G15 **Civitavecchia** *anc.* Centum Cellae, Trajani Portus. Lazio, C Italy
104 L10 **Civray** Vienne, W France
142 E14 **Çivril** Denizli, W Turkey
167 O5 **Cixian** Hebei, E China
143 R16 **Cizre** Şırnak, SE Turkey
Clacton *see* Clacton-on-Sea
99 Q21 **Clacton-on-Sea** *var.* Clacton. E England, UK
24 H5 **Claiborne, Lake** ⊠ Louisiana, S USA
104 L10 **Clain** ~ W France
9 Q11 **Claire, Lake** ◎ Alberta, C Canada
27 O6 **Clairemont** Texas, SW USA
36 M3 **Clair Engle Lake** ⊠ California, W USA
20 B15 **Clairton** Pennsylvania, NE USA
34 F7 **Clallam Bay** Washington, NW USA
105 P8 **Clamecy** Nièvre, C France
25 P5 **Clanton** Alabama, S USA
63 D17 **Clara** Entre Ríos, E Argentina
99 E18 **Clara** *Ir.* Clóirtheach. C Ireland
31 T9 **Clara City** Minnesota, N USA
63 D23 **Claraz** Buenos Aires, E Argentina
Clár Chlainne Mhuiris *see* Claremorris
190 I8 **Clare** South Australia
99 C19 **Clare** *Ir.* An Clár. *cultural region* W Ireland
99 C18 **Clare** ~ W Ireland
99 A16 **Clare Island** *Ir.* Cliara. *island* W Ireland
46 J12 **Claremont** C Jamaica
31 W10 **Claremont** Minnesota, N USA
21 N9 **Claremont** New Hampshire, NE USA
29 Q9 **Claremore** Oklahoma, C USA
99 C17 **Claremorris** *Ir.* Clár Chlainne Mhuiris. W Ireland
193 J16 **Clarence** Canterbury, South Island, NZ
193 J16 **Clarence** ~ South Island, NZ
67 F15 **Clarence Bay** *bay* Ascension Island, C Atlantic Ocean
65 H25 **Clarence, Isla** *island* S Chile
204 H2 **Clarence Island** *island* South Shetland Islands, Antarctica
191 V5 **Clarence River** ~ New South Wales, SE Australia
46 J5 **Clarence Town** Long Island, C Bahamas
29 W12 **Clarendon** Arkansas, C USA
27 O3 **Clarendon** Texas, SW USA
11 U12 **Clarenville** Newfoundland, Newfoundland and Labrador, SE Canada
9 Q17 **Claresholm** Alberta, SW Canada
31 T16 **Clarinda** Iowa, C USA
57 N5 **Clarines** Anzoátegui, NE Venezuela
31 V12 **Clarion** Iowa, C USA
20 C13 **Clarion** Pennsylvania, NE USA
199 L7 **Clarion Fracture Zone** *tectonic feature* NE Pacific Ocean
20 D13 **Clarion River** ~ Pennsylvania, NE USA
31 Q9 **Clark** South Dakota, N USA
38 K11 **Clarkdale** Arizona, SW USA
13 W4 **Clarke City** Québec, SE Canada
191 Q15 **Clarke Island** *island* Furneaux Group, Tasmania, SE Australia
189 X6 **Clarke Range** ▲ Queensland, E Australia
25 T2 **Clarkesville** Georgia, SE USA
31 S9 **Clarkfield** Minnesota, N USA
35 N7 **Clark Fork** Idaho, NW USA
35 N8 **Clark Fork** ~ Idaho/Montana, NW USA
41 Q12 **Clark, Lake** ◎ Alaska, USA
37 W12 **Clark Mountain** ▲ California, W USA
39 S3 **Clark Peak** ▲ Colorado, C USA
12 D14 **Clark, Point** *headland* Ontario, S Canada
23 S3 **Clarksburg** West Virginia, NE USA
24 K2 **Clarksdale** Mississippi, S USA
35 U12 **Clarks Fork Yellowstone River** ~ Montana/Wyoming, NW USA
25 V3 **Clarks Hall Lake** ◎ Georgia/South Carolina, SE USA
23 P13 **Clarks Hill Lake** *var.* J.Storm Thurmond Reservoir. ⊠ Georgia/South Carolina, SE USA
31 R14 **Clarkson** Nebraska, C USA
41 O13 **Clarks Point** Alaska, USA
20 I13 **Clarks Summit** Pennsylvania, NE USA
34 M10 **Clarkston** Washington, NW USA
46 J12 **Clark's Town** C Jamaica
29 T10 **Clarksville** Arkansas, C USA
33 P13 **Clarksville** Indiana, N USA
22 I8 **Clarksville** Tennessee, S USA
27 W5 **Clarksville** Texas, SW USA
23 U8 **Clarksville** Virginia, NE USA
23 U11 **Clarkton** North Carolina, SE USA
63 C24 **Claromecó** *var.* Balneario Claromecó. Buenos Aires, E Argentina
27 N3 **Claude** Texas, SW USA
Clausentum *see* Southampton
179 P7 **Claveria** Luzon, N Philippines
101 J20 **Clavier** Liège, E Belgium
25 W6 **Claxton** Georgia, SE USA
23 R4 **Clay** West Virginia, NE USA
29 N3 **Clay Center** Kansas, C USA
31 P16 **Clay Center** Nebraska, C USA
23 Y2 **Claymont** Delaware, NE USA
38 M14 **Claypool** Arizona, SW USA
25 R6 **Clayton** Alabama, S USA
25 T1 **Clayton** Georgia, SE USA
24 J5 **Clayton** Louisiana, S USA
29 Q12 **Clayton** Missouri, C USA
39 V9 **Clayton** New Mexico, SW USA
23 V9 **Clayton** North Carolina, SE USA
29 X5 **Clayton** Oklahoma, C USA
190 I4 **Clayton River** *seasonal river* South Australia
23 R7 **Claytor Lake** ⊠ Virginia, NE USA
29 P13 **Clear Boggy Creek** ~ Oklahoma, C USA
99 B22 **Clear, Cape** *var.* The Bill of Cape Clear, *Ir.* Ceann Cléire. *headland* SW Ireland
38 M12 **Clear Creek** ~ Arizona, SW USA
41 S12 **Cleare, Cape** *headland* Montague Island, Alaska, USA
20 E13 **Clearfield** Pennsylvania, NE USA
38 L2 **Clearfield** Utah, W USA
27 Q6 **Clear Fork Brazos River** ~ Texas, SW USA
33 T12 **Clear Fork Reservoir** ⊠ Ohio, N USA
9 N12 **Clear Hills** ▲ Alberta, SW Canada
31 V12 **Clear Lake** Iowa, C USA
31 R9 **Clear Lake** South Dakota, N USA
36 M6 **Clear Lake** ◎ California, W USA
24 G6 **Clear Lake** ⊠ Louisiana, S USA
36 M6 **Clearlake** California, W USA
37 P1 **Clear Lake Reservoir** ⊠ California, W USA
9 N16 **Clearwater** British Columbia, SW Canada
25 U12 **Clearwater** Florida, SE USA
9 R12 **Clearwater** ~ Alberta/Saskatchewan, C Canada
29 W7 **Clearwater Lake** ⊠ Missouri, C USA
35 N10 **Clearwater Mountains** ▲ Idaho, NW USA
35 N10 **Clearwater River** ~ Idaho, NW USA
31 S4 **Clearwater River** ~ Minnesota, N USA
27 T7 **Cleburne** Texas, SW USA
34 I9 **Cle Elum** Washington, NW USA
99 O17 **Cleethorpes** E England, UK
Cléire, Ceann *see* Clear, Cape
23 O11 **Clemson** South Carolina, SE USA
23 Q4 **Clendenin** West Virginia, NE USA
28 M9 **Cleo Springs** Oklahoma, C USA
Clerk Island *see* Onotoa
189 X8 **Clermont** Queensland, E Australia
13 S8 **Clermont** Québec, SE Canada
105 O4 **Clermont** Oise, N France
31 X12 **Clermont** Iowa, C USA
105 P11 **Clermont-Ferrand** Puy-de-Dôme, C France
105 Q15 **Clermont-l'Hérault** Hérault, S France
101 M22 **Clervaux** Diekirch, N Luxembourg
108 G6 **Cles** Trentino-Alto Adige, N Italy
190 H8 **Cleve** South Australia
Cleve *see* Kleve
25 T2 **Cleveland** Georgia, SE USA
24 K3 **Cleveland** Mississippi, S USA
33 T11 **Cleveland** Ohio, N USA
29 O9 **Cleveland** Oklahoma, C USA
22 L10 **Cleveland** Tennessee, S USA
27 W10 **Cleveland** Texas, SW USA
33 N7 **Cleveland** Wisconsin, N USA
33 O4 **Cleveland Cliffs Basin** ◎ Michigan, N USA
33 U11 **Cleveland Heights** Ohio, N USA
35 P6 **Cleveland, Mount** ▲ Montana, NW USA
Cleves *see* Kleve
99 B16 **Clew Bay** *Ir.* Cuan Mó. *inlet* W Ireland
25 Y14 **Clewiston** Florida, SE USA
Cliara *see* Clare Island
99 A17 **Clifden** *Ir.* An Clochán. W Ireland
39 O14 **Clifton** Arizona, SW USA
20 K14 **Clifton** New Jersey, NE USA
27 S8 **Clifton** Texas, SW USA
23 S6 **Clifton Forge** Virginia, NE USA
190 I1 **Clifton Hills** South Australia
9 S17 **Climax** Saskatchewan, S Canada
23 O8 **Clinch River** ~ Tennessee/Virginia, S USA
27 P12 **Cline** Texas, SW USA
23 N10 **Clingmans Dome** ▲ North Carolina/Tennessee, SE USA
26 H8 **Clint** Texas, SW USA
8 M16 **Clinton** British Columbia, SW Canada
12 E15 **Clinton** Ontario, S Canada
29 U10 **Clinton** Arkansas, C USA
32 L10 **Clinton** Illinois, N USA
31 Z14 **Clinton** Iowa, C USA
22 G7 **Clinton** Kentucky, S USA
24 I8 **Clinton** Louisiana, S USA
21 N11 **Clinton** Massachusetts, NE USA
33 R10 **Clinton** Michigan, N USA
24 K5 **Clinton** Mississippi, S USA
29 S5 **Clinton** Missouri, C USA
23 V10 **Clinton** North Carolina, SE USA
28 L10 **Clinton** Oklahoma, C USA
23 Q12 **Clinton** South Carolina, SE USA
22 M9 **Clinton** Tennessee, S USA
15 J7 **Clinton-Colden Lake** ◎ Northwest Territories, NW Canada
8 H5 **Clinton Creek** Yukon Territory, NW Canada
32 L13 **Clinton Lake** ⊠ Illinois, N USA
29 Q4 **Clinton Lake** ⊠ Kansas, N USA
23 T11 **Clio** South Carolina, SE USA
199 L17 **Clipperton Fracture Zone** *tectonic feature* E Pacific Ocean
200 N7 **Clipperton Island** ◇ *French dependency of French Polynesia* E Pacific Ocean
48 K6 **Clipperton Island** *island* E Pacific Ocean
1 F16 **Clipperton Seamounts** *undersea feature* E Pacific Ocean
104 J8 **Clisson** Loire-Atlantique, NW France
64 K7 **Clodomira** Santiago del Estero, N Argentina
Cloich na Coillte *see* Clonakilty
Clóirtheach *see* Clara
99 C21 **Clonakilty** *Ir.* Cloich na Coillte. SW Ireland
189 T6 **Cloncurry** Queensland, C Australia
99 F18 **Clondalkin** *Ir.* Cluain Dolcáin. E Ireland
99 E16 **Clones** *Ir.* Cluain Eois. N Ireland
99 D20 **Clonmel** *Ir.* Cluain Meala. S Ireland
102 G11 **Cloppenburg** Niedersachsen, NW Germany
31 W6 **Cloquet** Minnesota, N USA
39 S14 **Cloudcroft** New Mexico, SW USA
35 W12 **Cloud Peak** ▲ Wyoming, C USA
193 K14 **Cloudy Bay** *inlet* S outh Island, NZ
23 R10 **Clover** South Carolina, SE USA
36 M6 **Cloverdale** California, W USA
22 J5 **Cloverport** Kentucky, S USA
37 Q10 **Clovis** California, W USA
39 W12 **Clovis** New Mexico, SW USA
12 K13 **Cloyne** Ontario, SE Canada
Cluain Dolcáin *see* Clondalkin
Cluain Eois *see* Clones
Cluainín *see* Manorhamilton
Cluain Meala *see* Clonmel
118 H10 **Cluj** ◆ *county* NW Romania
Cluj *see* Cluj-Napoca
118 H10 **Cluj-Napoca** *Ger.* Klausenburg, *Hung.* Kolozsvár; *prev.* Cluj. Cluj, NW Romania
Clunia *see* Feldkirch
105 R10 **Cluny** Saône-et-Loire, C France
105 T10 **Cluses** Haute-Savoie, E France
108 E7 **Clusone** Lombardia, N Italy
27 W12 **Clute** Texas, SW USA
193 D23 **Clutha** ~ South Island, NZ
99 J18 **Clwyd** *cultural region* NE Wales, UK
193 D22 **Clyde** Otago, South Island, NZ
29 N3 **Clyde** Kansas, C USA
31 P2 **Clyde** North Dakota, N USA
33 S11 **Clyde** Ohio, N USA
27 Q7 **Clyde** Texas, SW USA
12 K13 **Clyde** ~ Ontario, SE Canada
98 J13 **Clyde** ~ W Scotland, UK
98 H12 **Clydebank** S Scotland, UK
98 H13 **Clyde, Firth of** *inlet* S Scotland, UK
35 S11 **Clyde Park** Montana, NW USA
106 I7 **Côa** ~ N Portugal
37 W16 **Coachella** California, W USA
37 W16 **Coachella Canal** *canal* California, W USA
42 I9 **Coacoyole** Durango, C Mexico
27 N7 **Coahoma** Texas, SW USA
8 K8 **Coal** ~ Yukon Territory, NW Canada
42 L14 **Coalcomán** *var.* Coalcomán de Matamoros. Michoacán de Ocampo, S Mexico
Coalcomán de Matamoros *see* Coalcomán
41 T8 **Coal Creek** Alaska, USA
9 Q17 **Coaldale** Alberta, SW Canada
29 P12 **Coalgate** Oklahoma, C USA
37 P11 **Coalinga** California, W USA
8 L9 **Coal River** British Columbia, W Canada
23 Q6 **Coal River** ~ West Virginia, NE USA
38 M2 **Coalville** Utah, W USA
60 E13 **Coari** Amazonas, N Brazil
61 D14 **Coari, Rio** ~ NW Brazil
83 J20 **Coast** ◆ *province* SE Kenya
Coast *see* Pwani
14 F11 **Coast Mountains** *Fr.* Chaîne Côtière. ▲ Canada/USA
17 F13 **Coast Ranges** ▲ W USA
98 I12 **Coatbridge** S Scotland, UK
44 B6 **Coatepeque** Quezaltenango, SW Guatemala
20 H16 **Coatesville** Pennsylvania, NE USA
13 Q13 **Coaticook** Québec, SE Canada
15 Mm6 **Coats Island** *island* Northwest Territories, NE Canada
205 O4 **Coats Land** *physical region* Antarctica
43 T14 **Coatzacoalcos** *var.* Quetzalcoalco; *prev.* Puerto México. Veracruz-Llave, E Mexico
43 S14 **Coatzacoalcos, Río** ~ SE Mexico
118 M15 **Cobadin** Constanţa, SW Romania
12 H9 **Cobalt** Ontario, S Canada
44 D5 **Cobán** Alta Verapaz, C Guatemala
191 O6 **Cobar** New South Wales, SE Australia
20 F12 **Cobb Hill** ▲ Pennsylvania, NE USA
1 D8 **Cobb Seamount** *undersea feature* E Pacific Ocean
12 K12 **Cobden** Ontario, SE Canada
99 D21 **Cobh** *Ir.* An Cóbh; *prev.* Cove of Cork, Queenstown. SW Ireland
59 J14 **Cobija** Pando, NW Bolivia
Coblence/Coblenz *see* Koblenz
20 J10 **Cobleskill** New York, NE USA
12 I15 **Cobourg** Ontario, SE Canada
189 P1 **Cobourg Peninsula** *headland* Northern Territory, N Australia
191 O10 **Cobram** Victoria, SE Australia
84 N13 **Cóbuè** Niassa, N Mozambique
103 K18 **Coburg** Bayern, SE Germany
21 Q5 **Coburn Mountain** ▲ Maine, NE USA

◆ Country ● Country Capital ◇ Dependent Territory ○ Dependent Territory Capital ◆ Administrative Region × International Airport ▲ Mountain ▲ Mountain Range Volcano ~ River ◎ Lake ⊠ Reservoir

Coca see Puerto Francisco de Orellana
59 H18 **Cocachacra** Arequipa, SW Peru
61 J17 **Cocalinho** Mato Grosso, W Brazil
Cocanada see Kākināda
107 S11 **Cocentaina** País Valenciano, E Spain
59 L18 **Cochabamba** hist. Oropeza. Cochabamba, C Bolivia
59 K18 **Cochabamba** ◆ department C Bolivia
59 L18 **Cochabamba, Cordillera de** ▲ C Bolivia
103 E18 **Cochem** Rheinland-Pfalz, W Germany
39 R6 **Cochetopa Hills** ▲ Colorado, C USA
161 G22 **Cochin** var. Kochi. Kerala, SW India
46 D5 **Cochinos, Bahía de** Eng. Bay of Pigs. bay SE Cuba
39 O16 **Cochise Head** ▲ Arizona, SW USA
25 U5 **Cochran** Georgia, SE USA
9 P16 **Cochrane** Alberta, SW Canada
10 G12 **Cochrane** Ontario, S Canada
65 G20 **Cochrane** Aisén, S Chile
9 U10 **Cochrane** ≈ Manitoba/Saskatchewan, C Canada
Cochrane, Lago see Pueyrredón, Lago
Cocibolca see Nicaragua, Lago de
Cockade State see Maryland
46 M6 **Cockburn Harbour** South Caicos, S Turks and Caicos Islands
12 C11 **Cockburn Island** island Ontario, S Canada
46 J3 **Cockburn Town** San Salvador, E Bahamas
23 X2 **Cockeysville** Maryland, NE USA
189 N12 **Cocklebiddy** Western Australia
46 I12 **Cockpit Country, The** physical region W Jamaica
45 S16 **Coclé** off. Provincia de Coclé. ◆ province C Panama
45 S15 **Coclé del Norte** Colón, C Panama
25 Y12 **Cocoa** Florida, SE USA
25 Y12 **Cocoa Beach** Florida, SE USA
81 D17 **Cocobeach** Estuaire, NW Gabon
46 G5 **Coco, Cayo** island C Cuba
157 Q19 **Coco Channel** strait Andaman Sea/Bay of Bengal
181 N6 **Coco-de-Mer Seamounts** undersea feature W Indian Ocean
38 K10 **Coconino Plateau** plain Arizona, SW USA
45 N6 **Coco, Río** var. Río Wanki, Segoviao Wangkí. ≈ Honduras/Nicaragua
181 T8 **Cocos (Keeling) Islands** ◇ Australian external territory E Indian Ocean
181 T7 **Cocos Basin** undersea feature E Indian Ocean
196 B17 **Cocos Island** island S Guam
Cocos Island Ridge see Cocos Ridge
133 S17 **Cocos Islands** island group E Indian Ocean
1 G15 **Cocos Plate** tectonic feature
200 Oo8 **Cocos Ridge** var. Cocos Island Ridge. undersea feature E Pacific Ocean
42 K13 **Cocula** Jalisco, SW Mexico
109 D17 **Coda Cavallo, Capo** headland Sardegna, Italy, C Mediterranean Sea
60 E13 **Codajás** Amazonas, N Brazil
Codazzi see Agustín Codazzi
21 Q12 **Cod, Cape** headland Massachusetts, NE USA
193 B25 **Codfish Island** island SW NZ
108 H9 **Codigoro** Emilia-Romagna, N Italy
11 P5 **Cod Island** island Newfoundland and Labrador, E Canada
118 J12 **Codlea** Ger. Zeiden, Hung. Feketehalom. Braşov, C Romania
60 M13 **Codó** Maranhão, E Brazil
108 E8 **Codogno** Lombardia, N Italy
118 M10 **Codrii** hill range C Moldova
47 W9 **Codrington** Barbuda, Antigua and Barbuda
108 J7 **Codroipo** Friuli-Venezia Giulia, NE Italy
30 M12 **Cody** Nebraska, C USA
35 U12 **Cody** Wyoming, C USA
23 P7 **Coeburn** Virginia, NE USA
56 E10 **Coello** Tolima, W Colombia
Coemba see Cuemba
189 V2 **Coen** Queensland, NE Australia
103 E14 **Coesfeld** Nordrhein-Westfalen, W Germany
34 M8 **Coeur d'Alene** Idaho, NW USA
34 M8 **Coeur d'Alene Lake** ⊠ Idaho, NW USA
100 O8 **Coevorden** Drenthe, NE Netherlands
8 H6 **Coffee Creek** Yukon Territory, W Canada
32 L15 **Coffeen Lake** ⊠ Illinois, N USA
24 L3 **Coffeeville** Mississippi, S USA
29 Q8 **Coffeyville** Kansas, C USA
190 G9 **Coffin Bay** South Australia
190 F9 **Coffin Bay Peninsula** peninsula South Australia
191 V5 **Coffs Harbour** New South Wales, SE Australia
107 R10 **Cofrentes** País Valenciano, E Spain
Cogîlnic see Kohyl'nyk
104 K11 **Cognac** anc. Compniacum. Charente, W France
108 B7 **Cogne** Valle d'Aosta, NW Italy
105 U16 **Cogolin** Var, SE France
107 O7 **Cogolludo** Castilla-La Mancha, C Spain
Cohalm see Rupea
20 F11 **Cohocton River** ≈ New York, NE USA
20 L10 **Cohoes** New York, NE USA
191 N10 **Cohuna** Victoria, SE Australia
45 P17 **Coiba, Isla de** island SW Panama
65 H23 **Coig, Río** ≈ S Argentina
65 G19 **Coihaique** var. Coyhaique. Aisén, S Chile
161 G21 **Coimbatore** Tamil Nādu, S India
106 G8 **Coimbra** anc. Conimbria, Conimbriga. Coimbra, W Portugal
106 G8 **Coimbra** ◆ district N Portugal
106 L15 **Coín** Andalucía, S Spain
59 J20 **Coipasa, Laguna** ◎ W Bolivia
59 J20 **Coipasa, Salar de** salt lake W Bolivia
Coira/Coire see Chur
Coirib, Loch see Corrib, Lough
56 K6 **Cojedes** off. Estado Cojedes. ◆ state N Venezuela
44 F7 **Cojutepeque** Cuscatlán, C El Salvador
35 S16 **Cokeville** Wyoming, C USA
190 M13 **Colac** Victoria, SE Australia
61 O20 **Colatina** Espírito Santo, SE Brazil
29 O13 **Colbert** Oklahoma, C USA
102 L12 **Colbitz-Letzinger Heide** heathland N Germany
28 I3 **Colby** Kansas, C USA
59 H17 **Colca, Río** ≈ SW Peru
99 P21 **Colchester** hist. Colneceaste, anc. Camulodunum. E England, UK
21 N13 **Colchester** Connecticut, NE USA
40 M16 **Cold Bay** Alaska, USA
9 R14 **Cold Lake** Alberta, SW Canada
9 R13 **Cold Lake** ◎ Alberta/Saskatchewan, S Canada
31 U8 **Cold Spring** Minnesota, N USA
27 W10 **Coldspring** Texas, SW USA
9 N17 **Coldstream** British Columbia, SW Canada
98 L13 **Coldstream** SE Scotland, UK
12 H13 **Coldwater** Ontario, S Canada
28 K7 **Coldwater** Kansas, C USA
33 Q10 **Coldwater** Michigan, N USA
27 N1 **Coldwater Creek** ≈ Oklahoma/Texas, SW USA
24 K2 **Coldwater River** ≈ Mississippi, S USA
191 O9 **Coleambally** New South Wales, SE Australia
21 O6 **Colebrook** New Hampshire, NE USA
29 T5 **Cole Camp** Missouri, C USA
41 T6 **Coleen River** ≈ Alaska, USA
9 P17 **Coleman** Alberta, SW Canada
27 Q8 **Coleman** Texas, SW USA
Çölemerik see Hakkâri
85 K22 **Colenso** KwaZulu/Natal, E South Africa
190 L12 **Coleraine** Victoria, SE Australia
99 F14 **Coleraine** Ir. Cúil Raithin. N Northern Ireland, UK
193 G18 **Coleridge, Lake** ◎ South Island, NZ
85 H24 **Colesberg** Northern Cape, C South Africa
24 H7 **Colfax** Louisiana, S USA
34 L9 **Colfax** Washington, NW USA
32 J6 **Colfax** Wisconsin, N USA
65 I19 **Colhué Huapí, Lago** ◎ S Argentina
47 Z6 **Colibris, Pointe des** headland Grande Terre, E Guadeloupe
108 D6 **Colico** Lombardia, N Italy
101 E14 **Colijnsplaat** Zeeland, SW Netherlands
42 L14 **Colima** Colima, S Mexico
42 K14 **Colima** ◆ state SW Mexico
42 L14 **Colima, Nevado de** ▲ C Mexico
61 M14 **Colinas** Maranhão, E Brazil
98 F10 **Coll** island W Scotland, UK
107 N7 **Collado Villalba** var. Villalba. Madrid, C Spain
191 R4 **Collarenebri** New South Wales, SE Australia
39 P5 **Collbran** Colorado, C USA
108 G12 **Colle di Val d'Elsa** Toscana, C Italy
41 R9 **College** Alaska, USA
34 K10 **College Place** Washington, NW USA
27 U10 **College Station** Texas, SW USA
191 P4 **Collerina** New South Wales, SE Australia
188 I13 **Collie** Western Australia
188 L4 **Collier Bay** bay Western Australia
22 F10 **Collierville** Tennessee, S USA
108 F11 **Collina, Passo della** pass C Italy
12 G14 **Collingwood** Ontario, S Canada
192 I13 **Collingwood** Tasman, South Island, NZ
194 M15 **Collingwood Bay** bay SE PNG
24 L7 **Collins** Mississippi, S USA
32 K15 **Collinsville** Illinois, N USA
29 P9 **Collinsville** Oklahoma, C USA
22 H10 **Collinwood** Tennessee, S USA
Collipo see Leiria
65 G14 **Collipulli** Araucanía, C Chile
99 D16 **Collooney** Ir. Cúil Mhuine. NW Ireland
31 R10 **Colman** South Dakota, N USA
105 U6 **Colmar** Ger. Kolmar. Haut-Rhin, NE France
106 M15 **Colmenar** Andalucía, S Spain
Colmenar see Colmenar de Oreja
107 O9 **Colmenar de Oreja** var. Colmenar. Madrid, C Spain
107 N7 **Colmenar Viejo** Madrid, C Spain
27 X9 **Colmesneil** Texas, SW USA
Cöln see Köln
Colneceaste see Colchester
42 C3 **Colnett** Baja California, NW Mexico
61 G15 **Colniza** Mato Grosso, W Brazil
Cologne see Köln
44 B6 **Colomba** Quezaltenango, SW Guatemala
Colomb-Béchar see Béchar
56 E11 **Colombia** Huila, C Colombia
56 G10 **Colombia** off. Republic of Colombia. ◆ republic N South America
66 E12 **Colombian Basin** undersea feature SW Caribbean Sea
Colombie-Britannique see British Columbia
13 T6 **Colombier** Québec, SE Canada
161 J25 **Colombo** ● (Sri Lanka) Western Province, W Sri Lanka
161 J25 **Colombo** ✕ Western Province, SW Sri Lanka
31 N11 **Colome** South Dakota, N USA
63 D18 **Colon** Entre Ríos, E Argentina
63 B19 **Colón** Buenos Aires, E Argentina
46 D5 **Colón** Matanzas, C Cuba
45 T14 **Colón** prev. Aspinwall. Colón, C Panama
44 K5 **Colón** ◆ department NE Honduras
45 S15 **Colón** off. Provincia de Colón. ◆ province N Panama
59 A16 **Colón, Archipiélago de** var. Islas de los Galápagos, Eng. Galapagos Islands, Tortoise Islands. island group Ecuador, E Pacific Ocean
46 K5 **Colonel Hill** Crooked Island, SE Bahamas
42 B3 **Colonet, Cabo** headland NW Mexico
196 G14 **Colonia** Yap, W Micronesia
63 D19 **Colonia** ◆ department SW Uruguay
Colonia see Kolonia, Micronesia
Colonia see Colonia del Sacramento, Uruguay
Colonia Agrippina see Köln
63 D20 **Colonia del Sacramento** var. Colonia. Colonia, SW Uruguay
64 L8 **Colonia Dora** Santiago del Estero, N Argentina
Colonia Julia Fanestris see Fano
23 W5 **Colonial Beach** Virginia, NE USA
23 V6 **Colonial Heights** Virginia, NE USA
200 Oo8 **Colón Ridge** undersea feature E Pacific Ocean
98 F12 **Colonsay** island W Scotland, UK
59 K22 **Colorada, Laguna** ◎ SW Bolivia
39 R6 **Colorado** off. State of Colorado; also known as Centennial State, Silver State. ◆ state C USA
65 H22 **Colorado, Cerro** ▲ S Argentina
27 O7 **Colorado City** Texas, SW USA
38 M7 **Colorado Plateau** plateau W USA
63 A24 **Colorado, Río** ≈ E Argentina
45 N12 **Colorado, Río** ≈ NE Costa Rica
Colorado, Río see Colorado River
18 Hh10 **Colorado River** var. Río Colorado. ≈ Mexico/USA
18 Ll15 **Colorado River** ≈ Texas, SW USA
37 W15 **Colorado River Aqueduct** aqueduct California, W USA
46 A4 **Colorados, Archipiélago de los** island group NW Cuba
64 J9 **Colorados, Desagües de los** ◎ W Argentina
39 T5 **Colorado Springs** Colorado, C USA
42 L11 **Colotlán** Jalisco, SW Mexico
59 L19 **Colquechaca** Potosí, C Bolivia
25 S7 **Colquitt** Georgia, SE USA
31 R11 **Colton** South Dakota, N USA
34 M10 **Colton** Washington, NW USA
37 P8 **Columbia** California, W USA
32 K16 **Columbia** Illinois, N USA
22 L7 **Columbia** Kentucky, S USA
24 J6 **Columbia** Louisiana, S USA
23 W3 **Columbia** Maryland, NE USA
24 L7 **Columbia** Mississippi, S USA
29 U4 **Columbia** Missouri, C USA
23 Y9 **Columbia** North Carolina, SE USA
20 G16 **Columbia** Pennsylvania, NE USA
23 Q12 **Columbia** state capital South Carolina, SE USA
22 I9 **Columbia** Tennessee, S USA
1 F9 **Columbia** ≈ Canada/USA
34 K9 **Columbia Basin** basin Washington, NW USA
207 Q10 **Columbia, Cape** headland Ellesmere Island, Northwest Territories, NE Canada
33 Q12 **Columbia City** Indiana, N USA
23 W3 **Columbia, District of** ◆ federal district NE USA
35 P7 **Columbia Falls** Montana, NW USA
9 O15 **Columbia Icefield** icefield Alberta/British Columbia, S Canada
9 O15 **Columbia, Mount** ▲ Alberta/British Columbia, SW Canada
9 N15 **Columbia Mountains** ▲ British Columbia, SW Canada
25 P4 **Columbiana** Alabama, S USA
33 V12 **Columbiana** Ohio, N USA
34 M14 **Columbia Plateau** plateau Idaho/Oregon, NW USA
31 P7 **Columbia Road Reservoir** ⊠ South Dakota, N USA
67 K16 **Columbia Seamount** undersea feature C Atlantic Ocean
85 D25 **Columbine, Cape** headland SW South Africa
107 U9 **Columbretes, Islas** island group E Spain
25 R5 **Columbus** Georgia, SE USA
33 P14 **Columbus** Indiana, N USA
29 R7 **Columbus** Kansas, C USA
25 N4 **Columbus** Mississippi, S USA
35 U11 **Columbus** Montana, NW USA
31 Q15 **Columbus** Nebraska, C USA
39 Q16 **Columbus** New Mexico, SW USA
23 P10 **Columbus** North Carolina, SE USA
30 K2 **Columbus** North Dakota, N USA
33 S13 **Columbus** state capital Ohio, N USA
27 U11 **Columbus** Texas, SW USA
32 L8 **Columbus** Wisconsin, N USA
33 R12 **Columbus Grove** Ohio, N USA
31 Y15 **Columbus Junction** Iowa, C USA
46 J3 **Columbus Point** headland Cat Island, C Bahamas
37 T8 **Columbus Salt Marsh** salt marsh Nevada, W USA
37 N6 **Colusa** California, W USA
34 L7 **Colville** Washington, NW USA
192 M5 **Colville, Cape** headland North Island, NZ
192 M5 **Colville Channel** channel North Island, NZ
41 P6 **Colville River** ≈ Alaska, USA
99 J18 **Colwyn Bay** N Wales, UK
108 H9 **Comacchio** var. Commachio; anc. Comactium. Emilia-Romagna, N Italy
108 H9 **Comacchio, Valli di** lagoon Adriatic Sea, N Mediterranean Sea
Comactium see Comacchio
43 V17 **Comalapa** Chiapas, SE Mexico
43 U15 **Comalcalco** Tabasco, SE Mexico
65 H16 **Comallo** Río Negro, SW Argentina
28 M12 **Comanche** Oklahoma, C USA
27 R8 **Comanche** Texas, SW USA
204 H2 **Comandante Ferraz** Brazilian research station Antarctica
64 N6 **Comandante Fontana** Formosa, N Argentina
65 I22 **Comandante Luis Peidra Buena** Santa Cruz, S Argentina
61 O18 **Comandatuba** Bahia, SE Brazil
118 K11 **Comănești** Hung. Kománfalva. Bacău, SW Romania
59 M19 **Comarapa** Santa Cruz, C Bolivia
118 J13 **Comarnic** Prahova, SE Romania
44 H6 **Comayagua** Comayagua, W Honduras
44 H6 **Comayagua** ◆ department W Honduras
44 I6 **Comayagua, Montañas de** ▲ C Honduras
23 R15 **Combahee River** ≈ South Carolina, SE USA
64 G10 **Combarbalá** Coquimbo, C Chile
105 S7 **Combeaufontaine** Haute-Saône, E France
99 G15 **Comber** Ir. An Comar. E Northern Ireland, UK
101 K20 **Comblain-au-Pont** Liège, E Belgium
104 I6 **Combourg** Ille-et-Vilaine, NW France
46 M9 **Comendador** prev. Elías Piña. W Dominican Republic
Comer See see Como, Lago di
27 R11 **Comfort** Texas, SW USA
159 V15 **Comilla** Ben. Kumillā. Chittagong, E Bangladesh
101 B18 **Comines** Hainaut, W Belgium
123 J16 **Comino** Malt. Kemmuna. island C Malta
109 D18 **Comino, Capo** headland Sardegna, Italy, C Mediterranean Sea
109 K25 **Comiso** Sicilia, Italy, C Mediterranean Sea
43 V16 **Comitán** var. Comitán de Domínguez. Chiapas, SE Mexico
Comitán de Domínguez see Comitán
Commachio see Comacchio
Commander Islands see Komandorskiye Ostrova
105 O10 **Commentry** Allier, C France
25 T2 **Commerce** Georgia, SE USA
29 R8 **Commerce** Oklahoma, C USA
27 V5 **Commerce** Texas, SW USA
39 T4 **Commerce City** Colorado, C USA
105 S5 **Commercy** Meuse, NE France
57 W9 **Commewijne** var. Commewyne. ◆ district NE Suriname
Commewyne see Commewijne
13 P8 **Commissaires, Lac des** ◎ Québec, SE Canada
66 A12 **Commissioner's Point** headland W Bermuda
15 L13 **Committee Bay** bay Northwest Territories, N Canada
108 D7 **Como** anc. Comum. Lombardia, N Italy
65 J19 **Comodoro Rivadavia** Chubut, SE Argentina
108 D6 **Como, Lago di** var. Lario, Eng. Lake Como, Ger. Comer See. ◎ N Italy
Como, Lake see Como, Lago di
42 E7 **Comondú** Baja California Sur, W Mexico
118 F12 **Comorâște** Hung. Komornok. Caraș-Severin, SW Romania
Comores, République Fédérale Islamique des see Comoros
161 G24 **Comorin, Cape** headland SE India
180 M8 **Comoro Basin** undersea feature SW Indian Ocean
70 K14 **Comoro Islands** island group W Indian Ocean
180 H13 **Comoros** off. Federal Islamic Republic of the Comoros, Fr. République Fédérale Islamique des Comores. ◆ republic W Indian Ocean
8 L17 **Comox** Vancouver Island, British Columbia, SW Canada
105 O4 **Compiègne** Oise, N France
Complutum see Alcalá de Henares
Compniacum see Cognac
42 K12 **Compostela** Nayarit, C Mexico
Compostella see Santiago
62 L11 **Comprida, Ilha** island S Brazil
119 N11 **Comrat** Rus. Komrat. S Moldova
27 O11 **Comstock** Texas, SW USA
33 P9 **Comstock Park** Michigan, N USA
199 Kk3 **Comstock Seamount** undersea feature N Pacific Ocean
Comum see Como
165 N17 **Cona** Xizang Zizhiqu, W China
78 H14 **Conakry** ● (Guinea) Conakry, SW Guinea
78 H14 **Conakry** ✕ Conakry, SW Guinea
Conamara see Connemara
Conca see Cuenca
27 Q12 **Concan** Texas, SW USA
104 F6 **Concarneau** Finistère, NW France
85 O17 **Conceição** Sofala, C Mozambique
61 K15 **Conceição do Araguaia** Pará, NE Brazil
60 F10 **Conceição do Maú** Roraima, W Brazil
63 D14 **Concepción** var. Concepcion. Corrientes, NE Argentina
64 J8 **Concepción** Tucumán, N Argentina
59 O17 **Concepción** Santa Cruz, E Bolivia
64 G13 **Concepción** Bío Bío, C Chile
56 E14 **Concepción** Putumayo, S Colombia
64 O5 **Concepción** var. Villa Concepción. Concepción, C Paraguay
64 O5 **Concepción** off. Departamento de Concepción. ◆ department E Paraguay
Concepción see La Concepción
Concepción de la Vega see La Vega
43 N9 **Concepción del Oro** Zacatecas, C Mexico
63 D18 **Concepción del Uruguay** Entre Ríos, E Argentina
44 K11 **Concepción, Volcán** ▲ SW Nicaragua
46 J4 **Conception Island** island C Bahamas
37 P14 **Conception, Point** headland California, W USA
56 H6 **Concha** Zulia, W Venezuela
62 L9 **Conchas** São Paulo, S Brazil
39 U11 **Conchas Dam** New Mexico, SW USA
39 U10 **Conchas Lake** ⊠ New Mexico, SW USA
104 M5 **Conches-en-Ouche** Eure, N France
39 N12 **Concho** Arizona, SW USA
42 J5 **Conchos, Río** ≈ NW Mexico
43 O8 **Conchos, Río** ≈ C Mexico
110 C8 **Concise** Vaud, W Switzerland
37 N8 **Concord** California, W USA
21 O9 **Concord** state capital New Hampshire, NE USA
23 R10 **Concord** North Carolina, SE USA
63 D17 **Concordia** Entre Ríos, E Argentina
56 D9 **Concordia** Antioquia, W Colombia
42 J10 **Concordia** Sinaloa, C Mexico
59 I19 **Concordia** Tacna, SW Peru
29 S4 **Concordia** Kansas, C USA
29 N3 **Concordia** Missouri, C USA
62 I13 **Concórdia** Santa Catarina, S Brazil
178 J7 **Con Cuông** Nghê An, N Vietnam
178 Jj16 **Côn Đao** var. Con Son. island S Vietnam
Condate see Rennes, Ille-et-Vilaine, France
Condate see St-Claude, Jura, France
Condate see Montereau-Faut-Yonne, Seine-St-Denis, France
31 P8 **Conde** South Dakota, N USA
44 J8 **Condega** Estelí, NW Nicaragua
105 P2 **Condé-sur-l'Escaut** Nord, N France
104 K5 **Condé-sur-Noireau** Calvados, N France
Condivincum see Nantes
191 P8 **Condobolin** New South Wales, SE Australia
104 L15 **Condom** Gers, S France
34 J11 **Condon** Oregon, NW USA
56 D9 **Condoto** Chocó, W Colombia
25 P7 **Conecuh River** ≈ Alabama/Florida, SE USA
108 H7 **Conegliano** Veneto, NE Italy
63 C19 **Conesa** Buenos Aires, E Argentina
12 F15 **Conestogo** ≈ Ontario, S Canada
195 O17 **Conflict Group** island group SE PNG
Confluentes see Koblenz
104 L10 **Confolens** Charente, W France
38 J4 **Confusion Range** ▲ Utah, W USA
64 N6 **Confuso, Río** ≈ C Paraguay
23 R12 **Congaree River** ≈ South Carolina, SE USA
Công Hoa Xa Hôi Chu Nghia Viêt Nam see Vietnam
166 K12 **Congjiang** prev. Bingmei. Guizhou, S China
81 G18 **Congo** off. Republic of the Congo, Fr. Moyen-Congo; prev. Middle Congo. ◆ republic C Africa
69 T11 **Congo** var. Kongo, Fr. Zaire. ≈ C Africa
Congo/Congo (Dem. Rep.)/Congo (Kinshasa) see Zaire
70 G12 **Congo Basin** drainage basin W Zaire
69 Q11 **Congo Canyon** var. Congo Seavalley, Congo Submarine Canyon. undersea feature E Atlantic Ocean
Congo Cone see Congo Fan
67 P15 **Congo Fan** var. Congo Cone. undersea feature E Atlantic Ocean
Coni see Cuneo
65 H18 **Cónico, Cerro** ▲ SW Argentina
Conimbria/Conimbriga see Coimbra
Conjeeveram see Kānchīpuram
9 R13 **Conklin** Alberta, C Canada
26 M1 **Conlen** Texas, SW USA
Con, Loch see Conn, Lough
Connacht see Connaught
99 B17 **Connaught** var. Connacht, Ir. Chonnacht, Cúige. cultural region W Ireland
33 V10 **Conneaut** Ohio, N USA
20 L13 **Connecticut** off. State of Connecticut; also known as Blue Law State, Constitution State, Land of Steady Habits, Nutmeg State. ◆ state NE USA
21 N8 **Connecticut** ≈ Canada/USA
21 O6 **Connecticut Lakes** lakes New Hampshire, NE USA
34 K9 **Connell** Washington, NW USA
99 B17 **Connemara** Ir. Conamara. physical region W Ireland
33 Q14 **Connersville** Indiana, N USA
99 B16 **Conn, Lough** Ir. Loch Con. ◎ W Ireland
37 X6 **Connors Pass** pass Nevada, W USA
189 X7 **Connors Range** ▲ Queensland, E Australia
58 E7 **Cononaco, Río** ≈ E Ecuador
31 W13 **Conrad** Iowa, C USA
35 R7 **Conrad** Montana, NW USA
27 W10 **Conroe** Texas, SW USA
27 V10 **Conroe, Lake** ⊠ Texas, SW USA
63 C17 **Conscripto Bernardi** Entre Ríos, E Argentina
61 M20 **Conselheiro Lafaiete** Minas Gerais, SE Brazil
Consentia see Cosenza
99 L14 **Consett** N England, UK
46 B5 **Consolación del Sur** Pinar del Río, W Cuba
Con Son see Côn Đao
9 R15 **Consort** Alberta, SW Canada
Constance see Konstanz
110 I6 **Constance, Lake** Ger. Bodensee. ◎ C Europe
106 G9 **Constância** Santarém, C Portugal
119 N14 **Constanța** var. Küstendje, Eng. Constanza, Ger. Konstanza, Turk. Küstence. Constanța, SE Romania
118 L14 **Constanța** ◆ county SE Romania
Constantia see Coutances, France
Constantia see Konstanz, Germany
106 K13 **Constantina** Andalucía, S Spain
76 L5 **Constantine** var. Qacentina, Ar. Qoussantîna. NE Algeria
41 O14 **Constantine, Cape** headland Alaska, USA
Constantinople see İstanbul
Constantiola see Oltenişa
Constanz see Konstanz
Constanza see Constanța
64 G13 **Constitución** Maule, C Chile
63 D17 **Constitución** Salto, N Uruguay
Constitution State see Connecticut
107 N10 **Consuegra** Castilla-La Mancha, C Spain
189 X9 **Consuelo Peak** ▲ Queensland, E Australia
58 E11 **Contamana** Loreto, N Peru
Contrasto, Colle del see Contrasto, Portella del
109 K23 **Contrasto, Portella del** var. Colle del Contrasto. pass Sicilia, Italy, C Mediterranean Sea
56 G8 **Contratación** Santander, C Colombia
104 M8 **Contres** Loir-et-Cher, C France
109 O17 **Conversano** Puglia, SE Italy
29 U11 **Conway** Arkansas, C USA
21 O8 **Conway** New Hampshire, NE USA
23 U13 **Conway** South Carolina, SE USA
27 N2 **Conway** Texas, SW USA
29 U11 **Conway, Lake** ⊠ Arkansas, C USA
29 N7 **Conway Springs** Kansas, C USA
99 J18 **Conwy** N Wales, UK
25 T3 **Conyers** Georgia, SE USA
Coo see Kos
190 F4 **Coober Pedy** South Australia
189 P2 **Cooinda** Northern Territory, N Australia
190 B6 **Cook** South Australia
31 W4 **Cook** Minnesota, N USA
203 N6 **Cook, Baie de** bay Moorea, W French Polynesia
8 J16 **Cook, Cape** headland Vancouver Island, British Columbia, SW Canada
39 Q15 **Cookes Peak** ▲ New Mexico, SW USA
22 L8 **Cookeville** Tennessee, S USA
183 P9 **Cook Fracture Zone** tectonic feature S Pacific Ocean
Cook, Grand Récif de see Cook, Récif de
41 Q12 **Cook Inlet** inlet Alaska, USA
203 X2 **Cook Island** island Line Islands, E Kiribati
202 J14 **Cook Islands** ◇ territory in free association with NZ S Pacific Ocean
193 E19 **Cook, Mount** prev. Aoraki, Aorangi. ▲ South Island, NZ
197 G4 **Cook, Récif de** var. Grand Récif de Cook. reef S New Caledonia
12 G14 **Cookstown** Ontario, S Canada
99 F15 **Cookstown** Ir. An Chorr Chríochach. C Northern Ireland, UK
193 K14 **Cook Strait** var. Raukawa. strait NZ
189 W3 **Cooktown** Queensland, NE Australia
191 P6 **Coolabah** New South Wales, SE Australia
190 J11 **Coola Coola Swamp** wetland South Australia
191 S7 **Coolah** New South Wales, SE Australia
191 P9 **Coolamon** New South Wales, SE Australia
191 T4 **Coolatai** New South Wales, SE Australia
188 K12 **Coolgardie** Western Australia
38 L14 **Coolidge** Arizona, SW USA
27 U8 **Coolidge** Texas, SW USA
191 Q11 **Cooma** New South Wales, SE Australia
Coomassie see Kumasi
191 R6 **Coonabarabran** New South Wales, SE Australia
190 J10 **Coonalpyn** South Australia
191 R6 **Coonamble** New South Wales, SE Australia
Coondapoor see Kundāpura
161 G21 **Coonoor** Tamil Nādu, SE India
31 U14 **Coon Rapids** Iowa, C USA
31 V8 **Coon Rapids** Minnesota, N USA
27 V5 **Cooper** Texas, SW USA
189 U9 **Cooper Creek** var. Barcoo, Cooper's Creek. seasonal river Queensland/South Australia
41 R12 **Cooper Landing** Alaska, USA
23 T14 **Cooper River** ≈ South Carolina, SE USA
Cooper's Creek see Cooper Creek
46 H1 **Coopers Town** Great Abaco, N Bahamas
20 J10 **Cooperstown** New York, NE USA
31 P4 **Cooperstown** North Dakota, N USA
33 P9 **Coopersville** Michigan, N USA
190 D7 **Coorabie** South Australia
25 Q3 **Coosa River** ≈ Alabama/Georgia, S USA
34 E14 **Coos Bay** Oregon, NW USA
191 Q9 **Cootamundra** New South Wales, SE Australia
99 E16 **Cootehill** Ir. Muinchille. N Ireland
Çop see Chop
59 J17 **Copacabana** La Paz, W Bolivia
65 G15 **Copahué, Volcán** ▲ C Chile
43 U16 **Copainalá** Chiapas, SE Mexico
34 F8 **Copalis Beach** Washington, NW USA
44 F6 **Copán** ◆ department W Honduras
Copán see Copán Ruinas
27 T14 **Copano Bay** bay NW Gulf of Mexico
44 F6 **Copán Ruinas** var. Copán. Copán, W Honduras
Copenhagen see København
109 Q19 **Copertino** Puglia, SE Italy
64 H7 **Copiapó** Atacama, N Chile
64 G8 **Copiapó, Bahía** bay N Chile
64 G7 **Copiapó, Río** ≈ N Chile
116 M12 **Çöpköy** Edirne, NW Turkey
190 I5 **Copley** South Australia
108 H9 **Copparo** Emilia-Romagna, C Italy
57 V10 **Coppename Rivier** var. Koppename. ≈ C Suriname
27 S9 **Copperas Cove** Texas, SW USA
84 J13 **Copperbelt** ◆ province C Zambia
41 S11 **Copper Center** Alaska, USA
15 I4 **Coppermine** var. Qurlurtuuq. Northwest Territories, NW Canada
15 I5 **Coppermine** ≈ Northwest Territories, N Canada
41 T11 **Copper River** ≈ Alaska, USA
Copper State see Arizona
118 I11 **Copşa Mică** Ger. Kleinkopisch, Hung. Kiskapus. Sibiu, C Romania
164 J14 **Coqên** Xizang Zizhiqu, W China
Coquilhatville see Mbandaka
34 E14 **Coquille** Oregon, NW USA
64 G9 **Coquimbo** Coquimbo, N Chile
64 G9 **Coquimbo** off. Región de Coquimbo. ◆ region C Chile
118 I15 **Corabia** Olt, S Romania
59 F17 **Coracora** Ayacucho, SW Peru
Cora Droma Rúisc see Carrick-on-Shannon
46 K9 **Corail** SW Haiti
191 V4 **Coraki** New South Wales, SE Australia
188 G8 **Coral Bay** Western Australia
25 Y16 **Coral Gables** Florida, SE USA
15 M5 **Coral Harbour** Southampton Island, Northwest Territories, NE Canada
199 I10 **Coral Sea** sea SW Pacific Ocean
182 M7 **Coral Sea Basin** undersea feature N Coral Sea
199 Hh10 **Coral Sea Islands** ◇ Australian external territory SW Pacific Ocean
190 M12 **Corangamite, Lake** ◎ Victoria, SE Australia
Corantijn Rivier see Courantyne River
20 B14 **Coraopolis** Pennsylvania, NE USA
109 N17 **Corato** Puglia, SE Italy
105 O17 **Corbières** ▲ S France
105 P8 **Corbigny** Nièvre, C France
23 N7 **Corbin** Kentucky, S USA
106 L14 **Corbones** ≈ SW Spain
Corcaigh see Cork
37 R11 **Corcoran** California, W USA
49 T14 **Corcovado, Golfo** gulf S Chile
65 G18 **Corcovado, Volcán** ▲ S Chile
106 F3 **Corcubión** Galicia, NW Spain
Corcyra Nigra see Korčula

◆ Country ● Country Capital ◇ Dependent Territory ○ Dependent Territory Capital ◆ Administrative Region ✕ International Airport ▲ Mountain ▲ Mountain Range ▲ Volcano ≈ River ◎ Lake ⊠ Reservoir

62 *Q9* **Cordeiro** Rio de Janeiro, SE Brazil
25 *T6* **Cordele** Georgia, SE USA
28 *L11* **Cordell** Oklahoma, C USA
105 *N14* **Cordes** Tarn, S France
64 *O6* **Cordillera** *off.* Departamento de la Cordillera. ◈ *department* C Paraguay
190 *K1* **Cordillo Downs** South Australia
64 *K10* **Córdoba** Córdoba, C Argentina
43 *R14* **Córdoba** Veracruz-Llave, E Mexico
106 *M13* **Córdoba** *var.* Cordoba, ***Eng.*** Cordova; ***anc.*** Corduba. Andalucía, SW Spain
64 *K11* **Córdoba** *off.* Provincia de Córdoba. ◈ *province* C Argentina
56 *D7* **Córdoba** *off.* Departamento de Córdoba. ◈ *province* NW Colombia
106 *L13* **Córdoba** ◈ *province* Andalucía, S Spain
64 *K10* **Córdoba, Sierras de** ▲▲ C Argentina
25 *O3* **Cordova** Alabama, S USA
41 *S12* **Cordova** Alaska, USA
Cordova/Corduba *see* Córdoba
Corentyne River *see* Courantyne River
Corfu *see* Kérkyra
106 *J9* **Coria** Extremadura, W Spain
106 *J14* **Coria del Río** Andalucía, S Spain
191 *S8* **Coricudgy, Mount** ▲ New South Wales, SE Australia
109 *N20* **Corigliano Calabro** Calabria, SW Italy
Corinium/Corinium Dobunorum *see* Cirencester
25 *N1* **Corinth** Mississippi, S USA
Corinth *see* Kórinthos
Corinth Canal *see* Dióryga Korinthou
Corinth, Gulf of/Corinthiacus Sinus *see* Korinthiakós Kólpos
Corinthus *see* Kórinthos
44 *I9* **Corinto** Chinandega, NW Nicaragua
99 *C21* **Cork** ***Ir.*** Corcaigh. S Ireland
99 *C21* **Cork** ***Ir.*** Corcaigh. *cultural region* SW Ireland
99 *C21* **Cork** ✕ SW Ireland
99 *D21* **Cork Harbour** ***Ir.*** Cuan Chorcaí. *inlet* SW Ireland
109 *I23* **Corleone** Sicilia, Italy, C Mediterranean Sea
116 *N13* **Çorlu** Tekirdağ, NW Turkey
116 *N12* **Çorlu Çayı** ≈ NW Turkey
Cormaiore *see* Courmayeur
9 *V13* **Cormorant** Manitoba, C Canada
25 *T2* **Cornelia** Georgia, SE USA
62 *J10* **Cornélio Procópio** Paraná, S Brazil
57 *V9* **Corneliskondre** Sipaliwini, N Suriname
32 *J5* **Cornell** Wisconsin, N USA
11 *S12* **Corner Brook** Newfoundland, Newfoundland and Labrador, E Canada
Corner Rise Seamounts *see* Corner Seamounts
66 *I9* **Corner Seamounts** *var.* Corner Rise Seamounts. *undersea feature* NW Atlantic Ocean
118 *M9* **Corneşti** ***Rus.*** Korneshty. C Moldova
Corneto *see* Tarquinia
Cornhusker State *see* Nebraska
29 *X8* **Corning** Arkansas, C USA
37 *N5* **Corning** California, W USA
31 *U15* **Corning** Iowa, C USA
20 *G11* **Corning** New York, NE USA
Corn Islands *see* Maíz, Islas del
109 *J14* **Corno Grande** ▲ C Italy
13 *N13* **Cornwall** Ontario, SE Canada
99 *H25* **Cornwall** *cultural region* SW England, UK
99 *G25* **Cornwall, Cape** *headland* SW England, UK
56 *J4* **Coro** *prev.* Santa Ana de Coro. Falcón, NW Venezuela
59 *J18* **Corocoro** La Paz, W Bolivia
59 *K17* **Coroico** La Paz, W Bolivia
192 *M5* **Coromandel** Waikato, North Island, NZ
161 *K20* **Coromandel Coast** *coast* E India
192 *M5* **Coromandel Peninsula** *peninsula* North Island, NZ
192 *M6* **Coromandel Range** ▲▲ North Island, NZ
179 *P12* **Coron** Busuanga Island, W Philippines
37 *T15* **Corona** California, W USA
39 *T12* **Corona** New Mexico, SW USA
9 *U17* **Coronach** Saskatchewan, S Canada
37 *U17* **Coronado** California, W USA
45 *N15* **Coronado, Bahía de** *bay* S Costa Rica
9 *R15* **Coronation** Alberta, SW Canada
15 *Ii4* **Coronation Gulf** *gulf* Northwest Territories, N Canada
204 *I1* **Coronation Island** *island* Antarctica
41 *X14* **Coronation Island** *island* Alexander Archipelago, Alaska, USA
63 *B18* **Coronda** Santa Fe, C Argentina
65 *F14* **Coronel** Bío Bío, C Chile
63 *D20* **Coronel Brandsen** *var.* Brandsen. Buenos Aires, E Argentina
64 *K4* **Coronel Cornejo** Salta, N Argentina
63 *B24* **Coronel Dorrego** Buenos Aires, E Argentina
64 *P6* **Coronel Oviedo** Caaguazú, SE Paraguay
63 *B23* **Coronel Pringles** Buenos Aires, E Argentina
63 *B23* **Coronel Suárez** Buenos Aires, E Argentina
63 *E22* **Coronel Vidal** Buenos Aires, E Argentina
57 *V9* **Coronie** ◈ *district* NW Suriname
59 *G17* **Coropuna, Nevado** ▲ S Peru
Çorovoda *see* Çorovodë
115 *L22* **Çorovodë** *var.* Çorovoda. Berat, S Albania
191 *P11* **Corowa** New South Wales, SE Australia
44 *G1* **Corozal** Corozal, N Belize
56 *E6* **Corozal** Sucre, NW Colombia
44 *G1* **Corozal** ◈ *district* N Belize
27 *T14* **Corpus Christi** Texas, SW USA
27 *T14* **Corpus Christi Bay** *inlet* Texas, SW USA
27 *R14* **Corpus Christi, Lake** ▣ Texas, SW USA
65 *F16* **Corral** Los Lagos, C Chile
107 *O9* **Corral de Almaguer** Castilla-La Mancha, C Spain
106 *K6* **Corrales** Castilla-León, N Spain
39 *R11* **Corrales** New Mexico, SW USA
Corrán Tuathail *see* Carrauntoohil
108 *F9* **Correggio** Emilia-Romagna, C Italy
179 *P11* **Corregidor Island** *island* NW Philippines
61 *M16* **Corrente** Piauí, E Brazil
61 *I19* **Correntes, Rio** ≈ SW Brazil
105 *N12* **Corrèze** ◈ *department* C France
99 *C17* **Corrib, Lough** ***Ir.*** Loch Coirib. ◎ W Ireland
63 *C14* **Corrientes** Corrientes, NE Argentina
63 *D15* **Corrientes** *off.* Provincia de Corrientes. ◈ *province* NE Argentina
46 *A5* **Corrientes, Cabo** *headland* W Cuba
42 *I13* **Corrientes, Cabo** *headland* SW Mexico
Corrientes, Provincia de *see* Corrientes
63 *C16* **Corrientes, Río** ≈ NE Argentina
58 *E8* **Corrientes, Río** ≈ Ecuador/Peru
27 *W9* **Corrigan** Texas, SW USA
57 *U9* **Corriverton** E Guyana
Corriza *see* Korçë
191 *Q11* **Corryong** Victoria, SE Australia
104 *F2* **Corse** ***Eng.*** Corsica. ◈ *region* France, C Mediterranean Sea
104 *E1* **Corse** ***Eng.*** Corsica. *island* France, C Mediterranean Sea
104 *F1* **Corse, Cap** *headland* Corse, France, C Mediterranean Sea
104 *E2* **Corse-du-Sud** ◈ *department* Corse, France, C Mediterranean Sea
31 *P11* **Corsica** South Dakota, N USA
Corsica *see* Corse
27 *U7* **Corsicana** Texas, SW USA
104 *F2* **Corte** Corse, France, C Mediterranean Sea
65 *G16* **Corte Alto** Los Lagos, S Chile
106 *I13* **Cortegana** Andalucía, S Spain
45 *N15* **Cortés** *var.* Ciudad Cortés. Puntarenas, SE Costa Rica
44 *G5* **Cortés** ◈ *department* NW Honduras
39 *P8* **Cortez** Colorado, C USA
Cortez, Sea of *see* California, Golfo de
108 *H6* **Cortina d'Ampezzo** Veneto, NE Italy
20 *H11* **Cortland** New York, NE USA
33 *V11* **Cortland** Ohio, N USA
108 *H12* **Cortona** Toscana, C Italy
78 *H13* **Corubal, Rio** ≈ E Guinea-Bissau
106 *G10* **Coruche** Santarém, C Portugal
Çoruh *see* Rize
143 *R11* **Çoruh Nehri** ***Geor.*** Chorokhi, ***Rus.*** Chorokh. ≈ Georgia/Turkey
142 *K12* **Çorum** *var.* Chorum. Çorum, N Turkey
142 *J12* **Çorum** *var.* Chorum. ◈ *province* N Turkey
61 *H19* **Corumbá** Mato Grosso do Sul, S Brazil
12 *D16* **Corunna** Ontario, S Canada
Corunna *see* A Coruña
34 *F12* **Corvallis** Oregon, NW USA
66 *M1* **Corvo** *var.* Ilha do Corvo. *island* Azores, Portugal, NE Atlantic Ocean
Corvo, Ilha do *see* Corvo
33 *O16* **Corydon** Indiana, N USA
31 *V16* **Corydon** Iowa, C USA
Cos *see* Kos
42 *I9* **Cosalá** Sinaloa, C Mexico
43 *R15* **Cosamaloapan** *var.* Cosamaloapan de Carpio. Veracruz-Llave, E Mexico
Cosamaloapan de Carpio *see* Cosamaloapan
109 *N21* **Cosenza** *anc.* Consentia. Calabria, SW Italy
33 *T13* **Coshocton** Ohio, N USA
44 *H9* **Cosigüina, Punta** *headland* NW Nicaragua
31 *T9* **Cosmos** Minnesota, N USA
105 *O8* **Cosne-sur-Loire** Nièvre, C France
110 *B9* **Cossonay** Vaud, W Switzerland
Cossyra *see* Pantelleria
49 *R4* **Costa, Cordillera de la** *var.* Cordillera de Venezuela. ▲▲ N Venezuela
44 *K13* **Costa Rica** *off.* Republic of Costa Rica. ◆ *republic* Central America
45 *N15* **Costeña, Fila** ▲▲ S Costa Rica
Costermansville *see* Bukavu
118 *I14* **Costeşti** Argeş, SW Romania
39 *S8* **Costilla** New Mexico, SW USA
37 *O7* **Cosumnes River** ≈ California, W USA
103 *O16* **Coswig** Sachsen, E Germany
103 *M14* **Coswig** Sachsen-Anhalt, E Germany
Cosyra *see* Pantelleria
179 *R16* **Cotabato** Mindanao, S Philippines
58 *C5* **Cotacachi** ▲ N Ecuador
59 *L21* **Cotagaita** Potosí, S Bolivia
105 *V15* **Côte d'Azur** *prev.* Nice. ✕ (Nice) Alpes-Maritimes, SE France
Côte d'Ivoire *see* Ivory Coast
105 *R8* **Côte d'Or** *cultural region* C France
105 *R7* **Côte d'Or** ◈ *department* E France
Côte Française des Somalis *see* Djibouti
104 *J4* **Cotentin** *peninsula* N France
104 *G6* **Côtes d'Armor** *prev.* Côtes-du-Nord. ◈ *department* NW France
Côtes-du Nord *see* Côtes d'Armor
Cöthen *see* Köthen
Côtière, Chaîne *see* Coast Mountains
42 *M13* **Cotija** *var.* Cotija de la Paz. Michoacán de Ocampo, SW Mexico
Cotija de la Paz *see* Cotija
79 *R16* **Cotonou** *var.* Kotonu. S Benin
79 *R16* **Cotonou** ✕ S Benin
58 *B6* **Cotopaxi** *prev.* León. ◈ *province* C Ecuador
58 *C6* **Cotopaxi** ⛰ N Ecuador
Cotrone *see* Crotone
99 *L21* **Cotswold Hills** *var.* Cotswolds. *hill range* S England, UK
Cotswolds *see* Cotswold Hills
34 *F13* **Cottage Grove** Oregon, NW USA
23 *S14* **Cottageville** South Carolina, SE USA
103 *P14* **Cottbus** *prev.* Kottbus. Brandenburg, E Germany
29 *U9* **Cotter** Arkansas, C USA
108 *A9* **Cottian Alps** ***Fr.*** Alpes Cottiennes, ***It.*** Alpi Cozie. ▲▲ France/Italy
Cottiennes, Alpes *see* Cottian Alps
Cotton State, The *see* Alabama
24 *G4* **Cotton Valley** Louisiana, S USA
38 *L12* **Cottonwood** Arizona, SW USA
34 *M10* **Cottonwood** Idaho, NW USA
31 *S9* **Cottonwood** Minnesota, N USA
27 *Q7* **Cottonwood** Texas, SW USA
29 *O5* **Cottonwood Falls** Kansas, C USA
38 *L3* **Cottonwood Heights** Utah, W USA
31 *S10* **Cottonwood River** ≈ Minnesota, N USA
47 *O9* **Cotuí** C Dominican Republic
27 *Q13* **Cotulla** Texas, SW USA
Cotyora *see* Ordu
104 *I11* **Coubre, Pointe de la** *headland* W France
20 *E12* **Coudersport** Pennsylvania, NE USA
13 *S9* **Coudres, Île aux** *island* Québec, SE Canada
190 *G11* **Couedic, Cape de** *headland* South Australia
Couentrey *see* Coventry
104 *I6* **Couesnon** ≈ NW France
34 *H10* **Cougar** Washington, NW USA
104 *L10* **Couhé** Vienne, W France
34 *K8* **Coulee City** Washington, NW USA
205 *Q15* **Coulman Island** *island* Antarctica
105 *P5* **Coulommiers** Seine-et-Marne, N France
12 *K11* **Coulonge** ≈ Québec, SE Canada
12 *K11* **Coulonge Est** ≈ Québec, SE Canada
37 *Q9* **Coulterville** California, W USA
40 *M9* **Council** Alaska, USA
34 *M12* **Council** Idaho, NW USA
31 *S15* **Council Bluffs** Iowa, C USA
29 *O5* **Council Grove** Kansas, C USA
29 *O5* **Council Grove Lake** ▣ Kansas, C USA
34 *G7* **Coupeville** Washington, NW USA
57 *U12* **Courantyne River** *var.* Corantijn Rivier, Corentyne River. ≈ Guyana/Suriname
101 *G21* **Courcelles** Hainaut, S Belgium
110 *C7* **Courgenay** Jura, NW Switzerland
130 *B2* **Courland Lagoon** ***Ger.*** Kurisches Haff, ***Rus.*** Kurskiy Zaliv. *lagoon* Lithuania/Russian Federation
120 *B12* **Courland Spit** ***Lith.*** Kuršių Nerija, ***Rus.*** Kurshskaya Kosa. *spit* Lithuania/Russian Federation
108 *A6* **Courmayeur** *prev.* Cormaiore. Valle d'Aosta, NW Italy
110 *D7* **Courroux** Jura, NW Switzerland
8 *K17* **Courtenay** Vancouver Island, British Columbia, SW Canada
23 *W7* **Courtland** Virginia, NE USA
27 *V10* **Courtney** Texas, SW USA
32 *J4* **Court Oreilles, Lac** ◎ Wisconsin, N USA
Courtrai *see* Kortrijk
101 *H19* **Court-Saint-Étienne** Walloon Brabant, C Belgium
24 *G6* **Coushatta** Louisiana, S USA
180 *I16* **Cousin** *island* Inner Islands, NE Seychelles
180 *I16* **Cousine** *island* Inner Islands, NE Seychelles
104 *J4* **Coutances** *anc.* Constantia. Manche, N France
104 *K12* **Coutras** Gironde, SW France
47 *U14* **Couva** Trinidad, Trinidad and Tobago
110 *B8* **Couvet** Neuchâtel, W Switzerland
101 *H22* **Couvin** Namur, S Belgium
118 *K12* **Covasna** ***Ger.*** Kowasna, ***Hung.*** Kovászna. Covasna, E Romania
118 *J11* **Covasna** ◈ *county* E Romania
12 *E12* **Cove Island** *island* Ontario, S Canada
36 *M5* **Covelo** California, W USA
99 *M20* **Coventry** *anc.* Couentrey. C England, UK
Cove of Cork *see* Cobh
23 *U5* **Covesville** Virginia, NE USA
106 *I8* **Covilhã** Castelo Branco, E Portugal
25 *T3* **Covington** Georgia, SE USA
33 *N13* **Covington** Indiana, N USA
22 *M3* **Covington** Kentucky, S USA
24 *K8* **Covington** Louisiana, S USA
33 *Q13* **Covington** Ohio, N USA
22 *F9* **Covington** Tennessee, S USA
23 *S6* **Covington** Virginia, NE USA
191 *Q8* **Cowal, Lake** *seasonal lake* New South Wales, SE Australia
9 *W15* **Cowan** Manitoba, S Canada
20 *F12* **Cowanesque River** ≈ New York/Pennsylvania, NE USA
188 *L12* **Cowan, Lake** ◎ Western Australia
13 *P13* **Cowansville** Québec, SE Canada
190 *H8* **Cowell** South Australia
99 *M23* **Cowes** S England, UK
29 *Q10* **Coweta** Oklahoma, C USA
1 *D6* **Cowie Seamount** *undersea feature* NE Pacific Ocean
34 *G10* **Cowlitz River** ≈ Washington, NW USA
23 *Q11* **Cowpens** South Carolina, SE USA
191 *R8* **Cowra** New South Wales, SE Australia
Coxen Hole *see* Roatán
61 *I19* **Coxim** Mato Grosso do Sul, S Brazil
61 *I19* **Coxim, Rio** ≈ SW Brazil
Coxin Hole *see* Roatán
159 *V17* **Cox's Bazar** Chittagong, S Bangladesh
78 *H14* **Coyah** Conakry, W Guinea
42 *K5* **Coyame** Chihuahua, N Mexico
26 *L9* **Coyanosa Draw** ≈ Texas, SW USA
Coyhaique *see* Coihaique
44 *C7* **Coyolate, Río** ≈ S Guatemala
Coyote State *see* South Dakota
42 *I10* **Coyotitán** Sinaloa, C Mexico
43 *N15* **Coyuca** *var.* Coyuca de Catalán. Guerrero, S Mexico
43 *O16* **Coyuca** *var.* Coyuca de Benítez. Guerrero, S Mexico
Coyuca de Benítez/Coyuca de Catalán *see* Coyuca
31 *N15* **Cozad** Nebraska, C USA
Cozie, Alpi *see* Cottian Alps
Cozmeni *see* Kitsman'
42 *E3* **Cozón, Cerro** ▲ NW Mexico
43 *Z12* **Cozumel** Quintana Roo, E Mexico
43 *Z12* **Cozumel, Isla** *island* SE Mexico
34 *K8* **Crab Creek** ≈ Washington, NW USA
46 *H12* **Crab Pond Point** *headland* W Jamaica
Cracovia/Cracow *see* Kraków
85 *I25* **Cradock** Eastern Cape, S South Africa
41 *Y14* **Craig** Prince of Wales Island, Alaska, USA
39 *Q3* **Craig** Colorado, C USA
99 *F15* **Craigavon** C Northern Ireland, UK
23 *T5* **Craigsville** Virginia, NE USA
103 *J21* **Crailsheim** Baden-Württemberg, S Germany
118 *H14* **Craiova** Dolj, SW Romania
8 *K12* **Cranberry Junction** British Columbia, SW Canada
20 *J8* **Cranberry Lake** ◎ New York, NE USA
9 *V13* **Cranberry Portage** Manitoba, C Canada
9 *P17* **Cranbrook** British Columbia, SW Canada
32 *M5* **Crandon** Wisconsin, N USA
34 *K14* **Crane** Oregon, NW USA
26 *M9* **Crane** Texas, SW USA
Crane *see* The Crane
27 *S8* **Cranfills Gap** Texas, SW USA
21 *O12* **Cranston** Rhode Island, NE USA
Cranz *see* Zelenogradsk
61 *L15* **Craolândia** Tocantins, E Brazil
104 *J7* **Craon** Mayenne, NW France
205 *V16* **Crary, Cape** *headland* Antarctica
Crasna *see* Kraszna
34 *G14* **Crater Lake** ◎ Oregon, NW USA
194 *I13* **Crater Mount** ▲ C PNG
35 *P14* **Craters of the Moon National Monument** *national park* Idaho, NW USA
61 *O14* **Crateús** Ceará, E Brazil
Crathis *see* Crati
109 *N20* **Crati** *anc.* Crathis. ≈ S Italy
9 *U16* **Craven** Saskatchewan, S Canada
56 *I8* **Cravo Norte** Arauca, E Colombia
30 *J12* **Crawford** Nebraska, C USA
27 *T8* **Crawford** Texas, SW USA
9 *O17* **Crawford Bay** British Columbia, SW Canada
67 *M19* **Crawford Seamount** *undersea feature* S Atlantic Ocean
33 *O13* **Crawfordsville** Indiana, N USA
25 *S9* **Crawfordville** Florida, SE USA
99 *O23* **Crawley** SE England, UK
35 *S10* **Crazy Mountains** ▲▲ Montana, NW USA
9 *T11* **Cree** ≈ Saskatchewan, C Canada
39 *R7* **Creede** Colorado, C USA
42 *I6* **Creel** Chihuahua, N Mexico
9 *S11* **Cree Lake** ◎ Saskatchewan, C Canada
9 *V13* **Creighton** Saskatchewan, C Canada
31 *Q13* **Creighton** Nebraska, C USA
105 *O4* **Creil** Oise, N France
108 *E8* **Crema** Lombardia, N Italy
108 *E8* **Cremona** Lombardia, N Italy
Creole State *see* Louisiana
114 *M10* **Crepaja** ***Hung.*** Cserépalja. Serbia, N Yugoslavia
105 *O4* **Crépy-en-Valois** Oise, N France
114 *B10* **Cres** ***It.*** Cherso. Primorje-Gorski Kotar, NW Croatia
114 *A11* **Cres** ***It.*** Cherso; ***anc.*** Crexa. *island* W Croatia
34 *H14* **Crescent** Oregon, NW USA
36 *K1* **Crescent City** California, W USA
25 *W10* **Crescent City** Florida, SE USA
178 *M10* **Crescent Group** *island group* C Paracel Islands
25 *W10* **Crescent Lake** ◎ Florida, SE USA
31 *X11* **Cresco** Iowa, C USA
63 *B18* **Crespo** Entre Ríos, E Argentina
56 *E5* **Crespo** ✕ (Cartagena) Bolívar, NW Colombia
105 *R13* **Crest** Drôme, E France
39 *R5* **Crested Butte** Colorado, C USA
33 *S12* **Crestline** Ohio, N USA
9 *O17* **Creston** British Columbia, SW Canada
31 *U15* **Creston** Iowa, C USA
35 *V16* **Creston** Wyoming, C USA
39 *S7* **Crestone Peak** ▲ Colorado, C USA
25 *P8* **Crestview** Florida, SE USA
123 *Gg10* **Cretan Trough** *undersea feature* Aegean Sea, C Mediterranean Sea
31 *R16* **Crete** Nebraska, C USA
Crete *see* Kríti
105 *O5* **Créteil** Val-de-Marne, N France
Crete, Sea of/Creticum, Mare *see* Kritikó Pélagos
107 *X4* **Creus, Cap de** *headland* NE Spain
105 *N10* **Creuse** ◈ *department* C France
104 *L9* **Creuse** ≈ C France
105 *T4* **Creutzwald** Moselle, NE France
107 *S12* **Crevillente** País Valenciano, E Spain
99 *L18* **Crewe** C England, UK
23 *V7* **Crewe** Virginia, NE USA
Crexa *see* Cres
45 *Q15* **Cricamola, Río** ≈ NW Panama
63 *K14* **Criciúma** Santa Catarina, S Brazil
98 *J11* **Crieff** C Scotland, UK
114 *B10* **Crikvenica** ***It.*** Cirquenizza; ***prev.*** Cirkvenica, Crjkvenica. Primorje-Gorski Kotar, NW Croatia
Crimea/Crimean Oblast *see* Krym, Respublika
103 *M16* **Crimmitschau** *var.* Krimmitschau. Sachsen, E Germany
118 *G11* **Crişcior** ***Hung.*** Kristyor. Hunedoara, W Romania
23 *Y5* **Crisfield** Maryland, NE USA
33 *P3* **Crisp Point** *headland* Michigan, N USA
61 *L19* **Cristalina** Goiás, C Brazil
46 *J7* **Cristal, Sierra del** ▲▲ E Cuba
45 *T14* **Cristóbal** Colón, C Panama
56 *F4* **Cristóbal Colón, Pico** ▲ N Colombia
Cristur/Cristuru Săcuiesc *see* Cristuru Secuiesc
118 *I11* **Cristuru Secuiesc** *prev.* Cristur, Cristuru Săcuiesc, Sitaş Cristuru, ***Ger.*** Kreutz, ***Hung.*** Székelykeresztúr, Szitás-Keresztúr. Harghita, C Romania
118 *F10* **Crişul Alb** *var.* Weisse Kreisch, ***Ger.*** Weisse Körös, ***Hung.*** Fehér-Körös. ≈ Hungary/Romania
118 *F10* **Crişul Negru** ***Ger.*** Schwarze Körös, ***Hung.*** Fekete-Körös. ≈ Hungary/Romania
118 *G10* **Crişul Repede** *var.* Schnelle Kreisch, ***Ger.*** Schnelle Körös, ***Hung.*** Sebes-Körös. ≈ Hungary/Romania
119 *N10* **Criuleni** ***Rus.*** Kriulyany. C Moldova
Crivadia Vulcanului *see* Vulcan
Crjkvenica *see* Crikvenica
115 *O17* **Crna Gora** ▲▲ FYR Macedonia/Yugoslavia
Crna Gora *see* Montenegro
115 *O20* **Crna Reka** ≈ S FYR Macedonia
Crni Drim *see* Black Drin
111 *V10* **Crni Vrh** ▲ NE Slovenia
111 *V13* **Črnomelj** ***Ger.*** Tschernembl. SE Slovenia
99 *A17* **Croagh Patrick** ***Ir.*** Cruach Phádraig. ▲ W Ireland
114 *D9* **Croatia** *off.* Republic of Croatia, ***Ger.*** Kroatien, ***SCr.*** Hrvatska. ◆ *republic* SE Europe
Croce, Picco di *see* Wilde Kreuzspitze
13 *P8* **Croche** ≈ Québec, SE Canada
175 *Nn3* **Crocker, Banjaran** *var.* Crocker Range. ▲▲ East Malaysia
Crocker Range *see* Crocker, Banjaran
27 *V9* **Crockett** Texas, SW USA
69 *V14* **Crocodile** *var.* Krokodil. ≈ N South Africa
Crocodile *see* Limpopo
22 *I7* **Crofton** Kentucky, S USA
31 *Q12* **Crofton** Nebraska, C USA
Croia *see* Krujë
105 *R16* **Croisette, Cap** *headland* SE France
104 *G8* **Croisic, Pointe du** *headland* NW France
105 *S13* **Croix Haute, Col de la** *pass* E France
13 *U5* **Croix, Pointe à la** *headland* Québec, SE Canada
12 *F13* **Croker, Cape** *headland* Ontario, S Canada
189 *P1* **Croker Island** *island* Northern Territory, N Australia
98 *I8* **Cromarty** N Scotland, UK
101 *M21* **Crombach** Liège, E Belgium
99 *Q18* **Cromer** E England, UK
193 *D22* **Cromwell** Otago, South Island, NZ
193 *H16* **Cronadun** West Coast, South Island, NZ
41 *O11* **Crooked Creek** Alaska, USA
46 *K5* **Crooked Island** *island* SE Bahamas
46 *J5* **Crooked Island Passage** *channel* SE Bahamas
34 *I13* **Crooked River** ≈ Oregon, NW USA
31 *R4* **Crookston** Minnesota, N USA
30 *I10* **Crooks Tower** ▲ South Dakota, N USA
33 *T14* **Crooksville** Ohio, N USA
191 *R9* **Crookwell** New South Wales, SE Australia
12 *L14* **Crosby** Ontario, SE Canada
99 *K17* **Crosby** *var.* Great Crosby. NW England, UK
31 *U6* **Crosby** Minnesota, N USA
30 *K2* **Crosby** North Dakota, N USA
27 *O5* **Crosbyton** Texas, SW USA
79 *V16* **Cross** ≈ Cameroon/Nigeria
25 *U10* **Cross City** Florida, SE USA
Crossen *see* Krosno Odrzańskie
29 *V14* **Crossett** Arkansas, C USA
99 *K15* **Cross Fell** ▲ N England, UK
9 *P16* **Crossfield** Alberta, SW Canada
23 *Q12* **Cross Hill** South Carolina, SE USA
21 *U6* **Cross Island** *island* Maine, NE USA
9 *X13* **Cross Lake** Manitoba, C Canada
24 *F5* **Cross Lake** ▣ Louisiana, S USA
38 *I12* **Crossman Peak** ▲ Arizona, SW USA
27 *Q7* **Cross Plains** Texas, SW USA
79 *V17* **Cross River** ◈ *state* SE Nigeria
22 *L9* **Crossville** Tennessee, S USA
33 *S8* **Croswell** Michigan, N USA
12 *K13* **Crotch Lake** ◎ Ontario, SE Canada
Croton/Crotona *see* Crotone
109 *O21* **Crotone** *var.* Cotrone; ***anc.*** Croton, Crotona. Calabria, SW Italy
35 *V11* **Crow Agency** Montana, NW USA
191 *U7* **Crowdy Head** *headland* New South Wales, SE Australia
27 *Q4* **Crowell** Texas, SW USA
191 *O6* **Crowl Creek** *seasonal river* New South Wales, SE Australia
24 *H9* **Crowley** Louisiana, S USA
37 *S9* **Crowley, Lake** ▣ California, W USA
29 *X10* **Crowleys Ridge** *hill range* Arkansas, C USA
194 *J11* **Crown Island** *island* N Papau New Guinea
33 *N11* **Crown Point** Indiana, N USA
39 *P10* **Crownpoint** New Mexico, SW USA
35 *R10* **Crow Peak** ▲ Montana, NW USA
9 *P17* **Crowsnest Pass** *pass* Alberta/British Columbia, SW Canada
31 *T6* **Crow Wing River** ≈ Minnesota, N USA
99 *O22* **Croydon** SE England, UK
181 *P11* **Crozet Basin** *undersea feature* S Indian Ocean
181 *O12* **Crozet Islands** *island group* French Southern and Antarctic Territories
181 *N12* **Crozet Plateau** *var.* Crozet Plateaus. *undersea feature* SW Indian Ocean
Crozet Plateaus *see* Crozet Plateau
104 *E6* **Crozon** Finistère, NW France
Cruacha Dubha, Na *see* Macgillycuddy's Reeks
Cruach Phádraig *see* Croagh Patrick
118 *M14* **Crucea** Constanţa, SE Romania
46 *E5* **Cruces** Cienfuegos, C Cuba
109 *O20* **Crucoli Torretta** Calabria, SW Italy
43 *P9* **Cruillas** Tamaulipas, C Mexico
66 *K9* **Cruiser Tablemount** *undersea feature* E Atlantic Ocean
63 *G14* **Cruz Alta** Rio Grande do Sul, S Brazil
46 *G8* **Cruz, Cabo** *headland* S Cuba
62 *N9* **Cruzeiro** São Paulo, S Brazil
62 *H10* **Cruzeiro do Oeste** Paraná, S Brazil
61 *A15* **Cruzeiro do Sul** Acre, W Brazil
25 *U11* **Crystal Bay** *bay* Florida, SE USA
190 *I8* **Crystal Brook** South Australia
9 *X17* **Crystal City** Manitoba, S Canada
29 *X5* **Crystal City** Missouri, C USA
27 *P13* **Crystal City** Texas, SW USA
32 *M4* **Crystal Falls** Michigan, N USA
25 *Q8* **Crystal Lake** Florida, SE USA
33 *O6* **Crystal Lake** ◎ Michigan, N USA
25 *V11* **Crystal River** Florida, SE USA
39 *Q5* **Crystal River** ≈ Colorado, C USA
24 *K6* **Crystal Springs** Mississippi, S USA
Csaca *see* Čadca
Csakathurn/Csáktornya *see* Čakovec
Csap *see* Chop
Csepén *see* Čepin
Cserépalja *see* Crepaja
Csermő *see* Cermei
Csíkszereda *see* Miercurea-Ciuc
113 *L24* **Csongrád** Csongrád, SE Hungary
113 *L24* **Csongrád** *off.* Csongrád Megye. ◈ *county* SE Hungary
113 *H22* **Csorna** Győr-Moson-Sopron, NW Hungary
Csucsa *see* Ciucea
113 *G25* **Csurgó** Somogy, SW Hungary
Csurog *see* Čurug
56 *L5* **Cúa** Miranda, N Venezuela
84 *C11* **Cuale** Malanje, NW Angola
69 *T12* **Cuando** *var.* Kwando. ≈ S Africa
85 *E15* **Cuando Cubango** *var.* Kuando-Kubango. ◈ *province* SE Angola
85 *E16* **Cuangar** Cuando Cubango, S Angola
84 *D11* **Cuango** Lunda Norte, NE Angola
84 *C10* **Cuango** Uíge, NW Angola
84 *C10* **Cuango** *var.* Kwango. ≈ Angola/Zaire *see also* Kwango
Cuan, Loch *see* Strangford Lough
84 *C12* **Cuanza** *var.* Kwanza. ≈ C Angola
84 *B11* **Cuanza Norte** *var.* Kuanza Norte. ◈ *province* NE Angola
84 *B12* **Cuanza Sul** *var.* Kuanza Sul. ◈ *province* NE Angola
63 *E16* **Cuareim, Río** *var.* Rio Quaraí. ≈ Brazil/Uruguay *see also* Quaraí, Rio
85 *D15* **Cuatir** ≈ S Angola
42 *M7* **Cuatro Ciénegas** *var.* Cuatro Ciénegas de Carranza. Coahuila de Zaragoza, NE Mexico
Cuatro Ciénegas de Carranza *see* Cuatro Ciénegas
42 *I6* **Cuauhtémoc** Chihuahua, N Mexico
43 *P14* **Cuautla** Morelos, S Mexico
106 *H12* **Cuba** Beja, S Portugal
29 *W6* **Cuba** Missouri, C USA
39 *R10* **Cuba** New Mexico, SW USA
46 *E6* **Cuba** *off.* Republic of Cuba. ◆ *republic* W West Indies
49 *O2* **Cuba** *island* W West Indies
84 *B13* **Cubal** Benguela, W Angola
85 *C15* **Cubango** *var.* Kuvango, ***Port.*** Vila Artur de Paiva, Vila da Ponte. Huíla, SW Angola
85 *D16* **Cubango** *var.* Kavango, Kavengo, Kubango, Okavango, Okavanggo. ≈ S Africa *see also* Okavango
56 *H8* **Cubará** Boyacá, N Colombia
142 *I12* **Çubuk** Ankara, N Turkey
85 *D14* **Cuchi** Cuando Cubango, C Angola
44 *C5* **Cuchumatanes, Sierra de los** ▲▲ W Guatemala
Cuculaya, Rio *see* Kukalaya, Rio
84 *E12* **Cucumbi** *prev.* Trás-os-Montes. Lunda Sul, NE Angola
56 *G7* **Cúcuta** *var.* San José de Cúcuta. Norte de Santander, N Colombia
33 *N9* **Cudahy** Wisconsin, N USA
161 *J21* **Cuddalore** Tamil Nādu, SE India
161 *I18* **Cuddapah** Andhra Pradesh, S India
106 *M6* **Cuéllar** Castilla-León, N Spain
84 *D13* **Cuemba** *var.* Coemba. Bié, C Angola
58 *B8* **Cuenca** Azuay, S Ecuador
107 *Q9* **Cuenca** *anc.* Conca. Castilla-La Mancha, C Spain
107 *P9* **Cuenca** ◈ *province* Castilla-La Mancha, C Spain
42 *L9* **Cuencamé** *var.* Cuencamé de Ceniceros. Durango, C Mexico
Cuencamé de Ceniceros *see* Cuencamé
107 *Q8* **Cuenca, Serrania de** ▲▲ C Spain
Cuera *see* Chur
107 *P5* **Cuerda del Pozo, Embalse de la** ▣ N Spain
43 *O14* **Cuernavaca** Morelos, S Mexico
27 *T12* **Cuero** Texas, SW USA
46 *I7* **Cueto** Holguín, E Cuba
43 *Q13* **Cuetzalán** *var.* Cuetzalán del Progreso. Puebla, S Mexico
Cuetzalán del Progreso *see* Cuetzalán
107 *Q14* **Cuevas de Almanzora** Andalucía, S Spain
107 *T8* **Cuevas de Vinromá** País Valenciano, E Spain
118 *H12* **Cugir** ***Hung.*** Kudzsir. Alba, SW Romania
61 *H18* **Cuiabá** *prev.* Cuyabá. *state capital* Mato Grosso, SW Brazil
61 *H19* **Cuiabá, Rio** ≈ SW Brazil
43 *R15* **Cuicatlán** *var.* San Juan Bautista Cuicatlán. Oaxaca, SE Mexico
203 *W16* **Cuidado, Punta** *headland* Easter Island, Chile, E Pacific Ocean
Cuidad Presidente Stroessner *see* Ciudad del Este
Cúige *see* Connaught
Cúige Laighean *see* Leinster
Cúige Mumhan *see* Munster
100 *L13* **Cuijck** Noord-Brabant, SE Netherlands
Cúil an tSúdaire *see* Portarlington
44 *D7* **Cuilapa** Santa Rosa, S Guatemala
44 *B5* **Cuilco, Río** ≈ W Guatemala
Cúil Mhuine *see* Collooney
Cúil Raithin *see* Coleraine
85 *C14* **Cuima** Huambo, C Angola
85 *E16* **Cuito** *var.* Kwito. ≈ SE Angola
85 *E15* **Cuíto Cuanavale** Cuando Cubango, E Angola
43 *N14* **Cuitzeo, Lago de** ◎ C Mexico
29 *W4* **Cuivre River** ≈ Missouri, C USA
Çuka *see* Çukë
174 *Hh4* **Cukai** *var.* Chukai, Kemaman. Terengganu, Peninsular Malaysia
115 *L23* **Çukë** *var.* Çuka. Vlorë, S Albania
Cularo *see* Grenoble
179 *Pp13* **Culasi** Panay Island, C Philippines
35 *Y7* **Culbertson** Montana, NW USA

◆ Country ● Country Capital ◇ Dependent Territory ○ Dependent Territory Capital ◈ Administrative Region ✕ International Airport ▲ Mountain ▲▲ Mountain Range ⛰ Volcano ≈ River ◎ Lake ▣ Reservoir

30 M16 **Culbertson** Nebraska, C USA
191 P10 **Culcairn** New South Wales, SE Australia
47 W5 **Culebra** var. Dewey. E Puerto Rico
47 W6 **Culebra, Isla de** island E Puerto Rico
39 T8 **Culebra Peak** ▲ Colorado, C USA
106 J5 **Culebra, Sierra de la** ▲▲ NW Spain
100 J12 **Culemborg** Gelderland, C Netherlands
143 V14 **Culfa** Rus. Dzhul'fa. SW Azerbaijan
191 P4 **Culgoa River** ≈ New South Wales/Queensland, SE Australia
42 I9 **Culiacán** var. Culiacán Rosales, Culiacán-Rosales. Sinaloa, C Mexico
Culiacán-Rosales/Culiacán Rosales see Culiacán
179 P13 **Culion Island** island Calamian Group, W Philippines
107 P14 **Cúllar-Baza** Andalucía, S Spain
107 S10 **Cullera** País Valenciano, E Spain
25 P3 **Cullman** Alabama, S USA
110 B10 **Cully** Vaud, W Switzerland
Culm see Chełmno
Culmsee see Chełmża
23 V4 **Culpeper** Virginia, NE USA
Culpepper Island see Darwin, Isla
193 I17 **Culverden** Canterbury, South Island, NZ
57 N5 **Cumaná** Sucre, NE Venezuela
57 O5 **Cumanacoa** Sucre, NE Venezuela
56 C13 **Cumbal, Nevado de** elevation S Colombia
23 O7 **Cumberland** Kentucky, S USA
23 U2 **Cumberland** Maryland, NE USA
23 V6 **Cumberland** Virginia, NE USA
197 A11 **Cumberland, Cape** var. Cape Nahoi. headland Espiritu Santo, N Vanuatu
9 V14 **Cumberland House** Saskatchewan, C Canada
25 W8 **Cumberland Island** island Georgia, SE USA
22 L7 **Cumberland, Lake** ⊟ Kentucky, S USA
16 O1 **Cumberland Peninsula** peninsula Baffin Island, Northwest Territories, NE Canada
1 K11 **Cumberland Plateau** plateau E USA
32 L1 **Cumberland Point** headland Michigan, N USA
23 O7 **Cumberland River** ≈ Kentucky/Tennessee, S USA
16 O2 **Cumberland Sound** inlet Baffin Island, Northwest Territories, NE Canada
98 I12 **Cumbernauld** S Scotland, UK
99 K15 **Cumbria** cultural region NW England, UK
99 K15 **Cumbrian Mountains** ▲▲ NW England, UK
25 S2 **Cumming** Georgia, SE USA
Cummin in Pommern see Kamień Pomorski
190 G9 **Cummins** South Australia
98 I13 **Cumnock** W Scotland, UK
42 G4 **Cumpas** Sonora, NW Mexico
142 H16 **Çumra** Konya, C Turkey
65 G15 **Cunco** Araucanía, C Chile
56 E9 **Cundinamarca** off. Departamento de Cundinamarca. ◈ province C Colombia
43 U15 **Cunduacán** Tabasco, SE Mexico
85 C16 **Cunene** ◈ province S Angola
85 A16 **Cunene** var. Kunene. ≈ Angola/Namibia see also Kunene
108 A9 **Cuneo** Fr. Coni. Piemonte, NW Italy
85 E15 **Cunjamba** Cuando Cubango, E Angola
189 V10 **Cunnamulla** Queensland, E Australia
94 K8 **Cuokkarašša** ▲ N Norway
108 B7 **Cuorgne** Piemonte, NE Italy
98 K11 **Cupar** E Scotland, UK
118 L8 **Cupcina** Rus. Kupchino; prev. Calinisc, Kalinisk. N Moldova
56 C8 **Cupica** Chocó, W Colombia
56 C8 **Cupica, Golfo de** gulf W Colombia
114 N13 **Ćuprija** Serbia, E Yugoslavia
Cura see Villa de Cura
47 P16 **Curaçao** island Netherlands Antilles
58 H13 **Curanja, Río** ≈ E Peru
58 F7 **Curaray, Río** ≈ Ecuador/Peru
118 K14 **Curcani** Călărași, SE Romania
190 H4 **Curdimurka** South Australia
105 P7 **Cure** ≈ C France
181 Y16 **Curepipe** C Mauritius
57 R6 **Curiapo** Delta Amacuro, NE Venezuela
Curia Rhaetorum see Chur
64 G12 **Curicó** Maule, C Chile
Curieta see Krk
180 I15 **Curieuse** island Inner Islands, NE Seychelles
61 C16 **Curitiba** Acre, W Brazil
62 K12 **Curitiba** prev. Curytiba. state capital Paraná, S Brazil
62 J13 **Curitibanos** Santa Catarina, S Brazil
191 S6 **Curlewis** New South Wales, SE Australia
190 J6 **Curnamona** South Australia
85 A15 **Curoca** ≈ SW Angola
191 T6 **Currabubula** New South Wales, SE Australia
61 Q14 **Currais Novos** Rio Grande do Norte, E Brazil
37 W7 **Currant** Nevada, W USA
37 W6 **Currant Mountain** ▲ Nevada, W USA
46 H2 **Current** Eleuthera Island, C Bahamas
29 W8 **Current River** ≈ Arkansas/Missouri, C USA
190 M14 **Currie** Tasmania, SE Australia
23 Y8 **Currituck** North Carolina, SE USA
23 Y8 **Currituck Sound** sound North Carolina, SE USA
41 R11 **Curry** Alaska, USA
Curtbunar see Tervel
118 I13 **Curtea de Argeș** var. Curtea-de-Arges. Argeș, S Romania
118 E10 **Curtici** Ger. Kurtitsch, Hung. Kürtös. Arad, W Romania
30 M16 **Curtis** Nebraska, C USA
106 H2 **Curtis-Estación** Galicia, NW Spain
191 O14 **Curtis Group** island group Tasmania, SE Australia
189 Y8 **Curtis Island** island Queensland, SE Australia
60 K11 **Curuá, Ilha do** island NE Brazil
49 U7 **Curuá, Rio** ≈ N Brazil
61 A14 **Curuçá, Rio** ≈ NW Brazil
114 L9 **Čurug** Hung. Csurog. Serbia, N Yugoslavia
63 D16 **Curuzú Cuatiá** Corrientes, NE Argentina
61 M19 **Curvelo** Minas Gerais, SE Brazil
20 E14 **Curwensville** Pennsylvania, NE USA
32 M3 **Curwood, Mount** ▲ Michigan, N USA
Curytiba see Curitiba
Curzola see Korčula
44 A10 **Cuscatlán** ◈ department C El Salvador
59 H15 **Cusco** var. Cuzco. Cusco, C Peru
59 H15 **Cusco** off. Departamento de Cusco; var. Cuzco. ◈ department C Peru
29 O9 **Cushing** Oklahoma, C USA
27 W8 **Cushing** Texas, SW USA
42 I6 **Cusihuiriachic** Chihuahua, N Mexico
105 P10 **Cusset** Allier, C France
25 S6 **Cusseta** Georgia, SE USA
30 J10 **Custer** South Dakota, N USA
Cüstrin see Kostrzyn
35 Q7 **Cut Bank** Montana, NW USA
Cutch, Gulf of see Kachchh, Gulf of
25 S8 **Cuthbert** Georgia, SE USA
9 S15 **Cut Knife** Saskatchewan, S Canada
25 Y16 **Cutler Ridge** Florida, SE USA
24 K10 **Cut Off** Louisiana, S USA
65 I15 **Cutral-Có** Neuquén, C Argentina
109 O21 **Cutro** Calabria, SW Italy
191 O4 **Cuttaburra Channels** seasonal river New South Wales, SE Australia
160 O12 **Cuttack** Orissa, E India
85 C15 **Cuvelai** Cunene, SW Angola
81 G18 **Cuvette** var. Région de la Cuvette. ◈ province C Congo
181 V9 **Cuvier Basin** undersea feature E Indian Ocean
181 U9 **Cuvier Plateau** undersea feature E Indian Ocean
84 B12 **Cuvo** ≈ W Angola
102 H9 **Cuxhaven** Niedersachsen, NW Germany
Cuyabá see Cuiabá
179 Pp13 **Cuyo East Pass** passage C Philippines
179 P13 **Cuyo West Pass** passage C Philippines
Cuyuni, Río see Cuyuni River
57 S8 **Cuyuni River** var. Río Cuyuni. ≈ Guyana/Venezuela
Cuzco see Cusco
99 K22 **Cwmbran** Wel. Cwmbrân. SW Wales, UK
30 K15 **C.W.McConaughy, Lake** ⊟ Nebraska, C USA
83 D20 **Cyangugu** SW Rwanda
112 D11 **Cybinka** Ger. Ziebingen. Zielona Góra, W Poland
Cyclades see Kykládes
Cydonia see Chaniá
Cymru see Wales
22 M5 **Cynthiana** Kentucky, S USA
9 S17 **Cypress Hills** ▲▲ Alberta/Saskatchewan, SW Canada
Cypro-Syrian Basin see Cyprus Basin
123 Mm1 **Cyprus** off. Republic of Cyprus, Gk. Kypros, Turk. Kıbrıs, Kıbrıs Cumhuriyeti. ◆ republic E Mediterranean Sea
86 L14 **Cyprus** Gk. Kypros, Turk. Kıbrıs. island E Mediterranean Sea
123 Gg10 **Cyprus Basin** var. Cypro-Syrian Basin. undersea feature E Mediterranean Sea
Cythera see Kýthira
Cythnos see Kýthnos
112 F9 **Czaplinek** Ger. Tempelburg. Koszalin, NW Poland
Czarna Woda see Wda
112 G8 **Czarne** Słupsk, NW Poland
112 G10 **Czarnków** Piła, NW Poland
113 E17 **Czech Republic** Cz. Česká Republika. ◆ republic C Europe
Czegléd see Cegléd
112 G12 **Czempiń** Poznań, W Poland
Czenstochau see Częstochowa
Czerkow see Čerchov
Czernowitz see Chernivtsi
112 I8 **Czersk** Bydgoszcz, NW Poland
113 J15 **Częstochowa** Ger. Czenstochau, Tschenstochau, Rus. Chenstokhov. Częstochowa, S Poland
113 J15 **Częstochowa** off. Województwo częstochowskie, Ger. Czenstochau, Tschenstochau, Rus. Chenstokhov. ◈ province S Poland
Częstochowskie, Województwo see Częstochowa
112 F10 **Człopa** Ger. Schloppe. Piła, W Poland
112 H8 **Człuchów** Ger. Schlochau. Słupsk, NW Poland

D

169 V9 **Da'an** var. Dalai. Jilin, NE China
13 S10 **Daaquam** Québec, SE Canada
Daawo, Webi see Dawa Wenz
56 I4 **Dabajuro** Falcón, NW Venezuela
79 N15 **Dabakala** NE Ivory Coast
Daban see Bairin Youqi
113 K23 **Dabas** Pest, C Hungary
166 L8 **Daba Shan** ▲▲ C China
146 J5 **Dabbāgh, Jabal** ▲ NW Saudi Arabia
56 D8 **Dabeiba** Antioquia, NW Colombia
166 L17 **Daben** Hainan, S China
160 E11 **Dabhoi** Gujarāt, W India
167 P8 **Dabie Shan** ▲▲ C China
78 J13 **Dabola** Haute-Guinée, C Guinea
79 N17 **Dabou** S Ivory Coast
112 P8 **Dąbrowa Białostocka** Białystok, NE Poland
113 M16 **Dąbrowa Tarnowska** Tarnów, SE Poland
121 M20 **Dabryn'** Rus. Dobryn'. Homyel'skaya Voblasts', SE Belorussia
165 P10 **Dabsan Hu** ◎ C China
167 Q13 **Dabu** prev. Huliao. Guangdong, S China
118 H15 **Dăbuleni** Dolj, SW Romania
Dacca see Dhaka
103 L23 **Dachau** Bayern, SE Germany
166 K8 **Dachuan** prev. Daxian, Da Xian. Sichuan, C China
Dacia Bank see Dacia Seamount
66 M10 **Dacia Seamount** var. Dacia Bank. undersea feature E Atlantic Ocean
39 T3 **Dacono** Colorado, C USA
Đặc Tô see Đak Tô
Dacura see Dákura
25 W12 **Dade City** Florida, SE USA
158 L10 **Dadeldhura** var. Dandeldhura. Far Western, W Nepal
25 Q5 **Dadeville** Alabama, S USA
105 N15 **Dadou** ≈ S France
160 D12 **Dādra and Nagar Haveli** ◈ union territory W India
155 P14 **Dādu** Sind, SE Pakistan
178 K11 **Da Du Bołoc** Kon Tum, C Vietnam
166 G9 **Dadu He** ≈ C China
Daegu see Taegu
Daerah Istimewa Aceh see Aceh
179 Q11 **Daet** Luzon, N Philippines
166 I11 **Dafang** Guizhou, S China
159 W11 **Dafla Hills** ▲▲ NE India
9 U15 **Dafoe** Saskatchewan, S Canada
78 G10 **Dagana** N Senegal
Dagana see Dahana, Tajikistan
Dagana see Massakory, Chad
120 K11 **Dagda** Krāslava, SE Latvia
Dagden see Hiiumaa
Dagden-Sund see Soela Väin
131 P16 **Dagestan, Respublika** prev. Dagestanskaya ASSR, Eng. Daghestan. ◈ autonomous republic SW Russian Federation
Dagestanskaya ASSR see Dagestan, Respublika
131 R17 **Dagestanskiye Ogni** Respublika Dagestan, SW Russian Federation
193 A23 **Dagg Sound** sound South Island, NZ
Daghestan see Dagestan, Respublika
147 Y8 **Daghmar** NE Oman
Dağliq Qarabağ see Nagornyy Karabakh
Dagö see Hiiumaa
56 D11 **Dagua** Valle del Cauca, W Colombia
166 H11 **Daguan** Yunnan, SW China
179 P9 **Dagupan** off. Dagupan City. Luzon, N Philippines
165 N16 **Dagzê** Xizang Zizhiqu, W China
153 Q13 **Dahana** Rus. Dagana, Dakhana. SW Tajikistan
169 V10 **Dahei Shan** ▲▲ N China
169 T7 **Da Hinggan Ling** Eng. Great Khingan Range. ▲▲ NE China
Dahlac Archipelago see Dahlak Archipelago
82 K9 **Dahlak Archipelago** var. Dahlac Archipelago. island group E Eritrea
25 T2 **Dahlonega** Georgia, SE USA
102 O14 **Dahme** Brandenburg, E Germany
103 O14 **Dahme** ≈ E Germany
147 O14 **Dahm, Ramlat** desert NW Yemen
160 E10 **Dāhod** prev. Dohad. Gujarāt, W India
Dahomey see Benin
164 G10 **Dahongliutan** Xinjiang Uygur Zizhiqu, NW China
Dahra see Dara
145 R2 **Dahūk** var. Dohuk, Kurd. Dihōk. N Iraq
118 J15 **Daia** Giurgiu, S Romania
171 L15 **Daigo** Ibaraki, Honshū, S Japan
169 O13 **Dai Hai** ◎ N China
Daihoku see T'aipei
185 X14 **Dai Island** island N Solomon Islands
177 G8 **Daik-u** Pegu, SW Myanmar
144 H9 **Dā'il** Dar'ā, S Syria
178 Kk12 **Đai Lanh** Khanh Hoa, S Vietnam
167 Q13 **Daimao Shan** ▲▲ SE China
107 N11 **Daimiel** Castilla-La Mancha, C Spain
117 F22 **Daimoniá** Pelopónnisos, S Greece
Dainan see T'ainan
27 W6 **Daingerfield** Texas, SW USA
Dainichi, Bá an see Dingle Bay
165 R13 **Dainkognubma** Xizang Zizhiqu, W China
171 Hh17 **Daiō-zaki** headland Honshū, SW Japan
Dairbhre see Valencia Island
63 B22 **Daireaux** Buenos Aires, E Argentina
Dairen see Dalian
77 W9 **Dairūṭ** var. Dayrūṭ. C Egypt
170 Ff12 **Dai-sen** ▲ Kyūshū, SW Japan
27 X10 **Daisetta** Texas, SW USA
199 Gg5 **Daitō-jima** island group
199 Gg5 **Daitō Ridge** undersea feature N Philippine Sea
167 N3 **Daixian** var. Dai Xian. Shanxi, C China
167 Q12 **Daiyun Shan** ▲▲ SE China
46 M8 **Dajabón** NW Dominican Republic
166 G8 **Dajin Chuan** ≈ C China
154 J6 **Dak** ◎ W Afghanistan
78 F11 **Dakar** ● (Senegal) W Senegal
78 F11 **Dakar** ✕ W Senegal
178 K11 **Đak Glây** Kon Tum, C Vietnam
Dakhana see Dahana
159 U16 **Dakhin Shahbazpur Island** island S Bangladesh
Dakhla see Ad Dakhla
78 F7 **Dakhlet Nouâdhibou** ◈ region NW Mauritania
Đak Lap see Kiên Đuc
178 K13 **Đak Nông** Đăc Lâc, S Vietnam
79 U11 **Dakoro** Maradi, S Niger
31 U12 **Dakota City** Iowa, C USA
31 R13 **Dakota City** Nebraska, C USA
115 M17 **Đakovica** var. Djakovica, Alb. Gjakovë. Serbia, S Yugoslavia
114 I10 **Đakovo** var. Djakovo, Hung. Diakovár. Osijek-Baranja, E Croatia
Dakshin see Deccan
178 K11 **Đak Tô** var. Đăc Tô. Kon Tum, C Vietnam
45 N7 **Dákura** var. Dacura. Región Autónoma Atlántico Norte, NE Nicaragua
97 I14 **Dal** Akershus, S Norway
84 E12 **Dala** Lunda Sul, E Angola
110 J8 **Dalaas** Vorarlberg, W Austria
78 I13 **Dalaba** Moyenne-Guinée, W Guinea
Dalai see Da'an
Dalain Hob see Ejin Qi
Dalai Nor see Hulun Nur
169 Q11 **Dalai Nur** salt lake N China
Dala-Jarna see Järna
97 M14 **Dalälven** ≈ C Sweden
142 D16 **Dalaman** Muğla, SW Turkey
142 C16 **Dalaman** ✕ Muğla, SW Turkey
142 D16 **Dalaman Çayı** ≈ SW Turkey
168 K11 **Dalandzadgad** Ömnögovĭ, S Mongolia
97 D17 **Dalane** physical region S Norway
201 Z2 **Dalap-Uliga-Djarrit** var. Delap-Uliga-Darrit, D-U-D. island group Ratak Chain, SE Marshall Islands
96 L13 **Dalarna** prev. Eng. Dalecarlia. cultural region C Sweden
97 P16 **Dalarö** Stockholm, C Sweden
178 Kk13 **Đa Lat** Lâm Đông, S Vietnam
168 J11 **Dalay** Ömnögovĭ, S Mongolia
154 L12 **Dālbandīn** var. Dāl Bandin. Baluchistān, SW Pakistan
97 J17 **Dalbosjön** lake bay S Sweden
189 Y10 **Dalby** Queensland, E Australia
96 D13 **Dale** Hordaland, S Norway
96 C12 **Dale** Sogn og Fjordane, S Norway
34 K12 **Dale** Oregon, NW USA
27 T11 **Dale** Texas, SW USA
Dalecarlia see Dalarna
23 W4 **Dale City** Virginia, NE USA
22 L8 **Dale Hollow Lake** ⊟ Kentucky/Tennessee, S USA
100 O8 **Dalen** Drenthe, NE Netherlands
97 E15 **Dalen** Telemark, S Norway
177 F4 **Daletme** Chin State, W Myanmar
25 Q7 **Daleville** Alabama, S USA
100 M9 **Dalfsen** Overijssel, E Netherlands
26 M1 **Dalhart** Texas, SW USA
11 O13 **Dalhousie** New Brunswick, SE Canada
158 I6 **Dalhousie** Himāchal Pradesh, N India
166 F12 **Dali** var. Xiaguan. Yunnan, SW China
Dali see Idálion
169 U14 **Dalian** var. Dairen, Dalien, Lüda, Ta-lien, Rus. Dalny. Liaoning, NE China
107 O15 **Dalías** Andalucía, S Spain
Dalien see Dalian
Dalijan see Delījān
114 J9 **Dalj** Hung. Dalja. Osijek-Baranja, E Croatia
Dalja see Dalj
34 F12 **Dallas** Oregon, NW USA
27 U6 **Dallas** Texas, SW USA
27 T7 **Dallas-Fort Worth** ✕ Texas, SW USA
160 K12 **Dalli Rājhara** Madhya Pradesh, C India
41 X15 **Dall Island** island Alexander Archipelago, Alaska, USA
40 M12 **Dall Lake** ◎ Alaska, USA
79 S12 **Dallol Bosso** seasonal river W Niger
147 U7 **Dalmā** island W UAE
115 E14 **Dalmacija** Eng. Dalmatia, Ger. Dalmatien, It. Dalmazia. cultural region S Croatia
Dalmatia/Dalmatien/Dalmazia see Dalmacija
127 Nn17 **Dal'negorsk** Primorskiy Kray, SE Russian Federation
127 Nn17 **Dal'nerechensk** Primorskiy Kray, SE Russian Federation
Dalny see Dalian
78 M16 **Daloa** C Ivory Coast
166 J11 **Dalou Shan** ▲▲ S China
189 X7 **Dalrymple Lake** ◎ Queensland, E Australia
12 H14 **Dalrymple Lake** ◎ Ontario, S Canada
189 X7 **Dalrymple, Mount** ▲ Queensland, E Australia
95 K20 **Dalsbruk** Fin. Taalintehdas. Turku-Pori, SW Finland
97 K19 **Dalsjöfors** Älvsborg, S Sweden
97 J17 **Dals Långed** var. Långed. Älvsborg, S Sweden
159 O15 **Dāltenganj** prev. Daltonganj. Bihār, N India
25 R2 **Dalton** Georgia, SE USA
Daltonganj see Dāltenganj
205 X14 **Dalton Iceberg Tongue** ice feature Antarctica
94 J1 **Dalvík** Nordhurland Eystra, N Iceland
37 N8 **Daly City** California, W USA
189 P2 **Daly River** ≈ Northern Territory, N Australia
189 Q3 **Daly Waters** Northern Territory, N Australia
121 F20 **Damachava** var. Damachova, Pol. Domaczewo, Rus. Domachëvo. Brestskaya Voblasts', SW Belorussia
Damachova see Damachava
79 W11 **Damagaram Takaya** Zinder, S Niger
160 D12 **Damān** Damān and Diu, W India
160 B12 **Damān and Diu** ◈ union territory W India
77 V7 **Damanhûr** anc. Hermopolis Parva. N Egypt
Damão see Damān
167 O1 **Damaqun Shan** ▲▲ E China
81 I15 **Damara** Ombella-Mpoko, S Central African Republic
85 D18 **Damaraland** physical region C Namibia
175 T15 **Damar, Kepulauan** var. Baraf Daja Islands, Kepulauan Barat Daya. island group C Indonesia
174 Gg4 **Damar Laut** Perak, Peninsular Malaysia
175 Tt15 **Damar, Pulau** island Maluku, E Indonesia
Damas see Dimashq
79 Y12 **Damasak** Borno, NE Nigeria
Damasco see Dimashq
23 Q8 **Damascus** Virginia, NE USA
Damascus see Dimashq
79 X13 **Damaturu** Yobe, NE Nigeria
175 Ss4 **Damau** Pulau Kaburuang, N Indonesia
149 O5 **Damāvand, Qolleh-ye** ▲ N Iran
84 B10 **Damba** Uíge, NW Angola
116 M12 **Dambaslar** Tekirdağ, NW Turkey
118 J13 **Dâmbovița** prev. Dîmbovița. ◈ county SE Romania
118 J13 **Dâmbovița** prev. Dîmbovița. ≈ S Romania
181 Y15 **D'Ambre, Île** island NE Mauritius
161 K24 **Dambulla** Central Province, C Sri Lanka
46 K9 **Dame-Marie** SW Haiti
46 J9 **Dame Marie, Cap** headland SW Haiti
149 Q4 **Dāmghān** Semnān, N Iran
Damietta see Dumyât
144 G10 **Dāmiyā** Al Balqā', NW Jordan
152 G11 **Damla** Dashkhovuzskiy Velayat, N Turkmenistan
Dammām see Ad Dammān
102 G12 **Damme** Niedersachsen, NW Germany
159 R15 **Dāmodar** ≈ NE India
160 J9 **Damoh** Madhya Pradesh, C India
79 P15 **Damongo** NW Ghana
144 G7 **Damoûr** var. Ad Dāmūr. W Lebanon
175 Pp7 **Dampal, Teluk** bay Sulawesi, C Indonesia
188 H7 **Dampier** Western Australia
188 H6 **Dampier Archipelago** island group Western Australia
176 Uu9 **Dampier, Selat** strait Irian Jaya, E Indonesia
194 L12 **Dampier Strait** strait NE PNG
147 U14 **Damqawt** var. Damqut. E Yemen
165 O13 **Dam Qu** ≈ C China
Damqut see Damqawt
178 Ii13 **Dâmrei, Chuŏr Phmun** Fr. Chaîne de l'Éléphant. ▲▲ SW Cambodia
110 C7 **Damvant** Jura, NW Switzerland
Damwâld see Damwoude
100 L5 **Damwoude** Fris. Damwâld. Friesland, N Netherlands
165 N15 **Damxung** Xizang Zizhiqu, W China
82 K11 **Danakil Desert** var. Afar Depression, Danakil Plain. desert E Africa
Danakil Plain see Danakil Desert
37 R8 **Dana, Mount** ▲ California, W USA
78 L16 **Danané** W Ivory Coast
178 Kk10 **Đa Nâng** prev. Tourane. Quang Nam-Đa Nâng, C Vietnam
179 Qq13 **Danao** var. Danao City. Cebu, C Philippines
166 G9 **Danba** Sichuan, C China
Danborg see Daneborg
20 L13 **Danbury** Connecticut, NE USA
27 W12 **Danbury** Texas, SW USA
37 X15 **Danby Lake** ◎ California, W USA
204 H4 **Danco Coast** physical region Antarctica
84 B11 **Dande** ≈ NW Angola
Dandeldhura see Dadeldhura
161 E17 **Dandeli** Karnātaka, W India
191 O12 **Dandenong** Victoria, SE Australia
169 V13 **Dandong** var. Tan-tung; prev. An-tung. Liaoning, NE China
207 Q14 **Daneborg** var. Danborg. N Greenland
27 V12 **Danevang** Texas, SW USA
Dänew see Deynau
12 L12 **Danford Lake** Québec, SE Canada
21 T4 **Danforth** Maine, NE USA
39 P3 **Danforth Hills** ▲▲ Colorado, C USA
Dangara see Danghara
165 V12 **Dangchang** Gansu, C China
Dangchengwan see Subei
84 B10 **Dange** Uíge, NW Angola
Dangerous Archipelago see Tuamotu, Îles
85 E26 **Danger Point** headland SW South Africa
153 Q13 **Danghara** Rus. Dangara. SW Tajikistan
165 P8 **Danghe Nanshan** ▲▲ W China
82 I12 **Dangila** var. Dānglā. NW Ethiopia
165 P8 **Dangjin Shankou** pass N China
Dangla see Tanggula Shan
Dānglā see Dangila, NW Ethiopia
Dangme Chu see Manās
159 Y11 **Dāngori** Assam, NE India
Dang Raek, Phanom/Dangrek, Chaîne des see Dângrêk, Chuŏr Phnum
178 Ii11 **Dângrêk, Chuŏr Phnum** var. Phanom Dang Raek, Phanom Dong Rak, Fr. Chaîne des Dangrek. ▲▲ Cambodia/Thailand
44 G3 **Dangriga** prev. Stann Creek. Stann Creek, E Belize
167 P6 **Dangshan** Anhui, E China
35 T15 **Daniel** Wyoming, C USA
85 H22 **Daniëlskuil** Northern Cape, N South Africa
21 N12 **Danielson** Connecticut, NE USA
128 M15 **Danilov** Yaroslavskaya Oblast', W Russian Federation
131 O9 **Danilovka** Volgogradskaya Oblast', SW Russian Federation
Danish West Indies see Virgin Islands (US)
166 L7 **Dan Jiang** ≈ C China
166 M7 **Danjiangkou Shuiku** ⊟ C China
147 W8 **Ḑank** var. Dhank. NW Oman
158 J7 **Dankhar** Himāchal Pradesh, N India
130 L6 **Dankov** Lipetskaya Oblast', W Russian Federation
44 J7 **Danlí** El Paraíso, S Honduras
Danmark see Denmark
Danmarksstraedet see Denmark Strait
97 O14 **Dannemora** Uppsala, C Sweden
20 L6 **Dannemora** New York, NE USA
102 K11 **Dannenberg** Niedersachsen, N Germany
192 N12 **Dannevirke** Manawatu-Wanganui, North Island, NZ
23 U8 **Dan River** ≈ Virginia, NE USA
178 Hh9 **Dan Sai** Loei, C Thailand
20 F10 **Dansville** New York, NE USA
Dantzig see Gdańsk
88 E12 **Danube** Bul. Dunav, Cz. Dunaj, Ger. Donau, Hung. Duna, Rom. Dunărea. ≈ C Europe
Danubian Plain see Dunavska Ravnina
177 Ff8 **Danubyu** Irrawaddy, SW Burma
Danum see Doncaster
21 P11 **Danvers** Massachusetts, NE USA
29 T11 **Danville** Arkansas, C USA
33 N13 **Danville** Illinois, N USA
33 O14 **Danville** Indiana, N USA
31 Y15 **Danville** Iowa, C USA
22 M6 **Danville** Kentucky, S USA
20 G14 **Danville** Pennsylvania, NE USA
23 T6 **Danville** Virginia, NE USA
166 L17 **Danxian** var. Dan Xian, Nada. Hainan, S China
Danzig see Gdańsk
Danziger Bucht see Danzig, Gulf of
112 J6 **Danzig, Gulf of** var. Gulf of Gdańsk, Ger. Danziger Bucht, Pol. Zakota Gdańska, Rus. Gdan'skaya Bukhta. gulf N Poland
166 F10 **Daocheng** Sichuan, C China
Daokou see Huaxian
106 H7 **Dão, Rio** ≈ N Portugal
Daosa see Dausa
79 Y7 **Dao Timmi** Agadez, NE Niger
166 M13 **Daoxian** var. Dao Xian. Hunan, S China
79 Q14 **Dapaong** N Togo
25 N8 **Daphne** Alabama, S USA
179 Qq15 **Dapitan** Mindanao, S Philippines
165 P9 **Da Qaidam** Qinghai, C China
169 V8 **Daqing** Heilongjiang, NE China
169 O13 **Daqing Shan** ▲▲ N China
Daqm see Duqm
145 T5 **Dāqūq** var. Tāwūq. N Iraq
78 G10 **Dara** var. Dahra. NW Senegal
144 H9 **Dar'ā** var. Der'a, Fr. Déraa. Dar'ā, SW Syria
144 H8 **Dar'ā** off. Muḩāfaẓat Dar'ā, var. Darā, Derá, Derrá. ◈ governorate S Syria
149 Q12 **Dārāb** Fārs, S Iran
118 K8 **Darabani** Botoșani, NW Romania
Daraj see Dirj
148 M8 **Dārān** Eşfahān, W Iran
178 Kk12 **Đa Răng, Sông** var. Ba. ≈ S Vietnam
126 Kk16 **Darasun** Chitinskaya Oblast', S Russian Federation
Daraut-Kurgan see Daroot-Korgon
79 W13 **Darazo** Bauchi, E Nigeria
145 S3 **Darband** N Iraq
145 V4 **Darband-i Khān, Sadd** dam NE Iraq
145 N1 **Darbāsīyah** var. Derbisîye. Al Ḩasakah, N Syria
120 C11 **Darbėnai** Kretinga, NW Lithuania
159 Q13 **Darbhanga** Bihār, N India
40 M9 **Darby, Cape** headland Alaska, USA
114 I9 **Darda** Hung. Dárda. Osijek-Baranja, E Croatia
29 T11 **Dardanelle** Arkansas, C USA
29 S11 **Dardanelle, Lake** ⊟ Arkansas, C USA
Dardanelles see Çanakkale Boğazı
Dardanelli see Çanakkale
Dar-el-Beida see Casablanca
142 M14 **Darende** Malatya, C Turkey
83 J22 **Dar es Salaam** Dar es Salaam, E Tanzania
83 J22 **Dar es Salaam** ✕ Pwani, E Tanzania
193 H18 **Darfield** Canterbury, South Island, NZ
108 F7 **Darfo** Lombardia, N Italy
82 B10 **Darfur** var. Darfur Massif. cultural region W Sudan
Darfur Massif see Darfur
152 J10 **Dargan-Ata** var. Darganata. Lebapskiy Velayat, NE Turkmenistan
Darganata see Dargan-Ata
149 T3 **Dargaz** var. Darreh Gaz; prev. Moḩammadābād. Khorāsān, NE Iran
145 U4 **Dargazayn** NE Iraq
191 P12 **Dargo** Victoria, SE Australia
168 K7 **Darhan** Bulgan, C Mongolia
169 N8 **Darhan** Hentiy, C Mongolia
168 L6 **Darhan** Selenge, N Mongolia
169 N12 **Darhan Muminggan Lianheqi** var. Bailingmiao. Nei Mongol Zizhiqu, N China
25 W7 **Darien** Georgia, SE USA
45 W16 **Darién** off. Provincia del Darién. ◈ province SE Panama
Darién, Golfo del see Darien, Gulf of
45 X14 **Darien, Gulf of** Sp. Golfo del Darién. gulf S Caribbean Sea
Darien, Isthmus of see Panamá, Istmo de
44 K9 **Dariense, Cordillera** ▲▲ C Nicaragua
45 W15 **Darién, Serranía del** ▲▲ Colombia/Panama
Dario see Ciudad Darío
Dariorigum see Vannes
Dariv see Darvi
Darj see Dirj
Darjeeling see Darjiling
159 S12 **Darjiling** prev. Darjeeling. West Bengal, NE India
Darkehnen see Ozersk
165 S12 **Darlag** Qinghai, C China
191 T3 **Darling Downs** hill range Queensland, E Australia
30 M2 **Darling, Lake** ⊟ North Dakota, N USA
188 I12 **Darling Range** ▲▲ Western Australia
190 L8 **Darling River** ≈ New South Wales, SE Australia
99 M15 **Darlington** N England, UK
23 T12 **Darlington** South Carolina, SE USA
32 K9 **Darlington** Wisconsin, N USA
112 G7 **Darłowo** Koszalin, NW Poland
103 G19 **Darmstadt** Hessen, SW Germany
77 S7 **Darnah** var. Dérna. NE Libya
105 S6 **Darney** Vosges, NE France
190 M7 **Darnick** New South Wales, SE Australia
205 Y6 **Darnley, Cape** headland Antarctica
107 R7 **Daroca** Aragón, NE Spain
153 S11 **Daroot-Korgon** var. Daraut-Kurgan. Oshskaya Oblast', SW Kyrgyzstan
63 A23 **Darragueira** var. Darregueira. Buenos Aires, E Argentina
Darregueira see Darragueira
Darreh Gaz see Dargaz
148 K7 **Darreh Shahr** var. Darreh-ye Shahr. Īlām, W Iran
Darreh-ye Shahr see Darreh Shahr
34 I7 **Darrington** Washington, NW USA
27 P1 **Darrouzett** Texas, SW USA
159 S15 **Darsana** var. Darshana. Khulna, N Bangladesh
Darshana see Darsana
102 M7 **Darss** peninsula NE Germany
102 M7 **Darsser Ort** headland NE Germany
99 J24 **Dart** ≈ SW England, UK
Dartang see Baqên
99 P22 **Dartford** SE England, UK
190 L12 **Dartmoor** Victoria, SE Australia
99 I24 **Dartmoor** moorland SW England, UK
11 Q15 **Dartmouth** Nova Scotia, SE Canada
99 J24 **Dartmouth** SW England, UK
13 Y6 **Dartmouth** ≈ Québec, SE Canada
191 Q11 **Dartmouth Reservoir** ◎ Victoria, SE Australia
Dartuch, Cabo see Artrutx, Cap d'
194 G15 **Daru** Western, SW PNG
114 G9 **Daruvar** Hung. Daruvár. Bjelovar-Bilogora, NE Croatia
152 F10 **Darvaza** Turkm. Derweze. Akhalskiy Velayat, C Turkmenistan
Darvaza see Darwoza
Darvazskiy Khrebet see Darvoz, Qatorkŭhi
168 F8 **Darvi** var. Dariv. Govĭ-Altay, W Mongolia
154 L9 **Darvīshān** var. Darweshan, Garmser. Helmand, S Afghanistan
153 R13 **Darvoz, Qatorkŭhi** Rus. Darvazskiy Khrebet. ▲▲ C Tajikistan
Darweshan see Darvīshān
65 J15 **Darwin** Río Negro, S Argentina
189 O1 **Darwin** prev. Palmerston, Port Darwin. territory capital Northern Territory, N Australia
67 D24 **Darwin** var. Darwin Settlement. East Falkland, Falkland Islands
64 H8 **Darwin, Cordillera** ▲▲ N Chile
59 B17 **Darwin, Volcán** ▲ Galapagos Islands, Ecuador, E Pacific Ocean
153 O10 **Darwoza** Rus. Darvaza. Jizzakh Wiloyati, C Uzbekistan
155 S8 **Darya Khān** Punjab, E Pakistan
151 O15 **Dar'yalyktakyr, Ravnina** plain S Kazakhstan
149 T11 **Dārzīn** Kermān, S Iran
166 L8 **Dashennongjia** ▲ C China
Dashhowuz see Dashkhovuz
Dashhowuz Welayaty see Dashkhovuzskiy Velayat
121 O16 **Dashkawka** Rus. Dashkovka. Mahilyowskaya Voblasts', E Belorussia
152 H8 **Dashkhovuz** Turkm. Dashhowuz; prev. Tashauz. Dashkhovuzskiy Velayat, N Turkmenistan
Dashkhovuz see Dashkhovuzskiy Velayat
152 E9 **Dashkhovuzskiy Velayat** var. Dashkhovuz, Turkm. Dashhowuz Welayaty. ◈ province N Turkmenistan
Dashköpri see Tashkepri
Dashkovka see Dashkawka
154 J15 **Dasht** ≈ SW Pakistan
Dashtidzhum see Dashtijum
153 R13 **Dashtijum** Rus. Dashtidzhum. SW Tajikistan
155 W7 **Daska** Punjab, NE Pakistan
Đa, Sông see Black River
79 R15 **Dassa** var. Dassa-Zoumé. S Benin
Dassa-Zoumé see Dassa
31 U8 **Dassel** Minnesota, N USA
158 H3 **Dastegil Sar** var. Disteghil Sār. ▲ N India
142 C16 **Datça** Muğla, SW Turkey
172 Nn6 **Date** Hokkaidō, NE Japan
160 I8 **Datia** prev. Duttia. Madhya Pradesh, C India
165 T10 **Datong** Qinghai, C China
167 N2 **Datong** var. Tatung, Ta-t'ung. Shanxi, C China
165 S9 **Datong He** ≈ C China
165 S9 **Datong Shan** ▲▲ C China

◆ Country
● Country Capital
◇ Dependent Territory
○ Dependent Territory Capital
◈ Administrative Region
✕ International Airport
▲ Mountain
▲▲ Mountain Range
▲ Volcano
≈ River
◎ Lake
⊟ Reservoir

174 Kk6 **Datu, Tanjung** *headland* Indonesia/Malaysia
Daua *see* Dawa Wenz
180 H16 **Dauban, Mount** ▲ Silhouette, NE Seychelles
155 T7 **Dāūd Khel** Punjab, E Pakistan
121 G15 **Daugai** Alytus, S Lithuania
Daugava *see* Western Dvina
120 J11 **Daugavpils** *Ger.* Dünaburg; *prev.* Rus. Dvinsk. *municipality* Daugvapils, SE Latvia
Dauka *see* Dawkah
Daulatabad *see* Malāyer
103 D18 **Daun** Rheinland-Pfalz, W Germany
161 E14 **Daund** *prev.* Dhond. Mahārāshtra, W India
178 Gg12 **Daung Kyun** *island* S Myanmar
9 W15 **Dauphin** Manitoba, S Canada
105 S13 **Dauphiné** *cultural region* E France
25 N9 **Dauphin Island** *island* Alabama, S USA
9 X15 **Dauphin River** Manitoba, S Canada
79 V12 **Daura** Katsina, N Nigeria
158 H12 **Dausa** *prev.* Daosa. Rājasthān, N India
Dauwa *see* Dawwah
143 Y10 **Däväçi** *Rus.* Divichi. NE Azerbaijan
161 F18 **Dāvangere** Karnātaka, W India
179 Rr16 **Davao** *off.* Davao City. Mindanao, S Philippines
179 Rr16 **Davao Gulf** *gulf* Mindanao, S Philippines
13 Q11 **Daveluyville** Québec, SE Canada
31 Z14 **Davenport** Iowa, C USA
34 L8 **Davenport** Washington, NW USA
45 P16 **David** Chiriquí, W Panama
13 O11 **David** ⚔ Québec, SE Canada
31 R15 **David City** Nebraska, C USA
David-Gorodok *see* Davyd-Haradok
9 T16 **Davidson** Saskatchewan, S Canada
23 R10 **Davidson** North Carolina, SE USA
28 K12 **Davidson** Oklahoma, C USA
41 S6 **Davidson Mountains** ▲ Alaska, USA
180 M8 **Davie Ridge** *undersea feature* W Indian Ocean
190 A1 **Davies, Mount** ▲ South Australia
37 O7 **Davis** California, W USA
29 N12 **Davis** Oklahoma, C USA
205 Y7 **Davis** *Australian research station* Antarctica
204 H3 **Davis Coast** *physical region* Antarctica
20 C16 **Davis, Mount** ▲ Pennsylvania, NE USA
26 K9 **Davis Mountains** ▲ Texas, SW USA
205 Z9 **Davis Sea** *sea* Antarctica
67 O20 **Davis Seamounts** *undersea feature* S Atlantic Ocean
206 M13 **Davis Strait** *strait* Baffin Bay/Labrador Sea
131 U5 **Davlekanovo** Respublika Bashkortostan, W Russian Federation
110 J9 **Davos** *Rmsch.* Tavau. Graubünden, E Switzerland
121 J20 **Davyd-Haradok** *Pol.* Dawidgródek, *Rus.* David-Gorodok. Brestskaya Voblasts', SW Belorussia
169 U12 **Dawa** Liaoning, NE China
147 O11 **Dawāsir, Wādī ad** *dry watercourse* S Saudi Arabia
83 K15 **Dawa Wenz** *var.* Daua, Webi Daawo. ⚔ E Africa
Dawaymah, Birkat ad *see* Umm al Baqar, Hawr
Dawei *see* Tavoy
121 K14 **Dawhinava** *Rus.* Dolginovo. Minskaya Voblasts', N Belorussia
Dawidgródek *see* Davyd-Haradok
147 V12 **Dawkah** *var.* Dauka. SW Oman
Dawlat Qaṭar *see* Qatar
26 M3 **Dawn** Texas, SW USA
146 M11 **Daws** Al Bāḩah, SW Saudi Arabia
8 H5 **Dawson** *var.* Dawson City. Yukon Territory, NW Canada
25 S6 **Dawson** Georgia, SE USA
31 S9 **Dawson** Minnesota, N USA
Dawson City *see* Dawson
9 N13 **Dawson Creek** British Columbia, W Canada
8 H7 **Dawson Range** ▲ Yukon Territory, W Canada
189 Y9 **Dawson River** ⚔ Queensland, E Australia
8 J15 **Dawsons Landing** British Columbia, SW Canada
22 I7 **Dawson Springs** Kentucky, S USA
25 S2 **Dawsonville** Georgia, SE USA
166 G8 **Dawu** Sichuan, C China
Dawu *see* Maqên
Dawukou *see* Shizuishan
147 Y10 **Dawwah** *var.* Dauwa. W Oman
104 J15 **Dax** *var.* Ax; *anc.* Aquae Augustae, Aquae Tarbelicae. Landes, SW France
Da Xian/Daxian *see* Dachuan
166 G9 **Daxue Shan** ▲ C China
166 G12 **Dayao** Yunnan, SW China
Dayishan *see* Gaoyou
191 N12 **Daylesford** Victoria, SE Australia
37 U10 **Daylight Pass** *pass* California, W USA
63 D17 **Daymán, Río** ⚔ N Uruguay
Dayr *see* Ad Dayr
144 G10 **Dayr 'Allā** *var.* Deir 'Alla. Al Balqā', N Jordan
145 N4 **Dayr az Zawr** *var.* Deir ez Zor. Dayr az Zawr, E Syria
144 M5 **Dayr az Zawr** *off.* Muḩāfaẓat Dayr az Zawr, *var.* Dayr Az-Zor. ◆ *governorate* E Syria
Dayr Az-Zor *see* Dayr az Zawr
Dayruṭ *see* Dairûṭ
9 Q15 **Daysland** Alberta, SW Canada
33 R14 **Dayton** Ohio, N USA
22 L10 **Dayton** Tennessee, S USA
27 W11 **Dayton** Texas, SW USA
34 L10 **Dayton** Washington, NW USA
25 X10 **Daytona Beach** Florida, SE USA
175 N10 **Dayu** Borneo, C Indonesia
167 O13 **Dayu Ling** ▲ S China
167 R7 **Da Yunhe** *Eng.* Grand Canal. *canal* E China
167 S11 **Dayu Shan** *island* SE China
166 J9 **Dazhu** Sichuan, C China
166 J9 **Dazu** Sichuan, C China
85 H24 **De Aar** Northern Cape, C South Africa
204 K5 **Deacon, Cape** *headland* Antarctica
41 R5 **Deadhorse** Alaska, USA
35 T12 **Dead Indian Peak** ▲ Wyoming, C USA
25 R9 **Dead Lake** ⊚ Florida, SE USA
46 J4 **Deadman's Cay** Long Island, C Bahamas
144 G11 **Dead Sea** *var.* Bahret Lut, Lacus Asphaltites, *Ar.* Al Baḩr al Mayyit, Baḩrat Lūt, *Heb.* Yam HaMelaḩ. *salt lake* Israel/Jordan
30 J9 **Deadwood** South Dakota, N USA
99 Q22 **Deal** SE England, UK
85 I22 **Dealesville** Free State, C South Africa
Dealnu *see* Tana/Teno
167 P10 **De'an** Jiangxi, S China
64 K9 **Deán Funes** Córdoba, C Argentina
204 L12 **Dean Island** *island* Antarctica
33 S10 **Dearborn** Michigan, N USA
29 R3 **Dearborn** Missouri, C USA
34 K9 **Deary** Idaho, NW USA
34 M9 **Deary** Washington, NW USA
8 J10 **Dease** ⚔ British Columbia, W Canada
8 J10 **Dease Lake** British Columbia, W Canada
37 U11 **Death Valley** California, W USA
37 U11 **Death Valley** *valley* California, W USA
104 L4 **Deauville** Calvados, N France
119 X7 **Debal'tseve** *Rus.* Debal'tsevo. Donets'ka Oblast', SE Ukraine
Debal'tsevo *see* Debal'tseve
115 M19 **Debar** *Ger.* Dibra, *Turk.* Debre. W FYR Macedonia
41 O9 **Debauch Mountain** ▲ Alaska, USA
De Behagle *see* Laï
27 X7 **De Berry** Texas, SW USA
131 T2 **Debesy** Udmurtskaya Respublika, NW Russian Federation
113 N16 **Dębica** Tarnów, SE Poland
De Bildt *see* De Bilt
100 J11 **De Bilt** *var.* De Bildt. Utrecht, C Netherlands
127 O9 **Debin** Magadanskaya Oblast', E Russian Federation
112 N13 **Dęblin** *Rus.* Ivangorod. Lublin, E Poland
112 D10 **Dębno** Gorzów, W Poland
41 S10 **Deborah, Mount** ▲ Alaska, USA
35 N8 **De Borgia** Montana, NW USA
Debra Birhan *see* Debre Birhan
Debra Marcos *see* Debre Mark'os
Debra Tabor *see* Debre Tabor
Debre *see* Debar
82 J13 **Debre Birhan** *var.* Debra Birhan. C Ethiopia
113 N22 **Debrecen** *Ger.* Debreczin, *Rom.* Debreţin; *prev.* Debreczen. Hajdú-Bihar, E Hungary
Debreczen/Debreczin *see* Debrecen
82 I12 **Debre Mark'os** *var.* Debra Marcos. NW Ethiopia
115 N19 **Debrešte** SW FYR Macedonia
82 J11 **Debre Tabor** *var.* Debra Tabor. NW Ethiopia
Debreţin *see* Debrecen
82 J13 **Debre Zeyt** C Ethiopia
115 L16 **Dečani** Serbia, S Yugoslavia
25 P2 **Decatur** Alabama, S USA
25 S3 **Decatur** Georgia, SE USA
32 L13 **Decatur** Illinois, N USA
33 Q12 **Decatur** Indiana, N USA
24 M5 **Decatur** Mississippi, S USA
31 S14 **Decatur** Nebraska, C USA
27 S6 **Decatur** Texas, SW USA
22 H9 **Decaturville** Tennessee, S USA
105 O13 **Decazeville** Aveyron, S France
161 H17 **Deccan** *Hind.* Dakshin. *plateau* C India
12 J8 **Decelles, Réservoir** ⊡ Québec, SE Canada
10 K2 **Déception** Québec, NE Canada
166 G11 **Dechang** Sichuan, C China
113 C15 **Děčín** *Ger.* Tetschen. Severní Čechy, NW Czech Republic
105 P9 **Decize** Nièvre, C France
100 I6 **De Cocksdorp** Noord-Holland, NW Netherlands
31 X11 **Decorah** Iowa, C USA
Dedeagaç/Dedeagach *see* Alexandroúpoli
196 C15 **Dededo** N Guam
100 N9 **Dedemsvaart** Overijssel, E Netherlands
21 O11 **Dedham** Massachusetts, NE USA
65 H19 **Dedo, Cerro** ▲ SW Argentina
79 O13 **Dédougou** W Burkina
128 G15 **Dedovichi** Pskovskaya Oblast', W Russian Federation
169 V6 **Dedu** *var.* Qingshan. Heilongjiang, NE China
161 J24 **Deduru Oya** ⚔ W Sri Lanka
85 N14 **Dedza** Central, S Malawi
85 N14 **Dedza Mountain** ▲ C Malawi
99 J16 **Dee** *Wel.* Afon Dyfrdwy. ⚔ England/Wales, UK
98 K9 **Dee** ⚔ NE Scotland, UK
Deep Bay *see* Chilumba
23 T3 **Deep Creek Lake** ⊡ Maryland, NE USA
38 J4 **Deep Creek Range** ▲ Utah, W USA
29 P10 **Deep Fork** ⚔ Oklahoma, C USA
12 J11 **Deep River** Ontario, SE Canada
23 T10 **Deep River** ⚔ North Carolina, SE USA
191 U4 **Deepwater** New South Wales, SE Australia
33 S14 **Deer Creek Lake** ⊚ Ohio, N USA
25 Z15 **Deerfield Beach** Florida, SE USA
41 N8 **Deering** Alaska, USA
40 M16 **Deer Island** *island* Alaska, USA
21 S7 **Deer Isle** *island* Maine, NE USA
11 S11 **Deer Lake** Newfoundland, Newfoundland and Labrador, SE Canada
101 D18 **Deerlijk** West-Vlaanderen, W Belgium
35 Q10 **Deer Lodge** Montana, NW USA
34 L8 **Deer Park** Washington, NW USA
31 U5 **Deer River** Minnesota, N USA
Deés *see* Dej
33 R11 **Defiance** Ohio, N USA
25 Q8 **De Funiak Springs** Florida, SE USA
97 L23 **Degeberga** Kristianstad, S Sweden
106 H12 **Degebe, Ribeira** ⚔ S Portugal
82 M13 **Degeh Bur** SE Ethiopia
13 U9 **Dégelis** Québec, SE Canada
79 U17 **Degema** Rivers, S Nigeria
97 L16 **Degerfors** Örebro, C Sweden
200 N16 **De Gerlache Seamounts** *undersea feature* SE Pacific Ocean
103 N21 **Deggendorf** Bayern, SE Germany
124 Nn2 **Değirmenlik** *Gk.* Kythréa. N Cyprus
82 I11 **Degoma** NW Ethiopia
De Gordyk *see* Gorredijk
29 T12 **De Gray Lake** ⊡ Arkansas, C USA
188 J6 **De Grey River** ⚔ Western Australia
130 M10 **Degtevo** Rostovskaya Oblast', SW Russian Federation
149 X13 **Dehak** Sīstān va Balūchestān, SE Iran
149 R9 **Deh 'Alī** Kermān, C Iran
149 T13 **Dehbārez** *var.* Rūdān. Hormozgān, S Iran
149 P10 **Deh Bīd** Fārs, C Iran
148 M10 **Deh Dasht** Kohkīlūyeh va Būyer Aḩmadī, SW Iran
77 N8 **Dehibat** SE Tunisia
Dehli *see* Delhi
148 K8 **Dehlorān** Īlām, W Iran
153 N13 **Dehqonobod** *Rus.* Dekhkanabad. Qashqadaryo Wiloyati, S Uzbekistan
158 J9 **Dehra Dūn** Uttar Pradesh, N India
159 O14 **Dehri** Bihār, N India
154 K10 **Deh Shū** *var.* Deshu. Helmand, S Afghanistan
101 D17 **Deinze** Oost-Vlaanderen, NW Belgium
Deir 'Alla *see* Dayr 'Allā
Deir ez Zor *see* Dayr az Zawr
Deirgeirt, Loch *see* Derg, Lough
118 H9 **Dej** *Hung.* Dés; *prev.* Deés. Cluj, NW Romania
97 K15 **Deje** Värmland, C Sweden
176 Y14 **De Jongs, Tanjung** *headland* Irian Jaya, SE Indonesia
De Jouwer *see* Joure
32 M10 **De Kalb** Illinois, N USA
24 M5 **De Kalb** Mississippi, S USA
27 W5 **De Kalb** Texas, SW USA
Dekéleia *see* Dhekéleia
81 K20 **Dekese** Kasai Occidental, C Zaire
Dekhkanabad *see* Dehqonobod
81 I14 **Dékoa** Kémo, C Central African Republic
100 H6 **De Koog** Noord-Holland, NW Netherlands
32 M9 **Delafield** Wisconsin, N USA
63 C23 **De La Garma** Buenos Aires, E Argentina
12 K10 **Delahey, Lac** ⊚ Québec, SE Canada
82 E11 **Delami** Southern Kordofan, C Sudan
25 X11 **De Land** Florida, SE USA
37 R12 **Delano** California, W USA
31 V8 **Delano** Minnesota, N USA
38 K6 **Delano Peak** ▲ Utah, W USA
Delap-Uliga-Darrit *see* Dalap-Uliga-Djarrit
154 L7 **Delārām** Farāh, SW Afghanistan
40 F17 **Delarof Islands** *island group* Aleutian Islands, Alaska, USA
32 M9 **Delavan** Wisconsin, N USA
33 S13 **Delaware** Ohio, N USA
20 I17 **Delaware** *off.* State of Delaware; also known as Blue Hen State, Diamond State, First State. ◆ *state* NE USA
20 I17 **Delaware Bay** *bay* NE USA
26 J8 **Delaware Mountains** ▲ Texas, SW USA
20 I12 **Delaware River** ⚔ NE USA
29 Q3 **Delaware River** ⚔ Kansas, C USA
20 J14 **Delaware Water Gap** *valley* New Jersey/Pennsylvania, NE USA
103 G14 **Delbrück** Nordrhein-Westfalen, W Germany
9 Q15 **Delburne** Alberta, SW Canada
180 M12 **Del Cano Rise** *undersea feature* SW Indian Ocean
115 Q18 **Delčevo** NE FYR Macedonia
Delcommune, Lac *see* Nzilo, Lac
100 O10 **Delden** Overijssel, E Netherlands
191 R12 **Delegate** New South Wales, SE Australia
De Lemmer *see* Lemmer
110 D7 **Delémont** *Ger.* Delsberg. Jura, NW Switzerland
27 R7 **De Leon** Texas, SW USA
117 F18 **Delfoí** Stereá Ellás, C Greece
100 G12 **Delft** Zuid-Holland, W Netherlands
161 J23 **Delft** *island* NW Sri Lanka
100 O5 **Delfzijl** Groningen, NE Netherlands
1 E9 **Delgada Fan** *undersea feature* NE Pacific Ocean
44 F7 **Delgado** San Salvador, SW El Salvador
84 Q12 **Delgado, Cabo** *headland* N Mozambique
82 E6 **Delgo** Northern, N Sudan
165 R10 **Delhi** *var.* Delingha. Qinghai, C China
158 I10 **Delhi** *var.* Dehli, *Hind.* Dilli; *hist.* Shahjahanabad. Delhi, N India
24 J5 **Delhi** Louisiana, S USA
20 J11 **Delhi** New York, NE USA
158 I10 **Delhi** ◆ *union territory* NW India
142 J17 **Deli Burnu** *headland* S Turkey
57 X10 **Délices** C French Guiana
142 J12 **Delice Çayı** ⚔ C Turkey
42 J6 **Delicias** *var.* Ciudad Delicias. Chihuahua, N Mexico
149 N7 **Delījān** *var.* Dalijan, Dilijan. Markazī, W Iran
114 P12 **Deli Jovan** ▲ E Yugoslavia
Déli-Kárpátok *see* Carpaţii Meridionali
15 H6 **Délįne** *prev.* Fort Franklin. Northwest Territories, NW Canada
Delingha *see* Delhi
13 Q7 **Delisle** Québec, SE Canada
9 T15 **Delisle** Saskatchewan, S Canada
103 M15 **Delitzsch** Sachsen, E Germany
35 Q12 **Dell** Montana, NW USA
26 I7 **Dell City** Texas, SW USA
105 U7 **Delle** Territoire-de-Belfort, E France
38 J9 **Dellenbaugh, Mount** ▲ Arizona, SW USA
31 R11 **Dell Rapids** South Dakota, N USA
23 Y4 **Delmar** Maryland, NE USA
20 K11 **Delmar** New York, NE USA
102 G11 **Delmenhorst** Niedersachsen, NW Germany
114 C9 **Delnice** Primorje-Gorski Kotar, NW Croatia
39 R7 **Del Norte** Colorado, C USA
41 N6 **De Long Mountains** ▲ Alaska, USA
191 P16 **Deloraine** Tasmania, SE Australia
9 W17 **Deloraine** Manitoba, S Canada
33 O12 **Delphi** Indiana, N USA
33 Q12 **Delphos** Ohio, N USA
25 Z15 **Delray Beach** Florida, SE USA
27 O12 **Del Rio** Texas, SW USA
Delsberg *see* Delémont
96 N11 **Delsbo** Gävleborg, C Sweden
39 P6 **Delta** Colorado, C USA
38 K5 **Delta** Utah, W USA
79 T17 **Delta** ◆ *state* S Nigeria
57 Q6 **Delta Amacuro** *off.* Territorio Delta Amacuro. ◆ *federal district* NE Venezuela
41 S9 **Delta Junction** Alaska, USA
25 X11 **Deltona** Florida, SE USA
191 T5 **Delungra** New South Wales, SE Australia
160 C12 **Delvāda** Gujarāt, W India
63 B21 **Del Valle** Buenos Aires, E Argentina
Delvina *see* Delvinë
117 C15 **Delvináki** *var.* Dhelvinákion; *prev.* Pogónion. Ípeiros, W Greece
115 L23 **Delvinë** *var.* Delvina, *It.* Delvino. Vlorë, S Albania
Delvino *see* Delvinë
118 I7 **Delyatyn** Ivano-Frankivs'ka Oblast', W Ukraine
131 U5 **Dëma** ⚔ W Russian Federation
107 O5 **Demanda, Sierra de la** ▲ W Spain
41 T5 **Demarcation Point** *headland* Alaska, USA
81 K21 **Demba** Kasai Occidental, C Zaire
180 H13 **Dembéni** Grande Comore, NW Comoros
81 M15 **Dembia** Mbomou, SE Central African Republic
Dembidollo *see* Dembī Dolo
82 H13 **Dembī Dolo** *var.* Dembidollo. W Ethiopia
158 K6 **Demchok** *var.* Dêmqog. China/India *see also* Dêmqog
158 L6 **Demchok** *var.* Dêmqog. *disputed region* China/India *see also* Dêmqog
100 I12 **De Meern** Utrecht, C Netherlands
101 I17 **Demer** ⚔ C Belgium
66 H12 **Demerara Plain** *undersea feature* W Atlantic Ocean
66 H12 **Demerara Plateau** *undersea feature* W Atlantic Ocean
57 T9 **Demerara River** ⚔ NE Guyana
130 H3 **Demidov** Smolenskaya Oblast', W Russian Federation
39 Q15 **Deming** New Mexico, SW USA
34 H6 **Deming** Washington, NW USA
60 E10 **Demini, Rio** ⚔ NW Brazil
142 D13 **Demirci** Manisa, W Turkey
115 P19 **Demir Kapija** *prev.* Železna Vrata. SE FYR Macedonia
116 N11 **Demirköy** Kırklareli, NW Turkey
102 N9 **Demmin** Mecklenburg-Vorpommern, NE Germany
25 O5 **Demopolis** Alabama, S USA
33 N11 **Demotte** Indiana, N USA
164 F13 **Dêmqog** *var.* Demchok. China/India *see also* Demchok
158 L6 **Dêmqog** *var.* Demchok. *disputed region* China/India *see also* Demchok
176 Yy10 **Demta** Irian Jaya, E Indonesia
125 G11 **Dem'yanka** ⚔ C Russian Federation
128 H15 **Demyansk** Novgorodskaya Oblast', W Russian Federation
125 Ff11 **Dem'yanskoye** Tyumenskaya Oblast', C Russian Federation
105 P2 **Denain** Nord, N France
41 S10 **Denali** Alaska, USA
Denali *see* McKinley, Mount
83 M14 **Denan** SE Ethiopia
Denau *see* Denow
99 J18 **Denbigh** *Wel.* Dinbych. NE Wales, UK
99 J18 **Denbigh** *cultural region* N Wales, UK
100 I6 **Den Burg** Noord-Holland, NW Netherlands
101 F18 **Dender** *Fr.* Dendre. ⚔ W Belgium
101 F18 **Denderleeuw** Oost-Vlaanderen, NW Belgium
101 F17 **Dendermonde** *Fr.* Termonde. Oost-Vlaanderen, NW Belgium
Dendre *see* Dender
204 I9 **Dendtler Island** *island* Antarctica
100 P10 **Denekamp** Overijssel, E Netherlands
79 W12 **Dengas** Zinder, S Niger
Dêngkagoin *see* Têwo
168 L13 **Dengkou** *var.* Bayan Gol. Nei Mongol Zizhiqu, N China
165 Q14 **Dêngqên** Xizang Zizhiqu, W China
Deng Xian *see* Dengzhou
166 M7 **Dengzhou** *prev.* Deng Xian. Henan, C China
Dengzhou *see* Penglai
Den Haag *see* 's-Gravenhage
100 N9 **Den Ham** Overijssel, E Netherlands
188 H10 **Denham** Western Australia
46 J12 **Denham, Mount** ▲ C Jamaica
24 J8 **Denham Springs** Louisiana, S USA
100 I7 **Den Helder** Noord-Holland, NW Netherlands
107 T11 **Denia** País Valenciano, E Spain
201 Q8 **Denig** W Nauru
191 N10 **Deniliquin** New South Wales, SE Australia
31 T14 **Denison** Iowa, C USA
27 U5 **Denison** Texas, SW USA
142 D15 **Denizli** Denizli, SW Turkey
142 D15 **Denizli** ◆ *province* SW Turkey
Denjong *see* Sikkim
191 S7 **Denman** New South Wales, SE Australia
205 Y10 **Denman Glacier** *glacier* Antarctica
23 R14 **Denmark** South Carolina, SE USA
97 G23 **Denmark** *off.* Kingdom of Denmark, *Dan.* Danmark; *anc.* Hafnia. ◆ *monarchy* N Europe
94 H1 **Denmark Strait** *var.* Danmarksstraedet. *strait* Greenland/Iceland
47 T11 **Dennery** E Saint Lucia
100 I7 **Den Oever** Noord-Holland, NW Netherlands
153 O13 **Denow** *Rus.* Denau. Surkhondaryo Wiloyati, S Uzbekistan
175 N16 **Denpasar** *prev.* Paloe. Bali, C Indonesia
118 E12 **Denta** Timiş, W Romania
23 Y3 **Denton** Maryland, NE USA
27 T6 **Denton** Texas, SW USA
195 O15 **D'Entrecasteaux Islands** *island group* SE PNG
39 T4 **Denver** *state capital* Colorado, C USA
18 K8 **Denver** ✕ Colorado, C USA
26 L6 **Denver City** Texas, SW USA
158 J9 **Deoband** Uttar Pradesh, N India
Deoghar *see* Devghar
160 E13 **Deolāli** Mahārāshtra, W India
160 I10 **Deori** Madhya Pradesh, C India
159 O12 **Deoria** Uttar Pradesh, N India
101 A17 **De Panne** West-Vlaanderen, W Belgium
56 M5 **Dependencia Federal** *off.* Territorio Dependencia Federal. ◆ *federal dependency* N Venezuela
Dependencia Federal, Territorio *see* Dependencia Federal
32 M7 **De Pere** Wisconsin, N USA
20 D10 **Depew** New York, NE USA
101 E17 **De Pinte** Oost-Vlaanderen, NW Belgium
27 V5 **Deport** Texas, SW USA
126 M7 **Deputatskiy** Respublika Sakha (Yakutiya), NE Russian Federation
29 S13 **De Queen** Arkansas, C USA
24 G8 **De Quincy** Louisiana, S USA
83 J20 **Dera** *spring/well* S Kenya
Der'a/Derá/Déraa *see* Dar'ā
155 S10 **Dera Ghāzi Khān** *var.* Dera Ghāzikhān. Punjab, C Pakistan
155 S8 **Dera Ismāīl Khān** North-West Frontier Province, C Pakistan
115 L16 **Đeravica** ▲ S Yugoslavia
118 L6 **Derazhnya** Khmel'nyts'ka Oblast', W Ukraine
131 R17 **Derbent** Respublika Dagestan, SW Russian Federation
153 N13 **Derbent** Surkhondaryo Wiloyati, S Uzbekistan
Derbisiye *see* Darbāsīyah
81 M15 **Derbissaka** Mbomou, SE Central African Republic
188 L4 **Derby** Western Australia
99 M19 **Derby** C England, UK
29 N7 **Derby** Kansas, C USA
99 L18 **Derbyshire** *cultural region* C England, UK
114 O11 **Đerdap** *physical region* E Yugoslavia
Dereli *see* Gónnoi
176 X11 **Derew** ⚔ Irian Jaya, E Indonesia
131 R8 **Dergachi** Saratovskaya Oblast', W Russian Federation
Dergachi *see* Derhachi
99 C19 **Derg, Lough** *Ir.* Loch Deirgeirt. ⊚ W Ireland
119 V5 **Derhachi** *Rus.* Dergachi. Kharkivs'ka Oblast', E Ukraine
24 G8 **De Ridder** Louisiana, S USA
143 P16 **Derik** Mardin, SE Turkey
85 E20 **Derm** Hardap, C Namibia
150 M14 **Dermentobe** *prev.* Dyurmen'tyube. Kzyl-Orda, S Kazakhstan
29 W14 **Dermott** Arkansas, C USA
Dérna *see* Darnah
Dernberg, Cape *see* Dolphin Head
24 J11 **Dernieres, Isles** *island group* Louisiana, S USA
Dernis *see* Drniš
104 I4 **Déroute, Passage de la** *strait* Channel Islands/France
Derrá *see* Dar'ā
Derry *see* Londonderry
Dertona *see* Tortona
Dertosa *see* Tortosa
82 H8 **Derudeb** Red Sea, NE Sudan
114 H10 **Derventa** N Bosnia and Herzegovina
191 O16 **Derwent Bridge** Tasmania, SE Australia
191 O17 **Derwent, River** ⚔ Tasmania, SE Australia
Derweze *see* Darvaza
Derżavinsk *see* Derzhavinsk
151 O9 **Derzhavinsk** *var.* Derżavinsk. Turgay, C Kazakhstan
Dés *see* Dej
59 J18 **Desaguadero** Puno, S Peru
59 J18 **Desaguadero, Río** ⚔ Bolivia/Peru
203 W9 **Désappointement, Îles du** *island group* Îles Tuamotu, C French Polynesia
29 W11 **Des Arc** Arkansas, C USA
12 C10 **Desbarats** Ontario, S Canada
64 H13 **Descabezado Grande, Volcán** ⩘ C Chile
42 B2 **Descanso** Baja California, NW Mexico
104 L9 **Descartes** Indre-et-Loire, C France
9 T13 **Deschambault Lake** ⊚ Saskatchewan, C Canada
Deschnaer Koppe *see* Velká Deštná
34 I11 **Deschutes River** ⚔ Oregon, NW USA
82 J12 **Desē** *var.* Desse, *It.* Dessie. N Ethiopia
65 I20 **Deseado, Río** ⚔ S Argentina
108 F8 **Desenzano del Garda** Lombardia, N Italy
38 K3 **Deseret Peak** ▲ Utah, W USA
66 P6 **Deserta Grande** *island* Madeira, Portugal, NE Atlantic Ocean
66 P6 **Desertas, Ilhas** *island group* Madeira, Portugal, NE Atlantic Ocean
37 X16 **Desert Center** California, W USA
37 V15 **Desert Hot Springs** California, W USA
12 K10 **Désert, Lac** ⊚ Québec, SE Canada
38 J2 **Desert Peak** ▲ Utah, W USA
33 R11 **Deshler** Ohio, N USA
Deshu *see* Deh Shū
Desiderii Fanum *see* St-Dizier
108 D7 **Desio** Lombardia, N Italy
117 E15 **Deskáti** *var.* Dheskáti. Dytikí Makedonía, N Greece
30 L2 **Des Lacs River** ⚔ North Dakota, N USA
29 X6 **Desloge** Missouri, C USA
9 Q12 **Desmarais** Alberta, W Canada
31 Q10 **De Smet** South Dakota, N USA
31 V14 **Des Moines** *state capital* Iowa, C USA
19 N8 **Des Moines River** ⚔ C USA
119 P4 **Desna** ⚔ Russian Federation/Ukraine
118 G14 **Desnăţui** ⚔ S Romania
65 F24 **Desolación, Isla** *island* S Chile
31 V14 **De Soto** Iowa, C USA
25 Q4 **De Soto Falls** *waterfall* Alabama, S USA
85 I25 **Despatch** Eastern Cape, S South Africa
107 N12 **Despeñaperros, Desfiladero de** *pass* S Spain
33 N10 **Des Plaines** Illinois, N USA
117 J21 **Despotikó** *island* Kykládes, Greece, Aegean Sea
114 N12 **Despotovac** Serbia, E Yugoslavia
103 M14 **Dessau** Sachsen-Anhalt, E Germany
Desse *see* Desē
101 J16 **Dessel** Antwerpen, N Belgium
Dessie *see* Desē
Destêrro *see* Florianópolis
25 P9 **Destin** Florida, SE USA
Deštná *see* Velká Deštná
200 Oo11 **Desventurados, Islas de los** *island group* W Chile
105 N1 **Desvres** Pas-de-Calais, N France
118 E12 **Deta** *Ger.* Detta. Timiş, W Romania
103 H14 **Detmold** Nordrhein-Westfalen, W Germany
33 S10 **Detroit** Michigan, N USA
27 W5 **Detroit** Texas, SW USA
33 S10 **Detroit** ⚔ Canada/USA
31 S6 **Detroit Lakes** Minnesota, N USA
33 S10 **Detroit Metropolitan** ✕ Michigan, N USA
Detta *see* Deta
178 J11 **Det Udom** Ubon Ratchathani, E Thailand
113 K20 **Detva** *Hung.* Gyeva. Stredné Slovensko, C Slovakia
160 G13 **Deūlgaon Rāja** Mahārāshtra, C India
101 L15 **Deurne** Noord-Brabant, SE Netherlands
101 H16 **Deurne** ✕ (Antwerpen) Antwerpen, N Belgium
Deutsch-Brod *see* Havlíčkův Brod
Deutschendorf *see* Poprad
Deutsch-Eylau *see* Iława
111 Y6 **Deutschkreutz** Burgenland, E Austria
Deutsch Krone *see* Wałcz
Deutschland/Deutschland, Bundesrepublik *see* Germany
111 V9 **Deutschlandsberg** Steiermark, SE Austria
Deutsch-Südwestafrika *see* Namibia
111 Y3 **Deutsch-Wagram** Niederösterreich, E Austria
Deux-Ponts *see* Zweibrücken
12 I11 **Deux Rivieres** Ontario, SE Canada
104 K9 **Deux-Sèvres** ◆ *department* W France
118 G11 **Deva** *Ger.* Diemrich, *Hung.* Déva. Hunedoara, W Romania
Deva *see* Chester
Devana *see* Aberdeen
Devana Castra *see* Chester
Đevđelija *see* Gevgelija
142 L12 **Deveci Dağları** ▲ N Turkey
143 P15 **Devegeçidi Barajı** ⊡ SE Turkey
142 K15 **Develi** Kayseri, C Turkey
100 M11 **Deventer** Overijssel, E Netherlands
13 O10 **Devenyns, Lac** ⊚ Québec, SE Canada
98 K8 **Deveron** ⚔ NE Scotland, UK
159 R14 **Devghar** *prev.* Deoghar. Bihār, NE India
29 R10 **Devil's Den** *plateau* Arkansas, C USA
37 R7 **Devils Gate** *pass* California, W USA
32 J2 **Devils Island** *island* Apostle Islands, Wisconsin, N USA
Devil's Island *see* Diable, Île du
31 P3 **Devils Lake** North Dakota, N USA
33 R10 **Devils Lake** ⊚ Michigan, N USA
31 O3 **Devils Lake** ⊚ North Dakota, N USA
37 W13 **Devils Playground** *desert* California, W USA
27 O11 **Devils River** ⚔ Texas, SW USA
35 Y12 **Devils Tower** ▲ Wyoming, C USA
116 I11 **Devin** *prev.* Dovlen. Plovdivska Oblast, SW Bulgaria
27 R12 **Devine** Texas, SW USA
158 H13 **Devli** Rājasthān, N India
Devne *see* Devnya
116 N8 **Devnya** *prev.* Devne. Varnenska Oblast, NE Bulgaria
33 U14 **Devola** Ohio, N USA
Devoll *see* Devollit, Lumi i
115 M21 **Devollit, Lumi i** *var.* Devoll. ⚔ SE Albania
9 Q14 **Devon** Alberta, SW Canada
99 I23 **Devon** *cultural region* SW England, UK
207 N10 **Devon Island** *prev.* North Devon Island. *island* Parry Islands, Northwest Territories, NE Canada
191 O16 **Devonport** Tasmania, SE Australia
142 H11 **Devrek** Zonguldak, N Turkey
160 G10 **Dewās** Madhya Pradesh, C India
De Westerein *see* Zwaagwesteinde
29 P8 **Dewey** Oklahoma, C USA
Dewey *see* Culebra
100 M8 **De Wijk** Drenthe, NE Netherlands
29 W12 **De Witt** Arkansas, C USA
31 Z14 **De Witt** Iowa, C USA
31 R16 **De Witt** Nebraska, C USA
99 M17 **Dewsbury** N England, UK
167 Q10 **Dexing** Jiangxi, S China
29 Y8 **Dexter** Missouri, C USA
39 U14 **Dexter** New Mexico, SW USA
166 I8 **Deyang** Sichuan, C China
190 C4 **Dey-Dey, Lake** *salt lake* South Australia
149 S7 **Deyhūk** Khorāsān, E Iran
152 K12 **Deynau** *var.* Dyanev, *Turkm.* Dänew. Lebapskiy Velayat, NE Turkmenistan
148 L8 **Dezfūl** *var.* Dizful. Khūzestān, SW Iran
133 X4 **Dezhneva, Mys** *headland* NE Russian Federation
167 P4 **Dezhou** Shandong, E China
Dezh Shāhpūr *see* Marīvān
Dhahran *see* Aẓ Ẓahrān
Dhahran Al Khobar *see* Aẓ Ẓahrān al Khubar
159 U14 **Dhaka** *prev.* Dacca. ● (Bangladesh) Dhaka, C Bangladesh
159 T15 **Dhaka** ◆ *division* C Bangladesh
Dhali *see* Idálion
147 O15 **Dhamār** W Yemen
160 K12 **Dhamtari** Madhya Pradesh, C India
159 Q15 **Dhanbād** Bihār, NE India
158 L10 **Dhangadhi** *var.* Dhangarhi. Far Western, W Nepal
Dhangarhi *see* Dhangadhi
Dhank *see* Ḑank
159 R12 **Dhankuta** Eastern, E Nepal
158 I6 **Dhaola Dhār** ▲ NE India
160 F10 **Dhār** Madhya Pradesh, C India
159 R12 **Dharan** *var.* Dharan Bazar. Eastern, E Nepal
161 H21 **Dhārāpuram** Tamil Nādu, SE India
161 H20 **Dharmapuri** Tamil Nādu, SE India
161 H18 **Dharmavaram** Andhra Pradesh, E India
160 M11 **Dharmjaygarh** Madhya Pradesh, C India
Dharmsāla *see* Dharmshāla
158 I7 **Dharmshāla** *prev.* Dharmsāla. Himāchal Pradesh, N India
161 F17 **Dhārwād** *prev.* Dharwar. Karnātaka, SW India
Dharwar *see* Dhārwād
159 O10 **Dhaulāgiri** ▲ C Nepal
83 L18 **Dheere Laaq** *var.* Lak Dera, *It.* Lach Dera. *seasonal river* Kenya/Somalia
124 O3 **Dhekéleia Sovereign Base Area** *UK military installation* E Cyprus
124 O3 **Dhekélia** *Eng.* Dhekelia, *Gk.* Dekéleia. *UK air base* SE Cyprus
Dhelvinákion *see* Delvináki
115 M22 **Dhëmbelit, Majae** ▲ S Albania
160 O12 **Dhenkānāl** Orissa, E India
Dheskáti *see* Deskáti
144 G11 **Dhībān** 'Ammān, NW Jordan
Dhidhimótikhon *see* Didymóteicho
Dhíkti Ori *see* Díkti
144 I12 **Dhirwah, Wādī adh** *dry watercourse* C Jordan
Dhístomon *see* Dístomo
Dhodhekánisos *see* Dodekánisos
Dhodhóni *see* Dodóni
Dhofar *see* Ẓufār
Dhomokós *see* Domokós
Dhond *see* Daund
161 H17 **Dhone** Andhra Pradesh, C India
160 B11 **Dhorāji** Gujarāt, W India
Dhrāma *see* Dráma
160 C10 **Dhrāngadhra** Gujarāt, W India
Dhrepanon, Akra *see* Drépano, Ákra
159 T13 **Dhubri** Assam, NE India
160 F12 **Dhule** *prev.* Dhulia. Mahārāshtra, C India
Dhulia *see* Dhule
Dhún Dealgan, Cuan *see* Dundalk Bay
Dhún Droma, Cuan *see* Dundrum Bay
Dhún na nGall, Bá *see* Donegal Bay
Dhū Shaykh *see* Qazānīyah
82 Q13 **Dhuudo** Bari, NE Somalia
83 N15 **Dhuusa Marreeb** *var.* Dusa Marreb, *It.* Dusa Mareb. Galguduud, C Somalia
117 J24 **Día** *island* SE Greece
57 Y9 **Diable, Île du** *var.* Devil's Island. *island* N French Guiana
13 N12 **Diable, Rivière du** ⚔ Québec, SE Canada

◆ Country
● Country Capital
◇ Dependent Territory
○ Dependent Territory Capital
◆ Administrative Region
✕ International Airport
▲ Mountain
▲ Mountain Range
⩘ Volcano
⚔ River
⊚ Lake
⊡ Reservoir

37 N8 **Diablo, Mount** ▲ California, W USA
37 O9 **Diablo Range** ▲▲ California, W USA
26 I8 **Diablo, Sierra** ▲▲ Texas, SW USA
47 O11 **Diablotins, Morne** ▲ N Dominica
79 N11 **Diafarabé** Mopti, C Mali
79 N11 **Diaka** ≈ SW Mali
Diakovár *see* Đakovo
78 I12 **Dialakoto** S Senegal
63 B18 **Diamante** Entre Ríos, E Argentina
64 I12 **Diamante, Río** ≈ C Argentina
61 M19 **Diamantina** Minas Gerais, SE Brazil
61 N17 **Diamantina, Chapada** ▲▲ E Brazil
181 U11 **Diamantina Fracture Zone** *tectonic feature* E Indian Ocean
189 T8 **Diamantina River** ≈ Queensland/South Australia
40 D9 **Diamond Head** *headland* Oahu, Hawaii, USA, C Pacific Ocean
39 P2 **Diamond Peak** ▲ Colorado, C USA
37 W5 **Diamond Peak** ▲ Nevada, W USA
Diamond State *see* Delaware
78 J11 **Diamou** Kayes, SW Mali
97 I23 **Dianalund** Vestsjælland, C Denmark
67 G25 **Diana's Peak** ▲ C Saint Helena
166 M16 **Dianbai** Guangdong, S China
166 G13 **Dian Chi** ⊠ SW China
108 B10 **Diano Marina** Liguria, NW Italy
79 R13 **Diapaga** E Burkina
Diarbekr *see* Diyarbakır
109 J15 **Diavolo, Passo del** *pass* C Italy
63 B18 **Díaz** Santa Fe, C Argentina
147 W6 **Dibā al Ḥiṣn** *var.* Dibāh, Dibba. Ash Shāriqah, NE UAE
145 S3 **Dībaga** N Iraq
Dibāh *see* Dibā al Ḥiṣn
81 L22 **Dibaya** Kasai Occidental, S Zaire
Dibba *see* Dibā al Ḥiṣn
205 W15 **Dibble Iceberg Tongue** *ice feature* Antarctica
115 L19 **Dibër** ◈ *district* E Albania
85 I20 **Dibete** Central, SE Botswana
27 W9 **Diboll** Texas, SW USA
Dibra *see* Debar
159 X11 **Dibrugarh** Assam, NE India
56 G4 **Dibulla** La Guajira, N Colombia
27 O5 **Dickens** Texas, SW USA
21 R2 **Dickey** Maine, NE USA
32 K9 **Dickeyville** Wisconsin, N USA
30 K5 **Dickinson** North Dakota, N USA
1 E6 **Dickins Seamount** *undersea feature* NE Pacific Ocean
29 O13 **Dickson** Oklahoma, C USA
22 I9 **Dickson** Tennessee, S USA
Dicle *see* Tigris
Dicsőszentmárton *see* Târnăveni
100 M12 **Didam** Gelderland, E Netherlands
169 Y8 **Didao** Heilongjiang, NE China
78 L12 **Didiéni** Koulikoro, W Mali
Didimo *see* Dídymo
Didimotiho *see* Didymóteicho
83 K17 **Didimtu** *spring/well* NE Kenya
69 U9 **Didinga Hills** ▲▲ S Sudan
9 Q16 **Didsbury** Alberta, SW Canada
158 G11 **Dīdwāna** Rājasthān, N India
117 G20 **Dídymo** *var.* Didimo. ▲ S Greece
116 L12 **Didymóteicho** *var.* Dhidhimótikhon, Didimotiho. Anatolikí Makedonía kai Thráki, NE Greece
105 S13 **Die** Drôme, E France
79 O13 **Diébougou** SW Burkina
Diedenhofen *see* Thionville
9 S16 **Diefenbaker, Lake** ⊠ Saskatchewan, S Canada
64 H7 **Diego de Almagro** Atacama, N Chile
65 F23 **Diego de Almagro, Isla** *island* S Chile
63 A20 **Diego de Alvear** Santa Fe, C Argentina
181 Q7 **Diego Garcia** *island* S British Indian Ocean Territory
Diégo-Suarez *see* Antsirañana
101 M23 **Diekirch** Diekirch, C Luxembourg
101 L23 **Diekirch** ◈ *district* N Luxembourg
78 K11 **Diéma** Kayes, W Mali
103 H15 **Diemel** ≈ W Germany
100 I10 **Diemen** Noord-Holland, C Netherlands
Diemrich *see* Deva
178 Ii6 **Điện Biên** *var.* Bien Bien, Dien Bien Phu. Lai Châu, N Vietnam
Dien Bien Phu *see* Điện Biên
178 Jj8 **Diên Châu** Nghê An, N Vietnam
101 K18 **Diepenbeek** Limburg, NE Belgium
100 N11 **Diepenheim** Overijssel, E Netherlands
100 M10 **Diepenveen** Overijssel, E Netherlands
102 G12 **Diepholz** Niedersachsen, NW Germany
104 M3 **Dieppe** Seine-Maritime, N France
100 M12 **Dieren** Gelderland, E Netherlands
29 S13 **Dierks** Arkansas, C USA
101 J17 **Diest** Vlaams Brabant, C Belgium
110 F7 **Dietikon** Zürich, NW Switzerland
105 R13 **Dieulefit** Drôme, E France
105 T5 **Dieuze** Moselle, NE France
121 H15 **Dieveniškės** Šalčininkai, SE Lithuania
100 N7 **Diever** Drenthe, NE Netherlands
103 F17 **Diez** Rheinland-Pfalz, W Germany
79 Y12 **Diffa** Diffa, SE Niger
79 Y10 **Diffa** ◈ *department* SE Niger
101 L25 **Differdange** Luxembourg, SW Luxembourg
11 O16 **Digby** Nova Scotia, SE Canada
28 J5 **Dighton** Kansas, C USA
Dignano d'Istria *see* Vodnjan
105 T14 **Digne** *var.* Digne-les-Bains. Alpes-de-Haute-Provence, SE France
Digne-les-Bains *see* Digne
Digoel *see* Digul, Sungai
105 Q10 **Digoin** Saône-et-Loire, C France
179 Rr16 **Digos** Mindanao, S Philippines
155 Q16 **Digri** Sind, SE Pakistan
176 Z13 **Digul Barat, Sungai** ≈ Irian Jaya, E Indonesia
176 Z14 **Digul, Sungai** *prev.* Digoel. ≈ Irian Jaya, E Indonesia
176 Z13 **Digul Timur, Sungai** ≈ Irian Jaya, E Indonesia
Dihang *see* Brahmaputra
159 X10 **Dihāng** ≈ NE India
Dihōk *see* Dahūk
83 L17 **Diinsoor** Bay, S Somalia
Dijlah *see* Tigris
101 H17 **Dijle** ≈ C Belgium
105 R8 **Dijon** *anc.* Dibio. Côte d'Or, C France
95 H14 **Dikanäs** Västerbotten, N Sweden
82 L12 **Dikhil** SW Djibouti
142 B13 **Dikili** İzmir, W Turkey
101 B17 **Diksmuide** *var.* Dixmuide, *Fr.* Dixmude. West-Vlaanderen, W Belgium
126 Hh6 **Dikson** Taymyrskiy (Dolgano-Nenetskiy) Avtonomnyy Okrug, N Russian Federation
117 K25 **Díkti** *var.* Dhíkti Ori. ▲▲ Kríti, Greece, E Mediterranean Sea
79 Z13 **Dikwa** Borno, NE Nigeria
83 J15 **Dīla** S Ethiopia
101 G18 **Dilbeek** Vlaams Brabant, C Belgium
175 S16 **Dili** *var.* Dilli, Dilly. Timor, C Indonesia
79 Y11 **Dilia** *var.* Dillia. ≈ SE Niger
Dilijan *see* Delījān
178 K13 **Di Linh** Lâm Đông, S Vietnam
103 G16 **Dillenburg** Hessen, W Germany
27 Q13 **Dilley** Texas, SW USA
Dilli *see* Delhi, India
Dilli *see* Dili, Indonesia
Dillia *see* Dilia
82 E11 **Dilling** *var.* Ad Dalanj. Southern Kordofan, C Sudan
103 D20 **Dillingen** Saarland, SW Germany
Dillingen *see* Dillingen an der Donau
103 J22 **Dillingen an der Donau** *var.* Dillingen. Bayern, S Germany
41 O13 **Dillingham** Alaska, USA
35 Q12 **Dillon** Montana, NW USA
23 T12 **Dillon** South Carolina, SE USA
33 T13 **Dillon Lake** ⊠ Ohio, N USA
Dilly *see* Dili
Dilman *see* Salmās
81 K24 **Dilolo** Shaba, S Zaire
117 J20 **Dílos** *island* Kykládes, Greece, Aegean Sea
147 Y11 **Ḑil', Ra's aḑ** *headland* E Oman
31 R5 **Dilworth** Minnesota, N USA
144 H7 **Dimashq** *var.* Ash Shām, Esh Sham, *Eng.* Damascus, *Fr.* Damas, *It.* Damasco. ● (Syria) Dimashq, SW Syria
144 I8 **Dimashq** *off.* Muḩāfaz̧at Dimashq, *var.* Damascus, *Ar.* Ash Sham, Ash Shām, Damasco, Esh Sham, *Fr.* Damas. ◈ *governorate* S Syria
144 I7 **Dimashq** ✕ Dimashq, S Syria
81 L21 **Dimbelenge** Kasai Occidental, C Zaire
79 N16 **Dimbokro** E Ivory Coast
190 L11 **Dimboola** Victoria, SE Australia
Dîmbovița *see* Dâmbovița
Dimitrov *see* Dymytrov
116 K11 **Dimitrovgrad** Khaskovska Oblast, S Bulgaria
131 R5 **Dimitrovgrad** Ul'yanovskaya Oblast', W Russian Federation
115 Q15 **Dimitrovgrad** *prev.* Caribrod. Serbia, SE Yugoslavia
Dimitrovo *see* Pernik
Dimlang *see* Vogel Peak
26 M3 **Dimmitt** Texas, SW USA
116 F7 **Dimovo** Oblast Montana, NW Bulgaria
61 A16 **Dimpolis** Acre, W Brazil
117 O23 **Dimyliá** Ródos, Dodekánisos, Greece, Aegean Sea
179 R13 **Dinagat** Dinagat Island, S Philippines
179 Rr13 **Dinagat Island** *island* S Philippines
159 S13 **Dinajpur** Rajshahi, NW Bangladesh
104 I6 **Dinan** Côtes d'Armor, NW France
101 I21 **Dinant** Namur, S Belgium
142 E15 **Dinar** Afyon, SW Turkey
114 F13 **Dinara** ▲ W Croatia
Dinara *see* Dinaric Alps
104 I5 **Dinard** Ille-et-Vilaine, NW France
114 F13 **Dinaric Alps** *var.* Dinara. ▲▲ Bosnia and Herzegovina/Croatia
149 N10 **Dīnār, Kūh-e** ▲ C Iran
Dinbych *see* Denbigh
161 H22 **Dindigul** Tamil Nādu, SE India
85 M19 **Dindiza** Gaza, S Mozambique
155 V7 **Dinga** Punjab, E Pakistan
81 H21 **Dinga** Bandundu, SW Zaire
164 L16 **Dinggyê** Xizang Zizhiqu, W China
99 A20 **Dingle** *Ir.* An Daingean. SW Ireland
99 A20 **Dingle Bay** *Ir.* Bá an Daingin. *bay* SW Ireland
20 I13 **Dingmans Ferry** Pennsylvania, NE USA
103 N22 **Dingofling** Bayern, SE Germany
179 P8 **Dingras** Luzon, N Philippines
78 J13 **Dinguiraye** Haute-Guinée, N Guinea
98 I8 **Dingwall** N Scotland, UK
165 V10 **Dingxi** Gansu, C China
167 Q7 **Dingyuan** Anhui, E China
167 O3 **Dingzhou** *prev.* Ding Xian. Hebei, E China
178 K6 **Đinh Lâp** Lang Sơn, N Vietnam
178 K14 **Đinh Quan** Đông Nai, S Vietnam
102 E13 **Dinkel** ≈ Germany/Netherlands
103 J21 **Dinkelsbühl** Bayern, S Germany
103 D14 **Dinslaken** Nordrhein-Westfalen, W Germany
37 R11 **Dinuba** California, W USA
23 W7 **Dinwiddie** Virginia, NE USA
100 N13 **Dinxperlo** Gelderland, E Netherlands
117 F14 **Dió** *anc.* Dium. *site of ancient city* Kentrikí Makedonía, N Greece
Diófás *see* Nucet
78 M12 **Dioïla** Koulikoro, W Mali
117 G19 **Dióryga Korinthou** *Eng.* Corinth Canal. *canal* S Greece
78 G12 **Diouloulou** SW Senegal
79 N11 **Dioura** Mopti, W Mali
78 G11 **Diourbel** W Senegal
158 L10 **Dipayal** Far Western, W Nepal
124 Oo2 **Dipkarpaz** *Gk.* Rizokarpaso, Rizokárpason. NE Cyprus
155 R17 **Diplo** Sind, SE Pakistan
179 Qq15 **Dipolog** *var.* Dipolog City. Mindanao, S Philippines
193 C23 **Dipton** Southland, South Island, NZ
79 O10 **Diré** Tombouctou, C Mali
82 L13 **Dirē Dawa** E Ethiopia
Dirfis *see* Dírfys
117 H18 **Dírfys** *var.* Dirfis. ▲▲ Évvioa, C Greece
77 N9 **Dirj** *var.* Daraj, Darj. W Libya
188 G10 **Dirk Hartog Island** *island* Western Australia
79 Y8 **Dirkou** Agadez, NE Niger
189 X11 **Dirranbandi** Queensland, E Australia
83 O16 **Dirri** Galguduud, C Somalia
Dirschau *see* Tczew
39 N6 **Dirty Devil River** ≈ Utah, W USA
34 E10 **Disappointment, Cape** *headland* Washington, NW USA
188 L8 **Disappointment, Lake** *salt lake* Western Australia
191 R12 **Disaster Bay** *bay* New South Wales, SE Australia
46 J11 **Discovery Bay** C Jamaica
190 K13 **Discovery Bay** *inlet* SE Australia
69 Y15 **Discovery II Fracture Zone** *tectonic feature* SW Indian Ocean
Discovery Seamount/Discovery Seamounts *see* Discovery Tablemount
67 O19 **Discovery Tablemount** *var.* Discovery Seamount, Discovery Seamounts. *undersea feature* SW Indian Ocean
110 G9 **Disentis** *Rmsch.* Mustér. Graubünden, S Switzerland
41 O10 **Dishna River** ≈ Alaska, USA
205 X4 **Dismal Mountains** ▲▲ Antarctica
30 M14 **Dismal River** ≈ Nebraska, C USA
Disna *see* Dzisna
101 L19 **Dison** Liège, E Belgium
159 V12 **Dispur** Assam, NE India
13 R11 **Disraeli** Québec, SE Canada
117 F18 **Dístomo** *prev.* Dhístomon. Stereá Ellás, C Greece
117 H18 **Dístos, Límni** ◎ Évvoia, C Greece
61 L18 **Distrito Federal** *Eng.* Federal District. ◈ *federal district* C Brazil
43 P14 **Distrito Federal** ◈ *federal district* S Mexico
56 L4 **Distrito Federal** *off.* Territorio Distrito Federal. ◈ *federal district* N Venezuela
Distrito Federal, Territorio *see* Distrito Federal
118 J10 **Ditrău** *Hung.* Ditró. Harghita, C Romania
Ditró *see* Ditrău
160 B12 **Diu** Damān and Diu, W India
179 Rr14 **Diuata Mountains** ▲▲ Mindanao, S Philippines
Dium *see* Dió
111 S13 **Divača** SW Slovenia
104 K5 **Dives** ≈ N France
Divichi *see* Däväçi
35 Q11 **Divide** Montana, NW USA
Divin *see* Dzivin
85 N18 **Divinhe** Sofala, E Mozambique
61 L20 **Divinópolis** Minas Gerais, SE Brazil
126 I14 **Divnogorsk** Krasnoyarskiy Kray, S Russian Federation
131 N13 **Divnoye** Stavropol'skiy Kray, SW Russian Federation
78 M17 **Divo** S Ivory Coast
Divodurum Mediomatricum *see* Metz
143 N13 **Divriği** Sivas, C Turkey
Diwaniyah *see* Ad Dīwānīyah
12 J10 **Dix Milles, Lac** ◎ Québec, SE Canada
12 M8 **Dix Milles, Lac des** ◎ Québec, SE Canada
Dixmude/Dixmuide *see* Diksmuide
37 N7 **Dixon** California, W USA
32 L10 **Dixon** Illinois, N USA
22 I6 **Dixon** Kentucky, S USA
29 V6 **Dixon** Missouri, C USA
39 S9 **Dixon** New Mexico, SW USA
41 Y15 **Dixon Entrance** *strait* Canada/USA
20 D14 **Dixonville** Pennsylvania, NE USA
143 T13 **Diyadin** Ağrı, E Turkey
145 V5 **Diyālá, Nahr** *var.* Rudkhaneh-ye Sīrvān, Sirwan. ≈ Iran/Iraq *see also* Sīrvān, Rudkhaneh-ye
143 P15 **Diyarbakır** *var.* Diarbekr; *anc.* Amida. Diyarbakır, SE Turkey
143 P15 **Diyarbakır** *var.* Diarbekr. ◈ *province* SE Turkey
Dizful *see* Dezfūl
81 F16 **Dja** ≈ SE Cameroon
Djadié *see* Zadié
79 X7 **Djado** Agadez, NE Niger
79 X6 **Djado, Plateau du** ▲▲ NE Niger
Djailolo *see* Halmahera, Pulau
Djajapura *see* Jayapura
Djakarta *see* Jakarta
Djakovica *see* Đakovica
Djakovo *see* Đakovo
81 G20 **Djambala** Plateaux, C Congo
Djambi *see* Jambi
Djambi *see* Hari, Batang, Sumatera, W Indonesia
76 M9 **Djanet** E Algeria
76 M11 **Djanet** *prev.* Fort Charlet. SE Algeria
Djatiwangi *see* Jatiwangi
Djaul *see* Dyaul Island
Djawa *see* Jawa
Djéblé *see* Jablah
80 I10 **Djédaa** Batha, C Chad
76 J6 **Djelfa** *var.* El Djelfa. N Algeria
81 M14 **Djéma** Haut-Mbomou, E Central African Republic
Djeneponto *see* Jeneponto
79 N12 **Djenné** *var.* Jenné. Mopti, C Mali
Djérablous *see* Jarābulus
Djerba *see* Jerba, Île de
81 F15 **Djérem** ≈ C Cameroon
Djevdjelija *see* Gevgelija
79 P11 **Djibo** N Burkina
82 L12 **Djibouti** *var.* Jibuti. ● (Djibouti) E Djibouti
82 L12 **Djibouti** *off.* Republic of Djibouti, *var.* Jibuti; *prev.* French Somaliland, French Territory of the Afars and Issas, *Fr.* Côte Française des Somalis, Territoire Français des Afars et des Issas. ◆ *republic* E Africa
82 L12 **Djibouti** ✕ C Djibouti
Djidjel/Djidjelli *see* Jijel
57 W10 **Djoemoe** Sipaliwini, C Suriname
Djokjakarta *see* Yogyakarta
81 K21 **Djoku-Punda** Kasai Occidental, S Zaire
81 K18 **Djolu** Equateur, N Zaire
Djorče Petrov *see* Đorče Petrov
81 F17 **Djoua** ≈ Congo/Gabon
79 R14 **Djougou** W Benin
81 F16 **Djoum** Sud, S Cameroon
80 I8 **Djourab, Erg du** *dunes* N Chad
81 P17 **Djugu** Haut-Zaïre, NE Zaire
Djumbir *see* Ďumbier
94 L3 **Djúpivogur** Austurland, SE Iceland
96 L13 **Djura** Kopparberg, C Sweden
Djurdjevac *see* Đurđevac
85 G18 **D'Kar** Ghanzi, NW Botswana
207 U6 **Dmitriya Lapteva, Proliv** *strait* N Russian Federation
130 J7 **Dmitriyev-L'govskiy** Kurskaya Oblast', W Russian Federation
Dmitriyevsk *see* Makiyivka
130 K3 **Dmitrov** Moskovskaya Oblast', W Russian Federation
Dmitrovichi *see* Dzmitravichy
130 J6 **Dmitrovsk-Orlovskiy** Orlovskaya Oblast', W Russian Federation
119 R3 **Dmytrivka** Chernihivs'ka Oblast', N Ukraine
Dnepr *see* Dnieper
Dneprodzerzhinsk *see* Dniprodzerzhyns'k
Dneprodzerzhinskoye Vodokhranilishche *see* Dniprodzerzhyns'ke Vodoskhovyshche
Dnepropetrovsk *see* Dnipropetrovs'k
Dnepropetrovskaya Oblast' *see* Dnipropetrovs'ka Oblast'
Dneprorudnoye *see* Dniprorudne
Dneprovskiy Liman *see* Dniprovs'kyy Lyman
Dneprovsko-Bugskiy Kanal *see* Dnyaprowska-Buhski, Kanal
Dnestr *see* Dniester
Dnestrovskiy Liman *see* Dnistrovs'kyy Lyman
88 H11 **Dnieper** *Bel.* Dnyapro, *Rus.* Dnepr, *Ukr.* Dnipro. ≈ E Europe
119 P3 **Dnieper Lowland** *Bel.* Prydnyaprowskaya Nizina, *Ukr.* Prydniprovs'ka Nyzovyna. *lowlands* Belorussia/Ukraine
118 M8 **Dniester** *Rom.* Nistru, *Rus.* Dnestr, *Ukr.* Dnister; *anc.* Tyras. ≈ Moldova/Ukraine
Dnipro *see* Dnieper
119 T7 **Dniprodzerzhyns'k** *Rus.* Dneprodzerzhinsk; *prev.* Kamenskoye. Dnipropetrovs'ka Oblast', E Ukraine
119 T7 **Dniprodzerzhyns'ke Vodoskhovyshche** *Rus.* Dneprodzerzhinskoye Vodokhranilishche. ⊠ C Ukraine
119 U7 **Dnipropetrovs'k** *Rus.* Dnepropetrovsk; *prev.* Yekaterinoslav. Dnipropetrovs'ka Oblast', E Ukraine
119 U8 **Dnipropetrovs'k** ✕ Dnipropetrovs'ka Oblast', S Ukraine
Dnipropetrovs'k *see* Dnipropetrovs'ka Oblast'
119 T7 **Dnipropetrovs'ka Oblast'** *var.* Dnipropetrovs'k, *Rus.* Dnepropetrovskaya Oblast'. ◈ *province* E Ukraine
119 U9 **Dniprorudne** *Rus.* Dneprorudnoye. Zaporiz'ka Oblast', SE Ukraine
119 Q11 **Dniprovs'kyy Lyman** *Rus.* Dneprovskiy Liman. *bay* S Ukraine
Dnister *see* Dniester
119 O11 **Dnistrovs'kyy Lyman** *Rus.* Dnestrovskiy Liman. *inlet* S Ukraine
128 G14 **Dno** Pskovskaya Oblast', W Russian Federation
Dnyapro *see* Dnieper
121 H20 **Dnyaprowska-Buhski, Kanal** *Rus.* Dneprovsko-Bugskiy Kanal. *canal* SW Belorussia
11 O14 **Doaktown** New Brunswick, SE Canada
80 H13 **Doba** Logone-Oriental, S Chad
120 E9 **Dobele** *Ger.* Doblen. Dobele, W Latvia
103 N16 **Döbeln** Sachsen, E Germany
176 Vv9 **Doberai, Jazirah** *Dut.* Vogelkop. *peninsula* Irian Jaya, E Indonesia
112 F10 **Dobiegniew** *Ger.* Woldenberg Neumark. Gorzów, W Poland
Doblen *see* Dobele
83 K18 **Dobli** *spring/well* SW Somalia
176 W13 **Dobo** Pulau Wamar, E Indonesia
114 H11 **Doboj** N Bosnia and Herzegovina
112 L8 **Dobre Miasto** *Ger.* Guttstadt. Olsztyn, N Poland
116 N7 **Dobrich** *Rom.* Bazargic; *prev.* Tolbukhin. Varnenska Oblast, NE Bulgaria
130 M8 **Dobrinka** Lipetskaya Oblast', W Russian Federation
130 M7 **Dobrinka** Volgogradskaya Oblast', SW Russian Federation
Dobrla Vas *see* Eberndorf
113 I15 **Dobrodzień** *Ger.* Guttentag. Częstochowa, S Poland
Dobrogea *see* Dobruja
119 W7 **Dobropillya** *Rus.* Dobropol'ye. Donets'ka Oblast', SE Ukraine
Dobropol'ye *see* Dobropillya
119 P8 **Dobrovelychkivka** Kirovohrads'ka Oblast', C Ukraine
Dobrudja/Dobrudzha *see* Dobruja
116 O7 **Dobruja** *var.* Dobrudja, *Bul.* Dobrudzha, *Rom.* Dobrogea. *physical region* Bulgaria/Romania
121 P19 **Dobrush** Homyel'skaya Voblasts', SE Belorussia
129 U14 **Dobryanka** Permskaya Oblast', NW Russian Federation
119 P2 **Dobryanka** Chernihivs'ka Oblast', N Ukraine
Dobryn' *see* Dabryn'
23 R8 **Dobson** North Carolina, SE USA
61 N20 **Doce, Rio** ≈ SE Brazil
95 I16 **Docksta** Västernorrland, C Sweden
43 N10 **Doctor Arroyo** Nuevo León, NE Mexico
64 L4 **Doctor Pedro P. Peña** Boquerón, W Paraguay
175 T7 **Dodaga** Pulau Halmahera, E Indonesia
161 G21 **Dodda Betta** ▲ S India
Dodecanese *see* Dodekánisos
117 M22 **Dodekánisos** *var.* Nóties Sporádes, *Eng.* Dodecanese; *prev.* Dhodhekánisos. *island group* SE Greece
28 J6 **Dodge City** Kansas, C USA
32 K9 **Dodgeville** Wisconsin, N USA
99 H25 **Dodman Point** *headland* SW England, UK
83 J14 **Dodola** S Ethiopia
83 H22 **Dodoma** ● (Tanzania) Dodoma, C Tanzania
83 H22 **Dodoma** ◈ *region* C Tanzania
117 C16 **Dodóni** *var.* Dhodhóni. *site of ancient city* Ípeiros, W Greece
35 U7 **Dodson** Montana, NW USA
27 P3 **Dodson** Texas, SW USA
100 M12 **Doesburg** Gelderland, E Netherlands
100 N12 **Doetinchem** Gelderland, E Netherlands
164 L12 **Dogai Coring** *var.* Lake Montcalm. ◎ W China
143 N15 **Doğanşehir** Malatya, C Turkey
86 E9 **Dogger Bank** *undersea feature* C North Sea
25 S10 **Dog Island** *island* Florida, SE USA
12 C7 **Dog Lake** ◎ Ontario, S Canada
108 B9 **Dogliani** Piemonte, NE Italy
170 G11 **Dōgo** *island* Oki-shotō, SW Japan
Do Gonbadān *see* Dow Gonbadān
79 S12 **Dogondoutchi** Dosso, SW Niger
Dōgo-san *see* Dōgo-yama
170 F13 **Dōgo-yama** *var.* Dōgo-san. ▲ Kyūshū, SW Japan
Dogrular *see* Pravda
143 T13 **Doğubayazıt** Ağrı, E Turkey
143 P12 **Doğu Karadeniz Dağları** *var.* Anadolu Dağları. ▲▲ NE Turkey
Doha *see* Ad Dawḩah
Dohad *see* Dāhod
Dohuk *see* Dahūk
165 N16 **Doilungdêqên** Xizang Zizhiqu, W China
116 F12 **Doïranis, Límnis** *Bul.* Ezero Doyransko. ◎ N Greece
Doire *see* Londonderry
101 H22 **Doische** Namur, S Belgium
61 P17 **Dois de Julho** ✕ (Salvador) Bahia, NE Brazil
62 H12 **Dois Vizinhos** Paraná, S Brazil
82 H10 **Doka** Gedaref, E Sudan
Doka *see* Kéita, Bahr
145 T3 **Dokan** *var.* Dūkān. E Iraq
96 H13 **Dokka** Oppland, S Norway
100 L5 **Dokkum** Friesland, N Netherlands
100 L5 **Dokkumer Ee** ≈ N Netherlands
78 K13 **Doko** Haute-Guinée, NE Guinea
Dokshitsy *see* Dokshytsy
120 K13 **Dokshytsy** *Rus.* Dokshitsy. Vitsyebskaya Voblasts', N Belorussia
119 X8 **Dokuchayevs'k** *var.* Dokuchayevsk. Donets'ka Oblast', SE Ukraine
Dolak, Pulau *see* Yos Sudarso, Pulau
31 P9 **Doland** South Dakota, N USA
65 J18 **Dolavón** Chaco, S Argentina
13 P6 **Dolbeau** Québec, SE Canada
104 I5 **Dol-de-Bretagne** Ille-et-Vilaine, NW France
66 J13 **Doldrums Fracture Zone** *tectonic feature* W Atlantic Ocean
105 S8 **Dôle** Jura, E France
99 J19 **Dolgellau** NW Wales, UK
Dolginovo *see* Dawhinava
Dolgi, Ostrov *see* Dolgiy, Ostrov
129 U2 **Dolgiy, Ostrov** *var.* Ostrov Dolgi. *island* NW Russian Federation
168 J9 **Dölgöön** Övörhangay, C Mongolia
109 C20 **Dolianova** Sardegna, Italy, C Mediterranean Sea
Dolina *see* Dolyna
127 Oo15 **Dolinsk** Ostrov Sakhalin, Sakhalinskaya Oblast', SE Russian Federation
Dolinskaya *see* Dolyns'ka
81 F21 **Dolisie** *prev.* Loubomo. Le Niari, S Congo
118 G14 **Dolj** ◈ *county* SW Romania
100 P5 **Dollard** *bay* NW Germany
204 J5 **Dolleman Island** *island* Antarctica
116 I8 **Dolni Dŭbnik** Loveshka Oblast, NW Bulgaria
116 F8 **Dolni Lom** Oblast Montana, NW Bulgaria
Dolnja Lendava *see* Lendava
116 K9 **Dolno Panicherevo** *var.* Panicherevo. Khaskovska Oblast, C Bulgaria
113 K18 **Dolný Kubín** *Hung.* Alsókubin. Stredné Slovensko, N Slovakia
108 H8 **Dolo** Veneto, NE Italy
Dolomites/Dolomiti *see* Dolomitiche, Alpi
108 H6 **Dolomitiche, Alpi** *var.* Dolomiti, *Eng.* Dolomites. ▲▲ NE Italy
Dolonnur *see* Duolun
168 K10 **Doloon** Ömnögovĭ, S Mongolia
63 D19 **Dolores** Buenos Aires, E Argentina
44 E3 **Dolores** Petén, N Guatemala
179 R12 **Dolores** Samar, C Philippines
107 S12 **Dolores** País Valenciano, E Spain
63 E21 **Dolores** Soriano, SW Uruguay
43 N12 **Dolores Hidalgo** *var.* Ciudad de Dolores Hidalgo. Guanajuato, C Mexico
15 Hh3 **Dolphin and Union Strait** *strait* Northwest Territories, N Canada
67 D23 **Dolphin, Cape** *headland* East Falkland, Falkland Islands
46 H12 **Dolphin Head** *hill* W Jamaica
85 B21 **Dolphin Head** *var.* Cape Dernberg. *headland* SW Namibia
112 G12 **Dolsk** *Ger.* Dolzig. Poznań, W Poland
178 J8 **Đô Lương** Nghê An, N Vietnam
118 I6 **Dolyna** *Rus.* Dolina. Ivano-Frankivs'ka Oblast', W Ukraine
119 R8 **Dolyns'ka** *Rus.* Dolinskaya. Kirovohrads'ka Oblast', S Ukraine
Dolzig *see* Dolsk
Domachëvo/Domaczewo *see* Damachava
119 P9 **Domanivka** Mykolayivs'ka Oblast', S Ukraine
159 S13 **Domar** Rajshahi, N Bangladesh
110 I9 **Domat/Ems** Graubünden, SE Switzerland
113 A18 **Domažlice** *Ger.* Taus. Západní Čechy, SW Czech Republic
131 X8 **Dombarovskiy** Orenburgskaya Oblast', W Russian Federation
96 G10 **Dombås** Oppland, S Norway
85 M17 **Dombe** Manica, C Mozambique
84 A13 **Dombe Grande** Benguela, C Angola
105 R10 **Dombes** *physical region* E France
176 Xx10 **Dombo** Irian Jaya, E Indonesia
113 I25 **Dombóvár** Tolna, S Hungary
101 D14 **Domburg** Zeeland, SW Netherlands
60 L13 **Dom Eliseu** Pará, NE Brazil
Domel Island *see* Letsôk-aw Kyun
105 O11 **Dôme, Puy de** ▲ C France
38 H13 **Dome Rock Mountains** ▲▲ Arizona, SW USA
Domesnes, Cape *see* Kolkasrags
64 G8 **Domeyko** Atacama, N Chile
64 H5 **Domeyko, Cordillera** ▲▲ N Chile
104 K5 **Domfront** Orne, N France
176 Xx10 **Dom, Gunung** ▲ Irian Jaya, E Indonesia
47 X11 **Dominica** *off.* Commonwealth of Dominica. ◆ *republic* E West Indies
49 S3 **Dominica** *island* Dominica
Dominica Channel *see* Martinique Passage
45 N15 **Dominical** Puntarenas, SE Costa Rica
47 Q8 **Dominican Republic** ◆ *republic* C West Indies
47 X11 **Dominica Passage** *passage* E Caribbean Sea
101 K14 **Dommel** ≈ S Netherlands
83 O14 **Domo** SE Ethiopia
130 L4 **Domodedovo** ✕ (Moskva) Moskovskaya Oblast', W Russian Federation
108 C6 **Domodossola** Piemonte, NE Italy
117 F17 **Domokós** *var.* Dhomokós. Stereá Ellás, C Greece
180 I14 **Domoni** Anjouan, SE Comoros
63 G16 **Dom Pedrito** Rio Grande do Sul, S Brazil
Dompoe *see* Dompu
175 Oo16 **Dompu** *prev.* Dompoe. Sumbawa, C Indonesia
Domschale *see* Domžale
64 H13 **Domuyo, Volcán** Ѫ W Argentina
111 U11 **Domžale** *Ger.* Domschale. C Slovenia
131 O10 **Don** *var.* Duna, Tanais. ≈ SW Russian Federation
98 K9 **Don** ≈ NE Scotland, UK
190 M11 **Donald** Victoria, SE Australia
24 J9 **Donaldsonville** Louisiana, S USA
25 S8 **Donalsonville** Georgia, SE USA
Donau *see* Danube
103 G23 **Donaueschingen** Baden-Württemberg, SW Germany
103 K22 **Donaumoos** *wetland* S Germany
103 K22 **Donauwörth** Bayern, S Germany
111 U7 **Donawitz** Steiermark, SE Austria
119 X7 **Donbass** *industrial region* Russian Federation/Ukraine
106 K11 **Don Benito** Extremadura, W Spain
99 M17 **Doncaster** *anc.* Danum. N England, UK
46 K12 **Don Christophers Point** *headland* C Jamaica
57 V9 **Donderkamp** Sipaliwini, NW Suriname
84 B12 **Dondo** Cuanza Norte, NW Angola
175 Q9 **Dondo** Sulawesi, N Indonesia
85 N17 **Dondo** Sofala, C Mozambique
175 Pp7 **Dondo, Teluk** *bay* Sulawesi, N Indonesia
161 K26 **Dondra Head** *headland* S Sri Lanka
Dondușani *see* Dondușeni
118 M8 **Dondușeni** *var.* Dondușani, *Rus.* Dondyushany. N Moldova
Dondyushany *see* Dondușeni
99 D15 **Donegal** *Ir.* Dún na nGall. NW Ireland
99 D14 **Donegal** *Ir.* Dún na nGall. *cultural region* NW Ireland
99 C15 **Donegal Bay** *Ir.* Bá Dhún na nGall. *bay* NW Ireland
86 K10 **Donets** ≈ Russian Federation/Ukraine
119 X8 **Donets'k** *Rus.* Donetsk; *prev.* Stalino. Donets'ka Oblast', E Ukraine
119 W8 **Donets'k** ✕ Donets'ka Oblast', E Ukraine
Donets'k *see* Donets'ka Oblast'
119 W8 **Donets'ka Oblast'** *var.* Donets'k, *Rus.* Donetskaya Oblast'; *prev.* Rus. Stalinskaya Oblast'. ◈ *province* SE Ukraine
Donetskaya Oblast' *see* Donets'ka Oblast'
69 P8 **Donga** ≈ Cameroon/Nigeria
163 O13 **Dongchuan** Yunnan, SW China
101 I14 **Dongen** Noord-Brabant, S Netherlands
166 K17 **Dongfang** *var.* Basuo. Hainan, S China
169 Z7 **Dongfanghong** Heilongjiang, NE China
169 W11 **Dongfeng** Jilin, NE China
175 P9 **Donggala** Sulawesi, C Indonesia
169 V13 **Donggou** Liaoning, NE China
167 O14 **Dongguan** Guangdong, S China
178 K9 **Đông Ha** Quang Tri, C Vietnam
Dong Hai *see* East China Sea
166 M16 **Donghai Dao** *island* S China
178 Jj9 **Đông Hơi** Quang Binh, C Vietnam
110 H10 **Dongio** Ticino, S Switzerland
Dongkan *see* Binhai
166 L11 **Dongkou** Hunan, S China
Dongliao *see* Liaoyuan
Dong-nai *see* Đông Nai, Sông
178 K13 **Đông Nai, Sông** *var.* Dong-nai, Dong Noi, Donnai. ≈ S Vietnam
167 O14 **Dongnan Qiuling** *plateau* SE China
169 Y9 **Dongning** Heilongjiang, NE China
Dong Noi *see* Đông Nai, Sông
85 C14 **Dongo** Huíla, C Angola
82 E7 **Dongola** *var.* Donqola, Dunqulah. Northern, N Sudan
81 I17 **Dongou** La Likouala, NE Congo
178 Jj13 **Đông Phu** Sông Be, S Vietnam
Dong Rak, Phanom *see* Dângrêk, Chuŏr Phnum
167 Q14 **Dongshan Dao** *island* SE China
169 N14 **Dongsheng** Nei Mongol Zizhiqu, N China
167 R7 **Dongtai** Jiangsu, E China
167 N10 **Dongting Hu** *var.* Tung-t'ing Hu. ◎ S China
167 P10 **Dongxiang** Jiangxi, S China
167 Q4 **Dongying** Shandong, E China
29 X8 **Doniphan** Missouri, C USA
8 G7 **Donjek** ≈ Yukon Territory, W Canada
114 E11 **Donji Lapac** Zadar-Knin, C Croatia
114 H8 **Donji Miholjac** Osijek-Baranja, NE Croatia
114 P12 **Donji Milanovac** Serbia, E Yugoslavia
114 G12 **Donji Vakuf** C Bosnia and Herzegovina
100 M6 **Donkerbroek** Friesland, N Netherlands
178 Hh11 **Don Muang** ✕ (Krung Thep) Nonthaburi, C Thailand
27 S17 **Donna** Texas, SW USA
13 Q10 **Donnacona** Québec, SE Canada
Donnai *see* Đông Nai, Sông
31 Y16 **Donnellson** Iowa, C USA
9 O13 **Donnelly** Alberta, W Canada
103 F19 **Donnersberg** ▲ W Germany
Donoso *see* Miguel de la Borda
107 P2 **Donostia-San Sebastián** País Vasco, N Spain
117 K21 **Donoússa** *island* Kykládes, Greece, Aegean Sea
37 P8 **Don Pedro Reservoir** ⊠ California, W USA
Donqola *see* Dongola
130 L5 **Donskoy** Tul'skaya Oblast', W Russian Federation
179 Q11 **Donsol** Luzon, N Philippines
83 L16 **Doolow** SE Ethiopia
41 Q7 **Doonerak, Mount** ▲ Alaska, USA
100 J12 **Doorn** Utrecht, C Netherlands
Doornik *see* Tournai
33 N6 **Door Peninsula** *peninsula* Wisconsin, N USA
82 P13 **Dooxo Nugaaleed** *var.* Nogal Valley. *valley* E Somalia
166 G8 **Do Qu** ≈ C China
108 B7 **Dora Baltea** *anc.* Duria Major. ≈ NW Italy
188 K7 **Dora, Lake** *salt lake* Western Australia
108 A8 **Dora Riparia** *anc.* Duria Minor. ≈ NW Italy
Dorbiljin *see* Emin
169 V8 **Dorbod** *var.* Dorbod Mongolzu Zizhixian, Talkang. Heilongjiang, NE China
Dorbod Mongolzu Zizhixian *see* Dorbod
115 N18 **Đorče Petrov** *var.* Djorče Petrov, Gorče Petrov. N FYR Macedonia
12 F16 **Dorchester** Ontario, S Canada
99 L24 **Dorchester** *anc.* Durnovaria. S England, UK
15 Mm4 **Dorchester, Cape** *headland* Baffin Island, Northwest Territories, NE Canada
85 D19 **Dordabis** Khomas, C Namibia
104 L12 **Dordogne** ◈ *department* SW France
105 N12 **Dordogne** ≈ W France
100 H13 **Dordrecht** *var.* Dordt, Dort. Zuid-Holland, SW Netherlands
Dordt *see* Dordrecht
105 P11 **Dore** ≈ C France
9 S13 **Doré Lake** Saskatchewan, C Canada
105 O12 **Dore, Monts** ▲▲ C France
103 M23 **Dorfen** Bayern, SE Germany
109 D18 **Dorgali** Sardegna, Italy, C Mediterranean Sea
168 F7 **Dörgön Nuur** ◎ NW Mongolia
79 Q12 **Dori** N Burkina
85 E24 **Doring** ≈ S South Africa
103 E16 **Dormagen** Nordrhein-Westfalen, W Germany
105 P4 **Dormans** Marne, N France
110 E6 **Dornach** Solothurn, NW Switzerland
Dorna Watra *see* Vatra Dornei
110 J7 **Dornbirn** Vorarlberg, W Austria
98 I7 **Dornoch** N Scotland, UK
98 J7 **Dornoch Firth** *inlet* N Scotland, UK
169 P7 **Dornod** ◈ *province* E Mongolia
169 N10 **Dornogovĭ** ◈ *province* SE Mongolia
79 P10 **Doro** Tombouctou, S Mali
118 L14 **Dorobanțu** Călărași, S Romania
113 J22 **Dorog** Komárom-Esztergom, N Hungary

◆ Country
● Country Capital
◇ Dependent Territory
○ Dependent Territory Capital
◈ Administrative Region
✕ International Airport
▲ Mountain
▲▲ Mountain Range
Ѫ Volcano
≈ River
◎ Lake
⊠ Reservoir

130 I4 Dorogobuzh Smolenskaya Oblast', W Russian Federation
118 K8 Dorohoi Botoșani, NE Romania
95 H15 Dorotea Västerbotten, N Sweden
Dorpat see Tartu
188 G10 Dorre Island island Western Australia
191 U5 Dorrigo New South Wales, SE Australia
37 N1 Dorris California, W USA
12 H13 Dorset Ontario, SE Canada
99 K23 Dorset cultural region S England, UK
103 E14 Dorsten Nordrhein-Westfalen, W Germany
Dort see Dordrecht
103 F15 Dortmund Nordrhein-Westfalen, W Germany
102 F12 Dortmund-Ems-Kanal canal W Germany
142 L17 Dörtyol Hatay, S Turkey
148 L7 Do Rūd var. Dow Rūd, Durud. Lorestān, W Iran
81 O15 Doruma Haut-Zaïre, N Zaire
13 O12 Dorval ✕ (Montréal) Québec, SE Canada
47 T5 Dos Bocas, Lago ◎ C Puerto Rico
106 K14 Dos Hermanas Andalucía, S Spain
Dospad Dagh see Rhodope Mountains
37 P10 Dos Palos California, W USA
116 I11 Dospat Plovdivska Oblast, SW Bulgaria
116 H11 Dospat, Yazovir ⊡ SW Bulgaria
102 M11 Dosse ~ NE Germany
79 S12 Dosso Dosso, SW Niger
79 S12 Dosso ◆ department SW Niger
150 G12 Dossor Atyrau, SW Kazakhstan
153 V9 Dostuk Narynskaya Oblast', C Kyrgyzstan
151 X13 Dostyk prev. Druzhba. Taldykorgan, SE Kazakhstan
25 R7 Dothan Alabama, S USA
41 T9 Dot Lake Alaska, USA
120 F12 Dotnuva Kėdainiai, C Lithuania
101 D19 Dottignies Hainaut, W Belgium
105 P2 Douai prev. Douay, anc. Duacum. Nord, N France
12 L9 Douaire, Lac ◎ Québec, SE Canada
81 D16 Douala var. Duala. Littoral, W Cameroon
81 D16 Douala ✕ Littoral, W Cameroon
104 F6 Douarnenez Finistère, NW France
104 E6 Douarnenez, Baie de bay NW France
Douay see Douai
27 O6 Double Mountain Fork Brazos River ~ Texas, SW USA
25 O3 Double Springs Alabama, S USA
105 T8 Doubs ◆ department E France
110 C8 Doubs ~ France/Switzerland
193 A22 Doubtful Sound sound South Island, NZ
192 J2 Doubtless Bay bay North Island, NZ
27 X9 Doucette Texas, SW USA
104 K8 Doué-la-Fontaine Maine-et-Loire, NW France
79 O11 Douentza Mopti, S Mali
67 D24 Douglas East Falkland, Falkland Islands
99 I16 Douglas ○ (Isle of Man) E Isle of Man
85 H23 Douglas Northern Cape, C South Africa
41 X13 Douglas Alexander Archipelago, Alaska, USA
39 O17 Douglas Arizona, SW USA
25 U7 Douglas Georgia, SE USA
35 Y15 Douglas Wyoming, C USA
8 J14 Douglas Channel channel British Columbia, W Canada
190 G3 Douglas Creek seasonal river South Australia
33 P5 Douglas Lake ◎ Michigan, N USA
23 O9 Douglas Lake ⊡ Tennessee, S USA
41 Q13 Douglas, Mount ▲ Alaska, USA
204 I6 Douglas Range ▲▲ Alexander Island, Antarctica
124 N10 Doukáto, Ákra headland Lefkáda, W Greece
105 O2 Doullens Somme, N France
Douma see Dūmā
81 F15 Doumé Est, E Cameroon
101 E21 Dour Hainaut, S Belgium
61 K18 Dourada, Serra ▲▲ S Brazil
61 I21 Dourados Mato Grosso do Sul, S Brazil
105 N5 Dourdan Essonne, N France
106 I6 Douro Sp. Duero. ~ Portugal/Spain see also Duero
106 G6 Douro Litoral former province N Portugal
Douvres see Dover
104 K15 Douze ~ SW France
191 P17 Dover Tasmania, SE Australia
99 Q22 Dover Fr. Douvres; Lat. Dubris Portus. SE England, UK
19 R8 Dover state capital Delaware, NE USA
21 P9 Dover New Hampshire, NE USA
20 J14 Dover New Jersey, NE USA
33 U12 Dover Ohio, N USA
22 H8 Dover Tennessee, S USA
99 Q23 Dover, Strait of var. Straits of Dover, Fr. Pas de Calais. strait England, UK/France
Dover, Straits of see Dover, Strait of
Dovlen see Devin
96 G11 Dovre Oppland, S Norway
96 G10 Dovrefjell plateau S Norway
Dovsk see Dowsk
85 M14 Dowa Central, C Malawi
33 O10 Dowagiac Michigan, N USA
149 N10 Dow Gonbadān var. Do Gonbadān, Gonbadān. Kohkīlūyeh va Būyer Aḥmadī, SW Iran
154 M2 Dowlatābād Fāryāb, N Afghanistan
99 G16 Down cultural region SE Northern Ireland, UK
35 R16 Downey Idaho, NW USA
37 P5 Downieville California, W USA
99 G16 Downpatrick Ir. Dún Pádraig. SE Northern Ireland, UK
28 M3 Downs Kansas, C USA
20 J12 Downsville New York, NE USA
Dow Rūd see Do Rūd
31 V12 Dows Iowa, C USA
121 O17 Dowsk Rus. Dovsk. Homyel'skaya Voblasts', SE Belorussia
37 Q4 Doyle California, W USA
20 I15 Doylestown Pennsylvania, NE USA
Doyransko, Ezero see Doïranis, Límnis
116 I8 Doyrentsi Loveshka Oblast, N Bulgaria
170 Ff11 Dōzen island Oki-shotō, SW Japan
12 K9 Dozois, Réservoir ⊡ Québec, SE Canada
76 D9 Drâa seasonal river S Morocco
Drâa, Hammada du see Dra, Hamada du
Drabble see José Enrique Rodó
119 Q5 Drabiv Cherkas'ka Voblast', C Ukraine
Drable see José Enrique Rodó
105 S13 Drac ~ E France
Drač/Drac see Durrës
62 I8 Dracena São Paulo, S Brazil
100 M6 Drachten Friesland, N Netherlands
94 H11 Drag Nordland, C Norway
118 L14 Dragalina Călărași, SE Romania
118 J14 Drăgănești-Vlașca Teleorman, S Romania
118 I13 Drăgășani Vâlcea, SW Romania
116 G9 Dragoman Sofiyska Oblast, W Bulgaria
117 L25 Dragonáda island SE Greece
Dragonera, Isla see Sa Dragonera
47 T14 Dragon's Mouths, The strait Trinidad and Tobago/Venezuela
97 J23 Dragør København, E Denmark
116 F10 Dragovishtsa Sofiyska Oblast, W Bulgaria
105 U15 Draguignan Var, SE France
76 E9 Dra, Hamada du var. Hammada du Drâa, Haut Plateau du Dra. plateau W Algeria
Dra, Haut Plateau du see Dra, Hamada du
121 H19 Drahichyn Pol. Drohiczyn Poleski, Rus. Drogichin. Brestskaya Voblasts', SW Belorussia
31 N4 Drake North Dakota, N USA
85 K23 Drakensberg ▲▲ Lesotho/South Africa
204 F3 Drake Passage passage Atlantic Ocean/Pacific Ocean
116 L8 Dralfa Razgradska Oblast, N Bulgaria
116 I12 Dráma var. Dhráma. Anatolikí Makedonía kai Thráki, NE Greece
Dramburg see Drawsko Pomorskie
97 H15 Drammen Buskerud, S Norway
97 H15 Drammensfjorden fjord S Norway
94 H1 Drangajökull ▲ NW Iceland
97 F16 Drangedal Telemark, S Norway
94 I2 Drangsnes Vestfirdhir, NW Iceland
Drann see Dravinja
111 T10 Drau var. Drava, Eng. Drave, Hung. Dráva. ~ C Europe see also Drava
86 I11 Drava var. Drau, Eng. Drave, Hung. Dráva. ~ C Europe see also Drau
Dráva see Drau/Drava
Drave see Drau/Drava
111 W10 Dravinja Ger. Drann. ~ NE Slovenia
111 V9 Dravograd Ger. Unterdrauburg; prev. Spodnji Dravograd. N Slovenia
112 F10 Drawa ~ NW Poland
112 F9 Drawno Gorzów, NW Poland
112 F9 Drawsko Pomorskie Ger. Dramburg. Koszalin, NW Poland
31 R3 Drayton North Dakota, N USA
9 P14 Drayton Valley Alberta, SW Canada
194 F10 Dreikikir East Sepik, NW PNG
Dreikirchen see Teiuș
100 N7 Drenthe ◆ province NE Netherlands
117 H15 Drépano, Ákra var. Akra Dhrepanon. headland N Greece
Drepanum see Trapani
12 D17 Dresden Ontario, S Canada
103 O16 Dresden Sachsen, E Germany
22 G8 Dresden Tennessee, S USA
120 M11 Dretun' Rus. Dretun'. Vitsyebskaya Voblasts', N Belorussia
104 M5 Dreux anc. Drocae, Durocasses. Eure-et-Loir, C France
96 I11 Drevsjø Hedmark, S Norway
24 K3 Drew Mississippi, S USA
112 F10 Drezdenko Ger. Driesen. Gorzów, W Poland
100 J12 Driebergen var. Driebergen-Rijsenburg. Utrecht, C Netherlands
Driebergen-Rijsenburg see Driebergen
Driesen see Drezdenko
99 N16 Driffield E England, UK
67 D25 Driftwood Point headland East Falkland, Falkland Islands
35 S14 Driggs Idaho, NW USA
Drin see Drinit, Lumi i
114 K12 Drina ~ Bosnia and Herzegovina/Yugoslavia
Drin, Gulf of see Drinit, Gjiri i
115 K18 Drinit, Gjiri i var. Pellg i Drinit, Eng. Gulf of Drin. gulf NW Albania
115 L17 Drinit, Lumi i var. Drin. ~ NW Albania
Drinit, Pellg i see Drinit, Gjiri i
Drinit të Zi, Lumi i see Black Drin
115 L22 Drino var. Drino, Drinos Pótamos, Alb. Lumi i Drinos. ~ Albania/Greece
Drinos, Lumi i/Drinos Pótamos see Drino
27 S11 Dripping Springs Texas, SW USA
27 S15 Driscoll Texas, SW USA
24 H5 Driskill Mountain ▲ Louisiana, S USA
Drissa see Drysa
96 G10 Driva ~ S Norway
114 E13 Drniš It. Dernis. Šibenik, S Croatia
97 H15 Drøbak Akershus, S Norway
118 G13 Drobeta-Turnu Severin prev. Turnu Severin. Mehedinți, SW Romania
Drocae see Dreux
118 M8 Drochia Rus. Drokiya. N Moldova
99 F17 Drogheda Ir. Droichead Átha. NE Ireland
Drogichin see Drahichyn
Drogobych see Drohobych
Drohiczyn Poleski see Drahichyn
118 H6 Drohobych Pol. Drohobycz, Rus. Drogobych. L'vivs'ka Oblast', NW Ukraine
Drohobycz see Drohobych
Droichead Átha see Drogheda
Droicheadna Bandan see Bandon
Droichead na Banna see Banbridge
Droim Mór see Dromore
Drokiya see Drochia
105 R13 Drôme ◆ department E France
105 S13 Drôme ~ E France
99 G15 Dromore Ir. Droim Mór. SE Northern Ireland, UK
108 A9 Dronero Piemonte, NE Italy
104 L12 Dronne ~ SW France
205 Q3 Dronning Maud Land physical region Antarctica
100 K6 Dronrijp Fris. Dronryp. Friesland, N Netherlands
Dronryp see Dronrijp
100 L9 Dronten Flevoland, C Netherlands
Drontheim see Trondheim
104 L13 Dropt ~ SW France
155 T4 Drosh North-West Frontier Province, NW Pakistan
Drossen see Ośno Lubuskie
Drug see Durg
152 I9 Drujba Rus. Druzhba. Khorazm Wiloyati, W Uzbekistan
120 I12 Drūkšiai ◎ NE Lithuania
Druk-yul see Bhutan
9 Q16 Drumheller Alberta, SW Canada
35 Q10 Drummond Montana, NW USA
33 R4 Drummond Island island Michigan, N USA
Drummond Island see Tabiteuea
23 X7 Drummond, Lake ◎ Virginia, NE USA
13 P12 Drummondville Québec, SE Canada
41 T11 Drum, Mount ▲ Alaska, USA
29 O9 Drumright Oklahoma, C USA
101 J14 Drunen Noord-Brabant, S Netherlands
Druskienniki see Druskininkai
121 F15 Druskininkai Pol. Druskienniki. Druskininskai, S Lithuania
100 K13 Druten Gelderland, SE Netherlands
120 K11 Druya Vitsyebskaya Voblasts', NW Belorussia
119 S2 Druzhba Sums'ka Oblast', NE Ukraine
Druzhba see Dostyk, Kazakhstan
Druzhba see Drujba, Uzbekistan
126 Mm7 Druzhina Respublika Sakha (Yakutiya), NE Russian Federation
119 X7 Druzhkivka Donets'ka Oblast', E Ukraine
114 E12 Drvar W Bosnia and Herzegovina
115 G15 Drvenik Split-Dalmacija, SE Croatia
116 K9 Dryanovo Loveshka Oblast, C Bulgaria
28 G7 Dry Cimarron River ~ Kansas/Oklahoma, C USA
10 B11 Dryden Ontario, C Canada
26 M11 Dryden Texas, SW USA
205 Q14 Drygalski Ice Tongue ice feature Antarctica
120 L11 Drysa Rus. Drissa. ~ N Belorussia
25 V17 Dry Tortugas island Florida, SE USA
81 D15 Dschang Ouest, W Cameroon
56 J5 Duaca Lara, N Venezuela
Duacum see Douai
Duala see Douala
47 N9 Duarte, Pico ▲ C Dominican Republic
146 J5 Ḍubā Tabūk, NW Saudi Arabia
Dubai see Dubayy
119 N9 Dubăsari Rus. Dubossary. NE Moldova
119 N9 Dubăsari Reservoir ⊡ NE Moldova
15 J8 Dubawnt ~ Northwest Territories, NW Canada
15 K7 Dubawnt Lake ◎ Northwest Territories, N Canada
32 L6 Du Bay, Lake ⊡ Wisconsin, N USA
147 U7 Dubayy Eng. Dubai. Dubayy, NE UAE
147 W7 Dubayy Eng. Dubai. ✕ Dubayy, NE UAE
191 R7 Dubbo New South Wales, SE Australia
110 G7 Dübendorf Zürich, NW Switzerland
99 F18 Dublin Ir. Baile Átha Cliath; anc. Eblana. ● (Ireland), E Ireland
25 U5 Dublin Georgia, SE USA
27 R7 Dublin Texas, SW USA
99 G18 Dublin Ir. Baile Átha Cliath; anc. Eblana. cultural region E Ireland
99 G18 Dublin Airport ✕ E Ireland
201 V12 Dublon var. Tonoas. island Chuuk Islands, C Micronesia
130 K2 Dubna Moskovskaya Oblast', W Russian Federation
113 G19 Dubňany Ger. Dubnian. Jižní Morava, SE Czech Republic
Dubnian see Dubňany
113 I19 Dubnica nad Váhom Hung. Máriatölgyes; prev. Dubnicz. Stredné Slovensko, NW Slovakia
Dubnicz see Dubnica nad Váhom
118 K4 Dubno Rivnens'ka Oblast', NW Ukraine
20 D13 Du Bois Pennsylvania, NE USA
35 R13 Dubois Idaho, NW USA
35 T14 Dubois Wyoming, C USA
Dubossary see Dubăsari
131 O10 Dubovka Volgogradskaya Oblast', SW Russian Federation
78 H14 Dubréka Guinée-Maritime, SW Guinea
12 B7 Dubreuilville Ontario, S Canada
Dubris Portus see Dover
121 L20 Dubrova Rus. Dubrova. Homyel'skaya Voblasts', SE Belorussia
130 I5 Dubrovka Bryanskaya Oblast', W Russian Federation
115 H16 Dubrovnik It. Ragusa. Dubrovnik-Neretva, SE Croatia
115 I16 Dubrovnik ✕ Dubrovnik-Neretva, SE Croatia
115 F16 Dubrovnik-Neretva off. Dubrovačko-Neretvanska Županija. ◆ province SE Croatia
Dubrovno see Dubrowna
118 L2 Dubrovytsya Rivnens'ka Oblast', NW Ukraine
121 O14 Dubrowna Rus. Dubrovno. Vitsyebskaya Voblasts', N Belorussia
31 Z13 Dubuque Iowa, C USA
120 E12 Dubysa ~ C Lithuania
178 K12 Đưc Cơ Gia Lai, C Vietnam
203 V12 Duc de Gloucester, Îles du Eng. Duke of Gloucester Islands. island group C French Polynesia
113 C15 Duchcov Ger. Dux. Severní Čechy, NW Czech Republic
39 N3 Duchesne Utah, W USA
203 P17 Ducie Island atoll E Pitcairn Islands
9 W15 Duck Bay Manitoba, S Canada
25 X17 Duck Key island Florida Keys, Florida, SE USA
9 T14 Duck Lake Saskatchewan, S Canada
9 V15 Duck Mountain ▲▲ Manitoba, S Canada
22 I9 Duck River ~ Tennessee, S USA
22 M10 Ducktown Tennessee, S USA
178 Kk11 Đưc Phô Quang Ngai, C Vietnam
178 Jj8 Đưc Tho Ha Tinh, N Vietnam
178 Kk13 Đưc Trong var. Liên Nghia. Lâm Đông, S Vietnam
D-U-D see Dalap-Uliga-Djarrit
101 M25 Dudelange var. Forge du Sud, Ger. Dudelingen. Luxembourg, S Luxembourg
Dudelingen see Dudelange
103 J15 Duderstadt Niedersachsen, C Germany
159 N15 Dūdhi Uttar Pradesh, N India
126 I8 Dudinka Taymyrskiy (Dolgano-Nenetskiy) Avtonomnyy Okrug, N Russian Federation
99 L20 Dudley C England, UK
160 G13 Dudna ~ C India
78 L16 Duékoué W Ivory Coast
106 M5 Dueñas Castilla-León, N Spain
106 K4 Duerna ~ NW Spain
107 O6 Duero Port. Douro. ~ Portugal/Spain see also Douro
Duesseldorf see Düsseldorf
23 P12 Due West South Carolina, SE USA
205 P11 Dufek Coast physical region Antarctica
101 H17 Duffel Antwerpen, C Belgium
37 S2 Duffer Peak ▲ Nevada, W USA
195 X7 Duff Islands island group E Solomon Islands
Dufour, Pizzo/Dufour, Punta see Dufour Spitze
110 E12 Dufour Spitze It. Pizzo Dufour, Punta Dufour. ▲ Italy/Switzerland
114 D9 Duga Resa Karlovac, C Croatia
24 H5 Dugdemona River ~ Louisiana, S USA
160 J12 Duggīpar Mahārāshtra, C India
114 B13 Dugi Otok var. Isola Grossa, It. Isola Lunga. island W Croatia
115 F14 Dugopolje Split-Dalmacija, S Croatia
166 L8 Du He ~ C China
56 M11 Duida, Cerro ▲ S Venezuela
Duinekerke see Dunkerque
103 E15 Duisburg prev. Duisburg-Hamborn. Nordrhein-Westfalen, W Germany
Duisburg-Hamborn see Duisburg
101 F14 Duiveland island SW Netherlands
100 M12 Duiven Gelderland, E Netherlands
145 W10 Dujaylah, Hawr ad ◎ S Iraq
83 L18 Dujuuma Shabeellaha Hoose, S Somalia
Dūkān see Dokan
41 Z14 Duke Island island Alexander Archipelago, Alaska, USA
Dukelský Priesmy/Dukelský Průsmyk see Dukla Pass
Duke of Gloucester Islands see Duc de Gloucester, Îles du
83 F14 Duk Faiwil Jonglei, SE Sudan
147 T7 Dukhān C Qatar
Dukhan Heights see Dukhān, Jabal
149 N16 Dukhān, Jabal var. Dukhan Heights. hill range S Qatar
131 Q7 Dukhovnitskoye Saratovskaya Oblast', W Russian Federation
130 H4 Dukhovshchina Smolenskaya Oblast', W Russian Federation
Dukielska, Przełęcz see Dukla Pass
113 N17 Dukla Krosno, SE Poland
Duklai Hág see Dukla Pass
113 N18 Dukla Pass Cz. Dukelský Průsmyk, Ger. Dukla-Pass, Hung. Duklai Hág, Pol. Przełęcz Dukielska, Slvk. Dukelský Priesmy. pass Poland/Slovakia
Dukou see Panzhihua
120 I12 Dūkštas Ignalina, E Lithuania
168 M8 Dulaan Hentiy, C Mongolia
165 R10 Dulan var. Qagan Us. Qinghai, C China
39 R8 Dulce New Mexico, SW USA
45 N16 Dulce, Golfo gulf S Costa Rica
Dulce, Golfo see Izabal, Lago de
44 K6 Dulce Nombre de Culmí Olancho, C Honduras
64 L9 Dulce, Río ~ C Argentina
126 M9 Dulgalakh ~ NE Russian Federation
116 M8 Dŭlgopol Varnenska Oblast, NE Bulgaria
159 V14 Dullabchara Assam, NE India
22 D3 Dulles ✕ (Washington DC) Virginia, NE USA
103 E14 Dülmen Nordrhein-Westfalen, W Germany
116 M7 Dulovo Razgradska Oblast, NE Bulgaria
31 W5 Duluth Minnesota, N USA
144 H7 Dūmā Fr. Douma. Dimashq, SW Syria
179 Pp16 Dumagasa Point headland Mindanao, S Philippines
179 Qq14 Dumaguete var. Dumagete City. Negros, C Philippines
174 Gg6 Dumai Sumatera, W Indonesia
191 T4 Dumaresq River ~ New South Wales/Queensland, SE Australia
29 W13 Dumas Arkansas, C USA
27 N1 Dumas Texas, SW USA
144 I7 Ḍumayr Dimashq, W Syria
98 I12 Dumbarton W Scotland, UK
98 I12 Dumbarton cultural region C Scotland, UK
197 J7 Dumbéa Province Sud, S New Caledonia
113 K19 Ďumbier Ger. Djumbir, Hung. Gyömbér. ▲ C Slovakia
118 I11 Dumbrăveni Ger. Elisabethstedt, Hung. Erzsébetváros; prev. Ebesfalva, Eppeschdorf, Ibașfalău. Sibiu, C Romania
118 L12 Dumbrăveni Vrancea, E Romania
99 J14 Dumfries S Scotland, UK
99 J14 Dumfries cultural region SW Scotland, UK
159 R15 Dumka Bihār, NE India
Dümmer see Dümmersee
102 G12 Dümmersee var. Dümmer. ◎ NW Germany
12 J11 Dumoine ~ Québec, SE Canada
12 J10 Dumoine, Lac ◎ Québec, SE Canada
205 V16 Dumont d'Urville French research station Antarctica
205 W15 Dumont d'Urville Sea S Pacific Ocean
12 K11 Dumont, Lac ◎ Québec, SE Canada
77 W7 Dumyât Eng. Damietta. N Egypt
Duna see Don, Russian Federation
Duna see Danube, C Europe
Düna see Western Dvina
Dünaburg see Daugavpils
113 J24 Dunaföldvár Tolna, C Hungary
Dunaj see Wien, Austria
Dunaj see Danube, C Europe
113 L18 Dunajec ~ S Poland
113 H21 Dunajská Streda Hung. Dunaszerdahely. Západné Slovensko, SW Slovakia
Dunapentele see Dunaújváros
Dunărea see Danube
118 M13 Dunărea Veche, Brațul ~ SE Romania
119 N13 Dunării, Delta delta SE Romania
Dunaszerdahely see Dunajská Streda
113 J23 Dunaújváros prev. Dunapentele, Sztálinváros. Fejér, C Hungary
Dunav see Danube
116 J8 Dunavska Ravnina Eng. Danubian Plain. plain N Bulgaria
116 G7 Dunavtsi Oblast Montana, NW Bulgaria
Dunayevtsy see Dunayivtsi
118 L7 Dunayivtsi Rus. Dunayevtsy. Khmel'nyts'ka Oblast', NW Ukraine
193 F22 Dunback Otago, South Island, NZ
8 L17 Duncan Vancouver Island, British Columbia, SW Canada
39 O15 Duncan Arizona, SW USA
28 M12 Duncan Oklahoma, C USA
Duncan Island see Pinzón, Isla
157 Q20 Duncan Passage strait Andaman Sea/Bay of Bengal
98 K6 Duncansby Head headland N Scotland, UK
12 G12 Dunchurch Ontario, S Canada
120 D7 Dundaga Talsi, NW Latvia
12 G14 Dundalk Ontario, S Canada
99 F16 Dundalk Ir. Dún Dealgan. NE Ireland
23 X3 Dundalk Maryland, NE USA
99 F16 Dundalk Bay Ir. Cuan Dhún Dealgan. bay NE Ireland
12 G16 Dundas Ontario, S Canada
188 L12 Dundas, Lake salt lake Western Australia
169 O7 Dundbürd Hentiy, E Mongolia
Dún Dealgan see Dundalk
13 N13 Dundee Québec, SE Canada
85 K22 Dundee KwaZulu/Natal, E South Africa
98 K11 Dundee E Scotland, UK
33 R10 Dundee Michigan, N USA
27 R5 Dundee Texas, SW USA
204 H3 Dundee Island island Antarctica
168 L9 Dundgovĭ ◆ province C Mongolia
99 G16 Dundrum Bay Ir. Cuan Dhún Droma. inlet NW Irish Sea
176 Y11 Dundu ~ Irian Jaya, E Indonesia
9 T15 Dundurn Saskatchewan, S Canada
168 E6 Dund-Us Hovd, W Mongolia
193 F23 Dunedin Otago, South Island, NZ
191 R7 Dunedoo New South Wales, SE Australia
99 D14 Dunfanaghy Ir. Dún Fionnachaidh. NW Ireland
98 J12 Dunfermline C Scotland, UK
Dún Fionnachaidh see Dunfanaghy
155 V10 Dunga Bunga Punjab, E Pakistan
99 F15 Dungannon Ir. Dún Geanainn. C Northern Ireland, UK
Dun Garbháin see Dungarvan
158 F15 Dūngarpur Rājasthān, N India
99 E21 Dungarvan Ir. Dun Garbháin. S Ireland
103 N21 Dungau cultural region SE Germany
Dún Geanainn see Dungannon
99 P23 Dungeness headland SE England, UK
65 I23 Dungeness, Punta headland S Argentina
Dungloe see Dunglow
99 D14 Dunglow var. Dungloe, Ir. An Clochán Liath. NW Ireland
191 T7 Dungog New South Wales, SE Australia
81 O16 Dungu Haut-Zaïre, NE Zaire
174 Hh3 Dungun var. Kuala Dungun. Terengganu, Peninsular Malaysia
82 I6 Dungûnab Red Sea, NE Sudan
13 P13 Dunham Québec, SE Canada
Dunheved see Launceston
Dunholme see Durham
169 X10 Dunhua Jilin, NE China
165 P8 Dunhuang Gansu, N China
190 L12 Dunkeld Victoria, SE Australia
105 O1 Dunkerque Eng. Dunkirk, Flem. Duinekerke; prev. Dunquerque. Nord, N France
99 K23 Dunkery Beacon ▲ SW England, UK
20 C11 Dunkirk New York, NE USA
Dunkirk see Dunkerque
79 P17 Dunkwa SW Ghana
99 G18 Dún Laoghaire Eng. Dunleary; prev. Kingstown. E Ireland
31 S14 Dunlap Iowa, C USA
22 L10 Dunlap Tennessee, S USA
Dunleary see Dún Laoghaire
Dún Mánmhaí see Dunmanway
99 B21 Dunmanway Ir. Dún Mánmhaí. SW Ireland
20 I13 Dunmore Pennsylvania, NE USA
23 U10 Dunn North Carolina, SE USA
Dún na nGall see Donegal
25 V11 Dunnellon Florida, SE USA
98 J6 Dunnet Head headland N Scotland, UK
31 N14 Dunning Nebraska, C USA
67 B24 Dunnose Head Settlement West Falkland, Falkland Islands
12 G17 Dunnville Ontario, S Canada
Dún Pádraig see Downpatrick
Dunquerque see Dunkerque
Dunqulah see Dongola
98 L12 Duns SE Scotland, UK
31 N2 Dunseith North Dakota, N USA
37 N2 Dunsmuir California, W USA
99 N21 Dunstable Lat. Durocobrivae. E England, UK
193 D21 Dunstan Mountains ▲▲ South Island, NZ
105 O9 Dun-sur-Auron Cher, C France
193 F21 Duntroon Canterbury, South Island, NZ
155 T10 Dunyāpur Punjab, E Pakistan
169 U5 Duobukur He ~ NE China
169 R12 Duolun var. Dolonnur. Nei Mongol Zizhiqu, N China
178 Ii14 Dương Đông Kiên Giang, S Vietnam
116 G10 Dupnitsa prev. Marek, Stanke Dimitrov. Sofiyska Oblast, W Bulgaria
30 L8 Dupree South Dakota, N USA
35 Q7 Dupuyer Montana, NW USA
147 Y11 Duqm var. Daqm. E Oman
53 X9 Duque de Caxias Rio de Janeiro, SE Brazil
65 F23 Duque de York, Isla island S Chile
189 N4 Durack Range ▲▲ Western Australia
Dura Europus see Aş Şāliḥīyah
142 K10 Durağan Sinop, N Turkey
105 S15 Durance ~ SE France
33 R9 Durand Michigan, N USA
32 I6 Durand Wisconsin, N USA
197 L7 Durand, Récif reef SE New Caledonia
42 K10 Durango var. Victoria de Durango. Durango, W Mexico
107 P3 Durango País Vasco, N Spain
39 Q8 Durango Colorado, C USA
42 J9 Durango ◆ state C Mexico
116 O7 Durankulak Rom. Răcari; prev. Blatnitsa, Duranulac. Varnenska Oblast, NE Bulgaria
24 L4 Durant Mississippi, S USA
29 P13 Durant Oklahoma, C USA
Duranulac see Durankulak
107 N6 Duratón ~ N Spain
63 E19 Durazno var. San Pedro de Durazno. Durazno, C Uruguay
63 E19 Durazno ◆ department C Uruguay
Durazzo see Durrës
85 K23 Durban var. Port Natal. KwaZulu/Natal, E South Africa
85 K23 Durban ✕ KwaZulu/Natal, E South Africa
120 C9 Durbe Ger. Durben. Liepāja, W Latvia
Durben see Durbe
101 K21 Durbuy Luxembourg, SE Belgium
107 N15 Dúrcal Andalucía, S Spain
114 F8 Đurđevac Ger. Sankt Georgen, Hung. Szentgyörgy; prev. Djurdjevac, Gjurgjevac. Koprivnica-Križevci, N Croatia
115 K15 Đurđevica Tara Montenegro, SW Yugoslavia
99 L24 Durdle Door natural arch S England, UK
164 L3 Düre Xinjiang Uygur Zizhiqu, W China
103 D16 Düren anc. Marcodurum. Nordrhein-Westfalen, W Germany
160 K12 Durg prev. Drug. Madhya Pradesh, C India
159 U13 Durgapur Dhaka, N Bangladesh
159 R15 Durgāpur West Bengal, NE India
12 F14 Durham Ontario, S Canada
99 M14 Durham hist. Dunholme. N England, UK
23 U9 Durham North Carolina, SE USA
99 L15 Durham cultural region N England, UK
174 Gg7 Duri Sumatera, W Indonesia
Duria Major see Dora Baltea
Duria Minor see Dora Riparia
Durlas see Thurles
147 P8 Ḍurmā Ar Riyāḍ, C Saudi Arabia
115 J15 Durmitor ▲ N Yugoslavia
98 H6 Durness N Scotland, UK
111 Y3 Dürnkrut Niederösterreich, E Austria
Durnovaria see Dorchester
Durobrivae see Rochester
Durocasses see Dreux
Durocobrivae see Dunstable
Durocortorum see Reims
Durostorum see Silistra
Durovernum see Canterbury
115 K20 Durrës var. Durrësi, Dursi, It. Durazzo, SCr. Drač, Turk. Draç. Durrës, W Albania
115 K19 Durrës ◆ district W Albania
Durrësi see Durrës
99 A21 Dursey Island Ir. Oileán Baoi. island SW Ireland
Dursi see Durrës
Durud see Do Rūd
116 P12 Durusu İstanbul, NW Turkey
116 O12 Durusu Gölü ◎ NW Turkey
144 I9 Durūz, Jabal ad ▲ SW Syria
192 K13 D'Urville Island island C NZ
176 Xx9 D'Urville, Tanjung headland Irian Jaya, E Indonesia
Dusa Mareb/Dusa Marreb see Dhuusa Marreeb
120 I11 Dusetos Zarasai, NE Lithuania
152 H14 Dushak Akhalskiy Velayat, S Turkmenistan
166 K12 Dushan Guizhou, S China
153 P13 Dushanbe var. Dyushambe; prev. Stalinabad, Taj. Stalinobod. ● (Tajikistan) W Tajikistan
153 P13 Dushanbe ✕ W Tajikistan
143 T9 Dushet'i E Georgia
20 H13 Dushore Pennsylvania, NE USA
193 A23 Dusky Sound sound South Island, NZ
103 E15 Düsseldorf var. Duesseldorf. Nordrhein-Westfalen, W Germany
153 P14 Dŭstí Rus. Dusti. SW Tajikistan
204 I9 Dustin Island island Antarctica
153 O10 Dŭstlik Jizzakh Wiloyati, C Uzbekistan
Dutch East Indies see Indonesia
Dutch Guiana see Suriname
40 L17 Dutch Harbor Unalaska Island, Alaska, USA
38 J3 Dutch Mount ▲ Utah, W USA
Dutch New Guinea see Irian Jaya
Dutch West Indies see Netherlands Antilles
85 H20 Dutlwe Kweneng, S Botswana
69 V16 Du Toit Fracture Zone tectonic feature SW Indian Ocean
129 U8 Dutovo Respublika Komi, NW Russian Federation
79 V13 Dutsan Wai var. Dutsen Wai. Kaduna, C Nigeria
79 W13 Dutse Jigawa, N Nigeria
Dutsen Wai see Dutsan Wai
Duttia see Datia
12 E17 Dutton Ontario, S Canada
38 L7 Dutton, Mount ▲ Utah, W USA
168 E7 Duut Hovd, W Mongolia
12 K11 Duval, Lac ◎ Québec, SE Canada
131 W3 Duvan Respublika Bashkortostan, W Russian Federation
144 L9 Duwaykhilat Satīḥ ar Ruwayshid seasonal river SE Jordan
Dux see Duchcov
166 J13 Duyang Shan ▲▲ S China
178 Jj15 Duyên Hai Tra Vinh, S Vietnam
166 K12 Duyun Guizhou, S China
142 G11 Düzce Bolu, NW Turkey
Duzdab see Zāhedān
Duzenkyr, Khrebet see Duzkyr, Khrebet
152 I16 Duzkyr, Khrebet prev. Khrebet Duzenkyr. ▲▲ S Turkmenistan
Dvina Bay see Chëshskaya Guba
Dvinsk see Daugavpils
128 L7 Dvinskaya Guba bay NW Russian Federation
114 E10 Dvor Sisak-Moslavina, C Croatia
119 W5 Dvorichna Kharkivs'ka Oblast', E Ukraine
113 F16 Dvůr Králové nad Labem Ger. Königinhof an der Elbe. Východní Čechy, NE Czech Republic
160 A10 Dwārka Gujarāt, W India
32 M12 Dwight Illinois, N USA
100 N8 Dwingeloo Drenthe, NE Netherlands
35 N10 Dworshak Reservoir ⊡ Idaho, NW USA
Dyal see Dyaul Island
Dyanev see Deynau
Dyatlovo see Dzyatlava
195 N9 Dyaul Island var. Djaul, Dyal. island NE PNG
22 G8 Dyer Tennessee, S USA
16 O1 Dyer, Cape headland Baffin Island, Northwest Territories, NE Canada
22 F8 Dyersburg Tennessee, S USA
31 Y13 Dyersville Iowa, C USA
99 I21 Dyfed cultural region SW Wales, UK
Dyfrdwy, Afon see Dee
Dyhernfurth see Brzeg Dolny
113 E19 Dyje var. Thaya. ~ Austria/Czech Republic see also Thaya
119 T5 Dykanska Poltavs'ka Oblast', C Ukraine
194 L15 Dyke Ackland Bay inlet E PNG
131 N16 Dykhtau ▲ SW Russian Federation
113 A16 Dyleń Ger. Tillenberg. ▲ NW Czech Republic
112 K9 Dylewska Góra ▲ N Poland
119 O4 Dymer Kyyivs'ka Oblast', N Ukraine
119 W7 Dymytrov Rus. Dimitrov. Donets'ka Oblast', SE Ukraine
113 O17 Dynów Przemyśl, SE Poland

◆ Country · ● Country Capital · ◇ Dependent Territory · ○ Dependent Territory Capital · ◆ Administrative Region · ✕ International Airport · ▲ Mountain · ▲▲ Mountain Range · Volcano · ~ River · ◎ Lake · ⊡ Reservoir

31 X13 Dysart Iowa, C USA
Dysna see Dzisna
117 D18 Dytikí Ellás Eng. Greece West. ◈ region C Greece
117 C14 Dytikí Makedonía Eng. Macedonia West. ◈ region N Greece
Dyurmen'tyube see Dermentobe
131 U4 Dyurtyuli Respublika Bashkortostan, W Russian Federation
Dyushambe see Dushanbe
168 J7 Dzaanhushuu Arhangay, C Mongolia
Dza Chu see Mekong
168 I8 Dzadgay Bayanhongor, C Mongolia
168 H8 Dzag Bayanhongor, C Mongolia
168 H10 Dzalaa Bayanhongor, C Mongolia
180 J14 Dzaoudzi E Mayotte
Dzaudzhikau see Vladikavkaz
168 G7 Dzavhan ◈ province NW Mongolia
168 G7 Dzavhan Gol ~ NW Mongolia
168 J7 Dzegstey Arhangay, C Mongolia
131 O3 Dzerzhinsk Nizhegorodskaya Oblast', W Russian Federation
Dzerzhinsk see Dzyarzhynsk, Belorussia
Dzerzhinsk see Dzerzhyns'k, Ukraine
Dzerzhinskiy see Nar'yan-Mar
151 W13 Dzerzhinskoye Taldykorgan, SE Kazakhstan
119 X7 Dzerzhyns'k Rus. Dzerzhinsk. Donets'ka Oblast', SE Ukraine
118 M5 Dzerzhyns'k Zhytomyrs'ka Oblast', N Ukraine
Dzhailgan see Jayilgan
151 N14 Dzhalagash Kaz. Zhalashash. Kzyl-Orda, S Kazakhstan
153 T10 Dzhalal-Abad Kir. Jalal-Abad. Dzhalal-Abadskaya Oblast', W Kyrgyzstan
153 S9 Dzhalal-Abadskaya Oblast' Kir. Jalal-Abad Oblasty. ◈ province W Kyrgyzstan
Dzhalilabad see Cälilabad
126 L15 Dzhalinda Amurskaya Oblast', SE Russian Federation
150 G9 Dzhambeyty Kaz. Zhympity. Zapadnyy Kazakhstan, W Kazakhstan
Dzhambul/Dzhambulskaya Oblast' see Zhambyl
Dzhankel'dy see Jangeldi
119 T12 Dzhankoy Respublika Krym, S Ukraine
151 V14 Dzhansugurov Kaz. Zhansügirov. Taldykorgan, SE Kazakhstan
153 R9 Dzhany-Bazar var. Yangibazar. Dzhalal-Abadskaya Oblast', W Kyrgyzstan
150 D9 Dzhanybek Kaz. Zhänibek. Zapadnyy Kazakhstan, W Kazakhstan
126 L8 Dzhardzhan Respublika Sakha (Yakutiya), NE Russian Federation
Dzharkurgan see Jarqürghon
119 S11 Dzharylhats'ka Zatoka gulf S Ukraine
Dzhayilgan see Jayilgan
152 B11 Dzhebel Turkm. Jebel. Balkanskiy Velayat, W Turkmenistan
153 T14 Dzhelandy SE Tajikistan
153 Y7 Dzhergalan Kir. Jyrgalan. Issyk-Kul'skaya Oblast', NE Kyrgyzstan
150 L8 Dzhetygara Kaz. Zhetiqara. Kustanay, NW Kazakhstan
Dzhezkazgan/Dzhezkazganskaya Oblast' see Zhezkazgan
152 J10 Dzhigirbent Turkm. Jigerbent. Lebapskiy Velayat, NE Turkmenistan
Dzhirgatal' see Jirgatol
Dzhizak see Jizzakh
Dzhizakskaya Oblast' see Jizzakh Wiloyati
127 N12 Dzhugdzhur, Khrebet ▲▲ E Russian Federation
Dzhul'fa see Culfa
Dzhuma see Juma
151 W14 Dzhungarskiy Alatau ▲▲ China/Kazakhstan
150 M14 Dzhusaly Kaz. Zholsaly. Kzyl-Orda, SW Kazakhstan
152 J12 Dzhynlykum, Peski desert E Turkmenistan
112 L9 Działdowo Ciechanów, C Poland
113 L16 Działoszyce Kielce, S Poland
43 X11 Dzidzantún Yucatán, E Mexico
113 G15 Dzierżoniów Ger. Reichenbach. Wałbrzych, SW Poland
43 X11 Dzilam de Bravo Yucatán, E Mexico
120 L12 Dzisna Rus. Disna. Vitsyebskaya Voblasts', N Belorussia
120 K12 Dzisna Lith. Dysna, Rus. Disna. ~ Belorussia/Lithuania
121 G20 Dzivin Rus. Divin. Brestskaya Voblasts', SW Belorussia
121 M15 Dzmitravichy Rus. Dmitrovichi. Minskaya Voblasts', C Belorussia
168 M8 Dzogsool Töv, C Mongolia
133 S8 Dzungaria var. Sungaria, Zungaria. physical region W China
Dzungarian Basin see Junggar Pendi
168 G5 Dzür Dzavhan, W Mongolia
169 Q8 Dzüünbulag Dornod, E Mongolia
169 O8 Dzüünbulag Sühbaatar, E Mongolia
168 H7 Dzuunmod Dzavhan, C Mongolia
168 L8 Dzuunmod Töv, C Mongolia
Dzüün Soyonï Nuruu see Eastern Sayans
168 F8 Dzüyl Govĭ-Altay, SW Mongolia
Dzvina see Western Dvina
121 J16 Dzyarzhynsk Rus. Dzerzhinsk; prev. Kaydanovo. Minskaya Voblasts', C Belorussia
121 H17 Dzyatlava Pol. Zdzięcioł, Rus. Dyatlovo. Hrodzyenskaya Voblasts', W Belorussia

E

E see Hubei
Éadan Doire see Edenderry
39 W6 Eads Colorado, C USA
39 O13 Eagar Arizona, SW USA
41 T8 Eagle Alaska, USA
11 S8 Eagle ~ Newfoundland and Labrador, E Canada
8 I3 Eagle ~ Yukon Territory, NW Canada
31 T7 Eagle Bend Minnesota, N USA
30 M8 Eagle Butte South Dakota, N USA
31 V12 Eagle Grove Iowa, C USA
21 R2 Eagle Lake Maine, NE USA
27 U11 Eagle Lake Texas, SW USA
10 A11 Eagle Lake ◎ Ontario, S Canada
37 P3 Eagle Lake ◎ California, W USA
21 R3 Eagle Lake ◎ Maine, NE USA
31 Y3 Eagle Mountain ▲ Minnesota, N USA
27 T6 Eagle Mountain Lake ⊡ Texas, SW USA
39 S9 Eagle Nest Lake ⊡ New Mexico, SW USA
27 P13 Eagle Pass Texas, SW USA
67 C25 Eagle Passage passage SW Atlantic Ocean
37 R8 Eagle Peak ▲ California, W USA
37 Q2 Eagle Peak ▲ California, W USA
39 P13 Eagle Peak ▲ New Mexico, SW USA
8 I4 Eagle Plain Yukon Territory, NW Canada
34 G15 Eagle Point Oregon, NW USA
195 N17 Eagle Point headland SE PNG
41 R11 Eagle River Alaska, USA
32 M2 Eagle River Michigan, N USA
32 L4 Eagle River Wisconsin, N USA
23 S6 Eagle Rock Virginia, NE USA
38 J13 Eagletail Mountains ▲▲ Arizona, SW USA
178 Kk12 Ea Hleo Đắc Lắc, S Vietnam
178 Kk12 Ea Kar Đắc Lắc, S Vietnam
Eanjum see Anjum
Eanodat see Enontekiö
10 B10 Ear Falls Ontario, C Canada
29 X10 Earle Arkansas, C USA
37 R12 Earlimart California, W USA
22 I6 Earlington Kentucky, S USA
12 H8 Earlton Ontario, S Canada
31 T13 Early Iowa, C USA
98 J11 Earn ~ N Scotland, UK
193 C21 Earnslaw, Mount ▲ South Island, NZ
26 M4 Earth Texas, SW USA
23 P11 Easley South Carolina, SE USA
East see Est
East Açores Fracture Zone see East Azores Fracture Zone
99 P19 East Anglia physical region E England, UK
13 Q12 East Angus Québec, SE Canada
East Antarctica see Greater Antarctica
20 E10 East Aurora New York, NE USA
East Australian Basin see Tasman Basin
East Azerbaijan see Āzarbāyjān-e Khāvarī
66 L9 East Azores Fracture Zone var. East Açores Fracture Zone. tectonic feature E Atlantic Ocean
24 M11 East Bay bay Louisiana, S USA
27 V11 East Bernard Texas, SW USA
31 V8 East Bethel Minnesota, N USA
East Borneo see Kalimantan Timur
99 P23 Eastbourne SE England, UK
13 R11 East-Broughton Québec, SE Canada
46 M6 East Caicos island E Turks and Caicos Islands
192 R7 East Cape headland North Island, NZ
182 M4 East Caroline Basin undersea feature SW Pacific Ocean
198 G5 East China Sea Chin. Dong Hai. sea W Pacific Ocean
99 P19 East Dereham E England, UK
32 J9 East Dubuque Illinois, N USA
9 S17 Eastend Saskatchewan, S Canada
200 Nn11 Easter Fracture Zone tectonic feature E Pacific Ocean
Easter Island see Pascua, Isla de
83 J18 Eastern ◈ province Kenya
159 Q12 Eastern ◈ zone E Nepal
84 L13 Eastern ◈ province E Zambia
85 H24 Eastern Cape off. Eastern Cape Province, Afr. Oos-Kaap. ◈ province SE South Africa
Eastern Desert see Sahara el Sharqîya
83 F15 Eastern Equatoria ◈ state SE Sudan
Eastern Euphrates see Murat Nehri
161 J17 Eastern Ghats ▲▲ SE India
194 I13 Eastern Highlands ◈ province C PNG
161 K25 Eastern Province ◈ province E Sri Lanka
Eastern Region see Ash Sharqiyah
126 I15 Eastern Sayans Mong. Dzüün Soyonï Nuruu, Rus. Vostochnyy Sayan. ▲▲ Mongolia/Russian Federation
Eastern Scheldt see Oosterschelde
Eastern Sierra Madre see Madre Oriental, Sierra
Eastern Transvaal see Mpumalanga
9 W14 Easterville Manitoba, C Canada
Easterwâlde see Oosterwolde
65 M23 East Falkland var. Soledad. island E Falkland Islands
21 P12 East Falmouth Massachusetts, NE USA
East Fayu see Fayu
East Flanders see Oost-Vlaanderen
41 S6 East Fork Chandalar River ~ Alaska, USA
31 U12 East Fork Des Moines River ~ Iowa/Minnesota, C USA
East Frisian Islands see Ostfriesische Inseln
20 K10 East Glenville New York, NE USA
31 R4 East Grand Forks Minnesota, N USA
99 O23 East Grinstead SE England, UK
20 M12 East Hartford Connecticut, NE USA
20 M13 East Haven Connecticut, NE USA
181 T9 East Indiaman Ridge undersea feature E Indian Ocean
133 V16 East Indies island group SE Asia
East Java see Jawa Timur
33 Q6 East Jordan Michigan, N USA
East Kalimantan see Kalimantan Timur
East Kazakhstan see Vostochnyy Kazakhstan
98 I12 East Kilbride S Scotland, UK
27 R7 Eastland Texas, SW USA
33 Q9 East Lansing Michigan, N USA
37 X11 East Las Vegas Nevada, W USA
99 M23 Eastleigh S England, UK
33 V12 East Liverpool Ohio, N USA
85 J25 East London Afr. Oos-Londen; prev. Emonti, Port Rex. Eastern Cape, S South Africa
98 K12 East Lothian cultural region SE Scotland, UK
10 I10 Eastmain Québec, E Canada
10 J10 Eastmain ~ Québec, C Canada
13 P13 Eastman Québec, SE Canada
25 U6 Eastman Georgia, SE USA
183 O3 East Mariana Basin undersea feature W Pacific Ocean
32 K11 East Moline Illinois, N USA
195 O12 East New Britain ◈ province E PNG
31 T15 East Nishnabotna River ~ Iowa, C USA
207 V12 East Novaya Zemlya Trough var. Novaya Zemlya Trough. undersea feature W Kara Sea
East Nusa Tenggara see Nusa Tenggara Timur
23 X4 Easton Maryland, NE USA
20 I14 Easton Pennsylvania, NE USA
200 N8 East Pacific Rise undersea feature E Pacific Ocean
East Pakistan see Bangladesh
33 V12 East Palestine Ohio, N USA
32 L12 East Peoria Illinois, N USA
25 S3 East Point Georgia, SE USA
21 U6 Eastport Maine, NE USA
29 Z8 East Prairie Missouri, C USA
21 O12 East Providence Rhode Island, NE USA
22 L11 East Ridge Tennessee, S USA
99 N16 East Riding cultural region N England, UK
20 F9 East Rochester New York, NE USA
32 K15 East Saint Louis Illinois, N USA
67 K21 East Scotia Basin undersea feature SE Scotia Sea
East Sea see Japan, Sea of
194 F11 East Sepik ◈ province NW PNG
181 N4 East Sheba Ridge undersea feature W Arabian Sea
East Siberian Sea see Vostochno-Sibirskoye More
20 I14 East Stroudsburg Pennsylvania, NE USA
East Tasmanian Rise/East Tasmania Plateau/East Tasmania Rise see East Tasman Plateau
199 Hh13 East Tasman Plateau var. East Tasmanian Rise, East Tasmania Plateau, East Tasmania Rise. undersea feature SW Tasman Sea
66 L7 East Thulean Rise undersea feature N Atlantic Ocean
East Timor see Timor Timur
23 Y6 Eastville Virginia, NE USA
37 R7 East Walker River ~ California/Nevada, W USA
190 D1 Eateringinna Creek ~ South Australia
39 T3 Eaton Colorado, C USA
13 Q12 Eaton ~ Québec, SE Canada
9 S16 Eatonia Saskatchewan, S Canada
33 Q10 Eaton Rapids Michigan, N USA
25 U4 Eatonton Georgia, SE USA
34 H9 Eatonville Washington, NW USA
32 J6 Eau Claire Wisconsin, N USA
Eau Claire, Lac à L' see St.Clair, Lake
10 J7 Eau Claire, Lac à l' ◎ Québec, SE Canada
32 I6 Eau Claire River ~ Wisconsin, N USA
196 J16 Eauripik Atoll atoll Caroline Islands, C Micronesia
199 H8 Eauripik Rise undersea feature W Pacific Ocean
104 K15 Eauze Gers, S France
43 P11 Ébano San Luis Potosí, C Mexico
99 K21 Ebbw Vale SE Wales, UK
81 E17 Ebebiyin NE Equatorial Guinea
97 H22 Ebeltoft Århus, C Denmark
111 X5 Ebenfurth Niederösterreich, E Austria
20 D14 Ebensburg Pennsylvania, NE USA
111 S5 Ebensee Oberösterreich, N Austria
103 H20 Eberbach Baden-Württemberg, SW Germany
124 Q9 Eber Gölü salt lake C Turkey
111 U9 Eberndorf Slvn. Dobrla Vas. Kärnten, S Austria
111 R4 Eberschwang Oberösterreich, N Austria
102 O11 Eberswalde-Finow Brandenburg, E Germany
Ebesfalva see Dumbrăveni
172 Oo5 Ebetsu var. Ebetu. Hokkaidō, NE Japan
Ebetu see Ebetsu
Ebinayon see Evinayong
164 I4 Ebinur Hu ◎ NW China
144 I3 Ebla Ar. Tell Mardīkh. site of ancient city Idlib, NW Syria
Eblana see Dublin
110 H7 Ebnat Sankt Gallen, NE Switzerland
109 L18 Eboli Campania, S Italy
81 E16 Ebolowa Sud, S Cameroon
81 N21 Ebombo Kasai Oriental, C Zaire
201 T9 Ebon Atoll var. Epoon. atoll Ralik Chain, S Marshall Islands
Ebora see Évora
Eboracum see York
Eborodunum see Yverdon
103 J19 Ebrach Bayern, C Germany
111 X5 Ebreichsdorf Niederösterreich, E Austria
107 S6 Ebro ~ NE Spain
107 N3 Ebro, Embalse del ⊡ N Spain
123 Hh8 Ebro Fan undersea feature W Mediterranean Sea
Eburacum see York
Ebusus see Eivissa
101 F20 Écaussinnes-d'Enghien Hainaut, SW Belgium
Ecbatana see Hamadān
23 Q6 Eccles West Virginia, NE USA
117 L14 Eceabat Çanakkale, NW Turkey
179 P9 Echague Luzon, N Philippines
Ech Cheliff/Ech Chleff see Chlef
Echeng see Ezhou
171 Kk13 Echigo-sanmyaku ▲▲ Honshū, C Japan
117 C18 Echinádes island group W Greece
116 J12 Echínos var. Ehinos, Ekhínos. Anatolikí Makedonía kai Thráki, NE Greece
171 H13 Echizen-misaki headland Honshū, SW Japan
Echmiadzin see Ejmiatsin
15 Hh5 Echo Bay Northwest Territories, NW Canada
37 Y11 Echo Bay Nevada, W USA
38 L9 Echo Cliffs cliff Arizona, SW USA
12 C10 Echo Lake ◎ Ontario, S Canada
37 Q7 Echo Summit ▲ California, W USA
12 L8 Échouani, Lac ◎ Québec, SE Canada
101 L17 Echt Limburg, SE Netherlands
103 H22 Echterdingen ✕ (Stuttgart) Baden-Württemberg, SW Germany
101 N24 Echternach Grevenmacher, E Luxembourg
191 N11 Echuca Victoria, SE Australia
106 L14 Ecija anc. Astigi. Andalucía, SW Spain
Eckengraf see Viesīte
102 I7 Eckernförde Schleswig-Holstein, N Germany
102 J7 Eckernförder Bucht inlet N Germany
104 L7 Écommoy Sarthe, NW France
12 L10 Écorce, Lac de l' ◎ Québec, SE Canada
13 Q8 Écorces, Rivière aux ~ Québec, SE Canada
58 C7 Ecuador off. Republic of Ecuador. ◆ republic NW South America
82 L10 Ed var. Edd. SE Eritrea
97 I17 Ed Älvsborg, S Sweden
100 I9 Edam Noord-Holland, C Netherlands
98 K4 Eday island NE Scotland, UK
27 S17 Edcouch Texas, SW USA
Edd see Ed
82 C11 Ed Da'ein Southern Darfur, W Sudan
82 G11 Ed Damazin var. Ad Damazīn. Blue Nile, E Sudan
82 G8 Ed Damer var. Ad Damar, Ad Dāmir. River Nile, NE Sudan
82 E8 Ed Debba Northern, N Sudan
82 F10 Ed Dueim var. Ad Duwaym, Ad Duwēm. White Nile, C Sudan
191 Q16 Eddystone Point headland Tasmania, SE Australia
99 I25 Eddystone Rocks rocks SW England, UK
31 W15 Eddyville Iowa, C USA
22 H7 Eddyville Kentucky, S USA
100 L12 Ede Gelderland, C Netherlands
79 T16 Ede Osun, SW Nigeria
81 D16 Edéa Littoral, SW Cameroon
113 M20 Edelény Borsod-Abaúj-Zemplén, NE Hungary
191 R12 Eden New South Wales, SE Australia
23 T8 Eden North Carolina, SE USA
27 P9 Eden Texas, SW USA
99 K14 Eden ~ NW England, UK
85 I23 Edenburg Free State, C South Africa
193 D24 Edendale Southland, South Island, NZ
99 E18 Edenderry Ir. Éadan Doire. C Ireland
190 L11 Edenhope Victoria, SE Australia
23 X8 Edenton North Carolina, SE USA
103 G16 Eder ~ NW Germany
176 Yy14 Ederah ~ Irian Jaya, E Indonesia
103 H15 Edersee ◎ W Germany
Edessa see Şanlıurfa
116 E13 Édessa var. Édhessa. Kentrikí Makedonía, N Greece
Edfu see Idfu
31 P16 Edgar Nebraska, C USA
21 P13 Edgartown Martha's Vineyard, Massachusetts, NE USA
41 X13 Edgecumbe, Mount ▲ Baranof Island, Alaska, USA
23 Q13 Edgefield South Carolina, SE USA
31 P6 Edgeley North Dakota, N USA
30 I11 Edgemont South Dakota, N USA
94 O3 Edgeøya island S Svalbard
29 Q4 Edgerton Kansas, C USA
31 S10 Edgerton Minnesota, N USA
23 X3 Edgewood Maryland, NE USA
27 V6 Edgewood Texas, SW USA
Édhessa see Édessa
31 V9 Edina Minnesota, N USA
29 U2 Edina Missouri, C USA
27 S17 Edinburg Texas, SW USA
67 M24 Edinburgh var. Settlement of Edinburgh. ○ (Tristan da Cunha) NW Tristan da Cunha
98 J12 Edinburgh ◐ S Scotland, UK
33 P14 Edinburgh Indiana, N USA
98 J12 Edinburgh ✕ S Scotland, UK
118 L8 Edineț var. Edineți, Rus. Yedintsy. NW Moldova
Edineți see Edineț
Edingen see Enghien
142 B9 Edirne Eng. Adrianople; anc. Adrianopolis, Hadrianopolis. Edirne, NW Turkey
142 B11 Edirne ◈ province NW Turkey
20 K15 Edison New Jersey, NE USA
23 S15 Edisto Island South Carolina, SE USA
23 R14 Edisto River ~ South Carolina, SE USA
35 S10 Edith, Mount ▲ Montana, NW USA
29 N10 Edmond Oklahoma, C USA
34 H8 Edmonds Washington, NW USA
9 Q14 Edmonton Alberta, SW Canada
22 K7 Edmonton Kentucky, S USA
9 Q14 Edmonton ✕ Alberta, SW Canada
31 P3 Edmore North Dakota, N USA
11 N13 Edmundston New Brunswick, SE Canada
27 U12 Edna Texas, SW USA
41 X14 Edna Bay Kosciusko Island, Alaska, USA
79 U16 Edo ◈ state S Nigeria
108 F6 Edolo Lombardia, N Italy
66 L6 Edoras Bank undersea feature C Atlantic Ocean
98 G7 Edrachillis Bay bay NW Scotland, UK
142 B12 Edremit Balıkesir, NW Turkey
142 B12 Edremit Körfezi gulf NW Turkey
97 P14 Edsbro Stockholm, C Sweden
96 N13 Edsbruk Kalmar, S Sweden
96 M12 Edsbyn Gävleborg, C Sweden
9 O14 Edson Alberta, SW Canada
64 K13 Eduardo Castex La Pampa, C Argentina
60 F12 Eduardo Gomes ✕ (Manaus) Amazonas, NW Brazil
Edwardesabad see Bannu
69 U9 Edward, Lake var. Albert Edward Nyanza, Edward Nyanza, Lac Idi Amin, Lake Rutanzige. ◎ Uganda/Zaire
Edward Nyanza see Edward, Lake
24 K5 Edwards Mississippi, S USA
27 O10 Edwards Plateau plain Texas, SW USA
32 J11 Edwards River ~ Illinois, N USA
32 K15 Edwardsville Illinois, N USA
205 O13 Edward VII Peninsula peninsula Antarctica
205 X4 Edward VIII Gulf bay Antarctica
8 J11 Edziza, Mount ▲ British Columbia, W Canada
41 N12 Eek Alaska, USA
101 D16 Eeklo var. Eekloo. Oost-Vlaanderen, NW Belgium
Eekloo see Eeklo
41 N12 Eek River ~ Alaska, USA
100 N6 Eelde Drenthe, NE Netherlands
36 L5 Eel River ~ California, W USA
33 P12 Eel River ~ Indiana, N USA
Eems see Ems
100 O4 Eemshaven Groningen, NE Netherlands
100 O5 Eems Kanaal canal NE Netherlands
100 M11 Eerbeek Gelderland, E Netherlands
101 C17 Eernegem West-Vlaanderen, W Belgium
101 J15 Eersel Noord-Brabant, S Netherlands
Eesti Vabariik see Estonia
197 C14 Éfaté Fr. Vaté; prev. Sandwich Island. island C Vanuatu
111 S4 Eferding Oberösterreich, N Austria
32 M15 Effingham Illinois, N USA
119 N15 Eforie-Nord Constanța, SE Romania
119 N15 Eforie Sud Constanța, E Romania
Efyrnwy, Afon see Vyrnwy
169 N7 Eg Hentiy, N Mongolia
107 P4 Ega ~ NE Spain
109 G23 Egadi, Isole island group S Italy
37 X6 Egan Range ▲▲ Nevada, W USA
12 K12 Eganville Ontario, SE Canada
Ege Denizi see Aegean Sea
41 O14 Egegik Alaska, USA
113 L21 Eger Ger. Erlau. Heves, NE Hungary
Eger see Cheb, Czech Republic
Eger see Ohře, Czech Republic/Germany
181 P8 Egeria Fracture Zone tectonic feature W Indian Ocean
97 C17 Egersund Rogaland, S Norway
110 J7 Egg Vorarlberg, NW Austria
103 H14 Egge-gebirge ▲▲ C Germany
111 Q4 Eggelsberg Oberösterreich, N Austria
111 W2 Eggenburg Niederösterreich, NE Austria
103 N22 Eggenfelden Bayern, SE Germany
20 J17 Egg Harbor City New Jersey, NE USA
67 G25 Egg Island island W Saint Helena
191 N14 Egg Lagoon Tasmania, SE Australia
101 I20 Éghezèe Namur, C Belgium
94 L2 Egilsstadhir Austurland, E Iceland
Egina see Aígina
Egindibulaq see Yegindybulak
Egio see Aígio
105 N12 Égletons Corrèze, C France
100 H9 Egmond aan Zee Noord-Holland, NW Netherlands
Egmont see Taranaki, Mount
192 J10 Egmont, Cape headland North Island, NZ
Egoli see Johannesburg
142 I15 Eğridir Gölü ◎ W Turkey
Egri Palanka see Kriva Palanka
97 G23 Egtved Vejle, C Denmark
127 Pp4 Egvekinot Chukotskiy Avtonomnyy Okrug, NE Russian Federation
77 V9 Egypt off. Arab Republic of Egypt, Ar. Jumhūrīyah Miṣr al 'Arabīyah; prev. United Arab Republic, anc. Aegyptus. ◆ republic NE Africa
32 L17 Egypt, Lake Of ⊡ Illinois, N USA
Ehen Hudag see Alxa Zuoqi
170 E15 Ehime off. Ehime-ken. ◈ prefecture Shikoku, SW Japan
103 I23 Ehingen Baden-Württemberg, S Germany
Ehinos see Echínos
23 R14 Ehrhardt South Carolina, SE USA
110 L7 Ehrwald Tirol, W Austria
203 W6 Eiao island Îles Marquises, NE French Polynesia
107 P2 Eibar País Vasco, N Spain
100 O11 Eibergen Gelderland, E Netherlands
111 V9 Eibiswald Steiermark, SE Austria
111 P8 Eichham ▲ SW Austria
103 J15 Eichsfeld hill range C Germany
103 K21 Eichstätt Bayern, SE Germany
102 H8 Eider ~ N Germany
96 E13 Eidfjord Hordaland, S Norway
96 D13 Eidfjorden fjord S Norway
96 F9 Eidsvåg Møre og Romsdal, S Norway
97 I14 Eidsvoll Akershus, S Norway
94 N2 Eidsvollfjellet ▲ NW Svalbard
Eier-Berg see Suur Munamägi
103 D18 Eifel plateau W Germany
110 E9 Eiger ▲ C Switzerland
98 G10 Eigg island W Scotland, UK
161 D24 Eight Degree Channel channel India/Maldives
46 G1 Eight Mile Rock Grand Bahama Island, N Bahamas
204 J9 Eights Coast physical region Antarctica
188 K6 Eighty Mile Beach beach Western Australia
101 L18 Eijsden Limburg, SE Netherlands
97 G15 Eikeren ◎ S Norway
Eil see Eyl
Eilat see Elat
191 O12 Eildon Victoria, SE Australia
191 O12 Eildon, Lake ◎ Victoria, SE Australia
82 E8 Eilei Northern Kordofan, C Sudan
103 N15 Eilenburg Sachsen, E Germany
96 H13 Eina Oppland, S Norway
103 I14 Einbeck Niedersachsen, C Germany
101 K15 Eindhoven Noord-Brabant, S Netherlands
110 G8 Einsiedeln Schwyz, NE Switzerland
Eipel see Ipel'
Éire see Ireland, Republic of
Éireann, Muir see Irish Sea
Eirik Outer Ridge see Eirik Ridge
66 I6 Eirik Ridge var. Eirik Outer Ridge. undersea feature E Labrador Sea
94 I3 Eiríksjökull ▲ C Iceland
61 B14 Eirunepé Amazonas, N Brazil
101 L17 Eisden Limburg, NE Belgium
85 I18 Eiseb ~ Botswana/Namibia
Eisen see Yŏngch'ŏn
103 J16 Eisenach Thüringen, C Germany
Eisenburg see Vasvár
111 U6 Eisenerz Steiermark, SE Austria
102 Q13 Eisenhüttenstadt Brandenburg, E Germany
111 U10 Eisenkappel Slvn. Železna Kapela. Kärnten, S Austria
Eisenmarkt see Hunedoara
111 Y5 Eisenstadt Burgenland, E Austria
Eishū see Yŏngju
121 H15 Eišiškes Šalčininkai, SE Lithuania
103 L15 Eisleben Sachsen-Anhalt, C Germany
202 I3 Eita Tarawa, W Kiribati
Eitape see Aitape
107 V11 Eivissa var. Iviza, Cast. Ibiza; anc. Ebusus. Eivissa, Spain, W Mediterranean Sea
107 V10 Eivissa var. Iviza, Cast. Ibiza; anc. Ebusus. island Islas Baleares, Spain, W Mediterranean Sea
107 R4 Ejea de los Caballeros Aragón, NE Spain
42 E8 Ejido Insurgentes Baja California Sur, W Mexico
168 I12 Ejin Qi var. Dalain Hob. Nei Mongol Zizhiqu, N China
Ejmiadzin see Ejmiatsin
143 T12 Ejmiatsin var. Ejmiadzin, Etchmiadzin, Rus. Echmiadzin. W Armenia
79 P16 Ejura C Ghana
43 R16 Ejutla var. Ejutla de Crespo. Oaxaca, SE Mexico
Ejutla de Crespo see Ejutla
35 Y10 Ekalaka Montana, NW USA
Ekapa see Cape Town
Ekaterinodar see Krasnodar
95 L20 Ekenäs Fin. Tammisaari. Uusimaa, SW Finland
Ekerem see Okarem
192 M13 Eketahuna Manawatu-Wanganui, North Island, NZ
Ekhínos see Echínos
127 P3 Ekiatapskiy Khrebet ▲▲ NE Russian Federation
151 T8 Ekibastuz Pavlodar, NE Kazakhstan
127 N14 Ekimchan Amurskaya Oblast', SE Russian Federation
97 O15 Ekoln ◎ C Sweden
82 I7 Ekowit Red Sea, NE Sudan
97 L19 Eksjö Jönköping, S Sweden
95 I15 Ekträsk Västerbotten, N Sweden
41 O13 Ekuk Alaska, USA
10 F9 Ekwan ~ Ontario, C Canada
41 O13 Ekwok Alaska, USA
177 G6 Ela Mandalay, C Myanmar
El Aaiun see El Ayoun
83 N15 Ēl Ābrēd E Ethiopia
117 F22 Elafónisos island S Greece
117 F22 Elafonísou, Porthmós strait S Greece
El-Aïoun see El Ayoun
77 U8 El 'Alamein var. Al 'Alamayn. N Egypt
43 Q12 El Alazán Veracruz-Llave, C Mexico
59 J18 El Alto var. La Paz. ✕ (La Paz) La Paz, W Bolivia
Elam see Īlām
El Amparo see El Amparo de Apure
56 I8 El Amparo de Apure var. El Amparo. Apure, C Venezuela
175 Ss12 Elara Pulau Ambelau, E Indonesia
El Araïch/El Araïche see Larache
42 D6 El Arco Baja California, NW Mexico
77 X7 El 'Arîsh var. Al 'Arīsh. NE Egypt
117 L25 Elása island SE Greece
El Asnam see Chlef
Elassón see Elassóna
117 E15 Elassóna prev. Elassón. Thessalía, C Greece
107 N2 El Astillero Cantabria, N Spain
144 F14 Elat var. Eilat, Elath. Southern, S Israel
Elat, Gulf of see Aqaba, Gulf of
Elath see Elat, Israel
Elath see Al 'Aqabah, Jordan
117 C17 Eláti ▲ Lefkáda, Iónioi Nísoi, Greece, C Mediterranean Sea
196 L16 Elato Atoll atoll Caroline Islands, C Micronesia
82 C7 El'Atrun Northern Darfur, NW Sudan
76 H6 El Ayoun var. El Aaiun, El-Aïoun, La Youne. NE Morocco
143 N14 Elâzığ var. Elâziz. Elâzığ, E Turkey
143 O14 Elâzığ var. Elâziz. ◈ province C Turkey
Elâziz see Elâzığ
25 Q7 Elba Alabama, S USA
108 E13 Elba, Isola d' island Archipelago Toscano, C Italy
56 F6 El Banco Magdalena, N Colombia
El Barco see O Barco
106 L8 El Barco de Ávila Castilla-León, N Spain
El Barco de Valdeorras see O Barco
144 H7 El Barouk, Jabal ▲ C Lebanon
115 L20 Elbasan var. Elbasani. Elbasan, C Albania
115 L20 Elbasan ◈ district C Albania
Elbasani see Elbasan
56 K6 El Baúl Cojedes, C Venezuela
88 D10 Elbe Cz. Labe. ~ Czech Republic/Germany
102 L13 Elbe-Havel-Kanal canal E Germany
102 K9 Elbe-Lübeck-Kanal canal N Germany
El Beni see Beni
144 H7 El Beqaa var. Al Biqā', Bekaa Valley. valley E Lebanon
27 R6 Elbert Texas, SW USA
39 R5 Elbert, Mount ▲ Colorado, C USA
25 U3 Elberton Georgia, SE USA
102 K11 Elbe-Seiten-Kanal canal N Germany
104 M4 Elbeuf Seine-Maritime, N France
Elbing see Elbląg
142 M15 Elbistan Kahramanmaraş, S Turkey
112 K7 Elbląg var. Elblag, Ger. Elbing. Elbląg, N Poland
112 J7 Elbląg off. Województwo Elbląskie, Ger. Elbing. ◈ province N Poland
Elbląskie, Województwo see Elbląg
45 N10 El Bluff Región Autónoma Atlántico Sur, SE Nicaragua
65 H17 El Bolsón Río Negro, W Argentina
107 P11 El Bonillo Castilla-La Mancha, C Spain
El Bordo see Patía

◆ Country
● Country Capital
◇ Dependent Territory
○ Dependent Territory Capital
◈ Administrative Region
✕ International Airport
▲ Mountain
▲▲ Mountain Range
Volcano
~ River
◎ Lake
⊡ Reservoir

El Boulaida/ El Boulaïda see Blida
9 T16 Elbow Saskatchewan, S Canada
31 S7 Elbow Lake Minnesota, N USA
131 N16 El'brus var. Gora El'brus. ▲ SW Russian Federation
El'brus, Gora see El'brus
130 M15 El'brusskiy Karachayevo-Cherkesskaya Respublika, SW Russian Federation
83 D14 El Buhayrat var. Lakes State. ◆ state S Sudan
El Bur see Ceel Buur
100 L10 Elburg Gelderland, E Netherlands
107 O6 El Burgo de Osma Castilla-León, C Spain
Elburz Mountains see Alborz, Reshteh-ye Kūhhā-ye
37 V17 El Cajon California, W USA
65 H22 El Calafate var. Calafate. Santa Cruz, S Argentina
57 Q8 El Callao Bolívar, E Venezuela
27 U12 El Campo Texas, SW USA
56 I7 El Cantón Barinas, W Venezuela
37 Q8 El Capitan ▲ California, W USA
56 H5 El Carmelo Zulia, NW Venezuela
64 J5 El Carmen Jujuy, NW Argentina
56 E5 El Carmen de Bolívar Bolívar, NW Colombia
57 O8 El Casabe Bolívar, SE Venezuela
44 M12 El Castillo de La Concepción Río San Juan, SE Nicaragua
El Cayo see San Ignacio
37 X17 El Centro California, W USA
57 N6 El Chaparro Anzoátegui, NE Venezuela
107 S12 Elche var. Elx-Elche; anc. Ilici, Lat. Illicis. País Valenciano, E Spain
107 Q12 Elche de la Sierra Castilla-La Mancha, C Spain
43 U15 El Chichonal, Volcán ✲ SE Mexico
42 C2 El Chinero Baja California, NW Mexico
189 R1 Elcho Island island Wessel Islands, Northern Territory, N Australia
65 H18 El Corcovado Chubut, SW Argentina
107 R12 Elda País Valenciano, E Spain
102 M10 Elde ∽ NE Germany
100 L12 Elden Gelderland, E Netherlands
83 J16 El Der spring/well S Ethiopia
El Dere see Ceel Dheere
42 E3 El Desemboque Sonora, NW Mexico
56 F5 El Difícil var. Ariguaní. Magdalena, N Colombia
126 Mm11 El'dikan Respublika Sakha (Yakutiya), NE Russian Federation
El Djazaïr see Alger
El Djelfa see Djelfa
31 X15 Eldon Iowa, C USA
29 U5 Eldon Missouri, C USA
56 E13 El Doncello Caquetá, S Colombia
31 W13 Eldora Iowa, C USA
62 G12 Eldorado Misiones, NE Argentina
42 I9 El Dorado Sinaloa, C Mexico
29 U14 El Dorado Arkansas, C USA
32 M17 Eldorado Illinois, N USA
29 O6 El Dorado Kansas, C USA
28 K12 Eldorado Oklahoma, C USA
27 O9 Eldorado Texas, SW USA
57 Q8 El Dorado Bolívar, E Venezuela
56 F10 El Dorado ✕ (Bogotá) Cundinamarca, C Colombia
El Dorado see California
29 O6 El Dorado Lake ▣ Kansas, C USA
29 S6 El Dorado Springs Missouri, C USA
83 H18 Eldoret Rift Valley, W Kenya
31 Z14 Eldridge Iowa, C USA
97 J21 Eldsberga Halland, S Sweden
27 R4 Electra Texas, SW USA
39 Q7 Electra Lake ▣ Colorado, C USA
40 B8 Eleele Haw. 'Ele'ele. Kauai, Hawaii, USA, C Pacific Ocean
Elefantes see Olifants
117 H19 Elefsína prev. Elevsís. Attikí, C Greece
117 G19 Eléftheres anc. Eleutherae. site of ancient city Attikí/Stereá Ellás, C Greece
116 I13 Eleftheroúpoli prev. Elevtheroúpolis. Anatolikí Makedonía kai Thráki, NE Greece
76 K7 El Eglab ⛰ SW Algeria
120 F10 Eleja Jelgava, C Latvia
Elek see Ilek
121 G14 Elektrėnai Kaišiadorys, SE Lithuania
130 L3 Elektrostal' Moskovskaya Oblast', W Russian Federation
83 H15 Elemi Triangle disputed region Kenya/Sudan
56 G16 El Encanto Amazonas, S Colombia
39 R14 Elephant Butte Reservoir ▣ New Mexico, SW USA
Éléphant, Chaîne de l' see Dâmrei, Chuŏr Phnum
204 G2 Elephant Island island South Shetland Islands, Antarctica
Elephant River see Olifants
El Escorial see San Lorenzo de El Escorial
Élesd see Aleşd
116 F11 Eleshnitsa ∽ W Bulgaria
143 S13 Eleşkirt Ağrı, E Turkey
44 F5 El Estor Izabal, E Guatemala
Eleutherae see Eléftheres
46 I2 Eleuthera Island island N Bahamas
39 S5 Elevenmile Canyon Reservoir ▣ Colorado, C USA
29 W8 Eleven Point River ∽ Arkansas/Missouri, C USA
Elevsís see Elefsína
Elevtheroúpolis see Eleftheroúpoli
77 W8 El Faiyûm var. Al Fayyūm. N Egypt
82 B10 El Fasher var. Al Fāshir. Northern Darfur, W Sudan
77 W8 El Fashn var. Al Fashn. C Egypt
El Ferrol/El Ferrol del Caudillo see Ferrol
41 W13 Elfin Cove Chichagof Island, Alaska, USA
107 W4 El Fluvià ∽ NE Spain
42 H7 El Fuerte Sinaloa, W Mexico
82 D11 El Fula Western Kordofan, C Sudan
El Gedaref see Gedaref
82 A10 El Geneina var. Ajjinena, Al-Genain, Al Junaynah. Western Darfur, W Sudan
98 J8 Elgin NE Scotland, UK
32 M10 Elgin Illinois, N USA
31 P14 Elgin Nebraska, C USA
37 Y9 Elgin Nevada, W USA
30 L6 Elgin North Dakota, N USA
28 M12 Elgin Oklahoma, C USA
27 T10 Elgin Texas, SW USA
127 N9 El'ginskiy Respublika Sakha (Yakutiya), NE Russian Federation
77 W8 El Gîza var. Al Jīzah, Gîza, Gizeh. N Egypt
76 J8 El Goléa var. Al Golea. C Algeria
42 D2 El Golfo de Santa Clara Sonora, NW Mexico
83 G18 Elgon, Mount ▲ E Uganda
96 I10 Elgpiggen ▲ S Norway
107 T4 El Grado Aragón, NE Spain
42 L6 El Guaje, Laguna ▣ NE Mexico
56 H6 El Guayabo Zulia, W Venezuela
79 O6 El Guettâra oasis N Mali
78 J6 El Ḥammâmi desert N Mauritania
78 M5 El Ḥank cliff N Mauritania
El Haseke see Al Ḥasakah
82 H10 El Hawata Gedaref, E Sudan
El Higo see Higos
176 Uu16 Eliase Pulau Selaru, E Indonesia
Elías Piña see Comendador
27 R6 Eliasville Texas, SW USA
Elichpur see Achalpur
39 V13 Elida New Mexico, SW USA
117 F18 Elikónas ⛰ C Greece
69 T10 Elila ∽ W Zaire
41 N9 Elim Alaska, USA
Elimberrum see Auch
Eliocroca see Lorca
63 B16 Elisa Santa Fe, C Argentina
Elisabethstedt see Dumbrăveni
Élisabethville see Lubumbashi
131 O13 Elista Respublika Kalmykiya, SW Russian Federation
190 I9 Elizabeth South Australia
23 Q3 Elizabeth West Virginia, NE USA
21 Q9 Elizabeth, Cape headland Maine, NE USA
23 Y8 Elizabeth City North Carolina, SE USA
23 P8 Elizabethton Tennessee, S USA
32 M17 Elizabethtown Illinois, N USA
22 K6 Elizabethtown Kentucky, S USA
20 L7 Elizabethtown New York, NE USA
23 U11 Elizabethtown North Carolina, SE USA
20 G15 Elizabethtown Pennsylvania, NE USA
76 E6 El-Jadida prev. Mazagan. W Morocco
El Jafr see Jafr, Qā' al
82 F11 El Jebelein White Nile, E Sudan
112 N8 Ełk Ger. Lyck. Suwałki, NE Poland
112 O8 Ełk ∽ NE Poland
31 Y12 Elkader Iowa, C USA
82 G9 El Kamlin Gezira, C Sudan
35 N11 Elk City Idaho, NW USA
28 K10 Elk City Oklahoma, C USA
29 P7 Elk City Lake ▣ Kansas, C USA
36 M5 Elk Creek California, W USA
30 J10 Elk Creek ∽ South Dakota, N USA
76 M5 El Kef var. Al Kāf, Le Kef. NW Tunisia
76 F7 El Kelâa Srarhna var. Kal al Sraghna. C Morocco
El Kerak see Al Karak
9 P17 Elkford British Columbia, SW Canada
El Khalil see Hebron
82 E7 El Khandaq Northern, N Sudan
77 W10 El Khârga var. Al Khārijah. C Egypt
33 P11 Elkhart Indiana, N USA
28 H7 Elkhart Kansas, C USA
27 V8 Elkhart Texas, SW USA
32 M7 Elkhart Lake ◎ Wisconsin, N USA
El Khartûm see Khartoum
39 Q3 Elkhead Mountains ⛰ Colorado, C USA
20 I12 Elk Hill ▲ Pennsylvania, NE USA
144 G8 El Khiyam var. Al Khiyām, Khiam. S Lebanon
31 S15 Elkhorn Nebraska, C USA
32 M9 Elkhorn Wisconsin, N USA
31 R14 Elkhorn River ∽ Nebraska, C USA
131 O16 El'khotovo Respublika Severnaya Osetiya, SW Russian Federation
116 L10 Elkhovo prev. Kizilagach. Burgaska Oblast, SE Bulgaria
23 R8 Elkin North Carolina, SE USA
23 S4 Elkins West Virginia, NE USA
205 X3 Elkins, Mount ▲ Antarctica
12 G8 Elk Lake Ontario, S Canada
110 L7 Elk Lake ◎ Michigan, N USA
20 F12 Elkland Pennsylvania, NE USA
37 W3 Elko Nevada, W USA
El Kôm see Al Kawm
9 R14 Elk Point Alberta, SW Canada
31 R12 Elk Point South Dakota, N USA
31 V8 Elk River Minnesota, N USA
22 J10 Elk River ∽ Alabama/Tennessee, S USA
23 R4 Elk River ∽ West Virginia, NE USA
22 I7 Elkton Kentucky, S USA
23 Y2 Elkton Maryland, NE USA
31 R10 Elkton South Dakota, N USA
22 I10 Elkton Tennessee, S USA
23 U5 Elkton Virginia, NE USA
El Kuneitra see Al Qunayṭirah
83 L15 El Kure SE Ethiopia
82 D12 El Lagowa Western Kordofan, C Sudan
41 S12 Ellamar Alaska, USA
Ellás see Greece
25 S6 Ellaville Georgia, SE USA
207 P9 Ellef Ringnes Island island Northwest Territories, N Canada
31 V10 Ellendale Minnesota, N USA
31 P7 Ellendale North Dakota, N USA
38 M6 Ellen, Mount ▲ Utah, W USA
34 I9 Ellensburg Washington, NW USA
20 K12 Ellenville New York, NE USA
Ellep see Lib
23 T10 Ellerbe North Carolina, SE USA
207 P10 Ellesmere Island island Queen Elizabeth Islands, Northwest Territories, N Canada
193 H19 Ellesmere, Lake ◎ South Island, NZ
99 K18 Ellesmere Port C England, UK
33 O14 Ellettsville Indiana, N USA
101 E19 Ellezelles Hainaut, SW Belgium
15 J4 Ellice ∽ Northwest Territories, NE Canada
Ellice Islands see Tuvalu
Ellichpur see Achalpur
23 W3 Ellicott City Maryland, NE USA
25 S2 Ellijay Georgia, SE USA
29 W7 Ellington Missouri, C USA
28 L5 Ellinwood Kansas, C USA
85 J24 Elliot Eastern Cape, SE South Africa
12 D10 Elliot Lake Ontario, S Canada
189 X6 Elliot, Mount ▲ Queensland, E Australia
23 T5 Elliott Knob ▲ Virginia, NE USA
28 K4 Ellis Kansas, C USA
190 F8 Elliston South Australia
24 M7 Ellisville Mississippi, S USA
107 V5 El Llobregat ∽ NE Spain
98 L9 Ellon NE Scotland, UK
Ellore see Elūru
23 S13 Elloree South Carolina, SE USA
28 M4 Ellsworth Kansas, C USA
21 S7 Ellsworth Maine, NE USA
32 I6 Ellsworth Wisconsin, N USA
28 M11 Ellsworth, Lake ▣ Oklahoma, C USA
204 K9 Ellsworth Land physical region Antarctica
204 L9 Ellsworth Mountains ⛰ Antarctica
103 J21 Ellwangen Baden-Württemberg, S Germany
20 B14 Ellwood City Pennsylvania, NE USA
110 H8 Elm Glarus, NE Switzerland
34 G9 Elma Washington, NW USA
124 Qq15 El Maḥalla el Kubra var. Al Maḥallah al Kubrá, Mahalla el Kubra. N Egypt
76 E9 El Mahbas var. Mahbés. SW Western Sahara
65 H17 El Maitén Chubut, W Argentina
142 E16 Elmalı Antalya, SW Turkey
82 G10 El Managil Gezira, C Sudan
56 M12 El Mango Amazonas, S Venezuela
77 W7 El Manṣûra var. Al Manṣūrah, Manṣûra. N Egypt
57 P8 El Manteco Bolívar, E Venezuela
31 O16 Elm Creek Nebraska, C USA
El Mediyya see Médéa
79 V9 Elméki Agadez, C Niger
110 K7 Elmen Tirol, W Austria
20 I16 Elmer New Jersey, NE USA
144 G6 El Mina var. Al Mīnā'. N Lebanon
77 W9 El Minya var. Al Minyā, Minya. C Egypt
12 F15 Elmira Ontario, S Canada
20 G11 Elmira New York, NE USA
38 K13 El Mirage Arizona, SW USA
31 O7 Elm Lake ▣ South Dakota, N USA
El Moján see San Rafael
107 N7 El Molar Madrid, C Spain
78 L7 El Mrâyer well C Mauritania
78 L5 El Mreïti well N Mauritania
78 L8 El Mreyyé desert E Mauritania
31 P8 Elm River ∽ North Dakota/South Dakota, N USA
102 I9 Elmshorn Schleswig-Holstein, N Germany
82 D12 El Muglad Western Kordofan, C Sudan
El Muwaqqar see Al Muwaqqar
12 G14 Elmvale Ontario, S Canada
32 K12 Elmwood Illinois, N USA
28 J8 Elmwood Oklahoma, C USA
105 P17 Elne anc. Illiberis. Pyrénées-Orientales, S France
56 F11 El Nevado, Cerro elevation C Colombia
179 Oo13 El Nido Palawan, W Philippines
64 I12 El Nihuil Mendoza, W Argentina
77 W7 El Nouzha ✕ (Alexandria) N Egypt
82 E10 El Obeid var. Al Obayyid, Al Ubayyiḍ. Northern Kordofan, C Sudan
43 O13 El Oro México, S Mexico
58 B8 El Oro ◆ province SW Ecuador
63 B19 Elortondo Santa Fe, C Argentina
56 J8 Elorza Apure, C Venezuela
El Ouâdi see El Oued
76 L7 El Oued var. Al Oued, El Ouâdi, El Wad. NE Algeria
38 L15 Eloy Arizona, SW USA
57 Q7 El Palmar Bolívar, E Venezuela
42 K8 El Palmito Durango, W Mexico
57 P7 El Pao Bolívar, E Venezuela
56 K5 El Pao Cojedes, N Venezuela
44 J7 El Paraíso El Paraíso, S Honduras
44 I7 El Paraíso ◆ department SE Honduras
32 L12 El Paso Illinois, N USA
26 G8 El Paso Texas, SW USA
26 G8 El Paso ✕ Texas, SW USA
107 U7 El Perello Cataluña, NE Spain
57 P5 El Pilar Sucre, NE Venezuela
44 F7 El Pital, Cerro ▲ El Salvador/Honduras
37 Q9 El Portal California, W USA
42 J3 El Porvenir Chihuahua, N Mexico
45 U14 El Porvenir San Blas, N Panama
107 W6 El Prat de Llobregat Cataluña, NE Spain
44 H5 El Progreso Yoro, NW Honduras
44 A2 El Progreso off. Departamento de El Progreso. ◆ department C Guatemala
El Progreso see Guastatoya
106 L9 El Puente del Arzobispo Castilla-La Mancha, C Spain
106 J15 El Puerto de Santa María Andalucía, S Spain
64 I8 El Puesto Catamarca, NW Argentina
El Qâhira see Cairo
77 V10 El Qaṣr var. Al Qaṣr. C Egypt
El Qatrani see Al Qaṭrānah
42 I10 El Quelite Sinaloa, C Mexico
64 G9 Elqui, Río ∽ N Chile
El Quneitra see Al Qunayṭirah
El Quseir see Al Quṣayr
El Quweira see Al Quwayrah
147 O15 El-Rahaba ✕ (Ṣan'ā') W Yemen
44 M10 El Rama Región Autónoma Atlántico Sur, SE Nicaragua
45 W16 El Real var. El Real de Santa María. Darién, SE Panama
El Real de Santa María see El Real
28 M10 El Reno Oklahoma, C USA
42 K9 El Rodeo Durango, C Mexico
106 J13 El Ronquillo Andalucía, S Spain
9 S16 Elrose Saskatchewan, S Canada
32 K8 Elroy Wisconsin, N USA
27 S17 Elsa Texas, SW USA
77 W8 El Ṣaff var. Aṣ Ṣaff. N Egypt
42 J10 El Salto Durango, C Mexico
44 D8 El Salvador off. Republica de El Salvador. ◆ republic Central America
56 K7 El Samán de Apure Apure, C Venezuela
12 D7 Elsas Ontario, S Canada
Elsass see Alsace
42 J5 El Sáuz Chihuahua, N Mexico
29 W4 Elsberry Missouri, C USA
47 P9 El Seibo var. Santa Cruz de El Seibo, Santa Cruz del Seibo. E Dominican Republic
44 B7 El Semillero Barra Nahualate Escuintla, SW Guatemala
Elsene see Ixelles
165 N11 Elsen Nur ◎ C China
38 L6 Elsinore Utah, W USA
Elsinore see Helsingør
101 L18 Elsloo Limburg, SE Netherlands
62 G13 El Soberbio Misiones, NE Argentina
57 N6 El Socorro Guárico, C Venezuela
56 L6 El Sombrero Guárico, N Venezuela
100 L10 Elspeet Gelderland, E Netherlands
100 L12 Elst Gelderland, E Netherlands
103 O15 Elsterwerda Brandenburg, E Germany
42 J4 El Sueco Chihuahua, N Mexico
El Suweida see As Suwaydā'
El Suweis see Suez
56 D12 El Tambo Cauca, SW Colombia
183 T13 Eltanin Fracture Zone tectonic feature SE Pacific Ocean
107 X5 El Ter ∽ NE Spain
192 K11 Eltham Taranaki, North Island, NZ
57 O6 El Tigre Anzoátegui, NE Venezuela
El Tigrito see San José de Guanipa
56 J5 El Tocuyo Lara, N Venezuela
131 Q10 El'ton Volgogradskaya Oblast', SW Russian Federation
34 K10 Eltopia Washington, NW USA
63 A18 El Trébol Santa Fe, C Argentina
42 J13 El Tuito Jalisco, SW Mexico
77 X8 El Ṭûr var. Aṭ Ṭūr. NE Egypt
161 K16 Elūru prev. Ellore. Andhra Pradesh, E India
120 H13 Elva Ger. Elwa. Tartumaa, SE Estonia
39 R9 El Vado Reservoir ▣ New Mexico, SW USA
45 S15 El Valle Coclé, C Panama
106 I11 Elvas Portalegre, C Portugal
56 K7 El Venado Apure, C Venezuela
107 V6 El Vendrell Cataluña, NE Spain
96 I13 Elverum Hedmark, S Norway
44 J9 El Viejo Chinandega, NW Nicaragua
56 G7 El Viejo, Cerro ▲ C Colombia
56 H6 El Vigía Mérida, NW Venezuela
107 Q4 El Villar de Arnedo La Rioja, N Spain
61 A14 Elvira Amazonas, W Brazil
Elwa see Elva
El Wad see El Oued
83 K17 El Wak North Eastern, NE Kenya
35 R7 Elwell, Lake ▣ Montana, NW USA
33 P13 Elwood Indiana, N USA
29 R3 Elwood Kansas, C USA
31 N16 Elwood Nebraska, C USA
Elx-Elche see Elche
99 O20 Ely E England, UK
31 X4 Ely Minnesota, N USA
37 X6 Ely Nevada, W USA
El Yopal see Yopal
33 T11 Elyria Ohio, N USA
47 S9 El Yunque ▲ E Puerto Rico
103 F23 Elz ∽ SW Germany
197 C14 Emae island Shepherd Islands, C Vanuatu
120 I5 Emajõgi Ger. Embach. ∽ SE Estonia
Emāmrūd see Shāhrūd
155 Q2 Emām Ṣāḥeb var. Emam Saheb, Hazarat Imam. Kunduz, NE Afghanistan
Emāmshahr see Shāhrūd
97 M20 Emån ∽ S Sweden
197 D14 Emao island C Vanuatu
150 J11 Emba Kaz. Embi. Aktyubinsk, W Kazakhstan
150 H12 Emba Kaz. Zhem. ∽ W Kazakhstan
Embach see Emajõgi
64 K5 Embarcación Salta, N Argentina
32 M15 Embarras River ∽ Illinois, N USA
Embi see Emba
83 I19 Embu Eastern, C Kenya
102 E10 Emden Niedersachsen, NW Germany
31 Q4 Emerado North Dakota, N USA
189 X8 Emerald Queensland, E Australia
Emerald Isle see Montserrat
59 J15 Emero, Río ∽ W Bolivia
9 Y17 Emerson Manitoba, S Canada
31 T15 Emerson Iowa, C USA
31 R13 Emerson Nebraska, C USA
38 M5 Emery Utah, W USA
Emesa see Ḥimṣ
142 E13 Emet Kütahya, W Turkey
194 G14 Emeti Western, SW PNG
37 V3 Emigrant Pass pass Nevada, W USA
80 I6 Emi Koussi ▲ N Chad
Emilia see Emilia-Romagna
43 V15 Emiliano Zapata Chiapas, SE Mexico
108 E9 Emilia-Romagna prev. Emilia, anc. Æmilia. ◆ region N Italy
164 J3 Emin var. Dorbiljin. Xinjiang Uygur Zizhiqu, NW China
155 W8 Eminābād Punjab, E Pakistan
22 L5 Eminence Kentucky, S USA
29 W7 Eminence Missouri, C USA
116 N9 Emine, Nos headland E Bulgaria
164 I3 Emin He ∽ NW China
195 N8 Emirau Island island N PNG
142 F13 Emirdağ Afyon, W Turkey
97 M21 Emmaboda Kalmar, S Sweden
120 E5 Emmaste Hiiumaa, W Estonia
20 I15 Emmaus Pennsylvania, NE USA
191 U4 Emmaville New South Wales, SE Australia
110 E9 Emme ∽ W Switzerland
100 L8 Emmeloord Flevoland, N Netherlands
100 O8 Emmen Drenthe, NE Netherlands
110 F8 Emmen Luzern, C Switzerland
103 F23 Emmendingen Baden-Württemberg, SW Germany
100 P8 Emmer-Compascuum Drenthe, NE Netherlands
103 D14 Emmerich Nordrhein-Westfalen, W Germany
31 U12 Emmetsburg Iowa, C USA
34 M14 Emmett Idaho, NW USA
40 M10 Emmonak Alaska, USA
Emona see Ljubljana
Emonti see East London
26 L12 Emory Peak ▲ Texas, SW USA
42 F6 Empalme Sonora, NW Mexico
85 L23 Empangeni KwaZulu/Natal, E South Africa
63 C14 Empedrado Corrientes, NE Argentina
199 I3 Emperor Seamounts undersea feature NW Pacific Ocean
199 J3 Emperor Trough undersea feature N Pacific Ocean
37 R4 Empire Nevada, W USA
Empire State of the South see Georgia
Emplawas see Amplawas
108 F11 Empoli Toscana, C Italy
29 P5 Emporia Kansas, C USA
23 W7 Emporia Virginia, NE USA
20 E13 Emporium Pennsylvania, NE USA
195 S12 Empress Augusta Bay inlet Bougainville Island, PNG
Empty Quarter see Ar Rub' al Khālī
102 E10 Ems Dut. Eems. ∽ NW Germany
102 F13 Emsdetten Nordrhein-Westfalen, NW Germany
Ems-Hunte Canal see Küstenkanal
102 F10 Ems-Jade-Kanal canal NW Germany
102 F11 Emsland cultural region NW Germany
190 D3 Emu Junction South Australia
169 T3 Emur He ∽ NE China
57 R8 Enachu Landing NW Guyana
95 F16 Enafors Jämtland, C Sweden
96 N11 Enånger Gävleborg, C Sweden
98 G7 Enard Bay bay NW Scotland, UK
Enareträsk see Inarijärvi
176 X12 Enarotali Irian Jaya, E Indonesia
171 I15 Ena-san ▲ Honshū, S Japan
144 E12 En 'Avedat well S Israel
172 P2 Enbetsu Hokkaidō, NE Japan
63 H16 Encantadas, Serra das ⛰ S Brazil
42 E7 Encantado, Cerro ▲ NW Mexico
64 P7 Encarnación Itapúa, S Paraguay
42 M12 Encarnación de Díaz Jalisco, SW Mexico
79 O17 Enchi SW Ghana
27 Q14 Encinal Texas, SW USA
37 U17 Encinitas California, W USA
27 S16 Encino Texas, SW USA
56 H6 Encontrados Zulia, NW Venezuela
190 I10 Encounter Bay inlet South Australia
63 F15 Encruzilhada Rio Grande do Sul, S Brazil
63 H16 Encruzilhada do Sul Rio Grande do Sul, S Brazil
113 M20 Encs Borsod-Abaúj-Zemplén, NE Hungary
199 M3 Endeavour Seamount undersea feature N Pacific Ocean
189 V1 Endeavour Strait strait Queensland, NE Australia
175 Q16 Endeh Flores, S Indonesia
97 G23 Endelave island C Denmark
203 T4 Enderbury Island atoll Phoenix Islands, C Kiribati
9 N16 Enderby British Columbia, SW Canada
205 W4 Enderby Land physical region Antarctica
181 N14 Enderby Plain undersea feature S Indian Ocean
31 Q6 Enderlin North Dakota, N USA
Endersdorf see Jędrzejów
30 K16 Enders Reservoir ▣ Nebraska, C USA
20 H11 Endicott New York, NE USA
41 P7 Endicott Mountains ⛰ Alaska, USA
120 I5 Endla Raba wetland C Estonia
119 T9 Enerhodar Zaporiz'ka Oblast', SE Ukraine
59 F14 Ene, Río ∽ C Peru
201 N4 Enewetak Atoll var. Ānewetak, Eniwetok. atoll Ralik Chain, W Marshall Islands
116 L13 Enez Edirne, NW Turkey
23 W8 Enfield North Carolina, SE USA
194 G12 Enga ◆ province W PNG
47 Q9 Engaño, Cabo headland E Dominican Republic
172 Q5 Engaru Hokkaidō, NE Japan
144 F11 'En Gedi Southern, E Israel
110 F9 Engelberg Unterwalden, C Switzerland
23 Y9 Engelhard North Carolina, SE USA
131 P8 Engel's Saratovskaya Oblast', W Russian Federation
103 G24 Engen Baden-Württemberg, SW Germany
Engeten see Aiud
174 H13 Enggano, Pulau island W Indonesia
82 J8 Enghershatu ▲ N Eritrea
101 F19 Enghien Dut. Edingen. Hainaut, SW Belgium
29 V12 England Arkansas, C USA
99 M20 England Lat. Anglia. national region UK
15 L2 Englefield, Cape headland Northwest Territories, NE Canada
12 H8 Englehart Ontario, S Canada
39 T4 Englewood Colorado, C USA
33 O16 English Indiana, N USA
41 Q13 English Bay Alaska, USA
English Bazar see Ingrāj Bāzār
99 N25 English Channel var. The Channel, Fr. la Manche. channel NW Europe
204 J7 English Coast physical region Antarctica
107 S11 Enguera País Valenciano, E Spain
120 E8 Engure Tukums, W Latvia
120 E8 Engures Ezers ◎ NW Latvia
143 R9 Enguri Rus. Inguri. ∽ NW Georgia
Engyum see Gangi
28 M9 Enid Oklahoma, C USA
24 L3 Enid Lake ▣ Mississippi, S USA
201 Y2 Enigu island Ratak Chain, SE Marshall Islands
Enikale Strait see Kerch Strait
153 Z8 Enil'chek Issyk-Kul'skaya Oblast', E Kyrgyzstan
117 F17 Enipéfs ∽ C Greece
172 O6 Eniwa Hokkaidō, NE Japan
172 O6 Eniwa-dake ▲ Hokkaidō, NE Japan
Eniwetok see Enewetak Atoll
Enkeldoorn see Chivhu
127 Nn11 Enken, Mys headland NE Russian Federation
100 J8 Enkhuizen Noord-Holland, NW Netherlands
111 Q4 Enknach ∽ N Austria
97 N15 Enköping Uppsala, C Sweden
109 K24 Enna var. Castrogiovanni, Henna. Sicilia, Italy, C Mediterranean Sea
82 D11 En Nahud Western Kordofan, C Sudan
144 F8 En Nâqoûra var. An Nāqūrah. SW Lebanon
En Nazira see Naẓerat
80 K8 Ennedi plateau E Chad
103 E15 Ennepetal Nordrhein-Westfalen, W Germany
191 P4 Enngonia New South Wales, SE Australia
99 C19 Ennis Ir. Inis. W Ireland
35 R11 Ennis Montana, NW USA
27 U7 Ennis Texas, SW USA
99 F20 Enniscorthy Ir. Inis Córthaidh. SE Ireland
99 E15 Enniskillen var. Inniskilling, Ir. Inis Ceithleann. SW Northern Ireland, UK
99 B19 Ennistimon Ir. Inis Díomáin. W Ireland
111 T4 Enns Oberösterreich, N Austria
111 T4 Enns ∽ C Austria
95 O16 Eno Pohjois-Karjala, SE Finland
26 M5 Enochs Texas, SW USA
95 N17 Enonkoski Mikkeli, SE Finland
94 K10 Enontekiö Lapp. Eanodat. Lappi, N Finland
23 Q11 Enoree South Carolina, SE USA
23 P11 Enoree River ∽ South Carolina, SE USA
20 M6 Enosburg Falls Vermont, NE USA
175 P11 Enrekang Sulawesi, C Indonesia
47 N10 Enriquillo SW Dominican Republic
47 N9 Enriquillo, Lago ◎ SW Dominican Republic
100 L9 Ens Flevoland, N Netherlands
100 P11 Enschede Overijssel, E Netherlands
42 B2 Ensenada Baja California, NW Mexico
103 E20 Ensheim ✕ (Saarbrücken) Saarland, W Germany
166 L9 Enshi Hubei, C China
171 Hh17 Enshū-nada gulf SW Japan
25 O8 Ensley Florida, SE USA
Enso see Svetogorsk
83 F18 Entebbe S Uganda
83 F18 Entebbe ✕ C Uganda
103 M18 Entenbühl ▲ Czech Republic/Germany
100 N10 Enter Overijssel, E Netherlands
25 Q7 Enterprise Alabama, S USA
34 L11 Enterprise Oregon, NW USA
38 J7 Enterprise Utah, W USA
34 J8 Entiat Washington, NW USA
107 P15 Entinas, Punta de las headland S Spain
110 F8 Entlebuch Luzern, W Switzerland
110 F8 Entlebuch valley C Switzerland
65 I22 Entrada, Punta headland S Argentina
105 O13 Entraygues-sur-Truyère Aveyron, S France
197 G3 Entrecasteaux, Récifs d' reef N New Caledonia
63 C17 Entre Ríos off. Provincia de Entre Ríos. ◆ province NE Argentina
44 K7 Entre Ríos, Cordillera ⛰ Honduras/Nicaragua
106 G9 Entroncamento Santarém, C Portugal
176 Z10 Entrop Irian Jaya, E Indonesia
79 V16 Enugu Enugu, S Nigeria
79 U16 Enugu ◆ state SE Nigeria
127 Pp3 Enurmino Chukotskiy Avtonomnyy Okrug, NE Russian Federation
56 E9 Envigado Antioquia, W Colombia
61 B15 Envira Amazonas, W Brazil
Enyélé see Enyellé
81 I16 Enyellé var. Enyélé. La Likouala, NE Congo
103 H21 Enz ∽ SW Germany
171 J16 Enzan Yamanashi, Honshū, S Japan
106 I2 Eo ∽ NW Spain
Eochaill see Youghal
Eochaille, Cuan see Youghal Bay
109 K22 Eolie, Isole var. Isole Lipari, Eng. Aeolian Islands, Lipari Islands. island group S Italy
201 U12 Eot island Chuuk, C Micronesia
117 J25 Epáno Archánes var. Áno Arkhánai; prev. Epáno Arkhánai. Kríti, Greece, E Mediterranean Sea
Epáno Arkhánai see Epáno Archánes
117 G14 Epanomí Kentrikí Makedonía, N Greece
100 M10 Epe Gelderland, E Netherlands
79 S16 Epe Lagos, S Nigeria
81 I17 Epéna La Likouala, NE Congo
Eperies/Eperjes see Prešov
105 Q4 Épernay anc. Sparnacum. Marne, N France
38 L5 Ephraim Utah, W USA
20 H15 Ephrata Pennsylvania, NE USA
34 J8 Ephrata Washington, NW USA
197 C13 Epi island C Vanuatu
107 R6 Épila Aragón, NE Spain
105 T6 Épinal Vosges, NE France
Epiphania see Ḥamāh
Epirus see Ípeiros
124 N4 Episkopí SW Cyprus
Episkopi Bay see Episkopí, Kólpos
124 N4 Episkopí, Kólpos var. Episkopi Bay. bay SE Cyprus
Epitoli see Pretoria
Epoon see Ebon Atoll
Eporedia see Ivrea
Eppeschdorf see Dumbrăveni
103 H21 Eppingen Baden-Württemberg, SW Germany
85 E18 Epukiro Omaheke, E Namibia
31 Y13 Epworth Iowa, C USA
149 O10 Eqlīd var. Iqlid. Fārs, C Iran
Equality State see Wyoming
81 J18 Equateur off. Région de l' Equateur. ◆ region N Zaire
157 K22 Equatorial Channel channel S Maldives
81 B17 Equatorial Guinea off. Republic of Equatorial Guinea. ◆ republic C Africa
194 H14 Era ∽ S PNG

◆ Country ● Country Capital ◇ Dependent Territory ○ Dependent Territory Capital ◆ Administrative Region ✕ International Airport ▲ Mountain ⛰ Mountain Range ✲ Volcano ∽ River ◎ Lake ▣ Reservoir

124 R13 **Eratosthenes Tablemount** *undersea feature* E Mediterranean Sea
Erautini *see* Johannesburg
194 H13 **Erave** Southern Highlands, W PNG
142 L12 **Erbaa** Tokat, N Turkey
103 E19 **Erbeskopf** ▲ W Germany
Erbil *see* Arbīl
124 Nn3 **Ercan** ✈ (Nicosia) N Cyprus
Ercegnovi *see* Herceg-Novi
143 T14 **Erçek Gölü** ◎ E Turkey
143 S14 **Erciş** Van, E Turkey
142 K14 **Erciyes Dağı** ***anc.*** Argaeus. ▲ C Turkey
113 J22 **Érd** ***Ger.*** Hanselbeck. Pest, C Hungary
169 X11 **Erdaobaihe** Jilin, NE China
165 O12 **Erdaogou** Qinghai, W China
169 X11 **Erdao Jiang** ▲▲ NE China
Erdăt-Sângeorz *see* Sângeorgiu de Pădure
142 C11 **Erdek** Balıkesir, NW Turkey
Erdély *see* Transylvania
Erdélyi-Havasok *see* Carpații Meridionali
142 J17 **Erdemli** İçel, S Turkey
168 K6 **Erdenet** Bulgan, N Mongolia
168 I8 **Erdenetsogt** Bayanhongor, C Mongolia
80 K7 **Erdi** *plateau* NE Chad
80 L7 **Erdi Ma** *desert* NE Chad
103 M23 **Erding** Bayern, SE Germany
Erdőszáda *see* Ardusat
Erdőszentgyörgy *see* Sângeorgiu de Pădure
104 I7 **Erdre** ≈ NW France
205 R13 **Erebus, Mount** ▲ Ross Island, Antarctica
63 H14 **Erechim** Rio Grande do Sul, S Brazil
169 O7 **Ereen Davaanï Nuruu** ▲▲ NE Mongolia
169 Q6 **Ereentsav** Dornod, NE Mongolia
142 I16 **Ereğli** Konya, S Turkey
117 A15 **Ereíkoussa** *island* Iónioi Nísoi, Greece, C Mediterranean Sea
169 O11 **Erenhot** ***var.*** Erlian. Nei Mongol Zizhiqu, NE China
106 M6 **Eresma** ≈ N Spain
117 K17 **Eresós** ***var.*** Eressós. Lésvos, E Greece
Eressós *see* Eresós
Erevan *see* Yerevan
Ereymentaū *see* Yermentau
101 K21 **Érezée** Luxembourg, SE Belgium
76 G7 **Erfoud** SE Morocco
103 D16 **Erft** ≈ W Germany
103 K16 **Erfurt** Thüringen, C Germany
143 P15 **Ergani** Dıyarbakır, SE Turkey
169 N11 **Ergel** Dornogovĭ, SE Mongolia
Ergene Irmağı *see* Ergene Çayı
168 L11 **Ergenetsogt** Ömnogövĭ, S Mongolia
142 C10 **Ergene Çayı** ***var.*** Ergene Irmağı. ≈ NW Turkey
120 I9 **Ērgļi** Madona, C Latvia
80 H11 **Erguig, Bahr** ≈ SW Chad
Ergun He *see* Argun
169 S5 **Ergun Youqi** Nei Mongol Zizhiqu, N China
169 T5 **Ergun Zuoqi** Nei Mongol Zizhiqu, N China
166 F12 **Er Hai** ⊠ SW China
106 K4 **Ería** ≈ NW Spain
82 H8 **Eriba** Kassala, NE Sudan
98 I6 **Eriboll, Loch** *inlet* NW Scotland, UK
67 Q18 **Erica Seamount** *undersea feature* SW Indian Ocean
109 H23 **Erice** Sicilia, Italy, C Mediterranean Sea
106 E10 **Ericeira** Lisboa, C Portugal
98 H10 **Ericht, Loch** ◎ C Scotland, UK
28 J11 **Erick** Oklahoma, C USA
20 B11 **Erie** Pennsylvania, NE USA
20 E9 **Erie Canal** *canal* New York, NE USA
Érié, Lac *see* Erie, Lake
33 T10 **Erie, Lake** ***Fr.*** Lac Érié. ◎ Canada/USA
Erigabo *see* Ceerigaabo
79 N8 **'Erîgât** *desert* N Mali
Erigavo *see* Ceerigaabo
94 P2 **Erik Eriksenstretet** *strait* E Svalbard
9 X15 **Eriksdale** Manitoba, S Canada
201 V6 **Erikub Atoll** ***var.*** Ādkup. *atoll* Ratak Chain, C Marshall Islands
Erimanthos *see* Erýmanthos
172 P8 **Erimo** Hokkaidō, NE Japan
172 Oo8 **Erimo-misaki** *headland* Hokkaidō, NE Japan
22 H8 **Erin** Tennessee, S USA
98 E9 **Eriskay** *island* NW Scotland, UK
Erithraí *see* Erythrés
82 I9 **Eritrea** ***off.*** State of Eritrea, ***Tig.*** Ērtra. ◆ *transitional government* E Africa
Erivan *see* Yerevan
103 D16 **Erkelenz** Nordrhein-Westfalen, W Germany
97 P15 **Erken** ◎ C Sweden
103 K19 **Erlangen** Bayern, S Germany
166 G9 **Erlang Shan** ▲ C China
Erlau *see* Eger
111 V5 **Erlauf** ≈ NE Austria
189 Q8 **Erldunda Roadhouse** Northern Territory, N Australia
Erlian *see* Erenhot
29 T15 **Erling, Lake** ⊠ Arkansas, USA
111 O8 **Erlsbach** Tirol, W Austria
Ermak *see* Aksu
100 K10 **Ermelo** Gelderland, C Netherlands
85 K21 **Ermelo** Mpumalanga, NE South Africa
142 H17 **Ermenek** Karaman, S Turkey
Érmihályfalva *see* Valea lui Mihai
117 G20 **Ermióni** Pelopónnisos, S Greece
117 J20 **Ermoúpoli** ***var.*** Hermoupolis; ***prev.*** Ermoúpolis. Sýros, Kykládes, Greece, Aegean Sea
Ermoúpolis *see* Ermoúpoli
Ernabella *see* Pukatja
161 G22 **Ernākulam** Kerala, SW India
104 J6 **Ernée** Mayenne, NW France
63 H14 **Ernestina, Barragem** ⊠ S Brazil
56 E4 **Ernesto Cortissoz** ✈ (Barranquilla) Atlántico, N Colombia
161 H21 **Erode** Tamil Nādu, SE India
Eroj *see* Iroj
85 C19 **Erongo** ◐ *district* W Namibia
101 F21 **Erquelinnes** Hainaut, S Belgium
76 G7 **Er-Rachidia** ***var.*** Ksar al Soule. E Morocco
82 E11 **Er Rahad** ***var.*** Ar Rahad. Northern Kordofan, C Sudan
Er Ramle *see* Ramla
85 O15 **Errego** Zambézia, NE Mozambique
Errenteria *see* Rentería
Er Rif/Er Riff *see* Rif
99 D14 **Errigal** ***Ir.*** An Earagail. ▲ N Ireland
99 A15 **Erris Head** ***Ir.*** Ceann Iorrais. *headland* W Ireland
197 D15 **Erromango** *island* S Vanuatu
Error Guyot *see* Error Tablemount
181 O4 **Error Tablemount** ***var.*** Error Guyot. *undersea feature* W Indian Ocean
82 G11 **Er Roseires** Blue Nile, E Sudan
Erseka *see* Ersekë
115 M22 **Ersekë** ***var.*** Erseka, Kolonjë. Korçë, SE Albania
Érsekújvár *see* Nové Zámky
31 S4 **Erskine** Minnesota, N USA
105 V6 **Erstein** Bas-Rhin, NE France
110 G9 **Erstfeld** Uri, C Switzerland
164 M3 **Ertai** Xinjiang Uygur Zizhiqu, NW China
130 M7 **Ertil'** Voronezhskaya Oblast', W Russian Federation
Ertis *see* Irtysh, C Asia
Ertis *see* Irtyshsk, Kazakhstan
164 K2 **Ertix He** ***Rus.*** Chërnyy Irtysh. ≈ China/Kazakhstan
Ērtra *see* Eritrea
23 P9 **Erwin** North Carolina, SE USA
116 L12 **Erydropótamos** ***Bul.*** Byala Reka. ≈ Bulgaria/Greece
117 E19 **Erýmanthos** ***var.*** Erimanthos. ▲ S Greece
117 G19 **Erythrés** ***prev.*** Erithraí. Stereá Ellás, C Greece
166 F12 **Eryuan** Yunnan, SW China
111 U6 **Erzbach** ≈ W Austria
Erzerum *see* Erzurum
103 N17 **Erzgebirge** ***Cz.*** Krušné Hory, ***Eng.*** Ore Mountains. ▲▲ Czech Republic/Germany *see also* Krušné Hory
126 I16 **Erzin** Respublika Tyva, S Russian Federation
143 O13 **Erzincan** ***var.*** Erzinjan. Erzincan, E Turkey
143 N13 **Erzincan** ***var.*** Erzinjan. ◐ *province* NE Turkey
Erzinjan *see* Erzincan
Erzsébetváros *see* Dumbrăveni
143 Q13 **Erzurum** ***prev.*** Erzerum. Erzurum, NE Turkey
143 Q12 **Erzurum** ***prev.*** Erzerum. ◐ *province* NE Turkey
195 N16 **Esa'ala** Normanby Island, SE PNG
172 Nn7 **Esan-misaki** *headland* Hokkaidō, N Japan
172 Pp3 **Esashi** Hokkaidō, NE Japan
171 M11 **Esashi** ***var.*** Esasi. Iwate, Honshū, C Japan
171 Mm6 **Esasho** Hokkaidō, N Japan
Esasi *see* Esashi
97 F23 **Esbjerg** Ribe, W Denmark
Esbo *see* Espoo
38 L7 **Escalante** Utah, W USA
38 M7 **Escalante River** ≈ Utah, W USA
12 L12 **Escalier, Réservoir l'** ⊠ Québec, SE Canada
42 K7 **Escalón** Chihuahua, N Mexico
106 M8 **Escalona** Castilla-La Mancha, C Spain
25 O8 **Escambia River** ≈ Florida, SE USA
33 N5 **Escanaba** Michigan, N USA
33 N4 **Escanaba River** ≈ Michigan, N USA
107 R8 **Escandón, Puerto de** *pass* E Spain
43 W14 **Escárcega** Campeche, SE Mexico
179 Pp7 **Escarpada Point** *headland* Luzon, N Philippines
25 N8 **Escatawpa River** ≈ Alabama/Mississippi, S USA
105 P2 **Escaut** ≈ N France
Escaut *see* Scheldt
101 M25 **Esch-sur-Alzette** Luxembourg, S Luxembourg
103 J15 **Eschwege** Hessen, C Germany
103 D16 **Eschweiler** Nordrhein-Westfalen, W Germany
Esclaves, Grand Lac des *see* Great Slave Lake
47 O8 **Escocesa, Bahía** *bay* N Dominican Republic
45 W15 **Escocés, Punta** *headland* NE Panama
37 U17 **Escondido** California, W USA
44 M10 **Escondido, Río** ≈ SE Nicaragua
13 S7 **Escoumins, Rivière des** ≈ Québec, SE Canada
39 O13 **Escudilla Mountain** ▲ Arizona, SW USA
42 J11 **Escuinapa** ***var.*** Escuinapa de Hidalgo. Sinaloa, C Mexico
Escuinapa de Hidalgo *see* Escuinapa
44 C6 **Escuintla** Escuintla, S Guatemala
43 V17 **Escuintla** Chiapas, SE Mexico
44 A2 **Escuintla** ***off.*** Departamento de Escuintla. ◐ *department* S Guatemala
13 W7 **Escuminac** ≈ Québec, SE Canada
81 D16 **Eséka** Centre, SW Cameroon
142 I12 **Esenboğa** ✈ (Ankara) Ankara, C Turkey
Esenguly *see* Gasan-Kuli
142 D17 **Eşen Çayı** ≈ SW Turkey
107 T4 **Ésera** ≈ NE Spain
149 N8 **Eşfahān** ***Eng.*** Isfahan; ***anc.*** Aspadana. Eşfahān, C Iran
149 O7 **Eşfahān** ***off.*** Ostān-e Eşfahān. ◐ *province* C Iran
107 N5 **Esgueva** ≈ N Spain
155 Q3 **Eshkamesh** Takhār, NE Afghanistan
155 T2 **Eshkāshem** Badakhshān, NE Afghanistan
85 L23 **Eshowe** KwaZulu/Natal, E South Africa
149 T5 **'Eshqābād** Khorāsān, NE Iran
Esh Sham *see* Dimashq
Esh Sharā *see* Ash Sharāh
Esik *see* Yesik
Esil *see* Ishim, Kazakhstan/Russian Federation
Esil *see* Yesil', Kazakhstan
191 V2 **Esk** Queensland, E Australia
192 O11 **Eskdale** Hawke's Bay, North Island, NZ
Eski Dzhumaya *see* Tŭrgovishte
94 L2 **Eskifjördhur** Austurland, E Iceland
145 S3 **Eski Kaļak** ***var.*** Askī Kalak, Kalak. N Iraq
97 N16 **Eskilstuna** Södermanland, C Sweden
14 G2 **Eskimo Lakes** *lakes* Northwest Territories, NW Canada
15 L8 **Eskimo Point** *headland* Northwest Territories, E Canada
Eskimo Point *see* Arviat
145 Q2 **Eski Mosul** N Iraq
153 T10 **Eski-Nookat** ***var.*** Iski-Nauket. Oshskaya Oblast', SW Kyrgyzstan
142 F12 **Eskişehir** ***var.*** Eskishehr. Eskişehir, W Turkey
142 F13 **Eskişehir** ***var.*** Eski shehr. ◐ *province* NW Turkey
Eskishehr *see* Eskişehir
106 K5 **Esla** ≈ NW Spain
148 J6 **Eslāmābād** ***var.*** Eslāmābād-e Gharb; ***prev.*** Harunabad, Shāhābād. Kermānshāhān, W Iran
Eslāmābād-e Gharb *see* Eslāmābād
154 J4 **Eslām Qal'eh** ***Pash.*** Islam Qala. Herāt, W Afghanistan
97 K23 **Eslöv** Malmöhus, S Sweden
149 S12 **Esmā'īlābād** Kermān, S Iran
149 U8 **Esmā'īlābād** Khorāsān, E Iran
142 D14 **Eşme** Uşak, W Turkey
46 G6 **Esmeralda** Camagüey, E Cuba
65 F21 **Esmeralda, Isla** *island* S Chile
58 B5 **Esmeraldas** Esmeraldas, N Ecuador
58 B5 **Esmeraldas** ◐ *province* NW Ecuador
Esna *see* Isna
12 B6 **Esnagi Lake** ◎ Ontario, S Canada
149 V14 **Espakeh** Sīstān va Balūchestān, SE Iran
105 O13 **Espalion** Aveyron, S France
España *see* Spain
12 E11 **Espanola** Ontario, S Canada
39 S10 **Espanola** New Mexico, SW USA
59 C18 **Española, Isla** ***var.*** Hood Island. *island* Galapagos Islands, Ecuador, E Pacific Ocean
106 M13 **Espejo** Andalucía, S Spain
96 C13 **Espeland** Hordaland, S Norway
102 G12 **Espelkamp** Nordrhein-Westfalen, NW Germany
40 M8 **Espenberg, Cape** *headland* Alaska, USA
188 L13 **Esperance** Western Australia
195 W15 **Esperance, Cape** *headland* Guadacanal, C Solomon Islands
59 P18 **Esperancita** Santa Cruz, E Bolivia
63 B17 **Esperanza** Santa Fe, C Argentina
42 G6 **Esperanza** Sonora, NW Mexico
26 H9 **Esperanza** Texas, SW USA
204 H3 **Esperanza** *Argentinian research station* Antarctica
106 E12 **Espichel, Cabo** *headland* S Portugal
56 E10 **Espinal** Tolima, C Colombia
50 K10 **Espinhaço, Serra do** ▲▲ SE Brazil
106 G6 **Espinho** Aveiro, N Portugal
61 N18 **Espinosa** Minas Gerais, SE Brazil
105 O15 **Espinouse** ▲▲ S France
62 Q8 **Espírito Santo** ***off.*** Estado do Espírito Santo. ◐ *state* E Brazil
197 B12 **Espiritu Santo** ***var.*** Santo. *island* W Vanuatu
43 Z13 **Espíritu Santo, Bahía del** *bay* SE Mexico
42 F9 **Espíritu Santo, Isla del** *island* W Mexico
43 Y12 **Espita** Yucatán, SE Mexico
13 Y7 **Espoir, Cap d'** *headland* Québec, SE Canada
Esponsede/Esponsende *see* Esposende
95 L20 **Espoo** ***Swe.*** Esbo. Uusimaa, S Finland
106 G5 **Esposende** ***var.*** Esponsede, Esponsende. Braga, N Portugal
85 M18 **Espungabera** Manica, SW Mozambique
65 H17 **Esquel** Chubut, SW Argentina
8 L17 **Esquimalt** Vancouver Island, British Columbia, SW Canada
63 C16 **Esquina** Corrientes, NE Argentina
44 E6 **Esquipulas** Chiquimula, SE Guatemala
44 K9 **Esquipulas** Matagalpa, C Nicaragua
96 I8 **Essandjøen** ◎ S Norway
76 E7 **Essaouira** ***prev.*** Mogador. W Morocco
Esseg *see* Osijek
Es Semara *see* Smara
101 G15 **Essen** Antwerpen, N Belgium
103 E15 **Essen** ***var.*** Essen an der Ruhr. Nordrhein-Westfalen, W Germany
Essen an der Ruhr *see* Essen
76 I5 **Es Senia** ✈ (Oran) NW Algeria
57 T8 **Essequibo Islands** *island group* N Guyana
57 T11 **Essequibo River** ≈ C Guyana
12 C18 **Essex** Ontario, S Canada
31 T16 **Essex** Iowa, C USA
99 P21 **Essex** *cultural region* E England, UK
33 R8 **Essexville** Michigan, N USA
103 H22 **Esslingen** ***var.*** Esslingen am Neckar. Baden-Württemberg, SW Germany
Esslingen am Neckar *see* Esslingen
105 N6 **Essonne** ◐ *department* N France
Es Suweida *see* As Suwaydā'
81 F16 **Est** ***Eng.*** East. ◐ *province* SE Cameroon
106 I1 **Estaca de Bares, Punta da** *point* NW Spain
26 M5 **Estacado, Llano** *plain* New Mexico/Texas, SW USA
65 K25 **Estados, Isla de los** ***prev. Eng.*** Staten Island. *island* S Argentina
149 P12 **Eşţahbān** Fārs, S Iran
12 F11 **Estaire** Ontario, S Canada
39 S12 **Estancia** New Mexico, SW USA
61 P16 **Estância** Sergipe, E Brazil
106 G7 **Estarreja** Aveiro, N Portugal
104 M17 **Estats, Pic d'** ***Sp.*** Pico d'Estats. ▲ France/Spain
Estats, Pico d' *see* Estats, Pic d'
85 K23 **Estcourt** KwaZulu/Natal, E South Africa
108 H8 **Este** ***anc.*** Ateste. Veneto, NE Italy
44 J9 **Estelí** Estelí, NW Nicaragua
44 J9 **Estelí** ◐ *department* NW Nicaragua
107 Q4 **Estella** Navarra, N Spain
31 R9 **Estelline** South Dakota, N USA
27 P4 **Estelline** Texas, SW USA
106 L14 **Estepa** Andalucía, S Spain
106 L16 **Estepona** Andalucía, S Spain
41 R9 **Ester** Alaska, USA
9 V16 **Esterhazy** Saskatchewan, S Canada
39 S3 **Estes Park** Colorado, C USA
9 V17 **Estevan** Saskatchewan, S Canada
31 T11 **Estherville** Iowa, C USA
23 R15 **Estill** South Carolina, SE USA
105 Q6 **Estissac** Aube, N France
13 T9 **Est, Lac de l'** ◎ Québec, SE Canada
Estland *see* Estonia
9 S16 **Eston** Saskatchewan, S Canada
120 G5 **Estonia** ***off.*** Republic of Estonia, ***Est.*** Eesti Vabariik, ***Ger.*** Estland, ***Latv.*** Igaunija; ***prev.*** Estonian SSR, ***Rus.*** Estonskaya SSR. ◆ *republic* NE Europe
Estonskaya SSR *see* Estonia
106 E11 **Estoril** Lisboa, W Portugal
61 L14 **Estreito** Maranhão, E Brazil
106 I8 **Estrela, Serra da** ▲▲ C Portugal
42 D3 **Estrella, Punta** *headland* NW Mexico
Estremadura *see* Extremadura
106 H11 **Estremoz** Évora, S Portugal
81 D18 **Estuaire** ***off.*** Province de l'Estuaire, ***var.*** L'Estuaire. ◐ *province* NW Gabon
Eszék *see* Osijek
113 I22 **Esztergom** ***Ger.*** Gran; ***anc.*** Strigonium. Komárom-Esztergom, N Hungary
158 K11 **Etah** Uttar Pradesh, N India
201 R17 **Etal Atoll** *atoll* Mortlock Islands, C Micronesia
101 K24 **Étalle** Luxembourg, SE Belgium
105 N6 **Étampes** Essonne, N France
190 J1 **Etamunbanie, Lake** *salt lake* South Australia
105 N1 **Étaples** Pas-de-Calais, N France
158 K12 **Etāwah** Uttar Pradesh, N India
13 R10 **Etchemin** ≈ Québec, SE Canada
Etchmiadzin *see* Ejmiatsin
42 G7 **Etchojoa** Sonora, NW Mexico
85 B16 **Etengua** Kunene, NW Namibia
101 K25 **Éthe** Luxembourg, SE Belgium
9 W15 **Ethelbert** Manitoba, S Canada
82 H12 **Ethiopia** ***off.*** Federal Democratic Republic of Ethiopia; ***prev.*** Abyssinia, People's Democratic Republic of Ethiopia. ◆ *republic* E Africa
82 I13 **Ethiopian Highlands** ***var.*** Ethiopian Plateau. *plateau* N Ethiopia
Ethiopian Plateau *see* Ethiopian Highlands
36 M2 **Etna** California, W USA
20 B14 **Etna** Pennsylvania, NE USA
96 G12 **Etna** ≈ S Norway
109 L24 **Etna, Monte** ***Eng.*** Mount Etna. ⛰ Sicilia, Italy, C Mediterranean Sea
Etna, Mount *see* Etna, Monte
97 C15 **Etne** Hordaland, S Norway
Etoliko *see* Aitolikó
41 Y14 **Etolin Island** *island* Alexander Archipelago, Alaska, USA
40 L12 **Etolin Strait** *strait* Alaska, USA
85 C17 **Etosha Pan** *salt lake* N Namibia
81 G18 **Etoumbi** Cuvette, NW Congo
22 M10 **Etowah** Tennessee, S USA
25 S2 **Etowah River** ≈ Georgia, SE USA
Etrek *see* Atrak
104 L3 **Étretat** Seine-Maritime, N France
116 H9 **Etropole** Sofiyska Oblast, W Bulgaria
Etsch *see* Adige
Et Tafila *see* Aţ Ţafīlah
101 M23 **Ettelbrück** Diekirch, C Luxembourg
201 V12 **Etten** *atoll* Chuuk Islands, C Micronesia
101 H14 **Etten-Leur** Noord-Brabant, S Netherlands
78 G7 **Et Tîdra** ***var.*** Ile Tîdra. *island* Dakhlet Nouâdhibou, NW Mauritania
103 G21 **Ettlingen** Baden-Württemberg, SW Germany
104 M2 **Eu** Seine-Maritime, N France
200 Rr16 **'Eua** ***prev.*** Middleburg Island. *island* Tongatapu Group, SE Tonga
200 R15 **Eua Iki** *island* Tongatapu Group, S Tonga
Euboea *see* Évvoia
189 O12 **Eucla** Western Australia
33 U11 **Euclid** Ohio, N USA
29 W14 **Eudora** Arkansas, C USA
29 Q4 **Eudora** Kansas, C USA
190 J9 **Eudunda** South Australia
25 R6 **Eufaula** Alabama, S USA
29 Q11 **Eufaula** Oklahoma, C USA
29 Q11 **Eufaula Lake** ***var.*** Eufaula Reservoir. ⊠ Oklahoma, C USA
Eufaula Reservoir *see* Eufaula Lake
34 F13 **Eugene** Oregon, NW USA
42 B6 **Eugenia, Punta** *headland* W Mexico
191 Q8 **Eugowra** New South Wales, SE Australia
106 I2 **Eume** ≈ NW Spain
106 H2 **Eume, Embalse do** ⊠ NW Spain
Eumolpias *see* Plovdiv
61 O18 **Eunápolis** Bahia, SE Brazil
24 H8 **Eunice** Louisiana, S USA
39 W15 **Eunice** New Mexico, SW USA
101 M19 **Eupen** Liège, E Belgium
139 Jj9 **Euphrates** ***Ar.*** Al Furāt, ***Turk.*** Firat Nehri. ≈ SW Asia
144 L3 **Euphrates Dam** *dam* N Syria
24 M4 **Eupora** Mississippi, S USA
95 K19 **Eura** Turku-Pori, SW Finland
95 K19 **Eurajoki** Turku-Pori, SW Finland
1 **Eurasian Plate** *tectonic feature*
104 L4 **Eure** ◐ *department* N France
104 M4 **Eure** ≈ N France
104 M6 **Eure-et-Loir** ◐ *department* C France
36 K3 **Eureka** California, W USA
29 P6 **Eureka** Kansas, C USA
35 O6 **Eureka** Montana, NW USA
37 V5 **Eureka** Nevada, W USA
31 O7 **Eureka** South Dakota, N USA
38 L4 **Eureka** Utah, W USA
34 K10 **Eureka** Washington, NW USA
29 S9 **Eureka Springs** Arkansas, C USA
190 K6 **Eurinilla Creek** *seasonal river* South Australia
191 O11 **Euroa** Victoria, SE Australia
180 M9 **Europa** *island* W Madagascar
106 L3 **Europa, Picos de** ▲▲ N Spain
106 L16 **Europa Point** *headland* S Gibraltar
86-87 **Europe** *continent*
100 F12 **Europoort** Zuid-Holland, W Netherlands
Euskadi *see* País Vasco
103 D17 **Euskirchen** Nordrhein-Westfalen, W Germany
25 W11 **Eustis** Florida, SE USA
190 M9 **Euston** New South Wales, SE Australia
25 N5 **Eutaw** Alabama, S USA
102 K8 **Eutin** Schleswig-Holstein, N Germany
8 K14 **Eutsuk Lake** ⊠ British Columbia, SW Canada
Euxine Sea *see* Black Sea
85 C16 **Evale** Cunene, SW Angola
39 T3 **Evans** Colorado, C USA
9 P14 **Evansburg** Alberta, SW Canada
31 X13 **Evansdale** Iowa, C USA
191 V4 **Evans Head** New South Wales, SE Australia
10 J11 **Evans, Lac** ◎ Québec, SE Canada
39 S5 **Evans, Mount** ▲ Colorado, C USA
15 Mm6 **Evans Strait** *strait* Northwest Territories, N Canada
33 N10 **Evanston** Illinois, N USA
35 S17 **Evanston** Wyoming, C USA
12 D11 **Evansville** Manitoulin Island, Ontario, S Canada
33 N16 **Evansville** Indiana, N USA
32 L9 **Evansville** Wisconsin, N USA
27 S8 **Evant** Texas, SW USA
149 P13 **Evaz** Fārs, S Iran
31 W4 **Eveleth** Minnesota, N USA
190 E3 **Evelyn Creek** *seasonal river* South Australia
189 Q2 **Evelyn, Mount** ▲ Northern Territory, N Australia
126 I11 **Evenkiyskiy Avtonomnyy Okrug** ◐ *autonomous district* N Russian Federation
191 R13 **Everard, Cape** *headland* Victoria, SE Australia
190 F6 **Everard, Lake** *salt lake* South Australia
190 C2 **Everard Ranges** ▲▲ South Australia
159 R11 **Everest, Mount** ***Chin.*** Qomolangma Feng, ***Nep.*** Sagarmatha. ▲ China/Nepal
20 E15 **Everett** Pennsylvania, NE USA
34 H7 **Everett** Washington, NW USA
101 E17 **Evergem** Oost-Vlaanderen, NW Belgium
25 X16 **Everglades City** Florida, SE USA
25 Y16 **Everglades, The** *wetland* Florida, SE USA
25 P7 **Evergreen** Alabama, S USA
39 T4 **Evergreen** Colorado, C USA
Evergreen State *see* Washington
99 L21 **Evesham** C England, UK
105 T10 **Évian-les-Bains** Haute-Savoie, E France
95 K16 **Evijärvi** Vaasa, W Finland
81 D17 **Evinayong** ***var.*** Ebinayon, Evinayoung. C Equatorial Guinea
Evinayoung *see* Evinayong
117 E18 **Évinos** ≈ C Greece
97 E17 **Evje** Aust-Agder, S Norway
Evmolpia *see* Plovdiv
106 H11 **Évora** ***anc.*** Ebora, ***Lat.*** Liberalitas Julia. Évora, C Portugal
106 G11 **Évora** ◐ *district* S Portugal
104 M4 **Évreux** ***anc.*** Civitas Eburovicum. Eure, N France
104 K6 **Évron** Mayenne, NW France
116 L13 **Évros** ***Bul.*** Maritsa, ***Turk.*** Meriç; ***anc.*** Hebrus. ≈ SE Europe *see also* Maritsa/Meriç
117 F21 **Evrótas** ≈ S Greece
105 O5 **Évry** Essonne, N France
27 O8 **E.V.Spence Reservoir** ⊠ Texas, SW USA
117 I18 **Évvoia** ***Lat.*** Euboea. *island* C Greece
40 D9 **Ewa Beach** Oahu, Hawaii, USA, C Pacific Ocean
34 L9 **Ewan** Washington, NW USA
46 K12 **Ewarton** C Jamaica
83 J18 **Ewaso Ng'iro** ***var.*** Nyiro. ≈ C Kenya
194 E13 **Ewe** ≈ W PNG
31 P13 **Ewing** Nebraska, C USA
204 J5 **Ewing Island** *island* Antarctica
67 P17 **Ewing Seamount** *undersea feature* E Atlantic Ocean
164 L6 **Ewirgol** Xinjiang Uygur Zizhiqu, W China
81 G19 **Ewo** Cuvette, W Congo
29 S3 **Excelsior Springs** Missouri, C USA
99 J23 **Exe** ≈ SW England, UK
204 L12 **Executive Committee Range** ▲▲ Antarctica
12 E16 **Exeter** Ontario, S Canada
99 J24 **Exeter** ***anc.*** Isca Damnoniorum. SW England, UK
37 R11 **Exeter** California, W USA
21 P10 **Exeter** New Hampshire, NE USA
Exin *see* Kcynia
31 T14 **Exira** Iowa, C USA
99 J23 **Exmoor** *moorland* SW England, UK
23 Y6 **Exmore** Virginia, NE USA
188 G8 **Exmouth** Western Australia
99 J24 **Exmouth** SW England, UK
188 G8 **Exmouth Gulf** *gulf* Western Australia
181 V8 **Exmouth Plateau** *undersea feature* E Indian Ocean
117 J20 **Exompourgo** *ancient monument* Tínos, Kykládes, Greece, Aegean Sea
106 I10 **Extremadura** ***var.*** Estremadura. ◐ *autonomous community* W Spain
106 F10 **Extremadura** *cultural and historical region* W Spain
80 F12 **Extrême-Nord** ***Eng.*** Extreme North. ◐ *province* N Cameroon
Extreme North *see* Extrême-Nord
46 I3 **Exuma Cays** *islets* C Bahamas
46 I3 **Exuma Sound** *sound* C Bahamas
83 H20 **Eyasi, Lake** ◎ N Tanzania
97 F17 **Eydehavn** Aust-Agder, S Norway
98 L12 **Eyemouth** SE Scotland, UK
98 G7 **Eye Peninsula** *peninsula* NW Scotland, UK
82 Q13 **Eyl** ***It.*** Eil. Nugaal, E Somalia
105 N11 **Eymoutiers** Haute-Vienne, C France
Eyo (lower course) *see* Uolo, Río
31 X10 **Eyota** Minnesota, N USA
190 H2 **Eyre Basin, Lake** *salt lake* South Australia
190 I1 **Eyre Creek** *seasonal river* Northern Territory/South Australia
182 L9 **Eyre, Lake** *salt lake* South Australia
193 C22 **Eyre Mountains** ▲▲ South Island, NZ
190 H3 **Eyre North, Lake** *salt lake* South Australia
190 G7 **Eyre Peninsula** *peninsula* South Australia
190 H4 **Eyre South, Lake** *salt lake* South Australia
63 D20 **Ezeiza** ✈ (Buenos Aires) Buenos Aires, E Argentina
Ezeres *see* Ezeriş
118 F12 **Ezeriş** ***Hung.*** Ezeres. Caraş-Severin, W Romania
167 O9 **Ezhou** ***prev.*** Echeng. Hubei, C China
129 R11 **Ezhva** Respublika Komi, NW Russian Federation
142 B12 **Ezine** Çanakkale, NW Turkey
Ezo *see* Hokkaidō
Ezra/Ezraa *see* Izra'

F

203 P7 **Faaa** Tahiti, W French Polynesia
203 P7 **Faaa** ✈ (Papeete) Tahiti, W French Polynesia
Faaborg *see* Fåborg
157 K19 **Faadhippolhu Atoll** ***var.*** Fadiffolu, Lhaviyani Atoll. *atoll* N Maldives
203 U10 **Faaite** *atoll* Îles Tuamotu, C French Polynesia
203 Q8 **Faaone** Tahiti, W French Polynesia
26 H8 **Fabens** Texas, SW USA
96 H12 **Fåberg** Oppland, S Norway
97 H24 **Fåborg** ***var.*** Faaborg. Fyn, C Denmark
108 I12 **Fabriano** Marche, C Italy
151 U16 **Fabrichnyy** Almaty, SE Kazakhstan
56 F10 **Facatativá** Cundinamarca, C Colombia
79 X9 **Fachi** Agadez, C Niger
196 B16 **Facpi Point** *headland* W Guam
20 I13 **Factoryville** Pennsylvania, NE USA
80 K8 **Fada** Borkou-Ennedi-Tibesti, E Chad
79 Q13 **Fada-Ngourma** E Burkina
126 Jj4 **Faddeya, Zaliv** *bay* N Russian Federation
126 M4 **Faddeyevskiy, Ostrov** *island* Novosibirskiye Ostrova, NE Russian Federation
147 W12 **Fadhī** S Oman
108 H10 **Faenza** ***anc.*** Faventia. Emilia-Romagna, N Italy
66 M5 **Faeroe-Iceland Ridge** *undersea feature* NW Norwegian Sea
66 M5 **Faeroe Islands** ***Dan.*** Færøerne, ***Faer.*** Føroyar. ◇ *Danish external territory* N Atlantic Ocean
88 C8 **Faeroe Islands** *island group* N Atlantic Ocean
Færøerne *see* Faeroe Islands
66 N6 **Faeroe-Shetland Trough** *undersea feature* NE Atlantic Ocean
106 H6 **Fafe** Braga, N Portugal
82 K13 **Fafen Shet'** ≈ E Ethiopia
200 Qq15 **Fafo** *island* Tongatapu Group, S Tonga
198 Bb8 **Fagaloa Bay** *bay* Upolu, E Western Samoa
198 B7 **Fagamālo** Savai'i, N Western Samoa
118 I12 **Făgăraş** ***Ger.*** Fogarasch, ***Hung.*** Fogaras. Braşov, C Romania
97 M20 **Fagerhult** Kalmar, S Sweden
96 G13 **Fagernes** Oppland, S Norway
94 I9 **Fagernes** Troms, N Norway
97 M14 **Fagersta** Västmanland, C Sweden
79 W13 **Faggo** ***var.*** Foggo. Bauchi, N Nigeria
Faghman *see* Fughmah
Fagibina, Lake *see* Faguibine, Lac
65 J25 **Fagnano, Lago** ◎ S Argentina
101 G22 **Fagne** *hill range* S Belgium
79 N10 **Faguibine, Lac** ***var.*** Lake Fagibina. ◎ NW Mali
Fahaheel *see* Al Fuḩayḩīl
Fahlun *see* Falun
149 U12 **Fahraj** Kermān, SE Iran
66 P5 **Faial** Madeira, Portugal, NE Atlantic Ocean
66 N2 **Faial** ***var.*** Ilha do Faial. *island* Azores, Portugal, NE Atlantic Ocean
Faial, Ilha do *see* Faial
110 G10 **Faido** Ticino, S Switzerland
Faifo *see* Hôi An
Failaka Island *see* Faylakah
202 G12 **Faioa, Île** *island* N Wallis and Futuna
189 W8 **Fairbairn Reservoir** ⊠ Queensland, E Australia
41 R9 **Fairbanks** Alaska, USA
23 U12 **Fair Bluff** North Carolina, SE USA
33 R14 **Fairborn** Ohio, N USA
25 S3 **Fairburn** Georgia, SE USA
32 M12 **Fairbury** Illinois, N USA
31 Q17 **Fairbury** Nebraska, C USA
31 T9 **Fairfax** Minnesota, N USA
29 O8 **Fairfax** Oklahoma, C USA
23 R14 **Fairfax** South Carolina, SE USA
37 N8 **Fairfield** California, W USA
35 O14 **Fairfield** Idaho, NW USA
32 M16 **Fairfield** Illinois, N USA
31 X15 **Fairfield** Iowa, C USA
35 R8 **Fairfield** Montana, NW USA
33 Q14 **Fairfield** Ohio, N USA
27 U8 **Fairfield** Texas, SW USA
29 T7 **Fair Grove** Missouri, C USA
21 P12 **Fairhaven** Massachusetts, NE USA
25 N8 **Fairhope** Alabama, S USA
98 L4 **Fair Isle** *island* NE Scotland, UK
193 F20 **Fairlie** Canterbury, South Island, NZ
31 U11 **Fairmont** Minnesota, N USA
31 Q16 **Fairmont** Nebraska, C USA
23 S3 **Fairmont** West Virginia, NE USA
33 P13 **Fairmount** Indiana, N USA
20 H10 **Fairmount** New York, NE USA
31 R7 **Fairmount** North Dakota, N USA
39 S5 **Fairplay** Colorado, C USA
20 F9 **Fairport** New York, NE USA
9 O12 **Fairview** Alberta, W Canada
28 L9 **Fairview** Oklahoma, C USA
38 L4 **Fairview** Utah, W USA
37 T6 **Fairview Peak** ▲ Nevada, W USA
196 H14 **Fais** *atoll* Caroline Islands, W Micronesia
155 U8 **Faisalābād** ***prev.*** Lyallpur. Punjab, NE Pakistan
Faisaliya *see* Fayşalīyah
30 L8 **Faith** South Dakota, N USA
159 N12 **Faizābād** Uttar Pradesh, N India
Faizabad/Faizābād *see* Feyẕābād
47 S9 **Fajardo** E Puerto Rico
145 R9 **Fajj, Wādī al** *dry watercourse* S Iraq
146 K4 **Fajr, Bi'r** *well* NW Saudi Arabia
203 W10 **Fakahina** *atoll* Îles Tuamotu, C French Polynesia
202 L10 **Fakaofo Atoll** *island* SE Tokelau
203 U10 **Fakarava** *atoll* Îles Tuamotu, C French Polynesia
131 T2 **Fakel** Udmurtskaya Respublika, NW Russian Federation
99 P19 **Fakenham** E England, UK
176 V11 **Fakfak** Irian Jaya, E Indonesia
176 V11 **Fakfak, Pegunungan** ▲▲ Irian Jaya, E Indonesia
159 T12 **Fakīragrām** Assam, NE India
116 M10 **Fakiyska Reka** ≈ SE Bulgaria

◆ Country
● Country Capital
◇ Dependent Territory
○ Dependent Territory Capital
◐ Administrative Region
✈ International Airport
▲ Mountain
▲▲ Mountain Range
⛰ Volcano
≈ River
◎ Lake
⊠ Reservoir

97 J24 **Fakse** Storstrøm, SE Denmark
97 J24 **Fakse Bugt** *bay* SE Denmark
97 J24 **Fakse Ladeplads** Storstrøm, SE Denmark
169 V11 **Faku** Liaoning, NE China
78 J14 **Falaba** N Sierra Leone
104 K5 **Falaise** Calvados, N France
116 H12 **Falakró** ▲ NE Greece
201 T12 **Falalu** *island* Chuuk, C Micronesia
177 Ff4 **Falam** Chin State, W Myanmar
149 N8 **Falāvarjān** Eşfahān, C Iran
118 M11 **Fălciu** Vaslui, E Romania
56 I4 **Falcón** *off.* Estado Falcón. ◆ *state* NW Venezuela
108 J12 **Falconara Marittima** Marche, C Italy
Falcone, Capo del *see* Falcone, Punta del
109 A16 **Falcone, Punta del** *var.* Capo del Falcone. *headland* Sardegna, Italy, C Mediterranean Sea
9 Y16 **Falcon Lake** Manitoba, S Canada
Falcon Lake *see* Falcón, Presa/Falcon Reservoir
43 O7 **Falcón, Presa** *var.* Falcon Lake, Falcon Reservoir. ⊠ Mexico/USA *see also* Falcon Reservoir
27 Q16 **Falcon Reservoir** *var.* Falcon Lake, Presa Falcón. ⊠ Mexico/USA *see also* Falcón, Presa
202 L10 **Fale** *island* Fakaofo Atoll, SE Tokelau
198 Aa7 **Faleālupo** Savai'i, NW Western Samoa
202 B10 **Falefatu** *island* Funafuti Atoll, C Tuvalu
198 Aa7 **Fālelima** Savai'i, NW Western Samoa
97 N18 **Falerum** Östergötland, S Sweden
Faleshty *see* Fălești
118 M9 **Fălești** *Rus.* Faleshty. NW Moldova
27 S15 **Falfurrias** Texas, SW USA
9 O13 **Falher** Alberta, W Canada
Falkenau an der Eger *see* Sokolov
97 J21 **Falkenberg** Halland, S Sweden
Falkenberg *see* Niemodlin
Falkenburg in Pommern *see* Złocieniec
102 N12 **Falkensee** Brandenburg, NE Germany
98 J12 **Falkirk** C Scotland, UK
67 I20 **Falkland Escarpment** *undersea feature* SW Atlantic Ocean
65 K24 **Falkland Islands** *var.* Falklands, Islas Malvinas. ◇ *UK dependent territory* SW Atlantic Ocean
49 W14 **Falkland Islands** *island group* SW Atlantic Ocean
67 I20 **Falkland Plateau** *var.* Argentine Rise. *undersea feature* SW Atlantic Ocean
Falklands *see* Falkland Islands
65 M23 **Falkland Sound** *var.* Estrecho de San Carlos. *strait* C Falkland Islands
Falknov nad Ohří *see* Sokolov
117 H21 **Falkonéra** *island* S Greece
97 K18 **Falköping** Skaraborg, S Sweden
145 U8 **Fallāḩ** E Iraq
37 U16 **Fallbrook** California, W USA
201 U12 **Falleallej Pass** *passage* Chuuk Islands, C Micronesia
95 J14 **Fällfors** Västerbotten, N Sweden
204 I6 **Fallières Coast** *physical region* Antarctica
102 I11 **Fallingbostel** Niedersachsen, NW Germany
35 X9 **Fallon** Montana, NW USA
37 S5 **Fallon** Nevada, W USA
21 O12 **Fall River** Massachusetts, NE USA
29 P6 **Fall River Lake** ⊠ Kansas, C USA
37 O3 **Fall River Mills** California, W USA
23 W4 **Falls Church** Virginia, NE USA
31 S17 **Falls City** Nebraska, C USA
27 S12 **Falls City** Texas, SW USA
Falluja *see* Al Fallūjah
79 S12 **Falmey** Dosso, SW Niger
47 W10 **Falmouth** Antigua, Antigua and Barbuda
46 J11 **Falmouth** W Jamaica
99 H25 **Falmouth** SW England, UK
22 M4 **Falmouth** Kentucky, S USA
21 P13 **Falmouth** Massachusetts, NE USA
23 W5 **Falmouth** Virginia, NE USA
201 U12 **Falos** *island* Chuuk, C Micronesia
85 E26 **False Bay** *Afr.* Valsbaai. *bay* SW South Africa
161 K17 **False Divi Point** *headland* E India
40 M16 **False Pass** Unimak Island, Alaska, USA
160 P12 **False Point** *headland* E India
107 U6 **Falset** Cataluña, NE Spain
97 I25 **Falster** *island* SE Denmark
97 J23 **Falsterbo** Malmöhus, S Sweden
118 K9 **Fălticeni** *Hung.* Falticsén. Suceava, NE Romania
Falticsén *see* Fălticeni
96 M13 **Falun** *var.* Fahlun. Kopparberg, C Sweden
Famagusta *see* Gazimağusa
Famagusta Bay *see* Gazimağusa Körfezi
64 I8 **Famatina** La Rioja, NW Argentina
101 J21 **Famenne** *physical region* SE Belgium
115 D22 **Fan** *var.* Fani. ~ N Albania
79 X15 **Fan** ~ E Nigeria
78 M12 **Fana** Koulikoro, SW Mali
117 K19 **Fána** *ancient harbor* Chíos, SE Greece
201 V13 **Fanan** *island* Chuuk, C Micronesia
201 U12 **Fanapanges** *island* Chuuk, C Micronesia
117 L20 **Fanári, Ákra** *headland* Ikaría, Dodekánisos, Greece, Aegean Sea
47 Q13 **Fancy** Saint Vincent, Saint Vincent and the Grenadines
180 I5 **Fandriana** Fianarantsoa, SE Madagascar
178 H6 **Fang** Chiang Mai, NW Thailand
82 E13 **Fangak** Jonglei, SE Sudan
203 W10 **Fangatau** *atoll* Îles Tuamotu, C French Polynesia
203 X12 **Fangataufa** *island* Îles Tuamotu, SE French Polynesia
200 Qq15 **Fanga Uta** *bay* S Tonga
167 N7 **Fangcheng** Henan, C China
166 K15 **Fangchenggang** *var.* Fangcheng Gezu Zizhixian; *prev.* Fangcheng. Guangxi Zhuangzu Zizhiqu, S China
167 S15 **Fangshan** S Taiwan
169 X8 **Fangzheng** Heilongjiang, NE China
Fani *see* Fan
121 K16 **Fanipal'** *Rus.* Fanipol'. Minskaya Voblasts', C Belarus
Fanipol' *see* Fanipal'
27 T13 **Fannin** Texas, SW USA
Fanning Island *see* Tabuaeran
96 G8 **Fannrem** Sør-Trøndelag, S Norway
108 I11 **Fano** *anc.* Colonia Julia Fanestris, Fanum Fortunae. Marche, C Italy
97 E23 **Fanø** *island* W Denmark
178 Ii5 **Fan Si Pan** ▲ N Vietnam
Fanum Fortunae *see* Fano
Fao *see* Al Fāw
147 W7 **Faq'** *var.* Al Faqa. Dubayy, E UAE
152 K12 **Farab** *Turkm.* Farap. Lebapskiy Velayat, NE Turkmenistan
204 H5 **Faraday** *UK research station* Antarctica
193 G16 **Faraday, Mount** ▲ South Island, NZ
81 P16 **Faradje** Haut-Zaïre, NE Zaire
Faradofay *see* Tôlañaro
180 I7 **Farafangana** Fianarantsoa, SE Madagascar
154 J7 **Farāh** *var.* Farah, Fararud. Farāh, W Afghanistan
154 K7 **Farāh** ◆ *province* W Afghanistan
154 J7 **Farāh Rūd** ~ W Afghanistan
196 K7 **Farallon de Medinilla** *island* C Northern Mariana Islands
196 J2 **Farallon de Pajaros** *var.* Uracas. *island* N Northern Mariana Islands
78 J14 **Faranah** Haute-Guinée, S Guinea
Farap *see* Farab
Fararud *see* Farāh
146 M13 **Farasān, Jazā'ir** *island group* SW Saudi Arabia
180 I5 **Faratsiho** Antananarivo, C Madagascar
196 K15 **Faraulep Atoll** *atoll* Caroline Islands, C Micronesia
101 H20 **Farciennes** Hainaut, S Belgium
107 O14 **Fardes** ~ S Spain
203 S10 **Fare** Huahine, W French Polynesia
99 M23 **Fareham** S England, UK
41 P11 **Farewell** Alaska, USA
192 H13 **Farewell, Cape** *headland* South Island, NZ
Farewell, Cape *see* Uummannarsuaq
192 I13 **Farewell Spit** *spit* South Island, NZ
97 I17 **Färgelanda** Älvsborg, S Sweden
153 S10 **Farghona** *Rus.* Fergana; *prev.* Novyy Margilan. Farghona Wiloyati, E Uzbekistan
Farghona Valley *see* Fergana Valley
153 R10 **Farghona Wiloyati** *Rus.* Ferganskaya Oblast'. ◆ *province* E Uzbekistan
Farghona, Wodii/Farghona Wodiysi *see* Fergana Valley
25 V8 **Fargo** Georgia, SE USA
31 R5 **Fargo** North Dakota, N USA
31 V10 **Faribault** Minnesota, N USA
158 J11 **Farīdabād** Haryāna, N India
158 H8 **Farīdkot** Punjab, NW India
159 T15 **Faridpur** Dhaka, C Bangladesh
124 N16 **Fārigh, Wādī al** ~ N Libya
180 I4 **Farihy Alaotra** ◎ C Madagascar
96 M11 **Färila** Gävleborg, C Sweden
106 E9 **Farilhões** *island* C Portugal
78 G12 **Farim** NW Guinea-Bissau
Farish *see* Forish
147 T11 **Fāris, Qalamat** *well* SE Saudi Arabia
97 N21 **Färjestaden** Kalmar, S Sweden
155 R2 **Farkhār** Takhār, NE Afghanistan
153 Q14 **Farkhor** *Rus.* Parkhar. SW Tajikistan
118 F12 **Fârliug** *prev.* Fîrliug, *Hung.* Furluk. Caraş-Severin, SW Romania
117 M21 **Farmakonísi** *island* Dodekánisos, Greece, Aegean Sea
32 M13 **Farmer City** Illinois, N USA
33 N14 **Farmersburg** Indiana, N USA
27 U6 **Farmersville** Texas, SW USA
24 H5 **Farmerville** Louisiana, S USA
31 X16 **Farmington** Iowa, C USA
21 Q6 **Farmington** Maine, NE USA
31 V9 **Farmington** Minnesota, N USA
29 X6 **Farmington** Missouri, C USA
21 O9 **Farmington** New Hampshire, NE USA
39 P9 **Farmington** New Mexico, SW USA
38 L2 **Farmington** Utah, W USA
23 W9 **Farmville** North Carolina, SE USA
23 U6 **Farmville** Virginia, NE USA
99 N22 **Farnborough** S England, UK
99 N22 **Farnham** S England, UK
8 J7 **Faro** Yukon Territory, W Canada
106 G14 **Faro** Faro, S Portugal
106 G14 **Faro** ◆ *district* S Portugal
106 G14 **Faro** ✕ Faro, S Portugal
80 F13 **Faro** ~ Cameroon/Nigeria
97 Q18 **Fårö** Gotland, SE Sweden
Faroe Bank Channel *see* Faroe Gap
Faro, Punta del *see* Peloro, Capo
97 Q18 **Fårösund** Gotland, SE Sweden
181 N7 **Farquhar Group** *island group* S Seychelles
20 B13 **Farrell** Pennsylvania, NE USA
158 K11 **Farrukhābād** Uttar Pradesh, N India
149 P11 **Fārs** *off.* Ostān-e Fārs; *anc.* Persis. ◆ *province* S Iran
117 F16 **Fársala** Thessalía, C Greece
149 R4 **Fārsīān** Māzandarān, N Iran
Fars, Khalīj-e *see* Persian Gulf
97 G21 **Farsø** Nordjylland, N Denmark
97 D18 **Farsund** Vest-Agder, S Norway
147 U14 **Fartak, Ra's** *headland* E Yemen
62 H13 **Fartura, Serra da** ▲ S Brazil
Farvel, Kap *see* Uummannarsuaq
26 L4 **Farwell** Texas, SW USA
204 I9 **Farwell Island** *island* Antarctica
158 L9 **Far Western** ◆ *zone* W Nepal
154 M3 **Fāryāb** ◆ *province* N Afghanistan
149 P12 **Fasā** Fārs, S Iran
147 U12 **Fasad, Ramlat** *desert* SW Oman
109 P17 **Fasano** Puglia, SE Italy
94 L3 **Fáskrúdhsfjördhur** Austurland, E Iceland
119 O5 **Fastiv** *Rus.* Fastov. Kyyivs'ka Oblast', NW Ukraine
99 B22 **Fastnet Rock** *Ir.* Carraig Aonair. *island* SW Ireland
Fastov *see* Fastiv
202 C9 **Fatato** *island* Funafuti Atoll, C Tuvalu
158 K12 **Fatehgarh** Uttar Pradesh, N India
155 U6 **Fatehjang** Punjab, E Pakistan
158 G11 **Fatehpur** Rājasthān, N India
158 L13 **Fatehpur** Uttar Pradesh, N India
130 J7 **Fatezh** Kurskaya Oblast', W Russian Federation
78 G11 **Fatick** W Senegal
106 G9 **Fátima** Santarém, W Portugal
142 M11 **Fatsa** Ordu, N Turkey
Fatshan *see* Foshan
202 D12 **Fatua, Pointe** *var.* Pointe Nord. *headland* Île Futuna, S Wallis and Futuna
203 X7 **Fatu Hiva** *island* Îles Marquises, NE French Polynesia
Fatunda *see* Fatundu
81 H21 **Fatundu** *var.* Fatunda. Bandundu, W Zaire
31 O8 **Faulkton** South Dakota, N USA
118 L13 **Făurei** *prev.* Filimon Sîrbu. Brăila, SE Romania
195 T13 **Fauro** *island* Shortland Islands, NW Solomon Islands
94 G12 **Fauske** Nordland, C Norway
9 P13 **Faust** Alberta, W Canada
101 L23 **Fauvillers** Luxembourg, SE Belgium
109 J24 **Favara** Sicilia, Italy, C Mediterranean Sea
Faventia *see* Faenza
109 G23 **Favignana, Isola** *island* Isole Egadi, S Italy
10 D8 **Fawn** ~ Ontario, SE Canada
Faxa Bay *see* Faxaflói
94 H3 **Faxaflói** *Eng.* Faxa Bay. *bay* W Iceland
80 I7 **Faya** *prev.* Faya-Largeau, Largeau. Borkou-Ennedi-Tibesti, N Chad
Faya-Largeau *see* Faya
197 J5 **Fayaoué** Province des Îles Loyauté, C New Caledonia
144 M5 **Fayḑāt** *hill range* E Syria
25 O3 **Fayette** Alabama, S USA
31 X12 **Fayette** Iowa, C USA
24 J6 **Fayette** Mississippi, S USA
29 U4 **Fayette** Missouri, C USA
29 S9 **Fayetteville** Arkansas, C USA
23 U10 **Fayetteville** North Carolina, SE USA
22 J10 **Fayetteville** Tennessee, S USA
27 U11 **Fayetteville** Texas, SW USA
23 R5 **Fayetteville** West Virginia, NE USA
147 R4 **Faylakah** *var.* Failaka Island. *island* E Kuwait
145 T10 **Fayşalīyah** *var.* Faisaliya. S Iraq
201 P15 **Fayu** *var.* East Fayu. *island* Hall Islands, C Micronesia
158 G8 **Fāzilka** Punjab, NW India
Fdérick *see* Fdérik
78 I6 **Fdérik** *var.* Fdérick, *Fr.* Fort Gouraud. Tiris Zemmour, NW Mauritania
Feabhail, Loch *see* Foyle, Lough
99 B20 **Feale** ~ SW Ireland
23 V12 **Fear, Cape** *headland* Bald Head Island, North Carolina, SE USA
37 O6 **Feather River** ~ California, W USA
193 M14 **Featherston** Wellington, North Island, NZ
104 L3 **Fécamp** Seine-Maritime, N France
Fédala *see* Mohammedia
63 D17 **Federación** Entre Ríos, E Argentina
63 D17 **Federal** Entre Ríos, E Argentina
79 T15 **Federal Capital District** ◆ *capital territory* C Nigeria
Federal Capital Territory *see* Australian Capital Territory
Federal District *see* Distrito Federal
23 Y4 **Federalsburg** Maryland, NE USA
76 M6 **Fedjaj, Chott el** *var.* Chott el Fejaj, Shaţţ al Fijāj. *salt lake* C Tunisia
96 B13 **Fedje** *island* S Norway
150 M7 **Fedorovka** Kustanay, N Kazakhstan
131 U6 **Fedorovka** Respublika Bashkortostan, W Russian Federation
Fëdory *see* Fyadory
119 U11 **Fedotova Kosa** *spit* SE Ukraine
201 V13 **Fefan** *atoll* Chuuk Islands, C Micronesia
113 O21 **Fehérgyarmat** Szabolcs-Szatmár-Bereg, E Hungary
Fehér-Körös *see* Crişul Alb
Fehértemplom *see* Bela Crkva
Fehérvölgy *see* Albac
102 L7 **Fehmarn** *island* N Germany
Fehmarnbelt *see* Femerbælt
111 X8 **Fehring** Steiermark, SE Austria
61 B15 **Feijó** Acre, W Brazil
192 M12 **Feilding** Manawatu-Wanganui, North Island, NZ
Feira *see* Feira de Santana
61 O17 **Feira de Santana** *var.* Feira. Bahia, E Brazil
111 X7 **Feistritz** ~ SE Austria
Feistritz *see* Ilirska Bistrica
167 P8 **Feixi** *prev.* Shangpaihe. Anhui, E China
Fejaj, Chott el *see* Fedjaj, Chott el
113 I23 **Fejér** *off.* Fejér Megye. ◆ *county* W Hungary
97 I24 **Fejø** *island* SE Denmark
142 K15 **Feke** Adana, S Turkey
Feketehalom *see* Codlea
Fekete-Körös *see* Crişul Negru
Felaniche *see* Felanitx
111 T3 **Feldaist** ~ N Austria
111 W8 **Feldbach** Steiermark, SE Austria
103 F24 **Feldberg** ▲ SW Germany
118 J12 **Feldioara** *Ger.* Marienburg, *Hung.* Földvár. Braşov, C Romania
110 I7 **Feldkirch** *anc.* Clunia. Vorarlberg, W Austria
111 S9 **Feldkirchen in Kärnten** *Slvn.* Trg. Kärnten, S Austria
Félegyháza *see* Kiskunfélegyháza
198 B8 **Feleolo** ✕ (Āpia) Upolu, C Western Samoa
106 H6 **Felgueiras** Porto, N Portugal
Felicitas Julia *see* Lisboa
180 J16 **Félicité** *island* Inner Islands, NE Seychelles
157 K20 **Felidhu Atoll** *atoll* C Maldives
43 Y13 **Felipe Carrillo Puerto** Quintana Roo, SE Mexico
99 Q21 **Felixstowe** E England, UK
105 N11 **Felletin** Creuse, C France
Fellin *see* Viljandi
Felsőbánya *see* Baia Sprie
Felsőmuzslya *see* Mužlja
Felsővisó *see* Vişeu de Sus
37 N10 **Felton** California, W USA
108 H7 **Feltre** Veneto, NE Italy
97 H25 **Femerbælt** *Ger.* Fehmarnbelt. *strait* Denmark/Germany
97 I24 **Femø** *island* SE Denmark
96 I10 **Femunden** ◎ S Norway
106 H2 **Fene** Galicia, NW Spain
12 I14 **Fenelon Falls** Ontario, SE Canada
201 U13 **Feneppi** *atoll* Chuuk Islands, C Micronesia
143 O11 **Fener Burnu** *headland* N Turkey
117 J14 **Fengári** ▲ Samothráki, E Greece
169 V13 **Fengcheng** *var.* Feng-cheng, Fenghwangcheng. Liaoning, NE China
166 K11 **Fenggang** *prev.* Longquan. Guizhou, S China
167 S9 **Fenghua** Zhejiang, SE China
Fenghwangcheng *see* Fengcheng
166 L9 **Fengjie** Sichuan, C China
166 M14 **Fengkai** *prev.* Jiankou. Guangdong, S China
167 T13 **Fenglin** *Jap.* Hōrin. C Taiwan
167 P1 **Fengning** *prev.* Dagezhen. Hebei, E China
166 E13 **Fengqing** Yunnan, SW China
167 O6 **Fengqiu** Henan, C China
167 Q2 **Fengrun** Hebei, E China
169 T4 **Fengshui Shan** ▲ NE China
167 P14 **Fengshun** Guangdong, S China
Fengtien *see* Liaoning, China
Fengtien *see* Shenyang, China
166 J7 **Fengxian** *var.* Feng Xian; *prev.* Shuangshipu. Shaanxi, C China
Fengxiang *see* Luobei
169 P13 **Fengzhen** Nei Mongol Zizhiqu, N China
166 M6 **Fen He** ~ C China
159 V15 **Feni** Chittagong, E Bangladesh
195 Q10 **Feni Islands** *island group* NE PNG
40 H17 **Fenimore Pass** *strait* Aleutian Islands, Alaska, USA
86 B9 **Feni Ridge** *undersea feature* N Atlantic Ocean
Fennern *see* Vändra
32 J9 **Fennimore** Wisconsin, N USA
180 J4 **Fenoarivo** Toamasina, E Madagascar
97 I24 **Fensmark** Storstrøm, SE Denmark
99 O19 **Fens, The** *wetland* E England, UK
33 R9 **Fenton** Michigan, N USA
202 K10 **Fenua Fala** *island* SE Tokelau
202 F12 **Fenuafo'ou, Île** *island* E Wallis and Futuna
202 L10 **Fenua Loa** *island* Fakaofo Atoll, E Tokelau
166 M4 **Fenyang** Shanxi, C China
119 U13 **Feodosiya** *var.* Kefe, *It.* Kaffa; *anc.* Theodosia. Respublika Krym, S Ukraine
96 I10 **Feragen** ◎ S Norway
76 L5 **Fer, Cap de** *headland* NE Algeria
33 O16 **Ferdinand** Indiana, N USA
Ferdinand *see* Montana, Bulgaria
Ferdinand *see* Mihail Kogălniceanu, Romania
Ferdinandsberg *see* Oţelu Roşu
149 T7 **Ferdows** *var.* Firdaus; *prev.* Tūn. Khorāsān, E Iran
105 Q5 **Fère-Champenoise** Marne, N France
Ferencz-Jósef Csúcs *see* Gerlachovský Štít
109 J16 **Ferentino** Lazio, C Italy
116 L13 **Féres** Anatolikí Makedonía kai Thráki, NE Greece
Fergana *see* Farghona
153 S10 **Fergana Valley** *var.* Farghona Valley, *Rus.* Ferganskaya Dolina, *Taj.* Wodii Farghona, *Uzb.* Farghona Wodiysi. *basin* Tajikistan/Uzbekistan
Ferganskaya Dolina *see* Fergana Valley
Ferganskaya Oblast' *see* Farghona Wiloyati
153 U9 **Ferganskiy Khrebet** ▲ C Kyrgyzstan
12 F15 **Fergus** Ontario, S Canada
31 S6 **Fergus Falls** Minnesota, N USA
195 N15 **Fergusson Island** *var.* Kaluwawa. *island* SE PNG
113 K22 **Ferihegy** ✕ (Budapest) Budapest, C Hungary
Ferizaj *see* Uroševac
79 N14 **Ferkessédougou** N Ivory Coast
111 T10 **Ferlach** *Slvn.* Borovlje. Kärnten, S Austria
99 E16 **Fermanagh** *cultural region* SW Northern Ireland, UK
108 J13 **Fermo** *anc.* Firmum Picenum. Marche, C Italy
106 J6 **Fermoselle** Castilla-León, N Spain
99 D20 **Fermoy** *Ir.* Mainistir Fhear Maí. SW Ireland
25 W8 **Fernandina Beach** Amelia Island, Florida, SE USA
59 A17 **Fernandina, Isla** *var.* Narborough Island. *island* Galapagos Islands, Ecuador, E Pacific Ocean
49 Y5 **Fernando de Noronha** *island* E Brazil
Fernando Po/Fernando Póo *see* Bioco, Isla de
62 J7 **Fernandópolis** São Paulo, S Brazil
106 M13 **Fernán Núñez** Andalucía, S Spain
85 Q14 **Fernão Veloso, Baia de** *bay* NE Mozambique
36 K3 **Ferndale** California, W USA
34 H6 **Ferndale** Washington, NW USA
9 P17 **Fernie** British Columbia, SW Canada
37 R5 **Fernley** Nevada, W USA
Ferozepore *see* Fīrozpur
109 N18 **Ferrandina** Basilicata, S Italy
108 G9 **Ferrara** *anc.* Forum Alieni. Emilia-Romagna, N Italy
123 H11 **Ferrat, Cap** *headland* NW Algeria
109 D20 **Ferrato, Capo** *headland* Sardegna, Italy, C Mediterranean Sea
106 G12 **Ferreira do Alentejo** Beja, S Portugal
58 B11 **Ferreñafe** Lambayeque, W Peru
110 C12 **Ferret** Valais, SW Switzerland
104 I13 **Ferret, Cap** *headland* W France
24 I6 **Ferriday** Louisiana, S USA
Ferro *see* Hierro
109 D16 **Ferro, Capo** *headland* Sardegna, Italy, C Mediterranean Sea
106 H2 **Ferrol** *var.* El Ferrol; *prev.* El Ferrol del Caudillo. Galicia, NW Spain
58 B12 **Ferrol, Península de** *peninsula* W Peru
38 M5 **Ferron** Utah, W USA
23 S7 **Ferrum** Virginia, NE USA
25 O8 **Ferry Pass** Florida, SE USA
Ferryville *see* Menzel Bourguiba
31 S4 **Fertile** Minnesota, N USA
Fertő *see* Neusiedler See
100 L5 **Ferwerd** *Fris.* Ferwert. Friesland, N Netherlands
Ferwert *see* Ferwerd
76 G6 **Fès** *Eng.* Fez. N Morocco
81 I22 **Feshi** Bandundu, SW Zaire
31 O4 **Fessenden** North Dakota, N USA
Festenberg *see* Twardogóra
29 X5 **Festus** Missouri, C USA
118 M14 **Feteşti** Ialomiţa, SE Romania
142 D17 **Fethiye** Muğla, SW Turkey
98 M1 **Fetlar** *island* NE Scotland, UK
97 I15 **Fetsund** Akershus, S Norway
10 L5 **Feuilles, Lac aux** ◎ Québec, E Canada
10 L5 **Feuilles, Rivière aux** ~ Québec, E Canada
101 M23 **Feulen** Diekirch, C Luxembourg
105 Q11 **Feurs** Loire, E France
97 F18 **Fevik** Aust-Agder, S Norway
126 Mm14 **Fevral'sk** Amurskaya Oblast', SE Russian Federation
155 S2 **Feyẕābād** *var.* Faizabad, Faizābād, Feyzābād, Fyzabad. Badakhshān, NE Afghanistan
Fez *see* Fès
99 J19 **Ffestiniog** NW Wales, UK
Fhóid Duibh, Cuan an *see* Blacksod Bay
64 I8 **Fiambalá** Catamarca, NW Argentina
180 I6 **Fianarantsoa** Fianarantsoa, C Madagascar
180 H6 **Fianarantsoa** ◆ *province* SE Madagascar
80 G12 **Fianga** Mayo-Kébbi, SW Chad
Ficce *see* Fichē
82 J12 **Fichē** *It.* Ficce. C Ethiopia
103 N17 **Fichtelberg** ▲ Czech Republic/Germany
103 M18 **Fichtelgebirge** ▲ SE Germany
103 M19 **Fichtelnaab** ~ SE Germany
108 E9 **Fidenza** Emilia-Romagna, N Italy
115 K21 **Fier** *var.* Fieri. Fier, SW Albania
115 K21 **Fier** ◆ *district* W Albania
Fieri *see* Fier
Fierza *see* Fierzë
115 L17 **Fierzë** *var.* Fierza. Shkodër, N Albania
115 L17 **Fierzës, Liqeni i** ◎ N Albania
110 F10 **Fiesch** Valais, SW Switzerland
108 G11 **Fiesole** Toscana, C Italy
144 G12 **Fīfah** Aţ Ţafīlah, W Jordan
98 K11 **Fife** *var.* Kingdom of Fife. *cultural region* E Scotland, UK
98 K11 **Fife Ness** *headland* E Scotland, UK
Fifteen Twenty Fracture Zone *see* Barracuda Fracture Zone
105 N13 **Figeac** Lot, S France
97 N19 **Figeholm** Kalmar, SE Sweden
Figig *see* Figuig
85 J18 **Figtree** Matabeleland South, SW Zimbabwe
106 F8 **Figueira da Foz** Coimbra, W Portugal
107 X4 **Figueres** Cataluña, E Spain
76 H7 **Figuig** *var.* Figig. E Morocco
Fijāj, Shaţţ al *see* Fedjaj, Chott el
197 J14 **Fiji** *off.* Sovereign Democratic Republic of Fiji, *Fij.* Viti. ◆ *republic* SW Pacific Ocean
197 J13 **Fiji** *island group* SW Pacific Ocean
183 Q8 **Fiji Plate** *tectonic feature*
107 P14 **Filabres, Sierra de los** ▲ SE Spain
85 K18 **Filabusi** Matabeleland South, S Zimbabwe
44 K13 **Filadelfia** Guanacaste, W Costa Rica
113 K20 **Fil'akovo** *Hung.* Fülek. Stredné Slovensko, S Slovakia
205 N5 **Filchner Ice Shelf** *ice shelf* Antarctica
12 J11 **Fildegrand** ~ Québec, SE Canada
35 O15 **Filer** Idaho, NW USA
Filevo *see* Vŭrbitsa
118 H14 **Filiaşi** Dolj, SW Romania
117 B16 **Filiátes** Ípeiros, W Greece
117 D21 **Filiatrá** Pelopónnisos, S Greece
109 K22 **Filicudi, Isola** *island* Isole Eolie, S Italy
147 Y10 **Filim** E Oman
Filimon Sîrbu *see* Făurei
79 S11 **Filingué** Tillabéri, W Niger
116 K13 **Filiourí** ~ NE Greece
116 I13 **Fílippoi** *anc.* Philippi. *site of ancient city* Anatolikí Makedonía kai Thráki, NE Greece
97 L15 **Filipstad** Värmland, C Sweden
110 I9 **Filisur** Graubünden, S Switzerland
96 E12 **Fillefjell** ▲ S Norway
37 R14 **Fillmore** California, W USA
38 K5 **Fillmore** Utah, W USA
12 J10 **Fils, Lac du** ◎ Québec, SE Canada
142 H11 **Filyos Çayı** ~ N Turkey
205 Q1 **Fimbul Ice Shelf** *ice shelf* Antarctica
205 Q2 **Fimbutheimen** *physical region* Antarctica
108 G9 **Finale Emilia** Emilia-Romagna, C Italy
108 C10 **Finale Ligure** Liguria, NW Italy
107 P14 **Fiñana** Andalucía, S Spain
180 I6 **Finandrahana** Fianarantsoa, SE Madagascar
23 S6 **Fincastle** Virginia, NE USA
101 M25 **Findel** ✕ (Luxembourg) Luxembourg, C Luxembourg
98 J9 **Findhorn** ~ N Scotland, UK
33 R12 **Findlay** Ohio, N USA
20 G11 **Finger Lakes** *lakes* New York, NE USA
85 L14 **Fingoè** Tete, NW Mozambique
142 E17 **Finike** Antalya, SW Turkey
104 F6 **Finistère** ◆ *department* NW France
194 J12 **Finisterre, Mount** ▲ C PNG
194 J12 **Finisterre Range** ▲ N PNG
189 Q8 **Finke** Northern Territory, N Australia
111 S10 **Finkenstein** Kärnten, S Austria
201 Y15 **Finkol, Mount** *var.* Mount Crozer. ▲ Kosrae, E Micronesia
95 L17 **Finland** *off.* Republic of Finland, *Fin.* Suomen Tasavalta, Suomi. ◆ *republic* N Europe
128 F12 **Finland, Gulf of** *Est.* Soome Laht, *Fin.* Suomenlahti, *Ger.* Finnischer Meerbusen, *Rus.* Finskiy Zaliv, *Swe.* Finska Viken. *gulf* E Baltic Sea
8 L11 **Finlay** ~ British Columbia, W Canada
191 O10 **Finley** New South Wales, SE Australia
31 Q4 **Finley** North Dakota, N USA
Finnischer Meerbusen *see* Finland, Gulf of
94 K9 **Finnmark** ◆ *county* N Norway
94 K9 **Finnmarksvidda** *physical region* N Norway
94 I9 **Finnsnes** Troms, N Norway
194 K13 **Finschhafen** Morobe, C PNG
96 E13 **Finse** Hordaland, S Norway
Finska Viken/Finskiy Zaliv *see* Finland, Gulf of
97 M17 **Finspång** Östergötland, S Sweden
110 F10 **Finsteraarhorn** ▲ Swtizerland
103 O14 **Finsterwalde** Brandenburg, E Germany
193 A23 **Fiordland** *physical region* South Island, NZ
108 E9 **Fiorenzuola d'Arda** Emilia-Romagna, C Italy
Firat Nehri *see* Euphrates
Firdaus *see* Ferdows
20 M14 **Fire Island** *island* New York, NE USA
108 G11 **Firenze** *Eng.* Florence; *anc.* Florentia. Toscana, C Italy
108 G10 **Firenzuola** Toscana, C Italy
12 C6 **Fire River** Ontario, S Canada
Fîrliug *see* Fârliug
63 B19 **Firmat** Santa Fe, C Argentina
105 Q12 **Firminy** Loire, E France
Firmum Picenum *see* Fermo
158 J12 **Fīrozābād** Uttar Pradesh, N India
158 G8 **Fīrozpur** *var.* Ferozepore. Punjab, NW India
First State *see* Delaware
149 O12 **Fīrūzābād** Fārs, S Iran
Fischamend *see* Fischamend Markt
111 Y4 **Fischamend Markt** *var.* Fischamend. Niederösterreich, NE Austria
111 W6 **Fischbacher Alpen** ▲ E Austria
Fischhausen *see* Primorsk
85 D21 **Fish** *var.* Vis. ~ S Namibia
85 F24 **Fish** *Afr.* Vis. ~ SW South Africa
9 X15 **Fisher Branch** Manitoba, S Canada
9 X15 **Fisher River** Manitoba, S Canada
21 N13 **Fishers Island** *island* New York, NE USA
39 U8 **Fishers Peak** ▲ Colorado, C USA
15 M6 **Fisher Strait** *strait* Northwest Territories, N Canada
99 H21 **Fishguard** *Wel.* Abergwaun. SW Wales, UK
21 R2 **Fish River Lake** ◎ Maine, NE USA
204 K6 **Fiske, Cape** *headland* Antarctica
105 P4 **Fismes** Marne, N France
106 F3 **Fisterra, Cabo** *headland* NW Spain
21 N11 **Fitchburg** Massachusetts, NE USA
98 L3 **Fitful Head** *headland* NE Scotland, UK
97 C14 **Fitjar** Hordaland, S Norway
198 Bb8 **Fito** ▲ Upolu, C Western Samoa
25 U6 **Fitzgerald** Georgia, SE USA
188 M5 **Fitzroy Crossing** Western Australia
65 G21 **Fitzroy, Monte** *var.* Cerro Chaltel. ▲ S Argentina
189 Y8 **Fitzroy River** ~ Queensland, E Australia
188 L5 **Fitzroy River** ~ Western Australia
12 E12 **Fitzwilliam Island** *island* Ontario, S Canada
109 J15 **Fiuggi** Lazio, C Italy
Fiume *see* Rijeka
109 H15 **Fiumicino** Lazio, C Italy
Fiumicino *see* Leonardo da Vinci
108 E10 **Fivizzano** Toscana, C Italy
81 O21 **Fizi** Sud Kivu, E Zaire
Fizuli *see* Füzuli
94 I11 **Fjällåsen** Norrbotten, N Sweden
97 G20 **Fjerritslev** Nordjylland, N Denmark
F.J.S. *see* Franz Josef Strauss
97 L16 **Fjugesta** Örebro, C Sweden
Fladstrand *see* Frederikshavn
39 V5 **Flagler** Colorado, C USA
25 X10 **Flagler Beach** Florida, SE USA
38 L11 **Flagstaff** Arizona, SW USA
67 H24 **Flagstaff Bay** *bay* Saint Helena, C Atlantic Ocean
21 P5 **Flagstaff Lake** ◎ Maine, NE USA
96 E13 **Flåm** Sogn og Fjordane, S Norway
13 O8 **Flamand** ~ Québec, SE Canada
32 J5 **Flambeau River** ~ Wisconsin, N USA
99 O16 **Flamborough Head** *headland* E England, UK
102 N13 **Fläming** *hill range* NE Germany
18 Ii7 **Flaming Gorge Reservoir** ⊠ Utah/Wyoming, NW USA
176 Xx13 **Flamingo, Teluk** *bay* N Arafura Sea
101 B18 **Flanders** *Dut.* Vlaanderen, *Fr.* Flandre. *cultural region* Belgium/France
Flandre *see* Flanders
31 R10 **Flandreau** South Dakota, N USA
98 D6 **Flannan Isles** *island group* NW Scotland, UK
30 M6 **Flasher** North Dakota, N USA
95 G15 **Flåsjön** ◎ N Sweden
41 O11 **Flat** Alaska, USA
14 G7 **Flat** ~ Northwest Territories, NW Canada
94 H1 **Flateyri** Vestfirdhir, Nw Iceland
35 P8 **Flathead Lake** ◎ Montana, NW USA
181 Y15 **Flat Island** *Fr.* Île Plate. *island* N Mauritius
179 N14 **Flat Island** *island* NE Spratly Islands
27 T11 **Flatonia** Texas, SW USA
193 M14 **Flat Point** *headland* North Island, NZ
29 X6 **Flat River** Missouri, C USA
33 P8 **Flat River** ~ Michigan, N USA
33 P14 **Flatrock River** ~ Indiana, N USA
34 E6 **Flattery, Cape** *headland* Washington, NW USA
66 B12 **Flatts Village** *var.* The Flatts Village. C Bermuda
110 H7 **Flawil** Sankt Gallen, NE Switzerland
99 N22 **Fleet** S England, UK
99 K16 **Fleetwood** NW England, UK
20 H15 **Fleetwood** Pennsylvania, NE USA
97 D18 **Flekkefjord** Vest-Agder, S Norway
23 N5 **Flemingsburg** Kentucky, S USA
20 J15 **Flemington** New Jersey, NE USA
66 I7 **Flemish Cap** *undersea feature* NW Atlantic Ocean
97 N16 **Flen** Södermanland, C Sweden

102 I6 **Flensburg** Schleswig-Holstein, N Germany
102 J6 **Flensburger Förde** *inlet* Denmark/Germany
104 K5 **Flers** Orne, N France
97 C14 **Flesland** ✕ (Bergen) Hordaland, S Norway
Flessingue *see* Vlissingen
23 P10 **Fletcher** North Carolina, SE USA
33 R6 **Fletcher Pond** ◎ Michigan, N USA
104 L15 **Fleurance** Gers, S France
110 B8 **Fleurier** Neuchâtel, W Switzerland
101 H20 **Fleurus** Hainaut, S Belgium
105 N7 **Fleury-les-Aubrais** Loiret, C France
100 K10 **Flevoland** ◈ *province* C Netherlands
Flickertail State *see* North Dakota
110 H9 **Flims** Glarus, NE Switzerland
190 F8 **Flinders Island** *island* Investigator Group, South Australia
191 P14 **Flinders Island** *island* Furneaux Group, Tasmania, SE Australia
190 I6 **Flinders Ranges** ▲▲ South Australia
189 U5 **Flinders River** ≈ Queensland, NE Australia
9 V13 **Flin Flon** Manitoba, C Canada
99 K18 **Flint** NE Wales, UK
33 R9 **Flint** Michigan, N USA
99 J18 **Flint** *cultural region* NE Wales, UK
29 O7 **Flint Hills** *hill range* Kansas, C USA
203 Y6 **Flint Island** *island* Line Islands, E Kiribati
25 S4 **Flint River** ≈ Georgia, SE USA
33 R9 **Flint River** ≈ Michigan, N USA
201 X12 **Flipper Point** *headland* C Wake Island
96 I13 **Flisa** Hedmark, S Norway
96 J13 **Flisa** ≈ S Norway
126 Hh4 **Flissingskiy, Mys** *headland* Novaya Zemlya, NW Russian Federation
Flitsch *see* Bovec
107 U6 **Flix** Cataluña, NE Spain
97 J19 **Floda** Älvsborg, S Sweden
103 O16 **Flöha** ≈ E Germany
27 O4 **Flomot** Texas, SW USA
31 V5 **Floodwood** Minnesota, N USA
32 M15 **Flora** Illinois, N USA
105 P14 **Florac** Lozère, S France
25 Q8 **Florala** Alabama, S USA
105 S4 **Florange** Moselle, NE France
Floreana, Isla *see* Santa María, Isla
25 O2 **Florence** Alabama, S USA
38 L14 **Florence** Arizona, SW USA
39 T6 **Florence** Colorado, C USA
29 O5 **Florence** Kansas, C USA
22 M4 **Florence** Kentucky, S USA
34 E13 **Florence** Oregon, NW USA
23 T12 **Florence** South Carolina, SE USA
27 S9 **Florence** Texas, SW USA
Florence *see* Firenze
56 E13 **Florencia** Caquetá, S Colombia
101 H21 **Florennes** Namur, S Belgium
Florentia *see* Firenze
65 J18 **Florentino Ameghino, Embalse** ▣ S Argentina
101 J24 **Florenville** Luxembourg, SE Belgium
44 E3 **Flores** Petén, N Guatemala
63 E19 **Flores** ◈ *department* S Uruguay
175 Pp16 **Flores** *island* Nusa Tenggara, C Indonesia
66 M1 **Flores** *island* Azores, Portugal, NE Atlantic Ocean
Floreshty *see* Floreşti
Flores, Lago de *see* Petén Itzá, Lago
Flores, Laut *see* Flores Sea
175 P15 **Flores Sea** *Ind.* Laut Flores. *sea* C Indonesia
118 M8 **Floreşti** *Rus.* Floreshty. N Moldova
27 S12 **Floresville** Texas, SW USA
61 N14 **Floriano** Piauí, E Brazil
63 K14 **Florianópolis** *prev.* Destêrro. *state capital* Santa Catarina, S Brazil
46 G6 **Florida** Camagüey, C Cuba
63 F19 **Florida** Florida, S Uruguay
63 F19 **Florida** ◈ *department* S Uruguay
25 U9 **Florida** *off.* State of Florida; also known as Peninsular State, Sunshine State. ◈ *state* SE USA
25 Y17 **Florida Bay** *bay* Florida, SE USA
56 G8 **Floridablanca** Santander, N Colombia
195 X15 **Florida Islands** *island group* C Solomon Islands
25 Y17 **Florida Keys** *island group* Florida, SE USA
39 Q16 **Florida Mountains** ▲▲ New Mexico, SW USA
66 D10 **Florida, Straits of** *strait* Atlantic Ocean/Gulf of Mexico
116 D13 **Flórina** *var.* Phlórina. Dytikí Makedonía, N Greece
29 X4 **Florissant** Missouri, C USA
96 C11 **Florø** Sogn og Fjordane, S Norway
117 L22 **Floúda, Ákra** *headland* Astypálaia, Kykládes, Greece, Aegean Sea
23 S7 **Floyd** Virginia, NE USA
27 N4 **Floydada** Texas, SW USA
Flüela Wisshorn *see* Weisshorn
100 K7 **Fluessen** ◎ N Netherlands
107 S5 **Flúmen** ≈ NE Spain
109 C20 **Flumendosa** ≈ Sardegna, Italy, C Mediterranean Sea
33 R9 **Flushing** Michigan, N USA
Flushing *see* Vlissingen
27 O6 **Fluvanna** Texas, SW USA
194 F14 **Fly** ≈ Indonesia/PNG
204 I10 **Flying Fish, Cape** *headland* Thurston Island, Antarctica
Flylân *see* Vlieland
200 Ss13 **Foa** *island* Ha'apai Group, C Tonga
9 U15 **Foam Lake** Saskatchewan, S Canada
115 J14 **Foča** SE Bosnia and Herzegovina
118 L12 **Focşani** Vrancea, E Romania
Fogaras/Fogarasch *see* Făgăraş
109 M16 **Foggia** Puglia, SE Italy
Foggo *see* Faggo
78 D10 **Fogo** *island* Ilhas de Sotavento, SW Cape Verde
11 U11 **Fogo Island** *island* Newfoundland and Labrador, E Canada
111 U7 **Fohnsdorf** Steiermark, SE Austria
102 G7 **Föhr** *island* NW Germany
106 F14 **Fóia** ▲ S Portugal
12 I10 **Foins, Lac aux** ◎ Québec, SE Canada
105 N17 **Foix** Ariège, S France
130 I5 **Fokino** Bryanskaya Oblast', W Russian Federation
Fola, Cnoc *see* Bloody Foreland
96 E13 **Folarskardnuten** ▲ S Norway
94 G11 **Folda** *fjord* C Norway
95 F14 **Foldereid** Nord-Trøndelag, C Norway
95 E14 **Foldfjorden** *fjord* C Norway
Földvár *see* Feldioara
117 J22 **Folégandros** *island* Kykládes, Greece, Aegean Sea
25 O9 **Foley** Alabama, S USA
31 U7 **Foley** Minnesota, N USA
12 E7 **Foleyet** Ontario, S Canada
97 D14 **Folgefonni** *glacier* S Norway
108 I13 **Foligno** Umbria, C Italy
99 Q23 **Folkestone** SE England, UK
25 W8 **Folkston** Georgia, SE USA
96 H10 **Folldal** Hedmark, S Norway
27 P1 **Follett** Texas, SW USA
108 F13 **Follonica** Toscana, C Italy
23 T15 **Folly Beach** South Carolina, SE USA
37 O7 **Folsom** California, W USA
118 M12 **Folteşti** Galaţi, E Romania
180 H14 **Fomboni** Mohéli, S Comoros
20 K10 **Fonda** New York, NE USA
9 S10 **Fond-du-Lac** Saskatchewan, C Canada
32 M8 **Fond du Lac** Wisconsin, N USA
9 T10 **Fond-du-Lac** ≈ Saskatchewan, C Canada
202 C9 **Fongafale** *var.* Funafuti. ● (Tuvalu) Funafuti Atoll, SE Tuvalu
202 G8 **Fongafale** *atoll* C Tuvalu
109 C18 **Fonni** Sardegna, Italy, C Mediterranean Sea
201 V12 **Fono** *island* Chuuk, C Micronesia
56 G4 **Fonseca** La Guajira, N Colombia
Fonseca, Golfo de *see* Fonseca, Gulf of
44 H8 **Fonseca, Gulf of** *Sp.* Golfo de Fonseca. *gulf* Central America
105 O6 **Fontainebleau** Seine-et-Marne, N France
65 G19 **Fontana, Lago** ◎ W Argentina
23 N10 **Fontana Lake** ▣ North Carolina, SE USA
109 L24 **Fontanarossa** ✕ (Catania) Sicilia, Italy, C Mediterranean Sea
9 N11 **Fontas** ≈ British Columbia, W Canada
60 D12 **Fonte Boa** Amazonas, N Brazil
104 J10 **Fontenay-le-Comte** Vendée, NW France
35 T16 **Fontenelle Reservoir** ▣ Wyoming, C USA
200 Ss12 **Fonualei** *island* Vava'u Group, N Tonga
113 H24 **Fonyód** Somogy, W Hungary
Foochow *see* Fuzhou
41 Q10 **Foraker, Mount** ▲ Alaska, USA
197 D14 **Forari** Éfaté, C Vanuatu
105 U4 **Forbach** Moselle, NE France
191 Q8 **Forbes** New South Wales, SE Australia
79 T17 **Forcados** Delta, S Nigeria
105 S14 **Forcalquier** Alpes-de-Haute-Provence, SE France
103 K19 **Forchheim** Bayern, SE Germany
176 V14 **Fordate, Pulau** *island* Kepulauan Tanimbar, E Indonesia
37 R13 **Ford City** California, W USA
96 D11 **Førde** Sogn og Fjordane, S Norway
33 N4 **Ford River** ≈ Michigan, N USA
191 O4 **Fords Bridge** New South Wales, SE Australia
22 J6 **Fordsville** Kentucky, S USA
29 U13 **Fordyce** Arkansas, C USA
78 I14 **Forécariah** Guinée-Maritime, SW Guinea
207 O14 **Forel, Mont** ▲ SE Greenland
9 R17 **Foremost** Alberta, SW Canada
12 D16 **Forest** Ontario, S Canada
24 L5 **Forest** Mississippi, S USA
33 S12 **Forest** Ohio, N USA
31 V11 **Forest City** Iowa, C USA
23 Q10 **Forest City** North Carolina, SE USA
34 G11 **Forest Grove** Oregon, NW USA
191 P17 **Forestier Peninsula** *peninsula* Tasmania, SE Australia
31 V8 **Forest Lake** Minnesota, N USA
25 S3 **Forest Park** Georgia, SE USA
31 Q3 **Forest River** ≈ North Dakota, N USA
13 T6 **Forestville** Québec, SE Canada
105 Q11 **Forez, Monts du** ▲▲ C France
98 K10 **Forfar** E Scotland, UK
28 J8 **Forgan** Oklahoma, C USA
Forge du Sud *see* Dudelange
103 J24 **Forggensee** ◎ S Germany
153 N10 **Forish** *Rus.* Farish. Jizzakh Wiloyati, C Uzbekistan
22 F9 **Forked Deer River** ≈ Tennessee, S USA
34 F7 **Forks** Washington, NW USA
94 N2 **Forlandsundet** *sound* W Svalbard
108 H10 **Forlì** *anc.* Forum Livii. Emilia-Romagna, N Italy
31 Q7 **Forman** North Dakota, N USA
99 K17 **Formby** NW England, UK
107 V11 **Formentera** *anc.* Ophiusa, *Lat.* Frumentum. *island* Islas Baleares, Spain, W Mediterranean Sea
Formentor, Cabo de *see* Formentor, Cap de
107 Y9 **Formentor, Cap de** *var.* Cabo de Formentor, Cape Formentor. *headland* Mallorca, Spain, W Mediterranean Sea
Formentor, Cape *see* Formentor, Cap de
109 J16 **Formia** Lazio, C Italy
64 O7 **Formosa** Formosa, NE Argentina
64 M6 **Formosa** *off.* Provincia de Formosa. ◈ *province* NE Argentina
Formosa/Formo'sa *see* Taiwan
61 I17 **Formosa, Serra** ▲▲ C Brazil
Formosa Strait *see* Taiwan Strait
97 H15 **Fornebu** ✕ (Oslo) Akershus, S Norway
27 U6 **Forney** Texas, SW USA
97 H21 **Fornæs** *headland* C Denmark
108 E9 **Fornovo di Taro** Emilia-Romagna, C Italy
119 T14 **Foros** Respublika Krym, S Ukraine
Føroyar *see* Faeroe Islands
98 J8 **Forres** NE Scotland, UK
29 X11 **Forrest City** Arkansas, C USA
41 Y15 **Forrester Island** *island* Alexander Archipelago, Alaska, USA
27 N7 **Forsan** Texas, SW USA
189 V5 **Forsayth** Queensland, NE Australia
97 L19 **Forserum** Jönköping, S Sweden
97 K15 **Forshaga** Värmland, C Sweden
95 L19 **Forssa** Häme, SW Finland
103 Q14 **Forst** *Lus.* Baršć Łužyca. Brandenburg, E Germany
191 U7 **Forster-Tuncurry** New South Wales, SE Australia
25 T4 **Forsyth** Georgia, SE USA
29 T8 **Forsyth** Missouri, C USA
35 W10 **Forsyth** Montana, NW USA
155 U11 **Fort Abbās** Punjab, E Pakistan
10 G10 **Fort Albany** Ontario, C Canada
58 L13 **Fortaleza** Pando, N Bolivia
60 P13 **Fortaleza** *prev.* Ceará. *state capital* Ceará, NE Brazil
61 D16 **Fortaleza** Rondônia, W Brazil
58 C13 **Fortaleza, Río** ≈ W Peru
Fort-Archambault *see* Sarh
23 U3 **Fort Ashby** West Virginia, NE USA
98 I9 **Fort Augustus** N Scotland, UK
Fort-Bayard *see* Zhanjiang
35 S8 **Fort Benton** Montana, NW USA
37 Q1 **Fort Bidwell** California, W USA
36 L5 **Fort Bragg** California, W USA
33 N16 **Fort Branch** Indiana, N USA
Fort-Bretonnet *see* Bousso
35 T17 **Fort Bridger** Wyoming, C USA
Fort-Cappolani *see* Tidjikja
Fort Charlet *see* Djanet
Fort-Chimo *see* Kuujjuaq
9 R10 **Fort Chipewyan** Alberta, C Canada
Fort Cobb Lake *see* Fort Cobb Reservoir
28 L11 **Fort Cobb Reservoir** *var.* Fort Cobb Lake. ▣ Oklahoma, C USA
39 T3 **Fort Collins** Colorado, C USA
12 K12 **Fort-Coulonge** Québec, SE Canada
Fort-Crampel *see* Kaga Bandoro
Fort-Dauphin *see* Tôlañaro
26 K10 **Fort Davis** Texas, SW USA
39 O10 **Fort Defiance** Arizona, SW USA
47 Q12 **Fort-de-France** *prev.* Fort-Royal. ○ (Martinique) W Martinique
47 P12 **Fort-de-France, Baie de** *bay* W Martinique
Fort de Kock *see* Bukittinggi
25 P6 **Fort Deposit** Alabama, S USA
31 U13 **Fort Dodge** Iowa, C USA
11 S10 **Forteau** Québec, E Canada
108 E11 **Forte dei Marmi** Toscana, C Italy
12 H17 **Fort Erie** Ontario, S Canada
188 H7 **Fortescue River** ≈ Western Australia
21 S2 **Fort Fairfield** Maine, NE USA
Fort-Foureau *see* Kousséri
10 A11 **Fort Frances** Ontario, S Canada
Fort Franklin *see* Déljne
25 R7 **Fort Gaines** Georgia, SE USA
39 T8 **Fort Garland** Colorado, C USA
23 P5 **Fort Gay** West Virginia, NE USA
Fort George *see* La Grande Rivière
29 Q10 **Fort Gibson** Oklahoma, C USA
29 Q9 **Fort Gibson Lake** ▣ Oklahoma, C USA
15 Gg5 **Fort Good Hope** *var.* Good Hope. Northwest Territories, NW Canada
25 V4 **Fort Gordon** Georgia, SE USA
Fort Gouraud *see* Fdérik
98 I11 **Forth** ≈ C Scotland, UK
Fort Hall *see* Murang'a
26 H8 **Fort Hancock** Texas, SW USA
Fort Hertz *see* Putao
98 K12 **Forth, Firth of** *estuary* E Scotland, UK
12 L14 **Forthton** Ontario, SE Canada
12 M8 **Fortier** ≈ Québec, SE Canada
Fortín General Eugenio Garay *see* General Eugenio A. Garay
Fort Jameson *see* Chipata
Fort Johnston *see* Mangochi
21 R1 **Fort Kent** Maine, NE USA
Fort-Lamy *see* Ndjamena
25 Z15 **Fort Lauderdale** Florida, SE USA
23 R11 **Fort Lawn** South Carolina, SE USA
15 Gg9 **Fort Liard** *var.* Liard. Northwest Territories, W Canada
46 M8 **Fort-Liberté** NE Haiti
23 N9 **Fort Loudoun Lake** ▣ Tennessee, S USA
39 T3 **Fort Lupton** Colorado, C USA
9 R12 **Fort MacKay** Alberta, C Canada
9 Q17 **Fort Macleod** *var.* MacLeod. Alberta, SW Canada
31 Y16 **Fort Madison** Iowa, C USA
Fort Manning *see* Mchinji
27 P9 **Fort McKavett** Texas, SW USA
9 R12 **Fort McMurray** Alberta, C Canada
14 Ff3 **Fort McPherson** *var.* McPherson. Northwest Territories, NW Canada
23 R11 **Fort Mill** South Carolina, SE USA
Fort-Millot *see* Ngouri
39 U3 **Fort Morgan** Colorado, C USA
25 W14 **Fort Myers** Florida, SE USA
25 W15 **Fort Myers Beach** Florida, SE USA
8 M10 **Fort Nelson** British Columbia, W Canada
8 M10 **Fort Nelson** ≈ British Columbia, W Canada
15 Gg6 **Fort Norman** *var.* Norman. Northwest Territories, NW Canada
25 Q2 **Fort Payne** Alabama, S USA
35 W7 **Fort Peck** Montana, NW USA
35 V8 **Fort Peck Lake** ▣ Montana, NW USA
25 Y13 **Fort Pierce** Florida, SE USA
31 N10 **Fort Pierre** South Dakota, N USA
83 E18 **Fort Portal** SW Uganda
15 Hh8 **Fort Providence** *var.* Providence. Northwest Territories, W Canada
9 U16 **Fort Qu'Appelle** Saskatchewan, S Canada
Fort-Repoux *see* Akjoujt
15 I8 **Fort Resolution** *var.* Resolution. Northwest Territories, W Canada
35 T13 **Fortress Mountain** ▲ Wyoming, C USA
Fort Rosebery *see* Mansa
Fort-Rousset *see* Owando
Fort-Royal *see* Fort-de-France
10 I10 **Fort Rupert** *prev.* Rupert House. Québec, SE Canada
14 G12 **Fort St.James** British Columbia, SW Canada
9 N12 **Fort St.John** British Columbia, W Canada
Fort Sandeman *see* Zhob
9 Q14 **Fort Saskatchewan** Alberta, SW Canada
29 R6 **Fort Scott** Kansas, C USA
10 E6 **Fort Severn** Ontario, C Canada
33 R12 **Fort Shawnee** Ohio, N USA
150 E14 **Fort-Shevchenko** Mangistau, W Kazakhstan
Fort-Sibut *see* Sibut
15 H8 **Fort Simpson** *var.* Simpson. Northwest Territories, W Canada
15 I9 **Fort Smith** *district capital* Northwest Territories, W Canada
29 R10 **Fort Smith** Arkansas, C USA
15 I7 **Fort Smith** ◈ *district* Northwest Territories, NW Canada
39 T13 **Fort Stanton** New Mexico, SW USA
26 L9 **Fort Stockton** Texas, SW USA
39 U12 **Fort Sumner** New Mexico, SW USA
28 K8 **Fort Supply** Oklahoma, C USA
28 K8 **Fort Supply Lake** ▣ Oklahoma, C USA
31 O10 **Fort Thompson** South Dakota, N USA
Fort-Trinquet *see* Bîr Mogreïn
107 R12 **Fortuna** Murcia, SE Spain
36 K3 **Fortuna** California, W USA
30 J2 **Fortuna** North Dakota, N USA
25 T5 **Fort Valley** Georgia, SE USA
9 P11 **Fort Vermilion** Alberta, W Canada
Fort Victoria *see* Masvingo
33 P13 **Fortville** Indiana, N USA
25 P9 **Fort Walton Beach** Florida, SE USA
33 P12 **Fort Wayne** Indiana, N USA
98 H10 **Fort William** N Scotland, UK
27 T6 **Fort Worth** Texas, SW USA
30 M7 **Fort Yates** North Dakota, N USA
41 S7 **Fort Yukon** Alaska, USA
Forum Alieni *see* Ferrara
Forum Julii *see* Fréjus
Forum Livii *see* Forlì
149 Q15 **Forūr, Jazīreh-ye** *island* S Iran
96 H7 **Fosen** *physical region* S Norway
167 N14 **Foshan** *var.* Fatshan, Fo-shan, Namhoi. Guangdong, S China
Fossa Claudia *see* Chioggia
108 B9 **Fossano** Piemonte, NW Italy
101 H21 **Fosses-la-Ville** Namur, S Belgium
34 J12 **Fossil** Oregon, NW USA
Foss Lake *see* Foss Reservoir
108 I11 **Fossombrone** Marche, C Italy
28 K10 **Foss Reservoir** *var.* Foss Lake. ▣ Oklahoma, C USA
31 S4 **Fosston** Minnesota, N USA
191 O13 **Foster** Victoria, SE Australia
9 T12 **Foster Lakes** ◎ Saskatchewan, C Canada
33 S12 **Fostoria** Ohio, N USA
81 D19 **Fougamou** Ngounié, C Gabon
104 J6 **Fougères** Ille-et-Vilaine, NW France
Fou-hsin *see* Fuxin
29 S14 **Fouke** Arkansas, C USA
98 K2 **Foula** *island* NE Scotland, UK
67 D24 **Foul Bay** *bay* East Falkland, Falkland Islands
99 P21 **Foulness Island** *island* SE England, UK
193 F15 **Foulwind, Cape** *headland* South Island, NZ
81 E15 **Foumban** Ouest, NW Cameroon
180 H13 **Foumbouni** Grande Comore, NW Comoros
205 N8 **Foundation Ice Stream** *glacier* Antarctica
39 T6 **Fountain** Colorado, C USA
38 L4 **Fountain Green** Utah, W USA
23 P11 **Fountain Inn** South Carolina, SE USA
29 S11 **Fourche LaFave River** ≈ Arkansas, C USA
35 Z13 **Four Corners** Wyoming, C USA
105 Q2 **Fourmies** Nord, N France
40 J17 **Four Mountains, Islands of** *island group* Aleutian Islands, Alaska, USA
181 P17 **Fournaise, Piton de la** ▲ SE Réunion
12 J8 **Fournière, Lac** ◎ Québec, SE Canada
117 L20 **Foúrnoi** *island* Dodekánisos, Greece, Aegean Sea
66 K13 **Four North Fracture Zone** *tectonic feature* W Atlantic Ocean
Fouron-Saint-Martin *see* Sint-Martens-Voeren
32 L3 **Fourteen Mile Point** *headland* Michigan, N USA
78 I13 **Fouta Djallon** *var.* Futa Jallon. ▲▲ W Guinea
193 C25 **Foveaux Strait** *strait* S NZ
37 Q11 **Fowler** California, W USA
39 U6 **Fowler** Colorado, C USA
33 N12 **Fowler** Indiana, N USA
190 D7 **Fowlers Bay** *bay* South Australia
27 R13 **Fowlerton** Texas, SW USA
148 M3 **Fowman** *var.* Fuman, Fumen. Gīlān, NW Iran
67 C25 **Fox Bay East** West Falkland, Falkland Islands
67 C25 **Fox Bay West** West Falkland, Falkland Islands
12 J14 **Foxboro** Ontario, SE Canada
9 O14 **Fox Creek** Alberta, W Canada
66 G5 **Foxe Basin** *sea* Northwest Territories, N Canada
66 G5 **Foxe Channel** *channel* Northwest Territories, N Canada
97 I16 **Foxen** ◎ C Sweden
16 N4 **Foxe Peninsula** *peninsula* Baffin Island, Northwest Territories, NE Canada
193 E19 **Fox Glacier** West Coast, South Island, NZ
40 L17 **Fox Islands** *island* Aleutian Islands, Alaska, USA
32 M10 **Fox Lake** Illinois, N USA
9 V12 **Fox Mine** Manitoba, C Canada
37 R3 **Fox Mountain** ▲ Nevada, W USA
67 E25 **Fox Point** *headland* East Falkland, Falkland Islands
32 M11 **Fox River** ≈ Illinois/Wisconsin, N USA
32 L7 **Fox River** ≈ Wisconsin, N USA
192 L13 **Foxton** Manawatu-Wanganui, North Island, NZ
9 S16 **Fox Valley** Saskatchewan, S Canada
9 W16 **Foxwarren** Manitoba, S Canada
99 E14 **Foyle, Lough** *Ir.* Loch Feabhail. *inlet* N Ireland
204 H5 **Foyn Coast** *physical region* Antarctica
106 I2 **Foz** Galicia, NW Spain
62 I12 **Foz do Areia, Represa de** ▣ S Brazil
61 A16 **Foz do Breu** Acre, W Brazil
85 A16 **Foz do Cunene** Namibe, SW Angola
62 G12 **Foz do Iguaçu** Paraná, S Brazil
60 C12 **Foz do Mamoriá** Amazonas, NW Brazil
107 T6 **Fraga** Aragón, NE Spain
46 F5 **Fragoso, Cayo** *island* C Cuba
63 G18 **Fraile Muerto** Cerro Largo, NE Uruguay
101 H21 **Fraire** Namur, S Belgium
101 L21 **Fraiture, Baraque de** *hill* SE Belgium
Frakštát *see* Hlohovec
207 S10 **Fram Basin** *var.* Amundsen Basin. *undersea feature* Arctic Ocean
101 F20 **Frameries** Hainaut, S Belgium
21 O11 **Framingham** Massachusetts, NE USA
62 L7 **Franca** São Paulo, S Brazil
197 G4 **Français, Récif des** *reef* W New Caledonia
109 K14 **Francavilla al Mare** Abruzzi, C Italy
109 P18 **Francavilla Fontana** Puglia, SE Italy
104 M8 **France** *off.* French Republic, *It./Sp.* Francia; *prev.* Gaul, Gaule, *Lat.* Gallia. ◆ *republic* W Europe
47 O8 **Francés Viejo, Cabo** *headland* NE Dominican Republic
81 F19 **Franceville** *var.* Massoukou, Masuku. Haut-Ogooué, E Gabon
81 F19 **Franceville** ✕ Haut-Ogooué, E Gabon
Francfort *see* Frankfurt am Main
105 T8 **Franche-Comté** ◈ *region* E France
Francia *see* France
31 O11 **Francis Case, Lake** ▣ South Dakota, N USA
62 H12 **Francisco Beltrão** Paraná, S Brazil
Francisco I. Madero *see* Villa Madero
63 A21 **Francisco Madero** Buenos Aires, E Argentina
44 H6 **Francisco Morazán** *prev.* Tegucigalpa. ◈ *department* C Honduras
85 J18 **Francistown** North East, NE Botswana
Franconian Forest *see* Frankenwald
Franconian Jura *see* Fränkische Alb
100 K6 **Franeker** *Fris.* Frjentsjer. Friesland, N Netherlands
Frankenalb *see* Fränkische Alb
103 H16 **Frankenberg** Hessen, C Germany
103 J20 **Frankenhöhe** *hill range* C Germany
33 R8 **Frankenmuth** Michigan, N USA
103 F20 **Frankenstein** *hill* W Germany
Frankenstein/Frankenstein in Schlesien *see* Ząbkowice Śląskie
103 G20 **Frankenthal** Rheinland-Pfalz, W Germany
103 L18 **Frankenwald** *Eng.* Franconian Forest. ▲▲ C Germany
46 J12 **Frankfield** C Jamaica
12 J14 **Frankford** Ontario, SE Canada
33 O13 **Frankfort** Indiana, N USA
29 O3 **Frankfort** Kansas, C USA
22 L5 **Frankfort** *state capital* Kentucky, S USA
Frankfort on the Main *see* Frankfurt am Main
Frankfurt *see* Słubice, Poland
Frankfurt *see* Frankfurt am Main, Germany
103 G18 **Frankfurt am Main** *var.* Frankfurt, *Fr.* Francfort; *prev. Eng.* Frankfort on the Main. Hessen, SW Germany
102 Q12 **Frankfurt an der Oder** Brandenburg, E Germany
103 L21 **Fränkische Alb** *var.* Frankenalb, *Eng.* Franconian Jura. ▲▲ S Germany
103 I18 **Fränkische Saale** ≈ C Germany
103 L19 **Fränkische Schweiz** *hill range* C Germany
25 R4 **Franklin** Georgia, SE USA
33 P14 **Franklin** Indiana, N USA
22 J7 **Franklin** Kentucky, S USA
24 I9 **Franklin** Louisiana, S USA
31 O17 **Franklin** Nebraska, C USA
23 N10 **Franklin** North Carolina, SE USA
20 C13 **Franklin** Pennsylvania, NE USA
22 J9 **Franklin** Tennessee, S USA
27 U9 **Franklin** Texas, SW USA
23 X7 **Franklin** Virginia, NE USA
23 T4 **Franklin** West Virginia, NE USA
32 M9 **Franklin** Wisconsin, N USA
15 H2 **Franklin Bay** *inlet* Northwest Territories, N Canada
34 K7 **Franklin D.Roosevelt Lake** ▣ Washington, NW USA
37 W4 **Franklin Lake** ◎ Nevada, W USA
193 B22 **Franklin Mountains** ▲▲ South Island, NZ
41 R5 **Franklin Mountains** ▲▲ Alaska, USA
41 N4 **Franklin, Point** *headland* Alaska, USA
191 O17 **Franklin River** ≈ Tasmania, SE Australia
15 K2 **Franklin Strait** *strait* Northwest Territories, N Canada
24 K8 **Franklinton** Louisiana, S USA
23 U9 **Franklinton** North Carolina, SE USA
Frankstadt *see* Frenštát pod Radhoštěm
27 V7 **Frankston** Texas, SW USA
35 U12 **Frannie** Wyoming, C USA
13 U5 **Franquelin** Québec, SE Canada
13 U5 **Franquelin** ≈ Québec, SE Canada
85 C18 **Fransfontein** Kunene, NW Namibia
95 H17 **Fränsta** Västernorrland, C Sweden
126 H1 **Frantsa-Iosifa, Zemlya** *Eng.* Franz Josef Land. *island group* N Russian Federation
193 E18 **Franz Josef Glacier** West Coast, South Island, NZ
Franz Josef Land *see* Frantsa-Iosifa, Zemlya
Franz-Josef Spitze *see* Gerlachovský Štít
103 L23 **Franz Josef Strauss** *abbrev.* F.J.S. ✕ (München) Bayern, SE Germany
109 A19 **Frasca, Capo della** *headland* Sardegna, Italy, C Mediterranean Sea
109 I15 **Frascati** Lazio, C Italy
9 N14 **Fraser** ≈ British Columbia, SW Canada
85 G24 **Fraserburg** Western Cape, SW South Africa
98 L8 **Fraserburgh** NE Scotland, UK
189 Z9 **Fraser Island** *var.* Great Sandy Island. *island* Queensland, E Australia
8 L14 **Fraser Lake** British Columbia, SW Canada
8 L15 **Fraser Plateau** *plateau* British Columbia, SW Canada
192 P10 **Frasertown** Hawke's Bay, North Island, NZ
101 E19 **Frasnes-lez-Buissenal** Hainaut, SW Belgium
110 I7 **Frastanz** Vorarlberg, NW Austria
12 B8 **Frater** Ontario, S Canada
Frauenbach *see* Baia Mare
Frauenburg *see* Saldus, Latvia
Frauenburg *see* Frombork, Poland
110 H6 **Frauenfeld** Thurgau, NE Switzerland
111 Z5 **Frauenkirchen** Burgenland, E Austria
63 D19 **Fray Bentos** Río Negro, W Uruguay
63 F19 **Fray Marcos** Florida, S Uruguay
31 S6 **Frazee** Minnesota, N USA
106 M5 **Frechilla** Castilla-León, N Spain
32 I4 **Frederic** Wisconsin, N USA
97 G23 **Fredericia** Vejle, C Denmark
23 W3 **Frederick** Maryland, NE USA
28 L12 **Frederick** Oklahoma, C USA
31 P7 **Frederick** South Dakota, N USA
31 X12 **Fredericksburg** Iowa, C USA
27 R10 **Fredericksburg** Texas, SW USA
23 W5 **Fredericksburg** Virginia, NE USA
41 X13 **Frederick Sound** *sound* Alaska , USA
29 X6 **Fredericktown** Missouri, C USA
62 H13 **Frederico Westphalen** Rio Grande do Sul, S Brazil
11 O15 **Fredericton** New Brunswick, SE Canada
97 I22 **Frederiksborg** *off.* Frederiksborgs Amt. ◈ *county* E Denmark
Frederikshåb *see* Paamiut
97 H19 **Frederikshavn** *prev.* Fladstrand. Nordjylland, N Denmark
97 J22 **Frederikssund** Frederiksborg, E Denmark
47 T9 **Frederiksted** Saint Croix, S Virgin Islands (US)
97 I22 **Frederiksværk** *var.* Frederiksværk og Hanehoved. Frederiksborg, E Denmark
Frederiksværk og Hanehoved *see* Frederiksværk
56 E9 **Fredonia** Antioquia, W Colombia
38 K8 **Fredonia** Arizona, SW USA
29 P7 **Fredonia** Kansas, C USA
20 C11 **Fredonia** New York, NE USA
37 P4 **Fredonyer Pass** *pass* California, W USA
95 I15 **Fredrika** Västerbotten, N Sweden
97 L14 **Fredriksberg** Kopparberg, C Sweden
Fredrikshald *see* Halden
Fredrikshamn *see* Hamina
97 H16 **Fredrikstad** Østfold, S Norway
32 K16 **Freeburg** Illinois, N USA
20 K15 **Freehold** New Jersey, NE USA
20 H14 **Freeland** Pennsylvania, NE USA
190 J5 **Freeling Heights** ▲ South Australia
37 Q7 **Freel Peak** ▲ California, W USA
16 T7 **Freels, Cape** *headland* Newfoundland, Newfoundland and Labrador, E Canada
31 Q11 **Freeman** South Dakota, N USA
46 G1 **Freeport** Grand Bahama Island, N Bahamas
32 L10 **Freeport** Illinois, N USA
27 W12 **Freeport** Texas, SW USA
46 G1 **Freeport** ✕ Grand Bahama Island, N Bahamas
27 R14 **Freer** Texas, SW USA
85 H22 **Free State** *off.* Free State Province; *prev.* Orange Free State, *Afr.* Oranje Vrystaat. ◈ *province* C South Africa
Free State *see* Maryland
78 G15 **Freetown** ● (Sierra Leone) W Sierra Leone
180 J16 **Frégate** *island* Inner Islands, NE Seychelles
106 J12 **Fregenal de la Sierra** Extremadura, W Spain
190 C2 **Fregon** South Australia
104 H5 **Fréhel, Cap** *headland* NW France
96 F8 **Frei** Møre og Romsdal, S Norway
103 O16 **Freiberg** Sachsen, E Germany
103 O16 **Freiberger Mulde** ≈ E Germany
Freiburg *see* Freiburg im Breisgau, Germany
Freiburg *see* Fribourg, Switzerland
103 F23 **Freiburg im Breisgau** *var.* Freiburg, *Fr.* Fribourg-en-Brisgau. Baden-Württemberg, SW Germany
Freiburg in Schlesien *see* Świebodzice
Freie Hansestadt Bremen *see* Bremen
Freie und Hansestadt Hamburg *see* Brandenburg
103 L22 **Freising** Bayern, SE Germany
111 T3 **Freistadt** Oberösterreich, N Austria
Freistadtl *see* Hlohovec
103 O16 **Freital** Sachsen, E Germany
Freiwaldau *see* Jeseník
106 J6 **Freixo de Espada à Cinta** Bragança, N Portugal
105 U15 **Fréjus** *anc.* Forum Julii. Var, SE France
188 I13 **Fremantle** Western Australia
37 N9 **Fremont** California, W USA
33 Q11 **Fremont** Indiana, N USA
31 W15 **Fremont** Iowa, C USA
33 P8 **Fremont** Michigan, N USA
31 R15 **Fremont** Nebraska, C USA
33 S11 **Fremont** Ohio, N USA
35 T14 **Fremont Peak** ▲ Wyoming, C USA
38 M6 **Fremont River** ≈ Utah, W USA
23 O9 **French Broad River** ≈ Tennessee, S USA
23 N5 **Frenchburg** Kentucky, S USA
20 C12 **French Creek** ≈ Pennsylvania, NE USA
34 K15 **Frenchglen** Oregon, NW USA
57 Y10 **French Guiana** *var.* Guiana, Guyane. ◇ *French overseas department* N South America
French Guinea *see* Guinea
33 O15 **French Lick** Indiana, N USA
193 J14 **French Pass** Marlborough, South Island, NZ

◆ Country ● Country Capital ◇ Dependent Territory ○ Dependent Territory Capital ◈ Administrative Region ✕ International Airport ▲ Mountain ▲▲ Mountain Range Volcano ≈ River ◎ Lake ▣ Reservoir

203 T11 **French Polynesia** ◇ French overseas territory C Polynesia
French Republic see France
12 F11 **French River** ≈ Ontario, S Canada
French Somaliland see Djibouti
181 P12 **French Southern and Antarctic Territories** Fr. Terres Australes et Antarctiques Françaises. ◇ French overseas territory S Indian Ocean
French Sudan see Mali
French Territory of the Afars and Issas see Djibouti
French Togoland see Togo
76 J6 **Frenda** NW Algeria
113 I18 **Frenštát pod Radhoštěm** Ger. Frankstadt. Severní Morava, E Czech Republic
78 M17 **Fresco** S Ivory Coast
205 U16 **Freshfield, Cape** headland Antarctica
42 L10 **Fresnillo** var. Fresnillo de González Echeverría. Zacatecas, C Mexico
Fresnillo de González Echeverría see Fresnillo
37 Q10 **Fresno** California, W USA
Freu, Cabo del see Freu, Cap des
107 Y9 **Freu, Cap des** var. Cabo del Freu. headland Mallorca, Spain, W Mediterranean Sea
103 G22 **Freudenstadt** Baden-Württemberg, SW Germany
Freudenthal see Bruntál
191 Q17 **Freycinet Peninsula** peninsula Tasmania, SE Australia
78 H14 **Fria** Guinée-Maritime, W Guinea
85 A17 **Fria, Cape** headland NW Namibia
37 Q10 **Friant** California, W USA
64 K8 **Frías** Santiago del Estero, N Argentina
110 D9 **Fribourg** Ger. Freiburg. Fribourg, W Switzerland
110 C9 **Fribourg** Ger. Freiburg. ◆ canton W Switzerland
Fribourg-en-Brisgau see Freiburg im Breisgau
34 G7 **Friday Harbor** San Juan Islands, Washington, NW USA
194 F11 **Frieda** ≈ NW PNG
Friedau see Ormož
103 K23 **Friedberg** Bayern, S Germany
103 H18 **Friedberg** Hessen, W Germany
Friedeberg Neumark see Strzelce Krajeńskie
Friedek-Mistek see Frýdek-Místek
Friedland see Pravdinsk
103 I24 **Friedrichshafen** Baden-Württemberg, S Germany
Friedrichstadt see Jaunjelgava
31 Q16 **Friend** Nebraska, C USA
Friendly Islands see Tonga
57 V9 **Friendship** Coronie, N Suriname
32 L7 **Friendship** Wisconsin, N USA
111 T8 **Friesach** Kärnten, S Austria
Friesche Eilanden see Frisian Islands
103 F22 **Friesenheim** Baden-Württemberg, SW Germany
Friesische Inseln see Frisian Islands
100 K6 **Friesland** ◆ province N Netherlands
62 Q10 **Frio, Cabo** headland SE Brazil
26 M3 **Friona** Texas, SW USA
44 L12 **Frío, Río** ≈ N Costa Rica
27 R13 **Frio River** ≈ Texas, SW USA
101 M25 **Frisange** Luxembourg, S Luxembourg
Frisches Haff see Vistula Lagoon
38 J6 **Frisco Peak** ▲ Utah, W USA
86 F9 **Frisian Islands** Dut. Friesche Eilanden, Ger. Friesische Inseln. island group N Europe
20 L12 **Frissell, Mount** ▲ Connecticut, NE USA
97 J19 **Fristad** Älvsborg, S Sweden
27 N2 **Fritch** Texas, SW USA
97 J19 **Fritsla** Älvsborg, S Sweden
103 H16 **Fritzlar** Hessen, C Germany
108 H6 **Friuli-Venezia Giulia** ◆ region NE Italy
Frjentsjer see Franeker
206 L13 **Frobisher Bay** inlet Baffin Island, Northwest Territories, NE Canada
Frobisher Bay see Iqaluit
9 S12 **Frobisher Lake** ◎ Saskatchewan, C Canada
96 G7 **Frohavet** sound C Norway
Frohenbruck see Veselí nad Lužnicí
111 V7 **Frohnleiten** Steiermark, SE Austria
101 G22 **Froidchapelle** Hainaut, S Belgium
131 O9 **Frolovo** Volgogradskaya Oblast', SW Russian Federation
112 K7 **Frombork** Ger. Frauenburg. Elbląg, N Poland
99 L22 **Frome** SW England, UK
190 J4 **Frome Creek** seasonal river South Australia
190 J6 **Frome Downs** South Australia
190 J5 **Frome, Lake** salt lake South Australia
Fronicken see Wronki
106 H10 **Fronteira** Portalegre, C Portugal
42 M7 **Frontera** Coahuila de Zaragoza, NE Mexico
43 U14 **Frontera** Tabasco, SE Mexico
42 G3 **Fronteras** Sonora, NW Mexico
105 Q16 **Frontignan** Hérault, S France
56 D8 **Frontino** Antioquia, NW Colombia
23 V4 **Front Royal** Virginia, NE USA
109 J16 **Frosinone** anc. Frusino. Lazio, C Italy
109 K16 **Frosolone** Molise, C Italy
27 U7 **Frost** Texas, SW USA
23 U2 **Frostburg** Maryland, NE USA
25 X13 **Frostproof** Florida, SE USA
Frostviken see Kvarnbergsvattnet
97 M15 **Frövi** Örebro, C Sweden
96 F7 **Frøya** island W Norway
39 P5 **Fruita** Colorado, C USA
30 J9 **Fruitdale** South Dakota, N USA
25 W11 **Fruitland Park** Florida, SE USA
Frumentum see Formentera
153 S11 **Frunze** Oshskaya Oblast', SW Kyrgyzstan
Frunze see Bishkek
119 O9 **Frunzivka** Odes'ka Oblast', SW Ukraine
Frusino see Frosinone
110 E9 **Frutigen** Bern, W Switzerland
113 I17 **Frýdek-Místek** Ger. Friedek-Mistek. Severní Morava, SE Czech Republic
200 Qq16 **Fua'amotu** Tongatapu, S Tonga
202 A9 **Fuafatu** island Funafuti Atoll, C Tuvalu
202 A9 **Fuagea** island Funafuti Atoll, C Tuvalu
202 B8 **Fualifeke** atoll C Tuvalu
202 A8 **Fualopa** island Funafuti Atoll, C Tuvalu
157 K22 **Fuammulah** var. Gnaviyani Atoll. atoll S Maldives
167 R11 **Fu'an** Fujian, SE China
Fu-chien see Fujian
Fu-chou see Fuzhou
170 F13 **Fuchū** var. Hutyû. Hiroshima, Honshū, SW Japan
166 M13 **Fuchuan** Guangxi Zhuangzu Zizhiqu, S China
172 N11 **Fudai** Iwate, Honshū, C Japan
167 S11 **Fuding** Fujian, SE China
83 J20 **Fudua** spring/well S Kenya
106 M16 **Fuengirola** Andalucía, S Spain
106 J12 **Fuente de Cantos** Extremadura, W Spain
106 J11 **Fuente del Maestre** Extremadura, W Spain
106 L12 **Fuente Obejuna** Andalucía, S Spain
106 L6 **Fuentesaúco** Castilla-León, N Spain
64 O3 **Fuerte Olimpo** var. Olimpo. Alto Paraguay, NE Paraguay
42 H8 **Fuerte, Río** ≈ C Mexico
66 Q11 **Fuerteventura** island Islas Canarias, Spain, NE Atlantic Ocean
147 S14 **Fughmah** var. Faghman, Fugma. C Yemen
94 M2 **Fuglehuken** headland W Svalbard
207 T15 **Fugløya Bank** undersea feature E Norwegian Sea
Fugma see Fughmah
83 K16 **Fugugo** spring/well NE Kenya
164 L2 **Fuhai** var. Burultokay. Xinjiang Uygur Zizhiqu, NW China
167 P10 **Fu He** ≈ S China
Fuhkien see Fujian
102 J9 **Fuhlsbüttel** ✕ (Hamburg) Hamburg, N Germany
103 L14 **Fuhne** ≈ C Germany
Fu-hsin see Fuxin
Fujairah see Al Fujayrah
171 J17 **Fuji** var. Huzi. Shizuoka, Honshū, S Japan
167 Q12 **Fujian** var. Fu-chien, Fuhkien, Fujian Sheng, Fukien, Min. ◆ province SE China
166 I9 **Fu Jiang** ≈ C China
Fujian Sheng see Fujian
171 Ii17 **Fujieda** var. Huzieda. Shizuoka, Honshū, S Japan
Fuji, Mount/Fujiyama see Fuji-san
169 Y7 **Fujin** Heilongjiang, NE China
171 J16 **Fujinomiya** var. Huzinomiya. Shizuoka, Honshū, S Japan
171 J16 **Fuji-san** var. Fujiyama, Eng. Mount Fuji. ▲ Honshū, SE Japan
171 Jj17 **Fujisawa** var. Huzisawa. Kanagawa, Honshū, S Japan
171 J16 **Fuji-Yoshida** var. Huziyosida. Yamanashi, Honshū, S Japan
172 Oo4 **Fukagawa** var. Hukagawa. Hokkaidō, NE Japan
164 L5 **Fukang** Xinjiang Uygur Zizhiqu, W China
171 M8 **Fukaura** Aomori, Honshū, C Japan
200 R15 **Fukave** island Tongatapu Group, S Tonga
Fukien see Fujian
171 Gg14 **Fukuchiyama** var. Hukutiyama. Kyōto, Honshū, SW Japan
170 B12 **Fukue** var. Hukue. Nagasaki, Fukue-jima, SW Japan
170 B12 **Fukue-jima** island Gotō-rettō, SW Japan
171 Hh13 **Fukui** var. Hukui. Fukui, Honshū, SW Japan
171 Hh14 **Fukui** off. Fukui-ken, var. Hukui. ◆ prefecture Honshū, SW Japan
170 C12 **Fukuoka** var. Hukuoka; hist. Najima. Fukuoka, Kyūshū, SW Japan
170 Cc13 **Fukuoka** off. Fukuoka-ken, var. Hukuoka. ◆ prefecture Kyūshū, SW Japan
171 L13 **Fukushima** var. Hukusima. Fukushima, Honshū, C Japan
171 Mm7 **Fukushima** Hokkaidō, NE Japan
171 Kk14 **Fukushima** off. Fukushima-ken, var. Hukusima. ◆ prefecture Honshū, C Japan
170 F14 **Fukuyama** var. Hukuyama. Hiroshima, Honshū, SW Japan
78 G13 **Fulacunda** C Guinea-Bissau
133 P8 **Fūlādī, Kūh-e** ▲ E Afghanistan
197 K16 **Fulaga** island Lau Group, E Fiji
103 I17 **Fulda** Hessen, C Germany
31 S10 **Fulda** Minnesota, N USA
103 I16 **Fulda** ≈ C Germany
Fülek see Fil'akovo
Fulin see Hanyuan
166 K10 **Fuling** Sichuan, C China
37 T15 **Fullerton** California, SE USA
31 P15 **Fullerton** Nebraska, C USA
110 M8 **Fulpmes** Tirol, W Austria
22 G8 **Fulton** Kentucky, S USA
25 N2 **Fulton** Mississippi, S USA
29 V4 **Fulton** Missouri, C USA
20 H9 **Fulton** New York, NE USA
Fuman/Fumen see Fowman
105 R3 **Fumay** Ardennes, N France
104 M13 **Fumel** Lot-et-Garonne, SW France
171 K17 **Funabashi** var. Hunabasi. Chiba, Honshū, S Japan
202 B10 **Funafara** atoll C Tuvalu
202 C9 **Funafuti** ✕ Funafuti Atoll, C Tuvalu
Funafuti see Fongafale
202 F8 **Funafuti Atoll** atoll C Tuvalu
202 B9 **Funangongo** atoll C Tuvalu
95 F17 **Funäsdalen** Jämtland, C Sweden
66 O6 **Funchal** Madeira, Portugal, NE Atlantic Ocean
66 P5 **Funchal** ✕ Madeira, Portugal, NE Atlantic Ocean
56 F5 **Fundación** Magdalena, N Colombia
106 I8 **Fundão** var. Fundáo. Castelo Branco, C Portugal
11 O16 **Fundy, Bay of** bay Canada/USA
Fünen see Fyn
56 C13 **Fúnes** Nariño, SW Colombia
Fünfkirchen see Pécs
85 M19 **Funhalouro** Inhambane, S Mozambique
167 R6 **Funing** Jiangsu, E China
166 I14 **Funing** Yunnan, SW China
166 M7 **Funiu Shan** ▲▲ C China
79 U13 **Funtua** Katsina, N Nigeria
167 R12 **Fuqing** Fujian, SE China
85 M14 **Furancungo** Tete, NW Mozambique
172 P5 **Furano** var. Hurano. Hokkaidō, NE Japan
118 I15 **Furculeşti** Teleorman, S Romania
Füred see Balatonfüred
172 Qq7 **Füren-ko** ◎ Hokkaidō, NE Japan
149 R12 **Fürg** Fārs, S Iran
Furluk see Fârliug
Fürmanov see Furmanovka
151 S15 **Furmanovka** Kaz. Fürmanov. Zhambyl, S Kazakhstan
150 E9 **Furmanovo** Zapadnyy Kazakhstan, W Kazakhstan
61 L20 **Furnas, Represa de** ⊠ SE Brazil
191 Q14 **Furneaux Group** island group Tasmania, SE Australia
Furnes see Veurne
166 I10 **Furong Jiang** ≈ S China
144 I5 **Furqlus** Ḥimṣ, W Syria
102 F12 **Fürstenau** Niedersachsen, NW Germany
111 X8 **Fürstenfeld** Steiermark, SE Austria
103 L23 **Fürstenfeldbruck** Bayern, S Germany
102 P12 **Fürstenwalde** Brandenburg, NE Germany
103 K20 **Fürth** Bayern, S Germany
111 W3 **Furth bei Göttweig** Niederösterreich, NW Austria
172 O4 **Furubira** Hokkaidō, NE Japan
96 L12 **Furudal** Kopparberg, C Sweden
171 I14 **Furukawa** Gifu, Honshū, SW Japan
171 M12 **Furukawa** var. Hurukawa. Miyagi, Honshū, C Japan
56 F10 **Fusagasugá** Cundinamarca, C Colombia
Fusan see Pusan
Fushë-Arëzi/Fushë-Arrësi see Fushë-Arrëz
115 L18 **Fushë-Arrëz** var. Fushë-Arëzi, Fushë-Arrësi. Shkodër, N Albania
Fushë-Kruja see Fushë-Krujë
115 K19 **Fushë-Krujë** var. Fushë-Kruja. Durrës, C Albania
169 V12 **Fushun** var. Fou-shan, Fu-shun. Liaoning, NE China
Fusin see Fuxin
110 G10 **Fusio** Ticino, S Switzerland
169 X11 **Fusong** Jilin, NE China
103 K24 **Füssen** Bayern, S Germany
166 K15 **Fusui** prev. Funan. Guangxi Zhuangzu Zizhiqu, S China
Futa Jallon see Fouta Djallon
65 G18 **Futaleufú** Los Lagos, S Chile
114 K10 **Futog** Serbia, NW Yugoslavia
171 K17 **Futtsu** var. Huttu. Chiba, Honshū, S Japan
197 E16 **Futuna** island S Vanuatu
202 D12 **Futuna, Île** island S Wallis and Futuna
167 Q11 **Futun Xi** ≈ SE China
166 L5 **Fuxian** var. Fu Xian. Shaanxi, C China
Fuxian see Wafangdian
166 G13 **Fuxian Hu** ◎ SW China
169 U12 **Fuxin** var. Fou-hsin, Fu-hsin, Fusin. Liaoning, NE China
Fuxing see Wangmo
167 P7 **Fuyang** Anhui, E China
167 O4 **Fuyang He** ≈ E China
169 U7 **Fuyu** Heilongjiang, NE China
Fuyu/Fu-yü see Songyuan
169 Z6 **Fuyuan** Heilongjiang, NE China
164 M3 **Fuyun** var. Koktokay. Xinjiang Uygur Zizhiqu, NW China
113 L22 **Füzesabony** Heves, E Hungary
167 R12 **Fuzhou** var. Foochow, Fu-chou. Fujian, SE China
Fuzhou see Linchuan
143 W13 **Füzuli** Rus. Fizuli. SW Azerbaijan
121 I20 **Fyadory** Rus. Fëdory. Brestskaya Voblasts', SW Belarus
97 G24 **Fyn** off. Fyns Amt, var. Fünen. ◆ county C Denmark
97 G23 **Fyn** Ger. Fünen. island C Denmark
98 H12 **Fyne, Loch** inlet W Scotland, UK
97 E16 **Fyresvatnet** ◎ S Norway
FYR Macedonia/FYROM see Macedonia, FYR
Fyzabad see Feyzābād

G

83 O14 **Gaalkacyo** var. Galka'yo, It. Galcaio. Mudug, C Somalia
Gabakly see Kabakly
116 H8 **Gabare** Oblast Montana, NW Bulgaria
104 K15 **Gabas** ≈ SW France
37 T7 **Gabbs** Nevada, W USA
84 B12 **Gabela** Cuanza Sul, W Angola
Gaberones see Gaborone
201 X14 **Gabert** island Caroline Islands, E Micronesia
76 M7 **Gabès** var. Qâbis. E Tunisia
76 M6 **Gabès, Golfe de** Ar. Khalīj Qābis. gulf E Tunisia
Gablonz an der Neisse see Jablonec nad Nisou
Gablös see Cavalese
81 E18 **Gabon** off. Gabonese Republic. ◆ republic C Africa
85 I20 **Gaborone** prev. Gaberones. ● (Botswana) South East, SE Botswana
85 I20 **Gaborone** ✕ South East, SE Botswana
106 K8 **Gabriel y Galán, Embalse de** ⊠ W Spain
149 U15 **Gābrīk, Rūd-e** ≈ SE Iran
116 J9 **Gabrovo** Loveshka Oblast, C Bulgaria
78 H12 **Gabú** prev. Nova Lamego. E Guinea-Bissau
31 O6 **Gackle** North Dakota, N USA
115 I15 **Gacko** S Bosnia and Herzegovina
161 F17 **Gadag** Karnātaka, W India
95 G15 **Gäddede** Jämtland, C Sweden
165 S12 **Gadê** Qinghai, C China
Gades/Gadier/Gadir/Gadire see Cádiz
107 P15 **Gádor, Sierra de** ▲▲ S Spain
155 S15 **Gadra** Sind, SE Pakistan
25 Q3 **Gadsden** Alabama, S USA
38 H15 **Gadsden** Arizona, SW USA
Gadyach see Hadyach
81 H15 **Gadzi** Mambéré-Kadéï, SW Central African Republic
118 J13 **Găeşti** Dâmboviţa, S Romania
109 J17 **Gaeta** Lazio, C Italy
109 J17 **Gaeta, Golfo di** var. Gulf of Gaeta. gulf C Italy
196 L14 **Gaferut** atoll Caroline Islands, W Micronesia
23 Q10 **Gaffney** South Carolina, SE USA
Gäfle see Gävle
Gäfleborg see Gävleborg
76 M6 **Gafsa** var. Qafşah. W Tunisia
Gafurov see Ghafurov
130 J3 **Gagarin** Smolenskaya Oblast', W Russian Federation
153 O10 **Gagarin** Jizzakh Wiloyati, C Uzbekistan
103 G21 **Gaggenau** Baden-Württemberg, SW Germany
196 F16 **Gagil Tamil** var. Gagil-Tomil. island Caroline Islands, W Micronesia
Gagil-Tomil see Gagil Tamil
131 O4 **Gagino** Nizhegorodskaya Oblast', W Russian Federation
109 Q19 **Gagliano del Capo** Puglia, SE Italy
96 L13 **Gagnef** Kopparberg, C Sweden
78 M17 **Gagnoa** C Ivory Coast
11 N10 **Gagnon** Québec, E Canada
Gago Coutinho see Lumbala N'Guimbo
175 Tt8 **Gag, Pulau** island E Indonesia
78 P3 **Gagra** NW Georgia
33 S13 **Gahanna** Ohio, N USA
149 R13 **Gahkom** Hormozgān, S Iran
Gahnpa see Ganta
59 Q19 **Gaíba, Laguna** ◎ E Bolivia
159 T13 **Gaibanda** var. Gaibandah. Rajshahi, NW Bangladesh
Gaibandah see Gaibanda
Gaibhlte, Cnoc Mór na n see Galtymore Mountain
111 R9 **Gail** ≈ S Austria
103 I21 **Gaildorf** Baden-Württemberg, S Germany
105 N15 **Gaillac** var. Gaillac-sur-Tarn. Tarn, S France
Gaillac-sur-Tarn see Gaillac
Gaillimh see Galway
Gaillimhe, Cuan na see Galway Bay
111 Q9 **Gailtaler Alpen** ▲▲ S Austria
65 J17 **Gaimán** Chaco, S Argentina
22 K8 **Gainesboro** Tennessee, S USA
25 V10 **Gainesville** Florida, SE USA
25 T2 **Gainesville** Georgia, SE USA
29 U8 **Gainesville** Missouri, C USA
27 T5 **Gainesville** Texas, SW USA
111 X5 **Gainfarn** Niederösterreich, NE Austria
99 N18 **Gainsborough** E England, UK
190 G6 **Gairdner, Lake** salt lake South Australia
94 L8 **Gaissane** ▲ N Norway
45 T15 **Gaital, Cerro** ▲ C Panama
23 W3 **Gaithersburg** Maryland, NE USA
169 U13 **Gaizhou** Liaoning, NE China
Gaiziņ see Gaiziņa Kalns
120 J9 **Gaiziņa Kalns** var. Gaiziņ. ▲ E Latvia
Gaja see Villeneuve-sur-Lot
174 L15 **Gajahmungkur, Danau** ◎ Jawa, S Indonesia
41 S10 **Gakona** Alaska, USA
Galaassiya see Galaosiye
Ğalāğil see Jalājil
Galam, Pulau see Gelam, Pulau
64 J6 **Galán, Cerro** ▲ NW Argentina
113 H21 **Galanta** Hung. Galánta. Západné Slovensko, SW Slovakia
152 L11 **Galaosiye** Rus. Galaassiya. Bukhoro Wiloyati, C Uzbekistan
59 B17 **Galápagos** off. Provincia de Galápagos. ◆ province Ecuador, E Pacific Ocean
199 M9 **Galapagos Fracture Zone** tectonic feature E Pacific Ocean
200 O10 **Galapagos Rise** undersea feature E Pacific Ocean
98 K13 **Galashiels** SE Scotland, UK
118 M12 **Galaţi** Ger. Galatz. Galaţi, E Romania
118 L12 **Galaţi** ◆ county E Romania
109 Q19 **Galatina** Puglia, SE Italy
109 Q19 **Galatone** Puglia, SE Italy
Galatz see Galaţi
23 R8 **Galax** Virginia, NE USA
Galaymor see Kala-i-Mor
Galcaio see Gaalkacyo
66 P11 **Gáldar** Gran Canaria, Islas Canarias, Spain, NE Atlantic Ocean
96 F11 **Galdhøpiggen** ▲ S Norway
42 I4 **Galeana** Chihuahua, N Mexico
43 O9 **Galeana** Nuevo León, NE Mexico
62 P9 **Galeão** ✕ (Rio de Janeiro) Rio de Janeiro, SE Brazil
175 T6 **Galela** Pulau Halmahera, E Indonesia
41 O9 **Galena** Alaska, USA
32 K10 **Galena** Illinois, N USA
29 R7 **Galena** Kansas, C USA
29 T8 **Galena** Missouri, C USA
47 V15 **Galeota Point** headland Trinidad, Trinidad and Tobago
107 P13 **Galera** Andalucía, S Spain
47 Y16 **Galera Point** headland Trinidad, Trinidad and Tobago
58 A5 **Galera, Punta** headland NW Ecuador
32 K12 **Galesburg** Illinois, N USA
32 J7 **Galesville** Wisconsin, N USA
20 F12 **Galeton** Pennsylvania, NE USA
118 H9 **Gâlgău** Hung. Galgó; prev. Gilgău. Sălaj, NW Romania
Galgó see Gâlgău
Galgóc see Hlohovec
83 N15 **Galguduud** off. Gobolka Galguduud. ◆ region E Somalia
143 Q9 **Gali** W Georgia
129 N14 **Galich** Kostromskaya Oblast', NW Russian Federation
116 H7 **Galiche** Oblast Montana, NW Bulgaria
106 H3 **Galicia** anc. Gallaecia. ◆ autonomous community NW Spain
66 M8 **Galicia Bank** undersea feature E Atlantic Ocean
Galilee see HaGalil
189 W7 **Galilee, Lake** ◎ Queensland, NE Australia
Galilee, Sea of see Tiberias, Lake
108 E11 **Galileo Galilei** ✕ (Pisa) Toscana, C Italy
33 S12 **Galion** Ohio, N USA
Galka'yo see Gaalkacyo
82 H11 **Gallabat** Gedaref, E Sudan
Gallaecia see Galicia
108 C7 **Gallarate** Lombardia, NW Italy
29 S2 **Gallatin** Missouri, C USA
22 J8 **Gallatin** Tennessee, S USA
35 R11 **Gallatin Peak** ▲ Montana, NW USA
35 R12 **Gallatin River** ≈ Montana/Wyoming, NW USA
161 J26 **Galle** prev. Point de Galle. Southern Province, SW Sri Lanka
107 S5 **Gállego** ≈ NE Spain
200 N9 **Gallego Rise** undersea feature E Pacific Ocean
Gallegos see Río Gallegos
65 H23 **Gallegos, Río** ≈ Argentina/Chile
Gallia see France
24 K10 **Galliano** Louisiana, S USA
116 G13 **Gallikós** ≈ N Greece
39 S12 **Gallinas Peak** ▲ New Mexico, SW USA
56 H3 **Gallinas, Punta** headland NE Colombia
39 T11 **Gallinas River** ≈ New Mexico, SW USA
109 Q19 **Gallipoli** Puglia, SE Italy
Gallipoli see Gelibolu
Gallipoli Peninsula see Gelibolu Yarımadası
33 T15 **Gallipolis** Ohio, N USA
94 J12 **Gällivare** Norrbotten, N Sweden
111 T4 **Gallneukirchen** Oberösterreich, N Austria
107 Q7 **Gallo** ≈ C Spain
95 G17 **Gällö** Jämtland, C Sweden
109 I23 **Gallo, Capo** headland Sicilia, Italy, C Mediterranean Sea
39 P13 **Gallo Mountains** ▲▲ New Mexico, SW USA
20 G8 **Galloo Island** island New York, NE USA
99 H15 **Galloway, Mull of** headland S Scotland, UK
39 P10 **Gallup** New Mexico, SW USA
107 R5 **Gallur** Aragón, NE Spain
Gâlma see Guelma
37 O8 **Galt** California, W USA
76 C10 **Galtat-Zemmour** C Western Sahara
97 G22 **Galten** Århus, C Denmark
99 D20 **Galtymore Mountain** Ir. Cnoc Mór na nGaibhlte. ▲ S Ireland
99 D20 **Galty Mountains** Ir. Na Gaibhlte. ▲▲ S Ireland
32 K11 **Galva** Illinois, N USA
27 X12 **Galveston** Texas, SW USA
27 W11 **Galveston Bay** inlet Texas, SW USA
27 W12 **Galveston Island** island Texas, SW USA
63 B18 **Gálvez** Santa Fe, C Argentina
99 C18 **Galway** Ir. Gaillimh. W Ireland
99 B18 **Galway** Ir. Gaillimh. cultural region W Ireland
99 B18 **Galway Bay** Ir. Cuan na Gaillimhe. bay W Ireland
85 F18 **Gam** Otjozondjupa, NE Namibia
194 G14 **Gama** ≈ SW PNG
171 Hh16 **Gamagōri** Aichi, Honshū, SW Japan
56 F7 **Gamarra** Cesar, N Colombia
Gámas see Kaamanen
164 L17 **Gamba** Xizang Zizhiqu, W China
79 P14 **Gambaga** NE Ghana
82 G13 **Gambēla** W Ethiopia
40 K10 **Gambell** Saint Lawrence Island, Alaska, USA
78 E12 **Gambia** off. Republic of The Gambia, The Gambia. ◆ republic W Africa
78 I12 **Gambia** Fr. Gambie. ≈ W Africa
66 K12 **Gambia Plain** undersea feature E Atlantic Ocean
Gambie see Gambia
33 T13 **Gambier** Ohio, N USA
203 Y13 **Gambier, Îles** island group E French Polynesia
190 G10 **Gambier Islands** island group South Australia
81 H19 **Gamboma** Plateaux, E Congo
81 G16 **Gamboula** Mambéré-Kadéï, SW Central African Republic
39 P10 **Gamerco** New Mexico, SW USA
143 V12 **Gamiş Dağı** ▲ W Azerbaijan
Gamlakarleby see Kokkola
97 N18 **Gamleby** Kalmar, S Sweden
Gammelstad see Gammelstaden
95 J14 **Gammelstaden** var. Gammelstad. Norrbotten, N Sweden
Gammouda see Sidi Bouzid
161 J25 **Gampaha** Western Province, W Sri Lanka
161 K25 **Gampola** Central Province, C Sri Lanka
176 Uu8 **Gam, Pulau** island E Indonesia
178 J5 **Gâm, Sông** ≈ N Vietnam
94 L7 **Gamvik** Finnmark, N Norway
156 H13 **Gan** Addu Atoll, C Maldives
Gan see Gansu, China
Gan see Jiangxi, China
Ganaane see Juba
39 O10 **Ganado** Arizona, SW USA
27 U12 **Ganado** Texas, SW USA
12 L14 **Gananoque** Ontario, SE Canada
Ganāveh see Bandar-e Gonāveh
143 V11 **Gäncä** Rus. Gyandzha; prev. Kirovabad, Yelisavetpol. W Azerbaijan
Ganchi see Ghonchí
Gand see Gent
84 B13 **Ganda** var. Mariano Machado, Port. Vila Mariano Machado. Benguela, W Angola
81 L22 **Gandajika** Kasai Oriental, S Zaire
159 O12 **Gandak** Nep. Nārāyāni. ≈ India/Nepal
11 U11 **Gander** Newfoundland, Newfoundland and Labrador, SE Canada
11 U11 **Gander** ✕ Newfoundland, Newfoundland and Labrador, E Canada
102 G11 **Ganderkesee** Niedersachsen, NW Germany
107 T7 **Gandesa** Cataluña, NE Spain
160 B10 **Gāndhīdhām** Gujarāt, W India
160 D10 **Gāndhīnagar** Gujarāt, W India
160 F9 **Gāndhi Sāgar** ◎ C India
107 T11 **Gandía** País Valenciano, E Spain
165 O10 **Gang** Qinghai, W China
158 G9 **Gangānagar** Rājasthān, NW India
158 I12 **Gangāpur** Rājasthān, N India
159 S17 **Ganga Sāgar** West Bengal, NE India
Gangavathi see Gangāwati
161 G17 **Gangāwati** var. Gangavathi. Karnātaka, C India
165 S9 **Gangca** var. Shaliuhe. Qinghai, C China
164 H14 **Gangdisê Shan** Eng. Kailas Range. ▲▲ W China
105 Q15 **Ganges** Hérault, S France
159 P13 **Ganges** Ben. Padma. ≈ Bangladesh/India see also Padma
Ganges Cone see Ganges Fan
181 S3 **Ganges Fan** var. Ganges Cone. undersea feature N Bay of Bengal
159 U17 **Ganges, Mouths of the** delta Bangladesh/India
109 K23 **Gangi** anc. Engyum. Sicilia, Italy, C Mediterranean Sea
158 K8 **Gangotri** Uttar Pradesh, N India
Gangra see Çankırı
159 S11 **Gangtok** Sikkim, N India
165 W11 **Gangu** Gansu, C China
169 U5 **Gan He** ≈ NE China
175 T9 **Gani** Pulau Halmahera, E Indonesia
167 O12 **Gan Jiang** ≈ S China
152 H15 **Gannaly** Akhalskiy Velayat, S Turkmenistan
169 U7 **Gannan** Heilongjiang, NE China
105 P10 **Gannat** Allier, C France
35 T14 **Gannett Peak** ▲ Wyoming, C USA
31 O10 **Gannvalley** South Dakota, N USA
111 Y3 **Gänserndorf** Niederösterreich, NE Austria
Gansos, Lago dos see Goose Lake
165 T9 **Gansu** var. Gan, Gansu Sheng, Kansu. ◆ province N China
Gansu Sheng see Gansu
78 K16 **Ganta** var. Gahnpa. NE Liberia
190 H11 **Gantheaume, Cape** headland South Australia
Gantsevichi see Hantsavichy
167 Q6 **Ganyu** var. Qingkou. Jiangsu, E China
150 D12 **Ganyushkino** Atyrau, SW Kazakhstan
167 O12 **Ganzhou** Jiangxi, S China
79 Q10 **Gao** Gao, E Mali
79 R10 **Gao** ◆ region SE Mali
167 O10 **Gao'an** Jiangxi, S China
167 N5 **Gaoping** Shanxi, C China
165 S8 **Gaotai** Gansu, N China
Gaoth Dobhair see Gweedore
79 O14 **Gaoua** SW Burkina
78 I13 **Gaoual** Moyenne-Guinée, N Guinea
Gaoxiong see Kaohsiung
167 R7 **Gaoyou** var. Dayishan. Jiangsu, E China
167 R7 **Gaoyou Hu** ◎ E China
166 M15 **Gaozhou** Guangdong, S China
105 T13 **Gap** anc. Vapincum. Hautes-Alpes, SE France
164 G13 **Gar** var. Gar Xincun. Xizang Zizhiqu, W China
Garabekevyul/Garabekewül see Karabekaul
Garabogazköl see Kara-Bogaz-Gol
45 V15 **Garachiné** Darién, SE Panama
45 V16 **Garachiné, Punta** headland SE Panama
Garagan see Karagan
56 G10 **Garagoa** Boyacá, C Colombia
Garagöl see Karagel'
Garagum see Garagumy
Garagum Kanaly see Garagumskiy Kanal
152 E12 **Garagumskiy Kanal** var. Kara Kum Canal, Karakumskiy Kanal, Turkm. Garagum Kanaly. canal C Turkmenistan
152 F12 **Garagumy** var. Qara Qum, Eng. Black Sand Desert, Kara Kum, Turkm. Garagum; prev. Peski Karakumy. desert C Turkmenistan
191 S4 **Garah** New South Wales, SE Australia
66 O11 **Garajonay** ▲ Gomera, Islas Canarias, Spain NE Atlantic Ocean
116 M8 **Gara Khitrino** Varnenska Oblast, NE Bulgaria
78 L13 **Garalo** Sikasso, SW Mali
Garam see Hron
Garamābnyyaz see Karamet-Niyaz
Garamszentkereszt see Žiar nad Hronom
79 Q13 **Garango** S Burkina
61 Q15 **Garanhuns** Pernambuco, E Brazil
196 H5 **Garapan** Saipan, S Northern Mariana Islands
Gárassavon see Kaaresuvanto
80 J13 **Garba** Bamingui-Bangoran, N Central African Republic
83 L16 **Garbahaarrey** It. Garba Harre. Gedo, SW Somalia
Garba Harre see Garbahaarrey
83 J18 **Garba Tula** Eastern, C Kenya
29 N9 **Garber** Oklahoma, C USA
36 L4 **Garberville** California, W USA
102 I12 **Garbsen** Niedersachsen, N Germany
62 K9 **Garça** São Paulo, S Brazil
106 L10 **García de Solá, Embalse de** ⊠ C Spain
105 Q14 **Gard** ◆ department S France
105 Q14 **Gard** ≈ S France
108 F7 **Garda, Lago di** var. Benaco, Eng. Lake Garda, Ger. Gardasee. ◎ NE Italy
Garda, Lake see Garda, Lago di
Gardan Divāl see Gardan Dīwāl
155 Q5 **Gardan Dīwāl** var. Gardan Divāl. Wardag, C Afghanistan
105 S15 **Gardanne** Bouches-du-Rhône, SE France
Gardasee see Garda, Lago di
102 L12 **Gardelegen** Sachsen-Anhalt, C Germany
12 B10 **Garden** ≈ Ontario, S Canada
25 X6 **Garden City** Georgia, SE USA
28 I6 **Garden City** Kansas, C USA
29 S5 **Garden City** Missouri, C USA
27 N8 **Garden City** Texas, SW USA
25 P3 **Gardendale** Alabama, S USA
33 P5 **Garden Island** island Michigan, N USA
24 M11 **Garden Island Bay** bay Louisiana, S USA
33 O5 **Garden Peninsula** peninsula Michigan, N USA
Garden State see New Jersey
97 I14 **Gardermoen** Akershus, S Norway
Gardeyz see Gardēz
155 Q6 **Gardēz** var. Gardeyz, Gordiaz. Paktīā, E Afghanistan
95 G14 **Gardiken** ◎ N Sweden
21 Q7 **Gardiner** Maine, NE USA
35 S12 **Gardiner** Montana, NW USA
21 N13 **Gardiners Island** island New York, NE USA
Gardner Island see Nikumaroro
21 T6 **Gardner Lake** ◎ Maine, NE USA
37 Q6 **Gardnerville** Nevada, W USA
Gardo see Qardho
108 F7 **Gardone Val Trompia** Lombardia, N Italy
Garegegasnjárga see Karigasniemi
40 F17 **Gareloi Island** island Aleutian Islands, Alaska, USA
108 B10 **Garessio** Piemonte, NE Italy
34 M9 **Garfield** Washington, NW USA
33 U11 **Garfield Heights** Ohio, N USA
Gargaliani see Gargaliánoi
117 D21 **Gargaliánoi** var. Gargaliani. Pelopónnisos, S Greece
109 N15 **Gargano, Promontorio del** headland SE Italy
110 J8 **Gargellen** Graubünden, W Switzerland
95 I14 **Gargnäs** Västerbotten, N Sweden

◆ Country ● Country Capital ◇ Dependent Territory ○ Dependent Territory Capital ◆ Administrative Region ✕ International Airport ▲ Mountain ▲▲ Mountain Range ⩙ Volcano ≈ River ◎ Lake ⊠ Reservoir

120 C11 **Gargždai** Gargždai, W Lithuania
160 J13 **Garhchiroli** Mahārāshtra, C India
159 O15 **Garhwa** Bihār, N India
176 Ww11 **Gariau** Irian Jaya, E Indonesia
85 E24 **Garies** Northern Cape, W South Africa
83 K19 **Garissa** Coast, E Kenya
23 V11 **Garland** North Carolina, SE USA
27 T6 **Garland** Texas, SW USA
38 L1 **Garland** Utah, W USA
108 D8 **Garlasco** Lombardia, N Italy
121 F14 **Garliava** Kaunas, S Lithuania
Garm *see* Gharm
148 M9 **Garm, Āb-e** ***var.*** Rūd-e Khersān. ≈ SW Iran
103 K25 **Garmisch-Partenkirchen** Bayern, S Germany
149 O5 **Garmsār** ***prev.*** Qishlaq. Semnān, N Iran
Garmser *see* Darvīshān
31 V12 **Garner** Iowa, C USA
23 U9 **Garner** North Carolina, SE USA
29 Q5 **Garnett** Kansas, C USA
101 M25 **Garnich** Luxembourg, SW Luxembourg
190 M8 **Garnpung, Lake** *salt lake* New South Wales, SE Australia
Garoe *see* Garoowe
Garoet *see* Garut
159 U13 **Gāro Hills** *hill range* NE India
104 K13 **Garonne** ***anc.*** Garumna. ≈ S France
82 P13 **Garoowe** ***var.*** Garoe. Nugaal, N Somalia
80 F12 **Garoua** ***var.*** Garua. Nord, N Cameroon
81 G14 **Garoua Boulaï** Est, E Cameroon
79 O10 **Garou, Lac** ◎ C Mali
194 M11 **Garove Island** *island* Witu Islands, C PNG
97 L16 **Garphyttan** Örebro, C Sweden
31 R11 **Garretson** South Dakota, N USA
33 Q11 **Garrett** Indiana, N USA
35 Q10 **Garrison** Montana, NW USA
30 M4 **Garrison** North Dakota, N USA
27 X8 **Garrison** Texas, SW USA
30 L4 **Garrison Dam** *dam* North Dakota, N USA
106 J9 **Garrovillas** Extremadura, W Spain
Garrygala *see* Kara-Kala
15 Jj6 **Garry Lake** ◎ Northwest Territories, N Canada
Gars *see* Gars am Kamp
111 W3 **Gars am Kamp** ***var.*** Gars. Niederösterreich, NE Austria
83 K20 **Garsen** Coast, S Kenya
Garshy *see* Karshi
12 F10 **Garson** Ontario, S Canada
111 T5 **Garsten** Oberösterreich, N Austria
Gartar *see* Qianning
104 M10 **Gartempe** ≈ C France
Gartog *see* Markam
Garua *see* Garoua
85 D21 **Garub** Karas, SW Namibia
Garumna *see* Garonne
174 Jj15 **Garut** ***prev.*** Garoet. Jawa, C Indonesia
193 C20 **Garvie Mountains** ⛰ South Island, NZ
112 N12 **Garwolin** Siedlce, E Poland
27 U12 **Garwood** Texas, SW USA
Gar Xincun *see* Gar
33 N11 **Gary** Indiana, N USA
27 X7 **Gary** Texas, SW USA
170 E12 **Garyū-san** ▲ Kyūshū, SW Japan
164 G13 **Gar Zangbo** ≈ W China
166 F8 **Garzê** Sichuan, C China
56 E12 **Garzón** Huila, S Colombia
152 B13 **Gasan-Kuli** ***var.*** Esenguly. Balkanskiy Velayat, W Turkmenistan
33 P13 **Gas City** Indiana, N USA
104 K15 **Gascogne** ***Eng.*** Gascony. *cultural region* S France
Gascogne, Golfe de *see* Gascony, Gulf of
28 V5 **Gasconade River** ≈ Missouri, C USA
Gascony *see* Gascogne
104 H15 **Gascony, Gulf of** ***var.*** Golfe de Gascogne. *gulf* France/Spain
188 H9 **Gascoyne Junction** Western Australia
181 V8 **Gascoyne Plain** *undersea feature* E Indian Ocean
188 H9 **Gascoyne River** ≈ Western Australia
199 I12 **Gascoyne Tablemount** *undersea feature* N Tasman Sea
69 U6 **Gash** ***var.*** Nahr al Qāsh. ≈ W Sudan
155 X3 **Gasherbrum** ▲ NE Pakistan
165 N9 **Gas Hu** ◎ C China
79 X12 **Gashua** Yobe, NE Nigeria
176 Uu9 **Gasim** Irian Jaya, E Indonesia
195 N12 **Gasmata** New Britain, E PNG
25 V14 **Gasparilla Island** *island* Florida, SE USA
174 Jj11 **Gaspar, Selat** *strait* W Indonesia
13 Y6 **Gaspé** Québec, SE Canada
13 Z6 **Gaspé, Cap de** *headland* Québec, SE Canada
13 X6 **Gaspé, Péninsule de** ***var.*** Péninsule de la Gaspésie. *peninsula* Québec, SE Canada
Gaspésie, Péninsule de la *see* Gaspé, Péninsule de
171 Ll12 **Gas-san** ▲ Honshū, C Japan
79 W15 **Gassol** Taraba, E Nigeria
Gastein *see* Badgastein
23 R10 **Gastonia** North Carolina, SE USA
23 V8 **Gaston, Lake** ▣ North Carolina/Virginia, SE USA
117 D19 **Gastoúni** Dytikí Ellás, S Greece
65 I17 **Gastre** Chubut, S Argentina
Gat *see* Ghāt
107 P15 **Gata, Cabo de** *headland* S Spain
Gata, Cape *see* Gátas, Akrotíri
107 T11 **Gata de Gorgos** País Valenciano, E Spain
118 E12 **Gătaia** ***Ger.*** Gataja, ***Hung.*** Gátalja; ***prev.*** Gáttája. Timiș, W Romania
Gataja/Gátalja *see* Gătaia
124 Nn4 **Gátas, Akrotíri** ***var.*** Cape Gata. *headland* S Cyprus
106 J8 **Gata, Sierra de** ⛰ W Spain
128 G13 **Gatchina** Leningradskaya Oblast', NW Russian Federation
23 P8 **Gate City** Virginia, NE USA
99 M14 **Gateshead** NE England, UK
15 Jj2 **Gateshead Island** *island* Northwest Territories, N Canada
23 X8 **Gatesville** North Carolina, SE USA
27 S8 **Gatesville** Texas, SW USA
12 L12 **Gatineau** Québec, SE Canada
12 L11 **Gatineau** ≈ Ontario/Québec, SE Canada
23 N9 **Gatlinburg** Tennessee, S USA
Gatooma *see* Kadoma
Gáttája *see* Gătaia
45 T14 **Gatún, Lago** ▣ C Panama
61 N14 **Gaturiano** Piauí, NE Brazil
99 O22 **Gatwick** ✕ (London) SE England, UK
197 J15 **Gau** ***prev.*** Ngau. *island* C Fiji
Gaua *see* Santa Maria
106 L16 **Gaucín** Andalucía, S Spain
Gauhāti *see* Guwāhāti
120 I8 **Gauja** ***Ger.*** Aa. ≈ Estonia/Latvia
120 I7 **Gaujiena** Alūksne, NE Latvia
Gaul/Gaule *see* France
96 H9 **Gauldalen** *valley* S Norway
23 R5 **Gauley River** ≈ West Virginia, NE USA
101 D19 **Gaurain-Ramecroix** Hainaut, SW Belgium
97 F15 **Gausta** ▲ S Norway
85 J21 **Gauteng** ***off.*** Gauteng Province; ***prev.*** Pretoria-Witwatersrand-Vereeniging. ⬖ *province* NE South Africa
Gauteng *see* Germiston, South Africa
Gauteng *see* Johannesburg, South Africa
176 Y10 **Gauttier, Pegunungan** ⛰ Irian Jaya, E Indonesia
149 P14 **Gāvbandī** Hormozgān, S Iran
117 H25 **Gavdopoúla** *island* SE Greece
117 H26 **Gávdos** *island* SE Greece
104 K16 **Gave de Pau** ***var.*** Gave-de-Pay. ≈ SW France
Gave-de-Pay *see* Gave de Pau
104 J16 **Gave d'Oloron** ≈ SW France
101 E18 **Gavere** Oost-Vlaanderen, NW Belgium
96 N13 **Gävle** ***var.*** Gäfle; ***prev.*** Gefle. Gävleborg, C Sweden
96 M11 **Gävleborg** ***var.*** Gäfleborg, Gefleborg. ⬖ *county* C Sweden
96 O13 **Gävlebukten** *bay* C Sweden
128 L16 **Gavrilov-Yam** Yaroslavskaya Oblast', W Russian Federation
195 P15 **Gawa Island** *island* SE Papau New Guinea
190 I9 **Gawler** South Australia
190 G7 **Gawler Ranges** *hill range* South Australia
Gawso *see* Goaso
168 H11 **Gaxun Nur** ◎ N China
159 P14 **Gaya** Bihār, N India
79 S13 **Gaya** Dosso, SW Niger
Gaya *see* Kyjov
33 Q6 **Gaylord** Michigan, N USA
31 U9 **Gaylord** Minnesota, N USA
189 Y9 **Gayndah** Queensland, E Australia
129 T12 **Gayny** Komi-Permyatskiy Avtonomnyy Okrug, NW Russian Federation
Gaysin *see* Haysyn
Gayvorno *see* Hayvoron
144 E11 **Gaza** ***Ar.*** Ghazzah, ***Heb.*** 'Azza. NE Gaza Strip
85 L20 **Gaza** ***off.*** Província de Gaza. ⬖ *province* SW Mozambique
152 I9 **Gaz-Achak** ***Turkm.*** Gazojak. Lebapskiy Velayat, NE Turkmenistan
Gazalkent *see* Ghazalkent
152 C11 **Gazandzhyk** ***Turkm.*** Gazanjyk; ***prev.*** Kazandzhik. Balkanskiy Velayat, W Turkmenistan
Gazanjyk *see* Gazandzhyk
79 V12 **Gazaoua** Maradi, S Niger
144 E11 **Gaza Strip** ***Ar.*** Qiṭā' Ghazzah. *disputed region* SW Asia
195 P11 **Gazelle Peninsula** *headland* New Britain, E PNG
197 J5 **Gazelle, Récif de la** *reef* C New Caledonia
Gazgan *see* Ghozghon
Gazi Antep *see* Gaziantep
142 M16 **Gaziantep** ***var.*** Gazi Antep; ***prev.*** Aintab, Antep. Gaziantep, S Turkey
142 M17 **Gaziantep** ***var.*** Gazi Antep. ⬖ *province* S Turkey
116 M13 **Gaziköy** Tekirdağ, NW Turkey
124 O3 **Gazimağusa** ***var.*** Famagusta, ***Gk.*** Ammóchostos. E Cyprus
124 Nn2 **Gazimağusa Körfezi** ***var.*** Famagusta Bay, ***Gk.*** Kólpos Ammóchostos. *bay* E Cyprus
152 K11 **Gazli** Bukhoro Wiloyati, C Uzbekistan
Gazojak *see* Gaz-Achak
81 K15 **Gbadolite** Equateur, NW Zaire
78 K16 **Gbanga** ***var.*** Gbarnga. N Liberia
Gbarnga *see* Gbanga
79 S14 **Gbéroubouè** ***var.*** Béroubouay. N Benin
79 W16 **Gboko** Benue, S Nigeria
Gcuwa *see* Butterworth
112 J7 **Gdańsk** ***Fr.*** Dantzig, ***Ger.*** Danzig. Gdańsk, N Poland
112 J7 **Gdańsk** ***off.*** Województwo Gdańskie, ***Fr.*** Dantzig, ***Ger.*** Danzig. ⬖ *province* N Poland
Gdan'skaya Bukhta/Gdańsk, Gulf of *see* Danzig, Gulf of
Gdańska, Zakota *see* Danzig, Gulf of
Gdańskie, Województwo *see* Gdańsk
Gdingen *see* Gdynia
128 F13 **Gdov** Pskovskaya Oblast', W Russian Federation
112 I6 **Gdynia** ***Ger.*** Gdingen. Gdańsk, N Poland
28 M10 **Geary** Oklahoma, C USA
Geavvú *see* Kevo
78 H12 **Gêba, Rio** ≈ C Guinea-Bissau
175 Tt8 **Gebe, Pulau** *island* E Indonesia
142 E11 **Gebze** Kocaeli, NW Turkey
124 O2 **Geçitkale** ***Gk.*** Lefkonico, Lefkónikon. NE Cyprus
82 H10 **Gedaref** ***var.*** Al Qaḍārif, El Gedaref. Gedaref, E Sudan
82 H10 **Gedaref** ⬖ *state* E Sudan
82 B11 **Gedid Ras el Fil** Southern Darfur, W Sudan
101 I23 **Gedinne** Namur, SE Belgium
142 E13 **Gediz** Kütahya, W Turkey
142 C14 **Gediz Nehri** ≈ W Turkey
83 N14 **Gedlegubē** SE Ethiopia
83 L17 **Gedo** ***off.*** Gobolka Gedo. ⬖ *region* SW Somalia
97 I25 **Gedser** Storstrøm, SE Denmark
101 I16 **Geel** ***var.*** Gheel. Antwerpen, N Belgium
191 N13 **Geelong** Victoria, SE Australia
Ge'e'mu *see* Golmud
101 I14 **Geertruidenberg** Noord-Brabant, S Netherlands
102 H10 **Geeste** ≈ NW Germany
102 J10 **Geesthacht** Schleswig-Holstein, N Germany
191 P17 **Geeveston** Tasmania, SE Australia
Gefle *see* Gävle
Gefleborg *see* Gävleborg
164 G13 **Gê'gyai** Xizang Zizhiqu, W China
79 X12 **Geidam** Yobe, NE Nigeria
9 T11 **Geikie** ≈ Saskatchewan, C Canada
96 F13 **Geilo** Buskerud, S Norway
96 E10 **Geiranger** Møre og Romsdal, S Norway
103 I22 **Geislingen** ***var.*** Geislingen an der Steige. Baden-Württemberg, SW Germany
Geislingen an der Steige *see* Geislingen
83 F20 **Geita** Mwanza, NW Tanzania
97 G15 **Geithus** Buskerud, S Norway
166 H14 **Gejiu** ***var.*** Kochiu. Yunnan, S China
Gëkdepe *see* Geok-Tepe
152 E9 **Geklengkui, Solonchak** ***var.*** Solonchak Goklenkuy. *salt marsh* NW Turkmenistan
83 D14 **Gel** ≈ W Sudan
109 K25 **Gela** ***prev.*** Terranova di Sicilia. Sicilia, Italy, C Mediterranean Sea
Gêladaindong *see* Glandaindong
83 N14 **Geladī** SE Ethiopia
174 Kk11 **Gelam, Pulau** ***var.*** Pulau Galam. *island* N Indonesia
100 L11 **Gelderland** ***prev. Eng.*** Guelders. ⬖ *province* E Netherlands
100 J13 **Geldermalsen** Gelderland, C Netherlands
103 D14 **Geldern** Nordrhein-Westfalen, W Germany
101 K15 **Geldrop** Noord-Brabant, SE Netherlands
101 L17 **Geleen** Limburg, SE Netherlands
130 K14 **Gelendzhik** Krasnodarskiy Kray, SW Russian Federation
Gelib *see* Jilib
142 B11 **Gelibolu** ***Eng.*** Gallipoli. Çanakkale, NW Turkey
117 L14 **Gelibolu Yarımadası** ***Eng.*** Gallipoli Peninsula. *peninsula* NW Turkey
Gelinting, Teluk *see* Geliting, Teluk
175 Qq16 **Geliting, Teluk** ***var.*** Teluk Gelinting. *bay* Nusa Tenggara, S Indonesia
83 O14 **Gellinsor** Mudug, C Somalia
103 H18 **Gelnhausen** Hessen, C Germany
103 E14 **Gelsenkirchen** Nordrhein-Westfalen, W Germany
85 C20 **Geluk** Hardap, SW Namibia
101 H20 **Gembloux** Namur, Belgium
194 I12 **Gembogl** Chimbu, C PNG
81 J16 **Gemena** Equateur, NW Zaire
101 L14 **Gemert** Noord-Brabant, SE Netherlands
142 E11 **Gemlik** Bursa, NW Turkey
Gem of the Mountains *see* Idaho
108 J6 **Gemona del Friuli** Friuli-Venezia Giulia, NE Italy
Gem State *see* Idaho
Genalē Wenz *see* Juba
174 Ll7 **Genali, Danau** ◎ Borneo, N Indonesia
101 G19 **Genappe** Walloon Brabant, C Belgium
143 P14 **Genç** Bingöl, E Turkey
Genck *see* Genk
100 M9 **Genemuiden** Overijssel, E Netherlands
65 K14 **General Acha** La Pampa, C Argentina
63 C21 **General Alvear** Buenos Aires, E Argentina
64 I12 **General Alvear** Mendoza, W Argentina
63 B20 **General Arenales** Buenos Aires, E Argentina
63 D21 **General Belgrano** Buenos Aires, E Argentina
204 H3 **General Bernardo O'Higgins** *Chilean research station* Antarctica
43 O8 **General Bravo** Nuevo León, NE Mexico
64 M7 **General Capdevila** Chaco, N Argentina
General Carrera, Lago *see* Buenos Aires, Lago
43 N9 **General Cepeda** Coahuila de Zaragoza, NE Mexico
65 K15 **General Conesa** Río Negro, E Argentina
63 G18 **General Enrique Martínez** Treinta y Tres, E Uruguay
64 L3 **General Eugenio A. Garay** ***var.*** Fortín General Eugenio Garay; ***prev.*** Yrendagüé. Nueva Asunción, NW Paraguay
63 C18 **General Galarza** Entre Ríos, E Argentina
63 E22 **General Guido** Buenos Aires, E Argentina
General José F.Uriburu *see* Zárate
63 E22 **General Juan Madariaga** Buenos Aires, E Argentina
43 O16 **General Juan N Alvarez** ✕ (Acapulco) Guerrero, S Mexico
63 B22 **General La Madrid** Buenos Aires, E Argentina
63 E21 **General Lavalle** Buenos Aires, E Argentina
General Machado *see* Camacupa
64 I8 **General Manuel Belgrano, Cerro** ▲ W Argentina
43 O8 **General Mariano Escobero** ✕ (Monterrey) Nuevo León, NE Mexico
63 B20 **General O'Brien** Buenos Aires, E Argentina
64 K13 **General Pico** La Pampa, C Argentina
64 M7 **General Pinedo** Chaco, N Argentina
63 B20 **General Pinto** Buenos Aires, E Argentina
63 E22 **General Pirán** Buenos Aires, E Argentina
45 N15 **General, Río** ≈ S Costa Rica
65 I15 **General Roca** Río Negro, C Argentina
179 Rr17 **General Santos** ***off.*** General Santos City. Mindanao, S Philippines
43 O9 **General Terán** Nuevo León, NE Mexico
116 N7 **General Toshevo** ***Rom.*** I.G.Duca, ***prev.*** Casim, Kasimköj. Varnenska Oblast, NE Bulgaria
63 B20 **General Viamonte** Buenos Aires, E Argentina
63 A20 **General Villegas** Buenos Aires, E Argentina
Gênes *see* Genova
20 E11 **Genesee River** ≈ New York/Pennsylvania, NE USA
32 K11 **Geneseo** Illinois, N USA
20 F10 **Geneseo** New York, NE USA
59 L14 **Geneshuaya, Río** ≈ N Bolivia
25 Q8 **Geneva** Alabama, S USA
32 M10 **Geneva** Illinois, N USA
31 Q16 **Geneva** Nebraska, C USA
20 G10 **Geneva** New York, NE USA
33 U10 **Geneva** Ohio, NE USA
Geneva *see* Genève
110 B10 **Geneva, Lake** ***Fr.*** Lac de Genève, Lac Léman, le Léman, ***Ger.*** Genfer See. ◎ France/Switzerland
110 A10 **Genève** ***Eng.*** Geneva, ***Ger.*** Genf, ***It.*** Ginevra. Genève, SW Switzerland
110 A11 **Genève** ***Eng.*** Geneva, ***Ger.*** Genf, ***It.*** Ginevra. ⬖ *canton* SW Switzerland
110 A10 **Genève** ***var.*** Geneva. ✕ Vaud, SW Switzerland
Genève, Lac de *see* Geneva, Lake
Genf *see* Genève
Genfer See *see* Geneva, Lake
169 S5 **Gen He** ≈ NE China
Genichesk *see* Heniches'k
106 L14 **Genil** ≈ S Spain
101 K18 **Genk** ***var.*** Genck. Limburg, NE Belgium
170 Cc12 **Genkai-nada** *gulf* Kyūshū, SW Japan
109 C19 **Gennargentu, Monti del** ▲ Sardegna, Italy, C Mediterranean Sea
101 M14 **Gennep** Limburg, SE Netherlands
32 M10 **Genoa** Illinois, N USA
31 Q15 **Genoa** Nebraska, C USA
Genoa *see* Genova
Genoa, Gulf of *see* Genova, Golfo di
108 D10 **Genova** ***Eng.*** Genoa, ***Fr.*** Gênes; ***anc.*** Genua. Liguria, NW Italy
108 D10 **Genova, Golfo di** ***Eng.*** Gulf of Genoa. *gulf* NW Italy
59 C17 **Genovesa, Isla** ***var.*** Tower Island. *island* Galapagos Islands, Ecuador, E Pacific Ocean
Genshū *see* Wŏnju
101 E17 **Gent** ***Eng.*** Ghent, ***Fr.*** Gand. Oost-Vlaanderen, NW Belgium
174 J15 **Genteng** Jawa, C Indonesia
102 M12 **Genthin** Sachsen-Anhalt, E Germany
29 R9 **Gentry** Arkansas, C USA
Genua *see* Genova
109 I15 **Genzano di Roma** Lazio, C Italy
Geokchay *see* Göyçay
152 F13 **Geok-Tepe** ***var.*** Gëkdepe, ***Turkm.*** Gökdepe. Akhalskiy Velayat, C Turkmenistan
126 Gg1 **Georga, Zemlya** ***Eng.*** George Land. *island* Zemlya Frantsa-Iosifa, N Russian Federation
85 G26 **George** Western Cape, S South Africa
31 S11 **George** Iowa, C USA
11 O5 **George** ≈ Newfoundland and Labrador/Québec, E Canada
67 C25 **George Island** *island* S Falkland Islands
191 R10 **George, Lake** ◎ New South Wales, SE Australia
83 E18 **George, Lake** ◎ SW Uganda
25 W10 **George, Lake** ◎ Florida, SE USA
20 L8 **George, Lake** ▣ New York, NE USA
George Land *see* Georga, Zemlya
Georgenburg *see* Jurbarkas
George River *see* Kangiqsualujjuaq
66 G8 **Georges Bank** *undersea feature* W Atlantic Ocean
193 A21 **George Sound** *sound* South Island, NZ
67 F15 **Georgetown** ○ (Ascension Island) NW Ascension Island
189 V5 **Georgetown** Queensland, NE Australia
191 P15 **George Town** Tasmania, SE Australia
46 I4 **George Town** Great Exuma Island, C Bahamas
46 D8 **George Town** ***var.*** Georgetown. ○ (Cayman Islands) Grand Cayman, SW Cayman Islands
78 H12 **Georgetown** E Gambia
57 T8 **Georgetown** ● (Guyana) N Guyana
173 Ff3 **George Town** ***var.*** Penang, Pinang. Pinang, Peninsular Malaysia
47 Y14 **Georgetown** Saint Vincent, Saint Vincent and the Grenadines
23 Y4 **Georgetown** Delaware, NE USA
25 R6 **Georgetown** Georgia, SE USA
22 M5 **Georgetown** Kentucky, S USA
23 T13 **Georgetown** South Carolina, SE USA
27 S10 **Georgetown** Texas, SW USA
57 T8 **Georgetown** ✕ N Guyana
205 U16 **George V Coast** *physical region* Antarctica
205 T15 **George V Land** *physical region* Antarctica
204 J7 **George VI Ice Shelf** *ice shelf* Antarctica
204 J6 **George VI Sound** *sound* Antarctica
27 S14 **George West** Texas, SW USA
143 R9 **Georgia** ***off.*** Republic of Georgia, ***Geor.*** Sak'art'velo, ***Rus.*** Gruzinskaya SSR, Gruziya; ***prev.*** Georgian SSR. ◆ *republic* SW Asia
25 S5 **Georgia** ***off.*** State of Georgia; also known as Empire State of the South, Peach State. ⬖ *state* SE USA
12 F12 **Georgian Bay** *lake bay* Ontario, S Canada
8 L17 **Georgia, Strait of** *strait* British Columbia, W Canada
Georgi Dimitrov *see* Kostenets
Georgi Dimitrov, Yazovir *see* Koprinka, Yazovir
116 M9 **Georgi Traykov, Yazovir** ▣ NE Bulgaria
Georgiu-Dezh *see* Liski
151 W10 **Georgiyevka** Semipalatinsk, E Kazakhstan
151 T6 **Georgiyevka** Zhambyl, SE Kazakhstan
131 N15 **Georgiyevsk** Stavropol'skiy Kray, SW Russian Federation
102 G13 **Georgsmarienhütte** Niedersachsen, NW Germany
205 O1 **Georg von Neumayer** *German research station* Antarctica
103 M16 **Gera** Thüringen, E Germany
103 K16 **Gera** ≈ C Germany
101 E19 **Geraardsbergen** Oost-Vlaanderen, SW Belgium
117 F21 **Geráki** Pelopónnisos, S Greece
29 W5 **Gerald** Missouri, C USA
49 V8 **Geral de Goiás, Serra** ⛰ E Brazil
193 G20 **Geraldine** Canterbury, South Island, NZ
188 H11 **Geraldton** Western Australia
10 E11 **Geraldton** Ontario, S Canada
62 J12 **Geral, Serra** ⛰ S Brazil
175 P16 **Gerampi** Sumbawa, S Indonesia
105 U6 **Gérardmer** Vosges, NE France
Gerasa *see* Jarash
Gerdauen *see* Zheleznodorozhnyy
41 Q11 **Gerdine, Mount** ▲ Alaska, USA
142 H11 **Gerede** Bolu, N Turkey
142 H11 **Gerede Çayı** ≈ N Turkey
154 M8 **Gereshk** Helmand, SW Afghanistan
103 L24 **Geretsried** Bayern, S Germany
107 P14 **Gérgal** Andalucía, S Spain
194 K13 **Gerhards, Cape** *headland* C PNG
30 I14 **Gering** Nebraska, C USA
37 R3 **Gerlach** Nevada, W USA
Gerlachfalvi Csúcs/Gerlachovka *see* Gerlachovský Štít
113 L18 **Gerlachovský Štít** ***var.*** Gerlachovka, ***Ger.*** Gerlsdorfer Spitze, ***Hung.*** Gerlachfalvi Csúcs; ***prev.*** Stalinov Štít, ***Ger.*** Franz-Josef Spitze, ***Hung.*** Ferencz-József Csúcs. ▲ N Slovakia
110 E8 **Gerlafingen** Solothurn, NW Switzerland
Gerlsdorfer Spitze *see* Gerlachovský Štít
145 V3 **Germak** E Iraq
German East Africa *see* Tanzania
Germanicopolis *see* Çankırı
Germanicum, Mare/German Ocean *see* North Sea
Germanovichi *see* Hyermanavichy
German Southwest Africa *see* Namibia
22 E10 **Germantown** Tennessee, S USA
103 I15 **Germany** ***off.*** Federal Republic of Germany, ***Ger.*** Bundesrepublik Deutschland, Deutschland. ◆ *federal republic* N Europe
103 L23 **Germering** Bayern, SE Germany
85 J21 **Germiston** ***var.*** Gauteng. Gauteng, NE South Africa
Gernika *see* Gernika-Lumo
107 P2 **Gernika-Lumo** ***var.*** Gernika, Guernica, Guernica y Lumo. País Vasco, N Spain
171 Ii15 **Gero** Gifu, Honshū, SW Japan
117 F22 **Geroliménas** Pelopónnisos, S Greece
107 W5 **Gerona** ⬖ *province* Cataluña, NE Spain
Gerona *see* Girona
101 H21 **Gerpinnes** Hainaut, S Belgium
104 L15 **Gers** ⬖ *department* S France
104 L14 **Gers** ≈ S France
Gerunda *see* Girona
142 K10 **Gerze** Sinop, N Turkey
164 I13 **Gêrzê** Xizang Zizhiqu, W China
Gesoriacum/Gessoriacum *see* Boulogne-sur-Mer
101 J21 **Gesves** Namur, SE Belgium
95 J20 **Geta** Åland, SW Finland
107 N8 **Getafe** Madrid, C Spain
97 J21 **Getinge** Halland, S Sweden
20 F16 **Gettysburg** Pennsylvania, NE USA
31 N8 **Gettysburg** South Dakota, N USA
204 K12 **Getz Ice Shelf** *ice shelf* Antarctica
143 S15 **Gevaş** Van, SE Turkey
Gevgeli *see* Gevgelija
115 Q20 **Gevgelija** ***var.*** Đevđelija, Djevdjelija, ***Turk.*** Gevgeli. SE FYR Macedonia
105 T10 **Gex** Ain, E France
94 I3 **Geysir** *physical region* SW Iceland
142 F11 **Geyve** Sakarya, NW Turkey
82 G10 **Gezira** ⬖ *state* E Sudan
111 V3 **Gföhl** Niederösterreich, N Austria
85 H22 **Ghaap Plateau** ***Afr.*** Ghaapplato. *plateau* C South Africa
Ghaapplato *see* Ghaap Plateau
Ghaba *see* Al Ghābah
144 J8 **Ghāb, Tall** ▲ SE Syria
145 Q9 **Ghadaf, Wādī al** *dry watercourse* C Iraq
Ghadamès *see* Ghadāmis
76 M9 **Ghadāmis** ***var.*** Ghadamès, Rhadames. W Libya
147 Y10 **Ghadan** E Oman
77 O10 **Ghaddūwah** C Libya
153 Q11 **Ghafurov** ***Rus.*** Gafurov; ***prev.*** Sovetabad. NW Tajikistan
159 N12 **Ghāghara** ≈ S Asia
155 P13 **Ghaibi Dero** Sind, SE Pakistan
147 Y10 **Ghalat** E Oman
153 O11 **Ghallaorol** Jizzakh Wiloyati, C Uzbekistan
145 W11 **Ghamūkah, Hawr** ◎ S Iraq
79 P15 **Ghana** ***off.*** Republic of Ghana. ◆ *republic* W Africa
147 X12 **Ghānah** *spring/well* S Oman
Ghanongga *see* Ranongga
Ghansi/Ghansiland *see* Ghanzi
85 F18 **Ghanzi** ***var.*** Khanzi. Ghanzi, W Botswana
85 G19 **Ghanzi** ***var.*** Ghansi, Ghansiland, Khanzi. ⬖ *district* C Botswana
69 T14 **Ghanzi** ***var.*** Knanzi. ≈ Botswana/South Africa
Ghap'an *see* Kapan
144 F13 **Gharandal** Ma'ān, SW Jordan
Gharbt, Jabal al *see* Liban, Jebel
76 K7 **Ghardaïa** N Algeria
145 U14 **Gharibīyah, Sha'īb al** ≈ S Iraq
153 R12 **Gharm** ***Rus.*** Garm. C Tajikistan
155 P17 **Gharo** Sind, SE Pakistan
145 W10 **Gharrāf, Shaṭṭ al** ≈ S Iraq
Gharvān *see* Gharyān
77 O7 **Gharyān** ***var.*** Gharvān. NW Libya
76 M11 **Ghāt** ***var.*** Gat. SW Libya
Ghawdex *see* Gozo
147 U8 **Ghayathi** Abū Ẓaby, W UAE
Ghazāl, Baḥr al *see* Ghazal, Bahr el
80 H9 **Ghazal, Bahr el** ***var.*** Soro. *seasonal river* C Chad
82 E13 **Ghazal, Bahr el** ***var.*** Baḥr al Ghazāl. ≈ S Sudan
153 Q9 **Ghazalkent** ***Rus.*** Gazalkent. Toshkent Wiloyati, E Uzbekistan
76 H6 **Ghazaouet** NW Algeria
158 J10 **Ghāziābād** Uttar Pradesh, N India
159 O13 **Ghāzīpur** Uttar Pradesh, N India
155 Q6 **Ghaznī** ***var.*** Ghazni. Ghaznī, E Afghanistan
155 P7 **Ghaznī** ⬖ *province* SE Afghanistan
Ghazzah *see* Gaza
Gheel *see* Geel
Ghelîzâne *see* Relizane
Ghent *see* Gent
Gheorghe Brațul *see* Sfântu Gheorghe, Brațul
Gheorghe Gheorghiu-Dej *see* Onești
118 J10 **Gheorgheni** ***prev.*** Gheorghieni, Sînt-Miclăuș, ***Ger.*** Niklasmarkt, ***Hung.*** Gyergyószentmiklós. Harghita, C Romania
Gheorghieni *see* Gheorgheni
118 H10 **Gherla** ***Ger.*** Neuschliss, ***Hung.*** Szamosújvár; ***prev.*** Armenierstadt. Cluj, NW Romania
Gheweifat *see* Ghuwayfāt
152 L11 **Ghijduwon** ***Rus.*** Gizhduvan. Bukhoro Wiloyati, C Uzbekistan
Ghilan *see* Gīlān
109 C18 **Ghilarza** Sardegna, Italy, C Mediterranean Sea
Ghilizane *see* Relizane
Ghimbi *see* Gīmbī
Ghiriș *see* Câmpia Turzii
104 F2 **Ghisonaccia** Corse, France, C Mediterranean Sea
Ghizo *see* Gizo
153 Q11 **Ghonchí** ***Rus.*** Ganchi. NW Tajikistan
Ghor *see* Ghowr
159 T13 **Ghoraghat** Rajshahi, NW Bangladesh
155 R13 **Ghotki** Sind, SE Pakistan
154 M5 **Ghowr** ***var.*** Ghor. ⬖ *province* C Afghanistan
152 M10 **Ghozghon** ***Rus.*** Gazgan. Nawoiy Wiloyati, C Uzbekistan
153 T13 **Ghŭdara** ***var.*** Gudara, ***Rus.*** Kudara. SE Tajikistan
159 R13 **Ghugri** ≈ N India
153 S14 **Ghund** ***Rus.*** Gunt. ≈ SE Tajikistan
Ghurdaqah *see* Hurghada
154 J5 **Ghūrīān** Herāt, W Afghanistan
147 T8 **Ghuwayfāt** ***var.*** Gheweifat. Abū Ẓaby, W UAE
123 Mm17 **Ghuzayyil, Sabkhat** *salt lake* N Libya
153 N13 **Ghuzor** ***Rus.*** Guzar. Qashqadaryo Wiloyati, S Uzbekistan
117 G17 **Giáltra** Évvoia, C Greece
Giamame *see* Jamaame
116 F13 **Giannitsá** ***var.*** Yiannitsá. Kentrikí Makedonía, N Greece
109 F14 **Giannutri, Isola di** *island* Archipelago Toscano, C Italy
98 F13 **Giant's Causeway** ***Ir.*** Clochán an Aifir. *lava flow* N Northern Ireland, UK
178 J15 **Gia Rai** Minh Hai, S Vietnam
109 L24 **Giarre** Sicilia, Italy, C Mediterranean Sea
46 I7 **Gibara** Holguín, E Cuba
31 O16 **Gibbon** Nebraska, C USA
34 K11 **Gibbon** Oregon, NW USA
35 P11 **Gibbonsville** Idaho, NW USA
66 A13 **Gibb's Hill** *hill* S Bermuda
94 I9 **Gibostad** Troms, N Norway
106 I14 **Gibraleón** Andalucía, S Spain
106 L16 **Gibraltar** ○ (Gibraltar) S Gibraltar
106 L16 **Gibraltar** ◇ *UK dependent territory* SW Europe
Gibraltar, Détroit de/Gibraltar, Estrecho de *see* Gibraltar, Strait of
106 J17 **Gibraltar, Strait of** ***Fr.*** Détroit de Gibraltar, ***Sp.*** Estrecho de Gibraltar. *strait* Atlantic Ocean/Mediterranean Sea
33 S11 **Gibsonburg** Ohio, N USA
32 M13 **Gibson City** Illinois, N USA
188 L8 **Gibson Desert** *desert* Western Australia
8 L17 **Gibsons** British Columbia, SW Canada
155 N12 **Gīdār** Baluchistān, SW Pakistan
161 I17 **Giddalūr** Andhra Pradesh, E India
27 U10 **Giddings** Texas, SW USA
29 Y8 **Gideon** Missouri, C USA
83 I15 **Gīdolē** SW Ethiopia
120 H13 **Giedraičiai** Molėtai, E Lithuania
105 O7 **Gien** Loiret, C France
103 G17 **Giessen** Hessen, W Germany
100 O6 **Gieten** Drenthe, NE Netherlands
25 Y13 **Gifford** Florida, SE USA
15 Ll1 **Gifford** ≈ Baffin Island, Northwest Territories, NE Canada
102 J12 **Gifhorn** Niedersachsen, N Germany
9 P13 **Gift Lake** Alberta, W Canada
171 Hh15 **Gifu** ***var.*** Gihu. Gifu, Honshū, SW Japan
171 I14 **Gifu** ***off.*** Gifu-ken, ***var.*** Gihu. ⬖ *prefecture* Honshū, SW Japan
130 M13 **Gigant** Rostovskaya Oblast', SW Russian Federation
42 E8 **Giganta, Sierra de la** ⛰ W Mexico
56 E12 **Gigante** Huila, S Colombia
116 I7 **Gigen** Loveshka Oblast, NW Bulgaria
Giggiga *see* Jijiga
98 G12 **Gigha Island** *island* SW Scotland, UK
109 E14 **Giglio, Isola del** *island* Archipelago Toscano, C Italy
Gihu *see* Gifu
106 L2 **Gijón** Asturias, NW Spain
83 D20 **Gikongoro** SW Rwanda
38 K14 **Gila Bend** Arizona, SW USA
38 J14 **Gila Bend Mountains** ⛰ Arizona, SW USA
39 N14 **Gila Mountains** ⛰ Arizona, SW USA
38 I15 **Gila Mountains** ⛰ Arizona, SW USA
148 M4 **Gīlān** ***off.*** Ostān-e Gīlān; ***var.*** Ghilan, Guilan. ⬖ *province* NW Iran
Gilani *see* Gnjilane
38 L14 **Gila River** ≈ Arizona, SW USA
31 W4 **Gilbert** Minnesota, N USA
Gilbert Islands *see* Tungaru
8 L16 **Gilbert, Mount** ▲ British Columbia, SW Canada
189 U4 **Gilbert River** ≈ Queensland, NE Australia
1 C6 **Gilbert Seamounts** *undersea feature* NE Pacific Ocean
35 S7 **Gildford** Montana, NW USA
85 P15 **Gilé** Zambézia, NE Mozambique
32 K4 **Gile Flowage** ◎ Wisconsin, N USA
190 G7 **Giles, Lake** *salt lake* South Australia
77 U12 **Gilf Kebir Plateau** ***Ar.*** Haḍabat al Jilf al Kabīr. *plateau* SW Egypt
191 R6 **Gilgandra** New South Wales, SE Australia
Gîlgău *see* Gâlgău
83 I19 **Gilgil** Rift Valley, SW Kenya
191 S4 **Gil Gil Creek** ≈ New South Wales, SE Australia
155 V3 **Gilgit** Jammu and Kashmir, NE Pakistan
155 V3 **Gilgit** ≈ N Pakistan
9 X11 **Gillam** Manitoba, C Canada
97 J22 **Gilleleje** Frederiksborg, E Denmark
32 K14 **Gillespie** Illinois, N USA
29 W13 **Gillett** Arkansas, C USA
35 X12 **Gillette** Wyoming, C USA
99 P22 **Gillingham** SE England, UK
205 X6 **Gillock Island** *island* Antarctica
181 O16 **Gillot** ✕ (St-Denis) N Réunion

◆ Country
● Country Capital
◇ Dependent Territory
○ Dependent Territory Capital
⬖ Administrative Region
✕ International Airport
▲ Mountain
⛰ Mountain Range
Volcano
≈ River
◎ Lake
▣ Reservoir

67 H25 **Gill Point** *headland* E Saint Helena
32 M12 **Gilman** Illinois, N USA
27 W6 **Gilmer** Texas, SW USA
Gilolo *see* Halmahera, Pulau
83 G14 **Gīlo Wenz** ≈ SW Ethiopia
37 O10 **Gilroy** California, W USA
194 H12 **Giluwe, Mount** ▲ W PNG
126 M14 **Gilyuy** ≈ SE Russian Federation
101 I14 **Gilze** Noord-Brabant, S Netherlands
172 O14 **Gima** Okinawa, Kume-jima, SW Japan
82 H13 **Gīmbī** *It.* Ghimbi. W Ethiopia
47 T12 **Gimie, Mount** ▲ C Saint Lucia
9 X16 **Gimli** Manitoba, S Canada
Gimma *see* Jīma
97 O14 **Gimo** Uppsala, C Sweden
104 L15 **Gimone** ≈ S France
Gimpoe *see* Gimpu
175 Pp9 **Gimpu** *prev.* Gimpoe. Sulawesi, C Indonesia
190 F5 **Gina** South Australia
Ginevra *see* Genève
101 J19 **Gingelom** Limburg, NE Belgium
188 I12 **Gingin** Western Australia
179 R14 **Gingoog** Mindanao, S Philippines
83 K14 **Gīnīr** S Ethiopia
Giohar *see* Jawhar
109 O17 **Gioia del Colle** Puglia, SE Italy
109 M22 **Gioia, Golfo di** *gulf* S Italy
Giona *see* Gkióna
117 I16 **Gioúra** *island* Vóreioi Sporádes, Greece, Aegean Sea
109 O17 **Giovinazzo** Puglia, SE Italy
Gipeswic *see* Ipswich
Gipuzkoa *see* Guipúzcoa
Giran *see* Ilan
32 K14 **Girard** Illinois, N USA
29 R7 **Girard** Kansas, C USA
27 O6 **Girard** Texas, SW USA
56 E10 **Girardot** Cundinamarca, C Colombia
180 M7 **Giraud Seamount** *undersea feature* SW Indian Ocean
85 A15 **Giraul** ≈ SW Angola
98 L9 **Girdle Ness** *headland* NE Scotland, UK
143 N11 **Giresun** *var.* Kerasunt; *anc.* Cerasus, Pharnacia. Giresun, NE Turkey
143 N12 **Giresun** *var.* Kerasunt. ◈ *province* NE Turkey
143 N12 **Giresun Dağları** ▲▲ N Turkey
77 X10 **Girga** *var.* Girgeh, Jirjā. C Egypt
Girgeh *see* Girga
Girgenti *see* Agrigento
194 H10 **Girgir, Cape** *headland* NW PNG
159 Q15 **Girīdīh** Bihār, NE India
191 P6 **Girilambone** New South Wales, SE Australia
Girin *see* Jilin
124 R12 **Girne** *Gk.* Kerýneia, Kyrenia. N Cyprus
107 X5 **Girona** *var.* Gerona; *anc.* Gerunda. Cataluña, NE Spain
104 J12 **Gironde** ◈ *department* SW France
104 J11 **Gironde** *estuary* SW France
107 V5 **Gironella** Cataluña, NE Spain
105 N15 **Girou** ≈ S France
99 H14 **Girvan** W Scotland, UK
26 M9 **Girvin** Texas, SW USA
192 Q9 **Gisborne** Gisborne, North Island, NZ
192 P9 **Gisborne** *off.* Gisborne District. ◈ *unitary authority* North Island, NZ
Giseifu *see* Ŭijŏngbu
Gisenye *see* Gisenyi
83 D19 **Gisenyi** *var.* Gisenye. NW Rwanda
97 K20 **Gislaved** Jönköping, S Sweden
105 N4 **Gisors** Eure, N France
Gissar *see* Hisor
153 P12 **Gissar Range** *Rus.* Gissarskiy Khrebet. ▲▲ Tajikistan/Uzbekistan
Gissarskiy Khrebet *see* Gissar Range
101 B16 **Gistel** West-Vlaanderen, W Belgium
110 F9 **Giswil** Unterwalden, C Switzerland
117 B16 **Gitánes** *ancient monument* Ípeiros, W Greece
83 E20 **Gitarama** C Rwanda
83 E20 **Gitega** C Burundi
Githio *see* Gýtheio
110 H11 **Giubiasco** Ticino, S Switzerland
108 K13 **Giulianova** Abruzzi, C Italy
Giulie, Alpi *see* Julian Alps
Giumri *see* Gyumri
118 M13 **Giurgeni** Ialomiţa, SE Romania
118 J15 **Giurgiu** Giurgiu, S Romania
118 J14 **Giurgiu** ◈ *county* SE Romania
97 F22 **Give** Vejle, C Denmark
105 R2 **Givet** Ardennes, N France
105 R11 **Givors** Rhône, E France
85 K19 **Giyani** Northern, NE South Africa
82 I13 **Giyon** C Ethiopia
Gîza/Gizeh *see* El Gîza
77 V8 **Giza, Pyramids of** *ancient monument* N Egypt
Gizhduvan *see* Ghijduwon
127 Oo8 **Gizhiga** Magadanskaya Oblast', E Russian Federation
127 Oo8 **Gizhiginskaya Guba** *bay* E Russian Federation
195 T14 **Gizo** Gizo, NW Solomon Islands
195 T14 **Gizo** *var.* Ghizo. *island* NW Solomon Islands
112 N7 **Giżycko** *Ger.* Lötzen. Suwałki, NE Poland
Gízymałów *see* Hrymayliv
Gjakovë *see* Đakovica
96 F12 **Gjende** ◎ S Norway
97 F17 **Gjerstad** Aust-Agder, S Norway
Gjilan *see* Gnjilane
Gjinokastër *see* Gjirokastër
115 L23 **Gjirokastër** *var.* Gjirokastra; *prev.* Gjinokastër, *Gk.* Argyrokastron, *It.* Argirocastro. Gjirokastër, S Albania
115 L22 **Gjirokastër** ◈ *district* S Albania
Gjirokastra *see* Gjirokastër
15 K3 **Gjoa Haven** King William Island, Northwest Territories, NW Canada
96 H13 **Gjøvik** Oppland, S Norway
115 J22 **Gjuhëzës, Kepi i** *headland* SW Albania
Gjurgjevac *see* Đurđevac
117 E18 **Gkióna** *var.* Giona. ▲▲ C Greece
124 Oo3 **Gkréko, Akrotíri** *var.* Cape Greco, Pidálion. *headland* E Cyprus
101 I18 **Glabbeek-Zuurbemde** Vlaams Brabant, C Belgium
11 R14 **Glace Bay** Cape Breton Island, Nova Scotia, SE Canada
9 O16 **Glacier** British Columbia, SW Canada
41 W12 **Glacier Bay** *inlet* Alaska, USA
34 I7 **Glacier Peak** ▲ Washington, NW USA
23 Q7 **Glade Spring** Virginia, NE USA
27 W7 **Gladewater** Texas, SW USA
189 Y8 **Gladstone** Queensland, E Australia
190 I8 **Gladstone** South Australia
9 X16 **Gladstone** Manitoba, S Canada
33 O5 **Gladstone** Michigan, N USA
29 R4 **Gladstone** Missouri, C USA
33 Q7 **Gladwin** Michigan, N USA
97 J15 **Glafsfjorden** ◎ C Sweden
94 H2 **Gláma** *physical region* NW Iceland
86 F7 **Gláma** ≈ SE Norway
114 F13 **Glamoč** W Bosnia and Herzegovina
99 J22 **Glamorgan** *cultural region* S Wales, UK
97 G24 **Glamsbjerg** Fyn, C Denmark
179 Rr17 **Glan** Mindanao, S Philippines
97 M17 **Glan** ◎ S Sweden
111 T9 **Glan** ≈ SE Austria
103 F19 **Glan** ≈ W Germany
165 N13 **Glandaindong** *var.* Gêladaindong. ▲ C China
Glaris *see* Glarus
110 H9 **Glarner Alpen** *Eng.* Glarus Alps. ▲▲ E Switzerland
110 H8 **Glarus** Glarus, E Switzerland
110 H9 **Glarus** *Fr.* Glaris. ◈ *canton* C Switzerland
Glarus Alps *see* Glarner Alpen
29 N3 **Glasco** Kansas, C USA
98 I12 **Glasgow** S Scotland, UK
22 K7 **Glasgow** Kentucky, S USA
29 T4 **Glasgow** Missouri, C USA
35 W7 **Glasgow** Montana, NW USA
23 T6 **Glasgow** Virginia, NE USA
98 I12 **Glasgow** ✕ W Scotland, UK
9 S14 **Glaslyn** Saskatchewan, S Canada
20 I16 **Glassboro** New Jersey, NE USA
26 L10 **Glass Mountains** ▲▲ Texas, SW USA
99 K23 **Glastonbury** SW England, UK
Glatz *see* Kłodzko
103 N16 **Glauchau** Sachsen, E Germany
Glavn'a Morava *see* Velika Morava
115 N16 **Glavnik** Serbia, S Yugoslavia
131 T1 **Glazov** Udmurtskaya Respublika, NW Russian Federation
Głda *see* Gwda
111 U8 **Gleinalpe** ▲▲ SE Austria
111 W8 **Gleisdorf** Steiermark, SE Austria
Gleiwitz *see* Gliwice
41 S11 **Glenallen** Alaska, USA
104 F7 **Glénan, Îles** *island group* NW France
193 G21 **Glenavy** Canterbury, South Island, NZ
8 H5 **Glenboyle** Yukon Territory, NW Canada
23 X3 **Glen Burnie** Maryland, NE USA
38 L8 **Glen Canyon** *canyon* Utah, W USA
38 L8 **Glen Canyon Dam** *dam* Arizona, SW USA
32 K15 **Glen Carbon** Illinois, N USA
12 E17 **Glencoe** Ontario, S Canada
85 K22 **Glencoe** KwaZulu/Natal, E South Africa
31 U9 **Glencoe** Minnesota, N USA
98 H10 **Glen Coe** *valley* N Scotland, UK
38 K13 **Glendale** Arizona, SW USA
37 S15 **Glendale** California, W USA
190 G5 **Glendambo** South Australia
35 Y8 **Glendive** Montana, NW USA
35 Y15 **Glendo** Wyoming, C USA
57 U10 **Glendor Mountains** ▲ C Guyana
190 K12 **Glenelg River** ≈ South Australia/Victoria, SE Australia
31 P4 **Glenfield** North Dakota, N USA
27 V12 **Glen Flora** Texas, SW USA
189 P7 **Glen Helen** Northern Territory, N Australia
191 U5 **Glen Innes** New South Wales, SE Australia
33 P6 **Glen Lake** ◎ Michigan, N USA
8 I7 **Glenlyon Peak** ▲ Yukon Territory, W Canada
39 N16 **Glenn, Mount** ▲ Arizona, SW USA
35 N15 **Glenns Ferry** Idaho, NW USA
25 W6 **Glennville** Georgia, SE USA
8 J10 **Glenora** British Columbia, W Canada
190 M11 **Glenorchy** Victoria, SE Australia
191 V5 **Glenreagh** New South Wales, SE Australia
35 X15 **Glenrock** Wyoming, C USA
98 K11 **Glenrothes** E Scotland, UK
20 L9 **Glens Falls** New York, NE USA
99 D14 **Glenties** *Ir.* Na Gleannta. NW Ireland
30 L5 **Glen Ullin** North Dakota, N USA
23 R4 **Glenville** West Virginia, NE USA
29 T12 **Glenwood** Arkansas, C USA
31 S15 **Glenwood** Iowa, C USA
31 T7 **Glenwood** Minnesota, N USA
38 L5 **Glenwood** Utah, W USA
32 I5 **Glenwood City** Wisconsin, N USA
39 Q4 **Glenwood Springs** Colorado, C USA
110 F10 **Gletsch** Valais, S Switzerland
Glevum *see* Gloucester
31 U14 **Glidden** Iowa, C USA
114 E9 **Glina** Sisak-Moslavina, NE Croatia
96 F11 **Glittertind** ▲ S Norway
113 J16 **Gliwice** *Ger.* Gleiwitz. Katowice, S Poland
38 M14 **Globe** Arizona, SW USA
Globino *see* Hlobyne
110 L9 **Glockturm** ▲ SW Austria
118 L9 **Glodeni** *Rus.* Glodyany. N Moldova
111 S9 **Glödnitz** Kärnten, S Austria
Glodyany *see* Glodeni
Glogau *see* Głogów
111 W6 **Gloggnitz** Niederösterreich, E Austria
112 F13 **Głogów** *Ger.* Glogau, Glogow. Legnica, W Poland
113 I16 **Głogówek** *Ger.* Oberglogau. Opole, SW Poland
94 G12 **Glomfjord** Nordland, C Norway
96 I12 **Glomma** *var.* Glommen. ≈ S Norway
Glommen *see* Glomma
95 I14 **Glommersträsk** Norrbotten, N Sweden
180 I1 **Glorieuses, Nosy** *island group* N Madagascar
67 C25 **Glorious Hill** *hill* East Falkland, Falkland Islands
40 J12 **Glory of Russia Cape** *headland* Saint Matthew Island, Alaska, USA
24 J7 **Gloster** Mississippi, S USA
191 U7 **Gloucester** New South Wales, SE Australia
194 L12 **Gloucester** New Britain, E PNG
99 L21 **Gloucester** *hist.* Caer Glou, *Lat.* Glevum. C England, UK
21 P10 **Gloucester** Massachusetts, NE USA
23 X6 **Gloucester** Virginia, NE USA
99 K21 **Gloucestershire** *cultural region* C England, UK
33 T14 **Glouster** Ohio, N USA
44 H3 **Glovers Reef** *reef* E Belize
20 K10 **Gloversville** New York, NE USA
112 K12 **Głowno** Łódź, C Poland
113 H16 **Głubczyce** *Ger.* Leobschütz. Opole, SW Poland
130 L11 **Glubokiy** Rostovskaya Oblast', SW Russian Federation
151 W9 **Glubokoye** Vostochnyy Kazakhstan, E Kazakhstan
Glubokoye *see* Hlybokaye
113 H16 **Głuchołazy** *Ger.* Ziegenhais. Opole, SW Poland
102 I9 **Glückstadt** Schleswig-Holstein, N Germany
Glukhov *see* Hlukhiv
Glushkevichi *see* Hlushkavichy
Glusk/Glussk *see* Hlusk
Glybokaya *see* Hlyboka
97 F21 **Glyngøre** Viborg, NW Denmark
131 Q9 **Gmelinka** Volgogradskaya Oblast', SW Russian Federation
111 U2 **Gmünd** Kärnten, S Austria
111 R8 **Gmünd** Niederösterreich, N Austria
Gmünd *see* Schwäbisch Gmünd
111 S5 **Gmunden** Oberösterreich, N Austria
Gmundner See *see* Traunsee
96 N10 **Gnarp** Gävleborg, C Sweden
111 W8 **Gnas** Steiermark, SE Austria
Gnesen *see* Gniezno
97 O16 **Gnesta** Södermanland, C Sweden
112 H11 **Gniezno** *Ger.* Gnesen. Poznań, C Poland
115 O17 **Gnjilane** *var.* Gilani, *Alb.* Gjilan. Serbia, S Yugoslavia
97 K20 **Gnosjö** Jönköping, S Sweden
161 E17 **Goa** *prev.* Old Goa, Vela Goa, Velha Goa. Goa, W India
161 E17 **Goa** *var.* Old Goa. ◈ *state* W India
44 H7 **Goascorán, Río** ≈ El Salvador/ Honduras
79 O16 **Goaso** *var.* Gawso. W Ghana
83 K14 **Goba** *It.* Gobbà. S Ethiopia
85 C20 **Gobabed** Erongo, W Namibia
85 E19 **Gobabis** Omaheke, E Namibia
Gobannium *see* Abergavenny
66 M7 **Goban Spur** *undersea feature* NW Atlantic Ocean
Gobbà *see* Goba
65 H21 **Gobernador Gregores** Santa Cruz, S Argentina
63 F14 **Gobernador Ingeniero Virasoro** Corrientes, NE Argentina
168 L12 **Gobi** *desert* China/Mongolia
170 G16 **Gobō** Wakayama, Honshū, SW Japan
103 D14 **Goch** Nordrhein-Westfalen, W Germany
85 E20 **Gochas** Hardap, S Namibia
161 I14 **Godāvari** *var.* Godavari. ≈ C India
161 L16 **Godāvari, Mouths of the** *delta* E India
13 V5 **Godbout** Québec, SE Canada
13 U5 **Godbout** ≈ Québec, SE Canada
13 U5 **Godbout Est** ≈ Québec, SE Canada
29 N6 **Goddard** Kansas, C USA
12 E15 **Goderich** Ontario, S Canada
Godhavn *see* Qeqertarsuaq
160 E10 **Godhra** Gujarāt, W India
Göding *see* Hodonín
113 K22 **Gödöllő** Pest, N Hungary
64 H11 **Godoy Cruz** Mendoza, W Argentina
9 Y11 **Gods** ≈ Manitoba, C Canada
9 Y13 **Gods Lake** Manitoba, C Canada
9 X13 **Gods Lake** ◎ Manitoba, C Canada
Godthaab/Godthåb *see* Nuuk
Godwin Austen, Mount *see* K2
Goede Hoop, Kaap de *see* Good Hope, Cape of
Goedgegun *see* Nhlangano
Goeie Hoop, Kaap die *see* Good Hope, Cape of
11 O7 **Goélands, Lac aux** ◎ Québec, SE Canada
100 E13 **Goeree** *island* SW Netherlands
101 F15 **Goes** Zeeland, SW Netherlands
Goettingen *see* Göttingen
21 O10 **Goffstown** New Hampshire, NE USA
12 E8 **Gogama** Ontario, S Canada
170 Ee12 **Gō-gawa** ≈ Honshū, SW Japan
32 L3 **Gogebic, Lake** ◎ Michigan, N USA
32 K3 **Gogebic Range** *hill range* Michigan/Wisconsin, N USA
143 V13 **Gogi, Mount** *Arm.* Gogi Lerr, *Az.* Küküdağ. ▲ Armenia/Azerbaijan
128 F12 **Gogland, Ostrov** *island* NW Russian Federation
113 I15 **Gogolin** Opole, SW Poland
Gogonou *see* Gogounou
79 S14 **Gogounou** *var.* Gogonou. N Benin
158 I10 **Gohāna** Haryāna, N India
61 K18 **Goianésia** Goiás, C Brazil
61 K18 **Goiânia** *prev.* Goyania. *state capital* Goiás, C Brazil
61 K18 **Goiás** Goiás, C Brazil
61 J18 **Goiás** *off.* Estado de Goiás; *prev.* Goiaz, Goyaz. ◈ *state* C Brazil
Goiaz *see* Goiás
165 R14 **Goinsargoin** Xizang Zizhiqu, W China
62 H10 **Goio-Erê** Paraná, SW Brazil
101 I15 **Goirle** Noord-Brabant, S Netherlands
106 H8 **Góis** Coimbra, N Portugal
171 Gg16 **Gojō** *var.* Gozyô. Nara, Honshū, SW Japan
171 M10 **Gojōme** Akita, Honshū, NW Japan
155 U9 **Gojra** Punjab, E Pakistan
170 D15 **Gokase-gawa** ≈ Kyūshū, SW Japan
142 A11 **Gökçeada** *var.* Imroz Adası, *Gk.* Imbros. *island* NW Turkey
Gökçeada *see* Imroz
Gökdepe *see* Geok-Tepe
142 I10 **Gökırmak** ≈ N Turkey
Goklenkuy, Solonchak *see* Geklengkui, Solonchak
142 C16 **Gökova Körfezi** *gulf* SW Turkey
142 K15 **Göksu** ≈ S Turkey
142 L15 **Göksun** Kahramanmaraş, C Turkey
142 I17 **Göksu Nehri** ≈ S Turkey
85 J16 **Gokwe** Midlands, NW Zimbabwe
96 F13 **Gol** Buskerud, S Norway
159 X12 **Golāghāt** Assam, NE India
112 H10 **Gołańcz** Piła, W Poland
144 G8 **Golan Heights** *Ar.* Al Jawlān, *Heb.* HaGolan. ▲ SW Syria
Golārā *see* Ārān
Golaya Pristan *see* Hola Prystan'
149 T11 **Golbāf** Kermān, C Iran
142 M15 **Gölbaşı** Adıyaman, S Turkey
111 P9 **Gölbner** ▲ SW Austria
32 M17 **Golconda** Illinois, N USA
37 T3 **Golconda** Nevada, W USA
142 E11 **Gölcük** Kocaeli, NW Turkey
110 I7 **Goldach** Sankt Gallen, NE Switzerland
112 N7 **Gołdap** *Ger.* Goldap. Suwałki, NE Poland
34 E15 **Gold Beach** Oregon, NW USA
Goldberg *see* Złotoryja
70 D12 **Gold Coast** *coastal region* S Ghana
191 V3 **Gold Coast** *cultural region* Queensland, E Australia
41 R10 **Gold Creek** Alaska, USA
9 O16 **Golden** British Columbia, SW Canada
39 T4 **Golden** Colorado, C USA
192 I13 **Golden Bay** *bay* South Island, NZ
29 R7 **Golden City** Missouri, C USA
34 I11 **Goldendale** Washington, NW USA
Goldener Tisch *see* Zlatý Stôl
46 L13 **Golden Grove** E Jamaica
12 J12 **Golden Lake** ◎ Ontario, SE Canada
24 K10 **Golden Meadow** Louisiana, S USA
47 V10 **Golden Rock** ✕ (Basseterre) Saint Kitts, Saint Kitts and Nevis
Golden State, The *see* California
85 K16 **Golden Valley** Mashonaland West, N Zimbabwe
37 U9 **Goldfield** Nevada, W USA
Goldingen *see* Kuldīga
Goldmarkt *see* Zlatna
8 K17 **Gold River** Vancouver Island, British Columbia, SW Canada
23 V10 **Goldsboro** North Carolina, SE USA
26 M8 **Goldsmith** Texas, SW USA
27 R8 **Goldthwaite** Texas, SW USA
143 R11 **Göle** Kars, NE Turkey
Golema Ada *see* Ostrovo
116 H9 **Golema Planina** ▲ W Bulgaria
116 F9 **Golemi Vrŭkh** ▲ W Bulgaria
112 D8 **Goleniów** *Ger.* Gollnow. Szczecin, NW Poland
37 Q14 **Goleta** California, W USA
45 O16 **Golfito** Puntarenas, SE Costa Rica
27 T13 **Goliad** Texas, SW USA
115 L14 **Golija** ▲▲ SW Yugoslavia
115 O16 **Goljak** ▲▲ SE Yugoslavia
142 M12 **Gölköy** Ordu, N Turkey
Gollel *see* Lavumisa
111 X3 **Göllersbach** ≈ NE Austria
Gollnow *see* Goleniów
Golmo *see* Golmud
165 P10 **Golmud** *var.* Ge'e'mu, Golmo, *Chin.* Ko-erh-mu. Qinghai, C China
104 F1 **Golo** ≈ Corse, France, C Mediterranean Sea
Golovanevsk *see* Holovanivs'k
Golovchin *see* Halowchyn
41 N9 **Golovin** Alaska, USA
148 M7 **Golpāyegān** *var.* Gulpaigan. Eşfahān, W Iran
Golshan *see* Ṭabas
Gol'shany *see* Hal'shany
98 J7 **Golspie** N Scotland, UK
114 O11 **Golubac** Serbia, NE Yugoslavia
112 J9 **Golub-Dobrzyń** Toruń, N Poland
151 S7 **Golubovka** Pavlodar, N Kazakhstan
84 B11 **Golungo Alto** Cuanza Norte, NW Angola
116 M8 **Golyama Kamchiya** ≈ E Bulgaria
116 L8 **Golyama Reka** ≈ N Bulgaria
116 H11 **Golyama Syutkya** ▲ SW Bulgaria
116 I12 **Golyam Perelik** ▲ S Bulgaria
116 I11 **Golyam Persenk** ▲ S Bulgaria
125 F12 **Golyshmanovo** Tyumenskaya Oblast', C Russian Federation
81 P19 **Goma** Nord Kivu, NE Zaire
171 Gg16 **Gomadan-zan** ▲ Honshū, SW Japan
Gomati *see* Gumti
79 X14 **Gombe** Bauchi, E Nigeria
69 U10 **Gombe** *var.* Igombe. ≈ E Tanzania
79 Y14 **Gombi** Adamawa, E Nigeria
Gombroon *see* Bandar-e 'Abbās
Gomel' *see* Homyel'
Gomel'skaya Oblast' *see* Homyel'skaya Voblasts'
66 N11 **Gomera** *island* Islas Canarias, Spain, NE Atlantic Ocean
42 I5 **Gómez Farias** Chihuahua, N Mexico
42 L8 **Gómez Palacio** Durango, C Mexico
164 J13 **Gomo** Xizang Zizhiqu, W China
175 T11 **Gomumu, Pulau** *see* Gomumu, Pulau
149 T6 **Gonābād** *var.* Gunabad. Khorāsān, NE Iran
46 L8 **Gonaïves** *var.* Les Gonaïves. N Haiti
126 M13 **Gonam** ≈ NE Russian Federation
46 L9 **Gonâve, Canal de la** *var.* Canal de Sud. *channel* N Caribbean Sea
46 K9 **Gonâve, Golfe de la** *gulf* N Caribbean Sea
Gonāveh *see* Bandar-e Gonāveh
46 K9 **Gonâve, Île de la** *island* C Haiti
Gonbadān *see* Dow Gonbadān
149 Q3 **Gonbad-e Kāvūs** *var.* Gunbad-i-Qawus. Māzandarān, N Iran
158 M12 **Gonda** Uttar Pradesh, N India
Gondar *see* Gonder
82 I11 **Gonder** *var.* Gondar. NW Ethiopia
80 J13 **Gondey** Moyen-Chari, S Chad
160 J12 **Gondia** Mahārāshtra, C India
106 G6 **Gondomar** Porto, NW Portugal
142 C12 **Gönen** Balıkesir, W Turkey
142 C12 **Gönen Çayı** ≈ NW Turkey
165 O15 **Gongbo'gyamda** Xizang Zizhiqu, W China
165 N16 **Gonggar** Xizang Zizhiqu, W China
166 G9 **Gongga Shan** ▲ C China
165 T10 **Gonghe** Qinghai, C China
164 I5 **Gongliu** *var.* Tokkuztara. Xinjiang Uygur Zizhiqu, NW China
79 W14 **Gongola** ≈ E Nigeria
Gongoleh State *see* Jonglei
191 P5 **Gongolgon** New South Wales, SE Australia
165 Q6 **Gongpoquan** Gansu, N China
166 I10 **Gongxian** *var.* Gong Xian. Sichuan, C China
Gongzhuling *see* Huaide
165 S14 **Gonjo** Xizang Zizhiqu, W China
109 B20 **Gonnesa** Sardegna, Italy, C Mediterranean Sea
Gonni/Gónnos *see* Gónnoi
117 F15 **Gónnoi** *var.* Gonni, Gónnos; *prev.* Dereli. Thessalía, C Greece
172 N9 **Gonohe** Aomori, Honshū, C Japan
170 Cc11 **Gōnoura** Nagasaki, Iki, SW Japan
37 O11 **Gonzales** California, W USA
24 J9 **Gonzales** Louisiana, S USA
27 T12 **Gonzales** Texas, SW USA
43 P11 **González** Tamaulipas, C Mexico
23 V6 **Goochland** Virginia, NE USA
195 N16 **Goodenough Bay** *inlet* SE PNG
205 X14 **Goodenough, Cape** *headland* Antarctica
195 N15 **Goodenough Island** *var.* Morata. *island* SE PNG
Good Hope *see* Fort Good Hope
41 N8 **Goodhope Bay** *bay* Alaska, USA
85 D26 **Good Hope, Cape of** *Afr.* Kaap de Goede Hoop, Kaap die Goeie Hoop. *headland* SW South Africa
Good Hope, Cape of *see* Yamsurba, Tanjung
8 K10 **Good Hope Lake** British Columbia, W Canada
85 E23 **Goodhouse** Northern Cape, W South Africa
35 O15 **Gooding** Idaho, NW USA
28 H3 **Goodland** Kansas, C USA
181 Y15 **Goodlands** NW Mauritius
22 J8 **Goodlettsville** Tennessee, S USA
41 N13 **Goodnews** Alaska, USA
27 O3 **Goodnight** Texas, SW USA
191 Q4 **Goodooga** New South Wales, SE Australia
31 N4 **Goodrich** North Dakota, N USA
27 W10 **Goodrich** Texas, SW USA
31 X10 **Goodview** Minnesota, N USA
28 H8 **Goodwell** Oklahoma, C USA
99 N17 **Goole** E England, UK
191 O8 **Goolgowi** New South Wales, SE Australia
190 I10 **Goolwa** South Australia
189 Y11 **Goondiwindi** Queensland, E Australia
100 O11 **Goor** Overijssel, E Netherlands
Goose Bay *see* Happy Valley-Goose Bay
35 V13 **Gooseberry Creek** ≈ Wyoming, C USA
23 S14 **Goose Creek** South Carolina, SE USA
65 M23 **Goose Green** East Falkland, Falkland Islands
17 G6 **Goose Lake** *var.* Lago dos Gansos. ◎ California/Oregon, W USA
31 Q4 **Goose River** ≈ North Dakota, N USA
159 T16 **Gopalganj** Dhaka, S Bangladesh
159 O12 **Gopālganj** Bihār, N India
Gopher State *see* Minnesota
103 I22 **Göppingen** Baden-Württemberg, SW Germany
112 G13 **Góra** *Ger.* Guhrau. Leszno, W Poland
112 M12 **Góra Kalwaria** Warszawa, C Poland
159 O12 **Gorakhpur** Uttar Pradesh, N India
Gorany *see* Harany
115 J14 **Goražde** SE Bosnia and Herzegovina
Gorbovichi *see* Harbavichy
Gorče Petrov *see* Đorče Petrov
1 E9 **Gorda Ridges** *undersea feature* NE Pacific Ocean
Gordiaz *see* Gardēz
80 K12 **Gordil** Vakaga, N Central African Republic
25 U5 **Gordon** Georgia, SE USA
30 K12 **Gordon** Nebraska, C USA
27 R7 **Gordon** Texas, SW USA
30 L13 **Gordon Creek** ≈ Nebraska, C USA
65 I25 **Gordon, Isla** *island* S Chile
191 O17 **Gordon, Lake** ◎ Tasmania, SE Australia
191 O17 **Gordon River** ≈ Tasmania, SE Australia
23 V5 **Gordonsville** Virginia, NE USA
82 H13 **Gorē** W Ethiopia
193 D24 **Gore** Southland, South Island, NZ
80 H13 **Goré** Logone-Oriental, S Chad
12 D11 **Gore Bay** Manitoulin Island, Ontario, S Canada
27 Q5 **Goree** Texas, SW USA
143 O11 **Görele** Giresun, NE Turkey
21 N6 **Gore Mountain** ▲ Vermont, NE USA
41 R13 **Gore Point** *headland* Alaska, USA
39 R4 **Gore Range** ▲▲ Colorado, C USA
99 F19 **Gorey** *Ir.* Guaire. SE Ireland
149 R12 **Gorgāb** Kermān, S Iran
149 Q4 **Gorgān** *var.* Astarabad, Astrabad, Gurgan; *prev.* Asterābād, *anc.* Hyrcania. Māzandarān, N Iran
149 Q4 **Gorgān, Rūd-e** ≈ N Iran
78 I10 **Gorgol** ◈ *region* S Mauritania
108 D12 **Gorgona, Isola di** *island* Archipelago Toscano, C Italy
21 P8 **Gorham** Maine, NE USA
143 T10 **Gori** C Georgia
100 I13 **Gorinchem** *var.* Gorkum. Zuid-Holland, C Netherlands
143 V13 **Goris** SE Armenia
128 K16 **Goritsy** Tverskaya Oblast', W Russian Federation
108 J7 **Gorizia** *Ger.* Görz. Friuli-Venezia Giulia, NE Italy
118 G13 **Gorj** ◈ *county* SW Romania
Gorjanci *see* Žumberačka Gora
Görkau *see* Jirkov
Gorki *see* Horki
Gor'kiy *see* Nizhniy Novgorod
Gor'kiy Reservoir *see* Gor'kovskoye Vodokhranilishche
125 D9 **Gor'kovskoye Vodokhranilishche** *Eng.* Gor'kiy Reservoir. ▣ W Russian Federation
Gorkum *see* Gorinchem
97 I23 **Gørlev** Vestsjælland, E Denmark
113 M17 **Gorlice** Nowy Sącz, S Poland
103 Q15 **Görlitz** Sachsen, E Germany
Görlitz *see* Zgorzelec
Gorlovka *see* Horlivka
27 R7 **Gorman** Texas, SW USA
23 T3 **Gormania** West Virginia, NE USA
Gorna Dzhumaya *see* Blagoevgrad
116 K8 **Gorna Oryakhovitsa** Loveshka Oblast, N Bulgaria
116 J8 **Gorna Studena** Loveshka Oblast, N Bulgaria
Gornja Mužlja *see* Mužlja
111 X9 **Gornja Radgona** *Ger.* Oberradkersburg. NE Slovenia
114 M13 **Gornji Milanovac** Serbia, C Yugoslavia
114 G13 **Gornji Vakuf** SW Bosnia and Herzegovina
126 H15 **Gorno-Altaysk** Respublika Altay, S Russian Federation
Gorno-Altayskaya Respublika *see* Altay, Respublika
126 K13 **Gorno-Chuyskiy** Irkutskaya Oblast', C Russian Federation
129 V14 **Gornozavodsk** Permskaya Oblast', NW Russian Federation
127 O16 **Gornozavodsk** Ostrov Sakhalin, Sakhalinskaya Oblast', SE Russian Federation
126 Gg15 **Gornyak** Altayskiy Kray, S Russian Federation
131 R8 **Gornyy** Saratovskaya Oblast', W Russian Federation
Gornyy Altay *see* Altay, Respublika
131 O10 **Gornyy Balykley** Volgogradskaya Oblast', SW Russian Federation
82 I13 **Goroch'an** ▲ W Ethiopia
Gorodenka *see* Horodenka
131 O3 **Gorodets** Nizhegorodskaya Oblast', W Russian Federation
Gorodets *see* Haradzyets
Gorodeya *see* Haradzyeya
131 P6 **Gorodishche** Penzenskaya Oblast', W Russian Federation
Gorodishche *see* Horodyshche
Gorodnya *see* Horodnya
Gorodok *see* Haradok
Gorodok/Gorodok Yagellonski *see* Horodok
130 M13 **Gorodovikovsk** Respublika Kalmykiya, SW Russian Federation
194 I12 **Goroka** Eastern Highlands, C PNG
Gorokhov *see* Horokhiv
131 N3 **Gorokhovets** Vladimirskaya Oblast', W Russian Federation
79 Q11 **Gorom-Gorom** NE Burkina
176 V12 **Gorong, Kepulauan** *island group* E Indonesia
85 M17 **Gorongosa** Sofala, C Mozambique
176 Uu12 **Gorong, Pulau** *island* Kepulauan Gorong, E Indonesia
175 R8 **Gorontalo** Sulawesi, C Indonesia
175 Qq8 **Gorontalo, Teluk** *bay* Sulawesi, C Indonesia
Gorontalo, Teluk *see* Tomini, Gulf of
112 L7 **Górowo Iławeckie** *Ger.* Landsberg. Olsztyn, N Poland
100 M7 **Gorredijk** *Fris.* De Gordyk. Friesland, N Netherlands
86 C14 **Gorringe Ridge** *undersea feature* E Atlantic Ocean
100 M11 **Gorssel** Gelderland, E Netherlands
111 T8 **Görtschitz** ≈ S Austria
Goryn *see* Horyn'
Görz *see* Gorizia
112 E10 **Gorzów** *off.* Województwo Gorzowskie. ◈ *province* W Poland
Gorzowskie, Województwo *see* Gorzów
112 E10 **Gorzów Wielkopolski** *Ger.* Landsberg, Landsberg an der Warthe. Gorzów, W Poland
110 G9 **Göschenen** Uri, C Switzerland
195 N16 **Goschen Strait** *strait* SE PNG
171 Kk13 **Gosen** Niigata, Honshū, C Japan
191 T8 **Gosford** New South Wales, SE Australia
33 P11 **Goshen** Indiana, N USA
20 K13 **Goshen** New York, NE USA
Goshoba *see* Koshoba
171 Mm8 **Goshogawara** *var.* Gosyogawara. Aomori, Honshū, C Japan
152 I8 **Goshquduq Qum** *var.* Tosquduq Qumlari, *Rus.* Peski Taskuduk. *desert* W Uzbekistan
103 J14 **Goslar** Niedersachsen, C Germany
29 Y9 **Gosnell** Arkansas, C USA
114 C11 **Gospić** Lika-Senj, C Croatia
99 N23 **Gosport** S England, UK
96 D9 **Gossa** *island* S Norway
110 H7 **Gossau** Sankt Gallen, NE Switzerland
101 G20 **Gosselies** *var.* Goss'lies. Hainaut, S Belgium
79 P10 **Gossi** Tombouctou, C Mali
Goss'lies *see* Gosselies
115 N18 **Gostivar** W FYR Macedonia
Gostomel' *see* Hostomel'
112 G12 **Gostyń** *var.* Gostyn. Leszno, W Poland
112 K11 **Gostynin** Płock, C Poland
Gosyogawara *see* Goshogawara
97 J18 **Göta Älv** ≈ S Sweden
97 N17 **Göta kanal** *canal* S Sweden
97 K18 **Götaland** *cultural region* S Sweden
97 H17 **Göteborg** *Eng.* Gothenburg. Göteborg och Bohus, S Sweden
97 H17 **Göteborg och Bohus** *var.* Göteborg and Bohus. ◈ *county* S Sweden
79 X16 **Gotel Mountains** ▲▲ E Nigeria
97 K17 **Götene** Skaraborg, S Sweden
Gotera *see* San Francisco
103 K16 **Gotha** Thüringen, C Germany
31 N15 **Gothenburg** Nebraska, C USA
Gothenburg *see* Göteborg
79 R12 **Gothèye** Tillabéri, SW Niger
Gothland *see* Gotland
97 P19 **Gotland** *var.* Gothland, Gottland. ◈ *county* SE Sweden
97 O18 **Gotland** *island* SE Sweden
170 B12 **Gotō-rettō** *island group* SW Japan
116 H12 **Gotse Delchev** *prev.* Nevrokop. Sofiyska Oblast, SW Bulgaria
97 P17 **Gotska Sandön** *island* SE Sweden
170 Ee12 **Gōtsu** *var.* Gôtu. Shimane, Honshū, SW Japan
103 I15 **Göttingen** *var.* Goettingen. Niedersachsen, C Germany
Gottland *see* Gotland
95 I16 **Gottne** Västernorrland, C Sweden
Gottschee *see* Kočevje
Gottwaldov *see* Zlín

◆ Country ● Country Capital ◇ Dependent Territory ○ Dependent Territory Capital ◈ Administrative Region ✕ International Airport ▲ Mountain ▲▲ Mountain Range Volcano ≈ River ◎ Lake ▣ Reservoir

Gôtu *see* Gōtsu
Goturdepe *see* Koturdepe
110 *I7* **Götzis** Vorarlberg, NW Austria
100 *H12* **Gouda** Zuid-Holland, C Netherlands
78 *I11* **Goudiri** *var.* Goudiry. E Senegal
Goudiry *see* Goudiri
79 *X12* **Goudoumaria** Diffa, S Niger
13 *R9* **Gouffre, Rivière du** ≈ Québec, SE Canada
67 *M19* **Gough Fracture Zone** *tectonic feature* S Atlantic Ocean
67 *M19* **Gough Island** *island* Tristan da Cunha, S Atlantic Ocean
13 *N8* **Gouin, Réservoir** ▣ Québec, SE Canada
12 *B10* **Goulais River** Ontario, S Canada
191 *R9* **Goulburn** New South Wales, SE Australia
191 *O11* **Goulburn River** ≈ Victoria, SE Australia
205 *O10* **Gould Coast** *physical region* Antarctica
Goulimime *see* Guelmime
116 *F13* **Gouménissa** Kentrikí Makedonía, N Greece
79 *O10* **Goundam** Tombouctou, NW Mali
80 *H12* **Goundi** Moyen-Chari, S Chad
80 *G12* **Gounou-Gaya** Mayo-Kébbi, SW Chad
79 *O12* **Gourci** *var.* Gourcy. NW Burkina
Gourcy *see* Gourci
104 *M13* **Gourdon** Lot, S France
79 *W11* **Gouré** Zinder, SE Niger
104 *G6* **Gourin** Morbihan, NW France
79 *P10* **Gourma-Rharous** Tombouctou, C Mali
105 *N4* **Gournay-en-Bray** Seine-Maritime, N France
80 *J6* **Gouro** Borkou-Ennedi-Tibesti, N Chad
106 *H8* **Gouveia** Guarda, N Portugal
20 *I7* **Gouverneur** New York, NE USA
101 *L21* **Gouvy** Luxembourg, E Belgium
47 *R14* **Gouyave** *var.* Charlotte Town. NW Grenada
Goverla, Gora *see* Hoverla, Hora
61 *N20* **Governador Valadares** Minas Gerais, SE Brazil
179 *Rr16* **Governor Generoso** Mindanao, S Philippines
46 *I2* **Governor's Harbour** Eleuthera Island, C Bahamas
168 *F9* **Govĭ-Altay** ◈ *province* SW Mongolia
168 *I10* **Govĭ Altayn Nuruu** ▲▲ S Mongolia
160 *L9* **Govind Ballabh Pant Sāgar** ▣ C India
158 *I7* **Govind Sagar** ▣ NE India
153 *N14* **Govurdak** ***Turkm.*** Gowurdak; *prev.* Guardak. Lebapskiy Velayat, E Turkmenistan
20 *D11* **Gowanda** New York, NE USA
154 *J10* **Gowd-e Zereh, Dasht-e** *var.* Guad-i-Zirreh. *marsh* SW Afghanistan
12 *F8* **Gowganda** Ontario, S Canada
12 *G8* **Gowganda Lake** ◎ Ontario, S Canada
31 *U13* **Gowrie** Iowa, C USA
Gowurdak *see* Govurdak
63 *C15* **Goya** Corrientes, NE Argentina
Goyania *see* Goiânia
143 *X11* **Göyçay** ***Rus.*** Geokchay. C Azerbaijan
Goymat *see* Koymat
Goymatdag *see* Koymatdag, Gory
142 *F12* **Göynük** Bolu, NW Turkey
172 *N12* **Goyō-san** ▲ Honshū, C Japan
80 *K11* **Goz Beïda** Ouaddaï, SE Chad
164 *H11* **Gozha Co** ◎ W China
123 *J15* **Gozo** ***Malt.*** Ghawdex. *island* N Malta
82 *H9* **Gōz Regeb** Kassala, NE Sudan
Gozyô *see* Gojō
85 *H25* **Graaff-Reinet** Eastern Cape, S South Africa
Graasten *see* Gråsten
78 *L17* **Grabo** SW Ivory Coast
114 *P11* **Grabovica** Serbia, E Yugoslavia
112 *I13* **Grabów nad Prosną** Kalisz, SW Poland
110 *I8* **Grabs** Sankt Gallen, NE Switzerland
114 *D12* **Gračac** Zadar-Knin, C Croatia
114 *I11* **Gračanica** NE Bosnia and Herzegovina
12 *L11* **Gracefield** Québec, SE Canada
101 *K19* **Grâce-Hollogne** Liège, E Belgium
25 *R8* **Graceville** Florida, SE USA
31 *R8* **Graceville** Minnesota, N USA
44 *G6* **Gracias** Lempira, W Honduras
Gracias *see* Lempira
44 *L5* **Gracias a Dios** ◈ *department* E Honduras
45 *O6* **Gracias a Dios, Cabo de** *headland* Honduras/Nicaragua
66 *O2* **Graciosa** *var.* Ilha Graciosa. *island* Azores, Portugal, NE Atlantic Ocean
66 *Q11* **Graciosa** *island* Islas Canarias, Spain, NE Atlantic Ocean
Graciosa, Ilha *see* Graciosa
114 *I11* **Gradačac** N Bosnia and Herzegovina
61 *J15* **Gradaús, Serra dos** ▲▲ C Brazil
106 *L3* **Gradefes** Castilla-León, N Spain
Gradizhsk *see* Hradyz'k
108 *J7* **Grado** Friuli-Venezia Giulia, NE Italy
106 *K2* **Grado** Asturias, N Spain
115 *P19* **Gradsko** C FYR Macedonia
39 *V11* **Grady** New Mexico, SW USA
114 *E8* **Grad Zagreb** ◈ *province* NC Croatia
31 *T12* **Graettinger** Iowa, C USA
103 *M23* **Grafing** Bayern, SE Germany
27 *S6* **Graford** Texas, SW USA
191 *V5* **Grafton** New South Wales, SE Australia
31 *Q3* **Grafton** North Dakota, N USA
23 *S3* **Grafton** West Virginia, NE USA
23 *T9* **Graham** North Carolina, SE USA
27 *R6* **Graham** Texas, SW USA
Graham Bell Island *see* Greem-Bell, Ostrov
8 *I13* **Graham Island** *island* Queen Charlotte Islands, British Columbia, SW Canada
21 *S6* **Graham Lake** ◎ Maine, NE USA
204 *H4* **Graham Land** *physical region* Antarctica
39 *N15* **Graham, Mount** ▲ Arizona, SW USA
Grahamstad *see* Grahamstown
85 *I25* **Grahamstown** ***Afr.*** Grahamstad. Eastern Cape, S South Africa
70 *C12* **Grain Coast** *coastal region* S Liberia
174 *Mm16* **Grajagan** Jawa, S Indonesia
174 *Mm16* **Grajagan, Teluk** *bay* Jawa, S Indonesia
61 *L14* **Grajaú** Maranhão, E Brazil
60 *M13* **Grajaú, Rio** ≈ NE Brazil
112 *O8* **Grajewo** Łomża, NE Poland
97 *F24* **Gram** Sønderjylland, SW Denmark
105 *N13* **Gramat** Lot, S France
24 *H5* **Grambling** Louisiana, S USA
117 *C14* **Grámmos** ▲▲ Albania/Greece
98 *I9* **Grampian Mountains** ▲▲ C Scotland, UK
190 *L12* **Grampians, The** ▲▲ Victoria, SE Australia
100 *O9* **Gramsbergen** Overijssel, E Netherlands
115 *L21* **Gramsh** *var.* Gramshi. Elbasan, C Albania
Gramshi *see* Gramsh
Gran *see* Hron, Slovakia
Gran *see* Esztergom, N Hungary
56 *F11* **Granada** Meta, C Colombia
44 *J10* **Granada** Granada, SW Nicaragua
107 *N14* **Granada** Andalucía, S Spain
39 *W6* **Granada** Colorado, C USA
44 *J11* **Granada** ◈ *department* SW Nicaragua
107 *N14* **Granada** ◈ *province* Andalucía, S Spain
65 *I21* **Gran Antiplanicie Central** *plain* S Argentina
99 *E17* **Granard** ***Ir.*** Gránard. C Ireland
65 *J20* **Gran Bajo** *basin* S Argentina
65 *J15* **Gran Bajo del Gualicho** *basin* E Argentina
65 *I21* **Gran Bajo de San Julián** *basin* SE Argentina
27 *S7* **Granbury** Texas, SW USA
13 *P12* **Granby** Québec, SE Canada
29 *S8* **Granby** Missouri, C USA
39 *S3* **Granby, Lake** ▣ Colorado, C USA
66 *O12* **Gran Canaria** *var.* Grand Canary. *island* Islas Canarias, Spain, NE Atlantic Ocean
49 *T11* **Gran Chaco** *var.* Chaco. *lowland plain* South America
47 *R14* **Grand Anse** SW Grenada
Grand-Anse *see* Portsmouth
46 *G1* **Grand Bahama Island** *island* N Bahamas
Grand Balé *see* Tui
105 *U7* **Grand Ballon** ***Ger.*** Ballon de Guebwiller. ▲ NE France
11 *T13* **Grand Bank** Newfoundland, Newfoundland and Labrador, SE Canada
66 *I7* **Grand Banks of Newfoundland** *undersea feature* NW Atlantic Ocean
Grand Bassa *see* Buchanan
79 *N17* **Grand-Bassam** *var.* Bassam. SE Ivory Coast
12 *E16* **Grand Bend** Ontario, S Canada
78 *L17* **Grand-Bérébi** *var.* Grand-Béréby. SW Ivory Coast
Grand-Béréby *see* Grand-Bérébi
47 *X11* **Grand-Bourg** Marie-Galante, SE Guadeloupe
46 *M6* **Grand Caicos** *var.* Middle Caicos. *island* C Turks and Caicos Islands
12 *K12* **Grand Calumet, Île du** *island* Québec, SE Canada
99 *E18* **Grand Canal** ***Ir.*** An Chanáil Mhór. *canal* C Ireland
Grand Canary *see* Gran Canaria
38 *K10* **Grand Canyon** Arizona, SW USA
38 *J9* **Grand Canyon** *canyon* Arizona, SW USA
Grand Canyon State *see* Arizona
46 *D8* **Grand Cayman** *island* SW Cayman Islands
9 *R14* **Grand Centre** Alberta, SW Canada
78 *L17* **Grand Cess** SE Liberia
110 *D12* **Grand Combin** ▲ S Switzerland
34 *K8* **Grand Coulee** Washington, NW USA
34 *J8* **Grand Coulee** *valley* Washington, NW USA
47 *X5* **Grand Cul-de-Sac Marin** *bay* N Guadeloupe
Grand Duchy of Luxembourg *see* Luxembourg
65 *I22* **Grande, Bahía** *bay* S Argentina
9 *N14* **Grande Cache** Alberta, W Canada
105 *U12* **Grande Casse** ▲ E France
180 *G12* **Grande Comore** *var.* Njazidja, Great Comoro. *island* NW Comoros
63 *G18* **Grande, Cuchilla** *hill range* E Uruguay
47 *S5* **Grande de Añasco, Río** ≈ W Puerto Rico
Grande de Chiloé, Isla *see* Chiloé, Isla de
60 *J12* **Grande de Gurupá, Ilha** *river island* NE Brazil
59 *K21* **Grande de Lipez, Río** ≈ SW Bolivia
47 *U6* **Grande de Loíza, Río** ≈ E Puerto Rico
47 *T5* **Grande de Manatí, Río** ≈ C Puerto Rico
44 *L9* **Grande de Matagalpa, Río** ≈ C Nicaragua
42 *K12* **Grande de Santiago, Río** *var.* Santiago. ≈ C Mexico
45 *O15* **Grande de Térraba, Río** *var.* Río Térraba. ≈ SE Costa Rica
10 *J9* **Grande Deux, Réservoir la** ▣ Québec, E Canada
62 *O10* **Grande, Ilha** *island* SE Brazil
9 *O13* **Grande Prairie** Alberta, W Canada
76 *I8* **Grand Erg Occidental** *desert* W Algeria
76 *L9* **Grand Erg Oriental** *desert* Algeria/Tunisia
61 *J20* **Grande, Rio** ≈ S Brazil
2 *F15* **Grande, Rio** *var.* Río Bravo, ***Sp.*** Río Bravo del Norte, Bravo del Norte. ≈ Mexico/USA
59 *M18* **Grande, Río** ≈ C Bolivia
13 *Y7* **Grande-Rivière** Québec, SE Canada
13 *Y6* **Grande Rivière** ≈ Québec, SE Canada
46 *M8* **Grande-Rivière-du-Nord** N Haiti
64 *K9* **Grande, Salina** *var.* Gran Salitral. *salt lake* C Argentina
13 *S7* **Grandes-Bergeronnes** Québec, SE Canada
49 *W6* **Grande, Serra** ▲▲ W Brazil
42 *K4* **Grande, Sierra** ▲▲ N Mexico
105 *S12* **Grandes Rousses** ▲▲ E France
65 *K17* **Grandes, Salinas** *salt lake* E Argentina
47 *Y5* **Grande Terre** *island* E West Indies
13 *X5* **Grande-Vallée** Québec, SE Canada
47 *Y5* **Grande Vigie, Pointe de la** *headland* Grande Terre, N Guadeloupe
11 *N14* **Grand Falls** New Brunswick, SE Canada
11 *T11* **Grand Falls** Newfoundland, Newfoundland and Labrador, SE Canada
26 *L9* **Grandfalls** Texas, SW USA
23 *P9* **Grandfather Mountain** ▲ North Carolina, SE USA
28 *L13* **Grandfield** Oklahoma, C USA
9 *N17* **Grand Forks** British Columbia, SW Canada
31 *R4* **Grand Forks** North Dakota, N USA
33 *O9* **Grand Haven** Michigan, N USA
Grandichi *see* Hrandzichy
31 *P15* **Grand Island** Nebraska, C USA
33 *O3* **Grand Island** *island* Michigan, N USA
24 *K10* **Grand Isle** Louisiana, S USA
67 *A23* **Grand Jason** *island* Jason Islands, NW Falkland Islands
39 *P5* **Grand Junction** Colorado, C USA
22 *F10* **Grand Junction** Tennessee, S USA
12 *J9* **Grand-Lac-Victoria** Québec, SE Canada
12 *J9* **Grand lac Victoria** ◎ Québec, SE Canada
79 *N17* **Grand-Lahou** *var.* Grand Lahu. S Ivory Coast
Grand Lahu *see* Grand-Lahou
39 *S3* **Grand Lake** Colorado, C USA
11 *S11* **Grand Lake** ◎ Newfoundland, Newfoundland and Labrador, E Canada
24 *G9* **Grand Lake** ◎ Louisiana, S USA
33 *R5* **Grand Lake** ◎ Michigan, N USA
33 *Q13* **Grand Lake** ▣ Ohio, N USA
29 *R9* **Grand Lake O' The Cherokees** *var.* Lake O' The Cherokees. ▣ Oklahoma, C USA
33 *Q9* **Grand Ledge** Michigan, N USA
104 *I8* **Grand-Lieu, Lac de** ◎ NW France
21 *U6* **Grand Manan Channel** *channel* Canada/USA
11 *O15* **Grand Manan Island** *island* New Brunswick, SE Canada
31 *Y4* **Grand Marais** Minnesota, N USA
13 *P10* **Grand-Mère** Québec, SE Canada
39 *P5* **Grand Mesa** ▲▲ Colorado, C USA
110 *C10* **Grand Muveran** ▲ W Switzerland
106 *G12* **Grândola** Setúbal, S Portugal
Grand Paradis *see* Gran Paradiso
197 *G4* **Grand Passage** *passage* N New Caledonia
79 *R16* **Grand-Popo** S Benin
31 *Z3* **Grand Portage** Minnesota, N USA
27 *T6* **Grand Prairie** Texas, SW USA
9 *W14* **Grand Rapids** Manitoba, C Canada
33 *P9* **Grand Rapids** Michigan, N USA
31 *V5* **Grand Rapids** Minnesota, N USA
197 *G5* **Grand Récif de Koumac** *reef* W New Caledonia
197 *J8* **Grand Récif Sud** *reef* S New Caledonia
12 *L10* **Grand-Remous** Québec, SE Canada
12 *F15* **Grand River** ≈ Ontario, S Canada
33 *P9* **Grand River** ≈ Michigan, N USA
29 *T3* **Grand River** ≈ Missouri, C USA
30 *M7* **Grand River** ≈ South Dakota, N USA
47 *Q11* **Grand' Rivière** N Martinique
34 *F11* **Grand Ronde** Oregon, NW USA
34 *L11* **Grand Ronde River** ≈ Oregon/Washington, NW USA
Grand-Saint-Bernard, Col du *see* Great Saint Bernard Pass
27 *V6* **Grand Saline** Texas, SW USA
57 *X10* **Grand-Santi** W French Guiana
Grandsee *see* Grandson
110 *B9* **Grandson** *prev.* Grandsee. Vaud, W Switzerland
180 *J16* **Grand Sœur** *island* Les Sœurs, NE Seychelles
35 *S14* **Grand Teton** ▲ Wyoming, C USA
33 *P5* **Grand Traverse Bay** *lake bay* Michigan, N USA
47 *N6* **Grand Turk** ○ (Turks and Caicos Islands) Grand Turk Island, S Turks and Caicos Islands
47 *N6* **Grand Turk Island** *island* SE Turks and Caicos Islands
105 *S13* **Grand Veymont** ▲ E France
9 *W15* **Grandview** Manitoba, S Canada
29 *R4* **Grandview** Missouri, C USA
38 *I10* **Grand Wash Cliffs** *cliff* Arizona, SW USA
12 *J8* **Granet, Lac** ◎ Québec, SE Canada
97 *L14* **Grangärde** Kopparberg, C Sweden
46 *H12* **Grange Hill** W Jamaica
98 *J12* **Grangemouth** C Scotland, UK
27 *T10* **Granger** Texas, SW USA
34 *J10* **Granger** Washington, NW USA
35 *T17* **Granger** Wyoming, C USA
Granges *see* Grenchen
97 *L14* **Grängesberg** Kopparberg, C Sweden
35 *N11* **Grangeville** Idaho, NW USA
8 *K13* **Granisle** British Columbia, SW Canada
32 *K15* **Granite City** Illinois, N USA
31 *S9* **Granite Falls** Minnesota, N USA
23 *Q9* **Granite Falls** North Carolina, SE USA
38 *K12* **Granite Mountain** ▲ Arizona, SW USA
35 *T12* **Granite Peak** ▲ Montana, NW USA
37 *T2* **Granite Peak** ▲ Nevada, W USA
38 *J3* **Granite Peak** ▲ Utah, W USA
Granite State *see* New Hampshire
109 *H24* **Granitola, Capo** *headland* Sicilia, Italy, C Mediterranean Sea
193 *H15* **Granity** West Coast, South Island, NZ
Gran Lago *see* Nicaragua, Lago de
65 *J18* **Gran Laguna Salada** ◎ S Argentina
Gran Malvina *see* West Falkland
97 *L18* **Gränna** Jönköping, S Sweden
107 *W5* **Granollers** *var.* Granollérs. Cataluña, NE Spain
108 *A7* **Gran Paradiso** ***Fr.*** Grand Paradis. ▲ NW Italy
Gran Pilastro *see* Hochfeiler
Gran Salitral *see* Grande, Salina
Gran San Bernardo, Passo di *see* Great Saint Bernard Pass
Gran Santiago *see* Santiago
109 *J14* **Gran Sasso d'Italia** ▲▲ C Italy
102 *N11* **Gransee** Brandenburg, NE Germany
30 *L15* **Grant** Nebraska, C USA
29 *R1* **Grant City** Missouri, C USA
99 *N19* **Grantham** E England, UK
67 *D24* **Grantham Sound** *sound* East Falkland, Falkland Islands
204 *K13* **Grant Island** *island* Antarctica
47 *Z14* **Grantley Adams** ✕ (Bridgetown) SE Barbados
37 *S7* **Grant, Mount** ▲ Nevada, W USA
98 *J9* **Grantown-on-Spey** N Scotland, UK
37 *W8* **Grant Range** ▲▲ Nevada, W USA
39 *Q11* **Grants** New Mexico, SW USA
32 *I4* **Grantsburg** Wisconsin, N USA
34 *F15* **Grants Pass** Oregon, NW USA
38 *K3* **Grantsville** Utah, W USA
23 *R4* **Grantsville** West Virginia, NE USA
104 *I5* **Granville** Manche, N France
9 *V12* **Granville Lake** ◎ Manitoba, C Canada
27 *V8* **Grapeland** Texas, SW USA
27 *T6* **Grapevine** Texas, SW USA
85 *K20* **Graskop** Mpumalanga, NE South Africa
97 *P14* **Gräsö** Uppsala, C Sweden
95 *I19* **Gräsö** *island* C Sweden
105 *U15* **Grasse** Alpes-Maritimes, SE France
20 *E14* **Grassflat** Pennsylvania, NE USA
35 *U9* **Grassrange** Montana, NW USA
20 *J6* **Grass River** ≈ New York, NE USA
37 *P6* **Grass Valley** California, W USA
191 *N14* **Grassy** Tasmania, SE Australia
30 *K4* **Grassy Butte** North Dakota, N USA
23 *R5* **Grassy Knob** ▲ West Virginia, NE USA
97 *G24* **Gråsten** *var.* Graasten. Sønderjylland, SW Denmark
97 *J18* **Grästorp** Skaraborg, S Sweden
Gratianopolis *see* Grenoble
111 *V8* **Gratwein** Steiermark, SE Austria
Gratz *see* Graz
110 *I9* **Graubünden** ***Fr.*** Grisons, ***It.*** Grigioni. ◈ *canton* SE Switzerland
Graudenz *see* Grudziądz
105 *N15* **Graulhet** Tarn, S France
107 *T4* **Graus** Aragón, NE Spain
63 *I16* **Gravataí** Rio Grande do Sul, S Brazil
100 *L13* **Grave** Noord-Brabant, SE Netherlands
9 *T17* **Gravelbourg** Saskatchewan, S Canada
105 *N1* **Gravelines** Nord, N France
Graven *see* Grez-Doiceau
12 *H13* **Gravenhurst** Ontario, S Canada
35 *O10* **Grave Peak** ▲ Idaho, NW USA
104 *I11* **Grave, Pointe de** *headland* W France
191 *S4* **Gravesend** New South Wales, SE Australia
99 *P22* **Gravesend** SE England, UK
109 *N17* **Gravina di Puglia** ***Eng.*** Gravina in Puglia. Puglia, SE Italy
Gravina in Puglia *see* Gravina di Puglia
105 *S8* **Gray** Haute-Saône, E France
25 *T4* **Gray** Georgia, SE USA
34 *F9* **Grayland** Washington, NW USA
41 *N10* **Grayling** Alaska, USA
33 *Q6* **Grayling** Michigan, N USA
34 *F9* **Grays Harbor** *inlet* Washington, NW USA
23 *O5* **Grayson** Kentucky, S USA
39 *S4* **Grays Peak** ▲ Colorado, C USA
32 *M16* **Grayville** Illinois, N USA
111 *V8* **Graz** *prev.* Gratz. Steiermark, SE Austria
106 *L15* **Grazalema** Andalucía, S Spain
115 *P15* **Grdelica** Serbia, SE Yugoslavia
46 *H1* **Great Abaco** *var.* Abaco Island. *island* N Bahamas
Great Admiralty Island *see* Manus Island
Great Alfold *see* Great Hungarian Plain
Great Ararat *see* Büyükağrı Dağı
189 *U8* **Great Artesian Basin** *lowlands* Queensland, C Australia
197 *I15* **Great Astrolabe Reef** *reef* Kadavu, SW Fiji
189 *O12* **Great Australian Bight** *bight* S Australia
66 *E11* **Great Bahama Bank** *undersea feature* E Gulf of Mexico
192 *M4* **Great Barrier Island** *island* N NZ
189 *X4* **Great Barrier Reef** *reef* Queensland, NE Australia
20 *L11* **Great Barrington** Massachusetts, NE USA
1 *F10* **Great Basin** *basin* W USA
15 *H5* **Great Bear Lake** ***Fr.*** Grand Lac de l'Ours. ◎ Northwest Territories, NW Canada
Great Belt *see* Storebælt
28 *L5* **Great Bend** Kansas, C USA
Great Bermuda *see* Bermuda
99 *A20* **Great Blasket Island** ***Ir.*** An Blascaod Mór. *island* SW Ireland
Great Britain *see* Britain
157 *Q23* **Great Channel** *channel* Andaman Sea/Indian Ocean
177 *F10* **Great Coco Island** *island* SW Myanmar
Great Crosby *see* Crosby
23 *X7* **Great Dismal Swamp** *wetland* North Carolina/Virginia, SE USA
35 *V16* **Great Divide Basin** *basin* Wyoming, C USA
189 *W7* **Great Dividing Range** ▲▲ NE Australia
12 *D12* **Great Duck Island** *island* Ontario, S Canada
Great Elder Reservoir *see* Waconda Lake
205 *V8* **Greater Antarctica** *var.* East Antarctica. *physical region* Antarctica
46 *G8* **Greater Antilles** *island group* West Indies
133 *V16* **Greater Sunda Islands** *var.* Sunda Islands. *island group* Indonesia
Greater Warsaw *see* Warszawa
192 *I1* **Great Exhibition Bay** *inlet* North Island, NZ
46 *H4* **Great Exuma Island** *island* C Bahamas
35 *R8* **Great Falls** Montana, NW USA
23 *R11* **Great Falls** South Carolina, SE USA
86 *F9* **Great Fisher Bank** *undersea feature* C North Sea
Great Glen *see* Mor, Glen
Great Grimsby *see* Grimsby
46 *I4* **Great Guana Cay** *island* C Bahamas
66 *I5* **Great Hellefiske Bank** *undersea feature* N Atlantic Ocean
113 *L24* **Great Hungarian Plain** *var.* Great Alfold, Plain of Hungary, ***Hung.*** Alföld. *plain* SE Europe
46 *L7* **Great Inagua** *var.* Inagua Islands. *island* S Bahamas
Great Indian Desert *see* Thar Desert
85 *G25* **Great Karoo** *var.* Great Karroo, High Veld, ***Afr.*** Groot Karoo, Hoë Karoo. *plateau region* S South Africa
Great Karroo *see* Great Karoo
Great Kei *see* Groot-Kei
Great Khingan Range *see* Da Hinggan Ling
12 *E11* **Great La Cloche Island** *island* Ontario, S Canada
191 *P16* **Great Lake** ◎ Tasmania, SE Australia
Great Lake *see* Tônlé Sap
16 *O16* **Great Lakes** *lakes* Ontario, Canada/USA
Great Lakes State *see* Michigan
99 *L20* **Great Malvern** W England, UK
192 *M5* **Great Mercury Island** *island* N NZ
Great Meteor Seamount *see* Great Meteor Tablemount
66 *K10* **Great Meteor Tablemount** *var.* Great Meteor Seamount. *undersea feature* E Atlantic Ocean
33 *Q14* **Great Miami River** ≈ Ohio, N USA
157 *Q24* **Great Nicobar** *island* Nicobar Islands, India, NE Indian Ocean
69 *T4* **Great Oasis, The** *var.* Khārga Oasis. *oasis* S Egypt
99 *O19* **Great Ouse** *var.* Ouse. ≈ E England, UK
191 *Q17* **Great Oyster Bay** *bay* Tasmania, SE Australia
46 *I13* **Great Pedro Bluff** *headland* W Jamaica
23 *T12* **Great Pee Dee River** ≈ North Carolina/South Carolina, SE USA
133 *W9* **Great Plain of China** *plain* E China
2 *F12* **Great Plains** *var.* High Plains. *plains* Canada/USA
39 *W6* **Great Plains Reservoirs** ▣ Colorado, C USA
21 *Q13* **Great Point** *headland* Nantucket Island, Massachusetts, NE USA
70 *I13* **Great Rift Valley** *var.* Rift Valley. *depression* Asia/Africa
83 *I23* **Great Ruaha** ≈ S Tanzania
20 *K10* **Great Sacandaga Lake** ▣ New York, NE USA
110 *C12* **Great Saint Bernard Pass** ***Fr.*** Col du Grand-Saint-Bernard, ***It.*** Passo di Gran San Bernardo. *pass* Italy/Switzerland
46 *F1* **Great Sale Cay** *island* N Bahamas
Great Salt Desert *see* Kavīr, Dasht-e
38 *K1* **Great Salt Lake** *salt lake* Utah, W USA
38 *J3* **Great Salt Lake Desert** *plain* Utah, W USA
28 *M8* **Great Salt Plains Lake** ▣ Oklahoma, C USA
77 *T9* **Great Sand Sea** *desert* Egypt/Libya
188 *L6* **Great Sandy Desert** *desert* Western Australia
Great Sandy Desert *see* Ar Rub' al Khālī
Great Sandy Island *see* Fraser Island
197 *I13* **Great Sea Reef** *reef* Vanua Levu, N Fiji
40 *H17* **Great Sitkin Island** *island* Aleutian Islands, Alaska, USA
15 *I8* **Great Slave Lake** ***Fr.*** Grand Lac des Esclaves. ◎ Northwest Territories, NW Canada
23 *O10* **Great Smoky Mountains** ▲▲ North Carolina/Tennessee, SE USA
8 *L11* **Great Snow Mountain** ▲ British Columbia, W Canada
66 *A12* **Great Sound** *bay* Bermuda, NW Atlantic Ocean
188 *M10* **Great Victoria Desert** *desert* South Australia/Western Australia
204 *H2* **Great Wall** *Chinese research station* South Shetland Islands, Antarctica
21 *T7* **Great Wass Island** *island* Maine, NE USA
99 *Q19* **Great Yarmouth** *var.* Yarmouth. E England, UK
145 *S1* **Great Zab** ***Ar.*** Az Zāb al Kabīr, ***Kurd.*** Zē-i Bādīnān, ***Turk.*** Büyükzap Suyu. ≈ Iraq/Turkey
97 *I17* **Grebbestad** Göteborg och Bohus, S Sweden
Grebenka *see* Hrebinka
44 *M13* **Grecia** Alajuela, C Costa Rica
63 *E18* **Greco** Río Negro, W Uruguay
Greco, Cape *see* Gkréko, Akrotíri
106 *L8* **Gredos, Sierra de** ▲▲ W Spain
20 *F9* **Greece** New York, NE USA
117 *E17* **Greece** *off.* Hellenic Republic, ***Gk.*** Ellás; *anc.* Hellas. ◆ *republic* SE Europe
Greece Central *see* Stereá Ellás
Greece West *see* Dytikí Ellás
39 *T3* **Greeley** Colorado, C USA
31 *P14* **Greeley** Nebraska, C USA
126 *Hh1* **Greem-Bell, Ostrov** ***Eng.*** Graham Bell Island. *island* Zemlya Frantsa-Iosifa, N Russian Federation
32 *M6* **Green Bay** Wisconsin, N USA
33 *N6* **Green Bay** *lake bay* Michigan/Wisconsin, N USA
23 *S5* **Greenbrier River** ≈ West Virginia, NE USA
31 *S2* **Greenbush** Minnesota, N USA
191 *R12* **Green Cape** *headland* New South Wales, SE Australia
33 *O14* **Greencastle** Indiana, N USA
20 *F16* **Greencastle** Pennsylvania, NE USA
29 *T2* **Green City** Missouri, C USA
23 *O9* **Greeneville** Tennessee, S USA
37 *O11* **Greenfield** California, W USA
33 *P14* **Greenfield** Indiana, N USA
31 *U15* **Greenfield** Iowa, C USA
20 *M11* **Greenfield** Massachusetts, NE USA
29 *S7* **Greenfield** Missouri, C USA
33 *S14* **Greenfield** Ohio, N USA
22 *G8* **Greenfield** Tennessee, S USA
32 *M9* **Greenfield** Wisconsin, N USA
29 *T9* **Green Forest** Arkansas, C USA
39 *T7* **Greenhorn Mountain** ▲ Colorado, C USA
Green Island *see* Lü Tao
195 *R10* **Green Islands** *var.* Nissan Islands. *island group* NE PNG
9 *S14* **Green Lake** Saskatchewan, C Canada
32 *L8* **Green Lake** ◎ Wisconsin, N USA
207 *O14* **Greenland** ***Dan.*** Grønland, ***Inuit*** Kalaallit Nunaat. ◇ *Danish external territory* NE North America
86 *D4* **Greenland** *island* NE North America
207 *R13* **Greenland Plain** *undersea feature* N Greenland Sea
94 *J1* **Greenland Sea** *sea* Arctic Ocean
39 *R4* **Green Mountain Reservoir** ▣ Colorado, C USA
20 *M8* **Green Mountains** ▲▲ Vermont, NE USA
Green Mountain State *see* Vermont
98 *H12* **Greenock** W Scotland, UK
41 *T5* **Greenough, Mount** ▲ Alaska, USA
194 *E10* **Green River** Sandaun, NW PNG
39 *N5* **Green River** Utah, W USA
35 *U17* **Green River** Wyoming, C USA
18 *Ii7* **Green River** ≈ W USA
32 *K11* **Green River** ≈ Illinois, N USA
22 *J7* **Green River** ≈ Kentucky, S USA
30 *K5* **Green River** ≈ North Dakota, N USA
39 *N6* **Green River** ≈ Utah, W USA
35 *T16* **Green River** ≈ Wyoming, C USA
22 *L7* **Green River Lake** ▣ Kentucky, S USA
25 *O5* **Greensboro** Alabama, S USA
25 *U3* **Greensboro** Georgia, SE USA
23 *T9* **Greensboro** North Carolina, SE USA
33 *P14* **Greensburg** Indiana, N USA
28 *K6* **Greensburg** Kansas, C USA
22 *L7* **Greensburg** Kentucky, S USA
20 *C15* **Greensburg** Pennsylvania, NE USA
39 *O13* **Greens Peak** ▲ Arizona, SW USA
23 *V12* **Green Swamp** *wetland* North Carolina, SE USA
23 *O4* **Greenup** Kentucky, S USA
38 *M16* **Green Valley** Arizona, SW USA
78 *K17* **Greenville** *var.* Sino, Sinoe. SE Liberia
25 *P6* **Greenville** Alabama, S USA
25 *T8* **Greenville** Florida, SE USA
25 *S4* **Greenville** Georgia, SE USA
32 *L15* **Greenville** Illinois, N USA
22 *I7* **Greenville** Kentucky, S USA
21 *Q5* **Greenville** Maine, NE USA
33 *P9* **Greenville** Michigan, N USA
24 *J4* **Greenville** Mississippi, S USA
23 *W9* **Greenville** North Carolina, SE USA
33 *Q13* **Greenville** Ohio, N USA
21 *O12* **Greenville** Rhode Island, NE USA
23 *P11* **Greenville** South Carolina, SE USA
27 *U6* **Greenville** Texas, SW USA
33 *T12* **Greenwich** Ohio, N USA
29 *S11* **Greenwood** Arkansas, C USA
33 *O14* **Greenwood** Indiana, N USA
24 *K4* **Greenwood** Mississippi, S USA
23 *P12* **Greenwood** South Carolina, SE USA
23 *Q12* **Greenwood, Lake** ▣ South Carolina, SE USA
23 *P11* **Greer** South Carolina, SE USA
29 *V10* **Greers Ferry Lake** ▣ Arkansas, C USA
29 *S13* **Greeson, Lake** ▣ Arkansas, C USA
31 *O12* **Gregory** South Dakota, N USA
190 *J3* **Gregory, Lake** *salt lake* South Australia
188 *J9* **Gregory Lake** ◎ W Australia
189 *V5* **Gregory Range** ▲▲ Queensland, E Australia
Greifenberg/Greifenberg in Pommern *see* Gryfice
Greifenhagen *see* Gryfino
102 *O8* **Greifswald** Mecklenburg-Vorpommern, NE Germany
102 *O8* **Greifswalder Bodden** *bay* NE Germany
111 *U4* **Grein** Oberösterreich, N Austria
103 *M17* **Greiz** Thüringen, C Germany
Gremicha/Gremiha *see* Gremikha
128 *M4* **Gremikha** *var.* Gremicha, Gremiha. Murmanskaya Oblast', NW Russian Federation
129 *V14* **Gremyachinsk** Permskaya Oblast', NW Russian Federation
97 *H21* **Grenå** *var.* Grenaa. Århus, C Denmark
Grenaa *see* Grenå
24 *L3* **Grenada** Mississippi, S USA
47 *W15* **Grenada** ◆ *commonwealth republic* SE West Indies
49 *S4* **Grenada** *island* Grenada
49 *R4* **Grenada Basin** *undersea feature* W Atlantic Ocean
24 *L3* **Grenada Lake** ▣ Mississippi, S USA
47 *Y14* **Grenadines, The** *island group* Grenada/St Vincent and the Grenadines
110 *D7* **Grenchen** ***Fr.*** Granges. Solothurn, NW Switzerland
191 *Q9* **Grenfell** New South Wales, SE Australia
9 *V16* **Grenfell** Saskatchewan, S Canada
94 *J1* **Grenivík** Nordhurland Eystra, N Iceland
105 *S12* **Grenoble** *anc.* Cularo, Gratianopolis. Isère, E France
30 *J2* **Grenora** North Dakota, N USA
94 *N8* **Grense-Jakobselv** Finnmark, N Norway
47 *S14* **Grenville** E Grenada
34 *G11* **Gresham** Oregon, NW USA
Gresk *see* Hresk
108 *B7* **Gressoney-St-Jean** Valle d'Aosta, NW Italy
24 *K9* **Gretna** Louisiana, S USA
23 *T7* **Gretna** Virginia, NE USA
100 *F13* **Grevelingen** *inlet* S North Sea
102 *F13* **Greven** Nordrhein-Westfalen, NW Germany
117 *D15* **Grevená** Dytikí Makedonía, N Greece
103 *D16* **Grevenbroich** Nordrhein-Westfalen, W Germany
101 *N24* **Grevenmacher** Grevenmacher, E Luxembourg
101 *M24* **Grevenmacher** ◈ *district* E Luxembourg

◆ Country
● Country Capital
◇ Dependent Territory
○ Dependent Territory Capital
◈ Administrative Region
✕ International Airport
▲ Mountain
▲▲ Mountain Range
Volcano
≈ River
◎ Lake
▣ Reservoir

102 K9 **Grevesmülhen** Mecklenburg-Vorpommern, N Germany
193 H16 **Grey** ∽ South Island, NZ
35 V12 **Greybull** Wyoming, C USA
35 U13 **Greybull River** ∽ Wyoming, C USA
67 A24 **Grey Channel** sound Falkland Islands
Greyerzer See see Gruyère, Lac de la
11 T10 **Grey Islands** island group Newfoundland and Labrador, E Canada
20 L10 **Greylock, Mount** ▲ Massachusetts, NE USA
193 G17 **Greymouth** West Coast, South Island, NZ
189 U10 **Grey Range** ▲ New South Wales/Queensland, E Australia
99 G18 **Greystones** Ir. Na Clocha Liatha. E Ireland
193 M14 **Greytown** Wellington, North Island, NZ
85 K23 **Greytown** KwaZulu/Natal, E South Africa
Greytown see San Juan del Norte
101 H19 **Grez-Doiceau** Dut. Graven. Walloon Brabant, C Belgium
117 J19 **Griá, Ákra** headland Ándros, Kykládes, Greece, Aegean Sea
131 N8 **Gribanovskiy** Voronezhskaya Oblast', W Russian Federation
80 I13 **Gribingui** ∽ N Central African Republic
37 O6 **Gridley** California, W USA
85 G23 **Griekwastad** Northern Cape, C South Africa
25 S4 **Griffin** Georgia, SE USA
191 O9 **Griffith** New South Wales, SE Australia
12 F13 **Griffith Island** island Ontario, S Canada
23 W10 **Grifton** North Carolina, SE USA
Grigioni see Graubünden
121 H14 **Grigiškes** Trakai, SE Lithuania
119 N10 **Grigoriopol** C Moldova
153 X7 **Grigor'yevka** Issyk-Kul'skaya Oblast', E Kyrgyzstan
200 Oo9 **Grijalva Ridge** undersea feature E Pacific Ocean
43 U15 **Grijalva, Río** var. Tabasco. ∽ Guatemala/Mexico
100 N5 **Grijpskerk** Groningen, NE Netherlands
85 C22 **Grillenthal** Karas, SW Namibia
81 J15 **Grimari** Ouaka, C Central African Republic
Grimaylov see Hrymayliv
101 G18 **Grimbergen** Vlaams Brabant, C Belgium
191 N15 **Grim, Cape** headland Tasmania, SE Australia
102 N8 **Grimmen** Mecklenburg-Vorpommern, NE Germany
12 G16 **Grimsby** Ontario, S Canada
99 O17 **Grimsby** prev. Great Grimsby. E England, UK
94 J1 **Grímsey** var. Grimsey. island N Iceland
9 O12 **Grimshaw** Alberta, W Canada
97 F18 **Grimstad** Aust-Agder, S Norway
94 H4 **Grindavík** Reykjanes, W Iceland
110 F9 **Grindelwald** Bern, S Switzerland
97 F23 **Grindsted** Ribe, W Denmark
31 W14 **Grinnell** Iowa, C USA
111 U10 **Grintavec** ▲ N Slovenia
190 H1 **Griselda, Lake** salt lake South Australia
Grisons see Graubünden
97 P14 **Grisslehamn** Stockholm, C Sweden
31 T15 **Griswold** Iowa, C USA
104 M1 **Griz Nez, Cap** headland N France
114 P13 **Grljan** Serbia, E Yugoslavia
114 E11 **Grmeč** ▲ NW Bosnia and Herzegovina
101 H16 **Grobbendonk** Antwerpen, N Belgium
Grobin see Grobiņa
120 C10 **Grobiņa** Ger. Grobin. Liepāja, W Latvia
85 K20 **Groblersdal** Mpumalanga, NE South Africa
85 G23 **Groblershoop** Northern Cape, W South Africa
Gródek Jagielloński see Horodok
111 Q6 **Grödig** Salzburg, W Austria
113 H15 **Grodków** Opole, SW Poland
Grodnenskaya Oblast' see Hrodzyenskaya Voblasts'
Grodno see Hrodna
112 L12 **Grodzisk Mazowiecki** Warszawa, C Poland
112 F12 **Grodzisk Wielkopolski** Poznań, W Poland
Grodzyanka see Hradzyanka
100 O12 **Groenlo** Gelderland, E Netherlands
85 E22 **Groenrivier** Karas, SE Namibia
27 U8 **Groesbeck** Texas, SW USA
100 L13 **Groesbeek** Gelderland, SE Netherlands
104 G7 **Groix, Îles de** island group NW France
112 M12 **Grójec** Radom, C Poland
67 K15 **Gröll Seamount** undersea feature C Atlantic Ocean
102 E13 **Gronau** var. Gronau in Westfalen. Nordrhein-Westfalen, NW Germany
Gronau in Westfalen see Gronau
95 F15 **Grong** Nord-Trøndelag, C Norway
97 N22 **Grönhögen** Kalmar, S Sweden
100 N5 **Groningen** Groningen, NE Netherlands
57 W9 **Groningen** Saramacca, N Suriname
100 N5 **Groningen** ◆ province NE Netherlands
Grønland see Greenland
110 H11 **Grono** Graubünden, S Switzerland
97 M20 **Grönskåra** Kalmar, S Sweden
27 O2 **Groom** Texas, SW USA
37 W9 **Groom Lake** ◎ Nevada, W USA
85 H25 **Groot** ∽ S South Africa
189 S2 **Groote Eylandt** island Northern Territory, N Australia
100 M6 **Grootegast** Groningen, NE Netherlands
85 D17 **Grootfontein** Otjozondjupa, N Namibia
85 E22 **Groot Karasberge** ▲ S Namibia
Groot Karoo see Great Karoo
85 J25 **Groot-Kei** Eng. Great Kei. ∽ S South Africa
47 T10 **Gros Islet** N Saint Lucia
46 L8 **Gros-Morne** NW Haiti
11 S11 **Gros Morne** ▲ Newfoundland, Newfoundland and Labrador, E Canada
105 R9 **Grosne** ∽ C France
47 S12 **Gros Piton** ▲ SW Saint Lucia
Grossa, Isola see Dugi Otok
Grossbetschkerek see Zrenjanin
Grosse Isper see Grosse Ysper
Grosse Kokel see Târnava Mare
103 M21 **Grosser Laaber** var. Grosse Laber. ∽ SE Germany
Grosse Laber see Grosser Laaber
Grosse Morava see Velika Morava
103 O15 **Grossenhain** Sachsen, E Germany
111 Y4 **Grossenzersdorf** Niederösterreich, NE Austria
103 O21 **Grosser Arber** ▲ SE Germany
103 K17 **Grosser Beerberg** ▲ C Germany
103 G18 **Grosser Feldberg** ▲ W Germany
111 O8 **Grosser Löffler** It. Monte Lovello. ▲ Austria/Italy
111 N8 **Grosser Möseler** var. Mesule. ▲ Austria/Italy
102 J8 **Grosser Plöner See** ◎ N Germany
103 O21 **Grosser Rachel** ▲ SE Germany
Grosser Sund see Suur Väin
13 V6 **Grosses-Roches** Québec, SE Canada
111 P8 **Grosses Weiesbachhorn** var. Wiesbachhorn. ▲ W Austria
108 F13 **Grosseto** Toscana, C Italy
103 M22 **Grosse Vils** ∽ SE Germany
111 U4 **Grosse Ysper** var. Grosse Isper. ∽ N Austria
103 G19 **Gross-Gerau** Hessen, W Germany
111 U3 **Gross Gerungs** Niederösterreich, N Austria
111 P8 **Grossglockner** ▲ W Austria
Grosskanizsa see Nagykanizsa
Gross-Karol see Carei
Grosskikinda see Kikinda
111 W9 **Grossklein** Steiermark, SE Austria
Grosskoppe see Velká Deštná
Grossmeseritsch see Velké Meziříčí
Grossmichel see Michalovce
103 H19 **Grossostheim** Bayern, C Germany
111 X7 **Grosspetersdorf** Burgenland, SE Austria
111 T5 **Grossraming** Oberösterreich, C Austria
103 P14 **Grossräschen** Brandenburg, E Germany
Grossrauschenbach see Revúca
Gross-Sankt-Johannis see Suure-Jaani
Gross-Schlatten see Abrud
111 V2 **Gross-Siegharts** Niederösterreich, N Austria
Gross-Skaisgirren see Bol'shakovo
Gross-Steffelsdorf see Rimavská Sobota
Gross Strehlitz see Strzelce Opolskie
111 O8 **Grossvenediger** ▲ W Austria
Grosswardein see Oradea
Gross Wartenberg see Syców
111 U11 **Grosuplje** C Slovenia
101 H17 **Grote Nete** ∽ N Belgium
96 E10 **Grotli** Oppland, S Norway
21 N13 **Groton** Connecticut, NE USA
31 P8 **Groton** South Dakota, N USA
109 P18 **Grottaglie** Puglia, SE Italy
109 L17 **Grottaminarda** Campania, S Italy
108 K13 **Grottammare** Marche, C Italy
23 U5 **Grottoes** Virginia, NE USA
Grou see Grouw
11 N10 **Groulx, Monts** ▲ Québec, E Canada
12 E7 **Groundhog** ∽ Ontario, S Canada
38 J1 **Grouse Creek** Utah, W USA
38 J1 **Grouse Creek Mountains** ▲ Utah, W USA
100 L6 **Grouw** Fris. Grou. Friesland, N Netherlands
29 R8 **Grove** Oklahoma, C USA
33 S13 **Grove City** Ohio, N USA
20 B13 **Grove City** Pennsylvania, NE USA
25 O6 **Grove Hill** Alabama, S USA
35 S15 **Grover** Wyoming, C USA
37 P13 **Grover City** California, W USA
27 Y11 **Groves** Texas, SW USA
21 O7 **Groveton** New Hampshire, NE USA
27 W9 **Groveton** Texas, SW USA
38 J15 **Growler Mountains** ▲ Arizona, SW USA
Grozdovo see Bratya Daskalovi
131 P16 **Groznyy** Chechenskaya Respublika, SW Russian Federation
Grubeshov see Hrubieszów
114 G9 **Grubišno Polje** Bjelovar-Bilogora, NE Croatia
Grudovo see Sredets
112 J9 **Grudziądz** Ger. Graudenz. Toruń, N Poland
27 R17 **Grulla** var. La Grulla. Texas, SW USA
42 K14 **Grullo** Jalisco, SW Mexico
69 V10 **Grumeti** ∽ N Tanzania
97 K16 **Grums** Värmland, C Sweden
111 S5 **Grünau im Almtal** Oberösterreich, N Austria
103 H17 **Grünberg** Hessen, W Germany
Grünberg/Grünberg in Schlesien see Zielona Góra
Grünberg in Schlesien see Zielona Góra
94 H3 **Grundarfjördhur** Vestfirdhir, W Iceland
23 P7 **Grundy** Virginia, NE USA
31 W13 **Grundy Center** Iowa, C USA
Grüneberg see Zielona Góra
27 N1 **Gruver** Texas, SW USA
110 C9 **Gruyère, Lac de la** Ger. Greyerzer See. ◎ SW Switzerland
110 C9 **Gruyères** Fribourg, W Switzerland
120 E11 **Gruzdžiai** Šiauliai, N Lithuania
Gruzinskaya SSR/Gruziya see Georgia
152 C10 **Gryada Akkyr** Turkm. Akgyr Erezi. hill range NW Turkmenistan
130 L7 **Gryazi** Lipetskaya Oblast', W Russian Federation
128 M14 **Gryazovets** Vologodskaya Oblast', NW Russian Federation
113 M17 **Grybów** Nowy Sącz, SE Poland
96 M13 **Grycksbo** Kopparberg, C Sweden
112 E8 **Gryfice** Ger. Greifenberg, Greifenberg in Pommern. Szczecin, NW Poland
112 D9 **Gryfino** Ger. Greifenhagen. Szczecin, NW Poland
94 H9 **Gryllefjord** Troms, N Norway
97 L15 **Grythyttan** Örebro, C Sweden
110 D10 **Gstaad** Bern, W Switzerland
45 P14 **Guabito** Bocas del Toro, NW Panama
46 G7 **Guacanayabo, Golfo de** gulf S Cuba
42 I7 **Guachochi** Chihuahua, N Mexico
106 J11 **Guadajira** ∽ SW Spain
106 M13 **Guadajoz** ∽ S Spain
42 L13 **Guadalajara** Jalisco, C Mexico
107 O8 **Guadalajara** Ar. Wad Al-Hajarah; anc. Arriaca. Castilla-La Mancha, C Spain
107 O7 **Guadalajara** ◆ province Castilla-La Mancha, C Spain
106 K12 **Guadalcanal** Andalucía, S Spain
195 W16 **Guadalcanal** off. Guadalcanal Province. ◆ province C Solomon Islands
195 W16 **Guadalcanal** island C Solomon Islands
107 O12 **Guadalén** ∽ S Spain
107 R13 **Guadalentín** ∽ SE Spain
106 K15 **Guadalete** ∽ SW Spain
107 O13 **Guadalimar** ∽ S Spain
107 P12 **Guadalmena** ∽ S Spain
106 L11 **Guadalmez** ∽ W Spain
107 S7 **Guadalope** ∽ E Spain
106 K13 **Guadalquivir** ∽ W Spain
106 J14 **Guadalquivir, Marismas del** var. Las Marismas. wetland SW Spain
42 M11 **Guadalupe** Zacatecas, C Mexico
59 E16 **Guadalupe** Ica, W Peru
106 L10 **Guadalupe** Extremadura, W Spain
38 L14 **Guadalupe** Arizona, SW USA
37 P13 **Guadalupe** California, W USA
199 Mm5 **Guadalupe** island NW Mexico
Guadalupe see Canelones
42 J3 **Guadalupe Bravos** Chihuahua, N Mexico
42 A4 **Guadalupe, Isla** island NW Mexico
39 U15 **Guadalupe Mountains** ▲ New Mexico/Texas, SW USA
26 J8 **Guadalupe Peak** ▲ Texas, SW USA
27 R11 **Guadalupe River** ∽ SW USA
106 K10 **Guadalupe, Sierra de** ▲ W Spain
42 K9 **Guadalupe Victoria** Durango, C Mexico
42 I8 **Guadalupe y Calvo** Chihuahua, N Mexico
107 N7 **Guadarrama** Madrid, C Spain
107 N7 **Guadarrama** ∽ C Spain
106 M7 **Guadarrama, Puerto de** pass C Spain
107 N9 **Guadarrama, Sierra de** ▲ C Spain
107 Q9 **Guadazaón** ∽ C Spain
47 X10 **Guadeloupe** ◇ French overseas department E West Indies
49 S3 **Guadeloupe** island group E West Indies
47 W10 **Guadeloupe Passage** passage E Caribbean Sea
106 H13 **Guadiana** ∽ Portugal/Spain
107 P13 **Guadiana Menor** ∽ S Spain
107 Q8 **Guadiela** ∽ C Spain
107 O14 **Guadix** Andalucía, S Spain
Guad-i-Zirreh see Gowd-e Zereh, Dasht-e
200 O13 **Guafo Fracture Zone** tectonic feature SE Pacific Ocean
65 F18 **Guafo, Isla** island S Chile
44 I6 **Guaimaca** Francisco Morazán, C Honduras
56 J12 **Guainía** off. Comisaría del Guainía. ◆ province E Colombia
56 K12 **Guainía, Río** ∽ Colombia/Venezuela
57 O9 **Guaiquinima, Cerro** elevation SE Venezuela
64 O7 **Guairá** off. Departamento del Guairá. ◆ department S Paraguay
62 G10 **Guaíra** Paraná, S Brazil
62 L7 **Guaíra** São Paulo, S Brazil
Guaire see Gorey
65 F18 **Guaiteca, Isla** island S Chile
46 G6 **Guajaba, Cayo** headland C Cuba
61 D16 **Guajará-Mirim** Rondônia, W Brazil
Guajira see La Guajira
56 H3 **Guajira, Península de la** peninsula N Colombia
44 J6 **Gualaco** Olancho, C Honduras
36 L7 **Gualala** California, W USA
44 E5 **Gualán** Zacapa, C Guatemala
63 C19 **Gualeguay** Entre Ríos, E Argentina
63 D18 **Gualeguaychú** Entre Ríos, E Argentina
63 C18 **Gualeguay, Río** ∽ E Argentina
65 K16 **Gualicho, Salina del** salt lake E Argentina
196 B15 **Guam** ◇ US unincorporated territory W Pacific Ocean
65 F19 **Guamblin, Isla** island Archipiélago de los Chonos, S Chile
63 A22 **Guaminí** Buenos Aires, E Argentina
42 H8 **Guamúchil** Sinaloa, C Mexico
56 H4 **Guana** var. Misión de Guana. Zulia, NW Venezuela
46 C4 **Guanabacoa** La Habana, W Cuba
44 K13 **Guanacaste** off. Provincia de Guanacaste. ◆ province NW Costa Rica
44 K12 **Guanacaste, Cordillera de** ▲ NW Costa Rica
42 J8 **Guanaceví** Durango, C Mexico
46 A5 **Guanahacabibes, Golfo de** gulf W Cuba
44 K4 **Guanaja, Isla de** island Islas de la Bahía, N Honduras
46 C4 **Guanajay** La Habana, W Cuba
43 N12 **Guanajuato** Guanajuato, C Mexico
42 M12 **Guanajuato** ◆ state C Mexico
56 J6 **Guanare** Portuguesa, N Venezuela
56 K7 **Guanare, Río** ∽ W Venezuela
56 J6 **Guanarito** Portuguesa, NW Venezuela
166 M3 **Guancen Shan** ▲ C China
64 I9 **Guandacol** La Rioja, W Argentina
46 A5 **Guane** Pinar del Río, W Cuba
167 N14 **Guangdong** var. Guangdong Sheng, Kuang-tung, Kwangtung, Yue. ◆ province S China
Guangdong Sheng see Guangdong
Guanghua see Laohekou
Guangju see Kwangju
166 I13 **Guangnan** Yunnan, SW China
Guangxi see Guangxi Zhuangzu Zizhiqu
166 K14 **Guangxi Zhuangzu Zizhiqu** var. Guangxi, Gui, Kuang-hsi, Kwangsi, Eng. Kwangsi Chuang Autonomous Region. ◆ autonomous region S China
166 J8 **Guangyuan** var. Kuang-yuan, Kwangyuan. Sichuan, C China
167 N14 **Guangzhou** var. Kuang-chou, Kwangchow, Eng. Canton. Guangdong, S China
61 N19 **Guanhães** Minas Gerais, SE Brazil
166 I12 **Guanling** var. Guanling Bouyeizu Miaozu Zizhixian. Guizhou, S China
Guanling Bouyeizu Miaozu Zizhixian see Guanling
57 N5 **Guanta** Anzoátegui, NE Venezuela
46 J8 **Guantánamo** Guantánamo, SE Cuba
166 H9 **Guanxian** var. Guan Xian. Sichuan, C China
167 Q6 **Guanyun** Jiangsu, E China
56 C12 **Guapí** Cauca, SW Colombia
45 N13 **Guápiles** Limón, NE Costa Rica
63 I15 **Guaporé** Rio Grande do Sul, S Brazil
49 S8 **Guaporé, Rio** var. Río Iténez. ∽ Bolivia/Brazil see also Iténez, Río
58 B7 **Guaranda** Bolívar, C Ecuador
62 H11 **Guaraniaçu** Paraná, S Brazil
61 O20 **Guarapari** Espírito Santo, SE Brazil
62 I12 **Guarapuava** Paraná, S Brazil
62 L8 **Guararapes** São Paulo, S Brazil
107 S4 **Guara, Sierra de** ▲ NE Spain
62 N10 **Guaratinguetá** São Paulo, S Brazil
106 I7 **Guarda** Guarda, N Portugal
106 I7 **Guarda** ◆ district N Portugal
Guardak see Govurdak
106 M3 **Guardo** Castilla-León, N Spain
106 K11 **Guareña** Extremadura, W Spain
62 J11 **Guaricana, Pico** ▲ S Brazil
56 L6 **Guárico** off. Estado Guárico. ◆ state N Venezuela
46 J7 **Guarico, Punta** headland E Cuba
56 L7 **Guárico, Río** ∽ C Venezuela
62 M10 **Guarujá** São Paulo, SE Brazil
63 L22 **Guarulhos** × (São Paulo) São Paulo, S Brazil
45 R17 **Guarumal** Veraguas, S Panama
Guasapa see Guasopa
42 H8 **Guasave** Sinaloa, C Mexico
56 I8 **Guasdualito** Apure, C Venezuela
57 Q7 **Guasipati** Bolívar, E Venezuela
195 Q15 **Guasopa** var. Guasapa. Woodlark Island, SE PNG
108 F9 **Guastalla** Emilia-Romagna, C Italy
44 D6 **Guastatoya** var. El Progreso. El Progreso, C Guatemala
44 D5 **Guatemala** off. Republic of Guatemala. ◆ republic Central America
44 A2 **Guatemala** off. Departamento de Guatemala. ◆ department S Guatemala
200 O7 **Guatemala Basin** undersea feature E Pacific Ocean
Guatemala City see Guatemala, Ciudad de
47 V14 **Guatuaro Point** headland Trinidad, Trinidad and Tobago
194 G14 **Guavi** ∽ SW PNG
56 G13 **Guaviare** off. Comisaría Guaviare. ◆ province S Colombia
56 J11 **Guaviare, Río** ∽ E Colombia
63 E15 **Guaviravi** Corrientes, NE Argentina
56 G12 **Guayabero, Río** ∽ SW Colombia
47 U6 **Guayama** E Puerto Rico
44 J7 **Guayambre, Río** ∽ S Honduras
Guayanas, Macizo de las see Guiana Highlands
47 V6 **Guayanés, Punta** headland E Puerto Rico
44 J6 **Guayape, Río** ∽ C Honduras
58 B7 **Guayaquil** var. Santiago de Guayaquil. Guayas, SW Ecuador
Guayaquil see Simon Bolivar
58 A8 **Guayaquil, Golfo de** var. Gulf of Guayaquil. gulf SW Ecuador
Guayaquil, Gulf of see Guayaquil, Golfo de
58 A7 **Guayas** ◆ province W Ecuador
64 N7 **Guaycurú, Río** ∽ NE Argentina
42 F6 **Guaymas** Sonora, NW Mexico
47 U5 **Guaynabo** E Puerto Rico
82 H12 **Guba** NW Ethiopia
152 H8 **Gubadag** Turkm. Tel'man; prev. Tel'mansk. Dashkhovuzskiy Velayat, N Turkmenistan
129 T1 **Guba Dolgaya** Nenetskiy Avtonomnyy Okrug, NW Russian Federation
129 V13 **Gubakha** Permskaya Oblast', NW Russian Federation
108 I12 **Gubbio** Umbria, C Italy
102 Q13 **Guben** var. Wilhelm-Pieck-Stadt. Brandenburg, E Germany
Guben see Gubin
112 D12 **Gubin** Ger. Guben. Zielona Góra, W Poland
130 K8 **Gubkin** Belgorodskaya Oblast', W Russian Federation
Gudara see Ghŭdara
107 S8 **Gúdar, Sierra de** ▲ E Spain
143 P8 **Gudaut'a** NW Georgia
96 G12 **Gudbrandsdalen** valley S Norway
97 G21 **Gudenå** var. Gudenaa. ∽ C Denmark
Gudenaa see Gudenå
131 P16 **Gudermes** Chechenskaya Respublika, SW Russian Federation
161 J18 **Gūdūr** Andhra Pradesh, E India
152 B13 **Gudurolum** Balkanskiy Velayat, W Turkmenistan
96 D13 **Gudvangen** Sogn og Fjordane, S Norway
105 U7 **Guebwiller** Haut-Rhin, NE France
Guéckédou see Guékédou
12 K8 **Guéguen, Lac** ◎ Québec, SE Canada
78 J15 **Guékédou** var. Guéckédou. Guinée-Forestière, S Guinea
43 R16 **Guelatao** Oaxaca, SE Mexico
Guelders see Gelderland
80 G11 **Guélengdeng** Mayo-Kébbi, W Chad
76 L5 **Guelma** var. Gâlma. NE Algeria
76 D8 **Guelmime** var. Goulimime. SW Morocco
12 G15 **Guelph** Ontario, S Canada
104 I7 **Guéméné-Penfao** Loire-Atlantique, NW France
104 I7 **Guer** Morbihan, NW France
80 I11 **Guéra** off. Préfecture du Guéra. ◆ prefecture S Chad
104 H8 **Guérande** Loire-Atlantique, NW France
80 K9 **Guéréda** Biltine, E Chad
105 N10 **Guéret** Creuse, C France
Guernica/Guernica y Lumo see Gernika-Lumo
35 Z15 **Guernsey** Wyoming, C USA
99 K25 **Guernsey** island Channel Islands, NW Europe
78 J10 **Guérou** Assaba, S Mauritania
27 R16 **Guerra** Texas, SW USA
43 O15 **Guerrero** ◆ state S Mexico
42 D6 **Guerrero Negro** Baja California Sur, NW Mexico
105 P9 **Gueugnon** Saône-et-Loire, C France
78 M17 **Guéyo** S Ivory Coast
109 L15 **Guglionesi** Molise, C Italy
196 K5 **Guguan** island C Northern Mariana Islands
Guhrau see Góra
Gui see Guangxi Zhuangzu Zizhiqu
Guiana see French Guiana
49 V4 **Guiana Basin** undersea feature W Atlantic Ocean
50 G6 **Guiana Highlands** var. Macizo de las Guayanas. ▲ N South America
Guiba see Juba
104 I7 **Guichen** Ille-et-Vilaine, NW France
63 E18 **Guichón** Paysandú, W Uruguay
79 U12 **Guidan-Roumji** Maradi, S Niger
Guidder see Guider
165 T10 **Guide** Qinghai, C China
80 F12 **Guider** var. Guidder. Nord, N Cameroon
78 I11 **Guidimaka** ◆ region S Mauritania
79 W12 **Guidimouni** Zinder, S Niger
78 G10 **Guier, Lac de** var. Lac de Guiers. ◎ N Senegal
166 L14 **Guigang** prev. Guixian, Gui Xian. Guangxi Zhuangzu Zizhiqu, S China
78 L16 **Guiglo** W Ivory Coast
56 L5 **Güigüe** Carabobo, N Venezuela
85 M20 **Guijá** Gaza, S Mozambique
44 E7 **Güija, Lago de** ◎ El Salvador/Guatemala
106 K8 **Guijuelo** Castilla-León, N Spain
Guilan see Gīlān
99 N22 **Guildford** SE England, UK
21 R5 **Guildford** Maine, NE USA
21 O7 **Guildhall** Vermont, NE USA
105 R13 **Guilherand** Ardèche, E France
166 L13 **Guilin** var. Kuei-lin, Kweilin. Guangxi Zhuangzu Zizhiqu, S China
10 J6 **Guillaume-Delisle, Lac** ◎ Québec, NE Canada
105 U13 **Guillestre** Hautes-Alpes, SE France
106 H6 **Guimarães** var. Guimaráes. Braga, N Portugal
60 D11 **Guimarães Rosas, Pico** ▲ NW Brazil
25 N3 **Guin** Alabama, S USA
Güina see Wina
78 I14 **Guinea** off. Republic of Guinea, var. Guinée; prev. French Guinea, People's Revolutionary Republic of Guinea. ◆ republic W Africa
66 N13 **Guinea Basin** undersea feature E Atlantic Ocean
78 E12 **Guinea-Bissau** off. Republic of Guinea-Bissau, Fr. Guinée-Bissau, Port. Guiné-Bissau; prev. Portuguese Guinea. ◆ republic W Africa
68 K7 **Guinea Fracture Zone** tectonic feature E Atlantic Ocean
66 O13 **Guinea, Gulf of** Fr. Golfe de Guinée. gulf E Atlantic Ocean
Guiné-Bissau see Guinea-Bissau
Guinée see Guinea
Guinée-Bissau see Guinea-Bissau
78 K15 **Guinée-Forestière** ◆ state SE Guinea
Guinée, Golfe de see Guinea, Gulf of
78 H13 **Guinée-Maritime** ◆ state W Guinea
46 C4 **Güines** La Habana, W Cuba
104 G5 **Guingamp** Côtes d'Armor, NW France
107 P3 **Guipúzcoa** Basq. Gipuzkoa. ◆ province País Vasco, N Spain
46 C5 **Güira de Melena** La Habana, W Cuba
76 G8 **Guir, Hamada du** desert Algeria/Morocco
57 P5 **Güiria** Sucre, NE Venezuela
166 L14 **Gui Shui** ∽ S China
106 H2 **Guitiriz** Galicia, NW Spain
79 N17 **Guitri** S Ivory Coast
179 R13 **Guiuan** Samar, C Philippines
Gui Xian/Guixian see Guigang
166 J12 **Guiyang** var. Kuei-Yang, Kuei-yang, Kueyang, Kweiyang; prev. Kweichu. Guizhou, S China
166 J12 **Guizhou** var. Guizhou Sheng, Kuei-chou, Kweichow, Qian. ◆ province S China
Guizhou Sheng see Guizhou
104 J13 **Gujan-Mestras** Gironde, SW France
160 B10 **Gujarāt** var. Gujerat. ◆ state W India
155 V6 **Gūjar Khān** Punjab, E Pakistan
Gujerat see Gujarāt
155 V7 **Gujrānwāla** Punjab, NE Pakistan
155 V7 **Gujrāt** Punjab, E Pakistan
165 U9 **Gulang** Gansu, C China
191 R6 **Gulargambone** New South Wales, SE Australia
161 G15 **Gulbarga** Karnātaka, C India
120 J8 **Gulbene** Ger. Alt-Schwanenburg. Gulbene, NE Latvia
153 U10 **Gul'cha** Kir. Gülchö. Oshskaya Oblast', SW Kyrgyzstan
Gülchö see Gul'cha
181 T10 **Gulden Draak Seamount** undersea feature E Indian Ocean
142 J16 **Gülek Boğazı** var. Cilician Gates. pass S Turkey
194 I14 **Gulf** ◆ province S PNG
25 O9 **Gulf Breeze** Florida, SE USA
25 V13 **Gulfport** Florida, SE USA
24 M9 **Gulfport** Mississippi, S USA
25 O9 **Gulf Shores** Alabama, S USA
Gulf, The see Persian Gulf
191 R7 **Gulgong** New South Wales, SE Australia
166 I11 **Gulin** Sichuan, C China
176 V12 **Gulir** Pulau Kasiui, E Indonesia
Gulistan see Guliston
153 P10 **Guliston** Rus. Gulistan. Sirdaryo Wiloyati, E Uzbekistan
169 T6 **Gulja Shan** ▲ NE China
Gulja see Yining
41 S11 **Gulkana** Alaska, USA
9 S17 **Gull Lake** Saskatchewan, S Canada
33 P10 **Gull Lake** ◎ Michigan, N USA
31 T6 **Gull Lake** ◎ Minnesota, N USA
97 L16 **Gullspång** Skaraborg, S Sweden
158 H5 **Gulmarg** Jammu and Kashmir, NW India
Gulpaigan see Golpāyegān
101 L18 **Gulpen** Limburg, SE Netherlands
151 S13 **Gul'shad** Kaz. Gulshat. Zhezkazgan, E Kazakhstan
Gulshat see Gul'shad
83 F17 **Gulu** N Uganda
116 K10 **Gŭlŭbovo** Khaskovska Oblast, C Bulgaria
116 I7 **Gulyantsi** Loveshka Oblast, NW Bulgaria
Gulyaypole see Hulyaypole
Guma see Pishan
81 K16 **Gumba** Equateur, NW Zaire
Gumbinnen see Gusev
83 H24 **Gumbiro** Ruvuma, S Tanzania
152 B11 **Gumdag** prev. Kum-Dag. Balkanskiy Velayat, W Turkmenistan
79 W12 **Gumel** Jigawa, N Nigeria
107 N5 **Gumiel de Hizán** Castilla-León, N Spain
194 I12 **Gumine** var. Gumire. Chimbu, C PNG
Gumire see Gumine
159 P16 **Gumla** Bihār, N India
Gumma see Gunma
103 F16 **Gummersbach** Nordrhein-Westfalen, W Germany
79 T13 **Gummi** Sokoto, NW Nigeria
Gumpolds see Humpolec
159 N13 **Gumti** var. Gomati. ∽ N India
Gümülcine/Gümüljina see Komotiní
Gümüşane see Gümüşhane
143 O12 **Gümüşhane** var. Gümüşane, Gumushkhane. Gümüşhane, NE Turkey
143 O12 **Gümüşhane** var. Gümüşane, Gumushkhane. ◆ province NE Turkey
Gumushkhane see Gümüşhane
176 W13 **Gumzai** Pulau Kola, E Indonesia
160 H9 **Guna** Madhya Pradesh, C India
Gunabad see Gonābād
Gunbad-i-Qawus see Gonbad-e Kāvūs
191 O9 **Gunbar** New South Wales, SE Australia
191 O9 **Gun Creek** seasonal river New South Wales, SE Australia
191 Q10 **Gundagai** New South Wales, SE Australia
81 K17 **Gundji** Equateur, N Zaire
161 G20 **Gundlupet** Karnātaka, W India
142 G16 **Gündoğmuş** Antalya, S Turkey
143 O14 **Güney Doğu Toroslar** ▲ SE Turkey
81 J21 **Gungu** Bandundu, SW Zaire
131 P17 **Gunib** Respublika Dagestan, SW Russian Federation
114 J11 **Gunja** Vukovar-Srijem, E Croatia
33 P9 **Gun Lake** ◎ Michigan, N USA
171 Jj15 **Gunma** off. Gunma-ken, var. Gumma. ◆ prefecture Honshū, S Japan
207 P15 **Gunnbjørn Fjeld** var. Gunnbjörns Bjerge. ▲ C Greenland
191 S6 **Gunnedah** New South Wales, SE Australia
181 Y15 **Gunner's Quoin** var. Coin de Mire. island N Mauritius
39 R6 **Gunnison** Colorado, C USA
38 L5 **Gunnison** Utah, W USA
39 P5 **Gunnison River** ∽ Colorado, C USA
23 X2 **Gunpowder River** ∽ Maryland, NE USA
Güns see Kőszeg
Gunsan see Kunsan
111 S4 **Gunskirchen** Oberösterreich, N Austria
Gunt see Ghund
161 H17 **Guntakal** Andhra Pradesh, C India
25 Q2 **Guntersville** Alabama, S USA
25 Q2 **Guntersville Lake** ⊡ Alabama, S USA
111 X4 **Guntramsdorf** Niederösterreich, E Austria
161 J16 **Guntūr** var. Guntur. Andhra Pradesh, SE India
173 F7 **Gunungsitoli** Pulau Nias, W Indonesia
161 M14 **Gunupur** Orissa, E India
103 J23 **Günz** ∽ S Germany
Gunzan see Kunsan
103 J22 **Günzburg** Bayern, S Germany
103 K21 **Gunzenhausen** Bayern, S Germany
167 P7 **Guoyang** Anhui, E China
118 G11 **Gurahonț** Hung. Honctő. Arad, W Romania
Gurahumora see Gura Humorului
118 K9 **Gura Humorului** Ger. Gurahumora. Suceava, NE Romania
164 K4 **Gurbantünggüt Shamo** desert W China
158 H7 **Gurdāspur** Punjab, N India
29 T13 **Gurdon** Arkansas, C USA
Gurdzhaani see Gurjaani
Gurgan see Gorgān
158 I10 **Gurgaon** Haryāna, N India
61 M15 **Gurguéia, Rio** ∽ NE Brazil
57 Q7 **Guri, Embalse de** ⊡ E Venezuela
143 V10 **Gurjaani** Rus. Gurdzhaani. E Georgia
111 T8 **Gurk** Kärnten, S Austria
111 T9 **Gurk** Slvn. Krka. ∽ S Austria
Gurkfeld see Krško
116 K9 **Gurkovo** prev. Kolupchii. Khaskovska Oblast, C Bulgaria
111 S9 **Gurktaler Alpen** ▲ S Austria
152 H8 **Gurlan** Rus. Gurlen. Khorazm Wiloyati, W Uzbekistan
Gurlen see Gurlan
85 M16 **Guro** Manica, C Mozambique
142 M14 **Gürün** Sivas, C Turkey
61 K16 **Gurupi** Tocantins, C Brazil
60 L12 **Gurupi, Rio** ∽ NE Brazil
158 E14 **Guru Sikhar** ▲ NW India
Gur'yev/Gur'yevskaya Oblast' see Atyrau
79 U13 **Gusau** Sokoto, N Nigeria
130 C3 **Gusev** Ger. Gumbinnen. Kaliningradskaya Oblast', W Russian Federation
152 J17 **Gushgy** prev. Kushka. Maryyskiy Velayat, S Turkmenistan
Gushiago see Gushiegu
79 Q14 **Gushiegu** var. Gushiago. NE Ghana
172 P15 **Gushikawa** Okinawa, Okinawa, SW Japan
115 L16 **Gusinje** Montenegro, SW Yugoslavia
126 Jj16 **Gusinoozersk** Respublika Buryatiya, S Russian Federation

◆ Country
● Country Capital
◇ Dependent Territory
○ Dependent Territory Capital
◆ Administrative Region
× International Airport
▲ Mountain
▲ Mountain Range
Volcano
∽ River
◎ Lake
⊡ Reservoir

130 M4 **Gus'-Khrustal'nyy** Vladimirskaya Oblast', W Russian Federation
109 B19 **Guspini** Sardegna, Italy, C Mediterranean Sea
111 X8 **Güssing** Burgenland, SE Austria
111 V6 **Gusswerk** Steiermark, E Austria
94 O2 **Gustav Adolf Land** *physical region* NE Svalbard
205 X5 **Gustav Bull Mountains** ▲ Antarctica
41 W13 **Gustavus** Alaska, USA
94 O1 **Gustav V Land** *physical region* NE Svalbard
37 P9 **Gustine** California, W USA
27 R8 **Gustine** Texas, SW USA
102 M9 **Güstrow** Mecklenburg-Vorpommern, NE Germany
97 N18 **Gusum** Östergötland, S Sweden
Guta/Gúta *see* Kolárovo
Gutenstein *see* Ravne na Koroškem
103 G14 **Gütersloh** Nordrhein-Westfalen, W Germany
29 N10 **Guthrie** Oklahoma, C USA
27 P5 **Guthrie** Texas, SW USA
31 U14 **Guthrie Center** Iowa, C USA
43 Q13 **Gutiérrez Zamora** Veracruz-Llave, E Mexico
Gutta *see* Kolárovo
31 Y12 **Guttenberg** Iowa, C USA
Guttentag *see* Dobrodzień
Guttstadt *see* Dobre Miasto
168 G8 **Guulin** Govĭ-Altay, C Mongolia
159 V12 **Guwāhāti** *prev.* Gauhāti. Assam, NE India
145 R3 **Guwēr** *var.* Al Kuwayr, Al Quwayr, Quwair. N Iraq
Guwlumayak *see* Kuuli-Mayak
57 R9 **Guyana** *off.* Cooperative Republic of Guyana; *prev.* British Guiana. ◆ *republic* N South America
23 P5 **Guyandotte River** West Virginia, NE USA
Guyane *see* French Guiana
Guyi *see* Sanjiang
28 H8 **Guymon** Oklahoma, C USA
152 K12 **Guynuk** Lebapskiy Velayat, NE Turkmenistan
23 O9 **Guyot, Mount** ▲ North Carolina/Tennessee, SE USA
191 U5 **Guyra** New South Wales, SE Australia
165 W10 **Guyuan** Ningxia, N China
Guzar *see* Ghuzor
124 N3 **Güzelyurt** *Gk.* Mórfou, Morphou. W Cyprus
124 N2 **Güzelyurt Körfezi** *var.* Morfou Bay, Morphou Bay, *Gk.* Kólpos Mórfou. *bay* W Cyprus
42 I3 **Guzmán** Chihuahua, N Mexico
121 B14 **Gvardeysk** *Ger.* Tapaiu. Kaliningradskaya Oblast', W Russian Federation
Gvardeyskoye *see* Hvardiys'ke
191 R5 **Gwabegar** New South Wales, SE Australia
154 J16 **Gwādar** *var.* Gwadur. Baluchistān, SW Pakistan
154 J16 **Gwādar East Bay** *bay* SW Pakistan
154 J16 **Gwādar West Bay** *bay* SW Pakistan
Gwadur *see* Gwādar
85 J17 **Gwai** Matabeleland North, W Zimbabwe
160 I7 **Gwalior** Madhya Pradesh, C India
85 J18 **Gwanda** Matabeleland South, SW Zimbabwe
81 N15 **Gwane** Haut-Zaïre, N Zaire
85 I17 **Gwayi** W Zimbabwe
112 G8 **Gwda** *var.* Głda, *Ger.* Küddow. NW Poland
99 C14 **Gweebarra Bay** *Ir.* Béal an Bheara. *inlet* W Ireland
99 D14 **Gweedore** *Ir.* Gaoth Dobhair. NW Ireland
Gwelo *see* Gweru
99 K21 **Gwent** *cultural region* S Wales, UK
85 K17 **Gweru** *prev.* Gwelo. Midlands, C Zimbabwe
31 Q7 **Gwinner** North Dakota, N USA
79 Y13 **Gwoza** Borno, NE Nigeria
Gwy *see* Wye
191 R4 **Gwydir River** New South Wales, SE Australia
99 I19 **Gwynedd** *var.* Gwyneth. *cultural region* NW Wales, UK
Gwyneth *see* Gwynedd
165 O16 **Gyaca** Xizang Zizhiqu, W China
Gya'gya *see* Saga
117 M22 **Gyalí** *var.* Yialí. *island* Dodekánisos, Greece, Aegean Sea
Gyandzha *see* Gäncä
164 M16 **Gyangzê** Xizang Zizhiqu, W China
164 L14 **Gyaring Co** ⊛ W China
165 Q12 **Gyaring Hu** ⊛ C China
117 I20 **Gyáros** *var.* Yioúra. *island* Kykládes, Greece, Aegean Sea
126 Hh7 **Gyda** Yamalo-Nenetskiy Avtonomnyy Okrug, N Russian Federation
126 H7 **Gydanskiy Poluostrov** *Eng.* Gyda Peninsula. *peninsula* N Russian Federation
Gyda Peninsula *see* /Gydanskiy Poluostrov
Gyéres *see* Câmpia Turzii
Gyergyószentmiklós *see* Gheorgheni
Gyergyótölgyes *see* Tulgheş
Gyertyámos *see* Cărpiniş
Gyeva *see* Detva
Gyigang *see* Zayü
97 I23 **Gyldenløves Høy** *hill range* C Denmark
189 Z10 **Gympie** Queensland, E Australia
177 Ff7 **Gyobingauk** Pegu, SW Myanmar
113 M23 **Gyomaendrőd** Békés, SE Hungary
Gyömbér *see* Ďumbier
113 L22 **Gyöngyös** Heves, NE Hungary
113 H22 **Győr** *Ger.* Raab; *Lat.* Arrabona. Győr-Moson-Sopron, NW Hungary
113 G22 **Győr-Moson-Sopron** *off.* Győr-Moson-Sopron Megye. ◆ *county* NW Hungary
9 X15 **Gypsumville** Manitoba, S Canada
10 M4 **Gyrfalcon Islands** *island group* Northwest Territories, NE Canada
97 N14 **Gysinge** Gävleborg, C Sweden
117 F22 **Gýtheio** *var.* Githio; *prev.* Yíthion. Pelopónnisos, S Greece
152 L13 **Gyuichbirleshik** Lebapskiy Velayat, E Turkmenistan
113 N24 **Gyula** *Rom.* Jula. Békés, SE Hungary
Gyulafehérvár *see* Alba Iulia
Gyulovo *see* Roza
143 T11 **Gyumri** *var.* Giumri, *Rus.* Kumayri; *prev.* Aleksandropol', Leninakan. W Armenia
152 D13 **Gyunuzyndag, Gora** ▲ W Turkmenistan
152 D12 **Gyzylarbat** *prev.* Kizyl-Arvat. Balkanskiy Velayat, W Turkmenistan
Gyzylbaydak *see* Krasnoye Znamya
Gyzyletrek *see* Kizyl-Atrek
Gyzylgaya *see* Kizyl-Kaya
Gyzylsu *see* Kizyl-Su

H

159 T12 **Ha** W Bhutan
Haabai *see* Ha'apai Group
101 H17 **Haacht** Vlaams Brabant, C Belgium
111 T4 **Haag** Niederösterreich, NE Austria
204 L8 **Haag Nunataks** ▲ Antarctica
94 N2 **Haakon VII Land** *physical region* NW Svalbard
100 O11 **Haaksbergen** Overijssel, E Netherlands
101 E14 **Haamstede** Zeeland, SW Netherlands
200 Ss13 **Ha'ano** *island* Ha'apai Group, C Tonga
200 Ss13 **Ha'apai Group** *var.* Haabai. *island group* C Tonga
95 L15 **Haapajärvi** Oulu, C Finland
95 L17 **Haapamäki** Keski-Suomi, C Finland
95 L15 **Haapavesi** Oulu, C Finland
203 N7 **Haapiti** Moorea, W French Polynesia
120 F4 **Haapsalu** *Ger.* Hapsal. Läänemaa, W Estonia
Ha'Arava *see* 'Arabah, Wādī al
Haarby *see* Hårby
100 H10 **Haarlem** *prev.* Harlem. Noord-Holland, W Netherlands
193 D19 **Haast** West Coast, South Island, NZ
193 C20 **Haast** South Island, NZ
193 D20 **Haast Pass** *pass* South Island, NZ
200 R16 **Ha'atua** 'Eau, E Tonga
155 P15 **Hab** SW Pakistan
147 W7 **Haba** *var.* Al Haba. Dubayy, NE UAE
164 K2 **Habahe** *var.* Kaba. Xinjiang Uygur Zizhiqu, NW China
147 U13 **Ḩabarūt** *var.* Habrut. SW Oman
83 J18 **Habaswein** North Eastern, NE Kenya
101 L24 **Habay-la-Neuve** Luxembourg, SE Belgium
145 S8 **Ḩabbānīyah, Buḩayrat** ⊛ C Iraq
Habelschwerdt *see* Bystrzyca Kłodzka
159 V14 **Habiganj** Chittagong, NE Bangladesh
169 Q12 **Habirag** Nei Mongol Zizhiqu, N China
97 L19 **Habo** Skaraborg, S Sweden
127 P16 **Habomai Islands** *island group* Kuril'skiye Ostrova, SE Russian Federation
172 P3 **Haboro** Hokkaidō, NE Japan
159 S16 **Habra** West Bengal, NE India
Habrut *see* Ḩabarūt
149 P17 **Ḩabshān** Abū Ẓaby, C UAE
56 E14 **Hacha** Putumayo, S Colombia
172 Ss13 **Hachijō** Tōkyō, Hachijō-jima, SE Japan
172 Ss13 **Hachijō-jima** *var.* Hatizyô Zima. *island* Izu-shotō, SE Japan
171 I14 **Hachiman** Gifu, Honshū, SW Japan
171 M9 **Hachimori** Akita, Honshū, C Japan
172 N10 **Hachinohe** Aomori, Honshū, C Japan
171 Jj16 **Hachiōji** *var.* Hatiôzi. Tōkyō, Honshū, S Japan
95 G17 **Hackås** Jämtland, C Sweden
20 K14 **Hackensack** New Jersey, NE USA
Hadama *see* Nazrēt
171 J16 **Hadano** Kanagawa, Honshū, S Japan
147 W13 **Ḩaḑbaram** S Oman
145 U13 **Ḩaddānīyah** *well* S Iraq
98 K12 **Haddington** SE Scotland, UK
147 Z8 **Ḩadd, Ra's al** *headland* NE Oman
Haded *see* Xadeed
79 W12 **Hadejia** Jigawa, N Nigeria
79 W12 **Hadejia** N Nigeria
144 F9 **Hadera** Haifa, C Israel
Hadersleben *see* Haderslev
97 G24 **Haderslev** *Ger.* Hadersleben. Sønderjylland, SW Denmark
157 J21 **Hadhdhunmathi Atoll** *var.* Haddummati Atoll, Laamu Atoll. *atoll* S Maldives
Hadhramaut *see* Ḩaḑramawt
147 W17 **Hadīboh** Suquṭrā, SE Yemen
164 K9 **Hadilik** Xinjiang Uygur Zizhiqu, W China
142 H16 **Hadım** Konya, S Turkey
146 K7 **Hadīyah** Al Madīnah, W Saudi Arabia
15 J1 **Hadley Bay** *bay* Victoria Island, Northwest Territories, N Canada
178 Jj6 **Ha Đông** *var.* Hadong. Ha Tây, N Vietnam
147 R15 **Ḩaḑramawt** *Eng.* Hadhramaut. ▲ S Yemen
Hadria *see* Adria
Hadrianopolis *see* Edirne
Hadria Picena *see* Apricena
97 G22 **Hadsten** Århus, C Denmark
97 G21 **Hadsund** Nordjylland, N Denmark
119 S4 **Hadyach** *Rus.* Gadyach. Poltavs'ka Oblast', NE Ukraine
114 I13 **Hadžići** SE Bosnia and Herzegovina
169 W14 **Haeju** S North Korea
Haerbin/Haerhpin/ Ha-erh-pin *see* Harbin
147 P5 **Ḩafar al Bāṭın** Ash Sharqīyah, N Saudi Arabia
9 T15 **Hafford** Saskatchewan, S Canada
142 M13 **Hafik** Sivas, N Turkey
155 V8 **Hāfizābād** Punjab, E Pakistan
94 H4 **Hafnarfjördhur** Reykjanes, W Iceland
Hafnia *see* København, Denmark
Hafnia *see* Denmark
Hafren *see* Severn
Hafun *see* Xaafuun
Hafun, Ras *see* Xaafuun, Raas
82 G10 **Hag 'Abdullah** Sinnar, E Sudan
83 K18 **Hagadera** North Eastern, E Kenya
144 G8 **HaGalil** *Eng.* Galilee. ▲ N Israel
12 G10 **Hagar** Ontario, S Canada
161 G18 **Hagari** *var.* Vedāvati. W India
102 M13 **Hagelberg** *hill* NE Germany
41 N14 **Hagemeister Island** *island* Alaska, USA
103 F15 **Hagen** Nordrhein-Westfalen, W Germany
102 K10 **Hagenow** Mecklenburg-Vorpommern, N Germany
8 K15 **Hagensborg** British Columbia, SW Canada
82 I13 **Hāgere Hiywet** *var.* Agere Hiywet, Ambo. C Ethiopia
35 O15 **Hagerman** Idaho, NW USA
39 U14 **Hagerman** New Mexico, SW USA
23 V2 **Hagerstown** Maryland, NE USA
12 G16 **Hagersville** Ontario, S Canada
104 J15 **Hagetmau** Landes, SW France
97 K14 **Hagfors** Värmland, C Sweden
95 G16 **Häggenås** Jämtland, C Sweden
170 Dd12 **Hagi** Yamaguchi, Honshū, SW Japan
178 J5 **Ha Giang** Ha Giang, N Vietnam
Hagios Evstrátios *see* Ágios Efstrátios
HaGolan *see* Golan Heights
105 T4 **Hagondange** Moselle, NE France
99 B18 **Hag's Head** *Ir.* Ceann Caillí. *headland* W Ireland
104 I3 **Hague, Cap de la** *headland* N France
105 V5 **Haguenau** Bas-Rhin, NE France
172 T16 **Hahajima-rettō** *island group* SE Japan
13 R8 **Há Há , Lac** ⊛ Québec, SE Canada
180 H13 **Hahaya** ✕ (Moroni) Grande Comore, NW Comoros
24 K9 **Hahnville** Louisiana, S USA
85 E22 **Haib** Karas, S Namibia
Haibak *see* Āybak
155 N15 **Haibo** SW Pakistan
169 U12 **Haicheng** Liaoning, NE China
Haida *see* Nový Bor
Haidarabad *see* Hyderābād
Haidenschaft *see* Ajdovščina
178 Jj6 **Hai Dương** Hai Hưng, N Vietnam
144 F9 **Haifa** ◆ *district* NW Israel
Haifa *see* Hefa
Haifa, Bay of *see* Hefa, Mifraz
167 P14 **Haifeng** Guangdong, S China
Haifong *see* Hai Phong
167 P3 **Hai He** E China
Haikang *see* Leizhou
166 L17 **Haikou** *var.* Hai-k'ou, Hoihow, *Fr.* Hoï-Hao. Hainan, S China
146 M6 **Ḩā'il** Ḩā'il, NW Saudi Arabia
147 N5 **Ḩā'il** *off.* Minṭaqah Ḩā'il. ◆ *province* N Saudi Arabia
Hai-la-erh *see* Hailar
169 S6 **Hailar** *var.* Hai-la-erh; *prev.* Hulun. Nei Mongol Zizhiqu, N China
169 S6 **Hailar He** NE China
35 P14 **Hailey** Idaho, NW USA
12 H9 **Haileybury** Ontario, S Canada
169 X9 **Hailin** Heilongjiang, NE China
Hā'il, Minṭaqah *see* Ḩā'il
Hailong *see* Meihekou
95 K14 **Hailuoto** *Swe.* Karlö. *island* W Finland
Haima *see* Haymā'
Haimen *see* Jiaojiang
166 M17 **Hainan** *var.* Hainan Sheng, Qiong. ◆ *province* S China
166 K17 **Hainan Dao** *island* S China
Hainan Sheng *see* Hainan
Hainan Strait *see* Qiongzhou Haixia
Hainasch *see* Ainaži
Hainau *see* Chojnów
101 E20 **Hainaut** ◆ *province* SW Belgium
Hainburg *see* Hainburg an der Donau
111 Z4 **Hainburg an der Donau** *var.* Hainburg. Niederösterreich, NE Austria
41 W12 **Haines** Alaska, USA
34 L12 **Haines** Oregon, NW USA
25 W12 **Haines City** Florida, SE USA
8 H8 **Haines Junction** Yukon Territory, W Canada
111 W4 **Hainfeld** Niederösterreich, NE Austria
103 N16 **Hainichen** Sachsen, E Germany
178 K6 **Hai Phong** *var.* Haifong, Haiphong. N Vietnam
167 S12 **Haitan Dao** *island* SE China
46 K8 **Haiti** *off.* Republic of Haiti. ◆ *republic* C West Indies
37 T11 **Haiwee Reservoir** ▣ California, W USA
82 I7 **Haiya** Red Sea, NE Sudan
165 T10 **Haiyan** Qinghai, W China
166 M13 **Haiyang Shan** ▲ S China
165 V10 **Haiyuan** Ningxia, N China
Hajda *see* Nový Bor
113 M22 **Hajdú-Bihar** *off.* Hajdú-Bihar Megye. ◆ *county* E Hungary
113 N22 **Hajdúböszörmény** Hajdú-Bihar, E Hungary
113 N22 **Hajdúhadház** Hajdú-Bihar, E Hungary
113 N21 **Hajdúnánás** Hajdú-Bihar, E Hungary
113 N22 **Hajdúszoboszló** Hajdú-Bihar, E Hungary
148 I3 **Ḩājī Ebrāhīm, Kūh-e** ▲ Iran/Iraq
171 Kk11 **Hajiki-zaki** *headland* Sado, C Japan
Hajîne *see* Abū Ḩardān
159 P13 **Hājīpur** Bihār, N India
147 N14 **Ḩajjah** W Yemen
145 U11 **Hajjama** S Iraq
149 R12 **Ḩājjīābād** Hormozgān, C Iran
145 U14 **Ḩājj, Thaqb al** *well* S Iraq
115 L16 **Hajla** ▲ SW Yugoslavia
112 P10 **Hajnówka** *Ger.* Hermhausen. Białystok, E Poland
177 Ff4 **Haka** Chin State, W Myanmar
Hakapehi *see* Punaauia
Hakâri *see* Hakkâri
143 T16 **Hakkâri** *var.* Çölemerik, Hakâri. Hakkâri, SE Turkey
143 T16 **Hakkâri** *var.* Hakkari. ◆ *province* SE Turkey
94 J12 **Hakkas** Norrbotten, N Sweden
171 Gg16 **Hakken-zan** ▲ Honshū, SW Japan
172 N9 **Hakkōda-san** ▲ Honshū, C Japan
172 Pp3 **Hako-dake** ▲ Hokkaidō, NE Japan
172 N7 **Hakodate** Hokkaidō, NE Japan
171 Ii12 **Hakui** Ishikawa, Honshū, SW Japan
202 B16 **Hakupu** SE Niue
171 I14 **Haku-san** ▲ Honshū, SW Japan
Hal *see* Halle
155 Q15 **Hāla** Sind, SE Pakistan
144 J3 **Ḩalab** *Eng.* Aleppo, *Fr.* Alep; *anc.* Beroea. Ḩalab, NW Syria
144 J3 **Ḩalab** *off.* Muḩāfaẓat Ḩalab, *var.* Aleppo, Halab. ◆ *governorate* NW Syria
144 J3 **Ḩalab** ✕ Ḩalab, NW Syria
147 O8 **Ḩalabān** *var.* Halibān. Ar Riyāḑ, C Saudi Arabia
145 V4 **Ḩalabja** NE Iraq
202 A16 **Halagigie Point** *headland* W Niue
77 Z11 **Halaib** SE Egypt
202 G12 **Halalo** Île Uvea, N Wallis and Futuna
Halandri *see* Chalándri
147 X13 **Ḩalāniyāt, Juzur al** *var.* Jazā'ir Bin Ghalfān, *Eng.* Kuria Muria Islands. *island group* S Oman
147 W13 **Ḩalānīyāt, Khalīj al** *Eng.* Kuria Muria Bay. *bay* S Oman
Halas *see* Kiskunhalas
40 G11 **Halawa** *Haw.* Hālawa. Hawaii, USA, C Pacific Ocean
40 F9 **Halawa, Cape** *headland* Molokai, Hawaii, USA, C Pacific Ocean
168 H6 **Halban** Hövsgöl, N Mongolia
103 K14 **Halberstadt** Sachsen-Anhalt, C Germany
192 M12 **Halcombe** Manawatu-Wanganui, North Island, NZ
97 I16 **Halden** *prev.* Fredrikshald. Østfold, S Norway
102 L13 **Haldensleben** Sachsen-Anhalt, C Germany
Háldi *see* Halti
159 S17 **Haldia** West Bengal, NE India
158 K10 **Haldwāni** Uttar Pradesh, N India
40 F10 **Haleakala** *crater* Maui, Hawaii, USA, C Pacific Ocean
27 N4 **Hale Center** Texas, SW USA
101 J18 **Halen** Limburg, NE Belgium
25 O2 **Haleyville** Alabama, S USA
79 O17 **Half Assini** SW Ghana
37 R8 **Half Dome** ▲ California, W USA
193 C25 **Halfmoon Bay** *var.* Oban. Stewart Island, Southland, NZ
190 E5 **Half Moon Lake** *salt lake* South Australia
169 R7 **Halhgol** Dornod, E Mongolia
Haliacmon *see* Aliákmonas
Halibān *see* Ḩalabān
12 I13 **Haliburton** Ontario, SE Canada
12 I12 **Haliburton Highlands** *var.* Madawaska Highlands. *hill range* Ontario, SE Canada
11 Q15 **Halifax** Nova Scotia, SE Canada
99 L17 **Halifax** N England, UK
23 W8 **Halifax** North Carolina, SE USA
23 U7 **Halifax** Virginia, NE USA
11 Q15 **Halifax** ✕ Nova Scotia, SE Canada
149 T13 **Halīl Rūd** *seasonal river* SE Iran
144 I6 **Ḩalīmah** ▲ Lebanon/Syria
168 G8 **Haliun** Govĭ-Altay, W Mongolia
120 I3 **Haljala** *Ger.* Halljal. Lääne-Virumaa, N Estonia
41 Q4 **Halkett, Cape** *headland* Alaska, USA
Halkida *see* Chalkída
98 J6 **Halkirk** N Scotland, UK
13 X7 **Hall** Québec, SE Canada
Hall *see* Schwäbisch Hall
95 H15 **Hälla** Västerbotten, N Sweden
98 J6 **Halladale** N Scotland, UK
97 J21 **Halland** ◆ *county* S Sweden
25 Z15 **Hallandale** Florida, SE USA
97 K22 **Hallandsås** *physical region* S Sweden
15 M2 **Hall Beach** Northwest Territories, N Canada
101 G19 **Halle** *Fr.* Hal. Vlaams Brabant, C Belgium
103 M15 **Halle** *var.* Halle an der Saale. Sachsen-Anhalt, C Germany
Halle an der Saale *see* Halle
37 W3 **Halleck** Nevada, W USA
97 L15 **Hällefors** Örebro, C Sweden
97 N16 **Hälleforsnäs** Södermanland, C Sweden
111 Q6 **Hallein** Salzburg, N Austria
103 L15 **Halle-Neustadt** Sachsen-Anhalt, C Germany
27 U12 **Hallettsville** Texas, SW USA
205 N4 **Halley** *UK research station* Antarctica
30 L4 **Halliday** North Dakota, N USA
39 S2 **Halligan Reservoir** ▣ Colorado, C USA
102 G7 **Halligen** *island group* N Germany
96 G13 **Hallingdal** *valley* S Norway
40 J12 **Hall Island** *island* Alaska, USA
Hall Island *see* Maiana
201 P15 **Hall Islands** *island group* C Micronesia
120 H6 **Halliste** S Estonia
Halljal *see* Haljala
95 I15 **Hällnäs** Västerbotten, N Sweden
31 R2 **Hallock** Minnesota, N USA
16 Oo3 **Hall Peninsula** *peninsula* Baffin Island, Northwest Territories, NE Canada
22 F9 **Halls** Tennessee, S USA
97 M16 **Hallsberg** Örebro, C Sweden
189 N5 **Halls Creek** Western Australia
190 L12 **Halls Gap** Victoria, SE Australia
97 N15 **Hallstahammar** Västmanland, C Sweden
111 R6 **Hallstatt** Salzburg, W Austria
111 R6 **Hallstatter See** ⊛ C Austria
97 P14 **Hallstavik** Stockholm, C Sweden
27 X7 **Hallsville** Texas, SW USA
105 P1 **Halluin** Nord, N France
Halmahera, Laut *see* Halmahera Sea
175 T7 **Halmahera, Pulau** *prev.* Djailolo, Gilolo, Jailolo. *island* E Indonesia
175 Tt8 **Halmahera Sea** *Ind.* Laut Halmahera. *sea* E Indonesia
97 J21 **Halmstad** Halland, S Sweden
175 T11 **Halong** Pulau Ambon, E Indonesia
121 N15 **Halowchyn** *Rus.* Golovchin. Mahilyowskaya Voblasts', E Belarus
97 H20 **Hals** Nordjylland, N Denmark
96 F8 **Halsa** Møre og Romsdal, S Norway
121 I15 **Hal'shany** *Rus.* Gol'shany. Hrodzyenskaya Voblasts', W Belarus
Hälsingborg *see* Helsingborg
31 R5 **Halstad** Minnesota, N USA
29 N6 **Halstead** Kansas, C USA
101 G15 **Halsteren** Noord-Brabant, S Netherlands
95 L16 **Halsua** Vaasa, W Finland
103 E14 **Haltern** Nordrhein-Westfalen, W Germany
94 J9 **Halti** *var.* Haltiatunturi, *Lapp.* Háldi. ▲ Finland/Norway
Haltiatunturi *see* Halti
118 J6 **Halych** Ivano-Frankivs'ka Oblast', W Ukraine
Halycus *see* Platani
105 P3 **Ham** Somme, N France
Hama *see* Ḩamāh
170 Ee12 **Hamada** Shimane, Honshū, SW Japan
148 L6 **Hamadān** *anc.* Ecbatana. Hamadān, W Iran
148 L6 **Hamadān** *off.* Ostān-e Hamadān. ◆ *province* W Iran
144 I5 **Ḩamāh** *var.* Hama; *anc.* Epiphania, *Bibl.* Hamath. Ḩamāh, W Syria
144 I5 **Ḩamāh** *off.* Muḩāfaẓat Ḩamāh, *var.* Hama. ◆ *governorate* C Syria
171 I17 **Hamakita** Shizuoka, Honshū, S Japan
172 O4 **Hamamasu** Hokkaidō, NE Japan
171 I17 **Hamamatsu** *var.* Hamamatu. Shizuoka, Honshū, S Japan
Hamamatu *see* Hamamatsu
172 Qq7 **Hamanaka** Hokkaidō, NE Japan
171 I17 **Hamana-ko** ⊛ Honshū, S Japan
96 I13 **Hamar** *prev.* Storhammer. Hedmark, S Norway
147 U10 **Ḩamārīr al Kidan, Qalamat** *well* E Saudi Arabia
170 G12 **Hamasaka** Hyōgo, Honshū, SW Japan
Hamath *see* Ḩamāh
172 Pp2 **Hamatonbetsu** Hokkaidō, NE Japan
161 K26 **Hambantota** Southern Province, SE Sri Lanka
194 G10 **Hambili** NW PNG
Hambourg *see* Hamburg
102 J9 **Hamburg** Hamburg, N Germany
29 V14 **Hamburg** Arkansas, C USA
31 S16 **Hamburg** Iowa, C USA
20 D10 **Hamburg** New York, NE USA
102 I10 **Hamburg** *Fr.* Hambourg. ◆ *state* N Germany
154 K5 **Hamdam Āb, Dasht-e** *Pash.* Dasht-i Hamdamab. ▲ W Afghanistan
Hamdamab, Dasht-i *see* Hamdam Āb, Dasht-e
20 M13 **Hamden** Connecticut, NE USA
146 K6 **Ḩamḑ, Wādī al** *dry watercourse* W Saudi Arabia
95 L18 **Häme** *Swe.* Tavastehus. ◆ *province* C Finland
95 K18 **Hämeenkyrö** Häme, SW Finland
95 L19 **Hämeenlinna** *Swe.* Tavastehus. Häme, SW Finland
HaMelah, Yam *see* Dead Sea
Hamelin *see* Hameln
102 I13 **Hameln** *Eng.* Hamelin. Niedersachsen, N Germany
188 I8 **Hamersley Range** ▲ Western Australia
169 Y12 **Hamgyŏng-sanmaek** ▲ N North Korea
169 X13 **Hamhŭng** C North Korea
165 O6 **Hami** *var.* Ha-mi, *Uigh.* Kumul, Qomul. Xinjiang Uygur Zizhiqu, NW China
145 X10 **Ḩāmid Amīn** E Iraq
147 W11 **Hamīdān, Khawr** *oasis* SE Saudi Arabia
144 H5 **Ḩamīdīyah** *var.* Hamîdîyé. Tarṭūs, W Syria
116 L12 **Hamidiye** Edirne, NW Turkey
Hamîdîyé *see* Ḩamīdīyah
190 L12 **Hamilton** Victoria, SE Australia
66 B12 **Hamilton** ○ (Bermuda) C Bermuda
12 G16 **Hamilton** Ontario, S Canada
192 M7 **Hamilton** Waikato, North Island, NZ
98 I12 **Hamilton** S Scotland, UK
25 N3 **Hamilton** Alabama, S USA
40 M10 **Hamilton** Alaska, USA
32 J13 **Hamilton** Illinois, N USA
29 S3 **Hamilton** Missouri, C USA
35 P10 **Hamilton** Montana, NW USA
27 S8 **Hamilton** Texas, SW USA
12 G16 **Hamilton** ✕ Ontario, SE Canada
66 I6 **Hamilton Bank** *undersea feature* SE Labrador Sea
190 E1 **Hamilton Creek** *seasonal river* South Australia
11 R8 **Hamilton Inlet** *inlet* Newfoundland and Labrador, E Canada
29 T12 **Hamilton, Lake** ▣ Arkansas, C USA
37 W6 **Hamilton, Mount** ▲ Nevada, W USA
77 S8 **Ḩamīm, Wādī al** NE Libya
95 N19 **Hamina** *Swe.* Fredrikshamn. Kymi, S Finland
9 W16 **Hamiota** Manitoba, S Canada
158 L13 **Hamīrpur** Uttar Pradesh, N India
Hamīs Musait *see* Khamīs Mushayt
23 T11 **Hamlet** North Carolina, SE USA
27 P6 **Hamlin** Texas, SW USA
23 P5 **Hamlin** West Virginia, NE USA
33 O7 **Hamlin Lake** ⊛ Michigan, N USA
103 F14 **Hamm** *var.* Hamm in Westfalen. Nordrhein-Westfalen, W Germany
Ḩammāmāt, Khalīj al *see* Hammamet, Golfe de
77 N5 **Hammamet, Golfe de** *Ar.* Khalīj al Ḩammāmāt. *gulf* NE Tunisia
145 R3 **Ḩammān al 'Alīl** N Iraq
145 X12 **Ḩammār, Hawr al** ⊛ SE Iraq
95 J20 **Hammarland** Åland, SW Finland
95 H16 **Hammarstrand** Jämtland, C Sweden
95 O17 **Hammaslahti** Pohjois-Karjala, SE Finland
101 F17 **Hamme** Oost-Vlaanderen, NW Belgium
102 H10 **Hamme** NW Germany
97 G22 **Hammel** Århus, C Denmark
103 I18 **Hammelburg** Bayern, C Germany
101 H18 **Hamme-Mille** Walloon Brabant, C Belgium
102 H10 **Hamme-Oste-Kanal** *canal* NW Germany
95 G16 **Hammerdal** Jämtland, C Sweden
94 K8 **Hammerfest** Finnmark, N Norway
103 D14 **Hamminkeln** Nordrhein-Westfalen, W Germany
Hamm in Westfalen *see* Hamm
28 K10 **Hammon** Oklahoma, C USA
33 N11 **Hammond** Indiana, N USA
24 K8 **Hammond** Louisiana, S USA
101 K20 **Hamoir** Liège, E Belgium
101 J21 **Hamois** Namur, SE Belgium
101 K16 **Hamont** Limburg, NE Belgium
193 F22 **Hampden** Otago, South Island, NZ
21 R6 **Hampden** Maine, NE USA
99 M23 **Hampshire** *cultural region* S England, UK
11 O15 **Hampton** New Brunswick, SE Canada
29 U14 **Hampton** Arkansas, C USA
31 V12 **Hampton** Iowa, C USA
21 P10 **Hampton** New Hampshire, NE USA
23 R14 **Hampton** South Carolina, SE USA
23 P8 **Hampton** Tennessee, S USA
23 X7 **Hampton** Virginia, NE USA
96 L11 **Hamra** Gävleborg, C Sweden
82 D10 **Hamrat esh Sheikh** Northern Kordofan, C Sudan
145 S5 **Ḩamrīn, Jabal** ▲ N Iraq
123 Jj16 **Hamrun** C Malta
178 K14 **Ham Thuân Nam** Binh Thuân, S Vietnam
176 Ww11 **Hamuku** Irian Jaya, E Indonesia
Hāmūn, Daryācheh-ye *see* Şāberī, Hāmūn-e/Sīstān, Daryācheh-ye
Hamwih *see* Southampton
40 G10 **Hana** *Haw.* Hāna. Maui, Hawaii, USA, C Pacific Ocean
23 S14 **Hanahan** South Carolina, SE USA
40 B8 **Hanalei** Kauai, Hawaii, USA, C Pacific Ocean
178 Kk10 **Ha Nam** Quang Nam-Đa Năng, C Vietnam
171 Mm11 **Hanamaki** Iwate, Honshū, C Japan
40 F10 **Hanamanioa, Cape** *headland* Maui, Hawaii, USA, C Pacific Ocean
202 B16 **Hanan** ✕ (Alofi) SW Niue
103 H18 **Hanau** Hessen, W Germany
15 J7 **Hanbury** Northwest Territories, NW Canada
Hânceşti *see* Hînceşti
8 M15 **Hanceville** British Columbia, SW Canada
25 P3 **Hanceville** Alabama, S USA
Hancewicze *see* Hantsavichy
166 L6 **Hancheng** Shaanxi, C China
23 V2 **Hancock** Maryland, NE USA
32 M3 **Hancock** Michigan, N USA
31 S8 **Hancock** Minnesota, N USA
20 I12 **Hancock** New York, NE USA
82 Q12 **Handa** Bari, NE Somalia
167 O5 **Handan** *var.* Han-tan. Hebei, E China
97 P16 **Handen** Stockholm, C Sweden
83 J22 **Handeni** Tanga, E Tanzania
39 Q7 **Handies Peak** ▲ Colorado, C USA
113 J19 **Handlová** *Ger.* Krickerhäu, *Hung.* Nyitrabánya; prev. *Ger.* Kriegerhaj. Stredné Slovensko, C Slovakia
171 K17 **Haneda** ✕ (Tōkyō) Tōkyō, Honshū, S Japan
144 F13 **HaNegev** *Eng.* Negev. *desert* S Israel
37 Q11 **Hanford** California, W USA
203 V16 **Hanga Roa** Easter Island, Chile, E Pacific Ocean
168 H7 **Hangayn Nuruu** ▲ C Mongolia
Hang-chou/Hangchow *see* Hangzhou
97 K20 **Hånger** Jönköping, S Sweden
Hangö *see* Hanko
167 R9 **Hangzhou** *var.* Hang-chou, Hangchow. Zhejiang, SE China
168 F5 **Hanhöhiy Uul** ▲ NW Mongolia
Hanhowuz *see* Khauz-Khan
143 P15 **Hani** Dıyarbakır, SE Turkey
Hania *see* Chaniá
147 R11 **Ḩanīsh al Kabīr, Jazīrat al** *island* SW Yemen
Hanka, Lake *see* Khanka, Lake
95 M17 **Hankasalmi** Keski-Suomi, C Finland
31 R7 **Hankinson** North Dakota, N USA
95 K20 **Hanko** *Swe.* Hangö. Uusimaa, SW Finland
Han-kou/Han-k'ou/Hankow *see* Wuhan
38 M6 **Hanksville** Utah, W USA
158 K6 **Hanle** Jammu and Kashmir, NW India
193 I17 **Hanmer Springs** Canterbury, South Island, NZ
9 R16 **Hanna** Alberta, SW Canada
29 V3 **Hannibal** Missouri, C USA
188 M3 **Hann, Mount** ▲ Western Australia
102 I12 **Hannover** *Eng.* Hanover. Niedersachsen, NW Germany
101 J19 **Hannut** Liège, C Belgium
97 L22 **Hanöbukten** *bay* S Sweden
178 Jj6 **Ha Nôi** *Eng.* Hanoi, *Fr.* Ha noï. ● (Vietnam) N Vietnam
12 F14 **Hanover** Ontario, S Canada
33 P15 **Hanover** Indiana, N USA
20 G16 **Hanover** Pennsylvania, NE USA
23 W6 **Hanover** Virginia, NE USA
Hanover *see* Hannover
65 G23 **Hanover, Isla** *island* S Chile
Hanselbeck *see* Érd
205 X5 **Hansen Mountains** ▲ Antarctica
166 M8 **Han Shui** C China
158 H10 **Hānsi** Haryāna, NW India
97 F20 **Hanstholm** Viborg, NW Denmark
Han-tan *see* Handan
164 H6 **Hantengri Feng** *var.* Pik Khan-Tengri. ▲ China/Kazakhstan *see also* Khan-Tengri, Pik
121 I18 **Hantsavichy** *Pol.* Hancewicze, *Rus.* Gantsevichi. Brestskaya Voblasts', SW Belarus
16 N2 **Hantzsch** Baffin Island, Northwest Territories, NE Canada
158 G9 **Hanumāngarh** Rājasthān, NW India
191 O9 **Hanwood** New South Wales, SE Australia
Hanyang *see* Caidian
Hanyang *see* Wuhan
166 H10 **Hanyuan** *var.* Fulin. Sichuan, C China
166 J7 **Hanzhong** Shaanxi, C China
203 W11 **Hao** *atoll* Îles Tuamotu, C French Polynesia
159 S16 **Hāora** *prev.* Howrah. West Bengal, NE India
80 K8 **Haouach, Ouadi** *dry watercourse* E Chad
Haoûârîne *see* Ḩawārīn
94 K13 **Haparanda** Norrbotten, N Sweden
27 N3 **Happy** Texas, SW USA
36 M1 **Happy Camp** California, W USA
11 Q9 **Happy Valley-Goose Bay** *prev.* Goose Bay. Newfoundland and Labrador, E Canada
Hapsal *see* Haapsalu
158 J10 **Hāpur** Uttar Pradesh, N India
144 F12 **HaQatan, HaMakhtesh** ▲ S Israel
146 I4 **Ḩaql** Tabūk, NW Saudi Arabia
176 Vv13 **Har** Pulau Kai Besar, E Indonesia
168 M8 **Haraat** Dundgovĭ, C Mongolia
147 R8 **Ḩaraḑ** *var.* Haradh. Ash Sharqīyah, E Saudi Arabia

◆ Country ● Country Capital ◇ Dependent Territory ○ Dependent Territory Capital ◆ Administrative Region ✕ International Airport ▲ Mountain ▲ Mountain Range Volcano River ⊛ Lake ▣ Reservoir

Haradh *see* Ḩaraḑ
120 *N12* **Haradok** *Rus.* Gorodok. Vitsyebskaya Voblasts', N Belarus
94 *J13* **Harads** Norrbotten, N Sweden
121 *G19* **Haradzyets** *Rus.* Gorodets. Brestskaya Voblasts', SW Belarus
121 *J17* **Haradzyeya** *Rus.* Gorodeya. Minskaya Voblasts', C Belarus
203 *V10* **Haraiki** *atoll* Îles Tuamotu, C French Polynesia
171 *Ll14* **Haramachi** Fukushima, Honshū, E Japan
120 *M12* **Harany** *Rus.* Gorany. Vitsyebskaya Voblasts', N Belarus
85 *L16* **Harare** *prev.* Salisbury. ● (Zimbabwe) Mashonaland East, NE Zimbabwe
85 *L16* **Harare** ✕ Mashonaland East, NE Zimbabwe
80 *J10* **Haraz-Djombo** Batha, C Chad
121 *O16* **Harbavichy** *Rus.* Gorbovichi. Mahilyowskaya Voblasts', E Belarus
78 *J16* **Harbel** W Liberia
169 *W8* **Harbin** *var.* Haerbin, Ha-erh-pin, Kharbin; *prev.* Haerhpin, Pingkiang, Pinkiang. Heilongjiang, NE China
33 *S7* **Harbor Beach** Michigan, N USA
11 *T13* **Harbour Breton** Newfoundland, Newfoundland and Labrador, E Canada
67 *D25* **Harbours, Bay of** *bay* East Falkland, Falkland Islands
97 *G24* **Hårby** *var.* Haarby. Fyn, C Denmark
38 *I13* **Harcuvar Mountains** ▲▲ Arizona, SW USA
110 *I7* **Hard** Vorarlberg, NW Austria
160 *H11* **Harda** Madhya Pradesh, C India
97 *D14* **Hardanger** *physical region* S Norway
97 *D14* **Hardangerfjorden** *fjord* S Norway
96 *E13* **Hardangerjøkulen** *glacier* S Norway
97 *E14* **Hardangervidda** *plateau* S Norway
85 *D20* **Hardap** ◈ *district* S Namibia
23 *R15* **Hardeeville** South Carolina, SE USA
100 *L5* **Hardegarijp** *Fris.* Hurdegaryp. Friesland, N Netherlands
100 *O9* **Hardenberg** Overijssel, E Netherlands
191 *Q9* **Harden-Murrumburrah** New South Wales, SE Australia
100 *K10* **Harderwijk** Gelderland, C Netherlands
32 *J14* **Hardin** Illinois, N USA
35 *V11* **Hardin** Montana, NW USA
25 *R5* **Harding, Lake** ⊞ Alabama/Georgia, SE USA
22 *J6* **Hardinsburg** Kentucky, S USA
100 *I13* **Hardinxveld-Giessendam** Zuid-Holland, C Netherlands
9 *R15* **Hardisty** Alberta, SW Canada
158 *L12* **Hardoi** Uttar Pradesh, N India
25 *U4* **Hardwick** Georgia, SE USA
29 *W9* **Hardy** Arkansas, C USA
96 *D10* **Hareid** Møre og Romsdal, S Norway
15 *Gg5* **Hare Indian** 〰 Northwest Territories, NW Canada
101 *D18* **Harelbeke** *var.* Harlebeke. West-Vlaanderen, W Belgium
Harem *see* Ḩārim
102 *E11* **Haren** Niedersachsen, NW Germany
100 *N6* **Haren** Groningen, NE Netherlands
82 *L13* **Hārer** E Ethiopia
97 *P14* **Harg** Uppsala, C Sweden
Hargeisa *see* Hargeysa
82 *M13* **Hargeysa** *var.* Hargeisa. Woqooyi Galbeed, NW Somalia
118 *J10* **Harghita** ◈ *county* NE Romania
27 *S17* **Hargill** Texas, SW USA
168 *J8* **Harhorin** Övörhangay, C Mongolia
165 *Q9* **Har Hu** ◎ C China
Hariana *see* Haryāna
147 *P15* **Ḩarīb** W Yemen
174 *I9* **Hari, Batang** *prev.* Djambi. 〰 Sumatera, W Indonesia
158 *J9* **Haridwār** *prev.* Hardwar. Uttar Pradesh, N India
161 *F18* **Harihar** Karnātaka, W India
193 *F18* **Harihari** West Coast, South Island, NZ
144 *I3* **Ḩārim** *var.* Harem. Idlib, W Syria
170 *G14* **Harima-nada** *sea* S Japan
100 *F13* **Haringvliet** *channel* SW Netherlands
100 *F13* **Haringvlietdam** *dam* SW Netherlands
155 *U5* **Harīpur** North-West Frontier Province, NW Pakistan
154 *J4* **Harīrūd** *var.* Tedzhen, *Turkm.* Tejen. 〰 Afghanistan/Iran *see also* Tedzhen
96 *J11* **Härjåhågnen** *Swe.* Härjahågnen, Härjehågna. ▲ Norway/Sweden
95 *K18* **Harjavalta** Turku-Pori, SW Finland
Härjehågna *see* Härjåhågnen
120 *G4* **Harjumaa** *off.* Harju Maakond. ◈ *province* NW Estonia
23 *X11* **Harkers Island** North Carolina, SE USA
145 *S1* **Harki** N Iraq
31 *T14* **Harlan** Iowa, C USA
23 *O7* **Harlan** Kentucky, S USA
31 *N17* **Harlan County Lake** ⊞ Nebraska, C USA
118 *L9* **Hârlău** *var.* Hirlău. Iaşi, NE Romania
Harlebeke *see* Harelbeke
35 *U7* **Harlem** Montana, NW USA
Harlem *see* Haarlem
97 *G22* **Harlev** Århus, C Denmark
100 *K6* **Harlingen** *Fris.* Harns. Friesland, N Netherlands
27 *T17* **Harlingen** Texas, SW USA
99 *O21* **Harlow** E England, UK
35 *T10* **Harlowton** Montana, NW USA
96 *N11* **Harmånger** Gävleborg, C Sweden
100 *I11* **Harmelen** Utrecht, C Netherlands
31 *X11* **Harmony** Minnesota, N USA
34 *J14* **Harney Basin** *basin* Oregon, NW USA
0 *F9* **Harney Basin** ▲▲ Oregon, NW USA
34 *J14* **Harney Lake** ◎ Oregon, NW USA
30 *J10* **Harney Peak** ▲ South Dakota, N USA
95 *H17* **Härnösand** *var.* Hernösand. Västernorrland, C Sweden
Harns *see* Harlingen
168 *F6* **Har Nuur** ◎ NW Mongolia
107 *P4* **Haro** La Rioja, N Spain
42 *F6* **Haro, Cabo** *headland* NW Mexico
96 *D9* **Harøy** *island* S Norway
99 *N21* **Harpenden** E England, UK
78 *L18* **Harper** *var.* Cape Palmas. NE Liberia
28 *M7* **Harper** Kansas, C USA
34 *L13* **Harper** Oregon, NW USA
27 *Q10* **Harper** Texas, SW USA
37 *U13* **Harper Lake** *salt flat* California, W USA
41 *T9* **Harper, Mount** ▲ Alaska, USA
97 *J21* **Harplinge** Halland, S Sweden
38 *J13* **Harquahala Mountains** ▲▲ Arizona, SW USA
147 *T15* **Ḩarrah** SE Yemen
10 *H11* **Harricana** 〰 Québec, SE Canada
22 *M9* **Harriman** Tennessee, S USA
11 *R11* **Harrington Harbour** Québec, E Canada
66 *B12* **Harrington Sound** *bay* Bermuda, NW Atlantic Ocean
98 *F8* **Harris** *physical region* NW Scotland, UK
29 *X10* **Harrisburg** Arkansas, C USA
32 *M17* **Harrisburg** Illinois, N USA
30 *I14* **Harrisburg** Nebraska, C USA
34 *F12* **Harrisburg** Oregon, NW USA
20 *G15* **Harrisburg** *state capital* Pennsylvania, NE USA
190 *F6* **Harris, Lake** ◎ South Australia
25 *W11* **Harris, Lake** ◎ Florida, SE USA
85 *J22* **Harrismith** Free State, E South Africa
29 *T9* **Harrison** Arkansas, C USA
33 *Q7* **Harrison** Michigan, N USA
30 *I12* **Harrison** Nebraska, C USA
41 *Q5* **Harrison Bay** *inlet* Alaska, USA
24 *I6* **Harrisonburg** Louisiana, S USA
23 *U4* **Harrisonburg** Virginia, NE USA
11 *R7* **Harrison, Cape** *headland* Newfoundland and Labrador, E Canada
29 *R5* **Harrisonville** Missouri, C USA
Harris Ridge *see* Lomonosov Ridge
199 *K3* **Harris Seamount** *undersea feature* N Pacific Ocean
98 *F8* **Harris, Sound of** *strait* NW Scotland, UK
33 *R6* **Harrisville** Michigan, N USA
23 *R3* **Harrisville** West Virginia, NE USA
22 *M6* **Harrodsburg** Kentucky, S USA
99 *M16* **Harrogate** N England, UK
27 *Q4* **Harrold** Texas, SW USA
29 *S5* **Harry S.Truman Reservoir** ⊞ Missouri, C USA
102 *G13* **Harsewinkel** Nordrhein-Westfalen, W Germany
118 *M14* **Hârşova** *prev.* Hîrşova. Constanţa, SE Romania
94 *H10* **Harstad** Troms, N Norway
33 *O8* **Hart** Michigan, N USA
26 *M4* **Hart** Texas, SW USA
8 *I5* **Hart** 〰 Yukon Territory, NW Canada
85 *F23* **Hartbees** 〰 C South Africa
111 *X7* **Hartberg** Steiermark, SE Austria
190 *I10* **Hart, Cape** *headland* South Australia
97 *E14* **Hårteigen** ▲ S Norway
25 *Q7* **Hartford** Alabama, S USA
29 *R11* **Hartford** Arkansas, C USA
20 *M12* **Hartford** *state capital* Connecticut, NE USA
22 *J6* **Hartford** Kentucky, S USA
33 *P10* **Hartford** Michigan, N USA
31 *R11* **Hartford** South Dakota, N USA
32 *M8* **Hartford** Wisconsin, N USA
33 *P13* **Hartford City** Indiana, N USA
31 *Q13* **Hartington** Nebraska, C USA
95 *G15* **Hartkjølen** ▲ C Norway
11 *N14* **Hartland** New Brunswick, SE Canada
99 *H23* **Hartland Point** *headland* SW England, UK
99 *M15* **Hartlepool** N England, UK
31 *T12* **Hartley** Iowa, C USA
26 *M1* **Hartley** Texas, SW USA
34 *J15* **Hart Mountain** ▲ Oregon, NW USA
181 *U10* **Hartog Ridge** *undersea feature* W Indian Ocean
95 *M18* **Hartola** Mikkeli, S Finland
69 *U14* **Harts** *var.* Hartz. 〰 N South Africa
25 *P2* **Hartselle** Alabama, S USA
25 *S3* **Hartsfield Atlanta** ✕ Georgia, SE USA
29 *Q11* **Hartshorne** Oklahoma, C USA
23 *S12* **Hartsville** South Carolina, SE USA
22 *K8* **Hartsville** Tennessee, S USA
29 *U7* **Hartville** Missouri, C USA
25 *U2* **Hartwell** Georgia, SE USA
23 *O11* **Hartwell Lake** ⊞ Georgia/South Carolina, SE USA
Hartz *see* Harts
Harunabad *see* Eslāmābād
168 *E6* **Har-Us** Hovd, W Mongolia
168 *E6* **Har Us Nuur** ◎ NW Mongolia
32 *M10* **Harvard** Illinois, N USA
31 *P16* **Harvard** Nebraska, C USA
39 *R5* **Harvard, Mount** ▲ Colorado, C USA
33 *N11* **Harvey** Illinois, N USA
31 *N4* **Harvey** North Dakota, N USA
99 *Q21* **Harwich** E England, UK
158 *H10* **Haryāna** *var.* Hariana. ◈ *state* N India
147 *Y9* **Ḩaryān, Ṭawī al** *spring/well* NE Oman
103 *J14* **Harz** ▲▲ C Germany
Hasakah *see* Al Ḩasakah
171 *M12* **Hasama** Miyagi, Honshū, C Japan
142 *J15* **Hasan Dağı** ▲ C Turkey
145 *T9* **Ḩasan Ibn Ḩassūn** C Iraq
155 *R6* **Ḩasan Khēl** *var.* Ahmad Khel. Paktiā, SE Afghanistan
102 *F12* **Hase** 〰 NW Germany
Haselberg *see* Krasnoznamensk
102 *F12* **Haselünne** Niedersachsen, NW Germany
168 *K9* **Hashaat** Dundgovĭ, C Mongolia
Hashemite Kingdom of Jordan *see* Jordan
145 *V8* **Hāshimah** E Iraq
171 *Gg16* **Hashimoto** *var.* Hasimoto. Wakayama, Honshū, SW Japan
147 *W13* **Ḩāsik** S Oman
155 *U10* **Hāsilpur** Punjab, E Pakistan
Hasimoto *see* Hashimoto
Hasiye *see* Ḩisyah
29 *Q10* **Haskell** Oklahoma, C USA
27 *Q6* **Haskell** Texas, SW USA
116 *M11* **Hasköy** Edirne, NW Turkey
97 *L24* **Hasle** Bornholm, E Denmark
99 *N23* **Haslemere** SE England, UK
104 *I16* **Hasparren** Pyrénées-Atlantiques, SW France
Hassakeh *see* Al Ḩasakah
161 *G19* **Hassan** Karnātaka, W India
38 *J13* **Hassayampa River** 〰 Arizona, SW USA
103 *J18* **Hassberge** *hill range* C Germany
96 *N10* **Hassela** Gävleborg, C Sweden
101 *J18* **Hasselt** Limburg, NE Belgium
100 *M9* **Hasselt** Overijssel, E Netherlands
Hassetché *see* Al Ḩasakah
103 *J18* **Hassfurt** Bayern, C Germany
76 *L9* **Hassi Bel Guebbour** E Algeria
76 *L8* **Hassi Messaoud** E Algeria
97 *K22* **Hässleholm** Kristianstad, S Sweden
Hasta Colonia/Hasta Pompeia *see* Asti
191 *O13* **Hastings** Victoria, SE Australia
192 *O11* **Hastings** Hawke's Bay, North Island, NZ
99 *P23* **Hastings** SE England, UK
33 *P9* **Hastings** Michigan, N USA
31 *W9* **Hastings** Minnesota, N USA
31 *P16* **Hastings** Nebraska, C USA
97 *K22* **Hästveda** Kristianstad, S Sweden
94 *J8* **Hasvik** Finnmark, N Norway
39 *V6* **Haswell** Colorado, C USA
168 *I10* **Hatansuudal** Bayanhongor, C Mongolia
169 *P9* **Hatavch** Sühbaatar, E Mongolia
142 *K17* **Hatay** ◈ *province* S Turkey
39 *R15* **Hatch** New Mexico, SW USA
38 *K7* **Hatch** Utah, W USA
22 *F9* **Hatchie River** 〰 Tennessee, S USA
118 *G12* **Haţeg** *Ger.* Wallenthal, *Hung.* Hátszeg; *prev.* Hatzeg, Hötzing. Hunedoara, SW Romania
172 *Oo17* **Hateruma-jima** *island* Yaeyama-shotō, SW Japan
191 *N8* **Hatfield** New South Wales, SE Australia
168 *I5* **Hatgal** Hövsgöl, N Mongolia
159 *V16* **Hathazari** Chittagong, SE Bangladesh
147 *T13* **Hathūt, Hişā'** *oasis* NE Yemen
178 *I13* **Ha Tiên** Kiên Giang, S Vietnam
178 *J8* **Ha Tinh** Ha Tinh, N Vietnam
Hatiōzi *see* Hachiōji
144 *F12* **Ḩatira, Haré** *hill range* S Israel
178 *J6* **Hat Lot** Sơn La, N Vietnam
47 *P16* **Hato Airport** ✕ (Willemstad) Curaçao, SW Netherlands Antilles
56 *H9* **Hato Corozal** Casanare, C Colombia
Hato del Volcán *see* Volcán
47 *P9* **Hato Mayor** E Dominican Republic
Hatra *see* Al Ḩaḑr
Hatria *see* Adria
Hátszeg *see* Haţeg
149 *R16* **Ḩattá** Dubayy, NE UAE
190 *L9* **Hattah** Victoria, SE Australia
100 *M9* **Hattem** Gelderland, E Netherlands
23 *Z10* **Hatteras** Hatteras Island, North Carolina, SE USA
23 *Rr10* **Hatteras, Cape** *headland* North Carolina, SE USA
23 *Z9* **Hatteras Island** *island* North Carolina, SE USA
66 *F10* **Hatteras Plain** *undersea feature* W Atlantic Ocean
95 *G14* **Hattfjelldal** Troms, N Norway
24 *M7* **Hattiesburg** Mississippi, S USA
31 *Q4* **Hatton** North Dakota, N USA
Hatton Bank *see* Hatton Ridge
66 *L6* **Hatton Ridge** *var.* Hatton Bank. *undersea feature* N Atlantic Ocean
203 *W6* **Hatutu** *island* Îles Marquises, NE French Polynesia
113 *K22* **Hatvan** Heves, NE Hungary
178 *H17* **Hat Yai** *var.* Ban Hat Yai. Songkhla, SW Thailand
Hatzeg *see* Haţeg
Hatzfeld *see* Jimbolia
82 *N13* **Haud** *plateau* Ethiopia/Somalia
97 *D18* **Hauge** Rogaland, S Norway
97 *C15* **Haugesund** Rogaland, S Norway
111 *X2* **Haugsdorf** Niederösterreich, NE Austria
192 *M9* **Hauhungaroa Range** ▲▲ North Island, NZ
97 *E15* **Haukeligrend** Telemark, S Norway
95 *L14* **Haukipudas** Oulu, C Finland
95 *M17* **Haukivesi** ◎ SE Finland
95 *M17* **Haukivuori** Mikkeli, SE Finland
Hauptkanal *see* Havelländ Grosse
195 *Z17* **Hauraha** San Cristobal, SE Solomon Islands
192 *L5* **Hauraki Gulf** *gulf* North Island, NZ
193 *B24* **Hauroko, Lake** ◎ South Island, NZ
178 *Jj15* **Hậu, Sông** 〰 S Vietnam
94 *N12* **Hautajärvi** Lappi, NE Finland
76 *F7* **Haut Atlas** *Eng.* High Atlas. ▲▲ C Morocco
104 *F1* **Haute-Corse** ◈ *department* Corse, France, C Mediterranean Sea
104 *L16* **Haute-Garonne** ◈ *department* S France
78 *J13* **Haute-Guinée** ◈ *state* NE Guinea
81 *K14* **Haute-Kotto** ◈ *prefecture* E Central African Republic
105 *P12* **Haute-Loire** ◈ *department* C France
105 *R6* **Haute-Marne** ◈ *department* N France
104 *M3* **Haute-Normandie** ◈ *region* N France
13 *U6* **Hauterive** Québec, SE Canada
105 *T13* **Hautes-Alpes** ◈ *department* SE France
105 *S7* **Haute-Saône** ◈ *department* E France
105 *T10* **Haute-Savoie** ◈ *department* E France
101 *M20* **Hautes Fagnes** *Ger.* Hohes Venn. ▲▲ E Belgium
104 *K16* **Hautes-Pyrénées** ◈ *department* S France
101 *L23* **Haute Sûre, Lac de la** ⊞ NW Luxembourg
104 *M11* **Haute-Vienne** ◈ *department* C France
21 *S8* **Haut, Isle au** *island* Maine, NE USA
81 *M14* **Haut-Mbomou** ◈ *préfecture* SE Central African Republic
105 *Q2* **Hautmont** Nord, N France
81 *F19* **Haut-Ogooué** *off.* Province du Haut-Ogooué, *var.* Le Haut-Ogooué. ◈ *province* SE Gabon
Haut-Ogooué, Le *see* Haut-Ogooué
105 *U7* **Haut-Rhin** ◈ *department* NE France
76 *I6* **Hauts Plateaux** *plateau* Algeria/Morocco
81 *M17* **Haut-Zaïre** *off.* Région du Haut-Zaïre. ◈ *region* NE Zaire
40 *D9* **Hauula** *Haw.* Hau'ula. Oahu, Hawaii, USA, C Pacific Ocean
103 *O22* **Hauzenberg** Bayern, SE Germany
32 *K13* **Havana** Illinois, N USA
Havana *see* La Habana
99 *N23* **Havant** S England, UK
37 *Y14* **Havasu, Lake** ⊞ Arizona/California, W USA
97 *J23* **Havdrup** Roskilde, E Denmark
102 *N10* **Havel** 〰 NE Germany
101 *J21* **Havelange** Namur, SE Belgium
102 *M11* **Havelberg** Sachsen-Anhalt, NE Germany
155 *U5* **Haveliān** North-West Frontier Province, NW Pakistan
102 *N12* **Havelländ Grosse** *var.* Hauptkanal. *canal* NE Germany
12 *J14* **Havelock** Ontario, SE Canada
193 *J14* **Havelock** Marlborough, South Island, NZ
23 *X11* **Havelock** North Carolina, SE USA
192 *O11* **Havelock North** Hawke's Bay, North Island, NZ
100 *M8* **Havelte** Drenthe, NE Netherlands
29 *N6* **Haven** Kansas, C USA
99 *H21* **Haverfordwest** SW Wales, UK
99 *P20* **Haverhill** E England, UK
21 *O10* **Haverhill** Massachusetts, NE USA
95 *G17* **Haverö** Västernorrland, C Sweden
113 *I17* **Havířov** Severní Morava, E Czech Republic
113 *E17* **Havlíčkův Brod** *Ger.* Deutsch-Brod; *prev.* Německý Brod. Východní Čechy, C Czech Republic
94 *K7* **Havøysund** Finnmark, N Norway
35 *T7* **Havre** Montana, NW USA
Havre *see* le Havre
101 *F20* **Havré** Hainaut, S Belgium
11 *P11* **Havre-St-Pierre** Québec, E Canada
142 *B10* **Havsa** Edirne, NW Turkey
40 *D8* **Hawaii** *off.* State of Hawaii; also known as Aloha State, Paradise of the Pacific. ◈ *state* USA, C Pacific Ocean
40 *G12* **Hawaii** *Haw.* Hawai'i. *island* Hawaiian Islands, USA, C Pacific Ocean
199 *K5* **Hawaiian Islands** *prev.* Sandwich Islands. *island group* Hawaii, USA, C Pacific Ocean
199 *Jj6* **Hawaiian Ridge** *undersea feature* N Pacific Ocean
199 *Kk6* **Hawaiian Trough** *undersea feature* N Pacific Ocean
31 *R12* **Hawarden** Iowa, C USA
Hawash *see* Āwash
145 *P6* **Hawbayn al Gharbīyah** C Iraq
193 *D21* **Hawea, Lake** ◎ South Island, NZ
192 *K11* **Hawera** Taranaki, North Island, NZ
22 *J5* **Hawesville** Kentucky, S USA
40 *G11* **Hawi** *Haw.* Hāwī. Hawaii, USA, C Pacific Ocean
98 *K13* **Hawick** SE Scotland, UK
145 *S4* **Ḩawījah** C Iraq
145 *Y10* **Ḩawīzah, Hawr al** ◎ S Iraq
193 *E21* **Hawkdun Range** ▲▲ South Island, NZ
192 *P10* **Hawke Bay** *bay* North Island, NZ
190 *I6* **Hawker** South Australia
192 *N11* **Hawke's Bay** *off.* Hawkes Bay Region. ◈ *region* North Island, NZ
155 *O16* **Hawkes Bay** *bay* SE Pakistan
13 *N12* **Hawkesbury** Ontario, SE Canada
Hawkeye State *see* Iowa
25 *T5* **Hawkinsville** Georgia, SE USA
12 *B7* **Hawk Junction** Ontario, S Canada
23 *N10* **Haw Knob** ▲ North Carolina/Tennessee, SE USA
23 *Q9* **Hawksbill Mountain** ▲ North Carolina, SE USA
35 *Z16* **Hawk Springs** Wyoming, C USA
Hawlēr *see* Arbīl
31 *S5* **Hawley** Minnesota, N USA
27 *P7* **Hawley** Texas, SW USA
147 *R14* **Ḩawrā'** C Yemen
145 *P7* **Ḩawrān, Wadi** *dry watercourse* W Iraq
23 *T9* **Haw River** 〰 North Carolina, SE USA
145 *U5* **Hawshqūrah** E Iraq
37 *S7* **Hawthorne** Nevada, W USA
39 *W3* **Haxtun** Colorado, C USA
191 *N9* **Hay** New South Wales, SE Australia
9 *O10* **Hay** 〰 W Canada
176 *U11* **Haya** Pulau Seram, E Indonesia
172 *N11* **Hayachine-san** ▲ Honshū, C Japan
105 *S4* **Hayange** Moselle, NE France
HaYarden *see* Jordan
Hayastani Hanrapetut'yun *see* Armenia
Hayasui-seto *see* Hōyo-kaikyō
41 *N9* **Haycock** Alaska, USA
38 *M14* **Hayden** Arizona, SW USA
39 *Q3* **Hayden** Colorado, C USA
30 *M10* **Hayes** South Dakota, N USA
9 *X13* **Hayes** 〰 Manitoba, C Canada
15 *Kk11* **Hayes** 〰 Northwest Territories, NE Canada
30 *M16* **Hayes Center** Nebraska, C USA
41 *S10* **Hayes, Mount** ▲ Alaska, USA
23 *R11* **Hayesville** North Carolina, SE USA
37 *X10* **Hayford Peak** ▲ Nevada, W USA
36 *M3* **Hayfork** California, W USA
Hayir, Qasr al *see* Ḩayr al Gharbī, Qaşr al
169 *P8* **Haylaastay** Sühbaatar, E Mongolia
12 *I12* **Hay Lake** ◎ Ontario, SE Canada
147 *X11* **Haymā'** *var.* Haima. C Oman
142 *H13* **Haymana** Ankara, C Turkey
144 *J7* **Ḩaymūr, Jabal** ▲▲ W Syria
Haynau *see* Chojnów
24 *G4* **Haynesville** Louisiana, S USA
25 *P6* **Hayneville** Alabama, S USA
116 *M12* **Hayrabolu** Tekirdağ, NW Turkey
142 *C10* **Hayrabolu Deresi** 〰 NW Turkey
144 *J6* **Ḩayr al Gharbī, Qaşr al** *var.* Qasr al Hayir, Qasr al Hir al Gharbi. *ruins* Ḩimş, C Syria
144 *L5* **Ḩayr ash Sharqī, Qaşr al** *var.* Qasr al Hir Ash Sharqī. *ruins* Ḩimş, C Syria
15 *Hh9* **Hay River** Northwest Territories, W Canada
28 *K4* **Hays** Kansas, C USA
30 *K12* **Hay Springs** Nebraska, C USA
67 *H25* **Haystack, The** ▲ NE Saint Helena
29 *N7* **Haysville** Kansas, C USA
119 *O7* **Haysyn** *Rus.* Gaysin. Vinnyts'ka Oblast', C Ukraine
29 *Y9* **Hayti** Missouri, C USA
31 *Q9* **Hayti** South Dakota, N USA
119 *O8* **Hayvoron** *Rus.* Gayvorno. Kirovohrads'ka Oblast', C Ukraine
37 *N9* **Hayward** California, W USA
32 *J4* **Hayward** Wisconsin, N USA
99 *O23* **Haywards Heath** SE England, UK
149 *S11* **Hazārān, Kūh-e** *var.* Kūh-e ā Hazr. ▲ SE Iran
Hazarat Imam *see* Emām Şāḩeb
23 *O7* **Hazard** Kentucky, S USA
143 *O15* **Hazar Gölü** ◎ C Turkey
159 *P15* **Hazārībāg** *var.* Hazāribāgh. Bihār, N India
Hazārībāgh *see* Hazārībāg
105 *O1* **Hazebrouck** Nord, N France
32 *K9* **Hazel Green** Wisconsin, N USA
199 *Ii10* **Hazel Holme Bank** *undersea feature* S Pacific Ocean
8 *K13* **Hazelton** British Columbia, SW Canada
31 *N6* **Hazelton** North Dakota, N USA
37 *R5* **Hazen** Nevada, W USA
30 *L5* **Hazen** North Dakota, N USA
40 *L12* **Hazen Bay** *bay* E Bering Sea
145 *S5* **Hazīm, Bi'r** *well* C Iraq
25 *V6* **Hazlehurst** Georgia, SE USA
24 *K6* **Hazlehurst** Mississippi, S USA
20 *K15* **Hazlet** New Jersey, NE USA
152 *I9* **Hazorasp** *Rus.* Khazarosp. Khorazm Wiloyati, W Uzbekistan
153 *R13* **Hazratishoh, Qatorkŭhi** *var.* Khrebet Khazretishi, *Rus.* Khrebet Khozretishi. ▲▲ S Tajikistan
Hazr, Kūh-e ā *see* Hazārān, Kūh-e
155 *U6* **Hazro** Punjab, E Pakistan
25 *R7* **Headland** Alabama, S USA
190 *C6* **Head of Bight** *headland* South Australia
35 *N10* **Headquarters** Idaho, NW USA
36 *M7* **Healdsburg** California, W USA
29 *N13* **Healdton** Oklahoma, C USA
191 *O12* **Healesville** Victoria, SE Australia
41 *R10* **Healy** Alaska, USA
181 *R13* **Heard and McDonald Islands** ◇ *Australian external territory* S Indian Ocean
xiii *R13* **Heard Island** *island* Heard and McDonald Islands, S Indian Ocean
27 *U9* **Hearne** Texas, SW USA
10 *F12* **Hearst** Ontario, S Canada
204 *J5* **Hearst Island** *island* Antarctica
Heart of Dixie *see* Alabama
30 *L5* **Heart River** 〰 North Dakota, N USA
33 *T13* **Heath** Ohio, N USA
191 *N11* **Heathcote** Victoria, SE Australia
99 *N22* **Heathrow** ✕ (London) SE England, UK
23 *X5* **Heathsville** Virginia, NE USA
29 *R11* **Heavener** Oklahoma, C USA
27 *R15* **Hebbronville** Texas, SW USA
169 *Q13* **Hebei** *var.* Hebei Sheng, Hopeh, Hopei, Ji; *prev.* Chihli. ◈ *province* E China
Hebei Sheng *see* Hebei
176 *U9* **Hebera** Irian Jaya, E Indonesia
38 *M3* **Heber City** Utah, W USA
29 *V10* **Heber Springs** Arkansas, C USA
167 *N5* **Hebi** Henan, C China
34 *F11* **Hebo** Oregon, NW USA
98 *F9* **Hebrides, Sea of the** *sea* NW Scotland, UK
11 *P5* **Hebron** Newfoundland and Labrador, E Canada
33 *N11* **Hebron** Indiana, N USA
31 *Q17* **Hebron** Nebraska, C USA
30 *L5* **Hebron** North Dakota, N USA
144 *F11* **Hebron** *var.* Al Khalīl, El Khalil, *Heb.* Hevron; *anc.* Kiriath-Arba. S West Bank
Hebrus *see* Évros/Maritsa/Meriç
97 *N14* **Heby** Västmanland, C Sweden
8 *I14* **Hecate Strait** *strait* British Columbia, W Canada
43 *W12* **Hecelchakán** Campeche, SE Mexico
166 *K13* **Hechi** *var.* Jinchengjiang. Guangxi Zhuangzu Zizhiqu, S China
103 *H23* **Hechingen** Baden-Württemberg, S Germany
101 *K17* **Hechtel** Limburg, NE Belgium
166 *J9* **Hechuan** Sichuan, C China
31 *P7* **Hecla** South Dakota, N USA
31 *T9* **Hector** Minnesota, N USA
95 *F17* **Hede** Jämtland, C Sweden
97 *M14* **Hedemora** Kopparberg, C Sweden
94 *K13* **Hedenäset** Norrbotten, N Sweden
97 *G23* **Hedensted** Vejle, C Denmark
97 *N14* **Hedesunda** Gävleborg, C Sweden
97 *N14* **Hedesundafjord** ◎ C Sweden
27 *O3* **Hedley** Texas, SW USA
96 *I12* **Hedmark** ◈ *county* S Norway
172 *Pp14* **Hedo-misaki** *headland* Okinawa, SW Japan
31 *X15* **Hedrick** Iowa, C USA
101 *L16* **Heel** Limburg, SE Netherlands
201 *Y12* **Heel Point** *point* Wake Island
100 *H9* **Heemskerk** Noord-Holland, W Netherlands
100 *M10* **Heerde** Gelderland, E Netherlands
100 *L7* **Heerenveen** *Fris.* It Hearrenfean. Friesland, N Netherlands
100 *I8* **Heerhugowaard** Noord-Holland, NW Netherlands
94 *O3* **Heer Land** *physical region* C Svalbard
101 *M18* **Heerlen** Limburg, SE Netherlands
101 *J19* **Heers** Limburg, NE Belgium
Heerwegen *see* Polkowice
100 *K13* **Heesch** Noord-Brabant, S Netherlands
101 *K15* **Heeze** Noord-Brabant, SE Netherlands
144 *F8* **Ḩefa** *var.* Haifa; *hist.* Caiffa, Caiphas, *anc.* Sycaminum. Haifa, N Israel
144 *F8* **Ḩefa, Mifraz** *Eng.* Bay of Haifa. *bay* N Israel
167 *Q8* **Hefei** *var.* Hofei; *hist.* Luchow. Anhui, E China
25 *R3* **Heflin** Alabama, S USA
169 *X7* **Hegang** Heilongjiang, NE China
171 *Ii11* **Hegura-jima** *island* SW Japan
Heguri-jima *see* Heigun-tō
Hei *see* Heilongjiang
102 *H8* **Heide** Schleswig-Holstein, N Germany
103 *G20* **Heidelberg** Baden-Württemberg, SW Germany
85 *J21* **Heidelberg** Gauteng, NE South Africa
24 *M6* **Heidelberg** Mississippi, S USA
Heidenheim *see* Heidenheim an der Brenz
103 *J22* **Heidenheim an der Brenz** *var.* Heidenheim. Baden-Württemberg, S Germany
111 *U2* **Heidenreichstein** Niederösterreich, N Austria
170 *E14* **Heigun-tō** *var.* Heguri-jima. *island* SW Japan
169 *W5* **Heihe** *prev.* Ai-hun. Heilongjiang, NE China
Hei-ho *see* Nagqu
85 *J22* **Heilbron** Free State, N South Africa
103 *H21* **Heilbronn** Baden-Württemberg, SW Germany
Heiligenbeil *see* Mamonovo
111 *Q8* **Heiligenblut** Tirol, W Austria
102 *K7* **Heiligenhafen** Schleswig-Holstein, N Germany
Heiligenkreuz *see* Žiar nad Hronom
103 *J15* **Heiligenstadt** Thüringen, C Germany
Heilong Jiang *see* Amur
169 *W8* **Heilongjiang** *var.* Hei, Heilongjiang Sheng, Hei-lung-chiang, Heilungkiang. ◈ *province* NE China
Heilongjiang Sheng *see* Heilongjiang
100 *H9* **Heiloo** Noord-Holland, NW Netherlands
Heilsberg *see* Lidzbark Warmiński
Hei-lung-chiang/Heilungkiang *see* Heilongjiang
94 *I4* **Heimaey** *var.* Heimaæy. *island* S Iceland
96 *H8* **Heimdal** Sør-Trøndelag, S Norway
Heinaste *see* Ainaži
95 *N17* **Heinävesi** Mikkeli, SE Finland
101 *M22* **Heinerscheid** Diekirch, N Luxembourg
100 *M10* **Heino** Overijssel, E Netherlands
95 *M18* **Heinola** Mikkeli, S Finland
103 *C16* **Heinsberg** Nordrhein-Westfalen, W Germany
169 *U12* **Heishan** Liaoning, NE China
166 *H8* **Heishui** Sichuan, C China
101 *H17* **Heist-op-den-Berg** Antwerpen, C Belgium
Heitō *see* P'ingtung
176 *Y14* **Heitske** Irian Jaya, E Indonesia
Hejanah *see* Al Hījānah
Hejaz *see* Al Ḩijāz
166 *M14* **He Jiang** 〰 S China
164 *K6* **Hejing** Xinjiang Uygur Zizhiqu, NW China
Héjjasfalva *see* Vânători
165 *S11* **Heka** Qinghai, W China
143 *N14* **Hekimhan** Malatya, C Turkey
94 *J4* **Hekla** ▲ S Iceland
112 *J6* **Hel** *Ger.* Hela. Gdańsk, N Poland
Hela *see* Hel
95 *F17* **Helagsfjället** ▲ C Sweden
165 *W8* **Helan** *var.* Xigang. Ningxia, N China
168 *K14* **Helan Shan** ▲▲ N China
101 *M16* **Helden** Limburg, SE Netherlands
29 *X12* **Helena** Arkansas, C USA
35 *R10* **Helena** *state capital* Montana, NW USA
98 *H12* **Helensburgh** W Scotland, UK
192 *K5* **Helensville** Auckland, North Island, NZ
97 *L20* **Helgasjön** ◎ S Sweden
102 *G8* **Helgoland** *Eng.* Heligoland. *island* NW Germany
Helgoland Bay *see* Helgoländer Bucht
102 *G8* **Helgoländer Bucht** *var.* Helgoland Bay, Heligoland Bight. *bay* NW Germany
Heligoland *see* Helgoland
Heligoland Bight *see* Helgoländer Bucht
Heliopolis *see* Baalbek
94 *I4* **Hella** Sudhurland, SW Iceland
Hellas *see* Greece
149 *N11* **Ḩelleh, Rūd-e** 〰 S Iran
100 *N10* **Hellendoorn** Overijssel, E Netherlands
Hellenic Republic *see* Greece
123 *Gg10* **Hellenic Trough** *undersea feature* Aegean Sea, C Mediterranean Sea
96 *E10* **Hellesylt** Møre og Romsdal, S Norway
100 *F13* **Hellevoetsluis** Zuid-Holland, SW Netherlands
107 *Q12* **Hellín** Castilla-La Mancha, C Spain
117 *H19* **Hellinikon** ✕ (Athína) Attikí, C Greece
34 *M12* **Hells Canyon** *valley* Idaho/Oregon, NW USA
154 *L9* **Helmand** ◈ *province* S Afghanistan
154 *K10* **Helmand, Daryā-ye** *var.* Rūd-e Hīrmand. 〰 Afghanistan/Iran *see also* Hīrmand, Rūd-e
Helmantica *see* Salamanca
103 *K15* **Helme** 〰 C Germany
101 *L15* **Helmond** Noord-Brabant, S Netherlands
98 *J7* **Helmsdale** N Scotland, UK
102 *K13* **Helmstedt** Niedersachsen, N Germany
169 *Y10* **Helong** Jilin, NE China
38 *M4* **Helper** Utah, W USA
102 *O10* **Helpter Berge** *hill* NE Germany
97 *J22* **Helsingborg** *prev.* Hälsingborg. Malmöhus, S Sweden
Helsingfors *see* Helsinki
97 *J22* **Helsingør** *Eng.* Elsinore. Frederiksborg, E Denmark
95 *M20* **Helsinki** *Swe.* Helsingfors. ● (Finland) Uusimaa, S Finland
99 *H25* **Helston** SW England, UK
Heltau *see* Cisnădie
63 *C17* **Helvecia** Santa Fe, C Argentina
99 *K15* **Helvellyn** ▲ NW England, UK
Helvetia *see* Switzerland
77 *W8* **Helwân** *var.* Hilwân, Hulwan, Hulwān. N Egypt
99 *N21* **Hemel Hempstead** E England, UK
37 *U16* **Hemet** California, W USA
31 *J13* **Hemingford** Nebraska, C USA
23 *T13* **Hemingway** South Carolina, SE USA

◆ Country
● Country Capital
◇ Dependent Territory
○ Dependent Territory Capital
◈ Administrative Region
✕ International Airport
▲ Mountain
▲▲ Mountain Range
Volcano
〰 River
◎ Lake
⊞ Reservoir

94 G13 Hemnesberget Nordland, C Norway
27 Y8 Hemphill Texas, SW USA
27 V11 Hempstead Texas, SW USA
97 P20 Hemse Gotland, SE Sweden
96 F13 Hemsedal valley S Norway
165 T11 Henan var. Henan Mongolzu Zizhixian, Yêgainnyin. Qinghai, C China
167 N6 Henan var. Henan Sheng, Honan, Yu. ◆ province C China
192 L4 Hen and Chickens island group N NZ
Henan Mongolzu Zizhixian/Henan Sheng see Henan
107 O7 Henares ↝ C Spain
171 M8 Henashi-zaki headland Honshū, C Japan
104 I16 Hendaye Pyrénées-Atlantiques, SW France
142 F11 Hendek Sakarya, NW Turkey
63 B21 Henderson Buenos Aires, E Argentina
22 I5 Henderson Kentucky, S USA
37 X11 Henderson Nevada, W USA
23 V8 Henderson North Carolina, SE USA
22 G10 Henderson Tennessee, S USA
27 W7 Henderson Texas, SW USA
32 J12 Henderson Creek ↝ Illinois, N USA
195 X16 Henderson Field ✕ (Honiara) Guadalcanal, C Solomon Islands
203 O17 Henderson Island atoll N Pitcairn Islands
23 O10 Hendersonville North Carolina, SE USA
22 J8 Hendersonville Tennessee, S USA
149 O14 Hendorābī, Jazīreh-ye island S Iran
57 V10 Hendrik Top var. Hendriktop. elevation C Suriname
Hendū Kosh see Hindu Kush
12 L12 Heney, Lac ⊚ Québec, SE Canada
194 I12 Henganofi Eastern Highlands, C PNG
Hengchow see Hengyang
167 S15 Hengchun S Taiwan
165 R16 Hengduan Shan ▲▲ SW China
100 N12 Hengelo Gelderland, E Netherlands
100 O10 Hengelo Overijssel, E Netherlands
Hengnan see Hengyang
167 N11 Hengshan Hunan, S China
166 L4 Hengshan Shaanxi, C China
167 O4 Hengshui Hebei, E China
167 N12 Hengyang var. Hengnan, Hengyang; prev. Hengchow. Hunan, S China
119 U11 Heniches'k Rus. Genichesk. Khersons'ka Oblast', S Ukraine
23 Z4 Henlopen, Cape headland Delaware, NE USA
Henna see Enna
96 M10 Hennan Gävleborg, C Sweden
104 G7 Hennebont Morbihan, NW France
32 L11 Hennepin Illinois, N USA
28 M9 Hennessey Oklahoma, C USA
102 N12 Hennigsdorf var. Hennigsdorf bei Berlin. Brandenburg, NE Germany
Hennigsdorf bei Berlin see Hennigsdorf
21 N9 Henniker New Hampshire, NE USA
27 S5 Henrietta Texas, SW USA
Henrique de Carvalho see Saurimo
32 L12 Henry Illinois, N USA
23 Y7 Henry, Cape headland Virginia, NE USA
29 P10 Henryetta Oklahoma, C USA
204 M7 Henry Ice Rise ice cap Antarctica
16 N1 Henry Kater, Cape headland Baffin Island, Northwest Territories, NE Canada
35 R13 Henrys Fork ↝ Idaho, NW USA
12 E15 Hensall Ontario, S Canada
102 I9 Henstedt-Ulzburg Schleswig-Holstein, N Germany
169 N7 Hentiy ◆ province N Mongolia
168 M7 Hentiyn Nuruu ▲▲ N Mongolia
191 P10 Henty New South Wales, SE Australia
177 Fj8 Henzada Irrawaddy, SW Myanmar
103 G19 Heppenheim Hessen, W Germany
34 J11 Heppner Oregon, NW USA
166 L15 Hepu prev. Lianzhou. Guangxi Zhuangzu Zizhiqu, S China
94 J2 Heradhsvötn ↝ C Iceland
Herakleion see Irákleio
154 K5 Herāt var. Herat; anc. Aria. Herāt, W Afghanistan
154 J5 Herāt ◆ province W Afghanistan
105 P14 Hérault ◆ department S France
105 P15 Hérault ↝ S France
9 T16 Herbert Saskatchewan, S Canada
193 F22 Herbert Otago, South Island, NZ
40 J17 Herbert Island island Aleutian Islands, Alaska, USA
194 I12 Herbert, Mount ▲ C PNG
Herbertshöhe see Kokopo
13 Q7 Hérbertville Québec, SE Canada
103 G17 Herborn Hessen, W Germany
115 I17 Herceg-Novi It. Castelnuovo; prev. Ercegnovi. Montenegro, SW Yugoslavia
9 X10 Herchmer Manitoba, C Canada
194 K14 Hercules Bay bay E PNG
94 K2 Herdhubreidh ▲ C Iceland
44 M13 Heredia Heredia, C Costa Rica
44 M12 Heredia off. Provincia de Heredia. ◆ province N Costa Rica
99 K21 Hereford W England, UK
26 M3 Hereford Texas, SW USA
13 Q13 Hereford, Mont ▲ Québec, SE Canada
99 K21 Herefordshire cultural region W England, UK
203 U11 Hereheretue atoll Îles Tuamotu, C French Polynesia
107 N10 Herencia Castilla-La Mancha, C Spain
101 H18 Herent Vlaams Brabant, C Belgium
101 I16 Herentals var. Herenthals. Antwerpen, N Belgium
Herenthals see Herentals
101 H17 Herenthout Antwerpen, N Belgium
97 J23 Herfølge Roskilde, E Denmark
102 G13 Herford Nordrhein-Westfalen, NW Germany
29 O5 Herington Kansas, C USA
110 H7 Herisau Fr. Hérisau. Appenzell Ausser Rhoden, NE Switzerland
Héristal see Herstal
101 J18 Herk-de-Stad Limburg, NE Belgium
Herkulesbad/Herkulesfürdő see Băile Herculane
Herlen Gol/Herlen He see Kerulen
37 Q4 Herlong California, W USA
99 L26 Herm island Channel Islands
111 R9 Hermagor Slvn. Šmohor. Kärnten, S Austria
31 S7 Herman Minnesota, N USA
98 L1 Herma Ness headland NE Scotland, UK
29 V4 Hermann Missouri, C USA
189 Q8 Hermannsburg Northern Territory, N Australia
Hermannstadt see Sibiu
96 E12 Hermansverk Sogn og Fjordane, S Norway
144 H6 Hermel var. Hirmil. NE Lebanon
Hermhausen see Hajnówka
191 P6 Hermidale New South Wales, SE Australia
57 X9 Herminadorp Sipaliwini, NE Suriname
34 K11 Hermiston Oregon, NW USA
29 T6 Hermitage Missouri, C USA
194 I8 Hermit Islands island group N PNG
27 O7 Hermleigh Texas, SW USA
144 G7 Hermon, Mount Ar. Jabal ash Shaykh. ▲ S Syria
Hermopolis Parva see Damanhûr
30 J10 Hermosa South Dakota, N USA
42 F5 Hermosillo Sonora, NW Mexico
Hermoupolis see Ermoúpoli
113 N20 Hernád var. Hornád, Ger. Kundert. ↝ Hungary/Slovakia
63 C18 Hernández Entre Ríos, E Argentina
25 V11 Hernando Florida, SE USA
24 L1 Hernando Mississippi, S USA
107 Q2 Hernani País Vasco, N Spain
101 F19 Herne Vlaams Brabant, C Belgium
103 E14 Herne Nordrhein-Westfalen, W Germany
97 F22 Herning Ringkøbing, W Denmark
Hernösand see Härnösand
124 Q13 Herodotus Basin undersea feature E Mediterranean Sea
124 Nn14 Herodotus Trough undersea feature C Mediterranean Sea
31 T11 Heron Lake Minnesota, N USA
Herowābād see Khalkhāl
97 G16 Herre Telemark, S Norway
31 N7 Herreid South Dakota, N USA
103 H22 Herrenberg Baden-Württemberg, S Germany
106 L14 Herrera Andalucía, S Spain
45 R17 Herrera off. Provincia de Herrera. ◆ province S Panama
106 L10 Herrera del Duque Extremadura, W Spain
106 M4 Herrera de Pisuerga Castilla-León, N Spain
43 Z13 Herrero, Punta headland SE Mexico
191 P16 Herrick Tasmania, SE Australia
32 L17 Herrin Illinois, N USA
22 M6 Herrington Lake ⊡ Kentucky, S USA
97 K18 Herrljunga Älvsborg, S Sweden
105 N16 Hers ↝ S France
8 I1 Herschel Island island Yukon Territory, NW Canada
101 I17 Herselt Antwerpen, C Belgium
20 G15 Hershey Pennsylvania, NE USA
101 K19 Herstal Fr. Héristal. Liège, E Belgium
99 O21 Hertford E England, UK
23 X8 Hertford North Carolina, SE USA
99 O21 Hertfordshire cultural region E England, UK
189 Z9 Hervey Bay Queensland, E Australia
103 O14 Herzberg Brandenburg, E Germany
101 E18 Herzele Oost-Vlaanderen, NW Belgium
103 K20 Herzogenaurach Bayern, SE Germany
111 W4 Herzogenburg Niederösterreich, NE Austria
Herzogenbusch see 's-Hertogenbosch
105 N2 Hesdin Pas-de-Calais, N France
166 K14 Heshan Guangxi Zhuangzu Zizhiqu, S China
165 X10 Heshui var. Xihuachi. Gansu, C China
101 M25 Hespérange Luxembourg, SE Luxembourg
37 U14 Hesperia California, W USA
39 P7 Hesperus Mountain ▲ Colorado, C USA
8 J6 Hess ↝ Yukon Territory, NW Canada
Hesse see Hessen
103 J21 Hesselberg ▲ S Germany
97 I22 Hesselø island E Denmark
103 H17 Hessen Eng./Fr. Hesse. ◆ state C Germany
199 Jj6 Hess Tablemount undersea feature C Pacific Ocean
29 N6 Hesston Kansas, C USA
99 K18 Heswall NW England, UK
159 P12 Hetauda Central, C Nepal
Hétfalu see Săcele
30 K7 Hettinger North Dakota, N USA
103 L14 Hettstedt Sachsen-Anhalt, C Germany
94 P3 Heuglin, Kapp headland SE Svalbard
195 Y16 Heuru San Cristobal, SE Solomon Islands
101 J17 Heusden Limburg, NE Belgium
100 J13 Heusden Noord-Brabant, S Netherlands
104 K3 Hève, Cap de la headland N France
101 H18 Heverlee Vlaams Brabant, C Belgium
113 L22 Heves Heves, NE Hungary
113 L22 Heves off. Heves Megye. ◆ county NE Hungary
Hevron see Hebron
47 Y13 Hewanorra ✕ (Saint Lucia) S Saint Lucia
166 M13 Hexian var. Babu, He Xian. Guangxi Zhuangzu Zizhiqu, S China
166 L6 Heyang Shaanxi, C China
Heydebrech see Kędzierzyn-Koźle
Heydekrug see Šilutė
99 K16 Heysham NW England, UK
167 O14 Heyuan Guangdong, S China
190 L12 Heywood Victoria, SE Australia
188 K3 Heywood Islands island group Western Australia
167 O6 Heze var. Caozhou. Shandong, E China
165 U11 Hezheng Gansu, C China
165 U11 Hezuozhen Gansu, C China
25 Z16 Hialeah Florida, SE USA
29 Q3 Hiawatha Kansas, C USA
38 M4 Hiawatha Utah, W USA
31 V4 Hibbing Minnesota, N USA
191 N17 Hibbs, Point headland Tasmania, SE Australia
Hibernia see Ireland
170 D12 Hibiki-nada inlet SW Japan
22 F8 Hickman Kentucky, S USA
23 Q9 Hickory North Carolina, SE USA
23 Q9 Hickory, Lake ⊚ North Carolina, SE USA
192 Q7 Hicks Bay Gisborne, North Island, NZ
27 S8 Hico Texas, SW USA
172 Oo6 Hidaka Hokkaidō, NE Japan
171 Gg13 Hidaka Hyōgo, Honshū, SW Japan
172 P7 Hidaka-sanmyaku ▲▲ Hokkaidō, NE Japan
43 O6 Hidalgo var. Villa Hidalgo. Coahuila de Zaragoza, NE Mexico
43 N8 Hidalgo Nuevo León, NE Mexico
43 O10 Hidalgo Tamaulipas, C Mexico
43 O13 Hidalgo ◆ state C Mexico
42 J7 Hidalgo del Parral var. Parral. Chihuahua, N Mexico
171 J14 Hida-sanmyaku ▲▲ Honshū, S Japan
102 N7 Hiddensee island NE Germany
82 G6 Hidiglib, Wadi ↝ NE Sudan
111 U6 Hieflau Salzburg, E Austria
197 H5 Hienghène Province Nord, C New Caledonia
Hierosolyma see Jerusalem
66 N12 Hierro var. Ferro. island Islas Canarias, Spain, NE Atlantic Ocean
170 Ee13 Higashi-Hiroshima var. Higasihirosima. Hiroshima, Honshū, SW Japan
171 J18 Higashi-Izu Shizuoka, Honshū, S Japan
171 Ll12 Higashine var. Higasine. Yamagata, Honshū, C Japan
170 C11 Higashi-suidō strait SW Japan
Higasihirosima see Higashi-Hiroshima
Higasine see Higashine
Higasiôsaka see Higashi-ōsaka
27 P1 Higgins Texas, SW USA
33 P7 Higgins Lake ⊚ Michigan, N USA
29 S4 Higginsville Missouri, C USA
High Atlas see Haut Atlas
32 M5 High Falls Reservoir ⊡ Wisconsin, N USA
46 K12 Highgate C Jamaica
27 X11 High Island Texas, SW USA
33 O5 High Island island Michigan, N USA
32 K15 Highland Illinois, N USA
33 N10 Highland Park Illinois, N USA
23 O10 Highlands North Carolina, SE USA
9 O11 High Level Alberta, W Canada
31 O9 Highmore South Dakota, N USA
179 Oo10 High Peak ▲ Luzon, N Philippines
High Plains see Great Plains
23 S9 High Point North Carolina, SE USA
20 J13 High Point hill New Jersey, NE USA
9 P13 High Prairie Alberta, W Canada
9 Q16 High River Alberta, SW Canada
23 S9 High Rock Lake ⊡ North Carolina, SE USA
25 V9 High Springs Florida, SE USA
High Veld see Great Karoo
99 J24 High Willhays ▲ SW England, UK
99 N22 High Wycombe prev. Chepping Wycombe, Chipping Wycombe. SE England, UK
43 P12 Higos var. El Higo. Veracruz-Llave, E Mexico
104 I16 Higuer, Cap headland NE Spain
47 R5 Higüero, Punta headland W Puerto Rico
47 P9 Higüey var. Salvaleón de Higüey. E Dominican Republic
202 G11 Hihifo ✕ (Matā'utu) Île Uvea, N Wallis and Futuna
83 N16 Hiiraan off. Gobolka Hiiraan. ◆ region C Somalia
120 E4 Hiiumaa off. Hiiumaa Maakond. ◆ province W Estonia
120 D4 Hiiumaa Ger. Dagden, Swe. Dagö. island W Estonia
Hijanah see Al Hījānah
107 S6 Híjar Aragón, NE Spain
170 E13 Hikari Yamaguchi, Honshū, SW Japan
170 Ff15 Hiketa Kagawa, Shikoku, SW Japan
171 Hh15 Hikone Shiga, Honshū, SW Japan
170 D13 Hiko-san ▲ Kyūshū, SW Japan
203 V10 Hikueru atoll Îles Tuamotu, C French Polynesia
192 K3 Hikurangi Northland, North Island, NZ
192 Q8 Hikurangi ▲ North Island, NZ
199 J13 Hikurangi Trench var. Hikurangi Trough. undersea feature SW Pacific Ocean
Hikurangi Trough see Hikurangi Trench
202 B15 Hikutavake NW Niue
124 Nn14 Hilāl, Ra's al headland N Libya
63 A24 Hilario Ascasubi Buenos Aires, E Argentina
103 K17 Hildburghausen Thüringen, C Germany
103 E15 Hilden Nordrhein-Westfalen, W Germany
102 I13 Hildesheim Niedersachsen, N Germany
35 T9 Hilger Montana, NW USA
Hili see Hilli
Hilla see Al Ḩillah
47 O14 Hillaby, Mount ▲ N Barbados
97 K19 Hillared Älvsborg, S Sweden
205 R12 Hillary Coast physical region Antarctica
44 G2 Hill Bank Orange Walk, N Belize
35 O14 Hill City Idaho, NW USA
28 K3 Hill City Kansas, C USA
31 V5 Hill City Minnesota, N USA
30 J10 Hill City South Dakota, N USA
67 C24 Hill Cove Settlement West Falkland, Falkland Islands
100 H10 Hillegom Zuid-Holland, W Netherlands
97 J22 Hillerød Frederiksborg, E Denmark
38 M7 Hillers, Mount ▲ Utah, W USA
159 S13 Hilli var. Hili. Rajshahi, NW Bangladesh
31 R11 Hills Minnesota, N USA
32 L14 Hillsboro Illinois, N USA
29 N5 Hillsboro Kansas, C USA
29 X5 Hillsboro Missouri, C USA
21 N10 Hillsboro New Hampshire, NE USA
39 Q14 Hillsboro New Mexico, SW USA
31 R4 Hillsboro North Dakota, N USA
33 R14 Hillsboro Ohio, N USA
34 G11 Hillsboro Oregon, NW USA
27 T8 Hillsboro Texas, SW USA
32 K8 Hillsboro Wisconsin, N USA
25 Y14 Hillsboro Canal canal Florida, SE USA
47 Y15 Hillsborough Carriacou, N Grenada
99 G15 Hillsborough E Northern Ireland, UK
23 U9 Hillsborough North Carolina, SE USA
33 Q10 Hillsdale Michigan, N USA
191 O8 Hillston New South Wales, SE Australia
23 R7 Hillsville Virginia, NE USA
98 L2 Hillswick NE Scotland, UK
Hill Tippera see Tripura
40 H11 Hilo Hawaii, USA, C Pacific Ocean
20 F9 Hilton New York, NE USA
12 C10 Hilton Beach Ontario, S Canada
23 R16 Hilton Head Island South Carolina, SE USA
23 R16 Hilton Head Island island South Carolina, SE USA
101 J15 Hilvarenbeek Noord-Brabant, S Netherlands
100 J11 Hilversum Noord-Holland, C Netherlands
Hilwān see Helwān
158 J7 Himāchal Pradesh ◆ state NW India
Himalaya/Himalaya Shan see Himalayas
158 M9 Himalayas var. Himalaya, Chin. Himalaya Shan. ▲▲ S Asia
179 Q14 Himamaylan Negros, C Philippines
95 K15 Himanka Vaasa, W Finland
Himara see Himarë
115 L23 Himarë var. Himara. Vlorë, S Albania
144 M2 Ḩimār, Wādī al dry watercourse N Syria
160 D9 Himatnagar Gujarāt, W India
111 Y4 Himberg Niederösterreich, E Austria
171 J14 Hime-gawa ↝ Honshū, S Japan
170 G14 Himeji var. Himezi. Hyōgo, Honshū, SW Japan
170 Dd13 Hime-jima island SW Japan
Himezi see Himeji
171 Ii13 Himi Toyama, Honshū, SW Japan
111 S9 Himmelberg Kärnten, S Austria
144 I5 Ḩimş var. Homs; anc. Emesa. Ḩimş, C Syria
144 K6 Ḩimş off. Muḩāfaẓat Ḩimş, var. Homs. ◆ governorate C Syria
144 I5 Ḩimş, Buḩayrat var. Buḩayrat Qaţţīnah. ⊚ W Syria
179 Rr15 Hinatuan Mindanao, S Philippines
119 N10 Hînceşti var. Hânceşti; prev. Kotovsk. C Moldova
46 M9 Hinche C Haiti
189 X5 Hinchinbrook Island island Queensland, NE Australia
41 S12 Hinchinbrook Island island Alaska, USA
99 M19 Hinckley C England, UK
31 V7 Hinckley Minnesota, N USA
38 K5 Hinckley Utah, W USA
20 J9 Hinckley Reservoir ⊡ New York, NE USA
158 I12 Hindaun Rājasthān, N India
Hindenburg/Hindenburg in Oberschlesien see Zabrze
Hindiya see Al Hindīyah
23 O6 Hindman Kentucky, S USA
190 L10 Hindmarsh, Lake ⊚ Victoria, SE Australia
193 G19 Hinds Canterbury, South Island, NZ
193 G19 Hinds ↝ South Island, NZ
97 H23 Hindsholm island C Denmark
155 S4 Hindu Kush Per. Hendū Kosh. ▲▲ Afghanistan/Pakistan
161 H19 Hindupur Andhra Pradesh, E India
9 O12 Hines Creek Alberta, W Canada
25 W6 Hinesville Georgia, SE USA
160 I12 Hinganghāt Mahārāshtra, C India
155 N15 Hingol ↝ SW Pakistan
160 H13 Hingoli Mahārāshtra, C India
143 R13 Hınıs Erzurum, E Turkey
94 O2 Hinlopenstretet strait N Svalbard
94 G10 Hinnøya island C Norway
170 D15 Hinokage Miyazaki, Kyūshū, SW Japan
170 F11 Hino-misaki headland Honshū, SW Japan
110 H10 Hinterrhein ↝ SW Switzerland
9 O14 Hinton Alberta, SW Canada
28 M10 Hinton Oklahoma, C USA
23 R6 Hinton West Virginia, NE USA
Hios see Chíos
43 N8 Hipolito Coahuila de Zaragoza, NE Mexico
Hipponium see Vibo Valentia
170 C12 Hirado Nagasaki, Hirado-shima, SW Japan
170 C12 Hirado-shima island SW Japan
171 Gg15 Hirakata Ōsaka, Honshū, SW Japan
172 P17 Hirakubo-saki headland Ishigaki-jima, SW Japan
160 M11 Hirākud Reservoir ⊡ E India
Hir al Gharbi, Qasr al see Ḩayr al Gharbī, Qaşr al
172 N9 Hiranai Aomori, Honshū, N Japan
172 Pp16 Hirara Okinawa, Miyako-jima, SW Japan
Qasr al Hir Ash Sharqī see Ḩayr ash Sharqī, Qaşr al
170 F12 Hirata Shimane, Honshū, SW Japan
171 Jj17 Hiratsuka var. Hiratuka. Kanagawa, Honshū, S Japan
Hiratuka see Hiratsuka
142 I13 Hirfanlı Barajı ⊡ C Turkey
161 G18 Hiriyūr Karnātaka, W India
Hîrlău see Hârlău
154 K10 Hīrmand, Rūd-e var. Daryā-ye Helmand. ↝ Afghanistan/Iran see also Helmand, Daryā-ye
Hirmil see Hermel
172 P8 Hiroo Hokkaidō, NE Japan
171 Mm9 Hirosaki Aomori, Honshū, C Japan
170 E13 Hiroshima var. Hirosima. Hiroshima, Honshū, SW Japan
170 Ee13 Hiroshima off. Hiroshima-ken, var. Hirosima. ◆ prefecture Honshū, SW Japan
Hirosima see Hiroshima
Hirschberg/Hirschberg im Riesengebirge/Hirschberg in Schlesien see Jelenia Góra
105 Q3 Hirson Aisne, N France
Hîrşova see Hârşova
97 G19 Hirtshals Nordjylland, N Denmark
171 H16 Hisai Mie, Honshū, SW Japan
158 H10 Hisār Haryāna, NW India
194 J15 Hisiu Central, SW PNG
153 P13 Hisor Rus. Gissar. W Tajikistan
Hispalis see Sevilla
Hispana/Hispania see Spain
46 M7 Hispaniola island Dominion Republic/Haiti
66 F11 Hispaniola Basin var. Hispaniola Trough. undersea feature SW Atlantic Ocean
Hispaniola Trough see Hispaniola Basin
Histonium see Vasto
145 R7 Hīt SW Iraq
170 D14 Hita Ōita, Kyūshū, SW Japan
171 L16 Hitachi var. Hitati. Ibaraki, Honshū, S Japan
171 L15 Hitachi-Ōta var. Hitatiôta. Ibaraki, Honshū, S Japan
Hitati see Hitachi
Hitatiôta see Hitachi-Ōta
99 O21 Hitchin E England, UK
203 Q7 Hitiaa Tahiti, W French Polynesia
170 Cc15 Hitoyoshi var. Hitoyosi. Kumamoto, Kyūshū, SW Japan
Hitoyosi see Hitoyoshi
96 F7 Hitra prev. Hitteren. island S Norway
Hitteren see Hitra
197 B10 Hiu island Torres Islands, N Vanuatu
171 K14 Hiuchi-ga-take ▲ Honshū, C Japan
170 Ee14 Hiuchi-nada gulf S Japan
203 X7 Hiva Oa island Îles Marquises, N French Polynesia
22 M10 Hiwassee Lake ⊡ North Carolina, SE USA
22 M10 Hiwassee River ↝ SE USA
97 H20 Hjallerup Nordjylland, N Denmark
97 M16 Hjälmaren Eng. Lake Hjalmar. ⊚ C Sweden
Hjalmar, Lake see Hjälmaren
97 C14 Hjellestad Hordaland, S Norway
97 D16 Hjelmeland Rogaland, S Norway
96 G10 Hjerkinn Oppland, S Norway
97 L18 Hjo Skaraborg, S Sweden
97 G19 Hjørring Nordjylland, N Denmark
178 H1 Hkakabo Razi ▲ Myanmar/China
178 H1 Hkring Bum ▲ N Myanmar
85 L21 Hlathikulu var. Hlatikulu. S Swaziland
Hlatikulu see Hlathikulu
Hliboka see Hlyboka
113 F17 Hlinsko var. Hlinsko v Čechách. Východní Čechy, C Czech Republic
Hlinsko v Čechách see Hlinsko
119 S6 Hlobyne Rus. Globino. Poltavs'ka Oblast', NE Ukraine
113 H20 Hlohovec Ger. Freistadtl, Hung. Galgóc; prev. Frakštát. Západné Slovensko, W Slovakia
85 J23 Hlotse var. Leribe. NW Lesotho
113 I17 Hlučín Ger. Hultschin, Pol. Hulczyn. Severní Morava, E Czech Republic
119 S2 Hlukhiv Rus. Glukhov. Sums'ka Oblast', NE Ukraine
121 K21 Hlushkavichy Rus. Glushkevichi. Homyel'skaya Voblasts', SE Belarus
121 L18 Hlusk Rus. Glusk, Glussk. Mahilyowskaya Voblasts', E Belarus
118 K8 Hlyboka Ger. Hliboka, Rus. Glybokaya. Chernivets'ka Oblast', W Ukraine
120 K13 Hlybokaye Rus. Glubokoye. Vitsyebskaya Voblasts', N Belarus
79 Q16 Ho SE Ghana
178 Jj6 Hoa Binh Hoa Binh, N Vietnam
85 E20 Hoachanas Hardap, C Namibia
Hoai Nhon see Bông Sơn
178 Jj8 Hoa Lac Quang Binh, C Vietnam
178 J5 Hoang Liên Sơn ▲▲ N Vietnam
85 B17 Hoanib ↝ NW Namibia
35 S15 Hoback Peak ▲ Wyoming, C USA
191 P17 Hobart prev. Hobarton, Hobart Town. state capital Tasmania, SE Australia
28 L11 Hobart Oklahoma, C USA
191 P17 Hobart ✕ Tasmania, SE Australia
Hobarton/Hobart Town see Hobart
39 W14 Hobbs New Mexico, SW USA
204 L12 Hobbs Coast physical region Antarctica
25 Z14 Hobe Sound Florida, SE USA
Hobicaurikány see Uricani
56 E12 Hobo Huila, S Colombia
101 G16 Hoboken Antwerpen, N Belgium
164 K3 Hoboksar var. Hoboksar Mongol Zizhixian. Xinjiang Uygur Zizhiqu, NW China
Hoboksar Mongol Zizhixian see Hoboksar
97 G21 Hobro Nordjylland, N Denmark
23 X10 Hobucken North Carolina, SE USA
97 O20 Hoburgen headland SE Sweden
83 P15 Hobyo It. Obbia. Mudug, E Somalia
111 R8 Hochalmspitze ▲ SW Austria
111 Q4 Hochburg Oberösterreich, N Austria
110 F8 Hochdorf Luzern, N Switzerland
111 N8 Hochfeiler It. Gran Pilastro. ▲ Austria/Italy
178 Jj14 Hô Chi Minh var. Ho Chi Minh City; prev. Saigon. S Vietnam
Ho Chi Minh City see Hô Chi Minh
110 I7 Höchst Vorarlberg, NW Austria
Höchstadt see Höchstadt an der Aisch
103 K19 Höchstadt an der Aisch var. Höchstadt. Bayern, C Germany
110 L9 Hochwilde It. L'Altissima. ▲ Austria/Italy
111 S7 Hochwildstelle ▲ C Austria
33 T14 Hocking River ↝ Ohio, N USA
Hoctúm see Hoctún
43 X12 Hoctún var. Hoctúm. Yucatán, E Mexico
Hodeida see Al Ḩudaydah
22 K6 Hodgenville Kentucky, S USA
9 T17 Hodgeville Saskatchewan, S Canada
78 L9 Hodh ech Chargui ◆ region E Mauritania
Hodh el Garbi see Hodh el Gharbi
78 J10 Hodh el Gharbi var. Hodh el Garbi. ◆ region S Mauritania
113 L25 Hódmezővásárhely Csongrád, SE Hungary
76 J6 Hodna, Chott El var. Chott el-Hodna, Ar. Shatt al-Hodna. salt lake N Algeria
Hodna, Shatt al- see Hodna, Chott El
113 G19 Hodonín Ger. Göding. Jižní Morava, SE Czech Republic
168 G6 Hödrögö Dzavhan, N Mongolia
Hodság/Hodschag see Odžaci
41 R7 Hodzana River ↝ Alaska, USA
Hoei see Huy
101 H19 Hoeilaart Vlaams Brabant, C Belgium
Hoë Karoo see Great Karoo
100 F12 Hoek van Holland Eng. Hook of Holland. Zuid-Holland, W Netherlands
100 L11 Hoenderloo Gelderland, E Netherlands
101 L18 Hoensbroek Limburg, SE Netherlands
169 Y11 Hoeryŏng NE North Korea
101 K18 Hoeselt Limburg, NE Belgium
100 K11 Hoevelaken Gelderland, C Netherlands
Hoey see Huy
103 M18 Hof Bayern, SE Germany
Höfdhakaupstadhur see Skagaströnd
Hofei see Hefei
103 G18 Hofheim am Taunus Hessen, W Germany
Hofmarkt see Odorheiu Secuiesc
94 L3 Höfn Austurland, SE Iceland
96 N13 Hofors Gävleborg, C Sweden
94 J6 Hofsjökull glacier C Iceland
94 J1 Hofsós Nordhurland Vestra, N Iceland
170 Dd13 Hōfu Yamaguchi, Honshū, SW Japan
Hofuf see Al Hufūf
97 J22 Höganäs Malmöhus, S Sweden
191 P14 Hogan Group island group Tasmania, SE Australia
25 R4 Hogansville Georgia, SE USA
41 P8 Hogatza River ↝ Alaska, USA
30 I14 Hogback Mountain ▲ Nebraska, C USA
97 G14 Høgevarde ▲ S Norway
Högfors see Karkkila
33 P5 Hog Island island Michigan, N USA
23 Y6 Hog Island island Virginia, NE USA
Hogoley Islands see Chuuk Islands
97 N20 Högsby Kalmar, S Sweden
38 K1 Hogup Mountains ▲▲ Utah, W USA
103 E17 Hohe Acht ▲ W Germany
Hohenelbe see Vrchlabí
110 I7 Hohenems Vorarlberg, W Austria
Hohenmauth see Vysoké Mýto
Hohensalza see Inowrocław
Hohenstadt see Zábřeh
Hohenstein in Ostpreussen see Olsztynek
22 I9 Hohenwald Tennessee, S USA
103 L17 Hohenwarte-Stausee ⊡ C Germany
Hohes Venn see Hautes Fagnes
111 Q8 Hohe Tauern ▲▲ W Austria
169 O13 Hohhot var. Huhehot, Huhuohaote, Mong. Kukukhoto; prev. Kweisui, Kwesui. Nei Mongol Zizhiqu, N China
105 U6 Hohneck ▲ NE France
79 Q16 Hohoe E Ghana
170 D12 Hōhoku Yamaguchi, Honshū, SW Japan
165 O11 Hoh Sai Hu ⊚ C China
165 N11 Hoh Xil Hu ⊚ C China
164 L11 Hoh Xil Shan ▲▲ W China
178 Kk10 Hôi An prev. Faifo. Quang Nam-Đa Nâng, C Vietnam
Hoï-Hao/Hoihow see Haikou
83 F17 Hoima W Uganda
28 L5 Hoisington Kansas, C USA
Hojagala see Khodzhakala
Hojambaz see Khodzhambas
97 H23 Højby Fyn, C Denmark
97 F24 Højer Sønderjylland, SW Denmark
170 Ee14 Hōjō var. Hôzyô. Ehime, Shikoku, SW Japan
192 J3 Hokianga Harbour inlet SE Tasman Sea
193 F17 Hokitika West Coast, South Island, NZ
172 P5 Hokkai-dō ◆ territory Hokkaidō, NE Japan
172 Oo5 Hokkaidō prev. Ezo, Yeso, Yezo. island NE Japan
97 G15 Hokksund Buskerud, S Norway
149 S4 Hokmābād Khorāsān, N Iran
Hokō see P'ohang
Hoko-guntō/Hoko-shotō see P'enghu Liehtao
143 T12 Hoktemberyan Rus. Oktemberyan. SW Armenia
96 F13 Hol Buskerud, S Norway
119 R11 Hola Prystan' Rus. Golaya Pristan. Khersons'ka Oblast', S Ukraine
97 I23 Holbæk Vestsjælland, E Denmark
168 G6 Holboo Dzavhan, W Mongolia
191 P10 Holbrook New South Wales, SE Australia
39 N11 Holbrook Arizona, SW USA
29 S5 Holden Missouri, C USA
38 K5 Holden Utah, W USA
29 O11 Holdenville Oklahoma, C USA
31 O16 Holdrege Nebraska, C USA
37 X3 Hole in the Mountain Peak ▲ Nevada, W USA
161 G20 Hole Narsipur Karnātaka, W India
113 H18 Holešov Ger. Holleschau. Jižní Morava, E Czech Republic
47 N14 Holetown prev. Jamestown. W Barbados
33 Q12 Holgate Ohio, N USA
46 I7 Holguín Holguín, SE Cuba
25 V12 Holiday Florida, SE USA
41 O12 Holitna River ↝ Alaska, USA
96 J13 Höljes Värmland, C Sweden
111 X3 Hollabrunn Niederösterreich, NE Austria
38 L3 Holladay Utah, W USA
9 X16 Holland Manitoba, S Canada

◆ Country ● Country Capital ◇ Dependent Territory ○ Dependent Territory Capital ◆ Administrative Region ✕ International Airport ▲ Mountain ▲▲ Mountain Range Volcano ↝ River ⊚ Lake ⊡ Reservoir

33 O9 **Holland** Michigan, N USA
27 T9 **Holland** Texas, SW USA
Holland *see* Netherlands
24 K4 **Hollandale** Mississippi, S USA
Hollandia *see* Jayapura
Hollandsch Diep *see* Hollands Diep
101 H14 **Hollands Diep** *var.* Hollandsch Diep. *channel* SW Netherlands
Holleschau *see* Holešov
27 R5 **Holliday** Texas, SW USA
20 E15 **Hollidaysburg** Pennsylvania, NE USA
23 S6 **Hollins** Virginia, NE USA
28 J12 **Hollis** Oklahoma, C USA
37 O10 **Hollister** California, W USA
29 T8 **Hollister** Missouri, C USA
95 M19 **Hollola** Häme, S Finland
100 K4 **Hollum** Friesland, N Netherlands
97 J23 **Höllviksnäs** Malmöhus, S Sweden
39 W6 **Holly** Colorado, C USA
33 R9 **Holly** Michigan, N USA
23 S14 **Holly Hill** South Carolina, SE USA
23 W11 **Holly Ridge** North Carolina, SE USA
24 L1 **Holly Springs** Mississippi, S USA
25 Z15 **Hollywood** Florida, SE USA
15 I2 **Holman** Victoria Island, Northwest Territories, N Canada
94 I2 **Hólmavík** Vestfirdhir, NW Iceland
32 J7 **Holmen** Wisconsin, N USA
25 R8 **Holmes Creek** ≈ Alabama/Florida, SE USA
97 H16 **Holmestrand** Vestfold, S Norway
95 J16 **Holmön** *island* N Sweden
97 E22 **Holmsland Klit** *beach* W Denmark
95 J16 **Holmsund** Västerbotten, N Sweden
97 Q18 **Holmudden** *headland* SE Sweden
194 L15 **Holnicote Bay** *headland* SW PNG
144 F10 **Holon** Tel Aviv, C Israel
119 P8 **Holovanivs'k** *Rus.* Golovanevsk. Kirovohrads'ka Oblast', C Ukraine
97 F21 **Holstebro** Ringkøbing, W Denmark
97 F23 **Holsted** Ribe, W Denmark
31 T13 **Holstein** Iowa, C USA
Holsteinborg/Holsteinsborg/Holstenborg/Holstensborg *see* Sisimiut
23 O8 **Holston River** ≈ Tennessee, S USA
33 Q9 **Holt** Michigan, N USA
100 N10 **Holten** Overijssel, E Netherlands
29 P3 **Holton** Kansas, C USA
29 U5 **Holts Summit** Missouri, C USA
37 X17 **Holtville** California, W USA
100 L5 **Holwerd** *Fris.* Holwert. Friesland, N Netherlands
Holwert *see* Holwerd
41 O11 **Holy Cross** Alaska, USA
39 R4 **Holy Cross, Mount Of The** ▲ Colorado, C USA
99 I18 **Holyhead** *Wel.* Caer Gybi. NW Wales, UK
99 H18 **Holy Island** *island* NW Wales, UK
98 L12 **Holy Island** *island* NE England, UK
39 W3 **Holyoke** Colorado, C USA
20 M11 **Holyoke** Massachusetts, NE USA
103 I14 **Holzminden** Niedersachsen, C Germany
83 G19 **Homa Bay** Nyanza, W Kenya
Homāyūnshahr *see* Khomeynīshahr
79 P11 **Hombori** Mopti, S Mali
103 E20 **Homburg** Saarland, SW Germany
16 Nn1 **Home Bay** *bay* Baffin Bay, Northwest Territories, NE Canada
Homenau *see* Humenné
41 Q13 **Homer** Alaska, USA
24 H4 **Homer** Louisiana, S USA
20 H10 **Homer** New York, NE USA
25 V7 **Homerville** Georgia, SE USA
25 Y16 **Homestead** Florida, SE USA
29 O9 **Hominy** Oklahoma, C USA
96 H8 **Hommelvik** Sør-Trøndelag, S Norway
97 C16 **Hommersåk** Rogaland, S Norway
161 H15 **Homnābād** Karnātaka, C India
24 J7 **Homochitto River** ≈ Mississippi, S USA
85 N20 **Homoine** Inhambane, SE Mozambique
114 O12 **Homoljske Planine** ▲ E Yugoslavia
Homonna *see* Humenné
Homs *see* Al Khums, Libya
Homs *see* Ḥimṣ, Syria
121 P19 **Homyel'** *Rus.* Gomel'. Homyel'skaya Voblasts', SE Belarus
120 L12 **Homyel'** Vitsyebskaya Voblasts', N Belarus
121 L19 **Homyel'skaya Voblasts'** *prev. Rus.* Gomel'skaya Oblast'. ◈ *province* SE Belarus
Honan *see* Henan, China
Honan *see* Luoyang, China
172 Pp6 **Honbetsu** Hokkaidō, NE Japan
Honctő *see* Gurahonț
56 E9 **Honda** Tolima, C Colombia
85 D24 **Hondeklip** *Afr.* Hondeklipbaai. Northern Cape, W South Africa
Hondeklipbaai *see* Hondeklip
9 Q13 **Hondo** Alberta, W Canada
170 C14 **Hondo** Kumamoto, Shimo-jima, SW Japan
27 Q12 **Hondo** Texas, SW USA
44 G1 **Hondo** ≈ Central America
Hondo *see* Honshū
44 G6 **Honduras** *off.* Republic of Honduras. ◆ *republic* Central America
Honduras, Golfo de *see* Honduras, Gulf of
44 H4 **Honduras, Gulf of** *Sp.* Golfo de Honduras. *gulf* W Caribbean Sea
9 V12 **Hone** Manitoba, C Canada
23 P12 **Honea Path** South Carolina, SE USA
97 H14 **Hønefoss** Buskerud, S Norway
33 S12 **Honey Creek** ≈ Ohio, N USA
27 V5 **Honey Grove** Texas, SW USA
37 Q4 **Honey Lake** ◎ California, W USA
104 L4 **Honfleur** Calvados, N France
Hon Gai *see* Hông Gai
167 O8 **Hong'an** *prev.* Huang'an. Hubei, C China
Hongay *see* Hông Gai
178 K6 **Hông Gai** *var.* Hon Gai, Hongay. Quang Ninh, N Vietnam
167 O15 **Honghai Wan** *bay* N South China Sea
Hông Hà, Sông *see* Red River
167 O7 **Hong He** ≈ C China
167 N9 **Hong Hu** ◎ C China
166 L11 **Hongjiang** Hunan, S China
167 O15 **Hong Kong** *Chin.* Xianggang. S China
165 P7 **Hongliuyuan** Gansu, N China
169 O9 **Hongor** Dornogovĭ, SE Mongolia
167 S8 **Hongqiao** ✕ (Shanghai) Shanghai Shi, E China
166 K14 **Hongshui He** ≈ S China
166 M5 **Hongtong** Shanxi, C China
170 G16 **Hongū** Wakayama, Honshū, SW Japan
Honguedo, Détroit d' *see* Honguedo Passage
13 Y5 **Honguedo Passage** *var.* Honguedo Strait, *Fr.* Détroit d'Honguedo. *strait* Québec, E Canada
Honguedo Strait *see* Honguedo Passage
Hongwan *see* Sunan
169 X13 **Hongwŏn** E North Korea
166 H7 **Hongyuan** *prev.* Hurama. Sichuan, C China
167 Q7 **Hongze Hu** *var.* Hung-tse Hu. ◎ E China
195 W16 **Honiara** ● (Solomon Islands) Guadalcanal, C Solomon Islands
171 Ll11 **Honjō** *var.* Honzyô. Akita, Honshū, C Japan
95 K18 **Honkajoki** Turku-Pori, SW Finland
171 Ii16 **Honkawane** Shizuoka, Honshū, S Japan
94 K7 **Honningsvåg** Finnmark, N Norway
97 I19 **Hönö** Göteborg och Bohus, S Sweden
40 G11 **Honokaa** *Haw.* Honoka'a. Hawaii, USA, C Pacific Ocean
40 G11 **Honokohau** *Haw.* Honokōhau. Hawaii, USA, C Pacific Ocean
40 D9 **Honolulu** ◈ Oahu, Hawaii, USA, C Pacific Ocean
40 H11 **Honomu** *Haw.* Honomū. Hawaii, USA, C Pacific Ocean
107 P10 **Honrubia** Castilla-La Mancha, C Spain
171 I15 **Honshū** *var.* Hondo, Honsyû. *island* SW Japan
Honsyû *see* Honshū
Honte *see* Westerschelde
Honzyô *see* Honjō
15 I5 **Hood** ≈ Northwest Territories, NW Canada
Hood Island *see* Española, Isla
34 H11 **Hood, Mount** ▲ Oregon, NW USA
194 K16 **Hood Point** *headland* S PNG
34 H11 **Hood River** Oregon, NW USA
100 H10 **Hoofddorp** Noord-Holland, W Netherlands
101 G15 **Hoogerheide** Noord-Brabant, S Netherlands
100 N8 **Hoogeveen** Drenthe, NE Netherlands
100 O6 **Hoogezand-Sappemeer** Groningen, NE Netherlands
100 J8 **Hoogkarspel** Noord-Holland, NW Netherlands
100 N5 **Hoogkerk** Groningen, NE Netherlands
100 G13 **Hoogvliet** Zuid-Holland, SW Netherlands
28 I8 **Hooker** Oklahoma, C USA
99 E21 **Hook Head** *Ir.* Rinn Duáin. *headland* SE Ireland
Hook of Holland *see* Hoek van Holland
168 J9 **Hoolt** Övörhangay, C Mongolia
41 W13 **Hoonah** Chichagof Island, Alaska, USA
40 L11 **Hooper Bay** Alaska, USA
33 N13 **Hoopeston** Illinois, N USA
97 K22 **Höör** Malmöhus, S Sweden
100 I9 **Hoorn** Noord-Holland, NW Netherlands
20 L10 **Hoosic River** ≈ New York, NE USA
Hoosier State *see* Indiana
37 Y11 **Hoover Dam** *dam* Arizona/Nevada, W USA
168 I9 **Höövör** Övörhangay, C Mongolia
143 Q11 **Hopa** Artvin, NE Turkey
20 J14 **Hopatcong** New Jersey, NE USA
8 M17 **Hope** British Columbia, SW Canada
41 R12 **Hope** Alaska, USA
29 T14 **Hope** Arkansas, C USA
33 P14 **Hope** Indiana, N USA
31 Q5 **Hope** North Dakota, N USA
11 Q7 **Hopedale** Newfoundland and Labrador, NE Canada
Hopeh/Hopei *see* Hebei
188 K13 **Hope, Lake** *salt lake* Western Australia
43 X13 **Hopelchén** Campeche, SE Mexico
23 U11 **Hope Mills** North Carolina, SE USA
191 O7 **Hope, Mount** New South Wales, SE Australia
94 P4 **Hopen** *island* SE Svalbard
207 Q4 **Hope, Point** *headland* Alaska, USA
10 M3 **Hopes Advance, Cap** *headland* Québec, NE Canada
190 L10 **Hopetoun** Victoria, SE Australia
85 H23 **Hopetown** Northern Cape, W South Africa
23 W6 **Hopewell** Virginia, NE USA
111 O7 **Hopfgarten im Brixental** Tirol, W Austria
189 N8 **Hopkins Lake** *salt lake* Western Australia
190 M12 **Hopkins River** ≈ Victoria, SE Australia
22 I7 **Hopkinsville** Kentucky, S USA
36 M6 **Hopland** California, W USA
97 G24 **Hoptrup** Sønderjylland, SW Denmark
34 F9 **Hoquiam** Washington, NW USA
31 R6 **Horace** North Dakota, N USA
143 R12 **Horasan** Erzurum, NE Turkey
103 G22 **Horb am Neckar** Baden-Württemberg, S Germany
97 K23 **Hörby** Malmöhus, S Sweden
45 P16 **Horconcitos** Chiriquí, W Panama
97 C14 **Hordaland** ◈ *county* S Norway
118 H13 **Horezu** Vâlcea, SW Romania
110 G7 **Horgen** Zürich, N Switzerland
168 I7 **Horgo** Arhangay, C Mongolia
Hōrin *see* Fenglin
169 O13 **Horinger** Nei Mongol Zizhiqu, N China
168 I9 **Horiult** Bayanhongor, C Mongolia
9 U17 **Horizon** Saskatchewan, S Canada
199 J10 **Horizon Bank** *undersea feature* S Pacific Ocean
199 Jj11 **Horizon Deep** *undersea feature* W Pacific Ocean
97 L14 **Hörken** Örebro, S Sweden
121 O15 **Horki** *Rus.* Gorki. Mahilyowskaya Voblasts', E Belarus
205 O10 **Horlick Mountains** ▲▲ Antarctica
119 X7 **Horlivka** *Rom.* Adâncata, *Rus.* Gorlovka. Donets'ka Oblast', E Ukraine
149 V11 **Hormak** Sīstān va Balūchestān, SE Iran
149 R13 **Hormozgān** *off.* Ostān-e Hormozgān. ◈ *province* S Iran
Hormoz, Tangeh-ye *see* Hormuz, Strait of
147 W6 **Hormuz, Strait of** *var.* Strait of Ormuz, *Per.* Tangeh-ye Hormoz. *strait* Iran/Oman
111 W2 **Horn** Niederösterreich, NE Austria
97 M18 **Horn** Östergötland, S Sweden
15 Hh8 **Horn** ≈ Northwest Territories, NW Canada
Hornád *see* Hernád
15 H3 **Hornaday** ≈ Northwest Territories, NW Canada
94 H13 **Hornavan** ◎ N Sweden
67 C24 **Hornby Mountains** *hill range* West Falkland, Falkland Islands
Horn, Cape *see* Hornos, Cabo de
99 O18 **Horncastle** E England, UK
97 N14 **Horndal** Kopparberg, C Sweden
95 I16 **Hörnefors** Västerbotten, N Sweden
20 F11 **Hornell** New York, NE USA
Horné Nové Mesto *see* Kysucké Nové Mesto
10 F12 **Hornepayne** Ontario, S Canada
96 D10 **Hornindalsvatnet** ◎ S Norway
103 G22 **Hornisgrinde** ▲ SW Germany
24 M9 **Horn Island** *island* Mississippi, S USA
65 J26 **Hornos, Cabo de** *Eng.* Cape Horn. *headland* S Chile
119 S10 **Hornostayivka** Khersons'ka Oblast', S Ukraine
191 T9 **Hornsby** New South Wales, SE Australia
99 O16 **Hornsea** E England, UK
96 O11 **Hornslandet** *peninsula* C Sweden
97 H22 **Hornslet** Århus, C Denmark
94 O4 **Hornsundtind** ▲ S Svalbard
Horochów *see* Horokhiv
118 J7 **Horodenka** *Rus.* Gorodenka. Ivano-Frankivs'ka Oblast', W Ukraine
119 Q2 **Horodnya** *Rus.* Gorodnya. Chernihivs'ka Oblast', NE Ukraine
118 K6 **Horodok** Khmel'nyts'ka Oblast', W Ukraine
118 H5 **Horodok** *Pol.* Gródek Jagielloński, *Rus.* Gorodok, Gorodok Yagellonski. L'vivs'ka Oblast', NW Ukraine
119 Q6 **Horodyshche** *Rus.* Gorodishche. Cherkas'ka Oblast', C Ukraine
172 P4 **Horokanai** Hokkaidō, NE Japan
118 J4 **Horokhiv** *Pol.* Horochów, *Rus.* Gorokhov. Volyns'ka Oblast', NW Ukraine
172 P7 **Horoshiri-dake** *var.* Horosiri Dake. ▲ Hokkaidō, N Japan
Horosiri Dake *see* Horoshiri-dake
113 C17 **Hořovice** *Ger.* Horowitz. Střední Čechy, W Czech Republic
Horowitz *see* Hořovice
169 T9 **Horqin Youyi Zhongqi** Nei Mongol Zizhiqu, NE China
169 U11 **Horqin Zuoyi Houqi** Nei Mongol Zizhiqu, N China
169 T9 **Horqin Zuoyi Zhongqi** Nei Mongol Zizhiqu, N China
64 O5 **Horqueta** Concepción, C Paraguay
57 O12 **Horqueta Minas** Amazonas, S Venezuela
97 J20 **Horred** Älvsborg, S Sweden
157 J19 **Horsburgh Atoll** *atoll* N Maldives
22 K7 **Horse Cave** Kentucky, S USA
39 V6 **Horse Creek** ≈ Colorado, C USA
29 S6 **Horse Creek** ≈ Missouri, C USA
20 G11 **Horseheads** New York, NE USA
39 P13 **Horse Mount** ▲ New Mexico, SW USA
97 G22 **Horsens** Vejle, C Denmark
67 F25 **Horse Pasture Point** *headland* W Saint Helena
35 N13 **Horseshoe Bend** Idaho, NW USA
38 L13 **Horseshoe Reservoir** ⊞ Arizona, SW USA
66 M9 **Horseshoe Seamounts** *undersea feature* E Atlantic Ocean
190 L11 **Horsham** Victoria, SE Australia
99 O23 **Horsham** SE England, UK
101 M15 **Horst** Limburg, SE Netherlands
66 N2 **Horta** Faial, Azores, Portugal, NE Atlantic Ocean
97 H16 **Horten** Vestfold, S Norway
113 M23 **Hortobágy-Berettyó** ≈ E Hungary
29 Q3 **Horton** Kansas, C USA
15 H3 **Horton** ≈ Northwest Territories, NW Canada
97 I23 **Hørve** Vestsjælland, E Denmark
97 L22 **Hörvik** Blekinge, S Sweden
144 E11 **Horvot Haluza** *ruins* Southern, S Israel
12 E7 **Horwood Lake** ◎ Ontario, S Canada
118 K4 **Horyn'** *Rus.* Goryn. ≈ NW Ukraine
83 I14 **Hosa'ina** *var.* Hosseina, *It.* Hosanna. SW Ethiopia
Hosanna *see* Hosa'ina
103 H18 **Hösbach** Bayern, C Germany
Hose Mountains *see* Hose, Pegunungan
174 Mm6 **Hose, Pegunungan** *var.* Hose Mountains. ▲▲ East Malaysia
154 L15 **Hoshāb** Baluchistān, SW Pakistan
160 H10 **Hoshangābād** Madhya Pradesh, C India
118 L4 **Hoshcha** Rivnens'ka Oblast', NW Ukraine
158 I7 **Hoshiārpur** Punjab, NW India
168 J7 **Höshööt** Arhangay, C Mongolia
101 M23 **Hosingen** Diekirch, NE Luxembourg
195 N12 **Hoskins** New Britain, E PNG
161 G17 **Hospet** Karnātaka, C India
106 K4 **Hospital de Orbigo** Castilla-León, N Spain
Hospitalet *see* L'Hospitalet de Llobregat
94 N13 **Hossa** Oulu, E Finland
Hosseina *see* Hosa'ina
Hosszúmezjő *see* Câmpulung Moldovenesc
65 I25 **Hoste, Isla** *island* S Chile
119 O4 **Hostomel'** *Rus.* Gostomel'. Kyyivs'ka Oblast', N Ukraine
161 H20 **Hosūr** Tamil Nādu, SE India
178 H8 **Hot** Chiang Mai, NW Thailand
164 G10 **Hotan** *var.* Khotan, *Chin.* Ho-t'ien. Xinjiang Uygur Zizhiqu, NW China
164 H9 **Hotan He** ≈ NW China
85 G22 **Hotazel** Northern Cape, N South Africa
39 Q5 **Hotchkiss** Colorado, C USA
37 V7 **Hot Creek Range** ▲▲ Nevada, W USA
Hote *see* Hoti
176 U11 **Hoti** *var.* Hote. Pulau Seram, E Indonesia
Ho-t'ien *see* Hotan
Hotin *see* Khotyn
95 H15 **Hoting** Jämtland, C Sweden
168 L14 **Hotong Qagan Nur** ◎ N China
168 J8 **Hotont** Arhangay, C Mongolia
29 T12 **Hot Springs** Arkansas, C USA
30 J11 **Hot Springs** South Dakota, N USA
23 S5 **Hot Springs** Virginia, NE USA
37 Q4 **Hot Springs Peak** ▲ California, W USA
29 T12 **Hot Springs Village** Arkansas, C USA
Hotspur Bank *see* Hotspur Seamount
67 J16 **Hotspur Seamount** *var.* Hotspur Bank. *undersea feature* C Atlantic Ocean
15 Hh6 **Hottah Lake** ◎ Northwest Territories, NW Canada
46 K9 **Hotte, Massif de la** ▲▲ SW Haiti
101 K21 **Hotton** Luxembourg, SE Belgium
Hötzing *see* Hațeg
197 I6 **Houaïlou** Province Nord, C New Caledonia
76 K5 **Houari Boumediène** ✕ (Alger) N Algeria
178 Hh6 **Houayxay** *var.* Ban Houayxay, Ban Houei Sai. Bokèo, N Laos
105 N5 **Houdan** Yvelines, N France
101 F20 **Houdeng-Goegnies** *var.* Houdeng-Gœgnies. Hainaut, S Belgium
104 K14 **Houeillès** Lot-et-Garonne, SW France
101 L22 **Houffalize** Luxembourg, SE Belgium
32 M3 **Houghton** Michigan, N USA
33 Q7 **Houghton Lake** Michigan, N USA
33 Q7 **Houghton Lake** ◎ Michigan, N USA
21 T3 **Houlton** Maine, NE USA
166 M5 **Houma** Shanxi, C China
200 Q15 **Houma** 'Eua, C Tonga
200 R16 **Houma** Tongatapu, S Tonga
24 J10 **Houma** Louisiana, S USA
200 Qq16 **Houma Taloa** *headland* Tongatapu, S Tonga
79 O13 **Houndé** SW Burkina
104 J12 **Hourtin-Carcans, Lac d'** ◎ SW France
38 J5 **House Range** ▲▲ Utah, W USA
8 K13 **Houston** British Columbia, SW Canada
41 R11 **Houston** Alaska, USA
31 X10 **Houston** Minnesota, N USA
24 M3 **Houston** Mississippi, S USA
29 V7 **Houston** Missouri, C USA
27 W11 **Houston** Texas, SW USA
27 W11 **Houston** ✕ Texas, SW USA
100 J12 **Houten** Utrecht, C Netherlands
101 K17 **Houthalen** Limburg, NE Belgium
101 I22 **Houyet** Namur, SE Belgium
97 H22 **Hov** Århus, C Denmark
97 L17 **Hova** Skaraborg, S Sweden
168 E6 **Hovd** *var.* Khovd. Hovd, W Mongolia
168 J10 **Hovd** Övörhangay, C Mongolia
168 E7 **Hovd** ◈ *province* W Mongolia
168 C5 **Hovd Gol** ≈ NW Mongolia
99 O23 **Hove** SE England, UK
31 N8 **Hoven** South Dakota, N USA
118 I8 **Hoverla, Hora** *Rus.* Gora Goverla. ▲ W Ukraine
168 H8 **Höviyn Am** Bayanhongor, C Mongolia
97 M21 **Hovmantorp** Kronoberg, S Sweden
169 N11 **Hövsgöl** Dornogovĭ, SE Mongolia
168 I5 **Hövsgöl** ◈ *province* N Mongolia
Hovsgol, Lake *see* Hövsgöl Nuur
168 J5 **Hövsgöl Nuur** *var.* Lake Hovsgol. ◎ N Mongolia
80 L9 **Howa, Ouadi** *var.* Wādi Howar. ≈ Chad/Sudan *see also* Howar, Wādi
29 P7 **Howard** Kansas, C USA
31 Q10 **Howard** South Dakota, N USA
27 N10 **Howard Draw** *valley* Texas, SW USA
31 U8 **Howard Lake** Minnesota, N USA
82 B8 **Howar, Wādi** *var.* Ouadi Howa. ≈ Chad/Sudan *see also* Howa, Ouadi
27 U5 **Howe** Texas, SW USA
191 R12 **Howe, Cape** *headland* New South Wales/Victoria, SE Australia
33 R9 **Howell** Michigan, N USA
30 L9 **Howes** South Dakota, N USA
85 K23 **Howick** KwaZulu/Natal, E South Africa
Howrah *see* Hāora
29 W9 **Hoxie** Arkansas, C USA
28 J3 **Hoxie** Kansas, C USA
103 I14 **Höxter** Nordrhein-Westfalen, W Germany
164 K6 **Hoxud** Xinjiang Uygur Zizhiqu, NW China
98 J5 **Hoy** *island* N Scotland, UK
45 S17 **Hoya, Cerro** ▲ S Panama
96 D12 **Høyanger** Sogn og Fjordane, S Norway
103 P15 **Hoyerswerda** Sachsen, E Germany
170 Dd15 **Hōyo-kaikyō** *var.* Hayasui-seto. *strait* SW Japan
106 J8 **Hoyos** Extremadura, W Spain
31 W4 **Hoyt Lakes** Minnesota, N USA
89 V2 **Hoyvík** Streymoy, N Faeroe Islands
143 O14 **Hozat** Tunceli, E Turkey
Hôzyô *see* Hōjō
113 F16 **Hradec Králové** *Ger.* Königgrätz. Východní Čechy, NE Czech Republic
113 B16 **Hradiště** *Ger.* Burgstadlberg. ▲ NW Czech Republic
119 R6 **Hradyz'k** *Rus.* Gradizhsk. Poltavs'ka Oblast', NE Ukraine
121 M16 **Hradzyanka** *Rus.* Grodzyanka. Mahilyowskaya Voblasts', E Belarus
121 F16 **Hrandzichy** *Rus.* Grandichi. Hrodzyenskaya Voblasts', W Belarus
113 H18 **Hranice** *Ger.* Mährisch-Weisskirchen. Severní Morava, E Czech Republic
114 I13 **Hrasnica** SE Bosnia and Herzegovina
111 V11 **Hrastnik** C Slovenia
143 U12 **Hrazdan** *Rus.* Razdan. C Armenia
143 T12 **Hrazdan** *var.* Zanga, *Rus.* Razdan. ≈ C Armenia
119 R5 **Hrebinka** *Rus.* Grebenka. Poltavs'ka Oblast', NE Ukraine
121 K17 **Hresk** *Rus.* Gresk. Minskaya Voblasts', C Belarus
Hrisoupoli *see* Chrysoúpoli
121 F16 **Hrodna** *Pol.* Grodno. Hrodzyenskaya Voblasts', W Belarus
121 F16 **Hrodzyenskaya Voblasts'** *prev. Rus.* Grodnenskaya Oblast'. ◈ *province* W Belarus
113 J21 **Hron** *Ger.* Gran, *Hung.* Garam. ≈ C Slovakia
113 Q14 **Hrubieszów** *Rus.* Grubeshov. Zamość, SE Poland
114 F13 **Hrvace** Split-Dalmacija, SE Croatia
Hrvatska *see* Croatia
Hrvatska Kostajnica *see* Kostajnica
118 K6 **Hrymayliv** *Pol.* Gízymałów, *Rus.* Grimaylov. Ternopil's'ka Oblast', W Ukraine
178 H4 **Hsenwi** Shan State, E Myanmar
Hsia-men *see* Xiamen
Hsiang-t'an *see* Xiangtan
Hsi Chiang *see* Xi Jiang
178 Gg6 **Hsihseng** Shan State, C Myanmar
167 S13 **Hsinchu** *municipality* N Taiwan
Hsing-k'ai Hu *see* Khanka, Lake
Hsining/Hsi-ning *see* Xining
Hsinking *see* Changchun
Hsin-yang *see* Xinyang
167 S14 **Hsinying** *var.* Sinying, *Jap.* Shinei. C Taiwan
178 Gg4 **Hsipaw** Shan State, C Myanmar
167 S13 **Hsüeh Shan** ▲ N Taiwan
Hu *see* Shanghai Shi
85 B18 **Huab** ≈ W Namibia
59 M21 **Huacaya** Chuquisaca, S Bolivia
59 J19 **Huachacalla** Oruro, SW Bolivia
165 X9 **Huachi** *var.* Rouyuanchengzi. Gansu, C China
59 N16 **Huachi, Laguna** ◎ N Bolivia
59 D14 **Huacho** Lima, W Peru
169 Y8 **Huachuan** Heilongjiang, NE China
169 P12 **Huade** Nei Mongol Zizhiqu, N China
169 W10 **Huadian** Jilin, NE China
58 E13 **Huagaruncho, Cordillera** ▲ C Peru
Hua Hin *see* Ban Hua Hin
203 S10 **Huahine** *island* Îles Sous le Vent, W French Polynesia
Huahua, Rio *see* Wawa, Río
178 I19 **Huai** ≈ E Thailand
167 P6 **Huaibei** Anhui, E China
169 V10 **Huaide** *var.* Gongzhuling. Jilin, NE China
163 T10 **Huai He** ≈ C China
166 L11 **Huaihua** Hunan, S China
167 N14 **Huaiji** Guangdong, S China
167 O2 **Huailai** *prev.* Shacheng. Hebei, E China
167 P7 **Huainan** *var.* Huai-nan, Hwainan. Anhui, E China
167 N2 **Huairen** Shanxi, C China
167 O7 **Huaiyang** Henan, C China
167 Q7 **Huaiyin** *var.* Qingjiang. Jiangsu, E China
178 Gg16 **Huai Yot** Trang, SW Thailand
43 Q15 **Huajuapan** *var.* Huajuapan de León. Oaxaca, SE Mexico
Huajuapan de León *see* Huajuapan
43 O9 **Hualahuises** Nuevo León, NE Mexico
38 I11 **Hualapai Mountains** ▲▲ Arizona, SW USA
38 I11 **Hualapai Peak** ▲ Arizona, SW USA
64 J7 **Hualfín** Catamarca, N Argentina
167 T13 **Hualien** *var.* Hwalien, *Jap.* Karen. C Taiwan
58 E10 **Huallaga, Río** ≈ N Peru
58 C11 **Huamachuco** La Libertad, C Peru
43 Q14 **Huamantla** Tlaxcala, S Mexico
84 C13 **Huambo** *Port.* Nova Lisboa. Huambo, C Angola
84 B13 **Huambo** ◈ *province* C Angola
43 P15 **Huamuxtitlán** Guerrero, S Mexico
65 H17 **Huancache, Sierra** ▲▲ SW Argentina
59 I17 **Huancané** Puno, SE Peru
59 F16 **Huancapi** Ayacucho, C Peru
59 E15 **Huancavelica** Huancavelica, SW Peru
59 E15 **Huancavelica** *off.* Departamento de Huancavelica. ◈ *department* W Peru
59 E14 **Huancayo** Junín, C Peru
59 K20 **Huanchaca, Cerro** ▲ S Bolivia
58 C12 **Huandoy, Nevado** ▲ W Peru
167 O8 **Huangchuan** Henan, C China
Huang Hai *see* Yellow Sea
163 Q8 **Huang He** *var.* Yellow River. ≈ C China
167 Q4 **Huanghe Kou** *delta* E China
166 L5 **Huangling** Shaanxi, C China
167 O9 **Huangpi** Hubei, C China
169 P13 **Huangqi Hai** ◎ N China
167 Q9 **Huang Shan** ▲ Anhui, E China
167 Q9 **Huangshan** *var.* Tunxi. Anhui, E China
167 O9 **Huangshi** *var.* Huang-shih, Hwangshih. Hubei, C China
Huang-shih *see* Huangshi
166 L5 **Huangtu Gaoyuan** *plateau* C China
63 B22 **Huanguelén** Buenos Aires, E Argentina
167 S10 **Huangyan** Zhejiang, SE China
165 T10 **Huangyuan** Qinghai, C China
165 T10 **Huangzhong** Qinghai, C China
169 W12 **Huanren** Liaoning, NE China
59 F15 **Huanta** Ayacucho, C Peru
58 E13 **Huánuco** Huánuco, C Peru
58 D13 **Huánuco** *off.* Departamento de Huánuco. ◈ *department* C Peru
59 K19 **Huanuni** Oruro, W Bolivia
165 X9 **Huan Xian** Gansu, C China
167 S12 **Huap'ing Yu** *island* N Taiwan
64 H3 **Huara** Tarapacá, N Chile
59 D14 **Huaral** Lima, W Peru
Huarás *see* Huaraz
58 D13 **Huaraz** *var.* Huarás. Ancash, W Peru
59 I16 **Huari Huari, Río** ≈ S Peru
58 C13 **Huarmey** Ancash, W Peru
42 H4 **Huásabas** Sonora, NW Mexico
58 D8 **Huasaga, Río** ≈ Ecuador/Peru
178 H16 **Hua Sai** Nakhon Si Thammarat, SW Thailand
58 D12 **Huascarán, Nevado** ▲ W Peru
64 G8 **Huasco** Atacama, N Chile
64 G8 **Huasco, Río** ≈ C Chile
165 S11 **Huashikia** Qinghai, W China
42 G7 **Huatabampo** Sonora, NW Mexico
165 W10 **Huating** Gansu, C China
178 Jj7 **Huatt, Phou** ▲ N Vietnam
43 Q14 **Huatusco** *var.* Huatusco de Chicuellar. Veracruz-Llave, C Mexico
Huatusco de Chicuellar *see* Huatusco
43 P13 **Huauchinango** Puebla, S Mexico
Huaunta *see* Wounta
43 R15 **Huautla** *var.* Huautla de Jiménez. Oaxaca, SE Mexico
Huautla de Jiménez *see* Huautla
167 O5 **Huaxian** *var.* Daokou, Hua Xian. Henan, C China
31 V13 **Hubbard** Iowa, C USA
27 U8 **Hubbard** Texas, SW USA
27 Q6 **Hubbard Creek Lake** ◎ Texas, SW USA
33 R6 **Hubbard Lake** ◎ Michigan, N USA
166 M9 **Hubei** *var.* E, Hubei Sheng, Hupeh, Hupei. ◈ *province* C China
Hubei Sheng *see* Hubei
111 P8 **Huben** Tirol, W Austria
33 R13 **Huber Heights** Ohio, N USA
161 F17 **Hubli** Karnātaka, SW India
169 X12 **Huch'ang** N North Korea
99 M18 **Hucknall** C England, UK
99 L17 **Huddersfield** N England, UK
97 O16 **Huddinge** Stockholm, C Sweden
96 N11 **Hudiksvall** Gävleborg, C Sweden
31 W13 **Hudson** Iowa, C USA
21 O11 **Hudson** Massachusetts, NE USA
33 Q11 **Hudson** Michigan, N USA
32 I6 **Hudson** Wisconsin, N USA
9 V14 **Hudson Bay** Saskatchewan, S Canada
10 G6 **Hudson Bay** *bay* NE Canada
205 T16 **Hudson, Cape** *headland* Antarctica
Hudson, Détroit d' *see* Hudson Strait
29 Q9 **Hudson, Lake** ⊞ Oklahoma, C USA
20 K9 **Hudson River** ≈ New Jersey/New York, NE USA
8 M12 **Hudson's Hope** British Columbia, W Canada
10 L2 **Hudson Strait** *Fr.* Détroit d'Hudson. *strait* Northwest Territories/Québec, NE Canada
Hudūd ash Shamālīyah, Minṭaqat al *see* Al Ḥudūd ash Shamālīyah
Hudur *see* Xuddur
178 K9 **Huê** Thưa Thiên-Huê, C Vietnam
106 J7 **Huebra** ≈ W Spain
26 H8 **Hueco Mountains** ▲▲ Texas, SW USA
118 G10 **Huedin** *Hung.* Bánffyhunyad. Cluj, NW Romania
42 J10 **Huehuento, Cerro** ▲ C Mexico
44 B5 **Huehuetenango** Huehuetenango, W Guatemala
44 B4 **Huehuetenango** *off.* Departamento de Huehuetenango. ◈ *department* W Guatemala
42 L11 **Huejuquilla** Jalisco, SW Mexico
43 P12 **Huejutla** *var.* Huejutla de Reyes. Hidalgo, C Mexico
Huejutla de Reyes *see* Huejutla
104 G6 **Huelgoat** Finistère, NW France
107 O13 **Huelma** Andalucía, S Spain
106 I14 **Huelva** *anc.* Onuba. Andalucía, SW Spain
106 I13 **Huelva** ◈ *province* Andalucía, SW Spain
106 J13 **Huelva** ≈ SW Spain
107 Q14 **Huercal-Overa** Andalucía, S Spain
39 Q9 **Huerfano Mountain** ▲ New Mexico, SW USA
39 T7 **Huerfano River** ≈ Colorado, C USA
107 S12 **Huertas, Cabo** *headland* SE Spain
107 R6 **Huerva** ≈ N Spain
107 S4 **Huesca** *anc.* Osca. Aragón, NE Spain
107 T4 **Huesca** ◈ *province* Aragón, NE Spain
107 P13 **Huéscar** Andalucía, S Spain
43 N15 **Huetamo** *var.* Huetamo de Núñez. Michoacán de Ocampo, SW Mexico
Huetamo de Núñez *see* Huetamo
107 P8 **Huete** Castilla-La Mancha, C Spain
25 P4 **Hueytown** Alabama, S USA
30 L16 **Hugh Butler Lake** ⊞ Nebraska, C USA
189 V6 **Hughenden** Queensland, NE Australia
190 A6 **Hughes** South Australia
41 P8 **Hughes** Alaska, USA
29 X11 **Hughes** Arkansas, C USA
27 W6 **Hughes Springs** Texas, SW USA
39 V5 **Hugo** Colorado, C USA
29 Q13 **Hugo** Oklahoma, C USA
29 Q13 **Hugo Lake** ⊞ Oklahoma, C USA
28 H7 **Hugoton** Kansas, C USA
Huhehot/Huhuohaote *see* Hohhot
167 R13 **Hui'an** Fujian, SE China
192 O9 **Huiarau Range** ▲ North Island, NZ
85 D22 **Huib-Hoch Plateau** *plateau* S Namibia
43 O13 **Huichapán** Hidalgo, C Mexico
Huicheng *see* Shexian
169 W13 **Hŭich'ŏn** C North Korea
56 E12 **Huila** *off.* Departamento del Huila. ◈ *province* S Colombia
85 B15 **Huíla** ◈ *province* SW Angola
56 D11 **Huila, Nevado del** *elevation* C Colombia
85 B15 **Huíla Plateau** *plateau* S Angola
166 G12 **Huili** Sichuan, C China
167 P4 **Huimin** Shandong, E China
169 W11 **Huinan** *var.* Chaoyang. Jilin, NE China
64 K12 **Huinca Renancó** Córdoba, C Argentina
165 V10 **Huining** Gansu, C China
166 J12 **Huishui** Guizhou, S China
104 L6 **Huisne** ≈ NW France
100 L12 **Huissen** Gelderland, SE Netherlands
165 N11 **Huiten Nur** ◎ C China

◆ Country
● Country Capital
◇ Dependent Territory
○ Dependent Territory Capital
◈ Administrative Region
✕ International Airport
▲ Mountain
▲▲ Mountain Range
Volcano
≈ River
◎ Lake
⊞ Reservoir

95 *K19* **Huittinen** Turku-Pori, SW Finland
43 *O15* **Huitzuco** *var.* Huitzuco de los Figueroa. Guerrero, S Mexico
Huitzuco de los Figueroa *see* Huitzuco
165 *W11* **Hui Xian** Gansu, C China
43 *V17* **Huixtla** Chiapas, SE Mexico
166 *H12* **Huize** Yunnan, SW China
100 *J10* **Huizen** Noord-Holland, C Netherlands
167 *O14* **Huizhou** Guangdong, S China
168 *J6* **Hujirt** Arhangay, C Mongolia
168 *J8* **Hujirt** Övörhangay, C Mongolia
168 *K8* **Hujrt** Töv, C Mongolia
Hukagawa *see* Fukagawa
Hŭksan-chedo *see* Hŭksan-gundo
169 *W17* **Hŭksan-gundo** *var.* Hŭksan-chedo. *island group* SW South Korea
Hukue *see* Fukue
Hukui *see* Fukui
85 *G20* **Hukuntsi** Kgalagadi, SW Botswana
Hukuoka *see* Fukuoka
Hukusima *see* Fukushima
Hukutiyama *see* Fukuchiyama
Hukuyama *see* Fukuyama
169 *W8* **Hulan** Heilongjiang, NE China
169 *W8* **Hulan He** ≈ NE China
33 *Q4* **Hulbert Lake** ◎ Michigan, N USA
Hulczyn *see* Hlučín
169 *Z8* **Hulin** Heilongjiang, NE China
169 *S9* **Hulingol** *prev.* Huolin Gol. Nei Mongol Zizhiqu, N China
12 *L12* **Hull** Québec, SE Canada
31 *S12* **Hull** Iowa, C USA
Hull *see* Kingston upon Hull
Hull Island *see* Orona
101 *F16* **Hulst** Zeeland, SW Netherlands
169 *Q7* **Hulstay** Dornod, NE Mongolia
Hultschin *see* Hlučín
97 *M19* **Hultsfred** Kalmar, S Sweden
Hulun *see* Hailar
Hu-lun Ch'ih *see* Hulun Nur
169 *Q6* **Hulun Nur** *var.* Hu-lun Ch'ih; *prev.* Dalai Nor. ◎ NE China
Hulwan/Hulwân *see* Helwân
119 *V8* **Hulyaypole** *Rus.* Gulyaypole. Zaporiz'ka Oblast', SE Ukraine
169 *V4* **Huma** Heilongjiang, NE China
47 *V6* **Humacao** E Puerto Rico
169 *U4* **Huma He** ≈ NE China
64 *J5* **Humahuaca** Jujuy, N Argentina
61 *E14* **Humaitá** Amazonas, N Brazil
64 *N7* **Humaitá** Neembucú, S Paraguay
85 *H26* **Humansdorp** Eastern Cape, S South Africa
29 *S6* **Humansville** Missouri, C USA
42 *J8* **Humaya, Río** ≈ C Mexico
85 *C16* **Humbe** Cunene, SW Angola
99 *N17* **Humber** *estuary* E England, UK
99 *N17* **Humberside** *cultural region* E England, UK
Humberto *see* Umberto
27 *W11* **Humble** Texas, SW USA
9 *U15* **Humboldt** Saskatchewan, S Canada
31 *U12* **Humboldt** Iowa, C USA
29 *Q6* **Humboldt** Kansas, C USA
31 *S17* **Humboldt** Nebraska, C USA
37 *S3* **Humboldt** Nevada, W USA
22 *G9* **Humboldt** Tennessee, S USA
36 *K3* **Humboldt Bay** *bay* California, W USA
37 *S4* **Humboldt Lake** ◎ Nevada, W USA
197 *J7* **Humboldt, Mont** ▲ S New Caledonia
37 *S4* **Humboldt River** ≈ Nevada, W USA
37 *T5* **Humboldt Salt Marsh** *wetland* Nevada, W USA
190 *P11* **Hume, Lake** ◎ New South Wales/Victoria, SE Australia
113 *N19* **Humenné** *Ger.* Homenau, *Hung.* Homonna. Východné Slovensko, E Slovakia
31 *V15* **Humeston** Iowa, C USA
56 *J5* **Humocaro Bajo** Lara, N Venezuela
31 *Q14* **Humphrey** Nebraska, C USA
37 *S9* **Humphreys, Mount** ▲ California, W USA
38 *L11* **Humphreys Peak** ▲ Arizona, SW USA
113 *E17* **Humpolec** *Ger.* Gumpolds, Humpoletz. Jižní Čechy, C Czech Republic
Humpoletz *see* Humpolec
95 *K19* **Humppila** Häme, SW Finland
34 *F8* **Humptulips** Washington, NW USA
44 *H7* **Humuya, Río** ≈ W Honduras
77 *P9* **Hūn** N Libya
Hunabasi *see* Funabashi
94 *I1* **Húnaflói** *bay* NW Iceland
166 *M11* **Hunan** *var.* Hunan Sheng, Xiang. ◈ *province* S China
Hunan Sheng *see* Hunan
169 *Y10* **Hunchun** Jilin, NE China
97 *I22* **Hundested** Frederiksborg, E Denmark
Hundred Mile House *see* 100 Mile House
118 *G12* **Hunedoara** *Ger.* Eisenmarkt, *Hung.* Vajdahunyad. Hunedoara, SW Romania
118 *G12* **Hunedoara** ◈ *county* W Romania
103 *I17* **Hünfeld** Hessen, C Germany
113 *H23* **Hungary** *off.* Republic of Hungary, *Ger.* Ungarn, *Hung.* Magyarország, *Rom.* Ungaria, *SCr.* Madarska, *Ukr.* Uhorshchyna; *prev.* Hungarian People's Republic. ◆ *republic* C Europe
Hungary, Plain of *see* Great Hungarian Plain
168 *F6* **Hungiy** Dzavhan, W Mongolia
169 *X13* **Hŭngnam** E North Korea
35 *P8* **Hungry Horse Reservoir** ▣ Montana, NW USA
Hungt'ou *see* Lan Yü
Hung-tse Hu *see* Hongze Hu
178 *J6* **Hưng Yên** Hai Hưng, N Vietnam
Hunjiang *see* Baishan
97 *I18* **Hunnebostrand** Göteborg och Bohus, S Sweden
103 *E19* **Hunsrück** ▲▲ W Germany
99 *P18* **Hunstanton** E England, UK
161 *G20* **Hunsūr** Karnātaka, E India
168 *I7* **Hunt** Arhangay, C Mongolia
102 *G12* **Hunte** ≈ NW Germany
31 *Q5* **Hunter** North Dakota, N USA
27 *S11* **Hunter** Texas, SW USA
193 *D20* **Hunter** ≈ South Island, NZ
191 *N15* **Hunter Island** *island* Tasmania, SE Australia
20 *K11* **Hunter Mountain** ▲ New York, NE USA
193 *B23* **Hunter Mountains** ▲▲ South Island, NZ
191 *S7* **Hunter River** ≈ New South Wales, SE Australia
34 *L7* **Hunters** Washington, NW USA
193 *F20* **Hunters Hills, The** *hill range* South Island, NZ
192 *M12* **Hunterville** Manawatu-Wanganui, North Island, NZ
33 *N16* **Huntingburg** Indiana, N USA
99 *O20* **Huntingdon** E England, UK
20 *E15* **Huntingdon** Pennsylvania, NE USA
22 *G9* **Huntingdon** Tennessee, S USA
99 *O20* **Huntingdonshire** *cultural region* C England, UK
33 *P12* **Huntington** Indiana, N USA
34 *L13* **Huntington** Oregon, NW USA
27 *X9* **Huntington** Texas, SW USA
38 *M5* **Huntington** Utah, W USA
23 *P5* **Huntington** West Virginia, NE USA
37 *T16* **Huntington Beach** California, W USA
37 *W4* **Huntington Creek** ≈ Nevada, W USA
192 *L7* **Huntly** Waikato, North Island, NZ
98 *K8* **Huntly** NE Scotland, UK
8 *K8* **Hunt, Mount** ▲ Yukon Territory, NW Canada
12 *H12* **Huntsville** Ontario, S Canada
25 *P2* **Huntsville** Alabama, S USA
29 *S9* **Huntsville** Arkansas, C USA
29 *U3* **Huntsville** Missouri, C USA
22 *M8* **Huntsville** Tennessee, S USA
27 *V10* **Huntsville** Texas, SW USA
38 *L2* **Huntsville** Utah, W USA
43 *W12* **Hunucmá** Yucatán, SE Mexico
155 *W3* **Hunza** *var.* Karīmābād. Jammu and Kashmir, NE Pakistan
155 *W3* **Hunza** ≈ NE Pakistan
Hunze *see* Oostermoers Vaart
164 *H4* **Huocheng** *var.* Shuiding. Xinjiang Uygur Zizhiqu, NW China
167 *N6* **Huojia** Henan, C China
Huolin Gol *see* Hulingol
197 *F3* **Huon** *reef* N New Caledonia
194 *K13* **Huon Gulf** *gulf* E PNG
194 *K13* **Huon Peninsula** *headland* C PNG
Huoshao Dao *see* Lü Tao
Huoshao Tao *see* Lan Yü
Hupeh/Hupei *see* Hubei
Hurano *see* Furano
97 *H14* **Hurdalssjøen** ◎ S Norway
12 *E13* **Hurd, Cape** *headland* Ontario, S Canada
Hurdegaryp *see* Hardegarijp
31 *N4* **Hurdsfield** North Dakota, N USA
168 *J7* **Hüremt** Bulgan, C Mongolia
168 *J8* **Hüremt** Övörhangay, C Mongolia
77 *X9* **Hurghada** *var.* Al Ghurdaqah, Ghurdaqah. E Egypt
69 *V9* **Huri Hills** ▲▲ NW Kenya
39 *P15* **Hurley** New Mexico, SW USA
32 *K4* **Hurley** Wisconsin, N USA
23 *Y4* **Hurlock** Maryland, NE USA
31 *P10* **Huron** South Dakota, N USA
33 *S6* **Huron, Lake** ◎ Canada/USA
33 *N3* **Huron Mountains** *hill range* Michigan, N USA
38 *J8* **Hurricane** Utah, W USA
23 *P5* **Hurricane** West Virginia, NE USA
38 *J8* **Hurricane Cliffs** *cliff* Arizona, SW USA
25 *V6* **Hurricane Creek** ≈ Georgia, SE USA
96 *E12* **Hurrungane** ▲ S Norway
103 *E16* **Hürth** Nordrhein-Westfalen, W Germany
Hurukawa *see* Furukawa
193 *I17* **Hurunui** ≈ South Island, NZ
97 *F21* **Hurup** Viborg, NW Denmark
119 *T14* **Hurzuf** Respublika Krym, S Ukraine
Huș *see* Huşi
94 *K1* **Húsavík** Nordhurland Eystra, NE Iceland
118 *M10* **Huşi** *var.* Huş. Vaslui, E Romania
97 *L19* **Huskvarna** Jönköping, S Sweden
41 *P8* **Huslia** Alaska, USA
Husn *see* Al Ḥuṣn
97 *C15* **Husnes** Hordaland, S Norway
96 *D8* **Hustadvika** *sea area* S Norway
Husté *see* Khust
102 *H7* **Husum** Schleswig-Holstein, N Germany
95 *I16* **Husum** Västernorrland, C Sweden
118 *K6* **Husyatyn** Ternopil's'ka Oblast', W Ukraine
Huszt *see* Khust
168 *K6* **Hutag** Bulgan, N Mongolia
28 *M6* **Hutchinson** Kansas, C USA
31 *U9* **Hutchinson** Minnesota, N USA
25 *Y13* **Hutchinson Island** *island* Florida, SE USA
38 *L11* **Hutch Mountain** ▲ Arizona, SW USA
147 *O14* **Ḥūth** NW Yemen
195 *R11* **Hutjena** Buka Island, NE PNG
111 *T8* **Hüttenberg** Kärnten, S Austria
27 *T10* **Hutto** Texas, SW USA
Huttu *see* Futtsu
110 *E8* **Huttwil** Bern, W Switzerland
164 *K5* **Hutubi** Xinjiang Uygur Zizhiqu, NW China
167 *N4* **Hutuo He** ≈ C China
Hutyû *see* Fuchū
193 *E20* **Huxley, Mount** ▲ South Island, NZ
101 *J20* **Huy** *Dut.* Hoei, Hoey. Liège, E Belgium
167 *R8* **Huzhou** *var.* Wuxing. Zhejiang, SE China
Huzi *see* Fuji
Huzieda *see* Fujieda
Huzinomiya *see* Fujinomiya
Huzisawa *see* Fujisawa
Huziyosida *see* Fuji-Yoshida
94 *I2* **Hvammstangi** Nordhurland Vestra, N Iceland
94 *K4* **Hvannadalshnúkur** ▲ S Iceland
115 *E15* **Hvar** *It.* Lesina. Split-Dalmacija, S Croatia
115 *F15* **Hvar** *It.* Lesina; *anc.* Pharus. *island* S Croatia
119 *T13* **Hvardiys'ke** *Rus.* Gvardeyskoye. Respublika Krym, S Ukraine
94 *I4* **Hveragerdhi** Sudhurland, SW Iceland
97 *E22* **Hvide Sande** Ringkøbing, W Denmark
94 *I3* **Hvitá** ≈ C Iceland
97 *G15* **Hvittingfoss** Buskerud, S Norway
94 *I4* **Hvolsvöllur** Sudhurland, SW Iceland
Hwach'ŏn-chŏsuji *see* P'aro-ho
Hwainan *see* Huainan
Hwalien *see* Hualien
85 *I16* **Hwange** *prev.* Wankie. Matabeleland North, W Zimbabwe
Hwang-Hae *see* Yellow Sea
Hwangshih *see* Huangshi
85 *L17* **Hwedza** Mashonaland East, E Zimbabwe
65 *G20* **Hyades, Cerro** ▲ S Chile
21 *Q12* **Hyannis** Massachusetts, NE USA
30 *L13* **Hyannis** Nebraska, C USA
168 *F6* **Hyargas Nuur** ◎ NW Mongolia
Hybla/Hybla Major *see* Paternò
41 *Y14* **Hydaburg** Prince of Wales Island, Alaska, USA
193 *F22* **Hyde** Otago, South Island, NZ
23 *O7* **Hyden** Kentucky, S USA
20 *K12* **Hyde Park** New York, NE USA
41 *Z14* **Hyder** Alaska, USA
161 *I15* **Hyderābād** *var.* Haidarabad. Andhra Pradesh, C India
155 *Q16* **Hyderābād** *var.* Haidarabad. Sind, SE Pakistan
105 *T16* **Hyères** Var, SE France
105 *T16* **Hyères, Îles d'** *island group* S France
120 *K12* **Hyermanavichy** *Rus.* Germanovichi. Vitsyebskaya Voblasts', N Belarus
169 *X12* **Hyesan** NE North Korea
8 *K8* **Hyland** ≈ Yukon Territory, NW Canada
97 *K20* **Hyltebruk** Halland, S Sweden
20 *D16* **Hyndman** Pennsylvania, NE USA
35 *P14* **Hyndman Peak** ▲ Idaho, NW USA
170 *G13* **Hyōgo** *off.* Hyōgo-ken. ◈ *prefecture* Honshū, SW Japan
170 *G13* **Hyōno-sen** ▲ Kyūshū, SW Japan
Hypanis *see* Kuban'
Hypsas *see* Belice
Hyrcania *see* Gorgān
38 *L1* **Hyrum** Utah, W USA
95 *N14* **Hyrynsalmi** Oulu, C Finland
35 *V10* **Hysham** Montana, NW USA
9 *N13* **Hythe** Alberta, W Canada
99 *Q23* **Hythe** SE England, UK
170 *D15* **Hyūga** Miyazaki, Kyūshū, SW Japan
Hyvinge *see* Hyvinkää
95 *L19* **Hyvinkää** *Swe.* Hyvinge. Uusimaa, S Finland

I

118 *J9* **Iacobeni** *Ger.* Jakobeny. Suceava, NE Romania
Iader *see* Zadar
180 *I7* **Iakora** Fianarantsoa, SE Madagascar
194 *H12* **Ialibu** Southern Highlands, W PNG
118 *K14* **Ialomiţa** *var.* Jalomitsa. ◈ *county* SE Romania
118 *K14* **Ialomiţa** ≈ SE Romania
119 *N10* **Ialoveni** *Rus.* Yaloveny. C Moldova
119 *N11* **Ialpug** *var.* Ialpugul Mare, *Rus.* Yalpug. ≈ Moldova/Ukraine
Ialpugul Mare *see* Ialpug
25 *T8* **Iamonia, Lake** ◎ Florida, SE USA
118 *L13* **Ianca** Brăila, SE Romania
118 *M10* **Iaşi** *Ger.* Jassy. Iaşi, NE Romania
118 *L9* **Iaşi** *Ger.* Jassy, Yassy. ◈ *county* NE Romania
116 *J13* **Íasmos** Anatolikí Makedonía kai Thráki, NE Greece
24 *H6* **Iatt, Lake** ▣ Louisiana, S USA
60 *B11* **Iauretê** Amazonas, NW Brazil
179 *Oo10* **Iba** Luzon, N Philippines
79 *S16* **Ibadan** Oyo, SW Nigeria
56 *E10* **Ibagué** Tolima, C Colombia
62 *J10* **Ibaiti** Paraná, S Brazil
179 *Pp12* **Ibajay** Panay Island, C Philippines
38 *J4* **Ibapah Peak** ▲ Utah, W USA
115 *M15* **Ibar** *Alb.* Ibër. ≈ C Yugoslavia
170 *F14* **Ibara** Okayama, Honshū, SW Japan
171 *Kk16* **Ibaraki** *off.* Ibaraki-ken. ◈ *prefecture* Honshū, S Japan
58 *C5* **Ibarra** *var.* San Miguel de Ibarra. Imbabura, N Ecuador
Ibaşfalău *see* Dumbrăveni
147 *O16* **Ibb** W Yemen
102 *F13* **Ibbenbüren** Nordrhein-Westfalen, NW Germany
81 *H16* **Ibenga** ≈ N Congo
Ibër *see* Ibar
59 *I14* **Iberia** Madre de Dios, E Peru
Iberia *see* Spain
68 *M1* **Iberian Basin** *undersea feature* E Atlantic Ocean
Iberian Mountains *see* Ibérico, Sistema
86 *D12* **Iberian Peninsula** *physical region* Portugal/Spain
66 *M8* **Iberian Plain** *undersea feature* E Atlantic Ocean
Ibérica, Cordillera *see* Ibérico, Sistema
107 *P6* **Ibérico, Sistema** *var.* Cordillera Ibérica, *Eng.* Iberian Mountains. ▲▲ NE Spain
10 *K7* **Iberville Lac d'** ◎ Québec, NE Canada
79 *T14* **Ibeto** Niger, W Nigeria
79 *W15* **Ibi** Taraba, C Nigeria
107 *S11* **Ibi** País Valenciano, E Spain
61 *L20* **Ibiá** Minas Gerais, SE Brazil
63 *F15* **Ibicuí, Rio** ≈ S Brazil
63 *C19* **Ibicuy** Entre Ríos, E Argentina
63 *F16* **Ibirapuitã** ≈ S Brazil
Ibiza *see* Eivissa
144 *J4* **Ibn Wardān, Qaṣr** *ruins* Ḥamāh, C Syria
Ibo *see* Sassandra
196 *E9* **Ibobang** Babeldaob, N Palau
176 *Vv11* **Ibonma** Irian Jaya, E Indonesia
61 *N17* **Ibotirama** Bahia, E Brazil
147 *Y8* **Ibrā** NE Oman
131 *Q4* **Ibresi** Chuvashskaya Respublika, W Russian Federation
147 *X8* **'Ibrī** NW Oman
170 *Bb16* **Ibusuki** Kagoshima, Kyūshū, SW Japan
59 *E16* **Ica** Ica, SW Peru
59 *E16* **Ica** *off.* Departamento de Ica. ◈ *department* SW Peru
60 *C11* **Içana** Amazonas, NW Brazil
Icaria *see* Ikaría
60 *B13* **Içá, Rio** *var.* Río Putumayo. ≈ NW South America *see also* Putumayo, Río
142 *I17* **İçel** *var.* Ichili. ◈ *province* S Turkey
94 *I3* **Iceland** *off.* Republic of Iceland, *Dan.* Island, *Icel.* Ísland. ◆ *republic* N Atlantic Ocean
88 *B6* **Iceland** *island* N Atlantic Ocean
66 *L5* **Iceland Basin** *undersea feature* N Atlantic Ocean
Icelandic Plateau *see* Iceland Plateau
207 *Q15* **Iceland Plateau** *var.* Icelandic Plateau. *undersea feature* S Greenland Sea
161 *E16* **Ichalkaranji** Mahārāshtra, W India
170 *Cc15* **Ichifusa-yama** ▲ Kyūshū, SW Japan
171 *K17* **Ichihara** *var.* Itihara. Chiba, Honshū, S Japan
Ichili *see* İçel
171 *I15* **Ichinomiya** *var.* Itinomiya. Aichi, Honshū, SW Japan
171 *Mm12* **Ichinoseki** *var.* Itinoseki. Iwate, Honshū, C Japan
119 *R3* **Ichnya** Chernihivs'ka Oblast', NE Ukraine
59 *L17* **Ichoa, Río** ≈ C Bolivia
I-ch'un *see* Yichun
Iconium *see* Konya
Iculisma *see* Angoulême
41 *U12* **Icy Bay** *inlet* Alaska, USA
41 *N5* **Icy Cape** *headland* Alaska, USA
41 *W13* **Icy Strait** *strait* Alaska, USA
29 *R13* **Idabel** Oklahoma, C USA
31 *T13* **Ida Grove** Iowa, C USA
79 *U16* **Idah** Kogi, S Nigeria
35 *N13* **Idaho** *off.* State of Idaho; also known as Gem of the Mountains, Gem State. ◈ *state* NW USA
35 *N14* **Idaho City** Idaho, NW USA
35 *R14* **Idaho Falls** Idaho, NW USA
124 *Nn3* **Idālion** *var.* Dali, Dhali. C Cyprus
27 *N5* **Idalou** Texas, SW USA
106 *I9* **Idanha-a-Nova** Castelo Branco, C Portugal
103 *E19* **Idar-Oberstein** Rheinland-Pfalz, SW Germany
120 *J3* **Ida-Virumaa** *off.* Ida-Viru Maakond. ◈ *province* NE Estonia
128 *J8* **Idel'** Respublika Kareliya, NW Russian Federation
81 *C15* **Idenao** Sud-Ouest, SW Cameroon
Idenburg-rivier *see* Taritatu, Sungai
Idensalmi *see* Iisalmi
168 *I6* **Ider** Hövsgöl, C Mongolia
77 *X10* **Idfu** *var.* Edfu. SE Egypt
Ídhi Óros *see* Ídi
Ídhra *see* Ýdra
173 *F3* **Idi** Sumatera, W Indonesia
117 *I25* **Ídi** *var.* Ídhi Óros. ▲▲ Kríti, Greece, E Mediterranean Sea
Idi Amin, Lac *see* Edward, Lake
108 *G10* **Idice** ≈ N Italy
78 *G9* **Idini** Trarza, W Mauritania
81 *J21* **Idiofa** Bandundu, SW Zaire
41 *O10* **Iditarod River** ≈ Alaska, USA
97 *M14* **Idkerberget** Kopparberg, C Sweden
144 *I3* **Idlib** Idlib, NW Syria
144 *I4* **Idlib** *off.* Muḥāfaẓat Idlib. ◈ *governorate* NW Syria
Idra *see* Ýdra
96 *J11* **Idre** Kopparberg, C Sweden
Idria *see* Idrija
111 *S11* **Idrija** *It.* Idria. W Slovenia
103 *G18* **Idstein** Hessen, W Germany
85 *J25* **Idutywa** Eastern Cape, SE South Africa
Idzhevan *see* Ijevan
120 *G9* **Iecava** Bauska, S Latvia
172 *P14* **Ie-jima** *var.* Ii-shima. *island* Nansei-shotō, SW Japan
101 *B18* **Ieper** *Fr.* Ypres. West-Vlaanderen, W Belgium
117 *K25* **Ierápetra** Kríti, Greece, E Mediterranean Sea
117 *G22* **Iérax, Ákra** *headland* S Greece
Ierisós *see* Ierissós
117 *H14* **Ierissós** *var.* Ierisós. Kentrikí Makedonía, N Greece
118 *I11* **Iernut** *Hung.* Radnót. Mureş, C Romania
108 *J12* **Iesi** *var.* Jesi. Marche, C Italy
Iesolo *see* Jesolo
196 *K16* **Ifalik Atoll** *atoll* Caroline Islands, C Micronesia
180 *I6* **Ifanadiana** Fianarantsoa, SE Madagascar
79 *T16* **Ife** Osun, SW Nigeria
79 *V8* **Iferouâne** Agadez, N Niger
Iferten *see* Yverdon
94 *L8* **Ifjord** Finnmark, N Norway
79 *R8* **Ifôghas, Adrar des** *var.* Adrar des Iforas. ▲▲ NE Mali
Iforas, Adrar des *see* Ifôghas, Adrar des
190 *D6* **Ifould lake** *salt lake* South Australia
76 *G6* **Ifrane** C Morocco
175 *T7* **Iga** Pulau Halmahera, E Indonesia
83 *G18* **Iganga** SE Uganda
62 *L7* **Igarapava** São Paulo, S Brazil
126 *Hh9* **Igarka** Krasnoyarskiy Kray, N Russian Federation
Igaunija *see* Estonia
I.G.Duca *see* General Toshevo
Igel *see* Jihlava
96 *N11* **Iggesund** Gävleborg, C Sweden
41 *P7* **Igikpak, Mount** ▲ Alaska, USA
41 *P13* **Igiugig** Alaska, USA
Iglau/Iglawa/Igława *see* Jihlava
109 *B20* **Iglesias** Sardegna, Italy, C Mediterranean Sea
131 *V4* **Iglino** Respublika Bashkortostan, W Russian Federation
Igló *see* Spišská Nová Ves
15 *Ll2* **Igloolik** Northwest Territories, N Canada
10 *B11* **Ignace** Ontario, S Canada
120 *I12* **Ignalina** Ignalina, E Lithuania
131 *Q5* **Ignatovka** Ul'yanovskaya Oblast', W Russian Federation
128 *K12* **Ignatovo** Vologodskaya Oblast', NW Russian Federation
116 *N11* **İğneada** Kırklareli, NW Turkey
124 *P7* **İğneada Burnu** *headland* NW Turkey
Igombe *see* Gombe
117 *B16* **Igoumenítsa** Ípeiros, W Greece
131 *T2* **Igra** Udmurtskaya Respublika, NW Russian Federation
125 *Ff9* **Igrim** Khanty-Mansiyskiy Avtonomnyy Okrug, N Russian Federation
62 *G12* **Iguaçu, Rio** *Sp.* Río Iguazú. ≈ Argentina/Brazil *see also* Iguazú, Río
61 *I22* **Iguaçu, Salto do** *Sp.* Cataratas del Iguazú; *prev.* Victoria Falls. *waterfall* Argentina/Brazil *see also* Iguazú, Cataratas del
43 *O15* **Iguala** *var.* Iguala de la Independencia. Guerrero, S Mexico
Iguala de la Independencia *see* Iguala
107 *V5* **Igualada** Cataluña, NE Spain
62 *G12* **Iguazú, Cataratas del** *Port.* Salto do Iguaçu, *prev.* Victoria Falls. *waterfall* Argentina/Brazil *see also* Iguaçu, Salto do
64 *Q6* **Iguazú, Río** *Port.* Rio Iguaçu. ≈ Argentina/Brazil *see also* Iguaçu, Rio
81 *D19* **Iguéla** Ogooué-Maritime, SW Gabon
Iguid, Erg *see* Iguidi, 'Erg
69 *M5* **Iguidi, 'Erg** *var.* Erg Iguid. *desert* Algeria/Mauritania
180 *K2* **Iharaña** *prev.* Vohémar. Antsiranana, NE Madagascar
157 *K18* **Ihavandippolhu Atoll** *var.* Ihavandiffulu Atoll. *atoll* N Maldives
168 *M11* **Ih Bulag** Ömnogövĭ, S Mongolia
172 *Pp14* **Iheya-jima** *island* Nansei-shotō, SW Japan
168 *L8* **Ihhayrhan** Töv, C Mongolia
180 *I6* **Ihosy** Fianarantsoa, S Madagascar
168 *L7* **Ihsüüj** Töv, C Mongolia
95 *L14* **Ii** Oulu, C Finland
171 *I16* **Iida** Nagano, Honshū, S Japan
171 *L13* **Iide-san** ▲ Honshū, C Japan
95 *M14* **Iijoki** ≈ C Finland
120 *J4* **Iisaku** *Ger.* Isaak. Ida-Virumaa, NE Estonia
95 *M16* **Iisalmi** *var.* Idensalmi. Kuopio, C Finland
171 *Jj14* **Iiyama** Nagano, Honshū, S Japan
170 *D13* **Iizuka** Fukuoka, Kyūshū, SW Japan
79 *S16* **Ijebu-Ode** Ogun, SW Nigeria
143 *U11* **Ijevan** *Rus.* Idzhevan. N Armenia
100 *H9* **IJmuiden** Noord-Holland, W Netherlands
100 *M12* **IJssel** *var.* Yssel. ≈ Netherlands/Germany
100 *J8* **IJsselmeer** *prev.* Zuider Zee. ◎ N Netherlands
100 *L9* **IJsselmuiden** Overijssel, E Netherlands
100 *I12* **IJsselstein** Utrecht, C Netherlands
63 *G14* **Ijuí** Rio Grande do Sul, S Brazil
63 *G14* **Ijuí, Rio** ≈ S Brazil
201 *R8* **Ijuw** NE Nauru
101 *E16* **IJzendijke** Zeeland, SW Netherlands
101 *A18* **Ijzer** ≈ W Belgium
95 *K18* **Ikaalinen** Häme, SW Finland
180 *I6* **Ikalamavony** Fianarantsoa, SE Madagascar
193 *G16* **Ikamatua** West Coast, South Island, NZ
79 *U16* **Ikare** Ondo, SW Nigeria
117 *L20* **Ikaría** *var.* Kariot, Nicaria, Nikaria; *anc.* Icaria. *island* Dodekánisos, Greece, Aegean Sea
97 *F22* **Ikast** Ringkøbing, W Denmark
192 *O9* **Ikawhenua Range** ▲▲ North Island, NZ
172 *Pp7* **Ikeda** Hokkaidō, NE Japan
170 *F15* **Ikeda** Tokushima, Shikoku, SW Japan
79 *S16* **Ikeja** Lagos, SW Nigeria
81 *L19* **Ikela** Equateur, C Zaire
116 *H10* **Ikhtiman** Sofiyska Oblast, W Bulgaria
170 *Cc12* **Iki** *island* SW Japan
131 *O13* **Iki Burul** Respublika Kalmykiya, SW Russian Federation
170 *C12* **Iki-suidō** *strait* SW Japan
170 *Bb12* **Ikitsuki-shima** *island* SW Japan
143 *P11* **İkizdere** Rize, NE Turkey
41 *P14* **Ikolik, Cape** *headland* Kodiak Island, Alaska, USA
79 *V17* **Ikom** Cross River, SE Nigeria
180 *I6* **Ikongo** *prev.* Fort-Carnot. Fianarantsoa, SE Madagascar
41 *P5* **Ikpikpuk River** ≈ Alaska, USA
202 *H1* **Iku** *prev.* Lone Tree Islet. *atoll* Tungaru, W Kiribati
171 *Gg14* **Ikuno** Hyōgo, Honshū, SW Japan
202 *H16* **Ikurangi** ▲ Rarotonga, S Cook Islands
176 *Xx12* **Ilaga** Irian Jaya, E Indonesia
179 *Pp8* **Ilagan** Luzon, N Philippines
148 *J7* **Īlām** *var.* Elam. Īlām, W Iran
148 *J8* **Īlām** *off.* Ostān-e Īlām. ◈ *province* W Iran
167 *T13* **Ilan** *Jap.* Giran. N Taiwan
152 *G9* **Ilanly Obvodnitel'nyy Kanal** *canal* N Turkmenistan
126 *Ii14* **Ilanskiy** Krasnoyarskiy Kray, S Russian Federation
110 *H9* **Ilanz** Graubünden, S Switzerland
79 *S16* **Ilaro** Ogun, SW Nigeria
59 *I17* **Ilave** Puno, S Peru
112 *K8* **Iława** *Ger.* Deutsch-Eylau. Olsztyn, N Poland
126 *Ll11* **Il'benge** Respublika Sakha (Yakutiya), NE Russian Federation
Ile *see* Ili
9 *S13* **Île-à-la-Crosse** Saskatchewan, C Canada
81 *J21* **Ilebo** *prev.* Port-Francqui. Kasai Occidental, W Zaire
105 *N5* **Île-de-France** ◈ *region* N France
150 *J9* **Ilek** *Kaz.* Elek. ≈ Kazakhstan/Russian Federation
Ilerda *see* Lleida
79 *T16* **Ilesha** Osun, SW Nigeria
197 *J5* **Îles Loyauté, Province des** ◈ *province* E New Caledonia
9 *X12* **Ilford** Manitoba, C Canada
99 *I23* **Ilfracombe** SW England, UK
142 *I11* **Ilgaz Dağları** ▲▲ N Turkey
142 *G15* **Ilgın** Konya, W Turkey
62 *I7* **Ilha Solteira** São Paulo, S Brazil
106 *G7* **Ílhavo** Aveiro, N Portugal
61 *O18* **Ilhéus** Bahia, E Brazil
133 *R7* **Ili** *Kaz.* Ile, *Rus.* Reka Ili. ≈ China/Kazakhstan
Ili *see* Ili He
118 *G11* **Ilia** *Hung.* Marosillye. Hunedoara, SW Romania
41 *P13* **Iliamna** Alaska, USA
41 *P13* **Iliamna Lake** ◎ Alaska, USA
143 *N13* **Iliç** Erzincan, C Turkey
Il'ichevsk *see* Şärur, Azerbaijan
Il'ichevsk *see* Illichivs'k, Ukraine
Ilici *see* Elche
39 *V2* **Iliff** Colorado, C USA
179 *R15* **Iligan** *off.* Iligan City. Mindanao, S Philippines
179 *R15* **Iligan Bay** *bay* S Philippines
164 *I5* **Ili He** *Rus.* Ili. ≈ China/Kazakhstan
58 *C6* **Iliniza** ▲ N Ecuador
Ilinski *see* Il'inskiy
129 *U14* **Il'inskiy** *var.* Ilinski. Permskaya Oblast', NW Russian Federation
127 *Oo15* **Il'inskiy** Ostrov Sakhalin, Sakhalinskaya Oblast', SE Russian Federation
20 *I10* **Ilion** New York, NE USA
40 *E9* **Ilio Point** *headland* Molokai, Hawaii, USA, C Pacific Ocean
111 *T13* **Ilirska Bistrica** *prev.* Bistrica, *Ger.* Feistritz, Illyrisch-Feistritz, *It.* Villa del Nevoso. SW Slovenia
143 *Q16* **Ilisu Barajı** ▣ SE Turkey
161 *G17* **Ilkal** Karnātaka, C India
99 *M19* **Ilkeston** C England, UK
123 *Jj17* **Il-Kullana** *headland* SW Malta
110 *J8* **Ill** ≈ W Austria
105 *U6* **Ill** ≈ NE France
64 *G10* **Illapel** Coquimbo, C Chile
Illaue Fartak Trench *see* Alula-Fartak Trench
190 *C2* **Illbillee, Mount** ▲ South Australia
104 *I6* **Ille-et-Vilaine** ◈ *department* NW France
79 *T11* **Illéla** Tahoua, SW Niger
103 *J24* **Iller** ≈ S Germany
103 *J23* **Illertissen** Bayern, S Germany
107 *N8* **Illescas** Castilla-La Mancha, C Spain
Ille-sur-la-Têt *see* Ille-sur-Têt
105 *O17* **Ille-sur-Têt** *var.* Ille-sur-la-Têt. Pyrénées-Orientales, S France
Illiberis *see* Elne
119 *P11* **Illichivs'k** *Rus.* Il'ichevsk. Odes'ka Oblast', SW Ukraine
Illicis *see* Elche
104 *M6* **Illiers-Combray** Eure-et-Loir, C France
32 *K12* **Illinois** *off.* State of Illinois; also known as Prairie State, Sucker State. ◈ *state* C USA
32 *J13* **Illinois River** ≈ Illinois, N USA
119 *N6* **Illintsi** Vinnyts'ka Oblast', C Ukraine
Illiturgis *see* Andújar
76 *M10* **Illizi** SE Algeria
29 *Y7* **Illmo** Missouri, C USA
Illur co *see* Lorca
Illuro *see* Mataró
Illyrisch-Feistritz *see* Ilirska Bistrica
103 *K16* **Ilm** ≈ C Germany
103 *K17* **Ilmenau** Thüringen, C Germany
128 *H14* **Il'men', Ozero** ◎ NW Russian Federation
59 *H18* **Ilo** Moquegua, SW Peru
179 *Q13* **Iloilo** *off.* Iloilo City. Panay Island, C Philippines
114 *K10* **Ilok** *Hung.* Újlak. Serbia, NW Yugoslavia
95 *O16* **Ilomantsi** Pohjois-Karjala, SE Finland
44 *F8* **Ilopango, Lago de** *volcanic lake* C El Salvador
79 *T15* **Ilorin** Kwara, W Nigeria
119 *X8* **Ilovays'k** *Rus.* Ilovaysk. Donets'ka Oblast', SE Ukraine
131 *O10* **Ilovlya** Volgogradskaya Oblast', SW Russian Federation
131 *O10* **Ilovlya** ≈ SW Russian Federation
127 *P8* **Il'pyrskiy** Koryakskiy Avtonomnyy Okrug, E Russian Federation
130 *K14* **Il'skiy** Krasnodarskiy Kray, SW Russian Federation
190 *B2* **Iltur** South Australia
176 *Y11* **Ilugwa** Irian Jaya, E Indonesia
Iluh *see* Batman
120 *I11* **Ilūkste** Daugvapils, SE Latvia
176 *Uu12* **Ilur** Pulau Gorong, E Indonesia
34 *F10* **Ilwaco** Washington, NW USA
152 *H8* **Il'yaly** *var.* Yylanly. Dashkhovuzskiy Velayat, N Turkmenistan
Ilyasbaba Burnu *see* Tekke Burnu
129 *U9* **Ilych** ≈ NW Russian Federation
103 *O21* **Ilz** ≈ SE Germany
113 *M14* **Iłża** Radom, SE Poland
170 *Ee14* **Imabari** *var.* Imaharu. Ehime, Shikoku, SW Japan
172 *N5* **Imagane** Hokkaidō, NE Japan
Imaharu *see* Imabari
171 *K15* **Imaichi** *var.* Imaiti. Tochigi, Honshū, S Japan
Imaiti *see* Imaichi
171 *Hh14* **Imajō** Fukui, Honshū, SW Japan
145 *R9* **Imām Ibn Hāshim** C Iraq
145 *T11* **Imān 'Abd Allāh** S Iraq
128 *J4* **Imandra, Ozero** ◎ NW Russian Federation
170 *E16* **Imano-yama** ▲ Shikoku, SW Japan
170 *C13* **Imari** Saga, Kyūshū, SW Japan
Imarssuak Mid-Ocean Seachannel *see* Imarssuak Seachannel
66 *J6* **Imarssuak Seachannel** *var.* Imarssuak Mid-Ocean Seachannel. *channel* N Atlantic Ocean
95 *N18* **Imatra** Kymi, SE Finland
171 *I15* **Imazu** Shiga, Honshū, SW Japan
58 *C6* **Imbabura** ◈ *province* N Ecuador
57 *R9* **Imbaimadai** W Guyana
63 *K14* **Imbituba** Santa Catarina, S Brazil
29 *W9* **Imboden** Arkansas, C USA
Imbros *see* Gökçeada
152 *B11* **Imeni 26 Bakinskikh Komissarov** *Turkm.* 26 Baku Komissarlary Adyndaky. Balkanskiy Velayat, W Turkmenistan
Imeni 26 Bakinskikh Komissarov *see* 26 Bakı Komissarı
129 *N13* **Imeni Babushkina** Vologodskaya Oblast', NW Russian Federation
130 *J7* **Imeni Karla Libknekhta** Kurskaya Oblast', W Russian Federation
152 *I14* **Imeni Mollanepesa** Maryyskiy Velayat, S Turkmenistan
127 *N14* **Imeni Poliny Osipenko** Khabarovskiy Kray, SE Russian Federation
152 *J15* **Imeni S.A.Niyazova** Maryyskiy Velayat, S Turkmenistan
Imeni Sverdlova Rudnik *see* Sverdlovs'k
196 *E9* **Imeong** Babeldaob, N Palau
83 *L14* **Imi** SE Ethiopia
117 *M21* **Imia** *Turk.* Kardak. *island* Dodekánisos, Greece, Aegean Sea
Imishli *see* İmişli
143 *X12* **İmişli** *Rus.* Imishli. C Azerbaijan
169 *X14* **Imjin-gang** ≈ North Korea/South Korea
37 *S3* **Imlay** Nevada, W USA
33 *S9* **Imlay City** Michigan, N USA
25 *X15* **Immokalee** Florida, SE USA
79 *U17* **Imo** ◈ *state* SE Nigeria
108 *G10* **Imola** Emilia-Romagna, N Italy
194 *E9* **Imonda** Sandaun, NW PNG
Imoschi *see* Imotski
115 *G14* **Imotski** *It.* Imoschi. Split-Dalmacija, SE Croatia
61 *L14* **Imperatriz** Maranhão, NE Brazil
108 *B10* **Imperia** Liguria, NW Italy
59 *E15* **Imperial** Lima, W Peru
37 *X17* **Imperial** California, W USA
30 *L16* **Imperial** Nebraska, C USA
26 *M9* **Imperial** Texas, SW USA

37 Y17 **Imperial Dam** dam California, W USA
81 I17 **Impfondo** La Likouala, NE Congo
159 X14 **Imphāl** Manipur, NE India
105 P9 **Imphy** Nièvre, C France
108 G11 **Impruneta** Toscana, C Italy
117 K15 **Imroz** var. Gökçeada. Çanakkale, NW Turkey
Imroz Adası see Gökçeada
110 L7 **Imst** Tirol, W Austria
42 F3 **Imuris** Sonora, NW Mexico
179 P11 **Imus** Luzon, N Philippines
171 J15 **Ina** Nagano, Honshū, S Japan
67 M18 **Inaccessible Island** island W Tristan da Cunha
117 F20 **Ínachos** S Greece
196 H6 **I Naftan, Puntan** headland Saipan, S Northern Mariana Islands
Inagua Islands see Great Inagua/Little Inagua
193 H15 **Inangahua** West Coast, South Island, NZ
176 V10 **Inanwatan** Irian Jaya, E Indonesia
59 I14 **Iñapari** Madre de Dios, E Peru
196 B17 **Inarajan** SE Guam
94 L10 **Inari** Lapp. Anár, Aanaar. Lappi, N Finland
94 L10 **Inarijärvi** Lapp. Aanaarjävri, Swe. Enareträsk. N Finland
94 L9 **Inarijoki** Lapp. Anárjohka. Finland/Norway
Ināu see Ineu
171 L14 **Inawashiro-ko** var. Inawasiro Ko. Honshū, C Japan
Inawasiro Ko see Inawashiro-ko
64 H7 **Inca de Oro** Atacama, N Chile
117 J15 **İnce Burnu** headland NW Turkey
142 K9 **İnce Burnu** headland N Turkey
142 I17 **İncekum Burnu** headland S Turkey
78 G7 **Inchiri** region NW Mauritania
169 X15 **Inch'ŏn** off. Inch'ŏn-gwangyŏksi, Jap. Jinsen; prev. Chemulpo. NW South Korea
85 M17 **Inchope** Manica, C Mozambique
Incoronata see Kornat
104 F2 **Incudine, Monte** Corse, France, C Mediterranean Sea
62 M10 **Indaiatuba** São Paulo, S Brazil
95 H17 **Indal** Västernorrland, C Sweden
95 H17 **Indalsälven** C Sweden
42 K8 **Inde** Durango, C Mexico
Indefatigable Island see Santa Cruz, Isla
37 S10 **Independence** California, W USA
31 X13 **Independence** Iowa, C USA
29 P7 **Independence** Kansas, C USA
22 M4 **Independence** Kentucky, S USA
29 R4 **Independence** Missouri, C USA
23 R8 **Independence** Virginia, NE USA
32 J7 **Independence** Wisconsin, N USA
207 R12 **Independence Fjord** fjord N Greenland
Independence Island see Malden Island
37 W2 **Independence Mountains** Nevada, W USA
59 K18 **Independencia** Cochabamba, C Bolivia
59 E16 **Independencia, Bahía de la** bay W Peru
118 M12 **Independenţa** Galaţi, SE Romania
Inderagiri see Indragiri, Sungai
Inderbor see Inderborskiy
150 F11 **Inderborskiy** Kaz. Inderbor. Atyrau, W Kazakhstan
157 I14 **India** off. Republic of India, var. Indian Union, Union of India, Hind. Bhārat. republic S Asia
India see Indija
20 D14 **Indiana** Pennsylvania, NE USA
33 N13 **Indiana** off. State of Indiana; also known as The Hoosier State. state N USA
33 O14 **Indianapolis** state capital Indiana, N USA
9 O10 **Indian Cabins** Alberta, W Canada
44 G1 **Indian Church** Orange Walk, N Belize
Indian Desert see Thar Desert
9 U16 **Indian Head** Saskatchewan, S Canada
33 O4 **Indian Lake** Michigan, N USA
20 K9 **Indian Lake** New York, NE USA
33 R13 **Indian Lake** Ohio, N USA
180-181 **Indian Ocean** ocean
31 V15 **Indianola** Iowa, C USA
24 K4 **Indianola** Mississippi, S USA
38 J6 **Indian Peak** Utah, W USA
25 Y13 **Indian River** lagoon Florida, SE USA
37 W10 **Indian Springs** Nevada, W USA
25 Y14 **Indiantown** Florida, SE USA
61 K19 **Indiara** Goiás, S Brazil
129 Q4 **Indiga** Nenetskiy Avtonomnyy Okrug, NW Russian Federation
126 Mm6 **Indigirka** NE Russian Federation
114 L10 **Indija** Hung. India; prev. Indjija. Serbia, N Yugoslavia
37 V16 **Indio** California, W USA
44 M12 **Indio, Río** SE Nicaragua
158 I10 **Indira Gandhi International** (Delhi) Delhi, N India
195 X15 **Indispensable Strait** strait C Solomon Islands
Indjija see Indija
133 Q13 **Indo-Australian Plate** tectonic feature
181 N11 **Indomed Fracture Zone** tectonic feature SW Indian Ocean
175 Nn12 **Indonesia** off. Republic of Indonesia, Ind. Republik Indonesia; prev. Dutch East Indies, Netherlands East Indies, United States of Indonesia. republic SE Asia
Indonesian Borneo see Kalimantan
160 G10 **Indore** Madhya Pradesh, C India
174 Hh8 **Indragiri, Sungai** var. Batang Kuantan, Inderagiri. Sumatera, W Indonesia
Indramajoe/Indramaju see Indramayu
174 K14 **Indramayu** prev. Indramajoe, Indramaju. Jawa, C Indonesia
161 K14 **Indrāvati** S India
105 N9 **Indre** department C France
104 M8 **Indre** C France
104 L8 **Indre-et-Loire** department C France
Indreville see Châteauroux
158 G3 **Indus** Chin. Yindu He; prev. Yin-tu Ho. S Asia
Indus Cone see Indus Fan
181 P3 **Indus Fan** var. Indus Cone. undersea feature N Arabian Sea
155 P17 **Indus, Mouths of the** delta S Pakistan
85 I24 **Indwe** Eastern Cape, SE South Africa
142 I10 **İnebolu** Kastamonu, N Turkey
79 P8 **I-n-Échaï** oasis C Mali
116 M13 **İnecik** Tekirdağ, NW Turkey
142 E12 **İnegöl** Bursa, NW Turkey
Inessa see Biancavilla
118 F10 **Ineu** Hung. Borosjenő; prev. Ināu. Arad, W Romania
Ineul/Ineu, Vîrful see Ineu, Vârful
118 J9 **Ineu, Vârful** var. Ineul; prev. Vîrful Ineu. N Romania
23 P6 **Inez** Kentucky, S USA
76 E8 **Inezgane** (Agadir) W Morocco
43 T17 **Inferior, Laguna** lagoon S Mexico
42 M15 **Infiernillo, Presa del** S Mexico
106 L2 **Infiesto** Asturias, N Spain
95 L20 **Ingå** Fin. Inkoo. Uusimaa, S Finland
79 U10 **Ingal** var. I-n-Gall. Agadez, C Niger
I-n-Gall see Ingal
101 C18 **Ingelmunster** West-Vlaanderen, W Belgium
81 I18 **Ingende** Equateur, W Zaire
64 L5 **Ingeniero Guillermo Nueva Juárez** Formosa, N Argentina
65 H16 **Ingeniero Jacobacci** Río Negro, C Argentina
12 F16 **Ingersoll** Ontario, S Canada
168 K6 **Ingettolgoy** Bulgan, N Mongolia
189 W5 **Ingham** Queensland, NE Australia
152 M11 **Ingichka** Samarqand Wiloyati, C Uzbekistan
99 L16 **Ingleborough** N England, UK
27 T14 **Ingleside** Texas, SW USA
192 K10 **Inglewood** Taranaki, North Island, NZ
37 S15 **Inglewood** California, W USA
126 Kk16 **Ingoda** S Russian Federation
103 L21 **Ingolstadt** Bayern, S Germany
35 Y9 **Ingomar** Montana, NW USA
11 R14 **Ingonish Beach** Cape Breton Island, Nova Scotia, SE Canada
159 S14 **Ingrāj Bāzār** prev. English Bazar. West Bengal, NE India
27 Q11 **Ingram** Texas, SW USA
205 X7 **Ingrid Christensen Coast** physical region Antarctica
76 K14 **I-n-Guezzam** S Algeria
Ingulets see Inhulets'
Inguri see Enguri
Ingushetia/Ingushetiya, Respublika see Ingushskaya Respublika
130 O15 **Ingushskaya Respublika** var. Respublika Ingushetiya, Eng. Ingushetia. autonomous republic SW Russian Federation
85 N20 **Inhambane** Inhambane, SE Mozambique
85 M20 **Inhambane** off. Província de Inhambane. province S Mozambique
85 N17 **Inhaminga** Sofala, C Mozambique
85 N20 **Inharrime** Inhambane, SE Mozambique
85 M18 **Inhassoro** Inhambane, E Mozambique
119 S9 **Inhulets'** Rus. Ingulets. Dnipropetrovs'ka Oblast', E Ukraine
119 R10 **Inhulets'** Rus. Ingulets. S Ukraine
107 Q10 **Iniesta** Castilla-La Mancha, C Spain
I-ning see Yining
56 K11 **Inírida, Río** E Colombia
Inis see Ennis
Inis Ceithleann see Enniskillen
Inis Córthaidh see Enniscorthy
Inis Díomáin see Ennistimon
99 A17 **Inishbofin** Ir. Inis Bó Finne. island W Ireland
99 B18 **Inisheer** var. Inishere, Ir. Inis Oírr. island W Ireland
Inishere see Inisheer
99 B18 **Inishmaan** Ir. Inis Meáin. island W Ireland
99 A18 **Inishmore** Ir. Árainn. island W Ireland
98 E13 **Inishtrahull** Ir. Inis Trá Tholl. island NW Ireland
99 A17 **Inishturk** Ir. Inis Toirc. island W Ireland
Inkoo see Ingå
193 J16 **Inland Kaikoura Range** South Island, NZ
Inland Sea see Seto-naikai
23 P11 **Inman** South Carolina, SE USA
110 L7 **Inn** C Europe
207 O11 **Innaanganeq** var. Kap York. headland NW Greenland
190 K2 **Innamincka** South Australia
96 J12 **Innbygda** S Norway
94 G12 **Inndyr** Nordland, C Norway
44 G3 **Inner Channel** inlet SE Belize
98 F11 **Inner Hebrides** island group W Scotland, UK
180 H15 **Inner Islands** var. Central Group. island group NE Seychelles
Inner Mongolia/Inner Mongolian Autonomous Region see Nei Mongol Zizhiqu
98 G8 **Inner Sound** strait NW Scotland, UK
102 J13 **Innerste** C Germany
189 W5 **Innisfail** Queensland, NE Australia
9 Q15 **Innisfail** Alberta, SW Canada
Inniskilling see Enniskillen
41 O11 **Innoko River** Alaska, USA
170 F14 **Innoshima** var. Innosima. Hiroshima, SW Japan
Innosima see Innoshima
Innsbruch see Innsbruck
110 M7 **Innsbruck** var. Innsbruch. Tirol, W Austria
81 I19 **Inongo** Bandundu, W Zaire
Inoucdjouac see Inukjuak
Inowrazlaw see Inowrocław
112 I10 **Inowrocław** Ger. Hohensalza; prev. Inowrazlaw. Bydgoszcz, C Poland
59 K18 **Inquisivi** La Paz, W Bolivia
Inrin see Yüanlin
79 O8 **I-n-Sâkâne, 'Erg** desert N Mali
76 J10 **I-n-Salah** var. In Salah. C Algeria
131 O5 **Insar** Respublika Mordoviya, W Russian Federation
201 X15 **Insiaf** Kosrae, E Micronesia
96 L13 **Insjön** Kopparberg, C Sweden
Insterburg see Chernyakhovsk
Insula see Lille
118 L13 **Însurăţei** Brăila, SE Romania
129 V6 **Inta** Respublika Komi, NW Russian Federation
79 R9 **I-n-Tebezas** Kidal, E Mali
Interamna see Teramo
Interamna Nahars see Terni
30 L11 **Interior** South Dakota, N USA
110 E9 **Interlaken** Bern, SW Switzerland
31 V2 **International Falls** Minnesota, N USA
178 Gg7 **Inthanon, Doi** NW Thailand
44 G7 **Intibucá** department SW Honduras
44 G8 **Intipucá** La Unión, SE El Salvador
63 B15 **Intiyaco** Santa Fe, C Argentina
118 K12 **Întorsura Buzăului** Ger. Bozau, Hung. Bodzafordulő. Covasna, E Romania
24 H9 **Intracoastal Waterway** inland waterway system Louisiana, S USA
27 V13 **Intracoastal Waterway** inland waterway system Texas, SW USA
110 G11 **Intragna** Ticino, S Switzerland
171 Kk17 **Inubō-zaki** headland Honshū, S Japan
170 D14 **Inukai** Ōita, Kyūshū, SW Japan
10 I5 **Inukjuak** var. Inoucdjouac; prev. Port Harrison. Québec, NE Canada
65 I24 **Inútil, Bahía** bay S Chile
Inuuvik see Inuvik
14 G3 **Inuvik** var. Inuuvik. district capital Northwest Territories, NW Canada
14 G3 **Inuvik** district Northwest Territories, NW Canada
171 I15 **Inuyama** Aichi, Honshū, SW Japan
58 G13 **Inuya, Río** E Peru
129 U13 **In'va** NW Russian Federation
98 H11 **Inveraray** W Scotland, UK
193 C24 **Invercargill** Southland, South Island, NZ
191 T5 **Inverell** New South Wales, SE Australia
98 I8 **Invergordon** N Scotland, UK
9 P16 **Invermere** British Columbia, SW Canada
11 R14 **Inverness** Cape Breton Island, Nova Scotia, SE Canada
98 I8 **Inverness** N Scotland, UK
25 V11 **Inverness** Florida, SE USA
98 I9 **Inverness** cultural region NW Scotland, UK
98 K9 **Inverurie** NE Scotland, UK
190 F8 **Investigator Group** island group South Australia
181 T7 **Investigator Ridge** undersea feature E Indian Ocean
190 H10 **Investigator Strait** strait South Australia
31 R11 **Inwood** Iowa, C USA
126 H16 **Inya** Respublika Altay, S Russian Federation
127 Nn10 **Inya** E Russian Federation
Inyanga see Nyanga
85 M16 **Inyangani** NE Zimbabwe
85 J17 **Inyathi** Matabeleland North, SW Zimbabwe
37 T12 **Inyokern** California, W USA
37 T10 **Inyo Mountains** California, W USA
131 P6 **Inza** Ul'yanovskaya Oblast', W Russian Federation
131 W5 **Inzer** Respublika Bashkortostan, W Russian Federation
131 N7 **Inzhavino** Tambovskaya Oblast', W Russian Federation
117 C16 **Ioánnina** var. Janina, Yannina. Ípeiros, W Greece
170 B17 **Iō-jima** var. Iwojima. island Nansei-shotō, SW Japan
128 L4 **Iokan'ga** NW Russian Federation
29 Q6 **Iola** Kansas, C USA
Iolcus see Iolkós
117 G16 **Iolkós** anc. Iolcus. site of ancient city Thessalía, C Greece
Iolotan' see Yëloten
85 A16 **Iona** Namibe, SW Angola
98 F11 **Iona** island W Scotland, UK
118 M15 **Ion Corvin** Constanţa, SE Romania
37 P7 **Ione** California, W USA
118 I13 **Ioneşti** Vâlcea, SW Romania
33 Q9 **Ionia** Michigan, N USA
Ionia Basin see Ionian Basin
123 Mm12 **Ionian Basin** var. Ionia Basin. undersea feature Ionian Sea, C Mediterranean Sea
Ionian Islands see Iónioi Nísoi
123 Mm11 **Ionian Sea** Gk. Iónio Pélagos, It. Mar Ionio. sea C Mediterranean Sea
117 B17 **Iónioi Nísoi** Eng. Ionian Islands. region W Greece
117 B17 **Iónioi Nísoi** Eng. Ionian Islands. island group W Greece
Ionio, Mar/Iónio Pélagos see Ionian Sea
Iordan see Jordan
143 U10 **Iori** var. Qabırrı. Azerbaijan/Georgia
Iorrais, Ceann see Erris Head
117 J22 **Íos** Íos, Kykládes, Greece, Aegean Sea
117 J22 **Íos** var. Nio. island Kykládes, Greece, Aegean Sea
24 G9 **Iowa** Louisiana, S USA
31 V13 **Iowa** off. State of Iowa; also known as The Hawkeye State. state C USA
31 Y14 **Iowa City** Iowa, C USA
31 V13 **Iowa Falls** Iowa, C USA
27 R4 **Iowa Park** Texas, SW USA
31 Y14 **Iowa River** Iowa, C USA
121 M19 **Ipa** Rus. Ipa. SE Belarus
61 N20 **Ipatinga** Minas Gerais, SE Brazil
131 N13 **Ipatovo** Stavropol'skiy Kray, SW Russian Federation
117 C16 **Ípeiros** Eng. Epirus. region W Greece
Ipek see Peć
113 J21 **Ipel'** var. Ipoly, Ger. Eipel. Hungary/Slovakia
56 C13 **Ipiales** Nariño, SW Colombia
201 V14 **Ipis** atoll Chuuk Islands, C Micronesia
61 A14 **Ipixuna** Amazonas, W Brazil
174 Gg4 **Ipoh** Perak, Peninsular Malaysia
Ipoly see Ipel'
197 D15 **Ipota** Erromango, S Vanuatu
81 K14 **Ippy** Ouaka, C Central African Republic
116 L13 **Ipsala** Edirne, NW Turkey
Ipsario see Ypsário
191 V3 **Ipswich** Queensland, E Australia
99 Q20 **Ipswich** hist. Gipeswic. E England, UK
31 O8 **Ipswich** South Dakota, N USA
Iput' see Iputs'
121 P18 **Iputs'** Rus. Iput'. Belarus/Russian Federation
16 O3 **Iqaluit** prev. Frobisher Bay. district capital Baffin Island, Northwest Territories, NE Canada
165 P9 **Iqe** Qinghai, W China
165 P9 **Iqe He** C China
Iqlid see Eqlīd
64 G3 **Iquique** Tarapacá, N Chile
58 G8 **Iquitos** Loreto, N Peru
27 N9 **Iraan** Texas, SW USA
81 K14 **Ira Banda** Haute-Kotto, E Central African Republic
172 Pp16 **Irabu-jima** island Miyako-shotō, SW Japan
57 Y9 **Iracoubo** N French Guiana
171 Hh17 **Irago-misaki** headland Honshū, SW Japan
62 H13 **Iraí** Rio Grande do Sul, S Brazil
116 G12 **Irákleia** Kentrikí Makedonía, N Greece
117 J21 **Irákleia** island Kykládes, Greece, Aegean Sea
117 J25 **Irákleio** var. Herakleion, Eng. Candia; prev. Iráklion. Kríti, Greece, E Mediterranean Sea
117 J25 **Irákleio** Kríti, Greece, E Mediterranean Sea
117 F15 **Irákleio** anc. Heracleum. castle Kentrikí Makedonía, N Greece
Iráklion see Irákleio
149 O7 **Iran** off. Islamic Republic of Iran; prev. Persia. republic SW Asia
61 F13 **Iranduba** Amazonas, NW Brazil
87 P13 **Iranian Plate** tectonic feature
149 Q9 **Iranian Plateau** var. Plateau of Iran. plateau N Iran
175 N6 **Iran, Pegunungan** var. Iran Mountains. Indonesia/Malaysia
Iran, Plateau of see Iranian Plateau
149 W13 **Īrānshahr** Sīstān va Balūchestān, SE Iran
57 P5 **Irapa** Sucre, NE Venezuela
43 N13 **Irapuato** Guanajuato, C Mexico
145 R7 **Iraq** off. Republic of Iraq, Ar. 'Irāq. republic SW Asia
62 J12 **Irati** Paraná, S Brazil
107 R3 **Irati** N Spain
129 T8 **Irayël'** Respublika Komi, NW Russian Federation
45 N13 **Irazú, Volcán** C Costa Rica
Irbenskiy Zaliv/Irbes Šaurums see Irbe Strait
120 D7 **Irbe Strait** Est. Kura Kurk, Latv. Irbes Šaurums, Rus. Irbenskiy Zaliv; prev. Est. Irbe Väin. strait Estonia/Latvia
Irbe Väin see Irbe Strait
144 G9 **Irbid** Irbid, N Jordan
144 G9 **Irbid** off. Muḥāfaẓat Irbid. governorate N Jordan
Irbīl see Arbīl
125 F11 **Irbit** Sverdlovskaya Oblast', C Russian Federation
111 S6 **Irdning** Steiermark, SE Austria
81 I18 **Irebu** Equateur, W Zaire
86 C9 **Ireland** Lat. Hibernia. island Ireland/UK
Ireland see Ireland, Republic of
66 A12 **Ireland Island North** island W Bermuda
66 A12 **Ireland Island South** island W Bermuda
99 D17 **Ireland, Republic of** off. Republic of Ireland, var. Ireland, Ir. Éire. republic NW Europe
129 V15 **Iren'** NW Russian Federation
193 A22 **Irene, Mount** South Island, NZ
Irgalem see Yirga 'Alem
150 L11 **Irgiz** Aktyubinsk, C Kazakhstan
Irian see New Guinea
Irian Barat see Irian Jaya
176 Y13 **Irian Jaya** var. Irian Barat, West Irian, West New Guinea; prev. Dutch New Guinea, Netherlands New Guinea. province E Indonesia
80 K9 **Iriba** Biltine, NE Chad
179 Q11 **Iriga** Luzon, N Philippines
131 X7 **Iriklinskoye Vodokhranilishche** W Russian Federation
83 H23 **Iringa** Iringa, C Tanzania
83 H23 **Iringa** region S Tanzania
172 O17 **Iriomote-jima** island Sakishima-shotō, SW Japan
44 L4 **Iriona** Colón, NE Honduras
49 U7 **Iriri** N Brazil
60 I13 **Iriri, Rio** C Brazil
Iris see Yeşilırmak
37 W9 **Irish, Mount** Nevada, W USA
99 H17 **Irish Sea** Ir. Muir Éireann. sea C British Isles
145 U12 **Irjal ash Shaykhīyah** S Iraq
153 U11 **Irkeshtam** Oshskaya Oblast', SW Kyrgyzstan
126 J16 **Irkut** S Russian Federation
126 Jj16 **Irkutsk** Irkutskaya Oblast', S Russian Federation
126 Jj13 **Irkutskaya Oblast'** province S Russian Federation
Irlir, Gora see Irlir Toghi
152 K8 **Irlir Toghi** var. Gora Irlir. N Uzbekistan
Irminger Basin see Reykjanes Basin
23 R12 **Irmo** South Carolina, SE USA
104 E6 **Iroise** sea NW France
201 X2 **Iroj** var. Eroj. island Ratak Chain, SE Marshall Islands
190 H7 **Iron Baron** South Australia
195 X15 **Iron Bottom Sound** sound C Solomon Islands
12 C10 **Iron Bridge** Ontario, S Canada
22 H10 **Iron City** Tennessee, S USA
12 I13 **Irondale** Ontario, SE Canada
190 H7 **Iron Knob** South Australia
32 M5 **Iron Mountain** Michigan, N USA
32 M4 **Iron River** Michigan, N USA
32 J3 **Iron River** Wisconsin, N USA
29 X6 **Ironton** Missouri, C USA
33 S15 **Ironton** Ohio, N USA
32 K4 **Ironwood** Michigan, N USA
10 H12 **Iroquois Falls** Ontario, S Canada
33 N12 **Iroquois River** Illinois/Indiana, N USA
171 Ii18 **Irō-zaki** headland Honshū, S Japan
Irpen' see Irpin'
119 O4 **Irpin'** Rus. Irpen'. Kyyivs'ka Oblast', N Ukraine
119 O4 **Irpin'** Rus. Irpen'. N Ukraine
147 Q16 **'Irqah** SW Yemen
177 F8 **Irrawaddy** var. Ayeyarwady. division SW Myanmar
177 G6 **Irrawaddy** var. Ayeyarwady. W Myanmar
177 F9 **Irrawaddy, Mouths of the** delta SW Myanmar
119 N4 **Irsha** N Ukraine
118 H7 **Irshava** Zakarpats'ka Oblast', W Ukraine
109 N18 **Irsina** Basilicata, S Italy
Irtish see Irtysh
133 R5 **Irtysh** var. Irtish, Kaz. Ertis. C Asia
151 S7 **Irtyshsk** Kaz. Ertis. Pavlodar, NE Kazakhstan
81 P17 **Irumu** Haut-Zaïre, E Zaire
107 Q2 **Irún** País Vasco, N Spain
Iruñea see Pamplona
107 Q3 **Irurzun** Navarra, N Spain
98 I13 **Irvine** W Scotland, UK
23 N6 **Irvine** Kentucky, S USA
27 T6 **Irving** Texas, SW USA
22 K5 **Irvington** Kentucky, S USA
Isaak see Iisaku
30 L8 **Isabel** South Dakota, N USA
195 W14 **Isabel** off. Isabel Province. province N Solomon Islands
179 Q17 **Isabela** Basilan Island, SW Philippines
47 S5 **Isabela** W Puerto Rico
47 N8 **Isabela, Cabo** headland NW Dominican Republic
59 A18 **Isabela, Isla** var. Albemarle Island. island Galapagos Islands, Ecuador, E Pacific Ocean
42 I12 **Isabela, Isla** island C Mexico
44 K9 **Isabella, Cordillera** NW Nicaragua
37 S12 **Isabella Lake** California, W USA
33 N2 **Isabelle, Point** headland Michigan, N USA
Isabel Segunda see Vieques
118 M13 **Isaccea** Tulcea, E Romania
94 H1 **Ísafjarðardjúp** inlet NW Iceland
94 H1 **Ísafjörður** Vestfirdhir, NW Iceland
170 C13 **Isahaya** Nagasaki, Kyūshū, SW Japan
155 S7 **Isa Khel** Punjab, E Pakistan
180 H7 **Isalo** var. Massif de L'Isalo. SW Madagascar
Isalo, Massif de L' see Isalo
81 K20 **Isandja** Kasai Occidental, C Zaire
197 D16 **Isangel** Tanna, S Vanuatu
81 M18 **Isangi** Haut-Zaïre, C Zaire
103 L24 **Isar** Austria/Germany
103 M23 **Isar-Kanal** canal SE Germany
Isbarta see Isparta
Isca Damnoniorum see Exeter
109 K18 **Ischia** var. Isola d'Ischia; anc. Aenaria. Campania, S Italy
109 J18 **Ischia, Isola d'** island S Italy
56 B12 **Iscuandé** var. Santa Bárbara. Nariño, SW Colombia
171 Hh16 **Ise** Mie, Honshū, SW Japan
102 J12 **Ise** N Germany
97 I23 **Isefjord** fjord E Denmark
Iseghem see Izegem
199 Jj17 **Iselin Seamount** undersea feature S Pacific Ocean
Isenhof see Püssi
108 E7 **Iseo** Lombardia, N Italy
105 U12 **Iseran, Col de l'** pass E France
105 S11 **Isère** department E France
105 S12 **Isère** E France
103 F15 **Iserlohn** Nordrhein-Westfalen, W Germany
109 K16 **Isernia** var. Æsernia. Molise, C Italy
171 Jj15 **Isesaki** Gunma, Honshū, S Japan
133 Q5 **Iset'** C Russian Federation
171 Hh16 **Ise-wan** bay S Japan
79 S15 **Iseyin** Oyo, W Nigeria
Isfahan see Eşfahān
153 Q11 **Isfana** Oshskaya Oblast', SW Kyrgyzstan
153 R11 **Isfara** N Tajikistan
155 O4 **Isfi Maidān** Ghowr, N Afghanistan
94 O3 **Isfjorden** fjord W Svalbard
Isha Baydhabo see Baydhabo
129 V11 **Isherim, Gora** NW Russian Federation
131 Q5 **Isheyevka** Ul'yanovskaya Oblast', W Russian Federation
172 Oo17 **Ishigaki** Okinawa, Ishigaki-jima, SW Japan
172 P17 **Ishigaki-jima** var. Isigaki Zima. island Sakishima-shotō, SW Japan
172 O5 **Ishikari** Hokkaidō, NE Japan
172 Oo5 **Ishikari-gawa** var. Isikari Gawa. Hokkaidō, NE Japan
172 O4 **Ishikari-wan** bay Hokkaidō, NE Japan
171 L14 **Ishikawa** Fukushima, Honshū, C Japan
172 Oo14 **Ishikawa** var. Isikawa. Okinawa, Okinawa, SW Japan
171 I13 **Ishikawa** off. Ishikawa-ken, var. Isikawa. prefecture Honshū, SW Japan
125 Ff12 **Ishim** Tyumenskaya Oblast', C Russian Federation
133 R6 **Ishim** Kaz. Esil. Kazakhstan/Russian Federation
131 V6 **Ishimbay** Respublika Bashkortostan, W Russian Federation
151 O9 **Ishimskoye** Turgay, C Kazakhstan
171 M13 **Ishinomaki** var. Isinomaki. Miyagi, Honshū, C Japan
171 Kk16 **Ishioka** var. Isioka. Ibaraki, Honshū, S Japan
170 Ee15 **Ishizuchi-san** Shikoku, SW Japan
Ishkashim see Ishkoshim
Ishkashimskiy Khrebet see Ishkoshim, Qatorkŭhi
153 S15 **Ishkoshim** Rus. Ishkashim. S Tajikistan
153 S15 **Ishkoshim, Qatorkŭhi** Rus. Ishkashimskiy Khrebet. SE Tajikistan
33 N4 **Ishpeming** Michigan, N USA
153 N11 **Ishtikhon** Rus. Ishtykhan. Samarqand Wiloyati, C Uzbekistan
Ishtykhan see Ishtikhon
159 T15 **Ishurdi** Rajshahi, W Bangladesh
63 G17 **Isidoro Noblia** Cerro Largo, NE Uruguay
104 J4 **Isigny-sur-Mer** Calvados, N France
Isikari Gawa see Ishikari-gawa
Isikawa see Ishikawa
142 C11 **Işıklar Dağı** NW Turkey
109 C19 **Isili** Sardegna, Italy, C Mediterranean Sea
125 Ff13 **Isil'kul'** Omskaya Oblast', C Russian Federation
Isinomaki see Ishinomaki
Isioka see Ishioka
83 I18 **Isiolo** Eastern, C Kenya
81 O16 **Isiro** Haut-Zaïre, NE Zaire
94 P2 **Isispynten** headland NE Svalbard
126 Ll11 **Isit** Respublika Sakha (Yakutiya), NE Russian Federation
155 O2 **Iskabad Canal** canal N Afghanistan
153 Q9 **Iskandar** Rus. Iskander. Toshkent Wiloyati, E Uzbekistan
Iskander see Iskandar
Iskār see Iskŭr
124 O2 **İskele** var. Trikomo, Gk. Tríkomon. E Cyprus
142 K17 **İskenderun** Eng. Alexandretta. Hatay, S Turkey
144 H2 **İskenderun Körfezi** Eng. Gulf of Alexandretta. gulf S Turkey
142 J11 **İskilip** Çorum, N Turkey
Iski-Nauket see Eski-Nookat
126 Gg14 **Iskitim** Novosibirskaya Oblast', C Russian Federation
116 J11 **Iskra** prev. Popovo. Khaskovska Oblast, S Bulgaria
116 G10 **Iskŭr** var. Iskār. NW Bulgaria
116 H10 **Iskŭr, Yazovir** prev. Yazovir Stalin. W Bulgaria
43 S15 **Isla** Veracruz-Llave, SE Mexico
121 J15 **Islach** Rus. Isloch'. C Belarus
106 H14 **Isla Cristina** Andalucía, S Spain
Isla de León see San Fernando
155 U6 **Islāmābād** (Pakistan) Federal Capital Territory Islāmābād, NE Pakistan
155 V6 **Islāmābād** Federal Capital Territory Islāmābād, NE Pakistan
Islamabad see Anantnāg
155 R17 **Islāmkot** Sind, SE Pakistan
25 Y17 **Islamorada** Florida Keys, Florida, SE USA
159 P14 **Islāmpur** Bihār, N India
Islam Qala see Eslām Qal'eh
Island/Ísland see Iceland
20 K16 **Island Beach** spit New Jersey, NE USA
21 S4 **Island Falls** Maine, NE USA
190 H6 **Island Lagoon** South Australia
9 Y13 **Island Lake** Manitoba, C Canada
31 W5 **Island Lake Reservoir** Minnesota, N USA
35 R13 **Island Park** Idaho, NW USA
21 N6 **Island Pond** Vermont, NE USA
192 K2 **Islands, Bay of** inlet North Island, NZ
105 R7 **Is-sur-Tille** Côte d'Or, C France
44 J3 **Islas de la Bahía** department N Honduras
67 L20 **Islas Orcadas Rise** undersea feature S Atlantic Ocean
98 F12 **Islay** island SW Scotland, UK
118 I15 **Islaz** Teleorman, S Romania
31 V7 **Isle** Minnesota, N USA
104 M12 **Isle** W France
99 I16 **Isle of Man** UK crown dependency NW Europe
23 X7 **Isle of Wight** Virginia, NE USA
99 M24 **Isle of Wight** cultural region S England, UK
203 Y3 **Isles Lagoon** Kiritimati, E Kiribati
39 R11 **Isleta Pueblo** New Mexico, SW USA
Isloch' see Islach
63 E19 **Ismael Cortinas** Flores, S Uruguay
Ismailia see Ismâ'ilîya
77 W7 **Ismâ'ilîya** var. Ismailia. N Egypt
Ismid see İzmit
77 X10 **Isna** var. Esna. SE Egypt
95 K18 **Isojoki** Vaasa, W Finland
84 M12 **Isoka** Northern, NE Zambia
Isola d'Ischia see Ischia
Isola d'Istria see Izola
Isonzo see Soča
13 U4 **Isoukustouc** Québec, SE Canada
142 F15 **Isparta** var. Isbarta. Isparta, SW Turkey
142 F15 **Isparta** var. Isbarta. province SW Turkey
116 M7 **Isperikh** prev. Kemanlar. Razgradska Oblast, NE Bulgaria
109 L26 **Ispica** Sicilia, Italy, C Mediterranean Sea
154 J14 **Ispikān** Baluchistān, SW Pakistan
143 Q12 **İspir** Erzurum, NE Turkey
144 E12 **Israel** off. State of Israel, var. Medinat Israel, Heb. Yisrael, Yisra'el. republic SW Asia
Issa see Vis
57 S9 **Issano** C Guyana
78 M16 **Issia** SW Ivory Coast
Issiq Köl see Issyk-Kul', Ozero
105 P11 **Issoire** Puy-de-Dôme, C France
105 N9 **Issoudun** anc. Uxellodunum. Indre, C France
83 H22 **Issuna** Singida, C Tanzania
Issyk see Yesik
Issyk-Kul' see Balykchy
153 X7 **Issyk-Kul', Ozero** var. Issiq Köl, Kir. Ysyk-Köl. E Kyrgyzstan
153 X7 **Issyk-Kul'skaya Oblast'** Kir. Ysyk-Köl Oblasty. province E Kyrgyzstan
155 Q7 **Istādeh-ye Moqor, Āb-e-** var. Āb-i-Istāda. SE Afghanistan
142 D11 **İstanbul** Bul. Tsarigrad, Eng. Istanbul; prev. Constantinople, anc. Byzantium. İstanbul, NW Turkey
116 P12 **İstanbul** province NW Turkey
116 P12 **İstanbul Boğazı** var. Bosporus Thracius, Eng. Bosphorus, Bosporus, Turk. Karadeniz Boğazı. strait NW Turkey
Istarska Županija see Istra
117 G19 **Isthmía** Pelopónnisos, S Greece
117 G17 **Istiaía** Évvoia, C Greece
56 D9 **Istmina** Chocó, W Colombia
25 W13 **Istokpoga, Lake** Florida, SE USA
114 A9 **Istra** off. Istarska županija. province NW Croatia
114 I10 **Istra** Eng. Istria, Ger. Istrien. cultural region NW Croatia
105 R15 **Istres** Bouches-du-Rhône, SE France
Istria/Istrien see Istra
179 R16 **Isulan** Mindanao, S Philippines
194 I11 **Isumrud Strait** strait N PNG
131 V7 **Isyangulovo** Respublika Bashkortostan, W Russian Federation
64 O6 **Itá** Central, S Paraguay
61 O17 **Itaberaba** Bahia, E Brazil
61 M20 **Itabira** prev. Presidente Vargas. Minas Gerais, SE Brazil
61 O18 **Itabuna** Bahia, E Brazil
61 J18 **Itacaiu** Mato Grosso, S Brazil
60 G12 **Itacoatiara** Amazonas, N Brazil
56 D9 **Itagüí** Antioquia, W Colombia
62 D13 **Itá Ibaté** Corrientes, NE Argentina
62 G11 **Itaipú, Represa de** Brazil/Paraguay
60 H13 **Itaituba** Pará, NE Brazil
62 K13 **Itajaí** Santa Catarina, S Brazil
Italia/Italiana, Republica/Italian Republic, The see Italy
Italian Somaliland see Somalia
27 T7 **Italy** Texas, SW USA
108 G12 **Italy** off. The Italian Republic, It. Italia, Republica Italiana. republic S Europe

Country · Country Capital · Dependent Territory · Dependent Territory Capital · Administrative Region · International Airport · Mountain · Mountain Range · Volcano · River · Lake · Reservoir

61 O19 **Itamaraju** Bahia, E Brazil
61 C14 **Itamarati** Amazonas, W Brazil
61 M19 **Itambé, Pico de** ▲ SE Brazil
171 Gg15 **Itami** ✕ (Ōsaka) Ōsaka, Honshū, SW Japan
117 H15 **Ítamos** ▲ N Greece
159 W11 **Itānagar** Arunāchal Pradesh, NE India
Itany see Litani
61 N19 **Itaobim** Minas Gerais, SE Brazil
61 P15 **Itaparica, Represa de** ⊠ E Brazil
60 M13 **Itapecuru-Mirim** Maranhão, E Brazil
62 Q8 **Itaperuna** Rio de Janeiro, SE Brazil
61 O18 **Itapetinga** Bahia, E Brazil
62 L10 **Itapetininga** São Paulo, S Brazil
62 K10 **Itapeva** São Paulo, S Brazil
49 W6 **Itapicuru, Rio** ≈ NE Brazil
61 O13 **Itapipoca** Ceará, E Brazil
62 M9 **Itapira** São Paulo, S Brazil
62 K8 **Itápolis** São Paulo, S Brazil
62 K10 **Itaporanga** São Paulo, S Brazil
64 P7 **Itapúa** *off.* Departamento de Itapúa. ◆ *department* SE Paraguay
61 E15 **Itapuã do Oeste** Rondônia, W Brazil
63 E15 **Itaqui** Rio Grande do Sul, S Brazil
62 K10 **Itararé** São Paulo, S Brazil
62 K10 **Itararé, Rio** ≈ S Brazil
160 H11 **Itārsi** Madhya Pradesh, C India
27 T7 **Itasca** Texas, SW USA
Itassi see Vieille Case
62 D13 **Itatí** Corrientes, NE Argentina
62 K10 **Itatinga** São Paulo, S Brazil
117 F18 **Itéas, Kólpos** *gulf* C Greece
59 N15 **Iténez, Río** *var.* Rio Guaporé. ≈ Bolivia/Brazil *see also* Guaporé, Rio
56 H11 **Iteviate, Río** ≈ C Colombia
102 I13 **Ith** *hill range* C Germany
33 Q8 **Ithaca** Michigan, N USA
20 H11 **Ithaca** New York, NE USA
117 C18 **Itháki** Itháki, Iónioi Nísoi, Greece, C Mediterranean Sea
117 C18 **Itháki** *island* Iónioi Nísoi, Greece, C Mediterranean Sea
It Hearrenfean see Heerenveen
Itihara see Ichihara
81 L17 **Itimbiri** ≈ N Zaire
Itinomiya see Ichinomiya
Itinoseki see Ichinoseki
41 Q5 **Itkilik River** ≈ Alaska, USA
171 J17 **Itō** Shizuoka, Honshū, S Japan
171 J13 **Itoigawa** Niigata, Honshū, C Japan
13 R6 **Itomamo, Lac** ⊚ Québec, SE Canada
172 Oo15 **Itoman** Okinawa, SW Japan
104 M5 **Iton** ≈ N France
59 M16 **Itonamas Río** ≈ NE Bolivia
Itoupé, Mont see Sommet Tabulaire
Itseqqortoormiit see Ittoqqortoormiit
24 K4 **Itta Bena** Mississippi, S USA
109 B17 **Ittiri** Sardegna, Italy, C Mediterranean Sea
207 Q14 **Ittoqqortoormiit** *var.* Itseqqortoormiit, *Dan.* Scoresbysund, *Eng.* Scoresby Sound. C Greenland
62 M10 **Itu** São Paulo, S Brazil
178 Mm14 **Itu Aba Island** *island* W Spratly Islands
56 D8 **Ituango** Antioquia, NW Colombia
61 A14 **Ituí, Rio** ≈ NW Brazil
81 O20 **Itula** Sud Kivu, E Zaire
61 K19 **Itumbiara** Goiás, C Brazil
57 T9 **Ituni** E Guyana
43 X13 **Iturbide** Campeche, SE Mexico
Ituri see Aruwimi
127 Pp16 **Iturup, Ostrov** *island* Kuril'skiye Ostrova, SE Russian Federation
62 L7 **Ituverava** São Paulo, S Brazil
61 C15 **Ituxi, Rio** ≈ W Brazil
63 E14 **Ituzaingó** Corrientes, NE Argentina
103 K18 **Itz** ≈ C Germany
102 I9 **Itzehoe** Schleswig-Holstein, N Germany
25 N2 **Iuka** Mississippi, S USA
62 I11 **Ivaiporã** Paraná, S Brazil
62 I11 **Ivaí, Rio** ≈ S Brazil
94 L10 **Ivalo** *Lapp.* Avveel, Avvil. Lappi, N Finland
94 L10 **Ivalojoki** *Lapp.* Avreel. ≈ N Finland
121 H20 **Ivanava** *Pol.* Janów, Janów Poleski, *Rus.* Ivanovo. Brestskaya Voblasts', SW Belarus
Ivangorod see Dęblin
Ivangrad see Berane
191 N7 **Ivanhoe** New South Wales, SE Australia
31 S9 **Ivanhoe** Minnesota, N USA
12 D8 **Ivanhoe** ≈ Ontario, S Canada
114 E8 **Ivanić-Grad** Sisak-Moslavina, N Croatia
119 T10 **Ivanivka** Khersons'ka Oblast', S Ukraine
119 P10 **Ivanivka** Odes'ka Oblast', SW Ukraine
115 L14 **Ivanjica** Serbia, C Yugoslavia
114 G11 **Ivanjska** NW Bosnia and Herzegovina
113 H21 **Ivanka** ✕ (Bratislava) Západné Slovensko, SW Slovakia
119 O3 **Ivankiv** *Rus.* Ivankov. Kyyivs'ka Oblast', N Ukraine
Ivankov see Ivankiv
41 O15 **Ivanof Bay** Alaska, USA
118 J7 **Ivano-Frankivs'k** *Ger.* Stanislau, *Pol.* Stanisławów, *Rus.* Ivano-Frankovsk; *prev.* Stanislav. Ivano-Frankivs'ka Oblast', W Ukraine
Ivano-Frankivs'k see Ivano-Frankivs'ka Oblast'
118 I7 **Ivano-Frankivs'ka Oblast'** *var.* Ivano-Frankivs'k, *Rus.* Ivano-Frankovskaya Oblast'; *prev.* Stanislavskaya Oblast'. ◆ *province* W Ukraine
Ivano-Frankovsk see Ivano-Frankivs'k
Ivano-Frankovskaya Oblast' see Ivano-Frankivs'ka Oblast'
128 M16 **Ivanovo** Ivanovskaya Oblast', W Russian Federation
Ivanovo see Ivanava
125 A16 **Ivanovskaya Oblast'** ◆ *province* W Russian Federation
37 X12 **Ivanpah Lake** ⊚ California, W USA
114 E7 **Ivanščica** ▲ NE Croatia
116 M8 **Ivanski** Varnenska Oblast, NE Bulgaria
131 R7 **Ivanteyevka** Saratovskaya Oblast', W Russian Federation
Ivantsevichi/Ivatsevichi see Ivatsevichy
118 I4 **Ivanychi** Volyns'ka Oblast', NW Ukraine
121 H18 **Ivatsevichy** *Pol.* Iwacewicze, *Rus.* Ivantsevichi, Ivatsevichi. Brestskaya Voblasts', SW Belarus
116 L12 **Ivaylovgrad** Khaskovska Oblast, S Bulgaria
116 K11 **Ivaylovgrad, Yazovir** ⊠ S Bulgaria
125 F10 **Ivdel'** Sverdlovskaya Oblast', C Russian Federation
Ivenets see Ivyanyets
118 L12 **Iveşti** Galaţi, E Romania
Ivigtut see Ivittuut
81 F18 **Ivindo** ≈ Congo/Gabon
61 I21 **Ivinheima** Mato Grosso do Sul, SW Brazil
206 M15 **Ivittuut** *var.* Ivigtut. S Greenland
Iviza see Eivissa
180 I6 **Ivohibe** Fianarantsoa, SE Madagascar
Ivoire, Côte d' see Ivory Coast
194 I14 **Ivori** ≈ S PNG
78 L15 **Ivory Coast** *off.* Republic of the Ivory Coast, *Fr.* Côte d'Ivoire, République de la Côte d'Ivoire. ◆ *republic* W Africa
70 C12 **Ivory Coast** *Fr.* Côte d'Ivoire. *coastal region* S Ivory Coast
97 L22 **Ivösjön** ⊚ S Sweden
108 B7 **Ivrea** *anc.* Eporedia. Piemonte, NW Italy
10 J2 **Ivujivik** Québec, NE Canada
121 J16 **Ivyanyets** *Rus.* Ivenets. Minskaya Voblasts', C Belarus
Iv'ye see Iwye
Iwacewicze see Ivatsevichy
172 N11 **Iwaizumi** Iwate, Honshū, NE Japan
171 Ll15 **Iwaki** Fukushima, Honshū, N Japan
171 Mm9 **Iwaki-san** ▲ Honshū, C Japan
170 E13 **Iwakuni** Yamaguchi, Honshū, SW Japan
172 Oo5 **Iwamizawa** Hokkaidō, NE Japan
172 Nn5 **Iwanai** Hokkaidō, NE Japan
171 Ll13 **Iwanuma** Miyagi, Honshū, C Japan
171 I17 **Iwata** Shizuoka, Honshū, S Japan
172 N10 **Iwate** Iwate, Honshū, N Japan
171 Mm11 **Iwate** *off.* Iwate-ken. ◆ *prefecture* Honshū, C Japan
171 Mm10 **Iwate-san** ▲ Honshū, C Japan
Iwje see Iwye
79 S16 **Iwo** Oyo, SW Nigeria
Iwojima see Iō-jima
121 I16 **Iwye** *Pol.* Iwje, *Rus.* Iv'ye. Hrodzyenskaya Voblasts', W Belarus
44 C4 **Ixcán, Río** ≈ Guatemala/Mexico
101 G18 **Ixelles** *Dut.* Elsene. Brussels, C Belgium
59 J16 **Ixiamas** La Paz, NW Bolivia
43 O13 **Ixmiquilpan** *var.* Ixmiquilpán. Hidalgo, C Mexico
85 K23 **Ixopo** KwaZulu/Natal, E South Africa
Ixtaccíhuatl, Volcán see Iztaccíhuatl, Volcán
42 M16 **Ixtapa** Guerrero, S Mexico
43 S16 **Ixtepec** Oaxaca, SE Mexico
42 K12 **Ixtlán** *var.* Ixtlán del Río. Nayarit, C Mexico
Ixtlán del Río see Ixtlán
125 F12 **Iyevlevo** Tyumenskaya Oblast', C Russian Federation
170 E14 **Iyo** Ehime, Shikoku, SW Japan
170 F15 **Iyomishima** *var.* Iyomisima. Ehime, Shikoku, SW Japan
Iyomisima see Iyomishima
170 Dd14 **Iyo-nada** *sea* S Japan
44 E4 **Izabal** *off.* Departamento de Izabal. ◆ *department* E Guatemala
44 F5 **Izabal, Lago de** *prev.* Golfo Dulce. ⊚ E Guatemala
149 O9 **Īzad Khvāst** Fārs, C Iran
43 X12 **Izamal** Yucatán, SE Mexico
131 Q16 **Izberbash** Respublika Dagestan, SW Russian Federation
101 C18 **Izegem** *prev.* Iseghem. West-Vlaanderen, W Belgium
148 M9 **Īzeh** Khūzestān, SW Iran
172 P14 **Izena-jima** *island* Nansei-shotō, SW Japan
116 N10 **Izgrev** Burgaska Oblast, SE Bulgaria
131 T2 **Izhevsk** *prev.* Ustinov. Udmurtskaya Respublika, NW Russian Federation
129 S7 **Izhma** Respublika Komi, NW Russian Federation
129 S7 **Izhma** ≈ NW Russian Federation
147 X8 **Izkī** NE Oman
Izmail see Izmayil
119 N13 **Izmayil** *Rus.* Izmail. Odes'ka Oblast', SW Ukraine
142 B14 **İzmir** *prev.* Smyrna. İzmir, W Turkey
142 C14 **İzmir** *prev.* Smyrna. ◆ *province* W Turkey
142 E11 **İzmit** *var.* Ismid; *anc.* Astacus. Kocaeli, NW Turkey
106 M14 **Iznájar** Andalucía, S Spain
106 M14 **Iznajar, Embalse de** ⊠ S Spain
107 N14 **Iznalloz** Andalucía, S Spain
142 E11 **İznik** Bursa, NW Turkey
142 E12 **İznik Gölü** ⊚ NW Turkey
130 M14 **Izobil'nyy** Stavropol'skiy Kray, SW Russian Federation
111 S13 **Izola** *It.* Isola d'Istria. SW Slovenia
144 H9 **Izra'** *var.* Ezra, Ezraa. Dar'ā, S Syria
43 P14 **Iztaccíhuatl, Volcán** *var.* Volcán Ixtaccíhuatal. Ⓥ S Mexico
44 C7 **Iztapa** Escuintla, SE Guatemala
Izúcar de Matamoros see Matamoros
171 J17 **Izu-hantō** *peninsula* Honshū, S Japan
170 C11 **Izuhara** Nagasaki, Tsushima, SW Japan
170 C15 **Izumi** Kagoshima, Kyūshū, SW Japan
171 Gg15 **Izumiōtsu** Ōsaka, Honshū, SW Japan
171 Gg15 **Izumi-Sano** Ōsaka, Honshū, SW Japan
170 F12 **Izumo** Shimane, Honshū, SW Japan
Izu Shichito see Izu-shotō
172 Ss13 **Izu-shotō** *var.* Izu Shichito. *island group* S Japan
199 H4 **Izu Trench** *undersea feature* NW Pacific Ocean
126 I4 **Izvestiy TsIK, Ostrova** *island* N Russian Federation
116 G10 **Izvor** Sofiyska Oblast, W Bulgaria
118 L5 **Izyaslav** Khmel'nyts'ka Oblast', W Ukraine
119 W6 **Izyum** Kharkivs'ka Oblast', E Ukraine

J

95 M18 **Jaala** Kymi, S Finland
146 J5 **Jabal ash Shifā** *desert* NW Saudi Arabia
147 U8 **Jabal az Ẓannah** *var.* Jebel Dhanna. Abū Ẓaby, W UAE
144 E11 **Jabalīya** *var.* Jabāliyah. NE Gaza Strip
Jabāliyah see Jabalīya
107 N11 **Jabalón** ≈ C Spain
160 J10 **Jabalpur** *prev.* Jubbulpore. Madhya Pradesh, C India
147 N15 **Jabal Zuuqar, Jazīrat** *var.* Az Zuqur. *island* SW Yemen
Jabat see Jabwot
144 J3 **Jabbūl, Sabkhat al** *salt flat* NW Syria
189 P1 **Jabiru** Northern Territory, N Australia
144 H4 **Jablah** *var.* Jeble, *Fr.* Djéblé. Al Lādhiqīyah, W Syria
114 C11 **Jablanac** Lika-Senj, W Croatia
115 H14 **Jablanica** SW Bosnia and Herzegovina
115 M20 **Jablanica** *Alb.* Mali i Jabllanicës, *var.* Malet e Jabllanicës. ▲ Albania/FYR Macedonia *see also* Jabllanicës, Mali i
Jabllanicës, Malet e see Jablanica/Jabllanicës, Mali i
115 M20 **Jabllanicës, Mali i** *var.* Malet e Jabllanicës, *Mac.* Jablanica. ▲ Albania/FYR Macedonia *see also* Jablanica
113 E15 **Jablonec nad Nisou** *Ger.* Gablonz an der Neisse. Severní Čechy, N Czech Republic
Jabłonków/Jablunkau see Jablunkov
112 J9 **Jabłonowo Pomorskie** Toruń, N Poland
113 J17 **Jablunkov** *Ger.* Jablunkau, *Pol.* Jabłonków. Severní Morava, E Czech Republic
61 Q15 **Jaboatão** Pernambuco, E Brazil
62 L8 **Jaboticabal** São Paulo, S Brazil
201 U7 **Jabwot** *var.* Jabat, Jebat, Jōwat. *island* Ralik Chain, S Marshall Islands
107 S4 **Jaca** Aragón, NE Spain
44 B4 **Jacaltenango** Huehuetenango, W Guatemala
61 G14 **Jacaré-a-Canga** Pará, NE Brazil
62 N10 **Jacareí** São Paulo, S Brazil
61 I18 **Jaciara** Mato Grosso, W Brazil
61 E15 **Jaciparaná** Rondônia, W Brazil
21 P5 **Jackman** Maine, NE USA
37 X1 **Jackpot** Nevada, W USA
22 M8 **Jacksboro** Tennessee, S USA
27 S6 **Jacksboro** Texas, SW USA
25 N7 **Jackson** Alabama, S USA
37 P7 **Jackson** California, W USA
25 T4 **Jackson** Georgia, SE USA
23 O6 **Jackson** Kentucky, S USA
24 J8 **Jackson** Louisiana, S USA
33 Q10 **Jackson** Michigan, N USA
31 T11 **Jackson** Minnesota, N USA
24 K5 **Jackson** *state capital* Mississippi, S USA
29 Y7 **Jackson** Missouri, C USA
23 W8 **Jackson** North Carolina, SE USA
33 T15 **Jackson** Ohio, NE USA
22 G9 **Jackson** Tennessee, S USA
35 S14 **Jackson** Wyoming, C USA
193 C19 **Jackson Bay** *bay* South Island, NZ
194 K16 **Jackson Field** ✕ (Port Moresby) Central/National Capital District, S PNG
193 C20 **Jackson Head** *headland* South Island, NZ
25 S8 **Jackson, Lake** ⊚ Florida, SE USA
35 S13 **Jackson Lake** ⊚ Wyoming, C USA
204 J6 **Jackson, Mount** ▲ Antarctica
39 U3 **Jackson Reservoir** ⊚ Colorado, C USA
25 Q3 **Jacksonville** Alabama, S USA
29 V11 **Jacksonville** Arkansas, C USA
25 W8 **Jacksonville** Florida, SE USA
32 K14 **Jacksonville** Illinois, N USA
23 W11 **Jacksonville** North Carolina, SE USA
27 W7 **Jacksonville** Texas, SW USA
25 X9 **Jacksonville Beach** Florida, SE USA
46 L9 **Jacmel** *var.* Jaquemel. S Haiti
Jacob see Nkayi
155 Q12 **Jacobābād** Sind, SE Pakistan
57 T11 **Jacobs Ladder Falls** *waterfall* S Guyana
47 O11 **Jaco, Pointe** *headland* N Dominica
13 Q9 **Jacques-Cartier** ≈ Québec, SE Canada
11 P11 **Jacques-Cartier, Détroit de** *var.* Jacques-Cartier Passage. *strait* Gulf of St. Lawrence/St. Lawrence River
13 W6 **Jacques-Cartier, Mont** ▲ Québec, SE Canada
Jacques-Cartier Passage see Jacques-Cartier, Détroit de
195 O12 **Jacquinot Bay** *inlet* New Britain, PNG
63 H16 **Jacuí, Rio** ≈ S Brazil
62 L11 **Jacupiranga** São Paulo, S Brazil
Jaddoûaâ see Jaddū'ah
102 G10 **Jade** ≈ NW Germany
102 G10 **Jadebusen** *bay* NW Germany
Jadotville see Likasi
Jadransko More/Jadransko Morje see Adriatic Sea
107 O7 **Jadraque** Castilla-La Mancha, C Spain
58 C10 **Jaén** Cajamarca, N Peru
107 N13 **Jaén** Andalucía, SW Spain
107 N13 **Jaén** ◆ *province* Andalucía, S Spain
161 J23 **Jaffna** Northern Province, N Sri Lanka
161 K23 **Jaffna Lagoon** *lagoon* N Sri Lanka
21 N10 **Jaffrey** New Hampshire, NE USA
144 H13 **Jafr, Qā' al** *var.* El Jafr. *salt pan* S Jordan
158 J9 **Jagādhri** Haryāna, N India
120 H4 **Jägala** *var.* Jägala Jõgi, *Ger.* Jaggowal. ≈ NW Estonia
Jägala Jõgi see Jägala
Jagannath see Puri
161 L14 **Jagdalpur** Madhya Pradesh, C India
169 U5 **Jagdaqi** Nei Mongol Zizhiqu, N China
Jägerndorf see Krnov
Jaggowal see Jägala
145 O2 **Jaghjaghah, Nahr** ≈ N Syria
179 Qq14 **Jagna** Bohol, C Philippines
114 N13 **Jagodina** *prev.* Svetozarevo. Serbia, C Yugoslavia
114 K12 **Jagodnja** ▲ W Yugoslavia
103 I20 **Jagst** ≈ SW Germany
161 I14 **Jagtiāl** Andhra Pradesh, C India
63 H18 **Jaguarão** Rio Grande do Sul, S Brazil
63 H18 **Jaguarão, Rio** *var.* Río Yaguarón. ≈ Brazil/Uruguay
62 K11 **Jaguariaíva** Paraná, S Brazil
46 D5 **Jagüey Grande** Matanzas, W Cuba
159 P14 **Jahānābād** Bihār, N India
Jahra see Al Jahrā'
149 P12 **Jahrom** *var.* Jahrum. Fārs, S Iran
Jahrum see Jahrom
Jailolo see Halmahera, Pulau
175 T8 **Jailolo, Selat** *strait* E Indonesia
Jainat see Chai Nat
Jainti see Jayanti
158 H12 **Jaipur** *prev.* Jeypore. Rājasthān, N India
159 T14 **Jaipur Hat** Rajshahi, NW Bangladesh
158 D11 **Jaisalmer** Rājasthān, NW India
160 O12 **Jājapur** Orissa, E India
149 R4 **Jājarm** Khorāsān, NE Iran
114 G12 **Jajce** W Bosnia and Herzegovina
Jajı see 'Alī Kheyl
85 D17 **Jakalsberg** Otjozondjupa, N Namibia
174 J14 **Jakarta** *prev.* Djakarta, *Dut.* Batavia. ● (Indonesia) Jawa, C Indonesia
8 I8 **Jakes Corner** Yukon Territory, W Canada
158 H9 **Jākhal** Haryāna, NW India
Jakobeny see Iacobeni
95 K16 **Jakobstad** *Fin.* Pietarsaari. Vaasa, W Finland
Jakobstadt see Jēkabpils
115 O18 **Jakupica** ▲ C FYR Macedonia
39 W15 **Jal** New Mexico, SW USA
147 P7 **Jalājil** *var.* Ğalāğıl. Ar Riyāḍ, C Saudi Arabia
Jalal-Abad see Dzhalal-Abad, Dzhalal-Abadskaya Oblast', W Kyrgyzstan
155 S5 **Jalālābād** *var.* Jalalabad, Jelalabad. Nangarhār, E Afghanistan
Jalal-Abad Oblasty see Dzhalal-Abadskaya Oblast'
155 V7 **Jalālpur** Punjab, E Pakistan
155 T11 **Jalālpur Pīrwāla** Punjab, E Pakistan
158 H8 **Jalandhar** *prev.* Jullundur. Punjab, N India
44 J7 **Jalán, Río** ≈ S Honduras
44 E6 **Jalapa** Jalapa, C Guatemala
44 J7 **Jalapa** Nueva Segovia, NW Nicaragua
44 A3 **Jalapa** *off.* Departamento de Jalapa. ◆ *department* SE Guatemala
44 E6 **Jalapa, Río** ≈ SE Guatemala
149 X13 **Jālaq** Sīstān va Balūchestān, SE Iran
95 K17 **Jalasjärvi** Vaasa, W Finland
155 O8 **Jaldak** Zābul, SE Afghanistan
62 J7 **Jales** São Paulo, S Brazil
160 P11 **Jaleshwar** *var.* Jaleswar. Orissa, NE India
Jaleswar see Jaleshwar
160 F12 **Jalgaon** Mahārāshtra, C India
145 W12 **Jalībah** S Iraq
145 W13 **Jalīb Shahāb** S Iraq
79 X15 **Jalingo** Taraba, E Nigeria
42 K13 **Jalisco** ◆ *state* SW Mexico
160 G13 **Jālna** Mahārāshtra, W India
Jalomitsa see Ialomiţa
107 R5 **Jalón** ≈ N Spain
158 E13 **Jālor** Rājasthān, N India
114 K11 **Jalovik** Serbia, W Yugoslavia
42 L12 **Jalpa** Zacatecas, C Mexico
159 S12 **Jalpāiguri** West Bengal, NE India
43 O12 **Jalpán** *var.* Jalpan. Querétaro de Arteaga, C Mexico
69 P2 **Jalta** *island* N Tunisia
77 S9 **Jālū** *var.* Jūlā. NE Libya
201 U8 **Jaluit Atoll** *var.* Jālwōj. *atoll* Ralik Chain, S Marshall Islands
Jālwōj see Jaluit Atoll
83 L18 **Jamaame** *It.* Giamame; *prev.* Margherita. Jubbada Hoose, S Somalia
79 W13 **Jamaare** ≈ NE Nigeria
46 G9 **Jamaica** ◆ *commonwealth republic* W West Indies
49 P3 **Jamaica** *island* W West Indies
46 I9 **Jamaica Channel** *channel* Haiti/Jamaica
159 T14 **Jamalpur** Dhaka, N Bangladesh
159 Q14 **Jamālpur** Bihār, NE India
174 I6 **Jamaluang** *var.* Jemaluang. Johor, Peninsular Malaysia
61 I14 **Jamanxim, Rio** ≈ C Brazil
58 B8 **Jambeli, Canal de** *channel* S Ecuador
101 I20 **Jambes** Namur, SE Belgium
174 Hh9 **Jambi** *var.* Telanaipura; *prev.* Djambi. Sumatera, W Indonesia
174 H9 **Jambi** *off.* Propinsi Jambi, *var.* Djambi. ◆ *province* W Indonesia
Jamdena see Yamdena, Pulau
10 H8 **James Bay** *bay* Ontario/Québec, E Canada
65 F19 **James, Isla** *island* Archipiélago de los Chonos, S Chile
189 Q8 **James Ranges** ▲ Northern Territory, C Australia
31 P8 **James River** ≈ North Dakota/South Dakota, N USA
23 X7 **James River** ≈ Virginia, NE USA
204 H4 **James Ross Island** *island* Antarctica
190 I8 **Jamestown** South Australia
67 G25 **Jamestown** ○ (Saint Helena) NW Saint Helena
37 P8 **Jamestown** California, W USA
22 L7 **Jamestown** Kentucky, S USA
20 D11 **Jamestown** New York, NE USA
31 P5 **Jamestown** North Dakota, N USA
22 L8 **Jamestown** Tennessee, S USA
Jamestown see Holetown
13 N10 **Jamet** ≈ Québec, SE Canada
43 Q17 **Jamiltepec** *var.* Santiago Jamiltepec. Oaxaca, SE Mexico
97 F20 **Jammerbugten** *bay* Skagerrak, E North Sea
158 H6 **Jammu** *prev.* Jummoo. Jammu and Kashmir, NW India
158 I5 **Jammu and Kashmir** *var.* Jammu-Kashmir, Kashmir. ◆ *state* NW India
155 V4 **Jammu and Kashmir** *disputed region* India/Pakistan
160 B10 **Jāmnagar** *prev.* Navanagar. Gujarāt, W India
155 T11 **Jāmpur** Punjab, E Pakistan
95 L18 **Jämsä** Keski-Suomi, C Finland
95 L18 **Jämsänkoski** Keski-Suomi, C Finland
159 Q16 **Jamshedpur** Bihār, NE India
96 K9 **Jämtland** ◆ *county* C Sweden
159 Q14 **Jamūi** Bihār, NE India
159 T14 **Jamuna** ≈ N Bangladesh
Jamuna see Brahmaputra
Jamundá see Nhamundá, Rio
56 D11 **Jamundí** Valle del Cauca, SW Colombia
159 Q12 **Janakpur** Central, C Nepal
61 N18 **Janaúba** Minas Gerais, SE Brazil
60 K11 **Janaucu, Ilha** *island* NE Brazil
149 Q7 **Jandaq** Eşfahān, C Iran
66 Q11 **Jandia, Punta de** *headland* Fuerteventura, Islas Canarias, Spain, NE Atlantic Ocean
61 B14 **Jandiatuba, Rio** ≈ NW Brazil
107 N12 **Jándula** ≈ S Spain
31 V10 **Janesville** Minnesota, N USA
32 L9 **Janesville** Wisconsin, N USA
155 N13 **Jangal** Baluchistān, SW Pakistan
85 N20 **Jangamo** Inhambane, SE Mozambique
161 J14 **Jangaon** Andhra Pradesh, C India
152 K10 **Jangeldi** *Rus.* Dzhankel'dy. Bukhoro Wiloyati, C Uzbekistan
159 S14 **Jangīpur** West Bengal, NE India
Janina see Ioánnina
Janischken see Joniškis
114 J11 **Janja** NE Bosnia and Herzegovina
Jankovac see Jánoshalma
207 Q15 **Jan Mayen** ◇ *Norwegian dependency* N Atlantic Ocean
86 D5 **Jan Mayen** *island* N Atlantic Ocean
207 R15 **Jan Mayen Fracture Zone** *tectonic feature* Greenland Sea/Norwegian Sea
207 R15 **Jan Mayen Ridge** *undersea feature* Greenland Sea/ Norwegian Sea
42 H3 **Janos** Chihuahua, N Mexico
113 K25 **Jánoshalma** *SCr.* Jankovac. Bács-Kiskun, S Hungary
Janów see Ivanava, Belarus
Janow/Janów see Jonava, Lithuania
112 H10 **Janowiec Wielkopolski** *Ger.* Janowitz. Bydgoszcz, C Poland
Janowitz see Janowiec Wielkopolski
113 O15 **Janów Lubelski** Tarnobrzeg, SE Poland
Janów Poleski see Ivanava
85 H25 **Jansenville** Eastern Cape, S South Africa
176 W12 **Jantan** Irian Jaya, E Indonesia
61 M18 **Januária** Minas Gerais, SE Brazil
Janūbīyah, Al Bādiyah al see Ash Shāmīyah
104 I7 **Janzé** Ille-et-Vilaine, NW France
160 F10 **Jaora** Madhya Pradesh, C India
171 H12 **Japan** *var.* Nippon, *Jap.* Nihon. ◆ *monarchy* E Asia
133 Y9 **Japan** *island group* E Asia
199 H3 **Japan Basin** *undersea feature* N Sea of Japan
133 Y8 **Japan, Sea of** *var.* East Sea, *Rus.* Yapanskoye More. *sea* NW Pacific Ocean
199 H4 **Japan Trench** *undersea feature* NW Pacific Ocean
Japen see Yapen, Pulau
61 A15 **Japiim** *var.* Máncio Lima. Acre, W Brazil
60 D12 **Japurá** Amazonas, N Brazil
60 C12 **Japurá, Rio** *var.* Río Caquetá, Yapurá. ≈ Brazil/Colombia *see also* Caquetá, Río
45 W17 **Jaqué** Darién, SE Panama
Jaquemel see Jacmel
Jarablos see Jarābulus
144 K2 **Jarābulus** *var.* Jarablos, Jerablus, *Fr.* Djérablous. Ḥalab, N Syria
62 K13 **Jaraguá do Sul** Santa Catarina, S Brazil
106 K9 **Jaraicejo** Extremadura, W Spain
106 K9 **Jaráiz de la Vera** Extremadura, W Spain
107 O7 **Jarama** ≈ C Spain
65 J20 **Jaramillo** Santa Cruz, SE Argentina
Jarandilla de la Vega see Jarandilla de la Vera
106 K8 **Jarandilla de la Vera** *var.* Jarandilla de la Vega. Extremadura, W Spain
155 V9 **Jarānwāla** Punjab, E Pakistan
144 G9 **Jarash** *var.* Jerash; *anc.* Gerasa. Irbid, NW Jordan
Jarbah, Jazīrat see Jerba, Île de
96 N13 **Järbo** Gävleborg, C Sweden
Jardan see Jordan
46 F7 **Jardines de la Reina, Archipiélago de los** *island group* C Cuba
168 J7 **Jargalant** Arhangay, C Mongolia
168 I8 **Jargalant** Bayanhongor, C Mongolia
168 D7 **Jargalant** Bayan-Ölgiy, W Mongolia
168 K6 **Jargalant** Bulgan, N Mongolia
168 G9 **Jargalant** Govĭ-Altay, W Mongolia
Jarid, Shaṭṭ al see Jerid, Chott el
60 I11 **Jari, Rio** *var.* Jary. ≈ N Brazil
147 N7 **Jarīr, Wādī al** *dry watercourse* C Saudi Arabia
Jarja see Yur'ya
96 L13 **Järna** *var.* Dala-Jarna. Kopparberg, C Sweden
97 O16 **Järna** Stockholm, C Sweden
104 K11 **Jarnac** Charente, W France
112 H12 **Jarocin** Kalisz, C Poland
113 F16 **Jaroměř** *Ger.* Jermer. Východní Čechy, NE Czech Republic
Jaroslau see Jarosław
113 O16 **Jarosław** *Ger.* Jaroslau, *Rus.* Yaroslav. Przemyśl, SE Poland
95 F16 **Järpen** Jämtland, C Sweden
153 O14 **Jarqŭrghon** *Rus.* Dzharkurgan. Surkhondaryo Wiloyati, S Uzbekistan
145 P2 **Jarrāh, Wadi** *dry watercourse* NE Syria
Jars, Plain of see Xiangkhoang, Plateau de
168 K14 **Jartai Yanchi** ⊚ N China
61 E16 **Jaru** Rondônia, W Brazil
169 T10 **Jarud Qi** Nei Mongol Zizhiqu, N China
120 I4 **Järva-Jaani** *Ger.* Sankt-Johannis. Järvamaa, N Estonia
120 G5 **Järvakandi** *Ger.* Jerwakant. Raplamaa, NW Estonia
120 H4 **Järvamaa** *off.* Järva Maakond. ◆ *province* N Estonia
95 L19 **Järvenpää** Uusimaa, S Finland
12 G17 **Jarvis** Ontario, S Canada
185 R8 **Jarvis Island** ◇ *US unincorporated territory* C Pacific Ocean
96 M11 **Järvsö** Gävleborg, C Sweden
Jary see Jari, Rio
114 M9 **Jaša Tomić** Serbia, NE Yugoslavia
114 D12 **Jasenice** Zadar-Knin, W Croatia
144 I11 **Jashshat al 'Adlah, Wādī al** *dry watercourse* C Jordan
79 Q16 **Jasikan** E Ghana
149 T15 **Jāsk** Hormozgān, SE Iran
152 F6 **Jasliq** *Rus.* Zhaslyk. Qoraqalpoghiston Respublikasi, NW Uzbekistan
113 N17 **Jasło** Krosno, SE Poland
9 U16 **Jasmin** Saskatchewan, S Canada
67 A23 **Jason Islands** *island group* NW Falkland Islands
204 I4 **Jason Peninsula** *peninsula* Antarctica
33 N15 **Jasonville** Indiana, N USA
9 O15 **Jasper** Alberta, SW Canada
12 L13 **Jasper** Ontario, SE Canada
25 O3 **Jasper** Alabama, S USA
29 T9 **Jasper** Arkansas, C USA
25 U8 **Jasper** Florida, SE USA
33 N16 **Jasper** Indiana, N USA
31 R11 **Jasper** Minnesota, N USA
29 S7 **Jasper** Missouri, C USA
22 K10 **Jasper** Tennessee, S USA
27 Y9 **Jasper** Texas, SW USA
9 O15 **Jasper National Park** *national park* Alberta/British Columbia, SW Canada
Jassy see Iaşi
115 N14 **Jastrebac** ▲ SE Yugoslavia
114 D9 **Jastrebarsko** Grad Zagreb, N Croatia
Jastrow see Jastrowie
112 G9 **Jastrowie** *Ger.* Jastrow. Piła, NW Poland
113 J17 **Jastrzębie-Zdrój** Katowice, S Poland
113 L22 **Jászapáti** Jász-Nagykun-Szolnok, E Hungary
113 L22 **Jászberény** Jász-Nagykun-Szolnok, E Hungary
113 L23 **Jász-Nagykun-Szolnok** *off.* Jász-Nagykun-Szolnok Megye. ◆ *county* E Hungary
61 J19 **Jataí** Goiás, C Brazil
60 G12 **Jatapu, Serra do** ▲ N Brazil
43 W16 **Jatate, Río** ≈ SE Mexico
155 P17 **Jāti** Sind, SE Pakistan
46 F6 **Jatibonico** Sancti Spíritus, C Cuba
174 Jj14 **Jatiluhur, Danau** ⊚ Jawa, S Indonesia
Jativa see Xátiva
174 K14 **Jatiwangi** *prev.* Djatiwangi. Jawa, C Indonesia
155 S11 **Jattoi** Punjab, E Pakistan
62 L9 **Jaú** São Paulo, S Brazil
60 F11 **Jauaperi, Rio** ≈ N Brazil
101 I19 **Jauche** Walloon Brabant, C Belgium
Jauer see Jawor
Jauf see Al Jawf
155 U7 **Jauharābād** Punjab, E Pakistan
59 E14 **Jauja** Junín, C Peru
43 O10 **Jaumave** Tamaulipas, C Mexico
120 H10 **Jaunjelgava** *Ger.* Friedrichstadt. Aizkraukle, S Latvia
Jaunlatgale see Pytalovo
120 I8 **Jaunpiebalga** Gulbene, NE Latvia
120 E9 **Jaunpils** Tukums, C Latvia
159 N13 **Jaunpur** Uttar Pradesh, N India
31 N8 **Java** South Dakota, N USA
Java see Jawa
107 R9 **Javalambre** ▲ E Spain
181 V7 **Java Ridge** *undersea feature* E Indian Ocean
61 A14 **Javari, Rio** *var.* Yavarí. ≈ Brazil/ Peru
169 O7 **Javarthushuu** Dornod, NE Mongolia
174 Kk13 **Java Sea** *Ind.* Laut Jawa. *sea* W Indonesia
181 U7 **Java Trench** *var.* Sunda Trench. *undersea feature* E Indian Ocean
107 T11 **Jávea** *var.* Xàbia. País Valenciano, E Spain
169 O7 **Javhlant** Hentiy, E Mongolia
65 G20 **Javier, Isla** *island* S Chile
115 L14 **Javor** ▲ Bosnia and Herzegovina/Yugoslavia
113 K20 **Javorie** *Hung.* Jávoros. ▲ S Slovakia
Jávoros see Javorie
95 J14 **Jävre** Norrbotten, N Sweden
174 K14 **Jawa** *Eng.* Java; *prev.* Djawa. *island* C Indonesia
174 J15 **Jawa Barat** *off.* Propinsi Jawa Barat, *Eng.* West Java. ◆ *province* S Indonesia
Jawa, Laut see Java Sea
145 R3 **Jawān** NW Iraq
174 Kk15 **Jawa Tengah** *off.* Propinsi Jawa Tengah, *Eng.* Central Java. ◆ *province* S Indonesia
174 Ll15 **Jawa Timur** *off.* Propinsi Jawa Timur, *Eng.* East Java. ◆ *province* S Indonesia
83 N17 **Jawhar** *var.* Jowhar, *It.* Giohar. Shabeellaha Dhexe, S Somalia
113 F14 **Jawor** *Ger.* Jauer. Legnica, W Poland
Jaworów see Yavoriv
113 J16 **Jaworzno** Katowice, S Poland
Jaxartes see Syr Darya
29 R9 **Jay** Oklahoma, C USA
Jayabum see Chaiyaphum
Jayanath see Chai Nat
159 T12 **Jayanti** *prev.* Jainti. West Bengal, NE India
176 Xx12 **Jaya, Puncak** *prev.* Puntjak Carstensz, Puntjak Sukarno. ▲ Irian Jaya, E Indonesia
176 Z10 **Jayapura** *var.* Djajapura, *Dut.* Hollandia; *prev.* Kotabaru, Sukarnapura. Irian Jaya, E Indonesia
176 Y12 **Jayawijaya, Pegunungan** ▲ Irian Jaya, E Indonesia
Jay Dairen see Dalian
Jayhawker State see Kansas
153 S12 **Jayilgan** *Rus.* Dzhailgan, Dzhayilgan. C Tajikistan
161 L14 **Jaypur** *var.* Jeypore, Jeypur. Orissa, E India
27 O6 **Jayton** Texas, SW USA
149 U13 **Jaz Mūrīān, Hāmūn** ⊚ SE Iran
144 M4 **Jazrah** Ar Raqqah, C Syria
144 G6 **Jbaïl** *var.* Jebeil, Jubayl, Jubeil; *anc.* Biblical Gebal, Bybles. W Lebanon
27 O7 **J.B.Thomas, Lake** ⊚ Texas, SW USA
Jdaïdé see Judaydah
37 X12 **Jean** Nevada, W USA
24 I9 **Jeanerette** Louisiana, S USA
46 L8 **Jean-Rabel** NW Haiti
149 T12 **Jebāl Bārez, Kūh-e** ▲ SE Iran
Jebat see Jabwot
79 T15 **Jebba** Kwara, W Nigeria
Jebeil see Jbaïl
118 E12 **Jebel** *Hung.* Széphely; *prev. Hung.* Zsebely. Timiş, W Romania
Jebel see Dzhebel
Jebel, Bahr el see White Nile
Jebel Dhanna see Jabal az Ẓannah
Jeble see Jablah
98 K13 **Jedburgh** SE Scotland, UK
Jedda see Jiddah
113 L15 **Jędrzejów** *Ger.* Endersdorf. Kielce, S Poland
102 K12 **Jeetze** *var.* Jeetzel. ≈ C Germany
Jeetzel see Jeetze

◆ Country ● Country Capital ◇ Dependent Territory ○ Dependent Territory Capital ◆ Administrative Region ✕ International Airport ▲ Mountain ▲ Mountain Range Ⓥ Volcano ≈ River ⊚ Lake ⊠ Reservoir

31 U14 **Jefferson** Iowa, C USA
23 Q8 **Jefferson** North Carolina, SE USA
27 X6 **Jefferson** Texas, SW USA
32 M9 **Jefferson** Wisconsin, N USA
29 U5 **Jefferson City** *state capital* Missouri, C USA
35 R10 **Jefferson City** Montana, NW USA
23 N9 **Jefferson City** Tennessee, S USA
37 U7 **Jefferson, Mount** ▲ Nevada, W USA
34 H12 **Jefferson, Mount** ▲ Oregon, NW USA
22 L5 **Jeffersontown** Kentucky, S USA
33 P16 **Jeffersonville** Indiana, N USA
35 V15 **Jeffrey City** Wyoming, C USA
79 T13 **Jega** Kebbi, NW Nigeria
Jehol *see* Chengde
64 P5 **Jejui-Guazú, Río** ∽ E Paraguay
120 I10 **Jēkabpils** *Ger.* Jakobstadt. Jēkabpils, S Latvia
25 W7 **Jekyll Island** *island* Georgia, SE USA
174 L11 **Jelai, Sungai** ∽ Borneo, N Indonesia
Jelalabad *see* Jalālābād
113 H14 **Jelcz-Laskowice** Wrocław, SW Poland
113 E14 **Jelenia Góra** *Ger.* Hirschberg, Hirschberg im Riesengebirge, Hirschberg in Riesengebirge, Hirschberg in Schlesien. Jelenia Góra, SW Poland
113 E14 **Jelenia Góra** *off.* Województwo Jeleniogórskie, *Ger.* Hirschberg, Hirschberg im Riesengebirge, Hirschberg in Schlesien. ◈ *province* SW Poland
Jeleniogórskie, Województwo *see* Jelenia Góra
159 S11 **Jelep La** *pass* N India
120 F9 **Jelgava** *Ger.* Mitau. Jelgava, C Latvia
114 L13 **Jelica** ▲ C Yugoslavia
22 M8 **Jellico** Tennessee, S USA
97 G23 **Jelling** Vejle, C Denmark
174 I15 **Jemaja, Pulau** *island* W Indonesia
Jemaluang *see* Jamaluang
101 E20 **Jemappes** Hainaut, S Belgium
174 M16 **Jember** *prev.* Djember. Jawa, C Indonesia
101 I20 **Jemeppe-sur-Sambre** Namur, S Belgium
39 R10 **Jemez Pueblo** New Mexico, SW USA
164 K2 **Jeminay** Xinjiang Uygur Zizhiqu, NW China
201 U5 **Jemo Island** *atoll* Ratak Chain, C Marshall Islands
175 Nn8 **Jempang, Danau** ◎ Borneo, N Indonesia
103 L16 **Jena** Thüringen, C Germany
24 I6 **Jena** Louisiana, S USA
110 I8 **Jenaz** Graubünden, SE Switzerland
111 N7 **Jenbach** Tirol, W Austria
175 P13 **Jeneponto** *prev.* Djeneponto. Sulawesi, C Indonesia
144 F9 **Jenin** N West Bank
23 P7 **Jenkins** Kentucky, S USA
29 P9 **Jenks** Oklahoma, C USA
Jenné *see* Djenné
111 X8 **Jennersdorf** Burgenland, SE Austria
24 H9 **Jennings** Louisiana, S USA
15 Jj4 **Jenny Lind Island** *island* Northwest Territories, N Canada
25 Y13 **Jensen Beach** Florida, SE USA
15 M2 **Jens Munk Island** *island* Northwest Territories, NE Canada
61 O17 **Jequié** Bahia, E Brazil
61 O18 **Jequitinhonha, Rio** ∽ E Brazil
Jerablus *see* Jarābulus
76 H6 **Jerada** NE Morocco
Jerash *see* Jarash
77 N7 **Jerba, Île de** *var.* Djerba, Jazīrat Jarbah. *island* E Tunisia
46 K9 **Jérémie** SW Haiti
Jerez *see* Jeréz de la Frontera, Spain
Jeréz *see* Jerez de García Salinas, Mexico
42 L11 **Jerez de García Salinas** *var.* Jeréz. Zacatecas, C Mexico
106 J15 **Jerez de la Frontera** *var.* Jerez; *prev.* Xeres. Andalucía, SW Spain
106 I12 **Jerez de los Caballeros** Extremadura, W Spain
Jergucati *see* Jorgucat
144 G10 **Jericho** *Ar.* Arīḥā, *Heb.* Yeriḥo. E West Bank
76 M7 **Jerid, Chott el** *var.* Shaṭṭ al Jarīd. *salt lake* SW Tunisia
191 O10 **Jerilderie** New South Wales, SE Australia
Jerischmarkt *see* Câmpia Turzii
94 K11 **Jerisjärvi** ◎ NW Finland
Jermer *see* Jaroměř
38 K11 **Jerome** Arizona, SW USA
35 O15 **Jerome** Idaho, NW USA
99 L26 **Jersey** *island* Channel Islands, NW Europe
20 K14 **Jersey City** New Jersey, NE USA
20 F13 **Jersey Shore** Pennsylvania, NE USA
32 K14 **Jerseyville** Illinois, N USA
106 K8 **Jerte** ∽ W Spain
144 F10 **Jerusalem** *Ar.* Al Quds, Al Quds ash Sharif, *Heb.* Yerushalayim; *anc.* Hierosolyma. ● (Israel) Jerusalem, NE Israel
144 G10 **Jerusalem** ◈ *district* E Israel
191 S10 **Jervis Bay** New South Wales, SE Australia
191 S10 **Jervis Bay Territory** ◈ *territory* SE Australia
Jerwakant *see* Järvakandi
111 S10 **Jesenice** *Ger.* Assling. NW Slovenia
113 H16 **Jeseník** *Ger.* Freiwaldau. Severní Morava, E Czech Republic
Jesi *see* Iesi
108 I8 **Jesolo** *var.* Iesolo. Veneto, NE Italy
Jesselton *see* Kota Kinabalu
97 I14 **Jessheim** Akershus, S Norway
159 T15 **Jessore** Khulna, W Bangladesh
25 W6 **Jesup** Georgia, SE USA
43 S15 **Jesús Carranza** Veracruz-Llave, SE Mexico
64 K10 **Jesús María** Córdoba, C Argentina
28 K6 **Jetmore** Kansas, C USA
105 Q2 **Jeumont** Nord, N France
97 H14 **Jevnaker** Oppland, S Norway
Jewe *see* Jõhvi
27 V9 **Jewett** Texas, SW USA
21 N12 **Jewett City** Connecticut, NE USA
Jewish Autonomous Oblast *see* Yevreyskaya Avtonomnaya Oblast'
Jeypore/Jeypur *see* Jaypur, Orissa, India
Jeypore *see* Jaipur, Rājasthān, India
115 L17 **Jezercës, Maja e** ▲ N Albania
113 B18 **Jezerní Hora** ▲ SW Czech Republic
160 F10 **Jhābua** Madhya Pradesh, C India
158 H14 **Jhālāwār** Rājasthān, N India
155 U9 **Jhang** *var.* Jhang Sadar, Jhang Sadr. Punjab, NE Pakistan
Jhang Sadar/Jhang Sadr *see* Jhang
158 J13 **Jhānsi** Uttar Pradesh, N India
160 M11 **Jhārsuguda** Orissa, E India
155 V7 **Jhelum** Punjab, NE Pakistan
133 P9 **Jhelum** ∽ E Pakistan
159 T15 **Jhenida** Dhaka, W Bangladesh
155 P16 **Jhimpir** Sind, SE Pakistan
Jhind *see* Jind
155 R16 **Jhudo** Sind, SE Pakistan
Jhumra *see* Chak Jhumra
158 H11 **Jhunjhunūn** Rājasthān, N India
Ji *see* Hebei, China
Ji *see* Jilin, China
159 S14 **Jiāganj** West Bengal, NE India
166 J7 **Jialing Jiang** ∽ C China
169 Y7 **Jiamusi** *var.* Chia-mu-ssu, Kiamusze. Heilongjiang, NE China
167 O11 **Ji'an** Jiangxi, S China
169 W12 **Ji'an** Jilin, NE China
169 T13 **Jianchang** Liaoning, NE China
166 F11 **Jianchuan** Yunnan, SW China
164 M4 **Jiangjunmiao** Xinjiang Uygur Zizhiqu, W China
166 K11 **Jiangkou** Guizhou, S China
167 Q12 **Jiangle** Fujian, SE China
167 N15 **Jiangmen** Guangdong, S China
167 Q10 **Jiangshan** Zhejiang, SE China
167 Q7 **Jiangsu** *var.* Chiang-su, Jiangsu Sheng, Kiangsu, Su. ◈ *province* E China
Jiangsu Sheng *see* Jiangsu
167 O11 **Jiangxi** *var.* Chiang-hsi, Gan, Jiangxi Sheng, Kiangsi. ◈ *province* S China
Jiangxi Sheng *see* Jiangxi
166 I8 **Jiangyou** *prev.* Zhongba. Sichuan, C China
167 N9 **Jianli** Hubei, C China
167 Q11 **Jian'ou** Fujian, SE China
169 S12 **Jianping** Liaoning, NE China
166 L9 **Jianshi** Hubei, C China
133 V11 **Jian Xi** ∽ SE China
167 Q11 **Jianyang** Fujian, SE China
166 I9 **Jianyang** Sichuan, C China
169 X10 **Jiaohe** Jilin, NE China
167 S10 **Jiaojiang** *var.* Haimen. Zhejiang, SE China
167 N6 **Jiaozuo** Henan, C China
167 Q7 **Jiashan** *var.* Mingguan. Anhui, SE China
164 F8 **Jiashi** *var.* Payzawat. Xinjiang Uygur Zizhiqu, NW China
160 L9 **Jiāwān** Madhya Pradesh, C India
167 S9 **Jiaxing** Zhejiang, SE China
Jiayi *see* Chiai
169 X6 **Jiayin** *var.* Chaoyang. Heilongjiang, NE China
165 R8 **Jiayuguan** Gansu, N China
144 M4 **Jibli** Ar Raqqah, C Syria
118 H9 **Jibou** *Hung.* Zsibó. Sălaj, NW Romania
147 Z9 **Jibsh, Ra's al** *headland* E Oman
Jibuti *see* Djibouti
113 E15 **Jičín** *Ger.* Jitschin. Východní Čechy, N Czech Republic
146 K10 **Jiddah** *Eng.* Jedda. Makkah, W Saudi Arabia
147 W11 **Jiddat al Ḥarāsīs** *desert* C Oman
94 K9 **Jiesjavrre** ◎ N Norway
166 M4 **Jiexiu** Shanxi, C China
167 P14 **Jieyang** Guangdong, S China
121 F14 **Jieznas** Prienai, S Lithuania
Jifa', Bi'r *see* Jif'īyah, Bi'r
147 P15 **Jif'īyah, Bi'r** *var.* Bi'r Jifa'. *well* C Yemen
79 W13 **Jigawa** ◈ *state* N Nigeria
Jigerbent *see* Dzhigirbent
46 I7 **Jiguaní** Granma, E Cuba
165 T12 **Jigzhi** Qinghai, C China
Jih-k'a-tse *see* Xigazê
113 E18 **Jihlava** *Ger.* Iglau, *Pol.* Igława. Jižní Morava, S Czech Republic
113 E18 **Jihlava** *var.* Igel, *Ger.* Iglawa. ∽ S Czech Republic
Jihočeský Kraj *see* Jižní Čechy
Jihomoravský Kraj *see* Jižní Morava
76 L5 **Jijel** *var.* Djidjel; *prev.* Djidjelli. NE Algeria
118 L9 **Jijia** ∽ N Romania
82 L13 **Jijiga** *It.* Giggiga. E Ethiopia
107 S12 **Jijona** *var.* Xixona. País Valenciano, E Spain
Jilf al Kabīr, Haḍabat al *see* Gilf Kebir Plateau
83 L18 **Jilib** *It.* Gelib. Jubbada Dhexe, S Somalia
169 W10 **Jilin** *var.* Chi-lin, Girin, Kirin; *prev.* Yungki, Yunki. Jilin, NE China
169 W10 **Jilin** *var.* Chi-lin, Girin, Ji, Jilin Sheng, Kirin. ◈ *province* NE China
169 W11 **Jilin Hada Ling** ▲ NE China
Jilin Sheng *see* Jilin
169 S4 **Jiliu He** ∽ NE China
107 Q6 **Jiloca** ∽ N Spain
83 I14 **Jīma** *var.* Jimma, *It.* Gimma. SW Ethiopia
46 M9 **Jimaní** W Dominican Republic
118 E11 **Jimbolia** *Ger.* Hatzfeld, *Hung.* Zsombolya. Timiş, W Romania
106 K16 **Jimena de la Frontera** Andalucía, S Spain
42 K7 **Jiménez** Chihuahua, N Mexico
43 N5 **Jiménez** Coahuila de Zaragoza, NE Mexico
43 P9 **Jiménez** *var.* Santander Jiménez. Tamaulipas, C Mexico
42 L10 **Jiménez del Teul** Zacatecas, C Mexico
79 Y14 **Jimeta** Adamawa, E Nigeria
Jimma *see* Jīma
164 M5 **Jimsar** Xinjiang Uygur Zizhiqu, NW China
20 I14 **Jim Thorpe** Pennsylvania, NE USA
Jin *see* Shanxi, China
Jin *see* Tianjin Shi, China
167 P5 **Jinan** *var.* Chinan, Chi-nan, Tsinan. Shandong, E China
165 T8 **Jinchang** Gansu, N China
167 N5 **Jincheng** Shanxi, C China
Jinchengjiang *see* Hechi
158 I9 **Jīnd** *prev.* Jhind. Haryāna, NW India
191 Q11 **Jindabyne** New South Wales, SE Australia
113 O18 **Jindřichův Hradec** *Ger.* Neuhaus. Jižní Čechy, S Czech Republic
Jing *see* Beijing Shi, China
Jing *see* Jinghe, China
165 X10 **Jingchuan** Gansu, C China
167 Q10 **Jingdezhen** Jiangxi, S China
167 O12 **Jinggangshan** Jiangxi, S China
167 P3 **Jinghai** Tianjin Shi, E China
166 K6 **Jing He** ∽ C China
164 I4 **Jinghe** *var.* Jing. Xinjiang Uygur Zizhiqu, NW China
166 F15 **Jinghong** *var.* Yunjinghong. Yunnan, SW China
166 M9 **Jingmen** Hubei, C China
169 X10 **Jingpo Hu** ◎ NE China
166 M8 **Jing Shan** ▲ C China
165 V9 **Jingtai** *var.* Yitiaoshan. Gansu, C China
166 J14 **Jingxi** Guangxi Zhuangzu Zizhiqu, S China
166 L12 **Jing Xian** Hunan, E China
Jing Xian *see* Jingzhou
169 W11 **Jingyu** Jilin, NE China
165 V10 **Jingyuan** Gansu, C China
166 L12 **Jingzhou** *var.* Jing Xian. Hunan, S China
167 R10 **Jinhua** Zhejiang, SE China
169 P13 **Jining** Nei Mongol Zizhiqu, N China
167 P5 **Jining** Shandong, E China
63 G18 **Jinja** S Uganda
167 O11 **Jin Jiang** ∽ S China
167 R13 **Jinjiang** *var.* Qingyang. Fujian, SE China
176 W14 **Jin, Kepulauan** *island group* E Indonesia
Jinmen Dao *see* Chinmen Tao
44 J9 **Jinotega** Jinotega, NW Nicaragua
44 K7 **Jinotega** ◈ *department* N Nicaragua
44 J11 **Jinotepe** Carazo, SW Nicaragua
166 L13 **Jinping** *prev.* Sanjiang. Guizhou, S China
166 H14 **Jinping** Yunnan, SW China
Jinsen *see* Inch'ŏn
166 J11 **Jinsha** Guizhou, S China
163 N12 **Jinsha Jiang** ∽ SW China
166 M10 **Jinshi** Hunan, S China
165 R7 **Jinta** Gansu, N China
179 Q12 **Jintotolo Channel** *channel* C Philippines
167 Q12 **Jin Xi** ∽ SE China
169 T13 **Jinxi** Liaoning, NE China
169 U14 **Jinxian** Liaoning, NE China
167 P6 **Jinxiang** Shandong, E China
167 P8 **Jinzhai** *prev.* Meishan. Anhui, E China
169 T12 **Jinzhou** *var.* Chin-chou, Chinchow; *prev.* Chinhsien. Liaoning, NE China
144 H12 **Jinz, Qā' al** ◎ C Jordan
49 S8 **Jiparaná, Rio** ∽ W Brazil
58 A7 **Jipijapa** Manabí, W Ecuador
44 F8 **Jiquilisco** Usulután, S El Salvador
153 S12 **Jirgatol** *Rus.* Dzhirgatal'. C Tajikistan
Jirjā *see* Girga
113 B15 **Jirkov** *Ger.* Görkau. Severní Čechy, NW Czech Republic
Jiroft *see* Sabzvārān
166 L11 **Jishou** Hunan, S China
Jisr ash Shadadi *see* Ash Shadādah
118 I14 **Jitaru** Olt, S Romania
Jitschin *see* Jičín
118 H14 **Jiu** *Ger.* Schil, Schyl, *Hung.* Zsil, Zsily. ∽ S Romania
167 R11 **Jiufeng Shan** ▲ SE China
167 P9 **Jiujiang** Jiangxi, S China
167 O10 **Jiuling Shan** ▲ S China
166 G10 **Jiulong** Sichuan, C China
167 Q13 **Jiulong Jiang** ∽ SE China
167 Q12 **Jiulong Xi** ∽ SE China
165 R8 **Jiuquan** Gansu, N China
166 K17 **Jiusuo** Hainan, S China
169 W10 **Jiutai** Jilin, NE China
166 K13 **Jiuwan Dashan** ▲ S China
154 I16 **Jiwani** Baluchistān, SW Pakistan
169 Y8 **Jixi** Heilongjiang, NE China
169 Y7 **Jixian** Heilongjiang, NE China
166 M5 **Jixian** *var.* Ji Xian. Shanxi, C China
Jiza *see* Al Jīzah
147 N13 **Jīzān** *var.* Qīzān. Jīzān, SW Saudi Arabia
147 N13 **Jīzān** *var.* Minṭaqat Jīzān. ◈ *province* SW Saudi Arabia
146 K6 **Jīzl, Wādī al** *dry watercourse* W Saudi Arabia
113 C18 **Jižní Čechy** *off.* Jihočeský Kraj. ◈ *region* S Czech Republic
113 F19 **Jižní Morava** *off.* Jihomoravský Kraj. ◈ *region* SE Czech Republic
170 Ff12 **Jizō-zaki** *headland* Honshū, SW Japan
147 U14 **Jiz', Wādī al** *dry watercourse* E Yemen
153 O11 **Jizzakh** *Rus.* Dzhizak. Jizzakh Wiloyati, C Uzbekistan
153 N10 **Jizzakh Wiloyati** *Rus.* Dzhizakskaya Oblast'. ◈ *province* C Uzbekistan
62 I13 **Joaçaba** Santa Catarina, S Brazil
Joal *see* Joal-Fadiout
78 F11 **Joal-Fadiout** *prev.* Joal. W Senegal
78 E10 **João Barrosa** Boa Vista, E Cape Verde
João Belo *see* Xai-Xai
João de Almeida *see* Chibia
61 Q15 **João Pessoa** *prev.* Paraíba. *state capital* Paraíba, E Brazil
27 X7 **Joaquin** Texas, SW USA
64 K6 **Joaquín V.González** Salta, N Argentina
Joazeiro *see* Juazeiro
Jo'burg *see* Johannesburg
111 O7 **Jochberger Ache** ∽ W Austria
Jo-ch'iang *see* Ruoqiang
94 K12 **Jock** Norrbotten, N Sweden
44 I5 **Jocón** Yoro, N Honduras
107 O13 **Jódar** Andalucía, S Spain
158 F12 **Jodhpur** Rājasthān, NW India
101 I19 **Jodoigne** Walloon Brabant, C Belgium
97 I22 **Jægerspris** Frederiksborg, E Denmark
95 O16 **Joensuu** Pohjois-Karjala, SE Finland
97 C17 **Jæren** *physical region* S Norway
29 W4 **Joes** Colorado, C USA
203 Z3 **Joe's Hill** *hill* Kiritimati, NE Kiribati
171 Jj13 **Jōetsu** *var.* Zyôetu. Niigata, Honshū, C Japan
85 M18 **Jofane** Inhambane, S Mozambique
161 E18 **Jog** *waterfall* W India
159 R12 **Jogbani** Bihār, NE India
120 I5 **Jõgeva** *Ger.* Laisholm. Jõgevamaa, E Estonia
120 I4 **Jõgevamaa** *off.* Jõgeva Maakond. ◈ *province* E Estonia
149 S4 **Joghatāy** Khorāsān, NE Iran
159 U12 **Jogīghopa** Assam, NE India
158 I7 **Jogindarnagar** Himāchal Pradesh, N India
Jogjakarta *see* Yogyakarta
171 Ii13 **Jōhana** Toyama, Honshū, SW Japan
85 J21 **Johannesburg** *var.* Egoli, Erautini, Gauteng, *abbrev.* Jo'burg. Gauteng, NE South Africa
37 T13 **Johannesburg** California, W USA
85 I21 **Johannesburg** ✕ Gauteng, NE South Africa
Johannisburg *see* Pisz
155 P14 **Johi** Sind, SE Pakistan
57 T13 **Johi Village** S Guyana
34 K13 **John Day** Oregon, NW USA
34 I11 **John Day River** ∽ Oregon, NW USA
20 L14 **John F Kennedy** ✕ (New York) Long Island, New York, NE USA
23 V8 **John H.Kerr Reservoir** *var.* Buggs Island Lake, Kerr Lake. ⊡ North Carolina/Virginia, SE USA
39 V6 **John Martin Reservoir** ⊡ Colorado, C USA
98 K6 **John o'Groats** N Scotland, UK
29 P5 **John Redmond Reservoir** ⊡ Kansas, C USA
41 Q7 **John River** ∽ Alaska, USA
28 H6 **Johnson** Kansas, C USA
20 M7 **Johnson** Vermont, NE USA
20 D13 **Johnsonburg** Pennsylvania, NE USA
20 H11 **Johnson City** New York, NE USA
23 P8 **Johnson City** Tennessee, S USA
27 R10 **Johnson City** Texas, SW USA
37 S12 **Johnsondale** California, W USA
8 I8 **Johnsons Crossing** Yukon Territory, W Canada
23 T13 **Johnsonville** South Carolina, SE USA
23 Q13 **Johnston** South Carolina, SE USA
199 K6 **Johnston Atoll** ◇ *US unincorporated territory* C Pacific Ocean
183 Q3 **Johnston Atoll** *atoll* C Pacific Ocean
32 L17 **Johnston City** Illinois, N USA
188 K12 **Johnston, Lake** *salt lake* Western Australia
33 S13 **Johnstown** Ohio, N USA
20 D15 **Johnstown** Pennsylvania, NE USA
174 Hh6 **Johor** *var.* Johore. ◈ *state* Peninsular Malaysia
Johor Baharu *see* Johor Bahru
174 I6 **Johor Bahru** *var.* Johor Baharu, Johore Bahru. Johor, Peninsular Malaysia
Johore *see* Johor
Johore Bahru *see* Johor Bahru
120 K3 **Jõhvi** *Ger.* Jewe. Ida-Virumaa, NE Estonia
105 P7 **Joigny** Yonne, C France
Joinvile *see* Joinville
62 K12 **Joinville** *var.* Joinvile. Santa Catarina, S Brazil
105 R6 **Joinville** Haute-Marne, N France
204 H3 **Joinville Island** *island* Antarctica
43 O15 **Jojutla** *var.* Jojutla de Juárez. Morelos, S Mexico
Jojutla de Juárez *see* Jojutla
94 I12 **Jokkmokk** Norrbotten, N Sweden
94 L2 **Jökulsá á Dal** ∽ E Iceland
94 K2 **Jökulsá á Fjöllum** ∽ NE Iceland
Jokyakarta *see* Yogyakarta
32 M11 **Joliet** Illinois, N USA
13 O11 **Joliette** Québec, SE Canada
179 Pp17 **Jolo** Jolo Island, SW Philippines
96 D11 **Jølstervatnet** ◎ S Norway
174 Ll15 **Jombang** *prev.* Djombang. Jawa, S Indonesia
165 R14 **Jomda** Xizang Zizhiqu, W China
58 A6 **Jome, Punta de** *headland* W Ecuador
120 G13 **Jonava** *Ger.* Janow, *Pol.* Janów. Jonava, C Lithuania
152 L11 **Jondor** *Rus.* Zhondor. Bukhoro Wiloyati, C Uzbekistan
165 V11 **Jonê** Gansu, C China
29 X9 **Jonesboro** Arkansas, C USA
25 S4 **Jonesboro** Georgia, SE USA
32 L17 **Jonesboro** Illinois, N USA
24 H5 **Jonesboro** Louisiana, S USA
23 P8 **Jonesboro** Tennessee, S USA
21 T6 **Jonesport** Maine, NE USA
1 J4 **Jones Sound** *channel* Northwest Territories, N Canada
24 I6 **Jonesville** Louisiana, S USA
33 Q10 **Jonesville** Michigan, N USA
23 Q11 **Jonesville** South Carolina, SE USA
83 F14 **Jonglei** Jonglei, SE Sudan
83 F14 **Jonglei** *var.* Gongoleh State. ◈ *state* SE Sudan
83 F14 **Jonglei Canal** *canal* S Sudan
120 F11 **Joniškėlis** Pasvalys, N Lithuania
120 F10 **Joniškis** *Ger.* Janischken. Joniškis, N Lithuania
97 L19 **Jönköping** Jönköping, S Sweden
97 K20 **Jönköping** ◈ *county* S Sweden
13 Q7 **Jonquière** Québec, SE Canada
43 V15 **Jonuta** Tabasco, SE Mexico
104 K12 **Jonzac** Charente-Maritime, W France
29 R7 **Joplin** Missouri, C USA
35 W8 **Jordan** Montana, NW USA
153 S11 **Jordan** *var.* Iordan, *Rus.* Jardan. Farghona Wiloyati, E Uzbekistan
144 H12 **Jordan** *off.* Hashemite Kingdom of Jordan, *Ar.* Al Mamlakah al Urdunīyah al Hāshimīyah, Al Urdunn; *prev.* Transjordan. ◆ *monarchy* SW Asia
144 G9 **Jordan** *Ar.* Urdunn, *Heb.* HaYarden. ∽ SW Asia
Jordan Lake *see* B.Everett Jordan Reservoir
113 K17 **Jordanów** Nowy Sącz, S Poland
34 M15 **Jordan Valley** Oregon, NW USA
144 G9 **Jordan Valley** *valley* N Israel
59 D15 **Jorge Chávez International** *var.* Lima. ✕ (Lima) Lima, W Peru
115 L23 **Jorgucat** *var.* Jergucati, Jorgucati. Gjirokastër, S Albania
Jorgucati *see* Jorgucat
159 X12 **Jorhāt** Assam, NE India
95 J14 **Jörn** Västerbotten, N Sweden
39 R14 **Jornada Del Muerto** *valley* New Mexico, SW USA
95 N17 **Joroinen** Mikkeli, SE Finland
97 C16 **Jørpeland** Rogaland, S Norway
79 W14 **Jos** Plateau, C Nigeria
179 Rr17 **Jose Abad Santos** *var.* Trinidad. Mindanao, S Philippines
63 F19 **José Batlle y Ordóñez** *var.* Batlle y Ordóñez. Florida, C Uruguay
65 H18 **José de San Martín** Chubut, S Argentina
63 E19 **José Enrique Rodó** *var.* Rodó, José E.Rodo; *prev.* Drabble, Drable. Soriano, SW Uruguay
José E.Rodo *see* José Enrique Rodó
Josefsdorf *see* Žabalj
46 C4 **José Martí** ✕ (La Habana) Cuidad de La Habana, N Cuba
63 F19 **José Pedro Varela** *var.* José P.Varela. Lavalleja, S Uruguay
189 N2 **Joseph Bonaparte Gulf** *gulf* N Australia
39 N11 **Joseph City** Arizona, SW USA
11 O9 **Joseph, Lake** ◎ Newfoundland and Labrador, E Canada
12 G13 **Joseph, Lake** ◎ Ontario, S Canada
194 I11 **Josephstaal** Madang, N PNG
José P.Varela *see* José Pedro Varela
61 J14 **José Rodrigues** Pará, N Brazil
158 K9 **Joshimath** Uttar Pradesh, N India
27 T7 **Joshua** Texas, SW USA
37 V15 **Joshua Tree** California, W USA
79 V14 **Jos Plateau** *plateau* C Nigeria
104 H6 **Josselin** Morbihan, NW France
Jos Sudarso *see* Yos Sudarso, Pulau
96 E11 **Jostedalsbreen** *glacier* S Norway
96 F12 **Jotunheimen** ▲ S Norway
144 G7 **Joûnié** *var.* Juniyah. W Lebanon
27 R13 **Jourdanton** Texas, SW USA
100 L7 **Joure** *Fris.* De Jouwer. Friesland, N Netherlands
95 M18 **Joutsa** Keski-Suomi, C Finland
95 N18 **Joutseno** Kymi, SE Finland
94 M12 **Joutsijärvi** Lappi, NE Finland
110 A9 **Joux, Lac de** ◎ W Switzerland
46 D5 **Jovellanos** Matanzas, W Cuba
159 V13 **Jowai** Meghālaya, NE India
Jowat *see* Jabwot
Jowhar *see* Jawhar
149 O12 **Jowkān** Fārs, S Iran
149 Q10 **Jowzam** Kermān, C Iran
155 N2 **Jowzjān** ◈ *province* N Afghanistan
Józseffalva *see* Žabalj
J.Storm Thurmond Reservoir *see* Clarks Hill Lake
47 T6 **Juana Díaz** C Puerto Rico
42 L9 **Juan Aldama** Zacatecas, C Mexico
1 E9 **Juan de Fuca Plate** *tectonic feature*
34 F7 **Juan de Fuca, Strait of** *strait* Canada/USA
Juan Fernandez Islands *see* Juan Fernández, Islas
200 Oo12 **Juan Fernández, Islas** *Eng.* Juan Fernandez Islands. *island group* W Chile
57 O4 **Juangriego** Nueva Esparta, NE Venezuela
58 D11 **Juanjuí** *var.* Juanjuy. San Martín, N Peru
Juanjuy *see* Juanjuí
95 N16 **Juankoski** Kuopio, C Finland
Juan Lacaze *see* Juan L.Lacaze
63 E20 **Juan L.Lacaze** *var.* Juan Lacaze, Puerto Sauce; *prev.* Sauce. Colonia, SW Uruguay
64 L5 **Juan Solá** Salta, N Argentina
65 F21 **Juan Stuven, Isla** *island* S Chile
61 H16 **Juará** Mato Grosso, W Brazil
43 N7 **Juárez** *var.* Villa Juárez. Coahuila de Zaragoza, NE Mexico
42 C2 **Juárez, Sierra de** ▲ NW Mexico
61 O15 **Juazeiro** *prev.* Joazeiro. Bahia, E Brazil
61 P14 **Juazeiro do Norte** Ceará, E Brazil
83 F15 **Juba** *var.* Jūbā. Bahr el Gabel, S Sudan
83 L17 **Juba** *Amh.* Genalē Wenz, *It.* Guiba, *Som.* Ganaane, Webi Jubba. ∽ Ethiopia/Somalia
204 H2 **Jubany** *Argentinian research station* Antarctica
Jubayl *see* Jbaïl
83 L18 **Jubbada Dhexe** *off.* Gobolka Jubbada Dhexe. ◈ *region* SW Somalia
83 K18 **Jubbada Hoose** ◈ *region* SW Somalia
Jubba, Webi *see* Juba
Jubbulpore *see* Jabalpur
Jubeil *see* Jbaïl
76 B9 **Juby, Cap** *headland* SW Morocco
107 R10 **Júcar** *var.* Jucar. ∽ C Spain
42 L12 **Juchipila** Zacatecas, C Mexico
43 S16 **Juchitán** *var.* Juchitán de Zaragosa. Oaxaca, SE Mexico
Juchitán de Zaragosa *see* Juchitán
144 G11 **Judaea** *cultural region* Israel/West Bank
144 F11 **Judaean Hills** *Heb.* Haré Yehuda. *hill range* E Israel
144 H8 **Judaydah** *Fr.* Jdaïdé. Dimashq, W Syria
145 P11 **Judayyidat Hāmir** S Iraq
111 U8 **Judenburg** Steiermark, C Austria
35 T8 **Judith River** ∽ Montana, NW USA
29 V11 **Judsonia** Arkansas, C USA
147 P14 **Jufrah, Wādī al** *dry watercourse* NW Yemen
Jugoslavija/Jugoslavija, Savezna Republika *see* Yugoslavia
44 K10 **Juigalpa** Chontales, S Nicaragua
167 T13 **Juishui** C Taiwan
102 E9 **Juist** *island* NW Germany
61 M21 **Juiz de Fora** Minas Gerais, SE Brazil
64 J5 **Jujuy** *off.* Provincia de Jujuy. ◈ *province* N Argentina
Jujuy *see* San Salvador de Jujuy
94 J11 **Jukkasjärvi** Norrbotten, N Sweden
Jula *see* Gyula, Hungary
Jūlā *see* Jālū, Libya
39 W2 **Julesburg** Colorado, C USA
Julia Beterrae *see* Béziers
59 I17 **Juliaca** Puno, SE Peru
189 U6 **Julia Creek** Queensland, C Australia
37 V17 **Julian** California, W USA
100 H7 **Julianadorp** Noord-Holland, NW Netherlands
111 S11 **Julian Alps** *Ger.* Julische Alpen, *It.* Alpi Giulie, *Slvn.* Julijske Alpe. ▲ Italy/Slovenia
57 V11 **Juliana Top** ▲ C Suriname
Julianehåb *see* Qaqortoq
Julijske Alpe *see* Julian Alps
42 J6 **Julimes** Chihuahua, N Mexico
Julio Briga *see* Bragança, Portugal
Juliobriga *see* Logroño, Spain
63 G15 **Júlio de Castilhos** Rio Grande do Sul, S Brazil
Juliomagus *see* Angers
Julische Alpen *see* Julian Alps
Jullundur *see* Jalandhar
153 N11 **Juma** *Rus.* Dzhuma. Samarqand Wiloyati, C Uzbekistan
167 O3 **Juma He** ∽ E China
83 L18 **Jumboo** Jubbada Hoose, S Somalia
37 Y11 **Jumbo Peak** ▲ Nevada, W USA
107 R12 **Jumilla** Murcia, SE Spain
159 N10 **Jumla** Mid Western, NW Nepal
Jummoo *see* Jammu
Jumna *see* Yamuna
Jumporn *see* Chumphon
32 K5 **Jump River** ∽ Wisconsin, N USA
160 B11 **Jūnāgadh** *var.* Junagarh. Gujarāt, W India
Junagarh *see* Jūnāgadh
167 Q6 **Junan** *prev.* Shizilu. Shandong, E China
64 G11 **Juncal, Cerro** ▲ C Chile
27 Q10 **Junction** Texas, SW USA
38 K6 **Junction** Utah, W USA
29 O4 **Junction City** Kansas, C USA
34 F13 **Junction City** Oregon, NW USA
62 M10 **Jundiaí** São Paulo, S Brazil
194 E13 **June** ∽ W PNG
41 X12 **Juneau** *state capital* Alaska, USA
32 M8 **Juneau** Wisconsin, N USA
107 U6 **Juneda** Cataluña, NE Spain
191 Q9 **Junee** New South Wales, SE Australia
37 R8 **June Lake** California, W USA
Jungbunzlau *see* Mladá Boleslav
164 L4 **Junggar Pendi** *Eng.* Dzungarian Basin. *basin* NW China
101 N24 **Junglinster** Grevenmacher, C Luxembourg
20 F14 **Juniata River** ∽ Pennsylvania, NE USA
63 B20 **Junín** Buenos Aires, E Argentina
59 E14 **Junín** Junín, C Peru
59 F14 **Junín** *off.* Departamento de Junín. ◈ *department* C Peru
65 H15 **Junín de los Andes** Neuquén, W Argentina
59 D14 **Junín, Lago de** ◎ C Peru
Juniyah *see* Joûnié
Junkseylon *see* Phuket
166 I11 **Junlian** Sichuan, C China
27 O11 **Juno** Texas, SW USA
94 J11 **Junosuando** Norrbotten, N Sweden
95 H16 **Junsele** Västernorrland, C Sweden
Junten *see* Sunch'ŏn
34 L14 **Juntura** Oregon, NW USA
95 N14 **Juntusranta** Oulu, E Finland
120 H11 **Juodupė** Rokiškis, NE Lithuania
121 H14 **Juozapinės Kalnas** ▲ SE Lithuania
101 K19 **Juprelle** Liège, E Belgium
82 D13 **Jur** ∽ C Sudan
105 S9 **Jura** ◈ *department* E France
110 C7 **Jura** ◈ *canton* NW Switzerland
110 B8 **Jura** *var.* Jura Mountains. ▲ France/Switzerland
98 G12 **Jura** *island* SW Scotland, UK
Juraciszki *see* Yuratsishki
56 C8 **Juradó** Chocó, NW Colombia
Jura Mountains *see* Jura
98 G12 **Jura, Sound of** *strait* W Scotland, UK
145 V15 **Juraybīyāt, Bi'r** *well* S Iraq
120 E13 **Jurbarkas** *Ger.* Georgenburg, Jurburg. Jurbarkas, W Lithuania
101 F20 **Jurbise** Hainaut, SW Belgium
Jurburg *see* Jurbarkas
120 F9 **Jūrmala** Rīga, C Latvia
176 Ww13 **Jursian, Pulau** *island* E Indonesia
60 D13 **Juruá** Amazonas, NW Brazil
50 F7 **Juruá, Rio** *var.* Río Yuruá. ∽ Brazil/Peru
61 G16 **Juruena** Mato Grosso, W Brazil
61 G16 **Juruena** ∽ W Brazil
171 Mm8 **Jūsan-ko** ◎ Honshū, C Japan
27 O6 **Justiceburg** Texas, SW USA
Justinianopolis *see* Kirşehir
64 K11 **Justo Daract** San Luis, C Argentina
61 C14 **Jutaí** Amazonas, W Brazil
60 C13 **Jutaí, Rio** ∽ NW Brazil
102 N13 **Jüterbog** Brandenburg, E Germany
44 E6 **Jutiapa** Jutiapa, S Guatemala
44 A3 **Jutiapa** *off.* Departamento de Jutiapa. ◈ *department* SE Guatemala
44 J6 **Juticalpa** Olancho, C Honduras
84 I13 **Jutila** North Western, NW Zambia
Jutland *see* Jylland
86 F8 **Jutland Bank** *undersea feature* SE North Sea
95 N16 **Juuka** Pohjois-Karjala, E Finland
95 N17 **Juva** Mikkeli, SE Finland
Juvavum *see* Salzburg
46 A6 **Juventud, Isla de la** *var.* Isla de Pinos, *Eng.* Isle of Youth; *prev.* The Isle of the Pines. *island* W Cuba
Ju Xian *see* Juxian
167 Q5 **Juxian** *var.* Ju Xian. Shandong, E China
167 P6 **Juye** Shandong, E China
115 O15 **Južna Morava** *Ger.* Südliche Morava. ∽ SE Yugoslavia
97 I23 **Jyderup** Vestsjælland, E Denmark
97 F22 **Jylland** *Eng.* Jutland. *peninsula* W Denmark
Jyrgalan *see* Dzhergalan
95 M17 **Jyväskylä** Keski-Suomi, C Finland

K

155 X3 **K2** *Chin.* Qogir Feng, *Eng.* Mount Godwin Austen. ▲ China/Pakistan
40 D9 **Kaaawa** *Haw.* Ka'a'wa. Oahu, Hawaii, USA, C Pacific Ocean
83 G16 **Kaabong** NE Uganda
Kaaden *see* Kadaň
57 V9 **Kaaimanston** Sipaliwini, N Suriname
152 G14 **Kaakhka** *var.* Kaka. Akhalskiy Velayat, S Turkmenistan
Kaala *see* Caála
197 H5 **Kaala-Gomen** Province Nord, W New Caledonia
94 L9 **Kaamanen** *Lapp.* Gámas. Lappi, N Finland
Kaapstad *see* Cape Town
Kaarasjoki *see* Karasjok
Kaaresuanto *see* Karesuando
94 J10 **Kaaresuvanto** *Lapp.* Gárassavon. Lappi, N Finland
95 K19 **Kaarina** Turku-Pori, SW Finland
101 I14 **Kaatsheuvel** Noord-Brabant, S Netherlands

◆ Country
● Country Capital
◇ Dependent Territory
○ Dependent Territory Capital
◈ Administrative Region
✕ International Airport
▲ Mountain
▲ Mountain Range
Volcano
∽ River
◎ Lake
⊡ Reservoir

95 N16 **Kaavi** Kuopio, C Finland
Ka'a'wa *see* Kaaawa
176 Y15 **Kaba** Irian Jaya, E Indonesia
Kaba *see* Habahe
175 Q13 **Kabaena, Pulau** *island* C Indonesia
175 Q13 **Kabaena, Selat** *strait* Sulawesi, C Indonesia
152 J11 **Kabakly** *Turkm.* Gabakly. Lebapskiy Velayat, NE Turkmenistan
78 J14 **Kabala** N Sierra Leone
83 E19 **Kabale** SW Uganda
57 U10 **Kabalebo Rivier** ≈ W Suriname
81 N22 **Kabalo** Shaba, SE Zaire
81 O21 **Kabambare** Maniema, E Zaire
197 K15 **Kabara** *prev.* Kambara. *island* Lau Group, E Fiji
Kabardino-Balkaria *see* Kabardino-Balkarskaya Respublika
130 M15 **Kabardino-Balkarskaya Respublika** *Eng.* Kabardino-Balkaria. ◆ *autonomous republic* SW Russian Federation
81 O19 **Kabare** Sud Kivu, E Zaire
176 Uu8 **Kabarei** Irian Jaya, E Indonesia
179 Q16 **Kabasalan** Mindanao, S Philippines
79 U15 **Kabba** Kogi, S Nigeria
94 I13 **Kåbdalis** Norrbotten, N Sweden
144 M6 **Kabd aş Şārim** *hill range* E Syria
12 B7 **Kabenung Lake** ◎ Ontario, S Canada
31 W3 **Kabetogama Lake** ◎ Minnesota, N USA
Kabia, Pulau *see* Kabin, Pulau
81 M22 **Kabinda** Kasai Oriental, SE Zaire
Kabinda *see* Cabinda
175 P13 **Kabin, Pulau** *var.* Pulau Kabia. *island* W Indonesia
175 Rr16 **Kabir** Pulau Pantar, S Indonesia
155 T10 **Kabīrwāla** Punjab, E Pakistan
176 U8 **Kable Bet** Irian Jaya, E Indonesia
80 I13 **Kabo** Ouham, NW Central African Republic
Kābol *see* Kābul
85 H14 **Kabompo** North Western, W Zambia
85 H14 **Kabompo** ≈ W Zambia
81 M22 **Kabongo** Shaba, SE Zaire
123 Kk12 **Kaboudia, Rass** *headland* E Tunisia
128 J14 **Kabozha** Novgorodskaya Oblast', W Russian Federation
149 U4 **Kabūd Gonbad** Khorāsān, NE Iran
148 L5 **Kabūd Rāhang** Hamadān, W Iran
84 L12 **Kabuko** Northern, NE Zambia
155 Q5 **Kābul** *var.* Kabul, *Per.* Kābol. ● (Afghanistan) Kābul, E Afghanistan
155 Q5 **Kābul** *Eng.* Kabul, *Per.* Kābol. ◆ *province* E Afghanistan
155 Q5 **Kābul** ✕ Kābul, E Afghanistan
155 R5 **Kabul** *var.* Daryā-ye Kābul. ≈ Afghanistan/Pakistan *see also* Kābul, Daryā-ye
155 S5 **Kābul, Daryā-ye** *var.* Kabul. ≈ Afghanistan/Pakistan *see also* Kabul
81 O25 **Kabunda** Shaba, SE Zaire
175 Ss4 **Kaburuang, Pulau** *island* Kepulauan Talaud, N Indonesia
82 G8 **Kabushiya** River Nile, NE Sudan
85 J14 **Kabwe** Central, C Zambia
194 K12 **Kabwum** Morobe, C PNG
115 N17 **Kačanik** Serbia, S Yugoslavia
176 U8 **Kacepi** Pulau Gebe, E Indonesia
120 F13 **Kačerginė** Kaunas, C Lithuania
119 S13 **Kacha** Respublika Krym, S Ukraine
160 A10 **Kachchh, Gulf of** *var.* Gulf of Cutch, Gulf of Kutch. *gulf* W India
160 I11 **Kachchhīdhāna** Madhya Pradesh, C India
155 Q11 **Kachchh, Rann of** *var.* Rann of Kachh, Rann of Kutch. *salt marsh* India/Pakistan
41 Q13 **Kachemak Bay** *bay* Alaska, USA
Kachh, Rann of *see* Kachchh, Rann of
79 V14 **Kachia** Kaduna, C Nigeria
178 Gg2 **Kachin State** ◆ *state* N Myanmar
151 T7 **Kachiry** Pavlodar, NE Kazakhstan
126 Jj15 **Kachug** Irkutskaya Oblast', S Russian Federation
143 Q11 **Kaçkar Dağları** ▲▲ NE Turkey
161 C21 **Kadamatt Island** *island* Lakshadweep, India, N Indian Ocean
113 B15 **Kadaň** *Ger.* Kaaden. Severní Čechy, NW Czech Republic
178 Gg12 **Kadan Kyun** *prev.* King Island. *island* Mergui Archipelago, S Myanmar
197 I16 **Kadavu** *prev.* Kandavu. *island* S Fiji
197 I15 **Kadavu Passage** *channel* S Fiji
81 G16 **Kadéï** ≈ Cameroon/Central African Republic
Kadhimain *see* Al Kāẓimīyah
Kadijica *see* Kadiytsa
116 M13 **Kadıköy Barajı** ▣ NW Turkey
190 I8 **Kadina** South Australia
142 H15 **Kadınhanı** Konya, C Turkey
78 M14 **Kadiolo** Sikasso, S Mali
142 L16 **Kadirli** Adana, S Turkey
116 G11 **Kadiytsa** *Mac.* Kadijica. ▲ Bulgaria/FYR Macedonia
30 L10 **Kadoka** South Dakota, N USA
131 N5 **Kadom** Ryazanskaya Oblast', W Russian Federation
85 K16 **Kadoma** *prev.* Gatooma. Mashonaland West, C Zimbabwe
82 E12 **Kadugli** Southern Kordofan, S Sudan
79 V14 **Kaduna** Kaduna, C Nigeria
79 V14 **Kaduna** ◆ *state* C Nigeria
79 V15 **Kaduna** ≈ N Nigeria
128 K14 **Kaduy** Vologodskaya Oblast', NW Russian Federation
160 E13 **Kadwa** ≈ W India
127 Nn9 **Kadykchan** Magadanskaya Oblast', E Russian Federation
Kadzharan *see* K'ajaran
129 T7 **Kadzherom** Respublika Komi, NW Russian Federation
153 X8 **Kadzhi-Say** *Kir.* Kajisay. Issyk-Kul'skaya Oblast', NE Kyrgyzstan
78 I10 **Kaédi** Gorgol, S Mauritania
80 G12 **Kaélé** Extrême-Nord, N Cameroon
40 C9 **Kaena Point** *headland* Oahu, Hawaii, USA, C Pacific Ocean
192 J2 **Kaeo** Northland, North Island, NZ
169 X14 **Kaesŏng** *var.* Kaesŏng-si. S North Korea
Kaesŏng-si *see* Kaesŏng
Kaewieng *see* Kavieng
81 L24 **Kafakumba** Shaba, S Zaire
Kafan *see* Kapan
79 V14 **Kafanchan** Kaduna, C Nigeria
Kaffa *see* Feodosiya
78 G11 **Kaffrine** C Senegal
Kafiau *see* Kofiau, Pulau
117 I19 **Kafiréas, Ákra** *headland* Évvoia, C Greece
117 I19 **Kafiréos, Stenó** *strait* Évvoia/Kykládes, Greece, Aegean Sea
Kafirnigan *see* Kofarnihon
Kafo *see* Kafu
Kafr ash Shaykh/Kafrel Sheik *see* Kafr el Sheikh
77 W7 **Kafr el Sheikh** *var.* Kafr ash Shaykh, Kafrel Sheik. N Egypt
83 F17 **Kafu** *var.* Kafo. ≈ W Uganda
85 J15 **Kafue** Lusaka, SE Zambia
85 I14 **Kafue** ≈ C Zambia
69 T13 **Kafue Flats** *plain* C Zambia
171 I13 **Kaga** Ishikawa, Honshū, SW Japan
81 J14 **Kaga Bandoro** *prev.* Fort-Crampel. Nana-Grébizi, C Central African Republic
83 E18 **Kagadi** W Uganda
40 H17 **Kagalaska Island** *island* Aleutian Islands, Alaska, USA
Kagan *see* Kogon
Kaganovichabad *see* Kolkhozobod
Kagarlyk *see* Kaharlyk
170 F15 **Kagawa** *off.* Kagawa-ken. ◆ *prefecture* Shikoku, SW Japan
160 J13 **Kagaznagar** Andhra Pradesh, C India
95 J14 **Kåge** Västerbotten, N Sweden
83 E19 **Kagera** *var.* Ziwa Magharibi, *Eng.* West Lake. ◆ *region* NW Tanzania
83 E19 **Kagera** *var.* Akagera. ≈ Rwanda/Tanzania *see also* Akagera
78 L5 **Kâgheţ** *var.* Karet. *physical region* N Mauritania
Kagi *see* Chiai
143 S12 **Kağızman** Kars, NE Turkey
196 I6 **Kagman Point** *headland* Saipan, S Northern Mariana Islands
170 Bb15 **Kagoshima** *var.* Kagosima. Kagoshima, Kyūshū, SW Japan
172 Qq14 **Kagoshima** *off.* Kagoshima-ken, *var.* Kagosima. ◆ *prefecture* Kyūshū, SW Japan
170 Bb16 **Kagoshima-wan** *bay* SW Japan
Kagosima *see* Kagoshima
194 H12 **Kagua** Southern Highlands, W PNG
Kagul *see* Cahul
Kagul, Ozero *see* Kahul, Ozero
40 B8 **Kahala Point** *headland* Kauai, Hawaii, USA, C Pacific Ocean
40 G12 **Kahaluu** *Haw.* Kahalu'u. Hawaii, USA, C Pacific Ocean
83 F21 **Kahama** Shinyanga, NW Tanzania
119 P5 **Kaharlyk** *Rus.* Kagarlyk. Kyyivs'ka Oblast', N Ukraine
174 Mm10 **Kahayan, Sungai** ≈ Borneo, C Indonesia
81 I22 **Kahemba** Bandundu, SW Zaire
193 A23 **Kaherekoau Mountains** ▲▲ South Island, NZ
149 W14 **Kahīrī** *var.* Kūhīrī. Sīstān va Balūchestān, SE Iran
103 L16 **Kahla** Thüringen, C Germany
103 G15 **Kahler Asten** ▲ W Germany
155 Q4 **Kahmard, Daryā-ye** *prev.* Darya-i-Surkhab. ≈ NE Afghanistan
149 T13 **Kahnūj** Kermān, SE Iran
29 V1 **Kahoka** Missouri, C USA
40 E10 **Kahoolawe** *island* Hawaii, USA, C Pacific Ocean
142 M16 **Kahramanmaraş** *var.* Kahraman Maraş, Maraş, Marash. Kahramanmaraş, S Turkey
142 L15 **Kahramanmaraş** *var.* Kahraman Maraş, Maraş, Marash. ◆ *province* C Turkey
155 T11 **Kahror** *var.* Kahror Pakka. Punjab, E Pakistan
Kahror Pakka *see* Kahror
143 N15 **Kâhta** Adıyaman, S Turkey
40 D8 **Kahuku** Oahu, Hawaii, USA, C Pacific Ocean
40 D8 **Kahuku Point** *headland* Oahu, Hawaii, USA, C Pacific Ocean
118 M12 **Kahul, Ozero** *var.* Lacul Cahul, *Rus.* Ozero Kagul. ◎ Moldova/Ukraine
149 V11 **Kahūrak** Sīstān va Balūchestān, SE Iran
192 G13 **Kahurangi Point** *headland* South Island, NZ
155 V6 **Kahūta** Punjab, E Pakistan
79 S14 **Kaiama** Kwara, W Nigeria
194 J12 **Kaiapit** Morobe, C PNG
193 I18 **Kaiapoi** Canterbury, South Island, NZ
38 K9 **Kaibab Plateau** *plain* Arizona, SW USA
171 Gg14 **Kaibara** Hyōgo, Honshū, SW Japan
176 Vv13 **Kai Besar, Pulau** *island* Kepulauan Kai, E Indonesia
38 L9 **Kaibito Plateau** *plain* Arizona, SW USA
164 K6 **Kaidu He** *var.* Karaxahar. ≈ NW China
57 S10 **Kaieteur Falls** *waterfall* C Guyana
167 O6 **Kaifeng** Henan, C China
192 J3 **Kaihu** Northland, North Island, NZ
176 V13 **Kai Kecil, Pulau** *island* Kepulauan Kai, E Indonesia
176 V14 **Kai, Kepulauan** *prev.* Kei Islands. *island group* Maluku, SE Indonesia
192 J3 **Kaikohe** Northland, North Island, NZ
193 J16 **Kaikoura** Canterbury, South Island, NZ
193 J16 **Kaikoura Peninsula** *peninsula* South Island, NZ
Kailas Range *see* Gangdisê Shan
166 K12 **Kaili** Guizhou, S China
40 F10 **Kailua** Maui, Hawaii, USA, C Pacific Ocean
40 G11 **Kailua** *var.* Kailua-Kona, Kona. Hawaii, USA, C Pacific Ocean
Kailua-Kona *see* Kailua
194 E13 **Kaim** ≈ W PNG
176 Y13 **Kaima** Irian Jaya, E Indonesia
192 M7 **Kaimai Range** ▲ North Island, NZ
116 E13 **Kaïmaktsalán** ▲ Greece/FYR Macedonia
193 C20 **Kaimanawa Mountains** ▲▲ North Island, NZ
120 E4 **Käina** *Ger.* Keinis; *prev.* Keina. Hiiumaa, W Estonia
111 V7 **Kainach** ≈ SE Austria
170 G16 **Kainan** Tokushima, Shikoku, SW Japan
170 Ff16 **Kainan** Wakayama, Honshū, SW Japan
194 J12 **Kainantu** Eastern Highlands, C PNG
153 U7 **Kaindy** *Kir.* Kayyngdy. Chuyskaya Oblast', N Kyrgyzstan
79 T14 **Kainji Dam** *dam* W Nigeria
Kainji Lake *see* Kainji Reservoir
79 T14 **Kainji Reservoir** *var.* Kainji Lake. ▣ W Nigeria
194 J14 **Kaintiba** *var.* Kamina. Gulf, S PNG
94 K12 **Kainulaisjärvi** Norrbotten, N Sweden
192 K5 **Kaipara Harbour** *harbor* North Island, NZ
158 I10 **Kairāna** Uttar Pradesh, N India
194 G9 **Kairiru Island** *island* NW PNG
76 M6 **Kairouan** *var.* Al Qayrawān. E Tunisia
Kaisaria *see* Kayseri
103 F20 **Kaiserslautern** Rheinland-Pfalz, SW Germany
120 G13 **Kaišiadorys** Kaišiadorys, S Lithuania
192 I2 **Kaitaia** Northland, North Island, NZ
167 O15 **Kai Tak** ✕ (Hong Kong) S China
193 E24 **Kaitangata** Otago, South Island, NZ
158 I9 **Kaithal** Haryāna, NW India
174 J11 **Kait, Tanjung** *headland* Sumatera, W Indonesia
40 E9 **Kaiwi Channel** *channel* Hawaii, USA, C Pacific Ocean
166 K9 **Kaixian** *var.* Kai Xian. Sichuan, C China
169 V11 **Kaiyuan** *var.* K'ai-yüan. Liaoning, NE China
166 H14 **Kaiyuan** Yunnan, SW China
41 O9 **Kaiyuh Mountains** ▲▲ Alaska, USA
95 M15 **Kajaani** *Swe.* Kajana. Oulu, C Finland
155 N7 **Kajakī, Band-e** ◎ C Afghanistan
Kajan *see* Kayan, Sungai
Kajana *see* Kajaani
143 V13 **K'ajaran** *Rus.* Kadzharan. SE Armenia
Kajisay *see* Kadzhi-Say
115 O20 **Kajmakčalan** ▲ S FYR Macedonia
Kajnar *see* Kaynar
155 N6 **Kajrān** Urūzgān, C Afghanistan
155 N5 **Kaj Rūd** ≈ C Afghanistan
Kaka *see* Kaakhka
10 C12 **Kakabeka Falls** Ontario, S Canada
85 F23 **Kakamas** Northern Cape, W South Africa
83 H18 **Kakamega** Western, W Kenya
114 H13 **Kakanj** C Bosnia and Herzegovina
193 F22 **Kakanui Mountains** ▲▲ South Island, NZ
192 K11 **Kakaramea** Taranaki, North Island, NZ
78 J16 **Kakata** C Liberia
192 M11 **Kakatahi** Manawatu-Wanganui, North Island, NZ
115 M23 **Kakavi** Gjirokastër, S Albania
153 O14 **Kakaydi** Surkhondaryo Wiloyati, S Uzbekistan
170 Ee13 **Kake** Hiroshima, Honshū, SW Japan
41 X13 **Kake** Kupreanof Island, Alaska, USA
175 R12 **Kakea** Pulau Wowoni, C Indonesia
171 Ii17 **Kakegawa** Shizuoka, Honshū, S Japan
172 Qq13 **Kakeromajima** Kagoshima, SW Japan
149 T6 **Kākhak** *var.* Kākhk. Khorāsān, E Iran
120 L11 **Kakhanavichy** *Rus.* Kokhanovichi. Vitsyebskaya Voblasts', N Belarus
41 P13 **Kakhonak** Alaska, USA
119 S10 **Kakhovka** Khersons'ka Oblast', S Ukraine
119 U9 **Kakhovs'ka Vodoskhovyshche** *Rus.* Kakhovskoye Vodokhranilishche. ▣ SE Ukraine
Kakhovskoye Vodokhranilishche *see* Kakhovs'ka Vodoskhovyshche
119 T11 **Kakhovs'kyy Kanal** *canal* S Ukraine
Kakia *see* Khakhea
161 L16 **Kākināda** *prev.* Cocanada. Andhra Pradesh, E India
Käkisalmi *see* Priozersk
170 G14 **Kakogawa** Hyōgo, Honshū, SW Japan
83 F18 **Kakoge** C Uganda
151 O7 **Kak, Ozero** ◎ N Kazakhstan
Ka-Krem *see* Malyy Yenisey
Kakshaal-Too, Khrebet *see* Kokshaal-Tau
41 S5 **Kaktovik** Alaska, USA
171 Ll13 **Kakuda** Miyagi, Honshū, C Japan
171 M11 **Kakunodate** Akita, Honshū, C Japan
Kalaallit Nunaat *see* Greenland
155 T7 **Kālābāgh** Punjab, E Pakistan
175 Rr16 **Kalabahi** Pulau Alor, S Indonesia
196 I5 **Kalabera** Saipan, S Northern Mariana Islands
85 G14 **Kalabo** Western, W Zambia
130 M9 **Kalach** Voronezhskaya Oblast', W Russian Federation
125 G13 **Kalachinsk** Omskaya Oblast', C Russian Federation
131 N10 **Kalach-na-Donu** Volgogradskaya Oblast', SW Russian Federation
177 F5 **Kaladan** ≈ W Myanmar
12 K14 **Kaladar** Ontario, SE Canada
40 G13 **Ka Lae** *var.* South Cape, South Point. *headland* Hawaii, USA, C Pacific Ocean
85 G19 **Kalahari Desert** *desert* Southern Africa
40 B8 **Kalaheo** *Haw.* Kalāheo. Kauai, Hawaii, USA, C Pacific Ocean
Kalaikhum *see* Qal'aikhum
152 J16 **Kala-i-Mor** *Turkm.* Galaymor. Maryyskiy Velayat, S Turkmenistan
95 K15 **Kalajoki** Oulu, W Finland
Kalak *see* Eski Kaļak
Kal al Sraghna *see* El Kelâa Srarhna
34 G10 **Kalama** Washington, NW USA
Kalámai *see* Kalámata
117 G14 **Kalamariá** Kentrikí Makedonía, N Greece
117 E21 **Kalámata** *prev.* Kalámai. Pelopónnisos, S Greece
33 P10 **Kalamazoo** Michigan, N USA
33 P9 **Kalamazoo River** ≈ Michigan, N USA
Kalambaka *see* Kalampáka
119 S13 **Kalamits'ka Zatoka** *Rus.* Kalamitskiy Zaliv. *gulf* S Ukraine
Kalamitskiy Zaliv *see* Kalamits'ka Zatoka
117 H18 **Kálamos** Attikí, C Greece
117 C18 **Kálamos** *island* Iónioi Nísoi, Greece, C Mediterranean Sea
117 D15 **Kalampáka** *var.* Kalambaka. Thessalía, C Greece
Kalan *see* Călan, Romania
Kalan *see* Tunceli, Turkey
119 S11 **Kalanchak** Khersons'ka Oblast', S Ukraine
175 Pp15 **Kalao, Pulau** *island* Kepulauan Bonerate, W Indonesia
175 Q15 **Kalaotoa, Pulau** *island* W Indonesia
161 J24 **Kala Oya** ≈ NW Sri Lanka
Kalarash *see* Călăraşi
95 H17 **Kälarne** Jämtland, C Sweden
149 V15 **Kalar Rūd** ≈ SE Iran
178 Ii9 **Kalasin** *var.* Muang Kalasin. Kalasin, E Thailand
155 O8 **Kalāt** *Per.* Qalāt. Zābul, S Afghanistan
155 O11 **Kalāt** *var.* Kelat, Khelat. Baluchistān, SW Pakistan
117 J14 **Kalathriá, Ákra** *headland* Samothráki, NE Greece
200 R17 **Kalau** *island* Tongatapu Group, SE Tonga
40 E9 **Kalaupapa** Molokai, Hawaii, USA, C Pacific Ocean
131 N13 **Kalaus** ≈ SW Russian Federation
Kalávrita *see* Kalávryta
117 E19 **Kalávryta** *var.* Kalávrita. Dytikí Ellás, S Greece
147 Y10 **Kalbān** W Oman
188 H11 **Kalbarri** Western Australia
151 X10 **Kalbinskiy Khrebet** *Kaz.* Qalba Zhotasy. ▲ E Kazakhstan
150 G10 **Kaldygayty** ≈ W Kazakhstan
142 I12 **Kalecik** Ankara, N Turkey
175 R13 **Kaledupa, Pulau** *island* Kepulauan Tukangbesi, C Indonesia
81 O19 **Kalehe** Sud Kivu, E Zaire
81 P22 **Kalemie** *prev.* Albertville. Shaba, SE Zaire
177 Ff3 **Kalemyo** Sagaing, W Myanmar
84 H12 **Kalene Hill** North Western, NW Zambia
Kale Sultanie *see* Çanakkale
128 I7 **Kalevala** Respublika Kareliya, NW Russian Federation
177 Ff3 **Kalewa** Sagaing, C Myanmar
Kalgan *see* Zhangjiakou
41 Q12 **Kalgin Island** *island* Alaska, USA
188 L12 **Kalgoorlie** Western Australia
Kali *see* Sārda
117 E17 **Kaliakoúda** ▲ C Greece
116 O8 **Kaliakra, Nos** *headland* NE Bulgaria
117 F19 **Kaliánoi** Pelopónnisos, S Greece
179 Q13 **Kalibo** Panay Island, C Philippines
117 N24 **Kalí Límni** ▲ Kárpathos, SE Greece
81 N20 **Kalima** Maniema, E Zaire
174 M8 **Kalimantan** *Eng.* Indonesian Borneo. *geopolitical region* Borneo, C Indonesia
174 L8 **Kalimantan Barat** *off.* Propinsi Kalimantan Barat, *Eng.* West Borneo, West Kalimantan. ◆ *province* N Indonesia
174 Mm11 **Kalimantan Selatan** *off.* Propinsi Kalimantan Selatan, *Eng.* South Borneo, South Kalimantan. ◆ *province* N Indonesia
174 M9 **Kalimantan Tengah** *off.* Propinsi Kalimantan Tengah, *Eng.* Central Borneo, Central Kalimantan. ◆ *province* N Indonesia
175 N7 **Kalimantan Timur** *off.* Propinsi Kalimantan Timur, *Eng.* East Borneo, East Kalimantan. ◆ *province* N Indonesia
Kálimnos *see* Kálymnos
159 S12 **Kālimpang** West Bengal, NE India
Kalinin *see* Tver', Russian Federation
Kalinin *see* Boldumsaz, Turkmenistan
Kalininabad *see* Kalininobod
130 B3 **Kaliningrad** Kaliningradskaya Oblast', W Russian Federation
Kaliningrad *see* Kaliningradskaya Oblast'
130 A3 **Kaliningradskaya Oblast'** *var.* Kaliningrad. ◆ *province and enclave* W Russian Federation
Kalinino *see* Tashir
153 P14 **Kalininobod** *Rus.* Kalininabad. SW Tajikistan
131 O8 **Kalininsk** Saratovskaya Oblast', W Russian Federation
Kalininsk *see* Boldumsaz
Kalinisk *see* Cupcina
121 M19 **Kalinkavichy** *Rus.* Kalinkovichi. Homyel'skaya Voblasts', SE Belarus
Kalinkovichi *see* Kalinkavichy
83 G18 **Kaliro** SE Uganda
Kalisch/Kalisch/Kalish/ Kaliskie, Województwo *see* Kalisz
35 O7 **Kalispell** Montana, NW USA
112 I13 **Kalisz** *Ger.* Kalisch, *Rus.* Kalish; *anc.* Calisia. Kalisz, C Poland
112 H13 **Kalisz** *off.* Województwo Kaliskie, *Ger.* Kalisch. ◆ *province* C Poland
112 F9 **Kalisz Pomorski** *Ger.* Kallies. Koszalin, NW Poland
130 M10 **Kalitva** ≈ SW Russian Federation
83 F21 **Kaliua** Tabora, C Tanzania
94 K13 **Kalix** Norrbotten, N Sweden
94 K12 **Kalixälven** ≈ N Sweden
94 J11 **Kalixfors** Norrbotten, N Sweden
151 T8 **Kalkaman** Pavlodar, NE Kazakhstan
Kalkandelen *see* Tetovo
189 O4 **Kalkarindji** Northern Territory, N Australia
33 P6 **Kalkaska** Michigan, N USA
95 F16 **Kall** Jämtland, C Sweden
201 X2 **Kallalen** *var.* Calalen. *island* Ratak Chain, SE Marshall Islands
120 J5 **Kallaste** *Ger.* Krasnogor. Tartumaa, SE Estonia
95 N16 **Kallavesi** ◎ SE Finland
117 F17 **Kallídromo** ▲ C Greece
Kallies *see* Kalisz Pomorski
97 M22 **Kallinge** Blekinge, S Sweden
117 L16 **Kalloní** Lésvos, E Greece
95 F16 **Kallsjön** ◎ C Sweden
97 N21 **Kalmar** *var.* Calmar. Kalmar, S Sweden
97 M19 **Kalmar** *var.* Calmar. ◆ *county* S Sweden
97 N20 **Kalmarsund** *strait* S Sweden
154 L16 **Kalmat, Khor** *Eng.* Kalmat Lagoon. *lagoon* SW Pakistan
Kalmat Lagoon *see* Kalmat, Khor
119 X9 **Kal'mius** ≈ E Ukraine
101 H15 **Kalmthout** Antwerpen, N Belgium
Kalmykia/Kalmykiya-Khal'mg Tangch, Respublika *see* Kalmykiya, Respublika
131 O12 **Kalmykiya, Respublika** *var.* Respublika Kalmykiya-Khal'mg Tangch, *Eng.* Kalmykia; *prev.* Kalmytskaya ASSR. ◆ *autonomous republic* SW Russian Federation
Kalmytskaya ASSR *see* Kalmykiya, Respublika
120 F9 **Kalnciems** Jelgava, C Latvia
116 L10 **Kalnitsa** ≈ SE Bulgaria
113 J24 **Kalocsa** Bács-Kiskun, S Hungary
116 J9 **Kalofer** Plovdivska Oblast, C Bulgaria
40 E10 **Kalohi Channel** *channel* C Pacific Ocean
85 I16 **Kalomo** Southern, S Zambia
31 X14 **Kalona** Iowa, C USA
117 K22 **Kalotási, Ákra** *headland* Amorgós, Kykládes, Greece, Aegean Sea
158 J8 **Kalpa** Himāchal Pradesh, N India
117 C15 **Kalpáki** Ípeiros, W Greece
161 C22 **Kalpeni Island** *island* Lakshadweep, India, N Indian Ocean
158 K13 **Kālpi** Uttar Pradesh, N India
164 G7 **Kalpin** Xinjiang Uygur Zizhiqu, NW China
152 K8 **Kalquduq** *Rus.* Kulkuduk. Nawoiy Wiloyati, N Uzbekistan
155 P16 **Kalri Lake** ◎ SE Pakistan
149 R5 **Kāl Shūr** N Iran
41 N11 **Kalskag** Alaska, USA
41 O9 **Kaltag** Alaska, USA
110 H7 **Kaltbrunn** Sankt Gallen, NE Switzerland
Kaltdorf *see* Pruszków
79 X14 **Kaltungo** Bauchi, E Nigeria
130 K4 **Kaluga** Kaluzhskaya Oblast', W Russian Federation
161 J26 **Kalu Ganga** ≈ S Sri Lanka
84 J13 **Kalulushi** Copperbelt, C Zambia
188 M2 **Kalumburu** Western Australia
97 H23 **Kalundborg** Vestsjælland, E Denmark
84 K11 **Kalungwishi** ≈ N Zambia
155 T8 **Kalūr Kot** Punjab, E Pakistan
118 I6 **Kalush** *Pol.* Kałusz. Ivano-Frankivs'ka Oblast', W Ukraine
Kałusz *see* Kalush
112 N11 **Kałuszyn** Siedlce, E Poland
161 J26 **Kalutara** Western Province, SW Sri Lanka
Kaluwawa *see* Fergusson Island
130 I5 **Kaluzhskaya Oblast'** ◆ *province* W Russian Federation
121 E14 **Kalvarija** *Pol.* Kalwaria. Marijampolė, S Lithuania
95 K15 **Kälviä** Vaasa, W Finland
111 U6 **Kalwang** Steiermark, E Austria
Kalwaria *see* Kalvarija
160 D13 **Kalyān** Mahārāshtra, W India
128 K16 **Kalyazin** Tverskaya Oblast', W Russian Federation
117 D18 **Kalydón** *anc.* Calydon. *site of ancient city* Dytikí Ellás, C Greece
117 M21 **Kálymnos** *var.* Kálimnos. Kálymnos, Dodekánisos, Greece, Aegean Sea
117 M21 **Kálymnos** *var.* Kálimnos. *island* Dodekánisos, Greece, Aegean Sea
119 O5 **Kalynivka** Kyyivs'ka Oblast', N Ukraine
119 N6 **Kalynivka** Vinnyts'ka Oblast', C Ukraine
44 M10 **Kama** *var.* Cama. Región Autónoma Atlántico Sur, SE Nicaragua
125 E9 **Kama** ≈ NW Russian Federation
172 N12 **Kamaishi** *var.* Kamaisi. Iwate, Honshū, C Japan
Kamaisi *see* Kamaishi
120 H13 **Kamajai** Molėtai, E Lithuania
120 H11 **Kamajai** Rokiškis, NE Lithuania
171 Jj17 **Kamakura** Kanagawa, Honshū, S Japan
155 U9 **Kamālia** Punjab, NE Pakistan
85 I14 **Kamalondo** North Western, NW Zambia
142 I13 **Kaman** Kirşehir, C Turkey
81 O20 **Kamanyola** Sud Kivu, E Zaire
147 N14 **Kamarān** *island* W Yemen
57 R9 **Kamarang** W Guyana
161 I14 **Kāmāreddi** *var.* Kamareddy. Andhra Pradesh, C India
Kamareddy *see* Kāmāreddi
Kama Reservoir *see* Kamskoye Vodokhranilishche
154 K13 **Kamarod** Baluchistān, SW Pakistan
175 R13 **Kamaru** Pulau Buton, C Indonesia
153 N12 **Kamashi** Qashqadaryo Wiloyati, S Uzbekistan
79 S13 **Kamba** Kebbi, NW Nigeria
Kambaeng Petch *see* Kamphaeng Phet
188 L12 **Kambalda** Western Australia
155 P13 **Kambar** *var.* Qambar. Sind, SE Pakistan
Kambara *see* Kabara
78 I14 **Kambia** W Sierra Leone
175 S16 **Kambing, Pulau** *island* S Indonesia
Kambos *see* Kámpos
81 N25 **Kambove** Shaba, SE Zaire
Kambryk *see* Cambrai
127 Pp10 **Kamchatka** ≈ E Russian Federation
Kamchatka *see* Kamchatka, Poluostrov
Kamchatka Basin *see* Komandorskaya Basin
127 P11 **Kamchatka, Poluostrov** *Eng.* Kamchatka. *peninsula* E Russian Federation
127 Pp11 **Kamchatskaya Oblast'** ◆ *province* E Russian Federation
127 Pp10 **Kamchatskiy Zaliv** *gulf* E Russian Federation
116 N9 **Kamchiya** ≈ E Bulgaria
116 L9 **Kamchiya, Yazovir** ◎ E Bulgaria
Kamdesh *see* Kāmdeysh
155 T4 **Kāmdeysh** *var.* Kamdesh. Kunar, E Afghanistan
170 Ee14 **Kamega-mori** ▲ Shikoku, SW Japan
120 M13 **Kamen'** *Rus.* Kamen'. Vitsyebskaya Voblasts', N Belarus
Kamenets *see* Kamyanyets
Kamenets-Podol'skaya Oblast' *see* Khmel'nyts'ka Oblast'
Kamenets-Podol'skiy *see* Kam"yanets'-Podil's'kyy
115 Q18 **Kamenica** NE FYR Macedonia
114 A11 **Kamenjak, Rt** *headland* NW Croatia
150 F8 **Kamenka** Zapadnyy Kazakhstan, NW Kazakhstan
129 O6 **Kamenka** Arkhangel'skaya Oblast', NW Russian Federation
130 L8 **Kamenka** Penzenskaya Oblast', W Russian Federation
131 O6 **Kamenka** Voronezhskaya Oblast', W Russian Federation
Kamenka *see* Camenca, Moldova
Kamenka *see* Kam"yanka, Ukraine
Kamenka-Bugskaya *see* Kam"yanka-Buz'ka
Kamenka Dneprovskaya *see* Kam"yanka-Dniprovs'ka
Kamen Kashirskiy *see* Kamin'-Kashyrs'kyy
126 Gg14 **Kamen'-na-Obi** Altayskiy Kray, S Russian Federation
130 L15 **Kamennomostskiy** Respublika Adygeya, SW Russian Federation
130 L11 **Kamenolomni** Rostovskaya Oblast', SW Russian Federation
131 P8 **Kamenskiy** Saratovskaya Oblast', W Russian Federation
127 P7 **Kamenskoye** Koryakskiy Avtonomnyy Okrug, E Russian Federation
Kamenskoye *see* Dniprodzerzhyns'k
130 L11 **Kamensk-Shakhtinskiy** Rostovskaya Oblast', SW Russian Federation
125 Ee11 **Kamensk-Ural'skiy** Sverdlovskaya Oblast', C Russian Federation
103 P15 **Kamenz** Sachsen, E Germany
171 Gg14 **Kameoka** Kyōto, Honshū, SW Japan
130 M3 **Kameshkovo** Vladimirskaya Oblast', W Russian Federation
171 H15 **Kameyama** Mie, Honshū, SW Japan
170 Cc10 **Kami-Agata** Nagasaki, Tsushima, SW Japan
35 N10 **Kamiah** Idaho, NW USA
Kamień Koszyrski *see* Kamin'-Kashyrs'kyy
112 H9 **Kamień Krajeński** *Ger.* Kamin in Westpreussen. Bydgoszcz, NW Poland
113 F15 **Kamienna Góra** *Ger.* Landeshut, Landeshut in Schlesien. Jelenia Góra, SW Poland
112 D8 **Kamień Pomorski** *Ger.* Cummin in Pommern. Szczecin, NW Poland
172 N7 **Kamiiso** Hokkaidō, NE Japan
81 L22 **Kamiji** Kasai Oriental, S Zaire
172 Pp5 **Kamikawa** Hokkaidō, NE Japan
170 Bb15 **Kami-Koshiki-jima** *island* SW Japan
81 M23 **Kamina** Shaba, S Zaire
Kamina *see* Kaintiba
44 C6 **Kaminaljuyú** *ruins* Guatemala, C Guatemala
Kamin in Westpreussen *see* Kamień Krajeński
118 J2 **Kamin'-Kashyrs'kyy** *Pol.* Kamień Koszyrski, *Rus.* Kamen Kashirskiy. Volyns'ka Oblast', NW Ukraine
172 N6 **Kaminokuni** Hokkaidō, NE Japan
171 Ll13 **Kaminoyama** Yamagata, Honshū, C Japan
171 Ii14 **Kamioka** Gifu, Honshū, SW Japan
41 Q13 **Kamishak Bay** *bay* Alaska, USA
172 Pp6 **Kami-Shihoro** Hokkaidō, NE Japan
Kamishli *see* Al Qāmishlī
Kamissar *see* Kamsar
170 Cc10 **Kami-Tsushima** Nagasaki, Tsushima, SW Japan
81 O20 **Kamituga** Sud Kivu, E Zaire
170 B17 **Kamiyaku** Kagoshima, Yaku-shima, SW Japan
9 N16 **Kamloops** British Columbia, SW Canada
109 G25 **Kamma** Sicilia, Italy, C Mediterranean Sea
199 Ii4 **Kammu Seamount** *undersea feature* N Pacific Ocean
111 U11 **Kamnik** *Ger.* Stein. C Slovenia
Kamniške Alpe *see* Savinjske Alpe
171 Kk13 **Kamo** Niigata, Honshū, C Japan
171 K17 **Kamogawa** Chiba, Honshū, S Japan
155 W8 **Kāmoke** Punjab, E Pakistan
84 L13 **Kamoto** Eastern, E Zambia
111 V3 **Kamp** ≈ N Austria
83 F18 **Kampala** ● (Uganda) S Uganda
174 H8 **Kampar, Sungai** ≈ Sumatera, W Indonesia
174 Ii10 **Kampa, Teluk** *bay* Pulau Bangka, W Indonesia
100 L9 **Kampen** Overijssel, E Netherlands
81 N20 **Kampene** Maniema, E Zaire
31 Q9 **Kampeska, Lake** ◎ South Dakota, N USA
178 Gg9 **Kamphaeng Phet** *var.* Kambaeng Petch. Kamphaeng Phet, W Thailand
Kampo *see* Campo, Cameroon
Kampo *see* Ntem, Cameroon/Equatorial Guinea
178 J13 **Kâmpóng Cham** *prev.* Kompong Cham. Kâmpóng Cham, C Cambodia
178 J13 **Kâmpóng Chhnăng** *prev.* Kompong. Kâmpóng Chhnăng, C Cambodia
178 Ii12 **Kâmpóng Khleăng** *prev.* Kompong Kleang. Siĕmréab, NW Cambodia
178 I14 **Kâmpóng Saôm** *prev.* Kompong Som, Sihanoukville. Kâmpóng Saôm, SW Cambodia
178 J13 **Kâmpóng Spoe** *prev.* Kompong Speu. Kâmpóng Spœ, S Cambodia
124 N3 **Kámpos** *var.* Kambos. NW Cyprus
178 Ii14 **Kâmpôt** Kâmpôt, SW Cambodia
Kamptee *see* Kāmthi
79 O14 **Kampti** SW Burkina
Kampuchea *see* Cambodia
174 L15 **Kampung Sirik** Sarawak, East Malaysia
176 Y13 **Kampung, Sungai** ≈ Irian Jaya, E Indonesia
176 Vv12 **Kamrau, Teluk** *bay* Irian Jaya, E Indonesia
9 V15 **Kamsack** Saskatchewan, S Canada
78 H13 **Kamsar** *var.* Kamissar. Guinée-Maritime, W Guinea
131 R4 **Kamskoye Ust'ye** Respublika Tatarstan, W Russian Federation
129 U14 **Kamskoye Vodokhranilishche** *var.* Kama Reservoir. ▣ NW Russian Federation
160 I12 **Kāmthi** *prev.* Kamptee. Mahārāshtra, C India
Kamuela *see* Waimea
172 Nn5 **Kamuenai** Hokkaidō, NE Japan
172 P7 **Kamui-dake** ▲ Hokkaidō, NE Japan
172 Nn4 **Kamui-misaki** *headland* Hokkaidō, NE Japan
45 O15 **Kámuk, Cerro** ▲ SE Costa Rica
176 Vv9 **Kamundan, Sungai** ≈ Irian Jaya, E Indonesia

◆ Country
● Country Capital
◇ Dependent Territory
○ Dependent Territory Capital
◆ Administrative Region
✕ International Airport
▲ Mountain
▲▲ Mountain Range
Volcano
≈ River
◎ Lake
▣ Reservoir

176 *X12* **Kamura, Sungai** ≈ Irian Jaya, E Indonesia
118 *K7* **Kam"yanets'-Podil's'kyy** ***Rus.*** Kamenets-Podol'skiy. Khmel'nyts'ka Oblast', W Ukraine
119 *Q6* **Kam"yanka** ***Rus.*** Kamenka. Cherkas'ka Oblast', C Ukraine
118 *I5* **Kam"yanka-Buz'ka** ***Rus.*** Kamenka-Bugskaya. L'vivs'ka Oblast', NW Ukraine
119 *T9* **Kam"yanka-Dniprovs'ka** ***Rus.*** Kamenka Dneprovskaya. Zaporiz'ka Oblast', SE Ukraine
121 *F19* **Kamyanyets** ***Rus.*** Kamenets. Brestskaya Voblasts', SW Belarus
131 *P9* **Kamyshin** Volgogradskaya Oblast', SW Russian Federation
125 *Ee11* **Kamyshlov** Sverdlovskaya Oblast', C Russian Federation
131 *Q13* **Kamyzyak** Astrakhanskaya Oblast', SW Russian Federation
10 *K8* **Kanaaupscow** ≈ Québec, C Canada
38 *K8* **Kanab** Utah, W USA
38 *K9* **Kanab Creek** ≈ Arizona/Utah, SW USA
197 *J13* **Kanacea** ***prev.*** Kanathea. Taveuni, N Fiji
197 *K14* **Kanacea** *island* Lau Group, E Fiji
40 *G17* **Kanaga Island** *island* Aleutian Islands, Alaska, USA
40 *G17* **Kanaga Volcano** ▲ Kanaga Island, Alaska, USA
171 *J17* **Kanagawa** ***off.*** Kanagawa-ken. ◆ *prefecture* Honshū, S Japan
11 *Q8* **Kanairiktok** ≈ Newfoundland and Labrador, E Canada
Kanaky *see* New Caledonia
81 *K22* **Kananga** ***prev.*** Luluabourg. Kasai Occidental, S Zaire
Kananur *see* Cannanore
Kanara *see* Karnātaka
38 *J7* **Kanarraville** Utah, W USA
131 *Q4* **Kanash** Chuvashskaya Respublika, W Russian Federation
Kanathea *see* Kanacea
23 *Q4* **Kanawha River** ≈ West Virginia, NE USA
171 *I15* **Kanayama** Gifu, Honshū, SW Japan
171 *I12* **Kanazawa** Ishikawa, Honshū, SW Japan
177 *G4* **Kanbalu** Sagaing, C Myanmar
177 *Ff8* **Kanbe** Yangon, SW Myanmar
178 *H11* **Kanchanaburi** Kanchanaburi, W Thailand
Kānchenjunga *see* Kangchenjunga
151 *V11* **Kanchingiz, Khrebet** ▲▲ E Kazakhstan
161 *J19* **Kānchīpuram** ***prev.*** Conjeeveram. Tamil Nādu, SE India
155 *N8* **Kandahār** ***Per.*** Qandahār. Kandahār, S Afghanistan
155 *N9* **Kandahār** ***Per.*** Qandahār. ◆ *province* SE Afghanistan
Kandalakša *see* Kandalaksha
128 *I5* **Kandalaksha** ***var.*** Kandalakša, ***Fin.*** Kantalahti. Murmanskaya Oblast', NW Russian Federation
Kandalaksha Gulf/Kandalakshskaya Guba *see* Kandalakshskiy Zaliv
128 *K6* **Kandalakshskiy Zaliv** ***var.*** Kandalakshskaya Guba, ***Eng.*** Kandalaksha Gulf. *bay* NW Russian Federation
Kandalangodi *see* Kandalengoti
85 *G17* **Kandalengoti** ***var.*** Kandalangodi. Ngamiland, NW Botswana
175 *N10* **Kandangan** Borneo, C Indonesia
Kandau *see* Kandava
120 *E8* **Kandava** ***Ger.*** Kandau. Tukums, W Latvia
Kandavu *see* Kadavu
79 *R14* **Kandé** ***var.*** Kanté. NE Togo
103 *F23* **Kandel** ▲ SW Germany
194 *G12* **Kandep** Enga, W PNG
155 *R12* **Kandhkot** Sind, SE Pakistan
79 *S13* **Kandi** N Benin
155 *P14* **Kandiāro** Sind, SE Pakistan
142 *F11* **Kandıra** Kocaeli, NW Turkey
191 *S8* **Kandos** New South Wales, SE Australia
154 *M16* **Kandrāch** ***var.*** Kanrach. Baluchistān, SW Pakistan
180 *I4* **Kandreho** Mahajanga, C Madagascar
194 *M12* **Kandrian** New Britain, E PNG
Kandukur *see* Kondukūr
161 *K25* **Kandy** Central Province, C Sri Lanka
20 *D12* **Kane** Pennsylvania, NE USA
66 *I11* **Kane Fracture Zone** *tectonic feature* NW Atlantic Ocean
Kanëka *see* Kanëvka
80 *G9* **Kanem** ***off.*** Préfecture du Kanem. ◆ *prefecture* W Chad
40 *D9* **Kaneohe** ***Haw.*** Kāne'ohe. Oahu, Hawaii, USA, C Pacific Ocean
Kanestron, Akra *see* Palioúri, Ákra
Kanëv *see* Kaniv
128 *M5* **Kanëvka** ***var.*** Kanëka. Murmanskaya Oblast', NW Russian Federation
130 *K13* **Kanevskaya** Krasnodarskiy Kray, SW Russian Federation
Kanevskoye Vodokhranilishche *see* Kanivs'ke Vodoskhovyshche
171 *Ll12* **Kaneyama** Yamagata, Honshū, C Japan
85 *G20* **Kang** Kgalagadi, C Botswana
78 *L13* **Kangaba** Koulikoro, SW Mali
142 *M13* **Kangal** Sivas, C Turkey
149 *O13* **Kangān** Būshehr, S Iran
149 *S15* **Kangān** Hormozgān, SE Iran
173 *G2* **Kangar** Perlis, Peninsular Malaysia
78 *L13* **Kangaré** Sikasso, S Mali
190 *F10* **Kangaroo Island** *island* South Australia
95 *M17* **Kangasniemi** Mikkeli, SE Finland
148 *K6* **Kangāvar** ***var.*** Kangāwar. Kermānshāhān, W Iran
Kangāwar *see* Kangāvar
159 *S11* **Kangchenjunga** ***var.*** Kānchenjunga. ▲ NE India
166 *G9* **Kangding** Sichuan, C China
175 *Nn14* **Kangean, Kepulauan** *island group* S Indonesia
175 *N14* **Kangean, Pulau** *island* Kepulauan Kangean, S Indonesia
69 *U8* **Kangen** ***var.*** Kengen. ≈ SE Sudan
207 *Q15* **Kangertittivaq** ***Dan.*** Scoresby Sund. *fjord* E Greenland
178 *H2* **Kangfang** Kachin State, N Myanmar
176 *Z13* **Kanggup** Irian Jaya, E Indonesia
169 *X12* **Kanggye** N North Korea
207 *P15* **Kangikajik** ***var.*** Kap Brewster. *headland* E Greenland
11 *N5* **Kangiqsualujjuaq** ***prev.*** George River, Port-Nouveau-Québec. Québec, E Canada
10 *L2* **Kangiqsujuaq** ***prev.*** Maricourt, Wakeham Bay. Québec, NE Canada
10 *M4* **Kangirsuk** ***prev.*** Bellin, Payne. Québec, E Canada
164 *J15* **Kangmar** Xizang Zizhiqu, W China
164 *M16* **Kangmar** Xizang Zizhiqu, W China
169 *Y14* **Kangnŭng** ***Jap.*** Kōryō. NE South Korea
81 *D18* **Kango** Estuaire, NW Gabon
158 *I7* **Kāngra** Himāchal Pradesh, NW India
159 *Q16* **Kangsabati Reservoir** ▣ N India
165 *O17* **Kangto** ▲ China/India
165 *W12* **Kang Xian** ***var.*** Zuitaizi. Gansu, C China
177 *Ff4* **Kani** Sagaing, C Myanmar
78 *M15* **Kani** NW Ivory Coast
81 *M23* **Kaniama** Shaba, S Zaire
Kanibadam *see* Konibodom
175 *O2* **Kanibongan** Sabah, East Malaysia
193 *F17* **Kaniere** West Coast, South Island, NZ
193 *G17* **Kaniere, Lake** ◎ South Island, NZ
196 *E17* **Kanifaay** Yap, W Micronesia
129 *O4* **Kanin Kamen'** ▲▲ NW Russian Federation
129 *N3* **Kanin Nos** Nenetskiy Avtonomnyy Okrug, NW Russian Federation
129 *N3* **Kanin Nos, Mys** *headland* NW Russian Federation
129 *O5* **Kanin, Poluostrov** *peninsula* NW Russian Federation
145 *V8* **Kānī Sakht** E Iraq
145 *T3* **Kānī Sulaymān** N Iraq
172 *N8* **Kanita** Aomori, Honshū, C Japan
119 *Q5* **Kaniv** ***Rus.*** Kanëv. Cherkas'ka Oblast', C Ukraine
190 *K11* **Kaniva** Victoria, SE Australia
119 *Q5* **Kanivs'ke Vodoskhovyshche** ***Rus.*** Kanevskoye Vodokhranilishche. ▣ C Ukraine
114 *L8* **Kanjiža** ***Ger.*** Altkanischa, ***Hung.*** Magyarkanizsa, Ókanizsa; ***prev.*** Stara Kanjiža. Serbia, N Yugoslavia
95 *K18* **Kankaanpää** Turku-Pori, SW Finland
32 *M12* **Kankakee** Illinois, N USA
33 *O11* **Kankakee River** ≈ Illinois/Indiana, N USA
78 *K14* **Kankan** Haute-Guinée, E Guinea
160 *K13* **Kānker** Madhya Pradesh, C India
78 *J10* **Kankossa** Assaba, S Mauritania
178 *Gg13* **Kanmaw Kyun** ***var.*** Kisseraing, Kithareng. *island* Mergui Archipelago, S Myanmar
170 *E13* **Kanmuri-yama** ▲ Kyūshū, SW Japan
23 *R10* **Kannapolis** North Carolina, SE USA
95 *L16* **Kannonkoski** Keski-Suomi, C Finland
Kannur *see* Cannanore
95 *K15* **Kannus** Vaasa, W Finland
79 *V13* **Kano** Kano, N Nigeria
79 *V13* **Kano** ◆ *state* N Nigeria
79 *V13* **Kano** ✕ Kano, N Nigeria
170 *F14* **Kan'onji** ***var.*** Kanonzi. Kagawa, Shikoku, SW Japan
Kanonzi *see* Kan'onji
28 *M5* **Kanopolis Lake** ▣ Kansas, C USA
38 *K5* **Kanosh** Utah, W USA
174 *Ll6* **Kanowit** Sarawak, East Malaysia
170 *Bb17* **Kanoya** Kagoshima, Kyūshū, SW Japan
158 *L13* **Kānpur** ***Eng.*** Cawnpore. Uttar Pradesh, N India
Kanrach *see* Kandrāch
171 *Gg15* **Kansai** ✕ (Ōsaka) Ōsaka, Honshū, SW Japan
29 *R9* **Kansas** Oklahoma, C USA
28 *L5* **Kansas** ***off.*** State of Kansas; also known as Jayhawker State, Sunflower State. ◆ *state* C USA
29 *R4* **Kansas City** Kansas, C USA
29 *R4* **Kansas City** Missouri, C USA
29 *R3* **Kansas City** ✕ Missouri, C USA
29 *P4* **Kansas River** ≈ Kansas, C USA
126 *I14* **Kansk** Krasnoyarskiy Kray, S Russian Federation
Kansu *see* Gansu
153 *V7* **Kant** Chuyskaya Oblast', N Kyrgyzstan
Kantalahti *see* Kandalaksha
178 *Gg16* **Kantang** ***var.*** Ban Kantang. Trang, SW Thailand
117 *H25* **Kántanos** Kríti, Greece, E Mediterranean Sea
79 *R12* **Kantchari** E Burkina
Kanté *see* Kandé
Kantemir *see* Cantemir
130 *L9* **Kantemirovka** Voronezhskaya Oblast', W Russian Federation
178 *J11* **Kantharalak** Si Sa Ket, E Thailand
Kantipur *see* Kathmandu
41 *Q9* **Kantishna River** ≈ Alaska, USA
171 *K16* **Kantō** *physical region* Honshū, SW Japan
203 *S3* **Kanton** ***var.*** Abariringa, Canton Island; ***prev.*** Mary Island. *atoll* Phoenix Islands, C Kiribati
171 *Jj15* **Kantō-sanchi** ▲▲ Honshū, S Japan
99 *C20* **Kanturk** ***Ir.*** Ceann Toirc. SW Ireland
57 *T11* **Kanuku Mountains** ▲▲ S Guyana
171 *Kk15* **Kanuma** Tochigi, Honshū, S Japan
85 *H20* **Kanye** Southern, SE Botswana
85 *H17* **Kanyu** Ngamiland, C Botswana
177 *G7* **Kanyutkwin** Pegu, C Myanmar
81 *M24* **Kanzenze** Shaba, SE Zaire
200 *Ss13* **Kao** *island* Kotu Group, W Tonga
167 *S14* **Kaohsiung** ***var.*** Gaoxiong, ***Jap.*** Takao, Takow. S Taiwan
167 *S14* **Kaohsiung** ✕ S Taiwan
Kaokaona *see* Kirakira
85 *B17* **Kaoko Veld** ▲▲ N Namibia
78 *G11* **Kaolack** ***var.*** Kaolak. W Senegal
Kaolak *see* Kaolack
Kaolan *see* Lanzhou
195 *W15* **Kaolo** San Jorge, N Solomon Islands
85 *H14* **Kaoma** Western, W Zambia
40 *B8* **Kapaa** ***Haw.*** Kapa'a. Kauai, Hawaii, USA, C Pacific Ocean
115 *J16* **Kapa Moračka** ▲ SW Yugoslavia
143 *V13* **Kapan** ***Rus.*** Kafan; ***prev.*** Ghap'an. SE Armenia
84 *L13* **Kapandashila** Northern, NE Zambia
81 *L23* **Kapanga** Shaba, S Zaire
151 *U15* **Kapchagay** ***Kaz.*** Kapshaghay. Almaty, SE Kazakhstan
151 *V15* **Kapchagayskoye Vodokhranilishche** ***Kaz.*** Qapshagay Böyeni. ▣ SE Kazakhstan
101 *F15* **Kapelle** Zeeland, SW Netherlands
101 *G16* **Kapellen** Antwerpen, N Belgium
97 *P15* **Kapellskär** Stockholm, C Sweden
83 *H18* **Kapenguria** Rift Valley, W Kenya
111 *V6* **Kapfenberg** Steiermark, C Austria
85 *J14* **Kapiri Mposhi** Central, C Zambia
155 *R4* **Kāpīsā** ◆ *province* E Afghanistan
10 *G10* **Kapiskau** ≈ Ontario, C Canada
192 *K13* **Kapiti Island** *island* C NZ
80 *K9* **Kapka, Massif du** ▲▲ E Chad
Kaplamada *see* Kaubalatmada, Gunung
24 *H9* **Kaplan** Louisiana, S USA
152 *E9* **Kaplangky, Plato** *ridge* Turkmenistan/Uzbekistan
113 *D19* **Kaplice** ***Ger.*** Kaplitz. Jižní Čechy, S Czech Republic
Kaplitz *see* Kaplice
Kapoche *see* Capoche
176 *U10* **Kapocol** Irian Jaya, E Indonesia
178 *Gg14* **Kapoe** Ranong, SW Thailand
Kapoeas *see* Kapuas, Sungai
83 *G15* **Kapoeta** Eastern Equatoria, SE Sudan
113 *I25* **Kapos** ≈ S Hungary
113 *H25* **Kaposvár** Somogy, SW Hungary
96 *H13* **Kapp** Oppland, S Norway
102 *I7* **Kappeln** Schleswig-Holstein, N Germany
Kaproncza *see* Koprivnica
111 *P7* **Kaprun** Salzburg, C Austria
Kapshaghay *see* Kapchagay
Kapstad *see* Cape Town
Kapsukas *see* Marijampolė
176 *Yy10* **Kaptiau** Irian Jaya, E Indonesia
121 *L19* **Kaptsevichy** ***Rus.*** Koptsevichi. Homyel'skaya Voblasts', SE Belarus
Kapuas Hulu, Banjaran/ Kapuas Hulu, Pegunungan *see* Kapuas Mountains
174 *M7* **Kapuas Mountains** ***Ind.*** Banjaran Kapuas Hulu, Pegunungan Kapuas Hulu. ▲▲ Indonesia/Malaysia
174 *Kk8* **Kapuas, Sungai** ≈ Borneo, N Indonesia
175 *N10* **Kapuas, Sungai** ***prev.*** Kapoeas. ≈ Borneo, C Indonesia
190 *J9* **Kapunda** South Australia
158 *H8* **Kapūrthala** Punjab, N India
174 *L14* **Kapur Utara, Pegugungan** ▲▲ Jawa, S Indonesia
10 *G12* **Kapuskasing** Ontario, S Canada
12 *D6* **Kapuskasing** ≈ Ontario, S Canada
131 *P11* **Kapustin Yar** Astrakhanskaya Oblast', SW Russian Federation
84 *K11* **Kaputa** Northern, NE Zambia
113 *G22* **Kapuvár** Győr-Moson-Sopron, NW Hungary
Kapydzhik, Gora *see* Qapiciğ Dağı
121 *J17* **Kapyl'** ***Rus.*** Kopyl'. Minskaya Voblasts', C Belarus
45 *N9* **Kara** ***var.*** Cara. Región Autónoma Atlántico Sur, E Nicaragua
79 *R14* **Kara** ***var.*** Lama-Kara. NE Togo
79 *Q14* **Kara** ≈ N Togo
153 *U7* **Kara-Balta** Chuyskaya Oblast', N Kyrgyzstan
150 *G11* **Karabau** Atyrau, W Kazakhstan
152 *E7* **Karabaur', Uval** ***Kaz.*** Korabavur Pastligi, ***Uzb.*** Qorabowur Kirlari. *physical region* Kazakhstan/Uzbekistan
152 *L13* **Karabekaul** ***var.*** Garabekevyul, ***Turkm.*** Garabekewül. Lebapskiy Velayat, E Turkmenistan
152 *K15* **Karabil', Vozvyshennost'** ▲▲ S Turkmenistan
152 *A9* **Kara-Bogaz-Gol** ***Turkm.*** Garabogazköl. Balkanskiy Velayat, NW Turkmenistan
152 *B9* **Kara-Bogaz-Gol, Zaliv** *bay* NW Turkmenistan
151 *R15* **Karaboget** ***Kaz.*** Qaraböget. Zhambyl, S Kazakhstan
142 *H11* **Karabük** Zonguldak, N Turkey
126 *Ii13* **Karabula** Krasnoyarskiy Kray, C Russian Federation
151 *V14* **Karabulak** ***Kaz.*** Qarabulaq. Taldykorgan, SE Kazakhstan
151 *Y11* **Karabulak** ***Kaz.*** Qarabulaq. Vostochnyy Kazakhstan, E Kazakhstan
151 *Q17* **Karabulak** ***Kaz.*** Qarabulaq. Yuzhnyy Kazakhstan, S Kazakhstan
142 *C17* **Kara Burnu** *headland* SW Turkey
150 *K10* **Karabutak** ***Kaz.*** Qarabutaq. Aktyubinsk, W Kazakhstan
142 *D12* **Karacabey** Bursa, NW Turkey
116 *O12* **Karacaköy** İstanbul, NW Turkey
116 *M12* **Karacaoğlan** Kırklareli, NW Turkey
Karachay-Cherkessia *see* Karachayevo-Cherkesskaya Respublika
130 *L15* **Karachayevo-Cherkesskaya Respublika** ***Eng.*** Karachay-Cherkessia. ◆ *autonomous republic* SW Russian Federation
130 *M15* **Karachayevsk** Karachayevo-Cherkesskaya Respublika, SW Russian Federation
130 *J6* **Karachev** Bryanskaya Oblast', W Russian Federation
155 *O16* **Karāchi** Sind, SE Pakistan
155 *O16* **Karāchi** ✕ Sind, S Pakistan
Karácsonkő *see* Piatra-Neamț
161 *E15* **Karād** Mahārāshtra, W India
142 *H16* **Karadağ** ▲ S Turkey
153 *T10* **Karadar'ya** ***Uzb.*** Qoradaryo. ≈ Kyrgyzstan/Uzbekistan
Karadeniz *see* Black Sea
Karadeniz Boğazı *see* İstanbul Boğazı
152 *B13* **Karadepe** Balkanskiy Velayat, W Turkmenistan
Karadzhar *see* Qorajar
Karaferiye *see* Véroia
152 *E13* **Karagan** ***Turkm.*** Garagan. Akhalskiy Velayat, C Turkmenistan
151 *R10* **Karaganda** ***Kaz.*** Qaraghandy. Karaganda, C Kazakhstan
151 *R10* **Karaganda** ***off.*** Karagandinskaya Oblast', ***Kaz.*** Qaraghandy Oblysy. ◆ *province* C Kazakhstan
Karagandinskaya Oblast' *see* Karaganda
151 *T10* **Karagayly** ***Kaz.*** Qaraghayly. Karaganda, C Kazakhstan
152 *A11* **Karagel'** ***Turkm.*** Garagöl. Balkanskiy Velayat, W Turkmenistan
127 *Pp8* **Karaginskiy, Ostrov** *island* E Russian Federation
207 *T1* **Karaginskiy Zaliv** *bay* E Russian Federation
143 *P13* **Karagöl Dağları** ▲▲ NE Turkey
116 *L13* **Karahisar** Edirne, NW Turkey
131 *V3* **Karaidel'** Respublika Bashkortostan, W Russian Federation
131 *V3* **Karaidel'skiy** Respublika Bashkortostan, W Russian Federation
116 *L13* **Karaidemir Barajı** ▣ NW Turkey
161 *J21* **Kāraikāl** Pondicherry, SE India
161 *I22* **Kāraikkudi** Tamil Nādu, SE India
151 *Y11* **Kara Irtysh** ***Rus.*** Chërnyy Irtysh. ≈ NE Kazakhstan
149 *N5* **Karaj** Tehrān, N Iran
174 *H5* **Karak** Pahang, Peninsular Malaysia
Karak *see* Al Karak
153 *T11* **Kara-Kabak** Oshskaya Oblast', SW Kyrgyzstan
152 *D12* **Kara-Kala** ***var.*** Garrygala. Balkanskiy Velayat, W Turkmenistan
Karakala *see* Oqqal'a
Karakalpakstan, Respublika *see* Qoraqalpoghiston Respublikasi
Karakalpakya *see* Qoraqalpoghiston
Karakax *see* Moyu
164 *G10* **Karakax He** ≈ NW China
124 *S9* **Karakaya Barajı** ▣ C Turkey
175 *Ss4* **Karakelang, Pulau** *island* N Indonesia
Karakılısse *see* Ağrı
Karak, Muḩāfaẓat al *see* Al Karak
Kara-Köl *see* Kara-Kul'
153 *Y7* **Karakol** ***prev.*** Przheval'sk. Issyk-Kul'skaya Oblast', NE Kyrgyzstan
153 *X8* **Karakol** ***var.*** Karakolka. Issyk-Kul'skaya Oblast', NE Kyrgyzstan
Karakolka *see* Karakol
155 *W2* **Karakoram Highway** *road* China/Pakistan
155 *Z3* **Karakoram Pass** ***Chin.*** Karakoram Shankou. *pass* C Asia
158 *I3* **Karakoram Range** ▲▲ C Asia
Karakoram Shankou *see* Karakoram Pass
Karaköse *see* Ağrı
151 *P14* **Karakoyyn, Ozero** ***Kaz.*** Qaraqoyyn. ◎ C Kazakhstan
85 *F19* **Karakubis** Ghanzi, W Botswana
153 *T9* **Kara-Kul'** ***Kir.*** Kara-Köl. Dzhalal-Abadskaya Oblast', W Kyrgyzstan
Karakul' *see* Qarokŭl, Tajikistan
Karakul' *see* Qorakŭl, Uzbekistan
153 *U10* **Kara-Kul'dzha** Oshskaya Oblast', SW Kyrgyzstan
131 *T3* **Karakulino** Udmurtskaya Respublika, NW Russian Federation
Karakul', Ozero *see* Qarokŭl
Kara Kum *see* Garagumy
Kara Kum Canal/Karakumskiy Kanal *see* Garagumskiy Kanal
Karakumy, Peski *see* Garagumy
85 *E17* **Karakuwisa** Okavango, NE Namibia
126 *Jj14* **Karam** Irkutskaya Oblast', S Russian Federation
Karamai *see* Karamay
175 *N13* **Karamain, Pulau** *island* N Indonesia
142 *I16* **Karaman** Karaman, S Turkey
142 *H16* **Karaman** ◆ *province* S Turkey
116 *M8* **Karamandere** ≈ NE Bulgaria
164 *J4* **Karamay** ***var.*** Karamai, Kelamayi, ***prev. Chin.*** K'o-la-ma-i. Xinjiang Uygur Zizhiqu, NW China
175 *Nn11* **Karambu** Borneo, N Indonesia
193 *H14* **Karamea** West Coast, South Island, NZ
193 *H14* **Karamea** ≈ South Island, NZ
193 *G15* **Karamea Bight** *gulf* South Island, NZ
152 *L14* **Karamet-Niyaz** ***Turkm.*** Garamäbnyyaz. Lebapskiy Velayat, E Turkmenistan
164 *K10* **Karamiran He** ≈ NW China
176 *Yy11* **Karamor, Pengunungan** ▲▲ Irian Jaya, E Indonesia
153 *S11* **Karamyk** Oshskaya Oblast', SW Kyrgyzstan
175 *Nn16* **Karangasem** Bali, S Indonesia
160 *H12* **Kāranja** Mahārāshtra, C India
158 *F9* **Karanpur** ***var.*** Karanpura. Rājasthān, NW India
Karanpura *see* Karanpur
Karánsebes/Karansebesch *see* Caransebeș
151 *T14* **Karaoy** ***Kaz.*** Qaraoy. Almaty, SE Kazakhstan
116 *N7* **Karapelit** ***Rom.*** Stejarul. Varnenska Oblast, NE Bulgaria
142 *I15* **Karapınar** Konya, C Turkey
85 *D22* **Karas** ◆ *district* S Namibia
153 *Y8* **Kara-Say** Issyk-Kul'skaya Oblast', NE Kyrgyzstan
85 *E22* **Karasburg** Karas, S Namibia
Kara Sea *see* Karskoye More
94 *L9* **Karasjok** ***Fin.*** Kaarasjoki. Finnmark, N Norway
94 *K9* **Karašjokka** ≈ N Norway
Kara Strait *see* Karskiye Vorota, Proliv
Kara Su *see* Mesta/Néstos
151 *N8* **Karasu** ***Kaz.*** Qarasū. Kustanay, N Kazakhstan
142 *F11* **Karasu** Sakarya, NW Turkey
Karasubazar *see* Bilohirs'k
125 *G14* **Karasuk** Novosibirskaya Oblast', C Russian Federation
151 *U13* **Karatal** ***Kaz.*** Qaratal. ≈ SE Kazakhstan
142 *K17* **Karataş** Adana, S Turkey
151 *Q16* **Karatau** ***Kaz.*** Qarataū. Zhambyl, S Kazakhstan
Karatau *see* Karatau, Khrebet
151 *P16* **Karatau, Khrebet** ***var.*** Karatau, ***Kaz.*** Qarataū. ▲▲ S Kazakhstan
150 *G13* **Karaton** ***Kaz.*** Qaraton. Atyrau, W Kazakhstan
170 *C12* **Karatsu** ***var.*** Karatu. Saga, Kyūshū, SW Japan
Karatu *see* Karatsu
126 *Hh7* **Karaul** Taymyrskiy (Dolgano-Nenetskiy) Avtonomnyy Okrug, N Russian Federation
Karaulbazar *see* Qorowulbozor
Karauzyak *see* Qoraŭzak
117 *D16* **Karáva** ▲ C Greece
Karavanke *see* Karawanken
117 *F22* **Karavás** Kýthira, S Greece
115 *J20* **Karavastasë, Laguna e** ***var.*** Kënet' e Karavastas, Kravasta Lagoon. *lagoon* W Albania
Karavastas, Kënet' e *see* Karavastasë, Laguna e
120 *I5* **Karavere** Tartumaa, E Estonia
117 *L23* **Karavonísia** *island* Kykládes, Greece, Aegean Sea
174 *Jj14* **Karawang** ***prev.*** Krawang. Jawa, C Indonesia
111 *T10* **Karawanken** ***Slvn.*** Karavanke. ▲▲ Austria/Yugoslavia
Karaxahar *see* Kaidu He
143 *R13* **Karayazı** Erzurum, NE Turkey
151 *Q12* **Karazhal** Zhezkazgan, C Kazakhstan
145 *S9* **Karbalā'** ***var.*** Kerbala, Kerbela. S Iraq
96 *L11* **Kårböle** Gävleborg, C Sweden
113 *M23* **Karcag** Jász-Nagykun-Szolnok, E Hungary
Kardak *see* Imia
116 *N7* **Kardam** Varnenska Oblast, NE Bulgaria
117 *M22* **Kardámaina** Kos, Dodekánisos, Greece, Aegean Sea
Kardamila *see* Kardámyla
117 *L18* **Kardámyla** ***var.*** Kardamila, Kardhámila. Chíos, E Greece
Kardeljevo *see* Ploče
Kardh *see* Qardho
Kardhámila *see* Kardámyla
Kardhítsa *see* Kardítsa
117 *E16* **Kardítsa** ***var.*** Kardhítsa. Thessalía, C Greece
120 *E4* **Kärdla** ***Ger.*** Kertel. Hiiumaa, W Estonia
Karelia *see* Kareliya, Respublika
121 *I16* **Karelichy** ***Pol.*** Korelicze, ***Rus.*** Korelichi. Hrodzyenskaya Voblasts', W Belarus
128 *I10* **Kareliya, Respublika** ***prev.*** Karel'skaya ASSR, ***Eng.*** Karelia. ◆ *autonomous republic* NW Russian Federation
Karel'skaya ASSR *see* Kareliya, Respublika
83 *E22* **Karema** Rukwa, W Tanzania
Karen *see* Hualien
85 *I14* **Karenda** Central, C Zambia
178 *Gg8* **Karen State** ***var.*** Kawthule State, Kayin State. ◆ *state* S Myanmar
94 *J10* **Karesuando** ***Lapp.*** Kaaresuanto. Norrbotten, N Sweden
Karet *see* Kâgheț
Kareyz-e-Elyās/Kārez Iliās *see* Kārīz-e Elyās
126 *Gg12* **Kargasok** Tomskaya Oblast', C Russian Federation
126 *Gg14* **Kargat** Novosibirskaya Oblast', C Russian Federation
142 *J11* **Kargı** Çorum, N Turkey
158 *I5* **Kargil** Jammu and Kashmir, NW India
Kargilik *see* Yecheng
128 *L11* **Kargopol'** Arkhangel'skaya Oblast', NW Russian Federation
112 *F12* **Kargowa** ***Ger.*** Unruhstadt. Zielona Góra, W Poland
79 *X13* **Kari** Bauchi, E Nigeria
85 *J15* **Kariba** Mashonaland West, N Zimbabwe
85 *J16* **Kariba, Lake** ▣ Zambia/Zimbabwe
172 *Nn5* **Kariba-yama** ▲ Hokkaidō, NE Japan
85 *C19* **Karibib** Erongo, C Namibia
Karies *see* Karyés
94 *L9* **Karigasniemi** ***Lapp.*** Garegegasnjárga. Lappi, N Finland
172 *P6* **Karikachi-tōge** *pass* Hokkaidō, NE Japan
192 *J2* **Karikari, Cape** *headland* North Island, NZ
Karīmābād *see* Hunza
174 *K10* **Karimata, Kepulauan** *island group* N Indonesia
174 *K9* **Karimata, Pulau** *island* Kepulauan Karimata, N Indonesia
174 *K10* **Karimata, Selat** *strait* W Indonesia
161 *I14* **Karīmnagar** Andhra Pradesh, C India
194 *I13* **Karimui** Chimbu, C PNG
174 *L13* **Karimunjawa, Pulau** *island* S Indonesia
82 *N12* **Karin** Woqooyi Galbeed, N Somalia
Kariot *see* Ikaría
95 *L20* **Karis** ***Fin.*** Karjaa. Uusimaa, SW Finland
Káristos *see* Kárystos
154 *J4* **Kārīz-e Elyās** ***var.*** Kareyz-e-Elyās, Kārez Iliās. Herāt, NW Afghanistan
Karjaa *see* Karis
151 *T10* **Karkaralinsk** ***Kaz.*** Qarqaraly. Karaganda, E Kazakhstan
194 *J11* **Karkar Island** *island* N PNG
149 *N7* **Karkas, Kūh-e** ▲▲ C Iran
148 *K8* **Karkheh, Rūd-e** ≈ SW Iran
117 *L20* **Karkinágrio** Ikaría, Dodekánisos, Greece, Aegean Sea
119 *R12* **Karkinits'ka Zatoka** ***Rus.*** Karkinitskiy Zaliv. *gulf* S Ukraine
Karkinitskiy Zaliv *see* Karkinits'ka Zatoka
95 *L19* **Karkkila** ***Swe.*** Högfors. Uusimaa, S Finland
95 *M19* **Kärkölä** Häme, S Finland
190 *G9* **Karkoo** South Australia
Karkūk *see* Kirkūk
120 *D5* **Kärla** ***Ger.*** Kergel. Saaremaa, W Estonia
Karleby *see* Kokkola
112 *F7* **Karlino** ***Ger.*** Körlin an der Persante. Koszalin, NW Poland
143 *Q13* **Karlıova** Bingöl, E Turkey
119 *U6* **Karlivka** Poltavs'ka Oblast', C Ukraine
Karl-Marx-Stadt *see* Chemnitz
Karlö *see* Hailuoto
114 *C11* **Karlobag** ***It.*** Carlopago. Lika-Senj, W Croatia
114 *D9* **Karlovac** ***Ger.*** Karlstadt, ***Hung.*** Károlyváros. Karlovac, C Croatia
114 *C10* **Karlovac** ***off.*** Karlovačka Županija. ◆ *province* C Croatia
Karlovačka Županija *see* Karlovac
116 *J9* **Karlovo** ***prev.*** Levskigrad. Plovdivska Oblast, C Bulgaria
113 *A16* **Karlovy Vary** ***Ger.*** Karlsbad; ***prev. Eng.*** Carlsbad. Západní Čechy, W Czech Republic
Karlsbad *see* Karlovy Vary
97 *L17* **Karlsborg** Skaraborg, S Sweden
Karlsburg *see* Alba Iulia
97 *L22* **Karlshamn** Blekinge, S Sweden
97 *L16* **Karlskoga** Örebro, C Sweden
97 *M22* **Karlskrona** Blekinge, S Sweden
103 *G21* **Karlsruhe** ***var.*** Carlsruhe. Baden-Württemberg, SW Germany
97 *K16* **Karlstad** Värmland, C Sweden
31 *R3* **Karlstad** Minnesota, N USA
103 *I18* **Karlstadt** Bayern, C Germany
Karlstadt *see* Karlovac
41 *Q14* **Karluk** Kodiak Island, Alaska, USA
Karluk *see* Qarluq
121 *O17* **Karma** ***Rus.*** Korma. Homyel'skaya Voblasts', SE Belarus
161 *F14* **Karmāla** Mahārāshtra, W India
152 *M11* **Karmana** Nawoiy Wiloyati, C Uzbekistan
144 *G8* **Karmi'él** ***var.*** Carmiel. Northern, N Israel
97 *B16* **Karmøy** *island* S Norway
158 *I9* **Karnāl** Haryāna, N India
159 *W15* **Karnaphuli Reservoir** ▣ NE India
161 *F17* **Karnātaka** ***var.*** Kanara; ***prev.*** Maisur, Mysore. ◆ *state* W India
27 *S13* **Karnes City** Texas, SW USA
111 *P9* **Karnische Alpen** ***It.*** Alpi Carniche. ▲▲ Austria/Italy
116 *M9* **Karnobat** Burgaska Oblast, E Bulgaria
111 *Q9* **Kärnten** ***off.*** Land Kärnten, ***Eng.*** Carinthi, ***Slvn.*** Koroška. ◆ *state* S Austria
Karnul *see* Kurnool
85 *K16* **Karoi** Mashonaland West, N Zimbabwe
Karol *see* Carei
Károly-Fehérvár *see* Alba Iulia
Károlyváros *see* Karlovac
179 *Qq15* **Karomatan** Mindanao, S Philippines
84 *M12* **Karonga** Northern, N Malawi
153 *W10* **Karool-Tëbë** Narynskaya Oblast', C Kyrgyzstan
190 *J9* **Karoonda** South Australia
155 *S9* **Karor** Punjab, E Pakistan
175 *P10* **Karosa** Sulawesi, C Indonesia
Karpasía/Karpas Peninsula *see* Kırpaşa
Karpaten *see* Carpathian Mountains
117 *L22* **Karpáthio Pélagos** *sea* Dodekánisos, Greece, Aegean Sea
117 *N24* **Kárpathos** Kárpathos, SE Greece
117 *N24* **Kárpathos** ***It.*** Scarpanto; ***anc.*** Carpathos, Carpathus. *island* SE Greece
Karpathos Strait *see* Karpathou, Stenó
117 *N24* **Karpathou, Stenó** ***var.*** Karpathos Strait, Scarpanto Strait. *strait* Dodekánisos, Greece, Aegean Sea
Karpaty *see* Carpathian Mountains
117 *E17* **Karpenísi** ***prev.*** Karpenísion. Stereá Ellás, C Greece
Karpenísion *see* Karpenísi
Karpilovka *see* Aktsyabrski
129 *O8* **Karpogory** Arkhangel'skaya Oblast', NW Russian Federation
188 *I7* **Karratha** Western Australia
143 *S12* **Kars** ***var.*** Qars. Kars, NE Turkey
143 *S12* **Kars** ***var.*** Qars. ◆ *province* NE Turkey
151 *O12* **Karsakpay** ***Kaz.*** Qarsaqbay. Zhezkazgan, C Kazakhstan
95 *L15* **Kärsämäki** Oulu, C Finland
Karsau *see* Kārsava
120 *K9* **Kārsava** ***Ger.*** Karsau; ***prev.*** Rus. Korsovka. Ludza, E Latvia
152 *A9* **Karshi** ***Turkm.*** Garshy. Balkanskiy Velayat, NW Turkmenistan
Karshi *see* Qarshi
Karshinskaya Step *see* Qarshi Chŭli
Karshinskiy Kanal *see* Qarshi Kanali
86 *I5* **Karskiye Vorota, Proliv** ***Eng.*** Kara Strait. *strait* N Russian Federation
126 *Gg5* **Karskoye More** ***Eng.*** Kara Sea. *sea* Arctic Ocean
95 *L17* **Karstula** Keski-Suomi, C Finland
131 *Q5* **Karsun** Ul'yanovskaya Oblast', W Russian Federation
125 *E12* **Kartaly** Chelyabinskaya Oblast', C Russian Federation
20 *E13* **Karthaus** Pennsylvania, NE USA
112 *I7* **Kartuzy** Gdańsk, NW Poland
172 *N10* **Karumai** Iwate, Honshū, C Japan
189 *U4* **Karumba** Queensland, NE Australia
148 *L10* **Kārūn** ***var.*** Rūd-e Kārūn. ≈ SW Iran
94 *K13* **Karungi** Norrbotten, N Sweden
94 *K13* **Karunki** Lappi, N Finland
Kārūn, Rūd-e *see* Kārūn
161 *H21* **Karūr** Tamil Nādu, SE India
95 *K17* **Karvia** Turku-Pori, SW Finland
113 *J17* **Karviná** ***Ger.*** Karwin, ***Pol.*** Karwina; ***prev.*** Nová Karvinná. Severní Morava, E Czech Republic
161 *E17* **Kārwār** Karnātaka, W India
110 *M7* **Karwendelgebirge** ▲▲ Austria/Germany
Karwin/Karwina *see* Karviná
117 *I14* **Karyés** ***var.*** Karies. Ágion Óros, N Greece
126 *Kk16* **Karymskoye** Chitinskaya Oblast', S Russian Federation
117 *I19* **Kárystos** ***var.*** Káristos. Évvoia, C Greece
142 *E17* **Kaş** Antalya, SW Turkey
41 *Y14* **Kasaan** Prince of Wales Island, Alaska, USA
170 *G14* **Kasai** Hyōgo, Honshū, SW Japan
81 *K21* **Kasai** ***var.*** Cassai, Kassai. ≈ Angola/Zaire
81 *K22* **Kasai Occidental** ***off.*** Région Kasai Occidental. ◆ *region* S Zaire
81 *L21* **Kasai Oriental** ***off.*** Région Kasai Oriental. ◆ *region* C Zaire
81 *L24* **Kasaji** Shaba, S Zaire
171 *Kk16* **Kasama** Ibaraki, Honshū, S Japan
84 *L12* **Kasama** Northern, N Zambia
Kasan *see* Koson
85 *H16* **Kasane** Chobe, NE Botswana
83 *E23* **Kasanga** Rukwa, W Tanzania
81 *G21* **Kasangulu** Bas-Zaïre, W Zaire
Kasansay *see* Kosonsoy
161 *E20* **Kāsaragod** Kerala, SW India
Kasargen *see* Kasari
120 *P13* **Kasari** ***var.*** Kasari Jõgi, ***Ger.*** Kasargen. ≈ W Estonia
Kasari Jõgi *see* Kasari
15 *K9* **Kasba Lake** ◎ Northwest Territories, NE Canada
Kaschau *see* Košice
170 *Bb16* **Kaseda** Kagoshima, Kyūshū, SW Japan
85 *I14* **Kasempa** North Western, NW Zambia
81 *O24* **Kasenga** Shaba, SE Zaire

◆ Country
● Country Capital
◇ Dependent Territory
○ Dependent Territory Capital
◆ Administrative Region
✕ International Airport
▲ Mountain
▲▲ Mountain Range
Volcano
≈ River
◎ Lake
▣ Reservoir

81 P17 **Kasenye** var. Kasenyi. Haut-Zaïre, NE Zaire
Kasenyi see Kasenye
83 E18 **Kasese** SW Uganda
81 O19 **Kasese** Maniema, E Zaire
158 J11 **Kāsganj** Uttar Pradesh, N India
149 U4 **Kashaf Rūd** River NE Iran
149 N7 **Kāshān** Eṣfahān, C Iran
130 M10 **Kashary** Rostovskaya Oblast', SW Russian Federation
41 O12 **Kashegelok** Alaska, USA
Kashgar see Kashi
164 E7 **Kashi** Chin. Kaxgar, K'o-shih, Uigh. Kashgar. Xinjiang Uygur Zizhiqu, NW China
171 Gg16 **Kashihara** var. Kasihara. Nara, Honshū, SW Japan
171 Kk17 **Kashima** Ibaraki, Honshū, S Japan
170 C13 **Kashima** var. Kasima. Saga, Kyūshū, SW Japan
171 L16 **Kashima-nada** gulf S Japan
128 K15 **Kashin** Tverskaya Oblast', W Russian Federation
158 K10 **Kāshīpur** Uttar Pradesh, N India
130 L4 **Kashira** Moskovskaya Oblast', W Russian Federation
171 K17 **Kashiwa** var. Kasiwa. Chiba, Honshū, S Japan
171 Jj13 **Kashiwazaki** var. Kasiwazaki. Niigata, Honshū, C Japan
Kashkadar'inskaya Oblast' see Qashqadaryo Wiloyati
149 T5 **Kāshmar** var. Turshiz; prev. Solṭānābād, Torshiz. Khorāsān, NE Iran
Kashmir see Jammu and Kashmir
155 R12 **Kashmor** Sind, SE Pakistan
155 S5 **Kashmūnd Ghar** Eng. Kashmund Range. Mountain range E Afghanistan
Kashmund Range see Kashmūnd Ghar
Kasi see Vārānasi
159 O12 **Kasia** Uttar Pradesh, N India
41 N12 **Kasigluk** Alaska, USA
Kasihara see Kashihara
41 R12 **Kasilof** Alaska, USA
Kasima see Kashima
Kasimköj see General Toshevo
130 M4 **Kasimov** Ryazanskaya Oblast', W Russian Federation
81 P18 **Kasindi** Nord Kivu, E Zaire
175 Ss8 **Kasiruta, Pulau** island Kepulauan Bacan, E Indonesia
84 M12 **Kasitu** River N Malawi
176 V12 **Kasiui, Pulau** island Kepulauan Watubela, E Indonesia
Kasiwa see Kashiwa
Kasiwazaki see Kashiwazaki
32 L14 **Kaskaskia River** River Illinois, N USA
95 J17 **Kaskinen** Swe. Kaskö. Vaasa, W Finland
Kaskö see Kaskinen
Kas Kong see Kŏng, Kaôh
9 O17 **Kaslo** British Columbia, SW Canada
Kåsmark see Kežmarok
174 M10 **Kasongan** Borneo, C Indonesia
81 N21 **Kasongo** Maniema, E Zaire
81 H22 **Kasongo-Lunda** Bandundu, SW Zaire
117 M24 **Kásos** island S Greece
Kasos Strait see Kasou, Stenó
117 M25 **Kasou, Stenó** var. Kasos Strait. strait Dodekánisos/Kríti, Greece, Aegean Sea
143 T10 **Kaspi** C Georgia
116 M8 **Kaspichan** Varnenska Oblast, NE Bulgaria
Kaspiy Mangy Oypaty see Caspian Depression
131 Q16 **Kaspiysk** Respublika Dagestan, SW Russian Federation
Kaspiyskiy see Lagan'
Kaspiyskoye More/Kaspiy Tengizi see Caspian Sea
Kassa see Košice
Kassai see Kasai
82 I9 **Kassala** Kassala, E Sudan
82 H9 **Kassala** state NE Sudan
117 G15 **Kassándra** prev. Pallíni; anc. Pallene. peninsula NE Greece
117 G15 **Kassándras, Ákra** headland N Greece
117 H15 **Kassándras, Kólpos** var. Kólpos Toronaíos. gulf N Greece
145 Y11 **Kassārah** E Iraq
103 I15 **Kassel** prev. Cassel. Hessen, C Germany
76 M6 **Kasserine** var. Al Qaṣrayn. W Tunisia
12 J14 **Kasshabog Lake** Lake Ontario, SE Canada
145 O5 **Kassīr, Sabkhat al** Lake E Syria
31 W10 **Kasson** Minnesota, N USA
117 C17 **Kassópi** site of ancient city Ípeiros, W Greece
117 N24 **Kastállou, Ákra** headland Kárpathos, SE Greece
142 I11 **Kastamonu** var. Castamoni, Kastamuni. Kastamonu, N Turkey
142 I10 **Kastamonu** var. Kastamuni. province N Turkey
Kastamuni see Kastamonu
117 E14 **Kastaneá** Kentrikí Makedonía, N Greece
117 H24 **Kastélli** Kríti, Greece, E Mediterranean Sea
Kastellórizon see Megísti
97 N21 **Kastlösa** Kalmar, S Sweden
117 D14 **Kastoría** Dytikí Makedonía, N Greece
130 K7 **Kastornoye** Kurskaya Oblast', W Russian Federation
117 I21 **Kástro** Sífnos, Kykládes, Greece, Aegean Sea
97 J23 **Kastrup** International airport (København) København, E Denmark
121 Q17 **Kastsyukovichy** Rus. Kostyukovichi. Mahilyowskaya Voblasts', E Belarus
121 O18 **Kastsyukowka** Rus. Kostyukovka. Homyel'skaya Voblasts', SE Belarus
170 Cc12 **Kasuga** Fukuoka, Kyūshū, SW Japan
171 I15 **Kasugai** Aichi, Honshū, SW Japan
83 E21 **Kasulu** Kigoma, W Tanzania
171 Gg13 **Kasumi** Hyōgo, Honshū, SW Japan
171 Kk16 **Kasumiga-ura** Lake Honshū, S Japan
131 R17 **Kasumkent** Respublika Dagestan, SW Russian Federation
84 M13 **Kasungu** Central, C Malawi
155 W9 **Kasūr** Punjab, E Pakistan
85 G15 **Kataba** Western, W Zambia
21 R4 **Katahdin, Mount** Mountain Maine, NE USA
81 M20 **Katako-Kombe** Kasai Oriental, C Zaire
41 T12 **Katalla** Alaska, USA
Katana see Qaṭanā
126 J12 **Katanga** River C Russian Federation
160 J11 **Katāngi** Madhya Pradesh, C India
188 J13 **Katanning** Western Australia
Katawaz see Zarghūn Shahr
157 Q22 **Katchall Island** island Nicobar Islands, India, NE Indian Ocean
117 F14 **Kateríni** Kentrikí Makedonía, N Greece
119 P7 **Katerynopil'** Cherkas'ka Oblast', C Ukraine
178 Gg3 **Katha** Sagaing, N Myanmar
189 P2 **Katherine** Northern Territory, N Australia
160 B11 **Kāthiāwār Peninsula** peninsula W India
159 P11 **Kathmandu** prev. Kantipur. Country capital (Nepal) Central, C Nepal
158 H7 **Kathua** Jammu and Kashmir, NW India
78 L12 **Kati** Koulikoro, SW Mali
159 R13 **Katihār** Bihār, NE India
192 N7 **Katikati** Bay of Plenty, North Island, NZ
85 H16 **Katima Mulilo** Caprivi, NE Namibia
79 N15 **Katiola** C Ivory Coast
203 V10 **Katiu** atoll Îles Tuamotu, C French Polynesia
119 N12 **Katlabukh, Ozero** Lake SW Ukraine
41 P14 **Katmai, Mount** Mountain Alaska, USA
160 J9 **Katni** Madhya Pradesh, C India
117 D19 **Káto Achaïa** var. Kato Ahaia, Káto Akhaía. Dytikí Ellás, S Greece
Kato Ahaia/Káto Akhaía see Káto Achaïa
124 Nn3 **Kato Lakatámeia** var. Kato Lakatamia. C Cyprus
Kato Lakatamia see Kato Lakatámeia
81 N22 **Katompi** Shaba, SE Zaire
85 K14 **Katondwe** Lusaka, C Zambia
116 H12 **Káto Nevrokópi** prev. Káto Nevrokópion. Anatolikí Makedonía kai Thráki, NE Greece
Káto Nevrokópion see Káto Nevrokópi
83 E18 **Katonga** River S Uganda
117 F15 **Káto Ólympos** Mountain range C Greece
117 D17 **Katoúna** Dytikí Ellás, C Greece
117 E19 **Káto Vlasiá** Dytikí Makedonía, S Greece
113 J16 **Katowice** Ger. Kattowitz. Katowice, S Poland
113 I16 **Katowice** off. Województwo Katowickie, Ger. Kattowitz. province S Poland
Katowickie, Województwo see Katowice
159 S15 **Kātoya** West Bengal, NE India
142 E16 **Katrançık Dağı** Mountain range SW Turkey
97 N16 **Katrineholm** Södermanland, C Sweden
98 I11 **Katrine, Loch** Lake C Scotland, UK
79 V12 **Katsina** Katsina, N Nigeria
79 U12 **Katsina** state N Nigeria
69 P8 **Katsina Ala** River S Nigeria
170 C11 **Katsumoto** Nagasaki, Iki, SW Japan
171 L16 **Katsuta** var. Katuta. Ibaraki, Honshū, S Japan
171 K17 **Katsuura** var. Katuura. Chiba, Honshū, S Japan
171 I14 **Katsuyama** var. Katuyama. Fukui, Honshū, SW Japan
170 Ff13 **Katsuyama** Okayama, Honshū, SW Japan
Kattakurgan see Kattaqŭrghon
153 N11 **Kattaqŭrghon** Rus. Kattakurgan. Samarqand Wiloyati, C Uzbekistan
117 O23 **Kattavía** Ródos, Dodekánisos, Greece, Aegean Sea
97 I21 **Kattegat** Dan. Kattegatt. strait N Europe
Kattegatt see Kattegat
97 P19 **Katthammarsvik** Gotland, SE Sweden
Kattowitz see Katowice
127 N17 **Katun'** River S Russian Federation
Katuta see Katsuta
Katuura see Katsuura
Katuyama see Katsuyama
Katwijk see Katwijk aan Zee
100 G11 **Katwijk aan Zee** var. Katwijk. Zuid-Holland, W Netherlands
40 B8 **Kauai** Haw. Kaua'i. island Hawaiian Islands, Hawaii, USA, C Pacific Ocean
40 C8 **Kauai Channel** channel Hawaii, USA, C Pacific Ocean
175 Ss11 **Kaubalatmada, Gunung** var. Kaplamada. Mountain Pulau Buru, E Indonesia
203 U10 **Kauehi** atoll Îles Tuamotu, C French Polynesia
Kauen see Kaunas
103 K24 **Kaufbeuren** Bayern, S Germany
27 U7 **Kaufman** Texas, SW USA
103 I15 **Kaufungen** Hessen, C Germany
95 K17 **Kauhajoki** Vaasa, W Finland
95 K16 **Kauhava** Vaasa, W Finland
32 M7 **Kaukauna** Wisconsin, N USA
94 L11 **Kaukonen** Lappi, N Finland
40 A8 **Kaulakahi Channel** channel Hawaii, USA, C Pacific Ocean
40 E9 **Kaunakakai** Molokai, Hawaii, USA, C Pacific Ocean
40 F12 **Kauna Point** headland Hawaii, USA, C Pacific Ocean
120 F13 **Kaunas** Ger. Kauen, Pol. Kowno; prev. Rus. Kovno. Kaunas, C Lithuania
194 H10 **Kaup** East Sepik, NW PNG
79 U12 **Kaura Namoda** Sokoto, NW Nigeria
Kaushany see Căuşeni
95 K16 **Kaustinen** Vaasa, W Finland
175 T7 **Kau, Teluk** bay Pulau Halmahera, E Indonesia
101 M23 **Kautenbach** Diekirch, NE Luxembourg
94 K10 **Kautokeino** Finnmark, N Norway
Kavadar see Kavadarci
115 P19 **Kavadarci** Turk. Kavadar. C FYR Macedonia
Kavaja see Kavajë
115 K20 **Kavajë** It. Cavaia, Kavaja. Tiranë, W Albania
116 M13 **Kavak Çayı** River NW Turkey
Kavakli see Topolovgrad
116 I13 **Kavála** prev. Kaválla. Anatolikí Makedonía kai Thráki, NE Greece
116 I13 **Kaválas, Kólpos** gulf Aegean Sea, NE Mediterranean Sea
127 Nn17 **Kavalerovo** Primorskiy Kray, SE Russian Federation
161 J17 **Kāvali** Andhra Pradesh, E India
Kaválla see Kavála
Kavango see Cubango/Okavango
161 C21 **Kavaratti** Lakshadweep, SW India
116 O8 **Kavarna** Varnenska Oblast, NE Bulgaria
120 G12 **Kavarskas** Anykščiai, E Lithuania
78 I13 **Kavendou** Mountain C Guinea
Kavengo see Cubango/Okavango
161 F20 **Kāveri** var. Cauvery. River S India
195 N9 **Kavieng** var. Kaewieng. NE PNG
85 H16 **Kavimba** Chobe, NE Botswana
85 I15 **Kavingu** Southern, S Zambia
149 Q6 **Kavīr, Dasht-e** var. Great Salt Desert. salt pan N Iran
Kavirondo Gulf see Winam Gulf
Kavkaz see Caucasus
97 K23 **Kävlinge** Malmöhus, S Sweden
197 I15 **Kavukavu Reef** var. Beqa Barrier Reef, Cakaubalavu Reef. reef Viti Levu, SW Fiji
84 G12 **Kavungo** Moxico, E Angola
171 M10 **Kawabe** Akita, Honshū, C Japan
171 K15 **Kawagoe** Saitama, Honshū, S Japan
171 K16 **Kawaguchi** var. Kawaguti. Saitama, Honshū, S Japan
Kawaguti see Kawaguchi
172 N11 **Kawai** Iwate, Honshū, C Japan
40 A8 **Kawaihoa Point** headland Niihau, Hawaii, USA, C Pacific Ocean
192 K3 **Kawakawa** Northland, North Island, NZ
84 I13 **Kawama** North Western, NW Zambia
84 K11 **Kawambwa** Luapula, N Zambia
170 F14 **Kawanoe** Ehime, Shikoku, SW Japan
160 K11 **Kawardha** Madhya Pradesh, C India
12 I14 **Kawartha Lakes** Lake Ontario, SE Canada
171 K17 **Kawasaki** Kanagawa, Honshū, S Japan
175 T9 **Kawassi** Pulau Obi, E Indonesia
172 N8 **Kawauchi** Aomori, Honshū, C Japan
192 L5 **Kawau Island** island N NZ
192 N10 **Kaweka Range** Mountain range North Island, NZ
Kawelecht see Puhja
176 Z13 **Kawentinkim** Irian Jaya, E Indonesia
192 O8 **Kawerau** Bay of Plenty, North Island, NZ
192 L8 **Kawhia** Waikato, North Island, NZ
192 K8 **Kawhia Harbour** inlet North Island, NZ
37 V8 **Kawich Peak** Mountain Nevada, W USA
37 V9 **Kawich Range** Mountain range Nevada, W USA
12 G12 **Kawigamog Lake** Lake Ontario, S Canada
175 Rr3 **Kawio, Kepulauan** island group N Indonesia
178 Gg9 **Kawkareik** Karen State, S Myanmar
29 O8 **Kaw Lake** Reservoir Oklahoma, C USA
177 G3 **Kawlin** Sagaing, N Myanmar
Kawm Umbū see Kôm Ombo
Kawthule State see Karen State
Kaxgar see Kashi
164 D7 **Kaxgar He** River NW China
164 J5 **Kax He** River NW China
79 P12 **Kaya** C Burkina
178 Gg7 **Kayah State** state C Myanmar
126 J7 **Kayak** Taymyrskiy (Dolgano-Nenetskiy) Avtonomnyy Okrug, N Russian Federation
41 T12 **Kayak Island** island Alaska, USA
116 M11 **Kayalıköy Barajı** Reservoir NW Turkey
177 G8 **Kayan** Yangon, SW Myanmar
161 G23 **Kāyankulam** Kerala, SW India
175 N6 **Kayan, Sungai** prev. Kajan. River Borneo, C Indonesia
150 F14 **Kaydak, Sor** salt flat SW Kazakhstan
Kaydanovo see Dzyarzhynsk
39 N9 **Kayenta** Arizona, SW USA
78 J11 **Kayes** Kayes, W Mali
78 J11 **Kayes** region SW Mali
Kayin State see Karen State
151 U10 **Kaynar** var. Kajnar. Semipalatinsk, E Kazakhstan
Kaynary see Căinari
85 H15 **Kayoya** Western, W Zambia
Kayrakkum see Qayroqqum
Kayrakkumskoye Vodokhranilishche see Qayroqqum, Obanbori
142 K14 **Kayseri** var. Kaisaria; anc. Caesarea Mazaca, Mazaca. Kayseri, C Turkey
142 K14 **Kayseri** var. Kaisaria. province C Turkey
38 L2 **Kaysville** Utah, W USA
126 Hh8 **Kayyerkan** Taymyrskiy (Dolgano-Nenetskiy) Avtonomnyy Okrug, N Russian Federation
Kayyngdy see Kaindy
12 L11 **Kazabazua** Québec, SE Canada
12 L12 **Kazabazua** River Québec, SE Canada
126 M7 **Kazach'ye** Respublika Sakha (Yakutiya), NE Russian Federation
Kazakdar'ya see Qozoqdaryo
152 E9 **Kazakhlyshor, Solonchak** var. Solonchak Shorkazakhly. salt marsh NW Turkmenistan
Kazakhskaya SSR/Kazakh Soviet Socialist Republic see Kazakhstan
151 R9 **Kazakhskiy Melkosopochnik** Eng. Kazakh Uplands, Kirghiz Steppe, Kaz. Saryarqa. uplands C Kazakhstan
150 L12 **Kazakhstan** off. Republic of Kazakhstan, var. Kazakstan, Kaz. Qazaqstan, Qazaqstan Respublikasy; prev. Kazakh Soviet Socialist Republic, Rus. Kazakhskaya SSR. Country republic C Asia
Kazakh Uplands see Kazakhskiy Melkosopochnik
Kazakstan see Kazakhstan
150 L14 **Kazalinsk** Kzyl-Orda, S Kazakhstan
131 R4 **Kazan'** Respublika Tatarstan, W Russian Federation
131 R4 **Kazan'** International airport Respublika Tatarstan, W Russian Federation
15 K8 **Kazan** River Northwest Territories, NW Canada
Kazandzhik see Gazandzhyk
119 R8 **Kazanka** Mykolayivs'ka Oblast', S Ukraine
Kazanketken see Qizqetkan
Kazanlik see Kazanlŭk
116 J9 **Kazanlŭk** prev. Kazanlik. Khaskovska Oblast, C Bulgaria
172 T17 **Kazan-rettō** Eng. Volcano Islands. island group SE Japan
125 F12 **Kazanskoye** Tyumenskaya Oblast', C Russian Federation
119 V12 **Kazantip, Mys** headland S Ukraine
153 U9 **Kazarman** Narynskaya Oblast', C Kyrgyzstan
Kazatin see Kozyatyn
Kazbegi see Kazbek
Kazbegi see Qazbegi
143 T9 **Kazbek** var. Kazbegi, Geor. Mqinvartsveri. Mountain N Georgia
84 M13 **Kazembe** Eastern, NE Zambia
149 N11 **Kāzerūn** Fārs, S Iran
129 R12 **Kazhym** Respublika Komi, NW Russian Federation
Kazi Ahmad see Qāzi Ahmad
Kazi Magomed see Qazimämmäd
142 H16 **Kazımkarabekir** Karaman, S Turkey
113 M20 **Kazincbarcika** Borsod-Abaúj-Zemplén, NE Hungary
121 H17 **Kazlowshchyna** Pol. Kozlowszczyzna, Rus. Kozlovshchina. Hrodzyenskaya Voblasts', W Belarus
121 E14 **Kazlų Rūda** Marijampolė, S Lithuania
150 E9 **Kaztalovka** Zapadnyy Kazakhstan, W Kazakhstan
81 K22 **Kazumba** Kasai Occidental, S Zaire
171 Mm10 **Kazuno** Akita, Honshū, C Japan
Kazvin see Qazvīn
120 J12 **Kaz'yany** Rus. Koz'yany. Vitsyebskaya Voblasts', NW Belarus
125 Ff9 **Kazym** River N Russian Federation
112 H10 **Kcynia** Ger. Exin. Bydgoszcz, W Poland
117 I20 **Kéa** Kéa, Kykládes, Greece, Aegean Sea
117 I20 **Kéa** prev. Kéos, anc. Ceos. island Kykládes, Greece, Aegean Sea
40 H11 **Keaau** Haw. Kea'au. Hawaii, USA, C Pacific Ocean
40 F11 **Keahole Point** headland Hawaii, USA, C Pacific Ocean
40 G12 **Kealakekua** Hawaii, USA, C Pacific Ocean
40 H11 **Kea, Mauna** Mountain Hawaii, USA, C Pacific Ocean
39 N10 **Keams** Arizona, SW USA
Kéamu see Anatom
31 O16 **Kearney** Nebraska, C USA
38 L3 **Kearns** Utah, W USA
117 H20 **Kéas, Stenó** strait SE Greece
143 O14 **Keban Barajı** dam C Turkey
143 O14 **Keban Barajı** Reservoir C Turkey
79 S13 **Kebbi** state NW Nigeria
78 G10 **Kébémèr** NW Senegal
76 M7 **Kebili** var. Qibilī. C Tunisia
144 H4 **Kebir, Nahr el** River NW Syria
82 A10 **Kebkabiya** Northern Darfur, W Sudan
94 I11 **Kebnekaise** Mountain N Sweden
83 M14 **K'ebrī Dehar** SE Ethiopia
154 K15 **Kech** River SW Pakistan
8 K10 **Kechika** River British Columbia, W Canada
113 K23 **Kecskemét** Bács-Kiskun, C Hungary
174 Gg2 **Kedah** state Peninsular Malaysia
120 F12 **Kėdainiai** Kėdainiai, C Lithuania
Kedder see Kehra
11 N13 **Kedgwick** New Brunswick, SE Canada
174 Ll15 **Kediri** Jawa, C Indonesia
176 Y10 **Kedir Sarmi** Irian Jaya, E Indonesia
169 V7 **Kedong** Heilongjiang, NE China
78 I12 **Kédougou** SE Senegal
126 Gg13 **Kedrovyy** Tomskaya Oblast', C Russian Federation
113 H16 **Kędzierzyn-Kozle** Ger. Heydebrech. Opole, SW Poland
14 G6 **Keele** River Northwest Territories, NW Canada
8 K6 **Keele Peak** Mountain Yukon Territory, NW Canada
Keelung see Chilung
21 N10 **Keene** New Hampshire, NE USA
101 H17 **Keerbergen** Vlaams Brabant, C Belgium
85 E21 **Keetmanshoop** Karas, S Namibia
10 A11 **Keewatin** Ontario, S Canada
31 V4 **Keewatin** Minnesota, N USA
15 K7 **Keewatin** off. District of Keewatin. district Northwest Territories, NE Canada
117 B18 **Kefallinía** var. Kefallonía. island Iónioi Nísoi, Greece, C Mediterranean Sea
Kefallonía see Kefallinía
117 M22 **Kéfalos** Kos, Dodekánisos, Greece, Aegean Sea
175 Rr17 **Kefamenanu** Timor, C Indonesia
144 F10 **Kefar Sava** Central, C Israel
Kefe see Feodosiya
79 V15 **Keffi** Plateau, C Nigeria
94 H4 **Keflavík** International airport (Reykjavík) Reykjanes, W Iceland
94 H4 **Keflavík** Reykjanes, W Iceland
Kegalee see Kegalla
161 J25 **Kegalla** var. Kegalee, Kegalle. Sabaragamuwa Province, C Sri Lanka
Kegalle see Kegalla
152 H7 **Kegayli** Rus. Kegeyli. Qoraqalpoghiston Respublikasi, W Uzbekistan
Kegel see Keila
151 W16 **Kegen** Almaty, SE Kazakhstan
Kegeyli see Kegayli
103 F22 **Kehl** Baden-Württemberg, SW Germany
120 H3 **Kehra** Ger. Kedder. Harjumaa, NW Estonia
119 U6 **Kehychivka** Kharkivs'ka Oblast', E Ukraine
99 L17 **Keighley** N England, UK
Kei Islands see Kai, Kepulauan
Keijō see Sŏul
120 G3 **Keila** Ger. Kegel. Harjumaa, NW Estonia
Keilberg see Klínovec
85 F23 **Keimoes** Northern Cape, W South Africa
Keina/Keinis see Käina
176 Yy14 **Keisak** Irian Jaya, E Indonesia
Keishū see Kyŏngju
79 T11 **Keïta** Tahoua, C Niger
80 J12 **Kéita, Bahr** var. Doka. River S Chad
95 M16 **Keitele** Lake C Finland
190 K10 **Keith** South Australia
98 K8 **Keith** NE Scotland, UK
28 K3 **Keith Sebelius Lake** Reservoir Kansas, C USA
34 G11 **Keizer** Oregon, NW USA
40 A8 **Kekaha** Kauai, Hawaii, USA, C Pacific Ocean
153 U10 **Këk-Art** prev. Alaykel', Alay-Kuu. Oshskaya Oblast', SW Kyrgyzstan
153 W10 **Këk-Aygyr** var. Keyaygyr. Narynskaya Oblast', C Kyrgyzstan
153 V9 **Këk-Dzhar** Narynskaya Oblast', C Kyrgyzstan
12 L8 **Kékek** River Québec, SE Canada
193 K15 **Kekerengu** Canterbury, South Island, NZ
113 L21 **Kékes** Mountain N Hungary
175 Rr17 **Kekneno, Gunung** Mountain Timor, S Indonesia
153 S9 **Këk-Tash** Kir. Kök-Tash. Dzhalal-Abadskaya Oblast', W Kyrgyzstan
83 M15 **K'elafo** SE Ethiopia
175 O6 **Kelai, Sungai** River Borneo, N Indonesia
Kelamayi see Karamay
Kelang see Klang
174 H3 **Kelantan** state Peninsular Malaysia
Kelantan see Kelantan, Sungai
174 H3 **Kelantan, Sungai** var. Kelantan. River Peninsular Malaysia
Kelat see Kalāt
Këlcyra see Këlcyrë
115 L22 **Këlcyrë** var. Këlcyra. Gjirokastër, S Albania
152 L14 **Kelifskiy Uzboy** salt marsh E Turkmenistan
143 O12 **Kelkit** Gümüşhane, NE Turkey
142 M12 **Kelkit Çayı** River N Turkey
79 W11 **Kellé** Zinder, S Niger
81 G18 **Kéllé** Cuvette, W Congo
151 P7 **Kellerovka** Kokshetau, N Kazakhstan
15 H1 **Kellett, Cape** headland Banks Island, Northwest Territories, NW Canada
33 S11 **Kelleys Island** island Ohio, N USA
35 N8 **Kellogg** Idaho, NW USA
94 M12 **Kelloselkä** Lappi, N Finland
99 F17 **Kells** Ir. Ceanannas. E Ireland
120 E12 **Kelmė** Kelmė, C Lithuania
101 M19 **Kelmis** var. La Calamine. Liège, E Belgium
80 H12 **Kélo** Tandjilé, SW Chad
85 I14 **Kelongwa** North Western, NW Zambia
9 N17 **Kelowna** British Columbia, SW Canada
9 X12 **Kelsey** Manitoba, C Canada
36 M6 **Kelseyville** California, W USA
98 K13 **Kelso** SE Scotland, UK
34 G10 **Kelso** Washington, NW USA
205 W15 **Keltie, Cape** headland Antarctica
Keltsy see Kielce
174 Hh6 **Keluang** var. Kluang. Johor, Peninsular Malaysia
174 I8 **Kelume** Pulau Lingga, W Indonesia
9 U15 **Kelvington** Saskatchewan, S Canada
128 J7 **Kem'** Respublika Kareliya, NW Russian Federation
128 I7 **Kem'** River NW Russian Federation
143 O13 **Kemah** Erzincan, E Turkey
143 N13 **Kemaliye** Erzincan, C Turkey
Kemaman see Cukai
Kemanlar see Isperikh
8 K14 **Kemano** British Columbia, SW Canada
Kemarat see Khemmarat
175 Qq9 **Kembani** Pulau Peleng, N Indonesia
142 F17 **Kemer** Antalya, SW Turkey
126 H14 **Kemerovo** prev. Shcheglovsk. Kemerovskaya Oblast', C Russian Federation
126 H14 **Kemerovskaya Oblast'** province S Russian Federation
94 L13 **Kemi** Lappi, NW Finland
94 M12 **Kemijärvi** Swe. Kemiträsk. Lappi, N Finland
94 M12 **Kemijärvi** Lake N Finland
94 L13 **Kemijoki** River NW Finland
153 V7 **Kemin** prev. Bystrovka. Chuyskaya Oblast', N Kyrgyzstan
94 L13 **Keminmaa** Lappi, NW Finland
Kemins Island see Nikumaroro
Kemiö see Kimito
Kemiträsk see Kemijärvi
131 P5 **Kemlya** Respublika Mordoviya, W Russian Federation
101 B18 **Kemmel** West-Vlaanderen, W Belgium
35 S16 **Kemmerer** Wyoming, C USA
Kemmuna see Comino
81 I14 **Kémo** prefecture S Central African Republic
27 U7 **Kemp** Texas, SW USA
95 L14 **Kempele** Oulu, C Finland
103 D15 **Kempen** Nordrhein-Westfalen, W Germany
27 Q5 **Kemp, Lake** Lake Texas, SW USA
205 W5 **Kemp Land** physical region Antarctica
27 S9 **Kempner** Texas, SW USA
46 H3 **Kemp's Bay** Andros Island, W Bahamas
191 U6 **Kempsey** New South Wales, SE Australia
103 J24 **Kempten** Bayern, S Germany
13 N9 **Kempt, Lac** Lake Québec, SE Canada
191 P17 **Kempton** Tasmania, SE Australia
160 J9 **Ken** River C India
41 R12 **Kenai** Alaska, USA
1 D5 **Kenai Mountains** Mountain range Alaska, USA
41 R12 **Kenai Peninsula** peninsula Alaska, USA
23 V11 **Kenansville** North Carolina, SE USA
124 Pp15 **Kenâyis, Râs el-** headland N Egypt
99 K16 **Kendal** NW England, UK
25 Y16 **Kendall** Florida, SE USA
15 Ll6 **Kendall, Cape** headland Northwest Territories, E Canada
20 J15 **Kendall Park** New Jersey, NE USA
33 Q11 **Kendallville** Indiana, N USA
175 Qq12 **Kendari** Sulawesi, C Indonesia
174 L10 **Kendawangan** Borneo, C Indonesia
174 Ll15 **Kendeng, Pegunungan** Mountain range Jawa, S Indonesia
160 O12 **Kendrāpāra** var. Kendrāparha. Orissa, E India
Kendrāparha see Kendrāpāra
160 O11 **Kendujhargarh** prev. Keonjihargarh. Orissa, E India
27 S13 **Kenedy** Texas, SW USA
152 E13 **Kënekesir** Turkm. Könekesir. Balkanskiy Velayat, W Turkmenistan
78 J15 **Kenema** SE Sierra Leone
31 P16 **Kenesaw** Nebraska, C USA
152 G8 **Këneurgench** Turkm. Köneürgench; prev. Kunya-Urgench. Dashkhovuzskiy Velayat, N Turkmenistan
81 H21 **Kenge** Bandundu, SW Zaire
Kengen see Kangen
178 Hh5 **Keng Tung** var. Kentung. Shan State, E Myanmar
85 F23 **Kenhardt** Northern Cape, W South Africa
78 J12 **Kéniéba** Kayes, W Mali
Kenimekh see Konimekh
175 Nn3 **Keningau** Sabah, East Malaysia
76 F6 **Kénitra** prev. Port-Lyautey. NW Morocco
23 V9 **Kenly** North Carolina, SE USA
99 B21 **Kenmare** Ir. Neidín. S Ireland
30 L2 **Kenmare** North Dakota, N USA
99 A21 **Kenmare River** Ir. An Ribhéar. inlet NE Atlantic Ocean
20 D10 **Kenmore** New York, NE USA
27 W8 **Kennard** Texas, SW USA
31 N10 **Kennebec** South Dakota, N USA
21 Q7 **Kennebec River** River Maine, NE USA
21 P9 **Kennebunk** Maine, NE USA
41 R13 **Kennedy Entrance** strait Alaska, USA
177 Ff3 **Kennedy Peak** Mountain W Myanmar
24 K9 **Kenner** Louisiana, S USA
188 I8 **Kenneth Range** Mountain range Western Australia
29 Y9 **Kennett** Missouri, C USA
20 I16 **Kennett Square** Pennsylvania, NE USA
34 K10 **Kennewick** Washington, NW USA
10 E11 **Kenogami** River Ontario, S Canada
13 Q7 **Kénogami, Lac** Lake Québec, SE Canada
12 G8 **Kenogami Lake** Ontario, S Canada
12 F7 **Kenogamissi Lake** Lake Ontario, S Canada
8 I6 **Keno Hill** Yukon Territory, NW Canada
10 A11 **Kenora** Ontario, S Canada
33 N9 **Kenosha** Wisconsin, N USA
11 P14 **Kensington** Prince Edward Island, SE Canada
28 L3 **Kensington** Kansas, C USA
34 H8 **Kent** Oregon, NW USA
26 J9 **Kent** Texas, SW USA
34 I11 **Kent** Washington, NW USA
99 P22 **Kent** cultural region SE England, UK
151 P16 **Kentau** Yuzhnyy Kazakhstan, S Kazakhstan
191 P14 **Kent Group** island group Tasmania, SE Australia
33 N12 **Kentland** Indiana, N USA
33 R12 **Kenton** Ohio, N USA
15 J4 **Kent Peninsula** peninsula Northwest Territories, N Canada
117 F14 **Kentrikí Makedonía** Eng. Macedonia Central. region N Greece
22 J6 **Kentucky** off. Commonwealth of Kentucky; also known as The Bluegrass State. state C USA
22 H8 **Kentucky Lake** Reservoir Kentucky/Tennessee, S USA
Kentung see Keng Tung
11 P15 **Kentville** Nova Scotia, SE Canada
24 K8 **Kentwood** Louisiana, S USA
33 P9 **Kentwood** Michigan, N USA
83 H17 **Kenya** off. Republic of Kenya. republic E Africa
Kenya, Mount see Kirinyaga
174 Hh3 **Kenyir, Tasik** var. Tasek Kenyir. Lake Peninsular Malaysia
31 W10 **Kenyon** Minnesota, N USA
31 Y16 **Keokuk** Iowa, C USA
Keonjihargarh see Kendujhargarh
Kéos see Kéa
31 X16 **Keosauqua** Iowa, C USA
31 X15 **Keota** Iowa, C USA
23 O11 **Keowee, Lake** Reservoir South Carolina, SE USA
128 I7 **Kepa** var. Kepe. Respublika Kareliya, NW Russian Federation
Kepe see Kepa
201 O13 **Kepirohi Falls** waterfall Pohnpei, E Micronesia
193 B22 **Kepler Mountains** Mountain range South Island, NZ
113 I14 **Kępno** Kalisz, C Poland
67 C24 **Keppel Island** island N Falkland Islands
Keppel Island see Niuatoputapu
67 C23 **Keppel Sound** sound N Falkland Islands
142 D12 **Kepsut** Balıkesir, NW Turkey
176 W12 **Kerai** Irian Jaya, E Indonesia
Kerak see Al Karak
161 F22 **Kerala** state S India
194 H10 **Keram** River N PNG
172 O14 **Kerama-rettō** island group SW Japan
191 N10 **Kerang** Victoria, SE Australia
Kerasunt see Giresun
117 H19 **Keratéa** var. Keratea. Attikí, C Greece
95 M19 **Kerava** Swe. Kervo. Uusimaa, S Finland
Kerbala/Kerbela see Karbalā'
34 F15 **Kerby** Oregon, NW USA
119 W12 **Kerch** Rus. Kerch'. Respublika Krym, SE Ukraine
Kerchens'ka Protska/Kerchenskiy Proliv see Kerch Strait
119 V13 **Kerchens'kyy Pivostriv** peninsula S Ukraine
124 R4 **Kerch Strait** var. Bosporus Cimmerius, Enikale Strait, Rus. Kerchenskiy Proliv, Ukr. Kerchens'ka Protska. strait Black Sea/Sea of Azov
158 K8 **Kerdārnāth** Uttar Pradesh, N India
Kerdilio see Kerdýlio
116 H13 **Kerdýlio** var. Kerdilio. Mountain N Greece
194 J14 **Kerema** Gulf, S PNG
Keremitlik see Lyulyakovo
142 I9 **Kerempe Burnu** headland N Turkey
82 J9 **Keren** var. Cheren. C Eritrea
27 U7 **Kerens** Texas, SW USA
192 M6 **Kerepehi** Waikato, North Island, NZ
151 P10 **Kerey, Ozero** Lake C Kazakhstan
Kergel see Kärla
181 Q12 **Kerguelen** island C French Southern and Antarctic Territories
181 Q13 **Kerguelen Plateau** undersea feature S Indian Ocean
117 C20 **Kerí** Zákynthos, Iónioi Nísoi, Greece, C Mediterranean Sea
83 H19 **Kericho** Rift Valley, W Kenya
192 K2 **Kerikeri** Northland, North Island, NZ
95 O17 **Kerimäki** Mikkeli, SE Finland
174 Gg10 **Kerinci, Danau** Lake Sumatera, W Indonesia
174 Gg9 **Kerinci, Gunung** Mountain Sumatera, W Indonesia
Keriya see Yutian
164 H9 **Keriya He** River NW China

◆ Country ● Country Capital ◇ Dependent Territory ○ Dependent Territory Capital ◆ Administrative Region ✕ International Airport ▲ Mountain ▲ Mountain Range Volcano River ◎ Lake ▣ Reservoir

100 J9 **Kerkbuurt** Noord-Holland, C Netherlands
100 J13 **Kerkdriel** Gelderland, C Netherlands
77 N6 **Kerkenah, Îles de** *var.* Kerkenna Islands, *Ar.* Juzur Qarqannah. *island group* E Tunisia
Kerkenna Islands *see* Kerkenah, Îles de
117 M20 **Kerketévs** ▲ Sámos, Dodekánisos, Greece, Aegean Sea
31 T8 **Kerkhoven** Minnesota, N USA
152 M14 **Kerki** Lebapskiy Velayat, E Turkmenistan
152 M14 **Kerkichi** Lebapskiy Velayat, E Turkmenistan
117 F16 **Kerkíneo** *prehistoric site* Thessalía, C Greece
116 G12 **Kerkinitis, Límni** ◎ N Greece
Kérkira *see* Kérkyra
101 M18 **Kerkrade** Limburg, SE Netherlands
Kerkuk *see* Kirkūk
117 B16 **Kerkyra** ✕ Kérkyra, Iónioi Nísoi, Greece, C Mediterranean Sea
117 B16 **Kérkyra** *var.* Kérkira, *Eng.* Corfu. Kérkyra, Iónioi Nísoi, Greece, C Mediterranean Sea
117 A16 **Kérkyra** *var.* Kérkira, *Eng.* Corfu. *island* Iónioi Nísoi, Greece, C Mediterranean Sea
199 Jj12 **Kermadec Islands** *island group* NZ, SW Pacific Ocean
183 R10 **Kermadec Ridge** *undersea feature* SW Pacific Ocean
183 R11 **Kermadec Trench** *undersea feature* SW Pacific Ocean
149 S10 **Kermān** *var.* Kirman; *anc.* Carmana. Kermān, C Iran
149 R11 **Kermān** *off.* Ostān-e Kermān, *var.* Kirman; *anc.* Carmania. ◆ *province* SE Iran
149 U12 **Kermān, Biābān-e** *var.* Kerman Desert. *desert* SE Iran
149 Q9 **Kermānshāh** Yazd, C Iran
Kermānshāh *see* Bākhtarān
148 J6 **Kermānshāhān** *off.* Ostān-e Kermānshāhān; *prev.* Bākhtarān. ◆ *province* W Iran
116 L10 **Kermen** Burgaska Oblast, E Bulgaria
26 L8 **Kermit** Texas, SW USA
23 P6 **Kermit** West Virginia, NE USA
23 S9 **Kernersville** North Carolina, SE USA
37 S12 **Kern River** ~ California, W USA
37 S12 **Kernville** California, W USA
117 K21 **Kéros** *island* Kykládes, Greece, Aegean Sea
78 K14 **Kérouané** Haute-Guinée, SE Guinea
103 D16 **Kerpen** Nordrhein-Westfalen, W Germany
152 I11 **Kerpichli** Lebapskiy Velayat, NE Turkmenistan
26 M1 **Kerrick** Texas, SW USA
Kerr Lake *see* John H.Kerr Reservoir
9 S15 **Kerrobert** Saskatchewan, S Canada
27 Q11 **Kerrville** Texas, SW USA
99 B20 **Kerry** *Ir.* Ciarraí. *cultural region* SW Ireland
23 S11 **Kershaw** South Carolina, SE USA
Kertel *see* Kärdla
97 H23 **Kerteminde** Fyn, C Denmark
169 Q7 **Kerulen** *Chin.* Herlen He, *Mong.* Herlen Gol. ~ China/Mongolia
Kervo *see* Kerava
Kerýneia *see* Girne
10 H11 **Kesagami Lake** ◎ Ontario, SE Canada
95 O17 **Kesälahti** Pohjois-Karjala, SE Finland
142 B11 **Keşan** Edirne, NW Turkey
171 Mm12 **Kesennuma** Miyagi, Honshū, C Japan
169 V7 **Keshan** Heilongjiang, NE China
32 M6 **Keshena** Wisconsin, N USA
142 I13 **Keskin** Kırıkkale, C Turkey
95 L17 **Keski-Suomi** *Swe.* Mellersta Finland. ◆ *province* C Finland
Késmárk *see* Kežmarok
128 I6 **Kesten'ga** *var.* Kest Enga. Respublika Kareliya, NW Russian Federation
100 K12 **Kesteren** Gelderland, C Netherlands
12 H14 **Keswick** Ontario, S Canada
99 K15 **Keswick** NW England, UK
113 H24 **Keszthely** Zala, SW Hungary
126 Hh13 **Ket'** ~ C Russian Federation
79 P17 **Keta** SE Ghana
174 Kk10 **Ketapang** Borneo, C Indonesia
131 O12 **Ketchenery** *prev.* Sovetskoye. Respublika Kalmykiya, SW Russian Federation
41 Y14 **Ketchikan** Revillagigedo Island, Alaska, USA
35 O14 **Ketchum** Idaho, NW USA
Kete/Kete Krakye *see* Kete-Krachi
79 Q15 **Kete-Krachi** *var.* Kete, Kete Krakye. E Ghana
100 L9 **Ketelmeer** *channel* E Netherlands
155 P17 **Keti Bandar** Sind, SE Pakistan
151 W16 **Ketmen', Khrebet** ▲ SE Kazakhstan
79 S16 **Kétou** SE Benin
112 M7 **Kętrzyn** *Ger.* Rastenburg. Olsztyn, NE Poland
99 N20 **Kettering** C England, UK
33 R14 **Kettering** Ohio, N USA
20 F13 **Kettle Creek** ~ Pennsylvania, NE USA
34 L7 **Kettle Falls** Washington, NW USA
12 D16 **Kettle Point** *headland* Ontario, S Canada
31 V6 **Kettle River** ~ Minnesota, N USA
194 E12 **Ketu** ~ W PNG
20 G10 **Keuka Lake** ◎ New York, NE USA
Keupriya *see* Primorsko
95 L17 **Keuruu** Keski-Suomi, C Finland
Kevevára *see* Kovin
94 L9 **Kevo** *Lapp.* Geavvú. Lappi, N Finland
46 M6 **Kew** North Caicos, N Turks and Caicos Islands
32 K11 **Kewanee** Illinois, N USA
33 N7 **Kewaunee** Wisconsin, N USA
32 M3 **Keweenaw Bay** ◎ Michigan, N USA
33 N2 **Keweenaw Peninsula** *peninsula* Michigan, N USA
33 N2 **Keweenaw Point** *headland* Michigan, N USA
31 N12 **Keya Paha River** ~ Nebraska/South Dakota, N USA
Keyaygyr *see* Këk-Aygyr
25 Z16 **Key Biscayne** Florida, SE USA
28 G8 **Keyes** Oklahoma, C USA
25 Y17 **Key Largo** Key Largo, Florida, SE USA
23 U3 **Keyser** West Virginia, NE USA
29 O9 **Keystone Lake** ⊟ Oklahoma, C USA
38 L16 **Keystone Peak** ▲ Arizona, SW USA
Keystone State *see* Pennsylvania
23 U7 **Keysville** Virginia, NE USA
29 T3 **Keytesville** Missouri, C USA
25 W17 **Key West** Florida Keys, Florida, SE USA
131 T1 **Kez** Udmurtskaya Respublika, NW Russian Federation
Kezdivásárhely *see* Târgu Secuiesc
126 J13 **Kezhma** Krasnoyarskiy Kray, C Russian Federation
113 L18 **Kežmarok** *Ger.* Käsmark, *Hung.* Késmárk. Východné Slovensko, NE Slovakia
85 F20 **Kgalagadi** ◆ *district* SW Botswana
85 I20 **Kgatleng** ◆ *district* SE Botswana
196 F8 **Kgkeklau** Babeldaob, N Palau
129 R6 **Khabarikha** *var.* Chabaricha. Respublika Komi, NW Russian Federation
127 N16 **Khabarovsk** Khabarovskiy Kray, SE Russian Federation
126 Mm12 **Khabarovskiy Kray** ◆ *territory* E Russian Federation
147 W7 **Khabb** Abū Ẓaby, E UAE
Khabour, Nahr al *see* Khābūr, Nahr al
Khabura *see* Al Khābūrah
145 N2 **Khābūr, Nahr al** *var.* Nahr al Khabour. ~ Syria/Turkey
Khachmas *see* Xaçmaz
82 B12 **Khadari** ~ W Sudan
147 X12 **Khādhil** *var.* Khudal. SE Oman
161 E14 **Khadki** *prev.* Kirkee. Mahārāshtra, W India
130 L14 **Khadyzhensk** Krasnodarskiy Kray, SW Russian Federation
116 N9 **Khadzhiyska Reka** ~ E Bulgaria
119 P10 **Khadzhybeys'kyy Lyman** ◎ SW Ukraine
144 K3 **Khafsah** Ḩalab, N Syria
158 M13 **Khaga** Uttar Pradesh, N India
159 Q13 **Khagaria** Bihār, NE India
155 Q13 **Khairpur** Sind, SE Pakistan
126 Hh15 **Khakasiya, Respublika** *prev.* Khakasskaya Avtonomnaya Oblast', *Eng.* Khakassia. ◆ *autonomous republic* C Russian Federation
Khakassia/Khakasskaya Avtonomnaya Oblast' *see* Khakasiya, Respublika
178 H9 **Kha Khaeng, Khao** ▲ W Thailand
85 G20 **Khakhea** *var.* Kakia. Southern, S Botswana
152 L13 **Khalach** Lebapskiy Velayat, E Turkmenistan
Khalándrion *see* Chalándri
131 W7 **Khalilovo** Orenburgskaya Oblast', W Russian Federation
Khalkabad *see* Khalqobod
148 L3 **Khalkhāl** *prev.* Herowābād. Ardabīl, NW Iran
Khalkidhikí *see* Chalkidikí
Khalkís *see* Chalkída
129 W3 **Khal'mer-Yu** Respublika Komi, NW Russian Federation
121 M14 **Khalopyenichy** *Rus.* Kholopenichi. Minskaya Voblasts', NE Belarus
152 H7 **Khalqobod** *Rus.* Khalkabad. Qoraqalpoghiston Respublikasi, W Uzbekistan
Khalturin *see* Orlov
147 Y10 **Khalūf** *var.* Al Khaluf. E Oman
160 K10 **Khamaria** Madhya Pradesh, C India
160 D11 **Khambhāt** Gujarāt, W India
160 C12 **Khambhāt, Gulf of** *Eng.* Gulf of Cambay. *gulf* W India
178 K10 **Khâm Đưc** Quang Nam-Đa Nāng, C Vietnam
160 G12 **Khāmgaon** Mahārāshtra, C India
147 O14 **Khamir** *var.* Khamr. W Yemen
147 N12 **Khamīs Mushayt** *var.* Hamïs Musait. 'Asīr, SW Saudi Arabia
126 L10 **Khampa** Respublika Sakha (Yakutiya), NE Russian Federation
Khamr *see* Khamir
85 C19 **Khan** ~ W Namibia
155 Q2 **Khānābād** Kunduz, NE Afghanistan
Khān Abou Châmâte/Khan Abou Ech Cham *see* Khān Abū Shāmāt
144 I7 **Khān Abū Shāmāt** *var.* Khān Abou Châmâte, Khan Abou Ech Cham. Dimashq, W Syria
Khān al Baghdādī *see* Al Baghdādī
Khān al Maḩāwīl *see* Al Maḩāwīl
145 T7 **Khān al Mashāhidah** C Iraq
145 T10 **Khān al Muşallá** S Iraq
145 U6 **Khānaqīn** E Iraq
145 T11 **Khān ar Ruḩbah** S Iraq
145 P2 **Khān as Sūr** N Iraq
145 T8 **Khān Āzād** C Iraq
160 N13 **Khandaparha** *prev.* Khandpara. Orissa, E India
Khandpara *see* Khandaparha
155 T2 **Khandūd** *var.* Khandud, Wakhan. Badakhshān, NE Afghanistan
160 G11 **Khandwa** Madhya Pradesh, C India
126 Mm10 **Khandyga** Respublika Sakha (Yakutiya), NE Russian Federation
155 T10 **Khānewāl** Punjab, NE Pakistan
155 S10 **Khāngarh** Punjab, E Pakistan
Khanh Hung *see* Soc Trăng
Khaniá *see* Chaniá
Khanka *see* Khonqa
169 Z8 **Khanka, Lake** *var.* Hsing-k'ai Hu, Lake Hanka, *Chin.* Xingkai Hu, *Rus.* Ozero Khanka. ◎ China/Russian Federation
Khanka, Ozero *see* Khanka, Lake
Khankendi *see* Xankändi
Khanlar *see* Xanlar
126 Kk10 **Khannya** ~ NE Russian Federation
155 S12 **Khānpur** Punjab, SE Pakistan
155 S12 **Khānpur** Punjab, E Pakistan
144 I4 **Khān Shaykhūn** *var.* Khan Sheikhun. Idlib, NW Syria
Khan Sheikhun *see* Khān Shaykhūn
151 S15 **Khantau** Zhambyl, S Kazakhstan
151 W16 **Khan Tengri, Pik** ▲ SE Kazakhstan
178 J9 **Khanthabouli** *prev.* Savannakhét. Savannakhét, S Laos
125 Ff10 **Khanty-Mansiysk** *prev.* Ostyako-Voguls'k. Khanty-Mansiyskiy Avtonomnyy Okrug, C Russian Federation
129 V8 **Khanty-Mansiyskiy Avtonomnyy Okrug** ◆ *autonomous district* C Russian Federation
145 R4 **Khānūqah** C Iraq
144 E11 **Khān Yūnis** *var.* Khān Yūnus. S Gaza Strip
Khān Yūnus *see* Khān Yūnis
Khanzi *see* Ghanzi
145 U5 **Khān Zūr** E Iraq
178 H10 **Khao Laem Reservoir** ⊟ W Thailand
126 Kk17 **Khapcheranga** Chitinskaya Oblast', S Russian Federation
131 Q12 **Kharabali** Astrakhanskaya Oblast', SW Russian Federation
159 R16 **Kharagpur** West Bengal, NE India
145 V11 **Kharā'ib 'Abd al Karīm** S Iraq
149 Q8 **Kharānaq** Yazd, C Iran
Kharbin *see* Harbin
152 H13 **Khardzhagaz** Akhalskiy Velayat, C Turkmenistan
Khārga Oasis *see* Great Oasis, The
160 F11 **Khargon** Madhya Pradesh, C India
155 V7 **Khāriān** Punjab, NE Pakistan
119 X8 **Kharisyz'k** Donets'ka Oblast', E Ukraine
119 V5 **Kharkiv** *Rus.* Khar'kov. Kharkivs'ka Oblast', NE Ukraine
119 V5 **Kharkiv** ✕ Kharkivs'ka Oblast', E Ukraine
Kharkiv *see* Kharkivs'ka Oblast'
119 U5 **Kharkivs'ka Oblast'** *var.* Kharkiv, *Rus.* Khar'kovskaya Oblast'. ◆ *province* E Ukraine
Khar'kov *see* Kharkiv
Khar'kovskaya Oblast' *see* Kharkivs'ka Oblast'
128 L3 **Kharlovka** Murmanskaya Oblast', NW Russian Federation
116 K11 **Kharmanli** Khaskovska Oblast, S Bulgaria
116 K11 **Kharmanliyska Reka** ~ S Bulgaria
128 M13 **Kharovsk** Vologodskaya Oblast', NW Russian Federation
82 F9 **Khartoum** *var.* El Khartûm, Khartum. ● (Sudan) Khartoum, C Sudan
82 F9 **Khartoum** ◆ *state* NE Sudan
82 F9 **Khartoum** ✕ Khartoum, C Sudan
82 F9 **Khartoum North** Khartoum, C Sudan
119 X8 **Khartsyz'k** *Rus.* Khartsyzsk. Donets'ka Oblast', SE Ukraine
Khartsyzsk *see* Khartsyz'k
Khartum *see* Khartoum
Khasab *see* Al Khaşab
127 N18 **Khasan** Primorskiy Kray, SE Russian Federation
131 P16 **Khasavyurt** Respublika Dagestan, SW Russian Federation
149 W12 **Khāsh** *prev.* Vāsht. Sīstān va Balūchestān, SE Iran
154 K8 **Khāsh, Dasht-e** *Eng.* Khash Desert. *desert* SW Afghanistan
Khash Desert *see* Khāsh, Dasht-e
Khashim Al Qirba/Khashm al Qirbah *see* Khashm el Girba
82 H9 **Khashm el Girba** *var.* Khashim Al Qirba, Khashm al Qirbah. Kassala, E Sudan
144 G14 **Khashsh, Jabal al** ▲ S Jordan
143 S10 **Khashuri** C Georgia
159 V13 **Khāsi Hills** *hill range* NE India
116 K11 **Khaskovo** Khaskovska Oblast, S Bulgaria
Khaskovo *see* Khaskovska Oblast
116 J11 **Khaskovska Oblast** *var.* Khaskovo. ◆ *province* S Bulgaria
126 J7 **Khatanga** Taymyrskiy (Dolgano-Nenetskiy) Avtonomnyy Okrug, N Russian Federation
126 J7 **Khatanga** ~ N Russian Federation
Khatanga, Gulf of *see* Khatangskiy Zaliv
126 Jj6 **Khatangskiy Zaliv** *var.* Gulf of Khatanga. *bay* N Russian Federation
147 W7 **Khatmat al Malāḩah** N Oman
149 S16 **Khaṭmat al Malāḩah** Ash Shāriqah, E UAE
Khātoûniyé *see* Khātūnīyah
127 Q6 **Khatyrka** Chukotskiy Avtonomnyy Okrug, NE Russian Federation
152 I14 **Khauz-Khan** *Turkm.* Hanhowuz. Akhalskiy Velayat, S Turkmenistan
152 I14 **Khauzkhanskoye Vodokhranilishche** ⊟ S Turkmenistan
Khavaling *see* Khovaling
Khavast *see* Khowos
145 W10 **Khawrah, Nahr al** ~ S Iraq
Khawr Barakah *see* Baraka
147 W7 **Khawr Fakkān** *var.* Khor Fakkan. Ash Shāriqah, NE UAE
146 L6 **Khaybar** Al Madīnah, NW Saudi Arabia
Khaybar, Kowtal-e *see* Khyber Pass
153 S11 **Khaydarkan** *var.* Khaydarken. Oshskaya Oblast', SW Kyrgyzstan
Khaydarken *see* Khaydarkan
129 U2 **Khaypudyrskaya Guba** *bay* NW Russian Federation
145 S1 **Khayrūzuk** E Iraq
Khazar, Baḩr-e/Khazar, Daryā-ye *see* Caspian Sea
Khazarosp *see* Hazorasp
Khazretishi, Khrebet *see* Hazratishoh, Qatorkŭhi
Khelat *see* Kalāt
76 F6 **Khemisset** NW Morocco
178 J10 **Khemmarat** *var.* Kemarat. Ubon Ratchathani, E Thailand
76 L6 **Khenchela** *var.* Khenchla. NE Algeria
Khenchla *see* Khenchela
76 G7 **Khénifra** C Morocco
Khersān, Rūd-e *see* Garm, Āb-e
119 R10 **Kherson** Khersons'ka Oblast', S Ukraine
Kherson *see* Khersons'ka Oblast'
119 S14 **Khersones, Mys** *Rus.* Mys Khersonesskiy. *headland* S Ukraine
Khersonesskiy, Mys *see* Khersones, Mys
119 R10 **Khersons'ka Oblast'** *var.* Kherson, *Rus.* Khersonskaya Oblast'. ◆ *province* S Ukraine
Khersonskaya Oblast' *see* Khersons'ka Oblast'
126 J7 **Kheta** Taymyrskiy (Dolgano-Nenetskiy) Avtonomnyy Okrug, N Russian Federation
126 J7 **Kheta** ~ N Russian Federation
178 Jj8 **Khe Ve** Quang Binh, C Vietnam
155 U7 **Khewra** Punjab, E Pakistan
Khiam *see* El Khiyam
128 J4 **Khibiny** ▲ NW Russian Federation
126 K16 **Khilok** Chitinskaya Oblast', S Russian Federation
126 K16 **Khilok** ~ S Russian Federation
130 K3 **Khimki** Moskovskaya Oblast', W Russian Federation
153 S12 **Khingov** *Rus.* Obi-Khingou. ~ C Tajikistan
Khíos *see* Chíos
155 R15 **Khipro** Sindh, SE Pakistan
145 S10 **Khirr, Wādī al** *dry watercourse* S Iraq
116 I10 **Khisarya** Plovdivska Oblast, C Bulgaria
Khiva *see* Khiwa
152 H9 **Khiwa** *Rus.* Khiva. Khorazm Wiloyati, W Uzbekistan
178 H9 **Khlong Khlung** Kamphaeng Phet, W Thailand
178 Gg16 **Khlong Thom** Krabi, SW Thailand
178 I12 **Khlung** Chantaburi, S Thailand
Khmel'nik *see* Khmil'nyk
Khmel'nitskaya Oblast' *see* Khmel'nyts'ka Oblast'
Khmel'nitskiy *see* Khmel 'nyts'kyy
118 K5 **Khmel'nyts'ka Oblast'** *var.* Khmel'nyts'kyy, *Rus.* Khmel'nitskaya Oblast'; *prev.* Kamenets-Podol'skaya Oblast'. ◆ *province* NW Ukraine
118 L6 **Khmel 'nyts'kyy** *Rus.* Khmel'nitskiy; *prev.* Proskurov. Khmel'nyts'ka Oblast', W Ukraine
Khmel'nyts'kyy *see* Khmel'nyts'ka Oblast'
118 M6 **Khmil'nyk** *Rus.* Khmel'nik. Vinnyts'ka Oblast', C Ukraine
143 R9 **Khobi** W Georgia
121 P15 **Khodasy** *Rus.* Khodosy. Mahilyowskaya Voblasts', E Belarus
118 I6 **Khodoriv** *Pol.* Chodorów, *Rus.* Khodorov. L'vivs'ka Oblast', NW Ukraine
Khodorov *see* Khodoriv
Khodosy *see* Khodasy
152 D12 **Khodzhakala** *Turkm.* Hojagala. Balkanskiy Velayat, W Turkmenistan
152 M13 **Khodzhambas** *Turkm.* Hojambaz. Lebapskiy Velayat, E Turkmenistan
Khodzhent *see* Khŭjand
Khodzheyli *see* Khŭjayli
Khoi *see* Khvoy
Khojend *see* Khŭjand
Khokand *see* Qŭqon
130 L8 **Khokhol'skiy** Voronezhskaya Oblast', W Russian Federation
178 Hh10 **Khok Samrong** Lop Buri, C Thailand
155 P2 **Kholm** *var.* Tashqurghan, *Pash.* Khulm. Balkh, N Afghanistan
128 H15 **Kholm** Novgorodskaya Oblast', W Russian Federation
Kholm *see* Chełm
Kholmech' *see* Kholmyech
127 Oo16 **Kholmsk** Ostrov Sakhalin, Sakhalinskaya Oblast', SE Russian Federation
121 O19 **Kholmyech** *Rus.* Kholmech'. Homyel'skaya Voblasts', SE Belarus
Kholopenichi *see* Khalopyenichy
85 D19 **Khomas** ◆ *district* C Namibia
85 D19 **Khomas Hochland** *var.* Khomasplato. *plateau* C Namibia
Khomasplato *see* Khomas Hochland
Khomein *see* Khomeyn
148 M7 **Khomeyn** *var.* Khomein, Khumain. Markazī, W Iran
149 N8 **Khomeynīshahr** *prev.* Homāyūnshahr. Eşfahān, C Iran
Khoms *see* Al Khums
Khong Sedone *see* Muang Khôngxédôn
178 I9 **Khon Kaen** *var.* Muang Khon Kaen. Khon Kaen, E Thailand
152 I9 **Khonqa** *Rus.* Khanka. Khorazm Wiloyati, W Uzbekistan
178 I9 **Khon San** Khon Kaen, E Thailand
127 N8 **Khonuu** Respublika Sakha (Yakutiya), NE Russian Federation
131 N8 **Khopër** *var.* Khoper. ~ SW Russian Federation
127 Nn16 **Khor** Khabarovskiy Kray, SE Russian Federation
127 Nn16 **Khor** ~ SE Russian Federation
149 S6 **Khorāsān** *off.* Ostān-e Khorāsān, *var.* Khorassan, Khurasan. ◆ *province* NE Iran
Khorassan *see* Khorāsān
Khorat *see* Nakhon Ratchasima
152 H9 **Khorazm Wiloyati** *Rus.* Khorezmskaya Oblast'. ◆ *province* W Uzbekistan
160 O13 **Khordha** *prev.* Khurda. Orissa, E India
129 U4 **Khorey-Ver** Nenetskiy Avtonomnyy Okrug, NW Russian Federation
Khorezmskaya Oblast' *see* Khorazm Wiloyati
Khor Fakkan *see* Khawr Fakkān
151 W15 **Khorgos** Taldykorgan, SE Kazakhstan
126 K16 **Khorinsk** Respublika Buryatiya, S Russian Federation
85 C18 **Khorixas** Kunene, NW Namibia
147 O17 **Khormaksar** *var.* Aden. ✕ ('Adan) SW Yemen
Khormal *see* Khurmāl
Khormuj *see* Khvormūj
Khorog *see* Khorugh
119 S5 **Khorol** Poltavs'ka Oblast', NE Ukraine
148 L7 **Khorramābād** *var.* Khurramabad. Lorestān, W Iran
148 K10 **Khorramshahr** *var.* Khurramshahr, Muhammerah; *prev.* Mohammerah. Khūzestān, SW Iran
153 S14 **Khorugh** *Rus.* Khorog. S Tajikistan
131 Q12 **Khosheutovo** Astrakhanskaya Oblast', SW Russian Federation
Khotan *see* Hotan
Khotimsk *see* Khotsimsk
Khotin *see* Khotyn
121 R16 **Khotsimsk** *Rus.* Khotimsk. Mahilyowskaya Voblasts', E Belarus
118 K7 **Khotyn** *Rom.* Hotin, *Rus.* Khotin. Chernivets'ka Oblast', W Ukraine
76 F7 **Khouribga** C Morocco
153 Q13 **Khovaling** *Rus.* Khavaling. SW Tajikistan
Khovd *see* Hovd
153 P11 **Khowos** *var.* Ursat'yevskaya, *Rus.* Khavast. Sirdaryo Wiloyati, E Uzbekistan
155 R6 **Khowst** Paktiā, E Afghanistan
Khoy *see* Khvoy
121 N20 **Khoyniki** *Rus.* Khoyniki. Homyel'skaya Voblasts', SE Belarus
Khozretishi, Khrebet *see* Hazratishoh, Qatorkŭhi
Khrisoúpolis *see* Chrysoúpoli
126 Mm6 **Khroma** ~ NE Russian Federation
150 J10 **Khromtau** *Kaz.* Khromtaū. Aktyubinsk, W Kazakhstan
Khrysokhou Bay *see* Chrysochoú, Kólpos
119 O7 **Khrystynivka** Cherkas'ka Oblast', C Ukraine
178 J10 **Khuang Nai** Ubon Ratchathani, E Thailand
Khudal *see* Khādhil
Khudat *see* Xudat
155 W9 **Khudiān** Punjab, E Pakistan
Khudzhand *see* Khŭjand
153 O13 **Khufar** Surkhondaryo Wiloyati, S Uzbekistan
85 G21 **Khuis** Kgalagadi, SW Botswana
153 Q11 **Khŭjand** *var.* Khodzhent, Khojend, *Rus.* Khudzhand; *prev.* Leninabad, *Taj.* Leninobod. N Tajikistan
152 H8 **Khŭjayli** *Rus.* Khodzheyli. Qoraqalpoghiston Respublikasi, W Uzbekistan
178 Ii11 **Khukhan** Si Sa Ket, E Thailand
Khulm *see* Kholm
159 T16 **Khulna** Khulna, SW Bangladesh
159 T16 **Khulna** ◆ *division* SW Bangladesh
Khumain *see* Khomeyn
Khums *see* Al Khums
155 W2 **Khunjerāb Pass** *Chin.* Kunjirap Daban. *pass* China/Pakistan *see also* Kunjirap Daban
159 P16 **Khunti** Bihār, N India
178 Gg7 **Khun Yuam** Mae Hong Son, NW Thailand
Khurais *see* Khurayş
Khurasan *see* Khorāsān
147 R7 **Khurayş** *var.* Khurais. Ash Sharqīyah, C Saudi Arabia
Khurda *see* Khordha
158 J11 **Khurja** Uttar Pradesh, N India
145 V4 **Khurmāl** *var.* Khormal. NE Iraq
Khurramabad *see* Khorramābād
Khurramshahr *see* Khorramshahr
155 U7 **Khushāb** Punjab, NE Pakistan
118 H8 **Khust** *Cz.* Chust, Husté, *Hung.* Huszt. Zakarpats'ka Oblast', W Ukraine
82 D11 **Khuwei** Western Kordofan, C Sudan
155 O13 **Khuzdār** Baluchistān, SW Pakistan
148 L9 **Khūzestān** *off.* Ostān-e Khūzestān, *var.* Khuzistan; *prev.* Arabistan, *anc.* Susiana. ◆ *province* SW Iran
Khuzistan *see* Khūzestān
155 R2 **Khvājeh Ghār** *var.* Khwajaghar, Khwaja-i-Ghar. Takhār, NE Afghanistan
131 Q7 **Khvalynsk** Saratovskaya Oblast', W Russian Federation
149 N12 **Khvormūj** *var.* Khormuj. Būshehr, S Iran
148 I2 **Khvoy** *var.* Khoi, Khoy. Āzarbāyjān-e Bākhtarī, NW Iran
Khwajaghar/Khwaja-i-Ghar *see* Khvājeh Ghār
155 S5 **Khyber Pass** *var.* Kowtal-e Khaybar. *pass* Afghanistan/Pakistan
195 V14 **Kia** Santa Isabel, N Solomon Islands
191 S10 **Kiama** New South Wales, SE Australia
179 R17 **Kiamba** Mindanao, S Philippines
81 O22 **Kiambi** Shaba, SE Zaire
29 Q12 **Kiamichi Mountains** ▲ Oklahoma, C USA
29 Q12 **Kiamichi River** ~ Oklahoma, C USA
12 M10 **Kiamika, Réservoir** ⊟ Québec, SE Canada
Kiamusze *see* Jiamusi
41 N7 **Kiana** Alaska, USA
Kiangmai *see* Chiang Mai
Kiang-ning *see* Nanjing
Kiangsi *see* Jiangxi
Kiangsu *see* Jiangsu
95 M14 **Kiantajärvi** ◎ E Finland
117 F19 **Kiáto** *prev.* Kiáton. Pelopónnisos, S Greece
Kiáton *see* Kiáto
Kiayi *see* Chiai
69 T9 **Kibali** *var.* Uele (upper course). ~ NE Zaire
81 E20 **Kibangou** Le Niari, SW Congo
Kibarty *see* Kybartai
94 M8 **Kiberg** Finnmark, N Norway
97 F22 **Kibæk** Ringkøbing, W Denmark
81 N20 **Kibombo** Maniema, E Zaire
83 E20 **Kibondo** Kigoma, NW Tanzania
83 J15 **Kibre Mengist** *var.* Adola. S Ethiopia
Kıbrıs/Kıbrıs Cumhuriyeti *see* Cyprus
83 E20 **Kibungo** *var.* Kibungu. SE Rwanda
Kibungu *see* Kibungo
115 N19 **Kičevo** SW FYR Macedonia
129 P13 **Kichmengskiy Gorodok** Vologodskaya Oblast', NW Russian Federation
32 J8 **Kickapoo River** ~ Wisconsin, N USA
9 P16 **Kicking Horse Pass** *pass* Alberta/British Columbia, SW Canada
79 R9 **Kidal** Kidal, C Mali
79 Q8 **Kidal** ◆ *region* NE Mali
179 R16 **Kidapawan** Mindanao, S Philippines
99 L20 **Kidderminster** C England, UK
78 I11 **Kidira** E Senegal
192 O11 **Kidnappers, Cape** *headland* North Island, NZ
102 J8 **Kiel** Schleswig-Holstein, N Germany
113 L15 **Kielce** *Rus.* Keltsy. Kielce, SE Poland
113 L15 **Kielce** *off.* Województwo Kieleckie, *Rus.* Keltsy. ◆ *province* SE Poland
Kieleckie, Województwo *see* Kielce
102 K7 **Kieler Bucht** *bay* N Germany
102 J7 **Kieler Förde** *inlet* N Germany
178 K13 **Kiên Đưc** *var.* Đak Lap. Đăc Lăc, S Vietnam
81 N24 **Kienge** Shaba, SE Zaire
195 S12 **Kieta** Bougainville Island, NE PNG
102 Q12 **Kietz** Brandenburg, NE Germany
Kiev *see* Kyyiv
Kiev Reservoir *see* Kyyivs'ke Vodoskhovyshche
78 J10 **Kiffa** Assaba, S Mauritania
117 H19 **Kifisiá** Attikí, C Greece
117 F18 **Kifisós** ~ C Greece
145 U5 **Kifrī** N Iraq
83 D20 **Kigali** ● (Rwanda) C Rwanda
83 E20 **Kigali** ✕ C Rwanda
143 P13 **Kiğı** Bingöl, E Turkey
83 E21 **Kigoma** Kigoma, W Tanzania
83 E21 **Kigoma** ◆ *region* W Tanzania
40 F10 **Kihei** *Haw.* Kihei. Maui, Hawaii, USA, C Pacific Ocean
95 K17 **Kihniö** Häme, SW Finland
120 F6 **Kihnu** *var.* Kihnu Saar, *Ger.* Kühnö. *island* SW Estonia
Kihnu Saar *see* Kihnu
40 A8 **Kii Landing** Niihau, Hawaii, USA, C Pacific Ocean
95 L14 **Kiiminki** Oulu, C Finland
171 H16 **Kii-Nagashima** *var.* Nagashima. Mie, Honshū, SW Japan
171 Gg16 **Kii-sanchi** ▲ Honshū, SW Japan
94 L11 **Kiistala** Lappi, N Finland
170 Ff16 **Kii-suidō** *strait* S Japan
172 R14 **Kikai-shima** *var.* Kikaiga-shima. *island* Nansei-shotō, SW Japan
114 M8 **Kikinda** *Ger.* Grosskikinda, *Hung.* Nagykikinda; *prev.* Velika Kikinda. Serbia, N Yugoslavia
Kikládhes *see* Kykládes
172 N7 **Kikonai** Hokkaidō, NE Japan
194 H14 **Kikori** Gulf, S PNG
194 G13 **Kikori** ~ W PNG
170 Cc14 **Kikuchi** *var.* Kikuti. Kumamoto, Kyūshū, SW Japan
Kikuti *see* Kikuchi
131 N8 **Kikvidze** Volgogradskaya Oblast', SW Russian Federation
12 I10 **Kikwissi, Lac** ◎ Québec, SE Canada
81 I21 **Kikwit** Bandundu, W Zaire
97 K15 **Kil** Värmland, C Sweden
96 N12 **Kilafors** Gävleborg, C Sweden
40 B8 **Kilauea** *Haw.* Kīlauea. Kauai, Hawaii, USA, C Pacific Ocean
40 H12 **Kilauea Caldera** *crater* Hawaii, USA, C Pacific Ocean
111 V4 **Kilb** Niederösterreich, C Austria
41 O12 **Kilbuck Mountains** ▲ Alaska, USA
169 Y12 **Kilchu** NE North Korea
99 F18 **Kilcock** *Ir.* Cill Choca. E Ireland
191 V2 **Kilcoy** Queensland, E Australia
99 F18 **Kildare** *Ir.* Cill Dara. E Ireland
99 F18 **Kildare** *Ir.* Cill Dara. *cultural region* E Ireland
128 K2 **Kil'din, Ostrov** *island* NW Russian Federation
27 W7 **Kilgore** Texas, SW USA
Kilien Mountains *see* Qilian Shan
116 K9 **Kilifarevo** Loveshka Oblast, C Bulgaria
83 K20 **Kilifi** Coast, SE Kenya
201 U9 **Kili Island** *var.* Kōle. *island* Ralik Chain, S Marshall Islands
155 V2 **Kilik Pass** *pass* Afghanistan/China
Kilimane *see* Quelimane
83 I21 **Kilimanjaro** ◆ *region* E Tanzania
83 I20 **Kilimanjaro** *var.* Uhuru Peak. ▲ NE Tanzania
Kilimbangara *see* Kolombangara
Kilinailau Islands *see* Tulun Islands
83 K23 **Kilindoni** Pwani, E Tanzania
120 H6 **Kilingi-Nõmme** *Ger.* Kurkund. Pärnumaa, SW Estonia
142 M17 **Kilis** Gaziantep, S Turkey
119 N12 **Kiliya** *Rom.* Chilia-Nouă. Odes'ka Oblast', SW Ukraine
99 B19 **Kilkee** *Ir.* Cill Chaoi. W Ireland
99 E19 **Kilkenny** *Ir.* Cill Chainnigh. S Ireland
99 E19 **Kilkenny** *Ir.* Cill Chainnigh. *cultural region* S Ireland
99 B18 **Kilkieran Bay** *Ir.* Cuan Chill Chiaráin. *bay* W Ireland
116 G13 **Kilkís** Kentrikí Makedonía, N Greece
99 C15 **Killala Bay** *Ir.* Cuan Chill Ala. *inlet* NW Ireland
9 R15 **Killam** Alberta, SW Canada
191 U3 **Killarney** Queensland, E Australia
9 W17 **Killarney** Manitoba, S Canada
12 E11 **Killarney** Ontario, S Canada
99 B20 **Killarney** *Ir.* Cill Airne. SW Ireland
30 K4 **Killdeer** North Dakota, N USA
30 J4 **Killdeer Mountains** ▲ North Dakota, N USA
47 V15 **Killdeer River** ~ Trinidad, Trinidad and Tobago
27 S9 **Killeen** Texas, SW USA
41 P6 **Killik River** ~ Alaska, USA
16 P4 **Killinek Island** *island* Northwest Territories, NE Canada
Killini *see* Kyllíni
117 C19 **Killínis, Ákra** *headland* S Greece
99 D15 **Killybegs** *Ir.* Na Cealla Beaga. NW Ireland
Kilmain *see* Quelimane
98 I13 **Kilmarnock** W Scotland, UK
23 X6 **Kilmarnock** Virginia, NE USA
129 S16 **Kil'mez'** Kirovskaya Oblast', NW Russian Federation
131 S2 **Kil'mez'** Udmurtskaya Respublika, NW Russian Federation
129 R16 **Kil'mez'** ~ NW Russian Federation
69 V11 **Kilombero** ~ S Tanzania
94 J10 **Kilpisjarvi** Lappi, N Finland
99 B19 **Kilrush** *Ir.* Cill Rois. W Ireland
81 O24 **Kilwa** Shaba, SE Zaire
Kilwa *see* Kilwa Kivinje
83 J24 **Kilwa Kivinje** *var.* Kilwa. Lindi, SE Tanzania
83 J24 **Kilwa Masoko** Lindi, SE Tanzania
176 Uu11 **Kilwo** Pulau Seram, E Indonesia
116 P12 **Kilyos** İstanbul, NW Turkey
39 V8 **Kim** Colorado, C USA
175 N3 **Kimanis, Teluk** *bay* Sabah, East Malaysia
190 H8 **Kimba** South Australia
30 I15 **Kimball** Nebraska, C USA
31 O11 **Kimball** South Dakota, N USA
81 I21 **Kimbao** Bandundu, SW Zaire
195 N12 **Kimbe** New Britain, E PNG

◆ Country ◇ Dependent Territory ◈ Administrative Region ▲ Mountain ☒ Volcano ◎ Lake
● Country Capital ○ Dependent Territory Capital ✕ International Airport ▲ Mountain Range ~ River ⊟ Reservoir

195 N11 Kimbe Bay inlet New Britain, E PNG
9 P17 Kimberley British Columbia, SW Canada
85 H23 Kimberley Northern Cape, C South Africa
188 M4 Kimberley Plateau plateau Western Australia
35 P15 Kimberly Idaho, NW USA
169 Y12 Kimch'aek prev. Sŏngjin. E North Korea
169 Y15 Kimch'ŏn C South Korea
169 Z16 Kim Hae var. Pusan. ✕ (Pusan) SE South Korea
Kími see Kými
95 K20 Kimito Swe. Kemiö. Turku-Pori, SW Finland
172 O6 Kimobetsu Hokkaidō, NE Japan
117 I21 Kímolos island Kykládes, Greece, Aegean Sea
117 I21 Kímolou Sífnou, Stenó strait Kykládes, Greece, Aegean Sea
130 L5 Kimovsk Tul'skaya Oblast', W Russian Federation
169 X15 Kimpo ✕ (Sŏul) NW South Korea
Kimpolung see Câmpulung Moldovenesc
128 K16 Kimry Tverskaya Oblast', W Russian Federation
81 H21 Kimvula Bas-Zaïre, SW Zaire
175 Nn2 Kinabalu, Gunung ▲ East Malaysia
Kinabatangan see Kinabatangan, Sungai
175 Oo3 Kinabatangan, Sungai var. Kinabatangan. ∾ East Malaysia
117 L21 Kínaros island Kykládes, Greece, Aegean Sea
9 O15 Kinbasket Lake ▣ British Columbia, SW Canada
98 I7 Kinbrace N Scotland, UK
12 E14 Kincardine Ontario, S Canada
98 K10 Kincardine cultural region E Scotland, UK
81 K21 Kinda Kasai Occidental, SE Zaire
81 M24 Kinda Shaba, SE Zaire
177 Ff3 Kindat Sagaing, N Myanmar
111 V6 Kindberg Steiermark, C Austria
24 H8 Kinder Louisiana, S USA
100 H13 Kinderdijk Zuid-Holland, SW Netherlands
99 M17 Kinder Scout ▲ C England, UK
9 S16 Kindersley Saskatchewan, S Canada
78 I14 Kindia Guinée-Maritime, SW Guinea
66 B11 Kindley Field air base E Bermuda
31 R6 Kindred North Dakota, N USA
81 N20 Kindu prev. Kindu-Port-Empain. Maniema, C Zaire
Kindu-Port-Empain see Kindu
131 S6 Kinel' Samarskaya Oblast', W Russian Federation
129 N15 Kineshma Ivanovskaya Oblast', W Russian Federation
King see King William's Town
146 K10 King Abdul Aziz ✕ (Makkah) Makkah, W Saudi Arabia
23 X6 King and Queen Court House Virginia, NE USA
King Charles Islands see Kong Karls Land
King Christian IX Land see Kong Christian IX Land
King Christian X Land see Kong Christian X Land
37 O11 King City California, W USA
29 R2 King City Missouri, C USA
40 M16 King Cove Alaska, USA
28 M10 Kingfisher Oklahoma, C USA
King Frederik VI Coast see Kong Frederik VI Kyst
King Frederik VIII Land see Kong Frederik VIII Land
67 B24 King George Bay bay West Falkland, Falkland Islands
204 G3 King George Island var. King George Land. island South Shetland Islands, Antarctica
10 I6 King George Islands island group Northwest Territories, C Canada
King George Land see King George Island
128 G13 Kingisepp Leningradskaya Oblast', NW Russian Federation
191 N14 King Island island Tasmania, SE Australia
8 J15 King Island island British Columbia, SW Canada
King Island see Kadan Kyun
Kingissepp see Kuressaare
147 Q7 King Khalid ✕ (Ar Riyāḍ) Ar Riyāḍ, C Saudi Arabia
37 S2 King Lear Peak ▲ Nevada, W USA
205 Y8 King Leopold and Queen Astrid Land physical region Antarctica
188 M4 King Leopold Ranges ▲ Western Australia
38 I11 Kingman Arizona, SW USA
28 M6 Kingman Kansas, C USA
199 K7 Kingman Reef ◇ US territory C Pacific Ocean
81 N20 Kingombe Maniema, E Zaire
190 F5 Kingoonya South Australia
204 J10 King Peninsula peninsula Antarctica
41 P13 King Salmon Alaska, USA
37 Q6 Kings Beach California, W USA
37 R11 Kingsburg California, W USA
190 I10 Kingscote South Australia
King's County see Offaly
204 H2 King Sejong South Korean research station Antarctica
191 T9 Kingsford Smith ✕ (Sydney) New South Wales, SE Australia
9 P17 Kingsgate British Columbia, SW Canada
25 W8 Kingsland Georgia, SE USA
31 S13 Kingsley Iowa, C USA
99 O19 King's Lynn var. Bishop's Lynn, Kings Lynn, Lynn, Lynn Regis. E England, UK
23 Q10 Kings Mountain North Carolina, SE USA
188 K4 King Sound sound Western Australia
39 N2 Kings Peak ▲ Utah, W USA
23 O8 Kingsport Tennessee, S USA
37 R11 Kings River ∾ California, W USA
191 P17 Kingston Tasmania, SE Australia
12 K14 Kingston Ontario, SE Canada
46 K13 Kingston ● (Jamaica) E Jamaica
193 C22 Kingston Otago, South Island, NZ
21 P12 Kingston Massachusetts, NE USA
29 S3 Kingston Missouri, C USA
20 K12 Kingston New York, NE USA
33 S14 Kingston Ohio, N USA
21 O13 Kingston Rhode Island, NE USA
22 M9 Kingston Tennessee, S USA
37 W12 Kingston Peak ▲ California, W USA
190 J11 Kingston Southeast South Australia
99 N17 Kingston upon Hull var. Hull. E England, UK
99 N22 Kingston upon Thames SE England, UK
47 P14 Kingstown ● (Saint Vincent and the Grenadines) Saint Vincent, Saint Vincent and the Grenadines
Kingstown see Dún Laoghaire
23 T13 Kingstree South Carolina, SE USA
66 L8 Kings Trough undersea feature E Atlantic Ocean
12 C18 Kingsville Ontario, S Canada
27 S15 Kingsville Texas, SW USA
23 W6 King William Virginia, NE USA
15 K3 King William Island island Northwest Territories, N Canada Arctic Ocean
85 I25 King William's Town var. King, Kingwilliamstown. Eastern Cape, S South Africa
23 T3 Kingwood West Virginia, NE USA
142 C13 Kınık İzmir, W Turkey
81 G21 Kinkala Le Pool, S Congo
171 Mm14 Kinka-san headland Honshū, C Japan
192 M8 Kinleith Waikato, North Island, NZ
97 J19 Kinna Älvsborg, S Sweden
98 L8 Kinnaird Head var. Kinnairds Head. headland NE Scotland, UK
97 K20 Kinnared Halland, S Sweden
Kinneret, Yam see Tiberias, Lake
161 K24 Kinniyai Eastern Province, NE Sri Lanka
95 L16 Kinnula Keski-Suomi, C Finland
12 I8 Kinojévis ∾ Québec, SE Canada
170 G16 Kino-kawa ∾ Honshū, SW Japan
9 U11 Kinoosao Saskatchewan, C Canada
101 L17 Kinrooi Limburg, NE Belgium
98 J11 Kinross C Scotland, UK
98 J11 Kinross cultural region C Scotland, UK
99 C21 Kinsale Ir. Cionn tSáile. SW Ireland
97 D14 Kinsarvik Hordaland, S Norway
81 G21 Kinshasa prev. Léopoldville. ● (Zaire) Kinshasa, W Zaire
81 G21 Kinshasa off. Ville de Kinshasa, var. Kinshasa City. ◈ region SW Zaire
81 G21 Kinshasa ✕ Kinshasa, SW Zaire
Kinshasa City see Kinshasa
119 U9 Kins'ka ∾ SE Ukraine
28 K6 Kinsley Kansas, C USA
23 W10 Kinston North Carolina, SE USA
79 P15 Kintampo W Ghana
190 B1 Kintore, Mount ▲ South Australia
98 G13 Kintyre peninsula W Scotland, UK
98 G13 Kintyre, Mull of headland W Scotland, UK
177 G4 Kin-u Sagaing, C Myanmar
10 G8 Kinushseo ∾ Ontario, C Canada
9 P13 Kinuso Alberta, W Canada
160 I13 Kinwat Mahārāshtra, C India
83 F16 Kinyeti ▲ S Sudan
103 I17 Kinzig ∾ SW Germany
197 J13 Kioa island N Fiji
Kioga, Lake see Kyoga, Lake
28 M8 Kiowa Kansas, C USA
29 P12 Kiowa Oklahoma, C USA
Kiparissia see Kyparissía
12 H10 Kipawa, Lac ◎ Québec, SE Canada
83 G24 Kipengere Range ▲ SW Tanzania
83 E23 Kipili Rukwa, W Tanzania
83 K20 Kipini Coast, SE Kenya
9 V16 Kipling Saskatchewan, S Canada
40 M13 Kipnuk Alaska, USA
99 F18 Kippure Ir. Cipiúr. ▲ E Ireland
81 N25 Kipushi Shaba, SE Zaire
195 Y17 Kirakira var. Kaokaona. San Cristobal, SE Solomon Islands
161 K14 Kirandul var. Bailādila. Madhya Pradesh, C India
161 I21 Kīranūr Tamil Nādu, SE India
121 N21 Kiraw Rus. Kirovo. Homyel'skaya Voblasts', SE Belarus
121 M17 Kirawsk Rus. Kirovsk; prev. Startsy. Mahilyowskaya Voblasts', E Belarus
120 F5 Kirbla Läänemaa, W Estonia
27 Y9 Kirbyville Texas, SW USA
116 M12 Kırcasalih Edirne, NW Turkey
111 W8 Kirchbach var. Kirchbach in Steiermark. Steiermark, SE Austria
Kirchbach in Steiermark see Kirchbach
110 H7 Kirchberg Sankt Gallen, NE Switzerland
111 S5 Kirchdorf an der Krems Oberösterreich, N Austria
Kirchheim see Kirchheim unter Teck
103 I22 Kirchheim unter Teck var. Kirchheim. Baden-Württemberg, SW Germany
Kirdzhali see Kŭrdzhali
126 Jj14 Kirenga ∾ S Russian Federation
126 Jj13 Kirensk Irkutskaya Oblast', C Russian Federation
Kirghizia see Kyrgyzstan
151 S16 Kirghiz Range Rus. Kirgizskiy Khrebet; prev. Alexander Range. ▲ Kazakhstan/Kyrgyzstan
Kirghiz SSR see Kyrgyzstan
Kirghiz Steppe see Kazakhskiy Melkosopochnik
Kirgizskaya SSR see Kyrgyzstan
Kirgizskiy Khrebet see Kirghiz Range
81 J19 Kiri Bandundu, W Zaire
Kiriath-Arba see Hebron
203 R3 Kiribati off. Republic of Kiribati. ◆ republic C Pacific Ocean
142 L17 Kırıkhan Hatay, S Turkey
142 I13 Kırıkkale Kırıkkale, C Turkey
142 C10 Kırıkkale ◈ province C Turkey
128 L13 Kirillov Vologodskaya Oblast', NW Russian Federation
Kirin see Jilin
83 I18 Kirinyaga prev. Mount Kenya. ⛰ C Kenya
128 H13 Kirishi var. Kirisi. Leningradskaya Oblast', NW Russian Federation
170 C16 Kirishima-yama ▲ Kyūshū, SW Japan
Kirisi see Kirishi
203 Y2 Kiritimati ✕ Kiritimati, E Kiribati
203 Y2 Kiritimati prev. Christmas Island. atoll Line Islands, E Kiribati
195 O15 Kiriwina Island Eng. Trobriand Island. island SE PNG
195 O15 Kiriwina Islands var. Trobriand Islands. island group S PNG
98 K12 Kirkcaldy E Scotland, UK
99 I14 Kirkcudbright S Scotland, UK
99 I14 Kirkcudbright cultural region S Scotland, UK
Kirkee see Khadki
94 M8 Kirkenes var. Kirkkoniemi. Finnmark, N Norway
97 I14 Kirkenær Hedmark, S Norway
94 J4 Kirkjubæjarklaustur Sudhurland, S Iceland
Kirk-Kilissa see Kırklareli
Kirkkoniemi see Kirkenes
95 L20 Kirkkonummi Swe. Kyrkslätt. Uusimaa, S Finland
12 G7 Kirkland Lake Ontario, S Canada
142 C9 Kırklareli prev. Kirk-Kilissa. Kırklareli, NW Turkey
142 I13 Kırklareli ◈ province NW Turkey
193 F20 Kirkliston Range ▲ South Island, NZ
12 D10 Kirkpatrick Lake ◎ Ontario, S Canada
205 Q11 Kirkpatrick, Mount ▲ Antarctica
29 U2 Kirksville Missouri, C USA
145 T4 Kirkūk var. Karkūk, Kerkuk. N Iraq
145 U7 Kir Kush E Iraq
98 K5 Kirkwall NE Scotland, UK
85 H25 Kirkwood Eastern Cape, S South Africa
29 X5 Kirkwood Missouri, C USA
Kirman see Kermān
Kir Moab/Kir of Moab see Al Karak
130 I5 Kirov Kaluzhskaya Oblast', W Russian Federation
129 R14 Kirov prev. Vyatka. Kirovskaya Oblast', NW Russian Federation
Kirov see Kirovskiy, Kazakhstan
Kirov see Kirova, Taldykorgan, Kazakhstan
151 U13 Kirova Kaz. Kīrov. Taldykorgan, SE Kazakhstan
Kirovabad see Gäncä, Azerbaijan
Kirovabad see Panj, Tajikistan
Kirovakan see Vanadzor
Kirovo see Kiraw, Belarus
Kirovo/Kirovograd see Kirovohrad, Ukraine
Kirovo see Beshariq, Uzbekistan
129 R14 Kirovo-Chepetsk Kirovskaya Oblast', NW Russian Federation
Kirovogradskaya Oblast'/Kirovohrad see Kirovohrads'ka Oblast'
119 R7 Kirovohrad Rus. Kirovograd; prev. Kirovo, Yelizavetgrad, Zinov'yevsk. Kirovohrads'ka Oblast', C Ukraine
119 P7 Kirovohrads'ka Oblast' var. Kirovohrad, Rus. Kirovogradskaya Oblast'. ◈ province C Ukraine
128 J4 Kirovsk Murmanskaya Oblast', NW Russian Federation
Kirovsk see Kirawsk, Belarus
Kirovsk see Babadaykhan, Turkmenistan
119 X7 Kirovs'k Luhans'ka Oblast', E Ukraine
125 Dd9 Kirovskaya Oblast' ◈ province NW Russian Federation
119 X8 Kirovs'ke Donets'ka Oblast', E Ukraine
119 U13 Kirovs'ke Rus. Kirovskoye. Respublika Krym, S Ukraine
151 V14 Kirovskiy Kaz. Kīrov. Taldykorgan, SE Kazakhstan
127 P12 Kirovskiy Kamchatskaya Oblast', E Russian Federation
Kirovskoye see Kyzyl-Adyr
Kirovskoye see Kirovs'ke
124 Oo2 Kırpaşa var. Karpas Peninsula, Gk. Karpasía. peninsula NE Cyprus
152 E11 Kirpili Akhalskiy Velayat, C Turkmenistan
98 K10 Kirriemuir E Scotland, UK
129 S13 Kirs Kirovskaya Oblast', NW Russian Federation
131 N7 Kirsanov Tambovskaya Oblast', W Russian Federation
142 J14 Kırşehir anc. Justinianopolis. Kırşehir, C Turkey
142 I13 Kırşehir ◈ province C Turkey
155 P4 Kirthar Range ▲ S Pakistan
39 P9 Kirtland New Mexico, SW USA
Kirun/Kirun' see Chilung
94 J11 Kiruna Norrbotten, N Sweden
81 M18 Kirundu Haut-Zaïre, NE Zaire
28 L3 Kirwin Reservoir ▣ Kansas, C USA
131 Q4 Kirya Chuvashskaya Respublika, W Russian Federation
171 K15 Kiryū Gunma, Honshū, S Japan
97 M18 Kisa Östergötland, S Sweden
171 Ll11 Kisakata Akita, Honshū, C Japan
Kisalföld see Little Alföld
81 L18 Kisangani prev. Stanleyville. Haut-Zaïre, NE Zaire
41 N12 Kisaralik River ∾ Alaska, USA
171 K17 Kisarazu Chiba, Honshū, S Japan
113 I22 Kisbér Komárom-Esztergom, NW Hungary
9 V17 Kisbey Saskatchewan, S Canada
126 H14 Kiselevsk Kemerovskaya Oblast', S Russian Federation
159 R13 Kishanganj Bihār, NE India
158 G12 Kishangarh Rājasthān, N India
Kishegyes see Mali Idoš
79 S15 Kishi Oyo, W Nigeria
Kishinev see Chişinău
Kishiözen see Malyy Uzen'
171 Gg15 Kishiwada var. Kisiwada. Ōsaka, Honshū, SW Japan
149 P14 Kish, Jazīreh-ye var. Qeys. island S Iran
158 I6 Kishtwār Jammu and Kashmir, NW India
83 H19 Kisii Nyanza, SW Kenya
83 J23 Kisiju Pwani, E Tanzania
Kisiwada see Kishiwada
Kisjenő see Chişineu-Criş
40 E17 Kiska Island island Aleutian Islands, Alaska, USA
Kiskapus see Copşa Mică
113 M22 Kiskőrei-víztároló ▣ E Hungary
Kis-Küküllo see Târnava Mică
113 L24 Kiskunfélegyháza var. Félegyháza. Bács-Kiskun, C Hungary
113 K25 Kiskunhalas var. Halas. Bács-Kiskun, S Hungary
113 K24 Kiskunmajsa Bács-Kiskun, S Hungary
131 N15 Kislovodsk Stavropol'skiy Kray, SW Russian Federation
83 L18 Kismaayo var. Chisimayu, Kismayu, It. Chisimaio. Jubbada Hoose, S Somalia
Kismayu see Kismaayo
171 Ii15 Kiso-sanmyaku ▲ Honshū, S Japan
Kisseraing see Kanmaw Kyun
78 K14 Kissidougou Guinée-Forestière, S Guinea
25 X12 Kissimmee Florida, SE USA
25 X12 Kissimmee, Lake ◎ Florida, SE USA
25 X13 Kissimmee River ∾ Florida, SE USA
9 V13 Kississing Lake ◎ Manitoba, C Canada
113 L24 Kistelek Csongrád, SE Hungary
Kistna see Krishna
113 M23 Kisújszállás Jász-Nagykun-Szolnok, E Hungary
170 F12 Kisuki Shimane, Honshū, SW Japan
83 H18 Kisumu prev. Port Florence. Nyanza, W Kenya
Kisutzaneustadtl see Kysucké Nové Mesto
113 O20 Kisvárda Ger. Kleinwardein. Szabolcs-Szatmár-Bereg, E Hungary
83 J24 Kiswere Lindi, SE Tanzania
Kiszucaújhely see Kysucké Nové Mesto
78 K12 Kita Kayes, W Mali
Kitab see Kitob
172 N5 Kitahiyama Hokkaidō, NE Japan
171 L15 Kita-Ibaraki Ibaraki, Honshū, S Japan
172 Ss17 Kita-Iō-jima Eng. San Alessandro. island SE Japan
171 Mm11 Kitakami Iwate, Honshū, C Japan
171 M13 Kitakami-gawa ∾ Honshū, C Japan
172 N11 Kitakami-sanchi ▲ Honshū, C Japan
171 L13 Kitakata Fukushima, Honshū, C Japan
170 D12 Kitakyūshū var. Kitakyûsyû. Fukuoka, Kyūshū, SW Japan
Kitakyûsyû see Kitakyūshū
83 H18 Kitale Rift Valley, W Kenya
172 Q5 Kitami Hokkaidō, NE Japan
172 Pp4 Kitami-sanchi ▲ Hokkaidō, NE Japan
171 Kk17 Kita-ura ◎ Honshū, S Japan
195 O15 Kitava Island island Kiriwina Islands, SE PNG
39 W5 Kit Carson Colorado, C USA
188 M12 Kitchener Western Australia
12 F16 Kitchener Ontario, S Canada
95 O17 Kitee Pohjois-Karjala, SE Finland
83 G16 Kitgum N Uganda
Kíthareng see Kanmaw Kyun
Kíthira see Kýthira
Kíthnos see Kýthnos
15 J3 Kitikmeot ◈ district Northwest Territories, N Canada
8 J13 Kitimat British Columbia, SW Canada
94 L11 Kitinen ∾ N Finland
153 N12 Kitob Rus. Kitab. Qashqadaryo Wiloyati, S Uzbekistan
118 K7 Kitsman' Ger. Kotzman, Rom. Cozmeni, Rus. Kitsman. Chernivets'ka Oblast', W Ukraine
170 Dd14 Kitsuki var. Kituki. Ōita, Kyūshū, SW Japan
20 C14 Kittanning Pennsylvania, NE USA
21 P10 Kittery Maine, NE USA
94 L11 Kittilä Lappi, N Finland
111 Z4 Kittsee Burgenland, E Austria
83 J19 Kitui Eastern, S Kenya
Kituki see Kitsuki
83 G22 Kitunda Tabora, C Tanzania
8 K13 Kitwanga British Columbia, SW Canada
84 J13 Kitwe var. Kitwe-Nkana. Copperbelt, C Zambia
Kitwe-Nkana see Kitwe
111 O7 Kitzbühel Tirol, W Austria
111 O7 Kitzbüheler Alpen ▲ W Austria
103 J19 Kitzingen Bayern, SE Germany
159 Q14 Kiul Bihār, NE India
194 E12 Kiunga Western, SW PNG
95 M16 Kiuruvesi Kuopio, C Finland
40 M7 Kivalina Alaska, USA
94 L13 Kivalo ridge C Finland
118 J3 Kivertsi Pol. Kiwerce, Rus. Kivertsy. Volyns'ka Oblast', NW Ukraine
Kivertsy see Kivertsi
95 L16 Kivijärvi Keski-Suomi, C Finland
97 L23 Kivik Kristianstad, S Sweden
120 J3 Kiviõli Ida-Virumaa, NE Estonia
Kivu, Lac see Kivu, Lake
69 U10 Kivu, Lake Fr. Lac Kivu. ◎ Rwanda/Zaire
194 G15 Kiwai Island island SW PNG
41 N8 Kiwalik Alaska, USA
Kiwerce see Kivertsi
Kiyev see Kyyiv
151 R10 Kiyevka Karaganda, C Kazakhstan
Kiyevskaya Oblast' see Kyyivs'ka Oblast'
Kiyevskoye Vodokhranilishche see Kyyivs'ke Vodoskhovyshche
142 D10 Kıyıköy Kırklareli, NW Turkey
151 O9 Kiyma Turgay, C Kazakhstan
129 V13 Kizel Permskaya Oblast', NW Russian Federation
129 O12 Kizema var. Kizëma. Arkhangel'skaya Oblast', NW Russian Federation
Kizilagach see Elkhovo
142 H12 Kızılcahamam Ankara, N Turkey
142 J10 Kızıl Irmak ∾ C Turkey
Kızılkoca see Şefaatli
Kizil Kum see Kyzyl Kum
143 P16 Kızıltepe Mardin, SE Turkey
Ki Zil Uzen see Qezel Owzan
131 Q16 Kizilyurt Respublika Dagestan, SW Russian Federation
131 Q15 Kizlyar Respublika Dagestan, SW Russian Federation
131 S3 Kizner Udmurtskaya Respublika, NW Russian Federation
Kizyl-Arvat see Gyzylarbat
152 B13 Kizyl-Atrek Turkm. Gyzyletrek. Balkanskiy Velayat, W Turkmenistan
152 D10 Kizyl-Kaya Turkm. Gyzylgaya. Balkanskiy Velayat, NW Turkmenistan
152 A10 Kizyl-Su Turkm. Gyzylsu. Balkanskiy Velayat, W Turkmenistan
97 H16 Kjerkøy island S Norway
Kjølen see Kölen
94 L7 Kjøllefjord Finnmark, N Norway
94 H11 Kjøpsvik Nordland, C Norway
174 I19 Klabat, Teluk bay Pulau Bangka, W Indonesia
114 I12 Kladanj E Bosnia and Herzegovina
176 Xx16 Kladar Irian Jaya, E Indonesia
113 C16 Kladno Střední Čechy, NW Czech Republic
114 P11 Kladovo Serbia, E Yugoslavia
178 Hh12 Klaeng Rayong, S Thailand
111 T9 Klagenfurt Slvn. Celovec. Kärnten, S Austria
120 B11 Klaipėda Ger. Memel. Klaipėda, NW Lithuania
174 M15 Klakah Jawa, C Indonesia
36 L2 Klamath California, W USA
34 H16 Klamath Falls Oregon, NW USA
36 M1 Klamath Mountains ▲ California/Oregon, W USA
36 L2 Klamath River ∾ California/Oregon, W USA
174 Gg5 Klang var. Kelang; prev. Port Swettenham. Selangor, Peninsular Malaysia
96 J13 Klarälven ∾ Norway/Sweden
113 B15 Klášterec nad Ohří Ger. Klösterle an der Eger. Severní Čechy, NW Czech Republic
174 L15 Klaten Jawa, C Indonesia
113 B18 Klatovy Ger. Klattau. Západní Čechy, SW Czech Republic
Klattau see Klatovy
Klausenburg see Cluj-Napoca
41 Y14 Klawock Prince of Wales Island, Alaska, USA
100 P8 Klazienaveen Drenthe, NE Netherlands
Kleck see Klyetsk
112 H11 Kłecko Poznań, W Poland
112 I11 Kleczew Konin, C Poland
8 L15 Kleena Kleene British Columbia, SW Canada
85 D20 Klein Aub Hardap, C Namibia
Kleine Donau see Mosoni-Duna
103 O14 Kleine Elster ∾ E Germany
Kleine Kokel see Târnava Mică
101 I16 Kleine Nete ∾ N Belgium
Kleines Ungarisches Tiefland see Little Alföld
85 E22 Klein Karas Karas, S Namibia
Kleinkopisch see Copşa Mică
Klein-Marien see Väike-Maarja
Kleinschlatten see Zlatna
85 D23 Kleinsee Northern Cape, W South Africa
Kleinwardein see Kisvárda
117 C16 Kleisoúra Ípeiros, W Greece
97 C17 Klepp Rogaland, S Norway
85 I22 Klerksdorp North-West, N South Africa
130 I5 Kletnya Bryanskaya Oblast', W Russian Federation
Kletsk see Klyetsk
103 D14 Kleve Eng. Cleves, Fr. Clèves; prev. Cleve. Nordrhein-Westfalen, W Germany
115 J16 Kličevo Montenegro, SW Yugoslavia
121 M16 Klichaw Rus. Klichev. Mahilyowskaya Voblasts', E Belarus
Klichev see Klichaw
121 Q16 Klimavichy Rus. Klimovichi. Mahilyowskaya Voblasts', E Belarus
116 M7 Kliment Varnenska Oblast, NE Bulgaria
Klimovichi see Klimavichy
95 G14 Klimpfjäll Västerbotten, N Sweden
130 K3 Klin Moskovskaya Oblast', W Russian Federation
115 M16 Klina Serbia, S Yugoslavia
113 B15 Klínovec Ger. Keilberg. ▲ NW Czech Republic
97 P19 Klintehamn Gotland, SE Sweden
131 R8 Klintsovka Saratovskaya Oblast', W Russian Federation
130 H6 Klintsy Bryanskaya Oblast', W Russian Federation
97 K22 Klippan Kristianstad, S Sweden
94 G13 Klippen Västerbotten, N Sweden
124 Nn3 Klírou W Cyprus
116 I9 Klisura Plovdivska Oblast, C Bulgaria
97 F20 Klitmøller Viborg, NW Denmark
114 F11 Ključ NW Bosnia and Herzegovina
113 I14 Kłobuck Częstochowa, S Poland
112 J11 Kłodawa Konin, C Poland
113 G16 Kłodzko Ger. Glatz. Wałbrzych, SW Poland
97 I14 Kløfta Akershus, S Norway
114 P12 Klokočevac Serbia, E Yugoslavia
120 G3 Klooga Ger. Lodensee. Harjumaa, NW Estonia
101 F15 Kloosterzande Zeeland, SW Netherlands
115 L19 Klos var. Klosi. Dibër, C Albania
Klosi see Klos
Klösterle an der Eger see Klášterec nad Ohří
111 X3 Klosterneuburg Niederösterreich, NE Austria
110 J9 Klosters Graubünden, SE Switzerland
110 G7 Kloten Zürich, N Switzerland
110 G7 Kloten ✕ (Zürich) Zürich, N Switzerland
102 K12 Klötze Sachsen-Anhalt, C Germany
10 K3 Klotz, Lac ◎ Québec, NE Canada
103 O15 Klotzsche ✕ (Dresden) Sachsen, E Germany
8 H7 Kluane Lake ◎ Yukon Territory, W Canada
Kluang see Keluang
113 I14 Kluczbork Ger. Kreuzburg, Kreuzburg in Oberschlesien. Opole, SW Poland
41 W12 Klukwan Alaska, USA
Klyastitsy see Klyastsitsy
120 L11 Klyastsitsy Rus. Klyastitsy. Vitsyebskaya Voblasts', N Belarus
131 T5 Klyavlino Samarskaya Oblast', W Russian Federation
86 K9 Klyaz'in ∾ W Russian Federation
131 N3 Klyaz'ma ∾ W Russian Federation
121 J17 Klyetsk Pol. Kleck, Rus. Kletsk. Minskaya Voblasts', SW Belarus
153 S8 Klyuchevka Talasskaya Oblast', NW Kyrgyzstan
127 Pp10 Klyuchevskaya Sopka, Vulkan ⛰ E Russian Federation
127 Pp10 Klyuchi Kamchatskaya Oblast', E Russian Federation
97 D17 Knaben Vest-Agder, S Norway
Knanzi see Ghanzi
97 K21 Knäred Halland, S Sweden
99 M16 Knaresborough N England, UK
116 H8 Knezha Oblast Montana, NW Bulgaria
27 O9 Knickerbocker Texas, SW USA
30 K5 Knife River ∾ North Dakota, N USA
8 K16 Knight Inlet inlet British Columbia, W Canada
41 S12 Knight Island island Alaska, USA
99 K20 Knighton E Wales, UK
37 O7 Knights Landing California, W USA
114 E13 Knin Zadar-Knin, S Croatia
27 Q12 Knippal Texas, SW USA
111 U7 Knittelfeld Steiermark, C Austria
97 O15 Knivsta Uppsala, C Sweden
115 P14 Knjaževac Serbia, E Yugoslavia
29 S4 Knob Noster Missouri, C USA
101 D15 Knokke-Heist West-Vlaanderen, NW Belgium
97 H20 Knøsen hill N Denmark
Knosós see Knossos
117 J25 Knossos Gk. Knosós. prehistoric site Kríti, Greece, E Mediterranean Sea
27 N7 Knott Texas, SW USA
204 K5 Knowles, Cape headland Antarctica
33 O11 Knox Indiana, N USA
31 O3 Knox North Dakota, N USA
20 C13 Knox Pennsylvania, NE USA
201 X8 Knox Atoll var. Ņadikdik, Narikrik. atoll Ratak Chain, SE Marshall Islands
8 H13 Knox, Cape headland Graham Island, British Columbia, SW Canada
27 P5 Knox City Texas, SW USA
205 Y11 Knox Coast physical region Antarctica
33 T12 Knox Lake ▣ Ohio, N USA
25 T5 Knoxville Georgia, SE USA
32 K12 Knoxville Illinois, N USA
31 W15 Knoxville Iowa, C USA
23 N9 Knoxville Tennessee, S USA
207 P11 Knud Rasmussen Land physical region N Greenland
Knüll see Knüllgebirge
103 I16 Knüllgebirge var. Knüll. ▲ C Germany
Knyazhevo see Sredishte
Knyazhitsy see Knyazhytsy
121 O15 Knyazhytsy Rus. Knyazhitsy. Mahilyowskaya Voblasts', E Belarus
85 G26 Knysna Western Cape, SW South Africa
176 V10 Koagas Irian Jaya, E Indonesia
Koartac see Quaqtaq
174 J10 Koba Pulau Bangka, W Indonesia
170 C16 Kobayashi var. Kobayasi. Miyazaki, Kyūshū, SW Japan
Kobayasi see Kobayashi
171 Gg14 Kōbe Hyōgo, Honshū, SW Japan
Kobelyaki see Kobelyaky
119 T6 Kobelyaky Rus. Kobelyaki. Poltavs'ka Oblast', NE Ukraine
97 J22 København Eng. Copenhagen; anc. Hafnia. ● (Denmark) Sjælland, København, E Denmark
97 J23 København off. Københavns Amt. ◈ county E Denmark
78 K10 Kobenni Hodh el Gharbi, S Mauritania
176 U11 Kobi Pulau Seram, E Indonesia
103 F17 Koblenz prev. Coblenz, Fr. Coblence, anc. Confluentes. Rheinland-Pfalz, W Germany
110 F6 Koblenz Aargau, N Switzerland
176 Ww11 Kobowre, Pegunungan ▲ Irian Jaya, E Indonesia
160 L11 Kobra Madhya Pradesh, C India
Kobrin see Kobryn
176 W14 Kobroor, Pulau island Kepulauan Aru, E Indonesia
121 G19 Kobryn Pol. Kobryn, Rus. Kobrin. Brestskaya Voblasts', SW Belarus
41 O7 Kobuk Alaska, USA
41 O7 Kobuk River ∾ Alaska, USA
143 Q10 K'obulet'i W Georgia
126 Ll10 Kobyay Respublika Sakha (Yakutiya), NE Russian Federation
142 E11 Kocaeli ◈ province NW Turkey
115 P18 Kočani NE FYR Macedonia
114 K12 Koceljevo Serbia, W Yugoslavia
111 U12 Kočevje Ger. Gottschee. S Slovenia
159 T12 Koch Bihār West Bengal, NE India
126 J10 Kochechum ∾ N Russian Federation
103 I20 Kocher ∾ SW Germany
129 T13 Kochevo Komi-Permyatskiy Avtonomnyy Okrug, NW Russian Federation
170 Ee15 Kōchi var. Kôti. Kōchi, Shikoku, SW Japan
170 Ee15 Kōchi off. Kōchi-ken, var. Kôti. ◈ prefecture Shikoku, SW Japan
Kochi see Cochin
Kochiu see Gejiu
Kochkor see Kochkorka
153 V8 Kochkorka Kir. Kochkor. Narynskaya Oblast', C Kyrgyzstan
129 V5 Kochmes Respublika Komi, NW Russian Federation
131 P15 Kochubey Respublika Dagestan, SW Russian Federation
117 I17 Kochýlas ▲ Skýros, Vóreioi Sporádes, Greece, Aegean Sea
112 O13 Kock Lublin, E Poland
83 J19 Kodacho spring/well S Kenya
161 K24 Koddiyar Bay bay NE Sri Lanka
41 Q14 Kodiak Kodiak Island, Alaska, USA
41 Q14 Kodiak Island island Alaska, USA
160 B12 Kodīnār Gujarāt, W India
128 M9 Kodino Arkhangel'skaya Oblast', NW Russian Federation
126 I13 Kodinsk Krasnoyarskiy Kray, C Russian Federation
82 F12 Kodok Upper Nile, SE Sudan
119 N8 Kodyma Odes'ka Oblast', SW Ukraine
101 B17 Koekelare West-Vlaanderen, W Belgium
Koeln see Köln
Koepang see Kupang
Ko-erh-mu see Golmud
101 J17 Koersel Limburg, NE Belgium
85 E21 Koës Karas, SE Namibia
Koetai see Mahakam, Sunga

◆ Country ● Country Capital ◇ Dependent Territory ○ Dependent Territory Capital ◈ Administrative Region ✕ International Airport ▲ Mountain ▲ Mountain Range ⛰ Volcano ∾ River ◎ Lake ▣ Reservoir

Koetaradja see Bandaaceh
38 I14 **Kofa Mountains** ▲▲ Arizona, SW USA
176 Z15 **Kofarau** Irian Jaya, E Indonesia
153 P13 **Kofarnihon** Rus. Kofarnikhon; prev. Ordzhonikidzeabad, Taj. Orjonikidzeobod, Yangi-Bazar. W Tajikistan
153 P14 **Kofarnihon** Rus. Kafirnigan. ≈ SW Tajikistan
Kofarnikhon see Kofarnihon
116 M11 **Kofçaz** Kırklareli, NW Turkey
176 U9 **Kofiau, Pulau** var. Kafiau. island Kepulauan Raja Ampat, E Indonesia
117 J25 **Kófinas** ▲ Kríti, Greece, E Mediterranean Sea
124 Nn4 **Kofínou** var. Kophinou. S Cyprus
111 V8 **Köflach** Steiermark, SE Austria
79 Q17 **Koforidua** SE Ghana
170 Ff12 **Kōfu** Tottori, Honshū, SW Japan
171 J15 **Kōfu** var. Kōhu. Yamanashi, Honshū, S Japan
171 K16 **Koga** Ibaraki, Honshū, S Japan
83 F22 **Koga** Tabora, C Tanzania
Kogălniceanu see Mihail Kogălniceanu
11 P6 **Kogaluk** ≈ Newfoundland and Labrador, E Canada
10 J4 **Kogaluk** ≈ Québec, NE Canada
126 Gg10 **Kogalym** Khanty-Mansiyskiy Avtonomnyy Okrug, C Russian Federation
97 J23 **Køge** Roskilde, E Denmark
97 J23 **Køge Bugt** bay E Denmark
79 U16 **Kogi** ◈ state C Nigeria
152 L11 **Kogon** Rus. Kagan. Bukhoro Wiloyati, C Uzbekistan
169 Y17 **Kŏgŭm-do** island S South Korea
Kőhalom see Rupea
155 T6 **Kohāt** North-West Frontier Province, NW Pakistan
120 G4 **Kohila** Ger. Koil. Raplamaa, NW Estonia
159 X13 **Kohīma** Nāgāland, E India
Koh I Noh see Büyükağrı Dağı
148 L10 **Kohkīlūyeh va Būyer Aḩmadī** off. Ostān-e Kohkīlūyeh va Būyer Aḩmadī, var. Boyer Ahmadī va Kohkīlūyeh. ◈ province SW Iran
Kohsān see Kūhestān
120 J3 **Kohtla-Järve** Ida-Virumaa, NE Estonia
Kōhu see Kōfu
119 N10 **Kohyl'nyk** Rom. Cogîlnic. ≈ Moldova/Ukraine
171 K13 **Koide** Niigata, Honshū, C Japan
8 G7 **Koidern** Yukon Territory, W Canada
78 J15 **Koidu** E Sierra Leone
120 I4 **Koigi** Järvamaa, C Estonia
Koil see Kohila
180 H13 **Koimbani** Grande Comore, NW Comoros
145 T3 **Koi Sanjaq** var. Koysanjaq, Küysanjaq. N Iraq
95 O16 **Koitere** ◎ E Finland
Koivisto see Primorsk
169 Z16 **Kŏje-do** Jap. Kyōsai-tō. island S South Korea
82 J13 **K'ok'a Hāyk'** ◎ C Ethiopia
Kokand see Qŭqon
190 F6 **Kokatha** South Australia
Kokcha see Kŭkcha
Kokchetav/Kokchetavskaya Oblast' see Kokshetau
95 K18 **Kokemäenjoki** ≈ SW Finland
176 X12 **Kokenau** var. Kokonau. Irian Jaya, E Indonesia
85 E22 **Kokerboom** Karas, SE Namibia
121 N14 **Kokhanava** Rus. Kokhanovo. Vitsyebskaya Voblasts', NE Belarus
Kokhanovichi see Kakhanavichy
Kokhanovo see Kokhanava
Kök-Janggak see Kok-Yangak
95 K16 **Kokkola** Swe. Karleby; prev. Swe. Gamlakarleby. Vaasa, W Finland
164 L3 **Kok Kuduk** well N China
120 H9 **Koknese** Aizkraukle, C Latvia
79 T13 **Koko** Kebbi, W Nigeria
194 K15 **Kokoda** Northern, S PNG
78 K12 **Kokofata** Kayes, W Mali
41 N6 **Kokolik River** ≈ Alaska, USA
33 O13 **Kokomo** Indiana, N USA
Kokonau see Kokenau
Koko Nor see Qinghai Hu, China
Koko Nor see Qinghai, China
195 P10 **Kokopo** var. Kopopo; prev. Herbertshöhe. New Britain, E PNG
151 X10 **Kokpekti** Kaz. Kökpekti. Semipalatinsk, E Kazakhstan
151 X11 **Kokpekti** ≈ E Kazakhstan
41 P9 **Kokrines** Alaska, USA
41 P9 **Kokrines Hills** ▲▲ Alaska, USA
151 P17 **Koksaray** Yuzhnyy Kazakhstan, S Kazakhstan
153 X9 **Kokshaal-Tau** Rus. Khrebet Kakshaal-Too. ▲▲ China/Kyrgyzstan
151 P7 **Kokshetau** Kaz. Kökshetaū; prev. Kokchetav. Kokshetau, N Kazakhstan
151 P7 **Kokshetau** off. Kokshetauskaya Oblast', Kaz. Kökshetaū Oblysy; prev. Kokchetavskaya Oblast'. ◈ province N Kazakhstan
Kökshetaū Oblysy/Kokshetauskaya Oblast' see Kokshetau
101 A17 **Koksijde** West-Vlaanderen, W Belgium
10 M5 **Koksoak** ≈ Québec, E Canada
85 K24 **Kokstad** KwaZulu/Natal, E South Africa
151 W15 **Koktal** Kaz. Köktal. Taldykorgan, SE Kazakhstan
151 Q12 **Koktas** ≈ C Kazakhstan
Kök-Tash see Këk-Tash
Koktokay see Fuyun
170 C16 **Kokubu** Kagoshima, Kyūshū, SW Japan
126 L15 **Kokuy** Chitinskaya Oblast', S Russian Federation
153 T9 **Kok-Yangak** Kir. Kök-Janggak. Dzhalal-Abadskaya Oblast', W Kyrgyzstan
164 F9 **Kokyar** Xinjiang Uygur Zizhiqu, W China
155 O13 **Kolāchi** var. Kulachi. ≈ SW Pakistan
78 J15 **Kolahun** N Liberia
175 Q12 **Kolaka** Sulawesi, C Indonesia
Kolam see Quilon
K'o-la-ma-i see Karamay
Kola Peninsula see Kol'skiy Poluostrov
161 H19 **Kolār** Karnātaka, E India
161 H19 **Kolār Gold Fields** Karnātaka, E India
94 K11 **Kolari** Lappi, NW Finland
113 I21 **Kolárovo** Ger. Gutta; prev. Guta, Hung. Gúta. Západné Slovensko, SW Slovakia
115 K16 **Kolašin** Montenegro, SW Yugoslavia
158 F11 **Kolāyat** Rājasthān, NW India
97 N15 **Kolbäck** Västmanland, C Sweden
Kolbcha see Kowbcha
207 Q15 **Kolbeinsey Ridge** undersea feature Denmark Strait/ Norwegian Sea
Kolberg see Kołobrzeg
97 H15 **Kolbotn** Akershus, S Norway
113 N16 **Kolbuszowa** Rzeszów, SE Poland
130 L3 **Kol'chugino** Vladimirskaya Oblast', W Russian Federation
78 H12 **Kolda** S Senegal
97 G23 **Kolding** Vejle, C Denmark
81 M17 **Kole** Haut-Zaïre, N Zaire
81 K20 **Kole** Kasai Oriental, SW Zaire
Kōle see Kili Island
86 F6 **Kölen** Nor. Kjølen. ▲▲ Norway/Sweden
Kolepom, Pulau see Yos Sudarso, Pulau
120 H3 **Kolga Laht** Ger. Kolko-Wiek. bay N Estonia
129 Q3 **Kolguyev, Ostrov** island NW Russian Federation
161 E16 **Kolhāpur** Mahārāshtra, SW India
157 K21 **Kolhumadulu Atoll** var. Kolumadulu Atoll, Thaa Atoll. atoll S Maldives
95 O16 **Koli** var. Kolinkylä. Pohjois-Karjala, E Finland
41 O13 **Koliganek** Alaska, USA
113 E16 **Kolín** Ger. Kolin. Střední Čechy, C Czech Republic
Kolinkylä see Koli
202 E12 **Koliu** Île Futuna, W Wallis and Futuna
120 E7 **Kolka** Talsi, NW Latvia
120 E7 **Kolkasrags** prev. Eng. Cape Domesnes. headland NW Latvia
Kolkhozabad see Kolkhozobod
153 P14 **Kolkhozobod** Rus. Kolkhozabad; prev. Kaganovichabad, Tugalan. SW Tajikistan
Kolki/Kołki see Kolky
Kolko-Wiek see Kolga Laht
118 K3 **Kolky** Pol. Kołki, Rus. Kolki. Volyns'ka Oblast', NW Ukraine
Kollam see Quilon
161 G20 **Kollegāl** Karnātaka, W India
100 M5 **Kollum** Friesland, N Netherlands
Kolmar see Colmar
103 E16 **Köln** var. Koeln, Eng./Fr. Cologne; prev. Cöln, anc. Colonia Agrippina, Oppidum Ubiorum. Nordrhein-Westfalen, W Germany
112 N9 **Kolno** Łomża, NE Poland
112 J12 **Koło** Konin, C Poland
40 B8 **Koloa** Haw. Kōloa. Kauai, Hawaii, USA, C Pacific Ocean
112 E7 **Kołobrzeg** Ger. Kolberg. Koszalin, NW Poland
130 H4 **Kolodnya** Smolenskaya Oblast', W Russian Federation
202 E13 **Kolofau, Mont** ⚲ Île Alofi, S Wallis and Futuna
129 O14 **Kologriv** Kostromskaya Oblast', NW Russian Federation
78 L12 **Kolokani** Koulikoro, W Mali
79 N13 **Koloko** W Burkina
195 U14 **Kolombangara** var. Kilimbangara, Nduke. island New Georgia Islands, NW Solomon Islands
Kolomea see Kolomyya
130 L4 **Kolomna** Moskovskaya Oblast', W Russian Federation
118 J7 **Kolomyya** Ger. Kolomea. Ivano-Frankivs'ka Oblast', W Ukraine
78 M13 **Kolondiéba** Sikasso, SW Mali
200 R15 **Kolonga** Tongatapu, S Tonga
201 U16 **Kolonia** var. Colonia. Pohnpei, E Micronesia
Kolonja see Kolonjë
115 K21 **Kolonjë** var. Kolonja. Fier, C Albania
Kolonjë see Ersekë
Kolotambu see Avuavu
200 Q15 **Kolovai** Tongatapu, S Tonga
175 R13 **Kolowanawatobo, Teluk** bay Pulau Buton, C Indonesia
Kolozsvár see Cluj-Napoca
114 C9 **Kolpa** Ger. Kulpa, SCr. Kupa. ≈ Croatia/Slovenia
126 H12 **Kolpashevo** Tomskaya Oblast', C Russian Federation
128 H13 **Kolpino** Leningradskaya Oblast', NW Russian Federation
102 M10 **Kölpinsee** ◎ NE Germany
128 K5 **Kol'skiy Poluostrov** Eng. Kola Peninsula. peninsula NW Russian Federation
131 T6 **Koltubanovskiy** Orenburgskaya Oblast', W Russian Federation
114 L11 **Kolubara** ≈ C Yugoslavia
Kolupchii see Gurkovo
112 K13 **Koluszki** Piotrków, C Poland
129 T6 **Kolva** ≈ NW Russian Federation
95 E14 **Kolvereid** Nord-Trøndelag, W Norway
154 L15 **Kolwa** Baluchistān, SW Pakistan
81 M24 **Kolwezi** Shaba, S Zaire
127 Nn7 **Kolyma** ≈ NE Russian Federation
Kolyma Lowland see Kolymskaya Nizmennost'
Kolyma Range/Kolymskiy, Khrebet see Kolymskoye Nagor'ye
127 Nn6 **Kolymskaya Nizmennost'** Eng. Kolyma Lowland. lowlands NE Russian Federation
127 Nn6 **Kolymskoye** Respublika Sakha (Yakutiya), NE Russian Federation
127 N17 **Kolymskoye Nagor'ye** var. Khrebet Kolymskiy, Eng. Kolyma Range. ▲▲ E Russian Federation
127 N17 **Kolyuchinskaya Guba** bay NE Russian Federation
151 W15 **Kol'zhat** Almaty, SE Kazakhstan
116 G8 **Kom** ▲ NW Bulgaria
82 I13 **Koma** C Ethiopia
79 X12 **Komadugu Gana** ≈ NE Nigeria
171 Ii15 **Komagane** Nagano, Honshū, S Japan
81 P17 **Komanda** Haut-Zaïre, NE Zaire
207 U1 **Komandorskaya Basin** var. Kamchatka Basin. undersea feature SW Bering Sea
129 Pp9 **Komandorskiye Ostrova** Eng. Commander Islands. island group E Russian Federation
Kománfalva see Comănești
113 I22 **Komárno** Ger. Komorn, Hung. Komárom. Západné Slovensko, SW Slovakia
113 I22 **Komárom** Komárom-Esztergom, NW Hungary
Komárom see Komárno
113 I22 **Komárom-Esztergom** off. Komárom-Esztergom Megye. ◈ county N Hungary
171 I13 **Komatsu** var. Komatu. Ishikawa, Honshū, SW Japan
170 Ff15 **Komatsushima** Tokushima, Shikoku, SW Japan
Komatu see Komatsu
85 D17 **Kombat** Otjozondjupa, N Namibia
Kombissiguiri see Kombissiri
79 P13 **Kombissiri** var. Kombissiguiri. C Burkina
196 E10 **Komebail Lagoon** lagoon N Palau
83 F20 **Kome Island** island N Tanzania
Komeyo see Wandai
176 W13 **Komfane** Pulau Wokam, E Indonesia
119 P10 **Kominternivs'ke** Odes'ka Oblast', SW Ukraine
129 R12 **Komi-Permyatskiy Avtonomnyy Okrug** ◈ autonomous district W Russian Federation
129 R8 **Komi, Respublika** ◈ autonomous republic NW Russian Federation
113 I25 **Komló** Baranya, SW Hungary
Kommunarsk see Alchevs'k
153 S12 **Kommunizm, Qullai** ▲ E Tajikistan
194 G12 **Komo** Southern Highlands, W PNG
175 P16 **Komodo** Pulau Komodo, S Indonesia
175 P16 **Komodo, Pulau** island Nusa Tenggara, S Indonesia
79 N15 **Komoé** var. Komoé Fleuve. ≈ E Ivory Coast
Komoé Fleuve see Komoé
77 X11 **Kôm Ombo** var. Kawm Umbū. SE Egypt
81 F20 **Komono** La Lékoumou, SW Congo
176 Y16 **Komoran** Irian Jaya, E Indonesia
176 Y16 **Komoran, Pulau** island E Indonesia
Komorn see Komárno
Komornok see Comorâște
171 J14 **Komoro** Nagano, Honshū, S Japan
Komosolabad see Komsomolobod
Komotau see Chomutov
116 K13 **Komotiní** var. Gümüljina, Turk. Gümülcine. Anatolikí Makedonía kai Thráki, NE Greece
115 K16 **Komovi** ▲▲ SW Yugoslavia
119 R8 **Kompaniyivka** Kirovohrads'ka Oblast', C Ukraine
194 H12 **Kompiam** Enga, W PNG
Kompong see Kâmpóng Chhnăng
Kompong Cham see Kâmpóng Cham
Kompong Kleang see Kâmpóng Khleăng
Kompong Som see Kâmpóng Saôm
Kompong Speu see Kâmpóng Spoe
Kompong Thom see Kâmpóng Thum
Komrat see Comrat
Komsomol see Komsomol'skiy, Atyrau, Kazakhstan
Komsomol see Komsomolets, Kustanay, Kazakhstan
150 L7 **Komsomolets** Kaz. Komsomol. Kustanay, N Kazakhstan
126 Ii2 **Komsomolets, Ostrov** island Severnaya Zemlya, N Russian Federation
150 F13 **Komsomolets, Zaliv** lake gulf SW Kazakhstan
153 Q12 **Komsomolobod** Rus. Komosolabad. C Tajikistan
128 M16 **Komsomol'sk** Ivanovskaya Oblast', W Russian Federation
119 S6 **Komsomol's'k** Poltavs'ka Oblast', C Ukraine
152 M11 **Komsomol'sk** Nawoiy Wiloyati, N Uzbekistan
150 G12 **Komsomol'skiy** Kaz. Komsomol. Atyrau, W Kazakhstan
129 W4 **Komsomol'skiy** Respublika Komi, NW Russian Federation
127 Nn15 **Komsomol'sk-na-Amure** Khabarovskiy Kray, SE Russian Federation
Komsomol'sk-na-Ustyurte see Komsomol'sk-Ustyurt
150 K10 **Komsomol'skoye** Aktyubinsk, NW Kazakhstan
131 Q8 **Komsomol'skoye** Saratovskaya Oblast', W Russian Federation
152 G6 **Komsomol'sk-Ustyurt** Rus. Komsomol'sk-na-Ustyurte. Qoraqalpoghiston Respublikasi, NW Uzbekistan
151 P10 **Kon** ≈ C Kazakhstan
Kona see Kailua
128 K16 **Konakovo** Tverskaya Oblast', W Russian Federation
149 V15 **Konārak** Sīstān va Balūchestān, SE Iran
Konarhā see Kunar
29 O11 **Konawa** Oklahoma, C USA
176 V9 **Konda** Irian Jaya, E Indonesia
125 Ff11 **Konda** ≈ C Russian Federation
160 L13 **Kondagaon** Madhya Pradesh, C India
12 K10 **Kondiaronk, Lac** ◎ Québec, SE Canada
188 J13 **Kondinin** Western Australia
83 H21 **Kondoa** Dodoma, C Tanzania
131 P6 **Kondol'** Penzenskaya Oblast', W Russian Federation
116 N10 **Kondolovo** Burgaska Oblast, SE Bulgaria
176 Z16 **Kondomirat** Irian Jaya, E Indonesia
128 J10 **Kondopoga** Respublika Kareliya, NW Russian Federation
Kondoz see Kunduz
161 J17 **Kondukūr** var. Kandukur. Andhra Pradesh, E India
Kondūz see Kunduz
197 H6 **Koné** Province Nord, W New Caledonia
Könekesir see Kënekesir
Köneürgench see Këneurgench
79 N15 **Kong** N Ivory Coast
41 S5 **Kongakut River** ≈ Alaska, USA
207 O14 **Kong Christian IX Land** Eng. King Christian IX Land. physical region SE Greenland
207 P13 **Kong Christian X Land** Eng. King Christian X Land. physical region E Greenland
207 N13 **Kong Frederik IX Land** Eng. King Frederik IX Land. physical region SW Greenland
207 Q12 **Kong Frederik VIII Land** Eng. King Frederik VIII Land. physical region NE Greenland
207 N15 **Kong Frederik VI Kyst** Eng. King Frederik VI Coast. physical region SE Greenland
178 I13 **Kông, Kaôh** prev. Kas Kong. island SW Cambodia
94 P2 **Kong Karls Land** Eng. King Charles Islands. island group SE Svalbard
83 G14 **Kong Kong** ≈ SE Sudan
Kongo see Congo
85 G16 **Kongola** Caprivi, NE Namibia
81 N21 **Kongolo** Shaba, E Zaire
83 F14 **Kongor** Jonglei, SE Sudan
207 Q14 **Kong Oscar Fjord** fjord E Greenland
79 P12 **Kongoussi** N Burkina
97 G15 **Kongsberg** Buskerud, S Norway
94 Q2 **Kongsøya** island Kong Karls Land, E Svalbard
97 I14 **Kongsvinger** Hedmark, S Norway
178 Jj11 **Kông, Tônle** Lao. Xê Kong. ≈ Cambodia/Laos
164 E8 **Kongur Shan** ▲ NW China
83 I22 **Kongwa** Dodoma, C Tanzania
Kong, Xê see Kông, Tônle
Konia see Konya
153 R11 **Konibodom** Rus. Kanibadam. N Tajikistan
113 K15 **Koniecpol** Częstochowa, S Poland
Konieh see Konya
Königgrätz see Hradec Králové
Königinhof an der Elbe see Dvůr Králové nad Labem
103 K23 **Königsbrunn** Bayern, S Germany
Königshütte see Chorzów
103 O24 **Königssee** ◎ SE Germany
111 S8 **Königstuhl** ▲ S Austria
111 U3 **Königswiesen** Oberösterreich, N Austria
103 E17 **Königswinter** Nordrhein-Westfalen, W Germany
152 M11 **Konimekh** Rus. Kenimekh. Nawoiy Wiloyati, N Uzbekistan
112 I12 **Konin** Ger. Kuhnau. Konin, C Poland
112 I12 **Konin** off. Województwo Konińskie. ◈ province C Poland
Koninkrijk der Nederlanden see Netherlands
Konińskie, Województwo see Konin
115 L24 **Konispol** var. Konispoli. Vlorë, S Albania
Konispoli see Konispol
117 C15 **Kónitsa** Ípeiros, W Greece
Konitz see Chojnice
110 D8 **Köniz** Bern, W Switzerland
115 H14 **Konjic** S Bosnia and Herzegovina
94 J10 **Könkämäälven** ≈ Finland/Sweden
161 D14 **Konkan** W India
85 D22 **Konkiep** ≈ S Namibia
78 I14 **Konkouré** ≈ W Guinea
79 O11 **Konna** Mopti, S Mali
195 P10 **Konogaiang, Mount** ▲ New Ireland, NE PNG
195 P10 **Konogogo** New Ireland, NE PNG
110 E9 **Konolfingen** Bern, W Switzerland
79 P16 **Konongo** C Ghana
195 O9 **Konos** New Ireland, NE PNG
128 M12 **Konosha** Arkhangel'skaya Oblast', NW Russian Federation
119 R3 **Konotop** Sums'ka Oblast', NE Ukraine
164 L7 **Konqi He** ≈ NW China
113 L14 **Końskie** Kielce, S Poland
Konstantinovka see Kostyantynivka
130 M11 **Konstantinovsk** Rostovskaya Oblast', SW Russian Federation
103 H24 **Konstanz** var. Constanz, Eng. Constance; hist. Kostnitz, anc. Constantia. Baden-Württemberg, S Germany
Konstanza see Constanța
79 T14 **Kontagora** Niger, W Nigeria
80 E13 **Kontcha** Nord, N Cameroon
101 G17 **Kontich** Antwerpen, N Belgium
95 O16 **Kontiolahti** Pohjois-Karjala, SE Finland
95 M15 **Kontiomäki** Oulu, C Finland
178 K11 **Kon Tum** var. Kontum. Kon Tum, C Vietnam
Konur see Sulakyurt
142 H15 **Konya** var. Konieh; prev. Konia, anc. Iconium. Konya, C Turkey
142 H15 **Konya** var. Konia, Konieh. ◈ province C Turkey
151 W15 **Konyrolen** Taldykorgan, SE Kazakhstan
83 I19 **Konza** Eastern, S Kenya
100 I9 **Koog aan den Zaan** Noord-Holland, C Netherlands
190 E7 **Koonibba** South Australia
33 O11 **Koontz Lake** Indiana, N USA
176 V8 **Koor** Irian Jaya, E Indonesia
191 R9 **Koorawatha** New South Wales, SE Australia
120 J5 **Koosa** Tartumaa, E Estonia
35 N7 **Kootenai** var. Kootenay. ≈ Canada/USA see also Kootenay
9 P17 **Kootenay** var. Kootenai. ≈ Canada/USA see also Kootenai
85 F24 **Kootjieskolk** Northern Cape, W South Africa
115 M15 **Kopaonik** ▲▲ S Yugoslavia
Kopar see Koper
94 K1 **Kópasker** Nordhurland Eystra, N Iceland
94 H4 **Kópavogur** Reykjanes, W Iceland
111 S13 **Koper** It. Capodistria; prev. Kopar. SW Slovenia
97 C16 **Kopervik** Rogaland, S Norway
Kopetdag, Khrebet see Koppeh Dāgh
125 Ee12 **Kopeysk** Kurganskaya Oblast', C Russian Federation
Kophinou see Kofínou
190 G8 **Kopi** South Australia
Kopiago see Lake Copiago
159 W12 **Kopili** ≈ NE India
97 M15 **Köping** Västmanland, C Sweden
115 K17 **Koplik** var. Kopliku. Shkodër, NW Albania
Kopliku see Koplik
Kopopo see Kokopo
96 I11 **Koppang** Hedmark, S Norway
97 L15 **Kopparberg** Örebro, C Sweden
96 J12 **Kopparberg** ◈ county C Sweden
149 S3 **Koppeh Dāgh** var. Khrebet Kopetdag. ▲▲ Iran/Turkmenistan
Koppename see Coppename Rivier
97 J15 **Koppom** Värmland, C Sweden
Kopreinitz see Koprivnica
116 K9 **Koprinka, Yazovir** prev. Yazovir Georgi Dimitrov. ⊠ C Bulgaria
114 F7 **Koprivnica** Ger. Kopreinitz, Hung. Kaproncza. Koprivnica-Križevci, N Croatia
114 F8 **Koprivnica-Križevci** off. Koprivničko-Križevačka Županija. ◈ province N Croatia
113 I17 **Kopřivnice** Ger. Nesselsdorf. Severní Morava, E Czech Republic
Köprülü see Veles
Koptsevichi see Kaptsevichy
Kopyl' see Kapyl'
121 O14 **Kopys'** Rus. Kopys'. Vitsyebskaya Voblasts', NE Belarus
115 M18 **Korab** ▲ Albania/FYR Macedonia
Korabavur Pastligi see Karabaur', Uval
83 M14 **K'orahē** SE Ethiopia
117 L16 **Kórakas, Ákra** headland Lésvos, E Greece
114 D9 **Korana** ≈ C Croatia
161 L14 **Korāput** Orissa, E India
Korat see Nakhon Ratchasima
178 I9 **Korat Plateau** plateau E Thailand
145 T1 **Kōrāwa, Sar-i** ▲ NE Iraq
103 H15 **Korbach** Hessen, C Germany
Korça see Korçë
115 M21 **Korçë** var. Korça, Gk. Korytsa, It. Corriza; prev. Koritsa. Korçë, SE Albania
115 M21 **Korçë** ◈ district SE Albania
115 G15 **Korčula** It. Curzola. Dubrovnik-Neretva, S Croatia
115 F15 **Korčula** It. Curzola; anc. Corcyra Nigra. island S Croatia
115 F15 **Korčulanski Kanal** channel S Croatia
148 J5 **Kordestān** off. Ostān-e Kordestān, var. Kurdestan. ◈ province W Iran
149 P4 **Kord Kūy** var. Kurd Kui. Māzandarān, N Iran
169 V13 **Korea Bay** bay China/ North Korea
Korea, Democratic People's Republic of see North Korea
176 Uu15 **Koreare** Pulau Yamdena, E Indonesia
Korea, Republic of see South Korea
169 Z17 **Korea Strait** Jap. Chōsen-kaikyō, Kor. Taehan-haehyŏp. channel Japan/South Korea
Korelichi/Korelicze see Karelichy
82 J11 **Korem** N Ethiopia
79 U11 **Korén Adoua** ≈ C Niger
130 I7 **Korenevo** Kurskaya Oblast', W Russian Federation
130 L13 **Korenovsk** Krasnodarskiy Kray, SW Russian Federation
118 L4 **Korets'** Pol. Korzec, Rus. Korets. Rivnens'ka Oblast', NW Ukraine
127 Pp8 **Korf** Koryakskiy Avtonomnyy Okrug, E Russian Federation
204 L7 **Korff Ice Rise** ice cap Antarctica
94 G13 **Korgen** Troms, N Norway
153 R9 **Korgon-Dĕbĕ** Dzhalal-Abadskaya Oblast', W Kyrgyzstan
78 M14 **Korhogo** N Ivory Coast
117 F19 **Korinthiakós Kólpos** Eng. Gulf of Corinth; anc. Corinthiacus Sinus. gulf C Greece
117 F19 **Kórinthos** Eng. Corinth; anc. Corinthus. Pelopónnisos, S Greece
115 M18 **Koritnik** ▲ S Yugoslavia
Koritsa see Korçë
171 L14 **Kōriyama** Fukushima, Honshū, C Japan
142 E16 **Korkuteli** Antalya, SW Turkey
164 K6 **Korla** Chin. K'u-erh-lo. Xinjiang Uygur Zizhiqu, NW China
126 H11 **Korliki** Khanty-Mansiyskiy Avtonomnyy Okrug, C Russian Federation
Körlin an der Persante see Karlino
Korma see Karma
12 D8 **Kormak** Ontario, S Canada
Kormakíti, Akrotíri/Kormakiti, Cape/ Kormakítis see Koruçam Burnu
113 G23 **Körmend** Vas, W Hungary
145 T5 **Kōrmōr** E Iraq
114 C13 **Kornat** It. Incoronata. island W Croatia
Korneshty see Cornești
111 X3 **Korneuburg** Niederösterreich, NE Austria
151 P7 **Korneyevka** Severnyy Kazakhstan, N Kazakhstan
97 I17 **Kornsjø** Østfold, S Norway
79 O11 **Koro** Mopti, S Mali
197 J14 **Koro** island C Fiji
194 F12 **Koroba** Southern Highlands, W PNG
130 K8 **Korocha** Belgorodskaya Oblast', W Russian Federation
142 H12 **Köroğlu Dağları** ▲▲ C Turkey
191 V6 **Korogoro Point** headland New South Wales, SE Australia
83 J21 **Korogwe** Tanga, E Tanzania
190 L13 **Koroit** Victoria, SE Australia
197 I15 **Korolevu** Viti Levu, W Fiji
202 J17 **Koromiri** island S Cook Islands
179 R16 **Koronadal** Mindanao, S Philippines
117 E22 **Koróni** Pelopónnisos, S Greece
116 G13 **Korónia, Límni** ◎ N Greece
112 I9 **Koronowo** Ger. Krone an der Brahe. Bydgoszcz, NW Poland
119 R2 **Korop** Chernihivs'ka Oblast', N Ukraine
117 H19 **Koropí** Attikí, C Greece
Koror see Oreor
Körös see Križevci
113 L23 **Kőrös** ≈ E Hungary
Kőrösbánya see Baia de Criș
197 J14 **Koro Sea** sea C Fiji
Koroška see Kärnten
119 N3 **Korosten'** Zhytomyrs'ka Oblast', NW Ukraine
Korostyshev see Korostyshiv
119 N4 **Korostyshiv** Rus. Korostyshev. Zhytomyrs'ka Oblast', N Ukraine
129 V3 **Korotaikha** ≈ NW Russian Federation
126 H9 **Korotchayevo** Yamalo-Nenetskiy Avtonomnyy Okrug, N Russian Federation
80 I8 **Koro Toro** Borkou-Ennedi-Tibesti, N Chad
41 N16 **Korovin Island** island Shumagin Islands, Alaska, USA
197 I14 **Korovou** Viti Levu, W Fiji
95 M17 **Korpilahti** Keski-Suomi, C Finland
94 K12 **Korpilombolo** Norrbotten, N Sweden
127 Oo16 **Korsakov** Ostrov Sakhalin, Sakhalinskaya Oblast', SE Russian Federation
95 J16 **Korsholm** Fin. Mustasaari. Vaasa, W Finland
97 I23 **Korsør** Vestsjælland, E Denmark
Korsovka see Kārsava
119 P6 **Korsun'-Shevchenkivs'kyy** Rus. Korsun'-Shevchenkovskiy. Cherkas'ka Oblast', C Ukraine
Korsun'-Shevchenkovskiy see Korsun'-Shevchenkivs'kyy
101 C17 **Kortemark** West-Vlaanderen, W Belgium
101 H18 **Kortenberg** Vlaams Brabant, C Belgium
101 K18 **Kortessem** Limburg, NE Belgium
101 E14 **Kortgene** Zeeland, SW Netherlands
82 F8 **Korti** Northern, N Sudan
101 C18 **Kortrijk** Fr. Courtrai. West-Vlaanderen, W Belgium
124 N2 **Koruçam Burnu** var. Cape Kormakiti, Kormakítis, Gk. Akrotíri Kormakíti. headland N Cyprus
191 O13 **Korumburra** Victoria, SE Australia
Koryak Range see Koryakskoye Nagor'ye
127 P8 **Koryakskiy Avtonomnyy Okrug** ◈ autonomous district E Russian Federation
Koryakskiy Khrebet see Koryakskoye Nagor'ye
127 Pp7 **Koryakskoye Nagor'ye** var. Koryakskiy Khrebet, Eng. Koryak Range. ▲▲ NE Russian Federation
129 P11 **Koryazhma** Arkhangel'skaya Oblast', NW Russian Federation
Kōryō see Kangnŭng
Korytsa see Korçë
119 Q2 **Koryukivka** Chernihivs'ka Oblast', N Ukraine
Korzec see Korets'
117 N21 **Kos** Kos, Dodekánisos, Greece, Aegean Sea
117 M21 **Kos** It. Coo; anc. Cos. island Dodekánisos, Greece, Aegean Sea
129 T12 **Kosa** Komi-Permyatskiy Avtonomnyy Okrug, NW Russian Federation
129 T13 **Kosa** ≈ NW Russian Federation
170 C11 **Kō-saki** headland Nagasaki, Tsushima, SW Japan
169 X13 **Kosan** SE North Korea
121 H18 **Kosava** Rus. Kosovo. Brestskaya Voblasts', SW Belarus
Kosch see Kose
150 G12 **Koschagyl** Kaz. Qosshaghyl. Atyrau, W Kazakhstan
112 G12 **Kościan** Ger. Kosten. Leszno, W Poland
112 I7 **Kościerzyna** Gdańsk, NW Poland
24 L4 **Kosciusko** Mississippi, S USA
191 R11 **Kosciusko, Mount** ▲ New South Wales, SE Australia
120 H4 **Kose** Ger. Kosch. Harjumaa, NW Estonia
116 G6 **Koshava** Oblast Montana, NW Bulgaria
153 U9 **Kosh-Dĕbĕ** var. Koshtebë. Narynskaya Oblast', C Kyrgyzstan
171 K16 **Koshigaya** var. Kosigaya. Saitama, Honshū, S Japan
K'o-shih see Kashi
170 B15 **Koshikijima-rettō** var. Kosikizima Rettô. island group SW Japan
151 W13 **Koshkarkol', Ozero** ◎ SE Kazakhstan
32 L9 **Koshkonong, Lake** ◎ Wisconsin, N USA
152 B10 **Koshoba** Turkm. Goshoba. Balkanskiy Velayat, NW Turkmenistan
171 J14 **Kōshoku** var. Kôsyoku. Nagano, Honshū, S Japan
Koshtebë see Kosh-Dĕbĕ
Kōshū see Kwangju
113 N19 **Košice** Ger. Kaschau, Hung. Kassa. Východné Slovensko, E Slovakia
Kosigaya see Koshigaya
Kosikizima Rettô see Koshikijima-rettō
159 R12 **Kosi Reservoir** ⊠ E Nepal
118 J8 **Kosiv** Ivano-Frankivs'ka Oblast', W Ukraine
151 O11 **Koskol'** Zhezkazgan, C Kazakhstan
129 Q9 **Koslan** Respublika Komi, NW Russian Federation
Köslin see Koszalin
152 M12 **Koson** Rus. Kasan. Qashqadaryo Wiloyati, S Uzbekistan
169 Y13 **Kosŏng** SE North Korea
153 S9 **Kosonsoy** Rus. Kasansay. Namangan Wiloyati, E Uzbekistan
115 M16 **Kosovo** prev. Autonomous Province of Kosovo and Metohija. cultural region S Yugoslavia
Kosovo see Kosava
Kosovo and Metohija, Autonomous Province of see Kosovo
115 N16 **Kosovo Polje** Serbia, S Yugoslavia
115 O16 **Kosovska Kamenica** Serbia, SE Yugoslavia
115 M16 **Kosovska Mitrovica** Alb. Mitrovicë; prev. Mitrovica, Titova Mitrovica. Serbia, S Yugoslavia
201 X17 **Kosrae** ◈ state E Micronesia
201 Y14 **Kosrae** prev. Kusaie. island Caroline Islands, E Micronesia
27 U9 **Kosse** Texas, SW USA
111 P6 **Kössen** Tirol, W Austria
78 M16 **Kossou, Lac de** ◎ C Ivory Coast
Kossukavak see Krumovgrad
114 F10 **Kostajnica** var. Hrvatska Kostajnica. Sisak-Moslavina, C Croatia
Kostamus see Kostomuksha
Kosten see Kościan
116 H10 **Kostenets** prev. Georgi Dimitrov. Sofiyska Oblast, W Bulgaria
82 F10 **Kosti** White Nile, C Sudan
Kostnitz see Konstanz
128 H7 **Kostomuksha** Fin. Kostamus. Respublika Kareliya, NW Russian Federation
118 K3 **Kostopil'** Rus. Kostopol'. Rivnens'ka Oblast', NW Ukraine
Kostopol' see Kostopil'
128 M15 **Kostroma** Kostromskaya Oblast', NW Russian Federation
129 N14 **Kostroma** ≈ NW Russian Federation
129 N14 **Kostromskaya Oblast'** ◈ province NW Russian Federation
112 D11 **Kostrzyn** Ger. Cüstrin, Küstrin. Gorzów, W Poland
112 H11 **Kostrzyn** Poznań, C Poland
119 X7 **Kostyantynivka** Rus. Konstantinovka. Donets'ka Oblast', SE Ukraine
Kostyukovichi see Kastsyukovichy

Kostyukovka see Kastsyukowka
Kôsyoku see Kôshoku
129 U6 **Kos'yu** Respublika Komi, NW Russian Federation
129 U6 **Kos'yu** ≈ NW Russian Federation
112 F7 **Koszalin** *Ger.* Köslin. Koszalin, NW Poland
112 F8 **Koszalin** *off.* Województwo Koszalińskie, *Ger.* Köslin. ⬖ *province* NW Poland
Koszalińskie, Województwo see Koszalin
113 F22 **Kőszeg** *Ger.* Güns. Vas, W Hungary
158 H13 **Kota** *prev.* Kotah. Rājasthān, N India
174 H9 **Kota Baru** Sumatera, W Indonesia
175 Nn11 **Kotabaru** Pulau Laut, C Indonesia
Kotabaru see Jayapura
174 H2 **Kota Bharu** *var.* Kota Baharu, Kota Bahru. Kelantan, Peninsular Malaysia
Kotaboemi see Kotabumi
174 Ii12 **Kotabumi** *prev.* Kotaboemi. Sumatera, W Indonesia
155 S10 **Kot Addu** Punjab, E Pakistan
Kotah see Kota
175 Nn2 **Kota Kinabalu** *prev.* Jesselton. Sabah, East Malaysia
175 Nn2 **Kota Kinabalu** × Sabah, East Malaysia
94 M12 **Kotala** Lappi, N Finland
Kotamobagoe see Kotamobagu
175 Rr7 **Kotamobagu** *prev.* Kotamobagoe. Sulawesi, C Indonesia
161 L14 **Kotapad** *var.* Kotapārh. Orissa, E India
Kotapārh see Kotapad
178 Gg17 **Ko Ta Ru Tao** *island* SW Thailand
174 L11 **Kotawaringin, Teluk** *bay* Borneo, C Indonesia
155 Q13 **Kot Diji** Sind, SE Pakistan
158 K9 **Kotdwāra** Uttar Pradesh, N India
129 Q14 **Kotel'nich** Kirovskaya Oblast', NW Russian Federation
131 N12 **Kotel'nikovo** Volgogradskaya Oblast', SW Russian Federation
126 Ll4 **Kotel'nyy, Ostrov** *island* Novosibirskiye Ostrova, N Russian Federation
119 T5 **Kotel'va** Poltavs'ka Oblast', C Ukraine
103 M14 **Köthen** *var.* Cöthen. Sachsen-Anhalt, C Germany
Kôti see Kôchi
83 G17 **Kotido** NE Uganda
95 N19 **Kotka** Kymi, S Finland
129 P11 **Kotlas** Arkhangel'skaya Oblast', NW Russian Federation
40 M10 **Kotlik** Alaska, USA
79 Q17 **Kotoka** × (Accra) S Ghana
Kotonu see Cotonou
115 J17 **Kotor** *It.* Cattaro. Montenegro, SW Yugoslavia
Kotor see Kotoriba
114 F7 **Kotoriba** *Hung.* Kotor. Medimurje, N Croatia
115 I17 **Kotorska, Boka** *It.* Bocche di Cattaro. *bay* Montenegro, SW Yugoslavia
114 H11 **Kotorsko** N Bosnia and Herzegovina
114 G11 **Kotor Varoš** N Bosnia and Herzegovina
Koto Sho/Kotosho see Lan Yü
130 M7 **Kotovsk** Tambovskaya Oblast', W Russian Federation
119 O9 **Kotovs'k** *Rus.* Kotovsk. Odes'ka Oblast', SW Ukraine
Kotovsk see Hînceşti
121 G16 **Kotra** *Rus.* Kotra. ≈ W Belarus
155 P16 **Kotri** Sind, SE Pakistan
111 Q9 **Kötschach** Kärnten, S Austria
161 K15 **Kottagūdem** Andhra Pradesh, E India
161 F21 **Kottappadi** Kerala, SW India
161 G23 **Kottayam** Kerala, SW India
Kottbus see Cottbus
Kotte see Sri Jayawardanapura
81 K15 **Kotto** ≈ Central African Republic/Zaire
200 S13 **Kotu Group** *island group* W Tonga
152 B11 **Koturdepe** *Turkm.* Goturdepe. Balkanskiy Velayat, W Turkmenistan
126 J9 **Kotuy** ≈ N Russian Federation
85 M16 **Kotwa** Mashonaland East, NE Zimbabwe
41 N7 **Kotzebue** Alaska, USA
40 M7 **Kotzebue Sound** *inlet* Alaska, USA
Kotzenan see Chocianów
Kotzman see Kitsman'
79 R14 **Kouandé** NW Benin
81 J15 **Kouango** Ouaka, S Central African Republic
79 O13 **Koudougou** C Burkina
100 K7 **Koudum** Friesland, N Netherlands
117 L25 **Koufonísi** *island* SE Greece
117 K21 **Koufonísi** *island* Kykládes, Greece, Aegean Sea
40 M8 **Kougarok Mountain** ▲ Alaska, USA
81 E20 **Kouilou** ≈ S Congo
16 N3 **Koukdjuak** ≈ Baffin Island, Northwest Territories, NE Canada
124 N4 **Koúklia** SW Cyprus
81 E19 **Koulamoutou** Ogooué-Lolo, C Gabon
78 L12 **Koulikoro** Koulikoro, SW Mali
78 L11 **Koulikoro** ⬖ *region* SW Mali
197 H5 **Koumac** Province Nord, W New Caledonia
171 J15 **Koumi** Nagano, Honshū, S Japan
80 I13 **Koumra** Moyen-Chari, S Chad
Kounadougou see Koundougou
78 M15 **Kounahiri** C Ivory Coast
78 I12 **Koundâra** Moyenne-Guinée, NW Guinea
79 N13 **Koundougou** *var.* Kounadougou. C Burkina
78 H11 **Koungheul** C Senegal
151 T13 **Kounradskiy** Zhezkazgan, SE Kazakhstan
27 X10 **Kountze** Texas, SW USA
79 Q13 **Koupéla** C Burkina
79 N13 **Kouri** Sikasso, SW Mali
57 Y9 **Kourou** N French Guiana
116 J12 **Kouroú** ≈ NE Greece
78 K14 **Kouroussa** Haute-Guinée, C Guinea
Kousseir see Al Quşayr
80 G11 **Kousséri** *prev.* Fort-Foureau. Extrême-Nord, NE Cameroon
Kouteifé see Al Quţayfah
78 M13 **Koutiala** Sikasso, S Mali
78 M14 **Kouto** NW Ivory Coast
95 M19 **Kouvola** Kymi, S Finland
81 G18 **Kouyou** ≈ C Congo
114 M10 **Kovačica** *Hung.* Antafalva; *prev.* Kovacsicza. Serbia, N Yugoslavia
Kovacsicza see Kovačica
Kővárhosszúfalu see Satulung
Kovászna see Covasna
128 I4 **Kovdor** Murmanskaya Oblast', NW Russian Federation
128 I5 **Kovdozero, Ozero** ◎ NW Russian Federation
118 J3 **Kovel'** *Pol.* Kowel. Volyns'ka Oblast', NW Ukraine
114 M11 **Kovin** *Hung.* Kevevára; *prev.* Temes-Kubin. Serbia, NE Yugoslavia
Kovno see Kaunas
131 N3 **Kovrov** Vladimirskaya Oblast', W Russian Federation
131 O5 **Kovylkino** Respublika Mordoviya, W Russian Federation
112 J11 **Kowal** Włocławek, C Poland
112 J9 **Kowalewo Pomorskie** *Ger.* Schönsee. Toruń, N Poland
Kowasna see Covasna
121 M16 **Kowbcha** *Rus.* Kolbcha. Mahilyowskaya Voblasts', E Belarus
Koweit see Kuwait
Kowel see Kovel'
193 F17 **Kowhitirangi** West Coast, South Island, NZ
167 O15 **Kowloon** *Chin.* Jiulong. Hong Kong, S China
Kowno see Kaunas
165 N7 **Kox Kuduk** *well* NW China
142 D16 **Köyceğiz** Muğla, SW Turkey
129 N6 **Koyda** Arkhangel'skaya Oblast', NW Russian Federation
152 D10 **Koymat** *Turkm.* Goymat. Balkanskiy Velayat, NW Turkmenistan
152 D10 **Koymatdag, Gory** *Turkm.* Goymatdag. *hill range* NW Turkmenistan
161 E15 **Koyna Reservoir** ▣ W India
171 M11 **Koyoshi-gawa** ≈ Honshū, C Japan
Koysanjaq see Koi Sanjaq
Koytash see Qŭytosh
41 N9 **Koyuk** Alaska, USA
41 N9 **Koyuk River** ≈ Alaska, USA
41 O9 **Koyukuk** Alaska, USA
41 O9 **Koyukuk River** ≈ Alaska, USA
142 J13 **Kozaklı** Nevşehir, C Turkey
170 F13 **Kōzan** Hiroshima, Honshū, SW Japan
142 K16 **Kozan** Adana, S Turkey
117 E14 **Kozáni** Dytikí Makedonía, N Greece
114 F10 **Kozara** ▲▲ NW Bosnia and Herzegovina
119 P3 **Kozelets'** *Rus.* Kozelets. Chernihivs'ka Oblast', NE Ukraine
119 S6 **Kozel'shchyna** Poltavs'ka Oblast', C Ukraine
130 J5 **Kozel'sk** Kaluzhskaya Oblast', W Russian Federation
Kozhikode see Calicut
129 V9 **Kozhimiz, Gora** ▲ NW Russian Federation
128 L9 **Kozhozero, Ozero** ◎ NW Russian Federation
129 T7 **Kozhva** *var.* Kozya. Respublika Komi, NW Russian Federation
129 T7 **Kozhva** ≈ NW Russian Federation
129 U6 **Kozhym** Respublika Komi, NW Russian Federation
112 N13 **Kozienice** Radom, C Poland
111 S13 **Kozina** SW Slovenia
116 H7 **Kozloduy** Oblast Montana, NW Bulgaria
131 Q3 **Kozlovka** Chuvashskaya Respublika, W Russian Federation
Kozlovshchina/Kozlowszczyzna see Kazlowshchyna
131 P3 **Koz'modem'yansk** Respublika Mariy El, W Russian Federation
118 J6 **Kozova** Ternopil's'ka Oblast', W Ukraine
115 P20 **Kožuf** ▲ S FYR Macedonia
172 S13 **Kōzu-shima** *island* E Japan
Kozya see Kozhva
Koz'yany see Kaz'yany
119 N5 **Kozyatyn** *Rus.* Kazatin. Vinnyts'ka Oblast', C Ukraine
79 Q16 **Kpalimé** *var.* Palimé. SW Togo
79 Q16 **Kpandu** E Ghana
101 F15 **Krabbendijke** Zeeland, SW Netherlands
178 Gg16 **Krabi** *var.* Muang Krabi. Krabi, SW Thailand
178 Gg14 **Kra Buri** Ranong, SW Thailand
178 Jj13 **Krâchéh** *prev.* Kratie. Krâchéh, E Cambodia
97 G17 **Kragerø** Telemark, S Norway
114 M13 **Kragujevac** Serbia, C Yugoslavia
Krainburg see Kranj
178 Gg14 **Kra, Isthmus of** *isthmus* Malaysia/Thailand
114 D12 **Krajina** *cultural region* SW Croatia
Krakatau, Pulau see Rakata, Pulau
Krakau see Kraków
113 L16 **Kraków** *Eng.* Cracow, *Ger.* Krakau; *anc.* Cracovia. Kraków, S Poland
113 K16 **Kraków** *off.* Województwo Krakowskie, *Eng.* Cracow, *Ger.* Krakau. ⬖ *province* S Poland
102 L9 **Krakower See** ◎ NE Germany
Krakowskie, Województwo see Kraków
178 Ii12 **Krâlănh** Siĕmréab, NW Cambodia
47 Q16 **Kralendijk** Bonaire, E Netherlands Antilles
114 B10 **Kraljevica** *It.* Porto Re. Primorje-Gorski Kotar, NW Croatia
114 M13 **Kraljevo** *prev.* Rankovićevo. Serbia, C Yugoslavia
Kralup an der Moldau see Kralupy nad Vltavou
113 C16 **Kralupy nad Vltavou** *Ger.* Kralup an der Moldau. Střední Čechy, NW Czech Republic
119 W7 **Kramators'k** *Rus.* Kramatorsk. Donets'ka Oblast', SE Ukraine
95 H17 **Kramfors** Västernorrland, C Sweden
117 D15 **Kranéa** Dytikí Makedonía, N Greece
110 M7 **Kranebitten** × (Innsbruck) Tirol, W Austria
117 G20 **Kranídi** Pelopónnisos, S Greece
111 T11 **Kranj** *Ger.* Krainburg. NW Slovenia
117 F16 **Krannón** *battleground* Thessalía, C Greece
Kranz see Zelenogradsk
114 D7 **Krapina** Krapina-Zagorje, N Croatia
114 E8 **Krapina** ≈ N Croatia
114 D8 **Krapina-Zagorje** *off.* Krapinsko-Zagorska Županija. ⬖ *province* N Croatia
116 L7 **Krapinets** ≈ NE Bulgaria
113 I15 **Krapkowice** *Ger.* Krappitz. Opole, SW Poland
Krappitz see Krapkowice
129 O12 **Krasavino** Vologodskaya Oblast', NW Russian Federation
125 Ff5 **Krasino** Novaya Zemlya, Arkhangel'skaya Oblast', N Russian Federation
127 N18 **Kraskino** Primorskiy Kray, SE Russian Federation
120 J11 **Krāslava** Krāslava, SE Latvia
121 M14 **Krasnaluki** *Rus.* Krasnoluki. Vitsyebskaya Voblasts', N Belarus
121 P17 **Krasnapollye** *Rus.* Krasnopol'ye. Mahilyowskaya Voblasts', E Belarus
130 L15 **Krasnaya Polyana** Krasnodarskiy Kray, SW Russian Federation
121 J18 **Krasnaya Slabada** *var.* Chyrvonaya Slabada, *Rus.* Krasnaya Sloboda. Minskaya Voblasts', S Belarus
Krasnaya Sloboda see Krasnaya Slabada
121 J15 **Krasnaye** *Rus.* Krasnoye. Minskaya Voblasts', C Belarus
113 O14 **Kraśnik** *Ger.* Kratznick. Lublin, E Poland
113 O14 **Kraśnik Fabryczny** Lublin, SE Poland
119 O9 **Krasni Okny** Odes'ka Oblast', SW Ukraine
151 P7 **Krasnoarmeysk** Kokshetau, N Kazakhstan
131 P8 **Krasnoarmeysk** Saratovskaya Oblast', W Russian Federation
Krasnoarmeysk see Krasnoarmiys'k
127 Oo4 **Krasnoarmeyskiy** Chukotskiy Avtonomnyy Okrug, NE Russian Federation
119 W7 **Krasnoarmiys'k** *Rus.* Krasnoarmeysk. Donets'ka Oblast', SE Ukraine
129 P11 **Krasnoborsk** Arkhangel'skaya Oblast', NW Russian Federation
130 K14 **Krasnodar** *prev.* Ekaterinodar, Yekaterinodar. Krasnodarskiy Kray, SW Russian Federation
130 K13 **Krasnodarskiy Kray** ⬖ *territory* SW Russian Federation
119 Z7 **Krasnodon** Luhans'ka Oblast', E Ukraine
Krasnogor see Kallaste
131 T2 **Krasnogorskoye** *Latv.* Sarkaņi. Udmurtskaya Respublika, NW Russian Federation
Krasnograd see Krasnohrad
Krasnogvardeysk see Bulunghur
130 M13 **Krasnogvardeyskoye** Stavropol'skiy Kray, SW Russian Federation
Krasnogvardeyskoye see Krasnohvardiys'ke
119 U6 **Krasnohrad** *Rus.* Krasnograd. Kharkivs'ka Oblast', E Ukraine
119 S12 **Krasnohvardiys'ke** *Rus.* Krasnogvardeyskoye. Respublika Krym, S Ukraine
126 L16 **Krasnokamensk** Chitinskaya Oblast', S Russian Federation
129 U14 **Krasnokamsk** Permskaya Oblast', W Russian Federation
131 U8 **Krasnokholm** Orenburgskaya Oblast', W Russian Federation
119 U5 **Krasnokuts'k** *Rus.* Krasnokutsk. Kharkivs'ka Oblast', E Ukraine
130 L7 **Krasnolesnyy** Voronezhskaya Oblast', W Russian Federation
Krasnoluki see Krasnaluki
Krasnoosol'skoye Vodokhranilishche see Chervonooskil's'ke Vodoskhovyshche
119 S11 **Krasnoperekops'k** *Rus.* Krasnoperekopsk. Respublika Krym, S Ukraine
119 U4 **Krasnopillya** Sums'ka Oblast', NE Ukraine
Krasnopol'ye see Krasnapollye
126 H9 **Krasnosel'kup** Yamalo-Nenetskiy Avtonomnyy Okrug, N Russian Federation
128 L5 **Krasnoshchel'ye** Murmanskaya Oblast', NW Russian Federation
131 T2 **Krasnoslobodsk** Respublika Mordoviya, W Russian Federation
131 O5 **Krasnoslobodsk** Volgogradskaya Oblast', SW Russian Federation
Krasnostav see Krasnystaw
125 F10 **Krasnotur'insk** Sverdlovskaya Oblast', C Russian Federation
125 E11 **Krasnoufimsk** Sverdlovskaya Oblast', C Russian Federation
125 Ee10 **Krasnoural'sk** Sverdlovskaya Oblast', C Russian Federation
131 V5 **Krasnousol'skiy** Respublika Bashkortostan, W Russian Federation
129 U12 **Krasnovishersk** Permskaya Oblast', NW Russian Federation
Krasnovodsk see Turkmenbashi
152 A10 **Krasnovodskiy Zaliv** *Turkm.* Krasnowodsk Aylagy. *lake gulf* W Turkmenistan
152 B10 **Krasnovodskoye Plato** *Turkm.* Krasnowodsk Platosy. *plateau* NW Turkmenistan
Krasnowodsk Aylagy see Krasnovodskiy Zaliv
Krasnowodsk Platosy see Krasnovodskoye Plato
126 Hh14 **Krasnoyarsk** Krasnoyarskiy Kray, S Russian Federation
131 X7 **Krasnoyarskiy** Orenburgskaya Oblast', W Russian Federation
126 I12 **Krasnoyarskiy Kray** ⬖ *territory* C Russian Federation
126 I14 **Krasnoyarskoye Vodokhranilishche** ▣ S Russian Federation
Krasnoye see Krasnaye
152 J15 **Krasnoye Znamya** *Turkm.* Gyzylbaydak. Maryyskiy Velayat, S Turkmenistan
129 R11 **Krasnozatonskiy** Respublika Komi, NW Russian Federation
120 D13 **Krasnoznamensk** *prev.* Lasdehnen, *Ger.* Haselberg. Kaliningradskaya Oblast', W Russian Federation
119 R11 **Krasnoznam"yans'kyy Kanal** *canal* S Ukraine
113 P14 **Krasnystaw** *Rus.* Krasnostav. Chełm, SE Poland
130 H4 **Krasnyy** Smolenskaya Oblast', W Russian Federation
131 P2 **Krasnyye Baki** Nizhegorodskaya Oblast', W Russian Federation
131 Q13 **Krasnyye Barrikady** Astrakhanskaya Oblast', SW Russian Federation
128 K15 **Krasnyy Kholm** Tverskaya Oblast', W Russian Federation
131 Q8 **Krasnyy Kut** Saratovskaya Oblast', W Russian Federation
Krasnyy Liman see Krasnyy Lyman
119 Y7 **Krasnyy Luch** *prev.* Krindachevka. Luhans'ka Oblast', E Ukraine
119 X6 **Krasnyy Lyman** *Rus.* Krasnyy Liman. Donets'ka Oblast', SE Ukraine
131 R3 **Krasnyy Steklovar** Respublika Mariy El, W Russian Federation
131 P8 **Krasnyy Tekstil'shchik** Saratovskaya Oblast', W Russian Federation
131 R13 **Krasnyy Yar** Astrakhanskaya Oblast', SW Russian Federation
Krassóvár see Caraşova
118 L5 **Krasyliv** Khmel'nyts'ka Oblast', W Ukraine
113 O21 **Kraszna** *Rom.* Crasna. ≈ Hungary/Romania
Kratie see Krâchéh
194 I13 **Kratke Range** ▲▲ C PNG
115 P17 **Kratovo** NE FYR Macedonia
Kratznick see Kraśnik
176 Yy11 **Krau** Irian Jaya, E Indonesia
178 Ii13 **Krâvanh, Chuŏr Phnum** *Eng.* Cardamom Mountains, *Fr.* Chaîne des Cardamomes. ▲▲ W Cambodia
Kravasta Lagoon see Karavastasë, Laguna e
Krawang see Karawang
Kraxatau see Rakata, Pulau
131 Q15 **Kraynovka** Respublika Dagestan, SW Russian Federation
120 D12 **Kražiai** Kelmė, C Lithuania
29 P11 **Krebs** Oklahoma, C USA
103 D15 **Krefeld** Nordrhein-Westfalen, W Germany
Kreisstadt see Krosno Odrzańskie
117 D17 **Kremastón, Technití Límni** ▣ C Greece
Kremenchug see Kremenchuk
Kremenchugskoye Vodokhranilishche/Kremenchuk Reservoir see Kremenchuts'ke Vodoskhovyshche
119 S6 **Kremenchuk** *Rus.* Kremenchug. Poltavs'ka Oblast', NE Ukraine
119 R6 **Kremenchuts'ke Vodoskhovyshche** *Eng.* Kremenchuk Reservoir, *Rus.* Kremenchugskoye Vodokhranilishche. ▣ C Ukraine
118 K5 **Kremenets'** *Pol.* Krzemieniec, *Rus.* Kremenets. Ternopil's'ka Oblast', W Ukraine
Kremennaya see Kreminna
119 X6 **Kreminna** *Rus.* Kremennaya. Luhans'ka Oblast', E Ukraine
39 R4 **Kremmling** Colorado, C USA
111 V3 **Krems** ≈ NE Austria
Krems see Krems an der Donau
111 W3 **Krems an der Donau** *var.* Krems. Niederösterreich, N Austria
Kremsier see Kroměříž
111 S4 **Kremsmünster** Oberösterreich, N Austria
40 M17 **Krenitzin Islands** *island* Aleutian Islands, Alaska, USA
Kresena see Kresna
116 G11 **Kresna** *var.* Kresena. Sofiyska Oblast, SW Bulgaria
114 O12 **Krespoljin** Serbia, E Yugoslavia
27 N4 **Kress** Texas, SW USA
127 Pp4 **Kresta, Zaliv** *bay* E Russian Federation
117 D20 **Kréstena** *prev.* Selinoús. Dytikí Ellás, S Greece
128 H14 **Kresttsy** Novgorodskaya Oblast', W Russian Federation
126 Kk11 **Krestyakh** Respublika Sakha (Yakutiya), NE Russian Federation
Kretikon Delagos see Kritikó Pélagos
120 C11 **Kretinga** *Ger.* Krottingen. Kretinga, NW Lithuania
Kreutz see Cristuru Secuiesc
Kreuz see Križevci, Croatia
Kreuz see Risti, Estonia
Kreuzburg/Kreuzburg in Oberschlesien see Kluczbork
Kreuzingen see Bol'shakovo
110 H6 **Kreuzlingen** Thurgau, NE Switzerland
103 K25 **Kreuzspitze** ▲ S Germany
103 F16 **Kreuztal** Nordrhein-Westfalen, W Germany
121 I15 **Kreva** *Rus.* Krevo. Hrodzyenskaya Voblasts', W Belarus
Krevo see Kreva
Kría Vrísi see Krýa Vrýsi
81 D16 **Kribi** Sud, SW Cameroon
Krichëv see Krychaw
Krickerhäu/Kriegerhaj see Handlová
111 W6 **Krieglach** Steiermark, E Austria
110 F8 **Kriens** Luzern, W Switzerland
Krimmitschau see Crimmitschau
100 H12 **Krimpen aan den IJssel** Zuid-Holland, SW Netherlands
Krindachevka see Krasnyy Luch
117 G25 **Kríos, Ákra** *headland* Kríti, Greece, E Mediterranean Sea
161 J16 **Krishna** *prev.* Kistna. ≈ C India
161 H20 **Krishnagiri** Tamil Nādu, SE India
161 K17 **Krishna, Mouths of the** *delta* SE India
159 S15 **Krishnanagar** West Bengal, N India
161 G20 **Krishnarājāsāgara Reservoir** ▣ W India
97 N19 **Kristdala** Kalmar, S Sweden
Kristiania see Oslo
97 E18 **Kristiansand** *var.* Christiansand. Vest-Agder, S Norway
97 L22 **Kristianstad** Kristianstad, S Sweden
97 J22 **Kristianstad** ⬖ *county* S Sweden
96 F8 **Kristiansund** *var.* Christiansund. Møre og Romsdal, S Norway
Kristiinankaupunki see Kristinestad
95 I14 **Kristineberg** Västerbotten, N Sweden
97 L16 **Kristinehamn** Värmland, C Sweden
95 J17 **Kristinestad** *Fin.* Kristiinankaupunki. Vaasa, W Finland
Kristyor see Crişcior
117 J25 **Kríti** *Eng.* Crete. ⬖ *region* Greece, Aegean Sea
117 J24 **Kríti** *Eng.* Crete. *island* Greece, Aegean Sea
117 J23 **Kritikó Pélagos** *var.* Kretikon Delagos, *Eng.* Sea of Crete; *anc.* Mare Creticum. *sea* Greece, Aegean Sea
Kriulyany see Criuleni
114 I12 **Krivaja** ≈ NE Bosnia and Herzegovina
Krivaja see Mali Idoš
115 P17 **Kriva Palanka** *Turk.* Eğri Palanka. NE FYR Macedonia
Krivichi see Kryvychy
116 H8 **Krivodol** Oblast Montana, NW Bulgaria
130 M10 **Krivorozh'ye** Rostovskaya Oblast', SW Russian Federation
Krivoshin see Kryvoshyn
Krivoy Rog see Kryvyy Rih
114 F7 **Križevci** *Ger.* Kreuz, *Hung.* Kőrös. Varaždin, NE Croatia
114 B10 **Krk** *It.* Veglia. Primorje-Gorski Kotar, NW Croatia
114 B10 **Krk** *It.* Veglia; *anc.* Curieta. *island* NW Croatia
111 V12 **Krka** ≈ SE Slovenia
Krka see Gurk
111 R11 **Krn** ▲ NW Slovenia
113 H16 **Krnov** *Ger.* Jägerndorf. Severní Morava, E Czech Republic
Kroatien see Croatia
97 G14 **Krøderen** Buskerud, S Norway
97 G14 **Krøderen** ◎ S Norway
Kroi see Krui
97 N17 **Krokek** Östergötland, S Sweden
Krokodil see Crocodile
95 G16 **Krokom** Jämtland, C Sweden
119 S2 **Krolevets'** *Rus.* Krolevets. Sums'ka Oblast', NE Ukraine
Królewska Huta see Chorzów
113 H18 **Kroměříž** *Ger.* Kremsier. Jižní Morava, E Czech Republic
100 I9 **Krommenie** Noord-Holland, C Netherlands
130 J6 **Kromy** Orlovskaya Oblast', W Russian Federation
103 L18 **Kronach** Bayern, E Germany
Krone an der Brahe see Koronowo
178 I13 **Krŏng Kaôh Kŏng** Kaôh Kŏng, SW Cambodia
97 K21 **Kronoberg** ⬖ *county* S Sweden
127 Pp11 **Kronotskiy Zaliv** *bay* E Russian Federation
205 O2 **Kronprinsesse Märtha Kyst** *physical region* Antarctica
205 V3 **Kronprins Olav Kyst** *physical region* Antarctica
128 G12 **Kronshtadt** Leningradskaya Oblast', NW Russian Federation
Kronstadt see Braşov
85 I22 **Kroonstad** Free State, C South Africa
126 Kk13 **Kropotkin** Irkutskaya Oblast', C Russian Federation
130 L14 **Kropotkin** Krasnodarskiy Kray, SW Russian Federation
Krośnieńskie, Województwo see Krosno
112 J11 **Krośniewice** Płock, C Poland
113 N17 **Krosno** *Ger.* Krossen. Krosno, SE Poland
113 N17 **Krosno** *off.* Województwo Krośnieńskie. ⬖ *province* SE Poland
112 E12 **Krosno Odrzańskie** *Ger.* Crossen, Kreisstadt. Zielona Góra, W Poland
Krossen see Krosno
Krotoschin see Krotoszyn
112 H13 **Krotoszyn** *Ger.* Krotoschin. Kalisz, C Poland
Krottingen see Kretinga
Krousón see Krousónas
117 J25 **Krousónas** *prev.* Krousón, Kroussón. Kríti, Greece, E Mediterranean Sea
Kroussón see Krousónas
Krraba see Krrabë
115 L20 **Krrabë** *var.* Krraba. Tiranë, C Albania
115 L17 **Krrabit, Mali i** ▲▲ N Albania
111 W12 **Krško** *Ger.* Gurkfeld; *prev.* Videm-Krško. E Slovenia
85 K19 **Kruger National Park** *national park* Northern, N South Africa
85 J21 **Krugersdorp** Gauteng, NE South Africa
40 D16 **Krugloi Point** *headland* Agattu Island, Alaska, USA
Krugloye see Kruhlaye
121 N15 **Kruhlaye** *Rus.* Krugloye. Mahilyowskaya Voblasts', E Belarus
174 I13 **Krui** *var.* Kroi. Sumatera, SW Indonesia
101 G16 **Kruibeke** Oost-Vlaanderen, N Belgium
85 G25 **Kruidfontein** Western Cape, SW South Africa
101 F15 **Kruiningen** Zeeland, SW Netherlands
Kruja see Krujë
115 L19 **Krujë** *var.* Kruja, *It.* Croia. Durrës, C Albania
Krulevshchina see Krulewshchyna
120 K13 **Krulewshchyna** *Rus.* Krulevshchina. Vitsyebskaya Voblasts', N Belarus
27 T6 **Krum** Texas, SW USA
103 J23 **Krumbach** Bayern, S Germany
115 M17 **Krumë** Kukës, NE Albania
Krummau see Český Krumlov
116 K12 **Krumovgrad** *prev.* Kossukavak. Khaskovska Oblast, S Bulgaria
116 K12 **Krumovitsa** ≈ S Bulgaria
116 L10 **Krumovo** Burgaska Oblast, SE Bulgaria
178 Hh11 **Krung Thep** *var.* Krung Thep Mahanakhon, *Eng.* Bangkok. ● (Thailand) Bangkok, C Thailand
178 Hh12 **Krung Thep, Ao** *var.* Bight of Bangkok. *bay* S Thailand
Krung Thep Mahanakhon see Krung Thep
121 M15 **Krupki** *Rus.* Krupki. Minskaya Voblasts', C Belarus
97 G24 **Kruså** *var.* Krusaa. Sønderjylland, SW Denmark
Krusaa see Kruså
15 I4 **Krusenstern, Cape** *headland* Northwest Territories, NW Canada
115 N14 **Kruševac** Serbia, C Yugoslavia
115 N19 **Kruševo** SW FYR Macedonia
113 A15 **Krušné Hory** *Eng.* Ore Mountains, *Ger.* Erzgebirge. ▲▲ Czech Republic/Germany *see also* Erzgebirge
41 W13 **Kruzof Island** *island* Alexander Archipelago, Alaska, USA
116 F13 **Krýa Vrýsi** *var.* Kría Vrísi. Kentrikí Makedonía, N Greece
121 P16 **Krychaw** *Rus.* Krichëv. Mahilyowskaya Voblasts', E Belarus
66 K11 **Krylov Seamount** *undersea feature* E Atlantic Ocean
Krym see Krym, Respublika
119 S13 **Krym, Respublika** *var.* Krym, *Eng.* Crimea, Crimean Oblast; *prev. Rus.* Krymskaya ASSR, Krymskaya Oblast'. ⬖ *province* SE Ukraine
130 K14 **Krymsk** Krasnodarskiy Kray, SW Russian Federation
Krymskaya ASSR/Krymskaya Oblast' see Krym, Respublika
119 T13 **Kryms'ki Hory** ▲▲ S Ukraine
119 T13 **Kryms'kyy Pivostriv** *peninsula* S Ukraine
113 M18 **Krynica** *Ger.* Tannenhof. Nowy Sącz, S Poland
119 P8 **Kryve Ozero** Odes'ka Oblast', SW Ukraine
121 I18 **Kryvoshyn** *Rus.* Krivoshin. Brestskaya Voblasts', SW Belarus
121 K14 **Kryvychy** *Rus.* Krivichi. Minskaya Voblasts', C Belarus
119 S8 **Kryvyy Rih** *Rus.* Krivoy Rog. Dnipropetrovs'ka Oblast', SE Ukraine
119 N8 **Kryzhopil'** Vinnyts'ka Oblast', C Ukraine
Krzemieniec see Kremenets'
113 J14 **Krzepice** Częstochowa, S Poland
112 F10 **Krzyż** Piła, W Poland
Ksar al Kabir see Ksar-el-Kebir
Ksar al Soule see Er-Rachidia
76 J5 **Ksar El Boukhari** N Algeria
76 G5 **Ksar-el-Kebir** *var.* Alcázar, Ksar al Kabir, Ksar-el-Kébir, *Ar.* Al-Kasr al-Kebir, Al-Qsar al-Kbir, *Sp.* Alcazarquivir. NW Morocco
112 H12 **Książ Wielkopolski** *Ger.* Xions. Poznań, W Poland
131 O3 **Kstovo** Nizhegorodskaya Oblast', W Russian Federation
174 Mm4 **Kuala Belait** W Brunei
Kuala Dungun see Dungun
174 M7 **Kualakerian** Borneo, C Indonesia
174 M10 **Kualakuayan** Borneo, C Indonesia
174 H4 **Kuala Lipis** Pahang, Peninsular Malaysia
174 H5 **Kuala Lumpur** ● (Malaysia) Kuala Lumpur, Peninsular Malaysia
Kuala Pelabohan Kelang see Pelabuhan Klang
175 Nn3 **Kuala Penyu** Sabah, East Malaysia
40 E9 **Kualapuu** *Haw.* Kualapu'u. Molokai, Hawaii, USA, C Pacific Ocean
173 G6 **Kuala, Sungai** ≈ Sumatera, W Indonesia
174 Hh3 **Kuala Terengganu** *var.* Kuala Trengganu. Terengganu, Peninsular Malaysia
174 Hh9 **Kualatungkal** Sumatera, W Indonesia
175 O3 **Kuamut, Sungai** ≈ East Malaysia
175 Qq7 **Kuandang** Sulawesi, N Indonesia
175 Qq7 **Kuandang, Teluk** *bay* Sulawesi, N Indonesia
169 V12 **Kuandian** Liaoning, NE China
Kuando-Kubango see Cuando Cubango
Kuang-chou see Guangzhou
Kuang-hsi see Guangxi Zhuangzu Zizhiqu
Kuang-tung see Guangdong
Kuang-yuan see Guangyuan
174 Hh4 **Kuantan** Pahang, Peninsular Malaysia
Kuantan, Batang see Indragiri, Sungai
Kuanza Norte see Cuanza Norte
Kuanza Sul see Cuanza Sul
Kuba see Quba
125 Aa12 **Kuban'** *var.* Hypanis. ≈ SW Russian Federation
Kubango see Cubango/Okavango
147 X8 **Kubārah** NW Oman
95 H16 **Kubbe** Västernorrland, C Sweden
82 A11 **Kubbum** Southern Darfur, W Sudan
128 L13 **Kubenskoye, Ozero** ◎ NW Russian Federation
170 Ee16 **Kubokawa** Kōchi, Shikoku, SW Japan
116 L7 **Kubrat** *prev.* Balbunar. Razgradska Oblast, NE Bulgaria
175 Oo15 **Kubu** Sumbawa, S Indonesia
114 O13 **Kučajske Planine** ▲▲ E Yugoslavia
172 Pp2 **Kuccharo-ko** ◎ Hokkaidō, N Japan
114 O11 **Kučevo** Serbia, NE Yugoslavia
Kuchan see Qūchān
174 L6 **Kuching** *prev.* Sarawak. Sarawak, East Malaysia
174 L7 **Kuching** × Sarawak, East Malaysia
170 Aa17 **Kuchinoerabu-jima** *island* Nansei-shotō, SW Japan
170 C13 **Kuchinotsu** Nagasaki, Kyūshū, SW Japan
111 Q6 **Kuchl** Salzburg, NW Austria
154 L9 **Kūchnay Darweyshān** Helmand, S Afghanistan
Kuchurgan see Kuchurhan
119 O9 **Kuchurhan** *Rus.* Kuchurgan. ≈ NE Ukraine
Kuçova see Kuçovë
115 L21 **Kuçovë** *var.* Kuçova; *prev.* Qyteti Stalin. Berat, C Albania
142 D11 **Küçük Çekmece** İstanbul, NW Turkey
170 Dd13 **Kudamatsu** *var.* Kudamatu. Yamaguchi, Honshū, SW Japan
Kudamatu see Kudamatsu
Kudara see Ghŭdara
175 O1 **Kudat** Sabah, East Malaysia
Küddow see Gwda
161 G17 **Kūdligi** Karnātaka, W India
Kudowa see Kudowa-Zdrój
113 F16 **Kudowa-Zdrój** *Ger.* Kudowa. Wałbrzych, SW Poland
119 P9 **Kudryavtsivka** Mykolayivs'ka Oblast', S Ukraine
174 L14 **Kudus** *prev.* Koedoes. Jawa, C Indonesia
129 T13 **Kudymkar** Komi-Permyatskiy Avtonomnyy Okrug, NW Russian Federation
Kudzsir see Cugir
Kuei-chou see Guizhou
Kuei-lin see Guilin
Kuei-yang see Guiyang
K'u-erh-lo see Korla
Kueyang see Guiyang
Kufa see Al Kūfah
142 E14 **Kūfiçayı** ≈ C Turkey
111 O6 **Kufstein** Tirol, W Austria
151 V14 **Kugaly** *Kaz.* Qoghaly. Taldykorgan, SE Kazakhstan
149 Y13 **Kūhak** Sīstān va Balūchestān, SE Iran
149 R9 **Kūhbonān** Kermān, C Iran
154 J5 **Kūhestān** *var.* Kohsān. Herāt, W Afghanistan
95 N15 **Kuhmo** Oulu, E Finland
95 L18 **Kuhmoinen** Keski-Suomi, C Finland
Kuhnau see Konin
Kühnö see Kihnu

◆ Country ● Country Capital ◇ Dependent Territory ○ Dependent Territory Capital ⬖ Administrative Region × International Airport ▲ Mountain ▲▲ Mountain Range Volcano ≈ River ◎ Lake ▣ Reservoir

149 O8 **Kūhpāyeh** Eşfahān, C Iran
178 H13 **Kui Buri** var. Ban Kui Nua. Prachuap Khiri Khan, SW Thailand
Kuibyshev see Kuybyshevskoye Vodokhranilishche
84 D13 **Kuito** Port. Silva Porto. Bié, C Angola
41 X14 **Kuiu Island** island Alexander Archipelago, Alaska, USA
94 L13 **Kuivaniemi** Oulu, C Finland
79 V14 **Kujama** Kaduna, C Nigeria
172 N10 **Kuji** var. Kuzi. Iwate, Honshū, C Japan
Kujto, Ozero see Kuyto, Ozero
Kujū-renzan see Kujū-san
170 D14 **Kujū-san** var. Kujū-renzan. ▲ Kyūshū, SW Japan
45 N7 **Kukalaya, Rio** var. Rio Cuculaya, Rio Kukulaya. ≈ NE Nicaragua
115 O16 **Kukavica** var. Vlajna. ▲ SE Yugoslavia
152 M10 **Kŭkcha** Rus. Kokcha. Bukhoro Wiloyati, C Uzbekistan
115 M18 **Kukës** var. Kukësi. Kukës, NE Albania
115 L18 **Kukës** ⬖ district NE Albania
Kukësi see Kukës
194 J14 **Kukipi** Gulf, S PNG
131 S3 **Kukmor** Respublika Tatarstan, W Russian Federation
Kukong see Shaoguan
41 N6 **Kukpowruk River** ≈ Alaska, USA
40 M6 **Kukpuk River** ≈ Alaska, USA
Kukukhoto see Hohhot
Kukulaya, Rio see Kukalaya, Rio
174 Hh7 **Kukup** Johor, Peninsular Malaysia
201 W12 **Kuku Point** headland NW Wake Island
152 G11 **Kukurtli** Akhalskiy Velayat, C Turkmenistan
Kül see Kül, Rūd-e
116 F7 **Kula** Oblast Montana, NW Bulgaria
142 D14 **Kula** Manisa, W Turkey
114 K9 **Kula** Serbia, NW Yugoslavia
155 S8 **Kulāchi** North-West Frontier Province, NW Pakistan
Kulachi see Kolāchi
150 F11 **Kulagino** Kaz. Kŭlagīno. Atyrau, W Kazakhstan
174 Hh6 **Kulai** Johor, Peninsular Malaysia
116 M7 **Kulak** ≈ NE Bulgaria
159 T11 **Kula Kangri** var. Kulhakangri. ▲ Bhutan/China
150 E13 **Kulaly, Ostrov** island SW Kazakhstan
153 V9 **Kulanak** Narynskaya Oblast', C Kyrgyzstan
152 B8 **Kulandag** ▲▲ W Turkmenistan
159 V14 **Kulaura** Chittagong, NE Bangladesh
120 D9 **Kuldīga** Ger. Goldingen. Kuldīga, W Latvia
Kuldja see Yining
Kul'dzhuktau, Gory see Quljuqtov-Toghi
131 N4 **Kulebaki** Nizhegorodskaya Oblast', W Russian Federation
114 E11 **Kulen Vakuf** NW Bosnia and Herzegovina
189 Q9 **Kulgera Roadhouse** Northern Territory, N Australia
Kulhakangri see Kula Kangri
131 T1 **Kuliga** Udmurtskaya Respublika, NW Russian Federation
Kulkuduk see Kalquduq
120 G4 **Kullamaa** Läänemaa, W Estonia
207 O12 **Kullorsuaq** var. Kuvdlorssuak. C Greenland
31 O6 **Kulm** North Dakota, N USA
Kulm see Chełmno
152 D12 **Kul'mach** Balkanskiy Velayat, W Turkmenistan
103 L18 **Kulmbach** Bayern, SE Germany
Kulmsee see Chełmża
153 Q14 **Kŭlob** Rus. Kulyab. SW Tajikistan
94 M13 **Kuloharju** Lappi, N Finland
129 N7 **Kuloy** Arkhangel'skaya Oblast', NW Russian Federation
129 N7 **Kuloy** ≈ NW Russian Federation
143 Q14 **Kulp** Diyarbakır, SE Turkey
Kulpa see Kolpa
79 P14 **Kulpawn** ≈ N Ghana
149 R13 **Kūl, Rūd-e** var. Kül. ≈ S Iran
150 G12 **Kul'sary** Kaz. Qulsary. Atyrau, W Kazakhstan
159 R15 **Kulti** West Bengal, NE India
95 G14 **Kultsjön** ◎ N Sweden
142 I14 **Kulu** Konya, W Turkey
127 Nn10 **Kulu** ≈ E Russian Federation
125 G14 **Kulunda** Altayskiy Kray, S Russian Federation
151 T7 **Kulunda Steppe** Kaz. Qulyndy Zhazyghy, Rus. Kulundinskaya Ravnina. grassland Kazakhstan/Russian Federation
Kulundinskaya Ravnina see Kulunda Steppe
190 M9 **Kulwin** Victoria, SE Australia
Kulyab see Kŭlob
119 Q3 **Kulykivka** Chernihivs'ka Oblast', N Ukraine
Kum see Qom
170 Ee15 **Kuma** Ehime, Shikoku, SW Japan
131 P14 **Kuma** ≈ SW Russian Federation
Kumafa see Kumawa, Pegunungan
171 K15 **Kumagaya** Saitama, Honshū, S Japan
172 N6 **Kumaishi** Hokkaidō, NE Japan
174 Ll11 **Kumai, Teluk** bay Borneo, C Indonesia
131 Y7 **Kumak** Orenburgskaya Oblast', W Russian Federation
176 Y9 **Kumamba, Kepulauan** island group E Indonesia
170 Cc14 **Kumamoto** Kumamoto, Kyūshū, SW Japan
170 C14 **Kumamoto** off. Kumamoto-ken. ⬖ prefecture Kyūshū, SW Japan
171 Gg17 **Kumano** Mie, Honshū, SW Japan
Kumanova see Kumanovo
115 O17 **Kumanovo** Turk. Kumanova. N FYR Macedonia
193 G17 **Kumara** West Coast, South Island, NZ
188 J8 **Kumarina Roadhouse** Western Australia
159 T15 **Kumarkhali** Khulna, W Bangladesh
79 P16 **Kumasi** prev. Coomassie. C Ghana
176 Vv11 **Kumawa, Pegunungan** var. Kumafa. ▲▲ Irian Jaya, E Indonesia
Kumayri see Gyumri
81 D15 **Kumba** Sud-Ouest, W Cameroon
116 N13 **Kumbağ** Tekirdağ, NW Turkey
161 J21 **Kumbakonam** Tamil Nādu, SE India
176 Z16 **Kumbe, Sungai** ≈ Irian Jaya, E Indonesia
Kum-Dag see Gumdag
172 O14 **Kume-jima** island Nansei-shotō, SW Japan
131 V6 **Kumertau** Respublika Bashkortostan, W Russian Federation
125 F11 **Kuminskiy** Khanty-Mansiyskiy Avtonomnyy Okrug, C Russian Federation
37 R4 **Kumiva Peak** ▲ Nevada, W USA
165 N8 **Kum Kuduk** well NW China
165 N7 **Kumkuduk** Xinjiang Uygur Zizhiqu, W China
Kumkurgan see Qumqurghon
97 M16 **Kumla** Örebro, C Sweden
142 E17 **Kumluca** Antalya, SW Turkey
102 N9 **Kummerower See** ◎ NE Germany
79 X14 **Kumo** Bauchi, E Nigeria
151 O13 **Kumola** ≈ C Kazakhstan
178 H1 **Kumon Range** ▲▲ N Myanmar
126 K14 **Kumora** Respublika Buryatiya, S Russian Federation
85 F22 **Kums** Karas, SE Namibia
161 E18 **Kumta** Karnātaka, W India
164 L6 **Kümük** Xinjiang Uygur Zizhiqu, W China
40 H12 **Kumukahi, Cape** headland Hawaii, USA, C Pacific Ocean
131 Q17 **Kumukh** Respublika Dagestan, SW Russian Federation
Kumul see Hami
131 N9 **Kumylzhenskaya** Volgogradskaya Oblast', SW Russian Federation
147 W6 **Kumzār** N Oman
155 S4 **Kunar** Per. Konarhā. ⬖ province E Afghanistan
Kunashiri see Kunashir, Ostrov
127 P16 **Kunashir, Ostrov** var. Kunashiri. island Kuril'skiye Ostrova, SE Russian Federation
120 I3 **Kunda** Lääne-Virumaa, NE Estonia
158 M13 **Kunda** Uttar Pradesh, N India
161 E19 **Kundāpura** var. Coondapoor. Karnātaka, W India
81 O24 **Kundelungu, Monts** ▲ S Zaire
Kundert see Hernád
194 I12 **Kundiawa** Chimbu, W PNG
Kundla see Sāvarkundla
174 Hh7 **Kundur, Pulau** island W Indonesia
155 Q2 **Kunduz** var. Kondoz, Kundūz, Qondūz, Per. Kondūz. Kunduz, NE Afghanistan
155 Q2 **Kunduz** Per. Kondūz. ⬖ province NE Afghanistan
Kuneitra see Al Qunayţirah
85 B18 **Kunene** ⬖ district NE Namibia
85 A16 **Kunene** var. Cunene. ≈ Angola/Namibia see also Cunene
Künes see Xinyuan
164 J5 **Künes He** ≈ NW China
97 I19 **Kungälv** Göteborg och Bohus, S Sweden
153 W7 **Kungei Ala-Tau** Rus. Khrebet Kyungëy Ala-Too, Kir. Küngöy Ala-Too. ▲▲ Kazakhstan/Kyrgyzstan
Küngöy Ala-Too see Kungei Ala-Tau
Kungrad see Qŭnghirot
97 J19 **Kungsbacka** Halland, S Sweden
97 I18 **Kungshamn** Göteborg och Bohus, S Sweden
97 M16 **Kungsör** Västmanland, C Sweden
81 J16 **Kungu** Equateur, NW Zaire
129 V15 **Kungur** Permskaya Oblast', NW Russian Federation
177 G9 **Kungyangon** Yangon, SW Myanmar
113 M22 **Kunhegyes** Jász-Nagykun-Szolnok, E Hungary
178 H5 **Kunhing** Shan State, E Myanmar
170 Cc15 **Kunimi-dake** ▲ Kyūshū, SW Japan
164 D9 **Kunjirap Daban** var. Khūnjerāb Pass. pass China/Pakistan see also Khūnjerāb Pass
Kunlun Mountains see Kunlun Shan
164 H10 **Kunlun Shan** Eng. Kunlun Mountains. ▲▲ NW China
165 P11 **Kunlun Shankou** pass C China
166 G13 **Kunming** var. K'un-ming; prev. Yunnan. Yunnan, SW China
172 N6 **Kunnui** Hokkaidō, NE Japan
169 X16 **Kunsan** var. Gunsan, Jap. Gunzan. W South Korea
113 L24 **Kunszentmárton** Jász-Nagykun-Szolnok, E Hungary
113 J23 **Kunszentmiklós** Bács-Kiskun, C Hungary
189 N3 **Kununurra** Western Australia
Kunya-Urgench see Këneurgench
Kunyé see Pins, Île des
174 Mm8 **Kunyi** Borneo, C Indonesia
103 I20 **Künzelsau** Baden-Württemberg, S Germany
167 S10 **Kuocang Shan** ▲▲ SE China
128 H5 **Kuoloyarvi** var. Luolajarvi. Murmanskaya Oblast', NW Russian Federation
95 N16 **Kuopio** Kuopio, C Finland
95 M16 **Kuopio** ⬖ province C Finland
95 K17 **Kuortane** Vaasa, W Finland
95 M18 **Kuortti** Mikkeli, S Finland
Kupa see Kolpa
175 R17 **Kupang** prev. Koepang. Timor, C Indonesia
41 Q5 **Kuparuk River** ≈ Alaska, USA
Kupchino see Cupcina
194 L16 **Kupiano** Central, S PNG
188 M4 **Kupingarri** Western Australia
125 G14 **Kupino** Novosibirskaya Oblast', C Russian Federation
120 H11 **Kupiškis** Kupiškis, NE Lithuania
116 L13 **Küplü** Edirne, NW Turkey
41 X13 **Kupreanof Island** island Alexander Archipelago, Alaska, USA
41 O16 **Kupreanof Point** headland Alaska, USA
114 G13 **Kupres** SW Bosnia and Herzegovina
119 W5 **Kup"yans'k** Rus. Kupyansk. Kharkivs'ka Oblast', E Ukraine
119 W5 **Kup"yans'k-Vuzlovyy** Kharkivs'ka Oblast', E Ukraine
164 I6 **Kuqa** Xinjiang Uygur Zizhiqu, NW China
Kür see Kura
143 W11 **Kura** Az. Kür, Geor. Mtkvari, Turk. Kura Nehri. ≈ SW Asia
57 R8 **Kuracki** NW Guyana
170 Ee13 **Kurahashi-jima** island SW Japan
Kura Kurk see Irbe Strait
153 Q10 **Kurama Range** Rus. Kuraminskiy Khrebet. ▲▲ Tajikistan/Uzbekistan
Kuraminskiy Khrebet see Kurama Range
Kura Nehri see Kura
176 Ww10 **Kuran, Kepulauan** island group E Indonesia
121 J14 **Kuranyets** Rus. Kurenets. Minskaya Voblasts', C Belarus
170 Ff14 **Kurashiki** var. Kurasiki. Okayama, Honshū, SW Japan
160 L10 **Kurasia** Madhya Pradesh, C India
Kurasiki see Kurashiki
170 G12 **Kurayoshi** var. Kurayosi. Tottori, Honshū, SW Japan
Kurayosi see Kurayoshi
169 X6 **Kurbin He** ≈ NE China
151 X10 **Kurchum** Kaz. Kürshim. Vostochnyy Kazakhstan, E Kazakhstan
151 Y10 **Kurchum** ≈ E Kazakhstan
143 X11 **Kürdämir** Rus. Kyurdamir. C Azerbaijan
Kurdestan see Kordestān
145 S1 **Kurdistan** cultural region SW Asia
Kurd Kui see Kord Küy
161 F15 **Kurduvādi** Mahārāshtra, W India
116 J11 **Kŭrdzhali** var. Kirdzhali. Khaskovska Oblast, S Bulgaria
116 J11 **Kŭrdzhali, Yazovir** ▣ S Bulgaria
170 Ee13 **Kure** Hiroshima, Honshū, SW Japan
199 J5 **Kure Atoll** var. Ocean Island. atoll Hawaiian Islands, Hawaii, USA, C Pacific Ocean
142 J10 **Küre Dağları** ▲▲ N Turkey
Kurenets see Kuranyets
120 E6 **Kuressaare** Ger. Arensburg; prev. Kingissepp. Saaremaa, W Estonia
126 J9 **Kureyka** Krasnoyarskiy Kray, N Russian Federation
126 J9 **Kureyka** ≈ N Russian Federation
151 P10 **Kurgal'dzhin, Ozero** ◎ C Kazakhstan
151 Q10 **Kurgal'dzhinskiy** Kaz. Qorghazhyn. Akmola, C Kazakhstan
125 F12 **Kurgan** Kurganskaya Oblast', C Russian Federation
130 L14 **Kurganinsk** Krasnodarskiy Kray, SW Russian Federation
125 Ee12 **Kurganskaya Oblast'** ⬖ province C Russian Federation
Kurgan-Tyube see Qŭrghonteppa
203 O2 **Kuria** prev. Woodle Island. island Tungaru, W Kiribati
Kuria Muria Bay see Ḩalāniyāt, Khalīj al
Kuria Muria Islands see Ḩalāniyāt, Juzur al
159 T13 **Kurigram** Rajshahi, N Bangladesh
176 Yy16 **Kurik** Irian Jaya, E Indonesia
95 K17 **Kurikka** Vaasa, W Finland
171 M12 **Kurikoma-yama** ▲ Honshū, C Japan
199 Hh3 **Kurile Basin** undersea feature NW Pacific Ocean
Kurile Islands see Kuril'skiye Ostrova
Kurile-Kamchatka Depression see Kurile Trench
199 Hh3 **Kurile Trench** var. Kurile-Kamchatka Depression. undersea feature NW Pacific Ocean
131 Q9 **Kurilovka** Saratovskaya Oblast', W Russian Federation
127 P15 **Kuril'sk** Kuril'skiye Ostrova, Sakhalinskaya Oblats', SE Russian Federation
127 Pp15 **Kuril'skiye Ostrova** Eng. Kurile Islands. island group SE Russian Federation
44 M9 **Kurinwas, Río** ≈ E Nicaragua
Kurisches Haff see Courland Lagoon
Kurkund see Kilingi-Nõmme
130 M4 **Kurlovskiy** Vladimirskaya Oblast', W Russian Federation
82 G12 **Kurmuk** Blue Nile, SE Sudan
Kurna see Al Qurnah
161 H17 **Kurnool** var. Karnul. Andhra Pradesh, S India
171 J13 **Kurobe** Toyama, Honshū, SW Japan
170 Cc13 **Kurogi** Fukuoka, Kyūshū, SW Japan
171 Mm9 **Kuroishi** var. Kuroisi. Aomori, Honshū, C Japan
Kuroisi see Kuroishi
171 Kk14 **Kuroiso** Tochigi, Honshū, S Japan
172 N5 **Kuromatsunai** Hokkaidō, NE Japan
172 Oo17 **Kuro-shima** island SW Japan
171 H16 **Kuroso-yama** ▲ Honshū, SW Japan
193 F21 **Kurow** Canterbury, South Island, NZ
176 Uu13 **Kur, Pulau** island E Indonesia
131 N15 **Kursavka** Stavropol'skiy Kray, SW Russian Federation
120 E11 **Kuršėnai** Šiauliai, N Lithuania
Kürshim see Kurchum
Kurshskaya Kosa/Kuršių Nerija see Courland Spit
130 J7 **Kursk** Kurskaya Oblast', W Russian Federation
130 I7 **Kurskaya Oblast'** ⬖ province W Russian Federation
Kurskiy Zaliv see Courland Lagoon
115 N15 **Kuršumlija** Serbia, S Yugoslavia
143 R15 **Kurtalan** Siirt, SE Turkey
125 Ee12 **Kurtamysh** Kurganskaya Oblast', C Russian Federation
Kurtbunar see Tervel
Kurt-Dere see Vŭlchidol
Kurtitsch/Kürtös see Curtici
151 U15 **Kurtty** ≈ SE Kazakhstan
95 L18 **Kuru** Häme, SW Finland
82 C13 **Kuru** ≈ W Sudan
116 M13 **Kuru Dağı** ▲▲ NW Turkey
164 L7 **Kuruktag** ▲▲ NW China
85 G22 **Kuruman** Northern Cape, N South Africa
69 T14 **Kuruman** ≈ W South Africa
170 Cc13 **Kurume** Fukuoka, Kyūshū, SW Japan
126 K15 **Kurumkan** Respublika Buryatiya, S Russian Federation
161 J25 **Kurunegala** North Western Province, C Sri Lanka
57 T10 **Kurupukari** C Guyana
129 U10 **Kur"ya** Respublika Komi, NW Russian Federation
150 E15 **Kuryk** prev. Yeraliyev. Mangistau, SW Kazakhstan
142 B15 **Kuşadası** Aydın, SW Turkey
117 M19 **Kuşadası Körfezi** gulf SW Turkey
170 Aa16 **Kusagaki-guntō** island SW Japan
Kusaie see Kosrae
151 T12 **Kusak** ≈ C Kazakhstan
Kusary see Qusar
178 Hh8 **Ku Sathan, Doi** ▲ NW Thailand
171 H15 **Kusatsu** var. Kusatu. Shiga, Honshū, SW Japan
Kusatu see Kusatsu
144 F11 **Kuseifa** Southern, C Israel
142 C12 **Kuş Gölü** ◎ NW Turkey
130 L12 **Kushchevskaya** Krasnodarskiy Kray, SW Russian Federation
171 H16 **Kushida-gawa** ≈ Honshū, SW Japan
170 Bb15 **Kushikino** var. Kusikino. Kagoshima, Kyūshū, SW Japan
170 C17 **Kushima** var. Kusima. Miyazaki, Kyūshū, SW Japan
170 G17 **Kushimoto** Wakayama, Honshū, SW Japan
172 Q7 **Kushiro** var. Kusiro. Hokkaidō, NE Japan
154 K4 **Kūshk** Herāt, W Afghanistan
152 J17 **Kushka** ≈ S Turkmenistan
Kushka see Gushgy
151 N8 **Kushmurun** Kaz. Qusmuryn. Kustanay, N Kazakhstan
151 N8 **Kushmurun, Ozero** Kaz. Qusmuryn. ◎ N Kazakhstan
131 U4 **Kushnarenkovo** Respublika Bashkortostan, W Russian Federation
Kushrabat see Qŭshrabot
159 T15 **Kushtia** Khulna, W Bangladesh
125 Ee10 **Kushva** Sverdlovskaya Oblast', C Russian Federation
Kusikino see Kushikino
Kusima see Kushima
Kusiro see Kushiro
40 M13 **Kuskokwim Bay** bay Alaska, USA
41 P11 **Kuskokwim Mountains** ▲▲ Alaska, USA
41 N12 **Kuskokwim River** ≈ Alaska, USA
110 G7 **Küsnacht** Zürich, N Switzerland
172 Qq6 **Kussharo-ko** var. Kussyaro. ◎ Hokkaidō, NE Japan
Küssnacht see Küssnacht am Rigi
110 F8 **Küssnacht am Rigi** var. Küssnacht. Schwyz, C Switzerland
Kussyaro see Kussharo-ko
150 M7 **Kustanay** Kaz. Qostanay. Kustanay, N Kazakhstan
150 L8 **Kustanay** off. Kustanayskaya Oblast', Kaz. Qostanay Oblysy. ⬖ province N Kazakhstan
Kustanayskaya Oblast' see Kustanay
Küstence/Küstendje see Constanţa
102 F11 **Küstenkanal** var. Ems-Hunte Canal. canal NW Germany
Küstrin see Kostrzyn
175 T7 **Kusu** Pulau Halmahera, E Indonesia
175 Nn16 **Kuta** Pulau Lombok, S Indonesia
145 T4 **Kutabān** N Iraq
142 E13 **Kütahya** prev. Kutaia. Kütahya, W Turkey
142 E13 **Kütahya** var. Kutaia. ⬖ province W Turkey
Kutai see Mahakam, Sungai
Kutaia see Kütahya
143 R9 **K'ut'aisi** W Georgia
Kūt al 'Amārah see Al Kūt
Kut al Hai/Kūt al Ḩayy see Al Ḩayy
Kut al Imara see Al Kūt
126 M12 **Kutana** Respublika Sakha (Yakutiya), NE Russian Federation
Kutaradja/Kutaraja see Bandaaceh
172 Nn5 **Kutchan** Hokkaidō, NE Japan
Kutch, Gulf of see Kachchh, Gulf of
Kutch, Rann of see Kachchh, Rann of
114 F9 **Kutina** Sisak-Moslavina, NE Croatia
114 H9 **Kutjevo** Požega-Slavonija, NE Croatia
113 E17 **Kutná Hora** Ger. Kuttenberg. Střední Čechy, C Czech Republic
112 K12 **Kutno** Płock, C Poland
Kuttenberg see Kutná Hora
81 I20 **Kutu** Bandundu, W Zaire
159 V17 **Kutubdia Island** island SE Bangladesh
82 B10 **Kutum** Northern Darfur, W Sudan
153 Y7 **Kuturgu** Issyk-Kul'skaya Oblast', E Kyrgyzstan
10 M5 **Kuujjuaq** prev. Fort-Chimo. Québec, E Canada
10 I7 **Kuujjuarapik** Québec, C Canada
152 A10 **Kuuli-Mayak** Turkm. Guwlumayak. Balkanskiy Velayat, NW Turkmenistan
120 I6 **Kuulse magi** ▲ S Estonia
94 N13 **Kuusamo** Oulu, E Finland
95 M19 **Kuusankoski** Kymi, S Finland
131 W7 **Kuvandyk** Orenburgskaya Oblast', W Russian Federation
Kuvango see Cubango
Kuvasay see Quwasoy
Kuvdlorssuak see Kullorsuaq
128 I16 **Kuvshinovo** Tverskaya Oblast', W Russian Federation
147 Q4 **Kuwait** off. State of Kuwait, var. Dawlat al Kuwait, Koweit, Kuweit. ◆ monarchy SW Asia
Kuwait see Al Kuwayt
Kuwait Bay see Kuwayt, Jūn al
Kuwait City see Al Kuwayt
Kuwait, Dawlat al see Kuwait
Kuwajleen see Kwajalein Atoll
171 H15 **Kuwana** Mie, Honshū, SW Japan
176 V9 **Kuwawin** Irian Jaya, E Indonesia
145 X9 **Kuwayt** E Iraq
148 K11 **Kuwayt, Jūn al** var. Kuwait Bay. bay E Kuwait
Kuweit see Kuwait
119 P10 **Kuyal'nyts'kyy Lyman** ◎ SW Ukraine
125 G13 **Kuybyshev** Novosibirskaya Oblast', C Russian Federation
Kuybyshev see Bolgar, Respublika Tatarstan, Russian Federation
Kuybyshev see Samara
119 W9 **Kuybysheve** Rus. Kuybyshevo. Zaporiz'ka Oblast', SE Ukraine
Kuybyshevo see Kuybysheve
Kuybyshev Reservoir see Kuybyshevskoye Vodokhranilishche
Kuybyshevskaya Oblast' see Samarskaya Oblast'
151 O7 **Kuybyshevskiy** Kokshetau, N Kazakhstan
131 R4 **Kuybyshevskoye Vodokhranilishche** var. Kuibyshev, Eng. Kuybyshev Reservoir. ▣ W Russian Federation
127 N9 **Kuydusun** Respublika Sakha (Yakutiya), NE Russian Federation
129 U16 **Kuyeda** Permskaya Oblast', NW Russian Federation
Küysanjaq see Koi Sanjaq
128 I7 **Kuyto, Ozero** var. Ozero Kujto. ◎ NW Russian Federation
164 J4 **Kuytun** Xinjiang Uygur Zizhiqu, NW China
126 J15 **Kuytun** Irkutskaya Oblast', S Russian Federation
126 Ii12 **Kuyumba** Evenkiyskiy Avtonomnyy Okrug, C Russian Federation
57 S12 **Kuyuwini Landing** S Guyana
Kuzi see Kuji
40 M9 **Kuzitrin River** ≈ Alaska, USA
131 P6 **Kuznetsk** Penzenskaya Oblast', W Russian Federation
118 K3 **Kuznetsovs'k** Rivnens'ka Oblast', NW Ukraine
128 K6 **Kuzomen'** Murmanskaya Oblast', NW Russian Federation
172 N10 **Kuzumaki** Iwate, Honshū, C Japan
94 H9 **Kvaløya** island N Norway
94 K8 **Kvalsund** Finnmark, N Norway
96 G11 **Kvam** Oppland, S Norway
131 X7 **Kvarkeno** Orenburgskaya Oblast', W Russian Federation
95 G15 **Kvarnbergsvattnet** var. Frostviken. ◎ N Sweden
114 A11 **Kvarner** var. Carnaro, It. Quarnero. gulf W Croatia
114 B11 **Kvarnerička Vrata** channel W Croatia
41 O14 **Kvichak Bay** bay Alaska, USA
94 H12 **Kvikkjokk** Norrbotten, N Sweden
97 D17 **Kvina** ≈ S Norway
94 Q1 **Kvitøya** island NE Svalbard
97 F16 **Kvitseid** Telemark, S Norway
97 H24 **Kværndrup** Fyn, C Denmark
81 H20 **Kwa** ≈ W Zaire
79 Q15 **Kwadwokurom** C Ghana
195 X14 **Kwailibesi** Malaita, N Solomon Islands
201 S6 **Kwajalein Atoll** var. Kuwajleen. atoll Ralik Chain, C Marshall Islands
57 W9 **Kwakoegron** Brokopondo, N Suriname
83 J21 **Kwale** Coast, S Kenya
79 U17 **Kwale** Delta, S Nigeria
81 H20 **Kwamouth** Bandundu, W Zaire
Kwando see Cuando
Kwangchow see Guangzhou
Kwangchu see Kwangju
169 X16 **Kwangju** off. Kwangju-gwangyŏksi, var. Guangju, Kwangchu, Jap. Kōshū. SW South Korea
81 H20 **Kwango** Port. Cuango. ≈ Angola/Zaire see also Cuango
Kwangsi/Kwangsi Chuang Autonomous Region see Guangxi Zhuangzu Zizhiqu
Kwangtung see Guangdong
Kwangyuan see Guangyuan
83 F17 **Kwania, Lake** ◎ C Uganda
Kwanza see Cuanza
79 S15 **Kwara** ⬖ state SW Nigeria
176 Ww11 **Kwatisore** Irian Jaya, E Indonesia
85 K22 **KwaZulu/Natal** off. KwaZulu/Natal Province; prev. Natal. ⬖ province E South Africa
Kweichow see Guizhou
Kweichu see Guiyang
Kweilin see Guilin
Kweisui see Hohhot
Kweiyang see Guiyang
85 K17 **Kwekwe** prev. Que Que. Midlands, C Zimbabwe
85 G20 **Kweneng** ⬖ district S Botswana
Kwesui see Hohhot
41 N12 **Kwethluk** Alaska, USA
41 N12 **Kwethluk River** ≈ Alaska, USA
112 J8 **Kwidzyń** Ger. Marienwerder. Elbląg, N Poland
40 M13 **Kwigillingok** Alaska, USA
194 K16 **Kwikila** Central, S PNG
81 I20 **Kwilu** ≈ W Zaire
Kwito see Cuito
176 V8 **Kwoka, Gunung** ▲ Irian Jaya, E Indonesia
80 I12 **Kyabé** Moyen-Chari, S Chad
191 O11 **Kyabram** Victoria, SE Australia
178 Gg9 **Kyaikkami** prev. Amherst. Mon State, S Myanmar
177 F9 **Kyaiklat** Irrawaddy, SW Myanmar
177 G8 **Kyaikto** Mon State, S Myanmar
126 Jj16 **Kyakhta** Respublika Buryatiya, S Russian Federation
190 G8 **Kyancutta** South Australia
177 F7 **Kyangin** Irrawaddy, SW Myanmar
178 J8 **Ky Anh** Ha Tinh, N Vietnam
177 F5 **Kyaukpadaung** Mandalay, C Myanmar
177 F6 **Kyaukpyu** Arakan State, W Myanmar
177 G5 **Kyaukse** Mandalay, C Myanmar
177 F8 **Kyaunggon** Irrawaddy, SW Myanmar
121 E14 **Kybartai** Pol. Kibarty. Vilkaviškis, S Lithuania
158 I7 **Kyelang** Himāchal Pradesh, NW India
113 G19 **Kyjov** Ger. Gaya. Jižní Morava, SE Czech Republic
117 J21 **Kykládes** var. Kikládhes, Eng. Cyclades. island group SE Greece
27 S11 **Kyle** Texas, SW USA
98 G9 **Kyle of Lochalsh** N Scotland, UK
103 D18 **Kyll** ≈ W Germany
117 F19 **Kyllíni** var. Killini. ▲ S Greece
117 H18 **Kými** prev. Kími. Évvoia, C Greece
95 N18 **Kymi** Swe. Kymmene. ⬖ province SE Finland
95 M19 **Kymijoki** ≈ S Finland
117 H18 **Kýmis, Ákra** headland Évvoia, C Greece
Kymmene see Kymi
129 W14 **Kyn** Permskaya Oblast', NW Russian Federation
191 N12 **Kyneton** Victoria, SE Australia
83 G17 **Kyoga, Lake** var. Lake Kioga. ◎ C Uganda
171 H13 **Kyōga-misaki** headland Honshū, SW Japan
191 V4 **Kyogle** New South Wales, SE Australia
169 W15 **Kyŏnggi-man** bay NW South Korea
169 Z16 **Kyŏngju** Jap. Keishū. SE South Korea
Kyŏngsŏng see Sŏul
Kyōsai-tō see Kŏje-do
83 F19 **Kyotera** S Uganda
171 H15 **Kyōto** Kyōto, Honshū, SW Japan
171 H14 **Kyōto** off. Kyōto-fu, var. Kyōto Hu. ⬖ urban prefecture Honshū, SW Japan
Kyōto-fu/Kyōto Hu see Kyōto
117 D21 **Kyparissía** var. Kiparissía. Pelopónnisos, S Greece
117 D20 **Kyparissiakós Kólpos** gulf S Greece
Kyperounda see Kyperoúnta
124 N3 **Kyperoúnta** var. Kyperounda. C Cyprus
Kypros see Cyprus
117 H16 **Kyrá Panagía** island Vóreioi Sporádes, Greece, Aegean Sea
Kyrenia see Girne
Kyrenia Mountains see Beşparmak Dağları
Kyrgyz Republic see Kyrgyzstan
153 U9 **Kyrgyzstan** off. Kyrgyz Republic, var. Kirghizia; prev. Kirgizskaya SSR, Kirghiz SSR, Republic of Kyrgyzstan. ◆ republic C Asia
102 M11 **Kyritz** Brandenburg, NE Germany
Kyrkslätt see Kirkkonummi
96 G8 **Kyrksæterøra** Sør-Trøndelag, S Norway
129 U8 **Kyrta** Respublika Komi, NW Russian Federation
125 Ee12 **Kyshtym** Chelyabinskaya Oblast', S Russian Federation
113 J18 **Kysucké Nové Mesto** prev. Horné Nové Mesto, Ger. Kisutzaneustadtl, Oberneustadtl, Hung. Kiszucaújhely. Stredné Slovensko, N Slovakia
119 N12 **Kytay, Ozero** ◎ SW Ukraine
117 F23 **Kýthira** var. Kíthira, It.Cerigo; Lat. Cythera. Kýthira, S Greece
117 F23 **Kýthira** var. Kíthira, It. Cerigo; Lat. Cythera. island S Greece
117 I20 **Kýthnos** Kýthnos, Kykládes, Greece, Aegean Sea
117 I20 **Kýthnos** var. Kíthnos, Thermiá, It. Termia; anc. Cythnos. island Kykládes, Greece, Aegean Sea
117 I20 **Kýthnou, Stenó** strait Kykládes, Greece, Aegean Sea
Kythréa see Değirmenlik
Kyungëy Ala-Too, Khrebet see Kungei Ala-Tau
Kyurdamir see Kürdämir
152 C11 **Kyuren, Gora** ▲ W Turkmenistan
172 C15 **Kyūshū** var. Kyûsyû. island SW Japan
199 Gg6 **Kyushu-Palau Ridge** var. Kyusyu-Palau Ridge. undersea feature W Pacific Ocean
170 Cc15 **Kyūshū-sanchi** ▲▲ Kyūshū, SW Japan
116 F10 **Kyustendil** anc. Pautalia. Sofiyska Oblast, W Bulgaria
Kyûsyû see Kyūshū
Kyusyu-Palau Ridge see Kyushu-Palau Ridge
126 L7 **Kyusyur** Respublika Sakha (Yakutiya), NE Russian Federation
191 P10 **Kywong** New South Wales, SE Australia
119 P4 **Kyyiv** Eng. Kiev, Rus. Kiyev. ● (Ukraine) Kyyivs'ka Oblast', N Ukraine
Kyyiv see Kyyivs'ka Oblast'
119 O4 **Kyyivs'ka Oblast'** var. Kyyiv, Rus. Kiyevskaya Oblast'. ⬖ province N Ukraine
119 P3 **Kyyivs'ke Vodoskhovyshche** Eng. Kiev Reservoir, Rus. Kiyevskoye Vodokhranilishche. ▣ N Ukraine
95 L16 **Kyyjärvi** Keski-Suomi, C Finland
126 I16 **Kyzyl** Respublika Tyva, C Russian Federation
153 S8 **Kyzyl-Adyr** prev. Kirovskoye. Talasskaya Oblast', NW Kyrgyzstan
151 V14 **Kyzylagash** Taldykorgan, SE Kazakhstan
152 C13 **Kyzylbair** Balkanskiy Velayat, W Turkmenistan
Kyzyl-Dzhiik, Pereval see Uzbel Shankou
151 S7 **Kyzylkak, Ozero** ◎ NE Kazakhstan
151 X11 **Kyzylkesek** Semipalatinsk, E Kazakhstan
153 S10 **Kyzyl-Kiya** Kir. Kyzyl-Kyya. Oshskaya Oblast', SW Kyrgyzstan
150 L11 **Kyzylkol', Ozero** ◎ C Kazakhstan
139 L8 **Kyzyl Kum** var. Kizil Kum, Qizil Qum, Uzb. Qizilqum. desert Kazakhstan/Uzbekistan
Kyzyl-Kyya see Kyzyl-Kiya
Kyzylrabat see Qizilrawbe
Kyzylrabot see Qizilrabot
Kyzylsu see Kyzyl-Suu
153 X7 **Kyzyl-Suu** prev. Pokrovka. Issyk-Kul'skaya Oblast', NE Kyrgyzstan
153 S12 **Kyzyl-Suu** var. Kyzylsu. ≈ Kyrgyzstan/Tajikistan
153 X8 **Kyzyl-Tuu** Issyk-Kul'skaya Oblast', E Kyrgyzstan
151 Q12 **Kyzylzhar** Kaz. Qyzylzhar. Zhezkazgan, C Kazakhstan
151 N15 **Kzyl-Orda** var. Qizil Orda, Kaz. Qyzylorda; prev. Perovsk. Kzyl-Orda, S Kazakhstan
150 L14 **Kzyl-Orda** off. Kzyl-Ordinskaya Oblast', Kaz. Qyzylorda Oblysy. ⬖ province S Kazakhstan
Kzyl-Ordinskaya Oblast' see Kzyl-Orda
151 R7 **Kzyltu** Kaz. Qyzyltū. Kokshetau, N Kazakhstan

L

111 X2 **Laa an der Thaya** Niederösterreich, NE Austria
65 K15 **La Adela** La Pampa, SE Argentina
Laagen see Numedalslågen
111 S5 **Laakirchen** Oberösterreich, N Austria
Laaland see Lolland
106 I11 **La Albuera** Extremadura, W Spain
107 O7 **La Alcarria** physical region C Spain
106 K14 **La Algaba** Andalucía, S Spain
107 P9 **La Almarcha** Castilla-La Mancha, C Spain
107 R6 **La Almunia de Doña Godina** Aragón, NE Spain
43 N5 **La Amistad, Presa** ▣ NW Mexico
120 F4 **Läänemaa** off. Lääne Maakond. ⬖ province NW Estonia

◆ Country ● Country Capital ◇ Dependent Territory ○ Dependent Territory Capital ⬖ Administrative Region ✕ International Airport ▲ Mountain ▲▲ Mountain Range Volcano ≈ River ◎ Lake ▣ Reservoir

120 I3 **Lääne-Virumaa** *off.* Lääne-Viru Maakond. ◈ *province* NE Estonia
64 J9 **La Antigua, Salina** *salt lake* W Argentina
101 E17 **Laarne** Oost-Vlaanderen, NW Belgium
82 O13 **Laas Caanood** Nugaal, N Somalia
43 O9 **La Ascensión** Nuevo León, NE Mexico
82 N12 **Laas Dhaareed** Woqooyi Galbeed, N Somalia
57 O4 **La Asunción** Nueva Esparta, NE Venezuela
Laatokka *see* Ladozhskoye Ozero
102 I13 **Laatzen** Niedersachsen, NW Germany
40 E9 **Laau Point** *headland* Molokai, Hawaii, USA, C Pacific Ocean
44 D6 **La Aurora** ✕ (Ciudad de Guatemala) Guatemala, C Guatemala
76 C9 **Laâyoune** *var.* Aaiún. ○ (Western Sahara) NW Western Sahara
130 L14 **Laba** ≈ SW Russian Federation
42 M6 **La Babia** Coahuila de Zaragoza, NE Mexico
13 R7 **La Baie** Québec, SE Canada
175 R16 **Labala** Pulau Lomblen, S Indonesia
64 K8 **La Banda** Santiago del Estero, N Argentina
La Banda Oriental *see* Uruguay
106 K4 **La Bañeza** Castilla-León, N Spain
42 M13 **La Barca** Jalisco, SW Mexico
42 K14 **La Barra de Navidad** Jalisco, C Mexico
197 J13 **Labasa** *prev.* Lambasa. Vanua Levu, N Fiji
179 Q15 **Labason** Mindanao, S Philippines
104 H8 **la Baule-Escoublac** Loire-Atlantique, NW France
Labe *see* Elbe
78 I13 **Labé** Moyenne-Guinée, NW Guinea
25 X14 **La Belle** Florida, SE USA
13 N11 **Labelle** Québec, SE Canada
8 H7 **Laberge, Lake** ◎ Yukon Territory, W Canada
Labes *see* Łobez
Labiau *see* Polessk
114 A10 **Labin** *It.* Albona. Istra, NW Croatia
130 L14 **Labinsk** Krasnodarskiy Kray, SW Russian Federation
107 X5 **La Bisbal d'Empordà** Cataluña, NE Spain
121 P16 **Labkovichy** *Rus.* Lobkovichi. Mahilyowskaya Voblasts', E Belarus
13 S4 **La Blache, Lac de** ◎ Québec, SE Canada
179 Q11 **Labo** Luzon, N Philippines
Laboehanbadjo *see* Labuhanbajo
Laborca *see* Laborec
113 N18 **Laborec** *Hung.* Laborca. ≈ E Slovakia
110 D11 **La Borgne** ≈ S Switzerland
47 T12 **Laborie** SW Saint Lucia
81 F21 **La Bouenza** ◈ *province* S Congo
104 J14 **Labouheyre** Landes, SW France
64 L12 **Laboulaye** Córdoba, C Argentina
11 Q7 **Labrador** *cultural region* Newfoundland and Labrador, SW Canada
66 I6 **Labrador Basin** *var.* Labrador Sea Basin. *undersea feature* Labrador Sea
11 N9 **Labrador City** Newfoundland and Labrador, E Canada
11 Q5 **Labrador Sea** *sea* NW Atlantic Ocean
Labrador Sea Basin *see* Labrador Basin
Labrang *see* Xiahe
56 G9 **Labranzagrande** Boyacá, C Colombia
47 U15 **La Brea** Trinidad, Trinidad and Tobago
61 D14 **Lábrea** Amazonas, N Brazil
13 S6 **Labrieville** Québec, SE Canada
104 K14 **Labrit** Landes, SW France
110 C9 **La Broye** ≈ SW Switzerland
105 N15 **Labruguière** Tarn, S France
174 I8 **Labu** Pulau Singkep, W Indonesia
175 N3 **Labuan** *var.* Victoria. Labuan, East Malaysia
175 N3 **Labuan** ◈ *federal territory* East Malaysia
Labuan *see* Labuan, Pulau
175 N3 **Labuan, Pulau** *var.* Labuan. *island* East Malaysia
173 Pp16 **Labuhanbajo** *prev.* Laboehanbadjo. Flores, S Indonesia
173 G6 **Labuhanbilik** Sumatera, N Indonesia
173 Ee5 **Labuhanhaji** Sumatera, W Indonesia
Labuk *see* Labuk, Sungai
Labuk Bay *see* Labuk, Teluk
175 O2 **Labuk, Sungai** *var.* Labuk. ≈ East Malaysia
175 Oo2 **Labuk, Teluk** *var.* Labuk Bay, Telukan Labuk. *bay* S Sulu Sea
Labuk, Telukan *see* Labuk, Teluk
177 Ff9 **Labutta** Irrawaddy, SW Myanmar
125 G8 **Labytnangi** Yamalo-Nenetskiy Avtonomnyy Okrug, N Russian Federation
80 F10 **Lac** *off.* Préfecture du Lac. ◈ *prefecture* W Chad
115 K19 **Laç** *var.* Laci. Lezhë, C Albania
59 K19 **Lacajahuira, Rio** ≈ W Bolivia
La Calamine *see* Kelmis
64 G11 **La Calera** Valparaíso, C Chile
11 P11 **Lac-Allard** Québec, E Canada
106 L13 **La Campana** Andalucía, S Spain
104 J12 **Lacanau** Gironde, SW France
44 C2 **Lacandón, Sierra del** ▲ Guatemala/Mexico
La Cañiza *see* A Cañiza
43 W16 **Lacantún, Río** ≈ SE Mexico
105 Q3 **la Capelle** Aisne, N France
114 K10 **Laćarak** Serbia, NW Yugoslavia
64 L11 **La Carlota** Córdoba, C Argentina
179 Q13 **La Carlota** Negros, S Philippines
106 L13 **La Carlota** Andalucía, S Spain
107 N12 **La Carolina** Andalucía, S Spain
105 O15 **Lacaune** Tarn, S France
13 P7 **Lac-Bouchette** Québec, SE Canada
Laccadive Islands/Laccadive Minicoy and Amindivi Islands, the *see* Lakshadweep
9 Y16 **Lac du Bonnet** Manitoba, S Canada
32 L4 **Lac du Flambeau** Wisconsin, N USA
13 P8 **Lac-Édouard** Québec, SE Canada
44 I4 **La Ceiba** Atlántida, N Honduras
56 E9 **La Ceja** Antioquia, W Colombia
190 J11 **Lacepede Bay** *bay* South Australia
34 G9 **Lacey** Washington, NW USA
105 P12 **la Chaise-Dieu** Haute-Loire, C France
116 G13 **Lachanás** Kentrikí Makedonía, N Greece
128 L11 **Lacha, Ozero** ◎ NW Russian Federation
105 O8 **la Charité-sur-Loire** Nièvre, C France
105 N9 **la Châtre** Indre, C France
110 C8 **La Chaux-de-Fonds** Neuchâtel, W Switzerland
Lach Dera *see* Dheere Laaq
110 G8 **Lachen** Schwyz, C Switzerland
191 Q8 **Lachlan River** ≈ New South Wales, SE Australia
45 T15 **La Chorrera** Panamá, C Panama
13 V7 **Lac-Humqui** Québec, SE Canada
13 N12 **Lachute** Québec, SE Canada
Lachyn *see* Laçın
Laci *see* Laç
143 W13 **Laçın** *Rus.* Lachyn. SW Azerbaijan
105 S16 **la Ciotat** *anc.* Citharista. Bouches-du-Rhône, SE France
20 D10 **Lackawanna** New York, NE USA
9 Q13 **Lac La Biche** Alberta, SW Canada
15 Hh7 **Lac La Martre** Northwest Territories, W Canada
13 R12 **Lac-Mégantic** *var.* Mégantic. Québec, SE Canada
Lacobriga *see* Lagos
42 G5 **La Colorada** Sonora, NW Mexico
9 Q15 **Lacombe** Alberta, SW Canada
32 L12 **Lacon** Illinois, N USA
45 P16 **La Concepción** *var.* Concepción. Chiriquí, W Panama
56 H5 **La Concepción** Zulia, NW Venezuela
56 H5 **La Concepción** Zulia, NW Venezuela
109 C19 **Laconi** Sardegna, Italy, C Mediterranean Sea
21 O9 **Laconia** New Hampshire, NE USA
63 H19 **La Coronilla** Rocha, E Uruguay
La Coruña *see* A Coruña
106 G2 **La Coruña** ◈ *province* Galicia, NW Spain
105 O11 **la Courtine** Creuse, C France
104 J16 **Lacq** Pyrénées-Atlantiques, SW France
13 P9 **La Croche** Québec, SE Canada
31 X3 **la Croix, Lac** ◎ Canada/USA
28 K5 **La Crosse** Kansas, C USA
23 V7 **La Crosse** Virginia, NE USA
34 L9 **La Crosse** Washington, NW USA
32 J7 **La Crosse** Wisconsin, N USA
56 C13 **La Cruz** Nariño, SW Colombia
44 K12 **La Cruz** Guanacaste, NW Costa Rica
42 I10 **La Cruz** Sinaloa, W Mexico
63 F19 **La Cruz** Florida, S Uruguay
44 M9 **La Cruz de Río Grande** Región Autónoma Atlántico Sur, E Nicaragua
56 J4 **La Cruz de Taratara** Falcón, N Venezuela
13 Q10 **Lac-St-Charles** Québec, SE Canada
42 M6 **La Cuesta** Coahuila de Zaragoza, NE Mexico
59 A17 **La Cumbra, Volcán** ⛰ Galapagos Islands, Ecuador, E Pacific Ocean
158 J5 **Ladākh Range** ▲ NE India
28 I5 **Ladder Creek** ≈ Kansas, C USA
47 X10 **la Désirade** *atoll* E Guadeloupe
Lādhiqīyah, Muḥāfaẓat al *see* Al Lādhiqīyah
85 F25 **Ladismith** Western Cape, SW South Africa
158 G11 **Lādnūn** Rājasthān, NW India
Ladoga, Lake *see* Ladozhskoye Ozero
117 E19 **Ládon** ≈ S Greece
56 E9 **La Dorada** Caldas, C Colombia
128 H11 **Ladozhskoye Ozero** *Eng.* Lake Ladoga, *Fin.* Laatokka. ◎ NW Russian Federation
39 R12 **Ladron Peak** ▲ New Mexico, SW USA
128 J11 **Ladva-Vetka** Respublika Kareliya, NW Russian Federation
191 Q15 **Lady Barron** Tasmania, SE Australia
12 G9 **Lady Evelyn Lake** ◎ Ontario, S Canada
25 W11 **Lady Lake** Florida, SE USA
8 L17 **Ladysmith** Vancouver Island, British Columbia, SW Canada
85 J22 **Ladysmith** KwaZulu/Natal, E South Africa
32 J5 **Ladysmith** Wisconsin, N USA
151 P9 **Ladyzhenka** Akmola, C Kazakhstan
194 K13 **Lae** Morobe, W PNG
201 R6 **Lae Atoll** *atoll* Ralik Chain, W Marshall Islands
42 C3 **La Encantada, Cerro de** ▲ NW Mexico
96 E12 **Lærdalsøyri** Sogn og Fjordane, S Norway
57 N11 **La Esmeralda** Amazonas, S Venezuela
44 G7 **La Esperanza** Intibucá, SW Honduras
32 K8 **La Farge** Wisconsin, N USA
25 R5 **Lafayette** Alabama, S USA
39 T4 **Lafayette** Colorado, C USA
25 R2 **La Fayette** Georgia, SE USA
33 O13 **Lafayette** Indiana, N USA
24 I9 **Lafayette** Louisiana, S USA
22 K8 **Lafayette** Tennessee, S USA
21 N7 **Lafayette, Mount** ▲ New Hampshire, NE USA
La Fe *see* Santa Fé
105 P3 **la Fère** Aisne, N France
104 L6 **la Ferté-Bernard** Sarthe, NW France
104 K5 **la Ferté-Macé** Orne, N France
105 N7 **la Ferté-St-Aubin** Loiret, C France
105 P5 **la Ferté-sous-Jouarre** Seine-et-Marne, N France
79 V15 **Lafia** Plateau, C Nigeria
79 T15 **Lafiagi** Kwara, W Nigeria
9 T17 **Lafleche** Saskatchewan, S Canada
104 K7 **la Flèche** Sarthe, NW France
111 X7 **Lafnitz** *Hung.* Lapines. ≈ Austria/Hungary
197 I6 **La Foa** Province Sud, S New Caledonia
22 M8 **La Follette** Tennessee, S USA
13 N12 **Lafontaine** Québec, SE Canada
24 K10 **Lafourche, Bayou** ≈ Louisiana, S USA
64 K6 **La Fragua** Santiago del Estero, N Argentina
56 H7 **La Fría** Táchira, NW Venezuela
106 J7 **La Fuente de San Esteban** Castilla-León, N Spain
194 G11 **Lagaip** ≈ W PNG
63 B15 **La Gallareta** Santa Fe, C Argentina
131 Q14 **Lagan'** *prev.* Kaspiyskiy. Respublika Kalmykiya, SW Russian Federation
97 L20 **Lagan** Kronoberg, S Sweden
97 K21 **Lågan** ≈ S Sweden
94 L2 **Lagarfljót** *var.* Lögurinn. ◎ E Iceland
39 R7 **La Garita Mountains** ▲ Colorado, C USA
179 P9 **Lagawe** Luzon, N Philippines
80 F13 **Lagdo** Nord, N Cameroon
80 F13 **Lagdo, Lac de** ◎ N Cameroon
102 H13 **Lage** Nordrhein-Westfalen, W Germany
96 H12 **Lågen** ≈ S Norway
62 J13 **Lages** Santa Catarina, S Brazil
155 R4 **Laghmān** ◈ *province* E Afghanistan
76 J6 **Laghouat** N Algeria
107 Q10 **La Gineta** Castilla-La Mancha, C Spain
117 E21 **Lagkáda** *var.* Langada. Pelopónnisos, S Greece
116 G13 **Lagkadás** *var.* Langades, Langadhás. Kentrikí Makedonía, N Greece
117 E20 **Lagkádia** *var.* Langádhia, Langadia. Pelopónnisos, S Greece
56 F6 **La Gloria** Cesar, N Colombia
43 O7 **La Gloria** Nuevo León, NE Mexico
94 N3 **Lågneset** *headland* W Svalbard
106 G14 **Lagoa** Faro, S Portugal
La Goagira *see* La Guajira
63 I14 **Lagoa Vermelha** Rio Grande do Sul, S Brazil
143 V10 **Lagodekhi** SE Georgia
44 C7 **La Gomera** Escuintla, S Guatemala
Lagone *see* Logone
109 M19 **Lagonegro** Basilicata, S Italy
65 G16 **Lago Ranco** Los Lagos, S Chile
79 S16 **Lagos** Lagos, SW Nigeria
106 F14 **Lagos** *anc.* Lacobriga. Faro, S Portugal
79 S16 **Lagos** ◈ *state* SW Nigeria
42 M12 **Lagos de Moreno** Jalisco, SW Mexico
Lagosta *see* Lastovo
76 A12 **Lagouira** SW Western Sahara
94 O1 **Lågøya** *island* N Svalbard
34 L11 **La Grande** Oregon, NW USA
105 Q14 **la Grande-Combe** Gard, S France
10 K9 **La Grande Rivière** *var.* Fort George. ≈ Québec, SE Canada
25 R4 **La Grange** Georgia, SE USA
33 P11 **Lagrange** Indiana, N USA
22 L5 **La Grange** Kentucky, S USA
29 V2 **La Grange** Missouri, C USA
23 V10 **La Grange** North Carolina, SE USA
27 U11 **La Grange** Texas, SW USA
107 N7 **La Granja** Castilla-León, N Spain
57 Q9 **La Gran Sabana** *grassland* E Venezuela
56 H7 **La Grita** Táchira, NW Venezuela
La Grulla *see* Grulla
13 R11 **La Guadeloupe** Québec, SE Canada
66 F12 **La Guaira** Distrito Federal, N Venezuela
56 G4 **La Guajira** *off.* Departamento de La Guajira, *var.* Guajira, La Goagira. ◈ *province* NE Colombia
196 I4 **Lagua Lichan, Punta** *headland* Saipan, S Northern Mariana Islands
20 K14 **La Guardia** ✕ (New York) Long Island, New York, NE USA
La Guardia/Laguardia *see* A Guardia
107 P4 **Laguardia** País Vasco, N Spain
La Gudiña *see* A Gudiña
105 O9 **la Guerche-sur-l'Aubois** Cher, C France
105 O13 **Laguiole** Aveyron, S France
L'Agulhas *see* Agulhas
63 K14 **Laguna** Santa Catarina, S Brazil
39 Q11 **Laguna** New Mexico, SW USA
37 T16 **Laguna Beach** California, W USA
37 Y17 **Laguna Dam** *dam* Arizona/California, W USA
42 L7 **Laguna El Rey** Coahuila de Zaragoza, N Mexico
37 V17 **Laguna Mountains** ▲ California, W USA
63 B17 **Laguna Paiva** Santa Fe, C Argentina
64 H3 **Lagunas** Tarapacá, N Chile
58 E9 **Lagunas** Loreto, N Peru
59 M20 **Lagunillas** Santa Cruz, SE Bolivia
56 H6 **Lagunillas** Mérida, NW Venezuela
46 C4 **La Habana** *var.* Havana. ● (Cuba) Ciudad de La Habana, W Cuba
175 Oo3 **Lahad Datu** Sabah, East Malaysia
175 Oo3 **Lahad Datu, Teluk** *var.* Telukan Lahad Datu, Teluk Darvel, Teluk Datu; *prev.* Darvel Bay. *bay* Sabah, East Malaysia
40 F10 **Lahaina** Maui, Hawaii, USA, C Pacific Ocean
174 Hh12 **Lahat** Sumatera, W Indonesia
La Haye *see* 's-Gravenhage
Lahej *see* Laḥij
64 G9 **La Higuera** Coquimbo, N Chile
147 S13 **Lahī, Ḥisā' al** *spring/well* NE Yemen
147 O16 **Laḥij** *var.* Laḥj, *Eng.* Lahej. SW Yemen
148 M3 **Lāhījān** Gīlān, NW Iran
121 I19 **Lahishyn** *Pol.* Lohiszyn, *Rus.* Logishin. Brestskaya Voblasts', SW Belarus
Laḥj *see* Laḥij
103 F18 **Lahn** ≈ W Germany
Lähn *see* Wleń
97 J21 **Laholm** Halland, S Sweden
97 J21 **Laholmsbukten** *bay* S Sweden
37 R6 **Lahontan Reservoir** ⊡ Nevada, W USA
155 W8 **Lahore** Punjab, NE Pakistan
155 W8 **Lahore** ✕ Punjab, E Pakistan
57 Q6 **La Horqueta** Delta Amacuro, NE Venezuela
121 K15 **Lahoysk** *Rus.* Logoysk. Minskaya Voblasts', C Belarus
103 F22 **Lahr** Baden-Württemberg, S Germany
95 M19 **Lahti** *Swe.* Lahtis. Häme, S Finland
Lahtis *see* Lahti
42 M14 **La Huacana** Michoacán de Ocampo, SW Mexico
42 K14 **La Huerta** Jalisco, SW Mexico
80 H12 **Laï** *prev.* Behagle, De Behagle. Tandjilé, S Chad
194 G12 **Laiagam** Enga, W PNG
Laibach *see* Ljubljana
178 I5 **Lai Châu** Lai Châu, N Vietnam
40 D9 **Laie** *Haw.* Lā'ie. Oahu, Hawaii, USA, C Pacific Ocean
104 L5 **l'Aigle** Orne, N France
105 Q7 **Laignes** Côte d'Or, C France
95 K17 **Laihia** Vaasa, W Finland
Laila *see* Laylā
85 F25 **Laingsburg** Western Cape, SW South Africa
111 U2 **Lainsitz** *Cz.* Lužnice. ≈ Austria/Czech Republic
98 I7 **Lairg** N Scotland, UK
83 I17 **Laisamis** Eastern, N Kenya
Laisberg *see* Leisi
131 R4 **Laishevo** Respublika Tatarstan, W Russian Federation
Laisholm *see* Jõgeva
94 H13 **Laisvall** Norrbotten, N Sweden
95 K19 **Laitila** Turku-Pori, SW Finland
167 P5 **Laiwu** Shandong, E China
167 R4 **Laixi** *var.* Shuiji. Shandong, E China
167 R4 **Laiyang** Shandong, E China
167 O3 **Laiyuan** Hebei, E China
167 R4 **Laizhou** *var.* Ye Xian. Shandong, E China
167 Q4 **Laizhou Wan** *var.* Laichow Bay. *bay* E China
39 S8 **La Jara** Colorado, C USA
63 I15 **Lajeado** Rio Grande do Sul, S Brazil
114 L12 **Lajkovac** Serbia, C Yugoslavia
113 K23 **Lajosmizse** Bács-Kiskun, C Hungary
Lajta *see* Leitha
42 I6 **La Junta** Chihuahua, N Mexico
39 V7 **La Junta** Colorado, C USA
94 J13 **Lakaträsk** Norrbotten, N Sweden
Lak Dera *see* Dheere Laaq
Lakeamu *see* Lakekamu
31 P12 **Lake Andes** South Dakota, N USA
24 H9 **Lake Arthur** Louisiana, S USA
197 L15 **Lakeba** *prev.* Lakemba. *island* Lau Group, E Fiji
197 L14 **Lakeba Passage** *channel* E Fiji
31 S10 **Lake Benton** Minnesota, N USA
25 V9 **Lake Butler** Florida, SE USA
191 P8 **Lake Cargelligo** New South Wales, SE Australia
24 G9 **Lake Charles** Louisiana, S USA
29 X9 **Lake City** Arkansas, C USA
39 Q7 **Lake City** Colorado, C USA
25 V9 **Lake City** Florida, SE USA
31 U13 **Lake City** Iowa, C USA
33 P7 **Lake City** Michigan, N USA
31 W9 **Lake City** Minnesota, N USA
23 T13 **Lake City** South Carolina, SE USA
31 Q7 **Lake City** South Dakota, N USA
22 M8 **Lake City** Tennessee, S USA
194 F12 **Lake Copiago** *var.* Kopiago. Southern Highlands, W PNG
8 L17 **Lake Cowichan** Vancouver Island, British Columbia, SW Canada
31 U10 **Lake Crystal** Minnesota, N USA
27 T6 **Lake Dallas** Texas, SW USA
99 K15 **Lake District** *physical region* NW England, UK
20 D10 **Lake Erie Beach** New York, NE USA
31 T11 **Lakefield** Minnesota, N USA
27 V6 **Lake Fork Reservoir** ⊡ Texas, SW USA
32 M9 **Lake Geneva** Wisconsin, N USA
20 L9 **Lake George** New York, NE USA
16 O4 **Lake Harbour** Baffin Island, Northwest Territories, NE Canada
38 I12 **Lake Havasu City** Arizona, SW USA
27 W12 **Lake Jackson** Texas, SW USA
194 J14 **Lakekamu** *var.* Lakeamu. ≈ S PNG
188 K13 **Lake King** Western Australia
194 F12 **Lake Kutubu** ◎ W PNG
25 V12 **Lakeland** Florida, SE USA
25 U7 **Lakeland** Georgia, SE USA
189 W4 **Lakeland Downs** Queensland, NE Australia
9 P16 **Lake Louise** Alberta, SW Canada
Lakemba *see* Lakeba
31 V11 **Lake Mills** Iowa, C USA
41 Q10 **Lake Minchumina** Alaska, USA
Lakemti *see* Nek'emtē
194 E13 **Lake Murray** Western, SW PNG
82 F5 **Nasser, Lake** *var.* Buhayrat Nasir, Buḥayrat Nāṣir, Buḥeiret Nâṣir. ◎ Egypt/Sudan
33 R9 **Lake Orion** Michigan, N USA
202 B16 **Lakepa** NE Niue
31 T11 **Lake Park** Iowa, C USA
20 K7 **Lake Placid** New York, NE USA
20 K9 **Lake Pleasant** New York, NE USA
36 M6 **Lakeport** California, W USA
31 Q10 **Lake Preston** South Dakota, N USA
24 J5 **Lake Providence** Louisiana, S USA
193 E20 **Lake Pukaki** Canterbury, South Island, NZ
191 Q12 **Lakes Entrance** Victoria, SE Australia
39 N12 **Lakeside** Arizona, SW USA
37 V17 **Lakeside** California, W USA
25 S9 **Lakeside** Florida, SE USA
30 K13 **Lakeside** Nebraska, C USA
34 E13 **Lakeside** Oregon, NW USA
23 W6 **Lakeside** Virginia, NE USA
Lakes State *see* El Buhayrat
Lake State *see* Michigan
193 F20 **Lake Tekapo** Canterbury, South Island, NZ
23 O10 **Lake Toxaway** North Carolina, SE USA
31 T13 **Lake View** Iowa, C USA
34 I16 **Lakeview** Oregon, NW USA
27 O3 **Lakeview** Texas, SW USA
29 W14 **Lake Village** Arkansas, C USA
25 W12 **Lake Wales** Florida, SE USA
39 T4 **Lakewood** Colorado, C USA
20 K15 **Lakewood** New Jersey, NE USA
20 C11 **Lakewood** New York, NE USA
33 T11 **Lakewood** Ohio, N USA
25 Y13 **Lakewood Park** Florida, SE USA
25 Z14 **Lake Worth** Florida, SE USA
158 H4 **Lake Wular** ◎ NE India
128 H11 **Lakhdenpokh'ya** Respublika Kareliya, NW Russian Federation
158 L11 **Lakhimpur** Uttar Pradesh, N India
160 J11 **Lakhnādon** Madhya Pradesh, C India
Lakhnau *see* Lucknow
160 A9 **Lakhpat** Gujarāt, W India
121 K19 **Lakhva** *Rus.* Lakhva. Brestskaya Voblasts', SW Belarus
28 I6 **Lakin** Kansas, C USA
155 S7 **Lakki Marwat** North-West Frontier Province, NW Pakistan
117 F21 **Lakonía** *historical region* S Greece
117 F22 **Lakonikós Kólpos** *gulf* S Greece
78 M17 **Lakota** S Ivory Coast
31 U11 **Lakota** Iowa, C USA
31 P3 **Lakota** North Dakota, N USA
Lak Sao *see* Ban Lakxao
94 L8 **Laksefjorden** *fjord* N Norway
94 K8 **Lakselv** Finnmark, N Norway
161 B21 **Lakshadweep** *prev.* the Laccadive, Minicoy and Amindivi Islands. ◈ *union territory* India, N Indian Ocean
161 C22 **Lakshadweep** *Eng.* Laccadive Islands. *island group* India, N Indian Ocean
159 S17 **Lakshmikāntapur** West Bengal, NE India
114 G11 **Laktaši** N Bosnia and Herzegovina
155 V7 **Lāla Mūsa** Punjab, NE Pakistan
la Laon *see* Laon
116 M11 **Lalapaşa** Edirne, NW Turkey
85 P14 **Lalaua** Nampula, N Mozambique
107 S10 **L'Alcúdia** *var.* L'Alcudia. País Valenciano, E Spain
81 F20 **La Lékoumou** ◈ *province* SW Congo
44 E8 **La Libertad** La Libertad, SW El Salvador
44 E3 **La Libertad** Petén, N Guatemala
44 H6 **La Libertad** Comayagua, SW Honduras
42 E4 **La Libertad** *var.* Puerto Libertad. Sonora, NW Mexico
44 K10 **La Libertad** Chontales, S Nicaragua
44 A9 **La Libertad** ◈ *department* SW El Salvador
58 B11 **La Libertad** *off.* Departamento de La Libertad. ◈ *department* W Peru
64 G11 **La Ligua** Valparaíso, C Chile
145 U5 **La'lī Khān** E Iraq
81 H16 **La Likouala** ◈ *province* NE Congo
106 H3 **Lalín** Galicia, NW Spain
104 L13 **Lalinde** Dordogne, SW France
106 K16 **La Línea** *var.* La Línea de la Concepción. Andalucía, S Spain
La Línea de la Concepción *see* La Línea
158 J14 **Lalitpur** Uttar Pradesh, N India
159 P11 **Lalitpur** Central, C Nepal
158 K10 **Lālkua** Uttar Pradesh, N India
9 R12 **La Loche** Saskatchewan, C Canada
104 M6 **la Loupe** Eure-et-Loir, C France
101 G20 **La Louvière** Hainaut, S Belgium
L'Altissima *see* Hochwilde
106 L14 **La Luisiana** Andalucía, S Spain
39 S14 **La Luz** New Mexico, SW USA
109 D16 **la Maddalena** Sardegna, Italy, C Mediterranean Sea
64 J7 **La Madrid** Tucumán, N Argentina
Lama-Kara *see* Kara
175 R16 **Lamakera, Selat** *strait* Nusa Tenggara, S Indonesia
13 S8 **La Malbaie** Québec, SE Canada
178 Jj10 **Lamam** Xékong, S Laos
107 P10 **La Mancha** *physical region* C Spain
la Manche *see* English Channel
197 C13 **Lamap** Malekula, C Vanuatu
39 W6 **Lamar** Colorado, C USA
29 S7 **Lamar** Missouri, C USA
23 S12 **Lamar** South Carolina, SE USA
109 C19 **La Marmora, Punta** ▲ Sardegna, Italy, C Mediterranean Sea
15 H7 **La Martre, Lac** ◎ Northwest Territories, NW Canada
58 D10 **Lamas** San Martín, N Peru
44 I5 **La Masica** Atlántida, NW Honduras
105 R12 **Lamastre** Ardèche, E France
La Matepec *see* Santa Ana, Volcán de
46 I7 **La Maya** Santiago de Cuba, E Cuba
111 S5 **Lambach** Oberösterreich, N Austria
173 Ff8 **Lambak** Pulau Pini, W Indonesia
104 H5 **Lamballe** Côtes d'Armor, NW France
81 D18 **Lambaréné** Moyen-Ogooué, W Gabon
Lambasa *see* Labasa
175 Q12 **Lambasina Besar, Pulau** *island* C Indonesia
58 B11 **Lambayeque** Lambayeque, W Peru
58 A10 **Lambayeque** *off.* Departamento de Lambayeque. ◈ *department* NW Peru
99 G17 **Lambay Island** *Ir.* Reachrainn. *island* E Ireland
195 O10 **Lambert, Cape** *headland* New Britain, E PNG
205 W6 **Lambert Glacier** *glacier* Antarctica
31 T10 **Lamberton** Minnesota, N USA
29 X4 **Lambert-Saint Louis** ✕ Missouri, C USA
33 R11 **Lambertville** Michigan, N USA
20 J15 **Lambertville** New Jersey, NE USA
175 Pp9 **Lambogo** Sulawesi, N Indonesia
108 D8 **Lambro** ≈ N Italy
15 H2 **Lambton, Cape** *headland* Banks Island, Northwest Territories, NW Canada
35 W11 **Lame Deer** Montana, NW USA
106 H6 **Lamego** Viseu, N Portugal
197 C13 **Lamen Bay** Épi, C Vanuatu
47 X6 **Lamentin** Basse Terre, N Guadeloupe
Lamentin *see* le Lamentin
190 K10 **Lameroo** South Australia
56 F10 **La Mesa** Cundinamarca, C Colombia
37 U17 **La Mesa** California, W USA
39 R16 **La Mesa** New Mexico, SW USA
27 N6 **Lamesa** Texas, SW USA
109 N21 **Lamezia** Calabria, SE Italy
197 I15 **Lami** Viti Levu, C Fiji
117 F17 **Lamía** Stereá Ellás, C Greece
179 Q17 **Lamitan** Basilan Island, SW Philippines
197 J14 **Lamiti** Gau, C Fiji
176 Uu8 **Lamlam** Irian Jaya, E Indonesia
196 B16 **Lamlam, Mount** ▲ SW Guam
111 Q6 **Lammer** ≈ E Austria
193 E23 **Lammerlaw Range** ▲ South Island, NZ
97 L20 **Lammhult** Kronoberg, S Sweden
95 L18 **Lammi** Häme, SW Finland
201 U11 **Lamoil** *island* Chuuk, C Micronesia
37 W3 **Lamoille** Nevada, W USA
20 M7 **Lamoille River** ≈ Vermont, NE USA
32 J13 **La Moine River** ≈ Illinois, N USA
179 Pp10 **Lamon Bay** *bay* Luzon, N Philippines
31 V16 **Lamoni** Iowa, C USA
37 R13 **Lamont** California, W USA
29 N8 **Lamont** Oklahoma, C USA
56 E13 **La Montañita** *var.* Montañita. Caquetá, S Colombia
45 N8 **La Mosquitia** *var.* Miskito Coast, *Eng.* Mosquito Coast. *coastal region* E Nicaragua
104 I9 **la Mothe-Achard** Vendée, NW France
196 L15 **Lamotrek Atoll** *atoll* Caroline Islands, C Micronesia
31 P6 **La Moure** North Dakota, N USA
178 H8 **Lampang** *var.* Muang Lampang. Lampang, NW Thailand
178 I9 **Lam Pao Reservoir** ⊡ E Thailand
27 S9 **Lampasas** Texas, SW USA
27 S9 **Lampasas River** ≈ Texas, SW USA
43 N7 **Lampazos** *var.* Lampazos de Naranjo. Nuevo León, NE Mexico
Lampazos de Naranjo *see* Lampazos
117 E19 **Lámpeia** Dytikí Ellás, S Greece
103 G19 **Lampertheim** Hessen, W Germany
99 I20 **Lampeter** SW Wales, UK
178 H7 **Lamphun** *var.* Lampun, Muang Lamphun. Lamphun, NW Thailand
9 X10 **Lamprey** Manitoba, C Canada
Lampun *see* Lamphun
174 I13 **Lampung** *off.* Propinsi Lampung. ◈ *province* SW Indonesia
174 Ii13 **Lampung, Teluk** *bay* Sumatera, SW Indonesia
130 K6 **Lamskoye** Lipetskaya Oblast', W Russian Federation
83 K20 **Lamu** Coast, SE Kenya
45 N14 **La Muerte, Cerro** ▲ C Costa Rica
105 S13 **la Mure** Isère, E France
39 S10 **Lamy** New Mexico, SW USA
121 J18 **Lan'** *Rus.* Lan'. ≈ C Belarus
40 E10 **Lanai** *Haw.* Lāna'i. *island* Hawaii, USA, C Pacific Ocean
40 E10 **Lanai City** Lanai, Hawaii, USA, C Pacific Ocean
101 L18 **Lanaken** Limburg, NE Belgium
179 R15 **Lanao, Lake** *var.* Lake Sultan Alonto. ◎ Mindanao, S Philippines
98 J12 **Lanark** S Scotland, UK
98 I13 **Lanark** *cultural region* C Scotland, UK
106 L9 **La Nava de Ricomalillo** Castilla-La Mancha, C Spain
178 Gg13 **Lanbi Kyun** *prev.* Sullivan Island. *island* Mergui Archipelago, S Myanmar
Lancang Jiang *see* Mekong
99 K17 **Lancashire** *cultural region* NW England, UK
13 N13 **Lancaster** Ontario, SE Canada
99 K16 **Lancaster** NW England, UK
37 T14 **Lancaster** California, W USA
22 M6 **Lancaster** Kentucky, S USA
29 U1 **Lancaster** Missouri, C USA
21 O7 **Lancaster** New Hampshire, NE USA
20 D10 **Lancaster** New York, NE USA
33 T14 **Lancaster** Ohio, N USA
20 H16 **Lancaster** Pennsylvania, NE USA
23 R11 **Lancaster** South Carolina, SE USA
27 U7 **Lancaster** Texas, SW USA
23 X5 **Lancaster** Virginia, NE USA
32 J9 **Lancaster** Wisconsin, N USA
207 N10 **Lancaster Sound** *sound* Northwest Territories, N Canada
Lan-chou/Lan-chow/Lanchow *see* Lanzhou
109 K14 **Lanciano** Abruzzi, C Italy
113 O16 **Łańcut** Rzeszów, SE Poland
174 Kk8 **Landak, Sungai** ≈ Borneo, N Indonesia
Landao *see* Lantau Island
Landau *see* Landau an der Isar, Bayern, Germany
Landau *see* Landau in der Pfalz, Rheinland-Pfalz, Germany
103 N22 **Landau an der Isar** *var.* Landau. Bayern, SE Germany
103 F20 **Landau in der Pfalz** *var.* Landau. Rheinland-Pfalz, SW Germany
Land Burgenland *see* Burgenland
110 K8 **Landeck** Tirol, W Austria
101 J19 **Landen** Vlaams Brabant, C Belgium
35 U15 **Lander** Wyoming, C USA
104 F5 **Landerneau** Finistère, NW France
97 K20 **Landeryd** Halland, S Sweden
104 J15 **Landes** ◈ *department* SW France
Landeshut/Landeshut in Schlesien *see* Kamienna Góra
107 R9 **Landete** Castilla-La Mancha, C Spain
101 M18 **Landgraaf** Limburg, SE Netherlands
104 F5 **Landivisiau** Finistère, NW France
Land of Enchantment *see* New Mexico
Land of Opportunity *see* Arkansas
Land of Steady Habits *see* Connecticut
Land of the Midnight Sun *see* Alaska
110 I8 **Landquart** Graubünden, SE Switzerland
110 J9 **Landquart** ≈ Austria/Switzerland
23 P10 **Landrum** South Carolina, SE USA
Landsberg *see* Górowo Iławeckie, Olsztyn, Poland
Landsberg *see* Gorzów Wielkopolski, Gorzów, Poland
103 K23 **Landsberg am Lech** Bayern, S Germany
Landsberg an der Warthe *see* Gorzów Wielkopolski
99 G25 **Land's End** *headland* SW England, UK
103 M22 **Landshut** Bayern, SE Germany
Landskron *see* Lanškroun

◆ Country ● Country Capital ◇ Dependent Territory ○ Dependent Territory Capital ◈ Administrative Region ✕ International Airport ▲ Mountain ▲ Mountain Range ⛰ Volcano ≈ River ◎ Lake ⊡ Reservoir

97 J22 **Landskrona** Malmöhus, S Sweden
100 I10 **Landsmeer** Noord-Holland, C Netherlands
97 J19 **Landvetter** ✈ (Göteborg) Göteborg och Bohus, S Sweden
Landwarów see Lentvaris
25 R5 **Lanett** Alabama, S USA
110 C8 **La Neuveville** var. Neuveville, Ger. Neuenstadt. Neuchâtel, W Switzerland
97 G21 **Langå** var. Langaa. Århus, C Denmark
Langaa see Langå
164 G14 **La'nga Co** ◎ W China
Langada see Lagkáda
Langades/Langadhás see Lagkadás
Langádhia/Langadia see Lagkádia
153 T14 **Langar** Rus. Lyangar. SE Tajikistan
152 M10 **Langar** Rus. Lyangar. Nawoiy Wiloyati, C Uzbekistan
148 M3 **Langarūd** Gīlān, NW Iran
9 V16 **Langbank** Saskatchewan, S Canada
31 P2 **Langdon** North Dakota, N USA
105 P12 **Langeac** Haute-Loire, C France
104 L8 **Langeais** Indre-et-Loire, C France
82 I8 **Langeb, Wadi** ≈ NE Sudan
Långed see Dals Långed
97 G25 **Langeland** island S Denmark
101 B18 **Langemark** West-Vlaanderen, W Belgium
103 G18 **Langen** Hessen, W Germany
103 J22 **Langenau** Baden-Württemberg, S Germany
9 V16 **Langenburg** Saskatchewan, S Canada
103 E16 **Langenfeld** Nordrhein-Westfalen, W Germany
110 L8 **Längenfeld** Tirol, W Austria
102 I12 **Langenhagen** Niedersachsen, N Germany
102 I12 **Langenhagen** ✈ (Hannover) Niedersachsen, NW Germany
111 W3 **Langenlois** Niederösterreich, NE Austria
110 E7 **Langenthal** Bern, NW Switzerland
111 W6 **Langenwang** Steiermark, E Austria
111 X3 **Langenzersdorf** Niederösterreich, E Austria
102 F9 **Langeoog** island NW Germany
126 Gg11 **Langepas** Khanty-Mansiyskiy Avtonomnyy Okrug, C Russian Federation
97 H23 **Langeskov** Fyn, C Denmark
97 G16 **Langesund** Telemark, S Norway
97 G17 **Langesundsfjorden** fjord S Norway
96 D10 **Langevågen** Møre og Romsdal, S Norway
167 P3 **Langfang** Hebei, E China
96 E9 **Langfjorden** fjord S Norway
31 Q8 **Langford** South Dakota, N USA
173 G6 **Langgapayung** Sumatera, W Indonesia
108 E9 **Langhirano** Emilia-Romagna, C Italy
99 K14 **Langholm** S Scotland, UK
94 I3 **Langjökull** glacier C Iceland
173 Ff2 **Langkawi, Pulau** island Peninsular Malaysia
175 R13 **Langkesi, Kepulauan** island group C Indonesia
178 Gg15 **Langkha Tuk, Khao** ▲ SW Thailand
12 L8 **Langlade** Québec, SE Canada
8 M17 **Langley** British Columbia, SW Canada
178 Jj7 **Lang Mô** Thanh Hoa, N Vietnam
Langnau see Langnau im Emmental
110 E8 **Langnau im Emmental** var. Langnau. Bern, W Switzerland
105 Q13 **Langogne** Lozère, S France
164 K16 **Langoi Kangri** ▲ W China
104 K13 **Langon** Gironde, SW France
La Ngounié see Ngounié
94 G10 **Langøya** island C Norway
164 G14 **Langqên Zangbo** ≈ China/India
105 S7 **Langres** Haute-Marne, N France
105 R8 **Langres, Plateau de** plateau C France
173 F4 **Langsa** Sumatera, W Indonesia
95 H16 **Långsele** Västernorrland, C Sweden
168 L12 **Lang Shan** ▲ N China
97 M14 **Långshyttan** Kopparberg, C Sweden
178 K5 **Lang Son** var. Langson. Lang Sơn, N Vietnam
178 Gg14 **Lang Suan** Chumphon, SW Thailand
95 J14 **Långträsk** Norrbotten, N Sweden
27 N11 **Langtry** Texas, SW USA
105 P16 **Languedoc** cultural region S France
105 P15 **Languedoc-Roussillon** ◆ region S France
29 X10 **L'Anguille River** ≈ Arkansas, C USA
95 I16 **Långviksmon** Västernorrland, N Sweden
103 K22 **Langweid** Bayern, S Germany
166 J8 **Langzhong** Sichuan, C China
Lan Hsü see Lan Yü
9 U15 **Lanigan** Saskatchewan, S Canada
118 K5 **Lanivtsi** Ternopil's'ka Oblast', W Ukraine
143 Y13 **Länkäran** Rus. Lenkoran'. S Azerbaijan
104 L16 **Lannemezan** Hautes-Pyrénées, S France
104 G5 **Lannion** Côtes d'Armor, NW France
12 M11 **L'Annonciation** Québec, SE Canada
107 V5 **L'Anoia** ≈ NE Spain
20 I15 **Lansdale** Pennsylvania, NE USA
12 L14 **Lansdowne** Ontario, SE Canada
158 K9 **Lansdowne** Uttar Pradesh, N India
32 M3 **L'Anse** Michigan, N USA
13 S7 **L'Anse-St-Jean** Québec, SE Canada
31 Y11 **Lansing** Iowa, C USA
29 R4 **Lansing** Kansas, C USA
33 Q9 **Lansing** state capital Michigan, N USA
94 J12 **Lansjärv** Norrbotten, N Sweden
113 G17 **Lanškroun** Ger. Landskron. Východní Čechy, E Czech Republic
178 Gg16 **Lanta, Ko** island S Thailand
167 O15 **Lantau Island** Cant. Tai Yue Shan, Chin. Landao. island Hong Kong, S China
Lan-ts'ang Chiang see Mekong
175 Q7 **Lanu** Sulawesi, N Indonesia
109 D19 **Lanusei** Sardegna, Italy, C Mediterranean Sea
104 H7 **Lanvaux, Landes de** physical region NW France
169 W8 **Lanxi** Heilongjiang, NE China
167 R10 **Lanxi** Zhejiang, SE China
La Nyanga see Nyanga
167 T15 **Lan Yü** var. Huoshao Tao, var. Hung't'ou, Lan Hsü, Lanyü, Eng. Orchid Island; prev. Kotosho, Koto Sho. island SE Taiwan
66 P11 **Lanzarote** island Islas Canarias, Spain, NE Atlantic Ocean
165 V10 **Lanzhou** var. Lan-chou, Lanchow, Lan-chow; prev. Kaolan. Gansu, C China
108 B8 **Lanzo Torinese** Piemonte, NE Italy
179 P8 **Laoag** Luzon, N Philippines
179 R12 **Laoang** Samar, C Philippines
178 J5 **Lao Cai** Lao Cai, N Vietnam
Laodicea/Laodicea ad Mare see Al Lādhiqīyah
Laoet see Laut, Pulau
169 T11 **Laoha He** ≈ NE China
166 M8 **Laohekou** prev. Guanghua. Hubei, C China
Laoi, An see Lee
99 E19 **Laois** prev. Leix, Queen's County. cultural region C Ireland
Laojunmiao see Yumen
169 W12 **Lao Ling** ▲ N China
66 O11 **La Oliva** var. Oliva. Fuerteventura, Islas Canarias, Spain, NE Atlantic Ocean
Lao, Loch see Belfast Lough
Lao Mangnai see Mangnai
105 P3 **Laon** var. la Laon; anc. Laudunum. Aisne, N France
Lao People's Democratic Republic see Laos
56 M3 **La Orchila, Isla** island N Venezuela
66 O11 **La Orotava** Tenerife, Islas Canarias, Spain, NE Atlantic Ocean
59 E14 **La Oroya** Junín, C Peru
178 I7 **Laos** off. Lao People's Democratic Republic. ◆ republic SE Asia
167 R5 **Laoshan Wan** bay E China
169 Y10 **Laoye Ling** ▲ NE China
62 J12 **Lapa** Paraná, S Brazil
105 P10 **Lapalisse** Allier, C France
56 F9 **La Palma** Cundinamarca, C Colombia
44 F7 **La Palma** Chalatenango, N El Salvador
45 W16 **La Palma** Darién, SE Panama
66 N11 **La Palma** island Islas Canarias, Spain, NE Atlantic Ocean
106 J14 **La Palma del Condado** Andalucía, S Spain
63 F18 **La Paloma** Durazno, C Uruguay
63 G20 **La Paloma** Rocha, E Uruguay
63 A21 **La Pampa** off. Provincia de La Pampa. ◆ province C Argentina
57 P8 **La Paragua** Bolívar, E Venezuela
121 O16 **Lapatsichy** Rus. Lopatichi. Mahilyowskaya Voblasts', E Belarus
63 C16 **La Paz** Entre Ríos, E Argentina
64 I11 **La Paz** Mendoza, C Argentina
59 J18 **La Paz** var. La Paz de Ayacucho. ● (Bolivia-legislative and administrative capital) La Paz, W Bolivia
44 H6 **La Paz** La Paz, SW Honduras
42 F9 **La Paz** Baja California Sur, NW Mexico
63 F20 **La Paz** Canelones, S Uruguay
59 J16 **La Paz** ◆ department W Bolivia
44 B9 **La Paz** ◆ department S El Salvador
44 G7 **La Paz** ◆ department SW Honduras
La Paz see El Alto, Bolivia
La Paz see Robles, Colombia
La Paz see La Paz Centro, Nicaragua
42 F9 **La Paz, Bahía de** bay W Mexico
44 I10 **La Paz Centro** var. La Paz. León, W Nicaragua
La Paz de Ayacucho see La Paz
56 J15 **La Pedrera** Amazonas, SE Colombia
33 S9 **Lapeer** Michigan, N USA
42 K6 **La Perla** Chihuahua, N Mexico
172 Pp1 **La Perouse Strait** Jap. Sōya-kaikyō, Rus. Proliv Laperuza. strait Japan/Russian Federation
65 I14 **La Perra, Salitral de** salt lake C Argentina
Laperuza, Proliv see La Perouse Strait
43 Q10 **La Pesca** Tamaulipas, C Mexico
42 M13 **La Piedad Cavadas** Michoacán de Ocampo, C Mexico
Lapines see Lafnitz
95 M16 **Lapinlahti** Kuopio, C Finland
Lápithos see Lapta
24 K9 **Laplace** Louisiana, S USA
47 X12 **La Plaine** SE Dominica
181 P16 **la Plaine-des-Palmistes** C Réunion
94 K11 **Lapland** Fin. Lappi, Swe. Lappland. cultural region N Europe
30 M8 **La Plant** South Dakota, N USA
63 D20 **La Plata** Buenos Aires, E Argentina
56 D12 **La Plata** Huila, SW Colombia
23 W4 **La Plata** Maryland, NE USA
La Plata see Sucre
47 U6 **la Plata, Río de** ≈ C Puerto Rico
107 W4 **La Pobla de Lillet** Cataluña, NE Spain
107 U4 **La Pobla de Segur** Cataluña, NE Spain
13 S9 **La Pocatière** Québec, SE Canada
106 L3 **La Pola de Gordón** Castilla-León, N Spain
33 O11 **La Porte** Indiana, N USA
20 H13 **Laporte** Pennsylvania, NE USA
31 X13 **La Porte City** Iowa, C USA
64 J8 **La Posta** Catamarca, C Argentina
42 E8 **La Poza Grande** Baja California Sur, W Mexico
95 K16 **Lappajärvi** Vaasa, W Finland
95 L16 **Lappajärvi** ◎ W Finland
95 N18 **Lappeenranta** Swe. Villmanstrand. Kymi, SE Finland
95 J17 **Lappfjärd** Fin. Lapväärtti. Vaasa, W Finland
94 L12 **Lappi** Swe. Lappland. ◆ province N Finland
Lappi see Lapland
Lappland see Lappi
Lappland see Lapland, N Europe
Lappo see Lapua
63 C23 **Laprida** Buenos Aires, E Argentina
27 P13 **La Pryor** Texas, SW USA
142 B11 **Lâpseki** Çanakkale, NW Turkey
124 Nn2 **Lapta** Gk. Lápithos. NW Cyprus
Laptev Sea see Laptevykh, More
126 Kk5 **Laptevykh, More** Eng. Laptev Sea. sea Arctic Ocean
95 K16 **Lapua** Swe. Lappo. Vaasa, W Finland
La Puebla see Sa Pobla
107 P3 **La Puebla de Arganzón** País Vasco, N Spain
106 L14 **La Puebla de Cazalla** Andalucía, S Spain
106 M9 **La Puebla de Montalbán** Castilla-La Mancha, C Spain
56 I6 **La Puerta** Trujillo, NW Venezuela
179 Qq13 **Lapu-Lapu** C Philippines
Lapurdum see Bayonne
42 E7 **La Purísima** Baja California Sur, W Mexico
Lapväärtti see Lappfjärd
112 O10 **Łapy** Białystok, E Poland
82 D6 **Laqiya Arba'in** Northern, NW Sudan
64 J4 **La Quiaca** Jujuy, N Argentina
109 J14 **L'Aquila** var. Aquila, Aquila degli Abruzzi. Abruzzi, C Italy
149 Q13 **Lār** Fārs, S Iran
56 J5 **Lara** off. Estado Lara. ◆ state NW Venezuela
106 G2 **Laracha** Galicia, NW Spain
76 G5 **Larache** var. al Araïch, El Araïch, El Araîche, anc. Lixus. NW Morocco
105 T14 **Laragne-Montéglin** Hautes-Alpes, SE France
106 M13 **La Rambla** Andalucía, S Spain
35 Y17 **Laramie** Wyoming, C USA
35 X15 **Laramie Mountains** ▲ Wyoming, C USA
35 Y16 **Laramie River** ≈ Wyoming, C USA
62 H12 **Laranjeiras do Sul** Paraná, S Brazil
Larantoeka see Larantuka
175 Qq16 **Larantuka** prev. Larantoeka. Flores, C Indonesia
176 V15 **Larat** Pulau Larat, E Indonesia
176 V15 **Larat, Pulau** island Kepulauan Tanimbar, E Indonesia
97 P19 **Lärbro** Gotland, SE Sweden
108 A9 **Larche, Col de** pass France/Italy
12 H8 **Larder Lake** Ontario, S Canada
107 O2 **Laredo** Cantabria, N Spain
27 Q15 **Laredo** Texas, SW USA
42 H9 **La Reforma** Sinaloa, W Mexico
100 N11 **Laren** Gelderland, E Netherlands
100 J11 **Laren** Noord-Holland, C Netherlands
104 K13 **la Réole** Gironde, SW France
La Réunion see Réunion
Largeau see Faya
105 U13 **l'Argentière-la-Bessée** Hautes-Alpes, SE France
155 O4 **Lar Gerd** var. Largird. Balkh, N Afghanistan
Largird see Lar Gerd
25 V12 **Largo** Florida, SE USA
39 Q9 **Largo, Canon** valley New Mexico, SW USA
46 D6 **Largo, Cayo** island W Cuba
25 Z17 **Largo, Key** island Florida Keys, Florida, SE USA
98 H12 **Largs** W Scotland, UK
104 I16 **la Rhune** var. Larrún. ▲ France/Spain see also Larrún
la Riege see Ariège
31 Q4 **Larimore** North Dakota, N USA
109 L15 **Larino** Molise, C Italy
Lario see Como, Lago di
64 J9 **La Rioja** La Rioja, NW Argentina
64 I9 **La Rioja** off. Provincia de La Rioja. ◆ province NW Argentina
107 O4 **La Rioja** ◆ autonomous community N Spain
117 F16 **Lárisa** var. Larissa. Thessalía, C Greece
Larissa see Lárisa
155 Q13 **Lārkāna** var. Larkhana. Sind, SE Pakistan
Larkhana see Lārkāna
Larnaca see Lárnaka
124 Nn3 **Lárnaka** var. Larnaca, Larnax. SE Cyprus
124 Nn3 **Lárnaka** ✈ SE Cyprus
Larnax see Lárnaka
99 G14 **Larne** Ir. Latharna. E Northern Ireland, UK
28 L5 **Larned** Kansas, C USA
106 L3 **La Robla** Castilla-León, N Spain
106 J10 **La Roca de la Sierra** Extremadura, W Spain
101 K22 **La Roche-en-Ardenne** Luxembourg, SE Belgium
104 L11 **la Rochefoucauld** Charente, W France
104 J10 **la Rochelle** anc. Rupella. Charente-Maritime, W France
104 I9 **la Roche-sur-Yon** prev. Bourbon Vendée, Napoléon-Vendée. Vendée, NW France
107 Q10 **La Roda** Castilla-La Mancha, C Spain
106 L14 **La Roda de Andalucía** Andalucía, S Spain
47 P9 **La Romana** E Dominican Republic
9 T13 **La Ronge** Saskatchewan, C Canada
9 U13 **La Ronge, Lac** ◎ Saskatchewan, C Canada
24 K10 **Larose** Louisiana, S USA
44 M7 **La Rosita** Región Autónoma Atlántico Norte, NE Nicaragua
189 Q3 **Larrimah** Northern Territory, N Australia
64 N11 **Larroque** Entre Ríos, E Argentina
107 Q2 **Larrún** Fr. la Rhune. ▲ France/Spain see also la Rhune
205 X6 **Lars Christensen Coast** physical region Antarctica
41 Q14 **Larsen Bay** Kodiak Island, Alaska, USA
204 I5 **Larsen Ice Shelf** ice shelf Antarctica
15 K3 **Larsen Sound** sound Northwest Territories, N Canada
La Rúa see A Rúa
104 K16 **Laruns** Pyrénées-Atlantiques, SW France
97 G16 **Larvik** Vestfold, S Norway
126 H11 **Lar'yak** Khanty-Mansiyskiy Avtonomnyy Okrug, C Russian Federation
La-sa see Lhasa
175 Tt11 **Lasahata** Pulau Seram, E Indonesia
Lasahau see Lasihao
39 O6 **La Sal** Utah, W USA
12 C17 **La Salle** Ontario, S Canada
32 L11 **La Salle** Illinois, N USA
47 O9 **Las Americas** ✈ (Santo Domingo) S Dominican Republic
81 G17 **La Sangha** ◆ province N Congo
39 V6 **Las Animas** Colorado, C USA
110 D10 **La Sarine** var. Sarine. ≈ SW Switzerland
110 B9 **La Sarraz** Vaud, W Switzerland
10 H12 **La Sarre** Québec, SE Canada
56 L3 **Las Aves, Islas** var. Islas de Aves. island group N Venezuela
57 N7 **Las Bonitas** Bolívar, C Venezuela
106 K15 **Las Cabezas de San Juan** Andalucía, S Spain
63 G19 **Lascano** Rocha, E Uruguay
64 I5 **Lascar, Volcán** ▲ N Chile
43 T15 **Las Choapas** var. Choapas. Veracruz-Llave, SE Mexico
39 R15 **Las Cruces** New Mexico, SW USA
Lasdehnen see Krasnoznamensk
107 V4 **La See d'Urgel** var. La Seu d'Urgell, Seo de Urgel. Cataluña, NE Spain
La Selle see Selle, Pic de la
64 G9 **La Serena** Coquimbo, C Chile
106 K11 **La Serena** physical region W Spain
La Seu d'Urgell see La See d'Urgel
105 T16 **la Seyne-sur-Mer** Var, SE France
63 D21 **Las Flores** Buenos Aires, E Argentina
64 H9 **Las Flores** San Juan, W Argentina
9 S14 **Lashburn** Saskatchewan, S Canada
64 I11 **Las Heras** Mendoza, W Argentina
178 Gg4 **Lashio** Shan State, E Myanmar
154 M8 **Lashkar Gāh** var. Lash-Kar-Gar'. Helmand, S Afghanistan
Lash-Kar-Gar' see Lashkar Gāh
175 Qq13 **Lasihao** var. Lasahau. Pulau Muna, C Indonesia
109 N21 **La Sila** ▲ SW Italy
64 H6 **La Silueta, Cerro** ▲ S Chile
44 L9 **La Sirena** Región Autónoma Atlántico Sur, E Nicaragua
112 J13 **Łask** Sieradz, C Poland
111 V11 **Laško** Ger. Tüffer. C Slovenia
65 H14 **Las Lajas** Neuquén, W Argentina
65 H15 **Las Lajas, Cerro** ▲ W Argentina
64 M6 **Las Lomitas** Formosa, N Argentina
43 V16 **Las Margaritas** Chiapas, SE Mexico
Las Marismas see Guadalquivir, Marismas del
56 M6 **Las Mercedes** Guárico, N Venezuela
44 F6 **Las Minas, Cerro** ▲ W Honduras
107 O11 **La Solana** Castilla-La Mancha, C Spain
47 Q14 **La Soufrière** ▲ Saint Vincent, Saint Vincent and the Grenadines
104 M10 **la Souterraine** Creuse, C France
64 N7 **Las Palmas** Chaco, N Argentina
45 Q16 **Las Palmas** Veraguas, W Panama
66 P12 **Las Palmas** var. Las Palmas de Gran Canaria. Gran Canaria, Islas Canarias, Spain, NE Atlantic Ocean
66 P12 **Las Palmas** ◆ province Islas Canarias, Spain, NE Atlantic Ocean
66 Q12 **Las Palmas** ✈ Gran Canaria, Islas Canarias, Spain, NE Atlantic Ocean
Las Palmas de Gran Canaria see Las Palmas
42 D6 **Las Palomas** Baja California Sur, W Mexico
107 P10 **Las Pedroñeras** Castilla-La Mancha, C Spain
108 E10 **La Spezia** Liguria, NW Italy
63 F20 **Las Piedras** Canelones, S Uruguay
65 J18 **Las Plumas** Chubut, S Argentina
63 B18 **Las Rosas** Santa Fe, C Argentina
Lassa see Lhasa
37 O4 **Lassen Peak** ▲ California, W USA
204 K6 **Lassiter Coast** physical region Antarctica
111 V9 **Lassnitz** ≈ SE Austria
13 O12 **L'Assomption** Québec, SE Canada
13 N11 **L'Assomption** ≈ Québec, SE Canada
45 S17 **Las Tablas** Los Santos, S Panama
Lastarria, Volcán see Azufre, Volcán
39 V4 **Last Chance** Colorado, C USA
Last Frontier, The see Alaska
9 U16 **Last Mountain Lake** ◎ Saskatchewan, S Canada
64 H9 **Las Tórtolas, Cerro** ▲ W Argentina
63 C14 **Las Toscas** Santa Fe, C Argentina
81 F19 **Lastoursville** Ogooué-Lolo, E Gabon
115 F16 **Lastovo** It. Lagosta. island SW Croatia
115 F16 **Lastovski Kanal** channel SW Croatia
42 E6 **Las Tres Vírgenes, Volcán** ▲ W Mexico
42 F4 **Las Trincheras** Sonora, NW Mexico
57 N8 **Las Trincheras** Bolívar, E Venezuela
46 H7 **Las Tunas** var. Victoria de las Tunas. Las Tunas, E Cuba
La Suisse see Switzerland
42 I5 **Las Varas** Chihuahua, N Mexico
42 J12 **Las Varas** Nayarit, C Mexico
64 L10 **Las Varillas** Córdoba, E Argentina
37 X11 **Las Vegas** Nevada, W USA
39 T10 **Las Vegas** New Mexico, SW USA
195 W8 **Lata** Nendö, Solomon Islands
11 R10 **La Tabatière** Québec, E Canada
58 C6 **Latacunga** Cotopaxi, C Ecuador
204 I7 **Latady Island** island Antarctica
56 E14 **La Tagua** Putumayo, S Colombia
Latakia see Al Lādhiqīyah
94 J10 **Lätäseno** ≈ NW Finland
12 H9 **Latchford** Ontario, S Canada
12 J13 **Latchford Bridge** Ontario, SE Canada
200 Ss12 **Late** island Vava'u Group, N Tonga
159 P15 **Lātehār** Bihār, N India
13 R7 **Laterrière** Québec, SE Canada
104 J13 **la Teste** Gironde, SW France
27 V8 **Latexo** Texas, SW USA
20 L10 **Latham** New York, NE USA
Latharna see Larne
110 B9 **La Thielle** var. Thièle. ≈ W Switzerland
29 R3 **Lathrop** Missouri, C USA
109 I16 **Latina** prev. Littoria. Lazio, C Italy
43 R14 **La Tinaja** Veracruz-Llave, S Mexico
108 J7 **Latisana** Friuli-Venezia Giulia, NE Italy
Latium see Lazio
117 K25 **Lató** site of ancient city Kríti, Greece, E Mediterranean Sea
197 J7 **La Tontouta** ✈ (Noumea) Province Sud, S New Caledonia
57 N4 **La Tortuga, Isla** var. Isla Tortuga. island N Venezuela
110 C10 **La Tour-de-Peilz** var. La Tour de Peilz. Vaud, SW Switzerland
105 S11 **la Tour-du-Pin** Isère, E France
104 J11 **la Tremblade** Charente-Maritime, W France
104 L10 **la Trimouille** Vienne, W France
44 J9 **La Trinidad** Estelí, NW Nicaragua
179 P9 **La Trinidad** Luzon, N Philippines
43 V16 **La Trinitaria** Chiapas, SE Mexico
47 Q11 **la Trinité** E Martinique
13 U7 **La Trinité-des-Monts** Québec, SE Canada
20 C15 **Latrobe** Pennsylvania, NE USA
191 P13 **La Trobe River** ≈ Victoria, SE Australia
Lattakia/Lattaquié see Al Lādhiqīyah
175 Tt11 **Latu** Pulau Seram, E Indonesia
13 P9 **La Tuque** Québec, SE Canada
161 G14 **Lātūr** Mahārāshtra, C India
120 G8 **Latvia** off. Republic of Latvia, Ger. Lettland, Latv. Latvija, Latvijas Republika; prev. Latvian SSR, Rus. Latviyskaya SSR. ◆ republic NE Europe
Latvian SSR/Latvija/LatvijasRepublika/Latviyskaya SSR see Latvia
195 O12 **Lau** New Britain, E PNG
183 R9 **Lau Basin** undersea feature S Pacific Ocean
103 O15 **Lauchhammer** Brandenburg, E Germany
Laudunum see Laon
Laudus see St-Lô
Lauenburg/Lauenburg in Pommern see Lębork
103 L20 **Lauf an der Pegnitz** Bayern, SE Germany
110 D7 **Laufen** Basel, NW Switzerland
111 P5 **Lauffen** Salzburg, NW Austria
94 I2 **Laugarbakki** Nordhurland Vestra, N Iceland
94 I4 **Laugarvatn** Sudhurland, SW Iceland
33 O3 **Laughing Fish Point** headland Michigan, N USA
197 L14 **Lau Group** island group E Fiji
Lauis see Lugano
95 M17 **Laukaa** Keski-Suomi, C Finland
120 D12 **Laukuva** Šilalė, W Lithuania
Laun see Louny
191 P16 **Launceston** Tasmania, SE Australia
99 I24 **Launceston** anc. Dunheved. SW England, UK
56 L7 **La Unión** Nariño, SW Colombia
44 H8 **La Unión** La Unión, SE El Salvador
44 I6 **La Unión** Olancho, C Honduras
42 M15 **La Unión** Guerrero, S Mexico
43 Y14 **La Unión** Quintana Roo, E Mexico
107 S13 **La Unión** Murcia, SE Spain
56 C13 **La Unión** Barinas, C Venezuela
44 B10 **La Unión** ◆ department E El Salvador
40 H11 **Laupahoehoe** Haw. Laupāhoehoe. Hawaii, USA, C Pacific Ocean
103 I23 **Laupheim** Baden-Württemberg, S Germany
189 W3 **Laura** Queensland, NE Australia
201 X2 **Laura** atoll Majuro Atoll, SE Marshall Islands
Laurana see Lovran
56 L8 **La Urbana** Bolívar, C Venezuela
23 Y4 **Laurel** Delaware, NE USA
25 V14 **Laurel** Florida, SE USA
23 W3 **Laurel** Maryland, NE USA
24 M6 **Laurel** Mississippi, S USA
35 U11 **Laurel** Montana, NW USA
31 R13 **Laurel** Nebraska, C USA
20 H15 **Laureldale** Pennsylvania, NE USA
20 C16 **Laurel Hill** ridge Pennsylvania, NE USA
31 T12 **Laurens** Iowa, C USA
23 P11 **Laurens** South Carolina, SE USA
13 P10 **Laurentian Highlands** var. Laurentian Mountains, Fr. Les Laurentides. plateau Newfoundland and Labrador/Québec, Canada
LaurentianMountains see Laurentian Highlands
13 O12 **Laurentides** Québec, SE Canada
Laurentides, Les see Laurentian Highlands
109 M19 **Lauria** Basilicata, S Italy
204 I1 **Laurie Island** island Antarctica
23 T11 **Laurinburg** North Carolina, SE USA
32 M2 **Laurium** Michigan, N USA
Lauru see Choiseul
110 B9 **Lausanne** It. Losanna. Vaud, SW Switzerland
103 Q16 **Lausche** Cz. Luže. ▲ Czech Republic/Germany see also Luže
103 Q16 **Lausitzer Bergland** var. Lausitzer Gebirge, Cz. Gory Lužyckie, Lužické Hory, Eng. Lusatian Mountains. ▲ E Germany
Lausitzer Gebirge see Lausitzer Bergland
Lausitzer Neisse see Neisse
105 T12 **Lautaret, Col du** pass SE France
65 G15 **Lautaro** Araucanía, C Chile
103 F21 **Lauter** ≈ W Germany
110 I7 **Lauterach** Vorarlberg, NW Austria
103 I17 **Lauterbach** Hessen, C Germany
110 E9 **Lauterbrunnen** Bern, C Switzerland
175 Nn12 **Laut Kecil, Kepulauan** island group N Indonesia
197 H14 **Lautoka** Viti Levu, W Fiji
175 Nn11 **Laut, Pulau** prev. Laoet. island Borneo, C Indonesia
174 Jj4 **Laut, Pulau** island Kepulauan Natuna, W Indonesia
175 Nn11 **Laut, Selat** strait Borneo, C Indonesia
173 F4 **Laut Tawar, Danau** ◎ Sumatera, NW Indonesia
201 V14 **Lauvergne Island** island Chuuk, C Micronesia
100 M5 **Lauwers Meer** ◎ N Netherlands
100 M4 **Lauwersoog** Groningen, NE Netherlands
104 M14 **Lauzerte** Tarn-et-Garonne, S France
27 U13 **Lavaca Bay** bay Texas, SW USA
27 U12 **Lavaca River** ≈ Texas, SW USA
13 O12 **Laval** Québec, SE Canada
104 J6 **Laval** Mayenne, NW France
13 T6 **Laval** ≈ Québec, SE Canada
63 F19 **Lavalleja** ◆ department S Uruguay
13 O12 **Lavaltrie** Québec, SE Canada
195 X17 **Lavanggu** Rennell, S Solomon Islands
149 O14 **Lāvān, Jazīreh-ye** island S Iran
111 U8 **Lavant** ≈ S Austria
120 G5 **Lavassaare** Ger. Lawassaar. Pärnumaa, SW Estonia
106 L3 **La Vecilla de Curueño** Castilla-León, N Spain
47 N8 **La Vega** var. Concepción de la Vega. C Dominican Republic
La Vela see La Vela de Coro
56 J4 **La Vela de Coro** var. La Vela. Falcón, N Venezuela
105 N17 **Lavelanet** Ariège, S France
109 M17 **Lavello** Basilicata, S Italy
38 J8 **La Verkin** Utah, W USA
28 J8 **Laverne** Oklahoma, C USA
27 S12 **La Vernia** Texas, SW USA
95 K18 **Lavia** Turku-Pori, SW Finland
56 L5 **La Victoria** Aragua, N Venezuela
12 I12 **Lavieille, Lake** ◎ Ontario, SE Canada
96 C12 **Lavik** Sogn og Fjordane, S Norway
La Vila Jojosa see Villajoyosa
35 U10 **Lavina** Montana, NW USA
204 H5 **Lavoisier Island** island Antarctica
25 U2 **Lavonia** Georgia, SE USA
105 R13 **la Voulte-sur-Rhône** Ardèche, E France
127 Q3 **Lavrentiya** Chukotskiy Avtonomnyy Okrug, NE Russian Federation
117 H20 **Lávrio** prev. Lávrion. Attikí, C Greece
Lávrion see Lávrio
85 L22 **Lavumisa** prev. Gollel. SE Swaziland
155 T4 **Lawarai Pass** pass N Pakistan
Lawassaar see Lavassaare
147 P16 **Lawdar** SW Yemen
27 Q7 **Lawn** Texas, SW USA
205 Y4 **Law Promontory** headland Antarctica
79 O14 **Lawra** NW Ghana
193 E23 **Lawrence** Otago, South Island, NZ
33 P14 **Lawrence** Indiana, N USA
29 Q4 **Lawrence** Kansas, C USA
21 O10 **Lawrence** Massachusetts, NE USA
22 L5 **Lawrenceburg** Kentucky, S USA
22 I10 **Lawrenceburg** Tennessee, S USA
25 T3 **Lawrenceville** Georgia, SE USA
33 N15 **Lawrenceville** Illinois, N USA
23 V7 **Lawrenceville** Virginia, NE USA
29 S3 **Lawson** Missouri, C USA
28 L12 **Lawton** Oklahoma, C USA
146 I4 **Lawz, Jabal al** ▲ NW Saudi Arabia
97 L16 **Laxå** Örebro, C Sweden
129 T5 **Laya** ≈ NW Russian Federation
59 I19 **La Yarada** Tacna, SW Peru
147 S15 **Layjūn** C Yemen
147 Q9 **Laylā** var. Laila. Ar Riyāḍ, C Saudi Arabia
25 P4 **Lay Lake** ⊡ Alabama, S USA
47 P14 **Layou** Saint Vincent, Saint Vincent and the Grenadines
La Youne see El Ayoun
199 Jj5 **Laysan Island** island Hawaiian Islands, Hawaii, USA, C Pacific Ocean
38 L2 **Layton** Utah, W USA
36 L5 **Laytonville** California, N USA
180 H17 **Lazare, Pointe** headland Mahé, NE Seychelles
127 O14 **Lazarev** Khabarovskiy Kray, SE Russian Federation
114 L12 **Lazarevac** Serbia, C Yugoslavia
Lazareva, Ostrov see Lazerew Oroli
67 N22 **Lazarev Sea** sea Antarctica
42 M15 **Lázaro Cárdenas** Michoacán de Ocampo, SW Mexico
121 F15 **Lazdijai** Lazdijai, S Lithuania
152 G5 **Lazerew Oroli** Rus. Ostrov Lazareva. island NW Uzbekistan
109 H15 **Lazio** anc. Latium. ◆ region C Italy
113 A16 **Lázně Kynžvart** Ger. Bad Königswart. Západní Čechy, W Czech Republic
Lazovsk see Sîngerei
178 Ii13 **Leach** Poŭthĭsăt, W Cambodia
29 X9 **Leachville** Arkansas, C USA
30 I9 **Lead** South Dakota, N USA
9 S16 **Leader** Saskatchewan, S Canada
21 S6 **Lead Mountain** ▲ Maine, NE USA
39 R5 **Leadville** Colorado, C USA
9 V12 **Leaf Rapids** Manitoba, C Canada
24 M7 **Leaf River** ≈ Mississippi, S USA
27 W11 **League City** Texas, SW USA
25 N7 **Leakesville** Mississippi, S USA
27 Q11 **Leakey** Texas, SW USA
Leal see Lihula
85 G15 **Lealui** Western, W Zambia
Leamhcán see Lucan
12 C18 **Leamington** Ontario, S Canada
Leamington/Leamington Spa see Royal Leamington Spa
Leammi see Lemmenjoki
27 S10 **Leander** Texas, SW USA
62 F13 **Leandro N.Alem** Misiones, NE Argentina
99 A20 **Leane, Lough** Ir. Loch Léin. ◎ SW Ireland
188 G8 **Learmonth** Western Australia
Leau see Zoutleeuw
L'Eau d'Heure see Plate Taille, Lac de la
202 D12 **Leava** Île Futuna, S Wallis and Futuna
29 R3 **Leavenworth** Kansas, C USA
34 I8 **Leavenworth** Washington, NW USA
29 R4 **Leawood** Kansas, C USA
112 H6 **Łeba** Ger. Leba. Słupsk, NW Poland
112 I6 **Łeba** Ger. Leba. ≈ N Poland
103 D20 **Lebach** Saarland, SW Germany
Łeba, Jezioro see Łebsko, Jezioro
179 R17 **Lebak** Mindanao, S Philippines
175 Oo11 **Lebani,Teluk** bay Sulawesi, C Indonesia
33 O13 **Lebanon** Indiana, N USA
22 L6 **Lebanon** Kentucky, S USA
29 U6 **Lebanon** Missouri, C USA

21 N9 **Lebanon** New Hampshire, NE USA
34 G12 **Lebanon** Oregon, NW USA
20 H15 **Lebanon** Pennsylvania, NE USA
22 J8 **Lebanon** Tennessee, S USA
23 P7 **Lebanon** Virginia, NE USA
144 G6 **Lebanon** *off.* Republic of Lebanon, *Ar.* Al Lubnān, *Fr.* Liban. ◆ *republic* SW Asia
22 K6 **Lebanon Junction** Kentucky, S USA
Lebanon, Mount *see* Liban, Jebel
152 J10 **Lebap** Lebapskiy Velayat, NE Turkmenistan
152 H11 **Lebapskiy Velayat** *Turkm.* Lebap Welayaty; *prev. Rus.* Chardzhevskaya Oblast', *Turkm.* Chärjew Oblasty. ◈ *province* E Turkmenistan
Lebap Welayaty *see* Lebapskiy Velayat
Lebasee *see* Łebsko, Jezioro
101 F17 **Lebbeke** Oost-Vlaanderen, NW Belgium
37 S14 **Lebec** California, W USA
Lebedin *see* Lebedyn
126 Ll12 **Lebedinyy** Respublika Sakha (Yakutiya), NE Russian Federation
130 L6 **Lebedyan'** Lipetskaya Oblast', W Russian Federation
119 T4 **Lebedyn** *Rus.* Lebedin. Sums'ka Oblast', NE Ukraine
10 I12 **Lebel-sur-Quévillon** Québec, SE Canada
94 L8 **Lebesby** Finnmark, N Norway
104 M9 **le Blanc** Indre, C France
29 P5 **Lebo** Kansas, C USA
81 L15 **Lebo** Haut-Zaïre, N Zaire
112 H6 **Lębork** *var.* Lębórk, *Ger.* Lauenburg, Lauenburg in Pommern. Słupsk, NW Poland
105 O17 **le Boulou** Pyrénées-Orientales, S France
110 A9 **Le Brassus** Vaud, W Switzerland
106 J15 **Lebrija** Andalucía, S Spain
112 G6 **Łebsko, Jezioro** *Ger.* Lebasee; *prev.* Jezioro Łeba. ◎ N Poland
65 F14 **Lebu** Bío Bío, C Chile
151 U8 **Lebyazh'ye** Pavlodar, NE Kazakhstan
106 F6 **Leça da Palmeira** Porto, N Portugal
105 U15 **le Cannet** Alpes-Maritimes, SE France
Le Cap *see* Cap-Haïtien
105 P2 **le Cateau-Cambrésis** Nord, N France
109 Q18 **Lecce** Puglia, SE Italy
108 D7 **Lecco** Lombardia, N Italy
31 V10 **Le Center** Minnesota, N USA
110 J7 **Lech** Vorarlberg, W Austria
103 K22 **Lech** ≈ Austria/Germany
117 D19 **Lechainá** *var.* Lehena, Lekhainá. Dytikí Ellás, S Greece
104 J11 **le Château d'Oléron** Charente-Maritime, W France
105 R3 **le Chesne** Ardennes, N France
105 R13 **le Cheylard** Ardèche, E France
110 K7 **Lechtaler Alpen** ▲▲ W Austria
102 H6 **Leck** Schleswig-Holstein, N Germany
12 L9 **Lecointre, Lac** ◎ Québec, SE Canada
24 H7 **Lecompte** Louisiana, S USA
105 Q9 **le Creusot** Saône-et-Loire, C France
Lecumberri *see* Lekunberri
112 P13 **Łęczna** Lublin, E Poland
112 J12 **Łęczyca** *Ger.* Lentschiza, *Rus.* Lenchitsa. Płock, C Poland
102 F10 **Leda** ≈ NW Germany
101 F17 **Lede** Oost-Vlaanderen, NW Belgium
106 K6 **Ledesma** Castilla-León, N Spain
47 Q12 **le Diamant** SW Martinique
180 J16 **Le Digue** *island* Inner Islands, NE Seychelles
105 Q10 **le Donjon** Allier, C France
104 M10 **le Dorat** Haute-Vienne, C France
Ledo Salinarius *see* Lons-le-Saunier
9 Q14 **Leduc** Alberta, SW Canada
127 Pp7 **Ledyanaya, Gora** ▲ E Russian Federation
99 C21 **Lee** *Ir.* An Laoi. ≈ SW Ireland
31 U5 **Leech Lake** ◎ Minnesota, N USA
28 K10 **Leedey** Oklahoma, C USA
99 M17 **Leeds** N England, UK
25 P4 **Leeds** Alabama, S USA
31 O3 **Leeds** North Dakota, N USA
100 N6 **Leek** Groningen, NE Netherlands
101 K15 **Leende** Noord-Brabant, SE Netherlands
102 F10 **Leer** Niedersachsen, NW Germany
100 J13 **Leerdam** Zuid-Holland, C Netherlands
100 K12 **Leersum** Utrecht, C Netherlands
25 W11 **Leesburg** Florida, SE USA
23 V3 **Leesburg** Virginia, NE USA
29 R4 **Lees Summit** Missouri, C USA
24 G7 **Leesville** Louisiana, S USA
27 S12 **Leesville** Texas, SW USA
33 U13 **Leesville Lake** ⊟ Ohio, N USA
Leesville Lake *see* Smith Mountain Lake
191 P9 **Leeton** New South Wales, SE Australia
100 L6 **Leeuwarden** *Fris.* Ljouwert. Friesland, N Netherlands
188 I14 **Leeuwin, Cape** *headland* Western Australia
37 R8 **Lee Vining** California, W USA
47 V8 **Leeward Islands** *island group* E West Indies
Leeward Islands *see* Vent, Îles Sous le, W French Polynesia
Leeward Islands *see* Sotavento, Ilhas de, Cape Verde
81 G20 **Léfini** ≈ SE Congo
Léfka *see* Lefke
117 C17 **Lefkáda** *prev.* Levkás. Lefkáda, Iónioi Nísoi, Greece, C Mediterranean Sea
117 B17 **Lefkáda** *It.* Santa Maura; *prev.* Levkás, *anc.* Leucas. *island* Iónioi Nísoi, Greece, C Mediterranean Sea
117 H25 **Lefká Óri** ▲▲ Kríti, Greece, E Mediterranean Sea
124 N3 **Lefke** *Gk.* Léfka. W Cyprus
117 B16 **Lefkímmi** *var.* Levkímmi. Kérkyra, Iónioi Nísoi, Greece, C Mediterranean Sea
Lefkonico/Lefkónikon *see* Geçitkale
Lefkoşa/Lefkosía *see* Nicosia
27 O2 **Lefors** Texas, SW USA
47 R12 **le François** E Martinique
188 L12 **Lefroy, Lake** *salt lake* Western Australia
Legaceaster *see* Chester
107 N8 **Leganés** Madrid, C Spain
179 Q11 **Legaspi** *off.* Legaspi City. Luzon, N Philippines
Leghorn *see* Livorno
112 M11 **Legionowo** Warszawa, C Poland
101 K24 **Léglise** Luxembourg, SE Belgium
108 G8 **Legnago** Lombardia, NE Italy
108 D7 **Legnano** Veneto, NE Italy
113 F14 **Legnica** *Ger.* Liegnitz. Legnica, W Poland
113 E14 **Legnica** *off.* Województwo Legnickie, *Ger.* Liegnitz. ◈ *province* W Poland
Legnickie, Województwo *see* Legnica
37 Q9 **Le Grand** California, W USA
105 Q15 **le Grau-du-Roi** Gard, S France
191 U3 **Legume** New South Wales, SE Australia
104 L4 **le Havre** *Eng.* Havre; *prev.* le Havre-de-Grâce. Seine-Maritime, N France
le Havre-de-Grâce *see* le Havre
Lehena *see* Lechainá
38 L3 **Lehi** Utah, W USA
20 I14 **Lehighton** Pennsylvania, NE USA
31 O6 **Lehr** North Dakota, N USA
40 A8 **Lehua Island** *island* Hawaiian Islands, Hawaii, USA, C Pacific Ocean
155 S9 **Leiāh** Punjab, NE Pakistan
111 W9 **Leibnitz** Steiermark, SE Austria
99 M19 **Leicester** *Lat.* Batae Coritanorum. C England, UK
99 M19 **Leicestershire** *cultural region* C England, UK
100 H11 **Leiden** *prev.* Leyden, *anc.* Lugdunum Batavorum. Zuid-Holland, W Netherlands
100 H11 **Leiderdorp** Zuid-Holland, W Netherlands
100 G11 **Leidschendam** Zuid-Holland, W Netherlands
101 D18 **Leie** *Fr.* Lys. ≈ Belgium/France
Leifear *see* Lifford
192 L4 **Leigh** Auckland, North Island, NZ
99 K17 **Leigh** NW England, UK
190 I5 **Leigh Creek** South Australia
25 O2 **Leighton** Alabama, S USA
99 M21 **Leighton Buzzard** E England, UK
Léim an Bhradáin *see* Leixlip
Léim an Mhadaidh *see* Limavady
Léime, Ceann *see* Loop Head, Ireland
Léime, Ceann *see* Slyne Head, Ireland
103 G20 **Leimen** Baden-Württemberg, SW Germany
102 I13 **Leine** ≈ NW Germany
103 J15 **Leinefelde** Thüringen, C Germany
Léin, Loch *see* Leane, Lough
99 D19 **Leinster** *Ir.* Cúige Laighean. *cultural region* E Ireland
99 F19 **Leinster, Mount** *Ir.* Stua Laighean. ▲ SE Ireland
121 F15 **Leipalingis** Lazdijai, S Lithuania
94 J12 **Leipojärvi** Norrbotten, N Sweden
33 R12 **Leipsic** Ohio, N USA
Leipsic *see* Leipzig
117 M20 **Leipsoí** *island* Dodekánisos, Greece, Aegean Sea
103 M15 **Leipzig** *Pol.* Lipsk; *hist.* Leipsic, *anc.* Lipsia. Sachsen, E Germany
103 M15 **Leipzig Halle** ✕ Sachsen, E Germany
106 G9 **Leiria** *anc.* Collipo. Leiria, C Portugal
106 F9 **Leiria** ◈ *district* C Portugal
97 C15 **Leirvik** Hordaland, S Norway
120 E5 **Leisi** *Ger.* Laisberg. Saaremaa, W Estonia
106 J3 **Leitariegos, Puerto de** *pass* NW Spain
22 J6 **Leitchfield** Kentucky, S USA
111 Y5 **Leitha** *Hung.* Lajta. ≈ Austria/Hungary
Leitir Ceanainn *see* Letterkenny
Leitmeritz *see* Litoměřice
Leitomischl *see* Litomyšl
99 D16 **Leitrim** *Ir.* Liatroim. *cultural region* NW Ireland
117 F18 **Leivádia** *prev.* Levádhia. Stereá Ellás, C Greece
Leix *see* Laois
99 F18 **Leixlip** *Eng.* Salmon Leap, *Ir.* Léim an Bhradáin. E Ireland
66 N8 **Leixões** Porto, N Portugal
167 N12 **Leiyang** Hunan, S China
166 L16 **Leizhou** *var.* Haikang. Guangdong, S China
166 L16 **Leizhou Bandao** *var.* Luichow Peninsula. *peninsula* S China
100 H13 **Lek** ≈ SW Netherlands
116 I13 **Lekánis** ▲▲ NE Greece
180 H13 **Le Kartala** ▲ Grande Comore, NW Comoros
Le Kef *see* El Kef
81 G20 **Lékéti, Monts de la** ▲▲ S Congo
Lekhainá *see* Lechainá
116 H8 **Lekhchevo** Oblast Montana, NW Bulgaria
94 G11 **Leknes** Nordland, C Norway
81 E21 **Le Kouilou** ◈ *province* SW Congo
96 L13 **Leksand** Kopparberg, C Sweden
128 H8 **Leksozero, Ozero** ◎ NW Russian Federation
107 Q3 **Lekunberri** *var.* Lecumberri. Navarra, N Spain
175 Tt6 **Lelai, Tanjung** *headland* Pulau Halmahera, N Indonesia
47 Q12 **le Lamentin** *var.* Lamentin. C Martinique
47 Q12 **le Lamentin** ✕ (Fort-de-France) C Martinique
33 P6 **Leland** Michigan, N USA
24 J4 **Leland** Mississippi, S USA
97 J16 **Lelång** *var.* Lelången. ◎ S Sweden
Lelången *see* Lelång
Lel'chitsy *see* Lyel'chytsy
le Léman *see* Geneva, Lake
27 O3 **Lelia Lake** Texas, SW USA
115 I14 **Lelija** ▲ SE Bosnia and Herzegovina
110 C8 **Le Locle** Neuchâtel, W Switzerland
201 Y14 **Lelu** Kosrae, E Micronesia
Lelu *see* Lelu Island
201 Y14 **Lelu Island** *var.* Lelu. *island* Kosrae, E Micronesia
57 W9 **Lelydorp** Wanica, N Suriname
100 K9 **Lelystad** Flevoland, C Netherlands
65 K25 **Le Maire, Estrecho de** *strait* S Argentina
174 Hh7 **Lemang** Pulau Rangsang, W Indonesia
195 R11 **Lemankoa** Buka Island, NE PNG
Léman, Lac *see* Geneva, Lake
104 L6 **le Mans** Sarthe, NW France
31 S12 **Le Mars** Iowa, C USA
174 I11 **Lematan, Air** ≈ Sumatera, W Indonesia
111 S3 **Lembach Im Mühlkreis** Oberösterreich, N Austria
103 G23 **Lemberg** ▲ SW Germany
Lemberg *see* L'viv
Lemdiyya *see* Médéa
124 Qq12 **Lemesós** *var.* Limassol. SW Cyprus
102 H13 **Lemgo** Nordrhein-Westfalen, W Germany
35 P13 **Lemhi Range** ▲▲ Idaho, NW USA
16 Oo2 **Lemieux Islands** *island group* Northwest Territories, NE Canada
175 Q7 **Lemito** Sulawesi, N Indonesia
94 L10 **Lemmenjoki** *Lapp.* Leammi. ≈ NE Finland
100 L7 **Lemmer** *Fris.* De Lemmer. Friesland, N Netherlands
30 L7 **Lemmon** South Dakota, N USA
38 M15 **Lemmon, Mount** ▲ Arizona, SW USA
Lemnos *see* Límnos
33 O14 **Lemon, Lake** ◎ Indiana, N USA
104 J5 **le Mont St-Michel** *castle* Manche, N France
37 Q11 **Lemoore** California, W USA
201 T13 **Lemotol Bay** *bay* Chuuk Islands, C Micronesia
47 Y5 **le Moule** *var.* Moule. Grande Terre, NE Guadeloupe
Lemovices *see* Limoges
Le Moyen-Ogooué *see* Moyen-Ogooué
10 M6 **le Moyne, Lac** ◎ Québec, E Canada
95 L18 **Lempäälä** Häme, SW Finland
44 E7 **Lempa, Río** ≈ Central America
44 F7 **Lempira** *prev.* Gracias. ◈ *department* SW Honduras
Lemsalu *see* Limbaži
109 N17 **Le Murge** ▲▲ SE Italy
129 V6 **Lemva** ≈ NW Russian Federation
97 F21 **Lemvig** Ringkøbing, W Denmark
177 Ff8 **Lemyethna** Irrawaddy, SW Myanmar
32 K10 **Lena** Illinois, N USA
133 V4 **Lena** ≈ NE Russian Federation
181 N13 **Lena Tablemount** *undersea feature* S Indian Ocean
Lenchitsa *see* Łęczyca
61 N17 **Lençóis** Bahia, E Brazil
62 K9 **Lençóis Paulista** São Paulo, S Brazil
178 Mm15 **Len Dao** *island* S Spratly Islands
111 Y9 **Lendava** *Ger.* Unterlimbach; *prev.* Dolnja Lendava. NE Slovenia
85 F20 **Lendepas** Hardap, SE Namibia
128 H9 **Lendery** Respublika Kareliya, NW Russian Federation
Lendum *see* Lens
29 R4 **Lenexa** Kansas, C USA
111 Q5 **Lengau** Oberösterreich, N Austria
151 Q17 **Lenger** Yuzhnyy Kazakhstan, S Kazakhstan
165 O9 **Lenghu** Qinghai, C China
165 T9 **Lenglong Ling** ▲ N China
110 D7 **Lengnau** Bern, W Switzerland
166 M12 **Lengshuitan** Hunan, S China
97 M20 **Lenhovda** Kronoberg, S Sweden
81 E20 **Le Niari** ◈ *province* SW Congo
Lenīn *see* Leninskoye, Kazakhstan
Lenin *see* Akdepe, Turkmenistan
Leninabad *see* Khŭjand
Leninakan *see* Gyumri
Lenina, Pik *see* Lenin Peak
119 V12 **Lenine** *Rus.* Lenino. Respublika Krym, S Ukraine
Lenīngor *see* Leninogorsk
153 Q13 **Leningrad** *Rus.* Leningradskiy; *prev.* Mŭ'minobod, *Rus.* Muminabad. SW Tajikistan
Leningrad *see* Sankt-Peterburg
130 L13 **Leningradskaya** Krasnodarskiy Kray, SW Russian Federation
205 S16 **Leningradskaya** *Russian research station* Antarctica
128 H12 **Leningradskaya Oblast'** ◈ *province* NW Russian Federation
Leningradskiy *see* Leningrad
Lenino *see* Lyenina, Belarus
Lenino *see* Lenine, Ukraine
Leninobod *see* Khŭjand
151 X9 **Leninogorsk** *Kaz.* Lenīngor. Vostochnyy Kazakhstan, E Kazakhstan
131 T5 **Leninogorsk** Respublika Tatarstan, W Russian Federation
153 T12 **Lenin Peak** *Rus.* Pik Lenina, *Taj.* Qullai Lenin. ▲ Kyrgyzstan/Tajikistan
153 S8 **Leninpol'** Talasskaya Oblast', NW Kyrgyzstan
Lenin, Qullai *see* Lenin Peak
131 P11 **Leninsk** Volgogradskaya Oblast', SW Russian Federation
Leninsk *see* Akdepe, Turkmenistan
Leninsk *see* Asaka, Uzbekistan
151 T8 **Leninskiy** Pavlodar, E Kazakhstan
126 H14 **Leninsk-Kuznetskiy** Kemerovskaya Oblast', S Russian Federation
151 N7 **Leninskoye** *Kaz.* Lenīn. Kustanay, N Kazakhstan
129 P15 **Leninskoye** Kirovskaya Oblast', NW Russian Federation
Leninsk-Turkmenski *see* Chardzhev
Leninváros *see* Tiszaújváros
Lenkoran' *see* Länkäran
103 F15 **Lenne** ≈ W Germany
103 G16 **Lennestadt** Nordrhein-Westfalen, W Germany
31 R11 **Lennox** South Dakota, N USA
65 J25 **Lennox, Isla** *Eng.* Lennox Island. *island* S Chile
Lennox Island *see* Lennox, Isla
23 Q9 **Lenoir** North Carolina, SE USA
22 M9 **Lenoir City** Tennessee, S USA
110 C7 **Le Noirmont** Jura, NW Switzerland
12 L9 **Lenôtre, Lac** ◎ Québec, SE Canada
31 U15 **Lenox** Iowa, C USA
105 O2 **Lens** *anc.* Lendum, Lentium. Pas-de-Calais, N France
126 Kk12 **Lensk** Respublika Sakha (Yakutiya), NE Russian Federation
113 F24 **Lenti** Zala, SW Hungary
Lentia *see* Linz
95 N14 **Lentiira** Oulu, E Finland
109 L25 **Lentini** *anc.* Leontini. Sicilia, Italy, C Mediterranean Sea
Lentium *see* Lens
Lentschiza *see* Łęczyca
95 N15 **Lentua** ◎ E Finland
121 H14 **Lentvaris** *Pol.* Landwarów. Trakai, SE Lithuania
110 F7 **Lenzburg** Aargau, N Switzerland
111 R5 **Lenzing** Oberösterreich, N Austria
79 P13 **Léo** SW Burkina
111 V7 **Leoben** Steiermark, C Austria
Leobschütz *see* Głubczyce
46 L9 **Léogâne** S Haiti
175 Q7 **Leok** Sulawesi, N Indonesia
31 O7 **Leola** South Dakota, N USA
99 K20 **Leominster** W England, UK
21 N11 **Leominster** Massachusetts, NE USA
31 V16 **Leon** Iowa, C USA
42 M12 **León** *var.* León de los Aldamas. Guanajuato, C Mexico
44 I10 **León** León, NW Nicaragua
106 L4 **León** Castilla-León, NW Spain
44 I9 **León** ◈ *department* W Nicaragua
106 K4 **León** ◈ *province* Castilla-León, NW Spain
León *see* Cotopaxi
104 I15 **Léon** Landes, SW France
27 V9 **Leona** Texas, SW USA
188 K11 **Leonara** Western Australia
27 U5 **Leonard** Texas, SW USA
Leonard Murray Mountains *see* Murray Range
109 H15 **Leonardo da Vinci** *prev.* Fiumicino. ✕ (Roma) Lazio, C Italy
23 X5 **Leonardtown** Maryland, NE USA
27 Q13 **Leona River** ≈ Texas, SW USA
43 Z11 **Leona Vicario** Quintana Roo, SE Mexico
103 H21 **Leonberg** Baden-Württemberg, SW Germany
64 M3 **León, Cerro** ▲ NW Paraguay
León de los Aldamas *see* León
111 T4 **Leonding** Oberösterreich, N Austria
109 I14 **Leonessa** Lazio, C Italy
109 K24 **Leonforte** Sicilia, Italy, C Mediterranean Sea
191 O13 **Leongatha** Victoria, SE Australia
117 F21 **Leonídi** Pelopónnisos, S Greece
106 J4 **León, Montes de** ▲▲ NW Spain
27 S8 **Leon River** ≈ Texas, SW USA
Leontini *see* Lentini
Léopold II, Lac *see* Mai-Ndombe, Lac
101 J17 **Leopoldsburg** Limburg, NE Belgium
Léopoldville *see* Kinshasa
28 I5 **Leoti** Kansas, C USA
118 M11 **Leova** *Rus.* Leovo. SW Moldova
Leovo *see* Leova
104 G8 **le Palais** Morbihan, NW France
29 X10 **Lepanto** Arkansas, C USA
174 J11 **Lepar, Pulau** *island* W Indonesia
106 I14 **Lepe** Andalucía, S Spain
Lepel' *see* Lyepyel'
85 I19 **Lephepe** Kweneng, SE Botswana
167 Q10 **Leping** Jiangxi, S China
Lépontiennes, Alpes/Lepontine, Alpi *see* Lepontine Alps
110 G10 **Lepontine Alps** *Fr.* Alpes Lépontiennes, *It.* Alpi Lepontine. ▲▲ Italy/Switzerland
81 G20 **Le Pool** ◈ *province* S Congo
181 O16 **le Port** NW Réunion
105 N1 **le Portel** Pas-de-Calais, N France
95 N17 **Leppävirta** Kuopio, C Finland
47 Q11 **le Prêcheur** NW Martinique
Lepsi *see* Lepsy
151 V13 **Lepsy** *Kaz.* Lepsi. Taldykorgan, SE Kazakhstan
151 V13 **Lepsy** *Kaz.* Lepsi. ≈ SE Kazakhstan
Le Puglie *see* Puglia
105 Q12 **le Puy** *prev.* le Puy-en-Velay, *hist.* Anicium, Podium Anicensis. Haute-Loire, C France
le Puy-en-Velay *see* le Puy
Le Raizet *see* le Raizet
47 X11 **le Raizet** *var.* Le Raizet. ✕ (Pointe-à-Pitre) Grande Terre, C Guadeloupe
109 J24 **Lercara Friddi** Sicilia, Italy, C Mediterranean Sea
80 G12 **Léré** Mayo-Kébbi, SW Chad
Leribe *see* Hlotse
108 E10 **Lerici** Liguria, NW Italy
56 I14 **Lérida** Vaupés, SE Colombia
107 U5 **Lérida** ◈ *province* Cataluña, NE Spain
Lérida *see* Lleida
107 N5 **Lerma** Castilla-León, N Spain
42 M13 **Lerma, Río** ≈ C Mexico
117 F20 **Lérna** *prehistoric site* Pelopónnisos, S Greece
47 R11 **le Robert** E Martinique
117 M21 **Léros** *island* Dodekánisos, Greece, Aegean Sea
32 L13 **Le Roy** Illinois, N USA
29 Q6 **Le Roy** Kansas, C USA
31 W11 **Le Roy** Minnesota, N USA
20 E10 **Le Roy** New York, NE USA
Lerrnayin Gharabakh *see* Nagornyy Karabakh
97 J19 **Lerum** Älvsborg, S Sweden
98 M2 **Lerwick** NE Scotland, UK
47 Y6 **les Abymes** *var.* Abymes. Grande Terre, C Guadeloupe
les Albères *see* Albères, Chaîne des
104 M4 **les Andelys** Eure, N France
47 Q12 **les Anses-d'Arlets** SW Martinique
107 U6 **Les Borges Blanques** *var.* Borjas Blancas. Cataluña, NE Spain
Lesbos *see* Lésvos
Les Cayes *see* Cayes
33 Q4 **Les Cheneaux Islands** *island* Michigan, N USA
105 T12 **les Écrins** ▲ E France
110 C10 **Le Sépey** Vaud, W Switzerland
13 T7 **Les Escoumins** Québec, SE Canada
Les Gonaïves *see* Gonaïves
Lesh/Leshi *see* Lezhë
166 H9 **Leshan** Sichuan, C China
110 D11 **Les Haudères** Valais, SW Switzerland
104 J9 **les Herbiers** Vendée, NW France
129 O8 **Leshukonskoye** Arkhangel'skaya Oblast', NW Russian Federation
Lesina *see* Hvar
109 M15 **Lesina, Lago di** ◎ SE Italy
116 K13 **Lesítse** ▲▲ NE Greece
96 G10 **Lesja** Oppland, S Norway
97 L15 **Lesjöfors** Värmland, C Sweden
113 O18 **Lesko** Krosno, SE Poland
115 O15 **Leskovac** Serbia, SE Yugoslavia
115 M22 **Leskovik** *var.* Leskoviku. Korçë, S Albania
Leskoviku *see* Leskovik
35 P14 **Leslie** Idaho, NW USA
33 Q10 **Leslie** Michigan, N USA
Leśna/Lesnaya *see* Lyasnaya
104 F5 **Lesneven** Finistère, NW France
114 J11 **Lešnica** Serbia, W Yugoslavia
129 S13 **Lesnoy** Kirovskaya Oblast', NW Russian Federation
126 I13 **Lesosibirsk** Krasnoyarskiy Kray, C Russian Federation
85 J23 **Lesotho** *off.* Kingdom of Lesotho; *prev.* Basutoland. ◆ *monarchy* S Africa
127 Nn17 **Lesozavodsk** Primorskiy Kray, SE Russian Federation
104 J12 **Lesparre-Médoc** Gironde, SW France
110 C8 **Les Ponts-de-Martel** Neuchâtel, W Switzerland
104 I9 **les Sables-d'Olonne** Vendée, NW France
111 S7 **Lessach** *var.* Lessachbach. ≈ E Austria
Lessachbach *see* Lessach
47 W11 **les Saintes** *var.* Îles des Saintes. *island group* S Guadeloupe
76 L5 **Les Salines** ✕ (Annaba) NE Algeria
101 J22 **Lesse** ≈ SE Belgium
97 M21 **Lessebo** Kronoberg, S Sweden
104 G4 **les Sept Îles** *island group* NW France
204 M10 **Lesser Antarctica** *var.* West Antarctica. *physical region* Antarctica
47 P15 **Lesser Antilles** *island group* E West Indies
143 T10 **Lesser Caucasus** *Rus.* Malyy Kavkaz. ▲▲ SW Asia
Lesser Khingan Range *see* Xiao Hinggan Ling
9 P13 **Lesser Slave Lake** ◎ Alberta, W Canada
Lesser Sunda Islands *see* Nusa Tenggara
101 E19 **Lessines** Hainaut, SW Belgium
105 R16 **les Stes-Maries-de-la-Mer** Bouches-du-Rhône, SE France
12 G15 **Lester B.Pearson** *var.* Toronto. ✕ (Toronto) Ontario, S Canada
31 U9 **Lester Prairie** Minnesota, N USA
95 L16 **Lestijärvi** Vaasa, W Finland
L'Estuaire *see* Estuaire
31 U9 **Le Sueur** Minnesota, N USA
110 B8 **Les Verrières** Neuchâtel, W Switzerland
117 L17 **Lésvos** *anc.* Lesbos. *island* E Greece
112 G12 **Leszno** *Ger.* Lissa. Leszno, W Poland
112 G13 **Leszno** *off.* Województwo Leszyńskie, *Ger.* Lissa. ◈ *province* W Poland
Leszyńskie, Województwo *see* Leszno
85 L20 **Letaba** Northern, NE South Africa
181 P17 **le Tampon** SW Réunion
99 O21 **Letchworth** E England, UK
113 G25 **Letenye** Zala, SW Hungary
9 Q17 **Lethbridge** Alberta, SW Canada
57 S11 **Lethem** S Guyana
85 H18 **Letiahau** ≈ W Botswana
56 J18 **Leticia** Amazonas, S Colombia
175 T15 **Leti, Kepulauan** *island group* E Indonesia
85 I18 **Letlhakane** Central, C Botswana
85 H20 **Letlhakeng** Kweneng, SE Botswana
116 J8 **Letnitsa** Loveshka Oblast, N Bulgaria
105 N1 **le Touquet-Paris-Plage** Pas-de-Calais, N France
177 G8 **Letpadan** Pegu, SW Myanmar
177 Ff6 **Letpan** Arakan State, W Myanmar
104 M2 **le Tréport** Seine-Maritime, N France
178 Gg13 **Letsôk-aw Kyun** *var.* Letsutan Island; *prev.* Domel Island. *island* Mergui Archipelago, S Myanmar
Letsutan Island *see* Letsôk-aw Kyun
99 E14 **Letterkenny** *Ir.* Leitir Ceanainn. NW Ireland
Lettland *see* Latvia
118 M6 **Letychiv** Khmel'nyts'ka Oblast', W Ukraine
Lëtzebuerg *see* Luxembourg
118 H14 **Leu** Dolj, SW Romania
Leucas *see* Lefkáda
105 P17 **Leucate** Aude, S France
105 P17 **Leucate, Étang de** ◎ S France
110 E10 **Leuk** Valais, SW Switzerland
110 E10 **Leukerbad** Valais, SW Switzerland
Leusden *see* Leusden-Centrum
100 K11 **Leusden-Centrum** *var.* Leusden. Utrecht, C Netherlands
Leutensdorf *see* Litvínov
Leutschau *see* Levoča
101 H18 **Leuven** *Fr.* Louvain, *Ger.* Löwen. Vlaams Brabant, C Belgium
101 I20 **Leuze** Namur, C Belgium
Leuze *see* Leuze-en-Hainaut
101 E19 **Leuze-en-Hainaut** *var.* Leuze. Hainaut, SW Belgium
Léva *see* Levice
Levádhia *see* Leivádia
94 L8 **Levajok** *var.* Lœvvajok. Finnmark, N Norway
38 L4 **Levan** Utah, W USA
95 E16 **Levanger** Nord-Trøndelag, C Norway
124 P14 **Levantine Basin** *undersea feature* E Mediterranean Sea
108 D10 **Levanto** Liguria, W Italy
109 H23 **Levanzo, Isola di** *island* Isole Egadi, S Italy
131 Q17 **Levashi** Respublika Dagestan, SW Russian Federation
26 M5 **Levelland** Texas, SW USA
41 P13 **Levelock** Alaska, USA
103 E16 **Leverkusen** Nordrhein-Westfalen, W Germany
113 J21 **Levice** *Ger.* Lewentz, Lewenz, *Hung.* Léva. Západné Slovensko, SW Slovakia
108 G6 **Levico Terme** Trentino-Alto Adige, N Italy
117 E20 **Levídi** Pelopónnisos, S Greece
105 P14 **le Vigan** Gard, S France
192 L13 **Levin** Manawatu-Wanganui, North Island, NZ
13 R10 **Lévis** *var.* Levis. Québec, SE Canada
23 P6 **Levisa Fork** ≈ Kentucky/Virginia, S USA
117 L21 **Levítha** *island* Kykládes, Greece, Aegean Sea
20 L14 **Levittown** Long Island, New York, NE USA
20 J15 **Levittown** Pennsylvania, NE USA
Levkás *see* Lefkáda
Levkímmi *see* Lefkímmi
113 L19 **Levoča** *Ger.* Leutschau, *Hung.* Locse. Východné Slovensko, NE Slovakia
Lévrier, Baie du *see* Nouâdhibou, Dakhlet
105 N9 **Levroux** Indre, C France
116 J8 **Levski** Loveshka Oblast, N Bulgaria
Levskigrad *see* Karlovo
130 L6 **Lev Tolstoy** Lipetskaya Oblast', W Russian Federation
197 I14 **Levuka** Ovalau, C Fiji
177 G6 **Lewe** Mandalay, C Myanmar
Lewentz/Lewenz *see* Levice
99 O23 **Lewes** SE England, UK
23 Z4 **Lewes** Delaware, NE USA
31 Q12 **Lewis And Clark Lake** ⊟ Nebraska/South Dakota, N USA
20 G14 **Lewisburg** Pennsylvania, NE USA
22 J10 **Lewisburg** Tennessee, S USA
23 S6 **Lewisburg** West Virginia, NE USA
98 F6 **Lewis, Butt of** *headland* NW Scotland, UK
98 F7 **Lewis, Isle of** *island* NW Scotland, UK
37 U4 **Lewis, Mount** ▲ Nevada, W USA
193 H16 **Lewis Pass** *pass* South Island, NZ
35 P7 **Lewis Range** ▲▲ Montana, NW USA
25 O3 **Lewis Smith Lake** ⊟ Alabama, S USA
34 M10 **Lewiston** Idaho, NW USA
21 P7 **Lewiston** Maine, NE USA
31 X10 **Lewiston** Minnesota, N USA
20 D9 **Lewiston** New York, NE USA
38 L1 **Lewiston** Utah, W USA
32 K13 **Lewistown** Illinois, N USA
35 T9 **Lewistown** Montana, NW USA
29 T14 **Lewisville** Arkansas, C USA
27 T6 **Lewisville** Texas, SW USA
27 T6 **Lewisville, Lake** ⊟ Texas, SW USA
Le Woleu-Ntem *see* Woleu-Ntem
25 U3 **Lexington** Georgia, SE USA
22 M5 **Lexington** Kentucky, S USA
24 L4 **Lexington** Mississippi, S USA
29 S4 **Lexington** Missouri, C USA
31 N16 **Lexington** Nebraska, C USA
22 J9 **Lexington** North Carolina, SE USA
29 N11 **Lexington** Oklahoma, C USA
23 R12 **Lexington** South Carolina, SE USA
22 G9 **Lexington** Tennessee, S USA
27 T10 **Lexington** Texas, SW USA
23 T6 **Lexington** Virginia, NE USA
23 X5 **Lexington Park** Maryland, NE USA
Leyden *see* Leiden
104 J14 **Leyre** ≈ SW France
179 R13 **Leyte** *island* C Philippines
179 R13 **Leyte Gulf** *gulf* E Philippines
113 O16 **Leżajsk** Rzeszów, SE Poland
Lezha *see* Lezhë
115 K18 **Lezhë** *var.* Lezha; *prev.* Lesh, Leshi. Lezhë, NW Albania
115 K18 **Lezhë** ◈ *district* NW Albania
105 O16 **Lézignan-Corbières** Aude, S France
130 J7 **L'gov** Kurskaya Oblast', W Russian Federation
165 P15 **Lhari** Xizang Zizhiqu, W China
165 N16 **Lhasa** *var.* La-sa, Lassa. Xizang Zizhiqu, W China
165 O15 **Lhasa He** ≈ W China
164 K16 **Lhazê** Xizang Zizhiqu, W China
164 K14 **Lhazhong** Xizang Zizhiqu, W China
173 F3 **Lhoksukon** Sumatera, W Indonesia
165 Q15 **Lhorong** Xizang Zizhiqu, W China
107 W6 **L'Hospitalet de Llobregat** *var.* Hospitalet. Cataluña, NE Spain
159 R11 **Lhotse** ▲ China/Nepal
165 N17 **Lhozhag** Xizang Zizhiqu, W China
165 O16 **Lhünzê** Xizang Zizhiqu, W China
165 N15 **Lhünzhub** *var.* Poindo. Xizang Zizhiqu, W China
178 H8 **Li** Lamphun, NW Thailand
Liancheng *see* Qinglong
179 Rr14 **Lianga** Mindanao, S Philippines
167 P12 **Liangcheng** Fujian, SE China
166 K9 **Liangping** Sichuan, C China
Liangzhou *see* Wuwei
167 O9 **Liangzi Hu** ⊟ C China
167 R12 **Lianjiang** Fujian, SE China
166 L15 **Lianjiang** Guangdong, S China
167 O13 **Lianping** Guangdong, S China
Lian Xian *see* Lianzhou
166 M11 **Lianyuan** *prev.* Lantian. Hunan, S China
167 Q6 **Lianyungang** *var.* Xinpu. Jiangsu, E China
167 N13 **Lianzhou** *var.* Linxian; *prev.* Lian Xian. Guangdong, S China
Liao *see* Liaoning
167 P5 **Liaocheng** Shandong, E China
169 U13 **Liaodong Bandao** *var.* Liaotung Peninsula. *peninsula* NE China
169 T13 **Liaodong Wan** *Eng.* Gulf of Lantung, Gulf of Liaotung. *gulf* NE China
169 U11 **Liao He** ≈ NE China
169 W12 **Liao Ling** ▲▲ NE China
169 U12 **Liaoning** *var.* Liao, Liaoning Sheng, Shengking; *hist.* Fengtien, Shenking. ◈ *province* NE China
Liaoning Sheng *see* Liaoning
Liaotung, Gulf of *see* Liaodong Wan
Liaotung Peninsula *see* Liaodong Bandao
169 V12 **Liaoyang** *var.* Liao-yang. Liaoning, NE China
169 V11 **Liaoyuan** *var.* Dongliao, Shuang-liao, *Jap.* Chengchiatun. Jilin, NE China
169 U12 **Liaozhong** Liaoning, NE China
Liaqatabad *see* Piplān
8 M10 **Liard** ≈ W Canada
Liard *see* Fort Liard
8 L10 **Liard River** British Columbia, W Canada
155 O15 **Liāri** Baluchistān, SW Pakistan
Liatroim *see* Leitrim
201 S6 **Lib** *var.* Ellep. *island* Ralik Chain, C Marshall Islands
Liban *see* Lebanon
144 H6 **Liban, Jebel** *Ar.* Jabal al Gharbt, Jabal Lubnān, *Eng.* Mount Lebanon. ▲▲ C Lebanon
Libau *see* Liepāja
35 N7 **Libby** Montana, NW USA
81 I16 **Libenge** Equateur, NW Zaire
28 I7 **Liberal** Kansas, C USA
29 R7 **Liberal** Missouri, C USA
Liberalitas Julia *see* Évora
113 D15 **Liberec** *Ger.* Reichenberg. Severní Čechy, N Czech Republic
44 K12 **Liberia** Guanacaste, NW Costa Rica

◆ Country
● Country Capital
◇ Dependent Territory
○ Dependent Territory Capital
◈ Administrative Region
✕ International Airport
▲ Mountain
▲▲ Mountain Range
Volcano
≈ River
◎ Lake
⊟ Reservoir

78 K17 Liberia off. Republic of Liberia. ◆ republic W Africa
63 D16 Libertad Corrientes, NE Argentina
63 E20 Libertad San José, S Uruguay
56 K6 Libertad Barinas, NW Venezuela
56 J7 Libertad Cojedes, N Venezuela
64 G12 Libertador off. Región del Libertador General Bernardo O'Higgins. ◆ region C Chile
Libertador General San Martín see Ciudad de Libertador General San Martín
22 L6 Liberty Kentucky, S USA
24 J7 Liberty Mississippi, S USA
29 R4 Liberty Missouri, C USA
20 J12 Liberty New York, NE USA
23 T9 Liberty North Carolina, SE USA
Libian Desert see Libyan Desert
101 J23 Libin Luxembourg, SE Belgium
166 K13 Libo Guizhou, S China
Libohova see Libohovë
115 L23 Libohovë var. Libohova. Gjirokastër, S Albania
83 K18 Liboi North Eastern, E Kenya
104 K13 Libourne Gironde, SW France
101 K23 Libramont Luxembourg, SE Belgium
115 M20 Librazhd var. Librazhdi. Elbasan, E Albania
Librazhdi see Librazhd
81 C18 Libreville ● (Gabon) Estuaire, NW Gabon
179 Rr15 Libuganon ∻ Mindanao, S Philippines
77 P10 Libya off. Socialist People's Libyan Arab Jamahiriya, Ar. Al Jamāhīrīyah al 'Arabīyah al Lībīyah ash Sha'bīyah al Ishtirākīyah; prev. Libyan Arab Republic. ◆ islamic state N Africa
77 T11 Libyan Desert var. Libian Desert, Ar. Aş Şahrā' al Lībīyah. desert N Africa
77 T8 Libyan Plateau var. Aḍ Diffah. plateau Egypt/Libya
Lībīyah, Aş Şahrā' al see Libyan Desert
64 G12 Licantén Maule, C Chile
109 J25 Licata anc. Phintias. Sicilia, Italy, C Mediterranean Sea
143 P14 Lice Diyarbakır, SE Turkey
99 L19 Lichfield C England, UK
85 N14 Lichinga Niassa, N Mozambique
111 V3 Lichtenau Niederösterreich, N Austria
85 I21 Lichtenburg North-West, N South Africa
103 K18 Lichtenfels Bayern, SE Germany
100 O12 Lichtenvoorde Gelderland, E Netherlands
Lichtenwald see Sevnica
101 C17 Lichtervelde West-Vlaanderen, W Belgium
166 L9 Lichuan Hubei, C China
29 V7 Licking Missouri, C USA
22 M4 Licking River ∻ Kentucky, S USA
114 C11 Lički Osik Lika-Senj, C Croatia
Ličko-Senjska Županija see Lika-Senj
109 K19 Licosa, Punta headland S Italy
121 H16 Lida Rus. Lida. Hrodzyenskaya Voblasts', W Belarus
95 H17 Liden Västernorrland, C Sweden
31 R7 Lidgerwood North Dakota, N USA
Lidhorikíon see Lidoríki
97 K21 Lidhult Kronoberg, S Sweden
97 P16 Lidingö Stockholm, C Sweden
97 K17 Lidköping Skaraborg, S Sweden
Lido di Iesolo see Lido di Jesolo
108 I8 Lido di Jesolo var. Lido di Iesolo. Veneto, NE Italy
109 H15 Lido di Ostia Lazio, C Italy
Lidokhorikion see Lidoríki
117 E18 Lidoríki prev. Lidhorikíon, Lidokhorikion. Stereá Ellás, C Greece
112 K9 Lidzbark Ciechanów, N Poland
112 L7 Lidzbark Warmiński Ger. Heilsberg. Olsztyn, N Poland
111 U3 Liebenau Oberösterreich, N Austria
189 P7 Liebig, Mount ▲ Northern Territory, C Australia
111 V8 Lieboch Steiermark, SE Austria
110 I8 Liechtenstein off. Principality of Liechtenstein. ◆ principality C Europe
101 F18 Liedekerke Vlaams Brabant, C Belgium
101 K19 Liège Dut. Luik, Ger. Lüttich. Liège, E Belgium
101 K20 Liège Dut. Luik. ◆ province E Belgium
Liegnitz see Legnica
95 O16 Lieksa Pohjois-Karjala, E Finland
120 F10 Lielupe ∻ Latvia/Lithuania
120 G9 Lielvārde Ogre, C Latvia
178 Kk14 Liên Hương var. Tuy Phong. Binh Thuận, S Vietnam
Liên Nghia see Đưc Trong
111 P9 Lienz Tirol, W Austria
120 B10 Liepāja Ger. Libau. Liepāja, W Latvia
101 H17 Lier Fr. Lierre. Antwerpen, N Belgium
97 H15 Lierbyen Buskerud, S Norway
101 L21 Lierneux Liège, E Belgium
Lierre see Lier
103 D18 Lieser ∻ W Germany
111 U7 Liesing ∻ E Austria
110 E6 Liestal Basel-Land, N Switzerland
Lietuva see Lithuania
Lievenhof see Līvāni
105 O2 Liévin Pas-de-Calais, N France
12 M9 Lièvre, Rivière du ∻ Québec, SE Canada
111 T6 Liezen Steiermark, C Austria
99 E14 Lifford Ir. Leifear. NW Ireland
197 K5 Lifou island Îles Loyauté, E New Caledonia
200 Ss13 Lifuka island Ha'apai Group, C Tonga
179 Q11 Ligao Luzon, N Philippines
Liger see Loire
44 H2 Lighthouse Reef reef E Belize
191 Q4 Lightning Ridge New South Wales, SE Australia
105 N9 Lignières Cher, C France
105 S5 Ligny-en-Barrois Meuse, NE France
85 P15 Ligonha ∻ NE Mozambique
33 P11 Ligonier Indiana, N USA
83 I25 Ligunga Ruvuma, S Tanzania
108 D9 Ligure, Appennino Eng. Ligurian Mountains. ▲ NW Italy
Ligure, Mar see Ligurian Sea
108 C9 Liguria ◆ region NW Italy
Ligurian Mountains see Ligure, Appennino
123 K6 Ligurian Sea Fr. Mer Ligurienne, It. Mar Ligure. sea N Mediterranean Sea
Ligurienne, Mer see Ligurian Sea
195 P9 Lihir Group island group NE PNG
195 P9 Lihir Island island Lihir Group, N PNG
40 B8 Lihue Haw. Lihu'e. Kauai, Hawaii, USA, C Pacific Ocean
120 F5 Lihula Ger. Leal. Läänemaa, W Estonia
128 I2 Liinakhamari var. Linacmamari. Murmanskaya Oblast', NW Russian Federation
Liivi Laht see Riga, Gulf of
166 F11 Lijiang var. Dayan, Lijiang Naxizu Zizhixian. Yunnan, SW China
114 C11 Lika-Senj off. Ličko-Senjska Županija. ◆ province W Croatia
81 N25 Likasi prev. Jadotville. Shaba, SE Zaire
81 L16 Likati Haut-Zaïre, N Zaire
8 M15 Likely British Columbia, SW Canada
159 Y11 Likhapāni Assam, NE India
128 J16 Likhoslavl' Tverskaya Oblast', W Russian Federation
201 U5 Likiep Atoll atoll Ratak Chain, C Marshall Islands
97 D18 Liknes Vest-Agder, S Norway
81 H18 Likouala ∻ N Congo
81 H18 Likouala aux Herbes ∻ E Congo
202 B16 Liku E Niue
Likupang, Selat see Bangka, Selat
29 Y8 Lilbourn Missouri, C USA
104 E1 l'Île-Rousse Corse, France, C Mediterranean Sea
111 W5 Lilienfeld Niederösterreich, NE Austria
167 N11 Liling Hunan, S China
97 J18 Lilla Edet Älvsborg, S Sweden
105 P1 Lille var. l'Isle, Dut. Rijssel, Flem. Ryssel; prev. Lisle, anc. Insula. Nord, N France
97 G24 Lillebælt var. Lille Bælt, Eng. Little Belt. strait S Denmark
104 L3 Lillebonne Seine-Maritime, N France
96 H12 Lillehammer Oppland, S Norway
105 O1 Lillers Pas-de-Calais, N France
97 F18 Lillesand Aust-Agder, S Norway
97 I15 Lillestrøm Akershus, S Norway
95 F18 Lillhärdal Jämtland, C Sweden
23 U10 Lillington North Carolina, SE USA
107 O9 Lillo Castilla-La Mancha, C Spain
8 M16 Lillooet British Columbia, SW Canada
85 M14 Lilongwe ● (Malawi) Central, W Malawi
85 M14 Lilongwe ✕ Central, W Malawi
85 M14 Lilongwe ∻ W Malawi
179 Q15 Liloy Mindanao, S Philippines
Lilybaeum see Marsala
190 J7 Lilydale South Australia
191 P16 Lilydale Tasmania, SE Australia
115 J14 Lim ∻ Bosnia and Herzegovina/Yugoslavia
59 D15 Lima ● (Peru) Lima, W Peru
96 K13 Lima Kopparberg, C Sweden
33 R12 Lima Ohio, NE USA
59 D14 Lima ◆ department W Peru
Lima see Jorge Chávez International
106 G5 Lima ∻ N Portugal
Lima see Limia
113 L17 Limanowa Nowy Sącz, S Poland
174 I8 Limas Pulau Sebangka, W Indonesia
Limassol see Lemesós
99 F14 Limavady Ir. Léim an Mhadaidh. NW Northern Ireland, UK
65 J14 Limay Mahuida La Pampa, C Argentina
65 H15 Limay, Río ∻ W Argentina
103 N16 Limbach-Oberfrohna Sachsen, E Germany
83 F22 Limba Limba ∻ C Tanzania
109 C17 Limbara, Monte ▲ Sardegna, Italy, C Mediterranean Sea
120 G7 Limbaži Est. Lemsalu. Limbaži, N Latvia
46 M8 Limbé N Haiti
175 Qq7 Limboto, Danau ⊚ Sulawesi, N Indonesia
101 L19 Limbourg Liège, E Belgium
101 K17 Limburg ◆ province NE Belgium
101 L16 Limburg ◆ province SE Netherlands
103 F17 Limburg an der Lahn Hessen, W Germany
96 K13 Limedsforsen Kopparberg, C Sweden
62 L9 Limeira São Paulo, S Brazil
99 C19 Limerick Ir. Luimneach. SW Ireland
99 C20 Limerick Ir. Luimneach. cultural region SW Ireland
21 S2 Limestone Maine, NE USA
27 U9 Limestone, Lake ⊚ Texas, SW USA
41 P12 Lime Village Alaska, USA
97 F20 Limfjorden fjord N Denmark
97 J23 Limhamn Malmöhus, S Sweden
106 H5 Limia Port. Lima. ∻ NW Spain
95 L14 Liminka Oulu, C Finland
Limín Vathéos see Sámos
117 G17 Límni Évvoia, C Greece
117 J15 Límnos anc. Lemnos. island E Greece
104 M11 Limoges anc. Augustoritum Lemovicensium, Lemovices. Haute-Vienne, C France
39 U5 Limon Colorado, C USA
45 O13 Limón var. Puerto Limón. Limón, E Costa Rica
44 K4 Limón Colón, NE Honduras
45 N13 Limón off. Provincia de Limón. ◆ province E Costa Rica
108 A10 Limone Piemonte Piemonte, NE Italy
Limones see Valdéz
Limonum see Poitiers
105 N11 Limousin ◆ region C France
105 N16 Limoux Aude, S France
85 L19 Limpopo var. Crocodile. ∻ S Africa
166 K17 Limu Ling ▲ S China
115 M20 Lin var. Lini. Elbasan, E Albania
Linacmamari see Liinakhamari
179 P13 Linapacan Island island W Philippines
64 G13 Linares Maule, C Chile
56 C13 Linares Nariño, SW Colombia
43 O9 Linares Nuevo León, NE Mexico
107 N12 Linares Andalucía, S Spain
109 G15 Linaro, Capo headland C Italy
108 D8 Linate ✕ (Milano) Lombardia, N Italy
166 F13 Lincang Yunnan, SW China
167 P11 Linchuan var. Fuzhou. Jiangxi, S China
63 B20 Lincoln Buenos Aires, E Argentina
193 H19 Lincoln Canterbury, South Island, NZ
99 N18 Lincoln anc. Lindum, Lindum Colonia. E England, UK
37 O6 Lincoln California, W USA
32 L13 Lincoln Illinois, N USA
28 M4 Lincoln Kansas, C USA
21 S5 Lincoln Maine, NE USA
29 T5 Lincoln Missouri, C USA
31 R16 Lincoln state capital Nebraska, C USA
34 F11 Lincoln City Oregon, NW USA
178 M10 Lincoln Island island E Paracel Islands
207 Q11 Lincoln Sea sea Arctic Ocean
99 N18 Lincolnshire cultural region E England, UK
23 R10 Lincolnton North Carolina, SE USA
27 V7 Lindale Texas, SW USA
103 I25 Lindau var. Lindau am Bodensee. Bayern, S Germany
Lindau am Bodensee see Lindau
126 L9 Linde ∻ NE Russian Federation
57 T9 Linden E Guyana
25 O6 Linden Alabama, S USA
22 H9 Linden Tennessee, S USA
27 X6 Linden Texas, SW USA
20 J16 Lindenwold New Jersey, NE USA
97 M15 Lindesberg Örebro, C Sweden
97 D18 Lindesnes headland S Norway
Líndhos see Líndos
83 K24 Lindi Lindi, SE Tanzania
83 J24 Lindi ◆ region SE Tanzania
81 N17 Lindi ∻ NE Zaire
169 V7 Lindian Heilongjiang, NE China
193 E21 Lindis Pass pass South Island, NZ
85 J22 Lindley Free State, C South Africa
97 J19 Lindome Göteborg och Bohus, S Sweden
Lindong see Bairin Zuoqi
117 O23 Líndos var. Líndhos. Ródos, Dodekánisos, Greece, Aegean Sea
12 I14 Lindsay Ontario, SE Canada
37 R11 Lindsay California, W USA
35 X8 Lindsay Montana, NW USA
29 N11 Lindsay Oklahoma, C USA
29 N5 Lindsborg Kansas, C USA
97 N21 Lindsdal Kalmar, S Sweden
175 Pp9 Lindu, Danau ⊚ Sulawesi, N Indonesia
Lindum/Lindum Colonia see Lincoln
203 W3 Line Islands island group E Kiribati
Linëvo see Linova
166 M5 Linfen var. Lin-fen. Shanxi, C China
161 F18 Linganamakki Reservoir ⊠ SW India
166 L17 Lingao Hainan, S China
179 Oo9 Lingayen Luzon, N Philippines
179 Oo9 Lingayen Gulf gulf Luzon, N Philippines
166 M6 Lingbao var. Guolüezhen. Henan, C China
96 N12 Lingbo Gävleborg, C Sweden
Lingeh see Bandar-e Langeh
102 E12 Lingen var. Lingen an der Ems. Niedersachsen, NW Germany
Lingen an der Ems see Lingen
174 Ii8 Lingga, Kepulauan island group W Indonesia
174 I8 Lingga, Pulau island Kepulauan Lingga, W Indonesia
12 J14 Lingham Lake ⊚ Ontario, SE Canada
96 M13 Linghed Kopparberg, C Sweden
35 Z15 Lingle Wyoming, C USA
20 G15 Linglestown Pennsylvania, NE USA
81 K18 Lingomo II Equateur, NW Zaire
166 L15 Lingshan Guangxi Zhuangzu Zizhiqu, S China
166 L17 Lingshui Hainan, S China
161 G16 Lingsugūr Karnātaka, C India
109 L23 Linguaglossa Sicilia, Italy, C Mediterranean Sea
78 H10 Linguère N Senegal
165 W8 Lingwu Ningxia, N China
Lingxi see Yongshun
167 O12 Lingxian var. Ling Xian. Hunan, S China
169 S12 Lingyuan Liaoning, NE China
169 U4 Linhai Heilongjiang, NE China
167 S10 Linhai var. Taizhou. Zhejiang, SE China
61 O20 Linhares Espírito Santo, SE Brazil
168 M13 Linhe Nei Mongol Zizhiqu, N China
Lini see Lin
145 S1 Līnik, Chiyā-ē ▲ N Iraq
97 M18 Linköping Östergötland, S Sweden
169 Y8 Linkou Heilongjiang, NE China
120 F11 Linkuva Pakruojis, N Lithuania
29 V5 Linn Missouri, C USA
27 S16 Linn Texas, SW USA
29 T2 Linneus Missouri, C USA
98 H10 Linnhe, Loch inlet W Scotland, UK
121 G19 Linova Rus. Linëvo. Brestskaya Voblasts', SW Belarus
167 O5 Linqing Shandong, E China
167 N6 Linruzhen Henan, C China
62 K8 Lins São Paulo, S Brazil
95 F17 Linsell Jämtland, C Sweden
166 J9 Linshui Sichuan, C China
46 K12 Linstead C Jamaica
165 U11 Lintan Gansu, N China
165 V11 Lintao Gansu, C China
13 S12 Lintère ∻ Québec, SE Canada
110 H8 Linth ∻ NW Switzerland
110 H8 Linthal Glarus, NE Switzerland
33 N15 Linton Indiana, N USA
31 N6 Linton North Dakota, N USA
169 R11 Linxi Nei Mongol Zizhiqu, N China
165 U11 Linxia var. Linxia Huizu Zizhizhou. Gansu, C China
Linxia Huizu Zizhizhou see Linxia
Linxian see Lianzhou
167 Q6 Linyi Shandong, S China
167 P4 Linyi Shandong, E China
166 M6 Linyi Shanxi, C China
111 T4 Linz anc. Lentia. Oberösterreich, N Austria
165 S8 Linze var. Shahepu. Gansu, N China
46 J13 Lionel Town C Jamaica
105 Q16 Lion, Golfe du Eng. Gulf of Lion, Gulf of Lions; anc. Sinus Gallicus. gulf S France
Lion, Gulf of/Lions, Gulf of see Lion, Golfe du
85 K16 Lions Den Mashonaland West, N Zimbabwe
12 F13 Lion's Head Ontario, S Canada
Lios Ceannúir, Bá see Liscannor Bay
Lios Mór see Lismore
Lios na gCearrbhach see Lisburn
Lios Tuathail see Listowel
81 G17 Liouesso La Sangha, N Congo
Liozno see Lyozna
179 P11 Lipa off. Lipa City. Luzon, N Philippines
27 S7 Lipan Texas, SW USA
Lipari Islands/Lipari, Isole see Eolie, Isole
109 L22 Lipari, Isola island Isole Eolie, S Italy
118 L8 Lipcani Rus. Lipkany. N Moldova
95 N17 Liperi Pohjois-Karjala, SE Finland
130 L7 Lipetsk Lipetskaya Oblast', W Russian Federation
130 K6 Lipetskaya Oblast' ◆ province W Russian Federation
59 K22 Lipez, Cordillera de ▲ SW Bolivia
112 E10 Lipiany Ger. Lippehne. Szczecin, W Poland
114 G9 Lipik Požega-Slavonija, NE Croatia
128 L12 Lipin Bor Vologodskaya Oblast', NW Russian Federation
166 L12 Liping Guizhou, S China
Lipkany see Lipcani
121 H15 Lipnishki Rus. Lipnishki. Hrodzyenskaya Voblasts', W Belarus
112 J10 Lipno Włocławek, C Poland
118 F11 Lipova Hung. Lippa. Arad, W Romania
Lipovets see Lypovets'
Lippa see Lipova
103 E14 Lippe ∻ W Germany
Lippehne see Lipiany
103 G14 Lippstadt Nordrhein-Westfalen, W Germany
27 P1 Lipscomb Texas, SW USA
Lipsia/Lipsk see Leipzig
112 P7 Lipsk Suwałki, NE Poland
Liptau-Sankt-Nikolaus/Liptószentmiklós see Liptovský Mikuláš
113 K19 Liptovský Mikuláš Ger. Liptau-Sankt-Nikolaus, Hung. Liptószentmiklós. Stredné Slovensko, N Slovakia
191 O13 Liptrap, Cape headland Victoria, SE Australia
166 L13 Lipu Guangxi Zhuangzu Zizhiqu, S China
147 X12 Liqbi S Oman
83 G17 Lira N Uganda
59 F15 Lircay Huancavelica, C Peru
109 J15 Liri ∻ C Italy
150 M8 Lisakovsk Kustanay, N Kazakhstan
81 K17 Lisala Equateur, N Zaire
106 F11 Lisboa Eng. Lisbon; anc. Felicitas Julia, Olisipo. ● (Portugal) Lisboa, W Portugal
106 F10 Lisboa ◆ Eng. Lisbon. district C Portugal
21 N7 Lisbon New Hampshire, NE USA
31 Q6 Lisbon North Dakota, N USA
Lisbon see Lisboa
21 Q8 Lisbon Falls Maine, NE USA
99 G15 Lisburn Ir. Lios na gCearrbhach. E Northern Ireland, UK
40 L6 Lisburne, Cape headland Alaska, USA
99 B19 Liscannor Bay Ir. Bá Lios Ceannúir. inlet W Ireland
115 Q18 Lisec ▲ E FYR Macedonia
166 F13 Lishe Jiang ∻ SW China
166 M4 Lishi Shanxi, C China
169 V10 Lishu Jilin, NE China
167 R10 Lishui Zhejiang, SE China
199 Jj5 Lisianski Island island Hawaiian Islands, Hawaii, USA, C Pacific Ocean
Lisichansk see Lysychans'k
104 L4 Lisieux anc. Noviomagus. Calvados, N France
130 L8 Liski prev. Georgiu-Dezh. Voronezhskaya Oblast', W Russian Federation
Lisle/l'Isle see Lille
105 N4 l'Isle-Adam Val-d'Oise, N France
105 R15 l'Isle-sur-la-Sorgue Vaucluse, SE France
13 S9 L'Islet Québec, SE Canada
190 M12 Lismore Victoria, SE Australia
99 D20 Lismore Ir. Lios Mór. S Ireland
Lissa see Vis, Croatia
Lissa see Leszno, Poland
100 H11 Lisse Zuid-Holland, W Netherlands
97 D18 Lista peninsula S Norway
97 D18 Listafjorden fjord S Norway
205 R13 Lister, Mount ▲ Antarctica
130 M8 Listopadovka Voronezhskaya Oblast', W Russian Federation
12 F15 Listowel Ontario, S Canada
99 B20 Listowel Ir. Lios Tuathail. SW Ireland
166 L14 Litang Guangxi Zhuangzu Zizhiqu, S China
166 F9 Litang Sichuan, C China
166 F10 Litang Qu ∻ C China
57 X12 Litani var. Itany. ∻ French Guiana/Suriname
144 G8 Lītani, Nahr el var. Nahr al Litant. ∻ C Lebanon
Litant, Nahr al see Lītani, Nahr el
Litauen see Lithuania
32 K14 Litchfield Illinois, N USA
31 U8 Litchfield Minnesota, N USA
38 K13 Litchfield Park Arizona, SW USA
191 S8 Lithgow New South Wales, SE Australia
117 I26 Líthino, Ákra headland Kríti, Greece, E Mediterranean Sea
120 D12 Lithuania off. Republic of Lithuania, Ger. Litauen, Lith. Lietuva, Pol. Litwa, Rus. Litva; prev. Lithuanian SSR, Rus. Litovskaya SSR. ◆ republic NE Europe
Lithuanian SSR see Lithuania
111 U11 Litija Ger. Littai. C Slovenia
20 H15 Lititz Pennsylvania, NE USA
117 F15 Litóchoro var. Litohoro, Litókhoron. Kentrikí Makedonía, N Greece
Litohoro/Litókhoron see Litóchoro
113 C15 Litoměřice Ger. Leitmeritz. Severní Čechy, N Czech Republic
113 F17 Litomyšl Ger. Leitomischl. Východní Čechy, NE Czech Republic
113 G17 Litovel Ger. Littau. Severní Morava, E Czech Republic
127 Nn15 Litovko Khabarovskiy Kray, SE Russian Federation
Litovskaya SSR see Lithuania
Littai see Litija
Littau see Litovel
46 G1 Little Abaco var. Abaco Island. island N Bahamas
113 I21 Little Alföld Ger. Kleines Ungarisches Tiefland, Hung. Kisalföld, Slvk. Podunajská Rovina. plain Hungary/Slovakia
157 Q20 Little Andaman island Andaman Islands, India, NE Indian Ocean
28 M5 Little Arkansas River ∻ Kansas, C USA
192 L4 Little Barrier Island island N NZ
Little Belt see Lillebælt
40 M11 Little Black River ∻ Alaska, USA
29 O2 Little Blue River ∻ Kansas/Nebraska, C USA
46 D8 Little Cayman island E Cayman Islands
9 X11 Little Churchill ∻ Manitoba, C Canada
177 Ee10 Little Coco Island island SW Myanmar
38 L10 Little Colorado River ∻ Arizona, SW USA
12 E11 Little Current Manitoulin Island, Ontario, S Canada
10 E11 Little Current ∻ Ontario, S Canada
40 L8 Little Diomede Island island Alaska, USA
46 J4 Little Exuma island C Bahamas
31 U7 Little Falls Minnesota, N USA
20 J10 Little Falls New York, NE USA
26 M5 Littlefield Texas, SW USA
31 V3 Littlefork Minnesota, N USA
31 V3 Little Fork River ∻ Minnesota, N USA
9 N16 Little Fort British Columbia, SW Canada
9 Y14 Little Grand Rapids Manitoba, C Canada
99 N23 Littlehampton SE England, UK
37 T2 Little Humboldt River ∻ Nevada, W USA
46 K6 Little Inagua var. Inagua Islands. island S Bahamas
23 Q4 Little Kanawha River ∻ West Virginia, NE USA
85 F25 Little Karoo plateau S South Africa
41 O16 Little Koniuji Island island Shumagin Islands, Alaska, USA
46 H12 Little London W Jamaica
11 R10 Little Mecatina Fr. Rivière du Petit Mécatina. ∻ Newfoundland and Labrador/Québec, E Canada
98 F8 Little Minch, The strait NW Scotland, UK
29 T13 Little Missouri River ∻ Arkansas, USA
30 J7 Little Missouri River ∻ NW USA
30 J3 Little Muddy River ∻ North Dakota, N USA
157 Q22 Little Nicobar island Nicobar Islands, India, NE Indian Ocean
29 R6 Little Osage River ∻ Missouri, C USA
99 P20 Little Ouse ∻ E England, UK
155 V2 Little Pamir Pash. Pāmīr-e Khord, Rus. Malyy Pamir. ▲ Afghanistan/Tajikistan
23 U12 Little Pee Dee River ∻ North Carolina/South Carolina, SE USA
29 V10 Little Red River ∻ Arkansas, C USA
Little Rhody see Rhode Island
193 I19 Little River Canterbury, South Island, NZ
23 U12 Little River South Carolina, SE USA
29 Y9 Little River ∻ Arkansas/Missouri, C USA
29 R13 Little River ∻ Arkansas/Oklahoma, USA
25 T7 Little River ∻ Georgia, SE USA
24 H6 Little River ∻ Louisiana, S USA
27 T10 Little River ∻ Texas, SW USA
29 V12 Little Rock state capital Arkansas, C USA
33 N8 Little Sable Point headland Michigan, N USA
105 U11 Little Saint Bernard Pass Fr. Col du Petit St-Bernard, It. Colle di Piccolo San Bernardo. pass France/Italy
38 K7 Little Salt Lake ⊚ Utah, W USA
188 K8 Little Sandy Desert desert Western Australia
31 S13 Little Sioux River ∻ Iowa, C USA
40 E17 Little Sitkin Island island Aleutian Islands, Alaska, USA
9 O13 Little Smoky Alberta, W Canada
9 O14 Little Smoky ∻ Alberta, W Canada
39 P3 Little Snake River ∻ Colorado, C USA
66 A12 Little Sound bay Bermuda, NW Atlantic Ocean
39 T4 Littleton Colorado, C USA
21 N7 Littleton New Hampshire, NE USA
20 D11 Little Valley New York, NE USA
32 M15 Little Wabash River ∻ Illinois, N USA
12 D10 Little White River ∻ Ontario, S Canada
30 M12 Little White River ∻ South Dakota, N USA
27 R5 Little Wichita River ∻ Texas, SW USA
148 I4 Little Zab Ar. Nahraz Zāb aş Şaghīr, Kurd. Zē-i Kōya, Per. Rūdkhāneh-ye Zāb-e Kūchek. ∻ Iran/Iraq
81 D15 Littoral ◆ province W Cameroon
Littoria see Latina
Litva/Litwa see Lithuania
113 B15 Litvínov Ger. Leutensdorf. Severní Čechy, NW Czech Republic
118 M6 Lityn Vinnyts'ka Oblast', C Ukraine
Liu-chou/Liuchow see Liuzhou
169 W11 Liuhe Jilin, NE China
Liukang Tenggaya, Kepulauan see Sabalana, Kepulauan
85 Q15 Liúpo Nampula, NE Mozambique
85 G14 Liuwa Plain plain W Zambia
166 L13 Liuzhou var. Liu-chou, Liuchow. Guangxi Zhuangzu Zizhiqu, S China
118 H8 Livada Hung. Sárköz. Satu Mare, NW Romania
117 J20 Liváda, Ákra headland Tínos, Kykládes, Greece, Aegean Sea
117 L21 Livádi island Kykládes, Greece, Aegean Sea
Livanátai see Livanátes
117 G18 Livanátes prev. Livanátai. Stereá Ellás, C Greece
120 I10 Līvāni Ger. Lievenhof. Preiļi, SE Latvia
67 E25 Lively Island island SE Falkland Islands
67 D25 Lively Sound sound SE Falkland Islands
41 R8 Livengood Alaska, USA
108 I7 Livenza ∻ NE Italy
37 O6 Live Oak California, W USA
25 U9 Live Oak Florida, SE USA
37 O9 Livermore California, W USA
22 I6 Livermore Kentucky, S USA
21 Q7 Livermore Falls Maine, NE USA
26 J10 Livermore, Mount ▲ Texas, SW USA
11 P16 Liverpool Nova Scotia, SE Canada
99 K17 Liverpool NW England, UK
191 S7 Liverpool Range ▲ New South Wales, SE Australia
98 J12 Livingston C Scotland, UK
25 N5 Livingston Alabama, S USA
37 P9 Livingston California, W USA
24 J8 Livingston Louisiana, S USA
35 S11 Livingston Montana, NW USA
22 L8 Livingston Tennessee, S USA
27 W9 Livingston Texas, SW USA
44 F4 Livingston Izabal, E Guatemala
85 I16 Livingstone var. Maramba. Southern, S Zambia
193 B22 Livingstone Mountains ▲ South Island, NZ
82 K13 Livingstone Mountains ▲ S Tanzania
84 N12 Livingstonia Northern, N Malawi
204 G4 Livingston Island island Antarctica
27 W9 Livingston, Lake ⊠ Texas, SW USA
114 F13 Livno SW Bosnia and Herzegovina
130 K7 Livny Orlovskaya Oblast', W Russian Federation
95 M14 Livojoki ∻ C Finland
33 R10 Livonia Michigan, N USA
108 E11 Livorno Eng. Leghorn. Toscana, C Italy
Livramento see Santana do Livramento
147 U8 Līwā var. Al Liwā'. oasis region S UAE
83 I24 Liwale Lindi, SE Tanzania
165 W9 Liwangbu Ningxia, N China
85 N15 Liwonde Southern, S Malawi
165 V11 Li Xian Gansu, C China
166 H8 Lixian var. Li Xian; prev. Zagunao. Sichuan, C China
Lixian Jiang see Black River
117 B18 Lixoúri prev. Lixoúrion. Kefallinía, Iónioi Nísoi, Greece, C Mediterranean Sea
Lixoúrion see Lixoúri
Lixus see Larache
35 U15 Lizard Head Peak ▲ Wyoming, C USA
99 H25 Lizard Point headland SW England, UK
114 L12 Ljig Serbia, C Yugoslavia
Ljouwert see Leeuwarden
Ljubelj see Loibl Pass
111 U11 Ljubljana Ger. Laibach, It. Lubiana; anc. Aemona, Emona. ● (Slovenia) C Slovenia
111 T11 Ljubljana ✕ C Slovenia
115 N17 Ljuboten ▲ S Yugoslavia
97 P19 Ljugarn Gotland, SE Sweden
86 G7 Ljungan ∻ N Sweden
95 F17 Ljungan ∻ C Sweden
97 K21 Ljungby Kronoberg, S Sweden
97 M17 Ljungsbro Östergötland, S Sweden
97 I18 Ljungskile Göteborg och Bohus, S Sweden
96 M11 Ljusdal Gävleborg, C Sweden
96 M11 Ljusnan ∻ C Sweden
96 N12 Ljusne Gävleborg, C Sweden
97 P15 Ljusterö Stockholm, C Sweden
111 X9 Ljutomer Ger. Luttenberg. NE Slovenia
65 G15 Llaima, Volcán ▲ S Chile
107 X4 Llançà var. Llansá. Cataluña, NE Spain
99 J21 Llandovery C Wales, UK
99 J20 Llandrindod Wells E Wales, UK
99 J18 Llandudno N Wales, UK
99 I21 Llanelli prev. Llanelly. SW Wales, UK
Llanelly see Llanelli
106 M2 Llanes Asturias, N Spain
99 K19 Llangollen NE Wales, UK
27 R10 Llano Texas, SW USA
27 Q10 Llano River ∻ Texas, SW USA
56 I9 Llanos physical region Colombia/Venezuela
65 G16 Llanquihue, Lago ⊚ S Chile
Llansá see Llançà
107 U5 Lleida Cast. Lérida; anc. Ilerda. Cataluña, NE Spain
Llera de Canales see Llera
106 K12 Llerena Extremadura, W Spain
107 S9 Llíria País Valenciano, E Spain
107 W4 Llivia Cataluña, NE Spain
107 O3 Llodio País Vasco, N Spain
107 X5 Lloret de Mar Cataluña, NE Spain
Llorri see Tossal de l'Orri
8 L11 Lloyd George, Mount ▲ British Columbia, W Canada
9 R14 Lloydminster Alberta/Saskatchewan, SW Canada
Lluchmayor see Llucmajor
38 L6 Loa Utah, W USA
174 Mm4 Loagan Bunut ⊚ East Malaysia
178 Mm14 Loaita Island island W Spratly Islands
40 G12 Loa, Mauna ▲ Hawaii, USA, C Pacific Ocean
Loanda see Luanda
81 J22 Loange ∻ S Zaire
81 E21 Loango Le Kouilou, S Congo
108 B10 Loano Liguria, NW Italy
64 H4 Loa, Río ∻ N Chile
85 I20 Lobatse var. Lobatsi. Kgatleng, SE Botswana
Lobatsi see Lobatse
103 Q15 Löbau Sachsen, E Germany
81 H16 Lobaye ◆ prefecture SW Central African Republic
81 I16 Lobaye ∻ SW Central African Republic
101 G21 Lobbes Hainaut, S Belgium
63 D23 Lobería Buenos Aires, E Argentina
112 F8 Lobez Ger. Labes. Szczecin, NW Poland
84 A13 Lobito Benguela, W Angola
Lobkovichi see Lakhavichy
Lob Nor see Lop Nur

◆ Country
● Country Capital
◇ Dependent Territory
○ Dependent Territory Capital
◆ Administrative Region
✕ International Airport
▲ Mountain
▲ Mountain Range
Volcano
∻ River
⊚ Lake
⊠ Reservoir

176 W11 Lobo Irian Jaya, E Indonesia
106 J11 Lobón Extremadura, W Spain
63 D20 Lobos Buenos Aires, E Argentina
42 E4 Lobos, Cabo headland NW Mexico
42 F6 Lobos, Isla island NW Mexico
Lobositz see Lovosice
Lobsens see Łobżenica
Loburi see Lop Buri
112 H9 Łobżenica Ger. Lobsens. Koszalin, W Poland
110 G11 Locarno Ger. Luggarus. Ticino, S Switzerland
98 E9 Lochboisdale NW Scotland, UK
100 N11 Lochem Gelderland, E Netherlands
104 M8 Loches Indre-et-Loire, C France
Loch Garman see Wexford
98 H12 Lochgilphead W Scotland, UK
98 H7 Lochinver N Scotland, UK
98 F8 Lochmaddy NW Scotland, UK
98 J10 Lochnagar ▲ C Scotland, UK
101 E17 Lochristi Oost-Vlaanderen, NW Belgium
98 H9 Lochy, Loch ⊚ N Scotland, UK
190 G8 Lock South Australia
99 J14 Lockerbie S Scotland, UK
29 S13 Lockesburg Arkansas, C USA
191 P10 Lockhart New South Wales, SE Australia
27 S11 Lockhart Texas, SW USA
20 F13 Lock Haven Pennsylvania, NE USA
27 N4 Lockney Texas, SW USA
102 O12 Löcknitz ↝ NE Germany
20 E9 Lockport New York, NE USA
178 Jj13 Lôc Ninh Sông Be, S Vietnam
109 N23 Locri Calabria, SW Italy
Locse see Levoča
29 T2 Locust Creek ↝ Missouri, C USA
25 P3 Locust Fork ↝ Alabama, S USA
29 Q9 Locust Grove Oklahoma, C USA
96 E11 Lodalskåpa ▲ S Norway
191 N10 Loddon River ↝ Victoria, SE Australia
Lodensee see Klooga
105 P15 Lodève anc. Luteva. Hérault, S France
128 I12 Lodeynoye Pole Leningradskaya Oblast', NW Russian Federation
35 V11 Lodge Grass Montana, NW USA
30 J15 Lodgepole Creek ↝ Nebraska/Wyoming, C USA
155 T11 Lodhrān Punjab, E Pakistan
108 D8 Lodi Lombardia, NW Italy
37 O8 Lodi California, W USA
33 T12 Lodi Ohio, N USA
94 H10 Lødingen Nordland, C Norway
81 L20 Lodja Kasai Oriental, C Zaire
39 O3 Lodore, Canyon of canyon Colorado, C USA
107 Q4 Lodosa Navarra, N Spain
83 H16 Lodwar Rift Valley, NW Kenya
112 K13 Łódź Rus. Lodz. Łódź, C Poland
112 K13 Łódź off. Województwo Łódzkie, Rus. Lodz. ◆ province C Poland
Łódzkie, Województwo see Łódź
178 I8 Loei var. Loey, Muang Loei. Loei, C Thailand
100 I11 Loenen Utrecht, C Netherlands
178 J9 Loeng Nok Tha Yasothon, E Thailand
85 F24 Loeriesfontein Northern Cape, W South Africa
97 H20 Læsø island N Denmark
Loewoek see Luwuk
Loey see Loei
78 J16 Lofa ↝ N Liberia
111 P6 Lofer Salzburg, C Austria
94 F11 Lofoten var. Lofoten Islands. island group C Norway
Lofoten Islands see Lofoten
97 N18 Loftahammar Kalmar, S Sweden
131 O10 Log Volgogradskaya Oblast', SW Russian Federation
79 S12 Loga Dosso, SW Niger
31 S14 Logan Iowa, C USA
28 K3 Logan Kansas, C USA
33 T14 Logan Ohio, N USA
38 L1 Logan Utah, W USA
23 P6 Logan West Virginia, NE USA
37 Y10 Logandale Nevada, W USA
21 O11 Logan International ✕ (Boston) Massachusetts, NE USA
9 N16 Logan Lake British Columbia, SW Canada
25 Q4 Logan Martin Lake ▣ Alabama, S USA
8 G8 Logan, Mount ▲ Yukon Territory, W Canada
34 I7 Logan, Mount ▲ Washington, NW USA
35 P7 Logan Pass pass Montana, NW USA
33 O12 Logansport Indiana, N USA
24 F6 Logansport Louisiana, S USA
Logar see Lowgar
69 R11 Loge ↝ NW Angola
Logishin see Lahishyn
Log na Coille see Lugnaquillia Mountain
80 G11 Logone var. Lagone. ↝ Cameroon/Chad
80 G13 Logone-Occidental off. Préfecture du Logone-Occidental. ◆ prefecture SW Chad
80 H13 Logone Occidental ↝ SW Chad
80 G13 Logone-Oriental off. Préfecture du Logone-Oriental. ◆ prefecture SW Chad
80 H13 Logone Oriental ↝ SW Chad
Logone Oriental see Pendé
L'Ogooué-Ivindo see Ogooué-Ivindo
L'Ogooué-Lolo see Ogooué-Lolo
L'Ogooué-Maritime see Ogooué-Maritime
Logoysk see Lahoysk
107 P4 Logroño anc. Vareia, Lat. Juliobriga. La Rioja, N Spain
106 L10 Logrosán Extremadura, W Spain
97 G20 Løgstør Nordjylland, N Denmark
97 H22 Løgten Århus, C Denmark
97 F24 Løgumkloster Sønderjylland, SW Denmark
Lögurinn see Lagarfljót
197 B10 Loh island Torres Islands, N Vanuatu
159 P15 Lohārdaga Bihār, N India
158 H10 Lohāru Haryāna, N India
103 D15 Lohausen ✕ (Düsseldorf) Nordrhein-Westfalen, W Germany
201 O14 Lohd Pohnpei, E Micronesia
194 I14 Lohiki ↝ S PNG
94 L12 Lohiniva Lappi, N Finland
Lohiszyn see Lahishyn
95 L20 Lohja var. Lojo. Uusimaa, S Finland
175 O8 Lohjanan Borneo, C Indonesia
27 Q9 Lohn Texas, SW USA
102 G12 Lohne Niedersachsen, NW Germany
Lohr see Lohr am Main
103 I18 Lohr am Main var. Lohr. Bayern, C Germany
111 T10 Loibl Pass Ger. Loiblpass, Slvn. Ljubelj. pass Austria/Slovenia
178 G6 Loi-Kaw Kayah State, C Myanmar
95 K19 Loimaa Turku-Pori, SW Finland
105 O6 Loing ↝ C France
178 I6 Loi, Phou ▲ N Laos
104 L7 Loir ↝ C France
105 Q11 Loire ◆ department E France
104 M7 Loire var. Liger. ↝ C France
104 I7 Loire-Atlantique ◆ department NW France
105 O7 Loiret ◆ department C France
104 M8 Loir-et-Cher ◆ department C France
103 L24 Loisach ↝ SE Germany
58 B9 Loja Loja, S Ecuador
106 M14 Loja Andalucía, S Spain
58 B9 Loja ◆ province S Ecuador
Lojo see Lohja
118 J4 Lokachi Volyns'ka Oblast', NW Ukraine
81 M20 Lokandu Maniema, C Zaire
94 M11 Lokan Tekojärvi ⊚ NE Finland
143 Z11 Lökbatan Rus. Lokbatan. E Azerbaijan
101 F17 Lokeren Oost-Vlaanderen, NW Belgium
Lokhvitsa see Lokhvytsya
119 S4 Lokhvytsya Rus. Lokhvitsa. Poltavs'ka Oblast', NE Ukraine
83 H17 Lokichar Rift Valley, NW Kenya
83 G16 Lokichokio Rift Valley, NW Kenya
83 H16 Lokitaung Rift Valley, NW Kenya
94 M11 Lokka Lappi, N Finland
96 G8 Løkken Verk Sør-Trøndelag, S Norway
128 G16 Loknya Pskovskaya Oblast', W Russian Federation
79 V15 Loko Plateau, S Nigeria
79 U15 Lokoja Kogi, C Nigeria
83 H17 Lokori Rift Valley, W Kenya
79 R16 Lokossa S Benin
120 I3 Loksa Ger. Loxa. Harjumaa, NW Estonia
16 P3 Loks Land island Northwest Territories, NE Canada
82 C13 Lol ↝ S Sudan
78 K15 Lola Guinée-Forestière, SE Guinea
37 Q5 Lola, Mount ▲ California, W USA
83 H20 Loliondo Arusha, NE Tanzania
97 H25 Lolland prev. Laaland. island S Denmark
195 O11 Lolobau Island island E PNG
175 T6 Loloda Utara, Kepulauan island group E Indonesia
81 E16 Lolodorf Sud, SW Cameroon
116 G7 Lom prev. Lom-Palanka. Oblast Montana, NW Bulgaria
116 G7 Lom ↝ NW Bulgaria
81 M19 Lomami ↝ C Zaire
59 F17 Lomas Arequipa, SW Peru
65 I23 Lomas, Bahía bay S Chile
63 D20 Lomas de Zamora Buenos Aires, E Argentina
63 D20 Loma Verde Buenos Aires, E Argentina
188 K4 Lombadina Western Australia
108 E6 Lombardia Eng. Lombardy. ◆ region N Italy
Lombardy see Lombardia
104 M15 Lombez Gers, S France
175 R15 Lomblen, Pulau island Nusa Tenggara, S Indonesia
181 W7 Lombok Basin undersea feature E Indian Ocean
175 Nn16 Lombok, Pulau island Nusa Tenggara, C Indonesia
175 Nn16 Lombok, Selat strait S Indonesia
79 Q16 Lomé ● (Togo) S Togo
79 Q16 Lomé ✕ S Togo
81 L19 Lomela Kasai Oriental, C Zaire
27 R9 Lometa Texas, SW USA
81 F16 Lomié Est, SE Cameroon
32 M8 Lomira Wisconsin, N USA
97 K23 Lomma Malmöhus, S Sweden
101 J16 Lommel Limburg, N Belgium
98 I11 Lomond, Loch ⊚ C Scotland, UK
207 R9 Lomonosov Ridge var. Harris Ridge, Rus. Khrebet Lomonsova. undersea feature Arctic Ocean
Lomonsova, Khrebet see Lomonosov Ridge
Lom-Palanka see Lom
Lomphat see Lumphăt
37 P14 Lompoc California, W USA
178 Hh9 Lom Sak var. Muang Lom Sak. Phetchabun, C Thailand
112 N9 Łomża Rus. Lomzha. Łomża, NE Poland
112 N9 Łomża off. Województwo Łomżyńskie, Rus. Lomzha. ◆ province NE Poland
Lomzha/Łomżyńskie, Województwo see Łomża
Lonaula see Lonāvale
161 D14 Lonāvale prev. Lonaula. Mahārāshtra, W India
65 G15 Loncoche Araucanía, C Chile
65 H14 Loncopue Neuquén, W Argentina
101 G17 Londerzeel Vlaams Brabant, C Belgium
Londinium see London
12 E16 London Ontario, S Canada
203 Y2 London Kiritimati, E Kiribati
99 O22 London anc. Augusta, Lat. Londinium. ● (UK) SE England, UK
23 N7 London Kentucky, S USA
33 S13 London Ohio, NE USA
27 Q10 London Texas, SW USA
99 O22 London City ✕ SE England, UK
99 E14 Londonderry var. Derry, Ir. Doire. NW Northern Ireland, UK
99 F14 Londonderry cultural region NW Northern Ireland, UK
188 M2 Londonderry, Cape headland Western Australia
65 H25 Londonderry, Isla island S Chile
45 O7 Londres, Cayos reef NE Nicaragua
62 I10 Londrina Paraná, S Brazil
29 N13 Lone Grove Oklahoma, C USA
12 E12 Lonely Island island Ontario, S Canada
37 T8 Lone Mountain ▲ Nevada, W USA
27 V6 Lone Oak Texas, SW USA
37 T11 Lone Pine California, W USA
Lone Star State see Texas
85 D14 Longa Cuando Cubango, C Angola
84 B12 Longa ↝ W Angola
85 E15 Longa ↝ SE Angola
169 W11 Longang Shan ⛰ NE China
207 S4 Longa, Proliv Eng. Long Strait. strait NE Russian Federation
46 J13 Long Bay bay W Jamaica
23 V13 Long Bay bay North Carolina/South Carolina, E USA
37 T16 Long Beach California, W USA
24 M9 Long Beach Mississippi, S USA
20 L14 Long Beach Long Island, New York, NE USA
34 F9 Long Beach Washington, NW USA
20 K16 Long Beach Island island New Jersey, NE USA
67 M25 Longbluff headland SW Tristan da Cunha
25 U13 Longboat Key island Florida, SE USA
20 K15 Long Branch New Jersey, NE USA
46 J5 Long Cay island SE Bahamas
167 P14 Longchuan prev. Laolong. Guangdong, S China
Longchuan Jiang see Shweli
34 K12 Long Creek Oregon, NW USA
165 W10 Longde Ningxia, N China
191 P16 Longford Tasmania, SE Australia
99 D17 Longford Ir. An Longfort. C Ireland
99 E17 Longford Ir. An Longfort. cultural region C Ireland
167 P1 Longhua Hebei, E China
175 Nn8 Longiram Borneo, C Indonesia
46 J4 Long Island island C Bahamas
10 H8 Long Island island Northwest Territories, C Canada
194 K11 Long Island var. Arop Island. island N PNG
20 L14 Long Island island New York, NE USA
Long Island see Bermuda
20 M14 Long Island Sound sound NE USA
166 K13 Long Jiang ↝ S China
169 U7 Longjiang Heilongjiang, NE China
169 Y10 Longjing var. Yanji. Jilin, NE China
167 R4 Longkou Shandong, E China
10 E11 Longlac Ontario, S Canada
21 S1 Long Lake ⊚ Maine, NE USA
33 O6 Long Lake ⊚ Michigan, N USA
33 R5 Long Lake ⊚ Michigan, N USA
31 N6 Long Lake ⊚ North Dakota, N USA
32 J4 Long Lake ▣ Wisconsin, N USA
101 K23 Longlier Luxembourg, SE Belgium
166 I13 Longlin var. Longlin Gezu Zizhixian. Guangxi Zhuangzu Zizhiqu, S China
39 T3 Longmont Colorado, C USA
31 N13 Long Pine Nebraska, C USA
Longping see Luodian
12 F17 Long Point headland Ontario, S Canada
12 K15 Long Point headland Ontario, SE Canada
192 P10 Long Point headland North Island, NZ
32 L2 Long Point headland Michigan, N USA
12 G17 Long Point Bay lake bay Ontario, S Canada
31 T7 Long Prairie Minnesota, N USA
11 S11 Long Range Mountains hill range Newfoundland, Newfoundland and Labrador, E Canada
67 H25 Long Range Point headland SE Saint Helena
189 V8 Longreach Queensland, E Australia
166 H7 Longriba Sichuan, C China
166 L10 Longshan Hunan, S China
39 S3 Longs Peak ▲ Colorado, C USA
Long Strait see Longa, Proliv
104 K8 Longué Maine-et-Loire, NW France
11 P11 Longue-Pointe Québec, E Canada
105 S4 Longuyon Meurthe-et-Moselle, NE France
27 W7 Longview Texas, SW USA
34 G10 Longview Washington, NW USA
67 H25 Longwood C Saint Helena
27 P7 Longworth Texas, SW USA
105 S3 Longwy Meurthe-et-Moselle, NE France
165 V11 Longxi Gansu, C China
178 J14 Long Xuyên var. Longxuyen. An Giang, S Vietnam
167 Q13 Longyan Fujian, SE China
94 O3 Longyearbyen ○ (Svalbard) Spitsbergen, W Svalbard
166 J15 Longzhou Guangxi Zhuangzu Zizhiqu, S China
102 F12 Löningen Niedersachsen, NW Germany
29 V11 Lonoke Arkansas, C USA
97 L21 Lönsboda Kristianstad, S Sweden
105 S9 Lons-le-Saunier anc. Ledo Salinarius. Jura, E France
33 O15 Loogootee Indiana, N USA
33 Q9 Looking Glass River ↝ Michigan, N USA
23 X11 Lookout, Cape headland North Carolina, SE USA
41 O6 Lookout Ridge ridge Alaska, USA
189 N11 Loongana Western Australia
101 I14 Loon op Zand Noord-Brabant, S Netherlands
99 A19 Loop Head Ir. Ceann Léime. headland W Ireland
111 V4 Loosdorf Niederösterreich, NE Austria
164 G10 Lop Xinjiang Uygur Zizhiqu, NW China
114 J11 Lopare NE Bosnia and Herzegovina
Lopatichi see Lapatsichy
131 Q15 Lopatin Respublika Dagestan, SW Russian Federation
131 P7 Lopatino Penzenskaya Oblast', W Russian Federation
178 Hh10 Lop Buri var. Loburi. Lop Buri, C Thailand
27 R16 Lopeno Texas, SW USA
Lopevi see Ulveah
81 C18 Lopez, Cap headland W Gabon
100 I12 Lopik Utrecht, C Netherlands
Lop Nor see Lop Nur
164 M7 Lop Nur var. Lob Nor, Lop Nor, Lo-pu Po. seasonal lake NW China
Lopnur see Yuli
81 K17 Lopori ↝ NW Zaire
100 O5 Loppersum Groningen, NE Netherlands
94 I8 Lopphavet sound N Norway
Lo-pu Po see Lop Nur
Lora see Lowrah
190 F3 Lora Creek seasonal river South Australia
106 K13 Lora del Río Andalucía, S Spain
154 M11 Lora, Hāmūn-i wetland SW Pakistan
33 T11 Lorain Ohio, N USA
27 O7 Loraine Texas, SW USA
33 R13 Loramie, Lake ⊚ Ohio, N USA
107 Q13 Lorca Ar. Lurka; anc. Eliocroca, Lat. Illur co. Murcia, S Spain
199 I12 Lord Howe Island island E Australia
Lord Howe Island see Ontong Java Atoll
183 O10 Lord Howe Rise undersea feature SW Pacific Ocean
199 I12 Lord Howe Seamounts undersea feature W Pacific Ocean
39 P15 Lordsburg New Mexico, SW USA
194 K8 Lorengau var. Lorungau. Manus Island, N PNG
27 N5 Lorenzo Texas, SW USA
148 K7 Lorestān off. Ostān-e Lorestān, var. Luristan. ◆ province W Iran
59 M17 Loreto Beni, N Bolivia
108 J12 Loreto Marche, C Italy
42 F8 Loreto Baja California Sur, W Mexico
42 M11 Loreto Zacatecas, C Mexico
58 E9 Loreto off. Departamento de Loreto. ◆ department NE Peru
83 K18 Lorian Swamp swamp E Kenya
56 E6 Lorica Córdoba, NW Colombia
104 G7 Lorient prev. l'Orient. Morbihan, NW France
113 K22 Lőrinci Heves, NE Hungary
12 G11 Loring Ontario, S Canada
35 V6 Loring Montana, NW USA
105 R13 Loriol-sur-Drôme Drôme, E France
23 U12 Loris South Carolina, SE USA
59 I18 Loriscota, Laguna ⊚ S Peru
191 N13 Lorne Victoria, SE Australia
98 G11 Lorn, Firth of inlet W Scotland, UK
Loro Sae see Timor Timur
103 F24 Lörrach Baden-Württemberg, S Germany
105 T5 Lorraine ◆ region NE France
Lorungau see Lorengau
96 L11 Los Gävleborg, C Sweden
37 P14 Los Alamos California, W USA
39 S10 Los Alamos New Mexico, SW USA
44 F5 Los Amates Izabal, E Guatemala
37 S15 Los Angeles California, W USA
37 S15 Los Angeles ✕ California, W USA
65 G14 Los Ángeles Bío Bío, C Chile
37 T13 Los Angeles Aqueduct aqueduct California, W USA
Losanna see Lausanne
65 H20 Los Antiguos Santa Cruz, SW Argentina
201 Q16 Losap Atoll atoll C Micronesia
37 P10 Los Banos California, W USA
106 K16 Los Barrios Andalucía, S Spain
64 L5 Los Blancos Salta, N Argentina
44 L12 Los Chiles Alajuela, NW Costa Rica
107 O2 Los Corrales de Buelna Cantabria, N Spain
27 T17 Los Fresnos Texas, SW USA
37 N9 Los Gatos California, W USA
112 O11 Łosice Biała Podlaska, E Poland
114 B11 Lošinj Ger. Lussin, It. Lussino. island W Croatia
Los Jardines see Ngetik Atoll
65 G15 Los Lagos Los Lagos, C Chile
65 F17 Los Lagos off. Región de los Lagos. ◆ region C Chile
Loslau see Wodzisław Śląski
66 N11 Los Llanos var. Los Llanos de Aridane. La Palma, Islas Canarias, Spain, NE Atlantic Ocean
Los Llanos de Aridane see Los Llanos
39 R11 Los Lunas New Mexico, SW USA
65 I16 Los Menucos Río Negro, C Argentina
42 H8 Los Mochis Sinaloa, C Mexico
37 N4 Los Molinos California, W USA
106 M9 Los Navalmorales Castilla-La Mancha, C Spain
27 S15 Los Olmos Creek ↝ Texas, SW USA
Losonc/Losontz see Lučenec
178 Jj5 Lô, Sông Chin. Panlong Jiang. ↝ China/Vietnam
46 B5 Los Palacios Pinar del Río, W Cuba
106 K14 Los Palacios y Villafranca Andalucía, S Spain
175 Ss16 Lospalos Timor, S Indonesia
39 R12 Los Pinos Mountains ⛰ New Mexico, SW USA
39 R11 Los Ranchos De Albuquerque New Mexico, SW USA
42 M14 Los Reyes Michoacán de Ocampo, SW Mexico
58 B7 Los Ríos ◆ province C Ecuador
66 O11 Los Rodeos ✕ (Santa Cruz de Ternerife) Tenerife, Islas Canarias, Spain, NE Atlantic Ocean
56 L4 Los Roques, Islas island group N Venezuela
45 S17 Los Santos Los Santos, S Panama
45 S17 Los Santos off. Provincia de Los Santos. ◆ province S Panama
Los Santos see Los Santos de Maimona
106 J12 Los Santos de Maimona var. Los Santos. Extremadura, W Spain
100 P10 Losser Overijssel, E Netherlands
98 J8 Lossiemouth NE Scotland, UK
63 B14 Los Tábanos Santa Fe, C Argentina
56 J4 Los Taques Falcón, N Venezuela
12 G11 Lost Channel Ontario, S Canada
56 L5 Los Teques Miranda, N Venezuela
37 Q12 Lost Hills California, W USA
38 I7 Lost Peak ▲ Utah, W USA
35 P11 Lost Trail Pass pass Montana, NW USA
195 N15 Losuia Kiriwina Island, SE PNG
64 G10 Los Vilos Coquimbo, C Chile
107 N10 Los Yébenes Castilla-La Mancha, C Spain
105 N13 Lot ◆ department S France
105 N13 Lot ↝ S France
65 F14 Lota Bío Bío, C Chile
83 G15 Lotagipi Swamp wetland Kenya/Sudan
104 K14 Lot-et-Garonne ◆ department SW France
85 K21 Lothair Mpumalanga, NE South Africa
35 R7 Lothair Montana, NW USA
81 L20 Loto Kasai Oriental, C Zaire
198 B8 Lotofagā Upolu, SE Western Samoa
110 E10 Lötschbergtunnel tunnel Valais, SW Switzerland
27 T9 Lott Texas, SW USA
128 H3 Lotta var. Lutto. ↝ Finland/Russian Federation
192 Q7 Lottin Point headland North Island, NZ
Lötzen see Giżycko
Loualaba see Lualaba
178 I6 Louangnamtha var. Luong Nam Tha. Louang Namtha, N Laos
178 I7 Louangphabang var. Louangphrabang, Luang Prabang. Louangphabang, N Laos
Louangphrabang see Louangphabang
204 H5 Loubet Coast physical region Antarctica
Loubomo see Dolisie
Louch see Loukhi
104 H6 Loudéac Côtes d'Armor, NW France
166 M11 Loudi Hunan, S China
81 F21 Loudima La Bouenza, S Congo
22 M9 Loudon Tennessee, S USA
33 T12 Loudonville Ohio, N USA
104 L8 Loudun Vienne, W France
104 K7 Loué Sarthe, NW France
78 G10 Louga NW Senegal
99 M19 Loughborough C England, UK
99 C18 Loughrea Ir. Baile Locha Riach. W Ireland
105 S9 Louhans Saône-et-Loire, C France
23 P5 Louisa Kentucky, S USA
23 V5 Louisa Virginia, NE USA
23 V9 Louisburg North Carolina, SE USA
27 U12 Louise Texas, SW USA
13 P11 Louiseville Québec, SE Canada
195 Q17 Louisiade Archipelago island group SE PNG
29 W3 Louisiana Missouri, C USA
24 G8 Louisiana off. State of Louisiana; also known as Creole State, Pelican State. ◆ state S USA
194 K9 Lou Island island N PNG
85 K19 Louis Trichardt Northern, NE South Africa
25 V4 Louisville Georgia, SE USA
32 M15 Louisville Illinois, N USA
22 K5 Louisville Kentucky, S USA
24 M4 Louisville Mississippi, S USA
31 S15 Louisville Nebraska, C USA
199 Jj12 Louisville Ridge undersea feature S Pacific Ocean
128 J6 Loukhi var. Louch. Respublika Kareliya, NW Russian Federation
81 H19 Loukoléla Cuvette, E Congo
106 G14 Loulé Faro, S Portugal
113 C16 Louny Ger. Laun. Severní Čechy, NW Czech Republic
31 O15 Loup City Nebraska, C USA
31 P15 Loup River ↝ Nebraska, C USA
13 S9 Loup, Rivière du ↝ Québec, SE Canada
10 K7 Loups Marins, Lacs des lakes Québec, NE Canada
104 K16 Lourdes Hautes-Pyrénées, S France
Lourenço Marques see Maputo
106 F11 Loures Lisboa, C Portugal
106 F10 Lourinhã Lisboa, C Portugal
117 C16 Loúros ↝ W Greece
106 G8 Lousã Coimbra, N Portugal
166 M10 Lou Shui ↝ C China
191 O5 Louth New South Wales, SE Australia
99 O18 Louth E England, UK
99 F17 Louth Ir. Lú. cultural region NE Ireland
117 H15 Loutrá Kentrikí Makedonía, N Greece
117 G19 Loutráki Pelopónnisos, S Greece
Louvain see Leuven
101 H19 Louvain-la Neuve Walloon Brabant, C Belgium
12 J8 Louvicourt Québec, SE Canada
104 M4 Louviers Eure, N France
32 K14 Lou Yaeger, Lake ▣ Illinois, N USA
95 J15 Lövånger Västerbotten, N Sweden
128 J14 Lovat' ↝ NW Russian Federation
115 J17 Lovćen ▲ S Yugoslavia
116 I8 Lovech Loveshka Oblast, NW Bulgaria
Lovech see Loveshka Oblast
27 V9 Lovelady Texas, SW USA
39 T3 Loveland Colorado, C USA
35 U12 Lovell Wyoming, C USA
Lovello, Monte see Grosser Löffler
37 S4 Lovelock Nevada, W USA
108 E7 Lovere Lombardia, N Italy
116 I8 Loveshka Oblast var. Lovech. ◆ province N Bulgaria
32 L10 Loves Park Illinois, N USA
28 M2 Lovewell Reservoir ▣ Kansas, C USA
95 M19 Loviisa Swe. Lovisa. Uusimaa, S Finland
39 V15 Loving New Mexico, SW USA
23 U6 Lovingston Virginia, NE USA
39 V14 Lovington New Mexico, SW USA
Lovisa see Loviisa
113 C15 Lovosice Ger. Lobositz. Severní Čechy, NW Czech Republic
128 K4 Lovozero Murmanskaya Oblast', NW Russian Federation
128 K4 Lovozero, Ozero ⊚ NW Russian Federation
114 B9 Lovran It. Laurana. Primorje-Gorski Kotar, NW Croatia
118 E11 Lovrin Ger. Lowrin. Timiș, W Romania
84 E10 Lóvua Lunda Norte, NE Angola
84 G12 Lóvua Moxico, E Angola
67 D25 Low Bay bay East Falkland, Falkland Islands
15 M6 Low, Cape headland Northwest Territories, E Canada
35 N10 Lowell Idaho, NW USA
21 O10 Lowell Massachusetts, NE USA
Löwen see Leuven
Löwenberg in Schlesien see Lwówek Śląski
Lower Austria see Niederösterreich
Lower Bann see Bann
Lower California see Baja California
Lower Danube see Niederösterreich
193 L14 Lower Hutt Wellington, North Island, NZ
41 N11 Lower Kalskag Alaska, USA
37 O1 Lower Klamath Lake ⊚ California, W USA
37 Q2 Lower Lake ⊚ California/Nevada, W USA
99 E15 Lower Lough Erne ⊚ SW Northern Ireland, UK
Lower Lusatia see Niederlausitz
Lower Normandy see Basse-Normandie, France
8 K9 Lower Post British Columbia, W Canada
31 T4 Lower Red Lake ⊚ Minnesota, N USA
Lower Rhine see Neder Rijn
Lower Saxony see Niedersachsen
Lower Tunguska see Nizhnyaya Tunguska
99 Q19 Lowestoft E England, UK
155 Q5 Lowgar var. Logar. ◆ province E Afghanistan
190 H7 Low Hill South Australia
112 K12 Łowicz Skierniewice, C Poland
35 N13 Lowman Idaho, NW USA
155 P8 Lowrah var. Lora. ↝ SE Afghanistan
Lowrin see Lovrin
191 N17 Low Rocky Point headland Tasmania, SE Australia
20 I8 Lowville New York, NE USA
Loxa see Loksa
190 K9 Loxton South Australia
83 G21 Loya Tabora, C Tanzania
32 K6 Loyal Wisconsin, N USA
20 G13 Loyalsock Creek ↝ Pennsylvania, NE USA
37 Q5 Loyalton California, W USA
Lo-yang see Luoyang
197 J6 Loyauté, Îles island group S New Caledonia
Loyev see Loyew
121 O20 Loyew Rus. Loyev. Homyel'skaya Voblasts', SE Belarus
129 S13 Loyno Kirovskaya Oblast', NW Russian Federation
105 P13 Lozère ◆ department S France
105 Q14 Lozère, Mont ▲ S France
114 J11 Loznica Serbia, W Yugoslavia
119 V7 Lozova Rus. Lozovaya. Kharkivs'ka Oblast', E Ukraine
Lozovaya see Lozova
107 N7 Lozoyuela Madrid, C Spain
Lœvvajok see Levajok
Lu see Shandong, China
Lú see Louth, Ireland
84 F12 Lucano Moxico, E Angola
81 N21 Lualaba Fr. Loualaba. ↝ SE Zaire
85 H14 Luampa Western, NW Zambia
85 H15 Luampa Kuta Western, W Zambia
167 P8 Lu'an Anhui, E China
106 K2 Luanco Asturias, N Spain
84 A11 Luanda var. Loanda, Port. São Paulo de Loanda. ● (Angola) Luanda, NW Angola
84 A11 Luanda ◆ province NW Angola
84 A11 Luanda ✕ Luanda, NW Angola
84 D12 Luando ↝ C Angola
Luang see Tapi, Mae Nam
85 G14 Luanginga var. Luanguinga. ↝ Angola/Zambia
178 Gg15 Luang, Khao ▲ SW Thailand
Luang Prabang see Louangphabang
178 I8 Luang Prabang Range Th. Thiukhaoluang Phrahang. ⛰ Laos/Thailand
178 H16 Luang, Thale lagoon S Thailand
Luangua, Rio see Luangwa
84 E11 Luangue ↝ NE Angola
Luanguinga see Luanginga
85 K15 Luangwa var. Aruângua. Lusaka, C Zambia
85 K14 Luangwa var. Aruângua, Rio Luangua. ↝ Mozambique/Zambia
167 Q2 Luan He ↝ E China
202 G11 Luaniva, Île island E Wallis and Futuna
167 P2 Luanping var. Anjiangying. Hebei, E China
84 J13 Luanshya Copperbelt, C Zambia
64 K13 Luan Toro La Pampa, C Argentina
167 Q2 Luanxian var. Luan Xian. Hebei, E China
84 J12 Luapula ◆ province N Zambia
81 O25 Luapula ↝ Zaire/Zambia
106 J2 Luarca Asturias, N Spain
174 Ll7 Luar, Danau ⊚ Borneo, N Indonesia
81 L25 Luashi Shaba, S Zaire
84 G12 Luau Port. Vila Teixeira de Sousa. Moxico, NE Angola
81 C16 Luba prev. San Carlos. Isla de Bioco, NW Equatorial Guinea
44 F4 Lubaantun ruins Toledo, S Belize
113 P16 Lubaczów var. Lúbaczów. Przemyśl, SE Poland
Lubale see Lubalo
84 E11 Lubalo Lunda Norte, NE Angola
84 E11 Lubalo var. Lubale. ↝ Angola/Zaire
120 J9 Lubāna Madona, E Latvia
Lubānas Ezers see Lubāns
179 P11 Lubang Island island N Philippines
85 B15 Lubango Port. Sá da Bandeira. Huíla, SW Angola
120 J9 Lubāns var. Lubānas Ezers. ⊚ E Latvia
81 M21 Lubao Kasai Oriental, C Zaire
112 O13 Lubartów Ger. Qumälisch. Lublin, E Poland
102 G13 Lübbecke Nordrhein-Westfalen, NW Germany
102 O13 Lübben Brandenburg, E Germany
103 P14 Lübbenau Brandenburg, E Germany
27 N5 Lubbock Texas, SW USA
Lubcz see Lyubcha
21 U6 Lubec Maine, NE USA
102 K9 Lübeck Schleswig-Holstein, N Germany
102 K8 Lübecker Bucht bay N Germany
81 M21 Lubefu Kasai Oriental, C Zaire
113 O14 Lubelska, Wyżyna plateau SE Poland
Lubelskie, Województwo see Lublin
Lubembe see Luembe

◆ Country ● Country Capital ◇ Dependent Territory ○ Dependent Territory Capital ◆ Administrative Region ✕ International Airport ▲ Mountain ⛰ Mountain Range Volcano ↝ River ⊚ Lake ▣ Reservoir

Lüben see Lubin
150 H9 **Lubenka** Zapadnyy Kazakhstan, W Kazakhstan
81 P18 **Lubero** Nord Kivu, E Zaire
81 L22 **Lubi** ≈ S Zaire
Lubiana see Ljubljana
112 J11 **Lubień Kujawski** Włocławek, C Poland
69 T11 **Lubilandji** ≈ S Zaire
112 F13 **Lubin** Ger. Lüben. Legnica, W Poland
113 O14 **Lublin** Rus. Lyublin. Lublin, E Poland
112 O13 **Lublin** off. Województwo Lubelskie, Rus. Lyublin. ❖ province E Poland
113 J15 **Lubliniec** Częstochowa, S Poland
Lubnān, Jabal see Liban, Jebel
119 R5 **Lubny** Poltavs'ka Oblast', NE Ukraine
Luboml see Lyuboml'
112 G11 **Luboń** Ger. Peterhof. Poznań, W Poland
112 D12 **Lubsko** Ger. Sommerfeld. Zielona Góra, W Poland
81 N24 **Lubudi** Shaba, SE Zaire
174 Hh11 **Lubuklinggau** Sumatera, W Indonesia
81 N25 **Lubumbashi** prev. Élisabethville. Shaba, SE Zaire
85 I14 **Lubungu** Central, C Zambia
81 N18 **Lubutu** Maniema, E Zaire
Luca see Lucca
84 C11 **Lucala** ≈ W Angola
12 E16 **Lucan** Ontario, S Canada
99 F18 **Lucan** Ir. Leamhcán. E Ireland
Lucanian Mountains see Lucano, Appennino
109 M18 **Lucano, Appennino** Eng. Lucanian Mountains. ▲ S Italy
84 F11 **Lucapa** var. Lukapa. Lunda Norte, NE Angola
31 V15 **Lucas** Iowa, C USA
63 C18 **Lucas González** Entre Ríos, E Argentina
67 C25 **Lucas Point** headland West Falkland, Falkland Islands
33 S15 **Lucasville** Ohio, N USA
108 F11 **Lucca** anc. Luca. Toscana, C Italy
42 H12 **Lucea** W Jamaica
99 H15 **Luce Bay** inlet SW Scotland, UK
24 M8 **Lucedale** Mississippi, S USA
179 Pp11 **Lucena** off. Lucena City. Luzon, N Philippines
106 M14 **Lucena** Andalucía, S Spain
107 S8 **Lucena del Cid** País Valenciano, E Spain
113 D15 **Lučenec** Ger. Losontz, Hung. Losonc. Stredné Slovensko, S Slovakia
Lucentum see Alicante
109 M16 **Lucera** Puglia, SE Italy
Lucerna/Lucerne see Luzern
Lucerne, Lake of see Vierwaldstätter See
42 J4 **Lucero** Chihuahua, N Mexico
127 Nn17 **Luchegorsk** Primorskiy Kray, SE Russian Federation
107 Q13 **Luchena** ≈ SE Spain
84 N13 **Lucheringo** var. Luchulingo. ≈ N Mozambique
Luchesa see Luchosa
Luchin see Luchyn
120 N13 **Luchosa** Rus. Luchesa. ≈ N Belarus
Luchow see Hefei
102 K11 **Lüchow** Mecklenburg-Vorpommern, N Germany
Luchulingo see Lucheringo
121 N17 **Luchyn** Rus. Luchin. Homyel'skaya Voblasts', SE Belarus
57 U11 **Lucie Rivier** ≈ W Suriname
190 K11 **Lucindale** South Australia
175 T13 **Lucipara, Kepulauan** island group E Indonesia
85 A14 **Lucira** Namibe, SW Angola
Łuck see Luts'k
103 O14 **Luckau** Brandenburg, E Germany
102 N13 **Luckenwalde** Brandenburg, E Germany
12 E15 **Lucknow** Ontario, S Canada
158 L12 **Lucknow** var. Lakhnau. Uttar Pradesh, N India
104 J10 **Luçon** Vendée, NW France
46 I7 **Lucrecia, Cabo** headland E Cuba
84 F13 **Lucusse** Moxico, E Angola
Lüda see Dalian
116 M9 **Luda Kamchiya** ≈ E Bulgaria
Ludasch see Luduş
116 J10 **Luda Yana** ≈ C Bulgaria
114 F7 **Ludbreg** Varaždin, N Croatia
31 P7 **Ludden** North Dakota, N USA
103 F15 **Lüdenscheid** Nordrhein-Westfalen, W Germany
85 C21 **Lüderitz** prev. Angra Pequena. Karas, SW Namibia
158 H8 **Ludhiāna** Punjab, N India
33 O7 **Ludington** Michigan, N USA
99 K20 **Ludlow** W England, UK
37 W14 **Ludlow** California, W USA
30 J7 **Ludlow** South Dakota, N USA
20 M9 **Ludlow** Vermont, NE USA
116 L7 **Ludogorie** physical region NE Bulgaria
25 W6 **Ludowici** Georgia, SE USA
Ludsan see Ludza
118 I10 **Luduş** Ger. Ludasch, Hung. Marosludas. Mureş, C Romania
97 M14 **Ludvika** Kopparberg, C Sweden
103 H21 **Ludwigsburg** Baden-Württemberg, SW Germany
102 O13 **Ludwigsfelde** Brandenburg, NE Germany
103 G20 **Ludwigshafen** var. Ludwigshafen am Rhein. Rheinland-Pfalz, W Germany
Ludwigshafen am Rhein see Ludwigshafen
103 L20 **Ludwigskanal** canal SE Germany
102 L10 **Ludwigslust** Mecklenburg-Vorpommern, N Germany
120 K10 **Ludza** Ger. Ludsan. Ludza, E Latvia
81 K21 **Luebo** Kasai Occidental, SW Zaire
27 Q6 **Lueders** Texas, SW USA
81 N20 **Lueki** Maniema, C Zaire
84 F10 **Luembe** var. Lubembe. ≈ Angola/Zaire
84 E13 **Luena** var. Lwena, Port. Luso. Moxico, E Angola
81 M24 **Luena** Shaba, SE Zaire
84 K12 **Luena** Northern, NE Zambia
84 F13 **Luena** ≈ E Angola
85 F16 **Luengue** ≈ SE Angola
69 V13 **Luenha** ≈ W Mozambique
85 G15 **Lueti** ≈ Angola/Zambia
166 J7 **Lüeyang** Shaanxi, C China
167 P14 **Lufeng** Guangdong, S China
81 N24 **Lufira** ≈ SE Zaire
81 N25 **Lufira, Lac de Retenue de la** var. Lac Tshangalele. ◎ SE Zaire
27 W8 **Lufkin** Texas, SW USA
84 L11 **Lufubu** ≈ N Zambia
128 G14 **Luga** Leningradskaya Oblast', NW Russian Federation
128 G13 **Luga** ≈ NW Russian Federation
Luganer See see Lugano, Lago di
110 H11 **Lugano** Ger. Lauis. Ticino, S Switzerland
110 H12 **Lugano, Lago di** var. Ceresio, Ger. Luganer See. ◎ S Switzerland
Lugansk see Luhans'k
197 B12 **Luganville** Espiritu Santo, C Vanuatu
Lugdunum see Lyon
Lugdunum Batavorum see Leiden
85 O15 **Lugela** Zambézia, NE Mozambique
85 O16 **Lugela** ≈ C Mozambique
84 P13 **Lugenda, Rio** ≈ N Mozambique
Luggarus see Locarno
Lugh Ganana see Luuq
99 G19 **Lugnaquillia Mountain** Ir. Log na Coille. ▲ E Ireland
108 H10 **Lugo** Emilia-Romagna, N Italy
106 I3 **Lugo** anc. Lugus Augusti. Galicia, NW Spain
106 I3 **Lugo** ❖ province Galicia, NW Spain
23 R12 **Lugoff** South Carolina, SE USA
118 F12 **Lugoj** Ger. Lugosch, Hung. Lugos. Timiş, W Romania
Lugos/Lugosch see Lugoj
151 S16 **Lugovoy** var. Lugovoye. Zhambyl, S Kazakhstan
Lugovoye see Lugovoy
164 I13 **Lugu** Xizang Zizhiqu, W China
Lugus Augusti see Lugo
Luguvallium/Luguvallum see Carlisle
119 Y7 **Luhans'k** Rus. Lugansk; prev. Voroshilovgrad. Luhans'ka Oblast', E Ukraine
119 Y7 **Luhans'k** ✕ Luhans'ka Oblast', E Ukraine
119 X6 **Luhans'ka Oblast'** var. Luhans'k; prev. Voroshilovgrad, Rus. Voroshilovgradskaya Oblast'. ❖ province E Ukraine
167 Q7 **Luhe** Jiangsu, E China
175 T11 **Luhu** Pulau Seram, E Indonesia
166 G8 **Luhuo** var. Zhaggo. Sichuan, C China
118 M3 **Luhyny** Zhytomyrs'ka Oblast', N Ukraine
85 G15 **Lui** ≈ W Zambia
85 G16 **Luiana** ≈ SE Angola
85 L15 **Luia, Rio** var. Ruya. ≈ Mozambique/Zimbabwe
Luichow Peninsula see Leizhou Bandao
Luik see Liège
84 C13 **Luimbale** Huambo, C Angola
Luimneach see Limerick
108 D6 **Luino** Lombardia, N Italy
84 E13 **Luio** ≈ E Angola
94 L11 **Luiro** ≈ NE Finland
81 N25 **Luishia** Shaba, SE Zaire
61 M19 **Luislândia do Oeste** Minas Gerais, SE Brazil
42 K5 **Luis L.León, Presa** ⊡ N Mexico
Luis Muñoz Marin see San Juan
205 N5 **Luitpold Coast** physical region Antarctica
81 K22 **Luiza** Kasai Occidental, S Zaire
63 D20 **Luján** Buenos Aires, E Argentina
81 N24 **Lukafu** Shaba, SE Zaire
Lukapa see Lucapa
114 I11 **Lukavac** NE Bosnia and Herzegovina
81 I20 **Lukenie** ≈ C Zaire
81 H19 **Lukolela** Equateur, W Zaire
121 M14 **Lukoml'skaye, Vozyera** Rus. Ozero Lukoml'skoye. ◎ N Belarus
Lukoml'skoye, Ozero see Lukoml'skaye, Vozyera
116 I8 **Lukovit** Loveshka Oblast, NW Bulgaria
112 O12 **Łuków** Ger. Bogendorf. Siedlce, E Poland
131 O4 **Lukoyanov** Nizhegorodskaya Oblast', W Russian Federation
81 N22 **Lukuga** ≈ SE Zaire
81 F21 **Lukula** Bas-Zaïre, SW Zaire
85 G14 **Lukulu** Western, NW Zambia
201 R17 **Lukunor Atoll** atoll Mortlock Islands, C Micronesia
84 J12 **Lukwesa** Luapula, NE Zambia
95 K14 **Luleå** Norrbotten, N Sweden
94 J13 **Luleälven** ≈ N Sweden
142 C10 **Lüleburgaz** Kırklareli, NW Turkey
166 M4 **Lüliang Shan** ▲ C China
81 O21 **Lulimba** Maniema, E Zaire
24 K9 **Luling** Louisiana, S USA
27 T11 **Luling** Texas, SW USA
81 I18 **Lulonga** ≈ NW Zaire
81 K22 **Lulua** ≈ S Zaire
Luluabourg see Kananga
198 Dd8 **Luma** Ta'ū, E American Samoa
174 M16 **Lumajang** Jawa, C Indonesia
164 G12 **Lumajangdong Co** ◎ W China
84 G13 **Lumbala Kaquengue** Moxico, E Angola
85 F14 **Lumbala N'Guimbo** var. Nguimbo, Port. Gago Coutinho, Vila Gago Coutinho. Moxico, E Angola
23 T11 **Lumber River** ≈ North Carolina/South Carolina, SE USA
Lumber State see Maine
24 L8 **Lumberton** Mississippi, S USA
23 U11 **Lumberton** North Carolina, SE USA
107 R4 **Lumbier** Navarra, N Spain
85 Q15 **Lumbo** Nampula, NE Mozambique
128 M4 **Lumbovka** Murmanskaya Oblast', NW Russian Federation
106 J7 **Lumbrales** Castilla-León, N Spain
159 W13 **Lumding** Assam, NE India
84 F12 **Lumege** var. Lumeje. Moxico, E Angola
Lumeje see Lumege
194 F10 **Lumi** Sandaun, NW PNG
101 J17 **Lummen** Limburg, NE Belgium
95 J20 **Lumparland** Åland, SW Finland
178 K12 **Lumphăt** prev. Lomphat. Rôtânôkiri, NE Cambodia
9 U16 **Lumsden** Saskatchewan, S Canada
193 C23 **Lumsden** Southland, South Island, NZ
174 J11 **Lumut, Tanjung** headland Sumatera, W Indonesia
163 P4 **Lün** Töv, C Mongolia
166 H13 **Lunan** var. Lunan Yizu Zizhixian. Yunnan, SW China
Lunan Yizu Zizhixian see Lunan
118 I13 **Lunca Corbului** Argeş, S Romania
97 K23 **Lund** Malmöhus, S Sweden
37 X6 **Lund** Nevada, W USA
84 D11 **Lunda Norte** ❖ province NE Angola
84 E12 **Lunda Sul** ❖ province NE Angola
84 M13 **Lundazi** Eastern, NE Zambia
97 G16 **Lunde** Telemark, S Norway
Lundenburg see Břeclav
97 C17 **Lundevatnet** ◎ S Norway
Lundi see Runde
99 I23 **Lundy** island SW England, UK
102 J10 **Lüneburg** Niedersachsen, N Germany
102 J11 **Lüneburger Heide** heathland NW Germany
105 Q15 **Lunel** Hérault, S France
103 F14 **Lünen** Nordrhein-Westfalen, W Germany
11 P16 **Lunenburg** Nova Scotia, SE Canada
23 V7 **Lunenburg** Virginia, NE USA
105 T5 **Lunéville** Meurthe-et-Moselle, NE France
85 I14 **Lunga** ≈ C Zambia
Lunga, Isola see Dugi Otok
164 H12 **Lungdo** Xizang Zizhiqu, W China
164 I14 **Lunggar** Xizang Zizhiqu, W China
78 I15 **Lungi** ✕ (Freetown) W Sierra Leone
Lungkiang see Qiqihar
Lungleh see Lunglei
159 W15 **Lunglei** prev. Lungleh. Mizoram, NE India
164 L15 **Lungsang** Xizang Zizhiqu, W China
84 E13 **Lungué-Bungo** var. Lungwebungu. ≈ Angola/Zambia see also Lungwebungu
85 G14 **Lungwebungu** var. Lungué-Bungo. ≈ Angola/Zambia see also Lungué-Bungo
158 F12 **Lūni** Rājasthān, N India
158 F12 **Lūni** ≈ N India
Luninets see Luninyets
37 S7 **Luning** Nevada, W USA
Luniniec see Luninyets
131 P6 **Lunino** Penzenskaya Oblast', W Russian Federation
121 J19 **Luninyets** Pol. Łuniniec, Rus. Luninets. Brestskaya Voblasts', SW Belarus
158 F10 **Lūnkaransar** Rājasthān, NW India
121 G17 **Lunna** Pol. Łunna, Rus. Lunna. Hrodzyenskaya Voblasts', W Belarus
78 I15 **Lunsar** W Sierra Leone
85 K14 **Lunsemfwa** ≈ C Zambia
164 J6 **Luntai** var. Bügür. Xinjiang Uygur Zizhiqu, NW China
100 K11 **Lunteren** Gelderland, C Netherlands
175 O16 **Lunyuk** Sumbawa, S Indonesia
111 U5 **Lunz am See** Niederösterreich, C Austria
169 Y7 **Luobei** var. Fengxiang. Heilongjiang, NE China
166 J13 **Luodian** var. Longping. Guizhou, S China
166 M15 **Luoding** Guangdong, S China
166 M6 **Luo He** ≈ C China
166 L5 **Luo He** ≈ C China
167 N7 **Luohe** Henan, C China
Luolajarvi see Kuoloyarvi
Luong Nam Tha see Louangnamtha
166 L13 **Luoqing Jiang** ≈ S China
167 O8 **Luoshan** Henan, C China
167 O12 **Luoxiao Shan** ▲ S China
167 N6 **Luoyang** var. Honan, Lo-yang. Henan, C China
167 R12 **Luoyuan** Fujian, SE China
81 F21 **Luozi** Bas-Zaïre, W Zaire
85 J17 **Lupane** Matabeleland North, W Zimbabwe
166 I12 **Lupanshui** prev. Shuicheng. Guizhou, S China
174 Ll7 **Lupar, Batang** ≈ East Malaysia
Lupatia see Altamura
118 G12 **Lupeni** Hung. Lupény. Hunedoara, SW Romania
Lupény see Lupeni
84 N13 **Lupiliche** Niassa, N Mozambique
85 E14 **Lupire** Cuando Cubango, E Angola
179 Rr16 **Lupon** Mindanao, S Philippines
81 L22 **Luputa** Kasai Oriental, S Zaire
123 Jj17 **Luqa** ✕ (Valletta) S Malta
165 U11 **Luqu** Gansu, C China
47 U5 **Luquillo, Sierra de** ▲ E Puerto Rico
28 L4 **Luray** Kansas, C USA
23 U4 **Luray** Virginia, NE USA
105 T7 **Lure** Haute-Saône, E France
84 D11 **Luremo** Lunda Norte, NE Angola
99 F15 **Lurgan** Ir. An Lorgain. S Northern Ireland, UK
59 K18 **Luribay** La Paz, W Bolivia
85 Q14 **Lúrio** Nampula, NE Mozambique
85 P14 **Lúrio, Rio** ≈ NE Mozambique
Luristan see Lorestān
Lurka see Lorca
85 J15 **Lusaka** ● (Zambia) Lusaka, SE Zambia
85 J15 **Lusaka** ❖ province C Zambia
85 J15 **Lusaka** ✕ Lusaka, C Zambia
81 L21 **Lusambo** Kasai Oriental, C Zaire
195 N14 **Lusancay Islands and Reefs** island group SE PNG
81 I21 **Lusanga** Bandundu, SW Zaire
81 N21 **Lusangi** Maniema, E Zaire
Lusatian Mountains see Lausitzer Bergland
Lushnja see Lushnjë
115 K21 **Lushnjë** var. Lushnja. Fier, C Albania
83 J21 **Lushoto** Tanga, E Tanzania
104 L10 **Lusignan** Vienne, W France
35 Z15 **Lusk** Wyoming, C USA
Luso see Luena
104 L10 **Lussac-les-Châteaux** Vienne, W France
Lussin/Lussino see Lošinj
Lussinpiccolo see Mali Lošinj
110 I7 **Lustenau** Vorarlberg, W Austria
167 T14 **Lü Tao** var. Huoshao Dao, Lütao, Eng. Green Island. island SE Taiwan
Lūt, Baḩrat/Lut, Bahret see Dead Sea
24 K9 **Lutcher** Louisiana, S USA
149 T9 **Lūt, Dasht-e** var. Kavīr-e Lūt. desert E Iran
85 F14 **Lutembo** Moxico, E Angola
Lutetia/Lutetia Parisiorum see Paris
Luteva see Lodève
12 G15 **Luther Lake** ◎ Ontario, S Canada
195 U13 **Luti** Choiseul Island, NW Solomon Islands
Lūt, Kavīr-e see Lūt, Dasht-e
99 N21 **Luton** SE England, UK
99 N21 **Luton** ✕ (London) SE England, UK
110 B10 **Lutry** Vaud, SW Switzerland
15 I8 **Łutselk'e** prev. Snowdrift. Northwest Territories, W Canada
31 Y4 **Lutsen** Minnesota, N USA
118 J4 **Luts'k** Pol. Łuck, Rus. Lutsk. Volyns'ka Oblast', NW Ukraine
Luttenberg see Ljutomer
Lüttich see Liège
85 G25 **Luttig** Western Cape, SW South Africa
Lutto see Lotta
84 E13 **Lutuai** Moxico, E Angola
119 Y7 **Lutuhyne** Luhans'ka Oblast', E Ukraine
176 Ww13 **Lutur, Pulau** island Kepulauan Aru, E Indonesia
25 V12 **Lutz** Florida, SE USA
Lutzow-Holm Bay see Lützow Holmbukta
205 V2 **Lützow Holmbukta** var. Lutzow-Holm Bay. bay Antarctica
83 L16 **Luuq** It. Lugh Ganana. Gedo, SW Somalia
94 M12 **Luusua** Lappi, NE Finland
25 Q6 **Luverne** Alabama, S USA
31 S11 **Luverne** Minnesota, N USA
81 O22 **Luvua** ≈ SE Zaire
84 F13 **Luvuei** Moxico, E Angola
83 H24 **Luwego** ≈ S Tanzania
84 K12 **Luwingu** Northern, NE Zambia
175 Qq9 **Luwuk** prev. Loewoek. Sulawesi, C Indonesia
25 N3 **Luxapalila Creek** ≈ Alabama/Mississippi, S USA
101 M25 **Luxembourg** ● (Luxembourg) Luxembourg, S Luxembourg
101 M25 **Luxembourg** off. Grand Duchy of Luxembourg, var. Lëtzebuerg, Luxemburg. ◆ monarchy NW Europe
101 J23 **Luxembourg** ❖ province SE Belgium
101 L24 **Luxembourg** ❖ district S Luxembourg
33 N6 **Luxemburg** Wisconsin, N USA
Luxemburg see Luxembourg
105 U7 **Luxeuil-les-Bains** Haute-Saône, E France
166 E13 **Luxi** prev. Mangshi. Yunnan, SW China
84 E10 **Luxico** ≈ Angola/Zaire
77 X10 **Luxor** Ar. Al Uqṣur. E Egypt
77 X10 **Luxor** ✕ C Egypt
166 M4 **Luya Shan** ▲ C China
104 J15 **Luy de Béarn** ≈ SW France
104 J15 **Luy de France** ≈ SW France
129 P12 **Luza** Kirovskaya Oblast', NW Russian Federation
129 Q12 **Luza** ≈ NW Russian Federation
106 I16 **Luz, Costa de la** coastal region SW Spain
113 K20 **Luže** var. Lausche. ▲ Czech Republic/Germany see also Lausche
110 F8 **Luzern** Fr. Lucerne, It. Lucerna. Luzern, C Switzerland
110 E8 **Luzern** Fr. Lucerne. ❖ canton C Switzerland
166 L13 **Luzhai** Guangxi Zhuangzu Zizhiqu, S China
120 K12 **Luzhki** Rus. Luzhki. Vitsyebskaya Voblasts', N Belarus
166 I10 **Luzhou** Sichuan, C China
Lužická Nisa see Neisse
Lužické Hory see Lausitzer Bergland
Lužnice see Lainsitz
179 Pp9 **Luzon** island N Philippines
179 Oo6 **Luzon Strait** strait Philippines/Taiwan
118 I5 **L'viv** Ger. Lemberg, Pol. Lwów, Rus. L'vov. L'vivs'ka Oblast', W Ukraine
L'viv see L'vivs'ka Oblast'
118 I4 **L'vivs'ka Oblast'** var. L'viv, Rus. L'vovskaya Oblast'. ❖ province NW Ukraine
L'vov see L'viv
L'vovskaya Oblast' see L'vivs'ka Oblast'
Lwena see Luena
Lwów see L'viv
112 F11 **Lwówek** Ger. Neustadt bei Pinne. Poznań, W Poland
113 E14 **Lwówek Śląski** Ger. Löwenberg in Schlesien. Jelenia Góra, SW Poland
121 I18 **Lyakhavichy** Rus. Lyakhovichi. Brestskaya Voblasts', SW Belarus
Lyakhovichi see Lyakhavichy
193 B22 **Lyall, Mount** ▲ South Island, NZ
Lyallpur see Faisalābād
125 G10 **Lyamin** ≈ C Russian Federation
Lyangar see Langar
125 G10 **Lyantor** Khanty-Mansiyskiy Avtonomnyy Okrug, C Russian Federation
128 H11 **Lyaskelya** Respublika Kareliya, NW Russian Federation
121 I18 **Lyasnaya** Rus. Lesnaya. Brestskaya Voblasts', SW Belarus
121 F19 **Lyasnaya** Pol. Leśna, Rus. Lesnaya. ≈ SW Belarus
128 H15 **Lychkovo** Novgorodskaya Oblast', W Russian Federation
Lyck see Ełk
95 I15 **Lycksele** Västerbotten, N Sweden
20 G13 **Lycoming Creek** ≈ Pennsylvania, NE USA
Lycopolis see Asyūt
205 N3 **Lyddan Island** island Antarctica
85 K20 **Lydenburg** Mpumalanga, NE South Africa
121 L20 **Lyel'chytsy** Rus. Lel'chitsy. Homyel'skaya Voblasts', SE Belarus
121 P14 **Lyenina** Rus. Lenino. Mahilyowskaya Voblasts', E Belarus
120 L13 **Lyepyel'** Rus. Lepel'. Vitsyebskaya Voblasts', N Belarus
27 S17 **Lyford** Texas, SW USA
97 E17 **Lygna** ≈ S Norway
20 G14 **Lykens** Pennsylvania, NE USA
117 E21 **Lykódimo** ▲ S Greece
99 K24 **Lyme Bay** bay S England, UK
99 K24 **Lyme Regis** S England, UK
112 L7 **Lyna** Ger. Alle. ≈ N Poland
31 P12 **Lynch** Nebraska, C USA
22 J10 **Lynchburg** Tennessee, S USA
23 T6 **Lynchburg** Virginia, NE USA
23 T12 **Lynches River** ≈ South Carolina, SE USA
34 H6 **Lynden** Washington, NW USA
190 I5 **Lyndhurst** South Australia
29 Q5 **Lyndon** Kansas, C USA
21 N7 **Lyndonville** Vermont, NE USA
97 D18 **Lyngdal** Vest-Agder, S Norway
94 I9 **Lyngen** inlet Arctic Ocean
97 G17 **Lyngør** Aust-Agder, S Norway
94 I9 **Lyngseidet** Troms, N Norway
21 P11 **Lynn** Massachusetts, NE USA
Lynn see King's Lynn
25 R9 **Lynn Haven** Florida, SE USA
9 V11 **Lynn Lake** Manitoba, C Canada
Lynn Regis see King's Lynn
120 I13 **Lyntupy** Rus. Lyntupy. Vitsyebskaya Voblasts', NW Belarus
105 R11 **Lyon** Eng. Lyons; anc. Lugdunum. Rhône, E France
15 H3 **Lyon, Cape** headland Northwest Territories, NW Canada
20 K6 **Lyon Mountain** ▲ New York, NE USA
105 Q11 **Lyonnais, Monts du** ▲ C France
67 N25 **Lyon Point** headland SE Tristan da Cunha
190 E5 **Lyons** South Australia
39 T3 **Lyons** Colorado, C USA
25 V6 **Lyons** Georgia, SE USA
28 M5 **Lyons** Kansas, C USA
31 R14 **Lyons** Nebraska, C USA
20 G10 **Lyons** New York, NE USA
Lyons see Lyon
120 O13 **Lyozna** Rus. Liozno. Vitsyebskaya Voblasts', NE Belarus
119 S4 **Lypova Dolyna** Sums'ka Oblast', NE Ukraine
119 N6 **Lypovets'** Rus. Lipovets. Vinnyts'ka Oblast', C Ukraine
Lys see Leie
113 I18 **Lysá Hora** ▲ E Czech Republic
97 D16 **Lysefjorden** fjord S Norway
97 I18 **Lysekil** Göteborg och Bohus, S Sweden
Lýsi see Akdoğan
35 V14 **Lysite** Wyoming, C USA
131 P3 **Lyskovo** Nizhegorodskaya Oblast', W Russian Federation
110 D8 **Lyss** Bern, W Switzerland
97 H22 **Lystrup** Århus, C Denmark
129 V14 **Lys'va** Permskaya Oblast', NW Russian Federation
119 P6 **Lysyanka** Cherkas'ka Oblast', C Ukraine
119 X6 **Lysychans'k** Rus. Lisichansk. Luhans'ka Oblast', E Ukraine
99 K17 **Lytham St Anne's** NW England, UK
193 I19 **Lyttelton** Canterbury, South Island, NZ
8 M17 **Lytton** British Columbia, SW Canada
121 L18 **Lyuban'** Rus. Lyuban'. Minskaya Voblasts', S Belarus
121 L18 **Lyubanskaye Vodaskhovishcha** ⊡ C Belarus
118 M5 **Lyubar** Zhytomyrs'ka Oblast', N Ukraine
Lyubashëvka see Lyubashivka
119 O8 **Lyubashivka** Rus. Lyubashëvka. Odes'ka Oblast', SW Ukraine
121 I16 **Lyubcha** Pol. Lubcz, Rus. Lyubcha. Hrodzyenskaya Voblasts', W Belarus
130 L4 **Lyubertsy** Moskovskaya Oblast', W Russian Federation
118 K2 **Lyubeshiv** Volyns'ka Oblast', NW Ukraine
128 M14 **Lyubim** Yaroslavskaya Oblast', NW Russian Federation
116 K11 **Lyubimets** Khaskovska Oblast, S Bulgaria
Lyublin see Lublin
118 I3 **Lyuboml'** Pol. Luboml. Volyns'ka Oblast', NW Ukraine
Lyubotin see Lyubotyn
119 U5 **Lyubotyn** Rus. Lyubotin. Kharkivs'ka Oblast', E Ukraine
130 I5 **Lyudinovo** Kaluzhskaya Oblast', W Russian Federation
131 T2 **Lyuk** Udmurtskaya Respublika, NW Russian Federation
116 M9 **Lyulyakovo** prev. Keremitlik. Burgaska Oblast, E Bulgaria
121 I18 **Lyusina** Rus. Lyusino. Brestskaya Voblasts', SW Belarus
Lyusino see Lyusina

M

144 G9 **Ma'ād** Irbid, N Jordan
Maalahti see Malax
Maale see Male'
144 G13 **Ma'ān** Ma'ān, SW Jordan
144 H13 **Ma'ān** off. Muḩāfaz̧at Ma'ān, var. Ma'an, Ma'ān. ❖ governorate S Jordan
95 M16 **Maaninka** Kuopio, C Finland
168 K7 **Maanĭt** Bulgan, C Mongolia
168 M8 **Maanĭt** Töv, C Mongolia
95 N15 **Maanselkä** Oulu, C Finland
167 Q8 **Ma'anshan** Anhui, E China
196 F16 **Maap** island Caroline Islands, W Micronesia
120 H3 **Maardu** Ger. Maart. Harjumaa, NW Estonia
Ma'aret-en-Nu'man see Ma'arrat an Nu'mān
101 K16 **Maarheeze** Noord-Brabant, SE Netherlands
Maarianhamina see Mariehamn
144 I4 **Ma'arrat an Nu'mān** var. Ma'aret-en-Nu'man, Fr. Maarret enn Naamâne. Idlib, NW Syria
Maarret enn Naamâne see Ma'arrat an Nu'mān
100 I11 **Maarssen** Utrecht, C Netherlands
Maart see Maardu
101 L17 **Maas** Fr. Meuse. ≈ W Europe see also Meuse
101 M15 **Maasbree** Limburg, SE Netherlands
101 L17 **Maaseik** prev. Maeseyck. Limburg, NE Belgium
179 R13 **Maasin** Leyte, C Philippines
101 L17 **Maasmechelen** Limburg, NE Belgium
100 G12 **Maassluis** Zuid-Holland, SW Netherlands
101 L18 **Maastricht** var. Maestricht; anc. Traietum ad Mosam, Traiectum Tungorum. Limburg, SE Netherlands
191 N18 **Maatsuyker Group** island group Tasmania, SE Australia
Maba see Qujiang
85 L20 **Mabalane** Gaza, S Mozambique
27 V7 **Mabank** Texas, SW USA
172 N10 **Mabechi-gawa** var. Mabuchi-gawa. ≈ Honshū, C Japan
99 O18 **Mablethorpe** E England, UK
176 W9 **Maboi** Irian Jaya, E Indonesia
85 M19 **Mabote** Inhambane, S Mozambique
34 J10 **Mabton** Washington, NW USA
Mabuchi-gawa see Mabechi-gawa
85 H20 **Mabutsane** Southern, S Botswana
65 G19 **Macá, Cerro** ▲ S Chile
62 Q9 **Macaé** Rio de Janeiro, SE Brazil
84 N13 **Macaloge** Niassa, N Mozambique
Macan see Bonerate, Kepulauan
167 N15 **Macao** Chin. Aomen, Port. Macau. ◇ Portugese special territory E Asia
106 H9 **Mação** Santarém, C Portugal
60 J11 **Macapá** state capital Amapá, N Brazil
45 S17 **Macaracas** Los Santos, S Panama
57 P6 **Macare, Caño** ≈ NE Venezuela
57 Q6 **Macareo, Caño** ≈ NE Venezuela
Macarsca see Makarska
MacArthur see Ormoc
190 L12 **Macarthur** Victoria, SE Australia
58 C7 **Macas** Morona Santiago, SE Ecuador
Macassar see Ujungpandang
61 Q14 **Macau** Rio Grande do Norte, E Brazil
Macau see Macao
Macău see Makó, Hungary
67 E24 **Macbride Head** headland East Falkland, Falkland Islands
25 V9 **Macclenny** Florida, SE USA
99 L18 **Macclesfield** C England, UK
198 F6 **Macclesfield Bank** undersea feature N South China Sea
MacCluer Gulf see Berau, Teluk
189 N7 **Macdonald, Lake** salt lake Western Australia
189 Q7 **Macdonnell Ranges** ▲ Northern Territory, C Australia
98 K8 **Macduff** NE Scotland, UK
106 I6 **Macedo de Cavaleiros** Bragança, N Portugal
Macedonia Central see Kentrikí Makedonía
Macedonia East and Thrace see Anatolikí Makedonía kai Thráki
116 E12 **Macedonia, FYR** off. the Former Yugoslav Republic of Macedonia, var. Macedonia, Mac. Makedonija, abbrev. FYR Macedonia, FYROM. ◆ republic SE Europe
Macedonia West see Dytikí Makedonía
61 Q16 **Maceió** state capital Alagoas, E Brazil
78 K15 **Macenta** Guinée-Forestière, SE Guinea
108 J12 **Macerata** Marche, C Italy
9 S11 **MacFarlane** ≈ Saskatchewan, C Canada
190 H7 **Macfarlane, Lake** var. Lake Mcfarlane. ◎ South Australia
Macgillicuddy's Reeks Mountains see Macgillycuddy's Reeks
99 B21 **Macgillycuddy's Reeks** var. Macgillicuddy's Reeks Mountains, Ir. Na Cruacha Dubha. ▲ SW Ireland
9 X16 **MacGregor** Manitoba, S Canada
155 O10 **Mach** Baluchistān, SW Pakistan
58 C6 **Machachi** Pichincha, C Ecuador
85 M19 **Machaila** Gaza, S Mozambique
Machaire Fíolta see Magherafelt
Machaire Rátha see Maghera
83 I19 **Machakos** Eastern, S Kenya
58 B8 **Machala** El Oro, SW Ecuador
85 J19 **Machaneng** Central, SE Botswana
85 M18 **Machanga** Sofala, E Mozambique
82 G13 **Machar Marshes** wetland SE Sudan
104 I8 **Machecoul** Loire-Atlantique, NW France
167 O8 **Macheng** Hubei, C China
161 J16 **Mācherla** Andhra Pradesh, C India
159 O11 **Machhapuchhre** ▲ C Nepal
21 T6 **Machias** Maine, NE USA
21 R3 **Machias River** ≈ Maine, NE USA
21 T6 **Machias River** ≈ Maine, NE USA
66 P5 **Machico** Madeira, Portugal, NE Atlantic Ocean
161 K16 **Machilīpatnam** var. Bandar Masulipatnam. Andhra Pradesh, E India
56 G5 **Machiques** Zulia, NW Venezuela
59 G15 **Machupicchu** Cusco, C Peru
85 M20 **Macia** var. Vila de Macia. Gaza, S Mozambique
Macías Nguema Biyogo see Bioco, Isla de
118 M13 **Măcin** Tulcea, SE Romania
191 T4 **Macintyre River** ≈ New South Wales/Queensland, SE Australia
189 Y7 **Mackay** Queensland, NE Australia
189 O7 **Mackay, Lake** salt lake Northern Territory/Western Australia
8 M13 **Mackenzie** British Columbia, W Canada
15 Gg6 **Mackenzie** ≈ Northwest Territories, NW Canada
205 Y6 **Mackenzie Bay** bay Antarctica
8 J1 **Mackenzie Bay** bay NW Canada
2 D8 **Mackenzie Delta** delta Northwest Territories, NW Canada
207 P8 **Mackenzie King Island** island Queen Elizabeth Islands, Northwest Territories, N Canada
14 G5 **Mackenzie Mountains** ▲ Northwest Territories, NW Canada
33 Q5 **Mackinac, Straits Of** ◎ Michigan, N USA
204 K5 **Mackintosh, Cape** headland Antarctica
9 R15 **Macklin** Saskatchewan, S Canada
191 V6 **Macksville** New South Wales, SE Australia
191 V5 **Maclean** New South Wales, SE Australia
85 J24 **Maclear** Eastern Cape, SE South Africa
191 U6 **Macleay River** ≈ New South Wales, SE Australia
MacLeod see Fort Macleod
188 G9 **Macleod, Lake** ◎ Western Australia
8 I6 **Macmillan** ≈ Yukon Territory, NW Canada
32 J12 **Macomb** Illinois, N USA
109 B18 **Macomer** Sardegna, Italy, C Mediterranean Sea
84 Q13 **Macomia** Cabo Delgado, NE Mozambique
25 T5 **Macon** Georgia, SE USA
25 N4 **Macon** Mississippi, S USA
29 U3 **Macon** Missouri, C USA

◆ Country ● Country Capital ◇ Dependent Territory ○ Dependent Territory Capital ❖ Administrative Region ✕ International Airport ▲ Mountain ▲ Mountain Range Volcano ≈ River ◎ Lake ⊡ Reservoir

105 R10 **Mâcon** *anc.* Matisco, Matisco Ædourum. Saône-et-Loire, C France
24 J6 **Macon, Bayou** ≈ Arkansas/ Louisiana, S USA
84 G13 **Macondo** Moxico, E Angola
85 M16 **Macossa** Manica, C Mozambique
9 T12 **Macoun Lake** ◎ Saskatchewan, C Canada
32 K14 **Macoupin Creek** ≈ Illinois, N USA
Macouria *see* Tonate
85 N18 **Macovane** Inhambane, SE Mozambique
191 N17 **Macquarie Harbour** *inlet* Tasmania, SE Australia
199 Ii15 **Macquarie Island** *island* NZ, SW Pacific Ocean
191 T8 **Macquarie, Lake** *lagoon* New South Wales, SE Australia
191 Q6 **Macquarie Marshes** *wetland* New South Wales, SE Australia
183 O13 **Macquarie Ridge** *undersea feature* SW Pacific Ocean
191 Q6 **Macquarie River** ≈ New South Wales, SE Australia
191 P17 **Macquarie River** ≈ Tasmania, SE Australia
205 V5 **Mac. Robertson Land** *physical region* Antarctica
99 C21 **Macroom** *Ir.* Maigh Chromtha. SW Ireland
44 G5 **Macuelizo** Santa Bárbara, NW Honduras
190 G2 **Macumba River** ≈ South Australia
59 I16 **Macusani** Puno, S Peru
58 E8 **Macusari, Río** ≈ N Peru
43 U15 **Macuspana** Tabasco, SE Mexico
144 G10 **Ma'dabā** *var.* Mādabā, Madeba; *anc.* Medeba. 'Ammān, NW Jordan
180 G2 **Madagascar** *off.* Democratic Republic of Madagascar, *Malg.* Madagasikara; *prev.* Malagasy Republic. ◆ *republic* W Indian Ocean
180 I5 **Madagascar** *island* W Indian Ocean
132 L17 **Madagascar Basin** *undersea feature* W Indian Ocean
132 L16 **Madagascar Plain** *undersea feature* W Indian Ocean
69 Y14 **Madagascar Plateau** *var.* Madagascar Ridge, Madagascar Rise, *Rus.* Madagaskarskiy Khrebet. *undersea feature* W Indian Ocean
Madagascar Ridge/ Madagascar Rise *see* Madagascar Plateau
Madagasikara *see* Madagascar
Madagaskarskiy Khrebet *see* Madagascar Plateau
66 N2 **Madalena** Pico, Azores, Portugal, NE Atlantic Ocean
79 Y6 **Madama** Agadez, NE Niger
116 J12 **Madan** Plovdivska Oblast, S Bulgaria
161 I19 **Madanapalle** Andhra Pradesh, E India
194 I11 **Madang** Madang, N PNG
194 I11 **Madang** ⬖ *province* N PNG
152 G7 **Madaniyat** *Rus.* Madeniyet. Qoraqalpoghiston Respublikasi, W Uzbekistan
Madanīyīn *see* Médenine
79 U11 **Madaoua** Tahoua, SW Niger
Madaras *see* Vtáčnik
159 U15 **Madaripur** Dhaka, C Bangladesh
79 U12 **Madarounfa** Maradi, S Niger
Mađarska *see* Hungary
152 B13 **Madau** *Turkm.* Madaw. Balkanskiy Velayat, W Turkmenistan
195 P15 **Madau Island** *island* SE PNG
Madaw *see* Madau
21 S1 **Madawaska** Maine, NE USA
12 J13 **Madawaska** ≈ Ontario, SE Canada
Madawaska Highlands *see* Haliburton Highlands
177 G4 **Madaya** Mandalay, C Myanmar
109 K17 **Maddaloni** Campania, S Italy
31 O3 **Maddock** North Dakota, N USA
101 I14 **Made** Noord-Brabant, S Netherlands
Madeba *see* Ma'dabā
66 L9 **Madeira** *var.* Ilha de Madeira. *island* Madeira, Portugal, NE Atlantic Ocean
Madeira, Ilha de *see* Madeira
66 O5 **Madeira Islands** *Port.* Região Autoónoma da Madeira. ⬖ *autonomous region* Madeira, Portugal, NE Atlantic Ocean
66 L9 **Madeira Plain** *undersea feature* E Atlantic Ocean
66 L9 **Madeira Ridge** *undersea feature* E Atlantic Ocean
61 F14 **Madeira, Rio** *Sp.* Río Madera. ≈ Bolivia/Brazil *see also* Madera, Río
103 J25 **Mädelegabel** ▲ Austria/ Germany
13 X6 **Madeleine** ≈ Québec, SE Canada
13 X5 **Madeleine, Cap de la** *headland* Québec, SE Canada
11 Q13 **Madeleine, Îles de la** *Eng.* Magdalen Islands. *island group* Québec, E Canada
31 U10 **Madelia** Minnesota, N USA
37 P3 **Madeline** California, W USA
32 K3 **Madeline Island** *island* Apostle Islands, Wisconsin, N USA
143 O15 **Maden** Elâzığ, SE Turkey
151 V12 **Madeniyet** Semipalatinsk, E Kazakhstan
Madeniyet *see* Madaniyat
42 H5 **Madera** Chihuahua, N Mexico
37 Q10 **Madera** California, W USA
58 L13 **Madera, Río** *Port.* Rio Madeira. ≈ Bolivia/Brazil *see also* Madeira, Rio
108 D6 **Madesimo** Lombardia, N Italy
147 O14 **Madhāb, Wādī** *dry watercourse* NW Yemen
159 R13 **Madhepura** *prev.* Madhipure. Bihār, NE India
Madhipure *see* Madhepura
159 Q13 **Madhubani** Bihār, N India
159 Q15 **Madhupur** Bihār, NE India
158 K15 **Madhya Pradesh** *prev.* Central Provinces and Berar. ⬖ *state* C India
59 K15 **Madidi, Río** ≈ W Bolivia
161 F20 **Madikeri** *prev.* Mercara. Karnātaka, W India
29 O13 **Madill** Oklahoma, C USA
81 G21 **Madimba** Bas-Zaïre, SW Zaire
144 M4 **Ma'dīn** Ar Raqqah, C Syria
Madīnah, Minţaqat al *see* Al Madīnah
78 M14 **Madinani** NW Ivory Coast
147 O17 **Madīnat ash Sha'b** *prev.* Al Ittiḥād. SW Yemen
144 K3 **Madīnat ath Thawrah** *var.* Ath Thawrah. Ar Raqqah, N Syria Asia
181 O6 **Madingley Rise** *undersea feature* W Indian Ocean
81 E21 **Madingo-Kayes** Le Kouilou, S Congo
81 F21 **Madingou** La Bouenza, S Congo
Madioen *see* Madiun
25 U8 **Madison** Florida, SE USA
25 T3 **Madison** Georgia, SE USA
33 P15 **Madison** Indiana, N USA
29 P6 **Madison** Kansas, C USA
21 Q6 **Madison** Maine, NE USA
31 S9 **Madison** Minnesota, N USA
24 K5 **Madison** Mississippi, S USA
31 Q14 **Madison** Nebraska, C USA
31 R10 **Madison** South Dakota, N USA
23 V5 **Madison** Virginia, NE USA
23 Q5 **Madison** West Virginia, NE USA
32 L9 **Madison** *state capital* Wisconsin, N USA
23 T6 **Madison Heights** Virginia, NE USA
22 M10 **Madisonville** Kentucky, S USA
22 I6 **Madisonville** Tennessee, S USA
27 V9 **Madisonville** Texas, SW USA
174 Ll15 **Madiun** *prev.* Madioen. Jawa, C Indonesia
Madjene *see* Majene
12 J14 **Madoc** Ontario, SE Canada
Madoera *see* Madura, Pulau
83 J18 **Mado Gashi** North Eastern, E Kenya
165 R11 **Madoi** Qinghai, C China
201 O13 **Madolenihmw** Pohnpei, E Micronesia
120 I9 **Madona** *Ger.* Modohn. Madona, E Latvia
109 J23 **Madonie** ⛰ Sicilia, Italy, C Mediterranean Sea
147 Y11 **Madrakah, Ra's** *headland* E Oman
161 J19 **Madras** *var.* Chennai. Tamil Nādu, S India
34 I12 **Madras** Oregon, NW USA
161 J19 **Madras** × Tamil Nādu, S India
Madras *see* Tamil Nādu
59 H14 **Madre de Dios** *off.* Departamento de Madre de Dios. ⬖ *department* E Peru
65 F22 **Madre de Dios, Isla** *island* S Chile
59 J14 **Madre de Dios, Río** ≈ Bolivia/Peru
27 T16 **Madre, Laguna** ◎ Texas, SW USA
43 Q9 **Madre, Laguna** *lagoon* NE Mexico
39 Q12 **Madre Mount** ▲ New Mexico, SW USA
107 N8 **Madrid** ● (Spain) Madrid, C Spain
31 V14 **Madrid** Iowa, C USA
107 N7 **Madrid** ⬖ *autonomous community* C Spain
107 N10 **Madridejos** Castilla-La Mancha, C Spain
106 L7 **Madrigal de las Altas Torres** Castilla-León, N Spain
106 K10 **Madrigalejo** Extremadura, W Spain
36 L3 **Mad River** ≈ California, W USA
44 J8 **Madriz** ⬖ *department* NW Nicaragua
106 K10 **Madroñera** Extremadura, W Spain
189 N12 **Madura** Western Australia
Madura *see* Madurai
161 H22 **Madurai** *prev.* Madura, Mathurai. Tamil Nādu, S India
174 M15 **Madura, Pulau** *prev.* Madoera. *island* C Indonesia
174 Mm15 **Madura, Selat** *strait* C Indonesia
131 Q17 **Madzhalis** Respublika Dagestan, SW Russian Federation
116 K12 **Madzharovo** Khaskovska Oblast, S Bulgaria
85 M14 **Madzimoyo** Eastern, E Zambia
171 K15 **Maebashi** *var.* Maebasi, Mayebashi. Gunma, Honshū, S Japan
Maebasi *see* Maebashi
178 Hh6 **Mae Chan** Chiang Rai, NW Thailand
178 Gg7 **Mae Hong Son** *var.* Maehongson, Muai To. Mae Hong Son, NW Thailand
Mae Nam Khong *see* Mekong
178 Hh7 **Mae Nam Nan** ≈ NW Thailand
178 H10 **Mae Nam Tha Chin** ≈ W Thailand
178 Hh7 **Mae Nam Yom** ≈ W Thailand
178 H7 **Mae Sariang** Mae Hong Son, NW Thailand
39 O3 **Maeser** Utah, W USA
Maeseyck *see* Maaseik
178 Gg9 **Mae Sot** *var.* Ban Mae Sot. Tak, W Thailand
Maestricht *see* Maastricht
178 H7 **Mae Suai** *var.* Ban Mae Suai. Chiang Rai, NW Thailand
178 H7 **Mae Tho, Doi** ▲ NW Thailand
180 I4 **Maevatanana** Mahajanga, C Madagascar
197 C12 **Maewo** *prev.* Aurora. *island* C Vanuatu
175 T8 **Mafa** Pulau Halmahera, E Indonesia
85 I23 **Mafeteng** W Lesotho
101 J21 **Maffe** Namur, SE Belgium
176 Y10 **Maffin** Irian Jaya, E Indonesia
191 P12 **Maffra** Victoria, SE Australia
83 K23 **Mafia** *island* E Tanzania
83 J23 **Mafia Channel** *sea waterway* E Tanzania
85 I21 **Mafikeng** North-West, N South Africa
62 J12 **Mafra** Santa Catarina, S Brazil
106 F10 **Mafra** Lisboa, C Portugal
149 Q17 **Mafraq** Abū Ẓaby, C UAE
Mafraq/Mafraq, Muḥāfaẓat al *see* Al Mafraq
127 O10 **Magadan** Magadanskaya Oblast', E Russian Federation
127 Nn8 **Magadanskaya Oblast'** ⬖ *province* E Russian Federation
110 G11 **Magadino** Ticino, S Switzerland
65 G23 **Magallanes** *off.* Región de Magallanes y de la Antártica Chilena. ⬖ *region* S Chile
Magallanes *see* Punta Arenas
Magallanes, Estrecho de *see* Magellan, Strait of
12 I10 **Maganasipi, Lac** ◎ Québec, SE Canada
56 F6 **Magangué** Bolívar, N Colombia
Magareva *see* Mangareva
79 V12 **Magaria** Zinder, S Niger
194 M16 **Magarida** Central, SW PNG
179 Pp9 **Magat** ≈ Luzon, N Philippines
29 T11 **Magazine Mountain** ▲ Arkansas, C USA
78 I15 **Magburaka** C Sierra Leone
126 M14 **Magdagachi** Amurskaya Oblast', SE Russian Federation
64 O12 **Magdalena** Buenos Aires, E Argentina
59 M15 **Magdalena** Beni, N Bolivia
42 F4 **Magdalena** Sonora, NW Mexico
39 Q13 **Magdalena** New Mexico, SW USA
56 F5 **Magdalena** *off.* Departamento del Magdalena. ⬖ *province* N Colombia
42 E9 **Magdalena, Bahía** *bay* W Mexico
65 G19 **Magdalena, Isla** *island* Archipiélago de los Chonos, S Chile
42 D8 **Magdalena, Isla** *island* W Mexico
49 P6 **Magdalena, Río** ≈ C Colombia
42 F4 **Magdalena, Río** ≈ NW Mexico
Magdalen Islands *see* Madeleine, Îles de la
102 L13 **Magdeburg** Sachsen-Anhalt, C Germany
24 L6 **Magee** Mississippi, S USA
174 Kk15 **Magelang** Jawa, C Indonesia
199 J7 **Magellan Rise** *undersea feature* C Pacific Ocean
65 H24 **Magellan, Strait of** *Sp.* Estrecho de Magallanes. *strait* Argentina/Chile
108 D7 **Magenta** Lombardia, NW Italy
Magerøy *see* Magerøya
94 K7 **Magerøya** *var.* Magerøy. *island* N Norway
170 B17 **Mage-shima** *island* Nansei-shotō, SW Japan
110 G11 **Maggia** Ticino, S Switzerland
110 G10 **Maggia** ≈ SW Switzerland
Maggiore, Lago *see* Maggiore, Lake
108 C6 **Maggiore, Lake** *It.* Lago Maggiore. ◎ Italy/Switzerland
46 I12 **Maggotty** W Jamaica
78 I10 **Maghama** Gorgol, S Mauritania
99 F14 **Maghera** *Ir.* Machaire Rátha. C Northern Ireland, UK
99 F15 **Magherafelt** *Ir.* Machaire Fíolta. C Northern Ireland, UK
196 H6 **Magicienne Bay** *bay* Saipan, S Northern Mariana Islands
107 O13 **Magina** ▲ S Spain
83 H24 **Magingo** Ruvuma, S Tanzania
126 Jj14 **Magistral'nyy** Irkutskaya Oblast', S Russian Federation
114 H11 **Maglaj** N Bosnia and Herzegovina
109 Q19 **Maglie** Puglia, SE Italy
38 L2 **Magna** Utah, W USA
Magnesia *see* Manisa
12 G12 **Magnetawan** ≈ Ontario, S Canada
125 Dd12 **Magnitogorsk** Chelyabinskaya Oblast', C Russian Federation
29 T14 **Magnolia** Arkansas, C USA
24 K7 **Magnolia** Mississippi, S USA
27 V10 **Magnolia** Texas, SW USA
Magnolia State *see* Mississippi
97 J15 **Magnor** Hedmark, S Norway
197 K14 **Mago** *prev.* Mango. *island* Lau Group, E Fiji
85 L15 **Màgoé** Tete, NW Mozambique
13 Q13 **Magog** Québec, SE Canada
85 J15 **Magoye** Southern, S Zambia
43 Q12 **Magozal** Veracruz-Llave, C Mexico
12 B7 **Magpie** ≈ Ontario, S Canada
9 Q17 **Magrath** Alberta, SW Canada
107 R10 **Magro** ≈ E Spain
78 I9 **Magta' Lahjar** *var.* Magta Lahjar, Magta' Lahjar, Magtá Lahjar. Brakna, SW Mauritania
85 L20 **Magude** Maputo, S Mozambique
79 Y12 **Magumeri** Borno, NE Nigeria
201 O14 **Magur Islands** *island group* Caroline Islands, C Micronesia
Magway *see* Magwe
177 Ff6 **Magwe** *var.* Magway. Magwe, W Myanmar
177 Ff6 **Magwe** *var.* Magway. ⬖ *division* C Myanmar
Magyar-Becse *see* Bečej
Magyarkanizsa *see* Kanjiža
Magyarország *see* Hungary
Magyarzsombor *see* Zimbor
148 J4 **Mahābād** *var.* Mehabad; *prev.* Sāūjbulāgh. Āzarbāyjān-e Bākhtarī, NW Iran
180 H5 **Mahabo** Toliara, W Madagascar
Maha Chai *see* Samut Sakhon
161 D14 **Mahād** Mahārāshtra, W India
83 N17 **Mahadday Weyne** Shabeellaha Dhexe, C Somalia
81 Q17 **Mahagi** Haut-Zaïre, NE Zaire
Mahāil *see* Muhāyil
180 I4 **Mahajamba** *seasonal river* NW Madagascar
158 G10 **Mahājan** Rājasthān, NW India
180 I3 **Mahajanga** *var.* Majunga. Mahajanga, NW Madagascar
180 I3 **Mahajanga** ⬖ *province* W Madagascar
180 I3 **Mahajanga** × Mahajanga, NW Madagascar
175 N7 **Mahakam, Sungai** *var.* Koetai, Kutai. ≈ Borneo, C Indonesia
85 I19 **Mahalapye** *var.* Mahalatswe. Central, SE Botswana
Mahalatswe *see* Mahalapye
Mahalla el Kubra *see* El Maḥalla el Kubra
175 Q10 **Mahalona** Sulawesi, C Indonesia
Mahameru *see* Semeru, Gunung
149 S11 **Mahān** Kermān, E Iran
160 N12 **Mahanādi** ≈ E India
180 J5 **Mahanoro** Toamasina, E Madagascar
159 P13 **Mahārājganj** Bihār, N India
160 G13 **Mahārāshtra** ⬖ *state* W India
Mahasaragam *see* Maha Sarakham
180 I4 **Mahavavy** *seasonal river* N Madagascar
161 K24 **Mahaweli Ganga** ≈ C Sri Lanka
Mahbés *see* El Mahbas
161 J15 **Mahbūbābād** Andhra Pradesh, E India
161 H16 **Mahbūbnagar** Andhra Pradesh, C India
146 M8 **Mahd adh Dhahab** Al Madīnah, W Saudi Arabia
57 S9 **Mahdia** C Guyana
77 N6 **Mahdia** *var.* Al Mahdīyah, Mehdia. NE Tunisia
161 F20 **Mahe** *Fr.* Mahé; *prev.* Mayyali. Pondicherry, SW India
180 I16 **Mahé** × Mahé, NE Seychelles
180 H16 **Mahé** *island* Inner Islands, NE Seychelles
181 Y17 **Mahebourg** SE Mauritius
158 I11 **Mahendragarh** Haryāna, N India
158 L10 **Mahendranagar** Far Western, W Nepal
83 I23 **Mahenge** Morogoro, SE Tanzania
193 F22 **Maheno** Otago, South Island, NZ
160 D9 **Mahesāna** Gujarāt, W India
160 F11 **Maheshwar** Madhya Pradesh, C India
157 F14 **Mahi** ≈ N India
192 Q10 **Mahia Peninsula** *peninsula* North Island, NZ
121 O16 **Mahilyow** *Rus.* Mogilëv. Mahilyowskaya Voblasts', E Belarus
121 M16 **Mahilyowskaya Voblasts'** *prev. Rus.* Mogilëvskaya Oblast'. ⬖ *province* E Belarus
203 P7 **Mahina** Tahiti, W French Polynesia
193 E23 **Mahinerangi, Lake** ◎ South Island, NZ
85 L22 **Mahlabatini** KwaZulu/Natal, E South Africa
177 G5 **Mahlaing** Mandalay, C Myanmar
111 X8 **Mahldorf** Steiermark, SE Austria
Mahmūd-e 'Erāqī *see* Maḥmūd-e Rāqī
155 R4 **Maḥmūd-e Rāqī** *var.* Mahmūd-e 'Erāqī. Kāpīsā, NE Afghanistan
Mahmudiya *see* Al Maḥmūdīyah
31 S5 **Mahnomen** Minnesota, N USA
158 K14 **Mahoba** Uttar Pradesh, N India
107 Z9 **Mahón** *Cat.* Maó, *Eng.* Port Mahon; *anc.* Portus Magonis. Menorca, Spain, W Mediterranean Sea
20 D14 **Mahoning Creek Lake** ▣ Pennsylvania, NE USA
107 Q10 **Mahora** Castilla-La Mancha, C Spain
Mähren *see* Moravia
Mährisch-Budwitz *see* Moravské Budějovice
Mährisch-Kromau *see* Moravský Krumlov
Mährisch-Neustadt *see* Uničov
Mährisch-Schönberg *see* Šumperk
Mährisch-Trübau *see* Moravská Třebová
Mährisch-Weisskirchen *see* Hranice
Māh-Shahr *see* Bandar-e Māhshahr
81 N19 **Mahulu** Maniema, E Zaire
160 C12 **Mahuva** Gujarāt, W India
116 N11 **Mahya Dağı** ▲ NW Turkey
107 T6 **Maials** *var.* Mayals. Cataluña, NE Spain
203 O2 **Maiana** *prev.* Hall Island. *atoll* Tungaru, W Kiribati
203 S11 **Maiao** *var.* Tapuaemanu, Tubuai-Manu. *island* Îles du Vent, W French Polynesia
56 H4 **Maicao** La Guajira, N Colombia
Mai Ceu/Mai Chio *see* Maych'ew
105 U8 **Maîche** Doubs, E France
99 N22 **Maidenhead** S England, UK
9 S15 **Maidstone** Saskatchewan, S Canada
99 P22 **Maidstone** SE England, UK
79 Y13 **Maiduguri** Borno, NE Nigeria
110 I8 **Maienfeld** Sankt Gallen, NE Switzerland
118 J12 **Măieruş** *Hung.* Szászmagyarós. Braşov, C Romania
Maigh Chromtha *see* Macroom
Maigh Eo *see* Mayo
57 N9 **Maigualida, Sierra** ⛰ S Venezuela
160 K9 **Maihar** Madhya Pradesh, C India
160 K11 **Maikala Range** ⛰ C India
69 T10 **Maiko** ≈ W Zaire
Mailand *see* Milano
158 L11 **Mailāni** Uttar Pradesh, N India
155 U10 **Māilsi** Punjab, E Pakistan
153 R8 **Maimak** Talasskaya Oblast', NW Kyrgyzstan
Maimāna *see* Meymaneh
Maimansingh *see* Mymensingh
176 Vv11 **Maimawa** Irian Jaya, E Indonesia
Maimuna *see* Al Maymūnah
103 G18 **Main** ≈ C Germany
117 F22 **Maïna** *ancient monument* Pelopónnisos, S Greece
117 E20 **Maínalo** ⛰ S Greece
103 L22 **Mainburg** Bayern, SE Germany
Main Camp *see* Banana
12 E12 **Main Channel** *lake channel* Ontario, S Canada
81 I20 **Mai-Ndombe, Lac** *prev.* Lac Léopold II. ◎ W Zaire
103 K20 **Main-Donau-Kanal** *canal* SE Germany
21 R6 **Maine** *off.* State of Maine; also known as Lumber State, Pine Tree State. ⬖ *state* NE USA
104 K6 **Maine** *cultural region* NW France
104 J7 **Maine-et-Loire** ⬖ *department* NW France
21 Q9 **Maine, Gulf of** *gulf* NE USA
79 X12 **Maïné-Soroa** Diffa, SE Niger
178 Gg1 **Maingkwan** *var.* Mungkawn. Kachin State, N Myanmar
Main Island *see* Bermuda
Mainistir Fhear Maí *see* Fermoy
Mainistirna Búille *see* Boyle
Mainistir na Corann *see* Midleton
Mainistir na Féile *see* Abbeyfeale
98 J5 **Mainland** *island* Orkney, N Scotland, UK
98 L2 **Mainland** *island* Shetland, NE Scotland, UK
165 P16 **Mainling** Xizang Zizhiqu, W China
158 K12 **Mainpuri** Uttar Pradesh, N India
105 N5 **Maintenon** Eure-et-Loir, C France
180 H4 **Maintirano** Mahajanga, W Madagascar
95 M15 **Mainua** Oulu, C Finland
103 G18 **Mainz** *Fr.* Mayence. Rheinland-Pfalz, SW Germany
78 I9 **Maio** *var.* Vila do Maio. Maio, S Cape Verde
78 E10 **Maio** *var.* Mayo. *island* Ilhas de Sotavento, SE Cape Verde
64 G12 **Maipo, Río** ≈ C Chile
64 H12 **Maipo, Volcán** ▲ W Argentina
63 E22 **Maipú** Buenos Aires, E Argentina
64 I11 **Maipú** Mendoza, E Argentina
64 H11 **Maipú** Santiago, C Chile
56 L5 **Maiquetía** Distrito Federal, N Venezuela
110 I10 **Maira** *It.* Mera. ≈ Italy/Switzerland
108 A9 **Maira** ≈ NW Italy
159 V12 **Mairābari** Assam, NE India
46 K7 **Maisí** Guantánamo, E Cuba
120 H13 **Maišiagala** Vilnius, SE Lithuania
159 V17 **Maiskhal Island** *island* SE Bangladesh
178 Gg13 **Mai Sombun** Chumphon, SW Thailand
Maisur *see* Karnātaka, India
Maisur *see* Mysore, India
191 T8 **Maitland** New South Wales, SE Australia
190 I9 **Maitland** South Australia
12 F15 **Maitland** ≈ Ontario, S Canada
205 R1 **Maitri** *Indian research station* Antarctica
165 N15 **Maizhokunggar** Xizang Zizhiqu, W China
45 O10 **Maíz, Islas del** *var.* Corn Islands. *island group* SE Nicaragua
171 H14 **Maizuru** Kyōto, Honshū, SW Japan
56 F6 **Majagual** Sucre, N Colombia
43 Z13 **Majahual** Quintana Roo, E Mexico
Majardah, Wādī *see* Medjerda, Oued/Mejerda
Mājeej *see* Mejit Island
175 P11 **Majene** *prev.* Madjene. Sulawesi, C Indonesia
45 V15 **Majé, Serranía de** ⛰ E Panama
114 I11 **Majevica** ⛰ NE Bosnia and Herzegovina
83 H15 **Majī** SW Ethiopia
147 X7 **Majīs** NW Oman
Majorca *see* Mallorca
Mājro *see* Majuro Atoll
Majunga *see* Mahajanga
201 Y3 **Majuro** × Majuro, SE Marshall Islands
201 Y2 **Majuro Atoll** *var.* Mājro. *atoll* Ratak Chain, SE Marshall Islands
201 X2 **Majuro Lagoon** *lagoon* Majuro Atoll, SE Marshall Islands
78 H11 **Maka** C Senegal
81 F20 **Makabana** Le Niari, SW Congo
40 D9 **Makaha** *Haw.* Mākaha. Oahu, Hawaii, USA, C Pacific Ocean
40 B8 **Makahuena Point** *headland* Kauai, Hawaii, USA, C Pacific Ocean
40 D9 **Makakilo City** Oahu, Hawaii, USA, C Pacific Ocean
85 H18 **Makalamabedi** Central, C Botswana
Makale *see* Mek'elē
164 K17 **Makalu** *Chin.* Makaru Shan. ▲ China/Nepal
83 G23 **Makampi** Mbeya, S Tanzania
151 X12 **Makanchi** *Kaz.* Maqanshy. Semipalatinsk, E Kazakhstan
44 M8 **Makantaka** Región Autónoma Atlántico Norte, NE Nicaragua
202 B16 **Makapu Point** *headland* W Niue
193 C24 **Makarewa** Southland, South Island, NZ
119 O4 **Makariv** Kyyivs'ka Oblast', N Ukraine
193 D20 **Makarora** ≈ South Island, NZ
127 Oo15 **Makarov** Ostrov Sakhalin, Sakhalinskaya Oblast', SE Russian Federation
207 R9 **Makarov Basin** *undersea feature* Arctic Ocean
199 Hh4 **Makarov Seamount** *undersea feature* W Pacific Ocean
115 F15 **Makarska** *It.* Macarsca. Split-Dalmacija, SE Croatia
Makaru Shan *see* Makalu
129 O15 **Makar'yev** Kostromskaya Oblast', NW Russian Federation
84 L11 **Makasa** Northern, NE Zambia
Makasar *see* Ujungpandang
Makasar, Selat *see* Makassar Straits
Makassar *see* Ujungpandang
198 Ff8 **Makassar Straits** *Ind.* Selat Makasar. *strait* C Indonesia
150 G12 **Makat** *Kaz.* Maqat. Atyrau, SW Kazakhstan
203 T10 **Makatea** *island* Îles Tuamotu, C French Polynesia
145 U7 **Makātū** E Iraq
180 H6 **Makay** *var.* Massif du Makay. ⛰ SW Madagascar
116 J12 **Makaza** *pass* Bulgaria/Greece
176 Uu9 **Makbon** Irian Jaya, E Indonesia
Makedonija *see* Macedonia, FYR
202 B16 **Makefu** W Niue
203 V10 **Makemo** *atoll* Îles Tuamotu, C French Polynesia
78 I15 **Makeni** C Sierra Leone
Makenzen *see* Orlyak
Makeyevka *see* Makiyivka
131 Q16 **Makhachkala** *prev.* Petrovsk-Port. Respublika Dagestan, SW Russian Federation
150 F11 **Makhambet** Atyrau, W Kazakhstan
Makharadze *see* Ozurget'i
145 W13 **Makhfar Al Buşayyah** S Iraq
145 R4 **Makhmūr** N Iraq
144 I11 **Makhrūq, Wadi al** *dry watercourse* E Jordan
145 R4 **Makḥūl, Jabal** ⛰ C Iraq
147 R13 **Makhyah, Wādī** *dry watercourse* N Yemen
176 W11 **Maki** Irian Jaya, E Indonesia
175 Ss8 **Makian, Pulau** *island* Maluku, E Indonesia
193 G21 **Makikihi** Canterbury, South Island, NZ
203 O2 **Makin** *prev.* Pitt Island. *atoll* Tungaru, W Kiribati
83 I20 **Makindu** Eastern, S Kenya
151 Q8 **Makinsk** Akmola, N Kazakhstan
195 Y17 **Makira** *off.* Makira Province. ⬖ *province* SE Solomon Islands
Makira *see* San Cristobal
119 X8 **Makiyivka** *Rus.* Makeyevka; *prev.* Dmitriyevsk. Donets'ka Oblast', E Ukraine
146 L10 **Makkah** *Eng.* Mecca. Makkah, W Saudi Arabia
146 M10 **Makkah** *var.* Minţaqat Makkah. ⬖ *province* W Saudi Arabia
11 R7 **Makkovik** Newfoundland and Labrador, NE Canada
100 K6 **Makkum** Friesland, N Netherlands
Mako *see* Makung
113 M25 **Makó** *Rom.* Macău. Csongrád, SE Hungary
12 G9 **Makobe Lake** ◎ Ontario, S Canada
197 I14 **Makogai** *island* C Fiji
81 F18 **Makokou** Ogooué-Ivindo, NE Gabon
83 G23 **Makongolosi** Mbeya, S Tanzania
83 E19 **Makota** SW Uganda
81 G18 **Makoua** Cuvette, C Congo
112 M10 **Maków Mazowiecki** Ostrołęka, E Poland
113 K17 **Maków Podhalański** Bielsko-Biała, S Poland
149 V14 **Makran** *cultural region* Iran/Pakistan
158 G12 **Makrāna** Rājasthān, N India
149 U15 **Makran Coast** *coastal region* SE Iran
121 F20 **Makrany** *Rus.* Mokrany. Brestskaya Voblasts', SW Belarus
Makrinoros *see* Makrynóros
117 H20 **Makrónisosi** *island* Kykládes, Greece, Aegean Sea
117 D17 **Makrynóros** *var.* Makrinoros. ⛰ C Greece
117 G19 **Makryplági** ▲ C Greece
Maksamaa *see* Maxmo
128 J15 **Maksatikha** *var.* Maksatha, Maksaticha. Tverskaya Oblast', W Russian Federation
160 G10 **Maksi** Madhya Pradesh, C India
148 I1 **Mākū** Āzarbāyjān-e Bākhtarī, NW Iran
159 Y11 **Mākum** Assam, NE India
Makun *see* Makung
167 R14 **Makung** *prev.* Mako, Makun. W Taiwan
170 Bb16 **Makurazaki** Kagoshima, Kyūshū, SW Japan
79 V15 **Makurdi** Benue, C Nigeria
125 F12 **Makushino** Kurganskaya Oblast', C Russian Federation
40 L17 **Makushin Volcano** ▲ Unalaska Island, Alaska, USA
85 K16 **Makwiro** Mashonaland West, N Zimbabwe
59 D15 **Mala** Lima, W Peru
Mala *see* Mallow, Ireland
Mala *see* Malaita, Solomon Islands
95 I14 **Malå** Västerbotten, N Sweden
202 G12 **Mala'atoli** Île Uvea, E Wallis and Futuna
179 Qq15 **Malabang** *see* Malabang
161 E21 **Malabār Coast** *coast* SW India
81 C16 **Malabo** *prev.* Santa Isabel. ● (Equatorial Guinea) Isla de Bioco, NW Equatorial Guinea
81 C16 **Malabo** × Isla de Bioco, N Equatorial Guinea
Malaca *see* Málaga
Malacca *see* Melaka
173 G4 **Malacca, Strait of** *Ind.* Selat Malaka. *strait* Indonesia/Malaysia
Malacka *see* Malacky
113 G20 **Malacky** *Hung.* Malacka. Západné Slovensko, W Slovakia
35 R16 **Malad City** Idaho, NW USA
119 Q4 **Mala Divytsya** Chernihivs'ka Oblast', N Ukraine
121 J15 **Maladzyechna** *Pol.* Molodeczno, *Rus.* Molodechno. Minskaya Voblasts', C Belarus
202 D12 **Malaee** Île Futuna, N Wallis and Futuna
39 V15 **Malaga** New Mexico, SW USA
56 G8 **Málaga** Santander, C Colombia
106 M15 **Málaga** *anc.* Malaca. Andalucía, S Spain
106 L15 **Málaga** ⬖ *province* Andalucía, S Spain
106 M15 **Málaga** × Andalucía, S Spain
Malagasy Republic *see* Madagascar
107 N10 **Malagón** Castilla-La Mancha, C Spain
99 G18 **Malahide** *Ir.* Mullach Íde. E Ireland
195 Y14 **Malaita** *off.* Malaita Province. ⬖ *province* N Solomon Islands
195 Y15 **Malaita** *var.* Mala. *island* N Solomon Islands
82 F13 **Malakal** Upper Nile, S Sudan
114 C10 **Mala Kapela** ⛰ NW Croatia
27 V7 **Malakoff** Texas, SW USA
Malakula *see* Malekula
155 V7 **Malakwāl** *var.* Mālikwāla. Punjab, E Pakistan
194 J12 **Malalamai** Madang, W PNG
194 J14 **Malalaua** Gulf, S PNG
175 Q11 **Malamala** Sulawesi, C Indonesia
174 M15 **Malang** Jawa, C Indonesia
85 O14 **Malanga** Niassa, N Mozambique
Malange *see* Malanje
94 I9 **Malangen** *sound* N Norway
84 C11 **Malanje** *var.* Malange. Malanje, NW Angola
84 C11 **Malanje** *var.* Malange. ⬖ *province* N Angola
154 M16 **Malān, Rās** *headland* SW Pakistan
79 S13 **Malanville** NE Benin
Malapane *see* Ozimek
161 F21 **Malappuram** Kerala, SW India
45 T17 **Mala, Punta** *headland* S Panama
97 N16 **Mälaren** ◎ C Sweden
64 H13 **Malargüe** Mendoza, W Argentina
12 J8 **Malartic** Québec, SE Canada
121 F20 **Malaryta** *Pol.* Maloryta, *Rus.* Malorita. Brestskaya Voblasts', SW Belarus
65 J19 **Malaspina** Chubut, SE Argentina
41 U12 **Malaspina Glacier** *glacier* Alaska, USA
143 N15 **Malatya** *anc.* Melitene. Malatya, SE Turkey
142 M14 **Malatya** ⬖ *province* C Turkey
119 Q7 **Mala Vyska** *Rus.* Malaya Viska. Kirovohrads'ka Oblast', S Ukraine
85 M14 **Malawi** *off.* Republic of Malaŵi; *prev.* Nyasaland, Nyasaland Protectorate. ◆ *republic* S Africa
Malawi, Lake *see* Nyasa, Lake
95 J17 **Malax** *Fin.* Maalahti. Vaasa, W Finland
128 H14 **Malaya Vishera** Novgorodskaya Oblast', W Russian Federation
Malaya Viska *see* Mala Vyska
179 R15 **Malaybalay** Mindanao, S Philippines
148 L6 **Malāyer** *prev.* Daulatabad. Hamadān, W Iran
174 Gg3 **Malay Peninsula** *peninsula* Malaysia/Thailand
174 I3 **Malaysia** *var.* Federation of Malaysia; *prev.* the separate territories of Federation of Malaya, Sarawak and Sabah (North Borneo) and Singapore. ◆ *monarchy* SE Asia
143 R14 **Malazgirt** Muş, E Turkey
13 R8 **Malbaie** ≈ Québec, SE Canada
79 T12 **Malbaza** Tahoua, S Niger
112 J7 **Malbork** *Ger.* Marienburg, Marienburg in Westpreussen. Elbląg, N Poland
102 N9 **Malchin** Mecklenburg-Vorpommern, N Germany
102 M9 **Malchiner See** ◎ NE Germany
Mālda *see* Māldah
101 D16 **Maldegem** Oost-Vlaanderen, NW Belgium
100 L13 **Malden** Gelderland, SE Netherlands
21 O11 **Malden** Massachusetts, NE USA
29 Y8 **Malden** Missouri, C USA
203 X4 **Malden Island** *prev.* Independence Island. *atoll* E Kiribati
181 Q6 **Maldives** *off.* Maldivian Divehi, Republic of Maldives. ◆ *republic* N Indian Ocean
Maldivian Divehi *see* Maldives
99 P21 **Maldon** E England, UK

◆ Country
● Country Capital
◇ Dependent Territory
○ Dependent Territory Capital
⬖ Administrative Region
× International Airport
▲ Mountain
⛰ Mountain Range
Volcano
≈ River
◎ Lake
▣ Reservoir

63 G20 **Maldonado** Maldonado, S Uruguay
63 G20 **Maldonado** ◈ *department* S Uruguay
43 P17 **Maldonado, Punta** *headland* S Mexico
157 K19 **Male'** *Div.* Maale ● (Maldives) Male' Atoll, C Maldives
108 G6 **Malè** Trentino-Alto Adige, N Italy
78 K13 **Maléa** *var.* Maléya. Haute-Guinée, NE Guinea
117 G22 **Maléas, Ákra** *headland* S Greece
117 L17 **Maléas, Ákra** *headland* Lésvos, E Greece
157 K19 **Male' Atoll** *var.* Kaafu Atoll. *atoll* C Maldives
Malebo, Pool *see* Stanley Pool
160 E12 **Mālegaon** Mahārāshtra, W India
83 F15 **Malek** Jonglei, S Sudan
197 B13 **Malekula** *var.* Malakula; *prev.* Mallicolo. *island* W Vanuatu
201 Y15 **Malem** Kosrae, E Micronesia
85 O15 **Malema** Nampula, N Mozambique
81 N23 **Malemba-Nkulu** Shaba, SE Zaire
195 Q10 **Malendok Island** *island* Tanga Islands, NE PNG
128 K9 **Malen'ga** Respublika Kareliya, NW Russian Federation
97 M20 **Målerås** Kalmar, S Sweden
105 O6 **Malesherbes** Loiret, C France
117 G18 **Malesína** Stereá Ellás, E Greece
Maléya *see* Maléa
131 O15 **Malgobek** Chechenskaya Respublika, SW Russian Federation
107 X5 **Malgrat de Mar** Cataluña, NE Spain
82 C9 **Malha** Northern Darfur, W Sudan
145 Q5 **Malḩāt** C Iraq
34 K14 **Malheur Lake** ◎ Oregon, NW USA
34 L14 **Malheur River** ≈ Oregon, NW USA
78 I13 **Mali** Moyenne-Guinée, NW Guinea
79 O9 **Mali** *off.* Republic of Mali, *Fr.* République du Mali; *prev.* French Sudan, Sudanese Republic. ◆ *republic* W Africa
175 S16 **Maliana** Timor, S Indonesia
178 H1 **Mali Hka** ≈ N Myanmar
Mali Idjoš *see* Mali Idoš
114 K8 **Mali Idoš** *var.* Mali Idjoš, *Hung.* Kishegyes; *prev.* Krivaja. Serbia, N Yugoslavia
114 K9 **Mali Kanal** *canal* N Yugoslavia
175 R8 **Maliku** Sulawesi, N Indonesia
Malik, Wadi al *see* Milk, Wadi el
Mālikwāla *see* Malakwal
178 Gg12 **Mali Kyun** *var.* Tavoy Island. *island* Mergui Archipelago, S Myanmar
97 M19 **Målilla** Kalmar, S Sweden
114 B11 **Mali Lošinj** *It.* Lussinpiccolo. Primorje-Gorski Kotar, W Croatia
Malin *see* Malyn
179 Q15 **Malindang, Mount** ▲ Mindanao, S Philippines
83 K20 **Malindi** Coast, SE Kenya
Malines *see* Mechelen
98 E13 **Malin Head** *Ir.* Cionn Mhálanna. *headland* NW Ireland
175 Pp7 **Malino, Gunung** ▲ Sulawesi, N Indonesia
115 M21 **Maliq** *var.* Maliqi. Korçë, SE Albania
Maliqi *see* Maliq
179 Rr16 **Malita** Mindanao, S Philippines
160 G12 **Malkāpur** Mahārāshtra, C India
142 B10 **Malkara** Tekirdağ, NW Turkey
121 J19 **Mal'kavichy** *Rus.* Mal'kovichi. Brestskaya Voblasts', SW Belarus
Malkiye *see* Al Mālikīyah
116 L11 **Malko Sharkovo, Yazovir** ⊠ SE Bulgaria
116 N11 **Malko Tŭrnovo** Burgaska Oblast, SE Bulgaria
Mal'kovichi *see* Mal'kavichy
191 R12 **Mallacoota** Victoria, SE Australia
98 G10 **Mallaig** N Scotland, UK
190 I9 **Mallala** South Australia
77 W9 **Mallawi** C Egypt
107 R5 **Mallén** Aragón, NE Spain
108 F5 **Malles Venosta** Trentino-Alto Adige, N Italy
Mallicolo *see* Malekula
111 Q8 **Mallnitz** Salzburg, S Austria
107 W9 **Mallorca** *Eng.* Majorca; *anc.* Baleares Major. *island* Islas Baleares, Spain, W Mediterranean Sea
99 C20 **Mallow** *Ir.* Mala. SW Ireland
95 E15 **Malm** Nord-Trøndelag, C Norway
97 L19 **Malmbäck** Jönköping, S Sweden
94 J12 **Malmberget** Norrbotten, N Sweden
101 M20 **Malmédy** Liège, E Belgium
85 E25 **Malmesbury** Western Cape, SW South Africa
97 N16 **Malmköping** Södermanland, C Sweden
97 K23 **Malmo** ✕ Malmöhus, S Sweden
97 K23 **Malmö** Malmöhus, S Sweden
97 K23 **Malmöhus** ◈ *county* S Sweden
47 Q16 **Malmok** *headland* Bonaire, S Netherlands Antilles
97 M18 **Malmslätt** Östergötland, S Sweden
129 R16 **Malmyzh** Kirovskaya Oblast', NW Russian Federation
58 A10 **Mal Nomre, Punta** *headland* NW Peru
197 B12 **Malo** *island* W Vanuatu
130 J7 **Maloarkhangel'sk** Orlovskaya Oblast', W Russian Federation
Maļoeļap *see* Maloelap Atoll
201 V6 **Maloelap Atoll** *var.* Maļoeļap. *atoll* E Marshall Islands
Maloenda *see* Malunda
110 I10 **Maloja** Graubünden, S Switzerland
84 L12 **Malole** Northern, NE Zambia
197 H13 **Malolo** *island* Mamanuca Group, W Fiji
197 H13 **Malolo Barrier Reef** *var.* Ro Ro Reef. *reef* W Fiji
179 P10 **Malolos** Luzon, N Philippines
20 K6 **Malone** New York, NE USA
81 K25 **Malonga** Shaba, S Zaire
113 L15 **Małopolska** *plateau* S Poland
Malorita/Maloryta *see* Malaryta
128 K9 **Maloshuyka** Arkhangel'skaya Oblast', NW Russian Federation
116 G10 **Mal'ovitsa** ▲ W Bulgaria
151 V15 **Malovodnoye** Almaty, SE Kazakhstan
96 C10 **Måløy** Sogn og Fjordane, S Norway
130 K4 **Maloyaroslavets** Kaluzhskaya Oblast', W Russian Federation
125 F6 **Malozemel'skaya Tundra** *physical region* NW Russian Federation
106 J10 **Malpartida de Cáceres** Extremadura, W Spain
106 K9 **Malpartida de Plasencia** Extremadura, W Spain
108 C7 **Malpensa** ✕ (Milano) Lombardia, N Italy
78 J6 **Malqteïr** *desert* N Mauritania
120 J10 **Malta** Rēzekne, SE Latvia
35 V7 **Malta** Montana, NW USA
123 Jj14 **Malta** *off.* Republic of Malta. ◆ *republic* C Mediterranean Sea
111 R8 **Malta** *var.* Maltabach. ≈ S Austria
123 L11 **Malta** *island* Malta, C Mediterranean Sea
Maltabach *see* Malta
Malta, Canale di *see* Malta Channel
123 L12 **Malta Channel** *It.* Canale di Malta. *strait* Italy/Malta
85 D20 **Maltahöhe** Hardap, SW Namibia
99 N16 **Malton** N England, UK
175 T11 **Maluku** *off.* Propinsi Maluku, *Dut.* Molukken, *Eng.* Moluccas. ◈ *province* E Indonesia
175 Ss9 **Maluku** *Dut.* Molukken, *Eng.* Moluccas; *prev.* Spice Islands. *island group* E Indonesia
Maluku, Laut *see* Molucca Sea
79 V13 **Malumfashi** Katsina, N Nigeria
175 P11 **Malunda** *prev.* Maloenda. Sulawesi, C Indonesia
96 K13 **Malung** Kopparberg, C Sweden
96 K13 **Malungsfors** Kopparberg, C Sweden
195 X14 **Maluu** *var.* Malu'u. Malaita, N Solomon Islands
161 D16 **Mālvan** Mahārāshtra, W India
Malventum *see* Benevento
29 U12 **Malvern** Arkansas, C USA
31 S15 **Malvern** Iowa, C USA
46 I13 **Malvern** ▲ W Jamaica
Malvinas, Islas *see* Falkland Islands
119 N4 **Malyn** *Rus.* Malin. Zhytomyrs'ka Oblast', N Ukraine
127 O5 **Malyy Anyuy** ≈ NE Russian Federation
131 O11 **Malyye Derbety** Respublika Kalmykiya, SW Russian Federation
Malyy Kavkaz *see* Lesser Caucasus
126 M5 **Malyy Lyakhovskiy, Ostrov** *island* NE Russian Federation
Malyy Pamir *see* Little Pamir
126 Jj4 **Malyy Taymyr, Ostrov** *island* Severnaya Zemlya, N Russian Federation
150 E10 **Malyy Uzen'** *Kaz.* Kishiözen. ≈ Kazakhstan/Russian Federation
126 I16 **Malyy Yenisey** *var.* Ka-Krem. ≈ S Russian Federation
126 K13 **Mama** Irkutskaya Oblast', C Russian Federation
131 S3 **Mamadysh** Respublika Tatarstan, W Russian Federation
119 N14 **Mamaia** Constanța, E Romania
197 G14 **Mamanuca Group** *island group* Yasawa Group, W Fiji
152 L13 **Mamash** Lebapskiy Velayat, E Turkmenistan
176 W11 **Mamasiware** Irian Jaya, E Indonesia
194 L14 **Mambare** ≈ S PNG
81 O17 **Mambasa** Haut-Zaïre, NE Zaire
176 Xx10 **Mamberamo, Sungai** ≈ Irian Jaya, E Indonesia
81 G15 **Mambéré** ≈ SW Central African Republic
81 G15 **Mambéré-Kadéï** ◈ *prefecture* SW Central African Republic
176 X9 **Mambetaloi** Irian Jaya, E Indonesia
Mambij *see* Manbij
81 H18 **Mambili** ≈ W Congo
85 N18 **Mambone** *var.* Nova Mambone. Inhambane, E Mozambique
179 P11 **Mamburao** Mindoro, N Philippines
180 I16 **Mamelles** *island* Inner Islands, NE Seychelles
101 M25 **Mamer** Luxembourg, SW Luxembourg
104 L6 **Mamers** Sarthe, NW France
81 D15 **Mamfe** Sud-Ouest, W Cameroon
151 P6 **Mamlyutka** Severnyy Kazakhstan, N Kazakhstan
38 M15 **Mammoth** Arizona, SW USA
35 S12 **Mammoth Hot Springs** Wyoming, C USA
Mamoedjoe *see* Mamuju
121 A14 **Mamonovo** *Ger.* Heiligenbeil. Kaliningradskaya Oblast', W Russian Federation
59 L14 **Mamoré, Río** ≈ Bolivia/Brazil
78 I14 **Mamou** Moyenne-Guinée, W Guinea
24 H8 **Mamou** Louisiana, S USA
180 I14 **Mamoudzou** ○ (Mayotte) C Mayotte
180 I3 **Mampikony** Mahajanga, N Madagascar
79 P16 **Mampong** C Ghana
112 M7 **Mamry, Jezioro** *Ger.* Mauersee. ◎ NE Poland
175 P10 **Mamuju** *prev.* Mamoedjoe. Sulawesi, S Indonesia
175 Oo10 **Mamuju, Teluk** *bay* Sulawesi, C Indonesia
85 F19 **Mamuno** Ghanzi, W Botswana
115 K19 **Mamuras** *var.* Mamurasi, Mamurras. Lezhë, C Albania
Mamurasi/Mamurras *see* Mamuras
78 L16 **Man** W Ivory Coast
57 X9 **Mana** NW French Guiana
58 A6 **Manabí** ◈ *province* W Ecuador
44 G4 **Manabique, Punta** *var.* Cabo Tres Puntas. *headland* E Guatemala
56 G11 **Manacacías, Río** ≈ C Colombia
60 F13 **Manacapuru** Amazonas, N Brazil
175 Rr6 **Manado** *prev.* Menado. Sulawesi, C Indonesia
196 H5 **Managaha** *island* S Northern Mariana Islands
101 G20 **Manage** Hainaut, S Belgium
44 J10 **Managua** ● (Nicaragua) Managua, W Nicaragua
44 J10 **Managua** ◈ *department* W Nicaragua
44 J10 **Managua** ✕ Managua, W Nicaragua
44 J10 **Managua, Lago de** *var.* Xolotlán. ◎ W Nicaragua
Manah *see* Bilād Manah
20 K16 **Manahawkin** New Jersey, NE USA
192 K11 **Manaia** Taranaki, North Island, NZ
180 J6 **Manakara** Fianarantsoa, SE Madagascar
158 J7 **Manāli** Himāchal Pradesh, NW India
133 U12 **Ma, Nam** *Vtn.* Sông Mã. ≈ Laos/Vietnam
Manama *see* Al Manāmah
194 I10 **Manam Island** *island* N PNG
69 Y13 **Mananara** ≈ SE Madagascar
190 M9 **Manangatang** Victoria, SE Australia
180 J6 **Mananjary** Fianarantsoa, SE Madagascar
78 L14 **Manankoro** Sikasso, SW Mali
78 J12 **Manantali, Lac de** ⊠ W Mali
Manáos *see* Manaus
193 B23 **Manapouri** Southland, South Island, NZ
193 B23 **Manapouri, Lake** ◎ South Island, NZ
60 F13 **Manaquiri** Amazonas, NW Brazil
Manar *see* Mannar
164 K5 **Manas** Xinjiang Uygur Zizhiqu, NW China
159 U12 **Manās** *var.* Dangme Chu. ≈ Bhutan/India
153 R8 **Manas, Gora** ▲ Kyrgyzstan/Uzbekistan
164 K3 **Manas Hu** ◎ NW China
159 P10 **Manaslu** ▲ C Nepal
39 S8 **Manassa** Colorado, C USA
23 W4 **Manassas** Virginia, NE USA
47 T5 **Manatí** C Puerto Rico
175 S16 **Manatuto** Timor, C Indonesia
194 L14 **Manau** Northern, S PNG
56 H4 **Manaure** La Guajira, N Colombia
60 F12 **Manaus** *prev.* Manáos. *state capital* Amazonas, NW Brazil
142 G17 **Manavgat** Antalya, SW Turkey
192 M13 **Manawatu** ≈ North Island, NZ
192 L11 **Manawatu-Wanganui** *off.* Manawatu-Wanganui Region. ◈ *region* North Island, NZ
176 Uu12 **Manawoka, Pulau** *island* Kepulauan Gorong, E Indonesia
179 Rr16 **Manay** Mindanao, S Philippines
144 K2 **Manbij** *var.* Mambij, *Fr.* Membidj. Ḩalab, N Syria
107 N13 **Mancha Real** Andalucía, S Spain
104 I4 **Manche** ◈ *department* N France
99 L17 **Manchester** *Lat.* Mancunium. NW England, UK
25 S5 **Manchester** Georgia, SE USA
31 Y13 **Manchester** Iowa, C USA
23 N7 **Manchester** Kentucky, S USA
21 O10 **Manchester** New Hampshire, NE USA
22 K10 **Manchester** Tennessee, S USA
20 M9 **Manchester** Vermont, NE USA
99 L18 **Manchester** ✕ NW England, UK
155 P15 **Manchhar Lake** ◎ SE Pakistan
Man-chou-li *see* Manzhouli
133 X7 **Manchurian Plain** *plain* NE China
Máncio Lima *see* Japiim
Mancunium *see* Manchester
154 J15 **Mand** Baluchistān, SW Pakistan
Mand *see* Mand, Rūd-e
83 H25 **Manda** Iringa, SW Tanzania
180 H6 **Mandabe** Toliara, W Madagascar
168 I5 **Mandal** Hövsgöl, N Mongolia
168 L7 **Mandal** Töv, C Mongolia
97 E18 **Mandal** Vest-Agder, S Norway
177 G5 **Mandalay** Mandalay, C Myanmar
177 G6 **Mandalay** ◈ *division* C Myanmar
168 L9 **Mandalgovĭ** Dundgovĭ, C Mongolia
145 V7 **Mandalī** E Iraq
97 E18 **Mandalselva** ≈ S Norway
30 M5 **Mandan** North Dakota, N USA
Mandargiri Hill *see* Mandār Hill
159 R14 **Mandār Hill** *prev.* Mandargiri Hill. Bihār, NE India
175 P11 **Mandar, Teluk** *bay* Sulawesi, C Indonesia
109 C19 **Mandas** Sardegna, Italy, C Mediterranean Sea
Mandasor *see* Mandsaur
83 L16 **Mandera** North Eastern, NE Kenya
35 V13 **Manderson** Wyoming, C USA
46 J12 **Mandeville** C Jamaica
24 K9 **Mandeville** Louisiana, S USA
158 I7 **Mandi** Himāchal Pradesh, NW India
78 K14 **Mandiana** Haute-Guinée, E Guinea
155 U10 **Mandi Būrewāla** *var.* Būrewāla. Punjab, E Pakistan
158 G9 **Mandi Dabwāli** Haryāna, NW India
Mandidzudzure *see* Chimanimani
85 M15 **Mandié** Manica, NW Mozambique
85 N14 **Mandimba** Niassa, N Mozambique
175 Ss9 **Mandioli, Pulau** *island* Kepulauan Bacan, E Indonesia
59 Q19 **Mandioré, Laguna** ◎ E Bolivia
160 J10 **Mandla** Madhya Pradesh, C India
85 M20 **Mandlakazi** *var.* Manjacaze. Gaza, S Mozambique
97 E24 **Mandø** *var.* Manø. *island* W Denmark
176 Ww9 **Mandori** Irian Jaya, E Indonesia
Mandoúdhion/Mandoudi *see* Mantoúdi
117 G19 **Mándra** Attikí, C Greece
180 I7 **Mandrare** ≈ S Madagascar
116 M10 **Mandra, Yazovir** *salt lake* SE Bulgaria
109 L23 **Mandrazzi, Portella** *pass* Sicilia, Italy, C Mediterranean Sea
180 J3 **Mandritsara** Mahajanga, N Madagascar
149 O13 **Mand, Rūd-e** *var.* Mand. ≈ S Iran
160 F9 **Mandsaur** *prev.* Mandasor. Madhya Pradesh, C India
160 F11 **Māndu** Madhya Pradesh, C India
175 Oo5 **Mandul, Pulau** *island* N Indonesia
85 G15 **Mandundu** Western, W Zambia
188 I13 **Mandurah** Western Australia
109 P18 **Manduria** Puglia, SE Italy
161 G20 **Mandya** Karnātaka, C India
79 P12 **Mané** C Burkina
108 E8 **Manerbio** Lombardia, NW Italy
Manevichi *see* Manevychi
118 K3 **Manevychi** *Pol.* Maniewicze, *Rus.* Manevichi. Volyns'ka Oblast', NW Ukraine
109 N16 **Manfredonia** Puglia, SE Italy
109 N16 **Manfredonia, Golfo di** *gulf* Adriatic Sea, N Mediterranean Sea
79 P13 **Manga** C Burkina
61 L16 **Mangabeiras, Chapada das** ▲ E Brazil
81 J20 **Mangai** Bandundu, W Zaire
202 L17 **Mangaia** *island group* S Cook Islands
192 M9 **Mangakino** Waikato, North Island, NZ
118 M15 **Mangalia** *anc.* Callatis. Constanța, SE Romania
80 J11 **Mangalmé** Guéra, SE Chad
161 E19 **Mangalore** Karnātaka, W India
203 Y13 **Mangareva** *var.* Magareva. *island* Îles Tuamotu, SE French Polynesia
85 I23 **Mangaung** Free State, C South Africa
Mangaung *see* Bloemfontein
160 K9 **Mangawān** Madhya Pradesh, C India
192 M11 **Mangaweka** Manawatu-Wanganui, North Island, NZ
192 N11 **Mangaweka** ▲ North Island, NZ
81 P17 **Mangbwalu** Haut-Zaïre, NE Zaire
103 L24 **Mangfall** ≈ SE Germany
174 K11 **Manggar** Pulau Belitung, W Indonesia
176 Vv12 **Manggawitu** Irian Jaya, E Indonesia
152 H8 **Manghit** *Rus.* Mangit. Qoraqalpoghiston Respublikasi, W Uzbekistan
177 G2 **Mangin Range** ▲ N Myanmar
145 R1 **Mangish** N Iraq
150 F15 **Mangistau** *Kaz.* Mangqystaū Oblysy; *prev.* Mangyshlaskaya. ◈ *province* SW Kazakhstan
Mangit *see* Manghit
56 A13 **Manglares, Cabo** *headland* SW Colombia
155 V6 **Mangla Reservoir** ⊠ NE Pakistan
165 N9 **Mangnai** *var.* Lao Mangnai. Qinghai, C China
Mango *see* Mago, Fiji
Mango *see* Sansanné-Mango, Togo
Mangoche *see* Mangochi
85 N14 **Mangochi** *var.* Mangoche; *prev.* Fort Johnston. Southern, SE Malawi
79 N14 **Mangodara** SW Burkina
180 H6 **Mangoky** ≈ W Madagascar
175 S10 **Mangole, Pulau** *island* Kepulauan Sula, E Indonesia
192 J2 **Mangonui** Northland, North Island, NZ
Mangqystaū Oblysy *see* Mangistau
Mangqystaū Shyghanaghy *see* Mangyshlakskiy Zaliv
106 H7 **Mangualde** Viseu, N Portugal
63 H18 **Mangueira, Lagoa** ◎ S Brazil
79 X6 **Manguéni, Plateau du** ▲ NE Niger
28 K11 **Mangum** Oklahoma, C USA
81 O18 **Manguredjipa** Nord Kivu, E Zaire
85 L16 **Mangwendi** Mashonaland East, E Zimbabwe
150 F15 **Mangyshlak, Plato** *plateau* SW Kazakhstan
150 E14 **Mangyshlakskiy Zaliv** *Kaz.* Mangqystaū Shyghanaghy. *gulf* SW Kazakhstan
Mangyshlaskaya *see* Mangistau
168 I5 **Manhan** Hövsgöl, N Mongolia
29 O4 **Manhattan** Kansas, C USA
101 L21 **Manhay** Luxembourg, SE Belgium
85 L21 **Manhiça** *prev.* Vila de Manhiça. Maputo, S Mozambique
85 L21 **Manhoca** Maputo, S Mozambique
61 N20 **Manhuaçu** Minas Gerais, SE Brazil
149 R11 **Mānī** Kermān, C Iran
56 H10 **Maní** Casanare, C Colombia
58 A6 **Manía, Bahía de** *bay* W Ecuador
85 M17 **Manica** *var.* Vila de Manica. Manica, W Mozambique
85 M17 **Manica** *off.* Província de Manica. ◈ *province* W Mozambique
85 L17 **Manicaland** ◈ *province* E Zimbabwe
13 U5 **Manic Deux, Réservoir** ⊠ Québec, SE Canada
Manich *see* Manych
61 F14 **Manicoré** Amazonas, N Brazil
11 N11 **Manicouagan** Québec, SE Canada
11 N11 **Manicouagan** ≈ Québec, SE Canada
13 U6 **Manicouagan, Péninsule de** *peninsula* Québec, SE Canada
11 N11 **Manicouagan, Réservoir** ◎ Québec, E Canada
13 T4 **Manic Trois, Réservoir** ⊠ Québec, SE Canada
81 M20 **Maniema** *off.* Région du Maniema. ◈ *region* E Zaire
Maniewicze *see* Manevychi
166 F8 **Maniganggo** Sichuan, C China
9 Y15 **Manigotagan** Manitoba, S Canada
159 R13 **Manihāri** Bihār, N India
203 U9 **Manihi** *island* Îles Tuamotu, C French Polynesia
202 L13 **Manihiki** *atoll* N Cook Islands
183 U8 **Manihiki Plateau** *undersea feature* C Pacific Ocean
206 M14 **Maniitsoq** *var.* Manîtsoq, *Dan.* Sukkertoppen. S Greenland
159 T15 **Manikganj** Dhaka, C Bangladesh
158 M14 **Mānikpur** Uttar Pradesh, N India
179 P11 **Manila** *off.* City of Manila. ● (Philippines) Luzon, N Philippines
29 Y9 **Manila** Arkansas, C USA
201 N16 **Manila Reef** *reef* W Micronesia
191 T6 **Manilla** New South Wales, SE Australia
200 Qq14 **Maniloa** *island* Tongatapu Group, S Tonga
127 P7 **Manily** Koryakskiy Avtonomnyy Okrug, E Russian Federation
176 Ww9 **Manim, Pulau** *island* E Indonesia
173 Ff8 **Maninjau, Danau** ◎ Sumatera, W Indonesia
159 W13 **Manipur** ◈ *state* NE India
159 X14 **Manipur Hills** *hill range* E India
142 C14 **Manisa** *var.* Manissa; *prev.* Saruhan, *anc.* Magnesia. Manisa, W Turkey
142 C13 **Manisa** *var.* Manissa. ◈ *province* W Turkey
Manissa *see* Manisa
33 O7 **Manistee** Michigan, N USA
33 P7 **Manistee River** ≈ Michigan, N USA
33 O4 **Manistique** Michigan, N USA
33 P4 **Manistique Lake** ◎ Michigan, N USA
9 W13 **Manitoba** ◈ *province* S Canada
9 X16 **Manitoba, Lake** ◎ Manitoba, S Canada
9 X17 **Manitou** Manitoba, S Canada
33 N2 **Manitou Island** *island* Michigan, N USA
12 H11 **Manitou Lake** ◎ Ontario, SE Canada
10 G15 **Manitoulin Island** *island* Ontario, S Canada
39 T5 **Manitou Springs** Colorado, C USA
12 G12 **Manitouwabing Lake** ◎ Ontario, S Canada
10 E12 **Manitouwadge** Ontario, S Canada
10 G15 **Manitowaning** Manitoulin Island, Ontario, S Canada
12 B7 **Manitowik Lake** ◎ Ontario, S Canada
33 N7 **Manitowoc** Wisconsin, N USA
Manîtsoq *see* Maniitsoq
145 O7 **Mānī', Wādī al** *dry watercourse* W Iraq
10 J14 **Maniwaki** Québec, SE Canada
176 X11 **Maniwori** Irian Jaya, E Indonesia
56 E10 **Manizales** Caldas, W Colombia
114 F11 **Manjača** ▲ NW Bosnia and Herzegovina
Manjacaze *see* Mandlakazi
188 J14 **Manjimup** Western Australia
111 V4 **Mank** Niederösterreich, C Austria
81 I17 **Mankanza** Equateur, NW Zaire
159 N12 **Mankāpur** Uttar Pradesh, N India
28 M3 **Mankato** Kansas, C USA
31 U10 **Mankato** Minnesota, N USA
119 O7 **Man'kivka** Cherkas'ka Oblast', C Ukraine
78 M15 **Mankono** C Ivory Coast
9 T17 **Mankota** Saskatchewan, S Canada
161 K23 **Mankulam** Northern Province, N Sri Lanka
41 Q9 **Manley Hot Springs** Alaska, USA
20 H10 **Manlius** New York, NE USA
107 W5 **Manlleu** Cataluña, NE Spain
31 V11 **Manly** Iowa, C USA
160 E13 **Manmād** Mahārāshtra, W India
190 J7 **Mannahill** South Australia
161 J23 **Mannar** *var.* Manar. Northern Province, NW Sri Lanka
161 I24 **Mannar, Gulf of** *gulf* India/Sri Lanka
161 J23 **Mannar Island** *island* N Sri Lanka
Mannersdorf *see* Mannersdorf am Leithagebirge
111 Y5 **Mannersdorf am Leithagebirge** *var.* Mannersdorf. Niederösterreich, E Austria
111 Y6 **Mannersdorf an der Rabnitz** Burgenland, E Austria
103 G20 **Mannheim** Baden-Württemberg, SW Germany
9 O12 **Manning** Alberta, W Canada
31 T14 **Manning** Iowa, C USA
30 K5 **Manning** North Dakota, N USA
23 S13 **Manning** South Carolina, SE USA
203 Y2 **Manning, Cape** *headland* Kiritimati, NE Kiribati
195 V13 **Manning Strait** *strait* NW Solomon Islands
23 S3 **Mannington** West Virginia, NE USA
190 A1 **Mann Ranges** ▲ South Australia
109 C19 **Mannu** ≈ Sardegna, Italy, C Mediterranean Sea
9 R14 **Mannville** Alberta, SW Canada
78 J15 **Mano** ≈ Liberia/Sierra Leone
Manø *see* Mandø
41 O13 **Manokotak** Alaska, USA
176 W9 **Manokwari** Irian Jaya, E Indonesia
81 N22 **Manono** Shaba, SE Zaire
27 T10 **Manor** Texas, SW USA
99 D16 **Manorhamilton** *Ir.* Cluainín. NW Ireland
105 S15 **Manosque** Alpes-de-Haute-Provence, SE France
10 L11 **Manouane, Lac** ◎ Québec, SE Canada
169 W12 **Manp'o** *var.* Manp'ojin. NW North Korea
Manp'ojin *see* Manp'o
203 T4 **Manra** *prev.* Sydney Island. *atoll* Phoenix Islands, C Kiribati
107 V5 **Manresa** Cataluña, NE Spain
158 H9 **Mānsa** Punjab, NW India
84 J12 **Mansa** *prev.* Fort Rosebery. Luapula, N Zambia
78 G12 **Mansa Konko** C Gambia
13 Q11 **Manseau** Québec, SE Canada
155 U5 **Mānsehra** North-West Frontier Province, NW Pakistan
15 Mm6 **Mansel Island** *island* Northwest Territories, NE Canada
191 O12 **Mansfield** Victoria, SE Australia
99 M18 **Mansfield** C England, UK
29 S11 **Mansfield** Arkansas, C USA
24 G6 **Mansfield** Louisiana, S USA
21 O12 **Mansfield** Massachusetts, NE USA
33 T12 **Mansfield** Ohio, N USA
20 G12 **Mansfield** Pennsylvania, NE USA
20 M7 **Mansfield, Mount** ▲ Vermont, NE USA
61 M16 **Mansidão** Bahia, E Brazil
104 L11 **Mansle** Charente, W France
78 G12 **Mansôa** C Guinea-Bissau
49 V8 **Manso, Rio** ≈ C Brazil
Mansûra *see* El Manṣûra
Mansurabad *see* Mehrān, Rūd-e
58 A6 **Manta** Manabí, W Ecuador
59 F14 **Mantaro, Río** ≈ C Peru
37 O8 **Manteca** California, W USA
56 J7 **Mantecal** Apure, C Venezuela
33 N11 **Manteno** Illinois, N USA
23 Y9 **Manteo** Roanoke Island, North Carolina, SE USA
Mantes-Gassicourt *see* Mantes-la-Jolie
105 N5 **Mantes-la-Jolie** *prev.* Mantes-Gassicourt, Mantes-sur-Seine, *anc.* Medunta. Yvelines, N France
Mantes-sur-Seine *see* Mantes-la-Jolie
38 L5 **Manti** Utah, W USA
Mantinea *see* Mantíneia
117 F20 **Mantíneia** *anc.* Mantinea. *site of ancient city* Pelopónnisos, S Greece
61 M21 **Mantiqueira, Serra da** ▲ S Brazil
31 W10 **Mantorville** Minnesota, N USA
117 G17 **Mantoúdi** *var.* Mandoudi; *prev.* Mandoúdhion. Évvoia, C Greece
Mantoue *see* Mantova
108 F8 **Mantova** *Eng.* Mantua, *Fr.* Mantoue. Lombardia, NW Italy
95 M19 **Mäntsälä** Uusimaa, S Finland
95 L17 **Mänttä** Häme, SW Finland
Mantua *see* Mantova
129 O14 **Manturovo** Kostromskaya Oblast', NW Russian Federation
95 M18 **Mäntyharju** Mikkeli, SE Finland
94 M13 **Mäntyjärvi** Lappi, N Finland
202 L16 **Manuae** *island* S Cook Islands
203 Q10 **Manuae** *atoll* Îles Sous le Vent, W French Polynesia
198 Dd8 **Manua Islands** *island group* E American Samoa
42 L5 **Manuel Benavides** Chihuahua, N Mexico
63 D21 **Manuel J.Cobo** Buenos Aires, E Argentina
60 M12 **Manuel Luís, Recife** *reef* E Brazil
63 F15 **Manuel Viana** Rio Grande do Sul, S Brazil
61 I14 **Manuel Zinho** Pará, N Brazil
203 V11 **Manuhangi** *atoll* Îles Tuamotu, C French Polynesia
193 E22 **Manuherikia** ≈ South Island, NZ
175 R11 **Manui, Pulau** *island* N Indonesia
Manukau *see* Manurewa
192 L6 **Manukau Harbour** *harbor* North Island, NZ
174 K14 **Manuk, Ci** ≈ Jawa, S Indonesia
176 U12 **Manuk, Pulau** *island* Maluku, E Indonesia
203 Z2 **Manulu Lagoon** ◎ Kiritimati, E Kiribati
190 J7 **Manunda Creek** *seasonal river* South Australia
59 K15 **Manupari, Río** ≈ N Bolivia
192 L6 **Manurewa** *var.* Manukau. Auckland, North Island, NZ
59 K15 **Manurimi, Río** ≈ NW Bolivia
194 I8 **Manus** ◈ *province* N PNG
194 J8 **Manus Island** *var.* Great Admiralty Island. *island* N PNG
176 U15 **Manuwui** Pulau Babar, E Indonesia
31 Q3 **Manvel** North Dakota, N USA
35 Z14 **Manville** Wyoming, C USA
24 G6 **Many** Louisiana, S USA
83 H21 **Manyara, Lake** ◎ NE Tanzania
130 L12 **Manych** *var.* Manich. ≈ SW Russian Federation
131 N13 **Manych-Gudilo, Ozero** *salt lake* SW Russian Federation
85 H14 **Manyinga** North Western, NW Zambia
107 O11 **Manzanares** Castilla-La Mancha, C Spain
46 H7 **Manzanillo** Granma, E Cuba
42 K14 **Manzanillo** Colima, SW Mexico
42 K14 **Manzanillo, Bahía** *bay* SW Mexico
39 S11 **Manzano Mountains** ▲ New Mexico, SW USA
39 R12 **Manzano Peak** ▲ New Mexico, SW USA
169 R6 **Manzhouli** *var.* Man-chou-li. Nei Mongol Zizhiqu, N China
Manzil Bū Ruqaybah *see* Menzel Bourguiba
145 X9 **Manziliyah** E Iraq
85 L21 **Manzini** *prev.* Bremersdorp. C Swaziland
85 L21 **Manzini** ✕ (Mbabane) C Swaziland
80 G10 **Mao** Kanem, W Chad
47 N8 **Mao** NW Dominican Republic
Maó *see* Mahón
Maoemere *see* Maumere
165 W9 **Maojing** Gansu, N China
176 Xx12 **Maoke, Pegunungan** *Dut.* Sneeuw-gebergte, *Eng.* Snow Mountains. ▲ Irian Jaya, E Indonesia
Maol Réidh, Caoc *see* Mweelrea
166 M15 **Maoming** Guangdong, S China
166 H8 **Maoxian** *var.* Mao Xian; *prev.* Fengyizhen. Sichuan, C China
85 L19 **Mapai** Gaza, SW Mozambique
164 H15 **Mapam Yumco** ◎ W China
85 I15 **Mapanza** Southern, S Zambia
56 J4 **Mapararí** Falcón, N Venezuela
43 U17 **Mapastepec** Chiapas, SE Mexico
175 O5 **Mapat, Pulau** *island* N Indonesia
176 Yy14 **Mapi** Irian Jaya, E Indonesia
176 Vv7 **Mapia, Kepulauan** *island group* E Indonesia
42 L8 **Mapimí** Durango, C Mexico
85 N19 **Mapinhane** Inhambane, SE Mozambique
57 N7 **Mapire** Monagas, NE Venezuela
9 S17 **Maple Creek** Saskatchewan, S Canada
33 Q9 **Maple River** ≈ Michigan, N USA
31 P7 **Maple River** ≈ North Dakota/South Dakota, N USA
31 S13 **Mapleton** Iowa, C USA
31 U10 **Mapleton** Minnesota, N USA
31 R5 **Mapleton** North Dakota, N USA
34 F13 **Mapleton** Oregon, NW USA
38 L3 **Mapleton** Utah, W USA
199 Ii5 **Mapmaker Seamounts** *undersea feature* N Pacific Ocean
194 G10 **Maprik** East Sepik, NW PNG
85 L21 **Maputo** *prev.* Lourenço Marques. ● (Mozambique) Maputo, S Mozambique
85 L21 **Maputo** ◈ *province* S Mozambique
85 L21 **Maputo** ✕ Maputo, S Mozambique
69 V14 **Maputo** ≈ S Mozambique
Maqanshy *see* Makanchi
Maqat *see* Makat
115 K19 **Maqë** ≈ NW Albania
115 M19 **Maqellarë** Dibër, C Albania
165 S12 **Maqên** *var.* Dawu. Qinghai, C China
165 S11 **Maqên Gangri** ▲ C China
165 U12 **Maqu** Gansu, C China
106 M9 **Maqueda** Castilla-La Mancha, C Spain
84 B9 **Maquela do Zombo** Uíge, NW Angola
65 I16 **Maquinchao** Río Negro, C Argentina
31 Z13 **Maquoketa** Iowa, C USA
31 Y13 **Maquoketa River** ≈ Iowa, C USA
12 F13 **Mar** Ontario, S Canada
97 F14 **Mår** ◎ S Norway
83 G19 **Mara** ◈ *region* N Tanzania
203 P8 **Maraa** Tahiti, W French Polynesia
60 D12 **Maraã** Amazonas, NW Brazil
203 O8 **Maraa, Pointe** *headland* Tahiti, W French Polynesia
61 K14 **Marabá** Pará, NE Brazil
56 H5 **Maracaibo** Zulia, NW Venezuela
Maracaibo, Gulf of *see* Venezuela, Golfo de

◆ Country ● Country Capital ◇ Dependent Territory ○ Dependent Territory Capital ◈ Administrative Region ✕ International Airport ▲ Mountain ▲ Mountain Range ⚠ Volcano ≈ River ◎ Lake ⊠ Reservoir

56 H5 **Maracaibo, Lago de** *var.* Lake Maracaibo. *inlet* NW Venezuela
Maracaibo, Lake *see* Maracaibo, Lago de
60 K10 **Maracá, Ilha de** *island* NE Brazil
61 H20 **Maracaju, Serra de** ▲ S Brazil
60 I11 **Maracanaquará, Planalto** ▲ NE Brazil
56 L5 **Maracay** Aragua, N Venezuela
Marada *see* Marādah
77 R9 **Marādah** *var.* Marada. N Libya
79 U12 **Maradi** Maradi, S Niger
79 U11 **Maradi** ◆ *department* S Niger
83 E21 **Maragarazi** *var.* Muragarazi. Burundi/Tanzania
Maragha *see* Marāgheh
148 J3 **Marāgheh** *var.* Maragha. Āžarbāyjān-e Khāvarī, NW Iran
147 P7 **Marāh** *var.* Marrāt. Ar Riyāḑ, C Saudi Arabia
57 N11 **Marahuaca, Cerro** ▲ S Venezuela
29 R5 **Marais des Cygnes River** Kansas/Missouri, C USA
60 L11 **Marajó, Baía de** *bay* N Brazil
61 K12 **Marajó, Ilha de** *island* N Brazil
203 O2 **Marakei** *atoll* Tungaru, W Kiribati
Marakesh *see* Marrakech
83 I18 **Maralal** Rift Valley, C Kenya
85 G21 **Maralaleng** Kgalagadi, S Botswana
151 U8 **Maraldy, Ozero** ◎ NE Kazakhstan
190 C5 **Maralinga** South Australia
179 R15 **Maramag** Mindanao, S Philippines
Máramarossziget *see* Sighetu Marmației
195 Y16 **Maramasike** *var.* Small Malaita. *island* N Solomon Islands
Maramba *see* Livingstone
204 H3 **Marambio** *Argentinian research station* Antarctica
118 H9 **Maramureș** ◆ *county* NW Romania
38 L15 **Marana** Arizona, SW USA
107 P7 **Maranchón** Castilla-La Mancha, C Spain
148 J2 **Marand** *var.* Merend. Āžarbāyjān-e Khāvarī, NW Iran
Marandellas *see* Marondera
60 L13 **Maranhão** *off.* Estado do Maranhão. ◆ *state* E Brazil
106 H10 **Maranhão, Barragem do** ⊠ C Portugal
155 O11 **Mārān, Koh-i** ▲ SW Pakistan
108 J7 **Marano, Laguna di** *lagoon* NE Italy
58 E9 **Marañón, Río** N Peru
104 J10 **Marans** Charente-Maritime, W France
85 M20 **Marão** Inhambane, S Mozambique
193 B23 **Mararoa** South Island, NZ
Maraş/Marash *see* Kahramanmaraş
109 M19 **Maratea** Basilicata, S Italy
106 G11 **Marateca** Setúbal, S Portugal
117 B20 **Marathiá, Ákra** *headland* Zákynthos, Iónioi Nísoi, Greece, C Mediterranean Sea
10 E12 **Marathon** Ontario, S Canada
25 Y17 **Marathon** Florida Keys, Florida, SE USA
26 L10 **Marathon** Texas, SW USA
Marathón *see* Marathónas
117 H19 **Marathónas** *prev.* Marathón. Attikí, C Greece
175 Oo6 **Maratua, Pulau** *island* N Indonesia
61 O18 **Maraú** Bahia, SE Brazil
149 R3 **Marāveh Tappeh** Māzandarān, N Iran
26 L11 **Maravillas Creek** Texas, SW USA
194 J13 **Marawaka** Eastern Highlands, C PNG
179 R15 **Marawi** Mindanao, S Philippines
Marbat *see* Mirbāţ
106 L16 **Marbella** Andalucía, S Spain
188 J7 **Marble Bar** Western Australia
38 L9 **Marble Canyon** *canyon* Arizona, SW USA
27 S10 **Marble Falls** Texas, SW USA
29 Y7 **Marble Hill** Missouri, C USA
35 T15 **Marbleton** Wyoming, C USA
Marburg *see* Maribor
Marburg *see* Marburg an der Lahn, Germany
103 H16 **Marburg an der Lahn** *hist.* Marburg. Hessen, W Germany
113 H23 **Marcal** W Hungary
47 G7 **Marcala** La Paz, SW Honduras
113 H24 **Marcali** Somogy, SW Hungary
85 A16 **Marca, Ponta da** *headland* SW Angola
61 I16 **Marcelândia** Mato Grosso, W Brazil
29 T3 **Marceline** Missouri, C USA
62 I13 **Marcelino Ramos** Rio Grande do Sul, S Brazil
57 Y12 **Marcel, Mont** ▲ S French Guiana
99 O19 **March** E England, UK
111 Z3 **March** *var.* Morava. C Europe *see also* Morava
108 I12 **Marche** *Eng.* Marches. ◆ *region* C Italy
105 N11 **Marche** *cultural region* C France
101 J21 **Marche-en-Famenne** Luxembourg, SE Belgium
106 K14 **Marchena** Andalucía, S Spain
59 B17 **Marchena, Isla** *var.* Bindloe Island. *island* Galapagos Islands, Ecuador, E Pacific Ocean
Marches *see* Marche
101 J20 **Marchin** Liège, E Belgium
189 S1 **Marchinbar Island** *island* Wessel Islands, Northern Territory, N Australia
64 L9 **Mar Chiquita, Laguna** ◎ C Argentina
105 Q10 **Marcigny** Saône-et-Loire, C France
25 W16 **Marco** Florida, SE USA
Marcodurum *see* Düren
61 O15 **Marcolândia** Pernambuco, E Brazil
108 I8 **Marco Polo** ✕ (Venezia) Veneto, NE Italy
Marcq *see* Mark
118 M8 **Mărculești** *Rus.* Markuleshty. N Moldova
31 S12 **Marcus** Iowa, C USA
41 S11 **Marcus Baker, Mount** ▲ Alaska, USA
199 Hh5 **Marcus Island** *var.* Minami Tori Shima. *island* E Japan
20 K8 **Marcy, Mount** ▲ New York, NE USA
155 T5 **Mardān** North-West Frontier Province, N Pakistan
65 N14 **Mar del Plata** Buenos Aires, E Argentina
143 Q16 **Mardin** Mardin, SE Turkey
143 Q16 **Mardin** ◆ *province* SE Turkey
143 Q16 **Mardin Dağları** ▲ SE Turkey
168 J9 **Mardzad** Övörhangay, C Mongolia
197 L6 **Maré** *island* Îles Loyauté, E New Caledonia
Marea Neagră *see* Black Sea
107 Z8 **Mare de Déu del Toro** ▲ Menorca, Spain, W Mediterranean Sea
189 W4 **Mareeba** Queensland, NE Australia
98 G8 **Maree, Loch** ◎ N Scotland, UK
Mareeq *see* Mereeg
Marek *see* Dupnitsa
78 J11 **Maréna** Kayes, W Mali
202 I2 **Marenanuka** *atoll* Tungaru, W Kiribati
31 X14 **Marengo** Iowa, C USA
104 J11 **Marennes** Charente-Maritime, W France
109 G23 **Marettimo, Isola** *island* Isole Egadi, S Italy
26 K10 **Marfa** Texas, SW USA
59 P17 **Marfil, Laguna** ◎ E Bolivia
Marganets *see* Marhanets'
27 Q4 **Margaret** Texas, SW USA
188 I14 **Margaret River** Western Australia
194 G12 **Margarima** Southern Highlands, W PNG
57 N4 **Margarita, Isla de** *island* N Venezuela
117 I25 **Margarítes** Kríti, Greece, E Mediterranean Sea
99 Q22 **Margate** *prev.* Mergate. SE England, UK
25 Z15 **Margate** Florida, SE USA
Margelan *see* Marghilon
105 P13 **Margeride, Montagnes de la** ▲ C France
Margherita *see* Jamaame
109 N16 **Margherita di Savoia** Puglia, SE Italy
Margherita, Lake *see* Ābaya Hāyk'
83 E18 **Margherita Peak** *Fr.* Pic Marguerite. ▲ Uganda/Zaire
155 O4 **Marghi** Bāmiān, N Afghanistan
153 S10 **Marghilon** *var.* Margelan, *Rus.* Margilan. Farghona Wiloyati, E Uzbekistan
118 G9 **Marghita** *Hung.* Margitta. Bihor, NW Romania
Margilan *see* Marghilon
118 K8 **Marginea** Suceava, NE Romania
Margitta *see* Marghita
154 K9 **Mārgow, Dasht-e** *desert* SW Afghanistan
101 L18 **Margraten** Limburg, SE Netherlands
8 M15 **Marguerite** British Columbia, SW Canada
204 I6 **Marguerite Bay** *bay* Antarctica
Marguerite, Pic *see* Margherita Peak
119 T9 **Marhanets'** *Rus.* Marganets. Dnipropetrovs'ka Oblast', E Ukraine
194 E15 **Mari** Western, SW PNG
203 R12 **Maria** *island* Îles Australes, SW French Polynesia
203 Y12 **Maria** *atoll* Groupe Actéon, SE French Polynesia
42 I12 **María Cleofas, Isla** *island* C Mexico
64 H4 **María Elena** *var.* Oficina María Elena. Antofagasta, N Chile
97 G21 **Mariager** Århus, C Denmark
63 C22 **María Ignacia** Buenos Aires, E Argentina
191 P17 **Maria Island** *island* Tasmania, SE Australia
42 H12 **María Madre, Isla** *island* C Mexico
42 I12 **María Magdalena, Isla** *island* C Mexico
199 H6 **Mariana Islands** *island group* Guam/Northern Mariana Islands
183 N3 **Mariana Trench** *var.* Challenger Deep. *undersea feature* W Pacific Ocean
159 X12 **Mariāni** Assam, NE India
29 X11 **Marianna** Arkansas, C USA
25 R8 **Marianna** Florida, SE USA
180 J16 **Marianne** *island* Inner Islands, NE Seychelles
97 M19 **Mariannelund** Jönköping, S Sweden
63 D15 **Mariano I.Loza** Corrientes, NE Argentina
Mariano Machado *see* Ganda
113 A16 **Mariánské Lázně** *Ger.* Marienbad. Západní Čechy, W Czech Republic
Máriaradna *see* Radna
35 S7 **Marias River** Montana, NW USA
Maria-Theresiopel *see* Subotica
Máriatölgyes *see* Dubnica nad Váhom
192 H1 **Maria van Diemen, Cape** *headland* North Island, NZ
111 V5 **Mariazell** Steiermark, E Austria
147 P15 **Mar'ib** W Yemen
97 I25 **Maribo** Storstrøm, S Denmark
111 W9 **Maribor** *Ger.* Marburg. NE Slovenia
Marica *see* Maritsa
37 R13 **Maricopa** California, W USA
Maricourt *see* Kangiqsujuaq
83 D15 **Maridi** Western Equatoria, SW Sudan
204 M11 **Marie Byrd Land** *physical region* Antarctica
199 L16 **Marie Byrd Seamount** *undersea feature* N Amundsen Sea
47 X11 **Marie-Galante** *var.* Ceyre to the Caribs. *island* SE Guadeloupe
47 Y6 **Marie-Galante, Canal de** *channel* S Guadeloupe
95 J20 **Mariehamn** *Fin.* Maarianhamina. Åland, SW Finland
46 C4 **Mariel** La Habana, W Cuba
101 H22 **Mariembourg** Namur, S Belgium
Marienbad *see* Mariánské Lázně
Marienburg *see* Alūksne, Latvia
Marienburg *see* Malbork, Poland
Marienburg *see* Feldioara, Romania
Marienburg in Westpreussen *see* Malbork
Marienhausen *see* Viļaka
85 D20 **Mariental** Hardap, SW Namibia
20 D13 **Marienville** Pennsylvania, NE USA
Marienwerder *see* Kwidzyń
60 C12 **Marié, Rio** NW Brazil
97 K17 **Mariestad** Skaraborg, S Sweden
25 S3 **Marietta** Georgia, SE USA
33 U14 **Marietta** Ohio, N USA
29 N13 **Marietta** Oklahoma, C USA
83 H18 **Marigat** Rift Valley, W Kenya
105 S16 **Marignane** Bouches-du-Rhône, SE France
Marignano *see* Melegnano
47 O11 **Marigot** NE Dominica
126 Hh14 **Mariinsk** Kemerovskaya Oblast', S Russian Federation
131 Q3 **Mariinskiy Posad** Respublika Mariy El, W Russian Federation
121 E14 **Marijampolė** *prev.* Kapsukas. Marijampolė, S Lithuania
116 G12 **Marikostenovo** Sofiyska Oblast, SW Bulgaria
62 J9 **Marília** São Paulo, S Brazil
84 D11 **Marimba** Malanje, NW Angola
145 T1 **Marī Mīlā** E Iraq
106 G4 **Marín** Galicia, NW Spain
37 N10 **Marina** California, W USA
Marina di Catanzaro *see* Catanzaro Marina
Mar"ina Gorka *see* Mar"ina Horka
121 L17 **Mar"ina Horka** *Rus.* Mar'ina Gorka. Minskaya Voblasts', C Belarus
179 Pp11 **Marinduque** *island* C Philippines
33 S9 **Marine City** Michigan, N USA
33 N6 **Marinette** Wisconsin, N USA
62 I10 **Maringá** Paraná, S Brazil
85 N16 **Maringuè** Sofala, C Mozambique
106 F9 **Marinha Grande** Leiria, C Portugal
109 I15 **Marino** Lazio, C Italy
61 A15 **Mário Lobão** Acre, W Brazil
25 O5 **Marion** Alabama, S USA
29 Y11 **Marion** Arkansas, C USA
32 L17 **Marion** Illinois, N USA
33 P13 **Marion** Indiana, N USA
31 X13 **Marion** Iowa, C USA
29 O5 **Marion** Kansas, C USA
22 H6 **Marion** Kentucky, S USA
23 P9 **Marion** North Carolina, SE USA
33 S12 **Marion** Ohio, N USA
23 T12 **Marion** South Carolina, SE USA
23 Q7 **Marion** Virginia, NE USA
29 O5 **Marion Lake** ⊠ Kansas, C USA
23 S13 **Marion, Lake** ⊠ South Carolina, SE USA
29 S8 **Marionville** Missouri, C USA
57 N7 **Maripa** Bolívar, E Venezuela
57 X11 **Maripasoula** W French Guiana
37 Q9 **Mariposa** California, W USA
63 G19 **Mariscala** Lavalleja, S Uruguay
64 M4 **Mariscal Estigarribia** Boquerón, NW Paraguay
58 C6 **Mariscal Sucre** *var.* Quito. ✕ (Quito) Pichincha, C Ecuador
32 K16 **Marissa** Illinois, N USA
105 U14 **Maritime Alps** *Fr.* Alpes Maritimes, *It.* Alpi Marittime. ▲ France/Italy
Maritimes, Alpes *see* Maritime Alps
Maritime Territory *see* Primorskiy Kray
116 K11 **Maritsa** *var.* Marica, *Gk.* Évros, *Turk.* Meriç; *anc.* Hebrus. SW Europe *see also* Évros/Meriç
Maritsa *see* Simeonovgrad
Marittime, Alpi *see* Maritime Alps
Maritzburg *see* Pietermaritzburg
197 C13 **Marium, Mount** ▲ Ambrym, C Vanuatu
119 X9 **Mariupol'** *prev.* Zhdanov. Donets'ka Oblast', SE Ukraine
57 Q6 **Mariusa, Caño** NE Venezuela
148 J5 **Marīvān** *prev.* Dezh Shāhpūr. Kordestān, W Iran
125 A16 **Mariy El, Respublika** *prev.* Mariyskaya ASSR. ◆ *autonomous republic* W Russian Federation
131 R3 **Mariyets** Respublika Mariy El, W Russian Federation
Mariyskaya ASSR *see* Mariy El, Respublika
120 G4 **Märjamaa** *Ger.* Merjama. Raplamaa, NW Estonia
101 I15 **Mark** *Fr.* Marcq. Belgium/Netherlands
83 N17 **Marka** *var.* Merca. Shabeellaha Hoose, S Somalia
151 Z10 **Markakol', Ozero** *Kaz.* Marqaköl. ◎ E Kazakhstan
78 M12 **Markala** Ségou, W Mali
165 S15 **Markam** *var.* Gartog. Xizang Zizhiqu, W China
97 K21 **Markaryd** Kronoberg, S Sweden
148 L7 **Markazī** *off.* Ostān-e Markazī. ◆ *province* W Iran
12 F14 **Markdale** Ontario, S Canada
29 X10 **Marked Tree** Arkansas, C USA
100 N11 **Markelo** Overijssel, E Netherlands
100 J9 **Markermeer** ◎ C Netherlands
99 N20 **Market Harborough** C England, UK
99 N18 **Market Rasen** E England, UK
126 Kk10 **Markha** NE Russian Federation
10 H16 **Markham** Ontario, S Canada
27 V12 **Markham** Texas, SW USA
194 J13 **Markham** C PNG
205 Q11 **Markham, Mount** ▲ Antarctica
112 M11 **Marki** Warszawa, C Poland
164 F8 **Markit** Xinjiang Uygur Zizhiqu, NW China
119 Y5 **Markivka** *Rus.* Markovka. Luhans'ka Oblast', E Ukraine
37 Q7 **Markleeville** California, W USA
100 L8 **Marknesse** Flevoland, N Netherlands
81 H14 **Markounda** *var.* Marcounda. Ouham, NW Central African Republic
Markovka *see* Markivka
127 P6 **Markovo** Chukotskiy Avtonomnyy Okrug, NE Russian Federation
131 P8 **Marks** Saratovskaya Oblast', W Russian Federation
24 K2 **Marks** Mississippi, S USA
24 I7 **Marksville** Louisiana, S USA
103 I19 **Marktheidenfeld** Bayern, C Germany
103 J24 **Marktoberdorf** Bayern, S Germany
103 M18 **Marktredwitz** Bayern, E Germany
Markt-Übelbach *see* Übelbach
29 V3 **Mark Twain Lake** ⊠ Missouri, C USA
Markuleshty *see* Mărculești
103 E14 **Marl** Nordrhein-Westfalen, W Germany
190 E2 **Marla** South Australia
189 Y8 **Marlborough** Queensland, E Australia
99 M22 **Marlborough** S England, UK
193 I15 **Marlborough** *off.* Marlborough District. ◆ *unitary authority* South Island, NZ
105 P3 **Marle** Aisne, N France
33 S8 **Marlette** Michigan, N USA
27 T9 **Marlin** Texas, SW USA
23 S5 **Marlinton** West Virginia, NE USA
28 M12 **Marlow** Oklahoma, C USA
161 E17 **Marmagao** Goa, W India
Marmanda *see* Marmande
104 L13 **Marmande** *anc.* Marmanda. Lot-et-Garonne, SW France
142 C11 **Marmara** Balıkesir, NW Turkey
142 D11 **Marmara Denizi** *Eng.* Sea of Marmara. *sea* NW Turkey
116 N13 **Marmaraereğlisi** Tekirdağ, NW Turkey
Marmara, Sea of *see* Marmara Denizi
142 C16 **Marmaris** Muğla, SW Turkey
30 J6 **Marmarth** North Dakota, N USA
23 Q5 **Marmet** West Virginia, NE USA
108 H5 **Marmolada, Monte** ▲ N Italy
106 M13 **Marmolejo** Andalucía, S Spain
12 J14 **Marmora** Ontario, SE Canada
41 Q14 **Marmot Bay** *bay* Alaska, USA
105 Q4 **Marne** ◆ *department* N France
105 Q4 **Marne** N France
143 U10 **Marneuli** *prev.* Borchalo, Sarvani. S Georgia
80 I13 **Maro** Moyen-Chari, S Chad
56 L12 **Maroa** Amazonas, S Venezuela
180 J3 **Maroantsetra** Toamasina, NE Madagascar
203 W11 **Marokau** *atoll* Îles Tuamotu, C French Polynesia
180 J5 **Marolambo** Toamasina, E Madagascar
180 J2 **Maromokotro** ▲ N Madagascar
85 L16 **Marondera** *prev.* Marandellas. Mashonaland East, NE Zimbabwe
57 X9 **Maroni** *Dut.* Marowijne. French Guiana/Suriname
191 V2 **Maroochydore-Mooloolaba** Queensland, E Australia
175 P13 **Maros** Sulawesi, C Indonesia
118 H11 **Maros** *var.* Mureș, Mureșul, *Ger.* Marosch, Mieresch. Hungary/Romania *see also* Mureș
Marosch *see* Maros/Mureș
Maroshévíz *see* Toplița
Marosillye *see* Ilia
Marosludas *see* Luduș
Marosújvár/Marosújvárakna *see* Ocna Mureș
Marosvásárhely *see* Târgu Mureș
203 V14 **Marotiri** *var.* Îlots de Bass, Morotiri. *island group* Îles Australes, SW French Polynesia
80 G12 **Maroua** Extrême-Nord, N Cameroon
57 X12 **Marouini Rivier** SE Suriname
180 I3 **Marovoay** Mahajanga, NW Madagascar
57 W9 **Marowijne** ◆ *district* NE Suriname
Marowijne *see* Maroni
Marqaköl *see* Markakol', Ozero
199 M9 **Marquesas Fracture Zone** *tectonic feature* E Pacific Ocean
Marquesas Islands *see* Marquises, Îles
25 W17 **Marquesas Keys** *island group* Florida, SE USA
31 Y12 **Marquette** Iowa, C USA
33 N3 **Marquette** Michigan, N USA
105 N1 **Marquise** Pas-de-Calais, N France
203 X7 **Marquises, Îles** *Eng.* Marquesas Islands. *island group* N French Polynesia
191 Q6 **Marra Creek** New South Wales, SE Australia
82 B10 **Marra Hills** *plateau* W Sudan
82 B11 **Marra, Jebel** ▲ W Sudan
76 E7 **Marrakech** *var.* Marakesh, *Eng.* Marrakesh; *prev.* Morocco. W Morocco
Marrakesh *see* Marrakech
Marrāt *see* Marāh
191 N15 **Marrawah** Tasmania, SE Australia
190 I4 **Marree** South Australia
83 L17 **Marrehan** ▲ SW Somalia
85 N17 **Marromeu** Sofala, C Mozambique
106 J17 **Marroquí, Punta** *headland* SW Spain
191 N8 **Marrowie Creek** *seasonal river* New South Wales, SE Australia
85 O14 **Marrupa** Niassa, N Mozambique
190 D1 **Marryat** South Australia
77 Y10 **Marsá 'Alam** SE Egypt
77 R8 **Marsá al Burayqah** *var.* Al Burayqah. N Libya
83 J17 **Marsabit** Eastern, N Kenya
109 H23 **Marsala** *anc.* Lilybaeum. Sicilia, Italy, C Mediterranean Sea
123 Jj17 **Marsaxlokk Bay** *bay* SE Malta
67 G15 **Mars Bay** *bay* Ascension Island, C Atlantic Ocean
103 H15 **Marsberg** Nordrhein-Westfalen, W Germany
9 R15 **Marsden** Saskatchewan, S Canada
100 H7 **Marsdiep** *strait* NW Netherlands
105 R16 **Marseille** *Eng.* Marseilles; *anc.* Massilia. Bouches-du-Rhône, SE France
Marseille-Marignane *see* Provence
32 M11 **Marseilles** Illinois, N USA
Marseilles *see* Marseille
78 J16 **Marshall** W Liberia
41 N11 **Marshall** Alaska, USA
29 U9 **Marshall** Arkansas, C USA
33 N14 **Marshall** Illinois, N USA
33 Q10 **Marshall** Michigan, N USA
31 S9 **Marshall** Minnesota, N USA
29 T4 **Marshall** Missouri, C USA
23 O9 **Marshall** North Carolina, SE USA
27 X6 **Marshall** Texas, SW USA
201 S4 **Marshall Islands** *off.* Republic of the Marshall Islands. ◆ *republic* W Pacific Ocean
183 Q3 **Marshall Islands** *island group* W Pacific Ocean
199 I7 **Marshall Seamounts** *undersea feature* SW Pacific Ocean
31 W13 **Marshalltown** Iowa, C USA
21 P12 **Marshfield** Massachusetts, NE USA
29 T7 **Marshfield** Missouri, C USA
32 K6 **Marshfield** Wisconsin, N USA
46 H1 **Marsh Harbour** Great Abaco, W Bahamas
21 S3 **Mars Hill** Maine, NE USA
23 P9 **Mars Hill** North Carolina, SE USA
24 H10 **Marsh Island** *island* Louisiana, S USA
23 S11 **Marshville** North Carolina, SE USA
13 W5 **Marsoui** Québec, SE Canada
13 R8 **Mars, Rivière à** Québec, SE Canada
97 O15 **Märsta** Stockholm, C Sweden
97 H24 **Marstal** Fyn, C Denmark
97 I19 **Marstrand** Göteborg och Bohus, S Sweden
27 U8 **Mart** Texas, SW USA
178 Gg9 **Martaban** *var.* Moktama. Mon State, S Myanmar
177 G9 **Martaban, Gulf of** *gulf* S Myanmar
109 Q19 **Martano** Puglia, SE Italy
Martapoera *see* Martapura
175 N11 **Martapura** *prev.* Martapoera. Borneo, C Indonesia
101 L23 **Martelange** Luxembourg, SE Belgium
116 L7 **Marten** Razgradska Oblast, NE Bulgaria
12 H10 **Marten River** Ontario, S Canada
9 T15 **Martensville** Saskatchewan, S Canada
Marteskirch *see* Târnăveni
Martes Tolosane *see* Martres-Tolosane
117 K25 **Mártha** Kríti, Greece, E Mediterranean Sea
191 Q6 **Marthaguy Creek** New South Wales, SE Australia
21 P13 **Martha's Vineyard** *island* Massachusetts, NE USA
110 C11 **Martigny** Valais, SW Switzerland
105 R16 **Martigues** Bouches-du-Rhône, SE France
113 J19 **Martin** *Ger.* Sankt Martin, *Hung.* Turócszentmárton; *prev.* Turčiansky Svätý Martin. Stredné Slovensko, NW Slovakia
30 L11 **Martin** South Dakota, N USA
22 G8 **Martin** Tennessee, S USA
107 S7 **Martín** E Spain
109 P18 **Martina Franca** Puglia, SE Italy
193 M14 **Martinborough** Wellington, North Island, NZ
27 S11 **Martindale** Texas, SW USA
37 N8 **Martinez** California, W USA
25 V3 **Martinez** Georgia, SE USA
43 Q13 **Martínez de La Torre** Veracruz-Llave, E Mexico
47 Y12 **Martinique** ◇ *French overseas department* E West Indies
1 O15 **Martinique** *island* E West Indies
Martinique Channel *see* Martinique Passage
47 X12 **Martinique Passage** *var.* Dominica Channel, Martinique Channel. *channel* Dominica/Martinique
25 Q5 **Martin Lake** ⊠ Alabama, S USA
117 G18 **Martíno** *prev.* Martínon. Stereá Ellás, C Greece
Martínon *see* Martíno
204 J11 **Martin Peninsula** *peninsula* Antarctica
41 S5 **Martin Point** *headland* Alaska, USA
111 V3 **Martinsberg** Niederösterreich, NE Austria
23 V3 **Martinsburg** West Virginia, NE USA
33 V13 **Martins Ferry** Ohio, N USA
Martinskirch *see* Târnăveni
33 O14 **Martinsville** Indiana, N USA
23 S8 **Martinsville** Virginia, NE USA
67 K16 **Martin Vaz, Ilhas** *island group* E Brazil
Martök *see* Martuk
192 M12 **Marton** Manawatu-Wanganui, North Island, NZ
107 N13 **Martos** Andalucía, S Spain
104 M16 **Martres-Tolosane** *var.* Martes Tolosane. Haute-Garonne, S France
94 M11 **Martti** Lappi, NE Finland
150 I9 **Martuk** *Kaz.* Martök. Aktyubinsk, NW Kazakhstan
143 U12 **Martuni** E Armenia
60 L11 **Marudá** Pará, E Brazil
175 O2 **Marudu, Teluk** *bay* East Malaysia
155 O8 **Ma'rūf** Kandahār, SE Afghanistan
170 F14 **Marugame** Kagawa, Shikoku, SW Japan
193 H16 **Maruia** South Island, NZ
100 M6 **Marum** Groningen, NE Netherlands
81 P23 **Marungu** ▲ SE Zaire
203 Y12 **Marutea** *atoll* Groupe Actéon, C French Polynesia
149 O11 **Marv Dasht** *var.* Mervdasht. Fārs, S Iran
105 P13 **Marvejols** Lozère, S France
29 X12 **Marvell** Arkansas, C USA
38 L6 **Marvine, Mount** ▲ Utah, W USA
145 Q7 **Marwānīyah** C Iraq
158 F13 **Mārwār** *var.* Marwar Junction. Rājasthān, N India
Marwar Junction *see* Mārwār
9 R14 **Marwayne** Alberta, SW Canada
152 I14 **Mary** *prev.* Merv. Maryyskiy Velayat, S Turkmenistan
Mary *see* Maryyskiy Velayat
189 Z9 **Maryborough** Queensland, E Australia
190 M11 **Maryborough** Victoria, SE Australia
Maryborough *see* Port Laoise
85 G23 **Marydale** Northern Cape, W South Africa
119 W8 **Mar"yinka** Donets'ka Oblast', E Ukraine
Mary Island *see* Kanton
23 W4 **Maryland** *off.* State of Maryland; also known as America in Miniature, Cockade State, Free State, Old Line State. ◆ *state* NE USA
27 P7 **Maryneal** Texas, SW USA
99 J15 **Maryport** NW England, UK
11 U13 **Marystown** Newfoundland, Newfoundland and Labrador, SE Canada
38 K6 **Marysvale** Utah, W USA
37 O6 **Marysville** California, W USA
29 O3 **Marysville** Kansas, C USA
33 S13 **Marysville** Michigan, N USA
33 S9 **Marysville** Ohio, N USA
34 H7 **Marysville** Washington, NW USA
29 R2 **Maryville** Missouri, C USA
23 N9 **Maryville** Tennessee, S USA
Mary Welayaty *see* Maryyskiy Velayat
152 I15 **Maryyskiy Velayat** *var.* Mary, *Turkm.* Mary Welayaty. ◆ *province* S Turkmenistan
Marzūq *see* Murzuq
176 V11 **Mas** Irian Jaya, E Indonesia
44 J11 **Masachapa** *var.* Puerto Masachapa. Managua, W Nicaragua
83 G19 **Masai Mara National Reserve** *reserve* C Kenya
83 I21 **Masai Steppe** *grassland* NW Tanzania
83 F19 **Masaka** SW Uganda
175 N13 **Masalembo Besar, Pulau** *island* S Indonesia
143 Y13 **Masallı** *Rus.* Masally. S Azerbaijan
Masally *see* Masallı
175 Pp10 **Masamba** Sulawesi, C Indonesia
Masampo *see* Masan
169 Y16 **Masan** *prev.* Masampo. S South Korea
Masandam Peninsula *see* Musandam Peninsula
83 J25 **Masasi** Mtwara, SE Tanzania
Masawa *see* Massawa
44 J10 **Masaya** Masaya, W Nicaragua
44 J10 **Masaya** ◆ *department* W Nicaragua
179 Q12 **Masbate** Masbate, N Philippines
179 Qq12 **Masbate** *island* C Philippines
76 I6 **Mascara** *var.* Mouaskar. NW Algeria
181 O7 **Mascarene Basin** *undersea feature* W Indian Ocean
181 O9 **Mascarene Islands** *island group* W Indian Ocean
181 N9 **Mascarene Plain** *undersea feature* W Indian Ocean
181 O7 **Mascarene Plateau** *undersea feature* W Indian Ocean
204 H5 **Mascart, Cape** *headland* Adelaide Island, Antarctica
64 J10 **Mascasín, Salinas de** *salt lake* C Argentina
42 K13 **Mascota** Jalisco, C Mexico
13 O12 **Mascouche** Québec, SE Canada
128 J9 **Masel'gskaya** Respublika Kareliya, NW Russian Federation
85 J23 **Maseru** ● (Lesotho) W Lesotho
85 J23 **Maseru** ✕ W Lesotho
Mashaba *see* Mashava
166 K14 **Mashan** Guangxi Zhuangzu Zizhiqu, S China
85 K17 **Mashava** *prev.* Mashaba. Masvingo, SE Zimbabwe
149 U4 **Mashhad** *var.* Meshed. Khorāsān, NE Iran
172 Oo4 **Mashike** Hokkaidō, NE Japan
Mashīz *see* Bardsīr
155 N14 **Mashkai** SW Pakistan
149 X13 **Māshkel** *var.* Rūd-i Māshkel, Rūd-e Māshkīd. Iran/Pakistan
154 K12 **Māshkel, Hāmūn-i** *salt marsh* SW Pakistan
Māshkel, Rūd-i/Māshkīd, Rūd-e *see* Māshkel
85 K15 **Mashonaland Central** ◆ *province* N Zimbabwe
85 K16 **Mashonaland East** ◆ *province* NE Zimbabwe
85 J16 **Mashonaland West** ◆ *province* NW Zimbabwe
Mashtagi *see* Maştağa
172 Qq6 **Mashū-ko** *var.* Masyû Ko. ◎ Hokkaidō, NE Japan
147 S14 **Masīlah, Wādī al** *dry watercourse* SE Yemen
81 I21 **Masi-Manimba** Bandundu, SW Zaire
83 F17 **Masindi** W Uganda
83 I19 **Masinga Reservoir** ⊠ S Kenya
179 Oo10 **Masinloc** Luzon, N Philippines
Masīra *see* Maşīrah, Jazīrat
Masīra, Gulf of *see* Maşīrah, Khalīj
147 Y10 **Maşīrah, Jazīrat** *var.* Masīra. *island* E Oman
147 Y10 **Maşīrah, Khalīj** *var.* Gulf of Masira. *bay* E Oman
Masis *see* Büyükağrı Dağı
81 O19 **Masisi** Nord Kivu, E Zaire
176 U11 **Masiwang** Pulau Seram, E Indonesia
Masjed-e Soleymān *see* Masjed Soleymān
148 L9 **Masjed Soleymān** *var.* Masjed-e Soleymān, Masjid-i Sulaiman. Khūzestān, SW Iran
Masjid-i Sulaiman *see* Masjed Soleymān
Maskat *see* Masqaţ
145 Q7 **Maskhān** C Iraq
147 X8 **Maskin** *var.* Miskin. NW Oman
99 B17 **Mask, Lough** *Ir.* Loch Measca. ◎ W Ireland
116 N10 **Maslen Nos** *headland* E Bulgaria
180 K3 **Masoala, Tanjona** *headland* NE Madagascar
Masohi *see* Amahai
33 Q9 **Mason** Michigan, N USA
33 R14 **Mason** Ohio, N USA
27 Q10 **Mason** Texas, SW USA
23 P4 **Mason** West Virginia, NE USA
193 B25 **Mason Bay** *bay* Stewart Island, NZ
31 V12 **Mason City** Iowa, C USA
32 K13 **Mason City** Illinois, N USA
Mā, Sông *see* Ma, Nam
20 B16 **Masontown** Pennsylvania, NE USA
147 Y8 **Masqaţ** *var.* Maskat, *Eng.* Muscat. ● (Oman) NE Oman
108 E10 **Massa** Toscana, C Italy
20 M11 **Massachusetts** *off.* Commonwealth of Massachusetts; also known as Bay State, Old Bay State, Old Colony State. ◆ *state* NE USA
21 P11 **Massachusetts Bay** *bay* Massachusetts, NE USA
37 R2 **Massacre Lake** ◎ Nevada, W USA
109 O18 **Massafra** Puglia, SE Italy
110 G11 **Massagno** Ticino, S Switzerland
80 G11 **Massaguet** Chari-Baguirmi, W Chad
Massakori *see* Massakory
80 G10 **Massakory** *var.* Massakori; *prev.* Dagana. Chari-Baguirmi, W Chad
80 H11 **Massalassef** Chari-Baguirmi, SW Chad
108 F13 **Massa Marittima** Toscana, C Italy
84 B11 **Massangano** Cuanza Norte, NW Angola
85 M18 **Massangena** Gaza, S Mozambique
82 J9 **Massawa** *var.* Masawa, *Amh.* Mits'iwa. E Eritrea
82 K9 **Massawa Channel** *channel* E Eritrea
20 J6 **Massena** New York, NE USA
80 H11 **Massenya** Chari-Baguirmi, SW Chad
8 I13 **Masset** Graham Island, British Columbia, SW Canada
104 L16 **Masseube** Gers, S France
12 E11 **Massey** Ontario, S Canada
105 P12 **Massiac** Cantal, C France
105 P12 **Massif Central** *plateau* C France
Massilia *see* Marseille
33 U12 **Massillon** Ohio, N USA
79 N12 **Massina** Ségou, W Mali
85 N19 **Massinga** Inhambane, SE Mozambique
85 L20 **Massingir** Gaza, SW Mozambique
205 Z10 **Masson Island** *island* Antarctica
Massoukou *see* Franceville
143 Z11 **Maştağa** *Rus.* Mashtagi, Mastaga. E Azerbaijan
Mastanli *see* Momchilgrad

◆ Country ● Country Capital ◇ Dependent Territory ○ Dependent Territory Capital ◆ Administrative Region ✕ International Airport ▲ Mountain ▲ Mountain Range ⁂ Volcano River ◎ Lake ⊠ Reservoir

2 M13 **Masterton** Wellington, North Island, NZ
M14 **Mastic** Long Island, New York, NE USA
5 O10 **Mastung** Baluchistān, SW Pakistan
1 J20 **Mastva** *Rus.* Mostva. ≈ SW Belarus
1 G17 **Masty** *Rus.* Mosty. Hrodzyenskaya Voblasts', W Belarus
0 E12 **Masuda** Shimane, Honshū, SW Japan
J11 **Masugnsbyn** Norrbotten, N Sweden
Masuku *see* Franceville
K17 **Masvingo** *prev.* Fort Victoria, Nyanda, Victoria. Masvingo, SE Zimbabwe
K18 **Masvingo** *prev.* Victoria. ⬖ *province* SE Zimbabwe
6 W10 **Maswaar, Pulau** *island* East Indies
4 H5 **Maşyāf** *Fr.* Misiaf. Ḥamāh, C Syria
Masyû Ko *see* Mashū-ko
2 E9 **Maszewo** Szczecin, NW Poland
5 I17 **Matabeleland North** ⬖ *province* W Zimbabwe
5 J18 **Matabeleland South** ⬖ *province* S Zimbabwe
O13 **Mataca** Niassa, N Mozambique
97 G13 **Matacawa Levu** *island* Yasawa Group, NW Fiji
2 G8 **Matachewan** Ontario, S Canada
1 F22 **Matadi** Bas-Zaïre, W Zaire
7 O4 **Matador** Texas, SW USA
4 J9 **Matagalpa** Matagalpa, C Nicaragua
4 K9 **Matagalpa** ⬖ *department* W Nicaragua
0 I12 **Matagami** Québec, S Canada
7 U13 **Matagorda** Texas, SW USA
7 U13 **Matagorda Bay** *inlet* Texas, SW USA
7 U14 **Matagorda Island** *island* Texas, SW USA
7 V13 **Matagorda Peninsula** *headland* Texas, SW USA
03 Q8 **Mataiea** Tahiti, W French Polynesia
03 T9 **Mataiva** *atoll* Îles Tuamotu, C French Polynesia
91 O7 **Matakana** New South Wales, SE Australia
92 N7 **Matakana Island** *island* NE NZ
5 C15 **Matala** Huíla, SW Angola
02 G12 **Matala'a Pointe** *headland* Île Uvea, N Wallis and Futuna
61 K25 **Matale** Central Province, C Sri Lanka
02 E12 **Matalesina, Pointe** *headland* Île Alofi, W Wallis and Futuna
8 I10 **Matam** NE Senegal
92 M8 **Matamata** Waikato, North Island, NZ
9 V12 **Matamey** Zinder, S Niger
2 L8 **Matamoros** Coahuila de Zaragoza, NE Mexico
3 P15 **Matamoros** *var.* Izúcar de Matamoros. Puebla, S Mexico
3 Q8 **Matamoros** Tamaulipas, C Mexico
175 Q10 **Matana, Danau** ◎ Sulawesi, C Indonesia
77 S13 **Ma'ţan as Sārah** SE Libya
4 J12 **Matanda** Luapula, N Zambia
3 J24 **Matandu** ≈ S Tanzania
13 V6 **Matane** Québec, SE Canada
13 V6 **Matane** ≈ Québec, SE Canada
79 S12 **Matankari** Dosso, SW Niger
41 R11 **Matanuska River** ≈ Alaska, USA
56 G7 **Matanza** Santander, N Colombia
46 D4 **Matanzas** Matanzas, NW Cuba
13 V7 **Matapédia** ≈ Québec, SE Canada
13 V6 **Matapédia, Lac** ◎ Québec, SE Canada
202 B17 **Mata Point** *headland* SE Niue
202 D12 **Matapu, Pointe** *headland* Île Futuna, W Wallis and Futuna
64 G12 **Mataquito, Río** ≈ C Chile
161 K26 **Matara** Southern Province, S Sri Lanka
117 D18 **Matarágka** *var.* Mataránga. Dytikí Ellás, C Greece
175 Nn16 **Mataram** Pulau Lombok, C Indonesia
Mataránga *see* Matarágka
189 Q3 **Mataranka** Northern Territory, N Australia
107 W6 **Mataró** *anc.* Illuro. Cataluña, E Spain
192 O8 **Matata** Bay of Plenty, North Island, NZ
198 Cc8 **Matātula, Cape** *headland* Tutuila, W American Samoa
193 D24 **Mataura** Southland, South Island, NZ
193 D24 **Mataura** ≈ South Island, NZ
Mata Uta *see* Matā'utu
202 G11 **Matā'utu** *var.* Mata Uta. ○ (Wallis and Futuna) Île Uvea, Wallis and Futuna
198 B8 **Matāutu** Upolu, C Western Samoa
202 G12 **Matā'utu, Baie de** *bay* Île Uvea, Wallis and Futuna
203 P7 **Mataval, Baie de** *bay* Tahiti, W French Polynesia
202 I16 **Matavera** Rarotonga, S Cook Islands
203 V16 **Mataveri** Easter Island, Chile, E Pacific Ocean
203 V17 **Mataveri** ✕ (Easter Island) Easter Island, Chile, E Pacific Ocean
192 P9 **Matawai** Gisborne, North Island, NZ
13 O10 **Matawin** ≈ Québec, SE Canada
151 V13 **Matay** Taldykorgan, SE Kazakhstan
12 K8 **Matchi-Manitou, Lac** ◎ Québec, SE Canada
43 O10 **Matehuala** San Luis Potosí, C Mexico
47 V13 **Matelot** Trinidad, Trinidad and Tobago
85 M15 **Matenge** Tete, NW Mozambique
109 O18 **Matera** Basilicata, S Italy
113 O21 **Mátészalka** Szabolcs-Szatmár-Bereg, E Hungary
176 Y10 **Matewar** Irian Jaya, E Indonesia
95 H17 **Matfors** Västernorrland, C Sweden
104 K11 **Matha** Charente-Maritime, W France
1 F15 **Mathematicians Seamounts** *undersea feature* E Pacific Ocean
23 X6 **Mathews** Virginia, NE USA
27 S14 **Mathis** Texas, SW USA
158 J11 **Mathura** *prev.* Muttra. Uttar Pradesh, N India
Mathurai *see* Madurai
179 Rr16 **Mati** Mindanao, S Philippines
Matianus *see* Orūmīyeh, Daryācheh-ye
Matiara *see* Matiāri
155 Q15 **Matiāri** *var.* Matiara. Sind, SE Pakistan
43 S16 **Matías Romero** Oaxaca, SE Mexico
45 O13 **Matina** Limón, E Costa Rica
12 D10 **Matinenda Lake** ◎ Ontario, S Canada
21 R8 **Matinicus Island** *island* Maine, NE USA
Matisco/Matisco Ædourum *see* Mâcon
155 Q16 **Mātli** Sind, SE Pakistan
99 M18 **Matlock** C England, UK
61 F18 **Mato Grosso** *prev.* Vila Bela da Santissima Trindade. Mato Grosso, W Brazil
61 G17 **Mato Grosso** *off.* Estado de Mato Grosso; *prev.* Matto Grosso. ⬖ *state* W Brazil
62 H8 **Mato Grosso do Sul** *off.* Estado de Mato Grosso do Sul. ⬖ *state* S Brazil
61 I18 **Mato Grosso, Planalto de** *plateau* C Brazil
106 G6 **Matosinhos** *prev.* Matozinhos. Porto, NW Portugal
57 Z10 **Matoury** NE French Guiana
Matozinhos *see* Matosinhos
113 L21 **Mátra** ▲▲ N Hungary
147 Y8 **Maţraḩ** *var.* Mutrah. NE Oman
118 L12 **Mătrăşeşti** Vrancea, E Romania
110 M8 **Matrei Am Brenner** Tirol, W Austria
111 P8 **Matrei in Osttirol** Tirol, W Austria
78 I15 **Matru** SW Sierra Leone
77 U7 **Maţrûḩ** *var.* Mersa Maţrûḩ; *anc.* Paraetonium. NW Egypt
172 Q13 **Matsubara** *var.* Matubara. Kagoshima, Tokuno-shima, SW Japan
171 K16 **Matsudo** *var.* Matudo. Chiba, Honshū, S Japan
170 F11 **Matsue** *var.* Matsuye, Matue. Shimane, Honshū, SW Japan
171 Mm7 **Matsumae** Hokkaidō, NE Japan
171 J14 **Matsumoto** *var.* Matumoto. Nagano, Honshū, S Japan
171 H16 **Matsusaka** *var.* Matsuzaka, Matusaka. Mie, Honshū, SW Japan
167 S12 **Matsu Tao** *Chin.* Mazu Dao. *island* NW Taiwan
Matsutō *see* Mattō
170 C12 **Matsuura** *var.* Matuura. Nagasaki, Kyūshū, SW Japan
170 Ee14 **Matsuyama** *var.* Matuyama. Ehime, Shikoku, SW Japan
Matsuye *see* Matsue
Matsuzaka *see* Matsusaka
171 J17 **Matsuzaki** Shizuoka, Honshū, S Japan
12 F8 **Mattagami** ≈ Ontario, S Canada
12 F8 **Mattagami Lake** ◎ Ontario, S Canada
64 K12 **Mattaldi** Córdoba, C Argentina
23 Y9 **Mattamuskeet, Lake** ◎ North Carolina, SE USA
23 W6 **Mattaponi River** ≈ Virginia, NE USA
12 I11 **Mattawa** Ontario, SE Canada
12 I11 **Mattawa** ≈ Ontario, SE Canada
21 S5 **Mattawamkeag** Maine, NE USA
21 S4 **Mattawamkeag Lake** ◎ Maine, NE USA
110 D11 **Matterhorn** *It.* Monte Cervino. ▲ Italy/Switzerland *see also* Cervino, Monte
37 W1 **Matterhorn** ▲ Nevada, W USA
34 L12 **Matterhorn** *var.* Sacajawea Peak. ▲ Oregon, NW USA
37 R8 **Matterhorn Peak** ▲ California, W USA
111 Y5 **Mattersburg** Burgenland, E Austria
110 E11 **Matter Vispa** ≈ S Switzerland
57 R7 **Matthews Ridge** N Guyana
46 K7 **Matthew Town** Great Inagua, S Bahamas
111 Q4 **Mattighofen** Oberösterreich, NW Austria
109 N16 **Mattinata** Puglia, SE Italy
147 T9 **Maţţī, Sabkhat** *salt flat* Saudi Arabia/UAE
20 M14 **Mattituck** Long Island, New York, NE USA
171 I13 **Mattō** *var.* Matsutō. Ishikawa, Honshū, SW Japan
Matto Grosso *see* Mato Grosso
32 M14 **Mattoon** Illinois, N USA
59 L16 **Mattos, Río** ≈ C Bolivia
Mattu *see* Metu
174 Ll5 **Matu** Sarawak, East Malaysia
59 E14 **Matucana** Lima, W Peru
Matudo *see* Matsudo
Matue *see* Matsue
197 J16 **Matuku** *island* S Fiji
114 B9 **Matulji** Primorje-Gorski Kotar, NW Croatia
Matumoto *see* Matsumoto
57 P5 **Maturín** Monagas, NE Venezuela
Matusaka *see* Matsusaka
Matuura *see* Matsuura
Matuyama *see* Matsuyama
130 K11 **Matveyev Kurgan** Rostovskaya Oblast', SW Russian Federation
131 O8 **Matyshevo** Volgogradskaya Oblast', SW Russian Federation
159 O13 **Mau** *var.* Maunāth Bhanjan. Uttar Pradesh, N India
85 O14 **Maúa** Niassa, N Mozambique
104 M17 **Maubermé, Pic de** *var.* Tuc de Moubermé, *Sp.* Pico Mauberme; *prev.* Tuc de Maubermé. ▲ France/Spain *see also* Moubermé, Tuc de
Maubermé, Pico *see* Maubermé, Pic de/ Moubermé, Tuc de
Maubermé, Tuc de *see* Maubermé, Pic de/ Moubermé, Tuc de
105 Q2 **Maubeuge** Nord, N France
177 Ff8 **Maubin** Irrawaddy, SW Myanmar
158 L13 **Maudaha** Uttar Pradesh, N India
191 N9 **Maude** New South Wales, SE Australia
205 P3 **Maudheimvidda** *physical region* Antarctica
67 N22 **Maud Rise** *undersea feature* S Atlantic Ocean
111 Q4 **Mauerkirchen** Oberösterreich, NW Austria
Mauersee *see* Mamry, Jezioro
196 K2 **Maug Islands** *island group* N Northern Mariana Islands
105 Q15 **Mauguio** Hérault, S France
199 Kk6 **Maui** *island* Hawaii, USA, C Pacific Ocean
202 M16 **Mauke** *atoll* S Cook Islands
64 G13 **Maule** *off.* Región del Maule. ⬖ *region* C Chile
104 J9 **Mauléon** Deux-Sèvres, W France
104 J16 **Mauléon-Licharre** Pyrénées-Atlantiques, SW France
64 G13 **Maule, Río** ≈ C Chile
65 G17 **Maullín** Los Lagos, S Chile
Maulmain *see* Moulmein
33 R11 **Maumee** Ohio, N USA
33 Q12 **Maumee River** ≈ Indiana/Ohio, N USA
29 U11 **Maumelle** Arkansas, C USA
29 T11 **Maumelle, Lake** ☒ Arkansas, C USA
175 Qq16 **Maumere** *prev.* Maoemere. Flores, S Indonesia
85 G17 **Maun** Ngamiland, C Botswana
Maunāth Bhanjan *see* Mau
Maunawai *see* Waimea
202 H16 **Maungaroa** ▲ Rarotonga, S Cook Islands
192 K3 **Maungatapere** Northland, North Island, NZ
192 K4 **Maungaturoto** Northland, North Island, NZ
203 R10 **Maupiti** *var.* Maurua. *island* Îles Sous le Vent, W French Polynesia
158 K14 **Mau Rānīpur** Uttar Pradesh, N India
24 K9 **Maurepas, Lake** ◎ Louisiana, S USA
105 T16 **Maures** ▲▲ SE France
105 O12 **Mauriac** Cantal, C France
Maurice *see* Mauritius
67 J20 **Maurice Ewing Bank** *undersea feature* SW Atlantic Ocean
190 C4 **Maurice, Lake** *salt lake* South Australia
20 I17 **Maurice River** ≈ New Jersey, NE USA
27 Y10 **Mauriceville** Texas, SW USA
100 K12 **Maurik** Gelderland, C Netherlands
78 H8 **Mauritania** *off.* Islamic Republic of Mauritania, *Ar.* Mūrītānīyah. ◆ *republic* W Africa
181 W15 **Mauritius** *off.* Republic of Mauritius, *Fr.* Maurice. ◆ *republic* W Indian Ocean
132 M17 **Mauritius** *island* W Indian Ocean
181 N9 **Mauritius Trench** *undersea feature* W Indian Ocean
104 H6 **Mauron** Morbihan, NW France
105 N13 **Maurs** Cantal, C France
Maurua *see* Maupiti
Maury Mid-Ocean Channel *see* Maury Seachannel
66 L6 **Maury Seachannel** *var.* Maury Mid-Ocean Channel. *undersea feature* N Atlantic Ocean
32 K8 **Mauston** Wisconsin, N USA
111 R8 **Mauterndorf** Salzburg, NW Austria
111 T4 **Mauthausen** Oberösterreich, N Austria
111 Q9 **Mauthen** Kärnten, S Austria
85 F15 **Mavinga** Cuando Cubango, SE Angola
85 M17 **Mavita** Manica, W Mozambique
117 K22 **Mavrópetra, Ákra** *headland* Thíra, Kykládes, Greece, Aegean Sea
117 F16 **Mavrovoúni** ▲ C Greece
192 Q8 **Mawhai Point** *headland* North Island, NZ
177 Ff3 **Mawlaik** Sagaing, C Myanmar
Mawlamyine *see* Moulmein
147 N14 **Mawr, Wādī** *dry watercourse* NW Yemen
205 X5 **Mawson** *Australian research station* Antarctica
205 X5 **Mawson Coast** *physical region* Antarctica
30 M4 **Max** North Dakota, N USA
43 W12 **Maxcanú** Yucatán, SE Mexico
Maxesibebi *see* Mount Ayliff
111 Q5 **Maxglan** ✕ (Salzburg) Salzburg, W Austria
95 K16 **Maxmo** *Fin.* Maksamaa. Vaasa, W Finland
23 T11 **Maxton** North Carolina, SE USA
27 R8 **May** Texas, SW USA
194 E10 **May** ≈ NW PNG
127 N17 **Maya** ≈ E Russian Federation
157 Q19 **Māyābandar** Andaman a nd Nicobar Islands, India, E Indian Ocean
Mayadin *see* Al Mayādīn
46 L5 **Mayaguana** *island* SE Bahamas
46 L5 **Mayaguana Passage** *passage* SE Bahamas
47 S6 **Mayagüez** W Puerto Rico
47 R6 **Mayagüez, Bahía de** *bay* W Puerto Rico
Mayals *see* Maials
81 G20 **Mayama** Le Pool, SE Congo
39 V8 **Maya, Mesa De** ▲ Colorado, C USA
149 R4 **Mayamey** Semnān, N Iran
44 F3 **Maya Mountains** *Sp.* Montañas Mayas. ▲▲ Belize/Guatemala
46 I7 **Mayarí** Holguín, E Cuba
Mayas, Montañas *see* Maya Mountains
20 I17 **May, Cape** *headland* New Jersey, NE USA
82 J11 **Maych'ew** *var.* Mai Chio, *It.* Mai Ceu. N Ethiopia
144 I2 **Maydān Ikbiz** Ḥalab, N Syria
155 Q5 **Maydān Shahr** Wardag, E Afghanistan
82 O12 **Maydh** Sanaag, N Somalia
Maydī *see* Mīdī
Mayebashi *see* Maebashi
Mayence *see* Mainz
104 K6 **Mayenne** Mayenne, NW France
104 J6 **Mayenne** ⬖ *department* NW France
104 J7 **Mayenne** ≈ N France
38 K12 **Mayer** Arizona, SW USA
24 J4 **Mayersville** Mississippi, S USA
9 P14 **Mayerthorpe** Alberta, SW Canada
23 S12 **Mayesville** South Carolina, SE USA
193 G19 **Mayfield** Canterbury, South Island, NZ
35 N14 **Mayfield** Idaho, NW USA
22 G7 **Mayfield** Kentucky, S USA
38 L5 **Mayfield** Utah, W USA
168 K9 **Mayhan** Övörhangay, C Mongolia
39 T14 **Mayhill** New Mexico, SW USA
151 T9 **Maykain** *Kaz.* Mayqayyng. Pavlodar, NE Kazakhstan
130 L14 **Maykop** Respublika Adygeya, SW Russian Federation
Maylibash *see* Maylybas
Mayli-Say *see* Mayluu-Suu
153 T9 **Mayluu-Suu** *prev.* Mayli-Say, *Kir.* Mayly-Say. Dzhalal-Abadskaya Oblast', W Kyrgyzstan
150 L14 **Maylybas** *prev.* Maylibash. Kzyl-Orda, S Kazakhstan
Mayly-Say *see* Mayluu-Suu
Maymana *see* Meymaneh
178 Gg5 **Maymyo** Mandalay, C Myanmar
127 P6 **Mayn** ≈ NE Russian Federation
131 Q5 **Mayna** Ul'yanovskaya Oblast', W Russian Federation
23 N8 **Maynardville** Tennessee, S USA
12 J13 **Maynooth** Ontario, SE Canada
8 I6 **Mayo** Yukon Territory, NW Canada
25 U9 **Mayo** Florida, SE USA
99 B16 **Mayo** *Ir.* Maigh Eo. *cultural region* W Ireland
Mayo *see* Maio
80 G12 **Mayo-Kébbi** *off.* Préfecture du Mayo-Kébbu, *var.* Mayo-Kébi. ⬖ *prefecture* SW Chad
Mayo-Kébi *see* Mayo-Kébbi
81 F19 **Mayoko** Le Niari, SW Congo
179 Q11 **Mayon Volcano** ⛰ Luzon, N Philippines
63 A24 **Mayor Buratovich** Buenos Aires, E Argentina
106 L4 **Mayorga** Castilla-León, N Spain
192 N6 **Mayor Island** *island* NE NZ
Mayor Pablo Lagerenza *see* Capitán Pablo Lagerenza
Mayor, Puig *see* Major, Puig
181 I14 **Mayotte** ◇ *French territorial collectivity* E Africa
Mayoumba *see* Mayumba
46 J13 **May Pen** C Jamaica
Mayqayyng *see* Maykain
179 P7 **Mayraira Point** *headland* Luzon, N Philippines
111 N8 **Mayrhofen** Tirol, W Austria
194 F10 **May River** East Sepik, NW PNG
126 Mm15 **Mayskiy** Amurskaya Oblast', SE Russian Federation
131 O15 **Mayskiy** Kabardino-Balkarskaya Respublika, SW Russian Federation
151 U9 **Mayskoye** Pavlodar, NE Kazakhstan
20 J17 **Mays Landing** New Jersey, NE USA
23 N4 **Maysville** Kentucky, S USA
29 R2 **Maysville** Missouri, C USA
176 Y14 **Mayu** *channel* Irian Jaya, E Indonesia
81 D20 **Mayumba** *var.* Mayoumba. Nyanga, S Gabon
175 Ss7 **Mayu, Pulau** *island* Maluku, E Indonesia
33 S8 **Mayville** Michigan, N USA
20 C11 **Mayville** New York, NE USA
31 Q4 **Mayville** North Dakota, N USA
126 M11 **Mayya** Respublika Sakha (Yakutiya), NE Russian Federation
Mayyali *see* Mahe
Mayyit, Al Baḩr al *see* Dead Sea
85 J15 **Mazabuka** Southern, S Zambia
Mazaca *see* Kayseri
Mazagan *see* El-Jadida
34 J7 **Mazama** Washington, NW USA
105 O15 **Mazamet** Tarn, S France
149 O4 **Māzandarān** *off.* Ostān-e Māzandarān. ⬖ *province* N Iran
162 F7 **Mazar** Xinjiang Uygur Zizhiqu, NW China
109 H24 **Mazara del Vallo** Sicilia, Italy, C Mediterranean Sea
155 O2 **Mazār-e Sharīf** *var.* Mazār-i Sharif. Balkh, N Afghanistan
Mazār-i Sharif *see* Mazār-e Sharīf
107 R13 **Mazarrón** Murcia, SE Spain
107 R14 **Mazarrón, Golfo de** *gulf* SE Spain
57 S9 **Mazaruni River** ≈ N Guyana
44 B6 **Mazatenango** Suchitepéquez, SW Guatemala
42 I10 **Mazatlán** Sinaloa, C Mexico
38 L12 **Mazatzal Mountains** ▲▲ Arizona, SW USA
120 D10 **Mažeikiai** Mažeikiai, NW Lithuania
120 D7 **Mazirbe** Talsi, NW Latvia
42 G5 **Mazocahui** Sonora, NW Mexico
59 I18 **Mazocruz** Puno, S Peru
Mazoe, Rio *see* Mazowe
81 N21 **Mazomeno** Maniema, E Zaire
165 Q6 **Mazong Shan** ▲ N China
85 L16 **Mazowe** *var.* Rio Mazoe. ≈ Mozambique/Zimbabwe
Mazra'a *see* Al Mazra'ah
144 G6 **Mazraat Kfar Debiâne** C Lebanon
120 H7 **Mazsalaca** *Est.* Väike-Salatsi, *Ger.* Salisburg. Valmiera, N Latvia
112 L9 **Mazury** *physical region* NE Poland
121 M20 **Mazyr** *Rus.* Mozyr'. Homyel'skaya Voblasts', SE Belarus
109 K25 **Mazzarino** Sicilia, Italy, C Mediterranean Sea
Mba *see* Ba
85 L21 **Mbabane** ● (Swaziland) NW Swaziland
Mbacké *see* Mbaké
79 N16 **Mbahiakro** E Ivory Coast
81 I16 **Mbaïki** *var.* M'Baiki. Lobaye, SW Central African Republic
81 F14 **Mbakaou, Lac de** ◎ C Cameroon
78 G11 **Mbaké** *var.* Mbacké. W Senegal
84 L11 **Mbala** *prev.* Abercorn. Northern, NE Zambia
85 J18 **Mbalabala** *prev.* Balla Balla. Matabeleland South, SW Zimbabwe
83 G18 **Mbale** E Uganda
81 E16 **Mbalmayo** *var.* M'Balmayo. Centre, S Cameroon
83 H25 **Mbamba Bay** Ruvuma, S Tanzania
81 I18 **Mbandaka** *prev.* Coquilhatville. Equateur, NW Zaire
84 B9 **M'Banza Congo** *var.* Mbanza Congo; *prev.* São Salvador, São Salvador do Congo. Zaire, NW Angola
81 G21 **Mbanza-Ngungu** Bas-Zaïre, W Zaire
69 V11 **Mbarangandu** ≈ E Tanzania
83 E19 **Mbarara** SW Uganda
81 L15 **Mbari** ≈ SE Central African Republic
83 I24 **Mbarika Mountains** ▲▲ S Tanzania
Mbatiki *see* Batiki
80 F13 **Mbé** Nord, N Cameroon
83 J24 **Mbemkuru** *var.* Mbwemkuru. ≈ S Tanzania
Mbengga *see* Beqa
180 H13 **Mbéni** Grande Comore, NW Comoros
85 K18 **Mberengwa** Midlands, S Zimbabwe
83 G24 **Mbeya** Mbeya, SW Tanzania
83 G23 **Mbeya** ⬖ *region* S Tanzania
81 E19 **Mbigou** Ngounié, C Gabon
Mbilua *see* Vella Lavella
81 F19 **Mbinda** Le Niari, SW Congo
81 D17 **Mbini** W Equatorial Guinea
Mbini *see* Uolo, Río
85 L18 **Mbizi** Masvingo, SE Zimbabwe
83 G23 **Mbogo** Mbeya, W Tanzania
81 N15 **Mboki** Haut-Mbomou, SE Central African Republic
81 G18 **Mbomo** Cuvette, NW Congo
81 L15 **Mbomou** ⬖ *prefecture* SE Central African Republic
Mbomou/M'Bomu/Mbomu *see* Bomu
78 F11 **Mbour** W Senegal
78 I10 **Mbout** Gorgol, S Mauritania
81 J14 **Mbrès** *var.* Mbrés. Nana-Grébizi, C Central African Republic
81 L22 **Mbuji-Mayi** *prev.* Bakwanga. Kasai Oriental, S Zaire
194 J9 **M'buke Islands** *island group* N PNG
83 H21 **Mbulu** Arusha, N Tanzania
194 K8 **M'bunai** *var.* Bunai. Manus Island, N PNG
64 N8 **Mburucuyá** Corrientes, NE Argentina
Mbutha *see* Buca
Mbwemkuru *see* Mbemkuru
83 G21 **Mbwikwe** Singida, C Tanzania
11 O15 **McAdam** New Brunswick, SE Canada
27 O5 **McAdoo** Texas, SW USA
37 V2 **McAfee Peak** ▲ Nevada, W USA
29 P11 **McAlester** Oklahoma, C USA
27 S17 **McAllen** Texas, SW USA
23 S11 **McBee** South Carolina, SE USA
9 N14 **McBride** British Columbia, SW Canada
26 M9 **McCamey** Texas, SW USA
35 R15 **McCammon** Idaho, NW USA
37 X11 **McCarran** ✕ (Las Vegas) Nevada, W USA
41 T11 **McCarthy** Alaska, USA
32 M5 **McCaslin Mountain** *hill* Wisconsin, N USA
27 O2 **McClellan Creek** ≈ Texas, SW USA
23 T14 **McClellanville** South Carolina, SE USA
15 Jj2 **McClintock Channel** *channel* Northwest Territories, N Canada
205 R12 **McClintock, Mount** ▲ Antarctica
37 N2 **McCloud** California, W USA
37 N3 **McCloud River** ≈ California, W USA
37 Q9 **McClure, Lake** ☒ California, W USA
207 O8 **McClure Strait** *strait* Northwest Territories, N Canada
31 N4 **McClusky** North Dakota, N USA
23 T11 **McColl** South Carolina, SE USA
24 K7 **McComb** Mississippi, S USA
20 E16 **McConnellsburg** Pennsylvania, NE USA
33 T14 **McConnelsville** Ohio, N USA
30 M17 **McCook** Nebraska, C USA
23 P13 **McCormick** South Carolina, SE USA
9 W16 **McCreary** Manitoba, S Canada
29 W11 **McCrory** Arkansas, C USA
27 T10 **McDade** Texas, SW USA
25 O8 **McDavid** Florida, SE USA
37 T1 **McDermitt** Nevada, W USA
25 S4 **McDonough** Georgia, SE USA
38 L12 **McDowell Mountains** ▲▲ Arizona, SW USA
22 H8 **McEwen** Tennessee, S USA
37 R12 **McFarland** California, W USA
Mcfarlane, Lake *see* Macfarlane, Lake
29 P12 **McGee Creek Lake** ☒ Oklahoma, C USA
29 W13 **McGehee** Arkansas, C USA
37 X5 **Mcgill** Nevada, W USA
12 K11 **McGillivray, Lac** ◎ Québec, SE Canada
41 P10 **Mcgrath** Alaska, USA
27 T8 **McGregor** Texas, SW USA
35 O12 **McGuire, Mount** ▲ Idaho, NW USA
85 M14 **Mchinji** *prev.* Fort Manning. Central, W Malawi
30 M7 **McIntosh** South Dakota, N USA
16 O3 **McKeand** ≈ Baffin Island, Northwest Territories, NE Canada
203 R4 **McKean Island** *island* Phoenix Islands, C Kiribati
32 J13 **McKee Creek** ≈ Illinois, N USA
20 C15 **Mckeesport** Pennsylvania, NE USA
23 V7 **McKenney** Virginia, NE USA
22 G8 **McKenzie** Tennessee, S USA
193 B20 **McKerrow, Lake** ◎ South Island, NZ
41 Q10 **McKinley, Mount** *var.* Denali. ▲ Alaska, USA
41 R10 **McKinley Park** Alaska, USA
36 K3 **McKinleyville** California, W USA
27 U6 **McKinney** Texas, SW USA
28 I5 **McKinney, Lake** ◎ Kansas, C USA
30 M7 **McLaughlin** South Dakota, N USA
27 O2 **McLean** Texas, SW USA
32 M16 **Mcleansboro** Illinois, N USA
9 O13 **McLennan** Alberta, W Canada
12 L9 **McLennan, Lac** ◎ Québec, SE Canada
8 M13 **McLeod Lake** British Columbia, W Canada
29 N10 **McLoud** Oklahoma, C USA
34 G15 **McLoughlin, Mount** ▲ Oregon, NW USA
39 U15 **McMillan, Lake** ☒ New Mexico, SW USA
34 G11 **McMinnville** Oregon, NW USA
22 K9 **McMinnville** Tennessee, S USA
205 R13 **McMurdo** *US research station* Antarctica
26 H9 **McNary** Texas, SW USA
39 N13 **Mcnary** Arizona, SW USA
29 N5 **McPherson** Kansas, C USA
McPherson *see* Fort McPherson
25 U6 **McRae** Georgia, SE USA
31 P4 **McVille** North Dakota, N USA
85 J25 **Mdantsane** Eastern Cape, SE South Africa
178 Jj6 **Me** Ninh Binh, N Vietnam
28 J7 **Meade** Kansas, C USA
41 O5 **Meade River** ≈ Alaska, USA
37 Y11 **Mead, Lake** ☒ Arizona/Nevada, W USA
26 M5 **Meadow** Texas, SW USA
9 S14 **Meadow Lake** Saskatchewan, C Canada
37 Y10 **Meadow Valley Wash** ≈ Nevada, W USA
24 J7 **Meadville** Mississippi, S USA
20 B12 **Meadville** Pennsylvania, NE USA
12 F14 **Meaford** Ontario, S Canada
Meáin, Inis *see* Inishmaan
106 G8 **Mealhada** Aveiro, N Portugal
11 R8 **Mealy Mountains** ▲▲ Newfoundland and Labrador, E Canada
9 O10 **Meander River** Alberta, W Canada
34 E11 **Meares, Cape** *headland* Oregon, NW USA
49 V6 **Mearim, Rio** ≈ NE Brazil
Measca, Loch *see* Mask, Lough
99 F17 **Meath** *Ir.* An Mhí. *cultural region* E Ireland
9 T14 **Meath Park** Saskatchewan, S Canada
105 O5 **Meaux** Seine-et-Marne, N France
23 T9 **Mebane** North Carolina, SE USA
176 W9 **Mebo, Gunung** ▲ Irian Jaya, E Indonesia
96 I8 **Mebonden** Sør-Trøndelag, S Norway
84 A10 **Mebridege** ≈ NW Angola
37 W16 **Mecca** California, W USA
Mecca *see* Makkah
31 Y14 **Mechanicsville** Iowa, C USA
20 L10 **Mechanicville** New York, NE USA
101 H17 **Mechelen** *Eng.* Mechlin, *Fr.* Malines. Antwerpen, C Belgium
196 C8 **Mecherchar** *var.* Eil Malk. *island* Palau Islands, Palau
103 D17 **Mechernich** Nordrhein-Westfalen, W Germany
130 L12 **Mechetinskaya** Rostovskaya Oblast', SW Russian Federation
116 J11 **Mechka** ≈ S Bulgaria
Mechlin *see* Mechelen
63 D23 **Mechongué** Buenos Aires, E Argentina
117 L14 **Mecidiye** Edirne, NW Turkey
103 I24 **Meckenbeuren** Baden-Württemberg, S Germany
102 L8 **Mecklenburger Bucht** *bay* N Germany
102 M10 **Mecklenburgische Seenplatte** *wetland* NE Germany
102 L9 **Mecklenburg-Vorpommern** ⬖ *state* NE Germany
85 Q15 **Meconta** Nampula, NE Mozambique
113 I25 **Mecsek** ▲▲ SW Hungary
85 P14 **Mecubúri** ≈ N Mozambique
85 Q14 **Mecúfi** Cabo Delgado, NE Mozambique
84 O13 **Mecula** Niassa, N Mozambique
173 Ff5 **Medan** Sumatera, E Indonesia
63 A24 **Médanos** *var.* Medanos. Buenos Aires, E Argentina
63 C19 **Médanos** Entre Ríos, E Argentina
161 K24 **Medawachchiya** North Central Province, N Sri Lanka
108 C8 **Mede** Lombardia, N Italy
76 J5 **Médéa** *var.* El Mediyya, Lemdiyya. N Algeria
Medeba *see* Ma'dabā
56 E8 **Medellín** Antioquia, NW Colombia
102 H9 **Medem** ≈ NW Germany
100 J8 **Medemblik** Noord-Holland, NW Netherlands
77 N7 **Médenine** *var.* Madanīyīn. SE Tunisia
78 G9 **Mederdra** Trarza, SW Mauritania
Medeshamstede *see* Peterborough
44 F4 **Medesto Mendez** Izabal, NE Guatemala
21 O11 **Medford** Massachusetts, NE USA
29 N8 **Medford** Oklahoma, C USA
34 G15 **Medford** Oregon, NW USA
32 K6 **Medford** Wisconsin, N USA
41 P10 **Medfra** Alaska, USA
118 M14 **Medgidia** Constanţa, SE Romania
Medgyes *see* Mediaş
62 G11 **Medianeira** Paraná, S Brazil
31 Y15 **Mediapolis** Iowa, C USA
118 I11 **Mediaş** *Ger.* Mediasch, *Hung.* Medgyes. Sibiu, C Romania
43 S15 **Medias Aguas** Veracruz-Llave, SE Mexico
Mediasch *see* Mediaş
108 G10 **Medicina** Emilia-Romagna, C Italy
35 X16 **Medicine Bow** Wyoming, C USA
39 S2 **Medicine Bow Mountains** ▲▲ Colorado/Wyoming, C USA
35 X16 **Medicine Bow River** ≈ Wyoming, C USA
9 R17 **Medicine Hat** Alberta, SW Canada
28 L7 **Medicine Lodge** Kansas, C USA
28 L7 **Medicine Lodge River** ≈ Kansas/Oklahoma, C USA
114 E7 **Međimurje** *off.* Međimurska Županija. ⬖ *province* N Croatia
Međimurska Županija *see* Međimurje
56 G10 **Medina** Cundinamarca, C Colombia
20 E9 **Medina** New York, NE USA
31 O5 **Medina** North Dakota, N USA
33 T11 **Medina** Ohio, N USA
27 Q11 **Medina** Texas, SW USA
Medina *see* Al Madīnah
123 Ll12 **Medina Bank** *undersea feature* C Mediterranean Sea
107 P6 **Medinaceli** Castilla-León, N Spain
106 L6 **Medina del Campo** Castilla-León, N Spain
106 L5 **Medina de Ríoseco** Castilla-León, N Spain
Médina Gonassé *see* Médina Gounas
78 H12 **Médina Gounas** *var.* Médina Gonassé. S Senegal
27 S12 **Medina River** ≈ Texas, SW USA
106 K16 **Medina Sidonia** Andalucía, S Spain
Medinat Israel *see* Israel
121 H14 **Medininkai** Vilnius, SE Lithuania
159 R16 **Medinīpur** West Bengal, NE India
Mediolanum *see* Saintes, France
Mediolanum *see* Milano, Italy
Mediomatrica *see* Metz
124 O13 **Mediterranean Ridge** *undersea feature* C Mediterranean Sea
123 L11 **Mediterranean Sea** *Fr.* Mer Méditerranée. *sea* Africa/Asia/Europe
Méditerranée, Mer *see* Mediterranean Sea
81 N17 **Medje** Haut-Zaïre, NE Zaire
123 K11 **Medjerda, Oued** *var.* Mejerda, Wādī Majardah. ≈ Algeria/ Tunisia *see also* Mejerda
116 G7 **Medkovets** Oblast Montana, NW Bulgaria
95 J15 **Medle** Västerbotten, N Sweden
131 W7 **Mednogorsk** Orenburgskaya Oblast', W Russian Federation
127 Qq9 **Mednyy, Ostrov** *island* E Russian Federation
104 J12 **Médoc** *cultural region* SW France
165 Q16 **Mêdog** Xizang Zizhiqu, W China

◆ Country
● Country Capital
◇ Dependent Territory
○ Dependent Territory Capital
⬖ Administrative Region
✕ International Airport
▲ Mountain
▲▲ Mountain Range
⛰ Volcano
≈ River
◎ Lake
☒ Reservoir

30 J5 **Medora** North Dakota, N USA
81 E17 **Médouneu** Woleu-Ntem, N Gabon
108 I7 **Meduna** ≈ NE Italy
Medunta see Mantes-la-Jolie
Medvedica see Medveditsa
128 J16 **Medveditsa** var. Medvedica. ≈ W Russian Federation
131 O9 **Medveditsa** ≈ SW Russian Federation
114 E8 **Medvednica** ▲ NE Croatia
129 R15 **Medvedok** Kirovskaya Oblast', NW Russian Federation
127 Nn5 **Medvezh'i, Ostrova** island group NE Russian Federation
128 J9 **Medvezh'yegorsk** Respublika Kareliya, NW Russian Federation
111 T11 **Medvode** Ger. Zwischenwässern. NW Slovenia
130 J4 **Medyn'** Kaluzhskaya Oblast', W Russian Federation
188 J10 **Meekatharra** Western Australia
39 Q4 **Meeker** Colorado, C USA
11 T12 **Meelpaeg Lake** ◎ Newfoundland, Newfoundland and Labrador, E Canada
Meenen see Menen
103 M16 **Meerane** Sachsen, E Germany
103 D15 **Meerbusch** Nordrhein-Westfalen, W Germany
100 I12 **Meerkerk** Zuid-Holland, C Netherlands
101 L18 **Meerssen** var. Mersen. Limburg, SE Netherlands
158 J10 **Meerut** Uttar Pradesh, N India
35 U13 **Meeteetse** Wyoming, C USA
101 K17 **Meeuwen** Limburg, NE Belgium
83 J16 **Mēga** S Ethiopia
83 J16 **Mēga Escarpment** escarpment S Ethiopia
Megála Kalívia see Megála Kalývia
117 E16 **Megála Kalývia** var. Megála Kalívia. Thessalía, C Greece
117 H14 **Megáli Panagiá** var. Megáli Panayía. Kentrikí Makedonía, N Greece
Megáli Panayía see Megáli Panagiá
Megáli Préspa, Límni see Prespa, Lake
116 K12 **Megálo Livádi** ▲ Bulgaria/Greece
117 E20 **Megalópoli** prev. Megalópolis. Pelopónnisos, S Greece
Megalópolis see Megalópoli
176 V9 **Megamo** Irian Jaya, E Indonesia
117 C18 **Meganísi** island Iónioi Nísoi, Greece, C Mediterranean Sea
Meganom, Mys see Mehanom, Mys
Mégantic see Lac-Mégantic
13 R12 **Mégantic, Mont** ▲ Québec, SE Canada
117 G19 **Mégara** Attikí, C Greece
27 R5 **Megargel** Texas, SW USA
100 K13 **Megen** Noord-Brabant, S Netherlands
159 U13 **Meghālaya** ◈ state NE India
159 U16 **Meghna** ≈ S Bangladesh
143 V14 **Meghri** Rus. Megri. SE Armenia
126 Gg11 **Megion** Khanty-Mansiyskiy Avtonomnyy Okrug, C Russian Federation
117 Q23 **Megísti** var. Kastellórizon. island SE Greece
Megri see Meghri
Mehabad see Mahābād
118 F13 **Mehadia** Hung. Mehádia. Caraş-Severin, SW Romania
94 L7 **Mehamn** Finnmark, N Norway
119 U13 **Mehanom, Mys** Rus. Mys Meganom. headland S Ukraine
155 P14 **Mehar** Sind, SE Pakistan
188 J8 **Meharry, Mount** ▲ Western Australia
Mehdia see Mahdia
118 G14 **Mehedinţi** ◈ county SW Romania
159 S15 **Meherpur** Khulna, W Bangladesh
23 W8 **Meherrin River** ≈ North Carolina/Virginia, SE USA
Meheso see Mī'ēso
203 T11 **Mehetia** island Îles du Vent, W French Polynesia
120 K6 **Mehikoorma** Tartumaa, E Estonia
Me Hka see Nmai Hka
149 N5 **Mehrabad** ✖ (Tehrān) Tehrān, N Iran
148 J7 **Mehrān** Īlām, W Iran
149 Q14 **Mehrān, Rūd-e** prev. Mansurabad. ≈ W Iran
149 Q9 **Mehrīz** Yazd, C Iran
155 R5 **Mehtarlām** var. Mehtar Lām, Meterlam, Methariam, Metharlam. Laghmān, E Afghanistan
105 N8 **Mehun-sur-Yèvre** Cher, C France
81 G14 **Meiganga** Adamaoua, NE Cameroon
166 H10 **Meigu** Sichuan, C China
169 W11 **Meihekou** var. Hailong. Jilin, NE China
101 L15 **Meijel** Limburg, SE Netherlands
177 G5 **Meiktila** Mandalay, C Myanmar
Meilbhe, Loch see Melvin, Lough
110 G7 **Meilen** Zürich, N Switzerland
Meilu see Wuchuan
167 T12 **Meinhua Yu** island N Taiwan
103 J17 **Meiningen** Thüringen, C Germany
110 F9 **Meiringen** Bern, S Switzerland
103 O15 **Meissen** var. Meißen. Sachsen, E Germany
103 I15 **Meissner** ▲ C Germany
101 K25 **Meix-devant-Virton** Luxembourg, SE Belgium
Mei Xian see Meizhou
167 P13 **Meizhou** var. Meixian, Mei Xian. Guangdong, S China
69 P2 **Mejerda** var. Oued Medjerda, Wādī Majardah. ≈ Algeria/Tunisia see also Medjerda, Oued
44 F7 **Mejicanos** San Salvador, C El Salvador
Méjico see Mexico
64 G5 **Mejillones** Antofagasta, N Chile
201 V5 **Mejit Island** var. Mājeej. island Ratak Chain, NE Marshall Islands
81 F17 **Mékambo** Ogooué-Ivindo, NE Gabon
82 J10 **Mek'elē** var. Makale. N Ethiopia
76 I10 **Mekerrhane, Sebkha** var. Sebkha Meqerghane, Sebkra Mekerrhane. salt flat C Algeria
Mekerrhane, Sebkra see Mekerrhane, Sebkha
78 G10 **Mékhé** NW Senegal
152 G14 **Mekhinli** Akhalskiy Velayat, C Turkmenistan
13 P9 **Mékinac, Lac** ◎ Québec, SE Canada
Meklong see Samut Songhram
76 G6 **Meknès** N Morocco
133 U12 **Mekong** var. Lan-ts'ang Chiang, Cam. Mékôngk, Chin. Lancang Jiang, Lao. Mènam Khong, Th. Mae Nam Khong, Tib. Dza Chu, Vtn. Sông Tiên Giang. ≈ SE Asia
Mekongga, Pegunungan see Mengkoka, Pegunungan
Mékôngk see Mekong
178 K15 **Mekong, Mouths of the** delta S Vietnam
40 L12 **Mekoryuk** Nunivak Island, Alaska, USA
79 R14 **Mékrou** ≈ N Benin
174 H6 **Melaka** var. Malacca. Melaka, Peninsular Malaysia
174 H6 **Melaka** var. Malacca. ◈ state Peninsular Malaysia
Melaka, Selat see Malacca, Strait of
183 O6 **Melanesia** island group W Pacific Ocean
183 P5 **Melanesian Basin** undersea feature W Pacific Ocean
175 Ss4 **Melanguane** Pulau Karakelang, N Indonesia
174 Ll8 **Melawi, Sungai** ≈ Borneo, N Indonesia
191 N12 **Melbourne** state capital Victoria, SE Australia
29 V9 **Melbourne** Arkansas, C USA
25 Y12 **Melbourne** Florida, SE USA
31 W14 **Melbourne** Iowa, C USA
94 G10 **Melbu** Nordland, C Norway
Melchor de Mencos see Ciudad Melchor de Mencos
65 F19 **Melchor, Isla** island Archipiélago de los Chonos, S Chile
42 M9 **Melchor Ocampo** Zacatecas, C Mexico
12 C11 **Meldrum Bay** Manitoulin Island, Ontario, S Canada
Meleda see Mljet
108 D8 **Melegnano** prev. Marignano. Lombardia, N Italy
196 F9 **Melekeok** var. Melekeiok. Babeldaob, N Palau
114 L9 **Melenci** Hung. Melencze. Serbia, N Yugoslavia
Melencze see Melenci
131 N4 **Melenki** Vladimirskaya Oblast', W Russian Federation
131 V6 **Meleuz** Respublika Bashkortostan, W Russian Federation
10 L6 **Mélèzes, Rivière aux** ≈ Québec, C Canada
80 I11 **Melfi** Guéra, S Chad
109 M17 **Melfi** Basilicata, S Italy
9 U14 **Melfort** Saskatchewan, S Canada
106 H4 **Melgaço** Viana do Castelo, N Portugal
107 N4 **Melgar de Fernamental** Castilla-León, N Spain
76 L6 **Melghir, Chott** var. Chott Melrhir. salt lake E Algeria
96 H8 **Melhus** Sør-Trøndelag, S Norway
106 H3 **Melide** Galicia, NW Spain
Meligalá see Meligalás
117 E21 **Meligalás** prev. Meligalá. Pelopónnisos, S Greece
62 L12 **Mel, Ilha do** island S Brazil
122 G11 **Melilla** anc. Rusaddir, Russadir. Melilla, Spain, N Africa
73 N1 **Melilla** enclave Spain, N Africa
65 G18 **Melimoyu, Monte** ▲ S Chile
175 N8 **Melintang, Danau** ◎ Borneo, N Indonesia
119 U7 **Melioratyvne** Dnipropetrovs'ka Oblast', E Ukraine
64 G11 **Melipilla** Santiago, C Chile
117 I25 **Mélissa, Ákra** headland Kríti, Greece, E Mediterranean Sea
15 Kk16 **Melita** Manitoba, S Canada
Melita see Mljet
Melitene see Malatya
109 M23 **Melito di Porto Salvo** Calabria, SW Italy
119 U10 **Melitopol'** Zaporiz'ka Oblast', SE Ukraine
111 V4 **Melk** Niederösterreich, NE Austria
97 K15 **Mellan-Fryken** ◎ C Sweden
101 E17 **Melle** Oost-Vlaanderen, NW Belgium
102 G13 **Melle** Niedersachsen, NW Germany
Mellersta Finland see Keski-Suomi
97 J17 **Mellerud** Älvsborg, S Sweden
104 K10 **Melle-sur-Bretonne** Deux-Sèvres, W France
31 P8 **Mellette** South Dakota, N USA
123 J16 **Mellieha** E Malta
82 B10 **Mellit** Northern Darfur, W Sudan
77 N7 **Mellita** ✖ SE Tunisia
65 G21 **Mellizo Sur, Cerro** ▲ S Chile
102 G9 **Mellum** island NW Germany
85 L22 **Melmoth** KwaZulu/Natal, E South Africa
113 D16 **Mělník** Ger. Melnik. Střední Čechy, NW Czech Republic
126 H13 **Mel'nikovo** Tomskaya Oblast', C Russian Federation
63 G18 **Melo** Cerro Largo, NE Uruguay
Melodunum see Melun
Melrhir, Chott see Melghir, Chott
191 P7 **Melrose** New South Wales, SE Australia
190 I7 **Melrose** South Australia
31 T7 **Melrose** Minnesota, N USA
35 Q11 **Melrose** Montana, NW USA
39 V12 **Melrose** New Mexico, SW USA
110 I8 **Mels** Sankt Gallen, NE Switzerland
Melsetter see Chimanimani
35 V9 **Melstone** Montana, NW USA
103 I16 **Melsungen** Hessen, C Germany
94 L12 **Meltaus** Lappi, NW Finland
99 N19 **Melton Mowbray** C England, UK
84 Q13 **Meluco** Cabo Delgado, NE Mozambique
105 O5 **Melun** anc. Melodunum. Seine-et-Marne, N France
82 F12 **Melut** Upper Nile, SE Sudan
29 P5 **Melvern Lake** ⊟ Kansas, C USA
9 V16 **Melville** Saskatchewan, S Canada
Melville Bay/Melville Bugt see Qimusseriarsuaq
47 O11 **Melville Hall** ✖ (Dominica) NE Dominica
189 O1 **Melville Island** island Northern Territory, N Australia
207 O8 **Melville Island** island Parry Islands, Northwest Territories, NW Canada
16 R7 **Melville, Lake** ◎ Newfoundland and Labrador, E Canada
15 Ll2 **Melville Peninsula** peninsula Northwest Territories, NE Canada
Melville Sound see Viscount Melville Sound
27 Q9 **Melvin** Texas, SW USA
99 D15 **Melvin, Lough** Ir. Loch Meilbhe. ◎ S Northern Ireland, UK/Ireland
174 M9 **Memala** Borneo, C Indonesia
115 L22 **Memaliaj** Gjirokastër, S Albania
85 Q14 **Memba** Nampula, NE Mozambique
85 Q14 **Memba, Baia de** inlet NE Mozambique
Membidj see Manbij
Memel see Neman, NE Europe
Memel see Klaipėda, Lithuania
103 J23 **Memmingen** Bayern, S Germany
29 U1 **Memphis** Missouri, C USA
22 E10 **Memphis** Tennessee, S USA
27 P3 **Memphis** Texas, SW USA
22 E10 **Memphis** ✖ Tennessee, S USA
13 Q13 **Memphrémagog, Lac** var. Lake Memphremagog. ◎ Canada/USA see also Memphremagog, Lake
21 N6 **Memphremagog, Lake** var. Lac Memphrémagog. ◎ Canada/USA see also Memphrémagog, Lac
119 Q2 **Mena** Chernihivs'ka Oblast', NE Ukraine
29 S12 **Mena** Arkansas, C USA
Menaam see Menaldum
Menado see Manado
108 D6 **Menaggio** Lombardia, N Italy
31 T6 **Menahga** Minnesota, N USA
79 R10 **Ménaka** Goa, E Mali
100 K5 **Menaldum** Fris. Menaam. Friesland, N Netherlands
Mènam Khong see Mekong
76 E7 **Menara** ✖ (Marrakech) C Morocco
27 Q9 **Menard** Texas, SW USA
199 M14 **Menard Fracture Zone** tectonic feature E Pacific Ocean
32 M7 **Menasha** Wisconsin, N USA
Mencezi Garagum see Tsentral'nyye Nizmennyye Garagumy
200 O10 **Mendaña Fracture Zone** tectonic feature E Pacific Ocean
174 M10 **Mendawai, Sungai** ≈ Borneo, C Indonesia
105 P13 **Mende** anc. Mimatum. Lozère, S France
83 J14 **Mendebo** ▲ C Ethiopia
82 J9 **Mendefera** prev. Adi Ugri. S Eritrea
207 S7 **Mendeleyev Ridge** undersea feature Arctic Ocean
131 T3 **Mendeleyevsk** Respublika Tatarstan, W Russian Federation
103 F15 **Menden** Nordrhein-Westfalen, W Germany
24 L6 **Mendenhall** Mississippi, S USA
40 L13 **Mendenhall, Cape** headland Nunivak Island, Alaska, USA
43 P9 **Méndez** var. Villa de Méndez. Tamaulipas, C Mexico
82 H13 **Mendi** W Ethiopia
194 G12 **Mendi** Southern Highlands, W PNG
99 K22 **Mendip Hills** var. Mendips. hill range S England, UK
Mendips see Mendip Hills
36 L6 **Mendocino** California, W USA
36 J3 **Mendocino, Cape** headland California, W USA
0 B8 **Mendocino Fracture Zone** tectonic feature NE Pacific Ocean
37 P10 **Mendota** California, W USA
32 L11 **Mendota** Illinois, N USA
32 K8 **Mendota, Lake** ◎ Wisconsin, N USA
64 I11 **Mendoza** Mendoza, W Argentina
64 I12 **Mendoza** off. Provincia de Mendoza. ◈ province W Argentina
110 H12 **Mendrisio** Ticino, S Switzerland
174 Hh7 **Mendung** Pulau Mendol, W Indonesia
56 I5 **Mene de Mauroa** Falcón, NW Venezuela
56 I5 **Mene Grande** Zulia, NW Venezuela
142 B14 **Menemen** İzmir, W Turkey
101 C18 **Menen** var. Meenen, Fr. Menin. West-Vlaanderen, W Belgium
169 Q8 **Menengiyn Tal** plain E Mongolia
201 R9 **Meneng Point** headland SW Nauru
94 L10 **Menesjärvi** Lapp. Menešjávri. Lappi, N Finland
Menešjávri see Menesjärvi
109 I24 **Menfi** Sicilia, Italy, C Mediterranean Sea
167 P7 **Mengcheng** Anhui, E China
166 F15 **Menghai** Yunnan, SW China
175 Q11 **Mengkoka, Pegunungan** var. Pegunungan Mekongga. ▲ Sulawesi, C Indonesia
166 F15 **Mengla** Yunnan, SW China
67 F24 **Menguera Point** headland East Falkland, Falkland Islands
166 M13 **Mengzhu Ling** ▲ S China
166 H14 **Mengzi** Yunnan, SW China
Menin see Menen
190 L7 **Menindee** New South Wales, SE Australia
190 L7 **Menindee Lake** ◎ New South Wales, SE Australia
190 J10 **Meningie** South Australia
105 O5 **Mennecy** Essonne, N France
31 Q12 **Menno** South Dakota, N USA
116 H13 **Menoíkio** ▲ NE Greece
33 N5 **Menominee** Michigan, N USA
32 M5 **Menominee River** ≈ Michigan/Wisconsin, N USA
32 M8 **Menomonee Falls** Wisconsin, N USA
32 I6 **Menomonie** Wisconsin, N USA
85 D14 **Menongue** var. Vila Serpa Pinto, Port. Serpa Pinto. Cuando Cubango, C Angola
123 I8 **Menorca** Eng. Minorca; anc. Balearis Minor. island Islas Baleares, Spain, W Mediterranean Sea
107 S13 **Menor, Mar** lagoon SE Spain
41 S10 **Mentasta Lake** ◎ Alaska, USA
41 S10 **Mentasta Mountains** ▲ Alaska, USA
173 Ff10 **Mentawai, Kepulauan** island group W Indonesia
173 G10 **Mentawai, Selat** strait W Indonesia
174 Ii10 **Mentok** Pulau Bangka, W Indonesia
105 V15 **Menton** It. Mentone. Alpes-Maritimes, SE France
26 K8 **Mentone** Texas, SW USA
Mentone see Menton
33 U11 **Mentor** Ohio, N USA
175 Nn7 **Menyapa, Gunung** ▲ Borneo, N Indonesia
165 T9 **Menyuan** var. Menyuan Huizu Zizhixian. Qinghai, C China
Menyuan Huizu Zizhixian see Menyuan
76 M5 **Menzel Bourguiba** var. Manzil Bū Ruqaybah; prev. Ferryville. N Tunisia
142 M15 **Menzelet Barajı** ⊟ C Turkey
131 T4 **Menzelinsk** Respublika Tatarstan, W Russian Federation
188 K11 **Menzies** Western Australia
205 V6 **Menzies, Mount** ▲ Antarctica
42 J6 **Meoqui** Chihuahua, N Mexico
85 N14 **Meponda** Niassa, NE Mozambique
100 M8 **Meppel** Drenthe, NE Netherlands
102 E12 **Meppen** Niedersachsen, NW Germany
Meqerghane, Sebkha see Mekerrhane, Sebkha
107 T6 **Mequinenza, Embalse de** ⊟ NE Spain
32 M8 **Mequon** Wisconsin, N USA
Mera see Maira
190 D3 **Meramangye, Lake** salt lake South Australia
29 W5 **Meramec River** ≈ Missouri, C USA
Meran see Merano
174 H10 **Merangin** ≈ Sumatera, W Indonesia
108 G5 **Merano** Ger. Meran. Trentino-Alto Adige, N Italy
174 H4 **Merapuh Lama** Pahang, Peninsular Malaysia
108 D7 **Merate** Lombardia, N Italy
175 Nn11 **Meratus, Pegunungan** ▲ Borneo, N Indonesia
176 Z16 **Merauke** Irian Jaya, E Indonesia
176 Z16 **Merauke, Sungai** ≈ Irian Jaya, E Indonesia
190 L9 **Merbein** Victoria, SE Australia
101 F21 **Merbes-le-Château** Hainaut, S Belgium
Merca see Marka
56 C13 **Mercaderes** Cauca, SW Colombia
Mercara see Madikeri
37 P9 **Merced** California, W USA
63 C20 **Mercedes** Buenos Aires, E Argentina
63 D15 **Mercedes** Corrientes, NE Argentina
64 J11 **Mercedes** prev. Villa Mercedes. San Luis, C Argentina
63 D19 **Mercedes** Soriano, SW Uruguay
27 S17 **Mercedes** Texas, SW USA
37 R9 **Merced Peak** ▲ California, W USA
37 P9 **Merced River** ≈ California, W USA
20 B13 **Mercer** Pennsylvania, NE USA
101 G18 **Merchtem** Vlaams Brabant, C Belgium
13 O13 **Mercier** Québec, SE Canada
27 Q9 **Mercury** Texas, SW USA
192 M5 **Mercury Islands** island group N New Zealand
21 O9 **Meredith** New Hampshire, NE USA
67 B25 **Meredith, Cape** headland West Falkland, Falkland Islands
39 V6 **Meredith, Lake** ◎ Colorado, C USA
27 N2 **Meredith, Lake** ⊟ Texas, SW USA
83 O16 **Mereeg** var. Mareeq, It. Meregh. Galguduud, E Somalia
119 V5 **Merefa** Kharkivs'ka Oblast', E Ukraine
Meregh see Mereeg
197 C11 **Mere Lava** island Banks Islands, N Vanuatu
101 E17 **Merelbeke** Oost-Vlaanderen, NW Belgium
Merend see Marand
127 Oo9 **Merenga** Magadanskaya Oblast', E Russian Federation
178 K12 **Mereuch** Môndól Kiri, E Cambodia
Mergate see Margate
150 F9 **Mergenevo** Zapadnyy Kazakhstan, NW Kazakhstan
178 Gg12 **Mergui** Tenasserim, S Myanmar
177 G12 **Mergui Archipelago** island group S Myanmar
116 L12 **Meriç** Edirne, NW Turkey
116 L12 **Meriç** Bul. Maritsa, Gk. Évros; anc. Hebrus. ≈ SE Europe see also Évros/Maritsa
43 X12 **Mérida** Yucatán, SW Mexico
106 J11 **Mérida** anc. Augusta Emerita. Extremadura, W Spain
56 I6 **Mérida** Mérida, W Venezuela
56 H7 **Mérida** off. Estado Mérida. ◈ state W Venezuela
20 M13 **Meriden** Connecticut, NE USA
24 M5 **Meridian** Mississippi, S USA
27 S8 **Meridian** Texas, SW USA
104 J13 **Mérignac** Gironde, SW France
104 J13 **Mérignac** ✖ (Bordeaux) Gironde, SW France
95 J18 **Merikarvia** Turku-Pori, SW Finland
191 R12 **Merimbula** New South Wales, SE Australia
190 L9 **Meringur** Victoria, SE Australia
Merín, Laguna see Mirim Lagoon
99 I19 **Merioneth** cultural region W Wales, UK
196 A11 **Merir** island Palau Islands, N Palau
196 B17 **Merizo** SW Guam
Merjama see Märjamaa
151 S16 **Merke** Zhambyl, S Kazakhstan
27 P7 **Merkel** Texas, SW USA
121 F15 **Merkinė** Varėna, S Lithuania
101 G16 **Merksem** Antwerpen, N Belgium
101 I15 **Merksplas** Antwerpen, N Belgium
Merkulovichi see Myerkulavichy
121 G15 **Merkys** ≈ S Lithuania
34 F15 **Merlin** Oregon, NW USA
63 C20 **Merlo** Buenos Aires, E Argentina
144 G8 **Meron, Haré** ▲ N Israel
76 K6 **Merouane, Chott** salt lake NE Algeria
82 F7 **Merowe** Northern, N Sudan
188 J12 **Merredin** Western Australia
98 I13 **Merrick** ▲ S Scotland, UK
34 H16 **Merrill** Oregon, NW USA
32 L5 **Merrill** Wisconsin, N USA
33 N11 **Merrillville** Indiana, N USA
21 O10 **Merrimack River** ≈ Massachusetts/New Hampshire, NE USA
30 L12 **Merriman** Nebraska, C USA
9 N17 **Merritt** British Columbia, SW Canada
25 Y12 **Merritt Island** Florida, SE USA
25 Y11 **Merritt Island** island Florida, SE USA
30 M12 **Merritt Reservoir** ⊟ Nebraska, C USA
191 S7 **Merriwa** New South Wales, SE Australia
191 O8 **Merriwagga** New South Wales, SE Australia
24 G8 **Merryville** Louisiana, S USA
82 K9 **Mersa Fatma** E Eritrea
104 M7 **Mer St-Aubin** Loir-et-Cher, C France
Mersa Maṭrûḥ see Maṭrûḥ
101 M24 **Mersch** Luxembourg, C Luxembourg
103 M15 **Merseburg** Sachsen-Anhalt, C Germany
Mersen see Meerssen
99 K18 **Mersey** ≈ NW England, UK
142 J17 **Mersin** İçel, S Turkey
174 I6 **Mersing** Johor, Peninsular Malaysia
120 E8 **Mērsrags** Talsi, NW Latvia
158 G12 **Merta** var. Merta City. Rājasthān, N India
Merta City see Merta
158 F12 **Merta Road** Rājasthān, N India
99 J21 **Merthyr Tydfil** S Wales, UK
106 H13 **Mértola** Beja, S Portugal
205 V16 **Mertz Glacier** glacier Antarctica
101 M24 **Mertzig** Diekirch, C Luxembourg
27 O9 **Mertzon** Texas, SW USA
83 I18 **Meru** Eastern, C Kenya
105 N4 **Méru** Oise, N France
83 I20 **Meru, Mount** ▲ NE Tanzania
Merv see Mary
Mervdasht see Marv Dasht
142 K11 **Merzifon** Amasya, N Turkey
103 D20 **Merzig** Saarland, SW Germany
38 L14 **Mesa** Arizona, SW USA
31 V4 **Mesabi Range** ▲ Minnesota, N USA
56 H6 **Mesa Bolívar** Mérida, NW Venezuela
109 Q18 **Mesagne** Puglia, SE Italy
41 P12 **Mesa Mountain** ▲ Alaska, USA
117 J25 **Mesará** lowland Kríti, Greece, E Mediterranean Sea
39 S14 **Mescalero** New Mexico, SW USA
103 G15 **Meschede** Nordrhein-Westfalen, W Germany
143 Q12 **Mescit Dağları** ▲ NE Turkey
201 V13 **Mesegon** island Chuuk, C Micronesia
Meseritz see Międzyrzecz
56 F11 **Mesetas** Meta, C Colombia
Meshchera Lowland see Meshcherskaya Nizina
130 M4 **Meshcherskaya Nizina** Eng. Meshchera Lowland. basin W Russian Federation
130 J5 **Meshchovsk** Kaluzhskaya Oblast', W Russian Federation
129 R9 **Meshchura** Respublika Komi, NW Russian Federation
Meshed see Mashhad
Meshed-i-Sar see Bābolsar
82 E13 **Meshra'er Req** Warab, S Sudan
39 R15 **Mesilla** New Mexico, SW USA
110 H10 **Mesocco** Ger. Misox. Ticino, S Switzerland
117 D18 **Mesolóngi** prev. Mesolóngion. Dytikí Ellás, W Greece
Mesolóngion see Mesolóngi
12 E8 **Mesomikenda Lake** ◎ Ontario, S Canada
63 D15 **Mesopotamia** var. Mesopotamia Argentina. physical region NE Argentina
Mesopotamia Argentina see Mesopotamia
37 Y10 **Mesquite** Nevada, W USA
84 Q13 **Messalo, Rio** var. Mualo. ≈ NE Mozambique
Messana/Messene see Messina
101 L25 **Messancy** Luxembourg, SE Belgium
109 M23 **Messina** var. Messana, Messene; anc. Zancle. Sicilia, Italy, C Mediterranean Sea
85 K19 **Messina** Northern, NE South Africa
Messina, Strait of see Messina, Stretto di
109 M23 **Messina, Stretto di** Eng. Strait of Messina. strait SW Italy
117 E21 **Messíni** Pelopónnisos, S Greece
117 E21 **Messinía** peninsula S Greece
117 E22 **Messiniakós Kólpos** gulf S Greece
126 H8 **Messoyakha** ≈ N Russian Federation
116 H11 **Mesta** Gk. Néstos, Turk. Kara Su. ≈ Bulgaria/Greece see also Néstos
Mestghanem see Mostaganem
143 R8 **Mestia** var. Mestiya. N Georgia
Mestiya see Mestia
117 K18 **Mestón, Ákra** headland Chíos, E Greece
108 H8 **Mestre** Veneto, NE Italy
61 M16 **Mestre, Espigão** ▲ E Brazil
174 Ii11 **Mesuji** ≈ Sumatera, W Indonesia
Mesule see Grosser Möseler
8 J10 **Meszah Peak** ▲ British Columbia, W Canada
56 G11 **Meta** off. Departamento del Meta. ◈ province C Colombia
13 Q8 **Metabetchouane** ≈ Québec, SE Canada
16 O4 **Meta Incognita Peninsula** peninsula Baffin Island, Northwest Territories, NE Canada
24 K9 **Metairie** Louisiana, S USA
34 M6 **Metaline Falls** Washington, NW USA
64 K6 **Metán** Salta, N Argentina
84 N13 **Metangula** Niassa, N Mozambique
44 E7 **Metapán** Santa Ana, NW El Salvador
56 K9 **Meta, Río** ≈ Colombia/Venezuela
108 I11 **Metauro** ≈ C Italy
82 H11 **Metema** NW Ethiopia
117 D15 **Metéora** religious building Thessalía, C Greece
67 O20 **Meteor Rise** undersea feature SW Indian Ocean
195 N9 **Meteran** New Hanover, NE PNG
Meterlam/Methariam/Metharlam see Mehtarlām
117 G20 **Methanon** peninsula S Greece
34 J6 **Methow River** ≈ Washington, NW USA
21 O10 **Methuen** Massachusetts, NE USA
193 G19 **Methven** Canterbury, South Island, NZ
Metis see Metz
115 G15 **Metković** Dubrovnik-Neretva, SE Croatia
41 Y14 **Metlakatla** Annette Island, Alaska, USA
111 V13 **Metlika** Ger. Möttling. SE Slovenia
111 T8 **Metnitz** Kärnten, S Austria
29 W13 **Meto, Bayou** ≈ Arkansas, C USA
174 Ii13 **Metro** Sumatera, W Indonesia
32 M17 **Metropolis** Illinois, N USA
Metropolitan see Santiago
37 N8 **Metropolitan Oakland** ✖ California, W USA
117 D15 **Métsovo** prev. Métsovon. Ípeiros, C Greece
Métsovon see Métsovo
25 V5 **Metter** Georgia, SE USA
101 H21 **Mettet** Namur, S Belgium
103 D20 **Mettlach** Saarland, SW Germany
Mettu see Metu
82 H13 **Metu** var. Mattu, Mettu. W Ethiopia
175 N7 **Metulang** Borneo, N Indonesia
144 G8 **Metulla** Northern, N Israel
150 G14 **Metvyy Kultuk, Sor** salt flat SW Kazakhstan
105 T4 **Metz** anc. Divodurum Mediomatricum, Mediomatrica, Metis. Moselle, NE France
103 H22 **Metzingen** Baden-Württemberg, S Germany
173 E4 **Meulaboh** Sumatera, W Indonesia
101 D18 **Meulebeke** West-Vlaanderen, W Belgium
105 U6 **Meurthe** ≈ NE France
105 S5 **Meurthe-et-Moselle** ◈ department NE France
105 S4 **Meuse** ◈ department NE France
86 F10 **Meuse** Dut. Maas. ≈ W Europe see also Maas
195 O11 **Mevelo** ≈ New Britain, C Papau New Guinea
Mexcala, Río see Balsas, Río
27 U8 **Mexia** Texas, SW USA
60 K11 **Mexiana, Ilha** island NE Brazil
42 C1 **Mexicali** Baja California, NW Mexico
28 K8 **Mexico** Missouri, C USA
20 H9 **Mexico** New York, NE USA
27 P15 **Mexico** off. United Mexican States, var. Méjico, México, Sp. Estados Unidos Mexicanos. ◆ federal republic N Central America
43 O14 **México** var. Ciudad de México, Eng. Mexico City. ● (Mexico) México, C Mexico
43 O13 **México** ◈ state S Mexico
1 J13 **Mexico Basin** var. Sigsbee Deep. undersea feature C Gulf of Mexico
Mexico City see México
México, Golfo de see Mexico, Gulf of
46 B4 **Mexico, Gulf of** Sp. Golfo de México. gulf W Atlantic Ocean
Meyadine see Al Mayādīn
41 Y14 **Meyers Chuck** Etolin Island, Alaska, USA
154 M3 **Meymaneh** var. Maimāna, Maymana. Fāryāb, NW Afghanistan
149 N7 **Meymeh** Eşfahān, C Iran
127 Pp6 **Meynypil'gyno** Chukotskiy Avtonomnyy Okrug, NE Russian Federation
110 A10 **Meyrin** Genève, SW Switzerland
177 Ff8 **Mezaligon** Irrawaddy, SW Myanmar
43 O15 **Mezcala** Guerrero, S Mexico
116 H8 **Mezdra** Oblast Montana, NW Bulgaria
105 P16 **Mèze** Hérault, S France
129 O6 **Mezen'** Arkhangel'skaya Oblast', NW Russian Federation
129 P8 **Mezen'** ≈ NW Russian Federation
Mezen, Bay of see Mezenskaya Guba
105 Q13 **Mézenc, Mont** ▲ C France
129 O8 **Mezenskaya Guba** var. Bay of Mezen. bay NW Russian Federation
125 Bb7 **Mezha** ≈ W Russian Federation
Mezha see Myazha
126 Hh15 **Mezhdurechensk** Kemerovskaya Oblast', S Russian Federation
125 F4 **Mezhdusharskiy, Ostrov** island Novaya Zemlya, N Russian Federation
Mezhëvo see Myezhava
Mezhgor'ye see Mizhhir"ya
119 V8 **Mezhova** Dnipropetrovs'ka Oblast', E Ukraine
8 J12 **Meziadin Junction** British Columbia, W Canada
113 G16 **Mezileské Sedlo** var. Przełęcz Międzyleska. ≈ Czech Republic/Poland
104 L14 **Mézin** Lot-et-Garonne, SW France
113 M24 **Mezőberény** Békés, SE Hungary
113 M25 **Mezőhegyes** Békés, SE Hungary
113 M25 **Mezőkovácsháza** Békés, SE Hungary
113 M21 **Mezőkövesd** Borsod-Abaúj-Zemplén, NE Hungary
Mezőtelegd see Tileagd
113 M23 **Mezőtúr** Jász-Nagykun-Szolnok, E Hungary
42 K10 **Mezquital** Durango, C Mexico
108 G6 **Mezzolombardo** Trentino-Alto Adige, N Italy
84 L13 **Mfuwe** Northern, N Zambia
123 J16 **Mġarr** Gozo, N Malta
130 H6 **Mglin** Bryanskaya Oblast', W Russian Federation
Mhálanna, Cionn see Malin Head
160 G10 **Mhow** Madhya Pradesh, C India
Miadzioł Nowy see Myadzyel
179 Q13 **Miagao** Panay Island, C Philippines
43 R17 **Miahuatlán** var. Miahuatlán de Porfirio Díaz. Oaxaca, SE Mexico
Miahuatlán de Porfirio Díaz see Miahuatlán
106 K10 **Miajadas** Extremadura, W Spain
Miajlar see Myājlār
38 M14 **Miami** Arizona, SW USA
25 Z16 **Miami** Florida, SE USA
29 R8 **Miami** Oklahoma, C USA
27 O2 **Miami** Texas, SW USA
25 Z16 **Miami** ✖ Florida, SE USA
25 Z16 **Miami Beach** Florida, SE USA
25 Y15 **Miami Canal** canal Florida, SE USA
33 R14 **Miamisburg** Ohio, N USA
155 U10 **Miān Channūn** Punjab, E Pakistan
148 J4 **Miāndowāb** var. Mianduab, Miyāndoāb. Āẕarbāyjān-e Bākhtarī, NW Iran
180 H5 **Miandrivazo** Toliara, C Madagascar
Mianduab see Miāndowāb
148 K3 **Mīāneh** var. Miyāneh. Āẕarbāyjān-e Khāvarī, NW Iran
155 O16 **Miāni Hōr** lagoon S Pakistan
166 G10 **Mianning** Sichuan, C China
155 T7 **Miānwāli** Punjab, NE Pakistan
166 J7 **Mianxian** var. Mian Xian. Shaanxi, C China
166 I8 **Mianyang** Sichuan, C China
Mianyang see Xiantao
167 R3 **Miaodao Qundao** island group E China

◆ Country ● Country Capital ◇ Dependent Territory ○ Dependent Territory Capital ◈ Administrative Region ✖ International Airport ▲ Mountain ▲ Mountain Range ✗ Volcano ≈ River ◎ Lake ⊟ Reservoir

167 S13 **Miaoli** N Taiwan
125 E12 **Miass** Chelyabinskaya Oblast', C Russian Federation
112 G8 **Miastko** *Ger.* Rummelsburg in Pommern. Słupsk, NW Poland
Miava *see* Myjava
9 O15 **Mica Creek** British Columbia, SW Canada
166 J7 **Micang Shan** ▲ C China
194 I12 **Michael, Mount** ▲ C PNG
Mi Chai *see* Nong Khai
113 O19 **Michalovce** *Ger.* Grossmichel, *Hung.* Nagymihály. Východné Slovensko, E Slovakia
101 M20 **Michel, Baraque** *hill* E Belgium
41 S5 **Michelson, Mount** ▲ Alaska, USA
47 P9 **Miches** E Dominican Republic
32 M4 **Michigamme, Lake** ◎ Michigan, N USA
32 M4 **Michigamme Reservoir** ▣ Michigan, N USA
33 N4 **Michigamme River** ♎ Michigan, N USA
33 O7 **Michigan** *off.* State of Michigan; also known as Great Lakes State, Lake State, Wolverine State. ◆ *state* N USA
33 O11 **Michigan City** Indiana, N USA
33 O8 **Michigan, Lake** ◎ N USA
33 P2 **Michipicoten Bay** *lake bay* Ontario, N Canada
12 A8 **Michipicoten Island** *island* Ontario, S Canada
12 B7 **Michipicoten River** Ontario, S Canada
Michurin *see* Tsarevo
130 M6 **Michurinsk** Tambovskaya Oblast', W Russian Federation
Mico, Punta/Mico, Punto *see* Monkey Point
44 L10 **Mico, Río** ♎ SE Nicaragua
47 T12 **Micoud** SE Saint Lucia
201 N16 **Micronesia** *off.* Federated States of Micronesia. ◆ *federation* W Pacific Ocean
183 P4 **Micronesia** *island group* W Pacific Ocean
174 Jj5 **Midai, Pulau** *island* Kepulauan Natuna, W Indonesia
Mid-Atlantic Cordillera *see* Mid-Atlantic Ridge
67 M17 **Mid-Atlantic Ridge** *var.* Mid-Atlantic Cordillera, Mid-Atlantic Rise, Mid-Atlantic Swell. *undersea feature* Atlantic Ocean
Mid-Atlantic Rise/ Mid-Atlantic Swell *see* Mid-Atlantic Ridge
101 E15 **Middelburg** Zeeland, SW Netherlands
85 H24 **Middelburg** Eastern Cape, S South Africa
85 K21 **Middelburg** Mpumalanga, NE South Africa
97 G23 **Middelfart** Fyn, C Denmark
100 G13 **Middelharnis** Zuid-Holland, SW Netherlands
101 B16 **Middelkerke** West-Vlaanderen, W Belgium
100 I9 **Middenbeemster** Noord-Holland, C Netherlands
100 I8 **Middenmeer** Noord-Holland, NW Netherlands
37 Q2 **Middle Alkali Lake** ◎ California, W USA
200 Nn6 **Middle America Trench** *undersea feature* E Pacific Ocean
157 P19 **Middle Andaman** *island* Andaman Islands, India, NE Indian Ocean
Middle Atlas *see* Moyen Atlas
23 R3 **Middlebourne** West Virginia, NE USA
25 W9 **Middleburg** Florida, SE USA
Middleburg Island *see* 'Eua
Middle Caicos *see* Grand Caicos
27 N8 **Middle Concho River** ♎ Texas, SW USA
Middle Congo *see* Congo
41 R6 **Middle Fork Chandalar River** ♎ Alaska, USA
41 Q7 **Middle Fork Koyukuk River** ♎ Alaska, USA
35 O12 **Middle Fork Salmon River** ♎ Idaho, NW USA
9 T15 **Middle Lake** Saskatchewan, S Canada
30 L13 **Middle Loup River** ♎ Nebraska, C USA
193 E22 **Middlemarch** Otago, South Island, NZ
33 T15 **Middleport** Ohio, N USA
31 U14 **Middle Raccoon River** ♎ Iowa, C USA
31 R3 **Middle River** ♎ Minnesota, N USA
23 N8 **Middlesboro** Kentucky, S USA
99 M15 **Middlesbrough** N England, UK
44 G3 **Middlesex** Stann Creek, C Belize
99 N22 **Middlesex** *cultural region* SE England, UK
11 P15 **Middleton** Nova Scotia, SE Canada
22 F10 **Middleton** Tennessee, S USA
32 L9 **Middleton** Wisconsin, N USA
41 S13 **Middleton Island** *island* Alaska, USA
36 M7 **Middletown** California, W USA
23 Y2 **Middletown** Delaware, NE USA
20 K15 **Middletown** New Jersey, NE USA
20 K13 **Middletown** New York, NE USA
33 R14 **Middletown** Ohio, N USA
20 G15 **Middletown** Pennsylvania, NE USA
147 N14 **Midi** *var.* Maydī. NW Yemen
105 O16 **Midi, Canal du** *canal* S France
104 K17 **Midi de Bigorre, Pic du** ▲ S France
104 K17 **Midi d'Ossau, Pic du** ▲ SW France
181 R7 **Mid-Indian Basin** *undersea feature* N Indian Ocean
181 P7 **Mid-Indian Ridge** *var.* Central Indian Ridge. *undersea feature* C Indian Ocean
105 N14 **Midi-Pyrénées** ◈ *region* S France
27 N8 **Midkiff** Texas, SW USA
12 G13 **Midland** Ontario, S Canada
33 R8 **Midland** Michigan, N USA
30 M10 **Midland** South Dakota, N USA
26 M8 **Midland** Texas, SW USA
85 K17 **Midlands** ◈ *province* C Zimbabwe
99 D21 **Midleton** *Ir.* Mainistir na Corann. SW Ireland
27 T7 **Midlothian** Texas, SW USA
98 K12 **Midlothian** *cultural region* S Scotland, UK
180 I7 **Midongy** Fianarantsoa, S Madagascar
104 K15 **Midou** ♎ SW France
199 I6 **Mid-Pacific Mountains** *var.* Mid-Pacific Seamounts. *undersea feature* NW Pacific Ocean
Mid-Pacific Seamounts *see* Mid-Pacific Mountains
179 R16 **Midsayap** Mindanao, S Philippines
38 L3 **Midway** Utah, W USA
199 Jj5 **Midway Islands** ◇ *US territory* C Pacific Ocean
35 X14 **Midwest** Wyoming, C USA
29 N10 **Midwest City** Oklahoma, C USA
158 M10 **Mid Western** ◈ *zone* W Nepal
100 P5 **Midwolda** Groningen, NE Netherlands
143 Q16 **Midyat** Mardin, SE Turkey
116 F8 **Midzhur** *SCr.* Midžor. ▲ Bulgaria/Yugoslavia *see also* Midžor
115 Q14 **Midžor** *Bul.* Midzhur. ▲ Bulgaria/Yugoslavia *see also* Midzhur
171 H16 **Mie** *off.* Mie-ken. ◈ *prefecture* Honshū, SW Japan
113 L16 **Miechów** Kielce, S Poland
112 F11 **Międzychód** *Ger.* Mitteldorf. Gorzów, W Poland
Międzyleska, Przełęcz *see* Mezileské Sedlo
112 O12 **Międzyrzec Podlaski** Biała Podlaska, E Poland
112 E11 **Międzyrzecz** *Ger.* Meseritz. Gorzów, W Poland
Mie-ken *see* Mie
104 L16 **Miélan** Gers, S France
113 N16 **Mielec** Rzeszów, SE Poland
97 L21 **Mien** ◎ S Sweden
43 O8 **Mier** Tamaulipas, C Mexico
118 J11 **Miercurea-Ciuc** *Ger.* Szeklerburg, *Hung.* Csíkszereda. Harghita, C Romania
106 K2 **Mieres** Asturias, NW Spain
Mieresch *see* Maros/Mureş
101 K15 **Mierlo** Noord-Brabant, SE Netherlands
43 O10 **Mier y Noriega** Nuevo León, NE Mexico
Mies *see* Stříbro
82 K13 **Mī'ēso** *var.* Meheso, Miesso. C Ethiopia
Miesso *see* Mī'ēso
112 D10 **Mieszkowice** *Ger.* Bärwalde Neumark. Szczecin, W Poland
20 G14 **Mifflinburg** Pennsylvania, NE USA
20 F14 **Mifflintown** Pennsylvania, NE USA
43 R15 **Miguel Alemán, Presa** ▣ SE Mexico
Miguel Asua *var.* Miguel Auza. Zacatecas, C Mexico
42 L9 (see above)
Miguel Auza *see* Miguel Asua
45 S15 **Miguel de la Borda** *var.* Donoso. Colón, C Panama
43 N13 **Miguel Hidalgo** ✕ (Guadalajara) Jalisco, SW Mexico
42 H7 **Miguel Hidalgo, Presa** ▣ W Mexico
118 J14 **Mihăileşti** Giurgiu, S Romania
118 M14 **Mihail Kogălniceanu** *var.* Kogălniceanu; *prev.* Caramurat, Ferdinand. Constanţa, SE Romania
119 N14 **Mihai Viteazu** Constanţa, SE Romania
142 G12 **Mihalıççık** Eskişehir, NW Turkey
170 Ee13 **Mihara** Hiroshima, Honshū, SW Japan
171 Jj17 **Mihara-yama** ⩘ Miyako-jima, SE Japan
107 S8 **Mijares** ♎ E Spain
100 I11 **Mijdrecht** Utrecht, C Netherlands
172 Oo5 **Mikasa** Hokkaidō, NE Japan
Mikashevichi *see* Mikashevichy
121 K19 **Mikashevichy** *Pol.* Mikaszewicze, *Rus.* Mikashevichi. Brestskaya Voblasts', SW Belarus
Mikaszewicze *see* Mikashevichy
171 Hh16 **Mikawa-wan** *bay* S Japan
Mikhailovgrad *see* Montana, Oblast
130 L5 **Mikhaylov** Ryazanskaya Oblast', W Russian Federation
Mikhaylovgrad *see* Montana/Montana, Oblast
205 Z8 **Mikhaylov Island** *island* Antarctica
151 T6 **Mikhaylovka** Pavlodar, N Kazakhstan
131 N9 **Mikhaylovka** Volgogradskaya Oblast', SW Russian Federation
Mikhaylovka *see* Mykhaylivka
170 G14 **Miki** Hyōgo, Honshū, SW Japan
83 K24 **Mikindani** Mtwara, SE Tanzania
95 N18 **Mikkeli** *Swe.* Sankt Michel. Mikkeli, SE Finland
95 N18 **Mikkeli** *Swe.* Sankt Michel, St.Michel. ◈ *province* C Finland
112 M8 **Mikołajki** *Ger.* Nikolaiken. Suwałki, NE Poland
Míkonos *see* Mýkonos
116 I9 **Mikre** Loveshka Oblast, C Bulgaria
116 C13 **Mikrí Préspa, Límni** ◎ N Greece
129 P4 **Mikulkin, Mys** *headland* NW Russian Federation
83 I23 **Mikumi** Morogoro, SE Tanzania
129 R10 **Mikun'** Respublika Komi, NW Russian Federation
171 Hh13 **Mikuni** Fukui, Honshū, SW Japan
171 Jj14 **Mikuni-tōge** *pass* Honshū, C Japan
172 Ss13 **Mikura-jima** *island* E Japan
31 V7 **Milaca** Minnesota, N USA
64 J10 **Milagro** La Rioja, C Argentina
58 B7 **Milagro** Guayas, SW Ecuador
33 P4 **Milakokia Lake** ◎ Michigan, N USA
32 J1 **Milan** Illinois, N USA
33 R10 **Milan** Michigan, N USA
29 T2 **Milan** Missouri, C USA
39 Q11 **Milan** New Mexico, SW USA
22 G9 **Milan** Tennessee, S USA
Milan *see* Milano
97 F15 **Miland** Telemark, S Norway
85 N15 **Milange** Zambézia, NE Mozambique
108 D8 **Milano** *Eng.* Milan, *Ger.* Mailand; *anc.* Mediolanum. Lombardia, N Italy
27 U10 **Milano** Texas, SW USA
142 C15 **Milas** Muğla, SW Turkey
121 K21 **Milashavichy** *Rus.* Milashevichi. Homyel'skaya Voblasts', SE Belarus
Milashevichi *see* Milashavichy
121 I18 **Milavidy** *Rus.* Milovidy. Brestskaya Voblasts', SW Belarus
109 L23 **Milazzo** *anc.* Mylae. Sicilia, Italy, C Mediterranean Sea
31 R8 **Milbank** South Dakota, N USA
21 T7 **Milbridge** Maine, NE USA
102 L11 **Milde** ♎ C Germany
12 F14 **Mildmay** Ontario, S Canada
190 L9 **Mildura** Victoria, SE Australia
143 X12 **Mil Düzü** *Rus.* Mil'skaya Ravnina, Mil'skaya Step'. *physical region* C Azerbaijan
166 H13 **Mile** Yunnan, SW China
Mile *see* Mili Atoll
189 Y10 **Miles** Queensland, E Australia
27 P8 **Miles** Texas, SW USA
35 X9 **Miles City** Montana, NW USA
9 U17 **Milestone** Saskatchewan, S Canada
109 N22 **Mileto** Calabria, SW Italy
109 K16 **Miletto, Monte** ▲ C Italy
20 M13 **Milford** Connecticut, NE USA
23 Y3 **Milford** *var.* Milford City. Delaware, NE USA
31 T11 **Milford** Iowa, C USA
21 S6 **Milford** Maine, NE USA
31 R16 **Milford** Nebraska, C USA
21 O10 **Milford** New Hampshire, NE USA
20 J13 **Milford** Pennsylvania, NE USA
27 T7 **Milford** Texas, SW USA
38 K6 **Milford** Utah, W USA
Milford *see* Milford Haven
Milford City *see* Milford
99 H21 **Milford Haven** *prev.* Milford. SW Wales, UK
29 O4 **Milford Lake** ▣ Kansas, C USA
193 B21 **Milford Sound** Southland, South Island, NZ
193 B21 **Milford Sound** *inlet* South Island, NZ
Milhau *see* Millau
Milḥ, Baḥr al *see* Razāzah, Buḥayrat ar
145 T10 **Milḥ, Wādī al** *dry watercourse* S Iraq
201 W8 **Mili Atoll** *var.* Mile. *atoll* Ratak Chain, SE Marshall Islands
112 H13 **Milicz** Wrocław, SW Poland
109 L25 **Militello in Val di Catania** Sicilia, Italy, C Mediterranean Sea
127 Pp11 **Mil'kovo** Kamchatskaya Oblast', E Russian Federation
9 R17 **Milk River** Alberta, SW Canada
46 J13 **Milk River** ♎ C Jamaica
35 W7 **Milk River** ♎ Montana, NW USA
82 D9 **Milk, Wadi el** *var.* Wadi al Malik. ♎ C Sudan
101 L14 **Mill** Noord-Brabant, SE Netherlands
105 P14 **Millau** *var.* Milhau; *anc.* Æmilianum. Aveyron, S France
12 I14 **Millbrook** Ontario, SE Canada
25 U4 **Milledgeville** Georgia, SE USA
10 C12 **Mille Lacs, Lac des** ◎ Ontario, S Canada
31 V6 **Mille Lacs Lake** ◎ Minnesota, N USA
25 V4 **Millen** Georgia, SE USA
31 O9 **Miller** South Dakota, N USA
32 K5 **Miller Dam Flowage** ◎ Wisconsin, N USA
41 U12 **Miller, Mount** ▲ Alaska, USA
130 L10 **Millerovo** Rostovskaya Oblast', SW Russian Federation
39 N17 **Miller Peak** ▲ Arizona, SW USA
33 T12 **Millersburg** Ohio, N USA
20 G15 **Millersburg** Pennsylvania, NE USA
193 D23 **Millers Flat** Otago, South Island, NZ
27 Q8 **Millersview** Texas, SW USA
108 B10 **Millesimo** Piemonte, NE Italy
15 Mm15 **Milles Lacs, Lac des** ◎ Ontario, SW Canada
27 Q13 **Millett** Texas, SW USA
105 N11 **Millevaches, Plateau de** *plateau* C France
190 K12 **Millicent** South Australia
100 M13 **Millingen aan den Rijn** Gelderland, SE Netherlands
22 E10 **Millington** Tennessee, S USA
21 R4 **Millinocket** Maine, NE USA
21 R4 **Millinocket Lake** ◎ Maine, NE USA
205 Z11 **Mill Island** *island* Antarctica
191 T3 **Millmerran** Queensland, E Australia
111 R9 **Millstatt** Kärnten, S Austria
99 B19 **Milltown Malbay** *Ir.* Sráid na Cathrach. W Ireland
20 J17 **Millville** New Jersey, NE USA
29 S13 **Millwood Lake** ▣ Arkansas, C USA
Milne Bank *see* Milne Seamounts
195 O17 **Milne Bay** ◈ *province* SE PNG
195 N17 **Milne Bay** *bay* SE PNG
66 J8 **Milne Seamounts** *var.* Milne Bank. *undersea feature* N Atlantic Ocean
31 Q6 **Milnor** North Dakota, N USA
21 R5 **Milo** Maine, NE USA
117 I22 **Mílos** Mílos, Kykládes, Greece, Aegean Sea
117 I22 **Mílos** *island* Kykládes, Greece, Aegean Sea
112 H11 **Miłosław** Poznań, C Poland
115 K19 **Milot** *var.* Miloti. Lezhë, C Albania
Miloti *see* Milot
119 Z5 **Milove** Luhans'ka Oblast', E Ukraine
Milovidy *see* Milavidy
190 L4 **Milparinka** New South Wales, SE Australia
37 N9 **Milpitas** California, W USA
Mil'skaya Ravnina/Mil'skaya Step' *see* Mil Düzü
12 G15 **Milton** Ontario, S Canada
193 E24 **Milton** Otago, South Island, NZ
23 Y4 **Milton** Delaware, NE USA
25 P8 **Milton** Florida, SE USA
20 G14 **Milton** Pennsylvania, NE USA
20 L7 **Milton** Vermont, NE USA
34 K11 **Milton-Freewater** Oregon, NW USA
99 N21 **Milton Keynes** SE England, UK
29 N3 **Miltonvale** Kansas, C USA
167 N10 **Miluo** Hunan, S China
32 M9 **Milwaukee** Wisconsin, N USA
Milyang *see* Miryang
Mimatum *see* Mende
39 Q15 **Mimbres Mountains** ▲ New Mexico, SW USA
190 D2 **Mimili** South Australia
104 J14 **Mimizan** Landes, SW France
Mimmaya *see* Minmaya
81 E19 **Mimongo** Ngounié, C Gabon
Min *see* Fujian
37 T7 **Mina** Nevada, W USA
149 S14 **Mīnāb** Hormozgān, SE Iran
Mīnā Baranīs *see* Berenice
155 R9 **Mīna Bāzār** Baluchistān, SW Pakistan
170 C15 **Minamata** Kumamoto, Kyūshū, SW Japan
172 Ss17 **Minami-Iō-jima** *Eng.* San Augustine. *island* SE Japan
172 Nn7 **Minami-Kayabe** Hokkaidō, NE Japan
170 B17 **Minamitane** Kagoshima, Tanega-shima, SW Japan
Minami Tori Shima *see* Marcus Island
64 J4 **Mina Pirquitas** Jujuy, NW Argentina
181 O3 **Mīnā' Qābūs** NE Oman
63 F19 **Minas** Lavalleja, S Uruguay
11 P15 **Minas Basin** *bay* Nova Scotia, SE Canada
63 F17 **Minas de Corrales** Rivera, NE Uruguay
46 A5 **Minas de Matahambre** Pinar del Río, W Cuba
106 J13 **Minas de Ríotinto** Andalucía, S Spain
62 K7 **Minas Gerais** *off.* Estado de Minas Gerais. ◈ *state* E Brazil
44 E5 **Minas, Sierra de las** ▲ E Guatemala
43 T15 **Minatitlán** Veracruz-Llave, E Mexico
177 Ff6 **Minbu** Magwe, W Myanmar
155 V10 **Minchinābād** Punjab, E Pakistan
65 G17 **Minchinmávida, Volcán** ▲ S Chile
98 G7 **Minch, The** *var.* North Minch. *strait* NW Scotland, UK
108 F8 **Mincio** *anc.* Mincius. ♎ N Italy
Mincius *see* Mincio
28 M11 **Minco** Oklahoma, C USA
179 Rr16 **Mindanao** *island* S Philippines
Mindanao Sea *see* Bohol Sea
103 J23 **Mindel** ♎ S Germany
103 J23 **Mindelheim** Bayern, S Germany
Mindello *see* Mindelo
78 C9 **Mindelo** *var.* Mindello; *prev.* Porto Grande. São Vicente, N Cape Verde
12 I13 **Minden** Ontario, SE Canada
102 H13 **Minden** *anc.* Minthun. Nordrhein-Westfalen, NW Germany
24 G5 **Minden** Louisiana, S USA
31 O16 **Minden** Nebraska, C USA
37 Q6 **Minden** Nevada, W USA
190 L8 **Mindona Lake** *seasonal lake* New South Wales, SE Australia
179 Pp12 **Mindoro** *island* N Philippines
179 P12 **Mindoro Strait** *strait* W Philippines
165 S9 **Mine** Gansu, N China
170 Dd12 **Mine** Yamaguchi, Honshū, SW Japan
99 E21 **Mine Head** *Ir.* Mionn Ard. *headland* S Ireland
99 J23 **Minehead** SW England, UK
61 J19 **Mineiros** Goiás, C Brazil
27 V6 **Mineola** Texas, SW USA
27 S13 **Mineral** Texas, SW USA
131 N15 **Mineral'nyye Vody** Stavropol'skiy Kray, SW Russian Federation
32 K9 **Mineral Point** Wisconsin, N USA
27 S6 **Mineral Wells** Texas, SW USA
38 K6 **Minersville** Utah, W USA
33 U12 **Minerva** Ohio, N USA
109 N17 **Minervino Murge** Puglia, SE Italy
105 O16 **Minervois** *physical region* S France
164 I10 **Minfeng** *var.* Niya. Xinjiang Uygur Zizhiqu, NW China
81 O25 **Minga** Shaba, SE Zaire
143 W11 **Mingäçevir** *Rus.* Mingechaur, Mingechevir. C Azerbaijan
143 W11 **Mingäçevir Su Anbarı** *Rus.* Mingechaurskoye Vodokhranilishche, Mingechevirskoye Vodokhranilishche. ▣ NW Azerbaijan
177 G8 **Mingaladon** ✕ (Yangon) Yangon, SW Myanmar
11 P11 **Mingan** Québec, E Canada
155 U5 **Mingāora** *var.* Mingora, Mongora. North-West Frontier Province, N Pakistan
152 K8 **Mingbuloq** *Rus.* Mynbulak. Nawoiy Wiloyati, N Uzbekistan
152 K9 **Mingbuloq Botighi** *Rus.* Vpadina Mynbulak. *depression* N Uzbekistan
Mingechaur/Mingechevir *see* Mingäçevir
Mingechaurskoye Vodokhranilishche/Mingech evirskoye Vodokhranilishche *see* Mingäçevir Su Anbarı
177 Ff4 **Mingin** Sagaing, C Myanmar
107 Q10 **Minglanilla** Castilla-La Mancha, C Spain
33 V13 **Mingo Junction** Ohio, N USA
Mingora *see* Mingāora
169 V7 **Mingshui** Heilongjiang, NE China
Mingteke Daban *see* Mintaka Pass
85 Q14 **Minguri** Nampula, NE Mozambique
165 U10 **Minhe** *var.* Shangchuankou. Qinghai, C China
177 Ff6 **Minhla** Magwe, W Myanmar
178 J15 **Minh Lương** Kiên Giang, S Vietnam
106 G5 **Minho** *Sp.* Miño. ♎ Portugal/Spain *see also* Miño
106 G5 **Minho** *former province* N Portugal
161 C24 **Minicoy Island** *island* SW India
35 P15 **Minidoka** Idaho, NW USA
120 C11 **Minija** ♎ W Lithuania
188 G9 **Minilya** Western Australia
12 E8 **Minisinakwa Lake** ◎ Ontario, S Canada
47 T12 **Ministre Point** *headland* S Saint Lucia
9 V15 **Minitonas** Manitoba, S Canada
Minius *see* Miño
167 R12 **Min Jiang** ♎ SE China
166 H10 **Min Jiang** ♎ C China
190 H9 **Minlaton** South Australia
172 N8 **Minmaya** *var.* Mimmaya. Aomori, Honshū, C Japan
79 U14 **Minna** Niger, C Nigeria
172 Pp16 **Minna-jima** *island* Sakishima-shotō, SW Japan
29 N4 **Minneapolis** Kansas, C USA
31 U9 **Minneapolis** Minnesota, N USA
15 Kk15 **Minnedosa** Manitoba, S Canada
28 J7 **Minneola** Kansas, C USA
31 S7 **Minnesota** *off.* State of Minnesota; also known as Gopher State, New England of the West, North Star State. ◆ *state* N USA
31 S9 **Minnesota River** ♎ Minnesota/South Dakota, N USA
31 V9 **Minnetonka** Minnesota, N USA
31 O3 **Minnewaukan** North Dakota, N USA
190 F7 **Minnipa** South Australia
106 H2 **Miño** Galicia, NW Spain
106 G5 **Miño** *var.* Mino, Minius, *Port.* Minho. ♎ Portugal/Spain *see also* Minho
171 Ii16 **Minobu** Yamanashi, Honshū, S Japan
32 L4 **Minocqua** Wisconsin, N USA
171 I15 **Minokamo** Gifu, Honshū, SW Japan
32 L12 **Minonk** Illinois, N USA
Minorca *see* Menorca
30 M3 **Minot** North Dakota, N USA
165 U8 **Minqin** Gansu, N China
121 J16 **Minsk** ● (Belarus) Minskaya Voblasts', C Belarus
121 L16 **Minsk** ✕ Minskaya Voblasts', C Belarus
Minskaya Oblast' *see* Minskaya Voblasts'
121 K16 **Minskaya Voblasts'** *prev.* Rus. Minskaya Oblast'. ◈ *province* C Belarus
121 J16 **Minskaya Wzvyshsha** ▲ C Belarus
112 N12 **Mińsk Mazowiecki** *var.* Nowo-Minsk. Siedlce, E Poland
33 Q13 **Minster** Ohio, N USA
81 F15 **Minta** Centre, C Cameroon
155 W2 **Mintaka Pass** *Chin.* Mingteke Daban. *pass* China/Pakistan
117 D20 **Mínthi** ▲ S Greece
Minthun *see* Minden
11 O14 **Minto** New Brunswick, SE Canada
8 H6 **Minto** Yukon Territory, W Canada
41 R9 **Minto** Alaska, USA
31 Q3 **Minto** North Dakota, N USA
10 K6 **Minto, Lac** ◎ Québec, C Canada
205 R16 **Minto, Mount** ▲ Antarctica
9 U17 **Minton** Saskatchewan, S Canada
201 R15 **Minto Reef** *atoll* Caroline Islands, C Micronesia
39 R4 **Minturn** Colorado, C USA
109 J16 **Minturno** Lazio, C Italy
126 Hh15 **Minusinsk** Krasnoyarskiy Kray, S Russian Federation
110 G11 **Minusio** Ticino, S Switzerland
81 E17 **Minvoul** Woleu-Ntem, N Gabon
147 R13 **Minwakh** N Yemen
165 V11 **Min Xian** *var.* Minxian. Gansu, C China
Minya *see* El Minya
33 R6 **Mio** Michigan, N USA
Mionn Ard *see* Mine Head
Miosnum, Pulau *see* Num, Pulau
176 Ww9 **Mios Num, Selat** *strait* Irian Jaya, E Indonesia
164 L5 **Miquan** Xinjiang Uygur Zizhiqu, NW China
121 I17 **Mir** Hrodzyenskaya Voblasts', W Belarus
108 H8 **Mira** Veneto, NE Italy
106 G13 **Mira** ♎ S Portugal
10 K15 **Mirabel** *var.* Montreal. ✕ (Montréal) Québec, SE Canada
62 Q8 **Miracema** Rio de Janeiro, SE Brazil
56 G9 **Miraflores** Boyacá, C Colombia
42 G10 **Miraflores** Baja California Sur, W Mexico
46 L9 **Miragoâne** S Haiti
161 E16 **Miraj** Mahārāshtra, W India
63 E23 **Miramar** Buenos Aires, E Argentina
105 R15 **Miramas** Bouches-du-Rhône, SE France
104 K12 **Mirambeau** Charente-Maritime, W France
104 L13 **Miramont-de-Guyenne** Lot-et-Garonne, SW France
117 L25 **Mirampéllou Kólpos** *gulf* Kríti, Greece, E Mediterranean Sea
164 L8 **Miran** Xinjiang Uygur Zizhiqu, NW China
56 M5 **Miranda** *off.* Estado Miranda. ◈ *state* N Venezuela
Miranda de Corvo *see* Miranda do Corvo
107 O3 **Miranda de Ebro** La Rioja, N Spain
106 G8 **Miranda do Corvo** *var.* Miranda de Corvo. Coimbra, N Portugal
106 J6 **Miranda do Douro** Bragança, N Portugal
104 L15 **Mirande** Gers, S France
106 I6 **Mirandela** Bragança, N Portugal
27 R15 **Mirando City** Texas, SW USA
108 G9 **Mirandola** Emilia-Romagna, N Italy
62 I8 **Mirandópolis** São Paulo, S Brazil
62 K8 **Mirassol** São Paulo, S Brazil
106 J3 **Miravalles** ▲ NW Spain
44 L12 **Miravalles, Volcán** ⩘ NW Costa Rica
147 W13 **Mirbāṭ** *var.* Marbat. S Oman
46 M9 **Mirebalais** C Haiti
105 T6 **Mirecourt** Vosges, NE France
105 N16 **Mirepoix** Ariège, S France
Mirgorod *see* Myrhorod
145 W10 **Mīr Ḥājī Khalīl** E Iraq
174 Mm4 **Miri** Sarawak, East Malaysia
79 W12 **Miria** Zinder, S Niger
190 F5 **Mirikata** South Australia
56 K4 **Mirimire** Falcón, N Venezuela
63 H18 **Mirim Lagoon** *var.* Lake Mirim, *Sp.* Laguna Merín. *lagoon* Brazil/Uruguay
Mirim, Lake *see* Mirim Lagoon
Mírina *see* Mýrina
180 H14 **Miringoni** Mohéli, S Comoros
149 W11 **Mīrjāveh** Sīstān va Balūchestān, SE Iran
205 Z9 **Mirny** *Russian research station* Antarctica
126 Jj11 **Mirnyy** Respublika Sakha (Yakutiya), NE Russian Federation
Mironovka *see* Myronivka
112 F9 **Mirosławiec** Piła, NW Poland
Mirovo *see* Vrattsa
102 N10 **Mirow** Mecklenburg-Vorpommern, N Germany
158 G6 **Mīrpur** Jammu and Kashmir, NW India
Mīrpur *see* New Mīrpur
155 P17 **Mīrpur Batoro** Sind, SE Pakistan
155 Q16 **Mīrpur Khās** Sind, SE Pakistan
155 P17 **Mīrpur Sakro** Sind, SE Pakistan
149 T14 **Mīr Shahdād** Hormozgān, S Iran
Mirtoan Sea *see* Mirtóo Pélagos
117 G21 **Mirtóo Pélagos** *Eng.* Mirtoan Sea; *anc.* Myrtoum Mare. *sea* S Greece
169 Z16 **Miryang** *var.* Milyang, *Jap.* Mitsuō. SE South Korea
Mirzachirla *see* Murzechirla
170 Dd14 **Misaki** Ehime, Shikoku, SW Japan
43 Q13 **Misantla** Veracruz-Llave, E Mexico
172 N9 **Misawa** Aomori, Honshū, C Japan
59 G14 **Mishagua, Río** ♎ C Peru
169 Z8 **Mishan** Heilongjiang, NE China
33 O11 **Mishawaka** Indiana, N USA
41 N6 **Misheguk Mountain** ▲ Alaska, USA
171 Jj17 **Mishima** *var.* Misima. Shizuoka, Honshū, S Japan
170 Dd11 **Mi-shima** *island* SW Japan
131 V4 **Mishkino** Respublika Bashkortostan, W Russian Federation
159 Y10 **Mishmi Hills** *hill range* NE India
167 N11 **Mi Shui** ♎ S China
Misiaf *see* Maṣyāf
109 J23 **Misilmeri** Sicilia, Italy, C Mediterranean Sea
Misima *see* Mishima
195 P17 **Misima Island** *island* SE PNG
Misión de Guana *see* Guana
62 F13 **Misiones** *off.* Provincia de Misiones. ◈ *province* NE Argentina
64 P8 **Misiones** *off.* Departamento de las Misiones. ◈ *department* S Paraguay
Misión San Fernando *see* San Fernando
Miskin *see* Maskin
Miskito Coast *see* La Mosquitia
45 O7 **Miskitos, Cayos** *island group* NE Nicaragua
113 M21 **Miskolc** Borsod-Abaúj-Zemplén, NE Hungary
175 Tt10 **Misool, Pulau** *island* Maluku, E Indonesia
Misox *see* Mesocco
31 Y3 **Misquah Hills** *hill range* Minnesota, N USA
77 P7 **Miṣrātah** *var.* Misurata. NW Libya
123 Ll15 **Miṣrātah, Rās** *headland* N Libya
12 C7 **Missanabie** Ontario, S Canada
60 E10 **Missão Catrimani** Roraima, N Brazil
12 D6 **Missinaibi** ♎ Ontario, S Canada
12 C7 **Missinaibi Lake** ◎ Ontario, S Canada
9 T13 **Missinipe** Saskatchewan, C Canada
30 M11 **Mission** South Dakota, N USA
27 S17 **Mission** Texas, SW USA
10 F10 **Missisa Lake** ◎ Ontario, C Canada
20 M6 **Missisquoi Bay** *lake bay* Canada/USA
12 C10 **Missisagi** ♎ Ontario, S Canada
12 G15 **Mississauga** Ontario, S Canada
33 P12 **Mississinewa Lake** ▣ Indiana, N USA
33 P12 **Mississinewa River** ♎ Indiana/Ohio, N USA
24 K4 **Mississippi** *off.* State of Mississippi; also known as Bayou State, Magnolia State. ◆ *state* SE USA
12 K13 **Mississippi** ♎ Ontario, SE Canada
24 M10 **Mississippi Delta** *delta* Louisiana, S USA
49 N1 **Mississippi Fan** *undersea feature* N Gulf of Mexico
12 L13 **Mississippi Lake** ◎ Ontario, SE Canada
1 J11 **Mississippi River** ♎ C USA
24 M9 **Mississippi Sound** *sound* Alabama/Mississippi, S USA
35 P9 **Missoula** Montana, NW USA
29 T5 **Missouri** *off.* State of Missouri; also known as Bullion State, Show Me State. ◆ *state* C USA
27 V11 **Missouri City** Texas, SW USA
1 J10 **Missouri River** ♎ C USA
13 Q6 **Mistassibi** ♎ Québec, SE Canada
13 P6 **Mistassini** Québec, SE Canada
13 P6 **Mistassini** ♎ Québec, SE Canada
10 J11 **Mistassini, Lac** ◎ Québec, SE Canada
111 Y3 **Mistelbach an der Zaya** Niederösterreich, NE Austria
109 L24 **Misterbianco** Sicilia, Italy, C Mediterranean Sea
97 N19 **Misterhult** Kalmar, S Sweden
59 H17 **Misti, Volcán** ▲ S Peru
Mistras *see* Mystrás
109 K23 **Mistretta** *anc.* Amestratus. Sicilia, Italy, C Mediterranean Sea
170 C14 **Misumi** Kumamoto, Kyūshū, SW Japan
170 Ee12 **Misumi** Shimane, Honshū, SW Japan
Misurata *see* Miṣrātah
85 O14 **Mitande** Niassa, N Mozambique
42 J13 **Mita, Punta de** *headland* C Mexico
57 W12 **Mitaraka, Massif du** ▲ NE South America
Mitau *see* Jelgava
189 X9 **Mitchell** Queensland, E Australia
12 E15 **Mitchell** Ontario, S Canada
30 I13 **Mitchell** Nebraska, C USA
34 J12 **Mitchell** Oregon, NW USA
31 P11 **Mitchell** South Dakota, N USA
25 P5 **Mitchell Lake** ▣ Alabama, S USA
33 P7 **Mitchell, Lake** ◎ Michigan, N USA
23 P9 **Mitchell, Mount** ▲ North Carolina, SE USA
189 V3 **Mitchell River** ♎ Queensland, NE Australia
99 D20 **Mitchelstown** *Ir.* Baile Mhistéala. SW Ireland
12 M9 **Mitchinamécus, Lac** ◎ Québec, SE Canada
Mitèmboni *see* Mitemele, Río
81 D17 **Mitemele, Río** *var.* Mitèmboni, Temboni, Utamboni. ♎ S Equatorial Guinea
155 S12 **Mithānkot** Punjab, E Pakistan
155 T7 **Mitha Tiwāna** Punjab, E Pakistan
155 R17 **Mithi** Sind, SE Pakistan
Míthimna *see* Míthymna
Mi Tho *see* My Tho
117 L16 **Míthymna** *var.* Míthimna. Lésvos, E Greece
202 L16 **Mitiaro** *island* S Cook Islands
Mitilíni *see* Mytilíni
13 U7 **Mitis** ♎ Québec, SE Canada
43 R16 **Mitla** Oaxaca, SE Mexico
171 Kk16 **Mito** Ibaraki, Honshū, S Japan
94 N2 **Mitra, Kapp** *headland* W Svalbard
192 M13 **Mitre** ▲ North Island, NZ
193 B21 **Mitre Peak** ▲ South Island, NZ
41 O15 **Mitrofania Island** *island* Alaska, USA
Mitrovica/Mitrowitz *see* Sremska Mitrovica, Serbia, Yugoslavia
Mitrovica/Mitrovicë *see* Kosovska Mitrovica, Serbia, Yugoslavia

◆ Country
● Country Capital
◇ Dependent Territory
○ Dependent Territory Capital
◈ Administrative Region
✕ International Airport
▲ Mountain
▲ Mountain Range
⩘ Volcano
♎ River
◎ Lake
▣ Reservoir

180 H12 **Mitsamiouli** Grande Comore, NW Comoros
180 I3 **Mitsinjo** Mahajanga, NW Madagascar
Mits'iwa *see* Massawa
180 H13 **Mitsoudjé** Grande Comore, NW Comoros
172 Oo7 **Mitsuishi** Hokkaidō, NE Japan
171 K13 **Mitsuke** *var.* Mituke. Niigata, Honshū, C Japan
Mitsuō *see* Miryang
170 Cc10 **Mitsushima** Nagasaki, Tsushima, SW Japan
102 G12 **Mittelandkanal** *canal* NW Germany
110 J7 **Mittelberg** Vorarlberg, NW Austria
Mitteldorf *see* Międzychód
Mittelstadt *see* Baia Sprie
Mitterburg *see* Pazin
111 P7 **Mittersill** Salzburg, NW Austria
103 N16 **Mittweida** Sachsen, E Germany
56 J13 **Mitú** Vaupés, SE Colombia
Mituke *see* Mitsuke
Mitumba, Chaîne des/Mitumba Range *see* Mitumba, Monts
81 O22 **Mitumba, Monts** *var.* Chaîne des Mitumba, Mitumba Range. ▲ E Zaire
81 N23 **Mitwaba** Shaba, SE Zaire
81 E18 **Mitzic** Woleu-Ntem, N Gabon
84 K11 **Miueru Wantipa, Lake** ◎ N Zambia
171 Jj17 **Miura** Kanagawa, Honshū, S Japan
171 M13 **Miyagi** *off.* Miyagi-ken. ◐ *prefecture* Honshū, C Japan
144 M7 **Miyāh, Wādī al** *dry watercourse* E Syria
172 Ss13 **Miyake** Tōkyō, Miyako-jima, SE Japan
172 N11 **Miyako** Iwate, Honshū, C Japan
172 Q16 **Miyako-jima** *island* Sakishima-shotō, SW Japan
170 C16 **Miyakonojō** *var.* Miyakonzyô. Miyazaki, Kyūshū, SW Japan
Miyakonzyô *see* Miyakonojō
172 Pp16 **Miyako-shotō** *island group* SW Japan
150 G11 **Miyaly** Atyrau, W Kazakhstan
Miyāndoāb *see* Mīāndowāb
Miyāneh *see* Mīāneh
170 C15 **Miyanojō** Kagoshima, Kyūshū, SW Japan
170 Cc16 **Miyazaki** Miyazaki, Kyūshū, SW Japan
170 C15 **Miyazaki** *off.* Miyazaki-ken. ◐ *prefecture* Kyūshū, SW Japan
171 H13 **Miyazu** Kyōto, Honshū, SW Japan
Miyory *see* Myory
170 F13 **Miyoshi** *var.* Miyosi. Hiroshima, Honshū, SW Japan
Miyosi *see* Miyoshi
Miza *see* Mizë
83 H14 **Mīzan Teferī** SW Ethiopia
Mizda *see* Mizdah
77 O8 **Mizdah** *var.* Mizda. NW Libya
115 K20 **Mizë** *var.* Miza. Fier, W Albania
99 A22 **Mizen Head** *Ir.* Carn Uí Néid. *headland* SW Ireland
118 H7 **Mizhhir"ya** *Rus.* Mezhgor'ye. Zakarpats'ka Oblast', W Ukraine
166 L4 **Mizhi** Shaanxi, C China
118 K13 **Mizil** Prahova, SE Romania
116 H7 **Miziya** Oblast Montana, NW Bulgaria
159 W15 **Mizo Hills** *hill range* E India
159 W15 **Mizoram** ◐ *state* NE India
144 F12 **Mizpe Ramon** Southern, S Israel
59 L19 **Mizque** Cochabamba, C Bolivia
59 M19 **Mizque, Río** ≈ C Bolivia
171 I15 **Mizunami** Gifu, Honshū, SW Japan
171 Mm12 **Mizusawa** Iwate, Honshū, C Japan
97 M18 **Mjölby** Östergötland, S Sweden
97 G15 **Mjøndalen** Buskerud, S Norway
97 J19 **Mjörn** ◎ S Sweden
96 I13 **Mjøsa** *var.* Mjøsen. ◎ S Norway
Mjøsen *see* Mjøsa
83 G21 **Mkalama** Singida, C Tanzania
82 K13 **Mkata** ≈ C Tanzania
85 K14 **Mkushi** Central, C Zambia
85 L22 **Mkuze** KwaZulu/Natal, E South Africa
83 J22 **Mkwaja** Tanga, E Tanzania
113 D16 **Mladá Boleslav** *Ger.* Jungbunzlau. Střední Čechy, N Czech Republic
114 M12 **Mladenovac** Serbia, C Yugoslavia
116 L11 **Mladinovo** Khaskovska Oblast, SE Bulgaria
115 O17 **Mlado Nagoričane** N FYR Macedonia
Mlanje *see* Mulanje
114 N12 **Mlava** ≈ E Yugoslavia
112 L9 **Mława** Ciechanów, C Poland
115 G16 **Mljet** *It.* Meleda; *anc.* Melita. *island* S Croatia
118 K4 **Mlyniv** Rivnens'ka Oblast', NW Ukraine
85 I21 **Mmabatho** North-West, N South Africa
85 I19 **Mmashoro** Central, E Botswana
46 J7 **Moa** Holguín, E Cuba
78 J15 **Moa** ≈ Guinea/Sierra Leone
39 O6 **Moab** Utah, W USA
189 V1 **Moa Island** *island* Queensland, NE Australia
197 J15 **Moala** *island* S Fiji
85 L21 **Moamba** Maputo, SW Mozambique
81 F19 **Moanda** *var.* Mouanda. Haut-Ogooué, SE Gabon
175 T16 **Moa, Pulau** *island* Kepulauan Leti, E Indonesia
85 M15 **Moatize** Tete, NW Mozambique
81 P22 **Moba** Shaba, E Zaire
171 K17 **Mobara** Chiba, Honshū, S Japan
Mobay *see* Montego Bay
81 K15 **Mobaye** Basse-Kotto, S Central African Republic
81 K15 **Mobayi-Mbongo** Equateur, NW Zaire
27 P2 **Mobeetie** Texas, SW USA
29 U3 **Moberly** Missouri, C USA
25 N8 **Mobile** Alabama, S USA
25 N9 **Mobile Bay** *bay* Alabama, S USA
25 N8 **Mobile River** ≈ Alabama, S USA
31 N8 **Mobridge** South Dakota, N USA
Mobutu Sese Seko, Lac *see* Albert, Lake
47 N8 **Moca** N Dominican Republic
Moçâmedes *see* Namibe
178 J6 **Môc Châu** Sơn La, N Vietnam
197 L15 **Moce** *island* Lau Group, E Fiji
Mocha *see* Al Mukhā
200 Oo13 **Mocha Fracture Zone** *tectonic feature* SE Pacific Ocean
65 F14 **Mocha, Isla** *island* C Chile
58 C12 **Moche, Río** ≈ W Peru
178 J14 **Môc Hoa** Long An, S Vietnam
85 I20 **Mochudi** Kgatleng, SE Botswana
84 Q13 **Mocímboa da Praia** *var.* Vila de Mocímboa da Praia. Cabo Delgado, N Mozambique
96 L13 **Mockfjärd** Kopparberg, C Sweden
23 R9 **Mocksville** North Carolina, SE USA
34 F8 **Moclips** Washington, NW USA
84 C13 **Moco** *var.* Morro de Môco. ▲ W Angola
56 D13 **Mocoa** Putumayo, SW Colombia
62 M8 **Mococa** São Paulo, S Brazil
Môco, Morro de *see* Môco
42 H8 **Mocorito** Sinaloa, C Mexico
42 J4 **Moctezuma** Chihuahua, N Mexico
43 N11 **Moctezuma** San Luis Potosí, C Mexico
42 G4 **Moctezuma** Sonora, NW Mexico
43 P12 **Moctezuma, Río** ≈ C Mexico
Mó, Cuan *see* Clew Bay
85 O16 **Mocuba** Zambézia, NE Mozambique
105 U12 **Modane** Savoie, E France
108 F9 **Modena** *anc.* Mutina. Emilia-Romagna, N Italy
38 I7 **Modena** Utah, W USA
37 O9 **Modesto** California, W USA
109 L25 **Modica** *anc.* Motyca. Sicilia, Italy, C Mediterranean Sea
81 K17 **Modjamboli** Equateur, N Zaire
111 X4 **Mödling** Niederösterreich, NE Austria
Modohn *see* Madona
169 N8 **Modot** Hentiy, C Mongolia
176 W12 **Modowi** Irian Jaya, E Indonesia
114 I12 **Modračko Jezero** ⊟ NE Bosnia and Herzegovina
114 I10 **Modriča** N Bosnia and Herzegovina
191 O13 **Moe** Victoria, SE Australia
Moearatewe *see* Muaratewe
Moei, Mae Nam *see* Thaungyin
96 H13 **Moelv** Hedmark, S Norway
94 I10 **Moen** Troms, N Norway
Moen *see* Weno, Micronesia
Möen *see* Møn, Denmark
Moena *see* Muna, Pulau
38 M10 **Moenkopi Wash** ≈ Arizona, SW USA
193 F22 **Moeraki Point** *headland* South Island, NZ
101 F16 **Moerbeke** Oost-Vlaanderen, NW Belgium
101 H14 **Moerdijk** Noord-Brabant, S Netherlands
Moero, Lac *see* Mweru, Lake
103 D15 **Moers** *var.* Mörs. Nordrhein-Westfalen, W Germany
Moesi *see* Musi, Air
Moeskroen *see* Mouscron
98 J13 **Moffat** S Scotland, UK
193 C22 **Moffat Peak** ▲ South Island, NZ
158 H8 **Moga** Punjab, N India
81 N19 **Moga** Sud Kivu, E Zaire
Mogadiscio/Mogadishu *see* Muqdisho
Mogador *see* Essaouira
106 J6 **Mogadouro** Bragança, N Portugal
171 Ll12 **Mogami-gawa** ≈ Honshū, C Japan
178 Gg2 **Mogaung** Kachin State, N Myanmar
112 L13 **Mogielnica** Radom, C Poland
Mogilëv *see* Mahilyow
Mogilev-Podol'skiy *see* Mohyliv-Podil's'kyy
Mogilëvskaya Oblast' *see* Mahilyowskaya Voblasts'
112 I11 **Mogilno** Bydgoszcz, C Poland
62 L9 **Mogi-Mirim** *var.* Moji-Mirim. São Paulo, S Brazil
85 Q15 **Mogincual** Nampula, NE Mozambique
116 E13 **Moglenítsas** ≈ N Greece
108 H8 **Mogliano Veneto** Veneto, NE Italy
115 M21 **Mogliçë** Korçë, SE Albania
126 L15 **Mogocha** Chitinskaya Oblast', S Russian Federation
126 H13 **Mogochin** Tomskaya Oblast', C Russian Federation
82 F13 **Mogogh** Jonglei, SE Sudan
176 Vv10 **Mogoi** Irian Jaya, E Indonesia
178 Gg4 **Mogok** Mandalay, C Myanmar
39 P14 **Mogollon Mountains** ▲ New Mexico, SW USA
38 M12 **Mogollon Rim** *cliff* Arizona, SW USA
63 E23 **Mogotes, Punta** *headland* E Argentina
44 J8 **Mogotón** ▲ NW Nicaragua
106 I14 **Moguer** Andalucía, S Spain
113 J26 **Mohács** Baranya, SW Hungary
193 C20 **Mohaka** ≈ North Island, NZ
30 M2 **Mohall** North Dakota, N USA
Moḥammadābād *see* Dargaz
76 F6 **Mohammedia** *prev.* Fédala. NW Morocco
76 F6 **Mohammed V** ✕ (Casablanca) W Morocco
Mohammerah *see* Khorramshahr
38 H10 **Mohave, Lake** ⊟ Arizona/Nevada, W USA
38 I12 **Mohave Mountains** ▲ Arizona, SW USA
38 I15 **Mohawk Mountains** ▲ Arizona, SW USA
20 J10 **Mohawk River** ≈ New York, NE USA
169 T3 **Mohe** Heilongjiang, NE China
97 L20 **Moheda** Kronoberg, S Sweden
180 H13 **Mohéli** *var.* Mwali, Mohilla, Mohila, *Fr.* Moili. *island* S Comoros
40 K12 **Mohican, Cape** *headland* Nunivak Island, Alaska, USA
Mohn *see* Muhu
103 G15 **Möhne** ≈ W Germany
103 G15 **Möhne-Stausee** ⊟ W Germany
94 P2 **Mohn, Kapp** *headland* NW Svalbard
207 S14 **Mohns Ridge** *undersea feature* Greenland Sea/Norwegian Sea
59 I17 **Moho** Puno, SW Peru
Mohokare *see* Caledon
97 L17 **Moholm** Skaraborg, S Sweden
38 J11 **Mohon Peak** ▲ Arizona, SW USA
83 J23 **Mohoro** Pwani, E Tanzania
Mohra *see* Moravice
Mohrungen *see* Morąg
118 M7 **Mohyliv-Podil's'kyy** *Rus.* Mogilev-Podol'skiy. Vinnyts'ka Oblast', C Ukraine
97 D17 **Moi** Rogaland, S Norway
197 I6 **Moindou** Province Sud, C New Caledonia
118 K11 **Moinești** *Hung.* Mojnest. Bacău, E Romania
Móinteach Mílic *see* Mountmellick
12 J14 **Moira** ≈ Ontario, SE Canada
94 G13 **Mo i Rana** Nordland, C Norway
159 X14 **Moirāng** Manipur, NE India
117 J25 **Moíres** Kríti, Greece, E Mediterranean Sea
120 H6 **Mõisaküla** *Ger.* Moiseküll. Viljandimaa, S Estonia
Moiseküll *see* Mõisaküla
13 W4 **Moisie** Québec, E Canada
13 W3 **Moisie** ≈ Québec, SE Canada
104 M14 **Moissac** Tarn-et-Garonne, S France
80 I13 **Moïssala** Moyen-Chari, S Chad
57 O7 **Moitaco** Bolívar, E Venezuela
97 P15 **Möja** Stockholm, C Sweden
107 Q14 **Mojácar** Andalucía, S Spain
37 T13 **Mojave** California, W USA
37 V13 **Mojave Desert** *plain* California, W USA
37 V13 **Mojave River** ≈ California, W USA
Moji-Mirim *see* Mogi-Mirim
115 K15 **Mojkovac** Montenegro, SW Yugoslavia
Mojnest *see* Moinești
174 Ll15 **Mojokerto** *prev.* Modjokerto. Jawa, C Indonesia
Mōka *see* Mooka
159 Q13 **Mokāma** *prev.* Mokameh, Mukama. Bihār, N India
81 O25 **Mokambo** Shaba, SE Zaire
Mokameh *see* Mokāma
40 D9 **Mokapu Point** *headland* Oahu, Hawaii, USA, C Pacific Ocean
192 L9 **Mokau** Waikato, North Island, NZ
192 L9 **Mokau** ≈ North Island, NZ
37 P7 **Mokelumne River** ≈ California, W USA
85 J23 **Mokhotlong** NE Lesotho
Mokil Atoll *see* Mwokil Atoll
97 N14 **Möklinta** Västmanland, C Sweden
192 L4 **Mokohinau Islands** *island group* N NZ
159 X12 **Mokokchūng** Nāgāland, NE India
80 F12 **Mokolo** Extrême-Nord, N Cameroon
193 D24 **Mokoreta** ≈ South Island, NZ
169 X17 **Mokp'o** *Jap.* Moppo. SW South Korea
115 L16 **Mokra Gora** ▲ S Yugoslavia
Mokrany *see* Makrany
131 O5 **Moksha** ≈ W Russian Federation
Moktama *see* Martaban
79 T14 **Mokwa** Niger, W Nigeria
101 J16 **Mol** *prev.* Moll. Antwerpen, N Belgium
109 O17 **Mola di Bari** Puglia, SE Italy
Molai *see* Moláoi
43 P13 **Molango** Hidalgo, C Mexico
117 F22 **Moláoi** *var.* Molai. Pelopónnisos, S Greece
43 Z12 **Molas del Norte, Punta** *var.* Punta Molas. *headland* SE Mexico
Molas, Punta *see* Molas del Norte, Punta
107 R11 **Molatón** ▲ C Spain
99 K18 **Mold** NE Wales, UK
Moldau *see* Moldova
Moldau *see* Vltava, Czech Republic
Moldavia *see* Moldova
Moldavian SSR/Moldavskaya SSR *see* Moldova
96 E9 **Molde** Møre og Romsdal, S Norway
Moldotau, Khrebet *see* Moldo-Too, Khrebet
153 V9 **Moldo-Too, Khrebet** *prev.* Khrebet Moldotau. ▲ C Kyrgyzstan
118 K9 **Moldova** ≈ N Romania
118 K9 **Moldova** *Eng.* Moldavia, *Ger.* Moldau. *former province* NE Romania
118 L9 **Moldova** *off.* Republic of Moldova, *var.* Moldavia; *prev.* Moldavian SSR, *Rus.* Moldavskaya SSR. ◆ *republic* SE Europe
118 F13 **Moldova Nouă** *Ger.* Neumoldowa, *Hung.* Újmoldova. Caraș-Severin, SW Romania
118 F13 **Moldova Veche** *Ger.* Altmoldowa, *Hung.* Ómoldova. Caraș-Severin, SW Romania
Moldoveanul *see* Vârful Moldoveanu
85 I20 **Molepolole** Kweneng, SE Botswana
46 L8 **Môle-St-Nicolas** NW Haiti
120 H13 **Molėtai** Molėtai, E Lithuania
109 O17 **Molfetta** Puglia, SE Italy
175 R8 **Molibagu** Sulawesi, N Indonesia
64 G12 **Molina** Maule, C Chile
107 Q7 **Molina de Aragón** Castilla-La Mancha, C Spain
107 R13 **Molina de Segura** Murcia, SE Spain
32 J11 **Moline** Illinois, N USA
29 P7 **Moline** Kansas, C USA
81 P23 **Moliro** Shaba, SE Zaire
109 K16 **Molise** ◐ *region* S Italy
97 K15 **Molkom** Värmland, C Sweden
Moll *see* Mol
111 Q9 **Möll** ≈ S Austria
97 J22 **Mölle** Malmöhus, S Sweden
59 H18 **Mollendo** Arequipa, SW Peru
107 U5 **Mollerussa** Cataluña, NE Spain
110 H8 **Mollis** Glarus, NE Switzerland
97 J19 **Mölndal** Göteborg och Bohus, S Sweden
97 J19 **Mölnlycke** Göteborg och Bohus, S Sweden
119 U9 **Molochans'k** *Rus.* Molochansk. Zaporiz'ka Oblast', SE Ukraine
119 U10 **Molochna** *Rus.* Molochnaya. ≈ S Ukraine
Molochnaya *see* Molochna
119 U10 **Molochnyy Lyman** *bay* N Black Sea
Molodechno/Molodeczno *see* Maladzyechna
205 V3 **Molodezhnaya** *Russian research station* Antarctica
128 J14 **Mologa** ≈ NW Russian Federation
40 E9 **Molokai** *Haw.* Molokaʻi. *island* Hawaii, USA, C Pacific Ocean
183 X3 **Molokai Fracture Zone** *tectonic feature* NE Pacific Ocean
128 K15 **Molokovo** Tverskaya Oblast', W Russian Federation
129 Q14 **Moloma** ≈ NW Russian Federation
191 R8 **Molong** New South Wales, SE Australia
85 H21 **Molopo** *seasonal river* Botswana/South Africa
117 F17 **Mólos** Stereá Ellás, C Greece
175 Q7 **Molosipat** Sulawesi, N Indonesia
Molotov *see* Severodvinsk, Arkhangel'skaya Oblast', Russian Federation
Molotov *see* Perm', Permskaya Oblast', Russian Federation
81 G17 **Moloundou** Est, SE Cameroon
105 U5 **Molsheim** Bas-Rhin, NE France
15 L12 **Molson Lake** ◎ Manitoba, C Canada
Moluccas *see* Maluku
175 Rr8 **Molucca Sea** *Ind.* Laut Maluku. *sea* E Indonesia
Molukken *see* Maluku
85 O15 **Molumbo** Zambézia, N Mozambique
176 Uu14 **Molu, Pulau** *island* Maluku, E Indonesia
85 P16 **Moma** Nampula, NE Mozambique
127 N17 **Moma** ≈ NE Russian Federation
176 Xx13 **Momats** ≈ Irian Jaya, E Indonesia
44 J11 **Mombacho, Volcán** ⛰ SW Nicaragua
83 K21 **Mombasa** Coast, SE Kenya
83 J21 **Mombasa** ✕ Coast, SE Kenya
Mombetsu *see* Monbetsu
176 Y16 **Mombum** Irian Jaya, E Indonesia
116 J12 **Momchilgrad** *prev.* Mastanli. Khaskovska Oblast, S Bulgaria
101 F23 **Momignies** Hainaut, S Belgium
56 E6 **Momil** Córdoba, NW Colombia
44 I10 **Momotombo, Volcán** ⛰ W Nicaragua
58 B5 **Mompiche, Ensenada de** *bay* NW Ecuador
81 K18 **Mompono** Equateur, NW Zaire
56 F6 **Mompós** Bolívar, NW Colombia
97 J24 **Møn** *prev.* Möen. *island* SE Denmark
38 L4 **Mona** Utah, W USA
Mona, Canal de la *see* Mona Passage
98 E8 **Monach Islands** *island group* NW Scotland, UK
105 V14 **Monaco** *var.* Monaco-Ville; *anc.* Monoecus. ● (Monaco) S Monaco
105 V14 **Monaco** *off.* Principality of Monaco. ◆ *monarchy* W Europe
Monaco *see* München
Monaco Basin *see* Canary Basin
Monaco-Ville *see* Monaco
98 I9 **Monadhliath Mountains** ▲ N Scotland, UK
57 O6 **Monagas** *off.* Estado Monagas. ◐ *state* NE Venezuela
99 F16 **Monaghan** *Ir.* Muineachán. N Ireland
99 E16 **Monaghan** *Ir.* Muineachán. *cultural region* N Ireland
45 S16 **Monagrillo** Herrera, S Panama
26 L8 **Monahans** Texas, SW USA
47 Q9 **Mona, Isla** *island* W Puerto Rico
47 Q9 **Mona Passage** *Sp.* Canal de la Mona. *channel* Dominican Republic/Puerto Rico
45 O14 **Mona, Punta** *headland* E Costa Rica
161 K25 **Monaragala** Uva Province, SE Sri Lanka
35 S9 **Monarch** Montana, NW USA
14 Ff14 **Monarch Mountain** ▲ British Columbia, SW Canada
Monasterio *see* Monesterio
Monasterzyska *see* Monastyrys'ka
Monastir *see* Bitola
Monastyriska *see* Monastyrys'ka
119 O7 **Monastyryshche** Cherkas'ka Oblast', C Ukraine
118 J6 **Monastyrys'ka** *Pol.* Monasterzyska, *Rus.* Monastyriska. Ternopil's'ka Oblast', W Ukraine
81 E15 **Monatélé** Centre, SW Cameroon
172 Q4 **Monbetsu** *var.* Mombetsu, Monbetu. Hokkaidō, NE Japan
Monbetu *see* Monbetsu
108 B8 **Moncalieri** Piemonte, NW Italy
106 G4 **Monção** Viana do Castelo, N Portugal
107 Q5 **Moncayo** ▲ N Spain
107 Q5 **Moncayo, Sierra del** ▲ N Spain
128 J4 **Monchegorsk** Murmanskaya Oblast', NW Russian Federation
103 D15 **Mönchengladbach** *prev.* München-Gladbach. Nordrhein-Westfalen, W Germany
106 F14 **Monchique** Faro, S Portugal
106 G14 **Monchique, Serra de** ▲ S Portugal
23 S14 **Moncks Corner** South Carolina, SE USA
43 N7 **Monclova** Coahuila de Zaragoza, NE Mexico
Moncorvo *see* Torre de Moncorvo
11 P14 **Moncton** New Brunswick, SE Canada
106 G8 **Mondego** ≈ N Portugal
106 F8 **Mondego, Cabo** *headland* N Portugal
106 I2 **Mondoñedo** Galicia, NW Spain
101 N25 **Mondorf-les-Bains** Grevenmacher, SE Luxembourg
104 M7 **Mondoubleau** Loir-et-Cher, C France
32 J6 **Mondovi** Wisconsin, N USA
108 B9 **Mondovì** Piemonte, NW Italy
107 P3 **Mondragón** *var.* Arrasate. País Vasco, N Spain
109 J17 **Mondragone** Campania, S Italy
111 R5 **Mondsee** ◎ N Austria
126 J16 **Mondy** Respublika Buryatiya, S Russian Federation
117 G22 **Monemvasía** Pelopónnisos, S Greece
20 B15 **Monessen** Pennsylvania, NE USA
106 J12 **Monesterio** *var.* Monasterio. Extremadura, W Spain
12 L8 **Monet** Québec, SE Canada
29 S8 **Monett** Missouri, C USA
29 X9 **Monette** Arkansas, C USA
12 G11 **Monetville** Ontario, S Canada
108 J7 **Monfalcone** Friuli-Venezia Giulia, NE Italy
106 H10 **Monforte** Portalegre, C Portugal
106 I4 **Monforte** Galicia, NW Spain
83 I24 **Monga** Lindi, SE Tanzania
81 L16 **Monga** Haut-Zaïre, N Zaire
83 F15 **Mongalla** Bahr el Gabel, S Sudan
159 U11 **Mongar** E Bhutan
178 K6 **Mong Cai** Quang Ninh, N Vietnam
188 I11 **Mongers Lake** *salt lake* Western Australia
195 U14 **Mongga** Kolombangara Island, NW Solomon Islands
178 Hh6 **Möng Hpayak** Shan State, E Myanmar
Monghyr *see* Munger
108 B10 **Mongioie** ▲ NW Italy
178 Gg5 **Möng Küng** Shan State, E Myanmar
Mongla *see* Mungla
196 C15 **Mongmong** C Guam
178 Gg6 **Möng Nai** Shan State, E Myanmar
80 I11 **Mongo** Guéra, C Chad
78 I14 **Mongo** ≈ N Sierra Leone
169 I8 **Mongolia** *Mong.* Mongol Uls. ◆ *republic* E Asia
133 V8 **Mongolia, Plateau of** *plateau* E Mongolia
Mongolküre *see* Zhaosu
Mongol Uls *see* Mongolia
81 E17 **Mongomo** E Equatorial Guinea
79 Y12 **Mongonu** *var.* Monguno. Borno, NE Nigeria
Mongora *see* Mingāora
80 K11 **Mongororo** Ouaddaï, SE Chad
Mongos, Chaîne des *see* Bongo, Massif des
81 I16 **Mongoumba** Lobaye, SW Central African Republic
Mongrove, Punta *see* Cayacal, Punta
85 G15 **Mongu** Western, W Zambia
78 I10 **Mônguel** Gorgol, SW Mauritania
Monguno *see* Mongonu
178 H4 **Möng Yai** Shan State, E Myanmar
178 Hh5 **Möng Yang** Shan State, E Myanmar
178 H3 **Möng Yu** Shan State, E Myanmar
168 K8 **Mönhbulag** Övörhangay, C Mongolia
Mönh Sarīdag *see* Munku-Sardyk, Gora
194 L15 **Moni** ≈ S Papau New Guinea
117 I15 **Moní Megístis Lávras** *monastery* Kentrikí Makedonía, N Greece
117 F18 **Moní Osíou Loúkas** *monastery* Stereá Ellás, C Greece
56 F9 **Moniquirá** Boyacá, C Colombia
105 Q12 **Monistrol-sur-Loire** Haute-Loire, C France
37 V7 **Monitor Range** ▲ Nevada, W USA
117 I14 **Moní Vatopedíou** *monastery* Kentrikí Makedonía, N Greece
179 Rr15 **Monkayo** Mindanao, S Philippines
Monkchester *see* Newcastle upon Tyne
85 N14 **Monkey Bay** Southern, SE Malawi
45 N11 **Monkey Point** *var.* Punta Mico, Punte Mono, Punto Mico. *headland* SE Nicaragua
Monkey River *see* Monkey River Town
44 G3 **Monkey River Town** *var.* Monkey River. Toledo, SE Belize
12 M13 **Monkland** Ontario, SE Canada
81 J19 **Monkoto** Equateur, NW Zaire
99 K21 **Monmouth** *Wel.* Trefynwy. SE Wales, UK
32 J12 **Monmouth** Illinois, N USA
34 F12 **Monmouth** Oregon, NW USA
99 K21 **Monmouth** *cultural region* SE Wales, UK
100 I10 **Monnickendam** Noord-Holland, C Netherlands
79 R15 **Mono** ≈ C Togo
Monoecus *see* Monaco
37 R8 **Mono Lake** ◎ California, W USA
117 O23 **Monólithos** Ródos, Dodekánisos, Greece, Aegean Sea
21 Q12 **Monomoy Island** *island* Massachusetts, NE USA
33 O12 **Monon** Indiana, N USA
31 Y12 **Monona** Iowa, C USA
32 L9 **Monona** Wisconsin, N USA
20 B15 **Monongahela** Pennsylvania, NE USA
20 B16 **Monongahela River** ≈ NE USA
109 P17 **Monopoli** Puglia, SE Italy
Mono, Punte *see* Monkey Point
113 K23 **Monor** Pest, C Hungary
Monostor *see* Beli Manastir
80 K8 **Monou** Borkou-Ennedi-Tibesti, NE Chad
107 S12 **Monóvar** País Valenciano, E Spain
107 R7 **Monreal del Campo** Aragón, NE Spain
109 I23 **Monreale** Sicilia, Italy, C Mediterranean Sea
25 T3 **Monroe** Georgia, SE USA
31 W14 **Monroe** Iowa, C USA
24 I5 **Monroe** Louisiana, S USA
33 S10 **Monroe** Michigan, N USA
20 K13 **Monroe** New York, NE USA
23 S11 **Monroe** North Carolina, SE USA
38 L6 **Monroe** Utah, W USA
34 H7 **Monroe** Washington, NW USA
32 L9 **Monroe** Wisconsin, N USA
29 V3 **Monroe City** Missouri, C USA
33 O15 **Monroe Lake** ⊟ Indiana, N USA
25 O7 **Monroeville** Alabama, S USA
20 C15 **Monroeville** Pennsylvania, NE USA
78 J16 **Monrovia** ● (Liberia) W Liberia
78 J16 **Monrovia** ✕ W Liberia
107 T7 **Monroyo** Aragón, NE Spain
101 F20 **Mons** *Dut.* Bergen. Hainaut, S Belgium
106 I8 **Monsanto** Castelo Branco, C Portugal
108 H8 **Monselice** Veneto, NE Italy
178 Gg9 **Mon State** ◐ *state* S Myanmar
100 G12 **Monster** Zuid-Holland, W Netherlands
97 N20 **Mönsterås** Kalmar, S Sweden
103 F17 **Montabaur** Rheinland-Pfalz, W Germany
108 G8 **Montagnana** Veneto, NE Italy
37 N1 **Montague** California, W USA
27 S5 **Montague** Texas, SW USA
191 S11 **Montague Island** *island* New South Wales, SE Australia
41 S12 **Montague Island** *island* Alaska, USA
41 S13 **Montague Strait** *strait* N Gulf of Alaska
104 J8 **Montaigu** Vendée, NW France
Montaigu *see* Scherpenheuvel
107 S7 **Montalbán** Aragón, NE Spain
108 G13 **Montalcino** Toscana, C Italy
106 H5 **Montalegre** Vila Real, N Portugal
116 G8 **Montana** *prev.* Ferdinand, Mikhaylovgrad. Oblast Montana, NW Bulgaria
110 D10 **Montana** Valais, SW Switzerland
41 R11 **Montana** Alaska, USA
35 T9 **Montana** *off.* State of Montana; also known as Mountain State, Treasure State. ◐ *state* NW USA
Montana *see* Montana, Oblast
116 G8 **Montana, Oblast** *var.* Montana; *prev.* Mikhailovgrad, Mikhaylovgrad. ◐ *province* NW Bulgaria
106 J10 **Montánchez** Extremadura, W Spain
Montañita *see* La Montañita
13 Q8 **Mont-Apica** Québec, SE Canada
106 G10 **Montargil** Portalegre, C Portugal
106 G10 **Montargil, Barragem de** ⊟ C Portugal
105 O7 **Montargis** Loiret, C France
105 O4 **Montataire** Oise, N France
104 M14 **Montauban** Tarn-et-Garonne, S France
21 N14 **Montauk** Long Island, New York, NE USA
21 N14 **Montauk Point** *headland* Long Island, New York, NE USA
105 Q7 **Montbard** Côte d'Or, C France
105 U7 **Montbéliard** Doubs, E France
27 W11 **Mont Belvieu** Texas, SW USA
107 U6 **Montblanc** *var.* Montblanch. Cataluña, NE Spain
Montblanch *see* Montblanc
105 Q11 **Montbrison** Loire, E France
Montcalm, Lake *see* Dogai Coring
105 Q9 **Montceau-les-Mines** Saône-et-Loire, C France
105 U12 **Mont Cenis, Col du** *pass* E France
104 K15 **Mont-de-Marsan** Landes, SW France
105 O3 **Montdidier** Somme, N France
197 J7 **Mont-Dore** Province Sud, S New Caledonia
22 K10 **Monteagle** Tennessee, S USA
59 M20 **Monteagudo** Chuquisaca, S Bolivia
43 R16 **Monte Albán** *ruins* Oaxaca, S Mexico
107 R11 **Montealegre del Castillo** Castilla-La Mancha, C Spain
61 N18 **Monte Azul** Minas Gerais, SE Brazil
12 M12 **Montebello** Québec, SE Canada
108 H7 **Montebelluna** Veneto, NE Italy
62 G13 **Montecarlo** Misiones, NE Argentina
63 D16 **Monte Caseros** Corrientes, NE Argentina
62 J13 **Monte Castelo** Santa Catarina, S Brazil
108 F11 **Montecatini Terme** Toscana, C Italy
44 H7 **Montecillos, Cordillera de** ▲ W Honduras
64 I12 **Monte Comén** Mendoza, W Argentina
46 M8 **Monte Cristi** *var.* San Fernando de Monte Cristi. NW Dominican Republic
60 C13 **Monte Cristo** Amazonas, W Brazil
109 E14 **Montecristo, Isola di** *island* Archipelago Toscano, C Italy
Monte Croce Carnico, Passo di *see* Plöcken Pass
60 J12 **Monte Dourado** Pará, NE Brazil
42 L11 **Monte Escobedo** Zacatecas, C Mexico
108 I13 **Montefalco** Umbria, C Italy
109 H14 **Montefiascone** Lazio, C Italy
107 N14 **Montefrío** Andalucía, S Spain
46 I11 **Montego Bay** *var.* Mobay. W Jamaica
Montego Bay *see* Sangster
106 J8 **Montehermoso** Extremadura, W Spain
106 F10 **Montejunto, Serra de** ▲ C Portugal
Monteleone di Calabria *see* Vibo Valentia
56 E7 **Montelíbano** Córdoba, NW Colombia
105 R13 **Montélimar** *anc.* Acunum Acusio, Montilium Adhemari. Drôme, E France
106 K15 **Montellano** Andalucía, S Spain
37 Y2 **Montello** Nevada, W USA
32 L8 **Montello** Wisconsin, N USA
65 J18 **Montemayor, Meseta de** *plain* SE Argentina
43 O9 **Montemorelos** Nuevo León, NE Mexico
106 G11 **Montemor-o-Novo** Évora, S Portugal
106 G8 **Montemor-o-Velho** *var.* Montemor-o-Vélho. Coimbra, N Portugal
106 H7 **Montemuro, Serra de** ▲ N Portugal
104 K12 **Montendre** Charente-Maritime, W France
63 I15 **Montenegro** Rio Grande do Sul, S Brazil
115 J16 **Montenegro** *Serb.* Crna Gora. ◐ *republic* SW Yugoslavia
64 G10 **Monte Patria** Coquimbo, N Chile
47 O9 **Monte Plata** E Dominican Republic
85 P14 **Montepuez** Cabo Delgado, N Mozambique
85 P14 **Montepuez** ≈ N Mozambique
108 G13 **Montepulciano** Toscana, C Italy
64 L6 **Monte Quemado** Santiago del Estero, N Argentina
105 O6 **Montereau-Faut-Yonne** *anc.* Condate. Seine-St-Denis, N France
37 N11 **Monterey** California, W USA
22 L9 **Monterey** Tennessee, S USA
23 T5 **Monterey** Virginia, NE USA
Monterey *see* Monterrey
37 N10 **Monterey Bay** *bay* California, W USA
56 D6 **Montería** Córdoba, NW Colombia
59 N18 **Montero** Santa Cruz, C Bolivia
64 J7 **Monteros** Tucumán, C Argentina
106 I5 **Monterrei** Galicia, NW Spain
43 O8 **Monterrey** *var.* Monterey. Nuevo León, NE Mexico
34 F9 **Montesano** Washington, NW USA
109 M19 **Montesano sulla Marcellana** Campania, S Italy
109 N16 **Monte Sant' Angelo** Puglia, SE Italy
61 O16 **Monte Santo** Bahia, E Brazil
109 D18 **Monte Santu, Capo di** *headland* Sardegna, Italy, C Mediterranean Sea
61 M19 **Montes Claros** Minas Gerais, SE Brazil
109 K14 **Montesilvano Marina** Abruzzi, C Italy
25 P4 **Montevallo** Alabama, S USA
108 G12 **Montevarchi** Toscana, C Italy
31 S9 **Montevideo** Minnesota, N USA
63 F20 **Montevideo** ● (Uruguay) Montevideo, S Uruguay
39 S7 **Monte Vista** Colorado, C USA
25 T5 **Montezuma** Georgia, SE USA
31 W14 **Montezuma** Iowa, C USA

◆ Country
● Country Capital
◇ Dependent Territory
○ Dependent Territory Capital
◐ Administrative Region
✕ International Airport
▲ Mountain
▲ Mountain Range
⛰ Volcano
≈ River
◎ Lake
⊟ Reservoir

28 J6 **Montezuma** Kansas, C USA
105 U12 **Montgenèvre, Col de** *pass* France/Italy
99 K20 **Montgomery** E Wales, UK
25 Q5 **Montgomery** *state capital* Alabama, S USA
31 V9 **Montgomery** Minnesota, N USA
20 G13 **Montgomery** Pennsylvania, NE USA
23 Q5 **Montgomery** West Virginia, NE USA
99 K19 **Montgomery** *cultural region* E Wales, UK
Montgomery *see* Sāhīwāl
29 V4 **Montgomery City** Missouri, C USA
37 S8 **Montgomery Pass** *pass* Nevada, W USA
104 K12 **Montguyon** Charente-Maritime, W France
110 C10 **Monthey** Valais, SW Switzerland
29 V13 **Monticello** Arkansas, C USA
25 T4 **Monticello** Florida, SE USA
25 T8 **Monticello** Georgia, SE USA
32 M13 **Monticello** Illinois, N USA
33 O12 **Monticello** Indiana, N USA
31 Y13 **Monticello** Iowa, C USA
22 L7 **Monticello** Kentucky, S USA
31 V8 **Monticello** Minnesota, N USA
24 K7 **Monticello** Mississippi, S USA
29 V2 **Monticello** Missouri, C USA
20 J12 **Monticello** New York, NE USA
39 O7 **Monticello** Utah, W USA
108 F8 **Montichiari** Lombardia, N Italy
104 M12 **Montignac** Dordogne, SW France
101 G21 **Montignies-le-Tilleul** *var.* Montigny-le-Tilleul. Hainaut, S Belgium
12 J8 **Montigny, Lac de** ◎ Québec, SE Canada
105 S6 **Montigny-le-Roi** Haute-Marne, N France
Montigny-le-Tilleul *see* Montignies-le-Tilleul
45 R16 **Montijo** Veraguas, S Panama
106 F11 **Montijo** Setúbal, W Portugal
106 J11 **Montijo** Extremadura, W Spain
Montilium Adhemari *see* Montélimar
106 M13 **Montilla** Andalucía, S Spain
104 L3 **Montivilliers** Seine-Maritime, N France
13 U7 **Mont-Joli** Québec, SE Canada
12 M10 **Mont-Laurier** Québec, SE Canada
13 X5 **Mont-Louis** Québec, SE Canada
105 N17 **Mont-Louis** *var.* Mont Louis. Pyrénées-Orientales, S France
105 O10 **Montluçon** Allier, C France
13 R10 **Montmagny** Québec, SE Canada
105 S3 **Montmédy** Meuse, NE France
105 P5 **Montmirail** Marne, N France
13 R9 **Montmorency** ≈ Québec, SE Canada
104 M10 **Montmorillon** Vienne, W France
109 J14 **Montorio al Vomano** Abruzzi, C Italy
106 M13 **Montoro** Andalucía, S Spain
35 S16 **Montpelier** Idaho, NW USA
31 P6 **Montpelier** North Dakota, N USA
20 M7 **Montpelier** *state capital* Vermont, NE USA
105 Q15 **Montpellier** Hérault, S France
104 L12 **Montpon-Ménestérol** Dordogne, SW France
12 G8 **Montreal** ≈ Ontario, S Canada
12 C8 **Montreal** ≈ Ontario, S Canada
Montreal *see* Mirabel
10 K15 **Montréal** *Eng.* Montreal. Québec, SE Canada
9 T14 **Montreal Lake** ◎ Saskatchewan, C Canada
12 B9 **Montreal River** Ontario, S Canada
105 N2 **Montreuil** Pas-de-Calais, N France
104 K8 **Montreuil-Bellay** Maine-et-Loire, NW France
110 C10 **Montreux** Vaud, SW Switzerland
110 B9 **Montricher** Vaud, W Switzerland
98 K10 **Montrose** E Scotland, UK
29 W14 **Montrose** Arkansas, C USA
39 Q6 **Montrose** Colorado, C USA
31 Y16 **Montrose** Iowa, C USA
20 H12 **Montrose** Pennsylvania, NE USA
23 X5 **Montross** Virginia, NE USA
13 O12 **Mont-St-Hilaire** Québec, SE Canada
105 S3 **Mont-St-Martin** Meurthe-et-Moselle, NE France
47 V10 **Montserrat** *var.* Emerald Isle. ◇ *UK dependent territory* E West Indies
107 V5 **Montserrat** ▲ NE Spain
106 M7 **Montuenga** Castilla-León, N Spain
101 M19 **Montzen** Liège, E Belgium
39 N8 **Monument Valley** *valley* Arizona/Utah, SW USA
177 G4 **Monywa** Sagaing, C Myanmar
108 D7 **Monza** Lombardia, N Italy
85 J15 **Monze** Southern, S Zambia
107 T5 **Monzón** Aragón, NE Spain
27 T9 **Moody** Texas, SW USA
100 L13 **Mook** Limburg, SE Netherlands
171 Kk15 **Mooka** *var.* Mōka. Tochigi, Honshū, S Japan
190 K3 **Moomba** South Australia
12 G13 **Moon** ≈ Ontario, S Canada
Moon *see* Muhu
189 Y10 **Moonie** Queensland, E Australia
198 B10 **Moonless Mountains** *undersea feature* E Pacific Ocean
190 L13 **Moonlight Head** *headland* Victoria, SE Australia
Moon-Sund *see* Väinameri
190 H8 **Moonta** South Australia
Moor *see* Mór
188 I12 **Moora** Western Australia
100 H12 **Moordrecht** Zuid-Holland, C Netherlands
35 T9 **Moore** Montana, NW USA
29 N11 **Moore** Oklahoma, C USA
27 R12 **Moore** Texas, SW USA
203 S10 **Moorea** *island* Îles du Vent, W French Polynesia
23 U3 **Moorefield** West Virginia, NE USA
25 X14 **Moore Haven** Florida, SE USA
188 J11 **Moore, Lake** ◎ Western Australia
21 N7 **Moore Reservoir** ⊡ New Hampshire/Vermont, NE USA
46 G1 **Moores Island** *island* N Bahamas
23 R10 **Mooresville** North Carolina, SE USA
31 R5 **Moorhead** Minnesota, N USA
24 K4 **Moorhead** Mississippi, S USA
176 Ww10 **Moor, Kepulauan** *island group* E Indonesia
101 F18 **Moorsel** Oost-Vlaanderen, C Belgium
101 C18 **Moorslede** West-Vlaanderen, W Belgium
20 L8 **Moosalamoo, Mount** ▲ Vermont, NE USA
103 M22 **Moosburg** Bayern, SE Germany
35 S14 **Moose** Wyoming, C USA
10 H11 **Moose** ≈ Ontario, S Canada
10 H10 **Moose Factory** Ontario, S Canada
21 Q4 **Moosehead Lake** ◎ Maine, NE USA
9 U16 **Moose Jaw** Saskatchewan, S Canada
9 V14 **Moose Lake** Manitoba, C Canada
31 W6 **Moose Lake** Minnesota, N USA
21 P6 **Mooselookmeguntic Lake** ◎ Maine, NE USA
41 R12 **Moose Pass** Alaska, USA
21 P5 **Moose River** ≈ Maine, NE USA
20 J9 **Moose River** ≈ New York, NE USA
9 V16 **Moosomin** Saskatchewan, S Canada
10 H10 **Moosonee** Ontario, SE Canada
21 N12 **Moosup** Connecticut, NE USA
85 N16 **Mopeia** Zambézia, NE Mozambique
Mopelia *see* Maupihaa
85 H18 **Mopipi** Central, C Botswana
Moppo *see* Mokp'o
79 N11 **Mopti** Mopti, C Mali
79 O11 **Mopti** ◐ *region* S Mali
59 H18 **Moquegua** Moquegua, SE Peru
59 H18 **Moquegua** *off.* Departamento de Moquegua. ◐ *department* S Peru
113 I23 **Mór** *Ger.* Moor. Fejér, C Hungary
80 G11 **Mora** Extrême-Nord, N Cameroon
106 G11 **Mora** Évora, S Portugal
107 N9 **Mora** Castilla-La Mancha, C Spain
96 L12 **Mora** Kopparberg, C Sweden
31 V7 **Mora** Minnesota, N USA
39 T10 **Mora** New Mexico, SW USA
115 J17 **Morača** ≈ SW Yugoslavia
158 K10 **Morādābād** Uttar Pradesh, N India
107 U6 **Móra d'Ebre** *var.* Mora de Ebro. Cataluña, NE Spain
Mora de Ebro *see* Móra d'Ebre
107 S8 **Mora de Rubielos** Aragón, NE Spain
180 H4 **Morafenobe** Mahajanga, W Madagascar
112 K8 **Morąg** *Ger.* Mohrungen. Olsztyn, N Poland
113 L25 **Mórahalom** Csongrád, S Hungary
107 N11 **Moral de Calatrava** Castilla-La Mancha, C Spain
65 G19 **Moraleda, Canal** *strait* SE Pacific Ocean
56 J3 **Morales** Bolívar, N Colombia
56 D12 **Morales** Cauca, SW Colombia
44 F5 **Morales** Izabal, E Guatemala
180 J5 **Moramanga** Toamasina, E Madagascar
29 Q6 **Moran** Kansas, C USA
27 Q7 **Moran** Texas, SW USA
189 X7 **Moranbah** Queensland, NE Australia
46 L13 **Morant Bay** E Jamaica
98 G10 **Morar, Loch** ◎ N Scotland, UK
Morata *see* Goodenough Island
107 Q12 **Moratalla** Murcia, SE Spain
110 C8 **Morat, Lac de** *Ger.* Murtensee. ◎ W Switzerland
86 I11 **Morava** *var.* March. ≈ C Europe *see also* March
Morava *see* Moravia, Czech Republic
Morava *see* Velika Morava, Yugoslavia
31 W15 **Moravia** Iowa, C USA
113 F18 **Moravia** *Cz.* Morava, *Ger.* Mähren. *cultural region* E Czech Republic
113 H17 **Moravice** *Ger.* Mohra. ≈ NE Czech Republic
Moravicza *see* Moraviţa
113 G17 **Moravská Třebová** *Ger.* Mährisch-Trübau. Východní Čechy, E Czech Republic
113 E19 **Moravské Budějovice** *Ger.* Mährisch-Budwitz. Jižní Morava, SE Czech Republic
113 F19 **Moravský Krumlov** *Ger.* Mährisch-Kromau. Jižní Morava, SE Czech Republic
Morawitza *see* Moraviţa
98 J8 **Moray** *cultural region* N Scotland, UK
98 J8 **Moray Firth** *inlet* N Scotland, UK
44 B10 **Morazán** ◐ *department* NE El Salvador
160 C10 **Morbi** Gujarāt, W India
104 G7 **Morbihan** ◐ *department* NW France
Mörbisch *see* Mörbisch am See
111 Y5 **Mörbisch am See** *var.* Mörbisch. Burgenland, E Austria
97 N21 **Mörbylånga** Kalmar, S Sweden
104 J14 **Morcenx** Landes, SW France
Morcheh Khort *see* Mürcheh Khvort
15 L16 **Morden** Manitoba, S Canada
Mordovia *see* Mordoviya, Respublika
131 N5 **Mordoviya, Respublika** *prev.* Mordovskaya ASSR, *Eng.* Mordovia, Mordvinia. ◐ *autonomous republic* W Russian Federation
130 M7 **Mordovo** Tambovskaya Oblast', W Russian Federation
Mordovskaya ASSR/ Mordvinia *see* Mordoviya, Respublika
Morea *see* Pelopónnisos
30 K8 **Moreau River** ≈ South Dakota, N USA
99 K16 **Morecambe** NW England, UK
99 K16 **Morecambe Bay** *inlet* NW England, UK
191 S4 **Moree** New South Wales, SE Australia
194 E15 **Morehead** Western, SW PNG
23 N5 **Morehead** Kentucky, S USA
194 E15 **Morehead** ≈ SW PNG
23 X11 **Morehead City** North Carolina, SE USA
29 Y8 **Morehouse** Missouri, C USA
110 E10 **Mörel** Valais, SW Switzerland
56 D13 **Morelia** Caquetá, S Colombia
43 N14 **Morelia** Michoacán de Ocampo, S Mexico
107 T7 **Morella** País Valenciano, E Spain
42 I7 **Morelos** Chihuahua, N Mexico
43 O15 **Morelos** ◐ *state* S Mexico
160 H7 **Morena** Madhya Pradesh, C India
106 L12 **Morena, Sierra** ⛰ S Spain
39 O14 **Morenci** Arizona, SW USA
33 R11 **Morenci** Michigan, N USA
118 J13 **Moreni** Dâmboviţa, S Romania
96 D9 **Møre og Romsdal** ◐ *county* S Norway
14 Ee12 **Moresby Island** *island* Queen Charlotte Islands, British Columbia, SW Canada
191 W2 **Moreton Island** *island* Queensland, E Australia
105 O3 **Moreuil** Somme, N France
37 V7 **Morey Peak** ▲ Nevada, W USA
129 U4 **More-Yu** ≈ NW Russian Federation
105 T9 **Morez** Jura, E France
Mórfou *see* Güzelyurt
Morfou Bay/Mórfou, Kólpos *see* Güzelyurt Körfezi
190 J8 **Morgan** South Australia
25 S7 **Morgan** Georgia, SE USA
27 S8 **Morgan** Texas, SW USA
24 J10 **Morgan City** Louisiana, S USA
22 H6 **Morganfield** Kentucky, S USA
37 O10 **Morgan Hill** California, W USA
23 Q9 **Morganton** North Carolina, SE USA
22 J7 **Morgantown** Kentucky, S USA
23 S2 **Morgantown** West Virginia, NE USA
110 B10 **Morges** Vaud, SW Switzerland
Morghāb, Daryā-ye *see* Murgab
98 I9 **Mor, Glen** *var.* Glen Albyn, Great Glen. *valley* N Scotland, UK
105 T5 **Morhange** Moselle, NE France
164 M5 **Mori** *var.* Mori Kazak Zizhixian. Xinjiang Uygur Zizhiqu, NW China
172 Nn6 **Mori** Hokkaidō, NE Japan
37 Y6 **Moriah, Mount** ▲ Nevada, W USA
39 S11 **Moriarty** New Mexico, SW USA
56 J12 **Morichal** Guainía, E Colombia
194 H14 **Morigio Island** *island* S PNG
Mori Kazak Zizhixian *see* Mori
169 U7 **Morin Dawa** *var.* Morin Dawa Daurzu Zizhiqi. Nei Mongol Zizhiqu, N China
Morin Dawa Daurzu Zizhiqi *see* Morin Dawa
15 I13 **Morinville** Alberta, SW Canada
171 Mm11 **Morioka** Iwate, Honshū, C Japan
191 T8 **Morisset** New South Wales, SE Australia
171 Mm10 **Moriyoshi-yama** ▲ Honshū, C Japan
94 K13 **Morjärv** Norrbotten, N Sweden
131 R3 **Morki** Respublika Mariy El, W Russian Federation
126 K10 **Morkoka** ≈ NE Russian Federation
104 F5 **Morlaix** Finistère, NW France
97 M20 **Mörlunda** Kalmar, S Sweden
109 N19 **Mormanno** Calabria, SW Italy
38 L11 **Mormon Lake** ◎ Arizona, SW USA
37 Y10 **Mormon Peak** ▲ Nevada, W USA
Mormon State *see* Utah
47 Y5 **Morne-à-l'Eau** Grande Terre, N Guadeloupe
31 Y15 **Morning Sun** Iowa, C USA
200 O14 **Mornington Abyssal Plain** *undersea feature* SE Pacific Ocean
65 F22 **Mornington, Isla** *island* S Chile
189 T4 **Mornington Island** *island* Wellesley Islands, Queensland, N Australia
117 E18 **Mórnos** ≈ C Greece
155 P14 **Moro** Sind, SE Pakistan
34 I11 **Moro** Oregon, NW USA
194 K14 **Morobe** Morobe, C PNG
194 J14 **Morobe** ◐ *province* C PNG
33 N12 **Morocco** Indiana, N USA
76 E8 **Morocco** *off.* Kingdom of Morocco, *Ar.* Al Mamlakah. ◆ *monarchy* N Africa
Morocco *see* Marrakech
83 I22 **Morogoro** Morogoro, E Tanzania
83 H24 **Morogoro** ◐ *region* SE Tanzania
179 Qq16 **Moro Gulf** *gulf* S Philippines
43 N13 **Moroleón** Guanajuato, C Mexico
180 H6 **Morombe** Toliara, W Madagascar
46 G5 **Morón** Ciego de Ávila, C Cuba
56 K5 **Morón** Carabobo, N Venezuela
Morón *see* Morón de la Frontera
169 N8 **Mörön** Hentiy, C Mongolia
168 I6 **Mörön** Hövsgöl, N Mongolia
58 D8 **Morona, Río** ≈ N Peru
58 C8 **Morona Santiago** ◐ *province* E Ecuador
180 H5 **Morondava** Toliara, W Madagascar
106 K14 **Morón de la Frontera** *var.* Morón. Andalucía, S Spain
180 G13 **Moroni** ● (Comoros) Grande Comore, NW Comoros
175 Tt6 **Morotai, Pulau** *island* Maluku, E Indonesia
175 T6 **Morotai, Selat** *strait* Maluku, E Indonesia
Morotiri *see* Marotiri
83 H17 **Moroto** NE Uganda
Morozov *see* Bratan
130 M11 **Morozovsk** Rostovskaya Oblast', SW Russian Federation
99 L14 **Morpeth** N England, UK
Morphou *see* Güzelyurt
Morphou Bay *see* Güzelyurt Körfezi
30 I13 **Morrill** Nebraska, C USA
29 U11 **Morrilton** Arkansas, C USA
9 Q16 **Morrin** Alberta, SW Canada
192 M7 **Morrinsville** Waikato, North Island, NZ
9 X16 **Morris** Manitoba, S Canada
32 M11 **Morris** Illinois, N USA
31 S8 **Morris** Minnesota, N USA
12 M13 **Morrisburg** Ontario, SE Canada
207 R11 **Morris Jesup, Kap** *headland* N Greenland
190 B1 **Morris, Mount** ▲ South Australia
32 K10 **Morrison** Illinois, N USA
38 K13 **Morristown** Arizona, SW USA
20 J14 **Morristown** New Jersey, NE USA
23 O8 **Morristown** Tennessee, S USA
44 L11 **Morrito** Río San Juan, SW Nicaragua
37 P13 **Morro Bay** California, W USA
97 L22 **Mörrum** Blekinge, S Sweden
85 N16 **Morrumbala** Zambézia, NE Mozambique
85 N20 **Morrumbene** Inhambane, SE Mozambique
97 F21 **Mors** *island* NW Denmark
Mörs *see* Moers
27 N1 **Morse** Texas, SW USA
131 N6 **Morshansk** Tambovskaya Oblast', W Russian Federation
104 L5 **Mortagne-au-Perche** Orne, N France
104 J8 **Mortagne-sur-Sèvre** Vendée, NW France
106 G8 **Mortágua** Viseu, N Portugal
104 J5 **Mortain** Manche, N France
108 C8 **Mortara** Lombardia, N Italy
61 J17 **Mortes, Rio das** ≈ C Brazil
190 M12 **Mortlake** Victoria, SE Australia
Mortlock Group *see* Takuu Islands
201 Q17 **Mortlock Islands** *prev.* Nomoi Islands. *island group* C Micronesia
31 T9 **Morton** Minnesota, N USA
24 L5 **Morton** Mississippi, S USA
26 M5 **Morton** Texas, SW USA
34 H9 **Morton** Washington, NW USA
1 D7 **Morton Seamount** *undersea feature* NE Pacific Ocean
47 U15 **Moruga** Trinidad, Trinidad and Tobago
191 P9 **Morundah** New South Wales, SE Australia
Moruroa *see* Mururoa
191 S11 **Moruya** New South Wales, SE Australia
105 Q8 **Morvan** *physical region* C France
193 G21 **Morven** Canterbury, South Island, NZ
191 O13 **Morwell** Victoria, SE Australia
129 N6 **Morzhovets, Ostrov** *island* NW Russian Federation
106 G4 **Mos** Galicia, NW Spain
130 J4 **Mosal'sk** Kaluzhskaya Oblast', W Russian Federation
103 H20 **Mosbach** Baden-Württemberg, SW Germany
97 E18 **Mosby** Vest-Agder, S Norway
35 V9 **Mosby** Montana, NW USA
34 M9 **Moscow** Idaho, NW USA
22 F10 **Moscow** Tennessee, S USA
Moscow *see* Moskva
103 D19 **Mosel** *Fr.* Moselle. ≈ W Europe *see also* Moselle
105 T4 **Moselle** ◐ *department* NE France
105 T6 **Moselle** *Ger.* Mosel. ≈ W Europe *see also* Mosel
34 K9 **Moses Lake** ◎ Washington, NW USA
85 I18 **Mosetse** Central, E Botswana
94 H4 **Mosfellsbær** Sudhurland, SW Iceland
193 F23 **Mosgiel** Otago, South Island, NZ
128 M11 **Mosha** ≈ NW Russian Federation
83 I20 **Moshi** Kilimanjaro, NE Tanzania
112 G12 **Mosina** Poznań, W Poland
32 L6 **Mosinee** Wisconsin, N USA
94 F13 **Mosjøen** Nordland, C Norway
127 Nn13 **Moskal'vo** Ostrov Sakhalin, Sakhalinskaya Oblast', SE Russian Federation
94 I13 **Moskosel** Norrbotten, N Sweden
130 K4 **Moskovskaya Oblast'** ◐ *province* W Russian Federation
Moskovskiy *see* Moskva
130 J3 **Moskva** *Eng.* Moscow. ● (Russian Federation) Gorod Moskva, W Russian Federation
153 Q14 **Moskva** *Rus.* Moskovskiy; *prev.* Chubek. SW Tajikistan
130 L4 **Moskva** ≈ W Russian Federation
85 I20 **Mosomane** Kgatleng, SE Botswana
Moson and Magyaróvár *see* Mosonmagyaróvár
113 H21 **Mosoni-Duna** *Ger.* Kleine Donau. ≈ NW Hungary
113 H21 **Mosonmagyaróvár** *Ger.* Wieselburg-Ungarisch-Altenburg; *prev.* Moson and Magyaróvár, *Ger.* Wieselburg and Ungarisch-Altenburg. Győr-Moson-Sopron, NW Hungary
Mospino *see* Mospyne
119 X8 **Mospyne** *Rus.* Mospino. Donets'ka Oblast', E Ukraine
56 B12 **Mosquera** Nariño, SW Colombia
39 U10 **Mosquero** New Mexico, SW USA
Mosquito Coast *see* La Mosquitia
33 U11 **Mosquito Creek Lake** ⊡ Ohio, N USA
Mosquito Gulf *see* Mosquitos, Golfo de los
25 X11 **Mosquito Lagoon** *wetland* Florida, SE USA
45 N10 **Mosquito, Punta** *headland* E Nicaragua
45 W14 **Mosquito, Punta** *headland* NE Panama
45 Q15 **Mosquitos, Golfo de los** *Eng.* Mosquito Gulf. *gulf* N Panama
97 H16 **Moss** Østfold, S Norway
Mossâmedes *see* Namibe
24 G8 **Moss Bluff** Louisiana, S USA
193 C23 **Mossburn** Southland, South Island, NZ
85 G26 **Mosselbaai** *var.* Mosselbai, *Eng.* Mossel Bay. Western Cape, SW South Africa
Mosselbai/Mossel Bay *see* Mosselbaai
81 F20 **Mossendjo** Le Niari, SW Congo
191 N8 **Mossgiel** New South Wales, SE Australia
103 H22 **Mössingen** Baden-Württemberg, S Germany
189 W4 **Mossman** Queensland, NE Australia
61 P14 **Mossoró** Rio Grande do Norte, NE Brazil
25 N9 **Moss Point** Mississippi, S USA
191 S9 **Moss Vale** New South Wales, SE Australia
34 G9 **Mossyrock** Washington, NW USA
113 B15 **Most** *Ger.* Brüx. Severní Čechy, NW Czech Republic
123 Jj16 **Mosta** *var.* Musta. C Malta
76 I5 **Mostaganem** *var.* Mestghanem. NW Algeria
115 H14 **Mostar** S Bosnia and Herzegovina
63 J17 **Mostardas** Rio Grande do Sul, S Brazil
118 K14 **Mostiştea** ≈ S Romania
Mostva *see* Mastva
Mosty *see* Masty
118 H5 **Mostys'ka** L'vivs'ka Oblast', W Ukraine
Mosul *see* Al Mawşil
97 F15 **Møsvatnet** ◎ S Norway
82 J12 **Mot'a** N Ethiopia
197 C10 **Mota** *island* Banks Islands, N Vanuatu
81 H16 **Motaba** ≈ N Congo
107 O10 **Mota del Cuervo** Castilla-La Mancha, C Spain
106 L5 **Mota del Marqués** Castilla-León, N Spain
44 F5 **Motagua, Río** ≈ Guatemala/Honduras
121 H19 **Motal'** Brestskaya Voblasts', SW Belarus
97 L17 **Motala** Östergötland, S Sweden
197 C10 **Mota Lava** *island* Banks Islands, N Vanuatu
203 X7 **Motane** *var.* Mohotani. *island* Îles Marquises, NE French Polynesia
158 K13 **Moth** Uttar Pradesh, N India
Mother of Presidents/ Mother of States *see* Virginia
98 I12 **Motherwell** C Scotland, UK
159 P12 **Motīhāri** Bihār, N India
107 Q10 **Motilla del Palancar** Castilla-La Mancha, C Spain
192 N7 **Motiti Island** *island* NE NZ
67 E25 **Motley Island** *island* SE Falkland Islands
85 J19 **Motloutse** ≈ E Botswana
43 V17 **Motozintla de Mendoza** Chiapas, SE Mexico
107 N15 **Motril** Andalucía, S Spain
118 G13 **Motru** Gorj, SW Romania
171 Mm5 **Motsuta-misaki** *headland* Hokkaidō, NE Japan
30 L6 **Mott** North Dakota, N USA
Möttling *see* Metlika
109 O18 **Mottola** Puglia, SE Italy
192 P8 **Motu** ≈ North Island, NZ
193 I14 **Motueka** Tasman, South Island, NZ
193 I14 **Motueka** ≈ South Island, NZ
Motu Iti *see* Tupai
43 X12 **Motul** *var.* Motul de Felipe Carrillo Puerto. Yucatán, SE Mexico
Motul de Felipe Carrillo Puerto *see* Motul
203 U17 **Motu Nui** *island* Easter Island, Chile, E Pacific Ocean
203 Q10 **Motu One** *var.* Bellingshausen. *atoll* Îles Sous le Vent, W French Polynesia
202 I16 **Motutapu** *island* E Cook Islands
200 R15 **Motu Tapu** *island* Tongatapu Group, S Tonga
192 L5 **Motutapu Island** *island* N NZ
Motyca *see* Modica
126 I13 **Motygino** Krasnoyarskiy Kray, C Russian Federation
Mouanda *see* Moanda
Mouaskar *see* Mascara
107 U3 **Moubermé, Tuc de** *Fr.* Pic de Maubermé, *Sp.* Pico Mauberme; *prev.* Tuc de Maubermé. ▲ France/Spain *see also* Maubermé, Pic de
47 N7 **Mouchoir Passage** *passage* SE Turks and Caicos Islands
78 I9 **Moudjéria** Tagant, SW Mauritania
110 C9 **Moudon** Vaud, W Switzerland
Mouhoun *see* Black Volta
81 E19 **Mouila** Ngounié, C Gabon
81 K14 **Mouka** Haute-Kotto, C Central African Republic
Moukden *see* Shenyang
191 N10 **Moulamein** New South Wales, SE Australia
Moulamein Creek *see* Billabong Creek
76 F6 **Moulay-Bousselham** NW Morocco
Moule *see* le Moule
82 M11 **Moulhoulé** N Djibouti
105 P9 **Moulins** Allier, C France
178 Gg9 **Moulmein** *var.* Maulmain, Mawlamyine. Mon State, S Myanmar
177 F9 **Moulmeingyun** Irrawaddy, SW Myanmar
76 G6 **Moulouya** *var.* Mulucha, Muluya, Mulwiya. *seasonal river* NE Morocco
25 O2 **Moulton** Alabama, S USA
31 W16 **Moulton** Iowa, C USA
27 T11 **Moulton** Texas, SW USA
25 T7 **Moultrie** Georgia, SE USA
23 S14 **Moultrie, Lake** ⊡ South Carolina, SE USA
24 K3 **Mound Bayou** Mississippi, S USA
32 L17 **Mound City** Illinois, N USA
29 R6 **Mound City** Kansas, C USA
29 Q2 **Mound City** Missouri, C USA
31 N7 **Mound City** South Dakota, N USA
80 H13 **Moundou** Logone-Occidental, SW Chad
29 P10 **Mounds** Oklahoma, C USA
23 R2 **Moundsville** West Virginia, NE USA
178 Ii12 **Moŭng Roessei** Bătdâmbâng, W Cambodia
Moun Hou *see* Black Volta
14 G5 **Mountain** ≈ Northwest Territories, NW Canada
39 S12 **Mountainair** New Mexico, SW USA
37 V1 **Mountain City** Nevada, W USA
23 Q8 **Mountain City** Tennessee, S USA
29 U7 **Mountain Grove** Missouri, C USA
29 U9 **Mountain Home** Arkansas, C USA
35 N15 **Mountain Home** Idaho, NW USA
27 Q11 **Mountain Home** Texas, SW USA
31 W4 **Mountain Iron** Minnesota, N USA
31 T10 **Mountain Lake** Minnesota, N USA
25 S3 **Mountain Park** Georgia, SE USA
37 W12 **Mountain Pass** *pass* California, W USA
29 T12 **Mountain Pine** Arkansas, C USA
41 Y14 **Mountain Point** Annette Island, Alaska, USA
Mountain State *see* Montana, USA
Mountain State *see* West Virginia, USA
29 V7 **Mountain View** Arkansas, C USA
40 H12 **Mountain View** Hawaii, USA, C Pacific Ocean
29 V10 **Mountain View** Missouri, C USA
40 M11 **Mountain Village** Alaska, USA
23 R8 **Mount Airy** North Carolina, SE USA
85 K24 **Mount Ayliff** *Xh.* Maxesibebi. Eastern Cape, SE South Africa
31 U16 **Mount Ayr** Iowa, C USA
190 J9 **Mount Barker** South Australia
188 J14 **Mount Barker** Western Australia
191 P11 **Mount Beauty** Victoria, SE Australia
12 E16 **Mount Brydges** Ontario, S Canada
33 N16 **Mount Carmel** Illinois, N USA
32 K10 **Mount Carroll** Illinois, N USA
33 S9 **Mount Clemens** Michigan, N USA
193 E19 **Mount Cook** Canterbury, South Island, NZ
85 L16 **Mount Darwin** Mashonaland Central, NE Zimbabwe
21 S7 **Mount Desert Island** *island* Maine, NE USA
25 W11 **Mount Dora** Florida, SE USA
190 G5 **Mount Eba** South Australia
27 W8 **Mount Enterprise** Texas, SW USA
190 J4 **Mount Fitton** South Australia
85 J24 **Mount Fletcher** Eastern Cape, SE South Africa
12 F15 **Mount Forest** Ontario, S Canada
190 K12 **Mount Gambier** South Australia
189 W5 **Mount Garnet** Queensland, NE Australia
23 P6 **Mount Gay** West Virginia, NE USA
33 S12 **Mount Gilead** Ohio, N USA
194 H12 **Mount Hagen** Western Highlands, C PNG
20 J16 **Mount Holly** New Jersey, NE USA
23 R10 **Mount Holly** North Carolina, SE USA
29 T12 **Mount Ida** Arkansas, C USA
189 T6 **Mount Isa** Queensland, C Australia
23 U4 **Mount Jackson** Virginia, NE USA
20 D12 **Mount Jewett** Pennsylvania, NE USA
20 L13 **Mount Kisco** New York, NE USA
20 B15 **Mount Lebanon** Pennsylvania, NE USA
190 J8 **Mount Lofty Ranges** ⛰ South Australia
188 J10 **Mount Magnet** Western Australia
192 N7 **Mount Maunganui** Bay of Plenty, North Island, NZ
99 E18 **Mountmellick** *Ir.* Móinteach Mílic. C Ireland
32 L10 **Mount Morris** Illinois, N USA
33 R9 **Mount Morris** Michigan, N USA
20 F10 **Mount Morris** New York, NE USA
20 B16 **Mount Morris** Pennsylvania, NE USA
32 K15 **Mount Olive** Illinois, N USA
23 V10 **Mount Olive** North Carolina, SE USA
23 N4 **Mount Olivet** Kentucky, S USA
31 Y15 **Mount Pleasant** Iowa, C USA
33 Q8 **Mount Pleasant** Michigan, N USA
20 C15 **Mount Pleasant** Pennsylvania, NE USA
23 T14 **Mount Pleasant** South Carolina, SE USA
22 I9 **Mount Pleasant** Tennessee, S USA
27 W6 **Mount Pleasant** Texas, SW USA
38 L4 **Mount Pleasant** Utah, W USA
65 N23 **Mount Pleasant** ✕ (Stanley) East Falkland, Falkland Islands
99 G25 **Mount's Bay** *inlet* SW England, UK
37 N2 **Mount Shasta** California, W USA
32 J13 **Mount Sterling** Illinois, N USA
23 N5 **Mount Sterling** Kentucky, S USA
20 E15 **Mount Union** Pennsylvania, NE USA
25 V6 **Mount Vernon** Georgia, SE USA
32 L16 **Mount Vernon** Illinois, N USA
22 M6 **Mount Vernon** Kentucky, S USA
29 S7 **Mount Vernon** Missouri, C USA
33 T13 **Mount Vernon** Ohio, N USA
34 H7 **Mount Vernon** Oregon, NW USA
27 W6 **Mount Vernon** Texas, SW USA
34 K13 **Mount Vernon** Washington, NW USA
22 L5 **Mount Washington** Kentucky, S USA
190 F8 **Mount Wedge** South Australia
32 L14 **Mount Zion** Illinois, N USA
189 Y9 **Moura** Queensland, NE Australia
60 F12 **Moura** Amazonas, NW Brazil
106 H12 **Moura** Beja, S Portugal
106 I12 **Mourão** Évora, S Portugal
78 L11 **Mourdiah** Koulikoro, W Mali
80 K7 **Mourdi, Dépression du** *desert lowland* Chad/Sudan
104 J16 **Mourenx** Pyrénées-Atlantiques, SW France
Mourgana *see* Mourgkána
117 C15 **Mourgkána** *var.* Mourgana. ▲ Albania/Greece
99 G16 **Mourne Mountains** *Ir.* Beanna Boirche. ⛰ SE Northern Ireland, UK
117 I15 **Moúrtzeflos, Ákra** *headland* Límnos, E Greece
101 C19 **Mouscron** *Dut.* Moeskroen. Hainaut, W Belgium
Mouse River *see* Souris River
80 H10 **Moussoro** Kanem, W Chad
105 T11 **Moûtiers** Savoie, E France
180 J14 **Moutsamoudou** *var.* Mutsamudu. Anjouan, SE Comoros
76 K11 **Mouydir, Monts de** ⛰ S Algeria
81 F20 **Mouyondzi** La Bouenza, S Congo
117 E16 **Mouzáki** *prev.* Mouzákion. Thessalía, C Greece
Mouzákion *see* Mouzáki
31 S13 **Moville** Iowa, C USA
84 E13 **Moxico** ◐ *province* E Angola
180 I14 **Moya** Anjouan, SE Comoros
42 L12 **Moyahua** Zacatecas, C Mexico
83 J16 **Moyalē** S Ethiopia
78 I15 **Moyamba** W Sierra Leone
76 G7 **Moyen Atlas** *Eng.* Middle Atlas. ⛰ N Morocco
80 H13 **Moyen-Chari** *off.* Préfecture du Moyen-Chari. ◐ *prefecture* S Chad
Moyen-Congo *see* Congo
85 J24 **Moyeni** *var.* Quthing. SW Lesotho
78 H13 **Moyenne-Guinée** ◐ *state* NW Guinea
81 D18 **Moyen-Ogooué** *off.* Province du Moyen-Ogooué, *var.* Le Moyen-Ogooué. ◐ *province* C Gabon
105 S4 **Moyeuvre-Grande** Moselle, NE France
35 N7 **Moyie Springs** Idaho, NW USA

◆ Country
● Country Capital
◇ Dependent Territory
○ Dependent Territory Capital
◐ Administrative Region
✕ International Airport
▲ Mountain
⛰ Mountain Range
Volcano
≈ River
◎ Lake
⊡ Reservoir

83 F16 **Moyo** NW Uganda
58 D10 **Moyobamba** San Martín, NW Peru
175 O16 **Moyo, Pulau** island S Indonesia
80 H10 **Moyto** Chari-Baguirmi, W Chad
164 G9 **Moyu** var. Karakax. Xinjiang Uygur Zizhiqu, NW China
126 Jj9 **Moyyero** ≈ N Russian Federation
151 Q15 **Moyynkum, Peski** Kaz. Moyynqum. desert S Kazakhstan
Moyynqum see Moyynkum, Peski
151 S12 **Moyynty** Zhezkazgan, C Kazakhstan
151 S12 **Moyynty** ≈ C Kazakhstan
Mozambika, Lakandranon' i see Mozambique Channel
85 M18 **Mozambique** off. Republic of Mozambique; prev. People's Republic of Mozambique, Portuguese East Africa. ◆ republic S Africa
Mozambique Basin see Natal Basin
Mozambique, Canal de see Mozambique Channel
85 P17 **Mozambique Channel** Fr. Canal de Mozambique, Mal. Lakandranon' i Mozambika. strait W Indian Ocean
180 L11 **Mozambique Escarpment** var. Mozambique Scarp. undersea feature SW Indian Ocean
180 L10 **Mozambique Plateau** var. Mozambique Rise. undersea feature SW Indian Ocean
Mozambique Rise see Mozambique Plateau
Mozambique Scarp see Mozambique Escarpment
131 O15 **Mozdok** Respublika Severnaya Osetiya, SW Russian Federation
59 K17 **Mozetenes, Serranías de** ⛰ C Bolivia
130 J4 **Mozhaysk** Moskovskaya Oblast', W Russian Federation
131 T3 **Mozhga** Udmurtskaya Respublika, NW Russian Federation
Mozyr' see Mazyr
81 P22 **Mpala** Shaba, E Zaire
81 G19 **Mpama** ≈ C Congo
83 E22 **Mpanda** Rukwa, W Tanzania
84 L11 **Mpande** Northern, NE Zambia
85 J18 **Mphoengs** Matabeleland South, SW Zimbabwe
83 F18 **Mpigi** S Uganda
84 L13 **Mpika** Northern, NE Zambia
85 J14 **Mpima** Central, C Zambia
84 J13 **Mpongwe** Copperbelt, C Zambia
84 K11 **Mporokoso** Northern, N Zambia
81 H20 **Mpouya** Plateaux, SE Congo
79 P16 **Mpraeso** C Ghana
84 L11 **Mpulungu** Northern, N Zambia
85 K21 **Mpumalanga** prev. Eastern Transvaal, Afr. Oos-Transvaal. ◈ province NE South Africa
85 D16 **Mpungu** Okavango, N Namibia
83 I22 **Mpwapwa** Dodoma, C Tanzania
Mqinvartsveri see Kazbek
112 M8 **Mrągowo** Ger. Sensburg. Olsztyn, NE Poland
131 V6 **Mrakovo** Respublika Bashkortostan, W Russian Federation
114 F12 **Mrkonjić Grad** W Bosnia and Herzegovina
112 H9 **Mrocza** Bydgoszcz, NW Poland
128 I14 **Msta** ≈ NW Russian Federation
Mtkvari see Kura
Mtoko see Mutoko
130 K6 **Mtsensk** Orlovskaya Oblast', W Russian Federation
83 K24 **Mtwara** Mtwara, SE Tanzania
83 J25 **Mtwara** ◈ region SE Tanzania
104 G14 **Mu** ▲ S Portugal
200 Qq15 **Mu'a** Tongatapu, S Tonga
Muai To see Mae Hong Son
85 P16 **Mualama** Zambézia, NE Mozambique
Mualo see Messalo, Rio
81 E22 **Muanda** Bas-Zaïre, SW Zaire
Muang Chiang Rai see Chiang Rai
178 J6 **Muang Ham** Houaphan, N Laos
178 J9 **Muang Hinboun** Khammouan, C Laos
Muang Kalasin see Kalasin
Muang Khammouan see Thakhèk
178 Jj11 **Muang Không** Champasak, S Laos
178 Jj10 **Muang Khôngxédôn** var. Khong Sedone. Salavan, S Laos
Muang Khon Kaen see Khon Kaen
178 Ii6 **Muang Khoua** Phôngsali, N Laos
Muang Krabi see Krabi
Muang Lampang see Lampang
Muang Lamphun see Lamphun
Muang Loei see Loei
Muang Lom Sak see Lom Sak
Muang Nakhon Sawan see Nakhon Sawan
178 I6 **Muang Namo** Oudômxai, N Laos
Muang Nan see Nan
178 Ii6 **Muang Ngoy** Louangphabang, N Laos
178 I5 **Muang Ou Tai** Phôngsali, N Laos
Muang Pak Lay see Pak Lay
Muang Pakxan see Pakxan
178 Jj10 **Muang Pakxong** Champasak, S Laos
178 Jj9 **Muang Phalan** var. Muang Phalane. Savannakhét, S Laos
Muang Phalane see Muang Phalan
Muang Phan see Phan
Muang Phayao see Phayao
Muang Phichit see Phichit
178 Jj9 **Muang Phin** Savannakhét, S Laos
Muang Phitsanulok see Phitsanulok
Muang Phrae see Phrae
Muang Roi Et see Roi Et
Muang Sakon Nakhon see Sakon Nakhon
Muang Samut Prakan see Samut Prakan
178 I6 **Muang Sing** Louang Namtha, N Laos
Muang Ubon see Ubon Ratchathani
Muang Uthai Thani see Uthai Thani
178 I7 **Muang Vangviang** Viangchan, C Laos
Muang Xaignabouri see Xaignabouli
Muang Xay see Xai
178 Jj9 **Muang Xépôn** var. Sepone. Savannakhét, S Laos
174 H6 **Muar** var. Bandar Maharani. Johor, Peninsular Malaysia
173 Ff6 **Muara** Sumatera, W Indonesia
174 Hh11 **Muarabeliti** Sumatera, W Indonesia
174 H9 **Muarabungo** Sumatera, W Indonesia
174 I11 **Muaraenim** Sumatera, W Indonesia
174 Mm8 **Muarajuloi** Borneo, C Indonesia
175 Nn9 **Muarakaman** Borneo, C Indonesia
173 Ff9 **Muarasigep** Pulau Siberut, W Indonesia
174 Hh9 **Muaratembesi** Sumatera, W Indonesia
175 N9 **Muaratewe** var. Muarateweh; prev. Moearatewe. Borneo, C Indonesia
Muarateweh see Muaratewe
175 O7 **Muarawahau** Borneo, C Indonesia
144 G13 **Mubārak, Jabal** ▲ S Jordan
159 N13 **Mubārakpur** Uttar Pradesh, N India
Mubarek see Muborak
83 F18 **Mubende** SW Uganda
79 Y14 **Mubi** Adamawa, NE Nigeria
152 M12 **Muborak** Rus. Mubarek. Qashqadaryo Wiloyati, S Uzbekistan
176 Vv9 **Mubrani** Irian Jaya, E Indonesia
69 U12 **Muchinga Escarpment** escarpment NE Zambia
131 N7 **Muchkapskiy** Tambovskaya Oblast', W Russian Federation
98 G10 **Muck** island W Scotland, UK
84 Q13 **Mucojo** Cabo Delgado, N Mozambique
84 F12 **Muconda** Lunda Sul, NE Angola
56 I10 **Muco, Río** ≈ E Colombia
85 O16 **Mucubela** Zambézia, NE Mozambique
44 J5 **Mucupina, Monte** ▲ N Honduras
142 J14 **Mucur** Kirşehir, C Turkey
149 U8 **Mūd** Khorāsān, E Iran
169 Y9 **Mudanjiang** var. Mu-tan-chiang. Heilongjiang, NE China
169 Y9 **Mudan Jiang** ≈ NE China
142 D11 **Mudanya** Bursa, NW Turkey
30 K8 **Mud Butte** South Dakota, N USA
161 G16 **Muddebihāl** Karnātaka, C India
29 P12 **Muddy Boggy Creek** ≈ Oklahoma, C USA
38 M6 **Muddy Creek** ≈ Utah, W USA
39 V7 **Muddy Creek Reservoir** ▣ Colorado, C USA
35 W15 **Muddy Gap** Wyoming, C USA
37 Y11 **Muddy Peak** ▲ Nevada, W USA
191 R7 **Mudgee** New South Wales, SE Australia
31 S3 **Mud Lake** ◎ Minnesota, N USA
31 P7 **Mud Lake Reservoir** ▣ South Dakota, N USA
178 Gg9 **Mudon** Mon State, S Myanmar
83 O14 **Mudug** off. Gobolka Mudug. ◈ region NE Somalia
83 O14 **Mudug** var. Mudugh. plain N Somalia
Mudugh see Mudug
85 Q15 **Muecate** Nampula, NE Mozambique
84 Q13 **Mueda** Cabo Delgado, NE Mozambique
44 L10 **Muelle de los Bueyes** Región Autónoma Atlántico Sur, SE Nicaragua
Muenchen see München
85 M14 **Muende** Tete, NW Mozambique
27 T5 **Muenster** Texas, SW USA
Muenster see Münster
45 O6 **Muerto, Cayo** reef NE Nicaragua
43 T17 **Muerto, Mar** lagoon SE Mexico
66 F11 **Muertos Trough** undersea feature N Caribbean Sea
85 H14 **Mufaya Kuta** Western, NW Zambia
84 J13 **Mufulira** Copperbelt, C Zambia
167 O10 **Mufu Shan** ⛰ C China
Mugalzhar Taūlary see Mugodzhary, Gory
143 Y12 **Muğan Düzü** Rus. Muganskaya Ravnina, Muganskaya Step'. physical region S Azerbaijan
Muganskaya Ravnina/Muganskaya Step' see Muğan Düzü
108 K8 **Múggia** Friuli-Venezia Giulia, NE Italy
159 N14 **Mughal Sarāi** Uttar Pradesh, N India
Mughla see Muğla
147 W11 **Mughshin** var. Muqshin. S Oman
153 S12 **Mughsu** Rus. Muksu. ≈ C Tajikistan
170 Ff16 **Mugi** Tokushima, Shikoku, SW Japan
142 C16 **Muğla** var. Mughla. Muğla, SW Turkey
142 C16 **Muğla** var. Mughla. ◈ province SW Turkey
150 J11 **Mugodzhary, Gory** Kaz. Mugalzhar Taūlary. ⛰ W Kazakhstan
85 O15 **Mugulama** Zambézia, NE Mozambique
145 U9 **Muḩammad** E Iraq
145 R8 **Muḩammadīyah** C Iraq
82 I6 **Muhammad Qol** Red Sea, NE Sudan
77 Y9 **Muḩammad, Râs** headland E Egypt
Muhammerah see Khorramshahr
146 M12 **Muhāyil** var. Mahāil. 'Asīr, SW Saudi Arabia
145 O7 **Muḩaywīr** W Iraq
103 H21 **Mühlacker** Baden-Württemberg, SW Germany
Mühlbach see Sebeş
Mühldorf see Mühldorf am Inn
103 N23 **Mühldorf am Inn** var. Mühldorf. Bayern, SE Germany
103 J15 **Mühlhausen** var. Mühlhausen in Thüringen. Thüringen, C Germany
Mühlhausen in Thüringen see Mühlhausen
205 Q2 **Mühlig-Hofmann Mountains** ⛰ Antarctica
95 L14 **Muhos** Oulu, C Finland
144 K6 **Muḩ, Sabkhat al** ◎ C Syria
120 E5 **Muhu** Ger. Mohn, Moon. island W Estonia
83 F19 **Muhutwe** Kagera, NW Tanzania
Muhu Väin see Väinameri
100 J10 **Muiden** Noord-Holland, C Netherlands
200 R15 **Mui Hopohoponga** headland Tongatapu, S Tonga
171 K14 **Muika** var. Muikamachi. Niigata, Honshū, C Japan
Muikamachi see Muika
Muinchille see Cootehill
Muineachán see Monaghan
99 F19 **Muine Bheag** Eng. Bagenalstown. SE Ireland
58 B5 **Muisne** Esmeraldas, NW Ecuador
85 P14 **Muite** Nampula, NE Mozambique
43 Z11 **Mujeres, Isla** island E Mexico
118 G7 **Mukacheve** Hung. Munkács, Rus. Mukachevo. Zakarpats'ka Oblast', W Ukraine
Mukachevo see Mukacheve
174 L15 **Mukah** Sarawak, East Malaysia
Mukalla see Al Mukallā
Mukama see Mokāma
Mukāshafa/Mukashshafah see Mukayshifah
172 Oo6 **Mu-kawa** ≈ Hokkaidō, NE Japan
145 S6 **Mukayshīfah** var. Mukāshafa, Mukashshafah. N Iraq
178 J9 **Mukdahan** Mukdahan, E Thailand
Mukden see Shenyang
172 Ss16 **Mukojima-rettō** Eng. Parry group. island group SE Japan
152 M14 **Mukry** Lebapskiy Velayat, E Turkmenistan
Muksu see Mughsu
159 U14 **Muktagacha** Dhaka, N Bangladesh
84 K13 **Mukuku** Central, C Zambia
84 K11 **Mukupa Kaoma** Northern, NE Zambia
83 I18 **Mukutan** Rift Valley, W Kenya
85 F16 **Mukwe** Caprivi, NE Namibia
107 R13 **Mula** Murcia, SE Spain
157 K20 **Mulaku Atoll** var. Meemu Atoll. atoll C Maldives
85 J15 **Mulalika** Lusaka, C Zambia
169 X8 **Mulan** Heilongjiang, NE China
85 N15 **Mulanje** var. Mlanje. Southern, S Malawi
42 H5 **Mulatos** Sonora, NW Mexico
25 P3 **Mulberry Fork** ≈ Alabama, S USA
41 P12 **Mulchatna River** ≈ Alaska, USA
129 W4 **Mul'da** Respublika Komi, NW Russian Federation
103 M14 **Mulde** ≈ E Germany
29 R10 **Muldrow** Oklahoma, C USA
42 E7 **Mulegé** Baja California Sur, W Mexico
110 I10 **Mulegns** Graubünden, S Switzerland
81 M21 **Mulenda** Kasai Oriental, C Zaire
26 M4 **Muleshoe** Texas, SW USA
85 O15 **Mulevala** Zambézia, NE Mozambique
191 P5 **Mulgoa Creek** seasonal river New South Wales, SE Australia
107 O15 **Mulhacén** var. Cerro de Mulhacén. ▲ S Spain
Mulhacén, Cerro de see Mulhacén
Mülhausen see Mulhouse
103 E24 **Mülheim** Baden-Württemberg, SW Germany
103 E15 **Mülheim** var. Mulheim an der Ruhr. Nordrhein-Westfalen, W Germany
Mulheim an der Ruhr see Mülheim
105 U7 **Mulhouse** Ger. Mülhausen. Haut-Rhin, NE France
166 G11 **Muli** var. Bowa, Muli Zangzu Zizhixian. Sichuan, C China
176 Y15 **Muli** channel Irian Jaya, E Indonesia
169 Y9 **Muling** Heilongjiang, NE China
Mullach Íde see Malahide
Mullaitivu see Mullaittivu
161 K23 **Mullaittivu** var. Mullaitivu. Northern Province, N Sri Lanka
35 N8 **Mullan** Idaho, NW USA
30 M13 **Mullen** Nebraska, C USA
191 Q6 **Mullengudgery** New South Wales, SE Australia
23 Q6 **Mullens** West Virginia, NE USA
Müller-gerbergte see Muller, Pegunungan
174 Mm7 **Muller, Pegunungan** Dut. Müller-gerbergte. ⛰ Borneo, C Indonesia
194 F12 **Muller Range** ⛰ W PNG
33 Q5 **Mullett Lake** ◎ Michigan, N USA
20 J16 **Mullica River** ≈ New Jersey, NE USA
27 R8 **Mullin** Texas, SW USA
99 E17 **Mullingar** Ir. An Muileann gCearr. C Ireland
23 T12 **Mullins** South Carolina, SE USA
98 G11 **Mull, Isle of** island W Scotland, UK
131 R5 **Mullovka** Ul'yanovskaya Oblast', W Russian Federation
97 K19 **Mullsjö** Skaraborg, S Sweden
191 V4 **Mullumbimby** New South Wales, SE Australia
85 H15 **Mulobezi** Western, SW Zambia
85 C15 **Mulondo** Huíla, SW Angola
85 G15 **Mulonga Plain** plain W Zambia
81 N23 **Mulongo** Shaba, SE Zaire
155 T10 **Multān** Punjab, E Pakistan
95 L17 **Multia** Keski-Suomi, C Finland
Mulucha see Moulouya
85 J14 **Mulungushi** Central, C Zambia
85 K14 **Mulungwe** Central, C Zambia
Muluya see Moulouya
29 N7 **Mulvane** Kansas, C USA
191 O10 **Mulwala** New South Wales, SE Australia
Mulwiya see Moulouya
190 K6 **Mulyungarie** South Australia
Mumbai see Bombay
85 D14 **Mumbué** Bié, C Angola
194 J13 **Mumeng** Morobe, C PNG
176 W9 **Mumi** Irian Jaya, E Indonesia
Muminabad/Mŭ'minobod see Leningrad
131 Q13 **Mumra** Astrakhanskaya Oblast', SW Russian Federation
43 X12 **Muna** Yucatán, SE Mexico
126 Kk9 **Muna** ≈ NE Russian Federation
158 C12 **Munābāo** Rājasthān, NW India
Munamägi see Suur Munamägi
175 Qq13 **Muna, Pulau** prev. Moena. island C Indonesia
175 Qq13 **Muna, Selat** strait Sulawesi, C Indonesia
103 L18 **Münchberg** Bayern, E Germany
103 L23 **München** var. Muenchen, Eng. Munich, It. Monaco. Bayern, SE Germany
München-Gladbach see Mönchengladbach
110 E6 **Münchenstein** Basel-Land, NW Switzerland
8 L10 **Muncho Lake** British Columbia, W Canada
33 P13 **Muncie** Indiana, N USA
20 G13 **Muncy** Pennsylvania, NE USA
195 U14 **Munda** New Georgia, NW Solomon Islands
9 Q14 **Mundare** Alberta, SW Canada
27 Q5 **Munday** Texas, SW USA
33 N10 **Mundelein** Illinois, N USA
103 I15 **Münden** Niedersachsen, C Germany
107 Q12 **Mundo** ≈ S Spain
194 L11 **Mundua Island** island Witu Islands, C PNG
84 B12 **Munenga** Cuanza Sul, NW Angola
107 P11 **Munera** Castilla-La Mancha, C Spain
22 E9 **Munford** Tennessee, S USA
22 K7 **Munfordville** Kentucky, S USA
190 D5 **Mungala** South Australia
85 M16 **Mungári** Manica, C Mozambique
81 O16 **Mungbere** Haut-Zaïre, NE Zaire
159 Q13 **Munger** prev. Monghyr. Bihār, NE India
190 I2 **Mungeranie** South Australia
Mu Nggava see Rennell
174 K6 **Mungguresak, Tanjung** headland Borneo, N Indonesia
Mungiki see Bellona
191 R4 **Mungindi** New South Wales, SE Australia
Mungkawn see Maingkwan
159 T16 **Mungla** var. Mongla. Khulna, S Bangladesh
84 C13 **Mungo** Huambo, W Angola
196 F16 **Munguuy Bay** bay Yap, W Micronesia
84 E13 **Munhango** Bié, C Angola
197 L14 **Munia** island Lau Group, E Fiji
Munich see München
107 S7 **Muniesa** Aragón, NE Spain
33 O4 **Munising** Michigan, N USA
Munkács see Mukacheve
97 I17 **Munkedal** Göteborg och Bohus, S Sweden
97 K15 **Munkfors** Värmland, C Sweden
126 J16 **Munku-Sardyk, Gora** var. Mönh Sarĭdag. ▲ Mongolia/Russian Federation
101 E18 **Munkzwalm** Oost-Vlaanderen, NW Belgium
178 J10 **Mun, Mae Nam** ≈ E Thailand
159 U15 **Munshiganj** Dhaka, C Bangladesh
110 D8 **Münsingen** Bern, W Switzerland
105 U6 **Munster** Haut-Rhin, NE France
102 J11 **Munster** Niedersachsen, NW Germany
99 B20 **Munster** Ir. Cúige Mumhan. cultural region S Ireland
102 F13 **Münster** var. Muenster, Münster in Westfalen. Nordrhein-Westfalen, W Germany
110 F10 **Münster** Valais, S Switzerland
Münsterberg in Schlesien see Ziębice
Münster in Westfalen see Münster
102 E13 **Münsterland** cultural region NW Germany
102 F13 **Münster-Osnabruck** ✕ Nordrhein-Westfalen, NW Germany
33 R4 **Munuscong Lake** ◎ Michigan, N USA
85 K17 **Munyati** ≈ C Zimbabwe
111 R3 **Münzkirchen** Oberösterreich, N Austria
94 K11 **Muodoslompolo** Norrbotten, N Sweden
94 M13 **Muojärvi** ◎ NE Finland
178 Jj6 **Mương Khên** Hoa Binh, N Vietnam
Muong Sai see Xai
178 I7 **Muong Xiang Ngeun** var. Xieng Ngeun. Louangphabang, N Laos
94 K11 **Muonio** Lappi, N Finland
Muonioälv/Muoniojoki see Muonionjoki
94 K11 **Muonionjoki** var. Muoniojoki, Swe. Muonioälv. ≈ Finland/Sweden
85 N17 **Mupa** ≈ C Mozambique
85 E16 **Mupini** Okavango, NE Namibia
82 F8 **Muqaddam, Wadi** ≈ N Sudan
144 K9 **Muqāṭ** Al Mafraq, E Jordan
147 X7 **Muqaz** N Oman
83 N17 **Muqdisho** Eng. Mogadishu, It. Mogadiscio. ● (Somalia) Banaadir, S Somalia
83 N17 **Muqdisho** ✕ Banaadir, E Somalia
Muqshin see Mughshin
111 T8 **Mur** SCr. Mura. ≈ C Europe
Mura see Mur
143 T14 **Muradiye** Van, E Turkey
Muragarazi see Maragarazi
171 L12 **Murakami** Niigata, Honshū, C Japan
65 G22 **Murallón, Cerro** ▲ S Argentina
83 E20 **Muramvya** C Burundi
83 I19 **Murang'a** prev. Fort Hall. Central, SW Kenya
83 H16 **Murangering** Rift Valley, NW Kenya
Murapara see Murupara
146 M5 **Murār, Bi'r al** well NW Saudi Arabia
129 Q13 **Murashi** Kirovskaya Oblast', NW Russian Federation
105 O12 **Murat** Cantal, C France
116 N12 **Muratlı** Tekirdağ, NW Turkey
143 R14 **Murat Nehri** var. Eastern Euphrates; anc. Arsanias. ≈ NE Turkey
109 D20 **Muravera** Sardegna, Italy, C Mediterranean Sea
171 Ll12 **Murayama** Yamagata, Honshū, C Japan
124 Oo15 **Muraysah, Ra's al** headland N Libya
106 I6 **Murça** Vila Real, N Portugal
82 Q11 **Murcanyo** Bari, NE Somalia
149 N8 **Mūrcheh Khvort** var. Morcheh Khort. Eşfahān, C Iran
193 H15 **Murchison** Tasman, South Island, NZ
193 B22 **Murchison Mountains** ⛰ South Island, NZ
188 I10 **Murchison River** ≈ Western Australia
107 R13 **Murcia** Murcia, SE Spain
107 Q13 **Murcia** ◈ autonomous community SE Spain
105 O13 **Mur-de-Barrez** Aveyron, S France
190 G8 **Murdinga** South Australia
30 M10 **Murdo** South Dakota, N USA
13 Q7 **Murdochville** Québec, SE Canada
111 W9 **Mureck** Steiermark, SE Austria
116 M13 **Mürefte** Tekirdağ, NW Turkey
118 I10 **Mureș** ◈ county N Romania
86 J11 **Mureș** var. Maros, Mureşul, Ger. Marosch, Mieresch. ≈ Hungary/Romania see also Maros
Mureşul see Maros/Mureş
104 M16 **Muret** Haute-Garonne, S France
29 T13 **Murfreesboro** Arkansas, C USA
23 W8 **Murfreesboro** North Carolina, SE USA
22 J9 **Murfreesboro** Tennessee, S USA
152 I14 **Murgab** prev. Murgap. Maryyskiy Velayat, S Turkmenistan
152 J16 **Murgab** var. Murghab, Pash. Daryā-ye Morghāb, Turkm. Murgap Deryasy. ≈ Afghanistan/Turkmenistan
Murgab see Murghob
Murgap/Murgap Deryasy see Murgab
116 H9 **Murgash** ▲ W Bulgaria
Murghab see Murgab
153 U13 **Murghob** Rus. Murgab. SE Tajikistan
153 U13 **Murghob** Rus. Murgab. ≈ SE Tajikistan
189 Z10 **Murgon** Queensland, E Australia
202 I16 **Muri** Rarotonga, S Cook Islands
110 F7 **Muri** Aargau, W Switzerland
110 D8 **Muri** var. Muri bei Bern. Bern, W Switzerland
106 K3 **Murias de Paredes** Castilla-León, N Spain
Muri bei Bern see Muri
84 F11 **Muriege** Lunda Sul, NE Angola
201 P14 **Murilo Atoll** atoll Hall Islands, C Micronesia
Mūrītānīyah see Mauritania
102 N10 **Müritz** var. Müritzee. ◎ NE Germany
Müritzee see Müritz
102 L10 **Müritz-Elde-Kanal** canal N Germany
192 K6 **Muriwai Beach** Auckland, North Island, NZ
94 J13 **Murjek** Norrbotten, N Sweden
128 J3 **Murmansk** Murmanskaya Oblast', NW Russian Federation
128 I4 **Murmanskaya Oblast'** ◈ province NW Russian Federation
207 V14 **Murmansk Rise** undersea feature SW Barents Sea
128 J3 **Murmashi** Murmanskaya Oblast', NW Russian Federation
130 M5 **Murmino** Ryazanskaya Oblast', W Russian Federation
103 K24 **Murnau** Bayern, SE Germany
104 E3 **Muro, Capo di** headland Corse, France, C Mediterranean Sea
109 M18 **Muro Lucano** Basilicata, S Italy
131 N4 **Murom** Vladimirskaya Oblast', W Russian Federation
125 G13 **Muromtsevo** Omskaya Oblast', C Russian Federation
172 Nn6 **Muroran** Hokkaidō, NE Japan
106 G3 **Muros** Galicia, NW Spain
106 F3 **Muros e Noia, Ría de** estuary NW Spain
170 F16 **Muroto** Kōchi, Shikoku, SW Japan
170 F16 **Muroto-zaki** headland Shikoku, SW Japan
118 L7 **Murovani Kurylivtsi** Vinnyts'ka Oblast', C Ukraine
112 G11 **Murowana Goślina** Poznań, W Poland
34 M14 **Murphy** Idaho, NW USA
23 N10 **Murphy** North Carolina, SE USA
37 P8 **Murphys** California, W USA
32 L17 **Murphysboro** Illinois, N USA
31 V15 **Murray** Iowa, C USA
22 H8 **Murray** Kentucky, S USA
190 J10 **Murray Bridge** South Australia
183 X2 **Murray Fracture Zone** tectonic feature NE Pacific Ocean
194 E13 **Murray, Lake** ◎ SW PNG
23 P12 **Murray, Lake** ▣ South Carolina, SE USA
8 K8 **Murray, Mount** ▲ Yukon Territory, NW Canada
194 H13 **Murray Range** var. Leonard Murray Mountains. ⛰ W PNG
Murray Range see Murray Ridge
181 O3 **Murray Ridge** var. Murray Range. undersea feature N Arabian Sea
191 N10 **Murray River** ≈ SE Australia
190 K10 **Murrayville** Victoria, SE Australia
155 U5 **Murree** Punjab, E Pakistan
103 I21 **Murrhardt** Baden-Württemberg, S Germany
191 O9 **Murrumbidgee River** ≈ New South Wales, SE Australia
85 P15 **Murrupula** Nampula, NE Mozambique
191 T7 **Murrurundi** New South Wales, SE Australia
111 X9 **Murska Sobota** Ger. Olsnitz. NE Slovenia
160 G12 **Murtajāpur** prev. Murtazapur. Mahārāshtra, C India
79 S16 **Murtala Muhammed** ✕ (Lagos) Ogun, SW Nigeria
Murtazapur see Murtajāpur
110 C8 **Murten** Neuchâtel, W Switzerland
Murtensee see Morat, Lac de
190 L11 **Murtoa** Victoria, SE Australia
94 N13 **Murtovaara** Oulu, E Finland
Murua Island see Woodlark Island
161 D14 **Murud** Mahārāshtra, W India
192 O9 **Murupara** var. Murapara. Bay of Plenty, North Island, NZ
203 X12 **Mururoa** var. Moruroa. atoll Îles Tuamotu, SE French Polynesia
Murviedro see Sagunto
160 J9 **Murwāra** Madhya Pradesh, N India
191 V4 **Murwillumbah** New South Wales, SE Australia
152 H11 **Murzechirla** prev. Mirzachirla. Akhalskiy Velayat, C Turkmenistan
Murzuk see Murzuq
77 O11 **Murzuq** var. Marzūq, Murzuk. SW Libya
Murzuq, Edeyin see Murzuq, Idhān
77 N11 **Murzuq, Ḩamādat** plateau W Libya
77 O11 **Murzuq, Idhān** var. Edeyin Murzuq. desert SW Libya
111 W6 **Mürzzuschlag** Steiermark, E Austria
143 Q14 **Muş** var. Mush. Muş, E Turkey
143 Q14 **Muş** var. Mush. ◈ province E Turkey
194 L16 **Musa** ≈ S PNG
120 G11 **Mūsa** ≈ Latvia/Lithuania
77 X8 **Mûsa, Gebel** ▲ NE Egypt
Musaiyib see Al Musayyib
Musa Khel see Mūsa Khel Bāzār
155 R9 **Mūsa Khel Bāzār** var. Musa Khel. Baluchistān, SW Pakistan
116 H10 **Musala** ▲ W Bulgaria
173 F6 **Musala, Pulau** island W Indonesia
85 I15 **Musale** Southern, S Zambia
147 Y9 **Muşalla** NE Oman
147 W6 **Musandam Peninsula** Ar. Masandam Peninsula. peninsula N Oman
Musay'īd see Umm Sa'īd
Muscat see Masqaṭ
Muscat and Oman see Oman
31 Y14 **Muscatine** Iowa, C USA
Muscat Sib Airport see Seeb
33 O15 **Muscatuck River** ≈ Indiana, N USA
194 G10 **Muschu Island** island NW PNG
32 K8 **Muscoda** Wisconsin, N USA
193 F19 **Musgrave, Mount** ▲ South Island, NZ
189 P9 **Musgrave Ranges** ⛰ South Australia
Mush see Muş
144 H12 **Mushayyish, Qaşr al** castle Ma'ān, C Jordan
81 H20 **Mushie** Bandundu, W Zaire
174 I11 **Musi, Air** prev. Moesi. ≈ Sumatera, W Indonesia
199 K5 **Musicians Seamounts** undersea feature N Pacific Ocean
56 D8 **Musinga, Alto** ▲ NW Colombia
31 T2 **Muskeg Bay** lake bay Minnesota, N USA
33 O8 **Muskegon** Michigan, N USA
33 O8 **Muskegon Heights** Michigan, N USA
33 P8 **Muskegon River** ≈ Michigan, N USA
33 T14 **Muskingum River** ≈ Ohio, N USA
97 P16 **Muskö** Stockholm, C Sweden
Muskogean see Tallahassee
29 Q10 **Muskogee** Oklahoma, C USA
12 H13 **Muskoka, Lake** ◎ Ontario, S Canada
82 H8 **Musmar** Red Sea, NE Sudan
85 K14 **Musofu** Central, C Zambia
83 G19 **Musoma** Mara, N Tanzania
84 L13 **Musoro** Central, C Zambia
194 M8 **Mussau Island** island NE PNG
100 P7 **Musselkanaal** Groningen, NE Netherlands
35 V9 **Musselshell River** ≈ Montana, NW USA
84 C12 **Mussende** Cuanza Sul, NW Angola
104 L12 **Mussidan** Dordogne, SW France
101 L25 **Musson** Luxembourg, SE Belgium
158 J9 **Mussoorie** Uttar Pradesh, N India
Musta see Mosta
158 M13 **Mustafābād** Uttar Pradesh, N India
142 D12 **Mustafakemalpaşa** Bursa, NW Turkey
Mustafa-Pasha see Svilengrad
83 M15 **Mustahīl** SE Ethiopia
26 M7 **Mustang Draw** valley Texas, SW USA
27 T14 **Mustang Island** island Texas, SW USA
Mustasaari see Korsholm
Mustér see Disentis
65 I19 **Musters, Lago** ◎ S Argentina
47 Y14 **Mustique** island C Saint Vincent and the Grenadines
120 I6 **Mustla** Viljandimaa, S Estonia
120 J4 **Mustvee** Ger. Tschorna. Jõgevamaa, E Estonia
44 L9 **Musún, Cerro** ▲ NE Nicaragua
191 T7 **Muswellbrook** New South Wales, SE Australia
113 M18 **Muszyna** Nowy Sącz, SE Poland
142 I17 **Mut** İçel, S Turkey
77 V10 **Mût** var. Mut. C Egypt
111 V9 **Muta** N Slovenia
202 B15 **Mutalau** N Niue
Mu-tan-chiang see Mudanjiang
84 I13 **Mutanda** North Western, NW Zambia
61 O17 **Mutá, Ponta do** headland E Brazil
85 L17 **Mutare** var. Mutari; prev. Umtali. Manicaland, E Zimbabwe
Mutari see Mutare
56 D8 **Mutatá** Antioquia, NW Colombia
Mutina see Modena
176 Z15 **Muting** Irian Jaya, E Indonesia
85 L16 **Mutoko** prev. Mtoko. Mashonaland East, NE Zimbabwe
83 J20 **Mutomo** Eastern, S Kenya
126 J12 **Mutoray** Evenkiyskiy Avtonomnyy Okrug, C Russian Federation
Mutrah see Maţraḩ
81 M24 **Mutshatsha** Shaba, S Zaire
172 Nn8 **Mutsu** var. Mutu. Aomori, Honshū, N Japan
172 N8 **Mutsu-wan** bay N Japan
110 E6 **Muttenz** Basel-Land, NW Switzerland
193 A26 **Muttonbird Islands** island group SW NZ
Mutu see Mutsu
85 O15 **Mutuáli** Nampula, N Mozambique
84 D13 **Mutumbo** Bié, C Angola
201 Y14 **Mutunte, Mount** var. Mount Buache. ▲ Kosrae, E Micronesia
161 K24 **Mutur** Eastern Province, E Sri Lanka
94 L13 **Muurola** Lappi, NW Finland
168 M14 **Mu Us Shamo** var. Ordos Desert. desert N China
84 B11 **Muxima** Bengo, NW Angola
128 I8 **Muyezerskiy** Respublika Kareliya, NW Russian Federation
83 E20 **Muyinga** NE Burundi
44 K9 **Muy Muy** Matagalpa, C Nicaragua
Muynak see Mŭynoq
152 G6 **Mŭynoq** Rus. Muynak. Qoraqalpoghiston Respublikasi, NW Uzbekistan
81 N22 **Muyumba** Shaba, SE Zaire
155 V5 **Muzaffarābād** Jammu and Kashmir, NE Pakistan
155 S10 **Muzaffargarh** Punjab, E Pakistan
158 J9 **Muzaffarnagar** Uttar Pradesh, N India
159 P13 **Muzaffarpur** Bihār, N India
164 H6 **Muzat He** ≈ W China
85 L15 **Muze** Tete, NW Mozambique
125 Ff8 **Muzhi** Yamalo-Nenetskiy Avtonomnyy Okrug, N Russian Federation
104 H7 **Muzillac** Morbihan, NW France
Muzkol, Khrebet see Muzqŭl, Qatorkŭhi
114 L9 **Mužlja** Hung. Felsőmuzslya; prev. Gornja Mužlja. Serbia, N Yugoslavia
56 F9 **Muzo** Boyacá, C Colombia
85 J15 **Muzoka** Southern, S Zambia
41 Y15 **Muzon, Cape** headland Dall Island, Alaska, USA
42 M6 **Múzquiz** Coahuila de Zaragoza, NE Mexico
153 U13 **Muzqŭl, Qatorkŭhi** Rus. Khrebet Muzkol. ⛰ SE Tajikistan
164 G10 **Muztag** ▲ NW China
164 D8 **Muztagata** ▲ NW China
164 K10 **Muztag Feng** var. Ulugh Muztag. ▲ W China

◆ Country ● Country Capital ◇ Dependent Territory ○ Dependent Territory Capital ◈ Administrative Region ✕ International Airport ▲ Mountain ⛰ Mountain Range Volcano ≈ River ◎ Lake ▣ Reservoir

85 K17 **Mvuma** *prev.* Umvuma. Midlands, C Zimbabwe
84 L13 **Mwanya** Eastern, E Zambia
83 G20 **Mwanza** Mwanza, NW Tanzania
81 N23 **Mwanza** Shaba, SE Zaire
83 F20 **Mwanza** ◈ *region* N Tanzania
84 M13 **Mwase Lundazi** Eastern, E Zambia
99 B17 **Mweelrea** *Ir.* Caoc Maol Réidh. ▲ W Ireland
81 K21 **Mweka** Kasai Occidental, C Zaire
84 K12 **Mwenda** Luapula, N Zambia
81 L22 **Mwene-Ditu** Kasai Oriental, S Zaire
85 L18 **Mwenezi** ∽ S Zimbabwe
81 O20 **Mwenga** Sud Kivu, E Zaire
84 K11 **Mweru, Lake** *var.* Lac Moero. ◎ Zaire/Zambia
84 H13 **Mwinilunga** North Western, NW Zambia
201 V16 **Mwokil Atoll** *var.* Mokil Atoll. *atoll* Caroline Islands, E Micronesia
Myadel' *see* Myadzyel
120 J13 **Myadzyel** *Pol.* Miadzioł Nowy, *Rus.* Myadel'. Minskaya Voblasts', N Belarus
158 C12 **Myājlār** *var.* Miajlar. Rājasthān, NW India
127 O9 **Myakit** Magadanskaya Oblast', E Russian Federation
25 W13 **Myakka River** ∽ Florida, SE USA
128 L14 **Myaksa** Vologodskaya Oblast', NW Russian Federation
191 U8 **Myall Lake** ◎ New South Wales, SE Australia
177 Ff7 **Myanaung** Irrawaddy, SW Myanmar
159 Y14 **Myanmar** *off.* Union of Myanmar, *var.* Burma. ◆ *military dictatorship* SE Asia
177 F9 **Myaungmya** Irrawaddy, SW Myanmar
120 N11 **Myazha** *Rus.* Mezha. Vitsyebskaya Voblasts', NE Belarus
121 O18 **Myerkulavichy** *Rus.* Merkulovichi. Homyel'skaya Voblasts', SE Belarus
121 N14 **Myezhava** *Rus.* Mezhëvo. Vitsyebskaya Voblasts', NE Belarus
177 Ff5 **Myingyan** Mandalay, C Myanmar
177 G5 **Myinmu** Sagaing, C Myanmar
178 Gg2 **Myitkyina** Kachin State, N Myanmar
177 G5 **Myittha** Mandalay, C Myanmar
113 H19 **Myjava** *Hung.* Miava. Západné Slovensko, W Slovakia
Myjeldino *see* Myyëldino
119 U9 **Mykhaylivka** *Rus.* Mikhaylovka. Zaporiz'ka Oblast', SE Ukraine
118 I5 **Mykolayiv** L'vivs'ka Oblast', W Ukraine
119 Q10 **Mykolayiv** *Rus.* Nikolayev. Mykolayivs'ka Oblast', S Ukraine
119 Q10 **Mykolayiv** ✕ Mykolayivs'ka Oblast', S Ukraine
Mykolayiv *see* Mykolayivs'ka Oblast'
119 P9 **Mykolayivka** Odes'ka Oblast', SW Ukraine
119 S13 **Mykolayivka** Respublika Krym, S Ukraine
119 P9 **Mykolayivs'ka Oblast'** *var.* Mykolayiv, *Rus.* Nikolayevskaya Oblast'. ◈ *province* S Ukraine
117 J20 **Mýkonos** Mýkonos, Kykládes, Greece, Aegean Sea
117 K20 **Mýkonos** *var.* Míkonos. *island* Kykládes, Greece, Aegean Sea
129 R7 **Myla** Respublika Komi, NW Russian Federation
Mylae *see* Milazzo
95 M19 **Myllykoski** Kymi, S Finland
159 U14 **Mymensingh** *var.* Maimansingh; *prev.* Nasirābād. Dhaka, N Bangladesh
95 K19 **Mynämäki** Turku-Pori, SW Finland
151 S14 **Mynaral** *Kaz.* Myngaral. Zhambyl, S Kazakhstan
Mynbulak *see* Mingbuloq
Mynbulak, Vpadina *see* Mingbuloq Botighi
Myngaral *see* Mynaral
177 F5 **Myohaung** Arakan State, W Myanmar
169 W13 **Myohyang-sanmaek** ▲▲ C North Korea
171 Jj13 **Myōkō-san** ▲ Honshū, S Japan
85 J15 **Myooye** Central, C Zambia
120 K12 **Myory** *prev.* Miyory. Vitsyebskaya Voblasts', N Belarus
94 J4 **Mýrdalsjökull** *glacier* S Iceland
94 G10 **Myre** Nordland, C Norway
119 S5 **Myrhorod** *Rus.* Mirgorod. Poltavs'ka Oblast', NE Ukraine
117 J15 **Mýrina** *var.* Mírina. Límnos, SE Greece
119 P5 **Myronivka** *Rus.* Mironovka. Kyyivs'ka Oblast', N Ukraine
23 U13 **Myrtle Beach** South Carolina, SE USA
34 F14 **Myrtle Creek** Oregon, NW USA
191 P11 **Myrtleford** Victoria, SE Australia
34 E14 **Myrtle Point** Oregon, NW USA
117 K25 **Mýrtos** Kríti, Greece, E Mediterranean Sea
Myrtoum Mare *see* Mirtóo Pélagos
95 G17 **Myrviken** Jämtland, C Sweden
97 I15 **Mysen** Østfold, S Norway
128 L15 **Myshkin** Yaroslavskaya Oblast', NW Russian Federation
113 K17 **Myślenice** Kraków, S Poland
112 D10 **Myślibórz** Gorzów, W Poland
161 G20 **Mysore** *var.* Maisur. Karnātaka, W India
Mysore *see* Karnātaka
117 F21 **Mystrás** *var.* Mistras. Pelopónnisos, S Greece
129 T12 **Mysy** Komi-Permyatskiy Avtonomnyy Okrug, NW Russian Federation
113 K15 **Myszków** Częstochowa, S Poland
178 Jj14 **My Tho** *var.* Mi Tho. Tiên Giang, S Vietnam
Mytilene *see* Mytilíni
117 L17 **Mytilíni** *var.* Mitilíni; *anc.* Mytilene. Lésvos, E Greece
130 K3 **Mytishchi** Moskovskaya Oblast', W Russian Federation
39 N3 **Myton** Utah, W USA
94 K2 **Mývatn** ◎ C Iceland
129 T11 **Myyëldino** *var.* Myjeldino. Respublika Komi, NW Russian Federation
84 M13 **Mzimba** Northern, NW Malawi
84 M12 **Mzuzu** Northern, N Malawi

N

103 M19 **Naab** ∽ SE Germany
100 G12 **Naaldwijk** Zuid-Holland, W Netherlands
40 G12 **Naalehu** *var.* Nā'ālehu. Hawaii, USA, C Pacific Ocean
95 K19 **Naantali** *Swe.* Nådendal. Turku-Pori, SW Finland
100 J10 **Naarden** Noord-Holland, C Netherlands
111 U4 **Naarn** ∽ N Austria
99 F18 **Naas** *Ir.* An Nás, Nás na Ríogh. C Ireland
94 M9 **Näätämöjoki** *Lapp.* Njávdám. ∽ NE Finland
85 E23 **Nababeep** *var.* Nababiep. Northern Cape, W South Africa
Nababiep *see* Nababeep
Nabadwip *see* Navadwīp
171 H16 **Nabari** Mie, Honshū, SW Japan
Nabatié/Nabatiyet et Tahta *see* Nabatîyé
144 G8 **Nabatîyé** *var.* An Nabatīyah at Taḥtā, Nabatié, Nabatiyet et Tahta. SW Lebanon
Nabatiyet et Tahta *see* Nabatîyé
197 I13 **Nabavatu** Vanua Levu, N Fiji
202 I2 **Nabeina** *island* Tungaru, W Kiribati
131 T4 **Naberezhnyye Chelny** *prev.* Brezhnev. Respublika Tatarstan, W Russian Federation
41 T10 **Nabesna** Alaska, USA
41 T10 **Nabesna River** ∽ Alaska, USA
77 N5 **Nabeul** *var.* Nābul. NE Tunisia
158 I9 **Nābha** Punjab, NW India
176 Ww11 **Nabire** Irian Jaya, E Indonesia
147 O15 **Nabī Shu'ayb, Jabal an** ▲ W Yemen
197 I13 **Nabiti** Vanua Levu, N Fiji
144 F10 **Nablus** *var.* Năbulus, *Heb.* Shekhem; *anc.* Neapolis, *Bibl.* Shechem. N West Bank
197 I13 **Nabouwalu** Vanua Levu, N Fiji
Nābul *see* Nabeul
Năbulus *see* Nablus
197 J13 **Nabuna** Vanua Levu, N Fiji
179 Rr15 **Nabunturan** Mindanao, S Philippines
85 Q14 **Nacala** Nampula, NE Mozambique
44 H8 **Nacaome** Valle, S Honduras
Na Cealla Beaga *see* Killybegs
Na-ch'ii *see* Nagqu
171 Gg17 **Nachikatsuura** *var.* Nachi-Katsuura. Wakayama, Honshū, SE Japan
83 J24 **Nachingwea** Lindi, SE Tanzania
113 F16 **Náchod** Východní Čechy, NE Czech Republic
Na Clocha Liatha *see* Greystones
42 G3 **Naco** Sonora, NW Mexico
27 X8 **Nacogdoches** Texas, SW USA
42 G4 **Nacozari de García** Sonora, NW Mexico
197 H13 **Nacula** *prev.* Nathula. *island* Yasawa Group, NW Fiji
Nada *see* Danxian
79 O14 **Nadawli** NW Ghana
106 I3 **Nadela** Galicia, NW Spain
Nådendal *see* Naantali
150 M7 **Nadezhdinka** *prev.* Nadezhdinskiy. Kustanay, N Kazakhstan
Nadezhdinskiy *see* Nadezhdinka
Nadgan *see* Nadqān, Qalamat
197 H14 **Nadi** *prev.* Nandi. Viti Levu, W Fiji
197 H14 **Nadi** *prev.* Nandi. ✕ Viti Levu, W Fiji
160 D10 **Nadiād** Gujarāt, W India
Ņadikdik *see* Knox Atoll
118 E11 **Nădlac** *Ger.* Nadlak, *Hung.* Nagylak. Arad, W Romania
Nadlak *see* Nădlac
76 H6 **Nador** *prev.* Villa Nador. NE Morocco
147 S9 **Nadqān, Qalamat** *var.* Nadgan. *well* E Saudi Arabia
113 N22 **Nádudvar** Hajdú-Bihar, E Hungary
123 J16 **Nadur** Gozo, N Malta
197 J13 **Naduri** *prev.* Nanduri. Vanua Levu, N Fiji
118 I7 **Nadvirna** *Pol.* Nadwórna, *Rus.* Nadvornaya. Ivano-Frankivs'ka Oblast', W Ukraine
128 J8 **Nadvoitsy** Respublika Kareliya, NW Russian Federation
Nadvornaya/Nadwórna *see* Nadvirna
126 Gg9 **Nadym** Yamalo-Nenetskiy Avtonomnyy Okrug, N Russian Federation
126 Gg9 **Nadym** ∽ C Russian Federation
194 J13 **Nadzab** Morobe, C PNG
79 X13 **Nafada** Bauchi, E Nigeria
110 H8 **Näfels** Glarus, NE Switzerland
117 E18 **Náfpaktos** *var.* Návpaktos. Dytikí Ellás, C Greece
117 F20 **Náfplio** *prev.* Návplion. Pelopónnisos, S Greece
145 U6 **Naft Khāneh** E Iraq
155 N13 **Nāg** Baluchistān, SW Pakistan
179 Q11 **Naga** *off.* Naga City; *prev.* Nueva Caceres. Luzon, N Philippines
Nagaarzê *see* Nagarzê
10 F11 **Nagagami** ∽ Ontario, S Canada
170 E14 **Nagahama** Ehime, Shikoku, SW Japan
171 Hh14 **Nagahama** Shiga, Honshū, SW Japan
159 X12 **Nāga Hills** ▲▲ NE India
171 Ll13 **Nagai** Yamagata, Honshū, C Japan
Na Gaibhlte *see* Galty Mountains
41 N16 **Nagai Island** *island* Shumagin Islands, Alaska, USA
159 X12 **Nāgāland** ◈ *state* NE India
171 Jj13 **Nagano** Nagano, Honshū, S Japan
171 J14 **Nagano** *off.* Nagano-ken. ◈ *prefecture* Honshū, S Japan
171 K13 **Nagaoka** Niigata, Honshū, C Japan
159 W12 **Nagaon** *prev.* Nowgong. Assam, NE India
161 J21 **Nāgappattinam** *var.* Negapatam, Negapattinam. Tamil Nādu, SE India
Nagara Nayok *see* Nakhon Nayok
Nagara Panom *see* Nakhon Phanom
Nagara Pathom *see* Nakhon Pathom
Nagara Sridharmaraj *see* Nakhon Si Thammarat
Nagara Svarga *see* Nakhon Sawan
161 H16 **Nāgārjuna Sāgar** ⊠ E India
44 I10 **Nagarote** León, SW Nicaragua
164 M16 **Nagarzê** *var.* Nagaarzê. Xizang Zizhiqu, W China
170 Bb13 **Nagasaki** Nagasaki, Kyūshū, SW Japan
170 Bb12 **Nagasaki** *off.* Nagasaki-ken. ◈ *prefecture* Kyūshū, SW Japan
170 Bb14 **Naga-shima** *island* SW Japan
170 Dd13 **Naga-shima** *island* SW Japan
Nagashima *see* Kii-Nagashima
170 Dd12 **Nagato** Yamaguchi, Honshū, SW Japan
158 F11 **Nāgaur** Rājasthān, NW India
160 F10 **Nāgda** Madhya Pradesh, C India
100 L8 **Nagele** Flevoland, N Netherlands
161 H24 **Nāgercoil** Tamil Nādu, SE India
159 X12 **Nāginimāra** Nāgāland, NE India
Na Gleannta *see* Glenties
172 P14 **Nago** Okinawa, Okinawa, SW Japan
160 K9 **Nāgod** Madhya Pradesh, C India
161 J26 **Nagoda** Southern Province, S Sri Lanka
103 G22 **Nagold** Baden-Württemberg, SW Germany
Nagorno-Karabakhskaya Avtonomnaya Oblast *see* Nagornyy Karabakh
126 Ll13 **Nagornyy** Respublika Sakha (Yakutiya), NE Russian Federation
143 V12 **Nagornyy Karabakh** *var.* Nagorno-Karabakhskaya Avtonomnaya Oblast , *Arm.* Lerrnayin Gharabakh, *Az.* Dağliq Qarabağ. *former autonomous region* SW Azerbaijan
129 R13 **Nagorsk** Kirovskaya Oblast', NW Russian Federation
171 Hh15 **Nagoya** Aichi, Honshū, SW Japan
160 I12 **Nāgpur** Mahārāshtra, C India
162 K10 **Nagqu** *Chin.* Na-ch'ii; *prev.* Hei-ho. Xizang Zizhiqu, W China
158 J8 **Nāg Tibba Range** ▲▲ N India
47 O8 **Nagua** NE Dominican Republic
113 H25 **Nagyatád** Somogy, SW Hungary
Nagybánya *see* Baia Mare
Nagybecskerek *see* Zrenjanin
Nagydisznód *see* Cisnădie
Nagyenyed *see* Aiud
113 N21 **Nagykálló** Szabolcs-Szatmár-Bereg, E Hungary
113 G25 **Nagykanizsa** *Ger.* Grosskanizsa. Zala, SW Hungary
Nagykároly *see* Carei
113 K22 **Nagykáta** Pest, C Hungary
Nagykikinda *see* Kikinda
113 K23 **Nagykőrös** Pest, C Hungary
Nagy-Küküllő *see* Târnava Mare
Nagylak *see* Nădlac
Nagymihály *see* Michalovce
Nagyrőce *see* Revúca
Nagysomkút *see* Şomcuta Mare
Nagysurány *see* Šurany
Nagyszalonta *see* Salonta
Nagyszeben *see* Sibiu
Nagyszentmiklós *see* Sânnicolau Mare
Nagyszöllös *see* Vynohradiv
Nagyszombat *see* Trnava
Nagytapolcsány *see* Topoľčany
Nagyvárad *see* Oradea
172 Oo15 **Naha** Okinawa, Okinawa, SW Japan
158 J8 **Nāhan** Himāchal Pradesh, NW India
Nahang, Rūd-e *see* Nihing
Nahariya *see* Nahariyya
144 F8 **Nahariyya** *var.* Nahariya. Northern, N Israel
148 L6 **Nahāvand** *var.* Nehavend. Hamadān, W Iran
103 F19 **Nahe** ∽ SW Germany
Na h-Iarmhidhe *see* Westmeath
201 O13 **Nahnalaud** ▲ Pohnpei, E Micronesia
Nahoi, Cape *see* Cumberland, Cape
65 H16 **Nahuel Huapi, Lago** ◎ W Argentina
25 W7 **Nahunta** Georgia, SE USA
42 J6 **Naica** Chihuahua, N Mexico
9 U15 **Naicam** Saskatchewan, S Canada
169 T11 **Naiman Qi** Nei Mongol Zizhiqu, N China
164 M4 **Naimin Bulak** *spring* NW China
11 P6 **Nain** Newfoundland and Labrador, NE Canada
149 P8 **Nā'īn** Eşfahān, C Iran
158 K10 **Naini Tāl** Uttar Pradesh, N India
160 J11 **Nainpur** Madhya Pradesh, C India
197 J14 **Nairai** *island* C Fiji
98 J8 **Nairn** N Scotland, UK
98 I8 **Nairn** *cultural region* NE Scotland, UK
83 I19 **Nairobi** ● (Kenya) Nairobi Area, S Kenya
83 I19 **Nairobi** ✕ Nairobi Area, S Kenya
84 P13 **Nairoto** Cabo Delgado, NE Mozambique
120 G3 **Naissaar** *island* N Estonia
Naissus *see* Niš
197 K13 **Naitaba** *var.* Naitauba; *prev.* Naitamba. *island* Lau Group, E Fiji
Naitamba/Naitauba *see* Naitaba
83 I19 **Naivasha** Rift Valley, SW Kenya
83 H19 **Naivasha, Lake** ◎ SW Kenya
Najaf *see* An Najaf
149 N8 **Najafābād** *var.* Nejafabad. Eşfahān, C Iran
147 N7 **Najd** *var.* Nejd. *cultural region* C Saudi Arabia
107 O4 **Nájera** La Rioja, N Spain
107 P4 **Najerilla** ∽ N Spain
158 J9 **Najībābād** Uttar Pradesh, N India
Najima *see* Fukuoka
169 Y11 **Najin** NE North Korea
145 T9 **Najm al Ḩassūn** C Iraq
147 O13 **Najrān** *var.* Abā as Su'ūd. Najrān, S Saudi Arabia
147 P12 **Najrān** *off.* Minţaqat al Najrān. ◈ *province* S Saudi Arabia
170 Bb12 **Nakadōri-jima** *island* Gotō-rettō, SW Japan
172 Pp3 **Nakagawa** Hokkaidō, NE Japan
171 Kk15 **Naka-gawa** ∽ Honshū, S Japan
40 F9 **Nakalele Pont** *headland* Maui, Hawaii, USA, C Pacific Ocean
170 D12 **Nakama** Fukuoka, Kyūshū, SW Japan
Nakambé *see* White Volta
Nakamti *see* Nek'emtē
170 E15 **Nakamura** Kōchi, Shikoku, SW Japan
195 O12 **Nakanai Mountains** ▲▲ New Britain, E PNG
171 Jj14 **Nakano** Nagano, Honshū, S Japan
170 Ff11 **Nakano-shima** *island* Oki-shotō, SW Japan
170 Ff12 **Nakano-umi** *var.* Naka-umi. ◎ Honshū, SW Japan
171 Mm8 **Nakasato** Aomori, Honshū, C Japan
172 P7 **Nakasatsunai** Hokkaidō, NE Japan
172 Qq7 **Nakashibetsu** Hokkaidō, NE Japan
83 F18 **Nakasongola** C Uganda
172 Pp3 **Nakatonbetsu** Hokkaidō, NE Japan
170 D13 **Nakatsu** *var.* Nakatu. Ōita, Kyūshū, SW Japan
171 I15 **Nakatsugawa** *var.* Nakatugawa. Gifu, Honshū, SW Japan
Nakatu *see* Nakatsu
Nakatugawa *see* Nakatsugawa
Naka-umi *see* Nakano-umi
172 O5 **Nakayama-tōge** *pass* Hokkaidō, NE Japan
Nakdong *see* Naktong-gang
Nakel *see* Nakło nad Notecią
82 J8 **Nakfa** N Eritrea
Nakhichevan' *see* Naxçıvan
127 Nn18 **Nakhodka** Primorskiy Kray, SE Russian Federation
126 H8 **Nakhodka** Yamalo-Nenetskiy Avtonomnyy Okrug, N Russian Federation
Nakhon Navok *see* Nakhon Nayok
178 Hh11 **Nakhon Nayok** *var.* Nagara Nayok, Nakhon Navok. Nakhon Nayok, C Thailand
178 H11 **Nakhon Pathom** *var.* Nagara Pathom, Nakorn Pathom. Nakhon Pathom, W Thailand
178 J9 **Nakhon Phanom** *var.* Nagara Panom. Nakhon Phanom, E Thailand
178 Hh10 **Nakhon Ratchasima** *var.* Khorat, Korat. Nakhon Ratchasima, E Thailand
178 H10 **Nakhon Sawan** *var.* Muang Nakhon Sawan, Nagara Svarga. Nakhon Sawan, W Thailand
178 H15 **Nakhon Si Thammarat** *var.* Nagara Sridharmaraj, Nakhon Sithamnaraj. Nakhon Si Thammarat, SW Thailand
Nakhon Sithamnaraj *see* Nakhon Si Thammarat
145 Y11 **Nakhrash** SE Iraq
8 I9 **Nakina** British Columbia, W Canada
112 H9 **Nakło nad Notecią** *Ger.* Nakel. Bydgoszcz, W Poland
41 P13 **Naknek** Alaska, USA
158 H8 **Nakodar** Punjab, NW India
84 M11 **Nakonde** Northern, NE Zambia
Nakorn Pathom *see* Nakhon Pathom
97 H24 **Nakskov** Storstrøm, SE Denmark
169 Y15 **Naktong-gang** *var.* Nakdong, *Jap.* Rakutō-kō. ∽ C South Korea
83 H18 **Nakuru** Rift Valley, SW Kenya
9 O17 **Nakusp** British Columbia, SW Canada
155 N15 **Nāl** ∽ W Pakistan
168 M7 **Nalayh** Töv, C Mongolia
159 V12 **Nalbāri** Assam, NE India
65 G19 **Nalcayec, Isla** *island* Archipiélago de los Chonos, S Chile
131 N15 **Nal'chik** Kabardino-Balkarskaya Respublika, SW Russian Federation
161 I16 **Nalgonda** Andhra Pradesh, C India
159 S14 **Nalhāti** West Bengal, NE India
159 U14 **Nalitabari** Dhaka, N Bangladesh
161 I17 **Nallamala Hills** ▲▲ E India
142 G12 **Nallıhan** Ankara, NW Turkey
106 K2 **Nalón** ∽ NW Spain
178 Gg3 **Nalong** Kachin State, N Myanmar
77 N8 **Nālūt** NW Libya
176 Uu12 **Nama** Pulau Manawoka, E Indonesia
201 Q16 **Nama** *island* C Micronesia
85 O16 **Namacurra** Zambézia, NE Mozambique
196 F9 **Namai Bay** *bay* Babeldaob, N Palau
31 W2 **Namakan Lake** ◎ Canada/USA
149 O6 **Namak, Daryācheh-ye** *marsh* N Iran
149 T6 **Namak, Kavīr-e** *salt pan* NE Iran
178 H6 **Namaklwe** Shan State, E Myanmar
Namaksār, Kowl-e/Namakzār, Daryācheh-ye *see* Namakzar
154 I5 **Namakzar** *Pash.* Daryācheh-ye Namakzār, Kowl-e Namaksār. *marsh* Afghanistan/Iran
176 W13 **Namalau** Pulau Jursian, E Indonesia
83 I20 **Namanga** Rift Valley, S Kenya
153 S10 **Namangan** Namangan Wiloyati, E Uzbekistan
Namanganskaya Oblast' *see* Namangan Wiloyati
153 R10 **Namangan Wiloyati** *Rus.* Namanganskaya Oblast'. ◈ *province* E Uzbekistan
85 Q14 **Namapa** Nampula, NE Mozambique
85 C21 **Namaqualand** *physical region* S Namibia
83 G18 **Namasagali** C Uganda
195 P10 **Namatanai** New Ireland, NE PNG
85 I14 **Nambala** Central, C Zambia
83 J23 **Nambanje** Lindi, SE Tanzania
176 Ww9 **Namber** Irian Jaya, E Indonesia
85 G16 **Nambiya** Ngamiland, N Botswana
191 V2 **Nambour** Queensland, E Australia
191 V6 **Nambucca Heads** New South Wales, SE Australia
165 N15 **Nam Co** ◎ W China
178 Ii5 **Nâm Cum** Lai Châu, N Vietnam
Namdik *see* Namorik Atoll
178 Jj6 **Nam Đinh** Nam Ha, N Vietnam
175 Tt11 **Namea, Tanjung** *headland* Pulau Seram, SE Indonesia
101 I20 **Namêche** Namur, SE Belgium
32 J4 **Namekagon Lake** ◎ Wisconsin, N USA
196 F10 **Namekakl Passage** *passage* Babeldaob, N Palau
Namen *see* Namur
85 P15 **Nametil** Nampula, NE Mozambique
169 X14 **Nam-gang** ∽ C North Korea
169 Y16 **Nam-gang** ∽ S South Korea
169 Y17 **Namhae-do** *Jap.* Nankai-tō. *island* S South Korea
Namhoi *see* Foshan
85 C19 **Namib Desert** *desert* W Namibia
85 A15 **Namibe** *Port.* Moçâmedes, Mossâmedes. Namibe, SW Angola
85 A15 **Namibe** ◈ *province* SE Angola
85 C18 **Namibia** *off.* Republic of Namibia, *var.* South West Africa, *Afr.* Suidwes-Afrika, *Ger.* Deutsch-Südwestafrika; *prev.* German Southwest Africa, South-West Africa. ◆ *republic* S Africa
67 O17 **Namibia Plain** *undersea feature* S Atlantic Ocean
171 Ll14 **Namie** Fukushima, Honshū, C Japan
171 Mm8 **Namioka** Aomori, Honshū, C Japan
42 I5 **Namiquipa** Chihuahua, N Mexico
165 P15 **Namjagbarwa Feng** ▲ W China
175 Ss11 **Namlea** Pulau Buru, E Indonesia
164 L16 **Namling** Xizang Zizhiqu, W China
Namnetes *see* Nantes
178 Ii8 **Nam Ngum** ∽ C Laos
Namo *see* Namu Atoll
191 R5 **Namoi River** ∽ New South Wales, SE Australia
201 Q17 **Namoluk Atoll** *atoll* Mortlock Islands, C Micronesia
201 O15 **Namonuito Atoll** *atoll* Caroline Islands, C Micronesia
201 T9 **Namorik Atoll** *var.* Namdik. *atoll* Ralik Chain, S Marshall Islands
178 Ii6 **Nam Ou** ∽ N Laos
34 M14 **Nampa** Idaho, NW USA
78 M11 **Nampala** Ségou, W Mali
169 W14 **Namp'o** SW North Korea
85 P15 **Nampula** Nampula, NE Mozambique
85 P15 **Nampula** *off.* Província de Nampula. ◈ *province* NE Mozambique
169 W13 **Namsan-ni** NW North Korea
Namslau *see* Namysłów
95 E15 **Namsos** Nord-Trøndelag, C Norway
95 F14 **Namsskogan** Nord-Trøndelag, C Norway
126 M10 **Namsty** Respublika Sakha (Yakutiya), NE Russian Federation
178 H6 **Nam Teng** ∽ E Myanmar
178 I6 **Nam Tha** ∽ N Laos
178 Gg4 **Namtu** Shan State, E Myanmar
8 J15 **Namu** British Columbia, SW Canada
201 T7 **Namu Atoll** *var.* Namo. *atoll* Ralik Chain, C Marshall Islands
197 K15 **Namuka-i-lau** *island* Lau Group, E Fiji
85 O15 **Namuli, Mont** ▲ NE Mozambique
85 P14 **Namuno** Cabo Delgado, N Mozambique
101 I20 **Namur** *Dut.* Namen. Namur, SE Belgium
101 H21 **Namur** *Dut.* Namen. ◈ *province* S Belgium
85 D17 **Namutoni** Kunene, N Namibia
169 Y16 **Namwŏn** *Jap.* Nangen. S South Korea
178 Mm14 **Namyit Island** *island* S Spratly Islands
113 H14 **Namysłów** *Ger.* Namslau. Opole, SW Poland
178 Hh7 **Nan** *var.* Muang Nan. Nan, NW Thailand
81 G15 **Nana** ∽ W Central African Republic
172 Nn7 **Nanae** Hokkaidō, NE Japan
81 I14 **Nana-Grébizi** ◈ *prefecture* N Central African Republic
8 L17 **Nanaimo** Vancouver Island, British Columbia, SW Canada
40 C9 **Nanakuli** *Haw.* Nānākuli. Oahu, Hawaii, USA, C Pacific Ocean
81 G15 **Nana-Mambéré** ◈ *prefecture* W Central African Republic
167 R13 **Nan'an** Fujian, SE China
191 U2 **Nanango** Queensland, E Australia
171 Ii12 **Nanao** Ishikawa, Honshū, SW Japan
167 Q14 **Nan'ao Dao** *island* S China
171 Ii11 **Nanatsu-shima** *island* SW Japan
58 F8 **Nanay, Río** ∽ NE Peru
166 J8 **Nanbu** Sichuan, C China
169 X7 **Nancha** Heilongjiang, NE China
167 P10 **Nanchang** *var.* Nan-ch'ang, Nanch'ang-hsien. Jiangxi, S China
Nanch'ang-hsien *see* Nanchang
167 P11 **Nancheng** Jiangxi, S China
Nan-ching *see* Nanjing
166 J9 **Nanchong** Sichuan, C China
166 J10 **Nanchuan** Sichuan, C China
105 T5 **Nancy** Meurthe-et-Moselle, NE France
193 A22 **Nancy Sound** *sound* South Island, NZ
158 L9 **Nanda Devi** ▲ NW India
44 J11 **Nandaime** Granada, SW Nicaragua
166 K13 **Nandan** Guangxi Zhuangzu Zizhiqu, S China
161 H14 **Nānded** Mahārāshtra, C India
170 G15 **Nanden** Hyōgo, Awaji-shima, SW Japan
191 S5 **Nandewar Range** ▲▲ New South Wales, SE Australia
Nandi *see* Nadi
166 E13 **Nanding He** ∽ China/Vietnam
Nándorhgy *see* Oţelu Roşu
160 E11 **Nandurbār** Mahārāshtra, W India
Nanduri *see* Naduri
161 I17 **Nandyāl** Andhra Pradesh, E India
167 P11 **Nanfeng** Jiangxi, S China
Nang *see* Nang Xian
81 E15 **Nanga Eboko** Centre, C Cameroon
Nangamesi, Teluk *see* Waingapu, Teluk
155 W4 **Nanga Parbat** ▲ India/Pakistan
174 L8 **Nangapinoh** Borneo, C Indonesia
155 R5 **Nangarhār** ◈ *province* E Afghanistan
174 M8 **Nangaserawai** *var.* Nangah Serawai. Borneo, C Indonesia
174 L9 **Nangatayap** Borneo, C Indonesia
Nangen *see* Namwŏn
105 P5 **Nangis** Seine-et-Marne, N France
169 X13 **Nangnim-sanmaek** ▲▲ C North Korea
167 O4 **Nangong** Hebei, E China
165 Q14 **Nangqên** Qinghai, C China
178 I11 **Nang Rong** Buri Ram, E Thailand
165 O16 **Nang Xian** *var.* Nang. Xizang Zizhiqu, W China
Nan Hai *see* South China Sea
166 L8 **Nan He** ∽ C China
166 F12 **Nanhua** Yunnan, SW China
Naniwa *see* Ōsaka
161 G20 **Nanjangūd** Karnātaka, W India
167 Q8 **Nanjing** *var.* Nan-ching, Nanking; *prev.* Chianning, Chian-ning, Kiang-ning. Jiangsu, E China
Nankai-tō *see* Namhae-do
167 O12 **Nankang** Jiangxi, S China
Nanking *see* Nanjing
170 F15 **Nankoku** Kōchi, Shikoku, SW Japan
167 N13 **Nan Ling** ▲▲ S China
166 L15 **Nanliu Jiang** ∽ S China
201 P13 **Nan Madol** *ruins* Temwen Island, E Micronesia
166 K15 **Nanning** *var.* Nan-ning; *prev.* Yung-ning. Guangxi Zhuangzu Zizhiqu, S China
206 M15 **Nanortalik** S Greenland
Nanouki *see* Aranuka
166 H13 **Nanpan Jiang** ∽ S China
158 M11 **Nānpāra** Uttar Pradesh, N India
167 Q12 **Nanping** *var.* Nan-p'ing; *prev.* Yenping. Fujian, SE China
166 I7 **Nanping** Sichuan, C China
167 R12 **Nanri Dao** *island* SE China
172 Q13 **Nansei-shotō** *Eng.* Ryukyu Islands. *island group* SW Japan
Nansei Syotō Trench *see* Ryukyu Trench
207 T10 **Nansen Basin** *undersea feature* Arctic Ocean
207 T10 **Nansen Cordillera** *var.* Arctic-Mid Oceanic Ridge, Nansen Ridge. *undersea feature* Arctic Ocean
Nansen Ridge *see* Nansen Cordillera
133 T9 **Nan Shan** ▲▲ C China
179 Nn14 **Nanshan Island** *island* E Spratly Islands
Nansha Qundao *see* Spratly Islands
10 K3 **Nantais, Lac** ◎ Québec, NE Canada
105 N5 **Nanterre** Hauts-de-Seine, N France
104 I8 **Nantes** *Bret.* Naoned; *anc.* Condivincum, Namnetes. Loire-Atlantique, NW France
12 G17 **Nanticoke** Ontario, S Canada
20 H13 **Nanticoke** Pennsylvania, NE USA
23 Y4 **Nanticoke River** ∽ Delaware/Maryland, NE USA
9 Q17 **Nanton** Alberta, SW Canada
167 S8 **Nantong** Jiangsu, E China
167 S13 **Nant'ou** W Taiwan
105 S10 **Nantua** Ain, E France
21 Q13 **Nantucket** Nantucket Island, Massachusetts, NE USA
21 Q13 **Nantucket Island** *island* Massachusetts, NE USA
21 Q13 **Nantucket Sound** *sound* Massachusetts, NE USA
84 P13 **Nantulo** Cabo Delgado, N Mozambique
201 O12 **Nanuh** Pohnpei, E Micronesia
197 K13 **Nanuku Passage** *channel* NE Fiji
202 D6 **Nanumaga** *var.* Nanumanga. *atoll* NW Tuvalu
Nanumanga *see* Nanumaga
202 D5 **Nanumea Atoll** *atoll* NW Tuvalu
61 O19 **Nanuque** Minas Gerais, SE Brazil
175 Ss4 **Nanusa, Kepulauan** *island group* N Indonesia
169 U4 **Nanweng He** ∽ NE China
166 I10 **Nanxi** Sichuan, C China
167 N10 **Nanxian** *var.* Nan Xian. Hunan, S China
167 N7 **Nanyang** *var.* Nan-yang. Henan, C China
167 P6 **Nanyang Hu** ◎ E China
171 L13 **Nan'yō** Yamagata, Honshū, C Japan
83 I18 **Nanyuki** Central, C Kenya
166 M8 **Nanzhang** Hubei, C China
107 T11 **Nao, Cabo de La** *headland* E Spain
10 M9 **Naococane, Lac** ◎ Québec, E Canada
159 S14 **Naogaon** Rajshahi, NW Bangladesh
Naokot *see* Naukot
197 C12 **Naone** Maewo, C Vanuatu
Naoned *see* Nantes
117 E14 **Náousa** Kentrikí Makedonía, N Greece
37 N8 **Napa** California, W USA
41 O11 **Napaimiut** Alaska, USA
41 N12 **Napakiak** Alaska, USA
126 H7 **Napalkovo** Yamalo-Nenetskiy Avtonomnyy Okrug, N Russian Federation
10 I16 **Napanee** Ontario, SE Canada
176 Ww11 **Napanwainami** Irian Jaya, E Indonesia
176 W11 **Napan-Yaur** Irian Jaya, E Indonesia
41 N12 **Napaskiak** Alaska, USA
178 Jj5 **Na Phac** Cao Băng, N Vietnam
176 Ww9 **Napido** Irian Jaya, E Indonesia
192 O11 **Napier** Hawke's Bay, North Island, NZ
205 X3 **Napier Mountains** ▲▲ Antarctica
13 O13 **Napierville** Québec, SE Canada
25 W15 **Naples** Florida, SE USA
27 W5 **Naples** Texas, SW USA
Naples *see* Napoli
166 I14 **Napo** Guangxi Zhuangzu Zizhiqu, S China
58 D6 **Napo** ◈ *province* NE Ecuador
31 O6 **Napoleon** North Dakota, N USA
33 R11 **Napoleon** Ohio, N USA
Napoléon-Vendée *see* la Roche-sur-Yon
24 J9 **Napoleonville** Louisiana, S USA
109 K17 **Napoli** *Eng.* Naples, *Ger.* Neapel; *anc.* Neapolis. Campania, S Italy
109 J18 **Napoli, Golfo di** *gulf* S Italy
59 F7 **Napo, Río** ∽ Ecuador/Peru
203 W9 **Napuka** *island* Îles Tuamotu, C French Polynesia
148 J3 **Naqadeh** Āzarbāyjān-e Bākhtarī, NW Iran
145 U6 **Naqnah** E Iraq
Nar *see* Nera
171 H15 **Nara** Nara, Honshū, SW Japan
78 L11 **Nara** Koulikoro, W Mali
171 Gg16 **Nara** *off.* Nara-ken. ◈ *prefecture* Honshū, SW Japan
155 R14 **Nāra Canal** *irrigation canal* S Pakistan
190 K11 **Naracoorte** South Australia
191 P8 **Naradhan** New South Wales, SE Australia
Naradhivas *see* Narathiwat
58 B8 **Naranjal** Guayas, W Ecuador
59 Q19 **Naranjos** Santa Cruz, E Bolivia
43 Q12 **Naranjos** Veracruz-Llave, E Mexico
165 Q6 **Naran Sebstein Bulag** *spring* NW China
149 X12 **Narānū** Sīstān va Balūchestān, SE Iran
170 Bb12 **Narao** Nagasaki, Nakadōri-jima, SW Japan

◆ Country
● Country Capital
◇ Dependent Territory
○ Dependent Territory Capital
◈ Administrative Region
✕ International Airport
▲ Mountain
▲▲ Mountain Range
Volcano
∽ River
◎ Lake
⊠ Reservoir

161 J16 **Narasaraopet** Andhra Pradesh, E India
164 J5 **Narat** Xinjiang Uygur Zizhiqu, W China
178 Hh17 **Narathiwat** var. Naradhivas. Narathiwat, SW Thailand
39 V10 **Nara Visa** New Mexico, SW USA
Nārāyāni see Gandak
Narbada see Narmada
Narbo Martius see Narbonne
105 P16 **Narbonne** anc. Narbo Martius. Aude, S France
Narborough Island see Fernandina, Isla
106 J2 **Narcea** ~ NW Spain
158 J9 **Narendranagar** Uttar Pradesh, N India
Nares Abyssal Plain see Nares Plain
66 G11 **Nares Plain** var. Nares Abyssal Plain. undersea feature NW Atlantic Ocean
207 P10 **Nares Strait** Dan. Nares Stræde. strait Canada/Greenland
Nares Stræde see Nares Strait
112 O9 **Narew** ~ E Poland
Narew see Naraw
161 F17 **Nargund** Karnātaka, W India
85 D20 **Narib** Hardap, S Namibia
Narikrik see Knox Atoll
56 B13 **Nariño** off. Departamento de Nariño. ❖ province SW Colombia
171 Kk17 **Narita** Chiba, Honshū, S Japan
171 Kk17 **Narita** ✈ (Tōkyō) Chiba, Honshū, S Japan
Narıya see An Nu'ayrīyah
158 J8 **Narkanda** Himāchal Pradesh, NW India
94 L13 **Narkaus** Lappi, NW Finland
160 E11 **Narmada** var. Narbada. ~ C India
158 H11 **Narnaul** var. Nārnaul. Haryāna, N India
109 I14 **Narni** Umbria, C Italy
109 J24 **Naro** Sicilia, Italy, C Mediterranean Sea
Narodichi see Narodychi
129 V7 **Narodnaya, Gora** ▲ NW Russian Federation
119 N3 **Narodychi** Rus. Narodichi. Zhytomyrs'ka Oblast', N Ukraine
130 J4 **Naro-Fominsk** Moskovskaya Oblast', W Russian Federation
83 H19 **Narok** Rift Valley, SW Kenya
106 H2 **Narón** Galicia, NW Spain
191 S11 **Narooma** New South Wales, SE Australia
Narova see Narva
Narovlya see Narowlya
155 W8 **Nārowāl** Punjab, E Pakistan
121 N20 **Narowlya** Rus. Narovlya. Homyel'skaya Voblasts', SE Belarus
95 J17 **Närpes** Fin. Närpiö. Vaasa, W Finland
Närpiö see Närpes
191 S5 **Narrabri** New South Wales, SE Australia
191 P9 **Narrandera** New South Wales, SE Australia
191 Q4 **Narran Lake** ◎ New South Wales, SE Australia
191 Q4 **Narran River** ~ New South Wales/Queensland, SE Australia
188 J13 **Narrogin** Western Australia
191 Q7 **Narromine** New South Wales, SE Australia
23 R6 **Narrows** Virginia, NE USA
206 M15 **Narsarsuaq** ✈ S Greenland
160 I10 **Narsimhapur** Madhya Pradesh, C India
Narsingdi see Narsinghdi
159 U15 **Narsinghdi** var. Narsingdi. Dhaka, C Bangladesh
160 H9 **Narsinghgarh** Madhya Pradesh, C India
169 Q11 **Nart** Nei Mongol Zizhiqu, N China
Nartës, Gjol i/Nartës, Laguna e see Nartës, Liqeni i
115 J22 **Nartës, Liqeni i** var. Gjol i Nartës, Laguna e Nartës. ◎ SW Albania
117 F17 **Narthāki** ▲ C Greece
131 O15 **Nartkala** Kabardino-Balkarskaya Respublika, SW Russian Federation
170 Ff15 **Naruto** Tokushima, Shikoku, SW Japan
120 K3 **Narva** Ida-Virumaa, NE Estonia
120 K4 **Narva** prev. Narova. ~ Estonia/Russian Federation
120 J3 **Narva Bay** Est. Narva Laht, Ger. Narwa-Bucht, Rus. Narvskiy Zaliv. bay Estonia/Russian Federation
Narva Laht see Narva Bay
128 F13 **Narva Reservoir** Est. Narva Veehoidla, Rus. Narvskoye Vodokhranilishche. ⊡ Estonia/Russian Federation
Narva Veehoidla see Narva Reservoir
94 H10 **Narvik** Nordland, C Norway
Narvskiy Zaliv see Narva Bay
Narvskoye Vodokhranilishche see Narva Reservoir
Narwa-Bucht see Narva Bay
158 I9 **Narwāna** Haryāna, NW India
129 R4 **Nar'yan-Mar** prev. Beloshchel'ye, Dzerzhinskiy. Nenetskiy Avtonomnyy Okrug, NW Russian Federation
126 H12 **Narym** Tomskaya Oblast', C Russian Federation
151 Y10 **Narymskiy Khrebet** Kaz. Naryn Zhotasy. ▲ E Kazakhstan
153 W9 **Naryn** Narynskaya Oblast', C Kyrgyzstan
153 U8 **Naryn** ~ Kyrgyzstan/Uzbekistan
151 W16 **Narynkol** Kaz. Narynqol. Almaty, SE Kazakhstan
Naryn Oblasty see Narynskaya Oblast'
Narynqol see Narynkol
153 V9 **Narynskaya Oblast'** Kir. Naryn Oblasty. ❖ province C Kyrgyzstan
Naryn Zhotasy see Narymskiy Khrebet
130 J6 **Naryshkino** Orlovskaya Oblast', W Russian Federation
97 L14 **Nås** Kopparberg, C Sweden
94 G13 **Nasa** ▲ C Norway
95 H16 **Nasåker** Västernorrland, C Sweden
197 J14 **Nasau** Koro, C Fiji
118 I9 **Năsăud** Ger. Nussdorf, Hung. Naszód. Bistrița-Năsăud, N Romania
105 P13 **Nasbinals** Lozère, S France
Na Sceirí see Skerries
Nase see Naze
193 E22 **Naseby** Otago, South Island, NZ
149 R10 **Nāșerīyeh** Kermān, C Iran
27 X5 **Nash** Texas, SW USA
160 E13 **Nāshik** prev. Nāsik. Mahārāshtra, W India
58 E7 **Nashiño, Río** ~ Ecuador/Peru
31 W12 **Nashua** Iowa, C USA
35 W7 **Nashua** Montana, NW USA
21 O10 **Nashua** New Hampshire, NE USA
29 S13 **Nashville** Arkansas, C USA
25 U7 **Nashville** Georgia, SE USA
32 L16 **Nashville** Illinois, N USA
33 O14 **Nashville** Indiana, N USA
23 V9 **Nashville** North Carolina, SE USA
22 J8 **Nashville** state capital Tennessee, S USA
22 J9 **Nashville** ✈ Tennessee, S USA
66 H10 **Nashville Seamount** undersea feature NW Atlantic Ocean
114 H9 **Našice** Požega-Slavonija, NE Croatia
112 M11 **Nasielsk** Ciechanów, C Poland
95 K18 **Näsijärvi** ◎ SW Finland
Nāsik see Nāshik
82 G13 **Nasir** Upper Nile, SE Sudan
155 Q12 **Nasīrābād** Baluchistān, SW Pakistan
154 J15 **Nasīrābād** Baluchistān, SW Pakistan
Nasīrābād see Mymensingh
Nasir, Buhayrat/Nâșir, Buḥeiret see Nasser, Lake
Nāsiri see Ahvāz
Nasiriya see An Nāṣirīyah
Nás na Ríogh see Naas
109 L23 **Naso** Sicilia, Italy, C Mediterranean Sea
Nasratabad see Zābol
8 J11 **Nass** ~ British Columbia, SW Canada
79 V15 **Nassarawa** Plateau, C Nigeria
46 H2 **Nassau** ● (Bahamas) New Providence, N Bahamas
46 H2 **Nassau** ✈ New Providence, C Bahamas
202 J13 **Nassau** island N Cook Islands
25 W8 **Nassau Sound** sound Florida, SE USA
110 L7 **Nassereith** Tirol, W Austria
97 L19 **Nässjö** Jönköping, S Sweden
101 K22 **Nassogne** Luxembourg, SE Belgium
10 J6 **Nastapoka Islands** island group Northwest Territories, C Canada
95 M19 **Nastola** Häme, S Finland
171 L14 **Nasu-dake** ▲ Honshū, S Japan
179 P11 **Nasugbu** Luzon, N Philippines
96 N11 **Näsviken** Gävleborg, C Sweden
Naszód see Năsăud
85 I17 **Nata** Central, NE Botswana
56 E11 **Natagaima** Tolima, C Colombia
61 Q14 **Natal** Rio Grande do Norte, E Brazil
173 Ff8 **Natal** Sumatera, N Indonesia
Natal see KwaZulu/Natal
181 L10 **Natal Basin** var. Mozambique Basin. undersea feature W Indian Ocean
27 R12 **Natalia** Texas, SW USA
69 W15 **Natal Valley** undersea feature SW Indian Ocean
Natanya see Netanya
149 O7 **Naṭanz** Eşfahān, C Iran
11 Q11 **Natashquan** Québec, E Canada
11 Q10 **Natashquan** ~ Newfoundland and Labrador/Québec, E Canada
24 J7 **Natchez** Mississippi, S USA
24 G6 **Natchitoches** Louisiana, S USA
110 E10 **Naters** Valais, S Switzerland
Nathanya see Netanya
94 O3 **Nathorst Land** physical region W Svalbard
Nathula see Nacula
194 J15 **National Capital District** ❖ province S PNG
37 U17 **National City** California, W USA
192 M10 **National Park** Manawatu-Wanganui, North Island, NZ
79 R14 **Natitingou** NW Benin
42 B5 **Natividad, Isla** island W Mexico
Natore see Nator
171 M13 **Natori** Miyagi, Honshū, C Japan
20 C14 **Natrona Heights** Pennsylvania, NE USA
83 H20 **Natron, Lake** ◎ Kenya/Tanzania
177 Ff7 **Nattalin** Pegu, C Myanmar
94 J12 **Nattavaara** Norrbotten, N Sweden
111 S3 **Natternbach** Oberösterreich, N Austria
97 M22 **Nättraby** Blekinge, S Sweden
174 K4 **Natuna Besar, Pulau** island Kepulauan Natuna, W Indonesia
Natuna Islands see Natuna, Kepulauan
174 Jj5 **Natuna, Kepulauan** var. Natuna Islands. island group W Indonesia
174 J6 **Natuna, Laut** sea W Indonesia
Natur see Nator
23 N6 **Natural Bridge** tourist site Kentucky, C USA
181 V11 **Naturaliste Fracture Zone** tectonic feature E Indian Ocean
182 J10 **Naturaliste Plateau** undersea feature E Indian Ocean
Nau see Nov
105 O14 **Naucelle** Aveyron, S France
85 D20 **Nauchas** Hardap, C Namibia
110 K9 **Nauders** Tirol, W Austria
Naugard see Nowogard
120 F12 **Naujamiestis** Panevėžys, C Lithuania
120 E10 **Naujoji Akmenė** Akmenė, NW Lithuania
155 R16 **Naukot** var. Naokot. Sind, SE Pakistan
103 L16 **Naumburg** var. Naumburg an der Saale. Sachsen-Anhalt, C Germany
Naumburg am Queis see Nowogrodziec
Naumburg an der Saale see Naumburg
203 W15 **Naunau** ancient monument Easter Island, Chile, E Pacific Ocean
144 G10 **Nā'ūr** 'Ammān, W Jordan
201 Q8 **Nauru** off. Republic of Nauru; prev. Pleasant Island. ◆ republic W Pacific Ocean
183 P5 **Nauru** island W Pacific Ocean
201 Q9 **Nauru International** ✈ S Nauru
Nausari see Navsāri
21 Q12 **Nauset Beach** beach Massachusetts, NE USA
Naushahra see Nowshera
155 P14 **Naushahro Fīroz** Sind, SE Pakistan
Naushara see Nowshera
197 I14 **Nausori** Viti Levu, W Fiji
58 F9 **Nauta** Loreto, N Peru
159 O12 **Nautanwa** Uttar Pradesh, N India
43 R13 **Nautla** Veracruz-Llave, E Mexico
Nauzad see Now Zād
43 N6 **Nava** Coahuila de Zaragoza, NE Mexico
Navabad see Navobod
106 L6 **Nava del Rey** Castilla-León, N Spain
159 S15 **Navadwīp** prev. Nabadwip. West Bengal, NE India
197 J14 **Navaga** Koro, W Fiji
106 M9 **Navahermosa** Castilla-La Mancha, C Spain
121 I16 **Navahrudak** Pol. Nowogródek, Rus. Novogrudok. Hrodzyenskaya Voblasts', W Belarus
121 I16 **Navahrudskaye Wzvyshsha** ▲ W Belarus
38 M8 **Navajo Mount** ▲ Utah, W USA
39 Q9 **Navajo Reservoir** ⊡ New Mexico, SW USA
179 Qq12 **Naval** Biliran Island, C Philippines
106 K9 **Navalmoral de la Mata** Extremadura, W Spain
106 K10 **Navalvillar de Pelea** Extremadura, W Spain
99 F17 **Navan** Ir. An Uaimh. E Ireland
Navanagar see Jāmnagar
120 L12 **Navapolatsk** Rus. Novopolotsk. Vitsyebskaya Voblasts', N Belarus
155 P6 **Nāvar, Dasht-e** Pash. Dasht-i-Nawar. desert C Afghanistan
127 Q5 **Navarin, Mys** headland NE Russian Federation
65 I25 **Navarino, Isla** island S Chile
107 Q4 **Navarra** Eng./Fr. Navarre. ❖ autonomous community N Spain
Navarre see Navarra
107 P4 **Navarrete** La Rioja, N Spain
63 C20 **Navarro** Buenos Aires, E Argentina
107 O12 **Navas de San Juan** Andalucía, S Spain
27 V10 **Navasota** Texas, SW USA
27 U9 **Navasota River** ~ Texas, SW USA
46 I9 **Navassa Island** ◇ US unincorporated territory C West Indies
121 L19 **Navasyolki** Rus. Novosëlki. Homyel'skaya Voblasts', SE Belarus
121 H17 **Navasyel'nya** Pol. Nowojelnia, Rus. Novoyel'nya. Hrodzyenskaya Voblasts', W Belarus
176 Yy11 **Naver** Irian Jaya, E Indonesia
120 H5 **Navesti** ~ C Estonia
106 J2 **Navia** Asturias, N Spain
106 J2 **Navia** ~ NW Spain
61 I21 **Naviraí** Mato Grosso do Sul, SW Brazil
197 G14 **Naviti** island Yasawa Group, NW Fiji
130 I6 **Navlya** Bryanskaya Oblast', W Russian Federation
197 J13 **Navoalevu** Vanua Levu, N Fiji
153 R12 **Navobod** Rus. Navabad, Novabad. C Tajikistan
153 P13 **Navobod** Rus. Navabad. W Tajikistan
Navoi see Nawoiy
Navoiyskaya Oblast' see Nawoiy Wiloyati
42 G7 **Navojoa** Sonora, NW Mexico
42 H9 **Navolat** var. Navolato. Sinaloa, C Mexico
Navolato see Navolat
197 C12 **Navonda** Ambae, C Vanuatu
Návpaktos see Náfpaktos
Návplion see Náfplio
79 P14 **Navrongo** N Ghana
160 D12 **Navsāri** var. Nausari. Gujarāt, W India
197 I15 **Navua** Viti Levu, W Fiji
144 H8 **Nawá** Dar'ā, S Syria
Nawabashah see Nawābshāh
159 S14 **Nawabganj** Rajshahi, NW Bangladesh
159 S14 **Nawābganj** Uttar Pradesh, N India
155 Q15 **Nawābshāh** var. Nawabashah. Sind, S Pakistan
159 P14 **Nawāda** Bihār, N India
158 H11 **Nawalgarh** Rājasthān, N India
Nawāl, Sabkhat an see Noual, Sebkhet en
Nawar, Dasht-i- see Nāvar, Dasht-e
178 Gg4 **Nawnghkio** var. Nawngkio. Shan State, C Myanmar
Nawngkio see Nawnghkio
152 M11 **Nawoiy** Rus. Navoi. Nawoiy Wiloyati, C Uzbekistan
152 K8 **Nawoiy Wiloyati** Rus. Navoiyskaya Oblast'. ❖ province N Uzbekistan
143 U13 **Naxçıvan** Rus. Nakhichevan'. SW Azerbaijan
166 I10 **Naxi** Sichuan, C China
117 K21 **Náxos** var. Naxos. Náxos, Kykládes, Greece, Aegean Sea
117 K21 **Náxos** island Kykládes, Greece, Aegean Sea
42 J11 **Nayarit** ❖ state C Mexico
197 K14 **Nayau** island Lau Group, E Fiji
149 S8 **Nāy Band** Khorāsān, E Iran
172 Pp4 **Nayoro** Hokkaidō, NE Japan
106 F9 **Nazaré** var. Nazare. Leiria, C Portugal
26 M4 **Nazareth** Texas, SW USA
Nazareth see Nazerat
181 O8 **Nazareth Bank** undersea feature W Indian Ocean
126 Hh14 **Nazarovo** Krasnoyarskiy Kray, S Russian Federation
42 K9 **Nazas** Durango, C Mexico
59 F16 **Nazca** Ica, S Peru
171 F12 **Nazca Plate** tectonic feature
200 Oo11 **Nazca Ridge** undersea feature E Pacific Ocean
172 R13 **Naze** var. Nase. Kagoshima, Amami-ōshima, SW Japan
144 G9 **Nazerat** Ar. En Nazira, Eng. Nazareth. Northern, N Israel
143 R14 **Nazik Gölü** ◎ E Turkey
142 C15 **Nazilli** Aydın, SW Turkey
143 P14 **Nazimiye** Tunceli, E Turkey
126 Gg11 **Nazino** Tomskaya Oblast', C Russian Federation
Nazinon see Red Volta
8 L15 **Nazko** British Columbia, SW Canada
131 O16 **Nazran'** Ingushskaya Respublika, SW Russian Federation
82 J13 **Nazrēt** var. Adama, Hadama. C Ethiopia
Nazwāh see Nizwā
125 Ff13 **Nazyvayevsk** Omskaya Oblast', C Russian Federation
84 J13 **Nchanga** Copperbelt, C Zambia
84 J11 **Nchelenge** Luapula, N Zambia
Ncheu see Ntcheu
Ndaghamcha, Sebkra de see Te-n-Dghâmcha, Sebkhet
83 G21 **Ndala** Tabora, C Tanzania
84 B11 **N'Dalatando** Port. Salazar, Vila Salazar. Cuanza Norte, NW Angola
79 S14 **Ndali** C Benin
83 E18 **Ndeke** SW Uganda
80 J13 **Ndélé** Bamingui-Bangoran, N Central African Republic
81 E19 **Ndendé** Ngounié, S Gabon
81 E20 **Ndindi** Nyanga, S Gabon
80 G11 **Ndjamena** var. N'Djamena; prev. Fort-Lamy. ● (Chad) Chari-Baguirmi, W Chad
80 G11 **Ndjamena** ✈ Chari-Baguirmi, W Chad
81 D18 **Ndjolé** Moyen-Ogooué, W Gabon
84 J13 **Ndola** Copperbelt, C Zambia
Ndrhamcha, Sebkha de see Te-n-Dghâmcha, Sebkhet
81 L15 **Ndu** Haut-Zaïre, N Zaire
83 H21 **Nduguti** Singida, C Tanzania
195 X16 **Nduindui** Guadalcanal, C Solomon Islands
Nduke see Kolombangara
117 F16 **Néa Anchíalos** var. Nea Anhialos, Néa Ankhíalos. Thessalía, C Greece
Nea Anhialos/Néa Ankhíalos see Néa Anchíalos
117 H18 **Néa Artáki** Évvoia, C Greece
99 F15 **Neagh, Lough** ◎ E Northern Ireland, UK
34 F7 **Neah Bay** Washington, NW USA
117 J22 **Néa Kaméni** island Kykládes, Greece, Aegean Sea
189 O8 **Neale, Lake** ◎ Northern Territory, C Australia
190 G2 **Neales River** seasonal river South Australia
117 G14 **Néa Moudanía** var. Néa Moudhaniá. Kentrikí Makedonía, N Greece
Néa Moudhaniá see Néa Moudanía
118 K10 **Neamț** ❖ county NE Romania
Neapel see Napoli
117 D14 **Neápoli** prev. Neápolis. Dytikí Makedonía, N Greece
117 K25 **Neápoli** Kríti, Greece, E Mediterranean Sea
117 G22 **Neápoli** Pelopónnisos, S Greece
Neapolis see Napoli, Italy
Neapolis see Nablus, West Bank
Neapolis see Neápoli, Greece
40 D16 **Near Islands** island group Aleutian Islands, Alaska, USA
99 J21 **Neath** S Wales, UK
116 H13 **Néa Zíchni** var. Néa Zíkhni; prev. Néa Zíkhna. Kentrikí Makedonía, NE Greece
Néa Zíkhna/Néa Zíkhni see Néa Zíchni
44 C5 **Nebaj** Quiché, W Guatemala
79 P13 **Nebbou** S Burkina
152 B11 **Nebitdag** Balkanskiy Velayat, W Turkmenistan
56 M13 **Neblina, Pico da** ▲ NW Brazil
128 I13 **Nebolchi** Novgorodskaya Oblast', W Russian Federation
38 L4 **Nebo, Mount** ▲ Utah, W USA
30 L14 **Nebraska** off. State of Nebraska; also known as Blackwater State, Cornhusker State, Tree Planters State. ❖ state C USA
31 S16 **Nebraska City** Nebraska, C USA
109 K23 **Nebrodi, Monti** var. Monti Caronie. ▲ Sicilia, Italy, C Mediterranean Sea
8 L14 **Nechako** ~ British Columbia, SW Canada
31 Q2 **Neche** North Dakota, N USA
27 V8 **Neches** Texas, SW USA
27 W8 **Neches River** ~ Texas, SW USA
103 H20 **Neckar** ~ SW Germany
103 H20 **Neckarsulm** Baden-Württemberg, SW Germany
199 K5 **Necker Island** island C British Virgin Islands
183 U3 **Necker Ridge** undersea feature N Pacific Ocean
63 D23 **Necochea** Buenos Aires, E Argentina
106 H2 **Neda** Galicia, NW Spain
117 E20 **Nédas** ~ S Greece
27 Y11 **Nederland** Texas, SW USA
Nederland see Netherlands
100 K12 **Neder Rijn** Eng. Lower Rhine. ~ C Netherlands
101 L16 **Nederweert** Limburg, SE Netherlands
97 G16 **Nedre Tokke** ◎ S Norway
Nedrigaylov see Nedryhayliv
119 S3 **Nedryhayliv** Rus. Nedrigaylov. Sums'ka Oblast', NE Ukraine
100 O11 **Neede** Gelderland, E Netherlands
35 T13 **Needle Mountain** ▲ Wyoming, C USA
37 Y14 **Needles** California, W USA
99 M24 **Needles, The** rocks Isle of Wight, S England, UK
64 O7 **Ñeembucú** off. Departamento de Ñeembucú. ❖ department SW Paraguay
32 M7 **Neenah** Wisconsin, N USA
9 W16 **Neepawa** Manitoba, S Canada
101 K16 **Neerpelt** Limburg, NE Belgium
76 M6 **Nefta** ✈ W Tunisia
130 L15 **Neftegorsk** Krasnodarskiy Kray, SW Russian Federation
131 U3 **Neftekamsk** Respublika Bashkortostan, W Russian Federation
131 O14 **Neftekumsk** Stavropol'skiy Kray, SW Russian Federation
125 G11 **Nefteyugansk** Khanty-Mansiyskiy Avtonomnyy Okrug, C Russian Federation
Neftezavodsk see Seydi
84 C10 **Negage** var. N'Gage. Uíge, NW Angola
Negapatam/Negapattinam see Nāgappattinam
175 N16 **Negara** Bali, Indonesia
175 N10 **Negara** Borneo, C Indonesia
Negara Brunei Darussalam see Brunei
33 N4 **Negaunee** Michigan, N USA
83 J15 **Negēlē** var. Negelli, It. Neghelli. S Ethiopia
Negelli see Negēlē
Negeri Pahang Darul Makmur see Pahang
Negeri Selangor Darul Ehsan see Selangor
174 H5 **Negeri Sembilan** var. Negri Sembilan. ❖ state Peninsular Malaysia
94 P3 **Negerpynten** headland S Svalbard
Negev see HaNegev
Neghelli see Negēlē
118 I12 **Negoiu** var. Negoiul. ▲ S Romania
Negoiul see Negoiu
84 P13 **Negomane** var. Negomano. Cabo Delgado, N Mozambique
Negomano see Negomane
161 J25 **Negombo** Western Province, SW Sri Lanka
Negoreloye see Nyeharelaye
114 P12 **Negotin** Serbia, E Yugoslavia
115 P19 **Negotino** C FYR Macedonia
106 G3 **Negreira** Galicia, NW Spain
118 L10 **Negrești** Vaslui, E Romania
Negrești see Negrești-Oaș
118 H8 **Negrești-Oaș** Hung. Avasfelsőfalu; prev. Negrești. Satu Mare, NE Romania
46 H12 **Negril** W Jamaica
Negri Sembilan see Negeri Sembilan
65 K15 **Negro, Río** ~ E Argentina
64 N7 **Negro, Río** ~ NE Argentina
59 N17 **Negro, Río** ~ E Bolivia
64 O5 **Negro, Río** ~ C Paraguay
50 F6 **Negro, Río** ~ N South America
63 E18 **Negro, Río** ~ Brazil/Uruguay
Negro, Río see Sico Tinto, Río, Honduras
Negro, Río see Chixoy, Río, Guatemala/Mexico
179 Q14 **Negros** island C Philippines
118 M15 **Negru Vodă** Constanța, SE Romania
11 P13 **Neguac** New Brunswick, SE Canada
12 B7 **Negwazu, Lake** ◎ Ontario, S Canada
Négyfalu see Săcele
34 F10 **Nehalem** Oregon, NW USA
34 F10 **Nehalem River** ~ Oregon, NW USA
Nehavend see Nahāvand
149 V9 **Nehbandān** Khorāsān, E Iran
169 V6 **Nehe** Heilongjiang, NE China
200 Ss12 **Neiafu** 'Uta Vava'u, N Tonga
47 N9 **Neiba** var. Neyba. SW Dominican Republic
Néid, Carn Uí see Mizen Head
94 M9 **Neiden** Finnmark, N Norway
Neidín see Kenmare
Néifinn see Nephin
105 S10 **Neige, Crêt de la** ▲ E France
181 O16 **Neiges, Piton des** ▲ C Réunion
13 R9 **Neiges, Rivière des** ~ Québec, SE Canada
166 I10 **Neijiang** Sichuan, C China
32 K6 **Neillsville** Wisconsin, N USA
Nei Monggol Zizhiqu/Nei Mongol see Nei Mongol Zizhiqu
169 Q10 **Nei Mongol Gaoyuan** plateau NE China
169 O12 **Nei Mongol Zizhiqu** var. Nei Mongol, Eng. Inner Mongolia, Inner Mongolian Autonomous Region; prev. Nei Monggol Zizhiqu. ❖ autonomous region N China
167 O4 **Neiqiu** Hebei, E China
Neiriz see Neyrīz
103 Q16 **Neisse** Cz. Lužická Nisa, Ger. Lausitzer Neisse, Pol. Nisa, Nysa Łużycka. ~ C Europe
Neisse see Nysa
56 E11 **Neiva** Huila, S Colombia
166 M7 **Neixiang** Henan, C China
Nejafabad see Najafābād
9 V9 **Nejanilini Lake** ◎ Manitoba, C Canada
Nejd see Najd
82 I13 **Nek'emtē** var. Lakemti, Nakamti. W Ethiopia
130 M9 **Nekhayevskiy** Volgogradskaya Oblast', SW Russian Federation
32 K7 **Nekoosa** Wisconsin, N USA
97 M24 **Neksø** Bornholm, E Denmark
117 C16 **Nekyomanteío** ancient monument Ípeiros, W Greece
106 H7 **Nelas** Viseu, N Portugal
128 H16 **Nelidovo** Tverskaya Oblast', W Russian Federation
31 P13 **Neligh** Nebraska, C USA
127 N12 **Nel'kan** Khabarovskiy Kray, E Russian Federation
94 M10 **Nellim** var. Nellimö, Lapp. Njellim. Lappi, N Finland
Nellimö see Nellim
161 J18 **Nellore** Andhra Pradesh, E India
127 O16 **Nel'ma** Khabarovskiy Kray, SE Russian Federation
63 B17 **Nelson** Santa Fe, C Argentina
9 O17 **Nelson** British Columbia, SW Canada
193 I14 **Nelson** Nelson, South Island, NZ
99 L17 **Nelson** NW England, UK
31 P17 **Nelson** Nebraska, C USA
193 J14 **Nelson** ❖ unitary authority South Island, NZ
9 X12 **Nelson** ~ Manitoba, C Canada
191 U8 **Nelson Bay** New South Wales, SE Australia
190 K13 **Nelson, Cape** headland Victoria, SE Australia
194 M15 **Nelson, Cape** headland S PNG
65 G23 **Nelson, Estrecho** strait SE Pacific Ocean
9 W12 **Nelson House** Manitoba, C Canada
32 J4 **Nelson Lake** ◎ Wisconsin, N USA
33 T14 **Nelsonville** Ohio, N USA
29 S2 **Nelsoon River** ~ Iowa/Missouri, C USA
85 K21 **Nelspruit** Mpumalanga, NE South Africa
78 L10 **Néma** Hodh ech Chargui, SE Mauritania
120 D13 **Neman** Ger. Ragnit. Kaliningradskaya Oblast', W Russian Federation
86 I9 **Neman** Bel. Nyoman, Ger. Memel, Lith. Nemunas, Pol. Niemen, Rus. Neman. ~ NE Europe
Nemausus see Nîmes
117 F19 **Neméa** Pelopónnisos, S Greece
Německý Brod see Havlíčkův Brod
12 D7 **Nemegosenda** ~ Ontario, S Canada
12 D8 **Nemegosenda Lake** ◎ Ontario, S Canada
121 H14 **Nemenčinė** Vilnius, SE Lithuania
Nemetocenna see Arras
Nemirov see Nemyriv
105 O6 **Nemours** Seine-et-Marne, N France
Nemunas see Neman
172 R7 **Nemuro** Hokkaidō, NE Japan
172 R7 **Nemuro-hantō** peninsula Hokkaidō, NE Japan
172 R6 **Nemuro-kaikyō** strait Japan/Russian Federation
172 R7 **Nemuro-wan** bay N Japan
118 H5 **Nemyriv** Rus. Nemirov. L'vivs'ka Oblast', NW Ukraine
119 N7 **Nemyriv** Rus. Nemirov. Vinnyts'ka Oblast', C Ukraine
99 D19 **Nenagh** Ir. An tAonach. C Ireland
41 R9 **Nenana** Alaska, USA
41 R9 **Nenana River** ~ Alaska, USA
195 W8 **Nendö** var. Swallow Island. island Santa Cruz Islands, E Solomon Islands
99 O19 **Nene** ~ E England, UK
129 R4 **Nenetskiy Avtonomnyy Okrug** ❖ autonomous district NW Russian Federation
203 W11 **Nengonengo** atoll Îles Tuamotu, C French Polynesia
169 U6 **Nen Jiang** var. Nonni. ~ NE China
169 V6 **Nenjiang** Heilongjiang, NE China
201 P16 **Neoch** atoll Caroline Islands, C Micronesia
117 D18 **Neochóri** Dytikí Ellás, C Greece
29 Q7 **Neodesha** Kansas, C USA
31 S14 **Neola** Iowa, C USA
117 M19 **Néon Karlovási** var. Néon Karlovásion. Sámos, Dodekánisos, Greece, Aegean Sea
Néon Karlovásion see Néon Karlovási
117 E16 **Néon Monastíri** Thessalía, C Greece
29 R8 **Neosho** Missouri, C USA
29 Q7 **Neosho River** ~ Kansas/Oklahoma, C USA
127 N17 **Nepa** ~ C Russian Federation
159 N10 **Nepal** off. Kingdom of Nepal. ◆ monarchy S Asia
158 M11 **Nepalganj** Mid Western, SW Nepal
12 L13 **Nepean** Ontario, SE Canada
38 L4 **Nephi** Utah, W USA
99 B16 **Nephin** Ir. Néifinn. ▲ W Ireland
69 T9 **Nepoko** ~ NE Zaire
20 K15 **Neptune** New Jersey, NE USA
190 G10 **Neptune Islands** island group South Australia
109 I14 **Nera** anc. Nar. ~ C Italy
104 L14 **Nérac** Lot-et-Garonne, SW France
113 D16 **Neratovice** Ger. Neratowitz. Střední Čechy, C Czech Republic
Neratowitz see Neratovice
126 L15 **Nercha** ~ S Russian Federation
126 L15 **Nerchinsk** Chitinskaya Oblast', S Russian Federation
126 L16 **Nerchinskiy Zavod** Chitinskaya Oblast', S Russian Federation
128 M15 **Nerekhta** Kostromskaya Oblast', NW Russian Federation
120 H10 **Nereta** Aizkraukle, S Latvia
108 K13 **Nereto** Abruzzi, C Italy
115 H15 **Neretva** ~ Bosnia and Herzegovina/Croatia
117 C17 **Nerikós** ruins Lefkáda, Iónioi Nísoi, Greece, C Mediterranean Sea
120 B12 **Neringa** Ger. Nidden; prev. Nida. Neringa, SW Lithuania
85 F15 **Neriquinha** Cuando Cubango, SE Angola
120 I13 **Neris** Bel. Viliya, Pol. Wilia; prev. Pol. Wilja. ~ Belarus/Lithuania
Neris see Viliya
107 N15 **Nerja** Andalucía, S Spain
128 L16 **Nerl'** ~ W Russian Federation
176 Vv13 **Nerong, Selat** strait Kepulauan Kai, E Indonesia
107 P12 **Nerpio** Castilla-La Mancha, C Spain
106 J13 **Nerva** Andalucía, S Spain
126 Ll13 **Neryungri** Respublika Sakha (Yakutiya), NE Russian Federation
100 L4 **Nes** Friesland, N Netherlands
96 G13 **Nesbyen** Buskerud, S Norway
94 L2 **Neskaupstadhur** Austurland, E Iceland
94 F13 **Nesna** Nordland, C Norway
28 K5 **Ness City** Kansas, C USA
Nesselsdorf see Kopřivnice
110 H7 **Nesslau** Sankt Gallen, NE Switzerland
98 I9 **Ness, Loch** ◎ N Scotland, UK
Nesterov see Zhovkva
116 I12 **Néstos** Bul. Mesta, Turk. Kara Su. ~ Bulgaria/Greece see also Mesta
97 C14 **Nesttun** Hordaland, S Norway
Nesvizh see Nyasvizh
144 F9 **Netanya** var. Natanya, Nathanya. Central, C Israel
100 I9 **Netherlands** off. Kingdom of the Netherlands, var. Holland, Dut. Koninkrijk der Nederlanden, Nederland. ◆ monarchy NW Europe
47 S9 **Netherlands Antilles** prev. Dutch West Indies. ◇ Dutch autonomous region S Caribbean Sea
Netherlands East Indies see Indonesia
Netherlands Guiana see Suriname
Netherlands New Guinea see Irian Jaya
118 L4 **Netishyn** Khmel'nyts'ka Oblast', W Ukraine
144 E11 **Netivot** Southern, S Israel
109 O21 **Neto** ~ S Italy
16 N2 **Nettilling Lake** ◎ Baffin Island, Northwest Territories, N Canada
31 V3 **Nett Lake** ◎ Minnesota, N USA
109 I16 **Nettuno** Lazio, C Italy
Netum see Noto
43 U16 **Netzahualcóyotl, Presa** ⊡ SE Mexico
Netze see Noteć
Neu Amerika see Puławy
Neubetsche see Novi Bečej
Neubidschow see Nový Bydžov
Neubistritz see Nová Bystřice
102 N9 **Neubrandenburg** Mecklenburg-Vorpommern, NE Germany
103 K22 **Neuburg an der Donau** Bayern, S Germany
110 C8 **Neuchâtel** Ger. Neuenburg. Neuchâtel, W Switzerland
110 C8 **Neuchâtel** Ger. Neuenburg. ❖ canton W Switzerland
110 C8 **Neuchâtel, Lac de** Ger. Neuenburger See. ◎ W Switzerland
Neudorf see Spišská Nová Ves
102 L10 **Neue Elde** canal N Germany
Neuenburg see Neuchâtel
Neuenburg an der Elbe see Nymburk
Neuenburger See see Neuchâtel, Lac de
110 F7 **Neuenhof** Aargau, N Switzerland
102 H11 **Neuenland** ✈ (Bremen) Bremen, NW Germany
Neuenstadt see La Neuveville
103 C18 **Neuerburg** Rheinland-Pfalz, W Germany
101 K24 **Neufchâteau** Luxembourg, SE Belgium
105 S6 **Neufchâteau** Vosges, NE France
104 M3 **Neufchâtel-en-Bray** Seine-Maritime, N France
111 S3 **Neufelden** Oberösterreich, N Austria
Neugradisk see Nova Gradiška
Neuhaus see Jindřichův Hradec

◆ Country
● Country Capital
◇ Dependent Territory
○ Dependent Territory Capital
❖ Administrative Region
✈ International Airport
▲ Mountain
▲ Mountain Range
Volcano
~ River
◎ Lake
⊡ Reservoir

Neuhäusel *see* Nové Zámky
110 G6 **Neuhausen** *var.* Neuhausen am Rheinfall. Schaffhausen, N Switzerland
Neuhausen am Rheinfall *see* Neuhausen
103 I17 **Neuhof** Hessen, C Germany
Neuhof *see* Zgierz
Neukuhren *see* Pionerskiy
Neu-Langenburg *see* Tukuyu
111 W4 **Neulengbach** Niederösterreich, NE Austria
115 G15 **Neum** S Bosnia and Herzegovina
Neumark *see* Nowy Targ, Nowy Sącz, Poland
Neumark *see* Nowe Miasto Lubawskie, Toruń, Poland
Neumarkt *see* Neumarkt im Hausruckkreis, Oberösterreich, Austria
Neumarkt *see* Neumarkt Am Wallersee, Salzburg, Austria
Neumarkt *see* Środa Śląska, Wrocław, Poland
Neumarkt *see* Târgu Secuiesc, Covasna, Romania
Neumarkt *see* Târgu Mureș, Mureș, Romania
111 Q5 **Neumarkt Am Wallersee** *var.* Neumarkt. Salzburg, NW Austria
111 R4 **Neumarkt im Hausruckkreis** *var.* Neumarkt. Oberösterreich, N Austria
103 L20 **Neumarkt in der Oberpfalz** Bayern, SE Germany
Neumarktl *see* Tržič
Neumoldowa *see* Moldova Nouă
102 J8 **Neumünster** Schleswig-Holstein, N Germany
111 X5 **Neunkirchen** *var.* Neunkirchen am Steinfeld. Niederösterreich, E Austria
103 E20 **Neunkirchen** Saarland, SW Germany
Neunkirchen am Steinfeld *see* Neunkirchen
Neuoderberg *see* Bohumín
65 I15 **Neuquén** Neuquén, SE Argentina
65 H14 **Neuquén** *off.* Provincia de Neuquén. ◆ *province* W Argentina
65 H14 **Neuquén, Río** ⚓ W Argentina
Neurode *see* Nowa Ruda
102 N11 **Neuruppin** Brandenburg, NE Germany
Neusalz an der Oder *see* Nowa Sól
Neu Sandec/Neusandez *see* Nowy Sącz
103 K22 **Neusäss** Bayern, S Germany
Neusatz *see* Novi Sad
Neuschliss *see* Gherla
23 N8 **Neuse River** ⚓ North Carolina, SE USA
111 Z5 **Neusiedl am See** Burgenland, E Austria
113 G22 **Neusiedler See** *Hung.* Fertő. ◎ Austria/Hungary
Neusohl *see* Banská Bystrica
103 D15 **Neuss** *anc.* Novaesium, Novesium. Nordrhein-Westfalen, W Germany
Neuss *see* Nyon
Neustadt *see* Neustadt an der Aisch, Bayern, Germany
Neustadt *see* Neustadt bei Coburg, Bayern, Germany
Neustadt *see* Prudnik, Opole, Poland
Neustadt *see* Baia Mare, Maramureș, Romania
102 I12 **Neustadt am Rübenberge** Niedersachsen, N Germany
103 J19 **Neustadt an der Aisch** *var.* Neustadt. Bayern, C Germany
Neustadt an der Haardt *see* Neustadt an der Weinstrasse
103 F20 **Neustadt an der Weinstrasse** *prev.* Neustadt an der Haardt, *hist.* Niewenstat, *anc.* Nova Civitas. Rheinland-Pfalz, SW Germany
103 K18 **Neustadt bei Coburg** *var.* Neustadt. Bayern, C Germany
Neustadt bei Pinne *see* Lwówek
Neustadt in Oberschlesien *see* Prudnik
Neustadtl *see* Novo Mesto
Neustadtl in Mähren *see* Nové Město na Moravě
Neustettin *see* Szczecinek
110 M8 **Neustift im Stubaital** *var.* Stubaital. Tirol, W Austria
102 N10 **Neustrelitz** Mecklenburg-Vorpommern, NE Germany
Neutitschein *see* Nový Jičín
Neutra *see* Nitra
103 J22 **Neu-Ulm** Bayern, S Germany
Neuveville *see* La Neuveville
105 N12 **Neuvic** Corrèze, C France
Neuwarp *see* Nowe Warpno
102 G9 **Neuwerk** *island* NW Germany
103 E17 **Neuwied** Rheinland-Pfalz, W Germany
Neuzen *see* Terneuzen
128 H12 **Neva** ⚓ NW Russian Federation
31 V14 **Nevada** Iowa, C USA
29 R6 **Nevada** Missouri, C USA
37 R5 **Nevada** *off.* State of Nevada; also known as Battle Born State, Sagebrush State, Silver State. ◆ *state* W USA
37 P6 **Nevada City** California, W USA
128 G16 **Nevel'** Pskovskaya Oblast', W Russian Federation
127 Oo16 **Nevel'sk** Ostrov Sakhalin, Sakhalinskaya Oblast', SE Russian Federation
126 Ll14 **Never** Amurskaya Oblast', SE Russian Federation
131 Q6 **Neverkino** Penzenskaya Oblast', W Russian Federation
105 P9 **Nevers** *anc.* Noviodunum. Nièvre, C France
20 J12 **Neversink River** ⚓ New York, NE USA
191 Q6 **Nevertire** New South Wales, SE Australia
115 H15 **Nevesinje** S Bosnia and Herzegovina
120 G12 **Nevėžis** ⚓ C Lithuania
130 M14 **Nevinnomyssk** Stavropol'skiy Kray, SW Russian Federation
47 W10 **Nevis** *island* Saint Kitts and Nevis
Nevoso, Monte *see* Snežnik
Nevrokop *see* Gotse Delchev
142 J14 **Nevşehir** *var.* Nevshehr. Nevşehir, C Turkey
142 J14 **Nevşehir** *var.* Nevshehr. ◆ *province* C Turkey
Nevshehr *see* Nevşehir
125 Ee11 **Nev'yansk** Sverdlovskaya Oblast', C Russian Federation
83 J25 **Newala** Mtwara, SE Tanzania
33 P16 **New Albany** Indiana, N USA
24 M2 **New Albany** Mississippi, S USA
31 Y11 **New Albin** Iowa, C USA
57 U8 **New Amsterdam** E Guyana
191 Q4 **New Angledool** New South Wales, SE Australia
23 Y2 **Newark** Delaware, NE USA
20 K14 **Newark** New Jersey, NE USA
20 G10 **Newark** New York, NE USA
33 T13 **Newark** Ohio, N USA
Newark *see* Newark-on-Trent
37 W5 **Newark Lake** ◎ Nevada, W USA
99 N18 **Newark-on-Trent** *var.* Newark. C England, UK
24 M7 **New Augusta** Mississippi, S USA
21 P12 **New Bedford** Massachusetts, NE USA
34 G11 **Newberg** Oregon, NW USA
23 X10 **New Bern** North Carolina, SE USA
22 F8 **Newbern** Tennessee, S USA
33 P4 **Newberry** Michigan, N USA
23 Q12 **Newberry** South Carolina, SE USA
20 F15 **New Bloomfield** Pennsylvania, NE USA
27 X5 **New Boston** Texas, SW USA
27 S11 **New Braunfels** Texas, SW USA
33 Q13 **New Bremen** Ohio, N USA
99 F18 **Newbridge** *Ir.* An Droichead Nua. C Ireland
20 B14 **New Brighton** Pennsylvania, NE USA
20 M12 **New Britain** Connecticut, NE USA
195 N13 **New Britain** *island* E PNG
199 Hh9 **New Britain Trench** *undersea feature* W Pacific Ocean
20 J15 **New Brunswick** New Jersey, NE USA
13 V8 **New Brunswick** *Fr.* Nouveau-Brunswick. ◆ *province* SE Canada
20 K13 **Newburgh** New York, NE USA
99 M22 **Newbury** S England, UK
21 P10 **Newburyport** Massachusetts, NE USA
79 T14 **New Bussa** Niger, W Nigeria
197 J4 **New Caledonia** *var.* Kanaky, *Fr.* Nouvelle-Calédonie. ◇ *French overseas territory* SW Pacific Ocean
197 H5 **New Caledonia** *island* SW Pacific Ocean
183 O10 **New Caledonia Basin** *undersea feature* W Pacific Ocean
191 T8 **Newcastle** New South Wales, SE Australia
11 O14 **Newcastle** New Brunswick, SE Canada
12 I15 **Newcastle** Ontario, SE Canada
99 C20 **Newcastle** *Ir.* An Caisleán Nua. SW Ireland
85 K22 **Newcastle** KwaZulu/Natal, E South Africa
99 G16 **Newcastle** *Ir.* An Caisleán Nua. SE Northern Ireland, UK
33 P13 **New Castle** Indiana, N USA
22 L5 **New Castle** Kentucky, S USA
29 N11 **Newcastle** Oklahoma, C USA
20 B13 **New Castle** Pennsylvania, NE USA
27 R6 **Newcastle** Texas, SW USA
38 J7 **Newcastle** Utah, W USA
23 S6 **New Castle** Virginia, NE USA
35 Z13 **Newcastle** Wyoming, C USA
47 W10 **Newcastle** ✈ Nevis, Saint Kitts and Nevis
99 L14 **Newcastle** ✈ NE England, UK
Newcastle *see* Newcastle upon Tyne
99 L18 **Newcastle-under-Lyme** C England, UK
99 M14 **Newcastle upon Tyne** *var.* Newcastle; *hist.* Monkchester, *Lat.* Pons Aelii. NE England, UK
189 Q4 **Newcastle Waters** Northern Territory, N Australia
Newchwang *see* Yingkou
20 K13 **New City** New York, NE USA
33 U13 **Newcomerstown** Ohio, N USA
20 G15 **New Cumberland** Pennsylvania, NE USA
23 R1 **New Cumberland** West Virginia, NE USA
158 I10 **New Delhi** ● (India) Delhi, N India
9 O17 **New Denver** British Columbia, SW Canada
30 J9 **Newell** South Dakota, N USA
23 Q13 **New Ellenton** South Carolina, SE USA
24 J6 **Newellton** Louisiana, S USA
30 K6 **New England** North Dakota, N USA
21 P8 **New England** *cultural region* NE USA
New England of the West *see* Minnesota
191 U5 **New England Range** ▲ New South Wales, SE Australia
66 G9 **New England Seamounts** *var.* Bermuda-New England Seamount Arc. *undersea feature* W Atlantic Ocean
40 M14 **Newenham, Cape** *headland* Alaska, USA
144 F11 **Newé Zohar** Southern, E Israel
20 D9 **Newfane** New York, NE USA
99 M23 **New Forest** *physical region* S England, UK
16 S8 **Newfoundland** *Fr.* Terre-Neuve. *island* Newfoundland and Labrador, SE Canada
11 R9 **Newfoundland and Labrador** *Fr.* Terre Neuve. ◆ *province* E Canada
67 J8 **Newfoundland Basin** *undersea feature* NW Atlantic Ocean
66 I8 **Newfoundland Ridge** *undersea feature* NW Atlantic Ocean
66 J8 **Newfoundland Seamounts** *undersea feature* N Sargasso Sea
20 G16 **New Freedom** Pennsylvania, NE USA
195 U14 **New Georgia** *island* New Georgia Islands, NW Solomon Islands
195 T15 **New Georgia Islands** *island group* NW Solomon Islands
195 U14 **New Georgia Sound** *var.* The Slot. *sound* E Solomon Sea
32 L9 **New Glarus** Wisconsin, N USA
11 Q15 **New Glasgow** Nova Scotia, SE Canada
New Goa *see* Panaji
194 D11 **New Guinea** *Dut.* Nieuw Guinea, *Ind.* Irian. *island* Indonesia/PNG
199 H9 **New Guinea Trench** *undersea feature* SW Pacific Ocean
34 I6 **Newhalem** Washington, NW USA
41 P13 **Newhalen** Alaska, USA
31 X13 **Newhall** Iowa, C USA
12 F16 **New Hamburg** Ontario, S Canada
21 N9 **New Hampshire** *off.* State of New Hampshire; also known as The Granite State. ◆ *state* NE USA
31 W12 **New Hampton** Iowa, C USA
195 N9 **New Hanover** *island* NE PNG
20 M13 **New Haven** Connecticut, NE USA
33 Q12 **New Haven** Indiana, N USA
29 W5 **New Haven** Missouri, C USA
99 P23 **Newhaven** SE England, UK
8 K13 **New Hazelton** British Columbia, SW Canada
New Hebrides *see* Vanuatu
183 P9 **New Hebrides Trench** *undersea feature* N Coral Sea
20 H15 **New Holland** Pennsylvania, NE USA
24 I9 **New Iberia** Louisiana, S USA
195 N10 **New Ireland** ◆ *province* NE PNG
195 P10 **New Ireland** *island* NE PNG
67 A24 **New Island** *island* W Falkland Islands
20 J15 **New Jersey** *off.* State of New Jersey; also known as The Garden State. ◆ *state* NE USA
20 C14 **New Kensington** Pennsylvania, NE USA
23 W6 **New Kent** Virginia, NE USA
29 O8 **Newkirk** Oklahoma, C USA
23 Q9 **Newland** North Carolina, SE USA
30 L6 **New Leipzig** North Dakota, N USA
12 H9 **New Liskeard** Ontario, S Canada
24 G7 **Newllano** Louisiana, S USA
21 N13 **New London** Connecticut, NE USA
31 Y15 **New London** Iowa, C USA
31 T8 **New London** Minnesota, N USA
29 V3 **New London** Missouri, C USA
32 M7 **New London** Wisconsin, N USA
29 Y8 **New Madrid** Missouri, C USA
188 J8 **Newman** Western Australia
204 M13 **Newman Island** *island* Antarctica
12 H15 **Newmarket** Ontario, S Canada
99 P20 **Newmarket** E England, UK
21 P10 **Newmarket** New Hampshire, NE USA
23 U4 **New Market** Virginia, NE USA
23 R2 **New Martinsville** West Virginia, NE USA
33 U14 **New Matamoras** Ohio, N USA
34 M12 **New Meadows** Idaho, NW USA
28 R12 **New Mexico** *off.* State of New Mexico; also known as Land of Enchantment, Sunshine State. ◆ *state* SW USA
155 V6 **New Mirpur** *var.* Mīrpur. Sind, SE Pakistan
25 S4 **Newnan** Georgia, SE USA
191 P17 **New Norfolk** Tasmania, SE Australia
24 K9 **New Orleans** Louisiana, S USA
24 K9 **New Orleans** ✈ Louisiana, S USA
20 K12 **New Paltz** New York, NE USA
33 U12 **New Philadelphia** Ohio, N USA
192 K10 **New Plymouth** Taranaki, North Island, NZ
99 M24 **Newport** S England, UK
99 K22 **Newport** SE Wales, UK
29 W10 **Newport** Arkansas, C USA
33 N13 **Newport** Indiana, N USA
22 M3 **Newport** Kentucky, S USA
31 W9 **Newport** Minnesota, N USA
34 F12 **Newport** Oregon, NW USA
21 O13 **Newport** Rhode Island, NE USA
23 O9 **Newport** Tennessee, S USA
21 N6 **Newport** Vermont, NE USA
34 M7 **Newport** Washington, NW USA
23 X7 **Newport News** Virginia, NE USA
99 N20 **Newport Pagnell** SE England, UK
25 U12 **New Port Richey** Florida, SE USA
31 V9 **New Prague** Minnesota, N USA
46 H3 **New Providence** *island* N Bahamas
99 H24 **Newquay** SW England, UK
99 I20 **New Quay** SW Wales, UK
31 V10 **New Richland** Minnesota, N USA
13 X7 **New-Richmond** Québec, SE Canada
33 R15 **New Richmond** Ohio, N USA
32 I5 **New Richmond** Wisconsin, N USA
44 G1 **New River** ⚓ N Belize
57 T12 **New River** ⚓ SE Guyana
23 R6 **New River** ⚓ West Virginia, NE USA
44 G1 **New River Lagoon** ◎ N Belize
24 J8 **New Roads** Louisiana, S USA
20 L14 **New Rochelle** New York, NE USA
31 O4 **New Rockford** North Dakota, N USA
99 P23 **New Romney** SE England, UK
99 F20 **New Ross** *Ir.* Ros Mhic Thriúin. SE Ireland
99 F16 **Newry** *Ir.* An tIúr. SE Northern Ireland, UK
30 M5 **New Salem** North Dakota, N USA
New Sarum *see* Salisbury
31 W14 **New Sharon** Iowa, C USA
New Siberian Islands *see* Novosibirskiye Ostrova
25 X11 **New Smyrna Beach** Florida, SE USA
191 O7 **New South Wales** ◆ *state* SE Australia
41 O13 **New Stuyahok** Alaska, USA
23 N8 **New Tazewell** Tennessee, S USA
40 M12 **Newtok** Alaska, USA
25 S7 **Newton** Georgia, SE USA
31 W14 **Newton** Iowa, C USA
29 N6 **Newton** Kansas, C USA
21 O11 **Newton** Massachusetts, NE USA
24 M5 **Newton** Mississippi, S USA
20 J14 **Newton** New Jersey, NE USA
23 R9 **Newton** North Carolina, SE USA
27 Y9 **Newton** Texas, SW USA
99 J24 **Newton Abbot** SW England, UK
98 K13 **Newton St Boswells** SE Scotland, UK
99 I14 **Newton Stewart** S Scotland, UK
94 O2 **Newtontoppen** ▲ C Svalbard
30 K3 **New Town** North Dakota, N USA
99 J20 **Newtown** E Wales, UK
99 G15 **Newtownabbey** *Ir.* Baile na Mainistreach. E Northern Ireland, UK
99 G15 **Newtownards** *Ir.* Baile Nua na hArda. SE Northern Ireland, UK
31 U10 **New Ulm** Minnesota, N USA
30 K10 **New Underwood** South Dakota, N USA
27 V10 **New Waverly** Texas, SW USA
20 K14 **New York** New York, NE USA
20 G10 **New York** ◆ *state* NE USA
37 X13 **New York Mountains** ▲ California, W USA
192 K12 **New Zealand** *abbrev.* NZ. ◆ *commonwealth republic* SW Pacific Ocean
129 O15 **Neya** Kostromskaya Oblast', NW Russian Federation
Neyba *see* Neiba
149 Q12 **Neyrīz** *var.* Neiriz, Niriz. Fārs, S Iran
149 T4 **Neyshābūr** *var.* Nishapur. Khorāsān, NE Iran
161 J21 **Neyveli** Tamil Nādu, SE India
Nezhin *see* Nizhyn
35 N10 **Nezperce** Idaho, NW USA
24 H8 **Nezpique, Bayou** ⚓ Louisiana, S USA
176 W14 **Ngabordamlu, Tanjung** *headland* Pulau Trangan, SE Indonesia
79 Y13 **Ngadda** ⚓ NE Nigeria
N'Gage *see* Negage
193 G16 **Ngahere** West Coast, South Island, NZ
79 Z12 **Ngala** Borno, NE Nigeria
85 G17 **Ngamiland** ◆ *district* N Botswana
164 K16 **Ngamring** Xizang Zizhiqu, W China
83 K19 **Ngangerabeli Plain** *plain* SE Kenya
164 I14 **Ngangla Ringco** ◎ W China
164 G13 **Nganglong Kangri** ▲ W China
164 K15 **Ngangzê Co** ◎ W China
81 F14 **Ngaoundéré** *var.* N'Gaoundéré. Adamaoua, N Cameroon
83 E20 **Ngara** Kagera, NW Tanzania
196 F8 **Ngardmau Bay** *bay* Babeldaob, N Palau
196 F7 **Ngaregur** *island* Palau Islands, N Palau
192 L7 **Ngaruawahia** Waikato, North Island, NZ
192 N11 **Ngaruroro** ⚓ North Island, NZ
202 I16 **Ngatangiia** Rarotonga, S Cook Islands
192 M6 **Ngatea** Waikato, North Island, NZ
177 F8 **Ngathainggyaung** Irrawaddy, SW Myanmar
Ngatik *see* Ngetik Atoll
Ngau *see* Gau
174 Ll15 **Ngawi** Jawa, S Indonesia
196 C7 **Ngcheangel** *var.* Kayangel Islands. *island* Palau Islands, N Palau
196 E10 **Ngchemiangel** Babeldaob, N Palau
196 C8 **Ngeaur** *var.* Angaur. *island* Palau Islands, S Palau
196 E10 **Ngerkeai** Babeldaob, N Palau
196 F9 **Ngermechau** Babeldaob, N Palau
196 C8 **Ngeruktabel** *prev.* Urukthapel. *island* Palau Islands, S Palau
196 F8 **Ngetbong** Babeldaob, N Palau
201 T17 **Ngetik Atoll** *var.* Ngatik; *prev.* Los Jardines. *atoll* Caroline Islands, E Micronesia
196 E10 **Ngetkip** Babeldaob, N Palau
Nggamea *see* Qamea
195 V15 **Nggatokae** *island* New Georgia Islands, NW Solomon Islands
85 C16 **N'Giva** *var.* Ondjiva, *Port.* Vila Pereira de Eça. Cunene, S Angola
81 G20 **Ngo** Plateaux, SE Congo
178 Jj7 **Ngoc Lac** Thanh Hoa, N Vietnam
81 G17 **Ngoko** ⚓ Cameroon/Congo
176 W14 **Ngoni, Tanjung** *headland* Maluku, Kepulauan Aru, SE Indonesia
83 H19 **Ngorengore** Rift Valley, SW Kenya
165 Q11 **Ngoring Hu** ◎ C China
Ngorolaka *see* Banifing
83 H20 **Ngorongoro Crater** *crater* N Tanzania
81 D19 **Ngounié** *off.* Province de la Ngounié, *var.* La Ngounié. ◆ *province* S Gabon
81 D19 **Ngounié** ⚓ Congo/Gabon
80 H10 **Ngoura** *var.* NGoura. Chari-Baguirmi, W Chad
80 G10 **Ngouri** *var.* NGouri; *prev.* Fort-Millot. Lac, W Chad
79 Y10 **Ngourti** Diffa, E Niger
79 Y11 **Nguigmi** *var.* N'Guigmi. Diffa, SE Niger
Nguimbo *see* Lumbala N'Guimbo
196 F15 **Ngulu Atoll** *atoll* Caroline Islands, W Micronesia
197 C14 **Nguna** *island* C Vanuatu
N'Gunza *see* Sumbe
175 N16 **Ngurah Rai** ✈ (Bali) Bali, S Indonesia
79 W12 **Nguru** Yobe, NE Nigeria
Ngwaketze *see* Southern
85 I16 **Ngweze** ⚓ S Zambia
85 M17 **Nhamatanda** Sofala, C Mozambique
60 G12 **Nhamundá, Rio** *var.* Jamundá, Yamundá. ⚓ N Brazil
62 J7 **Nhandeara** São Paulo, S Brazil
N'Harea *see* Nharêa
84 D12 **Nharêa** *var.* N'Harea, Nhareia. Bié, W Angola
Nhareia *see* Nharêa
178 Kk13 **Nha Trang** Khanh Hoa, S Vietnam
190 L11 **Nhill** Victoria, SE Australia
85 L22 **Nhlangano** *prev.* Goedgegun. SW Swaziland
189 S1 **Nhulunbuy** Northern Territory, N Australia
79 N10 **Niafounké** Tombouctou, W Mali
33 N5 **Niagara** Wisconsin, N USA
12 H16 **Niagara** ⚓ Ontario, S Canada
12 G15 **Niagara Escarpment** *hill range* Ontario, S Canada
12 H16 **Niagara Falls** Ontario, S Canada
20 D9 **Niagara Falls** New York, NE USA
16 Pp17 **Niagara Falls** *waterfall* Canada/USA
78 K12 **Niagassola** *var.* Nyagassola. Haute-Guinée, NE Guinea
79 R12 **Niamey** ● (Niger) Niamey, SW Niger
79 R12 **Niamey** ✈ Niamey, SW Niger
79 R14 **Niamtougou** N Togo
81 O16 **Niangara** Haut-Zaïre, NE Zaire
79 O10 **Niangay, Lac** ◎ E Mali
79 N14 **Niangoloko** SW Burkina
29 U6 **Niangua River** ⚓ Missouri, C USA
81 O17 **Nia-Nia** Haut-Zaïre, NE Zaire
21 N13 **Niantic** Connecticut, NE USA
169 U7 **Nianzishan** Heilongjiang, NE China
173 F7 **Nias, Pulau** *island* W Indonesia
84 O13 **Niassa** *off.* Província do Niassa. ◆ *province* N Mozambique
203 U10 **Niau** *island* Îles Tuamotu, C French Polynesia
97 G20 **Nibe** Nordjylland, N Denmark
201 Q8 **Nibok** N Nauru
120 C10 **Nīca** Liepāja, W Latvia
Nicaea *see* Nice
44 J9 **Nicaragua** *off.* Republic of Nicaragua. ◆ *republic* Central America
44 K11 **Nicaragua, Lago de** *var.* Cocibolca, Gran Lago, *Eng.* Lake Nicaragua. ◎ S Nicaragua
Nicaragua, Lake *see* Nicaragua, Lago de
66 D11 **Nicaraguan Rise** *undersea feature* NW Caribbean Sea
Nicaria *see* Ikaría
109 N21 **Nicastro** Calabria, SW Italy
105 V15 **Nice** *It.* Nizza; *anc.* Nicaea. Alpes-Maritimes, SE France
Nice *see* Côte d'Azur
Nicephorium *see* Ar Raqqah
10 M9 **Nichicun, Lac** ◎ Québec, E Canada
170 C17 **Nichinan** *var.* Nitinan. Miyazaki, Kyūshū, SW Japan
46 E4 **Nicholas Channel** *channel* N Cuba
Nicholas II Land *see* Severnaya Zemlya
155 U2 **Nicholas Range** *Pash.* Selseleh-ye Kūh-e Vākhān, *Taj.* Qatorkŭhi Vakhon. ▲ Afghanistan/Tajikistan
22 M6 **Nicholasville** Kentucky, S USA
46 G2 **Nicholls Town** Andros Island, NW Bahamas
23 U12 **Nichols** South Carolina, SE USA
57 U9 **Nickerie** ◆ *district* NW Suriname
57 V9 **Nickerie Rivier** ⚓ NW Suriname
157 P22 **Nicobar Islands** *island group* India, E Indian Ocean
118 L9 **Nicolae Bălcescu** Botoșani, NE Romania
13 P11 **Nicolet** Québec, SE Canada
13 Q12 **Nicolet** ⚓ Québec, SE Canada
33 Q4 **Nicolet, Lake** ◎ Michigan, N USA
31 U10 **Nicollet** Minnesota, N USA
63 F19 **Nico Pérez** Florida, S Uruguay
Nicopolis *see* Nikopol, Bulgaria
Nicopolis *see* Nikópoli, Greece
124 R12 **Nicosia** *Gk.* Lefkosía, *Turk.* Lefkoşa. ● (Cyprus) C Cyprus
109 K24 **Nicosia** Sicilia, Italy, C Mediterranean Sea
109 N22 **Nicotera** Calabria, SW Italy
44 K13 **Nicoya** Guanacaste, W Costa Rica
44 L14 **Nicoya, Golfo de** *gulf* W Costa Rica
44 L14 **Nicoya, Península de** *peninsula* NW Costa Rica
Nictheroy *see* Niterói
113 L15 **Nida** ⚓ S Poland
Nida *see* Neringa
Nidaros *see* Trondheim
110 D8 **Nidau** Bern, W Switzerland
103 H17 **Nidda** ⚓ W Germany
Nidden *see* Neringa
97 F17 **Nidelva** ⚓ S Norway
126 J10 **Nidym** Evenkiyskiy Avtonomnyy Okrug, N Russian Federation
112 L9 **Nidzica** *Ger.* Niedenburg. Olsztyn, N Poland
102 H6 **Niebüll** Schleswig-Holstein, N Germany
Niedenburg *see* Nidzica
101 N25 **Niederanven** Luxembourg, C Luxembourg
105 V4 **Niederbronn-les-Bains** Bas-Rhin, NE France
Niederdonau *see* Niederösterreich
111 S7 **Niedere Tauern** ▲ C Austria
103 P14 **Niederlausitz** *Eng.* Lower Lusatia. *physical region* E Germany
111 U5 **Niederösterreich** *off.* Land Niederösterreich, *Eng.* Lower Austria, *Ger.* Niederdonau; *prev.* Lower Danube. ◆ *state* NE Austria
102 G12 **Niedersachsen** *Eng.* Lower Saxony, *Fr.* Basse-Saxe. ◆ *state* NW Germany
81 D17 **Niefang** *var.* Sevilla de Niefang. NW Equatorial Guinea
85 G23 **Niekerkshoop** Northern Cape, W South Africa
101 G17 **Niel** Antwerpen, N Belgium
Niélé *see* Niellé
78 M14 **Niellé** *var.* Niélé. N Ivory Coast
81 O22 **Niemba** Shaba, E Zaire
113 G15 **Niemcza** *Ger.* Nimptsch. Wałbrzych, SW Poland
Niemen *see* Neman
94 J13 **Niemisel** Norrbotten, N Sweden
113 H15 **Niemodlin** *Ger.* Falkenberg. Opole, SW Poland
78 M13 **Niéna** Sikasso, SW Mali
102 H12 **Nienburg** Niedersachsen, N Germany
102 N13 **Nieplitz** ⚓ NE Germany
113 L16 **Niepołomice** Kraków, S Poland
103 D14 **Niers** ⚓ Germany/Netherlands
103 Q15 **Niesky** *Lus.* Niska. Sachsen, E Germany
Nieśwież *see* Nyasvizh
Nieuport *see* Nieuwpoort
100 O8 **Nieuw-Amsterdam** Drenthe, NE Netherlands
57 W9 **Nieuw Amsterdam** Commewijne, NE Suriname
101 M14 **Nieuw-Bergen** Limburg, SE Netherlands
100 O7 **Nieuw-Buinen** Drenthe, NE Netherlands
100 J12 **Nieuwegein** Utrecht, C Netherlands
100 P6 **Nieuwe Pekela** Groningen, NE Netherlands
100 P5 **Nieuweschans** Groningen, NE Netherlands
Nieuw Guinea *see* New Guinea
100 I11 **Nieuwkoop** Zuid-Holland, C Netherlands
100 M9 **Nieuwleusen** Overijssel, S Netherlands
100 J11 **Nieuw-Loosdrecht** Utrecht, C Netherlands
57 U9 **Nieuw Nickerie** Nickerie, NW Suriname
100 P5 **Nieuwolda** Groningen, NE Netherlands
101 B17 **Nieuwpoort** *var.* Nieuport. West-Vlaanderen, W Belgium
101 G14 **Nieuw-Vossemeer** Noord-Brabant, S Netherlands
100 P7 **Nieuw-Weerdinge** Drenthe, NE Netherlands
42 L10 **Nieves** Zacatecas, C Mexico
66 O11 **Nieves, Pico de las** ▲ Gran Canaria, Islas Canarias, Spain, NE Atlantic Ocean
105 P8 **Nièvre** ◆ *department* C France
Niewenstat *see* Neustadt an der Weinstrasse
142 J15 **Niğde** Niğde, C Turkey
142 J15 **Niğde** ◆ *province* C Turkey
85 J21 **Nigel** Gauteng, NE South Africa
79 V10 **Niger** *off.* Republic of Niger. ◆ *republic* W Africa
79 T14 **Niger** ◆ *state* C Nigeria
69 P8 **Niger** ⚓ W Africa
Niger Cone *see* Niger Fan
69 P9 **Niger Delta** *delta* S Nigeria
69 P9 **Niger Fan** *var.* Niger Cone. *undersea feature* E Atlantic Ocean
79 T13 **Nigeria** *off.* Federal Republic of Nigeria. ◆ *federal republic* W Africa
79 T17 **Niger, Mouths of the** *delta* S Nigeria
193 C24 **Nightcaps** Southland, South Island, NZ
12 F7 **Night Hawk Lake** ◎ Ontario, S Canada
67 M19 **Nightingale Island** *island* S Tristan da Cunha, S Atlantic Ocean
40 M12 **Nightmute** Alaska, USA
116 G13 **Nigrita** Kentrikí Makedonía, NE Greece
154 J15 **Nihing** *Per.* Rūd-e Nahang. ⚓ Iran/Pakistan
203 V10 **Nihiru** *atoll* Îles Tuamotu, C French Polynesia
Nihommatsu *see* Nihonmatsu
Nihon *see* Japan
171 L13 **Nihonmatsu** *var.* Nihommatsu, Nihonmatu. Fukushima, Honshū, C Japan
Nihonmatu *see* Nihonmatsu
64 I12 **Nihuil, Embalse del** ◎ W Argentina
171 K12 **Niigata** Niigata, Honshū, C Japan
171 K13 **Niigata** *off.* Niigata-ken. ◆ *prefecture* Honshū, C Japan
170 F15 **Niihama** Ehime, Shikoku, SW Japan
40 A8 **Niihau** *island* Hawaii, USA, C Pacific Ocean
172 Ss13 **Nii-jima** *island* E Japan
170 Ff13 **Niimi** Okayama, Honshū, SW Japan
171 Kk13 **Niitsu** *var.* Niitu. Niigata, Honshū, C Japan
Niitu *see* Niitsu
107 P15 **Níjar** Andalucía, S Spain
100 K11 **Nijkerk** Gelderland, C Netherlands
101 H16 **Nijlen** Antwerpen, N Belgium
100 L13 **Nijmegen** *Ger.* Nimwegen; *anc.* Noviomagus. Gelderland, SE Netherlands
100 N10 **Nijverdal** Overijssel, E Netherlands
202 G16 **Nikao** Rarotonga, S Cook Islands
Nikaria *see* Ikaría
128 I2 **Nikel'** Murmanskaya Oblast', NW Russian Federation
175 Rr17 **Nikiniki** Timor, S Indonesia
133 Q15 **Nikitin Seamount** *undersea feature* E Indian Ocean
79 S14 **Nikki** E Benin
171 Kk15 **Nikkō** *var.* Nikko. Tochigi, Honshū, S Japan
Niklasmarkt *see* Gheorgheni
41 P10 **Nikolai** Alaska, USA
Nikolaiken *see* Mikołajki
Nikolainkaupunki *see* Vaasa
Nikolayev *see* Mykolayiv
151 U15 **Nikolayevka** Almaty, SE Kazakhstan
151 O6 **Nikolayevka** Severnyy Kazakhstan, N Kazakhstan
131 P9 **Nikolayevsk** Volgogradskaya Oblast', SW Russian Federation
Nikolayevskaya Oblast' *see* Mykolayivs'ka Oblast'
127 Nn14 **Nikolayevsk-na-Amure** Khabarovskiy Kray, SE Russian Federation
131 P6 **Nikol'sk** Penzenskaya Oblast', W Russian Federation
129 O13 **Nikol'sk** Vologodskaya Oblast', NW Russian Federation
Nikol'sk *see* Ussuriysk
40 K17 **Nikolski** Umnak Island, Alaska, USA
Nikol'skiy *see* Satpayev
131 V7 **Nikol'skoye** Orenburgskaya Oblast', W Russian Federation
Nikol'sk-Ussuriyskiy *see* Ussuriysk
116 J7 **Nikopol** *anc.* Nicopolis. Loveshka Oblast, N Bulgaria
119 S9 **Nikopol'** Dnipropetrovs'ka Oblast', SE Ukraine
117 C17 **Nikópoli** *anc.* Nicopolis. *site of ancient city* Ípeiros, W Greece
142 M12 **Niksar** Tokat, N Turkey
149 V14 **Nīkshahr** Sīstān va Balūchestān, SE Iran
115 J16 **Nikšić** Montenegro, SW Yugoslavia
203 R4 **Nikumaroro** *prev.* Gardner Island, Kemins Island. *atoll* Phoenix Islands, C Kiribati
203 P3 **Nikunau** *var.* Nukunau; *prev.* Byron Island. *atoll* Tungaru, W Kiribati
161 G21 **Nilambūr** Kerala, SW India
37 X16 **Niland** California, W USA
69 T3 **Nile** *Ar.* Nahr an Nīl. ⚓ N Africa
82 G8 **Nile** *former province* NW Uganda
77 W7 **Nile Delta** *delta* N Egypt
69 T3 **Nile Fan** *undersea feature* E Mediterranean Sea
33 O11 **Niles** Michigan, N USA
33 V11 **Niles** Ohio, N USA
161 F20 **Nīleswaram** Kerala, SW India
12 K10 **Nilgaut, Lac** ◎ Québec, SE Canada
164 I5 **Nilka** Xinjiang Uygur Zizhiqu, NW China
Nîl, Nahr an *see* Nile
95 N16 **Nilsiä** Kuopio, C Finland
160 F9 **Nīmach** Madhya Pradesh, C India
158 G14 **Nimbāhera** Rājasthān, N India
78 L15 **Nimba, Monts** *var.* Nimba Mountains. ▲ W Africa
Nimba Mountains *see* Nimba, Monts
Nimburg *see* Nymburk
105 Q15 **Nîmes** *anc.* Nemausus, Nismes. Gard, S France
158 H11 **Nīm ka Thāna** Rājasthān, N India
191 R11 **Nimmitabel** New South Wales, SE Australia
Nimptsch *see* Niemcza
205 R11 **Nimrod Glacier** *glacier* Antarctica
Nimroze *see* Nīmrūz
154 K8 **Nīmrūz** *var.* Nimroze; *prev.* Chakhānsūr. ◆ *province* SW Afghanistan
83 F16 **Nimule** Eastern Equatoria, S Sudan
Nimwegen *see* Nijmegen
161 C23 **Nine Degree Channel** *channel* India/Maldives
20 G9 **Ninemile Point** *headland* New York, NE USA
181 S8 **Ninetyeast Ridge** *undersea feature* E Indian Ocean
191 P13 **Ninety Mile Beach** *beach* Victoria, SE Australia

192 I2 **Ninety Mile Beach** *beach* North Island, NZ
23 P12 **Ninety Six** South Carolina, SE USA
169 Y9 **Ning'an** Heilongjiang, NE China
167 S9 **Ningbo** *var.* Ning-po, Yin-hsien; *prev.* Ninghsien. Zhejiang, SE China
167 U12 **Ningde** Fujian, SE China
167 P12 **Ningdu** Jiangxi, S China
194 E12 **Ningerum** Western, SW PNG
167 R9 **Ningguo** Anhui, E China
167 S9 **Ninghai** Zhejiang, SE China
Ning-hsia *see* Ningxia
Ninghsien *see* Ningbo
166 J15 **Ningming** Guangxi Zhuangzu Zizhiqu, S China
166 H11 **Ningnan** Sichuan, C China
Ning-po *see* Ningbo
Ningsia/Ningsia Hui/ Ningsia Hui Autonomous Region *see* Ningxia
166 J5 **Ningxia** *off.* Ningxia Huizu Zizhiqu, *var.* Ning-hsia, Ningsia, *Eng.* Ningsia Hui, Ningsia Hui Autonomous Region. ◆ *autonomous region* N China
165 X10 **Ningxian** Gansu, N China
178 Jj7 **Ninh Binh** Ninh Binh, N Vietnam
178 Kk13 **Ninh Hoa** Khanh Hoa, S Vietnam
194 H7 **Ninigo Group** *island group* N PNG
41 Q12 **Ninilchik** Alaska, USA
29 N7 **Ninnescah River** ↝ Kansas, C USA
205 U16 **Ninnis Glacier** *glacier* Antarctica
172 N10 **Ninohe** Iwate, Honshū, C Japan
101 F18 **Ninove** Oost-Vlaanderen, C Belgium
179 P11 **Ninoy Aquino** ✕ (Manila) Luzon, N Philippines
Nio *see* Íos
31 P12 **Niobrara** Nebraska, C USA
30 M12 **Niobrara River** ↝ Nebraska/Wyoming, C USA
81 I20 **Nioki** Bandundu, W Zaire
78 M11 **Niono** Ségou, C Mali
78 K11 **Nioro** *var.* Nioro du Sahel. Kayes, W Mali
78 G11 **Nioro du Rip** SW Senegal
Nioro du Sahel *see* Nioro
104 K10 **Niort** Deux-Sèvres, W France
180 H14 **Nioumachoua** Mohéli, S Comoros
194 G12 **Nipa** Southern Highlands, W PNG
9 U14 **Nipawin** Saskatchewan, S Canada
10 D12 **Nipigon** Ontario, S Canada
10 D11 **Nipigon, Lake** ◎ Ontario, S Canada
9 S13 **Nipin** ↝ Saskatchewan, C Canada
12 G11 **Nipissing, Lake** ◎ Ontario, S Canada
37 P13 **Nipomo** California, W USA
Nippon *see* Japan
144 K6 **Niqniqiyah, Jabal an** ▲ C Syria
64 I9 **Niquivil** San Juan, W Argentina
176 Yy10 **Nirabotong** Irian Jaya, E Indonesia
171 J16 **Nirasaki** Yamanashi, Honshū, S Japan
Niriz *see* Neyrīz
161 I14 **Nirmal** Andhra Pradesh, C India
159 Q13 **Nirmāli** Bihār, NE India
115 O14 **Niš** *Eng.* Nish, *Ger.* Nisch; *anc.* Naissus. Serbia, SE Yugoslavia
106 H9 **Nisa** Portalegre, C Portugal
Nisa *see* Neisse
147 P4 **Niṣab** Al Ḥudūd ash Shamālīyah, N Saudi Arabia
147 Q15 **Niṣāb** *var.* Anṣāb. SW Yemen
115 P14 **Nišava** *Bul.* Nishava. ↝ Bulgaria/Yugoslavia *see also* Nishava
109 K25 **Niscemi** Sicilia, Italy, C Mediterranean Sea
Nisch/Nish *see* Niš
172 Nn5 **Niseko** Hokkaidō, NE Japan
Nishapur *see* Neyshābūr
116 G9 **Nishava** *var.* Nišava. ↝ Bulgaria/Yugoslavia *see also* Nišava
120 L11 **Nishcha** *Rus.* Nishcha. ↝ N Belarus
172 Qq7 **Nishibetsu-gawa** ↝ Hokkaidō, NE Japan
170 E13 **Nishi-gawa** ↝ Honshū, SW Japan
170 Ee13 **Nishi-Nōmi-jima** *var.* Nōmi-jima. *island* SW Japan
170 Bb17 **Nishinoomote** Kagoshima, Tanega-shima, SW Japan
172 Ss16 **Nishino-shima** *Eng.* Rosario. *island* Ogasawara-shotō, SE Japan
171 Hh16 **Nishio** *var.* Nisio. Aichi, Honshū, SW Japan
170 C13 **Nishi-Sonogi-hantō** *peninsula* Kyūshū, SW Japan
171 Gg14 **Nishiwaki** *var.* Nisiwaki. Hyōgo, Honshū, SW Japan
147 U14 **Nishtūn** SE Yemen
Nisiros *see* Nísyros
Nisiwaki *see* Nishiwaki
Niska *see* Niesky
115 O14 **Niška Banja** Serbia, SE Yugoslavia
10 D6 **Niskibi** ↝ Ontario, C Canada
113 O15 **Nisko** Tarnobrzeg, SE Poland
8 H7 **Nisling** ↝ Yukon Territory, W Canada
101 H22 **Nismes** Namur, S Belgium
Nismes *see* Nîmes
118 M10 **Nisporeni** *Rus.* Nisporeny. W Moldova
Nisporeny *see* Nisporeni
97 K20 **Nissan** ↝ S Sweden
195 R11 **Nissan Island** *island* Green Islands, NE PNG
Nissan Islands *see* Green Islands
97 F16 **Nisser** ◎ S Norway
97 E21 **Nissum Bredning** *inlet* NW Denmark
31 U6 **Nisswa** Minnesota, N USA
Nistru *see* Dniester
117 M22 **Nísyros** *var.* Nisiros. *island* Dodekánisos, Greece, Aegean Sea
120 H8 **Nītaure** Cēsis, C Latvia
62 P10 **Niterói** *prev.* Nictheroy. Rio de Janeiro, SE Brazil
12 F16 **Nith** ↝ Ontario, S Canada
98 J13 **Nith** ↝ S Scotland, UK
Nitinan *see* Nichinan
113 I21 **Nitra** *Ger.* Neutra, *Hung.* Nyitra. Západné Slovensko, SW Slovakia
113 I20 **Nitra** *Ger.* Neutra, *Hung.* Nyitra. ↝ W Slovakia
23 Q5 **Nitro** West Virginia, NE USA
125 F11 **Nitsa** ↝ C Russian Federation
97 H14 **Nittedal** Akershus, S Norway
Niuatobutabu *see* Niuatoputapu
200 S11 **Niuatoputapu** *var.* Niuatobutabu; *prev.* Keppel Island. *island* N Tonga
200 Q15 **Niu'Aunofa** *headland* Tongatapu, S Tonga
Niuchwang *see* Yingkou
202 B16 **Niue** ◇ *self-governing territory in free association with NZ* S Pacific Ocean
202 F10 **Niulakita** *var.* Nurakita. *atoll* S Tuvalu
202 E6 **Niutao** *atoll* NW Tuvalu
95 L15 **Nivala** Oulu, C Finland
104 I15 **Nive** ↝ SW France
101 G19 **Nivelles** Walloon Brabant, C Belgium
105 P8 **Nivernais** *cultural region* C France
13 N8 **Niverville, Lac** ◎ Québec, SE Canada
29 T7 **Nixa** Missouri, C USA
37 R5 **Nixon** Nevada, W USA
27 S12 **Nixon** Texas, SW USA
Niya *see* Minfeng
152 K12 **Niyazov** Lebapskiy Velayat, NE Turkmenistan
161 H14 **Nizāmābād** Andhra Pradesh, C India
161 H15 **Nizām Sāgar** ◎ C India
129 N16 **Nizhegorodskaya Oblast'** ◆ *province* W Russian Federation
126 K14 **Nizhneangarsk** Respublika Buryatiya, S Russian Federation
Nizhnegorskiy *see* Nyzhn'ohirs'kyy
131 S4 **Nizhnekamsk** Respublika Tatarstan, W Russian Federation
131 U3 **Nizhnekamskoye Vodokhranilishche** ⊠ W Russian Federation
127 O5 **Nizhnekolymsk** Respublika Sakha (Yakutiya), NE Russian Federation
127 N16 **Nizhne Leninskoye** Yevreyskaya Avtonomnaya Oblast', SE Russian Federation
126 Ii14 **Nizhneudinsk** Irkutskaya Oblast', S Russian Federation
126 Gg11 **Nizhnevartovsk** Khanty-Mansiyskiy Avtonomnyy Okrug, C Russian Federation
126 L16 **Nizhneyansk** Respublika Sakha (Yakutiya), NE Russian Federation
131 Q11 **Nizhniy Baskunchak** Astrakhanskaya Oblast', SW Russian Federation
126 M11 **Nizhniy Bestyakh** Respublika Sakha (Yakutiya), NE Russian Federation
131 O6 **Nizhniy Lomov** Penzenskaya Oblast', W Russian Federation
131 P3 **Nizhniy Novgorod** *prev.* Gor'kiy. Nizhegorodskaya Oblast', W Russian Federation
129 T8 **Nizhniy Odes** Respublika Komi, NW Russian Federation
Nizhniy Pyandzh *see* Panji Poyon
125 Ee11 **Nizhniy Tagil** Sverdlovskaya Oblast', C Russian Federation
129 T9 **Nizhnyaya-Omra** Respublika Komi, NW Russian Federation
129 P5 **Nizhnyaya Pesha** Nenetskiy Avtonomnyy Okrug, NW Russian Federation
125 F11 **Nizhnyaya Tavda** Tyumenskaya Oblast', C Russian Federation
126 Jj12 **Nizhnyaya Tunguska** *Eng.* Lower Tunguska. ↝ N Russian Federation
119 Q3 **Nizhyn** *Rus.* Nezhin. Chernihivs'ka Oblast', NE Ukraine
142 M17 **Nizip** Gaziantep, S Turkey
147 X8 **Nizwá** *var.* Nazwāh. NE Oman
Nizza *see* Nice
108 C9 **Nizza Monferrato** Piemonte, NE Italy
Njávdám *see* Näätämöjoki
Njellim *see* Nellim
83 H24 **Njombe** Iringa, S Tanzania
83 G23 **Njombe** ↝ C Tanzania
94 I10 **Njunis** ▲ N Norway
94 H17 **Njurunda** Västernorrland, C Sweden
96 N11 **Njutånger** Gävleborg, C Sweden
81 D14 **Nkambe** Nord-Ouest, NW Cameroon
Nkata Bay *see* Nkhata Bay
81 F21 **Nkayi** *prev.* Jacob. La Bouenza, S Congo
85 J17 **Nkayi** Matabeleland North, W Zimbabwe
84 N13 **Nkhata Bay** *var.* Nkata Bay. Northern, N Malawi
83 E22 **Nkonde** Kigoma, N Tanzania
81 D15 **Nkongsamba** *var.* N'Kongsamba. Littoral, W Cameroon
85 E16 **Nkurenkuru** Okavango, N Namibia
79 Q15 **Nkwanta** E Ghana
178 H1 **Nmai Hka** *var.* Me Hka. ↝ N Myanmar
Noardwâlde *see* Noordwolde
41 N7 **Noatak** Alaska, USA
41 N7 **Noatak River** ↝ Alaska, USA
Nobeji *see* Noheji
170 D15 **Nobeoka** Miyazaki, Kyūshū, SW Japan
29 N11 **Noble** Oklahoma, C USA
33 P13 **Noblesville** Indiana, N USA
172 O6 **Noboribetsu** *var.* Noboribetu. Hokkaidō, NE Japan
Noboribetu *see* Noboribetsu
61 H18 **Nobres** Mato Grosso, W Brazil
109 N21 **Nocera Terinese** Calabria, S Italy
42 I7 **Nochistlán** *var.* Asunción Nochixtlán. Oaxaca, SE Mexico
43 Q16 **Nochixtlán** *var.* Asunción Nochixtlán. Oaxaca, SE Mexico
27 S5 **Nocona** Texas, SW USA
65 K21 **Nodales, Bahía de los** *bay* S Argentina
29 Q2 **Nodaway River** ↝ Iowa/Missouri, C USA
29 R8 **Noel** Missouri, C USA
97 C17 **Nærbø** Rogaland, S Norway
97 I24 **Næstved** Storstrøm, SE Denmark
42 H3 **Nogales** Chihuahua, NW Mexico
42 F3 **Nogales** Sonora, NW Mexico
38 M17 **Nogales** Arizona, SW USA
Nogal Valley *see* Dooxo Nugaaleed
104 K15 **Nogaro** Gers, S France
112 J7 **Nogat** ↝ N Poland
170 D12 **Nōgata** Fukuoka, Kyūshū, SW Japan
131 P15 **Nogayskaya Step'** *steppe* SW Russian Federation
104 M6 **Nogent-le-Rotrou** Eure-et-Loir, C France
105 O4 **Nogent-sur-Oise** Oise, N France
105 P6 **Nogent-sur-Seine** Aube, N France
126 I10 **Noginsk** Evenkiyskiy Avtonomnyy Okrug, N Russian Federation
130 L3 **Noginsk** Moskovskaya Oblast', W Russian Federation
127 O14 **Nogliki** Ostrov Sakhalin, Sakhalinskaya Oblast', SE Russian Federation
171 I14 **Nōgōhaku-san** ▲ Honshū, SW Japan
168 D5 **Nogoonnuur** Bayan-Ölgiy, NW Mongolia
63 C18 **Nogoyá** Entre Ríos, E Argentina
113 K21 **Nógrád** *off.* Nógrád Megye. ◆ *county* N Hungary
107 U5 **Noguera Pallaresa** ↝ NE Spain
107 U4 **Noguera Ribagorçana** ↝ NE Spain
172 N9 **Noheji** *var.* Nobeji. Aomori, Honshū, C Japan
103 E19 **Nohfelden** Saarland, SW Germany
40 A8 **Nohili Point** *headland* Kauai, Hawaii, USA, C Pacific Ocean
106 G3 **Noia** Galicia, NW Spain
105 N16 **Noire, Montagne** ▲ S France
13 P12 **Noire, Rivière** ↝ Québec, SE Canada
12 J10 **Noire, Rivière** ↝ Québec, SE Canada
Noire, Rivière *see* Black River
104 G6 **Noires, Montagnes** ▲ NW France
104 H8 **Noirmoutier-en-l'Île** Vendée, NW France
104 H8 **Noirmoutier, Île de** *island* NW France
171 Jj17 **Nojima-zaki** *headland* Honshū, S Japan
195 W8 **Noka** Nendö, E Solomon Islands
85 G17 **Nokaneng** Ngamiland, NW Botswana
95 L18 **Nokia** Häme, SW Finland
154 K11 **Nok Kundi** Baluchistān, SW Pakistan
32 L14 **Nokomis** Illinois, N USA
32 K5 **Nokomis, Lake** ⊠ Wisconsin, N USA
80 G9 **Nokou** Kanem, W Chad
197 B12 **Nokuku** Espiritu Santo, W Vanuatu
97 J18 **Nol** Älvsborg, S Sweden
81 H16 **Nola** Sangha-Mbaéré, SW Central African Republic
27 P7 **Nolan** Texas, SW USA
129 R15 **Nolinsk** Kirovskaya Oblast', NW Russian Federation
194 F12 **Nomad** Western, SW Papau New Guinea
170 B15 **Noma-zaki** *headland* Kyūshū, SW Japan
42 K10 **Nombre de Dios** Durango, C Mexico
44 I5 **Nombre de Dios, Cordillera** ▲ N Honduras
40 M9 **Nome** Alaska, USA
31 Q6 **Nome** North Dakota, N USA
40 M9 **Nome, Cape** *headland* Alaska, USA
Nōmi-jima *see* Nishi-Nōmi-jima
12 M11 **Nominingue, Lac** ◎ Québec, SE Canada
Nomoi Islands *see* Mortlock Islands
170 Bb13 **Nomo-zaki** *headland* Kyūshū, SW Japan
200 S13 **Nomuka** *island* Nomuka Group, C Tonga
200 S14 **Nomuka Group** *island group* W Tonga
201 Q15 **Nomwin Atoll** *atoll* Hall Islands, C Micronesia
15 I8 **Nonacho Lake** ◎ Northwest Territories, NW Canada
Nondaburi *see* Nonthaburi
41 P12 **Nondalton** Alaska, USA
169 V10 **Nong'an** Jilin, NE China
178 I10 **Nong Bua Khok** Nakhon Ratchasima, C Thailand
178 I9 **Nong Bua Lamphu** Udon Thani, E Thailand
178 J7 **Nông Hèt** Xiangkhoang, N Laos
Nongkaya *see* Nong Khai
178 I8 **Nong Khai** *var.* Mi Chai, Nongkaya. Nong Khai, E Thailand
178 Gg15 **Nong Met** Surat Thani, SW Thailand
85 L22 **Nongoma** KwaZulu/Natal, E South Africa
178 Hh10 **Nong Phai** Phetchabun, C Thailand
159 U13 **Nongstoin** Meghālaya, NE India
85 C19 **Nonidas** Erongo, N Namibia
Nonni *see* Nen Jiang
42 I7 **Nonoava** Chihuahua, N Mexico
203 O3 **Nonouti** *prev.* Sydenham Island. *atoll* Tungaru, W Kiribati
178 Hh11 **Nonthaburi** *var.* Nondaburi, Nontha Buri. Nonthaburi, C Thailand
104 L11 **Nontron** Dordogne, SW France
189 P1 **Noonamah** Northern Territory, N Australia
30 K2 **Noonan** North Dakota, N USA
101 E14 **Noord-Beveland** *var.* North Beveland. *island* SW Netherlands
101 J14 **Noord-Brabant** *Eng.* North Brabant. ◆ *province* S Netherlands
100 H7 **Noorder Haaks** *spit* NW Netherlands
100 H9 **Noord-Holland** *Eng.* North Holland. ◆ *province* NW Netherlands
Noordhollandsch Kanaal *see* Noordhollands Kanaal
100 H8 **Noordhollands Kanaal** *var.* Noordhollandsch Kanaal. *canal* NW Netherlands
Noord-Kaap *see* Northern Cape
100 L8 **Noordoostpolder** *island* N Netherlands
47 P16 **Noordpunt** *headland* Curaçao, C Netherlands Antilles
100 I8 **Noord-Scharwoude** Noord-Holland, NW Netherlands
Noordwes *see* North-West
100 G11 **Noordwijk aan Zee** Zuid-Holland, W Netherlands
100 H11 **Noordwijkerhout** Zuid-Holland, W Netherlands
100 M7 **Noordwolde** *Fris.* Noardwâlde. Friesland, N Netherlands
Noordzee *see* North Sea
100 H10 **Noordzee-Kanaal** *canal* NW Netherlands
95 K18 **Noormarkku** *Swe.* Norrmark. Turku-Pori, SW Finland
41 N8 **Noorvik** Alaska, USA
8 J17 **Nootka Sound** *inlet* British Columbia, W Canada
84 A9 **Nóqui** Zaire, NW Angola
97 L15 **Nora** Örebro, C Sweden
153 Q13 **Norak** *Rus.* Nurek. W Tajikistan
16 P14 **Noranda** Québec, SE Canada
31 W12 **Nora Springs** Iowa, C USA
97 M14 **Norberg** Västmanland, C Sweden
12 K13 **Norcan Lake** ◎ Ontario, SE Canada
207 R12 **Nord** N Greenland
80 F13 **Nord** *Eng.* North. ◆ *province* N Cameroon
105 P2 **Nord** ◆ *department* N France
94 P1 **Nordaustlandet** *island* NE Svalbard
97 G24 **Nordborg** *Ger.* Nordburg. Sønderjylland, SW Denmark
Nordburg *see* Nordborg
97 F23 **Nordby** Ribe, W Denmark
9 P15 **Nordegg** Alberta, SW Canada
102 E9 **Norden** Niedersachsen, NW Germany
102 G10 **Nordenham** Niedersachsen, NW Germany
126 Ii4 **Nordenshel'da, Arkhipelag** *island group* N Russian Federation
94 O3 **Nordenskiold Land** *physical region* W Svalbard
102 E9 **Norderney** *island* NW Germany
102 J9 **Norderstedt** Schleswig-Holstein, N Germany
96 C11 **Nordfjord** *physical region* S Norway
96 D11 **Nordfjord** *fjord* S Norway
96 D11 **Nordfjordeid** Sogn og Fjordane, S Norway
94 G11 **Nordfold** Nordland, C Norway
Nordfriesische Inseln *see* North Frisian Islands
102 H7 **Nordfriesland** *cultural region* N Germany
103 K15 **Nordhausen** Thüringen, C Germany
27 T13 **Nordheim** Texas, SW USA
96 C13 **Nordhordland** *physical region* S Norway
102 E12 **Nordhorn** Niedersachsen, NW Germany
94 I1 **Nordhurfjördhur** Vestfirdhir, NW Iceland
94 J1 **Nordhurland Eystra** ◆ *region* N Iceland
94 I2 **Nordhurland Vestra** ◆ *region* N Iceland
180 H16 **Nord, Île du** *island* Inner Islands, NE Seychelles
97 F20 **Nordjylland** *off.* Nordjyllands Amt. ◆ *county* N Denmark
94 K7 **Nordkapp** *Eng.* North Cape. *headland* N Norway
94 O1 **Nordkapp** *headland* N Svalbard
94 L7 **Nordkinn** *headland* N Norway
81 N19 **Nord Kivu** *off.* Région du Nord Kivu. ◆ *region* E Zaire
94 G12 **Nordland** ◆ *county* C Norway
103 J21 **Nördlingen** Bayern, S Germany
95 I16 **Nordmaling** Västerbotten, N Sweden
97 K15 **Nordmark** Värmland, C Sweden
Nord, Mer du *see* North Sea
96 F8 **Nordmøre** *physical region* S Norway
102 I8 **Nord-Ostee-Kanal** *canal* N Germany
1 J3 **Nordostrundingen** *headland* NE Greenland
81 D14 **Nord-Ouest** *Eng.* North-West. ◆ *province* NW Cameroon
Nord-Ouest, Territoires du *see* Northwest Territories
105 N2 **Nord-Pas-de-Calais** ◆ *region* N France
103 F19 **Nordpfälzer Bergland** ▲ W Germany
Nord, Pointe *see* Fatua, Pointe
197 H5 **Nord, Province** ◆ *province* C New Caledonia
94 J9 **Nordreisa** Troms, N Norway
103 D14 **Nordrhein-Westfalen** *Eng.* North Rhine-Westphalia, *Fr.* Rhénanie du Nord-Westphalie. ◆ *state* W Germany
Nordsee/Nordsjøen/ Nordsøen *see* North Sea
102 H7 **Nordstrand** *island* N Germany
95 E15 **Nord-Trøndelag** ◆ *county* C Norway
99 E19 **Nore** *Ir.* An Fheoir. ↝ S Ireland
31 Q14 **Norfolk** Nebraska, C USA
23 X7 **Norfolk** Virginia, NE USA
99 P19 **Norfolk** *cultural region* E England, UK
199 Ii11 **Norfolk Island** ◇ *Australian external territory* SW Pacific Ocean
183 P9 **Norfolk Ridge** *undersea feature* W Pacific Ocean
29 U8 **Norfork Lake** ⊠ Arkansas/Missouri, C USA
100 N6 **Norg** Drenthe, NE Netherlands
Norge *see* Norway
97 D14 **Norheimsund** Hordaland, S Norway
27 S16 **Norias** Texas, SW USA
171 J14 **Norikura-dake** ▲ Honshū, S Japan
126 I8 **Noril'sk** Taymyrskiy (Dolgano-Nenetskiy) Avtonomnyy Okrug, N Russian Federation
12 I13 **Norland** Ontario, SE Canada
23 V8 **Norlina** North Carolina, SE USA
32 L13 **Normal** Illinois, N USA
29 N11 **Norman** Oklahoma, C USA
Norman *see* Fort Norman
195 O16 **Normanby Island** *island* SE PNG
Normandes, Îles *see* Channel Islands
60 G9 **Normandia** Roraima, N Brazil
104 L5 **Normandie** *Eng.* Normandy. *cultural region* N France
104 J5 **Normandie, Collines de** *hill range* NW France
Normandy *see* Normandie
27 V9 **Normangee** Texas, SW USA
23 Q10 **Norman, Lake** ⊠ North Carolina, SE USA
46 K13 **Norman Manley** ✕ (Kingston) E Jamaica
189 U5 **Norman River** ↝ Queensland, NE Australia
189 U4 **Normanton** Queensland, NE Australia
15 Gg5 **Norman Wells** Northwest Territories, NW Canada
10 H12 **Normétal** Québec, S Canada
9 V15 **Norquay** Saskatchewan, S Canada
96 N11 **Norra Dellen** ◎ C Sweden
Norra Karelen *see* Pohjois-Karjala
95 G15 **Norråker** Jämtland, C Sweden
96 N12 **Norrala** Gävleborg, C Sweden
Norra Ny *see* Stöllet
94 G13 **Norra Storjfjället** ▲ N Sweden
94 I13 **Norrbotten** ◆ *county* N Sweden
Nørre Aaby *see* Nørre Åby
97 G23 **Nørre Åby** *var.* Nørre Aaby. Fyn, C Denmark
97 I24 **Nørre Alslev** Storstrøm, SE Denmark
97 E23 **Nørre Nebel** Ribe, W Denmark
97 G20 **Nørresundby** Nordjylland, N Denmark
23 N8 **Norris Lake** ⊠ Tennessee, S USA
20 I15 **Norristown** Pennsylvania, NE USA
97 N17 **Norrköping** Östergötland, S Sweden
Norrmark *see* Noormarkku
96 N13 **Norrsundet** Gävleborg, C Sweden
97 P15 **Norrtälje** Stockholm, C Sweden
188 L12 **Norseman** Western Australia
95 I14 **Norsjö** Västerbotten, N Sweden
97 G16 **Norsjø** ◎ S Norway
126 Mm15 **Norsk** Amurskaya Oblast', SE Russian Federation
Norske Havet *see* Norwegian Sea
197 C13 **Norsup** Malekula, C Vanuatu
203 V15 **Norte, Cabo** *headland* Easter Island, Chile, E Pacific Ocean
56 F7 **Norte de Santander** *off.* Departamento de Norte de Santander. ◆ *province* N Colombia
63 E21 **Norte, Punta** *headland* E Argentina
23 R13 **North** South Carolina, SE USA
North *see* Nord
20 L10 **North Adams** Massachusetts, NE USA
115 L17 **North Albanian Alps** *Alb.* Bjeshkët e Namuna, *SCr.* Prokletije. ▲ Albania/Yugoslavia
99 M15 **Northallerton** N England, UK
188 J12 **Northam** Western Australia
85 J20 **Northam** Northern, N South Africa
1 **North America** *continent*
1 N12 **North American Basin** *undersea feature* W Sargasso Sea
1 C5 **North American Plate** *tectonic feature*
20 M11 **North Amherst** Massachusetts, NE USA
99 N20 **Northampton** C England, UK
99 M20 **Northamptonshire** *cultural region* C England, UK
157 P18 **North Andaman** *island* Andaman Islands, India, NE Indian Ocean
67 D25 **North Arm** East Falkland, Falkland Islands
23 Q13 **North Augusta** South Carolina, SE USA
181 W8 **North Australian Basin** *Fr.* Bassin Nord de l' Australie. *undersea feature* E Indian Ocean
33 R11 **North Baltimore** Ohio, N USA
9 T15 **North Battleford** Saskatchewan, S Canada
12 H11 **North Bay** Ontario, S Canada
10 H6 **North Belcher Islands** *island group* Belcher Islands, Northwest Territories, C Canada
31 R15 **North Bend** Nebraska, C USA
34 E14 **North Bend** Oregon, NW USA
98 K12 **North Berwick** SE Scotland, UK
North Beveland *see* Noord-Beveland
North Borneo *see* Sabah
191 P5 **North Bourke** New South Wales, SE Australia
North Brabant *see* Noord-Brabant
190 F2 **North Branch Neales** *seasonal river* South Australia
46 M6 **North Caicos** *island* NW Turks and Caicos Islands
28 L10 **North Canadian River** ↝ Oklahoma, C USA
33 U12 **North Canton** Ohio, N USA
11 R13 **North, Cape** *headland* Cape Breton Island, Nova Scotia, SE Canada
192 I1 **North Cape** *headland* North Island, NZ
195 N9 **North Cape** *headland* New Ireland, NE PNG
North Cape *see* Nordkapp
20 J17 **North Cape May** New Jersey, NE USA
10 C9 **North Caribou Lake** ◎ Ontario, C Canada
23 U10 **North Carolina** *off.* State of North Carolina; also known as Old North State, Tar Heel State, Turpentine State. ◆ *state* SE USA
North Celebes *see* Sulawesi Utara
161 J24 **North Central Province** ◆ *province* N Sri Lanka
33 S4 **North Channel** *lake channel* Canada/USA
99 G14 **North Channel** *strait* Northern Ireland/Scotland, UK
23 S14 **North Charleston** South Carolina, SE USA
33 N10 **North Chicago** Illinois, N USA
205 Y10 **Northcliffe Glacier** *glacier* Antarctica
33 Q14 **North College Hill** Ohio, N USA
27 O8 **North Concho River** ↝ Texas, SW USA
21 O8 **North Conway** New Hampshire, NE USA
29 V14 **North Crossett** Arkansas, C USA
30 L4 **North Dakota** *off.* State of North Dakota; also known as Flickertail State, Peace Garden State, Sioux State. ◆ *state* N USA
North Devon Island *see* Devon Island
99 O22 **North Downs** *hill range* SE England, UK
20 C11 **North East** Pennsylvania, NE USA
85 I18 **North East** ◆ *district* NE Botswana
67 G15 **North East Bay** *bay* Ascension Island, C Atlantic Ocean
40 L10 **Northeast Cape** *headland* Saint Lawrence Island, Alaska, USA
178 Mm13 **Northeast Cay** *island* NW Spratly Islands
83 J17 **North Eastern** ◆ *province* Kenya
North East Frontier Agency/North East Frontier Agency of Assam *see* Arunāchal Pradesh
67 E25 **North East Island** *island* E Falkland Islands
201 V11 **Northeast Island** *island* Chuuk, C Micronesia
46 L12 **North East Point** *headland* E Jamaica
46 L6 **Northeast Point** *headland* Great Inagua, S Bahamas
46 K5 **Northeast Point** *headland* Acklins Island, SE Bahamas
203 Z2 **Northeast Point** *headland* Kiritimati, E Kiribati
46 H2 **Northeast Providence Channel** *channel* N Bahamas
103 J14 **Northeim** Niedersachsen, C Germany
31 X14 **North English** Iowa, C USA
144 G8 **Northern** ◆ *district* N Israel
84 M12 **Northern** ◆ *region* N Malawi
194 L15 **Northern** ◆ *province* S PNG
85 J20 **Northern** *off.* Northern Province; *prev.* Northern Transvaal. ◆ *province* NE South Africa
82 D7 **Northern** ◆ *state* N Sudan
84 K12 **Northern** ◆ *province* NE Zambia
82 B13 **Northern Bahr el Ghazal** ◆ *state* SW Sudan
Northern Border Region *see* Al Ḥudūd ash Shamālīyah
85 F24 **Northern Cape** *off.* Northern Cape Province, *Afr.* Noord-Kaap. ◆ *province* W South Africa
202 K14 **Northern Cook Islands** *island group* N Cook Islands
82 B8 **Northern Darfur** ◆ *state* NW Sudan
Northern Dvina *see* Severnaya Dvina
99 F14 **Northern Ireland** *var.* The Six Counties. *political division* UK
82 D9 **Northern Kordofan** ◆ *state* C Sudan
197 K14 **Northern Lau Group** *island group* Lau Group, NE Fiji
196 K3 **Northern Mariana Islands** ◇ *US commonwealth territory* W Pacific Ocean
161 J23 **Northern Province** ◆ *province* N Sri Lanka
Northern Rhodesia *see* Zambia
Northern Sporades *see* Vóreioi Sporádes
190 D1 **Northern Territory** ◆ *territory* N Australia
Northern Transvaal *see* Northern
Northern Ural Hills *see* Severnyye Uvaly
86 I9 **North European Plain** *plain* N Europe
29 V2 **North Fabius River** ↝ Missouri, C USA
67 D24 **North Falkland Sound** *sound* N Falkland Islands
31 V9 **Northfield** Minnesota, N USA
21 O9 **Northfield** New Hampshire, NE USA
183 Q8 **North Fiji Basin** *undersea feature* N Coral Sea
99 Q22 **North Foreland** *headland* SE England, UK
37 P6 **North Fork American River** ↝ California, W USA
41 R7 **North Fork Chandalar River** ↝ Alaska, USA
30 K7 **North Fork Grand River** ↝ North Dakota/South Dakota, N USA
23 O6 **North Fork Kentucky River** ↝ Kentucky, S USA
41 Q7 **North Fork Koyukuk River** ↝ Alaska, USA
41 Q10 **North Fork Kuskokwim River** ↝ Alaska, USA
28 K11 **North Fork Red River** ↝ Oklahoma/Texas, SW USA
28 K3 **North Fork Solomon River** ↝ Kansas, C USA
25 W14 **North Fort Myers** Florida, SE USA
33 P5 **North Fox Island** *island* Michigan, N USA
102 G6 **North Frisian Islands** *var.* Nordfriesische Inseln. *island group* N Germany
207 N9 **North Geomagnetic Pole** *pole* Arctic Ocean
20 M13 **North Haven** Connecticut, NE USA
192 J5 **North Head** *headland* North Island, NZ
20 L6 **North Hero** Vermont, NE USA
37 O7 **North Highlands** California, W USA
North Holland *see* Noord-Holland
83 I16 **North Horr** Eastern, N Kenya
157 K21 **North Huvadhu Atoll** *var.* Gaafu Alifu Atoll. *atoll* S Maldives
67 A24 **North Island** *island* W Falkland Islands
192 N9 **North Island** *island* N NZ
23 U14 **North Island** *island* South Carolina, SE USA
33 O11 **North Judson** Indiana, N USA
North Kazakhstan *see* Severnyy Kazakhstan
33 V10 **North Kingsville** Ohio, N USA
169 Y13 **North Korea** *off.* Democratic People's Republic of Korea, *Kor.* Chosŏn-minjujuŭi-inmin-kanghwaguk. ◆ *republic* E Asia
159 X11 **North Lakhimpur** Assam, NE India
192 J3 **Northland** *off.* Northland Region. ◆ *region* North Island, NZ
199 J12 **Northland Plateau** *undersea feature* S Pacific Ocean
37 X11 **North Las Vegas** Nevada, W USA
33 O11 **North Liberty** Indiana, N USA
31 X14 **North Liberty** Iowa, C USA
29 V12 **North Little Rock** Arkansas, C USA
30 M13 **North Loup River** ↝ Nebraska, C USA
157 K18 **North Maalhosmadulu Atoll** *var.* North Malosmadulu Atoll, Raa Atoll. *atoll* N Maldives
33 U10 **North Madison** Ohio, N USA
33 P12 **North Manchester** Indiana, N USA
33 P6 **North Manitou Island** *island* Michigan, N USA
31 U10 **North Mankato** Minnesota, N USA
25 Z15 **North Miami** Florida, SE USA
157 K18 **North Miladummadulu Atoll** *atoll* N Maldives
North Minch *see* Minch, The
25 W15 **North Naples** Florida, SE USA
183 P8 **North New Hebrides Trench** *undersea feature* N Coral Sea
25 Y15 **North New River Canal** ↝ Florida, SE USA
157 K20 **North Nilandhe Atoll** *var.* Faafu Atoll. *atoll* C Maldives
38 L2 **North Ogden** Utah, W USA
North Ossetia *see* Severnaya Osetiya, Respublika
37 S10 **North Palisade** ▲ California, W USA
201 U11 **North Pass** *passage* Chuuk Islands, C Micronesia
30 M15 **North Platte** Nebraska, C USA
35 X17 **North Platte River** ↝ C USA
67 G14 **North Point** *headland* Ascension Island, C Atlantic Ocean
180 I16 **North Point** *headland* Mahé, NE Seychelles
33 S6 **North Point** *headland* Michigan, N USA
33 R5 **North Point** *headland* Michigan, N USA
41 S9 **North Pole** Alaska, USA
207 R9 **North Pole** *pole* Arctic Ocean
25 O4 **Northport** Alabama, S USA
25 W14 **North Port** Florida, SE USA
34 L6 **Northport** Washington, NW USA
34 L12 **North Powder** Oregon, NW USA
31 U13 **North Raccoon River** ↝ Iowa, C USA

◆ COUNTRY ● COUNTRY CAPITAL ◇ DEPENDENT TERRITORY ○ DEPENDENT TERRITORY CAPITAL ◆ ADMINISTRATIVE REGION ✕ INTERNATIONAL AIRPORT ▲ MOUNTAIN ▲ MOUNTAIN RANGE ⅄ VOLCANO ↝ RIVER ◎ LAKE ⊠ RESERVOIR

North Rhine-Westphalia *see* Nordrhein-Westfalen
99 M16 **North Riding** *cultural region* N England, UK
98 G5 **North Rona** *island* NW Scotland, UK
98 K4 **North Ronaldsay** *island* NE Scotland, UK
38 L2 **North Salt Lake** Utah, W USA
9 P15 **North Saskatchewan** ⟿ Alberta/Saskatchewan, S Canada
37 X5 **North Schell Peak** ▲ Nevada, W USA
North Scotia Ridge *see* South Georgia Ridge
88 D10 **North Sea** *Dan.* Nordsøen, *Dut.* Noordzee, *Fr.* Mer du Nord, *Ger.* Nordsee, *Nor.* Nordsjøen; *prev.* German Ocean, *Lat.* Mare Germanicum. *sea* NW Europe
37 T6 **North Shoshone Peak** ▲ Nevada, W USA
North Siberian Lowland/North Siberian Plain *see* Severo-Sibirskaya Nizmennost'
31 R13 **North Sioux City** South Dakota, N USA
98 K4 **North Sound, The** *sound* N Scotland, UK
191 T4 **North Star** New South Wales, SE Australia
North Star State *see* Minnesota
191 V3 **North Stradbroke Island** *island* Queensland, E Australia
North Sulawesi *see* Sulawesi Utara
North Sumatra *see* Sumatera Utara
12 D17 **North Sydenham** ⟿ Ontario, S Canada
20 H9 **North Syracuse** New York, NE USA
192 K9 **North Taranaki Bight** *gulf* North Island, NZ
202 I2 **North Tarawa** *atoll* Tungaru, W Kiribati
10 H9 **North Twin Island** *island* Northwest Territories, C Canada
98 E8 **North Uist** *island* NW Scotland, UK
99 L14 **Northumberland** *cultural region* N England, UK
189 Y7 **Northumberland Isles** *island group* Queensland, NE Australia
11 Q14 **Northumberland Strait** *strait* SE Canada
34 G14 **North Umpqua River** ⟿ Oregon, NW USA
47 Q13 **North Union** Saint Vincent, Saint Vincent and the Grenadines
8 L17 **North Vancouver** British Columbia, SW Canada
20 K9 **Northville** New York, NE USA
99 Q19 **North Walsham** E England, UK
41 T10 **Northway** Alaska, USA
85 G21 **North-West** *off.* North-West Province, *Afr.* Noordwes. ◆ *province* N South Africa
North-West *see* Nord-Ouest
66 I6 **Northwest Atlantic Mid-Ocean Canyon** *undersea feature* N Atlantic Ocean
188 G8 **North West Cape** *headland* Western Australia
40 J9 **Northwest Cape** *headland* Saint Lawrence Island, Alaska, USA
84 H13 **North Western** ◆ *province* W Zambia
161 J24 **North Western Province** ◆ *province* W Sri Lanka
155 U4 **North-West Frontier Province** ◆ *province* NW Pakistan
98 H8 **North West Highlands** ▲ N Scotland, UK
199 Hh4 **Northwest Pacific Basin** *undersea feature* NW Pacific Ocean
203 Y2 **Northwest Point** *headland* Kiritimati, E Kiribati
46 G1 **Northwest Providence Channel** *channel* N Bahamas
11 Q8 **North West River** Newfoundland and Labrador, E Canada
15 I5 **Northwest Territories** *Fr.* Territoires du Nord-Ouest. ◆ *territory* NW Canada
99 K18 **Northwich** C England, UK
27 Q5 **North Wichita River** ⟿ Texas, SW USA
20 J17 **North Wildwood** New Jersey, NE USA
23 R9 **North Wilkesboro** North Carolina, SE USA
21 P8 **North Windham** Maine, NE USA
207 Q6 **Northwind Plain** *undersea feature* Arctic Ocean
31 V11 **Northwood** Iowa, C USA
31 Q4 **Northwood** North Dakota, N USA
99 M15 **North York Moors** *moorland* N England, UK
27 V9 **North Zulch** Texas, SW USA
28 K2 **Norton** Kansas, C USA
33 S13 **Norton** Ohio, N USA
23 P7 **Norton** Virginia, NE USA
41 N9 **Norton Bay** *bay* Alaska, USA
Norton de Matos *see* Balombo
33 O9 **Norton Shores** Michigan, N USA
40 M10 **Norton Sound** *inlet* Alaska, USA
29 Q3 **Nortonville** Kansas, C USA
104 I8 **Nort-sur-Erdre** Loire-Atlantique, NW France
205 N2 **Norvegia, Cape** *headland* Antarctica
20 L13 **Norwalk** Connecticut, NE USA
31 V14 **Norwalk** Iowa, C USA
33 S11 **Norwalk** Ohio, N USA
21 P7 **Norway** Maine, NE USA
33 N5 **Norway** Michigan, N USA
95 E17 **Norway** *off.* Kingdom of Norway, *Nor.* Norge. ◆ *monarchy* N Europe
9 X13 **Norway House** Manitoba, C Canada
207 R16 **Norwegian Basin** *undersea feature* NW Norwegian Sea
86 D6 **Norwegian Sea** *Nor.* Norske Havet. *sea* NE Atlantic Ocean
207 S17 **Norwegian Trench** *undersea feature* NE North Sea
12 F16 **Norwich** Ontario, S Canada
99 Q19 **Norwich** E England, UK
21 N13 **Norwich** Connecticut, NE USA
20 I11 **Norwich** New York, NE USA
31 U9 **Norwood** Minnesota, N USA
33 Q15 **Norwood** Ohio, N USA
12 H11 **Nosbonsing, Lake** ◎ Ontario, S Canada
Nösen *see* Bistrița
172 P1 **Noshappu-misaki** *headland* Hokkaidō, NE Japan
171 M9 **Noshiro** *var.* Nosiro; *prev.* Noshirominato. Akita, Honshū, C Japan
Noshirominato/Nosiro *see* Noshiro
119 Q3 **Nosivka** *Rus.* Nosovka. Chernihivs'ka Oblast', NE Ukraine
69 T14 **Nosop** *var.* Nossob, Nossop. ⟿ Botswana/Namibia
129 S4 **Nosovaya** Nenetskiy Avtonomnyy Okrug, NW Russian Federation
Nosovka *see* Nosivka
149 V11 **Noşratābād** Sīstān va Balūchestān, E Iran
97 J18 **Nossebro** Skaraborg, S Sweden
98 K6 **Noss Head** *headland* N Scotland, UK
Nossi-Bé *see* Be, Nosy
85 E20 **Nossob** ⟿ E Namibia
Nossob/Nossop *see* Nosop
180 J2 **Nosy Be** ✕ Antsiraňana, N Madagascar
180 J6 **Nosy Varika** Fianarantsoa, SE Madagascar
12 L10 **Notawassi** ⟿ Québec, SE Canada
12 M9 **Notawassi, Lac** ◎ Québec, SE Canada
38 J5 **Notch Peak** ▲ Utah, W USA
112 G10 **Noteć** *Ger.* Netze. ⟿ NW Poland
Nóties Sporádes *see* Dodekánisos
117 J22 **Nótion Aigaíon** *Eng.* Aegean South. ◆ *region* E Greece
117 H18 **Nótios Evvoïkós Kólpos** *gulf* E Greece
117 B16 **Nótio Stenó Kérkyras** *strait* W Greece
109 L25 **Noto** *anc.* Netum. Sicilia, Italy, C Mediterranean Sea
171 J12 **Noto** Ishikawa, Honshū, SW Japan
97 G15 **Notodden** Telemark, S Norway
109 L25 **Noto, Golfo di** *gulf* Sicilia, Italy, C Mediterranean Sea
171 J12 **Noto-hantō** *peninsula* Honshū, SW Japan
171 J12 **Noto-jima** *island* SW Japan
172 Qq5 **Notoro-ko** ◎ Hokkaidō, NE Japan
11 T11 **Notre Dame Bay** *bay* Newfoundland, Newfoundland and Labrador, E Canada
13 P6 **Notre-Dame-de-Lorette** Québec, SE Canada
12 L11 **Notre-Dame-de-Pontmain** Québec, SE Canada
13 T8 **Notre-Dame-du-Lac** Québec, SE Canada
13 Q6 **Notre-Dame-du-Rosaire** Québec, SE Canada
13 U8 **Notre-Dame, Monts** ▲ Québec, S Canada
79 R16 **Notsé** S Togo
172 R7 **Notsuke-suidō** *strait* Japan/Russian Federation
172 R7 **Notsuke-zaki** *headland* Hokkaidō, NE Japan
12 G14 **Nottawasaga** ⟿ Ontario, S Canada
12 G14 **Nottawasaga Bay** *lake bay* Ontario, S Canada
10 I11 **Nottaway** ⟿ Québec, SE Canada
25 S1 **Nottely Lake** ⊞ Georgia, SE USA
97 H16 **Nøtterøy** *island* S Norway
99 M19 **Nottingham** C England, UK
16 N5 **Nottingham Island** *island* Northwest Territories, NE Canada
99 N18 **Nottinghamshire** *cultural region* C England, UK
23 V7 **Nottoway** Virginia, NE USA
23 V7 **Nottoway River** ⟿ Virginia, NE USA
78 G7 **Nouâdhibou** *prev.* Port-Étienne. Dakhlet Nouâdhibou, W Mauritania
78 G7 **Nouâdhibou** ✕ Dakhlet Nouâdhibou, W Mauritania
78 F7 **Nouâdhibou, Dakhlet** *prev.* Baie du Lévrier. *bay* W Mauritania
78 F7 **Nouâdhibou, Râs** *prev.* Cap Blanc. *headland* NW Mauritania
78 G9 **Nouakchott** ● (Mauritania) Nouakchott District, SW Mauritania
78 G9 **Nouakchott** ✕ Trarza, SW Mauritania
123 K13 **Noual, Sebkhet en** *var.* Sabkhat an Nawāl. *salt flat* C Tunisia
78 G8 **Nouâmghâr** *var.* Nouamrhar. Dakhlet Nouâdhibou, W Mauritania
Nouamrhar *see* Nouâmghâr
Nouă Sulița *see* Novoselytsya
197 I7 **Nouméa** ○ (New Caledonia) Province Sud, S New Caledonia
81 E15 **Noun** ⟿ C Cameroon
77 N12 **Nouna** W Burkina
85 H24 **Noupoort** Northern Cape, C South Africa
Nouveau-Brunswick *see* New Brunswick
Nouveau-Comptoir *see* Wemindji
13 P12 **Nouvel, Lacs** ◎ Québec, SE Canada
13 W7 **Nouvelle** Québec, SE Canada
13 W7 **Nouvelle** ⟿ Québec, SE Canada
Nouvelle-Calédonie *see* New Caledonia
Nouvelle Écosse *see* Nova Scotia
105 R3 **Nouzonville** Ardennes, N France
153 Q11 **Nov** *Rus.* Nau. NW Tajikistan
61 I21 **Nova Alvorada** Mato Grosso do Sul, SW Brazil
Novabad *see* Navobod
113 D19 **Nová Bystřice** *Ger.* Neubistritz. Jižní Čechy, S Czech Republic
118 H13 **Novaci** Gorj, SW Romania
Nova Civitas *see* Neustadt an der Weinstrasse
Novaesium *see* Neuss
62 H10 **Nova Esperança** Paraná, S Brazil
108 H11 **Novafeltria** Marche, C Italy
62 Q9 **Nova Friburgo** Rio de Janeiro, SE Brazil
84 D12 **Nova Gaia** *var.* Cambundi-Catembo. Malanje, NE Angola
111 S12 **Nova Gorica** W Slovenia
114 G10 **Nova Gradiška** *Ger.* Neugradisk, *Hung.* Újgradiska. Brod-Posavina, NE Croatia
62 K7 **Nova Granada** São Paulo, S Brazil
62 O10 **Nova Iguaçu** Rio de Janeiro, SE Brazil
119 S10 **Nova Kakhovka** *Rus.* Novaya Kakhovka. Khersons'ka Oblast', SE Ukraine
Nová Karvinná *see* Karviná
Nova Lamego *see* Gabú
Nova Lisboa *see* Huambo
114 C11 **Novalja** Lika-Senj, W Croatia
121 M14 **Novalukoml'** *Rus.* Novolukoml'. Vitsyebskaya Voblasts', N Belarus
Nova Mambone *see* Mambone
85 P16 **Nova Nabúri** Zambézia, NE Mozambique
119 Q9 **Nova Odesa** *var.* Novaya Odessa. Mykolayivs'ka Oblast', S Ukraine
62 H10 **Nova Olímpia** Paraná, S Brazil
63 I15 **Nova Prata** Rio Grande do Sul, S Brazil
12 H12 **Novar** Ontario, S Canada
108 C7 **Novara** *anc.* Novaria. Piemonte, NW Italy
Novaria *see* Novara
119 P7 **Novarkanels'k** Kirovohrads'ka Oblast', C Ukraine
11 P15 **Nova Scotia** *Fr.* Nouvelle Écosse. ◆ *province* SE Canada
1 M9 **Nova Scotia** *physical region* SE Canada
36 M8 **Novato** California, W USA
199 Jj8 **Nova Trough** *undersea feature* W Pacific Ocean
118 L7 **Nova Ushtsya** Khmel'nyts'ka Oblast', W Ukraine
85 M17 **Nova Vanduzi** Manica, C Mozambique
119 U5 **Nova Vodolaha** *Rus.* Novaya Vodolaga. Kharkivs'ka Oblast', E Ukraine
126 L13 **Novaya Chara** Chitinskaya Oblast', S Russian Federation
126 J14 **Novaya Igirma** Irkutskaya Oblast', C Russian Federation
Novaya Kakhovka *see* Nova Kakhovka
150 E10 **Novaya Kazanka** Zapadnyy Kazakhstan, W Kazakhstan
128 I12 **Novaya Ladoga** Leningradskaya Oblast', NW Russian Federation
125 Ee10 **Novaya Lyalya** Sverdlovskaya Oblast, C Russian Federation
131 R5 **Novaya Malykla** Ul'yanovskaya Oblast', W Russian Federation
Novaya Odessa *see* Nova Odesa
126 M4 **Novaya Sibir', Ostrov** *island* Novosibirskiye Ostrova, NE Russian Federation
Novaya Vodolaga *see* Nova Vodolaha
121 P17 **Novaya Yel'nya** *Rus.* Novaya Yel'nya. Mahilyowskaya Voblasts', E Belarus
125 G4 **Novaya Zemlya** *island group* N Russian Federation
Novaya Zemlya Trough *see* East Novaya Zemlya Trough
116 K10 **Nova Zagora** Burgaska Oblast, C Bulgaria
107 S12 **Novelda** País Valenciano, E Spain
113 H19 **Nové Mesto nad Váhom** *Ger.* Waagneustadtl, *Hung.* Vágújhely. Západné Slovensko, W Slovakia
113 F17 **Nové Město na Moravě** *Ger.* Neustadtl in Mähren. Jižní Morava, E Czech Republic
Novesium *see* Neuss
113 I21 **Nové Zámky** *Ger.* Neuhäusel, *Hung.* Érsekújvár. Západné Slovensko, SW Slovakia
125 C6 **Novgorod** Novgorodskaya Oblast', W Russian Federation
Novgorod-Severskiy *see* Novhorod-Sivers'kyy
125 C6 **Novgorodskaya Oblast'** ◆ *province* W Russian Federation
119 R8 **Novhorodka** Kirovohrads'ka Oblast', C Ukraine
119 R2 **Novhorod-Sivers'kyy** *Rus.* Novgorod-Severskiy. Chernihivs'ka Oblast', NE Ukraine
33 R10 **Novi** Michigan, N USA
Novi *see* Novi Vinodolski
114 L9 **Novi Bečej** *prev.* Új-Becse, Vološinovo, *Ger.* Neubetsche, *Hung.* Törökbecse. Serbia, N Yugoslavia
27 Q8 **Novice** Texas, SW USA
114 A9 **Novigrad** Istra, NW Croatia
116 G9 **Novi Iskŭr** Grad Sofiya, W Bulgaria
108 C9 **Novi Ligure** Piemonte, NW Italy
101 L22 **Noville** Luxembourg, SE Belgium
204 I10 **Noville Peninsula** *peninsula* Thurston Island, Antarctica
Noviodunum *see* Soissons, Aisne, France
Noviodunum *see* Nevers, Nièvre, France
Noviodunum *see* Nyon, Vaud, Switzerland
Noviomagus *see* Lisieux, France
Noviomagus *see* Nijmegen, Netherlands
116 M8 **Novi Pazar** Varnenska Oblast, NE Bulgaria
115 M15 **Novi Pazar** *Turk.* Yenipazar. Serbia, S Yugoslavia
114 K10 **Novi Sad** *Ger.* Neusatz, *Hung.* Újvidék. Serbia, N Yugoslavia
119 T6 **Novi Sanzhary** Poltavs'ka Oblast', C Ukraine
114 H12 **Novi Travnik** *prev.* Pučarevo. C Bosnia and Herzegovina
114 B10 **Novi Vinodolski** *var.* Novi. Primorje-Gorski Kotar, NW Croatia
60 F12 **Novo Airão** Amazonas, N Brazil
131 N14 **Novoaleksandrovsk** Stavropol'skiy Kray, SW Russian Federation
150 I10 **Novoalekseyevka** Aktyubinsk, W Kazakhstan
126 H14 **Novoaltaysk** Altayskiy Kray, S Russian Federation
131 N9 **Novoanninskiy** Volgogradskaya Oblast', SW Russian Federation
60 F13 **Novo Aripuanã** Amazonas, N Brazil
119 Y6 **Novoaydar** Luhans'ka Oblast', E Ukraine
119 X9 **Novoazovs'k** *Rus.* Novoazovsk. Donets'ka Oblast', E Ukraine
126 Mm16 **Novobureyskiy** Amurskaya Oblast', SE Russian Federation
131 Q3 **Novocheboksarsk** Chuvashskaya Respublika, W Russian Federation
131 R5 **Novocheremshansk** Ul'yanovskaya Oblast', W Russian Federation
130 L12 **Novocherkassk** Rostovskaya Oblast', SW Russian Federation
131 R6 **Novodevich'ye** Samarskaya Oblast', W Russian Federation
128 M8 **Novodvinsk** Arkhangel'skaya Oblast', NW Russian Federation
Novograd-Volynskiy *see* Novohrad-Volyns'kyy
Novogrudok *see* Navahrudak
63 I15 **Novo Hamburgo** Rio Grande do Sul, S Brazil
61 H16 **Novo Horizonte** Mato Grosso, W Brazil
62 K8 **Novo Horizonte** São Paulo, S Brazil
118 M4 **Novohrad-Volyns'kyy** *Rus.* Novograd-Volynskiy. Zhytomyrs'ka Oblast', N Ukraine
150 L14 **Novokazalinsk** *Kaz.* Zhangaqazaly. Kzyl-Orda, SW Kazakhstan
130 M8 **Novokhopersk** Voronezhskaya Oblast', W Russian Federation
131 R6 **Novokuybyshevsk** Samarskaya Oblast', W Russian Federation
126 H14 **Novokuznetsk** *prev.* Stalinsk. Kemerovskaya Oblast', S Russian Federation
205 R1 **Novolazarevskaya** *Russian research station* Antarctica
Novolukoml' *see* Novalukoml'
111 V12 **Novo Mesto** *Ger.* Rudolfswert; *prev. Ger.* Neustadtl. SE Slovenia
130 K15 **Novomikhaylovskiy** Krasnodarskiy Kray, SW Russian Federation
114 L8 **Novo Miloševo** Serbia, N Yugoslavia
Novomirgorod *see* Novomyrhorod
130 L5 **Novomoskovsk** Tul'skaya Oblast', W Russian Federation
119 U7 **Novomoskovs'k** *Rus.* Novomoskovsk. Dnipropetrovs'ka Oblast', E Ukraine
119 V8 **Novomykolayivka** Zaporiz'ka Oblast', SE Ukraine
119 Q7 **Novomyrhorod** *Rus.* Novomirgorod. Kirovohrads'ka Oblast', S Ukraine
126 I12 **Novonazimovo** Krasnoyarskiy Kray, C Russian Federation
131 N8 **Novonikolayevskiy** Volgogradskaya Oblast', SW Russian Federation
131 P10 **Novonikol'skoye** Volgogradskaya Oblast', SW Russian Federation
131 X7 **Novoorsk** Orenburgskaya Oblast', W Russian Federation
130 M13 **Novopokrovskaya** Krasnodarskiy Kray, SW Russian Federation
Novopolotsk *see* Navapolatsk
119 Y5 **Novopskov** Luhans'ka Oblast', E Ukraine
Novoradomsk *see* Radomsko
Novo Redondo *see* Sumbe
131 R8 **Novorepnoye** Saratovskaya Oblast', W Russian Federation
130 K14 **Novorossiysk** Krasnodarskiy Kray, SW Russian Federation
Novorossiyskiy *see* Novorossiyskoye
150 J10 **Novorossiyskoye** *prev.* Novorossiyskiy. Aktyubinsk, NW Kazakhstan
126 J6 **Novorybnaya** Taymyrskiy (Dolgano-Nenetskiy) Avtonomnyy Okrug, N Russian Federation
128 F15 **Novorzhev** Pskovskaya Oblast', W Russian Federation
Novoselitsa *see* Novoselytsya
119 S12 **Novoselivs'ke** Respublika Krym, S Ukraine
Novosëlki *see* Navasyolki
116 G6 **Novo Selo** Oblast Montana, NW Bulgaria
115 M14 **Novo Selo** Serbia, C Yugoslavia
118 K8 **Novoselytsya** *Rom.* Nouă Sulița, *Rus.* Novoselitsa. Chernivets'ka Oblast', W Ukraine
131 U7 **Novosergiyevka** Orenburgskaya Oblast', W Russian Federation
130 L11 **Novoshakhtinsk** Rostovskaya Oblast', SW Russian Federation
126 Gg14 **Novosibirsk** Novosibirskaya Oblast', C Russian Federation
125 G13 **Novosibirskaya Oblast'** ◆ *province* C Russian Federation
126 M4 **Novosibirskiye Ostrova** *Eng.* New Siberian Islands. *island group* N Russian Federation
130 K6 **Novosil'** Orlovskaya Oblast', W Russian Federation
128 G16 **Novosokol'niki** Pskovskaya Oblast', W Russian Federation
131 Q6 **Novospasskoye** Ul'yanovskaya Oblast', W Russian Federation
131 X8 **Novotroitsk** Orenburgskaya Oblast', W Russian Federation
Novotroitskoye *see* Brlik, Kazakhstan
Novotroitskoye *see* Novotroyits'ke, Ukraine
119 T11 **Novotroyits'ke** *Rus.* Novotroitskoye. Khersons'ka Oblast', S Ukraine
Novoukrainka *see* Novoukrayinka
119 Q8 **Novoukrayinka** *Rus.* Novoukrainka. Kirovohrads'ka Oblast', C Ukraine
131 Q5 **Novoul'yanovsk** Ul'yanovskaya Oblast', W Russian Federation
131 W8 **Novouralets** Orenburgskaya Oblast', W Russian Federation
Novo-Urgench *see* Urganch
118 I4 **Novovolyns'k** *Rus.* Novovolynsk. Volyns'ka Oblast', NW Ukraine
119 S9 **Novovorontsovka** Khersons'ka Oblast', S Ukraine
153 Y7 **Novovoznesenovka** Issyk-Kul'skaya Oblast', E Kyrgyzstan
129 R14 **Novovyatsk** Kirovskaya Oblast', NW Russian Federation
Novoyel'nya *see* Navayel'nya
119 O6 **Novozhyvotiv** Vinnyts'ka Oblast', C Ukraine
130 H6 **Novozybkov** Bryanskaya Oblast', W Russian Federation
114 F9 **Novska** Sisak-Moslavina, NE Croatia
Nový Bohumín *see* Bohumín
113 D15 **Nový Bor** *Ger.* Haida; *prev.* Bor u České Lípy, Hajda. Severní Čechy, N Czech Republic
113 E16 **Nový Bydžov** *Ger.* Neubidschow. Východní Čechy, N Czech Republic
121 G18 **Novy Dvor** *Rus.* Novyy Dvor. Hrodzyenskaya Voblasts', W Belarus
113 I17 **Nový Jičín** *Ger.* Neutitschein. Severní Morava, E Czech Republic
120 K12 **Novy Pahost** *Rus.* Novyy Pogost. Vitsyebskaya Voblasts', NW Belarus
Novyy Bug *see* Novyy Buh
119 R9 **Novyy Buh** *Rus.* Novyy Bug. Mykolayivs'ka Oblast', S Ukraine
119 Q4 **Novyy Bykiv** Chernihivs'ka Oblast', N Ukraine
Novyy Dvor *see* Novy Dvor
Novyye Aneny *see* Anenii Noi
131 P7 **Novyye Burasy** Saratovskaya Oblast', W Russian Federation
Novyy Margilan *see* Farghona
130 K8 **Novyy Oskol** Belgorodskaya Oblast', W Russian Federation
Novyy Pogost *see* Novy Pahost
131 R2 **Novyy Tor"yal** Respublika Mariy El, W Russian Federation
126 K14 **Novyy Uoyan** Respublika Buryatiya, S Russian Federation
126 Gg9 **Novyy Urengoy** Yamalo-Nenetskiy Avtonomnyy Okrug, N Russian Federation
127 N15 **Novyy Urgal** Khabarovskiy Kray, E Russian Federation
150 F15 **Novyy Uzen'** *Kaz.* Zhangaözen. Mangistau, W Kazakhstan
125 G12 **Novyy Vasyugan** Tomskaya Oblast', C Russian Federation
113 N16 **Nowa Dęba** Tarnobrzeg, SE Poland
113 G15 **Nowa Ruda** *Ger.* Neurode. Wałbrzych, SW Poland
112 F12 **Nowa Sól** *var.* Nowasól, *Ger.* Neusalz an der Oder. Zielona Góra, W Poland
29 Q8 **Nowata** Oklahoma, C USA
148 M6 **Nowbarān** Markazī, W Iran
112 J8 **Nowe** Bydgoszcz, N Poland
112 K9 **Nowe Miasto Lubawskie** *Ger.* Neumark. Toruń, N Poland
112 L13 **Nowe Miasto nad Pilicą** Radom, C Poland
112 D8 **Nowe Warpno** *Ger.* Neuwarp. Szczecin, NW Poland
Nowgong *see* Nagaon
112 E8 **Nowogard** *var.* Nowógard, *Ger.* Naugard. Szczecin, NW Poland
112 N9 **Nowogród** Łomża, NE Poland
Nowogródek *see* Navahrudak
113 E14 **Nowogrodziec** *Ger.* Naumburg am Queis. Jelenia Góra, SW Poland
Nowojelnia *see* Navayel'nya
Nowo-Minsk *see* Mińsk Mazowiecki
35 V13 **Nowood River** ⟿ Wyoming, C USA
Nowosądeckie, Województwo *see* Nowy Sącz
Nowo-Święciany *see* Švenčionėliai
191 S10 **Nowra-Bomaderry** New South Wales, SE Australia
155 T5 **Nowshera** *var.* Naushahra, Naushara. North-West Frontier Province, NE Pakistan
112 J7 **Nowy Dwór Gdański** *Ger.* Tiegenhof. Elbląg, N Poland
112 L11 **Nowy Dwór Mazowiecki** Warszawa, C Poland
113 M17 **Nowy Sącz** *Ger.* Neu Sandec. Nowy Sącz, S Poland
113 L18 **Nowy Sącz** *off.* Województwo Nowosądeckie, *Ger.* Neusandez. ◆ *province* S Poland
113 L18 **Nowy Targ** *Ger.* Neumark. Nowy Sącz, S Poland
112 F11 **Nowy Tomyśl** *var.* Nowy Tomysl. Poznań, W Poland
154 M7 **Now Zād** *var.* Nauzad. Helmand, S Afghanistan
25 N4 **Noxubee River** ⟿ Alabama/Mississippi, S USA
126 Gg10 **Noyabr'sk** Yamalo-Nenetskiy Avtonomnyy Okrug, N Russian Federation
104 L8 **Noyant** Maine-et-Loire, NW France
41 X14 **Noyes Island** *island* Alexander Archipelago, Alaska, USA
105 O3 **Noyon** Oise, N France
104 I7 **Nozay** Loire-Atlantique, NW France
84 L12 **Nsando** Northern, NE Zambia
85 N16 **Nsanje** Southern, S Malawi
79 Q17 **Nsawam** SE Ghana
84 K12 **Nsombo** Northern, NE Zambia
84 H13 **Ntambu** North Western, NW Zambia
85 N14 **Ntcheu** *var.* Ncheu. Central, S Malawi
81 D17 **Ntem** *prev.* Campo, Kampo. ⟿ Cameroon/Equatorial Guinea
85 I14 **Ntemwa** North Western, NW Zambia
Ntlenyana, Mount *see* Thabana Ntlenyana
81 I19 **Ntomba, Lac** *var.* Lac Tumba. ◎ NW Zaire
83 E19 **Ntungamo** SW Uganda
83 E18 **Ntusi** SW Uganda
85 H18 **Ntwetwe Pan** *salt lake* NE Botswana
95 M15 **Nuasjärvi** ◎ C Finland
82 F11 **Nuba Mountains** ▲ C Sudan
70 J9 **Nubian Desert** *desert* NE Sudan
118 G10 **Nucet** *Hung.* Diófás. Bihor, W Romania
Nu Chiang *see* Salween
151 U9 **Nuclear Testing Ground** *nuclear site* Pavlodar, E Kazakhstan
58 E9 **Nucuray, Río** ⟿ N Peru
27 R14 **Nueces River** ⟿ Texas, SW USA
9 V9 **Nueltin Lake** ◎ Manitoba/Northwest Territories, C Canada
101 K15 **Nuenen** Noord-Brabant, S Netherlands
64 G6 **Nuestra Señora, Bahía** *bay* N Chile
63 D14 **Nuestra Señora Rosario de Caa Catí** Corrientes, NE Argentina
56 J9 **Nueva Antioquia** Vichada, E Colombia
Nueva Caceres *see* Naga
43 O7 **Nueva Ciudad Guerrera** Tamaulipas, C Mexico
57 N4 **Nueva Esparta** *off.* Estado Nueva Esparta. ◆ *state* NE Venezuela
46 C5 **Nueva Gerona** Isla de la Juventud, S Cuba
44 H8 **Nueva Guadalupe** San Miguel, E El Salvador
44 M11 **Nueva Guinea** Región Autónoma Atlántico Sur, SE Nicaragua
63 D19 **Nueva Helvecia** Colonia, SW Uruguay
65 J25 **Nueva, Isla** *island* S Chile
42 M14 **Nueva Italia** Michoacán de Ocampo, SW Mexico
58 D6 **Nueva Loja** *var.* Lago Agrio. Sucumbíos, NE Ecuador
44 F6 **Nueva Ocotepeque** *prev.* Ocotepeque. Ocotepeque, W Honduras
63 D19 **Nueva Palmira** Colonia, SW Uruguay
43 N6 **Nueva Rosita** Coahuila de Zaragoza, NE Mexico
44 E7 **Nueva San Salvador** *prev.* Santa Tecla. La Libertad, SW El Salvador
44 J8 **Nueva Segovia** ◆ *department* NW Nicaragua
Nueva Tabarca *see* Plana, Isla
Nueva Villa de Padilla *see* Nuevo Padilla
63 B21 **Nueve de Julio** Buenos Aires, E Argentina
46 H6 **Nuevitas** Camagüey, E Cuba
63 D18 **Nuevo Berlín** Río Negro, W Uruguay
42 I4 **Nuevo Casas Grandes** Chihuahua, N Mexico
45 T14 **Nuevo Chagres** Colón, C Panama
43 W15 **Nuevo Coahuila** Campeche, E Mexico
65 K17 **Nuevo, Golfo** *gulf* S Argentina
43 O7 **Nuevo Laredo** Tamaulipas, NE Mexico
43 N8 **Nuevo León** ◆ *state* NE Mexico
43 P10 **Nuevo Padilla** *var.* Nueva Villa de Padilla. Tamaulipas, C Mexico
58 E6 **Nuevo Rocafuerte** Napo, E Ecuador
168 G6 **Nuga** Dzavhan, W Mongolia
82 O13 **Nugaal** *off.* Gobolka Nugaal. ◆ *region* N Somalia
193 E24 **Nugget Point** *headland* South Island, NZ
195 R9 **Nuguria Islands** *island group* E PNG
192 P10 **Nuhaka** Hawke's Bay, North Island, NZ
144 M10 **Nuhaydayn, Wādī an** *dry watercourse* W Iraq
202 E7 **Nui Atoll** *atoll* W Tuvalu
Nu Jiang *see* Salween
Nûk *see* Nuuk
190 G7 **Nukey Bluff** *hill* South Australia
Nukha *see* Şäki
127 O9 **Nukh Yablonevyy, Gora** ▲ E Russian Federation
195 T13 **Nukiki** Choiseul Island, NW Solomon Islands
194 F10 **Nuku** Sandaun, NW PNG
200 R15 **Nuku** *island* Tongatapu Group, NE Tonga
200 Qq15 **Nuku'alofa** Tongatapu, S Tonga
200 Qq15 **Nuku'alofa** ● (Tonga) Tongatapu, S Tonga
202 G12 **Nukuatea** *island* N Wallis and Futuna
202 F7 **Nukufetau Atoll** *atoll* C Tuvalu
202 G12 **Nukuhifala** *island* E Wallis and Futuna
203 W7 **Nuku Hiva** *island* Îles Marquises, NE French Polynesia
199 L19 **Nuku Hiva Island** *island* Îles Marquises, N French Polynesia
202 F9 **Nukulaelae Atoll** *var.* Nukulailai. *atoll* E Tuvalu
Nukulailai *see* Nukulaelae Atoll
202 G11 **Nukuloa** *island* N Wallis and Futuna
195 W10 **Nukumanu Islands** *prev.* Tasman Group. *island group* NE PNG
Nukunau *see* Nikunau
202 J9 **Nukunonu Atoll** *island* C Tokelau
202 J9 **Nukunonu Village** Nukunonu Atoll, C Tokelau
201 S18 **Nukuoro Atoll** *atoll* Caroline Islands, S Micronesia
152 H8 **Nukus** Qoraqalpoghiston Respublikasi, W Uzbekistan
202 G11 **Nukutapu** *island* N Wallis and Futuna
41 O9 **Nulato** Alaska, USA
41 O10 **Nulato Hills** ▲ Alaska, USA
107 T9 **Nules** País Valenciano, E Spain
Nuling *see* Sultan Kudarat
190 C6 **Nullarbor** South Australia
188 M11 **Nullarbor Plain** *plateau* South Australia/Western Australia
79 Y13 **Nulu'erhu Shan** ▲ N China
79 X14 **Numan** Adamawa, E Nigeria
171 K14 **Numata** Gunma, Honshū, S Japan
172 Oo4 **Numata** Hokkaidō, NE Japan
82 C13 **Numatinna** ⟿ W Sudan
171 J17 **Numazu** Shizuoka, Honshū, S Japan
97 F14 **Numedalen** *valley* S Norway
97 G14 **Numedalslågen** *var.* Laagen. ⟿ S Norway
95 L19 **Nummela** Uusimaa, S Finland
125 G9 **Numto** Khanty-Mansiyskiy Avtonomnyy Okrug, N Russian Federation
191 O11 **Numurkah** Victoria, SE Australia
Nunap Isua *see* Uummannarsuaq
56 H9 **Nunchia** Casanare, C Colombia
99 M20 **Nuneaton** C England, UK
159 W14 **Nungba** Manipur, NE India
40 L12 **Nunivak Island** *island* Alaska, USA
158 I5 **Nun Kun** ▲ NW India
100 L10 **Nunspeet** Gelderland, E Netherlands
109 C18 **Nuoro** Sardegna, Italy, C Mediterranean Sea
77 R12 **Nuqayy, Jabal** *hill range* S Libya
56 C9 **Nuquí** Chocó, W Colombia
149 O4 **Nūr** Māzandarān, N Iran
151 Q9 **Nura** ⟿ N Kazakhstan
149 N11 **Nūrābād** Fārs, C Iran
Nurakita *see* Niulakita
Nurata *see* Nurota
Nuratau, Khrebet *see* Nurota Tizmasi
142 L17 **Nur Dağları** ▲ S Turkey
Nurek *see* Norak
Nuremberg *see* Nürnberg
142 M15 **Nurhak** Kahramanmaraş, S Turkey
190 J9 **Nuriootpa** South Australia
131 S5 **Nurlat** Respublika Tatarstan, W Russian Federation
95 N15 **Nurmes** Pohjois-Karjala, E Finland
103 K20 **Nürnberg** *Eng.* Nuremberg. Bayern, S Germany
103 K20 **Nürnberg** ✕ Bayern, SE Germany
152 M10 **Nurota** *Rus.* Nurata. Nawoiy Wiloyati, C Uzbekistan
153 N10 **Nurota Tizmasi** *Rus.* Khrebet Nuratau. ▲ C Uzbekistan
155 T8 **Nūrpur** Punjab, E Pakistan
191 P6 **Nurri, Mount** *hill* New South Wales, SE Australia
27 T13 **Nursery** Texas, SW USA
175 P16 **Nusa Tenggara** *Eng.* Lesser Sunda Islands. *island group* C Indonesia
175 O15 **Nusa Tenggara Barat** *off.* Propinsi Nusa Tenggara Barat, *Eng.* West Nusa Tenggara. ◆ *province* S Indonesia
175 Q17 **Nusa Tenggara Timur** *off.* Propinsi Nusa Tenggara Timur, *Eng.* East Nusa Tenggara. ◆ *province* S Indonesia
176 Vv12 **Nusawulan** Irian Jaya, E Indonesia
143 Q16 **Nusaybin** *var.* Nisibin. Manisa, SE Turkey
41 O14 **Nushagak Bay** *bay* Alaska, USA
41 O13 **Nushagak Peninsula** *headland* Alaska, USA
41 O13 **Nushagak River** ⟿ Alaska, USA
166 E11 **Nu Shan** ▲ SW China
155 N11 **Nushki** Baluchistan, SW Pakistan

◆ Country ● Country Capital ◇ Dependent Territory ○ Dependent Territory Capital ◆ Administrative Region ✕ International Airport ▲ Mountain ▲ Mountain Range Volcano ⟿ River ◎ Lake ⊞ Reservoir

Nussdorf *see* Năsăud
114 *J9* **Nuštar** Vukovar-Srijem, E Croatia
101 *L18* **Nuth** Limburg, SE Netherlands
102 *N13* **Nuthe** ≈ NE Germany
Nutmeg State *see* Connecticut
41 *T10* **Nutzotin Mountains** ⛰ Alaska, USA
66 *I5* **Nuuk** *var.* Nûk, *Dan.* Godthaab, Godthåb. ○ (Greenland) SW Greenland
94 *L13* **Nuupas** Lappi, NW Finland
203 *O7* **Nuupere, Pointe** *headland* Moorea, W French Polynesia
203 *O7* **Nuuroa, Pointe** *headland* Tahiti, W French Polynesia
168 *M8* **Nüürst** Töv, C Mongolia
Nuwara *see* Nuwara Eliya
161 *K25* **Nuwara Eliya** *var.* Nuwara. Central Province, S Sri Lanka
190 *E7* **Nuyts Archipelago** *island group* South Australia
85 *F17* **Nxaunxau** Ngamiland, NW Botswana
41 *N12* **Nyac** Alaska, USA
125 *Ff10* **Nyagan'** Khanty-Mansiyskiy Avtonomnyy Okrug, N Russian Federation
Nyagassola *see* Niagassola
83 *I18* **Nyahururu** Central, W Kenya
190 *M10* **Nyah West** Victoria, SE Australia
164 *M15* **Nyainqêntanglha Feng** ▲ W China
165 *N15* **Nyainqêntanglha Shan** ⛰ W China
82 *B11* **Nyala** Southern Darfur, W Sudan
85 *M16* **Nyamapanda** Mashonaland East, NE Zimbabwe
83 *H25* **Nyamtumbo** Ruvuma, S Tanzania
Nyanda *see* Masvingo
128 *M11* **Nyandoma** Arkhangel'skaya Oblast', NW Russian Federation
85 *M16* **Nyanga** *prev.* Inyanga. Manicaland, E Zimbabwe
81 *D20* **Nyanga** *off.* Province de la Nyanga, *var.* La Nyanga. ⬖ *province* SW Gabon
81 *E20* **Nyanga** ≈ Congo/Gabon
83 *F20* **Nyantakara** Kagera, NW Tanzania
83 *G19* **Nyanza** ⬖ *province* W Kenya
83 *E21* **Nyanza-Lac** S Burundi
70 *J14* **Nyasa, Lake** *var.* Lake Malawi; *prev.* Lago Nyassa. ◎ E Africa
Nyasaland/Nyasaland Protectorate *see* Malawi
Nyassa, Lago *see* Nyasa, Lake
121 *J17* **Nyasvizh** *Pol.* Nieśwież, *Rus.* Nesvizh. Minskaya Voblasts', C Belarus
177 *G8* **Nyaunglebin** Pegu, SW Myanmar
177 *G5* **Nyaung-u** Magwe, C Myanmar
97 *H24* **Nyborg** Fyn, C Denmark
97 *N21* **Nybro** Kalmar, S Sweden
121 *J16* **Nyeharelaye** *Rus.* Negoreloye. Minskaya Voblasts', C Belarus
205 *W3* **Nye Mountains** ⛰ Antarctica
83 *I19* **Nyeri** Central, C Kenya
120 *M11* **Nyeshcharda, Vozyera** ◎ N Belarus
94 *O2* **Ny-Friesland** *physical region* N Svalbard
97 *L14* **Nyhammar** Kopparberg, C Sweden
166 *F7* **Nyikog Qu** ≈ C China
164 *L14* **Nyima** Xizang Zizhiqu, W China
85 *L14* **Nyimba** Eastern, E Zambia
165 *P16* **Nyingchi** Xizang Zizhiqu, W China
113 *O21* **Nyírbátor** Szabolcs-Szatmár-Bereg, E Hungary
113 *N21* **Nyíregyháza** Szabolcs-Szatmár-Bereg, NE Hungary
Nyiro *see* Ewaso Ng'iro
Nyitra *see* Nitra
Nyitrabánya *see* Handlová
95 *K16* **Nykarleby** *Fin.* Uusikaarlepyy. Vaasa, W Finland
97 *I25* **Nykøbing** Storstrøm, SE Denmark
97 *I22* **Nykøbing** Vestsjælland, C Denmark
97 *F21* **Nykøbing** Viborg, NW Denmark
97 *N17* **Nyköping** Södermanland, S Sweden
97 *L15* **Nykroppa** Värmland, C Sweden
Nyland *see* Uusimaa
85 *J20* **Nylstroom** Northern, NE South Africa
191 *P7* **Nymagee** New South Wales, SE Australia
191 *V5* **Nymboida** New South Wales, SE Australia
191 *U5* **Nymboida River** ≈ New South Wales, SE Australia
113 *D16* **Nymburk** *var.* Neuenburg an der Elbe, *Ger.* Nimburg. Střední Čechy, C Czech Republic
97 *O16* **Nynäshamn** Stockholm, C Sweden
191 *Q6* **Nyngan** New South Wales, SE Australia
Nyoman *see* Neman
110 *A10* **Nyon** *Ger.* Neuss; *anc.* Noviodunum. Vaud, SW Switzerland
81 *D16* **Nyong** ≈ SW Cameroon
105 *S14* **Nyons** Drôme, E France
81 *D14* **Nyos, Lac** *Eng.* Lake Nyos. ◎ NW Cameroon
Nyos, Lake *see* Nyos, Lac
129 *U11* **Nyrob** *var.* Nyrov. Permskaya Oblast', NW Russian Federation
Nyrov *see* Nyrob
113 *H15* **Nysa** *Ger.* Neisse. Opole, SW Poland
Nysa Łużycka *see* Neisse
Nyslott *see* Savonlinna
34 *M13* **Nyssa** Oregon, NW USA
Nystad *see* Uusikaupunki
97 *I25* **Nysted** Storstrøm, SE Denmark
129 *U14* **Nytva** Permskaya Oblast', NW Russian Federation
171 *Ll9* **Nyūdō-zaki** *headland* Honshū, C Japan
129 *P9* **Nyukhcha** Arkhangel'skaya Oblast', NW Russian Federation
128 *H8* **Nyuk, Ozero** *var.* Ozero Njuk. ◎ NW Russian Federation
129 *O12* **Nyuksenitsa** *var.* Njuksenica. Vologodskaya Oblast', NW Russian Federation
81 *O22* **Nyunzu** Shaba, SE Zaire
126 *Kk11* **Nyurba** Respublika Sakha (Yakutiya), NE Russian Federation
126 *Kk12* **Nyuya** Respublika Sakha (Yakutiya), NE Russian Federation
126 *K12* **Nyuya** ≈ NE Russian Federation
119 *T10* **Nyzhni Sirohozy** Khersons'ka Oblast', S Ukraine
119 *U12* **Nyzhn'ohirs'kyy** *Rus.* Nizhnegorskiy. Respublika Krym, S Ukraine
83 *G21* **Nzega** Tabora, C Tanzania
78 *K15* **Nzérékoré** Guinée-Forestière, SE Guinea
84 *A10* **N'Zeto** *prev.* Ambrizete. Zaire, NW Angola
81 *M24* **Nzilo, Lac** *prev.* Lac Delcommune. ◎ SE Zaire

O

31 *O11* **Oacoma** South Dakota, N USA
31 *N9* **Oahe Dam** *dam* South Dakota, N USA
30 *M9* **Oahe, Lake** ▣ North Dakota/South Dakota, N USA
40 *C9* **Oahu** *Haw.* O'ahu. *island* Hawaii, USA, C Pacific Ocean
172 *Qq6* **O-Akan-dake** ▲ Hokkaidō, NE Japan
190 *K8* **Oakbank** South Australia
21 *P13* **Oak Bluffs** Martha's Vineyard, New York, NE USA
38 *K4* **Oak City** Utah, W USA
39 *R3* **Oak Creek** Colorado, C USA
37 *P8* **Oakdale** California, W USA
24 *H8* **Oakdale** Louisiana, S USA
31 *P7* **Oakes** North Dakota, N USA
24 *J4* **Oak Grove** Louisiana, S USA
99 *N19* **Oakham** C England, UK
34 *H7* **Oak Harbor** Washington, NW USA
23 *R5* **Oak Hill** West Virginia, NE USA
37 *N8* **Oakland** California, W USA
31 *T15* **Oakland** Iowa, C USA
21 *Q7* **Oakland** Maine, NE USA
23 *T3* **Oakland** Maryland, NE USA
31 *R14* **Oakland** Nebraska, C USA
33 *N11* **Oak Lawn** Illinois, N USA
35 *P16* **Oakley** Idaho, NW USA
28 *I4* **Oakley** Kansas, C USA
33 *N10* **Oak Park** Illinois, N USA
9 *X16* **Oak Point** Manitoba, S Canada
34 *G13* **Oakridge** Oregon, NW USA
22 *M9* **Oak Ridge** Tennessee, S USA
192 *K10* **Oakura** Taranaki, North Island, NZ
24 *L7* **Oak Vale** Mississippi, S USA
12 *G16* **Oakville** Ontario, S Canada
27 *V8* **Oakwood** Texas, SW USA
193 *F22* **Oamaru** Otago, South Island, NZ
98 *F13* **Oa, Mull of** *headland* W Scotland, UK
175 *Q7* **Oan** Sulawesi, N Indonesia
193 *J17* **Oaro** Canterbury, South Island, NZ
37 *X2* **Oasis** Nevada, W USA
205 *S15* **Oates Land** *physical region* Antarctica
191 *P17* **Oatlands** Tasmania, SE Australia
38 *I11* **Oatman** Arizona, SW USA
43 *R16* **Oaxaca** *var.* Oaxaca de Juárez; *prev.* Antequera. Oaxaca, SE Mexico
43 *Q16* **Oaxaca** ⬖ *state* SE Mexico
Oaxaca de Juárez *see* Oaxaca
125 *G8* **Ob'** ≈ C Russian Federation
12 *G9* **Obabika Lake** ◎ Ontario, S Canada
Obagan *see* Ubagan
120 *M12* **Obal'** *Rus.* Obol'. Vitsyebskaya Voblasts', N Belarus
81 *E16* **Obala** Centre, SW Cameroon
12 *C6* **Oba Lake** ◎ Ontario, S Canada
171 *H14* **Obama** Fukui, Honshū, SW Japan
98 *H11* **Oban** W Scotland, UK
Oban *see* Halfmoon Bay
171 *Ll12* **Obanazawa** Yamagata, Honshū, C Japan
Obando *see* Puerto Inírida
106 *I4* **O Barco** *var.* El Barco, El Barco de Valdeorras, O Barco de Valdeorras. Galicia, NW Spain
O Barco de Valdeorras *see* O Barco
Obbia *see* Hobyo
95 *J16* **Obbola** Västerbotten, N Sweden
Obbrovazzo *see* Obrovac
Obchuga *see* Abchuha
Obdorsk *see* Salekhard
Óbecse *see* Bečej
120 *I11* **Obeliai** Rokiškis, NE Lithuania
62 *F13* **Oberá** Misiones, NE Argentina
110 *E8* **Oberburg** Bern, W Switzerland
111 *Q9* **Oberdrauburg** Salzburg, S Austria
Oberglogau *see* Głogówek
111 *W4* **Ober Grafendorf** Niederösterreich, NE Austria
103 *E15* **Oberhausen** Nordrhein-Westfalen, W Germany
Oberhollabrunn *see* Tulln
Oberlaibach *see* Vrhnika
103 *Q15* **Oberlausitz** *physical region* E Germany
28 *J2* **Oberlin** Kansas, C USA
24 *H8* **Oberlin** Louisiana, S USA
33 *T11* **Oberlin** Ohio, N USA
105 *U5* **Obernai** Bas-Rhin, NE France
111 *R4* **Obernberg am Inn** Oberösterreich, N Austria
Oberndorf *see* Oberndorf am Neckar
103 *G23* **Oberndorf am Neckar** *var.* Oberndorf. Baden-Württemberg, SW Germany
111 *Q5* **Oberndorf bei Salzburg** Salzburg, W Austria
Oberneustadtl *see* Kysucké Nové Mesto
191 *S8* **Oberon** New South Wales, SE Australia
111 *Q4* **Oberösterreich** *off.* Land Oberösterreich, *Eng.* Upper Austria. ⬖ *state* NW Austria
Oberpahlen *see* Põltsamaa
103 *M19* **Oberpfälzer Wald** ⛰ SE Germany
111 *Y6* **Oberpullendorf** Burgenland, E Austria
Oberradkersburg *see* Gornja Radgona
103 *G18* **Oberursel** Hessen, W Germany
111 *Q8* **Obervellach** Salzburg, S Austria
111 *X7* **Oberwart** Burgenland, SE Austria
Oberwischau *see* Vişeu de Sus
111 *T7* **Oberwölz** *var.* Oberwölz-Stadt. Steiermark, SE Austria
Oberwölz-Stadt *see* Oberwölz
33 *S13* **Obetz** Ohio, N USA
Ob', Gulf of *see* Obskaya Guba
56 *G8* **Obia** Santander, C Colombia
60 *H12* **Óbidos** Pará, NE Brazil
106 *F10* **Óbidos** Leiria, C Portugal
Obidovichi *see* Abidavichy
153 *Q13* **Obigarm** W Tajikistan
172 *P7* **Obihiro** Hokkaidō, NE Japan
Obi-Khingou *see* Khingov
153 *P13* **Obikiik** SW Tajikistan
115 *N16* **Obilić** Serbia, S Yugoslavia
131 *O12* **Obil'noye** Respublika Kalmykiya, SW Russian Federation
22 *F8* **Obion** Tennessee, S USA
22 *F8* **Obion River** ≈ Tennessee, S USA
175 *T9* **Obi, Pulau** *island* Maluku, E Indonesia
172 *Oo4* **Obira** Hokkaidō, NE Japan
175 *T9* **Obi, Selat** *strait* Maluku, E Indonesia
131 *N11* **Oblivskaya** Rostovskaya Oblast', SW Russian Federation
127 *N16* **Obluch'ye** Yevreyskaya Avtonomnaya Oblast', SE Russian Federation
130 *K4* **Obninsk** Kaluzhskaya Oblast', W Russian Federation
116 *J8* **Obnova** Loveshka Oblast, N Bulgaria
81 *N15* **Obo** Haut-Mbomou, E Central African Republic
82 *M11* **Obock** E Djibouti
Obol' *see* Obal'
Obolyanka *see* Abalyanka
176 *Vv11* **Obome** Irian Jaya, E Indonesia
112 *G11* **Oborniki** Poznań, W Poland
81 *G19* **Obouya** Cuvette, C Congo
130 *J8* **Oboyan'** Kurskaya Oblast', W Russian Federation
128 *M9* **Obozerskiy** Arkhangel'skaya Oblast', NW Russian Federation
114 *L11* **Obrenovac** Serbia, N Yugoslavia
114 *D12* **Obrovac** *It.* Obbrovazzo. Zadar-Knin, W Croatia
Obrovo *see* Abrova
37 *Q3* **Observation Peak** ▲ California, W USA
126 *H7* **Obskaya Guba** *Eng.* Gulf of Ob'. *gulf* N Russian Federation
181 *N13* **Ob' Tablemount** *undersea feature* S Indian Ocean
181 *T10* **Ob' Trench** *undersea feature* E Indian Ocean
79 *P16* **Obuasi** S Ghana
119 *P5* **Obukhiv** *Rus.* Obukhov. Kyyivs'ka Oblast', N Ukraine
Obukhov *see* Obukhiv
129 *U14* **Obva** ≈ NW Russian Federation
119 *V10* **Obytichna Kosa** *spit* SE Ukraine
119 *V10* **Obytichna Zatoka** *gulf* SE Ukraine
107 *O3* **Oca** ≈ N Spain
25 *W10* **Ocala** Florida, SE USA
42 *M7* **Ocampo** Coahuila de Zaragoza, NE Mexico
56 *G7* **Ocaña** Norte de Santander, N Colombia
107 *N9* **Ocaña** Castilla-La Mancha, C Spain
39 *T9* **Ocate** New Mexico, SW USA
Ocavango *see* Okavango
50 *D6* **Occidental, Cordillera** ⛰ Bolivia/Chile
50 *D6* **Occidental, Cordillera** ⛰ W Colombia
59 *D14* **Occidental, Cordillera** ⛰ W Peru
23 *Q6* **Oceana** West Virginia, NE USA
23 *Z4* **Ocean City** Maryland, NE USA
20 *J17* **Ocean City** New Jersey, NE USA
8 *K15* **Ocean Falls** British Columbia, SW Canada
Ocean Island *see* Kure Atoll
Ocean Island *see* Banaba
66 *J9* **Oceanographer Fracture Zone** *tectonic feature* NW Atlantic Ocean
37 *U17* **Oceanside** California, W USA
24 *M9* **Ocean Springs** Mississippi, S USA
Ocean State *see* Rhode Island
27 *O9* **O C Fisher Lake** ▣ Texas, SW USA
119 *Q10* **Ochakiv** *Rus.* Ochakov. Mykolayivs'ka Oblast', S Ukraine
Ochakov *see* Ochakiv
Ochamchira *see* Och'amch'ire
143 *Q9* **Och'amch'ire** *Rus.* Ochamchira. W Georgia
Ochansk *see* Okhansk
129 *T15* **Ocher** Permskaya Oblast', NW Russian Federation
117 *I19* **Óchi** ▲ Évvoia, C Greece
172 *R8* **Ochiishi-misaki** *headland* Hokkaidō, NE Japan
25 *S9* **Ochlockonee River** ≈ Florida/Georgia, SE USA
46 *K12* **Ocho Rios** C Jamaica
Ochrida *see* Ohrid
Ochrida, Lake *see* Ohrid, Lake
103 *J19* **Ochsenfurt** Bayern, C Germany
25 *U7* **Ocilla** Georgia, SE USA
96 *N13* **Ockelbo** Gävleborg, C Sweden
Ocker *see* Oker
97 *I19* **Öckerö** Göteborg och Bohus, S Sweden
25 *U6* **Ocmulgee River** ≈ Georgia, SE USA
118 *H11* **Ocna Mureş** *Hung.* Marosújvár; *prev.* Ocna Mureşului; prev. *Hung.* Marosújvárakna. Alba, C Romania
Ocna Mureşului *see* Ocna Mureş
118 *H11* **Ocna Sibiului** *Ger.* Salzburg, *Hung.* Vizakna. Sibiu, C Romania
118 *H13* **Ocnele Mari** *prev.* Vioara. Vâlcea, S Romania
118 *L7* **Ocniţa** *Rus.* Oknitsa. N Moldova
25 *U4* **Oconee, Lake** ▣ Georgia, SE USA
25 *U5* **Oconee River** ≈ Georgia, SE USA
32 *M9* **Oconomowoc** Wisconsin, N USA
32 *M6* **Oconto** Wisconsin, N USA
32 *M6* **Oconto Falls** Wisconsin, N USA
32 *M6* **Oconto River** ≈ Wisconsin, N USA
106 *I3* **O Corgo** Galicia, NW Spain
43 *V16* **Ocosingo** Chiapas, SE Mexico
44 *J8* **Ocotal** Nueva Segovia, NW Nicaragua
44 *F6* **Ocotepeque** ⬖ *department* W Honduras
Ocotepeque *see* Nueva Ocotepeque
42 *L13* **Ocotlán** Jalisco, SW Mexico
43 *R16* **Ocotlán** *var.* Ocotlán de Morelos. Oaxaca, SE Mexico
Ocotlán de Morelos *see* Ocotlán
43 *U16* **Ocozocuautla** Chiapas, SE Mexico
23 *Y10* **Ocracoke Island** *island* North Carolina, SE USA
104 *I3* **Octeville** Manche, N France
October Revolution Island *see* Oktyabr'skoy Revolyutsii, Ostrov
45 *R17* **Ocú** Herrera, S Panama
85 *Q14* **Ocua** Cabo Delgado, NE Mozambique
Ocumare *see* Ocumare del Tuy
56 *M5* **Ocumare del Tuy** *var.* Ocumare. Miranda, N Venezuela
79 *P17* **Oda** SE Ghana
170 *F12* **Ōda** *var.* Oda. Shimane, Honshū, SW Japan
94 *K3* **Ódadhahraun** *lava flow* C Iceland
176 *Y14* **Odammun** ≈ Irian Jaya, E Indonesia
171 *Mm9* **Ōdate** Akita, Honshū, C Japan
171 *J16* **Odawara** Kanagawa, Honshū, S Japan
97 *D14* **Odda** Hordaland, S Norway
97 *G22* **Odder** Århus, C Denmark
Oddur *see* Xuddur
31 *T13* **Odebolt** Iowa, C USA
106 *H14* **Odeleite** Faro, S Portugal
27 *Q4* **Odell** Texas, SW USA
27 *T14* **Odem** Texas, SW USA
106 *F13* **Odemira** Beja, S Portugal
142 *C14* **Ödemiş** İzmir, SW Turkey
Ödenburg *see* Sopron
85 *I22* **Odendaalsrus** Free State, C South Africa
Odenpäh *see* Otepää
97 *H23* **Odense** Fyn, C Denmark
103 *H19* **Odenwald** ⛰ W Germany
86 *H10* **Oder** *Cz./Pol.* Odra. ≈ C Europe
Oderberg *see* Bohumín
102 *P11* **Oderbruch** *wetland* Germany/Poland
Oderhaff *see* Szczeciński, Zalew
102 *O11* **Oder-Havel-Kanal** *canal* NE Germany
Oderhellen *see* Odorheiu Secuiesc
102 *P13* **Oder-Spree-Kanal** *canal* NE Germany
Odertal *see* Zdzieszowice
108 *I7* **Oderzo** Veneto, NE Italy
124 *Pp4* **Odesa** *Rus.* Odessa. Odes'ka Oblast', SW Ukraine
Odesa *see* Odes'ka Oblast'
97 *L18* **Ödeshög** Östergötland, S Sweden
119 *O9* **Odes'ka Oblast'** *var.* Odesa, *Rus.* Odesskaya Oblast'. ⬖ *province* SW Ukraine
26 *M8* **Odessa** Texas, SW USA
34 *K8* **Odessa** Washington, NW USA
Odessa *see* Odesa
Odesskaya Oblast' *see* Odes'ka Oblast'
125 *Ff13* **Odesskoye** Omskaya Oblast', C Russian Federation
Odessus *see* Varna
104 *F6* **Odet** ≈ NW France
106 *I14* **Odiel** ≈ SW Spain
78 *L14* **Odienné** NW Ivory Coast
179 *Pp12* **Odiongan** Tablas Island, C Philippines
118 *L12* **Odobeşti** Vrancea, E Romania
112 *H13* **Odolanów** *Ger.* Adelnau. Kalisz, SW Poland
178 *J13* **Ôdôngk** Kâmpóng Spoe, S Cambodia
27 *N6* **O'donnell** Texas, SW USA
100 *O7* **Odoorn** Drenthe, NE Netherlands
Odorhei *see* Odorheiu Secuiesc
118 *J11* **Odorheiu Secuiesc** *Ger.* Oderhellen, *Hung.* Vámosudvarhely; *prev.* Odorhei; *Ger.* Hofmarkt. Harghita, C Romania
Odra *see* Oder
114 *J9* **Odžaci** *Ger.* Hodschag, *Hung.* Hodság. Serbia, NW Yugoslavia
61 *N14* **Oeiras** Piauí, E Brazil
106 *F11* **Oeiras** Lisboa, C Portugal
103 *G14* **Oelde** Nordrhein-Westfalen, W Germany
30 *J11* **Oelrichs** South Dakota, N USA
Oels/Oels in Schlesien *see* Oleśnica
103 *M17* **Oelsnitz** Sachsen, E Germany
31 *X12* **Oelwein** Iowa, C USA
Oeniadae *see* Oiniádes
203 *N17* **Oeno Island** *atoll* Pitcairn Islands, C Pacific Ocean
Oesel *see* Saaremaa
110 *L7* **Oetz** *var.* Ötz. Tirol, W Austria
143 *P11* **Of** Trabzon, NE Turkey
32 *K15* **O'Fallon** Illinois, N USA
29 *W4* **O'Fallon** Missouri, C USA
109 *N16* **Ofanto** ≈ S Italy
99 *D18* **Offaly** *Ir.* Ua Uíbh Fhailí; *prev.* King's County. *cultural region* C Ireland
103 *H18* **Offenbach** *var.* Offenbach am Main. Hessen, W Germany
Offenbach am Main *see* Offenbach
103 *F22* **Offenburg** Baden-Württemberg, SW Germany
190 *C2* **Officer Creek** *seasonal river* South Australia
Oficina María Elena *see* María Elena
Oficina Pedro de Valdivia *see* Pedro de Valdivia
117 *K22* **Ofidoússa** *island* Kykládes, Greece, Aegean Sea
Ofiral *see* Sharm el Sheikh
94 *H10* **Ofotfjorden** *fjord* N Norway
198 *D8* **Ofu** *island* Manua Islands, E American Samoa
171 *Mm12* **Ōfunato** Iwate, Honshū, C Japan
171 *M10* **Oga** Akita, Honshū, C Japan
Ogaadeen *see* Ogadēn
171 *M11* **Ogachi** Akita, Honshū, C Japan
171 *M11* **Ogachi-tōge** *pass* Honshū, C Japan
83 *N14* **Ogadēn** *Som.* Ogaadeen. *plateau* Ethiopia/Somalia
171 *M10* **Oga-hantō** *peninsula* Honshū, C Japan
171 *Hh14* **Ōgaki** Gifu, Honshū, SW Japan
30 *L15* **Ogallala** Nebraska, C USA
174 *I12* **Ogan, Air** ≈ Sumatera, W Indonesia
172 *T16* **Ogasawara-shotō** *Eng.* Bonin Islands. *island group* SE Japan
12 *I9* **Ogascanane, Lac** ◎ Québec, SE Canada
172 *N9* **Ogawara-ko** ◎ Honshū, C Japan
79 *T15* **Ogbomosho** Oyo, W Nigeria
31 *U13* **Ogden** Iowa, C USA
38 *L2* **Ogden** Utah, W USA
20 *I6* **Ogdensburg** New York, NE USA
197 *L16* **Ogea Driki** *island* Lau Group, E Fiji
197 *L16* **Ogea Levu** *island* Lau Group, E Fiji
25 *W5* **Ogeechee River** ≈ Georgia, SE USA
Oger *see* Ogre
152 *F6* **Oghiyon Shŭrkhogi** *wetland* NW Uzbekistan
171 *K12* **Ogi** Niigata, Sado, C Japan
8 *H5* **Ogilvie** Yukon Territory, NW Canada
8 *H4* **Ogilvie** ≈ Yukon Territory, NW Canada
8 *H5* **Ogilvie Mountains** ⛰ Yukon Territory, NW Canada
Oginskiy Kanal *see* Ahinski Kanal
152 *B10* **Oglanly** Balkanskiy Velayat, W Turkmenistan
25 *T5* **Oglethorpe** Georgia, SE USA
25 *T2* **Oglethorpe, Mount** ▲ Georgia, SE USA
108 *F7* **Oglio** *anc.* Ollius. ≈ N Italy
105 *T8* **Ognon** ≈ E France
175 *Pp7* **Ogoamas, Pegunungan** ⛰ Sulawesi, N Indonesia
127 *N14* **Ogodzha** Amurskaya Oblast', S Russian Federation
79 *W16* **Ogoja** Cross River, S Nigeria
10 *C10* **Ogoki** ≈ Ontario, S Canada
10 *D11* **Ogoki Lake** ◎ Ontario, C Canada
168 *K10* **Ögöömör** Ömnogövĭ, S Mongolia
81 *F19* **Ogooué** ≈ Congo/Gabon
81 *E18* **Ogooué-Ivindo** *off.* Province de l'Ogooué-Ivindo, *var.* L'Ogooué-Ivindo. ⬖ *province* N Gabon
81 *E19* **Ogooué-Lolo** *off.* Province de l'Ogooué-Lolo, *var.* L'Ogooué-Lolo. ⬖ *province* C Gabon
81 *C19* **Ogooué-Maritime** *off.* Province de l'Ogooué-Maritime, *var.* L'Ogooué-Maritime. ⬖ *province* W Gabon
170 *Cc13* **Ogōri** Fukuoka, Kyūshū, SW Japan
170 *Dd13* **Ogōri** Yamaguchi, Honshū, SW Japan
116 *H7* **Ogosta** ≈ NW Bulgaria
114 *Q9* **Ogražden** *Bul.* Ograzhden. ⛰ Bulgaria/FYR Macedonia *see also* Ograzhden
116 *G12* **Ograzhden** *Mac.* Orgražden. ⛰ Bulgaria/FYR Macedonia *see also* Ogražden
120 *G9* **Ogre** *Ger.* Oger. Ogre, C Latvia
120 *H9* **Ogre** ≈ C Latvia
114 *C10* **Ogulin** Karlovac, NW Croatia
79 *S16* **Ogun** ⬖ *state* SW Nigeria
152 *A12* **Ogurdzhaly, Ostrov** *Turkm.* Ogurjaly Adasy. *island* W Turkmenistan
Ogurjaly Adasy *see* Ogurdzhaly, Ostrov
79 *U16* **Ogwashi-Uku** Delta, S Nigeria
193 *B23* **Ohai** Southland, South Island, NZ
153 *Q10* **Ohangaron** *Rus.* Akhangaran. Toshkent Wiloyati, E Uzbekistan
153 *Q10* **Ohangaron** *Rus.* Akhangaran. ≈ E Uzbekistan
85 *C16* **Ohangwena** ⬖ *district* N Namibia
171 *K17* **Ōhara** Chiba, Honshū, S Japan
32 *M10* **O'Hare** ✈ (Chicago) Illinois, N USA
172 *Nn8* **Ōhata** Aomori, Honshū, C Japan
192 *L13* **Ohau** Manawatu-Wanganui, North Island, NZ
193 *E20* **Ohau, Lake** ◎ South Island, NZ
Ohcejohka *see* Utsjoki
101 *J20* **Ohey** Namur, SE Belgium
203 *X15* **O'Higgins, Cabo** *headland* Easter Island, Chile, E Pacific Ocean
O'Higgins, Lago *see* San Martín, Lago
33 *S12* **Ohio** *off.* State of Ohio; also known as The Buckeye State. ⬖ *state* N USA
1 *L10* **Ohio River** ≈ N USA
Ohlau *see* Oława
103 *H16* **Ohm** ≈ C Germany
200 *R16* **Ohonua** 'Eua, E Tonga
25 *V5* **Ohoopee River** ≈ Georgia, SE USA
102 *L12* **Ohre** *Ger.* Eger. ≈ Czech Republic/Germany
Ohri *see* Ohrid
115 *M20* **Ohrid** *Turk.* Ochrida, Ohri. SW FYR Macedonia
115 *M20* **Ohrid, Lake** *var.* Lake Ochrida, *Alb.* Liqeni i Ohrit, *Mac.* Ohridsko Ezero. ◎ Albania/FYR Macedonia
Ohridsko Ezero/Ohrit, Liqeni i *see* Ohrid, Lake
192 *L9* **Ohura** Manawatu-Wanganui, North Island, NZ
60 *J9* **Oiapoque** Amapá, E Brazil
60 *J10* **Oiapoque, Rio** *var.* Fleuve l'Oyapok, Oyapock. ≈ Brazil/French Guiana *see also* Oyapok, Fleuve l'
13 *O9* **Oies, Île aux** *island* Québec, SE Canada
94 *L13* **Oijärvi** Oulu, C Finland
94 *L12* **Oikarainen** Lappi, N Finland
196 *F10* **Oikuul** Babeldaob, N Palau
20 *C13* **Oil City** Pennsylvania, NE USA
20 *C12* **Oil Creek** ≈ Pennsylvania, NE USA
37 *R13* **Oildale** California, W USA
Oileán Ciarral *see* Castleisland
Oil Islands *see* Chagos Archipelago
117 *D18* **Oiniádes** *anc.* Oeniadae. *site of ancient city* Dytikí Ellás, W Greece
117 *L18* **Oinoússes** *island* E Greece
Oírr, Inis *see* Inisheer
101 *J15* **Oirschot** Noord-Brabant, S Netherlands
105 *N4* **Oise** ⬖ *department* N France
105 *P3* **Oise** ≈ N France
101 *J14* **Oisterwijk** Noord-Brabant, S Netherlands
47 *O14* **Oistins** S Barbados
170 *D14* **Ōita** Ōita, Kyūshū, SW Japan
170 *D14* **Ōita** *off.* Ōita-ken. ⬖ *prefecture* Kyūshū, SW Japan
117 *E17* **Oíti** ▲ C Greece
172 *Oo6* **Oiwake** Hokkaidō, NE Japan
37 *R14* **Ojai** California, W USA
96 *K13* **Öje** Kopparberg, C Sweden
95 *J14* **Öjebyn** Norrbotten, N Sweden
170 *Bb12* **Ojika-jima** *island* SW Japan
42 *K5* **Ojinaga** Chihuahua, N Mexico
171 *K13* **Ojiya** *var.* Oziya. Niigata, Honshū, C Japan
42 *M11* **Ojo Caliente** *var.* Ojocaliente. Zacatecas, C Mexico
42 *D6* **Ojo de Liebre, Laguna** *var.* Laguna Scammon, Scammon Lagoon. *lagoon* W Mexico
64 *I7* **Ojos del Salado, Cerro** ▲ W Argentina
107 *R7* **Ojos Negros** Aragón, NE Spain
42 *M12* **Ojuelos de Jalisco** Aguascalientes, C Mexico
131 *N4* **Oka** ≈ W Russian Federation
85 *D19* **Okahandja** Otjozondjupa, C Namibia
192 *L9* **Okahukura** Manawatu-Wanganui, North Island, NZ
192 *J3* **Okaihau** Northland, North Island, NZ
85 *D18* **Okakarara** Otjozondjupa, N Namibia
11 *P5* **Okak Islands** *island group* Newfoundland and Labrador, E Canada
8 *M17* **Okanagan** ≈ British Columbia, SW Canada
9 *N17* **Okanagan Lake** ◎ British Columbia, SW Canada
Ókanizsa *see* Kanjiža
85 *C16* **Okankolo** Otjikoto, N Namibia
34 *K6* **Okanogan River** ≈ Washington, NW USA
194 *I13* **Okapa** Eastern Highlands, C PNG
85 *D18* **Okaputa** Otjozondjupa, N Namibia
155 *V9* **Okāra** Punjab, E Pakistan
28 *M10* **Okarche** Oklahoma, C USA
152 *B13* **Okarem** *Turkm.* Ekerem. Balkanskiy Velayat, W Turkmenistan
201 *X14* **Okat Harbor** *harbor* Kosrae, E Micronesia
24 *M5* **Okatibbee Creek** ≈ Mississippi, S USA
85 *C17* **Okaukuejo** Kunene, N Namibia
Okavanggo *see* Cubango/Okavango
85 *E17* **Okavango** ⬖ *district* NW Namibia
85 *G17* **Okavango** *var.* Cubango, Kavango, Kavengo, Kubango, Okavanggo, *Port.* Ocavango. ≈ S Africa *see also* Cubango
85 *G17* **Okavango Delta** *wetland* N Botswana
171 *J15* **Okaya** Nagano, Honshū, S Japan
170 *Ff14* **Okayama** Okayama, Honshū, SW Japan
170 *F13* **Okayama** *off.* Okayama-ken. ⬖ *prefecture* Honshū, SW Japan
171 *I16* **Okazaki** Aichi, Honshū, C Japan
112 *M12* **Okęcie** ✈ (Warszawa) Warszawa, C Poland
25 *Y13* **Okeechobee** Florida, SE USA
25 *Y14* **Okeechobee, Lake** ◎ Florida, SE USA
28 *M9* **Okeene** Oklahoma, C USA
25 *V8* **Okefenokee Swamp** *wetland* Georgia, SE USA
99 *J24* **Okehampton** SW England, UK
29 *P10* **Okemah** Oklahoma, C USA
79 *U16* **Okene** Kogi, S Nigeria
102 *K13* **Oker** *var.* Ocker. ≈ NW Germany
103 *J14* **Oker-Stausee** ◎ C Germany
127 *O13* **Okha** Ostrov Sakhalin, Sakhalinskaya Oblast', SE Russian Federation
129 *U15* **Okhansk** *var.* Ochansk. Permskaya Oblast', NW Russian Federation
127 *N10* **Okhota** ≈ E Russian Federation
127 *Nn11* **Okhotsk** Khabarovskiy Kray, E Russian Federation
199 *I2* **Okhotsk, Sea of** *sea* NW Pacific Ocean
119 *T4* **Okhtyrka** *Rus.* Akhtyrka. Sums'ka Oblast', NE Ukraine
199 *Gg6* **Oki-Daitō Ridge** *undersea feature* W Pacific Ocean
85 *E23* **Okiep** Northern Cape, W South Africa
Oki-guntō *see* Oki-shotō
170 *Ff11* **Oki-kaikyō** *strait* SW Japan
172 *P15* **Okinawa** Okinawa, SW Japan
172 *Oo14* **Okinawa** *off.* Okinawa-ken. ⬖ *prefecture* Okinawa, SW Japan
172 *Oo14* **Okinawa** *island* SW Japan
172 *Q14* **Okinoerabu-jima** *island* Nansei-shotō, SW Japan
170 *Dd15* **Okino-shima** *island* SW Japan
170 *Ff11* **Oki-shotō** *var.* Oki-guntō. *island group* SW Japan
79 *T16* **Okitipupa** Ondo, SW Nigeria
177 *G8* **Okkan** Pegu, SW Myanmar
29 *N10* **Oklahoma** *off.* State of Oklahoma; also known as The Sooner State. ⬖ *state* C USA
29 *N11* **Oklahoma City** *state capital* Oklahoma, C USA
27 *Q4* **Oklaunion** Texas, SW USA
25 *W10* **Oklawaha River** ≈ Florida, SE USA
29 *P10* **Okmulgee** Oklahoma, C USA
Oknitsa *see* Ocniţa
24 *M3* **Okolona** Mississippi, S USA
172 *Q4* **Okoppe** Hokkaidō, NE Japan
9 *Q16* **Okotoks** Alberta, SW Canada
82 *H6* **Oko, Wadi** ≈ NE Sudan
81 *G19* **Okoyo** Cuvette, W Congo
79 *S15* **Okpara** ≈ Benin/Nigeria
94 *J8* **Øksfjord** Finnmark, N Norway
176 *Z12* **Oksibil** Irian Jaya, E Indonesia
129 *R4* **Oksino** Nenetskiy Avtonomnyy Okrug, NW Russian Federation
94 *G13* **Oksskolten** ▲ C Norway
Oksu *see* Oqsu
150 *M8* **Oktaybr'skiy** Kustanay, N Kazakhstan
194 *E11* **Ok Tedi** Western, W PNG
Oktemberyan *see* Hoktemberyan
177 *G7* **Oktwin** Pegu, C Myanmar
150 *I10* **Oktyabr'sk** Aktyubinsk, W Kazakhstan
131 *R6* **Oktyabr'sk** Samarskaya Oblast', W Russian Federation
129 *N12* **Oktyabr'skiy** Arkhangel'skaya Oblast', NW Russian Federation
127 *Pp12* **Oktyabr'skiy** Kamchatskaya Oblast', E Russian Federation
131 *T5* **Oktyabr'skiy** Respublika Bashkortostan, W Russian Federation
131 *O11* **Oktyabr'skiy** Volgogradskaya Oblast', SW Russian Federation
Oktyabr'skiy *see* Aktsyabrski
131 *V7* **Oktyabr'skoye** Orenburgskaya Oblast', W Russian Federation
126 *J3* **Oktyabr'skoy Revolyutsii, Ostrov** *Eng.* October Revolution Island. *island* Severnaya Zemlya, N Russian Federation
170 *C15* **Ōkuchi** *var.* Ôkuti. Kagoshima, Kyūshū, SW Japan
Okulovka *see* Uglovka
171 *Mm5* **Okushiri-tō** *var.* Okusiri Tô. *island* NE Japan
Okusiri Tô *see* Okushiri-tō
79 *S15* **Okuta** Kwara, W Nigeria
Ôkuti *see* Ōkuchi
85 *F19* **Okwa** *var.* Chapman's. ≈ Botswana/Namibia
127 *O10* **Ola** Magadanskaya Oblast', E Russian Federation
29 *T11* **Ola** Arkansas, C USA
Ola *see* Ala
37 *T11* **Olacha Peak** ▲ California, W USA
94 *J1* **Ólafsfjördhur** Nordhurland Eystra, N Iceland
94 *H3* **Ólafsvík** Vesturland, W Iceland
Oláhbrettye *see* Bretea-Română
Oláhszentgyőrgy *see* Sângeorz-Băi
Oláh-Toplicza *see* Topliţa
37 *T11* **Olancha** California, W USA
44 *J5* **Olanchito** Yoro, C Honduras
44 *J6* **Olancho** ⬖ *department* E Honduras
97 *O20* **Öland** *island* S Sweden

◆ Country
● Country Capital
◇ Dependent Territory
○ Dependent Territory Capital
⬖ Administrative Region
✈ International Airport
▲ Mountain
⛰ Mountain Range
Volcano
≈ River
◎ Lake
▣ Reservoir

97 O19 **Ölands norra udde** *headland* S Sweden
97 N22 **Ölands södra udde** *headland* S Sweden
190 K7 **Olary** South Australia
29 R4 **Olathe** Kansas, C USA
63 C22 **Olavarría** Buenos Aires, E Argentina
94 O2 **Olav V Land** *physical region* C Svalbard
113 H14 **Oława** *Ger.* Ohlau. Wrocław, SW Poland
109 D17 **Olbia** *prev.* Terranova Pausania. Sardegna, Italy, C Mediterranean Sea
46 G5 **Old Bahama Channel** *channel* Bahamas/Cuba
Old Bay State/Old Colony State *see* Massachusetts
8 H2 **Old Crow** Yukon Territory, NW Canada
Old Dominion *see* Virginia
Oldeberkeap *see* Oldeberkoop
100 M7 **Oldeberkoop** *Fris.* Oldeberkeap. Friesland, N Netherlands
100 L10 **Oldebroek** Gelderland, E Netherlands
100 L8 **Oldemarkt** Overijssel, N Netherlands
96 E11 **Olden** Sogn og Fjordane, C Norway
102 G10 **Oldenburg** Niedersachsen, NW Germany
102 K8 **Oldenburg** Schleswig-Holstein, N Germany
100 P10 **Oldenzaal** Overijssel, E Netherlands
94 I9 **Olderdalen** Troms, N Norway
20 J8 **Old Forge** New York, NE USA
Old Goa *see* Goa
99 L17 **Oldham** NW England, UK
41 Q14 **Old Harbor** Kodiak Island, Alaska, USA
46 J13 **Old Harbour** C Jamaica
99 C22 **Old Head of Kinsale** *Ir.* An Seanchean. *headland* SW Ireland
22 J8 **Old Hickory Lake** ⊞ Tennessee, S USA
Old Line State *see* Maryland
Old North State *see* North Carolina
83 I17 **Ol Doinyo Lengeyo** ⛰ C Kenya
9 Q16 **Olds** Alberta, SW Canada
21 Q7 **Old Speck Mountain** ▲ Maine, NE USA
21 Q8 **Old Town** Maine, NE USA
9 T17 **Old Wives Lake** ◎ Saskatchewan, S Canada
168 J7 **Öldziyt** Arhangay, C Mongolia
169 N10 **Öldziyt** Dornogovĭ, SE Mongolia
196 H6 **Oleai** *var.* San Jose. Saipan, S Northern Mariana Islands
20 E11 **Olean** New York, NE USA
112 O7 **Olecko** *Ger.* Treuburg. Suwałki, NE Poland
108 C7 **Oleggio** Piemonte, NE Italy
126 L13 **Olëkma** Amurskaya Oblast', SE Russian Federation
126 L13 **Olëkma** ≈ C Russian Federation
126 L12 **Olëkminsk** Respublika Sakha (Yakutiya), NE Russian Federation
119 W7 **Oleksandrivka** Donets'ka Oblast', E Ukraine
119 R7 **Oleksandrivka** *Rus.* Aleksandrovka. Kirovohrads'ka Oblast', C Ukraine
119 Q9 **Oleksandrivka** Mykolayivs'ka Oblast', S Ukraine
119 S7 **Oleksandriya** *Rus.* Aleksandriya. Kirovohrads'ka Oblast', C Ukraine
95 B20 **Ølen** Hordaland, S Norway
128 J4 **Olenegorsk** Murmanskaya Oblast', NW Russian Federation
126 K8 **Olenëk** Respublika Sakha (Yakutiya), NE Russian Federation
126 J9 **Olenëk** ≈ NE Russian Federation
126 Kk6 **Olenëkskiy Zaliv** *bay* N Russian Federation
128 K6 **Olenitsa** Murmanskaya Oblast', NW Russian Federation
104 I11 **Oléron, Île d'** *island* W France
113 H14 **Oleśnica** *Ger.* Oels, Oels in Schlesien. Wrocław, SW Poland
113 I15 **Olesno** *Ger.* Rosenberg. Częstochowa, S Poland
118 M3 **Olevs'k** *Rus.* Olevsk. Zhytomyrs'ka Oblast', N Ukraine
127 Nn18 **Ol'ga** Primorskiy Kray, SE Russian Federation
189 P8 **Olga, Mount** ▲ Northern Territory, C Australia
94 P2 **Olgastretet** *strait* E Svalbard
168 D5 **Ölgiy** Bayan-Ölgiy, W Mongolia
97 F23 **Ølgod** Ribe, W Denmark
106 H14 **Olhão** Faro, S Portugal
95 L14 **Olhava** Oulu, C Finland
112 B12 **Olib** *It.* Ulbo. *island* W Croatia
85 B16 **Olifa** Kunene, NW Namibia
85 E20 **Olifants** *var.* Elephant River. ≈ E Namibia
85 E25 **Olifants** *var.* Elefantes. ≈ SW South Africa
85 G22 **Olifantshoek** Northern Cape, N South Africa
196 L15 **Olimarao Atoll** *atoll* Caroline Islands, C Micronesia
Ólimbos *see* Ólympos
Olimpo *see* Fuerte Olimpo
61 Q15 **Olinda** Pernambuco, E Brazil
Olinthos *see* Ólynthos
85 I20 **Oliphants Drift** Kgatleng, SE Botswana
Olisipo *see* Lisboa
Olita *see* Alytus
107 Q4 **Olite** Navarra, N Spain
62 K10 **Oliva** Córdoba, C Argentina
107 T11 **Oliva** País Valenciano, E Spain
106 I12 **Oliva de la Frontera** Extremadura, W Spain
Olivares *see* Olivares de Júcar
64 H9 **Olivares, Cerro de** ▲ N Chile
107 P9 **Olivares de Júcar** *var.* Olivares. Castilla-La Mancha, C Spain
24 L1 **Olive Branch** Mississippi, S USA
23 O5 **Olive Hill** Kentucky, S USA
37 O6 **Olivehurst** California, W USA
106 G7 **Oliveira de Azeméis** Aveiro, N Portugal
106 I11 **Olivenza** Extremadura, W Spain
9 N17 **Oliver** British Columbia, SW Canada
105 N7 **Olivet** Loiret, C France
31 Q12 **Olivet** South Dakota, N USA
31 T9 **Olivia** Minnesota, N USA
193 C20 **Olivine Range** ⛰ South Island, NZ
110 H10 **Olivone** Ticino, S Switzerland
Ölkeyek *see* Ul'kayak
131 O9 **Ol'khovka** Volgogradskaya Oblast', SW Russian Federation
113 K16 **Olkusz** Katowice, S Poland
24 I6 **Olla** Louisiana, S USA
64 I4 **Ollagüe, Volcán** *var.* Oyahue, Volcán Oyahue. ▲ N Chile
201 U13 **Ollan** *island* Chuuk, C Micronesia
196 F7 **Ollei** Babeldaob, N Palau
Ollius *see* Oglio
110 C10 **Ollon** Vaud, W Switzerland
153 Q10 **Olmaliq** *Rus.* Almalyk. Toshkent Wiloyati, E Uzbekistan
106 M6 **Olmedo** Castilla-León, N Spain
58 B10 **Olmos** Lambayeque, W Peru
Olmütz *see* Olomouc
32 M15 **Olney** Illinois, N USA
27 R5 **Olney** Texas, SW USA
97 L22 **Olofström** Blekinge, S Sweden
195 Y15 **Olomburi** Malaita, N Solomon Islands
113 H17 **Olomouc** *Ger.* Olmütz, *Pol.* Ołomuniec. Severní Morava, E Czech Republic
Olomuniec *see* Olomouc
125 Cc6 **Olonets** Respublika Kareliya, NW Russian Federation
179 P10 **Olongapo** *off.* Olongapo City. Luzon, N Philippines
104 J16 **Oloron-Ste-Marie** Pyrénées-Atlantiques, SW France
198 Dd8 **Olosega** *island* Manua Islands, E American Samoa
107 W4 **Olot** Cataluña, NE Spain
152 K12 **Olot** *Rus.* Alat. Bukhoro Wiloyati, C Uzbekistan
114 I12 **Olovo** E Bosnia and Herzegovina
126 Kk16 **Olovyannaya** Chitinskaya Oblast', S Russian Federation
127 Oo6 **Oloy** ≈ NE Russian Federation
103 F16 **Olpe** Nordrhein-Westfalen, W Germany
111 N8 **Olperer** ▲ SW Austria
Olshanka *see* Vil'shanka
Ol'shany *see* Al'shany
Olsnitz *see* Murska Sobota
100 M10 **Olst** Overijssel, E Netherlands
112 L8 **Olsztyn** *Ger.* Allenstein. Olsztyn, N Poland
112 L8 **Olsztyn** *off.* Województwo Olsztyńskie. ◈ *province* N Poland
112 L8 **Olsztynek** *Ger.* Hohenstein in Ostpreussen. Olsztyn, N Poland
Olsztyńskie, Województwo *see* Olsztyn
118 I14 **Olt** ◈ *county* SW Romania
118 I14 **Olt** *var.* Oltul, *Ger.* Alt. ≈ S Romania
110 E7 **Olten** Solothurn, NW Switzerland
118 K14 **Oltenița** *prev. Eng.* Oltenitsa, *anc.* Constantiola. Călărași, SE Romania
Oltenitsa *see* Oltenița
118 H14 **Olteț** ≈ S Romania
26 M4 **Olton** Texas, SW USA
143 R12 **Oltu** Erzurum, NE Turkey
Oltul *see* Olt
152 G7 **Oltynkŭl** Qoraqalpoghiston Respublikasi, NW Uzbekistan
167 S15 **Oluan Pi** *Eng.* Cape Olwanpi. *headland* S Taiwan
Ólubló *see* Stará Ľubovňa
143 R11 **Olur** Erzurum, NE Turkey
106 L15 **Olvera** Andalucía, S Spain
Ol'viopol' *see* Pervomays'k
Olwanpi, Cape *see* Oluan Pi
17 G2 **Olympia** *state capital* Washington, NW USA
117 D20 **Olympía** Dytikí Ellás, S Greece
190 H5 **Olympic Dam** South Australia
34 F7 **Olympic Mountains** ⛰ Washington, NW USA
124 R12 **Ólympos** *var.* Troodos, *Eng.* Mount Olympus. ▲ C Cyprus
117 F15 **Ólympos** *var.* Ólimbos, *Eng.* Mount Olympus. ▲ N Greece
117 L17 **Ólympos** ▲ Lésvos, E Greece
17 G1 **Olympus, Mount** ▲ Washington, NW USA
Olympus, Mount *see* Ólympos
117 G14 **Ólynthos** *var.* Olinthos; *anc.* Olynthus. *site of ancient city* Kentrikí Makedonía, N Greece
Olynthus *see* Ólynthos
119 Q3 **Olyshivka** Chernihivs'ka Oblast', N Ukraine
127 Q7 **Olyutorskiy, Mys** *headland* E Russian Federation
127 Pp8 **Olyutorskiy Zaliv** *bay* E Russian Federation
194 F11 **Om** ≈ W PNG
133 S6 **Om'** ≈ N Russian Federation
163 J13 **Oma** Xizang Zizhiqu, W China
172 N8 **Ōma** Aomori, Honshū, C Japan
129 P6 **Oma** ≈ NW Russian Federation
171 J14 **Ōmachi** *var.* Ōmati. Nagano, Honshū, S Japan
171 Ii17 **Omae-zaki** *headland* Honshū, S Japan
171 M11 **Ōmagari** Akita, Honshū, C Japan
99 E15 **Omagh** *Ir.* An Ómaigh. W Northern Ireland, UK
31 S15 **Omaha** Nebraska, C USA
85 E19 **Omaheke** ◈ *district* W Namibia
147 W10 **Oman** *off.* Sultanate of Oman, *Ar.* Salṭanat 'Umān; *prev.* Muscat and Oman. ◆ *monarchy* SW Asia
133 O10 **Oman Basin** *var.* Bassin d'Oman. *undersea feature* N Indian Ocean
Oman, Bassin d' *see* Oman Basin
133 N10 **Oman, Gulf of** *Ar.* Khalīj 'Umān. *gulf* N Arabian Sea
192 J3 **Omapere** Northland, North Island, NZ
193 E20 **Omarama** Canterbury, South Island, NZ
114 F11 **Omarska** NW Bosnia and Herzegovina
85 C18 **Omaruru** Erongo, NW Namibia
85 C19 **Omaruru** ≈ W Namibia
85 E17 **Omatako** ≈ NE Namibia
Ōmati *see* Ōmachi
85 E18 **Omawewozonyanda** Omaheke, E Namibia
172 N7 **Ōma-zaki** *headland* Honshū, C Japan
Omba *see* Ambae
Ombai *see* Alor, Pulau
175 Rr16 **Ombai, Selat** *strait* Nusa Tenggara, S Indonesia
85 C16 **Ombalantu** Omusati, N Namibia
81 H15 **Ombella-Mpoko** ◈ *prefecture* S Central African Republic
Ombetsu *see* Onbetsu
85 B17 **Ombombo** Kunene, NW Namibia
81 D19 **Omboué** Ogooué-Maritime, W Gabon
108 G13 **Ombrone** ≈ C Italy
82 F9 **Omdurman** *var.* Umm Durmān. Khartoum, C Sudan
171 Jj16 **Ōme** Tōkyō, Honshū, S Japan
108 C6 **Omegna** Piemonte, NE Italy
191 P12 **Omeo** Victoria, SE Australia
144 F11 **'Omer** Southern, C Israel
43 P16 **Ometepec** Guerrero, S Mexico
44 K11 **Ometepe, Isla de** *island* S Nicaragua
Om Hager *see* Om Hajer
82 I10 **Om Hajer** *var.* Om Hager. SW Eritrea
171 H14 **Ōmi-Hachiman** *var.* Ōmihachiman. Shiga, Honshū, SW Japan
8 L12 **Omineca Mountains** ⛰ British Columbia, W Canada
115 F14 **Omiš** *It.* Almissa. Split-Dalmacija, S Croatia
114 B10 **Omišalj** Primorje-Gorski Kotar, NW Croatia
170 Dd12 **Ōmi-shima** *island* SW Japan
85 D19 **Omitara** Khomas, C Namibia
43 O16 **Omitlán, Río** ≈ S Mexico
41 X14 **Ommaney, Cape** *headland* Baranof Island, Alaska, USA
100 N9 **Ommen** Overijssel, E Netherlands
168 K11 **Ömnögovĭ** ◈ *province* S Mongolia
203 X7 **Omoa** Fatu Hira, NE French Polynesia
Omo Botego *see* Omo Wenz
Ómoldova *see* Moldova Veche
127 O6 **Omolon** Chukotskiy Avtonomnyy Okrug, NE Russian Federation
127 O7 **Omolon** ≈ NE Russian Federation
126 L8 **Omoloy** ≈ NE Russian Federation
171 M10 **Omono-gawa** ≈ Honshū, C Japan
83 I14 **Omo Wenz** *var.* Omo Botego. ≈ Ethiopia/Kenya
125 Ff13 **Omsk** Omskaya Oblast', C Russian Federation
125 Ff12 **Omskaya Oblast'** ◈ *province* C Russian Federation
127 O8 **Omsukchan** Magadanskaya Oblast', E Russian Federation
172 Q4 **Ōmu** Hokkaidō, NE Japan
112 M9 **Omulew** ≈ NE Poland
118 J12 **Omul, Vârful** *prev.* Vîrful Omu. ▲ C Romania
85 D16 **Omundaungilo** Ohangwena, N Namibia
170 C13 **Ōmura** Nagasaki, Kyūshū, SW Japan
85 B17 **Omusati** ◈ *district* N Namibia
170 Cc13 **Ōmuta** Fukuoka, Kyūshū, SW Japan
129 S14 **Omutninsk** Kirovskaya Oblast', NW Russian Federation
Omu, Vîrful *see* Omul, Vârful
31 V7 **Onamia** Minnesota, N USA
23 Y5 **Onancock** Virginia, NE USA
12 E10 **Onaping Lake** ◎ Ontario, S Canada
32 M12 **Onarga** Illinois, N USA
13 R6 **Onatchiway, Lac** ◎ Québec, SE Canada
31 S14 **Onawa** Iowa, C USA
172 Pp7 **Onbetsu** *var.* Ombetsu. Hokkaidō, NE Japan
85 B16 **Oncócua** Cunene, SW Angola
107 S9 **Onda** País Valenciano, E Spain
113 N18 **Ondava** ≈ NE Slovakia
Ondjiva *see* N'Giva
79 T16 **Ondo** Ondo, SW Nigeria
79 T16 **Ondo** ◈ *state* SW Nigeria
169 N8 **Öndörhaan** Hentiy, E Mongolia
85 D18 **Ondundazongonda** Otjozondjupa, N Namibia
157 K21 **One and Half Degree Channel** *channel* S Maldives
197 L15 **Oneata** *island* Lau Group, E Fiji
128 L9 **Onega** Arkhangel'skaya Oblast', NW Russian Federation
125 Dd6 **Onega** ≈ NW Russian Federation
Onega Bay *see* Onezhskaya Guba
Onega, Lake *see* Onezhskoye Ozero
20 I10 **Oneida** New York, NE USA
22 M8 **Oneida** Tennessee, S USA
20 H9 **Oneida Lake** ◎ New York, NE USA
31 P13 **O'Neill** Nebraska, C USA
127 Pp13 **Onekotan, Ostrov** *island* Kuril'skiye Ostrova, SE Russian Federation
25 P3 **Oneonta** Alabama, S USA
20 J11 **Oneonta** New York, NE USA
202 I16 **Oneroa** *island* S Cook Islands
118 K11 **Onești** *Hung.* Onyest; *prev.* Gheorghe Gheorghiu-Dej. Bacău, E Romania
200 Qq15 **Onevai** *island* Tongatapu Group, S Tonga
110 A11 **Onex** Genève, SW Switzerland
128 K8 **Onezhskaya Guba** *Eng.* Onega Bay. *bay* NW Russian Federation
125 D6 **Onezhskoye Ozero** *Eng.* Lake Onega. ◎ NW Russian Federation
85 C16 **Ongandjera** Omusati, N Namibia
192 N12 **Ongaonga** Hawke's Bay, North Island, NZ
168 K9 **Ongi** Dundgovĭ, C Mongolia
168 J8 **Ongi** Övörhangay, C Mongolia
169 W14 **Ongjin** SW North Korea
161 J17 **Ongole** Andhra Pradesh, E India
168 K8 **Ongon** Övörhangay, C Mongolia
Ongtüstik Qazaqstan Oblysy *see* Yuzhnyy Kazakhstan
101 I21 **Onhaye** Namur, S Belgium
177 G8 **Onhne** Pegu, SW Myanmar
143 S9 **Oni** N Georgia
31 N9 **Onida** South Dakota, N USA
170 E15 **Onigajō-yama** ▲ Shikoku, SW Japan
180 H7 **Onilahy** ≈ S Madagascar
79 U16 **Onitsha** Anambra, S Nigeria
171 Gg14 **Ono** Hyōgo, Honshū, SW Japan
197 I15 **Ono** *island* SW Fiji
171 I14 **Ōno** Fukui, Honshū, SW Japan
170 D12 **Onoda** Yamaguchi, Honshū, SW Japan
197 L17 **Ono-i-lau** *island* SE Fiji
170 Cc13 **Ōnojō** *var.* Ōnozyô. Fukuoka, Kyūshū, SW Japan
126 K16 **Onokhoy** Respublika Buryatiya, S Russian Federation
170 F14 **Onomichi** *var.* Onomiti. Hiroshima, Honshū, SW Japan
Onomiti *see* Onomichi
169 O7 **Onon Gol** ≈ N Mongolia
Ononte *see* Orontes
57 N6 **Onoto** Anzoátegui, NE Venezuela
203 O3 **Onotoa** *prev.* Clerk Island. *atoll* Tungaru, W Kiribati
Ōnozyô *see* Ōnojō
97 I19 **Onsala** Halland, S Sweden
85 E23 **Onseepkans** Northern Cape, W South Africa
106 F4 **Ons, Illa de** *island* NW Spain
188 H7 **Onslow** Western Australia
23 W11 **Onslow Bay** *bay* North Carolina, E USA
100 P6 **Onstwedde** Groningen, NE Netherlands
170 Bb16 **On-take** ▲ Kyūshū, SW Japan
171 Ii15 **Ontake-san** ▲ Honshū, S Japan
37 T15 **Ontario** California, W USA
34 M13 **Ontario** Oregon, NW USA
10 D10 **Ontario** ◈ *province* S Canada
15 Gg2 **Ontario, Lake** ◎ Canada/USA
1 L9 **Ontario Peninsula** *peninsula* Canada/USA
Onteniente *see* Ontinyent
107 S11 **Ontinyent** *var.* Onteniente. País Valenciano, E Spain
95 N15 **Ontojärvi** ◎ E Finland
32 L3 **Ontonagon** Michigan, N USA
32 L3 **Ontonagon River** ≈ Michigan, N USA
195 W11 **Ontong Java Atoll** *prev.* Lord Howe Island. *atoll* N Solomon Islands
183 N5 **Ontong Java Rise** *undersea feature* W Pacific Ocean
Onuba *see* Huelva
57 W9 **Onverwacht** Para, N Suriname
Onyest *see* Onești
190 J7 **Oodla Wirra** South Australia
190 F2 **Oodnadatta** South Australia
190 C5 **Ooldea** South Australia
29 Q8 **Oologah Lake** ⊞ Oklahoma, C USA
Oos-Kaap *see* Eastern Cape
Oos-Londen *see* East London
101 E17 **Oostakker** Oost-Vlaanderen, NW Belgium
101 D15 **Oostburg** Zeeland, SW Netherlands
100 K9 **Oostelijk-Flevoland** *polder* C Netherlands
101 B16 **Oostende** *Eng.* Ostend, *Fr.* Ostende. West-Vlaanderen, NW Belgium
101 B16 **Oostende** ✕ West-Vlaanderen, NW Belgium
100 L12 **Oosterbeek** Gelderland, SE Netherlands
101 I14 **Oosterhout** Noord-Brabant, S Netherlands
100 O6 **Oostermoers Vaart** *var.* Hunze. ≈ NE Netherlands
101 F14 **Oosterschelde** *Eng.* Eastern Scheldt. *inlet* SW Netherlands
101 E14 **Oosterscheldedam** *dam* SW Netherlands
100 M7 **Oosterwolde** *Fris.* Easterwâlde. Friesland, N Netherlands
100 I9 **Oosthuizen** Noord-Holland, NW Netherlands
101 H16 **Oostmalle** Antwerpen, N Belgium
Oos-Transvaal *see* Mpumalanga
101 E15 **Oost-Souburg** Zeeland, SW Netherlands
101 E17 **Oost-Vlaanderen** *Eng.* East Flanders. ◈ *province* NW Belgium
100 J5 **Oost-Vlieland** Friesland, N Netherlands
100 F12 **Oostvoorne** Zuid-Holland, SW Netherlands
Ootacamund *see* Udagamandalam
100 O10 **Ootmarsum** Overijssel, E Netherlands
8 K14 **Ootsa Lake** ⊞ British Columbia, SW Canada
116 L8 **Opaka** Razgradska Oblast, N Bulgaria
81 M18 **Opala** Haut-Zaïre, C Zaire
129 Q13 **Oparino** Kirovskaya Oblast', NW Russian Federation
12 H8 **Opasatica, Lac** ◎ Québec, SE Canada
114 B9 **Opatija** *It.* Abbazia. Primorje-Gorski Kotar, NW Croatia
113 N15 **Opatów** Tarnobrzeg, SE Poland
113 I17 **Opava** *Ger.* Troppau. Severní Morava, E Czech Republic
113 H16 **Opava** *Ger.* Oppa. ≈ NE Czech Republic
Ópazova *see* Stara Pazova
194 L14 **Ope** ≈ S PNG
Ópécska *see* Pecica
12 E8 **Opeepeesway Lake** ◎ Ontario, S Canada
25 R5 **Opelika** Alabama, S USA
24 I8 **Opelousas** Louisiana, S USA
195 O11 **Open Bay** *bay* New Britain, E PNG
12 I12 **Opeongo Lake** ◎ Ontario, SE Canada
101 K17 **Opglabbeek** Limburg, NE Belgium
35 W6 **Opheim** Montana, NW USA
41 P10 **Ophir** Alaska, USA
Ophiusa *see* Formentera
81 N18 **Opienge** Haut-Zaïre, E Zaire
193 G20 **Opihi** ≈ South Island, NZ
10 J9 **Opinaca** ≈ Québec, C Canada
10 J10 **Opinaca, Réservoir** ⊞ Québec, E Canada
119 T5 **Opishnya** *Rus.* Oposhnya. Poltavs'ka Oblast', NE Ukraine
100 I8 **Opmeer** Noord-Holland, NW Netherlands
79 V17 **Opobo** Akwa Ibom, S Nigeria
128 F16 **Opochka** Pskovskaya Oblast', W Russian Federation
112 L13 **Opoczno** Piotrków, C Poland
113 I15 **Opole** *Ger.* Oppeln. Opole, SW Poland
113 H15 **Opole** *off.* Województwo Opolskie. ◈ *province* SW Poland
Opolskie, Województwo *see* Opole
150 G13 **Opornyy** Mangistau, SW Kazakhstan
Oporto *see* Porto
Oposhnya *see* Opishnya
192 P8 **Opotiki** Bay of Plenty, North Island, NZ
25 Q7 **Opp** Alabama, S USA
Oppa *see* Opava
96 G9 **Oppdal** Sør-Trøndelag, S Norway
Oppeln *see* Opole
109 N23 **Oppido Mamertina** Calabria, SW Italy
Oppidum Ubiorum *see* Köln
96 F12 **Oppland** ◈ *county* S Norway
120 J12 **Opsa** *Rus.* Opsa. Vitsyebskaya Voblasts', NW Belarus
28 I8 **Optima Lake** ⊞ Oklahoma, C USA
192 J11 **Opunake** Taranaki, North Island, NZ
203 N6 **Opunohu, Baie d'** *bay* Moorea, W French Polynesia
85 B17 **Opuwo** Kunene, NW Namibia
152 H6 **Oqqal'a** *var.* Akkala, *Rus.* Karakala. Qoraqalpoghiston Respublikasi, NW Uzbekistan
153 V13 **Oqsu** *Rus.* Oksu. ≈ SE Tajikistan
153 P14 **Oqtogh, Qatorkŭhi** *Rus.* Khrebet Aktau. ⛰ SW Tajikistan
152 M11 **Oqtosh** *Rus.* Aktash. Samarqand Wiloyati, C Uzbekistan
153 N11 **Oqtow Tizmasi** *Rus.* Khrebet Aktau. ⛰ C Uzbekistan
32 J12 **Oquawka** Illinois, N USA
150 J10 **Or'** *Kaz.* Or. ≈ Kazakhstan/Russian Federation
38 M15 **Oracle** Arizona, SW USA
118 F9 **Oradea** *prev.* Oradea Mare, *Ger.* Grosswardein, *Hung.* Nagyvárad. Bihor, NW Romania
Oradea Mare *see* Oradea
115 M17 **Orahovac** *Alb.* Rahovec. Serbia, S Yugoslavia
114 H9 **Orahovica** Virovitica-Podravina, NE Croatia
158 K13 **Orai** Uttar Pradesh, N India
94 K12 **Orajärvi** Lappi, NW Finland
Oral *see* Ural'sk
76 I5 **Oran** *var.* Ouahran, Wahran. NW Algeria
191 R8 **Orange** New South Wales, SE Australia
105 R14 **Orange** *anc.* Arausio. Vaucluse, SE France
27 Y10 **Orange** Texas, SW USA
23 V5 **Orange** Virginia, NE USA
23 R13 **Orangeburg** South Carolina, SE USA
60 J9 **Orange, Cabo** *headland* NE Brazil
31 S12 **Orange City** Iowa, C USA
Orange Cone *see* Orange Fan
180 J10 **Orange Fan** *var.* Orange Cone. *undersea feature* SW Indian Ocean
Orange Free State *see* Free State
27 S14 **Orange Grove** Texas, SW USA
20 K13 **Orange Lake** New York, NE USA
25 V10 **Orange Lake** ◎ Florida, SE USA
Orange Mouth/Orangemund *see* Oranjemund
25 W9 **Orange Park** Florida, SE USA194 M17
Orangerie Bay *bay* SE PNG
85 E23 **Orange River** *Afr.* Oranjerivier. ≈ S Africa
12 G15 **Orangeville** Ontario, S Canada
38 M5 **Orangeville** Utah, W USA
44 G1 **Orange Walk** Orange Walk, N Belize
44 F1 **Orange Walk** ◈ *district* NW Belize
102 N11 **Oranienburg** Brandenburg, NE Germany
100 O7 **Oranjekanaal** *canal* NE Netherlands
85 D23 **Oranjemund** *var.* Orangemund; *prev.* Orange Mouth. Karas, SW Namibia
Oranjerivier *see* Orange River
47 N16 **Oranjestad** ○ (Aruba) W Aruba
Oranje Vrystaat *see* Free State
176 W9 **Oransbari** Irian Jaya, E Indonesia
Orany *see* Varėna
85 H18 **Orapa** Central, C Botswana
144 F9 **Or 'Aqiva** Haifa, W Israel
114 I10 **Orašje** N Bosnia and Herzegovina
118 G11 **Orăștie** *Ger.* Broos, *Hung.* Szászváros. Hunedoara, W Romania
Orașul Stalin *see* Brașov
113 K18 **Orava** *Hung.* Árva, *Pol.* Orawa. ≈ N Slovakia
Oravainen *see* Oravais
95 K16 **Oravais** *Fin.* Oravainen. Vaasa, W Finland
Oravicabánya *see* Oravița
118 F13 **Oravița** *Ger.* Orawitza, *Hung.* Oravicabánya. Caraș-Severin, SW Romania
Orawa *see* Orava
193 B24 **Orawia** Southland, South Island, NZ
Orawitza *see* Oravița
105 P16 **Orb** ≈ S France
108 C9 **Orba** ≈ NW Italy
164 H12 **Orba Co** ◎ W China
110 B9 **Orbe** Vaud, W Switzerland
109 G14 **Orbetello** Toscana, C Italy
106 K3 **Órbigo** ≈ NW Spain
191 Q12 **Orbost** Victoria, SE Australia
97 O14 **Örbyhus** Uppsala, C Sweden
204 I1 **Orcadas** *Argentinian research station* South Orkney Islands, Antarctica
107 P12 **Orcera** Andalucía, S Spain
35 P9 **Orchard Homes** Montana, NW USA
39 P5 **Orchard Mesa** Colorado, C USA
20 D10 **Orchard Park** New York, NE USA
Orchid Island *see* Lan Yü
117 G18 **Orchómenos** *var.* Orhomenos, Orkhómenos; *prev.* Skripón, *anc.* Orchomenus. Stereá Ellás, C Greece
Orchomenus *see* Orchómenos
108 B7 **Orco** ≈ NW Italy
105 R8 **Or, Côte d'** *physical region* C France
31 O14 **Ord** Nebraska, C USA
Ordat' *see* Ordats'
121 O15 **Ordats'** *Rus.* Ordat'. Mahilyowskaya Voblasts', E Belarus
38 K8 **Orderville** Utah, W USA
106 H2 **Ordes** Galicia, NW Spain
37 V14 **Ord Mountain** ▲ California, W USA
Ordos Desert *see* Mu Us Shamo
196 B16 **Ordot** C Guam
143 N11 **Ordu** *anc.* Cotyora. Ordu, N Turkey
142 M11 **Ordu** ◈ *province* N Turkey
143 V14 **Ordubad** SW Azerbaijan
107 O3 **Orduña** País Vasco, N Spain
39 U6 **Ordway** Colorado, C USA
150 L8 **Ordzhonikidze** Kustanay, N Kazakhstan
119 T9 **Ordzhonikidze** Dnipropetrovs'ka Oblast', E Ukraine
Ordzhonikidze *see* Vladikavkaz, Russian Federation
Ordzhonikidze *see* Yenakiyeve, Ukraine
Ordzhonikidzeabad *see* Kofarnihon
57 U9 **Orealla** E Guyana
115 G15 **Orebić** *It.* Sabbioncello. Dubrovnik-Neretva, S Croatia
97 M16 **Örebro** Örebro, C Sweden
97 L16 **Örebro** ◈ *county* C Sweden
27 W6 **Ore City** Texas, SW USA
32 L10 **Oregon** Illinois, N USA
29 Q2 **Oregon** Missouri, C USA
33 R11 **Oregon** Ohio, N USA
34 H13 **Oregon** *off.* State of Oregon; also known as Beaver State, Sunset State, Valentine State, Webfoot State. ◈ *state* NW USA
34 G11 **Oregon City** Oregon, NW USA
97 P14 **Öregrund** Uppsala, C Sweden
Orekhov *see* Orikhiv
130 L3 **Orekhovo-Zuyevo** Moskovskaya Oblast', W Russian Federation
Orekhovsk *see* Arekhawsk
Orel *see* Orël
130 J6 **Orël** Orlovskaya Oblast', W Russian Federation
58 E11 **Orellana** Loreto, N Peru
106 L11 **Orellana, Embalse de** ⊞ W Spain
38 L3 **Orem** Utah, W USA
Ore Mountains *see* Erzgebirge/Krušné Hory
131 V7 **Orenburg** *prev.* Chkalov. Orenburgskaya Oblast', W Russian Federation
131 V7 **Orenburg** ✕ Orenburgskaya Oblast', W Russian Federation
131 T7 **Orenburgskaya Oblast'** ◈ *province* W Russian Federation
Orense *see* Ourense
196 E10 **Oreor** *var.* Koror. ● (Palau) Oreor, N Palau
196 E10 **Oreor** *var.* Koror. *island* N Palau
193 B24 **Orepuki** Southland, South Island, NZ
116 L12 **Orestiáda** *prev.* Orestiás. Anatolikí Makedonía kai Thráki, NE Greece
Orestiás *see* Orestiáda
Öresund/Øresund *see* Sound, The
193 C23 **Oreti** ≈ South Island, NZ
192 L5 **Orewa** Auckland, North Island, NZ
176 Y14 **Oreyabo** Irian Jaya, E Indonesia
67 A25 **Orford, Cape** *headland* West Falkland, Falkland Islands
46 B5 **Órganos, Sierra de los** ⛰ W Cuba
39 R15 **Organ Peak** ▲ New Mexico, SW USA
107 N9 **Orgaz** Castilla-La Mancha, C Spain
Orgeyev *see* Orhei
168 I6 **Orgil** Hövsgöl, C Mongolia
107 O15 **Orgiva** *var.* Orjiva. Andalucía, S Spain
168 I9 **Örgön** Bayanhongor, C Mongolia
119 N9 **Orhei** *var.* Orheiu, *Rus.* Orgeyev. N Moldova
Orheiu *see* Orhei
107 R3 **Orhi** *var.* Orhy, Pico de Orhy, Pic d'Orhy. ▲ France/Spain *see also* Orhy
Orhomenos *see* Orchómenos
168 L6 **Orhon Gol** ≈ N Mongolia
104 J16 **Orhy** *var.* Orhi, Pico de Orhy, Pic d'Orhy. ▲ France/Spain *see also* Orhi
Orhy, Pic d'/Orhy, Pico de *see* Orhi/Orhy
36 L2 **Orick** California, W USA
34 L6 **Orient** Washington, NW USA
50 D6 **Oriental, Cordillera** ⛰ Bolivia/Peru
50 D6 **Oriental, Cordillera** ⛰ C Colombia
59 H16 **Oriental, Cordillera** ⛰ C Peru
65 M15 **Oriente** Buenos Aires, E Argentina
107 R12 **Orihuela** País Valenciano, E Spain
119 V9 **Orikhiv** *Rus.* Orekhov. Zaporiz'ka Oblast', SE Ukraine
115 K22 **Orikum** *var.* Orikumi. Vlorë, SW Albania
Orikumi *see* Orikum
119 V6 **Oril'** *Rus.* Orel. ≈ E Ukraine
12 H14 **Orillia** Ontario, S Canada
95 M19 **Orimattila** Uusimaa, S Finland
35 Y15 **Orin** Wyoming, C USA
49 R4 **Orinoco, Río** ≈ Colombia/Venezuela
194 G15 **Oriomo** Western, SW PNG
32 K11 **Orion** Illinois, N USA
31 Q5 **Oriska** North Dakota, N USA
159 P17 **Orissa** ◈ *state* NE India
Orissaar *see* Orissaare
120 E5 **Orissaare** *Ger.* Orissaar. Saaremaa, W Estonia
109 B19 **Oristano** Sardegna, Italy, C Mediterranean Sea
109 A19 **Oristano, Golfo di** *gulf* Sardegna, Italy, C Mediterranean Sea
56 D13 **Orito** Putumayo, SW Colombia
95 L18 **Orivesi** Häme, SW Finland
95 N17 **Orivesi** ◎ SE Finland
60 H12 **Oriximiná** Pará, NE Brazil
43 Q14 **Orizaba** Veracruz-Llave, E Mexico
43 Q14 **Orizaba, Volcán Pico de** *var.* Citlaltépetl. ▲ S Mexico
97 I16 **Ørje** Østfold, S Norway
115 I16 **Orjen** ⛰ Bosnia and Herzegovina/Yugoslavia
Orjiva *see* Orgiva
96 G8 **Orkanger** Sør-Trøndelag, S Norway
96 G8 **Orkdalen** *valley* S Norway
97 K22 **Örkelljunga** Kristianstad, S Sweden
Orkhaniye *see* Botevgrad
Orkhómenos *see* Orchómenos
96 H9 **Orkla** ≈ S Norway
Orkney *see* Orkney Islands
67 J22 **Orkney Deep** *undersea feature* Scotia Sea/Weddell Sea
98 J4 **Orkney Islands** *var.* Orkney, Orkneys. *island group* N Scotland, UK
Orkneys *see* Orkney Islands
26 K8 **Orla** Texas, SW USA
37 N5 **Orland** California, W USA
25 X11 **Orlando** Florida, SE USA
25 X12 **Orlando** ✕ Florida, SE USA
109 K23 **Orlando, Capo d'** *headland* Sicilia, Italy, C Mediterranean Sea
Orlau *see* Orlová
105 N6 **Orléanais** *cultural region* C France
36 L2 **Orleans** California, W USA
21 Q12 **Orleans** Massachusetts, NE USA
105 N7 **Orléans** *anc.* Aurelianum. Loiret, C France
13 R10 **Orléans, Île d'** *island* Québec, SE Canada
Orléansville *see* Chlef
113 F16 **Orlice** *Ger.* Adler. ≈ NE Czech Republic
126 Ii15 **Orlik** Respublika Buryatiya, S Russian Federation
129 Q14 **Orlov** *prev.* Khalturin. Kirovskaya Oblast', NW Russian Federation
113 I17 **Orlová** *Ger.* Orlau, *Pol.* Orłowa. Severní Morava, S Czech Republic
Orlov, Mys *see* Orlovskiy, Mys
130 I6 **Orlovskaya Oblast'** ◈ *province* W Russian Federation

◆ Country · ● Country Capital · ◇ Dependent Territory · ○ Dependent Territory Capital · ◈ Administrative Region · ✕ International Airport · ▲ Mountain · ⛰ Mountain Range · ☒ Volcano · ≈ River · ◎ Lake · ⊞ Reservoir

128 *M5* **Orlovskiy, Mys** *var.* Mys Orlov. *headland* NW Russian Federation
Orłowa *see* Orlová
105 *O5* **Orly** ✕ (Paris) Essonne, N France
121 *G16* **Orlya** *Rus.* Orlya. Hrodzyenskaya Voblasts', W Belarus
116 *M7* **Orlyak** *prev.* Makenzen, Trubchular, *Rom.* Trupcilar. Varnenska Oblast, NE Bulgaria
154 *L16* **Ormāra** Baluchistān, SW Pakistan
179 *Qq13* **Ormoc** *off.* Ormoc City, *var.* MacArthur. Leyte, C Philippines
25 *X10* **Ormond Beach** Florida, SE USA
111 *X10* **Ormož** *Ger.* Friedau. NE Slovenia
12 *J13* **Ormsby** Ontario, SE Canada
99 *K17* **Ormskirk** NW England, UK
Ormsö *see* Vormsi
13 *N13* **Ormstown** Québec, SE Canada
Ormuz, Strait of *see* Hormuz, Strait of
105 *T8* **Ornans** Doubs, E France
104 *K5* **Orne** ◈ *department* N France
104 *K5* **Orne** ≈ N France
94 *G12* **Ørnes** Nordland, C Norway
112 *L7* **Orneta** Elbląg, N Poland
97 *P16* **Ornö** Stockholm, C Sweden
39 *Q3* **Orno Peak** ▲ Colorado, C USA
95 *I16* **Örnsköldsvik** Västernorrland, C Sweden
169 *X13* **Oro** E North Korea
47 *T6* **Orocovis** C Puerto Rico
56 *H10* **Orocué** Casanare, E Colombia
79 *N13* **Orodara** SW Burkina
107 *S4* **Oroel, Peña de** ▲ N Spain
35 *N10* **Orofino** Idaho, NW USA
168 *I9* **Orog Nuur** ◎ S Mongolia
37 *U14* **Oro Grande** California, W USA
39 *S15* **Orogrande** New Mexico, SW USA
203 *Q7* **Orohena, Mont** ⛰ Tahiti, W French Polynesia
Orolaunum *see* Arlon
Orol Dengizi *see* Aral Sea
201 *S15* **Oroluk Atoll** *atoll* Caroline Islands, C Micronesia
11 *O15* **Oromocto** New Brunswick, SE Canada
203 *S4* **Orona** *prev.* Hull Island. *atoll* Phoenix Islands, C Kiribati
203 *V17* **Orongo** *ancient monument* Easter Island, Chile, E Pacific Ocean
144 *I3* **Orontes** *var.* Ononte, *Ar.* Nahr el Aassi, Nahr al 'Āṣī. ≈ SW Asia
106 *L9* **Oropesa** Castilla-La Mancha, C Spain
107 *T8* **Oropesa** País Valenciano, E Spain
Oropeza *see* Cochabamba
169 *U5* **Oroqen Zizhiqi** Nei Mongol Zizhiqu, N China
179 *Qq15* **Oroquieta** *var.* Oroquieta City. Mindanao, S Philippines
42 *J8* **Oro, Río del** ≈ C Mexico
61 *O14* **Orós, Açude** ▣ E Brazil
109 *D18* **Orosei, Golfo di** *gulf* Tyrrhenian Sea, C Mediterranean Sea
113 *M24* **Orosháza** Békés, SE Hungary
Orosirá Rodhópis *see* Rhodope Mountains
113 *I22* **Oroszlány** Komárom-Esztergom, W Hungary
196 *B16* **Orote Peninsula** *peninsula* W Guam
127 *O9* **Orotukan** Magadanskaya Oblast', E Russian Federation
37 *O5* **Oroville** California, W USA
34 *K6* **Oroville** Washington, NW USA
37 *O5* **Oroville, Lake** ▣ California, W USA
0 *G15* **Orozco Fracture Zone** *tectonic feature* E Pacific Ocean
66 *I7* **Orphan Knoll** *undersea feature* NW Atlantic Ocean
31 *V3* **Orr** Minnesota, N USA
97 *M21* **Orrefors** Kalmar, S Sweden
190 *I7* **Orroroo** South Australia
33 *T12* **Orrville** Ohio, N USA
96 *L12* **Orsa** Kopparberg, C Sweden
Orschowa *see* Orşova
Orschütz *see* Orzyc
121 *O14* **Orsha** *Rus.* Orsha. Vitsyebskaya Voblasts', NE Belarus
131 *Q2* **Orshanka** Respublika Mariy El, W Russian Federation
110 *C11* **Orsières** Valais, SW Switzerland
125 *Dd13* **Orsk** Orenburgskaya Oblast', W Russian Federation
118 *F13* **Orşova** *Ger.* Orschowa, *Hung.* Orsova. Mehedinţi, SW Romania
96 *D10* **Ørsta** Møre og Romsdal, S Norway
97 *O15* **Örsundsbro** Uppsala, C Sweden
142 *D16* **Ortaca** Muğla, SW Turkey
109 *M16* **Orta Nova** Puglia, SE Italy
142 *I17* **Orta Toroslar** ▲ S Turkey
56 *E11* **Ortega** Tolima, W Colombia
106 *H1* **Ortegal, Cabo** *headland* NW Spain
Ortelsburg *see* Szczytno
104 *J15* **Orthez** Pyrénées-Atlantiques, SW France
59 *K14* **Orthon, Río** ≈ N Bolivia
62 *J10* **Ortigueira** Paraná, S Brazil
106 *H1* **Ortigueira** Galicia, NW Spain
108 *H5* **Ortisei** *Ger.* Sankt-Ulrich. Trentino-Alto Adige, N Italy
42 *F6* **Ortiz** Sonora, NW Mexico
56 *L5* **Ortiz** Guárico, N Venezuela
Ortler *see* Ortles
108 *F5* **Ortles** *Ger.* Ortler. ▲ N Italy
109 *K14* **Ortona** Abruzzi, C Italy
31 *R8* **Ortonville** Minnesota, N USA
153 *W8* **Orto-Tokoy** Issyk-Kul'skaya Oblast', NE Kyrgyzstan
95 *I15* **Örträsk** Västerbotten, N Sweden
102 *J12* **Örtze** ≈ NW Germany
Oruba *see* Aruba
148 *I3* **Orūmīyeh** *var.* Rizaiyeh, Urmia, Urmiyeh; *prev.* Reẓā'īyeh. Āẕarbāyjān-e Bākhtarī, NW Iran
148 *J3* **Orūmīyeh, Daryācheh-ye** *var.* Matianus, Sha Hi, Urumi Yeh, *Eng.* Lake Urmia; *prev.* Daryācheh-ye Reẓā'īyeh. ◎ NW Iran
59 *K19* **Oruro** Oruro, W Bolivia
59 *J19* **Oruro** ◈ *department* W Bolivia
97 *I18* **Orust** *island* S Sweden
Oruzgān/Orūzgān *see* Urūzgān
108 *H13* **Orvieto** *anc.* Velsuna. Umbria, C Italy
204 *K7* **Orville Coast** *physical region* Antarctica
116 *H7* **Oryakhovo** Oblast Montana, NW Bulgaria
Oryokko *see* Yalu
119 *R5* **Orzhytsya** Poltavs'ka Oblast', C Ukraine
112 *M9* **Orzyc** *Ger.* Orschütz. ≈ NE Poland
112 *N8* **Orzysz** *Ger.* Arys. Suwałki, NE Poland
96 *I10* **Os** Hedmark, S Norway
97 *C14* **Os** Hordaland, S Norway
129 *U15* **Osa** Permskaya Oblast', NW Russian Federation
31 *W11* **Osage** Iowa, C USA
29 *U5* **Osage Beach** Missouri, C USA
29 *P5* **Osage City** Kansas, C USA
29 *U7* **Osage Fork River** ≈ Missouri, C USA
29 *U5* **Osage River** ≈ Missouri, C USA
171 *Gg15* **Ōsaka** *hist.* Naniwa. Ōsaka, Honshū, SW Japan
171 *Gg15* **Ōsaka** *off.* Ōsaka-fu, *var.* Ōsaka Hu. ◈ *urban prefecture* Honshū, SW Japan
Ōsaka-fu/Ōsaka Hu *see* Ōsaka
151 *R10* **Osakarovka** Karaganda, C Kazakhstan
170 *G15* **Ōsaka-wan** *bay* SW Japan
31 *T7* **Osakis** Minnesota, N USA
45 *N16* **Osa, Península de** *peninsula* S Costa Rica
62 *M10* **Osasco** São Paulo, S Brazil
29 *R5* **Osawatomie** Kansas, C USA
28 *L3* **Osborne** Kansas, C USA
181 *S8* **Osborn Plateau** *undersea feature* E Indian Ocean
97 *L21* **Osby** Kristianstad, S Sweden
Osca *see* Huesca
94 *N2* **Oscar II Land** *physical region* W Svalbard
29 *Y10* **Osceola** Arkansas, C USA
31 *V15* **Osceola** Iowa, C USA
29 *S6* **Osceola** Missouri, C USA
31 *Q15* **Osceola** Nebraska, C USA
103 *N15* **Oschatz** Sachsen, E Germany
102 *K13* **Oschersleben** Sachsen-Anhalt, C Germany
33 *R7* **Oscoda** Michigan, N USA
Ösel *see* Saaremaa
96 *H6* **Osen** Sør-Trøndelag, S Norway
170 *Aa12* **Ōse-zaki** *headland* Fukue-jima, SW Japan
153 *T10* **Osh** Oshskaya Oblast', SW Kyrgyzstan
85 *C16* **Oshakati** Oshana, N Namibia
172 *Nn6* **Oshamanbe** Hokkaidō, NE Japan
85 *C16* **Oshana** ◈ *district* N Namibia
126 *Ii12* **Osharovo** Evenkiyskiy Avtonomnyy Okrug, N Russian Federation
12 *H15* **Oshawa** Ontario, SE Canada
171 *Mm13* **Oshika-hantō** *peninsula* Honshū, C Japan
85 *C16* **Oshikango** Ohangwena, N Namibia
Oshikoto *see* Otjikoto
170 *C12* **Ō-shima** *island* SW Japan
171 *M7* **Ō-shima** *island* NE Japan
171 *Jj17* **Ō-shima** *island* S Japan
170 *G17* **Ō-shima** *island* SW Japan
172 *N6* **Oshima-hantō** ▲ Hokkaidō, NE Japan
85 *D17* **Oshivelo** Otjikoto, N Namibia
30 *K14* **Oshkosh** Nebraska, C USA
32 *M7* **Oshkosh** Wisconsin, N USA
Oshmyany *see* Ashmyany
Osh Oblasty *see* Oshskaya Oblast'
79 *T16* **Oshogbo** Osun, W Nigeria
153 *S11* **Oshskaya Oblast'** *Kir.* Osh Oblasty. ◈ *province* SW Kyrgyzstan
81 *J20* **Oshwe** Bandundu, C Zaire
Osiek *see* Osijek
114 *I9* **Osijek** *prev.* Osiek, Osjek, *Ger.* Esseg, *Hung.* Eszék. Osijek-Baranja, E Croatia
114 *I9* **Osijek-Baranja** *off.* Osječko-Baranjska Županija. ◈ *province* E Croatia
108 *J12* **Osimo** Marche, C Italy
126 *H15* **Osinniki** Kemerovskaya Oblast', S Russian Federation
126 *J14* **Osinovka** Irkutskaya Oblast', C Russian Federation
Osintorf *see* Asintorf
114 *N11* **Osipaonica** Serbia, NE Yugoslavia
Osipenko *see* Berdyans'k
Osipovichi *see* Asipovichy
Osječko-Baranjska Županija *see* Osijek-Baranja
Osjek *see* Osijek
31 *W15* **Oskaloosa** Iowa, C USA
29 *Q4* **Oskaloosa** Kansas, C USA
97 *N20* **Oskarshamn** Kalmar, S Sweden
97 *J20* **Oskarström** Halland, S Sweden
12 *M8* **Oskélanéo** Québec, SE Canada
Öskemen *see* Ust'-Kamenogorsk
Oskil *see* Oskol
119 *W5* **Oskol** *Ukr.* Oskil. ≈ Russian Federation/Ukraine
95 *D20* **Oslo** *prev.* Christiania, Kristiania. ● (Norway) Oslo, S Norway
95 *D20* **Oslo** ◈ *county* S Norway
95 *D21* **Oslofjorden** *fjord* S Norway
161 *G15* **Osmānābād** Mahārāshtra, C India
142 *J11* **Osmancık** Çorum, N Turkey
142 *L16* **Osmaniye** Adana, S Turkey
97 *O16* **Ösmo** Stockholm, C Sweden
120 *E3* **Osmussaar** *island* W Estonia
102 *G13* **Osnabrück** Niedersachsen, NW Germany
112 *D11* **Ośno Lubuskie** *Ger.* Drossen. Gorzów, W Poland
Osogovske Planine *see* Osogovski Planina
115 *P18* **Osogovski Planina** *var.* Osogovske Planine, *Mac.* Osogovski Planini. ▲ Bulgaria/FYR Macedonia
Osogovski Planini *see* Osogovski Planina
172 *N8* **Osore-yama** ▲ Honshū, C Japan
Oşorhei *see* Târgu Mureş
63 *J16* **Osório** Rio Grande do Sul, S Brazil
65 *G16* **Osorno** Los Lagos, C Chile
106 *M4* **Osorno** Castilla-León, N Spain
9 *N17* **Osoyoos** British Columbia, SW Canada
56 *J6* **Ospino** Portuguesa, N Venezuela
100 *K13* **Oss** Noord-Brabant, S Netherlands
106 *H11* **Ossa** ▲ S Portugal
117 *F15* **Óssa** ▲ C Greece
25 *X6* **Ossabaw Island** *island* Georgia, SE USA
25 *X6* **Ossabaw Sound** *sound* Georgia, SE USA
191 *O16* **Ossa, Mount** ▲ Tasmania, SE Australia
106 *H11* **Ossa, Serra d'** ▲ SE Portugal
79 *U16* **Osse** ≈ S Nigeria
32 *J6* **Osseo** Wisconsin, N USA
111 *S9* **Ossiacher See** ◎ S Austria
20 *K13* **Ossining** New York, NE USA
96 *I12* **Ossjøen** ◎ S Norway
127 *P9* **Ossora** Koryakskiy Avtonomnyy Okrug, E Russian Federation
128 *I15* **Ostashkov** Tverskaya Oblast', W Russian Federation
102 *H9* **Oste** ≈ NW Germany
Ostee *see* Baltic Sea
Ostend/Ostende *see* Oostende
119 *P3* **Oster** Chernihivs'ka Oblast', N Ukraine
97 *O14* **Österbybruk** Uppsala, C Sweden
97 *M19* **Österbymo** Östergotland, S Sweden
96 *K12* **Österdalälven** ≈ C Sweden
96 *I12* **Østerdalen** *valley* S Norway
97 *L18* **Östergötland** ◈ *county* S Sweden
102 *H10* **Osterholz-Scharmbeck** Niedersachsen, NW Germany
Östermark *see* Teuva
Östermyra *see* Seinäjoki
Osterode/Osterode in Ostpreussen *see* Ostróda
103 *J14* **Osterode am Harz** Niedersachsen, C Germany
96 *C13* **Osterøy** *island* S Norway
Österreich *see* Austria
95 *G16* **Östersund** Jämtland, C Sweden
97 *N14* **Östervåla** Västmanland, C Sweden
103 *H22* **Ostfildern** Baden-Württemberg, SW Germany
97 *H16* **Østfold** ◈ *county* S Norway
102 *E9* **Ostfriesische Inseln** *Eng.* East Frisian Islands. *island group* NW Germany
102 *F10* **Ostfriesland** *historical region* NW Germany
97 *P14* **Östhammar** Uppsala, C Sweden
Ostia Aterni *see* Pescara
108 *G8* **Ostiglia** Lombardia, N Italy
97 *J14* **Östmark** Värmland, C Sweden
97 *K22* **Östra Ringsjön** ◎ S Sweden
113 *I17* **Ostrava** Severní Morava, E Czech Republic
112 *K8* **Ostróda** *Ger.* Osterode, Osterode in Ostpreussen. Olsztyn, N Poland
Ostrog/Ostróg *see* Ostroh
130 *L8* **Ostrogozhsk** Voronezhskaya Oblast', W Russian Federation
118 *L4* **Ostroh** *Pol.* Ostróg, *Rus.* Ostrog. Rivnens'ka Oblast', NW Ukraine
Ostrołęckie, Województwo *see* Ostrołęka
112 *N9* **Ostrołęka** *Ger.* Wiesenhof, *Rus.* Ostrolenka. Ostrołęka, NE Poland
112 *M10* **Ostrołęka** *off.* Województwo Ostrołęckie, *Rus.* Ostrolenka. ◈ *province* NE Poland
Ostrolenka *see* Ostrołęka
113 *A16* **Ostrov** *Ger.* Schlackenwerth. Západní Čechy, NW Czech Republic
128 *F15* **Ostrov** *Latv.* Austrava. Pskovskaya Oblast', W Russian Federation
Ostrovets *see* Ostrowiec Świętokrzyski
115 *M21* **Ostrovicës, Mali i** ▲ SE Albania
172 *T6* **Ostrov Iturup** *island* NE Russian Federation
116 *L7* **Ostrovo** *prev.* Golema Ada. Razgradska Oblast, NE Bulgaria
129 *N15* **Ostrovskoye** Kostromskaya Oblast', NW Russian Federation
Ostrów *see* Ostrów Wielkopolski
Ostrowiec *see* Ostrowiec Świętokrzyski
113 *M14* **Ostrowiec Świętokrzyski** *var.* Ostrowiec, *Rus.* Ostrovets. Kielce, SE Poland
112 *P13* **Ostrów Lubelski** Lublin, E Poland
112 *N10* **Ostrów Mazowiecka** *var.* Ostrów Mazowiecki. Ostrołęka, NE Poland
Ostrów Mazowiecki *see* Ostrów Mazowiecka
Ostrowo *see* Ostrów Wielkopolski
112 *H13* **Ostrów Wielkopolski** *var.* Ostrów, *Ger.* Ostrowo. Kalisz, C Poland
Ostryna *see* Astryna
112 *I13* **Ostrzeszów** Kalisz, C Poland
109 *P18* **Ostuni** Puglia, SE Italy
Ostyako-Voguls'k *see* Khanty-Mansiysk
Osum *see* Osumit, Lumi i
116 *I9* **Osŭm** ≈ N Bulgaria
170 *Bb17* **Ōsumi-hantō** ▲ Kyūshū, SW Japan
170 *Bb17* **Ōsumi-kaikyō** *strait* SW Japan
115 *L22* **Osumit, Lumi i** *var.* Osum. ≈ SE Albania
79 *T16* **Osun** ◈ *state* SW Nigeria
106 *L14* **Osuna** Andalucía, S Spain
62 *J8* **Osvaldo Cruz** São Paulo, S Brazil
Osveya *see* Asvyeya
20 *J7* **Oswegatchie River** ≈ New York, NE USA
29 *Q7* **Oswego** Kansas, C USA
20 *H9* **Oswego** New York, NE USA
99 *K19* **Oswestry** W England, UK
113 *J16* **Oświęcim** *Ger.* Auschwitz. Bielsko-Biała, S Poland
171 *K15* **Ōta** Gunma, Honshū, S Japan
193 *E22* **Otago** *off.* Otago Region. ◈ *region* South Island, NZ
193 *F23* **Otago Peninsula** *peninsula* South Island, NZ
170 *E13* **Ōtake** Hiroshima, Honshū, SW Japan
192 *L13* **Otaki** Wellington, North Island, NZ
171 *L14* **Ōtakine-yama** ▲ Honshū, C Japan
95 *M15* **Otanmäki** Oulu, C Finland
151 *T15* **Otar** Zhambyl, SE Kazakhstan
172 *O5* **Otaru** Hokkaidō, NE Japan
193 *C24* **Otatara** Southland, South Island, NZ
193 *C24* **Otautau** Southland, South Island, NZ
95 *M18* **Otava** Mikkeli, SE Finland
113 *B18* **Otava** *Ger.* Wottawa. ≈ SW Czech Republic
58 *C6* **Otavalo** Imbabura, N Ecuador
85 *D17* **Otavi** Otjozondjupa, N Namibia
171 *Kk15* **Ōtawara** Tochigi, Honshū, S Japan
85 *B16* **Otchinjau** Cunene, SW Angola
118 *F12* **Oţelu Roşu** *Ger.* Ferdinandsberg, *Hung.* Nándorhgy. Caras-Severin, SW Romania
193 *E21* **Otematata** Canterbury, South Island, NZ
120 *I6* **Otepää** *Ger.* Odenpäh. Valgamaa, SE Estonia
34 *K9* **Othello** Washington, NW USA
117 *A15* **Othonoí** *island* Iónioi Nísoi, Greece, C Mediterranean Sea
Othris *see* Óthrys
117 *F17* **Óthrys** *var.* Othris. ▲ C Greece
79 *Q14* **Oti** ≈ N Togo
42 *K10* **Otinapa** Durango, C Mexico
193 *G17* **Otira** West Coast, South Island, NZ
39 *V3* **Otis** Colorado, C USA
10 *L10* **Otish, Monts** ▲ Québec, E Canada
85 *C17* **Otjikondo** Kunene, N Namibia
85 *C17* **Otjikoto** *var.* Oshikoto. ◈ *district* N Namibia
85 *E18* **Otjinene** Omaheke, NE Namibia
85 *D18* **Otjiwarongo** Otjozondjupa, N Namibia
85 *D18* **Otjosondu** *var.* Otjosundu. Otjozondjupa, C Namibia
Otjosundu *see* Otjosondu
85 *D18* **Otjozondjupa** ◈ *district* C Namibia
114 *C11* **Otočac** Lika-Senj, W Croatia
172 *Pp6* **Otofuke-gawa** ≈ Hokkaidō, NE Japan
168 *M14* **Otog Qi** Nei Mongol Zizhiqu, N China
172 *Pp3* **Otoineppu** Hokkaidō, NE Japan
114 *J10* **Otok** Vukovar-Srijem, E Croatia
118 *K14* **Otopeni** ✕ (Bucureşti) Bucureşti, S Romania
192 *L8* **Otorohanga** Waikato, North Island, NZ
10 *D9* **Otoskwin** ≈ Ontario, C Canada
170 *F15* **Ōtoyo** Kōchi, Shikoku, SW Japan
97 *E16* **Otra** ≈ S Norway
109 *R19* **Otranto** Puglia, SE Italy
Otranto, Canale d' *see* Otranto, Strait of
109 *Q18* **Otranto, Strait of** *It.* Canale d'Otranto. *strait* Albania/Italy
113 *H18* **Otrokovice** *Ger.* Otrokowitz. Jižní Morava, SE Czech Republic
Otrokowitz *see* Otrokovice
33 *P10* **Otsego** Michigan, N USA
33 *Q6* **Otsego Lake** ◎ Michigan, N USA
20 *I11* **Otselic River** ≈ New York, NE USA
171 *H15* **Ōtsu** *var.* Ōtu. Shiga, Honshū, SW Japan
171 *Jj16* **Ōtsuki** *var.* Otuki. Yamanashi, Honshū, S Japan
96 *G11* **Otta** Oppland, S Norway
201 *U13* **Otta** *island* Chuuk, C Micronesia
96 *F11* **Otta** ≈ S Norway
201 *U13* **Otta Pass** *passage* Chuuk Islands, C Micronesia
97 *J22* **Ottarp** Malmöhus, S Sweden
12 *L12* **Ottawa** ● (Canada) Ontario, SE Canada
32 *L11* **Ottawa** Illinois, N USA
29 *Q5* **Ottawa** Kansas, C USA
33 *R12* **Ottawa** Ohio, N USA
12 *L12* **Ottawa** *var.* Uplands. ✕ Ontario, SE Canada
12 *M12* **Ottawa** *Fr.* Outaouais. ≈ Ontario/Québec, SE Canada
10 *I4* **Ottawa Islands** *island group* Northwest Territories, C Canada
20 *L8* **Otter Creek** ≈ Vermont, NE USA
38 *L6* **Otter Creek Reservoir** ▣ Utah, W USA
100 *L11* **Otterlo** Gelderland, E Netherlands
96 *D9* **Otterøya** *island* S Norway
31 *S6* **Otter Tail Lake** ◎ Minnesota, N USA
31 *R7* **Otter Tail River** ≈ Minnesota, C USA
97 *H23* **Otterup** Fyn, C Denmark
101 *H19* **Ottignies** Walloon Brabant, C Belgium
103 *L23* **Ottobrunn** Bayern, SE Germany
194 *I12* **Otto, Mount** ▲ C PNG
31 *X15* **Ottumwa** Iowa, C USA
Ōtu *see* Ōtsu
85 *B16* **Otuazuma** Kunene, NW Namibia
Otuki *see* Ōtsuki
79 *V16* **Oturkpo** Benue, S Nigeria
200 *Ss14* **Otu Tolu Group** *island group* SE Tonga
190 *M13* **Otway, Cape** *headland* Victoria, SE Australia
65 *H24* **Otway, Seno** *inlet* S Chile
110 *L8* **Ötztaler Ache** ≈ W Austria
110 *L9* **Ötztaler Alpen** *It.* Alpi Venoste. ▲ SW Austria
29 *T12* **Ouachita, Lake** ▣ Arkansas, C USA
29 *R11* **Ouachita Mountains** ▲ Arkansas/Oklahoma, C USA
29 *U13* **Ouachita River** ≈ Arkansas/Louisiana, C USA
Ouadaï *see* Ouaddaï
78 *J7* **Ouadâne** *var.* Ouadane. Adrar, C Mauritania
80 *K13* **Ouadda** Haute-Kotto, N Central African Republic
80 *J10* **Ouaddaï** *off.* Préfecture du Ouaddaï, *var.* Ouadaï, Wadai. ◈ *prefecture* SE Chad
79 *P13* **Ouagadougou** *var.* Wagadugu. ● (Burkina) C Burkina
79 *P13* **Ouagadougou** ✕ C Burkina
79 *O12* **Ouahigouya** NW Burkina
Ouahran *see* Oran
81 *J14* **Ouaka** ◈ *prefecture* C Central African Republic
81 *J15* **Ouaka** ≈ S Central African Republic
Oualam *see* Ouallam
78 *M9* **Oualâta** *var.* Oualata. Hodh ech Chargui, SE Mauritania
79 *R11* **Ouallam** *var.* Oualam. Tillabéri, W Niger
180 *H14* **Ouanani** Mohéli, S Comoros
57 *Z10* **Ouanary** E French Guiana
80 *L13* **Ouanda Djallé** Vakaga, NE Central African Republic
81 *N14* **Ouando** Haut-Mbomou, SE Central African Republic
81 *L15* **Ouango** Mbomou, S Central African Republic
79 *N14* **Ouangolodougou** *var.* Wangolodougou. N Ivory Coast
180 *I13* **Ouani** Anjouan, SE Comoros
81 *M15* **Ouara** ≈ E Central African Republic
78 *K7* **Ouarâne** *desert* C Mauritania
13 *O11* **Ouareau** ≈ Québec, SE Canada
76 *K7* **Ouargla** *var.* Wargla. NE Algeria
76 *F8* **Ouarzazate** S Morocco
79 *Q11* **Ouatagouna** Gao, E Mali
76 *G6* **Ouazzane** *var.* Ouezzane, *Ar.* Wazan, Wazzan. N Morocco
Oubangui *see* Ubangi
Oubangui-Chari *see* Central African Republic
Oubari, Edeyen d' *see* Awbārī, Idhān
100 *G13* **Oud-Beijerland** Zuid-Holland, SW Netherlands
100 *F13* **Ouddorp** Zuid-Holland, SW Netherlands
79 *P9* **Oudeïka** *oasis* C Mali
100 *G13* **Oude Maas** ≈ SW Netherlands
101 *E18* **Oudenaarde** *Fr.* Audenarde. Oost-Vlaanderen, SW Belgium
101 *H14* **Oudenbosch** Noord-Brabant, S Netherlands
100 *P6* **Oude Pekela** Groningen, NE Netherlands
Ouderkerk *see* Ouderkerk aan den Amstel
100 *I10* **Ouderkerk aan den Amstel** *var.* Ouderkerk. Noord-Holland, C Netherlands
100 *I6* **Oudeschild** Noord-Holland, NW Netherlands
101 *G14* **Oude-Tonge** Zuid-Holland, SW Netherlands
100 *I12* **Oudewater** Utrecht, C Netherlands
Oudjda *see* Oujda
100 *L5* **Oudkerk** Friesland, N Netherlands
104 *J7* **Oudon** ≈ NW France
100 *I9* **Oudorp** Noord-Holland, NW Netherlands
85 *G25* **Oudtshoorn** Western Cape, SW South Africa
101 *I16* **Oud-Turnhout** Antwerpen, N Belgium
76 *F7* **Oued-Zem** C Morocco
197 *H5* **Ouégoa** Province Nord, C New Caledonia
78 *L13* **Ouéléssébougou** *var.* Ouolosséboougou. Koulikoro, SW Mali
79 *N16* **Ouellé** E Ivory Coast
79 *R16* **Ouémé** ≈ C Benin
197 *J7* **Ouen, Île** *island* S New Caledonia
79 *O13* **Ouessa** S Burkina
104 *D5* **Ouessant, Île d'** *Eng.* Ushant. *island* NW France
81 *H17* **Ouésso** La Sangha, NW Congo
81 *D15* **Ouest** *Eng.* West. ◈ *province* W Cameroon
202 *G11* **Ouest, Baie del'** *bay* Wallis, Wallis and Futuna
13 *Y7* **Ouest, Pointe de l'** *headland* Québec, SE Canada
Ouezzane *see* Ouazzane
101 *K20* **Ouffet** Liège, E Belgium
81 *H14* **Ouham** ◈ *prefecture* NW Central African Republic
80 *I13* **Ouham** ≈ Central African Republic/Chad
81 *G14* **Ouham-Pendé** ◈ *prefecture* W Central African Republic
79 *R16* **Ouidah** *Eng.* Whydah, Wida. S Benin
76 *H6* **Oujda** *Ar.* Oudjda, Ujda. NE Morocco
78 *I7* **Oujeft** Adrar, C Mauritania
95 *L15* **Oulainen** Oulu, C Finland
Ould Yanja *see* Ould Yenjé
78 *J10* **Ould Yenjé** *var.* Ould Yanja. Guidimaka, S Mauritania
95 *L14* **Oulu** *Swe.* Uleåborg. Oulu, C Finland
95 *M14* **Oulu** *Swe.* Uleåborg. ◈ *province* N Finland
95 *L15* **Oulujärvi** *Swe.* Uleträsk. ◎ C Finland
95 *M14* **Oulujoki** *Swe.* Uleälv. ≈ C Finland
95 *L14* **Oulunsalo** Oulu, C Finland
108 *A8* **Oulx** Piemonte, NE Italy
80 *J9* **Oum-Chalouba** Borkou-Ennedi-Tibesti, NE Chad
78 *M16* **Oumé** C Ivory Coast
76 *F7* **Oum er Rbia** ≈ C Morocco
80 *J10* **Oum-Hadjer** Batha, E Chad
94 *K10* **Ounasjoki** ≈ N Finland
80 *J7* **Ounianga Kébir** Borkou-Ennedi-Tibesti, N Chad
Ouolossébougou *see* Ouéléssébougou
Oup *see* Auob
101 *K19* **Oupeye** Liège, E Belgium
101 *N21* **Our** ≈ NW Europe
39 *Q7* **Ouray** Colorado, C USA
105 *R7* **Ource** ≈ C France
106 *G9* **Ourém** Santarém, C Portugal
106 *H4* **Ourense** *Cast.* Orense; *Lat.* Aurium. Galicia, NW Spain
106 *I4* **Ourense** ◈ *province* Galicia, NW Spain
61 *O15* **Ouricuri** Pernambuco, E Brazil
62 *J9* **Ourinhos** São Paulo, S Brazil
106 *G13* **Ourique** Beja, S Portugal
61 *M20* **Ouro Preto** Minas Gerais, NE Brazil
Ours, Grand Lac de l' *see* Great Bear Lake
101 *K20* **Ourthe** ≈ E Belgium
171 *Mm11* **Ōu-sanmyaku** ▲ Honshū, C Japan
99 *M17* **Ouse** ≈ N England, UK
Ouse *see* Great Ouse
104 *H7* **Oust** ≈ NW France
Outaouais *see* Ottawa
13 *T4* **Outardes Quatre, Réservoir** ▣ Québec, SE Canada
13 *T5* **Outardes, Rivière aux** ≈ Québec, SE Canada
98 *E8* **Outer Hebrides** *var.* Western Isles. *island group* NW Scotland, UK
32 *K3* **Outer Island** *island* Apostle Islands, Wisconsin, N USA
37 *S16* **Outer Santa Barbara Passage** *passage* California, SW USA
106 *G3* **Outes** Galicia, NW Spain
85 *C18* **Outjo** Kunene, N Namibia
9 *T16* **Outlook** Saskatchewan, S Canada
95 *N16* **Outokumpu** Pohjois-Karjala, SE Finland
98 *M2* **Out Skerries** *island group* NE Scotland, UK
197 *J5* **Ouvéa** *island* Îles Loyauté, NE New Caledonia
105 *S14* **Ouvèze** ≈ SE France
190 *L9* **Ouyen** Victoria, SE Australia
41 *Q14* **Ouzinkie** Kodiak Island, Alaska, USA
143 *O13* **Ovacık** Tunceli, E Turkey
108 *C9* **Ovada** Piemonte, NE Italy
197 *I14* **Ovalau** *island* C Fiji
64 *G9* **Ovalle** Coquimbo, N Chile
85 *C17* **Ovamboland** *physical region* N Namibia
56 *L10* **Ovana, Cerro** ▲ S Venezuela
106 *G7* **Ovar** Aveiro, N Portugal
116 *L10* **Ovcharitsa, Yazovir** ▣ SE Bulgaria
56 *E6* **Ovejas** Sucre, NW Colombia
103 *E16* **Overath** Nordrhein-Westfalen, W Germany
100 *F13* **Overflakkee** *island* SW Netherlands
95 *F15* **Overhalla** Nord-Trøndelag, C Norway
101 *H19* **Overijse** Vlaams Brabant, C Belgium
100 *N10* **Overijssel** ◈ *province* E Netherlands
100 *M9* **Overijssels Kanaal** *canal* E Netherlands
94 *K13* **Överkalix** Norrbotten, N Sweden
29 *R4* **Overland Park** Kansas, C USA
101 *L14* **Overloon** Noord-Brabant, SE Netherlands
101 *K16* **Overpelt** Limburg, NE Belgium
37 *Y10* **Overton** Nevada, W USA
27 *W7* **Overton** Texas, SW USA
94 *K13* **Övertorneå** Norrbotten, N Sweden
97 *N18* **Överum** Kalmar, S Sweden
94 *G13* **Överuman** ◎ N Sweden
168 *H6* **Övgödiy** Dzavhan, C Mongolia
119 *P11* **Ovidiopol'** Odes'ka Oblast', SW Ukraine
118 *M14* **Ovidiu** Constanța, SE Romania
47 *N10* **Oviedo** SW Dominican Republic
106 *K2* **Oviedo** *anc.* Asturias. Asturias, NW Spain
106 *K2* **Oviedo** ✕ Asturias, N Spain
Ovilava *see* Wels
120 *D7* **Oviši** Ventspils, W Latvia
169 *P10* **Ovoot** Sühbaatar, SE Mongolia
163 *O4* **Övörhangay** ◈ *province* C Mongolia
96 *E12* **Øvre Årdal** Sogn og Fjordane, S Norway
97 *J14* **Övre Fryken** ◎ C Sweden
94 *J11* **Övre Soppero** Norrbotten, N Sweden
119 *N3* **Ovruch** Zhytomyrs'ka Oblast', N Ukraine
168 *J8* **Övt** Övörhangay, C Mongolia
193 *E24* **Owaka** Otago, South Island, NZ
81 *H18* **Owando** *prev.* Fort-Rousset. Cuvette, C Congo
171 *Gg17* **Owase** Mie, Honshū, SW Japan
29 *P9* **Owasso** Oklahoma, C USA
31 *V10* **Owatonna** Minnesota, N USA
181 *O4* **Owen Fracture Zone** *tectonic feature* W Arabian Sea
193 *H15* **Owen, Mount** ▲ South Island, NZ
193 *H15* **Owen River** Tasman, South Island, NZ
22 *I6* **Owensboro** Kentucky, S USA
37 *T11* **Owens Lake** *salt flat* California, W USA
12 *F14* **Owen Sound** Ontario, S Canada
12 *F13* **Owen Sound** ◎ Ontario, S Canada
37 *T10* **Owens River** ≈ California, W USA
194 *K15* **Owen Stanley Range** ▲ S PNG
29 *V5* **Owensville** Missouri, C USA
22 *M4* **Owenton** Kentucky, S USA
79 *U17* **Owerri** Imo, S Nigeria
192 *M10* **Owhango** Manawatu-Wanganui, North Island, NZ
23 *N5* **Owingsville** Kentucky, S USA
152 *K10* **Owminzatovo-Toshi** *Rus.* Gory Auminzatau. ▲ N Uzbekistan
79 *T16* **Owo** Ondo, SW Nigeria
33 *R9* **Owosso** Michigan, N USA
37 *V1* **Owyhee** Nevada, W USA
34 *L14* **Owyhee, Lake** ◎ Oregon, NW USA
34 *L15* **Owyhee River** ≈ Idaho/Oregon, NW USA
94 *K1* **Öxarfjördhur** *var.* Axarfjördhur. *fjord* N Iceland
96 *K12* **Oxberg** Kopparberg, C Sweden
9 *V17* **Oxbow** Saskatchewan, S Canada
97 *O17* **Oxelösund** Södermanland, S Sweden
193 *H18* **Oxford** Canterbury, South Island, NZ
99 *M21* **Oxford** *Lat.* Oxonia. S England, UK
25 *Q3* **Oxford** Alabama, S USA
24 *L2* **Oxford** Mississippi, S USA
31 *N16* **Oxford** Nebraska, C USA
20 *H16* **Oxford** New York, NE USA
23 *U8* **Oxford** North Carolina, SE USA
33 *Q14* **Oxford** Ohio, N USA
20 *I11* **Oxford** Pennsylvania, NE USA
9 *X12* **Oxford House** Manitoba, C Canada
31 *Y13* **Oxford Junction** Iowa, C USA
9 *X12* **Oxford Lake** ◎ Manitoba, C Canada
99 *M21* **Oxfordshire** *cultural region* S England, UK
Oxia *see* Oxyá
43 *X12* **Oxkutzcab** Yucatán, SE Mexico
37 *R15* **Oxnard** California, W USA
Oxonia *see* Oxford
12 *I12* **Oxtongue** ≈ Ontario, SE Canada
Oxus *see* Amu Darya
117 *E15* **Oxyá** *var.* Oxia. ▲ C Greece
171 *Ii13* **Oyabe** Toyama, Honshū, SW Japan
Oyahue/Oyahue, Volcán *see* Ollagüe, Volcán
171 *K16* **Oyama** Tochigi, Honshū, S Japan
49 *U5* **Oyapock** ≈ E French Guiana
Oyapock *see* Oiapoque, Rio
57 *Z10* **Oyapok, Baie de L'** *bay* Brazil/French Guiana
57 *Z11* **Oyapok, Fleuve l'** *var.* Oyapock, Rio Oiapoque. ≈ Brazil/French Guiana *see also* Oiapoque, Rio
81 *E17* **Oyem** Woleu-Ntem, N Gabon
9 *R16* **Oyen** Alberta, SW Canada
97 *I15* **Øyeren** ◎ S Norway
168 *G6* **Oygon** Dzavhan, N Mongolia
98 *I7* **Oykel** ≈ N Scotland, UK
127 *N9* **Oymyakon** Respublika Sakha (Yakutiya), NE Russian Federation
81 *H19* **Oyo** Cuvette, C Congo
79 *S15* **Oyo** Oyo, W Nigeria
79 *S15* **Oyo** ◈ *state* SW Nigeria
58 *D13* **Oyón** Lima, C Peru
105 *S10* **Oyonnax** Ain, E France
152 *L10* **Oyoqighitma** *Rus.* Ayakagytma. Bukhoro Wiloyati, C Uzbekistan
152 *M9* **Oyoqquduq** *Rus.* Ayakkuduk. Nawoiy Wiloyati, N Uzbekistan
34 *F9* **Oysterville** Washington, NW USA
97 *D14* **Øystese** Hordaland, S Norway
153 *U10* **Oy-Tal** Oshskaya Oblast', SW Kyrgyzstan
153 *T10* **Oy-Tal** ≈ SW Kyrgyzstan
151 *S16* **Oytal** Zhambyl, S Kazakhstan
Oyyl *see* Uil
179 *Qq15* **Ozamiz** Mindanao, S Philippines
Ozarichi *see* Azarychy
25 *R7* **Ozark** Alabama, S USA
29 *S10* **Ozark** Arkansas, C USA
29 *T8* **Ozark** Missouri, C USA
29 *T8* **Ozark Plateau** *plain* Arkansas/Missouri, C USA
29 *T6* **Ozarks, Lake of the** ▣ Missouri, C USA
199 *Jj11* **Ozbourn Seamount** *undersea feature* W Pacific Ocean
113 *L20* **Ózd** Borsod-Abaúj-Zemplén, NE Hungary
114 *D11* **Ozeblin** ▲ C Croatia
127 *Pp12* **Ozernovskiy** Kamchatskaya Oblast', E Russian Federation

◆ Country
● Country Capital
◇ Dependent Territory
○ Dependent Territory Capital
◈ Administrative Region
✕ International Airport
▲ Mountain
▲ Mountain Range
⛰ Volcano
≈ River
◎ Lake
▣ Reservoir

150 M7 **Ozërnoye** *var.* Ozërnyy. Kustanay, N Kazakhstan
Ozërnyy *see* Ozërnoye
117 D18 **Ozerós, Límni** ◎ W Greece
121 D14 **Ozersk** *prev.* Darkehnen, *Ger.* Angerapp. Kaliningradskaya Oblast', W Russian Federation
130 L4 **Ozery** Moskovskaya Oblast', W Russian Federation
Özgön *see* Uzgen
109 C17 **Ozieri** Sardegna, Italy, C Mediterranean Sea
113 I15 **Ozimek** *Ger.* Malapane. Opole, SW Poland
131 R8 **Ozinki** Saratovskaya Oblast', W Russian Federation
Oziya *see* Ojiya
27 O10 **Ozona** Texas, SW USA
Ozorkov *see* Ozorków
112 J12 **Ozorków** *Rus.* Ozorkov. Łódź, C Poland
170 E14 **Ōzu** Ehime, Shikoku, SW Japan
143 R10 **Ozurget'i** *prev.* Makharadze. W Georgia

P

101 J17 **Paal** Limburg, NE Belgium
197 C13 **Paama** *island* C Vanuatu
206 M14 **Paamiut** *var.* Pâmiut, *Dan.* Frederikshåb. S Greenland
178 Gg9 **Pa-an** Karen State, S Myanmar
103 L22 **Paar** ≈ SE Germany
85 E26 **Paarl** Western Cape, SW South Africa
95 L15 **Paavola** Oulu, C Finland
98 E8 **Pabbay** *island* NW Scotland, UK
175 P12 **Pabbiring, Kepulauan** *island group* C Indonesia
159 T15 **Pabna** Rajshahi, W Bangladesh
111 U4 **Pabneukirchen** Oberösterreich, N Austria
120 H13 **Pabradė** *Pol.* Podbrodzie. Švenčionys, SE Lithuania
58 L13 **Pacahuaras, Río** ≈ N Bolivia
Pacaraima, Sierra/Pacaraim, Serra *see* Pakaraima Mountains
58 B11 **Pacasmayo** La Libertad, W Peru
44 D6 **Pacaya, Volcán de** ♜ S Guatemala
117 K23 **Pachía** *island* Kykládes, Greece, Aegean Sea
109 L26 **Pachino** Sicilia, Italy, C Mediterranean Sea
58 F12 **Pachitea, Río** ≈ C Peru
160 I11 **Pachmarhi** Madhya Pradesh, C India
124 N4 **Páchna** *var.* Pakhna. SW Cyprus
117 H25 **Páchnes** ▲ Kríti, Greece, E Mediterranean Sea
56 F9 **Pacho** Cundinamarca, C Colombia
160 F12 **Pāchora** Mahārāshtra, C India
43 P13 **Pachuca** *var.* Pachuca de Soto. Hidalgo, C Mexico
Pachuca de Soto *see* Pachuca
29 W5 **Pacific** Missouri, C USA
199 Jj15 **Pacific-Antarctic Ridge** *undersea feature* S Pacific Ocean
34 F8 **Pacific Beach** Washington, NW USA
37 N10 **Pacific Grove** California, W USA
31 S15 **Pacific Junction** Iowa, C USA
198–200 **Pacific Ocean** *ocean*
133 Z10 **Pacific Plate** *tectonic feature*
115 J15 **Pačir** ▲ SW Yugoslavia
190 L5 **Packsaddle** New South Wales, SE Australia
34 H9 **Packwood** Washington, NW USA
Padalung *see* Phatthalung
175 Q12 **Padamarang, Pulau** *island* C Indonesia
173 G9 **Padang** Sumatera, W Indonesia
174 Hh5 **Padang Endau** Pahang, Peninsular Malaysia
Padangpandjang *see* Padangpanjang
173 G8 **Padangpanjang** *prev.* Padangpandjang. Sumatera, W Indonesia
173 Ff7 **Padangsidempuan** *prev.* Padangsidimpoean. Sumatera, W Indonesia
Padangsidimpoean *see* Padangsidempuan
128 I9 **Padany** Respublika Kareliya, NW Russian Federation
95 M18 **Padasjoki** Häme, SW Finland
59 M22 **Padcaya** Tarija, S Bolivia
103 H14 **Paderborn** Nordrhein-Westfalen, NW Germany
Padeşul/Padeş, Vîrful *see* Padeş, Vârful
118 F12 **Padeş, Vârful** *var.* Padeşul; *prev.* Vîrful Padeş. ▲ W Romania
114 L10 **Padinska Skela** Serbia, N Yugoslavia
Padma *see* Brahmaputra
159 S14 **Padma** *var.* Ganges. ≈ Bangladesh/India *see also* Ganges
108 H8 **Padova** *Eng.* Padua; *anc.* Patavium. Veneto, NE Italy
84 A10 **Padrão, Ponta do** *headland* NW Angola
27 T16 **Padre Island** *island* Texas, SW USA
106 G3 **Padrón** Galicia, NW Spain
120 K13 **Padsvillye** *Rus.* Podsvil'ye. Vitsyebskaya Voblasts', N Belarus
190 K11 **Padthaway** South Australia
Padua *see* Padova
22 G7 **Paducah** Kentucky, S USA
27 P4 **Paducah** Texas, SW USA
107 N15 **Padul** Andalucía, S Spain
203 P8 **Paea** Tahiti, W French Polynesia
193 L14 **Paekakariki** Wellington, North Island, NZ
169 X11 **Paektu-san** *var.* Baitou Shan. ▲ China/North Korea
169 V15 **Paengnyŏng-do** *island* NW South Korea
192 M7 **Paeroa** Waikato, North Island, NZ
56 D12 **Páez** Cauca, SW Colombia
123 Mm4 **Páfos** *var.* Paphos. W Cyprus
123 Mm4 **Páfos** ✕ SW Cyprus
85 L19 **Pafúri** Gaza, SW Mozambique
114 C12 **Pag** *It.* Pago. Lika-Senj, W Croatia
114 B11 **Pag** *It.* Pago. *island* C Croatia
179 Qq16 **Pagadian** Mindanao, S Philippines
173 G11 **Pagai Selatan, Pulau** *island* Kepulauan Mentawai, W Indonesia
173 Ff10 **Pagai Utara, Pulau** *island* Kepulauan Mentawai, W Indonesia
196 K4 **Pagan** *island* C Northern Mariana Islands
117 G16 **Pagasitikós Kólpos** *gulf* E Greece
38 L8 **Page** Arizona, SW USA
31 Q5 **Page** North Dakota, N USA
120 D13 **Pagėgiai** *Ger.* Pogegen. Šilutė, SW Lithuania
23 S11 **Pageland** South Carolina, SE USA
83 G16 **Pager** ≈ NE Uganda
155 Q5 **Paghmān** Kābul, E Afghanistan
Pago *see* Pag
196 C16 **Pago Bay** *bay* E Guam, W Pacific Ocean
117 M20 **Pagóndas** *var.* Pagóndhas. Sámos, Dodekánisos, Greece, Aegean Sea
Pagóndhas *see* Pagóndas
198 C8 **Pago Pago** ○ (American Samoa) Tutuila, W American Samoa
39 R8 **Pagosa Springs** Colorado, C USA
40 H12 **Pahala** *var.* Pāhala. Hawaii, USA, C Pacific Ocean
174 H4 **Pahang** *off.* Negeri Pahang Darul Makmur. ◈ *state* Peninsular Malaysia
Pahang *see* Pahang, Sungai
174 Hh5 **Pahang, Sungai** *var.* Pahang, Sungei Pahang. ≈ Peninsular Malaysia
155 S8 **Pahārpur** North-West Frontier Province, NW Pakistan
193 B24 **Pahia Point** *headland* South Island, NZ
192 M13 **Pahiatua** Manawatu-Wanganui, North Island, NZ
40 H12 **Pahoa** *Haw.* Pāhoa. Hawaii, USA, C Pacific Ocean
25 Y14 **Pahokee** Florida, SE USA
37 X9 **Pahranagat Range** ▲ Nevada, W USA
37 W11 **Pahrump** Nevada, W USA
Pahsien *see* Chongqing
37 V9 **Pahute Mesa** ▲ Nevada, W USA
178 H7 **Pai** Mae Hong Son, NW Thailand
40 F10 **Paia** *Haw.* Pā'ia. Maui, Hawaii, USA, C Pacific Ocean
Pai-ch'eng *see* Baicheng
120 H4 **Paide** *Ger.* Weissenstein. Järvamaa, N Estonia
99 J24 **Paignton** SW England, UK
192 K3 **Paihia** Northland, North Island, NZ
95 M18 **Päijänne** ◎ S Finland
116 F13 **Páïko** ▲ N Greece
59 M17 **Paila, Río** ≈ C Bolivia
178 I12 **Pailin** Bătdâmbâng, W Cambodia
56 F6 **Pailitas** Cesar, N Colombia
40 F9 **Pailolo Channel** *channel* Hawaii, USA, C Pacific Ocean
95 K19 **Paimio** *Swe.* Pemar. Turku-Pori, SW Finland
172 O17 **Paimi-saki** *var.* Yaeme-saki. *headland* Iriomote-jima, SW Japan
104 G5 **Paimpol** Côtes d'Armor, NW France
174 Gg9 **Painan** Sumatera, W Indonesia
65 G23 **Paine, Cerro** ▲ S Chile
33 U11 **Painesville** Ohio, N USA
33 S14 **Paint Creek** ≈ Ohio, N USA
38 L10 **Painted Desert** *desert* Arizona, SW USA
Paint Hills *see* Wemindji
32 M4 **Paint River** ≈ Michigan, N USA
27 P8 **Paint Rock** Texas, SW USA
23 O6 **Paintsville** Kentucky, S USA
Paisance *see* Piacenza
98 I12 **Paisley** W Scotland, UK
34 I15 **Paisley** Oregon, NW USA
107 R10 **País Valenciano** *var.* Valencia, *Cat.* València; *anc.* Valentia. ◈ *autonomous community* NE Spain
107 O3 **País Vasco** *Basq.* Euskadi, *Eng.* The Basque Country, *Sp.* Provincias Vascongadas. ◈ *autonomous community* N Spain
58 A9 **Paita** Piura, NW Peru
197 J7 **Païta** Province Sud, S New Caledonia
175 O1 **Paitan, Teluk** *bay* Sabah, East Malaysia
106 H7 **Paiva** ≈ N Portugal
94 K12 **Pajala** Norrbotten, N Sweden
106 K3 **Pajares, Puerto de** *pass* NW Spain
56 G9 **Pajárito** Boyacá, C Colombia
56 G4 **Pajaro** La Guajira, S Colombia
Pakanbaru *see* Pekanbaru
57 Q10 **Pakaraima Mountains** *var.* Serra Pacaraim, Sierra Pacaraima. ▲ N South America
178 Hh11 **Pak Chong** Nakhon Ratchasima, C Thailand
127 Pp7 **Pakhachi** Koryakskiy Avtonomnyy Okrug, E Russian Federation
Pakhna *see* Páchna
153 O11 **Pakhtakor** Jizzakh Wiloyati, C Uzbekistan
201 U16 **Pakin Atoll** *atoll* Caroline Islands, E Micronesia
155 Q12 **Pakistan** *off.* Islamic Republic of Pakistan, *var.* Islami Jamhuriya e Pakistan. ◆ *republic* S Asia
Pakistan, Islami Jamhuriya e *see* Pakistan
178 I8 **Pak Lay** *var.* Muang Pak Lay. Xaignabouli, C Laos
Paknam *see* Samut Prakan
177 Ff5 **Pakokku** Magwe, C Myanmar
112 I10 **Pakość** *Ger.* Pakosch. Bydgoszcz, C Poland
Pakosch *see* Pakość
155 V10 **Pākpattan** Punjab, E Pakistan
178 H16 **Pak Phanang** *var.* Ban Pak Phanang. Nakhon Si Thammarat, SW Thailand
114 G9 **Pakrac** *Hung.* Pakrácz. Požega-Slavonija, NE Croatia
Pakrácz *see* Pakrac
120 F11 **Pakruojis** Pakruojis, N Lithuania
113 J24 **Paks** Tolna, S Hungary
Pak Sane *see* Paksan
Paksé *see* Pakxé
178 I11 **Pak Thong Chai** Nakhon Ratchasima, C Thailand
155 R6 **Paktīā** ◈ *province* SE Afghanistan
155 Q7 **Paktīkā** ◈ *province* SE Afghanistan
175 Pp9 **Pakuli** Sulawesi, C Indonesia
83 F17 **Pakwach** NW Uganda
178 I8 **Pakxan** *var.* Muang Pakxan, Pak Sane. Bolikhamxai, C Laos
178 Jj10 **Pakxé** *var.* Paksé. Champasak, S Laos
80 G12 **Pala** Mayo-Kébbi, SW Chad
63 A17 **Palacios** Santa Fe, C Argentina
27 V13 **Palacios** Texas, SW USA
107 X5 **Palafrugell** Cataluña, NE Spain
109 L24 **Palagonia** Sicilia, Italy, C Mediterranean Sea
115 E17 **Palagruža** *It.* Pelagosa. *island* SW Croatia
117 G20 **Palaiá Epídavros** Pelopónnisos, S Greece
124 Nn3 **Palaichóri** *var.* Palekhori. C Cyprus
117 H25 **Palaiochóra** Kríti, Greece, E Mediterranean Sea
117 A15 **Palaiolastrítsa** *religious building* Kérkyra, Iónioi Nísoi, Greece, C Mediterranean Sea
117 J19 **Palaiópoli** Ándros, Kykládes, Greece, Aegean Sea
105 N5 **Palaiseau** Essonne, N France
Palakkad *see* Pālghāt
160 N11 **Pāla Laharha** Orissa, E India
85 G19 **Palamakoloi** Ghanzi, C Botswana
117 E16 **Palamás** Thessalía, C Greece
107 X5 **Palamós** Cataluña, NE Spain
120 J5 **Palamuse** *Ger.* Sankt-Bartholomäi. Jõgevamaa, E Estonia
191 Q14 **Palana** Tasmania, SE Australia
127 P9 **Palana** Koryakskiy Avtonomnyy Okrug, E Russian Federation
120 C11 **Palanga** *Ger.* Polangen. Palanga, NW Lithuania
149 V10 **Palangān, Kūh-e** ▲ E Iran
Palangkaraja *see* Palangkaraya
174 Mm10 **Palangkaraya** *prev.* Palangkaraja. Borneo, C Indonesia
161 H22 **Palani** Tamil Nādu, SE India
Palanka *see* Bačka Palanka
160 D9 **Pālanpur** Gujarāt, W India
Palantia *see* Palencia
85 I19 **Palapye** Central, SE Botswana
161 J19 **Pālār** ≈ SE India
106 H3 **Palas de Rei** Galicia, NW Spain
127 O10 **Palatka** Magadanskaya Oblast', E Russian Federation
25 W10 **Palatka** Florida, SE USA
196 B9 **Palau** *var.* Belau. ◆ *republic* W Pacific Ocean
133 Y14 **Palau Islands** *var.* Palau. *island group* N Palau
198 Aa8 **Palauli Bay** *bay* Savai'i, Western Samoa, C Pacific Ocean
178 Gg12 **Palaw** Tenasserim, S Myanmar
179 Oo15 **Palawan** *island* W Philippines
179 Oo15 **Palawan Passage** *passage* W Philippines
198 F7 **Palawan Trough** *undersea feature* S South China Sea
179 P10 **Palayan City** Luzon, N Philippines
161 H23 **Pālayankottai** Tamil Nādu, SE India
109 L25 **Palazzolo Acreide** *anc.* Acrae. Sicilia, Italy, C Mediterranean Sea
120 G3 **Paldiski** *prev.* Baltiski, *Eng.* Baltic Port, *Ger.* Baltischport. Harjumaa, NW Estonia
114 I13 **Pale** SE Bosnia and Herzegovina
Palekhori *see* Palaichóri
175 Q7 **Paleleh, Pegunungan** ▲ Sulawesi, N Indonesia
175 Qq7 **Paleleh, Teluk** *bay* Sulawesi, N Indonesia
174 I11 **Palembang** Sumatera, W Indonesia
65 G18 **Palena** Los Lagos, S Chile
65 G18 **Palena, Río** ≈ S Chile
106 M5 **Palencia** *anc.* Palantia, Pallantia. Castilla-León, NW Spain
106 M3 **Palencia** ◈ *province* Castilla-León, N Spain
37 X15 **Palen Dry Lake** ◎ California, W USA
43 V15 **Palenque** Chiapas, SE Mexico
43 V15 **Palenque** *var.* Ruinas de Palenque. *ruins* Chiapas, SE Mexico
47 O9 **Palenque, Punta** *headland* S Dominican Republic
Palenque, Ruinas de *see* Palenque
Palerme *see* Palermo
109 I23 **Palermo** *Fr.* Palerme; *anc.* Panhormus, Panormus. Sicilia, Italy, C Mediterranean Sea
27 V8 **Palestine** Texas, SW USA
27 V7 **Palestine, Lake** ⊡ Texas, SW USA
109 I15 **Palestrina** Lazio, C Italy
177 F5 **Paletwa** Chin State, W Myanmar
161 G21 **Pālghāt** *var.* Palakkad; *prev.* Pulicat. Kerala, SW India
158 F13 **Pāli** Rājasthān, N India
178 Gg16 **Palian** Trang, SW Thailand
201 O12 **Palikir** ● (Micronesia) Pohnpei, E Micronesia
179 R17 **Palimbang** Mindanao, S Philippines
Palimé *see* Kpalimé
109 L19 **Palinuro, Capo** *headland* S Italy
117 H15 **Palioúri, Ákra** *var.* Akra Kanestron. *headland* N Greece
35 R14 **Palisades Reservoir** ⊡ Idaho, NW USA
101 J23 **Paliseul** Luxembourg, SE Belgium
160 C11 **Pālitāna** Gujarāt, W India
120 F4 **Palivere** Läänemaa, W Estonia
43 V14 **Palizada** Campeche, SE Mexico
95 L18 **Pälkäne** Häme, SW Finland
161 J22 **Palk Strait** *strait* India/Sri Lanka
161 J23 **Pallai** Northern Province, NW Sri Lanka
Pallantia *see* Palencia
108 C6 **Pallanza** Piemonte, NE Italy
131 Q9 **Pallasovka** Volgogradskaya Oblast', SW Russian Federation
Pallene/Pallíni *see* Kassándra
193 L15 **Palliser Bay** *bay* North Island, NZ
193 L15 **Palliser, Cape** *headland* North Island, NZ
203 U9 **Palliser, Îles** *island group* Îles Tuamotu, C French Polynesia
107 X9 **Palma** *var.* Palma de Mallorca. Mallorca, Spain, W Mediterranean Sea
107 X9 **Palma** ✕ Mallorca, Spain, W Mediterranean Sea
84 Q12 **Palma** Cabo Delgado, N Mozambique
107 X10 **Palma, Badia de** *bay* Mallorca, Spain, W Mediterranean Sea
106 L13 **Palma del Río** Andalucía, S Spain
Palma de Mallorca *see* Palma
109 J25 **Palma di Montechiaro** Sicilia, Italy, C Mediterranean Sea
108 J7 **Palmanova** Friuli-Venezia Giulia, NE Italy
56 J7 **Palmarito** Apure, C Venezuela
45 N15 **Palmar Sur** Puntarenas, SE Costa Rica
62 I12 **Palmas** Paraná, S Brazil
61 K16 **Palmas do Tocantins** Tocantins, C Brazil
56 D11 **Palmaseca** ✕ (Cali) Valle del Cauca, SW Colombia
109 B21 **Palmas, Golfo di** *gulf* Sardegna, Italy, C Mediterranean Sea
46 I7 **Palma Soriano** Santiago de Cuba, E Cuba
25 Y12 **Palm Bay** Florida, SE USA
37 T14 **Palmdale** California, W USA
63 H14 **Palmeira das Missões** Rio Grande do Sul, S Brazil
84 A11 **Palmeirinhas, Ponta das** *headland* NW Angola
41 R11 **Palmer** Alaska, USA
21 N11 **Palmer** Massachusetts, NE USA
27 U7 **Palmer** Texas, SW USA
204 H4 **Palmer** *US research station* Antarctica
13 R11 **Palmer** ≈ Québec, SE Canada
39 T5 **Palmer Lake** Colorado, C USA
204 J6 **Palmer Land** *physical region* Antarctica
12 F15 **Palmerston** Ontario, SE Canada
193 F22 **Palmerston** Otago, South Island, NZ
202 K15 **Palmerston** *island* S Cook Islands
Palmerston *see* Darwin
192 M12 **Palmerston North** Manawatu-Wanganui, North Island, NZ
78 L18 **Palmes, Cap des** *headland* SW Ivory Coast
25 V13 **Palmetto** Florida, SE USA
Palmetto State *see* South Carolina
109 M22 **Palmi** Calabria, SW Italy
56 D11 **Palmira** Valle del Cauca, W Colombia
58 F8 **Palmira, Río** ≈ N Peru
63 D19 **Palmitas** Soriano, SW Uruguay
Palmnicken *see* Yantarnyy
37 V15 **Palm Springs** California, W USA
29 V2 **Palmyra** Missouri, C USA
20 G10 **Palmyra** New York, NE USA
20 G15 **Palmyra** Pennsylvania, NE USA
23 V5 **Palmyra** Virginia, NE USA
Palmyra *see* Tudmur
199 K7 **Palmyra Atoll** ◇ *US privately owned unincorporated territory* C Pacific Ocean
160 P12 **Palmyras Point** *headland* E India
37 N9 **Palo Alto** California, W USA
27 O1 **Palo Duro Creek** ≈ Texas, SW USA
Paloe *see* Palu
Paloe *see* Denpasar, Bali, C Indonesia
174 Hh6 **Paloh** Johor, Peninsular Malaysia
82 F12 **Paloich** Upper Nile, SE Sudan
42 I3 **Palomas** Chihuahua, N Mexico
109 I15 **Palombara Sabina** Lazio, C Italy
107 S13 **Palos, Cabo de** *headland* SE Spain
106 I14 **Palos de la Frontera** Andalucía, S Spain
62 G11 **Palotina** Paraná, S Brazil
34 M9 **Palouse** Washington, NW USA
34 L9 **Palouse River** ≈ Washington, NW USA
37 Y16 **Palo Verde** California, W USA
58 E16 **Palpa** Ica, W Peru
97 M16 **Pålsboda** Örebro, C Sweden
95 M15 **Paltamo** Oulu, C Finland
175 Pp9 **Palu** *prev.* Paloe. Sulawesi, C Indonesia
143 P14 **Palu** Elâzığ, E Turkey
175 Q16 **Palu, Pulau** *island* S Indonesia
175 P8 **Palu, Teluk** *bay* Sulawesi, C Indonesia
158 I11 **Palwal** Haryāna, N India
127 Oo4 **Palyavaam** ≈ NE Russian Federation
79 Q13 **Pama** SE Burkina
180 J14 **Pamandzi** ✕ (Mamoudzou) Petite-Terre, E Mayotte
Pamangkat *see* Pemangkat
149 R11 **Pā Mazār** Kermān, C Iran
85 N19 **Pambarra** Inhambane, SE Mozambique
176 Xx10 **Pamdai** Irian Jaya, E Indonesia
176 X10 **Pami** Irian Jaya, E Indonesia
105 N16 **Pamiers** Ariège, S France
153 T14 **Pamir** *var.* Daryā-ye Pāmīr, *Taj.* Dar"yoi Pomir. ≈ Afghanistan/Tajikistan *see also* Pāmīr, Daryā-ye
Pamir/Pāmīr, Daryā-ye *see* Pamirs
155 U1 **Pāmīr, Daryā-ye** *var.* Pamir, *Taj.* Dar"yoi Pomir. ≈ Afghanistan/Tajikistan *see also* Pamir
Pāmīr-e Khord *see* Little Pamir
133 Q8 **Pamirs** *Pash.* Daryā-ye Pāmīr, *Rus.* Pamir. ▲ C Asia
Pâmiut *see* Paamiut
23 X10 **Pamlico River** ≈ North Carolina, SE USA
23 Y10 **Pamlico Sound** *sound* North Carolina, SE USA
27 O2 **Pampa** Texas, SW USA
Pampa Aullagas, Lago *see* Poopó, Lago
63 B21 **Pampa Húmeda** *grassland* E Argentina
58 A10 **Pampa las Salinas** *salt lake* NW Peru
59 F15 **Pampas** Huancavelica, C Peru
64 K13 **Pampas** *plain* C Argentina
57 O4 **Pampatar** Nueva Esparta, NE Venezuela
Pampeluna *see* Pamplona
106 H8 **Pampilhosa da Serra** *var.* Pampilhosa de Serra. Coimbra, N Portugal
181 Y15 **Pamplemousses** N Mauritius
56 G7 **Pamplona** Norte de Santander, N Colombia
107 Q3 **Pamplona** *Basq.* Iruñea; *prev.* Pampeluna, *anc.* Pompaelo. Navarra, N Spain
116 I11 **Pamporovo** *prev.* Vasil Kolarov. Plovdivska Oblast, S Bulgaria
142 D15 **Pamukkale** Denizli, W Turkey
23 W5 **Pamunkey River** ≈ Virginia, NE USA
158 K5 **Pamzal** Jammu and Kashmir, NW India
32 L14 **Pana** Illinois, N USA
43 Y11 **Panabá** Yucatán, SE Mexico
37 Y8 **Panaca** Nevada, W USA
117 E19 **Panachaikó** ▲ S Greece
12 F11 **Panache Lake** ◎ Ontario, S Canada
116 I10 **Panagyurishte** Plovdivska Oblast, W Bulgaria
174 I14 **Panaitan, Pulau** *island* S Indonesia
174 Ii14 **Panaitan, Selat** *strait* Jawa, SW Indonesia
117 D18 **Panaitolikó** ▲ C Greece
161 E17 **Panaji** *var.* Pangim, Panjim, New Goa. Goa, W India
45 T14 **Panamá** *off.* Republic of Panama. ◆ *republic* Central America
45 T15 **Panamá** *var.* Ciudad de Panamá, *Eng.* Panama City. ● (Panama) Panamá, C Panama
45 U14 **Panamá** *off.* Provincia de Panamá. ◈ *province* E Panama
45 U15 **Panamá, Bahía de** *bay* N Gulf of Panama
200 Oo8 **Panama Basin** *undersea feature* E Pacific Ocean
45 T15 **Panama Canal** *canal* E Panama
25 R9 **Panama City** Florida, SE USA
45 T14 **Panama City** ✕ Panamá, C Panama
Panama City *see* Panamá
25 Q9 **Panama City Beach** Florida, SE USA
45 T17 **Panamá, Golfo de** *var.* Gulf of Panama. *gulf* S Panama
Panama, Gulf of *see* Panamá, Golfo de
Panama, Isthmus of *see* Panamá, Istmo de
45 T15 **Panamá, Istmo de** *Eng.* Isthmus of Panama; *prev.* Isthmus of Darien. *isthmus* E Panama
37 U11 **Panamint Range** ▲ California, W USA
109 L22 **Panarea, Isola** *island* Isole Eolie, S Italy
108 G9 **Panaro** ≈ N Italy
179 Q14 **Panay Gulf** *gulf* C Philippines
179 Pp13 **Panay Island** *island* C Philippines
37 W7 **Pancake Range** ▲ Nevada, W USA
114 M11 **Pančevo** *Ger.* Pantschowa, *Hung.* Pancsova. Serbia, N Yugoslavia
115 M15 **Pančićev Vrh** ▲ SW Yugoslavia
118 L12 **Panciu** Vrancea, E Romania
118 F10 **Pâncota** *Hung.* Pankota; *prev.* Pîncota. Arad, W Romania
Pancsova *see* Pančevo
85 N20 **Panda** Inhambane, SE Mozambique
176 X9 **Pandaidori, Kepulauan** *island group* E Indonesia
27 N11 **Pandale** Texas, SW USA
174 H7 **Pandang, Pulau** *island* W Indonesia
174 Kk9 **Pandang Tikar, Pulau** *island* N Indonesia
63 F20 **Pan de Azúcar** Maldonado, S Uruguay
120 H11 **Pandėlys** Rokiškis, NE Lithuania
161 F15 **Pandharpur** Mahārāshtra, W India
190 J1 **Pandie Pandie** South Australia
175 Pp9 **Pandiri** Sulawesi, C Indonesia
63 F20 **Pando** Canelones, S Uruguay
59 J14 **Pando** ◈ *department* N Bolivia
199 Ii10 **Pandora Bank** *undersea feature* W Pacific Ocean
97 G20 **Pandrup** Nordjylland, N Denmark
159 V12 **Pandu** Assam, NE India
81 J15 **Pandu** Equateur, NW Zaire
Paneas *see* Bāniyās
61 F15 **Panelas** Mato Grosso, W Brazil
120 G12 **Panevėžys** Panevėžys, C Lithuania
Panfilov *see* Zharkent
131 N9 **Panfilovo** Volgogradskaya Oblast', SW Russian Federation
81 N17 **Panga** Haut-Zaïre, N Zaire
200 Ss13 **Pangai** Lifuka, C Tonga
116 H13 **Pangaío** ▲ N Greece
81 G20 **Pangala** Le Pool, S Congo
83 J22 **Pangani** Tanga, E Tanzania
83 I21 **Pangani** ≈ NE Tanzania
195 U13 **Panggoe** Choiseul Island, NW Solomon Islands
81 N20 **Pangi** Maniema, E Zaire
194 H12 **Pangia** Southern Highlands, W PNG
Pangim *see* Panaji
173 F4 **Pangkalanbrandan** Sumatera, W Indonesia
Pangkalanbun *see* Pangkalanbuun
174 Ll10 **Pangkalanbuun** *var.* Pangkalanbun. Borneo, C Indonesia
174 J10 **Pangkalpinang** Pulau Bangka, W Indonesia
9 U17 **Pangman** Saskatchewan, S Canada
Pang-Nga *see* Phang-Nga
16 Nn2 **Pangnirtung** Baffin Island, Northwest Territories, NE Canada
158 K6 **Pangong Tso** *var.* Bangong Co. ◎ China/India *see also* Bangong Co
38 K7 **Panguitch** Utah, W USA
195 S12 **Panguna** Bougainville Island, NE PNG
179 Pp17 **Pangutaran Group** *island group* Sulu Archipelago, SW Philippines
27 N2 **Panhandle** Texas, SW USA
Panhormus *see* Palermo
176 X12 **Paniai, Danau** ◎ Irian Jaya, E Indonesia
81 L21 **Pania-Mutombo** Kasai Oriental, C Zaire
Panicherevo *see* Dolno Panicherevo
197 H5 **Panié, Mont** ▲ C New Caledonia
158 I10 **Pānīpat** Haryāna, N India
153 Q14 **Panj** *Rus.* Pyandzh; *prev.* Kirovabad. SW Tajikistan
153 P15 **Panj** *Rus.* Pyandzh. ≈ Afghanistan/Tajikistan
155 O5 **Panjāb** Bāmīān, C Afghanistan
153 O12 **Panjakent** *Rus.* Pendzhikent. W Tajikistan
154 L14 **Panjgūr** Baluchistān, SW Pakistan
Panjim *see* Panaji
169 U12 **Panjin** Liaoning, NE China
153 P14 **Panji Poyon** *Rus.* Nizhniy Pyandzh. SW Tajikistan
155 Q4 **Panjshīr** ≈ E Afghanistan
Pankota *see* Pâncota
79 W14 **Pankshin** Plateau, C Nigeria
169 Y10 **Pan Ling** ▲ N China
Panlong Jiang *see* Lô, Sông
160 J9 **Panna** Madhya Pradesh, C India
101 M16 **Panningen** Limburg, SE Netherlands
155 R13 **Pāno Āqil** Sind, SE Pakistan
124 Nn3 **Páno Léfkara** S Cyprus
124 N3 **Páno Panagiá** *var.* Pano Panayia. W Cyprus
Pano Panayia *see* Páno Panagiá
Panopolis *see* Akhmîm
31 U14 **Panora** Iowa, C USA
62 I8 **Panorama** São Paulo, S Brazil
117 I24 **Pánormos** Kríti, Greece, E Mediterranean Sea
Panormus *see* Palermo
169 W11 **Panshi** Jilin, NE China
61 H19 **Pantanal** *var.* Pantanalmato-Grossense. *swamp* SW Brazil
Pantanalmato-Grossense *see* Pantanal
63 H16 **Pântano Grande** Rio Grande do Sul, S Brazil
175 R16 **Pantar, Pulau** *island* Kepulauan Alor, S Indonesia
23 X9 **Pantego** North Carolina, SE USA
109 G25 **Pantelleria** *anc.* Cossyra, Cosyra. Sicilia, Italy, C Mediterranean Sea
109 G25 **Pantelleria, Isola di** *island* SW Italy
Pante Macassar/Pante Makassar *see* Pante Makasar
175 Rr17 **Pante Makasar** *var.* Pante Macassar, Pante Makassar. Timor, C Indonesia
158 K10 **Pantnagar** Uttar Pradesh, N India
117 A15 **Pantokrátoras** ▲ Kérkyra, Iónioi Nísoi, Greece, C Mediterranean Sea
Pantschowa *see* Pančevo
179 Rr16 **Pantukan** Mindanao, S Philippines
43 P11 **Pánuco** Veracruz-Llave, E Mexico
43 P11 **Pánuco, Río** ≈ C Mexico
166 I12 **Panxian** Guizhou, S China
173 G7 **Panyabungan** Sumatera, N Indonesia
79 W14 **Panyam** Plateau, C Nigeria
163 N13 **Panzhihua** *prev.* Dukou, Tu-k'ou. Sichuan, C China
81 I22 **Panzi** Bandundu, SW Zaire
44 E5 **Panzós** Alta Verapaz, E Guatemala
Pao-chi/Paoki *see* Baoji
Pao-king *see* Shaoyang
109 N20 **Paola** Calabria, SW Italy
123 Jj17 **Paola** E Malta
29 R5 **Paola** Kansas, C USA
33 O15 **Paoli** Indiana, N USA
197 D14 **Paonangisu** Éfaté, C Vanuatu
175 Tt11 **Paoni** *var.* Pauni. Pulau Seram, E Indonesia
39 Q5 **Paonia** Colorado, C USA
203 O7 **Paopao** Moorea, W French Polynesia
Pao-shan *see* Baoshan
Pao-ting *see* Baoding
Pao-t'ou/Paotow *see* Baotou
81 H14 **Paoua** Ouham-Pendé, W Central African Republic
Pap *see* Pop
113 H23 **Pápa** Veszprém, W Hungary
44 J12 **Papagayo, Golfo de** *gulf* NW Costa Rica
40 H11 **Papaikou** *var.* Pāpa'ikou. Hawaii, USA, C Pacific Ocean
43 R15 **Papaloapan, Río** ≈ S Mexico
192 L6 **Papakura** Auckland, North Island, NZ
43 Q13 **Papantla** *var.* Papantla de Olarte. Veracruz-Llave, E Mexico
Papantla de Olarte *see* Papantla
203 P8 **Papara** Tahiti, W French Polynesia
192 K4 **Paparoa** Northland, North Island, NZ
193 G16 **Paparoa Range** ▲ South Island, NZ
117 K20 **Pápas, Ákra** *headland* Ikaría, Dodekánisos, Greece, Aegean Sea
98 L2 **Papa Stour** *island* NE Scotland, UK
192 L6 **Papatoetoe** Auckland, North Island, NZ
193 E25 **Papatowai** Otago, South Island, NZ
98 K4 **Papa Westray** *island* NE Scotland, UK
203 T10 **Papeete** ○ (French Polynesia) Tahiti, W French Polynesia
102 F11 **Papenburg** Niedersachsen, NW Germany
100 H13 **Papendrecht** Zuid-Holland, SW Netherlands
203 Q7 **Papenoo** Tahiti, W French Polynesia
203 Q7 **Papenoo Rivière** ≈ Tahiti, W French Polynesia
203 N7 **Papetoai** Moorea, W French Polynesia
94 L3 **Papey** *island* E Iceland
Paphos *see* Páfos
42 H5 **Papigochic, Río** ≈ NW Mexico
120 E10 **Papilė** Akmenė, NW Lithuania
31 S15 **Papillion** Nebraska, C USA
13 T5 **Papinachois** ≈ Québec, SE Canada
194 I15 **Papua, Gulf of** *gulf* S PNG
194 H13 **Papua New Guinea** *off.* Independent State of Papua New Guinea; *prev.* Territory of Papua and New Guinea, *abbrev.* PNG. ◆ *commonwealth republic* NW Melanesia
199 H10 **Papua Plateau** *undersea feature* N Coral Sea
114 G9 **Papuk** ▲ NE Croatia
177 G8 **Papun** Karen State, S Myanmar
44 L14 **Paquera** Puntarenas, W Costa Rica
57 V9 **Para** ◈ *district* N Suriname
60 I13 **Pará** *off.* Estado do Pará. ◈ *state* NE Brazil
Pará *see* Belém
126 H12 **Parabel'** Tomskaya Oblast', C Russian Federation
188 I8 **Paraburdoo** Western Australia
59 E16 **Paracas, Península de** *peninsula* W Peru
61 L19 **Paracatu** Minas Gerais, NE Brazil
198 F7 **Paracel Islands** ◇ *disputed territory* SE Asia
190 I6 **Parachilna** South Australia
155 R6 **Pārachinār** North-West Frontier Province, NW Pakistan
114 N13 **Paraćin** Serbia, C Yugoslavia
12 K8 **Paradis** Québec, SE Canada
41 N11 **Paradise** *var.* Paradise Hill. Alaska, USA
37 O5 **Paradise** California, W USA
37 X11 **Paradise** Nevada, W USA
Paradise Hill *see* Paradise
39 R11 **Paradise Hills** New Mexico, SW USA
Paradise of the Pacific *see* Hawaii
38 L13 **Paradise Valley** Arizona, SW USA
37 T2 **Paradise Valley** Nevada, W USA
117 O22 **Paradísi** ✕ (Ródos) Ródos, Dodekánisos, Greece, Aegean Sea
176 X10 **Paradoi** Irian Jaya, E Indonesia
160 P12 **Pārādwīp** Orissa, E India
Paraetonium *see* Maţrūḩ
119 R4 **Parafiyivka** Chernihivs'ka Oblast', N Ukraine
38 K7 **Paragonah** Utah, W USA
29 X9 **Paragould** Arkansas, C USA
49 X8 **Paraguaçu** *var.* Paraguassú. ≈ E Brazil
62 J9 **Paraguaçu Paulista** São Paulo, S Brazil
56 H4 **Paraguaipoa** Zulia, NW Venezuela
64 O6 **Paraguarí** Paraguarí, S Paraguay
64 O7 **Paraguarí** *off.* Departamento de Paraguarí. ◈ *department* S Paraguay
57 O8 **Paragua, Río** ≈ SE Venezuela
59 O16 **Paraguá, Río** ≈ NE Bolivia

◆ Country ● Country Capital ◇ Dependent Territory ○ Dependent Territory Capital ◈ Administrative Region ✕ International Airport ▲ Mountain ▲ Mountain Range ♜ Volcano ≈ River ◎ Lake ⊡ Reservoir

Paraguassú *see* Paraguaçu
64 *N5* **Paraguay** ◆ *republic* C South America
49 *U10* **Paraguay** *var.* Río Paraguay. ≈ C South America
Parahiba/Parahyba *see* Paraíba
61 *P15* **Paraíba** *off.* Estado da Paraíba; *prev.* Parahiba, Parahyba. ◈ *state* E Brazil
Paraíba *see* João Pessoa
62 *P9* **Paraíba do Sul, Rio** ≈ SE Brazil
Parainen *see* Pargas
45 *N14* **Paraíso** Cartago, C Costa Rica
43 *U14* **Paraíso** Tabasco, SE Mexico
59 *O17* **Paraiso, Río** ≈ E Bolivia
Parajd *see* Praid
79 *S14* **Parakou** C Benin
124 *O3* **Paralimni** E Cyprus
117 *G18* **Paralímni, Límni** ◎ C Greece
194 *G15* **Parama Island** *island* SW PNG
57 *W8* **Paramaribo** ● (Suriname) Paramaribo, N Suriname
57 *W9* **Paramaribo** ◈ *district* N Suriname
57 *W9* **Paramaribo** ✕ Paramaribo, N Suriname
Paramithiá *see* Paramythiá
58 *C13* **Paramonga** Lima, W Peru
127 *Pp13* **Paramushir, Ostrov** *island* SE Russian Federation
117 *C16* **Paramythiá** *var.* Paramithiá. Ípeiros, W Greece
64 *M10* **Paraná** Entre Ríos, E Argentina
62 *H11* **Paraná** *off.* Estado do Paraná. ◈ *state* S Brazil
49 *U11* **Paraná** *var.* Alto Paraná. ≈ C South America
62 *K12* **Paranaguá** Paraná, S Brazil
61 *J20* **Paranaíba, Rio** ≈ E Brazil
63 *C19* **Paraná Ibicuy, Río** ≈ E Argentina
61 *H15* **Paranaíta** Mato Grosso, W Brazil
62 *H9* **Paranapanema, Rio** ≈ S Brazil
62 *K11* **Paranapiacaba, Serra do** ⛰ S Brazil
62 *H9* **Paranavaí** Paraná, S Brazil
149 *N5* **Parandak** Markazī, W Iran
116 *I12* **Paranéstio** Anatolikí Makedonía kai Thráki, NE Greece
203 *W11* **Paraoa** *atoll* Îles Tuamotu, C French Polynesia
192 *L13* **Paraparaumu** Wellington, North Island, NZ
59 *N20* **Parapeti, Río** ≈ SE Bolivia
56 *L10* **Paraque, Cerro** ▲ W Venezuela
160 *I11* **Parāsia** Madhya Pradesh, C India
117 *M23* **Paraspóri, Ákra** *headland* Kárpathos, SE Greece
62 *O10* **Parati** Rio de Janeiro, SE Brazil
61 *K14* **Parauapebas** Pará, N Brazil
105 *Q10* **Paray-le-Monial** Saône-et-Loire, C France
Parbatsar *see* Parvatsar
160 *G13* **Parbhani** Mahārāshtra, C India
102 *L10* **Parchim** Mecklenburg-Vorpommern, N Germany
Parchwitz *see* Prochowice
112 *P13* **Parczew** Biała Podlaska, E Poland
62 *L8* **Pardo, Rio** ≈ S Brazil
113 *E16* **Pardubice** *Ger.* Pardubitz. Východní Čechy, C Czech Republic
Pardubitz *see* Pardubice
121 *F16* **Parechcha** *Pol.* Porzecze, *Rus.* Porech'ye. Hrodzyenskaya Voblasts', W Belarus
61 *F17* **Parecis, Chapada dos** *var.* Serra dos Parecis. ⛰ W Brazil
Parecis, Serra dos *see* Parecis, Chapada dos
106 *M4* **Paredes de Nava** Castilla-León, N Spain
201 *U12* **Parem** *island* Chuuk, C Micronesia
201 *O12* **Parem Island** *island* E Micronesia
192 *I1* **Parengarenga Harbour** *inlet* North Island, NZ
13 *N8* **Parent** Québec, SE Canada
104 *J14* **Parentis-en-Born** Landes, SW France
Parenzo *see* Poreč
193 *G20* **Pareora** Canterbury, South Island, NZ
175 *P12* **Parepare** Sulawesi, C Indonesia
117 *B16* **Párga** Ípeiros, W Greece
95 *K20* **Pargas** *Swe.* Parainen. Turku-Pori, SW Finland
66 *O5* **Pargo, Ponta do** *headland* Madeira, Portugal, NE Atlantic Ocean
Paria, Golfo de *see* Paria, Gulf of
57 *N6* **Pariaguán** Anzoátegui, NE Venezuela
47 *X17* **Paria, Gulf of** *var.* Golfo de Paria. *gulf* Trinidad and Tobago/Venezuela
59 *I15* **Pariamanu, Río** ≈ E Peru
38 *L8* **Paria River** ≈ Utah, W USA
Parichi *see* Parychy
42 *M14* **Paricutín, Volcán** 🌋 C Mexico
45 *P16* **Parida, Isla** *island* SW Panama
57 *T8* **Parika** NE Guyana
95 *O18* **Parikkala** Kymi, SE Finland
60 *E10* **Parima, Serra** *var.* Sierra Parima. ⛰ Brazil/Venezuela *see also* Parima, Sierra
57 *N11* **Parima, Sierra** *var.* Serra Parima. ⛰ Brazil/Venezuela *see also* Parima, Serra
59 *F17* **Parinacochas, Laguna** ◎ SW Peru
49 *P8* **Pariñas, Punta** *headland* NW Peru
60 *H12* **Parintins** Amazonas, N Brazil
105 *O5* **Paris** *anc.* Lutetia, Lutetia Parisiorum, Parisii. ● (France) Paris, N France
203 *Y2* **Paris** Kiritimati, E Kiribati
29 *S11* **Paris** Arkansas, C USA
35 *S16* **Paris** Idaho, NW USA
33 *N14* **Paris** Illinois, N USA
22 *M5* **Paris** Kentucky, S USA
29 *V3* **Paris** Missouri, C USA
22 *H8* **Paris** Tennessee, S USA
27 *V5* **Paris** Texas, SW USA
Parisii *see* Paris
45 *S16* **Parita** Herrera, S Panama
45 *S16* **Parita, Bahía de** *bay* S Panama
Parkan/Párkány *see* Štúrovo
95 *K18* **Parkano** Häme, SW Finland
29 *N6* **Park City** Kansas, C USA
38 *L3* **Park City** Utah, W USA
38 *I12* **Parker** Arizona, SW USA
25 *R9* **Parker** Florida, SE USA
31 *R11* **Parker** South Dakota, N USA
37 *Z14* **Parker Dam** California, W USA
31 *W13* **Parkersburg** Iowa, C USA
23 *Q3* **Parkersburg** West Virginia, NE USA
31 *T7* **Parkers Prairie** Minnesota, N USA
179 *R17* **Parker Volcano** 🌋 Mindanao, S Philippines
189 *W13* **Parkes** New South Wales, SE Australia
32 *K4* **Park Falls** Wisconsin, N USA
Parkhar *see* Farkhor
12 *E16* **Parkhill** Ontario, S Canada
31 *T5* **Park Rapids** Minnesota, N USA
31 *Q3* **Park River** North Dakota, N USA
31 *Q11* **Parkston** South Dakota, N USA
8 *L17* **Parksville** Vancouver Island, British Columbia, SW Canada
39 *S3* **Parkview Mountain** ▲ Colorado, C USA
107 *N8* **Parla** Madrid, C Spain
31 *S8* **Parle, Lac qui** ▣ Minnesota, N USA
117 *F20* **Parlía Tyroú** Pelopónnisos, S Greece
161 *G14* **Parli Vaijnāth** Mahārāshtra, C India
108 *F9* **Parma** Emilia-Romagna, N Italy
33 *T11* **Parma** Ohio, N USA
Parnahyba *see* Parnaíba
60 *N13* **Parnaíba** *var.* Parnahyba. Piauí, E Brazil
67 *J14* **Parnaíba Ridge** *undersea feature* C Atlantic Ocean
60 *N13* **Parnaíba, Rio** ≈ NE Brazil
117 *F18* **Parnassós** ⛰ C Greece
193 *J17* **Parnassus** Canterbury, South Island, NZ
190 *H10* **Parndana** South Australia
117 *H19* **Párnitha** ⛰ C Greece
117 *F21* **Párnon** ⛰ S Greece
120 *G5* **Pärnu** *Ger.* Pernau, *Latv.* Pērnava; *prev.* Rus. Pernov. Pärnumaa, SW Estonia
120 *G6* **Pärnu** *var.* Parnu Jõgi, *Ger.* Pernau. ≈ SW Estonia
120 *G5* **Pärnu-Jaagupi** *Ger.* Sankt-Jakobi. Pärnumaa, SW Estonia
Parnu Jõgi *see* Pärnu
120 *G5* **Pärnu Laht** *Ger.* Pernauer Bucht. *bay* SW Estonia
120 *F5* **Pärnumaa** *off.* Pärnu Maakond. ◈ *province* SW Estonia
159 *T11* **Paro** W Bhutan
159 *T11* **Paro** ✕ (Thimphu) W Bhutan
193 *G17* **Paroa** West Coast, South Island, NZ
169 *X14* **P'aro-ho** *var.* Hwach'ŏn-chŏsuji. ▣ N South Korea
191 *N6* **Paroo River** *seasonal river* New South Wales/Queensland, SE Australia
Paropamisus Range *see* Sefīdkūh, Selseleh-ye
117 *J21* **Páros** Páros, Kykládes, Greece, Aegean Sea
117 *J21* **Páros** *island* Kykládes, Greece, Aegean Sea
38 *K7* **Parowan** Utah, W USA
105 *U13* **Parpaillon** ⛰ SE France
110 *I9* **Parpan** Graubünden, S Switzerland
64 *G13* **Parral** Maule, C Chile
Parral *see* Hidalgo del Parral
191 *T9* **Parramatta** New South Wales, SE Australia
23 *Y6* **Parramore Island** *island* Virginia, NE USA
42 *M8* **Parras** *var.* Parras de la Fuente. Coahuila de Zaragoza, NE Mexico
Parras de la Fuente *see* Parras
44 *M14* **Parrita** Puntarenas, S Costa Rica
12 *G13* **Parry Island** *island* Ontario, S Canada
207 *O9* **Parry Islands** *island group* Northwest Territories, NW Canada
12 *G12* **Parry Sound** Ontario, S Canada
112 *F7* **Parsęta** *Ger.* Persante. ≈ NW Poland
30 *L3* **Parshall** North Dakota, N USA
29 *Q7* **Parsons** Kansas, C USA
22 *H9* **Parsons** Tennessee, S USA
23 *T3* **Parsons** West Virginia, NE USA
Parsonstown *see* Birr
102 *P11* **Parsteiner See** ◎ NE Germany
109 *I24* **Partanna** Sicilia, Italy, C Mediterranean Sea
110 *J8* **Partenen** Graubünden, E Switzerland
104 *K9* **Parthenay** Deux-Sèvres, W France
97 *J19* **Partille** Göteborg och Bohus, S Sweden
109 *I23* **Partinico** Sicilia, Italy, C Mediterranean Sea
113 *I20* **Partizánske** *prev.* Šimonovany, *Hung.* Simony. Západné Slovensko, W Slovakia
60 *H11* **Paru de Oeste, Rio** ≈ N Brazil
190 *K9* **Paruna** South Australia
60 *I11* **Paru, Rio** ≈ N Brazil
Parvān *see* Parwān
161 *M14* **Pārvatipuram** Andhra Pradesh, E India
158 *G12* **Parvatsar** *prev.* Parbatsar. Rājasthān, N India
155 *Q5* **Parwān** *Per.* Parvān. ◈ *province* E Afghanistan
164 *I15* **Paryang** Xizang Zizhiqu, W China
121 *M18* **Parychy** *Rus.* Parichi. Homyel'skaya Voblasts', SE Belarus
85 *J21* **Parys** Free State, C South Africa
37 *T15* **Pasadena** California, W USA
27 *W11* **Pasadena** Texas, SW USA
58 *B8* **Pasaje** El Oro, SW Ecuador
143 *T9* **P'asanauri** N Georgia
173 *G10* **Pasapuat** Pulau Pagai Utara, W Indonesia
178 *Gg7* **Pasawng** Kayah State, C Myanmar
116 *L13* **Paşayiğit** Edirne, NW Turkey
25 *N9* **Pascagoula** Mississippi, S USA
24 *M8* **Pascagoula River** ≈ Mississippi, S USA
118 *F12* **Paşcani** *Hung.* Páskán. Iaşi, NE Romania
111 *T4* **Pasching** Oberösterreich, N Austria
34 *K10* **Pasco** Washington, NW USA
58 *E13* **Pasco** *off.* Departamento de Pasco. ◈ *department* C Peru
203 *N11* **Pascua, Isla de** *var.* Rapa Nui, *Eng.* Easter Island. *island* E Pacific Ocean
65 *G21* **Pascua, Río** ≈ S Chile
105 *N1* **Pas-de-Calais** ◈ *department* N France
102 *P10* **Pasewalk** Mecklenburg-Vorpommern, NE Germany
9 *T10* **Pasfield Lake** ◎ Saskatchewan, C Canada
Pa-shih Hai-hsia *see* Bashi Channel
Pashkeni *see* Bolyarovo
Pashmakli *see* Smolyan
179 *P10* **Pasig** Luzon, N Philippines
159 *X10* **Pāsighāt** Arunāchel Pradesh, NE India
143 *Q12* **Pasinler** Erzurum, NE Turkey
Pasi Oloy, Qatorkŭhi *see* Zaalayskiy Khrebet
44 *E3* **Pasión, Río de la** ≈ N Guatemala
174 *Gg10* **Pasirganting** Sumatera, W Indonesia
Pasirpangarayan *see* Bagansiapiapi
174 *H2* **Pasir Puteh** *var.* Pasir Putih. Kelantan, Peninsular Malaysia
174 *L6* **Pasir, Tanjung** *headland* East Malaysia
97 *N20* **Påskallavik** Kalmar, S Sweden
Páskán *see* Paşcani
112 *K7* **Pasłęk** *Ger.* Preußisch Holland. Elbląg, N Poland
112 *K7* **Pasłęka** *Ger.* Passarge. ≈ N Poland
154 *K16* **Pasni** Baluchistān, SW Pakistan
65 *I18* **Paso de Indios** Chubut, S Argentina
56 *L7* **Paso del Caballo** Guárico, N Venezuela
63 *E15* **Paso de los Libres** Corrientes, NE Argentina
63 *E18* **Paso de los Toros** Tacuarembó, C Uruguay
37 *P12* **Paso Robles** California, W USA
13 *Y7* **Paspébiac** Québec, SE Canada
9 *U14* **Pasquia Hills** ⛰ Saskatchewan, S Canada
155 *W7* **Pasrūr** Punjab, E Pakistan
32 *M1* **Passage Island** *island* Michigan, N USA
67 *B24* **Passage Islands** *island group* W Falkland Islands
15 *I1* **Passage Point** *headland* Banks Island, Northwest Territories, NW Canada
Passarge *see* Pasłęka
117 *C15* **Passarón** *ancient monument* Ípeiros, W Greece
Passarowitz *see* Požarevac
103 *O22* **Passau** Bayern, SE Germany
24 *M9* **Pass Christian** Mississippi, S USA
109 *L26* **Passero, Capo** *headland* Sicilia, Italy, C Mediterranean Sea
179 *Q13* **Passi** Panay Island, C Philippines
63 *H14* **Passo Fundo** Rio Grande do Sul, S Brazil
62 *H13* **Passo Fundo, Barragem de** ▣ S Brazil
63 *H15* **Passo Real, Barragem de** ▣ S Brazil
61 *L20* **Passos** Minas Gerais, NE Brazil
178 *M11* **Passu Keah** *island* S Paracel Islands
120 *J13* **Pastavy** *Pol.* Postawy, *Rus.* Postavy. Vitsyebskaya Voblasts', NW Belarus
58 *D7* **Pastaza** ◈ *province* E Ecuador
58 *D9* **Pastaza, Río** ≈ Ecuador/Peru
63 *A21* **Pasteur** Buenos Aires, E Argentina
13 *V3* **Pasteur** ≈ Québec, SE Canada
153 *Q12* **Pastigav** *Rus.* Pastigov. W Tajikistan
Pastigov *see* Pastigav
56 *C13* **Pasto** Nariño, SW Colombia
40 *M10* **Pastol Bay** *bay* Alaska, USA
39 *O8* **Pastora Peak** ▲ Arizona, SW USA
107 *O8* **Pastrana** Castilla-La Mancha, C Spain
174 *M15* **Pasuruan** *prev.* Pasoeroean. Jawa, C Indonesia
120 *F11* **Pasvalys** Pasvalys, N Lithuania
113 *K21* **Pásztó** Nógrád, N Hungary
201 *U12* **Pata** *var.* Patta. *atoll* Chuuk Islands, C Micronesia
38 *M16* **Patagonia** Arizona, SW USA
65 *H20* **Patagonia** *physical region* Argentina/Chile
Patalung *see* Phatthalung
160 *D9* **Pātan** Gujarāt, W India
160 *J10* **Pātan** Madhya Pradesh, C India
175 *Tt8* **Patani** Pulau Halmahera, E Indonesia
Patani *see* Pattani
13 *V7* **Patapédia Est** ≈ Québec, SE Canada
118 *K13* **Pătâriagele** *prev.* Pătîriagele. Buzău, SE Romania
Patavium *see* Padova
190 *I5* **Patawarta Hill** ▲ South Australia
190 *L10* **Patchewollock** Victoria, SE Australia
192 *K11* **Patea** Taranaki, North Island, NZ
192 *K11* **Patea** ≈ North Island, NZ
79 *U15* **Pategi** Kwara, C Nigeria
83 *K20* **Pate Island** *var.* Patta Island. *island* SE Kenya
107 *S10* **Paterna** País Valenciano, E Spain
111 *R9* **Paternion** *Slvn.* Špatrjan. Kärnten, S Austria
109 *L24* **Paternò** *anc.* Hybla, Hybla Major. Sicilia, Italy, C Mediterranean Sea
34 *J7* **Pateros** Washington, NW USA
20 *J14* **Paterson** New Jersey, NE USA
34 *J10* **Paterson** Washington, NW USA
193 *C25* **Paterson Inlet** *inlet* Stewart Island, NZ
100 *N6* **Paterswolde** Drenthe, NE Netherlands
158 *H7* **Pathānkot** Himāchal Pradesh, N India
Pathein *see* Bassein
35 *W15* **Pathfinder Reservoir** ▣ Wyoming, C USA
178 *Hh11* **Pathum Thani** *var.* Patumdhani, Prathum Thani. Pathum Thani, C Thailand
174 *L14* **Pati** Jawa, C Indonesia
56 *C12* **Patía** *var.* El Bordo. Cauca, SW Colombia
158 *I9* **Patiāla** *var.* Puttiala. Punjab, NW India
56 *B12* **Patía, Río** ≈ SW Colombia
175 *T8* **Patinti, Selat** *strait* Maluku, E Indonesia
196 *D15* **Pati Point** *headland* NE Guam
Pătîriagele *see* Pătâriagele
58 *C13* **Pativilca** Lima, W Peru
178 *Gg1* **Pātkai Bum** *var.* Patkai Range. ⛰ Myanmar/India
Patkai Range *see* Pātkai Bum
117 *L20* **Pátmos** Pátmos, Dodekánisos, Greece, Aegean Sea
117 *L20* **Pátmos** *island* Dodekánisos, Greece, Aegean Sea
159 *P13* **Patna** *var.* Azimabad. Bihār, N India
160 *M12* **Patnāgarh** Orissa, E India
179 *Pp13* **Patnongon** Panay Island, C Philippines
143 *S13* **Patnos** Ağrı, E Turkey
62 *H12* **Pato Branco** Paraná, S Brazil
33 *O16* **Patoka Lake** ◎ Indiana, N USA
94 *L9* **Patoniva** *Lapp.* Buoddobohki. Lappi, N Finland
115 *K21* **Patos** *var.* Patosi. Fier, SW Albania
Patos *see* Patos de Minas
61 *K19* **Patos de Minas** *var.* Patos. Minas Gerais, NE Brazil
Patosi *see* Patos
63 *I17* **Patos, Lagoa dos** *lagoon* S Brazil
64 *J9* **Patquía** La Rioja, C Argentina
117 *E19* **Pátra** *Eng.* Patras; *prev.* Pátrai. Dytikí Ellás, S Greece
Pátrai/Patras *see* Pátra
117 *D18* **Patraïkós Kólpos** *gulf* S Greece
94 *G2* **Patreksfjördhur** Vestfirdhir, W Iceland
26 *M7* **Patricia** Texas, SW USA
65 *F21* **Patricio Lynch, Isla** *island* S Chile
Patta *see* Pata
Patta Island *see* Pate Island
178 *Hh17* **Pattani** *var.* Patani. Pattani, SW Thailand
178 *Hh12* **Pattaya** Chon Buri, S Thailand
21 *S4* **Patten** Maine, NE USA
37 *O9* **Patterson** California, W USA
24 *J10* **Patterson** Louisiana, S USA
37 *R7* **Patterson, Mount** ▲ California, W USA
33 *P4* **Patterson, Point** *headland* Michigan, N USA
109 *L23* **Patti** Sicilia, Italy, C Mediterranean Sea
109 *L23* **Patti, Golfo di** *gulf* Sicilia, Italy, C Mediterranean Sea
95 *L14* **Pattijoki** Oulu, W Finland
199 *Mm5* **Patton Escarpment** *undersea feature* E Pacific Ocean
29 *S2* **Pattonsburg** Missouri, C USA
1 *D6* **Patton Seamount** *undersea feature* NE Pacific Ocean
8 *J12* **Pattullo, Mount** ▲ British Columbia, W Canada
Patuakhali *see* Patukhali
44 *M5* **Patuca, Río** ≈ E Honduras
159 *U16* **Patukhali** *var.* Patuakhali. Khulna, S Bangladesh
Patumdhani *see* Pathum Thani
42 *M14* **Pátzcuaro** Michoacán de Ocampo, SW Mexico
44 *C6* **Patzicía** Chimaltenango, S Guatemala
104 *K16* **Pau** Pyrénées-Atlantiques, SW France
104 *J12* **Pauillac** Gironde, SW France
177 *Ff5* **Pauk** Magwe, W Myanmar
15 *H3* **Paulatuk** Northwest Territories, NW Canada
44 *K5* **Paulayá, Río** ≈ NE Honduras
24 *M6* **Paulding** Mississippi, S USA
33 *Q12* **Paulding** Ohio, N USA
31 *S12* **Paullina** Iowa, C USA
61 *P15* **Paulo Afonso** Bahia, E Brazil
40 *M16* **Pauloff Harbor** *var.* Pavlor Harbour. Sanak Island, Alaska, USA
29 *N12* **Pauls Valley** Oklahoma, C USA
177 *Ff7* **Paungde** Pegu, C Myanmar
Pauni *see* Paoni
158 *K9* **Pauri** Uttar Pradesh, N India
Pautalia *see* Kyustendil
176 *Z11* **Pauwasi** ≈ Irian Jaya, E Indonesia
148 *J5* **Pāveh** Kermānshāhān, NW Iran
130 *L5* **Pavelets** Ryazanskaya Oblast', W Russian Federation
108 *D8* **Pavia** *anc.* Ticinum. Lombardia, N Italy
120 *C9* **Pāvilosta** Liepāja, W Latvia
129 *P14* **Pavino** Kostromskaya Oblast', NW Russian Federation
116 *J8* **Pavlikeni** Loveshka Oblast, N Bulgaria
151 *T8* **Pavlodar** Pavlodar, NE Kazakhstan
151 *S9* **Pavlodar** *off.* Pavlodarskaya Oblast', *Kaz.* Pavlodar Oblysy. ◈ *province* NE Kazakhstan
Pavlodar Oblysy/Pavlodarskaya Oblast' *see* Pavlodar
Pavlograd *see* Pavlohrad
119 *U7* **Pavlohrad** *Rus.* Pavlograd. Dnipropetrovs'ka Oblast', E Ukraine
Pavlor Harbour *see* Pauloff Harbor
151 *R9* **Pavlovka** Akmola, C Kazakhstan
131 *V4* **Pavlovka** Respublika Bashkortostan, W Russian Federation
131 *Q7* **Pavlovka** Ul'yanovskaya Oblast', W Russian Federation
131 *N3* **Pavlovo** Nizhegorodskaya Oblast', W Russian Federation
130 *L9* **Pavlovsk** Voronezhskaya Oblast', W Russian Federation
130 *L13* **Pavlovskaya** Krasnodarskiy Kray, SW Russian Federation
119 *S7* **Pavlysh** Kirovohrads'ka Oblast', C Ukraine
108 *F10* **Pavullo nel Frignano** Emilia-Romagna, C Italy
29 *P8* **Pawhuska** Oklahoma, C USA
23 *U13* **Pawleys Island** South Carolina, SE USA
178 *Gg6* **Pawn** ≈ C Myanmar
32 *K14* **Pawnee** Illinois, N USA
29 *O9* **Pawnee** Oklahoma, C USA
39 *U2* **Pawnee Buttes** ▲ Colorado, C USA
31 *S17* **Pawnee City** Nebraska, C USA
28 *K5* **Pawnee River** ≈ Kansas, C USA
33 *O10* **Paw Paw** Michigan, N USA
33 *O10* **Paw Paw Lake** Michigan, N USA
21 *O12* **Pawtucket** Rhode Island, NE USA
Pax Augusta *see* Badajoz
117 *I25* **Paximádia** *island* SE Greece
Pax Julia *see* Beja
117 *B16* **Paxoí** *island* Iónioi Nísoi, Greece, C Mediterranean Sea
41 *S10* **Paxson** Alaska, USA
32 *M13* **Paxton** Illinois, N USA
128 *J11* **Pay** Respublika Kareliya, NW Russian Federation
177 *G8* **Payagyi** Pegu, SW Myanmar
110 *C9* **Payerne** *Ger.* Peterlingen. Vaud, W Switzerland
34 *M13* **Payette** Idaho, NW USA
34 *M13* **Payette River** ≈ Idaho, NW USA
129 *V2* **Pay-Khoy, Khrebet** ⛰ NW Russian Federation
Payne *see* Kangirsuk
10 *K4* **Payne, Lac** ◎ Québec, NE Canada
31 *T8* **Paynesville** Minnesota, N USA
174 *M4* **Payong, Tanjung** *headland* East Malaysia
Payo Obispo *see* Chetumal
63 *D18* **Paysandú** Paysandú, W Uruguay
63 *D17* **Paysandú** ◈ *department* W Uruguay
104 *I7* **Pays de la Loire** ◈ *region* NW France
38 *L12* **Payson** Arizona, SW USA
38 *L4* **Payson** Utah, W USA
129 *W4* **Payyer, Gora** ▲ NW Russian Federation
Payzawat *see* Jiashi
143 *Q11* **Pazar** Rize, NE Turkey
142 *F10* **Pazarbaşı Burnu** *headland* NW Turkey
142 *M16* **Pazarcık** Kahramanmaraş, S Turkey
116 *I10* **Pazardzhik** *prev.* Tatar Pazardzhik. Plovdivska Oblast, SW Bulgaria
56 *H9* **Paz de Ariporo** Casanare, E Colombia
114 *A10* **Pazin** *Ger.* Mitterburg, *It.* Pisino. Istra, NW Croatia
44 *D7* **Paz, Río** ≈ El Salvador/Guatemala
115 *O18* **Pčinja** ≈ N FYR Macedonia
200 *Qq15* **Pea** Tongatapu, S Tonga
29 *O6* **Peabody** Kansas, C USA
9 *O12* **Peace** ≈ Alberta/British Columbia, W Canada
Peace Garden State *see* North Dakota
9 *Q10* **Peace Point** Alberta, C Canada
9 *O12* **Peace River** Alberta, W Canada
25 *W13* **Peace River** ≈ Florida, SE USA
9 *N17* **Peachland** British Columbia, SW Canada
38 *J10* **Peach Springs** Arizona, SW USA
Peach State *see* Georgia
25 *S4* **Peachtree City** Georgia, SE USA
201 *Y13* **Peacock Point** *point* SE Wake Island
99 *M18* **Peak District** *physical region* C England, UK
191 *Q7* **Peak Hill** New South Wales, SE Australia
67 *G15* **Peak, The** ▲ C Ascension Island
107 *O13* **Peal de Becerro** Andalucía, S Spain
201 *X11* **Peale Island** *island* N Wake Island
39 *O6* **Peale, Mount** ▲ Utah, W USA
41 *O4* **Peard Bay** *bay* Alaska, USA
25 *Q7* **Pea River** ≈ Alabama/Florida, S USA
27 *W11* **Pearland** Texas, SW USA
40 *D9* **Pearl City** Oahu, Hawaii, USA, C Pacific Ocean
40 *D9* **Pearl Harbor** *inlet* Oahu, Hawaii, USA, C Pacific Ocean
Pearl Islands *see* Perlas, Archipiélago de las
Pearl Lagoon *see* Perlas, Laguna de
24 *M5* **Pearl River** ≈ Louisiana/Mississippi, S USA
27 *Q13* **Pearsall** Texas, SW USA
25 *U7* **Pearson** Georgia, SE USA
27 *P4* **Pease River** ≈ Texas, SW USA
10 *F7* **Peawanuk** Ontario, C Canada
85 *P16* **Pebane** Zambézia, NE Mozambique
67 *C23* **Pebble Island** *island* N Falkland Islands
67 *C23* **Pebble Island Settlement** Pebble Island, N Falkland Islands
115 *L16* **Peć** *Alb.* Pejë, *Turk.* Ipek. Serbia, S Yugoslavia
27 *R8* **Pecan Bayou** ≈ Texas, SW USA
24 *H10* **Pecan Island** Louisiana, S USA
62 *L12* **Peças, Ilha das** *island* S Brazil
32 *L10* **Pecatonica River** ≈ Illinois/Wisconsin, N USA
110 *G10* **Peccia** Ticino, S Switzerland
Pechenegi *see* Pechenihy
Pechenezhskoye Vodokhranilishche *see* Pecheniz'ke Vodoskhovyshche
128 *I2* **Pechenga** *Fin.* Petsamo. Murmanskaya Oblast', NW Russian Federation
119 *V5* **Pechenihy** *Rus.* Pechenegi. Kharkivs'ka Oblast', E Ukraine
119 *V5* **Pecheniz'ke Vodoskhovyshche** *Rus.* Pechenezhskoye Vodokhranilishche. ▣ E Ukraine
129 *U7* **Pechora** Respublika Komi, NW Russian Federation
129 *R6* **Pechora** ≈ NW Russian Federation
Pechora Bay *see* Pechorskaya Guba
Pechora Sea *see* Pechorskoye More
129 *S3* **Pechorskaya Guba** *Eng.* Pechora Bay. *bay* NW Russian Federation
125 *Ff6* **Pechorskoye More** *Eng.* Pechora Sea. *sea* NW Russian Federation
118 *E11* **Pecica** *Ger.* Petschka, *Hung.* Ópécska. Arad, W Romania
26 *K8* **Pecos** Texas, SW USA
27 *N11* **Pecos River** ≈ New Mexico/Texas, SW USA
113 *I25* **Pécs** *Ger.* Fünfkirchen; *Lat.* Sopianae. Baranya, SW Hungary
45 *T17* **Pedasí** Los Santos, S Panama
Pedde *see* Pedja
191 *O17* **Pedder, Lake** ◎ Tasmania, SE Australia
46 *M10* **Pedernales** SW Dominican Republic
57 *Q5* **Pedernales** Delta Amacuro, NE Venezuela
27 *R10* **Pedernales River** ≈ Texas, SW USA
64 *H6* **Pedernales, Salar de** *salt lake* N Chile
Pedhoulas *see* Pedoulás
57 *X11* **Pédima** *var.* Malavate. SW French Guiana
190 *F1* **Pedirka** South Australia
175 *T7* **Pediwang** Pulau Halmahera, E Indonesia
120 *I5* **Pedja** *var.* Pedja Jõgi, *Ger.* Pedde. ≈ E Estonia
Pedja Jõgi *see* Pedja
124 *N3* **Pedoulás** *var.* Pedhoulas. W Cyprus
61 *N18* **Pedra Azul** Minas Gerais, NE Brazil
106 *I3* **Pedrafita, Porto de** *var.* Puerto de Piedrafita. *pass* NW Spain
78 *E9* **Pedra Lume** Sal, NE Cape Verde
45 *P16* **Pedregal** Chiriquí, W Panama
56 *J4* **Pedregal** Falcón, N Venezuela
42 *L9* **Pedriceña** Durango, C Mexico
62 *L11* **Pedro Barros** São Paulo, S Brazil
41 *Q13* **Pedro Bay** Alaska, USA
64 *H4* **Pedro de Valdivia** *var.* Oficina Pedro de Valdivia. Antofagasta, N Chile
64 *P4* **Pedro Juan Caballero** Amambay, E Paraguay
65 *L15* **Pedro Luro** Buenos Aires, E Argentina
107 *O10* **Pedro Muñoz** Castilla-La Mancha, C Spain
161 *J22* **Pedro, Point** *headland* NW Sri Lanka
190 *K9* **Peebinga** South Australia
98 *J13* **Peebles** SE Scotland, UK
33 *S15* **Peebles** Ohio, N USA
98 *J12* **Peebles** *cultural region* SE Scotland, UK
20 *K13* **Peekskill** New York, NE USA
99 *I16* **Peel** W Isle of Man
14 *Ff4* **Peel** ≈ Northwest Territories/Yukon Territory, NW Canada
15 *I1* **Peel Point** *headland* Victoria Island, Northwest Territories, NW Canada
15 *K1* **Peel Sound** *passage* Northwest Territories, N Canada
102 *N9* **Peene** ≈ NE Germany
101 *K17* **Peer** Limburg, NE Belgium
12 *H14* **Pefferlaw** Ontario, S Canada
193 *I18* **Pegasus Bay** *bay* South Island, NZ
123 *Mm3* **Pégeia** *var.* Peyia. SW Cyprus
111 *V7* **Peggau** Steiermark, SE Austria
103 *L19* **Pegnitz** Bayern, SE Germany
103 *L19* **Pegnitz** ≈ SE Germany
107 *T11* **Pego** País Valenciano, E Spain
177 *G8* **Pegu** *var.* Bago. Pegu, SW Myanmar
177 *G7* **Pegu** ◈ *division* S Myanmar
176 *W7* **Pegun, Pulau** *island* Kepulauan Mapia, E Indonesia
201 *N13* **Pehleng** Pohnpei, E Micronesia
116 *M12* **Pehlivanköy** Kırklareli, NW Turkey
79 *R14* **Péhonko** C Benin
63 *B21* **Pehuajó** Buenos Aires, E Argentina
Pei-ching *see* Beijing/Beijing Shi
102 *J13* **Peine** Niedersachsen, C Germany
Pei-p'ing *see* Beijing/Beijing Shi
Peipsi Järv/Peipus-See *see* Peipus, Lake
120 *J5* **Peipus, Lake** *Est.* Peipsi Järv, *Ger.* Peipus-See, *Rus.* Chudskoye Ozero. ◎ Estonia/Russian Federation
117 *H19* **Peiraías** *prev.* Piraiévs, *Eng.* Piraeus. Attikí, C Greece
Peisern *see* Pyzdry
62 *I8* **Peixe, Rio do** ≈ S Brazil
61 *I16* **Peixoto de Azevedo** Mato Grosso, W Brazil
174 *J8* **Pejantan, Pulau** *island* W Indonesia
Pejë *see* Peć
114 *N11* **Pek** ≈ E Yugoslavia
178 *Ii7* **Pèk** *var.* Xieng Khouang; *prev.* Xiangkhoang. Xiangkhoang, N Laos
174 *Kk14* **Pekalongan** Jawa, C Indonesia
174 *Gg7* **Pekanbaru** *var.* Pakanbaru. Sumatera, W Indonesia
32 *L12* **Pekin** Illinois, N USA
Peking *see* Beijing/Beijing Shi
Pelabohan Kelang/Pelabuhan Kelang *see* Pelabuhan Klang
173 *G5* **Pelabuhan Klang** *var.* Kuala Pelabohan Kelang, Pelabohan Kelang, Pelabuhan Kelang, Port Klang, Port Swettenham. Selangor, Peninsular Malaysia
174 *J15* **Pelabuhan Ratu, Teluk** *bay* Jawa, SW Indonesia
123 *L12* **Pelagie, Isole** *island group* SW Italy
Pelagosa *see* Palagruža
24 *L5* **Pelahatchie** Mississippi, S USA
175 *N11* **Pelaihari** *var.* Pleihari. Borneo, C Indonesia
105 *U14* **Pelat, Mont** ▲ SE France
118 *F12* **Peleaga, Vârful** *prev.* Vîrful Peleaga. ▲ W Romania
Peleaga, Vîrful *see* Peleaga, Vârful
126 *K12* **Peleduy** Respublika Sakha (Yakutiya), NE Russian Federation
12 *C18* **Pelee Island** *island* Ontario, S Canada
47 *Q11* **Pelée, Montagne** ▲ N Martinique
12 *D18* **Pelee, Point** *headland* Ontario, S Canada
175 *R9* **Pelei** Pulau Peleng, N Indonesia
Peleliu *see* Beliliou
175 *R9* **Peleng, Pulau** *island* Kepulauan Banggai, N Indonesia
175 *Qq9* **Peleng, Selat** *strait* Sulawesi, C Indonesia
25 *T7* **Pelham** Georgia, SE USA
113 *E18* **Pelhřimov** *Ger.* Pilgram. Jižní Čechy, S Czech Republic
41 *W13* **Pelican** Chichagof Island, Alaska, USA
203 *Z3* **Pelican Lagoon** ◎ Kiritimati, E Kiribati
31 *U6* **Pelican Lake** ◎ Minnesota, N USA
31 *V3* **Pelican Lake** ◎ Minnesota, N USA
32 *L5* **Pelican Lake** ◎ Wisconsin, N USA
46 *G1* **Pelican Point** Grand Bahama Island, N Bahamas
85 *B19* **Pelican Point** *headland* W Namibia
31 *S6* **Pelican Rapids** Minnesota, N USA
Pelican State *see* Louisiana
9 *U13* **Pelikan Narrows** Saskatchewan, C Canada
117 *L18* **Pelinaío** ▲ Chíos, E Greece
Pelinnaeum *see* Pelinnaío
117 *E16* **Pelinnaío** *anc.* Pelinnaeum. *ruins* Thessalía, C Greece
115 *N20* **Pelister** ▲ SW FYR Macedonia
115 *G15* **Pelješac** *peninsula* S Croatia
94 *M12* **Pelkosenniemi** Lappi, NE Finland
31 *W15* **Pella** Iowa, C USA
116 *F13* **Pélla** *site of ancient city* Kentrikí Makedonía, N Greece
25 *Q3* **Pell City** Alabama, S USA
63 *A22* **Pellegrini** Buenos Aires, E Argentina
94 *K12* **Pello** Lappi, NW Finland
102 *G7* **Pellworm** *island* N Germany
8 *H6* **Pelly** ≈ Yukon Territory, NW Canada
15 *L3* **Pelly Bay** Northwest Territories, N Canada
8 *I8* **Pelly Mountains** ⛰ Yukon Territory, W Canada
Pélmonostor *see* Beli Manastir
39 *P13* **Pelona Mountain** ▲ New Mexico, SW USA
Peloponnese/Peloponnesus *see* Pelopónnisos
117 *E20* **Pelopónnisos** *Eng.* Peloponnese. ◈ *region* S Greece
117 *E20* **Pelopónnisos** *var.* Morea, *Eng.* Peloponnese; *anc.* Peloponnesus. *peninsula* S Greece
109 *L23* **Peloritani, Monti** *anc.* Pelorus and Neptunius. ⛰ Sicilia, Italy, C Mediterranean Sea
109 *M22* **Peloro, Capo** *var.* Punta del Faro. *headland* S Italy
Pelorus and Neptunius *see* Peloritani, Monti
63 *H17* **Pelotas** Rio Grande do Sul, S Brazil
63 *I14* **Pelotas, Rio** ≈ S Brazil

◆ Country
● Country Capital
◇ Dependent Territory
○ Dependent Territory Capital
◈ Administrative Region
✕ International Airport
▲ Mountain
⛰ Mountain Range
🌋 Volcano
≈ River
◎ Lake
▣ Reservoir

94 *K10* **Peltovuoma** *Lapp.* Bealdovuopmi. Lappi, N Finland
125 *F10* **Pelym** ≈ C Russian Federation
21 *R4* **Pemadumcook Lake** ◎ Maine, NE USA
174 *Kk14* **Pemalang** Jawa, C Indonesia
174 *K7* **Pemangkat** *var.* Pamangkat. Borneo, C Indonesia
Pemar *see* Paimio
173 *Ff5* **Pematangsiantar** Sumatera, W Indonesia
85 *Q14* **Pemba** *prev.* Port Amelia, Porto Amélia. Cabo Delgado, NE Mozambique
83 *J22* **Pemba** ◈ *region* E Tanzania
83 *K21* **Pemba** *island* E Tanzania
85 *Q14* **Pemba, Baia de** *inlet* NE Mozambique
83 *J21* **Pemba Channel** *channel* E Tanzania
188 *J14* **Pemberton** Western Australia
8 *M16* **Pemberton** British Columbia, SW Canada
31 *Q2* **Pembina** North Dakota, N USA
31 *Q2* **Pembina** ≈ Canada/USA
9 *P15* **Pembina** ≈ Alberta, SW Canada
176 *Xx15* **Pembre** Irian Jaya, E Indonesia
12 *K12* **Pembroke** Ontario, SE Canada
99 *H21* **Pembroke** SW Wales, UK
25 *W6* **Pembroke** Georgia, SE USA
23 *U11* **Pembroke** North Carolina, SE USA
23 *R7* **Pembroke** Virginia, NE USA
99 *H21* **Pembroke** *cultural region* SW Wales, UK
Pembuang, Sungai *see* Seruyan, Sungai
45 *S15* **Peña Blanca, Cerro** ▲ C Panama
106 *K8* **Peña de Francia, Sierra de la** ⛰ W Spain
106 *G6* **Penafiel** *var.* Peñafiel. Porto, N Portugal
107 *N6* **Peñafiel** Castilla-León, N Spain
107 *S8* **Peñagolosa** ▲ E Spain
107 *N7* **Peñalara, Pico de** ▲ C Spain
175 *Nn5* **Penambo, Banjaran** *var.* Banjaran Tama Abu, Penambo Range. ⛰ Indonesia/Malaysia
Penambo Range *see* Penambo, Banjaran
43 *O10* **Peña Nevada, Cerro** ▲ C Mexico
Penang *see* Pinang, Pulau, Peninsular Malaysia
Penang *see* Pinang
Penang *see* George Town
62 *J8* **Penápolis** São Paulo, S Brazil
106 *L7* **Peñaranda de Bracamonte** Castilla-León, N Spain
107 *S8* **Peñarroya** ▲ E Spain
106 *L12* **Peñarroya-Pueblonuevo** Andalucía, S Spain
99 *K22* **Penarth** S Wales, UK
106 *K1* **Peñas, Cabo de** *headland* N Spain
65 *F20* **Penas, Golfo de** *gulf* S Chile
Pen-ch'i *see* Benxi
81 *H14* **Pendé** *var.* Logone Oriental. ≈ Central African Republic/Chad
78 *I14* **Pendembu** E Sierra Leone
31 *R13* **Pender** Nebraska, C USA
Penderma *see* Bandırma
34 *K11* **Pendleton** Oregon, NW USA
34 *M7* **Pend Oreille, Lake** ◎ Idaho, NW USA
34 *M7* **Pend Oreille River** ≈ Idaho/Washington, NW USA
Pendzhikent *see* Panjakent
Peneius *see* Pineiós
106 *G8* **Penela** Coimbra, N Portugal
12 *G13* **Penetanguishene** Ontario, S Canada
157 *H15* **Penganga** ≈ C India
167 *T12* **P'engchia Yu** *island* N Taiwan
81 *M21* **Penge** Kasai Oriental, C Zaire
Penghu Archipelago/ P'enghu Ch'üntao/Penghu Islands *see* P'enghu Liehtao
167 *R14* **P'enghu Liehtao** *var.* P'enghu Ch'üntao, Penghu Islands, *Eng.* Penghu Archipelago, Pescadores, *Jap.* Hoko-guntō, Hoko-shotō. *island group* W Taiwan
Penghu Shuidao/P'enghu Shuitao *see* Pescadores Channel
167 *R4* **Penglai** *var.* Dengzhou. Shandong, E China
Peng-pu *see* Bengbu
Penhsihu *see* Benxi
Penibético, Sistema *see* Béticos, Sistemas
106 *F10* **Peniche** Leiria, W Portugal
175 *Nn16* **Penida, Nusa** *island* S Indonesia
Peninsular State *see* Florida
107 *T8* **Peñíscola** País Valenciano, E Spain
42 *M13* **Pénjamo** Guanajuato, C Mexico
Penki *see* Benxi
104 *F7* **Penmarch, Pointe de** *headland* NW France
109 *L15* **Penna, Ponta della** *headland* C Italy
109 *K14* **Penne** Abruzzi, C Italy
Penner *see* Penneru
161 *J18* **Penneru** *var.* Penner. ≈ C India
190 *I10* **Penneshaw** South Australia
20 *C14* **Penn Hills** Pennsylvania, NE USA
Penninae, Alpes/Pennine, Alpi *see* Pennine Alps
110 *D11* **Pennine Alps** *Fr.* Alpes Pennines, *It.* Alpi Pennine; *Lat.* Alpes Penninae. ⛰ Italy/Switzerland
Pennine Chain *see* Pennines
99 *L15* **Pennines** *var.* Pennine Chain. ⛰ N England, UK
Pennines, Alpes *see* Pennine Alps
23 *O8* **Pennington Gap** Virginia, NE USA
20 *I16* **Penns Grove** New Jersey, NE USA
20 *I16* **Pennsville** New Jersey, NE USA
20 *E14* **Pennsylvania** *off.* Commonwealth of Pennsylvania; also known as The Keystone State. ◈ *state* NE USA
20 *G10* **Penn Yan** New York, NE USA
128 *H16* **Peno** Tverskaya Oblast', W Russian Federation
21 *R7* **Penobscot Bay** *bay* Maine, NE USA
21 *S5* **Penobscot River** ≈ Maine, NE USA
190 *K12* **Penola** South Australia
42 *K9* **Peñón Blanco** Durango, C Mexico
190 *E7* **Penong** South Australia
45 *S16* **Penonomé** Coclé, C Panama
202 *L13* **Penrhyn** *atoll* N Cook Islands
199 *Kk10* **Penrhyn Basin** *undersea feature* C Pacific Ocean
191 *S9* **Penrith** New South Wales, SE Australia
99 *K15* **Penrith** NW England, UK
25 *O9* **Pensacola** Florida, SE USA
25 *O9* **Pensacola Bay** *bay* Florida, SE USA
205 *N7* **Pensacola Mountains** ⛰ Antarctica
190 *L12* **Penshurst** Victoria, SE Australia
197 *C12* **Pentecost** *Fr.* Pentecôte. *island* C Vanuatu
13 *V4* **Pentecôte** ≈ Québec, SE Canada
Pentecôte *see* Pentecost
13 *V4* **Pentecôte, Lac** ◎ Québec, SE Canada
15 *Gg16* **Penticton** British Columbia, SW Canada
98 *J6* **Pentland Firth** *strait* N Scotland, UK
98 *J12* **Pentland Hills** *hill range* S Scotland, UK
175 *Rr10* **Penu** Pulau Taliabu, E Indonesia
161 *H18* **Penukonda** Andhra Pradesh, E India
177 *G7* **Penwegon** Pegu, C Surinam
26 *M8* **Penwell** Texas, SW USA
99 *J21* **Pen y Fan** ▲ SE Wales, UK
99 *L16* **Pen-y-ghent** ▲ N England, UK
175 *T12* **Penyu, Kepulauan** *island group* E Indonesia
131 *O6* **Penza** Penzenskaya Oblast', W Russian Federation
99 *G25* **Penzance** SW England, UK
131 *N6* **Penzenskaya Oblast'** ◈ *province* W Russian Federation
127 *P7* **Penzhina** ≈ E Russian Federation
127 *N17* **Penzhinskaya Guba** *bay* E Russian Federation
Penzig *see* Pieńsk
38 *K13* **Peoria** Arizona, SW USA
32 *L12* **Peoria** Illinois, N USA
32 *L12* **Peoria Heights** Illinois, N USA
33 *N11* **Peotone** Illinois, N USA
20 *J11* **Pepacton Reservoir** ⊞ New York, NE USA
78 *I15* **Pepel** W Sierra Leone
32 *I6* **Pepin, Lake** ⊞ Minnesota/Wisconsin, N USA
101 *L20* **Pepinster** Liège, E Belgium
115 *L20* **Peqin** *var.* Peqini. Elbasan, C Albania
Peqini *see* Peqin
42 *D7* **Pequeña, Punta** *headland* W Mexico
174 *I11* **Perabumulih** *var.* Prabumulih. Sumatera, W Indonesia
174 *Gg4* **Perak** ◈ *state* Peninsular Malaysia
174 *Gg4* **Perak, Sungai** ≈ Peninsular Malaysia
107 *R7* **Perales del Alfambra** Aragón, NE Spain
117 *C15* **Pérama** *var.* Perama. Ípeiros, W Greece
94 *M13* **Perä-Posio** Lappi, NE Finland
13 *Z6* **Percé** Québec, SE Canada
13 *Z6* **Percé, Rocher** *island* Québec, S Canada
104 *L5* **Perche, Collines de** ⛰ N France
111 *X4* **Perchtoldsdorf** Niederösterreich, NE Austria
188 *L6* **Percival Lakes** *lakes* Western Australia
107 *T3* **Perdido, Monte** ▲ NE Spain
25 *O8* **Perdido River** ≈ Alabama/Florida, S USA
Perece Vela Basin *see* West Mariana Basin
118 *G7* **Perechyn** Zakarpats'ka Oblast', W Ukraine
56 *E10* **Pereira** Risaralda, W Colombia
62 *I7* **Pereira Barreto** São Paulo, S Brazil
61 *G15* **Pereirinha** Pará, N Brazil
131 *N10* **Perelazovskiy** Volgogradskaya Oblast', SW Russian Federation
131 *S7* **Perelyub** Saratovskaya Oblast', W Russian Federation
33 *P7* **Pere Marquette River** ≈ Michigan, N USA
Peremyshl *see* Przemyśl
118 *I5* **Peremyshlyany** L'vivs'ka Oblast', W Ukraine
Pereshchepino *see* Pereshchepyne
118 *L9* **Pereshchepyne** *Rus.* Pereshchepino. Dnipropetrovs'ka Oblast', E Ukraine
128 *L16* **Pereslavl'-Zalesskiy** Yaroslavskaya Oblast', W Russian Federation
119 *Y7* **Pereval's'k** Luhans'ka Oblast', E Ukraine
131 *U7* **Perevolotskiy** Orenburgskaya Oblast', W Russian Federation
127 *Nn16* **Pereyaslavka** Khabarovskiy Kray, SE Russian Federation
Pereyaslav-Khmel'nitskiy *see* Pereyaslav-Khmel'nyts'kyy
119 *Q5* **Pereyaslav-Khmel'nyts'kyy** *Rus.* Pereyaslav-Khmel'nitskiy. Kyyivs'ka Oblast', N Ukraine
111 *U4* **Perg** Oberösterreich, N Austria
63 *B19* **Pergamino** Buenos Aires, E Argentina
108 *G6* **Pergine Valsugana** *Ger.* Persen. Trentino-Alto Adige, N Italy
31 *S6* **Perham** Minnesota, N USA
95 *L16* **Perho** Vaasa, W Finland
118 *E11* **Periam** *Ger.* Perjamosch, *Hung.* Perjámos. Timiş, W Romania
13 *Q6* **Péribonca** ≈ Québec, SE Canada
10 *L11* **Péribonca, Lac** ◎ Québec, SE Canada
13 *Q6* **Péribonca, Petite Rivière** ≈ Québec, SE Canada
13 *Q7* **Péribonka** Québec, SE Canada
42 *I9* **Pericos** Sinaloa, C Mexico
174 *Kk7* **Perigi** Borneo, C Indonesia
104 *L12* **Périgueux** *anc.* Vesuna. Dordogne, SW France
56 *G5* **Perijá, Serranía de** ⛰ Columbia/Venezuela
117 *H17* **Peristéra** *island* Vóreioi Sporádes, Greece, Aegean Sea
65 *H20* **Perito Moreno** Santa Cruz, S Argentina
161 *G22* **Periyāl** *var.* Periyār. ≈ SW India
Periyār *see* Periyāl
161 *G23* **Periyār Lake** ◎ S India
Perjámos/Perjamosch *see* Periam
29 *O9* **Perkins** Oklahoma, C USA
118 *L7* **Perkivtsi** Chernivets'ka Oblast', W Ukraine
45 *U15* **Perlas, Archipiélago de las** *Eng.* Pearl Islands. *island group* SE Panama
45 *O10* **Perlas, Cayos de** *reef* SE Nicaragua
45 *N9* **Perlas, Laguna de** *Eng.* Pearl Lagoon. *lagoon* E Nicaragua
45 *N10* **Perlas, Punta de** *headland* E Nicaragua
102 *L11* **Perleberg** Brandenburg, N Germany
Perlepe *see* Prilep
173 *G2* **Perlis** ◈ *state* Peninsular Malaysia
129 *U14* **Perm'** *prev.* Molotov. Permskaya Oblast', NW Russian Federation
115 *M22* **Përmet** *var.* Përmeti, Prëmet. Gjirokastër, S Albania
Përmeti *see* Përmet
129 *U15* **Permskaya Oblast'** ◈ *province* NW Russian Federation
61 *P15* **Pernambuco** *off.* Estado de Pernambuco. ◈ *state* E Brazil
Pernambuco *see* Recife
Pernambuco Abyssal Plain *see* Pernambuco Plain
49 *Y6* **Pernambuco Plain** *var.* Pernambuco Abyssal Plain. *undersea feature* E Atlantic Ocean
67 *K15* **Pernambuco Seamounts** *undersea feature* C Atlantic Ocean
190 *H6* **Pernatty Lagoon** *salt lake* South Australia
Pernau *see* Pärnu
Pernauer Bucht *see* Pärnu Laht
Pērnava *see* Pärnu
116 *G9* **Pernik** *prev.* Dimitrovo. Sofiyska Oblast, W Bulgaria
95 *K20* **Perniö** *Swe.* Bjärnå. Turku-Pori, SW Finland
111 *X5* **Pernitz** Niederösterreich, E Austria
Pernov *see* Pärnu
105 *O3* **Péronne** Somme, N France
12 *L8* **Péronne, Lac** ◎ Québec, SE Canada
108 *A8* **Perosa Argentina** Piemonte, NE Italy
43 *Q14* **Perote** Veracruz-Llave, E Mexico
Pérouse *see* Perugia
203 *W15* **Pérouse, Bahía de la** *bay* Easter Island, Chile, E Pacific Ocean
Perovsk *see* Kzyl-Orda
105 *O17* **Perpignan** Pyrénées-Orientales, S France
115 *M20* **Përrenjas** *var.* Përrenjasi, Prenjas, Prenjasi. Elbasan, E Albania
Përrenjasi *see* Përrenjas
94 *O2* **Perriertoppen** ▲ C Svalbard
27 *S6* **Perrin** Texas, SW USA
25 *Y16* **Perrine** Florida, SE USA
39 *S12* **Perro, Laguna del** ◎ New Mexico, SW USA
104 *G5* **Perros-Guirec** Côtes d'Armor, NW France
25 *T9* **Perry** Florida, SE USA
25 *T5* **Perry** Georgia, SE USA
31 *U14* **Perry** Iowa, C USA
20 *E10* **Perry** New York, NE USA
29 *N9* **Perry** Oklahoma, C USA
29 *Q3* **Perry Lake** ⊞ Kansas, C USA
33 *R11* **Perrysburg** Ohio, N USA
27 *O1* **Perryton** Texas, SW USA
41 *O15* **Perryville** Alaska, USA
29 *U11* **Perryville** Arkansas, C USA
29 *Y6* **Perryville** Missouri, C USA
Persante *see* Parsęta
Persen *see* Pergine Valsugana
Pershay *see* Pyarshai
119 *V7* **Pershotravens'k** Dnipropetrovs'ka Oblast', E Ukraine
119 *W9* **Pershotravneve** Donets'ka Oblast', E Ukraine
Persia *see* Iran
147 *T5* **Persian Gulf** *var.* The Gulf, *Ar.* Khalīj al 'Arabī, *Per.* Khalīj-e Fars. *gulf* SW Asia
Persis *see* Fārs
97 *K22* **Perstorp** Kristianstad, S Sweden
143 *O14* **Pertek** Tunceli, C Turkey
191 *P16* **Perth** Tasmania, SE Australia
188 *I13* **Perth** *state capital* Western Australia
12 *L13* **Perth** Ontario, SE Canada
98 *J11* **Perth** C Scotland, UK
188 *I12* **Perth** ✈ Western Australia
98 *J10* **Perth** *cultural region* C Scotland, UK
181 *V10* **Perth Basin** *undersea feature* SE Indian Ocean
105 *S15* **Pertuis** Vaucluse, SE France
104 *E3* **Pertusato, Capo** *headland* Corse, France, C Mediterranean Sea
32 *L11* **Peru** Illinois, N USA
33 *P12* **Peru** Indiana, N USA
59 *E13* **Peru** *off.* Republic of Peru. ◆ *republic* W South America
Peru *see* Beru
200 *Oo10* **Peru Basin** *undersea feature* E Pacific Ocean
200 *Oo9* **Peru-Chile Trench** *undersea feature* E Pacific Ocean
114 *F13* **Perućko Jezero** ◎ S Croatia
108 *H13* **Perugia** *Fr.* Pérouse; *anc.* Perusia. Umbria, C Italy
Perugia, Lake of *see* Trasimeno, Lago
63 *D15* **Perugorría** Corrientes, NE Argentina
62 *M11* **Peruíbe** São Paulo, S Brazil
161 *B21* **Perumalpār** *reef* India, N Indian Ocean
Perusia *see* Perugia
101 *D20* **Péruwelz** Hainaut, SW Belgium
143 *R15* **Pervari** Siirt, SE Turkey
131 *O4* **Pervomaysk** Nizhegorodskaya Oblast', W Russian Federation
119 *X7* **Pervomays'k** Luhans'ka Oblast', E Ukraine
119 *P8* **Pervomays'k** *prev.* Ol'viopol'. Mykolayivs'ka Oblast', S Ukraine
119 *S12* **Pervomays'ke** Respublika Krym, S Ukraine
131 *V7* **Pervomayskiy** Orenburgskaya Oblast', W Russian Federation
130 *M6* **Pervomayskiy** Tambovskaya Oblast', W Russian Federation
119 *V6* **Pervomays'kyy** Kharkivs'ka Oblast', E Ukraine
125 *E10* **Pervoural'sk** Sverdlovskaya Oblast', C Russian Federation
127 *Pp12* **Pervyy Kuril'skiy Proliv** *strait* E Russian Federation
101 *I19* **Perwez** Walloon Brabant, C Belgium
108 *I11* **Pesaro** *anc.* Pisaurum. Marche, C Italy
37 *N9* **Pescadero** California, W USA
Pescadores *see* P'enghu Liehtao
167 *S14* **Pescadores Channel** *var.* Penghu Shuidao, P'enghu Shuitao. *channel* W Taiwan
109 *K14* **Pescara** *anc.* Aternum, Ostia Aterni. Abruzzi, C Italy
109 *K15* **Pescara** ≈ C Italy
108 *F11* **Pescia** Toscana, C Italy
110 *C8* **Peseux** Neuchâtel, W Switzerland
129 *P6* **Pesha** ≈ NW Russian Federation
155 *T5* **Peshāwar** North-West Frontier Province, N Pakistan
155 *T6* **Peshāwar** ✈ North-West Frontier Province, N Pakistan
115 *M19* **Peshkopi** *var.* Peshkopia, Peshkopija. Dibër, NE Albania
Peshkopia/Peshkopija *see* Peshkopi
116 *I11* **Peshtera** Plovdivska Oblast, SW Bulgaria
33 *N6* **Peshtigo** Wisconsin, N USA
33 *N6* **Peshtigo River** ≈ Wisconsin, N USA
Peski *see* Pyeski
129 *S13* **Peskovka** Kirovskaya Oblast', NW Russian Federation
105 *S8* **Pesmes** Haute-Saône, E France
106 *H6* **Peso da Régua** *var.* Pêso da Regua. Vila Real, N Portugal
42 *F5* **Pesqueira** Sonora, NW Mexico
104 *J13* **Pessac** Gironde, SW France
113 *J23* **Pest** *off.* Pest Megye. ◈ *county* C Hungary
128 *J14* **Pestovo** Novgorodskaya Oblast', W Russian Federation
42 *M15* **Petacalco, Bahía** *bay* W Mexico
Petach-Tikva/Petah Tiqva *see* Petah Tiqwa
144 *F10* **Petah Tiqwa** *var.* Petach-Tikva, Petah Tiqva. Tel Aviv, C Israel
95 *L17* **Petäjävesi** Keski-Suomi, C Finland
24 *M7* **Petal** Mississippi, S USA
117 *I19* **Petalioí** *island* C Greece
117 *H19* **Petalión, Kólpos** *gulf* E Greece
117 *J19* **Pétalo** ▲ Ándros, Kykládes, Greece, Aegean Sea
36 *M8* **Petaluma** California, W USA
101 *L25* **Pétange** Luxembourg, SW Luxembourg
56 *M5* **Petare** Miranda, N Venezuela
43 *N16* **Petatlán** Guerrero, S Mexico
85 *L14* **Petauke** Eastern, E Zambia
12 *J12* **Petawawa** Ontario, SE Canada
12 *J11* **Petawawa** ≈ Ontario, SE Canada
Petchaburi *see* Phetchaburi
44 *D2* **Petén** *off.* Departamento del Petén. ◈ *department* N Guatemala
44 *D2* **Petén Itzá, Lago** *var.* Lago de Flores. ◎ N Guatemala
32 *K7* **Petenwell Lake** ⊞ Wisconsin, N USA
12 *D6* **Peterbell** Ontario, S Canada
190 *I7* **Peterborough** South Australia
12 *I14* **Peterborough** Ontario, SE Canada
99 *N20* **Peterborough** *prev.* Medeshamstede. E England, UK
21 *N10* **Peterborough** New Hampshire, NE USA
98 *L8* **Peterhead** NE Scotland, UK
Peterhof *see* Luboń
199 *Mm16* **Peter I Island** ◇ *Norwegian dependency* Antarctica
204 *H9* **Peter I Island** *var.* Peter I øy. *island* Antarctica
Peter I øy *see* Peter I Island
99 *M14* **Peterlee** N England, UK
Peterlingen *see* Payerne
207 *P14* **Petermann Bjerg** ▲ C Greenland
9 *S12* **Peter Pond Lake** ◎ Saskatchewan, C Canada
41 *X13* **Petersburg** Mytkof Island, Alaska, USA
32 *K13* **Petersburg** Illinois, N USA
33 *N16* **Petersburg** Indiana, N USA
31 *Q3* **Petersburg** North Dakota, N USA
27 *N5* **Petersburg** Texas, SW USA
23 *V7* **Petersburg** Virginia, NE USA
23 *T4* **Petersburg** West Virginia, NE USA
102 *H12* **Petershagen** Nordrhein-Westfalen, NW Germany
57 *S9* **Peters Mine** *var.* Peter's Mine. N Guyana
109 *O21* **Petilia Policastro** Calabria, SW Italy
46 *M9* **Pétionville** S Haiti
47 *X6* **Petit-Bourg** Basse Terre, C Guadeloupe
13 *Y5* **Petit-Cap** Québec, SE Canada
47 *Y6* **Petit Cul-de-Sac Marin** *bay* C Guadeloupe
10 *K7* **Petite Rivière de la Baleine** ≈ Québec, NE Canada
46 *M9* **Petite-Rivière-de-l'Artibonite** C Haiti
181 *X16* **Petite Rivière Noire, Piton de la** ▲ C Mauritius
13 *R9* **Petite-Rivière-St-François** Québec, SE Canada
46 *L9* **Petit-Goâve** S Haiti
Petitjean *see* Sidi-Kacem
11 *N10* **Petit Lac Manicouagan** ◎ Québec, E Canada
21 *T7* **Petit Manan Point** *headland* Maine, NE USA
Petit Mécatina, Rivière du *see* Little Mecatina
9 *N10* **Petitot** ≈ Alberta/British Columbia, W Canada
47 *S12* **Petit Piton** ▲ SW Saint Lucia
Petit-Popo *see* Aného
Petit St-Bernard, Col du *see* Little Saint Bernard Pass
11 *O8* **Petitsikapau Lake** ◎ Newfoundland and Labrador, E Canada
94 *L11* **Petkula** Lappi, N Finland
43 *X12* **Peto** Yucatán, SE Mexico
64 *G10* **Petorca** Valparaíso, C Chile
33 *Q5* **Petoskey** Michigan, N USA
144 *G14* **Petra** *archaeological site* Ma'ān, W Jordan
Petra *see* Wādī Mūsā
117 *F14* **Pétras, Sténa** *pass* N Greece
127 *Nn18* **Petra Velikogo, Zaliv** *bay* SE Russian Federation
Petrel *see* Petrer
12 *K15* **Petre, Point** *headland* Ontario, SE Canada
107 *S12* **Petrer** *var.* Petrel. País Valenciano, E Spain
129 *U11* **Petretsovo** Permskaya Oblast', NW Russian Federation
116 *G12* **Petrich** Sofiyska Oblast, SW Bulgaria
197 *H3* **Petrie, Récif** *reef* N New Caledonia
39 *N11* **Petrified Forest** *prehistoric site* Arizona, SW USA
Petrikau *see* Piotrków Trybunalski
Petrikov *see* Pyetrykaw
118 *H12* **Petrila** *Hung.* Petrilla. Hunedoara, W Romania
Petrilla *see* Petrila
114 *E9* **Petrinja** Sisak-Moslavina, C Croatia
Petroaleksandrovsk *see* Türtkül
Petrőcz *see* Bački Petrovac
128 *G12* **Petrodvorets** *Fin.* Pietarhovi. Leningradskaya Oblast', NW Russian Federation
Petrograd *see* Sankt-Peterburg
Petrokov *see* Piotrków Trybunalski
56 *G6* **Petrólea** Norte de Santander, NE Colombia
12 *D16* **Petrolia** Ontario, S Canada
27 *S4* **Petrolia** Texas, SW USA
61 *O15* **Petrolina** Pernambuco, E Brazil
47 *T6* **Petrona, Punta** *headland* C Puerto Rico
Petropavl *see* Petropavlovsk
119 *V7* **Petropavlivka** Dnipropetrovs'ka Oblast', E Ukraine
151 *P6* **Petropavlovsk** *Kaz.* Petropavl. Severnyy Kazakhstan, N Kazakhstan
127 *Pp11* **Petropavlovsk-Kamchatskiy** Kamchatskaya Oblast', E Russian Federation
62 *P9* **Petrópolis** Rio de Janeiro, SE Brazil
118 *H12* **Petroşani** *var.* Petroşeni, *Ger.* Petroschen, *Hung.* Petrozsény. Hunedoara, W Romania
Petroschen/Petroşeni *see* Petroşani
Petroskoi *see* Petrozavodsk
114 *N12* **Petrovac** Serbia, E Yugoslavia
Petrovac/Petrovácz *see* Bački Petrovac
115 *J17* **Petrovac na Moru** Montenegro, SW Yugoslavia
119 *S8* **Petrove** Kirovohrads'ka Oblast', C Ukraine
115 *O18* **Petrovec** C FYR Macedonia
Petrovgrad *see* Zrenjanin
131 *P7* **Petrovsk** Saratovskaya Oblast', W Russian Federation
128 *J9* **Petrovskiy Yam** Respublika Kareliya, NW Russian Federation
Petrovsk-Port *see* Makhachkala
126 *K16* **Petrovsk-Zabaykal'skiy** Chitinskaya Oblast', S Russian Federation
131 *P9* **Petrov Val** Volgogradskaya Oblast', SW Russian Federation
128 *J11* **Petrozavodsk** *Fin.* Petroskoi. Respublika Kareliya, NW Russian Federation
Petrozsény *see* Petroşani
85 *D20* **Petrusdal** Hardap, C Namibia
119 *T7* **Petrykivka** Dnipropetrovs'ka Oblast', E Ukraine
Petsamo *see* Pechenga
Petschka *see* Pecica
Pettau *see* Ptuj
111 *S5* **Pettenbach** Oberösterreich, C Austria
27 *S13* **Pettus** Texas, SW USA
125 *F13* **Petukhovo** Kurganskaya Oblast', C Russian Federation
Petuna *see* Songyuan
111 *R4* **Peuerbach** Oberösterreich, N Austria
64 *G12* **Peumo** Libertador, C Chile
173 *Ee3* **Peusangan, Krueng** ≈ Sumatera, NW Indonesia
127 *O4* **Pevek** Chukotskiy Avtonomnyy Okrug, NE Russian Federation
29 *X5* **Pevely** Missouri, C USA
Peyia *see* Pégeia
104 *J15* **Peyrehorade** Landes, SW France
128 *J14* **Peza** ≈ NW Russian Federation
105 *P16* **Pézenas** Hérault, S France
113 *H20* **Pezinok** *Ger.* Bösing, *Hung.* Bazin. Západné Slovensko, SW Slovakia
103 *L22* **Pfaffenhofen an der Ilm** Bayern, SE Germany
110 *G7* **Pfäffikon** Schwyz, C Switzerland
103 *F20* **Pfälzer Wald** *hill range* W Germany
103 *N22* **Pfarrkirchen** Bayern, SE Germany
103 *G21* **Pforzheim** Baden-Württemberg, SW Germany
103 *H24* **Pfullendorf** Baden-Württemberg, S Germany
110 *K8* **Pfunds** Tirol, W Austria
103 *G19* **Pfungstadt** Hessen, W Germany
85 *L20* **Phalaborwa** Northern, NE South Africa
158 *E11* **Phalodi** Rājasthān, NW India
158 *E12* **Phalsund** Rājasthān, NW India
161 *E15* **Phaltan** Mahārāshtra, W India
178 *Hh7* **Phan** *var.* Muang Phan. Chiang Rai, NW Thailand
178 *H14* **Phangan, Ko** *island* SW Thailand
178 *Gg15* **Phang-Nga** *var.* Pang-Nga, Phangnga. Phangnga, SW Thailand
Phan Rang/Phanrang *see* Phan Rang-Thap Cham
178 *Kk13* **Phan Rang-Thap Cham** *var.* Phanrang, Phan Rang, Phan Rang Thap Cham. Ninh Thuân, S Vietnam
178 *Kk14* **Phan Ri** Binh Thuân, S Vietnam
178 *K14* **Phan Thiêt** Binh Thuân, S Vietnam
Pharnacia *see* Giresun
27 *S17* **Pharr** Texas, SW USA
Pharus *see* Hvar
178 *H16* **Phatthalung** *var.* Padalung, Patalung. Phatthalung, SW Thailand
178 *Hh7* **Phayao** *var.* Muang Phayao. Phayao, NW Thailand
9 *U10* **Phelps Lake** ◎ Saskatchewan, C Canada
23 *X9* **Phelps Lake** ◎ North Carolina, SE USA
25 *R5* **Phenix City** Alabama, S USA
178 *Jj8* **Pheo** Quang Binh, C Vietnam
Phet Buri *see* Phetchaburi
178 *H12* **Phetchaburi** *var.* Bejraburi, Petchaburi, Phet Buri. Phetchaburi, SW Thailand
178 *Hh9* **Phichit** *var.* Bichitra, Muang Phichit, Pichit. Phichit, C Thailand
24 *M5* **Philadelphia** Mississippi, S USA
20 *I7* **Philadelphia** New York, NE USA
20 *I16* **Philadelphia** Pennsylvania, NE USA
20 *I16* **Philadelphia** ✈ Pennsylvania, NE USA
Philadelphia *see* 'Ammān
30 *L10* **Philip** South Dakota, N USA
101 *H22* **Philippeville** Namur, S Belgium
Philippeville *see* Skikda
23 *S3* **Philippi** West Virginia, NE USA
Philippi *see* Fílippoi
205 *Y9* **Philippi Glacier** *glacier* Antarctica
198 *G7* **Philippine Basin** *undersea feature* W Pacific Ocean
133 *X12* **Philippine Plate** *tectonic feature*
179 *Q13* **Philippines** *off.* Republic of the Philippines. ◆ *republic* SE Asia
133 *X13* **Philippines** *island group* W Pacific Ocean
179 *S12* **Philippine Sea** *sea* W Pacific Ocean
198 *G7* **Philippine Trench** *undersea feature* W Philippine Sea
85 *H23* **Philippolis** Free State, C South Africa
Philippopolis *see* Plovdiv, Bulgaria
Philippopolis *see* Shahbā', Syria
47 *V9* **Philipsburg** Sint Maarten, N Netherlands Antilles
35 *P10* **Philipsburg** Montana, NW USA
41 *R6* **Philip Smith Mountains** ⛰ Alaska, USA
158 *H8* **Phillaur** Punjab, N India
191 *N13* **Phillip Island** *island* Victoria, SE Australia
27 *N2* **Phillips** Texas, SW USA
32 *K5* **Phillips** Wisconsin, N USA
28 *K3* **Phillipsburg** Kansas, C USA
20 *I14* **Phillipsburg** New Jersey, NE USA
23 *S7* **Philpott Lake** ⊞ Virginia, NE USA
Phintias *see* Licata
178 *Hh9* **Phitsanulok** *var.* Bisnulok, Muang Phitsanulok, Pitsanulok. Phitsanulok, C Thailand
Phlórina *see* Flórina
Phnom Penh *see* Phnum Penh
178 *J13* **Phnum Penh** *var.* Phnom Penh. ● (Cambodia) Phnum Penh, S Cambodia
178 *J12* **Phnum Tbêng Meanchey** Preăh Vihéar, N Cambodia
38 *K13* **Phoenix** *state capital* Arizona, SW USA
Phoenix Island *see* Rawaki
203 *R3* **Phoenix Islands** *island group* C Kiribati
20 *I15* **Phoenixville** Pennsylvania, NE USA
85 *K22* **Phofung** *var.* Mont-aux-Sources. ▲ N Lesotho
178 *I10* **Phon** Khon Kaen, E Thailand
178 *I5* **Phôngsali** *var.* Phong Saly. Phôngsali, N Laos
Phong Saly *see* Phôngsali
178 *I8* **Phônhông** C Laos
178 *J5* **Phô Rang** Lao Cai, N Vietnam
Phort Láirge, Cuan *see* Waterford Harbour
178 *Gg10* **Phra Chedi Sam Ong** Kanchanaburi, W Thailand
178 *Hh8* **Phrae** *var.* Muang Phrae, Prae. Phrae, NW Thailand
Phra Nakhon Si Ayutthaya *see* Ayutthaya
177 *G15* **Phra Thong, Ko** *island* SW Thailand
Phu Cương *see* Thu Dâu Một
177 *G16* **Phuket** *var.* Bhuket, Puket, *Mal.* Ujung Salang; *prev.* Junkseylon, Salang. Phuket, SW Thailand
177 *G16* **Phuket** ✈ Phuket, SW Thailand
177 *G16* **Phuket, Ko** *island* SW Thailand
160 *N12* **Phulabāni** *prev.* Phulbani. Orissa, E India
Phulbani *see* Phulabāni
178 *K10* **Phu Lôc** Th,a Thiên-Huê, C Vietnam
178 *J14* **Phumĭ Banam** Prey Vêng, S Cambodia
178 *Ii13* **Phumĭ Chŏâm** Kâmpóng Spœ, SW Cambodia
178 *Jj11* **Phumĭ Kalêng** Stœng Trêng, NE Cambodia
178 *J12* **Phumĭ Kâmpóng Trâbêk** *prev.* Phum Kompong Trabek. Kâmpóng Thum, C Cambodia
178 *Ii12* **Phumĭ Koŭk Kduŏch** Bătdâmbâng, NW Cambodia
178 *K12* **Phumĭ Labăng** Rôtânôkiri, NE Cambodia
178 *J11* **Phumĭ Mlu Prey** Preăh Vihéar, N Cambodia
178 *Ii11* **Phumĭ Moŭng** Siĕmréab, NW Cambodia
178 *Ii13* **Phumĭ Prâmaôy** Poŭthĭsăt, W Cambodia
178 *I14* **Phumĭ Samĭt** Kaôh Kông, SW Cambodia
178 *Ii11* **Phumĭ Sâmraông** *prev.* Phum Samrong. Siĕmréab, NW Cambodia
178 *Jj12* **Phumĭ Siĕmbok** Stœng Trêng, N Cambodia
178 *Jj12* **Phumĭ Thalabârĭvăt** Stœng Trêng, N Cambodia
178 *Ii14* **Phumĭ Veal Renh** Kâmpôt, SW Cambodia
178 *I13* **Phumĭ Yeay Sên** Kaôh Kông, SW Cambodia
Phum Kompong Trabek *see* Phumĭ Kâmpóng Trâbêk
Phum Samrong *see* Phumĭ Sâmraông
178 *Kk11* **Phu My** Binh Đinh, C Vietnam
178 *J15* **Phung Hiêp** Cân Thơ, S Vietnam
159 *T12* **Phuntsholing** SW Bhutan
178 *J15* **Phươc Long** Minh Hai, S Vietnam
178 *Ii14* **Phu Quôc, Đao** *var.* Phu Quoc Island. *island* S Vietnam
Phu Quoc Island *see* Phu Quôc, Đao
178 *J6* **Phu Tho** Vinh Phu, N Vietnam
Phu Vinh *see* Tra Vinh
201 *T13* **Piaanu Pass** *passage* Chuuk Islands, C Micronesia
108 *E8* **Piacenza** *Fr.* Paisance; *anc.* Placentia. Emilia-Romagna, N Italy
109 *K14* **Pianella** Abruzzi, C Italy
109 *M15* **Pianosa, Isola** *island* Archipelago Toscano, C Italy
176 *Vv11* **Piar** Irian Jaya, E Indonesia
47 *U14* **Piarco** *var.* Port of Spain. ✈ (Port-of-Spain) Trinidad, Trinidad and Tobago
112 *M12* **Piaseczno** Warszawa, C Poland
118 *I15* **Piatra** Teleorman, S Romania
118 *L10* **Piatra-Neamţ** *Hung.* Karácsonkő. Neamţ, NE Romania
Piauhy *see* Piauí
61 *N15* **Piauí** *off.* Estado do Piauí; *prev.* Piauhy. ◈ *state* E Brazil
108 *I7* **Piave** ≈ NE Italy
109 *K24* **Piazza Armerina** *var.* Chiazza. Sicilia, Italy, C Mediterranean Sea
83 *G14* **Pibor** *Amh.* Pībor Wenz. ≈ Ethiopia/Sudan
83 *G14* **Pibor Post** Jonglei, SE Sudan
Pībor Wenz *see* Pibor
Pibrans *see* Příbram
38 *K11* **Picacho Butte** ▲ Arizona, SW USA
42 *D4* **Picachos, Cerro** ▲ NW Mexico
105 *O4* **Picardie** *Eng.* Picardy. ◈ *region* N France
Picardy *see* Picardie
24 *L8* **Picayune** Mississippi, S USA
Piccolo San Bernardo, Colle di *see* Little Saint Bernard Pass
64 *K5* **Pichanal** Salta, N Argentina
153 *P12* **Pichandar** W Tajikistan
29 *R8* **Picher** Oklahoma, C USA

◆ Country · ● Country Capital · ◇ Dependent Territory · ○ Dependent Territory Capital · ◈ Administrative Region · ✈ International Airport · ▲ Mountain · ⛰ Mountain Range · Volcano · ≈ River · ◎ Lake · ⊞ Reservoir

64 G12 **Pichilemu** Libertador, C Chile
42 F9 **Pichilingue** Baja California Sur, W Mexico
58 B6 **Pichincha** ◆ *province* N Ecuador
58 C6 **Pichincha** ▲ N Ecuador
Pichit *see* Phichit
43 U15 **Pichucalco** Chiapas, SE Mexico
24 L5 **Pickens** Mississippi, S USA
23 O11 **Pickens** South Carolina, SE USA
12 G11 **Pickerel** ≈ Ontario, S Canada
12 H15 **Pickering** Ontario, S Canada
99 N16 **Pickering** N England, UK
33 S13 **Pickerington** Ohio, N USA
10 C10 **Pickle Lake** Ontario, C Canada
31 P12 **Pickstown** South Dakota, N USA
27 V6 **Pickton** Texas, SW USA
25 N1 **Pickwick Lake** ▣ S USA
66 N2 **Pico** *var.* Ilha do Pico. *island* Azores, Portugal, NE Atlantic Ocean
65 J19 **Pico de Salamanca** Chubut, SE Argentina
1 P9 **Pico Fracture Zone** *tectonic feature* NW Atlantic Ocean
Pico, Ilha do *see* Pico
61 O14 **Picos** Piauí, E Brazil
65 I20 **Pico Truncado** Santa Cruz, SE Argentina
191 S9 **Picton** New South Wales, SE Australia
12 K15 **Picton** Ontario, SE Canada
193 K14 **Picton** Marlborough, South Island, NZ
65 H15 **Pićun Leufú, Arroyo** ≈ SW Argentina
Pidálion *see* Gkréko, Akrotíri
161 K25 **Pidurutalagala** ▲ S Sri Lanka
118 K6 **Pidvolochys'k** Ternopil's'ka Oblast', W Ukraine
109 K16 **Piedimonte Matese** Campania, S Italy
29 X7 **Piedmont** Missouri, C USA
23 P11 **Piedmont** South Carolina, SE USA
19 Q12 **Piedmont** *escarpment* E USA
Piedmont *see* Piemonte
33 U13 **Piedmont Lake** ▣ Ohio, N USA
106 M11 **Piedrabuena** Castilla-La Mancha, C Spain
Piedrafita, Puerto de *see* Pedrafita, Porto de
106 L8 **Piedrahita** Castilla-León, N Spain
43 N6 **Piedras Negras** *var.* Ciudad Porfirio Díaz. Coahuila de Zaragoza, NE Mexico
63 E21 **Piedras, Punta** *headland* E Argentina
59 I14 **Piedras, Río de las** ≈ E Peru
113 J16 **Piekary Śląskie** Katowice, S Poland
95 M17 **Pieksämäki** Mikkeli, SE Finland
111 V5 **Pielach** ≈ NE Austria
95 M16 **Pielavesi** Kuopio, C Finland
95 N16 **Pielinen** *var.* Pielisjärvi. ◎ E Finland
Pielisjärvi *see* Pielinen
108 A8 **Piemonte** *Eng.* Piedmont. ◆ *region* NW Italy
113 L18 **Pieniny** ⛰ S Poland
113 E14 **Pieńsk** *Ger.* Penzig. Jelenia Góra, SW Poland
31 Q13 **Pierce** Nebraska, C USA
9 R14 **Pierceland** Saskatchewan, C Canada
117 E14 **Piéria** ⛰ N Greece
31 N10 **Pierre** *state capital* South Dakota, N USA
104 K16 **Pierrefitte-Nestalas** Hautes-Pyrénées, S France
105 R14 **Pierrelatte** Drôme, E France
13 P11 **Pierreville** Québec, SE Canada
13 O7 **Pierriche** ≈ Québec, SE Canada
113 H20 **Piešt'any** *Ger.* Pistyan, *Hung.* Pöstyén. Západné Slovensko, W Slovakia
111 X5 **Piesting** ≈ E Austria
Pietarhovi *see* Petrodvorets
Pietari *see* Sankt-Peterburg
Pietarsaari *see* Jakobstad
85 K23 **Pietermaritzburg** *var.* Maritzburg. KwaZulu/Natal, E South Africa
85 K20 **Pietersburg** Northern, NE South Africa
109 K24 **Pietraperzia** Sicilia, Italy, C Mediterranean Sea
109 N22 **Pietra Spada, Passo della** *pass* SW Italy
85 K22 **Piet Retief** Mpumalanga, E South Africa
118 I9 **Pietrosul, Vârful** *prev.* Vîrful Pietrosu. ▲ N Romania
118 J10 **Pietrosul, Vârful** *prev.* Vîrful Pietrosu. ▲ N Romania
Pietrosu, Vîrful *see* Pietrosul, Vârful
108 I6 **Pieve di Cadore** Veneto, NE Italy
12 C18 **Pigeon Bay** *lake bay* Ontario, S Canada
29 X8 **Piggott** Arkansas, C USA
85 L21 **Piggs Peak** NW Swaziland
Pigs, Bay of *see* Cochinos, Bahía de
63 A23 **Pigüé** Buenos Aires, E Argentina
43 O12 **Piguícas** ▲ C Mexico
200 Qq15 **Piha Passage** *passage* S Tonga
Pihkva Järv *see* Pskov, Lake
95 N18 **Pihlajavesi** ◎ SE Finland
95 J18 **Pihlava** Turku-Pori, SW Finland
95 L16 **Pihtipudas** Keski-Suomi, C Finland
42 L14 **Pihuamo** Jalisco, SW Mexico
201 U11 **Piis Moen** *var.* Pis. *atoll* Chuuk Islands, C Micronesia
43 U17 **Pijijiapán** Chiapas, SE Mexico
100 G12 **Pijnacker** Zuid-Holland, W Netherlands
44 H5 **Pijol, Pico** ▲ NW Honduras
Pikaar *see* Bikar Atoll
128 I13 **Pikalevo** Leningradskaya Oblast', NW Russian Federation
196 M15 **Pikelot** *island* Caroline Islands, C Micronesia
32 M5 **Pike River** ≈ Wisconsin, N USA
39 T5 **Pikes Peak** ▲ Colorado, C USA
23 P6 **Pikeville** Kentucky, S USA
22 L9 **Pikeville** Tennessee, S USA
Pikinni *see* Bikini Atoll
81 H18 **Pikounda** La Sangha, C Congo
112 G9 **Piła** *Ger.* Schneidemühl. Piła, NW Poland
112 G10 **Piła** *off.* Województwo Pilski, *Ger.* Schneidemühl. ◆ *province* NW Poland
64 N6 **Pilagá, Riacho** ≈ NE Argentina
63 D20 **Pilar** Buenos Aires, E Argentina
64 N7 **Pilar** *var.* Villa del Pilar. Ñeembucú, S Paraguay
64 N6 **Pilcomayo, Río** ≈ C South America
153 R12 **Pildon** *Rus.* Pil'don. C Tajikistan
Piles *see* Pylés
Pilgram *see* Pelhřimov
179 Q11 **Pili** Luzon, N Philippines
158 L10 **Pīlībhīt** Uttar Pradesh, N India
112 M13 **Pilica** ≈ C Poland
117 G16 **Pílio** ⛰ C Greece
113 J22 **Pilisvörösvár** Pest, N Hungary
67 G15 **Pillar Bay** *bay* Ascension Island, C Atlantic Ocean
191 P17 **Pillar, Cape** *headland* Tasmania, SE Australia
Pillau *see* Baltiysk
191 R5 **Pilliga** New South Wales, SE Australia
46 H8 **Pilón** Granma, E Cuba
Pilos *see* Pýlos
9 W17 **Pilot Mound** Manitoba, S Canada
23 S8 **Pilot Mountain** North Carolina, SE USA
41 O14 **Pilot Point** Alaska, USA
27 T5 **Pilot Point** Texas, SW USA
34 K11 **Pilot Rock** Oregon, NW USA
40 M11 **Pilot Station** Alaska, USA
Pilsen *see* Plzeň
Pilski, Województwo *see* Piła
113 K18 **Pilsko** ▲ N Slovakia
Pilten *see* Piltene
120 D8 **Piltene** *Ger.* Pilten. Ventspils, W Latvia
113 M16 **Pilzno** Tarnów, SE Poland
Pilzno *see* Plzeň
39 N14 **Pima** Arizona, SW USA
60 H13 **Pimenta** Pará, N Brazil
61 F16 **Pimenta Bueno** Rondônia, W Brazil
58 B11 **Pimentel** Lambayeque, W Peru
107 S6 **Pina** Aragón, NE Spain
121 I20 **Pina** *Rus.* Pina. ≈ SW Belarus
42 E2 **Pinacate, Sierra del** ▲ NW Mexico
65 H22 **Pináculo, Cerro** ▲ S Argentina
203 X11 **Pinaki** *atoll* Îles Tuamotu, E French Polynesia
39 N15 **Pinaleno Mountains** ⛰ Arizona, SW USA
179 Pp12 **Pinamalayan** Mindoro, N Philippines
174 Kk8 **Pinang** Borneo, C Indonesia
173 G3 **Pinang** *var.* Penang. ◆ *state* Peninsular Malaysia
Pinang *see* Pinang, Pulau, Peninsular Malaysia
Pinang *see* George Town
173 G3 **Pinang, Pulau** *var.* Penang, Pinang; *prev.* Prince of Wales Island. *island* Peninsular Malaysia
46 B5 **Pinar del Río** Pinar del Río, W Cuba
116 N11 **Pınarhisar** Kırklareli, NW Turkey
179 P10 **Pinatubo, Mount** Ѫ Luzon, N Philippines
9 Y16 **Pinawa** Manitoba, S Canada
9 Q17 **Pincher Creek** Alberta, SW Canada
32 L16 **Pinckneyville** Illinois, N USA
Pîncota *see* Pâncota
113 L15 **Pińczów** Kielce, S Poland
155 U7 **Pind Dādan Khān** Punjab, E Pakistan
Píndhos/Píndhos Óros *see* Píndos
155 V8 **Pindi Bhattiān** Punjab, E Pakistan
155 U6 **Pindi Gheb** Punjab, E Pakistan
117 D15 **Píndos** *var.* Píndhos Óros, *Eng.* Pindus Mountains; *prev.* Píndhos. ⛰ C Greece
Pindus Mountains *see* Píndos
20 J16 **Pine Barrens** *physical region* New Jersey, NE USA
29 V12 **Pine Bluff** Arkansas, C USA
25 X11 **Pine Castle** Florida, SE USA
31 V7 **Pine City** Minnesota, N USA
189 P2 **Pine Creek** Northern Territory, N Australia
37 V4 **Pine Creek** ≈ Nevada, W USA
20 F13 **Pine Creek** ≈ Pennsylvania, NE USA
29 Q13 **Pine Creek Lake** ▣ Oklahoma, C USA
35 T15 **Pinedale** Wyoming, C USA
9 X15 **Pine Dock** Manitoba, S Canada
9 Y16 **Pine Falls** Manitoba, S Canada
37 R10 **Pine Flat Lake** ▣ California, W USA
129 N8 **Pinega** Arkhangel'skaya Oblast', NW Russian Federation
129 N8 **Pinega** ≈ NW Russian Federation
13 N12 **Pine Hill** Québec, SE Canada
9 T12 **Pinehouse Lake** ◎ Saskatchewan, C Canada
23 T10 **Pinehurst** North Carolina, SE USA
117 D19 **Pineiós** ≈ S Greece
117 E16 **Pineiós** *var.* Piniós; *anc.* Peneius. ≈ C Greece
31 W10 **Pine Island** Minnesota, N USA
25 V15 **Pine Island** *island* Florida, SE USA
204 K10 **Pine Island Glacier** *glacier* Antarctica
27 X9 **Pineland** Texas, SW USA
25 V13 **Pinellas Park** Florida, SE USA
8 M13 **Pine Pass** *pass* British Columbia, W Canada
15 I9 **Pine Point** Northwest Territories, W Canada
30 K12 **Pine Ridge** South Dakota, N USA
31 U6 **Pine River** Minnesota, N USA
33 Q8 **Pine River** ≈ Michigan, N USA
32 M4 **Pine River** ≈ Wisconsin, N USA
108 A8 **Pinerolo** Piemonte, NE Italy
27 W6 **Pines, Lake O' the** ▣ Texas, SW USA
Pines, The Isle of the *see* Juventud, Isla de la
Pine Tree State *see* Maine
23 N7 **Pineville** Kentucky, S USA
24 H7 **Pineville** Louisiana, S USA
29 R8 **Pineville** Missouri, C USA
23 R10 **Pineville** North Carolina, SE USA
23 Q6 **Pineville** West Virginia, NE USA
35 V8 **Piney Buttes** *physical region* Montana, NW USA
169 W9 **Ping'an** Jilin, NE China
166 H14 **Pingbian** *var.* Pingbian Miaozu Zizhixian. Yunnan, SW China
163 S9 **Pingdingshan** Henan, C China
167 R4 **Pingdu** Shandong, E China
201 W16 **Pingelap Atoll** *atoll* Caroline Islands, E Micronesia
166 K14 **Pingguo** Guangxi Zhuangzu Zizhiqu, S China
167 Q13 **Pinghe** Fujian, SE China
P'ing-hsiang *see* Pingxiang
167 N10 **Pingjiang** Hunan, S China
Pingkiang *see* Harbin
166 L8 **Pingli** Shaanxi, C China
165 W10 **Pingliang** *var.* P'ing-liang. Gansu, C China
165 W8 **Pingluo** Ningxia, N China
Pingma *see* Tiandong
178 H9 **Ping, Mae Nam** ≈ W Thailand
167 Q1 **Pingquan** Hebei, E China
31 P5 **Pingree** North Dakota, N USA
Pingsiang *see* Pingxiang
167 S14 **P'ingtung** *Jap.* Heitō. S Taiwan
166 I8 **Pingwu** Sichuan, C China
166 J15 **Pingxiang** Guangxi Zhuangzu Zizhiqu, S China
167 O11 **Pingxiang** *var.* P'ing-hsiang; *prev.* Pingsiang. Jiangxi, S China
167 S11 **Pingyang** Zhejiang, SE China
167 P5 **Pingyi** Shandong, E China
167 P5 **Pingyin** Shandong, E China
62 H13 **Pinhalzinho** Santa Catarina, S Brazil
62 I12 **Pinhão** Paraná, S Brazil
63 H17 **Pinheiro Machado** Rio Grande do Sul, S Brazil
106 I7 **Pinhel** Guarda, N Portugal
Piniós *see* Pineiós
195 R10 **Pinipel Island** *island* Green Islands, NE PNG
173 Ff8 **Pini, Pulau** *island* Kepulauan Batu, W Indonesia
111 Y7 **Pinka** ≈ SE Austria
111 X7 **Pinkafeld** Burgenland, SE Austria
Pinkiang *see* Harbin
8 M12 **Pink Mountain** British Columbia, W Canada
177 G3 **Pinlebu** Sagaing, N Burma
40 J12 **Pinnacle Island** *island* Alaska, USA
188 I12 **Pinnacles, The** *tourist site* Western Australia
190 K10 **Pinnaroo** South Australia
Pinne *see* Pniewy
102 I9 **Pinneberg** Schleswig-Holstein, N Germany
117 I15 **Pínnes, Ákra** *headland* N Greece
Pinos, Isla de *see* Juventud, Isla de la
37 R14 **Pinos, Mount** ▲ California, W USA
107 R12 **Pinoso** País Valenciano, E Spain
107 N14 **Pinos-Puente** Andalucía, S Spain
43 Q17 **Pinotepa Nacional** *var.* Santiago Pinotepa Nacional. Oaxaca, SE Mexico
116 F13 **Pínovo** ▲ N Greece
197 K7 **Pins, Île des** *var.* Kunyé. *island* E New Caledonia
121 I20 **Pinsk** *Pol.* Pińsk. Brestskaya Voblasts', SW Belarus
12 D18 **Pins, Pointe aux** *headland* Ontario, S Canada
59 B16 **Pinta, Isla** *var.* Abingdon. *island* Galapagos Islands, Ecuador, E Pacific Ocean
129 Q12 **Pinyug** Kirovskaya Oblast', NW Russian Federation
59 B17 **Pinzón, Isla** *var.* Duncan Island. *island* Galapagos Islands, Ecuador, E Pacific Ocean
37 Y8 **Pioche** Nevada, W USA
108 F13 **Piombino** Toscana, C Italy
1 C9 **Pioneer Fracture Zone** *tectonic feature* NE Pacific Ocean
126 Ii2 **Pioner, Ostrov** *island* Severnaya Zemlya, N Russian Federation
120 A13 **Pionerskiy** *Ger.* Neukuhren. Kaliningradskaya Oblast', W Russian Federation
112 N13 **Pionki** Radom, C Poland
192 L9 **Piopio** Waikato, North Island, NZ
113 J14 **Piotrków** *off.* Województwo Piotrkowskie. ◆ *province* C Poland
Piotrkowskie, Województwo *see* Piotrków
112 K13 **Piotrków Trybunalski** *Ger.* Petrikau, *Rus.* Petrokov. Piotrków, C Poland
158 F12 **Pīpār Road** Rājasthān, N India
117 I16 **Pipéri** *island* Vóreioi Sporádes, Greece, Aegean Sea
31 S10 **Pipestone** Minnesota, N USA
10 C9 **Pipestone** ≈ Ontario, C Canada
63 E21 **Pipinas** Buenos Aires, E Argentina
155 T7 **Piplān** *prev.* Liaqatabad. Punjab, E Pakistan
13 R5 **Pipmuacan, Réservoir** ▣ Québec, SE Canada
Piqan *see* Shanshan
33 R13 **Piqua** Ohio, N USA
107 P5 **Piqueras, Puerto de** *pass* N Spain
62 H11 **Piquiri, Rio** ≈ S Brazil
62 L9 **Piracicaba** São Paulo, S Brazil
Piraeus/Piraiévs *see* Peiraías
62 K10 **Piraju** São Paulo, S Brazil
62 K9 **Pirajuí** São Paulo, S Brazil
65 G21 **Pirámide, Cerro** ▲ S Chile
Piramiva *see* Pyramíva
111 R13 **Piran** *It.* Pirano. SW Slovenia
64 N6 **Pirané** Formosa, N Argentina
61 J18 **Piranhas** Goiás, S Brazil
Pirano *see* Piran
148 I4 **Pīrānshahr** Āžarbāyjān-e Bākhtarī, NW Iran
61 M19 **Pirapora** Minas Gerais, NE Brazil
62 I9 **Pirapòzinho** São Paulo, S Brazil
63 G19 **Piraraja** Lavalleja, S Uruguay
62 L9 **Pirassununga** São Paulo, S Brazil
47 V6 **Pirata, Monte** ▲ E Puerto Rico
62 I13 **Piratuba** Santa Catarina, S Brazil
116 I9 **Pirdop** *prev.* Strednogorie. Sofiyska Oblast, W Bulgaria
203 P7 **Pirea** Tahiti, W French Polynesia
61 K18 **Pirenópolis** Goiás, S Brazil
159 S13 **Pirganj** Rajshahi, NW Bangladesh
Pirgi *see* Pyrgí
Pírgos *see* Pýrgos
63 F20 **Piriápolis** Maldonado, S Uruguay
116 G11 **Pirin** ⛰ SW Bulgaria
Pirineos *see* Pyrenees
60 N13 **Piripiri** Piauí, E Brazil
120 H4 **Pirita** *var.* Pirita Jõgi. ≈ NW Estonia
Pirita Jõgi *see* Pirita
56 J6 **Píritu** Portuguesa, N Venezuela
95 L18 **Pirkkala** Häme, SW Finland
103 F20 **Pirmasens** Rheinland-Pfalz, SW Germany
103 P16 **Pirna** Sachsen, E Germany
Piroe *see* Piru
115 Q15 **Pirot** Serbia, SE Yugoslavia
158 H6 **Pīr Panjāl Range** ⛰ NE India
45 W16 **Pirre, Cerro** ▲ SE Panama
143 Y11 **Pirsaat** *Rus.* Pirsagat. ≈ E Azerbaijan
Pirsagat *see* Pirsaat
149 V11 **Pīr Shūrān, Selseleh-ye** ⛰ SE Iran
94 M12 **Pirttikoski** Lappi, N Finland
Pirttikylä *see* Pörtom
175 T11 **Piru** *prev.* Piroe. Pulau Seram, E Indonesia
Piryatin *see* Pyryatyn
Pis *see* Piis Moen
108 F11 **Pisa** *var.* Pisae. Toscana, C Italy
Pisae *see* Pisa
176 Uu10 **Pisang, Kepulauan** *island group* E Indonesia
176 Xx11 **Pisapa** Irian Jaya, E Indonesia
201 V12 **Pisar** *atoll* Chuuk Islands, C Micronesia
Pisaurum *see* Pesaro
12 M10 **Piscatosine, Lac** ◎ Québec, SE Canada
111 W7 **Pischeldorf** Steiermark, SE Austria
Pischk *see* Simeria
109 L19 **Pisciotta** Campania, S Italy
59 E16 **Pisco** Ica, SW Peru
118 G9 **Pişcolt** *Hung.* Piskolt. Satu Mare, NW Romania
59 E16 **Pisco, Río** ≈ E Peru
113 C18 **Písek** Jižní Čechy, SW Czech Republic
33 R14 **Pisgah** Ohio, N USA
164 F9 **Pishan** *var.* Guma. Xinjiang Uygur Zizhiqu, NW China
119 N8 **Pishchanka** Vinnyts'ka Oblast', C Ukraine
115 K21 **Pishë** Fier, SW Albania
149 X14 **Pīshīn** Sīstān va Balūchestān, SE Iran
155 O9 **Pishīn** North-West Frontier Province, NW Pakistan
155 N11 **Pishin Lora** *var.* Psein Lora, *Pash.* Pseyn Bowr. ≈ SW Pakistan
Pishma *see* Pizhma
Pishpek *see* Bishkek
175 Q13 **Pising** Pulau Kabaena, C Indonesia
Pisino *see* Pazin
Piski *see* Simeria
Piskolt *see* Pişcolt
153 Q9 **Piskom** *Rus.* Pskem. ≈ E Uzbekistan
Piskom Tizmasi *see* Pskemskiy Khrebet
37 P13 **Pismo Beach** California, W USA
79 P12 **Pissila** C Burkina
64 H8 **Pissis, Monte** ▲ N Argentina
43 X12 **Piste** Yucatán, E Mexico
109 O18 **Pisticci** Basilicata, S Italy
108 F11 **Pistoia** *anc.* Pistoria, Pistoriæ. Toscana, C Italy
34 E15 **Pistol River** Oregon, NW USA
Pistoria/Pistoriæ *see* Pistoia
13 U5 **Pistuacanis** ≈ Québec, SE Canada
Pistyan *see* Piešt'any
106 M5 **Pisuerga** ≈ N Spain
112 N8 **Pisz** *Ger.* Johannisburg. Suwałki, NE Poland
78 I13 **Pita** Moyenne-Guinée, NW Guinea
56 D12 **Pitalito** Huila, S Colombia
62 I11 **Pitanga** Paraná, S Brazil
190 M9 **Pitarpunga Lake** *salt lake* New South Wales, SE Australia
199 M11 **Pitcairn Island** *island* S Pitcairn Islands
199 M11 **Pitcairn Islands** ◇ *UK dependent territory* C Pacific Ocean
95 J14 **Piteå** Norrbotten, N Sweden
94 I13 **Piteälven** ≈ N Sweden
118 I13 **Pitești** Argeș, S Romania
Pithagorio *see* Pythagóreio
188 I12 **Pithara** Western Australia
105 N6 **Pithiviers** Loiret, C France
158 L9 **Pithorāgarh** Uttar Pradesh, N India
196 B16 **Piti** W Guam
108 G13 **Pitigliano** Toscana, C Italy
42 F3 **Pitiquito** Sonora, NW Mexico
Pitkäranta *see* Pitkyaranta
40 M11 **Pitkas Point** Alaska, USA
128 H11 **Pitkyaranta** *Fin.* Pitkäranta. Respublika Kareliya, NW Russian Federation
98 J10 **Pitlochry** C Scotland, UK
20 I16 **Pitman** New Jersey, NE USA
114 G8 **Pitomača** Koprivnica-Križevci, N Croatia
37 O2 **Pit River** ≈ California, W USA
65 G15 **Pitrufquén** Araucanía, S Chile
Pitsanulok *see* Phitsanulok
Pitschen *see* Byczyna
Pitsunda *see* Bichvint'a
111 X6 **Pitten** ≈ E Austria
8 J14 **Pitt Island** *island* British Columbia, W Canada
Pitt Island *see* Makin
24 M3 **Pittsboro** Mississippi, S USA
23 T9 **Pittsboro** North Carolina, SE USA
29 R7 **Pittsburg** Kansas, C USA
27 W6 **Pittsburg** Texas, SW USA
20 B14 **Pittsburgh** Pennsylvania, NE USA
32 J14 **Pittsfield** Illinois, N USA
21 R6 **Pittsfield** Maine, NE USA
20 L11 **Pittsfield** Massachusetts, NE USA
191 U3 **Pittsworth** Queensland, E Australia
64 I8 **Pituil** La Rioja, NW Argentina
58 A10 **Piura** Piura, NW Peru
58 A9 **Piura** *off.* Departamento de Piura. ◆ *department* NW Peru
37 S13 **Piute Peak** ▲ California, W USA
115 J15 **Piva** ≈ SW Yugoslavia
119 V5 **Pivdenne** Kharkivs'ka Oblast', E Ukraine
119 P8 **Pivdennyy Buh** *Rus.* Yuzhnyy Bug. ≈ S Ukraine
56 F5 **Pivijay** Magdalena, N Colombia
111 T13 **Pivka** *prev.* Šent Peter, *Ger.* Sankt Peter, *It.* San Pietro del Carso. SW Slovenia
119 U13 **Pivnichno-Kryms'kyy Kanal** *canal* S Ukraine
115 J15 **Pivsko Jezero** ◎ SW Yugoslavia
113 M18 **Piwniczna** Nowy Sącz, S Poland
37 R12 **Pixley** California, W USA
129 Q15 **Pizhma** *var.* Pishma. ≈ NW Russian Federation
11 U13 **Placentia** Newfoundland, Newfoundland and Labrador, SE Canada
Placentia *see* Piacenza
11 U13 **Placentia Bay** *inlet* Newfoundland, Newfoundland and Labrador, SE Canada
179 Qq12 **Placer** Masbate, N Philippines
37 P7 **Placerville** California, W USA
46 F5 **Placetas** Villa Clara, C Cuba
115 Q18 **Plačkovica** ⛰ E FYR Macedonia
38 L2 **Plain City** Utah, W USA
24 G4 **Plain Dealing** Louisiana, S USA
33 O14 **Plainfield** Indiana, N USA
20 K14 **Plainfield** New Jersey, NE USA
35 O8 **Plains** Montana, NW USA
26 L6 **Plains** Texas, SW USA
31 X10 **Plainview** Minnesota, N USA
31 Q13 **Plainview** Nebraska, C USA
27 N4 **Plainview** Texas, SW USA
28 K4 **Plainville** Kansas, C USA
117 L25 **Pláka, Ákra** *headland* Kríti, Greece, E Mediterranean Sea
117 J15 **Pláka, Ákra** *headland* Límnos, E Greece
115 N19 **Plakenska Planina** ⛰ SW FYR Macedonia
46 K5 **Plana Cays** *islets* SE Bahamas
107 S12 **Plana, Isla** *var.* Nueva Tabarca. *island* E Spain
61 L18 **Planaltina** Goiás, S Brazil
85 O14 **Planalto Moçambicano** *plateau* N Mozambique
114 N10 **Plandište** Serbia, NE Yugoslavia
102 N13 **Plane** ≈ NE Germany
56 E6 **Planeta Rica** Córdoba, NW Colombia
31 P11 **Plankinton** South Dakota, N USA
32 M11 **Plano** Illinois, N USA
27 U6 **Plano** Texas, SW USA
25 W12 **Plant City** Florida, SE USA
24 J9 **Plaquemine** Louisiana, S USA
106 K9 **Plasencia** Extremadura, W Spain
114 C10 **Plaški** Karlovac, C Croatia
115 N19 **Plasnica** SW FYR Macedonia
125 E12 **Plast** Chelyabinskaya Oblast', C Russian Federation
11 N14 **Plaster Rock** New Brunswick, SE Canada
109 J24 **Platani** *anc.* Halycus. ≈ Sicilia, Italy, C Mediterranean Sea
117 G17 **Plataniá** Thessalía, C Greece
117 G24 **Plátanos** Kríti, Greece, E Mediterranean Sea
67 H18 **Plata, Río de la** *var.* River Plate. *estuary* Argentina/Uruguay
79 V15 **Plateau** ◆ *state* C Nigeria
81 G19 **Plateaux** *var.* Région des Plateaux. ◆ *province* C Congo
94 P1 **Platen, Kapp** *headland* NE Svalbard
Plate, River *see* Plata, Río de la
101 G22 **Plate Taille, Lac de la** *var.* L'Eau d'Heure. ◎ SE Belgium
Plathe *see* Płoty
41 N13 **Platinum** Alaska, USA
56 F5 **Plato** Magdalena, N Colombia
31 O11 **Platte** South Dakota, N USA
29 R3 **Platte City** Missouri, C USA
Plattensee *see* Balaton
29 R3 **Platte River** ≈ Iowa/Missouri, USA
31 Q15 **Platte River** ≈ Nebraska, C USA
39 T3 **Platteville** Colorado, C USA
32 K9 **Platteville** Wisconsin, N USA
103 N21 **Plattling** Bayern, SE Germany
29 R3 **Plattsburg** Missouri, C USA
20 L6 **Plattsburgh** New York, NE USA
31 S15 **Plattsmouth** Nebraska, C USA
103 M17 **Plauen** *var.* Plauen im Vogtland. Sachsen, E Germany
Plauen im Vogtland *see* Plauen
102 M10 **Plauer See** ◎ NE Germany
115 L16 **Plav** Montenegro, SW Yugoslavia
120 I10 **Pļaviņas** *Ger.* Stockmannshof. Aizkraukle, S Latvia
130 K5 **Plavsk** Tul'skaya Oblast', W Russian Federation
43 Z12 **Playa del Carmen** Quintana Roo, E Mexico
42 J12 **Playa Los Corchos** Nayarit, SW Mexico
39 P16 **Playas Lake** ◎ New Mexico, SW USA
43 S15 **Playa Vicenté** Veracruz-Llave, SE Mexico
178 K11 **Plây Cu** *var.* Pleiku. Gia Lai, C Vietnam
30 L3 **Plaza** North Dakota, N USA
65 I15 **Plaza Huincul** Neuquén, C Argentina
38 L3 **Pleasant Grove** Utah, W USA
31 V14 **Pleasant Hill** Iowa, C USA
29 R4 **Pleasant Hill** Missouri, C USA
Pleasant Island *see* Nauru
38 K13 **Pleasant, Lake** ▣ Arizona, SW USA
21 P8 **Pleasant Mountain** ▲ Maine, NE USA
29 R5 **Pleasanton** Kansas, C USA
27 R12 **Pleasanton** Texas, SW USA
193 G20 **Pleasant Point** Canterbury, South Island, NZ
21 R5 **Pleasant River** ≈ Maine, NE USA
20 J17 **Pleasantville** New Jersey, NE USA
105 N12 **Pléaux** Cantal, C France
113 B19 **Plechý** *Ger.* Plöckenstein. ▲ Austria/Czech Republic
Pleebo *see* Plibo
Pleihari *see* Pelaihari
Pleiku *see* Plây Cu
103 M16 **Pleisse** ≈ E Germany
Plencia *see* Plentzia
192 O7 **Plenty, Bay of** *bay* North Island, NZ
35 Y6 **Plentywood** Montana, NW USA
107 O2 **Plentzia** *var.* Plencia. País Vasco, N Spain
104 H5 **Plérin** Côtes d'Armor, NW France
128 M10 **Plesetsk** Arkhangel'skaya Oblast', NW Russian Federation
Pleshchenitsy *see* Plyeshchanitsy
Pleskau *see* Pskov
Pleskauer See *see* Pskov, Lake
Pleskava *see* Pskov
114 E8 **Pleso International** ✕ (Zagreb) Grad Zagreb, NW Croatia
Pless *see* Pszczyna
13 Q11 **Plessisville** Québec, SE Canada
112 H12 **Pleszew** Kalisz, C Poland
10 L10 **Plétipi, Lac** ◎ Québec, SE Canada
103 F15 **Plettenberg** Nordrhein-Westfalen, W Germany
116 I8 **Pleven** *prev.* Plevna. Loveshka Oblast, N Bulgaria
Plevlja/Plevlje *see* Pljevlja
Plevna *see* Pleven
Plezzo *see* Bovec
Pliberk *see* Bleiburg
78 L17 **Plibo** *var.* Pleebo. SE Liberia
124 Oo13 **Pliny Trench** *undersea feature* C Mediterranean Sea
120 K13 **Plisa** *Rus.* Plissa. Vitsyebskaya Voblasts', N Belarus
Plissa *see* Plisa
114 D11 **Plitvica** Zadar-Knin, C Croatia
114 D11 **Plješevica** ⛰ C Croatia
115 K14 **Pljevlja** *prev.* Plevlja, Plevlje. Montenegro, N Yugoslavia
Ploça *see* Ploçë
Plocce *see* Ploče
115 G15 **Ploče** *It.* Plocce; *prev.* Kardeljevo. Dubrovnik-Neretva, SE Croatia
115 K22 **Ploçë** *var.* Ploça. Vlorë, SW Albania
112 K11 **Płock** *Ger.* Plozk. Płock, C Poland
112 K11 **Płock** *off.* Województwo Płockie, *Ger.* Plozk. ◆ *province* C Poland
111 Q10 **Plöcken Pass** *Ger.* Plöckenpass, *It.* Passo di Monte Croce Carnico. *pass* SW Austria
Plöckenstein *see* Plechý
Płockie, Województwo *see* Płock
101 B19 **Ploegsteert** Hainaut, W Belgium
104 H6 **Ploërmel** Morbihan, NW France
Ploești *see* Ploiești
118 K13 **Ploiești** *prev.* Ploești. Prahova, SE Romania
117 L17 **Plomári** *prev.* Plomárion. Lésvos, E Greece
Plomárion *see* Plomári
105 O12 **Plomb du Cantal** ▲ C France
191 V6 **Plomer, Point** *headland* New South Wales, SE Australia
102 J8 **Plön** Schleswig-Holstein, N Germany
112 L11 **Płońsk** Ciechanów, C Poland
121 J20 **Plotnitsa** *Rus.* Plotnitsa. Brestskaya Voblasts', SW Belarus
112 E8 **Płoty** *Ger.* Plathe. Szczecin, NW Poland
104 G7 **Plouay** Morbihan, NW France
113 D15 **Ploučnice** *Ger.* Polzen. ≈ NE Czech Republic
116 I10 **Plovdiv** *prev.* Eumolpias, *anc.* Evmolpia, Philippopolis, *Lat.* Trimontium. Plovdivska Oblast, C Bulgaria
Plovdiv *see* Plovdivska Oblast
116 I11 **Plovdivska Oblast** *var.* Plovdiv. ◆ *province* C Bulgaria
32 L6 **Plover** Wisconsin, N USA
Plozk *see* Płock
29 U11 **Plumerville** Arkansas, C USA
21 P10 **Plum Island** *island* Massachusetts, NE USA
34 M9 **Plummer** Idaho, NW USA
85 J18 **Plumtree** Matabeleland South, SW Zimbabwe
120 D11 **Plungė** Plungė, W Lithuania
115 J15 **Plužine** Montenegro, SW Yugoslavia
121 K14 **Plyeshchanitsy** *Rus.* Pleshchenitsy. Minskaya Voblasts', N Belarus
47 V10 **Plymouth** ○ (Montserrat) SW Montserrat
99 I24 **Plymouth** SW England, UK
33 O11 **Plymouth** Indiana, N USA
21 P12 **Plymouth** Massachusetts, NE USA
21 N8 **Plymouth** New Hampshire, NE USA
23 X9 **Plymouth** North Carolina, SE USA
32 M8 **Plymouth** Wisconsin, N USA
99 J20 **Plynlimon** ▲ C Wales, UK
128 G14 **Plyussa** Pskovskaya Oblast', W Russian Federation
113 B17 **Plzeň** *Ger.* Pilsen, *Pol.* Pilzno. Západní Čechy, W Czech Republic
112 F11 **Pniewy** *Ger.* Pinne. Poznań, W Poland
108 D8 **Po** ≈ N Italy
79 P13 **Pô** S Burkina
44 M13 **Poás, Volcán** Ѫ NW Costa Rica
79 S16 **Pobè** S Benin
127 N8 **Pobeda, Gora** ▲ NE Russian Federation
Pobeda Peak *see* Pobedy, Pik/Tomur Feng
153 Z7 **Pobedy, Pik** *var.* Pobeda Peak, *Chin.* Tomur Feng. ▲ China/Kyrgyzstan *see also* Tomur Feng
112 H11 **Pobiedziska** *Ger.* Pudewitz. Poznań, C Poland
Po, Bocche del *see* Po, Foci del
29 W9 **Pocahontas** Arkansas, C USA
31 U12 **Pocahontas** Iowa, C USA
35 Q15 **Pocatello** Idaho, NW USA
178 J13 **Pochentong** ✕ (Phnum Penh) Phnum Penh, S Cambodia
130 I6 **Pochep** Bryanskaya Oblast', W Russian Federation
130 H4 **Pochinok** Smolenskaya Oblast', W Russian Federation
43 R17 **Pochutla** *var.* San Pedro Pochutla. Oaxaca, SE Mexico
64 I6 **Pocitos, Salar** *var.* Salar Quiróm. *salt lake* NW Argentina
103 O22 **Pocking** Bayern, SE Germany
195 R17 **Pocklington Reef** *reef* SE PNG
199 Hh9 **Pocklington Trough** *undersea feature* W Pacific Ocean
29 R11 **Pocola** Oklahoma, C USA
23 Y5 **Pocomoke City** Maryland, NE USA
61 L21 **Poços de Caldas** Minas Gerais, NE Brazil
128 H14 **Podberez'ye** Novgorodskaya Oblast', NW Russian Federation
Podbrodzie *see* Pabradė
129 U8 **Podcher'ye** Respublika Komi, NW Russian Federation
113 E16 **Poděbrady** *Ger.* Podiebrad. Střední Čechy, C Czech Republic
176 Yy10 **Podena, Kepulauan** *island group* E Indonesia
130 L9 **Podgorenskiy** Voronezhskaya Oblast', W Russian Federation
115 J17 **Podgorica** *prev.* Titograd. Montenegro, SW Yugoslavia
115 K17 **Podgorica** ✕ Montenegro, SW Yugoslavia
111 T13 **Podgrad** SW Slovenia
Podiebrad *see* Poděbrady
118 M5 **Podil's'ka Vysochina** *plateau* W Ukraine
Podium Anicensis *see* le Puy
126 Ii11 **Podkamennaya Tunguska** *Eng.* Stony Tunguska. ≈ C Russian Federation
Pod Klošter *see* Arnoldstein
131 Q8 **Podlesnoye** Saratovskaya Oblast', W Russian Federation
130 K4 **Podol'sk** Moskovskaya Oblast', W Russian Federation
78 H10 **Podor** N Senegal
129 P12 **Podosinovets** Kirovskaya Oblast', NW Russian Federation
128 I12 **Podporozh'ye** Leningradskaya Oblast', NW Russian Federation
114 H9 **Podravska Slatina** *Hung.* Szlatina; *prev.* Slatina. Virovitica-Podravina, NE Croatia
114 J13 **Podromanlja** SE Bosnia and Herzegovina
Podsvil'ye *see* Padsvillye
118 L9 **Podu Iloaiei** *prev.* Podul Iloaiei. Iași, NE Romania
115 N15 **Podujevo** Serbia, S Yugoslavia
Podul Iloaiei *see* Podu Iloaiei
Podunajská Rovina *see* Little Alföld
128 M12 **Podyuga** Arkhangel'skaya Oblast', NW Russian Federation

◆ Country
● Country Capital
◇ Dependent Territory
○ Dependent Territory Capital
◆ Administrative Region
✕ International Airport
▲ Mountain
⛰ Mountain Range
Ѫ Volcano
≈ River
◎ Lake
▣ Reservoir

58 A9 **Poechos, Embalse** ◎ NW Peru
57 W10 **Poeketi** Sipaliwini, E Mynamar
102 L8 **Poel** island N Germany
85 M20 **Poelela, Lagoa** ◎ S Mozambique
Poerwodadi see Purwodadi
Poetovio see Ptuj
85 E23 **Pofadder** Northern Cape, W South Africa
108 I9 **Po, Foci del** var. Bocche del Po. ~ NE Italy
118 E12 **Pogănis** ~ W Romania
Pogegen see Pagėgiai
108 G12 **Poggibonsi** Toscana, C Italy
109 I14 **Poggio Mirteto** Lazio, C Italy
111 V4 **Pöggstall** Niederösterreich, N Austria
118 L13 **Pogoanele** Buzău, SE Romania
Pogónion see Delvináki
115 M21 **Pogradec** var. Pogradeci. Korçë, SE Albania
Pogradeci see Pogradec
127 N18 **Pogranichnyy** Primorskiy Kray, SE Russian Federation
40 M16 **Pogromni Volcano** ▲ Unimak Island, Alaska, USA
169 Z15 **P'ohang** Jap. Hokō. E South Korea
13 T9 **Pohénégamook, Lac** ◎ Québec, SE Canada
95 L20 **Pohja** Swe. Pojo. Uusimaa, SW Finland
Pohjanlahti see Bothnia, Gulf of
95 N16 **Pohjois-Karjala** Swe. Norra Karelen. ◈ province C Finland
201 U16 **Pohnpei** ◈ state E Micronesia
201 O12 **Pohnpei** ✕ Pohnpei, E Micronesia
201 O12 **Pohnpei** prev. Ponape Ascension Island. island E Micronesia
113 F19 **Pohořelice** Ger. Pohrlitz. Jižní Morava, SE Czech Republic
111 V10 **Pohorje** Ger. Bacher. ▲ N Slovenia
119 N6 **Pohrebyshche** Vinnyts'ka Oblast', C Ukraine
Pohrlitz see Pohořelice
175 Qq9 **Poh, Teluk** bay Sulawesi, C Indonesia
167 P9 **Po Hu** ⊡ E China
118 G15 **Poiana Mare** Dolj, S Romania
Poictiers see Poitiers
131 N6 **Poim** Penzenskaya Oblast', W Russian Federation
197 I6 **Poindimié** Province Nord, C New Caledonia
Poindo see Lhünzhub
205 Y13 **Poinsett, Cape** headland Antarctica
31 R9 **Poinsett, Lake** ◎ South Dakota, N USA
24 I10 **Point Au Fer Island** island Louisiana, S USA
41 X14 **Point Baker** Prince of Wales Island, Alaska, USA
27 U13 **Point Comfort** Texas, SW USA
Point de Galle see Galle
46 K10 **Pointe à Gravois** headland SW Haiti
24 L10 **Pointe a la Hache** Louisiana, S USA
47 Y6 **Pointe-à-Pitre** Grande Terre, C Guadeloupe
13 U7 **Pointe-au-Père** Québec, SE Canada
13 V5 **Pointe-aux-Anglais** Québec, SE Canada
47 T10 **Pointe Du Cap** headland N Saint Lucia
81 E21 **Pointe-Noire** Le Kouilou, S Congo
47 X6 **Pointe Noire** Basse Terre, W Guadeloupe
81 E21 **Pointe-Noire** ✕ Le Kouilou, S Congo
47 U15 **Point Fortin** Trinidad, Trinidad and Tobago
40 M6 **Point Hope** Alaska, USA
40 N5 **Point Lay** Alaska, USA
20 B16 **Point Marion** Pennsylvania, NE USA
20 K16 **Point Pleasant** New Jersey, NE USA
23 P4 **Point Pleasant** West Virginia, NE USA
47 R14 **Point Salines** ✕ (St.George's) SW Grenada
104 L9 **Poitiers** prev. Poictiers, anc. Limonum. Vienne, W France
104 K9 **Poitou** cultural region W France
104 K10 **Poitou-Charentes** ◈ region W France
105 N3 **Poix-de-Picardie** Somme, N France
Pojo see Pohja
39 S10 **Pojoaque** New Mexico, SW USA
158 E11 **Pokaran** Rājasthān, NW India
191 R4 **Pokataroo** New South Wales, SE Australia
121 P18 **Pokats'** Rus. Pokot'. ~ SE Belarus
31 V5 **Pokegama Lake** ◎ Minnesota, N USA
192 L6 **Pokeno** Waikato, North Island, NZ
159 O11 **Pokhara** Western, C Nepal
131 T6 **Pokhvistnevo** Samarskaya Oblast', W Russian Federation
57 W10 **Pokigron** Sipaliwini, C Suriname
94 L10 **Pokka** Lapp. Bohkká. Lappi, N Finland
81 N16 **Poko** Haut-Zaïre, NE Zaire
Pokot' see Pokats'
Po-ko-to Shan see Bogda Shan
153 S7 **Pokrovka** Talasskaya Oblast', NW Kyrgyzstan
Pokrovka see Kyzyl-Suu
126 M11 **Pokrovsk** Respublika Sakha (Yakutiya), NE Russian Federation
119 V8 **Pokrovs'ke** Rus. Pokrovskoye. Dnipropetrovs'ka Oblast', E Ukraine
Pokrovskoye see Pokrovs'ke
Pola see Pula
39 N10 **Polacca** Arizona, SW USA
106 L2 **Pola de Laviana** Asturias, N Spain
106 K2 **Pola de Lena** Asturias, N Spain
106 L2 **Pola de Siero** Asturias, N Spain
203 Y3 **Poland** Kiritimati, E Kiribati
112 H12 **Poland** off. Republic of Poland, var. Polish Republic, Pol. Polska, Rzeczpospolita Polska; prev. Pol. Polska Rzeczpospolita Ludowa, Polish People's Republic. ◆ republic C Europe
Polangen see Palanga
112 G7 **Polanów** Ger. Pollnow. Koszalin, NW Poland
142 H13 **Polatlı** Ankara, C Turkey
120 L12 **Polatsk** Rus. Polotsk. Vitsyebskaya Voblasts', N Belarus
112 F8 **Połczyn-Zdrój** Ger. Bad Polzin. Koszalin, NW Poland
152 I16 **Polekhatum** prev. Pul'-I-Khatum. Akhalskiy Velayat, S Turkmenistan
155 Q3 **Pol-e Khomrī** var. Pul-i-Khumri. Baghlān, NE Afghanistan
207 S10 **Pole Plain** undersea feature Arctic Ocean
149 P5 **Pol-e Safid** var. Pol-e-Sefid, Pul-i-Sefid. Māzandarān, N Iran
Pol-e-Sefid see Pol-e Safid
120 B13 **Polessk** Ger. Labiau. Kaliningradskaya Oblast', W Russian Federation
Polesskoye see Polis'ke
175 P11 **Polewali** Sulawesi, C Indonesia
116 G11 **Polezhan** ▲ SW Bulgaria
80 F13 **Poli** Nord, N Cameroon
Poli see Pólis
109 M19 **Policastro, Golfo di** gulf S Italy
112 D8 **Police** Ger. Politz. Szczecin, NW Poland
180 I17 **Police, Pointe** headland Mahé, NE Seychelles
117 L17 **Polichnítos** var. Polihnitos, Políkhnitos. Lésvos, E Greece
Poligiros see Polýgyros
109 P17 **Polignano a Mare** Puglia, SE Italy
105 S9 **Poligny** Jura, E France
Polihnitos see Polichnítos
Polikastro/Políkastron see Polýkastro
Políkhnitos see Polichnítos
116 K8 **Polikrayshte** Loveshka Oblast, N Bulgaria
179 Pp10 **Polillo Islands** island group N Philippines
111 Q9 **Polinik** ▲ SW Austria
123 Mm3 **Pólis** var. Poli. W Cyprus
Polish People's Republic see Poland
Polish Republic see Poland
119 O3 **Polis'ke** Rus. Polesskoye. Kyyivs'ka Oblast', N Ukraine
109 N22 **Polistena** Calabria, SW Italy
Politz see Police
Políyiros see Polýgyros
31 V14 **Polk City** Iowa, C USA
112 F13 **Polkowice** Ger. Heerwegen. Legnica, W Poland
161 G22 **Pollāchi** Tamil Nādu, SE India
111 W7 **Pöllau** Steiermark, SE Austria
201 T13 **Polle** atoll Chuuk Islands, C Micronesia
Pollensa see Pollença
Pollnow see Polanów
31 N7 **Pollock** South Dakota, N USA
94 L8 **Polmak** Finnmark, N Norway
32 L10 **Polo** Illinois, N USA
200 Qq15 **Poloa** island Tongatapu Group, N Tonga
44 E5 **Polochic, Río** ~ C Guatemala
Pologi see Polohy
119 V9 **Polohy** Rus. Pologi. Zaporiz'ka Oblast', SE Ukraine
12 M10 **Polonais, Lac des** ◎ Québec, SE Canada
63 G20 **Polonio, Cabo** headland E Uruguay
161 K24 **Polonnaruwa** North Central Province, C Sri Lanka
118 L5 **Polonne** Rus. Polonnoye. Khmel'nyts'ka Oblast', NW Ukraine
Polonnoye see Polonne
Polotsk see Polatsk
111 T7 **Pöls** var. Pölsbach. ~ E Austria
Pölsbach see Pöls
Polska/Polska, Rzeczpospolita/Polska Rzeczpospolita Ludowa see Poland
116 L10 **Polski Gradets** Burgaska Oblast, SE Bulgaria
116 K8 **Polsko Kosovo** Loveshka Oblast, N Bulgaria
35 P8 **Polson** Montana, NW USA
119 T6 **Poltava** Poltavs'ka Oblast', NE Ukraine
Poltava see Poltavs'ka Oblast'
119 R5 **Poltavs'ka Oblast'** var. Poltava, Rus. Poltavskaya Oblast'. ◈ province NE Ukraine
Poltoratsk see Ashgabat
Poltavskaya Oblast' see Poltavs'ka Oblast'
120 I5 **Põltsamaa** Ger. Oberpahlen. Jõgevamaa, E Estonia
120 I4 **Põltsamaa** var. Põltsamaa Jõgi. ~ C Estonia
Põltsamaa Jõgi see Põltsamaa
125 F10 **Polunochnoye** Sverdlovskaya Oblast', C Russian Federation
125 G8 **Poluy** ~ N Russian Federation
120 J6 **Põlva** Ger. Pölwe. Põlvamaa, SE Estonia
95 N16 **Polvijärvi** Pohjois-Karjala, SE Finland
Pölwe see Põlva
117 I22 **Polýaigos** island Kykládes, Greece, Aegean Sea
117 I22 **Polyaígou Folégandrou, Stenó** strait Kykládes, Greece, Aegean Sea
128 J3 **Polyarnyy** Murmanskaya Oblast', NW Russian Federation
129 W5 **Polyarnyy Ural** ▲ NW Russian Federation
117 G14 **Polýgyros** var. Poligiros, Políyiros. Kentrikí Makedonía, N Greece
116 F13 **Polýkastro** var. Polikastro; prev. Políkastron. Kentrikí Makedonía, N Greece
199 Kk9 **Polynesia** island group C Pacific Ocean
117 J15 **Polýochni** site of ancient city Límnos, E Greece
43 Y13 **Polyuc** Quintana Roo, E Mexico
111 V10 **Polzela** C Slovenia
Polzen see Ploučnice
176 Ww9 **Pom** Irian Jaya, E Indonesia
58 D12 **Pomabamba** Ancash, C Peru
193 D23 **Pomahaka** ~ South Island, NZ
108 F12 **Pomarance** Toscana, C Italy
106 G9 **Pombal** Leiria, C Portugal
78 D9 **Pombas** Santo Antão, NW Cape Verde
85 N19 **Pomene** Inhambane, SE Mozambique
112 G8 **Pomerania** cultural region Germany/Poland
112 D7 **Pomeranian Bay** Ger. Pommersche Bucht, Pol. Zatoka Pomorska. bay Germany/Poland
33 T15 **Pomeroy** Ohio, N USA
34 L10 **Pomeroy** Washington, NW USA
119 Q8 **Pomichna** Kirovohrads'ka Oblast', C Ukraine
195 O12 **Pomio** New Britain, E PNG
Pomir, Dar"yoi see Pamir/Pāmīr, Daryā-ye
29 T6 **Pomme de Terre Lake** ⊡ Missouri, C USA
31 S8 **Pomme de Terre River** ~ Minnesota, N USA
Pommersche Bucht see Pomeranian Bay
37 T15 **Pomona** California, W USA
116 N9 **Pomorie** Burgaska Oblast, E Bulgaria
Pomorska, Zatoka see Pomeranian Bay
129 Q4 **Pomorskiy Proliv** strait NW Russian Federation
Pomorze Zachodnie see Szczecin
129 T10 **Pomozdino** Respublika Komi, NW Russian Federation
Pompaelo see Pamplona
175 Q9 **Pompangeo, Pegunungan** ▲ Sulawesi, C Indonesia
25 Z15 **Pompano Beach** Florida, SE USA
109 K18 **Pompei** Campania, S Italy
35 V10 **Pompeys Pillar** Montana, NW USA
Ponape Ascension Island see Pohnpei
31 R13 **Ponca** Nebraska, C USA
29 O8 **Ponca City** Oklahoma, C USA
47 T6 **Ponce** C Puerto Rico
25 X10 **Ponce de Leon Inlet** inlet Florida, SE USA
24 K8 **Ponchatoula** Louisiana, S USA
28 M8 **Pond Creek** Oklahoma, C USA
161 J20 **Pondicherry** var. Puduchcheri, Fr. Pondichéry. Pondicherry, SE India
157 I20 **Pondicherry** var. Puduchcheri, Fr. Pondichéry. ◈ union territory India
Pondichéry see Pondicherry
207 N11 **Pond Inlet** Baffin Island, Northwest Territories, NE Canada
197 I6 **Ponérihouen** Province Nord, C New Caledonia
106 J4 **Ponferrada** Castilla-León, NW Spain
192 N13 **Pongaroa** Manawatu-Wanganui, North Island, NZ
178 I12 **Pong Nam Ron** Chantaburi, S Thailand
83 C14 **Pongo** ~ S Sudan
158 I7 **Pong Reservoir** ⊡ N India
113 N14 **Poniatowa** Lublin, E Poland
178 J13 **Pônley** Kâmpóng Chhnăng, C Cambodia
161 I20 **Ponnaiyār** ~ SE India
9 Q15 **Ponoka** Alberta, SW Canada
131 U6 **Ponomarevka** Orenburgskaya Oblast', W Russian Federation
174 L15 **Ponorogo** Jawa, C Indonesia
128 M5 **Ponoy** Murmanskaya Oblast', NW Russian Federation
125 E5 **Ponoy** ~ NW Russian Federation
104 K11 **Pons** Charente-Maritime, W France
Pons see Ponts
Pons Aelii see Newcastle upon Tyne
Pons Vetus see Pontevedra
101 G20 **Pont-à-Celles** Hainaut, S Belgium
104 K16 **Pontacq** Pyrénées-Atlantiques, SW France
66 P3 **Ponta Delgada** São Miguel, Azores, Portugal, NE Atlantic Ocean
66 P3 **Ponta Delgado** ✕ São Miguel, Azores, Portugal, NE Atlantic Ocean
66 N2 **Ponta do Pico** ▲ Pico, Azores, Portugal, NE Atlantic Ocean
62 J11 **Ponta Grossa** Paraná, S Brazil
105 S5 **Pont-à-Mousson** Meurthe-et-Moselle, NE France
105 T9 **Pontarlier** Doubs, E France
108 G11 **Pontassieve** Toscana, C Italy
104 L4 **Pont-Audemer** Eure, N France
24 K9 **Pontchartrain, Lake** ◎ Louisiana, S USA
104 I8 **Pontchâteau** Loire-Atlantique, NW France
105 R10 **Pont-de-Vaux** Ain, E France
106 G4 **Ponteareas** Galicia, NW Spain
108 J6 **Pontebba** Friuli-Venezia Giulia, NE Italy
106 G4 **Ponte Caldelas** Galicia, NW Spain
109 J16 **Pontecorvo** Lazio, C Italy
106 G5 **Ponte da Barca** Viana do Castelo, N Portugal
106 G5 **Ponte de Lima** Viana do Castelo, N Portugal
108 F11 **Pontedera** Toscana, C Italy
106 H10 **Ponte de Sor** Portalegre, C Portugal
106 H2 **Pontedeume** Galicia, NW Spain
108 F6 **Ponte di Legno** Lombardia, N Italy
9 T17 **Ponteix** Saskatchewan, S Canada
61 N20 **Ponte Nova** Minas Gerais, NE Brazil
61 G18 **Pontes e Lacerda** Mato Grosso, W Brazil
106 G4 **Pontevedra** anc. Pons Vetus. Galicia, NW Spain
106 G3 **Pontevedra** ◈ province Galicia, NW Spain
106 G4 **Pontevedra, Ría de** estuary NW Spain
32 M12 **Pontiac** Illinois, N USA
33 R9 **Pontiac** Michigan, N USA
174 Kk8 **Pontianak** Borneo, C Indonesia
109 I16 **Pontino, Agro** plain C Italy
Pontisarae see Pontoise
104 H6 **Pontivy** Morbihan, NW France
104 F6 **Pont-l'Abbé** Finistère, NW France
105 N4 **Pontoise** anc. Briva Isarae, Cergy-Pontoise, Pontisarae. Val-d'Oise, N France
9 W13 **Ponton** Manitoba, C Canada
104 J5 **Pontorson** Manche, N France
24 M2 **Pontotoc** Mississippi, S USA
27 R9 **Pontotoc** Texas, SW USA
108 E10 **Pontremoli** Toscana, C Italy
110 J10 **Pontresina** Graubünden, S Switzerland
107 U5 **Ponts** var. Pons. Cataluña, NE Spain
105 R14 **Pont-St-Esprit** Gard, S France
99 K21 **Pontypool** Wel. Pontypŵl. SE Wales, UK
99 J22 **Pontypridd** S Wales, UK
Pontypŵl see Pontypool
45 R17 **Ponuga** Veraguas, SE Panama
192 L6 **Ponui Island** island N NZ
121 K14 **Ponya** Rus. Ponya. ~ N Belarus
109 I17 **Ponziane, Isole** island C Italy
190 F7 **Poochera** South Australia
99 L24 **Poole** S England, UK
27 S6 **Poolville** Texas, SW USA
Poona see Pune
190 M8 **Pooncarie** New South Wales, SE Australia
191 N6 **Poopelloe Lake** seasonal lake New South Wales, SE Australia
59 K19 **Poopó** Oruro, C Bolivia
59 K19 **Poopó, Lago** var. Lago Pampa Aullagas. ◎ W Bolivia
192 L3 **Poor Knights Islands** island N NZ
41 P10 **Poorman** Alaska, USA
190 E3 **Pootnoura** South Australia
153 R10 **Pop** Rus. Pap. Namangan Wiloyati, E Uzbekistan
119 X7 **Popasna** Rus. Popasnaya. Luhans'ka Oblast', E Ukraine
Popasnaya see Popasna
56 D12 **Popayán** Cauca, SW Colombia
101 B18 **Poperinge** West-Vlaanderen, W Belgium
126 K7 **Popigay** Taymyrskiy (Dolgano-Nenetskiy) Avtonomnyy Okrug, N Russian Federation
126 Jj7 **Popigay** ~ N Russian Federation
119 O5 **Popil'nya** Zhytomyrs'ka Oblast', N Ukraine
190 K8 **Popiltah Lake** seasonal lake New South Wales, SE Australia
35 X7 **Poplar** Montana, NW USA
9 Y14 **Poplar** ~ Manitoba, C Canada
29 X8 **Poplar Bluff** Missouri, C USA
35 X6 **Poplar River** ~ Montana, NW USA
43 P14 **Popocatépetl** ▲ S Mexico
174 L16 **Popoh** Jawa, S Indonesia
81 H21 **Popokabaka** Bandundu, SW Zaire
109 J15 **Popoli** Abruzzi, C Italy
195 X16 **Popomanaseu, Mount** ▲ Guadalcanal, C Solomon Islands
194 L15 **Popondetta** Northern, S PNG
114 F9 **Popovača** Sisak-Moslavina, NE Croatia
116 J10 **Popovitsa** Loveshka Oblast, C Bulgaria
116 L8 **Popovo** Razgradska Oblast, N Bulgaria
Popovo see Iskra
Popper see Poprad
32 M5 **Popple River** ~ Wisconsin, N USA
113 L19 **Poprad** Ger. Deutschendorf, Hung. Poprád. Východné Slovensko, NE Slovakia
113 L18 **Poprad** Ger. Popper, Hung. Poprád. ~ Poland/Slovakia
113 L19 **Poprad-Tatry** ✕ (Poprad) Východné Slovensko, N Slovakia
23 X7 **Poquoson** Virginia, NE USA
155 O15 **Porāli** ~ SW Pakistan
192 N12 **Porangahau** Hawke's Bay, North Island, NZ
61 K17 **Porangatu** Goiás, C Brazil
121 G18 **Porazava** Pol. Porozow, Rus. Porozovo. Hrodzyenskaya Voblasts', W Belarus
160 A11 **Porbandar** Gujarāt, W India
8 I13 **Porcher Island** island British Columbia, SW Canada
106 M13 **Porcuna** Andalucía, S Spain
12 F7 **Porcupine** Ontario, S Canada
66 M6 **Porcupine Bank** undersea feature N Atlantic Ocean
9 V15 **Porcupine Hills** ▲ Manitoba/Saskatchewan, S Canada
32 L3 **Porcupine Mountains** hill range Michigan, N USA
66 M7 **Porcupine Plain** undersea feature E Atlantic Ocean
14 F4 **Porcupine River** ~ Canada/USA
108 I7 **Pordenone** anc. Portenau. Friuli-Venezia Giulia, NE Italy
56 H9 **Pore** Casanare, E Colombia
114 A9 **Poreč** It. Parenzo. Istra, NW Croatia
62 I9 **Porecatu** Paraná, S Brazil
Porech'ye see Parechcha
131 P4 **Poretskoye** Chuvashskaya Respublika, W Russian Federation
79 Q13 **Porga** N Benin
194 G12 **Porgera** Enga, W PNG
95 K18 **Pori** Swe. Björneborg. Turku-Pori, SW Finland
193 L14 **Porirua** Wellington, North Island, NZ
94 I12 **Porjus** Norrbotten, N Sweden
128 G14 **Porkhov** Pskovskaya Oblast', W Russian Federation
57 O4 **Porlamar** Nueva Esparta, NE Venezuela
104 I8 **Pornic** Loire-Atlantique, NW France
194 G12 **Poroma** Southern Highlands, W PNG
127 Oo15 **Poronaysk** Ostrov Sakhalin, Sakhalinskaya Oblast', SE Russian Federation
117 G20 **Póros** Póros, S Greece
117 C19 **Póros** Kefallinía, Iónioi Nísoi, Greece, C Mediterranean Sea
117 G20 **Póros** island S Greece
83 G24 **Poroto Mountains** ▲ SW Tanzania
114 B10 **Porozina** Primorje-Gorski Kotar, NW Croatia
Porozovo/Porozow see Porazava
205 X15 **Porpoise Bay** bay Antarctica
67 G15 **Porpoise Point** headland NE Ascension Island
67 C25 **Porpoise Point** headland East Falkland, Falkland Islands
110 C6 **Porrentruy** Jura, NW Switzerland
108 F10 **Porretta Terme** Emilia-Romagna, C Italy
106 G3 **Porriño** Galicia, NW Spain
94 L7 **Porsangen** fjord N Norway
94 K8 **Porsangerhalvøya** peninsula N Norway
97 G16 **Porsgrunn** Telemark, S Norway
142 E13 **Porsuk Çayı** ~ C Turkey
Porsy see Boldumsaz
59 N18 **Portachuelo** Santa Cruz, C Bolivia
190 I9 **Port Adelaide** South Australia
99 F15 **Portadown** Ir. Port An Dúnáin. S Northern Ireland, UK
33 P10 **Portage** Michigan, N USA
20 D15 **Portage** Pennsylvania, NE USA
32 K8 **Portage** Wisconsin, N USA
32 M3 **Portage Lake** ◎ Michigan, N USA
9 X16 **Portage la Prairie** Manitoba, S Canada
33 R11 **Portage River** ~ Ohio, N USA
29 Y8 **Portageville** Missouri, C USA
30 L2 **Portal** North Dakota, N USA
8 L17 **Port Alberni** Vancouver Island, British Columbia, SW Canada
12 E15 **Port Albert** Ontario, S Canada
106 I10 **Portalegre** anc. Ammaia, Amoea. Portalegre, E Portugal
106 H10 **Portalegre** ◈ district C Portugal
39 V12 **Portales** New Mexico, SW USA
41 X14 **Port Alexander** Baranof Island, Alaska, USA
85 I25 **Port Alfred** Eastern Cape, S South Africa
8 J16 **Port Alice** Vancouver Island, British Columbia, SW Canada
24 J8 **Port Allen** Louisiana, S USA
Port Amelia see Pemba
Port An Dúnáin see Portadown
34 G7 **Port Angeles** Washington, NW USA
46 L12 **Port Antonio** NE Jamaica
117 D16 **Pórta Panagiá** religious building Thessalía, C Greece
27 T14 **Port Aransas** Texas, SW USA
99 E18 **Portarlington** Ir. Cúil an tSúdaire. C Ireland
191 P17 **Port Arthur** Tasmania, SE Australia
18 Mm15 **Port Arthur** Texas, SW USA
98 G12 **Port Askaig** W Scotland, UK
190 I7 **Port Augusta** South Australia
46 M9 **Port-au-Prince** ● (Haiti) C Haiti
46 M9 **Port-au-Prince** ✕ E Haiti
24 I8 **Port Barre** Louisiana, S USA
157 Q19 **Port Blair** Andaman and Nicobar Islands, SE India
27 X12 **Port Bolivar** Texas, SW USA
107 X4 **Portbou** Cataluña, NE Spain
79 N17 **Port Bouet** ✕ (Abidjan) SE Ivory Coast
190 I8 **Port Broughton** South Australia
12 F17 **Port Burwell** Ontario, S Canada
10 G17 **Port Burwell** Québec, NE Canada
190 M13 **Port Campbell** Victoria, SE Australia
13 V4 **Port-Cartier** Québec, SE Canada
193 F23 **Port Chalmers** Otago, South Island, NZ
25 W14 **Port Charlotte** Florida, SE USA
40 L9 **Port Clarence** Alaska, USA
8 I13 **Port Clements** Graham Island, British Columbia, SW Canada
33 S11 **Port Clinton** Ohio, N USA
12 H17 **Port Colborne** Ontario, S Canada
13 Y7 **Port-Daniel** Québec, SE Canada
Port Darwin see Darwin
191 O17 **Port Davey** headland Tasmania, SE Australia
46 K8 **Port-de-Paix** NW Haiti
189 W4 **Port Douglas** Queensland, NE Australia
8 J13 **Port Edward** British Columbia, SW Canada
85 K24 **Port Edward** KwaZulu/Natal, SE South Africa
60 J12 **Portel** Pará, NE Brazil
106 H12 **Portel** Évora, S Portugal
12 E14 **Port Elgin** Ontario, S Canada
47 Y14 **Port Elizabeth** Bequia, Saint Vincent and the Grenadines
85 I26 **Port Elizabeth** Eastern Cape, S South Africa
98 G13 **Port Ellen** W Scotland, UK
Portenau see Pordenone
99 H16 **Port Erin** SW Isle of Man
47 Q13 **Porter Point** headland Saint Vincent, Saint Vincent and the Grenadines
193 G18 **Porters Pass** pass South Island, NZ
85 E25 **Porterville** Western Cape, SW South Africa
37 R12 **Porterville** California, W USA
Port-Étienne see Nouâdhibou
190 L13 **Port Fairy** Victoria, SE Australia
192 M4 **Port Fitzroy** Great Barrier Island, Auckland, NE NZ
Port Florence see Kisumu
Port-Francqui see Ilebo
81 C18 **Port-Gentil** Ogooué-Maritime, W Gabon
81 C18 **Port-Gentil** ✕ Ogooué-Maritime, W Gabon
190 I7 **Port Germein** South Australia
24 J6 **Port Gibson** Mississippi, S USA
41 Q13 **Port Graham** Alaska, USA
79 U17 **Port Harcourt** Rivers, S Nigeria
8 J16 **Port Hardy** Vancouver Island, British Columbia, SW Canada
Port Harrison see Inukjuak
11 R14 **Port Hawkesbury** Cape Breton Island, Nova Scotia, SE Canada
188 I6 **Port Hedland** Western Australia
41 O15 **Port Heiden** Alaska, USA
99 I19 **Porthmadog** var. Portmadoc. NW Wales, UK
12 I15 **Port Hope** Ontario, SE Canada
11 S9 **Port Hope Simpson** Newfoundland and Labrador, E Canada
67 C24 **Port Howard Settlement** West Falkland, Falkland Islands
33 T9 **Port Huron** Michigan, N USA
109 K17 **Portici** Campania, S Italy
143 Y13 **Port-Iliç** Rus. Port Il'ich. SE Azerbaijan
Port Il'ich see Port-Iliç
106 G14 **Portimão** var. Vila Nova de Portimão. Faro, S Portugal
27 T17 **Port Isabel** Texas, SW USA
20 J13 **Port Jervis** New York, NE USA
57 S7 **Port Kaituma** NW Guyana
130 K12 **Port Katon** Rostovskaya Oblast', SW Russian Federation
191 S9 **Port Kembla** New South Wales, SE Australia
190 F8 **Port Kenny** South Australia
Port Klang see Pelabuhan Klang
Port Láirge see Waterford
191 S8 **Portland** New South Wales, SE Australia
190 L13 **Portland** Victoria, SE Australia
192 K4 **Portland** Northland, North Island, NZ
33 Q13 **Portland** Indiana, N USA
21 P8 **Portland** Maine, NE USA
33 Q9 **Portland** Michigan, N USA
31 Q4 **Portland** North Dakota, N USA
34 G11 **Portland** Oregon, NW USA
22 J8 **Portland** Tennessee, S USA
27 T14 **Portland** Texas, SW USA
34 G11 **Portland** ✕ Oregon, NW USA
190 L13 **Portland Bay** bay Victoria, SE Australia
46 K13 **Portland Bight** bay S Jamaica
99 L24 **Portland Bill** var. Bill of Portland. headland S England, UK
Portland, Bill of see Portland Bill
191 P15 **Portland, Cape** headland Tasmania, SE Australia
8 J12 **Portland Inlet** inlet British Columbia, W Canada
192 P11 **Portland Island** island E NZ
67 F15 **Portland Point** headland SW Ascension Island
46 J13 **Portland Point** headland C Jamaica
105 P16 **Port-la-Nouvelle** Aude, S France
Portlaoighise see Port Laoise
99 E18 **Port Laoise** var. Portlaoise, Ir. Portlaoighise; prev. Maryborough. C Ireland
27 U13 **Port Lavaca** Texas, SW USA
190 G9 **Port Lincoln** South Australia
41 Q14 **Port Lions** Kodiak Island, Alaska, USA
78 I15 **Port Loko** W Sierra Leone
67 E24 **Port Louis** East Falkland, Falkland Islands
47 Y5 **Port-Louis** Grande Terre, N Guadeloupe
181 X16 **Port Louis** ● (Mauritius) NW Mauritius
Port Louis see Scarborough
Port-Lyautey see Kénitra
190 K12 **Port MacDonnell** South Australia
191 U7 **Port Macquarie** New South Wales, SE Australia
Portmadoc see Porthmadog
Port Mahon see Mahón
46 K12 **Port Maria** C Jamaica
8 K16 **Port McNeill** Vancouver Island, British Columbia, SW Canada
11 P11 **Port-Menier** Île d'Anticosti, Québec, E Canada
41 N15 **Port Moller** Alaska, USA
46 L13 **Port Morant** E Jamaica
46 K13 **Portmore** C Jamaica
194 I16 **Port Moresby** ● (PNG) Central/National Capital District, SW PNG
Port Natal see Durban
27 Y11 **Port Neches** Texas, SW USA
190 G9 **Port Neill** South Australia
13 S6 **Portneuf** ~ Québec, SE Canada
13 R6 **Portneuf, Lac** ◎ Québec, SE Canada
85 D23 **Port Nolloth** Northern Cape, W South Africa
20 J17 **Port Norris** New Jersey, NE USA
Port-Nouveau-Québec see Kangiqsualujjuaq
106 G6 **Porto** Eng. Oporto; anc. Portus Cale. Porto, NW Portugal
106 G6 **Porto** var. Pôrto. ◈ district N Portugal
106 G6 **Porto** ✕ Porto, W Portugal
63 I16 **Porto Alegre** var. Pôrto Alegre. state capital Rio Grande do Sul, S Brazil
Porto Alexandre see Tombua
84 B12 **Porto Amboim** Cuanza Sul, NW Angola
Porto Amélia see Pemba
Porto Bello see Portobelo
45 T14 **Portobelo** var. Porto Bello, Puerto Bello. Colón, N Panama
62 G10 **Pôrto Camargo** Paraná, S Brazil
27 U13 **Port O'Connor** Texas, SW USA
Pôrto de Mós see Porto de Moz
60 J12 **Porto de Moz** var. Pôrto de Mós. Pará, NE Brazil
66 O5 **Porto do Moniz** Madeira, Portugal, NE Atlantic Ocean
61 H16 **Porto dos Gaúchos** Mato Grosso, W Brazil
Porto Edda see Sarandë
109 J24 **Porto Empedocle** Sicilia, Italy, C Mediterranean Sea
61 H20 **Porto Esperança** Mato Grosso do Sul, SW Brazil
108 E13 **Portoferraio** Toscana, C Italy
98 G6 **Port of Ness** NW Scotland, UK
47 U14 **Port-of-Spain** ● (Trinidad and Tobago) Trinidad, Trinidad and Tobago
Port of Spain see Piarco
104 E2 **Porto, Golfe de** gulf Corse, France, C Mediterranean Sea
Porto Grande see Mindelo
108 I7 **Portogruaro** Veneto, NE Italy
37 P5 **Portola** California, W USA
197 B12 **Port-Olry** Espiritu Santo, C Vanuatu
95 J17 **Pörtom** Fin. Pirttikylä. Vaasa, W Finland
Port Omna see Portumna
61 G21 **Porto Murtinho** Mato Grosso do Sul, SW Brazil
61 K16 **Porto Nacional** Tocantins, C Brazil
79 S16 **Porto-Novo** ● (Benin) S Benin
25 X10 **Port Orange** Florida, SE USA
34 G8 **Port Orchard** Washington, NW USA
Porto Re see Kraljevica
34 E15 **Port Orford** Oregon, NW USA
Porto Rico see Puerto Rico
108 J13 **Porto San Giorgio** Marche, C Italy
109 F14 **Porto San Stefano** Toscana, C Italy
66 P5 **Porto Santo** var. Vila Baleira. Porto Santo, Madeira, Portugal, NE Atlantic Ocean
66 Q5 **Porto Santo** ✕ Porto Santo, Madeira, Portugal, NE Atlantic Ocean
66 P5 **Porto Santo** var. Ilha do Porto Santo. island Madeira, Portugal, NE Atlantic Ocean
62 H9 **Porto São José** Paraná, S Brazil
61 O19 **Porto Seguro** Bahia, E Brazil
109 B17 **Porto Torres** Sardegna, Italy, C Mediterranean Sea
61 J23 **Porto União** Santa Catarina, S Brazil
104 F3 **Porto-Vecchio** Corse, France, C Mediterranean Sea
61 E15 **Porto Velho** var. Velho. state capital Rondônia, W Brazil
58 A6 **Portoviejo** var. Puertoviejo. Manabí, W Ecuador
193 B26 **Port Pegasus** bay Stewart Island, NZ
12 H15 **Port Perry** Ontario, SE Canada
191 N12 **Port Phillip Bay** harbor Victoria, SE Australia
190 I8 **Port Pirie** South Australia
98 G9 **Portree** N Scotland, UK
Port Rex see East London
Port Rois see Portrush
46 K13 **Port Royal** E Jamaica
23 R15 **Port Royal** South Carolina, SE USA
23 R15 **Port Royal Sound** inlet South Carolina, SE USA
99 F14 **Portrush** Ir. Port Rois. N Northern Ireland, UK
77 W7 **Port Said** Ar. Būr Sa'īd. N Egypt
25 R9 **Port Saint Joe** Florida, SE USA
25 Y11 **Port Saint John** Florida, SE USA
85 K24 **Port St.Johns** Eastern Cape, SE South Africa
105 R16 **Port-St-Louis-du-Rhône** Bouches-du-Rhône, SE France
46 K10 **Port Salut** SW Haiti
67 E24 **Port Salvador** inlet East Falkland, Falkland Islands
67 D24 **Port San Carlos** East Falkland, Falkland Islands
11 S10 **Port Saunders** Newfoundland, Newfoundland and Labrador, SE Canada
85 K24 **Port Shepstone** KwaZulu/Natal, E South Africa
47 O11 **Portsmouth** var. Grand-Anse. NW Dominica
99 M24 **Portsmouth** S England, UK
21 P10 **Portsmouth** New Hampshire, NE USA

◆ Country
● Country Capital
◇ Dependent Territory
○ Dependent Territory Capital
◈ Administrative Region
✕ International Airport
▲ Mountain
▲ Mountain Range
▲ Volcano
~ River
◎ Lake
⊡ Reservoir

33 S15 **Portsmouth** Ohio, N USA
23 X7 **Portsmouth** Virginia, NE USA
12 E17 **Port Stanley** Ontario, S Canada
67 B25 **Port Stephens** *inlet* West Falkland, Falkland Islands
67 B25 **Port Stephens Settlement** West Falkland, Falkland Islands
99 F14 **Portstewart** *Ir.* Port Stíobhaird. N Northern Ireland, UK
Port Stíobhaird *see* Portstewart
82 I7 **Port Sudan** Red Sea, NE Sudan
24 L10 **Port Sulphur** Louisiana, S USA
Port Swettenham *see* Klang/Pelabuhan Klang
99 J22 **Port Talbot** S Wales, UK
94 L11 **Porttipahdan Tekojärvi** ◎ N Finland
34 G7 **Port Townsend** Washington, NW USA
106 H9 **Portugal** *off.* Republic of Portugal. ◆ *republic* SW Europe
107 O2 **Portugalete** País Vasco, N Spain
56 J6 **Portuguesa** *off.* Estado Portuguesa. ◈ *state* N Venezuela
Portuguese East Africa *see* Mozambique
Portuguese Guinea *see* Guinea-Bissau
Portuguese Timor *see* Timor Timur
Portuguese West Africa *see* Angola
99 D18 **Portumna** *Ir.* Port Omna. W Ireland
Portus Cale *see* Porto
Portus Magnus *see* Almería
Portus Magonis *see* Mahón
105 P17 **Port-Vendres** *var.* Port Vendres. Pyrénées-Orientales, S France
190 H9 **Port Victoria** South Australia
197 C14 **Port-Vila** *var.* Vila. ● (Vanuatu) Éfaté, C Vanuatu
190 I9 **Port Wakefield** South Australia
33 N8 **Port Washington** Wisconsin, N USA
59 J14 **Porvenir** Pando, NW Bolivia
65 I24 **Porvenir** Magallanes, S Chile
63 D18 **Porvenir** Paysandú, W Uruguay
95 M19 **Porvoo** *Swe.* Borgå. Uusimaa, S Finland
Porzecze *see* Parechcha
106 M10 **Porzuna** Castilla-La Mancha, C Spain
63 E14 **Posadas** Misiones, NE Argentina
106 L13 **Posadas** Andalucía, S Spain
Poschega *see* Slavonska Požega
110 J11 **Poschiavino** ≈ Italy/Switzerland
110 J10 **Poschiavo** *Ger.* Puschlav. Graubünden, S Switzerland
114 D12 **Posedarje** Zadar-Knin, W Croatia
Posen *see* Poznań
128 L14 **Poshekhon'ye** Yaroslavskaya Oblast', W Russian Federation
94 M13 **Posio** Lappi, NE Finland
Poskam *see* Zepu
Posnania *see* Poznań
175 Pp9 **Poso** Sulawesi, C Indonesia
61 P15 **Poço da Cruz, Açude** ⊠ E Brazil
175 Pp10 **Poso, Danau** ◎ Sulawesi, C Indonesia
143 R10 **Posof** Kars, NE Turkey
175 Pp9 **Poso, Sungai** ≈ Sulawesi, C Indonesia
27 R6 **Possum Kingdom Lake** ⊠ Texas, SW USA
27 N6 **Post** Texas, SW USA
Postavy/Postawy *see* Pastavy
10 I7 **Poste-de-la-Baleine** Québec, NE Canada
101 M17 **Posterholt** Limburg, SE Netherlands
85 G22 **Postmasburg** Northern Cape, N South Africa
Pôsto Diauarum *see* Campo de Diauarum
61 I16 **Pôsto Jacaré** Mato Grosso, W Brazil
111 T12 **Postojna** *Ger.* Adelsberg, *It.* Postumia. SW Slovenia
Postumia *see* Postojna
31 X12 **Postville** Iowa, C USA
Pöstyén *see* Piešťany
115 G14 **Posušje** SW Bosnia and Herzegovina
175 Pp16 **Pota** Flores, C Indonesia
117 G23 **Potamós** Antikýthira, S Greece
57 S9 **Potaru River** ≈ C Guyana
85 I21 **Potchefstroom** North-West, N South Africa
29 R11 **Poteau** Oklahoma, C USA
27 R12 **Poteet** Texas, SW USA
117 G14 **Poteídaia** *site of ancient city* Kentrikí Makedonía, N Greece
Potentia *see* Potenza
109 M18 **Potenza** *anc.* Potentia. Basilicata, S Italy
193 A24 **Poteriteri, Lake** ◎ South Island, NZ
106 M2 **Potes** Cantabria, N Spain
85 J20 **Potgietersrus** Northern, NE South Africa
27 S12 **Poth** Texas, SW USA
34 J9 **Potholes Reservoir** ⊠ Washington, NW USA
143 Q9 **P'ot'i** W Georgia
79 X13 **Potiskum** Yobe, NE Nigeria
34 M9 **Potlatch** Idaho, NW USA
35 N9 **Pot Mountain** ▲ Idaho, NW USA
115 H14 **Potoci** S Bosnia and Herzegovina
23 V3 **Potomac River** ≈ NE USA
29 W6 **Potosi** Missouri, C USA
59 L20 **Potosí** Potosí, S Bolivia
44 H9 **Potosí** Chinandega, NW Nicaragua
59 K21 **Potosí** ◈ *department* SW Bolivia
64 H7 **Potrerillos** Atacama, N Chile
44 H5 **Potrerillos** Cortés, NW Honduras
64 H8 **Potro, Cerro del** ▲ N Chile
102 N12 **Potsdam** Brandenburg, NE Germany
20 J7 **Potsdam** New York, NE USA
111 X5 **Pottendorf** Niederösterreich, E Austria
111 X5 **Pottenstein** Niederösterreich, E Austria
197 G4 **Pott, Île** *island* Îles Belep, W New Caledonia
20 I15 **Pottstown** Pennsylvania, NE USA
20 H14 **Pottsville** Pennsylvania, NE USA
161 L25 **Pottuvil** Eastern Province, SE Sri Lanka
155 U6 **Potwar Plateau** *plateau* NE Pakistan
104 J7 **Pouancé** Maine-et-Loire, W France
197 H5 **Pouébo** Province Nord, C New Caledonia
197 H6 **Pouembout** Province Nord, W New Caledonia
13 R6 **Poulin de Courval, Lac** ◎ Québec, SE Canada
20 L9 **Poultney** Vermont, NE USA
197 H5 **Poum** Province Nord, W New Caledonia
61 L21 **Pouso Alegre** Minas Gerais, NE Brazil
198 Bb8 **Poutasi** Upolu, SE Western Samoa
178 Ii12 **Poŭthĭsăt** *prev.* Pursat. W Cambodia
178 Ii13 **Poŭthĭsăt, Stœng** *prev.* Pursat. ≈ W Cambodia
104 J9 **Pouzauges** Vendée, NW France
Po, Valle del *see* Po Valley
108 F8 **Po Valley** *It.* Valle del Po. *valley* N Italy
113 I19 **Považská Bystrica** *Ger.* Waagbistritz, *Hung.* Vágbeszterce. Stredné Slovensko, NW Slovakia
128 J10 **Povenets** Respublika Kareliya, NW Russian Federation
192 Q9 **Poverty Bay** *inlet* North Island, NZ
114 K12 **Povlen** ▲▲ W Yugoslavia
106 G6 **Póvoa de Varzim** Porto, NW Portugal
131 N8 **Povorino** Voronezhskaya Oblast', W Russian Federation
Povungnituk *see* Puvirnituq
10 J3 **Povungnituk, Rivière de** ≈ Québec, NE Canada
12 H11 **Powassan** Ontario, S Canada
37 U17 **Poway** California, W USA
35 W14 **Powder River** Wyoming, C USA
35 Y10 **Powder River** ≈ Montana/Wyoming, NW USA
34 L12 **Powder River** ≈ Oregon, NW USA
35 W13 **Powder River Pass** *pass* Wyoming, C USA
35 U12 **Powell** Wyoming, C USA
67 I22 **Powell Basin** *undersea feature* NW Weddell Sea
38 M8 **Powell, Lake** ◎ Utah, W USA
39 R4 **Powell, Mount** ▲ Colorado, C USA
8 L17 **Powell River** British Columbia, SW Canada
33 N5 **Powers** Michigan, N USA
30 K2 **Powers Lake** North Dakota, N USA
23 V6 **Powhatan** Virginia, NE USA
33 V13 **Powhatan Point** Ohio, N USA
99 J20 **Powys** *cultural region* E Wales, UK
197 I6 **Poya** Province Nord, C New Caledonia
167 P10 **Poyang Hu** ◎ S China
126 Mm16 **Poyarkovo** Amurskaya Oblast', SE Russian Federation
32 L7 **Poygan, Lake** ◎ Wisconsin, N USA
111 Y2 **Poysdorf** Niederösterreich, NE Austria
114 N11 **Požarevac** *Ger.* Passarowitz. Serbia, NE Yugoslavia
43 Q13 **Poza Rica** *var.* Poza Rica de Hidalgo. Veracruz-Llave, E Mexico
Poza Rica de Hidalgo *see* Poza Rica
114 L13 **Požega** Serbia, W Yugoslavia
Požega *see* Slavonska Požega
114 H9 **Požega-Slavonija** *off.* Požeško-Slavonska Županija. ◈ *province* NE Croatia
129 U13 **Pozhva** Komi-Permyatskiy Avtonomnyy Okrug, NW Russian Federation
112 G11 **Poznań** *Ger.* Posen, Posnania. Poznań, W Poland
112 G11 **Poznań** *off.* Województwo Poznańskie, *Ger.* Posen, Posnania. ◈ *province* W Poland
Poznańskie, Województwo *see* Poznań
107 O13 **Pozo Alcón** Andalucía, S Spain
64 H3 **Pozo Almonte** Tarapacá, N Chile
106 L12 **Pozoblanco** Andalucía, S Spain
107 Q11 **Pozo Cañada** Castilla-La Mancha, C Spain
64 N5 **Pozo Colorado** Presidente Hayes, C Paraguay
65 J20 **Pozos, Punta** *headland* S Argentina
Pozsega *see* Slavonska Požega
Pozsony *see* Bratislava
57 N5 **Pozuelos** Anzoátegui, NE Venezuela
109 L26 **Pozzallo** Sicilia, Italy, C Mediterranean Sea
109 K17 **Pozzuoli** *anc.* Puteoli. Campania, S Italy
79 P17 **Pra** ≈ S Ghana
Prabumulih *see* Perabumulih
113 C19 **Prachatice** *Ger.* Prachatitz. Jižní Čechy, SW Czech Republic
Prachatitz *see* Prachatice
178 Hh11 **Prachin Buri** *var.* Prachinburi. Prachin Buri, C Thailand
Prachuab Girikhand *see* Prachuap Khiri Khan
178 H13 **Prachuap Khiri Khan** *var.* Prachuab Girikhand. Prachuap Khiri Khan, SW Thailand
113 H16 **Praděd** *Ger.* Altvater. ▲ NE Czech Republic
56 D11 **Pradera** Valle del Cauca, SW Colombia
105 O17 **Prades** Pyrénées-Orientales, S France
61 O19 **Prado** Bahia, SE Brazil
56 E11 **Prado** Tolima, C Colombia
Prae *see* Phrae
Prag/Praga/Prague *see* Praha
29 O10 **Prague** Oklahoma, C USA
113 D16 **Praha** *Eng.* Prague, *Ger.* Prag, *Pol.* Praga. ● (Czech Republic) Střední Čechy, NW Czech Republic
118 J13 **Prahova** ◈ *county* SE Romania
118 J13 **Prahova** ≈ S Romania
78 E10 **Praia** ● (Cape Verde) Santiago, S Cape Verde
85 M21 **Praia do Bilene** Gaza, S Mozambique
85 M20 **Praia do Xai-Xai** Gaza, S Mozambique
118 J10 **Praid** *Hung.* Parajd. Harghita, C Romania
28 J3 **Prairie Dog Creek** ≈ Kansas/Nebraska, C USA
32 J9 **Prairie du Chien** Wisconsin, N USA
29 S9 **Prairie Grove** Arkansas, C USA
33 P10 **Prairie River** ≈ Michigan, N USA
Prairie State *see* Illinois
27 V11 **Prairie View** Texas, SW USA
178 Ii11 **Prakhon Chai** Buri Ram, E Thailand
111 R4 **Pram** ≈ N Austria
111 S4 **Prambachkirchen** Oberösterreich, N Austria
120 H2 **Prangli** *island* N Estonia
160 J13 **Prānhita** ≈ C India
180 I15 **Praslin** *island* Inner Islands, NE Seychelles
117 O23 **Prasonísi, Ákra** *headland* Ródos, Dodekánisos, Greece, Aegean Sea
113 I14 **Praszka** Częstochowa, S Poland
121 M18 **Pratasy** *Rus.* Protasy. Homyel'skaya Voblasts', SE Belarus
178 I10 **Prathai** Nakhon Ratchasima, E Thailand
Prathet Thai *see* Thailand
Prathum Thani *see* Pathum Thani
65 F21 **Prat, Isla** *island* S Chile
108 G11 **Prato** Toscana, C Italy
105 O17 **Prats-de-Mollo-la-Preste** Pyrénées-Orientales, S France
28 L6 **Pratt** Kansas, C USA
110 E6 **Pratteln** Basel-Land, NW Switzerland
199 L2 **Pratt Seamount** *undersea feature* N Pacific Ocean
25 P5 **Prattville** Alabama, S USA
Praust *see* Pruszcz Gdański
116 M7 **Pravda** *prev.* Dogrular. Razgradska Oblast, NE Bulgaria
121 B14 **Pravdinsk** *Ger.* Friedland. Kaliningradskaya Oblast', W Russian Federation
106 K2 **Pravia** Asturias, N Spain
120 L12 **Prazaroki** *Rus.* Prozoroki. Vitsyebskaya Voblasts', N Belarus
Prázsmár *see* Prejmer
178 J11 **Preăh Vihéar** Preăh Vihéar, N Cambodia
118 J12 **Predeal** *Hung.* Predeál. Braşov, C Romania
111 S8 **Predlitz** Steiermark, SE Austria
9 V15 **Preeceville** Saskatchewan, S Canada
Preenkuln *see* Priekule
104 K6 **Pré-en-Pail** Mayenne, NW France
111 T4 **Pregarten** Oberösterreich, N Austria
56 H7 **Pregonero** Táchira, NW Venezuela
120 J10 **Preiļi** *Ger.* Preli. Preiļi, SE Latvia
118 J12 **Prejmer** *Ger.* Tartlau, *Hung.* Prázsmár. Braşov, S Romania
115 J16 **Prekornica** ▲▲ SW Yugoslavia
Preli *see* Preiļi
Prëmet *see* Përmet
102 M12 **Premnitz** Brandenburg, NE Germany
27 S15 **Premont** Texas, SW USA
115 H14 **Prenj** ▲▲ S Bosnia and Herzegovina
Prenjas/Prenjasi *see* Përrenjas
24 L7 **Prentiss** Mississippi, S USA
Preny *see* Prienai
102 O10 **Prenzlau** Brandenburg, NE Germany
126 Jj12 **Preobrazhenka** Irkutskaya Oblast', C Russian Federation
177 Ee9 **Preparis Island** *island* SW Myanmar
Prerau *see* Přerov
113 H18 **Přerov** *Ger.* Prerau. Severní Morava, E Czech Republic
Preschau *see* Prešov
12 M14 **Prescott** Ontario, SE Canada
38 K12 **Prescott** Arizona, SW USA
29 T13 **Prescott** Arkansas, C USA
34 L10 **Prescott** Washington, NW USA
32 H6 **Prescott** Wisconsin, N USA
193 A24 **Preservation Inlet** *inlet* South Island, NZ
114 O7 **Preševo** Serbia, SE Yugoslavia
31 N10 **Presho** South Dakota, N USA
60 M13 **Presidente Dutra** Maranhão, E Brazil
62 I8 **Presidente Epitácio** São Paulo, S Brazil
64 N5 **Presidente Hayes** *off.* Departamento de Presidente Hayes. ◈ *department* C Paraguay
62 I9 **Presidente Prudente** São Paulo, S Brazil
Presidente Stroessner *see* Ciudad del Este
Presidente Vargas *see* Itabira
62 I8 **Presidente Venceslau** São Paulo, S Brazil
199 L11 **President Thiers Seamount** *undersea feature* C Pacific Ocean
26 J11 **Presidio** Texas, SW USA
Preslav *see* Veliki Preslav
113 M19 **Prešov** *var.* Preschau, *Ger.* Eperies, *Hung.* Eperjes. Východné Slovensko, NE Slovakia
115 N20 **Prespa, Lake** *Alb.* Liqen i Prespës, *Gk.* Límni Megáli Préspa, Limni Prespa, *Mac.* Prespansko Ezero, *Serb.* Prespansko Jezero. ◎ SE Europe
Prespa, Limni/Prespansko Ezero/Prespansko Jezero/Prespës, Liqen i *see* Prespa, Lake
21 S2 **Presque Isle** Maine, NE USA
20 B11 **Presque Isle** *headland* Pennsylvania, NE USA
Pressburg *see* Bratislava
79 P17 **Prestea** SW Ghana
113 B17 **Přeštice** *Ger.* Pschestitz. Západní Čechy, W Czech Republic
99 K17 **Preston** NW England, UK
25 S6 **Preston** Georgia, SE USA
35 R16 **Preston** Idaho, NW USA
31 Z13 **Preston** Iowa, C USA
31 X11 **Preston** Minnesota, N USA
23 O6 **Prestonsburg** Kentucky, S USA
98 I13 **Prestwick** W Scotland, UK
85 J21 **Pretoria** *var.* Epitoli, Tshwane. ● (South Africa-administrative capital) Gauteng, NE South Africa
Pretoria-Witwatersrand-Vereeniging *see* Gauteng
Pretusha *see* Pretushë
115 M21 **Pretushë** *var.* Pretusha. Korçë, SE Albania
Preussisch Eylau *see* Bagrationovsk
Preussisch-Stargard *see* Starogard Gdański
Preußisch Holland *see* Pasłęk
117 C17 **Préveza** Ípeiros, W Greece
39 V3 **Prewitt Reservoir** ⊠ Colorado, C USA
178 J13 **Prey Vêng** Prey Vêng, S Cambodia
150 M12 **Priaral'skiye Karakumy, Peski** *desert* SW Kazakhstan
126 L16 **Priargunsk** Chitinskaya Oblast', S Russian Federation
40 K14 **Pribilof Islands** *island group* Alaska, USA
115 K14 **Priboj** Serbia, W Yugoslavia
113 C17 **Příbram** *Ger.* Pibrans. Střední Čechy, W Czech Republic
38 M4 **Price** Utah, W USA
39 N5 **Price River** ≈ Utah, W USA
25 N8 **Prichard** Alabama, S USA
27 R8 **Priddy** Texas, SW USA
107 P8 **Priego** Castilla-La Mancha, C Spain
106 M14 **Priego de Córdoba** Andalucía, S Spain
120 C10 **Priekule** *Ger.* Preenkuln. Liepāja, SW Latvia
120 C12 **Priekulė** *Ger.* Prökuls. Gargždai, W Lithuania
121 F14 **Prienai** *Pol.* Preny. Prienai, S Lithuania
85 G23 **Prieska** Northern Cape, C South Africa
34 M7 **Priest Lake** ◎ Idaho, NW USA
34 M7 **Priest River** Idaho, NW USA
106 M3 **Prieta, Peña** ▲ N Spain
42 J10 **Prieto, Cerro** ▲ C Mexico
113 J19 **Prievidza** *var.* Priewitz, *Ger.* Priwitz, *Hung.* Privigye. Stredné Slovensko, C Slovakia
Priewitz *see* Prievidza
114 F10 **Prijedor** NW Bosnia and Herzegovina
115 K14 **Prijepolje** Serbia, W Yugoslavia
Prikaspiyskaya Nizmennost' *see* Caspian Depression
115 O19 **Prilep** *Turk.* Perlepe. S FYR Macedonia
110 B9 **Prilly** Vaud, SW Switzerland
Priluki *see* Pryluky
64 L10 **Primero, Río** ≈ C Argentina
31 S12 **Primghar** Iowa, C USA
114 B9 **Primorje-Gorski Kotar** *off.* Primorsko-Goranska Županija. ◈ *province* NW Croatia
120 A13 **Primorsk** *Ger.* Fischhausen. Kaliningradskaya Oblast', W Russian Federation
128 G12 **Primorsk** *Fin.* Koivisto. Leningradskaya Oblast', NW Russian Federation
Primorsk/Primorskoye *see* Prymors'k
127 Nn17 **Primorskiy Kray** *prev. Eng.* Maritime Territory. ◈ *territory* SE Russian Federation
116 N10 **Primorsko** *prev.* Keupriya. Burgaska Oblast, SE Bulgaria
130 K13 **Primorsko-Akhtarsk** Krasnodarskiy Kray, SW Russian Federation
119 U13 **Primors'kyy** Respublika Krym, S Ukraine
115 D14 **Primošten** Šibenik, S Croatia
9 R13 **Primrose Lake** ◎ Saskatchewan, C Canada
9 T14 **Prince Albert** Saskatchewan, S Canada
85 G25 **Prince Albert** Western Cape, SW South Africa
15 I1 **Prince Albert Peninsula** *peninsula* Victoria Island, Northwest Territories, NW Canada
15 I3 **Prince Albert Sound** *inlet* Northwest Territories, N Canada
15 Mm2 **Prince Charles Island** *island* Northwest Territories, NE Canada
205 W6 **Prince Charles Mountains** ▲▲ Antarctica
Prince-Édouard, Île-du *see* Prince Edward Island
180 M13 **Prince Edward Fracture Zone** *tectonic feature* SW Indian Ocean
11 P14 **Prince Edward Island** *Fr.* Île-du Prince-Édouard. ◈ *province* SE Canada
11 Q14 **Prince Edward Island** *Fr.* Île-du Prince-Édouard. *island* SE Canada
181 M12 **Prince Edward Islands** *island group* S South Africa
23 X4 **Prince Frederick** Maryland, NE USA
8 M14 **Prince George** British Columbia, SW Canada
23 W6 **Prince George** Virginia, NE USA
207 O8 **Prince Gustaf Adolf Sea** *sea* Northwest Territories, N Canada
207 Q3 **Prince of Wales, Cape** *headland* Alaska, USA
189 V1 **Prince of Wales Island** *island* Queensland, E Australia
15 Jj1 **Prince of Wales Island** *island* Queen Elizabeth Islands, Northwest Territories, NW Canada
41 Y14 **Prince of Wales Island** *island* Alexander Archipelago, Alaska, USA
Prince of Wales Island *see* Pinang, Pulau
15 I1 **Prince of Wales Strait** *strait* Northwest Territories, N Canada
207 O8 **Prince Patrick Island** *island* Parry Islands, Northwest Territories, NW Canada
15 Kk1 **Prince Regent Inlet** *channel* Northwest Territories, N Canada
8 J13 **Prince Rupert** British Columbia, SW Canada
Prince's Island *see* Príncipe
23 Y5 **Princess Anne** Maryland, NE USA
205 R1 **Princess Astrid Kyst** *physical region* Antarctica
189 W2 **Princess Charlotte Bay** *bay* Queensland, NE Australia
205 W7 **Princess Elizabeth Land** *physical region* Antarctica
8 J14 **Princess Royal Island** *island* British Columbia, SW Canada
47 U15 **Princes Town** Trinidad, Trinidad and Tobago
9 N17 **Princeton** British Columbia, SW Canada
32 L11 **Princeton** Illinois, N USA
33 N16 **Princeton** Indiana, N USA
31 Z14 **Princeton** Iowa, C USA
22 H7 **Princeton** Kentucky, S USA
31 V8 **Princeton** Minnesota, N USA
29 S1 **Princeton** Missouri, C USA
20 J15 **Princeton** New Jersey, NE USA
23 R6 **Princeton** West Virginia, NE USA
41 S12 **Prince William Sound** *inlet* Alaska, USA
69 P9 **Príncipe** *var.* Príncipe Island, *Eng.* Prince's Island. *island* N Sao Tome and Principe
Príncipe Island *see* Príncipe
34 I13 **Prineville** Oregon, NW USA
30 J11 **Pringle** South Dakota, N USA
27 N1 **Pringle** Texas, SW USA
101 H14 **Prinsenbeek** Noord-Brabant, S Netherlands
100 L6 **Prinses Margriet Kanaal** *canal* N Netherlands
205 T2 **Prinsesse Ragnhild Kyst** *physical region* Antarctica
205 U2 **Prins Harald Kyst** *physical region* Antarctica
94 N2 **Prins Karls Forland** *island* W Svalbard
45 N8 **Prinzapolka** Región Autónoma Atlántico Norte, NE Nicaragua
44 L8 **Prinzapolka, Río** ≈ NE Nicaragua
125 Ff9 **Priob'ye** Khanty-Mansiyskiy Avtonomnyy Okrug, N Russian Federation
106 H1 **Prior, Cabo** *headland* NW Spain
31 V9 **Prior Lake** Minnesota, N USA
128 H11 **Priozersk** *Fin.* Käkisalmi. Leningradskaya Oblast', NW Russian Federation
121 J20 **Pripet** *Bel.* Prypyats', *Ukr.* Pryp"yat'. ≈ Belarus/Ukraine
121 J20 **Pripet Marshes** *wetland* Belarus/Ukraine
Prishtinë *see* Priština
130 J8 **Pristen'** Kurskaya Oblast', W Russian Federation
115 N16 **Priština** *Alb.* Prishtinë. Serbia, S Yugoslavia
102 M10 **Pritzwalk** Brandenburg, NE Germany
105 R13 **Privas** Ardèche, E France
109 I16 **Priverno** Lazio, C Italy
Privigye *see* Prievidza
114 C12 **Privlaka** Zadar-Knin, W Croatia
128 M15 **Privolzhsk** Ivanovskaya Oblast', NW Russian Federation
131 P7 **Privolzhskaya Vozvyshennost'** *var.* Volga Uplands. ▲▲ W Russian Federation
131 P8 **Privolzhskoye** Saratovskaya Oblast', W Russian Federation
Priwitz *see* Prievidza
131 N13 **Priyutnoye** Respublika Kalmykiya, SW Russian Federation
115 M17 **Prizren** *Alb.* Prizreni. Serbia, S Yugoslavia
Prizreni *see* Prizren
109 I24 **Prizzi** Sicilia, Italy, C Mediterranean Sea
115 P18 **Probištip** NE FYR Macedonia
174 M15 **Probolinggo** Jawa, C Indonesia
Probstberg *see* Wyszków
113 F14 **Prochowice** *Ger.* Parchwitz. Legnica, SW Poland
31 W5 **Proctor** Minnesota, N USA
27 R8 **Proctor** Texas, SW USA
27 R8 **Proctor Lake** ⊠ Texas, SW USA
161 I18 **Proddatūr** Andhra Pradesh, E India
106 H9 **Proença-a-Nova** Castelo Branco, C Portugal
97 I24 **Præstø** Storstrøm, SE Denmark
101 I21 **Profondeville** Namur, SE Belgium
43 W11 **Progreso** Yucatán, SE Mexico
126 Mm16 **Progress** Amurskaya Oblast', SE Russian Federation
131 O15 **Prokhladnyy** Kabardino-Balkarskaya Respublika, SW Russian Federation
Prokletije *see* North Albanian Alps
126 H14 **Prokop'yevsk** Kemerovskaya Oblast', S Russian Federation
Prōkuls *see* Priekulė
115 O15 **Prokuplje** Serbia, SE Yugoslavia
128 H14 **Proletariy** Novgorodskaya Oblast', W Russian Federation
130 M12 **Proletarsk** Rostovskaya Oblast', SW Russian Federation
130 J8 **Proletarskiy** Belgorodskaya Oblast', W Russian Federation
177 Ff7 **Prome** *var.* Pyè. Pegu, C Myanmar
62 J8 **Promissão** São Paulo, S Brazil
62 J8 **Promissão, Represa de** ⊠ S Brazil
129 V4 **Promyshlennyy** Respublika Komi, NW Russian Federation
121 O16 **Pronya** *Rus.* Pronya. ≈ E Belarus
8 M11 **Prophet River** British Columbia, W Canada
32 K11 **Prophetstown** Illinois, N USA
61 P16 **Propriá** Sergipe, E Brazil
104 E3 **Propriano** Corse, France, C Mediterranean Sea
Prościejów *see* Prostějov
Proskurov *see* Khmel 'nyts'kyy
116 H12 **Prosotsáni** Anatolikí Makedonía kai Thráki, NE Greece
179 Rr15 **Prosperidad** Mindanao, S Philippines
34 J10 **Prosser** Washington, NW USA
Prossnitz *see* Prostějov
113 G18 **Prostějov** *Ger.* Prossnitz, *Pol.* Prościejów. Jižní Morava, SE Czech Republic
119 V8 **Prosyana** Dnipropetrovs'ka Oblast', E Ukraine
113 L16 **Proszowice** Kraków, S Poland
Protasy *see* Pratasy
180 J11 **Protea Seamount** *undersea feature* SW Indian Ocean
117 D21 **Próti** *island* S Greece
116 N8 **Provadiya** Varnenska Oblast, NE Bulgaria
105 S15 **Provence** *prev.* Marseille-Marignane. ✕ (Marseille) Bouches-du-Rhône, SE France
105 T14 **Provence** *cultural region* SE France
105 T14 **Provence-Alpes-Côte d'Azur** ◈ *region* SE France
22 H6 **Providence** Kentucky, S USA
21 N12 **Providence** *state capital* Rhode Island, NE USA
38 L1 **Providence** Utah, W USA
Providence *see* Fort Providence
69 X10 **Providence Atoll** *var.* Providence. *atoll* S Seychelles
12 D12 **Providence Bay** Manitoulin Island, Ontario, S Canada
25 R6 **Providence Canyon** *valley* Alabama/Georgia, S USA
24 I5 **Providence, Lake** ◎ Louisiana, S USA
37 X13 **Providence Mountains** ▲▲ California, W USA
46 L6 **Providenciales** *island* W Turks and Caicos Islands
127 Q4 **Provideniya** Chukotskiy Avtonomnyy Okrug, NE Russian Federation
21 Q12 **Provincetown** Massachusetts, NE USA
105 P5 **Provins** Seine-et-Marne, N France
38 L3 **Provo** Utah, W USA
9 R15 **Provost** Alberta, SW Canada
114 G13 **Prozor** SW Bosnia and Herzegovina
Prozoroki *see* Prazaroki
62 I11 **Prudentópolis** Paraná, S Brazil
41 R5 **Prudhoe Bay** Alaska, USA
41 R4 **Prudhoe Bay** *bay* Alaska, USA
113 H16 **Prudnik** *Ger.* Neustadt, Neustadt in Oberschlesien. Opole, SW Poland
121 J16 **Prudy** *Rus.* Prudy. Minskaya Voblasts', C Belarus
103 D18 **Prüm** Rheinland-Pfalz, W Germany
103 D18 **Prüm** ≈ W Germany
Prusa *see* Bursa
112 J7 **Pruszcz Gdański** *Ger.* Praust. Gdańsk, N Poland
112 M12 **Pruszków** *Ger.* Kaltdorf. Warszawa, C Poland
118 K8 **Prut** *Ger.* Pruth. ≈ E Europe
Pruth *see* Prut
110 L8 **Prutz** Tirol, W Austria
Prużana *see* Pruzhany
121 G19 **Pruzhany** *Pol.* Prużana. Brestskaya Voblasts', SW Belarus
128 I11 **Pryazha** Respublika Kareliya, NW Russian Federation
119 U10 **Pryazovs'ke** Zaporiz'ka Oblast', SE Ukraine
Prychornomors'ka Nyzovyna *see* Black Sea Lowland
Prydniprovs'ka Nyzovyna/Prydnyaprowskaya Nizina *see* Dnieper Lowland
205 Y7 **Prydz Bay** *bay* Antarctica
119 R4 **Pryluky** *Rus.* Priluki. Chernihivs'ka Oblast', NE Ukraine
119 V10 **Prymors'k** *Rus.* Primorsk; *prev.* Primorskoye. Zaporiz'ka Oblast', SE Ukraine
29 Q9 **Pryor** Oklahoma, C USA
35 U11 **Pryor Creek** ≈ Montana, NW USA
Pryp"yat'/Prypyats' *see* Pripet
112 M10 **Przasnysz** Ostrołęka, NE Poland
113 K14 **Przedbórz** Piotrków, S Poland
Przemyskie, Województwo *see* Przemyśl
113 P17 **Przemyśl** *Rus.* Peremyshl. Przemyśl, SE Poland
113 O16 **Przemyśl** *off.* Województwo Przemyskie, *Rus.* Peremyshl. ◈ *province* SE Poland
113 O16 **Przeworsk** Przemyśl, SE Poland
Przheval'sk *see* Karakol
112 L13 **Przysucha** Radom, SE Poland
117 H18 **Psachná** *var.* Psahna, Psakhná. Évvoia, C Greece
Psahna/Psakhná *see* Psachná
117 K18 **Psará** *island* E Greece
117 I16 **Psathoúra** *island* Vóreioi Sporádes, Greece, Aegean Sea
Pschestitz *see* Přeštice
Psein Lora *see* Pishin Lora
119 S5 **Psël** ≈ Russian Federation/Ukraine
117 M21 **Psérimos** *island* Dodekánisos, Greece, Aegean Sea
Pseyn Bowr *see* Pishin Lora
Pskem *see* Piskom
153 R8 **Pskemskiy Khrebet** *Uzb.* Piskom Tizmasi. ▲▲ Kyrgyzstan/Uzbekistan
128 F14 **Pskov** *Ger.* Pleskau, *Latv.* Pleskava. Pskovskaya Oblast', W Russian Federation
120 K6 **Pskov, Lake** *Est.* Pihkva Järv, *Ger.* Pleskauer See, *Rus.* Pskovskoye Ozero. ◎ Estonia/Russian Federation
128 F15 **Pskovskaya Oblast'** ◈ *province* W Russian Federation
Pskovskoye Ozero *see* Pskov, Lake
114 G9 **Psunj** ▲▲ NE Croatia
113 J17 **Pszczyna** *Ger.* Pless. Katowice, S Poland
Ptačník/Ptacsnik *see* Vtáčnik
117 D17 **Ptéri** ▲ C Greece
Ptich' *see* Ptsich
117 E14 **Ptolemaïda** *prev.* Ptolemaïs. Dytikí Makedonía, N Greece
Ptolemaïs *see* Ptolemaïda, Greece
Ptolemaïs *see* 'Akko, Israel
123 Gg10 **Ptolemy Seamounts** *undersea feature* C Mediterranean Sea
121 M19 **Ptsich** *Rus.* Ptich'. Homyel'skaya Voblasts', SE Belarus
121 M18 **Ptsich** *Rus.* Ptich'. ≈ SE Belarus
111 X10 **Ptuj** *Ger.* Pettau; *anc.* Poetovio. NE Slovenia
194 E9 **Pua** ≈ NW PNG
63 A23 **Puán** Buenos Aires, E Argentina
198 B7 **Pu'apu'a** Savai'i, C Western Samoa
198 A7 **Puava, Cape** *headland* Savai'i, NW Western Samoa
58 F12 **Pucallpa** Ucayali, C Peru
59 J17 **Pucarani** La Paz, NW Bolivia
Pučarevo *see* Novi Travnik
163 U12 **Pucheng** Fujian, SE China
166 L6 **Pucheng** Shaanxi, C China
129 N16 **Puchezh** Ivanovskaya Oblast', W Russian Federation
113 I19 **Púchov** *Hung.* Puhó. Stredné Slovensko, NW Slovakia
118 J13 **Pucioasa** Dâmbovița, S Romania
112 I6 **Puck** Gdańsk, N Poland
32 L8 **Puckaway Lake** ◎ Wisconsin, N USA
65 G15 **Pucón** Araucanía, S Chile
95 M14 **Pudasjärvi** Oulu, C Finland
154 L8 **Pūdeh Tal, Shelleh-ye** ≈ SW Afghanistan
131 S1 **Pudem** Udmurtskaya Respublika, NW Russian Federation
Pudewitz *see* Pobiedziska
128 K11 **Pudozh** Respublika Kareliya, NW Russian Federation
99 M17 **Pudsey** N England, UK
Puduchcheri *see* Pondicherry
157 H21 **Pudukkottai** Tamil Nādu, SE India
176 Z10 **Pue** Irian Jaya, E Indonesia
43 P14 **Puebla** *var.* Puebla de Zaragoza. Puebla, S Mexico
43 P15 **Puebla** ◈ *state* S Mexico
106 L11 **Puebla de Alcocer** Extremadura, W Spain
Puebla de Don Fabrique *see* Puebla de Don Fadrique
107 P13 **Puebla de Don Fadrique** *var.* Puebla de Don Fabrique. Andalucía, S Spain
106 J11 **Puebla de la Calzada** Extremadura, W Spain
106 J5 **Puebla de Sanabria** Castilla-León, N Spain
106 I4 **Puebla de Trives** Galicia, NW Spain
Puebla de Zaragoza *see* Puebla
39 T6 **Pueblo** Colorado, C USA
39 N10 **Pueblo Colorado Wash** *valley* Arizona, SW USA
63 C16 **Pueblo Libertador** Corrientes, NE Argentina
42 J10 **Pueblo Nuevo** Durango, C Mexico
44 J8 **Pueblo Nuevo** Estelí, NW Nicaragua
56 J3 **Pueblo Nuevo** Falcón, N Venezuela
44 B6 **Pueblo Nuevo Tiquisate** *var.* Tiquisate. Escuintla, SW Guatemala
43 Q11 **Pueblo Viejo, Laguna de** *lagoon* E Mexico
65 J14 **Puelches** La Pampa, C Argentina
106 L14 **Puente-Genil** Andalucía, S Spain
107 Q3 **Puente la Reina** Navarra, N Spain
106 L12 **Puente Nuevo, Embalse de** ⊠ S Spain
59 D14 **Puente Piedra** Lima, W Peru
166 F14 **Pu'er** Yunnan, SW China
47 V6 **Puerca, Punta** *headland* E Puerto Rico
39 R12 **Puerco, Rio** ≈ New Mexico, SW USA
59 J17 **Puerto Acosta** La Paz, W Bolivia

◆ Country
● Country Capital
◇ Dependent Territory
○ Dependent Territory Capital
◈ Administrative Region
✕ International Airport
▲ Mountain
▲▲ Mountain Range
Volcano
≈ River
◎ Lake
⊠ Reservoir

65 G19 **Puerto Aisén** Aisén, S Chile
43 R17 **Puerto Ángel** Oaxaca, SE Mexico
43 T17 **Puerto Arista** Chiapas, SE Mexico
45 O16 **Puerto Armuelles** Chiriquí, SW Panama
Puerto Arrecife *see* Arrecife
56 D14 **Puerto Asís** Putumayo, SW Colombia
56 L9 **Puerto Ayacucho** Amazonas, SW Venezuela
59 C18 **Puerto Ayora** Galapagos Islands, Ecuador, E Pacific Ocean
59 C18 **Puerto Baquerizo Moreno** *var.* Baquerizo Moreno. Galapagos Islands, Ecuador, E Pacific Ocean
44 G4 **Puerto Barrios** Izabal, E Guatemala
Puerto Bello *see* Portobelo
56 F8 **Puerto Berrío** Antioquia, C Colombia
56 F9 **Puerto Boyaca** Boyacá, C Colombia
56 K4 **Puerto Cabello** Carabobo, N Venezuela
45 N7 **Puerto Cabezas** *var.* Bilwi. Región Autónoma Atlántico Norte, NE Nicaragua
56 L9 **Puerto Carreño** Vichada, E Colombia
56 E4 **Puerto Colombia** Atlántico, N Colombia
44 H4 **Puerto Cortés** Cortés, NW Honduras
56 J4 **Puerto Cumarebo** Falcón, N Venezuela
Puerto de Cabras *see* Puerto del Rosario
57 Q5 **Puerto de Hierro** Sucre, NE Venezuela
66 O11 **Puerto de la Cruz** Tenerife, Islas Canarias, Spain, NE Atlantic Ocean
66 Q11 **Puerto del Rosario** *var.* Puerto de Cabras. Fuerteventura, Islas Canarias, Spain, NE Atlantic Ocean
65 J20 **Puerto Deseado** Santa Cruz, SE Argentina
42 F8 **Puerto Escondido** Baja California Sur, W Mexico
43 R17 **Puerto Escondido** Oaxaca, SE Mexico
62 G12 **Puerto Esperanza** Misiones, NE Argentina
58 D6 **Puerto Francisco de Orellana** *var.* Coca. Napo, N Ecuador
56 H10 **Puerto Gaitán** Meta, C Colombia
Puerto Gallegos *see* Río Gallegos
62 G12 **Puerto Iguazú** Misiones, NE Argentina
58 F12 **Puerto Inca** Huánuco, N Peru
56 L11 **Puerto Inírida** *var.* Obando. Guainía, E Colombia
44 K13 **Puerto Jesús** Guanacaste, NW Costa Rica
43 Z11 **Puerto Juárez** Quintana Roo, SE Mexico
57 N5 **Puerto La Cruz** Anzoátegui, NE Venezuela
56 E14 **Puerto Leguízamo** Putumayo, S Colombia
45 N5 **Puerto Lempira** Gracias a Dios, E Honduras
Puerto Libertad *see* La Libertad
56 I11 **Puerto Limón** Meta, E Colombia
56 D13 **Puerto Limón** Putumayo, SW Colombia
Puerto Limón *see* Limón
107 N11 **Puertollano** Castilla-La Mancha, C Spain
65 K17 **Puerto Lobos** Chubut, SE Argentina
56 I3 **Puerto López** La Guajira, N Colombia
107 Q14 **Puerto Lumbreras** Murcia, SE Spain
43 V17 **Puerto Madero** Chiapas, SE Mexico
65 K17 **Puerto Madryn** Chubut, S Argentina
Puerto Magdalena *see* Bahía Magdalena
59 J15 **Puerto Maldonado** Madre de Dios, E Peru
Puerto Masachapa *see* Masachapa
Puerto México *see* Coatzacoalcos
65 G17 **Puerto Montt** Los Lagos, C Chile
43 Z12 **Puerto Morelos** Quintana Roo, SE Mexico
56 L10 **Puerto Nariño** Vichada, E Colombia
65 H23 **Puerto Natales** Magallanes, S Chile
45 X15 **Puerto Obaldía** San Blas, NE Panama
46 H6 **Puerto Padre** Las Tunas, E Cuba
56 L9 **Puerto Páez** Apure, C Venezuela
42 E3 **Puerto Peñasco** Sonora, NW Mexico
57 N5 **Puerto Píritu** Anzoátegui, NE Venezuela
47 N8 **Puerto Plata** *var.* San Felipe de Puerto Plata. N Dominican Republic
47 N8 **Puerto Plata** ✕ N Dominican Republic
Puerto Presidente Stroessner *see* Ciudad del Este
179 Oo14 **Puerto Princesa** *off.* Puerto Princesa City. Palawan, W Philippines
Puerto Princesa City *see* Puerto Princesa
Puerto Príncipe *see* Camagüey
Puerto Quellón *see* Quellón
62 F13 **Puerto Rico** Misiones, NE Argentina
59 K14 **Puerto Rico** Pando, N Bolivia
56 E12 **Puerto Rico** Caquetá, S Colombia
47 U5 **Puerto Rico** *off.* Commonwealth of Puerto Rico; *prev.* Porto Rico. ◇ *US commonwealth territory* C West Indies
66 F11 **Puerto Rico** *island* C West Indies
66 G11 **Puerto Rico Trench** *undersea feature* NE Caribbean Sea
56 I8 **Puerto Rondón** Arauca, E Colombia
Puerto San José *see* San José
65 J21 **Puerto San Julián** *var.* San Julián. Santa Cruz, SE Argentina
65 I22 **Puerto Santa Cruz** *var.* Santa Cruz. Santa Cruz, SE Argentina
Puerto Sauce *see* Juan L.Lacaze
59 Q20 **Puerto Suárez** Santa Cruz, E Bolivia
56 D13 **Puerto Umbría** Putumayo, SW Colombia
42 J13 **Puerto Vallarta** Jalisco, SW Mexico
65 G16 **Puerto Varas** Los Lagos, C Chile
44 M13 **Puerto Viejo** Heredia, NE Costa Rica
Puertoviejo *see* Portoviejo
59 B18 **Puerto Villamil** *var.* Villamil. Galapagos Islands, Ecuador, E Pacific Ocean
56 F8 **Puerto Wilches** Santander, N Colombia
65 H20 **Pueyrredón, Lago** *var.* Lago Cochrane. ◎ S Argentina
131 R7 **Pugachëv** Saratovskaya Oblast', W Russian Federation
131 T3 **Pugachëvo** Udmurtskaya Respublika, NW Russian Federation
34 H8 **Puget Sound** *sound* Washington, NW USA
109 O17 **Puglia** *var.* Le Puglie, *Eng.* Apulia. ◈ *region* SE Italy
109 N17 **Puglia, Canosa di** *anc.* Canusium. Puglia, SE Italy
120 I6 **Puhja** *Ger.* Kawelecht. Tartumaa, SE Estonia
Puhó *see* Púchov
107 V4 **Puigcerdà** Cataluña, NE Spain
Puigmal *see* Puigmal d'Err
105 N17 **Puigmal d'Err** *var.* Puigmal. ▲ S France
78 I16 **Pujehun** S Sierra Leone
Puka *see* Pukë
193 E20 **Pukaki, Lake** ◎ South Island, NZ
40 F10 **Pukalani** Maui, Hawaii, USA, C Pacific Ocean
202 J13 **Pukapuka** *atoll* N Cook Islands
203 X9 **Pukapuka** *atoll* Îles Tuamotu, E French Polynesia
Pukari Neem *see* Purekkari Neem
203 X11 **Pukarua** *var.* Pukaruha. *atoll* Îles Tuamotu, E French Polynesia
Pukaruha *see* Pukarua
12 A7 **Pukaskwa** ≈ Ontario, S Canada
9 V12 **Pukatawagan** Manitoba, C Canada
203 X16 **Pukatikei, Maunga** Ѫ Easter Island, Chile, E Pacific Ocean
190 C1 **Pukatja** *var.* Ernabella. South Australia
169 Y12 **Pukch'ŏng** E North Korea
115 L18 **Pukë** *var.* Puka. Shkodër, N Albania
192 L6 **Pukekohe** Auckland, North Island, NZ
192 L7 **Pukemiro** Waikato, North Island, NZ
202 D12 **Puke, Mont** ▲ Île Futuna, W Wallis and Futuna
Puket *see* Phuket
193 C20 **Puketeraki Range** ⛰ South Island, NZ
192 N13 **Puketoi Range** ⛰ North Island, NZ
193 F21 **Pukeuri Junction** Otago, South Island, NZ
121 L16 **Pukhavichy** *Rus.* Pukhovichi. Minskaya Voblasts', C Belarus
Pukhovichi *see* Pukhavichy
128 M10 **Puksoozero** Arkhangel'skaya Oblast', NW Russian Federation
114 A10 **Pula** *It.* Pola; *prev.* Pulj. Istra, NW Croatia
169 U14 **Pulandian** *var.* Xinjin. Liaoning, NE China
169 T14 **Pulandian Wan** *bay* NE China
179 Rr15 **Pulangi** ≈ Mindanao, S Philippines
201 O15 **Pulap Atoll** *atoll* Caroline Islands, C Micronesia
20 H9 **Pulaski** New York, NE USA
22 I10 **Pulaski** Tennessee, S USA
23 R7 **Pulaski** Virginia, NE USA
176 Yy13 **Pulau, Sungai** ≈ Irian Jaya, E Indonesia
112 N13 **Puławy** *Ger.* Neu Amerika. Lublin, E Poland
103 E16 **Pulheim** Nordrhein-Westfalen, W Germany
Pulicat *see* Pālghāt
161 J19 **Pulicat Lake** *lagoon* SE India
194 M12 **Pulie** ≈ New Britain, C PNG
Pul'-I-Khatum *see* Polekhatum
Pul-i-Khumri *see* Pol-e Khomrī
Pul-i-Sefid *see* Pol-e Safīd
Pulj *see* Pula
111 W2 **Pulkau** ≈ NE Austria
95 L15 **Pulkkila** Oulu, C Finland
125 Cc6 **Pul'kovo** ✕ (Sankt-Peterburg) Leningradskaya Oblast', NW Russian Federation
34 M9 **Pullman** Washington, NW USA
110 B10 **Pully** Vaud, SW Switzerland
42 F7 **Púlpita, Punta** *headland* W Mexico
112 M10 **Pułtusk** Ciechanów, C Poland
164 H10 **Pulu** Xinjiang Uygur Zizhiqu, W China
143 P13 **Pülümür** Tunceli, E Turkey
201 N16 **Pulusuk** *island* Caroline Islands, C Micronesia
201 N16 **Puluwat Atoll** *atoll* Caroline Islands, C Micronesia
27 N11 **Pumpville** Texas, SW USA
203 P7 **Punaauia** *var.* Hakapehi. Tahiti, W French Polynesia
58 B8 **Puná, Isla** *island* SW Ecuador
193 G16 **Punakaiki** West Coast, South Island, NZ
159 T11 **Punakha** C Bhutan
59 L18 **Punata** Cochabamba, C Bolivia
161 E14 **Pune** *prev.* Poona. Mahārāshtra, W India
85 M17 **Pungoè, Rio** *var.* Púnguè, Pungwe. ≈ C Mozambique
23 X10 **Pungo River** ≈ North Carolina, SE USA
Púnguè/Pungwe *see* Pungoè, Rio
81 N19 **Punia** Maniema, E Zaire
64 H8 **Punilla, Sierra de la** ⛰ W Argentina
167 P14 **Puning** Guangdong, S China
64 G10 **Punitaqui** Coquimbo, C Chile
158 H8 **Punjab** ◈ *state* NW India
155 T9 **Punjab** *prev.* West Punjab, Western Punjab. ◈ *province* E Pakistan
133 Q9 **Punjab Plains** *plain* N India
95 O17 **Punkaharju** *var.* Punkasalmi. Mikkeli, SE Finland
Punkasalmi *see* Punkaharju
59 I17 **Puno** Puno, SE Peru
59 H17 **Puno** *off.* Departamento de Puno. ◈ *department* S Peru
63 B24 **Punta Alta** Buenos Aires, E Argentina
65 H24 **Punta Arenas** *prev.* Magallanes. Magallanes, S Chile
47 T6 **Punta, Cerro de** ▲ C Puerto Rico
45 T15 **Punta Chame** Panamá, C Panama
59 G17 **Punta Colorada** Arequipa, SW Peru
42 F9 **Punta Coyote** Baja California Sur, W Mexico
64 G8 **Punta de Díaz** Atacama, N Chile
63 G20 **Punta del Este** Maldonado, S Uruguay
65 K17 **Punta Delgada** Chubut, SE Argentina
57 O5 **Punta de Mata** Monagas, NE Venezuela
57 O4 **Punta de Piedras** Nueva Esparta, NE Venezuela
44 F4 **Punta Gorda** Toledo, SE Belize
45 N11 **Punta Gorda** Región Autónoma Atlántico Sur, SE Nicaragua
25 W14 **Punta Gorda** Florida, SE USA
44 M11 **Punta Gorda, Río** ≈ SE Nicaragua
64 H6 **Punta Negra, Salar de** *salt lake* N Chile
42 D5 **Punta Prieta** Baja California, NW Mexico
44 L13 **Puntarenas** Puntarenas, W Costa Rica
44 L13 **Puntarenas** *off.* Provincia de Puntarenas. ◈ *province* W Costa Rica
56 J4 **Punto Fijo** Falcón, N Venezuela
107 S4 **Puntón de Guara** ▲ N Spain
20 D14 **Punxsutawney** Pennsylvania, NE USA
95 M14 **Puolanka** Oulu, C Finland
59 J17 **Pupuya, Nevado** ▲ W Bolivia
167 O10 **Puqi** Hubei, C China
59 F16 **Puquio** Ayacucho, S Peru
126 H9 **Pur** ≈ N Russian Federation
194 I13 **Purari** ≈ S PNG
29 N11 **Purcell** Oklahoma, C USA
9 O16 **Purcell Mountains** ⛰ British Columbia, SW Canada
107 P14 **Purchena** Andalucía, S Spain
29 S8 **Purdy** Missouri, C USA
120 I2 **Purekkari Neem** *prev.* Pukari Neem. *headland* N Estonia
39 U7 **Purgatoire River** ≈ Colorado, C USA
Purgstall *see* Purgstall an der Erlauf
111 V5 **Purgstall an der Erlauf** *var.* Purgstall. Niederösterreich, NE Austria
160 O13 **Puri** *var.* Jagannath. Orissa, E India
Puriramya *see* Buriram
111 X4 **Purkersdorf** Niederösterreich, NE Austria
100 I9 **Purmerend** Noord-Holland, C Netherlands
157 G16 **Pūrna** ≈ C India
Purnea *see* Pūrnia
159 R13 **Pūrnia** *prev.* Purnea. Bihār, NE India
Pursat *see* Poŭthĭsăt, Poŭthĭsăt, W Cambodia
Pursat *see* Poŭthĭsăt, Stœng, W Cambodia
Purulia *see* Puruliya
156 L13 **Puruliya** *prev.* Purulia. West Bengal, NE India
49 G7 **Purus, Rio** *Sp.* Río Purús. ≈ Brazil/Peru
194 G15 **Purutu Island** *island* SW PNG
95 N17 **Puruvesi** ◎ SE Finland
24 L7 **Purvis** Mississippi, S USA
116 J11 **Pŭrvomay** *prev.* Borisovgrad. Plovdivska Oblast, C Bulgaria
174 J14 **Purwakarta** *prev.* Poerwakarta. Jawa, C Indonesia
174 L15 **Purwodadi** *prev.* Poerwodadi. Jawa, C Indonesia
174 K15 **Purwokerto** *prev.* Poerwokerto. Jawa, C Indonesia
174 Kk15 **Purworejo** *prev.* Poerworedjo. Jawa, C Indonesia
22 H8 **Puryear** Tennessee, S USA
160 H13 **Pusad** Mahārāshtra, C India
169 Z16 **Pusan** *off.* Pusan-gwangyŏksi, *var.* Busan, *Jap.* Fusan. SE South Korea
173 Ee4 **Pusatgajo, Pegunungan** ⛰ Sumatera, NW Indonesia
Puschlav *see* Poschiavo
Pushkin *see* Tsarskoye Selo
131 Q8 **Pushkino** Saratovskaya Oblast', W Russian Federation
Pushkino *see* Biläsuvar
113 M22 **Püspökladány** Hajdú-Bihar, E Hungary
120 J3 **Püssi** *Ger.* Isenhof. Ida-Virumaa, NE Estonia
118 I5 **Pustomyty** L'vivs'ka Oblast', W Ukraine
128 F16 **Pustoshka** Pskovskaya Oblast', W Russian Federation
Pusztakalán *see* Călan
178 H1 **Putao** *prev.* Fort Hertz. Kachin State, N Mynamar
192 M8 **Putaruru** Waikato, North Island, NZ
Puteoli *see* Pozzuoli
167 R12 **Putian** Fujian, SE China
109 O17 **Putignano** Puglia, SE Italy
Putivl' *see* Putyvl'
43 Q16 **Putla** *var.* Putla de Guerrero. Oaxaca, SE Mexico
Putla de Guerrero *see* Putla
21 N12 **Putnam** Connecticut, NE USA
27 Q7 **Putnam** Texas, SW USA
20 M10 **Putney** Vermont, NE USA
113 L20 **Putnok** Borsod-Abaúj-Zemplén, NE Hungary
Putorana, Gory/Putorana Mountains *see* Putorana, Plato
126 Ii8 **Putorana, Plato** *var.* Gory Putorana, *Eng.* Putorana Mountains. ⛰ N Russian Federation
64 H2 **Putre** Tarapacá, N Chile
161 J24 **Puttalam** North Western Province, W Sri Lanka
161 J24 **Puttalam Lagoon** *lagoon* W Sri Lanka
101 H17 **Putte** Antwerpen, C Belgium
100 K11 **Putten** Gelderland, C Netherlands
102 K7 **Puttgarden** Schleswig-Holstein, N Germany
Puttiala *see* Patiāla
103 D20 **Püttlingen** Saarland, SW Germany
56 D14 **Putumayo** *off.* Intendencia del Putumayo. ◈ *province* S Colombia
50 E7 **Putumayo, Río** *var.* Rio Içá. ≈ NW South America *see also* Içá, Rio
174 K8 **Putus, Tanjung** *headland* Borneo, N Indonesia
118 J8 **Putyla** Chernivets'ka Oblast', W Ukraine
119 S3 **Putyvl'** *Rus.* Putivl'. Sums'ka Oblast', NE Ukraine
95 M18 **Puula** ◎ SE Finland
95 N18 **Puumala** Mikkeli, SE Finland
120 I5 **Puurmani** *Ger.* Talkhof. Jõgevamaa, E Estonia
101 G17 **Puurs** Antwerpen, N Belgium
Pu'uUla'ula *see* Red Hill
40 A8 **Puuwai** Niihau, Hawaii, USA, C Pacific Ocean
10 J4 **Puvirnituq** *prev.* Povungnituk. Québec, NE Canada
34 H8 **Puyallup** Washington, NW USA
167 O5 **Puyang** Henan, C China
167 R9 **Puyang Jiang** *var.* Tsien Tang. ≈ SE China
105 O11 **Puy-de-Dôme** ◈ *department* C France
105 N15 **Puylaurens** Tarn, S France
104 M13 **Puy-l'Evêque** Lot, S France
105 N17 **Puymorens, Col de** *pass* S France
58 C7 **Puyo** Pastaza, C Ecuador
193 A24 **Puysegur Point** *headland* South Island, NZ
154 J8 **Pūzak, Hāmūn-e** *Pash.* Hāmūn-i-Puzak. ◎ SW Afghanistan
Puzak, Hāmūn-i- *see* Pūzak, Hāmūn-e
83 J23 **Pwani** *Eng.* Coast. ◈ *region* E Tanzania
81 O23 **Pweto** Shaba, SE Zaire
99 I19 **Pwllheli** NW Wales, UK
201 O14 **Pwok** Pohnpei, E Micronesia
126 Gg10 **Pyakupur** ≈ N Russian Federation
128 M6 **Pyalitsa** Murmanskaya Oblast', NW Russian Federation
128 K10 **Pyal'ma** Respublika Kareliya, NW Russian Federation
Pyandzh *see* Panj
128 I6 **Pyaozero, Ozero** ◎ NW Russian Federation
177 Ff9 **Pyapon** Irrawaddy, SW Mynamar
121 J15 **Pyarshai** *Rus.* Pershay. Minskaya Voblasts', C Belarus
126 I6 **Pyasina** ≈ N Russian Federation
116 I10 **Pyasŭchnik, Yazovir** ⊠ C Bulgaria
125 B13 **Pyatigorsk** Stavropol'skiy Kray, SW Russian Federation
Pyatikhatki *see* P"yatykhatky
119 S7 **P"yatykhatky** *Rus.* Pyatikhatki. Dnipropetrovs'ka Oblast', E Ukraine
177 G6 **Pyawbwe** Mandalay, C Mynamar
131 T3 **Pychas** Udmurtskaya Respublika, NW Russian Federation
Pyè *see* Prome
177 F6 **Pyechin** Chin State, W Mynamar
121 G17 **Pyeski** *Rus.* Peski. Hrodzyenskaya Voblasts', W Belarus
121 L19 **Pyetrykaw** *Rus.* Petrikov. Homyel'skaya Voblasts', SE Belarus
95 M16 **Pyhajärvi** ◎ C Finland
95 O17 **Pyhäjärvi** ◎ SE Finland
95 L15 **Pyhäjoki** Oulu, W Finland
95 L15 **Pyhäjoki** ≈ W Finland
95 M15 **Pyhäntä** Oulu, C Finland
95 M16 **Pyhäsalmi** Oulu, C Finland
95 O17 **Pyhäselkä** ◎ SE Finland
95 M19 **Pyhtää** *Swe.* Pyttis. Kymi, S Finland
177 G6 **Pyinmana** Mandalay, C Mynamar
117 N24 **Pylés** *var.* Piles. Kárpathos, SE Greece
117 D21 **Pýlos** *var.* Pilos. Pelopónnisos, S Greece
20 B12 **Pymatuning Reservoir** ⊠ Ohio/Pennsylvania, NE USA
169 X15 **P'yŏngt'aek** NW South Korea
169 V14 **P'yŏngyang** *var.* P'yŏngyang-si, *Eng.* Pyongyang. ● (North Korea) SW North Korea
P'yŏngyang-si *see* P'yŏngyang
37 Q4 **Pyramid Lake** ◎ Nevada, W USA
39 P15 **Pyramid Mountains** ⛰ New Mexico, SW USA
39 R5 **Pyramid Peak** ▲ Colorado, C USA
117 D17 **Pyramíva** *var.* Piramiva. ▲ C Greece
Pyrenaei Montes *see* Pyrenees
88 B12 **Pyrenees** *Fr.* Pyrénées, *Sp.* Pirineos; *anc.* Pyrenaei Montes. ⛰ SW Europe
104 J16 **Pyrénées-Atlantiques** ◈ *department* SW France
105 N17 **Pyrénées-Orientales** ◈ *department* S France
117 L19 **Pyrgí** *var.* Pirgi. Chíos, E Greece
117 D20 **Pýrgos** *var.* Pírgos. Dytikí Ellás, S Greece
Pyritz *see* Pyrzyce
117 E19 **Pýrros** ≈ S Greece
119 R4 **Pyryatyn** *Rus.* Piryatin. Poltavs'ka Oblast', NE Ukraine
112 D9 **Pyrzyce** *Ger.* Pyritz. Szczecin, NW Poland
128 F15 **Pytalovo** *Latv.* Abrene; *prev.* Jaunlatgale. Pskovskaya Oblast', W Russian Federation
117 M20 **Pythagóreio** *var.* Pithagorio. Sámos, Dodekánisos, Greece, Aegean Sea
12 L11 **Pythonga, Lac** ◎ Québec, SE Canada
96 E10 **Pyttegga** ▲ S Norway
Pyttis *see* Pyhtää
177 G7 **Pyu** Pegu, C Mynamar
177 G8 **Pyuntaza** Pegu, SW Mynamar
159 N11 **Pyuthan** Mid Western, W Nepal
112 H12 **Pyzdry** *Ger.* Peisern. Konin, C Poland

Q

144 H13 **Qā' al Jafr** ◎ S Jordan
207 O11 **Qaanaaq** *var.* Qânâq, *Dan.* Thule. N Greenland
144 G7 **Qabb Eliâs** E Lebanon
Qabil *see* Al Qābil
Qabırrı *see* Iori
Qābis *see* Gabès
Qābis, Khalīj *see* Gabès, Golfe de
147 S14 **Qabr Hūd** C Yemen
Qacentina *see* Constantine
154 L4 **Qādes** Bādghīs, NW Afghanistan
145 T11 **Qādisīyah** S Iraq
Qadmoûs/Qadmūs *see* Al Qadmūs
149 O4 **Qā'emshahr** *prev.* 'Alīābad, Shāhī. Māzandarān, N Iran
149 U7 **Qā'en** *var.* Qain, Qāyen. Khorāsān, E Iran
147 U13 **Qafa** *spring/well* SW Oman
Qafṣah *see* Gafsa
169 V9 **Qagan Nur** ◎ NE China
169 Q11 **Qagan Nur** ◎ N China
Qagan Us *see* Dulan
164 H13 **Qagcaka** Xizang Zizhiqu, W China
Qahremānshahr *see* Bākhtarān
165 Q10 **Qaidam He** ≈ C China
162 L8 **Qaidam Pendi** *basin* C China
Qain *see* Qā'en
Qala Āhangarān *see* Chaghcharān
145 U3 **Qaļā Diza** *var.* Qal 'at Dīzah. NE Iraq
Qal'ah Sālih *see* Qal'at Şāliḩ
153 R13 **Qal'aikhum** *Rus.* Kalaikhum. S Tajikistan
Qala Nau *see* Qal'eh-ye Now
147 V17 **Qalansīyah** Suquṭrā, W Yemen
Qala Panja *see* Qal'eh-ye Panjeh
Qala Shāhar *see* Qal'eh Shahr
Qalāt *see* Kalāt
145 W9 **Qal'at Aḩmad** E Iraq
147 N11 **Qal'at Bīshah** 'Asīr, SW Saudi Arabia
144 H4 **Qal'at Burzay** Ḩamāh, W Syria
Qal 'at Dīzah *see* Qaļā Diza
145 W9 **Qal'at Ḩusayh** E Iraq
145 V10 **Qal'at Majnūnah** S Iraq
145 X11 **Qal'at Şāliḩ** *var.* Qal'ah Sālih. E Iraq
145 V10 **Qal'at Sukkar** SE Iraq
Qalba Zhotasy *see* Kalbinskiy Khrebet
149 Q12 **Qal'eh Biābān** Fārs, S Iran
155 N4 **Qal'eh Shahr** *Pash.* Qala Shāhar. Sar-e Pol, N Afghanistan
154 L4 **Qal'eh-ye Now** *var.* Qala Nau. Bādghīs, NW Afghanistan
155 T2 **Qal'eh-ye Panjeh** *var.* Qala Panja. Badakhshān, NE Afghanistan
Qamar Bay *see* Qamar, Ghubbat al
147 U14 **Qamar, Ghubbat al** *Eng.* Qamar Bay. *bay* Oman/Yemen
147 V13 **Qamar, Jabal al** ⛰ SW Oman
Qambar *see* Kambar
165 R14 **Qamdo** Xizang Zizhiqu, W China
197 K13 **Qamea** *prev.* Nggamea. *island* N Fiji
77 R7 **Qamīnis** NE Libya
Qamishly *see* Al Qāmishlī
Qânâq *see* Qaanaaq
Qandahār *see* Kandahār
82 Q11 **Qandala** Bari, NE Somalia
144 L2 **Qanṭārī** Ar Raqqah, N Syria
143 V13 **Qapiciğ Dağı** *Rus.* Gora Kapydzhik. ▲ SW Azerbaijan
164 H5 **Qapqal** *var.* Qapqal Xibe Zizhixian. Xinjiang Uygur Zizhiqu, NW China
Qapqal Xibe Zizhixian *see* Qapqal
Qapshagay Böyeni *see* Kapchagayskoye Vodokhranilishche
206 M15 **Qaqortoq** *Dan.* Julianehåb. S Greenland
77 U8 **Qâra** *var.* Qārah. NW Egypt
145 T4 **Qara Anjīr** N Iraq
Qarabāgh *see* Qarah Bāgh
Qaraböget *see* Karaboget
Qarabulaq *see* Karabulak
Qarabutaq *see* Karabutak
Qaraghandy/Qaraghandy Oblysy *see* Karaganda
Qaraghayly *see* Karagayly
145 U4 **Qara Gol** NE Iraq
Qārah *see* Qâra
154 J4 **Qarah Bāgh** *var.* Qarabāgh. Herāt, NW Afghanistan
144 G7 **Qaraoun, Lac de** *var.* Buḩayrat al Qir'awn. ◎ S Lebanon
Qaraoy *see* Karaoy
Qaraqoyyn *see* Karakoyyn, Ozero
Qara Qum *see* Garagumy
Qarasū *see* Karasu
Qaratal *see* Karatal
Qarataū *see* Karatau, Khrebet, Kazakhstan
Qarataū *see* Karatau, Zhambyl, Kazakhstan
Qaraton *see* Karaton
82 P13 **Qardho** *var.* Kardh, *It.* Gardo. Bari, N Somalia
148 M6 **Qareh Chāy** ≈ N Iran
148 K2 **Qareh Sū** ≈ NW Iran
Qariateïne *see* Al Qaryatayn
Qarkilik *see* Ruoqiang
153 O13 **Qarluq** *Rus.* Karluk. Surkhondaryo Wiloyati, S Uzbekistan
153 U12 **Qarokŭl** *Rus.* Karakul'. E Tajikistan
153 T12 **Qarokŭl** *Rus.* Ozero Karakul'. ◎ E Tajikistan
Qarqan *see* Qiemo
164 K9 **Qarqan He** ≈ NW China
Qarqannah, Juzur *see* Kerkenah, Îles de
Qarqaraly *see* Karkaralinsk
155 O1 **Qarqīn** Jowzjān, N Afghanistan
Qars *see* Kars
Qarsaqbay *see* Karsakpay
152 M12 **Qarshi** *Rus.* Karshi; *prev.* Bek-Budi. Qashqadaryo Wiloyati, S Uzbekistan
152 L12 **Qarshi Chŭli** *Rus.* Karshinskaya Step. *grassland* S Uzbekistan
152 M13 **Qarshi Kanali** *Rus.* Karshinskiy Kanal. *canal* Turkmenistan/Uzbekistan
Qaryatayn *see* Al Qaryatayn
152 M12 **Qashqadaryo Wiloyati** *Rus.* Kashkadar'inskaya Oblast'. ◈ *province* S Uzbekistan
Qasigianguit *see* Qasigiannguit
207 N13 **Qasigiannguit** *var.* Qasigianguit, *Dan.* Christianshåb. C Greenland
Qaşīm, Minţaqat *see* Al Qaşīm
145 P8 **Qaşr 'Amīj** C Iraq
145 R9 **Qaşr Darwīshāh** C Iraq
148 J6 **Qaşr-e Shīrīn** Kermānshāhān, W Iran
77 V10 **Qasr Farâfra** W Egypt
Qassim *see* Al Qaşīm
147 O16 **Qa'ṭabah** SW Yemen
144 H7 **Qaṭanā** *var.* Katana. Dimashq, S Syria
149 N15 **Qatar** *off.* State of Qatar, *Ar.* Dawlat Qaṭar. ◆ *monarchy* SW Asia
Qatrana *see* Al Qaṭrānah
149 Q12 **Qaṭrūyeh** Fārs, S Iran
Qattara Depression/Qaṭṭārah, Munkhafaḍ al *see* Qaṭṭâra, Monkhafad el
77 U8 **Qaṭṭâra, Monkhafad el** *var.* Munkhafaḍ al Qaṭṭārah, *Eng.* Qattara Depression. *desert* NW Egypt
Qaṭṭīnah, Buḩayrat *see* Ḩimş, Buḩayrat
Qaydār *see* Qeydār
Qāyen *see* Qā'en
153 Q11 **Qayroqqum** *Rus.* Kayrakkum. NW Tajikistan
153 Q10 **Qayroqqum, Obanbori** *Rus.* Kayrakkumskoye Vodokhranilishche. ⊠ NW Tajikistan
145 U7 **Qazānīyah** *var.* Dhū Shaykh. E Iraq
Qazaqstan/Qazaqstan Respublikasy *see* Kazakhstan
143 T9 **Qazbegi** *Rus.* Kazbegi. NE Georgia
155 P15 **Qāzi Ahmad** *var.* Kazi Ahmad. Sind, SE Pakistan
143 Y12 **Qazimämmäd** *Rus.* Kazi Magomed. SE Azerbaijan
Qazris *see* Cáceres
148 M4 **Qazvīn** *var.* Kazvin. Zanjān, NW Iran
197 K12 **Qelelevu Lagoon** *lagoon* NE Fiji
77 X10 **Qena** *var.* Qinā; *anc.* Caene, Caenepolis. E Egypt
115 L23 **Qeparo** Vlorë, S Albania
Qeqertarssuaq *see* Qeqertarsuaq
207 N13 **Qeqertarsuaq** *var.* Qeqertarssuaq, *Dan.* Godhavn. S Greenland
206 M13 **Qeqertarsuaq** *island* W Greenland
207 N13 **Qeqertarsuup Tunua** *Dan.* Disko Bugt. *inlet* W Greenland
Qerveh *see* Qorveh
149 S14 **Qeshm** Hormozgān, S Iran
149 R14 **Qeshm** *var.* Jazīreh-ye Qeshm, Qeshm Island. *island* S Iran
Qeshm Island/Qeshm, Jazīreh-ye *see* Qeshm
148 L4 **Qeydār** *var.* Qaydār. Zanjān, NW Iran
148 K5 **Qezel Owzan** *var.* Ki Zil Uzen, Qi Zil Uzun. ≈ NW Iran
148 L5 **Qezel Owzan, Rūd-e** ≈ NW Iran
Qian *see* Guizhou
Qian Gorlo *see* Qian Gorlos
169 V9 **Qian Gorlos** *var.* Qian Gorlo, Qian Gorlos Mongolzu Zizhixian, Qianguozhen. Jilin, NE China
Qian Gorlos Mongolzu Zizhixian/Qianguozhen *see* Qian Gorlos
167 N9 **Qianjiang** Hubei, C China
166 K10 **Qianjiang** Sichuan, C China
166 L14 **Qian Jiang** ≈ S China
166 G9 **Qianning** *var.* Gartar. Sichuan, C China
169 U13 **Qian Shan** ⛰ NE China
166 H10 **Qianwei** Sichuan, C China
166 J11 **Qianxi** Guizhou, S China
165 Q7 **Qiaowan** Gansu, N China
Qibilī *see* Kebili
164 K9 **Qiemo** *var.* Qarqan. Xinjiang Uygur Zizhiqu, NW China
166 J10 **Qijiang** Sichuan, C China
165 N5 **Qijiaojing** Xinjiang Uygur Zizhiqu, NW China
155 P9 **Qila Saifullāh** Baluchistān, SW Pakistan
165 S9 **Qilian** Qinghai, C China
140 Nn10 **Qilian Shan** *var.* Kilien Mountains. ⛰ N China
207 O11 **Qimusseriarsuaq** *Dan.* Melville Bugt, *Eng.* Melville Bay. *bay* NW Greenland
Qinā *see* Qena
165 W11 **Qin'an** Gansu, C China
Qing *see* Qinghai
169 W7 **Qing'an** Heilongjiang, NE China
167 R5 **Qingdao** *var.* Ching-Tao, Ch'ing-tao, Tsingtao, Tsintao, *Ger.* Tsingtau. Shandong, E China
169 V8 **Qinggang** Heilongjiang, NE China
Qinggil *see* Qinghe
165 P11 **Qinghai** *var.* Chinghai, Koko Nor, Qing, Qinghai Sheng, Tsinghai. ◈ *province* C China
165 S10 **Qinghai Hu** *var.* Ch'ing Hai, Tsing Hai, *Mong.* Koko Nor. ◎ C China
Qinghai Sheng *see* Qinghai
164 M3 **Qinghe** *var.* Qinggil. Xinjiang Uygur Zizhiqu, NW China
166 L4 **Qingjian** Shaanxi, C China
166 L9 **Qing Jiang** ≈ C China
Qingjiang *see* Huaiyin
Qingkou *see* Ganyu
166 I12 **Qinglong** *var.* Liancheng. Guizhou, S China
167 Q2 **Qinglong** Hebei, E China
Qingshan *see* Dedu
165 R12 **Qingshuihe** Qinghai, C China
Qingyang *see* Jinjiang
169 V11 **Qingyuan** Liaoning, NE China
164 L13 **Qingzang Gaoyuan** *var.* Xizang Gaoyuan, *Eng.* Plateau of Tibet. *plateau* W China
167 Q4 **Qingzhou** *prev.* Yidu. Shandong, E China
163 R9 **Qin He** ≈ C China
167 Q2 **Qinhuangdao** Hebei, E China
166 K7 **Qin Ling** ⛰ C China
Qin Xian *see* Qinxian
167 N5 **Qinxian** *var.* Qin Xian. Shanxi, C China
167 N6 **Qinyang** Henan, C China
166 K15 **Qinzhou** Guangxi Zhuangzu Zizhiqu, S China
Qiong *see* Hainan
166 L17 **Qionghai** *prev.* Jiaji. Hainan, S China
166 H9 **Qionglai** Sichuan, C China
166 H8 **Qionglai Shan** ⛰ C China
166 L17 **Qiongzhou Haixia** *var.* Hainan Strait. *strait* S China
169 U7 **Qiqihar** *var.* Ch'i-ch'i-ha-erh, Tsitsihar; *prev.* Lungkiang. Heilongjiang, NE China
149 P12 **Qīr** Fārs, S Iran
164 H10 **Qira** Xinjiang Uygur Zizhiqu, NW China
Qir'awn, Buḩayrat al *see* Qaraoun, Lac de
144 F11 **Qiryat Gat** Southern, C Israel
144 G8 **Qiryat Shemona** Northern, N Israel
Qishlaq *see* Garmsār
147 U14 **Qishn** SE Yemen
144 G9 **Qishon, Naḩal** ≈ N Israel
Qita Ghazzah *see* Gaza Strip
162 K5 **Qitai** Xinjiang Uygur Zizhiqu, NW China
169 Y8 **Qitaihe** Heilongjiang, NE China
147 W12 **Qitbīt, Wādī** *dry watercourse* S Oman
167 O5 **Qixian** *var.* Qi Xian, Zhaoge. Henan, C China
Qīzān *see* Jīzān
Qizil Orda *see* Kzyl-Orda
Qizil Qum/Qizilqum *see* Kyzyl Kum
153 V14 **Qizilrabot** *Rus.* Kyzylrabot. SE Tajikistan
152 J10 **Qizilrawbe** *Rus.* Kyzylrabat. Bukhoro Wiloyati, C Uzbekistan
Qi Zil Uzun *see* Qezel Owzan
145 S4 **Qizil Yār** N Iraq
152 G7 **Qizqetkan** *Rus.* Kazanketken. Qoraqalpoghiston Respublikasi, W Uzbekistan
Qoghaly *see* Kugaly
Qogir Feng *see* K2

149 N6 **Qom** *var.* Kum, Qum. Markazī, N Iran
Qomisheh *see* Shahreẓā
Qomolangma Feng *see* Everest, Mount
148 M7 **Qom, Rūd-e** ≈ C Iran
Qomsheh *see* Shahreẓā
Qomul *see* Hami
Qondūz *see* Kunduz
Qoqek *see* Tacheng
Qorabowur Kirlari *see* Karabaur', Uval
Qoradaryo *see* Karadar'ya
152 G6 **Qorajar** *Rus.* Karadzhar. Qoraqalpoghiston Respublikasi, NW Uzbekistan
152 K12 **Qorakŭl** *Rus.* Karakul'. Bukhoro Wiloyati, C Uzbekistan
152 E5 **Qoraqalpoghiston** *Rus.* Karakalpakya. Qoraqalpoghiston Respublikasi, NW Uzbekistan
152 G7 **Qoraqalpoghiston Respublikasi** *Rus.* Respublika Karakalpakstan. ◆ *autonomous republic* NW Uzbekistan
152 H7 **Qoraŭzak** *Rus.* Karauzyak. Qoraqalpoghiston Respublikasi, NW Uzbekistan
Qorghazhyn *see* Kurgal'dzhinskiy
144 H6 **Qornet es Saouda** ▲ NE Lebanon
152 L12 **Qorowulbozor** *Rus.* Karaulbazar. Bukhoro Wiloyati, C Uzbekistan
148 K5 **Qorveh** *var.* Qerveh, Qurveh. Kordestān, W Iran
Qosshaghyl *see* Koschagyl
Qostanay/Qostanay Oblysy *see* Kustanay
149 P12 **Qoṭbābād** Fārs, S Iran
149 R13 **Qoṭbābād** Hormozgān, S Iran
144 H6 **Qoubaïyât** *var.* Al Qubayyāt. N Lebanon
Qoussantîna *see* Constantine
164 K16 **Qowowuyag** *var.* Cho Oyu. ▲ China/Nepal *see also* Cho Oyu
152 H6 **Qozoqdaryo** *Rus.* Kazakdar'ya. Qoraqalpoghiston Respublikasi, NW Uzbekistan
21 N11 **Quabbin Reservoir** ⊞ Massachusetts, NE USA
102 F12 **Quakenbrück** Niedersachsen, NW Germany
20 I15 **Quakertown** Pennsylvania, NE USA
190 M10 **Quambatook** Victoria, SE Australia
27 Q4 **Quanah** Texas, SW USA
178 Kk11 **Quang Ngai** *var.* Quangngai, Quang Nghia. Quang Ngai, C Vietnam
Quang Nghia *see* Quang Ngai
178 K9 **Quang Tri** Quang Tri, C Vietnam
Quan Long *see* Ca Mau
158 L4 **Quanshuigou** China/India
167 R13 **Quanzhou** *var.* Ch'uan-chou, Tsinkiang; *prev.* Chin-chiang. Fujian, SE China
166 M12 **Quanzhou** Guangxi Zhuangzu Zizhiqu, S China
9 V16 **Qu'Appelle** ≈ Saskatchewan, S Canada
10 M3 **Quaqtaq** *prev.* Koartac. Québec, NE Canada
63 E16 **Quaraí** Rio Grande do Sul, S Brazil
61 H24 **Quaraí, Rio** *Sp.* Río Cuareim. ≈ Brazil/Uruguay *see also* Cuareim, Río
175 Pl10 **Quarles, Pegunungan** ▲ Sulawesi, C Indonesia
Quarnero *see* Kvarner
109 C20 **Quartu Sant' Elena** Sardegna, Italy, C Mediterranean Sea
31 X13 **Quasqueton** Iowa, C USA
181 X16 **Quatre Bornes** W Mauritius
180 I17 **Quatre Bornes** Mahé, NE Seychelles
143 X10 **Quba** *Rus.* Kuba. N Azerbaijan
Qubba *see* Ba'qūbah
149 T3 **Qūchān** *var.* Kuchan. Khorāsān, NE Iran
191 R10 **Queanbeyan** New South Wales, SE Australia
13 Q10 **Québec** *var.* Quebec. Québec, SE Canada
12 K10 **Québec** *var.* Quebec. ◆ *province* SE Canada
63 D17 **Quebracho** Paysandú, W Uruguay
103 K14 **Quedlinburg** Sachsen-Anhalt, C Germany
144 H10 **Queen Alia** ✕ ('Ammān) 'Ammān, C Jordan
8 L16 **Queen Bess, Mount** ▲ British Columbia, SW Canada
8 I14 **Queen Charlotte** British Columbia, SW Canada
67 B24 **Queen Charlotte Bay** *bay* West Falkland, Falkland Islands
8 H14 **Queen Charlotte Islands** *Fr.* Îles de la Reine-Charlotte. *island group* British Columbia, SW Canada
8 I15 **Queen Charlotte Sound** *sea area* British Columbia, W Canada
8 J16 **Queen Charlotte Strait** *strait* British Columbia, W Canada
29 U1 **Queen City** Missouri, C USA
27 X5 **Queen City** Texas, SW USA
207 O9 **Queen Elizabeth Islands** *Fr.* Îles de la Reine-Élisabeth. *island group* Northwest Territories, NW Canada
205 Y10 **Queen Mary Coast** *physical region* Antarctica
67 N24 **Queen Mary's Peak** ▲ C Tristan da Cunha
206 M8 **Queen Maud Gulf** *gulf* Arctic Ocean
205 P11 **Queen Maud Mountains** ▲ Antarctica
Queen's County *see* Laois
189 U7 **Queensland** ◆ *state* N Australia
199 Hh10 **Queensland Plateau** *undersea feature* N Coral Sea
191 O16 **Queenstown** Tasmania, SE Australia
193 C22 **Queenstown** Otago, South Island, NZ
85 I24 **Queenstown** Eastern Cape, S South Africa
Queenstown *see* Cobh
34 F8 **Queets** Washington, NW USA
63 D18 **Queguay Grande, Río** ≈ W Uruguay
61 O16 **Queimadas** Bahia, E Brazil
84 D11 **Quela** Malanje, NW Angola
85 O16 **Quelimane** *var.* Kilimane, Kilmain, Quilimane. Zambézia, NE Mozambique
65 G18 **Quellón** *var.* Puerto Quellón. Los Lagos, S Chile
Quelpart *see* Cheju-do
39 P12 **Quemado** New Mexico, SW USA
27 O12 **Quemado** Texas, SW USA
46 K7 **Quemado, Punta de** *headland* E Cuba
Quemoy *see* Chinmen Tao
64 K13 **Quemú Quemú** La Pampa, E Argentina
161 E17 **Quepem** Goa, W India
44 M14 **Quepos** Puntarenas, S Costa Rica
Que Que *see* Kwekwe
63 D23 **Quequén** Buenos Aires, E Argentina
63 D23 **Quequén Grande, Río** ≈ E Argentina
63 C23 **Quequén Salado, Río** ≈ E Argentina
Quera *see* Chur
43 N13 **Querétaro** Querétaro de Arteaga, C Mexico
42 F4 **Querobabi** Sonora, NW Mexico
44 M13 **Quesada** *var.* Ciudad Quesada, San Carlos. Alajuela, N Costa Rica
107 O13 **Quesada** Andalucía, S Spain
167 O7 **Queshan** Henan, C China
8 M15 **Quesnel** British Columbia, SW Canada
39 S9 **Questa** New Mexico, SW USA
104 H7 **Questembert** Morbihan, NW France
59 K22 **Quetena, Río** ≈ SW Bolivia
155 O10 **Quetta** Baluchistān, SW Pakistan
Quetzalcoalco *see* Coatzacoalcos
Quetzaltenango *see* Quezaltenango
58 B6 **Quevedo** Los Ríos, C Ecuador
44 B6 **Quezaltenango** *var.* Quetzaltenango. Quezaltenango, W Guatemala
44 A2 **Quezaltenango** *off.* Departamento de Quezaltenango, *var.* Quetzaltenango. ◆ *department* SW Guatemala
44 E6 **Quezaltepeque** Chiquimula, SE Guatemala
179 O15 **Quezon** Palawan, W Philippines
179 P10 **Quezon City** Luzon, N Philippines
167 P5 **Qufu** Shandong, E China
84 B12 **Quibala** Cuanza Sul, NW Angola
84 B11 **Quibaxe** *var.* Quibaxi. Cuanza Norte, NW Angola
Quibaxi *see* Quibaxe
56 D9 **Quibdó** Chocó, W Colombia
104 G7 **Quiberon** Morbihan, NW France
104 G7 **Quiberon, Baie de** *bay* NW France
56 J5 **Quíbor** Lara, N Venezuela
44 C4 **Quiché** *off.* Departamento del Quiché. ◆ *department* W Guatemala
101 E21 **Quiévrain** Hainaut, S Belgium
42 I9 **Quila** Sinaloa, C Mexico
85 B14 **Quilengues** Huíla, SW Angola
Quilimane *see* Quelimane
59 G15 **Quillabamba** Cusco, C Peru
59 L18 **Quillacollo** Cochabamba, C Bolivia
64 H4 **Quillagua** Antofagasta, N Chile
105 N17 **Quillan** Aude, S France
9 U15 **Quill Lakes** ⊙ Saskatchewan, S Canada
64 G11 **Quillota** Valparaíso, C Chile
161 G23 **Quilon** *var.* Kolam, Kollam. Kerala, SW India
189 V9 **Quilpie** Queensland, C Australia
155 O4 **Quil-Qala** Bāmīān, N Afghanistan
64 L7 **Quimilí** Santiago del Estero, C Argentina
59 O19 **Quimome** Santa Cruz, E Bolivia
104 F6 **Quimper** *anc.* Quimper Corentin. Finistère, NW France
Quimper Corentin *see* Quimper
104 G7 **Quimperlé** Finistère, NW France
34 F8 **Quinault** Washington, NW USA
34 F8 **Quinault River** ≈ Washington, NW USA
37 P5 **Quincy** California, W USA
25 S8 **Quincy** Florida, SE USA
32 I13 **Quincy** Illinois, N USA
21 O11 **Quincy** Massachusetts, NE USA
34 J9 **Quincy** Washington, NW USA
56 E10 **Quindío** *off.* Departamento del Quindío. ◆ *province* C Colombia
56 E10 **Quindío, Nevado del** ▲ C Colombia
64 J10 **Quines** San Luis, C Argentina
41 N13 **Quinhagak** Alaska, USA
78 G13 **Quinhámel** W Guinea-Bissau
Qui Nhon/Quinhon *see* Quy Nhon
Quinindé *see* Rosa Zárate
27 U6 **Quinlan** Texas, SW USA
63 H17 **Quinta** Rio Grande do Sul, S Brazil
107 O10 **Quintanar de la Orden** Castilla-La Mancha, C Spain
43 X13 **Quintana Roo** ◆ *state* SE Mexico
107 S6 **Quinto** Aragón, NE Spain
110 G10 **Quinto** Ticino, S Switzerland
29 Q11 **Quinton** Oklahoma, C USA
64 K12 **Quinto, Río** ≈ C Argentina
84 A10 **Quinzau** Zaire, NW Angola
12 H8 **Quinze, Lac des** ⊙ Québec, SE Canada
85 B15 **Quipungo** Huíla, C Angola
64 G13 **Quirihue** Bío Bío, C Chile
84 D12 **Quirima** Malanje, NW Angola
191 T6 **Quirindi** New South Wales, SE Australia
57 P5 **Quiriquire** Monagas, NE Venezuela
12 D10 **Quirke Lake** ⊙ Ontario, S Canada
63 B21 **Quiroga** Buenos Aires, E Argentina
106 I4 **Quiroga** Galicia, NW Spain
Quiróm, Salar *see* Pocitos, Salar
58 B9 **Quiroz, Río** ≈ NW Peru
84 Q13 **Quissanga** Cabo Delgado, NE Mozambique
85 M20 **Quissico** Inhambane, S Mozambique
27 O4 **Quitaque** Texas, SW USA
84 Q13 **Quiterajo** Cabo Delgado, NE Mozambique
25 T6 **Quitman** Georgia, SE USA
24 M6 **Quitman** Mississippi, S USA
27 V6 **Quitman** Texas, SW USA
58 C6 **Quito** ● (Ecuador) Pichincha, N Ecuador
Quito *see* Mariscal Sucre
60 P13 **Quixadá** Ceará, E Brazil
85 Q15 **Quixaxe** Nampula, NE Mozambique
166 J9 **Qu Jiang** ≈ C China
167 R10 **Qu Jiang** ≈ SE China
167 N13 **Qujiang** *prev.* Maba. Guangdong, S China
166 H12 **Qujing** Yunnan, SW China
152 L10 **Quljuqtov-Toghi** *Rus.* Gory Kul'dzhuktau. ▲ C Uzbekistan
Qulsary *see* Kul'sary
Qulyndy Zhazyghy *see* Kulunda Steppe
Qum *see* Qom
Qumälisch *see* Lubartów
165 P11 **Qumar He** ≈ C China
165 Q12 **Qumarlêb** Qinghai, C China
Qumisheh *see* Shahreẓā
153 O14 **Qumqurghon** *Rus.* Kumkurgan. Surkhondaryo Wiloyati, S Uzbekistan
Qunaytirah/Qunayṭirah, Muḥāfaẓat al/Qunaytra *see* Al Qunayṭirah
152 G7 **Qŭnghirot** *Rus.* Kungrad. Qoraqalpoghiston Respublikasi, NW Uzbekistan
201 V12 **Quoi** *island* Chuuk, C Micronesia
15 Kk6 **Quoich** ≈ Northwest Territories, NE Canada
85 E26 **Quoin Point** *headland* SW South Africa
190 I7 **Quorn** South Australia
153 R10 **Qŭqon** *var.* Khokand, *Rus.* Kokand. Farghona Wiloyati, E Uzbekistan
Qurein *see* Al Kuwayt
153 P14 **Qŭrghonteppa** *Rus.* Kurgan-Tyube. SW Tajikistan
Qurlurtuuq *see* Coppermine
Qurveh *see* Qorveh
Qusair *see* Quseir
143 X10 **Qusar** *Rus.* Kusary. NE Azerbaijan
Quṣayr *see* Al Quṣayr
77 Y10 **Quseir** *var.* Al Quṣayr, Qusair. E Egypt
148 I2 **Qūshchī** Āẕarbāyjān-e Bākhtarī, N Iran
153 N11 **Qŭshrabot** *Rus.* Kushrabat. Samarqand Wiloyati, C Uzbekistan
Qusmuryn *see* Kushmurun, Kustanay, Kazakhstan
Qusmuryn *see* Kushmurun, Ozero, Kazakhstan
Quṭayfah/Qutayfe/Quteife *see* Al Quṭayfah
Quthing *see* Moyeni
Quwair *see* Guwēr
153 S10 **Quwasoy** *Rus.* Kuvasay. Farghona Wiloyati, E Uzbekistan
Qu Xian *see* Quzhou
165 N16 **Qūxü** Xizang Zizhiqu, W China
178 Kk13 **Quy Chanh** Ninh Thuân, S Vietnam
178 Kk12 **Quy Nhon** *var.* Quinhon, Qui Nhon. Binh Đinh, C Vietnam
153 O11 **Qŭytosh** *Rus.* Koytash. Jizzakh Wiloyati, C Uzbekistan
167 R10 **Quzhou** *var.* Qu Xian. Zhejiang, SE China
Qyteti Stalin *see* Kuçovë
Qyzylorda/Qyzylorda Oblysy *see* Kzyl-Orda
Qyzyltū *see* Kzyltu
Qyzylzhar *see* Kyzylzhar

R

111 R4 **Raab** Oberösterreich, N Austria
111 X8 **Raab** *Hung.* Rába. ≈ Austria/Hungary *see also* Rába
Raab *see* Győr
111 V2 **Raabs an der Thaya** Niederösterreich, E Austria
95 L14 **Raahe** *Swe.* Brahestad. Oulu, W Finland
100 M10 **Raalte** Overijssel, E Netherlands
101 I14 **Raamsdonksveer** Noord-Brabant, S Netherlands
94 L12 **Raanujärvi** Lappi, NW Finland
98 G9 **Raasay** *island* NW Scotland, UK
120 H3 **Raasiku** *Ger.* Rasik. Harjumaa, NW Estonia
114 B11 **Rab** *It.* Arbe. Primorje-Gorski Kotar, NW Croatia
114 B11 **Rab** *It.* Arbe. *island* NW Croatia
175 P16 **Raba** Sumbawa, S Indonesia
113 G22 **Rába** *Ger.* Raab. ≈ Austria/Hungary *see also* Raab
114 A10 **Rabac** Istra, NW Croatia
106 I2 **Rábade** Galicia, NW Spain
82 F10 **Rabak** White Nile, C Sudan
194 M16 **Rabaraba** Milne Bay, SE PNG
104 K16 **Rabastens-de-Bigorre** Hautes-Pyrénées, S France
123 Jj17 **Rabat** W Malta
76 F6 **Rabat** *var.* al Dar al Baida. ● (Morocco) NW Morocco
Rabat *see* Victoria
195 P10 **Rabaul** New Britain, E PNG
Rabbah Ammon/Rabbath Ammon *see* 'Ammān
30 K8 **Rabbit Creek** ≈ South Dakota, N USA
12 H10 **Rabbit Lake** ⊙ Ontario, S Canada
197 K13 **Rabi** *prev.* Rambi. *island* N Fiji
146 K9 **Rābigh** Makkah, W Saudi Arabia
44 D5 **Rabinal** Baja Verapaz, C Guatemala
173 Ee6 **Rabi, Pulau** *island* NW Indonesia, East Indies
113 L17 **Rabka** Nowy Sącz, S Poland
161 F16 **Rabkavi** Karnātaka, W India
Râbniţa *see* Rîbniţa
111 Y6 **Rabnitz** ≈ E Austria
128 J7 **Rabocheostrovsk** Respublika Kareliya, NW Russian Federation
25 U1 **Rabun Bald** ▲ Georgia, SE USA
77 S11 **Rabyānah** SE Libya
77 S11 **Rabyānah, Ramlat** *var.* Rebiana Sand Sea, Ṣaḥrā' Rabyānah. *desert* SE Libya
Rabyānah, Ṣaḥrā' *see* Rabyānah, Ramlat
118 L11 **Răcăciuni** Bacău, E Romania
109 J24 **Racalmuto** Sicilia, Italy, C Mediterranean Sea
118 J14 **Răcari** Dâmboviţa, SE Romania
Răcari *see* Durankulak
118 F13 **Răcăşdia** *Hung.* Rakasd. Caraş-Severin, SW Romania
108 B9 **Racconigi** Piemonte, NE Italy
33 T15 **Raccoon Creek** ≈ Ohio, N USA
11 V13 **Race, Cape** *headland* Newfoundland, Newfoundland and Labrador, E Canada
24 K10 **Raceland** Louisiana, S USA
21 Q12 **Race Point** *headland* Massachusetts, NE USA
178 J15 **Rach Gia** Kiên Giang, S Vietnam
178 J14 **Rach Gia, Vinh** *bay* S Vietnam
78 J8 **Rachid** Tagant, C Mauritania
112 L10 **Raciąż** Ciechanów, C Poland
113 I16 **Racibórz** *Ger.* Ratibor. Katowice, S Poland
33 N9 **Racine** Wisconsin, N USA
12 D7 **Racine Lake** ⊙ Ontario, S Canada
113 J23 **Ráckeve** Pest, C Hungary
Rácz-Becse *see* Bečej
147 O15 **Radā'** *var.* Ridā'. W Yemen
115 O15 **Radan** ▲ SE Yugoslavia
65 J19 **Rada Tilly** Chubut, SE Argentina
118 K8 **Rădăuţi** *Ger.* Radautz, *Hung.* Rádóc. Suceava, N Romania
118 L8 **Rădăuţi-Prut** Botoşani, NE Romania
Radautz *see* Rădăuţi
Radbusa *see* Radbuza
113 A17 **Radbuza** *Ger.* Radbusa. ≈ SE Czech Republic
22 K6 **Radcliff** Kentucky, S USA
145 O2 **Radd, Wādī ar** *dry watercourse* N Syria
97 H16 **Råde** Østfold, S Norway
111 V11 **Radeče** *Ger.* Ratschach. C Slovenia
Radein *see* Radenci
118 J4 **Radekhiv** *Pol.* Radziechów, *Rus.* Radekhov. L'vivs'ka Oblast', W Ukraine
Radekhov *see* Radekhiv
111 X9 **Radenci** *Ger.* Radein; *prev.* Radinci. NE Slovenia
111 S9 **Radenthein** Kärnten, S Austria
23 R7 **Radford** Virginia, NE USA
160 C9 **Rādhanpur** Gujarāt, W India
Radinci *see* Radenci
131 Q6 **Radishchevo** Ul'yanovskaya Oblast', W Russian Federation
10 I9 **Radisson** Québec, E Canada
9 P16 **Radium Hot Springs** British Columbia, SW Canada
118 F11 **Radna** *Hung.* Máriaradna. Arad, W Romania
116 K10 **Radnevo** Khaskovska Oblast, C Bulgaria
99 J20 **Radnor** *cultural region* E Wales, UK
Radnót *see* Iernut
Rádóc *see* Rădăuţi
103 H24 **Radolfzell am Bodensee** Baden-Württemberg, S Germany
112 M13 **Radom** Radom, C Poland
112 M13 **Radom** *off.* Województwo Radomskie. ◆ *province* C Poland
118 I14 **Radomireşti** Olt, S Romania
Radomskie, Województwo *see* Radom
113 K14 **Radomsko** *Rus.* Novoradomsk. Piotrków, C Poland
119 N4 **Radomyshl'** Zhytomyrs'ka Oblast', N Ukraine
115 P19 **Radoviš** *prev.* Radovište. E FYR Macedonia
Radovište *see* Radoviš
96 B13 **Radøy** *island* S Norway
111 R7 **Radstadt** Salzburg, NW Austria
190 E8 **Radstock, Cape** *headland* South Australia
111 U10 **Raduha** ▲ N Slovenia
121 G15 **Radun'** *Rus.* Radun'. Hrodzyenskaya Voblasts', W Belarus
126 Gg11 **Raduzhnyy** Khanty-Mansiyskiy Avtonomnyy Okrug, C Russian Federation
120 F11 **Radviliškis** Radviliškis, N Lithuania
9 U17 **Radville** Saskatchewan, S Canada
146 K7 **Raḍwá, Jabal** ▲ W Saudi Arabia
113 P16 **Radymno** Przemyśl, SE Poland
118 J5 **Radyvyliv** Rivnens'ka Oblast', NW Ukraine
Radziechów *see* Radekhiv
112 I11 **Radziejów** Włocławek, C Poland
112 O12 **Radzyń Podlaski** Biała Podlaska, E Poland
15 Hh4 **Rae** ≈ Northwest Territories, NW Canada
158 M13 **Rāe Bareli** Uttar Pradesh, N India
15 Hh7 **Rae-Edzo** Northwest Territories, NW Canada
23 T11 **Raeford** North Carolina, SE USA
101 M19 **Raeren** Liège, E Belgium
15 Kk3 **Rae Strait** *strait* Northwest Territories, N Canada
192 L11 **Raetihi** Manawatu-Wanganui, North Island, NZ
203 U13 **Raevavae** *var.* Raivavae. *island* Îles Australes, SW French Polynesia
Rafa *see* Rafah
64 M10 **Rafaela** Santa Fe, E Argentina
144 E11 **Rafah** *var.* Rafa, Rafaḥ, *Heb.* Rafiaḥ, Raphiah. SW Gaza Strip
81 L15 **Rafaï** Mbomou, SE Central African Republic
147 O4 **Rafḥah** Al Ḥudūd ash Shamālīyah, N Saudi Arabia
Rafiaḥ *see* Rafah
149 R10 **Rafsanjān** Kermān, C Iran
82 B13 **Raga** Western Bahr el Ghazal, SW Sudan
21 S8 **Ragged Island** *island* Maine, NE USA
46 I5 **Ragged Island Range** *island group* S Bahamas
192 L7 **Raglan** Waikato, North Island, NZ
24 G8 **Ragley** Louisiana, S USA
Ragnit *see* Neman
109 K25 **Ragusa** Sicilia, Italy, C Mediterranean Sea
Ragusa *see* Dubrovnik
Ragusavecchia *see* Cavtat
175 Qq12 **Raha** Pulau Muna, C Indonesia
121 N17 **Rahachow** *Rus.* Rogachëv. Homyel'skaya Voblasts', SE Belarus
69 U6 **Rahad** *var.* Nahr ar Rahad. ≈ W Sudan
Rahad, Nahr ar *see* Rahad
Rahaeng *see* Tak
144 F11 **Rahat** Southern, C Israel
146 L8 **Rahaṭ, Ḥarrat** *lavaflow* W Saudi Arabia
155 S12 **Rahīmyār Khān** Punjab, SE Pakistan
97 I14 **Råholt** Akershus, S Norway
Rahovec *see* Orahovac
203 S10 **Raiatea** *island* Îles Sous le Vent, W French Polynesia
161 H16 **Rāichūr** Karnātaka, C India
Raidestos *see* Tekirdağ
159 S13 **Rāiganj** West Bengal, NE India
160 M11 **Raigarh** Madhya Pradesh, C India
175 Q18 **Raijua, Selat** *strait* Nusa Tenggara, S Indonesia
191 O16 **Railton** Tasmania, SE Australia
38 L8 **Rainbow Bridge** *natural arch* Utah, W USA
25 Q3 **Rainbow City** Alabama, S USA
9 N11 **Rainbow Lake** Alberta, W Canada
23 R5 **Rainelle** West Virginia, NE USA
34 G10 **Rainier** Oregon, NW USA
34 H9 **Rainier, Mount** ▲ Washington, NW USA
25 Q2 **Rainsville** Alabama, S USA
10 B11 **Rainy Lake** ⊙ Ontario, S Canada
31 U2 **Rainy Lake** ⊙ Minnesota, N USA
10 A11 **Rainy River** Ontario, C Canada
Raippaluoto *see* Replot
160 K12 **Raipur** Madhya Pradesh, C India
160 H10 **Raisen** Madhya Pradesh, C India
13 N13 **Raisin** ≈ Ontario, SE Canada
33 R11 **Raisin, River** ≈ Michigan, N USA
Raivavae *see* Raevavae
155 W9 **Rāiwind** Punjab, E Pakistan
176 U9 **Raja Ampat, Kepulauan** *island group* E Indonesia
161 L16 **Rājahmundry** Andhra Pradesh, E India
161 I18 **Rājampet** Andhra Pradesh, E India
Rajang *see* Rajang, Batang
174 Mm6 **Rajang, Batang** *var.* Rajang. ≈ East Malaysia
155 S11 **Rājanpur** Punjab, E Pakistan
161 H23 **Rājapālaiyam** Tamil Nādu, SE India
158 E12 **Rājasthān** ◆ *state* NW India
159 T15 **Rajbari** Dhaka, C Bangladesh
159 R12 **Rajbiraj** Eastern, E Nepal
160 G9 **Rājgarh** Madhya Pradesh, C India
158 H10 **Rājgarh** Rājasthān, NW India
159 P14 **Rājgīr** Bihār, N India
112 O8 **Rajgród** Łomża, NE Poland
160 L12 **Rājim** Madhya Pradesh, C India
114 C11 **Rajinac, Mali** ▲ W Croatia
160 B10 **Rājkot** Gujarāt, W India
159 R14 **Rājmahal** Bihār, NE India
159 Q14 **Rājmahāl Hills** *hill range* N India
160 K12 **Rāj Nāndgaon** Madhya Pradesh, C India
158 I8 **Rājpura** Punjab, NW India
159 S14 **Rajshahi** *prev.* Rampur Boalia. Rajshahi, W Bangladesh
159 S13 **Rajshahi** ◆ *division* NW Bangladesh
202 K13 **Rakahanga** *atoll* N Cook Islands
193 H19 **Rakaia** Canterbury, South Island, NZ
193 G19 **Rakaia** ≈ South Island, NZ
158 H3 **Rakaposhi** ▲ N India
Rakasd *see* Răcăşdia
174 Ii14 **Rakata, Pulau** *var.* Pulau Krakatau. *island* S Indonesia
164 K16 **Raka Zangbo** ≈ W China
147 U10 **Rakbah, Qalamat ar** *well* SE Saudi Arabia
Rakhine State *see* Arakan State
118 I8 **Rakhiv** Zakarpats'ka Oblast', W Ukraine
147 V13 **Rakhyūt** SW Oman
197 I14 **Rakiraki** Viti Levu, W Fiji
Rakka *see* Ar Raqqah
120 I4 **Rakke** Lääne-Virumaa, NE Estonia
97 I16 **Rakkestad** Østfold, S Norway
112 F12 **Rakoniewice** *Ger.* Rakwitz. Poznań, W Poland
Rakonitz *see* Rakovník
85 H18 **Rakops** Central, C Botswana
113 C16 **Rakovník** *Ger.* Rakonitz. Střední Čechy, W Czech Republic
116 J10 **Rakovski** Plovdivska Oblast, C Bulgaria
Rakutō-kō *see* Naktong-gang
120 I3 **Rakvere** *Ger.* Wesenberg. Lääne-Virumaa, N Estonia
Rakwitz *see* Rakoniewice
24 L6 **Raleigh** Mississippi, S USA
23 U9 **Raleigh** *state capital* North Carolina, SE USA
23 Y11 **Raleigh Bay** *bay* North Carolina, SE USA
23 U9 **Raleigh-Durham** ✕ North Carolina, SE USA
201 S6 **Ralik Chain** *island group* Ralik Chain, W Marshall Islands
27 N5 **Ralls** Texas, SW USA
20 G13 **Ralston** Pennsylvania, NE USA
147 O16 **Ramādah** W Yemen
Ramadi *see* Ar Ramādī
107 N2 **Ramales de la Victoria** Cantabria, N Spain
144 F10 **Ramallah** C West Bank
63 C19 **Ramallo** Buenos Aires, E Argentina
161 H20 **Rāmanagaram** Karnātaka, E India
161 I23 **Rāmanāthapuram** Tamil Nādu, SE India
160 N12 **Rāmapur** Orissa, E India
144 F10 **Ramat Gan** Tel Aviv, W Israel
105 T6 **Rambervillers** Vosges, NE France
Rambi *see* Rabi
105 N5 **Rambouillet** Yvelines, N France
194 L8 **Rambutyo Island** *island* N PNG
159 Q12 **Ramechhap** Central, C Nepal
191 R12 **Rame Head** *headland* Victoria, SE Australia
130 L4 **Ramenskoye** Moskovskaya Oblast', W Russian Federation
128 J15 **Rameshki** Tverskaya Oblast', W Russian Federation
159 P14 **Rāmgarh** Bihār, N India
158 D11 **Rāmgarh** Rājasthān, NW India
148 M9 **Rāmhormoz** *var.* Ram Hormuz, Ramuz. Khūzestān, SW Iran
Ram Hormuz *see* Rāmhormoz
Ram, Jebel *see* Ramm, Jabal
144 F10 **Ramla** *var.* Ramle, Ramleh, *Ar.* Er Ramle. Central, C Israel
Ramle/Ramleh *see* Ramla
144 F14 **Ramm, Jabal** *var.* Jebel Ram. ▲ SW Jordan
158 K10 **Rāmnagar** Uttar Pradesh, N India
97 N15 **Ramnäs** Västmanland, C Sweden
Râmnicul-Sărat *see* Râmnicu Sărat
118 L12 **Râmnicu Sărat** *prev.* Râmnicul-Sărat, Rîmnicu-Sărat. Buzău, E Romania
118 I13 **Râmnicu Vâlcea** *prev.* Rîmnicu Vîlcea. Vâlcea, C Romania
Ramokgwebana *see* Ramokgwebane
85 J18 **Ramokgwebane** *var.* Ramokgwebana. Central, NE Botswana
130 L7 **Ramon'** Voronezhskaya Oblast', W Russian Federation
37 V17 **Ramona** California, W USA
58 A10 **Ramón, Laguna** ⊙ NW Peru
12 G7 **Ramore** Ontario, S Canada
42 M11 **Ramos** San Luis Potosí, C Mexico
43 N8 **Ramos Arizpe** Coahuila de Zaragoza, NE Mexico
42 J9 **Ramos, Río de** ≈ C Mexico
41 R8 **Rampart** Alaska, USA
14 G5 **Ramparts** ≈ Northwest Territories, NW Canada
158 K10 **Rāmpur** Uttar Pradesh, N India
160 F9 **Rāmpura** Madhya Pradesh, C India
Rampur Boalia *see* Rajshahi
177 F6 **Ramree Island** *island* W Mynamar
147 W6 **Rams** *var.* Ar Rams. Ra's al Khaymah, NE UAE
149 N4 **Rāmsar** *prev.* Sakhtsar. Māzandarān, N Iran
95 H16 **Ramsele** Västernorrland, N Sweden
23 T9 **Ramseur** North Carolina, SE USA
99 I16 **Ramsey** NE Isle of Man
99 I16 **Ramsey Bay** *bay* NE Isle of Man
12 E9 **Ramsey Lake** ⊙ Ontario, S Canada
99 Q22 **Ramsgate** SE England, UK
96 M10 **Ramsjö** Gävleborg, C Sweden
160 I12 **Rāmtek** Mahārāshtra, C India
Ramtha *see* Ar Ramthā
194 H11 **Ramu** ≈ N PNG
Ramuz *see* Rāmhormoz
120 G12 **Ramygala** Panevėžys, C Lithuania
94 G12 **Rana** ≈ C Norway
158 H14 **Rāna Pratāp Sāgar** ⊙ N India
175 O2 **Ranau** Sabah, East Malaysia
174 I12 **Ranau, Danau** ⊙ Sumatera, W Indonesia
64 H12 **Rancagua** Libertador, C Chile
101 G22 **Rance** Hainaut, S Belgium
104 H6 **Rance** ≈ NW France
62 J9 **Rancharia** São Paulo, S Brazil
159 P15 **Rānchi** Bihār, N India
63 D21 **Ranchos** Buenos Aires, E Argentina
39 S9 **Ranchos De Taos** New Mexico, SW USA
65 G16 **Ranco, Lago** ⊙ C Chile
97 C16 **Randaberg** Rogaland, S Norway
31 U7 **Randall** Minnesota, N USA
109 L23 **Randazzo** Sicilia, Italy, C Mediterranean Sea
97 G21 **Randers** Århus, C Denmark
94 I12 **Randijaure** ⊙ N Sweden
23 T9 **Randleman** North Carolina, SE USA
21 O11 **Randolph** Massachusetts, NE USA
31 Q13 **Randolph** Nebraska, C USA
38 M1 **Randolph** Utah, W USA
102 P9 **Randow** ≈ NE Germany
97 H14 **Randsfjorden** ⊙ S Norway
94 K13 **Råneå** Norrbotten, N Sweden
78 H10 **Ranérou** C Senegal
193 E22 **Ranfurly** Otago, South Island, NZ
178 Hh17 **Rangae** Narathiwat, SW Thailand
159 V16 **Rangamati** Chittagong, SE Bangladesh
192 I2 **Rangaunu Bay** *bay* North Island, NZ
21 P6 **Rangeley** Maine, NE USA
39 O4 **Rangely** Colorado, C USA
27 R7 **Ranger** Texas, SW USA
12 C9 **Ranger Lake** Ontario, S Canada
12 C9 **Ranger Lake** ⊙ Ontario, S Canada
159 V12 **Rangia** Assam, NE India
193 I18 **Rangiora** Canterbury, South Island, NZ
203 T9 **Rangiroa** *atoll* Îles Tuamotu, W French Polynesia
192 N9 **Rangitaiki** ≈ North Island, NZ
193 F19 **Rangitata** ≈ South Island, NZ
192 M12 **Rangitikei** ≈ North Island, NZ
192 L6 **Rangitoto Island** *island* N NZ
Rangkasbitoeng *see* Rangkasbitung
174 Ii14 **Rangkasbitung** *prev.* Rangkasbitoeng. Jawa, SW Indonesia
178 Hh9 **Rang, Khao** ▲ C Thailand
153 V13 **Rangkŭl** *Rus.* Rangkul'. SE Tajikistan
Rangkul' *see* Rangkŭl
Rangoon *see* Yangon
159 T13 **Rangpur** Rajshahi, N Bangladesh
174 Hh7 **Rangsang, Pulau** *island* W Indonesia
161 F18 **Rānibennur** Karnātaka, W India
159 R15 **Rāniganj** West Bengal, NE India
155 Q13 **Rānīpur** Sind, SE Pakistan
Rāniyah *see* Rānya
27 N9 **Rankin** Texas, SW USA
15 L7 **Rankin Inlet** Northwest Territories, C Canada
191 P8 **Rankins Springs** New South Wales, SE Australia
Rankovićevo *see* Kraljevo
110 I7 **Rankweil** Vorarlberg, W Austria
Rann *see* Brežice
131 T8 **Ranneye** Orenburgskaya Oblast', W Russian Federation
98 I10 **Rannoch, Loch** ⊙ C Scotland, UK
203 U17 **Rano Kau** *var.* Rano Kao. *crater* Easter Island, Chile, E Pacific Ocean
178 Gg14 **Ranong** Ranong, SW Thailand
195 T14 **Ranongga** *var.* Ghanongga. *island* NW Solomon Islands
203 W16 **Rano Raraku** *ancient monument* Easter Island, Chile, E Pacific Ocean
176 W9 **Ransiki** Irian Jaya, E Indonesia
94 K12 **Rantajärvi** Norrbotten, N Sweden
95 N17 **Rantasalmi** Mikkeli, SE Finland
175 N11 **Rantau** Borneo, C Indonesia
174 Hh7 **Rantau, Pulau** *var.* Pulau Tebingtinggi. *island* W Indonesia
175 Pp11 **Rantepao** Sulawesi, C Indonesia
32 M13 **Rantoul** Illinois, N USA
95 L15 **Rantsila** Oulu, C Finland
94 L13 **Ranua** Lappi, NW Finland
145 T3 **Rānya** *var.* Rāniyah. NE Iraq
163 X3 **Raohe** Heilongjiang, NE China
76 H9 **Raoui, Erg er** *desert* W Algeria
199 L11 **Rapa** *island* Îles Australes, S French Polynesia
203 V14 **Rapa Iti** *island* Îles Australes, SW French Polynesia
108 D10 **Rapallo** Liguria, NW Italy
Rapa Nui *see* Pascua, Isla de
Raphiah *see* Rafah
23 V5 **Rapidan River** ≈ Virginia, NE USA
30 J10 **Rapid City** South Dakota, N USA
13 P8 **Rapide-Blanc** Québec, SE Canada
12 I8 **Rapide-Deux** Québec, SE Canada
120 K6 **Räpina** *Ger.* Rappin. Põlvamaa, SE Estonia
120 G4 **Rapla** *Ger.* Rappel. Raplamaa, NW Estonia
120 G4 **Raplamaa** *off.* Rapla Maakond. ◆ *province* NW Estonia
23 X6 **Rappahannock River** ≈ Virginia, NE USA
Rappel *see* Rapla
110 G7 **Rapperswil** Sankt Gallen, NE Switzerland
Rappin *see* Räpina
159 N12 **Rāpti** ≈ N India
59 K16 **Rapulo, Río** ≈ E Bolivia
Raqqah/Raqqah, Muḥāfaẓat al *see* Ar Raqqah
20 J8 **Raquette Lake** ⊙ New York, NE USA
20 J6 **Raquette River** ≈ New York, NE USA

◆ Country ● Country Capital ◇ Dependent Territory ○ Dependent Territory Capital ◆ Administrative Region ✕ International Airport ▲ Mountain ▲ Mountain Range ⛰ Volcano ≈ River ⊙ Lake ⊞ Reservoir

203 *V10* **Raraka** *atoll* Îles Tuamotu, C French Polynesia
203 *V10* **Raroia** *atoll* Îles Tuamotu, C French Polynesia
202 *H15* **Rarotonga** ✕ Rarotonga, S Cook Islands, C Pacific Ocean
202 *H16* **Rarotonga** *island* S Cook Islands, C Pacific Ocean
153 *P12* **Rarz** W Tajikistan
Ras al 'Ain *see* Ra's al 'Ayn
145 *N2* **Ra's al 'Ayn** ***var.*** Ras al 'Ain. Al Ḩasakah, N Syria
144 *H3* **Ra's al Basīţ** Al Lādhiqīyah, W Syria
Ra's al-Hafgī *see* Ra's al Khafjī
147 *R5* **Ra's al Khafjī** ***var.*** Ra's al-Hafgī. Ash Sharqīyah, NE Saudi Arabia
Ras al-Khaimah/Ras al Khaimah *see* Ra's al Khaymah
149 *R15* **Ra's al Khaymah** ***var.*** Ras al Khaimah. Ra's al Khaymah, NE UAE
149 *R15* **Ra's al Khaymah** ***var.*** Ras al-Khaimah. ✕ Ra's al Khaymah, NE UAE
144 *G13* **Ra's an Naqb** Ma'ān, S Jordan
63 *B26* **Rasa, Punta** *headland* E Argentina
176 *W10* **Rasawi** Irian Jaya, E Indonesia
Râşcani *see* Rişcani
82 *J10* **Ras Dashen Terara** ▲ N Ethiopia
157 *K19* **Rasdu Atoll** *atoll* C Maldives
120 *E12* **Raseiniai** Raseiniai, C Lithuania
77 *X8* **Râs Ghârib** E Egypt
168 *D6* **Rashaant** Bayan-Ölgiy, W Mongolia
168 *L10* **Rashaant** Dundgovĭ, C Mongolia
168 *J6* **Rashaant** Hövsgöl, N Mongolia
145 *Y11* **Rashīd** E Iraq
77 *V7* **Rashîd** ***Eng.*** Rosetta. N Egypt
148 *M3* **Rasht** ***var.*** Resht. Gīlān, NW Iran
145 *S2* **Rashwān** N Iraq
Rasik *see* Raasiku
115 *M15* **Raška** Serbia, C Yugoslavia
121 *P15* **Rasna** ***Rus.*** Ryasna. Mahilyowskaya Voblasts', E Belarus
118 *J12* **Râşnov** ***prev.*** Rîşno, Rozsnyó, ***Hung.*** Barcarozsnyó. Braşov, C Romania
120 *L11* **Rasony** ***Rus.*** Rossony. Vitsyebskaya Voblasts', N Belarus
Ra's Shamrah *see* Ugarit
131 *N7* **Rasskazovo** Tambovskaya Oblast', W Russian Federation
121 *O16* **Rasta** ∼ E Belarus
Rastadt *see* Rastatt
Rastâne *see* Ar Rastān
147 *S6* **Ra's Tannūrah** ***Eng.*** Ras Tanura. Ash Sharqīyah, NE Saudi Arabia
Ras Tanura *see* Ra's Tannūrah
103 *G21* **Rastatt** ***var.*** Rastadt. Baden-Württemberg, SW Germany
Rastenburg *see* Kętrzyn
155 *V7* **Rasūlnagar** Punjab, E Pakistan
201 *U6* **Ratak Chain** *island group* Ratak Chain, E Marshall Islands
121 *K15* **Ratamka** ***Rus.*** Ratomka. Minskaya Voblasts', C Belarus
95 *G17* **Ratan** Jämtland, C Sweden
158 *G11* **Ratangarh** Rājasthān, NW India
Rat Buri *see* Ratchaburi
178 *H11* **Ratchaburi** ***var.*** Rat Buri. Ratchaburi, W Thailand
31 *W15* **Rathbun Lake** ▣ Iowa, C USA
Ráth Caola *see* Rathkeale
177 *F5* **Rathedaung** Arakan State, W Mynamar
102 *M12* **Rathenow** Brandenburg, NE Germany
99 *C19* **Rathkeale** ***Ir.*** Ráth Caola. SW Ireland
98 *F13* **Rathlin Island** ***Ir.*** Reachlainn. *island* N Northern Ireland, UK
99 *C20* **Ráthluirc** ***Ir.*** An Ráth. SW Ireland
Ratibor *see* Racibórz
Ratisbon/Ratisbona/Ratisbonne *see* Regensburg
Rätische Alpen *see* Rhaetian Alps
40 *E17* **Rat Island** *island* Aleutian Islands, Alaska, USA
40 *E17* **Rat Islands** *island group* Aleutian Islands, Alaska, USA
160 *F10* **Ratlām** ***prev.*** Rutlam. Madhya Pradesh, C India
161 *D15* **Ratnāgiri** Mahārāshtra, W India
161 *K26* **Ratnapura** Sabaragamuwa Province, S Sri Lanka
118 *J2* **Ratne** ***Rus.*** Ratno. Volyns'ka Oblast', NW Ukraine
Ratno *see* Ratne
Ratomka *see* Ratamka
39 *U8* **Raton** New Mexico, SW USA
145 *O7* **Ratqah, Wādī ar** *dry watercourse* W Iraq
Ratschach *see* Radeče
178 *H17* **Rattaphum** Songkhla, SW Thailand
28 *L6* **Rattlesnake Creek** ∼ Kansas, C USA
96 *L13* **Rättvik** Kopparberg, C Sweden
102 *K9* **Ratzeburg** Mecklenburg-Vorpommern, N Germany
102 *K9* **Ratzeburger See** ◎ N Germany
8 *J10* **Ratz, Mount** ▲ British Columbia, SW Canada
63 *D22* **Rauch** Buenos Aires, E Argentina
43 *U16* **Raudales** Chiapas, SE Mexico
Raudhatain *see* Ar Rawḑatayn
Raudnitz an der Elbe *see* Roudnice nad Labem
94 *K1* **Raufarhöfn** Nordhurland Eystra, NE Iceland
96 *H13* **Raufoss** Oppland, S Norway
Raukawa *see* Cook Strait
192 *Q8* **Raukumara** ▲ North Island, NZ
199 *J12* **Raukumara Plain** *undersea feature* N Coral Sea
192 *P8* **Raukumara Range** ⛰ North Island, NZ
97 *F15* **Rauland** Telemark, S Norway
95 *J19* **Rauma** ***Swe.*** Raumo. Turku-Pori, SW Finland
96 *F10* **Rauma** ∼ S Norway
Raumo *see* Rauma
120 *H8* **Rauna** Cēsis, C Latvia
174 *Mm16* **Raung, Gunung** ▲ Jawa, S Indonesia
160 *N11* **Raurkela** ***prev.*** Rourkela. Orissa, E India
97 *J22* **Raus** Malmöhus, S Sweden
172 *R6* **Rausu** Hokkaidō, NE Japan
172 *R6* **Rausu-dake** ▲ Hokkaidō, NE Japan
95 *M17* **Rautalampi** Kuopio, C Finland
95 *N16* **Rautavaara** Kuopio, C Finland
118 *M9* **Raŭtel** ∼ C Moldova
95 *O18* **Rautjärvi** Kymi, SE Finland
Rautu *see* Sosnovo
203 *V11* **Ravahere** *atoll* Îles Tuamotu, C French Polynesia
109 *J25* **Ravanusa** Sicilia, Italy, C Mediterranean Sea
149 *S9* **Rāvar** Kermān, C Iran
153 *Q11* **Ravat** Oshskaya Oblast', SW Kyrgyzstan
20 *K11* **Ravena** New York, NE USA
108 *H10* **Ravenna** Emilia-Romagna, N Italy
31 *O15* **Ravenna** Nebraska, C USA
33 *U11* **Ravenna** Ohio, N USA
103 *I24* **Ravensburg** Baden-Württemberg, S Germany
189 *W4* **Ravenshoe** Queensland, NE Australia
188 *K13* **Ravensthorpe** Western Australia
23 *Q4* **Ravenswood** West Virginia, NE USA
155 *U9* **Rāvi** ∼ India/Pakistan
114 *C9* **Ravna Gora** Primorje-Gorski Kotar, NW Croatia
111 *U10* **Ravne na Koroškem** ***Ger.*** Gutenstein. N Slovenia
145 *P6* **Rāwah** W Iraq
203 *T4* **Rawaki** ***prev.*** Phoenix Island. *atoll* Phoenix Islands, C Kiribati
155 *U6* **Rāwalpindi** Punjab, NE Pakistan
112 *L13* **Rawa Mazowiecka** Skierniewice, C Poland
145 *T2* **Ŗawāndiz** ***var.*** Rawandoz, Rawāndūz. N Iraq
Rawandoz/Rawāndūz *see* Ŗawāndiz
176 *Vv9* **Rawarra** ∼ Irian Jaya, E Indonesia
176 *V9* **Rawas** Irian Jaya, E Indonesia
145 *O4* **Rawḑah** ◎ E Syria
112 *G13* **Rawicz** ***Ger.*** Rawitsch. Leszno, W Poland
Rawitsch *see* Rawicz
188 *M11* **Rawlinna** Western Australia
35 *W16* **Rawlins** Wyoming, C USA
65 *K17* **Rawson** Chubut, SE Argentina
165 *R16* **Rawu** Xizang Zizhiqu, W China
159 *P12* **Raxaul** Bihār, N India
30 *K3* **Ray** North Dakota, N USA
174 *M9* **Raya, Bukit** ▲ Borneo, C Indonesia
161 *I18* **Rāyachoti** Andhra Pradesh, E India
Rāyadrug *see* Rāyagarha
161 *M14* **Rāyagarha** ***prev.*** Rāyadrug. Orissa, E India
144 *H7* **Rayak** ***var.*** Rayaq, Riyāq. E Lebanon
Rayaq *see* Rayak
145 *T2* **Ŗāyat** E Iraq
174 *J10* **Raya, Tanjung** *headland* Pulau Bangka, W Indonesia
11 *R13* **Ray, Cape** *headland* Newfoundland, Newfoundland and Labrador, E Canada
126 *Mm16* **Raychikhinsk** Amurskaya Oblast', SE Russian Federation
131 *U5* **Rayevskiy** Respublika Bashkortostan, W Russian Federation
9 *Q17* **Raymond** Alberta, SW Canada
24 *K6* **Raymond** Mississippi, S USA
34 *F9* **Raymond** Washington, NW USA
191 *T8* **Raymond Terrace** New South Wales, SE Australia
27 *T17* **Raymondville** Texas, SW USA
9 *U16* **Raymore** Saskatchewan, S Canada
41 *Q8* **Ray Mountains** ⛰ Alaska, USA
24 *H9* **Rayne** Louisiana, S USA
43 *O12* **Rayón** San Luis Potosí, C Mexico
42 *G4* **Rayón** Sonora, NW Mexico
178 *Hh12* **Rayong** Rayong, S Thailand
27 *T5* **Ray Roberts, Lake** ◎ Texas, SW USA
20 *E15* **Raystown Lake** ▣ Pennsylvania, NE USA
147 *V13* **Raysūt** SW Oman
29 *R4* **Raytown** Missouri, C USA
24 *I5* **Rayville** Louisiana, S USA
148 *L5* **Razan** Hamadān, W Iran
145 *S9* **Razāzah, Buḩayrat ar** ***var.*** Baḩr al Milḩ. ◎ C Iraq
116 *L9* **Razboyna** ▲ E Bulgaria
Razdan *see* Hrazdan
Razdolnoye *see* Rozdol'ne
Razelm, Lacul *see* Razim, Lacul
145 *U2* **Ŗazga** E Iraq
116 *L8* **Razgrad** Razgradska Oblast, NE Bulgaria
Razgrad *see* Razgradska Oblast
116 *K7* **Razgradska Oblast** ***var.*** Razgrad. ⬖ *province* NE Bulgaria
119 *N13* **Razim, Lacul** ***prev.*** Lacul Razelm. *lagoon* NW Black Sea
116 *G11* **Razlog** Sofiyska Oblast, SW Bulgaria
120 *K10* **Rāznas Ezers** ◎ SE Latvia
104 *E6* **Raz, Pointe du** *headland* NW France
Reachlainn *see* Rathlin Island
Reachrainn *see* Lambay Island
99 *N22* **Reading** S England, UK
20 *H15* **Reading** Pennsylvania, NE USA
50 *C7* **Real, Cordillera** ⛰ C Ecuador
64 *K12* **Realicó** La Pampa, C Argentina
27 *R15* **Realitos** Texas, SW USA
110 *G9* **Realp** Uri, C Switzerland
178 *Ii12* **Reăng Kesei** Bătdâmbâng, W Cambodia
203 *Y11* **Reao** *atoll* Îles Tuamotu, French Polynesia
Reate *see* Rieti
188 *L11* **Rebecca, Lake** ◎ Western Australia
Rebiana Sand Sea *see* Rabyānah, Ramlat
128 *H8* **Reboly** Respublika Kareliya, NW Russian Federation
172 *P1* **Rebun** Rebun-tō, NE Japan
172 *P1* **Rebun-suidō** *strait* E Sea of Japan
172 *P1* **Rebun-tō** *island* NE Japan
108 *J12* **Recanati** Marche, C Italy
Rechitsa *see* Rechytsa
111 *Y7* **Rechnitz** Burgenland, SE Austria
121 *J20* **Rechytsa** ***Rus.*** Rechitsa. Brestskaya Voblasts', SW Belarus
121 *O19* **Rechytsa** ***Rus.*** Rechitsa. Homyel'skaya Voblasts', SE Belarus
61 *Q15* **Recife** ***prev.*** Pernambuco. *state capital* Pernambuco, E Brazil
85 *I26* **Recife, Cape** ***Afr.*** Kaap Recife. *headland* S South Africa
Recife, Kaap *see* Recife, Cape
180 *I16* **Récifs, Îles aux** *island* Inner Islands, NE Seychelles
103 *E14* **Recklinghausen** Nordrhein-Westfalen, W Germany
102 *M8* **Recknitz** ∼ NE Germany
101 *K23* **Recogne** Luxembourg, SE Belgium
63 *C15* **Reconquista** Santa Fe, C Argentina
205 *O6* **Recovery Glacier** *glacier* Antarctica
61 *G15* **Recreio** Mato Grosso, W Brazil
29 *X9* **Rector** Arkansas, C USA
112 *E9* **Recz** ***Ger.*** Reetz Neumark. Gorzów, NW Poland
101 *L24* **Redange** ***var.*** Redange-sur-Attert. Diekirch, W Luxembourg
Redange-sur-Attert *see* Redange
20 *C13* **Redbank Creek** ∼ Pennsylvania, NE USA
11 *S9* **Red Bay** Québec, E Canada
25 *N2* **Red Bay** Alabama, S USA
37 *N4* **Red Bluff** California, W USA
26 *J8* **Red Bluff Reservoir** ◎ New Mexico/Texas, SW USA
32 *K16* **Red Bud** Illinois, N USA
32 *J5* **Red Cedar River** ∼ Wisconsin, N USA
9 *R17* **Redcliff** Alberta, SW Canada
85 *K17* **Redcliff** Midlands, C Zimbabwe
190 *L9* **Red Cliffs** Victoria, SE Australia
31 *P17* **Red Cloud** Nebraska, C USA
24 *L8* **Red Creek** ∼ Mississippi, S USA
9 *P15* **Red Deer** Alberta, SW Canada
9 *Q16* **Red Deer** ∼ Alberta, SW Canada
41 *O11* **Red Devil** Alaska, USA
37 *N3* **Redding** California, W USA
99 *L20* **Redditch** W England, UK
31 *P9* **Redfield** South Dakota, N USA
26 *J12* **Redford** Texas, SW USA
47 *V13* **Redhead** Trinidad, Trinidad and Tobago
190 *I8* **Red Hill** South Australia
40 *F10* **Red Hill** ***Haw.*** Pu'uUla'ula. ▲ Maui, Hawaii, USA, C Pacific Ocean
28 *K7* **Red Hills** *hill range* Kansas, C USA
11 *T12* **Red Indian Lake** ◎ Newfoundland, Newfoundland and Labrador, E Canada
128 *J16* **Redkino** Tverskaya Oblast', W Russian Federation
10 *A10* **Red Lake** Ontario, C Canada
38 *I10* **Red Lake** *salt flat* Arizona, SW USA
31 *S4* **Red Lake Falls** Minnesota, N USA
31 *R4* **Red Lake River** ∼ Minnesota, N USA
37 *U15* **Redlands** California, W USA
20 *G16* **Red Lion** Pennsylvania, NE USA
35 *U11* **Red Lodge** Montana, NW USA
34 *H13* **Redmond** Oregon, NW USA
38 *L5* **Redmond** Utah, W USA
34 *H8* **Redmond** Washington, NW USA
Rednitz *see* Regnitz
31 *T15* **Red Oak** Iowa, C USA
20 *K12* **Red Oaks Mill** New York, NE USA
104 *I7* **Redon** Ille-et-Vilaine, NW France
47 *W10* **Redonda** *island* SW Antigua and Barbuda
106 *G4* **Redondela** Galicia, NW Spain
106 *H11* **Redondo** Évora, S Portugal
41 *Q12* **Redoubt Volcano** ▲ Alaska, USA
9 *Y16* **Red River** ∼ Canada/USA
133 *U12* **Red River** ***var.*** Yuan, ***Chin.*** Yuan Jiang, ***Vtn.*** Sông Hông Hà. ∼ China/Vietnam
27 *W4* **Red River** ∼ S USA
24 *H7* **Red River** ∼ Louisiana, S USA
32 *M6* **Red River** ∼ Wisconsin, N USA
Red Rock, Lake *see* Red Rock Reservoir
31 *W14* **Red Rock Reservoir** ***var.*** Lake Red Rock. ▣ Iowa, C USA
194 *J15* **Redscar Bay** *bay* S PNG
82 *H7* **Red Sea** ⬖ *state* NE Sudan
77 *Y9* **Red Sea** ***anc.*** Sinus Arabicus. *sea* Africa/Asia
23 *T11* **Red Springs** North Carolina, SE USA
15 *Gg6* **Redstone** ∼ Northwest Territories, NW Canada
9 *V17* **Redvers** Saskatchewan, S Canada
79 *P13* **Red Volta** ***var.*** Nazinon, ***Fr.*** Volta Rouge. ∼ Burkina/Ghana
9 *Q14* **Redwater** Alberta, SW Canada
30 *M16* **Red Willow Creek** ∼ Nebraska, C USA
31 *W9* **Red Wing** Minnesota, N USA
37 *N9* **Redwood City** California, W USA
31 *T9* **Redwood Falls** Minnesota, N USA
198 *Ff7* **Reed Bank** *undersea feature* C South China Sea
33 *P7* **Reed City** Michigan, N USA
30 *K6* **Reeder** North Dakota, N USA
37 *R11* **Reedley** California, W USA
35 *T11* **Reedpoint** Montana, NW USA
32 *K8* **Reedsburg** Wisconsin, N USA
34 *E13* **Reedsport** Oregon, NW USA
195 *X8* **Reef Islands** *island group* Santa Cruz Islands, E Solomon Islands
193 *H16* **Reefton** West Coast, South Island, NZ
22 *F8* **Reelfoot Lake** ◎ Tennessee, S USA
99 *D17* **Ree, Lough** ***Ir.*** Loch Rí. ◎ C Ireland
Reengus *see* Rīngas
37 *U4* **Reese River** ∼ Nevada, W USA
100 *M8* **Reest** ∼ E Netherlands
Reetz Neumark *see* Recz
143 *N13* **Refahiye** Erzincan, C Turkey
25 *N4* **Reform** Alabama, S USA
97 *K20* **Reftele** Jönköping, S Sweden
27 *T14* **Refugio** Texas, SW USA
112 *E8* **Rega** ∼ NW Poland
Regar *see* Tursunzoda
103 *O21* **Regen** Bayern, SE Germany
103 *M20* **Regen** ∼ SE Germany
103 *M21* **Regensburg** ***Eng.*** Ratisbon, ***Fr.*** Ratisbonne; ***hist.*** Ratisbona, ***anc.*** Castra Regina, Reginum. Bayern, SE Germany
103 *M21* **Regenstauf** Bayern, SE Germany
76 *I10* **Reggane** C Algeria
100 *N9* **Regge** ∼ E Netherlands
Reggio *see* Reggio nell' Emilia
Reggio Calabria *see* Reggio di Calabria
109 *M23* **Reggio di Calabria** ***var.*** Reggio Calabria, ***Gk.*** Rhegion; ***anc.*** Regium, Rhegium. Calabria, SW Italy
Reggio Emilia *see* Reggio nell' Emilia
108 *F9* **Reggio nell' Emilia** ***var.*** Reggio Emilia, ***abbrev.*** Reggio; ***anc.*** Regium Lepidum. Emilia-Romagna, N Italy
118 *I10* **Reghin** ***Ger.*** Sächsisch-Reen, ***Hung.*** Szászrégen; ***prev.*** Reghinul Săsesc, ***Ger.*** Sächsisch-Regen. Mureş, C Romania
Reghinul Săsesc *see* Reghin
9 *U16* **Regina** Saskatchewan, S Canada
9 *U16* **Regina** ✕ Saskatchewan, S Canada
57 *Z10* **Régina** E French Guiana
9 *U16* **Regina Beach** Saskatchewan, S Canada
Reginum *see* Regensburg
Registan *see* Rīgestān
62 *L11* **Registro** São Paulo, S Brazil
Regium *see* Reggio di Calabria
Regium Lepidum *see* Reggio nell' Emilia
103 *K19* **Regnitz** ***var.*** Rednitz. ∼ SE Germany
42 *K10* **Regocijo** Durango, W Mexico
106 *H12* **Reguengos de Monsaraz** Évora, S Portugal
103 *M18* **Rehau** Bayern, E Germany
85 *D19* **Rehoboth** Hardap, C Namibia
Rehoboth/Rehovoth *see* Reḩovot
23 *Z4* **Rehoboth Beach** Delaware, NE USA
144 *F10* **Reḩovot** ***var.*** Rehoboth, Rehovoth. Central, C Israel
83 *J20* **Rei** *spring/well* S Kenya
Reichenau *see* Rychnov nad Kněžnou, Czech Republic
Reichenau *see* Bogatynia, Poland
103 *M17* **Reichenbach** ***var.*** Reichenbach im Vogtland. Sachsen, E Germany
Reichenbach *see* Dzierżoniów
Reichenbach im Vogtland *see* Reichenbach
Reichenberg *see* Liberec
189 *O11* **Reid** Western Australia
25 *V6* **Reidsville** Georgia, SE USA
23 *T8* **Reidsville** North Carolina, SE USA
Reifnitz *see* Ribnica
99 *O22* **Reigate** SE England, UK
Reikjavik *see* Reykjavík
104 *I10* **Ré, Île de** *island* W France
39 *N15* **Reiley Peak** ▲ Arizona, SW USA
105 *Q4* **Reims** ***Eng.*** Rheims; ***anc.*** Durocortorum, Remi. Marne, N France
65 *G23* **Reina Adelaida, Archipiélago** *island group* S Chile
47 *O16* **Reina Beatrix** ✕ (Oranjestad) C Aruba
110 *F7* **Reinach** Aargau, W Switzerland
110 *E6* **Reinach** Basel-Land, NW Switzerland
66 *O11* **Reina Sofía** ✕ (Tenerife) Tenerife, Islas Canarias, Spain, NE Atlantic Ocean
31 *W13* **Reinbeck** Iowa, C USA
102 *J10* **Reinbek** Schleswig-Holstein, N Germany
9 *U12* **Reindeer** ∼ Saskatchewan, C Canada
9 *U11* **Reindeer Lake** ◎ Manitoba/Saskatchewan, C Canada
Reine-Charlotte, Îles de la *see* Queen Charlotte Islands
Reine-Élisabeth, Îles de la *see* Queen Elizabeth Islands
96 *F13* **Reineskarvet** ▲ S Norway
192 *H1* **Reinga, Cape** *headland* North Island, NZ
107 *N3* **Reinosa** Cantabria, N Spain
111 *R8* **Reisseck** ▲ S Austria
23 *W3* **Reisterstown** Maryland, NE USA
Reisui *see* Yŏsu
100 *N5* **Reitdiep** ∼ NE Netherlands
203 *V10* **Reitoru** *atoll* Îles Tuamotu, C French Polynesia
97 *M17* **Rejmyre** Östergötland, S Sweden
Reka *see* Rijeka
Reka Ili *see* Ili
97 *N16* **Rekarne** Västmanland, C Sweden
15 *Ii7* **Reliance** Northwest Territories, C Canada
35 *U16* **Reliance** Wyoming, C USA
76 *I5* **Relizane** ***var.*** Ghelîzâne, Ghilizane. NW Algeria
190 *I7* **Remarkable, Mount** ▲ South Australia
56 *E8* **Remedios** Antioquia, N Colombia
45 *Q16* **Remedios** Veraguas, W Panama
44 *D8* **Remedios, Punta** *headland* SW El Salvador
Remi *see* Reims
101 *N25* **Remich** Grevenmacher, SE Luxembourg
101 *J19* **Remicourt** Liège, E Belgium
12 *H8* **Rémigny, Lac** ◎ Québec, SE Canada
57 *Z10* **Rémire** NE French Guiana
131 *N13* **Remontnoye** Rostovskaya Oblast', SW Russian Federation
176 *V13* **Remoon** Pulau Kur, E Indonesia
101 *L20* **Remouchamps** Liège, E Belgium
105 *R15* **Remoulins** Gard, S France
181 *X16* **Rempart, Mont du** ***var.*** Mount Rempart. *hill* W Mauritius
103 *E15* **Remscheid** Nordrhein-Westfalen, W Germany
31 *S12* **Remsen** Iowa, C USA
96 *I12* **Rena** Hedmark, S Norway
96 *I11* **Rena** ∼ S Norway
Renaix *see* Ronse
120 *H7* **Rencēni** Valmiera, N Latvia
120 *D9* **Renda** Kuldīga, W Latvia
109 *N20* **Rende** Calabria, SW Italy
101 *K21* **Rendeux** Luxembourg, SE Belgium
Rendina *see* Rentína
32 *L16* **Rend Lake** ▣ Illinois, N USA
195 *U15* **Rendova** *island* New Georgia Islands, NW Solomon Islands
102 *I8* **Rendsburg** Schleswig-Holstein, N Germany
110 *B9* **Renens** Vaud, SW Switzerland
12 *K12* **Renfrew** Ontario, SE Canada
98 *I12* **Renfrew** *cultural region* SW Scotland, UK
174 *H8* **Rengat** Sumatera, W Indonesia
159 *W12* **Rengma Hills** ⛰ NE India
64 *H12* **Rengo** Libertador, C Chile
118 *M12* **Reni** Odes'ka Oblast', SW Ukraine
82 *F11* **Renk** Upper Nile, E Sudan
95 *L19* **Renko** Häme, SW Finland
100 *L12* **Renkum** Gelderland, SE Netherlands
190 *K9* **Renmark** South Australia
195 *W17* **Rennell** ***var.*** Mu Nggava. *island* S Solomon Islands
189 *Q4* **Renner Springs Roadhouse** Northern Territory, N Australia
104 *I6* **Rennes** ***Bret.*** Roazon; ***anc.*** Condate. Ille-et-Vilaine, NW France
205 *S16* **Rennick Glacier** *glacier* Antarctica
9 *Y16* **Rennie** Manitoba, S Canada
37 *Q5* **Reno** Nevada, W USA
108 *H10* **Reno** ∼ N Italy
37 *Q5* **Reno-Cannon** ✕ Nevada, W USA
85 *F24* **Renoster** ∼ SW South Africa
13 *T5* **Renouard, Lac** ◎ Québec, SE Canada
20 *F13* **Renovo** Pennsylvania, NE USA
167 *O3* **Renqiu** Hebei, E China
166 *I9* **Renshou** Sichuan, C China
33 *N12* **Rensselaer** Indiana, N USA
20 *L11* **Rensselaer** New York, NE USA
107 *Q2* **Rentería** ***Basq.*** Errenteria. País Vasco, N Spain
117 *E17* **Rentína** ***var.*** Rendina. Thessalía, C Greece
31 *T9* **Renville** Minnesota, N USA
79 *O13* **Réo** W Burkina
13 *O12* **Repentigny** Québec, SE Canada
152 *K13* **Repetek** Lebapskiy Velayat, E Turkmenistan
95 *J16* **Replot** ***Fin.*** Raippaluoto. *island* W Finland
Reppen *see* Rzepin
Reps *see* Rupea
29 *T7* **Republic** Missouri, C USA
34 *K7* **Republic** Washington, NW USA
29 *N3* **Republican River** ∼ Kansas/Nebraska, C USA
15 *Ll4* **Repulse Bay** Northwest Territories, N Canada
58 *F9* **Requena** Loreto, NE Peru
107 *R10* **Requena** País Valenciano, E Spain
105 *O14* **Réquista** Aveyron, S France
142 *M12* **Reşadiye** Tokat, N Turkey
Reschenpass *see* Resia, Passo di
Reschitza *see* Reşiţa
115 *N20* **Resen** ***Turk.*** Resne. SW FYR Macedonia
62 *J11* **Reserva** Paraná, S Brazil
9 *V15* **Reserve** Saskatchewan, S Canada
39 *P13* **Reserve** New Mexico, SW USA
Reshetilovka *see* Reshetylivka
119 *S6* **Reshetylivka** ***Rus.*** Reshetilovka. Poltavs'ka Oblast', NE Ukraine
Resht *see* Rasht
108 *F5* **Resia, Passo di** ***Ger.*** Reschenpass. *pass* Austria/Italy
Resicabánya *see* Reşiţa
64 *N7* **Resistencia** Chaco, NE Argentina
118 *F12* **Reşiţa** ***Ger.*** Reschitza, ***Hung.*** Resicabánya. Caraş-Severin, W Romania
Resne *see* Resen
207 *N9* **Resolute** Cornwallis Island, Northwest Territories, N Canada
Resolution *see* Fort Resolution
16 *P4* **Resolution Island** *island* Northwest Territories, NE Canada
193 *A23* **Resolution Island** *island* SW NZ
13 *W7* **Restigouche** Québec, SE Canada
9 *W17* **Reston** Manitoba, S Canada
12 *H11* **Restoule Lake** ◎ Ontario, S Canada
56 *F10* **Restrepo** Meta, C Colombia
44 *B6* **Retalhuleu** Retalhuleu, SW Guatemala
44 *A1* **Retalhuleu** ***off.*** Departamento de Retalhuleu. ⬖ *department* SW Guatemala
99 *N18* **Retford** C England, UK
105 *Q3* **Rethel** Ardennes, N France
Rethimno/Réthimnon *see* Réthymno
117 *I25* **Réthymno** ***var.*** Rethimno; ***prev.*** Réthimnon. Kríti, Greece, E Mediterranean Sea
Retiche, Alpi *see* Rhaetian Alps
101 *J16* **Retie** Antwerpen, N Belgium
113 *J21* **Rétság** Nógrád, N Hungary
111 *W2* **Retz** Niederösterreich, NE Austria
181 *N15* **Réunion** ***off.*** La Réunion. ◇ *French overseas department* W Indian Ocean
132 *L17* **Réunion** *island* W Indian Ocean
107 *U6* **Reus** Cataluña, E Spain
101 *J15* **Reusel** Noord-Brabant, S Netherlands
110 *F7* **Reuss** ∼ NW Switzerland
Reuţel *see* Ciuhuru
103 *H22* **Reutlingen** Baden-Württemberg, S Germany
110 *L7* **Reutte** Tirol, W Austria
101 *M16* **Reuver** Limburg, SE Netherlands
30 *K7* **Reva** South Dakota, N USA
Reval/Revel' *see* Tallinn
128 *J4* **Revda** Murmanskaya Oblast', NW Russian Federation
125 *Ee11* **Revda** Sverdlovskaya Oblast', C Russian Federation
105 *N16* **Revel** Haute-Garonne, S France
9 *O16* **Revelstoke** British Columbia, SW Canada
45 *N13* **Reventazón, Río** ∼ E Costa Rica
108 *G9* **Revere** Lombardia, N Italy
41 *Y14* **Revillagigedo Island** *island* Alexander Archipelago, Alaska, USA
105 *R3* **Revin** Ardennes, N France
94 *O3* **Revnosa** *headland* C Svalbard
Revolyutsii, Pik *see* Revolyutsiya, Qullai
153 *T13* **Revolyutsiya, Qullai** ***Rus.*** Pik Revolyutsii. ▲ SE Tajikistan
113 *L19* **Revúca** ***Ger.*** Grossrauschenbach, ***Hung.*** Nagyrőce. Východné Slovensko, E Slovakia
160 *K9* **Rewa** Madhya Pradesh, C India
158 *I11* **Rewāri** Haryāna, N India
35 *R14* **Rexburg** Idaho, NW USA
80 *G13* **Rey Bouba** Nord, NE Cameroon
94 *L3* **Reydharfjördhur** Austurland, E Iceland
59 *K16* **Reyes** Beni, NW Bolivia
36 *L8* **Reyes, Point** *headland* California, W USA
56 *B12* **Reyes, Punta** *headland* SW Colombia
142 *L17* **Reyhanlı** Hatay, S Turkey
45 *U16* **Rey, Isla del** *island* Archipiélago de las Perlas, SE Panama
94 *H2* **Reykhólar** Vestfirdhir, W Iceland
94 *K2* **Reykjahlídh** Nordhurland Eystra, NE Iceland
94 *I4* **Reykjanes** ⬖ *region* SW Iceland
207 *O16* **Reykjanes Basin** ***var.*** Irminger Basin. *undersea feature* N Atlantic Ocean
207 *N17* **Reykjanes Ridge** *undersea feature* N Atlantic Ocean
94 *H4* **Reykjavík** ***var.*** Reikjavik. ● (Iceland) Höfudhborgarsvaedhi, W Iceland
20 *D13* **Reynoldsville** Pennsylvania, NE USA
43 *P8* **Reynosa** Tamaulipas, C Mexico
Reẕa'īyeh *see* Orūmīyeh
Reẕā'īyeh, Daryācheh-ye *see* Orūmīyeh, Daryācheh-ye
104 *I8* **Rezé** Loire-Atlantique, NW France
120 *K10* **Rēzekne** ***Ger.*** Rositten; ***prev.*** Rus. Rezhitsa. Rēzekne, SE Latvia
Rezhitsa *see* Rēzekne
119 *N9* **Rezina** NE Moldova
116 *N11* **Rezovo** ***Turk.*** Rezve. Burgaska Oblast, SE Bulgaria
116 *N11* **Rezovska Reka** ***Turk.*** Rezve Deresi. ∼ Bulgaria/Turkey *see also* Rezve Deresi
Rezve *see* Rezovo
116 *N11* **Rezve Deresi** ***Bul.*** Rezovska Reka. ∼ Bulgaria/Turkey *see also* Rezovska Reka
Rhadames *see* Ghadāmis
Rhaedestus *see* Tekirdağ
110 *J10* **Rhaetian Alps** ***Fr.*** Alpes Rhétiques, ***Ger.*** Rätische Alpen, ***It.*** Alpi Retiche. ⛰ C Europe
110 *I8* **Rhätikon** ⛰ C Europe
103 *G14* **Rheda-Wiedenbrück** Nordrhein-Westfalen, W Germany
100 *M12* **Rheden** Gelderland, E Netherlands
Rhegion/Rhegium *see* Reggio di Calabria
Rheims *see* Reims
Rhein *see* Rhine
103 *E17* **Rheinbach** Nordrhein-Westfalen, W Germany
102 *F13* **Rheine** ***var.*** Rheine in Westfalen. Nordrhein-Westfalen, NW Germany
Rheine in Westfalen *see* Rheine
Rheinfeld *see* Rheinfelden
103 *F24* **Rheinfelden** Baden-Württemberg, S Germany
110 *E6* **Rheinfelden** ***var.*** Rheinfeld. Aargau, N Switzerland
103 *E17* **Rheinisches Schiefergebirge** ***var.*** Rhine State Uplands, ***Eng.*** Rhenish Slate Mountains. ⛰ W Germany
103 *D18* **Rheinland-Pfalz** ***Eng.*** Rhineland-Palatinate, ***Fr.*** Rhénanie-Palatinat. ⬖ *state* W Germany
103 *G18* **Rhein/Main** ✕ (Frankfurt am Main) Hessen, W Germany
Rhénanie du Nord-Westphalie *see* Nordrhein-Westfalen
Rhénanie-Palatinat *see* Rheinland-Pfalz
100 *K12* **Rhenen** Utrecht, C Netherlands
Rhenish Slate Mountains *see* Rheinisches Schiefergebirge
Rhétiques, Alpes *see* Rhaetian Alps
102 *N10* **Rhin** ∼ NE Germany
Rhin *see* Rhine
86 *F10* **Rhine** ***Dut.*** Rijn, ***Fr.*** Rhin, ***Ger.*** Rhein. ∼ W Europe
32 *L5* **Rhinelander** Wisconsin, N USA
Rhineland-Palatinate *see* Rheinland-Pfalz
Rhine State Uplands *see* Rheinisches Schiefergebirge
102 *N11* **Rhinkanal** *canal* NE Germany
83 *F17* **Rhino Camp** NW Uganda
76 *D7* **Rhir, Cap** *headland* W Morocco
108 *D7* **Rho** Lombardia, N Italy
21 *N12* **Rhode Island** ***off.*** State of Rhode Island and Providence Plantations; also known as Little Rhody, Ocean State. ⬖ *state* NE USA
21 *O13* **Rhode Island** *island* Rhode Island, NE USA
21 *O13* **Rhode Island Sound** *sound* Maine/Rhode Island, NE USA
Rhodes *see* Ródos
Rhode-Saint-Genèse *see* Sint-Genesius-Rode
86 *L14* **Rhodes Basin** *undersea feature* E Mediterranean Sea
Rhodesia *see* Zimbabwe
116 *I12* **Rhodope Mountains** ***var.*** Rodhópi Óri, ***Bul.*** Rhodope Planina, Rodopi, ***Gk.*** Orosirá Rodhópis, ***Turk.*** Dospad Dagh. ⛰ Bulgaria/Greece
Rhodope Planina *see* Rhodope Mountains
Rhodos *see* Ródos
103 *I18* **Rhön** ⛰ C Germany
99 *J21* **Rhondda** S Wales, UK
105 *Q10* **Rhône** ⬖ *department* E France
88 *C12* **Rhône** ∼ France/Switzerland
105 *R12* **Rhône-Alpes** ⬖ *region* E France
123 *J6* **Rhône Fan** *undersea feature* W Mediterranean Sea
100 *G13* **Rhoon** Zuid-Holland, SW Netherlands
98 *G9* **Rhum** ***var.*** Rum. *island* W Scotland, UK
Rhuthun *see* Ruthin
99 *J18* **Rhyl** NE Wales, UK
61 *K18* **Rialma** Goiás, S Brazil
106 *L3* **Riaño** Castilla-León, N Spain
107 *O9* **Riansáres** ∼ C Spain
158 *H6* **Riāsi** Jammu and Kashmir, NW India
174 *Gg7* **Riau** ***off.*** Propinsi Riau. ⬖ *province* W Indonesia
Riau Archipelago *see* Riau, Kepulauan
174 *I8* **Riau, Kepulauan** ***var.*** Riau Archipelago, ***Dut.*** Riouw-Archipel. *island group* W Indonesia
107 *O6* **Riaza** Castilla-León, N Spain
107 *N6* **Riaza** ∼ N Spain
83 *K17* **Riba** *spring/well* NE Kenya
106 *H4* **Ribadavia** Galicia, NW Spain
106 *J2* **Ribadeo** Galicia, NW Spain
106 *L2* **Ribadesella** Asturias, N Spain
106 *G10* **Ribatejo** *former province* C Portugal
149 *Q8* **Ribaţ-e Rīzāb** Yazd, C Iran
85 *P15* **Ribáuè** Nampula, N Mozambique
99 *K17* **Ribble** ∼ NW England, UK
97 *F23* **Ribe** Ribe, W Denmark
97 *F23* **Ribe** ***off.*** Ribe Amt, ***var.*** Ripen. ⬖ *county* W Denmark
106 *G3* **Ribeira** Galicia, NW Spain
66 *O5* **Ribeira Brava** Madeira, Portugal, NE Atlantic Ocean
66 *P3* **Ribeira Grande** São Miguel, Azores, Portugal, NE Atlantic Ocean
62 *L8* **Ribeirão Preto** São Paulo, S Brazil
62 *L11* **Ribeira, Rio** ∼ S Brazil
109 *I24* **Ribera** Sicilia, Italy, C Mediterranean Sea
59 *L14* **Riberalta** Beni, N Bolivia
107 *W4* **Ribes de Freser** Cataluña, NE Spain
32 *L6* **Rib Mountain** ▲ Wisconsin, N USA
111 *U12* **Ribnica** ***Ger.*** Reifnitz. S Slovenia
119 *N9* **Rîbniţa** ***var.*** Râbniţa, ***Rus.*** Rybnitsa. NE Moldova
102 *M8* **Ribnitz-Damgarten** Mecklenburg-Vorpommern, NE Germany

◆ Country ● Country Capital
◇ Dependent Territory ○ Dependent Territory Capital
⬖ Administrative Region ✕ International Airport
▲ Mountain ⛰ Mountain Range
Volcano ∼ River
◎ Lake ▣ Reservoir

113 D16 **Říčany** Ger. Ritschan. Střední Čechy, W Czech Republic
31 U7 **Rice** Minnesota, N USA
32 J5 **Rice Lake** Wisconsin, N USA
12 I15 **Rice Lake** ◎ Ontario, SE Canada
12 E8 **Rice Lake** ◎ Ontario, S Canada
25 V3 **Richard B.Russell Lake** ▣ Georgia, SE USA
27 U6 **Richardson** Texas, SW USA
9 R11 **Richardson** ≈ Alberta, C Canada
8 I3 **Richardson Mountains** ▲ Yukon Territory, NW Canada
193 C21 **Richardson Mountains** ▲ South Island, NZ
44 F3 **Richardson Peak** ▲ SE Belize
78 G10 **Richard Toll** N Senegal
30 L5 **Richardton** North Dakota, N USA
12 F13 **Rich, Cape** headland Ontario, S Canada
104 L8 **Richelieu** Indre-et-Loire, C France
35 P15 **Richfield** Idaho, NW USA
38 K5 **Richfield** Utah, W USA
20 J10 **Richfield Springs** New York, NE USA
20 M6 **Richford** Vermont, NE USA
29 R6 **Rich Hill** Missouri, C USA
11 P14 **Richibucto** New Brunswick, SE Canada
110 G8 **Richisau** Glarus, NE Switzerland
25 S6 **Richland** Georgia, SE USA
29 U6 **Richland** Missouri, C USA
27 U8 **Richland** Texas, SW USA
34 K10 **Richland** Washington, NW USA
32 K8 **Richland Center** Wisconsin, N USA
23 W11 **Richlands** North Carolina, SE USA
23 Q7 **Richlands** Virginia, NE USA
27 R9 **Richland Springs** Texas, SW USA
191 S8 **Richmond** New South Wales, SE Australia
8 L17 **Richmond** British Columbia, SW Canada
12 L13 **Richmond** Ontario, SE Canada
13 Q12 **Richmond** Québec, SE Canada
193 I14 **Richmond** Tasman, South Island, NZ
37 N8 **Richmond** California, W USA
33 Q14 **Richmond** Indiana, N USA
22 M6 **Richmond** Kentucky, S USA
29 S4 **Richmond** Missouri, C USA
27 V11 **Richmond** Texas, SW USA
38 L1 **Richmond** Utah, W USA
23 W6 **Richmond** state capital Virginia, NE USA
12 H15 **Richmond Hill** Ontario, S Canada
193 J15 **Richmond Range** ▲ South Island, NZ
29 S12 **Rich Mountain** ▲ Arkansas, C USA
33 S13 **Richwood** Ohio, N USA
23 R5 **Richwood** West Virginia, NE USA
106 K5 **Ricobayo, Embalse de** ▣ NW Spain
Ricomagus see Riom
Ridā' see Radā'
100 H13 **Ridderkerk** Zuid-Holland, SW Netherlands
35 N16 **Riddle** Idaho, NW USA
34 F14 **Riddle** Oregon, NW USA
12 L13 **Rideau** ≈ Ontario, SE Canada
37 T12 **Ridgecrest** California, W USA
20 L13 **Ridgefield** Connecticut, NE USA
24 K5 **Ridgeland** Mississippi, S USA
23 R15 **Ridgeland** South Carolina, SE USA
22 F8 **Ridgely** Tennessee, S USA
12 D17 **Ridgetown** Ontario, S Canada
Ridgeway see Ridgway
23 R12 **Ridgeway** South Carolina, SE USA
20 D13 **Ridgway** var. Ridgeway. Pennsylvania, NE USA
9 W16 **Riding Mountain** ▲ Manitoba, S Canada
Ried see Ried im Innkreis
111 R4 **Ried im Innkreis** var. Ried. Oberösterreich, NW Austria
111 X8 **Riegersburg** Steiermark, SE Austria
110 E6 **Riehen** Basel-Stadt, NW Switzerland
101 K18 **Riemst** Limburg, NE Belgium
94 J9 **Rieppe** ▲ N Norway
103 O15 **Riesa** Sachsen, E Germany
65 H24 **Riesco, Isla** island S Chile
109 K25 **Riesi** Sicilia, Italy, C Mediterranean Sea
85 F25 **Riet** ≈ SW South Africa
85 I23 **Riet** ≈ SW South Africa
120 D11 **Rietavas** Plungė, W Lithuania
85 F19 **Rietfontein** Omaheke, E Namibia
109 I14 **Rieti** anc. Reate. Lazio, C Italy
86 D14 **Rif** var. Er Rif, Er Riff, Riff. ▲ N Morocco
Riff see Rif
39 Q4 **Rifle** Colorado, C USA
33 R7 **Rifle River** ≈ Michigan, N USA
83 H18 **Rift Valley** ◆ province Kenya
Rift Valley see Great Rift Valley
120 F9 **Riga** Eng. Riga. ● (Latvia) Rīga, C Latvia
Rigaer Bucht see Riga, Gulf of
120 F6 **Riga, Gulf of** Est. Liivi Laht, Ger. Rigaer Bucht, Latv. Rīgas Jūras Līcis, Rus. Rizhskiy Zaliv; prev. Est. Riia Laht. gulf Estonia/Latvia
149 U12 **Rīgān** Kermān, SE Iran
Rīgas Jūras Līcis see Riga, Gulf of
13 N12 **Rigaud** ≈ Ontario/Québec, SE Canada
35 R14 **Rigby** Idaho, NW USA
154 M10 **Rīgestān** var. Registan. desert region S Afghanistan
34 M11 **Riggins** Idaho, NW USA
11 R8 **Rigolet** Newfoundland and Labrador, NE Canada
80 G9 **Rig-Rig** Kanem, W Chad
120 F4 **Riguldi** Läänemaa, W Estonia
Riia Laht see Riga, Gulf of
95 L19 **Riihimäki** Häme, S Finland
205 O2 **Riiser-Larsen Ice Shelf** ice shelf Antarctica
205 U2 **Riiser-Larsen Peninsula** peninsula Antarctica
67 P22 **Riiser-Larsen Sea** sea Antarctica
42 D2 **Riíto** Sonora, NW Mexico
114 B9 **Rijeka** Ger. Sankt Veit am Flaum, It. Fiume, Slvn. Reka; anc. Tarsatica. Primorje-Gorski Kotar, NW Croatia
101 I14 **Rijen** Noord-Brabant, S Netherlands
101 H15 **Rijkevorsel** Antwerpen, N Belgium
Rijn see Rhine
100 G11 **Rijnsburg** Zuid-Holland, W Netherlands
Rijssel see Lille
100 N10 **Rijssen** Overijssel, E Netherlands
100 G12 **Rijswijk** Eng. Ryswick. Zuid-Holland, W Netherlands
94 I10 **Riksgränsen** Norrbotten, N Sweden
172 Q6 **Rikubetsu** Hokkaidō, NE Japan
171 Mm12 **Rikuzen-Takata** Iwate, Honshū, C Japan
29 O4 **Riley** Kansas, C USA
101 I17 **Rillaar** Vlaams Brabant, C Belgium
Rí, Loch see Ree, Lough
116 G11 **Rilska Reka** ≈ W Bulgaria
79 T12 **Rima** ≈ N Nigeria
147 N7 **Rimah, Wādī ar** var. Wādī ar Rummah. dry watercourse C Saudi Arabia
Rimaszombat see Rimavská Sobota
203 R12 **Rimatara** island Îles Australes, SW French Polynesia
113 L20 **Rimavská Sobota** Ger. Gross-Steffelsdorf, Hung. Rimaszombat. Stredné Slovensko, SE Slovakia
9 Q15 **Rimbey** Alberta, SW Canada
97 P15 **Rimbo** Stockholm, C Sweden
97 M18 **Rimforsa** Östergötland, S Sweden
108 I11 **Rimini** anc. Ariminum. Emilia-Romagna, N Italy
Rîmnicu-Sărat see Râmnicu Sărat
Rîmnicu Vîlcea see Râmnicu Vâlcea
155 Y3 **Rimo Muztāgh** ▲ India/Pakistan
13 U7 **Rimouski** Québec, SE Canada
164 M16 **Rinbung** Xizang Zizhiqu, W China
168 I5 **Rinchinlhümbe** Hövsgöl, N Mongolia
64 I5 **Rincón, Cerro** ▲ N Chile
106 M15 **Rincón de la Victoria** Andalucía, S Spain
Rincón del Bonete, Lago Artificial de see Río Negro, Embalse del
107 Q4 **Rincón de Soto** La Rioja, N Spain
96 G8 **Rindal** Møre og Romsdal, S Norway
117 J20 **Ríneia** island Kykládes, Greece, Aegean Sea
158 H11 **Rīngas** prev. Reengus, Rīngus. Rājasthān, N India
97 H24 **Ringe** Fyn, C Denmark
96 H11 **Ringebu** Oppland, S Norway
Ringen see Rõngu
195 U14 **Ringgi** Kolombangara Island, NW Solomon Islands
25 R1 **Ringgold** Georgia, SE USA
24 G5 **Ringgold** Louisiana, S USA
27 S5 **Ringgold** Texas, SW USA
97 E22 **Ringkøbing** Ringkøbing, W Denmark
97 E21 **Ringkøbing** off. Ringkøbing Amt. ◆ county W Denmark
97 E22 **Ringkøbing Fjord** fjord W Denmark
35 S10 **Ringling** Montana, NW USA
29 N13 **Ringling** Oklahoma, C USA
96 H13 **Ringsaker** Hedmark, S Norway
97 I23 **Ringsted** Vestsjælland, E Denmark
Rīngus see Rīngas
94 I9 **Ringvassøy** island N Norway
20 K13 **Ringwood** New Jersey, NE USA
Rinn Duáin see Hook Head
102 H13 **Rinteln** Niedersachsen, NW Germany
Rio see Rio de Janeiro
117 E18 **Río** Dytikí Ellás, S Greece
58 C7 **Riobamba** Chimborazo, C Ecuador
62 P9 **Rio Bonito** Rio de Janeiro, SE Brazil
61 C16 **Rio Branco** state capital Acre, W Brazil
63 H18 **Río Branco** Cerro Largo, NE Uruguay
Rio Branco, Território de see Roraima
43 P8 **Río Bravo** Tamaulipas, C Mexico
65 G16 **Río Bueno** Los Lagos, C Chile
57 P5 **Río Caribe** Sucre, NE Venezuela
56 M5 **Río Chico** Miranda, N Venezuela
65 H18 **Río Cisnes** Aisén, S Chile
62 L9 **Rio Claro** São Paulo, S Brazil
47 V14 **Rio Claro** Trinidad, Trinidad and Tobago
56 J5 **Río Claro** Lara, N Venezuela
65 K15 **Río Colorado** Río Negro, E Argentina
64 K11 **Río Cuarto** Córdoba, C Argentina
62 P10 **Rio de Janeiro** var. Rio. state capital Rio de Janeiro, SE Brazil
62 P9 **Rio de Janeiro** off. Estado do Rio de Janeiro. ◆ state SE Brazil
45 R17 **Río de Jesús** Veraguas, S Panama
36 K3 **Rio Dell** California, W USA
62 K13 **Rio do Sul** Santa Catarina, S Brazil
65 I23 **Río Gallegos** var. Gallegos, Puerto Gallegos. Santa Cruz, S Argentina
63 I18 **Rio Grande** var. São Pedro do Rio Grande do Sul. Rio Grande do Sul, S Brazil
26 I9 **Rio Grande** ≈ Texas, SW USA
65 J24 **Río Grande** Tierra del Fuego, S Argentina
42 L10 **Río Grande** Zacatecas, C Mexico
44 J9 **Río Grande** León, NW Nicaragua
47 V5 **Río Grande** E Puerto Rico
27 R17 **Rio Grande City** Texas, SW USA
61 P14 **Rio Grande do Norte** off. Estado do Rio Grande do Norte. ◆ state E Brazil
63 G15 **Rio Grande do Sul** off. Estado do Rio Grande do Sul. ◆ state S Brazil
67 M17 **Rio Grande Fracture Zone** tectonic feature C Atlantic Ocean
67 J18 **Rio Grande Gap** undersea feature S Atlantic Ocean
Rio Grande Plateau see Rio Grande Rise
67 J18 **Rio Grande Rise** var. Rio Grande Plateau. undersea feature SW Atlantic Ocean
56 G4 **Ríohacha** La Guajira, N Colombia
45 S16 **Río Hato** Coclé, C Panama
27 T17 **Rio Hondo** Texas, SW USA
58 D10 **Rioja** San Martín, N Peru
43 Y11 **Río Lagartos** Yucatán, SE Mexico
105 P11 **Riom** anc. Ricomagus. Puy-de-Dôme, C France
106 F10 **Rio Maior** Santarém, C Portugal
105 O12 **Riom-ès-Montagnes** Cantal, C France
62 J12 **Rio Negro** Paraná, S Brazil
65 I15 **Río Negro** off. Provincia de Río Negro. ◆ province C Argentina
63 D18 **Río Negro** ◆ department W Uruguay
49 V12 **Río Negro, Embalse del** var. Lago Artificial de Rincón del Bonete. ▣ C Uruguay
109 M17 **Rionero in Vulture** Basilicata, S Italy
143 S9 **Rioni** ≈ W Georgia
107 P12 **Riópar** Castilla-La Mancha, C Spain
63 H16 **Rio Pardo** Rio Grande do Sul, S Brazil
39 R11 **Rio Rancho Estates** New Mexico, SW USA
44 L11 **Río San Juan** ◆ department S Nicaragua
56 E9 **Riosucio** Caldas, W Colombia
56 C7 **Ríosucio** Chocó, NW Colombia
64 K10 **Río Tercero** Córdoba, C Argentina
56 J5 **Río Tocuyo** Lara, N Venezuela
Riouw-Archipel see Riau, Kepulauan
61 J19 **Rio Verde** Goiás, C Brazil
43 O12 **Río Verde** var. Rioverde. San Luis Potosí, C Mexico
37 O8 **Rio Vista** California, W USA
114 M11 **Ripanj** Serbia, N Yugoslavia
108 J13 **Ripatransone** Marche, C Italy
Ripen see Ribe
24 M2 **Ripley** Mississippi, S USA
33 R15 **Ripley** Ohio, N USA
22 F9 **Ripley** Tennessee, S USA
23 Q4 **Ripley** West Virginia, NE USA
107 W4 **Ripoll** Cataluña, NE Spain
99 M16 **Ripon** N England, UK
32 M7 **Ripon** Wisconsin, N USA
109 L24 **Riposto** Sicilia, Italy, C Mediterranean Sea
101 L14 **Rips** Noord-Brabant, SE Netherlands
56 D9 **Risaralda** off. Departamento de Risaralda. ◆ province C Colombia
118 L8 **Rîşcani** var. Râşcani, Rus. Ryshkany. NW Moldova
158 J9 **Rishikesh** Uttar Pradesh, N India
172 P2 **Rishiri-suidō** strait E Sea of Japan
172 Oo2 **Rishiri-tō** var. Risiri Tô. island NE Japan
172 P2 **Rishiri-yama** ✕ Rishiri-tō, NE Japan
27 R7 **Rising Star** Texas, SW USA
33 Q15 **Rising Sun** Indiana, N USA
Risiri Tô see Rishiri-tō
104 L4 **Risle** ≈ N France
Rişno see Râşnov
29 V13 **Rison** Arkansas, C USA
97 G17 **Risør** Aust-Agder, S Norway
94 H10 **Risøyhamn** Nordland, C Norway
103 I23 **Riss** ≈ S Germany
120 G4 **Risti** Ger. Kreuz. Läänemaa, W Estonia
13 V8 **Ristigouche** ≈ Québec, SE Canada
95 N18 **Ristiina** Mikkeli, SE Finland
95 N14 **Ristijärvi** Oulu, C Finland
196 C14 **Ritidian Point** headland N Guam
Ritschan see Říčany
37 R9 **Ritter, Mount** ▲ California, W USA
33 T12 **Rittman** Ohio, N USA
34 L9 **Ritzville** Washington, NW USA
108 F7 **Riva** var. Riva del Garda. Trentino-Alto Adige, N Italy
63 A21 **Rivadavia** Buenos Aires, E Argentina
Riva del Garda see Riva
108 B8 **Rivarolo Canavese** Piemonte, W Italy
44 K11 **Rivas** Rivas, SW Nicaragua
44 J11 **Rivas** ◆ department SW Nicaragua
105 R11 **Rive-de-Gier** Loire, E France
63 A22 **Rivera** Buenos Aires, E Argentina
63 F16 **Rivera** Rivera, NE Uruguay
63 F17 **Rivera** ◆ department NE Uruguay
37 P9 **Riverbank** California, W USA
78 K17 **River Cess** SW Liberia
30 M4 **Riverdale** North Dakota, N USA
32 I6 **River Falls** Wisconsin, N USA
9 T16 **Riverhurst** Saskatchewan, S Canada
191 O10 **Riverina** physical region New South Wales, SE Australia
82 G8 **River Nile** ◆ state NE Sudan
65 F19 **Rivero, Isla** island Archipiélago de los Chonos, S Chile
9 W16 **Rivers** Manitoba, S Canada
79 U17 **Rivers** ◆ state S Nigeria
193 D23 **Riversdale** Southland, South Island, NZ
85 F26 **Riversdale** Western Cape, SW South Africa
37 U15 **Riverside** California, W USA
27 W9 **Riverside** Texas, SW USA
39 U3 **Riverside Reservoir** ▣ Colorado, C USA
8 K15 **Rivers Inlet** British Columbia, SW Canada
8 K15 **Rivers Inlet** inlet British Columbia, SW Canada
9 X15 **Riverton** Manitoba, S Canada
193 C24 **Riverton** Southland, South Island, NZ
32 L13 **Riverton** Illinois, N USA
38 L3 **Riverton** Utah, W USA
35 V15 **Riverton** Wyoming, C USA
12 G10 **River Valley** Ontario, S Canada
11 P14 **Riverview** New Brunswick, SE Canada
105 O17 **Rivesaltes** Pyrénées-Orientales, S France
38 H11 **Riviera** Arizona, SW USA
27 S15 **Riviera** Texas, SW USA
25 Z14 **Riviera Beach** Florida, SE USA
13 Q10 **Rivière-à-Pierre** Québec, SE Canada
13 T9 **Rivière-Bleue** Québec, SE Canada
13 T8 **Rivière-du-Loup** Québec, SE Canada
181 Y15 **Rivière du Rempart** NE Mauritius
47 R12 **Rivière-Pilote** S Martinique
181 O17 **Rivière St-Etienne, Point de la** headland SW Réunion
11 S10 **Rivière-St-Paul** Québec, E Canada
Rivière Sèche see Bel Air
118 K4 **Rivne** Pol. Równe, Rus. Rovno. Rivnens'ka Oblast', NW Ukraine
Rivne see Rivnens'ka Oblast'
118 K3 **Rivnens'ka Oblast'** var. Rivne, Rus. Rovenskaya Oblast'. ◆ province NW Ukraine
108 B8 **Rivoli** Piemonte, NW Italy
165 Q14 **Riwoqê** Xizang Zizhiqu, W China
101 H19 **Rixensart** Walloon Brabant, C Belgium
Riyadh/Riyāḍ, Minţaqat ar see Ar Riyāḍ
Riyāq see Rayak
Rizaiyeh see Orūmīyeh
143 P11 **Rize** Rize, NE Turkey
143 P11 **Rize** prev. Çoruh. ◆ province NE Turkey
167 R5 **Rizhao** Shandong, E China
Rizhskiy Zaliv see Riga, Gulf of
Rizokarpaso/Rizokárpason see Dipkarpaz
109 O21 **Rizzuto, Capo** headland S Italy
97 F15 **Rjukan** Telemark, S Norway
96 D16 **Rjuven** ▲ S Norway
78 H9 **Rkîz** Trarza, W Mauritania
97 H14 **Roa** Oppland, S Norway
107 N5 **Roa** Castilla-León, N Spain
47 T9 **Road Town** ○ (British Virgin Islands) Tortola, C British Virgin Islands
98 F6 **Roag, Loch** inlet NW Scotland, UK
39 O5 **Roan Cliffs** cliff Colorado/Utah, W USA
23 P9 **Roan High Knob** var. Roan Mountain. ▲ North Carolina/Tennessee, SE USA
Roan Mountain see Roan High Knob
105 Q10 **Roanne** anc. Rodunma. Loire, E France
25 R4 **Roanoke** Alabama, S USA
23 S7 **Roanoke** Virginia, NE USA
23 Z9 **Roanoke Island** island North Carolina, SE USA
23 W8 **Roanoke Rapids** North Carolina, SE USA
23 X9 **Roanoke River** ≈ North Carolina/Virginia, SE USA
39 O4 **Roan Plateau** plain Utah, W USA
39 R5 **Roaring Fork River** ≈ Colorado, C USA
27 O5 **Roaring Springs** Texas, SW USA
44 J4 **Roatán** var. Coxen Hole, Coxin Hole. Islas de la Bahía, N Honduras
44 I4 **Roatán, Isla de** island Islas de la Bahía, N Honduras
Roat Kampuchea see Cambodia
Roazon see Rennes
149 T7 **Robāţ-e Chāh Gonbad** Khorāsān, E Iran
149 R7 **Robāţ-e Khān** Khorāsān, C Iran
149 T7 **Robāţ-e Khvosh Āb** Khorāsān, E Iran
149 R8 **Robāţ-e Posht-e Bādām** Khorāsān, NE Iran
183 S8 **Robbie Ridge** undersea feature W Pacific Ocean
23 T10 **Robbins** North Carolina, SE USA
191 N15 **Robbins Island** island Tasmania, SE Australia
23 N10 **Robbinsville** North Carolina, SE USA
190 J12 **Robe** South Australia
23 W9 **Robersonville** North Carolina, SE USA
27 P8 **Robert Lee** Texas, SW USA
37 V5 **Roberts Creek Mountain** ▲ Nevada, W USA
95 J15 **Robertsfors** Västerbotten, N Sweden
29 R11 **Robert S.Kerr Reservoir** ▣ Oklahoma, C USA
40 L12 **Roberts Mountain** ▲ Nunivak Island, Alaska, USA
85 F26 **Robertson** Western Cape, SW South Africa
204 H4 **Robertson Island** island Antarctica
78 J16 **Robertsport** W Liberia
190 J8 **Robertstown** South Australia
Robert Williams see Caála
13 P7 **Roberval** Québec, SE Canada
33 N15 **Robinson** Illinois, N USA
200 Oo12 **Róbinson Crusoe, Isla** island Islas Juan Fernández, Chile, E Pacific Ocean
188 J9 **Robinson Range** ▲ Western Australia
194 L16 **Robinson River** Central, S PNG
190 M9 **Robinvale** Victoria, SE Australia
107 P11 **Robledo** Castilla-La Mancha, C Spain
56 G5 **Robles** var. La Paz, Robles La Paz. Cesar, N Colombia
Robles La Paz see Robles
9 V15 **Roblin** Manitoba, S Canada
195 U13 **Rob Roy** island NW Solomon Islands
9 S17 **Robsart** Saskatchewan, S Canada
9 N15 **Robson, Mount** ▲ British Columbia, SW Canada
27 T14 **Robstown** Texas, SW USA
27 P6 **Roby** Texas, SW USA
106 E11 **Roca, Cabo da** headland C Portugal
Rocadas see Xangongo
43 S14 **Roca Partida, Punta** headland C Mexico
49 X6 **Rocas, Atol das** island E Brazil
109 L18 **Roccadaspide** var. Rocca d'Aspide. Campania, S Italy
109 K15 **Roccaraso** Abruzzi, C Italy
108 H10 **Rocca San Casciano** Emilia-Romagna, C Italy
108 G13 **Roccastrada** Toscana, C Italy
63 G20 **Rocha** Rocha, E Uruguay
63 G19 **Rocha** ◆ department E Uruguay
99 L17 **Rochdale** NW England, UK
104 L11 **Rochechouart** Haute-Vienne, C France
101 J22 **Rochefort** Namur, SE Belgium
104 J11 **Rochefort** var. Rochefort sur Mer. Charente-Maritime, W France
Rochefort sur Mer see Rochefort
129 N10 **Rochegda** Arkhangel'skaya Oblast', NW Russian Federation
32 L10 **Rochelle** Illinois, N USA
27 Q9 **Rochelle** Texas, SW USA
11 P13 **Rocher Percé** island Rocher Percé, Québec, E Canada
13 V3 **Rochers Ouest, Rivière aux** ≈ Québec, SE Canada
99 O22 **Rochester** anc. Durobrivae. SE England, UK
33 O12 **Rochester** Indiana, N USA
31 W10 **Rochester** Minnesota, N USA
21 O9 **Rochester** New Hampshire, NE USA
20 F9 **Rochester** New York, NE USA
27 P5 **Rochester** Texas, SW USA
33 S9 **Rochester Hills** Michigan, N USA
Rocheuses, Montagnes/Rockies see Rocky Mountains
66 M6 **Rockall** island UK, N Atlantic Ocean
66 L6 **Rockall Bank** undersea feature N Atlantic Ocean
86 B8 **Rockall Rise** undersea feature N Atlantic Ocean
86 C9 **Rockall Trough** undersea feature N Atlantic Ocean
37 U2 **Rock Creek** ≈ Nevada, W USA
27 T10 **Rockdale** Texas, SW USA
205 N12 **Rockefeller Plateau** plateau Antarctica
32 K11 **Rock Falls** Illinois, N USA
25 Q5 **Rockford** Alabama, S USA
32 L10 **Rockford** Illinois, N USA
13 Q12 **Rock Forest** Québec, SE Canada
9 T17 **Rockglen** Saskatchewan, S Canada
189 Y8 **Rockhampton** Queensland, E Australia
23 R11 **Rock Hill** South Carolina, SE USA
188 I13 **Rockingham** Western Australia
23 T11 **Rockingham** North Carolina, SE USA
32 J11 **Rock Island** Illinois, N USA
27 U12 **Rock Island** Texas, SW USA
12 C10 **Rock Lake** Ontario, S Canada
31 O2 **Rock Lake** North Dakota, N USA
12 J12 **Rock Lake** ◎ Ontario, SE Canada
12 M12 **Rockland** Ontario, SE Canada
21 R7 **Rockland** Maine, NE USA
190 L11 **Rocklands Reservoir** ▣ Victoria, SE Australia
37 O7 **Rocklin** California, W USA
25 R3 **Rockmart** Georgia, SE USA
33 N16 **Rockport** Indiana, N USA
29 Q1 **Rock Port** Missouri, C USA
27 T14 **Rockport** Texas, SW USA
34 I7 **Rockport** Washington, NW USA
31 S11 **Rock Rapids** Iowa, C USA
32 K11 **Rock River** ≈ Illinois/Wisconsin, N USA
46 I3 **Rock Sound** Eleuthera Island, C Bahamas
35 U17 **Rock Springs** Wyoming, C USA
27 P11 **Rocksprings** Texas, SW USA
57 T9 **Rockstone** C Guyana
31 S12 **Rock Valley** Iowa, C USA
33 N14 **Rockville** Indiana, N USA
23 W3 **Rockville** Maryland, NE USA
27 U6 **Rockwall** Texas, SW USA
31 U13 **Rockwell City** Iowa, C USA
33 S10 **Rockwood** Michigan, N USA
22 M9 **Rockwood** Tennessee, S USA
27 Q8 **Rockwood** Texas, SW USA
39 U6 **Rocky Ford** Colorado, C USA
12 D9 **Rocky Island Lake** ◎ Ontario, S Canada
23 V9 **Rocky Mount** North Carolina, SE USA
23 S7 **Rocky Mount** Virginia, NE USA
35 Q8 **Rocky Mountain** ▲ Montana, NW USA
9 P15 **Rocky Mountain House** Alberta, SW Canada
39 T3 **Rocky Mountain National Park** national park Colorado, C USA
2 E12 **Rocky Mountains** var. Rockies, Fr. Montagnes Rocheuses. ▲ Canada/USA
44 H1 **Rocky Point** headland NE Belize
85 A17 **Rocky Point** headland NW Namibia
97 F14 **Rødberg** Buskerud, S Norway
97 I25 **Rødby** Storstrøm, SE Denmark
97 I25 **Rødbyhavn** Storstrøm, SE Denmark
11 T10 **Roddickton** Newfoundland, Newfoundland and Labrador, SE Canada
97 F23 **Rødding** Sønderjylland, SW Denmark
97 M22 **Rödeby** Blekinge, S Sweden
100 N6 **Roden** Drenthe, NE Netherlands
64 H9 **Rodeo** San Juan, W Argentina
105 O14 **Rodez** anc. Segodunum. Aveyron, S France
Rodholívos see Rodolívos
Rodhópi Óri see Rhodope Mountains
Ródhos/Rodi see Ródos
109 N15 **Rodi Garganico** Puglia, SE Italy
103 N20 **Roding** Bayern, SE Germany
115 J19 **Rodinit, Kepi i** headland W Albania
118 I9 **Rodnei, Munţii** ▲ N Romania
192 L4 **Rodney, Cape** headland North Island, NZ
40 L9 **Rodney, Cape** headland Alaska, USA
128 M16 **Rodniki** Ivanovskaya Oblast', W Russian Federation
121 Q16 **Rodnya** Rus. Rodnya. Mahilyowskaya Voblasts', E Belarus
Rodó see José Enrique Rodó
116 H13 **Rodolívos** var. Rodholívos. Kentrikí Makedonía, NE Greece
Rodopi see Rhodope Mountains
117 O22 **Ródos** var. Ródhos, Eng. Rhodes, It. Rodi. Ródos, Dodekánisos, Greece, Aegean Sea
117 O22 **Ródos** var. Ródhos, Eng. Rhodes, It. Rodi; anc. Rhodos. island Dodekánisos, Greece, Aegean Sea
Rodosto see Tekirdağ
61 A14 **Rodrigues** Amazonas, W Brazil
181 P8 **Rodrigues** var. Rodriquez. island E Mauritius
Rodriquez see Rodrigues
Rodunma see Roanne
188 I7 **Roebourne** Western Australia
85 J20 **Roedtan** Northern, NE South Africa
100 H11 **Roelofarendsveen** Zuid-Holland, W Netherlands
Roepat see Rupat, Pulau
Roer see Rur
101 M16 **Roermond** Limburg, SE Netherlands
101 C18 **Roeselare** Fr. Roulers; prev. Rousselaere. West-Vlaanderen, W Belgium
15 L5 **Roes Welcome Sound** strait Northwest Territories, N Canada
Roeteng see Ruteng
Rofreit see Rovereto
Rogachëv see Rahachow
59 L15 **Rogagua, Laguna** ◎ NW Bolivia
97 C16 **Rogaland** ◆ county S Norway
27 Y9 **Roganville** Texas, SW USA
111 W11 **Rogaška Slatina** Ger. Rohitsch-Sauerbrunn; prev. Rogatec-Slatina. E Slovenia
Rogatec-Slatina see Rogaška Slatina
114 J13 **Rogatica** SE Bosnia and Herzegovina
Rogatin see Rohatyn
95 F17 **Rogen** ◎ C Sweden
29 S9 **Rogers** Arkansas, C USA
31 P5 **Rogers** North Dakota, N USA
27 T9 **Rogers** Texas, SW USA
33 R5 **Rogers City** Michigan, N USA
Roger Simpson Island see Abemama
37 T14 **Rogers Lake** salt flat California, W USA
23 Q8 **Rogers, Mount** ▲ Virginia, NE USA
35 O16 **Rogerson** Idaho, NW USA
9 O16 **Rogers Pass** pass British Columbia, SW Canada
23 O8 **Rogersville** Tennessee, S USA
101 L16 **Roggel** Limburg, SE Netherlands
Roggeveen see Roggewein, Cabo
200 Nn12 **Roggeveen Basin** undersea feature E Pacific Ocean
203 X16 **Roggewein, Cabo** var. Roggeveen. headland Easter Island, Chile, E Pacific Ocean
104 F1 **Rogliano** Corse, France, C Mediterranean Sea
109 N21 **Rogliano** Calabria, SW Italy
94 G12 **Rognan** Nordland, C Norway
102 K10 **Rögnitz** ≈ N Germany
Rogozhina/Rogozhinë see Rrogozhinë
112 G10 **Rogoźno** Piła, NW Poland
34 E15 **Rogue River** ≈ Oregon, NW USA
118 I6 **Rohatyn** Rus. Rogatin. Ivano-Frankivs'ka Oblast', W Ukraine
201 O14 **Rohi** Pohnpei, E Micronesia
Rohitsch-Sauerbrunn see Rogaška Slatina
155 Q13 **Rohri** Sind, SE Pakistan
158 I10 **Rohtak** Haryāna, N India
Roi Ed see Roi Et
178 Ii10 **Roi Et** var. Muang Roi Et, Roi Ed. Roi Et, E Thailand
203 U9 **Roi Georges, Îles du** island group Îles Tuamotu, C French Polynesia
159 Y10 **Roing** Arunāchal Pradesh, NE India
120 E7 **Roja** Talsi, NW Latvia
63 B20 **Rojas** Buenos Aires, E Argentina
155 R12 **Rojhān** Punjab, E Pakistan
43 Q12 **Rojo, Cabo** headland C Mexico
47 Q10 **Rojo, Cabo** headland W Puerto Rico
173 G7 **Rokan Kanan, Sungai** ≈ Sumatera, W Indonesia
173 G7 **Rokan Kiri, Sungai** ≈ Sumatera, W Indonesia
Rokha see Rokhah
155 R4 **Rokhah** var. Rokha. Kāpīsā, E Afghanistan
120 I11 **Rokiškis** Rokiškis, NE Lithuania
172 Nn9 **Rokkasho** Aomori, Honshū, C Japan
113 B17 **Rokycany** Ger. Rokytzan. Západní Čechy, W Czech Republic
119 P6 **Rokytne** Kyyivs'ka Oblast', N Ukraine
118 L3 **Rokytne** Rivnens'ka Oblast', NW Ukraine
Rokytzan see Rokycany
164 L11 **Rola Co** ◎ W China
31 V13 **Roland** Iowa, C USA
97 D15 **Røldal** Hordaland, S Norway
100 O7 **Rolde** Drenthe, NE Netherlands
31 O2 **Rolette** North Dakota, N USA
29 V6 **Rolla** Missouri, C USA
31 O2 **Rolla** North Dakota, N USA
110 A10 **Rolle** Vaud, W Switzerland
189 X8 **Rolleston** Queensland, E Australia
193 H19 **Rolleston** Canterbury, South Island, NZ
193 G18 **Rolleston Range** ▲ South Island, NZ
12 H8 **Rollet** Québec, SE Canada
24 J4 **Rolling Fork** Mississippi, S USA
22 L6 **Rolling Fork** ≈ Kentucky, S USA
12 J11 **Rolphton** Ontario, SE Canada
Röm see Rømø
189 X10 **Roma** Queensland, E Australia
109 I15 **Roma** Eng. Rome. ● (Italy) Lazio, C Italy
97 P19 **Roma** Gotland, SE Sweden
23 T14 **Romain, Cape** headland South Carolina, SE USA
11 P11 **Romaine** ≈ Newfoundland and Labrador/Québec, E Canada
27 R17 **Roma Los Saenz** Texas, SW USA
116 H8 **Roman** Oblast Montana, NW Bulgaria
118 L10 **Roman** Hung. Románvásár. Neamţ, NE Romania
66 M13 **Romanche Fracture Zone** tectonic feature E Atlantic Ocean
63 C15 **Romang** Santa Fe, C Argentina
175 T15 **Romang, Pulau** var. Pulau Roma. island Kepulauan Damar, E Indonesia
175 Ss15 **Romang, Selat** strait Nusa Tenggara, S Indonesia
113 O24 **Romania** Bul. Rumŭniya, Ger. Rumänien, Hung. Románia, Rom. România, SCr. Rumunjska, Ukr. Rumuniya; prev. Republica Socialistă România, Roumania, Rumania, Socialist Republic of Romania, Rom. Romînia. ◆ republic SE Europe
119 T14 **Roman-Kash** ▲ S Ukraine
25 W16 **Romano, Cape** headland Florida, SE USA
46 G5 **Romano, Cayo** island C Cuba
126 Kk15 **Romanovka** Respublika Buryatiya, S Russian Federation
131 N8 **Romanovka** Saratovskaya Oblast', W Russian Federation
110 I6 **Romanshorn** Thurgau, NE Switzerland
105 R12 **Romans-sur-Isère** Drôme, E France
201 U12 **Romanum** island Chuuk, C Micronesia
Románvásár see Roman
41 S5 **Romanzof Mountains** ▲ Alaska, USA
Roma, Pulau see Romang, Pulau
105 S4 **Rombas** Moselle, NE France
176 Xx10 **Rombebai, Danau** ◎ Irian Jaya, E Indonesia
25 R2 **Rome** Georgia, SE USA
20 I9 **Rome** New York, NE USA
Rome see Roma
33 S9 **Romeo** Michigan, N USA
Römerstadt see Rýmařov
Rometan see Romitan
105 P5 **Romilly-sur-Seine** Aube, N France
Romînia see Romania
152 L11 **Romitan** Rus. Rometan. Bukhoro Wiloyati, C Uzbekistan
23 U3 **Romney** West Virginia, NE USA
119 S4 **Romny** Sums'ka Oblast', NE Ukraine
97 E24 **Rømø** Ger. Röm. island SW Denmark

◆ Country
● Country Capital
◇ Dependent Territory
○ Dependent Territory Capital
◆ Administrative Region
✈ International Airport
▲ Mountain
▲ Mountain Range
✕ Volcano
≈ River
◎ Lake
▣ Reservoir

119 S5 **Romodan** Poltavs'ka Oblast', NE Ukraine
131 P5 **Romodanovo** Respublika Mordoviya, W Russian Federation
Romorantin see Romorantin-Lanthenay
105 N8 **Romorantin-Lanthenay** var. Romorantin. Loir-et-Cher, C France
174 Hh5 **Rompin, Sungai** ~ Peninsular Malaysia
96 F9 **Romsdal** physical region S Norway
96 F10 **Romsdalen** valley S Norway
96 E9 **Romsdalsfjorden** fjord S Norway
35 P8 **Ronan** Montana, NW USA
61 M14 **Roncador** Maranhão, E Brazil
195 W12 **Roncador Reef** reef N Solomon Islands
61 J17 **Roncador, Serra do** ▲▲ C Brazil
23 S6 **Ronceverte** West Virginia, NE USA
109 H14 **Ronciglione** Lazio, C Italy
106 L15 **Ronda** Andalucía, S Spain
96 G11 **Rondane** ▲▲ S Norway
106 L15 **Ronda, Serranía de** ▲▲ S Spain
97 H22 **Rønde** Århus, C Denmark
Rŏndik see Rongrik Atoll
61 E16 **Rondônia** off. Estado de Rondônia; prev. Território de Rondônia. ◐ state W Brazil
61 I18 **Rondonópolis** Mato Grosso, W Brazil
96 G11 **Rondslottet** ▲ S Norway
97 P20 **Ronehamn** Gotland, SE Sweden
166 L13 **Rong'an** var. Chang'an, Rongan. Guangxi Zhuangzu Zizhiqu, S China
201 R4 **Rongelap Atoll** var. Rōnļap. atoll Ralik Chain, NW Marshall Islands
Rongerik see Rongrik Atoll
166 L13 **Rong Jiang** ~ S China
166 K12 **Rongjiang** prev. Guzhou. Guizhou, S China
Rong, Kas see Rŭng, Kaôh
178 Hh8 **Rong Kwang** Phrae, NW Thailand
201 T4 **Rongrik Atoll** var. Rōņdik, Rongerik. atoll Ralik Chain, N Marshall Islands
201 X2 **Rongrong** island SE Marshall Islands
166 L13 **Rongshui** var. Rongshui Miaozu Zizhixian. Guangxi Zhuangzu Zizhiqu, S China
Rongshui Miaozu Zizhixian see Rongshui
120 I6 **Rõngu** Ger. Ringen. Tartumaa, SE Estonia
166 L15 **Rongxian** var. Rong Xian. Guangxi Zhuangzu Zizhiqu, S China
Roniu see Ronui, Mont
201 N13 **Ronkiti** Pohnpei, E Micronesia
Rōnļap see Rongelap Atoll
97 L24 **Rønne** Bornholm, E Denmark
97 M22 **Ronneby** Blekinge, S Sweden
204 J7 **Ronne Entrance** inlet Antarctica
204 L6 **Ronne Ice Shelf** ice shelf Antarctica
101 E19 **Ronse** Fr. Renaix. Oost-Vlaanderen, SW Belgium
203 R8 **Ronui, Mont** var. Roniu. ✶ Tahiti, W French Polynesia
32 K14 **Roodhouse** Illinois, N USA
85 C19 **Rooibank** Erongo, W Namibia
Rooke Island see Umboi Island
67 N24 **Rookery Point** headland NE Tristan da Cunha
176 W10 **Roon, Pulau** island E Indonesia
181 V7 **Roo Rise** undersea feature E Indian Ocean
158 J9 **Roorkee** Uttar Pradesh, N India
101 H15 **Roosendaal** Noord-Brabant, S Netherlands
27 P10 **Roosevelt** Texas, SW USA
39 N3 **Roosevelt** Utah, W USA
49 T8 **Roosevelt** ~ W Brazil
205 O13 **Roosevelt Island** island Antarctica
8 L10 **Roosevelt, Mount** ▲ British Columbia, W Canada
9 P17 **Roosville** British Columbia, SW Canada
31 X10 **Root River** ~ Minnesota, N USA
113 N16 **Ropczyce** Rzeszów, SE Poland
189 Q3 **Roper Bar** Northern Territory, N Australia
26 M5 **Ropesville** Texas, SW USA
104 K14 **Roquefort** Landes, SW France
63 C21 **Roque Pérez** Buenos Aires, E Argentina
60 E10 **Roraima** off. Estado de Roraima; prev. Território de Rio Branco, Território de Roraima. ◐ state N Brazil
60 F9 **Roraima, Mount** ▲ N South America
176 X10 **Rori** Irian Jaya, E Indonesia
Ro Ro Reef see Malolo Barrier Reef
96 I9 **Røros** Sør-Trøndelag, S Norway
110 I7 **Rorschach** Sankt Gallen, NE Switzerland
95 E14 **Rørvik** Nord-Trøndelag, C Norway
121 G17 **Ros'** Rus. Ross'. Hrodzyenskaya Voblasts', W Belarus
121 G17 **Ros'** Rus. Ross'. ~ W Belarus
119 O6 **Ros'** ~ N Ukraine
46 K7 **Rosa, Lake** ◎ Great Inagua, S Bahamas
34 M9 **Rosalia** Washington, NW USA
203 W15 **Rosalia, Punta** headland Easter Island, Chile, E Pacific Ocean
47 P12 **Rosalie** E Dominica
37 T14 **Rosamond** California, W USA
37 S14 **Rosamond Lake** salt flat California, W USA
63 B18 **Rosario** Santa Fe, C Argentina
42 J11 **Rosario** Sinaloa, C Mexico
42 G6 **Rosario** Sonora, NW Mexico
64 O6 **Rosario** San Pedro, C Paraguay
63 E20 **Rosario** Colonia, SW Uruguay
56 H5 **Rosario** Zulia, NW Venezuela
Rosario see Rosarito
42 B4 **Rosario, Bahía del** bay NW Mexico
64 K6 **Rosario de la Frontera** Salta, N Argentina
63 C18 **Rosario del Tala** Entre Ríos, E Argentina
63 F16 **Rosário do Sul** Rio Grande do Sul, S Brazil
61 H18 **Rosário Oeste** Mato Grosso, W Brazil
42 E7 **Rosarito** Baja California, NW Mexico
42 B1 **Rosarito** var. Rosario. Baja California, NW Mexico
42 E7 **Rosarito** Baja California Sur, W Mexico
106 L9 **Rosarito, Embalse del** ▣ W Spain
109 N22 **Rosarno** Calabria, SW Italy
58 B5 **Rosa Zárate** var. Quinindé. Esmeraldas, SW Ecuador
Roscianum see Rossano
31 O8 **Roscoe** South Dakota, N USA
27 P7 **Roscoe** Texas, SW USA
104 F5 **Roscoff** Finistère, NW France
Ros Comáin see Roscommon
99 C17 **Roscommon** Ir. Ros Comáin. C Ireland
33 Q7 **Roscommon** Michigan, N USA
99 C17 **Roscommon** Ir. Ros Comáin. cultural region C Ireland
Ros. Cré see Roscrea
99 D19 **Roscrea** Ir. Ros. Cré. C Ireland
47 X12 **Roseau** prev. Charlotte Town. ● (Dominica) SW Dominica
31 S2 **Roseau** Minnesota, N USA
181 Y16 **Rose Belle** SE Mauritius
191 O16 **Rosebery** Tasmania, SE Australia
23 U11 **Roseboro** North Carolina, SE USA
27 T9 **Rosebud** Texas, SW USA
35 W10 **Rosebud Creek** ~ Montana, NW USA
34 F14 **Roseburg** Oregon, NW USA
24 J3 **Rosedale** Mississippi, S USA
101 H21 **Rosée** Namur, S Belgium
57 U8 **Rose Hall** E Guyana
181 X16 **Rose Hill** W Mauritius
82 H12 **Roseires, Reservoir** var. Lake Rusayris. ▣ E Sudan
Rosenau see Rožnov pod Radhoštěm, Czech Republic
Rosenau see Rožňava, Slovakia
27 V11 **Rosenberg** Texas, SW USA
Rosenberg see Olesno, Poland
Rosenberg see Ružomberok, Slovakia
102 I10 **Rosengarten** Niedersachsen, N Germany
103 M24 **Rosenheim** Bayern, S Germany
Rosenhof see Zilupe
107 X4 **Roses** Cataluña, NE Spain
107 X4 **Roses, Golf de** gulf NE Spain
109 K14 **Roseto degli Abruzzi** Abruzzi, C Italy
9 S16 **Rosetown** Saskatchewan, S Canada
Rosetta see Rashîd
37 O7 **Roseville** California, W USA
32 J12 **Roseville** Illinois, N USA
31 V8 **Roseville** Minnesota, N USA
31 R7 **Rosholt** South Dakota, N USA
108 F12 **Rosignano Marittimo** Toscana, C Italy
118 I14 **Roşiori de Vede** Teleorman, S Romania
116 K8 **Rositsa** ~ N Bulgaria
Rositten see Rēzekne
97 J23 **Roskilde** Roskilde, E Denmark
97 I23 **Roskilde** off. Roskilde Amt. ◐ county E Denmark
Ros Láir see Rosslare
130 H5 **Roslavl'** Smolenskaya Oblast', W Russian Federation
34 I8 **Roslyn** Washington, NW USA
101 K14 **Rosmalen** Noord-Brabant, S Netherlands
Ros Mhic Thriúin see New Ross
115 P19 **Rosoman** C FYR Macedonia
104 F6 **Rosporden** Finistère, NW France
193 F17 **Ross** West Coast, South Island, NZ
8 J7 **Ross** ~ Yukon Territory, W Canada
Ross' see Ros'
98 H8 **Ross and Cromarty** cultural region N Scotland, UK
109 O20 **Rossano** anc. Roscianum. Calabria, SW Italy
24 L5 **Ross Barnett Reservoir** ▣ Mississippi, S USA
9 W16 **Rossburn** Manitoba, S Canada
12 H13 **Rosseau** Ontario, S Canada
12 H13 **Rosseau, Lake** ◎ Ontario, S Canada
195 R17 **Rossel Island** prev. Yela Island. island SE PNG
205 P12 **Ross Ice Shelf** ice shelf Antarctica
11 P16 **Rossignol, Lake** ◎ Nova Scotia, SE Canada
85 C19 **Rössing** Erongo, W Namibia
205 Q14 **Ross Island** island Antarctica
Rossitten see Rybachiy
Rossiyskaya Federatsiya see Russian Federation
9 N17 **Rossland** British Columbia, SW Canada
99 F20 **Rosslare** Ir. Ros Láir. SE Ireland
99 F20 **Rosslare Harbour** Wexford, SE Ireland
103 M14 **Rosslau** Sachsen-Anhalt, E Germany
78 G10 **Rosso** Trarza, SW Mauritania
104 X14 **Rosso, Cap** headland Corse, France, C Mediterranean Sea
95 H16 **Rosson** Jämtland, C Sweden
99 K21 **Ross-on-Wye** W England, UK
Rossony see Rasony
130 L9 **Rossosh'** Voronezhskaya Oblast', W Russian Federation
189 Q7 **Ross River** Northern Territory, N Australia
8 J7 **Ross River** Yukon Territory, W Canada
205 O15 **Ross Sea** sea Antarctica
25 R1 **Rossville** Georgia, SE USA
Rostak see Ar Rustāq
149 P14 **Rostāq** Hormozgān, S Iran
119 N5 **Rostavytsya** ~ N Ukraine
9 T15 **Rosthern** Saskatchewan, S Canada
102 M8 **Rostock** Mecklenburg-Vorpommern, NE Germany
128 L16 **Rostov** Yaroslavskaya Oblast', W Russian Federation
Rostov see Rostov-na-Donu
130 L12 **Rostov-na-Donu** var. Rostov, Eng. Rostov-on-Don. Rostovskaya Oblast', SW Russian Federation
Rostov-on-Don see Rostov-na-Donu
130 L10 **Rostovskaya Oblast'** ◐ province SW Russian Federation
94 G13 **Røsvatnet** ◎ C Norway
94 J14 **Rosvik** Norrbotten, N Sweden
25 S3 **Roswell** Georgia, SE USA
39 U14 **Roswell** New Mexico, SW USA
96 K12 **Rot** Kopparberg, C Sweden
103 I23 **Rot** ~ S Germany
106 J15 **Rota** Andalucía, S Spain
196 K9 **Rota** island S Northern Mariana Islands
27 P6 **Rotan** Texas, SW USA
Rotcher Island see Tamana
102 I11 **Rotenburg** Niedersachsen, NW Germany
Rotenburg see Rotenburg an der Fulda
103 I16 **Rotenburg an der Fulda** var. Rotenburg. Thüringen, C Germany
103 L18 **Roter Main** ~ E Germany
103 K20 **Roth** Bayern, SE Germany
103 G16 **Rothaargebirge** ▲▲ W Germany
Rothenburg see Rothenburg ob der Tauber
103 J20 **Rothenburg ob der Tauber** var. Rothenburg. Bayern, S Germany
204 H6 **Rothera** UK research station Antarctica
193 I17 **Rotherham** Canterbury, South Island, NZ
99 M17 **Rotherham** N England, UK
98 H12 **Rothesay** W Scotland, UK
110 E7 **Rothrist** Aargau, N Switzerland
204 H6 **Rothschild Island** island Antarctica
175 Qq18 **Roti, Pulau** island S Indonesia
Roti, Pulau see Rote, Pulau
175 R18 **Roti, Selat** strait Nusa Tenggara, S Indonesia
191 O8 **Roto** New South Wales, SE Australia
192 N8 **Rotoiti, Lake** ◎ North Island, NZ
Rotomagus see Rouen
109 N19 **Rotondella** Basilicata, S Italy
104 E2 **Rotondo, Monte** ▲ Corse, France, C Mediterranean Sea
193 I15 **Rotoroa, Lake** ◎ South Island, NZ
192 N8 **Rotorua** Bay of Plenty, North Island, NZ
192 N8 **Rotorua, Lake** ◎ North Island, NZ
103 N22 **Rott** ~ SE Germany
110 F10 **Rotten** ~ S Switzerland
111 T6 **Rottenmann** Steiermark, E Austria
100 H12 **Rotterdam** Zuid-Holland, SW Netherlands
20 K10 **Rotterdam** New York, NE USA
97 M21 **Rottnen** ◎ S Sweden
100 N4 **Rottumeroog** island Waddeneilanden, NE Netherlands
100 N4 **Rottumerplaat** island Waddeneilanden, NE Netherlands
103 G23 **Rottweil** Baden-Württemberg, S Germany
203 O7 **Rotui, Mont** ✶ Moorea, W French Polynesia
105 P1 **Roubaix** Nord, N France
113 C15 **Roudnice nad Labem** Ger. Raudnitz an der Elbe. Severní Čechy, N Czech Republic
104 M4 **Rouen** anc. Rotomagus. Seine-Maritime, N France
176 Y11 **Rouffaer Reserves** reserve Irian Jaya, E Indonesia
Rouffaer-Rivier see Tariku, Sungai
13 N10 **Rouge, Rivière** ~ Québec, SE Canada
22 J6 **Rough River** ~ Kentucky, S USA
22 J6 **Rough River Lake** ▣ Kentucky, S USA
Rouhaïbé see Ar Ruḩaybah
104 K11 **Rouillac** Charente, W France
Roulers see Roeselare
Roumania see Romania
181 Y15 **Round Island** var. Île Ronde. island NE Mauritius
12 J12 **Round Lake** ◎ Ontario, SE Canada
37 U7 **Round Mountain** Nevada, W USA
27 R10 **Round Mountain** Texas, SW USA
191 U5 **Round Mountain** ▲ New South Wales, SE Australia
27 S10 **Round Rock** Texas, SW USA
35 U10 **Roundup** Montana, NW USA
57 Y10 **Roura** NE French Guiana
Rourkela see Raurkela
98 J4 **Rousay** island N Scotland, UK
Rousselaere see Roeselare
105 O17 **Roussillon** cultural region S France
13 V7 **Routhierville** Québec, SE Canada
101 K25 **Rouvroy** Luxembourg, SE Belgium
12 I7 **Rouyn-Noranda** Québec, SE Canada
Rouyuanchengzi see Huachi
94 L12 **Rovaniemi** Lappi, N Finland
108 E7 **Rovato** Lombardia, N Italy
129 N11 **Rovdino** Arkhangel'skaya Oblast', NW Russian Federation
Roven'ki see Roven'ky
119 Y8 **Roven'ky** var. Roven'ki. Luhans'ka Oblast', E Ukraine
Rovenskaya Oblast' see Rivnens'ka Oblast'
Rovenskaya Sloboda see Rovyenskaya Slabada
108 G7 **Rovereto** Ger. Rofreit. Trentino-Alto Adige, N Italy
178 J12 **Rôviĕng Tbong** Preăh Vihéar, N Cambodia
Rovigno see Rovinj
108 H8 **Rovigo** Veneto, NE Italy
114 A10 **Rovinj** It. Rovigno. Istra, NW Croatia
56 E10 **Rovira** Tolima, C Colombia
Rovno see Rivne
131 P9 **Rovnoye** Saratovskaya Oblast', W Russian Federation
84 Q12 **Rovuma, Rio** var. Ruvuma. ~ Mozambique/Tanzania see also Ruvuma
121 O19 **Rovyenskaya Slabada** Rus. Rovenskaya Sloboda. Homyel'skaya Voblasts', SE Belarus
191 R5 **Rowena** New South Wales, SE Australia
23 T11 **Rowland** North Carolina, SE USA
15 M1 **Rowley** ~ Baffin Island, Northwest Territories, NE Canada
15 M2 **Rowley Island** island Northwest Territories, NE Canada
181 W8 **Rowley Shoals** reef NW Australia
179 Pp12 **Roxas** Mindoro, N Philippines
179 Q13 **Roxas City** Panay Island, C Philippines
23 U8 **Roxboro** North Carolina, SE USA
193 D23 **Roxburgh** Otago, South Island, NZ
98 K13 **Roxburgh** cultural region SE Scotland, UK
190 H5 **Roxby Downs** South Australia
97 M17 **Roxen** ◎ S Sweden
27 V5 **Roxton** Texas, SW USA
13 P12 **Roxton-Sud** Québec, SE Canada
35 U8 **Roy** Montana, NW USA
39 U10 **Roy** New Mexico, SW USA
99 E17 **Royal Canal** Ir. An Chanáil Ríoga. canal C Ireland
32 L1 **Royale, Isle** island Michigan, N USA
39 S6 **Royal Gorge** valley Colorado, C USA
99 M20 **Royal Leamington Spa** var. Leamington, Leamington Spa. C England, UK
99 O23 **Royal Tunbridge Wells** var. Tunbridge Wells. SE England, UK
26 L9 **Royalty** Texas, SW USA
104 J11 **Royan** Charente-Maritime, W France
67 B24 **Roy Cove Settlement** West Falkland, Falkland Islands
105 O3 **Roye** Somme, N France
97 H15 **Røyken** Buskerud, S Norway
95 F14 **Røyrvik** Nord-Trøndelag, C Norway
27 U6 **Royse City** Texas, SW USA
99 O21 **Royston** E England, UK
25 U2 **Royston** Georgia, SE USA
116 L10 **Roza** prev. Gyulovo. Burgaska Oblast, E Bulgaria
115 L16 **Rožaje** Montenegro, SW Yugoslavia
112 M10 **Różan** Ostrołęka, E Poland
119 O10 **Rozdil'na** Odes'ka Oblast', SW Ukraine
119 S12 **Rozdol'ne** Rus. Razdolnoye. Respublika Krym, S Ukraine
151 Q9 **Rozhdestvenka** Akmola, C Kazakhstan
118 I6 **Rozhnyativ** Ivano-Frankivs'ka Oblast', W Ukraine
118 J3 **Rozhyshche** Volyns'ka Oblast', NW Ukraine
Roznau am Radhost see Rožnov pod Radhoštěm
113 L19 **Rožňava** Ger. Rosenau, Hung. Rozsnyó. Východné Slovensko, E Slovakia
118 K10 **Roznov** Neamţ, NE Romania
113 I18 **Rožnov pod Radhoštěm** Ger. Rosenau, Roznau am Radhost. Severní Morava, E Czech Republic
Rózsahegy see Ružomberok
Rozsnyó see Râşnov, Romania
Rozsnyó see Rožňava, Slovakia
115 K18 **Rranxë** Shkodër, NW Albania
115 L18 **Rrëshen** var. Rresheni, Rrshen. Lezhë, C Albania
Rresheni see Rrëshen
Rrogozhina see Rrogozhinë
115 K20 **Rrogozhinë** var. Rogozhina, Rogozhinë, Rrogozhina. Tiranë, W Albania
Rrshen see Rrëshen
114 O13 **Rtanj** ▲ E Yugoslavia
131 O7 **Rtishchevo** Saratovskaya Oblast', W Russian Federation
192 N12 **Ruahine Range** var. Ruarine. ▲▲ North Island, NZ
193 L14 **Ruamahanga** ~ North Island, NZ
Ruanda see Rwanda
192 M10 **Ruapehu, Mount** ▲ North Island, NZ
193 C25 **Ruapuke Island** island SW NZ
Ruarine see Ruahine Range
192 O9 **Ruatahuna** Bay of Plenty, North Island, NZ
192 Q8 **Ruatoria** Gisborne, North Island, NZ
192 K4 **Ruawai** Northland, North Island, NZ
13 N8 **Ruban** ~ Québec, SE Canada
83 I22 **Rubeho Mountains** ▲▲ C Tanzania
172 Q5 **Rubeshibe** Hokkaidō, NE Japan
Rubezhnoye see Rubizhne
115 L18 **Rubik** Lezhë, C Albania
56 H7 **Rubio** Táchira, W Venezuela
119 X6 **Rubizhne** Rus. Rubezhnoye. Luhans'ka Oblast', E Ukraine
83 F20 **Rubondo Island** island N Tanzania
126 Gg15 **Rubtsovsk** Altayskiy Kray, S Russian Federation
41 P9 **Ruby** Alaska, USA
37 W3 **Ruby Dome** ▲ Nevada, W USA
37 W4 **Ruby Lake** ◎ Nevada, W USA
37 W4 **Ruby Mountains** ▲▲ Nevada, W USA
35 Q12 **Ruby Range** ▲▲ Montana, NW USA
120 C10 **Rucava** Liepāja, SW Latvia
Rūdān see Dehbārez
Rudelstadt see Ciechanowiec
Rudensk see Rudzyensk
121 G14 **Rūdiškės** Trakai, S Lithuania
97 H24 **Rudkøbing** Fyn, C Denmark
127 Nn17 **Rudnaya Pristan'** Primorskiy Kray, SE Russian Federation
151 V14 **Rudnichnyy** Kaz. Rŭdnīchnyy. Taldykorgan, SE Kazakhstan
129 S13 **Rudnichnyy** Kirovskaya Oblast', NW Russian Federation
116 N9 **Rudnik** Varnenska Oblast, E Bulgaria
Rudny see Rudnyy
130 H4 **Rudnya** Smolenskaya Oblast', W Russian Federation
131 O8 **Rudnya** Volgogradskaya Oblast', SW Russian Federation
150 M7 **Rudnyy** var. Rudny. Kustanay, N Kazakhstan
126 Hh1 **Rudol'fa, Ostrov** island Zemlya Frantsa-Iosifa, NW Russian Federation
83 H16 **Rudolf, Lake** var. Lake Turkana. ◎ N Kenya
Rudolfswert see Novo Mesto
103 L17 **Rudolstadt** Thüringen, C Germany
33 Q4 **Rudyard** Michigan, N USA
35 S7 **Rudyard** Montana, NW USA
121 K16 **Rudzyensk** Rus. Rudensk. Minskaya Voblasts', C Belarus
106 L6 **Rueda** Castilla-León, N Spain
116 F10 **Ruen** ▲ Bulgaria/FYR Macedonia
82 G10 **Rufa'a** Gezira, C Sudan
104 L10 **Ruffec** Charente, W France
23 R14 **Ruffin** South Carolina, SE USA
83 J23 **Rufiji** ~ E Tanzania
63 A20 **Rufino** Santa Fe, C Argentina
78 F11 **Rufisque** W Senegal
85 K14 **Rufunsa** Lusaka, C Zambia
120 J9 **Rugāji** Balvi, E Latvia
167 R7 **Rugao** Jiangsu, E China
99 M20 **Rugby** C England, UK
31 N3 **Rugby** North Dakota, N USA
102 N7 **Rügen** headland NE Germany
Ruhaybeh see Ar Ruḩaybah
167 N7 **Ru He** ~ C China
83 E19 **Ruhengeri** NW Rwanda
Ruhja see Rūjiena
102 M10 **Ruhner Berg** hill N Germany
120 F7 **Ruhnu** var. Ruhnu Saar, Swe. Runö. island SW Estonia
Ruhnu Saar see Ruhnu
103 G15 **Ruhr** ~ W Germany
93 V6 **Ruhr Valley** industrial region W Germany
167 S11 **Rui'an** var. Rui an. Zhejiang, SE China
167 P10 **Ruichang** Jiangxi, S China
26 J11 **Ruidosa** Texas, SW USA
39 S14 **Ruidoso** New Mexico, SW USA
167 P12 **Ruijin** Jiangxi, S China
166 D13 **Ruili** Yunnan, SW China
100 N8 **Ruinen** Drenthe, NE Netherlands
101 D17 **Ruiselede** West-Vlaanderen, W Belgium
66 P5 **Ruivo de Santana, Pico** ▲ Madeira, Portugal, NE Atlantic Ocean
42 J12 **Ruiz** Nayarit, SW Mexico
56 E10 **Ruiz, Nevado del** ✶ W Colombia
144 J9 **Rujaylah, Ḩarrat ar** salt lake N Jordan
Rujen see Rūjiena
120 H7 **Rūjiena** Est. Ruhja, Ger. Rujen. Valmiera, N Latvia
81 I18 **Ruki** ~ W Zaire
83 E22 **Rukwa** ◐ region SW Tanzania
83 F23 **Rukwa, Lake** ◎ SE Tanzania
27 P6 **Rule** Texas, SW USA
24 K3 **Ruleville** Mississippi, S USA
Rum see Rhum
114 K10 **Ruma** Serbia, N Yugoslavia
Rumadiya see Ar Ramādī
147 Q7 **Rumāh** Ar Riyāḑ, C Saudi Arabia
Rumaitha see Ar Rumaythah
Rumania/Rumänien see Romania
Rumänisch-Sankt-Georgen see Sângeorz-Băi
145 Y13 **Rumaylah** SE Iraq
145 P2 **Rumaylah, Wādī** dry watercourse NE Syria
176 V10 **Rumbati** Irian Jaya, E Indonesia
83 E14 **Rumbek** El Buhayrat, S Sudan
176 W10 **Rumberpon, Pulau** island E Indonesia
Rumburg see Rumburk
113 D14 **Rumburk** Ger. Rumburg. Severní Čechy, N Czech Republic
46 J4 **Rum Cay** island C Bahamas
101 M26 **Rumelange** Luxembourg, S Luxembourg
101 D20 **Rumes** Hainaut, SW Belgium
21 P7 **Rumford** Maine, NE USA
112 I6 **Rumia** Gdańsk, N Poland
115 J17 **Rumija** ▲▲ SW Yugoslavia
105 T11 **Rumilly** Haute-Savoie, E France
145 O6 **Rūmiyah** W Iraq
Rummah, Wādī ar see Rimah, Wādī ar
Rummelsburg in Pommern see Miastko
172 Oo4 **Rumoi** Hokkaidō, NE Japan
84 M12 **Rumphi** var. Rumpi. Northern, N Malawi
Rumpi see Rumphi
31 V7 **Rum River** ~ Minnesota, N USA
196 F16 **Rumung** island Caroline Islands, W Micronesia
Rumuniya/Rumŭniya/Rumunjska see Romania
193 G16 **Runanga** West Coast, South Island, NZ
192 P7 **Runaway, Cape** headland North Island, NZ
99 K18 **Runcorn** C England, UK
120 K10 **Rundāni** Ludza, E Latvia
85 L18 **Runde** var. Lundi. ~ SE Zimbabwe
85 E16 **Rundu** var. Runtu. Okavango, NE Namibia
95 I16 **Rundvik** Västerbotten, N Sweden
83 G20 **Runere** Mwanza, N Tanzania
27 S13 **Runge** Texas, SW USA
178 I14 **Rŭng, Kaôh** prev. Kas Rong. island SW Cambodia
81 O16 **Rungu** Haut-Zaïre, NE Zaire
83 F23 **Rungwa** Rukwa, W Tanzania
83 G22 **Rungwa** Singida, C Tanzania
96 M13 **Runn** ◎ C Sweden
26 M4 **Running Water Draw** valley New Mexico/Texas, SW USA
Runö see Ruhnu
Runtu see Rundu
201 V12 **Ruo** island Caroline Islands, C Micronesia
164 L9 **Ruoqiang** var. Jo-ch'iang, Uigh. Charkhlik, Charkhliq, Qarkilik. Xinjiang Uygur Zizhiqu, NW China
165 S7 **Ruo Shui** ~ N China
95 L18 **Ruovesi** Häme, SW Finland
114 B9 **Rupa** Primorje-Gorski Kotar, NW Croatia
190 M11 **Rupanyup** Victoria, SE Australia
174 H6 **Rupat, Pulau** prev. Roepat. island W Indonesia
174 Gg6 **Rupat, Selat** strait Sumatera, W Indonesia
118 J11 **Rupea** Ger. Reps, Hung. Kőhalom; prev. Cohalm. Braşov, C Romania
101 G17 **Rupel** ~ N Belgium
Rupella see la Rochelle
35 P15 **Rupert** Idaho, NW USA
23 R5 **Rupert** West Virginia, NE USA
Rupert House see Fort Rupert
10 J10 **Rupert, Rivière de** ~ Québec, C Canada
204 M13 **Ruppert Coast** physical region Antarctica
102 N11 **Ruppiner Kanal** canal NE Germany
57 S11 **Rupununi River** ~ S Guyana
103 D16 **Rur** Dut. Roer. ~ Germany/Netherlands
60 H13 **Rurópolis Presidente Medici** Pará, N Brazil
203 S12 **Rurutu** island Îles Australes, SW French Polynesia
Rusaddir see Melilla
85 L17 **Rusape** Manicaland, E Zimbabwe
Rusayris, Lake see Roseires, Reservoir
Ruschuk/Rusçuk see Ruse
116 K7 **Ruse** var. Ruschuk, Rustchuk, Turk. Rusçuk. Razgradska Oblast, N Bulgaria
111 W10 **Ruše** NE Slovenia
116 K7 **Rusenski Lom** ~ N Bulgaria
99 G17 **Rush** Ir. An Ros. E Ireland
167 S4 **Rushan** var. Xiacun. Shandong, E China
Rushan see Rŭshon
Rushanskiy Khrebet see Rushon, Qatorkŭhi
31 V7 **Rush City** Minnesota, N USA
39 V5 **Rush Creek** ~ Colorado, C USA
31 X10 **Rushford** Minnesota, N USA
160 N13 **Rushikulya** ~ E India
12 D8 **Rush Lake** ◎ Ontario, S Canada
32 M7 **Rush Lake** ◎ Wisconsin, N USA
30 J10 **Rushmore, Mount** ▲ South Dakota, N USA
153 S13 **Rŭshon** Rus. Rushan. S Tajikistan
153 S14 **Rushon, Qatorkŭhi** Rus. Rushanskiy Khrebet. ▲▲ SE Tajikistan
28 M12 **Rush Springs** Oklahoma, C USA
47 V15 **Rushville** Trinidad, Trinidad and Tobago
32 J13 **Rushville** Illinois, N USA
30 K12 **Rushville** Nebraska, C USA
191 O11 **Rushworth** Victoria, SE Australia
27 W8 **Rusk** Texas, SW USA
95 I14 **Rusksele** Västerbotten, N Sweden
120 C12 **Rusnė** Šilutė, W Lithuania
116 M10 **Rusokastrenska Reka** ~ E Bulgaria
Russadir see Melilla
111 X3 **Russbach** ~ NE Austria
9 V16 **Russell** Manitoba, S Canada
192 K2 **Russell** Northland, North Island, NZ
28 L4 **Russell** Kansas, C USA
23 O4 **Russell** Kentucky, S USA
195 W15 **Russell Islands** island group C Solomon Islands
22 L7 **Russell Springs** Kentucky, S USA
25 O2 **Russellville** Alabama, S USA
29 T11 **Russellville** Arkansas, C USA
22 J7 **Russellville** Kentucky, S USA
103 G18 **Rüsselsheim** Hessen, W Germany
94 K8 **Russenes** Finnmark, N Norway
Russia see Russian Federation
Russian America see Alaska
127 N17 **Russian Federation** off. Russian Federation, var. Russia, Latv. Krievija, Rus. Rossiyskaya Federatsiya. ◆ republic Asia/Europe
41 N11 **Russian Mission** Alaska, USA
36 M7 **Russian River** ~ California, W USA
204 L13 **Russkaya** Russian research station Antarctica
126 H3 **Russkaya Gavan'** Novaya Zemlya, Arkhangel'skaya Oblast', N Russian Federation
126 J4 **Russkiy, Ostrov** island N Russian Federation
111 Y5 **Rust** Burgenland, E Austria
Rustaq see Ar Rustāq
143 U10 **Rust'avi** SE Georgia
23 T7 **Rustburg** Virginia, NE USA
Rustchuk see Ruse
94 L8 **Rustefjelbma** Finnmark, N Norway
85 I21 **Rustenburg** North-West, N South Africa
24 H5 **Ruston** Louisiana, S USA
83 E21 **Rutana** SE Burundi
64 I4 **Rutana, Volcán** ▲ N Chile
Rutanzige, Lake see Edward, Lake
Rutba see Ar Ruṭbah
106 M14 **Rute** Andalucía, S Spain
175 Pp16 **Ruteng** prev. Roeteng. Flores, C Indonesia
204 L8 **Rutford Ice Stream** ice feature Antarctica
37 X6 **Ruth** Nevada, W USA
103 G15 **Rüthen** Nordrhein-Westfalen, W Germany
12 D17 **Rutherford** Ontario, S Canada
23 Q10 **Rutherfordton** North Carolina, SE USA
99 J18 **Ruthin** Wel. Rhuthun. NE Wales, UK
110 G7 **Rüti** Zürich, N Switzerland
Rutlam see Ratlām
20 M9 **Rutland** Vermont, NE USA
99 N19 **Rutland** cultural region C England, UK
23 N8 **Rutledge** Tennessee, S USA
164 G12 **Rutog** var. Rutok. Xizang Zizhiqu, W China
Rutok see Rutog
81 P19 **Rutshuru** Nord Kivu, E Zaire
100 L8 **Rutten** Flevoland, N Netherlands
131 Q17 **Rutul** Respublika Dagestan, SW Russian Federation
95 L14 **Ruukki** Oulu, C Finland
100 N11 **Ruurlo** Gelderland, E Netherlands
149 S15 **Ru'ūs al Jibāl** headland Oman/UAE
144 I7 **Ru'ūs aṭ Ṭiwāl, Jabal** ▲▲ W Syria
83 H25 **Ruvuma** ◐ region SE Tanzania
83 I25 **Ruvuma** var. Rio Rovuma. ~ Mozambique/Tanzania see also Rovuma, Rio
Ruwais see Ar Ruways
144 L9 **Ruwayshid, Wadi ar** dry watercourse NE Jordan
147 Z10 **Ruways, Ra's ar** headland E Oman
81 P18 **Ruwenzori** ▲▲ Uganda/Zaire
147 Y8 **Ruwī** NE Oman
116 F9 **Ruy** ▲ Bulgaria/Yugoslavia
Ruya see Luia, Rio
83 E20 **Ruyigi** E Burundi
131 P5 **Ruzayevka** Respublika Mordoviya, W Russian Federation
121 G18 **Ruzhany** Rus. Ruzhany. Brestskaya Voblasts', SW Belarus
116 I10 **Rŭzhevo Konare** var. Rŭzhevo Konare. Plovdivska Oblast, C Bulgaria
Ruzhin see Ruzhyn
116 G7 **Ruzhintsi** Oblast Montana, NW Bulgaria
119 N5 **Ruzhyn** Rus. Ruzhin. Zhytomyrs'ka Oblast', N Ukraine
113 K19 **Ružomberok** Ger. Rosenberg, Hung. Rózsahegy. Stredné Slovensko, N Slovakia
113 C16 **Ruzyně** ✕ (Praha) Praha, C Czech Republic
83 D19 **Rwanda** off. Rwandese Republic; prev. Ruanda. ◆ republic C Africa
Rwandese Republic see Rwanda
97 G22 **Ry** Århus, C Denmark
Ryasna see Rasna
130 L5 **Ryazan'** Ryazanskaya Oblast', W Russian Federation
130 L5 **Ryazanskaya Oblast'** ◐ province W Russian Federation
130 M6 **Ryazhsk** Ryazanskaya Oblast', W Russian Federation
120 B13 **Rybachiy** Ger. Rossitten. Kaliningradskaya Oblast', W Russian Federation
128 J2 **Rybachiy, Poluostrov** peninsula NW Russian Federation
Rybach'ye see Balykchy
128 L15 **Rybinsk** prev. Andropov. Yaroslavskaya Oblast', W Russian Federation
128 K14 **Rybinskoye Vodokhranilishche** Eng. Rybinsk Reservoir, Rybinsk Sea. ▣ W Russian Federation
Rybinsk Reservoir/Rybinsk Sea see Rybinskoye Vodokhranilishche

◆ Country ● Country Capital ◇ Dependent Territory ○ Dependent Territory Capital ◐ Administrative Region ✕ International Airport ▲ Mountain ▲▲ Mountain Range ✶ Volcano ~ River ◎ Lake ▣ Reservoir

113 I16 **Rybnik** Katowice, S Poland
Rybnitsa see Rîbniţa
113 F16 **Rychnov nad Kněžnou** Ger. Reichenau. Východní Čechy, NE Czech Republic
112 I12 **Rychwał** Konin, C Poland
9 O13 **Rycroft** Alberta, W Canada
97 L21 **Ryd** Kronoberg, S Sweden
97 L20 **Rydaholm** Jönköping, S Sweden
204 I8 **Rydberg Peninsula** peninsula Antarctica
99 P23 **Rye** SE England, UK
35 T10 **Ryegate** Montana, NW USA
37 S3 **Rye Patch Reservoir** ⊡ Nevada, W USA
97 D15 **Ryfylke** physical region S Norway
97 H16 **Rygge** Østfold, S Norway
112 N13 **Ryki** Lublin, E Poland
Rykovo see Yenakiyeve
130 I7 **Ryl'sk** Kurskaya Oblast', W Russian Federation
191 S8 **Rylstone** New South Wales, SE Australia
113 H17 **Rýmařov** Ger. Römerstadt. Severní Morava, E Czech Republic
150 E11 **Ryn-Peski** desert W Kazakhstan
171 K12 **Ryōtsu** var. Ryôtu. Niigata, Sado, C Japan
Ryôtu see Ryōtsu
112 K10 **Rypin** Włocławek, C Poland
Ryshkany see Rîşcani
Ryssel see Lille
Ryswick see Rijswijk
97 M24 **Rytterknægten** hill E Denmark
171 Kk16 **Ryūgasaki** Ibaraki, Honshū, S Japan
198 G5 **Ryukyu Trench** var. Nansei Syotō Trench. undersea feature S East China Sea
112 D11 **Rzepin** Ger. Reppen. Gorzów, W Poland
113 N16 **Rzeszów** Rzeszów, SE Poland
113 N16 **Rzeszów** off. Województwo Rzeszowskie. ◈ province SE Poland
Rzeszowskie, Województwo see Rzeszów
128 I16 **Rzhev** Tverskaya Oblast', W Russian Federation
Rzhishchev see Rzhyshchiv
119 P5 **Rzhyshchiv** Rus. Rzhishchev. Kyyivs'ka Oblast', N Ukraine

S

144 E11 **Sa'ad** Southern, W Israel
111 P7 **Saalach** ≈ W Austria
103 L14 **Saale** ≈ C Germany
103 L17 **Saalfeld** var. Saalfeld an der Saale. Thüringen, C Germany
Saalfeld see Zalewo
Saalfeld an der Saale see Saalfeld
110 C8 **Saane** ≈ W Switzerland
103 D19 **Saar** Fr. Sarre. ≈ France/Germany
103 E20 **Saarbrücken** Fr. Sarrebruck. Saarland, SW Germany
Saarburg see Sarrebourg
Saare see Saaremaa
120 D6 **Sääre** var. Sjar. Saaremaa, W Estonia
120 D5 **Saaremaa** off. Saare Maakond. ◈ province W Estonia
120 E6 **Saaremaa** Ger. Oesel, Ösel; prev. Saare. island W Estonia
94 L12 **Saarenkylä** Lappi, N Finland
Saargemund see Sarreguemines
95 L17 **Saarijärvi** Keski-Suomi, C Finland
Saar in Mähren see Žďár nad Sázavou
94 M10 **Saariselkä** Lapp. Suoločielgi. Lappi, N Finland
94 L10 **Saariselkä** hill range NE Finland
103 D20 **Saarland** Fr. Sarre. ◈ state SW Germany
Saarlautern see Saarlouis
103 D20 **Saarlouis** prev. Saarlautern. Saarland, SW Germany
110 E11 **Saaser Vispa** ≈ S Switzerland
143 X12 **Saatlı** Rus. Saatly. C Azerbaijan
Saatly see Saatlı
Saaz see Žatec
176 X9 **Saba** Irian Jaya, E Indonesia
47 V9 **Saba** island N Netherlands Antilles
144 J7 **Sab' Ābār** var. Sab'a Biyar, Sa'b Bi'ār. Ḥimş, C Syria
Sab'a Biyar see Sab' Ābār
114 K11 **Šabac** Serbia, W Yugoslavia
107 W5 **Sabadell** Cataluña, E Spain
171 Hh13 **Sabae** Fukui, Honshū, SW Japan
175 O3 **Sabah** prev. British North Borneo, North Borneo. ◈ state East Malaysia
174 Gg4 **Sabak** var. Sabak Bernam. Selangor, Peninsular Malaysia
Sabak Bernam see Sabak
40 D16 **Sabak, Cape** headland Agattu Island, Alaska, USA
83 J20 **Sabaki** ≈ S Kenya
175 P14 **Sabalana, Kepulauan** var. Kepulauan Liukang Tenggaya. island group C Indonesia
148 L2 **Sabalān, Kuhhā-ye** ▲ NW Iran
160 H7 **Sabalgarh** Madhya Pradesh, C India
46 E4 **Sabana, Archipiélago de** island group C Cuba
44 H7 **Sabanagrande** var. Sabana Grande. Francisco Morazán, S Honduras
56 E5 **Sabanalarga** Atlántico, N Colombia
43 W14 **Sabancuy** Campeche, SE Mexico
47 N8 **Sabaneta** NW Dominican Republic
56 J4 **Sabaneta** Falcón, N Venezuela
196 H4 **Sabaneta, Puntan** prev. Ushi Point. headland Saipan, S Northern Mariana Islands
176 Y12 **Sabang** Irian Jaya, E Indonesia
118 L10 **Săbăoani** Neamţ, NE Romania
161 J26 **Sabaragamuwa Province** ◈ province C Sri Lanka
Sabaria see Szombathely
160 D10 **Sābarmati** ≈ NW India
175 T6 **Sabatai** Pulau Morotai, E Indonesia
147 Q15 **Sab'atayn, Ramlat as** desert C Yemen
109 I16 **Sabaudia** Lazio, C Italy
59 J19 **Sabaya** Oruro, S Bolivia
Sa'b Bi'ār see Sab' Ābār
Sabbioncello see Orebić
154 I8 **Šāberī, Hāmūn-e** var. Daryācheh-ye Hāmūn, Daryācheh-ye Sīstān. ◎ Afghanistan/Iran see also Sīstān, Daryācheh-ye
29 P2 **Sabetha** Kansas, C USA
77 P10 **Sabhā** C Libya
69 V13 **Sabi** var. Rio Save. ≈ Mozambique/Zimbabwe see also Save, Rio
120 E8 **Sabile** Ger. Zabeln. Talsi, NW Latvia
33 R14 **Sabina** Ohio, N USA
42 I3 **Sabinal** Chihuahua, N Mexico
27 Q12 **Sabinal** Texas, SW USA
27 Q11 **Sabinal River** ≈ Texas, SW USA
107 S4 **Sabiñánigo** Aragón, NE Spain
43 N6 **Sabinas** Coahuila de Zaragoza, NE Mexico
43 O8 **Sabinas Hidalgo** Nuevo León, NE Mexico
43 N6 **Sabinas, Río** ≈ NE Mexico
24 F9 **Sabine Lake** ◎ Louisiana/Texas, S USA
94 O3 **Sabine Land** physical region C Svalbard
27 W7 **Sabine River** ≈ Louisiana/Texas, SW USA
143 X12 **Sabirabad** C Azerbaijan
Sabkha see As Sabkhah
179 P12 **Sablayan** Mindoro, N Philippines
11 P16 **Sable, Cape** headland Newfoundland and Labrador, SE Canada
25 X17 **Sable, Cape** headland Florida, SE USA
11 R16 **Sable Island** island Nova Scotia, SE Canada
12 L11 **Sables, Lac des** ◎ Québec, SE Canada
12 E10 **Sables, Rivière aux** ≈ Ontario, S Canada
104 K7 **Sable-sur-Sarthe** Sarthe, NW France
129 U7 **Sablya, Gora** ▲ NW Russian Federation
79 U14 **Sabon Birnin Gwari** Kaduna, C Nigeria
79 V11 **Sabon Kafi** Zinder, C Niger
106 I6 **Sabor, Rio** ≈ N Portugal
12 J8 **Sabourin, Lac** ◎ Québec, SE Canada
104 J14 **Sabres** Landes, SW France
205 X13 **Sabrina Coast** physical region Antarctica
146 M11 **Sabt al Ulayā** 'Asīr, SW Saudi Arabia
106 I8 **Sabugal** Guarda, N Portugal
31 Z13 **Sabula** Iowa, C USA
147 N13 **Şabyā** Jīzān, SW Saudi Arabia
Sabzawar see Sabzevār
Sabzawaran see Sabzvārān
149 S4 **Sabzevār** var. Sabzawar. Khorāsān, NE Iran
149 T12 **Sabzvārān** var. Sabzawaran; prev. Jiroft. Kermān, SE Iran
Sacajawea Peak see Matterhorn
84 C9 **Sacandica** Uíge, NW Angola
44 A2 **Sacatepéquez** off. Departamento de Sacatepéquez. ◈ department S Guatemala
106 F11 **Sacavém** Lisboa, W Portugal
31 T13 **Sac City** Iowa, C USA
107 P8 **Sacedón** Castilla-La Mancha, C Spain
118 J12 **Săcele** Ger. Vierdörfer, Hung. Négyfalu; prev. Ger. Sieben Dörfer, Hung. Hétfalu. Braşov, C Romania
10 C8 **Sachigo** Ontario, C Canada
10 C7 **Sachigo** ≈ Ontario, C Canada
10 C8 **Sachigo Lake** ◎ Ontario, C Canada
169 Y16 **Sach'ŏn** Jap. Sansenhō; prev. Samch'ŏnpŏ. S South Korea
103 O15 **Sachsen** Eng. Saxony, Fr. Saxe. ◈ state E Germany
103 K14 **Sachsen-Anhalt** Eng. Saxony-Anhalt. ◈ state C Germany
111 R9 **Sachsenburg** Salzburg, S Austria
Sachsenfeld see Žalec
15 H1 **Sachs Harbour** Banks Island, Northwest Territories, N Canada
Sächsisch-Reen/Sächsisch-Regen see Reghin
20 H8 **Sackets Harbor** New York, NE USA
11 P14 **Sackville** New Brunswick, SE Canada
21 P9 **Saco** Maine, NE USA
21 P8 **Saco River** ≈ Maine/New Hampshire, NE USA
37 O7 **Sacramento** state capital California, W USA
39 T14 **Sacramento Mountains** ⛰ New Mexico, SW USA
37 N6 **Sacramento River** ≈ California, W USA
37 N5 **Sacramento Valley** valley California, W USA
38 I10 **Sacramento Wash** valley Arizona, SW USA
107 N15 **Sacratif, Cabo** headland S Spain
118 F9 **Săcueni** prev. Săcuieni, Hung. Székelyhíd. Bihor, W Romania
Săcuieni see Săcueni
107 R4 **Sádaba** Aragón, NE Spain
Sá da Bandeira see Lubango
144 I6 **Şadad** Ḥimş, W Syria
147 O13 **Şa'dah** NW Yemen
170 Dd14 **Sadamisaki-hinto** peninsula Shikoku, SW Japan
175 P12 **Sadang, Sungai** ≈ Sulawesi, C Indonesia
178 H17 **Sadao** Songkhla, SW Thailand
148 L8 **Sadd-e Dez, Daryācheh-ye** ◎ W Iran
21 S3 **Saddleback Mountain** hill Maine, NE USA
21 P6 **Saddleback Mountain** ▲ Maine, NE USA
178 J114 **Sa Đec** Đông Thap, S Vietnam
147 W13 **Sadḥ** S Oman
78 J11 **Sadiola** Kayes, W Mali
155 R12 **Sādiqābād** Punjab, E Pakistan
159 Y10 **Sadiya** Assam, NE India
145 W9 **Sa'dīyah, Hawr as** ◎ E Iraq
171 K12 **Sado** var. Sadoga-shima. island C Japan
Sadoga-shima see Sado
106 F12 **Sado, Rio** ≈ S Portugal
116 I8 **Sadovets** Loveshka Oblast, N Bulgaria
131 O11 **Sadovoye** Respublika Kalmykiya, SW Russian Federation
107 W9 **Sa Dragonera** var. Isla Dragonera. island Islas Baleares, Spain, W Mediterranean Sea
97 H20 **Sæby** Nordjylland, N Denmark
107 P9 **Saelices** Castilla-La Mancha, C Spain
Saena Julia see Siena
Saetabicula see Alzira
116 O12 **Safaalan** Tekirdağ, NW Turkey
Safad see Ẕefat
Şafāqis see Sfax
198 B8 **Safata Bay** bay Upolu, Western Samoa, C Pacific Ocean
Safed see Ẕefat
Safed, Āb-i- see Sefīd, Darya-ye
145 X11 **Şaffāf, Ḥawr aş** wetland S Iraq
97 J16 **Säffle** Värmland, C Sweden
39 N15 **Safford** Arizona, SW USA
76 E7 **Safi** W Morocco
149 V9 **Safīdābeh** Khorāsān, E Iran
148 M4 **Safīd, Rūd-e** ≈ NW Iran
130 I4 **Safonovo** Smolenskaya Oblast', W Russian Federation
142 H11 **Safranbolu** Zonguldak, N Turkey
145 Y13 **Safwān** SE Iraq
164 J16 **Saga** var. Gya'gya. Xizang Zizhiqu, W China
170 Cc13 **Saga** Saga, Kyūshū, SW Japan
170 Cc13 **Saga** off. Saga-ken. ◈ prefecture Kyūshū, SW Japan
171 Ll12 **Sagae** Yamagata, Honshū, C Japan
177 G5 **Sagaing** Sagaing, C Mynamar
177 G3 **Sagaing** ◈ division N Mynamar
171 Jj16 **Sagamihara** Kanagawa, Honshū, S Japan
171 Jj17 **Sagami-nada** inlet SW Japan
171 Jj17 **Sagami-wan** bay SW Japan
Sagan see Żagań
31 Y3 **Saganaga Lake** ◎ Minnesota, N USA
161 F18 **Sāgar** Karnātaka, W India
160 I9 **Sāgar** prev. Saugor. Madhya Pradesh, C India
13 S8 **Sagard** Québec, SE Canada
Sagarmatha see Everest, Mount
179 Qq13 **Sagay** Negros, C Philippines
Sagebrush State see Nevada
149 V11 **Sāghand** Yazd, C Iran
21 N14 **Sag Harbor** Long Island, New York, NE USA
Saghez see Saqqez
33 R8 **Saginaw** Michigan, N USA
33 R8 **Saginaw Bay** lake bay Michigan, N USA
150 H11 **Sagiz** Atyrau, W Kazakhstan
66 H6 **Saglek Bank** undersea feature W Labrador Sea
11 P5 **Saglek Bay** bay SW Labrador Sea
Saglouc/Sagluk see Salluit
104 E2 **Sagonne, Golfe de** gulf Corse, France, C Mediterranean Sea
107 P13 **Sagra** ▲ S Spain
106 F14 **Sagres** Faro, S Portugal
39 S7 **Saguache** Colorado, C USA
46 J7 **Sagua de Tánamo** Holguín, E Cuba
46 E5 **Sagua la Grande** Villa Clara, C Cuba
13 R7 **Saguenay** ≈ Québec, SE Canada
76 C9 **Saguia al Hamra** var. As Saqia al Hamra. ≈ N Western Sahara
Sagunt/Saguntum see Sagunto
107 S9 **Sagunto** var. Sagunt, Ar. Murviedro; anc. Saguntum. País Valenciano, E Spain
144 H10 **Saḥāb** 'Ammān, NW Jordan
56 E6 **Sahagún** Córdoba, NW Colombia
106 L4 **Sahagún** Castilla-León, N Spain
147 X8 **Saḥam** N Oman
70 F9 **Sahara** desert Libya/Algeria
77 U9 **Sahara el Gharbîya** var. Aş Şaḥrā' al Gharbīyah, Eng. Western Desert. desert C Egypt
77 X9 **Sahara el Sharqîya** var. Aş Şaḥrā' ash Sharqīyah, Eng. Arabian Desert, Eastern Desert. desert E Egypt
Saharan Atlas see Atlas Saharien
158 J9 **Sahāranpur** Uttar Pradesh, N India
66 L10 **Saharan Seamounts** var. Saharian Seamounts. undersea feature E Atlantic Ocean
159 Q13 **Saharsa** Bihār, NE India
69 O7 **Sahel** physical region C Africa
159 R14 **Sāhibganj** Bihār, NE India
145 Q7 **Şāḥilīyah** C Iraq
144 H4 **Şāḥilīyah, Jibāl as** ⛰ NW Syria
116 M13 **Şahin** Tekirdağ, NW Turkey
155 U8 **Sāhīwāl** Punjab, E Pakistan
155 U9 **Sāhīwāl** prev. Montgomery. Punjab, E Pakistan
147 W11 **Saḥmah, Ramlat as** desert C Oman
145 T13 **Şaḥrā' al Ḥijārah** desert S Iraq
42 H5 **Sahuaripa** Sonora, NW Mexico
38 M16 **Sahuarita** Arizona, SW USA
42 L13 **Sahuayo** var. Sahuayo de José Mariá Morelos; prev. Sahuayo de Díaz, Sahuayo de Porfirio Díaz. Michoacán de Ocampo, SW Mexico
Sahuayo de Díaz/Sahuayo de José Mariá Morelos/Sahuayo de Porfirio Díaz see Sahuayo
181 W8 **Sahul Shelf** undersea feature N Timor Sea
178 Hh17 **Sai Buri** Pattani, SW Thailand
76 I6 **Saïda** NW Algeria
144 G7 **Saïda** var. Şaydā, Sayida; anc. Sidon. W Lebanon
Sa'īdābād see Sīrjān
82 B13 **Sa'id Bundas** Western Bahr el Ghazal, SW Sudan
194 J12 **Saidor** Madang, N PNG
159 S13 **Saidpur** var. Syedpur. Rajshahi, NW Bangladesh
110 C7 **Saignelégier** Jura, NW Switzerland
170 G11 **Saigō** Shimane, Dōgo, SW Japan
Saigon see Hô Chi Minh
168 I12 **Saihan Toroi** Nei Mongol Zizhiqu, N China
Saihon Tal see Sonid Youqi
Sai Hun see Syr Darya
94 M11 **Saija** Lappi, NE Finland
170 Ee14 **Saijō** Ehime, Shikoku, SW Japan
170 Dd15 **Saiki** Ōita, Kyūshū, SW Japan
176 Uu9 **Sailolof** Irian Jaya, E Indonesia
95 N18 **Saimaa** ◎ SE Finland
95 N18 **Saimaa Canal** Fin. Saimaan Kanava, Rus. Saymenskiy Kanal. canal Finland/Russian Federation
Saimaan Kanava see Saimaa Canal
42 L10 **Saín Alto** Zacatecas, C Mexico
98 L12 **St Abb's Head** headland SE Scotland, UK
9 Y16 **St.Adolphe** Manitoba, S Canada
105 O15 **St-Affrique** Aveyron, S France
13 Q10 **St-Agapit** Québec, SE Canada
99 O21 **St Albans** anc. Verulamium. E England, UK
20 L6 **Saint Albans** Vermont, NE USA
23 Q5 **Saint Albans** West Virginia, NE USA
99 M24 **St Alban's Head** var. St.Aldhelm's Head. headland S England, UK
9 Q14 **St.Albert** Alberta, SW Canada
St. Aldhelm's Head see St Alban's Head
13 S8 **St-Alexandre** Québec, SE Canada
13 O11 **St-Alexis-des-Monts** Québec, SE Canada
105 P2 **St-Amand-les-Eaux** Nord, N France
105 O9 **St-Amand-Montrond** var. St-Amand-Mont-Rond. Cher, C France
13 Q7 **St-Ambroise** Québec, SE Canada
181 P16 **St-André** NE Réunion
12 M12 **St-André-Avellin** Québec, SE Canada
104 K12 **St-André-de-Cubzac** Gironde, SW France
98 K11 **St Andrews** E Scotland, UK
25 Q9 **Saint Andrews Bay** bay Florida, SE USA
25 W7 **Saint Andrew Sound** sound Georgia, SE USA
Saint Anna Trough see Svyataya Anna Trough
46 J11 **St.Ann's Bay** C Jamaica
11 T10 **St.Anthony** Newfoundland, Newfoundland and Labrador, SE Canada
35 R13 **Saint Anthony** Idaho, NW USA
190 M11 **Saint Arnaud** Victoria, SE Australia
193 I15 **St.Arnaud Range** ⛰ South Island, NZ
13 T8 **St-Arsène** Québec, SE Canada
11 R10 **St-Augustin** Québec, E Canada
25 X9 **Saint Augustine** Florida, SE USA
99 H24 **St Austell** SW England, UK
105 T4 **St-Avold** Moselle, NE France
105 N17 **St-Barthélemy** ▲ S France
104 L17 **St-Béat** Haute-Garonne, S France
99 I15 **St Bees Head** headland NW England, UK
181 P16 **St-Benoit** E Réunion
105 T13 **St-Bonnet** Hautes-Alpes, SE France
St.Botolph's Town see Boston
99 G21 **St Brides Bay** inlet SW Wales, UK
104 H5 **St-Brieuc** Côtes d'Armor, NW France
104 H5 **St-Brieuc, Baie de** bay NW France
104 L7 **St-Calais** Sarthe, NW France
13 Q10 **St-Casimir** Québec, SE Canada
12 H16 **St.Catharines** Ontario, S Canada
47 S14 **St.Catherine, Mount** ▲ N Grenada
66 C11 **St Catherine Point** headland E Bermuda
25 X6 **Saint Catherines Island** island Georgia, SE USA
99 M24 **St Catherine's Point** headland S England, UK
105 N13 **St-Céré** Lot, S France
110 A10 **St.Cergue** Vaud, W Switzerland
105 R11 **St-Chamond** Loire, E France
35 S16 **Saint Charles** Idaho, NW USA
29 X4 **Saint Charles** Missouri, C USA
105 P13 **St-Chély-d'Apcher** Lozère, S France
Saint Christopher-Nevis see Saint Kitts and Nevis
33 S9 **Saint Clair** Michigan, N USA
12 D17 **St.Clair** ≈ Canada/USA
191 O17 **St.Clair, Lake** ◎ Tasmania, SE Australia
12 C17 **St.Clair, Lake** var. Lac à L'eau Claire. ◎ Canada/USA
33 S10 **Saint Clair Shores** Michigan, N USA
105 S10 **St-Claude** anc. Condate. Jura, E France
47 X6 **St-Claude** Basse Terre, SW Guadeloupe
25 X12 **Saint Cloud** Florida, SE USA
31 U8 **Saint Cloud** Minnesota, N USA
47 T9 **Saint Croix** island S Virgin Islands (US)
32 J4 **Saint Croix Flowage** ⊡ Wisconsin, N USA
21 T5 **Saint Croix River** ≈ Canada/USA
31 W7 **Saint Croix River** ≈ Minnesota/Wisconsin, N USA
47 S14 **St.David's** SE Grenada
99 H21 **St David's** SW Wales, UK
99 G21 **St David's Head** headland SW Wales, UK
66 C12 **St David's Island** island E Bermuda
181 O16 **St-Denis** ○ (Réunion) NW Réunion
105 U6 **St-Dié** Vosges, NE France
105 R5 **St-Dizier** anc. Desiderii Fanum. Haute-Marne, N France
13 N11 **St-Donat** Québec, SE Canada
13 N11 **Ste-Adèle** Québec, SE Canada
13 N11 **Ste-Agathe-des-Monts** Québec, SE Canada
9 Y16 **Ste.Anne** Manitoba, S Canada
47 R12 **Ste-Anne** Grande Terre, E Guadeloupe
47 Y6 **Ste-Anne** SE Martinique
180 I16 **Sainte Anne** island Inner Islands, NE Seychelles
13 Q10 **Ste-Anne** ≈ Québec, SE Canada
13 W6 **Ste-Anne-des-Monts** Québec, SE Canada
12 M10 **Ste-Anne-du-Lac** Québec, SE Canada
13 U4 **Ste-Anne, Lac** ◎ Québec, SE Canada
13 S10 **Ste-Apolline** Québec, SE Canada
13 U7 **Ste-Blandine** Québec, SE Canada
13 R10 **Ste-Claire** Québec, SE Canada
13 Q10 **Ste-Croix** Québec, SE Canada
110 B8 **Ste.Croix** Vaud, SW Switzerland
105 P14 **Ste-Énimie** Lozère, S France
29 Y6 **Sainte Genevieve** Missouri, C USA
105 S12 **St-Egrève** Isère, E France
41 T12 **Saint Elias, Cape** headland Kayak Island, Alaska, USA
41 U11 **Saint Elias, Mount** ▲ Alaska, USA
8 G8 **Saint Elias Mountains** ⛰ Canada/USA
57 Y10 **St-Élie** N French Guiana
105 O10 **St-Eloy-les-Mines** Puy-de-Dôme, C France
13 S7 **Ste-Maguerite Nord-Est** ≈ Québec, SE Canada
13 R7 **Ste-Marguerite** ≈ Québec, SE Canada
13 V4 **Ste-Marguerite, Pointe** headland Québec, SE Canada
13 V3 **Ste-Marguesite** ≈ Québec, SE Canada
13 R10 **Ste-Marie** Québec, SE Canada
47 Q11 **Ste-Marie** NE Martinique
181 P16 **Ste-Marie** NE Réunion
105 U6 **Ste-Marie-aux-Mines** Haut-Rhin, NE France
10 J14 **Ste-Marie, Lac** ⊡ Québec, S Canada
180 K4 **Sainte Marie, Nosy** island E Madagascar
104 L8 **Ste-Maure-de-Touraine** Indre-et-Loire, C France
105 R4 **Ste-Menehould** Marne, NE France
Ste-Perpétue see Ste-Perpétue-de-l'Islet
13 S9 **Ste-Perpétue-de-l'Islet** var. Ste-Perpétue. Québec, SE Canada
47 X11 **Ste-Rose** Basse Terre, N Guadeloupe
181 P16 **Ste-Rose** E Réunion
9 W15 **Ste.Rose du Lac** Manitoba, S Canada
104 J11 **Saintes** anc. Mediolanum. Charente-Maritime, W France
47 X7 **Saintes, Canal des** channel SW Guadeloupe
Saintes, Îles des see les Saintes
181 P16 **Ste-Suzanne** N Réunion
13 P10 **Ste-Thècle** Québec, SE Canada
105 Q12 **St-Étienne** Loire, E France
104 M4 **St-Étienne-du-Rouvray** Seine-Maritime, N France
Saint Eustatius see Sint Eustatius
12 M11 **Ste-Véronique** Québec, SE Canada
13 T7 **St-Fabien** Québec, SE Canada
13 P7 **St-Félicien** Québec, SE Canada
13 O11 **St-Félix-de-Valois** Québec, SE Canada
104 F1 **St-Florent** Corse, France, C Mediterranean Sea
104 F1 **St-Florent, Golfe de** gulf Corse, France, C Mediterranean Sea
105 P6 **St-Florentin** Yonne, C France
105 N9 **St-Florent-sur-Cher** Cher, C France
105 P12 **St-Flour** Cantal, C France
28 H2 **Saint Francis** Kansas, C USA
85 H26 **St.Francis, Cape** headland S South Africa
29 X10 **Saint Francis River** ≈ Arkansas/Missouri, C USA
24 J8 **Saint Francisville** Louisiana, S USA
13 Q12 **St-François** ≈ Québec, SE Canada
47 Y6 **St-François** Grande Terre, E Guadeloupe
13 R11 **St-François, Lac** ◎ Québec, SE Canada
29 X7 **Saint Francois Mountains** ⛰ Missouri, C USA
St-Gall/Saint Gall/St.Gallen see Sankt Gallen
104 L16 **St-Gaudens** Haute-Garonne, S France
13 R12 **St-Gédéon** Québec, SE Canada
189 X10 **Saint George** Queensland, E Australia
66 B12 **St George** N Bermuda
40 K15 **Saint George** Saint George Island, Alaska, USA
23 S14 **Saint George** South Carolina, SE USA
38 J8 **Saint George** Utah, W USA
11 R12 **St.George, Cape** headland Newfoundland, Newfoundland and Labrador, E Canada
195 P11 **St.George, Cape** headland New Ireland, NE PNG
40 J15 **Saint George Island** island Pribilof Islands, Alaska, US
40 J15 **Saint George Island** island Pribilof Islands, Alaska, USA
25 S10 **Saint George Island** island Florida, SE USA
101 J19 **Saint-Georges** Liège, E Belgium
13 R11 **St-Georges** Québec, SE Canada
57 Z11 **St-Georges** E French Guiana
47 R14 **St.George's** ● (Grenada) SW Grenada
11 R12 **St.George's Bay** inlet Newfoundland, Newfoundland and Labrador, E Canada
99 G21 **Saint George's Channel** channel Ireland/Wales, UK
195 P10 **St.George's Channel** channel NE PNG
66 B11 **St George's Island** island E Bermuda
101 I21 **Saint-Gérard** Namur, S Belgium
Saint-Germain see St-Germain-en-Laye
13 P12 **St-Germain-de-Grantham** Québec, SE Canada
105 N5 **St-Germain-en-Laye** var. St-Germain. Yvelines, N France
104 H8 **St-Gildas, Pointe du** headland NW France
105 R15 **St-Gilles** Gard, S France
104 I9 **St-Gilles-Croix-de-Vie** Vendée, NW France
181 O16 **St-Gilles-les-Bains** W Réunion
104 M16 **St-Girons** Ariège, S France
Saint Gotthard see Szentgotthárd
110 G9 **St.Gotthard Tunnel** tunnel Ticino, S Switzerland
99 H22 **St Govan's Head** headland SW Wales, UK
36 M7 **Saint Helena** California, W USA
67 F24 **Saint Helena** ◇ UK dependent territory C Atlantic Ocean
69 O12 **Saint Helena** island C Atlantic Ocean
85 E25 **St.Helena Bay** bay SW South Africa
67 M16 **Saint Helena Fracture Zone** tectonic feature C Atlantic Ocean
36 M7 **Saint Helena, Mount** ▲ California, W USA
23 S15 **Saint Helena Sound** inlet South Carolina, SE USA
33 Q7 **Saint Helen, Lake** ◎ Michigan, N USA
191 Q16 **Saint Helens** Tasmania, SE Australia
99 K18 **St Helens** NW England, UK
34 G10 **Saint Helens** Oregon, NW USA
34 H10 **Saint Helens, Mount** ※ Washington, NW USA
99 L26 **St Helier** ○ (Jersey) S Jersey, Channel Islands
13 S9 **St-Hilarion** Québec, SE Canada
101 K22 **Saint-Hubert** Luxembourg, SE Belgium
13 T8 **St-Hubert** Québec, SE Canada
13 P12 **St-Hyacinthe** Québec, SE Canada
St.Iago de la Vega see Spanish Town
33 Q4 **Saint Ignace** Michigan, N USA
13 O10 **St-Ignace-du-Lac** Québec, SE Canada
10 D12 **St.Ignace Island** island Ontario, S Canada
110 C7 **St.Imier** Bern, W Switzerland
99 G25 **St Ives** SW England, UK
31 U10 **Saint James** Minnesota, N USA
8 I15 **St.James, Cape** headland Graham Island, British Columbia, SW Canada
13 O13 **St-Jean** var. St-Jean-sur-Richelieu. Québec, SE Canada
57 X9 **St-Jean** NW French Guiana
13 R8 **St-Jean** ≈ Québec, SE Canada
Saint-Jean-d'Acre see 'Akko
104 K11 **St-Jean-d'Angély** Charente-Maritime, W France
105 N7 **St-Jean-de-Braye** Loiret, C France
104 I16 **St-Jean-de-Luz** Pyrénées-Atlantiques, SW France
105 T12 **St-Jean-de-Maurienne** Savoie, E France
104 I9 **St-Jean-de-Monts** Vendée, NW France
105 Q14 **St-Jean-du-Gard** Gard, S France
13 Q7 **St-Jean, Lac** ◎ Québec, SE Canada
104 I16 **St-Jean-Pied-de-Port** Pyrénées-Atlantiques, SW France
13 S9 **St-Jean-Port-Joli** Québec, SE Canada
St-Jean-sur-Richelieu see St-Jean
13 N12 **St-Jérôme** Québec, SE Canada
27 T5 **Saint Jo** Texas, SW USA
11 O15 **St.John** New Brunswick, SE Canada
28 L6 **Saint John** Kansas, C USA
78 K16 **Saint John** ≈ C Liberia
47 T9 **Saint John** island C Virgin Islands (US)
24 I6 **Saint John, Lake** ◎ Louisiana, S USA
21 Q2 **Saint John** Fr. Saint-John. ≈ Canada/USA
47 W10 **St John's** ● (Antigua and Barbuda) Antigua, Antigua and Barbuda
11 V12 **St.John's** Newfoundland, Newfoundland and Labrador, E Canada
39 O12 **Saint Johns** Arizona, SW USA
33 Q9 **Saint Johns** Michigan, N USA
11 V12 **St.John's** ✕ Newfoundland, Newfoundland and Labrador, E Canada
25 X11 **Saint Johns River** ≈ Florida, SE USA
47 N12 **St.Joseph** W Dominica
181 P17 **St-Joseph** S Réunion
24 J6 **Saint Joseph** Louisiana, S USA
33 O10 **Saint Joseph** Michigan, N USA
29 R3 **Saint Joseph** Missouri, C USA
22 I10 **Saint Joseph** Tennessee, S USA
24 R9 **Saint Joseph Bay** bay Florida, SE USA
13 R11 **St-Joseph-de-Beauce** Québec, SE Canada
10 C10 **St.Joseph, Lake** ◎ Ontario, C Canada
33 Q11 **Saint Joseph River** ≈ N USA
12 C11 **Saint Joseph's Island** island Ontario, S Canada
13 N11 **St-Jovite** Québec, SE Canada
123 Jj16 **St Julian's** N Malta
St-Julien see St-Julien-en-Genevois
105 T10 **St-Julien-en-Genevois** var. St-Julien. Haute-Savoie, E France
104 M11 **St-Junien** Haute-Vienne, C France
105 Q11 **St-Just-St-Rambert** Loire, E France
98 D8 **St Kilda** island NW Scotland, UK
47 V10 **Saint Kitts** island Saint Kitts and Nevis
47 U10 **Saint Kitts and Nevis** off. Federation of Saint Christopher and Nevis, var. Saint Christopher-Nevis. ◆ commonwealth republic E West Indies
9 X16 **St.Laurent** Manitoba, S Canada
St-Laurent see St-Laurent-du-Maroni
57 X9 **St-Laurent-du-Maroni** var. St-Laurent. NW French Guiana
St-Laurent, Fleuve see St.Lawrence
104 J12 **St-Laurent-Médoc** Gironde, SW France
11 N12 **St.Lawrence** Fr. Fleuve St-Laurent. ≈ Canada/USA
11 Q12 **St.Lawrence, Gulf of** gulf NW Atlantic Ocean
40 K10 **Saint Lawrence Island** island Alaska, USA
12 M14 **Saint Lawrence River** ≈ Canada/USA
101 L25 **Saint-Léger** Luxembourg, SE Belgium
11 N14 **St.Léonard** New Brunswick, SE Canada
13 P11 **St-Léonard** Québec, SE Canada
181 O17 **St-Leu** W Réunion
104 J4 **St-Lô** anc. Briovera, Laudus. Manche, N France
9 T15 **St.Louis** Saskatchewan, S Canada
105 V7 **St-Louis** Haut-Rhin, NE France
181 O17 **St-Louis** S Réunion
78 G10 **Saint Louis** NW Senegal
29 X4 **Saint Louis** Missouri, C USA
31 W5 **Saint Louis River** ≈ Minnesota, N USA
105 T7 **St-Loup-sur-Semouse** Haute-Saône, E France
13 O12 **St-Luc** Québec, SE Canada
47 X13 **Saint Lucia** ◆ commonwealth republic SE West Indies
49 S3 **Saint Lucia** island SE West Indies
85 L22 **St.Lucia, Cape** headland E South Africa
47 Y13 **Saint Lucia Channel** channel Martinique/Saint Lucia
85 L22 **St.Lucia Estuary** KwaZulu/Natal, E South Africa
25 Y14 **Saint Lucie Canal** canal Florida, SE USA
25 Z13 **Saint Lucie Inlet** inlet Florida, SE USA
98 L2 **St Magnus Bay** bay N Scotland, UK
104 K10 **St-Maixent-l'École** Deux-Sèvres, W France
9 Y16 **St.Malo** Manitoba, S Canada
104 I5 **St-Malo** Ille-et-Vilaine, NW France
104 H4 **St-Malo, Golfe de** gulf NW France
46 L9 **St-Marc** C Haiti
46 L9 **St-Marc, Canal de** channel W Haiti
105 S12 **St-Marcellin-le-Mollard** Isère, E France
98 K5 **St Margaret's Hope** NE Scotland, UK
34 M9 **Saint Maries** Idaho, NW USA
25 T9 **Saint Marks** Florida, SE USA
110 D11 **St.Martin** Valais, SW Switzerland
Saint Martin see Sint Maarten
33 O5 **Saint Martin Island** island Michigan, N USA
24 I9 **Saint Martinville** Louisiana, S USA
193 E20 **St.Mary, Mount** ▲ South Island, NZ

◆ Country
● Country Capital
◇ Dependent Territory
○ Dependent Territory Capital
◈ Administrative Region
✕ International Airport
▲ Mountain
⛰ Mountain Range
※ Volcano
≈ River
◎ Lake
⊡ Reservoir

194 K14 St.Mary, Mount ▲ S PNG
190 I6 Saint Mary Peak ▲ South Australia
191 Q16 Saint Marys Tasmania, SE Australia
12 E16 St.Marys Ontario, S Canada
40 M11 Saint Marys Alaska, USA
25 W8 Saint Marys Georgia, SE USA
29 P4 Saint Marys Kansas, C USA
33 Q4 Saint Marys Ohio, N USA
23 R3 Saint Marys West Virginia, NE USA
25 W8 Saint Marys River ~ Florida/Georgia, SE USA
33 Q4 Saint Marys River ~ Michigan, N USA
104 D6 St-Mathieu, Pointe headland NW France
40 J12 Saint Matthew Island island Alaska, USA
23 R13 Saint Matthews South Carolina, SE USA
St.Matthew's Island see Zadetkyi Kyun
194 M8 St.Matthias Group island group NE PNG
110 C11 St.Maurice Valais, SW Switzerland
13 P9 St-Maurice ~ Québec, SE Canada
104 J13 St-Médard-en-Jalles Gironde, SW France
41 N10 Saint Michael Alaska, USA
St.Michel see Mikkeli
13 N10 St-Michel-des-Saints Québec, SE Canada
105 S5 St-Mihiel Meuse, NE France
110 J10 St.Moritz Ger. Sankt Moritz, Rmsch. San Murezzan. Graubünden, SE Switzerland
104 H8 St-Nazaire Loire-Atlantique, NW France
Saint Nicholas see São Nicolau
Saint-Nicolas see Sint-Niklaas
105 N1 St-Omer Pas-de-Calais, N France
104 J11 Saintonge cultural region W France
13 S9 St-Pacôme Québec, SE Canada
13 S10 St-Pamphile Québec, SE Canada
13 S9 St-Pascal Québec, SE Canada
12 J11 St-Patrice, Lac ◎ Québec, SE Canada
9 R14 St.Paul Alberta, SW Canada
181 O16 St-Paul NW Réunion
40 K14 Saint Paul Saint Paul Island, Alaska, USA
31 V8 Saint Paul state capital Minnesota, N USA
31 P15 Saint Paul Nebraska, C USA
23 P7 Saint Paul Virginia, NE USA
79 Q17 Saint Paul, Cape headland S Ghana
105 O17 St-Paul-de-Fenouillet Pyrénées-Orientales, S France
67 K14 Saint Paul Fracture Zone tectonic feature E Atlantic Ocean
40 J14 Saint Paul Island island Pribilof Islands, Alaska, USA
104 J15 St-Paul-les-Dax Landes, SW France
23 U11 Saint Pauls North Carolina, SE USA
Saint Paul's Bay see San Pawl il-Bahar
203 R16 St Paul's Point headland Pitcairn Island, Pitcairn Islands
31 U10 Saint Peter Minnesota, N USA
99 L26 St Peter Port ○ (Guernsey) C Guernsey, Channel Islands
25 V13 Saint Petersburg Florida, SE USA
Saint Petersburg see Sankt-Peterburg
25 V13 Saint Petersburg Beach Florida, SE USA
181 P17 St-Philippe SE Réunion
47 Q11 St-Pierre NW Martinique
181 O17 St-Pierre SW Réunion
11 S13 St-Pierre and Miquelon Fr. Îles St-Pierre et Miquelon. ◇ French territorial collectivity NE North America
13 P11 St-Pierre, Lac ◎ Québec, SE Canada
104 F5 St-Pol-de-Léon Finistère, NW France
105 O2 St-Pol-sur-Ternoise Pas-de-Calais, N France
St. Pons see St-Pons-de-Thomières
105 O16 St-Pons-de-Thomières var. St.Pons. Hérault, S France
105 P10 St-Pourçain-sur-Sioule Allier, C France
13 S11 St-Prosper Québec, SE Canada
105 P3 St-Quentin Aisne, N France
13 R10 St-Raphaël Québec, SE Canada
105 U15 St-Raphaël Var, SE France
13 Q10 St-Raymond Québec, SE Canada
35 Q9 Saint Regis Montana, NW USA
20 J7 Saint Regis River ~ New York, NE USA
105 R15 St-Rémy-de-Provence Bouches-du-Rhône, SE France
13 V6 St-René-de-Matane Québec, SE Canada
104 M9 St-Savin Vienne, W France
13 S8 St-Siméon Québec, SE Canada
25 X7 Saint Simons Island island Georgia, SE USA
203 Y2 Saint Stanislas Bay bay Kiritimati, E Kiribati
11 O15 St.Stephen New Brunswick, SE Canada
41 X12 Saint Terese Alaska, USA
12 E17 St.Thomas Ontario, S Canada
31 Q2 Saint Thomas North Dakota, N USA
47 T9 Saint Thomas island W Virgin Islands (US)
Saint Thomas see São Tomé, Sao Tome and Principe
Saint Thomas see Charlotte Amalie, Virgin Islands (US)
13 P10 St-Tite Québec, SE Canada
Saint-Trond see Sint-Truiden
105 U16 St-Tropez Var, SE France
Saint Ubes see Setúbal
104 L3 St-Valéry-en-Caux Seine-Maritime, N France
105 Q9 St-Vallier Saône-et-Loire, C France
108 B7 St-Vincent Valle d'Aosta, NW Italy
47 Q14 Saint Vincent island N Saint Vincent and the Grenadines
Saint Vincent see São Vicente
47 W14 Saint Vincent and the Grenadines ◆ commonwealth republic SE West Indies
Saint Vincent, Cape see São Vicente, Cabo de
104 I15 St-Vincent-de-Tyrosse Landes, SW France
190 I9 Saint Vincent, Gulf gulf South Australia
25 R10 Saint Vincent Island island Florida, SE USA
47 T12 Saint Vincent Passage passage Saint Lucia/Saint Vincent and the Grenadines
191 N18 Saint Vincent, Point headland Tasmania, SE Australia
Saint-Vith see Sankt-Vith
9 S14 St.Walburg Saskatchewan, S Canada
St Wolfgangsee see Wolfgangsee
104 M11 St-Yrieix-la-Perche Haute-Vienne, C France
Saint Yves see Setúbal
13 Y5 St-Yvon Québec, SE Canada
196 H5 Saipan island ● (Northern Mariana Islands) S Northern Mariana Islands
196 H6 Saipan Channel channel S Northern Mariana Islands
196 H6 Saipan International Airport × Saipan, S Northern Mariana Islands
76 G6 Sais × (Fès) C Morocco
Saishū see Cheju
Saishū see Cheju-do
104 J16 Saison ~ SW France
174 L7 Sai, Sungai ~ Borneo, N Indonesia
171 Jj16 Saitama off. Saitama-ken. ◐ prefecture Honshū, S Japan
170 Cc16 Saito Miyazaki, Kyūshū, SW Japan
Saiyid Abid see Sayyid 'Abīd
59 J19 Sajama, Nevado ▲ W Bolivia
147 V13 Sājir, Ras headland S Oman
113 M20 Sajószentpéter Borsod-Abaúj-Zemplén, NE Hungary
85 F24 Sak ~ SW South Africa
83 J18 Saka Coast, E Kenya
178 I11 Sa Kaeo Prachin Buri, C Thailand
171 Gg15 Sakai Ōsaka, Honshū, SW Japan
170 F14 Sakaide Kagawa, Shikoku, SW Japan
170 Ff12 Sakaiminato Tottori, Honshū, SW Japan
146 M3 Sakākah Al Jawf, NW Saudi Arabia
30 L4 Sakakawea, Lake ▣ North Dakota, N USA
10 J9 Sakami, Lac ◎ Québec, C Canada
81 O26 Sakania Shaba, SE Zaire
152 K12 Sakar Lebapskiy Velayat, E Turkmenistan
180 H7 Sakaraha Toliara, SW Madagascar
152 I14 Sakar-Chaga Turkm. Sakarchäge. Maryyskiy Velayat, C Turkmenistan
Sakarchäge see Sakar-Chaga
Sak'art'velo see Georgia
142 F11 Sakarya ◐ province NW Turkey
142 F12 Sakarya Nehri ~ NW Turkey
171 Ll11 Sakata Yamagata, Honshū, C Japan
126 L9 Sakha (Yakutiya), Respublika var. Respublika Yakutiya, Yakutiya, Eng. Yakutia. ◐ autonomous republic NE Russian Federation
Sakhalin see Sakhalin, Ostrov
127 Oo14 Sakhalin, Ostrov var. Sakhalin. island SE Russian Federation
127 P14 Sakhalinskaya Oblast' ◐ province SE Russian Federation
127 Nn13 Sakhalinskiy Zaliv gulf E Russian Federation
Sakhnovshchina see Sakhnovshchyna
119 U6 Sakhnovshchyna Rus. Sakhnovshchina. Kharkivs'ka Oblast', E Ukraine
Sakhon Nakhon see Sakon Nakhon
Sakhtsar see Rāmsar
Saki see Saky
143 W10 Şäki Rus. Sheki; prev. Nukha. NW Azerbaijan
120 E13 Šakiai Ger. Schaken. Šakiai, S Lithuania
176 Z16 Sakiramke Irian Jaya, E Indonesia
172 Oo16 Sakishima-shotō var. Sakisima Syotō. island group SW Japan
Sakiz see Saqqez
Sakiz-Adasi see Chíos
161 F19 Sakleshpur Karnātaka, E India
178 J9 Sakon Nakhon var. Muang Sakon Nakhon, Sakhon Nakhon. Sakon Nakhon, E Thailand
155 P15 Sakrand Sind, SE Pakistan
85 F24 Sak River Afr. Sakrivier. Northern Cape, W South Africa
Sakrivier see Sak River
Saksaul'skiy see Saksaul'skoye
150 K13 Saksaul'skoye prev. Saksaul'skiy, Kaz. Sekseüil. Kzyl-Orda, S Kazakhstan
97 I25 Sakskøbing Storstrøm, SE Denmark
171 Jj15 Saku Nagano, Honshū, S Japan
171 K16 Sakura Chiba, Honshū, S Japan
119 S13 Saky Rus. Saki. Respublika Krym, S Ukraine
78 E9 Sal island Ilhas de Barlavento, NE Cape Verde
131 N12 Sal ~ SW Russian Federation
113 I21 Sal'a Hung. Sellye, Vágsellye. Západné Slovensko, SW Slovakia
97 N15 Sala Västmanland, C Sweden
175 Qq11 Salabangka, Kepulauan island group N Indonesia
13 N13 Salaberry-de-Valleyfield var. Valleyfield. Québec, SE Canada
120 G7 Salacgrīva Est. Salatsi. Limbaži, N Latvia
109 M18 Sala Consilina Campania, S Italy
42 C2 Salada, Laguna ◎ NW Mexico
63 D14 Saladas Corrientes, NE Argentina
63 C21 Saladillo Buenos Aires, E Argentina
63 B16 Saladillo, Río ~ C Argentina
27 T9 Salado Texas, SW USA
65 J16 Salado, Arroyo ~ SE Argentina
39 Q12 Salado, Rio ~ New Mexico, SW USA
63 D21 Salado, Río ~ E Argentina
64 J12 Salado, Río ~ C Argentina
43 N7 Salado, Río ~ NE Mexico
149 N6 Salafchegān var. Sarafjagān. Tehrān, C Iran
79 Q15 Salaga C Ghana
198 Aa7 Sala'ilua Savai'i, W Western Samoa
118 G9 Sălaj ◐ county NW Romania
85 H20 Salajwe Kweneng, SE Botswana
80 H9 Salal Kanem, W Chad
82 I6 Salala Red Sea, NE Sudan
147 V13 Şalālah SW Oman
44 D5 Salamá Baja Verapaz, C Guatemala
44 J6 Salamá Olancho, C Honduras
64 G10 Salamanca Coquimbo, C Chile
43 N13 Salamanca Guanajuato, C Mexico
106 K7 Salamanca anc. Helmantica, Salmantica. Castilla-León, NW Spain
20 D11 Salamanca New York, NE USA
106 J7 Salamanca ◐ province Castilla-León, W Spain
65 J19 Salamanca, Pampa de plain S Argentina
80 J12 Salamat off. Préfecture du Salamat. ◐ prefecture SE Chad
80 I12 Salamat, Bahr ~ S Chad
56 F5 Salamina Magdalena, N Colombia
117 G19 Salamína var. Salamís. Salamína, C Greece
117 G19 Salamína island C Greece
Salamís see Salamína
144 I5 Salamīyah var. As Salamīyah. Ḩamāh, W Syria
33 P12 Salamonie Lake ▣ Indiana, N USA
33 P12 Salamonie River ~ Indiana, N USA
Salang see Phuket
198 Bb8 Salani Upolu, SE Western Samoa
120 C11 Salantai Kretinga, NW Lithuania
106 K2 Salas Asturias, N Spain
107 O5 Salas de los Infantes Castilla-León, N Spain
104 M16 Salat ~ S France
201 V13 Salat island Chuuk, C Micronesia
174 L15 Salatiga Jawa, C Indonesia
201 V13 Salat Pass passage W Pacific Ocean
Salatsi see Salacgrīva
178 Jj10 Salavan var. Saravan, Saravane. Salavan, S Laos
131 V6 Salavat Respublika Bashkortostan, W Russian Federation
58 C12 Salaverry La Libertad, N Peru
176 Uu9 Salawati, Pulau island E Indonesia
200 Nn11 Sala y Gomez island Chile, E Pacific Ocean
Sala y Gomez Fracture Zone see Sala y Gomez Ridge
200 O11 Sala y Gomez Ridge var. Sala y Gomez Fracture Zone. tectonic feature SE Pacific Ocean
63 A22 Salazar Buenos Aires, E Argentina
56 G7 Salazar Norte de Santander, N Colombia
Salazar see N'Dalatando
181 P16 Salazie C Réunion
105 N8 Salbris Loir-et-Cher, C France
59 G15 Salcantay, Nevado ▲ C Peru
47 O8 Salcedo N Dominican Republic
41 S9 Salcha River ~ Alaska, USA
121 H15 Šalčininkai Šalčininkai, SE Lithuania
Saldae see Béjaïa
56 E11 Saldaña Tolima, C Colombia
106 M4 Saldaña Castilla-León, N Spain
85 E25 Saldanha Western Cape, SW South Africa
Salduba see Zaragoza
63 B23 Saldungaray Buenos Aires, E Argentina
120 D9 Saldus Ger. Frauenburg. Saldus, W Latvia
191 P13 Sale Victoria, SE Australia
76 F6 Salé NW Morocco
76 F6 Salé × (Rabat) W Morocco
Salehābād see Andīmeshk
174 Ii10 Saleh, Air ~ Sumatera, W Indonesia
175 Oo16 Saleh, Teluk bay Nusa Tenggara, S Indonesia
125 G8 Salekhard prev. Obdorsk. Yamalo-Nenetskiy Avtonomnyy Okrug, N Russian Federation
198 B7 Sālelologa Savai'i, C Western Samoa
161 H21 Salem Tamil Nādu, SE India
29 V9 Salem Arkansas, C USA
32 L15 Salem Illinois, N USA
33 P15 Salem Indiana, N USA
21 P11 Salem Massachusetts, NE USA
29 V6 Salem Missouri, C USA
20 I16 Salem New Jersey, NE USA
33 U12 Salem Ohio, N USA
34 G12 Salem state capital Oregon, NW USA
31 Q11 Salem South Dakota, N USA
38 L4 Salem Utah, W USA
23 S7 Salem Virginia, NE USA
23 R3 Salem West Virginia, NE USA
109 H23 Salemi Sicilia, Italy, C Mediterranean Sea
Salemy see As Sālimī
96 K12 Sälen Kopparberg, C Sweden
109 Q18 Salentina, Campi Puglia, SE Italy
109 Q18 Salentina, Penisola peninsula SE Italy
109 L18 Salerno anc. Salernum. Campania, S Italy
109 L18 Salerno, Golfo di Eng. Gulf of Salerno. gulf S Italy
Salerno, Gulf of see Salerno, Golfo di
Salernum see Salerno
99 K17 Salford NW England, UK
Salgir see Salhyr
113 K21 Salgótarján Nógrád, N Hungary
61 O15 Salgueiro Pernambuco, E Brazil
Salhiyé see Aş Şāliḩīyah
96 C13 Salhus Hordaland, S Norway
119 T12 Salhyr Rus. Salgir. ~ S Ukraine
175 S4 Salibabu, Pulau island N Indonesia
39 S6 Salida Colorado, C USA
104 J15 Salies-de-Béarn Pyrénées-Atlantiques, SW France
142 C14 Salihli Manisa, W Turkey
121 K18 Salihorsk Rus. Soligorsk. Minskaya Voblasts', S Belarus
121 K18 Salihorskaye Vodaskhovishcha ▣ C Belarus
85 N14 Salima Central, C Malawi
177 Ff5 Salin Magwe, W Myanmar
29 N4 Salina Kansas, C USA
38 L5 Salina Utah, W USA
43 S17 Salina Cruz Oaxaca, SE Mexico
109 L22 Salina, Isola island Isole Eolie, S Italy
46 J5 Salina Point headland Acklins Island, SE Bahamas
58 A7 Salinas Guayas, W Ecuador
42 M11 Salinas var. Salinas de Hidalgo. San Luis Potosí, C Mexico
47 T6 Salinas C Puerto Rico
37 O10 Salinas California, W USA
Salinas, Cabo de see Salines, Cap de ses
Salinas de Hidalgo see Salinas
84 A13 Salinas, Ponta das headland W Angola
47 O10 Salinas, Punta headland S Dominican Republic
Salinas, Río see Chixoy, Río
37 O11 Salinas River ~ California, W USA
24 H6 Saline Lake ◎ Louisiana, S USA
27 R17 Salineno Texas, SW USA
29 V14 Saline River ~ Arkansas, C USA
32 M17 Saline River ~ Illinois, N USA
29 N4 Saline River ~ Kansas, C USA
107 X10 Salines, Cap de ses var. Cabo de Salinas. headland Mallorca, Spain, W Mediterranean Sea
Salisburg see Mazsalaca
47 O12 Salisbury var. Baroui. W Dominica
99 M23 Salisbury var. New Sarum. S England, UK
23 Y4 Salisbury Maryland, NE USA
29 T3 Salisbury Missouri, C USA
23 S9 Salisbury North Carolina, SE USA
Salisbury see Harare
16 N5 Salisbury Island island Northwest Territories, NE Canada
Salisbury, Lake see Bisina, Lake
99 L23 Salisbury Plain plain S England, UK
23 R14 Salkehatchie River ~ South Carolina, SE USA
144 I9 Şalkhad As Suwaydā', SW Syria
94 M12 Salla Lappi, NE Finland
105 U11 Sallanches Haute-Savoie, E France
107 V5 Sallent Cataluña, NE Spain
63 A22 Salliqueló Buenos Aires, E Argentina
29 R10 Sallisaw Oklahoma, C USA
82 I7 Sallom Red Sea, NE Sudan
10 J2 Salluit prev. Saglouc, Sagluk. Québec, NE Canada
Sallūm, Khalīj as see Salûm, Gulf of
11 S11 Sally's Cove Newfoundland, Newfoundland and Labrador, E Canada
145 W9 Salmān Bin 'Ārāzah E Iraq
Salmantica see Salamanca
148 I2 Salmās prev. Dilman, Shāpūr. Āžarbāyjān-e Bākhtarī, NW Iran
128 I11 Salmi Respublika Kareliya, NW Russian Federation
35 P12 Salmon Idaho, NW USA
9 N16 Salmon Arm British Columbia, SW Canada
199 Jj5 Salmon Bank undersea feature N Pacific Ocean
Salmon Leap see Leixlip
36 L2 Salmon Mountains ⛰ California, W USA
12 J15 Salmon Point headland Ontario, SE Canada
35 N11 Salmon River ~ Idaho, NW USA
20 K6 Salmon River ~ New York, NE USA
35 N12 Salmon River Mountains ⛰ Idaho, NW USA
20 I9 Salmon River Reservoir ▣ New York, NE USA
95 K19 Salo Turku-Pori, SW Finland
108 F7 Salò Lombardia, N Italy
Salona/Salonae see Solin
105 S15 Salon-de-Provence Bouches-du-Rhône, SE France
Salonica/Salonika see Thessaloníki
117 I14 Salonikós, Ákra headland Thásos, E Greece
118 F10 Salonta Hung. Nagyszalonta. Bihor, W Romania
106 I9 Salor ~ W Spain
107 U6 Salou Cataluña, NE Spain
78 H11 Saloum ~ C Senegal
44 H4 Sal, Punta headland NW Honduras
94 N3 Salpynten headland W Svalbard
144 I3 Salqīn Idlib, W Syria
95 F14 Salsbruket Nord-Trøndelag, C Norway
130 M13 Sal'sk Rostovskaya Oblast', SW Russian Federation
109 K25 Salso ~ Sicilia, Italy, C Mediterranean Sea
109 J25 Salso ~ Sicilia, Italy, C Mediterranean Sea
108 E9 Salsomaggiore Terme Emilia-Romagna, N Italy
Salt see As Salt
64 J6 Salta Salta, NW Argentina
64 K6 Salta off. Provincia de Salta. ◐ province N Argentina
99 I24 Saltash SW England, UK
26 I8 Salt Basin basin Texas, SW USA
9 V16 Saltcoats Saskatchewan, S Canada
32 L13 Salt Creek ~ Illinois, N USA
26 J9 Salt Draw ~ Texas, SW USA
99 F21 Saltee Islands island group SE Ireland
94 G12 Saltfjorden inlet C Norway
26 I8 Salt Flat Texas, SW USA
27 P3 Salt Fork ~ Texas, SW USA
29 N8 Salt Fork Arkansas River ~ Oklahoma, C USA
33 T13 Salt Fork Lake ▣ Ohio, N USA
28 J11 Salt Fork Red River ~ Oklahoma, C USA
97 J23 Saltholm island E Denmark
43 N8 Saltillo Coahuila de Zaragoza, NE Mexico
190 L5 Salt Lake salt lake New South Wales, SE Australia
39 V15 Salt Lake ◎ New Mexico, SW USA
38 K2 Salt Lake City state capital Utah, W USA
63 C20 Salto Buenos Aires, E Argentina
63 D17 Salto Salto, N Uruguay
63 E17 Salto ◐ department N Uruguay
109 I14 Salto ~ C Italy
64 Q6 Salto del Guairá Canindeyú, E Paraguay
63 D17 Salto Grande, Embalse de var. Lago de Salto Grande. ▣ Argentina/Uruguay
Salto Grande, Lago de see Salto Grande, Embalse de
37 W16 Salton Sea ◎ California, W USA
62 I12 Salto Santiago, Represa de ▣ S Brazil
155 U7 Salt Range ⛰ E Pakistan
38 M13 Salt River ~ Arizona, SW USA
22 L5 Salt River ~ Kentucky, S USA
29 V3 Salt River ~ Missouri, C USA
97 F17 Saltrød Aust-Agder, S Norway
97 P16 Saltsjöbaden Stockholm, C Sweden
23 Q7 Saltville Virginia, NE USA
Saluces/Saluciae see Saluzzo
23 Q12 Saluda South Carolina, SE USA
23 X6 Saluda Virginia, NE USA
23 Q12 Saluda River ~ South Carolina, SE USA
175 R10 Salue Timpaus, Selat var. Selat Banggai. strait N Banda Sea
77 T7 Salûm var. As Sallūm. NW Egypt
158 F14 Sālumbar Rājasthān, N India
77 T7 Salûm, Gulf of Ar. Khalīj as Sallūm. gulf Egypt/Libya
175 Q7 Salumpaga Sulawesi, N Indonesia
161 M14 Sālūr Andhra Pradesh, E India
57 Y9 Salut, Îles du island group N French Guiana
108 A9 Saluzzo Fr. Saluces; anc. Saluciae. Piemonte, NW Italy
65 F23 Salvación, Bahía bay S Chile
61 P17 Salvador prev. São Salvador. Bahia, E Brazil
67 E24 Salvador East Falkland, Falkland Islands
24 K10 Salvador, Lake ◎ Louisiana, S USA
Salvaleón de Higüey see Higüey
106 F10 Salvaterra de Magos Santarém, C Portugal
43 N13 Salvatierra Guanajuato, C Mexico
107 P3 Salvatierra Basq. Agurain. País Vasco, N Spain
Salwa/Salwah see As Salwā
178 H5 Salween Bur. Thanlwin, Chin. Nu Chiang, Nu Jiang. ~ SE Asia
143 Y12 Salyan Rus. Sal'yany. SE Azerbaijan
159 N11 Salyan var. Sallyana. Mid Western, W Nepal
Sal'yany see Salyan
23 O6 Salyersville Kentucky, S USA
111 V6 Salza ~ E Austria
111 Q7 Salzach ~ Austria/Germany
111 Q6 Salzburg anc. Juvavum. Salzburg, N Austria
111 O8 Salzburg off. Land Salzburg. ◐ state C Austria
Salzburg see Ocna Sibiului
Salzburg Alps see Salzburger Kalkalpen
111 Q7 Salzburger Kalkalpen Eng. Salzburg Alps. ⛰ C Austria
102 J13 Salzgitter prev. Watenstedt-Salzgitter. Niedersachsen, C Germany
103 G14 Salzkotten Nordrhein-Westfalen, W Germany
102 K11 Salzwedel Sachsen-Anhalt, N Germany
158 D11 Sām Rājasthān, NW India
106 K2 Sama var. Sama de Langreo. Asturias, N Spain
56 G9 Samacá Boyacá, C Colombia
42 I7 Samachique Chihuahua, N Mexico
147 Y8 Şamad NE Oman
Sama de Langreo see Sama
59 M19 Samaipata Santa Cruz, C Bolivia
178 Jj11 Samakhixai var. Attapu, Attopeu. Attapu, S Laos
Samakov see Samokov
44 B6 Samalá, Río ~ SW Guatemala
42 J3 Samalayuca Chihuahua, N Mexico
179 Q17 Samales Group island group Sulu Archipelago, SW Philippines
161 L16 Sāmalkot Andhra Pradesh, E India
47 P8 Samaná var. Santa Bárbara de Samaná. E Dominican Republic
47 P8 Samaná, Bahía de bay E Dominican Republic
46 K4 Samana Cay island SE Bahamas
142 K17 Samandağı Hatay, S Turkey
155 P3 Samangān ◐ province N Afghanistan
Samangān see Āybak
172 P8 Samani Hokkaidō, NE Japan
56 C13 Samaniego Nariño, SW Colombia
179 R12 Samar island C Philippines
131 S6 Samara prev. Kuybyshev. Samarskaya Oblast', W Russian Federation
131 S6 Samara × Samarskaya Oblast', W Russian Federation
131 T7 Samara ~ W Russian Federation
119 V7 Samara ~ E Ukraine
195 N17 Samarai Milne Bay, SE PNG
Samarang see Semarang
144 G9 Samarian Hills hill range N Israel
56 L9 Samariapo Amazonas, C Venezuela
175 O8 Samarinda Borneo, C Indonesia
Samarkand see Samarqand
Samarkandskaya Oblast' see Samarqand Wiloyati
Samarkandski/Samarkandskoye see Temirtau
Samarobriva see Amiens
153 N11 Samarqand Rus. Samarkand. Samarqand Wiloyati, C Uzbekistan
152 M11 Samarqand Wiloyati Rus. Samarkandskaya Oblast'. ◐ province C Uzbekistan
145 S6 Sāmarrā' C Iraq
131 R7 Samarskaya Oblast' prev. Kuybyshevskaya Oblast'. ◐ province W Russian Federation
159 Q13 Samastipur Bihār, N India
78 L14 Samatiguila NW Ivory Coast
121 Q17 Samatsevichy Rus. Samotevichi. Mahilyowskaya Voblasts', E Belarus
Samawa see As Samāwah
143 Y11 Şamaxı Rus. Shemakha. C Azerbaijan
158 H6 Samba Jammu and Kashmir, NW India
81 K18 Samba Equateur, NW Zaire
81 N21 Samba Maniema, E Zaire
175 Oo6 Sambaliung, Pegunungan ⛰ Borneo, N Indonesia
160 M11 Sambalpur Orissa, E India
69 X12 Sambao ~ W Madagascar
174 Kk7 Sambas, Sungai ~ Borneo, N Indonesia
180 K2 Sambava Antsirañana, NE Madagascar
176 Ww9 Samberi Irian Jaya, E Indonesia
158 J10 Sambhal Uttar Pradesh, N India
158 H12 Sāmbhar Salt Lake ◎ N India
109 N21 Sambiase Calabria, SW Italy
118 H5 Sambir Rus. Sambor. L'vivs'ka Oblast', NW Ukraine
84 C13 Sambo Huambo, C Angola
Sambor see Sambir
63 E21 Samborombón, Bahía bay NE Argentina
101 H20 Sambre ~ Belgium/France
45 V16 Sambú, Río ~ SE Panama
169 Z14 Samch'ŏk Jap. Sanchoku. NE South Korea
Samch'ŏnpŏ see Sach'ŏn
83 I21 Same Kilimanjaro, NE Tanzania
110 J10 Samedan Ger. Samaden. Graubünden, S Switzerland
84 K12 Samfya Luapula, N Zambia
147 W13 Samḩān, Jabal ⛰ SW Oman
117 C18 Sámi Kefallinía, Iónioi Nísoi, Greece, C Mediterranean Sea
58 F10 Samiria, Río ~ N Peru
Samirum see Semirom
143 V11 Şämkir Rus. Shamkhor. NW Azerbaijan
178 J7 Sam, Nam Vtn. Sông Chu. ~ Laos/Vietnam
Samnān see Semnān
Sam Neua see Xam Nua
77 P10 Samnū C Libya
198 C8 Sāmoa island group American Samoa/Western Samoa
183 Y9 Samoa Basin undersea feature W Pacific Ocean
Sāmoa-i-Sisifo see Western Samoa
114 D8 Samobor Grad Zagreb, N Croatia
116 H10 Samokov var. Samakov. Sofiyska Oblast, W Bulgaria
113 H21 Šamorín Ger. Sommerein, Hung. Somorja. Západné Slovensko, SW Czech Republic
117 M19 Sámos prev. Limín Vathéos. Sámos, Dodekánisos, Greece, Aegean Sea
117 M20 Sámos island Dodekánisos, Greece, Aegean Sea
Samosch see Szamos
173 Ff5 Samosir, Pulau island W Indonesia
Samotevichi see Samatsevichy
Samothrace see Samothráki
117 K14 Samothráki Samothráki, NE Greece
117 J14 Samothráki anc. Samothrace. island NE Greece
117 A15 Samothráki island Iónioi Nísoi, Greece, C Mediterranean Sea
Samotschin see Szamocin
174 M10 Sampit Borneo, C Indonesia
174 M10 Sampit, Sungai ~ Borneo, N Indonesia
Sampoku see Sanpoku
195 P11 Sampun New Britain, E PNG
81 N24 Sampwe Shaba, SE Zaire
27 X8 Sam Rayburn Reservoir ▣ Texas, SW USA
178 I6 Sam Sao, Phou ⛰ Laos/Thailand
97 H22 Samsø island E Denmark
97 H23 Samsø Bælt channel E Denmark
178 Jj7 Sâm Sơn Thanh Hoa, N Vietnam
142 L11 Samsun anc. Amisus. Samsun, N Turkey
142 K11 Samsun ◐ province N Turkey
143 R9 Samtredia W Georgia
61 E15 Samuel, Represa de ▣ W Brazil
178 H15 Samui, Ko island SW Thailand
Samundari see Samundri
155 U9 Samundri var. Samundari. Punjab, E Pakistan
143 X10 Samur ~ Azerbaijan/Russian Federation
143 Y11 Samur-Abşeron Kanalı Rus. Samur-Apsheronskiy Kanal. canal E Azerbaijan
Samur-Apsheronskiy Kanal see Samur-Abşeron Kanalı
178 Hh11 Samut Prakan var. Muang Samut Prakan, Paknam. Samut Prakan, C Thailand
178 H11 Samut Sakhon var. Maha Chai, Samut Sakorn, Tha Chin. Samut Sakhon, C Thailand
Samut Sakorn see Samut Sakhon
178 H11 Samut Songhram prev. Meklong. Samut Songkhram, SW Thailand
79 N12 San Ségou, C Mali
113 O15 San ~ SE Poland
147 O15 Şan'ā' Eng. Sana. ● (Yemen) W Yemen
114 F11 Sana ~ NW Bosnia and Herzegovina
82 O12 Sanaag off. Gobolka Sanaag. ◐ region N Somalia
116 J8 Sanadinovo Loveshka Oblast, N Bulgaria
205 P1 Sanae South African research station Antarctica
145 Y10 Sanāf, Hawr as ◎ S Iraq
81 E15 Sanaga ~ C Cameroon
56 D12 San Agustín Huila, SW Colombia
179 S16 San Agustin, Cape headland Mindanao, S Philippines
39 Q13 San Agustin, Plains of plain New Mexico, SW USA
40 M16 Sanak Island island Aleutian Islands, Alaska, USA
200 P11 San Ambrosio, Isla Eng. San Ambrosio Island. island W Chile
San Ambrosio Island see San Ambrosio, Isla
175 S10 Sanana Pulau Sanana, E Indonesia
175 S10 Sanana, Pulau island Maluku, E Indonesia
148 K5 Sanandaj prev. Sinneh. Kordestān, W Iran
37 P8 San Andreas California, W USA
2 C13 San Andreas Fault fault W USA
56 G8 San Andrés Santander, C Colombia
63 C20 San Andrés de Giles Buenos Aires, E Argentina
39 R14 San Andres Mountains ⛰ New Mexico, SW USA
43 S15 San Andrés Tuxtla var. Tuxtla. Veracruz-Llave, E Mexico
27 P8 San Angelo Texas, SW USA
109 A20 San Antioco, Isola di island W Italy
44 F4 San Antonio Toledo, S Belize
64 G11 San Antonio Valparaíso, C Chile
196 H6 San Antonio Saipan, S Northern Mariana Islands
39 R13 San Antonio New Mexico, SW USA
27 R12 San Antonio Texas, SW USA
56 M11 San Antonio Amazonas, S Venezuela
56 I7 San Antonio Barinas, C Venezuela
57 O5 San Antonio Monagas, NE Venezuela
27 S12 San Antonio × Texas, SW USA
San Antonio see San Antonio del Táchira
107 V11 San Antonio Abad Eivissa, Spain, W Mediterranean Sea
27 U13 San Antonio Bay inlet Texas, SW USA
63 E22 San Antonio, Cabo headland E Argentina
46 A5 San Antonio, Cabo de headland W Cuba
107 T11 San Antonio, Cabo de headland E Spain

◆ Country ● Country Capital ◇ Dependent Territory ○ Dependent Territory Capital ◐ Administrative Region × International Airport ▲ Mountain ⛰ Mountain Range ☀ Volcano ~ River ◎ Lake ▣ Reservoir

56 *H7* **San Antonio de Caparo** Táchira, W Venezuela
64 *J5* **San Antonio de los Cobres** Salta, NE Argentina
56 *H7* **San Antonio del Táchira** *var.* San Antonio. Táchira, W Venezuela
37 *T15* **San Antonio, Mount** ▲ California, W USA
65 *K16* **San Antonio Oeste** Río Negro, E Argentina
27 *T13* **San Antonio River** ≈ Texas, SW USA
56 *J5* **Sanare** Lara, N Venezuela
105 *T16* **Sanary-sur-Mer** Var, SE France
27 *X8* **San Augustine** Texas, SW USA
147 *T13* **Sanāw** *var.* Sanaw. NE Yemen
43 *O11* **San Bartolo** San Luis Potosí, C Mexico
109 *L16* **San Bartolomeo in Galdo** Campania, S Italy
108 *K13* **San Benedetto del Tronto** Marche, C Italy
44 *E3* **San Benito** Petén, N Guatemala
27 *T17* **San Benito** Texas, SW USA
56 *E6* **San Benito Abad** Sucre, N Colombia
37 *P11* **San Benito Mountain** ▲ California, W USA
37 *O10* **San Benito River** ≈ California, W USA
110 *H10* **San Bernardino** Graubünden, S Switzerland
37 *U15* **San Bernardino** California, W USA
110 *H10* **San Bernardino, Passo del** *pass* SE Switzerland
64 *H11* **San Bernardo** Santiago, C Chile
42 *J8* **San Bernardo** Durango, C Mexico
170 *F12* **Sanbe-san** ▲ Kyūshū, SW Japan
42 *J12* **San Blas** Nayarit, C Mexico
42 *H8* **San Blas** Sinaloa, C Mexico
45 *V14* **San Blas** *off.* Comarca de San Blas. ◈ *special territory* NE Panama
45 *U14* **San Blas, Archipiélago de** *island group* NE Panama
25 *Q10* **San Blas, Cape** *headland* Florida, SE USA
45 *V14* **San Blas, Cordillera de** ⛰ NE Panama
64 *J8* **San Blas de los Sauces** Catamarca, NW Argentina
108 *G8* **San Bonifacio** Veneto, NE Italy
31 *S12* **Sanborn** Iowa, C USA
42 *M7* **San Buenaventura** Coahuila de Zaragoza, NE Mexico
107 *S5* **San Caprasio** ▲ N Spain
61 *L21* **San Carlos** São Paulo, SE Brazil
64 *G13* **San Carlos** Bío Bío, C Chile
42 *E9* **San Carlos** Baja California Sur, W Mexico
43 *N5* **San Carlos** Coahuila de Zaragoza, NE Mexico
43 *P9* **San Carlos** Tamaulipas, C Mexico
44 *L12* **San Carlos** Río San Juan, S Nicaragua
45 *T16* **San Carlos** Panamá, C Panama
179 *P9* **San Carlos** *off.* San Carlos City. Luzon, N Philippines
38 *M14* **San Carlos** Arizona, SW USA
63 *G20* **San Carlos** Maldonado, S Uruguay
56 *K5* **San Carlos** Cojedes, N Venezuela
San Carlos *see* Quesada, Costa Rica
San Carlos *see* Luba, Equatorial Guinea
63 *B17* **San Carlos Centro** Santa Fe, C Argentina
179 *Q13* **San Carlos City** Negros, C Philippines
San Carlos de Ancud *see* Ancud
65 *H16* **San Carlos de Bariloche** Río Negro, SW Argentina
63 *B21* **San Carlos de Bolívar** Buenos Aires, E Argentina
56 *H6* **San Carlos del Zulia** Zulia, W Venezuela
56 *L12* **San Carlos de Río Negro** Amazonas, S Venezuela
San Carlos, Estrecho de *see* Falkland Sound
38 *M14* **San Carlos Reservoir** ▣ Arizona, SW USA
44 *M12* **San Carlos, Río** ≈ N Costa Rica
67 *D24* **San Carlos Settlement** East Falkland, Falkland Islands
63 *C23* **San Cayetano** Buenos Aires, E Argentina
105 *O8* **Sancerre** Cher, C France
164 *G7* **Sanchakou** Xinjiang Uygur Zizhiqu, NW China
Sanchoku *see* Samch'ŏk
43 *O12* **San Ciro** San Luis Potosí, C Mexico
107 *P10* **San Clemente** Castilla-La Mancha, C Spain
37 *T16* **San Clemente** California, W USA
63 *E21* **San Clemente del Tuyú** Buenos Aires, E Argentina
37 *S17* **San Clemente Island** *island* Channel Islands, California, W USA
105 *O9* **Sancoins** Cher, C France
195 *Z17* **San Cristobal** *var.* Makira. *island* SE Solomon Islands
63 *B16* **San Cristóbal** Santa Fe, C Argentina
46 *B4* **San Cristóbal** Pinar del Río, W Cuba
47 *O9* **San Cristóbal** *var.* Benemérita de San Cristóbal. S Dominican Republic
56 *H7* **San Cristóbal** Táchira, W Venezuela
San Cristóbal *see* San Cristóbal de Las Casas
43 *U16* **San Cristóbal de Las Casas** *var.* San Cristóbal. Chiapas, SE Mexico
200 *Oo8* **San Cristóbal, Isla** *var.* Chatham Island. *island* Galapagos Islands, Ecuador, E Pacific Ocean
44 *D5* **San Cristóbal Verapaz** Alta Verapaz, C Guatemala
46 *F6* **Sancti Spíritus** Sancti Spíritus, C Cuba
105 *O11* **Sancy, Puy de** ▲ C France
97 *D15* **Sand** Rogaland, S Norway
175 *Oo2* **Sandakan** Sabah, East Malaysia
190 *K9* **Sandalwood** South Australia
Sandalwood Island *see* Sumba, Pulau
96 *D11* **Sandane** Sogn og Fjordane, S Norway
116 *G12* **Sandanski** *prev.* Sveti Vrach. Sofiyska Oblast, SW Bulgaria
78 *J11* **Sandaré** Kayes, W Mali
97 *J19* **Sandared** Älvsborg, S Sweden
96 *N12* **Sandarne** Gävleborg, C Sweden
194 *E10* **Sandaun** *prev.* West Sepik. ◈ *province* NW PNG
98 *K4* **Sanday** *island* NE Scotland, UK
179 *N14* **Sand Cay** *island* W Spratly Islands
33 *P15* **Sand Creek** ≈ Indiana, N USA
97 *H15* **Sande** Vestfold, S Norway
97 *H16* **Sandefjord** Vestfold, S Norway
79 *O15* **Sandégué** E Ivory Coast
79 *P14* **Sandema** N Ghana
39 *O11* **Sanders** Arizona, SW USA
26 *M11* **Sanderson** Texas, SW USA
25 *U4* **Sandersville** Georgia, SE USA
94 *H4* **Sandgerdhi** Sudhurland, SW Iceland
30 *K14* **Sand Hills** ⛰ Nebraska, C USA
27 *S14* **Sandia** Texas, SW USA
37 *T17* **San Diego** California, W USA
27 *S14* **San Diego** Texas, SW USA
142 *F14* **Sandıklı** Afyon, W Turkey
158 *L12* **Sandīla** Uttar Pradesh, N India
123 *J15* **San Dimitri, Ras** *var.* San Dimitri Point. *headland* Gozo, NW Malta
174 *Gg11* **Sanding, Selat** *strait* W Indonesia
32 *J3* **Sand Island** *island* Apostle Islands, Wisconsin, N USA
97 *C16* **Sandnes** Rogaland, S Norway
94 *F13* **Sandnessjøen** Nordland, C Norway
81 *L24* **Sandoa** Shaba, S Zaire
113 *N15* **Sandomierz** *Rus.* Sandomir. Tarnobrzeg, SE Poland
Sandomir *see* Sandomierz
56 *C13* **Sandoná** Nariño, SW Colombia
108 *I7* **San Donà di Piave** Veneto, NE Italy
128 *K14* **Sandovo** Tverskaya Oblast', W Russian Federation
177 *Ff7* **Sandoway** Arakan State, W Burma
99 *M24* **Sandown** S England, UK
41 *N16* **Sand Point** Popof Island, Alaska, USA
67 *N24* **Sand Point** *headland* E Tristan da Cunha
33 *R7* **Sand Point** *headland* Michigan, N USA
34 *M7* **Sandpoint** Idaho, NW USA
95 *H14* **Sandsele** Västerbotten, N Sweden
8 *I14* **Sandspit** Moresby Island, British Columbia, SW Canada
29 *P9* **Sand Springs** Oklahoma, C USA
31 *W7* **Sandstone** Minnesota, N USA
38 *K15* **Sand Tank Mountains** ⛰ Arizona, SW USA
33 *S8* **Sandusky** Michigan, N USA
33 *S11* **Sandusky** Ohio, N USA
33 *S12* **Sandusky River** ≈ Ohio, N USA
85 *D22* **Sandverhaar** Karas, S Namibia
97 *L24* **Sandvig** Bornholm, E Denmark
97 *H15* **Sandvika** Akershus, S Norway
96 *N13* **Sandviken** Gävleborg, C Sweden
32 *M11* **Sandwich** Illinois, N USA
Sandwich Island *see* Éfaté
Sandwich Islands *see* Hawaiian Islands
159 *V16* **Sandwip Island** *island* SE Bangladesh
9 *U12* **Sandy Bay** Saskatchewan, C Canada
191 *N16* **Sandy Cape** *headland* Tasmania, SE Australia
178 *Mm14* **Sandy Cay** *island* NW Spratly Islands
38 *L3* **Sandy City** Utah, W USA
33 *U12* **Sandy Creek** ≈ Ohio, N USA
23 *O5* **Sandy Hook** Kentucky, S USA
20 *K15* **Sandy Hook** *headland* New Jersey, NE USA
152 *J15* **Sandykachi** *Turkm.* Sandykgachy. Maryyskiy Velayat, S Turkmenistan
Sandykgachy *see* Sandykachi
152 *L13* **Sandykly, Peski** *desert* E Turkmenistan
9 *Q13* **Sandy Lake** Alberta, W Canada
10 *B8* **Sandy Lake** Ontario, C Canada
10 *B8* **Sandy Lake** ◎ Ontario, C Canada
25 *S3* **Sandy Springs** Georgia, SE USA
26 *H8* **San Elizario** Texas, SW USA
101 *L25* **Sanem** Luxembourg, SW Luxembourg
44 *K5* **San Esteban** Olancho, C Honduras
107 *O6* **San Esteban de Gormaz** Castilla-León, N Spain
42 *E5* **San Esteban, Isla** *island* NW Mexico
San Eugenio/San Eugenio del Cuareim *see* Artigas
64 *H11* **San Felipe** *var.* San Felipe de Aconcagua. Valparaíso, C Chile
42 *D3* **San Felipe** Baja California, NW Mexico
42 *N12* **San Felipe** Guanajuato, C Mexico
56 *K5* **San Felipe** Yaracuy, NW Venezuela
46 *B5* **San Felipe, Cayos de** *island group* W Cuba
San Felipe de Aconcagua *see* San Felipe
San Felipe de Puerto Plata *see* Puerto Plata
39 *R11* **San Felipe Pueblo** New Mexico, SW USA
San Feliú de Guixols *see* Sant Feliu de Guíxols
200 *Oo11* **San Félix, Isla** *Eng.* San Felix Island. *island* W Chile
San Felix Island *see* San Félix, Isla
56 *L11* **San Fernanado de Atabapo** Amazonas, S Venezuela
42 *C4* **San Fernando** *var.* Misión San Fernando. Baja California, NW Mexico
43 *P9* **San Fernando** Tamaulipas, C Mexico
179 *P9* **San Fernando** Luzon, N Philippines
179 *P10* **San Fernando** Luzon, N Philippines
106 *J16* **San Fernando** *prev.* Isla de León. Andalucía, S Spain
47 *U14* **San Fernando** Trinidad, Trinidad and Tobago
37 *S15* **San Fernando** California, W USA
56 *L7* **San Fernando** *var.* San Fernando de Apure. Apure, C Venezuela
San Fernando de Apure *see* San Fernando
64 *L8* **San Fernando del Valle de Catamarca** *var.* Catamarca. Catamarca, NW Argentina
San Fernando de Monte Cristi *see* Monte Cristi
43 *P9* **San Fernando, Río** ≈ C Mexico
25 *X11* **Sanford** Florida, SE USA
21 *P9* **Sanford** Maine, NE USA
23 *T10* **Sanford** North Carolina, SE USA
27 *N2* **Sanford** Texas, SW USA
41 *T10* **Sanford, Mount** ▲ Alaska, USA
44 *G8* **San Francisco** *var.* Gotera, San Francisco Gotera. Morazán, E El Salvador
45 *R16* **San Francisco** Veraguas, C Panama
179 *Pp11* **San Francisco** *var.* Aurora. Luzon, N Philippines
37 *L8* **San Francisco** California, W USA
56 *H5* **San Francisco** Zulia, NW Venezuela
36 *M8* **San Francisco** ✈ California, W USA
37 *N9* **San Francisco Bay** *bay* California, W USA
63 *C24* **San Francisco de Bellocq** Buenos Aires, E Argentina
42 *I6* **San Francisco de Borja** Chihuahua, N Mexico
44 *J6* **San Francisco de la Paz** Olancho, C Honduras
42 *J7* **San Francisco del Oro** Chihuahua, N Mexico
42 *M12* **San Francisco del Rincón** Jalisco, SW Mexico
47 *O8* **San Francisco de Macorís** C Dominican Republic
San Francisco de Satipo *see* Satipo
San Francisco Gotera *see* San Francisco
San Francisco Telixtlahuaca *see* Telixtlahuaca
109 *K23* **San Fratello** Sicilia, Italy, C Mediterranean Sea
San Fructuoso *see* Tacuarembó
84 *C12* **Sanga** Cuanza Sul, NW Angola
58 *C5* **San Gabriel** Carchi, N Ecuador
165 *S15* **Sa'ngain** Xizang Zizhiqu, W China
160 *E13* **Sangamner** Mahārāshtra, W India
158 *H12* **Sāngāner** Rājasthān, N India
Sangan, Koh-i- *see* Sangān, Kūh-e
155 *N6* **Sangān, Kūh-e** *Pash.* Koh-i-Sangan. ⛰ C Afghanistan
126 *Ll10* **Sangar** Respublika Sakha (Yakutiya), NE Russian Federation
175 *O8* **Sangasanga** Borneo, C Indonesia
105 *N1* **Sangatte** Pas-de-Calais, N France
109 *B19* **San Gavino Monreale** Sardegna, Italy, C Mediterranean Sea
59 *D16* **Sangayan, Isla** *island* W Peru
32 *L14* **Sangchris Lake** ▣ Illinois, N USA
175 *P15* **Sangeang, Pulau** *island* S Indonesia
118 *I10* **Sângeorgiu de Pădure** *prev.* Erdăt-Sângeorz, Sîngeorgiu de Pădure, *Hung.* Erdőszentgyörgy. Mureș, C Romania
118 *I9* **Sângeorz-Băi** *var.* Singeroz Băi, *Ger.* Rumänisch-Sankt-Georgen, *Hung.* Oláhszentgyőrgy; *prev.* Sîngeorz-Băi. Bistrița-Năsăud, N Romania
37 *R10* **Sanger** California, W USA
27 *T5* **Sanger** Texas, SW USA
Sângerei *see* Sîngerei
103 *L15* **Sangerhausen** Sachsen-Anhalt, C Germany
47 *S6* **San Germán** W Puerto Rico
San Germano *see* Cassino
167 *N2* **Sanggan He** ≈ E China
175 *Oo16* **Sanggar, Teluk** *bay* Nusa Tenggara, S Indonesia
174 *L8* **Sanggau** Borneo, C Indonesia
81 *H16* **Sangha** ≈ Central African Republic/Congo
81 *G16* **Sangha-Mbaéré** ◈ *prefecture* SW Central African Republic
155 *Q15* **Sānghar** Sind, SE Pakistan
117 *F22* **Sangiás** ▲ S Greece
Sangihe, Kepulauan *see* Sangir, Kepulauan
175 *S4* **Sangihe, Pulau** *var.* Sangir. *island* N Indonesia
56 *G8* **San Gil** Santander, C Colombia
108 *F12* **San Gimignano** Toscana, C Italy
154 *M8* **Sangīn** *var.* Sangin. Helmand, S Afghanistan
109 *O21* **San Giovanni in Fiore** Calabria, SW Italy
109 *M16* **San Giovanni Rotondo** Puglia, SE Italy
108 *G12* **San Giovanni Valdarno** Toscana, C Italy
Sangir *see* Sangihe, Pulau
175 *Rr6* **Sangir, Kepulauan** *var.* Kepulauan Sangihe. *island group* N Indonesia
168 *K9* **Sangiyn Dalay** Dundgovĭ, C Mongolia
168 *H9* **Sangiyn Dalay** Govĭ-Altay, C Mongolia
168 *K11* **Sangiyn Dalay** Ömnogövĭ, S Mongolia
168 *K8* **Sangiyn Dalay** Övörhangay, C Mongolia
169 *Y15* **Sangju** *Jap.* Shōshū. C South Korea
178 *Ii11* **Sangkha** Surin, E Thailand
175 *Oo7* **Sangkulirang** Borneo, N Indonesia
175 *Oo7* **Sangkulirang, Teluk** *bay* Borneo, N Indonesia
161 *E16* **Sāngli** Mahārāshtra, W India
81 *E16* **Sangmélima** Sud, S Cameroon
37 *V15* **San Gorgonio Mountain** ▲ California, W USA
39 *T8* **Sangre de Cristo Mountains** ⛰ Colorado/New Mexico, C USA
63 *A20* **San Gregorio** Santa Fe, C Argentina
63 *F18* **San Gregorio de Polanco** Tacuarembó, C Uruguay
47 *V14* **Sangre Grande** Trinidad, Trinidad and Tobago
165 *N16* **Sangri** Xizang Zizhiqu, W China
158 *H9* **Sangrūr** Punjab, NW India
46 *I11* **Sangster** *off.* Sir Donald Sangster International Airport, *var.* Montego Bay. ✈ (Montego Bay) W Jamaica
61 *G17* **Sangue, Rio do** ≈ W Brazil
107 *R4* **Sangüesa** Navarra, N Spain
63 *C16* **San Gustavo** Entre Ríos, E Argentina
Sangyuan *see* Wuqiao
42 *C6* **San Hipólito, Punta** *headland* W Mexico
25 *W15* **Sanibel** Sanibel Island, Florida, SE USA
25 *V15* **Sanibel Island** *island* Florida, SE USA
62 *F13* **San Ignacio** Misiones, NE Argentina
44 *F2* **San Ignacio** *prev.* Cayo, El Cayo. Cayo, W Belize
59 *L16* **San Ignacio** Beni, N Bolivia
59 *O18* **San Ignacio** Santa Cruz, E Bolivia
44 *M14* **San Ignacio** *var.* San Ignacio de Acosta. San José, W Costa Rica
42 *E6* **San Ignacio** Baja California Sur, W Mexico
42 *J10* **San Ignacio** Sinaloa, W Mexico
58 *B9* **San Ignacio** Cajamarca, N Peru
San Ignacio de Acosta *see* San Ignacio
42 *D7* **San Ignacio, Laguna** *lagoon* W Mexico
10 *I6* **Sanikiluaq** Belcher Islands, Northwest Territories, C Canada
179 *Pp9* **San Ildefonso Peninsula** *peninsula* Luzon, N Philippines
Saniquillie *see* Sanniquellie
63 *D20* **San Isidro** Buenos Aires, E Argentina
45 *N14* **San Isidro** *var.* San Isidro de El General. San José, SE Costa Rica
San Isidro de El General *see* San Isidro
56 *E5* **San Jacinto** Bolívar, N Colombia
37 *U16* **San Jacinto** California, W USA
37 *V15* **San Jacinto Peak** ▲ California, W USA
63 *F14* **San Javier** Misiones, NE Argentina
63 *C16* **San Javier** Santa Fe, C Argentina
107 *S13* **San Javier** Murcia, SE Spain
63 *D18* **San Javier** Río Negro, W Uruguay
63 *C16* **San Javier, Río** ≈ C Argentina
166 *L12* **Sanjiang** *var.* Guyi, Sanjiang Dongzu Zizhixian. Guangxi Zhuangzu Zizhiqu, S China
Sanjiang Dongzu Zizhixian *see* Sanjiang
171 *Kk13* **Sanjō** *var.* Sanzyô. Niigata, Honshū, C Japan
59 *M15* **San Joaquín** Beni, N Bolivia
57 *O6* **San Joaquín** Anzoátegui, NE Venezuela
37 *O9* **San Joaquin River** ≈ California, W USA
37 *P10* **San Joaquin Valley** *valley* California, W USA
63 *A18* **San Jorge** Santa Fe, C Argentina
195 *W15* **San Jorge** *island* N Solomon Islands
42 *D3* **San Jorge, Bahía de** *bay* NW Mexico
65 *J19* **San Jorge, Golfo** *var.* Gulf of San Jorge. *gulf* S Argentina
San Jorge, Gulf of *see* San Jorge, Golfo
196 *K8* **San Jose** Tinian, S Northern Mariana Islands
179 *Pp12* **San Jose** Mindoro, N Philippines
37 *N9* **San Jose** California, W USA
63 *F14* **San José** Misiones, NE Argentina
59 *P19* **San José** *var.* San José de Chiquitos. Santa Cruz, E Bolivia
44 *M14* **San José** ● (Costa Rica) San José, C Costa Rica
44 *C7* **San José** *var.* Puerto San José. Escuintla, S Guatemala
42 *G6* **San José** Sonora, NW Mexico
107 *U11* **San José** Eivissa, Spain, W Mediterranean Sea
56 *H5* **San José** Zulia, NW Venezuela
44 *M14* **San José** *off.* Provincia de San José. ◈ *province* W Costa Rica
63 *E19* **San José** ◈ *department* S Uruguay
44 *M13* **San José** ✈ Alajuela, C Costa Rica
San José *see* San José del Guaviare, Colombia
San José *see* San José de Mayo, S Uruguay
179 *P9* **San Jose City** Luzon, N Philippines
179 *Pp13* **San Jose de Buenavista** Panay Island, C Philippines
San José de Cúcuta *see* Cúcuta
63 *D16* **San José de Feliciano** Entre Ríos, E Argentina
57 *O6* **San José de Guanipa** *var.* El Tigrito. Anzoátegui, NE Venezuela
64 *I9* **San José de Jáchal** San Juan, W Argentina
42 *G10* **San José del Cabo** Baja California Sur, W Mexico
56 *G12* **San José del Guaviare** *var.* San José. Guaviare, S Colombia
63 *E20* **San José de Mayo** *var.* San José. San José, S Uruguay
56 *I10* **San José de Ocuné** Vichada, E Colombia
43 *O9* **San José de Raíces** Nuevo León, NE Mexico
65 *K17* **San José, Golfo** *gulf* E Argentina
42 *F9* **San José, Isla** *island* W Mexico
45 *U16* **San José, Isla** *island* SE Panama
27 *U14* **San Jose Island** *island* Texas, SW USA
64 *I10* **San Juan** San Juan, W Argentina
47 *N9* **San Juan** *var.* San Juan de la Maguana. C Dominican Republic
59 *E17* **San Juan** Ica, S Peru
47 *U5* **San Juan** ○ (Puerto Rico) NE Puerto Rico
64 *H10* **San Juan** *off.* Provincia de San Juan. ◈ *province* W Argentina
47 *U5* **San Juan** *var.* Luis Muñoz Marin. ✈ NE Puerto Rico
San Juan *see* San Juan de los Morros
64 *O7* **San Juan Bautista** Misiones, S Paraguay
37 *O10* **San Juan Bautista** California, W USA
San Juan Bautista *see* Villahermosa
San Juan Bautista Cuicatlán *see* Cuicatlán
San Juan Bautista Tuxtepec *see* Tuxtepec
81 *C17* **San Juan, Cabo** *headland* S Equatorial Guinea
107 *S12* **San Juan de Alicante** País Valenciano, E Spain
56 *H7* **San Juan de Colón** Táchira, NW Venezuela
42 *L9* **San Juan de Guadalupe** Durango, C Mexico
San Juan de la Maguana *see* San Juan
56 *G4* **San Juan del Cesar** La Guajira, N Colombia
42 *L15* **San Juan de Lima, Punta** *headland* SW Mexico
44 *I8* **San Juan de Limay** Estelí, NW Nicaragua
45 *N12* **San Juan del Norte** *var.* Greytown. Río San Juan, SE Nicaragua
56 *K4* **San Juan de los Cayos** Falcón, N Venezuela
42 *M12* **San Juan de los Lagos** Jalisco, C Mexico
56 *L5* **San Juan de los Morros** *var.* San Juan. Guárico, N Venezuela
42 *K9* **San Juan del Río** Durango, C Mexico
43 *O13* **San Juan del Río** Querétaro de Arteaga, C Mexico
44 *J11* **San Juan del Sur** Rivas, SW Nicaragua
56 *M9* **San Juan de Manapiare** Amazonas, S Venezuela
42 *E7* **San Juanico** Baja California Sur, W Mexico
42 *D7* **San Juanico, Punta** *headland* W Mexico
34 *G6* **San Juan Islands** *island group* Washington, NW USA
42 *I6* **San Juanito** Chihuahua, N Mexico
42 *I12* **San Juanito, Isla** *island* C Mexico
39 *R8* **San Juan Mountains** ⛰ Colorado, C USA
56 *E5* **San Juan Nepomuceno** Bolívar, NW Colombia
46 *E5* **San Juan, Pico** ▲ C Cuba
203 *W15* **San Juan, Punta** *headland* Easter Island, Chile, E Pacific Ocean
44 *M12* **San Juan, Río** ≈ Costa Rica/Nicaragua
43 *S15* **San Juan, Río** ≈ SE Mexico
39 *O8* **San Juan River** ≈ Colorado/Utah, W USA
San Julián *see* Puerto San Julián
63 *B17* **San Justo** Santa Fe, C Argentina
111 *W5* **Sankt Aegyd am Neuwalde** Niederösterreich, E Austria
111 *U9* **Sankt Andrä** *Slvn.* Šent Andraž. Kärnten, S Austria
Sankt Andrä *see* Szentendre
Sankt Anna *see* Sântana
110 *K8* **Sankt Anton am Arlberg** Vorarlberg, W Austria
103 *E16* **Sankt Augustin** Nordrhein-Westfalen, W Germany
Sankt-Bartholomäi *see* Palamuse
103 *F24* **Sankt Blasien** Baden-Württemberg, SW Germany
111 *R3* **Sankt Florian am Inn** Oberösterreich, N Austria
110 *I7* **Sankt Gallen** *var.* St.Gallen, *Eng.* Saint Gall, *Fr.* St-Gall. Sankt Gallen, NE Switzerland
110 *H8* **Sankt Gallen** *var.* St.Gallen, Eng, Saint Gall, *Fr.* St-Gall. ◈ *canton* NE Switzerland
110 *J8* **Sankt Gallenkirch** Vorarlberg, W Austria
111 *Q5* **Sankt Georgen** Salzburg, N Austria
Sankt Georgen *see* Đurđevac, Croatia
Sankt-Georgen *see* Sfântu Gheorghe, Romania
111 *R6* **Sankt Gilgen** Salzburg, NW Austria
Sankt Gotthard *see* Szentgotthárd
103 *E20* **Sankt Ingbert** Saarland, SW Germany
Sankt-Jakobi *see* Viru-Jaagupi, Lääne-Virumaa, Estonia
Sankt-Jakobi *see* Pärnu-Jaagupi, Pärnumaa, Estonia
Sankt Johann *see* Sankt Johann in Tirol
111 *T7* **Sankt Johann am Tauern** Steiermark, E Austria
111 *Q7* **Sankt Johann im Pongau** Salzburg, NW Austria
111 *P6* **Sankt Johann in Tirol** *var.* Sankt Johann. Tirol, W Austria
Sankt-Johannis *see* Järva-Jaani
110 *L8* **Sankt Leonhard** Tirol, W Austria
Sankt Margarethen *see* Sankt Margarethen im Burgenland
111 *Y5* **Sankt Margarethen im Burgenland** *var.* Sankt Margarethen. Burgenland, E Austria
Sankt Martin *see* Martin
111 *X8* **Sankt Martin an der Raab** Burgenland, SE Austria
111 *U7* **Sankt Michael in Obersteiermark** Steiermark, SE Austria
Sankt Michel *see* Mikkeli
Sankt Moritz *see* St.Moritz
110 *E11* **Sankt Niklaus** Valais, S Switzerland
111 *S7* **Sankt Nikolai** *var.* Sankt Nikolai im Sölktal. Steiermark, SE Austria
Sankt Nikolai im Sölktal *see* Sankt Nikolai
111 *U9* **Sankt Paul** *var.* Sankt Paul im Lavanttal. Kärnten, S Austria
Sankt Paul im Lavanttal *see* Sankt Paul
Sankt Peter *see* Pivka
111 *W9* **Sankt Peter am Ottersbach** Steiermark, SE Austria
128 *J13* **Sankt-Peterburg** *prev.* Leningrad, Petrograd, *Eng.* Saint Petersburg, *Fin.* Pietari. Leningradskaya Oblast', NW Russian Federation
102 *H8* **Sankt Peter-Ording** Schleswig-Holstein, N Germany
111 *V4* **Sankt Pölten** Niederösterreich, N Austria
111 *W7* **Sankt Ruprecht** *var.* Sankt Ruprecht an der Raab. Steiermark, SE Austria
Sankt Ruprecht an der Raab *see* Sankt Ruprecht
Sankt-Ulrich *see* Ortisei
111 *T4* **Sankt Valentin** Niederösterreich, C Austria
Sankt Veit am Flaum *see* Rijeka
111 *T9* **Sankt Veit an der Glan** *Slvn.* Šent Vid. Kärnten, S Austria
101 *M21* **Sankt-Vith** *var.* Saint-Vith. Liège, E Belgium
103 *E20* **Sankt Wendel** Saarland, SW Germany
111 *R6* **Sankt Wolfgang** Salzburg, NW Austria
81 *K21* **Sankuru** ≈ C Zaire
42 *D8* **San Lázaro, Cabo** *headland* W Mexico
143 *O16* **Şanlıurfa** *prev.* Sanli Urfa, Urfa, *anc.* Edessa. Şanlıurfa, S Turkey
143 *O16* **Şanlıurfa** *prev.* Urfa. ◈ *province* SE Turkey
143 *O16* **Şanlıurfa Yaylası** *plateau* SE Turkey
63 *B18* **San Lorenzo** Santa Fe, C Argentina
59 *M21* **San Lorenzo** Tarija, S Bolivia
58 *C5* **San Lorenzo** Esmeraldas, N Ecuador
44 *H8* **San Lorenzo** Valle, S Honduras
107 *N8* **San Lorenzo de El Escorial** *var.* El Escorial. Madrid, C Spain
42 *E5* **San Lorenzo, Isla** *island* NW Mexico
59 *C14* **San Lorenzo, Isla** *island* W Peru
65 *G20* **San Lorenzo, Monte** ▲ S Argentina
42 *I9* **San Lorenzo, Río** ≈ C Mexico
106 *J15* **Sanlúcar de Barrameda** Andalucía, S Spain
106 *J14* **Sanlúcar la Mayor** Andalucía, S Spain
42 *F11* **San Lucas** Baja California Sur, NW Mexico
42 *E6* **San Lucas** *var.* Cabo San Lucas. Baja California Sur, W Mexico
42 *G11* **San Lucas, Cabo** *var.* San Lucas Cape. *headland* W Mexico
San Lucas Cape *see* San Lucas, Cabo
64 *J11* **San Luis** San Luis, C Argentina
44 *E4* **San Luis** Petén, NE Guatemala
42 *D2* **San Luis** *var.* San Luis Río Colorado. Sonora, NW Mexico
44 *M7* **San Luis** Región Autónoma Atlántico Norte, NE Nicaragua
38 *H15* **San Luis** Arizona, SW USA
39 *T8* **San Luis** Colorado, C USA
56 *J4* **San Luis** Falcón, N Venezuela
64 *J11* **San Luis** *off.* Provincia de San Luis. ◈ *province* C Argentina
43 *N12* **San Luis de la Paz** Guanajuato, C Mexico
42 *K8* **San Luis del Cordero** Durango, C Mexico
42 *D4* **San Luis, Isla** *island* NW Mexico
44 *E6* **San Luis Jilotepeque** Jalapa, SE Guatemala
59 *M16* **San Luis, Laguna de** ◎ NW Bolivia
37 *P13* **San Luis Obispo** California, W USA
39 *R7* **San Luis Peak** ▲ Colorado, C USA
43 *N11* **San Luis Potosí** San Luis Potosí, C Mexico
43 *N11* **San Luis Potosí** ◈ *state* C Mexico
37 *O10* **San Luis Reservoir** ▣ California, W USA
San Luis Río Colorado *see* San Luis
39 *S8* **San Luis Valley** *basin* Colorado, C USA
109 *C19* **Sanluri** Sardegna, Italy, C Mediterranean Sea
63 *D23* **San Manuel** Buenos Aires, E Argentina
38 *M15* **San Manuel** Arizona, SW USA
108 *F11* **San Marcello Pistoiese** Toscana, C Italy
109 *N20* **San Marco Argentano** Calabria, SW Italy
56 *E6* **San Marcos** Sucre, N Colombia
44 *M14* **San Marcos** San José, C Costa Rica
44 *B5* **San Marcos** San Marcos, W Guatemala
44 *F6* **San Marcos** Ocotepeque, SW Honduras
43 *O16* **San Marcos** Guerrero, S Mexico
27 *S11* **San Marcos** Texas, SW USA
44 *A5* **San Marcos** *off.* Departamento de San Marcos. ◈ *department* W Guatemala
San Marcos de Arica *see* Arica
42 *E6* **San Marcos, Isla** *island* W Mexico
108 *H11* **San Marino** ● (San Marino) C San Marino
108 *I11* **San Marino** *off.* Republic of San Marino. ◆ *republic* S Europe
64 *I11* **San Martín** Mendoza, C Argentina
56 *F11* **San Martín** Meta, C Colombia
58 *D11* **San Martín** *off.* Departamento de San Martín. ◈ *department* C Peru
204 *I5* **San Martín** *Argentinian research station* Antarctica
65 *H16* **San Martín de los Andes** Neuquén, W Argentina
106 *M8* **San Martín de Valdeiglesias** Madrid, C Spain
65 *G21* **San Martín, Lago** *var.* Lago O'Higgins. ◎ S Argentina
108 *H6* **San Martino di Castrozza** Trentino-Alto Adige, N Italy
59 *N16* **San Martín, Río** ≈ N Bolivia
San Martín Texmelucan *see* Texmelucan
37 *N9* **San Mateo** California, W USA
57 *O6* **San Mateo** Anzoátegui, NE Venezuela
44 *B4* **San Mateo Ixtatán** Huehuetenango, W Guatemala
59 *Q18* **San Matías** Santa Cruz, E Bolivia
65 *K16* **San Matías, Golfo** *var.* Gulf of San Matías. *gulf* E Argentina
San Matías, Gulf of *see* San Matías
13 *O8* **Sanmaur** Québec, SE Canada
167 *T10* **Sanmen Wan** *bay* E China
166 *M6* **Sanmenxia** *var.* Shan Xian. Henan, C China
Sânmiclăuș Mare *see* Sânnicolau Mare
63 *D14* **San Miguel** Corrientes, NE Argentina
59 *L16* **San Miguel** Beni, N Bolivia
44 *G8* **San Miguel** San Miguel, SE El Salvador
42 *L6* **San Miguel** Coahuila de Zaragoza, N Mexico
42 *J9* **San Miguel** *var.* San Miguel de Cruces. Durango, C Mexico
45 *U16* **San Miguel** Panamá, SE Panama
37 *P12* **San Miguel** California, W USA
44 *B9* **San Miguel** ◈ *department* E El Salvador
43 *N13* **San Miguel de Allende** Guanajuato, C Mexico
San Miguel de Cruces *see* San Miguel
San Miguel de Ibarra *see* Ibarra
63 *D21* **San Miguel del Monte** Buenos Aires, E Argentina
64 *J7* **San Miguel de Tucumán** *var.* Tucumán. Tucumán, N Argentina
45 *V16* **San Miguel, Golfo de** *gulf* S Panama
37 *P15* **San Miguel Island** *island* California, W USA
44 *L11* **San Miguelito** Río San Juan, S Nicaragua
45 *T15* **San Miguelito** Panamá, C Panama
59 *N18* **San Miguel, Río** ≈ E Bolivia
58 *D6* **San Miguel, Río** ≈ Colombia/Ecuador
42 *I7* **San Miguel, Río** ≈ N Mexico
44 *G8* **San Miguel, Volcán de** Ѫ SE El Salvador
167 *Q12* **Sanming** Fujian, SE China
108 *F11* **San Miniato** Toscana, C Italy
San Murezzan *see* St.Moritz
Sannār *see* Sennar
109 *M15* **Sannicandro Garganico** Puglia, SE Italy
42 *H6* **San Nicolás** Sonora, NW Mexico
63 *C19* **San Nicolás de los Arroyos** Buenos Aires, E Argentina
37 *R16* **San Nicolas Island** *island* Channel Islands, California, W USA
Sânnicolaul-Mare *see* Sânnicolau Mare

◆ Country
● Country Capital
◇ Dependent Territory
○ Dependent Territory Capital
◈ Administrative Region
✈ International Airport
▲ Mountain
⛰ Mountain Range
Ѫ Volcano
≈ River
◎ Lake
▣ Reservoir

118 E11 **Sânnicolau Mare** *var.* Sânnicolaul-Mare, *Hung.* Nagyszentmiklós; *prev.* Sânmiclăuş Mare, Sînnicolau Mare. Timiş, W Romania
126 L15 **Sannikova, Proliv** *strait* NE Russian Federation
78 K16 **Sanniquellie** *var.* Saniquillie. NE Liberia
172 N9 **Sannohe** Aomori, Honshū, C Japan
Sanntaler Alpen *see* Savinjske Alpe
171 K15 **Sano** Tochigi, Honshū, S Japan
113 O17 **Sanok** Krosno, SE Poland
56 E5 **San Onofre** Sucre, NW Colombia
59 K21 **San Pablo** Potosí, S Bolivia
179 P11 **San Pablo** *off.* San Pablo City. Luzon, N Philippines
San Pablo Balleza *see* Balleza
37 N8 **San Pablo Bay** *bay* California, W USA
42 C6 **San Pablo, Punta** *headland* W Mexico
45 R16 **San Pablo, Río** ≈ C Panama
179 Q11 **San Pascual** Burias Island, C Philippines
123 Jj16 **San Pawl il-Bahar** *Eng.* Saint Paul's Bay. E Malta
63 C19 **San Pedro** Buenos Aires, E Argentina
64 K5 **San Pedro** Jujuy, N Argentina
62 G13 **San Pedro** Misiones, NE Argentina
44 H1 **San Pedro** Corozal, NE Belize
42 L8 **San Pedro** *var.* San Pedro de las Colonias. Coahuila de Zaragoza, NE Mexico
64 O5 **San Pedro** San Pedro, SE Paraguay
64 O6 **San Pedro** *off.* Departamento de San Pedro. ◈ *department* C Paraguay
79 N16 **San Pedro** ✕ (Yamoussoukro) C Ivory Coast
46 G6 **San Pedro** ≈ C Cuba
San Pedro *see* San Pedro del Pinatar
78 M17 **San-Pédro** S Ivory Coast
44 D5 **San Pedro Carchá** Alta Verapaz, C Guatemala
37 S16 **San Pedro Channel** *channel* California, W USA
64 I5 **San Pedro de Atacama** Antofagasta, N Chile
San Pedro de Durazno *see* Durazno
42 G5 **San Pedro de la Cueva** Sonora, NW Mexico
San Pedro de las Colonias *see* San Pedro
58 B11 **San Pedro de Lloc** La Libertad, NW Peru
107 S13 **San Pedro del Pinatar** *var.* San Pedro. Murcia, SE Spain
47 P9 **San Pedro de Macorís** SE Dominican Republic
42 C3 **San Pedro Mártir, Sierra** ▲▲ NW Mexico
San Pedro Pochutla *see* Pochutla
44 D2 **San Pedro, Río** ≈ Guatemala/Mexico
42 K10 **San Pedro, Río** ≈ C Mexico
106 J10 **San Pedro, Sierra de** ▲▲ W Spain
44 G5 **San Pedro Sula** Cortés, NW Honduras
San Pedro Tapanatepec *see* Tapanatepec
64 I4 **San Pedro, Volcán** ▲ N Chile
108 E7 **San Pellegrino Terme** Lombardia, N Italy
27 T16 **San Perlita** Texas, SW USA
San Pietro *see* Supetar
San Pietro del Carso *see* Pivka
109 A20 **San Pietro, Isola di** *island* W Italy
34 K7 **Sanpoil River** ≈ Washington, NW USA
171 L12 **Sanpoku** *var.* Sampoku. Niigata, Honshū, C Japan
42 C3 **San Quintín** Baja California, NW Mexico
42 B3 **San Quintín, Bahía de** *bay* NW Mexico
42 B3 **San Quintín, Cabo** *headland* NW Mexico
64 I12 **San Rafael** Mendoza, W Argentina
43 N9 **San Rafael** Nuevo León, NE Mexico
36 M8 **San Rafael** California, W USA
39 Q11 **San Rafael** New Mexico, SW USA
56 H4 **San Rafael** *var.* El Moján. Zulia, NW Venezuela
44 J8 **San Rafael del Norte** Jinotega, NW Nicaragua
44 J10 **San Rafael del Sur** Managua, SW Nicaragua
38 M5 **San Rafael Knob** ▲ Utah, W USA
37 Q14 **San Rafael Mountains** ▲▲ California, W USA
44 M13 **San Ramón** Alajuela, C Costa Rica
59 E14 **San Ramón** Junín, C Peru
63 F19 **San Ramón** Canelones, S Uruguay
64 K5 **San Ramón de la Nueva Orán** Salta, N Argentina
59 O16 **San Ramón, Río** ≈ E Bolivia
108 B11 **San Remo** Liguria, NW Italy
56 J3 **San Román, Cabo** *headland* NW Venezuela
63 C15 **San Roque** Corrientes, NE Argentina
196 I4 **San Roque** Saipan, S Northern Mariana Islands
106 K16 **San Roque** Andalucía, S Spain
27 R9 **San Saba** Texas, SW USA
27 Q9 **San Saba River** ≈ Texas, SW USA
63 D17 **San Salvador** Entre Ríos, E Argentina
44 F7 **San Salvador** ● (El Salvador) San Salvador, SW El Salvador
44 A10 **San Salvador** ◈ *department* C El Salvador
44 F8 **San Salvador** ✕ La Paz, S El Salvador
46 K4 **San Salvador** *prev.* Watlings Island. *island* E Bahamas
64 J5 **San Salvador de Jujuy** *var.* Jujuy. Jujuy, N Argentina
44 F7 **San Salvador, Volcán de** ☒ C El Salvador
79 Q14 **Sansanné-Mango** *var.* Mango. N Togo
47 S5 **San Sebastián** W Puerto Rico
65 J24 **San Sebastián, Bahía** *bay* S Argentina
Sansenhō *see* Sach'ŏn
108 H12 **Sansepolcro** Toscana, C Italy
109 M16 **San Severo** Puglia, SE Italy
114 F11 **Sanski Most** NW Bosnia and Herzegovina
176 Ww9 **Sansundi** Irian Jaya, E Indonesia
106 K11 **Santa Amalia** Extremadura, W Spain
62 F13 **Santa Ana** Misiones, NE Argentina
59 L16 **Santa Ana** Beni, N Bolivia
44 E7 **Santa Ana** Santa Ana, NW El Salvador
42 F4 **Santa Ana** Sonora, NW Mexico
37 T16 **Santa Ana** California, W USA
57 N6 **Santa Ana** Nueva Esparta, NE Venezuela
44 A9 **Santa Ana** ◈ *department* NW El Salvador
Santa Ana de Coro *see* Coro
44 E7 **Santa Ana, Volcán de** *var.* La Matepec. ☒ W El Salvador
42 J7 **Santa Barbara** Chihuahua, N Mexico
37 Q14 **Santa Barbara** California, W USA
44 G6 **Santa Bárbara** Santa Bárbara, W Honduras
56 L11 **Santa Bárbara** Amazonas, S Venezuela
56 I7 **Santa Bárbara** Barinas, W Venezuela
44 F5 **Santa Bárbara** ◈ *department* NW Honduras
Santa Bárbara *see* Iscuandé
37 Q15 **Santa Barbara Channel** *channel* California, W USA
Santa Bárbara de Samaná *see* Samaná
37 R16 **Santa Barbara Island** *island* Channel Islands, California, W USA
56 E5 **Santa Catalina** Bolívar, N Colombia
45 R15 **Santa Catalina** Bocas del Toro, W Panama
37 T17 **Santa Catalina, Gulf of** *gulf* California, W USA
42 F8 **Santa Catalina, Isla** *island* W Mexico
37 S16 **Santa Catalina Island** *island* Channel Islands, California, W USA
43 N8 **Santa Catarina** Nuevo León, NE Mexico
62 H13 **Santa Catarina** *off.* Estado de Santa Catarina. ◈ *state* S Brazil
Santa Catarina de Tepehuanes *see* Tepehuanes
62 L13 **Santa Catarina, Ilha de** *island* S Brazil
47 Q16 **Santa Catherina** Curaçao, C Netherlands Antilles
44 K5 **Santa Clara** Villa Clara, C Cuba
37 N9 **Santa Clara** California, W USA
38 J8 **Santa Clara** Utah, W USA
Santa Clara *see* Santa Clara de Olimar
63 F18 **Santa Clara de Olimar** *var.* Santa Clara. Cerro Largo, NE Uruguay
63 A17 **Santa Clara de Saguier** Santa Fe, C Argentina
Santa Coloma *see* Santa Coloma de Gramenet
107 X5 **Santa Coloma de Farners** *var.* Santa Coloma de Farnés. Cataluña, NE Spain
Santa Coloma de Farnés *see* Santa Coloma de Farners
107 W6 **Santa Coloma de Gramanet** *var.* Santa Coloma. Cataluña, NE Spain
106 G2 **Santa Comba** Galicia, NW Spain
Santa Comba *see* Uaco Cungo
106 H8 **Santa Comba Dão** Viseu, N Portugal
84 C10 **Santa Cruz** Uíge, NW Angola
59 N19 **Santa Cruz** *var.* Santa Cruz de la Sierra. Santa Cruz, C Bolivia
64 G12 **Santa Cruz** Libertador, C Chile
44 K13 **Santa Cruz** Guanacaste, W Costa Rica
46 I12 **Santa Cruz** W Jamaica
66 P6 **Santa Cruz** Madeira, Portugal, NE Atlantic Ocean
37 N10 **Santa Cruz** California, W USA
65 H20 **Santa Cruz** *off.* Provincia de Santa Cruz. ◈ *province* S Argentina
59 O18 **Santa Cruz** ◈ *department* E Bolivia
Santa Cruz *see* Viru-Viru
Santa Cruz *see* Puerto Santa Cruz
Santa Cruz Barillas *see* Barillas
61 O18 **Santa Cruz Cabrália** Bahia, E Brazil
Santa Cruz de El Seibo *see* El Seibo
66 N11 **Santa Cruz de la Palma** La Palma, Islas Canarias, Spain, NE Atlantic Ocean
Santa Cruz de la Sierra *see* Santa Cruz
107 O9 **Santa Cruz de la Zarza** Castilla-La Mancha, C Spain
44 C5 **Santa Cruz del Quiché** Quiché, W Guatemala
107 N8 **Santa Cruz del Retamar** Castilla-La Mancha, C Spain
Santa Cruz del Seibo *see* El Seibo
46 G7 **Santa Cruz del Sur** Camagüey, C Cuba
107 O11 **Santa Cruz de Mudela** Castilla-La Mancha, C Spain
66 Q11 **Santa Cruz de Tenerife** Tenerife, Islas Canarias, Spain, NE Atlantic Ocean
66 P11 **Santa Cruz de Tenerife** ◈ *province* Islas Canarias, Spain, NE Atlantic Ocean
62 K9 **Santa Cruz do Rio Pardo** São Paulo, S Brazil
63 H15 **Santa Cruz do Sul** Rio Grande do Sul, S Brazil
59 C17 **Santa Cruz, Isla** *var.* Indefatigable Island, Isla Chávez. *island* Galapagos Islands, Ecuador, E Pacific Ocean
42 F8 **Santa Cruz, Isla** *island* W Mexico
37 Q15 **Santa Cruz Island** *island* California, W USA
195 X8 **Santa Cruz Islands** *island group* E Solomon Islands
65 I22 **Santa Cruz, Río** ≈ S Argentina
38 L15 **Santa Cruz River** ≈ Arizona, SW USA
63 C17 **Santa Elena** Entre Ríos, E Argentina
44 F2 **Santa Elena** Cayo, W Belize
27 R16 **Santa Elena** Texas, SW USA
58 A7 **Santa Elena, Bahía de** *bay* W Ecuador
57 R10 **Santa Elena de Uairén** Bolívar, E Venezuela
44 K12 **Santa Elena, Península** *peninsula* NW Costa Rica
58 A7 **Santa Elena, Punta** *headland* W Ecuador
106 L11 **Santa Eufemia** Andalucía, S Spain
109 N21 **Santa Eufemia, Golfo di** *gulf* S Italy
107 S4 **Santa Eulalia de Gállego** Aragón, NE Spain
107 V11 **Santa Eulalia del Río** Eivissa, Spain, W Mediterranean Sea
63 B17 **Santa Fe** Santa Fe, C Argentina
107 N14 **Santa Fe** Andalucía, S Spain
39 S10 **Santa Fe** *state capital* New Mexico, SW USA
63 B15 **Santa Fe** *off.* Provincia de Santa Fe. ◈ *province* C Argentina
Santa Fe *see* Bogotá
46 C6 **Santa Fé** *var.* La Fe. Isla de la Juventud, W Cuba
45 R16 **Santa Fé** Veraguas, C Panama
Santa Fe de Bogotá *see* Bogotá
62 J7 **Santa Fé do Sul** São Paulo, S Brazil
59 B18 **Santa Fe, Isla** *var.* Barrington Island. *island* Galapagos Islands, Ecuador, E Pacific Ocean
25 V9 **Santa Fe River** ≈ Florida, SE USA
61 M15 **Santa Filomena** Piauí, E Brazil
42 G10 **Santa Genoveva** ▲ W Mexico
159 S14 **Santahar** Rajshahi, NW Bangladesh
62 G11 **Santa Helena** Paraná, S Brazil
56 J5 **Santa Inés** Lara, N Venezuela
65 G24 **Santa Inés, Isla** *island* S Chile
64 J13 **Santa Isabel** La Pampa, C Argentina
45 U14 **Santa Isabel** Colón, N Panama
195 W14 **Santa Isabel** *var.* Bughotu. *island* N Solomon Islands
Santa Isabel *see* Malabo
60 D11 **Santa Isabel do Rio Negro** Amazonas, NW Brazil
63 C15 **Santa Lucia** Corrientes, NE Argentina
59 I17 **Santa Lucía** Puno, S Peru
63 F20 **Santa Lucía** *var.* Santa Lucia. Canelones, S Uruguay
44 B6 **Santa Lucía Cotzumalguapa** Escuintla, SW Guatemala
109 L23 **Santa Lucia del Mela** Sicilia, Italy, C Mediterranean Sea
37 O11 **Santa Lucia Range** ▲▲ California, W USA
42 D9 **Santa Margarita, Isla** *island* W Mexico
63 G15 **Santa Maria** Rio Grande do Sul, S Brazil
37 P13 **Santa Maria** California, W USA
66 Q4 **Santa Maria** ✕ Santa Maria, Azores, Portugal, NE Atlantic Ocean
66 P3 **Santa Maria** *island* Azores, Portugal, NE Atlantic Ocean
197 C11 **Santa Maria** *var.* Gaua. *island* Banks Islands, N Vanuatu
64 J7 **Santa María** Catamarca, N Argentina
Santa María Asunción Tlaxiaco *see* Tlaxiaco
42 G9 **Santa María, Bahía** *bay* W Mexico
85 L21 **Santa Maria, Cabo de** *headland* S Mozambique
106 G15 **Santa Maria, Cabo de** *headland* S Portugal
46 J4 **Santa Maria, Cape** *headland* Long Island, C Bahamas
109 J17 **Santa Maria Capua Vetere** Campania, S Italy
61 M17 **Santa Maria da Vitória** Bahia, E Brazil
57 N9 **Santa Maria de Erebato** Bolívar, SE Venezuela
106 G7 **Santa Maria de Feira** Aveiro, N Portugal
57 N6 **Santa María de Ipire** Guárico, C Venezuela
Santa Maria del Buen Aire *see* Buenos Aires
42 J8 **Santa María del Oro** Durango, C Mexico
43 N12 **Santa María del Río** San Luis Potosí, C Mexico
Santa Maria di Castellabate *see* Castellabate
109 Q20 **Santa Maria di Leuca, Capo** *headland* SE Italy
110 K10 **Santa Maria im Münstertal** Graubünden, SE Switzerland
59 B18 **Santa María, Isla** *var.* Isla Floreana, Charles Island. *island* Galapagos Islands, Ecuador, E Pacific Ocean
42 J3 **Santa María, Laguna de** ◎ N Mexico
63 G16 **Santa Maria, Rio** ≈ S Brazil
45 R16 **Santa María, Río** ≈ C Panama
38 J12 **Santa Maria River** ≈ Arizona, SW USA
109 G15 **Santa Marinella** Lazio, C Italy
56 F4 **Santa Marta** Magdalena, N Colombia
106 J11 **Santa Marta** Extremadura, W Spain
Santa Maura *see* Lefkáda
37 S15 **Santa Monica** California, W USA
118 F10 **Sântana** *Ger.* Sankt Anna, *Hung.* Újszentanna; *prev.* Sîntana. Arad, W Romania
63 F16 **Santana, Coxilha de** *hill range* S Brazil
63 H16 **Santana da Boa Vista** Rio Grande do Sul, S Brazil
63 F16 **Santana do Livramento** *prev.* Livramento. Rio Grande do Sul, S Brazil
107 N2 **Santander** Cantabria, N Spain
56 F8 **Santander** *off.* Departamento de Santander. ◈ *province* C Colombia
Santander Jiménez *see* Jiménez
Sant'Andrea *see* Svetac
109 B20 **Sant'Antioco** Sardegna, Italy, C Mediterranean Sea
Santañy *see* Santanyí
106 J13 **Santa Olalla del Cala** Andalucía, S Spain
37 R15 **Santa Paula** California, W USA
38 L4 **Santaquin** Utah, W USA
60 I12 **Santarém** Pará, N Brazil
106 G10 **Santarém** *anc.* Scalabis. Santarém, W Portugal
106 G10 **Santarém** ◈ *district* C Portugal
46 F4 **Santaren Channel** *channel* W Bahamas
56 K10 **Santa Rita** Vichada, E Colombia
196 B16 **Santa Rita** SW Guam
44 H5 **Santa Rita** Cortés, NW Honduras
42 E9 **Santa Rita** Baja California Sur, W Mexico
56 H5 **Santa Rita** Zulia, NW Venezuela
61 I19 **Santa Rita de Araguaia** Goiás, S Brazil
Santa Rita de Cassia *see* Cássia
63 D14 **Santa Rosa** Corrientes, NE Argentina
64 K13 **Santa Rosa** La Pampa, C Argentina
63 G14 **Santa Rosa** Rio Grande do Sul, S Brazil
60 E10 **Santa Rosa** Roraima, N Brazil
58 B8 **Santa Rosa** El Oro, SW Ecuador
59 I16 **Santa Rosa** Puno, S Peru
36 M7 **Santa Rosa** California, W USA
39 U11 **Santa Rosa** New Mexico, SW USA
57 O6 **Santa Rosa** Anzoátegui, NE Venezuela
44 A3 **Santa Rosa** *off.* Departamento de Santa Rosa. ◈ *department* SE Guatemala
Santa Rosa *see* Santa Rosa de Copán
65 J15 **Santa Rosa, Bajo de** *basin* E Argentina
44 F6 **Santa Rosa de Copán** *var.* Santa Rosa. Copán, W Honduras
56 E8 **Santa Rosa de Osos** Antioquia, C Colombia
37 Q15 **Santa Rosa Island** *island* California, W USA
25 O9 **Santa Rosa Island** *island* Florida, SE USA
42 E6 **Santa Rosalía** Baja California Sur, W Mexico
56 K6 **Santa Rosalía** Portuguesa, NW Venezuela
196 C15 **Santa Rosa, Mount** ▲ NE Guam
37 V16 **Santa Rosa Mountains** ▲▲ California, W USA
37 T2 **Santa Rosa Range** ▲▲ Nevada, W USA
64 M8 **Santa Sylvina** Chaco, N Argentina
Santa Tecla *see* Nueva San Salvador
63 B19 **Santa Teresa** Santa Fe, C Argentina
61 O20 **Santa Teresa** Espírito Santo, SE Brazil
63 E21 **Santa Teresita** Buenos Aires, E Argentina
63 H19 **Santa Vitória do Palmar** Rio Grande do Sul, S Brazil
37 Q14 **Santa Ynez River** ≈ California, W USA
Sant Carles de la Rápida *see* Sant Carles de la Ràpita
107 U7 **Sant Carles de la Ràpita** *var.* Sant Carles de la Rápida. Cataluña, NE Spain
107 W5 **Sant Celoni** Cataluña, NE Spain
37 U17 **Santee** California, W USA
23 T13 **Santee River** ≈ South Carolina, SE USA
42 K15 **San Telmo, Punta** *headland* SW Mexico
109 O17 **Santeramo in Colle** Puglia, SE Italy
109 M23 **San Teresa di Riva** Sicilia, Italy, C Mediterranean Sea
107 X5 **Sant Feliu de Guíxols** *var.* San Feliú de Guixols. Cataluña, NE Spain
107 W6 **Sant Feliu de Llobregat** Cataluña, NE Spain
108 C7 **Santhià** Piemonte, NE Italy
63 F15 **Santiago** Rio Grande do Sul, S Brazil
64 H11 **Santiago** *var.* Gran Santiago. ● (Chile) Santiago, C Chile
47 N8 **Santiago** *var.* Santiago de los Caballeros. N Dominican Republic
42 G10 **Santiago** Baja California Sur, W Mexico
43 O8 **Santiago** Nuevo León, NE Mexico
45 R16 **Santiago** Veraguas, S Panama
59 E16 **Santiago** Ica, SW Peru
106 G3 **Santiago** *var.* Santiago de Compostela, *Eng.* Compostella; *anc.* Campus Stellae. Galicia, NW Spain
64 H11 **Santiago** *off.* Región Metropolitana de Santiago, *var.* Metropolitan. ◈ *region* C Chile
64 H11 **Santiago** ✕ Santiago, C Chile
106 G3 **Santiago** ✕ Galicia, NW Spain
78 D10 **Santiago** *var.* São Tiago. *island* Ilhas de Sotavento, S Cape Verde
Santiago *see* Santiago de Cuba, Cuba
Santiago *see* Grande de Santiago, Río, Mexico
44 B6 **Santiago Atitlán** Sololá, SW Guatemala
45 Q16 **Santiago, Cerro** ▲ W Panama
Santiago de Compostela *see* Santiago
46 I8 **Santiago de Cuba** *var.* Santiago. Santiago de Cuba, E Cuba
Santiago de Guayaquil *see* Guayaquil
64 K8 **Santiago del Estero** Santiago del Estero, C Argentina
63 A15 **Santiago del Estero** *off.* Provincia de Santiago del Estero. ◈ *province* N Argentina
42 I8 **Santiago de los Caballeros** Sinaloa, W Mexico
Santiago de los Caballeros *see* Santiago, Dominican Republic
Santiago de los Caballeros *see* Guatemala, Guatemala
44 F8 **Santiago de María** Usulután, SE El Salvador
106 F12 **Santiago do Cacém** Setúbal, S Portugal
42 J12 **Santiago Ixcuintla** Nayarit, C Mexico
Santiago Jamiltepec *see* Jamiltepec
26 L11 **Santiago Mountains** ▲▲ Texas, SW USA
42 J9 **Santiago Papasquiaro** Durango, C Mexico
Santiago Pinotepa Nacional *see* Pinotepa Nacional
58 C8 **Santiago, Río** ≈ N Peru
42 M10 **San Tiburcio** Zacatecas, C Mexico
107 N2 **Santillana** Cantabria, N Spain
56 I5 **San Timoteo** Zulia, NW Venezuela
Santi Quaranta *see* Sarandë
Santissima Trinidad *see* Chilung
107 O12 **Santisteban del Puerto** Andalucía, S Spain
107 U7 **Sant Jordi, Golf de** *gulf* NE Spain
107 T8 **Sant Mateu** País Valenciano, E Spain
27 S7 **Santo** Texas, SW USA
Santo *see* Espiritu Santo
62 M10 **Santo Amaro, Ilha de** *island* SE Brazil
53 W10 **Santo André** São Paulo, S Brazil
63 G14 **Santo Ângelo** Rio Grande do Sul, S Brazil
78 C9 **Santo Antão** *island* Ilhas de Barlavento, N Cape Verde
62 J10 **Santo Antônio da Platina** Paraná, S Brazil
60 C13 **Santo Antônio do Içá** Amazonas, N Brazil
59 Q18 **Santo Corazón, Río** ≈ E Bolivia
46 E5 **Santo Domingo** Villa Clara, C Cuba
47 O9 **Santo Domingo** *prev.* Ciudad Trujillo. ● (Dominican Republic) SE Dominican Republic
42 E8 **Santo Domingo** Baja California Sur, W Mexico
42 M10 **Santo Domingo** San Luis Potosí, C Mexico
44 L10 **Santo Domingo** Chontales, S Nicaragua
107 P4 **Santo Domingo de la Calzada** La Rioja, N Spain
58 B6 **Santo Domingo de los Colorados** Pichincha, NW Ecuador
Santo Domingo Tehuantepec *see* Tehuantepec
57 O6 **San Tomé** Anzoátegui, NE Venezuela
San Tomé de Guayana *see* Ciudad Guayana
107 R13 **Santomera** Murcia, SE Spain
107 O2 **Santoña** Cantabria, N Spain
Santorin/Santoríni *see* Thíra
62 M10 **Santos** São Paulo, S Brazil
67 J17 **Santos Plateau** *undersea feature* SW Atlantic Ocean
106 G6 **Santo Tirso** Porto, N Portugal
42 B2 **Santo Tomás** Baja California, NW Mexico
44 L10 **Santo Tomás** Chontales, S Nicaragua
44 G5 **Santo Tomás de Castilla** Izabal, E Guatemala
42 B2 **Santo Tomás, Punta** *headland* NW Mexico
59 H16 **Santo Tomás, Río** ≈ C Peru
59 B18 **Santo Tomás, Volcán** ☒ Galapagos Islands, Ecuador, E Pacific Ocean
63 F14 **Santo Tomé** Corrientes, NE Argentina
Santo Tomé de Guayana *see* Ciudad Guayana
100 H10 **Santpoort** Noord-Holland, W Netherlands
Santurce *see* Santurtzi
107 O2 **Santurtzi** *var.* Santurce, Santurzi. País Vasco, N Spain
Santurzi *see* Santurtzi
65 G20 **San Valentín, Cerro** ▲ S Chile
44 F8 **San Vicente** San Vicente, C El Salvador
42 C2 **San Vicente** Baja California, NW Mexico
196 H6 **San Vicente** Saipan, S Northern Mariana Islands
44 B9 **San Vicente** ◈ *department* E El Salvador
106 I10 **San Vicente de Alcántara** Extremadura, W Spain
107 N2 **San Vicente de Barakaldo** *var.* Baracaldo. País Vasco, N Spain
59 E15 **San Vicente de Cañete** *var.* Cañete. Lima, W Peru
106 M2 **San Vicente de la Barquera** Cantabria, N Spain
56 E12 **San Vicente del Caguán** Caquetá, S Colombia
44 F8 **San Vicente, Volcán de** ☒ C El Salvador
45 O15 **San Vito** Puntarenas, SE Costa Rica
108 I7 **San Vito al Tagliamento** Friuli-Venezia Giulia, NE Italy
109 H23 **San Vito, Capo** *headland* Sicilia, Italy, C Mediterranean Sea
109 P18 **San Vito dei Normanni** Puglia, SE Italy
166 L17 **Sanya** *var.* Ya Xian. Hainan, S China
85 J16 **Sanyati** ≈ N Zimbabwe
27 Q16 **San Ygnacio** Texas, SW USA
166 L6 **Sanyuan** Shaanxi, C China
126 Ll12 **Sanyyakhtakh** Respublika Sakha (Yakutiya), NE Russian Federation
84 C10 **Sanza Pombo** Uíge, NW Angola
Sanzyō *see* Sanjō
106 G14 **São Bartolomeu de Messines** Faro, S Portugal
62 M10 **São Bernardo do Campo** São Paulo, S Brazil
63 F15 **São Borja** Rio Grande do Sul, S Brazil
106 H14 **São Brás de Alportel** Faro, S Portugal
62 M10 **São Caetano do Sul** São Paulo, S Brazil
62 L9 **São Carlos** São Paulo, S Brazil
61 P16 **São Cristóvão** Sergipe, E Brazil
63 F15 **São Francisco de Assis** Rio Grande do Sul, S Brazil
60 K13 **São Félix** Pará, NE Brazil
São Félix *see* São Félix do Araguaia
61 J16 **São Félix do Araguaia** *var.* São Félix. Mato Grosso, W Brazil
61 J14 **São Félix do Xingu** Pará, NE Brazil
62 Q9 **São Fidélis** Rio de Janeiro, SE Brazil
78 D10 **São Filipe** Fogo, S Cape Verde
62 K12 **São Francisco do Sul** Santa Catarina, S Brazil
62 K12 **São Francisco, Ilha de** *island* S Brazil
61 P16 **São Francisco, Rio** ≈ E Brazil
63 G16 **São Gabriel** Rio Grande do Sul, S Brazil
62 P10 **São Gonçalo** Rio de Janeiro, SE Brazil
83 H23 **Sao Hill** Iringa, S Tanzania
62 R9 **São João da Barra** Rio de Janeiro, SE Brazil
106 G7 **São João da Madeira** Aveiro, N Portugal
60 M12 **São João de Cortês** Maranhão, E Brazil
61 M21 **São João del Rei** Minas Gerais, NE Brazil
61 N15 **São João do Piauí** Piauí, E Brazil
61 N14 **São João dos Patos** Maranhão, E Brazil
60 C11 **São Joaquim** Amazonas, NW Brazil
63 J14 **São Joaquim** Santa Catarina, S Brazil
62 L7 **São Joaquim da Barra** São Paulo, S Brazil
66 N2 **São Jorge** *island* Azores, Portugal, NE Atlantic Ocean
63 K14 **São José** Santa Catarina, S Brazil
62 M8 **São José do Rio Pardo** São Paulo, S Brazil
62 K8 **São José do Rio Preto** São Paulo, S Brazil
62 N10 **São Jose dos Campos** São Paulo, S Brazil
63 I17 **São Lourenço do Sul** Rio Grande do Sul, S Brazil
60 F11 **São Luís** Roraima, N Brazil
60 M12 **São Luís** *state capital* Maranhão, NE Brazil
60 M12 **São Luís, Ilha de** *island* NE Brazil
63 F14 **São Luiz Gonzaga** Rio Grande do Sul, S Brazil
106 I10 **São Mamede** ▲ C Portugal
São Mandol *see* São Manuel, Rio
49 U8 **Sao Manuel** ≈ C Brazil
61 H15 **São Manuel, Rio** *var.* São Mandol, Teles Pirés. ≈ C Brazil
60 C11 **São Marcelino** Amazonas, NW Brazil
60 N12 **São Marcos, Baía de** *bay* N Brazil
61 O20 **São Mateus** Espírito Santo, SE Brazil
62 J12 **São Mateus do Sul** Paraná, S Brazil
66 P3 **São Miguel** *island* Azores, Portugal, NE Atlantic Ocean
62 G13 **São Miguel d'Oeste** Santa Catarina, S Brazil
47 P9 **Saona, Isla** *island* SE Dominican Republic
180 H12 **Saondzou** ▲ Grande Comore, NW Comoros
105 R10 **Saône** ≈ E France
105 Q9 **Saône-et-Loire** ◈ *department* C France
78 D9 **São Nicolau** *Eng.* Saint Nicholas. *island* Ilhas de Barlavento, N Cape Verde
62 M10 **São Paulo** *state capital* São Paulo, S Brazil
62 K9 **São Paulo** *off.* Estado de São Paulo. ◈ *state* S Brazil
São Paulo de Loanda *see* Luanda
São Pedro do Rio Grande do Sul *see* Rio Grande
106 H7 **São Pedro do Sul** Viseu, N Portugal
66 K13 **São Pedro e São Paulo** *undersea feature* C Atlantic Ocean
61 M14 **São Raimundo das Mangabeiras** Maranhão, E Brazil
61 Q14 **São Roque, Cabo de** *headland* E Brazil
São Salvador/São Salvador do Congo *see* M'Banza Congo, Zaire, Angola
São Salvador *see* Salvador, Brazil
62 N10 **São Sebastião, Ilha de** *island* S Brazil
85 N19 **São Sebastião, Ponta** *headland* C Mozambique
106 F13 **São Teotónio** Beja, S Portugal
São Tiago *see* Santiago
81 B18 **São Tomé** ● (Sao Tome and Principe) São Tomé, S Sao Tome and Principe
81 B18 **São Tomé** ✕ São Tomé, S Sao Tome and Principe
81 B18 **São Tomé** *Eng.* Saint Thomas. *island* S Sao Tome and Principe
81 B17 **Sao Tome and Principe** *off.* Democratic Republic of Sao Tome and Principe. ◆ *republic* E Atlantic Ocean
76 H9 **Saoura, Oued** ≈ NW Algeria
62 M10 **São Vicente** *Eng.* Saint Vincent. São Paulo, S Brazil
66 O5 **São Vicente** Madeira, Portugal, NE Atlantic Ocean
78 C9 **São Vicente** *Eng.* Saint Vincent. *island* Ilhas de Barlavento, N Cape Verde
São Vicente, Cabo de *see* São Vicente, Cabo de
106 F14 **São Vicente, Cabo de** *Eng.* Cape Saint Vincent, *Port.* Cabo de São Vicente. *headland* S Portugal
Sápai *see* Sápes
Sapaleri, Cerro *see* Zapaleri, Cerro
175 Tt11 **Saparau, Pulau** *island* C Indonesia
Saparoea *see* Saparua
175 Tt11 **Saparua** *prev.* Saparoea. Pulau Saparau, C Indonesia
174 Hh8 **Sapat** Sumatera, W Indonesia
79 U17 **Sapele** Delta, S Nigeria
25 X7 **Sapelo Island** *island* Georgia, SE USA
25 X7 **Sapelo Sound** *sound* Georgia, SE USA
116 K13 **Sápes** *var.* Sápai. Anatolikí Makedonía kai Thráki, NE Greece
175 P16 **Sape, Selat** *strait* Nusa Tenggara, S Indonesia
117 D22 **Sapiéntza** *island* S Greece
63 I15 **Sapiranga** Rio Grande do Sul, S Brazil
116 K13 **Sápka** ▲ NE Greece
58 D11 **Saposoa** San Martín, N Peru
121 F16 **Sapotskin** *Pol.* Sopockinie, *Rus.* Sopotskin. Hrodzyenskaya Voblasts', W Belarus
79 P13 **Sapoui** *var.* Sapouy. S Burkina
Sapouy *see* Sapoui
144 F12 **Sappir** Southern, S Israel
172 O5 **Sapporo** Hokkaidō, NE Japan
109 M19 **Sapri** Campania, S Italy
174 Mm15 **Sapulu, Pulau** *island* S Indonesia
29 P9 **Sapulpa** Oklahoma, C USA
148 J4 **Saqqez** *var.* Saghez, Sakiz, Saqqiz. Kordestān, NW Iran
Saqqiz *see* Saqqez
145 U8 **Sarābādī** E Iraq
178 Hh11 **Sara Buri** *var.* Saraburi. Saraburi, C Thailand
26 K9 **Saragosa** Texas, SW USA
Saragossa *see* Zaragoza
Saragt *see* Serakhs
58 B8 **Saraguro** Loja, S Ecuador
130 M6 **Sarai** Ryazanskaya Oblast', W Russian Federation
Sarāi *see* Saray
160 M12 **Saraipāli** Madhya Pradesh, C India
155 T9 **Sarāi Sidhu** Punjab, E Pakistan
95 M15 **Säräisniemi** Oulu, C Finland
115 I14 **Sarajevo** ● (Bosnia and Herzegovina) SE Bosnia and Herzegovina
114 I13 **Sarajevo** ✕ C Bosnia and Herzegovina
149 V4 **Sarakhs** Khorāsān, NE Iran
117 H17 **Sarakíniko, Ákra** *headland* Évvoia, C Greece
117 I18 **Sarakinó** *island* Vóreioi Sporádes, Greece, Aegean Sea
131 V7 **Saraktash** Orenburgskaya Oblast', W Russian Federation
32 L15 **Sara, Lake** ▣ Illinois, N USA
25 N8 **Saraland** Alabama, S USA
57 V9 **Saramacca** ◈ *district* N Suriname
57 V10 **Saramacca Rivier** ≈ C Suriname
177 G2 **Saramati** ▲ N Myanmar
151 R10 **Saran'** *Kaz.* Saran. Karaganda, C Kazakhstan
20 K7 **Saranac Lake** New York, NE USA
20 K7 **Saranac River** ≈ New York, NE USA
Saranda *see* Sarandë
115 L23 **Sarandë** *var.* Saranda, *It.* Porto Edda; *prev.* Santi Quaranta. Vlorë, S Albania

◆ Country
● Country Capital
◇ Dependent Territory
○ Dependent Territory Capital
◈ Administrative Region
✕ International Airport
▲ Mountain
▲▲ Mountain Range
☒ Volcano
≈ River
◎ Lake
▣ Reservoir

63 H14 **Sarandi** Rio Grande do Sul, S Brazil
63 F19 **Sarandí del Yí** Durazno, C Uruguay
63 F19 **Sarandí Grande** Florida, S Uruguay
179 Rr17 **Sarangani Islands** *island group* S Philippines
131 P5 **Saransk** Respublika Mordoviya, W Russian Federation
117 C14 **Sarantáporos** ≈ N Greece
116 H9 **Sarantsi** Sofiyska Oblast, W Bulgaria
131 T3 **Sarapul** Udmurtskaya Respublika, NW Russian Federation
Sarâqeb *see* Sarāqib
144 I3 **Sarāqib** ***Fr.*** Sarâqeb. Idlib, N Syria
56 J5 **Sarare** Lara, N Venezuela
57 O10 **Sarariña** Amazonas, S Venezuela
149 S10 **Sar Ashk** Kermān, C Iran
25 V13 **Sarasota** Florida, SE USA
119 O11 **Sarata** Odes'ka Oblast', SW Ukraine
118 I10 **Sărăţel** ***Hung.*** Szeretfalva. Bistriţa-Năsăud, N Romania
27 X10 **Saratoga** Texas, SW USA
20 K10 **Saratoga Springs** New York, NE USA
131 P8 **Saratov** Saratovskaya Oblast', W Russian Federation
131 P8 **Saratovskaya Oblast'** ⬖ *province* W Russian Federation
131 Q7 **Saratovskoye Vodokhranilishche** ▣ W Russian Federation
Saravan/Saravane *see* Salavan
194 K12 **Sarawaget Range** ***var.*** Saruwaged Range. ⛰ C PNG
174 M5 **Sarawak** ⬖ *state* East Malaysia
Sarawak *see* Kuching
145 U6 **Sarāy** ***var.*** Sarāi. E Iraq
142 D10 **Saray** Tekirdağ, NW Turkey
78 J12 **Saraya** SE Senegal
149 W14 **Sarbāz** Sīstān va Balūchestān, SE Iran
149 U8 **Sarbīsheh** Khorāsān, E Iran
113 J24 **Sárbogárd** Fejér, C Hungary
Şărcad *see* Sarkad
29 S7 **Sarcoxie** Missouri, C USA
158 L11 **Sārda** ***Nep.*** Kali. ≈ India/Nepal
158 G10 **Sardārshahr** Rājasthān, NW India
109 C18 **Sardegna** ***Eng.*** Sardinia. ⬖ *region* Italy, C Mediterranean Sea
109 A18 **Sardegna** ***Eng.*** Sardinia. *island* Italy, C Mediterranean Sea
44 K13 **Sardinal** Guanacaste, NW Costa Rica
56 G7 **Sardinata** Norte de Santander, N Colombia
Sardinia *see* Sardegna
123 K8 **Sardinia-Corsica Trough** *undersea feature* Tyrrhenian Sea, C Mediterranean Sea
24 L2 **Sardis** Mississippi, S USA
24 L2 **Sardis Lake** ▣ Mississippi, S USA
29 P12 **Sardis Lake** ▣ Oklahoma, C USA
94 H12 **Sarek** ⛰ N Sweden
155 N3 **Sar-e Pol** ***var.*** Sar-i-Pul. Sar-e Pol, N Afghanistan
155 O3 **Sar-e Pol** ⬖ *province* N Afghanistan
Sar-e Pol *see* Sar-e Pol-e Žahāb
148 J6 **Sar-e Pol-e Žahāb** ***var.*** Sar-e Pol, Sar-i Pul. Kermānshāhān, W Iran
176 Ww10 **Sarera, Teluk** ***var.*** Teluk Irian. *bay* W Pacific Ocean
153 T13 **Sarez, Kŭli** ***Rus.*** Sarezskoye Ozero. ◎ SE Tajikistan
Sarezskoye Ozero *see* Sarez, Kŭli
66 G10 **Sargasso Sea** *sea* W Atlantic Ocean
155 U8 **Sargodha** Punjab, NE Pakistan
80 I13 **Sarh** ***prev.*** Fort-Archambault. Moyen-Chari, S Chad
149 P4 **Sārī** ***var.*** Sari, Sāri. Māzandarān, N Iran
117 N23 **Saría** *island* SE Greece
Sariasiya *see* Sariosiyo
42 F3 **Saric** Sonora, NW Mexico
196 K6 **Sarigan** *island* C Northern Mariana Islands
142 D14 **Sarıgöl** Manisa, SW Turkey
145 T6 **Sārihah** E Iraq
143 R12 **Sarıkamış** Kars, NE Turkey
174 L6 **Sarikei** Sarawak, East Malaysia
153 U12 **Sarikol Range** ***Rus.*** Sarykol'skiy Khrebet. ⛰ China/Tajikistan
189 Y7 **Sarina** Queensland, NE Australia
Sarine *see* La Sarine
107 S5 **Sariñena** Aragón, NE Spain
153 O13 **Sariosiyo** ***Rus.*** Sariasiya. Surkhondaryo Wiloyati, S Uzbekistan
Sar-i-Pul *see* Sar-e Pol, Afghanistan
Sar-i Pul *see* Sar-e Pol-e Žahāb, Iran
Sariqamish Kŭli *see* Sarykamyshkoye Ozero
155 V1 **Sarī Qŭl** ***Rus.*** Ozero Zurkul', ***Taj.*** Zŭrkŭl. ◎ Afghanistan/Tajikistan *see also* Zŭrkŭl
77 Q12 **Sarīr Tībistī** ***var.*** Serir Tibesti. *desert* S Libya
27 S15 **Sarita** Texas, SW USA
169 W14 **Sariwŏn** SW North Korea
116 P12 **Sarıyer** İstanbul, NW Turkey
99 L26 **Sark** ***Fr.*** Sercq. *island* Channel Islands
113 N24 **Sarkad** ***Rom.*** Şărcad. Békés, SE Hungary
151 W14 **Sarkand** Taldykorgan, SW Kazakhstan
Sarkaṇi *see* Krasnogorskoye
158 D11 **Sarkāri Tala** Rājasthān, NW India
142 G15 **Şarkîkaraağaç** ***var.*** Şarki Karaağaç. İsparta, SW Turkey
142 L13 **Şarkışla** Sivas, C Turkey
142 C11 **Şarköy** Tekirdağ, NW Turkey
Sárköz *see* Livada
Sarlat *see* Sarlat-la-Canéda
104 M13 **Sarlat-la-Canéda** ***var.*** Sarlat. Dordogne, SW France
111 S3 **Sarleinsbach** Oberösterreich, N Austria
176 Y10 **Sarmi** Irian Jaya, E Indonesia
65 I19 **Sarmiento** Chubut, S Argentina
65 H25 **Sarmiento, Monte** ▲ S Chile
96 J11 **Särna** Kopparberg, C Sweden
110 F8 **Sarnen** Obwalden, C Switzerland
110 F9 **Sarner See** ◎ C Switzerland
12 D16 **Sarnia** Ontario, S Canada
118 L3 **Sarny** Rivnens'ka Oblast', NW Ukraine
175 Q10 **Saroako** Sulawesi, C Indonesia
120 L13 **Sarochyna** ***Rus.*** Sorochino. Vitsyebskaya Voblasts', N Belarus
174 Hh10 **Sarolangun** Sumatera, W Indonesia
172 Q5 **Saroma** Hokkaidō, NE Japan
172 Q5 **Saroma-ko** ◎ Hokkaidō, NE Japan
Saronic Gulf *see* Saronikós Kólpos
117 H20 **Saronikós Kólpos** ***Eng.*** Saronic Gulf. *gulf* S Greece
108 D7 **Saronno** Lombardia, N Italy
142 B11 **Saros Körfezi** *gulf* NW Turkey
113 N20 **Sárospatak** Borsod-Abaúj-Zemplén, NE Hungary
131 P12 **Sarpa** Respublika Kalmykiya, SW Russian Federation
131 P12 **Sarpa, Ozero** ◎ SW Russian Federation
115 M18 **Šar Planina** ⛰ FYR Macedonia/Yugoslavia
97 I16 **Sarpsborg** Østfold, S Norway
145 U5 **Sarqaḷā** N Iraq
105 U4 **Sarralbe** Moselle, NE France
Sarre *see* Saar, France/Germany
Sarre *see* Saarland, Germany
105 U5 **Sarrebourg** ***Ger.*** Saarburg. Moselle, NE France
Sarrebruck *see* Saarbrücken
105 U4 **Sarreguemines** ***prev.*** Saargemund. Moselle, NE France
106 I3 **Sarria** Galicia, NW Spain
107 S8 **Sarrión** Aragón, NE Spain
44 F4 **Sarstoon** ***Sp.*** Río Sarstún. ≈ Belize/Guatemala
Sarstún, Río *see* Sarstoon
126 M9 **Sartang** ≈ NE Russian Federation
104 E3 **Sartène** Corse, France, C Mediterranean Sea
104 K7 **Sarthe** ⬖ *department* NW France
104 K7 **Sarthe** ≈ N France
117 H15 **Sárti** Kentrikí Makedonía, N Greece
172 Pp2 **Sarufutsu** Hokkaidō, NE Japan
172 Oo7 **Saru-gawa** ≈ Hokkaidō, NE Japan
Saruhan *see* Manisa
158 G9 **Sarūpsar** Rājasthān, NW India
143 U13 **Şärur** ***prev.*** Il'ichevsk. SW Azerbaijan
Saruwaged Range *see* Sarawaget Range
Sarvani *see* Marneuli
113 G23 **Sárvár** Vas, W Hungary
149 P11 **Sarvestān** Fārs, S Iran
176 X9 **Sarwon** Irian Jaya, E Indonesia
151 P17 **Saryagach** ***Kaz.*** Saryaghash. Yuzhnyy Kazakhstan, S Kazakhstan
Saryaghash *see* Saryagach
Saryarqa *see* Kazakhskiy Melkosopochnik
153 W8 **Sary-Bulak** Narynskaya Oblast', C Kyrgyzstan
153 U10 **Sary-Bulak** Oshskaya Oblast', SW Kyrgyzstan
119 S14 **Sarych, Mys** *headland* S Ukraine
153 Z7 **Sary-Dzhaz** ***var.*** Aksu He. ≈ China/Kyrgyzstan *see also* Aksu He
151 T14 **Saryesik-Atyrau, Peski** *desert* E Kazakhstan
150 G13 **Sarykamys** ***Kaz.*** Saryqamys. Mangistau, SW Kazakhstan
152 F8 **Sarykamyshkoye Ozero** ***Uzb.*** Sariqamish Kŭli. *salt lake* Kazakhstan/Uzbekistan
Sarykol'skiy Khrebet *see* Sarikol Range
150 M10 **Sarykopa, Ozero** ◎ C Kazakhstan
151 V15 **Saryozek** ***Kaz.*** Saryözek. Taldykorgan, SE Kazakhstan
Saryqamys *see* Sarykamys
151 S13 **Saryshagan** ***Kaz.*** Saryshahan. Zhezkazgan, SE Kazakhstan
Saryshahan *see* Saryshagan
151 O13 **Sarysu** ≈ S Kazakhstan
153 T11 **Sary-Tash** Oshskaya Oblast', SW Kyrgyzstan
152 J15 **Saryyazynskoye Vodokhranilishche** ▣ S Turkmenistan
108 E10 **Sarzana** Liguria, NW Italy
42 F3 **Sásabe** ***var.*** Aduana del Sásabe. Sonora, NW Mexico
196 B17 **Sasalaguan, Mount** ▲ S Guam
159 O14 **Sasarām** Bihār, N India
195 W14 **Sasari, Mount** ▲ Santa Isabel, N Solomon Islands
170 C12 **Sasebo** Nagasaki, Kyūshū, SW Japan
12 I9 **Saseginaga, Lac** ◎ Québec, SE Canada
Saseno *see* Sazan
9 R13 **Saskatchewan** ⬖ *province* SW Canada
9 U14 **Saskatchewan** ≈ Manitoba/Saskatchewan, C Canada
9 T15 **Saskatoon** Saskatchewan, S Canada
9 T15 **Saskatoon** ✕ Saskatchewan, S Canada
126 K7 **Saskylakh** Respublika Sakha (Yakutiya), NE Russian Federation
44 L7 **Saslaya, Cerro** ▲ N Nicaragua
40 G17 **Sasmik, Cape** *headland* Tanaga Island, Alaska, USA
121 N19 **Sasnovy Bor** ***Rus.*** Sosnovyy Bor. Homyel'skaya Voblasts', SE Belarus
131 N5 **Sasovo** Ryazanskaya Oblast', W Russian Federation
27 S12 **Saspamco** Texas, SW USA
111 W9 **Sass** ***var.*** Sassbach. ≈ SE Austria
78 M17 **Sassandra** S Ivory Coast
78 M17 **Sassandra** ***var.*** Ibo, Sassandra Fleuve. ≈ S Ivory Coast
Sassandra Fleuve *see* Sassandra
109 B17 **Sassari** Sardegna, Italy, C Mediterranean Sea
Sassbach *see* Sass
100 H11 **Sassenheim** Zuid-Holland, W Netherlands
Sassmacken *see* Valdemārpils
102 O7 **Sassnitz** Mecklenburg-Vorpommern, NE Germany
101 E16 **Sas van Gent** Zeeland, SW Netherlands
151 W12 **Sasykkol', Ozero** ◎ E Kazakhstan
119 O12 **Sasyk Kunduk, Ozero** ◎ SW Ukraine
78 J12 **Satadougou** Kayes, SW Mali
107 V11 **Sa Talaiassa** ▲ Eivissa, Spain, W Mediterranean Sea
170 B17 **Sata-misaki** *headland* Kyūshū, SW Japan
28 I7 **Satanta** Kansas, C USA
161 E15 **Sātāra** Mahārāshtra, W India
198 Aa7 **Sātaua** Savai'i, NW Western Samoa
196 M16 **Satawal** *island* Caroline Islands, C Micronesia
201 R17 **Satawan Atoll** *atoll* Mortlock Islands, C Micronesia
25 Y12 **Satellite Beach** Florida, SE USA
97 M14 **Säter** Kopparberg, C Sweden
Sathmar *see* Satu Mare
25 V7 **Satilla River** ≈ Georgia, SE USA
59 F14 **Satipo** ***var.*** San Francisco de Satipo. Junín, C Peru
125 E11 **Satka** Chelyabinskaya Oblast', C Russian Federation
159 T16 **Satkhira** Khulna, SW Bangladesh
160 K9 **Satna** ***prev.*** Sutna. Madhya Pradesh, C India
105 R11 **Satolas** ✕ (Lyon) Rhône, E France
113 N20 **Sátoraljaújhely** Borsod-Abaúj-Zemplén, NE Hungary
151 O12 **Satpayev** ***prev.*** Nikol'skiy. Zhezkazgan, C Kazakhstan
160 G11 **Sātpura Range** ⛰ C India
170 Bb16 **Satsuma-hantō** *peninsula* Kyūshū, SW Japan
178 Hh12 **Sattahip** ***var.*** Ban Sattahip, Ban Sattahipp. Chon Buri, S Thailand
94 L11 **Sattanen** Lappi, NE Finland
Satul *see* Satun
118 H9 **Satulung** ***Hung.*** Kővárhosszúfalu. Maramureş, N Romania
Satul-Vechi *see* Staro Selo
118 G8 **Satu Mare** ***Ger.*** Sathmar, ***Hung.*** Szatmárrnémeti. Satu Mare, NW Romania
118 G8 **Satu Mare** ⬖ *county* NW Romania
178 H17 **Satun** ***var.*** Satul, Setul. Satun, SW Thailand
198 Aa8 **Satupaiteau** Savai'i, W Western Samoa
Sau *see* Sava
12 F14 **Sauble** ≈ Ontario, S Canada
12 F13 **Sauble Beach** Ontario, S Canada
63 C16 **Sauce** Corrientes, NE Argentina
Sauce *see* Juan L.Lacaze
38 K15 **Sauceda Mountains** ⛰ Arizona, SW USA
63 C17 **Sauce de Luna** Entre Ríos, E Argentina
65 L15 **Sauce Grande, Río** ≈ E Argentina
42 K6 **Saucillo** Chihuahua, N Mexico
97 D15 **Sauda** Rogaland, S Norway
94 J2 **Saudhárkrókur** Nordhurland Vestra, N Iceland
147 P9 **Saudi Arabia** ***off.*** Kingdom of Saudi Arabia, ***Ar.*** Al 'Arabīyah as Su'ūdīyah, Al Mamlakah al 'Arabīyah as Su'ūdīyah. ◆ *monarchy* SW Asia
103 D19 **Sauer** ***var.*** Sûre. ≈ NW Europe *see also* Sûre
103 F15 **Sauerland** *forest* W Germany
12 F14 **Saugeen** ≈ Ontario, S Canada
20 K12 **Saugerties** New York, NE USA
Saugor *see* Sāgar
8 K15 **Saugstad, Mount** ▲ British Columbia, SW Canada
Sāūjbulāgh *see* Mahābād
104 J11 **Saujon** Charente-Maritime, W France
31 T7 **Sauk Centre** Minnesota, N USA
32 L8 **Sauk City** Wisconsin, N USA
176 Vv8 **Sau Korem** Irian Jaya, E Indonesia
31 U7 **Sauk Rapids** Minnesota, N USA
57 Y11 **Saül** C French Guiana
105 O7 **Sauldre** ≈ C France
103 I23 **Saulgau** Baden-Württemberg, SW Germany
105 Q8 **Saulieu** Côte d'Or, C France
120 G8 **Saulkrasti** Rīga, C Latvia
13 S6 **Sault-aux-Cochons, Rivière du** ≈ Québec, SE Canada
33 Q4 **Sault Sainte Marie** Michigan, N USA
10 F14 **Sault Ste.Marie** Ontario, S Canada
202 E13 **Sauma, Pointe** *headland* Île Alofi, W Wallis and Futuna
176 Uu15 **Saumlaki** ***var.*** Saumlakki. Pulau Yamdena, E Indonesia
Saumlakki *see* Saumlaki
13 R12 **Saumon, Rivière au** ≈ Québec, SE Canada
104 K8 **Saumur** Maine-et-Loire, NW France
193 F23 **Saunders, Cape** *headland* South Island, NZ
205 N13 **Saunders Coast** *physical region* Antarctica
67 B23 **Saunders Island** *island* NW Falkland Islands
67 C24 **Saunders Island Settlement** Saunders Island, NW Falkland Islands
84 F11 **Saurimo** ***Port.*** Henrique de Carvalho, Vila Henrique de Carvalho. Lunda Sul, NE Angola
57 S11 **Sauriwaunawa** S Guyana
176 V8 **Sausapor** Irian Jaya, E Indonesia
84 D12 **Sautar** Malanje, NW Angola
47 S13 **Sauteurs** N Grenada
104 K13 **Sauveterre-de-Guyenne** Gironde, SW France
121 O14 **Sava** ***Rus.*** Sava. Mahilyowskaya Voblasts', E Belarus
86 H11 **Sava** ***Eng.*** Save, ***Ger.*** Sau, ***Hung.*** Száva. ≈ SE Europe
44 J5 **Savá** Colón, N Honduras
35 Y8 **Savage** Montana, NW USA
191 N16 **Savage River** Tasmania, SE Australia
198 Aa7 **Savai'i** *island* NW Western Samoa
79 R15 **Savalou** S Benin
32 K10 **Savanna** Illinois, N USA
25 X6 **Savannah** Georgia, SE USA
29 R2 **Savannah** Missouri, C USA
22 H10 **Savannah** Tennessee, S USA
23 O12 **Savannah River** ≈ Georgia/South Carolina, SE USA
Savannakhét *see* Khanthabouli
46 H12 **Savanna-La-Mar** W Jamaica
10 B10 **Savant Lake** ◎ Ontario, S Canada
161 F17 **Savanūr** Karnātaka, W India
95 J16 **Sävar** Västerbotten, N Sweden
Savaria *see* Szombathely
160 C11 **Sāvarkundla** ***var.*** Kundla. Gujarāt, W India
118 F11 **Săvârşin** ***Hung.*** Soborsin; ***prev.*** Săvîrşin. Arad, W Romania
142 C13 **Savaştepe** Balıkesir, W Turkey
Savat *see* Sawot
85 N18 **Save** Inhambane, E Mozambique
104 L16 **Save** ≈ S France
85 L17 **Save** ***var.*** Sabi. ≈ Mozambique/Zimbabwe *see also* Sabi
Save *see* Sava
79 R15 **Savè** SE Benin
148 M6 **Sāveh** Markazī, W Iran
118 L8 **Săveni** Botoşani, NE Romania
105 N16 **Saverdun** Ariège, S France
105 U5 **Saverne** ***var.*** Zabern; ***anc.*** Tres Tabernae. Bas-Rhin, NE France
Savichi *see* Savichy
121 O21 **Savichy** ***Rus.*** Savichi. Homyel'skaya Voblasts', SE Belarus
108 B9 **Savigliano** Piemonte, NW Italy
Savigsivik *see* Savissivik
Savinichi *see* Savinichy
121 Q16 **Savinichy** ***Rus.*** Savinichi. Mahilyowskaya Voblasts', E Belarus
111 T10 **Savinjske Alpe** ***var.*** Kamniške Alpe, Sanntaler Alpen, ***Ger.*** Steiner Alpen. ⛰ N Slovenia
Savinski *see* Savinskiy
125 Dd6 **Savinskiy** ***var.*** Savinski. Arkhangel'skaya Oblast', NW Russian Federation
108 H11 **Savio** ≈ C Italy
Săvîrşin *see* Săvârşin
207 O11 **Savissivik** ***var.*** Savigsivik. N Greenland
95 N18 **Savitaipale** Kymi, SE Finland
115 J15 **Šavnik** Montenegro, SW Yugoslavia
195 W15 **Savo** *island* C Solomon Islands
110 I9 **Savognin** Graubünden, S Switzerland
105 T12 **Savoie** ⬖ *department* E France
108 C10 **Savona** Liguria, NW Italy
95 N17 **Savonlinna** ***Swe.*** Nyslott. Mikkeli, SE Finland
95 N17 **Savonranta** Mikkeli, SE Finland
40 K10 **Savoonga** Saint Lawrence Island, Alaska, USA
32 M13 **Savoy** Illinois, N USA
119 O8 **Savran'** Odes'ka Oblast', SW Ukraine
143 R11 **Şavşat** Artvin, NE Turkey
97 L19 **Sävsjö** Jönköping, S Sweden
Savu, Kepulauan *see* Sawu, Kepulauan
94 M11 **Savukoski** Lappi, NE Finland
Savu, Pulau *see* Sawu, Pulau
197 J13 **Savusavu** Vanua Levu, N Fiji
175 Q17 **Savu Sea** ***Ind.*** Laut Sawu. *sea* S Indonesia
85 H17 **Savute** Chobe, N Botswana
145 N7 **Şawāb, 'Uqlat** *well* W Iraq
144 M7 **Sawāb, Wādī as** *dry watercourse* W Iraq
158 H13 **Sawāi Mādhopur** Rājasthān, N India
175 Tt10 **Sawai, Teluk** *bay* Pulau Seram, E Indonesia
Sawakin *see* Suakin
178 Ii9 **Sawang Daen Din** Sakon Nakhon, E Thailand
178 H8 **Sawankhalok** ***var.*** Swankalok. Sukhothai, NW Thailand
171 Kk17 **Sawara** Chiba, Honshū, S Japan
171 Jj12 **Sawasaki-bana** *headland* Sado, C Japan
39 R5 **Sawatch Range** ⛰ Colorado, C USA
147 N12 **Sawdā', Jabal** ▲ SW Saudi Arabia
77 P9 **Sawdā', Jabal as** ⛰ C Libya
Sawdirī *see* Sodiri
176 W9 **Saweba, Tanjung** *headland* Irian Jaya, E Indonesia
99 F14 **Sawel** ▲ C Northern Ireland, UK
Sawhāj *see* Sohâg
79 O15 **Sawla** N Ghana
153 P11 **Sawot** ***Rus.*** Savat. Sirdaryo Wiloyati, E Uzbekistan
147 X12 **Şawqirah** ***var.*** Suqrah. S Oman
147 X12 **Şawqirah, Dawḩat** ***var.*** Ghubbat Sawqirah, Sukra Bay, Suqrah Bay. *bay* S Oman
Sawqirah, Ghubbat *see* Şawqirah, Dawḩat
191 V5 **Sawtell** New South Wales, SE Australia
144 K7 **Şawt, Wādī aş** *dry watercourse* S Syria
175 Q18 **Sawu, Kepulauan** ***var.*** Kepulauan Savu. *island group* S Indonesia
Sawu, Laut *see* Savu Sea
175 Qq18 **Sawu, Pulau** ***var.*** Pulau Savu. *island* Kepulauan Sawu, S Indonesia
107 S12 **Sax** País Valenciano, E Spain
Saxe *see* Sachsen
110 C11 **Saxon** Valais, SW Switzerland
Saxony *see* Sachsen
Saxony-Anhalt *see* Sachsen-Anhalt
79 R12 **Say** Niamey, SW Niger
13 V7 **Sayabec** Québec, SE Canada
Sayaboury *see* Xaignabouli
151 U12 **Sayak** ***Kaz.*** Sayaq. Zhezkazgan, E Kazakhstan
59 D14 **Sayán** Lima, W Peru
126 Hh15 **Sayanogorsk** Respublika Khakasiya, S Russian Federation
126 J15 **Sayansk** Irkutskaya Oblast', S Russian Federation
133 T6 **Sayanskiy Khrebet** ⛰ S Russian Federation
Sayaq *see* Sayak
152 K13 **Sayat** Lebapskiy Velayat, E Turkmenistan
44 D3 **Sayaxché** Petén, N Guatemala
Şaydā/Sayida *see* Saïda
147 T15 **Sayḩūt** E Yemen
31 U14 **Saylorville Lake** ▣ Iowa, C USA
Saymenskiy Kanal *see* Saimaa Canal
169 N10 **Saynshand** Dornogovĭ, SE Mongolia
168 J11 **Saynshand** Ömnögovĭ, S Mongolia
168 F7 **Sayn-Ust** Govĭ-Altay, W Mongolia
Say-Ötesh *see* Say-Utës
144 J7 **Şayqal, Baḩr** ◎ S Syria
Sayrab *see* Sayrob
164 H4 **Sayram Hu** ◎ NW China
28 K11 **Sayre** Oklahoma, C USA
20 H12 **Sayre** Pennsylvania, NE USA
20 K15 **Sayreville** New Jersey, NE USA
153 N13 **Sayrob** ***Rus.*** Sayrab. Surkhondaryo Wiloyati, S Uzbekistan
42 L13 **Sayula** Jalisco, SW Mexico
147 R14 **Say 'ūn** ***var.*** Saywūn. C Yemen
150 G14 **Say-Utës** ***Kaz.*** Say-Ötesh. Mangistau, SW Kazakhstan
8 K16 **Sayward** Vancouver Island, British Columbia, SW Canada
Saywūn *see* Say 'ūn
Sayyāl *see* As Sayyāl
145 U8 **Sayyid 'Abīd** ***var.*** Saiyid Abid. E Iraq
115 J22 **Sazan** ***var.*** Ishulli i Sazanit, ***It.*** Saseno. *island* SW Albania
Sazanit, Ishulli i *see* Sazan
Sazau/Sazawa *see* Sázava
113 E17 **Sázava** ***var.*** Sazau, ***Ger.*** Sazawa. ≈ C Czech Republic
128 J14 **Sazonovo** Vologodskaya Oblast', NW Russian Federation
104 G6 **Scaër** Finistère, NW France
99 J15 **Scafell Pike** ▲ NW England, UK
Scalabis *see* Santarém
98 M2 **Scalloway** N Scotland, UK
40 M11 **Scammon Bay** Alaska, USA
Scammon Lagoon/ Scammon, Laguna *see* Ojo de Liebre, Laguna
86 F7 **Scandinavia** *geophysical region* NW Europe
Scania *see* Skåne
98 K5 **Scapa Flow** *sea basin* N Scotland, UK
109 K26 **Scaramia, Capo** *headland* Sicilia, Italy, C Mediterranean Sea
12 H15 **Scarborough** Ontario, SE Canada
47 Z16 **Scarborough** ***prev.*** Port Louis. Tobago, Trinidad and Tobago
99 N16 **Scarborough** N England, UK
193 I17 **Scargill** Canterbury, South Island, NZ
98 E7 **Scarp** *island* NW Scotland, UK
Scarpanto *see* Kárpathos
Scarpanto Strait *see* Karpathou, Stenó
109 G25 **Scauri** Sicilia, Italy, C Mediterranean Sea
Scealg, Bá na *see* Ballinskelligs Bay
Scebeli *see* Shebeli
102 K10 **Schaale** ≈ N Germany
102 K9 **Schaalsee** ◎ N Germany
101 G18 **Schaerbeek** Brussels, C Belgium
110 G6 **Schaffhausen** ***Fr.*** Schaffhouse. Schaffhausen, N Switzerland
110 G6 **Schaffhausen** ***Fr.*** Schaffhouse. ⬖ *canton* N Switzerland
Schaffhouse *see* Schaffhausen
100 I8 **Schagen** Noord-Holland, NW Netherlands
Schaken *see* Šakiai
100 M10 **Schalkhaar** Overijssel, E Netherlands
111 R3 **Schärding** Oberösterreich, N Austria
102 G9 **Scharhörn** *island* NW Germany
Schässburg *see* Sighişoara
Schaulen *see* Šiauliai
32 M10 **Schaumburg** Illinois, N USA
Schebschi Mountains *see* Shebshi Mountains
100 P6 **Scheemda** Groningen, NE Netherlands
102 I10 **Scheessel** Niedersachsen, NW Germany
11 N8 **Schefferville** Québec, E Canada
Schelde *see* Scheldt
101 D18 **Scheldt** ***Dut.*** Schelde, ***Fr.*** Escaut. ≈ W Europe
37 X5 **Schell Creek Range** ⛰ Nevada, W USA
20 K10 **Schenectady** New York, NE USA
101 I17 **Scherpenheuvel** ***Fr.*** Montaigu. Vlaams Brabant, C Belgium
100 K11 **Scherpenzeel** Gelderland, C Netherlands
27 S12 **Schertz** Texas, SW USA
100 G11 **Scheveningen** Zuid-Holland, W Netherlands
100 G12 **Schiedam** Zuid-Holland, SW Netherlands
101 M24 **Schieren** Diekirch, NE Luxembourg
100 M4 **Schiermonnikoog** ***Fris.*** Skiermûntseach. Friesland, N Netherlands
100 M4 **Schiermonnikoog** ***Fris.*** Skiermûntseach. *island* Waddeneilanden, N Netherlands
101 K14 **Schijndel** Noord-Brabant, S Netherlands
Schil *see* Jiu
101 H16 **Schilde** Antwerpen, N Belgium
Schillen *see* Zhilino
105 V5 **Schiltigheim** Bas-Rhin, NE France
108 G7 **Schio** Veneto, NE Italy
100 H10 **Schiphol** ✕ (Amsterdam) Noord-Holland, C Netherlands
Schippenbeil *see* Sępopol
Schiria *see* Şiria
Schivelbein *see* Świdwin
117 D22 **Schíza** *island* S Greece
183 U3 **Schjetman Reef** *reef* Antarctica
Schlackenwerth *see* Ostrov
111 R7 **Schladming** Steiermark, SE Austria
Schlan *see* Slaný
Schlanders *see* Silandro
102 I7 **Schlei** *inlet* N Germany
103 D17 **Schleiden** Nordrhein-Westfalen, W Germany
195 P9 **Schleinitz Range** ⛰ New Ireland, N PNG
Schlelau *see* Szydłowiec
102 I7 **Schleswig** Schleswig-Holstein, N Germany
31 T13 **Schleswig** Iowa, C USA
102 H8 **Schleswig-Holstein** ⬖ *state* N Germany
Schlettstadt *see* Sélestat
110 F7 **Schlieren** Zürich, N Switzerland
Schlochau *see* Człuchów
Schloppe *see* Człopa
103 I18 **Schlüchtern** Hessen, C Germany
103 J17 **Schmalkalden** Thüringen, C Germany
111 W2 **Schmida** ≈ NE Austria
67 P19 **Schmidt-Ott Seamount** ***var.*** Schmitt-Ott Seamount, Schmitt-Ott Tablemount. *undersea feature* SW Indian Ocean
Schmiegel *see* Śmigiel
Schmitt-Ott Seamount/ Schmitt-Ott Tablemount *see* Schmidt-Ott Seamount
13 V3 **Schmon** ≈ Québec, SE Canada
103 M18 **Schneeberg** ▲ W Germany
Schneeberg *see* Snežnik
Schnee-Eifel *see* Schneifel
Schneekoppe *see* Sněžka
Schneidemühl *see* Piła
103 D18 **Schneifel** ***var.*** Schnee-Eifel. *plateau* W Germany
Schnelle Körös/Schnelle Kreisch *see* Crişul Repede
102 I11 **Schneverdingen** ***var.*** Schneverdingen (Wümme). Niedersachsen, NW Germany
Schneverdingen (Wümme) *see* Schneverdingen
Schoden *see* Skuodas
20 K10 **Schoharie** New York, NE USA
20 K11 **Schoharie Creek** ≈ New York, NE USA
117 J21 **Schoinoússa** *island* Kykládes, Greece, Aegean Sea
102 L13 **Schönebeck** Sachsen-Anhalt, C Germany
Schöneck *see* Skarszewy
102 O12 **Schönefeld** ✕ (Berlin) Berlin, NE Germany
103 K24 **Schongau** Bayern, S Germany
102 K13 **Schöningen** Niedersachsen, C Germany
Schönlanke *see* Trzcianka
Schönsee *see* Kowalewo Pomorskie
33 P10 **Schoolcraft** Michigan, N USA
100 O8 **Schoonebeek** Drenthe, NE Netherlands
100 I12 **Schoonhoven** Zuid-Holland, C Netherlands
100 H8 **Schoorl** Noord-Holland, NW Netherlands
Schooten *see* Schoten
103 F24 **Schopfheim** Baden-Württemberg, SW Germany
103 I21 **Schorndorf** Baden-Württemberg, S Germany
102 F10 **Schortens** Niedersachsen, NW Germany
101 H16 **Schoten** ***var.*** Schooten. Antwerpen, N Belgium
191 Q17 **Schouten Island** *island* Tasmania, SE Australia
194 H9 **Schouten Islands** *island group* NW PNG
100 E13 **Schouwen** *island* SW Netherlands
47 Q12 **Schœlcher** W Martinique
Schreiberhau *see* Szklarska Poręba
111 U2 **Schrems** Niederösterreich, E Austria
103 L22 **Schrobenhausen** Bayern, SE Germany
20 L8 **Schroon Lake** ◎ New York, NE USA
110 J8 **Schruns** Vorarlberg, W Austria
Schubin *see* Szubin
27 U11 **Schulenburg** Texas, SW USA
Schuls *see* Scuol
110 E8 **Schüpfheim** Luzern, C Switzerland
37 S6 **Schurz** Nevada, W USA
103 I24 **Schussen** ≈ S Germany
Schüttenhofen *see* Sušice
31 R15 **Schuyler** Nebraska, C USA
20 L10 **Schuylerville** New York, NE USA
103 K20 **Schwabach** Bayern, SE Germany
Schwabenalb *see* Schwäbische Alb
103 I23 **Schwäbische Alb** ***var.*** Schwabenalb, ***Eng.*** Swabian Jura. ⛰ S Germany
103 I22 **Schwäbisch Gmünd** ***var.*** Gmünd. Baden-Württemberg, SW Germany
103 I21 **Schwäbisch Hall** ***var.*** Hall. Baden-Württemberg, SW Germany
103 H16 **Schwalm** ≈ C Germany
111 V9 **Schwanberg** Steiermark, SE Austria
110 H8 **Schwanden** Glarus, E Switzerland
103 M20 **Schwandorf** Bayern, SE Germany
111 S5 **Schwanenstadt** Oberösterreich, NW Austria
174 M9 **Schwaner, Pegunungan** ⛰ Borneo, N Indonesia
111 W5 **Schwarza** ≈ E Austria
111 P9 **Schwarzach** ≈ S Austria
103 M20 **Schwarzach** ***Cz.*** Černice. ≈ Czech Republic/Germany
Schwarzach *see* Schwarzach im Pongau, Austria
Schwarzach *see* Svratka, Czech Republic
111 Q7 **Schwarzach im Pongau** ***var.*** Schwarzach. Salzburg, NW Austria
Schwarzawa *see* Svratka
103 N14 **Schwarze Elster** ≈ E Germany
Schwarze Körös *see* Crişul Negru
110 D9 **Schwarzenburg** Bern, W Switzerland
85 D21 **Schwarzrand** ⛰ S Namibia
103 G23 **Schwarzwald** ***Eng.*** Black Forest. ⛰ SW Germany
Schwarzwasser *see* Wda
41 P7 **Schwatka Mountains** ⛰ Alaska, USA
111 N7 **Schwaz** Tirol, W Austria
111 Y4 **Schwechat** Niederösterreich, NE Austria
111 Y4 **Schwechat** ✕ (Wien) Wien, E Austria
102 P11 **Schwedt** Brandenburg, NE Germany
103 D19 **Schweich** Rheinland-Pfalz, SW Germany
Schweidnitz *see* Świdnica
103 J18 **Schweinfurt** Bayern, SE Germany
Schweiz *see* Switzerland
102 L9 **Schwerin** Mecklenburg-Vorpommern, N Germany
Schwerin *see* Skwierzyna
102 L9 **Schweriner See** ◎ N Germany
Schwertberg *see* Świecie
103 F15 **Schwerte** Nordrhein-Westfalen, W Germany
Schwiebus *see* Świebodzin
102 P13 **Schwielochsee** ◎ NE Germany
Schwihau *see* Švihov
Schwiz *see* Schwyz
110 G8 **Schwyz** ***var.*** Schwiz. Schwyz, C Switzerland
110 G8 **Schwyz** ***var.*** Schwiz. ⬖ *canton* C Switzerland
12 J11 **Schyan** ≈ Québec, SE Canada
Schyl *see* Jiu
109 I24 **Sciacca** Sicilia, Italy, C Mediterranean Sea
Sciasciamana *see* Shashemenē
109 L26 **Scicli** Sicilia, Italy, C Mediterranean Sea
99 F25 **Scilly, Isles of** *island group* SW England, UK
113 H17 **Ścinawa** ***Ger.*** Steinau an der Elbe. Legnica, SW Poland
Scio *see* Chíos
33 S14 **Scioto River** ≈ Ohio, N USA
38 L5 **Scipio** Utah, W USA
35 X6 **Scobey** Montana, NW USA
191 T7 **Scone** New South Wales, SE Australia
Scoresby Sound/ Scoresbysund *see* Ittoqqortoormiit
Scoresby Sund *see* Kangertittivaq
Scorno, Punta dello *see* Caprara, Punta
36 K3 **Scotia** California, W USA
49 Y14 **Scotia Plate** *tectonic feature*
49 V15 **Scotia Ridge** *undersea feature* S Atlantic Ocean
204 H2 **Scotia Sea** *sea* SW Atlantic Ocean
31 Q12 **Scotland** South Dakota, N USA
27 R5 **Scotland** Texas, SW USA
98 H11 **Scotland** *national region* UK
23 W8 **Scotland Neck** North Carolina, SE USA
205 R13 **Scott Base** *NZ research station* Antarctica
8 J16 **Scott, Cape** *headland* Vancouver Island, British Columbia, SW Canada
28 I5 **Scott City** Kansas, C USA
29 Y7 **Scott City** Missouri, C USA
205 R14 **Scott Coast** *physical region* Antarctica
20 C15 **Scottdale** Pennsylvania, NE USA
205 Y11 **Scott Glacier** *glacier* Antarctica
205 Q17 **Scott Island** *island* Antarctica

◆ Country
● Country Capital
◇ Dependent Territory
○ Dependent Territory Capital
⬖ Administrative Region
✕ International Airport
▲ Mountain
⛰ Mountain Range
Volcano
≈ River
◎ Lake
▣ Reservoir

28 L11 **Scott, Mount** ▲ Oklahoma, USA
34 G15 **Scott, Mount** ▲ Oregon, NW USA
36 M1 **Scott River** ≈ California, W USA
30 I13 **Scottsbluff** Nebraska, C USA
25 Q2 **Scottsboro** Alabama, S USA
33 P15 **Scottsburg** Indiana, N USA
191 P16 **Scottsdale** Tasmania, SE Australia
38 L13 **Scottsdale** Arizona, SW USA
47 O12 **Scotts Head Village** *var.* Cachacrou. S Dominica
199 Jj17 **Scott Shoal** *undersea feature* S Pacific Ocean
22 K7 **Scottsville** Kentucky, S USA
31 U14 **Scranton** Iowa, C USA
20 I13 **Scranton** Pennsylvania, NE USA
194 G10 **Screw** ≈ NW PNG
31 R14 **Scribner** Nebraska, C USA
Scrobesbyrig' *see* Shrewsbury
12 I14 **Scugog** ≈ Ontario, SE Canada
12 I14 **Scugog, Lake** ◎ Ontario, SE Canada
99 N17 **Scunthorpe** E England, UK
110 K9 **Scuol** *Ger.* Schuls. Graubünden, E Switzerland
Scupi *see* Skopje
Scutari *see* Shkodër
115 K17 **Scutari, Lake** *Alb.* Liqeni i Shkodrës, *SCr.* Skadarsko Jezero. ◎ Albania/Yugoslavia
Scyros *see* Skýros
Scythopolis *see* Bet She'an
27 U13 **Seadrift** Texas, SW USA
23 Y4 **Seaford** *var.* Seaford City. Delaware, NE USA
Seaford City *see* Seaford
12 E15 **Seaforth** Ontario, S Canada
26 M6 **Seagraves** Texas, SW USA
9 X9 **Seal** ≈ Manitoba, C Canada
190 M10 **Sea Lake** Victoria, SE Australia
85 G26 **Seal, Cape** *headland* S South Africa
67 D26 **Sea Lion Islands** *island group* SE Falkland Islands
21 S8 **Seal Island** *island* Maine, NE USA
27 V11 **Sealy** Texas, SW USA
37 X12 **Searchlight** Nevada, W USA
29 V11 **Searcy** Arkansas, C USA
21 R7 **Searsport** Maine, NE USA
37 N10 **Seaside** California, W USA
34 F10 **Seaside** Oregon, NW USA
20 K16 **Seaside Heights** New Jersey, NE USA
34 H8 **Seattle** Washington, NW USA
34 H9 **Seattle-Tacoma** ✈ Washington, NW USA
193 J16 **Seaward Kaikoura Range** ▲▲ South Island, NZ
44 J9 **Sébaco** Matagalpa, W Nicaragua
21 P8 **Sebago Lake** ◎ Maine, NE USA
176 V11 **Sebakor, Teluk** *bay* Irian Jaya, E Indonesia
Sebangan, Sungai *see* Sebangau Besar, Sungai
174 M11 **Sebangan, Teluk** *bay* Borneo, C Indonesia
174 Mm11 **Sebanganu, Teluk** *bay* Borneo, C Indonesia
174 Mm11 **Sebangau Besar, Sungai** *var.* Sungai Sebangan. ≈ Borneo, N Indonesia
174 I8 **Sebanglea, Pulau** *island* W Indonesia
Sebaste/Sebastia *see* Sivas
25 Y12 **Sebastian** Florida, SE USA
42 C5 **Sebastían Vizcaíno, Bahía** *bay* NW Mexico
21 R6 **Sebasticook Lake** ◎ Maine, NE USA
36 M7 **Sebastopol** California, W USA
Sebastopol *see* Sevastopol'
175 Oo4 **Sebatik, Pulau** *island* N Indonesia
21 R5 **Sebec Lake** ◎ Maine, NE USA
78 K12 **Sébékoro** Kayes, W Mali
Sebenico *see* Šibenik
42 G6 **Seberi, Cerro** ▲ NW Mexico
118 H11 **Sebeş** *Ger.* Mühlbach, *Hung.* Szászsebes; *prev.* Sebeşu Săsesc. Alba, W Romania
Sebes-Körös *see* Crişul Repede
Sebeşu Săsesc *see* Sebeş
33 R8 **Sebewaing** Michigan, N USA
128 F16 **Sebezh** Pskovskaya Oblast', W Russian Federation
143 N12 **Şebinkarahisar** Giresun, N Turkey
118 F11 **Sebiş** *Hung.* Borossebes. Arad, W Romania
Sebkra Azz el Matti *see* Azzel Matti, Sebkha
21 Q4 **Seboomook Lake** ◎ Maine, NE USA
76 G6 **Sebou** *var.* Sebu. ≈ N Morocco
22 I6 **Sebree** Kentucky, S USA
25 X13 **Sebring** Florida, SE USA
Sebta *see* Ceuta
Sebu *see* Sebou
175 Nn11 **Sebuku, Pulau** *island* N Indonesia
175 Oo4 **Sebuku, Teluk** *bay* Borneo, N Indonesia
176 Vv10 **Sebyar** ≈ Irian Jaya, E Indonesia
108 F10 **Secchia** ≈ N Italy
8 L17 **Sechelt** British Columbia, SW Canada
58 C12 **Sechin, Río** ≈ W Peru
58 A10 **Sechura, Bahía de** *bay* NW Peru
193 A22 **Secretary Island** *island* SW NZ
161 I15 **Secunderābād** *var.* Sikandarabad. Andhra Pradesh, C India
59 L17 **Sécure, Río** ≈ C Bolivia
120 D10 **Seda** Mažeikiai, NW Lithuania
29 T5 **Sedalia** Missouri, C USA
105 R3 **Sedan** Ardennes, N France
29 P7 **Sedan** Kansas, C USA
107 N3 **Sedano** Castilla-León, N Spain
106 H10 **Seda, Ribeira de** *stream* C Portugal
193 K15 **Seddon** Marlborough, South Island, NZ
193 H15 **Seddonville** West Coast, South Island, NZ
149 U7 **Sedeh** Khorāsān, E Iran
144 E11 **Sederot** Southern, S Israel
67 B23 **Sedge Island** *island* NW Falkland Islands
78 G12 **Sédhiou** SW Senegal
9 U16 **Sedley** Saskatchewan, S Canada
Sedlez *see* Siedlce
125 G12 **Sednel'nikovo** Omskaya Oblast', C Russian Federation
119 Q2 **Sedniv** Chernihivs'ka Oblast', N Ukraine
38 L11 **Sedona** Arizona, SW USA
Sedunum *see* Sion
120 F12 **Šeduva** Radviliškis, N Lithuania
147 Y8 **Seeb** *var.* Muscat Sīb Airport. ✈ (Masqaţ) NE Oman
Seeb *see* As Sīb
110 M7 **Seefeld in Tirol** Tirol, W Austria
85 E22 **Seeheim Noord** Karas, S Namibia
Seeland *see* Sjælland
205 N9 **Seelig, Mount** ▲ Antarctica
Seeonee *see* Seoni
168 E6 **Seer** Hovd, W Mongolia
104 L5 **Sées** Orne, N France
103 J14 **Seesen** Niedersachsen, C Germany
Seesker Höhe *see* Szeskie Wzgórza
102 J10 **Seevetal** Niedersachsen, N Germany
111 V6 **Seewiesen** Steiermark, E Austria
142 J13 **Şefaatli** *var.* Kızılkoca. Yozgat, C Turkey
155 N3 **Sefīd, Darya-ye** *Pash.* Āb-i-Safed. ≈ N Afghanistan
154 K5 **Sefīdkūh, Selseleh-ye** *Eng.* Paropamisus Range. ▲▲ W Afghanistan
76 G6 **Sefrou** N Morocco
193 E19 **Sefton, Mount** ▲ South Island, NZ
176 U10 **Segaf, Kepulauan** *island group* E Indonesia
175 Oo3 **Segama, Sungai** ≈ East Malaysia
174 Hh6 **Segamat** Johor, Peninsular Malaysia
79 S13 **Ségbana** NE Benin
Segestica *see* Sisak
Segesvár *see* Sighişoara
176 Uu9 **Seget** Irian Jaya, E Indonesia
Segewold *see* Sigulda
128 J9 **Segezha** Respublika Kareliya, NW Russian Federation
Seghedin *see* Szeged
Segna *see* Senj
109 I16 **Segni** Lazio, C Italy
Segodunum *see* Rodez
107 S9 **Segorbe** País Valenciano, E Spain
78 M12 **Ségou** *var.* Segu. Ségou, C Mali
78 M12 **Ségou** ◈ *region* SW Mali
56 E8 **Segovia** Antioquia, N Colombia
107 N7 **Segovia** Castilla-León, C Spain
106 M6 **Segovia** ◈ *province* Castilla-León, N Spain
Segoviao Wangkí *see* Coco, Río
128 J9 **Segozero, Ozero** ◎ NW Russian Federation
107 U5 **Segre** ≈ NE Spain
104 J7 **Segré** Maine-et-Loire, NW France
Segu *see* Ségou
40 I17 **Seguam Island** *island* Aleutian Islands, Alaska, USA
40 I17 **Seguam Pass** *strait* Aleutian Islands, Alaska, USA
79 Y7 **Séguédine** Agadez, NE Niger
78 M15 **Séguéla** W Ivory Coast
27 S11 **Seguin** Texas, SW USA
40 E17 **Segula Island** *island* Aleutian Islands, Alaska, USA
64 K10 **Segundo, Río** ≈ C Argentina
107 Q12 **Segura** ≈ S Spain
85 G18 **Sehithwa** Ngamiland, N Botswana
160 H10 **Sehore** Madhya Pradesh, C India
195 O16 **Sehulea** Normanby Island, S PNG
155 P15 **Sehwān** Sind, SE Pakistan
111 V8 **Seiersberg** Steiermark, SE Austria
28 L9 **Seiling** Oklahoma, C USA
105 S9 **Seille** ≈ E France
101 J20 **Seilles** Namur, SE Belgium
95 K17 **Seinäjoki** *Swe.* Östermyra. Vaasa, W Finland
10 B12 **Seine** ≈ Ontario, S Canada
104 M4 **Seine** ≈ N France
104 K4 **Seine, Baie de la** *bay* N France
Seine, Banc de la *see* Seine Seamount
105 O5 **Seine-et-Marne** ◈ *department* N France
104 L3 **Seine-Maritime** ◈ *department* N France
86 B14 **Seine Plain** *undersea feature* E Atlantic Ocean
86 B15 **Seine Seamount** *var.* Banc de la Seine. *undersea feature* E Atlantic Ocean
104 E6 **Sein, Île de** *island* NW France
176 Y12 **Seinma** Irian Jaya, E Indonesia
Seisbierrum *see* Sexbierum
111 U5 **Seitenstetten Markt** Niederösterreich, C Austria
Seiyu *see* Chŏnju
97 H22 **Sejerø** *island* E Denmark
112 P7 **Sejny** Suwałki, NE Poland
174 Ii13 **Sekampung, Way** ≈ Sumatera, SW Indonesia
83 G20 **Seke** Shinyanga, N Tanzania
171 I15 **Seki** Gifu, Honshū, SW Japan
167 U12 **Sekibi-sho** *island* China/Japan/Taiwan
172 Pp5 **Sekihoku-tōge** *pass* Hokkaidō, NE Japan
Sekondi *see* Sekondi-Takoradi
79 P17 **Sekondi-Takoradi** *var.* Sekondi. S Ghana
82 J11 **Sek'ot'a** N Ethiopia
Sekseūil *see* Saksaul'skoye
34 I9 **Selah** Washington, NW USA
174 Gg5 **Selangor** *var.* Negeri Selangor Darul Ehsan. ◈ *state* Peninsular Malaysia
Selânik *see* Thessaloníki
174 Hh7 **Selapanjang** Pulau Rantau, W Indonesia
178 Ii10 **Selaphum** Roi Et, E Thailand
176 Uu16 **Selaru, Pulau** *island* Kepulauan Tanimbar, E Indonesia
176 Vv11 **Selassi** Irian Jaya, E Indonesia
173 G3 **Selatan, Selat** *strait* Peninsular Malaysia
41 N8 **Selawik** Alaska, USA
41 N8 **Selawik Lake** ◎ Alaska, USA
175 Pp13 **Selayar, Selat** *strait* Sulawesi, C Indonesia
97 C14 **Selbjørnsfjorden** *fjord* S Norway
96 H8 **Selbusjøen** ◎ S Norway
99 M17 **Selby** N England, UK
31 N8 **Selby** South Dakota, N USA
23 Z4 **Selbyville** Delaware, NE USA
142 B15 **Selçuk** *var.* Akıncılar. İzmir, SW Turkey
41 Q13 **Seldovia** Alaska, USA
109 M18 **Sele** *anc.* Silarius. ≈ S Italy
44 B5 **Selegua, Río** ≈ W Guatemala
133 X7 **Selemdzha** ≈ SE Russian Federation
133 U7 **Selenga** *Mong.* Selenge Mörön. ≈ Mongolia/Russian Federation
168 K6 **Selenge** Bulgan, N Mongolia
168 J6 **Selenge** Hövsgöl, N Mongolia
81 I19 **Selenge** Bandundu, W Zaire
168 L6 **Selenge** ◈ *province* N Mongolia
Selenge Mörön *see* Selenga
126 Jj16 **Selenginsk** Respublika Buryatiya, S Russian Federation
Selenica *see* Selenicë
115 K22 **Selenicë** *var.* Selenica. Vlorë, SW Albania
126 M7 **Selennyakh** ≈ NE Russian Federation
102 J8 **Selenter See** ◎ N Germany
Sele Sound *see* Soela Väin
105 U6 **Sélestat** *Ger.* Schlettstadt. Bas-Rhin, NE France
Selety *see* Sileti
Seleucia *see* Silifke
94 I4 **Selfoss** Sudhurland, SW Iceland
30 M7 **Selfridge** North Dakota, N USA
78 I15 **Seli** ≈ N Sierra Leone
78 I11 **Sélibabi** *var.* Sélibaby. Guidimaka, S Mauritania
Sélibaby *see* Sélibabi
Selidovka/Selidovo *see* Selydove
128 I15 **Seliger, Ozero** ◎ W Russian Federation
38 J11 **Seligman** Arizona, SW USA
29 S8 **Seligman** Missouri, C USA
82 E6 **Selima Oasis** *oasis* N Sudan
78 L13 **Sélingué, Lac de** ⊟ S Mali
Selinoús *see* Kréstena
20 G14 **Selinsgrove** Pennsylvania, NE USA
Selishche *see* Syelishcha
128 I16 **Selizharovo** Tverskaya Oblast', W Russian Federation
96 C10 **Selje** Sogn og Fjordane, S Norway
9 X16 **Selkirk** Manitoba, S Canada
98 K13 **Selkirk** SE Scotland, UK
98 K13 **Selkirk** *cultural region* SE Scotland, UK
9 O16 **Selkirk Mountains** ▲▲ British Columbia, SW Canada
200 Oo12 **Selkirk Rise** *undersea feature* SE Pacific Ocean
117 F21 **Sellasía** Pelopónnisos, S Greece
46 M9 **Selle, Pic de la** *var.* La Selle. ▲ SE Haiti
104 M8 **Selles-sur-Cher** Loir-et-Cher, C France
38 K16 **Sells** Arizona, SW USA
Sellye *see* Sal'a
25 P5 **Selma** Alabama, S USA
37 Q11 **Selma** California, W USA
22 G10 **Selmer** Tennessee, S USA
181 N17 **Sel, Pointe au** *headland* W Réunion
Selseleh-ye Kūh-e Vākhān *see* Nicholas Range
131 S2 **Selty** Udmurtskaya Respublika, NW Russian Federation
Selukwe *see* Shurugwi
64 L9 **Selva** Santiago del Estero, N Argentina
9 T9 **Selwyn Lake** ◎ Northwest Territories/Saskatchewan, C Canada
15 Gg2 **Selwyn Mountains** ▲▲ Yukon Territory, NW Canada
189 T6 **Selwyn Range** ▲▲ Queensland, C Australia
119 W8 **Selydove** *var.* Selidovka, *Rus.* Selidovo. Donets'ka Oblast', SE Ukraine
Selzaete *see* Zelzate
Seman *see* Semanit, Lumi i
174 Ii13 **Semangka, Teluk** *bay* Sumatera, SW Indonesia
174 I13 **Semangka, Way** ≈ Sumatera, SW Indonesia
115 D22 **Semanit, Lumi i** *var.* Seman. ≈ W Albania
174 Kk14 **Semarang** *var.* Samarang. Jawa, C Indonesia
174 Kk6 **Sematan** Sarawak, East Malaysia
175 Qq17 **Semau, Pulau** *island* S Indonesia
175 Nn8 **Semayang, Danau** ◎ Borneo, N Indonesia
175 O4 **Sembakung, Sungai** ≈ Borneo, N Indonesia
81 G17 **Sembé** La Sangha, NW Congo
Semberong *see* Semberong, Sungai
174 Hh6 **Semberong, Sungai** *var.* Semberong. ≈ Peninsular Malaysia
174 M10 **Sembulu, Danau** ◎ Borneo, N Indonesia
Semendria *see* Smederevo
119 R1 **Semenivka** Chernihivs'ka Oblast', N Ukraine
119 S6 **Semenivka** *Rus.* Semenovka. Poltavs'ka Oblast', NE Ukraine
131 O3 **Semenov** Nizhegorodskaya Oblast', W Russian Federation
Semenovka *see* Semenivka
174 M16 **Semeru, Gunung** *var.* Mahameru. ▲ Jawa, S Indonesia
Semey/Semey Oblysy *see* Semipalatinsk
Semezhevo *see* Syemyezhava
130 L7 **Semiluki** Voronezhskaya Oblast', W Russian Federation
35 W16 **Seminoe Reservoir** ⊟ Wyoming, C USA
29 O11 **Seminole** Oklahoma, C USA
26 M6 **Seminole** Texas, SW USA
25 S8 **Seminole, Lake** ⊟ Florida/Georgia, SE USA
150 M8 **Semiozernoye** Kustanay, N Kazakhstan
151 V9 **Semipalatinsk** *Kaz.* Semey. Semipalatinsk, E Kazakhstan
151 V11 **Semipalatinsk** *off.* Semipalatinskaya Oblast', *Kaz.* Semey Oblysy. ◈ *province* E Kazakhstan
149 O9 **Semīrom** *var.* Samirum. Eşfahān, C Iran
40 F17 **Semisopochnoi Island** *island* Aleutian Islands, Alaska, USA
174 Ll7 **Semitau** Borneo, C Indonesia
83 E18 **Semliki** ≈ Uganda/Zaire
149 P5 **Semnān** *var.* Samnān. Semnān, N Iran
149 Q5 **Semnān** *off.* Ostān-e Semnān. ◈ *province* N Iran
101 K24 **Semois** ≈ SE Belgium
110 E8 **Sempacher See** ◎ C Switzerland
Sena *see* Vila de Sena
32 L12 **Senachwine Lake** ◎ Illinois, N USA
61 O14 **Senador Pompeu** Ceará, E Brazil
Sena Gallica *see* Senigallia
61 C15 **Sena Madureira** Acre, W Brazil
161 L25 **Senanayake Samudra** ◎ E Sri Lanka
85 G15 **Senanga** Western, SW Zambia
29 Y9 **Senath** Missouri, C USA
24 L2 **Senatobia** Mississippi, S USA
170 C15 **Sendai** Kagoshima, Kyūshū, SW Japan
171 M13 **Sendai** Miyagi, Honshū, C Japan
170 Bb15 **Sendai-gawa** ≈ Kyūshū, SW Japan
171 M14 **Sendai-wan** *bay* E Japan
103 J23 **Senden** Bayern, S Germany
160 F11 **Sendhwa** Madhya Pradesh, C India
113 H21 **Senec** *Ger.* Wartberg, *Hung.* Szenc; *prev.* Szempcz. Západné Slovensko, W Slovakia
29 P3 **Seneca** Kansas, C USA
29 R8 **Seneca** Missouri, C USA
34 K13 **Seneca** Oregon, NW USA
23 O11 **Seneca** South Carolina, SE USA
20 G11 **Seneca Lake** ◎ New York, NE USA
33 U13 **Senecaville Lake** ⊟ Ohio, N USA
78 G11 **Senegal** *off.* Republic of Senegal, *Fr.* Sénégal. ◆ *republic* W Africa
78 H9 **Senegal** *Fr.* Sénégal. ≈ W Africa
33 O4 **Seney Marsh** *wetland* Michigan, N USA
103 P14 **Senftenberg** Brandenburg, E Germany
84 L11 **Senga Hill** Northern, NE Zambia
164 G13 **Sênggê Zangbo** ≈ W China
176 Z11 **Senggi** Irian Jaya, E Indonesia
131 R5 **Sengiley** Ul'yanovskaya Oblast', W Russian Federation
65 I19 **Senguerr, Río** ≈ S Argentina
85 J16 **Sengwa** ≈ C Zimbabwe
Senia *see* Senj
113 H19 **Senica** *Ger.* Senitz, *Hung.* Szenice. Západné Slovensko, W Slovakia
Seniça *see* Sjenica
108 J11 **Senigallia** *anc.* Sena Gallica. Marche, C Italy
142 F15 **Senirkent** İsparta, SW Turkey
Senitz *see* Senica
114 C10 **Senj** *Ger.* Zengg, *It.* Segna; *anc.* Senia. Lika-Senj, NW Croatia
169 O10 **Senj** Dornogovĭ, SE Mongolia
94 H9 **Senja** *prev.* Senjen. *island* N Norway
Senjen *see* Senja
167 U12 **Senkaku-shotō** *island group* SW Japan
143 R12 **Şenkaya** Erzurum, NE Turkey
85 I16 **Senkobo** Southern, S Zambia
105 O4 **Senlis** Oise, N France
178 K13 **Senmonorom** Môndól Kiri, E Cambodia
82 G10 **Sennar** *var.* Sannār. Sinnar, C Sudan
Senno *see* Syanno
Senones *see* Sens
111 W11 **Senovo** E Slovenia
105 P6 **Sens** *anc.* Agendicum, Senones. Yonne, C France
Sensburg *see* Mrągowo
178 J12 **Sên, Stœng** ≈ C Cambodia
44 F7 **Sensuntepeque** Cabañas, NE El Salvador
114 L8 **Senta** *Hung.* Zenta. Serbia, N Yugoslavia
Šent Andraž *see* Sankt Andrä
176 Z10 **Sentani, Danau** ◎ Irian Jaya, E Indonesia
30 J5 **Sentinel Butte** ▲ North Dakota, N USA
8 M13 **Sentinel Peak** ▲ British Columbia, W Canada
61 N16 **Sento Sé** Bahia, E Brazil
Šent Peter *see* Pivka
Šent Vid *see* Sankt Veit an der Glan
194 E10 **Senu** ≈ NW PNG
Seo de Urgel *see* La See d'Urgel
160 I7 **Seondha** Madhya Pradesh, C India
160 J11 **Seoni** *prev.* Seeonee. Madhya Pradesh, C India
Seoul *see* Sŏul
192 I13 **Separation Point** *headland* South Island, NZ
175 O7 **Sepasu** Borneo, N Indonesia
194 F10 **Sepik** ≈ Indonesia/PNG
Sepone *see* Muang Xépôn
112 M7 **Sępopol** *Ger.* Schippenbeil. Olsztyn, N Poland
118 F10 **Şepreuş** *Hung.* Seprős. Arad, W Romania
Seprős *see* Şepreuş
Şepşi-Sângeorz/Sepsiszentgyőrgy *see* Sfântu Gheorghe
13 W4 **Sept-Îles** Québec, SE Canada
107 N6 **Sepúlveda** Castilla-León, N Spain
174 Ii12 **Seputih, Way** ≈ Sumatera, SW Indonesia
106 K8 **Sequeros** Castilla-León, N Spain
106 L5 **Sequillo** ≈ NW Spain
34 G7 **Sequim** Washington, NW USA
37 S11 **Sequoia National Park** *national park* California, W USA
143 Q14 **Şerafettin Dağları** ▲▲ E Turkey
131 N10 **Serafimovich** Volgogradskaya Oblast', SW Russian Federation
175 Rr6 **Serai** Sulawesi, N Indonesia
101 K19 **Seraing** Liège, E Belgium
Sêraitang *see* Baima
Serajgonj *see* Shirajganj Ghat
152 I15 **Serakhs** *var.* Saragt. Akhalskiy Velayat, S Turkmenistan
176 X10 **Serami** Irian Jaya, E Indonesia
Seram, Laut *see* Ceram Sea
Serampore/Serampur *see* Shrīrāmpur
175 Tt11 **Seram, Pulau** *var.* Serang, *Eng.* Ceram. *island* Maluku, E Indonesia
174 J14 **Serang** Jawa, C Indonesia
Serang *see* Seram, Pulau
174 Kk6 **Serasan, Pulau** *island* Kepulauan Natuna, W Indonesia
174 Kk6 **Serasan, Selat** *strait* Indonesia/Malaysia
114 M12 **Serbia** *Ger.* Serbien, *Serb.* Srbija. ◈ *republic* Yugoslavia
Serbien *see* Serbia
Sercq *see* Sark
Serdica *see* Sofiya
131 O7 **Serdobsk** Penzenskaya Oblast', W Russian Federation
151 X9 **Serebryansk** Vostochnyy Kazakhstan, E Kazakhstan
126 Ll13 **Serebryanyy Bor** Respublika Sakha (Yakutiya), NE Russian Federation
113 H20 **Sered'** *Hung.* Szered. Západné Slovensko, SW Slovakia
119 S1 **Seredyna-Buda** Sums'ka Oblast', NE Ukraine
120 E13 **Seredžius** Jurbarkas, C Lithuania
142 I14 **Şereflikoçhisar** Ankara, C Turkey
108 D7 **Seregno** Lombardia, N Italy
105 P7 **Serein** ≈ C France
174 H5 **Seremban** Negeri Sembilan, Peninsular Malaysia
83 H20 **Serengeti Plain** *plain* N Tanzania
84 K13 **Serenje** Central, E Zambia
Seres *see* Sérres
118 J5 **Seret** ≈ W Ukraine
Seret/Sereth *see* Siret
117 I21 **Serfopoúla** *island* Kykládes, Greece, Aegean Sea
131 P4 **Sergach** Nizhegorodskaya Oblast', W Russian Federation
31 S13 **Sergeant Bluff** Iowa, C USA
169 P7 **Sergelen** Dornod, NE Mongolia
169 O9 **Sergelen** Sühbaatar, E Mongolia
173 F4 **Sergeulangit, Pegunungan** ▲▲ Sumatera, NW Indonesia
126 I4 **Sergeya Kirova, Ostrova** *island* N Russian Federation
Sergeyevichi *see* Syarhyeyevichy
151 O7 **Sergeyevka** Severnyy Kazakhstan, N Kazakhstan
Sergiopol *see* Ayaguz
61 P16 **Sergipe** *off.* Estado de Sergipe. ◈ *state* E Brazil
130 L3 **Sergiyev Posad** Moskovskaya Oblast', W Russian Federation
128 K5 **Sergozero, Ozero** ◎ NW Russian Federation
174 L7 **Serian** Sarawak, East Malaysia
174 J13 **Seribu, Kepulauan** *island group* S Indonesia
117 I21 **Sérifos** *anc.* Seriphos. *island* Kykládes, Greece, Aegean Sea
117 I21 **Sérifou, Stenó** *strait* SE Greece
142 F16 **Serik** Antalya, SW Turkey
108 E7 **Serio** ≈ N Italy
Seriphos *see* Sérifos
Serir Tibesti *see* Sarīr Tībistī
131 S5 **Sernovodsk** Samarskaya Oblast', W Russian Federation
131 R2 **Sernur** Respublika Mariy El, W Russian Federation
112 M11 **Serock** Warszawa, C Poland
63 B18 **Serodino** Santa Fe, C Argentina
Seroei *see* Serui
107 P14 **Serón** Andalucía, S Spain
101 E14 **Serooskerke** Zeeland, SW Netherlands
107 T6 **Seròs** Cataluña, NE Spain
125 F10 **Serov** Sverdlovskaya Oblast', C Russian Federation
85 I19 **Serowe** Central, SE Botswana
106 H13 **Serpa** Beja, S Portugal
Serpa Pinto *see* Menongue
190 A4 **Serpentine Lakes** *salt lake* South Australia
47 T15 **Serpent's Mouth, The** *Sp.* Boca de la Serpiente. *strait* Trinidad and Tobago/Venezuela
Serpiente, Boca de la *see* Serpent's Mouth, The
130 K4 **Serpukhov** Moskovskaya Oblast', W Russian Federation
62 K13 **Serra do Mar** ▲▲ S Brazil
Sérrai *see* Sérres
109 N22 **Serra San Bruno** Calabria, SW Italy
105 S14 **Serres** Hautes-Alpes, SE France
116 H13 **Sérres** *var.* Seres; *prev.* Sérrai. Kentrikí Makedonía, NE Greece
64 J9 **Serrezuela** Córdoba, C Argentina
61 O16 **Serrinha** Bahia, E Brazil
61 M19 **Serro** *var.* Sêrro. Minas Gerais, NE Brazil
Sêrro *see* Serro
Sert *see* Siirt
Sertá *see* Sertã
106 H9 **Sertã** *var.* Sertá. Castelo Branco, C Portugal
62 L8 **Sertãozinho** São Paulo, S Brazil
166 F7 **Sêrtar** Sichuan, C China
176 X10 **Serui** *prev.* Seroei. Irian Jaya, E Indonesia
85 J19 **Serule** Central, E Botswana
174 Ll10 **Seruyan, Sungai** *var.* Sungai Pembuang. ≈ Borneo, N Indonesia
117 E14 **Sérvia** Dytikí Makedonía, N Greece
166 E7 **Sêrxü** Sichuan, C China
126 Mm15 **Seryshevo** Amurskaya Oblast', SE Russian Federation
Sé San *see* San, Tônle
Sesana *see* Sežana
175 Nn5 **Sesayap, Sungai** ≈ Borneo, N Indonesia
Sesdlets *see* Siedlce
81 N17 **Sese** Haut-Zaïre, N Zaire
83 F18 **Sese Islands** *island group* S Uganda
175 T9 **Sesepe** Pulau Obi, E Indonesia
85 H16 **Sesheke** *var.* Sesheko. Western, SE Zambia
Sesheko *see* Sesheke
108 C8 **Sesia** *anc.* Sessites. ≈ NW Italy
106 F11 **Sesimbra** Setúbal, S Portugal
117 N22 **Sesklió** *island* Dodekánisos, Greece, Aegean Sea
32 L16 **Sesser** Illinois, N USA
Sessites *see* Sesia
108 G11 **Sesto Fiorentino** Toscana, C Italy
108 E7 **Sesto San Giovanni** Lombardia, N Italy
108 A8 **Sestriere** Piemonte, NE Italy
108 D10 **Sestri Levante** Liguria, NW Italy
109 C20 **Sestu** Sardegna, Italy, C Mediterranean Sea
114 E8 **Sesvete** Grad Zagreb, N Croatia
120 G12 **Šeta** Kėdainiai, C Lithuania
Setabis *see* Xátiva
172 N5 **Setana** Hokkaidō, NE Japan
105 Q16 **Sète** *prev.* Cette. Hérault, S France
60 J11 **Sete Ilhas** Amapá, NE Brazil
61 L20 **Sete Lagoas** Minas Gerais, NE Brazil
62 G10 **Sete Quedas, Ilha das** *island* S Brazil
94 I10 **Setermoen** Troms, N Norway
97 E17 **Setesdal** *valley* S Norway
45 W16 **Setetule, Cerro** ▲ SE Panama
23 Q5 **Seth** West Virginia, NE USA
Setia *see* Sezze
76 K5 **Sétif** *var.* Stif. N Algeria
171 I15 **Seto** Aichi, Honshū, SW Japan
170 F14 **Seto-naikai** *Eng.* Inland Sea. *sea* S Japan
172 Qq13 **Setouchi** *var.* Setoushi. Kagoshima, Amami-Ō-shima, SW Japan
76 F6 **Settat** W Morocco
81 D20 **Setté Cama** Ogooué-Maritime, SW Gabon
9 W13 **Setting Lake** ◎ Manitoba, C Canada
99 L16 **Settle** N England, UK
201 Y12 **Settlement** E Wake Island
106 F11 **Setúbal** *Eng.* Saint Ubes, Saint Yves. Setúbal, W Portugal
106 F11 **Setúbal** ◈ *district* S Portugal
106 F12 **Setúbal, Baía de** *bay* W Portugal
Setul *see* Satun
10 B10 **Seul, Lac** ◎ Ontario, S Canada
105 R8 **Seurre** Côte d'Or, C France
143 U11 **Sevan** C Armenia
143 V12 **Sevana Lich** *Eng.* Lake Sevan, *Rus.* Ozero Sevan. ◎ E Armenia
Sevan, Lake/Sevan, Ozero *see* Sevana Lich
79 N11 **Sévaré** Mopti, C Mali
119 S14 **Sevastopol'** *Eng.* Sebastopol. Respublika Krym, S Ukraine
27 R14 **Seven Sisters** Texas, SW USA
8 K13 **Seven Sisters Peaks** ▲ British Columbia, SW Canada
101 M15 **Sevenum** Limburg, SE Netherlands
105 P14 **Séverac-le-Château** Aveyron, S France
12 H13 **Severn** ≈ Ontario, S Canada
99 L21 **Severn** *Wel.* Hafren. ≈ England/Wales, UK
129 O11 **Severnaya Dvina** *var.* Northern Dvina. ≈ NW Russian Federation
131 N16 **Severnaya Osetiya, Respublika** *Eng.* North Ossetia; *prev.* Severo-Osetinskaya SSR. ◈ *autonomous republic* SW Russian Federation
125 F9 **Severnaya Sos'va** ≈ N Russian Federation
127 N17 **Severnaya Zemlya** *var.* Nicholas II Land. *island group* N Russian Federation
113 C15 **Severní Čechy** *off.* Severočeský Kraj. ◈ *region* NW Czech Republic
113 H17 **Severní Morava** *off.* Severomoravský Kraj. ◈ *region* E Czech Republic
131 T5 **Severnoye** Orenburgskaya Oblast', W Russian Federation
37 S3 **Severn Troughs Range** ▲▲ Nevada, W USA
129 W3 **Severnyy** Respublika Komi, NW Russian Federation
150 I13 **Severnyy Chink Ustyurta** ▲▲ W Kazakhstan
129 Q13 **Severnyye Uvaly** *var.* Northern Ural Hills. *hill range* NW Russian Federation
151 O6 **Severnyy Kazakhstan** *off.* Severo-Kazakhstanskaya Oblast', *var.* North Kazakhstan, *Kaz.* Soltüstik Qazaqstan Oblysy. ◈ *province* N Kazakhstan
129 V9 **Severnyy Ural** ▲▲ NW Russian Federation
Severo-Alichurskiy Khrebet *see* Alichuri Shimolí, Qatorkŭhi
126 K14 **Severobaykal'sk** Respublika Buryatiya, S Russian Federation
Severočeský Kraj *see* Severní Čechy
Severodonetsk *see* Syeverodonets'k
128 M8 **Severodvinsk** *prev.* Molotov, Sudostroy. Arkhangel'skaya Oblast', NW Russian Federation
Severo-Kazakhstanskaya Oblast' *see* Severnyy Kazakhstan
127 Pp13 **Severo-Kuril'sk** Sakhalinskaya Oblast', SE Russian Federation
Severomoravský Kraj *see* Severní Morava
128 J3 **Severomorsk** Murmanskaya Oblast', NW Russian Federation
Severo-Osetinskaya SSR *see* Severnaya Osetiya, Respublika
126 J6 **Severo-Sibirskaya Nizmennost'** *var.* North Siberian Plain, *Eng.* North Siberian Lowland. *lowlands* N Russian Federation
125 Ee10 **Severoural'sk** Sverdlovskaya Oblast', C Russian Federation
126 I12 **Severo-Yeniseyskiy** Krasnoyarskiy Kray, C Russian Federation
130 M11 **Severskiy Donets** *Ukr.* Sivers'kyy Donets'. ≈ Russian Federation/Ukraine *see also* Sivers'kyy Donets'
94 M9 **Sevettijärvi** Lappi, N Finland
38 M5 **Sevier Bridge Reservoir** ⊟ Utah, W USA
38 J4 **Sevier Desert** *plain* Utah, W USA
38 J5 **Sevier Lake** ◎ Utah, W USA
23 N9 **Sevierville** Tennessee, S USA
106 J14 **Sevilla** *Eng.* Seville; *anc.* Hispalis. Andalucía, SW Spain
106 J13 **Sevilla** ◈ *province* Andalucía, SW Spain
Sevilla de Niefang *see* Niefang
45 O16 **Sevilla, Isla** *island* SW Panama
Seville *see* Sevilla
116 J9 **Sevlievo** Loveshka Oblast, C Bulgaria
Sevluš/Sevlyush *see* Vynohradiv
111 V11 **Sevnica** *Ger.* Lichtenwald. E Slovenia
130 I7 **Sevsk** Bryanskaya Oblast', W Russian Federation
78 J15 **Sewa** ≈ E Sierra Leone
41 R12 **Seward** Alaska, USA
31 R15 **Seward** Nebraska, C USA
8 G8 **Seward Glacier** *glacier* Yukon Territory, W Canada
207 Q3 **Seward Peninsula** *peninsula* Alaska, USA
Seward's Folly *see* Alaska
64 H12 **Sewell** Libertador, C Chile
100 K5 **Sexbierum** *Fris.* Seisbierrum. Friesland, N Netherlands
9 O13 **Sexsmith** Alberta, W Canada
43 W13 **Seybaplaya** Campeche, SE Mexico
181 N6 **Seychelles** *off.* Republic of Seychelles. ◆ *republic* W Indian Ocean
69 Z9 **Seychelles** *island group* NE Seychelles
181 N6 **Seychelles Bank** *var.* Le Banc des Seychelles. *undersea feature* W Indian Ocean
Seychelles, Le Banc des *see* Seychelles Bank
180 H17 **Seychellois, Morne** ▲ Mahé, NE Seychelles
94 L2 **Seydhisfjördhur** Austurland, E Iceland
152 J12 **Seydi** *prev.* Neftezavodsk. Lebapskiy Velayat, E Turkmenistan
142 G16 **Seydişehir** Konya, SW Turkey
142 J13 **Seyfe Gölü** ◎ C Turkey
Seyhan *see* Adana
142 K16 **Seyhan Barajı** ⊟ S Turkey
142 K17 **Seyhan Nehri** ≈ S Turkey
142 F13 **Seyitgazi** Eskişehir, W Turkey
130 J7 **Seym** ≈ W Russian Federation
119 S3 **Seym** ≈ N Ukraine
127 O9 **Seymchan** Magadanskaya Oblast', E Russian Federation
116 N12 **Seymen** Tekirdağ, NW Turkey
191 O11 **Seymour** Victoria, SE Australia
85 I25 **Seymour** Eastern Cape, S South Africa
31 W16 **Seymour** Iowa, C USA
29 U7 **Seymour** Missouri, C USA
27 Q5 **Seymour** Texas, SW USA
116 M12 **Şeytan Deresi** ≈ NW Turkey
111 S12 **Sežana** *It.* Sesana. SW Slovenia
105 P5 **Sézanne** Marne, N France
109 I16 **Sezze** *anc.* Setia. Lazio, C Italy
117 H25 **Sfákia** Kríti, Greece, E Mediterranean Sea
117 D21 **Sfaktiría** *island* S Greece

◆ Country
● Country Capital
◇ Dependent Territory
○ Dependent Territory Capital
◈ Administrative Region
✈ International Airport
▲ Mountain
▲▲ Mountain Range
Volcano
≈ River
◎ Lake
⊟ Reservoir

118 J11 **Sfântu Gheorghe** *Ger.* Sankt-Georgen, *Hung.* Sepsiszentgyörgy; *prev.* Şepşi-Sângeorz, Sfintu Gheorghe. Covasna, C Romania
119 N13 **Sfântu Gheorghe, Braţul** *var.* Gheorghe Braţul. ~ E Romania
77 N6 **Sfax** *Ar.* Şafāqis. E Tunisia
77 N6 **Sfax** × E Tunisia
Sfintu Gheorghe *see* Sfântu Gheorghe
100 H13 **'s-Gravendeel** Zuid-Holland, SW Netherlands
100 F11 **'s-Gravenhage** *var.* Den Haag, *Eng.* The Hague, *Fr.* La Haye. ● (Netherlands-seat of government) Zuid-Holland, W Netherlands
100 G12 **'s-Gravenzande** Zuid-Holland, W Netherlands
Shaan/Shaanxi Sheng *see* Shaanxi
165 X11 **Shaanxi** *var.* Shaan, Shaanxi Sheng, Shan-hsi, Shenshi, Shensi. ◆ *province* C China
Shaartuz *see* Shahrtuz
81 L24 **Shaba** *off.* Région du Shaba. ◆ *region* SE Zaire
Shabani *see* Zvishavane
83 N17 **Shabeellaha Dhexe** *off.* Gobolka Shabeellaha Dhexe. ◆ *region* E Somalia
83 L17 **Shabeellaha Hoose** *off.* Gobolka Shabeellaha Hoose. ◆ *region* S Somalia
Shabeelle, Webi *see* Shebeli
116 O7 **Shabla** Varnenska Oblast, NE Bulgaria
116 O7 **Shabla, Nos** *headland* NE Bulgaria
11 N9 **Shabogama Lake** ◎ Newfoundland and Labrador, E Canada
81 N20 **Shabunda** Sud Kivu, E Zaire
147 Q15 **Shabwah** C Yemen
164 F8 **Shache** *var.* Yarkant. Xinjiang Uygur Zizhiqu, NW China
Shacheng *see* Huailai
205 R12 **Shackleton Coast** *physical region* Antarctica
205 Z10 **Shackleton Ice Shelf** *ice shelf* Antarctica
Shaddādī *see* Ash Shadādah
30 K7 **Shadehill Reservoir** ⊟ South Dakota, N USA
125 Ee12 **Shadrinsk** Kurganskaya Oblast', C Russian Federation
33 O12 **Shafer, Lake** ⊟ Indiana, N USA
37 R13 **Shafter** California, W USA
26 J11 **Shafter** Texas, SW USA
99 L23 **Shaftesbury** S England, UK
193 F22 **Shag** ~ South Island, NZ
151 V9 **Shagan** ~ E Kazakhstan
41 O11 **Shageluk** Alaska, USA
126 I16 **Shagonar** Respublika Tyva, S Russian Federation
193 F22 **Shag Point** *headland* South Island, NZ
150 J12 **Shagyray, Plato** *plain* SW Kazakhstan
Shāhābād *see* Eslāmābād
174 H5 **Shah Alam** Selangor, Peninsular Malaysia
119 O12 **Shahany, Ozero** ◎ SW Ukraine
144 H9 **Shahbā'** *anc.* Philippopolis. As Suwaydā', S Syria
Shahbān *see* Ad Dayr
155 P17 **Shāhbandar** Sind, SE Pakistan
155 P13 **Shāhdādkot** Sind, SW Pakistan
149 T10 **Shahdād, Namakzār-e** *salt pan* E Iran
155 Q15 **Shāhdādpur** Sind, SE Pakistan
160 K10 **Shahdol** Madhya Pradesh, C India
167 N7 **Sha He** ~ C China
Shahepu *see* Linze
159 N13 **Shāhganj** Uttar Pradesh, N India
158 C11 **Shāhgarh** Rājasthān, NW India
Sha Hi *see* Orūmīyeh, Daryācheh-ye, Iran
Shāhī *see* Qā'emshahr, Māzandarān, Iran
145 Q6 **Shāhimah** *var.* Shahma. C Iraq
Shahjahanabad *see* Delhi
158 L11 **Shāhjahānpur** Uttar Pradesh, N India
Shahma *see* Shāhimah
155 U7 **Shāhpur** Punjab, E Pakistan
Shāhpur *see* Shāhpur Chākar
158 G13 **Shāhpura** Rājasthān, N India
155 Q15 **Shāhpur Chākar** *var.* Shāhpur. Sind, SE Pakistan
154 M5 **Shahrak** Ghowr, C Afghanistan
149 Q11 **Shahr-e Bābak** Kermān, C Iran
149 N8 **Shahr-e Kord** *var.* Shahr Kord. Chahār Maḩall va Bakhtīārī, C Iran
149 O9 **Shahreẓā** *var.* Qomisheh, Qumisheh, Shahriza; *prev.* Qomsheh. Eşfahān, C Iran
153 S10 **Shahrikhon** *Rus.* Shakhrikhan. Andijon Wiloyati, E Uzbekistan
153 N12 **Shahrisabz** *Rus.* Shakhrisabz. Qashqadaryo Wiloyati, S Uzbekistan
153 P11 **Shahriston** *Rus.* Shakhristan. NW Tajikistan
Shahriza *see* Shahreẓā
Shahr-i-Zabul *see* Zābol
Shahr Kord *see* Shahr-e Kord
153 P14 **Shahrtuz** *Rus.* Shaartuz. SW Tajikistan
149 Q4 **Shāhrūd** *prev.* Emāmrūd, Emāmshahr. Semnān, N Iran
Shahsavār/Shahsawar *see* Tonekābon
Shaidara *see* Step' Nardara
Shaikh Ābid *see* Shaykh 'Ābid
Shaikh Fāris *see* Shaykh Fāris
Shaikh Najm *see* Shaykh Najm
144 K5 **Sha'īr, Jabal** ▲ C Syria
160 G10 **Shājāpur** Madhya Pradesh, C India
82 J8 **Shakal, Ras** *headland* NE Sudan
Shakhdarinskiy Khrebet *see* Shokhdara, Qatorkŭhi
Shakhrikhan *see* Shahrikhon
Shakhrisabz *see* Shahrisabz
Shakhristan *see* Shahriston
119 X8 **Shakhtars'k** *Rus.* Shakhtërsk. Donets'ka Oblast', SE Ukraine
127 O15 **Shakhtersk** Ostrov Sakhalin, Sakhalinskaya Oblast', SE Russian Federation
Shakhtërsk *see* Shakhtars'k
151 R10 **Shakhtinsk** Karaganda, C Kazakhstan
130 L11 **Shakhty** Rostovskaya Oblast', SW Russian Federation
131 P2 **Shakhun'ya** Nizhegorodskaya Oblast', W Russian Federation
79 S15 **Shaki** Oyo, W Nigeria
83 J15 **Shakīso** S Ethiopia
119 X8 **Shakmars'k** Donets'ka Oblast', E Ukraine
31 V9 **Shakopee** Minnesota, N USA
172 Nn5 **Shakotan-hantō** *peninsula* Hokkaidō, NE Japan
172 O4 **Shakotan-misaki** *headland* Hokkaidō, NE Japan
41 N9 **Shaktoolik** Alaska, USA
83 J14 **Shala Hāyk'** ◎ C Ethiopia
128 M10 **Shalakusha** Arkhangel'skaya Oblast', NW Russian Federation
151 U8 **Shalday** Pavlodar, NE Kazakhstan
131 P16 **Shali** Chechenskaya Respublika, SW Russian Federation
147 W12 **Shalim** *var.* Shelim. S Oman
Shaliuhe *see* Gangca
150 F9 **Shalkar, Ozero** *prev.* Chelkar, Ozero. ◎ W Kazakhstan
23 V12 **Shallotte** North Carolina, SE USA
27 N5 **Shallowater** Texas, SW USA
128 K11 **Shal'skiy** Respublika Kareliya, NW Russian Federation
166 F9 **Shaluli Shan** ▲ C China
83 F22 **Shama** ~ C Tanzania
9 Z11 **Shamattawa** Manitoba, C Canada
10 F8 **Shamattawa** ~ Ontario, C Canada
Shām, Bādiyat ash *see* Syrian Desert
Shamiya *see* Ash Shāmīyah
147 X8 **Shām, Jabal ash** *var.* Jebel Sham. ▲ NW Oman
Sham, Jebel *see* Shām, Jabal ash
Shamkhor *see* Şämkir
20 G14 **Shamokin** Pennsylvania, NE USA
27 P2 **Shamrock** Texas, SW USA
Sha'nabī, Jabal ash *see* Chambi, Jebel
145 Y12 **Shanāwah** E Iraq
165 T8 **Shandan** Gansu, N China
Shandī *see* Shendi
167 Q5 **Shandong** *var.* Lu, Shandong Sheng, Shantung. ◆ *province* E China
167 R4 **Shandong Bandao** *var.* Shantung Peninsula. *peninsula* E China
Shandong Peninsula *see* Shandong Bandao
Shandong Sheng *see* Shandong
145 U8 **Shandrūkh** E Iraq
85 J17 **Shangani** ~ W Zimbabwe
167 O15 **Shangchuan Dao** *island* S China
Shangchuankou *see* Minhe
169 P12 **Shangdu** Nei Mongol Zizhiqu, N China
167 O11 **Shanggao** Jiangxi, S China
167 S8 **Shanghai** *var.* Shang-hai. Shanghai Shi, E China
Shanghai *see* Shanghai Shi
167 S8 **Shanghai Shi** *var.* Hu, Shanghai. ◆ *municipality* E China
167 P13 **Shanghang** Fujian, SE China
166 K14 **Shanglin** Guangxi Zhuangzu Zizhiqu, S China
85 G15 **Shangombo** Western, W Zambia
167 O6 **Shangqiu** *var.* Zhuji. Henan, C China
167 Q10 **Shangrao** Jiangxi, S China
167 S9 **Shangyu** *var.* Baiguan. Zhejiang, SE China
169 X9 **Shangzhi** Heilongjiang, NE China
166 L7 **Shangzhou** *var.* Shang Xian. Shaanxi, C China
169 W9 **Shanhetun** Heilongjiang, NE China
Shan-hsi *see* Shaanxi, China
Shan-hsi *see* Shanxi, China
165 O6 **Shankou** Xinjiang Uygur Zizhiqu, W China
192 M13 **Shannon** Manawatu-Wanganui, North Island, NZ
99 B19 **Shannon** × W Ireland
99 C17 **Shannon** *Ir.* An tSionainn. ~ W Ireland
178 H6 **Shan Plateau** *plateau* E Myanmar
164 M6 **Shanshan** *var.* Piqan. Xinjiang Uygur Zizhiqu, NW China
Shansi *see* Shanxi
178 Gg5 **Shan State** ◆ *state* E Myanmar
Shantar Islands *see* Shantarskiye Ostrova
127 N13 **Shantarskiye Ostrova** *Eng.* Shantar Islands. *island group* E Russian Federation
167 Q14 **Shantou** *var.* Shan-t'ou, Swatow. Guangdong, S China
Shantung *see* Shandong
Shantung Peninsula *see* Shandong Bandao
169 O14 **Shanxi** *var.* Jin, Shan-hsi, Shansi, Shanxi Sheng. ◆ *province* C China
Shan Xian *see* Sanmenxia
167 P6 **Shanxian** *var.* Shan Xian. Shandong, E China
Shanxi Sheng *see* Shanxi
166 L7 **Shanyang** Shaanxi, C China
167 O13 **Shaoguan** *var.* Shao-kuan, *Cant.* Kukong; *prev.* Ch'u-chiang. Guangdong, S China
Shao-kuan *see* Shaoguan
167 Q11 **Shaowu** Fujian, SE China
167 S9 **Shaoxing** Zhejiang, SE China
166 M12 **Shaoyang** *prev.* Tangdukou. Hunan, S China
166 M11 **Shaoyang** *var.* Baoqing, Shao-yang; *prev.* Pao-king. Hunan, S China
98 K5 **Shapinsay** *island* NE Scotland, UK
129 S4 **Shapkina** ~ NW Russian Federation
Shāpūr *see* Salmās
164 M4 **Shaqiuhe** Xinjiang Uygur Zizhiqu, W China
145 T2 **Shaqlāwa** *var.* Shaqlāwah. E Iraq
Shaqlāwah *see* Shaqlāwa
144 I8 **Shaqqā** As Suwaydā', S Syria
147 P7 **Shaqrā'** Ar Riyāḑ, C Saudi Arabia
Shaqrā *see* Shuqrah
155 O6 **Sharan** Urūzgān, SE Afghanistan
Sharaqpur *see* Sharqpur
Sharbaqty *see* Shcherbakty
147 X12 **Sharbatāt** S Oman
147 X12 **Sharbithāt, Ras** *var.* Ra's Sharbatāt. *headland* S Oman
12 K14 **Sharbot Lake** Ontario, SE Canada
Shardara Dalasy *see* Step' Nardara
168 H6 **Sharga** Govĭ-Altay, W Mongolia
168 F8 **Sharga** Hövsgöl, N Mongolia
118 M7 **Sharhorod** Vinnyts'ka Oblast', C Ukraine
168 K10 **Sharhulsan** Ömnögovĭ, S Mongolia
172 Qq6 **Shari** Hokkaidō, NE Japan
Shari *see* Chari
145 T6 **Shārī, Buḩayrat** ◎ C Iraq
Sharjah *see* Ash Shāriqah
120 K12 **Sharkawshchyna** *var.* Sharkowshchyna, *Pol.* Szarkowszczyzna, *Rus.* Sharkovshchina. Vitsyebskaya Voblasts', NW Belarus
188 G9 **Shark Bay** *bay* Western Australia
147 Y9 **Sharkh** E Oman
Sharkovshchina/Sharkowshchyna *see* Sharkawshchyna
131 U6 **Sharlyk** Orenburgskaya Oblast', W Russian Federation
Sharm ash Shaykh *see* Sharm el Sheikh
77 Y9 **Sharm el Sheikh** *var.* Ofiral, Sharm ash Shaykh. E Egypt
20 B13 **Sharon** Pennsylvania, NE USA
28 H4 **Sharon Springs** Kansas, C USA
33 Q14 **Sharonville** Ohio, N USA
Sharourah *see* Sharūrah
31 O10 **Sharpe, Lake** ⊟ South Dakota, N USA
Sharqī, Al Jabal ash/Sharqi, Jebel esh *see* Anti-Lebanon
Sharqīyah, Al Minṭaqah ash *see* Ash Sharqīyah
144 I6 **Sharqīyat an Nabk, Jabal** ▲ W Syria
155 W8 **Sharqpur** *var.* Sharaqpur. Punjab, E Pakistan
147 Q13 **Sharūrah** *var.* Sharourah. Najrān, S Saudi Arabia
129 O14 **Shar'ya** Kostromskaya Oblast', NW Russian Federation
151 V15 **Sharyn** *var.* Charyn. ~ SE Kazakhstan
Sharyn *see* Charyn
85 J18 **Shashe** Central, NE Botswana
85 J18 **Shashe** *var.* Shashi. ~ Botswana/Zimbabwe
83 J14 **Shashemenē** *var.* Shashemenne, Shashhamana, *It.* Sciasciamana. S Ethiopia
Shashemenne/Shashhamana *see* Shashemenē
166 M9 **Shashi** *var.* Sha-shih, Shasi. Hubei, C China
Shashi *see* Shashe
Sha-shih/Shasi *see* Shashi
37 N3 **Shasta Lake** ⊟ California, W USA
37 N2 **Shasta, Mount** ▲ California, W USA
131 O4 **Shatki** Nizhegorodskaya Oblast', W Russian Federation
152 J13 **Shatlyk** Maryyskiy Velayat, C Turkmenistan
Shatra *see* Ash Shaṭrah
121 K17 **Shatsk** *Rus.* Shatsk. Minskaya Voblasts', C Belarus
131 N5 **Shatsk** Ryazanskaya Oblast', W Russian Federation
28 J9 **Shattuck** Oklahoma, C USA
151 P16 **Shaul'der** Yuzhnyy Kazakhstan, S Kazakhstan
9 S17 **Shaunavon** Saskatchewan, S Canada
Shavat *see* Showot
164 K4 **Shawan** Xinjiang Uygur Zizhiqu, NW China
12 G12 **Shawanaga** Ontario, S Canada
32 M6 **Shawano** Wisconsin, N USA
32 M6 **Shawano Lake** ◎ Wisconsin, N USA
13 P10 **Shawinigan** *prev.* Shawinigan Falls. Québec, SE Canada
Shawinigan Falls *see* Shawinigan
13 P10 **Shawinigan-Sud** Québec, SE Canada
144 J5 **Shawmarīyah, Jabal ash** ▲ C Syria
29 O11 **Shawnee** Oklahoma, C USA
12 K12 **Shawville** Québec, SE Canada
Shaykh *see* Ash Shakk
145 W9 **Shaykh 'Ābid** *var.* Shaikh Ābid. E Iraq
145 Y10 **Shaykh Fāris** *var.* Shaikh Fāris. E Iraq
145 T7 **Shaykh Ḩātim** E Iraq
Shaykh, Jabal ash *see* Hermon, Mount
145 X10 **Shaykh Najm** *var.* Shaikh Najm. E Iraq
145 W9 **Shaykh Sa'd** E Iraq
153 T14 **Shazud** SE Tajikistan
121 N18 **Shchadryn** *Rus.* Shchedrin. Homyel'skaya Voblasts', SE Belarus
121 H18 **Shchara** ~ SW Belarus
Shchedrin *see* Shchadryn
Shcheglovsk *see* Kemerovo
130 K5 **Shchëkino** Tul'skaya Oblast', W Russian Federation
129 S7 **Shchel'yayur** Respublika Komi, NW Russian Federation
151 U8 **Shcherbakty** *Kaz.* Sharbaqty. Pavlodar, E Kazakhstan
130 K7 **Shchigry** Kurskaya Oblast', W Russian Federation
Shchitkovichi *see* Shchytkavichy
119 Q2 **Shchors** Chernihivs'ka Oblast', N Ukraine
119 T8 **Shchors'k** Dnipropetrovs'ka Oblast', E Ukraine
Shchuchin *see* Shchuchyn
151 Q7 **Shchuchinsk** *prev.* Shchuchye. Kokshetau, N Kazakhstan
Shchuchye *see* Shchuchinsk
121 G16 **Shchuchyn** *Pol.* Szczuczyn Nowogródzki, *Rus.* Shchuchin. Hrodzyenskaya Voblasts', W Belarus
121 K17 **Shchytkavichy** *Rus.* Shchitkovichi. Minskaya Voblasts', C Belarus
126 H15 **Shebalino** Respublika Altay, S Russian Federation
130 J9 **Shebekino** Belgorodskaya Oblast', W Russian Federation
Shebelē Wenz, Wabē *see* Shebeli
83 L14 **Shebeli** *Amh.* Wabē Shebelē Wenz, *It.* Scebeli, *Som.* Webi Shabeelle. ~ Ethiopia/Somalia
115 M20 **Shebenikut, Maja e** ▲ E Albania
155 N2 **Sheberghān** *var.* Shibarghān, Shiberghan, Shiberghān. Jowzjān, N Afghanistan
150 F14 **Shebir** Mangistau, SW Kazakhstan
33 N8 **Sheboygan** Wisconsin, N USA
79 X15 **Shebshi Mountains** *var.* Schebschi Mountains. ▲ E Nigeria
Shechem *see* Nablus
Shedadi *see* Ash Shadādah
11 P14 **Shediac** New Brunswick, SE Canada
130 L15 **Shedok** Krasnodarskiy Kray, SW Russian Federation
82 N12 **Sheekh** Woqooyi Galbeed, N Somalia
40 M11 **Sheenjek River** ~ Alaska, USA
98 D13 **Sheep Haven** *Ir.* Cuan na gCaorach. *inlet* N Ireland
37 X10 **Sheep Range** ▲ Nevada, W USA
100 M13 **'s-Heerenberg** Gelderland, E Netherlands
99 P22 **Sheerness** SE England, UK
11 Q15 **Sheet Harbour** Nova Scotia, SE Canada
193 H18 **Sheffield** Canterbury, South Island, NZ
99 M18 **Sheffield** N England, UK
25 O2 **Sheffield** Alabama, S USA
31 V12 **Sheffield** Iowa, C USA
27 N10 **Sheffield** Texas, SW USA
65 H22 **Shehuen, Río** ~ S Argentina
Shekhem *see* Nablus
155 V8 **Shekhūpura** Punjab, NE Pakistan
Sheki *see* Şäki
128 L14 **Sheksna** Vologodskaya Oblast', NW Russian Federation
127 O4 **Shelagskiy, Mys** *headland* NE Russian Federation
29 V3 **Shelbina** Missouri, C USA
11 P16 **Shelburne** Nova Scotia, SE Canada
12 G14 **Shelburne** Ontario, S Canada
35 R7 **Shelby** Montana, NW USA
23 Q10 **Shelby** North Carolina, SE USA
33 S12 **Shelby** Ohio, N USA
32 L14 **Shelbyville** Illinois, N USA
33 P14 **Shelbyville** Indiana, N USA
22 L5 **Shelbyville** Kentucky, S USA
29 V2 **Shelbyville** Missouri, C USA
22 J10 **Shelbyville** Tennessee, S USA
27 X8 **Shelbyville** Texas, SW USA
32 L14 **Shelbyville, Lake** ⊟ Illinois, N USA
31 S12 **Sheldon** Iowa, C USA
40 M11 **Sheldons Point** Alaska, USA
126 J16 **Shelekhov** Irkutskaya Oblast', C Russian Federation
Shelekhov Gulf *see* Shelikhova, Zaliv
127 Oo9 **Shelikhova, Zaliv** *Eng.* Shelekhov Gulf. *gulf* E Russian Federation
41 P14 **Shelikof Strait** *strait* Alaska, USA
Shelim *see* Shalim
9 T14 **Shellbrook** Saskatchewan, S Canada
30 L3 **Shell Creek** ~ North Dakota, N USA
Shellif *see* Chelif, Oued
24 I10 **Shell Keys** *island group* Louisiana, S USA
32 J4 **Shell Lake** Wisconsin, N USA
31 W12 **Shell Rock** Iowa, C USA
193 C26 **Shelter Point** *headland* Stewart Island, NZ
20 L13 **Shelton** Connecticut, NE USA
34 G8 **Shelton** Washington, NW USA
Shemakha *see* Şamaxı
151 W9 **Shemonaikha** Vostochnyy Kazakhstan, E Kazakhstan
131 Q4 **Shemursha** Chuvashskaya Respublika, W Russian Federation
40 D16 **Shemya Island** *island* Aleutian Islands, Alaska, USA
31 T16 **Shenandoah** Iowa, C USA
23 U4 **Shenandoah** Virginia, NE USA
23 U4 **Shenandoah Mountains** *ridge* West Virginia, NE USA
23 V3 **Shenandoah River** ~ West Virginia, NE USA
79 W15 **Shendam** Plateau, C Nigeria
82 G8 **Shendi** *var.* Shandī. River Nile, NE Sudan
78 I15 **Shenge** SW Sierra Leone
151 U15 **Shengel'dy** Almaty, SE Kazakhstan
115 K18 **Shëngjin** *var.* Shëngjini. Lezhë, NW Albania
Shëngjini *see* Shëngjin
Shengking *see* Liaoning
Sheng Xian/Shengxian *see* Shengzhou
167 S9 **Shengzhou** *var.* Shengxian, Sheng Xian. Zhejiang, SE China
Shenking *see* Liaoning
129 N11 **Shenkursk** Arkhangel'skaya Oblast', NW Russian Federation
166 L3 **Shenmu** Shaanxi, C China
115 L19 **Shën Noj i Madh** ▲ C Albania
Shenshi/Shensi *see* Shaanxi
169 V12 **Shenyang** *Chin.* Shen-yang, *Eng.* Moukden, Mukden; *prev.* Fengtien. Liaoning, NE China
167 O15 **Shenzhen** Guangdong, S China
160 G8 **Sheopur** Madhya Pradesh, C India
118 L5 **Shepetivka** *Rus.* Shepetovka. Khmel'nyts'ka Oblast', NW Ukraine
Shepetovka *see* Shepetivka
27 W10 **Shepherd** Texas, SW USA
197 D14 **Shepherd Islands** *island group* C Vanuatu
22 K5 **Shepherdsville** Kentucky, S USA
191 O11 **Shepparton** Victoria, SE Australia
99 P22 **Sheppey, Isle of** *island* SE England, UK
Sherabad *see* Sherobod
99 L23 **Sherborne** S England, UK
78 H16 **Sherbro Island** *island* SW Sierra Leone
13 Q12 **Sherbrooke** Québec, SE Canada
31 T11 **Sherburn** Minnesota, N USA
80 H6 **Sherda** Borkou-Ennedi-Tibesti, N Chad
82 G7 **Shereik** River Nile, N Sudan
130 K3 **Sheremet'yevo** × (Moskva) Moskovskaya Oblast', W Russian Federation
159 P14 **Shergāti** Bihār, N India
29 U12 **Sheridan** Arkansas, C USA
35 W12 **Sheridan** Wyoming, C USA
190 G8 **Sheringa** South Australia
126 L16 **Sherlovaya Gora** Chitinskaya Oblast', S Russian Federation
27 U5 **Sherman** Texas, SW USA
204 J10 **Sherman Island** *island* Antarctica
21 S4 **Sherman Mills** Maine, NE USA
31 O15 **Sherman Reservoir** ⊟ Nebraska, C USA
153 N14 **Sherobod** *Rus.* Sherabad. Surkhondaryo Wiloyati, S Uzbekistan
153 O13 **Sherobod** *Rus.* Sherabad. ~ S Uzbekistan
159 T14 **Sherpur** Dhaka, N Bangladesh
39 T4 **Sherrelwood** Colorado, C USA
101 J14 **'s-Hertogenbosch** *Fr.* Bois-le-Duc, *Ger.* Herzogenbusch. Noord-Brabant, S Netherlands
30 M2 **Sherwood** North Dakota, N USA
9 Q14 **Sherwood Park** Alberta, SW Canada
58 F13 **Sheshea, Río** ~ E Peru
149 T5 **Sheshtamad** Khorāsān, NE Iran
31 S10 **Shetek, Lake** ◎ Minnesota, N USA
98 M2 **Shetland Islands** *island group* NE Scotland, UK
150 F14 **Shetpe** Mangistau, SW Kazakhstan
160 C11 **Shetrunji** ~ W India
Shevchenko *see* Aktau
119 W5 **Shevchenkove** Kharkivs'ka Oblast', E Ukraine
83 H14 **Shewa Gīmīra** SW Ethiopia
167 Q9 **Shexian** *var.* Huicheng, She Xian. Anhui, E China
167 R6 **Sheyang** *prev.* Hede. Jiangsu, E China
31 O4 **Sheyenne** North Dakota, N USA
31 P4 **Sheyenne River** ~ North Dakota, N USA
98 G7 **Shiant Islands** *island group* NW Scotland, UK
127 Pp14 **Shiashkotan, Ostrov** *island* Kuril'skiye Ostrova, SE Russian Federation
33 R9 **Shiawassee River** ~ Michigan, N USA
147 R14 **Shibām** C Yemen
Shibarghān *see* Sheberghān
171 Kk12 **Shibata** *var.* Sibata. Niigata, Honshū, C Japan
172 Qq7 **Shibecha** Hokkaidō, NE Japan
Shiberghan/Shiberghān *see* Sheberghān
172 Qq6 **Shibetsu** Hokkaidō, N Japan
172 Pp4 **Shibetsu** *var.* Sibetu. Hokkaidō, NE Japan
172 P5 **Shibetsu** *var.* Sibetu. Hokkaidō, NE Japan
Shibh Jazīrat Sīnā' *see* Sinai
Shibīn al Kawm *see* Shibîn el Kôm
77 W8 **Shibîn el Kôm** *var.* Shibīn al Kawm. N Egypt
149 O13 **Shīb, Kūh-e** ▲ S Iran
10 D8 **Shibogama Lake** ◎ Ontario, C Canada
Shibotsu-jima *see* Zelënyy, Ostrov
171 K14 **Shibukawa** *var.* Sibukawa. Gunma, Honshū, S Japan
170 Bb16 **Shibushi** Kagoshima, Kyūshū, SW Japan
170 C17 **Shibushi-wan** *bay* SW Japan
172 N9 **Shichinohe** Aomori, Honshū, C Japan
201 U13 **Shichiyo Islands** *island group* Chuuk, C Micronesia
Shickshock Mountains *see* Chic-Chocs, Monts
151 S9 **Shiderti** ~ N Kazakhstan
151 S8 **Shiderty** Pavlodar, NE Kazakhstan
98 G10 **Shiel, Loch** ◎ N Scotland, UK
171 H15 **Shiga** *off.* Shiga-ken, *var.* Siga. ◆ *prefecture* Honshū, SW Japan
Shigatse *see* Xigazê
147 U13 **Shiḩan** *oasis* NE Yemen
Shih-chia-chuang *see* Shijiazhuang
164 K4 **Shihezi** Xinjiang Uygur Zizhiqu, NW China
Shihmen *see* Shijiazhuang
Shiichi *see* Shyichy
115 K19 **Shijak** *var.* Shijaku. Durrës, W Albania
Shijaku *see* Shijak
167 O4 **Shijiazhuang** *var.* Shih-chia-chuang; *prev.* Shihmen. Hebei, E China
172 Nn7 **Shikabe** Hokkaidō, NE Japan
155 Q13 **Shikārpur** Sind, S Pakistan
201 V12 **Shiki Islands** *island group* Chuuk, C Micronesia
170 Ee15 **Shikoku** *var.* Sikoku. *island* SW Japan
199 Gg6 **Shikoku Basin** *var.* Sikoku Basin. *undersea feature* N Philippine Sea
170 Ee15 **Shikoku-sanchi** ▲ Shikoku, SW Japan
172 S7 **Shikotan, Ostrov** *Jap.* Shikotan-tō. *island* NE Russian Federation
Shikotan-tō *see* Shikotan, Ostrov
172 O6 **Shikotsu-ko** *var.* Sikotu Ko. ◎ Hokkaidō, NE Japan
83 N15 **Shilabo** SE Ethiopia
131 X7 **Shil'da** Orenburgskaya Oblast', W Russian Federation
145 V3 **Shilēr, Āw-e** ~ E Iraq
159 S12 **Shiliguri** *prev.* Siliguri. West Bengal, NE India
126 Kk16 **Shilka** Chitinskaya Oblast', S Russian Federation
133 V7 **Shilka** ~ S Russian Federation
20 H15 **Shillington** Pennsylvania, NE USA
159 V13 **Shillong** Meghālaya, NE India
130 M5 **Shilovo** Ryazanskaya Oblast', W Russian Federation
170 C14 **Shimabara** *var.* Simabara. Nagasaki, Kyūshū, SW Japan
170 C14 **Shimabara-wan** *bay* SW Japan
171 Ii17 **Shimada** *var.* Simada. Shizuoka, Honshū, S Japan
170 Ee12 **Shimane** *off.* Shimane-ken, *var.* Simane. ◆ *prefecture* Honshū, SW Japan
170 F11 **Shimane-hantō** *peninsula* Honshū, SW Japan
126 M15 **Shimanovsk** Amurskaya Oblast', SE Russian Federation
Shimbir Berris *see* Shimbiris
82 O12 **Shimbiris** *var.* Shimbir Berris. ▲ N Somalia
172 P6 **Shimizu** Hokkaidō, NE Japan
171 Ii16 **Shimizu** *var.* Simizu. Shizuoka, Honshū, S Japan
158 I8 **Shimla** *prev.* Simla. Himāchal Pradesh, N India
Shimminato *see* Shinminato
171 J18 **Shimoda** *var.* Simoda. Shizuoka, Honshū, S Japan
171 Kk16 **Shimodate** *var.* Simodate. Ibaraki, Honshū, S Japan
161 F18 **Shimoga** Karnātaka, W India
170 Bb14 **Shimo-jima** *island* SW Japan
170 B15 **Shimo-Koshiki-jima** *island* SW Japan
83 J21 **Shimoni** Coast, S Kenya
170 D12 **Shimonoseki** *var.* Simonoseki; *hist.* Akamagaseki, Bakan. Yamaguchi, Honshū, SW Japan
171 Kk16 **Shimotsuma** *var.* Simotuma. Ibaraki, Honshū, S Japan
128 G14 **Shimsk** Novgorodskaya Oblast', NW Russian Federation
171 Jj14 **Shinano-gawa** *var.* Sinano Gawa. ~ Honshū, C Japan
147 W7 **Shināş** N Oman
154 J6 **Shīndand** Farāh, W Afghanistan
Shinei *see* Hsinying
27 T12 **Shiner** Texas, SW USA
178 Gg1 **Shingbwiyang** Kachin State, N Myanmar
151 W11 **Shingozha** Semipalatinsk, E Kazakhstan
171 Gg17 **Shingū** *var.* Singû. Wakayama, Honshū, SW Japan
12 F8 **Shining Tree** Ontario, S Canada
170 F12 **Shinji-ko** *var.* Sinzi-ko. ◎ Honshū, SW Japan
171 Ll12 **Shinjō** *var.* Sinzyô. Yamagata, Honshū, C Japan
98 I7 **Shin, Loch** ◎ N Scotland, UK
171 Ii13 **Shinminato** *var.* Shimminato, Sinminato. Toyama, Honshū, SW Japan
170 Dd12 **Shinnanyō** *var.* Shin-Nan'yō, Sinn'anyô. Yamaguchi, Honshū, SW Japan
23 S3 **Shinnston** West Virginia, NE USA
144 I6 **Shinshār** *Fr.* Chinnchâr. Ḩimş, W Syria
171 I16 **Shinshiro** *var.* Sinsiro. Aichi, Honshū, SW Japan
Shinshū *see* Chinju
172 P6 **Shintoku** Hokkaidō, NE Japan
83 G20 **Shinyanga** Shinyanga, NW Tanzania
83 G20 **Shinyanga** ◆ *region* N Tanzania
171 M13 **Shiogama** *var.* Siogama. Miyagi, Honshū, C Japan
171 J15 **Shiojiri** *var.* Sioziri. Nagano, Honshū, S Japan
170 G17 **Shiono-misaki** *headland* Honshū, SW Japan
171 Ll15 **Shioya-zaki** *headland* Honshū, C Japan
116 J9 **Shipchenski Prokhod** *pass* C Bulgaria
166 G14 **Shiping** Yunnan, SW China
11 P13 **Shippagan** *var.* Shippegan. New Brunswick, SE Canada
Shippegan *see* Shippagan
20 F15 **Shippensburg** Pennsylvania, NE USA
39 O9 **Ship Rock** ▲ New Mexico, SW USA
39 P9 **Shiprock** New Mexico, SW USA
13 R6 **Shipshaw** ~ Québec, SE Canada
127 Pp11 **Shipunskiy, Mys** *headland* E Russian Federation
166 K7 **Shiquan** Shaanxi, C China
126 Hh14 **Shira** Respublika Khakasiya, S Russian Federation
170 G16 **Shirahama** Wakayama, Honshū, SW Japan
159 T14 **Shirajganj Ghat** *var.* Serajgonj, Sirajganj. Rajshahi, C Bangladesh
171 Mm7 **Shirakami-misaki** *headland* Hokkaidō, NE Japan
171 L14 **Shirakawa** *var.* Sirakawa. Fukushima, Honshū, C Japan
171 Ii13 **Shirakawa** Gifu, Honshū, SW Japan
171 K14 **Shirane-san** ▲ Honshū, S Japan
171 J16 **Shirane-san** ▲ Honshū, S Japan
172 Pp7 **Shiranuka** Hokkaidō, NE Japan
172 O6 **Shiraoi** Hokkaidō, NE Japan
205 N12 **Shirase Coast** *physical region* Antarctica
172 Pp5 **Shirataki** Hokkaidō, NE Japan
149 O11 **Shīrāz** *var.* Shīrāz. Fārs, S Iran
85 N15 **Shire** *var.* Chire. ~ Malawi/Mozambique
168 G7 **Shiree** Dzavhan, W Mongolia
169 O9 **Shireet** Sühbaatar, SE Mongolia
172 R6 **Shiretoko-hantō** *headland* Hokkaidō, NE Japan
172 R5 **Shiretoko-misaki** *headland* Hokkaidō, NE Japan
131 N5 **Shiringushi** Respublika Mordoviya, W Russian Federation
154 M3 **Shīrīn Tagāb** Fāryāb, N Afghanistan
155 N2 **Shīrīn Tagāb** ~ N Afghanistan
172 Nn8 **Shiriya-zaki** *headland* Honshū, C Japan
150 J12 **Shirkala, Gryada** *plain* W Kazakhstan
171 Ll13 **Shiroishi** *var.* Siroisi. Miyagi, Honshū, C Japan
Shirokoye *see* Shyroke
171 K12 **Shirone** *var.* Sirone. Niigata, Honshū, C Japan
171 I14 **Shirotori** Gifu, Honshū, SW Japan
171 J13 **Shirouma-dake** ▲ Honshū, S Japan
207 T1 **Shirshov Ridge** *undersea feature* W Bering Sea
Shirshütür *see* Shirshyutyur, Peski
152 K12 **Shirshyutyur, Peski** *Turkm.* Shirshütür. *desert* E Turkmenistan
149 T3 **Shīrvān** *var.* Shīrwān. Khorāsān, NE Iran
Shirwa, Lake *see* Chilwa, Lake
Shirwān *see* Shīrvān
165 N5 **Shisanjianfang** Xinjiang Uygur Zizhiqu, W China
40 M16 **Shishaldin Volcano** ▲ Unimak Island, Alaska, USA
Shishchitsy *see* Shyshchytsy
40 M8 **Shishmaref** Alaska, USA
Shisur *see* Ash Shişar
171 I16 **Shitara** Aichi, Honshū, SW Japan
158 D12 **Shiv** Rājasthān, NW India
160 H8 **Shivpuri** Madhya Pradesh, C India
38 J9 **Shivwits Plateau** *plain* Arizona, SW USA
Shiwālik Range *see* Siwalik Range
166 M8 **Shiyan** Hubei, C China
166 H13 **Shizong** Yunnan, SW China
171 Mm13 **Shizugawa** Miyagi, Honshū, NE Japan
165 W8 **Shizuishan** *var.* Dawukou. Ningxia, N China
172 Oo7 **Shizunai** Hokkaidō, NE Japan
171 Ii16 **Shizuoka** *var.* Sizuoka. Shizuoka, Honshū, S Japan
171 Ii16 **Shizuoka** *off.* Shizuoka-ken, *var.* Sizuoka. ◆ *prefecture* Honshū, S Japan
Shklov *see* Shklow
121 N15 **Shklow** *Rus.* Shklov. Mahilyowskaya Voblasts', E Belarus
115 K18 **Shkodër** *var.* Shkodra, *It.* Scutari, *SCr.* Skadar. Shkodër, NW Albania
115 K17 **Shkodër** ◆ *district* NW Albania
Shkodra *see* Shkodër
Shkodrës, Liqeni i *see* Scutari, Lake
Shkumbi/Shkumbin *see* Shkumbinit, Lumi i
115 L20 **Shkumbinit, Lumi i** *var.* Shkumbi, Shkumbin. ~ C Albania
Shligigh, Cuan *see* Sligo Bay
126 I2 **Shmidta, Ostrov** *island* Severnaya Zemlya, N Russian Federation
191 S10 **Shoalhaven River** ~ New South Wales, SE Australia
9 W16 **Shoal Lake** Manitoba, S Canada
33 O15 **Shoals** Indiana, N USA
171 F13 **Shōbara** *var.* Syōbara. Hiroshima, Honshū, SW Japan
170 Ff14 **Shōdo-shima** *island* SW Japan
171 Ii13 **Shō-gawa** ~ Honshū, SW Japan
Shōka *see* Changhua
126 J3 **Shokal'skogo, Proliv** *strait* N Russian Federation
172 Oo4 **Shokanbetsu-dake** Ж Hokkaidō, NE Japan
153 T14 **Shokhdara, Qatorkŭhi** *Rus.* Shakhdarinskiy Khrebet. ▲ SE Tajikistan
151 N9 **Sholaksay** Kustanay, N Kazakhstan
Sholāpur *see* Solāpur
Sholdaneshty *see* Şoldăneşti

◆ Country ● Country Capital ◇ Dependent Territory ○ Dependent Territory Capital ◆ Administrative Region × International Airport ▲ Mountain ▲ Mountain Range Ж Volcano ~ River ◎ Lake ⊟ Reservoir

Shoqpar *see* Chokpar
161 *G21* **Shoranūr** Kerala, SW India
161 *G16* **Shorāpur** Karnātaka, C India
32 *M11* **Shorewood** Illinois, N USA
Shorkazakhly, Solonchak *see* Kazakhlyshor, Solonchak
151 *Q9* **Shortandy** Akmola, C Kazakhstan
Shortepa/Shor Tepe *see* Shūr Tappeh
195 *S13* **Shortland Island** *var.* Alu. *island* Shortland Islands, NW Solomon Islands
195 *T13* **Shortland Islands** *island group* NW Solomon Islands
Shosambetsu *see* Shosanbetsu
172 *P3* **Shosanbetsu** *var.* Shosambetsu. Hokkaidō, NE Japan
35 *O15* **Shoshone** Idaho, NW USA
37 *T6* **Shoshone Mountains** ▲▲ Nevada, W USA
35 *U12* **Shoshone River** ≈ Wyoming, C USA
85 *I19* **Shoshong** Central, SE Botswana
35 *V14* **Shoshoni** Wyoming, C USA
Shōshū *see* Sangju
119 *S2* **Shostka** Sums'ka Oblast', NE Ukraine
193 *C21* **Shotover** ≈ South Island, NZ
39 *N12* **Show Low** Arizona, SW USA
Show Me State *see* Missouri
152 *H9* **Showot** *Rus.* Shavat. Khorazm Wiloyati, W Uzbekistan
129 *O4* **Shoyna** Nenetskiy Avtonomnyy Okrug, NW Russian Federation
128 *M11* **Shozhma** Arkhangel'skaya Oblast', NW Russian Federation
119 *Q7* **Shpola** Cherkas'ka Oblast', N Ukraine
Shqipëria/Shqipërisë, Republika e *see* Albania
24 *G5* **Shreveport** Louisiana, S USA
99 *K19* **Shrewsbury** *hist.* Scrobesbyrig'. W England, UK
158 *D11* **Shri Mohangarh** *prev.* Sri Mohangorh. Rājasthān, NW India
159 *S16* **Shrīrāmpur** *prev.* Serampore, Serampur. West Bengal, NE India
99 *K19* **Shropshire** *cultural region* W England, UK
151 *S16* **Shu** *Kaz.* Shū. Zhambyl, SE Kazakhstan
Shū *see* Chu
166 *G13* **Shuangbai** Yunnan, SW China
169 *W9* **Shuangcheng** Heilongjiang, NE China
166 *E14* **Shuangjiang** Yunnan, SW China
169 *U10* **Shuangliao** *var.* Zhengjiatun. Jilin, NE China
Shuang-liao *see* Liaoyuan
169 *Y7* **Shuangyashan** *var.* Shuang-ya-shan. Heilongjiang, NE China
Shu'aymiah *see* Shu'aymīyah
147 *W12* **Shu'aymīyah** *var.* Shu'aymiah. S Oman
150 *I10* **Shubarkuduk** *Kaz.* Shubarqudyq. Aktyubinsk, W Kazakhstan
Shubarqudyq *see* Shubarkuduk
151 *N12* **Shubar-Tengiz, Ozero** ◎ C Kazakhstan
41 *S5* **Shublik Mountains** ▲▲ Alaska, USA
Shubrā al Khaymah *see* Shubrâ el Kheima
124 *Qq16* **Shubrâ el Kheima** *var.* Shubrā al Khaymah. N Egypt
164 *E8* **Shufu** Xinjiang Uygur Zizhiqu, NW China
153 *S14* **Shughnon, Qatorkŭhi** *Rus.* Shugnanskiy Khrebet. ▲▲ SE Tajikistan
Shugnanskiy Khrebet *see* Shughnon, Qatorkŭhi
167 *Q6* **Shu He** ≈ E China
Shuiding *see* Huocheng
Shuiji *see* Laixi
Shū-Ile Taūlary *see* Chu-Iliyskiye Gory
155 *T10* **Shujāābād** Punjab, E Pakistan
169 *W9* **Shulan** Jilin, NE China
164 *E8* **Shule** Xinjiang Uygur Zizhiqu, NW China
Shuleh *see* Shule He
165 *Q8* **Shule He** *var.* Shuleh, Sulo. ≈ C China
32 *K9* **Shullsburg** Wisconsin, N USA
41 *N16* **Shumagin Islands** *island group* Alaska, USA
152 *G7* **Shumanay** Qoraqalpoghiston Respublikasi, W Uzbekistan
116 *M8* **Shumen** Varnenska Oblast, NE Bulgaria
131 *P4* **Shumerlya** Chuvashskaya Respublika, W Russian Federation
125 *Ee12* **Shumikha** Kurganskaya Oblast', C Russian Federation
120 *M12* **Shumilina** *Rus.* Shumilino. Vitsyebskaya Voblasts', NE Belarus
Shumilino *see* Shumilina
127 *Pp12* **Shumshu, Ostrov** *island* SE Russian Federation
118 *K5* **Shums'k** Ternopil's'ka Oblast', W Ukraine
41 *O7* **Shungnak** Alaska, USA
Shunsen *see* Ch'unch'ŏn
166 *M3* **Shuo Xian** Shanxi, NE China
Shuo Xian/Shuoxian *see* Shuozhou
167 *N3* **Shuozhou** *var.* Shuoxian; *prev.* Shuo Xian. Shanxi, C China
147 *P16* **Shuqrah** *var.* Shaqrā. SW Yemen
Shurab *see* Shŭrob
153 *O14* **Shŭrchi** *Rus.* Shurchi. Surkhondaryo Wiloyati, S Uzbekistan
153 *R11* **Shŭrob** *Rus.* Shurab. NW Tajikistan
149 *T10* **Shūr, Rūd-e** ≈ E Iran
155 *O2* **Shūr Tappeh** *var.* Shortepa, Shor Tepe. Balkh, N Afghanistan
85 *K17* **Shurugwi** *prev.* Selukwe. Midlands, C Zimbabwe
148 *L8* **Shūsh** *anc.* Susa, *Bibl.* Shushan. Khūzestān, SW Iran
Shushan *see* Shūsh
148 *L9* **Shūshtar** *var.* Shustar, Shushter. Khūzestān, SW Iran
Shushter/Shustar *see* Shūshtar
147 *T9* **Shuṭfah, Qalamat** *well* E Saudi Arabia
145 *V9* **Shuwayjah, Hawr ash** *var.* Hawr as Suwayqiyah. ◎ E Iraq
128 *M16* **Shuya** Ivanovskaya Oblast', W Russian Federation
41 *Q14* **Shuyak Island** *island* Alaska, USA
177 *G4* **Shwebo** Sagaing, C Myanmar
177 *Ff7* **Shwedaung** Pegu, W Myanmar
177 *G8* **Shwegyin** Pegu, SW Myanmar
178 *Gg4* **Shweli** *Chin.* Longchuan Jiang. ≈ Myanmar/China
177 *G6* **Shwemyo** Mandalay, C Myanmar
Shyghys Qazagastan Oblysy *see* Vostochnyy Kazakhstan
Shyghys Qongyrat *see* Vostochno-Kounradskiy
121 *M19* **Shyichy** *Rus.* Shiichi. Homyel'skaya Voblasts', SE Belarus
151 *Q17* **Shymkent** *prev.* Chimkent. Yuzhnyy Kazakhstan, S Kazakhstan
Shyngghyrlaū *see* Chingirlau
158 *J5* **Shyok** Jammu and Kashmir, NW India
119 *S9* **Shyroke** *Rus.* Shirokoye. Dnipropetrovs'ka Oblast', E Ukraine
119 *O9* **Shyryayeve** Odes'ka Oblast', SW Ukraine
119 *S5* **Shyshaky** Poltavs'ka Oblast', C Ukraine
121 *K17* **Shyshchytsy** *Rus.* Shishchitsy. Minskaya Voblasts', C Belarus
155 *Y3* **Siachen Muztāgh** ▲▲ NE Pakistan
Siadehan *see* Tākestān
154 *M13* **Siāhān Range** ▲▲ W Pakistan
148 *I1* **Sīāh Chashmeh** Āžarbāyjān-e Bākhtarī, N Iran
155 *W7* **Siālkot** Punjab, NE Pakistan
194 *K12* **Sialum** Morobe, C PNG
Siam *see* Thailand
Siam, Gulf of *see* Thailand, Gulf of
Sian *see* Xi'an
Siang *see* Brahmaputra
Siangtan *see* Xiangtan
174 *J5* **Siantan, Pulau** *island* Kepulauan Anambas, W Indonesia
56 *H11* **Siare, Río** ≈ C Colombia
179 *Rr13* **Siargao Island** *island* S Philippines
194 *K12* **Siassi** Umboi Island, C PNG
117 *D14* **Siátista** Dytikí Makedonía, N Greece
177 *Ff4* **Siatlai** Chin State, W Myanmar
179 *Q15* **Siaton** Negros, C Philippines
179 *Q15* **Siaton Point** *headland* Negros, C Philippines
120 *F11* **Šiauliai** *Ger.* Schaulen. Šiauliai, N Lithuania
175 *S5* **Siau, Pulau** *island* N Indonesia
85 *J15* **Siavonga** Southern, SE Zambia
Siazan' *see* Siyäzän
Sibah *see* As Sībah
109 *N20* **Sibari** Calabria, S Italy
Sibata *see* Shibata
131 *X6* **Sibay** Respublika Bashkortostan, W Russian Federation
95 *M19* **Sibbo** *Fin.* Sipoo. Uusimaa, S Finland
114 *D13* **Šibenik** *It.* Sebenico. Šibenik, S Croatia
114 *E13* **Šibenik** *off.* Šibenska Županija. ◈ *province* S Croatia
Šibenska Županija *see* Šibenik
Siberia *see* Sibir'
Siberoet *see* Siberut, Pulau
173 *Ff9* **Siberut, Pulau** *prev.* Siberoet. *island* Kepulauan Mentawai, W Indonesia
173 *Ff9* **Siberut, Selat** *strait* W Indonesia
Sibetu *see* Shibetsu
155 *P11* **Sibi** Baluchistān, SW Pakistan
194 *F15* **Sibidiri** Western, SW PNG
126 *K10* **Sibir'** *var.* Siberia. *physical region* NE Russian Federation
81 *F20* **Sibiti** La Lékoumou, S Congo
83 *G21* **Sibiti** ≈ C Tanzania
118 *I12* **Sibiu** *Ger.* Hermannstadt, *Hung.* Nagyszeben. Sibiu, C Romania
118 *I11* **Sibiu** ◈ *county* C Romania
31 *S11* **Sibley** Iowa, C USA
173 *Ff6* **Sibolga** Sumatera, W Indonesia
173 *Ff6* **Sibolga, Teluk** *var.* Teluk Tapanuli. *bay* Sumatera, W Indonesia
174 *Ll6* **Sibu** Sarawak, East Malaysia
Sibukawa *see* Shibukawa
44 *G2* **Sibun** ≈ E Belize
81 *I15* **Sibut** *prev.* Fort-Sibut. Kémo, S Central African Republic
179 *P17* **Sibutu** *island* SW Philippines
179 *P17* **Sibutu Passage** *passage* SW Philippines
179 *Q12* **Sibuyan Island** *island* C Philippines
179 *Q12* **Sibuyan Sea** *sea* C Philippines
201 *U1* **Sibylla Island** *island* N Marshall Islands
9 *N16* **Sicamous** British Columbia, SW Canada
Sichelburger Gerbirge *see* Žumberačka Gora
178 *H15* **Sichon** *var.* Ban Sichon, Si Chon. Nakhon Si Thammarat, SW Thailand
166 *H9* **Sichuan** *var.* Chuan, Sichuan Sheng, Ssu-ch'uan, Szechuan, Szechwan. ◈ *province* C China
166 *I9* **Sichuan Pendi** *basin* C China
Sichuan Sheng *see* Sichuan
105 *S16* **Sicie, Cap** *headland* SE France
109 *J24* **Sicilia** *Eng.* Sicily; *anc.* Trinacria. ◈ *region* Italy, C Mediterranean Sea
109 *M24* **Sicilia** *Eng.* Sicily; *anc.* Trinacria. *island* Italy, C Mediterranean Sea
Sicilian Channel *see* Sicily, Strait of
Sicily *see* Sicilia
109 *H24* **Sicily, Strait of** *var.* Sicilian Channel. *strait* C Mediterranean Sea
44 *K5* **Sico Tinto, Río** *var.* Río Negro. ≈ NE Honduras
59 *H16* **Sicuani** Cusco, S Peru
114 *J10* **Šid** Serbia, NW Yugoslavia
117 *A15* **Sidári** Kérkyra, Iónioi Nísoi, Greece, C Mediterranean Sea
174 *Kk8* **Sidas** Borneo, C Indonesia
100 *O5* **Siddeburen** Groningen, NE Netherlands
160 *D9* **Siddhapur** *prev.* Siddhpur, Sidhpur. Gujarāt, W India
Siddhpur *see* Siddhapur
161 *I15* **Siddipet** Andhra Pradesh, C India
195 *O17* **Sideia Island** *island* SE PNG
175 *Pp12* **Sidenreng, Danau** ◎ Sulawesi, C Indonesia
79 *N14* **Sidéradougou** SW Burkina
109 *N23* **Siderno** Calabria, SW Italy
Siders *see* Sierre
160 *L9* **Sidhi** Madhya Pradesh, C India
Sidhirókastron *see* Sidirókastro
Sidhpur *see* Siddhapur
Sīdī al Hānī', Sabkhat *see* Sidi el Hani, Sebkhet de
77 *U7* **Sîdi Barrâni** NW Egypt
76 *I6* **Sidi Bel Abbès** *var.* Sidi bel Abbès, Sidi-Bel-Abbès. NW Algeria
76 *E7* **Sidi-Bennour** W Morocco
76 *M6* **Sidi Bouzid** *var.* Gammouda, Sīdī Bu Zayd. C Tunisia
123 *K12* **Sidi el Hani, Sebkhet de** *var.* Sabkhat Sīdī al Hānī'. *salt flat* NE Tunisia
76 *D8* **Sidi-Ifni** SW Morocco
76 *G6* **Sidi-Kacem** *prev.* Petitjean. N Morocco
116 *G12* **Sidirókastro** *prev.* Sidhirókastron. Kentrikí Makedonía, NE Greece
204 *L12* **Sidley, Mount** ▲ Antarctica
31 *S16* **Sidney** Iowa, C USA
35 *Y7* **Sidney** Montana, NW USA
30 *J15* **Sidney** Nebraska, C USA
20 *I11* **Sidney** New York, NE USA
33 *R13* **Sidney** Ohio, N USA
25 *T2* **Sidney Lanier, Lake** ⊡ Georgia, SE USA
Sidon *see* Saïda
126 *Hh9* **Sidorovsk** Yamalo-Nenetskiy Avtonomnyy Okrug, N Russian Federation
Sidra/Sidra, Gulf of *see* Surt, Khalīj, N Libya
Sidra *see* Surt, N Libya
Sīdī Bu Zayd *see* Sidi Bouzid
Siebenbürgen *see* Transylvania
Sieben Dörfer *see* Săcele
112 *O12* **Siedlce** *Ger.* Sedlez, *Rus.* Sesdlets. Siedlce, E Poland
112 *N11* **Siedlce** *off.* Województwo Siedleckie, *var.* Syedlets, *Ger.* Sedlez. ◈ *province* E Poland
Siedleckie, Województwo *see* Siedlce
103 *E16* **Sieg** ≈ W Germany
103 *F16* **Siegen** Nordrhein-Westfalen, W Germany
111 *X4* **Sieghartskirchen** Niederösterreich, E Austria
112 *O11* **Siemiatycze** Białystok, E Poland
178 *Jj11* **Siĕmpang** Stœ̆ng Trêng, NE Cambodia
178 *Ii12* **Siĕmréab** *prev.* Siemreap. Siĕmréab, NW Cambodia
Siemreap *see* Siĕmréab
108 *G12* **Siena** *Fr.* Sienne; *anc.* Saena Julia. Toscana, C Italy
Sienne *see* Siena
94 *K12* **Sieppijärvi** Lappi, NW Finland
112 *J13* **Sieradz** Sieradz, C Poland
112 *J13* **Sieradz** *off.* Województwo Sieradzkie. ◈ *province* C Poland
Sieradzkie, Województwo *see* Sieradz
112 *K10* **Sierpc** Płock, C Poland
26 *I9* **Sierra Blanca** Texas, SW USA
39 *S14* **Sierra Blanca Peak** ▲ New Mexico, SW USA
37 *P5* **Sierra City** California, W USA
65 *I16* **Sierra Colorada** Río Negro, S Argentina
64 *I13* **Sierra del Nevado** ▲▲ W Argentina
107 *P13* **Sierra de Segura** ▲▲ S Spain
65 *J16* **Sierra Grande** Río Negro, E Argentina
78 *G15* **Sierra Leone** *off.* Republic of Sierra Leone. ◆ *republic* W Africa
66 *M13* **Sierra Leone Basin** *undersea feature* E Atlantic Ocean
68 *K8* **Sierra Leone Fracture Zone** *tectonic feature* E Atlantic Ocean
Sierra Leone Ridge *see* Sierra Leone Rise
66 *L13* **Sierra Leone Rise** *var.* Sierra Leone Ridge, Sierra Leone Schwelle. *undersea feature* E Atlantic Ocean
Sierra Leone Schwelle *see* Sierra Leone Rise
43 *U17* **Sierra Madre** *var.* Sierra de Soconusco. ▲▲ Guatemala/Mexico
179 *Pp9* **Sierra Madre** ▲▲ Luzon, N Philippines
39 *R2* **Sierra Madre** ▲▲ Colorado/Wyoming, C USA
1 *H15* **Sierra Madre del Sur** ▲▲ S Mexico
1 *G13* **Sierra Madre Occidental** *var.* Western Sierra Madre. ▲▲ C Mexico
1 *H13* **Sierra Madre Oriental** *var.* Eastern Sierra Madre. ▲▲ C Mexico
46 *H8* **Sierra Maestra** ▲▲ E Cuba
42 *L7* **Sierra Mojada** Coahuila de Zaragoza, NE Mexico
107 *O14* **Sierra Nevada** ▲▲ S Spain
37 *P6* **Sierra Nevada** ▲▲ W USA
56 *F4* **Sierra Nevada de Santa Marta** ▲▲ NE Colombia
44 *K5* **Sierra Río Tinto** ▲▲ NE Honduras
26 *J10* **Sierra Vieja** ▲▲ Texas, SW USA
39 *N16* **Sierra Vista** Arizona, SW USA
110 *D10* **Sierre** *Ger.* Siders. Valais, SW Switzerland
38 *L16* **Sierrita Mountains** ▲▲ Arizona, SW USA
Siete Moai *see* Ahu Akivi
78 *M15* **Sifié** W Ivory Coast
117 *I21* **Sífnos** *anc.* Siphnos. *island* Kykládes, Greece, Aegean Sea
117 *I21* **Sífnou, Stenó** *strait* SE Greece
Siga *see* Shiga
197 *H15* **Sigatoka** *prev.* Singatoka. Viti Levu, W Fiji
105 *P16* **Sigean** Aude, S France
Sighet *see* Sighetu Marmației
118 *I8* **Sighetu Marmației** *var.* Sighet, Sighetul Marmației, *Hung.* Máramarossziget. Maramureș, N Romania
Sighetul Marmației *see* Sighetu Marmației
118 *I11* **Sighișoara** *Ger.* Schässburg, *Hung.* Segesvár. Mureș, C Romania
173 *E3* **Sigli** Sumatera, W Indonesia
94 *J1* **Siglufjördhur** Nordhurland Vestra, N Iceland
103 *H23* **Sigmaringen** Baden-Württemberg, S Germany
103 *N20* **Signalberg** ▲ SE Germany
38 *I13* **Signal Peak** ▲ Arizona, SW USA
Signan *see* Xi'an
204 *H1* **Signy** *UK research station* South Orkney Islands, Antarctica
31 *X15* **Sigourney** Iowa, C USA
117 *K17* **Sígri, Ákra** *headland* Lésvos, E Greece
Sigsbee Deep *see* Mexico Basin
49 *N2* **Sigsbee Escarpment** *undersea feature* N Gulf of Mexico
58 *C8* **Sigsig** Azuay, S Ecuador
97 *O15* **Sigtuna** Stockholm, C Sweden
44 *H6* **Siguatepeque** Comayagua, W Honduras
107 *P7* **Sigüenza** Castilla-La Mancha, C Spain
107 *R4* **Sigües** Aragón, NE Spain
78 *K13* **Siguiri** Haute-Guinée, NE Guinea
120 *G8* **Sigulda** *Ger.* Segewold. Rīga, C Latvia
Sihanoukville *see* Kâmpóng Saôm
110 *G8* **Sihlsee** ◎ NW Switzerland
95 *K18* **Siikainen** Turku-Pori, SW Finland
95 *M16* **Siilinjärvi** Kuopio, C Finland
143 *R15* **Siirt** *var.* Sert; *anc.* Tigranocerta. Siirt, SE Turkey
143 *R15* **Siirt** *var.* Sert. ◈ *province* SE Turkey
195 *Z15* **Sikaiana** *var.* Stewert Islands. *island group* W Solomon Islands
Sikandarabad *see* Secunderābād
158 *J11* **Sikandra Rao** Uttar Pradesh, N India
8 *M11* **Sikanni Chief** British Columbia, W Canada
8 *M11* **Sikanni Chief** ≈ British Columbia, W Canada
158 *H11* **Sīkar** Rājasthān, N India
78 *M13* **Sikasso** Sikasso, S Mali
78 *L13* **Sikasso** ◈ *region* SW Mali
178 *Gg3* **Sikaw** Kachin State, C Myanmar
85 *H14* **Sikelenge** Western, W Zambia
29 *Y7* **Sikeston** Missouri, C USA
95 *J14* **Sikfors** Norrbotten, N Sweden
127 *O16* **Sikhote-Alin', Khrebet** ▲▲ SE Russian Federation
Siking *see* Xi'an
117 *J22* **Síkinos** *island* Kykládes, Greece, Aegean Sea
159 *S11* **Sikkim** *Tib.* Denjong. ◈ *state* N India
113 *I26* **Siklós** Baranya, SW Hungary
Sikoku *see* Shikoku
Sikoku Basin *see* Shikoku Basin
85 *G14* **Sikongo** Western, W Zambia
Sikotu Ko *see* Shikotsu-ko
Sikouri/Sikoúrion *see* Sykoúri
126 *L7* **Siktyakh** Respublika Sakha (Yakutiya), NE Russian Federation
120 *D12* **Šilalė** Šilalė, W Lithuania
108 *G5* **Silandro** *Ger.* Schlanders. Trentino-Alto Adige, N Italy
43 *N12* **Silao** Guanajuato, C Mexico
Silarius *see* Sele
179 *Q13* **Silay** *off.* Silay City. Negros, C Philippines
159 *W14* **Silchar** Assam, NE India
110 *G9* **Silenen** Uri, C Switzerland
23 *T9* **Siler City** North Carolina, SE USA
35 *U11* **Silesia** Montana, NW USA
112 *F13* **Silesia** *physical region* SW Poland
76 *K12* **Silet** S Algeria
151 *R8* **Sileti** *var.* Selety. ≈ N Kazakhstan
Siletitengiz *see* Siletiteniz, Ozero
151 *R7* **Siletiteniz, Ozero** *Kaz.* Siletitengiz. ◎ N Kazakhstan
180 *H16* **Silhouette** *island* Inner Islands, SE Seychelles
142 *I17* **Silifke** *anc.* Seleucia. İçel, S Turkey
Siliguri *see* Shiliguri
162 *J10* **Siling Co** ◎ W China
Silinhot *see* Xilinhot
198 *Aa7* **Silisili** ▲ Savai'i, C Western Samoa
116 *M6* **Silistra** *var.* Silistria; *anc.* Durostorum. Razgradska Oblast, NE Bulgaria
Silistria *see* Silistra
142 *D10* **Silivri** İstanbul, NW Turkey
96 *L13* **Siljan** ◎ C Sweden
97 *G22* **Silkeborg** Århus, C Denmark
110 *M8* **Sill** ≈ W Austria
107 *S10* **Silla** País Valenciano, E Spain
64 *H3* **Sillajguay, Cordillera** ▲ N Chile
120 *K3* **Sillamäe** *Ger.* Sillamäggi. Ida-Virumaa, NE Estonia
Sillamäggi *see* Sillamäe
Sillein *see* Žilina
111 *P9* **Sillian** Tirol, W Austria
114 *B10* **Šilo** Primorje-Gorski Kotar, NW Croatia
29 *R9* **Siloam Springs** Arkansas, C USA
27 *X10* **Silsbee** Texas, SW USA
149 *W15* **Sīlūp, Rūd-e** ≈ SE Iran
120 *C12* **Šilutė** *Ger.* Heydekrug. Šilutė, W Lithuania
143 *Q15* **Silvan** Diyarbakır, SE Turkey
110 *J10* **Silvaplana** Graubünden, S Switzerland
Silva Porto *see* Kuito
60 *M12* **Silva, Recife do** *reef* E Brazil
160 *D12* **Silvassa** Dādra and Nagar Haveli, W India
31 *X4* **Silver Bay** Minnesota, N USA
39 *P15* **Silver City** New Mexico, SW USA
20 *D10* **Silver Creek** New York, NE USA
39 *N12* **Silver Creek** ≈ Arizona, SW USA
29 *P4* **Silver Lake** Kansas, C USA
34 *I14* **Silver Lake** Oregon, NW USA
37 *T9* **Silver Peak Range** ▲▲ Nevada, W USA
23 *W3* **Silver Spring** Maryland, NE USA
Silver State *see* Nevada
Silver State *see* Colorado
39 *Q7* **Silverton** Colorado, C USA
20 *K16* **Silverton** New Jersey, NE USA
34 *G11* **Silverton** Oregon, NW USA
27 *N4* **Silverton** Texas, SW USA
106 *G14* **Silves** Faro, S Portugal
56 *D12* **Silvia** Cauca, SW Colombia
110 *J9* **Silvrettagruppe** ▲▲ Austria/Switzerland
Sily-Vajdej *see* Vulcan
110 *L7* **Silz** Tirol, W Austria
180 *I13* **Sima** Anjouan, SE Comoros
Simabara *see* Shimabara
Simada *see* Shimada
85 *H15* **Simakando** Western, W Zambia
Simane *see* Shimane
121 *L20* **Simanichy** *Rus.* Simonichi. Homyel'skaya Voblasts', SE Belarus
166 *F14* **Simao** Yunnan, SW China
159 *P12* **Simara** Central, C Nepal
12 *I8* **Simard, Lac** ◎ Québec, SE Canada
142 *D13* **Simav** Kütahya, W Turkey
142 *D13* **Simav Çayı** ≈ NW Turkey
81 *L18* **Simba** Haut-Zaïre, N Zaire
194 *H11* **Simbai** Madang, N PNG
195 *O9* **Simberi Island** *island* Tabar Islands, N PNG
Simbirsk *see* Ul'yanovsk
12 *F17* **Simcoe** Ontario, S Canada
12 *H14* **Simcoe, Lake** ◎ Ontario, S Canada
82 *J11* **Sīmēn** ▲▲ N Ethiopia
116 *K11* **Simeonovgrad** *prev.* Maritsa. Khaskovska Oblast, S Bulgaria
118 *G11* **Simeria** *Ger.* Pischk, *Hung.* Piski. Hunedoara, W Romania
109 *L24* **Simeto** ≈ Sicilia, Italy, C Mediterranean Sea
173 *E5* **Simeulue, Pulau** *island* NW Indonesia
119 *T13* **Simferopol'** Respublika Krym, S Ukraine
119 *T13* **Simferopol'** ✕ Respublika Krym, S Ukraine
Simi *see* Sými
158 *M9* **Simikot** Far Western, NW Nepal
56 *F7* **Simití** Bolívar, N Colombia
116 *G11* **Simitli** Sofiyska Oblast, SW Bulgaria
37 *S15* **Simi Valley** California, W USA
Simizu *see* Shimizu
Simla *see* Shimla
Şimlăul Silvaniei/Şimleul Silvaniei *see* Şimleu Silvaniei
118 *G9* **Şimleu Silvaniei** *Hung.* Szilágşomlyó; *prev.* Şimlăul Silvaniei, Şimleul Silvaniei. Sălaj, NW Romania
Simmer *see* Simmerbach
103 *E19* **Simmerbach** *var.* Simmer. ≈ W Germany
103 *F18* **Simmern** Rheinland-Pfalz, W Germany
24 *I7* **Simmesport** Louisiana, S USA
121 *F14* **Simnas** Alytus, S Lithuania
94 *L13* **Simo** Lappi, NW Finland
Simoda *see* Shimoda
Simodate *see* Shimodate
94 *M13* **Simojärvi** ◎ N Finland
94 *L13* **Simojoki** ≈ NW Finland
43 *U15* **Simojovel** *var.* Simojovel de Allende. Chiapas, SE Mexico
Simojovel de Allende *see* Simojovel
58 *B7* **Simon Bolivar** *var.* Guayaquil. ✕ (Quayaquil) Guayas, W Ecuador
56 *L5* **Simon Bolívar** ✕ (Caracas) Distrito Federal, N Venezuela
Simonichi *see* Simanichy
12 *M12* **Simon, Lac** ◎ Québec, SE Canada
Simonoseki *see* Shimonoseki
Šimonovany *see* Partizánske
Simonstad *see* Simon's Town
85 *E26* **Simon's Town** *var.* Simonstad. Western Cape, SW South Africa
Simony *see* Partizánske
Simotuma *see* Shimotsuma
173 *F6* **Simpangkaman, Sungai** ≈ Sumatera, NW Indonesia
173 *F5* **Simpangkiri, Sungai** ≈ Sumatera, NW Indonesia
Simpeln *see* Simplon
101 *M18* **Simpelveld** Limburg, SE Netherlands
110 *E11* **Simplon** *var.* Simpeln. Valais, SW Switzerland
110 *E11* **Simplon Pass** *pass* S Switzerland
108 *C6* **Simplon Tunnel** *tunnel* Italy/Switzerland
Simpson *see* Fort Simpson
190 *G1* **Simpson Desert** *desert* Northern Territory/South Australia
8 *J9* **Simpson Peak** ▲ British Columbia, W Canada
15 *L3* **Simpson Peninsula** *peninsula* Northwest Territories, NE Canada
23 *P11* **Simpsonville** South Carolina, SE USA
97 *L23* **Simrishamn** Kristianstad, S Sweden
127 *Pp15* **Simushir, Ostrov** *island* Kuril'skiye Ostrova, SE Russian Federation
Sīnā'/Sinai Peninsula *see* Sinai
173 *Ee6* **Sinabang** Sumatera, W Indonesia
83 *N15* **Sina Dhaqa** Galguduud, C Somalia
77 *X8* **Sinai** *var.* Sinai Peninsula, *Ar.* Shibh Jazīrat Sīnā', Sīnā'. *physical region* NE Egypt
118 *J12* **Sinaia** Prahova, SE Romania
196 *B16* **Sinajana** C Guam
42 *H8* **Sinaloa** ◈ *state* C Mexico
56 *H4* **Sinamaica** Zulia, NW Venezuela
169 *X14* **Sinan-ni** SE North Korea
Sinano Gawa *see* Shinano-gawa
Sīnāwan *see* Sīnāwin
77 *N8* **Sīnāwin** *var.* Sīnāwan. NW Libya
85 *J16* **Sinazongwe** Southern, S Zambia
177 *Ff6* **Sinbaungwe** Magwe, W Myanmar
177 *Ff5* **Sinbyugyun** Magwe, W Myanmar
56 *E6* **Since** Sucre, NW Colombia
56 *E6* **Sincelejo** Sucre, NW Colombia
177 *F5* **Sinchaingbyin** *var.* Zullapara. Arakan State, W Myanmar
25 *U4* **Sinclair, Lake** ⊡ Georgia, SE USA
8 *M14* **Sinclair Mills** British Columbia, SW Canada
178 *Mm15* **Sin Cowe East Island** *island* S Spratly Islands
178 *Mm15* **Sin Cowe Island** *island* SW Spratly Islands
155 *Q14* **Sind** *var.* Sindh. ◈ *province* SE Pakistan
160 *I8* **Sind** ≈ N India
97 *H19* **Sindal** Nordjylland, N Denmark
179 *Q15* **Sindañgan** Mindanao, S Philippines
81 *D19* **Sindara** Ngounié, W Gabon
158 *E13* **Sindari** *prev.* Sindri. Rājasthān, N India
175 *Q16* **Sindeh, Teluk** *bay* Nusa Tenggara, C Indonesia
116 *N8* **Sindel** Varnenska Oblast, NE Bulgaria
103 *H22* **Sindelfingen** Baden-Württemberg, SW Germany
161 *G16* **Sindgi** Karnātaka, C India
Sindh *see* Sind
120 *G5* **Sindi** *Ger.* Zintenhof. Pärnumaa, SW Estonia
142 *C13* **Sındırgı** Balıkesir, W Turkey
79 *N14* **Sindou** SW Burkina
Sindri *see* Sindari
155 *T9* **Sind Sāgar Doāb** *desert* E Pakistan
130 *M11* **Sinegorskiy** Rostovskaya Oblast', SW Russian Federation
127 *O9* **Sinegor'ye** Magadanskaya Oblast', E Russian Federation
116 *O12* **Sinekli** İstanbul, NW Turkey
106 *F12* **Sines** Setúbal, S Portugal
106 *F12* **Sines, Cabo de** *headland* S Portugal
94 *L12* **Sinettä** Lappi, NW Finland
195 *P11* **Sinewit, Mount** ▲ New Britain, C PNG
82 *G11* **Singa** *var.* Sinja, Sinjah. Sinnar, E Sudan
80 *J12* **Singako** Moyen-Chari, S Chad
Singan *see* Xi'an
174 *I7* **Singapore** ● (Singapore) S Singapore
174 *I7* **Singapore** *off.* Republic of Singapore. ◆ *republic* SE Asia
174 *I7* **Singapore Strait** *var.* Strait of Singapore, *Mal.* Selat Singapura. *strait* Indonesia/Singapore
Singapore, Strait of/Singapura, Selat *see* Singapore Strait
175 *N16* **Singaraja** Bali, C Indonesia
Singatoka *see* Sigatoka
178 *H10* **Sing Buri** *var.* Singhaburi. Sing Buri, C Thailand
103 *H24* **Singen** Baden-Württemberg, S Germany
Sîngeorgiu de Pădure *see* Sângeorgiu de Pădure
Sîngeorz-Băi/Singeroz Băi *see* Sângeorz-Băi
118 *M9* **Sîngerei** *var.* Sângerei; *prev.* Lazovsk. N Moldova
Singhaburi *see* Sing Buri
83 *H21* **Singida** Singida, C Tanzania
83 *G22* **Singida** ◈ *region* C Tanzania
Singidunum *see* Beograd
177 *G2* **Singkaling Hkamti** Sagaing, N Myanmar
175 *Pp12* **Singkang** Sulawesi, C Indonesia
174 *Gg8* **Singkarak, Danau** ◎ Sumatera, W Indonesia
174 *K7* **Singkawang** Borneo, C Indonesia
174 *I8* **Singkep, Pulau** *island* Kepulauan Lingga, W Indonesia
173 *F6* **Singkilbaru** Sumatera, W Indonesia
191 *T7* **Singleton** New South Wales, SE Australia
Singora *see* Songkhla
Singû *see* Shingū
Sining *see* Xining
109 *D17* **Siniscola** Sardegna, Italy, C Mediterranean Sea
115 *F14* **Sinj** Split-Dalmacija, SE Croatia
Sinja/Sinjah *see* Singa
Sinjajevina *see* Sinjavina
145 *P3* **Sinjār** NW Iraq
145 *P2* **Sinjār, Jabal** ▲▲ N Iraq
115 *K15* **Sinjavina** *var.* Sinjajevina. ▲▲ SW Yugoslavia
82 *I7* **Sinkat** Red Sea, NE Sudan
Sinkiang/Sinkiang Uighur Autonomous Region *see* Xinjiang Uygur Zizhiqu
Sînmartin *see* Târnăveni
169 *V13* **Sinmi-do** *island* NW North Korea
Sinminato *see* Shinminato
103 *I18* **Sinn** ≈ C Germany
Sinnamarie *see* Sinnamary
57 *Y9* **Sinnamary** *var.* Sinnamarie. N French Guiana
Sinn'anyô *see* Shinnanyō
82 *G11* **Sinnar** ◈ *state* E Sudan
Sinneh *see* Sanandaj
20 *E13* **Sinnemahoning Creek** ≈ Pennsylvania, NE USA
Sînnicolau Mare *see* Sânnicolau Mare
Sino/Sinoe *see* Greenville
Sinoe, Lacul *see* Sinoie, Lacul
Sinoia *see* Chinhoyi
119 *N14* **Sinoie, Lacul** *prev.* Lacul Sinoe. *lagoon* SE Romania
61 *H16* **Sinop** Mato Grosso, W Brazil
142 *K10* **Sinop** *anc.* Sinope. Sinop, N Turkey
142 *J10* **Sinop** ◈ *province* N Turkey
142 *K10* **Sinop Burnu** *headland* N Turkey
Sinope *see* Sinop
169 *Y12* **Sinp'o** E North Korea
103 *H20* **Sinsheim** Baden-Württemberg, SW Germany
Sinsiro *see* Shinshiro
Sîntana *see* Sântana
174 *L8* **Sintang** Borneo, C Indonesia
101 *F14* **Sint Annaland** Zeeland, SW Netherlands
100 *L5* **Sint Annaparochie** Friesland, N Netherlands
47 *V9* **Sint Eustatius** *Eng.* Saint Eustatius. *island* N Netherlands Antilles
101 *G19* **Sint-Genesius-Rode** *Fr.* Rhode-Saint-Genèse. Vlaams Brabant, C Belgium
101 *F16* **Sint-Gillis-Waas** Oost-Vlaanderen, N Belgium
101 *H17* **Sint-Katelijne-Waver** Antwerpen, C Belgium
101 *E18* **Sint-Lievens-Houtem** Oost-Vlaanderen, NW Belgium
47 *V9* **Sint Maarten** *Eng.* Saint Martin. *island* N Netherlands Antilles
101 *F14* **Sint Maartensdijk** Zeeland, SW Netherlands
101 *L19* **Sint-Martens-Voeren** *Fr.* Fouron-Saint-Martin. Limburg, NE Belgium
101 *J14* **Sint-Michielsgestel** Noord-Brabant, S Netherlands
Sînt-Miclăuș *see* Gheorgheni
47 *O16* **Sint Nicholaas** S Aruba
101 *F16* **Sint-Niklaas** *Fr.* Saint-Nicolas. Oost-Vlaanderen, N Belgium
101 *K14* **Sint-Oedenrode** Noord-Brabant, S Netherlands
27 *T14* **Sinton** Texas, SW USA
101 *G14* **Sint Philipsland** Zeeland, SW Netherlands
101 *G19* **Sint-Pieters-Leeuw** Vlaams Brabant, C Belgium
106 *E11* **Sintra** *prev.* Cintra. Lisboa, W Portugal
101 *J18* **Sint-Truiden** *Fr.* Saint-Trond. Limburg, NE Belgium
101 *H14* **Sint Willebrord** Noord-Brabant, S Netherlands
169 *V13* **Sinŭiju** W North Korea
82 *P13* **Sinujiif** Nugaal, NE Somalia
Sinus Aelaniticus *see* Aqaba, Gulf of
Sinus Gallicus *see* Lion, Golfe du
Sinyang *see* Xinyang
Sinyavka *see* Sinyawka
121 *I18* **Sinyawka** *Rus.* Sinyavka. Minskaya Voblasts', SW Belarus
126 *Ll11* **Sinyaya** ≈ NE Russian Federation
Sinying *see* Hsinying
Sinyukha *see* Synyukha
Sinzi-ko *see* Shinji-ko
Sinzyô *see* Shinjō
113 *I24* **Sió** ≈ W Hungary
179 *Q16* **Siocon** Mindanao, S Philippines
Siogama *see* Shiogama
85 *G15* **Sioma** Western, SW Zambia
110 *D11* **Sion** *Ger.* Sitten; *anc.* Sedunum. Valais, SW Switzerland
105 *O11* **Sioule** ≈ C France
31 *S12* **Sioux Center** Iowa, C USA
31 *R13* **Sioux City** Iowa, C USA
31 *R11* **Sioux Falls** South Dakota, N USA
10 *B11* **Sioux Lookout** Ontario, S Canada
31 *T12* **Sioux Rapids** Iowa, C USA
Sioux State *see* North Dakota
Sioziri *see* Shiojiri
179 *Q14* **Sipalay** Negros, C Philippines
57 *V11* **Sipaliwini** ◈ *district* S Suriname
47 *U15* **Siparia** Trinidad, Trinidad and Tobago
Siphnos *see* Sífnos
169 *V11* **Siping** *var.* Ssu-p'ing, Szeping; *prev.* Ssu-p'ing-chieh. Jilin, NE China

◆ Country
● Country Capital
◇ Dependent Territory
○ Dependent Territory Capital
◈ Administrative Region
✕ International Airport
▲ Mountain
▲▲ Mountain Range
Volcano
≈ River
◎ Lake
⊡ Reservoir

9 X12 **Sipiwesk** Manitoba, C Canada
9 W13 **Sipiwesk Lake** ◎ Manitoba, C Canada
205 O11 **Siple Coast** *physical region* Antarctica
204 K12 **Siple Island** *island* Antarctica
204 K13 **Siple, Mount** ▲ Siple Island, Antarctica
Sipoo *see* Sibbo
114 G12 **Šipovo** W Bosnia and Herzegovina
25 O4 **Sipsey River** ≈ Alabama, S USA
173 Ff10 **Sipura, Pulau** *island* W Indonesia
0 G16 **Siqueiros Fracture Zone** *tectonic feature* E Pacific Ocean
44 L10 **Siquia, Río** ≈ SE Nicaragua
179 Qq14 **Siquijor Island** *island* C Philippines
45 N13 **Siquirres** Limón, E Costa Rica
56 J5 **Siquisique** Lara, N Venezuela
161 G19 **Sīra** Karnātaka, W India
97 D16 **Sira** ≈ S Norway
178 Hh12 **Siracha** *var.* Ban Si Racha, Si Racha. Chon Buri, S Thailand
109 L25 **Siracusa** *Eng.* Syracuse. Sicilia, Italy, C Mediterranean Sea
Sirajganj *see* Shirajganj Ghat
Sirakawa *see* Shirakawa
9 N14 **Sir Alexander, Mount** ▲ British Columbia, W Canada
143 O12 **Şiran** Gümüşhane, NE Turkey
79 Q12 **Sirba** ≈ E Burkina
149 O17 **Şīr Banī Yās** *island* W UAE
97 D17 **Sirdalsvatnet** ◎ S Norway
Sir Darya/Sirdaryo *see* Syr Darya
153 O11 **Sirdaryo Wiloyati** *Rus.* Syrdar'inskaya Oblast'. ◈ *province* E Uzbekistan
Sir Donald Sangster International Airport *see* Sangster
194 H13 **Sirebi** ≈ S PNG
189 S3 **Sir Edward Pellew Group** *island group* Northern Territory, NE Australia
118 K8 **Siret** *Ger.* Sereth, *Hung.* Szeret. Suceava, N Romania
118 K8 **Siret** *var.* Siretul, *Ger.* Sereth, *Rus.* Seret, *Ukr.* Siret. ≈ Romania/Ukraine
Siretul *see* Siret
146 K3 **Sirḥān, Wādī as** *dry watercourse* Jordan/Saudi Arabia
158 I8 **Sirhind** Punjab, N India
118 F11 **Şiria** *Ger.* Schiria. Arad, W Romania
Siria *see* Syria
149 S14 **Sīrīk** Hormozgān, SE Iran
178 Hh8 **Sirikit Reservoir** ◎ N Thailand
60 K12 **Sirituba, Ilha** *island* NE Brazil
176 Ww11 **Siriwo** ≈ Irian Jaya, E Indonesia
149 R11 **Sīrjān** *prev.* Sa'īdābād. Kermān, S Iran
190 H9 **Sir Joseph Banks Group** *island group* South Australia
94 K11 **Sirkka** Lappi, N Finland
Sirna *see* Sýrna
143 R16 **Şırnak** Şırnak, SE Turkey
143 S16 **Şırnak** ◈ *province* SE Turkey
Siroisi *see* Shiroishi
161 J14 **Sironcha** Mahārāshtra, C India
Sirone *see* Shirone
Síros *see* Sýros
Sirotino *see* Sirotsina
120 M12 **Sirotsina** *Rus.* Sirotino. Vitsyebskaya Voblasts', N Belarus
158 H9 **Sirsa** Haryāna, NW India
181 Y17 **Sir Seewoosagur Ramgoolam** ✕ (Port Louis) SE Mauritius
161 E18 **Sirsi** Karnātaka, W India
Sirte *see* Surt
190 A2 **Sir Thomas, Mount** ▲ South Australia
Sirti, Gulf of *see* Surt, Khalīj
148 J5 **Sīrvān, Rūdkhāneh-ye** *var.* Nahr Diyālá, Sirwan. ≈ Iran/Iraq *see also* Diyālá, Nahr
120 H13 **Širvintos** Širvintos, SE Lithuania
Sirwan *see* Diyālá, Nahr/Sīrvān, Rūdkhāneh-ye
9 N15 **Sir Wilfrid Laurier, Mount** ▲ British Columbia, SW Canada
12 M10 **Sir-Wilfrid, Mont** ▲ Québec, SE Canada
Sisačko-Moslavačka Županija *see* Sisak-Moslavina
114 E9 **Sisak** *var.* Siscia, *Ger.* Sissek, *Hung.* Sziszek; *anc.* Segestica. Sisak-Moslavina, C Croatia
178 J10 **Si Sa Ket** *var.* Sisaket, Sri Saket. Si Sa Ket, E Thailand
114 E9 **Sisak-Moslavina** *off.* Sisačko-Moslavačka Županija. ◈ *province* C Croatia
178 H8 **Si Satchanala** Sukhothai, NW Thailand
Siscia *see* Sisak
176 W10 **Sisember** Irian Jaya, E Indonesia
85 G22 **Sishen** Northern Cape, NW South Africa
143 V13 **Sisian** SE Armenia
207 N13 **Sisimiut** *var.* Holsteinborg, Holsteinsborg, Holstenborg, Holstensborg. S Greenland
32 M1 **Siskiwit Bay** *lake bay* Michigan, N USA
36 L1 **Siskiyou Mountains** ▲▲ California/Oregon, W USA
178 I12 **Sisŏphŏn** Bătdâmbâng, NW Cambodia
110 E7 **Sissach** Basel-Land, NW Switzerland
194 F9 **Sissano** Sandaun, NW PNG
Sissek *see* Sisak
31 R7 **Sisseton** South Dakota, N USA
149 W9 **Sīstān, Daryācheh-ye** *var.* Daryācheh-ye Hāmūn, Hāmūn-e Şāberī. ◎ Afghanistan/Iran *see also* Şāberī, Hāmūn-e
149 V12 **Sīstān va Balūchestān** *off.* Ostān-e Sīstān va Balūchestān, *var.* Balūchestān va Sīstān. ◈ *province* SE Iran
105 T14 **Sisteron** Alpes-de-Haute-Provence, SE France
34 H13 **Sisters** Oregon, NW USA
67 G15 **Sisters Peak** ▲ N Ascension Island
23 R3 **Sistersville** West Virginia, NE USA
Sistova *see* Svishtov
Sitakund *see* Sitakunda
159 V16 **Sitakunda** *var.* Sitakund. Chittagong, SE Bangladesh
159 P12 **Sītāmarhi** Bihār, N India
158 L11 **Sītāpur** Uttar Pradesh, N India
Sitaş Cristuru *see* Cristuru Secuiesc
117 L25 **Siteía** *var.* Sitía. Kríti, Greece, E Mediterranean Sea
107 V6 **Sitges** Cataluña, NE Spain
117 H15 **Sithoniá** *peninsula* NE Greece
Sitía *see* Siteía
56 F4 **Sitionuevo** Magdalena, N Colombia
41 X13 **Sitka** Baranof Island, Alaska, USA
41 Q15 **Sitkinak Island** *island* Trinity Islands, Alaska, USA
177 G7 **Sittang** *var.* Sittoung. ≈ S Myanmar
101 L17 **Sittard** Limburg, SE Netherlands
Sitten *see* Sion
110 H7 **Sitter** ≈ NW Switzerland
111 U10 **Sittersdorf** Kärnten, S Austria
Sittoung *see* Sittang
177 F6 **Sittwe** *var.* Akyab. Arakan State, W Myanmar
174 Mm15 **Situbondo** *prev.* Sitoebondo. Jawa, C Indonesia
44 L8 **Siuna** Región Autónoma Atlántico Norte, NE Nicaragua
159 R15 **Siuri** West Bengal, NE India
Siut *see* Asyût
126 M15 **Sivaki** Amurskaya Oblast', SE Russian Federation
142 M13 **Sivas** *anc.* Sebastia, Sebaste. Sivas, C Turkey
142 M13 **Sivas** ◈ *province* C Turkey
143 O15 **Siverek** Şanlıurfa, S Turkey
119 X6 **Sivers'k** Donets'ka Oblast', E Ukraine
128 G13 **Siverskiy** Leningradskaya Oblast', NW Russian Federation
119 X6 **Sivers'kyy Donets'** *Rus.* Severskiy Donets. ≈ Russian Federation/Ukraine *see also* Severskiy Donets
129 W5 **Sivomaskinskiy** Respublika Komi, NW Russian Federation
142 G13 **Sivrihisar** Eskişehir, W Turkey
101 F22 **Sivry** Hainaut, S Belgium
127 Pp9 **Sivuchiy, Mys** *headland* E Russian Federation
77 U9 **Siwa** *var.* Sīwah. NW Egypt
Sīwah *see* Siwa
158 J9 **Siwalik Range** *var.* Shiwālik Range. ▲▲ India/Nepal
159 O13 **Siwān** Bihār, N India
45 O14 **Sixaola, Río** ≈ Costa Rica/Panama
Six Counties, The *see* Northern Ireland
105 T16 **Six-Fours-les-Plages** Var, SE France
167 Q7 **Sixian** *var.* Si Xian. Anhui, E China
24 J9 **Six Mile Lake** ◎ Louisiana, S USA
145 V3 **Siyāh Gūz** E Iraq
161 L25 **Siyambalanduwa** Uva Province, SE Sri Lanka
143 Y10 **Siyäzän** *Rus.* Siazan'. NE Azerbaijan
Sizebolu *see* Sozopol
Sizuoka *see* Shizuoka
Sjar *see* Sääre
115 L15 **Sjenica** *Turk.* Seniça. Serbia, SW Yugoslavia
96 G11 **Sjoa** ≈ S Norway
97 K23 **Sjöbo** Malmöhus, S Sweden
97 I24 **Sjælland** *Eng.* Zealand, *Ger.* Seeland. *island* E Denmark
96 E9 **Sjøholt** Møre og Romsdal, S Norway
94 O1 **Sjuøyane** *island group* N Svalbard
Skadar *see* Shkodër
Skadarsko Jezero *see* Scutari, Lake
119 R11 **Skadovs'k** Khersons'ka Oblast', S Ukraine
94 I2 **Skagaströnd** *prev.* Höfdhakaupstadhur. Nordhurland Vestra, N Iceland
97 H19 **Skagen** Nordjylland, N Denmark
Skagerak *see* Skagerrak
97 L16 **Skagern** ◎ C Sweden
207 T17 **Skagerrak** *var.* Skagerak. *channel* N Europe
96 G12 **Skaget** ▲ S Norway
34 H7 **Skagit River** ≈ Washington, NW USA
41 W12 **Skagway** Alaska, USA
94 K8 **Skaidi** Finnmark, N Norway
117 F21 **Skála** Pelopónnisos, S Greece
118 K6 **Skalat** *Pol.* Skałat. Ternopil's'ka Oblast', W Ukraine
97 J22 **Skälderviken** *inlet* Denmark/Sweden
94 I12 **Skalka** ◎ N Sweden
116 I12 **Skalotí** Anatolikí Makedonía kai Thráki, NE Greece
97 G22 **Skanderborg** Århus, C Denmark
97 K22 **Skåne** *prev. Eng.* Scania. *cultural region* S Sweden
77 N6 **Skanès** ✕ (Sousse) E Tunisia
97 C15 **Skånevik** Hordaland, S Norway
97 M18 **Skänninge** Östergötland, S Sweden
97 J23 **Skanör** Malmöhus, S Sweden
117 H17 **Skantzoúra** *island* Vóreioi Sporádes, Greece, Aegean Sea
97 K18 **Skara** Skaraborg, S Sweden
97 J18 **Skaraborg** ◈ *county* S Sweden
97 M17 **Skärblacka** Östergötland, S Sweden
97 I18 **Skärhamn** Göteborg och Bohus, S Sweden
97 I14 **Skarnes** Hedmark, S Norway
121 M21 **Skarodnaye** *Rus.* Skorodnoye. Homyel'skaya Voblasts', SE Belarus
112 I8 **Skarszewy** *Ger.* Schöneck. Gdańsk, NW Poland
113 M14 **Skarżysko-Kamienna** Kielce, SE Poland
97 K16 **Skattkärr** Värmland, C Sweden
120 D12 **Skaudvilė** Tauragė, SW Lithuania
94 J12 **Skaulo** Norrbotten, N Sweden
113 K17 **Skawina** Kraków, S Poland
8 K12 **Skeena** ≈ British Columbia, SW Canada
8 J11 **Skeena Mountains** ▲▲ British Columbia, W Canada
99 O18 **Skegness** E England, UK
94 J4 **Skeidharársandur** *coast* S Iceland
95 J15 **Skellefteå** Västerbotten, N Sweden
95 I14 **Skellefteälven** ≈ N Sweden
95 J15 **Skelleftehamn** Västerbotten, N Sweden
27 O2 **Skellytown** Texas, SW USA
97 J19 **Skene** Älvsborg, S Sweden
99 G17 **Skerries** *Ir.* Na Sceirí. E Ireland
97 H15 **Ski** Akershus, S Norway
117 G17 **Skíathos** Skíathos, Vóreioi Sporádes, Greece, Aegean Sea
117 G17 **Skíathos** *island* Vóreioi Sporádes, Greece, Aegean Sea
29 P9 **Skiatook** Oklahoma, C USA
29 P9 **Skiatook Lake** ⊞ Oklahoma, C USA
99 B22 **Skibbereen** *Ir.* An Sciobairín. SW Ireland
94 I9 **Skibotn** Troms, N Norway
121 F16 **Skidal'** *Rus.* Skidel'. Hrodzyenskaya Voblasts', W Belarus
99 K15 **Skiddaw** ▲ NW England, UK
Skidel' *see* Skidal'
27 T14 **Skidmore** Texas, SW USA
97 G16 **Skien** Telemark, S Norway
Skiermûntseach *see* Schiermonnikoog
112 L12 **Skierniewice** Skierniewice, C Poland
112 K12 **Skierniewice** *off.* Województwo Skierniewickie. ◈ *province* C Poland
Skierniewickie, Województwo *see* Skierniewice
76 L5 **Skikda** *prev.* Philippeville. NE Algeria
32 M16 **Skillet Fork** ≈ Illinois, N USA
97 L19 **Skillingaryd** Jönköping, S Sweden
117 B19 **Skinári, Ákra** *headland* Zákynthos, Iónioi Nísoi, Greece, C Mediterranean Sea
97 M15 **Skinnskatteberg** Västmanland, C Sweden
190 M12 **Skipton** Victoria, SE Australia
99 L16 **Skipton** N England, UK
Skiropoula *see* Skyropoúla
Skíros *see* Skýros
97 F21 **Skive** Viborg, NW Denmark
96 F11 **Skjåk** Oppland, S Norway
94 K2 **Skjálfandafljót** ≈ C Iceland
97 F22 **Skjern** Ringkøbing, W Denmark
97 F22 **Skjern Å** *var.* Skjern Aa. ≈ W Denmark
Skjern Aa *see* Skjern Å
94 G12 **Skjerstad** Nordland, C Norway
94 I8 **Skjervøy** Troms, N Norway
94 I10 **Skjold** Troms, N Norway
113 I17 **Skoczów** Bielsko-Biała, S Poland
97 I24 **Skælskør** Vestsjælland, E Denmark
111 T11 **Škofja Loka** *Ger.* Bischoflack. NW Slovenia
96 N12 **Skog** Gävleborg, C Sweden
97 K16 **Skoghall** Värmland, C Sweden
33 N10 **Skokie** Illinois, N USA
118 H6 **Skole** L'vivs'ka Oblast', W Ukraine
117 D19 **Skóllis** ▲ S Greece
178 J13 **Skon** Kâmpóng Cham, C Cambodia
117 H17 **Skópelos** Skópelos, Vóreioi Sporádes, Greece, Aegean Sea
117 H17 **Skópelos** *island* Vóreioi Sporádes, Greece, Aegean Sea
130 L5 **Skopin** Ryazanskaya Oblast', W Russian Federation
115 N18 **Skopje** *var.* Üsküb, *Turk.* Üsküp; *prev.* Skoplje, *anc.* Scupi. ● (FYR Macedonia) N FYR Macedonia
115 O18 **Skopje** ✕ N FYR Macedonia
Skoplje *see* Skopje
112 I8 **Skórcz** *Ger.* Skurz. Gdańsk, N Poland
Skorodnoye *see* Skarodnaye
95 H16 **Skorped** Västernorrland, C Sweden
97 G21 **Skørping** Nordjylland, N Denmark
97 K18 **Skövde** Skaraborg, S Sweden
126 Ll14 **Skovorodino** Amurskaya Oblast', SE Russian Federation
21 Q6 **Skowhegan** Maine, NE USA
9 W15 **Skownan** Manitoba, S Canada
96 H13 **Skreia** Oppland, S Norway
Skripón *see* Orchómenos
120 H9 **Skrīveri** Aizkraukle, S Latvia
120 J11 **Skrudaliena** Daugvapils, SE Latvia
120 D9 **Skrunda** Kuldīga, W Latvia
97 C16 **Skudeneshavn** Rogaland, S Norway
85 L20 **Skukuza** Mpumalanga, NE South Africa
99 B22 **Skull** *Ir.* An Scoil. SW Ireland
24 L3 **Skuna River** ≈ Mississippi, S USA
31 X15 **Skunk River** ≈ Iowa, C USA
120 C10 **Skuodas** *Ger.* Schoden, *Pol.* Szkudy. Skuodas, NW Lithuania
97 K23 **Skurup** Malmöhus, S Sweden
Skurz *see* Skórcz
116 H8 **Skŭt** ≈ NW Bulgaria
96 O13 **Skutskär** Uppsala, C Sweden
Skvira *see* Skvyra
119 O5 **Skvyra** *Rus.* Skvira. Kyyivs'ka Oblast', N Ukraine
41 Q11 **Skwentna** Alaska, USA
112 E11 **Skwierzyna** *Ger.* Schwerin. Gorzów, W Poland
98 G9 **Skye, Isle of** *island* NW Scotland, UK
34 I8 **Skykomish** Washington, NW USA
Skylge *see* Terschelling
65 F19 **Skyring, Peninsula** *peninsula* S Chile
65 H24 **Skyring, Seno** *inlet* S Chile
117 H17 **Skyropoúla** *var.* Skiropoula. *island* Vóreioi Sporádes, Greece, Aegean Sea
117 I17 **Skýros** *var.* Skíros. Skýros, Vóreioi Sporádes, Greece, Aegean Sea
117 I17 **Skýros** *var.* Skíros; *anc.* Scyros. *island* Vóreioi Sporádes, Greece, Aegean Sea
120 J12 **Slabodka** *Rus.* Slobodka. Vitsyebskaya Voblasts', NW Belarus
97 I23 **Slagelse** Vestsjælland, E Denmark
95 I14 **Slagnäs** Norrbotten, N Sweden
174 Kk15 **Slamet, Gunung** ▲ Jawa, S Indonesia
41 T10 **Slana** Alaska, USA
99 F20 **Slaney** *Ir.* An tSláine. ≈ SE Ireland
118 J13 **Slănic** Prahova, SE Romania
118 K11 **Slănic Moldova** Bacău, E Romania
115 H16 **Slano** Dubrovnik-Neretva, SE Croatia
128 F13 **Slantsy** Leningradskaya Oblast', NW Russian Federation
113 C16 **Slaný** *Ger.* Schlan. Střední Čechy, NW Czech Republic
10 C10 **Slate Falls** Ontario, S Canada
29 T4 **Slater** Missouri, C USA
118 I14 **Slatina** Olt, S Romania
Slatina *see* Podravska Slatina
27 N5 **Slaton** Texas, SW USA
97 H14 **Slattum** Akershus, S Norway
9 R10 **Slave** ≈ Alberta/Northwest Territories, C Canada
70 E12 **Slave Coast** *coastal region* W Africa
9 P13 **Slave Lake** Alberta, SW Canada
125 G14 **Slavgorod** Altayskiy Kray, S Russian Federation
Slavgorod *see* Slawharad
Slavonia *see* Slavonija
114 G9 **Slavonija** *Eng.* Slavonia, *Ger.* Slawonien, *Hung.* Szlavonia, Szlavonország. *cultural region* NE Croatia
114 H9 **Slavonska Požega** *prev.* Požega, *Ger.* Poschega, *Hung.* Pozsega. Požega-Slavonija, NE Croatia
114 H10 **Slavonski Brod** *Ger.* Brod, *Hung.* Bród; *prev.* Brod, Brod na Savi. Brod-Posavina, NE Croatia
118 L4 **Slavuta** Khmel'nyts'ka Oblast', NW Ukraine
119 P2 **Slavutych** Chernihivs'ka Oblast', N Ukraine
127 N18 **Slavyanka** Primorskiy Kray, SE Russian Federation
116 J8 **Slavyanovo** Loveshka Oblast, N Bulgaria
Slavyansk *see* Slov"yans'k
130 K14 **Slavyansk-na-Kubani** Krasnodarskiy Kray, SW Russian Federation
121 N20 **Slavyechna** *Rus.* Slovechna. ≈ Belarus/Ukraine
121 O16 **Slawharad** *Rus.* Slavgorod. Mahilyowskaya Voblasts', E Belarus
112 G7 **Sławno** Słupsk, NW Poland
Slawonien *see* Slavonija
31 S10 **Slayton** Minnesota, N USA
99 N18 **Sleaford** E England, UK
99 A20 **Slea Head** *Ir.* Ceann Sléibhe. *headland* SW Ireland
98 G9 **Sleat, Sound of** *strait* NW Scotland, UK
Sledyuki *see* Slyedzyuki
10 I5 **Sleeper Islands** *island group* Northwest Territories, C Canada
33 O6 **Sleeping Bear Point** *headland* Michigan, N USA
31 T10 **Sleepy Eye** Minnesota, N USA
41 O11 **Sleetmute** Alaska, USA
Sléibhe, Ceann *see* Slea Head
Slēmānī *see* As Sulaymānīyah
205 O5 **Slessor Glacier** *glacier* Antarctica
24 L9 **Slidell** Louisiana, S USA
20 K12 **Slide Mountain** ▲ New York, NE USA
100 I13 **Sliedrecht** Zuid-Holland, C Netherlands
123 Jj16 **Sliema** N Malta
99 G16 **Slieve Donard** ▲ SE Northern Ireland, UK
Sligeach *see* Sligo
99 D16 **Sligo** *Ir.* Sligeach. NW Ireland
99 C16 **Sligo** *Ir.* Sligeach. *cultural region* NW Ireland
99 C15 **Sligo Bay** *Ir.* Cuan Shligigh. *inlet* NW Ireland
20 B13 **Slippery Rock** Pennsylvania, NE USA
97 P19 **Slite** Gotland, SE Sweden
116 L9 **Sliven** *var.* Slivno. Burgaska Oblast, E Bulgaria
116 G9 **Slivnitsa** Sofiyska Oblast, W Bulgaria
Slivno *see* Sliven
116 L7 **Slivo Pole** Razgradska Oblast, NE Bulgaria
31 S13 **Sloan** Iowa, C USA
37 X12 **Sloan** Nevada, W USA
Slobodka *see* Slabodka
129 R14 **Slobodskoy** Kirovskaya Oblast', NW Russian Federation
Slobodzeya *see* Slobozia
119 O10 **Slobozia** *Rus.* Slobodzeya. E Moldova
118 L14 **Slobozia** Ialomiţa, SE Romania
100 O5 **Slochteren** Groningen, NE Netherlands
121 H17 **Slonim** *Pol.* Słonim, *Rus.* Slonim. Hrodzyenskaya Voblasts', W Belarus
100 K7 **Sloter Meer** ◎ N Netherlands
Slot, The *see* New Georgia Sound
99 N22 **Slough** S England, UK
113 J20 **Slovakia** *off.* Slovenská Republika, *Ger.* Slowakei, *Hung.* Szlovákia, *Slvk.* Slovensko. ◆ *republic* C Europe
Slovak Ore Mountains *see* Slovenské Rudohorie
Slovechna *see* Slavyechna
111 S12 **Slovenia** *off.* Republic of Slovenia, *Ger.* Slowenien, *Slvn.* Slovenija. ◆ *republic* SE Europe
Slovenija *see* Slovenia
111 V10 **Slovenj Gradec** *Ger.* Windischgraz. N Slovenia
111 W10 **Slovenska Bistrica** *Ger.* Windischfeistritz. NE Slovenia
111 W10 **Slovenska Konjice** E Slovenia
Slovenská Republika *see* Slovakia
113 K20 **Slovenské Rudohorie** *Eng.* Slovak Ore Mountains, *Ger.* Slowakisches Erzgebirge, Ungarisches Erzgebirge. ▲▲ C Slovakia
Slovensko *see* Slovakia
119 Y7 **Slov"yanoserbs'k** Luhans'ka Oblast', E Ukraine
119 W6 **Slov"yans'k** *Rus.* Slavyansk. Donets'ka Oblast', E Ukraine
Slowakei *see* Slovakia
Slowakisches Erzgebirge *see* Slovenské Rudohorie
Slowenien *see* Slovenia
112 D11 **Słubice** *Ger.* Frankfurt. Gorzów, W Poland
121 K19 **Sluch** *Rus.* Sluch'. ≈ C Belarus
118 L4 **Sluch** ≈ NW Ukraine
101 D16 **Sluis** Zeeland, SW Netherlands
114 D10 **Slunj** *Hung.* Szluin. Karlovac, C Croatia
112 I11 **Słupca** Konin, C Poland
112 G6 **Słupia** *Ger.* Stolpe. ≈ NW Poland
112 G6 **Słupsk** *Ger.* Stolp. Słupsk, NW Poland
112 G7 **Słupsk** *off.* Województwo Słupskie, *Ger.* Stolp. ◈ *province* NW Poland
Słupskie, Województwo *see* Słupsk
121 K18 **Slutsk** *Rus.* Slutsk. Minskaya Voblasts', S Belarus
121 O16 **Slyedzyuki** *Rus.* Sledyuki. Mahilyowskaya Voblasts', E Belarus
99 A17 **Slyne Head** *Ir.* Ceann Léime. *headland* W Ireland
126 J16 **Slyudyanka** Irkutskaya Oblast', S Russian Federation
29 U14 **Smackover** Arkansas, C USA
97 L20 **Småland** *cultural region* S Sweden
97 K20 **Smålandsstenar** Jönköping, S Sweden
Small Malaita *see* Maramasike
11 O8 **Smallwood Reservoir** ◎ Newfoundland and Labrador, S Canada
121 N14 **Smalyany** *Rus.* Smolyany. Vitsyebskaya Voblasts', NE Belarus
121 L15 **Smalyavichy** *Rus.* Smolevichi. Minskaya Voblasts', C Belarus
76 C9 **Smara** *var.* Es Semara. N Western Sahara
121 I14 **Smarhon'** *Pol.* Smorgonie, *Rus.* Smorgon'. Hrodzyenskaya Voblasts', W Belarus
114 M11 **Smederevo** *Ger.* Semendria. Serbia, N Yugoslavia
114 M12 **Smederevska Palanka** Serbia, C Yugoslavia
97 M14 **Smedjebacken** Kopparberg, C Sweden
118 L13 **Smeeni** Buzău, SE Romania
Smela *see* Smila
109 D16 **Smeralda, Costa** *cultural region* Sardegna, Italy, C Mediterranean Sea
113 J22 **Śmigiel** *Ger.* Schmiegel. Leszno, W Poland
119 Q6 **Smila** *Rus.* Smela. Cherkas'ka Oblast', C Ukraine
100 N7 **Smilde** Drenthe, NE Netherlands
9 S16 **Smiley** Saskatchewan, S Canada
27 T12 **Smiley** Texas, SW USA
Smilten *see* Smiltene
120 I8 **Smiltene** *Ger.* Smilten. Valka, N Latvia
127 O14 **Smirnykh** Ostrov Sakhalin, Sakhalinskaya Oblast', SE Russian Federation
9 Q13 **Smith** Alberta, W Canada
41 P4 **Smith Bay** *bay* Alaska, USA
10 I3 **Smith, Cape** *headland* Québec, NE Canada
28 L3 **Smith Center** Kansas, C USA
8 K13 **Smithers** British Columbia, SW Canada
23 V10 **Smithfield** North Carolina, SE USA
38 L1 **Smithfield** Utah, W USA
23 X7 **Smithfield** Virginia, NE USA
10 I3 **Smith Island** *island* Northwest Territories, C Canada
Smith Island *see* Sumisu-jima
22 H7 **Smithland** Kentucky, S USA
23 T7 **Smith Mountain Lake** *var.* Leesville Lake. ⊞ Virginia, NE USA
36 L1 **Smith River** California, W USA
35 R9 **Smith River** ≈ Montana, NW USA
12 L13 **Smiths Falls** Ontario, SE Canada
35 N13 **Smiths Ferry** Idaho, NW USA
22 K7 **Smiths Grove** Kentucky, S USA
191 N15 **Smithton** Tasmania, SE Australia
20 L14 **Smithtown** Long Island, New York, NE USA
22 K9 **Smithville** Tennessee, S USA
27 T11 **Smithville** Texas, SW USA
Šmohor *see* Hermagor
37 Q4 **Smoke Creek Desert** *desert* Nevada, W USA
9 O14 **Smoky** ≈ Alberta, W Canada
190 E7 **Smoky Bay** South Australia
191 V6 **Smoky Cape** *headland* New South Wales, SE Australia
28 L4 **Smoky Hill River** ≈ Kansas, C USA
28 L4 **Smoky Hills** *hill range* Kansas, C USA
9 Q14 **Smoky Lake** Alberta, SW Canada
96 E8 **Smøla** *island* W Norway
130 H4 **Smolensk** Smolenskaya Oblast', W Russian Federation
130 H4 **Smolenskaya Oblast'** ◈ *province* W Russian Federation
Smolensk-Moscow Upland *see* Smolensko-Moskovskaya Vozvyshennost'
130 J3 **Smolensko-Moskovskaya Vozvyshennost'** *var.* Smolensk-Moscow Upland. ▲▲ W Russian Federation
Smolevichi *see* Smalyavichy
117 C15 **Smolikás** ▲ W Greece
116 I12 **Smolyan** *prev.* Pashmakli. Plovdivska Oblast, S Bulgaria
Smolyany *see* Smalyany
35 S15 **Smoot** Wyoming, C USA
10 G12 **Smooth Rock Falls** Ontario, S Canada
Smorgon'/Smorgonie *see* Smarhon'
97 K23 **Smygehamn** Malmöhus, S Sweden
204 I7 **Smyley Island** *island* Antarctica
23 Y3 **Smyrna** Delaware, NE USA
25 S3 **Smyrna** Georgia, SE USA
22 J9 **Smyrna** Tennessee, S USA
Smyrna *see* İzmir
176 W10 **Snabai** Irian Jaya, E Indonesia
99 I16 **Snaefell** ▲ C Isle of Man
94 H3 **Snaefellsjökull** ▲ W Iceland
8 J4 **Snake** ≈ Yukon Territory, NW Canada
31 O8 **Snake Creek** ≈ South Dakota, N USA
191 P13 **Snake Island** *island* Victoria, SE Australia
37 Y6 **Snake Range** ▲▲ Nevada, W USA
34 K10 **Snake River** ≈ NW USA
31 V6 **Snake River** ≈ Minnesota, N USA
30 L12 **Snake River** ≈ Nebraska, C USA
35 Q14 **Snake River Plain** *plain* Idaho, NW USA
15 I7 **Snare** ≈ Northwest Territories, NW Canada
95 F15 **Snåsa** Nord-Trøndelag, C Norway
23 O8 **Sneedville** Tennessee, S USA
100 K6 **Sneek** Friesland, N Netherlands
Sneeuw-gebergte *see* Maoke, Pegunungan
97 F22 **Snejbjerg** Ringkøbing, C Denmark
126 I8 **Snezhnogorsk** Taymyrskiy (Dolgano-Nenetskiy) Avtonomnyy Okrug, N Russian Federation
Snezhnoye *see* Snizhne
113 G15 **Sněžka** *Ger.* Schneekoppe. ▲ N Czech Republic
111 T13 **Snežnik** *Ger.* Schneeberg, *It.* Monte Nevoso. ▲ SW Slovenia
112 N8 **Śniardwy, Jezioro** *Ger.* Spirdingsee. ◎ NE Poland
Sniečkus *see* Visaginas
119 R10 **Snihurivka** Mykolayivs'ka Oblast', S Ukraine
118 I5 **Snilow** ✕ (L'viv) L'vivs'ka Oblast', W Ukraine
113 O19 **Snina** *Hung.* Szinna. Východné Slovensko, E Slovakia
119 Y8 **Snizhne** *Rus.* Snezhnoye. Donets'ka Oblast', SE Ukraine
94 J3 **Snækollur** ▲ C Iceland
96 G10 **Snøhetta** *var.* Snohetta. ▲ S Norway
94 G12 **Snøtinden** ▲ C Norway
99 I18 **Snowdon** ▲ NW Wales, UK
99 I18 **Snowdonia** ▲▲ NW Wales, UK
15 Ii8 **Snowdrift** ≈ Northwest Territories, NW Canada
Snowdrift *see* Łutselk'e
39 N12 **Snowflake** Arizona, SW USA
23 Y5 **Snow Hill** Maryland, NE USA
23 W10 **Snow Hill** North Carolina, SE USA
204 H3 **Snowhill Island** *island* Antarctica
9 V13 **Snow Lake** Manitoba, C Canada
39 R5 **Snowmass Mountain** ▲ Colorado, C USA
20 M10 **Snow, Mount** ▲ Vermont, NE USA
36 M5 **Snow Mountain** ▲ California, W USA
Snow Mountains *see* Maoke, Pegunungan
35 N7 **Snowshoe Peak** ▲ Montana, NW USA
190 I8 **Snowtown** South Australia
38 K1 **Snowville** Utah, W USA
37 X3 **Snow Water Lake** ◎ Nevada, W USA
191 Q11 **Snowy Mountains** ▲▲ New South Wales/Victoria, SE Australia
191 Q12 **Snowy River** ≈ New South Wales/Victoria, SE Australia
46 K5 **Snug Corner** Acklins Island, SE Bahamas
178 Jj13 **Snuŏl** Krâchéh, E Cambodia
118 J7 **Snyatyn** *Rus.* Snyatyn. Ivano-Frankivs'ka Oblast', W Ukraine
28 L12 **Snyder** Oklahoma, C USA
27 O6 **Snyder** Texas, SW USA
180 H3 **Soalala** Mahajanga, W Madagascar
180 J4 **Soanierana-Ivongo** Toamasina, E Madagascar
175 Ss7 **Soasiu** *var.* Tidore. Pulau Tidore, E Indonesia
56 G8 **Soatá** Boyacá, C Colombia
180 I5 **Soavinandriana** Antananarivo, C Madagascar
176 Yy12 **Soba** Irian Jaya, E Indonesia
79 V13 **Soba** Kaduna, C Nigeria
169 Y16 **Sobaek-sanmaek** ▲▲ S South Korea
82 F13 **Sobat** ≈ E Sudan
176 Z12 **Sobger, Sungai** ≈ Irian Jaya, E Indonesia
176 W10 **Sobiei** Irian Jaya, E Indonesia
130 M3 **Sobinka** Vladimirskaya Oblast', W Russian Federation
131 S7 **Sobolevo** Orenburgskaya Oblast', W Russian Federation
Soborsin *see* Săvârşin
170 D15 **Sobo-san** ▲ Kyūshū, SW Japan
113 G14 **Sobótka** Wrocław, SW Poland
61 O15 **Sobradinho** Bahia, E Brazil
Sobradinho, Barragem de *see* Sobradinho, Represa de
61 O16 **Sobradinho, Represa de** *var.* Barragem de Sobradinho. ⊞ E Brazil
60 O13 **Sobral** Ceará, E Brazil
107 T4 **Sobrarbe** *physical region* NE Spain
111 R10 **Soča** *It.* Isonzo. ≈ Italy/Slovenia
112 L11 **Sochaczew** Skierniewice, C Poland
130 L15 **Sochi** Krasnodarskiy Kray, SW Russian Federation
116 G13 **Sochós** *var.* Sohos, Sokhós. Kentrikí Makedonía, N Greece
203 R11 **Société, Archipel de la** *var.* Archipel de Tahiti, Îles de la Société, *Eng.* Society Islands. *island group* W French Polynesia
Société, Îles de la/Society Islands *see* Société, Archipel de la
23 T11 **Society Hill** South Carolina, SE USA
183 W9 **Society Ridge** *undersea feature* C Pacific Ocean
64 I5 **Socompa, Volcán** ▲ N Chile
Soconusco, Sierra de *see* Sierra Madre
56 G8 **Socorro** Santander, C Colombia
39 R13 **Socorro** New Mexico, SW USA
Socotra *see* Suquţrā
178 Jj15 **Soc Trăng** *var.* Khanh *Hung.* Soc Trăng, S Vietnam
107 P10 **Socuéllamos** Castilla-La Mancha, C Spain
37 W13 **Soda Lake** *salt flat* California, W USA
94 L11 **Sodankylä** Lappi, N Finland
Sodari *see* Sodiri
35 R15 **Soda Springs** Idaho, NW USA
Soddo/Soddu *see* Sodo
22 L10 **Soddy Daisy** Tennessee, S USA
97 N14 **Söderfors** Uppsala, C Sweden
96 N12 **Söderhamn** Gävleborg, C Sweden
97 N17 **Söderköping** Östergötland, S Sweden
97 N17 **Södermanland** ◈ *county* C Sweden
97 O16 **Södertälje** Stockholm, C Sweden
82 D10 **Sodiri** *var.* Sawdirī, Sodari. Northern Kordofan, C Sudan
83 I14 **Sodo** *var.* Soddo, Soddu. SW Ethiopia
96 N11 **Södra Dellen** ◎ C Sweden
97 M19 **Södra Vi** Kalmar, S Sweden
20 G9 **Sodus Point** *headland* New York, NE USA
175 Rr17 **Soe** *prev.* Soë. Timor, C Indonesia
174 J14 **Soekarno-Hatta** ✕ (Jakarta) Jawa, S Indonesia
Soëla-Sund *see* Soela Väin
120 E5 **Soela Väin** *prev. Eng.* Sele Sound, *Ger.* Dagden-Sund, Soëla-Sund. *strait* W Estonia
Soemba *see* Sumba, Pulau
Soembawa *see* Sumbawa
Soemenep *see* Sumenep
Soengaipenoeh *see* Sungaipenuh
Soerabaja *see* Surabaya
103 G14 **Soest** Nordrhein-Westfalen, W Germany
100 J11 **Soest** Utrecht, C Netherlands
102 F11 **Soeste** ≈ NW Germany
100 J11 **Soesterberg** Utrecht, C Netherlands
117 E16 **Sofádes** *var.* Sofádhes. Thessalía, C Greece
Sofádhes *see* Sofádes
85 N18 **Sofala** Sofala, C Mozambique
85 N17 **Sofala** ◈ *province* C Mozambique
85 N18 **Sofala, Baia de** *bay* E Mozambique
180 J3 **Sofia** *seasonal river* NW Madagascar
Sofia *see* Sofiya
117 G19 **Sofikó** Pelopónnisos, S Greece
Sofi-Kurgan *see* Sopu-Korgon
116 G10 **Sofiya** *var.* Sophia, *Eng.* Sofia; *Lat.* Serdica. ● (Bulgaria) Grad Sofiya, W Bulgaria
116 G9 **Sofiya** ✕ Grad Sofiya, W Bulgaria
Sofiya *see* Sofiyska Oblast
116 G9 **Sofiya, Grad** ◈ *municipality* W Bulgaria
Sofiyevka *see* Sofiyivka
119 S8 **Sofiyivka** *Rus.* Sofiyevka. Dnipropetrovs'ka Oblast', E Ukraine
127 Nn14 **Sofiysk** Khabarovskiy Kray, SE Russian Federation
127 N14 **Sofiysk** Khabarovskiy Kray, SE Russian Federation
116 F10 **Sofiyska Oblast** *var.* Sofiya. ◈ *province* W Bulgaria
128 I6 **Sofporog** Respublika Kareliya, NW Russian Federation
172 Ss15 **Sōfu-gan** *island* Izu-shotō, SE Japan

◆ Country ● Country Capital ◇ Dependent Territory ○ Dependent Territory Capital ◈ Administrative Region ✕ International Airport ▲ Mountain ▲▲ Mountain Range ⛰ Volcano ≈ River ◎ Lake ⊞ Reservoir

Sog see Sog Xian
56 G9 Sogamoso Boyacá, C Colombia
142 I11 Soğanlı Çayı ≈ N Turkey
96 E12 Sogn physical region S Norway
96 E12 Sogndal var. Sogndalsfjøra. Sogn og Fjordane, S Norway
Sogndalsfjøra see Sogndal
97 E18 Søgne Vest-Agder, S Norway
96 D12 Sognefjorden fjord NE North Sea
96 C12 Sogn Og Fjordane ◐ county S Norway
179 R13 Sogod Leyte, C Philippines
168 I11 Sogo Nur ◎ N China
165 T12 Sogruma Qinghai, W China
169 X17 Sŏgwip'o S South Korea
162 K10 Sog Xian var. Sog. Xizang Zizhiqu, W China
77 X10 Sohâg var. Sawhāj, Suliag. C Egypt
Sohar see Şuḩār
66 H9 Sohm Plain undersea feature NW Atlantic Ocean
102 H7 Soholmer Au ≈ N Germany
Sohos see Sochós
Sohrau see Żory
101 F20 Soignies Hainaut, SW Belgium
165 R15 Soila Xizang Zizhiqu, W China
105 P4 Soissons anc. Augusta Suessionum, Noviodunum. Aisne, N France
170 Ff14 Sōja Okayama, Honshū, SW Japan
158 F13 Sojat Rājasthān, N India
169 W13 Sŏjosŏn-man inlet W North Korea
118 I4 Sokal' Rus. Sokal. L'vivs'ka Oblast', NW Ukraine
169 Y14 Sokch'o N South Korea
142 B15 Söke Aydın, SW Turkey
201 N12 Sokehs Island island E Micronesia
81 M24 Sokele Shaba, SE Zaire
153 R11 Sokh Uzb. Sŭkh. ≈ Kyrgyzstan/Uzbekistan
Sokh see Sŭkh
Sokhós see Sochós
143 Q8 Sokhumi Rus. Sukhumi. NW Georgia
115 O14 Sokobanja Serbia, E Yugoslavia
79 R15 Sokodé C Togo
127 O10 Sokol Magadanskaya Oblast', E Russian Federation
128 M13 Sokol Vologodskaya Oblast', NW Russian Federation
112 P9 Sokółka Białystok, NE Poland
78 M11 Sokolo Ségou, W Mali
113 A16 Sokolov Ger. Falkenau an der Eger; prev. Falknov nad Ohří. Západní Čechy, W Czech Republic
113 O16 Sokołów Małopolski Rzeszów, SE Poland
112 O11 Sokołów Podlaski Siedlce, E Poland
78 G11 Sokone W Senegal
79 T12 Sokoto Sokoto, NW Nigeria
79 T12 Sokoto ◐ state NW Nigeria
79 S12 Sokoto ≈ NW Nigeria
Sokotra see Suquṭrā
153 U7 Sokuluk Chuyskaya Oblast', N Kyrgyzstan
118 L7 Sokyryany Chernivets'ka Oblast', W Ukraine
97 C16 Sola Rogaland, S Norway
197 C10 Sola Vanua Lava, N Vanuatu
97 C17 Sola ✕ (Stavanger) Rogaland, S Norway
83 H18 Solai Rift Valley, W Kenya
176 Y15 Solaka Irian Jaya, E Indonesia
158 I8 Solan Himāchal Pradesh, N India
193 A25 Solander Island island SW NZ
Solano see Bahía Solano
161 F15 Solāpur var. Sholāpur. Mahārāshtra, W India
95 H16 Solberg Västernorrland, C Sweden
118 K9 Solca Ger. Solka. Suceava, N Romania
107 O16 Sol, Costa del coastal region S Spain
108 F5 Solda Trentino-Alto Adige, N Italy
119 N9 Şoldăneşti Rus. Sholdaneshty. N Moldova
Soldau see Wkra
110 L8 Sölden Tirol, W Austria
29 P3 Soldier Creek ≈ Kansas, C USA
41 R12 Soldotna Alaska, USA
112 I10 Solec Kujawski Bydgoszcz, W Poland
63 B16 Soledad Santa Fe, C Argentina
57 Y11 Soledad Atlántico, N Colombia
37 O11 Soledad California, W USA
57 O7 Soledad Anzoátegui, NE Venezuela
Soledad see East Falkland
63 H15 Soledade Rio Grande do Sul, S Brazil
104 F2 Solenzara Corse, France, C Mediterranean Sea
Soleure see Solothurn
96 C12 Solheim Hordaland, S Norway
129 N14 Soligalich Kostromskaya Oblast', NW Russian Federation
Soligorsk see Salihorsk
99 L20 Solihull C England, UK
129 U13 Solikamsk Permskaya Oblast', NW Russian Federation
131 V8 Sol'-Iletsk Orenburgskaya Oblast', W Russian Federation
59 G17 Solimana, Nevado ▲ S Peru
60 E13 Solimões, Rio ≈ C Brazil
115 E14 Solin It. Salona; anc. Salonae. Split-Dalmacija, S Croatia
103 E15 Solingen Nordrhein-Westfalen, W Germany
Solka see Solca
95 H16 Sollefteå Västernorrland, C Sweden
97 O15 Sollentuna Stockholm, C Sweden
96 L13 Sollerön Kopparberg, C Sweden
103 I14 Solling hill range C Germany
97 O16 Solna Stockholm, C Sweden
130 K3 Solnechnogorsk Moskovskaya Oblast', W Russian Federation
127 Nn15 Solnechnyy Khabarovskiy Kray, SE Russian Federation
127 N11 Solnechnyy Respublika Sakha (Yakutiya), NE Russian Federation
96 H11 Sølnkletten ▲ S Norway
109 L17 Solofra Campania, S Italy
174 Gg9 Solok Sumatera, W Indonesia
44 C6 Sololá Sololá, W Guatemala
44 A2 Sololá off. Departamento de Sololá. ◐ department SW Guatemala
83 J16 Sololo Eastern, N Kenya
44 C4 Soloma Huehuetenango, W Guatemala
40 M9 Solomon Alaska, USA
29 N4 Solomon Kansas, C USA
195 U16 Solomon Islands prev. British Solomon Islands Protectorate. ◆ commonwealth republic W Pacific Ocean
195 T12 Solomon Islands island group PNG/Solomon Islands
28 M3 Solomon River ≈ Kansas, C USA
199 Hh9 Solomon Sea sea W Pacific Ocean
33 U11 Solon Ohio, N USA
119 T8 Solone Dnipropetrovs'ka Oblast', E Ukraine
175 R16 Solor, Kepulauan island group S Indonesia
130 M4 Solotcha Ryazanskaya Oblast', W Russian Federation
110 D7 Solothurn Fr. Soleure. Solothurn, NW Switzerland
110 D7 Solothurn Fr. Soleure. ◐ canton NW Switzerland
128 J7 Solovetskiye Ostrova island group NW Russian Federation
107 V5 Solsona Cataluña, NE Spain
115 E14 Šolta It. Solta. island S Croatia
Solţānābād see Kāshmar
148 L4 Solţānīyeh Zanjān, NW Iran
102 I11 Soltau Niedersachsen, NW Germany
128 G14 Sol'tsy Novgorodskaya Oblast', W Russian Federation
Soltūstik Qazaqstan Oblysy see Severnyy Kazakhstan
Solun see Thessaloníki
115 O19 Solunska Glava ▲ C FYR Macedonia
97 L22 Sölvesborg Blekinge, S Sweden
99 J15 Solway Firth inlet England/Scotland, UK
84 I13 Solwezi North Western, NW Zambia
171 Ll14 Sōma Fukushima, Honshū, C Japan
142 C13 Soma Manisa, W Turkey
83 O15 Somalia off. Somali Democratic Republic, Som. Jamuuriyada Demuqraadiga Soomaaliyeed, Soomaaliya; prev. Italian Somaliland, Somaliland Protectorate. ◆ republic E Africa
181 N6 Somali Basin undersea feature W Indian Ocean
69 Y8 Somali Plain undersea feature W Indian Ocean
114 J8 Sombor Hung. Zombor. Serbia, NW Yugoslavia
101 H20 Sombreffe Namur, S Belgium
42 L10 Sombrerete Zacatecas, C Mexico
47 V8 Sombrero island N Anguilla
157 Q21 Sombrero Channel channel Nicobar Islands, India
118 H9 Şomcuta Mare Hung. Nagysomkút; prev. Somcuta Mare. Maramureş, N Romania
178 I19 Somdet Kalasin, E Thailand
101 L15 Someren Noord-Brabant, SE Netherlands
95 L19 Somero Turku-Pori, SW Finland
35 P7 Somers Montana, NW USA
66 A12 Somerset var. Somerset Village. W Bermuda
39 Q5 Somerset Colorado, C USA
22 M7 Somerset Kentucky, S USA
21 O12 Somerset Massachusetts, NE USA
99 K23 Somerset cultural region SW England, UK
Somerset East see Somerset-Oos
66 A12 Somerset Island island W Bermuda
207 N9 Somerset Island island Queen Elizabeth Islands, Northwest Territories, NW Canada
Somerset Nile see Victoria Nile
85 I25 Somerset-Oos Eng. Somerset East. Eastern Cape, S South Africa
85 E26 Somerset-Wes Eng. Somerset West. Western Cape, SW South Africa
Somerset West see Somerset-Wes
Somers Islands see Bermuda
20 J17 Somers Point New Jersey, NE USA
21 P9 Somersworth New Hampshire, NE USA
38 I15 Somerton Arizona, SW USA
20 J14 Somerville New Jersey, NE USA
22 F10 Somerville Tennessee, S USA
27 U10 Somerville Texas, SW USA
27 T10 Somerville Lake ⊡ Texas, SW USA
Someş/Somesch/Someşul see Szamos
105 N2 Somme ◐ department N France
105 N2 Somme ≈ N France
97 L18 Sommen Jönköping, S Sweden
97 M18 Sommen ◎ S Sweden
103 K16 Sömmerda Thüringen, C Germany
Sommerein see Šamorín
Sommerfeld see Lubsko
57 Y11 Sommet Tabulaire var. Mont Itoupé. ▲ S French Guiana
113 H25 Somogy off. Somogy Megye. ◐ county SW Hungary
Somorja see Šamorín
107 N7 Somosierra, Puerto de pass N Spain
197 J13 Somosomo Taveuni, N Fiji
44 I9 Somotillo Chinandega, NW Nicaragua
44 J8 Somoto Madriz, NW Nicaragua
112 I11 Sompolno Konin, C Poland
107 S3 Somport var. Puerto de Somport, Fr. Col du Somport; anc. Summus Portus. pass France/Spain see also Somport, Col du
104 J17 Somport, Col du var. Puerto de Somport, Sp. Somport; anc. Summus Portus. pass France/Spain see also Somport
Somport, Puerto de see Somport/Somport, Col du
101 K15 Son Noord-Brabant, S Netherlands
97 H15 Son Buskerud, S Norway
160 L9 Son var. Sone. ≈ C India
45 R16 Soná Veraguas, W Panama
160 M12 Sonapur prev. Sonepur. Orissa, E India
176 Vv10 Sonar Irian Jaya, E Indonesia
97 G24 Sønderborg Ger. Sonderburg. Sønderjylland, SW Denmark
Sonderburg see Sønderborg
97 F24 Sønderjylland off. Sønderjyllands Amt. ◐ county SW Denmark
103 K15 Sondershausen Thüringen, C Germany
207 N14 Søndre Strømfjord ✕ W Greenland
108 E6 Sondrio Lombardia, N Italy
Sone see Son
Sonepur see Sonapur
59 K22 Sonequera ▲ S Bolivia
178 Kk12 Sông Câu Phu Yên, C Vietnam
178 J15 Sông Đôc Minh Hai, S Vietnam
83 H25 Songea Ruvuma, S Tanzania
176 Z11 Songgato, Sungai ≈ Irian Jaya, E Indonesia
169 X10 Songhua Hu ◎ NE China
169 Y7 Songhua Jiang var. Sungari. ≈ NE China
167 S8 Songjiang Shanghai Shi, E China
Sŏngjin see Kimch'aek
178 H17 Songkhla var. Songkla, Mal. Singora. Songkhla, SW Thailand
Songkla see Songkhla
169 T13 Song Ling ▲ NE China
169 W14 Songnim SW North Korea
84 B10 Songo Uíge, NW Angola
85 M15 Songo Tete, NW Mozambique
81 F21 Songololo Bas-Zaïre, SW Zaire
166 H7 Songpan prev. Sungpu. Sichuan, C China
169 Y17 Sŏngsan S South Korea
167 R11 Songxi Fujian, SE China
166 M6 Songxian var. Song Xian. Henan, C China
167 R10 Songyin Zhejiang, SE China
169 V9 Songyuan var. Fu-yü, Petuna; prev. Fuyu. Jilin, NE China
169 P11 Sonid Youqi var. Saihon Tal. Nei Mongol Zizhiqu, N China
169 P11 Sonid Zuoqi Nei Mongol Zizhiqu, N China
158 I10 Sonīpat Haryāna, N India
95 M15 Sonkajärvi Kuopio, C Finland
178 J6 Sơn La Sơn La, N Vietnam
155 O16 Sonmiāni Baluchistān, S Pakistan
155 O16 Sonmiāni Bay bay S Pakistan
103 K18 Sonneberg Thüringen, C Germany
103 N24 Sonntagshorn ▲ Austria/Germany
Sonoita see Sonoyta
42 E3 Sonoita, Rio var. Río Sonoyta. ≈ Mexico/USA
37 N7 Sonoma California, W USA
37 T3 Sonoma Peak ▲ Nevada, W USA
37 P8 Sonora California, W USA
27 O10 Sonora Texas, SW USA
42 F5 Sonora ◐ state NW Mexico
37 X17 Sonoran Desert var. Desierto de Altar. desert Mexico/USA see also Altar, Desierto de
42 G5 Sonora, Río ≈ NW Mexico
42 E2 Sonoyta var. Sonoita. Sonora, NW Mexico
Sonoyta, Río see Sonoita, Rio
148 K6 Sonqor var. Sunqur. Kermānshāhān, W Iran
107 N9 Sonseca var. Sonseca con Casalgordo. Castilla-La Mancha, C Spain
Sonseca con Casalgordo see Sonseca
56 E9 Sonsón Antioquia, W Colombia
44 E7 Sonsonate Sonsonate, W El Salvador
44 A9 Sonsonate ◐ department SW El Salvador
196 A10 Sonsorol Islands island group S Palau
114 J9 Sonta Hung. Szond; prev. Szonta. Serbia, NW Yugoslavia
178 J6 Sơn Tây var. Sontay. Ha Tây, N Vietnam
103 J25 Sonthofen Bayern, S Germany
Soochow see Suzhou
Soomaaliya/Soomaaliyeed, Jamuuriyada Demuqraadiga see Somalia
Soome Laht see Finland, Gulf of
Sooner State see Oklahoma
25 V5 Soperton Georgia, SE USA
178 J6 Sop Hao Houaphan, N Laos
Sophia see Sofiya
175 Tt5 Sopi Pulau Morotai, E Indonesia
Sopianae see Pécs
176 Vv11 Sopinusa Irian Jaya, E Indonesia
175 Tt5 Sopi, Tanjung headland Pulau Morotai, N Indonesia
83 B14 Sopo ≈ W Sudan
Sopockinie/Sopotskin see Sapotskino
116 I9 Sopot Plovdivska Oblast, C Bulgaria
112 I7 Sopot Ger. Zoppot. Gdańsk, N Poland
178 H8 Sop Prap var. Ban Sop Prap. Lampang, NW Thailand
113 G22 Sopron Ger. Ödenburg. Győr-Moson-Sopron, NW Hungary
153 U11 Sopu-Korgon var. Sofi-Kurgan. Oshskaya Oblast', SW Kyrgyzstan
158 H5 Sopur Jammu and Kashmir, NW India
109 J15 Sora Lazio, C Italy
160 N13 Sorada Orissa, E India
95 H17 Söråker Västernorrland, C Sweden
59 J17 Sorata La Paz, W Bolivia
Sorau/Sorau in der Niederlausitz see Żary
107 Q14 Sorbas Andalucía, S Spain
Sord/Sórd Choluim Chille see Swords
13 O11 Sorel Québec, SE Canada
191 P17 Sorell Tasmania, SE Australia
191 O17 Sorell, Lake ◎ Tasmania, SE Australia
108 E8 Soresina Lombardia, N Italy
97 D14 Sørfjorden fjord S Norway
96 N11 Sörforsa Gävleborg, C Sweden
105 R14 Sorgues Vaucluse, SE France
142 K13 Sorgun Yozgat, C Turkey
107 P5 Soria Castilla-León, N Spain
107 P6 Soria ◐ province Castilla-León, N Spain
63 D19 Soriano Soriano, SW Uruguay
63 D19 Soriano ◐ department SW Uruguay
94 O4 Sørkapp headland SW Svalbard
149 T5 Sorkh, Kūh-e ▲ NE Iran
Soro see Ghazal, Bahr el
97 I23 Sorø Vestsjælland, E Denmark
118 M8 Soroca Rus. Soroki. N Moldova
62 L10 Sorocaba São Paulo, S Brazil
Sorochino see Sarochyna
131 T7 Sorochinsk Orenburgskaya Oblast', W Russian Federation
Soroki see Soroca
196 H15 Sorol atoll Caroline Islands, W Micronesia
176 Uu9 Sorong Irian Jaya, E Indonesia
83 G17 Soroti C Uganda
Sørøy see Sørøya
94 J8 Sørøya var. Sørøy. island N Norway
106 G11 Sorraia, Rio ≈ C Portugal
94 I10 Sørreisa Troms, N Norway
109 K18 Sorrento anc. Surrentum. Campania, S Italy
106 H10 Sor, Ribeira de stream C Portugal
205 T3 Sør Rondane Mountains ▲ Antarctica
95 H14 Sorsele Västerbotten, N Sweden
109 B17 Sorso Sardegna, Italy, C Mediterranean Sea
179 Qq11 Sorsogon Luzon, N Philippines
107 U4 Sort Cataluña, NE Spain
128 H11 Sortavala Respublika Kareliya, NW Russian Federation
109 L25 Sortino Sicilia, Italy, C Mediterranean Sea
94 G10 Sortland Nordland, C Norway
96 G9 Sør-Trøndelag ◐ county S Norway
97 I15 Sørumsand Akershus, S Norway
120 D6 Sõrve Säär headland SW Estonia
97 K22 Sösdala Kristianstad, S Sweden
107 R4 Sos del Rey Católico Aragón, NE Spain
95 F15 Sösjöfjällen ▲ C Sweden
130 K7 Sosna ≈ W Russian Federation
64 H12 Sosneado, Cerro ▲ W Argentina
129 S9 Sosnogorsk Respublika Komi, NW Russian Federation
128 J8 Sosnovets Respublika Kareliya, NW Russian Federation
Sosnovets see Sosnowiec
131 Q3 Sosnovka Chuvashskaya Respublika, W Russian Federation
129 S16 Sosnovka Kirovskaya Oblast', NW Russian Federation
128 M6 Sosnovka Murmanskaya Oblast', NW Russian Federation
130 M6 Sosnovka Tambovskaya Oblast', W Russian Federation
128 H12 Sosnovo Fin. Rautu. Leningradskaya Oblast', NW Russian Federation
126 K15 Sosnovo-Ozerskoye Respublika Buryatiya, S Russian Federation
Sosnovyy Bor see Sasnovy Bor
113 J16 Sosnowiec Ger. Sosnowitz, Rus. Sosnovets. Katowice, S Poland
Sosnowitz see Sosnowiec
119 R2 Sosnytsya Chernihivs'ka Oblast', N Ukraine
111 V10 Šoštanj N Slovenia
125 F10 Sos'va Sverdlovskaya Oblast', C Russian Federation
56 D12 Sotará, Volcán S Colombia
78 D10 Sotavento, Ilhas de var. Leeward Islands. island group S Cape Verde
95 N15 Sotkamo Oulu, C Finland
43 P10 Soto la Marina Tamaulipas, C Mexico
43 P10 Soto la Marina, Río ≈ C Mexico
43 X12 Sotuta Yucatán, SE Mexico
81 F17 Souanké La Sangha, NW Congo
78 M17 Soubré S Ivory Coast
117 H24 Soúda var. Soúdha, Eng. Suda. Kríti, Greece, E Mediterranean Sea
Soúdha see Soúda
Soueida see As Suwaydā'
116 L12 Souflí prev. Souflíon. Anatolikí Makedonía kai Thráki, NE Greece
Souflíon see Souflí
47 S11 Soufrière W Saint Lucia
47 X6 Soufrière ▲ Basse Terre, S Guadeloupe
104 M13 Souillac Lot, S France
181 Y17 Souillac S Mauritius
76 M5 Souk Ahras NE Algeria
76 E6 Souk-el-Arba-Rharb var. Souk el Arba du Rharb, Souk-el-Arba-du-Rharb, Souk-el-Arba-el-Rhab. NW Morocco
Soukhné see As Sukhnah
169 X14 Sŏul off. Sŏul-t'ŭkpyŏlsi, Eng. Seoul, Jap. Keijō; prev. Kyŏngsŏng. ● (South Korea) NW South Korea
104 J11 Soulac-sur-Mer Gironde, SW France
101 L19 Soumagne Liège, E Belgium
20 M14 Sound Beach Long Island, New York, NE USA
97 J22 Sound, The Dan. Øresund, Swe. Öresund. strait Denmark/Sweden
117 H20 Soúnio, Ákra headland C Greece
144 F8 Soûr var. Şūr; anc. Tyre. SW Lebanon
Sources, Mont-aux- see Phofung
106 G8 Soure Coimbra, N Portugal
9 W17 Souris Manitoba, S Canada
11 Q14 Souris Prince Edward Island, SE Canada
30 L2 Souris River var. Mouse River. ≈ Canada/USA
27 X10 Sour Lake Texas, SW USA
117 F17 Sourpi Thessalía, C Greece
106 H11 Sousel Portalegre, C Portugal
77 N6 Sousse var. Sūsah. NE Tunisia
12 H11 South ≈ Ontario, S Canada
South see Sud
85 G23 South Africa off. Republic of South Africa, Afr. Suid-Afrika. ◆ republic S Africa
48-49 South America continent
2 J18 South American Plate tectonic feature
99 M23 Southampton hist. Hamwih, Lat. Clausentum. S England, UK
21 N14 Southampton Long Island, New York, NE USA
15 M5 Southampton Island island Northwest Territories, NE Canada
157 P20 South Andaman island Andaman Islands, India, NE Indian Ocean
11 Q6 South Aulatsivik Island island Newfoundland and Labrador, E Canada
190 E4 South Australia ◐ state S Australia
South Australian Abyssal Plain see South Australian Plain
199 Gg13 South Australian Basin undersea feature SW Indian Ocean
181 X12 South Australian Plain var. South Australian Abyssal Plain. undersea feature SE Indian Ocean
39 R13 South Baldy ▲ New Mexico, SW USA
25 Y14 South Bay Florida, SE USA
12 E12 South Baymouth Manitoulin Island, Ontario, S Canada
32 L10 South Beloit Illinois, N USA
33 O11 South Bend Indiana, N USA
27 R6 South Bend Texas, SW USA
34 F9 South Bend Washington, NW USA
South Beveland see Zuid-Beveland
South Borneo see Kalimantan Selatan
23 U7 South Boston Virginia, NE USA
190 F2 South Branch Neales seasonal river South Australia
23 U3 South Branch Potomac River ≈ West Virginia, NE USA
193 H19 Southbridge Canterbury, South Island, NZ
21 N12 Southbridge Massachusetts, NE USA
191 P17 South Bruny Island island Tasmania, SE Australia
20 L7 South Burlington Vermont, NE USA
46 M6 South Caicos island S Turks and Caicos Islands
South Cape see Ka Lae
25 V3 South Carolina off. State of South Carolina; also known as The Palmetto State. ◐ state SE USA
South Carpathians see Carpaţii Meridionali
South Celebes see Sulawesi Selatan
23 Q5 South Charleston West Virginia, NE USA
198 F7 South China Basin undersea feature SE South China Sea
198 F7 South China Sea Chin. Nan Hai, Ind. Laut Cina Selatan, Vtn. Biên Đông. sea SE Asia
35 Z10 South Dakota off. State of South Dakota; also known as The Coyote State, Sunshine State. ◐ state N USA
25 X10 South Daytona Florida, SE USA
39 R10 South Domingo Pueblo New Mexico, SW USA
99 N23 South Downs hill range SE England, UK
85 I21 South East ◐ district SE Botswana
67 H15 South East Bay bay Ascension Island, C Atlantic Ocean
191 O17 South East Cape headland Tasmania, SE Australia
40 K10 Southeast Cape headland Saint Lawrence Island, Alaska, USA
South-East Celebes see Sulawesi Tenggara
198 G14 Southeast Indian Ridge undersea feature Indian Ocean/Pacific Ocean
Southeast Island see Tagula Island
199 Mm16 Southeast Pacific Basin var. Belling Hausen Mulde. undersea feature SE Pacific Ocean
67 H15 South East Point headland SE Ascension Island
191 O14 South East Point headland Victoria, S Australia
203 Z3 South East Point headland Kiritimati, NE Kiribati
46 L5 Southeast Point headland Mayaguana, SE Bahamas
South-East Sulawesi see Sulawesi Tenggara
9 U12 Southend Saskatchewan, C Canada
99 P22 Southend-on-Sea E England, UK
85 H20 Southern var. Bangwaketse, Ngwaketze. ◐ district SE Botswana
144 E13 Southern ◐ district S Israel
85 N15 Southern ◐ region S Malawi
85 I15 Southern ◐ province S Zambia
193 E19 Southern Alps ▲ South Island, NZ
202 K15 Southern Cook Islands island group S Cook Islands
188 K12 Southern Cross Western Australia
82 A12 Southern Darfur ◐ state W Sudan
194 F13 Southern Highlands ◐ province W PNG
9 V11 Southern Indian Lake ◎ Manitoba, C Canada
82 E11 Southern Kordofan ◐ state C Sudan
197 L15 Southern Lau Group island group Lau Group, SE Fiji
xii-xiii Southern Ocean ocean
23 T10 Southern Pines North Carolina, SE USA
161 J26 Southern Province ◐ province S Sri Lanka
98 I13 Southern Uplands ▲ S Scotland, UK
Southern Urals see Yuzhnyy Ural
191 P16 South Esk River ≈ Tasmania, SE Australia
9 U16 Southey Saskatchewan, S Canada
29 V2 South Fabius River ≈ Missouri, C USA
33 S10 Southfield Michigan, N USA
199 J11 South Fiji Basin undersea feature S Pacific Ocean
99 Q22 South Foreland headland SE England, UK
37 P7 South Fork American River ≈ California, W USA
30 K7 South Fork Grand River ≈ South Dakota, N USA
37 T12 South Fork Kern River ≈ California, W USA
41 Q7 South Fork Koyukuk River ≈ Alaska, USA
41 Q11 South Fork Kuskokwim River ≈ Alaska, USA
28 H2 South Fork Republican River ≈ C USA
28 L3 South Fork Solomon River ≈ Kansas, C USA
33 P5 South Fox Island island Michigan, N USA
22 G8 South Fulton Tennessee, S USA
205 U10 South Geomagnetic Pole pole Antarctica
67 J20 South Georgia island South Georgia and the South Sandwich Islands, SW Atlantic Ocean
67 K21 South Georgia and the South Sandwich Islands ◇ UK dependent territory SW Atlantic Ocean
49 Y14 South Georgia Ridge var. North Scotia Ridge. undersea feature SW Atlantic Ocean
189 Q1 South Goulburn Island island Northern Territory, N Australia
159 U16 South Hatia Island island SE Bangladesh
33 O10 South Haven Michigan, N USA
23 V7 South Hill Virginia, NE USA
South Holland see Zuid-Holland
23 P8 South Holston Lake ⊡ Tennessee/Virginia, S USA
183 N1 South Honshu Ridge undersea feature W Pacific Ocean
28 M6 South Hutchinson Kansas, C USA
157 K21 South Huvadhu Atoll var. Gaafu Dhaalu Atoll. atoll S Maldives
181 U14 South Indian Basin undersea feature Indian Ocean/Pacific Ocean
9 W11 South Indian Lake Manitoba, C Canada
83 I17 South Island island NW Kenya
193 C20 South Island island S NZ
67 B23 South Jason island Jason Islands, NW Falkland Islands
South Kalimantan see Kalimantan Selatan
South Kazakhstan see Yuzhnyy Kazakhstan
169 X15 South Korea off. Republic of Korea, Kor. Taehan Min'guk. ◆ republic E Asia
37 Q6 South Lake Tahoe California, W USA
27 N6 Southland Texas, SW USA
193 B23 Southland off. Southland Region. ◐ region South Island, NZ
31 N15 South Loup River ≈ Nebraska, C USA
157 K19 South Maalhosmadulu Atoll var. Baa Atoll. atoll N Maldives
12 E15 South Maitland ≈ Ontario, S Canada
198 F9 South Makassar Basin undersea feature E Java Sea
33 O6 South Manitou Island island Michigan, N USA
157 K18 South Miladummadulu Atoll atoll N Maldives
23 X8 South Mills North Carolina, SE USA
14 G7 South Nahanni ≈ Northwest Territories, NW Canada
41 P13 South Naknek Alaska, USA
12 M13 South Nation ≈ Ontario, SE Canada
46 F9 South Negril Point headland W Jamaica
157 K20 South Nilandhe Atoll var. Dhaalu Atoll. atoll C Maldives
38 L2 South Ogden Utah, W USA
20 M14 Southold Long Island, New York, NE USA
204 H1 South Orkney Islands island group Antarctica
143 S9 South Ossetia former autonomous region SW Georgia
South Pacific Basin see Southwest Pacific Basin
21 P7 South Paris Maine, NE USA
35 U15 South Pass pass Wyoming, C USA
201 U13 South Pass passage Chuuk Islands, C Micronesia
22 K10 South Pittsburg Tennessee, S USA
30 K15 South Platte River ≈ Colorado/Nebraska, C USA
33 T16 South Point Ohio, N USA
67 G15 South Point headland S Ascension Island
33 R6 South Point headland Michigan, N USA
South Point see Ka Lae
191 P17 Southport Tasmania, SE Australia
99 K17 Southport NW England, UK
23 V12 Southport North Carolina, SE USA
21 P8 South Portland Maine, NE USA
12 H12 South River Ontario, S Canada
23 U11 South River ≈ North Carolina, SE USA
98 K5 South Ronaldsay island NE Scotland, UK
38 L2 South Salt Lake Utah, W USA
67 L21 South Sandwich Islands island group SE South Georgia and South Sandwich Islands
67 K21 South Sandwich Trench undersea feature SW Atlantic Ocean
9 S16 South Saskatchewan ≈ Alberta/Saskatchewan, S Canada
67 I21 South Scotia Ridge undersea feature S Scotia Sea
9 V10 South Seal ≈ Manitoba, C Canada
204 G4 South Shetland Islands island group Antarctica
67 H22 South Shetland Trough undersea feature Atlantic Ocean/Pacific Ocean
99 M14 South Shields NE England, UK
31 R13 South Sioux City Nebraska, C USA
199 I10 South Solomon Trench undersea feature W Pacific Ocean
191 V3 South Stradbroke Island island Queensland, E Australia
South Sulawesi see Sulawesi Selatan
South Sumatra see Sumatera Selatan
192 K11 South Taranaki Bight bight SE Tasman Sea
202 I3 South Tarawa atoll Tungaru, N Kiribati
South Tasmania Plateau see Tasman Plateau
38 M15 South Tucson Arizona, SW USA
10 H9 South Twin Island island Northwest Territories, C Canada
98 E9 South Uist island NW Scotland, UK
South-West see Sud-Ouest
South-West Africa/South West Africa see Namibia
67 F15 South West Bay bay Ascension Island, C Atlantic Ocean
191 N18 South West Cape headland Tasmania, SE Australia
193 B26 South West Cape headland Stewart Island, NZ
40 J10 Southwest Cape headland Saint Lawrence Island, Alaska, USA
178 Mm13 Southwest Cay island NW Spratly Islands
Southwest Indian Ocean Ridge see Southwest Indian Ridge
181 N11 Southwest Indian Ridge var. Southwest Indian Ocean Ridge. undersea feature SW Indian Ocean
199 Kk13 Southwest Pacific Basin var. South Pacific Basin. undersea feature SE Pacific Ocean
46 H2 Southwest Point headland Great Abaco, N Bahamas
203 X3 South West Point headland Kiritimati, NE Kiribati
67 G25 South West Point headland SW Saint Helena
27 P5 South Wichita River ≈ Texas, SW USA
99 Q20 Southwold E England, UK
21 Q12 South Yarmouth Massachusetts, NE USA
118 J10 Sovata Hung. Szováta. Mureş, C Romania
109 N22 Soverato Calabria, SW Italy
Sovetabad see Ghafurov
130 C2 Sovetsk Ger. Tilsit. Kaliningradskaya Oblast', W Russian Federation
129 Q15 Sovetsk Kirovskaya Oblast', NW Russian Federation
131 N10 Sovetskaya Rostovskaya Oblast', SW Russian Federation
127 O15 Sovetskaya Gavan' Khabarovskiy Kray, SE Russian Federation
125 F10 Sovetskiy Khanty-Mansiyskiy Avtonomnyy Okrug, C Russian Federation

◆ Country ● Country Capital ◇ Dependent Territory ○ Dependent Territory Capital ◐ Administrative Region ✕ International Airport ▲ Mountain ▲ Mountain Range Volcano ≈ River ◎ Lake ⊡ Reservoir

Sovetskoye *see* Ketchenery
152 *I15* **Sovet"yab** ***prev.*** Sovet"yap. Akhalskiy Velayat, S Turkmenistan
Sovet"yap *see* Sovet"yab
119 *U12* **Sovyets'kyy** Respublika Krym, S Ukraine
85 *I18* **Sowa** *var.* Sua. Central, NE Botswana
85 *I18* **Sowa Pan** *salt lake* NE Botswana
176 *Ww9* **Sowek** Irian Jaya, E Indonesia
85 *J21* **Soweto** Gauteng, NE South Africa
Sōya-kaikyō *see* La Perouse Strait
172 *Pp1* **Sōya-misaki** *headland* Hokkaidō, NE Japan
129 *N7* **Soyana** ≈ NW Russian Federation
152 *A8* **Soye, Mys** *var.* Mys Suz. *headland* NW Turkmenistan
84 *A10* **Soyo** Zaire, NW Angola
82 *J10* **Soyra** ▲ C Eritrea
Sozaq *see* Suzak
121 *P16* **Sozh** ***Rus.*** Sozh. ≈ NE Europe
116 *N10* **Sozopol** ***prev.*** Sizebolu, ***anc.*** Apollonia. Burgaska Oblast, SE Bulgaria
180 *J15* **Sœurs, Les** *island group* Inner Islands, W Seychelles
101 *L20* **Spa** Liège, E Belgium
204 *I7* **Spaatz Island** *island* Antarctica
150 *M14* **Space Launching Centre** *space station* Kzyl-Orda, S Kazakhstan
107 *O7* **Spain** ***off.*** Kingdom of Spain, ***Sp.*** España; ***anc.*** Hispania, Iberia, ***Lat.*** Hispana. ◆ *monarchy* SW Europe
Spalato *see* Split
99 *O19* **Spalding** E England, UK
12 *D11* **Spanish** Ontario, S Canada
38 *L3* **Spanish Fork** Utah, W USA
66 *B12* **Spanish Point** *headland* C Bermuda
12 *E9* **Spanish River** ≈ Ontario, S Canada
46 *K13* **Spanish Town** ***hist.*** St.Iago de la Vega. C Jamaica
117 *H24* **Spánta, Ákra** *headland* Kríti, Greece, E Mediterranean Sea
37 *Q5* **Sparks** Nevada, W USA
Sparnacum *see* Épernay
97 *N16* **Sparreholm** Södermanland, C Sweden
25 *U4* **Sparta** Georgia, SE USA
32 *J7* **Sparta** Illinois, N USA
33 *P9* **Sparta** Michigan, N USA
23 *R8* **Sparta** North Carolina, SE USA
22 *L9* **Sparta** Tennessee, S USA
32 *K16* **Sparta** Wisconsin, N USA
Sparta *see* Spárti
23 *Q11* **Spartanburg** South Carolina, SE USA
122 *F10* **Spartel, Cap** *headland* N Morocco
117 *F21* **Spárti** ***Eng.*** Sparta. Pelopónnisos, S Greece
109 *B21* **Spartivento, Capo** *headland* Sardegna, Italy, C Mediterranean Sea
9 *P17* **Sparwood** British Columbia, SW Canada
130 *I4* **Spas-Demensk** Kaluzhskaya Oblast', W Russian Federation
130 *M4* **Spas-Klepiki** Ryazanskaya Oblast', W Russian Federation
127 *N17* **Spassk-Dal'niy** Primorskiy Kray, SE Russian Federation
130 *M5* **Spassk-Ryazanskiy** Ryazanskaya Oblast', W Russian Federation
117 *H19* **Spáta** Attikí, C Greece
124 *O12* **Spátha, Ákra** *headland* Kríti, Greece, E Mediterranean Sea
Špatrjan *see* Paternion
30 *I9* **Spearfish** South Dakota, N USA
27 *O1* **Spearman** Texas, SW USA
67 *C25* **Speedwell Island** *island* S Falkland Islands
67 *C25* **Speedwell Island Settlement** S Falkland Islands
67 *G25* **Speery Island** *island* S Saint Helena
47 *N14* **Speightstown** NW Barbados
108 *I13* **Spello** Umbria, C Italy
41 *R12* **Spenard** Alaska, USA
Spence Bay *see* Taloyoak
33 *O14* **Spencer** Indiana, N USA
31 *T12* **Spencer** Iowa, C USA
31 *P12* **Spencer** Nebraska, C USA
23 *S9* **Spencer** North Carolina, SE USA
22 *L9* **Spencer** Tennessee, S USA
23 *Q4* **Spencer** West Virginia, NE USA
32 *K6* **Spencer** Wisconsin, N USA
190 *G10* **Spencer, Cape** *headland* South Australia
41 *V13* **Spencer, Cape** *headland* Alaska, USA
190 *H9* **Spencer Gulf** *gulf* South Australia
20 *F9* **Spencerport** New York, NE USA
33 *Q12* **Spencerville** Ohio, N USA
117 *E17* **Spercheiáda** *var.* Sperhiada, Sperkhiás. Stereá Ellás, C Greece
117 *E17* **Spercheiós** ≈ C Greece
Sperhiada *see* Spercheiáda
97 *G14* **Sperillen** ◎ S Norway
Sperkhiás *see* Spercheiáda
103 *I18* **Spessart** *hill range* C Germany
Spétsai *see* Spétses
117 *G21* **Spétses** ***prev.*** Spétsai. Spétses, S Greece
117 *G21* **Spétses** *island* S Greece
98 *J8* **Spey** ≈ NE Scotland, UK
103 *G20* **Speyer** ***Eng.*** Spires; ***anc.*** Civitas Nemetum, Spira. Rheinland-Pfalz, SW Germany
103 *G20* **Speyerbach** ≈ W Germany
109 *N20* **Spezzano Albanese** Calabria, SW Italy
Spice Islands *see* Maluku
102 *F9* **Spiekeroog** *island* NW Germany
111 *W9* **Spielfeld** Steiermark, SE Austria
67 *N21* **Spiess Seamount** *undersea feature* S Atlantic Ocean
110 *E9* **Spiez** Bern, W Switzerland
100 *G13* **Spijkenisse** Zuid-Holland, SW Netherlands
41 *T6* **Spike Mountain** ▲ Alaska, USA
117 *I25* **Spíli** Kríti, Greece, E Mediterranean Sea
110 *D10* **Spillgerten** ▲ W Switzerland
120 *F9* **Spilva** ✕ (Rīga) Rīga, C Latvia
109 *N17* **Spinazzola** Puglia, SE Italy
155 *O9* **Spīn Būldak** Kandahār, S Afghanistan
Spira *see* Speyer
Spirdingsee *see* Śniardwy, Jezioro
Spires *see* Speyer
31 *T11* **Spirit Lake** Iowa, C USA
31 *T11* **Spirit Lake** ◎ Iowa, C USA
9 *N13* **Spirit River** Alberta, W Canada
9 *S14* **Spiritwood** Saskatchewan, S Canada
29 *R11* **Spiro** Oklahoma, C USA
113 *L19* **Spišská Nová Ves** ***Ger.*** Neudorf, Zipser Neudorf, ***Hung.*** Igló. Východné Slovensko, E Slovakia
143 *T11* **Spitak** NW Armenia
94 *O2* **Spitsbergen** *island* NW Svalbard
Spittal *see* Spittal an der Drau
111 *R9* **Spittal an der Drau** ***var.*** Spittal. Kärnten, S Austria
111 *V3* **Spitz** Niederösterreich, NE Austria
96 *D9* **Spjelkavik** Møre og Romsdal, S Norway
27 *W10* **Splendora** Texas, SW USA
115 *E14* **Split** ***It.*** Spalato. Split-Dalmacija, S Croatia
115 *E14* **Split** ✕ Split-Dalmacija, S Croatia
115 *E14* **Split-Dalmacija** ***off.*** Splitsko-Dalmatinska Županija. ◈ *province* S Croatia
9 *X12* **Split Lake** ◎ Manitoba, C Canada
Splitsko-Dalmatinska Županija *see* Split-Dalmacija
110 *H10* **Splügen** Graubünden, S Switzerland
Spodnji Dravograd *see* Dravograd
27 *P12* **Spofford** Texas, SW USA
120 *J11* **Špoģi** Daugvapils, SE Latvia
34 *L8* **Spokane** Washington, NW USA
34 *L8* **Spokane River** ≈ Washington, NW USA
108 *I13* **Spoleto** Umbria, C Italy
32 *I4* **Spooner** Wisconsin, N USA
32 *K12* **Spoon River** ≈ Illinois, N USA
23 *W5* **Spotsylvania** Virginia, NE USA
34 *L8* **Sprague** Washington, NW USA
178 *Ll16* **Spratly Island** *island* SW Spratly Islands
198 *Ff7* **Spratly Islands** ***Chin.*** Nansha Qundao. ◇ *disputed territory* SE Asia
34 *J12* **Spray** Oregon, NW USA
114 *I11* **Spreča** ≈ N Bosnia and Herzegovina
102 *P13* **Spree** ≈ E Germany
102 *P13* **Spreewald** *wetland* NE Germany
103 *P14* **Spremberg** Brandenburg, E Germany
27 *W11* **Spring** Texas, SW USA
33 *Q10* **Spring Arbor** Michigan, N USA
85 *E23* **Springbok** Northern Cape, W South Africa
20 *I15* **Spring City** Pennsylvania, NE USA
22 *L9* **Spring City** Tennessee, S USA
38 *L4* **Spring City** Utah, W USA
37 *W3* **Spring Creek** Nevada, W USA
29 *S9* **Springdale** Arkansas, C USA
33 *Q14* **Springdale** Ohio, N USA
102 *I13* **Springe** Niedersachsen, N Germany
39 *U9* **Springer** New Mexico, SW USA
39 *W7* **Springfield** Colorado, C USA
25 *W5* **Springfield** Georgia, SE USA
32 *K14* **Springfield** *state capital* Illinois, N USA
22 *L6* **Springfield** Kentucky, S USA
20 *M12* **Springfield** Massachusetts, NE USA
31 *T10* **Springfield** Minnesota, N USA
29 *T7* **Springfield** Missouri, C USA
33 *R13* **Springfield** Ohio, N USA
34 *G13* **Springfield** Oregon, NW USA
31 *Q12* **Springfield** South Dakota, N USA
22 *J8* **Springfield** Tennessee, S USA
20 *M9* **Springfield** Vermont, NE USA
32 *K14* **Springfield, Lake** ▣ Illinois, N USA
57 *T8* **Spring Garden** NE Guyana
32 *K8* **Spring Green** Wisconsin, N USA
31 *X11* **Spring Grove** Minnesota, N USA
11 *P15* **Springhill** Nova Scotia, SE Canada
25 *V12* **Spring Hill** Florida, SE USA
29 *R4* **Spring Hill** Kansas, C USA
24 *G4* **Springhill** Louisiana, S USA
22 *I9* **Spring Hill** Tennessee, S USA
23 *U10* **Spring Lake** North Carolina, SE USA
26 *M4* **Springlake** Texas, SW USA
37 *W11* **Spring Mountains** ⛰ Nevada, W USA
67 *B24* **Spring Point** West Falkland, Falkland Islands
29 *W9* **Spring River** ≈ Arkansas/Missouri, C USA
29 *S7* **Spring River** ≈ Missouri/Oklahoma, C USA
85 *J21* **Springs** Gauteng, NE South Africa
193 *H16* **Springs Junction** West Coast, South Island, NZ
189 *X8* **Springsure** Queensland, E Australia
31 *W11* **Spring Valley** Minnesota, N USA
20 *K13* **Spring Valley** New York, NE USA
31 *N12* **Springview** Nebraska, C USA
20 *D11* **Springville** New York, NE USA
38 *L3* **Springville** Utah, W USA
Sprottau *see* Szprotawa
13 *V4* **Sproule, Pointe** *headland* Québec, SE Canada
9 *Q14* **Spruce Grove** Alberta, SW Canada
23 *T4* **Spruce Knob** ▲ West Virginia, NE USA
37 *X3* **Spruce Mountain** ▲ Nevada, W USA
23 *P9* **Spruce Pine** North Carolina, SE USA
100 *G13* **Spui** ≈ SW Netherlands
109 *O19* **Spulico, Capo** *headland* S Italy
27 *O5* **Spur** Texas, SW USA
99 *O17* **Spurn Head** *headland* E England, UK
101 *H20* **Spy** Namur, S Belgium
97 *I15* **Spydeberg** Østfold, S Norway
193 *J17* **Spy Glass Point** *headland* South Island, NZ
8 *L17* **Squamish** British Columbia, SW Canada
21 *O8* **Squam Lake** ◎ New Hampshire, NE USA
21 *S2* **Squa Pan Mountain** ▲ Maine, NE USA
41 *N16* **Squaw Harbor** Unga Island, Alaska, USA
12 *E11* **Squaw Island** *island* Ontario, S Canada
109 *O22* **Squillace, Golfo di** *gulf* S Italy
109 *Q18* **Squinzano** Puglia, SE Italy
174 *L15* **Sragen** Jawa, C Indonesia
Sráid na Cathrach *see* Milltown Malbay
178 *Jj11* **Srâlau** Stœng Trêng, N Cambodia
Srath an Urláir *see* Stranorlar
114 *G10* **Srbac** N Bosnia and Herzegovina
Srbija *see* Serbia
114 *K9* **Srbobran** ***var.*** Bácsszenttamás, ***Hung.*** Szenttamás. Serbia, N Yugoslavia
178 *Ii14* **Srê Âmběl** Kaôh Kông, SW Cambodia
114 *K13* **Srebrenica** E Bosnia and Herzegovina
114 *I11* **Srebrenik** NE Bosnia and Herzegovina
116 *M10* **Sredets** ***prev.*** Grudovo. Burgaska Oblast, SE Bulgaria
116 *K10* **Sredets** ***prev.*** Syulemeshlii. Khaskovska Oblast, C Bulgaria
116 *M10* **Sredetska Reka** ≈ SE Bulgaria
127 *P9* **Sredinnyy Khrebet** ⛰ E Russian Federation
116 *N7* **Sredishte** ***Rom.*** Beibunar; ***prev.*** Knyazhevo. Varnenska Oblast, NE Bulgaria
116 *I10* **Sredna Gora** ⛰ C Bulgaria
127 *N7* **Srednekolymsk** Respublika Sakha (Yakutiya), NE Russian Federation
130 *K7* **Srednerusskaya Vozvyshennost'** ***Eng.*** Central Russian Upland. ⛰ W Russian Federation
126 *Ii9* **Srednesibirskoye Ploskogor'ye** ***var.*** Central Siberian Uplands, ***Eng.*** Central Siberian Plateau. ⛰ N Russian Federation
129 *V13* **Sredniy Ural** ⛰ NW Russian Federation
178 *Jj13* **Srê Khtŭm** Môndól Kiri, E Cambodia
113 *G17* **Śrem** Poznań, W Poland
114 *K10* **Sremska Mitrovica** ***prev.*** Mitrovica, ***Ger.*** Mitrowitz. Serbia, NW Yugoslavia
178 *Ii11* **Srêng, Stœng** ≈ NW Cambodia
178 *Ii11* **Srê Noy** Siĕmréab, NW Cambodia
Srepok, Sông *see* Srêpôk, Tônle
178 *K12* **Srêpôk, Tônle** ***var.*** Sông Srepok. ≈ Cambodia/Vietnam
126 *L15* **Sretensk** Chitinskaya Oblast', S Russian Federation
174 *Ll7* **Sri Aman** Sarawak, East Malaysia
119 *R4* **Sribne** Chernihivs'ka Oblast', N Ukraine
161 *I25* **Sri Jayawardanapura** ***var.*** Sri Jayawardenepura; ***prev.*** Kotte. Western Province, W Sri Lanka
161 *M14* **Srīkākulam** Andhra Pradesh, E India
161 *I25* **Sri Lanka** ***off.*** Democratic Socialist Republic of Sri Lanka; ***prev.*** Ceylon. ◆ *republic* S Asia
139 *Mm15* **Sri Lanka** *island* S Asia
159 *V14* **Srimangal** Chittagong, E Bangladesh
Sri Mohangorh *see* Shri Mohangarh
158 *H5* **Srīnagar** Jammu and Kashmir, N India
178 *H10* **Srinagarind Reservoir** ◎ W Thailand
161 *F19* **Sringeri** Karnātaka, W India
161 *K25* **Sri Pada** ***Eng.*** Adam's Peak. ▲ S Sri Lanka
Sri Saket *see* Si Sa Ket
113 *G14* **Sroda Śląska** ***Ger.*** Neumarkt. Wrocław, SW Poland
112 *H12* **Środa Wielkopolska** Poznań, W Poland
Ssu-ch'uan *see* Sichuan
Ssu-p'ing/Ssu-p'ing-chieh *see* Siping
Stablo *see* Stavelot
101 *G15* **Stabroek** Antwerpen, N Belgium
Stackeln *see* Strenči
98 *I5* **Stack Skerry** *island* N Scotland, UK
96 *C10* **Stad** *peninsula* S Norway
102 *I9* **Stade** Niedersachsen, NW Germany
111 *R5* **Stadl-Paura** Oberösterreich, NW Austria
121 *L20* **Stadolichy** ***Rus.*** Stodolichi. Homyel'skaya Voblasts', SE Belarus
100 *P7* **Stadskanaal** Groningen, NE Netherlands
103 *H16* **Stadtallendorf** Hessen, C Germany
103 *K23* **Stadtbergen** Bayern, S Germany
110 *G7* **Stäfa** Zürich, NE Switzerland
97 *K23* **Staffanstorp** Malmöhus, S Sweden
103 *K18* **Staffelstein** Bayern, C Germany
99 *L19* **Stafford** C England, UK
28 *L6* **Stafford** Kansas, C USA
23 *W4* **Stafford** Virginia, NE USA
99 *L19* **Staffordshire** *cultural region* C England, UK
21 *N12* **Stafford Springs** Connecticut, NE USA
117 *H14* **Stágira** Kentrikí Makedonía, N Greece
120 *G7* **Staicele** Limbaži, N Latvia
Ştaierdorf-Anina *see* Anina
111 *V8* **Stainz** Steiermark, SE Austria
Stájerlakanina *see* Anina
119 *Y7* **Stakhanov** Luhans'ka Oblast', E Ukraine
110 *E11* **Stalden** Valais, SW Switzerland
Stalin *see* Varna
Stalinabad *see* Dushanbe
Stalingrad *see* Volgograd
Staliniri *see* Ts'khinvali
Stalino *see* Donets'k
Stalinobod *see* Dushanbe
Stalinov Štít *see* Gerlachovský Štít
Stalinsk *see* Novokuznetsk
Stalinskaya Oblast' *see* Donets'ka Oblast'
Stalinski Zaliv *see* Varnenski Zaliv
Stalin, Yazovir *see* Iskŭr, Yazovir
113 *N15* **Stalowa Wola** Tarnobrzeg, SE Poland
116 *I11* **Stamboliyski** Plovdivska Oblast, C Bulgaria
116 *J8* **Stamboliyski, Yazovir** ▣ N Bulgaria
99 *N19* **Stamford** E England, UK
20 *L14* **Stamford** Connecticut, NE USA
27 *P6* **Stamford** Texas, SW USA
27 *Q6* **Stamford, Lake** ▣ Texas, SW USA
110 *I10* **Stampa** Graubünden, SE Switzerland
Stampalia *see* Astypálaia
29 *T14* **Stamps** Arkansas, C USA
94 *G11* **Stamsund** Nordland, C Norway
29 *R2* **Stanberry** Missouri, C USA
205 *O3* **Stancomb-Wills Glacier** *glacier* Antarctica
85 *K21* **Standerton** Mpumalanga, E South Africa
33 *R7* **Standish** Michigan, N USA
22 *M6* **Stanford** Kentucky, S USA
35 *S9* **Stanford** Montana, NW USA
97 *P19* **Stånga** Gotland, SE Sweden
96 *I13* **Stange** Hedmark, S Norway
85 *L23* **Stanger** KwaZulu/Natal, E South Africa
Stanimaka *see* Asenovgrad
Stanislau *see* Ivano-Frankivs'k
37 *P8* **Stanislaus River** ≈ California, W USA
Stanislav *see* Ivano-Frankivs'k
Stanislavskaya Oblast' *see* Ivano-Frankivs'ka Oblast'
Stanisławów *see* Ivano-Frankivs'k
Stanke Dimitrov *see* Dupnitsa
191 *O15* **Stanley** Tasmania, SE Australia
67 *E24* **Stanley** ***var.*** Port Stanley. ○ (Falkland Islands) East Falkland, Falkland Islands
35 *O13* **Stanley** Idaho, NW USA
30 *L3* **Stanley** North Dakota, N USA
23 *U4* **Stanley** Virginia, NE USA
32 *J6* **Stanley** Wisconsin, N USA
81 *G21* **Stanley Pool** ***var.*** Pool Malebo. ◎ Congo/Zaire
161 *H20* **Stanley Reservoir** ▣ S India
Stanleyville *see* Kisangani
44 *G3* **Stann Creek** ◈ *district* SE Belize
Stann Creek *see* Dangriga
127 *N17* **Stanovoy Khrebet** ⛰ SE Russian Federation
110 *F8* **Stans** Unterwalden, C Switzerland
99 *O21* **Stansted** ✕ (London) Essex, E England, UK
191 *U4* **Stanthorpe** Queensland, E Australia
23 *N6* **Stanton** Kentucky, S USA
33 *Q8* **Stanton** Michigan, N USA
31 *Q14* **Stanton** Nebraska, C USA
30 *L5* **Stanton** North Dakota, N USA
27 *N7* **Stanton** Texas, SW USA
34 *H7* **Stanwood** Washington, NW USA
119 *Y7* **Stanychno-Luhans'ke** Luhans'ka Oblast', E Ukraine
110 *K7* **Stanzach** Tirol, W Austria
100 *M9* **Staphorst** Overijssel, E Netherlands
12 *D18* **Staples** Ontario, S Canada
31 *T6* **Staples** Minnesota, N USA
30 *M14* **Stapleton** Nebraska, C USA
27 *S8* **Star** Texas, SW USA
113 *M14* **Starachowice** Kielce, SE Poland
Stara Kanjiža *see* Kanjiža
113 *M18* **Stará L'ubovňa** ***Ger.*** Altlublau, ***Hung.*** Ólubló. Východné Slovensko, E Slovakia
114 *L10* **Stara Pazova** ***Ger.*** Altpasua, ***Hung.*** Ópazova. Serbia, N Yugoslavia
Stara Planina *see* Balkan Mountains
116 *L9* **Stara Reka** ≈ C Bulgaria
118 *M5* **Stara Synyava** Khmel'nyts'ka Oblast', W Ukraine
118 *I2* **Stara Vyzhivka** Volyns'ka Oblast', NW Ukraine
Staraya Belitsa *see* Staraya Byelitsa
121 *M14* **Staraya Byelitsa** ***Rus.*** Staraya Belitsa. Vitsyebskaya Voblasts', NE Belarus
131 *R5* **Staraya Mayna** Ul'yanovskaya Oblast', W Russian Federation
121 *O18* **Staraya Rudnya** ***Rus.*** Staraya Rudnya. Homyel'skaya Voblasts', SE Belarus
128 *H14* **Staraya Russa** Novgorodskaya Oblast', W Russian Federation
116 *K10* **Stara Zagora** ***Lat.*** Augusta Trajana. Khaskovska Oblast, C Bulgaria
31 *S8* **Starbuck** Minnesota, N USA
203 *W4* **Starbuck Island** ***prev.*** Volunteer Island. *island* E Kiribati
29 *V13* **Star City** Arkansas, C USA
114 *F13* **Staretina** ⛰ W Bosnia and Herzegovina
Stargard in Pommern *see* Stargard Szczeciński
112 *E9* **Stargard Szczeciński** ***Ger.*** Stargard in Pommern. Szczecin, NW Poland
195 *Z17* **Star Harbour** *harbor* San Cristobal, SE Solomon Islands
Stari Bečej *see* Bečej
115 *F15* **Starigrad** ***It.*** Cittavecchia. Split-Dalmacija, S Croatia
175 *Qq12* **Staring, Teluk** ***var.*** Teluk Wawosungu. *bay* Sulawesi, C Indonesia
128 *J16* **Staritsa** Tverskaya Oblast', W Russian Federation
25 *V9* **Starke** Florida, SE USA
24 *M4* **Starkville** Mississippi, S USA
194 *E11* **Star Mountains** ***Ind.*** Pegunungan Sterren. ⛰ Indonesia/PNG
103 *L23* **Starnberg** Bayern, SE Germany
103 *L24* **Starnberger See** ◎ SE Germany
Starobel'sk *see* Starobil's'k
119 *X8* **Starobesheve** Donets'ka Oblast', E Ukraine
119 *Y6* **Starobil's'k** ***Rus.*** Starobel'sk. Luhans'ka Oblast', E Ukraine
Starobin *see* Starobyn
121 *K18* **Starobyn** ***Rus.*** Starobin. Minskaya Voblasts', S Belarus
130 *H6* **Starodub** Bryanskaya Oblast', W Russian Federation
112 *I8* **Starogard Gdański** ***Ger.*** Preussisch-Stargard. Gdańsk, N Poland
151 *P16* **Staroikan** Yuzhnyy Kazakhstan, S Kazakhstan
Starokonstantinov *see* Starokostyantyniv
118 *L5* **Starokostyantyniv** ***Rus.*** Starokonstantinov. Khmel'nyts'ka Oblast', NW Ukraine
130 *K12* **Starominskaya** Krasnodarskiy Kray, SW Russian Federation
116 *L7* **Staro Selo** ***Rom.*** Satul-Vechi; ***prev.*** Star-Smil. Razgradska Oblast, NE Bulgaria
130 *K12* **Staroshcherbinovskaya** Krasnodarskiy Kray, SW Russian Federation
131 *V6* **Starosubkhangulovo** Respublika Bashkortostan, W Russian Federation
37 *S4* **Star Peak** ▲ Nevada, W USA
Star-Smil *see* Staro Selo
99 *J25* **Start Point** *headland* SW England, UK
Startsy *see* Kirawsk
Starum *see* Stavoren
121 *L18* **Staryya Darohi** ***Rus.*** Staryye Dorogi. Minskaya Voblasts', S Belarus
Staryye Dorogi *see* Staryya Darohi
131 *T2* **Staryye Zyatsy** Udmurtskaya Respublika, NW Russian Federation
119 *U13* **Staryy Krym** Respublika Krym, S Ukraine
130 *K8* **Staryy Oskol** Belgorodskaya Oblast', W Russian Federation
118 *H6* **Staryy Sambir** L'vivs'ka Oblast', W Ukraine
103 *L14* **Stassfurt** ***var.*** Staßfurt. Sachsen-Anhalt, C Germany
113 *M15* **Staszów** Tarnobrzeg, SE Poland
31 *W13* **State Center** Iowa, C USA
20 *E14* **State College** Pennsylvania, NE USA
20 *K15* **Staten Island** *island* New York, NE USA
Staten Island *see* Estados, Isla de los
25 *U8* **Statenville** Georgia, SE USA
25 *W5* **Statesboro** Georgia, SE USA
States, The *see* United States of America
23 *R9* **Statesville** North Carolina, SE USA
97 *G16* **Stathelle** Telemark, S Norway
32 *K15* **Staunton** Illinois, N USA
23 *T5* **Staunton** Virginia, NE USA
97 *C16* **Stavanger** Rogaland, S Norway
101 *L21* **Stavelot** ***Dut.*** Stablo. Liège, E Belgium
97 *G16* **Stavern** Vestfold, S Norway
Stavers Island *see* Vostok Island
100 *J7* **Stavoren** ***Fris.*** Starum. Friesland, N Netherlands
130 *M14* **Stavropol'** ***prev.*** Voroshilovsk. Stavropol'skiy Kray, SW Russian Federation
Stavropol' *see* Tol'yatti
130 *M14* **Stavropol'skaya Vozvyshennost'** ⛰ SW Russian Federation
130 *M14* **Stavropol'skiy Kray** ◈ *territory* SW Russian Federation
117 *H14* **Stavrós** Kentrikí Makedonía, N Greece
117 *J24* **Stavrós, Ákra** *headland* Kríti, Greece, E Mediterranean Sea
117 *K21* **Stavrós, Ákra** *headland* Náxos, Kykládes, Greece, Aegean Sea
116 *I12* **Stavroúpoli** ***prev.*** Stavroúpolis. Anatolikí Makedonía kai Thráki, NE Greece
Stavroúpolis *see* Stavroúpoli
119 *O6* **Stavyshche** Kyyivs'ka Oblast', N Ukraine
190 *M11* **Stawell** Victoria, SE Australia
112 *N9* **Stawiski** Łomża, NE Poland
12 *G14* **Stayner** Ontario, S Canada
39 *R3* **Steamboat Springs** Colorado, C USA
22 *M8* **Stearns** Kentucky, S USA
41 *N10* **Stebbins** Alaska, USA
110 *K7* **Steeg** Tirol, W Austria
29 *Y9* **Steele** Missouri, C USA
31 *N5* **Steele** North Dakota, N USA
204 *J5* **Steele Island** *island* Antarctica
32 *K16* **Steeleville** Illinois, N USA
29 *W6* **Steelville** Missouri, C USA
101 *G14* **Steenbergen** Noord-Brabant, S Netherlands
Steenkool *see* Bintuni
9 *O10* **Steen River** Alberta, W Canada
100 *M8* **Steenwijk** Overijssel, N Netherlands
67 *A23* **Steeple Jason** *island* Jason Islands, NW Falkland Islands
182 *J8* **Steep Point** *headland* Western Australia
118 *L9* **Ştefăneşti** Botoşani, NE Romania
Stefanie, Lake *see* Ch'ew Bahir
15 *J1* **Stefansson Island** *island* Northwest Territories, N Canada
119 *O10* **Ştefan Vodă** ***Rus.*** Suvorovo. SE Moldova
65 *H18* **Steffen, Cerro** ▲ S Chile
110 *D9* **Steffisburg** Bern, C Switzerland
97 *J24* **Stege** Storstrøm, SE Denmark
118 *G10* **Ştei** ***Hung.*** Vaskohsziklás. Bihor, W Romania
Steier *see* Steyr
Steierdorf/Steierdorf-Anina *see* Anina
111 *T7* **Steiermark** ***off.*** Land Steiermark, ***Eng.*** Styria. ◈ *state* C Austria
103 *J19* **Steigerwald** *hill range* C Germany
101 *L17* **Stein** Limburg, SE Netherlands
Stein *see* Stein an der Donau, Austria
Stein *see* Kamnik, Slovenia
110 *M8* **Steinach** Tirol, W Austria
Steinamanger *see* Szombathely
111 *W3* **Stein an der Donau** ***var.*** Stein. Niederösterreich, NE Austria
Steinau an der Elbe *see* Ścinawa
9 *Y16* **Steinbach** Manitoba, S Canada
Steiner Alpen *see* Savinjske Alpe
101 *L24* **Steinfort** Luxembourg, W Luxembourg
102 *H12* **Steinhuder Meer** ◎ NW Germany
95 *E15* **Steinkjer** Nord-Trøndelag, C Norway
Stejarul *see* Karapelit
101 *F16* **Stekene** Oost-Vlaanderen, NW Belgium
85 *E26* **Stellenbosch** Western Cape, SW South Africa
100 *F13* **Stellendam** Zuid-Holland, SW Netherlands
41 *T12* **Steller, Mount** ▲ Alaska, USA
104 *F1* **Stello, Monte** ▲ Corse, France, C Mediterranean Sea
108 *F5* **Stelvio, Passo dello** *pass* Italy/Switzerland
105 *R3* **Stenay** Meuse, NE France
102 *L12* **Stendal** Sachsen-Anhalt, C Germany
120 *E8* **Stende** Talsi, NW Latvia
190 *H10* **Stenhouse Bay** South Australia
97 *J23* **Stenløse** Frederiksborg, E Denmark
97 *L19* **Stensjön** Jönköping, S Sweden
97 *K18* **Stenstorp** Skaraborg, S Sweden
97 *I18* **Stenungsund** Göteborg och Bohus, S Sweden
Stepanakert *see* Xankändi
143 *T11* **Step'anavan** N Armenia
102 *K9* **Stepenitz** ≈ N Germany
31 *O10* **Stephan** South Dakota, N USA
31 *R3* **Stephen** Minnesota, N USA
29 *T14* **Stephens** Arkansas, C USA
192 *J13* **Stephens, Cape** *headland* D'Urville Island, Marlborough, SW NZ
23 *V3* **Stephens City** Virginia, NE USA
190 *L6* **Stephens Creek** New South Wales, SE Australia
192 *K13* **Stephens Island** *island* C NZ
33 *N5* **Stephenson** Michigan, N USA
11 *S12* **Stephenville** Newfoundland, Newfoundland and Labrador, SE Canada
27 *S7* **Stephenville** Texas, SW USA
151 *P17* **Step' Nardara** ***Kaz.*** Shardara Dalasy; ***prev.*** Shaidara. *grassland* S Kazakhstan
131 *O15* **Stepnoye** Stavropol'skiy Kray, SW Russian Federation
151 *Q8* **Stepnyak** Kokshetau, N Kazakhstan
198 *C9* **Steps Point** *headland* Tutuila, W American Samoa
117 *F17* **Stereá Ellás** ***Eng.*** Greece Central. ◈ *region* C Greece
85 *J24* **Sterkspruit** Eastern Cape, SE South Africa
131 *U6* **Sterlibashevo** Respublika Bashkortostan, W Russian Federation
41 *R12* **Sterling** Alaska, USA
39 *V3* **Sterling** Colorado, C USA
32 *K11* **Sterling** Illinois, N USA
28 *M5* **Sterling** Kansas, C USA
27 *O8* **Sterling City** Texas, SW USA
33 *S9* **Sterling Heights** Michigan, N USA
23 *W3* **Sterling Park** Virginia, NE USA
39 *V2* **Sterling Reservoir** ▣ Colorado, C USA
24 *I5* **Sterlington** Louisiana, S USA
131 *U6* **Sterlitamak** Respublika Bashkortostan, W Russian Federation
Sternberg *see* Šternberk
113 *H17* **Šternberk** ***Ger.*** Sternberg. Severní Morava, E Czech Republic
147 *V17* **Stēroh** Suquṭrā, S Yemen
112 *G11* **Stęszew** Poznań, W Poland
Stettin *see* Szczecin
Stettiner Haff *see* Szczeciński, Zalew
9 *Q15* **Stettler** Alberta, SW Canada
33 *V13* **Steubenville** Ohio, N USA
99 *O21* **Stevenage** E England, UK
25 *Q1* **Stevenson** Alabama, S USA
34 *H11* **Stevenson** Washington, NW USA
190 *E1* **Stevenson Creek** *seasonal river* South Australia
41 *Q13* **Stevenson Entrance** *strait* Alaska, USA
32 *L6* **Stevens Point** Wisconsin, N USA
41 *R8* **Stevens Village** Alaska, USA
35 *P10* **Stevensville** Montana, NW USA
95 *E25* **Stevns Klint** *headland* E Denmark
8 *J12* **Stewart** British Columbia, W Canada
8 *J6* **Stewart** ≈ Yukon Territory, NW Canada
8 *I6* **Stewart Crossing** Yukon Territory, NW Canada
65 *H25* **Stewart, Isla** *island* S Chile
193 *B25* **Stewart Island** *island* S NZ
189 *W6* **Stewart, Mount** ▲ Queensland, E Australia
8 *H6* **Stewart River** Yukon Territory, NW Canada
29 *R3* **Stewartsville** Missouri, C USA
9 *S16* **Stewart Valley** Saskatchewan, S Canada
31 *W10* **Stewartville** Minnesota, N USA
Steyerlak-Anina *see* Anina
111 *T5* **Steyr** ***var.*** Steier. Oberösterreich, N Austria
111 *T5* **Steyr** ≈ NW Austria
31 *P11* **Stickney** South Dakota, N USA
100 *L5* **Stiens** Friesland, N Netherlands
Stif *see* Sétif
29 *Q11* **Stigler** Oklahoma, C USA
109 *N18* **Stigliano** Basilicata, S Italy
97 *N17* **Stigtomta** Södermanland, C Sweden
8 *I11* **Stikine** ≈ British Columbia, W Canada
Stilida/Stilís *see* Stylída
97 *G22* **Stilling** Århus, C Denmark
31 *W8* **Stillwater** Minnesota, N USA
29 *O9* **Stillwater** Oklahoma, C USA
37 *S5* **Stillwater Range** ⛰ Nevada, W USA
20 *I8* **Stillwater Reservoir** ▣ New York, NE USA
109 *O22* **Stilo, Punta** *headland* S Italy
29 *R10* **Stilwell** Oklahoma, C USA
115 *N17* **Štimlje** Serbia, S Yugoslavia
27 *N1* **Stinnett** Texas, SW USA
115 *P18* **Štip** E FYR Macedonia
Stira *see* Stýra
98 *J12* **Stirling** C Scotland, UK
98 *I12* **Stirling** *cultural region* C Scotland, UK
188 *J14* **Stirling Range** ⛰ Western Australia
95 *E16* **Stjørdal** Nord-Trøndelag, C Norway
Stochód *see* Stokhid
103 *H24* **Stockach** Baden-Württemberg, S Germany
27 *S12* **Stockdale** Texas, SW USA
111 *X3* **Stockerau** Niederösterreich, NE Austria
95 *H20* **Stockholm** ● (Sweden) Stockholm, C Sweden
97 *O15* **Stockholm** ◈ *county* C Sweden
Stockmannshof *see* Pļaviņas
99 *L18* **Stockport** NW England, UK
67 *K15* **Stocks Seamount** *undersea feature* C Atlantic Ocean
37 *O8* **Stockton** California, W USA
28 *L3* **Stockton** Kansas, C USA
29 *S6* **Stockton** Missouri, C USA
32 *K3* **Stockton Island** *island* Apostle Islands, Wisconsin, N USA
29 *S7* **Stockton Lake** ▣ Missouri, C USA
99 *M15* **Stockton-on-Tees** ***var.*** Stockton on Tees. N England, UK
26 *M10* **Stockton Plateau** *plain* Texas, SW USA
30 *M16* **Stockville** Nebraska, C USA
95 *H17* **Stöde** Västernorrland, C Sweden
Stodolichi *see* Stadolichy
178 *Jj12* **Stœng Trêng** ***prev.*** Stung Treng. Stœng Trêng, NE Cambodia
115 *M19* **Stogovo Karaorman** ⛰ W FYR Macedonia
Stoke *see* Stoke-on-Trent
99 *L19* **Stoke-on-Trent** ***var.*** Stoke. C England, UK
190 *M15* **Stokes Point** *headland* Tasmania, SE Australia
118 *J2* **Stokhid** ***Pol.*** Stochód, ***Rus.*** Stokhod. ≈ NW Ukraine
Stokhod *see* Stokhid
94 *I4* **Stokkseyri** Sudhurland, SW Iceland
94 *G10* **Stokmarknes** Nordland, C Norway
Stol *see* Veliki Krš
115 *H15* **Stolac** S Bosnia and Herzegovina
Stolbce *see* Stowbtsy
103 *D16* **Stolberg** ***var.*** Stolberg im Rheinland. Nordrhein-Westfalen, W Germany
Stolberg im Rheinland *see* Stolberg
126 *L5* **Stolbovoy, Ostrov** *island* NE Russian Federation
Stolbtsy *see* Stowbtsy
Stołeczne Warszawskie, Województwo *see* Warszawa

◆ Country
● Country Capital
◇ Dependent Territory
○ Dependent Territory Capital
◈ Administrative Region
✕ International Airport
▲ Mountain
⛰ Mountain Range
Volcano
≈ River
◎ Lake
▣ Reservoir

121 *J20* **Stolin** *Rus.* Stolin. Brestskaya Voblasts', SW Belarus
97 *K14* **Stöllet** ***var.*** Norra Ny. Värmland, C Sweden
Stolp *see* Słupsk
Stolpe *see* Słupia
Stolpmünde *see* Ustka
117 *F15* **Stómio** Thessalía, C Greece
12 *J11* **Stonecliffe** Ontario, SE Canada
98 *L10* **Stonehaven** NE Scotland, UK
99 *M23* **Stonehenge** *ancient monument* Wiltshire, S England, UK
25 *T3* **Stone Mountain** ▲ Georgia, SE USA
9 *X16* **Stonewall** Manitoba, S Canada
23 *S3* **Stonewood** West Virginia, NE USA
12 *D17* **Stoney Point** Ontario, S Canada
94 *H10* **Stonglandseidet** Troms, N Norway
67 *N25* **Stonybeach Bay** *bay* Tristan da Cunha, SE Atlantic Ocean
37 *N5* **Stony Creek** ≈ California, W USA
67 *N25* **Stonyhill Point** *headland* S Tristan da Cunha
12 *I14* **Stony Lake** ◎ Ontario, SE Canada
9 *Q14* **Stony Plain** Alberta, SW Canada
23 *R9* **Stony Point** North Carolina, SE USA
20 *G8* **Stony Point** *headland* New York, NE USA
9 *T10* **Stony Rapids** Saskatchewan, C Canada
41 *P11* **Stony River** Alaska, USA
Stony Tunguska *see* Podkamennaya Tunguska
10 *G10* **Stooping** ≈ Ontario, C Canada
102 *I9* **Stör** ≈ N Germany
97 *M15* **Storå** Örebro, S Sweden
97 *J16* **Stora Gla** ◎ C Sweden
97 *I16* **Stora Le** *Nor.* Store Le. ◎ Norway/Sweden
94 *I12* **Stora Lulevatten** ◎ N Sweden
94 *H13* **Storavan** ◎ N Sweden
95 *I20* **Storby** Åland, SW Finland
96 *E10* **Stordalen** Møre og Romsdal, S Norway
Storebelt *see* Storebælt
97 *H23* **Storebælt** ***var.*** Store Bælt, ***Eng.*** Great Belt, Storebelt. *channel* Baltic Sea/Kattegat
97 *M19* **Storebro** Kalmar, S Sweden
97 *J24* **Store Heddinge** Storstrøm, SE Denmark
Store Le *see* Stora Le
95 *E16* **Støren** Sør-Trøndelag, S Norway
97 *B14* **Store Sotra** *island* S Norway
94 *O4* **Storfjorden** *fjord* S Norway
97 *L15* **Storfors** Värmland, C Sweden
94 *G13* **Storforshei** Nordland, C Norway
Storhammer *see* Hamar
102 *L10* **Störkanal** *canal* N Germany
95 *F16* **Storlien** Jämtland, C Sweden
191 *P17* **Storm Bay** *inlet* Tasmania, SE Australia
31 *T12* **Storm Lake** Iowa, C USA
31 *S13* **Storm Lake** ◎ Iowa, C USA
98 *G7* **Stornoway** NW Scotland, UK
Storojineț *see* Storozhynets'
94 *P1* **Storøya** *island* NE Svalbard
129 *S10* **Storozhevsk** Respublika Komi, NW Russian Federation
Storozhinets *see* Storozhynets'
118 *K8* **Storozhynets'** ***Ger.*** Storozynetz, ***Rom.*** Storojineț, ***Rus.*** Storozhinets. Chernivets'ka Oblast', W Ukraine
Storozynetz *see* Storozhynets'
94 *H11* **Storriten** ▲ C Norway
21 *N12* **Storrs** Connecticut, NE USA
96 *I11* **Storsjøen** ◎ S Norway
96 *N13* **Storsjön** ◎ C Sweden
95 *F16* **Storsjön** ◎ C Sweden
94 *I9* **Storsteinnes** Troms, N Norway
97 *I24* **Storstrøm** ***off.*** Storstrøms Amt. ◈ *county* SE Denmark
95 *J14* **Storsund** Norrbotten, N Sweden
95 *F16* **Storsylen** ▲ S Norway
94 *H11* **Stortoppen** ▲ N Sweden
95 *H14* **Storuman** Västerbotten, N Sweden
95 *H14* **Storuman** ◎ N Sweden
96 *N13* **Storvik** Gävleborg, C Sweden
97 *O14* **Storvreta** Uppsala, C Sweden
31 *V13* **Story City** Iowa, C USA
9 *V17* **Stoughton** Saskatchewan, S Canada
21 *O11* **Stoughton** Massachusetts, NE USA
32 *L9* **Stoughton** Wisconsin, N USA
99 *L23* **Stour** ≈ E England, UK
99 *P21* **Stour** ≈ S England, UK
29 *T5* **Stover** Missouri, C USA
97 *G21* **Støvring** Nordjylland, N Denmark
121 *J17* **Stowbtsy** ***Pol.*** Stolbce, ***Rus.*** Stolbtsy. Minskaya Voblasts', C Belarus
27 *X11* **Stowell** Texas, SW USA
99 *P20* **Stowmarket** E England, UK
116 *N8* **Stozher** Varnenska Oblast, NE Bulgaria
99 *E14* **Strabane** ***Ir.*** An Srath Bán. W Northern Ireland, UK
123 *Gg10* **Strabo Trench** *undersea feature* C Mediterranean Sea
29 *T7* **Strafford** Missouri, C USA
191 *N17* **Strahan** Tasmania, SE Australia
113 *C18* **Strakonice** ***Ger.*** Strakonitz. Jižní Čechy, SW Czech Republic
Strakonitz *see* Strakonice
102 *N8* **Stralsund** Mecklenburg-Vorpommern, NE Germany
101 *L16* **Stramproy** Limburg, SE Netherlands
85 *E26* **Strand** Western Cape, SW South Africa
96 *E10* **Stranda** Møre og Romsdal, S Norway
99 *G15* **Strangford Lough** ***Ir.*** Loch Cuan. *inlet* E Northern Ireland, UK
97 *N16* **Strängnäs** Södermanland, C Sweden
99 *E14* **Stranorlar** ***Ir.*** Srath an Urláir. NW Ireland
99 *H14* **Stranraer** S Scotland, UK
9 *U16* **Strasbourg** Saskatchewan, S Canada
105 *V5* **Strasbourg** ***Ger.*** Strassburg; ***anc.*** Argentoratum. Bas-Rhin, NE France
39 *U4* **Strasburg** Colorado, C USA
31 *N7* **Strasburg** North Dakota, N USA
33 *U12* **Strasburg** Ohio, N USA
23 *U3* **Strasburg** Virginia, NE USA
119 *N10* **Strășeni** ***var.*** Strasheny. C Moldova
Strasheny *see* Strășeni
111 *T8* **Strassburg** Kärnten, S Austria
Strassburg *see* Strasbourg, France
Strassburg *see* Aiud, Romania
101 *M25* **Strassen** Luxembourg, S Luxembourg
111 *R5* **Strasswalchen** Salzburg, C Austria
12 *F16* **Stratford** Ontario, S Canada
192 *K10* **Stratford** Taranaki, North Island, NZ
37 *Q11* **Stratford** California, W USA
31 *V13* **Stratford** Iowa, C USA
29 *O12* **Stratford** Oklahoma, C USA
27 *N1* **Stratford** Texas, SW USA
32 *K6* **Stratford** Wisconsin, N USA
Stratford *see* Stratford-upon-Avon
99 *M20* **Stratford-upon-Avon** ***var.*** Stratford. C England, UK
191 *O17* **Strathgordon** Tasmania, SE Australia
9 *Q16* **Strathmore** Alberta, SW Canada
37 *R11* **Strathmore** California, W USA
12 *E16* **Strathroy** Ontario, S Canada
98 *I6* **Strathy Point** *headland* N Scotland, UK
39 *W4* **Stratton** Colorado, C USA
21 *P6* **Stratton** Maine, NE USA
20 *M10* **Stratton Mountain** ▲ Vermont, NE USA
103 *N21* **Straubing** Bayern, SE Germany
94 *G12* **Straumen** Nordland, C Norway
102 *O12* **Strausberg** Brandenburg, E Germany
34 *K13* **Strawberry Mountain** ▲ Oregon, NW USA
31 *X12* **Strawberry Point** Iowa, C USA
38 *M3* **Strawberry Reservoir** ▣ Utah, W USA
38 *M4* **Strawberry River** ≈ Utah, W USA
27 *R7* **Strawn** Texas, SW USA
115 *P17* **Straža** ▲ Bulgaria/ FYR Macedonia
113 *I19* **Strážov** ***Hung.*** Sztrazsó. ▲ NW Slovakia
190 *F7* **Streaky Bay** South Australia
190 *E7* **Streaky Bay** *bay* South Australia
32 *L12* **Streator** Illinois, N USA
Streckenbach *see* Świdnik
113 *J19* **Stredné Slovensko** ◈ *region* C Slovakia
113 *C17* **Střední Čechy** ***off.*** Středočeský Kraj. ◈ *region* W Czech Republic
Strednogorie *see* Pirdop
31 *O6* **Streeter** North Dakota, N USA
27 *U8* **Streetman** Texas, SW USA
118 *G13* **Strehaia** Mehedinți, SW Romania
Strehlen *see* Strzelin
116 *I10* **Strelcha** Plovdivska Oblast, C Bulgaria
126 *I13* **Strelka** Krasnoyarskiy Kray, C Russian Federation
128 *L6* **Strel'na** ≈ NW Russian Federation
120 *H7* **Strenči** ***Ger.*** Stackeln. Valka, N Latvia
110 *K8* **Strengen** Tirol, W Austria
108 *C6* **Stresa** Piemonte, NE Italy
Streshin *see* Streshyn
121 *N18* **Streshyn** ***Rus.*** Streshin. Homyel'skaya Voblasts', SE Belarus
126 *Gg11* **Strezhevoy** Tomskaya Oblast', C Russian Federation
97 *G23* **Strib** Fyn, C Denmark
113 *A17* **Stříbro** ***Ger.*** Mies. Západní Čechy, W Czech Republic
194 *E13* **Strickland** ≈ SW PNG
Striegau *see* Strzegom
Strigonium *see* Esztergom
100 *H13* **Strijen** Zuid-Holland, SW Netherlands
65 *H21* **Strobel, Lago** ◎ S Argentina
63 *B25* **Stroeder** Buenos Aires, E Argentina
117 *C20* **Strofádes** *island* Iónioi Nísoi, Greece, C Mediterranean Sea
Strofilia *see* Strofyliá
117 *G17* **Strofyliá** ***var.*** Strofilia. Évvoia, C Greece
102 *O10* **Strom** ≈ NE Germany
109 *L22* **Stromboli** ⋀ Isola Stromboli, SW Italy
109 *L22* **Stromboli, Isola** *island* Isole Eolie, S Italy
98 *H9* **Stromeferry** N Scotland, UK
98 *J5* **Stromness** N Scotland, UK
96 *N11* **Strömsbruk** Gävleborg, C Sweden
31 *Q15* **Stromsburg** Nebraska, C USA
97 *K21* **Strömsnäsbruk** Kronoberg, S Sweden
97 *I17* **Strömstad** Göteborg och Bohus, S Sweden
95 *G16* **Strömsund** Jämtland, C Sweden
95 *G15* **Ströms Vattudal** *valley* N Sweden
29 *V14* **Strong** Arkansas, C USA
Strongilí *see* Strongylí
109 *O21* **Strongoli** Calabria, SW Italy
33 *T11* **Strongsville** Ohio, N USA
117 *Q23* **Strongylí** ***var.*** Strongilí. *island* SE Greece
98 *K5* **Stronsay** *island* NE Scotland, UK
99 *L21* **Stroud** C England, UK
29 *O10* **Stroud** Oklahoma, C USA
20 *I14* **Stroudsburg** Pennsylvania, NE USA
97 *F21* **Struer** Ringkøbing, W Denmark
115 *M20* **Struga** SW FYR Macedonia
Strugi-Kranyse *see* Strugi-Krasnyye
128 *G14* **Strugi-Krasnyye** ***var.*** Strugi-Kranyse. Pskovskaya Oblast', W Russian Federation
116 *G11* **Struma** ***Gk.*** Strymónas. ≈ Bulgaria/ Greece *see also* Strymónas
99 *G21* **Strumble Head** *headland* SW Wales, UK
115 *Q19* **Strumeshnitsa** ***Mac.*** Strumica. ≈ Bulgaria/FYR Macedonia
115 *Q19* **Strumica** E FYR Macedonia
Strumica *see* Strumeshnitsa
116 *G11* **Strumyani** Sofiyska Oblast, SW Bulgaria
33 *V12* **Struthers** Ohio, N USA
116 *I10* **Stryama** ≈ C Bulgaria
116 *G13* **Strymónas** ***Bul.*** Struma. ≈ Bulgaria/Greece *see also* Struma
117 *H14* **Strymonikós Kólpos** *gulf* N Greece
118 *I6* **Stryy** L'vivs'ka Oblast', NW Ukraine
118 *H6* **Stryy** ≈ W Ukraine
113 *F14* **Strzegom** ***Ger.*** Striegau. Wałbrzych, SW Poland
112 *E10* **Strzelce Krajeńskie** ***Ger.*** Friedeberg Neumark. Gorzów, W Poland
113 *I15* **Strzelce Opolskie** ***Ger.*** Gross Strehlitz. Opole, SW Poland
190 *K3* **Strzelecki Creek** *seasonal river* South Australia
190 *J3* **Strzelecki Desert** *desert* South Australia
113 *G15* **Strzelin** ***Ger.*** Strehlen. Wrocław, SW Poland
112 *I11* **Strzelno** Bydgoszcz, C Poland
113 *N17* **Strzyżów** Rzeszów, SE Poland
Stua Laighean *see* Leinster, Mount
25 *Y13* **Stuart** Florida, SE USA
31 *U14* **Stuart** Iowa, C USA
31 *O13* **Stuart** Nebraska, C USA
23 *S8* **Stuart** Virginia, NE USA
8 *L13* **Stuart** ≈ British Columbia, SW Canada
41 *N10* **Stuart Island** *island* Alaska, USA
8 *L13* **Stuart Lake** ◎ British Columbia, SW Canada
193 *B22* **Stuart Mountains** ▲▲ South Island, NZ
190 *F3* **Stuart Range** *hill range* South Australia
Stubaital *see* Neustift im Stubaital
97 *I24* **Stubbekøbing** Storstrøm, SE Denmark
47 *P14* **Stubbs** Saint Vincent, Saint Vincent and the Grenadines
111 *V6* **Stübming** ≈ E Austria
116 *J11* **Studen Kladenets, Yazovir** ▣ S Bulgaria
193 *G21* **Studholme** Canterbury, South Island, NZ
Stuhlweissenberg *see* Székesfehérvár
Stuhm *see* Sztum
10 *C7* **Stull Lake** ◎ Ontario, C Canada
Stung Treng *see* Stœng Trêng
130 *L4* **Stupino** Moskovskaya Oblast', W Russian Federation
29 *U4* **Sturgeon** Missouri, C USA
12 *G10* **Sturgeon** ≈ Ontario, S Canada
33 *N6* **Sturgeon Bay** Wisconsin, N USA
12 *G11* **Sturgeon Falls** Ontario, S Canada
10 *C11* **Sturgeon Lake** ◎ Ontario, S Canada
32 *M3* **Sturgeon River** ≈ Michigan, N USA
22 *H6* **Sturgis** Kentucky, S USA
33 *P11* **Sturgis** Michigan, N USA
30 *J9* **Sturgis** South Dakota, N USA
114 *D10* **Šturlić** NW Bosnia and Herzegovina
113 *J22* **Štúrovo** ***Hung.*** Párkány; ***prev.*** Parkan. Západné Slovensko, S Slovakia
190 *L4* **Sturt, Mount** *hill* New South Wales, SE Australia
189 *P4* **Sturt Plain** *plain* Northern Territory, N Australia
189 *T9* **Sturt Stony Desert** *desert* South Australia
85 *J25* **Stutterheim** Eastern Cape, S South Africa
103 *H21* **Stuttgart** Baden-Württemberg, SW Germany
29 *W12* **Stuttgart** Arkansas, C USA
94 *H2* **Stykkishólmur** Vesturland, W Iceland
117 *F17* **Stylída** ***var.*** Stilida, Stilís. Stereá Ellás, C Greece
118 *K2* **Styr** ***Rus.*** Styr'. ≈ Belarus/Ukraine
117 *I19* **Stýra** ***var.*** Stira. Évvoia, C Greece
Styria *see* Steiermark
Su *see* Jiangsu
Sua *see* Sowa
175 *S17* **Suai** Timor, C Indonesia
56 *G9* **Suaita** Santander, C Colombia
82 *I7* **Suakin** ***var.*** Sawakin. Red Sea, NE Sudan
167 *T13* **Suao** ***Jap.*** Suō. N Taiwan
Suao *see* Suau
42 *G6* **Suaqui Grande** Sonora, NW Mexico
63 *A16* **Suardi** Santa Fe, C Argentina
56 *D11* **Suárez** Cauca, SW Colombia
195 *N17* **Suau** ***var.*** Suao. Suaul Island, SE PNG
120 *G12* **Subačius** Kupiškis, NE Lithuania
174 *Jj14* **Subang** ***prev.*** Soebang. Jawa, C Indonesia
174 *Gg5* **Subang** ✕ (Kuala Lumpur) Pahang, Peninsular Malaysia
133 *S10* **Subansiri** ≈ NE India
120 *I11* **Subate** Daugvapils, SE Latvia
145 *N5* **Subaykhān** Dayr az Zawr, E Syria
165 *P8* **Subei** ***var.*** Dangchengwan, Subei Mongolzu Zizhixian. Gansu, N China
Subei Mongolzu Zizhixian *see* Subei
174 *K5* **Subi Besar, Pulau** *island* Kepulauan Natuna, W Indonesia
Subiyah *see* Aş Şubayḩīyah
28 *I7* **Sublette** Kansas, C USA
114 *K8* **Subotica** ***Ger.*** Maria-Theresiopel, ***Hung.*** Szabadka. Serbia, N Yugoslavia
118 *K9* **Suceava** ***Ger.*** Suczawa, ***Hung.*** Szucsava. Suceava, NE Romania
118 *J9* **Suceava** ◈ *county* NE Romania
118 *K9* **Suceava** ***Ger.*** Suczawa. ≈ N Romania
114 *E12* **Sučevići** Zadar-Knin, C Croatia
113 *K17* **Sucha Beskidzka** Bielsko-Biała, S Poland
113 *M14* **Suchedniów** Kielce, SE Poland
44 *A2* **Suchitepéquez** ***off.*** Departamento de Suchitepéquez. ◈ *department* SW Guatemala
Su-chou *see* Suzhou
Suchow *see* Suzhou, Jiangsu, China
Suchow *see* Xuzhou, Jiangsu, China
99 *D17* **Suck** ≈ C Ireland
Sucker State *see* Illinois
194 *M16* **Suckling, Mount** ▲ S PNG
59 *L19* **Sucre** ***hist.*** Chuquisaca, La Plata. ● (Bolivia-legal capital) Chuquisaca, S Bolivia
56 *E6* **Sucre** Santander, N Colombia
58 *A7* **Sucre** Manabí, W Ecuador
56 *E6* **Sucre** ***off.*** Departamento de Sucre. ◈ *province* N Colombia
57 *O5* **Sucre** ***off.*** Estado Sucre. ◈ *state* NE Venezuela
58 *D6* **Sucumbíos** ◈ *province* NE Ecuador
115 *G15* **Sućuraj** Split-Dalmacija, S Croatia
60 *K10* **Sucuriju** Amapá, NE Brazil
Suczawa *see* Suceava
81 *E16* **Sud** ***Eng.*** South. ◈ *province* S Cameroon
128 *K13* **Suda** ≈ NW Russian Federation
Suda *see* Soúda
119 *U13* **Sudak** Respublika Krym, S Ukraine
26 *M4* **Sudan** Texas, SW USA
82 *C10* **Sudan** ***off.*** Republic of Sudan, ***Ar.*** Jumhuriyat as-Sudan; ***prev.*** Anglo-Egyptian Sudan. ◆ *republic* N Africa
Sudanese Republic *see* Mali
Sudan, Jumhuriyat as- *see* Sudan
12 *F10* **Sudbury** Ontario, S Canada
99 *P20* **Sudbury** E England, UK
Sud, Canal de *see* Gonâve, Canal de la
82 *E13* **Sudd** *swamp region* S Sudan
102 *K10* **Sude** ≈ N Germany
Sudest Island *see* Tagula Island
113 *E15* **Sudeten** ***var.*** Sudetes, Sudetic Mountains, Cz./Pol. Sudety. ▲▲ Czech Republic/Poland
Sudetes/Sudetic Mountains/ Sudety *see* Sudeten
94 *G1* **Sudhureyri** Vestfirdhir, NW Iceland
94 *J4* **Sudhurland** ◈ *region* S Iceland
176 *Xx12* **Sudirman, Pegunungan** ▲▲ Irian Jaya, E Indonesia
128 *M15* **Sudislavl'** Kostromskaya Oblast', NW Russian Federation
Südkarpaten *see* Carpații Meridionali
81 *N20* **Sud Kivu** ***off.*** Région Sud Kivu. ◈ *region* E Zaire
Südliche Morava *see* Južna Morava
102 *E12* **Süd-Nord-Kanal** *canal* NW Germany
130 *M3* **Sudogda** Vladimirskaya Oblast', W Russian Federation
Sudostroy *see* Severodvinsk
81 *C15* **Sud-Ouest** ***Eng.*** South-West. ◈ *province* W Cameroon
181 *X17* **Sud Ouest, Pointe** *headland* SW Mauritius
197 *J7* **Sud, Province** ◈ *province* S New Caledonia
130 *J8* **Sudzha** Kurskaya Oblast', W Russian Federation
83 *D15* **Sue** ≈ S Sudan
107 *S10* **Sueca** País Valenciano, E Spain
116 *I10* **Sŭedinenie** Plovdivska Oblast, C Bulgaria
Suero *see* Alzira
77 *X8* **Suez** ***Ar.*** As Suways, El Suweis. NE Egypt
77 *W7* **Suez Canal** ***Ar.*** Qanāt as Suways. *canal* NE Egypt
77 *X8* **Suez, Gulf of** ***Ar.*** Khalīj as Suways. *gulf* NE Egypt
9 *R17* **Suffield** Alberta, SW Canada
23 *X7* **Suffolk** Virginia, NE USA
99 *P20* **Suffolk** *cultural region* E England, UK
148 *J2* **Şūfīān** Āžarbāyjān-e Khāvarī, N Iran
33 *N12* **Sugar Creek** ≈ Illinois, N USA
32 *L13* **Sugar Creek** ≈ Illinois, N USA
33 *R3* **Sugar Island** *island* Michigan, N USA
27 *V11* **Sugar Land** Texas, SW USA
21 *P6* **Sugarloaf Mountain** ▲ Maine, NE USA
67 *G24* **Sugar Loaf Point** *headland* N Saint Helena
142 *G16* **Suğla Gölü** ◎ SW Turkey
127 *O8* **Sugoy** ≈ E Russian Federation
153 *U11* **Sugum, Gora** ▲ SW Kyrgyzstan
164 *F7* **Sugun** Xinjiang Uygur Zizhiqu, W China
175 *O2* **Sugut, Sungai** ≈ East Malaysia
165 *O9* **Suhai Hu** ◎ C China
168 *K14* **Suhait** Nei Mongol Zizhiqu, N China
147 *X7* **Şuḩār** ***var.*** Sohar. N Oman
168 *L6* **Sühbaatar** Selenge, N Mongolia
169 *P9* **Sühbaatar** ◈ *province* E Mongolia
103 *K17* **Suhl** Thüringen, C Germany
110 *F7* **Suhr** Aargau, N Switzerland
167 *O12* **Suichuan** Jiangxi, S China
Suid-Afrika *see* South Africa
166 *L4* **Suide** Shaanxi, C China
Suidwes-Afrika *see* Namibia
169 *Y9* **Suifenhe** Heilongjiang, NE China
Suigen *see* Suwŏn
169 *W8* **Suihua** Heilongjiang, NE China
Súilí, Loch *see* Swilly, Lough
167 *Q6* **Suining** Jiangsu, E China
166 *I9* **Suining** Sichuan, C China
105 *Q4* **Suippes** Marne, N France
99 *E20* **Suir** ***Ir.*** An tSiúir. ≈ S Ireland
171 *Gg15* **Suita** Ōsaka, Honshū, SW Japan
166 *L16* **Suixi** Guangdong, S China
Sui Xian *see* Suizhou
169 *T13* **Suizhong** Liaoning, NE China
167 *N8* **Suizhou** ***prev.*** Sui Xian. Hubei, C China
155 *P17* **Sujāwal** Sind, SE Pakistan
174 *Jj14* **Sukabumi** ***prev.*** Soekaboemi. Jawa, C Indonesia
174 *Kk9* **Sukadana, Teluk** *bay* Borneo, W Indonesia
171 *Ll14* **Sukagawa** Fukushima, Honshū, C Japan
Sukarnapura *see* Jayapura
Sukarno, Puntjak *see* Jaya, Puncak
153 *R11* **Sŭkh** ***Rus.*** Sokh. Farghona Wiloyati, E Uzbekistan
Sŭkh *see* Sokh
116 *N8* **Sukha Reka** ≈ NE Bulgaria
130 *J5* **Sukhinichi** Kaluzhskaya Oblast', W Russian Federation
Sukhne *see* As Sukhnah
133 *Q4* **Sukhona** ***var.*** Tot'ma. ≈ NW Russian Federation
178 *H9* **Sukhothai** ***var.*** Sukotai. Sukhothai, W Thailand
Sukhumi *see* Sokhumi
Sukkertoppen *see* Maniitsoq
155 *Q13* **Sukkur** Sind, SE Pakistan
Sukotai *see* Sukhothai
Sukra Bay *see* Şawqirah, Dawḩat
129 *V15* **Suksun** Permskaya Oblast', NW Russian Federation
170 *E16* **Sukumo** Kōchi, Shikoku, SW Japan
96 *B12* **Sula** *island* S Norway
129 *Q5* **Sula** ≈ NW Russian Federation
119 *R5* **Sula** ≈ N Ukraine
44 *H6* **Sulaco, Río** ≈ NW Honduras
Sulaimaniya *see* As Sulaymānīyah
155 *S10* **Sulaimān Range** ▲▲ C Pakistan
131 *Q16* **Sulak** Respublika Dagestan, SW Russian Federation
131 *Q16* **Sulak** ≈ SW Russian Federation
175 *Rr10* **Sula, Kepulauan** *island group* C Indonesia
142 *I12* **Sulakyurt** ***var.*** Konur. Kırıkkale, N Turkey
175 *R17* **Sulamu** Timor, S Indonesia
98 *F5* **Sula Sgeir** *island* NW Scotland, UK
175 *Pp10* **Sulawesi** ***Eng.*** Celebes. *island* C Indonesia
Sulawesi, Laut *see* Celebes Sea
175 *P11* **Sulawesi Selatan** ***off.*** Propinsi Sulawesi Selatan, ***Eng.*** South Celebes, South Sulawesi. ◈ *province* C Indonesia
175 *Q9* **Sulawesi Tengah** ***off.*** Propinsi Sulawesi Tengah, ***Eng.*** Central Celebes, Central Sulawesi. ◈ *province* N Indonesia
175 *Q11* **Sulawesi Tenggara** ***off.*** Propinsi Sulawesi Tenggara, ***Eng.*** South-East Celebes, South-East Sulawesi. ◈ *province* C Indonesia
175 *Qq7* **Sulawesi Utara** ***off.*** Propinsi Sulawesi Utara, ***Eng.*** North Celebes, North Sulawesi. ◈ *province* N Indonesia
145 *T5* **Sulaymān Beg** N Iraq
97 *D15* **Suldalsvatnet** ◎ S Norway
112 *E12* **Sulechów** ***Ger.*** Züllichau. Zielona Góra, W Poland
112 *E11* **Sulęcin** Gorzów, W Poland
79 *U14* **Suleja** Niger, C Nigeria
113 *K14* **Sulejów** Piotrków, S Poland
98 *I5* **Sule Skerry** *island* N Scotland, UK
Suliag *see* Sohâg
78 *J16* **Sulima** S Sierra Leone
119 *O13* **Sulina** Tulcea, SE Romania
119 *N13* **Sulina Brațul** ≈ SE Romania
102 *H12* **Sulingen** Niedersachsen, NW Germany
94 *H12* **Suliskongen** ▲ C Norway
94 *H12* **Sulitjelma** Nordland, C Norway
58 *A9* **Sullana** Piura, NW Peru
25 *N3* **Sulligent** Alabama, S USA
32 *M14* **Sullivan** Illinois, N USA
33 *N15* **Sullivan** Indiana, N USA
29 *W5* **Sullivan** Missouri, C USA
Sullivan Island *see* Lanbi Kyun
98 *M1* **Sullom Voe** NE Scotland, UK
105 *O7* **Sully-sur-Loire** Loiret, C France
Sulmo *see* Sulmona
109 *K15* **Sulmona** ***anc.*** Sulmo. Abruzzi, C Italy
Sulo *see* Shule He
116 *M11* **Süloğlu** Edirne, NW Turkey
24 *G9* **Sulphur** Louisiana, S USA
29 *O12* **Sulphur** Oklahoma, C USA
30 *K9* **Sulphur Creek** ≈ South Dakota, N USA
26 *M5* **Sulphur Draw** ≈ Texas, SW USA
27 *W5* **Sulphur River** ≈ Arkansas/Texas, SW USA
27 *V6* **Sulphur Springs** Texas, SW USA
26 *M6* **Sulphur Springs Draw** ≈ Texas, SW USA
12 *D8* **Sultan** Ontario, S Canada
Sultānābād *see* Arāk
Sultan Alonto, Lake *see* Lanao, Lake
142 *G15* **Sultan Dağları** ▲▲ C Turkey
116 *N13* **Sultanköy** Tekirdağ, NW Turkey
179 *R16* **Sultan Kudarat** ***var.*** Nuling. Mindanao, S Philippines
158 *M13* **Sultānpur** Uttar Pradesh, N India
179 *Pp17* **Sulu Archipelago** *island group* SW Philippines
198 *Ff7* **Sulu Basin** *undersea feature* SE South China Sea
Sülüktü *see* Sulyukta
Sulu, Laut *see* Sulu Sea
175 *Pp1* **Sulu Sea** ***Ind.*** Laut Sulu. *sea* SW Philippines
151 *O15* **Sulutobe** ***Kaz.*** Sulūtöbe. Kzyl-Orda, S Kazakhstan
153 *Q11* **Sulyukta** ***Kir.*** Sülüktü. Oshskaya Oblast', SW Kyrgyzstan
Sulz *see* Sulz am Neckar
103 *G22* **Sulz am Neckar** ***var.*** Sulz. Baden-Württemberg, SW Germany
103 *L20* **Sulzbach-Rosenberg** Bayern, SE Germany
205 *N13* **Sulzberger Bay** *bay* Antarctica
Sumail *see* Summēl
115 *F15* **Sumartin** Split-Dalmacija, S Croatia
34 *H6* **Sumas** Washington, NW USA
174 *Gg7* **Sumatera** ***Eng.*** Sumatra. *island* W Indonesia
173 *G9* **Sumatera Barat** ***off.*** Propinsi Sumatera Barat, ***Eng.*** West Sumatra. ◈ *province* W Indonesia
174 *Hh11* **Sumatera Selatan** ***off.*** Propinsi Sumatera Selatan, ***Eng.*** South Sumatra. ◈ *province* W Indonesia
173 *Ff6* **Sumatera Utara** ***off.*** Propinsi Sumatera Utara, ***Eng.*** North Sumatra. ◈ *province* W Indonesia
Sumatra *see* Sumatera
Šumava *see* Bohemian Forest
Sumayl *see* Summēl
145 *U7* **Sumayr al Muḩammad** E Iraq
175 *P17* **Sumba, Pulau** ***Eng.*** Sandalwood Island; ***prev.*** Soemba. *island* Nusa Tenggara, C Indonesia
152 *D12* **Sumbar** ≈ W Turkmenistan
175 *P16* **Sumba, Selat** *strait* Nusa Tenggara, S Indonesia
175 *Oo16* **Sumbawa** ***prev.*** Soembawa. *island* Nusa Tenggara, C Indonesia
175 *O16* **Sumbawabesar** Sumbawa, S Indonesia
83 *F23* **Sumbawanga** Rukwa, W Tanzania
84 *B12* **Sumbe** ***prev.*** N'Gunza, ***Port.*** Novo Redondo. Cuanza Sul, W Angola
98 *M3* **Sumburgh Head** *headland* NE Scotland, UK
113 *H23* **Sümeg** Veszprém, W Hungary
82 *C12* **Sumeih** Southern Darfur, S Sudan
174 *Mm14* **Sumenep** ***prev.*** Soemenep. Pulau Madura, C Indonesia
Sumgait *see* Sumqayıt, Azerbaijan
Sumgait *see* Sumqayıtçay, Azerbaijan
172 *Ss14* **Sumisu-jima** ***Eng.*** Smith Island. *island* SE Japan
145 *Q2* **Summēl** ***var.*** Sumail, Sumayl. N Iraq
33 *O5* **Summer Island** *island* Michigan, N USA
34 *H15* **Summer Lake** ◎ Oregon, NW USA
9 *N17* **Summerland** British Columbia, SW Canada
11 *P14* **Summerside** Prince Edward Island, SE Canada
23 *R5* **Summersville** West Virginia, NE USA
23 *R5* **Summersville Lake** ▣ West Virginia, NE USA
23 *S13* **Summerton** South Carolina, SE USA
25 *R2* **Summerville** Georgia, SE USA
23 *S14* **Summerville** South Carolina, SE USA
41 *R10* **Summit** Alaska, USA
37 *V6* **Summit Mountain** ▲ Nevada, W USA
39 *R8* **Summit Peak** ▲ Colorado, C USA
Summus Portus *see* Somport, Col du
31 *X12* **Sumner** Iowa, C USA
24 *K3* **Sumner** Mississippi, S USA
193 *H17* **Sumner, Lake** ◎ South Island, NZ
39 *U12* **Sumner, Lake** ▣ New Mexico, SW USA
171 *Kk13* **Sumon-dake** ▲ Honshū, C Japan
170 *G15* **Sumoto** Hyōgo, Awaji-shima, SW Japan
113 *G17* **Šumperk** ***Ger.*** Mährisch-Schönberg. Severní Morava, E Czech Republic
44 *F7* **Sumpul, Río** ≈ El Salvador/Honduras
143 *Z11* **Sumqayıt** ***Rus.*** Sumgait. E Azerbaijan
143 *Y11* **Sumqayıtçay** ***Rus.*** Sumgait. ≈ E Azerbaijan
153 *R9* **Sumsar** Dzhalal-Abadskaya Oblast', W Kyrgyzstan
119 *S3* **Sums'ka Oblast'** ***var.*** Sumy, ***Rus.*** Sumskaya Oblast'. ◈ *province* NE Ukraine
Sumskaya Oblast' *see* Sums'ka Oblast'
128 *J8* **Sumskiy Posad** Respublika Kareliya, NW Russian Federation
23 *S12* **Sumter** South Carolina, SE USA
119 *T3* **Sumy** Sums'ka Oblast', NE Ukraine
Sumy *see* Sums'ka Oblast'
165 *Q15* **Sumzom** Xizang Zizhiqu, W China
129 *R15* **Suna** Kirovskaya Oblast', NW Russian Federation
128 *I10* **Suna** ≈ NW Russian Federation
172 *Oo5* **Sunagawa** Hokkaidō, NE Japan
159 *V13* **Sunamganj** Chittagong, NE Bangladesh
165 *S8* **Sunan** ***var.*** Hongwan, Sunan Yugurzu Zizhixian. Gansu, N China
169 *W14* **Sunan** ✕ (P'yŏngyang) SW North Korea
Sunan Yugurzu Zizhixian *see* Sunan
21 *N9* **Sunapee Lake** ◎ New Hampshire, NE USA
145 *P4* **Sunaysilah** *salt marsh* N Iraq
22 *M8* **Sunbright** Tennessee, S USA
35 *R6* **Sunburst** Montana, NW USA
191 *N12* **Sunbury** Victoria, SE Australia
23 *X8* **Sunbury** North Carolina, SE USA
20 *G14* **Sunbury** Pennsylvania, NE USA
63 *A17* **Sunchales** Santa Fe, C Argentina
169 *W13* **Sunch'ŏn** SW North Korea
169 *Y16* **Sunch'ŏn** ***Jap.*** Junten. S South Korea
38 *K13* **Sun City** Arizona, SW USA
21 *O9* **Suncook** New Hampshire, NE USA
Sunda Islands *see* Greater Sunda Islands
35 *Z12* **Sundance** Wyoming, C USA
160 *M11* **Sundargarh** Orissa, E India
174 *Ii14* **Sunda, Selat** *strait* Jawa/Sumatera, SW Indonesia
133 *U15* **Sunda Shelf** *undersea feature* S South China Sea
Sunda Trench *see* Java Trench
133 *U17* **Sunda Trough** *undersea feature* E Indian Ocean
97 *O16* **Sundbyberg** Stockholm, C Sweden
99 *M14* **Sunderland** ***var.*** Wearmouth. NE England, UK
103 *F15* **Sundern** Nordrhein-Westfalen, W Germany
142 *F12* **Sündiken Dağları** ▲▲ C Turkey
26 *M5* **Sundown** Texas, SW USA
9 *P16* **Sundre** Alberta, SW Canada
12 *H12* **Sundridge** Ontario, S Canada
95 *H17* **Sundsvall** Västernorrland, C Sweden
28 *H4* **Sunflower, Mount** ▲ Kansas, C USA
Sunflower State *see* Kansas
174 *Gg4* **Sungai Bernam** ≈ Peninsular Malaysia
174 *Ii12* **Sungaibuntu** Sumatera, SW Indonesia
174 *Gg9* **Sungaidareh** Sumatera, W Indonesia
178 *Hh17* **Sungai Kolok** ***var.*** Sungai Ko-Lok. Narathiwat, SW Thailand
174 *Gg10* **Sungaipenuh** ***prev.*** Soengaipenoeh. Sumatera, W Indonesia
174 *Kk8* **Sungaipinyuh** Borneo, C Indonesia
Sungari *see* Songhua Jiang
Sungaria *see* Dzungaria
Sungei Pahang *see* Pahang, Sungai
178 *Hh8* **Sung Men** Phrae, NW Thailand
85 *M15* **Sungo** Tete, NW Mozambique
174 *Ii10* **Sungsang** Sumatera, W Indonesia
116 *M9* **Sungurlare** Burgaska Oblast, E Bulgaria
142 *J12* **Sungurlu** Çorum, N Turkey
114 *F9* **Sunja** Sisak-Moslavina, C Croatia
159 *Q12* **Sun Koshi** ≈ E Nepal
96 *F9* **Sunndalen** *valley* S Norway
96 *F9* **Sunndalsøra** Møre og Romsdal, S Norway
97 *K15* **Sunne** Värmland, C Sweden
97 *O15* **Sunnersta** Uppsala, C Sweden
96 *C11* **Sunnfjord** *physical region* S Norway
97 *C15* **Sunnhordland** *physical region* S Norway
96 *D10* **Sunnmøre** *physical region* S Norway
39 *N4* **Sunnyside** Utah, W USA
34 *J10* **Sunnyside** Washington, NW USA
37 *N9* **Sunnyvale** California, W USA
32 *L8* **Sun Prairie** Wisconsin, N USA
Sunqur *see* Sonqor
27 *N1* **Sunray** Texas, SW USA

◆ Country ● Country Capital ◇ Dependent Territory ○ Dependent Territory Capital ◈ Administrative Region ✕ International Airport ▲ Mountain ▲▲ Mountain Range ⋀ Volcano ≈ River ◎ Lake ▣ Reservoir

24 I8 **Sunset** Louisiana, S USA
27 S5 **Sunset** Texas, SW USA
Sunset State see Oregon
189 Z10 **Sunshine Coast** cultural region Queensland, E Australia
Sunshine State see Florida, USA
Sunshine State see New Mexico, USA
Sunshine State see South Dakota, USA
126 Kk11 **Suntar** Respublika Sakha (Yakutiya), NE Russian Federation
41 R10 **Suntrana** Alaska, USA
154 J15 **Suntsar** Baluchistān, SW Pakistan
169 W15 **Sunwi-do** island SW North Korea
169 W6 **Sunwu** Heilongjiang, NE China
79 O16 **Sunyani** W Ghana
Suō see Suao
95 M17 **Suolahti** Keski-Suomi, C Finland
Suoločielgi see Saariselkä
Suomenlahti see Finland, Gulf of
Suomen Tasavalta/Suomi see Finland
95 N14 **Suomussalmi** Oulu, E Finland
170 D13 **Suō-nada** sea SW Japan
95 M17 **Suonenjoki** Kuopio, C Finland
178 Jj13 **Suŏng** Kâmpóng Cham, C Cambodia
128 I10 **Suoyarvi** Respublika Kareliya, NW Russian Federation
Supanburi see Suphan Buri
59 D14 **Supe** Lima, W Peru
13 V7 **Supérieur, Lac** ◎ Québec, SE Canada
Supérieur, Lac see Superior, Lake
38 M14 **Superior** Arizona, SW USA
35 O9 **Superior** Montana, NW USA
31 P17 **Superior** Nebraska, C USA
32 I3 **Superior** Wisconsin, N USA
43 S17 **Superior, Laguna** lagoon S Mexico
33 N2 **Superior, Lake** Fr. Lac Supérieur. ◎ Canada/USA
38 L13 **Superstition Mountains** ⛰ Arizona, SW USA
115 F14 **Supetar** It. San Pietro. Split-Dalmacija, S Croatia
178 H11 **Suphan Buri** var. Supanburi. Suphan Buri, W Thailand
176 W9 **Supiori, Pulau** island E Indonesia
196 K2 **Supply Reef** reef N Northern Mariana Islands
205 O7 **Support Force Glacier** glacier Antarctica
143 R10 **Sup'sa** var. Supsa. ≈ W Georgia
Sūq 'Abs see 'Abs
145 W12 **Sūq ash Shuyūkh** SE Iraq
144 H4 **Şuqaylibīyah** Ḩamāh, W Syria
167 Q6 **Suqian** Jiangsu, E China
Suqrah see Şawqirah
Suqrah Bay see Şawqirah, Dawḩat
147 V16 **Suquṭrā** var. Sokotra, Eng. Socotra. island SE Yemen
147 Z8 **Şūr** NE Oman
Şūr see Soûr
131 P5 **Sura** Penzenskaya Oblast', W Russian Federation
131 P4 **Sura** ≈ W Russian Federation
155 N12 **Sūrāb** Baluchistān, SW Pakistan
Surabaja see Surabaya
174 M15 **Surabaya** prev. Soerabaja, Surabaja. Jawa, C Indonesia
97 N15 **Surahammar** Västmanland, C Sweden
174 L15 **Surakarta** Eng. Solo; prev. Soerakarta. Jawa, S Indonesia
Surakhany see Suraxanı
179 R17 **Surallah** Mindanao, S Philippines
143 S10 **Surami** C Georgia
149 X13 **Sūrān** Sīstān va Balūchestān, SE Iran
113 I21 **Šurany** Hung. Nagysurány. Západné Slovensko, SW Slovakia
160 D12 **Sūrat** Gujarāt, W India
Suratdhani see Surat Thani
158 G9 **Sūratgarh** Rājasthān, NW India
178 Gg15 **Surat Thani** var. Suratdhani. Surat Thani, SW Thailand
121 Q16 **Suraw** Rus. Surov. ≈ E Belarus
143 Z11 **Suraxanı** Rus. Surakhany. E Azerbaijan
147 Y11 **Surayr** E Oman
144 K2 **Suraysāt** Ḩalab, N Syria
120 O12 **Surazh** Rus. Surazh. Vitsyebskaya Voblasts', NE Belarus
130 H6 **Surazh** Bryanskaya Oblast', W Russian Federation
203 V17 **Sur, Cabo** headland Easter Island, Chile, E Pacific Ocean
114 L11 **Surčin** Serbia, N Yugoslavia
118 H9 **Surduc** Hung. Szurduk. Sălaj, NW Romania
115 P16 **Surdulica** Serbia, SE Yugoslavia
101 L24 **Sûre** var. Sauer. ≈ W Europe see also Sauer
160 C10 **Surendranagar** Gujarāt, W India
20 K16 **Surf City** New Jersey, NE USA
191 V3 **Surfers Paradise** Queensland, E Australia
23 U13 **Surfside Beach** South Carolina, SE USA
104 J10 **Surgères** Charente-Maritime, W France
125 G11 **Surgut** Khanty-Mansiyskiy Avtonomnyy Okrug, C Russian Federation
126 Hh10 **Surgutikha** Krasnoyarskiy Kray, N Russian Federation
100 M6 **Surhuisterveen** Friesland, N Netherlands
107 V5 **Súria** Cataluña, NE Spain
149 P10 **Sūrīān** Fārs, S Iran
161 J15 **Suriāpet** Andhra Pradesh, C India
179 R14 **Surigao** Mindanao, S Philippines
178 Ii11 **Surin** Surin, E Thailand
Surinam see Suriname
57 U11 **Suriname** off. Republic of Surinam, var. Surinam; prev. Dutch Guiana, Netherlands Guiana. ◆ republic N South America
Sūrīya/Sūrīyah, Al-Jumhūrīyah al-'Arabīyah as- see Syria
Surkhab, Darya-i- see Kahmard, Daryā-ye
Surkhandar'inskaya Oblast' see Surkhondaryo Wiloyati
Surkhandar'ya see Surkhondaryo
Surkhet see Birendranagar
153 R12 **Surkhob** ≈ C Tajikistan
153 P13 **Surkhondaryo** Rus. Surkhandar'ya. ≈ Tajikistan/Uzbekistan
153 N13 **Surkhondaryo Wiloyati** Rus. Surkhandar'inskaya Oblast'. ◐ province S Uzbekistan
143 P11 **Sürmene** Trabzon, NE Turkey
Surov see Suraw
131 N11 **Surovikino** Volgogradskaya Oblast', SW Russian Federation
126 Jj14 **Surovo** Irkutskaya Oblast', S Russian Federation
37 N11 **Sur, Point** headland California, W USA
197 F3 **Surprise, Île** island N New Caledonia
63 E22 **Sur, Punta** headland E Argentina
Surrentum see Sorrento
30 M3 **Surrey** North Dakota, N USA
99 O22 **Surrey** cultural region SE England, UK
23 X7 **Surry** Virginia, NE USA
110 F8 **Sursee** Luzern, W Switzerland
131 P6 **Sursk** Penzenskaya Oblast', W Russian Federation
131 P5 **Surskoye** Ul'yanovskaya Oblast', W Russian Federation
77 P8 **Surt** var. Sidra, Sirte. N Libya
97 I19 **Surte** Göteborg och Bohus, S Sweden
77 Q8 **Surt, Khalīj** Eng. Gulf of Sidra, Gulf of Sirti, Sidra. gulf N Libya
94 I5 **Surtsey** island S Iceland
143 N17 **Suruç** Şanlıurfa, S Turkey
171 Ii17 **Suruga-wan** bay SE Japan
174 Hh10 **Surulangun** Sumatera, W Indonesia
Süs see Susch
108 A8 **Susa** Piemonte, NE Italy
170 E12 **Susa** Yamaguchi, Honshū, SW Japan
Susa see Shūsh
115 E16 **Sušac** It. Cazza. island SW Croatia
Sūsah see Sousse
170 Ee15 **Susaki** Kōchi, Shikoku, SW Japan
170 G17 **Susami** Wakayama, Honshū, SW Japan
148 K9 **Sūsangerd** var. Susangird. Khūzestān, SW Iran
Susangird see Sūsangerd
37 P4 **Susanville** California, W USA
110 J9 **Susch** var. Süs. Graubünden, SE Switzerland
143 N12 **Suşehri** Sivas, N Turkey
Susiana see Khūzestān
113 B18 **Sušice** Ger. Schüttenhofen. Západní Čechy, SW Czech Republic
41 R11 **Susitna** Alaska, USA
41 R11 **Susitna River** ≈ Alaska, USA
131 Q3 **Suslonger** Respublika Mariy El, W Russian Federation
107 N14 **Suspiro del Moro, Puerto del** pass S Spain
20 H16 **Susquehanna River** ≈ New York/Pennsylvania, NE USA
11 O15 **Sussex** New Brunswick, SE Canada
20 J13 **Sussex** New Jersey, NE USA
23 W7 **Sussex** Virginia, NE USA
99 O23 **Sussex** cultural region S England, UK
191 S10 **Sussex Inlet** New South Wales, SE Australia
101 L17 **Susteren** Limburg, SE Netherlands
8 K12 **Sustut Peak** ▲ British Columbia, W Canada
127 Nn9 **Susuman** Magadanskaya Oblast', E Russian Federation
196 H6 **Susupe** Saipan, S Northern Mariana Islands
142 D12 **Susurluk** Balıkesir, NW Turkey
116 M13 **Susuzmüsellim** Tekirdağ, NW Turkey
142 F15 **Sütçüler** Isparta, SW Turkey
118 L13 **Şuţeşti** Brăila, SE Romania
85 F25 **Sutherland** Western Cape, SW South Africa
30 L15 **Sutherland** Nebraska, C USA
98 I7 **Sutherland** cultural region N Scotland, UK
193 B21 **Sutherland Falls** waterfall South Island, NZ
34 F14 **Sutherlin** Oregon, NW USA
155 V10 **Sutlej** ≈ India/Pakistan
Sutna see Satna
37 P7 **Sutter Creek** California, W USA
41 R11 **Sutton** Alaska, USA
31 Q16 **Sutton** Nebraska, C USA
23 R4 **Sutton** West Virginia, NE USA
12 H8 **Sutton** ≈ Ontario, C Canada
99 M19 **Sutton Coldfield** C England, UK
23 R4 **Sutton Lake** ⊡ West Virginia, NE USA
13 P13 **Sutton, Monts** hill range Québec, SE Canada
10 F8 **Sutton Ridges** ⛰ Ontario, C Canada
172 Nn5 **Suttsu** Hokkaidō, NE Japan
41 P15 **Sutwik Island** island Alaska, USA
168 K7 **Süüj** Bulgan, C Mongolia
120 H5 **Suure-Jaani** Ger. Gross-Sankt-Johannis. Viljandimaa, S Estonia
120 J7 **Suur Munamägi** var. Munamägi, Ger. Eier-Berg. ▲ SE Estonia
120 F5 **Suur Väin** Ger. Grosser Sund. strait W Estonia
153 U8 **Suusamyr** Chuyskaya Oblast', C Kyrgyzstan
197 I13 **Suva** ● (Fiji) Viti Levu, W Fiji
197 I13 **Suva** ✕ Viti Levu, C Fiji
115 N18 **Suva Gora** ⛰ W FYR Macedonia
120 H11 **Suvainiškis** Rokiškis, NE Lithuania
Suvalkai/Suvalki see Suwałki
115 P15 **Suva Planina** ⛰ SE Yugoslavia
115 M17 **Suva Reka** Serbia, S Yugoslavia
130 K5 **Suvorov** Tul'skaya Oblast', W Russian Federation
119 N12 **Suvorove** Odes'ka Oblast', SW Ukraine
Suvorovo see Ştefan Vodă
171 J15 **Suwa** Nagano, Honshū, S Japan
Suwaik see As Suwayq
Suwaira see Aş Şuwayrah
112 O7 **Suwałki** Lith. Suvalkai, Rus. Suvalki. Suwałki, NE Poland
112 N8 **Suwałki** off. Województwo Suwalskie, Lith. Suvalkai, Rus. Suvalki. ◐ province NE Poland
Suwalskie, Województwo see Suwałki
178 Ii10 **Suwannaphum** Roi Et, E Thailand
25 V8 **Suwannee River** ≈ Florida/Georgia, SE USA
Şuwār see Aş Şuwār
202 K14 **Suwarrow** atoll N Cook Islands
Suwaydá/Suwaydā', Muḩāfaẓat as see As Suwaydā'
149 R16 **Suwaydān** var. Sweihan. Abū Ẓaby, E UAE
Suwayqiyah, Hawr as see Shuwayjah, Hawr ash
Suways, Khalīj as see Suez, Gulf of
Suways, Qanāt as see Suez Canal
Suweida see As Suwaydā'
Suweon see Suwŏn
169 X15 **Suwŏn** var. Suweon, Jap. Suigen. NW South Korea
Su Xian see Suzhou
149 R14 **Sūzā** Hormozgān, S Iran
151 P15 **Suzak** Kaz. Sozaq. Yuzhnyy Kazakhstan, S Kazakhstan
Suzaka see Suzuka
130 M3 **Suzdal'** Vladimirskaya Oblast', W Russian Federation
167 R8 **Suzhou** var. Su Xian. Anhui, E China
167 P7 **Suzhou** var. Soochow, Su-chou, Suchow; prev. Wuhsien. Jiangsu, E China
Suz, Mys see Soye, Mys
171 J12 **Suzu** Ishikawa, Honshū, SW Japan
171 Hh16 **Suzuka** Mie, Honshū, SW Japan
171 Jj14 **Suzuka** var. Suzaka. Nagano, Honshū, S Japan
171 J12 **Suzu-misaki** headland Honshū, SW Japan
Svågälv see Svågan
96 M10 **Svågan** var. Svågälv. ≈ C Sweden
Svalava/Svaljava see Svalyava
94 O2 **Svalbard** ◇ Norwegian dependency Arctic Ocean
94 J2 **Svalbardhs** Nordhurland Eystra, N Iceland
97 K22 **Svalöv** Malmöhus, S Sweden
118 H7 **Svalyava** Cz. Svalava, Svaljava, Hung. Szolyva. Zakarpats'ka Oblast', W Ukraine
94 O2 **Svanbergfjellet** ▲ C Svalbard
97 M24 **Svaneke** Bornholm, E Denmark
97 L22 **Svängsta** Blekinge, S Sweden
97 J16 **Svanskog** Värmland, C Sweden
97 L16 **Svartå** Örebro, C Sweden
97 L15 **Svartälven** ≈ C Sweden
94 G12 **Svartisen** glacier C Norway
119 X6 **Svatove** Rus. Svatovo. Luhans'ka Oblast', E Ukraine
Svatovo see Svatove
Sväty Kríž nad Hronom see Žiar nad Hronom
178 Ii12 **Svay Chék, Stœng** ≈ Cambodia/Thailand
178 Jj14 **Svay Riĕng** Svay Riĕng, S Cambodia
94 O3 **Sveagruva** Spitsbergen, W Svalbard
97 K23 **Svedala** Malmöhus, S Sweden
120 H12 **Svėdesai** Anykščiai, NE Lithuania
95 G18 **Sveg** Jämtland, C Sweden
120 C12 **Švėkšna** Šilutė, W Lithuania
96 C11 **Svelgen** Sogn og Fjordane, S Norway
97 H15 **Svelvik** Vestfold, S Norway
120 I13 **Švenčionėliai** Pol. Nowo-Święciany. Švenčionys, SE Lithuania
120 I13 **Švenčionys** Pol. Swięciany. Švenčionys, SE Lithuania
97 H24 **Svendborg** Fyn, C Denmark
97 K19 **Svenljunga** Älvsborg, S Sweden
94 P2 **Svenskøya** island E Svalbard
95 G17 **Svenstavik** Jämtland, C Sweden
97 G20 **Svenstrup** Nordjylland, N Denmark
120 H12 **Šventoji** ≈ C Lithuania
119 Z8 **Sverdlovs'k** Rus. Sverdlovsk; prev. Imeni Sverdlova Rudnik. Luhans'ka Oblast', E Ukraine
Sverdlovsk see Yekaterinburg
131 W2 **Sverdlovskaya Oblast'** ◐ province C Russian Federation
126 Hh5 **Sverdrup, Ostrov** island N Russian Federation
Sverige see Sweden
115 D15 **Svetac** prev. Sveti Andrea, It. Sant'Andrea. island SW Croatia
Sveti Andrea see Svetac
Sveti Nikola see Sveti Nikole
115 O18 **Sveti Nikole** prev. Sveti Nikola. C FYR Macedonia
Sveti Vrach see Sandanski
127 O16 **Svetlaya** Primorskiy Kray, SE Russian Federation
130 B2 **Svetlogorsk** Kaliningradskaya Oblast', W Russian Federation
126 I9 **Svetlogorsk** Krasnoyarskiy Kray, N Russian Federation
Svetlogorsk see Svyetlahorsk
131 N14 **Svetlograd** Stavropol'skiy Kray, SW Russian Federation
Svetlovodsk see Svitlovods'k
121 A14 **Svetlyy** Ger. Zimmerbude. Kaliningradskaya Oblast', W Russian Federation
131 Y8 **Svetlyy** Orenburgskaya Oblast', W Russian Federation
128 G11 **Svetogorsk** Fin. Enso. Leningradskaya Oblast', NW Russian Federation
Svetozarevo see Jagodina
113 B18 **Švihov** Ger. Schwihau. Západní Čechy, W Czech Republic
114 E13 **Svilaja** ⛰ SE Croatia
114 N12 **Svilajnac** Serbia, C Yugoslavia
116 L11 **Svilengrad** prev. Mustafa-Pasha. Khaskovska Oblast, SE Bulgaria
Svinecea Mare, Munte see Svinecea Mare, Vârful
118 F13 **Svinecea Mare, Vârful** var. Munte Svinecea Mare. ▲ SW Romania
153 N14 **Svintsovyy Rudnik** Turkm. Swintsowyy Rudnik. Lebapskiy Velayat, E Turkmenistan
120 I13 **Svir** Rus. Svir'. Minskaya Voblasts', NW Belarus
128 I12 **Svir'** canal NW Russian Federation
Svir', Ozero see Svir, Vozyera
121 I14 **Svir, Vozyera** Rus. Ozero Svir'. ◎ C Belarus
116 J7 **Svishtov** prev. Sistova. Loveshka Oblast, N Bulgaria
121 F18 **Svislach** Pol. Świsłocz, Rus. Svisloch'. Hrodzyenskaya Voblasts', W Belarus
121 M17 **Svislach** Rus. Svisloch'. Mahilyowskaya Voblasts', E Belarus
121 L17 **Svislach** Rus. Svisloch'. ≈ E Belarus
Svisloch' see Svislach
113 F17 **Svitavy** Ger. Zwittau. Východní Čechy, E Czech Republic
119 S6 **Svitlovods'k** Rus. Svetlovodsk. Kirovohrads'ka Oblast', C Ukraine
Svizzera see Switzerland
126 Mm15 **Svobodnyy** Amurskaya Oblast', SE Russian Federation
116 G9 **Svoge** Sofiyska Oblast, W Bulgaria
94 G11 **Svolvær** Nordland, C Norway
113 F18 **Svratka** Ger. Schwarzach, Schwarzawa. ≈ SE Czech Republic
115 P14 **Svrljig** Serbia, E Yugoslavia
207 U10 **Svyataya Anna Trough** var. Saint Anna Trough. undersea feature N Kara Sea
128 M4 **Svyatoy Nos, Mys** headland NW Russian Federation
126 M5 **Svyatoy Nos, Mys** headland NE Russian Federation
121 N18 **Svyetlahorsk** Rus. Svetlogorsk. Homyel'skaya Voblasts', SE Belarus
Swabian Jura see Schwäbische Alb
99 P19 **Swaffham** E England, UK
25 V5 **Swainsboro** Georgia, SE USA
85 C19 **Swakop** ≈ W Namibia
85 C19 **Swakopmund** Erongo, W Namibia
99 M15 **Swale** ≈ N England, UK
Swallow Island see Nendö
101 M16 **Swalmen** Limburg, SE Netherlands
10 G8 **Swan** ≈ Ontario, C Canada
99 L24 **Swanage** S England, UK
190 M10 **Swan Hill** Victoria, SE Australia
9 P13 **Swan Hills** Alberta, W Canada
67 D24 **Swan Island** island C Falkland Islands
Swankalok see Sawankhalok
31 U10 **Swan Lake** ◎ Minnesota, N USA
23 Y10 **Swanquarter** North Carolina, SE USA
190 J9 **Swan Reach** South Australia
9 V15 **Swan River** Manitoba, S Canada
191 P17 **Swansea** Tasmania, SE Australia
99 J22 **Swansea** Wel. Abertawe. S Wales, UK
23 R13 **Swansea** South Carolina, SE USA
21 S7 **Swans Island** island Maine, NE USA
30 L17 **Swanson Lake** ⊡ Nebraska, C USA
33 R11 **Swanton** Ohio, N USA
112 G11 **Swarzędz** Poznań, W Poland
Swatow see Shantou
85 L22 **Swaziland** off. Kingdom of Swaziland. ◆ monarchy S Africa
95 G18 **Sweden** off. Kingdom of Sweden, Swe. Sverige. ◆ monarchy N Europe
Swedru see Agona Swedru
27 V12 **Sweeny** Texas, SW USA
35 R6 **Sweetgrass** Montana, NW USA
34 G12 **Sweet Home** Oregon, NW USA
27 T12 **Sweet Home** Texas, SW USA
29 T4 **Sweet Springs** Missouri, C USA
22 M10 **Sweetwater** Tennessee, S USA
27 P7 **Sweetwater** Texas, SW USA
35 V15 **Sweetwater River** ≈ Wyoming, C USA
Sweihan see Suwaydān
85 F26 **Swellendam** Western Cape, SW South Africa
113 G15 **Świdnica** Ger. Schweidnitz. Wałbrzych, SW Poland
113 O14 **Świdnik** Ger. Streckenbach. Lublin, E Poland
112 F8 **Świdwin** Ger. Schivelbein. Koszalin, NW Poland
113 F15 **Świebodzice** Ger. Freiburg in Schlesien, Swiebodzice. Wałbrzych, SW Poland
112 E11 **Świebodzin** Ger. Schwiebus. Zielona Góra, W Poland
Święciany see Švenčionys
112 I9 **Świecie** Ger. Schwertberg. Bydgoszcz, N Poland
9 T16 **Swift Current** Saskatchewan, S Canada
100 K9 **Swifterbant** Flevoland, C Netherlands
191 Q12 **Swifts Creek** Victoria, SE Australia
98 E13 **Swilly, Lough** Ir. Loch Súilí. inlet N Ireland
99 M22 **Swindon** S England, UK
Swinemünde see Świnoujście
112 D8 **Świnoujście** Ger. Swinemünde. Szczecin, NW Poland
Swintsowyy Rudnik see Svintsovyy Rudnik
Świsłocz see Svislach
Swiss Confederation see Switzerland
110 E9 **Switzerland** off. Swiss Confederation, Fr. La Suisse, Ger. Schweiz, It. Svizzera; anc. Helvetia. ◆ federal republic C Europe
99 F17 **Swords** Ir. Sord, Sórd Choluim Chille. E Ireland
20 H13 **Swoyersville** Pennsylvania, NE USA
128 I10 **Syamozera, Ozero** ◎ NW Russian Federation
128 M13 **Syamzha** Vologodskaya Oblast', NW Russian Federation
120 N13 **Syanno** Rus. Senno. Vitsyebskaya Voblasts', NE Belarus
121 K16 **Syarhyeyevichy** Rus. Sergeyevichi. Minskaya Voblasts', C Belarus
128 I12 **Syas'stroy** Leningradskaya Oblast', NW Russian Federation
Sycaminum see Hefa
32 M10 **Sycamore** Illinois, N USA
130 J3 **Sychëvka** Smolenskaya Oblast', W Russian Federation
113 H14 **Syców** Ger. Gross Wartenberg. Kalisz, SW Poland
12 E17 **Sydenham** ≈ Ontario, S Canada
Sydenham Island see Nonouti
191 T9 **Sydney** state capital New South Wales, SE Australia
11 R14 **Sydney** Cape Breton Island, Nova Scotia, SE Canada
Sydney Island see Manra
11 R14 **Sydney Mines** Cape Breton Island, Nova Scotia, SE Canada
Syedlets see Siedlce
Syedpur see Saidpur
121 K18 **Syelishcha** Rus. Selishche. Minskaya Voblasts', C Belarus
121 J18 **Syemyezhava** Rus. Semezhevo. Minskaya Voblasts', C Belarus
Syene see Aswân
119 X6 **Syeverodonets'k** Rus. Severodonetsk. Luhans'ka Oblast', E Ukraine
167 T6 **Syiao Shan** island SE China
102 H11 **Syke** Niedersachsen, NW Germany
96 D10 **Sykkylven** Møre og Romsdal, S Norway
117 F15 **Sykoúri** var. Sikouri; prev. Sikoúrion. Thessalía, C Greece
129 R11 **Syktyvkar** prev. Ust'-Sysol'sk. Respublika Komi, NW Russian Federation
25 Q4 **Sylacauga** Alabama, S USA
Sylarna see Sylene
96 J9 **Sylene** Swe. Sylarna. ▲ Norway/Sweden
159 V14 **Sylhet** Chittagong, NE Bangladesh
102 G6 **Sylt** island NW Germany
23 O10 **Sylva** North Carolina, SE USA
129 V15 **Sylva** ≈ NW Russian Federation
25 W5 **Sylvania** Georgia, SE USA
33 R11 **Sylvania** Ohio, N USA
9 Q15 **Sylvan Lake** Alberta, SW Canada
35 T13 **Sylvan Pass** pass Wyoming, C USA
25 T7 **Sylvester** Georgia, SE USA
27 P6 **Sylvester** Texas, SW USA
8 L11 **Sylvia, Mount** ▲ British Columbia, W Canada
126 Hh12 **Sym** ≈ C Russian Federation
117 N22 **Sými** var. Simi. island Dodekánisos, Greece, Aegean Sea
119 U8 **Synel'nykove** Dnipropetrovs'ka Oblast', E Ukraine
129 U6 **Synya** Respublika Komi, NW Russian Federation
119 P7 **Synyukha** Rus. Sinyukha. ≈ S Ukraine
Syôbara see Shōbara
205 V2 **Syowa** Japanese research station Antarctica
28 H6 **Syracuse** Kansas, C USA
31 S16 **Syracuse** Nebraska, C USA
20 H10 **Syracuse** New York, NE USA
Syracuse see Siracusa
Syrdar'inskaya Oblast' see Sirdaryo Wiloyati
Syrdariya see Syr Darya
150 L14 **Syr Darya** var. Sai Hun, Sir Darya, Syrdarya, Kaz. Syrdariya, Rus. Syrdar'ya, Uzb. Sirdaryo; anc. Jaxartes. ≈ C Asia
153 P10 **Syrdar'ya** Sirdaryo Wiloyati, E Uzbekistan
144 J6 **Syria** off. Syrian Arab Republic, var. Siria, Syrie, Ar. Al-Jumhūrīyah al-'Arabīyah as-Sūrīyah, Sūrīya. ◆ republic SW Asia
144 L9 **Syrian Desert** Ar. Al Hamad, Bādiyat ash Shām. desert SW Asia
Syrie see Syria
117 L22 **Sýrna** var. Sirna. island Kykládes, Greece, Aegean Sea
117 I20 **Sýros** var. Síros. island Kykládes, Greece, Aegean Sea
95 M18 **Sysmä** Mikkeli, S Finland
129 R12 **Sysola** ≈ NW Russian Federation
Syulemeshlii see Sredets
131 S2 **Syumsi** Udmurtskaya Respublika, NW Russian Federation
116 K10 **Syuyutliyka** ≈ C Bulgaria
Syvash, Zaliv see Syvash, Zatoka
119 U12 **Syvash, Zatoka** Rus. Zaliv Syvash. inlet S Ukraine
131 Q6 **Syzran'** Samarskaya Oblast', W Russian Federation
Szabadka see Subotica
113 N21 **Szabolcs-Szatmár-Bereg** off. Szabolcs-Szatmár-Bereg Megye. ◐ county E Hungary
112 G10 **Szamocin** Ger. Samotschin. Piła, W Poland
118 H8 **Szamos** var. Someş, Someşul, Ger. Samosch, Somesch. ≈ Hungary/Romania
Szamosújvár see Gherla
112 G11 **Szamotuły** Poznań, W Poland
Szarkowszczyzna see Sharkawshchyna
113 M24 **Szarvas** Békés, SE Hungary
Szászmagyarós see Măieruş
Szászrégen see Reghin
Szászsebes see Sebeş
Szászváros see Orăştie
Szatmárrnémeti see Satu Mare
Száva see Sava
113 P15 **Szczebrzeszyn** Zamość, SE Poland
112 D9 **Szczecin** Eng./Ger. Stettin. Szczecin, NW Poland
112 D9 **Szczecin** off. Województwo Szczecińskie; prev. Pomorze Zachodnie. ◐ province NW Poland
112 G8 **Szczecinek** Ger. Neustettin. Koszalin, NW Poland
Szczecińskie, Województwo see Szczecin
112 D8 **Szczeciński, Zalew** var. Stettiner Haff, Ger. Oderhaff. bay Germany/Poland
113 K15 **Szczekociny** Częstochowa, S Poland
112 N8 **Szczuczyn** Łomża, NE Poland
Szczuczyn Nowogródzki see Shchuchyn
112 M8 **Szczytno** Ger. Ortelsburg. Olsztyn, NE Poland
Szechuan/Szechwan see Sichuan
113 K21 **Szécsény** Nógrád, N Hungary
113 L25 **Szeged** Ger. Szegedin, Rom. Seghedin. Csongrád, SE Hungary
Szegedin see Szeged
113 N23 **Szeghalom** Békés, SE Hungary
Székelyhid see Săcueni
Székelykeresztúr see Cristuru Secuiesc
113 I23 **Székesfehérvár** Ger. Stuhlweissenberg; anc. Alba Regia. Fejér, W Hungary
Szeklerburg see Miercurea-Ciuc
Szekler Neumarkt see Târgu Secuiesc
113 J25 **Szekszárd** Tolna, S Hungary
Szempcz/Szenc see Senec
Szenice see Senica
Szentágota see Agnita
113 J22 **Szentendre** Ger. Sankt Andrä. Pest, N Hungary
113 L24 **Szentes** Csongrád, SE Hungary
113 F23 **Szentgotthárd** Eng. Saint Gotthard, Ger. Sankt Gotthard. Vas, W Hungary
Szentgyörgy see Đurđevac
Szenttamás see Srbobran
Széphely see Jebel
Szeping see Siping
Szered see Sered'
113 N21 **Szerencs** Borsod-Abaúj-Zemplén, NE Hungary
Szeret see Siret
Szeretfalva see Sărăţel
112 N7 **Szeskie Wzgórza** Ger. Seesker Höhe. hill NE Poland
113 H25 **Szigetvár** Baranya, SW Hungary
Szilágysomlyó see Şimleu Silvaniei
Szinna see Snina
Sziszek see Sisak
Szitás-Keresztúr see Cristuru Secuiesc
113 E15 **Szklarska Poręba** Ger. Schreiberhau. Jelenia Góra, SW Poland
Szkudy see Skuodas
Szlatina see Podravska Slatina
Szlavonia/Szlavonország see Slavonija
Szlovákia see Slovakia
Szluin see Slunj
113 L23 **Szolnok** Jász-Nagykun-Szolnok, C Hungary
Szolyva see Svalyava
113 G23 **Szombathely** Ger. Steinamanger; anc. Sabaria, Savaria. Vas, W Hungary
Szond/Szonta see Sonta
Szováta see Sovata
112 F13 **Szprotawa** Ger. Sprottau. Zielona Góra, W Poland
Sztálinváros see Dunaújváros
Sztrazsó see Strážov
112 J8 **Sztum** Ger. Stuhm. Elbląg, N Poland
112 H10 **Szubin** Ger. Schubin. Bydgoszcz, W Poland
Szucsava see Suceava
Szurduk see Surduc
113 M14 **Szydłowiec** Ger. Schlelau. Radom, C Poland

T

Taalintehdas see Dalsbruk
179 P11 **Taal, Lake** ◎ Luzon, NW Philippines
Taastrup see Tåstrup
113 I24 **Tab** Somogy, W Hungary
179 Q11 **Tabaco** Luzon, N Philippines
194 M7 **Tabalo** Mussau Island, NE PNG
106 K5 **Tábara** Castilla-León, N Spain
195 P9 **Tabar Island** island Tabar Islands, N PNG
195 P9 **Tabar Islands** island group NE PNG
Tabariya, Bahrat see Tiberias, Lake
149 S7 **Ţabas** var. Golshan. Khorāsān, C Iran
45 P15 **Tabasará, Serranía de** ⛰ W Panama
43 U15 **Tabasco** ◐ state SE Mexico
Tabasco see Grijalva, Río
131 Q2 **Tabashino** Respublika Mariy El, W Russian Federation
60 B13 **Tabatinga** Amazonas, N Brazil
76 G9 **Tabelbala** W Algeria
9 Q17 **Taber** Alberta, SW Canada
176 W14 **Taberfane** Pulau Trangan, E Indonesia
97 L19 **Taberg** Jönköping, S Sweden
Tabibuga see Tabibuga
194 H12 **Tabibuga** var. Tabibug. Western Highlands, C PNG
203 O3 **Tabiteuea** prev. Drummond Island. atoll Tungaru, W Kiribati
179 Q12 **Tablas Island** island C Philippines
179 Pp12 **Tablas Strait** strait C Philippines
194 M16 **Table Bay** bay SE PNG
192 Q10 **Table Cape** headland North Island, NZ
11 S13 **Table Mountain** ▲ Newfoundland, Newfoundland and Labrador, E Canada
181 P17 **Table, Pointe de la** headland SE Réunion
29 S8 **Table Rock Lake** ⊡ Arkansas/Missouri, C USA
38 K14 **Table Top** ▲ Arizona, SW USA
194 J13 **Tabletop, Mount** ▲ C PNG
126 Mm5 **Tabor** Respublika Sakha (Yakutiya), NE Russian Federation
31 S15 **Tabor** Iowa, C USA
113 D18 **Tábor** Jižní Čechy, SW Czech Republic
83 F21 **Tabora** Tabora, W Tanzania
83 F21 **Tabora** ◐ region C Tanzania
23 U12 **Tabor City** North Carolina, SE USA
153 Q10 **Taboshar** NW Tajikistan
78 L18 **Tabou** var. Tabu. S Ivory Coast
148 J2 **Tabrīz** var. Tebriz; anc. Tauris. Āžarbāyjān-e Khāvarī, NW Iran
Tabu see Tabou
203 W1 **Tabuaeran** prev. Fanning Island. atoll Line Islands, E Kiribati
194 E11 **Tabubil** Western, SW PNG
179 P8 **Tabuk** Luzon, N Philippines
146 J4 **Tabūk** Tabūk, NW Saudi Arabia
146 J5 **Tabūk** off. Minţaqat Tabūk. ◐ province NW Saudi Arabia
197 B12 **Tabwemasana, Mount** ▲ Espiritu Santo, W Vanuatu
97 O15 **Täby** Stockholm, C Sweden
43 N14 **Tacámbaro** Michoacán de Ocampo, SW Mexico
44 A5 **Tacaná, Volcan** (volcano) Guatemala/Mexico
45 X16 **Tacarcuna, Cerro** ▲ SE Panama
Tachau see Tachov
164 J3 **Tacheng** var. Qoqek. Xinjiang Uygur Zizhiqu, NW China
56 H7 **Táchira** off. Estado Táchira. ◐ state W Venezuela
167 T13 **Tachoshui** N Taiwan
113 A17 **Tachov** Ger. Tachau. Západní Čechy, W Czech Republic
179 R13 **Tacloban** off. Tacloban City. Leyte, C Philippines
59 I19 **Tacna** Tacna, SE Peru
59 H18 **Tacna** off. Departamento de Tacna. ◐ department S Peru
34 H8 **Tacoma** Washington, NW USA
20 L11 **Taconic Range** ⛰ NE USA
64 L6 **Taco Pozo** Formosa, N Argentina
59 M20 **Tacsara, Cordillera de** ⛰ S Bolivia
63 F17 **Tacuarembó** prev. San Fructuoso. Tacuarembó, C Uruguay
63 E18 **Tacuarembó** ◐ department C Uruguay
63 F17 **Tacuarembó, Río** ≈ C Uruguay
85 I14 **Tacuali** North Western, NW Zambia
179 R16 **Tacurong** Mindanao, S Philippines

◆ Country ● Country Capital ◇ Dependent Territory ○ Dependent Territory Capital ◐ Administrative Region ✕ International Airport ▲ Mountain ⛰ Mountain Range (volcano) Volcano ≈ River ◎ Lake ⊡ Reservoir

171 *Kk13* **Tadamu-gawa** ≈ Honshū, C Japan
79 *V8* **Tadek** ≈ NW Niger
76 *J9* **Tademaït, Plateau du** *plateau* C Algeria
197 *K6* **Tadine** Province des Îles Loyauté, E New Caledonia
82 *L11* **Tadjoura** E Djibouti
82 *M11* **Tadjoura, Golfe de** *Eng.* Gulf of Tajura. *inlet* E Djibouti
Tadmor/Tadmur *see* Tudmur
9 *W10* **Tadoule Lake** ◎ Manitoba, C Canada
13 *S8* **Tadoussac** Québec, SE Canada
161 *H18* **Tādpatri** Andhra Pradesh, E India
Tadzhikabad *see* Tojikobod
Tadzhikistan *see* Tajikistan
169 *Y14* **T'aebaek-sanmaek** ▲▲ E South Korea
169 *V15* **Taechŏng-do** *island* NW South Korea
169 *X13* **Taedong-gang** ≈ C North Korea
169 *Y16* **Taegu** *off.* Taegu-gwangyŏksi, *var.* Daegu, *Jap.* Taikyū. SE South Korea
Taehan-haehyŏp *see* Korea Strait
Taehan Min'guk *see* South Korea
169 *Y15* **Taejŏn** *off.* Taejŏn-gwangyŏksi, *Jap.* Taiden. C South Korea
200 *T11* **Tafahi** *island* N Tonga
107 *Q4* **Tafalla** Navarra, N Spain
77 *M12* **Tafassâsset, Oued** ≈ SE Algeria
79 *W7* **Tafassâsset, Ténéré du** *desert* N Niger
57 *U11* **Tafelberg** ▲ S Suriname
99 *J21* **Taff** ≈ SE Wales, UK
Tafila/Ţafīlah, Muḩāfaẓat aţ *see* Aţ Ţafīlah
79 *N15* **Tafiré** N Ivory Coast
148 *M6* **Tafresh** Markazī, W Iran
149 *Q9* **Taft** Yazd, C Iran
37 *R13* **Taft** California, W USA
27 *T14* **Taft** Texas, SW USA
149 *W12* **Taftān, Kūh-e** ▲ SE Iran
37 *R13* **Taft Heights** California, W USA
201 *Y14* **Tafunsak** Kosrae, E Micronesia
198 *Aa8* **Tāga** Savai'i, SW Western Samoa
155 *N3* **Tagāb** Kāpīsā, E Afghanistan
41 *O8* **Tagagawik River** ≈ Alaska, USA
171 *M13* **Tagajō** *var.* Tagazyô. Miyagi, Honshū, C Japan
130 *K12* **Taganrog** Rostovskaya Oblast', SW Russian Federation
130 *K12* **Taganrog, Gulf of** *Rus.* Taganrogskiy Zaliv, *Ukr.* Tahanroz'ka Zatoka. *gulf* Russian Federation/Ukraine
Taganrogskiy Zaliv *see* Taganrog, Gulf of
78 *J8* **Tagant** ◈ *region* C Mauritania
154 *M14* **Tagas** Baluchistān, SW Pakistan
170 *D13* **Tagawa** Fukuoka, Kyūshū, SW Japan
179 *P11* **Tagaytay** Luzon, N Philippines
Tagazyô *see* Tagajō
179 *Qq14* **Tagbilaran** *var.* Tagbilaran City. Bohol, C Philippines
108 *B10* **Taggia** Liguria, NW Italy
79 *V9* **Taghouaji, Massif de** ▲ C Niger
109 *J15* **Tagliacozzo** Lazio, C Italy
108 *J7* **Tagliamento** ≈ NE Italy
179 *R15* **Tagoloan** Mindanao, S Philippines
155 *N3* **Tagow Bāy** *var.* Bai. Sar-e Pol, N Afghanistan
Tagtabazar *see* Takhtabazar
61 *L17* **Taguatinga** Tocantins, C Brazil
195 *Q17* **Tagula** Tagula Island, SE PNG
195 *P17* **Tagula Island** *prev.* Southeast Island, Sudest Island. *island* SE PNG
179 *Rr15* **Tagum** Mindanao, S Philippines
56 *C7* **Tagún, Cerro** *elevation* Colombia/Panama
107 *P7* **Tagus** *Port.* Rio Tejo, *Sp.* Río Tajo. ≈ Portugal/Spain
66 *M9* **Tagus Plain** *undersea feature* E Atlantic Ocean
203 *S10* **Tahaa** *island* Îles Sous le Vent, W French Polynesia
203 *U10* **Tahanea** *atoll* Îles Tuamotu, C French Polynesia
Tahanroz'ka Zatoka *see* Taganrog, Gulf of
171 *I16* **Tahara** Aichi, Honshū, SW Japan
76 *K12* **Tahat** ▲ SE Algeria
169 *V12* **Ta He** ≈ NE China
169 *U4* **Tahe** Heilongjiang, NE China
168 *G9* **Tahilt** Govĭ-Altay, W Mongolia
203 *T10* **Tahiti** *island* Îles du Vent, W French Polynesia
Tahiti, Archipel de *see* Société, Archipel de la
120 *E4* **Tahkuna nina** *headland* W Estonia
154 *K12* **Tāhlāb** ≈ W Pakistan
154 *K12* **Tāhlāb, Dasht-i** *desert* SW Pakistan
29 *R10* **Tahlequah** Oklahoma, C USA
37 *Q6* **Tahoe City** California, W USA
37 *P6* **Tahoe, Lake** ◎ California/Nevada, W USA
Tahoena *see* Tahuna
27 *N6* **Tahoka** Texas, SW USA
34 *F8* **Taholah** Washington, NW USA
79 *T11* **Tahoua** Tahoua, W Niger
79 *T11* **Tahoua** ◈ *department* W Niger
33 *P3* **Tahquamenon Falls** *waterfall* Michigan, N USA
33 *P4* **Tahquamenon River** ≈ Michigan, N USA
145 *V10* **Taḩrīr** S Iraq
8 *K17* **Tahsis** Vancouver Island, British Columbia, SW Canada
Tahta *see* Takhta
77 *W9* **Ṭahta** C Egypt
142 *L15* **Tahtalı Dağları** ▲▲ C Turkey
59 *I14* **Tahuamanu, Río** ≈ Bolivia/Peru
58 *F13* **Tahuanía, Río** ≈ E Peru
203 *X7* **Tahuata** *island* Îles Marquises, NE French Polynesia
175 *S6* **Tahulandang, Pulau** *island* N Indonesia
175 *S5* **Tahuna** *prev.* Tahoena. Pulau Sangihe, N Indonesia
176 *Yy10* **Tahun, Danau** *see* Tahun, Danau
78 *L17* **Taï** SW Ivory Coast
167 *P5* **Tai'an** Shandong, E China
203 *R8* **Taiarapu, Presqu'île de** *peninsula* Tahiti, W French Polynesia
Taibad *see* Tāybād
166 *K7* **Taibai Shan** ▲ C China
107 *Q12* **Taibilla, Sierra de** ▲▲ S Spain
169 *Q12* **Taibus Qi** *var.* Baochang. Nei Mongol Zizhiqu, N China
Taichū *see* T'aichung
167 *S13* **T'aichung** *Jap.* Taichū; *prev.* Taiwan. C Taiwan
Taiden *see* Taejŏn
193 *E23* **Taieri** ≈ South Island, NZ
117 *E21* **Taïgetos** ▲▲ S Greece
167 *N4* **Taihang Shan** ▲▲ C China
192 *M11* **Taihape** Manawatu-Wanganui, North Island, NZ
167 *O7* **Taihe** Anhui, E China
167 *O12* **Taihe** Jiangxi, S China
Taihoku *see* T'aipei
167 *R8* **Tai Hu** ◎ E China
167 *P9* **Taihu** Anhui, E China
167 *O6* **Taikang** Henan, C China
172 *P7* **Taiki** Hokkaidō, NE Japan
177 *Ff8* **Taikkyi** Yangon, SW Myanmar
Taikyū *see* Taegu
169 *U8* **Tailai** Heilongjiang, NE China
173 *Ff10* **Taileleo** Pulau Siberut, W Indonesia
190 *J10* **Tailem Bend** South Australia
98 *I8* **Tain** N Scotland, UK
167 *S14* **T'ainan** *Jap.* Tainan; *prev.* Dainan. S Taiwan
117 *E22* **Taínaro, Ákra** *headland* S Greece
167 *Q11* **Taining** Fujian, SE China
203 *W7* **Taiohae** *prev.* Madisonville. Nuku Hiva, NE French Polynesia
167 *T13* **T'aipei** *Jap.* Taihoku; *prev.* Daihoku. ● (Taiwan) N Taiwan
174 *Gg3* **Taiping** Perak, Peninsular Malaysia
169 *S8* **Taiping Ling** ▲ NE China
172 *N6* **Taisei** Hokkaidō, NE Japan
170 *F12* **Taisha** Shimane, Honshū, SW Japan
111 *R4* **Taiskirchen** Oberösterreich, NW Austria
65 *F20* **Taitao, Peninsula de** *peninsula* S Chile
Taitō *see* T'aitung
167 *T14* **T'aitung** *Jap.* Taitō. S Taiwan
94 *M13* **Taivalkoski** Oulu, E Finland
95 *K19* **Taivassalo** Turku-Pori, SW Finland
167 *T14* **Taiwan** *off.* Republic of China, *var.* Formosa, Formo'sa. ◆ *republic* E Asia
140 *Q11* **Taiwan** *var.* Formosa. *island* E Asia
Taiwan *see* T'aichung
T'aiwan Haihsia/Taiwan Haixia *see* Taiwan Strait
Taiwan Shan *see* Chungyang Shanmo
167 *R13* **Taiwan Strait** *var.* Formosa Strait, *Chin.* T'aiwan Haihsia, Taiwan Haixia. *strait* China/Taiwan
167 *N4* **Taiyuan** *prev.* T'ai-yuan, T'ai-yüan, Yangku. Shanxi, C China
167 *R7* **Taizhou** Jiangsu, E China
Taizhou *see* Linhai
147 *O16* **Ta'izz** SW Yemen
147 *O16* **Ta'izz** ✕ SW Yemen
77 *P12* **Tajarhī** SW Libya
153 *P13* **Tajikistan** *off.* Republic of Tajikistan, *Rus.* Tadzhikistan, *Taj.* Jumhurii Tojikiston; *prev.* Tajik S.S.R. ◆ *republic* C Asia
Tajik S.S.R *see* Tajikistan
171 *Kk14* **Tajima** Fukushima, Honshū, C Japan
Tajoe *see* Tayu
Tajo, Río *see* Tagus
44 *B5* **Tajumulco, Volcán** ▲ W Guatemala
107 *P7* **Tajuña** ≈ C Spain
Tajura, Gulf of *see* Tadjoura, Golfe de
178 *H9* **Tak** *var.* Rahaeng. Tak, W Thailand
201 *U4* **Taka Atoll** *var.* Tōke. *atoll* Ratak Chain, N Marshall Islands
171 *L16* **Takahagi** Ibaraki, Honshū, S Japan
170 *Ff13* **Takahashi** *var.* Takahasi. Okayama, Honshū, SW Japan
170 *F13* **Takahashi-gawa** ≈ Honshū, SW Japan
Takahasi *see* Takahashi
201 *P12* **Takaieu Island** *island* E Micronesia
192 *I13* **Takaka** Tasman, South Island, NZ
175 *P13* **Takalar** Sulawesi, C Indonesia
170 *Ff14* **Takamatsu** *var.* Takamatu. Kagawa, Shikoku, SW Japan
Takamatu *see* Takamatsu
170 *Cc14* **Takamori** Kumamoto, Kyūshū, SW Japan
170 *Cc16* **Takanabe** Miyazaki, Kyūshū, SW Japan
175 *O16* **Takan, Gunung** ▲ Pulau Sumba, S Indonesia
171 *M9* **Takanosu** Akita, Honshū, C Japan
Takao *see* Kaohsiung
171 *Ii13* **Takaoka** Toyama, Honshū, SW Japan
192 *N12* **Takapau** Hawke's Bay, North Island, NZ
203 *U9* **Takapoto** *atoll* Îles Tuamotu, C French Polynesia
192 *L5* **Takapuna** Auckland, North Island, NZ
171 *Gg14* **Takarazuka** Hyōgo, Honshū, SW Japan
203 *U9* **Takaroa** *atoll* Îles Tuamotu, C French Polynesia
171 *Jj15* **Takasaki** Gunma, Honshū, S Japan
171 *Gg15* **Takatsuki** *var.* Takatuki. Ōsaka, Honshū, SW Japan
Takatuki *see* Takatsuki
171 *Ii14* **Takayama** Gifu, Honshū, SW Japan
171 *Hh13* **Takefu** *var.* Takehu. Fukui, Honshū, SW Japan
170 *F14* **Takehara** Hiroshima, Honshū, SW Japan
Takehu *see* Takefu
170 *C13* **Takeo** Saga, Kyūshū, SW Japan
Takeo *see* Takêv
170 *B17* **Take-shima** *island* Nansei-shotō, SW Japan
148 *M5* **Tākestān** *var.* Takistan; *prev.* Siadehan. Zanjān, W Iran
170 *D14* **Taketa** Ōita, Kyūshū, SW Japan
178 *J14* **Takêv** *prev.* Takeo. Takêv, S Cambodia
178 *Hh10* **Tak Fah** Nakhon Sawan, C Thailand
145 *T13* **Takhādīd** *well* S Iraq
155 *R3* **Takhār** ◈ *province* NE Afghanistan
Takhiatash *see* Takhiatosh
152 *H8* **Takhiatosh** *Rus.* Takhiatash. Qoraqalpoghiston Respublikasi, W Uzbekistan
178 *J13* **Ta Khmau** Kândal, S Cambodia
152 *H9* **Takhta** *Turkm.* Tahta. Dashkhovuzskiy Velayat, N Turkmenistan
152 *J16* **Takhtabazar** *var.* Tagtabazar. Maryyskiy Velayat, S Turkmenistan
151 *O8* **Takhtabrod** Kokshetau, N Kazakhstan
152 *H7* **Takhtakŭpir** *Rus.* Takhtakupyr. Qoraqalpoghiston Respublikasi, NW Uzbekistan
Takhtakupyr *see* Takhtakŭpir
148 *M8* **Takht-e Shāh, Kūh-e** ▲ C Iran
79 *V12* **Takiéta** Zinder, S Niger
15 *I5* **Takijuq Lake** ◎ Northwest Territories, NW Canada
172 *P4* **Takikawa** Hokkaidō, NE Japan
172 *Pp4* **Takinoue** Hokkaidō, NE Japan
Takistan *see* Tākestān
193 *B23* **Takitimu Mountains** ▲▲ South Island, NZ
Takkaze *see* Tekezē
172 *N10* **Takko** Aomori, Honshū, C Japan
8 *L13* **Takla Lake** ◎ British Columbia, SW Canada
Takla Makan Desert *see* Taklimakan Shamo
164 *H9* **Taklimakan Shamo** *Eng.* Takla Makan Desert. *desert* NW China
178 *Jj12* **Takôk** Môndól Kiri, E Cambodia
175 *P9* **Takolekaju, Pegunungan** ▲▲ Sulawesi, N Indonesia
41 *P10* **Takotna** Alaska, USA
Takow *see* Kaohsiung
126 *Kk14* **Taksimo** Respublika Buryatiya, S Russian Federation
170 *Cc13* **Taku** Saga, Kyūshū, SW Japan
8 *I10* **Taku** ≈ British Columbia, W Canada
177 *G15* **Takua Pa** *var.* Ban Takua Pa. Phangnga, SW Thailand
79 *W16* **Takum** Taraba, E Nigeria
203 *V10* **Takume** *atoll* Îles Tuamotu, C French Polynesia
202 *L16* **Takutea** *island* S Cook Islands
195 *U11* **Takuu Islands** *prev.* Mortlock Group. *island group* NE PNG
121 *L18* **Tal'** *Rus.* Tal'. Minskaya Voblasts', S Belarus
42 *L13* **Tala** Jalisco, C Mexico
63 *F19* **Tala** Canelones, S Uruguay
Talabriga *see* Aveiro, Portugal
Talabriga *see* Talavera de la Reina, Spain
121 *N14* **Talachyn** *Rus.* Tolochin. Vitsyebskaya Voblasts', NE Belarus
155 *U7* **Talagang** Punjab, E Pakistan
161 *J23* **Talaimannar** Northern Province, NW Sri Lanka
119 *R3* **Talalayivka** Chernihivs'ka Oblast', N Ukraine
45 *O15* **Talamanca, Cordillera de** ▲▲ S Costa Rica
58 *A9* **Talara** Piura, NW Peru
106 *L11* **Talarrubias** Extremadura, W Spain
153 *S8* **Talas** Talasskaya Oblast', NW Kyrgyzstan
153 *S8* **Talas** ≈ NW Kyrgyzstan
195 *N11* **Talasea** New Britain, E PNG
Talas Oblasty *see* Talasskaya Oblast'
153 *S8* **Talasskaya Oblast'** *Kir.* Talas Oblasty. ◈ *province* NW Kyrgyzstan
153 *S8* **Talasskiy Alatau, Khrebet** ▲▲ Kazakhstan/Kyrgyzstan
Talat *see* Maha Sarakham
79 *U12* **Talata Mafara** Sokoto, N Nigeria
175 *Ss4* **Talaud, Kepulauan** *island group* E Indonesia
106 *M9* **Talavera de la Reina** *anc.* Caesarobriga, Talabriga. Castilla-La Mancha, C Spain
106 *J11* **Talavera la Real** Extremadura, W Spain
194 *L12* **Talawe, Mount** ▲ New Britain, C PNG
25 *S5* **Talbotton** Georgia, SE USA
191 *R7* **Talbragar River** ≈ New South Wales, SE Australia
64 *G13* **Talca** Maule, C Chile
64 *F13* **Talcahuano** Bío Bío, C Chile
160 *N12* **Tālcher** Orissa, E India
27 *W5* **Talco** Texas, SW USA
151 *V14* **Taldykorgan** *Kaz.* Taldyqorghan; *prev.* Taldy-Kurgan. Taldykorgan, SE Kazakhstan
151 *U13* **Taldykorgan** *off.* Taldykorganskaya Oblast'; *prev.* Taldy-Kurganskaya Oblast'. ◈ *province* SE Kazakhstan
Taldykorganskaya Oblast'/Taldy-Kurgan/ Taldy-Kurganskaya Oblast'/Taldyqorghan *see* Taldykorgan
153 *Y7* **Taldy-Suu** Issyk-Kul'skaya Oblast', E Kyrgyzstan
153 *U10* **Taldy-Suu** Oshskaya Oblast', SW Kyrgyzstan
Tal-e Khosravī *see* Yāsūj
200 *Ss14* **Taleki Tonga** *island* Otu Tolu Group, C Tonga
200 *Ss13* **Taleki Vavu'u** *island* Otu Tolu Group, C Tonga
104 *J13* **Talence** Gironde, SW France
151 *U16* **Talgar** *Kaz.* Talghar. Almaty, SE Kazakhstan
Talghar *see* Talgar
175 *Rr10* **Taliabu, Pulau** *island* Kepulauan Sula, C Indonesia
117 *L22* **Taliarós, Ákra** *headland* Astypálaia, Kykládes, Greece, Aegean Sea
Ta-lien *see* Dalian
29 *Q12* **Talihina** Oklahoma, C USA
Talimardzhan *see* Tollimarjon
Talin *see* T'alin
143 *T12* **T'alin** *Rus.* Talin; *prev.* Verin T'alin. W Armenia
83 *E15* **Tali Post** Bahr el Gabel, S Sudan
Taliq-an *see* Tāloqān
Talış Dağları *see* Talish Mountains
148 *L2* **Talish Mountains** *Az.* Talış Dağları, *Per.* Kūhhā-ye Ţavālesh, *Rus.* Talyshskiye Gory. ▲▲ Azerbaijan/Iran
125 *F11* **Talitsa** Sverdlovskaya Oblast', C Russian Federation
175 *O16* **Taliwang** Sumbawa, C Indonesia
121 *L17* **Tal'ka** *Rus.* Tal'ka. Minskaya Voblasts', C Belarus
Talkang *see* Dorbod
41 *R11* **Talkeetna** Alaska, USA
41 *R11* **Talkeetna Mountains** ▲▲ Alaska, USA
Talkhof *see* Puurmani
94 *H2* **Tálknafjördhur** Vestfirdhir, W Iceland
145 *Q3* **Tall 'Abţah** N Iraq
144 *M2* **Tall Abyaḑ** *var.* Tell Abiad. Ar Raqqah, N Syria
25 *Q4* **Talladega** Alabama, S USA
145 *Q2* **Tall 'Afar** N Iraq
25 *S8* **Tallahassee** *prev.* Muskogean. *state capital* Florida, SE USA
24 *L2* **Tallahatchie River** ≈ Mississippi, S USA
Tall al Abyaḑ *see* At Tall al Abyaḑ
145 *W12* **Tall al Laḩm** S Iraq
191 *P11* **Tallangatta** Victoria, SE Australia
25 *R4* **Tallapoosa River** ≈ Alabama/Georgia, S USA
105 *T13* **Tallard** Hautes-Alpes, SE France
145 *Q3* **Tall ash Sha'īr** N Iraq
25 *Q5* **Tallassee** Alabama, S USA
145 *R4* **Tall 'Azbah** NW Iraq
144 *I5* **Tall Bīsah** Ḩimş, W Syria
145 *R3* **Tall Ḩassūnah** N Iraq
145 *Q2* **Tall Ḩuqnah** *var.* Tell Huqnah. N Iraq
Tallin *see* Tallinn
120 *G3* **Tallinn** *Ger.* Reval, *Rus.* Tallin; *prev.* Revel. ● (Estonia) Harjumaa, NW Estonia
120 *H3* **Tallinn** ✕ Harjumaa, NW Estonia
144 *H5* **Tall Kalakh** *var.* Tell Kalakh. Ḩimş, C Syria
145 *R2* **Tall Kayf** NW Iraq
Tall Kūchak *see* Tall Kūshik
145 *X3* **Tall Kūshik** *var.* Tall Kūchak. Al Ḩasakah, E Syria
33 *U12* **Tallmadge** Ohio, N USA
24 *J5* **Tallulah** Louisiana, S USA
145 *Q2* **Tall 'Uwaynāt** NW Iraq
145 *Q2* **Tall Ẓāhir** N Iraq
126 *H14* **Tal'menka** Altayskiy Kray, S Russian Federation
126 *I8* **Talnakh** Taymyrskiy (Dolgano-Nenetskiy) Avtonomnyy Okrug, N Russian Federation
119 *P7* **Tal'ne** *Rus.* Tal'noye. Cherkas'ka Oblast', C Ukraine
Tal'noye *see* Tal'ne
82 *E12* **Talodi** Southern Kordofan, C Sudan
196 *B16* **Talofofo** SE Guam
196 *B16* **Talofofo Bay** *bay* SE Guam
28 *L9* **Taloga** Oklahoma, C USA
127 *O10* **Talon** Magadanskaya Oblast', E Russian Federation
12 *H11* **Talon, Lake** ◎ Ontario, S Canada
155 *R2* **Tāloqān** *var.* Taliq-an. Takhār, NE Afghanistan
130 *M8* **Talovaya** Voronezhskaya Oblast', W Russian Federation
175 *Qq10* **Talowa, Teluk** *bay* Sulawesi, C Indonesia
15 *Kk3* **Taloyoak** *prev.* Spence Bay. Northwest Territories, N Canada
27 *Q8* **Talpa** Texas, SW USA
42 *K13* **Talpa de Allende** Jalisco, C Mexico
25 *S9* **Talquin, Lake** ⊟ Florida, SE USA
Talsen *see* Talsi
168 *H9* **Talshand** Govĭ-Altay, C Mongolia
120 *E8* **Talsi** *Ger.* Talsen. Talsi, NW Latvia
149 *V11* **Tal Sīāh** Sīstān va Balūchestān, SE Iran
64 *G6* **Taltal** Antofagasta, N Chile
15 *I8* **Taltson** ≈ Northwest Territories, NW Canada
174 *H8* **Taluk** Sumatera, W Indonesia
94 *J8* **Talvik** Finnmark, N Norway
190 *M7* **Talyawalka Creek** ≈ New South Wales, SE Australia
Talyshskiye Gory *see* Talish Mountains
31 *W14* **Tama** Iowa, C USA
Tama Abu, Banjaran *see* Penambo, Banjaran
175 *N5* **Tamabo, Banjaran** ▲▲ East Malaysia
202 *B16* **Tamakautoga** SW Niue
131 *N7* **Tamala** Penzenskaya Oblast', W Russian Federation
79 *P15* **Tamale** C Ghana
170 *Cc13* **Tamana** Kumamoto, Kyūshū, SW Japan
203 *P3* **Tamana** *prev.* Rotcher Island. *atoll* Tungaru, W Kiribati
170 *Ff14* **Tamano** Okayama, Honshū, SW Japan
76 *K12* **Tamanrasset** *var.* Tamenghest. S Algeria
76 *J13* **Tamanrasset** *wadi* Algeria/ Mali
177 *G2* **Tamanthi** Sagaing, N Myanmar
99 *I24* **Tamar** ≈ SW England, UK
Tamar *see* Tudmur
56 *H9* **Támara** Casanare, C Colombia
56 *F7* **Tamar, Alto de** ▲ C Colombia
181 *X16* **Tamarin** E Mauritius
107 *T5* **Tamarite de Litera** *var.* Tararite de Llitera. Aragón, NE Spain
113 *I24* **Tamási** Tolna, S Hungary
Tamatave *see* Toamasina
43 *O9* **Tamaulipas** ◈ *state* C Mexico
43 *P10* **Tamaulipas, Sierra de** ▲ C Mexico
58 *F12* **Tamaya, Río** ≈ E Peru
42 *I9* **Tamazula** Durango, C Mexico
42 *L14* **Tamazula** Jalisco, C Mexico
Tamazulápam *see* Tamazulapán
43 *Q15* **Tamazulapán** *var.* Tamazulápam. Oaxaca, SE Mexico
43 *P12* **Tamazunchale** San Luis Potosí, C Mexico
78 *H11* **Tambacounda** SE Senegal
85 *M16* **Tambara** Manica, C Mozambique
175 *Pp9* **Tambarana** Sulawesi, N Indonesia
79 *T13* **Tambawel** Sokoto, NW Nigeria
195 *W15* **Tambea** Guadalcanal, C Solomon Islands
174 *Jj7* **Tambelan, Kepulauan** *island group* W Indonesia
59 *E15* **Tambo de Mora** Ica, W Peru
63 *E17* **Tambores** Paysandú, W Uruguay
59 *F14* **Tambo, Río** ≈ C Peru
58 *F7* **Tamboryacu, Río** ≈ N Peru
130 *M7* **Tambov** Tambovskaya Oblast', W Russian Federation
130 *L6* **Tambovskaya Oblast'** ◈ *province* W Russian Federation
106 *H3* **Tambre** ≈ NW Spain
175 *Nn3* **Tambunan** Sabah, East Malaysia
83 *C15* **Tambura** Western Equatoria, SW Sudan
175 *P8* **Tambu, Teluk** *bay* Sulawesi, C Indonesia
Tâmchaket *see* Tâmchekket
78 *J9* **Tâmchekket** *var.* Tâmchaket. Hodh el Gharbi, S Mauritania
178 *Jj7* **Tam Điệp** Ninh Binh, N Vietnam
Tamdybulak *see* Tomdibuloq
56 *H8* **Tame** Arauca, C Colombia
106 *H6* **Tâmega, Rio** *Sp.* Río Támega. ≈ Portugal/Spain
117 *H20* **Tamélos, Ákra** *headland* Kéa, Kykládes, Greece, Aegean Sea
Tamenghest *see* Tamanrasset
79 *V8* **Tamgak, Adrar** ▲ C Niger
78 *I13* **Tamgue** ▲ NW Guinea
43 *Q12* **Tamiahua** Veracruz-Llave, E Mexico
43 *Q12* **Tamiahua, Laguna de** *lagoon* E Mexico
25 *Y16* **Tamiami Canal** *canal* Florida, SE USA
196 *F17* **Tamil Harbor** *harbor* Yap, W Micronesia
161 *H21* **Tamil Nādu** *prev.* Madras. ◈ *state* SE India
101 *H20* **Tamines** Namur, S Belgium
118 *E12* **Tamiš** *Ger.* Temesch, *Hung.* Temes, *SCr.* Tamiš. ≈ Romania/Yugoslavia
178 *Kk10* **Tam Ky** Quang Nam-Đa Nẵng, C Vietnam
Tammerfors *see* Tampere
Tammisaari *see* Ekenäs
97 *N14* **Tämnaren** ◎ C Sweden
203 *Q7* **Tamotoe, Passe** *passage* Tahiti, W French Polynesia
25 *V12* **Tampa** Florida, SE USA
25 *V12* **Tampa** ✕ Florida, SE USA
25 *V13* **Tampa Bay** *bay* Florida, SE USA
95 *L18* **Tampere** *Swe.* Tammerfors. Häme, SW Finland
43 *Q11* **Tampico** Tamaulipas, C Mexico
175 *Qq12* **Tampo** Pulau Muna, C Indonesia
178 *Kk11* **Tam Quan** Binh Đinh, C Vietnam
176 *V9* **Tamrau, Pegunungan** ▲▲ Irian Jaya, E Indonesia
168 *J13* **Tamsag Muchang** Nei Mongol Zizhiqu, N China
Tamsal *see* Tamsalu
120 *I4* **Tamsalu** *Ger.* Tamsal. Lääne-Virumaa, NE Estonia
111 *S8* **Tamsweg** Salzburg, SW Austria
177 *Ff3* **Tamu** Sagaing, N Myanmar
43 *P12* **Tamuín** San Luis Potosí, C Mexico
196 *C15* **Tamuning** NW Guam
191 *T6* **Tamworth** New South Wales, SE Australia
99 *M19* **Tamworth** C England, UK
94 *L8* **Tana** Finnmark, N Norway
94 *M8* **Tana** *var.* Tenojoki, *Fin.* Teno, *Lapp.* Dealnu. ≈ Finland/Norway *see also* Teno
83 *K19* **Tana** ≈ SE Kenya
170 *G17* **Tanabe** Wakayama, Honshū, SW Japan
41 *T10* **Tanacross** Alaska, USA
94 *L7* **Tanafjorden** *fjord* N Norway
40 *G17* **Tanaga Island** *island* Aleutian Islands, Alaska, USA
40 *G17* **Tanaga Volcano** ▲ Tanaga Island, Alaska, USA
109 *M18* **Tanagro** ≈ S Italy
82 *H11* **T'ana Hāyk'** *Eng.* Lake Tana. ◎ NW Ethiopia
173 *F8* **Tanahbela, Pulau** *island* Kepulauan Batu, W Indonesia
175 *Pp15* **Tanahjampea, Pulau** *island* W Indonesia
173 *Ff8* **Tanahmasa, Pulau** *island* Kepulauan Batu, W Indonesia
Tanais *see* Don
158 *L10* **Tanakpur** Uttar Pradesh, N India
Tana, Lake *see* T'ana Hāyk'
189 *P5* **Tanami Desert** *desert* Northern Territory, N Australia
178 *Jj14* **Tân An** Long An, S Vietnam
41 *Q9* **Tanana** Alaska, USA
Tananarive *see* Antananarivo
41 *Q9* **Tanana River** ≈ Alaska, USA
97 *C16* **Tananger** Rogaland, S Norway
196 *H5* **Tanapag** Saipan, S Northern Mariana Islands
196 *H5* **Tanapag, Puetton** *bay* Saipan, S Northern Mariana Islands
108 *C9* **Tanaro** ≈ N Italy
169 *Y12* **Tanch'ŏn** E North Korea
42 *M14* **Tancitaro, Cerro** ⊼ C Mexico
159 *N12* **Tānda** Uttar Pradesh, N India
79 *O15* **Tanda** E Ivory Coast
179 *Rr14* **Tandag** Mindanao, S Philippines
118 *L14* **Ţăndărei** Ialomiţa, SE Romania
65 *N14* **Tandil** Buenos Aires, E Argentina
80 *H12* **Tandjilé** *off.* Préfecture du Tandjilé. ◈ *prefecture* SW Chad
Tandjoeng *see* Tanjung
Tandjoengpandan *see* Tanjungpandan
Tandjoengpinang *see* Tanjungpinang
Tandjoengredeb *see* Tanjungredeb
155 *Q16* **Tando Allāhyār** Sind, SE Pakistan
155 *Q17* **Tando Bāgo** Sind, SE Pakistan
155 *Q16* **Tando Muhammad Khān** Sind, SE Pakistan
190 *L7* **Tandou Lake** *seasonal lake* New South Wales, SE Australia
96 *L11* **Tandsjöborg** Gävleborg, C Sweden
161 *H15* **Tāndūr** Andhra Pradesh, C India
170 *Bb17* **Tanega-shima** *island* Nansei-shotō, SW Japan
172 *N10* **Taneichi** Iwate, Honshū, C Japan
Tanen Taunggyi *see* Tane Range
178 *H8* **Tane Range** *Bur.* Tanen Taunggyi. ▲▲ W Thailand
113 *P15* **Tanew** ≈ SE Poland
23 *W2* **Taneytown** Maryland, NE USA
76 *H12* **Tanezrouft** *desert* Algeria/Mali
144 *L7* **Ţanf, Jabal aţ** ▲ SE Syria
83 *J20* **Tanga** Tanga, E Tanzania
83 *I22* **Tanga** ◈ *region* E Tanzania
159 *T14* **Tangail** Dhaka, C Bangladesh
195 *Q9* **Tanga Islands** *island group* NE PNG
161 *K26* **Tangalla** Southern Province, S Sri Lanka
Tanganyika and Zanzibar *see* Tanzania
70 *J13* **Tanganyika, Lake** ◎ E Africa
58 *E7* **Tangarana, Río** ≈ N Peru
195 *W16* **Tangarare** Guadalcanal, C Solomon Islands
203 *V16* **Tangaroa, Maunga** ⊼ Easter Island, Chile, E Pacific Ocean
76 *G5* **Tanger** *var.* Tangiers, Tangier, *Fr./Ger.* Tangerk, *Sp.* Tánger; *anc.* Tingis. NW Morocco
174 *J14* **Tangerang** Jawa, C Indonesia
Tangerk *see* Tanger
102 *M12* **Tangermünde** Sachsen-Anhalt, C Germany
162 *K10* **Tanggula Shan** *var.* Dangla, Tangla Range. ▲▲ W China
165 *N13* **Tanggula Shan** ▲ W China
Tanggulashan *see* Tuotuoheyan
162 *K10* **Tanggula Shankou** *pass* W China
167 *N7* **Tanghe** Henan, C China
155 *T5* **Tangi** North-West Frontier Province, NW Pakistan
Tangier *see* Tanger
23 *Y5* **Tangier Island** *island* Virginia, NE USA
Tangiers *see* Tanger
24 *K8* **Tangipahoa River** ≈ Louisiana, S USA
Tangla Range *see* Tanggula Shan
171 *H13* **Tango-hantō** *peninsula* Honshū, SW Japan
162 *I10* **Tangra Yumco** *var.* Tangro Tso. ◎ W China
Tangro Tso *see* Tangra Yumco
163 *T7* **Tangshan** *var.* T'ang-shan. Hebei, E China
179 *Qq15* **Tangub** *var.* Tangub City. Mindanao, S Philippines
79 *R14* **Tanguiéta** NW Benin
169 *X7* **Tangwang He** ≈ NE China
169 *X7* **Tangyuan** Heilongjiang, NE China
94 *M11* **Tanhua** Lappi, N Finland
176 *Uu16* **Tanimbar, Kepulauan** *island group* Maluku, E Indonesia
Tanintharyi *see* Tenasserim
145 *U4* **Tānjarō** ≈ E Iraq
133 *T15* **Tanjong Piai** *headland* Peninsular Malaysia
Tanjore *see* Thanjāvūr
175 *N10* **Tanjung** *prev.* Tandjoeng. Borneo, C Indonesia
175 *Oo6* **Tanjungbatu** Borneo, N Indonesia
Tanjungkarang *see* Bandarlampung
174 *J11* **Tanjunglabu** Pulau Lepar, W Indonesia
174 *J10* **Tanjungpandan** *prev.* Tandjoengpandan. Pulau Belitung, W Indonesia
174 *I7* **Tanjungpinang** *prev.* Tandjoengpinang. Pulau Bintan, W Indonesia
175 *O6* **Tanjungredeb** *var.* Tanjungredep; *prev.* Tandjoengredeb. Borneo, C Indonesia
Tanjungredep *see* Tanjungredeb
155 *S8* **Tank** North-West Frontier Province, NW Pakistan
197 *D16* **Tanna** *island* S Vanuatu
95 *F17* **Tännäs** Jämtland, C Sweden
Tannenhof *see* Krynica
110 *K7* **Tannheim** Tirol, W Austria
Tannu-Tuva *see* Tyva, Respublika
175 *Rr10* **Tano** Pulau Taliabu, E Indonesia
79 *O17* **Tano** ≈ S Ghana
158 *D10* **Tanot** Rājasthān, NW India
79 *V11* **Tanout** Zinder, C Niger
43 *P12* **Tanquián** San Luis Potosí, C Mexico
79 *R13* **Tansarga** E Burkina
178 *Jj14* **Tan Son Nhat** ✕ (Hồ Chí Minh) Tây Ninh, S Vietnam
77 *V8* **Tanta** *var.* Tantā, Tantâ. N Egypt
76 *D9* **Tan-Tan** SW Morocco
43 *P12* **Tantoyuca** Veracruz-Llave, E Mexico
158 *J12* **Tāntpur** Uttar Pradesh, N India
Tan-tung *see* Dandong
40 *M12* **Tanunak** Alaska, USA
177 *Ff5* **Ta-nyaung** Magwe, W Myanmar
178 *J5* **Tân Yên** Tuyên Quang, N Vietnam
83 *F22* **Tanzania** *off.* United Republic of Tanzania, *Swa.* Jamhuri ya Muungano wa Tanzania; *prev.* German East Africa, Tanganyika and Zanzibar. ◆ *republic* E Africa
Tanzania, Jamhuri ya Muungano wa *see* Tanzania
169 *U9* **Tao'an** *var.* Taoan, Taonan. Jilin, NE China
169 *T8* **Tao'er He** ≈ NE China
165 *U11* **Tao He** ≈ C China
T'aon-an *see* Baicheng
Taongi *see* Bokaak Atoll
109 *M23* **Taormina** *anc.* Tauromenium. Sicilia, Italy, C Mediterranean Sea
39 *S9* **Taos** New Mexico, SW USA
Taoudenit *see* Taoudenni
79 *O6* **Taoudenni** *var.* Taoudenit. Tombouctou, N Mali
76 *G6* **Taounate** N Morocco
167 *S13* **T'aoyüan** *Jap.* Tōen. N Taiwan
120 *I3* **Tapa** *Ger.* Taps. Lääne-Virumaa, NE Estonia
43 *V17* **Tapachula** Chiapas, SE Mexico
Tapaiu *see* Gvardeysk
61 *H14* **Tapajós, Rio** *var.* Tapajóz. ≈ NW Brazil
Tapajóz *see* Tapajós, Rio
63 *C21* **Tapalqué** *var.* Tapalquén. Buenos Aires, E Argentina
Tapalquén *see* Tapalqué
Tapanahoni *see* Tapanahony Rivier
57 *W11* **Tapanahony Rivier** *var.* Tapanahoni. ≈ E Suriname
43 *T16* **Tapanatepec** *var.* San Pedro Tapanatepec. Oaxaca, SE Mexico
193 *D23* **Tapanui** Otago, South Island, NZ
Tapanuli, Teluk *see* Sibolga, Teluk
61 *E14* **Tapauá** Amazonas, N Brazil
49 *R7* **Tapauá, Rio** ≈ W Brazil
193 *I14* **Tapawera** Tasman, South Island, NZ
63 *I16* **Tapes** Rio Grande do Sul, S Brazil
78 *K16* **Tapeta** C Liberia
160 *H11* **Tāpi** *prev.* Tāpti. ≈ W India
106 *J2* **Tapia de Casariego** Asturias, N Spain
58 *F10* **Tapiche, Río** ≈ N Peru
178 *Gg15* **Tapi, Mae Nam** *var.* Luang. ≈ SW Thailand
194 *K14* **Tapini** Central, S PNG
Tapirapecó, Serra *see* Tapirapecó, Sierra
57 *N13* **Tapirapecó, Sierra** *Port.* Serra Tapirapecó. ▲▲ Brazil/Venezuela
79 *R13* **Tapoa** ≈ Benin/Niger

◆ Country ● Country Capital ◆ Country ● Country Capital ◇ Dependent Territory ○ Dependent Territory Capital ◈ Administrative Region ✕ International Airport ▲ Mountain ▲▲ Mountain Range ⊼ Volcano ≈ River ◎ Lake ⊟ Reservoir

196 H5 **Tapochau, Mount** ▲ Saipan, S Northern Mariana Islands
113 H24 **Tapolca** Veszprém, W Hungary
23 X5 **Tappahannock** Virginia, NE USA
33 U13 **Tappan Lake** ⊡ Ohio, N USA
171 Mm7 **Tappi-zaki** *headland* Honshū, C Japan
Taps *see* Tapa
Tāpti *see* Tāpi
193 J16 **Tapuaenuku** ▲ South Island, NZ
179 Pp17 **Tapul Group** *island group* Sulu Archipelago, SW Philippines
60 E11 **Tapurmcuará** *var.* Tapuruquara. Amazonas, NW Brazil
Tapuruquara *see* Tapurmcuará
198 C9 **Taputapu, Cape** *headland* Tutuila, W American Samoa
147 W13 **Ṭāqah** S Oman
145 T3 **Taqtaq** N Iraq
63 J15 **Taquara** Rio Grande do Sul, S Brazil
61 H19 **Taquari, Rio** ≈ C Brazil
62 L8 **Taquaritinga** São Paulo, S Brazil
125 G12 **Tara** Omskaya Oblast', C Russian Federation
85 I16 **Tara** Southern, S Zambia
115 J15 **Tara** ≈ SW Yugoslavia
114 K13 **Tara** ▲ W Yugoslavia
79 W15 **Taraba** ◈ *state* E Nigeria
79 X15 **Taraba** ≈ E Nigeria
77 O7 **Ṭarābulus** *var.* Ṭarābulus al Gharb, *Eng.* Tripoli. ● (Libya) NW Libya
77 O7 **Ṭarābulus** ✕ NW Libya
Ṭarābulus/Ṭarābulus ash Shām *see* Tripoli
Ṭarābulus al Gharb *see* Ṭarābulus
107 O7 **Taracena** Castilla-La Mancha, C Spain
119 N12 **Taraclia** *Rus.* Tarakilya. S Moldova
145 V10 **Tarād al Kahf** SE Iraq
191 R10 **Tarago** New South Wales, SE Australia
174 Jj15 **Taraju** Jawa, S Indonesia
176 Vv11 **Tarak** Irian Jaya, E Indonesia
175 O5 **Tarakan** Borneo, C Indonesia
175 O5 **Tarakan, Pulau** *island* N Indonesia
Tarakilya *see* Taraclia
172 Pp16 **Tarama-jima** *island* Sakishima-shotō, SW Japan
192 K10 **Taranaki** *off.* Taranaki Region. ◈ *region* North Island, NZ
192 K10 **Taranaki, Mount** *var.* Egmont. ▲ North Island, NZ
107 O9 **Tarancón** Castilla-La Mancha, C Spain
196 M15 **Tarang Reef** *reef* C Micronesia
98 E7 **Taransay** *island* NW Scotland, UK
109 P18 **Taranto** *var.* Tarentum. Puglia, SE Italy
109 O19 **Taranto, Golfo di** *Eng.* Gulf of Taranto. *gulf* S Italy
Taranto, Gulf of *see* Taranto, Golfo di
64 G3 **Tarapacá** *off.* Región de Tarapacá. ◈ *region* N Chile
195 Y16 **Tarapaina** Maramasike Island, N Solomon Islands
58 D10 **Tarapoto** San Martín, N Peru
144 M6 **Ṭaraq an Na'jah** *hill range* E Syria
144 M6 **Ṭaraq Sidāwī** *hill range* E Syria
105 Q11 **Tarare** Rhône, E France
Tararite de Llitera *see* Tamarite de Litera
192 M13 **Tararua Range** ▲ North Island, NZ
157 Q22 **Tarāsa Dwip** *island* Nicobar Islands, India, NE Indian Ocean
105 Q15 **Tarascon** Bouches-du-Rhône, SE France
104 M17 **Tarascon-sur-Ariège** Ariège, S France
119 P6 **Tarashcha** Kyyivs'ka Oblast', N Ukraine
59 L18 **Tarata** Cochabamba, C Bolivia
59 I18 **Tarata** Tacna, SW Peru
202 H2 **Tarawa** *atoll* Tungaru, W Kiribati
61 B15 **Tarauacá** Acre, W Brazil
61 B15 **Tarauacá, Rio** ≈ NW Brazil
203 Q8 **Taravao** Tahiti, W French Polynesia
203 R8 **Taravao, Baie de** *bay* Tahiti, W French Polynesia
203 Q8 **Taravao, Isthme de** *isthmus* Tahiti, W French Polynesia
104 E3 **Taravo** ≈ Corse, France, C Mediterranean Sea
202 J3 **Tarawa** ✕ Tarawa, W Kiribati
202 H2 **Tarawa** *atoll* Tungaru, W Kiribati
192 N10 **Tarawera** Hawke's Bay, North Island, NZ
192 N8 **Tarawera, Lake** ◎ North Island, NZ
192 N8 **Tarawera, Mount** ▲ North Island, NZ
107 S8 **Tarayuela** ▲ N Spain
107 Q5 **Tarazona** Aragón, NE Spain
107 Q10 **Tarazona de la Mancha** Castilla-La Mancha, C Spain
151 X12 **Tarbagatay, Khrebet** ▲ China/Kazakhstan
98 J8 **Tarbat Ness** *headland* N Scotland, UK
155 U5 **Tarbela Reservoir** ⊡ N Pakistan
98 H12 **Tarbert** W Scotland, UK
98 F7 **Tarbert** Western Isles, NW Scotland, UK
104 K16 **Tarbes** *anc.* Bigorra. Hautes-Pyrénées, S France
23 W9 **Tarboro** North Carolina, SE USA
Tarca *see* Torysa
108 J6 **Tarcento** Friuli-Venezia Giulia, NE Italy
190 F5 **Tarcoola** South Australia
107 S5 **Tardienta** Aragón, NE Spain
104 L11 **Tardoire** ≈ W France
191 U7 **Taree** New South Wales, SE Australia
94 K12 **Tärendö** Norrbotten, N Sweden
Tarentum *see* Taranto
76 C9 **Tarfaya** SW Morocco
118 J13 **Târgoviște** *prev.* Tîrgoviște. Dâmbovița, S Romania
118 M12 **Târgu Bujor** *prev.* Tîrgu Bujor. Galați, E Romania
118 H13 **Târgu Cărbunești** *prev.* Tîrgu. Gorj, SW Romania
118 L9 **Târgu Frumos** *prev.* Tîrgu Frumos. Iași, NE Romania
118 H13 **Targu Jui** *prev.* Tîrgu Jiu. Gorj, W Romania
118 H9 **Târgu Lăpuș** *prev.* Tîrgu Lăpuș. Maramureș, N Romania
Târgul-Neamț *see* Târgu-Neamț
Târgul-Săcuiesc *see* Târgu Secuiesc
118 I10 **Târgu Mureș** *prev.* Oșorhei, Tîrgu Mures, *Ger.* Neumarkt, *Hung.* Marosvásárhely. Mureș, C Romania
118 K9 **Târgu-Neamț** *var.* Târgul-Neamț; *prev.* Tîrgu-Neamț. Neamț, NE Romania
118 K11 **Târgu Ocna** *Hung.* Aknavásár; *prev.* Tîrgu Ocna. Bacău, E Romania
118 K11 **Târgu Secuiesc** *Ger.* Neumarkt, Szekler Neumarkt, *Hung.* Kezdivásárhely; *prev.* Chezdi-Oșorheiu, Târgul-Săcuiesc, Tîrgu Secuiesc. Covasna, E Romania
151 X10 **Targyn** Vostochnyy Kazakhstan, E Kazakhstan
Tar Heel State *see* North Carolina
194 G12 **Tari** Southern Highlands, W PNG
149 P17 **Ṭarīf** Abū Ẓaby, C UAE
106 K16 **Tarifa** Andalucía, S Spain
86 C14 **Tarifa, Punta de** *headland* SW Spain
59 M21 **Tarija** Tarija, S Bolivia
59 M21 **Tarija** ◈ *department* S Bolivia
147 R14 **Tarīm** C Yemen
Tarim Basin *see* Tarim Pendi
83 G19 **Tarime** Mara, N Tanzania
133 S8 **Tarim He** ≈ NW China
165 H8 **Tarim Pendi** *Eng.* Tarim Basin. *basin* NW China
155 N7 **Tarīn Kowt** *var.* Terinkot. Urūzgān, C Afghanistan
175 Pp10 **Taripa** Sulawesi, C Indonesia
176 Z11 **Taritatu, Sungai** *prev.* Idenburg-rivier. ≈ Irian Jaya, E Indonesia
119 Q12 **Tarkhankut, Mys** *headland* S Ukraine
29 Q1 **Tarkio** Missouri, C USA
126 H9 **Tarko-Sale** Yamalo-Nenetskiy Avtonomnyy Okrug, N Russian Federation
79 P17 **Tarkwa** S Ghana
179 P10 **Tarlac** Luzon, N Philippines
97 F22 **Tarm** Ringkøbing, W Denmark
59 E14 **Tarma** Junín, C Peru
105 N15 **Tarn** ◈ *department* S France
105 M15 **Tarn** ≈ S France
113 L22 **Tarna** ≈ C Hungary
94 G13 **Tärnaby** Västerbotten, N Sweden
155 P8 **Tarnak Rūd** ≈ SE Afghanistan
118 J11 **Târnava Mare** *Ger.* Grosse Kokel, *Hung.* Nagy-Küküllő; *prev.* Tîrnava Mare. ≈ S Romania
118 I11 **Târnava Mică** *Ger.* Kleine Kokel, *Hung.* Kis-Küküllo; *prev.* Tîrnava Mică. ≈ C Romania
118 I11 **Târnăveni** *Ger.* Marteskirch, Martinskirch, *Hung.* Dicsőszentmárton; *prev.* Sînmartin, Tîrnăveni. Mureș, C Romania
104 L14 **Tarn-et-Garonne** ◈ *department* S France
113 P18 **Tarnica** ▲ SE Poland
113 N15 **Tarnobrzeg** Tarnobrzeg, SE Poland
113 N15 **Tarnobrzeg** *off.* Województwo Tarnobrzeskie. ◈ *province* SE Poland
Tarnobrzeskie, Województwo *see* Tarnobrzeg
129 N12 **Tarnogskiy Gorodok** Vologodskaya Oblast', NW Russian Federation
Tarnopol *see* Ternopil'
113 M16 **Tarnów** Tarnów, SE Poland
113 M16 **Tarnów** *off.* Województwo Tarnowskie. ◈ *province* SE Poland
Tarnowice/Tarnowitz *see* Tarnowskie Góry
113 J16 **Tarnowskie Góry** *var.* Tarnowice, Tarnowskie Gory, *Ger.* Tarnowitz. Katowice, S Poland
Tarnowskie, Województwo *see* Tarnów
97 N14 **Tärnsjö** Västmanland, C Sweden
108 E9 **Taro** ≈ NW Italy
195 Q10 **Taron** New Ireland, NE PNG
76 E8 **Taroudannt** *var.* Taroudant. SW Morocco
Taroudant *see* Taroudannt
25 V12 **Tarpon, Lake** ◎ Florida, SE USA
25 V12 **Tarpon Springs** Florida, SE USA
109 G14 **Tarquinia** *anc.* Tarquinii; *hist.* Corneto. Lazio, C Italy
Tarquinii *see* Tarquinia
Tarraco *see* Tarragona
78 D10 **Tarrafal** Santiago, S Cape Verde
107 V6 **Tarragona** *anc.* Tarraco. Cataluña, E Spain
107 T7 **Tarragona** ◈ *province* Cataluña, NE Spain
191 O17 **Tarraleah** Tasmania, SE Australia
25 P3 **Tarrant City** Alabama, S USA
193 D21 **Tarras** Otago, South Island, NZ
Tarrasa *see* Terrassa
107 U5 **Tàrrega** *var.* Tarrega. Cataluña, NE Spain
23 W9 **Tar River** ≈ North Carolina, SE USA
Tarsatica *see* Rijeka
142 J17 **Tarsus** İçel, S Turkey
64 K4 **Tartagal** Salta, N Argentina
143 V12 **Tärtär** *Rus.* Terter. ≈ SW Azerbaijan
104 J15 **Tartas** Landes, SW France
145 Q6 **Tārtasah** C Iraq
Tartlau *see* Prejmer
Tartous/Tartouss *see* Ṭarṭūs
120 J5 **Tartu** *Ger.* Dorpat; *prev.* Rus. Yurev, Yur'yev. Tartumaa, SE Estonia
120 I5 **Tartumaa** *off.* Tartu Maakond. ◈ *province* E Estonia
144 H5 **Ṭarṭūs** *Fr.* Tartouss; *anc.* Tortosa. Ṭarṭūs, W Syria
144 H5 **Ṭarṭūs** *off.* Muḥāfaẓat Ṭarṭūs, *var.* Tartous, Tartus. ◈ *governorate* W Syria
170 Bb16 **Tarumizu** Kagoshima, Kyūshū, SW Japan
130 K4 **Tarusa** Kaluzhskaya Oblast', W Russian Federation
173 G9 **Tarusan** Sumatera, W Indonesia
119 N11 **Tarutyne** Odes'ka Oblast', SW Ukraine
168 I7 **Tarvagatyn Nuruu** ▲ N Mongolia
108 J6 **Tarvisio** Friuli-Venezia Giulia, NE Italy
Tarvisium *see* Treviso
59 O16 **Tarvo, Río** ≈ E Bolivia
12 G8 **Tarzwell** Ontario, S Canada
42 K5 **Tasajera, Sierra de la** ▲ N Mexico
151 S13 **Tasaral** Zhezkazgan, C Kazakhstan
Tasbōget *see* Tasbuget
151 N15 **Tasbuget** *Kaz.* Tasbōget. Kzyl-Orda, S Kazakhstan
110 E11 **Tasch** Valais, SW Switzerland
Tasek Kenyir *see* Kenyir, Tasik
126 Hh16 **Tashanta** Respublika Altay, S Russian Federation
Tashauz *see* Dashkhovuz
Tashi Chho Dzong *see* Thimphu
159 U11 **Tashigang** E Bhutan
143 T11 **Tashir** *prev.* Kalinino. N Armenia
149 Q11 **Ṭashk, Daryācheh-ye** ◎ C Iran
Tashkent *see* Toshkent
Tashkentskaya Oblast' *see* Toshkent Wiloyati
152 J16 **Tashkepri** *Turkm.* Dashköpri. Maryyskiy Velayat, S Turkmenistan
Tash-Kömür *see* Tash-Kumyr
153 S9 **Tash-Kumyr** *Kir.* Tash-Kömür. Dzhalal-Abadskaya Oblast', W Kyrgyzstan
131 T7 **Tashla** Orenburgskaya Oblast', W Russian Federation
Tashqurghan *see* Kholm
126 H15 **Tashtagol** Kemerovskaya Oblast', S Russian Federation
174 Jj15 **Tasikmalaya** *prev.* Tasikmalaja. Jawa, C Indonesia
97 H24 **Tåsinge** *island* C Denmark
10 M5 **Tasiujaq** Québec, E Canada
127 Nn9 **Taskan** Magadanskaya Oblast', E Russian Federation
79 W11 **Tasker** Zinder, C Niger
151 W12 **Taskesken** Semipalatinsk, E Kazakhstan
142 J10 **Taşköprü** Kastamonu, N Turkey
Taskuduk, Peski *see* Goshquduq Qum
195 N9 **Taskul** New Ireland, NE PNG
143 S13 **Taşlıçay** Ağrı, E Turkey
193 H14 **Tasman** *off.* Tasman District. ◈ *unitary authority* South Island, NZ
199 I14 **Tasman Basin** *var.* East Australian Basin. *undersea feature* S Tasman Sea
193 I14 **Tasman Bay** *inlet* South Island, NZ
199 Hh14 **Tasman Fracture Zone** *tectonic feature* S Indian Ocean
193 E19 **Tasman Glacier** *glacier* South Island, NZ
Tasman Group *see* Nukumanu Islands
191 N15 **Tasmania** *prev.* Van Diemen's Land. ◈ *state* SE Australia
191 Q16 **Tasmania** *island* SE Australia
193 H14 **Tasman Mountains** ▲ South Island, NZ
191 P17 **Tasman Peninsula** *peninsula* Tasmania, SE Australia
199 Hh13 **Tasman Plain** *undersea feature* W Tasman Sea
199 Hh14 **Tasman Plateau** *var.* South Tasmania Plateau. *undersea feature* SW Tasman Sea
199 Ii14 **Tasman Sea** *sea* SW Pacific Ocean
118 G9 **Tășnad** *Ger.* Trestenberg, Trestendorf, *Hung.* Tasnád. Satu Mare, NW Romania
142 L11 **Taşova** Amasya, N Turkey
79 T10 **Tassara** Tahoua, W Niger
10 K4 **Tassialouc, Lac** ◎ Québec, C Canada
Tassili du Hoggar *see* Tassili ta-n-Ahaggar
76 L11 **Tassili-n-Ajjer** *plateau* E Algeria
76 K14 **Tassili ta-n-Ahaggar** *var.* Tassili du Hoggar. *plateau* S Algeria
61 M15 **Tasso Fragoso** Maranhão, E Brazil
97 J23 **Tåstrup** *var.* Taastrup. København, E Denmark
151 O9 **Tasty-Taldy** Turgay, C Kazakhstan
149 W10 **Tāsūkī** Sīstān va Balūchestān, SE Iran
113 I22 **Tata** *Ger.* Totis. Komárom-Esztergom, NW Hungary
76 E8 **Tata** SW Morocco
Tataaihoa, Pointe *see* Vénus, Pointe
113 I22 **Tatabánya** Komárom-Esztergom, NW Hungary
203 X10 **Tatakoto** *atoll* Îles Tuamotu, E French Polynesia
77 N7 **Tataouine** *var.* Taṭāwīn. SE Tunisia
57 O5 **Tataracual, Cerro** ▲ NE Venezuela
119 O12 **Tatarbunary** Odes'ka Oblast', SW Ukraine
121 M17 **Tatarka** *Rus.* Tatarka. Mahilyowskaya Voblasts', E Belarus
Tatar Pazardzhik *see* Pazardzhik
125 G13 **Tatarsk** Novosibirskaya Oblast', C Russian Federation
Tatarskaya ASSR *see* Tatarstan, Respublika
127 O15 **Tatarskiy Proliv** *Eng.* Tatar Strait. *strait* SE Russian Federation
131 R4 **Tatarstan, Respublika** *prev.* Tatarskaya ASSR. ◈ *autonomous republic* W Russian Federation
Tatar Strait *see* Tatarskiy Proliv
195 O9 **Tatau Island** *island* Tabar Islands, N PNG
Taṭāwīn *see* Tataouine
175 P8 **Tate** Sulawesi, N Indonesia
171 Jj17 **Tateyama** Chiba, Honshū, S Japan
171 J14 **Tate-yama** ▲ Honshū, S Japan
147 N11 **Tathlīth** 'Asīr, S Saudi Arabia
147 O11 **Tathlīth, Wādī** *dry watercourse* S Saudi Arabia
191 R11 **Tathra** New South Wales, SE Australia
131 P8 **Tatishchevo** Saratovskaya Oblast', W Russian Federation
41 S12 **Tatitlek** Alaska, USA
8 L15 **Tatla Lake** British Columbia, SW Canada
124 O2 **Tatlısu** *Gk.* Akanthoú. N Cyprus
9 Z10 **Tatnam, Cape** *headland* Manitoba, C Canada
Tatra/Tátra *see* Tatra Mountains
113 K18 **Tatra Mountains** *Ger.* Tatra, *Hung.* Tátra, *Pol./Slvk.* Tatry. ▲ Poland/Slovakia
Tatry *see* Tatra Mountains
170 G14 **Tatsuno** *var.* Tatuno. Hyōgo, Honshū, SW Japan
151 S16 **Tatti** *var.* Tatty. Zhambyl, S Kazakhstan
Tatty *see* Tatti
62 L10 **Tatuí** São Paulo, S Brazil
39 V14 **Tatum** New Mexico, SW USA
27 X7 **Tatum** Texas, SW USA
Ta-t'ung/Tatung *see* Datong
Tatuno *see* Tatsuno
143 R14 **Tatvan** Bitlis, SE Turkey
97 C16 **Tau** Rogaland, S Norway
198 Dd8 **Ta'ū** *var.* Tau. *island* Manua Islands, E American Samoa
200 R14 **Tau** *island* Tongatapu Group, N Tonga
61 O14 **Tauá** Ceará, E Brazil
62 N10 **Taubaté** São Paulo, S Brazil
103 I19 **Tauber** ≈ SW Germany
103 I19 **Tauberbischofsheim** Baden-Württemberg, C Germany
150 E14 **Tauchik** *Kaz.* Taūshyq. Mangistau, SW Kazakhstan
203 W10 **Tauere** *atoll* Îles Tuamotu, C French Polynesia
103 H17 **Taufstein** ▲ C Germany
202 I17 **Taukoka** *island* SE Cook Islands
151 T15 **Taukum, Peski** *desert* SE Kazakhstan
192 L10 **Taumarunui** Manawatu-Wanganui, North Island, NZ
61 A15 **Taumaturgo** Acre, W Brazil
29 X6 **Taum Sauk Mountain** ▲ Missouri, C USA
85 H22 **Taung** North-West, N South Africa
177 G6 **Taungdwingyi** Magwe, C Myanmar
178 Gg6 **Taunggyi** Shan State, C Myanmar
177 G5 **Taungtha** Mandalay, C Myanmar
177 F7 **Taungup** Arakan State, W Myanmar
155 S9 **Taunsa** Punjab, E Pakistan
99 K23 **Taunton** SW England, UK
21 O12 **Taunton** Massachusetts, NE USA
103 F18 **Taunus** ▲ W Germany
103 G18 **Taunusstein** Hessen, W Germany
192 N9 **Taupo** Waikato, North Island, NZ
192 M9 **Taupo, Lake** ◎ North Island, NZ
111 R8 **Taurach** *var.* Taurachbach. ≈ E Austria
Taurachbach *see* Taurach
120 D12 **Tauragė** *Ger.* Tauroggen. Tauragė, SW Lithuania
56 G10 **Tauramena** Casanare, C Colombia
192 N7 **Tauranga** Bay of Plenty, North Island, NZ
13 O10 **Taureau, Réservoir** ⊡ Québec, SE Canada
109 N22 **Taurianova** Calabria, SW Italy
Tauris *see* Tabrīz
192 I2 **Tauroa Point** *headland* North Island, NZ
Tauroggen *see* Tauragė
Tauromenium *see* Taormina
Taurus Mountains *see* Toros Dağları
Taus *see* Domažlice
Taūshyq *see* Tauchik
107 R5 **Tauste** Aragón, NE Spain
203 V16 **Tautara, Motu** *island* Easter Island, Chile, E Pacific Ocean
203 R8 **Tautira** Tahiti, W French Polynesia
Tauz *see* Tovuz
Ṭavālesh, Kūhhā-ye *see* Talish Mountains
142 D15 **Tavas** Denizli, SW Turkey
Tavastehus *see* Häme, Finland
Tavastehus *see* Hämeenlinna, Finland
Tavau *see* Davos
125 F11 **Tavda** Sverdlovskaya Oblast', C Russian Federation
125 F11 **Tavda** ≈ C Russian Federation
107 T11 **Tavernes de la Valldigna** País Valenciano, E Spain
83 J20 **Taveta** Coast, S Kenya
197 J13 **Taveuni** *island* N Fiji
153 R13 **Tavildara** *Rus.* Tavil'dara, Tovil'-Dora. C Tajikistan
168 L8 **Tavin** Dundgovĭ, C Mongolia
106 H14 **Tavira** Faro, S Portugal
99 I24 **Tavistock** SW England, UK
178 Gg11 **Tavoy** *var.* Dawei. Tenasserim, S Myanmar
Tavoy Island *see* Mali Kyun
125 Ff13 **Tavricheskoye** Omskaya Oblast', C Russian Federation
117 E16 **Tavropoú, Techníti Límni** ⊡ C Greece
142 E13 **Tavşanlı** Kütahya, NW Turkey
197 H14 **Tavua** Viti Levu, W Fiji
197 I16 **Tavuki** Kadavu, SW Fiji
99 J23 **Taw** ≈ SW England, UK
193 L14 **Tawa** Wellington, North Island, NZ
27 V6 **Tawakoni, Lake** ⊡ Texas, SW USA
159 V11 **Tawang** Arunāchal Pradesh, NE India
174 L16 **Tawang, Teluk** *bay* Jawa, S Indonesia
33 R7 **Tawas Bay** ◎ Michigan, N USA
33 R7 **Tawas City** Michigan, N USA
175 Oo4 **Tawau** Sabah, East Malaysia
147 U10 **Ṭawīl, Qalamat aṭ** *well* SE Saudi Arabia
179 P17 **Tawitawi** *island* Tawitawi Group, SW Philippines
179 Pp17 **Tawitawi Group** *island group* Sulu Archipelago, SW Philippines
Ṭawkar *see* Tokar
Tāwūq *see* Dāqūq
Tawzar *see* Tozeur
43 O15 **Taxco** *var.* Taxco de Alarcón. Guerrero, S Mexico
Taxco de Alarcón *see* Taxco
164 D9 **Taxkorgan** *var.* Taxkorgan Tajik Zizhixian. Xinjiang Uygur Zizhiqu, NW China
Taxkorgan Tajik Zizhixian *see* Taxkorgan
98 J10 **Tay** ≈ C Scotland, UK
176 V13 **Tayandu, Kepulauan** *island group* E Indonesia
149 V6 **Tāybād** *var.* Taibad, Tāyyebād, Tayyebāt. Khorāsān, NE Iran
Taybert at Turkz *see* Ṭayyibat at Turkī
128 J3 **Taybola** Murmanskaya Oblast', NW Russian Federation
83 M16 **Tayeeglow** Bakool, C Somalia
98 K11 **Tay, Firth of** *inlet* E Scotland, UK
126 H13 **Tayga** Kemerovskaya Oblast', S Russian Federation
168 G8 **Taygan** Govĭ-Altay, C Mongolia
127 Oo9 **Taygonos, Mys** *headland* E Russian Federation
98 I11 **Tay, Loch** ◎ C Scotland, UK
9 N12 **Taylor** British Columbia, W Canada
31 O14 **Taylor** Nebraska, C USA
20 I13 **Taylor** Pennsylvania, NE USA
27 T10 **Taylor** Texas, SW USA
39 Q11 **Taylor, Mount** ▲ New Mexico, SW USA
39 R5 **Taylor Park Reservoir** ⊡ Colorado, C USA
39 R6 **Taylor River** ≈ Colorado, C USA
23 P11 **Taylors** South Carolina, SE USA
22 L5 **Taylorsville** Kentucky, S USA
23 R6 **Taylorsville** North Carolina, SE USA
32 L14 **Taylorville** Illinois, N USA
146 K5 **Taymā'** Tabūk, NW Saudi Arabia
126 Jj11 **Taymura** ≈ C Russian Federation
126 Kk6 **Taymylyr** Respublika Sakha (Yakutiya), NE Russian Federation
126 J5 **Taymyr, Ozero** ◎ N Russian Federation
126 J5 **Taymyr, Poluostrov** *peninsula* N Russian Federation
126 Ii7 **Taymyrskiy (Dolgano-Nenetskiy) Avtonomnyy Okrug** *var.* Taymyrskiy Avtonomnyy Okrug. ◈ *autonomous district* N Russian Federation
178 Jj13 **Tây Ninh** Tây Ninh, S Vietnam
126 Ii14 **Tayshet** Irkutskaya Oblast', S Russian Federation
179 Oo13 **Taytay** Palawan, W Philippines
174 L14 **Tayu** *prev.* Tajoe. Jawa, C Indonesia
Tāyybād/Tayyebāt *see* Tāybād
144 L5 **Ṭayyibah** *var.* At Taybé. Ḥimṣ, C Syria
144 I4 **Ṭayyibat at Turkī** *var.* Taybert at Turkz. Ḥamāh, W Syria
126 H9 **Taz** ≈ N Russian Federation
76 G6 **Taza** NE Morocco
145 T4 **Tāza Khurmātū** E Iraq
171 M10 **Tazawa-ko** ◎ Honshū, C Japan
Taz, Bay of *see* Tazovskaya Guba
23 N8 **Tazewell** Tennessee, S USA
23 Q7 **Tazewell** Virginia, NE USA
Tazimi *see* Tajimi
77 S11 **Tāzirbū** SE Libya
41 S11 **Tazlina Lake** ◎ Alaska, USA
126 H7 **Tazovskaya Guba** *Eng.* Bay of Taz. *bay* N Russian Federation
126 H8 **Tazovskiy** Yamalo-Nenetskiy Avtonomnyy Okrug, N Russian Federation
143 U10 **T'bilisi** *Eng.* Tiflis. ● (Georgia) SE Georgia
143 T10 **T'bilisi** ✕ S Georgia
81 E14 **Tchabal Mbabo** ▲ NW Cameroon
Tchad *see* Chad
Tchad, Lac *see* Chad, Lake
79 S15 **Tchaourou** E Benin
81 E20 **Tchibanga** Nyanga, S Gabon
Tchien *see* Zwedru
79 Z6 **Tchigaï, Plateau du** ▲ NE Niger
79 V9 **Tchighozérine** Agadez, C Niger
79 T10 **Tchin-Tabaradene** Tahoua, W Niger
80 G13 **Tcholliré** Nord, NE Cameroon
Tchongking *see* Chongqing
24 K4 **Tchula** Mississippi, S USA
112 I7 **Tczew** *Ger.* Dirschau. Gdańsk, N Poland
118 I10 **Teaca** *Ger.* Tekendorf, *Hung.* Teke; *prev. Ger.* Teckendorf. Bistrița-Năsăud, N Romania
42 J11 **Teacapán** Sinaloa, C Mexico
202 A10 **Teafuafou** *island* Funafuti Atoll, C Tuvalu
27 U8 **Teague** Texas, SW USA
203 R9 **Teahupoo** Tahiti, W French Polynesia
202 H15 **Te Aiti Point** *headland* Rarotonga, S Cook Islands
67 D24 **Teal Inlet** East Falkland, Falkland Islands
193 B22 **Te Anau** Southland, South Island, NZ
193 B22 **Te Anau, Lake** ◎ South Island, NZ
43 U15 **Teapa** Tabasco, SE Mexico
192 Q7 **Te Araroa** Gisborne, North Island, NZ
192 M7 **Te Aroha** Waikato, North Island, NZ
Teate *see* Chieti
202 A9 **Te Ava Fuagea** *channel* Funafuti Atoll, SE Tuvalu
202 B8 **Te Ava I Te Lape** *channel* Funafuti Atoll, SE Tuvalu
202 B9 **Te Ava Pua Pua** *channel* Funafuti Atoll, SE Tuvalu
192 M8 **Te Awamutu** Waikato, North Island, NZ
176 Xx9 **Teba** Irian Jaya, E Indonesia
106 L15 **Teba** Andalucía, S Spain
130 M15 **Teberda** Karachayevo-Cherkesskaya Respublika, SW Russian Federation
76 M6 **Tébessa** NE Algeria
64 O7 **Tebicuary, Río** ≈ S Paraguay
174 Hh11 **Tebingtinggi** Sumatera, W Indonesia
173 Ff5 **Tebingtinggi** Sumatera, N Indonesia
Tebingtinggi, Pulau *see* Rantau, Pulau
Tebriz *see* Tabrīz
143 U9 **Tebulos Mt'a** *Rus.* Gora Tebulosmta. ▲ Georgia/Russian Federation
Tebulosmta, Gora *see* Tebulos Mt'a
43 Q14 **Tecamachalco** Puebla, S Mexico
42 B1 **Tecate** Baja California, NW Mexico
142 M13 **Tecer Dağları** ▲ C Turkey
105 O17 **Tech** ≈ S France
79 P16 **Techiman** W Ghana
119 N15 **Techirghiol** Constanța, SE Romania
76 A12 **Techla** *var.* Techlé. SW Western Sahara
Techlé *see* Techla
65 H18 **Tecka, Sierra de** ▲ SW Argentina
Teckendorf *see* Teaca
42 K13 **Tecolotlán** Jalisco, SW Mexico
42 K14 **Tecomán** Colima, SW Mexico
37 V12 **Tecopa** California, W USA
42 G5 **Tecoripa** Sonora, NW Mexico
43 N16 **Tecpan** *var.* Tecpan de Galeana. Guerrero, S Mexico
Tecpan de Galeana *see* Tecpan
42 J11 **Tecuala** Nayarit, C Mexico
118 L12 **Tecuci** Galați, E Romania
33 R10 **Tecumseh** Michigan, N USA
31 S16 **Tecumseh** Nebraska, C USA
29 O11 **Tecumseh** Oklahoma, C USA
194 E12 **Tedi** ≈ W PNG
152 H14 **Tedzhen** *Turkm.* Tejen. Akhalskiy Velayat, S Turkmenistan
152 I15 **Tedzhen** *Per.* Harīrūd, *Turkm.* Tejen. ≈ Afghanistan/Iran *see also* Harīrūd
152 H15 **Tedzhenstroy** *Turkm.* Tejenstroy. Akhalskiy Velayat, S Turkmenistan
168 I7 **Teel** Arhangay, C Mongolia
99 L15 **Tees** ≈ N England, UK
12 E15 **Teeswater** Ontario, S Canada
202 A10 **Tefala** *island* Funafuti Atoll, C Tuvalu
60 D13 **Tefé** Amazonas, N Brazil
76 K11 **Tefedest** ▲ S Algeria
142 E16 **Tefenni** Burdur, SW Turkey
60 D13 **Tefé, Rio** ≈ NW Brazil
174 Kk14 **Tegal** Jawa, C Indonesia
102 O12 **Tegel** ✕ (Berlin) Berlin, NE Germany
101 M15 **Tegelen** Limburg, SE Netherlands
103 L24 **Tegernsee** ◎ SE Germany
109 M18 **Teggiano** Campania, S Italy
79 U14 **Tegina** Niger, C Nigeria
197 B10 **Tegua** *island* Torres Islands, N Vanuatu
44 I7 **Tegucigalpa** ● (Honduras) Francisco Morazán, SW Honduras
44 H7 **Tegucigalpa** ✕ Central District, C Honduras
Tegucigalpa *see* Central District, Honduras
Tegucigalpa *see* Francisco Morazán, Honduras
79 U9 **Teguidda-n-Tessoumt** Agadez, C Niger
66 Q11 **Teguise** Lanzarote, Islas Canarias, Spain, NE Atlantic Ocean
126 Hh13 **Tegul'det** Tomskaya Oblast', C Russian Federation
37 S13 **Tehachapi** California, W USA
37 S13 **Tehachapi Mountains** ▲ California, W USA
Tehama *see* Tihāmah
Teheran *see* Tehrān
79 O14 **Téhini** NE Ivory Coast
149 N5 **Tehrān** *var.* Teheran. ● (Iran) Tehrān, N Iran
149 N6 **Tehrān** *off.* Ostān-e Tehrān, *var.* Tehran. ◈ *province* N Iran
158 K9 **Tehri** Uttar Pradesh, N India
Tehri *see* Tikamgarh
43 Q15 **Tehuacán** Puebla, S Mexico
43 S17 **Tehuantepec** *var.* Santo Domingo Tehuantepec. Oaxaca, SE Mexico
43 S17 **Tehuantepec, Golfo de** *var.* Gulf of Tehuantepec. *gulf* S Mexico
Tehuantepec, Gulf of *see* Tehuantepec, Golfo de
Tehuantepec, Isthmus of *see* Tehuantepec, Istmo de
43 T16 **Tehuantepec, Istmo de** *var.* Isthmus of Tehuantepec. *isthmus* SE Mexico
1 I16 **Tehuantepec Ridge** *undersea feature* E Pacific Ocean
43 S16 **Tehuantepec, Río** ≈ SE Mexico
203 W10 **Tehuata** *atoll* Îles Tuamotu, C French Polynesia
66 O11 **Teide, Pico de** ▲ Gran Canaria, Islas Canarias, Spain, NE Atlantic Ocean
99 I21 **Teifi** ≈ SW Wales, UK
82 B9 **Teiga Plateau** *plateau* W Sudan
99 J24 **Teignmouth** SW England, UK
Teisen *see* Chech'ŏn
118 H1 **Teiuș** *Ger.* Dreikirchen, *Hung.* Tövis. Alba, C Romania
175 N16 **Tejakula** Bali, C Indonesia
Tejen *see* Harīrūd/Tedzhen
Tejenstroy *see* Tedzhenstroy
37 S14 **Tejon Pass** *pass* California, W USA
Tejo, Rio *see* Tagus
43 O14 **Tejupilco** *var.* Tejupilco de Hidalgo. México, S Mexico
Tejupilco de Hidalgo *see* Tejupilco
192 P7 **Te Kaha** Bay of Plenty, North Island, NZ
31 S14 **Tekamah** Nebraska, C USA
192 I1 **Te Kao** Northland, North Island, NZ
193 F20 **Tekapo** ≈ South Island, NZ
193 F19 **Tekapo, Lake** ◎ South Island, NZ
192 P9 **Te Karaka** Gisborne, North Island, NZ
192 L7 **Te Kauwhata** Waikato, North Island, NZ
43 X12 **Tekax** *var.* Tekax de Álvaro Obregón. Yucatán, SE Mexico
Tekax de Álvaro Obregón *see* Tekax
Teke/Tekendorf *see* Teaca
142 A14 **Teke Burnu** *headland* W Turkey
116 M12 **Teke Deresi** ≈ NW Turkey
152 D10 **Tekedzhik, Gory** *hill range* NW Turkmenistan
151 V14 **Tekeli** Taldykorgan, SE Kazakhstan
151 R7 **Teke, Ozero** ◎ N Kazakhstan
164 I5 **Tekes** Xinjiang Uygur Zizhiqu, NW China
151 W16 **Tekes** Almaty, SE Kazakhstan
Tekes *see* Tekes He
164 H5 **Tekes He** *Rus.* Tekes. ≈ China/Kazakhstan
82 I10 **Tekezē** *var.* Takkaze. ≈ Eritrea/Ethiopia
Tekhtin *see* Tsyakhtsin
142 C10 **Tekirdağ** *It.* Rodosto; *anc.* Bisanthe, Raidestos, Rhaedestus. Tekirdağ, NW Turkey
142 C10 **Tekirdağ** ◈ *province* NW Turkey
161 N14 **Tekkali** Andhra Pradesh, E India
117 K15 **Tekke Burnu** *Turk.* İlyasbaba Burnu. *headland* NW Turkey
143 Q13 **Tekman** Erzurum, NE Turkey
34 M9 **Tekoa** Washington, NW USA
202 H16 **Te Kou** ▲ Rarotonga, S Cook Islands
Tekrit *see* Tikrīt
175 R9 **Teku** Sulawesi, N Indonesia
192 L9 **Te Kuiti** Waikato, North Island, NZ
44 H4 **Tela** Atlántida, NW Honduras
144 F12 **Telalim** Southern, S Israel
Telanaipura *see* Jambi
143 U10 **T'elavi** E Georgia
144 F10 **Tel Aviv** ◈ *district* W Israel
Tel Aviv-Jaffa *see* Tel Aviv-Yafo
144 F10 **Tel Aviv-Yafo** *var.* Tel Aviv-Jaffa. Tel Aviv, C Israel
144 F10 **Tel Aviv-Yafo** ✕ Tel Aviv, C Israel

◆ COUNTRY
● COUNTRY CAPITAL
◇ DEPENDENT TERRITORY
○ DEPENDENT TERRITORY CAPITAL
◈ ADMINISTRATIVE REGION
✕ INTERNATIONAL AIRPORT
▲ MOUNTAIN
▲ MOUNTAIN RANGE
⩚ VOLCANO
≈ RIVER
◎ LAKE
⊡ RESERVOIR

113 E18 **Telč** Ger. Teltsch. Jižní Morava, S Czech Republic
194 E11 **Telefomin** Sandaun, NW PNG
8 J10 **Telegraph Creek** British Columbia, W Canada
202 B10 **Telele** island Funafuti Atoll, C Tuvalu
62 J11 **Telêmaco Borba** Paraná, S Brazil
97 E15 **Telemark** ◆ county S Norway
64 J13 **Telén** La Pampa, C Argentina
Teleneshty see Teleneşti
118 M9 **Teleneşti** Rus. Teleneshty. C Moldova
106 J4 **Teleno, El** ▲ NW Spain
175 O8 **Telen, Sungai** ≈ Borneo, C Indonesia
118 I15 **Teleorman** ◆ county S Romania
118 I14 **Teleorman** ≈ S Romania
27 V5 **Telephone** Texas, SW USA
37 U11 **Telescope Peak** ▲ California, W USA
Teles Pirés see São Manuel, Rio
99 L19 **Telford** C England, UK
110 L7 **Telfs** Tirol, W Austria
44 I9 **Telica** León, NW Nicaragua
44 J6 **Telica, Río** ≈ C Honduras
78 I13 **Télimélé** Guinée-Maritime, W Guinea
45 O14 **Telire, Río** ≈ Costa Rica/ Panama
116 I8 **Telish** prev. Azizie. Loveshka Oblast, NW Bulgaria
43 R16 **Telixtlahuaca** var. San Francisco Telixtlahuaca. Oaxaca, SE Mexico
8 K13 **Telkwa** British Columbia, SW Canada
27 P4 **Tell** Texas, SW USA
Tell Abiad see Tall Abyaḍ
Tell Abiad/Tell Abyad see At Tall al Abyaḍ
Tell 'Annz see Al 'Anz
Tell Bâz see Tall Bāz
Tell Brâk see Tall Birāk
33 O16 **Tell City** Indiana, N USA
40 M9 **Teller** Alaska, USA
Tell Huqnah see Tall Ḥuqnah
161 F20 **Tellicherry** var. Thalassery. Kerala, SW India
22 M10 **Tellico Plains** Tennessee, S USA
Tell Kalakh see Tall Kalakh
Tell Mardīkh see Ebla
56 E11 **Tello** Huila, C Colombia
Tell Shagher Bazar see Jāghir Bāzār
Tell Shedadi see Ash Shadādah
Tell Tamr see Tall Tamir
39 Q7 **Telluride** Colorado, C USA
Tel'man/Tel'mansk see Gubadag
119 X9 **Tel'manove** Donets'ka Oblast', E Ukraine
168 H6 **Telmen Nuur** ◎ NW Mongolia
Teloekbetoeng see Bandarlampung
43 O15 **Teloloapán** Guerrero, S Mexico
Telo Martius see Toulon
129 V8 **Telposiz, Gora** ▲ NW Russian Federation
Telschen see Telšiai
65 J17 **Telsen** Chubut, S Argentina
120 D11 **Telšiai** Ger. Telschen. Telšiai, NW Lithuania
Teltsch see Telč
Telukbetung see Bandarlampung
173 F7 **Telukdalam** Pulau Nias, W Indonesia
12 H9 **Temagami** Ontario, S Canada
12 G9 **Temagami, Lake** ◎ Ontario, S Canada
202 H16 **Te Manga** ▲ Rarotonga, S Cook Islands
Temanggoeng see Temanggung
174 Kk15 **Temanggung** prev. Temanggoeng. Jawa, S Indonesia
203 W12 **Tematangi** atoll Îles Tuamotu, S French Polynesia
43 X11 **Temax** Yucatán, SE Mexico
176 X12 **Tembagapura** Irian Jaya, E Indonesia
133 U5 **Tembenchi** ≈ N Russian Federation
174 Hh10 **Tembesi, Sungai** ≈ Sumatera, W Indonesia
57 P6 **Temblador** Monagas, NE Venezuela
107 N9 **Tembleque** Castilla-La Mancha, C Spain
Temboni see Mitemele, Río
37 U16 **Temecula** California, W USA
174 Gg3 **Temengor, Tasik** ◎ Peninsular Malaysia
114 L9 **Temerin** Serbia, N Yugoslavia
Temes/Temesch see Tamiš
Temeschburg/Temeschwar see Timişoara
Temes-Kubin see Kovin
Temesmóra see Moraviţa
Temesvár/Temeswar see Timişoara
Teminaboean see Teminabuan
176 V9 **Teminabuan** prev. Teminaboean. Irian Jaya, E Indonesia
151 P17 **Temirlanovka** Yuzhnyy Kazakhstan, S Kazakhstan
151 R10 **Temirtau** prev. Samarkandski, Samarkandskoye. Karaganda, C Kazakhstan
12 H10 **Témiscaming** Québec, SE Canada
Témiscamingue, Lac see Timiskaming, Lake
13 T8 **Témiscouata, Lac** ◎ Québec, SE Canada
131 N5 **Temnikov** Respublika Mordoviya, W Russian Federation
203 Y13 **Temoe** island Îles Gambier, E French Polynesia
191 Q9 **Temora** New South Wales, SE Australia
42 H7 **Témoris** Chihuahua, W Mexico
42 I5 **Temósachic** Chihuahua, N Mexico
195 W8 **Temotu** off. Temotu Province. ◆ province E Solomon Islands
38 L14 **Tempe** Arizona, SW USA
175 P12 **Tempe, Danau** ◎ Sulawesi, C Indonesia
Tempelburg see Czaplinek
109 C17 **Tempio Pausania** Sardegna, Italy, C Mediterranean Sea
44 K12 **Tempisque, Río** ≈ NW Costa Rica
27 T9 **Temple** Texas, SW USA
102 O12 **Templehof** ✈ (Berlin) Berlin, NE Germany
99 D19 **Templemore** Ir. An Teampall Mór. C Ireland
102 O11 **Templin** Brandenburg, NE Germany
43 P12 **Tempoal** var. Tempoal de Sánchez. Veracruz-Llave, E Mexico
Tempoal de Sánchez see Tempoal
43 P13 **Tempoal, Río** ≈ C Mexico
85 E14 **Tempué** Moxico, C Angola
130 J14 **Temryuk** Krasnodarskiy Kray, SW Russian Federation
101 G17 **Temse** Oost-Vlaanderen, N Belgium
65 F15 **Temuco** Araucanía, C Chile
193 G20 **Temuka** Canterbury, South Island, NZ
201 P13 **Temwen Island** island E Micronesia
58 C6 **Tena** Napo, C Ecuador
43 W13 **Tenabo** Campeche, E Mexico
Tenaghau see Aola
27 X7 **Tenaha** Texas, SW USA
41 X13 **Tenake** Chichagof Island, Alaska, USA
161 K16 **Tenāli** Andhra Pradesh, E India
Tenan see Ch'ŏnan
43 O14 **Tenancingo** var. Tenencingo de Degollado. México, S Mexico
203 X12 **Tenararo** island Groupe Actéon, SE French Polynesia
178 Gg12 **Tenasserim** Tenasserim, S Myanmar
178 H11 **Tenasserim** var. Tanintharyi. ◆ division S Myanmar
100 O5 **Ten Boer** Groningen, NE Netherlands
99 I21 **Tenby** SW Wales, UK
82 K11 **Tendaho** NE Ethiopia
105 V14 **Tende** Alpes Maritimes, SE France
157 Q20 **Ten Degree Channel** strait Andaman and Nicobar Islands, India, E Indian Ocean
82 F11 **Tendelti** White Nile, E Sudan
78 G8 **Te-n-Dghâmcha, Sebkhet** var. Sebkha de Ndrhamcha, Sebkra de Ndaghamcha. salt lake W Mauritania
171 Ll12 **Tendō** Yamagata, Honshū, C Japan
76 H7 **Tendrara** NE Morocco
119 Q11 **Tendrivs'ka Kosa** spit S Ukraine
119 Q11 **Tendrivs'ka Zatoka** gulf S Ukraine
Tenencingo de Degollado see Tenancingo
79 N11 **Ténenkou** Mopti, C Mali
79 W9 **Ténéré** physical region C Niger
79 W9 **Ténére, Erg du** desert C Niger
66 O11 **Tenerife** island Islas Canarias, Spain, NE Atlantic Ocean
76 J5 **Ténès** NW Algeria
175 Oo15 **Tengah, Kepulauan** island group C Indonesia
175 O8 **Tenggarong** Borneo, C Indonesia
168 J15 **Tengger Shamo** desert N China
174 I4 **Tenggul, Pulau** island Peninsular Malaysia
Tengiz Köl see Tengiz, Ozero
151 P9 **Tengiz, Ozero** Kaz. Tengiz Köl. salt lake C Kazakhstan
78 M14 **Tengréla** var. Tingréla. N Ivory Coast
166 M14 **Tengxian** var. Teng Xian. Guangxi Zhuangzu Zizhiqu, S China
204 H2 **Teniente Rodolfo Marsh** Chilean research station South Shetland Islands, Antarctica
34 G9 **Tenino** Washington, NW USA
114 I9 **Tenja** Osijek-Baranja, E Croatia
196 B16 **Tenjo, Mount** ▲ W Guam
161 H23 **Tenkāsi** Tamil Nādu, SE India
81 N24 **Tenke** Shaba, SE Zaire
Tenke see Tinca
126 M7 **Tenkeli** Respublika Sakha (Yakutiya), NE Russian Federation
29 R10 **Tenkiller Ferry Lake** ▣ Oklahoma, C USA
79 Q13 **Tenkodogo** S Burkina
189 Q5 **Tennant Creek** Northern Territory, C Australia
22 G9 **Tennessee** off. State of Tennessee; also known as The Volunteer State. ◆ state SE USA
39 R5 **Tennessee Pass** pass Colorado, C USA
22 H10 **Tennessee River** ≈ S USA
25 N2 **Tennessee Tombigbee Waterway** canal Alabama/Mississippi, S USA
101 K22 **Tenneville** Luxembourg, SE Belgium
94 M11 **Tenniöjoki** ≈ NE Finland
94 L9 **Teno** var. Tenojoki, Lapp. Dealnu, Nor. Tana. ≈ Finland/Norway see also Tana
Tenojoki see Tana/Teno
175 Nn3 **Tenom** Sabah, East Malaysia
Tenos see Tínos
43 V15 **Tenosique** var. Tenosique de Pino Suárez. Tabasco, SE Mexico
Tenosique de Pino Suárez see Tenosique
171 H15 **Tenri** Nara, Honshū, SW Japan
171 I16 **Tenryū** Shizuoka, Honshū, C Japan
172 Ii15 **Tenryū-gawa** ≈ Honshū, C Japan
24 I6 **Tensas River** ≈ Louisiana, S USA
25 O8 **Tensaw River** ≈ Alabama, S USA
76 E7 **Tensift** seasonal river W Morocco
175 Pp10 **Tentena** var. Tenteno. Sulawesi, C Indonesia
Tenteno see Tentena
191 U4 **Tenterfield** New South Wales, SE Australia
25 X16 **Ten Thousand Islands** island group Florida, SE USA
62 H9 **Teodoro Sampaio** São Paulo, S Brazil
61 N19 **Teófilo Otoni** var. Theophilo Ottoni. Minas Gerais, NE Brazil
118 K5 **Teofipol'** Khmel'nyts'ka Oblast', W Ukraine
203 Q8 **Teohatu** Tahiti, W French Polynesia
43 P14 **Teotihuacán** ruins México, S Mexico
Teotilán see Teotitlán del Camino
43 Q15 **Teotitlán del Camino** var. Teotilán. Oaxaca, S Mexico
202 G12 **Tepa** Île Uvea, E Wallis and Futuna
203 P8 **Tepaee, Récif** reef Tahiti, W French Polynesia
42 L14 **Tepalcatepec** Michoacán de Ocampo, SW Mexico
202 A16 **Tepa Point** headland SW Niue
42 L13 **Tepatitlán** var. Tepatitlán de Morelos. Jalisco, SW Mexico
Tepatitlán de Morelos see Tepatitlán
42 J9 **Tepehuanes** var. Santa Catarina de Tepehuanes. Durango, C Mexico
Tepelena see Tepelenë
115 L22 **Tepelenë** var. Tepelena, It. Tepeleni. Gjirokastër, S Albania
Tepeleni see Tepelenë
42 K12 **Tepic** Nayarit, C Mexico
113 C15 **Teplice** Ger. Teplitz; prev. Teplice-Šanov, Teplitz-Schönau. Severní Čechy, NW Czech Republic
Teplice-Šanov/Teplitz/Teplitz-Schönau see Teplice
119 O7 **Teplyk** Vinnyts'ka Oblast', C Ukraine
126 Mm10 **Teplyy Klyuch** Respublika Sakha (Yakutiya), NE Russian Federation
42 E5 **Tepoca, Cabo** headland NW Mexico
203 W9 **Tepoto** island Îles du Désappointement, C French Polynesia
94 L11 **Tepsa** Lappi, N Finland
202 B8 **Tepuka** atoll Funafuti Atoll, C Tuvalu
192 N7 **Te Puke** Bay of Plenty, North Island, NZ
42 L13 **Tequila** Jalisco, SW Mexico
43 O13 **Tequisquiapan** Querétaro de Arteaga, C Mexico
106 J5 **Tera** ≈ NW Spain
79 Q12 **Téra** Tillabéri, W Niger
203 V1 **Teraina** prev. Washington Island. atoll Line Islands, E Kiribati
83 F15 **Terakeka** Bahr el Gabel, S Sudan
109 J14 **Teramo** anc. Interamna. Abruzzi, C Italy
100 P7 **Ter Apel** Groningen, NE Netherlands
106 H11 **Tera, Ribeira de** ≈ S Portugal
193 K14 **Terawhiti, Cape** headland North Island, NZ
100 N12 **Terborg** Gelderland, E Netherlands
143 P13 **Tercan** Erzincan, NE Turkey
66 Q2 **Terceira** ✈ Terceira, Azores, Portugal, NE Atlantic Ocean
66 Q2 **Terceira** var. Ilha Terceira. island Azores, Portugal, NE Atlantic Ocean
Terceira, Ilha see Terceira
118 K6 **Terebovlya** Ternopil's'ka Oblast', W Ukraine
131 O15 **Terek** ≈ SW Russian Federation
Terekhovka see Tsyerakhowka
153 R9 **Terek-Say** Dzhalal-Abadskaya Oblast', W Kyrgyzstan
174 Hh3 **Terengganu** var. Trengganu. ◆ state Peninsular Malaysia
131 X7 **Terensay** Orenburgskaya Oblast', W Russian Federation
60 N13 **Teresina** var. Therezina. state capital Piauí, NE Brazil
62 P9 **Teresópolis** Rio de Janeiro, SE Brazil
112 P12 **Terespol** Biała Podlaska, E Poland
203 V16 **Terevaka, Maunga** ⛰ Easter Island, Chile, E Pacific Ocean
105 P3 **Tergnier** Aisne, N France
45 O14 **Teribe, Río** ≈ NW Panama
128 K3 **Teriberka** Murmanskaya Oblast', NW Russian Federation
Terijoki see Zelenogorsk
Terinkot see Tarīn Kowt
Terisaqqan see Tersakkan
26 K12 **Terlingua** Texas, SW USA
26 K11 **Terlingua Creek** ≈ Texas, SW USA
64 K7 **Termas de Río Hondo** Santiago del Estero, N Argentina
142 M11 **Terme** Samsun, N Turkey
Termez see Termiz
Termia see Kýthnos
109 J23 **Termini Imerese** anc. Thermae Himerenses. Sicilia, Italy, C Mediterranean Sea
43 V14 **Términos, Laguna de** lagoon SE Mexico
79 X10 **Termit-Kaoboul** Zinder, C Niger
153 O14 **Termiz** Rus. Termez. Surkhondaryo Wiloyati, S Uzbekistan
109 L15 **Termoli** Molise, C Italy
Termonde see Dendermonde
100 P5 **Termunten** Groningen, NE Netherlands
175 T7 **Ternate** Pulau Ternate, E Indonesia
175 Ss7 **Ternate, Pulau** island E Indonesia
111 T5 **Ternberg** Oberösterreich, N Austria
101 E15 **Terneuzen** var. Neuzen. Zeeland, SW Netherlands
127 O17 **Terney** Primorskiy Kray, SE Russian Federation
109 I14 **Terni** anc. Interamna Nahars. Umbria, C Italy
111 X6 **Ternitz** Niederösterreich, E Austria
119 V7 **Ternivka** Dnipropetrovs'ka Oblast', E Ukraine
118 K6 **Ternopil'** Pol. Tarnopol, Rus. Ternopol'. Ternopil's'ka Oblast', W Ukraine
Ternopil' see Ternopil's'ka Oblast'
118 I6 **Ternopil's'ka Oblast'** var. Ternopil', Rus. Ternopol'skaya Oblast'. ◆ province NW Ukraine
Ternopol' see Ternopil'
Ternopol'skaya Oblast' see Ternopil's'ka Oblast'
127 Oo15 **Terpeniya, Mys** headland Ostrov Sakhalin, SE Russian Federation
127 Oo15 **Terpeniya, Zaliv** inlet Ostrov Sakhalin, SE Russian Federation
Térraba, Río see Grande de Térraba, Río
8 J13 **Terrace** British Columbia, W Canada
10 D12 **Terrace Bay** Ontario, S Canada
109 I16 **Terracina** Lazio, C Italy
95 F14 **Terråk** Troms, N Norway
28 M13 **Terral** Oklahoma, C USA
109 B19 **Terralba** Sardegna, Italy, C Mediterranean Sea
Terranova di Sicilia see Gela
Terranova Pausania see Olbia
107 W5 **Terrassa** Cast. Tarrasa. Cataluña, E Spain
13 O12 **Terrebonne** Québec, SE Canada
24 J11 **Terrebonne Bay** bay Louisiana, SE USA
33 N14 **Terre Haute** Indiana, N USA
27 U6 **Terrell** Texas, SW USA
Terre-Neuve see Newfoundland
Terre Neuve see Newfoundland and Labrador
35 Q14 **Terreton** Idaho, NW USA
105 T7 **Territoire-de-Belfort** ◆ department E France
35 X9 **Terry** Montana, NW USA
30 J9 **Terry Peak** ▲ South Dakota, N USA
142 H14 **Tersakan Gölü** ◎ C Turkey
151 O10 **Tersakkan** Kaz. Terisaqqan. ≈ C Kazakhstan
100 J4 **Terschelling** Fris. Skylge. island Waddeneilanden, N Netherlands
80 H10 **Tersef** Chari-Baguirmi, C Chad
153 X8 **Terskey Ala-Too, Khrebet** ⛰ Kazakhstan/Kyrgyzstan
Terter see Tärtär
107 R8 **Teruel** anc. Turba. Aragón, E Spain
107 R7 **Teruel** ◆ province Aragón, E Spain
116 M7 **Tervel** prev. Kurtbunar, Rom. Curtbunar. Varnenska Oblast, NE Bulgaria
95 M16 **Tervo** Kuopio, C Finland
94 L13 **Tervola** Lappi, NW Finland
Tervueren see Tervuren
101 H18 **Tervuren** var. Tervueren. Vlaams Brabant, C Belgium
114 H11 **Tešanj** N Bosnia and Herzegovina
Teschen see Cieszyn
85 M19 **Tesenane** Inhambane, S Mozambique
82 I9 **Teseney** var. Tessenei. W Eritrea
41 P5 **Teshekpuk Lake** ◎ Alaska, USA
168 K6 **Teshig** Bulgan, N Mongolia
172 Q6 **Teshikaga** Hokkaidō, NE Japan
172 P2 **Teshio** Hokkaidō, NE Japan
172 P2 **Teshio-gawa** var. Tesio Gawa. ≈ Hokkaidō, NE Japan
172 P3 **Teshio-sanchi** ⛰ Hokkaidō, NE Japan
Těšín see Cieszyn
Tesio Gawa see Teshio-gawa
168 F5 **Tesiyn Gol** var. Tes-Khem. ≈ Mongolia/Russian Federation see also Tes-Khem
133 T7 **Tes-Khem** var. Tesiyn Gol. ≈ Mongolia/Russian Federation see also Tesiyn Gol
114 H11 **Teslić** N Bosnia and Herzegovina
8 I9 **Teslin** Yukon Territory, W Canada
8 I8 **Teslin** ≈ British Columbia/Yukon Territory, W Canada
79 Q8 **Tessalit** Kidal, NE Mali
79 V12 **Tessaoua** Maradi, S Niger
101 J17 **Tessenderlo** Limburg, NE Belgium
Tessenei see Teseney
12 L7 **Tessier, Lac** ◎ Québec, SE Canada
Tessin see Ticino
99 M23 **Test** ≈ S England, UK
Testama see Tõstamaa
57 P4 **Testigos, Islas los** island group N Venezuela
39 S10 **Tesuque** New Mexico, SW USA
105 O17 **Têt** var. Tet. ≈ S France
56 G5 **Tetas, Cerro de las** ▲ NW Venezuela
85 M15 **Tete** Tete, NW Mozambique
85 M15 **Tete** off. Província de Tete. ◆ province NW Mozambique
9 N15 **Tête Jaune Cache** British Columbia, SW Canada
192 O8 **Te Teko** Bay of Plenty, North Island, NZ
195 U15 **Tetepare** island New Georgia Islands, NW Solomon Islands
Teterev see Teteriv
118 M5 **Teteriv** Rus. Teterev. ≈ N Ukraine
102 M9 **Teterow** Mecklenburg-Vorpommern, NE Germany
116 I9 **Teteven** Loveshka Oblast, W Bulgaria
203 T10 **Tetiaroa** atoll Îles du Vent, W French Polynesia
107 P14 **Tetica de Bacares** ▲ S Spain
Tetiyev see Tetiyiv
119 O6 **Tetiyiv** Rus. Tetiyev. Kyyivs'ka Oblast', N Ukraine
41 T10 **Tetlin** Alaska, USA
35 R8 **Teton River** ≈ Montana, NW USA
76 G5 **Tétouan** var. Tetouan, Tetuán. N Morocco
Tetova/Tetovë see Tetovo
116 L7 **Tetovo** Razgradska Oblast, NE Bulgaria
115 N18 **Tetovo** Alb. Tetova, Tetovë, Turk. Kalkandelen. NW FYR Macedonia
117 E20 **Tetrázio** ⛰ S Greece
Tetschen see Děčín
Tetuán see Tétouan
203 Q8 **Tetufera, Mont** ▲ Tahiti, W French Polynesia
131 R4 **Tetyushi** Respublika Tatarstan, W Russian Federation
110 I7 **Teufen** Sankt Gallen, NE Switzerland
42 L12 **Teul** var. Teul de Gonzáles Ortega. Zacatecas, C Mexico
109 B21 **Teulada** Sardegna, Italy, C Mediterranean Sea
Teul de Gonzáles Ortega see Teul
9 X16 **Teulon** Manitoba, S Canada
44 I7 **Teupasenti** El Paraíso, S Honduras
172 Oo3 **Teuri-tō** island NE Japan
102 G13 **Teutoburger Wald** Eng. Teutoburg Forest. hill range NW Germany
Teutoburg Forest see Teutoburger Wald
95 K17 **Teuva** Swe. Östermark. Vaasa, W Finland
109 H15 **Tevere** Eng. Tiber. ≈ C Italy
144 G9 **Teverya** var. Tiberias. Northern, N Israel
98 K13 **Teviot** ≈ SE Scotland, UK
Tevli see Tewli
125 Ff12 **Tevriz** Omskaya Oblast', C Russian Federation
193 B24 **Te Waewae Bay** bay South Island, NZ
99 L21 **Tewkesbury** C England, UK
121 F19 **Tewli** Rus. Tevli. Brestskaya Voblasts', SW Belarus
165 U12 **Têwo** var. Dêngkagoin. Gansu, C China
27 U12 **Texana, Lake** ◎ Texas, SW USA
29 S14 **Texarkana** Arkansas, C USA
27 X5 **Texarkana** Texas, SW USA
27 N9 **Texas** off. State of Texas; also known as The Lone Star State. ◆ state S USA
27 W12 **Texas City** Texas, SW USA
43 P14 **Texcoco** México, C Mexico
100 I6 **Texel** island Waddeneilanden, NW Netherlands
28 H8 **Texhoma** Oklahoma, C USA
27 N1 **Texhoma** Texas, SW USA
39 W12 **Texico** New Mexico, SW USA
26 L1 **Texline** Texas, SW USA
43 P14 **Texmelucan** var. San Martín Texmelucan. Puebla, S Mexico
29 O13 **Texoma, Lake** ▣ Oklahoma/Texas, C USA
27 N9 **Texon** Texas, SW USA
126 I12 **Teya** Krasnoyarskiy Kray, C Russian Federation
85 J23 **Teyateyaneng** NW Lesotho
128 M16 **Teykovo** Ivanovskaya Oblast', W Russian Federation
128 M16 **Teza** ≈ W Russian Federation
43 Q13 **Teziutlán** Puebla, S Mexico
159 W12 **Tezpur** Assam, NE India
15 L8 **Tha-Anne** ≈ Northwest Territories, NE Canada
85 K23 **Thabana Ntlenyana** var. Thabantshonyana, Mount Ntlenyana. ▲ E Lesotho
Thabantshonyana see Thabana Ntlenyana
85 J23 **Thaba Putsoa** ▲ C Lesotho
178 I8 **Tha Bo** Nong Khai, E Thailand
105 T12 **Thabor, Pic du** ▲ E France
Tha Chin see Samut Sakhon
177 G7 **Thagaya** Pegu, C Myanmar
Thai, Ao see Thailand, Gulf of
178 Jj6 **Thai Binh** Thai Binh, N Vietnam
178 Jj7 **Thai Hoa** Nghê An, N Vietnam
178 Hh10 **Thailand** off. Kingdom of Thailand, Th. Prathet Thai; prev. Siam. ◆ monarchy SE Asia
178 Hh13 **Thailand, Gulf of** var. Gulf of Siam, Th. Ao Thai, Vtn. Vinh Thai Lan. gulf SE Asia
Thai Lan, Vinh see Thailand, Gulf of
178 Jj6 **Thai Nguyên** Băc Thai, N Vietnam
178 J9 **Thakhèk** prev. Muang Khammouan. Khammouan, C Laos
159 S13 **Thakurgaon** Rajshahi, NW Bangladesh
155 S6 **Thal** North-West Frontier Province, NW Pakistan
177 G16 **Thalang** Phuket, SW Thailand
Thalassery see Tellicherry
178 I10 **Thalat Khae** Nakhon Ratchasima, C Thailand
111 Q5 **Thalgau** Salzburg, NW Austria
110 G7 **Thalwil** Zürich, NW Switzerland
85 I20 **Thamaga** Kweneng, SE Botswana
Thamarīd see Thamarīt
147 V13 **Thamarīt** var. Thamarīd, Thumrayt. SW Oman
147 P16 **Thamar, Jabal** ▲ SW Yemen
192 M6 **Thames** Waikato, North Island, NZ
12 D17 **Thames** ≈ Ontario, S Canada
99 O22 **Thames** ≈ S England, UK
192 M6 **Thames, Firth of** gulf North Island, NZ
12 D17 **Thamesville** Ontario, S Canada
147 S13 **Thamūd** N Yemen
178 Gg9 **Thanbyuzayat** Mon State, S Myanmar
158 I9 **Thānesar** Haryāna, NW India
178 Jj7 **Thanh Hoa** Thanh Hoa, N Vietnam
Thanintari Taungdan see Bilauktaung Range
161 I21 **Thanjāvūr** prev. Tanjore. Tamil Nādu, SE India
Thanlwin see Salween
105 U7 **Thann** Haut-Rhin, NE France
178 H16 **Tha Nong Phrom** Phatthalung, SW Thailand
178 H13 **Thap Sakae** var. Thap Sakau. Prachuap Khiri Khan, SW Thailand
Thap Sakau see Thap Sakae
100 L10 **'t Harde** Gelderland, E Netherlands
158 D11 **Thar Desert** var. Great Indian Desert, Indian Desert. desert India/Pakistan
189 V10 **Thargomindah** Queensland, C Australia
156 D11 **Thar Pārkar** desert SE Pakistan
145 S7 **Tharthār al Furāt, Qanāt ath** canal C Iraq
145 R7 **Tharthār, Buḥayrat ath** ◎ C Iraq
145 R5 **Tharthār, Wādī ath** dry watercourse N Iraq
178 Gg14 **Tha Sae** Chumphon, SW Thailand
178 H15 **Tha Sala** Nakhon Si Thammarat, SW Thailand
116 I13 **Thásos** Thásos, E Greece
117 I14 **Thásos** island E Greece
39 N14 **Thatcher** Arizona, SW USA
178 Jj5 **Thât Khê** var. Trâng Dinh. Lang Sơn, N Vietnam
178 Gg9 **Thaton** Mon State, S Myanmar
178 J9 **That Phanom** Nakhon Phanom, E Thailand
178 Ii10 **Tha Tum** Surin, E Thailand
105 P16 **Thau, Bassin de** var. Étang de Thau. ◎ S France
Thau, Étang de see Thau, Bassin de
177 G3 **Thaungdut** Sagaing, N Myanmar
178 Gg8 **Thaungyin** Th. Mae Nam Moei. ≈ Myanmar/Thailand
178 J9 **Tha Uthen** Nakhon Phanom, E Thailand
111 W2 **Thaya** var. Dyje. ≈ Austria/Czech Republic see also Dyje
29 V8 **Thayer** Missouri, C USA
177 Ff7 **Thayetmyo** Magwe, C Myanmar
35 S15 **Thayne** Wyoming, C USA
177 G6 **Thazi** Mandalay, C Myanmar
Thebes see Thíva
46 L5 **The Carlton** var. Abraham Bay. Mayaguana, SE Bahamas
47 O14 **The Crane** var. Crane. S Barbados
34 I11 **The Dalles** Oregon, NW USA
30 M14 **Thedford** Nebraska, C USA
The Hague see 's-Gravenhage
Theiss see Tisa/Tisza
15 Jj6 **Thelon** ≈ Northwest Territories, N Canada
9 V15 **Theodore** Saskatchewan, S Canada
25 N8 **Theodore** Alabama, S USA
38 L13 **Theodore Roosevelt Lake** ▣ Arizona, SW USA
Theodosia see Feodosiya
Theophilo Ottoni see Teófilo Otoni
15 K13 **The Pas** Manitoba, C Canada
33 T14 **The Plains** Ohio, N USA
Thera see Thíra
180 H17 **Thérèse, Île** island Inner Islands, NE Seychelles
Therezina see Teresina
117 L20 **Thérma** Ikaría, Dodekánisos, Greece, Aegean Sea
Thermae Himerenses see Termini Imerese
Thermae Pannonicae see Baden
Thermaic Gulf/Thermaicus Sinus see Thermaïkós Kólpos
123 Gg10 **Thermaïkós Kólpos** Eng. Thermaic Gulf; anc. Thermaicus Sinus. gulf N Greece
Thermiá see Kýthnos
117 L17 **Thermís** Lésvos, E Greece
117 E18 **Thérmo** Dytikí Ellás, C Greece
35 V14 **Thermopolis** Wyoming, C USA
191 P10 **The Rock** New South Wales, SE Australia
205 O5 **Theron Mountains** ⛰ Antarctica
117 G18 **Thespiés** Stereá Ellás, C Greece
117 E16 **Thessalía** Eng. Thessaly. ◆ region C Greece
12 C10 **Thessalon** Ontario, S Canada
117 G14 **Thessaloníki** Eng. Salonica, Salonika, SCr. Solun, Turk. Selânik. Kentrikí Makedonía, N Greece
117 G14 **Thessaloníki** ✈ Kentrikí Makedonía, N Greece
Thessaly see Thessalía
86 B12 **Theta Gap** undersea feature E Atlantic Ocean
99 P20 **Thetford** E England, UK
13 R11 **Thetford-Mines** Québec, SE Canada
115 K17 **Theth** var. Thethi. Shkodër, N Albania
Thethi see Theth
101 L20 **Theux** Liège, E Belgium
47 V9 **The Valley** ○ (Anguilla) E Anguilla
29 N10 **The Village** Oklahoma, C USA
27 W10 **The Woodlands** Texas, SW USA
Thiamis see Thýamis
Thian Shan see Tien Shan
24 J9 **Thibodaux** Louisiana, S USA
31 S3 **Thief Lake** ◎ Minnesota, N USA
31 S3 **Thief River** ≈ Minnesota, C USA
31 S3 **Thief River Falls** Minnesota, N USA
Thièle see La Thielle
34 G14 **Thielsen, Mount** ▲ Oregon, NW USA
Thielt see Tielt
108 G7 **Thiene** Veneto, NE Italy
Thienen see Tienen
105 P11 **Thiers** Puy-de-Dôme, C France
78 F11 **Thiès** W Senegal
83 I19 **Thika** Central, S Kenya
Thikombia see Cikobia
157 K18 **Thiladhunmathi Atoll** var. Tiladummati Atoll. atoll N Maldives
Thimbu see Thimphu
159 T11 **Thimphu** var. Thimbu; prev. Tashi Chho Dzong. ● (Bhutan) W Bhutan
94 H2 **Thingeyri** Vestfirdhir, NW Iceland
94 I3 **Thingvellir** Sudhurland, SW Iceland
197 J6 **Thio** Province Sud, C New Caledonia
105 T4 **Thionville** Ger. Diedenhofen. Moselle, NE France
117 K22 **Thíra** Thíra, Kykládes, Greece, Aegean Sea
117 K22 **Thíra** prev. Santorin, Santoríni, anc. Thera. island Kykládes, Greece, Aegean Sea
117 J22 **Thirasía** island Kykládes, Greece, Aegean Sea
99 M16 **Thirsk** N England, UK
12 F12 **Thirty Thousand Islands** island group Ontario, S Canada
Thiruvanathapuram see Trivandrum
97 F20 **Thisted** Viborg, NW Denmark
Thistil Fjord see Thistilfjördhur
94 L1 **Thistilfjördhur** var. Thistil Fjord. fjord NE Iceland
190 G9 **Thistle Island** island South Australia
Thithia see Cicia
179 N14 **Thitu Island** island NW Spratly Islands
Thiukhaoluang Phrahang see Luang Prabang Range
117 G18 **Thíva** Eng. Thebes; prev. Thívai. Stereá Ellás, C Greece
Thívai see Thíva
104 M12 **Thiviers** Dordogne, SW France
94 J4 **Thjórsá** ≈ C Iceland
15 L9 **Thlewiaza** ≈ Northwest Territories, NE Canada
15 J9 **Thoa** ≈ Northwest Territories, NW Canada
101 G14 **Tholen** Zeeland, SW Netherlands
101 F14 **Tholen** island SW Netherlands
28 L10 **Thomas** Oklahoma, C USA
23 T3 **Thomas** West Virginia, NE USA
29 U3 **Thomas Hill Reservoir** ▣ Missouri, C USA
25 S5 **Thomaston** Georgia, SE USA
21 R7 **Thomaston** Maine, NE USA
27 T12 **Thomaston** Texas, SW USA
25 O6 **Thomasville** Alabama, S USA
25 T8 **Thomasville** Georgia, SE USA
23 S9 **Thomasville** North Carolina, SE USA
37 N5 **Thomes Creek** ≈ California, W USA
9 W12 **Thompson** Manitoba, C Canada
31 R4 **Thompson** North Dakota, N USA
0 F8 **Thompson** ≈ Alberta/British Columbia, SW Canada
35 O8 **Thompson Falls** Montana, NW USA
31 Q10 **Thompson, Lake** ◎ South Dakota, N USA
36 M3 **Thompson Peak** ▲ California, W USA
29 S2 **Thompson River** ≈ Missouri, C USA
193 A22 **Thompson Sound** sound South Island, NZ
15 Hh1 **Thomsen** ≈ Banks Island, Northwest Territories, NW Canada
25 V4 **Thomson** Georgia, SE USA
105 T10 **Thonon-les-Bains** Haute-Savoie, E France
105 O15 **Thoré** var. Thore. ≈ S France
39 P11 **Thoreau** New Mexico, SW USA

◆ Country ● Country Capital ◇ Dependent Territory ○ Dependent Territory Capital ◆ Administrative Region ✈ International Airport ▲ Mountain ⛰ Mountain Range Volcano ≈ River ◎ Lake ▣ Reservoir

Thorenburg *see* Turda
94 J3 **Thórisvatn** ◎ C Iceland
94 P4 **Thor, Kapp** *headland* S Svalbard
94 I4 **Thorlákshöfn** Sudhurland, SW Iceland
Thorn *see* Toruń
27 T10 **Thorndale** Texas, SW USA
12 H10 **Thorne** Ontario, S Canada
99 J14 **Thornhill** S Scotland, UK
27 U8 **Thornton** Texas, SW USA
Thornton Island *see* Caroline Island
12 H16 **Thorold** Ontario, S Canada
34 I9 **Thorp** Washington, NW USA
205 S3 **Thorshavnheiane** *physical region* Antarctica
94 L1 **Thórshöfn** Nordhurland Eystra, NE Iceland
Thospitis *see* Van Gölü
178 J14 **Thốt Nốt** Cần Thơ, S Vietnam
104 K8 **Thouars** Deux-Sèvres, W France
159 X14 **Thoubal** Manipur, NE India
104 K9 **Thouet** ≈ W France
Thoune *see* Thun
20 H7 **Thousand Islands** *island* Canada/USA
37 S15 **Thousand Oaks** California, W USA
116 J13 **Thracian Sea** *Gk.* Thrakikó Pélagos; *anc.* Thracium Mare. *sea* Greece/Turkey
Thracium Mare/Thrakikó Pélagos *see* Thracian Sea
Thrá Lí, Bá *see* Tralee Bay
35 R11 **Three Forks** Montana, NW USA
9 Q16 **Three Hills** Alberta, SW Canada
191 N15 **Three Hummock Island** *island* Tasmania, SE Australia
192 H1 **Three Kings Islands** *island group* N NZ
183 P10 **Three Kings Rise** *undersea feature* W Pacific Ocean
79 O18 **Three Points, Cape** *headland* S Ghana
33 P10 **Three Rivers** Michigan, N USA
27 S13 **Three Rivers** Texas, SW USA
85 G24 **Three Sisters** Northern Cape, SW South Africa
34 H13 **Three Sisters** ▲ Oregon, NW USA
195 Z16 **Three Sisters Islands** *island group* SE Solomon Islands
Thrissur *see* Trichūr
27 Q6 **Throckmorton** Texas, SW USA
188 M10 **Throssell, Lake** *salt lake* Western Australia
117 K25 **Thrýptis** ▲ Kríti, Greece, E Mediterranean Sea
178 Jj14 **Thu Dầu Một** *var.* Phu Cuong. Sông Be, S Vietnam
178 Jj6 **Thu Do** ✕ (Ha Nôi) Ha Nôi, N Vietnam
101 G21 **Thuin** Hainaut, S Belgium
155 Q12 **Thul** Sind, SE Pakistan
Thule *see* Qaanaaq
85 J18 **Thuli** *var.* Tuli. ≈ S Zimbabwe
Thumrayt *see* Thamarīt
110 D9 **Thun** *Fr.* Thoune. Bern, W Switzerland
10 C12 **Thunder Bay** Ontario, S Canada
32 M1 **Thunder Bay** *lake bay* S Canada
33 R6 **Thunder Bay** *lake bay* Michigan, N USA
33 R6 **Thunder Bay River** ≈ Michigan, N USA
29 N11 **Thunderbird, Lake** ▣ Oklahoma, C USA
30 L8 **Thunder Butte Creek** ≈ South Dakota, N USA
110 E9 **Thuner See** ◎ C Switzerland
178 H16 **Thung Song** *var.* Cha Mai. Nakhon Si Thammarat, SW Thailand
110 H7 **Thur** ≈ N Switzerland
110 G6 **Thurgau** *Fr.* Thurgovie. ◈ *canton* NE Switzerland
Thurgovie *see* Thurgau
Thuringe *see* Thüringen
110 J7 **Thüringen** Vorarlberg, W Austria
103 J17 **Thüringen** *Eng.* Thuringia, *Fr.* Thuringe. ◈ *state* C Germany
103 J17 **Thüringer Wald** *Eng.* Thuringian Forest. ▲▲ C Germany
Thuringia *see* Thüringen
Thuringian Forest *see* Thüringer Wald
99 D19 **Thurles** *Ir.* Durlas. S Ireland
23 W2 **Thurmont** Maryland, NE USA
Thurø *see* Thurø By
97 H24 **Thurø By** *var.* Thurø. Fyn, C Denmark
12 M12 **Thurso** Québec, SE Canada
98 J6 **Thurso** N Scotland, UK
204 I10 **Thurston Island** *island* Antarctica
110 I9 **Thusis** Graubünden, S Switzerland
117 C15 **Thýamis** *var.* Thiamis. ≈ W Greece
97 E21 **Thyborøn** *var.* Tyborøn. Ringkøbing, W Denmark
205 U3 **Thyer Glacier** *glacier* Antarctica
117 L20 **Thýmaina** *island* Dodekánisos, Greece, Aegean Sea
85 N15 **Thyolo** *var.* Cholo. Southern, S Malawi
191 U6 **Tia** New South Wales, SE Australia
56 H5 **Tía Juana** Zulia, NW Venezuela
166 J14 **Tiandong** *var.* Pingma. Guangxi Zhuangzu Zizhiqu, S China
167 O3 **Tianjin** *var.* Tientsin. Tianjin Shi, E China
Tianjin *see* Tianjin Shi
167 P3 **Tianjin Shi** *var.* Jin, Tianjin, T'ien-ching, Tientsin. ◈ *municipality* E China
165 S10 **Tianjun** *var.* Xinyuan. Qinghai, C China
166 J13 **Tianlin** *prev.* Leli. Guangxi Zhuangzu Zizhiqu, S China
Tian Shan *see* Tien Shan
165 W11 **Tianshui** Gansu, C China
156 I7 **Tianshuihai** Xinjiang Uygur Zizhiqu, W China
167 S10 **Tiantai** Zhejiang, SE China
166 J14 **Tianyang** Guangxi Zhuangzu Zizhiqu, S China
165 U9 **Tianzhu** *var.* Tianzhu Zangzu Zizhixian. Gansu, C China
Tianzhu Zangzu Zizhixian *see* Tianzhu
203 Q7 **Tiarei** Tahiti, W French Polynesia
76 J6 **Tiaret** *var.* Tihert. NW Algeria
Tiâs *see* Tiyās
79 N17 **Tiassalé** S Ivory Coast
198 Bb8 **Ti'avea** Upolu, SE Western Samoa
Tiba *see* Chiba
62 J11 **Tibagi** *var.* Tibají. Paraná, S Brazil
62 J10 **Tibagi, Rio** *var.* Rio Tibají. ≈ S Brazil
Tibají *see* Tibagi
Tibají, Rio *see* Tibagi, Rio
145 Q9 **Tibal, Wādī** *dry watercourse* S Iraq
56 G9 **Tibaná** Boyacá, C Colombia
81 F14 **Tibati** Adamaoua, N Cameroon
78 K15 **Tibé, Pic de** ▲ SE Guinea
Tiber *see* Tevere, Italy
Tiber *see* Tivoli, Italy
Tiberias *see* Teverya
144 G8 **Tiberias, Lake** *var.* Chinnereth, Sea of Bahr Tabariya, Sea of Galilee, *Ar.* Bahrat Tabariya, *Heb.* Yam Kinneret. ◎ N Israel
69 Q5 **Tibesti** *var.* Tibesti Massif, *Ar.* Tibistī. ▲▲ N Africa
Tibesti Massif *see* Tibesti
Tibetan Autonomous Region *see* Xizang Zizhiqu
Tibet, Plateau of *see* Qingzang Gaoyuan
Tibistī *see* Tibesti
12 K7 **Tiblemont, Lac** ◎ Québec, SE Canada
145 X9 **Ţīb, Nahr aţ** ≈ S Iraq
Tibnī *see* At Tibnī
190 L4 **Tibooburra** New South Wales, SE Australia
97 L18 **Tibro** Skaraborg, S Sweden
42 E5 **Tiburón, Isla** *var.* Isla del Tiburón. *island* NW Mexico
Tiburón, Isla del *see* Tiburón, Isla
25 W14 **Tice** Florida, SE USA
Tichau *see* Tychy
116 L8 **Ticha, Yazovir** ◎ NE Bulgaria
78 K9 **Tichit** *var.* Tichitt. Tagant, C Mauritania
Tichitt *see* Tichit
110 G11 **Ticino** *Fr./Ger.* Tessin. ◈ *canton* S Switzerland
108 D8 **Ticino** ≈ Italy/Switzerland
110 H11 **Ticino** *Ger.* Tessin. ≈ SW Switzerland
Ticinum *see* Pavia
43 X12 **Ticul** Yucatán, SE Mexico
97 K18 **Tidaholm** Skaraborg, S Sweden
Tidjikdja *see* Tidjikja
78 J8 **Tidjikja** *var.* Tidjikdja; *prev.* Fort-Cappolani. Tagant, C Mauritania
Tidore *see* Soasiu
175 Ss7 **Tidore, Pulau** *island* E Indonesia
Tidra, Ile *see* Et Tîdra
79 N16 **Tiébissou** *var.* Tiebissou. C Ivory Coast
169 V11 **Tiefa** Liaoning, NE China
110 I9 **Tiefencastel** Graubünden, S Switzerland
Tiegenhof *see* Nowy Dwór Gdański
T'ieh-ling *see* Tieling
100 K13 **Tiel** Gelderland, C Netherlands
169 W7 **Tieli** Heilongjiang, NE China
169 V11 **Tieling** *var.* T'ieh-ling. Liaoning, NE China
158 L4 **Tielongtan** China/India
101 D17 **Tielt** *var.* Thielt. West-Vlaanderen, W Belgium
T'ien-ching *see* Tianjin Shi
101 I18 **Tienen** *var.* Thienen, *Fr.* Tirlemont. Vlaams Brabant, C Belgium
Tiên Giang, Sông *see* Mekong
153 X9 **Tien Shan** *Chin.* Thian Shan, Tian Shan, T'ien Shan, *Rus.* Tyan'-Shan'. ▲▲ C Asia
Tientsin *see* Tianjin
Tientsin *see* Tianjin Shi
178 K6 **Tiên Yên** Quang Ninh, N Vietnam
97 O14 **Tierp** Uppsala, C Sweden
64 H7 **Tierra Amarilla** Atacama, N Chile
39 R9 **Tierra Amarilla** New Mexico, SW USA
43 R15 **Tierra Blanca** Veracruz-Llave, E Mexico
43 O16 **Tierra Colorada** Guerrero, S Mexico
65 J17 **Tierra Colorada, Bajo de la** *basin* SE Argentina
65 I25 **Tierra del Fuego** *off.* Provincia de la Tierra del Fuego. ◈ *province* S Argentina
65 J24 **Tierra del Fuego** *island* Argentina/Chile
56 D7 **Tierralta** Córdoba, NW Colombia
106 K9 **Tiétar** ≈ W Spain
62 L10 **Tietê** São Paulo, S Brazil
62 J8 **Tietê, Rio** ≈ S Brazil
34 I9 **Tieton** Washington, NW USA
34 J6 **Tiffany Mountain** ▲ Washington, NW USA
33 S12 **Tiffin** Ohio, N USA
33 Q11 **Tiffin River** ≈ Ohio, N USA
Tiflis *see* T'bilisi
25 U7 **Tifton** Georgia, SE USA
175 Ss11 **Tifu** Pulau Buru, E Indonesia
197 K6 **Tiga, Île** *island* Îles Loyauté, W New Caledonia
40 L17 **Tigalda Island** *island* Aleutian Islands, Alaska, USA
117 I15 **Tigáni, Ákra** *headland* Límnos, E Greece
175 O1 **Tiga Tarok** Sabah, East Malaysia
119 O10 **Tighina** *Rus.* Bendery; *prev.* Bender. E Moldova
127 P10 **Tigil'** Koryakskiy Avtonomnyy Okrug, E Russian Federation
151 X9 **Tigiretskiy Khrebet** ▲▲ E Kazakhstan
81 F14 **Tignère** Adamaoua, N Cameroon
11 P14 **Tignish** Prince Edward Island, SE Canada
Tigranocerta *see* Siirt
43 O11 **Tigre, Cerro del** ▲ C Mexico
58 F8 **Tigre, Río** ≈ N Peru
145 X10 **Tigris** *Ar.* Dijlah, *Turk.* Dicle. ≈ Iraq/Turkey
78 G9 **Tiguent** Trarza, SW Mauritania
76 M10 **Tiguentourine** E Algeria
79 V10 **Tiguidit, Falaise de** *ridge* C Niger
147 N13 **Tihāmah** *var.* Tehama. *plain* Saudi Arabia/Yemen
Tihert *see* Tiaret
Ti-hua/Tihwa *see* Ürümqi
43 Q13 **Tihuatlán** Veracruz-Llave, E Mexico
42 B1 **Tijuana** Baja California, NW Mexico
44 E2 **Tikal** Petén, N Guatemala
160 I9 **Tīkamgarh** *prev.* Tehri. Madhya Pradesh, C India
164 L7 **Tikanlik** Xinjiang Uygur Zizhiqu, NW China
79 P12 **Tikaré** N Burkina
41 O12 **Tikchik Lakes** *lakes* Alaska, USA
203 T9 **Tikehau** *atoll* Îles Tuamotu, C French Polynesia
203 V9 **Tikei** *island* Îles Tuamotu, C French Polynesia
125 B12 **Tikhoretsk** Krasnodarskiy Kray, SW Russian Federation
128 I13 **Tikhvin** Leningradskaya Oblast', NW Russian Federation
199 Ll10 **Tiki Basin** *undersea feature* S Pacific Ocean
78 K13 **Tikinsso** ≈ NE Guinea
192 Q8 **Tikitiki** Gisborne, North Island, NZ
81 D16 **Tiko** Sud-Ouest, SW Cameroon
145 S6 **Tikrīt** *var.* Tekrit. N Iraq
128 I8 **Tiksha** Respublika Kareliya, NW Russian Federation
128 I6 **Tikshozero, Ozero** ◎ NW Russian Federation
126 L7 **Tiksi** Respublika Sakha (Yakutiya), NE Russian Federation
173 G8 **Tiku** Sumatera, W Indonesia
44 A6 **Tilapa** San Marcos, SW Guatemala
44 L13 **Tilarán** Guanacaste, NW Costa Rica
101 J14 **Tilburg** Noord-Brabant, S Netherlands
12 D17 **Tilbury** Ontario, S Canada
190 K4 **Tilcha** South Australia
Tilcha Creek *see* Callabonna Creek
31 Q14 **Tilden** Nebraska, C USA
27 R13 **Tilden** Texas, SW USA
12 H10 **Tilden Lake** Ontario, S Canada
118 G9 **Tileagd** *Hung.* Mezőtelegd. Bihor, W Romania
79 Q8 **Tilemsi, Vallée de** ≈ C Mali
127 Pp8 **Tilichiki** Koryakskiy Avtonomnyy Okrug, E Russian Federation
Tiligul *see* Tilihul
Tiligul'skiy Liman *see* Tilihul's'kyy Lyman
119 P9 **Tilihul** *Rus.* Tiligul. ≈ SW Ukraine
119 P10 **Tilihul's'kyy Lyman** *Rus.* Tiligul'skiy Liman. ◎ S Ukraine
Tilimsen *see* Tlemcen
Tilio Martius *see* Toulon
79 R11 **Tillabéri** *var.* Tillabéry. Tillabéri, W Niger
79 R11 **Tillabéri** ◈ *department* SW Niger
Tillabéry *see* Tillabéri
34 F11 **Tillamook** Oregon, NW USA
34 E11 **Tillamook Bay** *inlet* Oregon, NW USA
157 Q22 **Tillanchāng Dwīp** *island* Nicobar Islands, India, NE Indian Ocean
97 N15 **Tillberga** Västmanland, C Sweden
Tillenberg *see* Dyleň
23 S10 **Tillery, Lake** ▣ North Carolina, SE USA
79 T10 **Tillia** Tahoua, W Niger
25 N8 **Tillmans Corner** Alabama, S USA
12 F17 **Tillsonburg** Ontario, S Canada
117 N22 **Tílos** *island* Dodekánisos, Greece, Aegean Sea
191 N5 **Tilpa** New South Wales, SE Australia
Tilsit *see* Sovetsk
33 N13 **Tilton** Illinois, N USA
130 K7 **Tim** Kurskaya Oblast', W Russian Federation
56 D12 **Timaná** Huila, S Colombia
Timan Ridge *see* Timanskiy Kryazh
129 Q6 **Timanskiy Kryazh** *Eng.* Timan Ridge. *ridge* NW Russian Federation
193 G20 **Timaru** Canterbury, South Island, NZ
131 S6 **Timashevo** Samarskaya Oblast', W Russian Federation
130 K13 **Timashevsk** Krasnodarskiy Kray, SW Russian Federation
Timbaki/Timbákion *see* Tympáki
24 K10 **Timbalier Bay** *bay* Louisiana, S USA
24 K11 **Timbalier Island** *island* Louisiana, S USA
194 K12 **Timbe** ≈ C Papau New Guinea
78 L10 **Timbedgha** *var.* Timbédra. Hodh ech Chargui, SE Mauritania
Timbédra *see* Timbedgha
34 G10 **Timber** Oregon, NW USA
189 O3 **Timber Creek** Northern Territory, N Australia
30 M8 **Timber Lake** South Dakota, N USA
56 D12 **Timbío** Cauca, SW Colombia
56 C12 **Timbiquí** Cauca, SW Colombia
85 O17 **Timbue, Ponta** *headland* C Mozambique
Timbuktu *see* Tombouctou
176 Vv10 **Timbuni, Sungai** ≈ Irian Jaya, E Indonesia
175 Oo4 **Timbun Mata, Pulau** *island* E Malaysia
79 P8 **Timétrine** *var.* Ti-n-Kâr. *oasis* C Mali
Timfi *see* Týmfi
Timfristos *see* Tymfristós
79 V9 **Timia** Agadez, C Niger
176 X12 **Timika** Irian Jaya, E Indonesia
76 I9 **Timimoun** C Algeria
Timiris, Cap *see* Timirist, Râs
78 F8 **Timirist, Râs** *var.* Cap Timiris. *headland* NW Mauritania
151 O7 **Timiryazevo** Severnyy Kazakhstan, N Kazakhstan
118 E11 **Timiş** ◈ *county* SW Romania
12 H9 **Timiskaming, Lake** *Fr.* Lac Témiscamingue. ◎ Ontario/Québec, SE Canada
118 E11 **Timi Soara** ✕ Timiş, SW Romania
118 E11 **Timişoara** *Ger.* Temeschwar, Temeswar, *Hung.* Temesvár; *prev.* Temeschburg. Timiş, W Romania
Timkovichi *see* Tsimkavichy
79 U8 **Ti-m-Meghsoï** ≈ NW Niger
102 K8 **Timmerdorfer Strand** Schleswig-Holstein, N Germany
12 F7 **Timmins** Ontario, S Canada
23 S12 **Timmonsville** South Carolina, SE USA
32 K5 **Timms Hill** ▲ Wisconsin, N USA
176 Vv9 **Timoforo** ≈ Irian Jaya, E Indonesia
114 P12 **Timok** ≈ E Yugoslavia
60 N13 **Timon** Maranhão, E Brazil
175 Rr17 **Timor** *island* Nusa Tenggara, C Indonesia
175 S17 **Timor Sea** *sea* E Indian Ocean
175 S16 **Timor Timur** *off.* Propinsi Timor Timur, *var.* Loro Sae, *Eng.* East Timor; *prev.* Portuguese Timor. ◈ *province* S Indonesia
Timor Trench *see* Timor Trough
198 G9 **Timor Trough** *var.* Timor Trench. *undersea feature* NE Timor Sea
63 A21 **Timote** Buenos Aires, E Argentina
56 I6 **Timotes** Mérida, NW Venezuela
27 X8 **Timpson** Texas, SW USA
126 Ll13 **Timpton** ≈ NE Russian Federation
95 H17 **Timrå** Västernorrland, C Sweden
22 J10 **Tims Ford Lake** ▣ Tennessee, S USA
174 Hh7 **Timun** Pulau Kundur, C Indonesia
174 H3 **Timur, Banjaran** ▲▲ Peninsular Malaysia
179 R17 **Tinaca Point** *headland* Mindanao, S Philippines
56 K5 **Tinaco** Cojedes, N Venezuela
66 Q11 **Tinajo** Lanzarote, Islas Canarias, Spain, NE Atlantic Ocean
195 W8 **Tinakula** *island* Santa Cruz Islands, E Solomon Islands
56 K5 **Tinaquillo** Cojedes, N Venezuela
118 F10 **Tinca** *Hung.* Tenke. Bihor, W Romania
161 J20 **Tindivanam** Tamil Nādu, SE India
76 E9 **Tindouf** W Algeria
76 E9 **Tindouf, Sebkha de** *salt lake* W Algeria
106 J2 **Tineo** Asturias, N Spain
79 R9 **Ti-n-Essako** Kidal, E Mali
191 T5 **Tingha** New South Wales, SE Australia
Tingis *see* Tanger
Tinglett *see* Tinglev
97 F24 **Tinglev** *Ger.* Tinglett. Sønderjylland, SW Denmark
58 E12 **Tingo María** Huánuco, C Peru
Tingréla *see* Tengréla
164 K16 **Tingri** *var.* Xêgar. Xizang Zizhiqu, W China
97 M21 **Tingsryd** Kronoberg, S Sweden
97 P19 **Tingstäde** Gotland, SE Sweden
64 H12 **Tinguiririca, Volcán** ▲ C Chile
96 F9 **Tingvoll** Møre og Romsdal, S Norway
194 M9 **Tingwon Island** *island* N PNG
196 K8 **Tinian** *island* S Northern Mariana Islands
Ti-n-Kâr *see* Timétrine
Tinnevelly *see* Tirunelveli
97 G15 **Tinnoset** Telemark, S Norway
97 F15 **Tinnsjø** ◎ S Norway
Tino *see* Chino
117 J20 **Tínos** Tínos, Kykládes, Greece, Aegean Sea
117 J20 **Tínos** *anc.* Tenos. *island* Kykládes, Greece, Aegean Sea
159 R14 **Tinpahar** Bihār, NE India
124 O14 **Tin, Ra's al** *headland* N Libya
159 X11 **Tinsukia** Assam, NE India
78 K10 **Tintâne** Hodh el Gharbi, S Mauritania
64 L7 **Tintina** Santiago del Estero, N Argentina
190 K10 **Tintinara** South Australia
106 I14 **Tinto** ≈ SW Spain
79 S8 **Ti-n-Zaouâtene** Kidal, NE Mali
Tiobraid Árann *see* Tipperary
30 K3 **Tioga** North Dakota, N USA
20 G12 **Tioga** Pennsylvania, NE USA
27 T5 **Tioga** Texas, SW USA
37 Q8 **Tioga Pass** *pass* California, W USA
20 G12 **Tioga River** ≈ New York/Pennsylvania, NE USA
176 Y11 **Tiom** Irian Jaya, E Indonesia
Tioman Island *see* Tioman, Pulau
174 I5 **Tioman, Pulau** *var.* Tioman Island. *island* Peninsular Malaysia
20 C12 **Tionesta** Pennsylvania, NE USA
20 D12 **Tionesta Creek** ≈ Pennsylvania, NE USA
173 G11 **Tiop** Pulau Pagai Selatan, W Indonesia
175 Qq12 **Tioro, Selat** *var.* Tiworo. *strait* Sulawesi, C Indonesia
79 O12 **Tiou** NW Burkina
20 H11 **Tioughnioga River** ≈ New York, NE USA
176 U10 **Tip** Irian Jaya, E Indonesia
76 J5 **Tipasa** *var.* Tipaza. N Algeria
Tipaza *see* Tipasa
44 J10 **Tipitapa** Managua, W Nicaragua
33 R13 **Tipp City** Ohio, N USA
33 O12 **Tippecanoe River** ≈ Indiana, N USA
99 D20 **Tipperary** *Ir.* Tiobraid Árann. S Ireland
99 D19 **Tipperary** *Ir.* Tiobraid Árann. *cultural region* S Ireland
37 R12 **Tipton** California, W USA
33 P13 **Tipton** Indiana, N USA
31 Y14 **Tipton** Iowa, C USA
29 U5 **Tipton** Missouri, C USA
38 I10 **Tipton, Mount** ▲ Arizona, SW USA
22 F8 **Tiptonville** Tennessee, S USA
10 E12 **Tip Top Mountain** ▲ Ontario, S Canada
161 G19 **Tiptūr** Karnātaka, W India
Tiquisate *see* Pueblo Nuevo Tiquisate
60 L13 **Tiracambu, Serra do** ▲▲ E Brazil
Tirana *see* Tiranë
115 K19 **Tirana Rinas** ✕ Durrës, W Albania
115 L20 **Tiranë** *var.* Tirana. ● (Albania) Tiranë, C Albania
115 K20 **Tiranë** ◈ *district* W Albania
146 I5 **Tirān, Jazīrat** *island* Egypt/Saudi Arabia
108 F6 **Tirano** Lombardia, N Italy
190 I2 **Tirari Desert** *desert* South Australia
119 O10 **Tiraspol** *Rus.* Tiraspol'. E Moldova
192 M8 **Tirau** Waikato, North Island, NZ
142 C14 **Tire** İzmir, SW Turkey
143 O11 **Tirebolu** Giresun, N Turkey
98 F11 **Tiree** *island* W Scotland, UK
Tîrgovişte *see* Târgovişte
Tîrgu *see* Târgu Cărbuneşti
Tîrgu Bujor *see* Târgu Bujor
Tîrgu Frumos *see* Târgu Frumos
Tîrgu Jiu *see* Targu Jui
Tîrgu Lăpuş *see* Târgu Lăpuş
Tîrgu Mures *see* Târgu Mureş
Tîrgu-Neamţ *see* Târgu-Neamţ
Tîrgu Ocna *see* Târgu Ocna
Tîrgu Secuiesc *see* Târgu Secuiesc
155 T3 **Tirich Mīr** ▲ NW Pakistan
78 J5 **Tiris Zemmour** ◈ *region* N Mauritania
Tirlemont *see* Tienen
131 W5 **Tirlyanskiy** Respublika Bashkortostan, W Russian Federation
Tîrnava Mare *see* Târnava Mare
Tîrnava Mică *see* Târnava Mică
Tîrnăveni *see* Târnăveni
Tírnavos *see* Týrnavos
Tirnovo *see* Veliko Tŭrnovo
160 J11 **Tirodi** Madhya Pradesh, C India
110 K8 **Tirol** *off.* Land Tirol, *var.* Tyrol, *It.* Tirolo. ◈ *state* W Austria
Tirolo *see* Tirol
Tirreno, Mare *see* Tyrrhenian Sea
109 B19 **Tirso** ≈ Sardegna, Italy, C Mediterranean Sea
97 H22 **Tirstrup** ✕ (Århus) Århus, C Denmark
161 I21 **Tiruchchirāppalli** *prev.* Trichinopoly. Tamil Nādu, SE India
161 H23 **Tirunelveli** *var.* Tinnevelly. Tamil Nādu, SE India
161 J19 **Tirupati** Andhra Pradesh, E India
161 I20 **Tiruppattūr** Tamil Nādu, SE India
161 H21 **Tiruppur** Tamil Nādu, SW India
161 I20 **Tiruvannāmalai** Tamil Nādu, SE India
114 L10 **Tisa** *Ger.* Theiss, *Hung.* Tisza, *Rus.* Tissa, *Ukr.* Tysa. ≈ SE Europe *see also* Tisza
Tischnowitz *see* Tišnov
9 U14 **Tisdale** Saskatchewan, S Canada
29 O13 **Tishomingo** Oklahoma, C USA
97 M17 **Tisnaren** ◎ S Sweden
113 F18 **Tišnov** *Ger.* Tischnowitz. Jižní Morava, SE Czech Republic
Tissa *see* Tisa/Tisza
76 J6 **Tissemsilt** N Algeria
159 S12 **Tista** ≈ NE India
114 L8 **Tisza** *Ger.* Theiss, *Rom./Slvn./SCr.* Tisa, *Rus.* Tissa, *Ukr.* Tysa. ≈ SE Europe *see also* Tisa
113 L23 **Tiszaföldvár** Jász-Nagykun-Szolnok, E Hungary
113 M22 **Tiszafüred** Jász-Nagykun-Szolnok, E Hungary
113 L23 **Tiszakécske** Bács-Kiskun, C Hungary
113 M21 **Tiszaújváros** *prev.* Leninváros. Borsod-Abaúj-Zemplén, NE Hungary
113 N21 **Tiszavasvári** Szabolcs-Szatmár-Bereg, NE Hungary
Titibu *see* Chichibu
59 I17 **Titicaca, Lake** ◎ Bolivia/Peru
202 H17 **Titikaveka** Rarotonga, S Cook Islands
160 M13 **Titilāgarh** Orissa, E India
174 Gg4 **Titiwangsa, Banjaran** ▲▲ Peninsular Malaysia
Titograd *see* Podgorica
Titose *see* Chitose
Titova Mitrovica *see* Kosovska Mitrovica
Titovo Užice *see* Užice
115 M18 **Titov Vrv** ▲ NW FYR Macedonia
96 F7 **Titran** Sør-Trøndelag, S Norway
33 Q8 **Tittabawassee River** ≈ Michigan, N USA
118 J13 **Titu** Dâmboviţa, S Romania
81 M16 **Titule** Haut-Zaïre, N Zaire
25 X11 **Titusville** Florida, SE USA
20 C12 **Titusville** Pennsylvania, NE USA
78 G11 **Tivaouane** W Senegal
115 I17 **Tivat** Montenegro, SW Yugoslavia
12 E14 **Tiverton** Ontario, S Canada
99 J23 **Tiverton** SW England, UK
21 O12 **Tiverton** Rhode Island, NE USA
109 I15 **Tivoli** *anc.* Tiber. Lazio, C Italy
27 U13 **Tivoli** Texas, SW USA
176 W11 **Tiwarra** Irian Jaya, E Indonesia
147 Z8 **Ţīwī** NE Oman
Tiworo *see* Tioro, Selat
176 Ww12 **Tiyo, Pegunungan** ▲▲ Irian Jaya, E Indonesia
43 Y11 **Tizimín** Yucatán, SE Mexico
76 K5 **Tizi Ouzou** *var.* Tizi-Ouzou. N Algeria
76 D8 **Tiznit** SW Morocco
115 I14 **Tjentište** SE Bosnia and Herzegovina
Tjepoe/Tjepu *see* Cepu
100 L7 **Tjeukemeer** ◎ N Netherlands
Tjiamis *see* Ciamis
Tjiandjoer *see* Cianjur
Tjilatjap *see* Cilacap
Tjiledoeg *see* Ciledug
97 F23 **Tjæreborg** Ribe, W Denmark
97 I18 **Tjörn** *island* S Sweden
94 O3 **Tjuvfjorden** *fjord* S Svalbard
Tkvarcheli *see* Tqvarch'eli
42 L8 **Tlahualillo** Durango, N Mexico
43 P14 **Tlalnepantla** México, C Mexico
43 Q13 **Tlapacoyán** Veracruz-Llave, E Mexico
43 P16 **Tlapa de Comonfort** Guerrero, S Mexico
42 L13 **Tlaquepaque** Jalisco, C Mexico
Tlascala *see* Tlaxcala
43 P14 **Tlaxcala** *var.* Tlascala, Tlaxcala de Xicohténcatl. Tlaxcala, C Mexico
43 P14 **Tlaxcala** ◈ *state* S Mexico
Tlaxcala de Xicohténcatl *see* Tlaxcala
43 P14 **Tlaxco** *var.* Tlaxco de Morelos. Tlaxcala, S Mexico
Tlaxco de Morelos *see* Tlaxco
43 Q16 **Tlaxiaco** *var.* Santa María Asunción Tlaxiaco. Oaxaca, S Mexico
76 I6 **Tlemcen** *var.* Tilimsen, Tlemsen. NW Algeria
Tlemsen *see* Tlemcen
144 L4 **Tlété Ouâte Rharbi, Jebel** ▲ N Syria
118 J7 **Tlumach** Ivano-Frankivs'ka Oblast', W Ukraine
131 P17 **Tlyarata** Respublika Dagestan, SW Russian Federation
118 K10 **Toaca, Vârful** *prev.* Vîrful Toaca. ▲ NE Romania
Toaca, Vîrful *see* Toaca, Vârful
197 C13 **Toak** Ambrym, C Vanuatu
180 J4 **Toamasina** *var.* Tamatave. Toamasina, E Madagascar
180 J4 **Toamasina** ◈ *province* E Madagascar
180 J4 **Toamasina** ✕ Toamasina, E Madagascar
23 X6 **Toano** Virginia, NE USA
203 U10 **Toau** *atoll* Îles Tuamotu, C French Polynesia
47 T6 **Toa Vaca, Embalse** ▣ C Puerto Rico
64 K13 **Toay** La Pampa, C Argentina
165 R14 **Toba** Xizang Zizhiqu, W China
171 Hh16 **Toba** Mie, Honshū, SW Japan
173 Ff5 **Toba, Danau** ◎ Sumatera, W Indonesia
47 Y16 **Tobago** *island* NE Trinidad and Tobago
155 Q9 **Toba Kākar Range** ▲▲ NW Pakistan
175 T10 **Tobalai, Selat** *strait* Maluku, E Indonesia
175 Q9 **Tobamawu** Sulawesi, N Indonesia
107 Q12 **Tobarra** Castilla-La Mancha, C Spain
155 U9 **Toba Tek Singh** Punjab, E Pakistan
175 T6 **Tobelo** Pulau Halmahera, E Indonesia
12 E12 **Tobermory** Ontario, S Canada
98 G10 **Tobermory** W Scotland, UK
172 Oo5 **Tōbetsu** Hokkaidō, NE Japan
188 M6 **Tobin Lake** ◎ Western Australia
9 U14 **Tobin Lake** ◎ Saskatchewan, C Canada
37 T4 **Tobin, Mount** ▲ Nevada, W USA
171 L10 **Tobi-shima** *island* C Japan
174 J11 **Toboali** Pulau Bangka, W Indonesia
150 M8 **Tobol** *Kaz.* Tobyl. Kustanay, N Kazakhstan
150 L8 **Tobol** *Kaz.* Tobyl. ≈ Kazakhstan/Russian Federation
125 F11 **Tobol'sk** Tyumenskaya Oblast', C Russian Federation
Tobruch/Tobruk *see* Ţubruq
129 R3 **Tobseda** Nenetskiy Avtonomnyy Okrug, NW Russian Federation
Tobyl *see* Tobol
129 Q6 **Tobysh** ≈ NW Russian Federation
56 F10 **Tocaima** Cundinamarca, C Colombia
61 K16 **Tocantins** *off.* Estado do Tocantins. ◈ *state* C Brazil
61 K15 **Tocantins, Rio** ≈ N Brazil
25 T2 **Toccoa** Georgia, SE USA
171 K15 **Tochigi** *var.* Totigi. Tochigi, Honshū, S Japan
171 Kk15 **Tochigi** *off.* Tochigi-ken, *var.* Totigi. ◈ *prefecture* Honshū, S Japan
171 K13 **Tochio** *var.* Totio. Niigata, Honshū, C Japan
97 I15 **Töcksfors** Värmland, C Sweden
44 J5 **Tocoa** Colón, N Honduras
64 H4 **Tocopilla** Antofagasta, N Chile
64 I4 **Tocorpuri, Cerro de** ▲ Bolivia/Chile
191 O10 **Tocumwal** New South Wales, SE Australia
56 K4 **Tocuyo de La Costa** Falcón, NW Venezuela
158 H13 **Toda Rāisingh** Rājasthān, N India
108 H13 **Todi** Umbria, C Italy
110 G9 **Tödi** ▲ NE Switzerland
176 Uu9 **Todlo** Irian Jaya, E Indonesia
172 N12 **Todoga-saki** *headland* Honshū, C Japan
61 P17 **Todos os Santos, Baía de** *bay* E Brazil
42 F10 **Todos Santos** Baja California Sur, W Mexico
42 B2 **Todos Santos, Bahía de** *bay* NW Mexico
Toeal *see* Tual
Toeban *see* Tuban
Toekang Besi Eilanden *see* Tukangbesi, Kepulauan
Tōen *see* T'aoyüan
193 D25 **Toetoes Bay** *bay* South Island, NZ
9 Q14 **Tofield** Alberta, SW Canada
8 K17 **Tofino** Vancouver Island, British Columbia, SW Canada
201 X17 **Tofol** Kosrae, E Micronesia
97 J20 **Tofta** Halland, S Sweden
97 H15 **Tofte** Buskerud, S Norway
97 F24 **Toftlund** Sønderjylland, SW Denmark
200 S13 **Tofua** *island* Ha'apai Group, C Tonga
197 B10 **Toga** *island* Torres Islands, N Vanuatu
171 Kk17 **Tōgane** Chiba, Honshū, S Japan
82 N13 **Togdheer** *off.* Gobolka Togdheer. ◈ *region* NW Somalia
Toghyzaq *see* Toguzak
171 Ii12 **Togi** Ishikawa, Honshū, SW Japan
41 N13 **Togiak** Alaska, USA
175 Qq8 **Togian, Kepulauan** *island group* C Indonesia
79 Q15 **Togo** *off.* Togolese Republic; *prev.* French Togoland. ◆ *republic* W Africa
168 F8 **Tögrög** Govĭ-Altay, SW Mongolia
168 E7 **Tögrög** Hovd, W Mongolia
Togton-heyan *see* Tuotuoheyan
150 L7 **Toguzak** *Kaz.* Toghyzaq. ≈ Kazakhstan/Russian Federation
39 P10 **Tohatchi** New Mexico, SW USA
203 O7 **Tohiea, Mont** ▲ Moorea, W French Polynesia
95 O17 **Tohmajärvi** Pohjois-Karjala, SE Finland
143 N14 **Tohma Çayı** ≈ C Turkey
95 L16 **Toholampi** Vaasa, W Finland
168 M10 **Töhöm** Dornogovĭ, SE Mongolia
25 X12 **Tohopekaliga, Lake** ◎ Florida, SE USA
171 J17 **Toi** Shizuoka, Honshū, S Japan
202 B15 **Toi** N Niue
95 L19 **Toijala** Häme, SW Finland
175 Qq9 **Toima** Sulawesi, N Indonesia
170 C17 **Toi-misaki** *headland* Kyūshū, SW Japan
175 Rr17 **Toineke** Timor, S Indonesia
Toirc, Inis *see* Inishturk
37 U6 **Toiyabe Range** ▲▲ Nevada, W USA
Tojikiston, Jumhurii *see* Tajikistan
153 R12 **Tojikobod** *Rus.* Tadzhikabad. C Tajikistan
170 F13 **Tōjō** Hiroshima, Honshū, SW Japan
41 T10 **Tok** Alaska, USA
172 P5 **Tokachi-dake** ▲ Hokkaidō, NE Japan

◆ Country ● Country Capital ◇ Dependent Territory ○ Dependent Territory Capital ◈ Administrative Region ✕ International Airport ▲ Mountain ▲▲ Mountain Range ▲ Volcano ≈ River ◎ Lake ▣ Reservoir

172 Pp7 **Tokachi-gawa** *var.* Tokati Gawa. ≈ Hokkaidō, NE Japan
171 Hh16 **Tōkai** Aichi, Honshū, SW Japan
113 N21 **Tokaj** Borsod-Abaúj-Zemplén, NE Hungary
171 Jj13 **Tōkamachi** Niigata, Honshū, C Japan
193 D25 **Tokanui** Southland, South Island, NZ
82 I7 **Tokar** *var.* Ṭawkar. Red Sea, NE Sudan
142 L12 **Tokat** Tokat, N Turkey
142 L12 **Tokat** ◆ *province* N Turkey
Tokati Gawa *see* Tokachi-gawa
169 X15 **Tŏkchŏk-gundo** *island group* NW South Korea
Tōke *see* Taka Atoll
202 J9 **Tokelau** ◇ *NZ overseas territory* W Polynesia
Tőketerebes *see* Trebišov
Tokhtamyshbek *see* Tŭkhtamish
26 M6 **Tokio** Texas, SW USA
Tokio *see* Tōkyō
201 W11 **Toki Point** *point* NW Wake Island
Tokkuztara *see* Gongliu
153 V7 **Tokmak** *Kir.* Tokmok. Chuyskaya Oblast', N Kyrgyzstan
119 V9 **Tokmak** *var.* Velykyy Tokmak. Zaporiz'ka Oblast', SE Ukraine
Tokmok *see* Tokmak
192 Q8 **Tokomaru Bay** Gisborne, North Island, NZ
171 Hh16 **Tokoname** Aichi, Honshū, SW Japan
172 Qq5 **Tokoro** Hokkaidō, NE Japan
192 M8 **Tokoroa** Waikato, North Island, NZ
172 Q6 **Tokoro-gawa** ≈ Hokkaidō, NE Japan
78 K14 **Tokounou** Haute-Guinée, C Guinea
40 M12 **Toksook Bay** Alaska, USA
Toksu *see* Xinhe
Toksum *see* Toksun
164 L6 **Toksun** *var.* Toksum. Xinjiang Uygur Zizhiqu, NW China
153 T8 **Toktogul** Talasskaya Oblast', NW Kyrgyzstan
153 T9 **Toktogul'skoye Vodokhranilishche** ⊡ W Kyrgyzstan
Toktomush *see* Tŭkhtamish
200 Ss12 **Toku** *island* Vava'u Group, N Tonga
172 Qq14 **Tokunoshima** Kagoshima, Tokuno-shima, SW Japan
172 Q14 **Tokuno-shima** *island* Nansei-shotō, SW Japan
170 Ff15 **Tokushima** *var.* Tokusima. Tokushima, Shikoku, SW Japan
170 F15 **Tokushima** *off.* Tokushima-ken, *var.* Tokusima. ◆ *prefecture* Shikoku, SW Japan
Tokusima *see* Tokushima
170 E13 **Tokuyama** Yamaguchi, Honshū, SW Japan
171 Jj16 **Tōkyō** *var.* Tokio. ● (Japan) Tōkyō, Honshū, S Japan
171 J15 **Tōkyō** *off.* Tōkyō-to. ◆ *capital district* Honshū, S Japan
171 K17 **Tōkyō-wan** *bay* S Japan
151 T12 **Tokyrau** ≈ C Kazakhstan
155 O3 **Tokzār** *Pash.* Tukzār. Sar-e Pol, N Afghanistan
201 U12 **Tol** *atoll* Chuuk Islands, C Micronesia
192 Q9 **Tolaga Bay** Gisborne, North Island, NZ
180 I7 **Tôlañaro** *prev.* Faradofay, Fort-Dauphin. Toliara, SE Madagascar
168 D6 **Tolbo** Bayan-Ölgiy, W Mongolia
Tolbukhin *see* Dobrich
62 G11 **Toledo** Paraná, S Brazil
56 G8 **Toledo** Norte de Santander, N Colombia
179 Qq13 **Toledo** *off.* Toledo City. Cebu, C Philippines
107 N9 **Toledo** *anc.* Toletum. Castilla-La Mancha, C Spain
32 M14 **Toledo** Illinois, N USA
31 W13 **Toledo** Iowa, C USA
33 R11 **Toledo** Ohio, N USA
34 F12 **Toledo** Oregon, NW USA
34 G9 **Toledo** Washington, NW USA
44 F3 **Toledo** ◆ *district* S Belize
106 M9 **Toledo** ◆ *province* Castilla-La Mancha, C Spain
27 Y7 **Toledo Bend Reservoir** ⊡ Louisiana/Texas, SW USA
106 M10 **Toledo, Montes de** ▲ C Spain
108 J12 **Tolentino** Marche, C Italy
Toletum *see* Toledo
96 H10 **Tolga** Hedmark, S Norway
164 J3 **Toli** Xinjiang Uygur Zizhiqu, NW China
180 H7 **Toliara** *var.* Toliary; *prev.* Tuléar. Toliara, SW Madagascar
180 H7 **Toliara** ◆ *province* SW Madagascar
Toliary *see* Toliara
56 D11 **Tolima** *off.* Departamento del Tolima. ◆ *province* C Colombia
175 Pp7 **Tolitoli** Sulawesi, C Indonesia
97 K22 **Tollarp** Kristianstad, S Sweden
102 N9 **Tollense** ≈ NE Germany
102 N10 **Tollensesee** ⊚ NE Germany
38 K13 **Tolleson** Arizona, SW USA
152 M13 **Tollimarjon** *Rus.* Talimardzhan. Qashqadaryo Wiloyati, S Uzbekistan
Tolmein *see* Tolmin
108 J6 **Tolmezzo** Friuli-Venezia Giulia, NE Italy
111 S11 **Tolmin** *Ger.* Tolmein, *It.* Tolmino. W Slovenia
Tolmino *see* Tolmin
113 J25 **Tolna** *Ger.* Tolnau. Tolna, S Hungary
113 I24 **Tolna** *off.* Tolna Megye. ◆ *county* SW Hungary
Tolnau *see* Tolna
81 I20 **Tolo** Bandundu, W Zaire
Tolochin *see* Talachyn
202 D12 **Toloke** Île Futuna, W Wallis and Futuna
32 M13 **Tolono** Illinois, N USA
107 Q3 **Tolosa** País Vasco, N Spain
Tolosa *see* Toulouse
175 Qq10 **Tolo, Teluk** *bay* Sulawesi, C Indonesia
41 R9 **Tolovana River** ≈ Alaska, USA
127 Oo10 **Tolstoy, Mys** *headland* E Russian Federation
65 G15 **Toltén** Araucanía, C Chile
65 G15 **Toltén, Río** ≈ S Chile
56 E6 **Tolú** Sucre, NW Colombia
43 O14 **Toluca** *var.* Toluca de Lerdo. México, S Mexico
Toluca de Lerdo *see* Toluca
43 O14 **Toluca, Nevado de** ⛰ C Mexico
131 R6 **Tol'yatti** *prev.* Stavropol'. Samarskaya Oblast', W Russian Federation
126 H14 **Tom'** ≈ S Russian Federation
29 O12 **Toma** NW Burkina
32 K7 **Tomah** Wisconsin, N USA
32 L5 **Tomahawk** Wisconsin, N USA
119 T8 **Tomakivka** Dnipropetrovs'ka Oblast', E Ukraine
172 O6 **Tomakomai** Hokkaidō, NE Japan
172 P3 **Tomamae** Hokkaidō, NE Japan
106 G9 **Tomar** Santarém, W Portugal
127 O15 **Tomari** Ostrov Sakhalin, Sakhalinskaya Oblast', SE Russian Federation
117 C16 **Tómaros** ▲ W Greece
Tomaschow *see* Tomaszów Lubelski, Poland
Tomaschow *see* Tomaszów Mazowiecki, Poland
63 E16 **Tomás Gomensoro** Artigas, N Uruguay
119 N7 **Tomashpil'** Vinnyts'ka Oblast', C Ukraine
Tomaszów *see* Tomaszów Mazowiecki
113 P15 **Tomaszów Lubelski** *Ger.* Tomaschow. Zamość, SE Poland
Tomaszów Mazowiecka *see* Tomaszów Mazowiecki
112 L13 **Tomaszów Mazowiecki** *var.* Tomaszów Mazowiecka; *prev.* Tomaszów, *Ger.* Tomaschow. Piotrków, C Poland
42 J13 **Tomatlán** Jalisco, C Mexico
170 F12 **Tombara** Shimane, Honshū, SW Japan
83 F15 **Tombe** Jonglei, S Sudan
25 N4 **Tombigbee River** ≈ Alabama/Mississippi, S USA
84 A10 **Tomboco** Zaire, NW Angola
79 O10 **Tombouctou** *Eng.* Timbuktu. Tombouctou, N Mali
79 N9 **Tombouctou** ◆ *region* W Mali
39 N16 **Tombstone** Arizona, SW USA
85 A15 **Tombua** *Port.* Porto Alexandre. Namibe, SW Angola
85 J19 **Tom Burke** Northern, NE South Africa
152 L9 **Tomdibuloq** *Rus.* Tamdybulak. Nawoiy Wiloyati, N Uzbekistan
152 L9 **Tomditow-Toghi** ▲ N Uzbekistan
64 G13 **Tomé** Bío Bío, C Chile
60 L12 **Tomé-Açu** Pará, NE Brazil
97 L23 **Tomelilla** Kristianstad, S Sweden
107 O10 **Tomelloso** Castilla-La Mancha, C Spain
12 H10 **Tomiko Lake** ⊚ Ontario, S Canada
79 N12 **Tominian** Ségou, C Mali
175 Pp8 **Tomini, Gulf of** *var.* Teluk Tomini; *prev.* Teluk Gorontalo. *bay* Sulawesi, C Indonesia
Tomini, Teluk *see* Tomini, Gulf of
172 Ll15 **Tomioka** Fukushima, Honshū, C Japan
172 Jj15 **Tomioka** Gunma, Honshū, S Japan
115 G14 **Tomislavgrad** SW Bosnia and Herzegovina
189 O9 **Tomkinson Ranges** ▲ South Australia/Western Australia
126 Ll12 **Tommot** Respublika Sakha (Yakutiya), NE Russian Federation
175 Rr7 **Tomohon** Sulawesi, N Indonesia
56 K9 **Tomo, Río** ≈ E Colombia
115 L21 **Tomorrit, Mali i** ▲ S Albania
9 S17 **Tompkins** Saskatchewan, S Canada
22 K8 **Tompkinsville** Kentucky, S USA
175 Pp7 **Tompo** Sulawesi, N Indonesia
188 I8 **Tom Price** Western Australia
126 H13 **Tomsk** Tomskaya Oblast', C Russian Federation
126 Gg12 **Tomskaya Oblast'** ◆ *province* C Russian Federation
20 K16 **Toms River** New Jersey, NE USA
Tom Steed Lake *see* Tom Steed Reservoir
28 L12 **Tom Steed Reservoir** *var.* Tom Steed Lake. ⊡ Oklahoma, C USA
176 Vv10 **Tomu** Irian Jaya, E Indonesia
194 F13 **Tomu** ≈ W PNG
164 H6 **Tomur Feng** *var.* Pik Pobedy, Pobeda Peak. ▲ China/Kyrgyzstan *see also* Pobedy, Pik
201 N13 **Tomworoahlang** Pohnpei, E Micronesia
43 U17 **Tonalá** Chiapas, SE Mexico
108 F6 **Tonale, Passo del** *pass* N Italy
171 Ii13 **Tonami** Toyama, Honshū, SW Japan
60 C12 **Tonantins** Amazonas, W Brazil
34 K6 **Tonasket** Washington, NW USA
57 Y9 **Tonate** *var.* Macouria. N French Guiana
20 D10 **Tonawanda** New York, NE USA
175 Rr7 **Tondano** Sulawesi, C Indonesia
175 Rr7 **Tondano, Danau** ⊚ Sulawesi, N Indonesia
106 H7 **Tondela** Viseu, N Portugal
97 F24 **Tønder** *Ger.* Tondern. Sønderjylland, SW Denmark
Tondern *see* Tønder
171 K16 **Tone-gawa** ≈ Honshū, S Japan
149 N4 **Tonekābon** *var.* Shahsawar, Tonkābon; *prev.* Shahsavār. Māzandarān, N Iran
Tonezh *see* Tonyezh
200 S15 **Tonga** *off.* Kingdom of Tonga, *var.* Friendly Islands. ◆ *monarchy* SW Pacific Ocean
183 R9 **Tonga** *island group* SW Pacific Ocean
85 K23 **Tongaat** KwaZulu/Natal, E South Africa
167 Q13 **Tong'an** *var.* Tong an. Fujian, SE China
29 Q4 **Tonganoxie** Kansas, C USA
41 Y13 **Tongass National Forest** *reserve* Alaska, USA
200 Qq16 **Tongatapu** ✕ Tongatapu, S Tonga
200 R15 **Tongatapu** *island* Tongatapu Group, S Tonga
200 S14 **Tongatapu Group** *island group* S Tonga
183 S9 **Tonga Trench** *undersea feature* S Pacific Ocean
167 N8 **Tongbai Shan** ▲ C China
167 P8 **Tongcheng** Anhui, E China
166 L6 **Tongchuan** Shaanxi, C China
166 L12 **Tongdao** *var.* Tongdao Dongzu Zizhixian; *prev.* Shuangjiang. Hunan, S China
165 T11 **Tongde** Qinghai, C China
101 K19 **Tongeren** *Fr.* Tongres. Limburg, NE Belgium
Tonggou *see* Tongyu
169 Y14 **Tonghae** NE South Korea
166 G13 **Tonghai** Yunnan, SW China
169 X8 **Tonghe** Heilongjiang, NE China
169 W11 **Tonghua** Jilin, NE China
194 L8 **Tong Island** *island* N PNG
169 Z6 **Tongjiang** Heilongjiang, NE China
169 Y13 **Tongjosŏn-man** *prev.* Broughton Bay. *bay* E North Korea
169 V7 **Tongken He** ≈ NE China
178 K7 **Tongking, Gulf of** *Chin.* Beibu Wan, *Vtn.* Vinh Bắc Bộ. *gulf* China/Vietnam
169 U10 **Tongliao** Nei Mongol Zizhiqu, N China
167 Q9 **Tongling** Anhui, E China
167 R9 **Tonglu** Zhejiang, SE China
197 D14 **Tongoa** *island* Shepherd Islands, S Vanuatu
64 G9 **Tongoy** Coquimbo, C Chile
166 L11 **Tongren** Guizhou, S China
165 T11 **Tongren** Qinghai, C China
Tongres *see* Tongeren
159 U11 **Tongsa** *var.* Tongsa Dzong. C Bhutan
Tongsa Dzong *see* Tongsa
Tongshan *see* Xuzhou
165 P12 **Tongtian He** ≈ C China
98 I6 **Tongue** N Scotland, UK
46 H3 **Tongue of the Ocean** *strait* C Bahamas
35 X10 **Tongue River** ≈ Montana, NW USA
35 W11 **Tongue River Resevoir** ⊡ Montana, NW USA
165 V11 **Tongwei** Gansu, C China
165 W9 **Tongxin** Ningxia, N China
169 U9 **Tongyu** *var.* Tonggou. Jilin, NE China
166 J11 **Tongzi** Guizhou, S China
42 G5 **Tónichi** Sonora, NW Mexico
83 D14 **Tonj** Warab, SW Sudan
158 H13 **Tonk** Rājasthān, N India
Tonkābon *see* Tonekābon
29 N8 **Tonkawa** Oklahoma, C USA
178 Ii12 **Tônlé Sap** *Eng.* Great Lake. ⊚ W Cambodia
104 L14 **Tonneins** Lot-et-Garonne, SW France
105 Q7 **Tonnerre** Yonne, C France
Tonoas *see* Dublon
37 U8 **Tonopah** Nevada, W USA
170 Ff14 **Tonoshō** Okayama, Shōdo-shima, SW Japan
45 S17 **Tonosí** Los Santos, S Panama
97 H16 **Tønsberg** Vestfold, S Norway
41 T11 **Tonsina** Alaska, USA
97 D17 **Tonstad** Vest-Agder, S Norway
200 S14 **Tonumea** *island* Nomuka Group, W Tonga
143 O11 **Tonya** Trabzon, NE Turkey
121 K20 **Tonyezh** *Rus.* Tonezh. Homyel'skaya Voblasts', SE Belarus
38 L3 **Tooele** Utah, W USA
126 Ii15 **Toora-Khem** Respublika Tyva, S Russian Federation
191 O5 **Toorale East** New South Wales, SE Australia
85 H25 **Toorberg** ▲ S South Africa
120 G5 **Tootsi** Pärnumaa, SW Estonia
191 U3 **Toowoomba** Queensland, E Australia
29 Q4 **Topeka** *state capital* Kansas, C USA
113 M18 **Topľa** *Hung.* Toplya. ≈ NE Slovakia
126 H14 **Topki** Kemerovskaya Oblast', S Russian Federation
Toplicza *see* Toplița
118 J10 **Toplița** *Ger.* Töplitz, *Hung.* Maroshévíz; *prev.* Toplița Română, *Hung.* Oláh-Toplicza, Toplicza. Harghita, C Romania
Toplița Română/Töplitz *see* Toplița
Toplya *see* Topľa
113 I20 **Topoľčany** *Hung.* Nagytapolcsány. Západné Slovensko, W Slovakia
42 G8 **Topolobampo** Sinaloa, C Mexico
118 I13 **Topoloveni** Argeș, S Romania
116 L11 **Topolovgrad** *prev.* Kavakli. Burgaska Oblast, SE Bulgaria
Topolya *see* Bačka Topola
128 I6 **Topozero, Ozero** ⊚ NW Russian Federation
34 J10 **Toppenish** Washington, NW USA
189 P4 **Top Springs Roadhouse** Northern Territory, N Australia
201 U11 **Tora** *island* Chuuk, C Micronesia
Toraigh *see* Tory Island
201 U11 **Tora Island Pass** *passage* Chuuk Islands, C Micronesia
149 U5 **Torbat-e Ḩeydarīyeh** *var.* Turbat-i-Haidari. Khorāsān, NE Iran
149 V5 **Torbat-e Jām** *var.* Turbat-i-Jam. Khorāsān, NE Iran
41 Q11 **Torbert, Mount** ▲ Alaska, USA
33 P6 **Torch Lake** ⊚ Michigan, N USA
Törcsvár *see* Bran
Torda *see* Turda
106 L6 **Tordesillas** Castilla-León, N Spain
94 K13 **Töre** Norrbotten, N Sweden
97 L17 **Töreboda** Skaraborg, S Sweden
97 J21 **Torekov** Kristianstad, S Sweden
94 O3 **Torell Land** *physical region* SW Svalbard
119 Y8 **Torez** Donets'ka Oblast', SE Ukraine
103 N14 **Torgau** Sachsen, E Germany
Torgay *see* Turgay
Torgay Üstirti *see* Turgayskaya Stolovaya Strana
Torghay/Torghay Oblysy *see* Turgay
97 N22 **Torhamn** Blekinge, S Sweden
101 C17 **Torhout** West-Vlaanderen, W Belgium
108 B8 **Torino** *Eng.* Turin. Piemonte, NW Italy
172 Q13 **Tori-shima** *island* Izu-shotō, SE Japan
83 F16 **Torit** Eastern Equatoria, S Sudan
195 O11 **Toriu** New Britain, E PNG
154 M4 **Torkestān, Selseleh-ye Band-e** *var.* Bandi-i Turkistan. ▲ NW Afghanistan
106 L7 **Tormes** ≈ W Spain
Tornacum *see* Tournai
Torneå *see* Tornio
94 K12 **Torneälven** *var.* Tornionjoki, *Fin.* Tornionjoki. ≈ Finland/Sweden
94 I11 **Torneträsk** ⊚ N Sweden
11 O4 **Torngat Mountains** ▲ Newfoundland and Labrador, NE Canada
26 H8 **Tornillo** Texas, SW USA
94 K13 **Tornio** *Swe.* Torneå. Lappi, NW Finland
Tornionjoki/Tornionjoki *see* Torneälven
63 B23 **Tornquist** Buenos Aires, E Argentina
106 L6 **Toro** Castilla-León, N Spain
64 H9 **Toro, Cerro del** ▲ N Chile
79 R12 **Torodi** Tillabéri, SW Niger
Törökbecse *see* Novi Bečej
195 S12 **Torokina** Bougainville Island, NE PNG
113 L23 **Törökszentmiklós** Jász-Nagykun-Szolnok, E Hungary
44 G7 **Torola, Río** ≈ El Salvador/Honduras
Toronaíos, Kólpos *see* Kassándras, Kólpos
12 H15 **Toronto** Ontario, S Canada
33 V12 **Toronto** Ohio, N USA
Toronto *see* Lester B.Pearson
29 P6 **Toronto Lake** ⊡ Kansas, C USA
37 V16 **Toro Peak** ▲ California, W USA
128 H16 **Toropets** Tverskaya Oblast', W Russian Federation
83 G18 **Tororo** E Uganda
142 H16 **Toros Dağları** *Eng.* Taurus Mountains. ▲ S Turkey
191 N13 **Torquay** Victoria, SE Australia
99 J24 **Torquay** SW England, UK
106 M5 **Torquemada** Castilla-León, N Spain
37 S16 **Torrance** California, W USA
106 G12 **Torrão** Setúbal, S Portugal
106 H8 **Torre, Alto da** ▲ C Portugal
109 K18 **Torre Annunziata** Campania, S Italy
107 T8 **Torreblanca** País Valenciano, E Spain
106 L15 **Torrecilla** ▲ S Spain
107 P4 **Torrecilla en Cameros** La Rioja, N Spain
107 N13 **Torredelcampo** Andalucía, S Spain
109 K17 **Torre del Greco** Campania, S Italy
106 I6 **Torre de Moncorvo** *var.* Moncorvo, Tôrre de Moncorvo. Bragança, N Portugal
106 J9 **Torrejoncillo** Extremadura, W Spain
107 O8 **Torrejón de Ardoz** Madrid, C Spain
107 N7 **Torrelaguna** Madrid, C Spain
107 N2 **Torrelavega** Cantabria, N Spain
109 M16 **Torremaggiore** Puglia, SE Italy
106 M15 **Torremolinos** Andalucía, S Spain
190 I6 **Torrens, Lake** *salt lake* South Australia
Torrent/Torrent de l'Horta *see* Torrente
107 S10 **Torrente** *var.* Torrent, Torrent de l'Horta. País Valenciano, E Spain
42 L8 **Torreón** Coahuila de Zaragoza, NE Mexico
107 R13 **Torre Pacheco** Murcia, SE Spain
108 A8 **Torre Pellice** Piemonte, NE Italy
107 O13 **Torreperogil** Andalucía, S Spain
63 J15 **Torres** Rio Grande do Sul, S Brazil
Torrès, Îles *see* Torres Islands
197 B10 **Torres Islands** *Fr.* Îles Torrès. *island group* N Vanuatu
106 G9 **Torres Novas** Santarém, C Portugal
189 V1 **Torres Strait** *strait* Australia/PNG
106 F10 **Torres Vedras** Lisboa, C Portugal
107 S13 **Torrevieja** País Valenciano, E Spain
194 F9 **Torricelli Mountains** ▲ NW PNG
98 G8 **Torridon, Loch** *inlet* NW Scotland, UK
108 D9 **Torriglia** Liguria, NW Italy
106 M9 **Torrijos** Castilla-La Mancha, C Spain
20 L12 **Torrington** Connecticut, NE USA
35 Z15 **Torrington** Wyoming, C USA
95 F16 **Torröjen** *var.* Torrön. ⊚ C Sweden
Torrön *see* Torröjen
107 N15 **Torrox** Andalucía, S Spain
96 N13 **Torsåker** Gävleborg, C Sweden
97 N21 **Torsås** Kalmar, S Sweden
97 J14 **Torsby** Värmland, C Sweden
97 N16 **Torshälla** Södermanland, C Sweden
Torshiz *see* Kāshmar
47 T9 **Tortola** *island* C British Virgin Islands
108 D9 **Tortona** *anc.* Dertona. Piemonte, NW Italy
109 L23 **Tortorici** Sicilia, Italy, C Mediterranean Sea
107 U7 **Tortosa** *anc.* Dertosa. Cataluña, E Spain
Tortosa *see* Ṭarṭūs
107 U7 **Tortosa, Cap** *headland* E Spain
46 L8 **Tortue, Île de la** *var.* Tortuga Island. *island* N Haiti
57 Y10 **Tortue, Montagne** ▲ C French Guiana
Tortuga, Isla *see* La Tortuga, Isla
Tortuga Island *see* Tortue, Île de la
56 C11 **Tortugas, Golfo** *gulf* W Colombia
47 T5 **Tortuguero, Laguna** *lagoon* N Puerto Rico
143 Q12 **Tortum** Erzurum, NE Turkey
Torugart, Pereval *see* Turugart Shankou
143 O12 **Torul** Gümüşhane, NE Turkey
112 J10 **Toruń** *Ger.* Thorn. Toruń, C Poland
112 J9 **Toruń** *off.* Województwo Toruńskie, *Ger.* Thorn. ◆ *province* N Poland
Toruńskie, Województwo *see* Toruń
97 K20 **Torup** Halland, S Sweden
120 I6 **Tõrva** *Ger.* Törwa. Valgamaa, S Estonia
Törwa *see* Tõrva
98 D13 **Tory Island** *Ir.* Toraigh. *island* NW Ireland
113 N19 **Torysa** *Hung.* Tarca. ≈ NE Slovakia
Törzburg *see* Bran
128 J16 **Torzhok** Tverskaya Oblast', W Russian Federation
170 Ee15 **Tosa** Kōchi, Shikoku, SW Japan
170 E16 **Tosa-Shimizu** *var.* Tosasimizu. Kōchi, Shikoku, SW Japan
Tosasimizu *see* Tosa-Shimizu
170 Ee16 **Tosa-wan** *bay* SW Japan
85 H21 **Tosca** North-West, N South Africa
108 F12 **Toscana** *Eng.* Tuscany. ◆ *region* C Italy
109 E14 **Toscano, Archipelago** *Eng.* Tuscan Archipelago. *island group* C Italy
108 G10 **Tosco-Emiliano, Appennino** *Eng.* Tuscan-Emilian Mountains. ▲ C Italy
Toshetu *see* Tongshih
171 J18 **To-shima** *island* Izu-shotō, SE Japan
153 Q9 **Toshkent** *Eng./Rus.* Tashkent. ● (Uzbekistan) Toshkent Wiloyati, E Uzbekistan
153 Q9 **Toshkent** ✕ Toshkent Wiloyati, E Uzbekistan
153 P9 **Toshkent Wiloyati** *Rus.* Tashkentskaya Oblast'. ◆ *province* E Uzbekistan
128 H13 **Tosno** Leningradskaya Oblast', NW Russian Federation
165 Q10 **Toson Hu** ⊚ C China
168 H6 **Tosontsengel** Dzavhan, NW Mongolia
Tosquduq Qumlari *see* Goshquduq Qum
107 U4 **Tossal de l'Orri** *var.* Llorri. ▲ NE Spain
63 A15 **Tostado** Santa Fe, C Argentina
120 F6 **Tõstamaa** *Ger.* Testama. Pärnumaa, SW Estonia
102 I10 **Tostedt** Niedersachsen, NW Germany
142 J11 **Tosya** Kastamonu, N Turkey
97 F15 **Totak** ⊚ S Norway
107 R13 **Totana** Murcia, SE Spain
96 H13 **Toten** *physical region* S Norway
85 G18 **Toteng** Ngamiland, C Botswana
104 M3 **Tôtes** Seine-Maritime, N France
Totigi *see* Tochigi
Totio *see* Tochio
Totis *see* Tata
201 U13 **Totiw** *island* Chuuk, C Micronesia
129 N13 **Tot'ma** *var.* Totma. Vologodskaya Oblast', NW Russian Federation
Tot'ma *see* Sukhona
57 V9 **Totness** Coronie, N Suriname
44 C5 **Totonicapán** Totonicapán, W Guatemala
44 A2 **Totonicapán** *off.* Departamento de Totonicapán. ◆ *department* W Guatemala
63 B18 **Totoras** Santa Fe, C Argentina
197 K15 **Totoya** *island* S Fiji
191 Q7 **Tottenham** New South Wales, SE Australia
171 Gg13 **Tottori** Tottori, Honshū, SW Japan
170 Ff13 **Tottori** *off.* Tottori-ken. ◆ *prefecture* Honshū, SW Japan
78 I6 **Touâjil** Tiris Zemmour, N Mauritania
78 L15 **Touba** W Ivory Coast
78 G11 **Touba** W Senegal
76 E7 **Toubkal, Jbel** ▲ W Morocco
34 K10 **Touchet** Washington, NW USA
105 P7 **Toucy** Yonne, C France
79 O12 **Tougan** W Burkina
76 L7 **Touggourt** NE Algeria
79 Q12 **Tougouri** N Burkina
78 J13 **Tougué** Moyenne-Guinée, NW Guinea
78 K12 **Toukoto** Kayes, W Mali
105 S5 **Toul** Meurthe-et-Moselle, NE France
78 L16 **Touléplеu** *var.* Toulobli. W Ivory Coast
167 S14 **Touliu** C Taiwan
13 U3 **Toulnustouc** ≈ Québec, SE Canada
Toulobli *see* Touléplеu
105 T16 **Toulon** *anc.* Telo Martius, Tilio Martius. Var, SE France
32 K12 **Toulon** Illinois, N USA
104 M15 **Toulouse** *anc.* Tolosa. Haute-Garonne, S France
104 M15 **Toulouse** ✕ Haute-Garonne, S France
79 N16 **Toumodi** C Ivory Coast
76 G9 **Tounassine, Hamada** *hill range* W Algeria
177 G7 **Toungoo** Pegu, C Myanmar
104 L8 **Touraine** *cultural region* C France
Tourane *see* Đà Nẵng
105 P1 **Tourcoing** Nord, N France
106 F2 **Touriñán, Cabo** *headland* NW Spain
78 J6 **Tourine** Tiris Zemmour, N Mauritania
104 J3 **Tourlaville** Manche, N France
101 D19 **Tournai** *var.* Tournay, *Dut.* Doornik; *anc.* Tornacum. Hainaut, SW Belgium
104 L16 **Tournay** Hautes-Pyrénées, S France
Tournay *see* Tournai
105 R12 **Tournon** Ardèche, E France
105 R9 **Tournus** Saône-et-Loire, C France
61 Q14 **Touros** Rio Grande do Norte, E Brazil
104 L8 **Tours** *anc.* Caesarodunum, Turoni. Indre-et-Loire, C France
191 Q17 **Tourville, Cape** *headland* Tasmania, SE Australia
168 L8 **Töv** ◆ *province* C Mongolia
56 H7 **Tovar** Mérida, NW Venezuela
130 L5 **Tovarkovskiy** Tul'skaya Oblast', W Russian Federation
Tovil'-Dora *see* Tavildara
Tövis *see* Teiuș
143 V11 **Tovuz** *Rus.* Tauz. W Azerbaijan
172 N9 **Towada** Aomori, Honshū, C Japan
172 N9 **Towada-ko** *var.* Towada Ko. ⊚ Honshū, C Japan
192 K3 **Towai** Northland, North Island, NZ
20 H12 **Towanda** Pennsylvania, NE USA
31 W4 **Tower** Minnesota, N USA
175 Pp8 **Towera** Sulawesi, N Indonesia
Tower Island *see* Genovesa, Isla
188 M13 **Tower Peak** ▲ Western Australia
37 U11 **Towne Pass** *pass* California, W USA
31 N3 **Towner** North Dakota, N USA
35 R10 **Townsend** Montana, NW USA
189 X6 **Townsville** Queensland, NE Australia
Towoeti Meer *see* Towuti, Danau
175 Q10 **Towori, Teluk** *bay* Sulawesi, C Indonesia
154 K4 **Towraghoudi** Herāt, NW Afghanistan
23 X3 **Towson** Maryland, NE USA
175 Q11 **Towuti, Danau** *Dut.* Towoeti Meer. ⊚ Sulawesi, C Indonesia
Toxkan He *see* Ak-say
26 K9 **Toyah** Texas, SW USA
172 Nn6 **Tōya-ko** ⊚ Hokkaidō, NE Japan
171 Ii13 **Toyama** Toyama, Honshū, SW Japan
171 Ii13 **Toyama** *off.* Toyama-ken. ◆ *prefecture* Honshū, SW Japan
171 J13 **Toyama-wan** *bay* W Japan
170 F16 **Tōyo** Ehime, Shikoku, SW Japan
170 Ee14 **Tōyo** Kōchi, Shikoku, SW Japan
Toyohara *see* Yuzhno-Sakhalinsk
171 Hh16 **Toyohashi** *var.* Toyohasi. Aichi, Honshū, SW Japan
Toyohasi *see* Toyohashi
171 I16 **Toyokawa** Aichi, Honshū, SW Japan
171 Gg13 **Toyooka** Hyōgo, Honshū, SW Japan
171 Kk12 **Toyosaka** Niigata, Honshū, C Japan
171 I16 **Toyota** Aichi, Honshū, SW Japan
172 Pp2 **Toyotomi** Hokkaidō, NE Japan
170 Dd12 **Toyoura** Yamaguchi, Honshū, SW Japan
Toytepa *see* Tuytepa
76 M6 **Tozeur** *var.* Tawzar. W Tunisia
41 Q8 **Tozi, Mount** ▲ Alaska, USA
143 Q9 **Tqvarch'eli** *Rus.* Tkvarcheli. NW Georgia
Trâblous *see* Tripoli
143 O11 **Trabzon** *Eng.* Trebizond; *anc.* Trapezus. Trabzon, NE Turkey
143 O11 **Trabzon** *Eng.* Trebizond. ◆ *province* NE Turkey
11 P13 **Tracadie** New Brunswick, SE Canada
Trachenberg *see* Żmigród
13 O11 **Tracy** Québec, SE Canada
37 O8 **Tracy** California, W USA
31 S10 **Tracy** Minnesota, N USA
22 K10 **Tracy City** Tennessee, S USA
108 D7 **Tradate** Lombardia, N Italy
86 F6 **Traena Bank** *undersea feature* E Norwegian Sea
31 W13 **Traer** Iowa, C USA
106 J16 **Trafalgar, Cabo de** *headland* SW Spain
Traiectum ad Mosam/Traiectum Tungorum *see* Maastricht
Tráigh Mhór *see* Tramore
9 O17 **Trail** British Columbia, SW Canada
60 B11 **Traíra, Serra do** ▲ NW Brazil
111 V5 **Traisen** Niederösterreich, NE Austria
111 W4 **Traisen** ≈ NE Austria
111 X4 **Traiskirchen** Niederösterreich, NE Austria
Trajani Portus *see* Civitavecchia
Trajectum ad Rhenum *see* Utrecht
121 H14 **Trakai** *Ger.* Traken, *Pol.* Troki. Trakai, SE Lithuania
Traken *see* Trakai
99 B20 **Tralee** *Ir.* Trá Lí. SW Ireland
99 A20 **Tralee Bay** *Ir.* Bá Thrá Lí. *bay* SW Ireland
Trá Lí *see* Tralee
Trälleborg *see* Trelleborg
Tralles *see* Aydın
63 J16 **Tramandaí** Rio Grande do Sul, S Brazil
110 C7 **Tramelan** Bern, W Switzerland
Trá Mhór *see* Tramore
99 E20 **Tramore** *Ir.* Tráigh Mhór, Trá Mhór. S Ireland
97 L18 **Tranås** Jönköping, S Sweden
64 J7 **Trancas** Tucumán, N Argentina
106 I7 **Trancoso** Guarda, N Portugal
97 H22 **Tranebjerg** Århus, C Denmark
97 K19 **Tranemo** Älvsborg, S Sweden
178 Gg16 **Trang** Trang, S Thailand
176 W14 **Trangan, Pulau** *island* Kepulauan Aru, E Indonesia
Trâng Dinh *see* Thất Khê
191 Q7 **Trangie** New South Wales, SE Australia
96 K12 **Trängslet** Kopparberg, C Sweden
109 N16 **Trani** Puglia, SE Italy
63 F17 **Tranqueras** Rivera, NE Uruguay
65 G17 **Tranqui, Isla** *island* S Chile
41 V6 **Trans-Alaska pipeline** *oil pipeline* Alaska, USA
205 Q10 **Transantarctic Mountains** ▲ Antarctica
Transcarpathian Oblast *see* Zakarpats'ka Oblast'
Transilvania *see* Transylvania
Transilvaniei, Alpi *see* Carpații Meridionali
Transjordan *see* Jordan
180 L11 **Transkei Basin** *undersea feature* SW Indian Ocean
127 N17 **Trans-Siberian Railway** *railroad* Russian Federation
Transsylvanische Alpen/Transylvanian Alps *see* Carpații Meridionali
96 K12 **Transtrand** Kopparberg, C Sweden
118 G10 **Transylvania** *Eng.* Ardeal, Transilvania, *Ger.* Siebenbürgen, *Hung.* Erdély. *cultural region* NW Romania
178 Jj15 **Tra Ôn** Vinh Long, S Vietnam
109 H23 **Trapani** *anc.* Drepanum. Sicilia, Italy, C Mediterranean Sea
178 J12 **Trâpeăng Vêng** Kâmpóng Thum, C Cambodia
Trapezus *see* Trabzon
116 L9 **Trapoklovo** Burgaska Oblast, E Bulgaria
191 P13 **Traralgon** Victoria, SE Australia
78 H9 **Trarza** ◆ *region* SW Mauritania
Trasimenischersee *see* Trasimeno, Lago
108 H12 **Trasimeno, Lago** *Eng.* Lake of Perugia, *Ger.* Trasimenischersee. ⊚ C Italy
97 J20 **Träslövsläge** Halland, S Sweden
Trás-os-Montes *see* Cucumbi
106 I6 **Trás-os-Montes e Alto Douro** *former province* N Portugal
178 I13 **Trat** *var.* Bang Phra. Trat, S Thailand
Trá Tholl, Inis *see* Inishtrahull
Traù *see* Trogir
111 T4 **Traun** Oberösterreich, N Austria
111 S5 **Traun** ≈ N Austria
Traun, Lake *see* Traunsee
103 N23 **Traunreut** Bayern, SE Germany
111 S5 **Traunsee** *var.* Gmundner See, *Eng.* Lake Traun. ⊚ N Austria
Trautenau *see* Trutnov

◆ Country ● Country Capital ◇ Dependent Territory ○ Dependent Territory Capital ◆ Administrative Region ✕ International Airport ▲ Mountain ▲ Mountain Range ⛰ Volcano ≈ River ⊚ Lake ⊡ Reservoir

23 P11 **Travelers Rest** South Carolina, SE USA
190 L8 **Travellers Lake** seasonal lake New South Wales, SE Australia
33 P6 **Traverse City** Michigan, N USA
31 R7 **Traverse, Lake** ◎ Minnesota/South Dakota, N USA
193 I16 **Travers, Mount** ▲ South Island, NZ
9 P17 **Travers Reservoir** ⊠ Alberta, SW Canada
178 Jj15 **Tra Vinh** var. Phu Vinh. Tra Vinh, S Vietnam
27 S10 **Travis, Lake** ⊠ Texas, SW USA
114 H12 **Travnik** C Bosnia and Herzegovina
111 V11 **Trbovlje** Ger. Trifail. C Slovenia
25 V13 **Treasure Island** Florida, SE USA
Treasure State see Montana
195 S14 **Treasury Islands** island group NW Solomon Islands
108 D9 **Trebbia** anc. Trebia. ≈ NW Italy
102 N8 **Trebel** ≈ NE Germany
105 O16 **Trèbes** Aude, S France
Trebia see Trebbia
113 F18 **Třebíč** Ger. Trebitsch. Jižní Morava, S Czech Republic
115 I16 **Trebinje** S Bosnia and Herzegovina
Trebišnica see Trebišnjica
115 H16 **Trebišnjica** var. Trebišnica. ≈ S Bosnia and Herzegovina
113 N20 **Trebišov** Hung. Tőketerebes. Východné Slovensko, E Slovakia
Trebitsch see Třebíč
Trebizond see Trabzon
Trebnitz see Trzebnica
111 V12 **Trebnje** SE Slovenia
113 D19 **Třeboň** Ger. Wittingau. Jižní Čechy, S Czech Republic
106 J15 **Trebujena** Andalucía, S Spain
102 I7 **Treene** ≈ N Germany
Tree Planters State see Nebraska
111 S9 **Treffen** Kärnten, S Austria
Trefynwy see Monmouth
104 G5 **Tréguier** Côtes d'Armor, NW France
63 G18 **Treinta y Tres** Treinta y Tres, E Uruguay
63 F18 **Treinta y Tres** ◈ department E Uruguay
116 F9 **Treklyanska Reka** ≈ W Bulgaria
175 R10 **Treko, Kepulauan** island group N Indonesia
104 K8 **Trélazé** Maine-et-Loire, NW France
65 K17 **Trelew** Chubut, SE Argentina
97 K23 **Trelleborg** var. Trälleborg. Malmöhus, S Sweden
115 P15 **Trem** ▲ SE Yugoslavia
13 N11 **Tremblant, Mont** ▲ Québec, SE Canada
101 H17 **Tremelo** Vlaams Brabant, C Belgium
109 M15 **Tremiti, Isole** island group SE Italy
32 K12 **Tremont** Illinois, N USA
38 L1 **Tremonton** Utah, W USA
107 U4 **Tremp** Cataluña, NE Spain
32 J7 **Trempealeau** Wisconsin, N USA
13 P8 **Trenche** ≈ Québec, SE Canada
13 O7 **Trenche, Lac** ◎ Québec, SE Canada
113 I19 **Trenčín** Ger. Trentschin, Hung. Trencsén. Západné Slovensko, W Slovakia
Trencsén see Trenčín
Trengganu see Terengganu
63 A21 **Trenque Lauquen** Buenos Aires, E Argentina
12 J14 **Trent** ≈ Ontario, SE Canada
99 N18 **Trent** ≈ England, UK
Trent see Trento
108 F5 **Trentino-Alto Adige** prev. Venezia Tridentina. ◈ region N Italy
108 G6 **Trento** Eng. Trent, Ger. Trient; anc. Tridentum. Trentino-Alto Adige, N Italy
12 J15 **Trenton** Ontario, SE Canada
25 V10 **Trenton** Florida, SE USA
25 R1 **Trenton** Georgia, SE USA
33 S10 **Trenton** Michigan, N USA
29 S2 **Trenton** Missouri, C USA
30 M17 **Trenton** Nebraska, C USA
20 J15 **Trenton** state capital New Jersey, NE USA
23 W10 **Trenton** North Carolina, SE USA
22 G9 **Trenton** Tennessee, S USA
38 L1 **Trenton** Utah, W USA
Trentschin see Trenčín
Treptow an der Rega see Trzebiatów
63 C23 **Tres Arroyos** Buenos Aires, E Argentina
63 J15 **Três Cachoeiras** Rio Grande do Sul, S Brazil
108 E7 **Trescore Balneario** Lombardia, N Italy
43 V17 **Tres Cruces, Cerro** ▲ SE Mexico
59 K18 **Tres Cruces, Cordillera** ▲▲ W Bolivia
115 N18 **Treska** ≈ NW FYR Macedonia
115 I14 **Treskavica** ▲ SE Bosnia and Herzegovina
61 J20 **Três Lagoas** Mato Grosso do Sul, SW Brazil
42 H12 **Tres Marías, Islas** island group C Mexico
61 M19 **Três Marias, Represa** ⊠ SE Brazil
65 F20 **Tres Montes, Península** headland S Chile
107 O3 **Trespaderne** Castilla-León, N Spain
62 G13 **Três Passos** Rio Grande do Sul, S Brazil
63 A23 **Tres Picos, Cerro** ▲ E Argentina
65 G17 **Tres Picos, Cerro** ▲ SW Argentina
62 I12 **Três Pinheiros** Paraná, S Brazil
61 M21 **Três Pontas** Minas Gerais, SE Brazil
Tres Puntas, Cabo see Manabique, Punta
62 P9 **Três Rios** Rio de Janeiro, SE Brazil
Tres Tabernae see Saverne
Trestenberg/Trestendorf see Tăşnad
43 R15 **Tres Valles** Veracruz-Llave, SE Mexico
96 H12 **Tretten** Oppland, S Norway
Treuburg see Olecko
103 K21 **Treuchtlingen** Bayern, S Germany
102 N13 **Treuenbrietzen** Brandenburg, E Germany
97 F16 **Treungen** Telemark, S Norway
65 H17 **Trevelín** Chubut, SW Argentina
Treves/Trèves see Trier
108 I13 **Trevi** Umbria, C Italy
108 E7 **Treviglio** Lombardia, N Italy
106 J4 **Trevinca, Peña** ▲ NW Spain
107 P3 **Treviño** Castilla-León, N Spain
108 I7 **Treviso** anc. Tarvisium. Veneto, NE Italy
99 G24 **Trevose Head** headland SW England, UK
Trg see Feldkirchen in Kärnten
191 P17 **Triabunna** Tasmania, SE Australia
23 W4 **Triangle** Virginia, NE USA
85 L18 **Triangle** Masvingo, SE Zimbabwe
117 L23 **Tría Nisía** island Kykládes, Greece, Aegean Sea
Triberg see Triberg im Schwarzwald
103 G23 **Triberg im Schwarzwald** var. Triberg. Baden-Württemberg, SW Germany
159 P11 **Tribhuvan** ✕ (Kathmandu) Central, C Nepal
56 C9 **Tribugá, Golfo de** gulf W Colombia
189 W4 **Tribulation, Cape** headland Queensland, NE Australia
110 M8 **Tribulaun** ▲ SW Austria
9 U17 **Tribune** Saskatchewan, S Canada
28 H5 **Tribune** Kansas, C USA
109 N18 **Tricarico** Basilicata, S Italy
109 Q19 **Tricase** Puglia, SE Italy
Trichinopoly see Tiruchchirāppalli
117 D18 **Trichonída, Límni** ◎ C Greece
161 G22 **Trichūr** var. Thrissur. Kerala, SW India
Tricorno see Triglav
191 O8 **Trida** New South Wales, SE Australia
37 S1 **Trident Peak** ▲ Nevada, W USA
Tridentum/Trient see Trento
111 T6 **Trieben** Steiermark, SE Austria
103 D19 **Trier** Eng. Treves, Fr. Trèves; anc. Augusta Treverorum. Rheinland-Pfalz, SW Germany
108 K7 **Trieste** Slvn. Trst. Friuli-Venezia Giulia, NE Italy
Trieste, Golfo di/Triest, Golf von see Trieste, Gulf of
108 J8 **Trieste, Gulf of** Cro. Tršćanski Zaljev, Ger. Golf von Triest, It. Golfo di Trieste, Slvn. Tržaški Zaliv. gulf S Europe
111 W4 **Triesting** ≈ W Austria
Trifail see Trbovlje
118 L9 **Trifeşti** Iaşi, NE Romania
111 S10 **Triglav** It. Tricorno. ▲ NW Slovenia
106 I14 **Trigueros** Andalucía, S Spain
117 E16 **Tríkala** prev. Trikkala. Thessalía, C Greece
117 E17 **Trikeriótis** ≈ C Greece
Trikkala see Tríkala
99 F17 **Trim** Ir. Baile Átha Troim. E Ireland
110 E7 **Trimbach** Solothurn, NW Switzerland
111 Q5 **Trimmelkam** Oberösterreich, N Austria
31 U11 **Trimont** Minnesota, N USA
Trimontium see Plovdiv
Trinacria see Sicilia
161 K24 **Trincomalee** var. Trinkomali. Eastern Province, NE Sri Lanka
67 K16 **Trindade, Ilha da** island Brazil, W Atlantic Ocean
49 Y9 **Trindade Spur** undersea feature SW Atlantic Ocean
113 J17 **Třinec** Ger. Trzynietz. Severní Morava, E Czech Republic
59 M16 **Trinidad** Beni, N Bolivia
56 H9 **Trinidad** Casanare, E Colombia
46 E6 **Trinidad** Sancti Spíritus, C Cuba
39 U8 **Trinidad** Colorado, C USA
63 E19 **Trinidad** Flores, S Uruguay
47 Y17 **Trinidad** island C Trinidad and Tobago
Trinidad see Jose Abad Santos
47 Y16 **Trinidad and Tobago** off. Republic of Trinidad and Tobago. ◆ republic SE West Indies
65 F22 **Trinidad, Golfo** gulf S Chile
63 B24 **Trinidad, Isla** island E Argentina
109 N16 **Trinitapoli** Puglia, SE Italy
57 X10 **Trinité, Montagnes de la** ▲▲ C French Guiana
27 W9 **Trinity** Texas, SW USA
11 U12 **Trinity Bay** inlet Newfoundland, Newfoundland and Labrador, E Canada
41 P15 **Trinity Islands** island group Alaska, USA
37 N2 **Trinity Mountains** ▲▲ California, W USA
37 S4 **Trinity Peak** ▲ Nevada, W USA
37 S5 **Trinity Range** ▲▲ Nevada, W USA
37 N2 **Trinity River** ≈ California, W USA
27 V8 **Trinity River** ≈ Texas, SW USA
Trinkomali see Trincomalee
181 Y15 **Triolet** NW Mauritius
109 O20 **Trionto, Capo** headland S Italy
173 Ee4 **Tripa, Krueng** ≈ Sumatera, NW Indonesia
117 J16 **Tripití, Ákra** headland Ágios Efstrátios, E Greece
144 G6 **Tripoli** var. Tarābulus, Ṭarābulus ash Shām, Trâblous; anc. Tripolis. N Lebanon
31 X12 **Tripoli** Iowa, C USA
Tripoli see Ṭarābulus
117 F20 **Trípoli** prev. Trípolis. Pelopónnisos, S Greece
Tripolis see Tripoli, Lebanon
Trípolis see Trípoli, Greece
31 Q12 **Tripp** South Dakota, N USA
159 V15 **Tripura** var. Hill Tippera. ◈ state NE India
110 K8 **Trisanna** ≈ W Austria
102 H8 **Trischen** island NW Germany
67 M24 **Tristan da Cunha** ◇ dependency of Saint Helena SE Atlantic Ocean
69 P15 **Tristan da Cunha** island SE Atlantic Ocean
67 L18 **Tristan da Cunha Fracture Zone** tectonic feature S Atlantic Ocean
178 J14 **Tri Tôn** An Giang, S Vietnam
178 Ll11 **Triton Island** island S Paracel Islands
161 G24 **Trivandrum** var. Thiruvanathapuram. Kerala, SW India
113 H20 **Trnava** Ger. Tyrnau, Hung. Nagyszombat. Západné Slovensko, W Slovakia
Trnovo see Veliko Tŭrnovo
Trobriand Island see Kiriwina Island
Trobriand Islands see Kiriwina Islands
9 Q16 **Trochu** Alberta, SW Canada
111 U7 **Trofaiach** Steiermark, SE Austria
95 F14 **Trofors** Troms, N Norway
115 E14 **Trogir** It. Traù. Split-Dalmacija, S Croatia
114 F13 **Troglav** ▲ Bosnia and Herzegovina/Croatia
109 M16 **Troia** Puglia, SE Italy
109 K24 **Troina** Sicilia, Italy, C Mediterranean Sea
181 O16 **Trois-Bassins** W Réunion
103 E17 **Troisdorf** Nordrhein-Westfalen, W Germany
76 H5 **Trois Fourches, Cap des** headland NE Morocco
13 T8 **Trois-Pistoles** Québec, SE Canada
101 L21 **Trois-Ponts** Liège, E Belgium
13 P11 **Trois-Rivières** Québec, SE Canada
57 Y12 **Trois Sauts** S French Guiana
101 M22 **Troisvierges** Diekirch, N Luxembourg
125 Ee12 **Troitsk** Chelyabinskaya Oblast', S Russian Federation
129 T9 **Troitsko-Pechorsk** Respublika Komi, NW Russian Federation
131 V7 **Troitskoye** Orenburgskaya Oblast', W Russian Federation
Troki see Trakai
96 F9 **Trolla** ▲ S Norway
97 J18 **Trollhättan** Älvsborg, S Sweden
96 G9 **Trollheimen** ▲ S Norway
96 E9 **Trolltindane** ▲ S Norway
60 H11 **Trombetas, Rio** ≈ NE Brazil
132 L16 **Tromelin, Île** island N Réunion
94 I9 **Troms** ◈ county N Norway
94 I9 **Tromsø** Fin. Tromssa. Troms, N Norway
86 F5 **Tromsøflaket** undersea feature W Barents Sea
Tromssa see Tromsø
96 H10 **Tron** ▲ S Norway
37 U12 **Trona** California, W USA
65 G16 **Tronador, Cerro** ▲ S Chile
96 H8 **Trondheim** Ger. Drontheim; prev. Nidaros, Trondhjem. Sør-Trøndelag, S Norway
96 H7 **Trondheimsfjorden** fjord S Norway
Trondhjem see Trondheim
109 J14 **Tronto** ≈ C Italy
Troodos see Ólympos
124 N3 **Troódos** var. Troodos Mountains. ▲▲ C Cyprus
Troodos Mountains see Troódos
98 I13 **Troon** W Scotland, UK
109 M22 **Tropea** Calabria, SW Italy
38 L7 **Tropic** Utah, W USA
66 L10 **Tropic Seamount** var. Banc du Tropique. undersea feature E Atlantic Ocean
Tropique, Banc du see Tropic Seamount
Tropoja see Tropojë
115 L17 **Tropojë** var. Tropoja. Kukës, N Albania
Troppau see Opava
97 O16 **Trosa** Södermanland, C Sweden
120 H12 **Troškūnai** Anykščiai, E Lithuania
103 G23 **Trossingen** Baden-Württemberg, SW Germany
119 T4 **Trostyanets'** Rus. Trostyanets. Sums'ka Oblast', NE Ukraine
119 N7 **Trostyanets'** Rus. Trostyanets. Vinnyts'ka Oblast', C Ukraine
118 L11 **Trotuş** ≈ E Romania
46 M8 **Trou-du-Nord** N Haiti
27 W7 **Troup** Texas, SW USA
15 H8 **Trout** ≈ Northwest Territories, NW Canada
35 N8 **Trout Creek** Montana, NW USA
34 H10 **Trout Lake** Washington, NW USA
10 B9 **Trout Lake** ◎ Ontario, S Canada
35 T12 **Trout Peak** ▲ Wyoming, C USA
104 L4 **Trouville** Calvados, N France
99 L22 **Trowbridge** S England, UK
25 Q6 **Troy** Alabama, S USA
29 Q3 **Troy** Kansas, C USA
29 W4 **Troy** Missouri, C USA
20 L10 **Troy** New York, NE USA
23 S10 **Troy** North Carolina, SE USA
33 R13 **Troy** Ohio, N USA
27 T9 **Troy** Texas, SW USA
116 J9 **Troyan** Loveshka Oblast, C Bulgaria
116 J9 **Troyanski Prokhod** pass N Bulgaria
151 N6 **Troyebratskiy** Severnyy Kazakhstan, N Kazakhstan
105 Q6 **Troyes** anc. Augustobona Tricassium. Aube, N France
119 X5 **Troyits'ke** Luhans'ka Oblast', E Ukraine
37 W7 **Troy Peak** ▲ Nevada, W USA
115 G15 **Trpanj** Dubrovnik-Neretva, S Croatia
Tršćanski Zaljev see Trieste, Gulf of
Trst see Trieste
115 N14 **Trstenik** Serbia, C Yugoslavia
130 I6 **Trubchevsk** Bryanskaya Oblast', W Russian Federation
Trubchular see Orlyak
Truc Giang see Bên Tre
39 S10 **Truchas Peak** ▲ New Mexico, SW USA
149 P16 **Trucial Coast** physical region C UAE
Trucial States see United Arab Emirates
37 Q6 **Truckee** California, W USA
37 R5 **Truckee River** ≈ Nevada, W USA
131 Q13 **Trudfront** Astrakhanskaya Oblast', SW Russian Federation
12 I9 **Truite, Lac à la** ◎ Québec, SE Canada
44 K4 **Trujillo** Colón, NE Honduras
58 C12 **Trujillo** La Libertad, NW Peru
106 K10 **Trujillo** Extremadura, W Spain
56 I6 **Trujillo** Trujillo, NW Venezuela
56 I6 **Trujillo** off. Estado Trujillo. ◈ state W Venezuela
Truk see Chuuk
Truk Islands see Chuuk Islands
31 U10 **Truman** Minnesota, N USA
29 X10 **Trumann** Arkansas, C USA
38 J9 **Trumbull, Mount** ▲ Arizona, SW USA
116 F9 **Trŭn** Sofiyska Oblast, W Bulgaria
191 Q8 **Trundle** New South Wales, SE Australia
133 U13 **Trung Phân** physical region S Vietnam
Trupcilar see Orlyak
11 Q15 **Truro** Nova Scotia, SE Canada
99 H25 **Truro** SW England, UK
27 P5 **Truscott** Texas, SW USA
118 K9 **Truşeşti** Botoşani, NE Romania
118 H6 **Truskavets'** L'vivs'ka Oblast', W Ukraine
97 H22 **Trustrup** Århus, C Denmark
8 M11 **Trutch** British Columbia, W Canada
39 Q14 **Truth Or Consequences** New Mexico, SW USA
113 F15 **Trutnov** Ger. Trautenau. Východní Čechy, NE Czech Republic
105 P13 **Truyère** ≈ C France
116 K9 **Tryavna** Loveshka Oblast, C Bulgaria
30 M14 **Tryon** Nebraska, C USA
96 J12 **Trysil** Hedmark, S Norway
96 I11 **Trysilelva** ≈ S Norway
114 D10 **Tržac** NW Bosnia and Herzegovina
Tržaški Zaliv see Trieste, Gulf of
112 G10 **Trzcianka** Ger. Schönlanke. Piła, NW Poland
112 E7 **Trzebiatów** Ger. Treptow an der Rega. Szczecin, NW Poland
113 G14 **Trzebnica** Ger. Trebnitz. Wrocław, SW Poland
111 T10 **Tržič** Ger. Neumarktl. NW Slovenia
Trzynietz see Třinec
Tsabong see Tshabong
168 G7 **Tsagaanchuluut** Dzavhan, C Mongolia
169 P7 **Tsagaanders** Dornod, NE Mongolia
169 S8 **Tsagaannuur** Dornod, E Mongolia
168 G8 **Tsagaan-Olom** Govĭ-Altay, C Mongolia
168 J8 **Tsagaan-Ovoo** Övörhangay, C Mongolia
168 D5 **Tsagaantüngi** Bayan-Ölgiy, NW Mongolia
131 P12 **Tsagan Aman** Respublika Kalmykiya, SW Russian Federation
25 V11 **Tsala Apopka Lake** ◎ Florida, SE USA
Tsamkong see Zhanjiang
Tsangpo see Brahmaputra
168 L9 **Tsant** Dundgovĭ, C Mongolia
85 G17 **Tsao** Ngamiland, NW Botswana
180 I4 **Tsaratanana** Mahajanga, C Madagascar
116 N10 **Tsarevo** prev. Michurin. Burgaska Oblast, SE Bulgaria
Tsarigrad see Istanbul
Tsaritsyn see Volgograd
128 G13 **Tsarskoye Selo** prev. Pushkin. Leningradskaya Oblast', NW Russian Federation
119 T7 **Tsarychanka** Dnipropetrovs'ka Oblast', E Ukraine
85 H21 **Tsatsu** Southern, S Botswana
83 J20 **Tsavo** Coast, S Kenya
85 E21 **Tsawisis** Karas, S Namibia
Tschakathurn see Čakovec
Tschaslau see Čáslav
Tschenstochau see Częstochowa
Tschernembl see Črnomelj
30 K6 **Tschida, Lake** ⊠ North Dakota, N USA
Tschorna see Mustvee
85 I17 **Tsebanana** Central, NE Botswana
168 G8 **Tseel** Govĭ-Altay, SW Mongolia
130 M13 **Tselina** Rostovskaya Oblast', SW Russian Federation
Tselinograd/Tselinogradskaya Oblast see Akmola
168 J6 **Tsengel** Hövsgöl, N Mongolia
168 E7 **Tsenher** Hovd, W Mongolia
152 E12 **Tsentral'nyye Nizmennyye Garagumy** Turkm. Merkezi Garagum. desert C Turkmenistan
85 E21 **Tses** Karas, S Namibia
Tseshevlya see Tsyeshawlya
168 E7 **Tsetsegnuur** Hovd, W Mongolia
168 J7 **Tsetserleg** Arhangay, C Mongolia
79 R16 **Tsévié** S Togo
85 G21 **Tshabong** var. Tsabong. Kgalagadi, SW Botswana
85 G20 **Tshane** Kgalagadi, SW Botswana
Tshangalele, Lac see Lufira, Lac de Retenue de la
85 H17 **Tshauxaba** Central, C Botswana
81 F21 **Tshela** Bas-Zaïre, W Zaire
81 K22 **Tshibala** Kasai Occidental, S Zaire
81 J22 **Tshikapa** Kasai Occidental, SW Zaire
81 L22 **Tshilenge** Kasai Oriental, S Zaire
81 L24 **Tshimbalanga** Shaba, S Zaire
81 L22 **Tshimbulu** Kasai Occidental, S Zaire
Tshiumbe see Chiumbe
81 M21 **Tshofa** Kasai Oriental, C Zaire
81 K18 **Tshuapa** ≈ C Zaire
Tshwane see Pretoria
116 G7 **Tsibritsa** ≈ NW Bulgaria
Tsien Tang see Puyang Jiang
116 I12 **Tsiganski Gradishte** ▲ Bulgaria/Greece
14 G3 **Tsiigehtchic** prev. Arctic Red River. Northwest Territories, NW Canada
129 Q7 **Tsil'ma** ≈ NW Russian Federation
121 J17 **Tsimkavichy** Rus. Timkovichi. Minskaya Voblasts', C Belarus
130 M11 **Tsimlyansk** Rostovskaya Oblast', SW Russian Federation
131 N11 **Tsimlyanskoye Vodokhranilishche** var. Tsimlyansk Vodoskhovshche, Eng. Tsimlyansk Reservoir ⊠ SW Russian Federation
Tsimlyansk Reservoir see Tsimlyanskoye Vodokhranilishche
Tsimlyansk Vodoskhovshche see Tsimlyanskoye Vodokhranilishche
Tsinan see Jinan
Tsing Hai see Qinghai Hu, China
Tsinghai see Qinghai, China
Tsingtao/Tsingtau see Qingdao
Tsingyuan see Baoding
Tsinkiang see Quanzhou
Tsintao see Qingdao
85 D17 **Tsintsabis** Otjikoto, N Namibia
180 H8 **Tsiombe** var. Tsihombe. Toliara, S Madagascar
126 Kk14 **Tsipa** ≈ S Russian Federation
180 H5 **Tsiribihina** ≈ W Madagascar
180 I5 **Tsiroanomandidy** Antananarivo, C Madagascar
201 U13 **Tsis** island Chuuk, C Micronesia
Tsitsihar see Qiqihar
131 Q3 **Tsivil'sk** Chuvashskaya Respublika, W Russian Federation
143 T9 **Ts'khinvali** prev. Staliniri. C Georgia
121 J19 **Tsna** ≈ SW Belarus
128 I15 **Tsna** var. Zna. ≈ W Russian Federation
168 K11 **Tsoohor** Ömnögovĭ, S Mongolia
171 H16 **Tsu** var. Tu. Mie, Honshū, SW Japan
171 K13 **Tsubame** var. Tubame. Niigata, Honshū, C Japan
171 Ii13 **Tsubata** Ishikawa, Honshū, SW Japan
172 Q6 **Tsubetsu** Hokkaidō, NE Japan
171 Kk16 **Tsuchiura** var. Tutiura. Ibaraki, Honshū, S Japan
172 N7 **Tsugaru-kaikyō** strait N Japan
171 Kk13 **Tsugawa** Niigata, Honshū, C Japan
172 Oo5 **Tsukigata** Hokkaidō, NE Japan
170 Dd15 **Tsukumi** var. Tukumi. Ōita, Kyūshū, SW Japan
168 E5 **Tsul-Ulaan** Bayan-Ölgiy, W Mongolia
85 D17 **Tsumeb** Otjikoto, N Namibia
85 F17 **Tsumkwe** Otjozondjupa, NE Namibia
170 Cc16 **Tsuno** Miyazaki, Kyūshū, SW Japan
170 D11 **Tsuno-shima** island SW Japan
171 H14 **Tsuruga** var. Turuga. Fukui, Honshū, SW Japan
170 F15 **Tsurugi-san** ▲ Shikoku, SW Japan
170 Dd15 **Tsurumi-zaki** headland Kyūshū, SW Japan
171 L11 **Tsuruoka** var. Turuoka. Yamagata, Honshū, C Japan
171 Hh15 **Tsushima** var. Tusima. Aichi, Honshū, SW Japan
170 C10 **Tsushima** var. Tsushima-tō, Tusima. island group SW Japan
Tsushima-tō see Tsushima
170 E12 **Tsuwano** Shimane, Honshū, SW Japan
170 Ff13 **Tsuyama** var. Tuyama. Okayama, Honshū, SW Japan
85 G19 **Tswaane** Ghanzi, W Botswana
121 N16 **Tsyakhtsin** Rus. Tekhtin. Mahilyowskaya Voblasts', E Belarus
121 P19 **Tsyerakhowka** Rus. Terekhovka. Homyel'skaya Voblasts', SE Belarus
121 I17 **Tsyeshawlya** Rus. Cheshevlya, Tseshevlya. Brestskaya Voblasts', SW Belarus
Tsyurupinsk see Tsyurupyns'k
119 R10 **Tsyurupyns'k** Rus. Tsyurupinsk. Khersons'ka Oblast', S Ukraine
Tu see Tsu
194 H13 **Tua** ≈ C PNG
Tuaim see Tuam
192 L6 **Tuakau** Waikato, North Island, NZ
99 C17 **Tuam** Ir. Tuaim. W Ireland
193 K14 **Tuamarina** Marlborough, South Island, NZ
Tuamotu, Archipel des see Tuamotu, Îles
199 M10 **Tuamotu Fracture Zone** tectonic feature E Pacific Ocean
203 W9 **Tuamotu, Îles** var. Archipel des Tuamotu, Dangerous Archipelago, Tuamotu Islands. island group N French Polynesia
Tuamotu Islands see Tuamotu, Îles
183 X10 **Tuamotu Ridge** undersea feature C Pacific Ocean
178 I5 **Tuần Giao** Lai Châu, N Vietnam
179 P8 **Tuao** Luzon, N Philippines
202 B15 **Tuapa** NW Niue
45 N7 **Tuapí** Región Autónoma Atlántico Norte, NE Nicaragua
130 K15 **Tuapse** Krasnodarskiy Kray, SW Russian Federation
175 Nn2 **Tuaran** Sabah, East Malaysia
106 I6 **Tua, Rio** ≈ N Portugal
198 B7 **Tuasivi** Savai'i, C Western Samoa
193 B24 **Tuatapere** Southland, South Island, NZ
38 M9 **Tuba City** Arizona, SW USA
144 H11 **Ṭubah, Qaṣr aṭ** castle Ma'ān, C Jordan
Tubame see Tsubame
174 Ll14 **Tuban** prev. Toeban. Jawa, C Indonesia
147 O16 **Tuban, Wādī** dry watercourse SW Yemen
63 K14 **Tubarão** Santa Catarina, S Brazil
100 O10 **Tubbergen** Overijssel, E Netherlands
Tubeke see Tubize
103 H22 **Tübingen** var. Tuebingen. Baden-Württemberg, SW Germany
131 W6 **Tubinskiy** Respublika Bashkortostan, W Russian Federation
101 G19 **Tubize** Dut. Tubeke. Walloon Brabant, C Belgium
78 J16 **Tubmanburg** NW Liberia
179 Qq15 **Tubod** Mindanao, S Philippines
77 T7 **Ṭubruq** Eng. Tobruk, It. Tobruch. NE Libya
203 T13 **Tubuai** island Îles Australes, SW French Polynesia
Tubuai, Îles/Tubuai Islands see Australes, Îles
42 F3 **Tubutama** Sonora, NW Mexico
56 K4 **Tucacas** Falcón, N Venezuela
61 P16 **Tucano** Bahia, E Brazil
59 P19 **Tucavaca, Río** ≈ E Bolivia
112 H8 **Tuchola** Bydgoszcz, NW Poland
113 M17 **Tuchów** Tarnów, SE Poland
25 S3 **Tucker** Georgia, SE USA
29 W10 **Tuckerman** Arkansas, C USA
66 B12 **Tucker's Town** E Bermuda
Tuckum see Tukums
38 M15 **Tucson** Arizona, SW USA
64 J7 **Tucumán** off. Provincia de Tucumán. ◈ province N Argentina
Tucumán see San Miguel de Tucumán
39 V11 **Tucumcari** New Mexico, SW USA
60 H13 **Tucunaré** Pará, N Brazil
57 Q6 **Tucupita** Delta Amacuro, NE Venezuela
60 K13 **Tucuruí, Represa de** ⊠ NE Brazil
112 F9 **Tuczno** Piła, NW Poland
Tuddo see Tudu
107 Q5 **Tudela** Basq. Tutera; anc. Tutela. Navarra, N Spain
106 M6 **Tudela de Duero** Castilla-León, N Spain
144 K6 **Tudmur** var. Tadmur, Tamar, Gk. Palmyra; Bibl. Tadmor. Ḥimṣ, C Syria
120 J4 **Tudu** Ger. Tuddo. Lääne-Virumaa, NE Estonia
Tuebingen see Tübingen
126 H16 **Tuekta** Respublika Altay, S Russian Federation
106 I5 **Tuela, Rio** ≈ N Portugal
159 X12 **Tuensang** Nāgāland, NE India
142 L15 **Tufanbeyli** Adana, C Turkey
Tüffer see Laško
194 M15 **Tufi** Northern, S PNG
199 L3 **Tufts Plain** undersea feature N Pacific Ocean
Tugalan see Kolkhozobod
69 V14 **Tugela** ≈ SE South Africa
23 P6 **Tug Fork** ≈ S USA
41 P15 **Tugidak Island** island Trinity Islands, Alaska, USA
179 P8 **Tuguegarao** Luzon, N Philippines
127 N13 **Tugur** Khabarovskiy Kray, SE Russian Federation
167 P4 **Tuhai He** ≈ E China
106 G4 **Tui** Galicia, NW Spain
79 O13 **Tui** var. Grand Balé. ≈ W Burkina
59 J16 **Tuichi, Río** ≈ W Bolivia
66 Q11 **Tuineje** Fuerteventura, Islas Canarias, Spain, NE Atlantic Ocean
45 X16 **Tuira, Río** ≈ SE Panama
Tuisarkan see Tūysarkān
Tujiabu see Yongxiu
131 W5 **Tukan** Respublika Bashkortostan, W Russian Federation
175 R13 **Tukangbesi, Kepulauan** Dut. Toekang Besi Eilanden. island group C Indonesia
153 V13 **Tŭkhtamish** Rus. Toktomush, prev. Tokhtamyshbek. SE Tajikistan
192 O12 **Tukituki** ≈ North Island, NZ
Tu-k'ou see Panzhihua
124 N15 **Tūkrah** NE Libya
14 G2 **Tuktoyaktuk** Northwest Territories, NW Canada
173 Ff6 **Tuktuk** Pulau Samosir, W Indonesia
Tukumi see Tsukumi
120 E9 **Tukums** Ger. Tuckum. Tukums, W Latvia
83 G24 **Tukuyu** prev. Neu-Langenburg. Mbeya, S Tanzania
Tukzār see Tokzār
43 O13 **Tula** var. Tula de Allende. Hidalgo, C Mexico
43 O11 **Tula** Tamaulipas, C Mexico
130 K5 **Tula** Tul'skaya Oblast', W Russian Federation
Tulach Mhór see Tullamore
Tula de Allende see Tula
165 N10 **Tulage Ar Gol** ≈ W China
195 X15 **Tulaghi** var. Tulagi. Florida Islands, C Solomon Islands
Tulagi see Tulaghi
43 P13 **Tulancingo** Hidalgo, C Mexico
37 R11 **Tulare** California, W USA
31 P9 **Tulare** South Dakota, N USA
37 Q12 **Tulare Lake Bed** salt flat California, W USA
39 S14 **Tularosa** New Mexico, SW USA
39 P13 **Tularosa Mountains** ▲▲ New Mexico, SW USA
39 S15 **Tularosa Valley** basin New Mexico, SW USA
85 E25 **Tulbagh** Western Cape, SW South Africa
58 C5 **Tulcán** Carchi, N Ecuador
119 N13 **Tulcea** Tulcea, E Romania
119 N13 **Tulcea** ◈ county SE Romania
Tul'chin see Tul'chyn
119 N7 **Tul'chyn** Rus. Tul'chin. Vinnyts'ka Oblast', C Ukraine
Tuléar see Toliara
37 O1 **Tulelake** California, W USA
118 J10 **Tulgheş** Hung. Gyergyótölgyes. Harghita, C Romania
Tul'govichi see Tul'havichy
121 N20 **Tul'havichy** Rus. Tul'govichi. Homyel'skaya Voblasts', SE Belarus
Tuli see Thuli
27 N4 **Tulia** Texas, SW USA
22 J10 **Tullahoma** Tennessee, S USA
191 N12 **Tullamarine** ✕ (Melbourne) Victoria, SE Australia
191 Q7 **Tullamore** New South Wales, SE Australia
99 E18 **Tullamore** Ir. Tulach Mhór. C Ireland
105 N12 **Tulle** anc. Tutela. Corrèze, C France
111 X3 **Tulln** var. Oberhollabrunn. Niederösterreich, NE Austria
111 W4 **Tulln** ≈ NE Austria
24 H6 **Tullos** Louisiana, S USA
99 F19 **Tullow** Ir. An Tullach. SE Ireland
189 W5 **Tully** Queensland, NE Australia
128 J3 **Tuloma** ≈ NW Russian Federation
116 K10 **Tulovo** Khaskovska Oblast, C Bulgaria
29 P9 **Tulsa** Oklahoma, C USA
159 N11 **Tulsipur** Mid Western, W Nepal
130 K6 **Tul'skaya Oblast'** ◈ province W Russian Federation
130 L14 **Tul'skiy** Respublika Adygeya, SW Russian Federation
194 K8 **Tulu** Manus Island, N PNG
56 D10 **Tuluá** Valle del Cauca, W Colombia
118 M12 **Tuluceşti** Galaţi, E Romania
41 N12 **Tuluksak** Alaska, USA
43 Z12 **Tulum, Ruinas de** ruins Quintana Roo, SE Mexico
126 Ii15 **Tulun** Irkutskaya Oblast', S Russian Federation
174 Ll15 **Tulungagung** prev. Toeloengagoeng. Jawa, C Indonesia
195 S11 **Tulun Islands** var. Kilinailau Islands; prev. Carteret Islands. island group NE PNG
130 M4 **Tuma** Ryazanskaya Oblast', W Russian Federation
56 B12 **Tumaco** Nariño, SW Colombia
56 B12 **Tumaco, Bahía de** bay SW Colombia
Tuman-gang see Tumen
44 L8 **Tuma, Río** ≈ N Nicaragua
97 O16 **Tumba** Stockholm, C Sweden
Tumba, Lac see Ntomba, Lac
174 M9 **Tumbangsenamang** Borneo, C Indonesia
191 Q10 **Tumbarumba** New South Wales, SE Australia
58 A8 **Tumbes** Tumbes, NW Peru
58 A9 **Tumbes** off. Departamento de Tumbes. ◈ department NW Peru
21 P5 **Tumbledown Mountain** ▲ Maine, NE USA
9 N13 **Tumbler Ridge** British Columbia, W Canada
178 I12 **Tumbŏt, Phnum** ▲ W Cambodia
190 G9 **Tumby Bay** South Australia
169 Y10 **Tumen** Jilin, NE China

◆ Country ● Country Capital ◇ Dependent Territory ○ Dependent Territory Capital ◈ Administrative Region ✕ International Airport ▲ Mountain ▲▲ Mountain Range ⁂ Volcano ≈ River ◎ Lake ⊠ Reservoir

169 Y11 **Tumen** *Chin.* Tumen Jiang, *Kor.* Tumen-gang, *Rus.* Tumyn'tszyan. ≈ E Asia
Tumen Jiang *see* Tumen
57 Q8 **Tumeremo** Bolívar, E Venezuela
161 G19 **Tumkūr** Karnātaka, W India
98 I10 **Tummel** ≈ C Scotland, UK
196 B15 **Tumon Bay** *bay* W Guam
79 P14 **Tumu** NW Ghana
60 I10 **Tumuc Humac Mountains** *var.* Serra Tumucumaque. ▲ N South America
Tumucumaque, Serra *see* Tumuc Humac Mountains
191 Q10 **Tumut** New South Wales, SE Australia
Tumyn'tszyan *see* Tumen
Tūn *see* Ferdows
47 U14 **Tunapuna** Trinidad, Trinidad and Tobago
62 K11 **Tunas** Paraná, S Brazil
Tunbridge Wells *see* Royal Tunbridge Wells
116 L11 **Tunca Nehri** *Bul.* Tundzha. ≈ Bulgaria/Turkey *see also* Tundzha
143 O14 **Tunceli** *var.* Kalan. Tunceli, E Turkey
143 O14 **Tunceli** ◐ *province* C Turkey
158 J12 **Tūndla** Uttar Pradesh, N India
83 I25 **Tunduru** Ruvuma, S Tanzania
116 L10 **Tundzha** *Turk.* Tunca Nehri. ≈ Bulgaria/Turkey *see also* Tunca Nehri
161 H17 **Tungabhadra** ≈ S India
161 F17 **Tungabhadra Reservoir** ◎ S India
203 P2 **Tungaru** *prev.* Gilbert Islands. *island group* W Kiribati
179 Q16 **Tungawan** Mindanao, S Philippines
174 Hh9 **Tungkal** ≈ Sumatera, W Indonesia
T'ung-shan *see* Xuzhou
167 Q16 **Tungsha Tao** *Chin.* Dongsha Qundao, *Eng.* Pratas Island. *island* S Taiwan
167 S13 **Tungshih** *Jap.* Tōsei. N Taiwan
14 G7 **Tungsten** Northwest Territories, W Canada
Tung-t'ing Hu *see* Dongting Hu
58 A13 **Tungurahua** ◐ *province* C Ecuador
97 F14 **Tunhovdfjorden** ◎ S Norway
24 K2 **Tunica** Mississippi, S USA
77 N5 **Tunis** *var.* Tūnis. ● (Tunisia) NE Tunisia
77 N5 **Tunis, Golfe de** *Ar.* Khalīj Tūnis. *gulf* NE Tunisia
77 N6 **Tunisia** *off.* Republic of Tunisia, *Ar.* Al Jumhūrīyah at Tūnisīyah, *Fr.* République Tunisienne. ◆ *republic* N Africa
Tūnisīyah, Al Jumhūrīyah at *see* Tunisia
Tūnis, Khalīj *see* Tunis, Golfe de
56 G9 **Tunja** Boyacá, C Colombia
95 F14 **Tunnsjøen** ◎ C Norway
41 N12 **Tuntutuliak** Alaska, USA
153 U8 **Tunuk** Chuyskaya Oblast', C Kyrgyzstan
11 Q6 **Tunungayualok Island** *island* Newfoundland and Labrador, E Canada
64 H11 **Tunuyán** Mendoza, W Argentina
64 I11 **Tunuyán, Río** ≈ W Argentina
Tunxi *see* Huangshan
37 P9 **Tuolumne River** ≈ California, W USA
Tuong Buong *see* Tương Đương
178 J7 **Tương Đương** *var.* Tuong Buong. Nghê An, N Vietnam
166 I13 **Tuoniang Jiang** ≈ S China
165 N12 **Tuotuo He** ≈ C China
165 O12 **Tuotuoheyan** *var.* Tanggulashan, Togton-heyan. Qinghai, C China
Tüp *see* Tyup
62 J9 **Tupã** São Paulo, S Brazil
203 S10 **Tupai** *var.* Motu Iti. *atoll* Îles Sous le Vent, W French Polynesia
63 G15 **Tupanciretã** Rio Grande do Sul, S Brazil
24 M2 **Tupelo** Mississippi, S USA
126 L14 **Tupik** Chitinskaya Oblast', S Russian Federation
61 K18 **Tupiraçaba** Goiás, S Brazil
59 L21 **Tupiza** Potosí, S Bolivia
9 N13 **Tupper** British Columbia, W Canada
20 J8 **Tupper Lake** ◎ New York, NE USA
64 H11 **Tupungato, Volcán** ▲ W Argentina
169 T9 **Tuquan** Nei Mongol Zizhiqu, N China
56 C13 **Túquerres** Nariño, SW Colombia
159 U13 **Tura** Meghālaya, NE India
126 J10 **Tura** Evenkiyskiy Avtonomnyy Okrug, N Russian Federation
125 F11 **Tura** ≈ C Russian Federation
146 M10 **Turabah** Makkah, W Saudi Arabia
57 O8 **Turagua, Cerro** ▲ C Venezuela
192 L12 **Turakina** Manawatu-Wanganui, North Island, NZ
193 K15 **Turakirae Head** *headland* North Island, NZ
194 G13 **Turama** ≈ S PNG
126 I15 **Turan** Respublika Tyva, S Russian Federation
192 M10 **Turangi** Waikato, North Island, NZ
152 F11 **Turan Lowland** *var.* Turan Plain, *Kaz.* Turan Oypaty, *Rus.* Turanskaya Nizmennost', *Turk.* Turan Pesligi, *Uzb.* Turon Pasttekisligi. *plain* C Asia
Turan Oypaty/Turan Pesligi/ Turan Plain/Turanskaya Nizmennost' *see* Turan Lowland
144 K7 **Ţurāq al 'Ilab** *hill range* S Syria
121 K20 **Turaw** *Rus.* Turov. Homyel'skaya Voblasts', SE Belarus
146 L2 **Ţurayf** Al Ḩudūd ash Shamālīyah, NW Saudi Arabia
Turba *see* Teruel
56 E5 **Turbaco** Bolívar, N Colombia
154 K15 **Turbat** Baluchistān, SW Pakistan
Turbat-i-Haidari *see* Torbat-e Ḩeydarīyeh
Turbat-i-Jam *see* Torbat-e Jām
56 D7 **Turbo** Antioquia, NW Colombia
Turčianský Svätý Martin *see* Martin
118 H10 **Turda** *Ger.* Thorenburg, *Hung.* Torda. Cluj, NW Romania
148 M7 **Ţūreh** Markazī, W Iran
203 X12 **Tureia** *atoll* Îles Tuamotu, SE French Polynesia
112 I12 **Turek** Konin, C Poland
95 L19 **Turenki** Häme, SW Finland
Turfan *see* Turpan
151 R8 **Turgay** *Kaz.* Torghay. Akmola, W Kazakhstan
151 N10 **Turgay** *off.* Turgayskaya Oblast', *Kaz.* Torghay Oblysy. ◐ *province* C Kazakhstan
151 N10 **Turgay** *Kaz.* Torgay. ≈ C Kazakhstan
150 M8 **Turgayskaya Stolovaya Strana** *Kaz.* Torgay Üstirti. *plateau* Kazakhstan/Russian Federation
Turgel *see* Türi
116 L8 **Türgovishte** *prev.* Eski Dzhumaya. Razgradska Oblast, NE Bulgaria
142 C14 **Turgutlu** Manisa, W Turkey
142 L12 **Turhal** Tokat, N Turkey
120 H4 **Türi** *Ger.* Turgel. Järvamaa, N Estonia
107 S9 **Turia** ≈ E Spain
60 M12 **Turiaçu** Maranhão, E Brazil
Turin *see* Torino
118 I3 **Turiys'k** Volyns'ka Oblast', NW Ukraine
Turja *see* Tur"ya
126 K15 **Turka** Respublika Buryatiya, S Russian Federation
118 H6 **Turka** L'vivs'ka Oblast', W Ukraine
Turkana, Lake *see* Rudolf, Lake
151 P16 **Turkestan** *Kaz.* Türkistan. Yuzhnyy Kazakhstan, S Kazakhstan
153 Q12 **Turkestan Range** *Rus.* Turkestanskiy Khrebet. ▲ C Asia
Turkestanskiy Khrebet *see* Turkestan Range
113 M23 **Túrkeve** Jász-Nagykun-Szolnok, E Hungary
27 O4 **Turkey** Texas, SW USA
142 H14 **Turkey** *off.* Republic of Turkey, *Turk.* Türkiye Cumhuriyeti. ◆ *republic* SW Asia
189 N4 **Turkey Creek** Western Australia
28 M9 **Turkey Creek** ≈ Oklahoma, C USA
39 T9 **Turkey Mountains** ▲ New Mexico, SW USA
31 X11 **Turkey River** ≈ Iowa, C USA
131 N7 **Turki** Saratovskaya Oblast', W Russian Federation
Türkistan *see* Turkestan
Turkistan, Bandi-i *see* Torkestān, Selseleh-ye Band-e
Türkiye Cumhuriyeti *see* Turkey
Türkmen Aylagy *see* Turkmenskiy Zaliv
152 A10 **Turkmenbashi** *prev.* Krasnovodsk. Balkanskiy Velayat, W Turkmenistan
Türkmengala *see* Turkmen-kala
152 G13 **Turkmenistan** *off.* Turkmenistan; *prev.* Turkmenskaya Soviet Socialist Republic. ◆ *republic* C Asia
152 J14 **Turkmen-kala** *Turkm.* Türkmengala; *prev.* Turkmen-Kala. Maryyskiy Velayat, S Turkmenistan
Turkmenskaya Soviet Socialist Republic *see* Turkmenistan
152 A11 **Turkmenskiy Zaliv** *Turkm.* Türkmen Aylagy. *lake gulf* W Turkmenistan
142 L16 **Türkoğlu** Kahramanmaraş, S Turkey
46 L6 **Turks and Caicos Islands** ◇ *UK dependent territory* N West Indies
66 G10 **Turks and Caicos Islands** *island group* N West Indies
47 N6 **Turks Islands** *island group* SE Turks and Caicos Islands
95 K19 **Turku** *Swe.* Åbo. Turku-Pori, SW Finland
Turku ja Pori *see* Turku-Pori
95 K19 **Turku-Pori** *var.* Turku ja Pori, *Swe.* Åbo-Björneborg. ◐ *province* SW Finland
83 H17 **Turkwel** *seasonal river* NW Kenya
29 P9 **Turley** Oklahoma, C USA
37 P9 **Turlock** California, W USA
120 I12 **Turmantas** Zarasai, NE Lithuania
Turmberg *see* Wieżyca
192 N13 **Turnagain, Cape** *headland* North Island, NZ
Turnau *see* Turnov
44 H2 **Turneffe Islands** *island group* E Belize
20 M11 **Turners Falls** Massachusetts, NE USA
9 P16 **Turner Valley** Alberta, SW Canada
101 I16 **Turnhout** Antwerpen, N Belgium
111 V5 **Turnitz** Niederösterreich, E Austria
9 S12 **Turnor Lake** ◎ Saskatchewan, C Canada
113 E15 **Turnov** *Ger.* Turnau. Východní Čechy, N Czech Republic
Tŭrnovo *see* Veliko Tŭrnovo
118 I15 **Turnu Măgurele** *var.* Turnu-Măgurele. Teleorman, S Romania
Turnu Severin *see* Drobeta-Turnu Severin
Turócszentmárton *see* Martin
Turoni *see* Tours
Turon Pasttekisligi *see* Turan Lowland
Turov *see* Turaw
Turpakkla *see* Turpoqqal'a
164 M6 **Turpan** *var.* Turfan. Xinjiang Uygur Zizhiqu, NW China
Turpan Depression *see* Turpan Pendi
164 M6 **Turpan Pendi** *Eng.* Turpan Depression. *depression* NW China
164 M5 **Turpan Zhan** Xinjiang Uygur Zizhiqu, W China
Turpentine State *see* North Carolina
152 J10 **Turpoqqal'a** *Rus.* Turpakkla. Khorazm Wiloyati, W Uzbekistan
46 H8 **Turquino, Pico** ▲ E Cuba
29 Y10 **Turrell** Arkansas, C USA
45 N14 **Turrialba** Cartago, E Costa Rica
98 K8 **Turriff** NE Scotland, UK
145 V7 **Tursāq** E Iraq
Turshiz *see* Kāshmar
Tursunzade *see* Tursunzoda
153 P13 **Tursunzoda** *Rus.* Tursunzade; *prev.* Regar. W Tajikistan
168 J4 **Turt** Hövsgöl, N Mongolia
152 I9 **Turtkŭl** *Rus.* Turtkul'; *prev.* Petroaleksandrovsk. Qoraqalpoghiston Respublikasi, W Uzbekistan
31 O9 **Turtle Creek** ≈ South Dakota, N USA
32 K4 **Turtle Flambeau Flowage** ⊡ Wisconsin, N USA
9 S14 **Turtleford** Saskatchewan, S Canada
30 M4 **Turtle Lake** North Dakota, N USA
94 K12 **Turtola** Lappi, NW Finland
126 Jj10 **Turu** ≈ N Russian Federation
Turuga *see* Tsuruga
153 V10 **Turugart Pass** *pass* China/Kyrgyzstan
164 E7 **Turugart Shankou** *var.* Pereval Torugart. *pass* China/Kyrgyzstan
126 Hh9 **Turukhan** ≈ N Russian Federation
126 I9 **Turukhansk** Krasnoyarskiy Kray, N Russian Federation
145 N3 **Ţurumbah** *well* NE Syria
Turuoka *see* Tsuruoka
150 H14 **Turush** Mangistau, SW Kazakhstan
62 K7 **Turvo, Rio** ≈ S Brazil
118 J2 **Tur"ya** *Pol.* Turja, *Rus.* Tur'ya. ≈ NW Ukraine
25 O4 **Tuscaloosa** Alabama, S USA
25 O4 **Tuscaloosa, Lake** ◎ Alabama, S USA
Tuscan Archipelago *see* Toscano, Archipelago
Tuscan-Emilian Mountains *see* Tosco-Emiliano, Appennino
Tuscany *see* Toscana
37 V2 **Tuscarora** Nevada, W USA
20 F15 **Tuscarora Mountain** *ridge* Pennsylvania, NE USA
32 M14 **Tuscola** Illinois, N USA
27 P7 **Tuscola** Texas, SW USA
25 O2 **Tuscumbia** Alabama, S USA
94 O4 **Tusenøyane** *island group* S Svalbard
150 K13 **Tushybas, Zaliv** *prev.* Zaliv Paskevicha. *lake gulf* SW Kazakhstan
Tusima *see* Tsushima
176 Z14 **Tusirah** Irian Jaya, E Indonesia
25 Q5 **Tuskegee** Alabama, S USA
96 E8 **Tustna** *island* S Norway
41 R12 **Tustumena Lake** ◎ Alaska, USA
112 K13 **Tuszyn** Piotrków, C Poland
143 S13 **Tutak** Ağrı, E Turkey
193 C20 **Tutamoe Range** ▲ North Island, NZ
Tutasev *see* Tutayev
128 L15 **Tutayev** *var.* Tutasev. Yaroslavskaya Oblast', W Russian Federation
Tutela *see* Tulle, France
Tutela *see* Tudela, Spain
Tutera *see* Tudela
161 H23 **Tuticorin** Tamil Nādu, SE India
115 L15 **Tutin** Serbia, S Yugoslavia
192 O10 **Tutira** Hawke's Bay, North Island, NZ
Tutiura *see* Tsuchiura
126 Ii10 **Tutonchny** Evenkiyskiy Avtonomnyy Okrug, N Russian Federation
116 L6 **Tutrakan** Razgradska Oblast, NE Bulgaria
31 N5 **Tuttle** North Dakota, N USA
28 M11 **Tuttle** Oklahoma, C USA
29 O3 **Tuttle Creek Lake** ⊡ Kansas, C USA
103 H23 **Tuttlingen** Baden-Württemberg, S Germany
175 Ss16 **Tutuala** Timor, S Indonesia
198 Cc9 **Tutuila** *island* W American Samoa
85 I18 **Tutume** Central, E Botswana
41 N7 **Tututalak Mountain** ▲ Alaska, USA
24 K3 **Tutwiler** Mississippi, S USA
168 L8 **Tuul Gol** ≈ N Mongolia
95 O16 **Tuupovaara** Pohjois-Karjala, SE Finland
Tuva *see* Tyva, Respublika
202 E7 **Tuvalu** *prev.* Ellice Islands. ◆ *commonwealth republic* SW Pacific Ocean
197 L17 **Tuvana-i-Colo** *prev.* Tuvana-i-Tholo. *island* Lau Group, SE Fiji
197 L18 **Tuvana-i-Ra** *island* Lau Group, SE Fiji
Tuvana-i-Tholo *see* Tuvana-i-Colo
Tuvinskaya ASSR *see* Tyva, Respublika
197 L14 **Tuvuca** *prev.* Tuvutha. *island* Lau Group, E Fiji
Tuvutha *see* Tuvuca
147 P9 **Ţuwayq, Jabal** ▲ C Saudi Arabia
144 H13 **Ţuwayyil ash Shihāq** *desert* S Jordan
9 U16 **Tuxford** Saskatchewan, S Canada
178 K13 **Tu Xoay** Đăc Lăc, S Vietnam
42 L14 **Tuxpan** Jalisco, C Mexico
42 J12 **Tuxpan** Nayarit, C Mexico
43 Q12 **Tuxpán** *var.* Tuxpán de Rodríguez Cano. Veracruz-Llave, E Mexico
Tuxpán de Rodríguez Cano *see* Tuxpán
43 R15 **Tuxtepec** *var.* San Juan Bautista Tuxtepec. Oaxaca, S Mexico
43 U16 **Tuxtla** *var.* Tuxtla Gutiérrez. Chiapas, SE Mexico
Tuxtla *see* San Andrés Tuxtla
Tuxtla Gutiérrez *see* Tuxtla
Tuyama *see* Tsuyama
178 Jj5 **Tuyên Quang** Tuyên Quang, N Vietnam
178 K14 **Tuy Hoa** Binh Thuân, S Vietnam
178 Kk12 **Tuy Hoa** Phu Yên, S Vietnam
131 U5 **Tuymazy** Respublika Bashkortostan, W Russian Federation
148 L6 **Tūysarkān** *var.* Tuisarkan, Tuyserkān. Hamadān, W Iran
Tuyserkān *see* Tūysarkān
153 Q10 **Tuytepa** *Rus.* Toytepa. Toshkent Wiloyati, E Uzbekistan
151 W16 **Tuyuk** *Kaz.* Tuyyq. Taldykorgan, SE Kazakhstan
Tuyyq *see* Tuyuk
142 I14 **Tuz Gölü** ◎ C Turkey
129 Q15 **Tuzha** Kirovskaya Oblast', NW Russian Federation
115 K17 **Tuzi** Montenegro, SW Yugoslavia
145 T5 **Ţūz Khurmātū** N Iraq
114 I11 **Tuzla** NE Bosnia and Herzegovina
119 N15 **Tuzla** Constanţa, SE Romania
143 T12 **Tuzluca** Kars, NE Turkey
97 J20 **Tvååker** Halland, S Sweden
97 F17 **Tvedestrand** Aust-Agder, S Norway
128 J16 **Tver'** *prev.* Kalinin. Tverskaya Oblast', W Russian Federation
130 I15 **Tverskaya Oblast'** ◐ *province* W Russian Federation
128 I15 **Tvertsa** ≈ W Russian Federation
112 H13 **Twardogóra** *Ger.* Festenberg. Wrocław, SW Poland
12 J14 **Tweed** Ontario, SE Canada
98 K13 **Tweed** ≈ England/Scotland, UK
100 O7 **Tweede-Exloërmond** Drenthe, NE Netherlands
191 V3 **Tweed Heads** New South Wales, SE Australia
100 M11 **Twello** Gelderland, E Netherlands
37 W15 **Twentynine Palms** California, W USA
27 P9 **Twin Buttes Reservoir** ⊡ Texas, SW USA
35 O15 **Twin Falls** Idaho, NW USA
41 N13 **Twin Hills** Alaska, USA
9 O11 **Twin Lakes** Alberta, W Canada
35 O12 **Twin Peaks** ▲ Idaho, NW USA
193 I14 **Twins, The** ▲ South Island, NZ
31 S5 **Twin Valley** Minnesota, N USA
102 G11 **Twistringen** Niedersachsen, NW Germany
193 E20 **Twizel** Canterbury, South Island, NZ
31 X5 **Two Harbors** Minnesota, N USA
9 R14 **Two Hills** Alberta, SW Canada
33 N7 **Two Rivers** Wisconsin, N USA
118 H8 **Tyachiv** Zakarpats'ka Oblast', W Ukraine
Tyan'-Shan' *see* Tien Shan
177 Ff3 **Tyao** ≈ Myanmar/India
Tyas *see* Tiyās
119 R6 **Tyas'myn** ≈ N Ukraine
25 X6 **Tybee Island** Georgia, SE USA
Tyborøn *see* Thyborøn
113 J16 **Tychy** *Ger.* Tichau. Katowice, S Poland
113 O16 **Tyczyn** Rzeszów, SE Poland
96 I8 **Tydal** Sør-Trøndelag, S Norway
117 H24 **Tyflós** ≈ Kríti, Greece, E Mediterranean Sea
23 S3 **Tygart Lake** ⊡ West Virginia, NE USA
126 M15 **Tygda** Amurskaya Oblast', SE Russian Federation
23 Q11 **Tyger River** ≈ South Carolina, SE USA
34 I11 **Tygh Valley** Oregon, NW USA
96 F12 **Tyin** ◎ S Norway
31 S10 **Tyler** Minnesota, N USA
27 W7 **Tyler** Texas, SW USA
27 W7 **Tyler, Lake** ⊡ Texas, SW USA
24 K7 **Tylertown** Mississippi, S USA
Tylos *see* Bahrain
126 Gg12 **Tym** ≈ C Russian Federation
117 C15 **Týmfi** *var.* Timfi. ▲ W Greece
117 E17 **Tymfristós** *var.* Timfristos. ▲ C Greece
127 O14 **Tymovskoye** Ostrov Sakhalin, Sakhalinskaya Oblast', SE Russian Federation
117 J25 **Tympáki** *var.* Timbaki; *prev.* Timbákion. Kríti, Greece, E Mediterranean Sea
126 Ll14 **Tynda** Amurskaya Oblast', SE Russian Federation
31 Q12 **Tyndall** South Dakota, N USA
99 L14 **Tyne** ≈ N England, UK
99 M14 **Tynemouth** NE England, UK
99 L14 **Tyneside** *cultural region* NE England, UK
96 H10 **Tynset** Hedmark, S Norway
41 Q12 **Tyonek** Alaska, USA
Tyôsi *see* Chôshi
Tyras *see* Dniester, Moldova/Ukraine
Tyras *see* Bilhorod-Dnistrovs'kyy, Ukraine
Tyre *see* Soûr
97 G14 **Tyrifjorden** ◎ S Norway
97 K22 **Tyringe** Kristianstad, S Sweden
127 N15 **Tyrma** Khabarovskiy Kray, SE Russian Federation
Tyrnau *see* Trnava
117 F15 **Týrnavos** *var.* Tírnavos. Thessalía, C Greece
131 N16 **Tyrnyauz** Kabardino-Balkarskaya Respublika, SW Russian Federation
Tyrol *see* Tirol
20 E14 **Tyrone** Pennsylvania, NE USA
99 E15 **Tyrone** *cultural region* W Northern Ireland, UK
190 M10 **Tyrrell, Lake** *salt lake* Victoria, SE Australia
86 H14 **Tyrrhenian Basin** *undersea feature* Tyrrhenian Sea, C Mediterranean Sea
123 L9 **Tyrrhenian Sea** *It.* Mare Tirreno. *sea* N Mediterranean Sea
Tysa *see* Tisa/Tisza
118 J7 **Tysmenytsya** Ivano-Frankivs'ka Oblast', W Ukraine
97 C14 **Tysnesøya** *island* S Norway
97 C14 **Tysse** Hordaland, S Norway
97 D14 **Tyssedal** Hordaland, S Norway
97 O17 **Tystberga** Södermanland, C Sweden
120 E12 **Tytuvėnai** Kelmė, C Lithuania
150 D14 **Tyub-Karagan, Mys** *headland* SW Kazakhstan
153 V8 **Tyugel'-Say** Narynskaya Oblast', C Kyrgyzstan
125 Ff13 **Tyukalinsk** Omskaya Oblast', C Russian Federation
131 V7 **Tyul'gan** Orenburgskaya Oblast', W Russian Federation
125 F11 **Tyumen'** Tyumenskaya Oblast', C Russian Federation
125 Ff10 **Tyumenskaya Oblast'** ◐ *province* C Russian Federation
126 Kk10 **Tyung** ≈ NE Russian Federation
153 Y7 **Tyup** *Kir.* Tüp. Issyk-Kul'skaya Oblast', NE Kyrgyzstan
126 I16 **Tyva, Respublika** *prev.* Tannu-Tuva, Tuva, Tuvinskaya ASSR. ◐ *autonomous republic* C Russian Federation
119 N7 **Tyvriv** Vinnyts'ka Oblast', C Ukraine
99 J21 **Tywi** ≈ S Wales, UK
99 I19 **Tywyn** W Wales, UK
85 K20 **Tzaneen** Northern, NE South Africa
Tzekung *see* Zigong
43 X12 **Tzucacab** Yucatán, SE Mexico

U

84 B12 **Uaco Cungo** *var.* Waku Kungo, *Port.* Santa Comba. Cuanza Sul, C Angola
UAE *see* United Arab Emirates
203 X7 **Ua Huka** *island* Îles Marquises, NE French Polynesia
60 E10 **Uaiacás** Roraima, N Brazil
Uamba *see* Wamba
Uanle Uen *see* Wanlaweyn
203 W7 **Ua Pu** *island* Îles Marquises, NE French Polynesia
83 L17 **Uar Garas** *spring/well* SW Somalia
60 G12 **Uatumã, Rio** ≈ C Brazil
Ua Uíbh Fhailí *see* Offaly
60 C11 **Uaupés, Rio** *var.* Río Vaupés. ≈ Brazil/Colombia *see also* Vaupés, Río
151 X9 **Uba** ≈ E Kazakhstan
151 N6 **Ubagan** *Kaz.* Obagan. ≈ Kazakhstan/Russian Federation
195 N12 **Ubai** New Britain, E PNG
81 J15 **Ubangi** *Fr.* Oubangui. ≈ C Africa
Ubangi-Shari *see* Central African Republic
118 M3 **Ubarts'** *Ukr.* Ubort'. ≈ Belarus/Ukraine *see also* Ubort'
56 F9 **Ubaté** Cundinamarca, C Colombia
62 N10 **Ubatuba** São Paulo, S Brazil
155 R12 **Ubauro** Sind, SE Pakistan
179 Qq14 **Ubay** Bohol, C Philippines
105 U14 **Ubaye** ≈ SE France
Ubayid, Wadi al *see* Ubayyiḍ, Wādī al
145 N8 **Ubaylah** W Iraq
145 O10 **Ubayyiḍ, Wādī al** *var.* Wadi al Ubayid. *dry watercourse* SW Iraq
100 L13 **Ubbergen** Gelderland, E Netherlands
170 Dd13 **Ube** Yamaguchi, Honshū, SW Japan
107 O13 **Úbeda** Andalucía, S Spain
111 V7 **Übelbach** *var.* Markt-Übelbach. Steiermark, SE Austria
61 L20 **Uberaba** Minas Gerais, SE Brazil
59 Q19 **Uberaba, Laguna** ◎ E Bolivia
61 K19 **Uberlândia** Minas Gerais, SE Brazil
103 H24 **Überlingen** Baden-Württemberg, S Germany
79 U16 **Ubiaja** Edo, S Nigeria
106 K3 **Ubiña, Peña** ▲ NW Spain
59 H17 **Ubinas, Volcán** ▲ S Peru
Ubol Rajadhani/Ubol Ratchathani *see* Ubon Ratchathani
178 Ii9 **Ubolratna Reservoir** ⊡ C Thailand
178 J10 **Ubon Ratchathani** *var.* Muang Ubon, Ubol Rajadhani, Ubol Ratchathani, Udon Ratchathani. Ubon Ratchathani, E Thailand
121 L20 **Ubort'** *Bel.* Ubarts'. ≈ Belarus/Ukraine *see also* Ubarts'
106 K15 **Ubrique** Andalucía, S Spain
Ubsu-Nur, Ozero *see* Uvs Nuur
81 M18 **Ubundu** Haut-Zaïre, C Zaire
143 X11 **Ucar** *Rus.* Udzhary. C Azerbaijan
58 G13 **Ucayali** *off.* Departamento de Ucayali. ◐ *department* E Peru
58 F10 **Ucayali, Río** ≈ C Peru
Uccle *see* Ukkel
152 J13 **Uch-Adzhi** *Turkm.* Üchajy. Maryyskiy Velayat, C Turkmenistan
Üchajy *see* Uch-Adzhi
131 X4 **Uchaly** Respublika Bashkortostan, W Russian Federation
151 W13 **Ucharal** *Kaz.* Üsharal. Taldykorgan, E Kazakhstan
170 C17 **Uchinoura** Kagoshima, Kyūshū, SW Japan
172 Nn6 **Uchiura-wan** *bay* NW Pacific Ocean
Uchkuduk *see* Uchquduq
Uchkurghan *see* Uchqŭrgon
152 K8 **Uchquduq** *Rus.* Uchkuduk. Nawoiy Wiloyati, N Uzbekistan
153 S9 **Uchqŭrgon** *Rus.* Uchkurghan. Namangan Wiloyati, E Uzbekistan
Uchsay *see* Uchsoy
152 G6 **Uchsoy** *Rus.* Uchsay. Qoraqalpoghiston Respublikasi, NW Uzbekistan
Uchtagan Gumy *see* Uchtagan, Peski
152 D10 **Uchtagan, Peski** *Turkm.* Uchtagan Gumy. *desert* NW Turkmenistan
126 Mm12 **Uchur** ≈ E Russian Federation
102 O10 **Uckermark** *cultural region* E Germany
8 K17 **Ucluelet** Vancouver Island, British Columbia, SW Canada
126 Ii14 **Uda** ≈ S Russian Federation
126 Mm13 **Uda** ≈ E Russian Federation
126 K9 **Udachnyy** Respublika Sakha (Yakutiya), NE Russian Federation
161 G21 **Udagamandalam** *var.* Udhagamandalam; *prev.* Ootacamund. Tamil Nādu, SW India
158 F14 **Udaipur** *prev.* Oodeypore. Rājasthān, N India
Udayadhani *see* Uthai Thani
149 N16 **'Udayd, Khawr al** *var.* Khor al Udeid. *inlet* Qatar/Saudi Arabia
114 D11 **Udbina** Zadar-Knin, C Croatia
97 I18 **Uddevalla** Göteborg och Bohus, S Sweden
Uddjaur *see* Uddjaure
94 H13 **Uddjaure** *var.* Uddjaur. ◎ N Sweden
Udeid, Khor al *see* 'Udayd, Khawr al
101 K14 **Uden** Noord-Brabant, SE Netherlands
Uden *see* Udenhout
101 J14 **Udenhout** *var.* Uden. Noord-Brabant, S Netherlands
161 H14 **Udgīr** Mahārāshtra, C India
Udhagamandalam *see* Udagamandalam
158 H6 **Udhampur** Jammu and Kashmir, NW India
145 X14 **'Udhaybah, 'Uqlat al** *well* S Iraq
108 J7 **Udine** *anc.* Utina. Friuli-Venezia Giulia, NE Italy
183 T14 **Udintsev Fracture Zone** *tectonic feature* S Pacific Ocean
Udipi *see* Udupi
Udmurtia *see* Udmurtskaya Respublika
131 S2 **Udmurtskaya Respublika** *Eng.* Udmurtia. ◐ *autonomous republic* NW Russian Federation
128 J15 **Udomlya** Tverskaya Oblast', W Russian Federation
Udon Ratchathani *see* Ubon Ratchathani
178 Ii9 **Udon Thani** *var.* Ban Mak Khaeng, Udordhani. Udon Thani, N Thailand
Udordhani *see* Udon Thani
201 U12 **Udot** *atoll* Chuuk Islands, C Micronesia
127 N13 **Udskaya Guba** *bay* E Russian Federation
161 E19 **Udupi** *var.* Udipi. Karnātaka, SW India
Udzhary *see* Ucar
175 Q9 **Uebonti, Teluk** *bay* Sulawesi, C Indonesia
102 O9 **Uecker** ≈ NE Germany
102 P9 **Ueckermünde** Mecklenburg-Vorpommern, NE Germany
171 J14 **Ueda** *var.* Uyeda. Nagano, Honshū, S Japan
81 L16 **Uele** *var.* Welle. ≈ NE Zaire
Uele (upper course) *see* Uolo, Río, Equatorial Guinea/Gabon
Uele (upper course) *see* Kibali, Zaire
127 Q3 **Uelen** Chukotskiy Avtonomnyy Okrug, NE Russian Federation
102 J11 **Uelzen** Niedersachsen, N Germany
171 H15 **Ueno** Mie, Honshū, SW Japan
131 V4 **Ufa** Respublika Bashkortostan, W Russian Federation
131 V4 **Ufa** ≈ W Russian Federation
152 A10 **Ufra** Balkanskiy Velayat, NW Turkmenistan
85 C18 **Ugab** ≈ C Namibia
120 D8 **Ugāle** Ventspils, NW Latvia
83 F17 **Uganda** *off.* Republic of Uganda. ◆ *republic* E Africa
144 G4 **Ugarit** *Ar.* Ra's Shamrah. *site of ancient city* Al Lādhiqīyah, NW Syria
41 O14 **Ugashik** Alaska, USA
109 Q19 **Ugento** Puglia, SE Italy
107 O15 **Ugíjar** Andalucía, S Spain
105 T11 **Ugine** Savoie, E France
127 O15 **Uglegorsk** Ostrov Sakhalin, Sakhalinskaya Oblast', SE Russian Federation
129 V13 **Ugleural'skiy** Permskaya Oblast', NW Russian Federation
128 L15 **Uglich** Yaroslavskaya Oblast', W Russian Federation
128 I14 **Uglovka** *var.* Okulovka. Novgorodskaya Oblast', W Russian Federation
127 Pp5 **Ugol'nyye Kopi** Chukotskiy Avtonomnyy Okrug, NE Russian Federation
130 I4 **Ugra** ≈ W Russian Federation
153 V9 **Ugyut** Narynskaya Oblast', C Kyrgyzstan
113 H19 **Uherské Hradiště** *Ger.* Ungarisch-Hradisch. Jižní Morava, SE Czech Republic
113 H19 **Uherský Brod** *Ger.* Ungarisch-Brod. Jižní Morava, SE Czech Republic
113 B17 **Úhlava** *Ger.* Angel. ≈ W Czech Republic
Uhorshchyna *see* Hungary
33 T13 **Uhrichsville** Ohio, N USA
Uhuru Peak *see* Kilimanjaro
98 G8 **Uig** N Scotland, UK
84 B10 **Uíge** *Port.* Carmona, Vila Marechal Carmona. Uíge, NW Angola
84 B10 **Uíge** ◐ *province* N Angola
200 Ss13 **Uiha** *island* Ha'apai Group, C Tonga
201 U13 **Uijec** *island* Chuuk, C Micronesia
169 X14 **Ŭijŏngbu** *Jap.* Giseifu. NW South Korea
150 H10 **Uil** *Kaz.* Oyyl. Aktyubinsk, W Kazakhstan
150 H10 **Uil** *Kaz.* Oyyl. ≈ W Kazakhstan
38 M3 **Uinta Mountains** ▲ Utah, W USA
85 C18 **Uis** Erongo, NW Namibia
85 I25 **Uitenhage** Eastern Cape, S South Africa
100 H9 **Uitgeest** Noord-Holland, W Netherlands
100 I11 **Uithoorn** Noord-Holland, C Netherlands
100 O4 **Uithuizen** Groningen, NE Netherlands
100 O4 **Uithuizermeeden** Groningen, NE Netherlands
201 R6 **Ujae Atoll** *var.* Wūjae. *atoll* Ralik Chain, W Marshall Islands
Ujain *see* Ujjain
113 I16 **Ujazd** Opole, SW Poland
Új-Becse *see* Novi Bečej
Ujda *see* Oujda
201 N5 **Ujelang Atoll** *var.* Wujlān. *atoll* Ralik Chain, W Marshall Islands
113 N21 **Újfehértó** Szabolcs-Szatmár-Bereg, E Hungary
Újgradiska *see* Nova Gradiška
171 H15 **Uji** *var.* Uzi. Kyōto, Honshū, SW Japan
170 Aa16 **Uji-guntō** *island* Nansei-shotō, SW Japan
83 E21 **Ujiji** Kigoma, W Tanzania
160 G10 **Ujjain** *prev.* Ujain. Madhya Pradesh, C India
Újlak *see* Ilok
'Ujmān *see* 'Ajmān
Újmoldova *see* Moldova Nouă
Újszentanna *see* Sântana
175 P13 **Ujungpandang** *var.* Macassar, Makassar; *prev.* Makasar. Sulawesi, C Indonesia
Ujung Salang *see* Phuket
Újvidék *see* Novi Sad
160 E11 **Ukāi Reservoir** ⊡ W India
83 G19 **Ukara Island** *island* N Tanzania
'Ukash, Wādī *see* 'Akāsh, Wādī
83 F19 **Ukerewe Island** *island* N Tanzania
145 S9 **Ukhayḍhir** C Iraq
159 X13 **Ukhrul** Manipur, NE India
129 S9 **Ukhta** Respublika Komi, NW Russian Federation
36 L6 **Ukiah** California, W USA
34 K12 **Ukiah** Oregon, NW USA
101 G18 **Ukkel** *Fr.* Uccle. Brussels, C Belgium
120 G13 **Ukmergė** *Pol.* Wiłkomierz. Ukmergė, C Lithuania
Ukraina *see* Ukraine
118 L6 **Ukraine** *off.* Ukraine, *Rus.* Ukraina, *Ukr.* Ukrayina; *prev.* Ukrainian Soviet Socialist Republic, Ukrainskaya S.S.R. ◆ *republic* SE Europe
Ukrainskay S.S.R/ Ukrayina *see* Ukraine
84 B13 **Uku** Cuanza Sul, NW Angola
170 Bb12 **Uku-jima** *island* Gotō-rettō, SW Japan
85 F20 **Ukwi** Kgalagadi, SW Botswana
120 M13 **Ula** *Rus.* Ulla. Vitsyebskaya Voblasts', N Belarus
142 C16 **Ula** Muğla, SW Turkey
120 M13 **Ula** *Rus.* Ulla. ≈ N Belarus
168 L7 **Ulaanbaatar** *Eng.* Ulan Bator. ● (Mongolia) Töv, C Mongolia
169 N8 **Ulaan-Ereg** Hentiy, E Mongolia

◆ Country ● Country Capital ◇ Dependent Territory ○ Dependent Territory Capital ◐ Administrative Region ✕ International Airport ▲ Mountain ▲ Mountain Range ▲ Volcano ≈ River ◎ Lake ⊡ Reservoir

168 E5 **Ulaangom** Uvs, NW Mongolia
168 E7 **Ulaantolgoy** Hovd, W Mongolia
168 I8 **Ulaan-Uul** Bayanhongor, C Mongolia
169 O10 **Ulaan-Uul** Dornogovĭ, SE Mongolia
165 R10 **Ulan** Qinghai, C China
Ulan Bator *see* Ulaanbaatar
168 L13 **Ulan Buh Shamo** *desert* N China
Ulanhad *see* Chifeng
169 T8 **Ulanhot** Nei Mongol Zizhiqu, N China
131 Q14 **Ulan Khol** Respublika Kalmykiya, SW Russian Federation
168 M13 **Ulansuhai Nur** ◎ N China
126 Jj16 **Ulan-Ude** *prev.* Verkhneudinsk. Respublika Buryatiya, S Russian Federation
165 N12 **Ulan Ul Hu** ◎ C China
195 Z16 **Ulawa Island** *island* SE Solomon Islands
144 J7 **'Ulayyānīyah, Bi'r al** *var.* Al Hilbeh. *well* S Syria
127 Nn13 **Ul'banskiy Zaliv** *strait* E Russian Federation
Ulbo *see* Olib
115 J18 **Ulcinj** Montenegro, SW Yugoslavia
169 O7 **Uldz** Hentiy, NE Mongolia
Uleåborg *see* Oulu
Uleälv *see* Oulujoki
97 G16 **Ulefoss** Telemark, S Norway
Uleträsk *see* Oulujärvi
115 L19 **Ulëz** *var.* Ulëza. Dibër, C Albania
Ulëza *see* Ulëz
97 F22 **Ulfborg** Ringkøbing, W Denmark
100 N13 **Ulft** Gelderland, E Netherlands
168 G7 **Uliastay** Dzavhan, W Mongolia
196 F8 **Ulimang** Babeldaob, N Palau
69 T10 **Ulindi** ≈ W Zaire
196 H14 **Ulithi Atoll** *atoll* Caroline Islands, W Micronesia
114 N10 **Uljma** Serbia, NE Yugoslavia
150 L11 **Ul'kayak** *Kaz.* Ölkeyek. ≈ C Kazakhstan
151 Q7 **Ul'ken-Karoy, Ozero** ◎ N Kazakhstan
Ülkenözen *see* Bol'shoy Uzen'
Ülkenqobda *see* Bol'shaya Khobda
106 G3 **Ulla** ≈ NW Spain
Ulla *see* Ula
191 S10 **Ulladulla** New South Wales, SE Australia
159 T14 **Ullapara** Rajshahi, W Bangladesh
98 H7 **Ullapool** N Scotland, UK
97 J20 **Ullared** Halland, S Sweden
107 T7 **Ulldecona** Cataluña, NE Spain
94 I9 **Ullsfjorden** *fjord* N Norway
99 K15 **Ullswater** ◎ NW England, UK
103 I22 **Ulm** Baden-Württemberg, S Germany
35 R8 **Ulm** Montana, NW USA
191 V5 **Ulmarra** New South Wales, SE Australia
118 K13 **Ulmeni** Buzău, C Romania
118 K14 **Ulmeni** Călăraşi, S Romania
44 L7 **Ulmukhuás** Región Autónoma Atlántico Norte, NE Nicaragua
196 C8 **Ulong** *var.* Aulong. *island* Palau Islands, N Palau
85 N14 **Ulonguè** *var.* Ulongwé. Tete, NW Mozambique
Ulongwé *see* Ulonguè
97 K19 **Ulricehamn** Älvsborg, S Sweden
100 N5 **Ulrum** Groningen, NE Netherlands
169 Z16 **Ulsan** *Jap.* Urusan. SE South Korea
96 D10 **Ulsteinvik** Møre og Romsdal, S Norway
99 D15 **Ulster** ◈ *province* Northern Ireland, UK/Ireland
175 S5 **Ulu** Pulau Siau, N Indonesia
126 Ll12 **Ulu** Respublika Sakha (Yakutiya), NE Russian Federation
44 H5 **Ulúa, Río** ≈ NW Honduras
142 D12 **Ulubat Gölü** ◎ NW Turkey
142 E12 **Uludağ** ▲ NW Turkey
Ulugh Muztag *see* Muztag Feng
164 D7 **Ulugqat** Xinjiang Uygur Zizhiqu, W China
142 J16 **Ulukışla** Niğde, S Turkey
201 O15 **Ulul** *island* Caroline Islands, C Micronesia
85 L22 **Ulundi** KwaZulu/Natal, E South Africa
164 M3 **Ulungur He** ≈ NW China
164 K2 **Ulungur Hu** ◎ NW China
189 P8 **Uluru** *var.* Ayers Rock. *rocky outcrop* Northern Territory, C Australia
197 D13 **Ulveah** *var.* Lopevi. *island* C Vanuatu
99 K16 **Ulverston** NW England, UK
191 O16 **Ulverstone** Tasmania, SE Australia
96 D13 **Ulvik** Hordaland, S Norway
95 J18 **Ulvila** Turku-Pori, SW Finland
119 O8 **Ulyanivka** *Rus.* Ul'yanovka. Kirovohrads'ka Oblast', C Ukraine
Ul'yanovka *see* Ulyanivka
131 Q5 **Ul'yanovsk** *prev.* Simbirsk. Ul'yanovskaya Oblast', W Russian Federation
131 Q5 **Ul'yanovskaya Oblast'** ◈ *province* W Russian Federation
151 S10 **Ul'yanovskiy** Karaganda, C Kazakhstan
Ul'yanovskiy Kanal *see* Ul'yanow Kanali
152 M13 **Ul'yanow Kanali** *Rus.* Ul'yanovskiy Kanal. *canal* Turkmenistan/Uzbekistan
Ulyshylanshyq *see* Uly-Zhylanshyk
28 H6 **Ulysses** Kansas, C USA
151 O12 **Ulytau, Gory** ⛰ C Kazakhstan
126 K14 **Ulyunkhan** Respublika Buryatiya, S Russian Federation
151 N11 **Uly-Zhylanshyk** *Kaz.* Ulyshylanshyq. ≈ C Kazakhstan
114 A9 **Umag** *It.* Umago. Istra, NW Croatia
Umago *see* Umag
201 V13 **Uman** *atoll* Chuuk Islands, C Micronesia
119 O7 **Uman'** *Rus.* Uman. Cherkas'ka Oblast', C Ukraine
43 W12 **Umán** Yucatán, SE Mexico
Umanak/Umanaq *see* Uummannaq
'Umān, Khalīj *see* Oman, Gulf of
'Umān, Salṭanat *see* Oman
176 Ww12 **Umari** Irian Jaya, E Indonesia
160 K10 **Umaria** Madhya Pradesh, C India
155 R16 **Umarkot** Sind, SE Pakistan
196 B17 **Umatac** SW Guam
196 A17 **Umatac Bay** *bay* SW Guam
145 S6 **Umayqah** C Iraq
128 J5 **Umba** Murmanskaya Oblast', NW Russian Federation
144 I8 **Umbāshī, Khirbat al** *ruins* As Suwaydā', S Syria
82 A12 **Umbelasha** ≈ W Sudan
108 H12 **Umbertide** Umbria, C Italy
63 B17 **Umberto** *var.* Humberto. Santa Fe, C Argentina
194 K11 **Umboi Island** *var.* Rooke Island. *island* C PNG
128 J4 **Umbozero, Ozero** ◎ NW Russian Federation
108 H13 **Umbria** ◈ *region* C Italy
Umbrian-Machigian Mountains *see* Umbro-Marchigiano, Appennino
108 I12 **Umbro-Marchigiano, Appennino** *Eng.* Umbrian-Machigian Mountains. ⛰ C Italy
95 J16 **Umeå** Västerbotten, N Sweden
95 H14 **Umeälven** ≈ N Sweden
41 Q5 **Umiat** Alaska, USA
85 K23 **Umlazi** KwaZulu/Natal, E South Africa
145 X10 **Umm al Baqar, Hawr** *var.* Birkat ad Dawaymah. *spring* S Iraq
147 U12 **Umm al Ḥayt, Wādī** *var.* Wādī Amilḥayt. *seasonal river* SW Oman
Umm al Qaiwain *see* Umm al Qaywayn
149 R15 **Umm al Qaywayn** *var.* Umm al Qaiwain. Umm al Qaywayn, NE UAE
145 Q5 **Umm al Ṭūz** C Iraq
144 J3 **Umm 'Āmūd** Ḥalab, N Syria
147 Y10 **Umm ar Ruṣāṣ** *var.* Umm Ruṣayṣ. W Oman
147 X9 **Ummas Samīn** *salt flat* C Oman
147 V9 **Umm az Zumūl** *oasis* E Saudi Arabia
82 A9 **Umm Buru** Western Darfur, W Sudan
82 A12 **Umm Dafag** Southern Darfur, W Sudan
Umm Durmān *see* Omdurman
144 F9 **Umm el Fahm** Haifa, N Israel
82 F9 **Umm Inderab** Northern Kordofan, C Sudan
82 C10 **Umm Keddada** Northern Darfur, W Sudan
146 J7 **Umm Lajj** Tabūk, W Saudi Arabia
144 L10 **Umm Maḥfur** ≈ N Jordan
145 Y13 **Umm Qaṣr** SE Iraq
Umm Ruṣayṣ *see* Umm ar Ruṣāṣ
82 F11 **Umm Ruwaba** *var.* Umm Ruwābah, Um Ruwāba. Northern Kordofan, C Sudan
Umm Ruwābah *see* Umm Ruwaba
149 N16 **Umm Sa'īd** *var.* Musay'īd. S Qatar
144 K10 **Umm Ṭuways, Wādī** *dry watercourse* N Jordan
40 J17 **Umnak Island** *island* Aleutian Islands, Alaska, USA
34 F13 **Umpqua River** ≈ Oregon, NW USA
84 D13 **Umpulo** Bié, C Angola
160 I12 **Umred** Mahārāshtra, C India
145 Y10 **Umr Sawān, Hawr** ◎ S Iraq
Um Ruwāba *see* Umm Ruwaba
Umtali *see* Mutare
85 J24 **Umtata** Eastern Cape, SE South Africa
79 V17 **Umuahia** Abia, SW Nigeria
62 H10 **Umuarama** Paraná, S Brazil
Umvuma *see* Mvuma
85 K18 **Umzingwani** ≈ S Zimbabwe
114 D11 **Una** ≈ Bosnia and Herzegovina/Croatia
114 E12 **Unac** ≈ W Bosnia and Herzegovina
25 T6 **Unadilla** Georgia, SE USA
20 I10 **Unadilla River** ≈ New York, NE USA
61 L18 **Unaí** Minas Gerais, SE Brazil
41 N10 **Unalakleet** Alaska, USA
40 K17 **Unalaska Island** *island* Aleutian Islands, Alaska, USA
193 I16 **Una, Mount** ▲ South Island, NZ
84 N13 **Unango** Niassa, N Mozambique
Unao *see* Unnão
94 L12 **Unari** Lappi, N Finland
147 O6 **'Unayzah** *var.* Anaiza. Al Qaṣīm, C Saudi Arabia
144 L10 **'Unayzah, Jabal** ▲ Jordan/Saudi Arabia
Unci *see* Almería
59 K19 **Uncía** Potosí, C Bolivia
39 Q7 **Uncompahgre Peak** ▲ Colorado, C USA
39 P6 **Uncompahgre Plateau** *plain* Colorado, C USA
97 L17 **Unden** ◎ S Sweden
30 M4 **Underwood** North Dakota, N USA
176 Uu11 **Undur** Pulau Seram, E Indonesia
194 M11 **Unea Island** *island* C PNG
130 H6 **Unecha** Bryanskaya Oblast', W Russian Federation
41 N16 **Unga** Unga Island, Alaska, USA
Ungaria *see* Hungary
191 P8 **Ungarie** New South Wales, SE Australia
Ungarisch-Brod *see* Uherský Brod
Ungarisches Erzgebirge *see* Slovenské Rudohorie
Ungarisch-Hradisch *see* Uherské Hradiště
Ungarn *see* Hungary
10 M4 **Ungava Bay** *bay* Québec, E Canada
10 J2 **Ungava, Péninsule d'** *peninsula* Québec, SE Canada
Ungeny *see* Ungheni
118 M9 **Ungheni** *Rus.* Ungeny. W Moldova
Unguja *see* Zanzibar
Üngüz Angyrsyndaky Garagum *see* Zaunguzkiye Garagumy
152 H11 **Unguz, Solonchakovyye Vpadiny** *salt marsh* C Turkmenistan
Ungvár *see* Uzhhorod
62 I12 **União da Vitória** Paraná, S Brazil
113 G17 **Uničov** *Ger.* Mährisch-Neustadt. Severní Morava, E Czech Republic
112 J12 **Uniejów** Konin, C Poland
114 A11 **Unije** *island* W Croatia
40 L16 **Unimak Island** *island* Aleutian Islands, Alaska, USA
40 L16 **Unimak Pass** *strait* Aleutian Islands, Alaska, USA
29 W5 **Union** Missouri, C USA
34 L12 **Union** Oregon, NW USA
23 Q11 **Union** South Carolina, SE USA
23 R6 **Union** West Virginia, NE USA
64 J12 **Unión** San Luis, C Argentina
63 B25 **Unión, Bahía** *bay* E Argentina
33 Q13 **Union City** Indiana, N USA
33 Q10 **Union City** Michigan, N USA
20 C12 **Union City** Pennsylvania, NE USA
22 G8 **Union City** Tennessee, S USA
34 G14 **Union Creek** Oregon, NW USA
85 G25 **Uniondale** Western Cape, SW South Africa
42 K13 **Unión de Tula** Jalisco, SW Mexico
32 M9 **Union Grove** Wisconsin, N USA
47 Y15 **Union Island** *island* S Saint Vincent and the Grenadines
48 K5 **Union Reefs** *reef* SW Mexico
0 D7 **Union Seamount** *undersea feature* NE Pacific Ocean
25 Q6 **Union Springs** Alabama, S USA
22 H6 **Uniontown** Kentucky, S USA
20 C16 **Uniontown** Pennsylvania, NE USA
29 T1 **Unionville** Missouri, C USA
147 V8 **United Arab Emirates** *Ar.* Al Imārāt al 'Arabīyah al Muttaḥidah, *abbrev.* UAE; *prev.* Trucial States. ◆ *federation* SW Asia
United Arab Republic *see* Egypt
99 H14 **United Kingdom** *off.* UK of Great Britain and Northern Ireland, *abbrev.* UK. ◆ *monarchy* NW Europe
United Mexican States *see* Mexico
United Provinces *see* Uttar Pradesh
18 L9 **United States of America** *off.* United States of America, *var.* America, The States, *abbrev.* U.S., USA. ◆ *federal republic*
128 J10 **Unitsa** Respublika Kareliya, NW Russian Federation
9 S15 **Unity** Saskatchewan, S Canada
Unity State *see* Wahda
107 Q8 **Universales, Montes** ⛰ C Spain
29 X4 **University City** Missouri, C USA
197 B13 **Unmet** Malekula, C Vanuatu
103 F15 **Unna** Nordrhein-Westfalen, W Germany
158 L12 **Unnão** *prev.* Unao. Uttar Pradesh, N India
197 D15 **Unpongkor** Erromango, S Vauautu
Unruhstadt *see* Kargowa
98 M1 **Unst** *island* NE Scotland, UK
103 K16 **Unstrut** ≈ C Germany
Unterdrauburg *see* Dravograd
Unterlimbach *see* Lendava
103 L23 **Unterschleissheim** Bayern, SE Germany
103 H24 **Untersee** ◎ Germany/Switzerland
102 O10 **Unterueckersee** ◎ NE Germany
110 F9 **Unterwalden** ◈ *canton* C Switzerland
57 N12 **Unturán, Sierra de** ⛰ Brazil/Venezuela
165 N11 **Unuli Horog** Qinghai, W China
142 M11 **Ünye** Ordu, W Turkey
Unza *see* Unzha
129 O14 **Unzha** *var.* Unza. ≈ NW Russian Federation
81 E17 **Uolo, Río** *var.* Eyo (lower course), Mbini, Uele (upper course), Woleu; *prev.* Benito. ≈ Equatorial Guinea/Gabon
57 Q10 **Uonán** Bolívar, SE Venezuela
167 T12 **Uotsuri-shima** *island* China/Japan/Taiwan
171 J13 **Uozu** Toyama, Honshū, SW Japan
44 L12 **Upala** Alajuela, NW Costa Rica
57 P7 **Upata** Bolívar, E Venezuela
81 M23 **Upemba, Lac** ◎ SE Zaire
207 O12 **Upernavik** *var.* Upernivik. C Greenland
Upernivik *see* Upernavik
85 F22 **Upington** Northern Cape, W South Africa
Uplands *see* Ottawa
198 Bb8 **Upolu** *island* SE Western Samoa
40 G11 **Upolu Point** *headland* Hawaii, USA, C Pacific Ocean
Upper Austria *see* Oberösterreich
Upper Bann *see* Bann
12 M13 **Upper Canada Village** *tourist site* Ontario, SE Canada
20 I16 **Upper Darby** Pennsylvania, NE USA
30 L2 **Upper Des Lacs Lake** ⊞ North Dakota, N USA
193 L14 **Upper Hutt** Wellington, North Island, NZ
31 X11 **Upper Iowa River** ≈ Iowa, C USA
34 H15 **Upper Klamath Lake** ◎ Oregon, NW USA
36 M6 **Upper Lake** California, W USA
37 Q1 **Upper Lake** ◎ California, W USA
8 K9 **Upper Liard** Yukon Territory, W Canada
99 E16 **Upper Lough Erne** ◎ SW Northern Ireland, UK
82 F12 **Upper Nile** ◈ *state* E Sudan
31 T3 **Upper Red Lake** ◎ Minnesota, N USA
33 S12 **Upper Sandusky** Ohio, N USA
Upper Volta *see* Burkina
97 O15 **Upplandsväsby** *var.* Upplands Väsby. Stockholm, C Sweden
97 O15 **Uppsala** Uppsala, C Sweden
97 O14 **Uppsala** ◈ *county* C Sweden
40 J12 **Upright Cape** *headland* Saint Matthew Island, Alaska, USA
22 K6 **Upton** Kentucky, S USA
35 Y13 **Upton** Wyoming, C USA
147 N7 **'Uqlat aş Şuqūr** Al Qaşīm, W Saudi Arabia
Uqturpan *see* Wushi
56 C7 **Urabá, Golfo de** *gulf* NW Colombia
Uracas *see* Farallon de Pajaros
Uradar'ya *see* Ŭradaryo
153 N13 **Ŭradaryo** *Rus.* Uradar'ya. ≈ S Uzbekistan
168 M13 **Urad Qianqi** *var.* Xishanzui. Nei Mongol Zizhiqu, N China
171 Jj17 **Uraga-suidō** *strait* S Japan
172 Pp7 **Urahoro** Hokkaidō, NE Japan
172 Oo8 **Urakawa** Hokkaidō, NE Japan
131 X6 **Ural** *Kaz.* Zayyq. ≈ Kazakhstan/Russian Federation
191 T6 **Uralla** New South Wales, SE Australia
Ural Mountains *see* Ural'skiye Gory
150 F8 **Ural'sk** *Kaz.* Oral. Zapadnyy Kazakhstan, NW Kazakhstan
Ural'skaya Oblast' *see* Zapadnyy Kazakhstan
131 W5 **Ural'skiye Gory** *var.* Ural'skiy Khrebet, *Eng.* Ural Mountains. ⛰ Kazakhstan/Russian Federation
Ural'skiy Khrebet *see* Ural'skiye Gory
144 I3 **Urām aş Şughrá** Ḥalab, N Syria
191 P10 **Urana** New South Wales, SE Australia
191 V6 **Uranga** New South Wales, SE Australia
9 S10 **Uranium City** Saskatchewan, C Canada
60 F10 **Uraricoera** Roraima, N Brazil
49 S5 **Uraricoera, Rio** ≈ N Brazil
Ura-Tyube *see* Ŭroteppa
171 K16 **Urawa** Saitama, Honshū, S Japan
125 F10 **Uray** Khanty-Mansiyskiy Avtonomnyy Okrug, C Russian Federation
147 R7 **'Uray'irah** Ash Sharqīyah, E Saudi Arabia
32 M13 **Urbana** Illinois, N USA
33 R13 **Urbana** Ohio, N USA
31 V14 **Urbandale** Iowa, C USA
108 I11 **Urbania** Marche, C Italy
176 Uu8 **Urbinasopon** Irian Jaya, E Indonesia
108 I11 **Urbino** Marche, C Italy
59 H16 **Urcos** Cusco, S Peru
150 D10 **Urda** Zapadnyy Kazakhstan, W Kazakhstan
107 N10 **Urda** Castilla-La Mancha, C Spain
168 E7 **Urdgol** Hovd, W Mongolia
Urdunn *see* Jordan
151 X12 **Urdzhar** *Kaz.* Ürzhar. Semipalatinsk, E Kazakhstan
99 L16 **Ure** ≈ N England, UK
121 K18 **Urechcha** *Rus.* Urech'ye. Minskaya Voblasts', S Belarus
Urech'ye *see* Urechcha
131 P2 **Uren'** Nizhegorodskaya Oblast', W Russian Federation
126 H9 **Urengoy** Yamalo-Nenetskiy Avtonomnyy Okrug, N Russian Federation
192 K10 **Urenui** Taranaki, North Island, NZ
197 B10 **Ureparapara** *island* Banks Islands, N Vanuatu
42 G5 **Ures** Sonora, NW Mexico
Urfa *see* Şanlıurfa
152 H9 **Urganch** *Rus.* Urgench; *prev.* Novo-Urgench. Khorazm Wiloyati, W Uzbekistan
Urgench *see* Urganch
142 J14 **Ürgüp** Nevşehir, C Turkey
153 O12 **Urgut** Samarqand Wiloyati, C Uzbekistan
164 K3 **Urho** Xinjiang Uygur Zizhiqu, W China
158 G5 **Uri** Jammu and Kashmir, NW India
110 G9 **Uri** ◈ *canton* C Switzerland
56 F11 **Uribe** Meta, C Colombia
56 H4 **Uribia** La Guajira, N Colombia
118 G12 **Uricani** *Hung.* Hobicaurikány. Hunedoara, SW Romania
59 M21 **Uriondo** Tarija, S Bolivia
42 I7 **Urique** Chihuahua, N Mexico
42 I7 **Urique, Río** ≈ N Mexico
58 E9 **Urityacu, Río** ≈ N Peru
151 N7 **Uritskiy** Kustanay, N Kazakhstan
100 K8 **Urk** Flevoland, N Netherlands
142 B14 **Urla** İzmir, W Turkey
118 K13 **Urlaţi** Prahova, SE Romania
131 V4 **Urman** Respublika Bashkortostan, W Russian Federation
153 P12 **Urmetan** W Tajikistan
Urmia *see* Orūmīyeh
Urmia, Lake *see* Orūmīyeh, Daryācheh-ye
Urmiyeh *see* Orūmīyeh
115 N17 **Uroševac** *Alb.* Ferizaj. Serbia, S Yugoslavia
153 P11 **Ŭroteppa** *Rus.* Ura-Tyube. NW Tajikistan
56 D8 **Urrao** Antioquia, W Colombia
Ursat'yevskaya *see* Khowos
168 I11 **Urt** Ömnogovĭ, S Mongolia
131 X7 **Urtazym** Orenburgskaya Oblast', W Russian Federation
61 K18 **Uruaçu** Goiás, C Brazil
42 M14 **Uruapan** *var.* Uruapan del Progreso. Michoacán de Ocampo, SW Mexico
Uruapan del Progreso *see* Uruapan
59 G15 **Urubamba, Cordillera** ⛰ C Peru
59 G14 **Urubamba, Río** ≈ C Peru
60 G12 **Urucará** Amazonas, N Brazil
63 E16 **Uruguaiana** Rio Grande do Sul, S Brazil
Uruguai, Rio *see* Uruguay
63 E18 **Uruguay** *off.* Oriental Republic of Uruguay; *prev.* La Banda Oriental. ◆ *republic* E South America
63 E15 **Uruguay** *var.* Rio Uruguai, Río Uruguay. ≈ E South America
Uruguay, Río *see* Uruguay
Uruk *see* Erech
Urumchi *see* Ürümqi
164 L5 **Ürümqi** *var.* Tihwa, Urumchi, Urumqi, Urumtsi, Wu-lu-k'o-mu-shi, Wu-lu-mu-ch'i; *prev.* Ti-hua. *autonomous region capital* Xinjiang Uygur Zizhiqu, NW China
Urumtsi *see* Ürümqi
Urundi *see* Burundi
196 C15 **Uruno Point** *headland* NW Guam
127 P15 **Urup, Ostrov** *island* Kuril'skiye Ostrova, SE Russian Federation
147 P11 **'Uruq al Mawārid** *desert* S Saudi Arabia
Urusan *see* Ulsan
131 T5 **Urussu** Respublika Tatarstan, W Russian Federation
192 K10 **Uruti** Taranaki, North Island, NZ
59 K19 **Uru Uru, Lago** ◎ W Bolivia
57 P9 **Uruyén** Bolívar, SE Venezuela
155 O7 **Ūrūzgān** *var.* Oruzgān, Orūzgān. Urūzgān, C Afghanistan
155 N6 **Urūzgān** *Per.* Orūzgān. ◈ *province* C Afghanistan
172 P6 **Uryū-gawa** ≈ Hokkaidō, NE Japan
172 P4 **Uryū-ko** ◎ Hokkaidō, NE Japan
131 N8 **Uryupinsk** Volgogradskaya Oblast', SW Russian Federation
Ürzhar *see* Urdzhar
129 R16 **Urzhum** Kirovskaya Oblast', NW Russian Federation
118 K13 **Urziceni** Ialomiţa, SE Romania
U.S./USA *see* United States of America
170 D13 **Usa** Ōita, Kyūshū, SW Japan
121 L16 **Usa** *Rus.* Usa. ≈ C Belarus
129 T6 **Usa** ≈ NW Russian Federation
142 E14 **Uşak** *prev.* Ushak. Uşak, W Turkey
142 D14 **Uşak** *var.* Ushak. ◈ *province* W Turkey
85 C19 **Usakos** Erongo, W Namibia
83 J21 **Usambara Mountains** ⛰ NE Tanzania
83 G23 **Usangu Flats** *wetland* SW Tanzania
67 D24 **Usborne, Mount** ▲ East Falkland, Falkland Islands
102 O8 **Usedom** *island* NE Germany
101 M24 **Useldange** Diekirch, C Luxembourg
120 L12 **Ushacha** *Rus.* Ushacha. Vitsyebskaya Voblasts', N Belarus
Ushachi *see* Ushachy
120 L13 **Ushachy** *Rus.* Ushachi. Vitsyebskaya Voblasts', N Belarus
Ushak *see* Uşak
126 I2 **Ushakova, Ostrov** *island* Severnaya Zemlya, N Russian Federation
Ushant *see* Ouessant, Île d'
Üsharal *see* Ucharal
170 Bb14 **Ushibuka** *var.* Usibuka. Kumamoto, Shimo-jima, SW Japan
Ushi Point *see* Sabaneta, Puntan
151 V14 **Ushtobe** *Kaz.* Üshtöbe. Taldykorgan, SE Kazakhstan
65 I25 **Ushuaia** Tierra del Fuego, S Argentina
41 R10 **Usibelli** Alaska, USA
Usibuka *see* Ushibuka
194 I12 **Usino** Madang, N PNG
129 U6 **Usinsk** Respublika Komi, NW Russian Federation
99 K22 **Usk** *Wel.* Wysg. ≈ SE Wales, UK
Uskočke Planine/Uskokengebirge *see* Žumberačka Gora
Üsküb *see* Skopje
116 M11 **Üsküpdere** Kırklareli, NW Turkey
130 L7 **Usman'** Lipetskaya Oblast', W Russian Federation
120 D8 **Usmas Ezers** ◎ NW Latvia
129 U13 **Usol'ye** Permskaya Oblast', NW Russian Federation
126 J15 **Usol'ye-Sibirskoye** Irkutskaya Oblast', C Russian Federation
43 T16 **Uspanapa, Río** ≈ SE Mexico
151 R11 **Uspenskiy** Zhezkazgan, C Kazakhstan
105 O11 **Ussel** Corrèze, C France
169 Z6 **Ussuri** *var.* Usuri, Wusuri, *Chin.* Wusuli Jiang. ≈ China/Russian Federation
127 Nn18 **Ussuriysk** *prev.* Nikol'sk, Nikol'sk-Ussuriyskiy, Voroshilov. Primorskiy Kray, SE Russian Federation
142 J10 **Usta Burnu** *headland* N Turkey
155 P13 **Usta Muhammad** Baluchistān, SW Pakistan
126 K15 **Ust'-Barguzin** Respublika Buryatiya, S Russian Federation
127 P12 **Ust'-Bol'sheretsk** Kamchatskaya Oblast', E Russian Federation
131 N9 **Ust'-Buzulukskaya** Volgogradskaya Oblast', SW Russian Federation
110 G7 **Uster** Zürich, NE Switzerland
109 I22 **Ustica, Isola d'** *island* S Italy
126 J13 **Ust'-Ilimsk** Irkutskaya Oblast', C Russian Federation
113 C15 **Ústí nad Labem** *Ger.* Aussig. Severní Čechy, N Czech Republic
113 F17 **Ústí nad Orlicí** *Ger.* Wildenschwert. Východní Čechy, E Czech Republic
Ustinov *see* Izhevsk
115 J14 **Ustiprača** SE Bosnia and Herzegovina
125 Ff12 **Ust'-Ishim** Omskaya Oblast', C Russian Federation
112 G6 **Ustka** *Ger.* Stolpmünde. Słupsk, NW Poland
127 Pp10 **Ust'-Kamchatsk** Kamchatskaya Oblast', E Russian Federation
151 X9 **Ust'-Kamenogorsk** *Kaz.* Öskemen. Vostochnyy Kazakhstan, E Kazakhstan
127 Oo10 **Ust'-Khayryuzovo** Koryakskiy Avtonomnyy Okrug, E Russian Federation
126 H16 **Ust'-Koksa** Respublika Altay, S Russian Federation
129 S11 **Ust'-Kulom** Respublika Komi, NW Russian Federation
126 Jj14 **Ust'-Kut** Irkutskaya Oblast', C Russian Federation
126 M7 **Ust'-Kuyga** Respublika Sakha (Yakutiya), NE Russian Federation
130 L14 **Ust'-Labinsk** Krasnodarskiy Kray, SW Russian Federation
126 Mm11 **Ust'-Maya** Respublika Sakha (Yakutiya), NE Russian Federation
127 N9 **Ust'-Nera** Respublika Sakha (Yakutiya), NE Russian Federation
126 Ll13 **Ust'-Nyukzha** Amurskaya Oblast', S Russian Federation
126 Kk6 **Ust'-Olenëk** Respublika Sakha (Yakutiya), NE Russian Federation
127 O10 **Ust'-Omchug** Magadanskaya Oblast', E Russian Federation
126 Jj15 **Ust'-Ordynskiy** Ust'-Ordynskiy Buryatskiy Avtonomnyy Okrug, S Russian Federation
126 J15 **Ust'-Ordynskiy Buryatskiy Avtonomnyy Okrug** ◈ *autonomous district* S Russian Federation
129 N8 **Ust'-Pinega** Arkhangel'skaya Oblast', NW Russian Federation
126 Hh8 **Ust'-Port** Taymyrskiy (Dolgano-Nenetskiy) Avtonomnyy Okrug, N Russian Federation
116 L11 **Ustrem** *prev.* Vakav. Burgaska Oblast, SE Bulgaria
113 O18 **Ustrzyki Dolne** Krosno, SE Poland
Ust'-Sysol'sk *see* Syktyvkar
129 R7 **Ust'-Tsil'ma** Respublika Komi, NW Russian Federation
Ust Urt *see* Ustyurt Plateau
129 O11 **Ust'ya** ≈ NW Russian Federation
119 R8 **Ustynivka** Kirovohrads'ka Oblast', C Ukraine
150 H15 **Ustyurt Plateau** *var.* Ust Urt, *Uzb.* Ustyurt Platosi. *plateau* Kazakhstan/Uzbekistan
Ustyurt Platosi *see* Ustyurt Plateau
128 K14 **Ustyuzhna** Vologodskaya Oblast', NW Russian Federation
164 J4 **Usu** Xinjiang Uygur Zizhiqu, NW China
175 Q10 **Usu** Sulawesi, C Indonesia
170 Dd14 **Usuki** Ōita, Kyūshū, SW Japan
44 G8 **Usulután** Usulután, SE El Salvador
44 B9 **Usulután** ◈ *department* SE El Salvador
43 W16 **Usumacinta, Río** ≈ Guatemala/Mexico
Usumbura *see* Bujumbura
Usuri *see* Ussuri
176 X12 **Uta** Irian Jaya, E Indonesia
38 K5 **Utah** *off.* State of Utah; also known as Beehive State, Mormon State. ◈ *state* W USA
38 L3 **Utah Lake** ◎ Utah, W USA
Utaidhani *see* Uthai Thani
95 M14 **Utajärvi** Oulu, C Finland
Utamboni *see* Mitemele, Río
Utaradit *see* Uttaradit
173 G3 **Utara, Selat** *strait* Peninsular Malaysia
172 P5 **Utashinai** *var.* Utasinai. Hokkaidō, NE Japan
Utasinai *see* Utashinai
176 X12 **Uta, Sungai** ≈ Irian Jaya, E Indonesia
200 Ss12 **'Uta Vava'u** *island* Vava'u Group, N Tonga
39 V9 **Ute Creek** ≈ New Mexico, SW USA
120 H12 **Utena** Utena, E Lithuania
39 V10 **Ute Reservoir** ⊞ New Mexico, SW USA
178 H10 **Uthai Thani** *var.* Muang Uthai Thani, Udayadhani, Utaidhani. Uthai Thani, W Thailand
155 O15 **Uthal** Baluchistān, SW Pakistan
20 I10 **Utica** New York, NE USA
107 R10 **Utiel** País Valenciano, E Spain
9 O13 **Utikuma Lake** ◎ Alberta, W Canada
44 I4 **Utila, Isla de** *island* Islas de la Bahía, N Honduras
Utina *see* Udine
61 O17 **Utinga** Bahia, E Brazil
Utirik *see* Utrik Atoll
97 M22 **Utlängan** *island* S Sweden
119 U11 **Utlyuts'kyy Lyman** *bay* S Ukraine
170 Cc14 **Uto** Kumamoto, Kyūshū, SW Japan
97 P16 **Utö** Stockholm, C Sweden
27 Q12 **Utopia** Texas, SW USA
100 J11 **Utrecht** *Lat.* Trajectum ad Rhenum. Utrecht, C Netherlands
85 K22 **Utrecht** KwaZulu/Natal, E South Africa
100 I11 **Utrecht** ◈ *province* C Netherlands
106 K14 **Utrera** Andalucía, S Spain
201 V4 **Utrik Atoll** *var.* Utirik, Utrōk, Utrōnk. *atoll* Ratak Chain, N Marshall Islands
Utrōk/Utrōnk *see* Utrik Atoll
97 B16 **Utsira** *island* SW Norway
94 L8 **Utsjoki** *var.* Ohcejohka. Lappi, N Finland
171 Kk15 **Utsunomiya** *var.* Utunomiya. Tochigi, Honshū, S Japan
131 P13 **Utta** Respublika Kalmykiya, SW Russian Federation
178 Hh8 **Uttaradit** *var.* Utaradit. Uttaradit, N Thailand
158 J8 **Uttarkāshi** Uttar Pradesh, N India
158 K11 **Uttar Pradesh** *prev.* United Provinces, United Provinces of Agra and Oudh. ◈ *state* N India
47 T5 **Utuado** C Puerto Rico
164 K3 **Utubulak** Xinjiang Uygur Zizhiqu, W China
41 N5 **Utukok River** ≈ Alaska, USA
Utunomiya *see* Utsunomiya
195 X9 **Utupua** *island* Santa Cruz Islands, E Soloman Islands
150 G9 **Utva** ≈ NW Kazakhstan
201 Y15 **Utwe** Kosrae, E Micronesia
201 X15 **Utwe Harbor** *harbor* Kosrae, E Micronesia
168 J7 **Uubulan** Arhangay, C Mongolia
120 G6 **Uulu** Pärnumaa, SW Estonia
207 N13 **Uummannaq** *var.* Umanak, Umanaq. C Greenland
206 L16 **Uummannarsuaq** *var.* Nunap Isua, *Dan.* Kap Farvel, *Eng.* Cape Farewell. *headland* S Greenland
168 E4 **Üüreg Nuur** ◎ NW Mongolia
Uusikaarlepyy *see* Nykarleby
95 J19 **Uusikaupunki** *Swe.* Nystad. Turku-Pori, SW Finland
95 L19 **Uusimaa** *Swe.* Nyland. ◈ *province* S Finland
131 S2 **Uva** Udmurtskaya Respublika, NW Russian Federation
115 L14 **Uvac** ≈ W Yugoslavia
27 Q12 **Uvalde** Texas, SW USA
161 K25 **Uva Province** ◈ *province* SE Sri Lanka
121 O18 **Uvaravichy** *Rus.* Uvarovichi. Homyel'skaya Voblasts', SE Belarus
56 J11 **Uvá, Río** ≈ E Colombia
Uvarovichi *see* Uvaravichy
131 N7 **Uvarovo** Tambovskaya Oblast', W Russian Federation
125 Ff11 **Uvat** Tyumenskaya Oblast', C Russian Federation
202 G12 **Uvea, Île** *island* N Wallis and Futuna
83 E21 **Uvinza** Kigoma, W Tanzania
81 O20 **Uvira** Sud Kivu, E Zaire
168 E5 **Uvs** ◈ *province* NW Mongolia
168 F5 **Uvs Nuur** *var.* Ozero Ubsu-Nur. ◎ Mongolia/Russian Federation
170 E15 **Uwa** Ehime, Shikoku, SW Japan
170 E15 **Uwajima** *var.* Uwazima. Ehime, Shikoku, SW Japan
82 B5 **'Uwaynāt, Jabal al** *var.* Jebel Uweinat. ▲ Libya/Sudan
Uwazima *see* Uwajima
Uweinat, Jebel *see* 'Uwaynāt, Jabal al
176 Z14 **Uwimmerah, Sungai** ≈ Irian Jaya, E Indonesia
12 H14 **Uxbridge** Ontario, S Canada
Uxellodunum *see* Issoudun
168 M15 **Uxin Qi** Nei Mongol Zizhiqu, N China
43 X12 **Uxmal, Ruinas** *ruins* Yucatán, SE Mexico
133 Q5 **Uy** ≈ Kazakhstan/Russian Federation
150 K15 **Uyaly** Kzyl-Orda, S Kazakhstan
126 Mm7 **Uyandina** ≈ NE Russian Federation
126 I14 **Uyar** Krasnoyarskiy Kray, S Russian Federation
168 L10 **Üydzen** Ömnogovĭ, S Mongolia
Uyeda *see* Ueda
126 Hh3 **Uyedineniya, Ostrov** *island* N Russian Federation
79 V17 **Uyo** Akwa Ibom, S Nigeria
168 D8 **Üyönch** Hovd, W Mongolia
151 Q15 **Uyuk** Zhambyl, S Kazakhstan
147 V13 **'Uyūn** SW Oman
59 K20 **Uyuni** Potosí, W Bolivia
59 J20 **Uyuni, Salar de** *wetland* SW Bolivia

◆ Country
● Country Capital
◇ Dependent Territory
○ Dependent Territory Capital
◈ Administrative Region
✕ International Airport
▲ Mountain
⛰ Mountain Range
Volcano
≈ River
◎ Lake
⊞ Reservoir

152 I9 **Uzbekistan** *off.* Republic of Uzbekistan. ◆ *republic* C Asia
164 D8 **Uzbel Shankou** *Rus.* Pereval Kyzyl-Dzhiik. *pass* China/Tajikistan
121 J17 **Uzda** *Rus.* Uzda. Minskaya Voblasts', C Belorussia
105 N12 **Uzerche** Corrèze, C France
105 R14 **Uzès** Gard, S France
153 T10 **Uzgen** *Kir.* Özgön. Oshskaya Oblast', SW Kyrgyzstan
119 O3 **Uzh** ≈ N Ukraine
Uzhgorod *see* Uzhhorod
118 G7 **Uzhhorod** *Rus.* Uzhgorod; *prev.* Ungvár. Zakarpats'ka Oblast', W Ukraine
126 Hh14 **Uzhur** Krasnoyarskiy Kray, S Russian Federation
Uzi *see* Uji
114 K13 **Užice** *prev.* Titovo Užice. Serbia, W Yugoslavia
Uzin *see* Uzyn
130 L5 **Uzlovaya** Tul'skaya Oblast', W Russian Federation
110 H7 **Uznach** Sankt Gallen, NE Switzerland
151 U16 **Uzunagach** Almaty, SE Kazakhstan
142 B10 **Uzunköprü** Edirne, NW Turkey
120 D11 **Užventis** Kelmė, C Lithuania
119 P5 **Uzyn** *Rus.* Uzin. Kyyivs'ka Oblast', N Ukraine

V

Vääksy *see* Asikkala
85 H23 **Vaal** ≈ C South Africa
95 M14 **Vaala** Oulu, C Finland
95 N19 **Vaalimaa** Kymi, SE Finland
101 M19 **Vaals** Limburg, SE Netherlands
95 J16 **Vaasa** *Swe.* Vasa; *prev.* Nikolainkaupunki. Vaasa, W Finland
95 K17 **Vaasa** *Swe.* Vasa. ◐ *province* C Finland
100 L10 **Vaassen** Gelderland, E Netherlands
120 G11 **Vabalninkas** Biržai, NE Lithuania
Vabkent *see* Wobkent
113 J22 **Vác** *Ger.* Waitzen. Pest, N Hungary
63 I14 **Vacaria** Rio Grande do Sul, S Brazil
37 N7 **Vacaville** California, W USA
105 R15 **Vaccarès, Étang de** ◎ SE France
46 L10 **Vache, Île à** *island* SW Haiti
181 Y16 **Vacoas** W Mauritius
34 G10 **Vader** Washington, NW USA
96 D12 **Vadheim** Sogn og Fjordane, S Norway
124 O3 **Vadili** *Gk.* Vatilí. C Cyprus
160 D11 **Vadodara** *prev.* Baroda. Gujarāt, W India
94 M8 **Vadsø** *Fin.* Vesisaari. Finnmark, N Norway
97 L17 **Vadstena** Östergötland, S Sweden
110 I8 **Vaduz** ● (Liechtenstein) W Liechtenstein
Vág *see* Váh
129 N12 **Vaga** ≈ NW Russian Federation
96 G11 **Vågåmo** Oppland, S Norway
114 D12 **Vaganski Vrh** ▲ W Croatia
Vágbeszterce *see* Považská Bystrica
97 L19 **Vaggeryd** Jönköping, S Sweden
195 U14 **Vaghena** *var.* Wagina. *island* NW Solomon Islands
97 O16 **Vagnhärad** Södermanland, C Sweden
106 G7 **Vagos** Aveiro, N Portugal
Vágsellye *see* Sal'a
94 H10 **Vågsfjorden** *fjord* N Norway
96 C10 **Vågsøy** *island* S Norway
Vágújhely *see* Nové Mesto nad Váhom
113 I21 **Váh** *Ger.* Waag, *Hung.* Vág. ≈ W Slovakia
95 K16 **Vähäkyrö** Vaasa, W Finland
203 X11 **Vahitahi** *atoll* Îles Tuamotu, E French Polynesia
Vaidei *see* Vulcan
24 L4 **Vaiden** Mississippi, S USA
161 I23 **Vaigai** ≈ SE India
203 V16 **Vaihu** Easter Island, Chile, E Pacific Ocean
120 I6 **Väike Emajõgi** ≈ S Estonia
120 I4 **Väike-Maarja** *Ger.* Klein-Marien. Lääne-Virumaa, NE Estonia
Väike-Salatsi *see* Mazsalaca
39 R4 **Vail** Colorado, C USA
200 Qq15 **Vaina** Tongatapu, S Tonga
120 E5 **Väinameri** *prev.* Muhu Väin, *Ger.* Moon-Sund. *sea* E Baltic Sea
95 N19 **Vainikkala** Kymi, SE Finland
120 D10 **Vaiņode** Liepāja, SW Latvia
161 H23 **Vaippār** ≈ SE India
203 W11 **Vairaatea** *atoll* Îles Tuamotu, C French Polynesia
203 R8 **Vairao** Tahiti, W French Polynesia
105 R14 **Vaison-la-Romaine** Vaucluse, SE France
202 G11 **Vaitupu** Île Uvea, E Wallis and Futuna
202 F7 **Vaitupu** *atoll* C Tuvalu
Vajdahunyad *see* Hunedoara
Vajdej *see* Vulcan
80 K12 **Vakaga** ◐ *prefecture* NE Central African Republic
116 H10 **Vakarel** Sofiyska Oblast, W Bulgaria
Vakav *see* Ustrem
143 O11 **Vakfıkebir** Trabzon, NE Turkey
126 H11 **Vakh** ≈ C Russian Federation
Vakhon, Qatorkŭhi *see* Nicholas Range
153 P14 **Vakhsh** SW Tajikistan
153 Q12 **Vakhsh** ≈ SW Tajikistan
131 P1 **Vakhtan** Nizhegorodskaya Oblast', W Russian Federation
96 C13 **Vaksdal** Hordaland, S Norway
129 O8 **Vaksha** ≈ NW Russian Federation
195 O15 **Vakuta Island** *island* Kiriwina Islands, SE PNG
Valachia *see* Wallachia
110 D11 **Valais** *Ger.* Wallis. ◐ *canton* SW Switzerland
115 M21 **Valamarës, Mali i** ▲ SE Albania
131 S2 **Valamaz** Udmurtskaya Respublika, NW Russian Federation
115 Q19 **Valandovo** SE FYR Macedonia
113 I18 **Valašské Meziříčí** *Ger.* Wallachisch-Meseritsch, *Pol.* Wałeckie Międzyrzecze. Severní Morava, E Czech Republic
117 I17 **Valáxa** *island* Vóreioi Sporádes, Greece, Aegean Sea
97 K16 **Vålberg** Värmland, C Sweden
118 H12 **Vâlcea** *prev.* Vîlcea. ◐ *county* SW Romania
65 J16 **Valcheta** Río Negro, E Argentina
13 P12 **Valcourt** Québec, SE Canada
Valdai Hills *see* Valdayskaya Vozvyshennost'
106 M3 **Valdavia** ≈ N Spain
128 I15 **Valday** Novgorodskaya Oblast', W Russian Federation
128 I15 **Valdayskaya Vozvyshennost'** *var.* Valdai Hills. *hill range* W Russian Federation
106 L9 **Valdecañas, Embalse de** ⊟ W Spain
120 E8 **Valdemārpils** *Ger.* Sassmacken. Talsi, NW Latvia
97 N18 **Valdemarsvik** Östergötland, S Sweden
107 N8 **Valdemoro** Madrid, C Spain
107 O11 **Valdepeñas** Castilla-La Mancha, C Spain
106 L5 **Valderaduey** ≈ NE Spain
106 L5 **Valderas** Castilla-León, N Spain
107 T7 **Valderrobres** *var.* Vall-de-roures. Aragón, NE Spain
65 K17 **Valdés, Península** *peninsula* SE Argentina
41 S11 **Valdez** Alaska, USA
58 C5 **Valdéz** *var.* Limones. Esmeraldas, NW Ecuador
Valdia *see* Weldiya
105 U11 **Val d'Isère** Savoie, E France
65 G15 **Valdivia** Los Lagos, C Chile
Valdivia Bank *see* Valdivia Seamount
67 P17 **Valdivia Seamount** *var.* Valdivia Bank. *undersea feature* E Atlantic Ocean
105 N4 **Val-d'Oise** ◐ *department* N France
12 J8 **Val-d'Or** Québec, SE Canada
25 U8 **Valdosta** Georgia, SE USA
96 G13 **Valdres** *physical region* S Norway
34 L13 **Vale** Oregon, NW USA
118 F9 **Valea lui Mihai** *Hung.* Érmihályfalva. Bihor, NW Romania
9 N15 **Valemount** British Columbia, SW Canada
61 O17 **Valença** Bahia, E Brazil
106 G4 **Valença do Minho** Viana do Castelo, N Portugal
61 N14 **Valença do Piauí** Piauí, E Brazil
105 N8 **Valençay** Indre, C France
105 R13 **Valence** *anc.* Valentia, Valentia Julia, Ventia. Drôme, E France
107 S10 **Valencia** País Valenciano, E Spain
56 K5 **Valencia** Carabobo, N Venezuela
107 R10 **Valencia** *Cat.* València. ◐ *province* País Valenciano, E Spain
107 S10 **Valencia** ✕ Valencia, E Spain
València/Valencia *see* País Valenciano
106 I10 **Valencia de Alcántara** Extremadura, W Spain
106 L4 **Valencia de Don Juan** Castilla-León, N Spain
107 U9 **Valencia, Golfo de** *var.* Gulf of Valencia. *gulf* E Spain
Valencia, Gulf of *see* Valencia, Golfo de
99 A21 **Valencia Island** *Ir.* Dairbhre. *island* SW Ireland
105 P2 **Valenciennes** Nord, N France
118 K13 **Vălenii de Munte** Prahova, SE Romania
Valentia *see* Valence, France
Valentia *see* País Valenciano
Valentia Julia *see* Valence
105 T8 **Valentigney** Doubs, E France
30 M12 **Valentine** Nebraska, C USA
26 J10 **Valentine** Texas, SW USA
Valentine State *see* Oregon
108 C8 **Valenza** Piemonte, NW Italy
96 I13 **Våler** Hedmark, S Norway
56 I6 **Valera** Trujillo, NW Venezuela
199 K13 **Valerie Guyot** *undersea feature* S Pacific Ocean
Valetta *see* Valletta
120 I7 **Valga** *Ger.* Walk, *Latv.* Valka. Valgamaa, S Estonia
120 I7 **Valgamaa** *off.* Valga Maakond. ◐ *province* S Estonia
45 Q15 **Valiente, Península** *peninsula* NW Panama
104 E3 **Valinco, Golfe de** *gulf* Corse, France, C Mediterranean Sea
114 L12 **Valjevo** Serbia, W Yugoslavia
94 L9 **Valjok** Finnmark, N Norway
120 I7 **Valka** *Ger.* Walk. Valka, N Latvia
Valka *see* Valga
95 L18 **Valkeakoski** Häme, SW Finland
95 M19 **Valkeala** Kymi, S Finland
101 L18 **Valkenburg** Limburg, SE Netherlands
101 K15 **Valkenswaard** Noord-Brabant, S Netherlands
121 G15 **Valkininkai** Varėna, S Lithuania
119 U5 **Valky** Kharkivs'ka Oblast', E Ukraine
43 Y12 **Valladolid** Yucatán, SE Mexico
106 M5 **Valladolid** Castilla-León, NW Spain
106 L5 **Valladolid** ◐ *province* Castilla-León, N Spain
105 U15 **Vallauris** Alpes-Maritimes, SE France
Vall-de-roures *see* Valderrobres
107 S9 **Vall d'Uxó** País Valenciano, E Spain
97 E16 **Valle** Aust-Agder, S Norway
107 N2 **Valle** Cantabria, N Spain
44 H8 **Valle** ◐ *department* S Honduras
107 N8 **Vallecas** Madrid, C Spain
39 Q8 **Vallecito Reservoir** ⊟ Colorado, C USA
108 A7 **Valle d'Aosta** ◐ *region* NW Italy
43 O14 **Valle de Bravo** México, S Mexico
57 N5 **Valle de Guanape** Anzoátegui, N Venezuela
56 M6 **Valle de La Pascua** Guárico, N Venezuela
56 B11 **Valle del Cauca** *off.* Departamento del Valle del Cauca. ◐ *province* W Colombia
43 N13 **Valle de Santiago** Guanajuato, C Mexico
42 J7 **Valle de Zaragoza** Chihuahua, N Mexico
56 G5 **Valledupar** Cesar, N Colombia
78 G10 **Vallée de Ferlo** ≈ NW Senegal
59 M19 **Vallegrande** Santa Cruz, C Bolivia
43 P8 **Valle Hermoso** Tamaulipas, C Mexico
37 N8 **Vallejo** California, W USA
64 G8 **Vallenar** Atacama, N Chile
97 O15 **Vallentuna** Stockholm, C Sweden
123 I12 **Valletta** *prev.* Valetta. ● (Malta) E Malta
29 N6 **Valley Center** Kansas, C USA
31 Q5 **Valley City** North Dakota, N USA
34 I15 **Valley Falls** Oregon, NW USA
Valleyfield *see* Salaberry-de-Valleyfield
23 S4 **Valley Head** West Virginia, NE USA
27 T8 **Valley Mills** Texas, SW USA
77 W10 **Valley of the Kings** *ancient monument* E Egypt
31 R11 **Valley Springs** South Dakota, N USA
22 K5 **Valley Station** Kentucky, S USA
9 O13 **Valleyview** Alberta, W Canada
27 T5 **Valley View** Texas, SW USA
63 C21 **Vallimanca, Arroyo** ≈ E Argentina
109 M19 **Vallo della Lucania** Campania, S Italy
110 B9 **Vallorbe** Vaud, W Switzerland
107 V6 **Valls** Cataluña, NE Spain
96 N11 **Vallsta** Gävleborg, C Sweden
96 N12 **Vallvik** Gävleborg, C Sweden
9 T17 **Val Marie** Saskatchewan, S Canada
120 H7 **Valmiera** *Est.* Volmari, *Ger.* Wolmar. Valmiera, N Latvia
107 N3 **Valnera** ▲ N Spain
104 J3 **Valognes** Manche, N France
Valona *see* Vlorë
Valona Bay *see* Vlorës, Gjiri i
106 G6 **Valongo** *var.* Valongo de Gaia. Porto, N Portugal
Valongo de Gaia *see* Valongo
106 M5 **Valoria la Buena** Castilla-León, N Spain
121 J15 **Valozhyn** *Pol.* Wołożyn, *Rus.* Volozhin. Minskaya Voblasts', C Belorussia
106 I5 **Valpaços** Vila Real, N Portugal
25 P8 **Valparaiso** Florida, SE USA
33 N11 **Valparaiso** Indiana, N USA
64 G11 **Valparaíso** Valparaíso, C Chile
42 L11 **Valparaíso** Zacatecas, C Mexico
64 G11 **Valparaíso** *off.* Región de Valparaíso. ◐ *region* C Chile
Valpo *see* Valparaíso
114 I9 **Valpovo** *Hung.* Valpó. Osijek-Baranja, E Croatia
105 R14 **Valréas** Vaucluse, SE France
Vals *see* Vals-Platz
160 D12 **Valsād** *prev.* Bulsar. Gujarāt, W India
Valsbaai *see* False Bay
176 Uu10 **Valse Pisang, Kepulauan** *island group* E Indonesia
110 H9 **Vals-Platz** *var.* Vals. Graubünden, S Switzerland
176 Xx16 **Vals, Tanjung** *headland* Irian Jaya, SE Indonesia
95 N15 **Valtimo** Pohjois-Karjala, E Finland
117 D17 **Váltou** ▲ C Greece
131 O12 **Valuyevka** Rostovskaya Oblast', SW Russian Federation
130 K9 **Valuyki** Belgorodskaya Oblast', W Russian Federation
38 L2 **Val Verda** Utah, W USA
66 N12 **Valverde** Hierro, Islas Canarias, Spain, NE Atlantic Ocean
106 I13 **Valverde del Camino** Andalucía, S Spain
97 G23 **Vamdrup** Vejle, C Denmark
96 L12 **Våmhus** Kopparberg, C Sweden
95 K18 **Vammala** Turku-Pori, SW Finland
Vámosudvarhely *see* Odorheiu Secuiesc
143 S14 **Van** Van, E Turkey
27 V7 **Van** Texas, SW USA
143 T14 **Van** ◐ *province* E Turkey
143 T11 **Vanadzor** *prev.* Kirovakan. N Armenia
27 U5 **Van Alstyne** Texas, SW USA
35 W10 **Vananda** Montana, NW USA
118 I11 **Vânători** *Hung.* Héjjasfalva; *prev.* Vînători. Mureș, C Romania
203 W12 **Vanavana** *atoll* Îles Tuamotu, SE French Polynesia
Vana-Vändra *see* Vändra
126 J12 **Vanavara** Evenkiyskiy Avtonomnyy Okrug, C Russian Federation
13 Q8 **Van Bruyssel** Québec, SE Canada
29 R10 **Van Buren** Arkansas, C USA
21 S1 **Van Buren** Maine, NE USA
29 W7 **Van Buren** Missouri, C USA
21 T5 **Vanceboro** Maine, NE USA
23 W10 **Vanceboro** North Carolina, SE USA
23 O4 **Vanceburg** Kentucky, S USA
Vanch *see* Vanj
8 L17 **Vancouver** British Columbia, SW Canada
34 G11 **Vancouver** Washington, NW USA
8 L17 **Vancouver** ✕ British Columbia, SW Canada
8 K16 **Vancouver Island** *island* British Columbia, SW Canada
Vanda *see* Vantaa
176 Xx11 **Van Daalen** ≈ Irian Jaya, E Indonesia
32 L15 **Vandalia** Illinois, N USA
29 V3 **Vandalia** Missouri, C USA
33 R13 **Vandalia** Ohio, N USA
27 U13 **Vanderbilt** Texas, SW USA
33 Q10 **Vandercook Lake** Michigan, N USA
8 L14 **Vanderhoof** British Columbia, SW Canada
20 K8 **Vanderwhacker Mountain** ▲ New York, NE USA
189 P1 **Van Diemen Gulf** *gulf* Northern Territory, N Australia
Van Diemen's Land *see* Tasmania
120 H5 **Vändra** *Ger.* Fennern; *prev.* Vana-Vändra. Pärnumaa, SW Estonia
Vandsburg *see* Więcbork
36 L4 **Van Duzen River** ≈ California, W USA
120 F13 **Vandžiogala** Kaunas, C Lithuania
43 N10 **Vanegas** San Luis Potosí, C Mexico
Vaner, Lake *see* Vänern
97 K17 **Vänern** *Eng.* Lake Vaner; *prev.* Lake Vener. ◎ S Sweden
97 J18 **Vänersborg** Älvsborg, S Sweden
96 F12 **Vang** Oppland, S Norway
180 I7 **Vangaindrano** Fianarantsoa, SE Madagascar
143 S14 **Van Gölü** *Eng.* Lake Van; *anc.* Thospitis. *salt lake* E Turkey
195 V15 **Vangunu** *island* New Georgia Islands, NW Solomon Islands
26 J9 **Van Horn** Texas, SW USA
195 X9 **Vanikolo** *var.* Vanikoro. *island* Santa Cruz Islands, E Solomon Islands
Vanikoro *see* Vanikolo
194 E9 **Vanimo** Sandaun, NW PNG
127 O15 **Vanino** Khabarovskiy Kray, SE Russian Federation
161 G19 **Vānīvilāsa Sāgara** ◎ SW India
153 S13 **Vanj** *Rus.* Vanch. S Tajikistan
118 G14 **Vânju Mare** *prev.* Vinju Mare. Mehedinți, SW Romania
127 P3 **Vankarem** Chukotskiy Avtonomnyy Okrug, NE Russian Federation
13 N12 **Vankleek Hill** Ontario, SE Canada
Van, Lake *see* Van Gölü
94 I8 **Vanna** *island* N Norway
95 I16 **Vännäs** Västerbotten, N Sweden
95 I15 **Vännäsby** Västerbotten, N Sweden
104 H7 **Vannes** *anc.* Dariorigum. Morbihan, NW France
105 T12 **Vanoise, Massif de la** ▲ E France
176 Xx10 **Van Rees, Pegunungan** ▲ Irian Jaya, E Indonesia
85 E24 **Vanrhynsdorp** Western Cape, SW South Africa
23 P7 **Vansant** Virginia, NE USA
96 L13 **Vansbro** Kopparberg, C Sweden
97 D18 **Vanse** Vest-Agder, S Norway
15 M4 **Vansittart Island** *island* Northwest Territories, NE Canada
95 M20 **Vantaa** *Swe.* Vanda. Uusimaa, S Finland
95 L19 **Vantaa** ✕ (Helsinki) Uusimaa, S Finland
34 J9 **Vantage** Washington, NW USA
197 K14 **Vanua Balavu** *prev.* Vanua Mbalavu. *island* Lau Group, E Fiji
197 C10 **Vanua Lava** *island* Banks Islands, N Vanuatu
197 J12 **Vanua Levu** *island* N Fiji
197 J12 **Vanua Levu Barrier Reef** *reef* C Fiji
Vanua Mbalavu *see* Vanua Balavu
197 B10 **Vanuatu** *off.* Republic of Vanuatu; *prev.* New Hebrides. ◆ *republic* SW Pacific Ocean
183 P8 **Vanuatu** *island group* SW Pacific Ocean
197 K15 **Vanua Vatu** *island* Lau Group, E Fiji
33 Q12 **Van Wert** Ohio, N USA
197 K7 **Vao** Province Sud, S New Caledonia
Vapincum *see* Gap
119 N7 **Vapnyarka** Vinnyts'ka Oblast', C Ukraine
105 T15 **Var** ◐ *department* SE France
105 U14 **Var** ≈ SE France
97 J18 **Vara** Skaraborg, S Sweden
Varadinska Županija *see* Varaždin
120 J10 **Varakļāni** Madona, C Latvia
108 C7 **Varallo** Piemonte, NE Italy
149 O5 **Varāmīn** *var.* Veramin. Tehrān, N Iran
159 N14 **Vārānasi** *prev.* Banaras, Benares, *hist.* Kasi. Uttar Pradesh, N India
129 T3 **Varandey** Nenetskiy Avtonomnyy Okrug, NW Russian Federation
94 M8 **Varangerbotn** Finnmark, N Norway
94 M8 **Varangerfjorden** *fjord* N Norway
94 M8 **Varangerhalvøya** *peninsula* N Norway
Varannó *see* Vranov nad Topl'ou
109 M15 **Varano, Lago di** ◎ SE Italy
120 J13 **Varapayeva** *Rus.* Voropayevo. Vitsyebskaya Voblasts', NW Belorussia
Varasd *see* Varaždin
114 E7 **Varaždin** *Ger.* Warasdin, *Hung.* Varasd. Varaždin, N Croatia
114 E7 **Varaždin** *off.* Varadinska Županija. ◐ *province* E Croatia
108 C10 **Varazze** Liguria, NW Italy
97 J20 **Varberg** Halland, S Sweden
Vardak *see* Wardag
115 Q19 **Vardar** *Gk.* Axiós. ≈ FYR Macedonia/Greece *see also* Axiós
97 F23 **Varde** Ribe, W Denmark
143 V12 **Vardenis** E Armenia
94 N8 **Vardø** *Fin.* Vuoreija. Finnmark, N Norway
117 E18 **Vardoúsia** ▲ C Greece
Vareia *see* Logroño
102 G10 **Varel** Niedersachsen, NW Germany
121 G15 **Varėna** *Pol.* Orany. Varėna, S Lithuania
13 O12 **Varennes** Québec, SE Canada
105 P10 **Varennes-sur-Allier** Allier, C France
114 I12 **Vareš** E Bosnia and Herzegovina
108 D7 **Varese** Lombardia, N Italy
118 J12 **Vârful Moldoveanu** *var.* Moldoveanul; *prev.* Vîrful Moldoveanu. ▲ C Romania
Varganzi *see* Warganza
97 J18 **Vårgårda** Älvsborg, S Sweden
125 F12 **Vargashi** Kurganskaya Oblast', C Russian Federation
97 J18 **Vargön** Älvsborg, S Sweden
97 C17 **Varhaug** Rogaland, S Norway
95 N17 **Varkaus** Kuopio, C Finland
94 J2 **Varmahlíð** Nordhurland Vestra, N Iceland
97 J15 **Värmland** ◐ *county* C Sweden
97 K16 **Värmlandsnäs** *peninsula* S Sweden
116 N8 **Varna** *prev.* Stalin, *anc.* Odessus. Varnenska Oblast, NE Bulgaria
116 N8 **Varna** ✕ Varnenska Oblast, NE Bulgaria
Varna *see* Varnenska Oblast
97 L20 **Värnamo** Jönköping, S Sweden
116 M7 **Varnenska Oblast** *var.* Varna. ◐ *province* NE Bulgaria
116 N8 **Varnenski Zaliv** *prev.* Stalinski Zaliv. *bay* E Bulgaria
116 N8 **Varnensko Ezero** *estuary* E Bulgaria
120 D11 **Varniai** Telšiai, W Lithuania
Varnoús *see* Baba
113 D14 **Varnsdorf** *Ger.* Warnsdorf. Severní Čechy, N Czech Republic
113 I23 **Várpalota** Veszprém, W Hungary
Varshava *see* Warszawa
120 K6 **Värska** Põlvamaa, SE Estonia
100 N12 **Varsseveld** Gelderland, E Netherlands
117 D19 **Vartholomió** *prev.* Vartholomión. Dytikí Ellás, S Greece
Vartholomión *see* Vartholomió
143 Q14 **Varto** Muş, E Turkey
97 K18 **Vartofta** Skaraborg, S Sweden
95 O17 **Värtsilä** Pohjois-Karjala, E Finland
Värtsilä *see* Vyartsilya
119 R4 **Varva** Chernihivs'ka Oblast', NE Ukraine
61 H18 **Várzea Grande** Mato Grosso, SW Brazil
108 D9 **Varzi** Lombardia, N Italy
Varzimanor Ayni *see* Ayní
128 K5 **Varzuga** ≈ NW Russian Federation
105 P8 **Varzy** Nièvre, C France
113 G23 **Vas** *off.* Vas Megye. ◐ *county* W Hungary
Vasa *see* Vaasa
202 A9 **Vasafua** *island* Funafuti Atoll, C Tuvalu
113 O21 **Vásárosnamény** Szabolcs-Szatmár-Bereg, E Hungary
106 H13 **Vascão, Ribeira de** ≈ S Portugal
118 G10 **Vașcău** *Hung.* Vaskoh. Bihor, NE Romania
Vascongadas, Provincias *see* País Vasco
Vashess Bay *see* Vaskess Bay
Vāsht *see* Khāsh
Vasilevichi *see* Vasilyevichy
117 G14 **Vasiliká** Kentrikí Makedonía, NE Greece
117 C18 **Vasilikí** Lefkáda, Iónioi Nísoi, Greece, C Mediterranean Sea
117 K25 **Vasilikí** Kríti, Greece, E Mediterranean Sea
121 G16 **Vasilishki** *Pol.* Wasiliszki, *Rus.* Vasilishki. Hrodzyenskaya Voblasts', W Belorussia
Vasil Kolarov *see* Pamporovo
Vasil'kov *see* Vasyl'kiv
121 N19 **Vasilyevichy** *Rus.* Vasilevichi. Homyel'skaya Voblasts', SE Belorussia
203 Y3 **Vaskess Bay** *var.* Vashess Bay. *bay* Kiritimati, E Kiribati
Vaskoh *see* Vașcău
Vaskohsziklás *see* Ștei
118 M10 **Vaslui** Vaslui, C Romania
118 L11 **Vaslui** ◐ *county* NE Romania
33 R8 **Vassar** Michigan, N USA
97 E15 **Vassdalseggi** ▲ S Norway
62 P9 **Vassouras** Rio de Janeiro, SE Brazil
94 H11 **Vastenjaure** ◎ N Sweden
97 N15 **Västerås** Västmanland, C Sweden
95 G15 **Västerbotten** ◐ *county* N Sweden
96 K12 **Västerdalälven** ≈ C Sweden
97 O16 **Västerhaninge** Stockholm, C Sweden
96 M10 **Västernorrland** ◐ *county* C Sweden
97 N19 **Västervik** Kalmar, S Sweden
97 M15 **Västmanland** ◐ *county* C Sweden
109 L15 **Vasto** *anc.* Histonium. Abruzzi, C Italy
97 J16 **Västra Silen** ◎ S Sweden
113 G23 **Vasvár** *Ger.* Eisenburg. Vas, W Hungary
119 U9 **Vasylivka** Zaporiz'ka Oblast', SE Ukraine
119 O5 **Vasyl'kiv** *Rus.* Vasil'kov. Kyyivs'ka Oblast', N Ukraine
126 Gg12 **Vasyugan** ≈ C Russian Federation
105 N8 **Vatan** Indre, C France
Vaté *see* Éfaté
109 G15 **Vatican City** *off.* Vatican City State. ◆ *papal state* S Europe
109 M22 **Vaticano, Capo** *headland* S Italy
Vatilí *see* Vadili
94 K3 **Vatnajökull** *glacier* SE Iceland
97 P15 **Vätö** Stockholm, C Sweden
197 L16 **Vatoa** *island* Lau Group, SE Fiji
180 J5 **Vatomandry** Toamasina, E Madagascar
118 J9 **Vatra Dornei** *Ger.* Dorna Watra. Suceava, NE Romania
118 J9 **Vatra Moldoviței** Suceava, NE Romania
Vatter, Lake *see* Vättern
97 L18 **Vättern** *Eng.* Lake Vatter; *prev.* Lake Vetter. ◎ S Sweden
197 H14 **Vatukoula** Viti Levu, W Fiji
197 H15 **Vatulele** *island* SW Fiji
119 P7 **Vatutine** Cherkas'ka Oblast', C Ukraine
197 J14 **Vatu Vara** *island* Lau Group, E Fiji
105 R14 **Vaucluse** ◐ *department* SE France
105 S5 **Vaucouleurs** Meuse, NE France
110 B9 **Vaud** *Ger.* Waadt. ◐ *canton* SW Switzerland
13 N12 **Vaudreuil** Québec, SE Canada
39 T12 **Vaughn** New Mexico, SW USA
56 I14 **Vaupés** *off.* Comisaría del Vaupés. ◐ *province* SE Colombia
56 J13 **Vaupés, Río** *var.* Rio Uaupés. ≈ Brazil/Colombia *see also* Uaupés, Rio
105 Q15 **Vauvert** Gard, S France
9 R17 **Vauxhall** Alberta, SW Canada
101 K23 **Vaux-sur-Sûre** Luxembourg, SE Belgium
180 J4 **Vavatenina** Toamasina, E Madagascar
200 Ss12 **Vava'u Group** *island group* N Tonga
78 M16 **Vavoua** W Ivory Coast
131 S2 **Vavozh** Udmurtskaya Respublika, NW Russian Federation
161 K23 **Vavuniya** Northern Province, N Sri Lanka
121 G17 **Vawkavysk** *Pol.* Wołkowysk, *Rus.* Volkovysk. Hrodzyenskaya Voblasts', W Belorussia
121 F17 **Vawkavyskaye Wzvyshsha** *Rus.* Volkovyskiye Vysoty. *hill range* W Belorussia
97 P15 **Vaxholm** Stockholm, C Sweden
97 L21 **Växjö** *var.* Vexiö. Kronoberg, S Sweden
129 T1 **Vaygach, Ostrov** *island* NW Russian Federation
143 V13 **Vayk'** *prev.* Azizbekov. SE Armenia
129 P8 **Vazhgort** *prev.* Chasovo. Respublika Komi, NW Russian Federation
47 V10 **V.C.Bird** ✕ (St John's) Antigua, Antigua and Barbuda
31 Q7 **Veblen** South Dakota, N USA
100 N9 **Vecht** *Ger.* Vechte. ≈ Germany/Netherlands *see also* Vechte
102 G12 **Vechta** Niedersachsen, NW Germany
102 E12 **Vechte** *Dut.* Vecht. ≈ Germany/Netherlands *see also* Vecht
120 I8 **Vecpiebalga** Cēsis, C Latvia
120 G9 **Vecumnieki** Bauska, C Latvia
Vedāvati *see* Hagari
97 J20 **Veddige** Halland, S Sweden
118 J15 **Vedea** ≈ S Romania
131 P16 **Vedeno** Chechenskaya Respublika, SW Russian Federation
197 H14 **Ve Drala Reef** *reef* N Fiji
97 C16 **Vedvågen** Rogaland, S Norway
100 O6 **Veendam** Groningen, NE Netherlands
100 K12 **Veenendaal** Utrecht, C Netherlands
101 E14 **Veere** Zeeland, SW Netherlands
26 M2 **Vega** Texas, SW USA
94 E13 **Vega** *island* C Norway
47 T5 **Vega Baja** C Puerto Rico
40 D17 **Vega Point** *headland* Kiska Island, Alaska, USA
97 F17 **Vegår** ◎ S Norway
101 K14 **Veghel** Noord-Brabant, S Netherlands
Veglia *see* Krk
116 E13 **Vegorítis, Límni** ◎ N Greece
9 Q14 **Vegreville** Alberta, SW Canada
97 K21 **Veinge** Halland, S Sweden
63 B21 **Veinticinco de Mayo** *var.* 25 de Mayo. Buenos Aires, E Argentina
65 I14 **Veinticinco de Mayo** La Pampa, C Argentina
121 F15 **Veisiejai** Lazdijai, S Lithuania
97 F23 **Vejen** Ribe, W Denmark
106 K16 **Vejer de la Frontera** Andalucía, S Spain
97 G23 **Vejle** Vejle, C Denmark
97 F23 **Vejle** *off.* Vejle Amt. ◐ *county* C Denmark
116 M7 **Vekilski** Varnenska Oblast, NE Bulgaria
56 G3 **Vela, Cabo de la** *headland* NE Colombia
Vela Goa *see* Goa
115 F15 **Vela Luka** Dubrovnik-Neretva, S Croatia
63 G19 **Velázquez** Rocha, E Uruguay
103 E15 **Velbert** Nordrhein-Westfalen, W Germany
111 S9 **Velden** Kärnten, S Austria
Veldes *see* Bled
101 K15 **Veldhoven** Noord-Brabant, S Netherlands
114 C11 **Velebit** ▲ C Croatia
116 N11 **Veleka** ≈ SE Bulgaria
111 V10 **Velenje** *Ger.* Wöllan. N Slovenia
202 E12 **Vele, Pointe** *headland* Île Futuna, S Wallis and Futuna
115 O18 **Veles** *Turk.* Köprülü. C FYR Macedonia
115 M20 **Velešta** SW FYR Macedonia
117 F16 **Velestíno** *prev.* Velestínon. Thessalía, C Greece
Velestínon *see* Velestíno
Velevshchina *see* Vyelyewshchyna
56 F9 **Vélez** Santander, C Colombia
107 Q13 **Vélez Blanco** Andalucía, S Spain
106 M17 **Vélez de la Gomera, Peñon de** *island group* S Spain
107 N15 **Vélez-Málaga** Andalucía, S Spain
107 Q13 **Vélez Rubio** Andalucía, S Spain
Velha Goa *see* Goa
Velho *see* Porto Velho
114 E8 **Velika Gorica** Grad Zagreb, N Croatia
114 C9 **Velika Kapela** ▲ NW Croatia
Velika Kikinda *see* Kikinda
114 D10 **Velika Kladuša** NW Bosnia and Herzegovina
114 N11 **Velika Morava** *var.* Glavn'a Morava, Morava, *Ger.* Grosse Morava. ≈ C Yugoslavia
114 N12 **Velika Plana** Serbia, C Yugoslavia
127 Pp5 **Velikaya** ≈ NE Russian Federation
128 F15 **Velikaya** ≈ W Russian Federation
Velikaya Berestovitsa *see* Vyalikaya Byerastavitsa
Velikaya Lepetikha *see* Velyka Lepetykha
Veliki Bečkerek *see* Zrenjanin
114 P12 **Veliki Krš** *var.* Stol. ▲ E Yugoslavia
116 L8 **Veliki Preslav** *prev.* Preslav. Varnenska Oblast, NE Bulgaria
114 B9 **Veliki Risnjak** ▲ NW Croatia
114 J13 **Veliki Stolac** ▲ E Bosnia and Herzegovina
Velikiy Bor *see* Vyaliki Bor
128 G16 **Velikiye Luki** Pskovskaya Oblast', W Russian Federation
129 P12 **Velikiy Ustyug** Vologodskaya Oblast', NW Russian Federation
114 N11 **Veliko Gradište** Serbia, NE Yugoslavia
161 I18 **Velikonda Range** ▲ SE India
116 K9 **Veliko Tŭrnovo** *prev.* Tirnovo, Trnovo, Tŭrnovo. Loveshka Oblast, N Bulgaria
Velikovec *see* Völkermarkt
129 R5 **Velikovisochnoye** Nenetskiy Avtonomnyy Okrug, NW Russian Federation
78 H12 **Vélingara** C Senegal
78 H11 **Vélingara** S Senegal
116 H11 **Velingrad** Plovdivska Oblast, SW Bulgaria
130 H3 **Velizh** Smolenskaya Oblast', W Russian Federation
113 F16 **Velká Deštná** *var.* Deštná, Grosskoppe, *Ger.* Deschnaer Koppe. ▲ NE Czech Republic
113 F18 **Velké Meziříčí** *Ger.* Grossmeseritsch. Jižní Morava, SE Czech Republic
94 N1 **Velkomstpynten** *headland* NW Svalbard
113 K21 **Veľký Krtíš** Stredné Slovensko, S Slovakia
195 T14 **Vella Lavella** *var.* Mbilua. *island* New Georgia Islands, NW Solomon Islands
109 I15 **Velletri** Lazio, C Italy
97 K23 **Vellinge** Malmöhus, S Sweden
161 I19 **Vellore** Tamil Nādu, SE India
Velobriga *see* Viana do Castelo
117 G21 **Velopoúla** *island* S Greece
100 M12 **Velp** Gelderland, SE Netherlands
Velsen *see* Velsen-Noord
100 H9 **Velsen-Noord** *var.* Velsen. Noord-Holland, W Netherlands
129 N12 **Vel'sk** *var.* Velsk. Arkhangel'skaya Oblast', NW Russian Federation
Velsuna *see* Orvieto

100 K10 **Veluwemeer** *lake channel* C Netherlands
30 M3 **Velva** North Dakota, N USA
117 E14 **Velvendós** *var.* Velvendos. Dytikí Makedonía, N Greece
119 S5 **Velyka Bahachka** Poltavs'ka Oblast', C Ukraine
119 S9 **Velyka Lepetykha** *Rus.* Velikaya Lepetikha. Khersons'ka Oblast', S Ukraine
119 O10 **Velyka Mykhaylivka** Odes'ka Oblast', SW Ukraine
119 W8 **Velyka Novosilka** Donets'ka Oblast', E Ukraine
119 S9 **Velyka Oleksandrivka** Khersons'ka Oblast', S Ukraine
119 T4 **Velyka Pysanivka** Sums'ka Oblast', NE Ukraine
118 G6 **Velykyy Bereznyy** Zakarpats'ka Oblast', W Ukraine
119 W4 **Velykyy Burluk** Kharkivs'ka Oblast', E Ukraine
Velykyy Tokmak *see* Tokmak
181 P7 **Vema Fracture Zone** *tectonic feature* W Indian Ocean
67 P18 **Vema Seamount** *undersea feature* SW Indian Ocean
95 F17 **Vemdalen** Jämtland, C Sweden
97 N19 **Vena** Kalmar, S Sweden
43 N11 **Venado** San Luis Potosí, C Mexico
64 L11 **Venado Tuerto** Entre Ríos, E Argentina
63 A19 **Venado Tuerto** Santa Fe, C Argentina
109 K16 **Venafro** Molise, C Italy
57 Q9 **Venamo, Cerro** ▲ E Venezuela
108 B8 **Venaria** Piemonte, NW Italy
105 U15 **Vence** Alpes-Maritimes, SE France
106 H5 **Venda Nova** Vila Real, N Portugal
106 G11 **Vendas Novas** Évora, S Portugal
104 J9 **Vendée** ◈ *department* NW France
105 Q6 **Vendeuvre-sur-Barse** Aube, NE France
104 M7 **Vendôme** Loir-et-Cher, C France
Venedig *see* Venezia
Vener, Lake *see* Vänern
108 I8 **Veneta, Laguna** *lagoon* NE Italy
Venetia *see* Venezia
41 S7 **Venetie** Alaska, USA
108 H8 **Veneto** *var.* Venezia Euganea. ◈ *region* NE Italy
116 M7 **Venets** Varnenska Oblast, NE Bulgaria
130 L5 **Venev** Tul'skaya Oblast', W Russian Federation
108 I8 **Venezia** *Eng.* Venice, *Fr.* Venise, *Ger.* Venedig; anc.Venetia. Veneto, NE Italy
Venezia Euganea *see* Veneto
Venezia, Golfo di *see* Venice, Gulf of
Venezia Tridentina *see* Trentino-Alto Adige
56 K8 **Venezuela** *off.* Republic of Venezuela; *prev.* Estados Unidos de Venezuela, United States of Venezuela. ◆ *republic* N South America
Venezuela, Cordillera de *see* Costa, Cordillera de la
56 I4 **Venezuela, Golfo de** *Eng.* Gulf of Maracaibo, Gulf of Venezuela. *gulf* NW Venezuela
Venezuela, Gulf of *see* Venezuela, Golfo de
66 F11 **Venezuelan Basin** *undersea feature* E Caribbean Sea
161 D16 **Vengurla** Mahārāshtra, W India
41 O15 **Veniaminof, Mount** ▲ Alaska, USA
25 V14 **Venice** Florida, SE USA
24 L10 **Venice** Louisiana, S USA
Venice *see* Venezia
108 J8 **Venice, Gulf of** *It.* Golfo di Venezia, *Slvn.* Beneški Zaliv. *gulf* N Adriatic Sea
Venise *see* Venezia
96 K13 **Venjan** Kopparberg, C Sweden
96 K13 **Venjansjön** ◎ C Sweden
161 J18 **Venkatagiri** Andhra Pradesh, E India
101 M15 **Venlo** *prev.* Venloo. Limburg, SE Netherlands
Venloo *see* Venlo
97 E18 **Vennesla** Vest-Agder, S Norway
109 M17 **Venosa** *anc.* Venusia. Basilicata, S Italy
Venoste, Alpi *see* Ötztaler Alpen
Venraij *see* Venray
101 M14 **Venray** *var.* Venraij. Limburg, SE Netherlands
120 C8 **Venta** *Ger.* Windau. ≈ Latvia/Lithuania
Venta Belgarum *see* Winchester
42 G9 **Ventana, Punta Arena de la** *var.* Punta de la Ventana. *headland* W Mexico
Ventana, Punta de la *see* Ventana, Punta Arena de la
63 B23 **Ventana, Sierra de la** *hill range* E Argentina
Ventia *see* Valence
203 S11 **Vent, Îles du** *var.* Windward Islands. *island group* Archipel de la Société, W French Polynesia
203 R10 **Vent, Îles Sous le** *var.* Leeward Islands. *island group* Archipel de la Société, W French Polynesia
108 B11 **Ventimiglia** Liguria, NW Italy
99 M24 **Ventnor** S England, UK
20 J17 **Ventnor City** New Jersey, NE USA
105 S14 **Ventoux, Mont** ▲ SE France
120 C8 **Ventspils** *Ger.* Windau. Ventspils, NW Latvia
56 M10 **Ventuari, Río** ≈ S Venezuela
37 R15 **Ventura** California, W USA
190 F8 **Venus Bay** South Australia
Venusia *see* Venosa
203 P7 **Vénus, Pointe** *var.* Pointe Tataaihoa. *headland* Tahiti, W French Polynesia
43 V16 **Venustiano Carranza** Chiapas, SE Mexico
43 N7 **Venustiano Carranza, Presa** ⊞ NE Mexico
63 B15 **Vera** Santa Fe, C Argentina
107 Q14 **Vera** Andalucía, S Spain
65 K18 **Vera, Bahía** *bay* E Argentina
43 R14 **Veracruz** *var.* Veracruz Llave. Veracruz-Llave, E Mexico
43 Q13 **Veracruz-Llave** *var.* Veracruz. ◈ *state* E Mexico
45 Q16 **Veraguas** *off.* Provincia de Veraguas. ◈ *province* W Panama
Veramin *see* Varāmīn
160 B12 **Verāval** Gujarāt, W India
108 C6 **Verbania** Piemonte, NW Italy
109 N20 **Verbicaro** Calabria, SW Italy
110 D11 **Verbier** Valais, SW Switzerland
Vercellae *see* Vercelli
108 C8 **Vercelli** *anc.* Vercellae. Piemonte, NW Italy
105 S13 **Vercors** *physical region* E France
95 E16 **Verdalsøra** Nord-Trøndelag, C Norway
Verde, Cabo *see* Cape Verde
46 J5 **Verde, Cape** *headland* Long Island, C Bahamas
106 M2 **Verde, Costa** *coastal region* N Spain
Verde Grande, Río/Verde Grande y de Belem, Río *see* Verde, Río
102 H11 **Verden** Niedersachsen, NW Germany
61 J19 **Verde, Rio** ≈ SE Brazil
59 P16 **Verde, Río** ≈ Bolivia/Brazil
42 M12 **Verde, Río** *var.* Río Verde Grande, Río Verde Grande y de Belem. ≈ C Mexico
43 Q16 **Verde, Río** ≈ SE Mexico
38 L13 **Verde River** ≈ Arizona, SW USA
Verdhikoúsa/Verdhikoússa *see* Verdikoússa
29 Q8 **Verdigris River** ≈ Kansas/Oklahoma, C USA
117 E15 **Verdikoússa** *var.* Verdhikoúsa, Verdhikoússa. Thessalía, C Greece
105 S15 **Verdon** ≈ SE France
13 O12 **Verdun** Québec, SE Canada
105 S4 **Verdun** *var.* Verdun-sur-Meuse; *anc.* Verodunum. Meuse, NE France
Verdun-sur-Meuse *see* Verdun
85 J21 **Vereeniging** Gauteng, NE South Africa
Veremeyki *see* Vyeramyeyki
129 T14 **Vereshchagino** Permskaya Oblast', NW Russian Federation
78 G14 **Verga, Cap** *headland* W Guinea
63 G18 **Vergara** Treinta y Tres, E Uruguay
110 G11 **Vergeletto** Ticino, S Switzerland
20 L8 **Vergennes** Vermont, NE USA
Veria *see* Véroia
106 I5 **Verín** Galicia, NW Spain
Verin T'alin *see* T'alin
120 K6 **Veriora** Põlvamaa, SE Estonia
119 T7 **Verkhivtseve** Dnipropetrovs'ka Oblast', E Ukraine
131 W3 **Verkhiye Kigi** Respublika Bashkortostan, W Russian Federation
Verkhnedvinsk *see* Vyerkhnyadzvinsk
126 Hh11 **Verkhneimbatsk** Krasnoyarskiy Kray, N Russian Federation
128 I3 **Verkhnetulomskiy** Murmanskaya Oblast', NW Russian Federation
128 I3 **Verkhnetulomskoye Vodokhranilishche** ⊞ NW Russian Federation
Verkhneudinsk *see* Ulan-Ude
126 L11 **Verkhnevilyuysk** Respublika Sakha (Yakutiya), NE Russian Federation
131 W5 **Verkhniy Avzyan** Respublika Bashkortostan, W Russian Federation
131 Q11 **Verkhniy Baskunchak** Astrakhanskaya Oblast', SW Russian Federation
119 T9 **Verkhniy Rohachyk** Khersons'ka Oblast', S Ukraine
126 Ll12 **Verkhnyaya Amga** Respublika Sakha (Yakutiya), NE Russian Federation
129 V6 **Verkhnyaya Inta** Respublika Komi, NW Russian Federation
126 I6 **Verkhnyaya Taymyra** ≈ N Russian Federation
129 O10 **Verkhnyaya Toyma** Arkhangel'skaya Oblast', NW Russian Federation
130 K6 **Verkhov'ye** Orlovskaya Oblast', W Russian Federation
118 I8 **Verkhovyna** Ivano-Frankivs'ka Oblast', W Ukraine
126 M8 **Verkhoyansk** Respublika Sakha (Yakutiya), NE Russian Federation
126 L8 **Verkhoyanskiy Khrebet** ▲▲ NE Russian Federation
119 T7 **Verkhn'odniprovs'k** Dnipropetrovs'ka Oblast', E Ukraine
103 G14 **Verl** Nordrhein-Westfalen, NW Germany
94 N1 **Verlegenhuken** *headland* N Svalbard
84 A9 **Vermelha, Ponta** *headland* NW Angola
105 P7 **Vermenton** Yonne, C France
9 R14 **Vermilion** Alberta, SW Canada
33 T11 **Vermilion** Ohio, N USA
24 I10 **Vermilion Bay** *bay* Louisiana, S USA
31 V4 **Vermilion Lake** ◎ Minnesota, N USA
12 F9 **Vermilion River** ≈ Ontario, S Canada
32 L12 **Vermilion River** ≈ Illinois, N USA
31 R12 **Vermillion** South Dakota, N USA
31 R12 **Vermillion River** ≈ South Dakota, N USA
13 O9 **Vermillon, Rivière** ≈ Québec, SE Canada
117 E14 **Vérmio** ▲▲ N Greece
20 L8 **Vermont** *off.* State of Vermont; also known as The Green Mountain State. ◈ *state* NE USA
115 K16 **Vermosh** *var.* Vermoshi. Shkodër, N Albania
Vermoshi *see* Vermosh
39 O3 **Vernal** Utah, W USA
12 G11 **Verner** Ontario, S Canada
104 M5 **Verneuil-sur-Avre** Eure, N France
116 D13 **Vérno** ▲▲ N Greece
9 N17 **Vernon** British Columbia, SW Canada
104 M4 **Vernon** Eure, N France
25 N3 **Vernon** Alabama, S USA
33 P15 **Vernon** Indiana, N USA
27 Q4 **Vernon** Texas, SW USA
34 G10 **Vernonia** Oregon, NW USA
12 G12 **Vernon, Lake** ◎ Ontario, S Canada
24 G7 **Vernon Lake** ⊞ Louisiana, S USA
25 Y13 **Vero Beach** Florida, SE USA
Verőcze *see* Virovitica
Verodunum *see* Verdun
117 E14 **Véroia** *var.* Veria, Vérroia, *Turk.* Karaferiye. Kentrikí Makedonía, N Greece
108 E8 **Verolanuova** Lombardia, N Italy
12 K14 **Verona** Ontario, SE Canada
108 G8 **Verona** Veneto, NE Italy
31 P6 **Verona** North Dakota, N USA
32 L9 **Verona** Wisconsin, N USA
63 E20 **Verónica** Buenos Aires, E Argentina
24 J9 **Verret, Lake** ◎ Louisiana, S USA
Vérroia *see* Véroia
195 P10 **Verron Range** ▲▲ New Ireland, NE PNG
105 N5 **Versailles** Yvelines, N France
33 P15 **Versailles** Indiana, N USA
22 M5 **Versailles** Kentucky, S USA
29 U5 **Versailles** Missouri, C USA
33 Q13 **Versailles** Ohio, N USA
Versecz *see* Vršac
110 A10 **Versoix** Genève, SW Switzerland
13 Z6 **Verte, Pointe** *headland* Québec, SE Canada
113 I22 **Vértes** ▲▲ NW Hungary
46 G6 **Vertientes** Camagüey, C Cuba
116 G13 **Vertískos** ▲▲ N Greece
104 I8 **Vertou** Loire-Atlantique, NW France
Verulamium *see* St Albans
101 L19 **Verviers** Liège, E Belgium
104 F1 **Vescovato** Corse, France, C Mediterranean Sea
101 L20 **Vesdre** ≈ E Belgium
119 U10 **Vesele** *Rus.* Veseloye. Zaporiz'ka Oblast', S Ukraine
113 D18 **Veselí nad Lužnicí** *var.* Weseli an der Lainsitz, *Ger.* Frohenbruck. Jižní Čechy, S Czech Republic
116 M9 **Veselinovo** Varnenska Oblast, E Bulgaria
130 L12 **Veselovskoye Vodokhranilishche** ⊞ SW Russian Federation
Veseloye *see* Vesele
119 Q9 **Veselynove** Mykolayivs'ka Oblast', S Ukraine
Veseya *see* Vyasyeya
130 M10 **Veshenskaya** Rostovskaya Oblast', SW Russian Federation
131 Q5 **Veshkayma** Ul'yanovskaya Oblast', W Russian Federation
Vesisaari *see* Vadsø
Vesontio *see* Besançon
105 T7 **Vesoul** *anc.* Vesulium, Vesulum. Haute-Saône, E France
97 J20 **Vessigebro** Halland, S Sweden
97 D17 **Vest-Agder** ◈ *county* S Norway
25 P4 **Vestavia Hills** Alabama, S USA
86 F6 **Vesterålen** *island* N Norway
94 G10 **Vesterålen** *island group* N Norway
89 W3 **Vestervig** Viborg, NW Denmark
94 H2 **Vestfirdhir** ◈ *region* NW Iceland
94 G11 **Vestfjorden** *fjord* C Norway
97 G16 **Vestfold** ◈ *county* S Norway
94 I4 **Vestmannaeyjar** Sudhurland, S Iceland
96 E9 **Vestnes** Møre og Romsdal, S Norway
97 I23 **Vestsjælland** *off.* Vestsjællands Amt. ◈ *county* E Denmark
94 H3 **Vesturland** ◈ *region* W Iceland
94 G11 **Vestvågøy** *island* C Norway
Vesulium/Vesulum *see* Vesoul
Vesuna *see* Périgueux
109 K17 **Vesuvio** *Eng.* Vesuvius. ※ S Italy
Vesuvius *see* Vesuvio
128 K14 **Ves'yegonsk** Tverskaya Oblast', W Russian Federation
113 I23 **Veszprém** *Ger.* Veszprim. Veszprém, W Hungary
113 H23 **Veszprém** *off.* Veszprém Megye. ◈ *county* W Hungary
Veszprim *see* Veszprém
Vetka *see* Vyetka
97 M19 **Vetlanda** Jönköping, S Sweden
131 P1 **Vetluga** Nizhegorodskaya Oblast', W Russian Federation
129 P14 **Vetluga** ≈ NW Russian Federation
129 O14 **Vetluzhskiy** Kostromskaya Oblast', NW Russian Federation
131 P2 **Vetluzhskiy** Nizhegorodskaya Oblast', W Russian Federation
109 H14 **Vetralla** Lazio, C Italy
116 M9 **Vetren** *prev.* Zhitarovo. Burgaska Oblast, E Bulgaria
116 M8 **Vetrino** Varnenska Oblast, NE Bulgaria
Vetrino *see* Vyetryna
126 I6 **Vetrovaya, Gora** ▲ N Russian Federation
Vetter, Lake *see* Vättern
108 J13 **Vettore, Monte** ▲ C Italy
101 A17 **Veurne** *var.* Furnes. West-Vlaanderen, W Belgium
33 Q15 **Vevay** Indiana, N USA
110 C10 **Vevey** *Ger.* Vivis; *anc.* Vibiscum. Vaud, SW Switzerland
Vexiö *see* Växjö
105 S13 **Veynes** Hautes-Alpes, SE France
105 N11 **Vézère** ≈ W France
116 I9 **Vezhen** ▲ C Bulgaria
142 K11 **Vezirköprü** Samsun, N Turkey
59 J18 **Viacha** La Paz, W Bolivia
29 R10 **Vian** Oklahoma, C USA
Viana de Castelo *see* Viana do Castelo
106 H12 **Viana do Alentejo** Évora, S Portugal
106 I4 **Viana do Bolo** Galicia, NW Spain
106 G5 **Viana do Castelo** *var.* Viana de Castelo; *anc.* Velobriga. Viana do Castelo, NW Portugal
106 G5 **Viana do Castelo** *var.* Viana de Castelo. ◈ *district* N Portugal
100 J12 **Vianen** Zuid-Holland, C Netherlands
178 I8 **Viangchan** *Eng./Fr.* Vientiane. ● (Laos) C Laos
178 I6 **Viangphoukha** *var.* Vieng Pou Kha. Louang Namtha, N Laos
106 K13 **Viar** ≈ SW Spain
108 E11 **Viareggio** Toscana, C Italy
105 O14 **Viaur** ≈ S France
Vibiscum *see* Vevey
97 G21 **Viborg** Viborg, NW Denmark
31 R12 **Viborg** South Dakota, N USA
97 F21 **Viborg** *off.* Viborg Amt. ◈ *county* NW Denmark
109 N22 **Vibo Valentia** *prev.* Monteleone di Calabria; *anc.* Hipponium. Calabria, SW Italy
107 W5 **Vic** *var.* Vich; *anc.* Ausa, Vicus Ausonensis. Cataluña, NE Spain
104 K16 **Vic-en-Bigorre** Hautes-Pyrénées, S France
42 K10 **Vicente Guerrero** Durango, C Mexico
43 P10 **Vicente Guerrero, Presa** *var.* Presa de las Adjuntas. ⊞ NE Mexico
Vicentia *see* Vicenza
108 G8 **Vicenza** *anc.* Vicentia. Veneto, NE Italy
Vich *see* Vic
56 J10 **Vichada** *off.* Comisaría del Vichada. ◈ *province* E Colombia
56 K10 **Vichada, Río** ≈ E Colombia
63 G17 **Vichadero** Rivera, NE Uruguay
Vichegda *see* Vychegda
128 M16 **Vichuga** Ivanovskaya Oblast', W Russian Federation
105 P10 **Vichy** Allier, C France
28 K9 **Vici** Oklahoma, C USA
33 P10 **Vicksburg** Michigan, N USA
24 J5 **Vicksburg** Mississippi, S USA
105 O12 **Vic-sur-Cère** Cantal, C France
31 X14 **Victor** Iowa, C USA
61 I21 **Víctor** Mato Grosso do Sul, SW Brazil
190 I10 **Victor Harbor** South Australia
63 C18 **Victoria** Entre Ríos, E Argentina
8 L17 **Victoria** Vancouver Island, British Columbia, SW Canada
47 R14 **Victoria** NW Grenada
44 H6 **Victoria** Yoro, NW Honduras
123 J16 **Victoria** *var.* Rabat. Gozo, NW Malta
118 I12 **Victoria** *Ger.* Viktoriastadt. Brașov, C Romania
180 H17 **Victoria** ● (Seychelles) Mahé, SW Seychelles
27 U13 **Victoria** Texas, SW USA
191 N12 **Victoria** ◈ *state* SE Australia
182 K7 **Victoria** ≈ Western Australia
Victoria *see* Labuan, East Malaysia
Victoria *see* Masvingo, Zimbabwe
Victoria Bank *see* Vitória Seamount
9 Y15 **Victoria Beach** Manitoba, S Canada
Victoria de Durango *see* Durango
Victoria de las Tunas *see* Las Tunas
85 I16 **Victoria Falls** Matabeleland North, W Zimbabwe
85 I16 **Victoria Falls** ✕ Matabeleland North, W Zimbabwe
85 I16 **Victoria Falls** *waterfall* Zambia/Zimbabwe
Victoria Falls *see* Iguaçu, Salto do
65 F19 **Victoria, Isla** *island* Archipiélago de los Chonos, S Chile
15 J2 **Victoria Island** *island* Northwest Territories, NW Canada
190 L8 **Victoria, Lake** ◎ New South Wales, SE Australia
70 J13 **Victoria, Lake** *var.* Victoria Nyanza. ◎ E Africa
205 S13 **Victoria Land** *physical region* Antarctica
177 F5 **Victoria, Mount** ▲ W Burma
197 I14 **Victoria, Mount** ▲ Viti Levu, W Fiji
194 K15 **Victoria, Mount** ▲ S PNG
83 F17 **Victoria Nile** *var.* Somerset Nile. ≈ C Uganda
Victoria Nyanza *see* Victoria, Lake
44 G3 **Victoria Peak** ▲ SE Belize
193 H16 **Victoria Range** ▲▲ South Island, NZ
189 O3 **Victoria River** ≈ Northern Territory, N Australia
189 P3 **Victoria River Roadhouse** Northern Territory, N Australia
13 Q11 **Victoriaville** Québec, SE Canada
Victoria-Wes *see* Victoria West
85 G24 **Victoria West** *Afr.* Victoria-Wes. Northern Cape, W South Africa
64 J13 **Victorica** La Pampa, C Argentina
205 T3 **Victor, Mount** ▲ Antarctica
37 U14 **Victorville** California, W USA
64 G9 **Vicuña** Coquimbo, N Chile
64 K11 **Vicuña Mackenna** Córdoba, C Argentina
Vicus Ausonensis *see* Vic
Vicus Elbii *see* Viterbo
35 X7 **Vida** Montana, NW USA
25 V6 **Vidalia** Georgia, SE USA
24 J7 **Vidalia** Louisiana, S USA
97 F22 **Videbæk** Ringkøbing, C Denmark
62 I13 **Videira** Santa Catarina, S Brazil
118 J14 **Videle** Teleorman, S Romania
Videm-Krško *see* Krško
Vídeň *see* Wien
106 H12 **Vidigueira** Beja, S Portugal
116 J9 **Vidima** ≈ N Bulgaria
116 G7 **Vidin** *anc.* Bononia. Oblast Montana, NW Bulgaria
160 H10 **Vidisha** Madhya Pradesh, C India
27 Y10 **Vidor** Texas, SW USA
97 L20 **Vidöstern** ◎ S Sweden
94 J13 **Vidsel** Norrbotten, N Sweden
120 H9 **Vidzemes Augstiene** ▲ C Latvia
120 J12 **Vidzy** *Rus.* Vidzy. Vitsyebskaya Voblasts', NW Belorussia
65 L16 **Viedma** Río Negro, E Argentina
65 H22 **Viedma, Lago** ◎ S Argentina
47 O11 **Vieille Case** *var.* Itassi. N Dominica
106 M2 **Vieja, Peña** ▲ N Spain
42 E4 **Viejo, Cerro** ▲ NW Mexico
58 B9 **Viejo, Cerro** ▲ N Peru
120 E10 **Viekšniai** Akmenė, NW Lithuania
107 U3 **Vielha** *var.* Viella. Cataluña, NE Spain
Viella *see* Vielha
101 L21 **Vielsalm** Luxembourg, E Belgium
Vieng Pou Kha *see* Viangphoukha
25 T6 **Vienna** Georgia, SE USA
32 L17 **Vienna** Illinois, N USA
29 V5 **Vienna** Missouri, C USA
23 Q3 **Vienna** West Virginia, NE USA
Vienna *see* Wien, Austria
Vienna *see* Vienne, France
105 R11 **Vienne** *anc.* Vienna. Isère, E France
104 L10 **Vienne** ◈ *department* W France
104 L9 **Vienne** ≈ W France
Vientiane *see* Viangchan
Vientos, Paso de los *see* Windward Passage
47 V6 **Vieques** *var.* Isabel Segunda. E Puerto Rico
47 V6 **Vieques, Isla de** *island* E Puerto Rico
47 V6 **Vieques, Pasaje de** *passage* E Puerto Rico
47 V5 **Vieques, Sonda de** *sound* E Puerto Rico
Vierdörfer *see* Săcele
95 M15 **Vieremä** Kuopio, C Finland
101 M14 **Vierlingsbeek** Noord-Brabant, SE Netherlands
103 G20 **Viernheim** Hessen, W Germany
103 D15 **Viersen** Nordrhein-Westfalen, W Germany
110 G8 **Vierwaldstätter See** *Eng.* Lake of Lucerne. ◎ C Switzerland
105 N8 **Vierzon** Cher, C France
42 L8 **Viesca** Coahuila de Zaragoza, NE Mexico
120 H10 **Viesīte** *Ger.* Eckengraf. Jēkabpils, S Latvia
109 N15 **Vieste** Puglia, SE Italy
178 J9 **Vietnam** *off.* Socialist Republic of Vietnam, *Vtn.* Công Hoa Xa Hôi Chu Nghia Việt Nam. ◆ *republic* SE Asia
178 J5 **Việt Quang** Ha Giang, N Vietnam
Vietri *see* Việt Tri
178 J6 **Việt Tri** *var.* Vietri. Vinh Phu, N Vietnam
32 L4 **Vieux Desert, Lac** ◎ Michigan/Wisconsin, N USA
47 Y13 **Vieux Fort** S Saint Lucia
47 X6 **Vieux-Habitants** Basse Terre, SW Guadeloupe
121 G14 **Vievis** Kaišiadorys, S Lithuania
179 P8 **Vigan** Luzon, N Philippines
108 D8 **Vigevano** Lombardia, N Italy
109 N18 **Viggiano** Basilicata, S Italy
60 L12 **Vigia** Pará, NE Brazil
43 Y12 **Vigía Chico** Quintana Roo, SE Mexico
47 T11 **Vigie** ✕ (Castries) NE Saint Lucia
104 K17 **Vignemale** *var.* Pic de Vignemale. ▲ France/Spain
Vignemale, Pic de *see* Vignemale
108 G10 **Vignola** Emilia-Romagna, C Italy
106 G4 **Vigo** Galicia, NW Spain
106 G4 **Vigo, Ría de** *estuary* NW Spain
96 D9 **Vigra** *island* S Norway
97 C17 **Vigrestad** Rogaland, S Norway
95 L15 **Vihanti** Oulu, C Finland
155 U10 **Vihāri** Punjab, E Pakistan
104 K8 **Vihiers** Maine-et-Loire, NW France
113 O19 **Vihorlat** ▲ E Slovakia
95 L19 **Vihti** Uusimaa, S Finland
Viipuri *see* Vyborg
95 M16 **Viitasaari** Keski-Suomi, C Finland
120 K3 **Viivikonna** Ida-Virumaa, NE Estonia
161 K16 **Vijayawāda** *prev.* Bezwada. Andhra Pradesh, SE India
Vijosa/Vijosë *see* Aóos, Albania/Greece
Vijosa/Vijosë *see* Vjosës, Lumi i, Albania/Greece
Vik *see* Vikøyri
94 J4 **Vík** Sudhurland, S Iceland
96 L13 **Vika** Kopparberg, C Sweden
94 L12 **Vikajärvi** Lappi, N Finland
96 L13 **Vikarbyn** Kopparberg, C Sweden
97 J22 **Viken** Malmöhus, S Sweden
97 L17 **Viken** ◎ C Sweden
97 G15 **Vikersund** Buskerud, S Norway
126 J14 **Vikhorevka** Irkutskaya Oblast', S Russian Federation
116 G11 **Vikhren** ▲ SW Bulgaria
9 R15 **Viking** Alberta, SW Canada
86 E7 **Viking Bank** *undersea feature* N North Sea
97 M14 **Vikmanshyttan** Kopparberg, C Sweden
96 D12 **Vikøyri** *var.* Vik. Sogn og Fjordane, S Norway
95 H17 **Viksjö** Västernorrland, C Sweden
Viktoriastadt *see* Victoria
Vila *see* Port-Vila
Vila Arriaga *see* Bibala
Vila Artur de Paiva *see* Cubango
Vila Bela da Santissima Trindade *see* Mato Grosso
60 B12 **Vila Bittencourt** Amazonas, NW Brazil
Vila da Ponte *see* Cubango
66 O2 **Vila da Praia da Vitória** Terceira, Azores, Portugal, NE Atlantic Ocean
Vila de Aljustrel *see* Cangamba
Vila de Almoster *see* Chiange
Vila de João Belo *see* Xai-Xai
Vila de Macia *see* Macia
Vila de Manhiça *see* Manhiça
Vila de Manica *see* Manica
Vila de Mocímboa da Praia *see* Mocímboa da Praia
85 N16 **Vila de Sena** *var.* Sena. Sofala, C Mozambique
106 F14 **Vila do Bispo** Faro, S Portugal
106 G6 **Vila do Conde** Porto, NW Portugal
Vila do Maio *see* Maio
66 P3 **Vila do Porto** Santa Maria, Azores, Portugal, NE Atlantic Ocean
85 K15 **Vila do Zumbo** *prev.* Vila do Zumbu, Zumbo. Tete, NW Mozambique
Vila do Zumbu *see* Vila do Zumbo
106 I6 **Vila Flor** *var.* Vila Flôr. Bragança, N Portugal
107 V6 **Vilafranca del Penedès** *var.* Villafranca del Panadés. Cataluña, NE Spain
106 F10 **Vila Franca de Xira** *var.* Vilafranca de Xira. Lisboa, C Portugal
Vila Gago Coutinho *see* Lumbala N'Guimbo
106 G3 **Vilagarcía de Arousa** *var.* Villagarcía de Arosa. Galicia, NW Spain
Vila General Machado *see* Camacupa
Vila Henrique de Carvalho *see* Saurimo
104 I7 **Vilaine** ≈ NW France
Vila João de Almeida *see* Chibia
120 K8 **Viļaka** *Ger.* Marienhausen. Balvi, NE Latvia
106 I2 **Vilalba** Galicia, NW Spain
Vila Marechal Carmona *see* Uíge
Vila Mariano Machado *see* Ganda
180 G3 **Vilanandro, Tanjona** *headland* W Madagascar
Vilanculos *see* Vilankulo
120 J10 **Viļāni** Rēzekne, E Latvia
85 N19 **Vilankulo** *var.* Vilanculos. Inhambane, E Mozambique
Vila Norton de Matos *see* Balombo
106 G6 **Vila Nova de Famalicão** *var.* Vila Nova de Famalicao. Braga, N Portugal
106 I6 **Vila Nova de Foz Côa** *var.* Vila Nova de Fozcôa. Guarda, N Portugal
106 F6 **Vila Nova de Gaia** Porto, NW Portugal
Vila Nova de Portimão *see* Portimão
107 V6 **Vilanova i La Geltrú** Cataluña, NE Spain
Vila Pereira de Eça *see* N'Giva
106 H6 **Vila Pouca de Aguiar** Vila Real, N Portugal
106 H6 **Vila Real** *var.* Vila Rial. Vila Real, N Portugal
106 H6 **Vila Real** ◈ *district* N Portugal
107 T9 **Vila-real de los Infantes** *var.* Villarreal. País Valenciano, E Spain
106 H14 **Vila Real de Santo Antóni›** Faro, S Portugal
106 J7 **Vilar Formoso** Guarda, N Portugal
Vila Rial *see* Vila Real
61 J15 **Vila Rica** Mato Grosso, W Brazil
Vila Robert Williams *see* Caála
Vila Salazar *see* N'Dalatando
Vila Serpa Pinto *see* Menongue
Vila Teixeira da Silva *see* Bailundo
Vila Teixeira de Sousa *see* Luau
106 H9 **Vila Velha de Ródão** Castelo Branco, C Portugal
106 G5 **Vila Verde** Braga, N Portugal
106 H11 **Vila Viçosa** Évora, S Portugal
59 G15 **Vilcabamba, Cordillera de** ▲▲ C Peru
Vîlcea *see* Vâlcea
126 Hh1 **Vil'cheka, Zemlya** *Eng.* Wilczek Land. *island* Zemlya Frantsa-Iosifa, NW Russian Federation
97 F22 **Vildbjerg** Ringkøbing, C Denmark
Vileyka *see* Vilyeyka
95 H15 **Vilhelmina** Västerbotten, N Sweden
61 F17 **Vilhena** Rondônia, W Brazil
117 G19 **Vília** Attikí, C Greece
Viliya *see* Viliya
121 I14 **Viliya** *Lith.* Neris, *Rus.* Viliya. ≈ W Belorussia
Viliya *see* Neris
120 H5 **Viljandi** *Ger.* Fellin. Viljandimaa, S Estonia
120 H5 **Viljandimaa** *off.* Viljandi Maakond. ◈ *province* SW Estonia
121 E14 **Vilkaviškis** *Pol.* Wyłkowyszki. Vilkaviškis, SW Lithuania
120 F13 **Vilkija** Kaunas, C Lithuania
207 V9 **Vil'kitskogo, Proliv** *strait* N Russian Federation
Vilkovo *see* Vylkove
59 L21 **Villa Abecia** Chuquisaca, S Bolivia
Villa Acuña *see* Ciudad Acuña
42 J4 **Villa Ahumada** Chihuahua, N Mexico
47 O9 **Villa Altagracia** C Dominican Republic
58 L13 **Villa Bella** Beni, N Bolivia
106 J3 **Villablino** Castilla-León, N Spain
56 K6 **Villa Bruzual** Portuguesa, N Venezuela
107 O9 **Villacañas** Castilla-La Mancha, C Spain
107 O12 **Villacarrillo** Andalucía, S Spain
106 M7 **Villacastín** Castilla-León, N Spain
Villa Cecilia *see* Ciudad Madero
111 S9 **Villach** *Slvn.* Beljak. Kärnten, S Austria
109 B20 **Villacidro** Sardegna, Italy, C Mediterranean Sea
Villa Concepción *see* Concepción
106 L4 **Villada** Castilla-León, N Spain
42 M10 **Villa de Cos** Zacatecas, C Mexico
56 L5 **Villa de Cura** *var.* Cura. Aragua, N Venezuela
Villa del Nevoso *see* Ilirska Bistrica
Villa del Pilar *see* Pilar
106 M13 **Villa del Río** Andalucía, S Spain
Villa de Méndez *see* Méndez
44 H6 **Villa de San Antonio** Comayagua, W Honduras
107 N4 **Villadiego** Castilla-León, N Spain
107 T8 **Villafames** País Valenciano, E Spain
43 U16 **Villa Flores** Chiapas, SE Mexico
106 J3 **Villafranca del Bierzo** Castilla-León, N Spain
107 S8 **Villafranca del Cid** País Valenciano, E Spain
106 J11 **Villafranca de los Barros** Extremadura, W Spain
107 N10 **Villafranca de los Caballeros** Castilla-La Mancha, C Spain
Villafranca del Panadés *see* Vilafranca del Penedès
108 F8 **Villafranca di Verona** Veneto, NE Italy
109 J23 **Villafrati** Sicilia, Italy, C Mediterranean Sea
Villagarcía de Arosa *see* Vilagarcía de Arousa
43 O9 **Villagrán** Tamaulipas, C Mexico
63 C17 **Villaguay** Entre Ríos, E Argentina
64 O6 **Villa Hayes** Presidente Hayes, S Paraguay
43 U15 **Villahermosa** *prev.* San Juan Bautista. Tabasco, SE Mexico
107 O11 **Villahermosa** Castilla-La Mancha, C Spain
66 O11 **Villahermoso** Gomera, Islas Canarias, Spain, NE Atlantic Ocean
Villa Hidalgo *see* Hidalgo
107 T12 **Villajoyosa** *var.* La Vila Jojosa. País Valenciano, E Spain
Villa Juárez *see* Juárez
Villalba *see* Collado Villalba
43 N8 **Villaldama** Nuevo León, NE Mexico
106 L5 **Villalón de Campos** Castilla-León, N Spain
63 A25 **Villalonga** Buenos Aires, E Argentina
106 L5 **Villalpando** Castilla-León, N Spain
42 K9 **Villa Madero** *var.* Francisco I.Madero. Durango, C Mexico
43 O9 **Villa Mainero** Tamaulipas, C Mexico
Villamaña *see* Villamañán
106 L4 **Villamañán** *var.* Villamaña. Castilla-León, N Spain

◆ Country
● Country Capital
◇ Dependent Territory
○ Dependent Territory Capital
◈ Administrative Region
✕ International Airport
▲ Mountain
▲▲ Mountain Range
※ Volcano
≈ River
◎ Lake
⊞ Reservoir

64 L10 **Villa María** Córdoba, C Argentina
63 C17 **Villa María Grande** Entre Ríos, E Argentina
59 K21 **Villa Martín** Potosí, SW Bolivia
106 K15 **Villamartin** Andalucía, S Spain
64 J8 **Villa Mazán** La Rioja, NW Argentina
Villa Mercedes *see* Mercedes
Villamil *see* Puerto Villamil
Villa Nador *see* Nador
56 G5 **Villanueva** La Guajira, N Colombia
44 H5 **Villanueva** Cortés, NW Honduras
42 L11 **Villanueva** Zacatecas, C Mexico
44 I9 **Villa Nueva** Chinandega, NW Nicaragua
39 T11 **Villanueva** New Mexico, SW USA
106 M12 **Villanueva de Córdoba** Andalucía, S Spain
107 O12 **Villanueva del Arzobispo** Andalucía, S Spain
106 K11 **Villanueva de la Serena** Extremadura, W Spain
106 L5 **Villanueva del Campo** Castilla-León, N Spain
107 O11 **Villanueva de los Infantes** Castilla-La Mancha, C Spain
63 C14 **Villa Ocampo** Santa Fe, C Argentina
42 J8 **Villa Ocampo** Durango, C Mexico
42 J7 **Villa Orestes Pereyra** Durango, C Mexico
107 N3 **Villarcayo** Castilla-León, N Spain
106 L5 **Villardefrades** Castilla-León, N Spain
107 S9 **Villar del Arzobispo** País Valenciano, E Spain
107 Q6 **Villaroya de la Sierra** Aragón, NE Spain
Villarreal *see* Vila-real de los Infantes
64 P6 **Villarrica** Guairá, SE Paraguay
65 G15 **Villarrica, Volcán** ⛰ S Chile
107 P10 **Villarrobledo** Castilla-La Mancha, C Spain
107 N10 **Villarrubia de los Ojos** Castilla-La Mancha, C Spain
20 J17 **Villas** New Jersey, NE USA
107 O3 **Villasana de Mena** Castilla-León, N Spain
109 M23 **Villa San Giovanni** Calabria, S Italy
63 D18 **Villa San José** Entre Ríos, E Argentina
Villa Sanjurjo *see* Al-Hoceïma
107 P6 **Villasayas** Castilla-León, N Spain
109 C20 **Villasimius** Sardegna, Italy, C Mediterranean Sea
43 N6 **Villa Unión** Coahuila de Zaragoza, NE Mexico
42 K10 **Villa Unión** Durango, C Mexico
42 J10 **Villa Unión** Sinaloa, C Mexico
64 K12 **Villa Valeria** Córdoba, C Argentina
107 N8 **Villaverde** Madrid, C Spain
56 F10 **Villavicencio** Meta, C Colombia
106 L2 **Villaviciosa** Asturias, N Spain
106 L12 **Villaviciosa de Cordoba** Andalucía, S Spain
59 L22 **Villazón** Potosí, S Bolivia
12 J8 **Villebon, Lac** ⊚ Québec, SE Canada
Ville de Kinshasa *see* Kinshasa
104 J5 **Villedieu-les-Poëles** Manche, N France
Villefranche *see* Villefranche-sur-Saône
105 N16 **Villefranche-de-Lauragais** Haute-Garonne, S France
105 N14 **Villefranche-de-Rouergue** Aveyron, S France
105 R10 **Villefranche-sur-Saône** *var.* Villefranche. Rhône, E France
12 H9 **Ville-Marie** Québec, SE Canada
104 M15 **Villemur-sur-Tarn** Haute-Garonne, S France
107 S11 **Villena** País Valenciano, E Spain
Villeneuve-d'Agen *see* Villeneuve-sur-Lot
104 L13 **Villeneuve-sur-Lot** *var.* Villeneuve-d'Agen; *hist.* Gajac. Lot-et-Garonne, SW France
105 P6 **Villeneuve-sur-Yonne** Yonne, C France
24 H8 **Ville Platte** Louisiana, S USA
105 R11 **Villeurbanne** Rhône, E France
103 G23 **Villingen-Schwenningen** Baden-Württemberg, S Germany
31 T15 **Villisca** Iowa, C USA
Villmanstrand *see* Lappeenranta
Vilna *see* Vilnius
121 H14 **Vilnius** *Pol.* Wilno, *Ger.* Wilna; *prev.* Rus. Vilna. ● (Lithuania) Vilnius, SE Lithuania
121 H14 **Vilnius** ✕ Vilnius, SE Lithuania
119 S7 **Vil'nohirs'k** Dnipropetrovs'ka Oblast', E Ukraine
119 U8 **Vil'nyans'k** Zaporiz'ka Oblast', SE Ukraine
95 L17 **Vilppula** Häme, SW Finland
103 M20 **Vils** ⤳ SE Germany
120 C5 **Vilsandi Saar** *island* W Estonia
119 P8 **Vil'shanka** *Rus.* Olshanka. Kirovohrads'ka Oblast', C Ukraine
103 O22 **Vilshofen** Bayern, SE Germany
161 J20 **Viluppuram** Tamil Nādu, SE India
115 I16 **Vilusi** Montenegro, SW Yugoslavia
101 G18 **Vilvoorde** *Fr.* Vilvorde. Vlaams Brabant, C Belgium
Vilvorde *see* Vilvoorde
121 J14 **Vilyeyka** *Pol.* Wilejka, *Rus.* Vileyka. Minskaya Voblasts', NW Belorussia
126 Kk11 **Vilyuy** ⤳ NE Russian Federation
126 L10 **Vilyuysk** Respublika Sakha (Yakutiya), NE Russian Federation
126 K11 **Vilyuyskoye Vodokhranilishche** ⊡ NE Russian Federation
106 G2 **Vimianzo** Galicia, NW Spain
97 M19 **Vimmerby** Kalmar, S Sweden
104 L5 **Vimoutiers** Orne, N France
95 L16 **Vimpeli** Vaasa, W Finland
81 G14 **Vina** ⤳ Cameroon/Chad
64 G11 **Viña del Mar** Valparaíso, C Chile
21 R8 **Vinalhaven Island** *island* Maine, NE USA
107 T8 **Vinaròs** País Valenciano, E Spain
Vînători *see* Vânători
33 N15 **Vincennes** Indiana, N USA
205 Y12 **Vincennes Bay** *bay* Antarctica
27 O7 **Vincent** Texas, SW USA
97 H24 **Vindeby** Fyn, C Denmark
95 I15 **Vindeln** Västerbotten, N Sweden
97 F21 **Vinderup** Ringkøbing, C Denmark
Vindhya Mountains *see* Vindhya Range
159 N14 **Vindhya Range** *var.* Vindhya Mountains. ▲ N India
Vindobona *see* Wien
22 K6 **Vine Grove** Kentucky, S USA
20 J17 **Vineland** New Jersey, NE USA
118 E11 **Vinga** Arad, W Romania
97 M16 **Vingåker** Södermanland, C Sweden
178 Jj8 **Vinh** Nghê An, N Vietnam
106 I5 **Vinhais** Bragança, N Portugal
178 K9 **Vinh Linh** Quang Tri, C Vietnam
Vinh Loi *see* Bac Liêu
178 Jj14 **Vinh Long** *var.* Vinhlong. Vinh Long, S Vietnam
115 Q18 **Vinica** NE FYR Macedonia
111 V13 **Vinica** SE Slovenia
116 G8 **Vinishte** Oblast Montana, NW Bulgaria
29 Q8 **Vinita** Oklahoma, C USA
Vinju Mare *see* Vânju Mare
100 I11 **Vinkeveen** Utrecht, C Netherlands
118 L6 **Vin'kivtsi** Khmel'nyts'ka Oblast', W Ukraine
114 I10 **Vinkovci** *Ger.* Winkowitz, *Hung.* Vinkovcze. Vukovar-Srijem, E Croatia
Vinkovcze *see* Vinkovci
Vinnitsa *see* Vinnytsya
Vinnitskaya Oblast'/Vinnytsya *see* Vinnyts'ka Oblast'
118 M7 **Vinnyts'ka Oblast'** *var.* Vinnytsya, *Rus.* Vinnitskaya Oblast'. ◆ *province* C Ukraine
119 N6 **Vinnytsya** *Rus.* Vinnitsa. Vinnyts'ka Oblast', C Ukraine
119 N6 **Vinnytsya** ✕ Vinnyts'ka Oblast', N Ukraine
Vinogradov *see* Vynohradiv
204 L8 **Vinson Massif** ▲ Antarctica
96 G11 **Vinstra** Oppland, S Norway
118 K12 **Vintilă Vodă** Buzău, SE Romania
31 X13 **Vinton** Iowa, C USA
24 F9 **Vinton** Louisiana, S USA
161 J17 **Vinukonda** Andhra Pradesh, E India
Vioara *see* Ocnele Mari
85 E23 **Vioolsdrif** Northern Cape, SW South Africa
84 M13 **Viphya Mountains** ▲ C Malawi
179 Qq11 **Virac** Catanduanes Island, N Philippines
128 K8 **Virandozero** Respublika Kareliya, NW Russian Federation
143 P16 **Viranşehir** Şanlıurfa, SE Turkey
160 D13 **Virār** Mahārāshtra, W India
9 W16 **Virden** Manitoba, S Canada
32 K14 **Virden** Illinois, N USA
Virdois *see* Virrat
104 J5 **Vire** Calvados, N France
104 J4 **Vire** ⤳ N France
85 A15 **Virei** Namibe, SW Angola
Virful Moldoveanu *see* Vârful Moldoveanu
37 R5 **Virgina Peak** ▲ Nevada, W USA
47 U9 **Virgin Gorda** *island* C British Virgin Islands
85 I22 **Virginia** Free State, C South Africa
32 K13 **Virginia** Illinois, N USA
31 W4 **Virginia** Minnesota, N USA
23 T6 **Virginia** *off.* Commonwealth of Virginia; also known as Mother of Presidents, Mother of States, Old Dominion. ◆ *state* NE USA
23 Y7 **Virginia Beach** Virginia, NE USA
35 R11 **Virginia City** Montana, NW USA
37 Q6 **Virginia City** Nevada, W USA
12 H8 **Virginiatown** Ontario, S Canada
Virgin Islands *see* British Virgin Islands
47 T9 **Virgin Islands (US)** *var.* Virgin Islands of the United States; *prev.* Danish West Indies. ◇ *US unincorporated territory* E West Indies
47 T9 **Virgin Passage** *passage* Puerto Rico/Virgin Islands (US)
37 Y10 **Virgin River** ⤳ Nevada/Utah, W USA
Virihaur *see* Virihaure
94 H12 **Virihaure** *var.* Virihaur. ⊚ N Sweden
178 Jj11 **Virôchey** Rôtânôkiri, NE Cambodia
95 N19 **Virolahti** Kymi, S Finland
32 J8 **Viroqua** Wisconsin, N USA
114 G8 **Virovitica** *Ger.* Virovititz, *Hung.* Verőcze; *prev. Ger.* Werowitz. Virovitica-Podravina, NE Croatia
114 G8 **Virovitica-Podravina** *off.* Virovitičko-Podravska Županija. ◆ *province* NE Croatia
Virovititz *see* Virovitica
115 J17 **Virpazar** Montenegro, SW Yugoslavia
95 L17 **Virrat** *Swe.* Virdois. Häme, SW Finland
97 M20 **Virserum** Kalmar, S Sweden
101 K25 **Virton** Luxembourg, SE Belgium
120 F5 **Virtsu** *Ger.* Werder. Läänemaa, W Estonia
58 C12 **Virú** La Libertad, C Peru
Virudhunagar *see* Virudunagar
161 H23 **Virudunagar** *var.* Virudhunagar. Tamil Nādu, SE India
120 I3 **Viru-Jaagupi** *Ger.* Sankt-Jakobi. Lääne-Virumaa, NE Estonia
59 N19 **Viru-Viru** *var.* Santa Cruz. ✕ (Santa Cruz) Santa Cruz, C Bolivia
115 E15 **Vis** *It.* Lissa; *anc.* Issa. *island* S Croatia
Vis *see* Fish
120 I12 **Visaginas** *prev.* Sniečkus. Ignalina, E Lithuania
161 M15 **Visākhapatnam** Andhra Pradesh, SE India
37 R11 **Visalia** California, W USA
Višău *see* Vişeu
179 Qq12 **Visayan Sea** *sea* C Philippines
97 P19 **Visby** *Ger.* Wisby. Gotland, SE Sweden
207 N9 **Viscount Melville Sound** *prev.* Melville Sound. *sound* Northwest Territories, N Canada
101 L19 **Visé** Liège, E Belgium
114 K13 **Višegrad** SE Bosnia and Herzegovina
60 L12 **Viseu** Pará, NE Brazil
106 H7 **Viseu** *prev.* Vizeu. Viseu, N Portugal
106 H7 **Viseu** *var.* Vizeu. ◆ *district* N Portugal
118 I8 **Vişeu** *Hung.* Visó; *prev.* Višău. ⤳ NW Romania
118 I8 **Vişeu de Sus** *var.* Vişeul de Sus, *Ger.* Oberwischau, *Hung.* Felsővisó. Maramureş, N Romania
Vişeul de Sus *see* Vişeu de Sus
129 R10 **Vishera** ⤳ NW Russian Federation
97 J19 **Viskafors** Älvsborg, S Sweden
97 J20 **Viskan** ⤳ S Sweden
97 L21 **Vislanda** Kronoberg, S Sweden
Vislinskiy Zaliv *see* Vistula Lagoon
Visó *see* Vişeu
114 H13 **Visoko** C Bosnia and Herzegovina
108 A9 **Viso, Monte** ▲ NW Italy
110 E10 **Visp** Valais, SW Switzerland
110 E10 **Vispa** ⤳ S Switzerland
97 M21 **Vissefjärda** Kalmar, S Sweden
102 I11 **Visselhövede** Niedersachsen, NW Germany
97 G23 **Vissenbjerg** Fyn, C Denmark
37 U17 **Vista** California, W USA
60 C11 **Vista Alegre** Amazonas, NW Brazil
116 J13 **Vistonída, Límni** ⊚ NE Greece
Vistula *see* Wisła
121 A14 **Vistula Lagoon** *Ger.* Frisches Haff, *Pol.* Zalew Wiślany, *Rus.* Vislinskiy Zaliv. *lagoon* Poland/Russian Federation
116 I8 **Vit** ⤳ NW Bulgaria
Vitebsk *see* Vitsyebsk
Vitebskaya Oblast' *see* Vitsyebskaya Voblasts'
109 H14 **Viterbo** *anc.* Vicus Elbii. Lazio, C Italy
114 H12 **Vitez** C Bosnia and Herzegovina
178 J15 **Vi Thanh** Cân Thơ, S Vietnam
Viti *see* Fiji
194 K12 **Vitiaz Strait** *strait* NE PNG
106 J7 **Vitigudino** Castilla-León, N Spain
197 H15 **Viti Levu** *island* W Fiji
126 Kk14 **Vitim** ⤳ C Russian Federation
126 Kk13 **Vitimskiy** Irkutskaya Oblast', C Russian Federation
111 V2 **Vitis** Niederösterreich, N Austria
Vitoria *see* Vitoria-Gasteiz
61 O20 **Vitória** Espírito Santo, SE Brazil
Vitoria Bank *see* Vitória Seamount
61 N18 **Vitória da Conquista** Bahia, E Brazil
107 P3 **Vitoria-Gasteiz** *var.* Vitoria, *Eng.* Vittoria. País Vasco, N Spain
67 J16 **Vitória Seamount** *var.* Victoria Bank, Vitoria Bank. *undersea feature* C Atlantic Ocean
114 F13 **Vitorog** ▲ SW Bosnia and Herzegovina
104 J6 **Vitré** Ille-et-Vilaine, NW France
105 R5 **Vitry-le-François** Marne, N France
116 D13 **Vítsoi** ▲ N Greece
120 N13 **Vitsyebsk** *Rus.* Vitebsk. Vitsyebskaya Voblasts', NE Belorussia
120 K13 **Vitsyebskaya Voblasts'** *prev.* Rus. Vitebskaya Oblast'. ◆ *province* N Belorussia
94 J11 **Vittangi** Norrbotten, N Sweden
105 R8 **Vitteaux** Côte d'Or, C France
105 S6 **Vittel** Vosges, NE France
97 N15 **Vittinge** Västmanland, C Sweden
109 K25 **Vittoria** Sicilia, Italy, C Mediterranean Sea
Vittoria *see* Vitoria-Gasteiz
108 I7 **Vittorio Veneto** Veneto, NE Italy
183 Q9 **Vitu Levu** *island* W Fiji
199 Jj7 **Vityaz Seamount** *undersea feature* C Pacific Ocean
183 Q7 **Vityaz Trench** *undersea feature* W Pacific Ocean
110 G8 **Vitznau** Luzern, W Switzerland
106 I1 **Viveiro** Galicia, NW Spain
107 S9 **Viver** País Valenciano, E Spain
105 Q13 **Viverais, Monts du** ▲ C France
126 Ii10 **Vivi** ⤳ N Russian Federation
24 F4 **Vivian** Louisiana, S USA
31 N10 **Vivian** South Dakota, N USA
105 R13 **Viviers** Ardèche, E France
Vivis *see* Vevey
85 K19 **Vivo** Northern, NE South Africa
104 L10 **Vivonne** Vienne, W France
197 G14 **Viwa** *island* Yasawa Group, NW Fiji
Vizakna *see* Ocna Sibiului
107 O2 **Vizcaya** *Basq.* Bizkaia. ◆ *province* País Vasco, N Spain
Vizcaya, Golfo de *see* Biscay, Bay of
142 C10 **Vize** Kırklareli, NW Turkey
126 I2 **Vize, Ostrov** *island* Severnaya Zemlya, N Russian Federation
Vizeu *see* Viseu
161 M15 **Vizianagaram** *var.* Vizianagram. Andhra Pradesh, E India
Vizianagram *see* Vizianagaram
105 S12 **Vizille** Isère, E France
129 R11 **Vizinga** Respublika Komi, NW Russian Federation
118 M13 **Viziru** Brăila, SE Romania
115 K21 **Vjosës, Lumi i** *var.* Vijosa, Vijosë, *Gk.* Aóos. ⤳ Albania/Greece *see also* Aóos
101 H18 **Vlaams Brabant** ◆ *province* C Belgium
Vlaanderen *see* Flanders
100 G12 **Vlaardingen** Zuid-Holland, SW Netherlands
118 F10 **Vlădeasa, Vârful** *prev.* Vîrful Vlădeasa. ▲ NW Romania
Vlădeasa, Vîrful *see* Vlădeasa, Vârful
115 P16 **Vladičin Han** Serbia, SE Yugoslavia
131 O16 **Vladikavkaz** *prev.* Dzaudzhikau, Ordzhonikidze. Respublika Severnaya Osetiya, SW Russian Federation
130 M3 **Vladimir** Vladimirskaya Oblast', W Russian Federation
150 M7 **Vladimirovka** Kustanay, N Kazakhstan
Vladimirovka *see* Yuzhno-Sakhalinsk
130 L3 **Vladimirskaya Oblast'** ◆ *province* W Russian Federation
130 I3 **Vladimirskiy Tupik** Smolenskaya Oblast', W Russian Federation
Vladimir-Volynskiy *see* Volodymyr-Volyns'kyy
127 Nn18 **Vladivostok** Primorskiy Kray, SE Russian Federation
119 U13 **Vladyslavivka** Respublika Krym, S Ukraine
100 P6 **Vlagtwedde** Groningen, NE Netherlands
Vlajna *see* Kukavica
114 J12 **Vlasenica** E Bosnia and Herzegovina
114 G12 **Vlašić** ▲ C Bosnia and Herzegovina
113 D17 **Vlašim** *Ger.* Wlaschim. Střední Čechy, C Czech Republic
115 P15 **Vlasotince** Serbia, SE Yugoslavia
126 Ll7 **Vlasovo** Respublika Sakha (Yakutiya), NE Russian Federation
100 I11 **Vleuten** Utrecht, C Netherlands
100 I5 **Vlieland** *Fris.* Flylân. *island* Waddeneilanden, N Netherlands
100 I5 **Vliestroom** *strait* NW Netherlands
101 J14 **Vlijmen** Noord-Brabant, S Netherlands
101 E15 **Vlissingen** *Eng.* Flushing, *Fr.* Flessingue. Zeeland, SW Netherlands
Vlodava *see* Włodawa
Vlonë/Vlora *see* Vlorë
115 K22 **Vlorë** *prev.* Vlonë, *It.* Valona, Vlora. Vlorë, SW Albania
115 K22 **Vlorë** ◆ *district* SW Albania
115 K22 **Vlorës, Gjiri i** *var.* Valona Bay. *bay* SW Albania
Vlotslavsk *see* Włocławek
113 C16 **Vltava** *Ger.* Moldau. ⤳ W Czech Republic
130 K3 **Vnukovo** ✕ (Moskva) Gorod Moskva, W Russian Federation
27 Q9 **Voca** Texas, SW USA
111 R5 **Vöcklabruck** Oberösterreich, NW Austria
114 D13 **Vodice** Šibenik, S Croatia
128 K10 **Vodlozero, Ozero** ⊚ NW Russian Federation
114 A10 **Vodnjan** *It.* Dignano d'Istria. Istra, NW Croatia
129 S9 **Vodnyy** Respublika Komi, NW Russian Federation
97 G20 **Vodskov** Nordjylland, N Denmark
94 H4 **Vogar** Sudhurland, SW Iceland
195 N16 **Vogel, Cape** *headland* SE PNG
Vogelkop *see* Doberai, Jazirah
79 X15 **Vogel Peak** *prev.* Dim lang. ▲ E Nigeria
103 H17 **Vogelsberg** ▲ C Germany
108 D8 **Voghera** Lombardia, N Italy
114 I13 **Vogošća** SE Bosnia and Herzegovina
103 M17 **Vogtland** *historical region* E Germany
129 V12 **Vogul'skiy Kamen', Gora** ▲ NW Russian Federation
197 H6 **Voh** Province Nord, C New Caledonia
Vohémar *see* Iharaña
180 H8 **Vohimena, Tanjona** *Fr.* Cap Sainte Marie. *headland* S Madagascar
180 J6 **Vohipeno** Fianarantsoa, SE Madagascar
120 H5 **Võhma** *Ger.* Wöchma. Viljandimaa, S Estonia
83 J20 **Voi** Coast, S Kenya
78 K15 **Voinjama** N Liberia
105 S12 **Voiron** Isère, E France
111 V8 **Voitsberg** Steiermark, SE Austria
97 F24 **Vojens** *Ger.* Woyens. Sønderjylland, SW Denmark
114 K9 **Vojvodina** *Ger.* Wojwodina. *cultural region* N Yugoslavia
13 S6 **Volant** ⤳ Québec, SE Canada
Volaterrae *see* Volterra
45 P15 **Volcán** *var.* Hato del Volcán. Chiriquí, W Panama
Volchansk *see* Vovchans'k
Volchya *see* Vovcha
96 D10 **Volda** Møre og Romsdal, S Norway
100 J9 **Volendam** Noord-Holland, C Netherlands
128 L15 **Volga** Yaroslavskaya Oblast', W Russian Federation
31 R10 **Volga** South Dakota, N USA
125 Gc11 **Volga** ⤳ NW Russian Federation
Volga-Baltic Waterway *see* Volgo-Baltiyskiy Kanal
Volga Hills/Volga Uplands *see* Privolzhskaya Vozvyshennost'
128 L13 **Volgo-Baltiyskiy Kanal** *Eng.* Volga-Baltic Waterway. *canal* NW Russian Federation
130 M12 **Volgodonsk** Rostovskaya Oblast', SW Russian Federation
131 O10 **Volgograd** *prev.* Stalingrad, Tsaritsyn. Volgogradskaya Oblast', SW Russian Federation
131 N9 **Volgogradskaya Oblast'** ◆ *province* SW Russian Federation
131 P10 **Volgogradskoye Vodokhranilishche** ⊡ SW Russian Federation
103 J19 **Volkach** Bayern, C Germany
111 U9 **Völkermarkt** *Slvn.* Velikovec. Kärnten, S Austria
128 I12 **Volkhov** Leningradskaya Oblast', NW Russian Federation
103 D20 **Völklingen** Saarland, SW Germany
Volkovysk *see* Vawkavysk
Volkovyskiye Vysoty *see* Vawkavyskaye Wzvyshsha
85 K22 **Volksrust** Mpumalanga, E South Africa
100 L8 **Vollenhove** Overijssel, N Netherlands
121 L16 **Volma** *Rus.* Volma. ⤳ C Belorussia
Volmari *see* Valmiera
119 W9 **Volnovakha** Donets'ka Oblast', SE Ukraine
118 K6 **Volochys'k** Khmel'nyts'ka Oblast', W Ukraine
119 O6 **Volodarka** Kyyivs'ka Oblast', N Ukraine
119 W9 **Volodars'ke** Donets'ka Oblast', E Ukraine
131 R13 **Volodarskiy** Astrakhanskaya Oblast', SW Russian Federation
151 P7 **Volodarskoye** Kokshetau, N Kazakhstan
119 N8 **Volodars'k-Volyns'kyy** Zhytomyrs'ka Oblast', N Ukraine
118 K3 **Volodymerets'** Rivnens'ka Oblast', NW Ukraine
118 I3 **Volodymyr-Volyns'kyy** *Pol.* Włodzimierz, *Rus.* Vladimir-Volynskiy. Volyns'ka Oblast', NW Ukraine
128 L14 **Vologda** Vologodskaya Oblast', W Russian Federation
128 L12 **Vologodskaya Oblast'** ◆ *province* NW Russian Federation
130 K3 **Volokolamsk** Moskovskaya Oblast', W Russian Federation
130 K9 **Volokonovka** Belgorodskaya Oblast', W Russian Federation
117 G16 **Vólos** Thessalía, C Greece
128 M11 **Voloshka** Arkhangel'skaya Oblast', NW Russian Federation
Vološinovo *see* Novi Bečej
118 H7 **Volovets'** Zakarpats'ka Oblast', W Ukraine
116 K7 **Volovo** Razgradska Oblast, N Bulgaria
Volozhin *see* Valozhyn
131 Q7 **Vol'sk** Saratovskaya Oblast', W Russian Federation
79 Q17 **Volta** ⤳ SE Ghana
Volta Blanche *see* White Volta
79 P16 **Volta, Lake** ⊡ SE Ghana
Volta Noire *see* Black Volta
62 O9 **Volta Redonda** Rio de Janeiro, SE Brazil
Volta Rouge *see* Red Volta
108 F12 **Volterra** *anc.* Volaterrae. Toscana, C Italy
109 K17 **Volturno** ⤳ S Italy
115 I15 **Volujak** ▲ SW Yugoslavia
Volunteer Island *see* Starbuck Island
67 F24 **Volunteer Point** *headland* East Falkland, Falkland Islands
Volunteer State *see* Tennessee
116 H13 **Vólvi, Límni** ⊚ N Greece
Volyn *see* Volyns'ka Oblast'
118 I3 **Volyns'ka Oblast'** *var.* Volyn, *Rus.* Volynskaya Oblast'. ◆ *province* NW Ukraine
131 Q3 **Volzhsk** Respublika Mariy El, W Russian Federation
Volynskaya Oblast' *see* Volyns'ka Oblast'
131 O10 **Volzhskiy** Volgogradskaya Oblast', SW Russian Federation
180 I7 **Vondrozo** Fianarantsoa, SE Madagascar
116 K9 **Voneshta Voda** Loveshka Oblast, N Bulgaria
41 P10 **Von Frank Mountain** ▲ Alaska, USA
117 C17 **Vónitsa** Dytikí Ellás, W Greece
120 J6 **Võnnu** *Ger.* Wendau. Tartumaa, SE Estonia
100 G12 **Voorburg** Zuid-Holland, W Netherlands
100 H11 **Voorschoten** Zuid-Holland, W Netherlands
100 M11 **Voorst** Gelderland, E Netherlands
100 K11 **Voorthuizen** Gelderland, C Netherlands
94 L2 **Vopnafjördhur** Austurland, E Iceland
94 L2 **Vopnafjördhur** *bay* E Iceland
Vora *see* Vorë
121 H15 **Voranava** *Pol.* Werenów, *Rus.* Voronovo. Hrodzyenskaya Voblasts', W Belorussia
110 I8 **Vorarlberg** *off.* Land Vorarlberg. ◆ *state* W Austria
111 X7 **Vorau** Steiermark, E Austria
100 N11 **Vorden** Gelderland, E Netherlands
110 H9 **Vorderrhein** ⤳ SE Switzerland
94 J2 **Vordhufell** ▲ N Iceland
97 I24 **Vordingborg** Storstrøm, SE Denmark
115 K19 **Vorë** *var.* Vora. Tiranë, W Albania
117 H17 **Vóreioi Sporádes** *var.* Vórioi Sporádhes, *Eng.* Northern Sporades. *island group* E Greece
117 J17 **Vóreion Aigaíon** *Eng.* Aegean North. ◆ *region* SE Greece
117 G18 **Voreiós Evvoïkós Kólpos** *gulf* E Greece
207 S16 **Voring Plateau** *undersea feature* N Norwegian Sea
Vórioi Sporádhes *see* Vóreioi Sporádes
129 W4 **Vorkuta** Respublika Komi, NW Russian Federation
97 I14 **Vorma** ⤳ S Norway
120 E4 **Vormsi** *var.* Vormsi Saar, *Ger.* Worms, Swed. Ormsö. *island* W Estonia
Vormsi Saar *see* Vormsi
126 Hh12 **Vorogovo** Krasnoyarskiy Kray, C Russian Federation
131 N7 **Vorona** ⤳ W Russian Federation
130 L7 **Voronezh** Voronezhskaya Oblast', W Russian Federation
130 L7 **Voronezh** ⤳ W Russian Federation
130 K8 **Voronezhskaya Oblast'** ◆ *province* W Russian Federation
Voronovitsya *see* Voronovytsya
Voronovo *see* Voranava
119 N6 **Voronovytsya** *Rus.* Voronovitsya. Vinnyts'ka Oblast', C Ukraine
126 Hh7 **Vorontsovo** Taymyrskiy (Dolgano-Nenetskiy) Avtonomnyy Okrug, N Russian Federation
128 K3 **Voron'ya** ⤳ NW Russian Federation
Voropayevo *see* Varapayeva
Voroshilov *see* Ussuriysk
Voroshilovgrad *see* Luhans'k, Ukraine
Voroshilovgrad *see* Luhans'ka Oblast', Ukraine
Voroshilovgradskaya Oblast' *see* Luhans'ka Oblast'
Voroshilovsk *see* Stavropol', Russian Federation
Voroshilovsk *see* Alchevs'k, Ukraine
143 V13 **Vorotan** *Az.* Bärgușad. ⤳ Armenia/Azerbaijan
131 P3 **Vorotynets** Nizhegorodskaya Oblast', W Russian Federation
119 S3 **Vorozhba** Sums'ka Oblast', NE Ukraine
119 T5 **Vorskla** ⤳ Russian Federation/Ukraine
101 I17 **Vorst** Antwerpen, N Belgium
85 G21 **Vorstershoop** North-West, N South Africa
120 H6 **Võrtsjärv** *Ger.* Wirz-See. ⊚ SE Estonia
120 J7 **Võru** *Ger.* Werro. Võrumaa, SE Estonia
153 R11 **Vorukh** N Tajikistan
120 I7 **Võrumaa** *off.* Võru Maakond. ◆ *province* SE Estonia
85 G24 **Vosburg** Northern Cape, W South Africa
153 Q14 **Vose'** *Rus.* Vose; *prev.* Aral. SW Tajikistan
105 S6 **Vosges** ◆ *department* NE France
105 U6 **Vosges** ▲ NE France
128 K13 **Voskresenkoye** Vologodskaya Oblast', NW Russian Federation
130 L4 **Voskresensk** Moskovskaya Oblast', W Russian Federation
131 P2 **Voskresenskoye** Nizhegorodskaya Oblast', W Russian Federation
131 V6 **Voskresenskoye** Respublika Bashkortostan, W Russian Federation
96 D13 **Voss** Hordaland, S Norway
96 D13 **Voss** *physical region* S Norway
101 I16 **Vosselaar** Antwerpen, N Belgium
96 D13 **Vosso** ⤳ S Norway
Vostochno-Kazakhstanskaya Oblast' *see* Vostochnyy Kazakhstan
151 T12 **Vostochno-Kounradskiy** *Kaz.* Shyghys Qongyrat. Zhezkazgan, C Kazakhstan
127 N4 **Vostochno-Sibirskoye More** *Eng.* East Siberian Sea. *sea* Arctic Ocean
151 X10 **Vostochnyy Kazakhstan** *off.* Vostochno-Kazakhstanskaya Oblast', *var.* East Kazakhstan, *Kaz.* Shyghys Qazagastan Oblysy. ◆ *province* E Kazakhstan
Vostochnyy Sayan *see* Eastern Sayans
Vostock Island *see* Vostok Island
205 U10 **Vostok** *Russian research station* Antarctica
203 X5 **Vostok Island** *var.* Vostock Island; *prev.* Stavers Island. *island* Line Islands, SE Kiribati
131 T2 **Votkinsk** Udmurtskaya Respublika, NW Russian Federation
129 U15 **Votkinskoye Vodokhranilishche** *var.* Votkinsk Reservoir. ⊡ NW Russian Federation
Votkinsk Reservoir *see* Votkinskoye Vodokhranilishche
62 J7 **Votuporanga** São Paulo, S Brazil
106 H7 **Vouga, Rio** ⤳ N Portugal
117 E14 **Voúrinos** ▲ N Greece
117 G24 **Voúxa, Ákra** *headland* Kríti, Greece, E Mediterranean Sea
105 R4 **Vouziers** Ardennes, N France
119 V7 **Vovcha** *Rus.* Volchya. ⤳ E Ukraine
119 V4 **Vovchans'k** *Rus.* Volchansk. Kharkivs'ka Oblast', E Ukraine
105 N6 **Voves** Eure-et-Loir, C France
81 M14 **Vovodo** ⤳ S Central African Republic
96 M12 **Voxna** Gävleborg, C Sweden
96 L11 **Voxnan** ⤳ C Sweden
116 F7 **Voynishka Reka** ⤳ NW Bulgaria
129 T9 **Voyvozh** Respublika Komi, NW Russian Federation
128 M12 **Vozhega** Vologodskaya Oblast', NW Russian Federation
128 L12 **Vozhe, Ozero** ⊚ NW Russian Federation
119 Q9 **Voznesens'k** *Rus.* Voznesensk. Mykolayivs'ka Oblast', S Ukraine
128 J12 **Voznesen'ye** Leningradskaya Oblast', NW Russian Federation
150 J14 **Vozrozhdeniya, Ostrov** *Uzb.* Wozrojdeniye Oroli. *island* Kazakhstan/Uzbekistan
97 G20 **Vrå** *var.* Vraa. Nordjylland, N Denmark
Vraa *see* Vrå
116 H9 **Vrachesh** Sofiyska Oblast, NW Bulgaria
117 C19 **Vrachíonas** ▲ Zákynthos, Iónioi Nísoi, Greece, C Mediterranean Sea
119 P8 **Vradiyivka** Mykolayivs'ka Oblast', S Ukraine
115 G14 **Vran** ▲ SW Bosnia and Herzegovina
118 K12 **Vrancea** ◆ *county* E Romania
153 T14 **Vrang** SE Tajikistan
127 Oo2 **Vrangelya, Ostrov** *Eng.* Wrangel Island. *island* NE Russian Federation
114 H13 **Vranica** ▲ C Bosnia and Herzegovina
115 O16 **Vranje** Serbia, SE Yugoslavia
Vranov *see* Vranov nad Topľou
113 N19 **Vranov nad Topľou** *var.* Vranov, *Hung.* Varannó. Východné Slovensko, E Slovakia
116 H8 **Vratsa** Oblast Montana, NW Bulgaria
116 F10 **Vrattsa** *prev.* Mirovo. Sofiyska Oblast, W Bulgaria
114 G11 **Vrbanja** ⤳ NW Bosnia and Herzegovina
114 K9 **Vrbas** Serbia, NW Yugoslavia
114 G13 **Vrbas** ⤳ N Bosnia and Herzegovina
114 E8 **Vrbovec** Grad Zagreb, N Croatia
114 C9 **Vrbovsko** Primorje-Gorski Kotar, NW Croatia
113 E15 **Vrchlabí** *Ger.* Hohenelbe. Východní Čechy, NE Czech Republic
85 J22 **Vrede** Free State, E South Africa
102 E13 **Vreden** Nordrhein-Westfalen, NW Germany
85 E25 **Vredenburg** Western Cape, SW South Africa
101 I23 **Vresse-sur-Semois** Namur, SE Belgium
97 L16 **Vretstorp** Örebro, C Sweden
115 G15 **Vrgorac** *prev.* Vrhgorac. Split-Dalmacija, SE Croatia
Vrhgorac *see* Vrgorac
111 T12 **Vrhnika** *Ger.* Oberlaibach. W Slovenia
161 I21 **Vriddhāchalam** Tamil Nādu, SE India
100 N6 **Vries** Drenthe, NE Netherlands
100 O10 **Vriezenveen** Overijssel, E Netherlands
97 L20 **Vrigstad** Jönköping, S Sweden
110 H9 **Vrin** Graubünden, S Switzerland
114 E13 **Vrlika** Split-Dalmacija, S Croatia
115 M14 **Vrnjačka Banja** Serbia, C Yugoslavia
Vrondádhes/Vrondados *see* Vrontádos
117 L18 **Vrontádos** *var.* Vrondados; *prev.* Vrondádhes. Chíos, E Greece
100 N9 **Vroomshoop** Overijssel, E Netherlands
114 N10 **Vršac** *Ger.* Werschetz, *Hung.* Versecz. Serbia, NE Yugoslavia
114 M10 **Vršački Kanal** *canal* N Yugoslavia
85 H21 **Vryburg** North-West, N South Africa

◆ Country
● Country Capital
◇ Dependent Territory
○ Dependent Territory Capital
◆ Administrative Region
✕ International Airport
▲ Mountain
▲ Mountain Range
⛰ Volcano
⤳ River
⊚ Lake
⊡ Reservoir

85 K22 **Vryheid** KwaZulu/Natal, E South Africa
113 I18 **Vsetín** *Ger.* Wsetin. Severní Morava, E Czech Republic
113 J20 **Vtáčnik** *Hung.* Madaras, Ptacsnik; *prev.* Ptačnik. ▲ W Slovakia
Vuadil' *see* Wodil
Vuanggava *see* Vuaqava
197 K15 **Vuaqava** *prev.* Vuanggava. *island* Lau Group, SE Fiji
116 I11 **Vŭcha** ∾ SW Bulgaria
115 N16 **Vučitrn** Serbia, S Yugoslavia
101 J14 **Vught** Noord-Brabant, S Netherlands
119 W8 **Vuhledar** Donets'ka Oblast', E Ukraine
114 I9 **Vuka** ∾ E Croatia
115 K17 **Vukël** *var.* Vukli. Shkodër, N Albania
Vukli *see* Vukël
114 J9 **Vukovar** *Hung.* Vukovár. Vukovar-Srijem, E Croatia
114 I10 **Vukovar-Srijem** *off.* Vukovarsko-Srijemska Županija. ◆ *province* E Croatia
129 U8 **Vuktyl** Respublika Komi, NW Russian Federation
9 Q17 **Vulcan** Alberta, SW Canada
118 G12 **Vulcan** *Ger.* Wulkan, *Hung.* Zsilyvajdevulkán; *prev.* Crivadia Vulcanului, Vaidei, *Hung.* Sily-Vajdej, Vajdej. Hunedoara, W Romania
118 M12 **Vulcănești** *Rus.* Vulkaneshty. S Moldova
109 L22 **Vulcano, Isola** *island* Isole Eolie, S Italy
116 G7 **Vŭlchedrŭm** Oblast Montana, NW Bulgaria
116 N8 **Vŭlchidol** *prev.* Kurt-Dere. Varnenska Oblast, NE Bulgaria
Vulkaneshty *see* Vulcănești
38 J13 **Vulture Mountains** ▲ Arizona, SW USA
178 K14 **Vung Tau** *prev. Fr.* Cape Saint Jacques, Cap Saint-Jacques. Ba Ria-Vung Tau, S Vietnam
197 I15 **Vunisea** Kadavu, SE Fiji
Vuohčču *see* Vuotso
95 N15 **Vuokatti** Oulu, C Finland
95 M15 **Vuolijoki** Oulu, C Finland
94 J13 **Vuollerim** Norrbotten, N Sweden
Vuoreija *see* Vardø
94 L10 **Vuotso** *Lapp.* Vuohčču. Lappi, N Finland
116 J11 **Vŭrbitsa** *prev.* Filevo. Khaskovska Oblast, S Bulgaria
116 J12 **Vŭrbitsa** ∾ S Bulgaria
131 Q4 **Vurnary** Chuvashskaya Respublika, W Russian Federation
116 G8 **Vŭrshets** Oblast Montana, NW Bulgaria
121 F17 **Vyalikaya Byerastavitsa** *Pol.* Brzostowica Wielka, *Rus.* Bol'shaya Berëstovitsa; *prev.* Velikaya Berestovitsa. Hrodzyenskaya Voblasts', SW Belarus
121 N20 **Vyaliki Bor** *Rus.* Velikiy Bor. Homyel'skaya Voblasts', SE Belarus
121 J18 **Vyaliki Rozhan** *Rus.* Bol'shoy Rozhan. Minskaya Voblasts', S Belarus
128 H10 **Vyartsilya** *Fin.* Värtsilä. Respublika Kareliya, NW Russian Federation
121 K17 **Vyasyeya** *Rus.* Veseya. Minskaya Voblasts', C Belarus
129 R15 **Vyatka** ∾ NW Russian Federation
Vyatka *see* Kirov
129 S16 **Vyatskiye Polyany** Kirovskaya Oblast', NW Russian Federation
127 Nn16 **Vyazemskiy** Khabarovskiy Kray, SE Russian Federation
130 I4 **Vyaz'ma** Smolenskaya Oblast', W Russian Federation
131 N3 **Vyazniki** Vladimirskaya Oblast', W Russian Federation
131 O8 **Vyazovka** Volgogradskaya Oblast', SW Russian Federation
121 J14 **Vyazyn'** *Rus.* Vyazyn'. Minskaya Voblasts', NW Belarus
128 G11 **Vyborg** *Fin.* Viipuri. Leningradskaya Oblast', NW Russian Federation
129 P11 **Vychegda** *var.* Vichegda. ∾ NW Russian Federation
113 L18 **Východné Slovensko** ◆ *region* E Slovakia
113 E16 **Východní Čechy** *off.* Východočeský Kraj. ◆ *region* N Czech Republic
126 Jj16 **Vydrino** Respublika Buryatiya, S Russian Federation
121 L14 **Vyelyewshchyna** *Rus.* Velevshchina. Vitsyebskaya Voblasts', N Belarus
121 P16 **Vyeramyeyki** *Rus.* Veremeyki. Mahilyowskaya Voblasts', E Belarus
120 K11 **Vyerkhnyadzvinsk** *Rus.* Verkhnedvinsk. Vitsyebskaya Voblasts', N Belarus
121 P18 **Vyetka** *Rus.* Vetka. Homyel'skaya Voblasts', SE Belarus
120 L12 **Vyetryna** *Rus.* Vetrino. Vitsyebskaya Voblasts', N Belarus
Vygonovskoye, Ozero *see* Vyhanawskaye, Vozyera
128 J9 **Vygozero, Ozero** ◎ NW Russian Federation
Vyhanashchanskaye Vozyera *see* Vyhanawskaye, Vozyera
121 I18 **Vyhanawskaye, Vozyera** *var.* Vyhanashchanskaye Vozyera, *Rus.* Ozero Vygonovskoye. ◎ SW Belarus
131 N4 **Vyksa** Nizhegorodskaya Oblast', W Russian Federation
119 O12 **Vylkove** *Rus.* Vilkovo. Odes'ka Oblast', SW Ukraine
129 R9 **Vym'** ∾ NW Russian Federation
118 H8 **Vynohradiv** *Cz.* Sevluš, *Hung.* Nagyszőllős, *Rus.* Vinogradov; *prev.* Sevlyush. Zakarpats'ka Oblast', W Ukraine
128 G13 **Vyritsa** Leningradskaya Oblast', NW Russian Federation
99 J19 **Vyrnwy** *Wel.* Afon Efyrnwy. ∾ E Wales, UK
151 X9 **Vyshe Ivanovskiy Belak, Gora** ▲ E Kazakhstan
119 P4 **Vyshhorod** Kyyivs'ka Oblast', N Ukraine
128 I15 **Vyshniy Volochek** Tverskaya Oblast', W Russian Federation
113 G18 **Vyškov** *Ger.* Wischau. Jižní Morava, SE Czech Republic
113 F17 **Vysoké Mýto** *Ger.* Hohenmauth. Východní Čechy, E Czech Republic
119 S9 **Vysokopillya** Khersons'ka Oblast', S Ukraine
130 K3 **Vysokovsk** Moskovskaya Oblast', W Russian Federation
128 K12 **Vytegra** Vologodskaya Oblast', NW Russian Federation
118 J8 **Vyzhnytsya** Chernivets'ka Oblast', W Ukraine

W

79 O14 **Wa** NW Ghana
Waadt *see* Vaud
Waag *see* Váh
Waagbistritz *see* Považská Bystrica
Waagneustadtl *see* Nové Mesto nad Váhom
83 M16 **Waajid** Gedo, SW Somalia
100 L13 **Waal** ∾ S Netherlands
197 G4 **Waala** Province Nord, W New Caledonia
101 I14 **Waalwijk** Noord-Brabant, S Netherlands
101 E16 **Waarschoot** Oost-Vlaanderen, NW Belgium
194 G12 **Wabag** Enga, W PNG
197 I15 **Wabano** ∾ Québec, SE Canada
9 P11 **Wabasca** ∾ Alberta, SW Canada
33 P12 **Wabash** Indiana, N USA
31 X9 **Wabasha** Minnesota, N USA
33 N13 **Wabash River** ∾ N USA
12 C7 **Wabatongushi Lake** ◎ Ontario, S Canada
83 L15 **Wabē Gestro Wenz** ∾ SE Ethiopia
12 B9 **Wabos** Ontario, S Canada
9 W13 **Wabowden** Manitoba, C Canada
112 J9 **Wąbrzeźno** Toruń, N Poland
194 G14 **Wabuda Island** *island* SW PNG
23 U12 **Waccamaw River** ∾ South Carolina, SE USA
25 U11 **Waccasassa Bay** *bay* Florida, SE USA
101 F16 **Wachtebeke** Oost-Vlaanderen, NW Belgium
27 T8 **Waco** Texas, SW USA
28 M3 **Waconda Lake** *var.* Great Elder Reservoir. ⊡ Kansas, C USA
Wadai *see* Ouaddaï
Wad Al-Hajarah *see* Guadalajara
171 Gg13 **Wadayama** Hyōgo, Honshū, SW Japan
82 D10 **Wad Banda** Western Kordofan, C Sudan
77 P9 **Waddān** NW Libya
100 J4 **Waddeneilanden** *Eng.* West Frisian Islands. *island group* N Netherlands
100 J6 **Waddenzee** *var.* Wadden Zee. *sea* SE North Sea
8 L16 **Waddington, Mount** ▲ British Columbia, SW Canada
100 H12 **Waddinxveen** Zuid-Holland, C Netherlands
9 U15 **Wadena** Saskatchewan, S Canada
31 T6 **Wadena** Minnesota, N USA
110 G7 **Wädenswil** Zürich, N Switzerland
23 S11 **Wadesboro** North Carolina, SE USA
161 G16 **Wādi** Karnātaka, C India
144 G10 **Wādī as Sīr** *var.* Wadi es Sir. 'Ammān, NW Jordan
Wadi es Sir *see* Wādī as Sīr
82 F5 **Wadi Halfa** *var.* Wādī Ḥalfā'. Northern, N Sudan
144 G13 **Wādī Mūsā** *var.* Petra. Ma'ān, S Jordan
25 V4 **Wadley** Georgia, SE USA
Wad Madanī *see* Wad Medani
82 G10 **Wad Medani** *var.* Wad Madanī. Gezira, C Sudan
82 F10 **Wad Nimr** White Nile, C Sudan
172 Q14 **Wadomari** Kagoshima, Okinoerabu-jima, SW Japan
113 K17 **Wadowice** Bielsko-Biała, S Poland
37 R5 **Wadsworth** Nevada, W USA
33 T12 **Wadsworth** Ohio, N USA
27 T11 **Waelder** Texas, SW USA
Waereghem *see* Waregem
169 U13 **Wafangdian** *var.* Fuxian. Fu Xian. Liaoning, NE China
175 S11 **Waflia** Pulau Buru, E Indonesia
Wagadugu *see* Ouagadougou
100 K12 **Wageningen** Gelderland, SE Netherlands
57 V9 **Wageningen** Nickerie, NW Suriname
15 L15 **Wager Bay** *inlet* Northwest Territories, N Canada
176 Y10 **Wageseri** Irian Jaya, E Indonesia
191 P10 **Wagga Wagga** New South Wales, SE Australia
188 J13 **Wagin** Western Australia
Wagina *see* Vaghena
110 H8 **Wagitaler See** ◎ SW Switzerland
31 P12 **Wagner** South Dakota, N USA
29 Q9 **Wagoner** Oklahoma, C USA
39 U10 **Wagon Mound** New Mexico, SW USA
34 J14 **Wagontire** Oregon, NW USA
112 H10 **Wągrowiec** Piła, NW Poland
155 U6 **Wāh** Punjab, NE Pakistan
176 U10 **Wahai** Pulau Seram, E Indonesia
175 O7 **Wahau, Sungai** ∾ Borneo, C Indonesia
Wahaybah, Ramlat Al *see* Wahībah, Ramlat Āl
82 D13 **Wahda** *var.* Unity State. ◆ *state* S Sudan
40 D9 **Wahiawa** *Haw.* Wahiawā. Oahu, Hawaii, USA, C Pacific Ocean
Wahībah, Ramlat Ahl *see* Wahībah, Ramlat Āl
147 Y9 **Wahībah, Ramlat Āl** *var.* Ramlat Ahl Wahībah, Ramlat Al Wahaybah, *Eng.* Wahibah Sands. *desert* N Oman
Wahibah Sands *see* Wahībah, Ramlat Āl
103 E16 **Wahn** ✕ (Köln) Nordrhein-Westfalen, W Germany
31 R15 **Wahoo** Nebraska, C USA
31 R6 **Wahpeton** North Dakota, N USA
Wahran *see* Oran
38 J6 **Wah Wah Mountains** ▲ Utah, W USA
40 D9 **Waialua** Oahu, Hawaii, USA, C Pacific Ocean
40 D9 **Waianae** *Haw.* Wai'anae. Oahu, Hawaii, USA, C Pacific Ocean
192 Q8 **Waiapu** ∾ North Island, NZ
193 I17 **Waiau** Canterbury, South Island, NZ
193 I17 **Waiau** ∾ South Island, NZ
193 B23 **Waiau** ∾ South Island, NZ
103 H21 **Waiblingen** Baden-Württemberg, S Germany
Waidhofen *see* Waidhofen an der Ybbs, Niederösterreich, Austria
Waidhofen *see* Waidhofen an der Thaya, Niederösterreich, Austria
111 V2 **Waidhofen an der Thaya** *var.* Waidhofen. Niederösterreich, NE Austria
111 U5 **Waidhofen an der Ybbs** *var.* Waidhofen. Niederösterreich, E Austria
176 Uu8 **Waigeo, Pulau** *island* Maluku, E Indonesia
192 L5 **Waiheke Island** *island* N NZ
192 M7 **Waihi** Waikato, North Island, NZ
193 C20 **Waihou** ∾ North Island, NZ
Waikaboebak *see* Waikabubak
175 P17 **Waikabubak** *prev.* Waikaboebak. Pulau Sumba, C Indonesia
193 D23 **Waikaia** ∾ South Island, NZ
193 D23 **Waikaka** Southland, South Island, NZ
192 L13 **Waikanae** Wellington, North Island, NZ
192 M7 **Waikare, Lake** ◎ North Island, NZ
192 O9 **Waikaremoana, Lake** ◎ North Island, NZ
193 I17 **Waikari** Canterbury, South Island, NZ
192 L8 **Waikato** *off.* Waikato Region. ◆ *region* North Island, NZ
192 M8 **Waikato** ∾ North Island, NZ
190 J9 **Waikerie** South Australia
193 F23 **Waikouaiti** Otago, South Island, NZ
40 H11 **Wailea** Hawaii, USA, C Pacific Ocean
40 F10 **Wailuku** Maui, Hawaii, USA, C Pacific Ocean
193 H18 **Waimakariri** ∾ South Island, NZ
40 D9 **Waimanalo Beach** Oahu, Hawaii, USA, C Pacific Ocean
193 G15 **Waimangaroa** West Coast, South Island, NZ
193 G21 **Waimate** Canterbury, South Island, NZ
40 G11 **Waimea** *var.* Kamuela. Hawaii, USA, C Pacific Ocean
40 D9 **Waimea** *var.* Maunawai. Oahu, Hawaii, USA, C Pacific Ocean
40 B8 **Waimea** Kauai, Hawaii, USA, C Pacific Ocean
101 M20 **Waimes** Liège, E Belgium
160 J11 **Wainganga** *var.* Wain River. ∾ C India
Waingapoe *see* Waingapu
175 Pp17 **Waingapu** *prev.* Waingapoe. Pulau Sumba, C Indonesia
57 S7 **Waini** ∾ N Guyana
57 S7 **Waini Point** *headland* NW Guyana
Wain River *see* Wainganga
9 R15 **Wainwright** Alberta, SW Canada
41 O5 **Wainwright** Alaska, USA
192 K4 **Waiotira** Northland, North Island, NZ
192 M11 **Waiouru** Manawatu-Wanganui, North Island, NZ
176 X11 **Waipa** Irian Jaya, E Indonesia
192 L8 **Waipa** ∾ North Island, NZ
192 P9 **Waipaoa** ∾ North Island, NZ
193 D25 **Waipapa Point** *headland* South Island, NZ
193 I18 **Waipara** Canterbury, South Island, NZ
192 N12 **Waipawa** Hawke's Bay, North Island, NZ
192 K4 **Waipu** Northland, North Island, NZ
192 N12 **Waipukurau** Hawke's Bay, North Island, NZ
176 Vv13 **Wair** Pulau Kai Besar, E Indonesia
Wairakai *see* Wairakei
192 N9 **Wairakei** *var.* Wairakai. Waikato, North Island, NZ
193 M14 **Wairarapa, Lake** ◎ North Island, NZ
193 J15 **Wairau** ∾ South Island, NZ
192 P10 **Wairoa** Hawke's Bay, North Island, NZ
192 P10 **Wairoa** ∾ North Island, NZ
192 J4 **Wairoa** ∾ North Island, NZ
192 N9 **Waitahanui** Waikato, North Island, NZ
192 M6 **Waitakaruru** Waikato, North Island, NZ
193 F21 **Waitaki** ∾ South Island, NZ
192 K10 **Waitara** Taranaki, North Island, NZ
192 M7 **Waitoa** Waikato, North Island, NZ
192 L8 **Waitomo Caves** Waikato, North Island, NZ
192 L11 **Waitotara** Taranaki, North Island, NZ
192 L11 **Waitotara** ∾ North Island, NZ
34 L10 **Waitsburg** Washington, NW USA
Waitzen *see* Vác
192 L6 **Waiuku** Auckland, North Island, NZ
171 J12 **Wajima** *var.* Wazima. Ishikawa, Honshū, SW Japan
83 K17 **Wajir** North Eastern, NE Kenya
83 I14 **Waka** SW Ethiopia
81 J17 **Waka** Equateur, NW Zaire
12 D9 **Wakami Lake** ◎ Ontario, S Canada
170 G13 **Wakasa** Tottori, Honshū, SW Japan
171 H13 **Wakasa-wan** *bay* C Japan
193 C22 **Wakatipu, Lake** ◎ South Island, NZ
9 T15 **Wakaw** Saskatchewan, S Canada
197 I14 **Wakaya** *island* C Fiji
170 Ff15 **Wakayama** Wakayama, Honshū, SW Japan
170 G16 **Wakayama** *off.* Wakayama-ken. ◆ *prefecture* Honshū, SW Japan
28 K4 **Wa Keeney** Kansas, C USA
193 I14 **Wakefield** Tasman, South Island, NZ
99 M17 **Wakefield** N England, UK
29 O4 **Wakefield** Kansas, C USA
32 L4 **Wakefield** Michigan, N USA
23 U9 **Wake Forest** North Carolina, SE USA
Wakeham Bay *see* Kangiqsujuaq
201 Y11 **Wake Island** ◇ US *unincorporated territory* NW Pacific Ocean
201 Y12 **Wake Island** ✕ NW Pacific Ocean
201 Y12 **Wake Island** *atoll* NW Pacific Ocean
201 X12 **Wake Lagoon** *lagoon* Wake Island, NW Pacific Ocean
177 Ff9 **Wakema** Irrawaddy, SW Myanmar
Wakhan *see* Khandūd
170 Ff15 **Waki** Tokushima, Shikoku, SW Japan
172 N8 **Wakinosawa** Aomori, Honshū, C Japan
172 Pp1 **Wakkanai** Hokkaidō, NE Japan
85 K22 **Wakkerstroom** Mpumalanga, E South Africa
12 C10 **Wakomata Lake** ◎ Ontario, S Canada
191 N10 **Wakool** New South Wales, SE Australia
Wakra *see* Al Wakrah
Waku Kungo *see* Uaco Cungo
195 S12 **Wakunai** Bougainville Island, NE PNG
Walachei/Walachia *see* Wallachia
175 Pp12 **Walanae, Sungai** ∾ Sulawesi, C Indonesia
161 K26 **Walawe Ganga** ∾ S Sri Lanka
113 F15 **Wałbrzych** *Ger.* Waldenburg, Waldenburg in Schlesien. Wałbrzych, SW Poland
113 F15 **Wałbrzych** *off.* Województwo Wałbrzyskie, *Ger.* Waldenburg, Waldenburg in Schlesien. ◆ *province* SW Poland
Wałbrzyskie, Województwo *see* Wałbrzych
191 T6 **Walcha** New South Wales, SE Australia
103 K24 **Walchensee** ◎ SE Germany
101 D14 **Walcheren** *island* SW Netherlands
31 Z14 **Walcott** Iowa, C USA
35 W16 **Walcott** Wyoming, C USA
101 G21 **Walcourt** Namur, S Belgium
112 G9 **Wałcz** *Ger.* Deutsch Krone. Piła, NW Poland
110 H7 **Wald** Zürich, N Switzerland
111 U3 **Waldaist** ∾ N Austria
188 I9 **Waldburg Range** ▲ Western Australia
39 R3 **Walden** Colorado, C USA
20 K13 **Walden** New York, NE USA
Waldenburg/Waldenburg in Schlesien *see* Wałbrzych
9 T15 **Waldheim** Saskatchewan, S Canada
Waldia *see* Weldiya
103 M23 **Waldkraiburg** Bayern, SE Germany
29 T14 **Waldo** Arkansas, C USA
25 V9 **Waldo** Florida, SE USA
21 R7 **Waldoboro** Maine, NE USA
23 W4 **Waldorf** Maryland, NE USA
34 F12 **Waldport** Oregon, NW USA
29 S11 **Waldron** Arkansas, C USA
205 Y13 **Waldron, Cape** *headland* Antarctica
103 F24 **Waldshut-Tiengen** Baden-Württemberg, S Germany
175 Qq9 **Walea, Selat** *strait* Sulawesi, C Indonesia
Wałeckie Międzyrzecze *see* Valašské Meziříčí
110 H8 **Walensee** ◎ NW Switzerland
40 L8 **Wales** Alaska, USA
99 J20 **Wales** *Wel.* Cymru. *national region* UK
15 L13 **Wales Island** *island* Northwest Territories, NE Canada
79 P14 **Walewale** N Ghana
101 M24 **Walferdange** Luxembourg, C Luxembourg
191 Q5 **Walgett** New South Wales, SE Australia
204 K10 **Walgreen Coast** *physical region* Antarctica
31 Q2 **Walhalla** North Dakota, N USA
23 O11 **Walhalla** South Carolina, SE USA
81 O19 **Walikale** Nord Kivu, E Zaire
194 G9 **Walis Island** *island* NW PNG
Walk *see* Valga, Estonia
Walk *see* Valka, Latvia
31 U5 **Walker** Minnesota, N USA
13 V4 **Walker, Lac** ◎ Québec, SE Canada
37 S7 **Walker Lake** ◎ Nevada, W USA
37 R6 **Walker River** ∾ Nevada, W USA
30 K10 **Wall** South Dakota, N USA
181 U9 **Wallaby Plateau** *undersea feature* E Indian Ocean
35 N8 **Wallace** Idaho, NW USA
23 V11 **Wallace** North Carolina, SE USA
12 D17 **Wallaceburg** Ontario, S Canada
24 F5 **Wallace Lake** ⊡ Louisiana, S USA
9 P13 **Wallace Mountain** ▲ Alberta, W Canada
118 J14 **Wallachia** *var.* Walachia, *Ger.* Walachei, *Rom.* Valachia. *cultural region* S Romania
Wallachisch-Meseritsch *see* Valašské Meziříčí
191 U4 **Wallangarra** New South Wales, SE Australia
190 I8 **Wallaroo** South Australia
34 L10 **Walla Walla** Washington, NW USA
47 V9 **Wallblake** ✕ (The Valley) C Anguilla
103 H19 **Walldürn** Baden-Württemberg, SW Germany
102 F12 **Wallenhorst** Niedersachsen, NW Germany
Wallenthal *see* Hațeg
111 S4 **Wallern** Oberösterreich, N Austria
Wallern *see* Wallern im Burgenland
111 Z5 **Wallern im Burgenland** *var.* Wallern. Burgenland, E Austria
20 M9 **Wallingford** Vermont, NE USA
27 V11 **Wallis** Texas, SW USA
Wallis *see* Valais
199 Jj10 **Wallis and Futuna** *Fr.* Territoire de Wallis et Futuna. ◇ *French overseas territory* C Pacific Ocean
110 G7 **Wallisellen** Zürich, N Switzerland
202 H11 **Wallis, Îles** *island group* N Wallis and Futuna
101 H19 **Walloon Brabant** ◆ *province* C Belgium
33 Q5 **Walloon Lake** ◎ Michigan, N USA
34 K10 **Wallula** Washington, NW USA
34 K10 **Wallula, Lake** ◎ Washington, NW USA
23 S8 **Walnut Cove** North Carolina, SE USA
37 N8 **Walnut Creek** California, W USA
28 K5 **Walnut Creek** ∾ Kansas, C USA
29 W9 **Walnut Ridge** Arkansas, C USA
27 S7 **Walnut Springs** Texas, SW USA
190 L10 **Walpeup** Victoria, SE Australia
197 L7 **Walpole, Île** *island* SE New Caledonia
41 N13 **Walrus Islands** *island group* Alaska, USA
99 L19 **Walsall** C England, UK
39 T7 **Walsenburg** Colorado, C USA
9 S17 **Walsh** Alberta, SW Canada
39 W7 **Walsh** Colorado, C USA
102 I11 **Walsrode** Niedersachsen, NW Germany
Waltenberg *see* Zalău
23 R14 **Walterboro** South Carolina, SE USA
Walter F. George Lake *see* Walter F. George Reservoir
25 R6 **Walter F. George Reservoir** *var.* Walter F. George Lake. ⊡ Alabama/Georgia, SE USA
28 M12 **Walters** Oklahoma, C USA
103 J16 **Waltershausen** Thüringen, C Germany
181 N10 **Walters Shoal** *var.* Walters Shoals. *reef* S Madagascar
Walters Shoals *see* Walters Shoal
24 M3 **Walthall** Mississippi, S USA
22 M4 **Walton** Kentucky, S USA
20 J11 **Walton** New York, NE USA
81 O20 **Walungu** Sud Kivu, E Zaire
Walvisbaai *see* Walvis Bay
85 C19 **Walvis Bay** *Afr.* Walvisbaai. Erongo, NW Namibia
85 B19 **Walvis Bay** *bay* NW Namibia
Walvish Ridge *see* Walvis Ridge
67 O17 **Walvis Ridge** *var.* Walvish Ridge. *undersea feature* E Atlantic Ocean
176 Yy15 **Wamal** Irian Jaya, E Indonesia
176 W13 **Wamar, Pulau** *island* Kepulauan Aru, E Indonesia
79 V15 **Wamba** Plateau, C Nigeria
81 O17 **Wamba** Haut-Zaïre, NE Zaire
81 H22 **Wamba** *var.* Uamba. ∾ Angola/Zaire
29 P4 **Wamego** Kansas, C USA
20 I10 **Wampsville** New York, NE USA
44 K6 **Wampú, Río** ∾ E Honduras
176 Xx16 **Wan** Irian Jaya, E Indonesia
Wan *see* Anhui
191 N4 **Wanaaring** New South Wales, SE Australia
193 D21 **Wanaka** Otago, South Island, NZ
193 D20 **Wanaka, Lake** ◎ South Island, NZ
176 Ww12 **Wanapiri** Irian Jaya, E Indonesia
12 F9 **Wanapitei** ∾ Ontario, S Canada
12 F10 **Wanapitei Lake** ◎ Ontario, S Canada
20 K14 **Wanaque** New Jersey, NE USA
176 V9 **Wanau** Irian Jaya, E Indonesia
193 F22 **Wanbrow, Cape** *headland* South Island, NZ
Wanchuan *see* Zhangjiakou
176 X11 **Wandai** *var.* Komeyo. Irian Jaya, E Indonesia
169 Z8 **Wanda Shan** ▲ NE China
207 R11 **Wandel Sea** *sea* Arctic Ocean
166 D13 **Wanding** *var.* Wandingzhen. Yunnan, SW China
Wandingzhen *see* Wanding
176 Z14 **Wandip** Irian Jaya, E Indonesia
101 H20 **Wanfercée-Baulet** Hainaut, S Belgium
192 L12 **Wanganui** Manawatu-Wanganui, North Island, NZ
192 L11 **Wanganui** ∾ North Island, NZ
191 P11 **Wangaratta** Victoria, SE Australia
166 J8 **Wangcang** *prev.* Fengjiaba. Sichuan, C China
Wangda *see* Zogang
103 I24 **Wangen im Allgäu** Baden-Württemberg, S Germany
Wangerin *see* Węgorzyno
102 F9 **Wangerooge** *island* NW Germany
176 Ww11 **Wanggar** Irian Jaya, E Indonesia
166 J13 **Wangmo** *var.* Fuxing. Guizhou, S China
Wangolodougou *see* Ouangolodougou
167 S9 **Wangpan Yang** *sea* E China
169 Y10 **Wangqing** Jilin, NE China
178 I9 **Wang Saphung** Loei, C Thailand
178 H6 **Wan Hsa-la** Shan State, E Myanmar
57 W9 **Wanica** ◆ *district* N Suriname
81 M18 **Wanie-Rukula** Haut-Zaïre, C Zaire
Wankie *see* Hwange
Wanki, Río *see* Coco, Río
83 N17 **Wanlaweyn** *var.* Wanle Weyn, *It.* Uanle Uen. Shabeellaha Hoose, SW Somalia
Wanle Weyn *see* Wanlaweyn
188 I12 **Wanneroo** Western Australia
166 L17 **Wanning** Hainan, S China
178 I8 **Wanon Niwat** Sakon Nakhon, E Thailand
161 H16 **Wanparti** Andhra Pradesh, C India
Wansen *see* Wiązów
166 L11 **Wanshan** Guizhou, S China
101 M14 **Wanssum** Limburg, SE Netherlands
192 N12 **Wanstead** Hawke's Bay, North Island, NZ
166 K9 **Wanxian** Sichuan, C China
196 F16 **Wanyaan** Yap, Micronesia
166 K8 **Wanyuan** Sichuan, C China
167 O11 **Wanzai** Jiangxi, S China
101 J20 **Wanze** Liège, E Belgium
33 R12 **Wapakoneta** Ohio, N USA
10 D7 **Wapaseese** ∾ Ontario, C Canada
34 I10 **Wapato** Washington, NW USA
31 Y15 **Wapello** Iowa, C USA
194 H12 **Wapenamanda** Enga, W PNG
9 N13 **Wapiti** ∾ Alberta/British Columbia, SW Canada
29 X7 **Wappapello Lake** ⊡ Missouri, C USA
20 K13 **Wappingers Falls** New York, NE USA
31 X13 **Wapsipinicon River** ∾ Iowa, C USA
194 G14 **Wapumba Island** *island* SW PNG
12 L9 **Waqes** ∾ Québec, SE Canada
166 H7 **Waqên** Sichuan, C China
23 Q7 **War** West Virginia, NE USA
82 D13 **Warab** Warab, SW Sudan
83 D14 **Warab** ◆ *state* SW Sudan
161 J15 **Warangal** Andhra Pradesh, C India
Warasdin *see* Varaždin
191 O16 **Waratah** Tasmania, SE Australia
191 O14 **Waratah Bay** *bay* Victoria, SE Australia
103 H15 **Warburg** Nordrhein-Westfalen, W Germany
190 I1 **Warburton Creek** *seasonal river* South Australia
188 M9 **Warburton** Western Australia
101 M20 **Warche** ∾ E Belgium
155 P5 **Wardag** *var.* Wardak, *Per.* Vardak. ◆ *province* E Afghanistan
Wardak *see* Wardag
34 K9 **Warden** Washington, NW USA
160 I12 **Wardha** Mahārāshtra, W India
194 L14 **Ward Hunt, Cape** *headland* S PNG
195 N16 **Ward Hunt Strait** *strait* S PNG
123 J16 **Wardija, Ras il-** *var.* Wardija Point. *headland* Gozo, NW Malta
145 P3 **Wardiyah** N Iraq
193 E19 **Ward, Mount** ▲ South Island, NZ
176 Ww9 **Wardo** Irian Jaya, E Indonesia
8 L11 **Ware** British Columbia, W Canada
101 D18 **Waregem** *var.* Waereghem. West-Vlaanderen, W Belgium
101 J19 **Waremme** Liège, E Belgium
102 N10 **Waren** Mecklenburg-Vorpommern, NE Germany
176 X10 **Waren** Irian Jaya, E Indonesia
103 F14 **Warendorf** Nordrhein-Westfalen, W Germany
23 P12 **Ware Shoals** South Carolina, SE USA
100 N4 **Warffum** Groningen, NE Netherlands
83 O15 **Wargalo** Mudug, E Somalia
152 M12 **Warganza** *Rus.* Varganzi. Qashqadaryo Wiloyati, S Uzbekistan
Wargla *see* Ouargla
194 K14 **Waria** ∾ S PNG
191 T4 **Warialda** New South Wales, SE Australia
160 F13 **Wāri Godri** Mahārāshtra, C India
176 W11 **Warika** Irian Jaya, E Indonesia
176 W13 **Warilau** Pulau Warilau, E Indonesia
176 Ww13 **Warilau, Pulau** *island* Kepulauan Aru, E Indonesia
178 J10 **Warin Chamrap** Ubon Ratchathani, E Thailand
27 R11 **Waring** Texas, SW USA
41 O8 **Waring Mountains** ▲ Alaska, USA
112 M12 **Warka** Radom, E Poland
192 L5 **Warkworth** Auckland, North Island, NZ
176 V8 **Warmandi** Irian Jaya, E Indonesia
85 E22 **Warmbad** Karas, S Namibia
100 H8 **Warmenhuizen** Noord-Holland, NW Netherlands
99 L22 **Warminster** S England, UK
20 I15 **Warminster** Pennsylvania, NE USA
37 V8 **Warm Springs** Nevada, W USA
34 H12 **Warm Springs** Oregon, NW USA
23 S5 **Warm Springs** Virginia, NE USA
102 M8 **Warnemünde** Mecklenburg-Vorpommern, NE Germany
29 Q10 **Warner** Oklahoma, C USA
37 Q2 **Warner Mountains** ▲ California, W USA
25 T5 **Warner Robins** Georgia, SE USA
59 N18 **Warnes** Santa Cruz, C Bolivia
102 M9 **Warnow** ∾ NE Germany
Warnsdorf *see* Varnsdorf
100 M11 **Warnsveld** Gelderland, E Netherlands
176 Uu10 **Waromge, Teluk** *bay* Irian Jaya, E Indonesia
160 I13 **Warora** Mahārāshtra, C India
190 L11 **Warracknabeal** Victoria, SE Australia
191 O13 **Warragul** Victoria, SE Australia
191 O4 **Warrego River** *seasonal river* New South Wales/Queensland, E Australia
191 Q6 **Warren** New South Wales, SE Australia
9 X16 **Warren** Manitoba, S Canada
29 V14 **Warren** Arkansas, C USA
33 S10 **Warren** Michigan, N USA
31 R3 **Warren** Minnesota, N USA
33 U11 **Warren** Ohio, N USA
20 D12 **Warren** Pennsylvania, NE USA
27 X10 **Warren** Texas, SW USA
99 G16 **Warrenpoint** *Ir.* An Pointe. SE Northern Ireland, UK
29 S4 **Warrensburg** Missouri, C USA
85 H22 **Warrenton** Northern Cape, N South Africa
25 U4 **Warrenton** Georgia, SE USA
29 W4 **Warrenton** Missouri, C USA
23 V8 **Warrenton** North Carolina, SE USA
23 V4 **Warrenton** Virginia, NE USA
79 U17 **Warri** Delta, S Nigeria
99 L18 **Warrington** C England, UK
25 O9 **Warrington** Florida, SE USA
25 P3 **Warrior** Alabama, S USA
190 L13 **Warrnambool** Victoria, SE Australia
31 T2 **Warroad** Minnesota, N USA
191 S6 **Warrumbungle Range** ▲ New South Wales, SE Australia
160 J12 **Wārsa** Mahārāshtra, C India
33 P11 **Warsaw** Indiana, N USA
22 L4 **Warsaw** Kentucky, S USA
29 T5 **Warsaw** Missouri, C USA
20 E10 **Warsaw** New York, NE USA
23 V10 **Warsaw** North Carolina, SE USA
23 X5 **Warsaw** Virginia, NE USA
Warsaw/Warschau *see* Warszawa
83 N17 **Warshiikh** Shabeellaha Dhexe, C Somalia
103 G15 **Warstein** Nordrhein-Westfalen, W Germany
112 M11 **Warszawa** *Eng.* Warsaw, *Ger.* Warschau, *Rus.* Varshava. ● (Poland) Warszawa, C Poland
112 L11 **Warszawa** *off.* Województwo Stołeczne Warszawskie, *Eng.* Greater Warsaw. ◆ *province* C Poland
112 J13 **Warta** Sieradz, C Poland
112 D11 **Warta** *Ger.* Warthe. ∾ W Poland
Wartberg *see* Senec
22 M9 **Wartburg** Tennessee, S USA
110 J7 **Warth** Vorarlberg, NW Austria
Warthe *see* Warta
175 O9 **Waru** Borneo, C Indonesia
176 Uu11 **Waru** Pulau Seram, E Indonesia
145 N6 **Wa'r, Wādī al** *dry watercourse* E Syria
191 U3 **Warwick** Queensland, E Australia
13 Q11 **Warwick** Québec, SE Canada
99 M20 **Warwick** C England, UK
20 K13 **Warwick** New York, NE USA
31 P4 **Warwick** North Dakota, N USA

◆ COUNTRY ● COUNTRY CAPITAL ◇ DEPENDENT TERRITORY ○ DEPENDENT TERRITORY CAPITAL ◆ ADMINISTRATIVE REGION ✕ INTERNATIONAL AIRPORT ▲ MOUNTAIN ▲ MOUNTAIN RANGE ∆ VOLCANO ∾ RIVER ◎ LAKE ⊡ RESERVOIR

21 O12 **Warwick** Rhode Island, NE USA
99 L20 **Warwickshire** *cultural region* C England, UK
12 G14 **Wasaga Beach** Ontario, S Canada
79 U13 **Wasagu** Kebbi, NW Nigeria
38 M2 **Wasatch Range** ⛰ W USA
37 R12 **Wasco** California, W USA
31 V10 **Waseca** Minnesota, N USA
12 H13 **Washago** Ontario, S Canada
21 S2 **Washburn** Maine, NE USA
30 M5 **Washburn** North Dakota, N USA
32 K3 **Washburn** Wisconsin, N USA
33 S14 **Washburn Hill** *hill* Ohio, N USA
160 H13 **Wāshīm** Mahārāshtra, C India
99 M14 **Washington** NE England, UK
25 U3 **Washington** Georgia, SE USA
32 L12 **Washington** Illinois, N USA
33 N15 **Washington** Indiana, N USA
31 X15 **Washington** Iowa, C USA
29 O3 **Washington** Kansas, C USA
29 W5 **Washington** Missouri, C USA
23 X9 **Washington** North Carolina, SE USA
20 B15 **Washington** Pennsylvania, NE USA
27 V10 **Washington** Texas, SW USA
38 J8 **Washington** Utah, W USA
23 V4 **Washington** Virginia, NE USA
34 I9 **Washington** *off.* State of Washington; also known as Chinook State, Evergreen State. ◐ *state* NW USA
Washington *see* Washington Court House
33 S14 **Washington Court House** *var.* Washington. Ohio, NE USA
23 W4 **Washington DC** ● (USA) District of Columbia, NE USA
33 O5 **Washington Island** *island* Wisconsin, N USA
Washington Island *see* Teraina
21 O7 **Washington, Mount** ▲ New Hampshire, NE USA
28 M11 **Washita River** ~ Oklahoma/Texas, C USA
99 O18 **Wash, The** *inlet* E England, UK
34 L9 **Washtucna** Washington, NW USA
Wasiliszki *see* Vasilishki
112 P9 **Wasilków** Białystok, NE Poland
41 R11 **Wasilla** Alaska, USA
57 U9 **Wasjabo** Sipaliwini, NW Surinam
9 X11 **Waskaiowaka Lake** ◎ Manitoba, C Canada
9 T14 **Waskesiu Lake** Saskatchewan, C Canada
27 X7 **Waskom** Texas, SW USA
112 G13 **Wąsosz** Leszno, SW Poland
44 M6 **Waspam** *var.* Waspán. Región Autónoma Atlántico Norte, NE Nicaragua
Waspán *see* Waspam
172 P4 **Wassamu** Hokkaidō, NE Japan
110 G9 **Wassen** Uri, C Switzerland
100 G11 **Wassenaar** Zuid-Holland, W Netherlands
101 N24 **Wasserbillig** Grevenmacher, E Luxembourg
Wasserburg *see* Wasserburg am Inn
103 M23 **Wasserburg am Inn** *var.* Wasserburg. Bayern, SE Germany
103 I17 **Wasserkuppe** ▲ C Germany
105 R5 **Wassy** Haute-Marne, N France
175 Pp12 **Watampone** *var.* Bone. Sulawesi, C Indonesia
175 Ss11 **Watawa** Pulau Buru, E Indonesia
Watenstedt-Salzgitter *see* Salzgitter
20 M13 **Waterbury** Connecticut, NE USA
23 R11 **Wateree Lake** ⊡ South Carolina, SE USA
23 R12 **Wateree River** ~ South Carolina, SE USA
99 E20 **Waterford** *Ir.* Port Láirge. S Ireland
33 S9 **Waterford** Michigan, N USA
99 E20 **Waterford** *Ir.* Port Láirge. *cultural region* S Ireland
99 E21 **Waterford Harbour** *Ir.* Cuan Phort Láirge. *inlet* S Ireland
100 G12 **Wateringen** Zuid-Holland, W Netherlands
101 G19 **Waterloo** Walloon Brabant, C Belgium
12 F16 **Waterloo** Ontario, S Canada
13 P12 **Waterloo** Québec, SE Canada
32 K16 **Waterloo** Illinois, N USA
31 X13 **Waterloo** Iowa, C USA
20 G10 **Waterloo** New York, NE USA
32 L4 **Watersmeet** Michigan, N USA
25 V9 **Watertown** Florida, SE USA
20 I8 **Watertown** New York, NE USA
31 R9 **Watertown** South Dakota, N USA
32 M8 **Watertown** Wisconsin, N USA
24 L3 **Water Valley** Mississippi, S USA
29 O3 **Waterville** Kansas, C USA
19 Ss4 **Waterville** Maine, NE USA
31 V10 **Waterville** Minnesota, N USA
20 I10 **Waterville** New York, NE USA
12 E16 **Watford** Ontario, S Canada
99 N21 **Watford** SE England, UK
30 K4 **Watford City** North Dakota, N USA
147 X12 **Wāṭif** S Oman
20 G11 **Watkins Glen** New York, NE USA
Watlings Island *see* San Salvador
176 V13 **Watnil** Pulau Kai Kecil, E Indonesia
28 M10 **Watonga** Oklahoma, C USA
9 T16 **Watrous** Saskatchewan, S Canada
39 T10 **Watrous** New Mexico, SW USA
81 P16 **Watsa** Haut-Zaïre, NE Zaire
33 N12 **Watseka** Illinois, N USA
81 J19 **Watsikengo** Equateur, C Zaire
190 C5 **Watson** South Australia
9 U15 **Watson** Saskatchewan, S Canada
205 O10 **Watson Escarpment** ⛰ Antarctica
8 K9 **Watson Lake** Yukon Territory, W Canada
37 N10 **Watsonville** California, W USA
178 I8 **Wattay** ✕ (Viangchan) Viangchan, C Laos
111 N7 **Wattens** Tirol, W Austria
22 M9 **Watts Bar Lake** ⊡ Tennessee, S USA
110 H7 **Wattwil** Sankt Gallen, NE Switzerland
176 Uu12 **Watubela, Kepulauan** *island group* E Indonesia
103 N24 **Watzmann** ▲ SE Germany
194 J13 **Wau** Morobe, C PNG
83 D14 **Wau** *var.* Wāw. Western Bahr el Ghazal, S Sudan
31 Q8 **Waubay** South Dakota, N USA
31 Q8 **Waubay Lake** ◎ South Dakota, N USA
191 U7 **Wauchope** New South Wales, SE Australia
25 W13 **Wauchula** Florida, SE USA
32 M10 **Wauconda** Illinois, N USA
190 J7 **Waukaringa** South Australia
33 N10 **Waukegan** Illinois, N USA
32 M9 **Waukesha** Wisconsin, N USA
31 X11 **Waukon** Iowa, C USA
32 L8 **Waunakee** Wisconsin, N USA
32 L7 **Waupaca** Wisconsin, N USA
32 M8 **Waupun** Wisconsin, N USA
28 M13 **Waurika** Oklahoma, C USA
28 M12 **Waurika Lake** ⊡ Oklahoma, C USA
32 L6 **Wausau** Wisconsin, N USA
33 R11 **Wauseon** Ohio, N USA
32 L7 **Wautoma** Wisconsin, N USA
32 M9 **Wauwatosa** Wisconsin, N USA
24 L9 **Waveland** Mississippi, S USA
99 Q20 **Waveney** ~ E England, UK
192 L11 **Waverley** Taranaki, North Island, NZ
31 W12 **Waverly** Iowa, C USA
29 T4 **Waverly** Missouri, C USA
31 R15 **Waverly** Nebraska, C USA
20 G12 **Waverly** New York, NE USA
22 H8 **Waverly** Tennessee, S USA
23 W7 **Waverly** Virginia, NE USA
101 H19 **Wavre** Walloon Brabant, C Belgium
177 G8 **Waw** Pegu, SW Burma
Wāw *see* Wau
12 B7 **Wawa** Ontario, S Canada
79 T14 **Wawa** Niger, W Nigeria
77 Q11 **Wāw al Kabīr** S Libya
45 N7 **Wawa, Río** *var.* Rio Huahua. ~ NE Nicaragua
194 G13 **Wawoi** ~ SW PNG
Wawosungu, Teluk *see* Staring, Teluk
27 T7 **Waxahachie** Texas, SW USA
164 L9 **Waxxari** Xinjiang Uygur Zizhiqu, NW China
197 H14 **Waya** *island* Yasawa Group, NW Fiji
25 V7 **Waycross** Georgia, SE USA
188 K10 **Way, Lake** ◎ Western Australia
33 P9 **Wayland** Michigan, N USA
31 R13 **Wayne** Nebraska, C USA
20 K14 **Wayne** New Jersey, NE USA
23 P5 **Wayne** West Virginia, NE USA
25 V4 **Waynesboro** Georgia, SE USA
24 M7 **Waynesboro** Mississippi, S USA
22 H10 **Waynesboro** Tennessee, S USA
23 U5 **Waynesboro** Virginia, NE USA
20 B16 **Waynesburg** Pennsylvania, NE USA
29 U6 **Waynesville** Missouri, C USA
23 O10 **Waynesville** North Carolina, SE USA
28 L8 **Waynoka** Oklahoma, C USA
Wazan *see* Ouazzane
Wazima *see* Wajima
155 V7 **Wazīrābād** Punjab, NE Pakistan
Wazzan *see* Ouazzane
112 I8 **Wda** *var.* Czarna Woda, *Ger.* Schwarzwasser. ~ N Poland
197 K6 **Wé** Province des Îles Loyauté, E New Caledonia
99 O23 **Weald, The** *lowlands* SE England, UK
194 E15 **Weam** Western, SW PNG
99 L15 **Wear** ~ N England, UK
Wearmouth *see* Sunderland
28 L10 **Weatherford** Oklahoma, C USA
27 S6 **Weatherford** Texas, SW USA
36 M3 **Weaverville** California, W USA
29 R7 **Webb City** Missouri, C USA
198 G9 **Weber Basin** *undersea feature* S Ceram Sea
Webfoot State *see* Oregon
20 F9 **Webster** New York, NE USA
31 Q8 **Webster** South Dakota, N USA
31 V13 **Webster City** Iowa, C USA
29 X5 **Webster Groves** Missouri, C USA
23 S4 **Webster Springs** *var.* Addison. West Virginia, NE USA
175 T8 **Weda, Teluk** *bay* Pulau Halmahera, E Indonesia
67 B25 **Weddell Island** *island* W Falkland Islands
67 K22 **Weddell Plain** *undersea feature* SW Atlantic Ocean
67 K23 **Weddell Sea** *sea* SW Atlantic Ocean
67 B25 **Weddell Settlement** Weddell Island, W Falkland Islands
190 M11 **Wedderburn** Victoria, SE Australia
102 I9 **Wedel** Schleswig-Holstein, N Germany
94 N3 **Wedel Jarlsberg Land** *physical region* SW Svalbard
102 I12 **Wedemark** Niedersachsen, NW Germany
8 M17 **Wedge Mountain** ▲ British Columbia, SW Canada
25 R4 **Wedowee** Alabama, S USA
176 Vv13 **Weduar** Pulau Kai Besar, E Indonesia
176 Vv14 **Weduar, Tanjung** *headland* Pulau Kai Besar, SE Indonesia
37 N2 **Weed** California, W USA
13 Q12 **Weedon Centre** Québec, SE Canada
20 E13 **Weedville** Pennsylvania, NE USA
102 F10 **Weener** Niedersachsen, NW Germany
31 S16 **Weeping Water** Nebraska, C USA
101 L16 **Weert** Limburg, SE Netherlands
100 I10 **Weesp** Noord-Holland, C Netherlands
191 S5 **Wee Waa** New South Wales, SE Australia
112 N7 **Węgorzewo** *Ger.* Angerburg. Suwałki, NE Poland
112 E9 **Węgorzyno** *Ger.* Wangerin. Szczecin, NW Poland
112 N11 **Węgrów** *Ger.* Bingerau. Siedlce, E Poland
100 N5 **Wehe-Den Hoorn** Groningen, NE Netherlands
100 M12 **Wehl** Gelderland, E Netherlands
Wehlau *see* Znamensk
173 E2 **Weh, Pulau** *island* NW Indonesia
Wei *see* Weifang
167 P1 **Weichang** *prev.* Zhuizishan. Hebei, E China
Weichsel *see* Wisła
103 M16 **Weida** Thüringen, C Germany
Weiden *see* Weiden in der Oberpfalz
103 M19 **Weiden in der Oberpfalz** *var.* Weiden. Bayern, SE Germany
167 Q4 **Weifang** *var.* Wei, Wei-fang; *prev.* Weihsien. Shandong, E China
167 S4 **Weihai** Shandong, E China
166 K6 **Wei He** ~ C China
Weihsien *see* Weifang
103 G17 **Weilburg** Hessen, W Germany
103 K24 **Weilheim** Bayern, SE Germany
191 P4 **Weilmoringle** New South Wales, SE Australia
103 L16 **Weimar** Thüringen, C Germany
27 U11 **Weimar** Texas, SW USA
166 L6 **Weinan** Shaanxi, C China
110 H6 **Weinfelden** Thurgau, NE Switzerland
103 I24 **Weingarten** Baden-Württemberg, S Germany
103 G20 **Weinheim** Baden-Württemberg, SW Germany
166 H11 **Weining** *var.* Weining Yizu Huizu Miaozu Zizhixian. Guizhou, S China
Weining Yizu Huizu Miaozu Zizhixian *see* Weining
189 V2 **Weipa** Queensland, NE Australia
9 Y11 **Weir River** Manitoba, C Canada
23 R1 **Weirton** West Virginia, NE USA
34 M13 **Weiser** Idaho, NW USA
166 F12 **Weishan** Yunnan, SW China
167 P6 **Weishan Hu** ◎ E China
103 M15 **Weisse Elster** *Eng.* White Elster. ~ Czech Republic/Germany
Weisse Körös/Weisse Kreisch *see* Crişul Alb
110 L7 **Weissenbach am Lech** Tirol, W Austria
103 K21 **Weissenburg** Bayern, SE Germany
Weissenburg *see* Wissembourg, France
Weissenburg *see* Alba Iulia, Romania
103 M15 **Weissenfels** *var.* Weißenfels. Sachsen-Anhalt, C Germany
111 R9 **Weissensee** ◎ S Austria
Weissenstein *see* Paide
110 E11 **Weisshorn** *var.* Flüela Wisshorn. ▲ SW Switzerland
Weisskirchen *see* Bela Crkva
25 R3 **Weiss Lake** ⊡ Alabama, S USA
103 Q14 **Weisswasser** *Lus.* Běla Woda. Sachsen, E Germany
101 M22 **Weiswampach** Diekirch, N Luxembourg
111 U2 **Weitra** Niederösterreich, N Austria
167 O4 **Weixian** *var.* Wei Xian. Hebei, E China
165 V11 **Weiyuan** Gansu, C China
166 F14 **Weiyuan Jiang** ~ SW China
111 W7 **Weiz** Steiermark, SE Austria
166 K16 **Weizhou Dao** *island* S China
112 I6 **Wejherowo** Gdańsk, NW Poland
29 Q8 **Welch** Oklahoma, C USA
26 M6 **Welch** Texas, SW USA
23 Q6 **Welch** West Virginia, NE USA
47 O14 **Welchman Hall** C Barbados
82 J11 **Weldiya** *var.* Waldia, *It.* Valdia. N Ethiopia
23 W8 **Weldon** North Carolina, SE USA
27 V9 **Weldon** Texas, SW USA
101 M19 **Welkenraedt** Liège, E Belgium
199 L2 **Welker Seamount** *undersea feature* N Pacific Ocean
85 I22 **Welkom** Free State, C South Africa
12 H16 **Welland** Ontario, S Canada
12 G16 **Welland** ~ Ontario, S Canada
99 O19 **Welland** ~ C England, UK
12 H17 **Welland Canal** *canal* Ontario, S Canada
161 K25 **Wellawaya** Uva Province, SE Sri Lanka
Welle *see* Uele
189 T4 **Wellesley Islands** *island group* Queensland, N Australia
101 J22 **Wellin** Luxembourg, SE Belgium
99 N20 **Wellingborough** C England, UK
191 R7 **Wellington** New South Wales, SE Australia
12 J15 **Wellington** Ontario, SE Canada
193 L14 **Wellington** ● (NZ) Wellington, North Island, NZ
85 E26 **Wellington** Western Cape, SW South Africa
39 T2 **Wellington** Colorado, C USA
29 N7 **Wellington** Kansas, C USA
37 R7 **Wellington** Nevada, W USA
33 T11 **Wellington** Ohio, N USA
27 P3 **Wellington** Texas, SW USA
38 M4 **Wellington** Utah, W USA
193 M14 **Wellington** *off.* Wellington Region. ◐ *region* North Island, NZ
193 L14 **Wellington** ✕ Wellington, North Island, NZ
Wellington *see* Wellington, Isla
65 F22 **Wellington, Isla** *var.* Wellington. *island* S Chile
191 P12 **Wellington, Lake** ◎ Victoria, SE Australia
31 X14 **Wellman** Iowa, C USA
26 M6 **Wellman** Texas, SW USA
99 K22 **Wells** SW England, UK
31 V11 **Wells** Minnesota, N USA
37 X2 **Wells** Nevada, W USA
27 W8 **Wells** Texas, SW USA
20 F12 **Wellsboro** Pennsylvania, NE USA
23 R1 **Wellsburg** West Virginia, NE USA
192 K4 **Wellsford** Auckland, North Island, NZ
188 L9 **Wells, Lake** ◎ Western Australia
189 N4 **Wells, Mount** ▲ Western Australia
99 P18 **Wells-next-the-Sea** E England, UK
33 T15 **Wellston** Ohio, N USA
29 O10 **Wellston** Oklahoma, C USA
20 E11 **Wellsville** New York, NE USA
33 V12 **Wellsville** Ohio, N USA
38 L1 **Wellsville** Utah, W USA
38 I14 **Wellton** Arizona, SW USA
111 S4 **Wels** *anc.* Ovilava. Oberösterreich, N Austria
101 K15 **Welschap** ✕ (Eindhoven) Noord-Brabant, S Netherlands
102 P10 **Welse** ~ NE Germany
24 H9 **Welsh** Louisiana, S USA
99 K19 **Welshpool** *Wel.* Y Trallwng. E Wales, UK
99 O21 **Welwyn Garden City** SE England, UK
81 K18 **Wema** Equateur, NW Zaire
83 G21 **Wembere** ~ C Tanzania
9 N13 **Wembley** Alberta, W Canada
10 I9 **Wemindji** *prev.* Nouveau-Comptoir, Paint Hills. Québec, C Canada
101 G18 **Wemmel** Vlaams Brabant, C Belgium
34 J8 **Wenatchee** Washington, NW USA
166 M17 **Wenchang** Hainan, S China
167 R11 **Wencheng** *prev.* Daxue. Zhejiang, SE China
79 P16 **Wenchi** W Ghana
Wen-chou/Wenchow *see* Wenzhou
166 H8 **Wenchuan** *prev.* Weizhou. Sichuan, C China
Wendau *see* Võnnu
Wenden *see* Cēsis
167 S4 **Wendeng** Shandong, E China
83 J14 **Wendo** S Ethiopia
38 J2 **Wendover** Utah, W USA
12 D9 **Wenebegon** ~ Ontario, S Canada
12 D8 **Wenebegon Lake** ◎ Ontario, S Canada
110 E9 **Wengen** Bern, W Switzerland
167 O13 **Wengyuan** *prev.* Longxian. Guangdong, S China
Wenmen Island *see* Wolf, Isla
201 P15 **Weno** *prev.* Moen. Chuuk, C Micronesia
201 V12 **Weno** *prev.* Moen. *atoll* Chuuk Islands, C Micronesia
164 H4 **Wenquan** Qinghai, C China
165 N13 **Wenquan** *var.* Arixang. Xinjiang Uygur Zizhiqu, NW China
166 H14 **Wenshan** Yunnan, SW China
164 H6 **Wensu** Xinjiang Uygur Zizhiqu, W China
190 L8 **Wentworth** New South Wales, SE Australia
29 W4 **Wentzville** Missouri, C USA
165 V12 **Wen Xian** Gansu, C China
167 S10 **Wenzhou** *var.* Wen-chou, Wenchow. Zhejiang, SE China
36 L4 **Weott** California, W USA
101 I20 **Wépion** Namur, SE Belgium
102 O11 **Werbellinsee** ◎ NE Germany
101 L21 **Werbomont** Liège, E Belgium
85 G20 **Werda** Kgalagadi, S Botswana
Werder *see* Virtsu
83 N14 **Werdēr** SE Ethiopia
Werenów *see* Voranava
176 V11 **Weri** Irian Jaya, E Indonesia
100 I13 **Werkendam** Noord-Brabant, S Netherlands
103 M20 **Wernberg-Köblitz** Bayern, SE Germany
103 J18 **Werneck** Bayern, C Germany
103 K14 **Wernigerode** Sachsen-Anhalt, C Germany
Werowitz *see* Virovitica
103 J16 **Werra** ~ C Germany
191 N12 **Werribee** Victoria, SE Australia
191 T6 **Werris Creek** New South Wales, SE Australia
Werro *see* Võru
Werschetz *see* Vršac
103 K23 **Wertach** ~ S Germany
103 I19 **Wertheim** Baden-Württemberg, SW Germany
100 J8 **Wervershoof** Noord-Holland, NW Netherlands
Wervicq *see* Wervik
101 C18 **Wervik** *var.* Wervicq, Werwick. West-Vlaanderen, W Belgium
Werwick *see* Wervik
103 D14 **Wesel** Nordrhein-Westfalen, W Germany
Weseli an der Lainsitz *see* Veselí nad Lužnicí
Wesenberg *see* Rakvere
102 H12 **Weser** ~ NW Germany
Wes-Kaap *see* Western Cape
27 S17 **Weslaco** Texas, SW USA
12 J13 **Weslemkoon Lake** ◎ Ontario, SE Canada
189 R1 **Wessel Islands** *island group* Northern Territory, N Australia
31 P9 **Wessington** South Dakota, N USA
31 P10 **Wessington Springs** South Dakota, N USA
27 T8 **West** Texas, SW USA
West *see* Ouest
32 M9 **West Allis** Wisconsin, N USA
190 E8 **Westall, Point** *headland* South Australia
West Antarctica *see* Lesser Antarctica
12 G11 **West Arm** Ontario, S Canada
West Azerbaijan *see* Āzarbāyjān-e Bākhtarī
144 F10 **West Bank** *disputed region* SW Asia
9 N17 **Westbank** British Columbia, SW Canada
12 E11 **West Bay** Manitoulin Island, Ontario, S Canada
24 L11 **West Bay** *bay* Louisiana, S USA
32 M8 **West Bend** Wisconsin, N USA
159 R16 **West Bengal** ◐ *state* NE India
West Borneo *see* Kalimantan Barat
31 Y14 **West Branch** Iowa, C USA
33 R7 **West Branch** Michigan, N USA
20 F13 **West Branch Susquehanna River** ~ Pennsylvania, NE USA
99 L20 **West Bromwich** C England, UK
21 P8 **Westbrook** Maine, NE USA
31 T10 **Westbrook** Minnesota, N USA
31 Y15 **West Burlington** Iowa, C USA
98 L2 **West Burra** *island* NE Scotland, UK
32 J8 **Westby** Wisconsin, N USA
46 L6 **West Caicos** *island* W Turks and Caicos Islands
193 A24 **West Cape** *headland* South Island, NZ
182 L4 **West Caroline Basin** *undersea feature* SW Pacific Ocean
20 I16 **West Chester** Pennsylvania, NE USA
193 E18 **West Coast** *off.* West Coast Region. ◐ *region* South Island, NZ
27 V12 **West Columbia** Texas, SW USA
31 W10 **West Concord** Minnesota, N USA
31 V14 **West Des Moines** Iowa, C USA
39 Q6 **West Elk Peak** ▲ Colorado, C USA
46 F1 **West End** Grand Bahama Island, N Bahamas
46 F1 **West End Point** *headland* Grand Bahama Island, N Bahamas
100 O7 **Westerbork** Drenthe, NE Netherlands
100 N3 **Westereems** *strait* Germany/Netherlands
100 O9 **Westerhaar-Vriezenveensewijk** Overijssel, E Netherlands
102 G6 **Westerland** Schleswig-Holstein, N Germany
101 I17 **Westerlo** Antwerpen, N Belgium
21 N13 **Westerly** Rhode Island, NE USA
83 G18 **Western** ◐ *province* W Kenya
159 N11 **Western** ◐ *zone* C Nepal
194 E14 **Western** ◐ *province* SW PNG
195 T14 **Western** *off.* Western Province. ◐ *province* NW Solomon Islands
85 G15 **Western** ◐ *province* SW Zambia
188 K8 **Western Australia** ◐ *state* W Australia
82 A13 **Western Bahr el Ghazal** ◐ *state* SW Sudan
Western Bug *see* Bug
85 F25 **Western Cape** *off.* Western Cape Province, *Afr.* Wes-Kaap. ◐ *province* SW South Africa
82 A11 **Western Darfur** ◐ *state* W Sudan
Western Desert *see* Sahara el Gharbîya
120 G9 **Western Dvina** *Bel.* Dzvina, *Ger.* Düna, *Latv.* Daugava, *Rus.* Zapadnaya Dvina. ~ W Europe
83 D15 **Western Equatoria** ◐ *state* SW Sudan
161 E16 **Western Ghats** ⛰ SW India
194 G12 **Western Highlands** ◐ *province* C PNG
Western Isles *see* Outer Hebrides
82 C12 **Western Kordofan** ◐ *state* C Sudan
23 T3 **Westernport** Maryland, NE USA
161 J26 **Western Province** ◐ *province* SW Sri Lanka
76 B10 **Western Sahara** ◇ *disputed territory* N Africa
198 Bb7 **Western Samoa** *off.* Independent State of Western Samoa, *var.* Sāmoa-i-Sisifo. ◆ *monarchy* W Polynesia
Western Sayans *see* Zapadnyy Sayan
Western Scheldt *see* Westerschelde
Western Sierra Madre *see* Madre Occidental, Sierra
101 E15 **Westerschelde** *Eng.* Western Scheldt; *prev.* Honte. *inlet* S North Sea
33 S13 **Westerville** Ohio, N USA
103 F17 **Westerwald** ⛰ W Germany
67 C25 **West Falkland** *var.* Gran Malvina. *island* W Falkland Islands
31 R5 **West Fargo** North Dakota, N USA
196 M15 **West Fayu Atoll** *atoll* Caroline Islands, C Micronesia
20 C11 **Westfield** New York, NE USA
32 L7 **Westfield** Wisconsin, N USA
West Flanders *see* West-Vlaanderen
29 S10 **West Fork** Arkansas, C USA
31 P16 **West Fork Big Blue River** ~ Nebraska, C USA
31 U12 **West Fork Des Moines River** ~ Iowa/Minnesota, C USA
27 S5 **West Fork Trinity River** ~ Texas, SW USA
32 L16 **West Frankfort** Illinois, N USA
100 I8 **West-Friesland** *physical region* NW Netherlands
West Frisian Islands *see* Waddeneilanden
21 T5 **West Grand Lake** ◎ Maine, NE USA
20 M12 **West Hartford** Connecticut, NE USA
20 M13 **West Haven** Connecticut, NE USA
29 X12 **West Helena** Arkansas, C USA
30 M2 **Westhope** North Dakota, N USA
205 Y8 **West Ice Shelf** *ice shelf* Antarctica
49 R2 **West Indies** *island group* SE North America
West Irian *see* Irian Jaya
West Java *see* Jawa Barat
38 L3 **West Jordan** Utah, W USA
West Kalimantan *see* Kalimantan Barat
101 D14 **Westkapelle** Zeeland, SW Netherlands
33 O13 **West Lafayette** Indiana, N USA
33 T13 **West Lafayette** Ohio, N USA
West Lake *see* Kagera
31 Y14 **West Liberty** Iowa, C USA
23 O5 **West Liberty** Kentucky, S USA
Westliche Morava *see* Zapadna Morava
15 I13 **Westlock** Alberta, SW Canada
12 E17 **West Lorne** Ontario, S Canada
98 J12 **West Lothian** *cultural region* S Scotland, UK
101 H16 **Westmalle** Antwerpen, N Belgium
199 H6 **West Mariana Basin** *var.* Perece Vela Basin. *undersea feature* W Pacific Ocean
99 E17 **Westmeath** *Ir.* An Iarmhí, Na h-Iarmhidhe. *cultural region* C Ireland
29 Y11 **West Memphis** Arkansas, C USA
23 W2 **Westminster** Maryland, NE USA
23 O11 **Westminster** South Carolina, SE USA
24 I5 **West Monroe** Louisiana, S USA
20 D15 **Westmont** Pennsylvania, NE USA
29 O3 **Westmoreland** Kansas, C USA
37 W17 **Westmorland** California, W USA
194 L11 **West New Britain** ◐ *province* E PNG
West New Guinea *see* Irian Jaya
85 K18 **West Nicholson** Matabeleland South, S Zimbabwe
31 T14 **West Nishnabotna River** ~ Iowa, C USA
183 P11 **West Norfolk Ridge** *undersea feature* W Pacific Ocean
27 P12 **West Nueces River** ~ Texas, SW USA
West Nusa Tenggara *see* Nusa Tenggara Barat
31 T11 **West Okoboji Lake** ◎ Iowa, C USA
35 R16 **Weston** Idaho, NW USA
23 R4 **Weston** West Virginia, NE USA
99 J22 **Weston-super-Mare** SW England, UK
25 Z14 **West Palm Beach** Florida, SE USA
196 E9 **West Passage** *passage* Babeldaob, N Palau
25 O9 **West Pensacola** Florida, SE USA
29 V8 **West Plains** Missouri, C USA
37 P7 **West Point** California, W USA
25 R5 **West Point** Georgia, SE USA
24 M3 **West Point** Mississippi, S USA
31 R14 **West Point** Nebraska, C USA
23 X6 **West Point** Virginia, NE USA
190 G10 **West Point** *headland* South Australia
67 B24 **Westpoint Island Settlement** Westpoint Island, NW Falkland Islands
25 R4 **West Point Lake** ⊡ Alabama/Georgia, SE USA
99 B16 **Westport** *Ir.* Cathair na Mart. W Ireland
193 G15 **Westport** West Coast, South Island, NZ
34 F10 **Westport** Oregon, NW USA
34 F9 **Westport** Washington, NW USA
33 S15 **West Portsmouth** Ohio, N USA
West Punjab *see* Punjab
9 V14 **Westray** Manitoba, C Canada
98 J4 **Westray** *island* NE Scotland, UK
12 F9 **Westree** Ontario, S Canada
99 L16 **West Riding** *cultural region* N England, UK
West River *see* Xi Jiang
32 J7 **West Salem** Wisconsin, N USA
67 H21 **West Scotia Ridge** *undersea feature* W Scotia Sea
West Sepik *see* Sandaun
181 N4 **West Sheba Ridge** *undersea feature* W Indian Ocean
West Siberian Plain *see* Zapadno-Sibirskaya Ravnina
33 S11 **West Sister Island** *island* Ohio, N USA
West-Skylge *see* West-Terschelling
West Sumatra *see* Sumatera Barat
100 J5 **West-Terschelling** *Fris.* West-Skylge. Friesland, N Netherlands
66 J7 **West Thulean Rise** *undersea feature* N Atlantic Ocean
31 X12 **West Union** Iowa, C USA
33 R15 **West Union** Ohio, N USA
23 R3 **West Union** West Virginia, NE USA
33 N13 **Westville** Illinois, N USA
23 R3 **West Virginia** *off.* State of West Virginia; also known as The Mountain State. ◐ *state* NE USA
101 A17 **West-Vlaanderen** *Eng.* West Flanders. ◐ *province* W Belgium
37 R7 **West Walker River** ~ California/Nevada, W USA
37 P4 **Westwood** California, W USA
191 P9 **West Wyalong** New South Wales, SE Australia
179 N14 **West York Island** *island* N Spratly Islands
175 S15 **Wetar, Pulau** *island* Kepulauan Damar, E Indonesia
175 Ss16 **Wetar, Selat** *var.* Wetar Strait. *strait* Nusa Tenggara, S Indonesia
Wetar Strait *see* Wetar, Selat
9 Q15 **Wetaskiwin** Alberta, SW Canada
83 K21 **Wete** Pemba, E Tanzania
177 G4 **Wetlet** Sagaing, C Burma
39 T6 **Wet Mountains** ⛰ Colorado, C USA
103 E15 **Wetter** Nordrhein-Westfalen, W Germany
103 H17 **Wetter** ~ W Germany
101 F17 **Wetteren** Oost-Vlaanderen, NW Belgium
110 F7 **Wettingen** Aargau, N Switzerland
29 P11 **Wetumka** Oklahoma, C USA
25 Q5 **Wetumpka** Alabama, S USA
110 G7 **Wetzikon** Zürich, N Switzerland
103 G17 **Wetzlar** Hessen, W Germany
101 C18 **Wevelgem** West-Vlaanderen, W Belgium
40 M6 **Wevok** *var.* Wewuk. Alaska, USA
25 R9 **Wewahitchka** Florida, SE USA
194 G10 **Wewak** East Sepik, NW PNG
29 O11 **Wewoka** Oklahoma, C USA
Wewuk *see* Wevok
99 F20 **Wexford** *Ir.* Loch Garman. SE Ireland
99 F20 **Wexford** *Ir.* Loch Garman. *cultural region* SE Ireland
32 L7 **Weyauwega** Wisconsin, N USA
9 U17 **Weyburn** Saskatchewan, S Canada
Weyer *see* Weyer Markt
111 U5 **Weyer Markt** *var.* Weyer. Oberösterreich, N Austria
102 H11 **Weyhe** Niedersachsen, NW Germany
99 L24 **Weymouth** S England, UK
21 P11 **Weymouth** Massachusetts, NE USA
101 H18 **Wezembeek-Oppem** Vlaams Brabant, C Belgium
100 M9 **Wezep** Gelderland, E Netherlands
192 M9 **Whakamaru** Waikato, North Island, NZ
192 O8 **Whakatane** Bay of Plenty, North Island, NZ
192 O8 **Whakatane** ~ North Island, NZ
15 L7 **Whale Cove** Northwest Territories, C Canada
98 M2 **Whalsay** *island* NE Scotland, UK
192 L11 **Whangaehu** ~ North Island, NZ
192 M6 **Whangamata** Waikato, North Island, NZ
192 Q9 **Whangara** Gisborne, North Island, NZ
192 K3 **Whangarei** Northland, North Island, NZ
192 K3 **Whangaruru Harbour** *inlet* North Island, NZ
27 V12 **Wharton** Texas, SW USA
181 U8 **Wharton Basin** *var.* West Australian Basin. *undersea feature* E Indian Ocean
193 E18 **Whataroa** West Coast, South Island, NZ
192 K6 **Whatipu** Auckland, North Island, NZ
35 Y16 **Wheatland** Wyoming, C USA
12 D18 **Wheatley** Ontario, S Canada
32 M10 **Wheaton** Illinois, N USA
31 R7 **Wheaton** Minnesota, N USA
39 T4 **Wheat Ridge** Colorado, C USA
27 P2 **Wheeler** Texas, SW USA
25 O2 **Wheeler Lake** ⊡ Alabama, S USA
37 Y6 **Wheeler Peak** ▲ Nevada, W USA
39 T9 **Wheeler Peak** ▲ New Mexico, SW USA
33 S15 **Wheelersburg** Ohio, N USA

◆ Country ● Country Capital ◇ Dependent Territory ○ Dependent Territory Capital ◐ Administrative Region ✕ International Airport ▲ Mountain ⛰ Mountain Range Ж Volcano ~ River ◎ Lake ⊡ Reservoir

23 R2 **Wheeling** West Virginia, NE USA
99 L16 **Whernside** ▲ N England, UK
190 F9 **Whidbey, Point** *headland* South Australia
188 I7 **Whim Creek** Western Australia
8 L17 **Whistler** British Columbia, SW Canada
23 W8 **Whitakers** North Carolina, SE USA
12 H15 **Whitby** Ontario, S Canada
99 N15 **Whitby** N England, UK
8 G6 **White** ≈ Yukon Territory, W Canada
11 T11 **White Bay** *bay* Newfoundland, Newfoundland and Labrador, E Canada
22 I8 **White Bluff** Tennessee, S USA
30 J6 **White Butte** ▲ North Dakota, N USA
21 R5 **White Cap Mountain** ▲ Maine, NE USA
24 J9 **White Castle** Louisiana, S USA
190 M5 **White Cliffs** New South Wales, SE Australia
33 P8 **White Cloud** Michigan, N USA
9 P14 **Whitecourt** Alberta, SW Canada
27 O2 **White Deer** Texas, SW USA
White Elster *see* Weisse Elster
26 M5 **Whiteface** Texas, SW USA
20 K7 **Whiteface Mountain** ▲ New York, NE USA
31 W5 **Whiteface Reservoir** ⊟ Minnesota, N USA
35 O7 **Whitefish** Montana, NW USA
33 N9 **Whitefish Bay** Wisconsin, N USA
33 Q3 **Whitefish Bay** *lake bay* Canada/USA
12 E11 **Whitefish Falls** Ontario, S Canada
12 B7 **Whitefish Lake** ◎ Ontario, S Canada
31 U6 **Whitefish Lake** ◎ Minnesota, C USA
33 Q3 **Whitefish Point** *headland* Michigan, N USA
33 O4 **Whitefish River** ≈ Michigan, N USA
27 O4 **Whiteflat** Texas, SW USA
29 V12 **White Hall** Arkansas, C USA
32 K14 **White Hall** Illinois, N USA
33 O8 **Whitehall** Michigan, N USA
20 L9 **Whitehall** New York, NE USA
33 S13 **Whitehall** Ohio, N USA
32 J7 **Whitehall** Wisconsin, N USA
99 J15 **Whitehaven** NW England, UK
8 I8 **Whitehorse** *territory capital* Yukon Territory, W Canada
192 O7 **White Island** *island* NE NZ
12 K13 **White Lake** ◎ Ontario, SE Canada
24 H10 **White Lake** ◎ Louisiana, S USA
195 N12 **Whiteman Range** ▲ New Britain, E PNG
191 Q15 **Whitemark** Tasmania, SE Australia
37 S9 **White Mountains** ▲ California/Nevada, W USA
21 N7 **White Mountains** ▲ Maine/New Hampshire, NE USA
82 F11 **White Nile** ◐ *state* C Sudan
69 U7 **White Nile** *var.* Bahr el Jebel. ≈ S Sudan
83 E14 **White Nile** *Ar.* Al Baḩr al Abyaḑ, An Nīl al Abyaḑ, Bahr el Jebel. ≈ SE Sudan
27 W5 **White Oak Creek** ≈ Texas, SW USA
8 H9 **White Pass** *pass* Canada/USA
34 I9 **White Pass** *pass* Washington, NW USA
23 O9 **White Pine** Tennessee, S USA
20 K14 **White Plains** New York, NE USA
30 M11 **White River** South Dakota, N USA
29 W12 **White River** ≈ Arkansas, SE USA
39 P3 **White River** ≈ Colorado/Utah, C USA
33 N15 **White River** ≈ Indiana, N USA
33 O8 **White River** ≈ Michigan, N USA
30 K11 **White River** ≈ South Dakota, N USA
27 O5 **White River** ≈ Texas, SW USA
20 M8 **White River** ≈ Vermont, NE USA
39 N13 **Whiteriver** Arizona, SW USA
27 O5 **White River Lake** ⊟ Texas, SW USA
34 H11 **White Salmon** Washington, NW USA
20 I10 **Whitesboro** New York, NE USA
27 T5 **Whitesboro** Texas, SW USA
23 O7 **Whitesburg** Kentucky, S USA
White Sea *see* Beloye More
White Sea-Baltic Canal/White Sea Canal *see* Belomorsko-Baltiyskiy Kanal
65 I25 **Whiteside, Canal** *channel* S Chile
35 S10 **White Sulphur Springs** Montana, NW USA
23 R6 **White Sulphur Springs** West Virginia, NE USA
22 J6 **Whitesville** Kentucky, S USA
34 I10 **White Swan** Washington, NW USA
23 U12 **Whiteville** North Carolina, SE USA
22 F10 **Whiteville** Tennessee, S USA
79 Q13 **White Volta** *var.* Nakambé, *Fr.* Volta Blanche. ≈ Burkina/Ghana
32 M9 **Whitewater** Wisconsin, N USA
39 P14 **Whitewater Baldy** ▲ New Mexico, SW USA
25 X17 **Whitewater Bay** *bay* Florida, SE USA
33 Q14 **Whitewater River** ≈ Indiana/Ohio, N USA
9 V16 **Whitewood** Saskatchewan, S Canada
30 J9 **Whitewood** South Dakota, N USA
27 U5 **Whitewright** Texas, SW USA
99 I15 **Whithorn** S Scotland, UK
192 M6 **Whitianga** Waikato, North Island, NZ
21 N11 **Whitinsville** Massachusetts, NE USA
22 M8 **Whitley City** Kentucky, S USA
23 Q11 **Whitmire** South Carolina, SE USA
33 R10 **Whitmore Lake** Michigan, N USA
205 N9 **Whitmore Mountains** ▲ Antarctica
12 I12 **Whitney** Ontario, SE Canada
27 T8 **Whitney** Texas, SW USA
27 S8 **Whitney, Lake** ⊟ Texas, SW USA
37 S11 **Whitney, Mount** ▲ California, W USA
189 Y6 **Whitsunday Group** *island group* Queensland, E Australia
27 S6 **Whitt** Texas, SW USA
31 U12 **Whittemore** Iowa, C USA
41 R12 **Whittier** Alaska, USA
37 T15 **Whittier** California, W USA
85 I25 **Whittlesea** Eastern Cape, S South Africa
22 K10 **Whitwell** Tennessee, S USA
15 J9 **Wholdaia Lake** ◎ Northwest Territories, NW Canada
190 H7 **Whyalla** South Australia
Whydah *see* Ouidah
12 F13 **Wiarton** Ontario, S Canada
175 Q11 **Wiau** Sulawesi, C Indonesia
113 H15 **Wiązów** *Ger.* Wansen. Wrocław, SW Poland
35 Y8 **Wibaux** Montana, NW USA
29 N6 **Wichita** Kansas, C USA
27 R5 **Wichita Falls** Texas, SW USA
28 L11 **Wichita Mountains** ▲ Oklahoma, C USA
27 R5 **Wichita River** ≈ Texas, SW USA
98 K6 **Wick** N Scotland, UK
38 K13 **Wickenburg** Arizona, SW USA
26 L8 **Wickett** Texas, SW USA
188 I7 **Wickham** Western Australia
190 M14 **Wickham, Cape** *headland* Tasmania, SE Australia
22 G7 **Wickliffe** Kentucky, S USA
99 G19 **Wicklow** *Ir.* Cill Mhantáin. E Ireland
99 F19 **Wicklow** *Ir.* Cill Mhantáin. *cultural region* E Ireland
99 G19 **Wicklow Head** *Ir.* Ceann Chill Mhantáin. *headland* E Ireland
99 F18 **Wicklow Mountains** *Ir.* Sléibhte Chill Mhantáin. ▲ E Ireland
12 H10 **Wicksteed Lake** ◎ Ontario, S Canada
Wida *see* Ouidah
67 G15 **Wideawake Airfield** ✕ (Georgetown) SW Ascension Island
195 P11 **Wide Bay** *bay* New Britain, PNG
175 T19 **Widi, Kepulauan** *island group* E Indonesia
99 K18 **Widnes** C England, UK
112 H9 **Więcbork** *Ger.* Vandsburg. Bydgoszcz, NW Poland
103 E17 **Wied** ≈ W Germany
103 F16 **Wiehl** Nordrhein-Westfalen, W Germany
113 L17 **Wieliczka** Kraków, S Poland
113 J14 **Wieluń** Sieradz, C Poland
111 X4 **Wien** *Eng.* Vienna, *Hung.* Bécs, *Slvk.* Vídeň, *Slvn.* Dunaj; *anc.* Vindobona. ● (Austria) Wien, NE Austria
111 X4 **Wien** *off.* Land Wien, *Eng.* Vienna. ◐ *state* NE Austria
111 X5 **Wiener Neustadt** Niederösterreich, E Austria
112 G7 **Wieprza** *Ger.* Wipper. ≈ NW Poland
100 O10 **Wierden** Overijssel, E Netherlands
100 I7 **Wieringerwerf** Noord-Holland, NW Netherlands
Wieruschow *see* Wieruszów
113 I14 **Wieruszów** *Ger.* Wieruschow. Kalisz, SW Poland
111 V9 **Wies** Steiermark, SE Austria
Wiesbachhorn *see* Grosses Wiesbachhorn
103 G18 **Wiesbaden** Hessen, W Germany
Wieselburg and Ungarisch-Altenburg/Wieselburg-Ungarisch-Altenburg *see* Mosonmagyaróvár
Wiesenhof *see* Ostrołęka
103 G20 **Wiesloch** Baden-Württemberg, SW Germany
102 F10 **Wiesmoor** Niedersachsen, NW Germany
112 I7 **Wieżyca** *Ger.* Turmberg. *hill* Gdańsk, N Poland
99 L17 **Wigan** NW England, UK
39 U3 **Wiggins** Colorado, C USA
24 M8 **Wiggins** Mississippi, S USA
Wigorna Ceaster *see* Worcester
99 I14 **Wigtown** S Scotland, UK
99 H14 **Wigtown** *cultural region* SW Scotland, UK
99 I15 **Wigtown Bay** *bay* SW Scotland, UK
100 L13 **Wijchen** Gelderland, SE Netherlands
94 N1 **Wijdefjorden** *fjord* NW Svalbard
100 M10 **Wijhe** Overijssel, E Netherlands
100 J12 **Wijk bij Duurstede** Utrecht, C Netherlands
100 J13 **Wijk en Aalburg** Noord-Brabant, S Netherlands
101 H16 **Wijnegem** Antwerpen, N Belgium
12 E11 **Wikwemikong** Manitoulin Island, Ontario, S Canada
110 H7 **Wil** Sankt Gallen, NE Switzerland
31 R16 **Wilber** Nebraska, C USA
34 K8 **Wilbur** Washington, NW USA
29 Q11 **Wilburton** Oklahoma, C USA
190 M6 **Wilcannia** New South Wales, SE Australia
20 D12 **Wilcox** Pennsylvania, NE USA
Wilczek Land *see* Vil'cheka, Zemlya
111 U6 **Wildalpen** Steiermark, E Austria
33 O13 **Wildcat Creek** ≈ Indiana, N USA
110 L9 **Wilde Kreuzspitze** *It.* Picco di Croce. ▲ Austria/Italy
Wildenschwert *see* Ústí nad Orlicí
100 O6 **Wildervank** Groningen, NE Netherlands
102 G11 **Wildeshausen** Niedersachsen, NW Germany
110 D10 **Wildhorn** ▲ SW Switzerland
9 R17 **Wild Horse** Alberta, SW Canada
29 N12 **Wildhorse Creek** ≈ Oklahoma, C USA
30 L14 **Wild Horse Hill** ▲ Nebraska, C USA
111 W8 **Wildon** Steiermark, SE Austria
26 M2 **Wildorado** Texas, SW USA
31 R6 **Wild Rice River** ≈ Minnesota/North Dakota, N USA
Wilejka *see* Vilyeyka
205 Y9 **Wilhelm II Coast** *physical region* Antarctica
205 X9 **Wilhelm II Land** *physical region* Antarctica
57 U11 **Wilhelmina Gebergte** ▲ C Surinam
20 B13 **Wilhelm, Lake** ⊟ Pennsylvania, NE USA
194 I12 **Wilhelm, Mount** ▲ C PNG
94 O2 **Wilhelmøya** *island* C Svalbard
Wilhelm-Pieck-Stadt *see* Guben
111 W4 **Wilhelmsburg** Niederösterreich, E Austria
102 G10 **Wilhelmshaven** Niedersachsen, NW Germany
Wilia/Wilja *see* Neris
20 H13 **Wilkes Barre** Pennsylvania, NE USA
23 R9 **Wilkesboro** North Carolina, SE USA
205 W15 **Wilkes Coast** *physical region* Antarctica
201 W12 **Wilkes Island** *island* N Wake Island
205 X12 **Wilkes Land** *physical region* Antarctica
9 S15 **Wilkie** Saskatchewan, S Canada
204 I6 **Wilkins Ice Shelf** *ice shelf* Antarctica
190 D4 **Wilkinsons Lakes** *salt lake* South Australia
Wilkomierz *see* Ukmergė
190 K11 **Willalooka** South Australia
34 G11 **Willamette River** ≈ Oregon, NW USA
191 O8 **Willandra Billabong Creek** *seasonal river* New South Wales, SE Australia
34 F9 **Willapa Bay** *inlet* Washington, NW USA
29 T7 **Willard** Missouri, C USA
39 S12 **Willard** New Mexico, SW USA
33 S12 **Willard** Ohio, N USA
38 L1 **Willard** Utah, W USA
195 N11 **Willaumez Peninsula** *headland* New Britain, E PNG
39 N15 **Willcox** Arizona, SW USA
39 N16 **Willcox Playa** *salt flat* Arizona, SW USA
101 G17 **Willebroek** Antwerpen, C Belgium
47 P16 **Willemstad** ○ (Netherlands Antilles) Curaçao, Netherlands Antilles
101 G14 **Willemstad** Noord-Brabant, S Netherlands
9 S11 **William** ≈ Saskatchewan, C Canada
25 O6 **William "Bill" Dannelly Reservoir** ⊟ Alabama, S USA
190 G3 **William Creek** South Australia
189 T15 **William, Mount** ▲ South Australia
38 K11 **Williams** Arizona, SW USA
31 X14 **Williamsburg** Iowa, C USA
22 M8 **Williamsburg** Kentucky, S USA
33 R15 **Williamsburg** Ohio, N USA
23 X6 **Williamsburg** Virginia, NE USA
8 M15 **Williams Lake** British Columbia, SW Canada
23 P6 **Williamson** West Virginia, NE USA
33 N13 **Williamsport** Indiana, N USA
20 G13 **Williamsport** Pennsylvania, NE USA
23 W9 **Williamston** North Carolina, SE USA
23 P11 **Williamston** South Carolina, SE USA
22 M4 **Williamstown** Kentucky, S USA
20 L10 **Williamstown** Massachusetts, NE USA
20 J16 **Willingboro** New Jersey, NE USA
9 Q14 **Willingdon** Alberta, SW Canada
27 W10 **Willis** Texas, SW USA
110 F8 **Willisau** Luzern, W Switzerland
85 F24 **Williston** Northern Cape, W South Africa
25 V10 **Williston** Florida, SE USA
30 J3 **Williston** North Dakota, N USA
23 Q13 **Williston** South Carolina, SE USA
8 L12 **Williston Lake** ⊟ British Columbia, W Canada
36 L5 **Willits** California, W USA
31 T8 **Willmar** Minnesota, N USA
8 K11 **Will, Mount** ▲ British Columbia, W Canada
33 T11 **Willoughby** Ohio, N USA
9 U17 **Willow Bunch** Saskatchewan, S Canada
34 J11 **Willow Creek** ≈ Oregon, NW USA
41 R11 **Willow Lake** Alaska, USA
15 H7 **Willowlake** ≈ Northwest Territories, NW Canada
85 H25 **Willowmore** Eastern Cape, S South Africa
32 L5 **Willow Reservoir** ⊟ Wisconsin, N USA
37 N5 **Willows** California, W USA
29 V7 **Willow Springs** Missouri, C USA
190 I7 **Wilmington** South Australia
23 Y2 **Wilmington** Delaware, NE USA
23 V12 **Wilmington** North Carolina, SE USA
33 R14 **Wilmington** Ohio, N USA
22 M6 **Wilmore** Kentucky, S USA
31 R8 **Wilmot** South Dakota, N USA
Wilna/Wilno *see* Vilnius
103 G16 **Wilnsdorf** Nordrhein-Westfalen, W Germany
101 G16 **Wilrijk** Antwerpen, N Belgium
102 I10 **Wilseder Berg** *hill* NW Germany
69 Z12 **Wilshaw Ridge** *undersea feature* W Indian Ocean
23 V9 **Wilson** North Carolina, SE USA
27 N5 **Wilson** Texas, SW USA
190 A7 **Wilson Bluff** *headland* South Australia/Western Australia
37 Y7 **Wilson Creek Range** ▲ Nevada, W USA
25 O1 **Wilson Lake** ⊟ Alabama, S USA
28 M4 **Wilson Lake** ⊟ Kansas, SE USA
39 P7 **Wilson, Mount** ▲ Colorado, C USA
191 P13 **Wilsons Promontory** *peninsula* Victoria, SE Australia
31 Y14 **Wilton** Iowa, C USA
21 P7 **Wilton** Maine, NE USA
30 M5 **Wilton** North Dakota, N USA
99 L22 **Wiltshire** *cultural region* S England, UK
101 M23 **Wiltz** Diekirch, NW Luxembourg
188 K9 **Wiluna** Western Australia
101 M23 **Wilwerwiltz** Diekirch, NE Luxembourg
31 P5 **Wimbledon** North Dakota, N USA
44 K7 **Wina** *var.* Güina. Jinotega, N Nicaragua
33 O12 **Winamac** Indiana, N USA
83 G19 **Winam Gulf** *var.* Kavirondo Gulf. *gulf* SW Kenya
85 I22 **Winburg** Free State, C South Africa
21 N10 **Winchendon** Massachusetts, NE USA
12 M13 **Winchester** Ontario, SE Canada
99 M23 **Winchester** *hist.* Wintanceaster, *Lat.* Venta Belgarum. S England, UK
34 M10 **Winchester** Idaho, NW USA
32 J14 **Winchester** Illinois, N USA
33 Q13 **Winchester** Indiana, N USA
22 M5 **Winchester** Kentucky, S USA
20 M10 **Winchester** New Hampshire, NE USA
22 K10 **Winchester** Tennessee, S USA
23 V3 **Winchester** Virginia, NE USA
101 L22 **Wincrange** Diekirch, NW Luxembourg
8 I5 **Wind** ≈ Yukon Territory, NW Canada
191 S8 **Windamere, Lake** ◎ New South Wales, SE Australia
Windau *see* Ventspils, Latvia
Windau *see* Venta, Latvia/Lithuania
20 D15 **Windber** Pennsylvania, NE USA
25 T3 **Winder** Georgia, SE USA
99 K15 **Windermere** NW England, UK
12 C7 **Windermere Lake** ◎ Ontario, S Canada
33 U11 **Windham** Ohio, N USA
85 D19 **Windhoek** *Ger.* Windhuk. ● (Namibia) Khomas, C Namibia
85 D20 **Windhoek** ✕ Khomas, C Namibia
Windhuk *see* Windhoek
13 O8 **Windigo** Québec, SE Canada
13 O8 **Windigo** ≈ Québec, SE Canada
Windischfeistritz *see* Slovenska Bistrica
111 T6 **Windischgarsten** Oberösterreich, W Austria
Windischgraz *see* Slovenj Gradec
39 T16 **Wind Mountain** ▲ New Mexico, SW USA
31 T10 **Windom** Minnesota, N USA
39 Q7 **Windom Peak** ▲ Colorado, C USA
189 U9 **Windorah** Queensland, C Australia
39 O10 **Window Rock** Arizona, SW USA
33 N9 **Wind Point** *headland* Wisconsin, N USA
35 U14 **Wind River** ≈ Wyoming, C USA
11 P15 **Windsor** Nova Scotia, SE Canada
12 C18 **Windsor** Ontario, S Canada
13 Q12 **Windsor** Québec, SE Canada
99 N22 **Windsor** S England, UK
39 T3 **Windsor** Colorado, C USA
20 M12 **Windsor** Connecticut, NE USA
29 T5 **Windsor** Missouri, C USA
23 X9 **Windsor** North Carolina, SE USA
20 M12 **Windsor Locks** Connecticut, NE USA
27 R5 **Windthorst** Texas, SW USA
47 Z14 **Windward Islands** *island group* E West Indies
Windward Islands *see* Vent, Îles du, Archipel de la Société, French Polynesia
Windward Islands *see* Barlavento, Ilhas de, Cape Verde
46 K8 **Windward Passage** *Sp.* Paso de los Vientos. *channel* Cuba/Haiti
57 T9 **Wineperu** C Guyana
25 O3 **Winfield** Alabama, S USA
31 Y15 **Winfield** Iowa, C USA
29 O7 **Winfield** Kansas, C USA
27 W6 **Winfield** Texas, SW USA
23 Q4 **Winfield** West Virginia, NE USA
31 N5 **Wing** North Dakota, N USA
191 U7 **Wingham** New South Wales, SE Australia
10 G16 **Wingham** Ontario, S Canada
35 T8 **Winifred** Montana, NW USA
10 F7 **Winisk** Ontario, C Canada
10 E8 **Winisk** ≈ Ontario, S Canada
10 E9 **Winisk Lake** ◎ Ontario, C Canada
26 L8 **Wink** Texas, SW USA
38 M14 **Winkelman** Arizona, SW USA
9 X17 **Winkler** Manitoba, S Canada
111 Q9 **Winklern** Tirol, W Austria
Winkowitz *see* Vinkovci
34 G9 **Winlock** Washington, NW USA
79 P17 **Winneba** SE Ghana
31 U11 **Winnebago** Minnesota, N USA
31 R13 **Winnebago** Nebraska, C USA
32 M7 **Winnebago, Lake** ◎ Wisconsin, N USA
32 M7 **Winneconne** Wisconsin, N USA
37 T3 **Winnemucca** Nevada, W USA
37 R4 **Winnemucca Lake** ◎ Nevada, W USA
103 H21 **Winnenden** Baden-Württemberg, SW Germany
31 N11 **Winner** South Dakota, N USA
35 V9 **Winnett** Montana, NW USA
12 I9 **Winneway** Québec, SE Canada
24 H6 **Winnfield** Louisiana, S USA
31 U4 **Winnibigoshish, Lake** ◎ Minnesota, N USA
27 X11 **Winnie** Texas, SW USA
9 Y16 **Winnipeg** Manitoba, S Canada
9 X16 **Winnipeg** ✕ Manitoba, S Canada
1 J8 **Winnipeg** ≈ Manitoba, S Canada
9 X16 **Winnipeg Beach** Manitoba, S Canada
9 W14 **Winnipeg, Lake** ◎ Manitoba, C Canada
9 W15 **Winnipegosis** Manitoba, S Canada
9 W15 **Winnipegosis, Lake** ◎ Manitoba, C Canada
21 O8 **Winnipesaukee, Lake** ◎ New Hampshire, NE USA
24 I6 **Winnsboro** Louisiana, S USA
23 R12 **Winnsboro** South Carolina, SE USA
27 W6 **Winnsboro** Texas, SW USA
31 X10 **Winona** Minnesota, N USA
24 L4 **Winona** Mississippi, S USA
29 W7 **Winona** Missouri, C USA
27 W7 **Winona** Texas, SW USA
20 M7 **Winooski River** ≈ Vermont, NE USA
100 P6 **Winschoten** Groningen, NE Netherlands
102 J10 **Winsen** Niedersachsen, N Germany
38 M11 **Winslow** Arizona, SW USA
21 Q7 **Winslow** Maine, NE USA
20 M12 **Winsted** Connecticut, NE USA
34 F14 **Winston** Oregon, NW USA
23 S9 **Winston Salem** North Carolina, SE USA
100 N5 **Winsum** Groningen, NE Netherlands
Wintanceaster *see* Winchester
25 W11 **Winter Garden** Florida, SE USA
8 J16 **Winter Harbour** Vancouver Island, British Columbia, SW Canada
25 W12 **Winter Haven** Florida, SE USA
25 X11 **Winter Park** Florida, SE USA
27 P8 **Winters** Texas, SW USA
31 U15 **Winterset** Iowa, C USA
100 O12 **Winterswijk** Gelderland, E Netherlands
110 G6 **Winterthur** Zürich, NE Switzerland
31 U9 **Winthrop** Minnesota, N USA
34 J7 **Winthrop** Washington, NW USA
189 V7 **Winton** Queensland, E Australia
193 C24 **Winton** Southland, South Island, NZ
23 X8 **Winton** North Carolina, SE USA
103 K15 **Wipper** ≈ C Germany
103 K14 **Wipper** ≈ C Germany
Wipper *see* Wieprza
176 Vv9 **Wiriagar, Sungai** ≈ Irian Jaya, E Indonesia
190 G6 **Wirraminna** South Australia
190 F4 **Wirrida** South Australia
190 F7 **Wirrulla** South Australia
Wirsitz *see* Wyrzysk
Wirz-See *see* Võrtsjärv
99 O19 **Wisbech** E England, UK
Wisby *see* Visby
21 Q8 **Wiscasset** Maine, NE USA
Wischau *see* Vyškov
32 J5 **Wisconsin** *off.* State of Wisconsin; *also known as* The Badger State. ◐ *state* N USA
32 L8 **Wisconsin Dells** Wisconsin, N USA
32 L8 **Wisconsin, Lake** ⊟ Wisconsin, N USA
32 L7 **Wisconsin Rapids** Wisconsin, N USA
32 L7 **Wisconsin River** ≈ Wisconsin, N USA
35 P11 **Wisdom** Montana, NW USA
23 P7 **Wise** Virginia, NE USA
41 Q7 **Wiseman** Alaska, USA
98 J12 **Wishaw** W Scotland, UK
31 O6 **Wishek** North Dakota, N USA
34 I11 **Wishram** Washington, NW USA
113 J17 **Wisła** Bielsko-Biała, S Poland
112 K11 **Wisła** *Eng.* Vistula, *Ger.* Weichsel. ≈ C Poland
Wiślany, Zalew *see* Vistula Lagoon
113 M16 **Wisłoka** ≈ SE Poland
102 L9 **Wismar** Mecklenburg-Vorpommern, N Germany
31 R14 **Wisner** Nebraska, C USA
105 V4 **Wissembourg** *var.* Weissenburg. Bas-Rhin, NE France
32 J6 **Wissota, Lake** ⊟ Wisconsin, N USA
99 O18 **Witham** ≈ E England, UK
99 O17 **Withernsea** E England, UK
39 Q13 **Withington, Mount** ▲ New Mexico, SW USA
25 U8 **Withlacoochee River** ≈ Florida/Georgia, SE USA
112 H11 **Witkowo** Konin, C Poland
99 M21 **Witney** S England, UK
103 E15 **Witten** Nordrhein-Westfalen, W Germany
103 N14 **Wittenberg** Sachsen-Anhalt, E Germany
32 L6 **Wittenberg** Wisconsin, N USA
102 L11 **Wittenberge** Brandenburg, N Germany
105 U7 **Wittenheim** Haut-Rhin, NE France
188 I7 **Wittenoom** Western Australia
Wittingau *see* Třeboň
102 K12 **Wittingen** Niedersachsen, C Germany
103 E18 **Wittlich** Rheinland-Pfalz, SW Germany
102 F9 **Wittmund** Niedersachsen, NW Germany
102 M10 **Wittstock** Brandenburg, NE Germany
194 M11 **Witu Islands** *island group* E PNG
112 O7 **Wiżajny** Suwałki, NE Poland
57 W10 **W.J. van Blommesteinmeer** ⊟ E Surinam
112 L11 **Wkra** *Ger.* Soldau. ≈ C Poland
112 I6 **Władysławowo** Gdańsk, N Poland
Wlaschim *see* Vlašim
113 E14 **Wleń** *Ger.* Lähn. Jelenia Góra, SW Poland
112 J11 **Włocławek** *Ger./Rus.* Vlotslavsk. Włocławek, C Poland
112 I11 **Włocławek** *off.* Województwo Włocławskie, *Ger./Rus.* Vlotslavsk. ◐ *province* C Poland
Włocławskie, Województwo *see* Włocławek
112 P13 **Włodawa** *Rus.* Vlodava. Chełm, SE Poland
Włodzimierz *see* Volodymyr-Volyns'kyy
113 K15 **Włoszczowa** Kielce, S Poland
85 C19 **Wlotzkasbaken** Erongo, W Namibia
152 L11 **Wobkent** *Rus.* Vabkent. Bukhoro Wiloyati, C Uzbekistan
13 R12 **Woburn** Québec, SE Canada
21 O11 **Woburn** Massachusetts, NE USA
Wocheiner Feistritz *see* Bohinjska Bistrica
Wöchma *see* Võhma
153 S11 **Wodil** *var.* Vuadil'. Farghona Wiloyati, E Uzbekistan
189 V14 **Wodonga** Victoria, SE Australia
113 I17 **Wodzisław Śląski** *Ger.* Loslau. Katowice, S Poland
100 I11 **Woerden** Zuid-Holland, C Netherlands
100 I8 **Wognum** Noord-Holland, NW Netherlands
Wohlau *see* Wołów
110 F7 **Wohlen** Aargau, NW Switzerland
205 R2 **Wohlthat Mountains** ▲ Antarctica
176 W9 **Woinui, Selat** *strait* Irian Jaya, E Indonesia
194 K15 **Woitape** Central, S PNG
Wōjjā *see* Wotje Atoll
Wojwodina *see* Vojvodina
176 W13 **Wokam, Pulau** *island* Kepulauan Aru, E Indonesia
99 N22 **Woking** SE England, UK
Woldenberg Neumark *see* Dobiegniew
196 K15 **Woleai Atoll** *atoll* Caroline Islands, W Micronesia
Woleu *see* Uolo, Río
81 E17 **Woleu-Ntem** *off.* Province du Woleu-Ntem, *var.* Le Woleu-Ntem. ◐ *province* W Gabon
34 F15 **Wolf Creek** Oregon, NW USA
28 K9 **Wolf Creek** ≈ Oklahoma/Texas, SW USA
39 R7 **Wolf Creek Pass** *pass* Colorado, C USA
21 O9 **Wolfeboro** New Hampshire, NE USA
27 U5 **Wolfe City** Texas, SW USA
12 L15 **Wolfe Island** *island* Ontario, SE Canada
103 M14 **Wolfen** Sachsen-Anhalt, E Germany
102 J13 **Wolfenbüttel** Niedersachsen, C Germany
111 T4 **Wolfern** Oberösterreich, N Austria
111 Q6 **Wolfgangsee** *var.* Abersee, St Wolfgangsee. ◎ N Austria
41 P9 **Wolf Mountain** ▲ Alaska, USA
35 X7 **Wolf Point** Montana, NW USA
24 L8 **Wolf River** ≈ Mississippi, S USA
32 M7 **Wolf River** ≈ Wisconsin, N USA
111 U9 **Wolfsberg** Kärnten, SE Austria
102 K12 **Wolfsburg** Niedersachsen, N Germany
59 B17 **Wolf, Volcán** ⛰ Galapagos Islands, Ecuador, E Pacific Ocean
102 O8 **Wolgast** Mecklenburg-Vorpommern, NE Germany
110 F8 **Wolhusen** Luzern, W Switzerland
112 D8 **Wolin** *Ger.* Wollin. Szczecin, NW Poland
111 Y3 **Wolkersdorf** Niederösterreich, NE Austria
Wołkowysk *see* Vawkavysk
Wöllan *see* Velenje
15 I2 **Wollaston, Cape** *headland* Victoria Island, Northwest Territories, NW Canada
65 J25 **Wollaston, Isla** *island* S Chile
9 U11 **Wollaston Lake** Saskatchewan, C Canada
9 T10 **Wollaston Lake** ◎ Saskatchewan, C Canada
15 I3 **Wollaston Peninsula** *peninsula* Victoria Island, Northwest Territories, NW Canada
Wollin *see* Wolin
191 S9 **Wollongong** New South Wales, SE Australia
Wolmar *see* Valmiera
102 L13 **Wolmirstedt** Sachsen-Anhalt, C Germany
112 M11 **Wołomin** Warszawa, C Poland
112 G13 **Wołów** *Ger.* Wohlau. Wrocław, SW Poland
Wołożyn *see* Valozhyn
12 G11 **Wolseley Bay** Ontario, S Canada
31 P10 **Wolsey** South Dakota, N USA
112 F12 **Wolsztyn** Zielona Góra, W Poland
100 M7 **Wolvega** *Fris.* Wolvegea. Friesland, N Netherlands
Wolvegea *see* Wolvega
99 K19 **Wolverhampton** C England, UK
Wolverine State *see* Michigan
101 G18 **Wolvertem** Vlaams Brabant, C Belgium
101 H16 **Wommelgem** Antwerpen, N Belgium
176 W11 **Wondiwoi, Pegunungan** ▲ Irian Jaya, E Indonesia
194 J13 **Wonenara** *var.* Wonerara. Eastern Highlands, C PNG
Wonerara *see* Wonenara
Wongalara Lake *see* Wongalarroo Lake
191 N6 **Wongalarroo Lake** *var.* Wongalara Lake. *seasonal lake* New South Wales, SE Australia
169 Y15 **Wŏnju** *Jap.* Genshū. N South Korea
8 M12 **Wonowon** British Columbia, W Canada
169 X13 **Wŏnsan** SE North Korea
191 O13 **Wonthaggi** Victoria, SE Australia
25 N2 **Woodall Mountain** ▲ Mississippi, S USA
25 W7 **Woodbine** Georgia, SE USA
31 S14 **Woodbine** Iowa, C USA
20 J17 **Woodbine** New Jersey, NE USA
23 W4 **Woodbridge** Virginia, NE USA
191 V4 **Woodburn** New South Wales, SE Australia
34 G11 **Woodburn** Oregon, NW USA
22 K9 **Woodbury** Tennessee, S USA
191 V5 **Wooded Bluff** *headland* New South Wales, SE Australia
191 V3 **Woodenbong** New South Wales, SE Australia
37 R11 **Woodlake** California, W USA
37 N7 **Woodland** California, W USA
21 T5 **Woodland** Maine, NE USA
34 G10 **Woodland** Washington, NW USA
39 T5 **Woodland Park** Colorado, C USA
195 P15 **Woodlark Island** *var.* Murua Island. *island* SE PNG
Woodle Island *see* Kuria
9 T17 **Wood Mountain** ▲ Saskatchewan, S Canada
32 K15 **Wood River** Illinois, N USA
31 P16 **Wood River** Nebraska, C USA
41 R9 **Wood River** ≈ Alaska, USA
41 O13 **Wood River Lakes** *lakes* Alaska, USA
190 C1 **Woodroffe, Mount** ▲ South Australia
23 P11 **Woodruff** South Carolina, SE USA
32 K4 **Woodruff** Wisconsin, N USA
27 T14 **Woodsboro** Texas, SW USA
33 U13 **Woodsfield** Ohio, N USA
189 P4 **Woods, Lake** ◎ Northern Territory, N Australia
9 Z16 **Woods, Lake of the** *Fr.* Lac des Bois. ◎ Canada/USA
27 Q6 **Woodson** Texas, SW USA
11 N14 **Woodstock** New Brunswick, SE Canada
12 F16 **Woodstock** Ontario, S Canada
32 M10 **Woodstock** Illinois, N USA
20 M9 **Woodstock** Vermont, NE USA
23 U4 **Woodstock** Virginia, NE USA
21 N8 **Woodsville** New Hampshire, NE USA

◆ Country
● Country Capital
◇ Dependent Territory
○ Dependent Territory Capital
◐ Administrative Region
✕ International Airport
▲ Mountain
▲ Mountain Range
⛰ Volcano
≈ River
◎ Lake
⊟ Reservoir

192 M12 **Woodville** Manawatu-Wanganui, North Island, NZ
24 J7 **Woodville** Mississippi, S USA
27 X9 **Woodville** Texas, SW USA
28 K9 **Woodward** Oklahoma, C USA
31 O5 **Woodworth** North Dakota, N USA
176 Y12 **Woogi** Irian Jaya, E Indonesia
176 Ww9 **Wool** Irian Jaya, E Indonesia
191 V5 **Woolgoolga** New South Wales, E Australia
190 H6 **Woomera** South Australia
21 O12 **Woonsocket** Rhode Island, NE USA
31 P10 **Woonsocket** South Dakota, N USA
33 T12 **Wooster** Ohio, N USA
82 L12 **Woqooyi Galbeed** *off.* Gobolka Woqooyi Galbeed. ◈ *region* NW Somalia
110 E8 **Worb** Bern, C Switzerland
85 F26 **Worcester** Western Cape, SW South Africa
99 L20 **Worcester** *hist.* Wigorna Ceaster. W England, UK
21 N11 **Worcester** Massachusetts, NE USA
99 L20 **Worcestershire** *cultural region* C England, UK
34 H16 **Worden** Oregon, NW USA
111 O6 **Wörgl** Tirol, W Austria
176 Ww14 **Workai, Pulau** *island* Kepulauan Aru, E Indonesia
99 J15 **Workington** NW England, UK
100 K7 **Workum** Friesland, N Netherlands
35 V13 **Worland** Wyoming, C USA
Wormatia *see* Worms
101 N25 **Wormeldange** Grevenmacher, E Luxembourg
100 I9 **Wormer** Noord-Holland, C Netherlands
103 G19 **Worms** *anc.* Augusta Vangionum, Borbetomagus, Wormatia. Rheinland-Pfalz, SW Germany
Worms *see* Vormsi
103 K21 **Wörnitz** ~ S Germany
103 G21 **Wörth** Rheinland-Pfalz, SW Germany
27 U8 **Wortham** Texas, SW USA
111 S9 **Worther See** ◎ S Austria
99 O23 **Worthing** SE England, UK
31 S11 **Worthington** Minnesota, N USA
33 S13 **Worthington** Ohio, N USA
37 W8 **Worthington Peak** ▲ Nevada, W USA
176 Y12 **Wosi** Irian Jaya, E Indonesia
176 W11 **Wosimi** Irian Jaya, E Indonesia
201 R5 **Wotho Atoll** *var.* Wōtto. *atoll* Ralik Chain, W Marshall Islands
201 V5 **Wotje Atoll** *var.* Wōjjā. *atoll* Ratak Chain, E Marshall Islands
Wotoe *see* Wotu
Wottawa *see* Otava
Wōtto *see* Wotho Atoll
175 Pp10 **Wotu** *prev.* Wotoe. Sulawesi, C Indonesia
100 K11 **Woudenberg** Utrecht, C Netherlands
100 I13 **Woudrichem** Noord-Brabant, S Netherlands
45 N8 **Wounta** *var.* Huaunta. Región Autónoma Atlántico Norte, NE Nicaragua
175 R12 **Wowoni, Pulau** *island* C Indonesia
175 Qq12 **Wowoni, Selat** *strait* Sulawesi, C Indonesia
83 J17 **Woyamdero Plain** *plain* E Kenya
Woyens *see* Vojens
Wozrojdeniye Oroli *see* Vozrozhdeniya, Ostrov
Wrangel Island *see* Vrangelya, Ostrov
41 Y13 **Wrangell** Wrangell Island, Alaska, USA
40 C15 **Wrangell, Cape** *headland* Attu Island, Alaska, USA
41 S11 **Wrangell, Mount** ▲ Alaska, USA
41 T11 **Wrangell Mountains** ▲▲ Alaska, USA
207 S7 **Wrangel Plain** *undersea feature* Arctic Ocean
98 H6 **Wrath, Cape** *headland* N Scotland, UK
39 W3 **Wray** Colorado, C USA
46 K13 **Wreck Point** *headland* C Jamaica
85 C23 **Wreck Point** *headland* W South Africa
25 V4 **Wrens** Georgia, SE USA
99 K18 **Wrexham** NE Wales, UK
29 R13 **Wright City** Oklahoma, C USA
204 J12 **Wright Island** *island* Antarctica
11 N9 **Wright, Mont** ▲ Québec, E Canada
27 X5 **Wright Patman Lake** ⊞ Texas, SW USA
38 M16 **Wrightson, Mount** ▲ Arizona, SW USA
25 U5 **Wrightsville** Georgia, SE USA
23 W12 **Wrightsville Beach** North Carolina, SE USA
37 T15 **Wrightwood** California, W USA
15 Gg7 **Wrigley** Northwest Territories, W Canada
113 G14 **Wrocław** *Eng./Ger.* Breslau. Wrocław, SW Poland
113 G14 **Wrocław** *off.* Województwo Wrocławskie. ◈ *province* SW Poland
Wrocławskie, Województwo *see* Wrocław
112 F10 **Wronki** *Ger.* Fronicken. Piła, NW Poland
112 H11 **Września** Poznań, C Poland
112 F12 **Wschowa** Leszno, W Poland
Wsetin *see* Vsetín
188 I12 **Wubin** Western Australia
169 W9 **Wuchang** Heilongjiang, NE China
Wuchang *see* Wuhan
Wu-chou/Wuchow *see* Wuzhou
166 M16 **Wuchuan** *var.* Meilu. Guangdong, S China
166 K10 **Wuchuan** *prev.* Duru. Guizhou, S China
169 O13 **Wuchuan** Nei Mongol Zizhiqu, N China
169 V6 **Wudalianchi** Heilongjiang, NE China
165 O11 **Wudaoliang** Qinghai, C China
147 Q13 **Wuday'ah** *spring/well* S Saudi Arabia
79 V13 **Wudil** Kano, N Nigeria
166 G12 **Wuding** Yunnan, SW China
166 L4 **Wuding He** ~ C China
190 G8 **Wudinna** South Australia
163 P10 **Wudu** Gansu, C China
166 L9 **Wufeng** Hubei, C China
167 O11 **Wugong Shan** ▲▲ S China
163 P7 **Wuhai** Nei Mongol Zizhiqu, N China
167 O9 **Wuhan** *var.* Han-kou, Han-k'ou, Hanyang, Wuchang, Wu-han; *prev.* Hankow. Hubei, C China
167 Q7 **Wuhe** Anhui, E China
Wuhsi/Wu-hsi *see* Wuxi
Wuhsien *see* Suzhou
167 Q8 **Wuhu** *var.* Wu-na-mu. Anhui, E China
Wūjae *see* Ujae Atoll
166 K11 **Wu Jiang** ~ C China
Wujlān *see* Ujelang Atoll
79 W15 **Wukari** Taraba, E Nigeria
166 H11 **Wulian Feng** ▲▲ SW China
166 F13 **Wuliang Shan** ▲▲ SW China
176 U15 **Wuliaru, Pulau** *island* Kepulauan Tanimbar, E Indonesia
166 K11 **Wuling Shan** ▲▲ S China
111 Y5 **Wulka** ~ E Austria
Wulkan *see* Vulcan
111 T3 **Wullowitz** Oberösterreich, N Austria
Wu-lu-k'o-mu-shi/Wu-lu-mu-ch'i *see* Ürümqi
81 D14 **Wum** Nord-Ouest, NE Cameroon
166 H12 **Wumeng Shan** ▲▲ SW China
166 K14 **Wuming** Guangxi Zhuangzu Zizhiqu, S China
102 I10 **Wümme** ~ NW Germany
Wu-na-mu *see* Wuhu
176 Y11 **Wunen** Irian Jaya, E Indonesia
10 D9 **Wunnummin Lake** ◎ Ontario, C Canada
82 D13 **Wun Rog** Warab, S Sudan
103 M18 **Wunsiedel** Bayern, E Germany
102 I12 **Wunstorf** Niedersachsen, NW Germany
177 G3 **Wuntho** Sagaing, N Burma
103 F15 **Wupper** ~ W Germany
103 E15 **Wuppertal** *prev.* Barmen-Elberfeld. Nordrhein-Westfalen, W Germany
166 K5 **Wuqi** Shaanxi, C China
167 P4 **Wuqiao** *var.* Sangyuan. Hebei, E China
103 L23 **Würm** ~ SE Germany
79 T12 **Wurno** Sokoto, NW Nigeria
103 I19 **Würzburg** Bayern, SW Germany
103 N15 **Wurzen** Sachsen, E Germany
166 L9 **Wu Shan** ▲ C China
164 G7 **Wushi** *var.* Uqturpan. Xinjiang Uygur Zizhiqu, NW China
Wusih *see* Wuxi
67 N18 **Wüst Seamount** *undersea feature* S Atlantic Ocean
Wusuli Jiang/Wusuri *see* Ussuri
167 N3 **Wutai Shan** ▲ C China
166 H10 **Wutongqiao** Sichuan, C China
165 P6 **Wutongwozi Quan** *spring* NW China
194 E9 **Wutung** Sandaun, NW PNG
101 H15 **Wuustwezel** Antwerpen, N Belgium
194 G8 **Wuvulu Island** *island* NW PNG
165 U9 **Wuwei** *var.* Liangzhou. Gansu, C China
167 R8 **Wuxi** *var.* Wuhsi, Wu-hsi, Wusih. Jiangsu, E China
Wuxing *see* Huzhou
166 L14 **Wuxuan** Guangxi Zhuangzu Zizhiqu, S China
166 K11 **Wuyang He** ~ S China
169 X6 **Wuyiling** Heilongjiang, NE China
163 T12 **Wuyi Shan** ▲▲ SE China
167 Q11 **Wuyishan** *prev.* Chong'an. Fujian, SE China
168 M13 **Wuyuan** Nei Mongol Zizhiqu, N China
166 L17 **Wuzhi Shan** ▲ S China
165 W8 **Wuzhong** Ningxia, N China
166 M14 **Wuzhou** *var.* Wu-chou, Wuchow. Guangxi Zhuangzu Zizhiqu, S China
20 H12 **Wyalusing** Pennsylvania, NE USA
190 M10 **Wycheproof** Victoria, SE Australia
99 K21 **Wye** *Wel.* Gwy. ~ England/Wales, UK
Wyłkowyszki *see* Vilkaviškis
99 P19 **Wymondham** E England, UK
31 R17 **Wymore** Nebraska, C USA
190 E5 **Wynbring** South Australia
189 N3 **Wyndham** Western Australia
31 R6 **Wyndmere** North Dakota, N USA
29 X11 **Wynne** Arkansas, C USA
29 N12 **Wynnewood** Oklahoma, C USA
191 O15 **Wynyard** Tasmania, SE Australia
9 U15 **Wynyard** Saskatchewan, S Canada
35 V11 **Wyola** Montana, NW USA
190 A4 **Wyola Lake** *salt lake* South Australia
33 P9 **Wyoming** Michigan, N USA
35 V14 **Wyoming** *off.* State of Wyoming; also known as The Equality State. ◈ *state* C USA
35 S15 **Wyoming Range** ▲▲ Wyoming, C USA
191 T8 **Wyong** New South Wales, SE Australia
112 G9 **Wyrzysk** *Ger.* Wirsitz. Piła, W Poland
Wysg *see* Usk
112 O10 **Wysokie Mazowieckie** Łomża, E Poland
112 M11 **Wyszków** *Ger.* Probstberg. Ostrołęka, NE Poland
112 L11 **Wyszogród** Płock, C Poland
23 R7 **Wytheville** Virginia, NE USA

X

82 Q12 **Xaafuun** *It.* Hafun. Bari, NE Somalia
82 Q12 **Xaafuun, Raas** *var.* Ras Hafun. *headland* NE Somalia
Xábia *see* Jávea
44 C4 **Xaclbal, Río** *var.* Xalbal. ~ Guatemala/Mexico
143 Y10 **Xaçmaz** *Rus.* Khachmas. N Azerbaijan
82 O12 **Xadeed** *var.* Haded. *physical region* N Somalia
165 O14 **Xagquka** Xizang Zizhiqu, W China
178 I6 **Xai** *var.* Muang Xay, Muong Sai. Oudômxai, N Laos
164 F10 **Xaidulla** Xinjiang Uygur Zizhiqu, W China
178 I7 **Xaignabouli** *prev.* Muang Xaignabouri, *Fr.* Sayaboury. Xaignabouli, N Laos
178 J7 **Xai Lai Leng, Phou** ▲ Laos/Vietnam
164 L15 **Xainza** Xizang Zizhiqu, W China
164 L16 **Xaitongmoin** Xizang Zizhiqu, W China
85 M20 **Xai-Xai** *prev.* João Belo, Vila de João Bel. Gaza, S Mozambique
Xalbal *see* Xaclbal, Río
82 P13 **Xalin** Nugaal, N Somalia
178 J6 **Xam Nua** *var.* Sam Neua. Houaphan, N Laos
84 D11 **Xá-Muteba** *Port.* Cinco de Outubro. Lunda Norte, NE Angola
85 C16 **Xangongo** *Port.* Rocadas. Cunene, SW Angola
143 W12 **Xankändi** *Rus.* Khankendi; *prev.* Stepanakert. SW Azerbaijan
143 V11 **Xanlar** *Rus.* Khanlar. NW Azerbaijan
116 J13 **Xánthi** Anatolikí Makedonía kai Thráki, NE Greece
62 H13 **Xanxerê** Santa Catarina, S Brazil
83 O15 **Xarardheere** Mudug, E Somalia
133 W8 **Xar Moron** ~ NE China
Xarra *see* Xarrë
115 L23 **Xarrë** *var.* Xarra. Vlorë, S Albania
84 D12 **Xassengue** Lunda Sul, NW Angola
107 S11 **Xátiva** *var.* Jativa; *anc.* Setabis. País Valenciano, E Spain
Xauen *see* Chefchaouen
62 K10 **Xavantes, Represa de** *var.* Represa de Chavantes. ⊞ S Brazil
164 I7 **Xayar** Xinjiang Uygur Zizhiqu, W China
Xäzär Dänizi *see* Caspian Sea
178 Jj9 **Xé Bangfai** ~ C Laos
178 Jj10 **Xé Banghiang** *var.* Bang Hieng. ~ S Laos
Xégar *see* Tingri
33 R14 **Xenia** Ohio, N USA
Xeres *see* Jeréz de la Frontera
117 E15 **Xeriás** ~ C Greece
117 G17 **Xeró** ▲ Évvoia, C Greece
85 H18 **Xhumo** Central, C Botswana
167 N15 **Xiachuan Dao** *island* S China
Xiacun *see* Rushan
Xiaguan *see* Dali
165 U11 **Xiahe** *var.* Labrang. Gansu, C China
167 Q13 **Xiamen** *var.* Hsia-men; *prev.* Amoy. Fujian, SE China
166 L6 **Xi'an** *var.* Changan, Sian, Signan, Siking, Singan, Xian. Shaanxi, C China
166 L10 **Xianfeng** Hubei, C China
Xiang *see* Hunan
167 N7 **Xiangcheng** Henan, C China
166 F10 **Xiangcheng** *prev.* Qagchêng. Sichuan, C China
166 M8 **Xiangfan** *var.* Xiangyang. Hubei, C China
167 N10 **Xiang Jiang** ~ S China
Xiangkhoang *see* Pèk
178 Ii7 **Xiangkhoang, Plateau de** *var.* Plain of Jars. *plateau* N Laos
167 N11 **Xiangtan** *var.* Hsiang-t'an, Siangtan. Hunan, S China
167 N11 **Xiangxiang** Hunan, S China
Xiangyang *see* Xiangfan
167 S10 **Xianju** Zhejiang, SE China
167 K8 **Xianshui He** ~ C China
167 N9 **Xiantao** *var.* Mianyang. Hubei, C China
167 R10 **Xianxia Ling** ▲▲ SE China
166 K6 **Xianyang** Shaanxi, C China
164 L5 **Xiaocaohu** Xinjiang Uygur Zizhiqu, W China
169 W6 **Xiao Hinggan Ling** *Eng.* Lesser Khingan Range. ▲▲ NE China
166 M6 **Xiao Shan** ▲▲ C China
166 M12 **Xiao Shui** ~ S China
167 P6 **Xiaoxian** *var.* Xiao Xian. Anhui, E China
166 G11 **Xichang** Sichuan, C China
43 P11 **Xicoténcatl** Tamaulipas, C Mexico
Xieng Khouang *see* Pèk
Xieng Ngeun *see* Muong Xiang Ngeun
165 X10 **Xifeng** Gansu, C China
166 J11 **Xifeng** Guizhou, S China
Xigang *see* Helan
164 L16 **Xigazê** *var.* Jih-k'a-tse, Shigatse, Xigaze. Xizang Zizhiqu, W China
166 I8 **Xi He** ~ C China
165 W11 **Xihe** Gansu, C China
Xihuachi *see* Heshui
165 Q7 **Xijian Quan** *spring* NW China
165 W10 **Xiji** Ningxia, N China
166 M14 **Xi Jiang** *var.* Hsi Chiang, *Eng.* West River. ~ S China
166 K15 **Xijin Shuiku** ⊞ S China
Xilaganí *see* Xylaganí
166 I13 **Xilin** *prev.* Bada. Guangxi Zhuangzu Zizhiqu, S China
169 Q10 **Xilinhot** *var.* Silinhot. Nei Mongol Zizhiqu, N China
Xilokastro *see* Xylókastro
Xin *see* Xinjiang Uygur Zizhiqu
167 R10 **Xin'anjiang Shuiku** ⊞ SE China
Xin'anzhen *see* Xinyi
169 Q7 **Xin Barag Youqi** *var.* Altan Emel. Nei Mongol Zizhiqu, N China
169 R7 **Xin Barag Zuoqi** *var.* Amgalang. Nei Mongol Zizhiqu, N China
169 W12 **Xinbin** Liaoning, NE China
167 O7 **Xincai** Henan, C China
165 V8 **Xincheng** *var.* Yinchuanzhan. Ningxia, N China
167 O13 **Xinfeng** Jiangxi, S China
167 O14 **Xinfengjiang Shuiku** ⊞ S China
169 T13 **Xingcheng** Liaoning, NE China
84 E11 **Xinge** Lunda Norte, NE Angola
167 P12 **Xingguo** Jiangxi, S China
165 S11 **Xinghai** Qinghai, C China
167 R7 **Xinghua** Jiangsu, E China
Xingkai Hu *see* Khanka, Lake
167 P13 **Xingning** Guangdong, S China
166 I13 **Xingren** Guizhou, S China
167 O4 **Xingtai** Hebei, E China
61 J14 **Xingu, Rio** ~ C Brazil
165 P6 **Xingxingxia** Xinjiang Uygur Zizhiqu, NW China
166 I13 **Xingyi** Guizhou, S China
164 I6 **Xinhe** *var.* Toksu. Xinjiang Uygur Zizhiqu, NW China
Xin Hot *see* Abag Qi
165 T10 **Xining** *var.* Hsining, Hsi-ning, Sining. *province capital* Qinghai, C China
167 O4 **Xinji** *prev.* Shulu. Hebei, E China
167 P10 **Xinjian** Jiangxi, S China
Xinjiang *see* Xinjiang Uygur Zizhiqu
168 D8 **Xinjiang Uygur Zizhiqu** *var.* Sinkiang, Sinkiang Uighur Autonomous Region, Xin, Xinjiang. ◈ *autonomous region* NW China
166 H9 **Xinjin** Sichuan, C China
Xinjin *see* Pulandian
169 U12 **Xinmin** Liaoning, NE China
166 M12 **Xinning** Hunan, S China
Xinpu *see* Lianyungang
167 P5 **Xinwen** *prev.* Suncun. Shandong, E China
Xin Xian *see* Xinzhou
167 N6 **Xinxiang** Henan, C China
167 O8 **Xinyang** *var.* Hsin-yang, Sinyang. Henan, C China
167 Q6 **Xinyi** *var.* Xin'anzhen. Jiangsu, E China
167 Q6 **Xinyi He** ~ E China
167 O11 **Xinyu** Jiangxi, S China
164 I5 **Xinyuan** *var.* Künes. Xinjiang Uygur Zizhiqu, NW China
Xinyuan *see* Tianjun
168 M14 **Xinzhao Shan** ▲ N China
167 N3 **Xinzhou** *var.* Xin Xian. Shanxi, C China
106 H4 **Xinzo de Limia** Galicia, NW Spain
Xions *see* Książ Wielkopolski
167 O7 **Xiping** Henan, C China
165 T11 **Xiqing Shan** ▲▲ C China
61 N16 **Xique-Xique** Bahia, E Brazil
117 E14 **Xirovoúni** ▲ N Greece
Xishanzui *see* Urad Qianqi
166 I11 **Xishui** Guizhou, S China
167 O9 **Xishui** Hubei, C China
169 R10 **Xi Ujimqin Qi** *var.* Bayan Ul Hot. Nei Mongol Zizhiqu, N China
166 K11 **Xiushan** Sichuan, C China
167 O10 **Xiu Shui** ~ S China
164 J16 **Xixabangma Feng** ▲ W China
166 M7 **Xixia** Henan, C China
Xixona *see* Jijona
Xizang *see* Xizang Zizhiqu
Xizang Gaoyuan *see* Qingzang Gaoyuan
166 E9 **Xizang Zizhiqu** *var.* Thibet, Tibetan Autonomous Region, Xizang, *Eng.* Tibet. ◈ *autonomous region* W China
169 U14 **Xizhong Dao** *island* N China
Xolotlán *see* Managua, Lago de
165 N9 **Xorkol** Xinjiang Uygur Zizhiqu, NW China
43 X14 **Xpujil** Quintana Roo, E Mexico
Xuancheng *see* Xuanzhou
178 Jj9 **Xuân Đuc** Quang Binh, C Vietnam
166 L9 **Xuan'en** Hubei, C China
166 K8 **Xuanhan** Sichuan, C China
167 O2 **Xuanhua** Hebei, E China
167 P4 **Xuanhui He** ~ E China
167 Q8 **Xuanzhou** *var.* Xuancheng. Anhui, E China
167 N7 **Xuchang** Henan, C China
143 X10 **Xudat** *Rus.* Khudat. NE Azerbaijan
83 M16 **Xuddur** *var.* Hudur, *It.* Oddur. Bakool, SW Somalia
82 O13 **Xudun** Nugaal, N Somalia
166 L11 **Xuefeng Shan** ▲▲ S China
44 F2 **Xunantunich** *ruins* Cayo, W Belize
169 W6 **Xun He** ~ NE China
166 L7 **Xun He** ~ C China
166 L14 **Xun Jiang** ~ S China
169 W5 **Xunke** Heilongjiang, NE China
167 P13 **Xunwu** Jiangxi, S China
167 O3 **Xushui** Hebei, E China
166 L16 **Xuwen** Guangdong, S China
166 I11 **Xuyong** *var.* Yongning. Sichuan, C China
167 P6 **Xuzhou** *var.* Hsu-chou, Suchow, Tongshan; *prev.* T'ung-shan. Jiangsu, E China
116 K13 **Xylaganí** *var.* Xilaganí. Anatolikí Makedonía kai Thráki, NE Greece
117 F19 **Xylókastro** *var.* Xilokastro. Pelopónnisos, S Greece

Y

166 H9 **Ya'an** *var.* Yaan. Sichuan, C China
190 L10 **Yaapeet** Victoria, SE Australia
81 D15 **Yabassi** Littoral, W Cameroon
83 J15 **Yabēlo** S Ethiopia
172 Pp5 **Yabetsu-gawa** *var.* Yûbetsu-gawa. ~ Hokkaidō, NE Japan
116 H9 **Yablanitsa** Loveshka Oblast, W Bulgaria
45 N7 **Yablis** Región Autónoma Atlántico Norte, NE Nicaragua
126 Kk16 **Yablonovyy Khrebet** ▲▲ S Russian Federation
168 J14 **Yabrai Shan** ▲▲ NE China
47 U5 **Yabucoa** E Puerto Rico
197 K14 **Yacata** *island* Lau Group, E Fiji
166 J11 **Yachi He** ~ S China
34 H10 **Yacolt** Washington, NW USA
56 M10 **Yacuaray** Amazonas, S Venezuela
59 M22 **Yacuiba** Tarija, S Bolivia
59 K16 **Yacuma, Río** ~ C Bolivia
161 H16 **Yādgīr** Karnātaka, C India
23 R8 **Yadkin River** ~ North Carolina, SE USA
23 R9 **Yadkinville** North Carolina, SE USA
131 P3 **Yadrin** Chuvashskaya Respublika, W Russian Federation
197 I13 **Yadua** *prev.* Yandua. *island* NW Fiji
172 Oo17 **Yaeyama-shotō** *var.* Yaegama-shotō. *island group* SW Japan
77 O8 **Yafran** NW Libya
197 L15 **Yagasa Cluster** *island group* Lau Group, E Fiji
172 Oo3 **Yagashiri-tō** *island* NE Japan
67 H21 **Yaghan Basin** *undersea feature* SE Pacific Ocean
127 Nn9 **Yagodnoye** Magadanskaya Oblast', E Russian Federation
Yagotin *see* Yahotyn
80 G12 **Yagoua** Extrême-Nord, NE Cameroon
165 Q11 **Yagradagzê Shan** ▲ C China
Yaguachi *see* Yaguachi Nuevo
58 B7 **Yaguachi Nuevo** *var.* Yaguachi. Guayas, W Ecuador
Yaguarón, Río *see* Jaguarão, Rio
171 I16 **Yahagi-gawa** ~ Honshū, SW Japan
119 Q11 **Yahorlyts'kyy Lyman** *bay* S Ukraine
119 Q5 **Yahotyn** *Rus.* Yagotin. Kyyivs'ka Oblast', N Ukraine
42 L12 **Yahualica** Jalisco, SW Mexico
81 L17 **Yahuma** Haut-Zaïre, N Zaire
142 K15 **Yahyalı** Kayseri, C Turkey
178 Gg15 **Yai, Khao** ▲ SW Thailand
171 Kk15 **Yaita** Tochigi, Honshū, S Japan
171 I17 **Yaizu** Shizuoka, Honshū, S Japan
166 G9 **Yajiang** Sichuan, C China
121 O14 **Yakawlyevichi** *Rus.* Yakovlevichi. Vitsyebskaya Voblasts', NE Belorussia
169 S6 **Yakeshi** Nei Mongol Zizhiqu, N China
34 I9 **Yakima** Washington, NW USA
34 J10 **Yakima River** ~ Washington, NW USA
116 G7 **Yakimovo** Oblast Montana, NW Bulgaria
Yakkabag *see* Yakkabogh
153 N12 **Yakkabogh** *Rus.* Yakkabag. Qashqadaryo Wiloyati, S Uzbekistan
154 L12 **Yakmach** Baluchistān, SW Pakistan
79 O12 **Yako** W Burkina
41 W13 **Yakobi Island** *island* Alexander Archipelago, Alaska, USA
81 K16 **Yakoma** Equateur, N Zaire
116 H11 **Yakoruda** Sofiyska Oblast, SW Bulgaria
Yakovlevichi *see* Yakawlyevichi
131 T2 **Yakshur-Bod'ya** Udmurtskaya Respublika, NW Russian Federation
172 N6 **Yakumo** Hokkaidō, NE Japan
170 B17 **Yaku-shima** *island* Nansei-shotō, SW Japan
41 V12 **Yakutat** Alaska, USA
41 U12 **Yakutat Bay** *inlet* Alaska, USA
Yakutia/Yakutiya/Yakutiya, Respublika *see* Sakha (Yakutiya), Respublika
126 M11 **Yakutsk** Respublika Sakha (Yakutiya), NE Russian Federation
178 Hh17 **Yala** Yala, SW Thailand
190 D6 **Yalata** South Australia
33 S9 **Yale** Michigan, N USA
188 I11 **Yalgoo** Western Australia
116 O12 **Yalıköy** İstanbul, NW Turkey
81 L14 **Yalinga** Haute-Kotto, C Central African Republic
121 M17 **Yalizava** *Rus.* Yelizovo. Mahilyowskaya Voblasts', E Belorussia
46 L13 **Yallahs Hill** ▲ E Jamaica
24 L3 **Yalobusha River** ~ Mississippi, S USA
81 H15 **Yaloké** Ombella-Mpoko, W Central African Republic
166 E7 **Yalong Jiang** ~ C China
142 E11 **Yalova** İstanbul, NW Turkey
Yaloveny *see* Ialoveni
Yalpug *see* Ialpug
Yalpug, Ozero *see* Yalpuh, Ozero
119 N12 **Yalpuh, Ozero** *Rus.* Ozero Yalpug. ◎ SW Ukraine
119 T14 **Yalta** Respublika Krym, S Ukraine
169 W12 **Yalu** *Chin.* Yalu Jiang, *Jap.* Oryokko, *Kor.* Amnok-kang. ~ China/North Korea
Yalu Jiang *see* Yalu
125 F12 **Yalutorovsk** Tyumenskaya Oblast', C Russian Federation
142 F14 **Yalvaç** Isparta, SW Turkey
172 N12 **Yamada** Iwate, Honshū, C Japan
170 Cc14 **Yamaga** Kumamoto, Kyūshū, SW Japan
171 L12 **Yamagata** Yamagata, Honshū, C Japan
171 Ll12 **Yamagata** *off.* Yamagata-ken. ◈ *prefecture* Honshū, C Japan
170 Bb16 **Yamagawa** Kagoshima, Kyūshū, SW Japan
170 Dd12 **Yamaguchi** *var.* Yamaguti. Yamaguchi, Honshū, SW Japan
170 Dd12 **Yamaguchi** *off.* Yamaguchi-ken, *var.* Yamaguti. ◈ *prefecture* Honshū, SW Japan
Yamaguti *see* Yamaguchi
129 X5 **Yamalo-Nenetskiy Avtonomnyy Okrug** ◈ *autonomous district* N Russian Federation
126 Gg6 **Yamal, Poluostrov** *peninsula* N Russian Federation
171 J16 **Yamanashi** *off.* Yamanashi-ken, *var.* Yamanasi. ◈ *prefecture* Honshū, S Japan
Yamanasi *see* Yamanashi
Yamanīyah, Al Jumhūrīyah al *see* Yemen
131 W5 **Yamantau** ▲ W Russian Federation
126 K16 **Yamarovka** Chitinskaya Oblast', S Russian Federation
Yamasaki *see* Yamazaki
13 P12 **Yamaska** ~ Québec, SE Canada
171 Jj17 **Yamato** Kanagawa, Honshū, S Japan
199 Gg4 **Yamato Ridge** *undersea feature* S Sea of Japan
170 G14 **Yamazaki** *var.* Yamasaki. Hyōgo, Honshū, SW Japan
191 V5 **Yamba** New South Wales, SE Australia
83 D16 **Yambio** *var.* Yambiyo. Western Equatoria, S Sudan
Yambiyo *see* Yambio
116 L10 **Yambol** *Turk.* Yanboli. Burgaska Oblast, E Bulgaria
81 M17 **Yambuya** Haut-Zaïre, N Zaire
176 Uu15 **Yamdena, Pulau** *prev.* Jamdena. *island* Kepulauan Tanimbar, E Indonesia
171 Cc13 **Yame** Fukuoka, Kyūshū, SW Japan
177 G6 **Yamethin** Mandalay, C Burma
194 G11 **Yaminbot** East Sepik, NW PNG
171 L15 **Yamizo-san** ▲ Honshū, C Japan
189 U9 **Yamma Yamma, Lake** ◎ Queensland, C Australia
78 M16 **Yamoussoukro** ● (Ivory Coast) C Ivory Coast
39 P3 **Yampa River** ~ Colorado, C USA
119 S2 **Yampil'** Sums'ka Oblast', NE Ukraine
118 M8 **Yampil'** Vinnyts'ka Oblast', C Ukraine
127 Oo10 **Yamsk** Magadanskaya Oblast', E Russian Federation
158 J8 **Yamuna** *prev.* Jumna. ~ N India
158 I9 **Yamunānagar** Haryāna, N India
Yamundá *see* Nhamundá, Rio
151 U8 **Yamyshevo** Pavlodar, NE Kazakhstan
165 N16 **Yamzho Yumco** ◎ W China
126 Ll6 **Yana** ~ NE Russian Federation
195 P15 **Yanaba Island** *island* SE PNG
170 C13 **Yanagawa** Fukuoka, Kyūshū, SW Japan
170 E13 **Yanai** Yamaguchi, Honshū, SW Japan
161 L16 **Yanam** *var.* Yanaon. Pondicherry, E India
166 L5 **Yan'an** *var.* Yanan. Shaanxi, C China
Yanaon *see* Yanam
131 U3 **Yanaul** Respublika Bashkortostan, W Russian Federation
120 O12 **Yanavichy** *Rus.* Yanovichi. Vitsyebskaya Voblasts', NE Belorussia
Yanboli *see* Yambol
146 K8 **Yanbu' al Baḥr** Al Madīnah, W Saudi Arabia
23 T8 **Yanceyville** North Carolina, SE USA
167 R7 **Yancheng** Jiangsu, E China
165 W8 **Yanchi** Ningxia, N China
166 L5 **Yanchuan** Shaanxi, C China
191 O10 **Yanco Creek** *seasonal river* New South Wales, SE Australia
191 O6 **Yanda Creek** *seasonal river* New South Wales, SE Australia
190 K4 **Yandama Creek** *seasonal river* New South Wales/South Australia
167 S11 **Yandang Shan** ▲▲ SE China
197 G5 **Yandé, Île** *island* Îles Belep, W New Caledonia
Yandua *see* Yadua
165 O6 **Yandun** Xinjiang Uygur Zizhiqu, W China
78 L13 **Yanfolila** Sikasso, SW Mali
81 M18 **Yangambi** Haut-Zaïre, N Zaire
164 M15 **Yangbajain** Xizang Zizhiqu, W China
Yangchow *see* Yangzhou
166 M15 **Yangchun** Guangdong, S China
167 N2 **Yanggao** Shanxi, C China
Yanggeta *see* Yaqeta
Yangiabad *see* Yangiobod
Yangibazar *see* Dzhany-Bazar, Kyrgyzstan
Yangi-Bazar *see* Kofarnihon, Tajikistan
Yangiklshak *see* Yangiqishloq
152 M13 **Yangi-Nishon** *Rus.* Yangi-Nishan. Qashqadaryo Wiloyati, S Uzbekistan
153 Q9 **Yangiobod** *Rus.* Yangiabad. Toshkent Wiloyati, E Uzbekistan
153 O10 **Yangiqishloq** *Rus.* Yangiklshak. Jizzakh Wiloyati, C Uzbekistan
153 P11 **Yangiyer** Sirdaryo Wiloyati, E Uzbekistan
153 P9 **Yangiyŭl** *Rus.* Yangiyul'. Toshkent Wiloyati, E Uzbekistan
166 M15 **Yangjiang** Guangdong, S China
Yangku *see* Taiyuan
Yang-Nishan *see* Yangi-Nishon
177 G9 **Yangon** *Eng.* Rangoon. ● (Burma) Yangon, S Burma
177 G8 **Yangon** *Eng.* Rangoon. ◈ *division* SW Burma
166 K17 **Yangpu Gang** *harbour* Hainan, S China
167 N4 **Yangquan** Shanxi, C China
167 N13 **Yangshan** Guangdong, S China
178 Kk13 **Yang Sin, Chu** ▲ S Vietnam
Yangtze *see* Chang Jiang, C China
Yangtze Kiang *see* Chang Jiang
166 G11 **Yangyuan** Sichuan, C China
167 R7 **Yangzhou** *var.* Yangchow. Jiangsu, E China
166 L5 **Yan He** ~ C China
169 Y10 **Yanji** Jilin, NE China
Yanji *see* Longjing
31 Q12 **Yankton** South Dakota, N USA
Yannina *see* Ioánnina
126 M6 **Yano-Indigirskaya Nizmennost'** *plain* NE Russian Federation
Yanovichi *see* Yanavichy
161 K24 **Yan Oya** ~ N Sri Lanka
164 K6 **Yanqi** *var.* Yanqi Huizu Zizhixian. Xinjiang Uygur Zizhiqu, NW China
Yanqi Huizu Zizhixian *see* Yanqi
167 P2 **Yan Shan** ▲▲ E China
167 Q10 **Yanshan** Jiangxi, S China
166 H14 **Yanshan** *prev.* Hekou. Yunnan, SW China
169 X8 **Yanshou** Heilongjiang, NE China
126 Ll6 **Yanskiy Zaliv** *bay* N Russian Federation
191 O4 **Yantabulla** New South Wales, SE Australia
167 R4 **Yantai** *var.* Yan-t'ai; *prev.* Chefoo, Chih-fu. Shandong, E China
120 A13 **Yantarnyy** *Ger.* Palmnicken. Kaliningradskaya Oblast', W Russian Federation
116 J9 **Yantra** Loveshka Oblast, N Bulgaria
116 K9 **Yantra** ~ N Bulgaria
167 P5 **Yanzhou** Shandong, E China
81 E16 **Yaoundé** *var.* Yaunde. ● (Cameroon) Centre, S Cameroon
196 I14 **Yap** ◈ *state* W Micronesia
196 F16 **Yap** *island* Caroline Islands, W Micronesia
59 M18 **Yapacani, Rio** ~ C Bolivia
176 Ww12 **Yapa Kopra** Irian Jaya, E Indonesia
Yapan *see* Yapen, Selat
Yapanskoye More *see* Japan, Sea of
79 P15 **Yapei** N Ghana
10 M10 **Yapeitso, Mont** ▲ Québec, E Canada
176 X10 **Yapen, Pulau** *prev.* Japen. *island* E Indonesia
176 X9 **Yapen, Selat** *var.* Yapan. *strait* Irian Jaya, E Indonesia
63 E15 **Yapeyú** Corrientes, NE Argentina
142 I11 **Yapraklı** Çankırı, N Turkey
182 M3 **Yap Trench** *var.* Yap Trough. *undersea feature* SE Philippine Sea
Yap Trough *see* Yap Trench
Yapurá *see* Caquetá, Río, Brazil/Colombia
Yapurá *see* Japurá, Rio, Brazil/Colombia
176 U11 **Yaputih** Pulau Seram, E Indonesia
197 I13 **Yaqaga** *island* N Fiji
197 H13 **Yaqeta** *prev.* Yanggeta. *island* Yasawa Group, NW Fiji
42 G6 **Yaqui** Sonora, NW Mexico
34 E12 **Yaquina Bay** *bay* Oregon, NW USA
42 G6 **Yaqui, Río** ~ NW Mexico
176 Y14 **Yar** *channel* Irian Jaya, E Indonesia

◆ Country ● Country Capital ◇ Dependent Territory ○ Dependent Territory Capital ◈ Administrative Region ✈ International Airport ▲ Mountain ▲▲ Mountain Range Volcano ~ River ◎ Lake ⊞ Reservoir

56 K5 **Yaracuy** *off.* Estado Yaracuy. ◐ *state* NW Venezuela
152 E13 **Yaradzhi** *Turkm.* Yarajy. Akhalskiy Velayat, C Turkmenistan
Yarajy *see* Yaradzhi
129 Q15 **Yaransk** Kirovskaya Oblast', NW Russian Federation
142 F17 **Yardımcı Burnu** *headland* SW Turkey
99 Q19 **Yare** ≈ E England, UK
129 S9 **Yarega** Respublika Komi, NW Russian Federation
118 I7 **Yaremcha** Ivano-Frankivs'ka Oblast', W Ukraine
201 Q9 **Yaren** SW Nauru
129 Q10 **Yarensk** Arkhangel'skaya Oblast', NW Russian Federation
161 F16 **Yargatti** Karnātaka, W India
171 Ii14 **Yariga-take** ▲ Honshū, S Japan
147 O15 **Yarim** W Yemen
56 F14 **Yarí, Río** ≈ SW Colombia
56 K5 **Yaritagua** Yaracuy, N Venezuela
Yarkand *see* Yarkant He
Yarkant *see* Shache
164 E9 **Yarkant He** *var.* Yarkand. ≈ NW China
155 U3 **Yarkhūn** ≈ NW Pakistan
Yarlung Zangbo Jiang *see* Brahmaputra
118 L6 **Yarmolyntsi** Khmel'nyts'ka Oblast', W Ukraine
169 T11 **Yar Moron** ≈ N China
11 O16 **Yarmouth** Nova Scotia, SE Canada
Yarmouth *see* Great Yarmouth
Yaroslav *see* Jarosław
128 L15 **Yaroslavl'** Yaroslavskaya Oblast', W Russian Federation
128 K14 **Yaroslavskaya Oblast'** ◐ *province* W Russian Federation
126 Kk12 **Yaroslavskiy** Respublika Sakha (Yakutiya), NE Russian Federation
191 P13 **Yarram** Victoria, SE Australia
191 O11 **Yarrawonga** Victoria, SE Australia
190 L4 **Yarriarraburra Swamp** *wetland* New South Wales, SE Australia
126 Gg8 **Yar-Sale** Yamalo-Nenetskiy Avtonomnyy Okrug, N Russian Federation
126 I12 **Yartsevo** Krasnoyarskiy Kray, C Russian Federation
130 I4 **Yartsevo** Smolenskaya Oblast', W Russian Federation
56 E8 **Yarumal** Antioquia, NW Colombia
197 H13 **Yasawa** *island* Yasawa Group, NW Fiji
197 G13 **Yasawa Group** *island group* NW Fiji
79 V12 **Yashi** Katsina, N Nigeria
79 S14 **Yashikera** Kwara, W Nigeria
153 T14 **Yashilkŭl** *Rus.* Ozero Yashil'kul'. ◎ SE Tajikistan
Yashil'kul', Ozero *see* Yashilkŭl
171 Ll11 **Yashima** Akita, Honshū, C Japan
170 Dd14 **Ya-shima** *island* SW Japan
170 Ee14 **Yashiro-jima** *island* SW Japan
131 P13 **Yashkul'** Respublika Kalmykiya, SW Russian Federation
152 F13 **Yashlyk** Akhalskiy Velayat, C Turkmenistan
Yasinovataya *see* Yasynuvata
116 N10 **Yasna Polyana** Burgaska Oblast, SE Bulgaria
126 M14 **Yasnyy** Amurskaya Oblast', SE Russian Federation
178 J10 **Yasothon** Yasothon, E Thailand
191 R10 **Yass** New South Wales, SE Australia
Yassy *see* Iaşi
170 Ff12 **Yasugi** Shimane, Honshū, SW Japan
149 N10 **Yāsūj** *var.* Yesuj; *prev.* Tal-e Khosravī. Kohkīlūyeh va Būyer Aḩmadī, C Iran
142 M11 **Yasun Burnu** *headland* N Turkey
119 X8 **Yasynuvata** *Rus.* Yasinovataya. Donets'ka Oblast', SE Ukraine
142 C15 **Yatağan** Muğla, SW Turkey
171 M9 **Yatate-tōge** *pass* Honshū, C Japan
197 J7 **Yaté** Province Sud, S New Caledonia
29 P6 **Yates Center** Kansas, C USA
193 B21 **Yates Point** *headland* South Island, NZ
15 Kk7 **Yathkyed Lake** ◎ Northwest Territories, NE Canada
176 U15 **Yatoke** Pulau Babar, E Indonesia
81 M18 **Yatolema** Haut-Zaïre, N Zaire
171 J15 **Yatsuga-take** ▲ Honshū, S Japan
170 C14 **Yatsushiro** *var.* Yatusiro. Kumamoto, Kyūshū, SW Japan
170 C15 **Yatsushiro-kai** *bay* SW Japan
144 F11 **Yatta** *var.* Yuta. S West Bank
83 J20 **Yatta Plateau** *plateau* SE Kenya
Yatusiro *see* Yatsushiro
59 F17 **Yauca, Río** ≈ SW Peru
47 S6 **Yauco** W Puerto Rico
176 Xx9 **Yauke** Irian Jaya, E Indonesia
Yaunde *see* Yaoundé
Yavan *see* Yovon
Yavarí *see* Javari, Rio
58 G9 **Yavari Mirim, Río** ≈ NE Peru
42 G7 **Yavaros** Sonora, NW Mexico
160 N13 **Yavatmāl** Mahārāshtra, C India
56 M9 **Yaví, Cerro** ▲ C Venezuela
45 W16 **Yaviza** Darién, SE Panama
144 F10 **Yavne** Central, W Israel
118 H5 **Yavoriv** *Pol.* Jaworów, *Rus.* Yavorov. L'vivs'ka Oblast', NW Ukraine
Yavorov *see* Yavoriv
170 E15 **Yawatahama** Ehime, Shikoku, SW Japan
Ya Xian *see* Sanya
142 L17 **Yayladağı** Hatay, S Turkey
129 V13 **Yayva** Permskaya Oblast', NW Russian Federation
129 V12 **Yayva** ≈ NW Russian Federation
149 Q9 **Yazd** *var.* Yezd. Yazd, C Iran
149 Q8 **Yazd** *off.* Ostān-e Yazd, *var.* Yezd. ◐ *province* C Iran
Yazgulemskiy Khrebet *see* Yazgulom, Qatorkŭhi
153 S13 **Yazgulom, Qatorkŭhi** *Rus.* Yazgulemskiy Khrebet. ▲▲ S Tajikistan
24 K5 **Yazoo City** Mississippi, S USA
24 K5 **Yazoo River** ≈ Mississippi, S USA
131 Q5 **Yazykovo** Ul'yanovskaya Oblast', W Russian Federation
111 U4 **Ybbs** Niederösterreich, NE Austria
111 U4 **Ybbs** ≈ C Austria
97 G22 **Yding Skovhøj** *hill* C Denmark
117 G20 **Ýdra** *var.* Ídhra, Idra. Ýdra, S Greece
117 G21 **Ýdra** *var.* Ídhra. *island* S Greece
117 G20 **Ýdras, Kólpos** *strait* S Greece
178 Gg10 **Ye** Mon State, S Burma
191 O12 **Yea** Victoria, SE Australia
80 I5 **Yebbi-Bou** Borkou-Ennedi-Tibesti, N Chad
164 F9 **Yecheng** *var.* Kargilik. Xinjiang Uygur Zizhiqu, NW China
107 R11 **Yecla** Murcia, SE Spain
42 H6 **Yécora** Sonora, NW Mexico
Yedintsy *see* Edineţ
128 J13 **Yefimovskiy** Leningradskaya Oblast', NW Russian Federation
176 Uu9 **Yeflio** Irian Jaya, E Indonesia
130 K6 **Yefremov** Tul'skaya Oblast', W Russian Federation
Yêgainnyin *see* Henan
143 U12 **Yeghegis** *Rus.* Yekhegis. ≈ C Armenia
151 T10 **Yegindybulak** *Kaz.* Egindibulaq. Karaganda, C Kazakhstan
130 L4 **Yegor'yevsk** Moskovskaya Oblast', W Russian Federation
Yehuda, Haré *see* Judaean Hills
83 E15 **Yei** ≈ S Sudan
167 P8 **Yeji** *var.* Yejiaji. Anhui, E China
Yejiaji *see* Yeji
125 Ee11 **Yekaterinburg** *prev.* Sverdlovsk. Sverdlovskaya Oblast', C Russian Federation
Yekaterinodar *see* Krasnodar
Yekaterinoslav *see* Dnipropetrovs'k
126 Mm15 **Yekaterinoslavka** Amurskaya Oblast', SE Russian Federation
131 O7 **Yekaterinovka** Saratovskaya Oblast', W Russian Federation
78 K16 **Yekepa** NE Liberia
131 T3 **Yelabuga** Respublika Tatarstan, W Russian Federation
Yela Island *see* Rossel Island
131 O8 **Yelan'** Volgogradskaya Oblast', SW Russian Federation
119 Q9 **Yelanets'** *Rus.* Yelanets. Mykolayivs'ka Oblast', S Ukraine
125 G13 **Yelanka** Novosibirskaya Oblast', C Russian Federation
127 Nn15 **Yel'ban'** Khabarovskiy Kray, E Russian Federation
130 L7 **Yelets** Lipetskaya Oblast', W Russian Federation
129 W4 **Yeletskiy** Respublika Komi, NW Russian Federation
78 J11 **Yélimané** Kayes, W Mali
Yelisavetpol *see* Gäncä
Yelizavetgrad *see* Kirovohrad
127 O13 **Yelizavety, Mys** *headland* SE Russian Federation
127 Pp11 **Yelizovo** Kamchatskaya Oblast', E Russian Federation
Yelizovo *see* Yalizava
131 S5 **Yelkhovka** Samarskaya Oblast', W Russian Federation
98 M1 **Yell** *island* NE Scotland, UK
161 E17 **Yellāpur** Karnātaka, W India
9 U17 **Yellow Grass** Saskatchewan, S Canada
Yellowhammer State *see* Alabama
9 O15 **Yellowhead Pass** *pass* Alberta/British Columbia, SW Canada
15 Hh8 **Yellowknife** *territory capital* Northwest Territories, W Canada
15 I7 **Yellowknife** ≈ Northwest Territories, NW Canada
194 F10 **Yellow River** ≈ NW PNG
25 P8 **Yellow River** ≈ Alabama/Florida, S USA
32 I4 **Yellow River** ≈ Wisconsin, N USA
32 J6 **Yellow River** ≈ Wisconsin, N USA
32 K7 **Yellow River** ≈ Wisconsin, N USA
Yellow River *see* Huang He
163 V8 **Yellow Sea** *Chin.* Huang Hai, *Kor.* Hwang-Hae. *sea* E Asia
35 S13 **Yellowstone Lake** ◎ Wyoming, C USA
35 T13 **Yellowstone National Park** *national park* Wyoming, NW USA
35 Y8 **Yellowstone River** ≈ Montana/Wyoming, NW USA
98 L1 **Yell Sound** *strait* N Scotland, UK
29 U9 **Yellville** Arkansas, C USA
126 Hh11 **Yelogay** ≈ C Russian Federation
152 J14 **Yëloten** *prev.* Iolotan', *Turkm.* Yolöten. Maryyskiy Velayat, S Turkmenistan
121 M20 **Yel'sk** *Rus.* Yel'sk. Homyel'skaya Voblasts', SE Belorussia
79 T13 **Yelwa** Kebbi, W Nigeria
125 Ee12 **Yemanzhelinsk** Chelyabinskaya Oblast', C Russian Federation
23 R15 **Yemassee** South Carolina, SE USA
147 O15 **Yemen** *off.* Republic of Yemen, *Ar.* Al Jumhūrīyah al Yamanīyah, Al Yaman. ◆ *republic* SW Asia
118 M4 **Yemil'chyne** Zhytomyrs'ka Oblast', N Ukraine
128 M10 **Yemtsa** Arkhangel'skaya Oblast', NW Russian Federation
128 M10 **Yemtsa** ≈ NW Russian Federation
129 R10 **Yemva** *prev.* Zheleznodorozhnyy. Respublika Komi, NW Russian Federation
119 X7 **Yenakiyeve** *Rus.* Yenakiyevo; *prev.* Ordzhonikidze, Rykovo. Donets'ka Oblast', E Ukraine
Yenakiyevo *see* Yenakiyeve
177 Ff6 **Yenangyaung** Magwe, W Burma
178 Jj5 **Yên Bai** Yên Bai, N Vietnam
191 P9 **Yenda** New South Wales, SE Australia
176 W10 **Yende** Irian Jaya, E Indonesia
79 Q14 **Yendi** NE Ghana
164 E8 **Yengisar** Xinjiang Uygur Zizhiqu, NW China
124 O3 **Yeniboğaziçi** *var.* Ayios Seryios, *Gk.* Ágios Sérgios. E Cyprus
124 Oo2 **Yenierenköy** *var.* Yialousa, *Gk.* Agialoúsa. NE Cyprus
Yenipazar *see* Novi Pazar
142 E12 **Yenişehir** Bursa, NW Turkey
Yenisei Bay *see* Yeniseyskiy Zaliv
126 Hh8 **Yenisey** ≈ Mongolia/Russian Federation
126 I13 **Yeniseysk** Krasnoyarskiy Kray, C Russian Federation
207 W10 **Yeniseyskiy Zaliv** *var.* Yenisei Bay. *bay* N Russian Federation
131 Q12 **Yenotayevka** Astrakhanskaya Oblast', SW Russian Federation
128 L4 **Yenozero, Ozero** ◎ NW Russian Federation
Yenping *see* Nanping
41 Q11 **Yentna River** ≈ Alaska, USA
188 M10 **Yeo, Lake** *salt lake* Western Australia
191 R7 **Yeoval** New South Wales, SE Australia
99 K23 **Yeovil** SW England, UK
42 H6 **Yepachic** Chihuahua, N Mexico
189 Y8 **Yeppoon** Queensland, E Australia
130 M5 **Yeraktur** Ryazanskaya Oblast', W Russian Federation
Yeraliyev *see* Kuryk
152 F12 **Yerbent** Akhalskiy Velayat, C Turkmenistan
126 Jj12 **Yerbogachen** Irkutskaya Oblast', C Russian Federation
143 T12 **Yerevan** *var.* Erevan, *Eng.* Erivan. ● (Armenia) C Armenia
143 U12 **Yerevan** ✕ C Armenia
131 O12 **Yergeni** *hill range* SW Russian Federation
Yeriho *see* Jericho
37 R6 **Yerington** Nevada, W USA
142 J13 **Yerköy** Yozgat, C Turkey
116 L13 **Yerlisu** Edirne, NW Turkey
Yermak *see* Aksu
151 R9 **Yermentau** *Kaz.* Ereymentaū. Jermentau. Akmola, C Kazakhstan
151 R9 **Yermentau, Gory** ▲ C Kazakhstan
129 R5 **Yermitsa** Respublika Komi, NW Russian Federation
37 V14 **Yermo** California, W USA
126 Ll14 **Yerofey Pavlovich** Amurskaya Oblast', SE Russian Federation
101 F15 **Yerseke** Zeeland, SW Netherlands
131 Q8 **Yershov** Saratovskaya Oblast', W Russian Federation
129 P9 **Yërtom** Respublika Komi, NW Russian Federation
58 D13 **Yerupaja, Nevado** ▲ C Peru
Yerushalayim *see* Jerusalem
107 R4 **Yesa, Embalse de** ▣ NE Spain
151 V15 **Yesik** *Kaz.* Esik; *prev.* Issyk. Almaty, SE Kazakhstan
151 O8 **Yesil'** *Kaz.* Esil. Turgay, N Kazakhstan
142 K15 **Yeşilhisar** Kayseri, C Turkey
142 L11 **Yeşilırmak** *anc.* Iris. ≈ N Turkey
39 U12 **Yeso** New Mexico, SW USA
Yeso *see* Hokkaidō
131 N15 **Yessentuki** Stavropol'skiy Kray, SW Russian Federation
126 J9 **Yessey** Evenkiyskiy Avtonomnyy Okrug, N Russian Federation
107 P12 **Yeste** Castilla-La Mancha, C Spain
Yesuj *see* Yāsūj
191 T4 **Yetman** New South Wales, SE Australia
78 L4 **Yetti** *physical region* N Mauritania
177 G4 **Ye-u** Sagaing, C Burma
104 H9 **Yeu, Île d'** *island* NW France
Yevlakh *see* Yevlax
143 W11 **Yevlax** *Rus.* Yevlakh. C Azerbaijan
119 S13 **Yevpatoriya** Respublika Krym, S Ukraine
125 B17 **Yevreyskaya Avtonomnaya Oblast'** *Eng.* Jewish Autonomous Oblast. ◐ *autonomous province* SE Russian Federation
130 K12 **Yeya** ≈ SW Russian Federation
164 I10 **Yeyik** Xinjiang Uygur Zizhiqu, W China
130 K12 **Yeysk** Krasnodarskiy Kray, SW Russian Federation
Yezd *see* Yazd
Yezerishche *see* Yezyaryshcha
Yezo *see* Hokkaidō
120 N11 **Yezyaryshcha** *Rus.* Yezerishche. Vitsyebskaya Voblasts', NE Belorussia
Yialí *see* Gyalí
Yialousa *see* Yenierenköy
169 V7 **Yi'an** Heilongjiang, NE China
Yiannitsá *see* Giannitsá
166 I10 **Yibin** Sichuan, C China
164 K13 **Yibug Caka** ◎ W China
166 M9 **Yichang** Hubei, C China
166 L5 **Yichuan** Shaanxi, C China
163 W3 **Yichun** Heilongjiang, NE China
169 X6 **Yichun** *var.* I-ch'un. Heilongjiang, NE China
167 O11 **Yichun** Jiangxi, S China
Yidu *see* Qingzhou
196 C15 **Yigo** NE Guam
167 Q5 **Yi He** ≈ E China
169 X8 **Yilan** Heilongjiang, NE China
142 C9 **Yıldız Dağları** ▲▲ NW Turkey
142 L13 **Yıldızeli** Sivas, N Turkey
169 U4 **Yilehuli Shan** ▲▲ NE China
169 S7 **Yimin He** ≈ NE China
165 W8 **Yinchuan** *var.* Yinch'uan, Yin-ch'uan, Yinchwan. Ningxia, N China
Yinchuanzhan *see* Xincheng
Yinchwan *see* Yinchuan
Yindu He *see* Indus
167 N14 **Yingde** Guangdong, S China
167 O7 **Ying He** ≈ C China
169 U13 **Yingkou** *var.* Ying-k'ou, Yingkow; *prev.* Newchwang, Niuchwang. Liaoning, NE China
Yingkow *see* Yingkou
167 N8 **Yingshan** Hubei, C China
167 P9 **Yingshan** Hubei, C China
167 Q10 **Yingtan** Jiangxi, S China
Yin-hsien *see* Ningbo
164 H5 **Yining** *var.* I-ning, *Uigh.* Gulja, Kuldja. Xinjiang Uygur Zizhiqu, NW China
166 K11 **Yinjiang** Guizhou, S China
177 Ff4 **Yinmabin** Sagaing, C Burma
169 N13 **Yin Shan** ▲▲ N China
Yin-tu Ho *see* Indus
165 P15 **Yi'ong Zangbo** ≈ W China
Yioúra *see* Gyáros
83 J14 **Yirga 'Alem** *It.* Irgalem. S Ethiopia
63 E19 **Yí, Río** ≈ C Uruguay
83 E14 **Yirol** El Buhayrat, S Sudan
Yirshi *see* Yirxie
169 S8 **Yirxie** *prev.* Yirshi. Nei Mongol Zizhiqu, N China
167 Q5 **Yishui** Shandong, E China
Yisrael/Yisra'el *see* Israel
Yíthion *see* Gýtheio
Yitiaoshan *see* Jingtai
169 W10 **Yitong** Jilin, NE China
165 P5 **Yiwu** *var.* Aratürük. Xinjiang Uygur Zizhiqu, NW China
169 U12 **Yiwulü Shan** ▲ N China
169 T12 **Yi Xian** Liaoning, NE China
167 N10 **Yiyang** Hunan, S China
167 Q10 **Yiyang** Jiangxi, S China
167 N13 **Yizhang** Hunan, S China
95 K19 **Yläne** Turku-Pori, SW Finland
95 L14 **Yli-Ii** Oulu, C Finland
95 L14 **Ylikiiminki** Oulu, C Finland
94 N13 **Yli-Kitka** ◎ NE Finland
95 K17 **Ylistaro** Vaasa, W Finland
94 K13 **Ylitornio** Lappi, NW Finland
95 L15 **Ylivieska** Oulu, W Finland
95 L18 **Ylöjärvi** Häme, SW Finland
97 N17 **Yngaren** ◎ C Sweden
27 T12 **Yoakum** Texas, SW USA
79 X13 **Yobe** ◐ *state* NE Nigeria
172 Nn4 **Yobetsu-dake** ⛰ Hokkaidō, NE Japan
176 Xx10 **Yobi** Irian Jaya, E Indonesia
82 L11 **Yoboki** C Djibouti
170 C12 **Yobuko** Saga, Kyūshū, SW Japan
24 M4 **Yockanookany River** ≈ Mississippi, S USA
24 L2 **Yocona River** ≈ Mississippi, S USA
176 Yy15 **Yodom** Irian Jaya, E Indonesia
174 Kk15 **Yogyakarta** *prev.* Djokjakarta, Jogjakarta, Jokyakarta. Jawa, C Indonesia
174 Kk16 **Yogyakarta** *off.* Daerah Istimewa Yogyakarta, *var.* Djokjakarta, Jogjakarta, Jokyakarta. ◐ *autonomous district* S Indonesia
172 O5 **Yoichi** Hokkaidō, NE Japan
44 G6 **Yojoa, Lago de** ◎ NW Honduras
81 G16 **Yokadouma** Est, SE Cameroon
171 H15 **Yōkaichi** *var.* Yôkaiti. Shiga, Honshū, SW Japan
Yôkaiti *see* Yōkaichi
171 H15 **Yokkaichi** *var.* Yokkaiti. Mie, Honshū, SW Japan
Yokkaiti *see* Yokkaichi
81 E15 **Yoko** Centre, C Cameroon
172 Qq12 **Yokoate-jima** *island* Nansei-shotō, SW Japan
172 N9 **Yokohama** Aomori, Honshū, C Japan
171 Jj16 **Yokohama** Kanagawa, Honshū, S Japan
171 Jj17 **Yokosuka** Kanagawa, Honshū, S Japan
170 F12 **Yokota** Shimane, Honshū, SW Japan
171 M11 **Yokote** Akita, Honshū, C Japan
172 Nn7 **Yokotsu-dake** ▲ Hokkaidō, NE Japan
79 Y14 **Yola** Adamawa, E Nigeria
81 L19 **Yolombo** Equateur, C Zaire
Yolöten *see* Yëloten
176 W10 **Yomber** Irian Jaya, E Indonesia
172 T16 **Yome-jima** *island* Ogasawara-shotō, SE Japan
78 K16 **Yomou** Guinée-Forestière, SE Guinea
176 Y15 **Yomuka** Irian Jaya, E Indonesia
196 C16 **Yona** E Guam
170 Ff12 **Yonago** Tottori, Honshū, SW Japan
172 O17 **Yonaguni** Okinawa, SW Japan
172 Nn16 **Yonaguni-jima** *island* Nansei-shotō, SW Japan
172 Pp14 **Yonaha-dake** ▲ Okinawa, SW Japan
169 X14 **Yonan** SW North Korea
171 L13 **Yonezawa** Yamagata, Honshū, C Japan
167 Q12 **Yong'an** *var.* Yongan. Fujian, SE China
165 T9 **Yongchang** Gansu, N China
167 P7 **Yongcheng** Henan, C China
169 Z15 **Yŏngch'ŏn** *Jap.* Eisen. SE South Korea
166 J10 **Yongchuan** Sichuan, C China
165 U10 **Yongdeng** Gansu, C China
133 W9 **Yongding He** ≈ E China
167 P11 **Yongfeng** Jiangxi, S China
164 L5 **Yongfengqu** Xinjiang Uygur Zizhiqu, W China
169 X13 **Yŏnghŭng** E North Korea
165 U10 **Yongjing** Gansu, C China
169 Y15 **Yŏngju** *Jap.* Eishū. C South Korea
Yongning *see* Xuyong
166 E12 **Yongping** Yunnan, SW China
166 G12 **Yongren** Yunnan, SW China
166 L10 **Yongshun** *var.* Lingxi. Hunan, S China
167 P10 **Yongxiu** *var.* Tujiabu. Jiangxi, S China
166 M12 **Yongzhou** Hunan, S China
20 K14 **Yonkers** New York, NE USA
105 Q7 **Yonne** ◐ *department* C France
105 P6 **Yonne** ≈ C France
56 H9 **Yopal** *var.* El Yopal. Casanare, C Colombia
164 E8 **Yopurga** *var.* Yukuriawat. Xinjiang Uygur Zizhiqu, NW China
188 J12 **York** Western Australia
99 M16 **York** *anc.* Eboracum, Eburacum. N England, UK
25 N5 **York** Alabama, S USA
31 Q15 **York** Nebraska, C USA
20 G16 **York** Pennsylvania, NE USA
23 R11 **York** South Carolina, SE USA
12 J13 **York** ≈ Ontario, SE Canada
13 X6 **York** ≈ Québec, SE Canada
189 V1 **York, Cape** *headland* Queensland, NE Australia
190 I9 **Yorke Peninsula** *peninsula* South Australia
190 I9 **Yorketown** South Australia
21 P9 **York Harbor** Maine, NE USA
23 X6 **York River** ≈ Virginia, NE USA
99 M16 **Yorkshire** *cultural region* N England, UK
99 L16 **Yorkshire Dales** *physical region* N England, UK
9 V16 **Yorkton** Saskatchewan, S Canada
27 T12 **Yorktown** Texas, SW USA
23 X6 **Yorktown** Virginia, NE USA
32 M11 **Yorkville** Illinois, N USA
44 I5 **Yoro** Yoro, C Honduras
44 H5 **Yoro** ◐ *department* N Honduras
172 Pp14 **Yoron-jima** *island* Nansei-shotō, SW Japan
79 N13 **Yorosso** Sikasso, S Mali
37 R8 **Yosemite National Park** *national park* California, W USA
170 Ff14 **Yoshii-gawa** ≈ Honshū, SW Japan
170 Ff15 **Yoshino-gawa** *var.* Yosino Gawa. ≈ Shikoku, SW Japan
131 Q3 **Yoshkar-Ola** Respublika Mariy El, W Russian Federation
Yosino Gawa *see* Yoshino-gawa
176 Y15 **Yos Sudarso, Pulau** *var.* Pulau Dolak, Pulau Kolepom; *prev.* Jos Sudarso. *island* E Indonesia
176 Z10 **Yos Sudarso, Teluk** *bay* Irian Jaya, E Indonesia
169 Y17 **Yŏsu** *Jap.* Reisui. S South Korea
172 Nn5 **Yotei-zan** ▲ Hokkaidō, NE Japan
99 D21 **Youghal** *Ir.* Eochaill. S Ireland
99 D21 **Youghal Bay** *Ir.* Cuan Eochaille. *inlet* S Ireland
20 C15 **Youghiogheny River** ≈ Pennsylvania, NE USA
166 K14 **You Jiang** ≈ S China
191 Q9 **Young** New South Wales, SE Australia
9 T15 **Young** Saskatchewan, S Canada
63 E18 **Young** Río Negro, W Uruguay
190 G5 **Younghusband, Lake** *salt lake* South Australia
190 J10 **Younghusband Peninsula** *peninsula* South Australia
192 Q10 **Young Nicks Head** *headland* North Island, NZ
193 D20 **Young Range** ▲▲ South Island, NZ
203 Q15 **Young's Rock** *island* Pitcairn Island, Pitcairn Islands
9 R16 **Youngstown** Alberta, SW Canada
33 V12 **Youngstown** Ohio, N USA
165 N9 **Youshashan** Qinghai, C China
Youth, Isle of *see* Juventud, Isla de la
79 N11 **Youvarou** Mopti, C Mali
166 K10 **Youyang** Sichuan, C China
169 Y7 **Youyi** Heilongjiang, NE China
153 P13 **Yovon** *Rus.* Yavan. SW Tajikistan
142 J13 **Yozgat** Yozgat, C Turkey
142 K13 **Yozgat** ◐ *province* C Turkey
64 O6 **Ypacaraí** *var.* Ypacaray. Central, S Paraguay
Ypacaray *see* Ypacaraí
64 P5 **Ypané, Río** ≈ C Paraguay
Ypres *see* Ieper
116 I13 **Ypsário** *var.* Ipsario. ▲ Thásos, E Greece
33 R10 **Ypsilanti** Michigan, N USA
36 M1 **Yreka** California, W USA
Yrendagüé *see* General Eugenio A. Garay
195 N8 **Ysabel Channel** *channel* N PNG
12 K8 **Yser, Lac** ◎ Québec, SE Canada
153 Y8 **Yshtyk** Issyk-Kul'skaya Oblast', E Kyrgyzstan
Yssel *see* IJssel
105 Q12 **Yssingeaux** Haute-Loire, C France
97 K23 **Ystad** Malmöhus, S Sweden
Ysyk-Köl *see* Balykchy, Kyrgyzstan
Ysyk-Köl *see* Issyk-Kul', Ozero, Kyrgyzstan
Ysyk-Köl Oblasty *see* Issyk-Kul'skaya Oblast'
98 L8 **Ythan** ≈ NE Scotland, UK
Y Trallwng *see* Welshpool
96 C13 **Ytre Arna** Hordaland, S Norway
96 B12 **Ytre Sula** *island* S Norway
95 G17 **Ytterhogdal** Jämtland, C Sweden
126 M10 **Ytyk-Kyuyel'** Respublika Sakha (Yakutiya), NE Russian Federation
Yu *see* Henan
Yuan Jiang *see* Red River
167 S13 **Yüanlin** *Jap.* Inrin. C Taiwan
167 N3 **Yuanping** Shanxi, C China
167 O11 **Yuan Shui** ≈ S China
170 G16 **Yuasa** Wakayama, Honshū, SW Japan
194 H10 **Yuat** ≈ N PNG
37 O6 **Yuba City** California, W USA
172 Oo6 **Yūbari** Hokkaidō, NE Japan
172 P6 **Yūbari-sanchi** ▲▲ Hokkaidō, NE Japan
37 O6 **Yuba River** ≈ California, W USA
82 H13 **Yubdo** W Ethiopia
172 Q5 **Yūbetsu** Hokkaidō, NE Japan
Yūbetsu-gawa *see* Yabetsu-gawa
43 X12 **Yucatán** ◐ *state* SE Mexico
49 O3 **Yucatan Basin** *var.* Yucatan Deep. *undersea feature* N Caribbean Sea
Yucatán, Canal de *see* Yucatan Channel
43 Y10 **Yucatan Channel** *Sp.* Canal de Yucatán. *channel* Cuba/Mexico
Yucatan Deep *see* Yucatan Basin
Yucatan Peninsula *see* Yucatán, Península de
43 X13 **Yucatán, Península de** *Eng.* Yucatan Peninsula. *peninsula* Guatemala/Mexico
38 I11 **Yucca** Arizona, SW USA
37 V15 **Yucca Valley** California, W USA
167 P4 **Yucheng** Shandong, E China
167 N4 **Yuci** Shanxi, C China
133 X5 **Yudoma** ≈ E Russian Federation
167 P12 **Yudu** Jiangxi, C China
Yue *see* Guangdong
166 M12 **Yuecheng Ling** ▲▲ S China
189 P7 **Yuendumu** Northern Territory, N Australia
166 H10 **Yuexi** Sichuan, C China
167 N10 **Yueyang** Hunan, S China
129 U14 **Yug** Permskaya Oblast', NW Russian Federation
129 P13 **Yug** ≈ NW Russian Federation
127 N11 **Yugorenok** Respublika Sakha (Yakutiya), NE Russian Federation
125 F10 **Yugorsk** Khanty-Mansiyskiy Avtonomnyy Okrug, C Russian Federation
125 G6 **Yugorskiy Poluostrov** *peninsula* NW Russian Federation
114 M13 **Yugoslavia** *off.* Federal Republic of Yugoslavia, *SCr.* Jugoslavija, Savezna Republika Jugoslavija. ◆ *federal republic* SE Europe
152 K14 **Yugo-Vostochnyye Garagumy** *prev.* Yugo-Vostochnyye Karakumy. *desert* E Turkmenistan
Yugo-Vostochnyye Karakumy *see* Yugo-Vostochnyye Garagumy
167 S10 **Yuhuan Dao** *island* SE China
166 L14 **Yu Jiang** ≈ S China
127 Nn7 **Yukagirskoye Ploskogor'ye** *plateau* NE Russian Federation
120 L11 **Yukhavichy** *Rus.* Yukhovichi. Vitsyebskaya Voblasts', N Belorussia
130 J4 **Yukhnov** Kaluzhskaya Oblast', W Russian Federation
Yukhovichi *see* Yukhavichy
81 J20 **Yuki** *var.* Yuki Kengunda. Bandundu, W Zaire
Yuki Kengunda *see* Yuki
28 M10 **Yukon** Oklahoma, C USA
1 F4 **Yukon** ≈ Canada/USA
Yukon *see* Yukon Territory
41 S7 **Yukon Flats** *salt flat* Alaska, USA
14 F5 **Yukon Territory** *var.* Yukon, *Fr.* Territoire du Yukon. ◐ *territory* NW Canada
143 T16 **Yüksekova** Hakkâri, SE Turkey
126 Jj11 **Yukta** Evenkiyskiy Avtonomnyy Okrug, C Russian Federation
170 Dd13 **Yukuhashi** *var.* Yukuhasi. Fukuoka, Kyūshū, SW Japan
Yukuhasi *see* Yukuhashi
Yukuriawat *see* Yopurga
129 O9 **Yula** ≈ NW Russian Federation
189 P8 **Yulara** Northern Territory, N Australia
131 W6 **Yuldybayevo** Respublika Bashkortostan, W Russian Federation
25 W8 **Yulee** Florida, SE USA
164 K7 **Yuli** *var.* Lopnur. Xinjiang Uygur Zizhiqu, NW China
167 T14 **Yüli** C Taiwan
166 L15 **Yulin** Guangxi Zhuangzu Zizhiqu, S China
166 L4 **Yulin** Shaanxi, C China
167 T14 **Yü Shan** ▲ C Taiwan
166 F11 **Yulongxue Shan** ▲ SW China
38 H14 **Yuma** Arizona, SW USA
39 W3 **Yuma** Colorado, C USA
56 K5 **Yumare** Yaracuy, N Venezuela
65 G14 **Yumbel** Bío Bío, C Chile
81 N19 **Yumbi** Maniema, E Zaire
165 R8 **Yumen** *var.* Laojunmiao, Yümen. Gansu, N China
165 Q7 **Yumenzhen** Gansu, N China
164 J3 **Yumin** Xinjiang Uygur Zizhiqu, NW China
Yun *see* Yunnan
142 G14 **Yunak** Konya, W Turkey
47 O8 **Yuna, Río** ≈ E Dominican Republic
40 I17 **Yunaska Island** *island* Aleutian Islands, Alaska, USA
166 M6 **Yuncheng** Shanxi, C China
59 L18 **Yungas** *physical region* E Bolivia
Yungki *see* Jilin
Yung-ning *see* Nanning
166 I12 **Yun Gui Gaoyuan** *plateau* SW China
Yunjinghong *see* Jinghong
166 M15 **Yunkai Dashan** ▲▲ S China
Yunki *see* Jilin
166 E11 **Yun Ling** ▲▲ SW China
167 N9 **Yunmeng** Hubei, C China
163 N14 **Yunnan** *var.* Yun, Yunnan Sheng, Yünnan, Yun-nan. ◐ *province* SW China
Yunnan *see* Kunming
Yunnan Sheng *see* Yunnan
170 Cc15 **Yunomae** Kumamoto, Kyūshū, SW Japan
167 N8 **Yun Shui** ≈ C China
190 J7 **Yunta** South Australia
167 Q14 **Yunxiao** Fujian, SE China
166 K9 **Yunyang** Sichuan, C China
200 Nn10 **Yupanqui Basin** *undersea feature* E Pacific Ocean
Yuratishki *see* Yuratsishki
121 I15 **Yuratsishki** *Pol.* Juraciszki, *Rus.* Yuratishki. Hrodzyenskaya Voblasts', W Belorussia
Yurev *see* Tartu
126 H14 **Yurga** Kemerovskaya Oblast', S Russian Federation
58 E10 **Yurimaguas** Loreto, N Peru
131 P3 **Yurino** Respublika Mariy El, W Russian Federation
43 N13 **Yuriria** Guanajuato, C Mexico
129 T13 **Yurla** Komi-Permyatskiy Avtonomnyy Okrug, NW Russian Federation
Yuruá, Río *see* Juruá, Rio
116 M13 **Yürük** Tekirdağ, NW Turkey
164 G10 **Yurungkax He** ≈ W China
129 Q14 **Yur'ya** *var.* Jarja. Kirovskaya Oblast', NW Russian Federation
Yur'yev *see* Tartu
129 N16 **Yur'yevets** Ivanovskaya Oblast', W Russian Federation
130 M3 **Yur'yev-Pol'skiy** Vladimirskaya Oblast', W Russian Federation
119 V7 **Yur"yivka** Dnipropetrovs'ka Oblast', E Ukraine
126 K6 **Yuryung-Khaya** Respublika Sakha (Yakutiya), NE Russian Federation
44 I7 **Yuscarán** El Paraíso, S Honduras
167 P12 **Yu Shan** ▲ S China
128 I7 **Yushkozero** Respublika Kareliya, NW Russian Federation
165 R13 **Yushu** Qinghai, C China
131 P12 **Yusta** Respublika Kalmykiya, SW Russian Federation
128 I10 **Yustozero** Respublika Kareliya, NW Russian Federation
143 Q11 **Yusufeli** Artvin, NE Turkey
170 E15 **Yusuhara** Kōchi, Shikoku, SW Japan
129 T14 **Yus'va** Permskaya Oblast', NW Russian Federation
Yuta *see* Yatta
167 P2 **Yutian** Hebei, E China
164 H10 **Yutian** *var.* Keriya. Xinjiang Uygur Zizhiqu, NW China
64 K5 **Yuto** Jujuy, NW Argentina
64 P7 **Yuty** Caazapá, S Paraguay
166 G13 **Yuxi** Yunnan, SW China
167 O2 **Yuxian** *prev.* Yu Xian. Hebei, E China
171 M11 **Yuzawa** Akita, Honshū, C Japan
129 N16 **Yuzha** Ivanovskaya Oblast', W Russian Federation
Yuzhno-Alichurskiy Khrebet *see* Alichuri Janubí, Qatorkŭhi
Yuzhno-Kazakhstanskaya Oblast' *see* Yuzhnyy Kazakhstan
127 Oo15 **Yuzhno-Sakhalinsk** *Jap.* Toyohara; *prev.* Vladimirovka. Ostrov Sakhalin, Sakhalinskaya Oblast', SE Russian Federation
131 P14 **Yuzhno-Sukhokumsk** Respublika Dagestan, SW Russian Federation
125 Ee12 **Yuzhnoural'sk** Chelyabinskaya Oblast', C Russian Federation
126 I13 **Yuzhno-Yeniseyskiy** Krasnoyarskiy Kray, C Russian Federation
151 Z10 **Yuzhnyy Altay, Khrebet** ▲▲ E Kazakhstan
Yuzhnyy Bug *see* Pivdennyy Buh
151 O15 **Yuzhnyy Kazakhstan** *off.* Yuzhno-Kazakhstanskaya Oblast', *Eng.* South Kazakhstan, *Kaz.* Ongtüstik Qazaqstan Oblysy; *prev.* Chimkentskaya Oblast'. ◐ *province* S Kazakhstan
127 Oo10 **Yuzhnyy, Mys** *headland* E Russian Federation
131 W6 **Yuzhnyy Ural** *var.* Southern Urals. ▲▲ W Russian Federation
165 V10 **Yuzhong** Gansu, C China
Yuzhou *see* Chongqing
105 N5 **Yvelines** ◐ *department* N France
110 B9 **Yverdon** *var.* Yverdon-les-Bains, *Ger.* Iferten; *anc.* Eborodunum. Vaud, W Switzerland
Yverdon-les-Bains *see* Yverdon
104 M3 **Yvetot** Seine-Maritime, N France
Yylanly *see* Il'yaly

◆ Country ● Country Capital ◇ Dependent Territory ○ Dependent Territory Capital ◐ Administrative Region ✕ International Airport ▲ Mountain ▲▲ Mountain Range ⛰ Volcano ≈ River ◎ Lake ▣ Reservoir

Z

53 T12 **Zaalayskiy Khrebet** *Taj.* Qatorkŭhi Pasi Oloy. ▲▲ Kyrgyzstan/Tajikistan
Zaamin *see* Zomin
Zaandam *see* Zaanstad
00 I10 **Zaanstad** *prev.* Zaandam. Noord-Holland, C Netherlands
Zabadani *see* Az Zabdānī
21 L18 **Zabalatstsye** *Rus.* Zabolot'ye. Homyel'skaya Voblasts', SE Belarus
14 L9 **Žabalj** *Ger.* Josefsdorf, *Hung.* Zsablya; *prev.* Józseffalva;. Serbia, N Yugoslavia
Zāb aş Şaghīr, Nahraz *see* Little Zab
26 L16 **Zabaykal'sk** Chitinskaya Oblast', S Russian Federation
Zāb-e Kūchek, Rūdkhāneh-ye *see* Little Zab
Zabeln *see* Sabile
Zabéré *see* Zabré
Zabern *see* Saverne
47 N16 **Zabīd** W Yemen
47 O16 **Zabīd, Wādī** *dry watercourse* SW Yemen
Žabinka *see* Zhabinka
Ząbkowice *see* Ząbkowice Śląskie
13 G15 **Ząbkowice Śląskie** *var.* Ząbkowice, *Ger.* Frankenstein, Frankenstein in Schlesien. Wałbrzych, SW Poland
12 P10 **Zabłudów** Białystok, NE Poland
14 D8 **Zabok** Krapina-Zagorje, N Croatia
49 W9 **Zābol** *var.* Shahr-i-Zabul, Zabul; *prev.* Nasratabad. Sīstān va Balūchestān, E Iran
Zābol *see* Zābul
49 W13 **Zābolī** Sīstān va Balūchestān, SE Iran
Zabolot'ye *see* Zabalatstsye
9 Q13 **Zabré** *var.* Zabéré. S Burkina
13 G17 **Zábřeh** *Ger.* Hohenstadt. Severní Morava, E Czech Republic
13 J16 **Zabrze** *Ger.* Hindenburg, Hindenburg in Oberschlesien. Katowice, S Poland
55 O7 **Zābul** *Per.* Zābol. ◈ *province* SE Afghanistan
Zabul *see* Zābol
4 E6 **Zacapa** Zacapa, E Guatemala
4 A3 **Zacapa** *off.* Departamento de Zacapa. ◈ *department* E Guatemala
2 M14 **Zacapú** Michoacán de Ocampo, SW Mexico
3 V14 **Zacatal** Campeche, SE Mexico
2 M11 **Zacatecas** Zacatecas, C Mexico
2 L10 **Zacatecas** ◈ *state* C Mexico
4 F8 **Zacatecoluca** La Paz, S El Salvador
3 P15 **Zacatepec** Morelos, S Mexico
3 Q13 **Zacatlán** Puebla, S Mexico
50 F8 **Zachagansk** Zapadnyy Kazakhstan, NW Kazakhstan
17 D20 **Zacháro** *var.* Zaharo, Zakháro. Dytikí Ellás, S Greece
4 J8 **Zachary** Louisiana, S USA
19 U6 **Zachepylivka** Kharkivs'ka Oblast', E Ukraine
Zachist'ye *see* Zachystsye
21 L14 **Zachystsye** *Rus.* Zachist'ye. Minskaya Voblasts', NW Belarus
2 L13 **Zacoalco** *var.* Zacoalco de Torres. Jalisco, SW Mexico
Zacoalco de Torres *see* Zacoalco
3 P13 **Zacualtipán** Hidalgo, C Mexico
14 C12 **Zadar** *It.* Zara; *anc.* Iader. Zadar-Knin, W Croatia
14 C12 **Zadar-Knin** *off.* Zadarsko-Kninska Županija. ◈ *province* SW Croatia
77 G14 **Zadetkyi Kyun** *var.* St. Matthew's Island. *island* Mergui Archipelago, S Myanmar
9 Q9 **Zadié** *var.* Djadié. ≈ NE Gabon
65 Q13 **Zadoi** Qinghai, C China
30 L7 **Zadonsk** Lipetskaya Oblast', W Russian Federation
7 X8 **Za'farâna** E Egypt
55 W7 **Zafarwāl** Punjab, E Pakistan
24 P1 **Zafer Burnu** *var.* Cape Andreas, Cape Apostolas Andreas, *Gk.* Akrotíri Apostólou Andréa. *headland* NE Cyprus
09 J23 **Zafferano, Capo** *headland* Sicilia, Italy, C Mediterranean Sea
16 M7 **Zafirovo** Razgradska Oblast, NE Bulgaria
17 L23 **Zaforá** *island* Kykládes, Greece, Aegean Sea
06 J12 **Zafra** Extremadura, W Spain
12 E13 **Żagań** *var.* Zagań, Żegań, *Ger.* Sagan. Zielona Góra, W Poland
20 F10 **Žagarė** *Pol.* Żagory. Joniškis, N Lithuania
7 W7 **Zagazig** *var.* Az Zaqāzīq. N Egypt
5 M5 **Zaghouan** *var.* Zaghwān. NE Tunisia
Zaghwān *see* Zaghouan
17 G16 **Zagorá** Thessalía, C Greece
Zagorod'ye *see* Zaharoddzye
Żagory *see* Žagarė
Zágráb *see* Zagreb
14 E8 **Zagreb** *Ger.* Agram, *Hung.* Zágráb. ● (Croatia) Grad Zagreb, N Croatia
48 L7 **Zāgros, Kūhhā-ye** *Eng.* Zagros Mountains. ▲▲ W Iran
Zagros Mountains *see* Zāgros, Kūhhā-ye
14 O12 **Žagubica** Serbia, E Yugoslavia
13 L22 **Zagyva** ≈ N Hungary
Zaharo *see* Zacháro
21 G19 **Zaharoddzye** *Rus.* Zagorod'ye. *physical region* SW Belarus
149 W11 **Zāhedān** *var.* Zahidan; *prev.* Duzdab. Sīstān va Balūchestān, SE Iran
Zahidan *see* Zāhedān
Zaḩlah *see* Zahlé
144 H7 **Zahlé** *var.* Zaḩlah. C Lebanon
Zähmet *see* Zakhmet
113 O20 **Záhony** Szabolcs-Szatmár-Bereg, NE Hungary
147 N13 **Z̧ahrān** 'Asīr, S Saudi Arabia
145 R12 **Z̧ahrat al Baţn** *hill range* S Iraq
123 I12 **Zahrez Chergui** *var.* Zahrez Chergúi. *marsh* N Algeria
131 S4 **Zainsk** Respublika Tatarstan, W Russian Federation
81 K19 **Zaire** *now called* Congo (Dem. Rep.), *off.* Republic of Zaire; *prev.* Belgian Congo, Congo (Kinshasa). ◆ *republic* C Africa
84 A10 **Zaire** *prev.* Congo. ◈ *province* NW Angola
Zaire *see* Congo
114 P13 **Zaječar** Serbia, E Yugoslavia
85 L18 **Zaka** Masvingo, E Zimbabwe
126 J16 **Zakamensk** Respublika Buryatiya, S Russian Federation
118 G7 **Zakarpats'ka Oblast'** *Eng.* Transcarpathian Oblast, *Rus.* Zakarpatskaya Oblast'. ◈ *province* W Ukraine
Zakarpatskaya Oblast' *see* Zakarpats'ka Oblast'
Zakataly *see* Zaqatala
Zakháro *see* Zacháro
Zakhidnyy Buh/Zakhodni Buh *see* Bug
152 J14 **Zakhmet** *Turkm.* Zähmet. Maryyskiy Velayat, C Turkmenistan
145 Q1 **Zākhō** *var.* Zākhū. N Iraq
Zākhū *see* Zākhō
Zákinthos *see* Zákynthos
113 L18 **Zakopane** Nowy Sącz, S Poland
80 J12 **Zakouma** Salamat, S Chad
117 L25 **Zákros** Kríti, Greece, E Mediterranean Sea
117 C19 **Zákynthos** *var.* Zákinthos. Zákynthos, W Greece
117 C20 **Zákynthos** *var.* Zákinthos, *It.* Zante. *island* Iónioi Nísoi, Greece, C Mediterranean Sea
117 C19 **Zakýnthou, Porthmós** *strait* SW Greece
113 G24 **Zala** *off.* Zala Megye. ◈ *county* W Hungary
113 G24 **Zala** ≈ W Hungary
144 M4 **Zalābiyah** Dayr az Zawr, C Syria
113 G24 **Zalaegerszeg** Zala, W Hungary
106 K11 **Zalamea de la Serena** Extremadura, W Spain
106 J13 **Zalamea la Real** Andalucía, S Spain
169 U7 **Zalantun** *var.* Butha Qi. Nei Mongol Zizhiqu, N China
126 J15 **Zalari** Irkutskaya Oblast', S Russian Federation
113 G23 **Zalaszentgrót** Zala, SW Hungary
Zalatna *see* Zlatna
118 G9 **Zalău** *Ger.* Waltenberg, *Hung.* Zilah; prev. *Ger.* Zillenmarkt. Sălaj, NW Romania
111 V10 **Žalec** *Ger.* Sachsenfeld. C Slovenia
119 S9 **Zalenodol's'k** Dnipropetrovs'ka Oblast', E Ukraine
112 K8 **Zalewo** *Ger.* Saalfeld. Olsztyn, N Poland
147 N9 **Z̧alim** Makkah, W Saudi Arabia
82 A11 **Zalingei** *var.* Zalinje. Western Darfur, W Sudan
Zalinje *see* Zalingei
118 K7 **Zalishchyky** Ternopil's'ka Oblast', W Ukraine
Zallah *see* Zillah
100 J13 **Zaltbommel** Gelderland, C Netherlands
128 H15 **Zaluch'ye** Novgorodskaya Oblast', NW Russian Federation
Zamak *see* Zamakh
147 Q14 **Zamakh** *var.* Zamak. N Yemen
142 K15 **Zamantı Irmağı** ≈ C Turkey
Zambesi/Zambeze *see* Zambezi
85 G14 **Zambezi** North Western, W Zambia
85 K15 **Zambezi** *var.* Zambesi, *Port.* Zambeze. ≈ S Africa
85 O15 **Zambézia** *off.* Província da Zambézia. ◈ *province* C Mozambique
85 I14 **Zambia** *off.* Republic of Zambia; *prev.* Northern Rhodesia. ◆ *republic* S Africa
179 Q16 **Zamboanga** *off.* Zamboanga City. Mindanao, S Philippines
56 E5 **Zambrano** Bolívar, N Colombia
112 N10 **Zambrów** Łomża, E Poland
85 L14 **Zambué** Tete, NW Mozambique
79 T13 **Zamfara** ≈ NW Nigeria
Zamojskie, Województwo *see* Zamość
58 C9 **Zamora** Zamora Chinchipe, S Ecuador
106 K6 **Zamora** Castilla-León, NW Spain
106 K5 **Zamora** ◈ *province* Castilla-León, NW Spain
Zamora *see* Barinas
58 A13 **Zamora Chinchipe** ◈ *province* S Ecuador
42 M13 **Zamora de Hidalgo** Michoacán de Ocampo, SW Mexico
113 P15 **Zamość** *Rus.* Zamoste. Zamość, SE Poland
113 P15 **Zamość** *off.* Województwo Zamojskie, *Rus.* Zamoste. ◈ *province* SE Poland
Zamoste *see* Zamość
166 G7 **Zamtang** *prev.* Gamda. Sichuan, C China
77 O8 **Zamzam, Wādī** *dry watercourse* NW Libya
81 F20 **Zanaga** La Lékoumou, S Congo
43 T16 **Zanatepec** Oaxaca, SE Mexico
107 P9 **Záncara** ≈ C Spain
Zancle *see* Messina
164 G14 **Zanda** Xizang Zizhiqu, W China
100 H10 **Zandvoort** Noord-Holland, W Netherlands
41 P8 **Zane Hills** *hill range* Alaska, USA
33 T13 **Zanesville** Ohio, N USA
Zanga *see* Hrazdan
148 L4 **Zanjān** *var.* Zenjan, Zinjan. Zanjān, NW Iran
148 L4 **Zanjān** *off.* Ostān-e Zanjān, *var.* Zenjan, Zinjan. ◈ *province* NW Iran
Zante *see* Zákynthos
83 J22 **Zanzibar** Zanzibar, E Tanzania
83 J22 **Zanzibar** ◈ *region* E Tanzania
83 J22 **Zanzibar** *Swa.* Unguja. *island* E Tanzania
83 J22 **Zanzibar Channel** *channel* E Tanzania
171 Ll13 **Zaō-san** ▲ Honshū, C Japan
167 N8 **Zaoyang** Hubei, C China
126 I14 **Zaozernyy** Krasnoyarskiy Kray, S Russian Federation
167 Q6 **Zaozhuang** Shandong, E China
30 L4 **Zap** North Dakota, N USA
114 L13 **Zapadna Morava** *Ger.* Westliche Morava. ≈ C Yugoslavia
128 H16 **Zapadnaya Dvina** Tverskaya Oblast', W Russian Federation
Zapadnaya Dvina *see* Western Dvina
113 H20 **Západné Slovensko** ◈ *region* W Slovakia
113 A17 **Západní Čechy** *off.* Západočeský Kraj. ◈ *region* W Czech Republic
126 H10 **Zapadno-Sibirskaya Ravnina** *Eng.* West Siberian Plain. *plain* C Russian Federation
Zapadnyy Bug *see* Bug
150 E9 **Zapadnyy Kazakhstan** *off.* Zapadno-Kazakhstanskaya Oblast', *Eng.* West Kazakhstan, *Kaz.* Batys Qazaqstan Oblysy; *prev.* Ural'skaya Oblast'. ◈ *province* NW Kazakhstan
126 Hh15 **Zapadnyy Sayan** *Eng.* Western Sayans. ▲▲ S Russian Federation
65 H15 **Zapala** Neuquén, W Argentina
64 I4 **Zapaleri, Cerro** *var.* Cerro Sapaleri. ▲ N Chile
27 Q16 **Zapata** Texas, SW USA
46 D5 **Zapata, Península de** *peninsula* W Cuba
63 G19 **Zapicán** Lavalleja, S Uruguay
67 J19 **Zapiola Ridge** *undersea feature* SW Atlantic Ocean
67 L19 **Zapiola Seamount** *undersea feature* S Atlantic Ocean
128 I2 **Zapolyarnyy** Murmanskaya Oblast', NW Russian Federation
119 U8 **Zaporizhzhya** *Rus.* Zaporozh'ye; *prev.* Aleksandrovsk. Zaporiz'ka Oblast', SE Ukraine
Zaporizhzhya *see* Zaporiz'ka Oblast'
119 U9 **Zaporiz'ka Oblast'** *var.* Zaporizhzhya, *Rus.* Zaporozhskaya Oblast'. ◈ *province* SE Ukraine
Zaporozhskaya Oblast' *see* Zaporiz'ka Oblast'
Zaporozh'ye *see* Zaporizhzhya
42 L14 **Zapotiltic** Jalisco, SW Mexico
164 G13 **Zapung** Xizang Zizhiqu, W China
143 V10 **Zaqatala** *Rus.* Zakataly. NW Azerbaijan
165 P13 **Zaqên** Qinghai, W China
165 Q13 **Za Qu** ≈ C China
142 M13 **Zara** Sivas, C Turkey
Zara *see* Zadar
Zarafshan *see* Zarafshon
153 P12 **Zarafshon** *Rus.* Zeravshan. W Tajikistan
152 L9 **Zarafshon** *Rus.* Zarafshan. Nawoiy Wiloyati, N Uzbekistan
Zarafshon *see* Zeravshan
153 O12 **Zarafshon, Qatorkŭhi** *Rus.* Zeravshanskiy Khrebet, *Uzb.* Zarafshon Tizmasi. ▲▲ Tajikistan/Uzbekistan
Zarafshon Tizmasi *see* Zarafshon, Qatorkŭhi
56 E7 **Zaragoza** Antioquia, N Colombia
42 I5 **Zaragoza** Chihuahua, N Mexico
43 N6 **Zaragoza** Coahuila de Zaragoza, NE Mexico
43 O10 **Zaragoza** Nuevo León, NE Mexico
107 R5 **Zaragoza** *Eng.* Saragossa; *anc.* Caesaraugusta, Salduba. Aragón, NE Spain
107 R6 **Zaragoza** ◈ *province* Aragón, NE Spain
107 R5 **Zaragoza** × Aragón, NE Spain
149 S10 **Zarand** Kermān, C Iran
154 J9 **Zaranj** Nīmrūz, SW Afghanistan
120 I11 **Zarasai** Zarasai, E Lithuania
64 N12 **Zárate** *prev.* General José F.Uriburu. Buenos Aires, E Argentina
107 Q2 **Zarautz** *var.* Zarauz. País Vasco, N Spain
Zarauz *see* Zarautz
Zaravecchia *see* Biograd na Moru
Zarāyīn *see* Zarēn
130 L4 **Zaraysk** Moskovskaya Oblast', W Russian Federation
57 N6 **Zaraza** Guárico, N Venezuela
Zarbdar *see* Zarbdor
153 P11 **Zarbdor** *Rus.* Zarbdar. Jizzakh Wiloyati, C Uzbekistan
148 M8 **Zard Kūh** ▲ SW Iran
128 I5 **Zarechensk** Murmanskaya Oblast', NW Russian Federation
155 Q7 **Zareh Sharan** Paktīkā, E Afghanistan
41 Y14 **Zarembo Island** *island* Alexander Archipelago, Alaska, USA
145 V4 **Zarēn** *var.* Zarāyīn. E Iraq
155 Q7 **Zarghūn Shahr** *var.* Katawaz. Paktīkā, SE Afghanistan
79 V13 **Zaria** Kaduna, C Nigeria
118 K2 **Zarichne** Rivnens'ka Oblast', NW Ukraine
126 H14 **Zarinsk** Altayskiy Kray, S Russian Federation
118 J12 **Zărneşti** *Hung.* Zernest. Braşov, C Romania
117 J25 **Zarós** Kríti, Greece, E Mediterranean Sea
102 O9 **Zarow** ≈ NE Germany
Zarqa/Zarqā', Muḩāfaz̧at az *see* Az Zarqā'
113 G20 **Záruby** ▲ W Slovakia
58 B8 **Zaruma** El Oro, SW Ecuador
112 E13 **Żary** *Ger.* Sorau, Sorau in der Niederlausitz. Zielona Góra, W Poland
56 D10 **Zarzal** Valle del Cauca, W Colombia
44 I7 **Zarzalar, Cerro** ▲ S Honduras
158 I5 **Zāskār** ≈ NE India
158 I5 **Zāskār Range** ▲▲ NE India
121 K15 **Zaslawye** Minskaya Voblasts', C Belarus
118 K7 **Zastavna** Chernivets'ka Oblast', W Ukraine
113 B16 **Žatec** *Ger.* Saaz. Severní Čechy, NW Czech Republic
Zaumgarten *see* Chrzanów
152 G10 **Zaunguzskiye Garagumy** *Turkm.* Üngüz Angyrsyndaky Garagum. *desert* N Turkmenistan
27 X9 **Zavalla** Texas, SW USA
101 H18 **Zaventem** Vlaams Brabant, C Belgium
101 H18 **Zaventem** × (Brussel/Bruxelles) Vlaams Brabant, C Belgium
Zavertse *see* Zawiercie
116 L7 **Zavet** Razgradska Oblast, NE Bulgaria
131 O12 **Zavetnoye** Rostovskaya Oblast', SW Russian Federation
162 M3 **Zavhan Gol** ≈ W Mongolia
114 H12 **Zavidovići** N Bosnia and Herzegovina
126 Mm16 **Zavitinsk** Amurskaya Oblast', SE Russian Federation
125 F12 **Zavodoukovsk** Tyumenskaya Oblast', C Russian Federation
Zawia *see* Az Zāwiyah
113 K15 **Zawiercie** *Rus.* Zavertse. Katowice, S Poland
77 P11 **Zawīlah** *var.* Zuwaylah, *It.* Zueila. C Libya
144 I4 **Zāwīyah, Jabal az** ▲▲ NW Syria
111 Y3 **Zaya** ≈ NE Austria
177 G8 **Zayatkyi** Pegu, C Myanmar
151 Y11 **Zaysan** Vostochnyy Kazakhstan, E Kazakhstan
Zaysan Köl *see* Zaysan, Ozero
151 Y11 **Zaysan, Ozero** *Kaz.* Zaysan Köl. ◎ E Kazakhstan
165 R16 **Zayü** *var.* Gyigang. Xizang Zizhiqu, W China
Zayyq *see* Ural
46 F6 **Zaza** ≈ C Cuba
118 K5 **Zbarazh** Ternopil's'ka Oblast', W Ukraine
118 J5 **Zboriv** Ternopil's'ka Oblast', W Ukraine
113 F18 **Zbraslav** Jižní Morava, SE Czech Republic
118 K6 **Zbruch** ≈ W Ukraine
Ždár *see* Žd'ár nad Sázavou
113 F17 **Žd'ár nad Sázavou** *Ger.* Saar in Mähren; *prev.* Žd'ár. Jižní Morava, C Czech Republic
118 K4 **Zdolbuniv** *Pol.* Zdolbunów, *Rus.* Zdolbunov. Rivnens'ka Oblast', NW Ukraine
Zdolbunov/Zdolbunów *see* Zdolbuniv
112 J13 **Zduńska Wola** Sieradz, C Poland
119 O4 **Zdvizh** ≈ N Ukraine
Zdzięciół *see* Dzyatlava
113 I16 **Zdzieszowice** *Ger.* Odertal. Opole, SW Poland
Zealand *see* Sjælland
196 K6 **Zealandia Bank** *undersea feature* C Pacific Ocean
65 H20 **Zeballos, Monte** ▲ S Argentina
85 K20 **Zebediela** Northern, NE South Africa
115 L18 **Zebë, Mal** *var.* Mali i Zebës. ▲ NE Albania
Zebës, Mali i *see* Zebë, Mal
23 V9 **Zebulon** North Carolina, SE USA
114 K8 **Žednik** *Hung.* Bácsjózseffalva. Serbia, N Yugoslavia
101 C15 **Zeebrugge** West-Vlaanderen, NW Belgium
191 N16 **Zeehan** Tasmania, SE Australia
101 L14 **Zeeland** Noord-Brabant, SE Netherlands
31 N7 **Zeeland** North Dakota, N USA
101 E14 **Zeeland** ◈ *province* SW Netherlands
85 I21 **Zeerust** North-West, N South Africa
100 K10 **Zeewolde** Flevoland, C Netherlands
144 G8 **Z̲efat** *var.* Safed, *Ar.* Safad. Northern, N Israel
Żegań *see* Żagań
Zehden *see* Cedynia
102 O11 **Zehdenick** Brandenburg, NE Germany
Zē-i Bādīnān *see* Great Zab
Zeiden *see* Codlea
152 M14 **Zeidskoye Vodokhranilishche** ⊡ E Turkmenistan
Zē-i Kōya *see* Little Zab
189 P7 **Zeil, Mount** ▲ Northern Territory, C Australia
100 J12 **Zeist** Utrecht, C Netherlands
103 M16 **Zeitz** Sachsen-Anhalt, E Germany
165 T11 **Zêkog** Qinghai, C China
Zelaya Norte *see* Atlántico Norte, Región Autónoma
Zelaya Sur *see* Atlántico Sur, Región Autónoma
101 F17 **Zele** Oost-Vlaanderen, NW Belgium
112 N12 **Żelechów** Siedlce, E Poland
115 H14 **Zelena Glava** ▲ SE Bosnia and Herzegovina
115 I14 **Zelengora** ▲▲ S Bosnia and Herzegovina
128 I5 **Zelenoborskiy** Murmanskaya Oblast', NW Russian Federation
131 R3 **Zelenodol'sk** Respublika Tatarstan, W Russian Federation
128 G12 **Zelenogorsk** *Fin.* Terijoki. Leningradskaya Oblast', NW Russian Federation
130 K3 **Zelenograd** Moskovskaya Oblast', W Russian Federation
120 B13 **Zelenogradsk** *Ger.* Cranz, Kranz. Kaliningradskaya Oblast', W Russian Federation
131 O15 **Zelenokumsk** Stavropol'skiy Kray, SW Russian Federation
172 Rr7 **Zelënyy, Ostrov** *var.* Shibotsu-jima. *island* NE Russian Federation
Železna Kapela *see* Eisenkappel
Železna Vrata *see* Demir Kapija
114 L11 **Železniki** Serbia, N Yugoslavia
100 N12 **Zelhem** Gelderland, E Netherlands
115 N18 **Želino** NW FYR Macedonia
115 M14 **Željin** ▲▲ C Yugoslavia
103 K17 **Zella-Mehlis** Thüringen, C Germany
111 P7 **Zell am See** *var.* Zell-am-See. Salzburg, S Austria
111 N7 **Zell am Ziller** Tirol, W Austria
Zelle *see* Celle
111 W2 **Zellerndorf** Niederösterreich, NE Austria
111 U7 **Zeltweg** Steiermark, S Austria
121 G17 **Zel'va** *Pol.* Zelwa. Hrodzyenskaya Voblasts', W Belarus
120 H13 **Želva** Ukmergė, C Lithuania
Zelwa *see* Zel'va
101 E16 **Zelzate** *var.* Selzaete. Oost-Vlaanderen, NW Belgium
120 E11 **Žemaičių Aukštumas** *physical region* W Lithuania
120 C12 **Žemaičių Naumiestis** Šilutė, SW Lithuania
Zembin *see* Zyembin
131 N6 **Zemetchino** Penzenskaya Oblast', W Russian Federation
81 M15 **Zémio** Haut-Mbomou, E Central African Republic
43 R16 **Zempoaltepec, Cerro** ▲ SE Mexico
101 G17 **Zemst** Vlaams Brabant, C Belgium
114 L11 **Zemun** Serbia, N Yugoslavia
Zendajan *see* Zendeh Jan
154 J5 **Zendeh Jan** *var.* Zendajan, Zindajān. Herāt, NW Afghanistan
Zengg *see* Senj
114 H12 **Zenica** C Bosnia and Herzegovina
Zenjan *see* Zanjān
Zen'kov *see* Zin'kiv
Zenshū *see* Chŏnju
Zenta *see* Senta
170 Ff14 **Zentsūji** *var.* Zentûzi. Kagawa, Shikoku, SW Japan
Zentûzi *see* Zentsūji
84 B11 **Zenza do Itombe** Cuanza Norte, NW Angola
114 H12 **Žepče** N Bosnia and Herzegovina
25 W12 **Zephyrhills** Florida, SE USA
199 J10 **Zephyr Reef** *reef* Antarctica
164 F9 **Zepu** *var.* Poskam. Xinjiang Uygur Zizhiqu, NW China
153 Q12 **Zeravshan** *Taj./Uzb.* Zarafshon. ≈ Tajikistan/Uzbekistan
Zeravshan *see* Zarafshon
Zeravshanskiy Khrebet *see* Zarafshon, Qatorkŭhi
103 M14 **Zerbst** Sachsen-Anhalt, E Germany
151 P8 **Zerenda** Kokshetau, N Kazakhstan
112 H12 **Żerków** Kalisz, C Poland
110 E11 **Zermatt** Valais, SW Switzerland
Zernest *see* Zărneşti
110 J9 **Zernez** Graubünden, SE Switzerland
130 L12 **Zernograd** Rostovskaya Oblast', SW Russian Federation
Zestafoni *see* Zestap'oni
143 S9 **Zestap'oni** *Rus.* Zestafoni. C Georgia
100 H12 **Zestienhoven** × (Rotterdam) Zuid-Holland, SW Netherlands
115 J16 **Zeta** ≈ SW Yugoslavia
15 J2 **Zeta Lake** ◎ Victoria Island, Northwest Territories, N Canada
100 L12 **Zetten** Gelderland, SE Netherlands
103 M17 **Zeulenroda** Thüringen, C Germany
102 H10 **Zeven** Niedersachsen, NW Germany
100 M12 **Zevenaar** Gelderland, SE Netherlands
101 H14 **Zevenbergen** Noord-Brabant, S Netherlands
126 M14 **Zeya** Amurskaya Oblast', SE Russian Federation
133 X6 **Zeya** ≈ SE Russian Federation
Zeya Reservoir *see* Zeyskoye Vodokhranilishche
149 T11 **Zeynalābād** Kermān, C Iran
126 M14 **Zeyskoye Vodokhranilishche** *Eng.* Zeya Reservoir. ⊡ SE Russian Federation
106 H8 **Zêzere** ≈ C Portugal
Zgerzh *see* Zgierz
144 H6 **Zgharta** N Lebanon
112 K12 **Zgierz** *Ger.* Neuhof, *Rus.* Zgerzh. Łódź, C Poland
113 E14 **Zgorzelec** *Ger.* Görlitz. Jelenia Góra, SW Poland
Zhabdün *see* Zhongba
121 F19 **Zhabinka** *Pol.* Żabinka, *Rus.* Zhabinka. Brestskaya Voblasts', SW Belarus
Zhaggo *see* Luhuo
165 R15 **Zhag'yab** Xizang Zizhiqu, W China
150 L9 **Zhailma** *Kaz.* Zhayylma. Kustanay, N Kazakhstan
151 V16 **Zhalanash** Almaty, SE Kazakhstan
Zhalashash *see* Dzhalagash
151 S7 **Zhalauly, Ozero** ◎ NE Kazakhstan
121 G16 **Zhaludok** *Rus.* Zheludok. Hrodzyenskaya Voblasts', W Belarus
Zhaman-Akkol', Ozero *see* Akkol', Ozero
151 R16 **Zhambyl** *prev.* Aulie Ata, Auliye-Ata, Dzhambul. Zhambyl, S Kazakhstan
151 Q14 **Zhambyl** *off.* Zhambylskaya Oblast', *Kaz.* Zhambyl Oblysy; *prev.* Dzhambulskaya Oblast'. ◈ *province* S Kazakhstan
Zhambyl Oblysy/Zhambylskaya Oblast' *see* Zhambyl
Zhamo *see* Bomi
151 S12 **Zhamshy** ≈ C Kazakhstan
150 M15 **Zhanadar'ya** Kzyl-Orda, S Kazakhstan
151 O15 **Zhanakorgan** *Kaz.* Zhangaqorghan. Kzyl-Orda, S Kazakhstan
165 N16 **Zhanang** Xizang Zizhiqu, W China
151 T12 **Zhanaortalyk** Zhezkazgan, C Kazakhstan
151 Q16 **Zhanatas** Zhambyl, S Kazakhstan
Zhangaözen *see* Novyy Uzen'
Zhangaqazaly *see* Novokazalinsk
Zhangaqorghan *see* Zhanakorgan
167 O2 **Zhangbei** Hebei, E China
Zhangdian *see* Zibo
169 X9 **Zhangguangcai Ling** ▲▲ NE China
151 W10 **Zhangiztobe** Semipalatinsk, E Kazakhstan
165 W11 **Zhangjiachuan** Gansu, N China
166 L10 **Zhangjiajie** *var.* Dayong. Hunan, S China
167 O2 **Zhangjiakou** *var.* Changkiakow, Zhang-chia-k'ou, *Eng.* Kalgan; *prev.* Wanchuan. Hebei, E China
167 Q13 **Zhangping** Fujian, SE China
167 Q13 **Zhangpu** Fujian, SE China
169 U11 **Zhangwu** Liaoning, NE China
165 S8 **Zhangye** Gansu, N China
167 Q13 **Zhangzhou** Fujian, SE China
169 W6 **Zhan He** ≈ NE China
Zhänibek *see* Dzhanybek
166 L16 **Zhanjiang** *var.* Chanchiang, Chan-chiang, *Cant.* Tsamkong, *Fr.* Fort-Bayard. Guangdong, S China
Zhansügirov *see* Dzhansugurov
169 V8 **Zhaodong** Heilongjiang, NE China
Zhaoge *see* Qixian
166 H11 **Zhaojue** Sichuan, C China
167 N14 **Zhaoqing** Guangdong, S China
164 H5 **Zhaosu** *var.* Mongolküre. Xinjiang Uygur Zizhiqu, NW China
166 H11 **Zhaotong** Yunnan, SW China
169 V9 **Zhaoyuan** Heilongjiang, NE China
169 V9 **Zhaozhou** Heilongjiang, NE China
151 X13 **Zharbulak** Semipalatinsk, E Kazakhstan
164 J15 **Zhari Namco** ◎ W China
150 I12 **Zharkamys** *Kaz.* Zharqamys. Aktyubinsk, W Kazakhstan
151 W15 **Zharkent** *prev.* Panfilov. Taldykorgan, SE Kazakhstan
128 H17 **Zharkovskiy** Tverskaya Oblast', W Russian Federation
151 W11 **Zharma** Semipalatinsk, E Kazakhstan
150 F14 **Zharmysh** Mangistau, SW Kazakhstan
Zharqamys *see* Zharkamys
120 L13 **Zhary** *Rus.* Zhary. Vitsyebskaya Voblasts', N Belarus
Zhaslyk *see* Jasliq
126 Ll11 **Zhatay** Respublika Sakha (Yakutiya), NE Russian Federation
164 J14 **Zhaxi Co** ◎ W China
Zhayylma *see* Zhailma
Zhdanov *see* Beyläqan, Azerbaijan
Zhdanov *see* Mariupol', Ukraine
Zhe *see* Zhejiang
167 R10 **Zhejiang** *var.* Che-chiang, Chekiang, Zhe, Zhejiang Sheng. ◈ *province* SE China
Zhejiang Sheng *see* Zhejiang
151 S7 **Zhelezinka** Pavlodar, N Kazakhstan
121 C14 **Zheleznodorozhnyy** *Ger.* Gerdauen. Kaliningradskaya Oblast', W Russian Federation
126 J13 **Zheleznodorozhnyy** Irkutskaya Oblast', C Russian Federation
Zheleznodorozhnyy *see* Yemva
130 J7 **Zheleznogorsk** Kurskaya Oblast', W Russian Federation
126 Jj14 **Zheleznogorsk-Ilimskiy** Irkutskaya Oblast', S Russian Federation
131 N15 **Zheleznovodsk** Stavropol'skiy Kray, SW Russian Federation
Zhëltyye Vody *see* Zhovti Vody
Zheludok *see* Zhaludok
Zhem *see* Emba
166 K7 **Zhenba** Shaanxi, C China
166 I13 **Zhenfeng** Guizhou, S China
Zhengjiatun *see* Shuangliao
165 X10 **Zhengning** Gansu, N China
169 Q12 **Zhengxiangbai Qi** Nei Mongol Zizhiqu, N China
167 N6 **Zhengzhou** *var.* Ch'eng-chou, Chengchow; *prev.* Chenghsien. Henan, C China
167 R8 **Zhenjiang** *var.* Chenkiang. Jiangsu, E China
169 U9 **Zhenlai** Jilin, NE China
166 I11 **Zhenxiong** Yunnan, SW China
166 K11 **Zhenyuan** *prev.* Wuyang. Guizhou, S China
167 R11 **Zherong** Fujian, SE China
Zhetiqara *see* Dzhetygara
150 F15 **Zhetybay** Mangistau, SW Kazakhstan
166 M11 **Zhexi Shuiku** ⊡ C China
151 O12 **Zhezdy** Zhezkazgan, C Kazakhstan
151 O12 **Zhezkazgan** *Kaz.* Zhezqazghan; *prev.* Dzhezkazgan. Zhezkazgan, C Kazakhstan
151 O13 **Zhezkazgan** *off.* Zhezkazganskaya Oblast', *Kaz.* Zhezqazghan Oblysy; *prev.* Dzhezkazganskaya Oblast'. ◈ *province* C Kazakhstan
Zhezkazganskaya Oblast'/Zhezqazghan/Zhezqazghan Oblysy *see* Zhezkazgan
166 M9 **Zhicheng** Hubei, C China
Zhidachov *see* Zhydachiv
165 Q12 **Zhidoi** Qinghai, C China
126 Jj15 **Zhigalovo** Irkutskaya Oblast', S Russian Federation
126 L9 **Zhigansk** Respublika Sakha (Yakutiya), NE Russian Federation
131 R6 **Zhigulevsk** Samarskaya Oblast', W Russian Federation
120 D13 **Zhilino** *Ger.* Schillen. Kaliningradskaya Oblast', W Russian Federation
131 O8 **Zhirnovsk** Volgogradskaya Oblast', SW Russian Federation
Zhitarovo *see* Vetren
Zhitkovichi *see* Zhytkavichy
131 P10 **Zhitkur** Volgogradskaya Oblast', SW Russian Federation
Zhitomir *see* Zhytomyr
Zhitomirskaya Oblast' *see* Zhytomyrs'ka Oblast'
130 J5 **Zhizdra** Kaluzhskaya Oblast', W Russian Federation
121 N18 **Zhlobin** Homyel'skaya Voblasts', SE Belarus
Zhmerinka *see* Zhmerynka
118 M7 **Zhmerynka** *Rus.* Zhmerinka. Vinnyts'ka Oblast', C Ukraine
155 R9 **Zhob** *var.* Fort Sandeman. Baluchistān, SW Pakistan
155 R8 **Zhob** ≈ C Pakistan
Zhodino *see* Zhodzina
121 L15 **Zhodzina** *Rus.* Zhodino. Minskaya Voblasts', C Belarus
126 Mm3 **Zhokhova, Ostrov** *island* Novosibirskiye Ostrova, NE Russian Federation
Zholkev/Zholkva *see* Zhovkva
Zholsaly *see* Dzhusaly
Zhondor *see* Jondor
164 I15 **Zhongba** *var.* Zhabdün. Xizang Zizhiqu, W China
166 F11 **Zhongdian** Yunnan, SW China
Zhonghua Renmin Gongheguo *see* China
165 V9 **Zhongning** Ningxia, N China
167 N15 **Zhongshan** Guangdong, S China
205 X7 **Zhongshan** *Chinese research station* Antarctica
166 M6 **Zhongtiao Shan** ▲▲ C China
165 V9 **Zhongwei** Ningxia, N China
166 K9 **Zhongxian** *var.* Zhong Xian. Sichuan, C China
167 N9 **Zhongxiang** Hubei, C China
167 O7 **Zhoukou** *var.* Zhoukouzhen. Henan, C China
Zhoukouzhen *see* Zhoukou
167 S9 **Zhoushan** Zhejiang, S China
167 S9 **Zhoushan Qundao** *Eng.* Zhoushan Islands. *island group* SE China
118 I5 **Zhovkva** *Pol.* Żółkiew, *Rus.* Zholkev, Zholkva; *prev.* Nesterov. L'vivs'ka Oblast', NW Ukraine
119 S7 **Zhovti Vody** *Rus.* Zhëltyye Vody. Dnipropetrovs'ka Oblast', E Ukraine
119 Q10 **Zhovtneve** *Rus.* Zhovtnevoye. Mykolayivs'ka Oblast', S Ukraine
Zhovtnevoye *see* Zhovtneve
116 K9 **Zhrebchevo, Yazovir** ⊡ C Bulgaria
169 V13 **Zhuanghe** Liaoning, NE China
165 W11 **Zhuanglang** Gansu, C China
151 P15 **Zhuantobe** *Kaz.* Zhūantöbe. Yuzhnyy Kazakhstan, S Kazakhstan
167 Q5 **Zhucheng** Shandong, E China
165 V12 **Zhugqu** Gansu, C China
167 N15 **Zhuhai** Guangdong, S China
Zhuizishan *see* Weichang
Zhuji *see* Shangqiu

◆ Country
● Country Capital
◇ Dependent Territory
○ Dependent Territory Capital
◈ Administrative Region
× International Airport
▲ Mountain
▲▲ Mountain Range
Volcano
≈ River
◎ Lake
⊡ Reservoir

130 *I5* **Zhukovka** Bryanskaya Oblast', W Russian Federation
167 *O3* **Zhuozhou** *prev.* Zhuo Xian. Hebei, E China
168 *L14* **Zhuozi Shan** ▲ N China
Zhuravichi *see* Zhuravichy
121 *O17* **Zhuravichy** ***Rus.*** Zhuravichi. Homyel'skaya Voblasts', SE Belarus
151 *Q8* **Zhuravlevka** Akmola, N Kazakhstan
119 *Q4* **Zhurivka** Kyyivs'ka Oblast', N Ukraine
150 *J11* **Zhuryn** Aktyubinsk, W Kazakhstan
151 *T15* **Zhusandala, Step'** *grassland* SE Kazakhstan
166 *L8* **Zhushan** Hubei, C China
167 *N11* **Zhuzhou** Hunan, S China
118 *I6* **Zhydachiv** ***Pol.*** Żydaczów, ***Rus.*** Zhidachov. L'vivs'ka Oblast', NW Ukraine
Zhympity *see* Dzhambeyty
121 *K19* **Zhytkavichy** ***Rus.*** Zhitkovichi. Homyel'skaya Voblasts', SE Belarus
119 *N4* **Zhytomyr** ***Rus.*** Zhitomir. Zhytomyrs'ka Oblast', NW Ukraine
Zhytomyr *see* Zhytomyrs'ka Oblast'
118 *M4* **Zhytomyrs'ka Oblast'** ***var.*** Zhytomyr, ***Rus.*** Zhitomirskaya Oblast'. ◈ *province* N Ukraine
159 *U15* **Zia** ✈ (Dhaka) Dhaka, C Bangladesh
113 *J20* **Žiar nad Hronom** ***var.*** Sväty Kríž nad Hronom, ***Ger.*** Heiligenkreuz, ***Hung.*** Garamszentkereszt. Stredné Slovensko, W Slovakia
167 *Q4* **Zibo** ***var.*** Zhangdian. Shandong, E China
166 *L4* **Zichang** ***prev.*** Wayaobu. Shaanxi, C China
Zichenau *see* Ciechanów
113 *G15* **Ziębice** ***Ger.*** Münsterberg in Schlesien. Wałbrzych, SW Poland
Ziebingen *see* Cybinka
Ziegenhais *see* Głuchołazy
112 *E12* **Zielona Góra** ***Ger.*** Grünberg, Grünberg in Schlesien, Grüneberg. Zielona Góra, W Poland
112 *E12* **Zielona Góra** ***off.*** Województwo Zielonogórskie. ◈ *province* W Poland
Zielonogórskie, Województwo *see* Zielona Góra
101 *F14* **Zierikzee** Zeeland, SW Netherlands
166 *I10* **Zigong** ***var.*** Tzekung. Sichuan, C China
78 *G12* **Ziguinchor** SW Senegal
43 *N16* **Zihuatanejo** Guerrero, S Mexico
Zilah *see* Zalău
131 *W7* **Zilair** Respublika Bashkortostan, W Russian Federation
142 *L12* **Zile** Tokat, N Turkey
113 *J18* **Žilina** ***Ger.*** Sillein, ***Hung.*** Zsolna. Stredné Slovensko, NW Slovakia
77 *Q9* **Zillah** ***var.*** Zallah. C Libya
Zillenmarkt *see* Zalău
111 *N7* **Ziller** ≈ W Austria
Zillertal Alps *see* Zillertaler Alpen
111 *N8* **Zillertaler Alpen** ***Eng.*** Zillertal Alps, ***It.*** Alpi Aurine. ▲▲ Austria/Italy
120 *K10* **Zilupe** ***Ger.*** Rosenhof. Ludza, E Latvia
126 *J15* **Zima** Irkutskaya Oblast', S Russian Federation
43 *O13* **Zimapán** Hidalgo, C Mexico
85 *I16* **Zimba** Southern, S Zambia
85 *J17* **Zimbabwe** ***off.*** Republic of Zimbabwe; ***prev.*** Rhodesia. ◆ *republic* S Africa
118 *H10* **Zimbor** ***Hung.*** Magyarzsombor. Sălaj, NW Romania
Zimmerbude *see* Svetlyy
118 *J15* **Zimnicea** Teleorman, S Romania
116 *L9* **Zimnitsa** Burgaska Oblast, E Bulgaria
131 *N12* **Zimovniki** Rostovskaya Oblast', SW Russian Federation
Zindajān *see* Zendeh Jan
79 *V12* **Zinder** Zinder, S Niger
79 *W11* **Zinder** ◈ *department* S Niger
79 *P12* **Ziniaré** C Burkina
Zinjan *see* Zanjān
147 *P16* **Zinjibār** SW Yemen
119 *T4* **Zin'kiv** ***var.*** Zen'kov. Poltavs'ka Oblast', NE Ukraine
Zinov'yevsk *see* Kirovohrad
Zintenhof *see* Sindi
33 *N10* **Zion** Illinois, N USA
56 *F10* **Zipaquirá** Cundinamarca, C Colombia
Zipser Neudorf *see* Spišská Nová Ves
113 *H23* **Zirc** Veszprém, W Hungary
115 *D14* **Žirje** ***It.*** Zuri. *island* S Croatia
Zirknitz *see* Cerknica
110 *M7* **Zirl** Tirol, W Austria
103 *K20* **Zirndorf** Bayern, SE Germany
166 *M11* **Zi Shui** ≈ C China
111 *Y3* **Zistersdorf** Niederösterreich, NE Austria
43 *O14* **Zitácuaro** Michoacán de Ocampo, SW Mexico
103 *Q16* **Zittau** Sachsen, E Germany
114 *I12* **Živinice** E Bosnia and Herzegovina
Ziwa Magharibi *see* Kagera
83 *J14* **Ziway Hāyk'** ◎ C Ethiopia
167 *N12* **Zixing** Hunan, S China
131 *W7* **Ziyanchurino** Orenburgskaya Oblast', W Russian Federation
166 *K8* **Ziyang** Shaanxi, C China
113 *I20* **Zlaté Moravce** ***Hung.*** Aranyosmarót. Západné Slovensko, SW Slovakia
114 *K13* **Zlatibor** ▲▲ W Yugoslavia
116 *L9* **Zlati Voyvoda** Burgaska Oblast, E Bulgaria
118 *G11* **Zlatna** ***Ger.*** Kleinschlatten, ***Hung.*** Zalatna; prev. ***Ger.*** Goldmarkt. Alba, C Romania
116 *I8* **Zlatna Panega** Loveshka Oblast, NW Bulgaria
116 *N8* **Zlatni Pyasŭtsi** Varnenska Oblast, NE Bulgaria
125 *E11* **Zlatoust** Chelyabinskaya Oblast', C Russian Federation
113 *M19* **Zlatý Stôl** ***Ger.*** Goldener Tisch, ***Hung.*** Aranyosasztal. ▲ C Slovakia
115 *P18* **Zletovo** NE FYR Macedonia
113 *H18* **Zlín** ***prev.*** Gottwaldov. Jižní Morava, SE Czech Republic
77 *O7* **Zlīţan** W Libya
112 *F9* **Złocieniec** ***Ger.*** Falkenburg in Pommern. Koszalin, NW Poland
112 *J13* **Złoczew** Sieradz, S Poland
Złoczów *see* Zolochiv
113 *F14* **Złotoryja** ***Ger.*** Goldberg. Legnica, W Poland
112 *G9* **Złotów** Piła, NW Poland
126 *Gg15* **Zmeinogorsk** Altayskiy Kray, S Russian Federation
112 *G13* **Żmigród** ***Ger.*** Trachenberg. Wrocław, SW Poland
130 *J6* **Zmiyevka** Orlovskaya Oblast', W Russian Federation
119 *V5* **Zmiyiv** Kharkivs'ka Oblast', E Ukraine
Zna *see* Tsna
Znaim *see* Znojmo
130 *M7* **Znamenka** Tambovskaya Oblast', W Russian Federation
Znamenka *see* Znam"yanka
121 *C14* **Znamensk** ***Ger.*** Wehlau. Kaliningradskaya Oblast', W Russian Federation
125 *Ff12* **Znamenskoye** Omskaya Oblast', C Russian Federation
119 *R7* **Znam"yanka** ***Rus.*** Znamenka. Kirovohrads'ka Oblast', C Ukraine
112 *H10* **Żnin** Bydgoszcz, W Poland
113 *F19* **Znojmo** ***Ger.*** Znaim. Jižní Morava, S Czech Republic
81 *N16* **Zobia** Haut-Zaïre, N Zaire
85 *N15* **Zóbuè** Tete, NW Mozambique
100 *G12* **Zoetermeer** Zuid-Holland, W Netherlands
110 *E7* **Zofingen** Aargau, N Switzerland
165 *R15* **Zogang** ***var.*** Wangda. Xizang Zizhiqu, W China
108 *E7* **Zogno** Lombardia, N Italy
148 *M10* **Zohreh, Rūd-e** ≈ SW Iran
166 *H7* **Zoigê** Sichuan, C China
Zółkiew *see* Zhovkva
110 *D8* **Zollikofen** Bern, W Switzerland
Zolochev *see* Zolochiv
119 *U4* **Zolochiv** ***Rus.*** Zolochev. Kharkivs'ka Oblast', E Ukraine
118 *J5* **Zolochiv** ***Pol.*** Złoczów, ***Rus.*** Zolochev. L'vivs'ka Oblast', W Ukraine
119 *X7* **Zolote** ***Rus.*** Zolotoye. Luhans'ka Oblast', E Ukraine
119 *Q6* **Zolotonosha** Cherkas'ka Oblast', C Ukraine
Zolotoye *see* Zolote
Zólyom *see* Zvolen
85 *N15* **Zomba** Southern, S Malawi
Zombor *see* Sombor
101 *D17* **Zomergem** Oost-Vlaanderen, NW Belgium
153 *P11* **Zomin** ***Rus.*** Zaamin. Jizzakh Wiloyati, C Uzbekistan
81 *I15* **Zongo** Equateur, N Zaire
142 *G10* **Zonguldak** Zonguldak, NW Turkey
142 *H10* **Zonguldak** ◈ *province* NW Turkey
101 *K17* **Zonhoven** Limburg, NE Belgium
148 *J2* **Zonūz** Āzarbāyjān-e Khāvarī, NW Iran
104 *F3* **Zonza** Corse, France, C Mediterranean Sea
Zoppot *see* Sopot
Zorgho *see* Zorgo
79 *Q13* **Zorgo** ***var.*** Zorgho. C Burkina
106 *K10* **Zorita** Extremadura, W Spain
153 *U14* **Zorkŭl** ***Rus.*** Ozero Zorkul'. ◎ SE Tajikistan
Zorkul', Ozero *see* Zorkŭl
58 *A8* **Zorritos** Tumbes, N Peru
113 *J16* **Żory** ***var.*** Zory, ***Ger.*** Sohrau. Katowice, S Poland
78 *K15* **Zorzor** N Liberia
101 *E18* **Zottegem** Oost-Vlaanderen, NW Belgium
79 *R15* **Zou** ≈ S Benin
80 *H6* **Zouar** Borkou-Ennedi-Tibesti, N Chad
78 *J6* **Zouérat** ***var.*** Zouérate, Zouîrât. Tiris Zemmour, N Mauritania
Zouérate *see* Zouérat
Zoug *see* Zug
Zouîrât *see* Zouérat
78 *M16* **Zoukougbeu** C Ivory Coast
100 *M5* **Zoutkamp** Groningen, NE Netherlands
101 *J18* **Zoutleeuw** ***Fr.*** Leau. Vlaams Brabant, C Belgium
114 *L9* **Zrenjanin** ***prev.*** Petrovgrad, Veliki Bečkerek, ***Ger.*** Grossbetschkerek, ***Hung.*** Nagybecskerek. Serbia, N Yugoslavia
114 *E10* **Zrinska Gora** ▲▲ C Croatia
Zsablya *see* Žabalj
103 *N16* **Zschopau** ≈ E Germany
Zsebely *see* Jebel
Zsibó *see* Jibou
Zsil/Zsily *see* Jiu
Zsilyvajdevulkán *see* Vulcan
Zsolna *see* Žilina
Zsombolya *see* Jimbolia
Zsupanya *see* Županja
57 *N7* **Zuata** Anzoátegui, NE Venezuela
107 *N14* **Zubia** Andalucía, S Spain
67 *P16* **Zubov Seamount** *undersea feature* E Atlantic Ocean
128 *I16* **Zubtsov** Tverskaya Oblast', W Russian Federation
110 *M8* **Zuckerhütl** ▲ SW Austria
Zueila *see* Zawīlah
78 *M16* **Zuénoula** C Ivory Coast
107 *S5* **Zuera** Aragón, NE Spain
147 *V13* **Ẓufār** ***Eng.*** Dhofar. *physical region* SW Oman
110 *G8* **Zug** ***Fr.*** Zoug. Zug, C Switzerland
110 *G8* **Zug** ***Fr.*** Zoug. ◈ *canton* C Switzerland
143 *R9* **Zugdidi** W Georgia
110 *G8* **Zuger See** ◎ NW Switzerland
103 *K25* **Zugspitze** ▲ S Germany
101 *E15* **Zuid-Beveland** ***var.*** South Beveland. *island* SW Netherlands
100 *K10* **Zuidelijk-Flevoland** *polder* C Netherlands
Zuider Zee *see* IJsselmeer
100 *G12* **Zuid-Holland** ***Eng.*** South Holland. ◈ *province* W Netherlands
100 *N5* **Zuidhorn** Groningen, NE Netherlands
100 *O6* **Zuidlaardermeer** ◎ NE Netherlands
100 *O6* **Zuidlaren** Drenthe, NE Netherlands
101 *K14* **Zuid-Willemsvaart Kanaal** *canal* S Netherlands
100 *N8* **Zuidwolde** Drenthe, NE Netherlands
Zuitaizi *see* Kang Xian
107 *O14* **Zújar** Andalucía, S Spain
106 *L11* **Zújar** ≈ W Spain
106 *L11* **Zújar, Embalse del** ▣ W Spain
82 *J9* **Zula** E Eritrea
56 *G6* **Zulia** ***off.*** Estado Zulia. ◈ *state* NW Venezuela
Zullapara *see* Sinchaingbyin
Züllichau *see* Sulechów
107 *P3* **Zumárraga** País Vasco, N Spain
111 *W12* **Žumberačka Gora** ***var.*** Uskočke Planine, Žumberak, ***Ger.*** Uskokengebirge, ***Slvn.*** Gorjanci; ***prev.*** Sichelburger Gerbirge. ▲▲ Croatia/Slovenia
Žumberak *see* Žumberačka Gora
204 *K7* **Zumberge Coast** *coastal feature* Antarctica
Zumbo *see* Vila do Zumbo
31 *W10* **Zumbro Falls** Minnesota, N USA
31 *W10* **Zumbro River** ≈ Minnesota, N USA
31 *W10* **Zumbrota** Minnesota, N USA
101 *H15* **Zundert** Noord-Brabant, S Netherlands
Zungaria *see* Dzungaria
79 *U14* **Zungeru** Niger, C Nigeria
39 *O11* **Zuni** New Mexico, SW USA
39 *P11* **Zuni Mountains** ▲▲ New Mexico, SW USA
166 *J11* **Zunyi** Guizhou, S China
166 *J15* **Zuo Jiang** ≈ China/Vietnam
110 *J9* **Zuoz** Graubünden, SE Switzerland
114 *I10* **Županja** ***Hung.*** Zsupanya. Vukovar-Srijem, E Croatia
115 *M17* **Žur** Serbia, S Yugoslavia
131 *T2* **Zura** Udmurtskaya Respublika, NW Russian Federation
145 *V8* **Zurbāţīyah** E Iraq
Zuri *see* Žirje
110 *F7* **Zürich** ***Eng./Fr.*** Zurich, ***It.*** Zurigo. Zürich, N Switzerland
110 *G6* **Zürich** ***Eng./Fr.*** Zurich. ◈ *canton* N Switzerland
Zurich, Lake *see* Zürichsee
110 *G7* **Zürichsee** ***Eng.*** Lake Zurich. ◎ NE Switzerland
Zurigo *see* Zürich
155 *V1* **Zŭrkŭl** ***Pash.*** Sarī Qūl, ***Rus.*** Ozero Zurkul'. ◎ Afghanistan/Tajikistan *see also* Sarī Qūl
Zurkul', Ozero *see* Sarī Qūl/Zŭrkŭl
112 *K10* **Żuromin** Ciechanów, N Poland
110 *J8* **Zürs** Vorarlberg, W Austria
79 *T13* **Zuru** Kebbi, W Nigeria
110 *F6* **Zurzach** Aargau, N Switzerland
103 *J22* **Zusam** ≈ S Germany
100 *M11* **Zutphen** Gelderland, E Netherlands
77 *N7* **Zuwārah** NW Libya
Zuwaylah *see* Zawīlah
129 *R14* **Zuyevka** Kirovskaya Oblast', NW Russian Federation
167 *N10* **Zuzhou** Hunan, S China
Zvenigorodka *see* Zvenyhorodka
119 *P6* **Zvenyhorodka** ***Rus.*** Zvenigorodka. Cherkas'ka Oblast', C Ukraine
126 *Jj14* **Zvezdnyy** Irkutskaya Oblast', C Russian Federation
85 *K18* **Zvishavane** ***prev.*** Shabani. Matabeleland South, S Zimbabwe
113 *J20* **Zvolen** ***Ger.*** Altsohl, ***Hung.*** Zólyom. Stredné Slovensko, C Slovakia
114 *J12* **Zvornik** E Bosnia and Herzegovina
100 *M5* **Zwaagwesteinde** ***Fris.*** De Westerein. Friesland, N Netherlands
100 *H10* **Zwanenburg** Noord-Holland, C Netherlands
100 *L8* **Zwarte Meer** ◎ N Netherlands
100 *M9* **Zwarte Water** ≈ N Netherlands
100 *M8* **Zwartsluis** Overijssel, E Netherlands
78 *L17* **Zwedru** ***var.*** Tchien. E Liberia
100 *O8* **Zweeloo** Drenthe, NE Netherlands
103 *E20* **Zweibrücken** ***Fr.*** Deux-Ponts; ***Lat.*** Bipontium. Rheinland-Pfalz, SW Germany
110 *D9* **Zweisimmen** Fribourg, W Switzerland
103 *M15* **Zwenkau** Sachsen, E Germany
111 *V3* **Zwettl** Wien, NE Austria
111 *T3* **Zwettl an der Rodl** Oberösterreich, N Austria
101 *D18* **Zwevegem** West-Vlaanderen, W Belgium
103 *M17* **Zwickau** Sachsen, E Germany
103 *O21* **Zwiesel** Bayern, SE Germany
100 *H13* **Zwijndrecht** Zuid-Holland, SW Netherlands
103 *N16* **Zwikauer Mulde** ≈ E Germany
Zwischenwässern *see* Medvode
Zwittau *see* Svitavy
112 *N13* **Zwoleń** Radom, SE Poland
100 *M9* **Zwolle** Overijssel, E Netherlands
24 *G6* **Zwolle** Louisiana, S USA
112 *K12* **Żychlin** Płock, C Poland
Żydaczów *see* Zhydachiv
121 *L14* **Zyembin** ***Rus.*** Zembin. Minskaya Voblasts', C Belarus
Zyôetu *see* Jōetsu
112 *L12* **Żyrardów** Skierniewice, C Poland
127 *Nn8* **Zyryanka** Respublika Sakha (Yakutiya), NE Russian Federation
151 *Y9* **Zyryanovsk** Vostochnyy Kazakhstan, E Kazakhstan
113 *J17* **Żywiec** ***Ger.*** Bäckermühle Schulzenmühle. Bielsko-Biała, S Poland

◆ COUNTRY
● COUNTRY CAPITAL
◇ DEPENDENT TERRITORY
○ DEPENDENT TERRITORY CAPITAL
◈ ADMINISTRATIVE REGION
✈ INTERNATIONAL AIRPORT
▲ MOUNTAIN
▲▲ MOUNTAIN RANGE
VOLCANO
≈ RIVER
◎ LAKE
▣ RESERVOIR

PICTURE CREDITS

DORLING KINDERSLEY *would like to express their thanks to the following individuals, companies and institutions for their help in preparing this atlas.*

Earth Resource Mapping Ltd., *Egham, Surrey*
Brian Groombridge, World Conservation Monitoring Centre, *Cambridge*
The British Library, *London*
British Library of Political and Economic Science, *London*
The British Museum, *London*
The City Business Library, *London*
King's College, *London*
National Meteorological Library and Archive, *Bracknell*
The Printed Word, *London*
The Royal Geographical Society, *London*
University of London Library
Paul Beardmore
Philip Boyes
Hayley Crockford
Alistair Dougal
Reg Grant
Louise Keane
Zoe Livesley
Laura Porter
Andy Summers

Every effort has been made to trace the copyright holders and we apologize in advance for any unintentional omissions. We would be pleased to insert the appropriate acknowledgement in any subsequent edition of this publication.

Adams Picture Library: 88CLA. **G. Andrews:** 194CR. **Ardea, London Ltd:** K. Ghana 156C; M. Iijima 140TC; R. Waller 154TCR. **Aspect Picture Library:** P. Carmichael 137CRB, 166TR; G. Tompkinson 202CRA. **Axiom Photographic Agency:** C. Bradley 154CA, 165CA; J. Holmes xiv CRA, xxxvii CRB, xxiv BCR, 156TCR, 172TL, 172BR; J. Morris 77TL, 77CRB; J. Spaull 134BL. **Bridgeman Art Library:** Collection of the Earl of Pembroke, Wilton House xx BC. **J. Allan Cash Ltd:** 8BC, 62CL, 71CL, 73CL, 74CRB, 78BC, 89BL, 111BR, 144BCL, 147TL, 160CR, 186BR, 189TR. **Bruce Coleman Ltd:** 100CLB; S. Alden 199BR; Atlantide xxxvi TCR, 144BR; E. Bjurstrom 147BR; T. Buchholz xv CL, 130CA; J. Burton xxiii CRi; J. Cancalosi 189AR; B. J. Coates 199BC; B. Coleman 65TL; B. & C. Colhoun 38CR; A. Compost xxiii CBRi; Dr S. Coyne 47TL; G. Cubitt xvi TL, 173BCL, 186TR, 192TR; P. Davey xxxvii CLB, 123CBL; N. Devore 197CBL; S.J. Doylee xxii CRii; H. Flygare xvii CA; M.P. & L. Fogden 17C; J. Foott Productions xxiii CBRii, 9 CRA; M. Freeman 93CRB; G. Gualco 146C; B. Henderson 201CR; Dr.C. Henneghien 71C; C. Hughes 71BCL; J. Johnson 41CR, 207TR; J. Jurka 93CLA; S. J. Krasemann 35TR; H. Lange 8CRA, 70CA; L. Lee Rue III 157BCL; C.C. Lockwood 34BC; M. McCoy 195TR; L.C. Marigo xxii BC, xxxvii CLA, 88CB; J. Murray xv C, 187BR; Orion Press 172TR; Orion Service & Trading Co. 171tr; C. Ott 18BL; Dr. E. Pott 42CLA, 89CB, 95BL, 204 CLB; F. Prenzel 197C, 201CB; M. Read 44BR, 45CRB; H. Reinhard xxii CRi, xxxvii TCR, 204BR; J. Shaw xix TL; K.N. Swenson 204BC; P. Terry 117TL; N.Tomalin 56BCL; H. Van Den Berg 71CR; P. Van Gaalen 88TR; 102CL U. Walz; P. Ward 80CLA; S. Widstrand 59TR; K. Wothe 93 CLB, 181TCL; J.T. Wright 131BR. **Colorific!:** Black Star/ M. Koene 57TR; J. Prupp 167BCR; R. Rogers 59BR; M. Yamashita 179CA; Matrix/R. Caputo 80CB. **Comstock:** 110CRB. **D. Cousens:** 153CRA. **Sue Cunningham Photography:** 53CR. **James Davis Travel Photography:** 11C, 21BC, 58CRB, 59CLA, 63BCL, 122CB, 164BC, 187CRA, 203BR. **George Dunnet:** 128CA. **Environmental Picture Library:** C. Westwood 130CL. **Eye Ubiquitous:** L. Fordyce 10CLA; L. Johnstone 6CRA, 32C; S. Miller xxi CA; M. Southern 75BLA. **FFOTOGRAFF:** C. Aithie 137CL; N. Tapsell 164CL. **G.S.F. Picture Library:** xvi BR, xvi BRA, 110BR, 126BR; Solarfilma 99TC. **Robert Harding Picture Library:** xvii TL, xxiv CR, xxx CLA, 13CR, 13CRA, 39CB, 41CLA, 52BL, 101TC, 116TC, 125BR, 138CLA, 148CB, 149TL, 153TR, 173CA, 173CB, 177BR; P.G. Adam 11CLA; D. Atchison-Jones 72CLB; J. Bayne 74CB; Bildagentur Schuster 82CRA; Bowman 52BR, 55CA, 64CL, 72CRA; C. Campbell xxi BC; R. Cundy 71BR; R. Frerck 53BL; G. Corrigan 165CRB, 167CRB; Delu 81CRB; Financial Times 148BR; T. Gervis 7CR; I. Griffiths xxx CL, 79TL; T. Hall 177CRA; D. Harney 148CA; G. Hellier xv CR, 135BL; F. Jackson 143BCR; P. Koch 145TR; S. Massif xv CB; A. Mills 90CLB; L. Murray 116TL; G. Renner 76CB, 204C; R. Richardson 120CB; E. Rooney 128TR; Sassoon xxiv CL, 154CBL; P. Scholey 184TR; M. Short 143TL; E. Simanor XXXVII CR; V. Southwell 145CR; J. Strachan 44TR, 136BCR; C. Tokeley 140CLA; A.C. Waltham xvii CLB, xxii CLiii, 144CR, 167C; Westlight 39CR; N. Wheeler 145CBL. **Paul Harris:** 126TL, 174TC. **The Hutchison Library:** 6BL, 140BCL; P .Collomb 143CR; C. Dodwell 139TR; N. Durrell McKenna xxxvi BCR; S. Errington 72CB; P. Hellyer 148BC; J. Horner xxxvi TCL; R.I. Lloyd 134CRA; J. Nowell 135CLB, 149TCR; A. Zvoznikov xxii CLii. **The Image Bank:** 89BR; A. Becker xxiv BL; J. Banagan 202CB; K. Forest 169TR; P. Hendrie 174BCL; M. Isy-Schwart 201C, 203CL; M. Khansa 124BR; T. Madison 177CR; C. Molyneux xxii CRiii; K. Mori 201TC; C. Navajas xviii TR; Ocean Inc.199CBL; S. Proehl 6CLB;T. Rakke xix TR, 99CL; M. Reitz 206CA; M. Romanelli 177BL; G.A. Rossi 157BCR, 184CLB; B. Roussel 111TL; S. Satushek xvii BC; J. Van Os xvii TC; Bullaty/Lomeo xxiv TCL; Stockphotos/ J. M. Spielman xxiv TCR. **Images Colour Library:** xxii CLi, 21BR, 39TL, 46TL, 64TC, 93BR, 156CL, 171CL, 172CRA, 188CA. **Impact Photos:** J. & G. Andrews 194BL; G. Buthaud 100BC; S. Franklin 130BL; A. Indge xxxvii TCL; C. Jones xxxi CB, 72BL; A. Le Garsmeur 137CR; V. Nemirousky 143BR; J. Nicholl 78TR; C. Penn 197BR; G. Sweeney xvii BR, 206TR; 206CB. **JVZ Picture Library:** T. Nilson 135TC. **Magnum Photos:** Abbas 85CR, 142C; S. Franklin 134CBR; D. Hurn 4CB; P. Jones-Griffiths 203BL; H. Kubota xvi CBA; S. McCurry 75CLA, 137BCR; F. Maer xvi BL; G. Rodger 76TR; C. Steele Perkins 74BL. **Frank Lane Picture Agency:** xxi TC, 95TL; J. Holmes xiv BL; Silvestris 181TCR; D. Smith xxii BCL; A. Wharton xxiii BL; W. Wisniewsli 126TC, 205BR. **Mountain Camera:** J. Cleare 159TR; C. Monteath 159CR. **Nature Photographers Ltd:** E.A. Janes 114CB. **Network Photographers Ltd:** Rapho/C. Sappa 121BR. **Natural History Photographic Agency:** N.J. Dennis xxiii CLi; D. Heuchlin xxiii CLA; S. Krasemann 13BL; 27BR, 40TR; R. Tidman 166CLB; D. Tomlinson 151CR. **Nottingham Trent University:** T. Waltham xiv CA, xv BR. **Novosti:** 150CLB. **OSF:** D. Allan xxii TR; H.R. Bardarson xviii CB; D. Bown xxiii CBLii; M. Brown 146BL; M. Colbeck 153CAR; L. Gould xxiii CRA; D. Guravich xxiii TR; M. Hill 59TL, 205TR; C. Menteath 140T; S. Osolinski 84CA; R. Packwood 74CA; M. Pitts 187TC; N. Rosing xxiii CBLi, 9TR, 207BR; D. Simonson 59C; R. Toms xxiiiBR; K. Wothe xvii CLA, xxi BL; Okapia/ P. Hammer-schmidy 89CL; Survival Anglia/C. Catton 143TR. **Panos Pictures:** B. Aris 137C; P. Barker xxciv BR; T. Bolstao 159BR; N. Cooper 84CB, 159TC; J.L. Dugast 177CB, 178BCR; J. Hartley 92C, 75CRA; J. Holmes 155BCR; J. Morris 78CRB; M. Rose 152TR; D. Sansoni 161C; L.C. Stowers 169TL. **Pictor International Ltd:** xiv BR, xv CRB, xix TC, xx CL, 19BR, 22TR, 22CRB, 24CL, 25CB, 28C, 29CB, 32CRA, 36BR, 36CR, 36CB, 40C, 40CRB, 100TC, 101TR, 108CLB, 177TCR, 178BR, 179CR, 188BL, 193TL. **Pictures Colour Library:** xxi BCL, xxii BR, xxxvi BCL, 6BR, 13TR, 17TR, 21TL, 22BL, 26C, 26CLA, 29TR, 34TR, 38CB, 43CA, 45CRA, 70BL, 92CRA, 101BR, 108CRB, 108CA, 108TR 109CLA, 170BC, 171BR, 199CL. **Planet Earth Pictures:** D. Barrett 154CB, 192CA; R. Coomber 17BL; G. Douwma 201BL; E. Edmonds 181BR; H.C. Heap 124TR; J. Lythgoe 206BL; A. Mounter 137BCR, 180CR; M. Potts 6CA; P. Scoones xx TR; D. Tackitt 180BR; J. Waters 55BCL. **Popperfoto/Reuters:** J. Drake xxxii CL. **Rex Features Ltd:** 170CR; Antelope xxxii CLB; M. Friedel xxi CR; I. McIlgorm xxx CBR; J. Shelley xxx CR; Sipa Press: xxx CRA; Sipa Press/Ali xxxx CBL; Chamussy 184BL. **Russia & Republics Picture Library:** M. Wadlow 120CA, 121CB, 128TL,128C, 128CB, 128BR,130TR. **SCR Library:** J. King 151BR. **Science Photo Library:** CNES, 1990 Distribution Spot Images 137BL; Earth Satellite Corporation xix CRA, XXXI CR; F. Gohier xi CR; J. Heseltine xvi TC; K. Kent xv CLB; P. Menzell xv BL; NASA x BC; D. Parker xiv CB; Peter Arnold Inc./ R.J. Wainscoat xi BC; University Of Cambridge Collection Air Pix 89CLB; D. Weintraub xi BL. **South American Pictures:** 59BL, 64TR; Guyana Space Centre 52TR; R. Francis 54BL; T. Morrison 52CR, 54TR, 56TR, 62BL, 63C. **Southampton Oceanography:** xviii BL. **Sovfoto/ Eastfoto:** xxxii CBR. **Spectrum Colour Library:** 52BC, 166BC. **Still Pictures:** C. Caldicott 79TR; A. Crump 197CL; M. & C. Denis-Huot xxii BL, 80TC, 83BL; M. Edwards xxi AR, 55BL, 71CLB, 99CR, 161BR; J. Frebet 55LCB; M. Gunther 123BR; E. Parker 54CL; R. Seitre 137CA,138TL 138BL. **Frank Spooner Pictures:** A. Zamur 115BR; Diard/ Photo News 115CB; Figaro/Torrengo 80TR; Gamma-Liaison: 28CRB; Gamma-Liaison/E. Baitel xxxii BCL; Bernstein xxxi CL; Contrast 114TR; C. Hires xxxii CLA; D. Marleen 115BL; Nickelsberg xxxii TR; P. Piel xxx CA; N. Quidu 135CLA; L. Sazy xxxii BCR; H. Stucke 196CBL, 202CA; Vogel 140BL. **Tony Stone Images:** xxxvi TR, 7BL; 11CRB; 41BR; 4CRA, 103TR; 109 TL, 111CL, 111CRB, 137BR, 170CLB, 171CR, 188CB; 189BR, 196BC, 199T; G. Allison 20TR , 33CR, 195CR; D. Armand 12CLA; D. Austen 188TR, 194CL, 195CL; J. Beatty 76CL; O. Benn xxxvi BR; K. Biggs xxi TL; R. Bradbury 46BR; R.A. Butcher xxxvi TL; J. Callahan xxxvii CRA; P. Chesley 193BCL, 196C; W. Clay 32BL, 33CRA; C. Condina 43C; J. Cornish 108BL; T. Craddock xxiv TR; P. Degginger 38C; Demetrio 5BR; N. DeVore xxiv BCL; A. Diesendruck 62BR; S. Egan 89CRA; R. Elliott xxii BCR; S. Elmore 21C; R. Frerck 122TR; J. Garrett 75CR; S. Grandadam 12BR; C. Harvey 71TL; G. Hellier 172CR; D. Hughes xxxi CBR; A. Husmo 93TC; G. Irvine 33BL; G. Johnso xvii TR, 138CLB; A. Kehr 115CA; R. Koskas xvi TR; J. Lawrence 77CRA; L. Lefkowitz 7CA; M. Lewis 47CLA; S. Mayman 57BR; Murray & Assoc. 47CR; N. Parfitt xxxvii CL, 70TCR, 83TL; R. Passmore 123T N. Press xvi CB; E. Pritchard 90CA, 92C; T. Raymond 23BL; L. Resnick 76BR; M. Rogers 82CRB; C. Saule 92CRA; 7CLA; S. Schulhoff xxiv TL; D. Schultz 7CLA; P. Seaward 36C; M. Segal 34BL; V. Shenai 158CL; R. Sherman 28CLA; H. Sitton 142CR; R. Smith 58CA; S. Studd; 110CLAH. Strand 65TR; P. Tweedie 185CR; L. Ulrich 19BL; M. Vines 19TL; A.B. Wadham 62CR; J. Warden 65BCL; R. Wells 25CR, 200BL; G. Yeowell 36BL. **Telegraph Colour Library:** 63TCR, 63BR; J. Sims 28BR. **Topham Picturepoint Ltd:** xxxi CBL, 137BCL, 139CR, 168BR, 174TR, 176BC. **Travel Ink:** Andrew Cowin 90TR. **Trip:** 146BR, 150CA, 161CR; B. Ashe 165TR; D. Cole 202CR, 202BCL; D. Davis 91BL; I. Deineko xxxi TR; J. Dennis 24BL; Dinodia 160CL; A. Gasson 155CR; W. Jacobs 45TL, 56BL, 185BC, 186CLA, 193CBR, 197BL; P. Kingsbury 114C; T. Knight 185BR; V. Kolpakov 153BL; T. Noorits 89TL, 121TR, 152CL; R. Power 43TR; N. Ray 176C; E. Smith 191TL, 191BC; V. Sidoropolev 151TR. **Woodfin Camp Associates Inc.:** 94CRB. **World Pictures:** xv CA, xvii CRA, 25CL, 25BR, 26BL, 37BL, 42TR, 53T, 73BL, 82TCR 84TR, 85BL, 88BR, 100BR, 102TC, 103TC, 123CB, 124B 167BCL, 168CLB, 180CBL, 180BC, 187BL, 190CB, 191C, 192CL, 193CR. **ZEFA:** xvi BC, xvii CB, xviii CL, 11BL, 12TC, 17CA, 23TL, 24BR, 27BL, 34TC, 38BR, 71CLA, 81BL, 83BR, 89CRB, 94C, 100C, 100CLA, 101BL, 102BR, 108TL, 120CRA, 122BL, 126CRB, 128CLA, 170CA, 191CR; Anatol 115TR; Barone 116BR; Brandenburg 5CLA; A.J Brown 46TR; H. J. Clauss 57CLB; Damm 73CB; Evert 94BR; J. Fields 197CRA; R. Frerck 4BLB; G. Heil 58BR; K. Helbig 117TR; Hunt 8CB; Kitchin 8TR; Dr. H. Kramarz 7CLB, 126CRA; Mehlio 161BL; J.F. Raga 26TR; Rossenbach 122CA; T. Stewart 11TR, 21CR; Streichan 91TL; Sunak 56BR, 168TR; B. Zaunders 42CB. **Additional Photography:** G. Dann; H. Taylor; J. Young

NORTH AMERICA

CANADA
PAGES 8–16

UNITED STATES OF AMERICA
PAGES 17–41

MEXICO
PAGES 42–43

BELIZE
PAGES 44–45

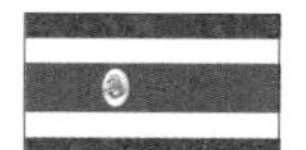
COSTA RICA
PAGES 44–45

EL SALVADOR
PAGES 44–45

GUATEMALA
PAGES 44–45

HONDURAS
PAGES 44–45

GRENADA
PAGES 46–47

HAITI
PAGES 46–47

JAMAICA
PAGES 46–47

ST. KITTS & NEVIS
PAGES 46–47

ST. LUCIA
PAGES 46–47

ST. VINCENT & THE GRENADINES
PAGES 46–47

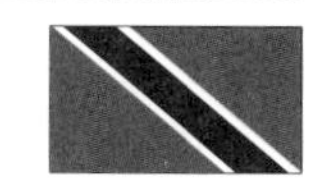
TRINIDAD & TOBAGO
PAGES 46–47

SOUTH AM

COLOMBI
PAGES 56–5

URUGUAY
PAGES 62–63

CHILE
PAGES 64–65

PARAGUAY
PAGES 64–65

AFRICA

ALGERIA
PAGES 76–77

EGYPT
PAGES 76–77

LIBYA
PAGES 76–77

MOROCCO
PAGES 76–77

TUNISIA
PAGES 76–7

LIBERIA
PAGES 78–79

MALI
PAGES 78–79

MAURITANIA
PAGES 78–79

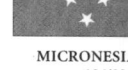
NIGER
PAGES 78–79

NIGERIA
PAGES 78–79

SENEGAL
PAGES 78–79

SIERRA LEONE
PAGES 78–79

TOGO
PAGES 78–79

BURUNDI
PAGES 82–83

DJIBOUTI
PAGES 82–83

ERITREA
PAGES 82–83

ETHIOPIA
PAGES 82–83

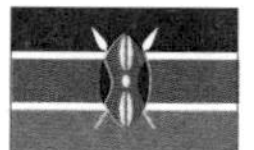
KENYA
PAGES 82–83

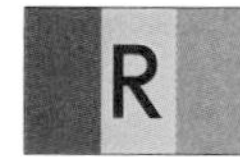
R
RWANDA
PAGES 82–83

SOMALIA
PAGES 82–83

SUDAN
PAGES 82–83

SOUTH AFRICA
PAGES 84–85

SWAZILAND
PAGES 84–85

ZAMBIA
PAGES 84–85

ZIMBABWE
PAGES 84–85

EUROPE

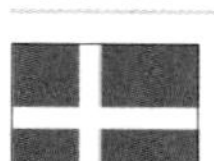
DENMARK
PAGES 94–97

FINLAND
PAGES 94–95

ICELAND
PAGES 94–95

NORWA
PAGES 94–

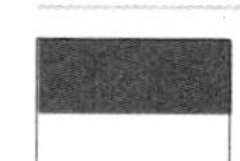
MONACO
PAGES 104–105

ANDORRA
PAGES 106–107

PORTUGAL
PAGES 106–107

SPAIN
PAGES 106–107

ITALY
PAGES 108–109

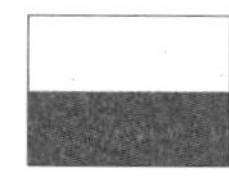
SAN MARINO
PAGES 108–109

VATICAN CITY
PAGES 108–109

AUSTRIA
PAGES 110–

BOSNIA & HERZEGOVINA
PAGES 114–115

CROATIA
PAGES 114–115

MACEDONIA
PAGES 114–115

YUGOSLAVIA
PAGES 114–115

BULGARIA
PAGES 116–117

GREECE
PAGES 116–117

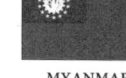

MOLDOVA
PAGES 118–119

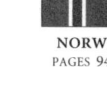
ROMANI
PAGES 118–

ASIA

ARMENIA
PAGES 142–143

AZERBAIJAN
PAGES 142–143

GEORGIA
PAGES 142–143

TURKEY
PAGES 142–143/116–117

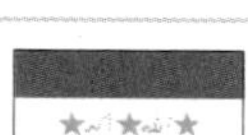
IRAQ
PAGES 144–145

ISRAEL
PAGES 144–145

JORDAN
PAGES 144–145

LEBANO
PAGES 144–

IRAN
PAGES 148–149

KAZAKHSTAN
PAGES 150–151

KYRGYSTAN
PAGES 152–153

TAJIKISTAN
PAGES 152–153

TURKMENISTAN
PAGES 152–153

UZBEKISTAN
PAGES 152–153

AFGHANISTAN
PAGES 154–155

PAKISTA
PAGES 154–

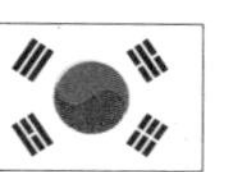
SOUTH KOREA
PAGES 162–163/168–169

TAIWAN
PAGES 166–167

JAPAN
PAGES 170–172

BRUNEI
PAGES 173–176

INDONESIA
PAGES 173–176

MALAYSIA
PAGES 173–176

SINGAPORE
PAGES 173–176

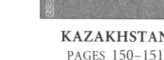

MYANMAR
PAGES 177–17

MAURITIUS
PAGES 180–181

SEYCHELLES
PAGES 180–181

AUSTRALASIA & OCEANIA

AUSTRALIA
PAGES 188–191

NEW ZEALAND
PAGES 192–193

PAPUA NEW GUINEA
PAGES 194–195

SOLOMON ISLANDS
PAGES 194–195

MARSHALL ISLANDS
PAGES 196/201

MICRONESIA
PAGES 196/20